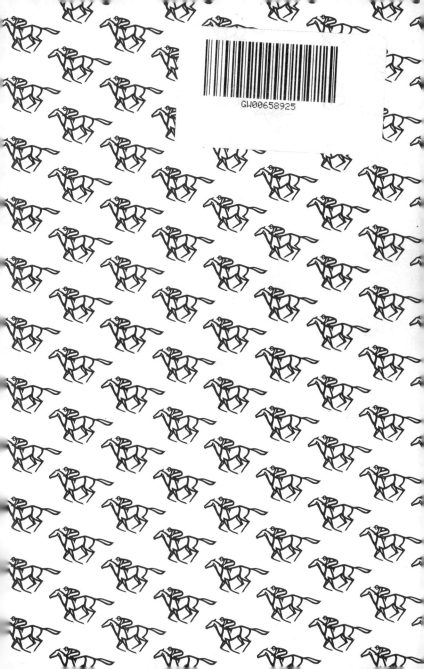

GW00658925

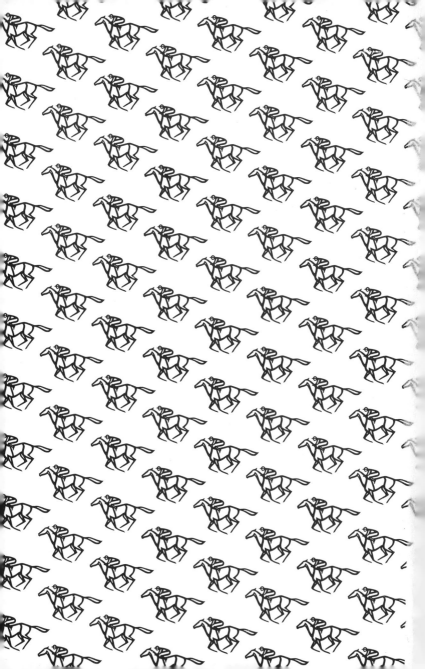

AGE, WEIGHT & DISTANCE TABLE

For use with Timeform Ratings

Dist	Age	Mar	Apr	May	June	July	Aug	Sep	Oct	Nov
5f	4	10-0	10-0	10-0	10-0	10-0	10-0	10-0	10-0	10-0
	3	9-0	9-2	9-4	9-6	9-8	9-10	9-11	9-12	9-13
	2	6-8	6-13	7-3	7-7	7-11	8-1	8-5	8-8	8-11
6f	4	9-13	10-0	10-0	10-0	10-0	10-0	10-0	10-0	10-0
	3	8-11	9-0	9-2	9-4	9-6	9-8	9-10	9-11	9-12
	2			6-13	7-3	7-7	7-11	8-1	8-5	8-8
7f	4	9-12	9-13	10-0	10-0	10-0	10-0	10-0	10-0	10-0
	3	8-8	8-11	9-0	9-2	9-4	9-6	9-8	9-10	9-11
	2					7-4	7-8	7-12	8-2	8-5
1m	4	9-11	9-12	9-13	10-0	10-0	10-0	10-0	10-0	10-0
	3	8-6	8-9	8-12	9-1	9-3	9-5	9-7	9-9	9-10
	2							7-9	7-13	8-2
9f	4	9-11	9-12	9-13	9-13	10-0	10-0	10-0	10-0	10-0
	3	8-4	8-7	8-10	8-13	9-2	9-4	9-6	9-8	9-9
1¼m	4	9-10	9-11	9-12	9-13	10-0	10-0	10-0	10-0	10-0
	3	8-2	8-5	8-8	8-11	9-0	9-3	9-5	9-7	9-8
11f	4	9-9	9-11	9-12	9-13	10-0	10-0	10-0	10-0	10-0
	3	8-0	8-4	8-7	8-10	8-13	9-2	9-4	9-6	9-7
1½m	4	9-9	9-10	9-11	9-12	9-13	10-0	10-0	10-0	10-0
	3	7-12	8-2	8-5	8-8	8-11	9-0	9-3	9-5	9-7
13f	4	9-8	9-10	9-11	9-12	9-13	9-13	10-0	10-0	10-0
	3	7-11	8-1	8-4	8-7	8-10	8-13	9-2	9-4	9-6
1¾m	4	9-7	9-9	9-10	9-12	9-13	9-13	10-0	10-0	10-0
	3	7-9	7-13	8-3	8-6	8-9	8-12	9-1	9-3	9-5
15f	4	9-6	9-8	9-10	9-11	9-12	9-13	10-0	10-0	10-0
	3	7-8	7-12	8-2	8-5	8-8	8-11	9-0	9-2	9-4
2m	4	9-6	9-8	9-10	9-11	9-12	9-13	10-0	10-0	10-0
	3	7-7	7-11	8-1	8-5	8-8	8-11	9-0	9-2	9-4
2¼m	4	9-6	9-8	9-9	9-11	9-12	9-13	10-0	10-0	10-0
	3	7-6	7-10	8-0	8-4	8-7	8-10	8-13	9-1	9-3
2½m	4	9-5	9-7	9-9	9-10	9-11	9-12	9-13	10-0	10-0
	3	7-5	7-9	7-13	8-3	8-6	8-9	8-12	9-1	9-3

For 5-y-o's and older, use 10-0 in all cases

1

The Sporting Life

WINS EVERY YEAR

The Sporting Life

Curragh Bloodstock Agency

OUR RECENT GROUP 1 PURCHASES

*CARROLL HOUSE

*EUROBIRD   *ALYDARESS

*JALMOOD   *HIGH HAWK

*MTOTO   *PEN BAL LADY

*PARK EXPRESS   *PERSIAN BOY

*MISTER MAJESTIC

*WASSL

Carroll House was purchased by the CBA as a foal for 15,000 Gns and resold as a yearling for 32,000 Gns. His 4 Group 1 wins include Prix de l'Arc de Triomphe and his total earnings are over £850,000.

IRELAND	ENGLAND
Main Street, Newbridge, Co. Kildare.	'Crossways' 23 The Avenue, Newmarket, Suffolk CB8 9AA
Tel: (045) 31402 Telex: 60665 Fax: (045) 32720	Tel: (0638) 662620 or 663791 Telex: 81426 Fax: (0638) 661658

4

RACEHORSES
OF 1989

A Timeform Publication   Price £59.00

A Timeform Publication

Compiled and produced under the direction of
Reg Griffin

by members of the Timeform Organisation

G. Greetham, B.A., G. F. Walton, Dip.A.D.
(Directors), J. D. Newton, B.A. (Editor-in-Chief),
D. P. Adams (Editor), R. J. C. Austen, B.A., G.
Crowther, G. J. Cunningham, LL.B., W. Hughes,
G. M. Johnstone, P. A. Muncaster, B.Sc., G. J.
North, B.Sc., N. Townsend, B.A. and C. S.
Williams

© Portway Press Limited 1990

ISBN 0 900599 50 2

CONTENTS

FOREWORD

"Racehorses of 1989" deals individually, in alphabetical sequence, with every horse that ran under Jockey Club Rules in 1989, plus a number of foreign-trained horses that did not race here. For each of these horses is given (1) its age, colour and sex, (2) its breeding, (3) a form summary giving details of all its performances during the past two seasons, (4) a rating of its merit, (5) a commentary upon its racing or general characteristics as a racehorse, with some suggestions, perhaps, regarding its potentialities in 1990 and (6) the name of the trainer in whose charge it was on the last occasion it ran. For each two-year-old the foaling date is also given.

The book is published with a twofold purpose. Firstly, it is designed to provide the betting man with data for practical use in analysing the racing programmes from day to day, and instructions as to its use in this capacity will be found in the Explanatory Notes which follow this Foreword; and secondly, the book is intended to have some permanent value as a review of the exploits and achievements of the more notable of our thoroughbreds in 1989. Thus, while the commentaries upon the vast majority of the horses are, of necessity, in note form, the best horses are more critically examined, and the short essays upon them are illustrated by half-tone portraits and photographs of the finishes of some of the races in which they were successful.

The attention of foreign buyers of British bloodstock, and others who are concerned with Timeform Ratings as a measure of absolute racing class in terms of a standard scale, is drawn to the section headed "The Level of the Ratings" in the Explanatory Notes.

February, 1990

Home of ZILZAL and SHADEED

Enquiries to:
M.H. Goodbody, **Gainsborough Stud,** Woolton Hill, Newbury, Berkshire.
Telephone: (0635) 253273. Fax: (0635) 254690. Telex: 849436.
or
Allen Kershaw, Gainsborough Farm, Rt.1 Steele Road, Versailles, Kentucky 40383.
Telephone: (606) 873 8918. Fax: (606) 873 2462. Telex: 852529.

INDEX TO PHOTOGRAPHS

PORTRAITS & SNAPSHOTS

10

11

Mountain Kingdom ...	5 b.h.	Exceller– Star In The North (Northern Dancer)	*John Crofts*	585
Mukddaam	2 b.c.	Danzig– Height of Fashion (Bustino)	*W. W. Rouch & Co.*	590
Musical Bliss	3 b.f.	The Minstrel–Bori (Quadrangle)	*John Crofts*	594
Nabeel Dancer	4 b.c.	Northern Dancer– Prayers'n Promises (Foolish Pleasure)	*John Crofts*	602
Nashwan	3 ch.c.	Blushing Groom– Height of Fashion (Bustino)	*W. W. Rouch & Co.*	612
N C Owen	3 b.c.	Bustino–Neenah (Bold Lad (Ire))	*John Crofts*	616
Observation Post	3 b.c.	Shirley Heights–Godzilla (Gyr)	*Rex Coleman*	637
Old Vic	3 b.c.	Sadler's Wells–Cockade (Derring-Do)	*John Crofts*	645
Opening Verse	3 ch.c.	The Minstrel–Shy Dawn (Grey Dawn II)	*Camilla Russell*	650
Ozone Friendly	2 ch.f.	Green Forest–Kristana (Kris)	*Rex Coleman*	659
Pass The Peace	3 b.f.	Alzao–Lover's Rose (King Emperor)	*John Crofts*	664
Pelorus	4 b.c.	High Top–St Isabel (Saint Crespin II)	*John Crofts*	670
Per Quod	4 b.g.	Lyllos–Allegedly (Sir Ivor)	*John Crofts*	673
Petillante	2 gr.f.	Petong–French Bugle (Bleep-Bleep)	*John Crofts*	675
Petite Ile	3 b.f.	Ile de Bourbon–Aces Full (Round Table)	*Jacqueline O'Brien*	678
Phantom Breeze	3 b.c.	Vision–Ask The Wind (Run The Gantlet)	*Jacqueline O'Brien*	680
Polish Precedent	3 b.c.	Danzig–Past Example (Buckpasser)	*John Crofts*	696
Princess Sobieska	3 b.f.	Niniski–Rexana (Relko)	*Rex Coleman*	708
Prorutori	3 b.c.	Providential– Miss Flower Belle (Torsion)	*John Crofts*	711
Qathif	2 b.c.	Riverman–Al Bayan (Northern Dancer)	*John Crofts*	714
Qirmazi	2 ch.f.	Riverman– Cream'N Crimson (Vaguely Noble)	*John Crofts*	715
Raj Waki	2 b.c.	Miswaki–Script Approval (Silent Screen)	*Rex Coleman*	723
Relief Pitcher	3 b.c.	Welsh Term– Bases Loaded (Northern Dancer)	*W. W. Rouch & Co.*	734
Reprimand	4 b.c.	Mummy's Pet– Just You Wait (Nonoalco)	*Camilla Russell*	736
Robellation	2 b.c.	Robellino–Vexation (Vice Regent)	*Rex Coleman*	744
Rock City	2 br.c.	Ballad Rock– Rimosa's Pet (Petingo)	*W. W. Rouch & Co.*	749
Routilante	2 b.f.	Rousillon– Danseuse Classique (Northern Dancer)	*W. W. Rouch & Co.*	759
Royal Academy	2 b.c.	Nijinsky–Crimson Saint (Crimson Satan)	*Jacqueline O'Brien*	760
Russian Bond	3 b.c.	Danzig–Somfas (What A Pleasure)	*Camilla Russell*	770
Sadeem	6 ch.h.	Forli–Miss Mazepah (Nijinsky)	*Rex Coleman*	775

Safawan	3 ch.c.	Young Generation–Safita (Habitat)	*John Crofts*	777
Saint Andrews	5 b.h.	Kenmare–Hardiona (Hard To Beat)	*P. Bertrand*	780
Samoan	3 b.c.	Diesis–Pago Dancer (Pago Pago)	*Camilla Russell*	786
Saratogan	3 ch.c.	El Gran Senor–Patia (Don)	*Jacqueline O'Brien*	792
Serious Trouble	3 ch.c.	Good Times– Silly Woman (Silly Season)	*John Crofts*	805
Shaadi	3 b.c.	Danzig–Unfurled (Hoist The Flag)	*John Crofts*	810
Silver Fling	4 br.f.	The Minstrel– Royal Dilemma (Buckpasser)	*W. W. Rouch & Co.*	835
Snow Bride	3 ch.f.	Blushing Groom–Awaasif (Snow Knight)	*Camilla Russell*	848
Somethingdifferent	2 b.c.	Green Forest– Try Something New (Hail The Pirates)	*John Crofts*	853
Spinning	2 br.c.	Glint of Gold–Strathspey (Jimmy Reppin)	*W. W. Rouch & Co.*	860
Squill	4 b.c.	Stop The Music– River Rose (Riverman)	*John Crofts*	865
Stadler	2 b.c.	Sadler's Wells– Santa Roseanna (Caracol)	*Jacqueline O'Brien*	866
Star Lift	5 ch.h.	Mill Reef–Seneca (Chaparral)	*John Crofts*	870
Statoblest	3 b.c.	Ahonoora–Statira (Skymaster)	*John Crofts*	873
Teach Dha Mhile	2 b.c.	Kampala–Mittens (Run The Gantlet)	*Jacqueline O'Brien*	901
Terimon	3 gr.c.	Bustino–Nicholas Grey (Track Spare)	*John Crofts*	906
The Caretaker	2 b.f.	Caerleon–Go Feather Go (Go Marching)	*Jacqueline O'Brien*	910
Tigani	3 b.c.	Good Times– She Who Dares (Bellypha)	*Rex Coleman*	917
Torjoun	3 ch.c.	Green Dancer–Tarsila (High Top)	*John Crofts*	929
Two Timing	3 b.c.	Blushing Groom– Social Column (Vaguely Noble)	*W. W. Rouch & Co.*	943
Unfuwain	4 b.c.	Northern Dancer– Height of Fashion (Bustino)	*W. W. Rouch & Co.*	948
Upward Trend	3 ch.f.	Salmon Leap– Ivory Home (Home Guard)	*Jacqueline O'Brien*	951
Warning	4 b.c.	Known Fact– Slightly Dangerous (Roberto)	*Rex Coleman*	966
Warrshan	3 b.c.	Northern Dancer– Secret Asset (Graustark)	*John Crofts*	969
Wedding Bouquet	2 b.f.	Kings Lake– Doff The Derby (Master Derby)	*Jacqueline O'Brien*	971
Weld	3 ch.c.	Kalaglow–Meliora (Crowned Prince)	*John Crofts*	973
Zayyani	3 b.c.	Darshaan–Zariya (Blushing Groom)	*W. W. Rouch & Co.*	998
Zero Watt	5 b.h.	Little Current– Ruby Tuesday (T V Lark)	*Rex Coleman*	999

RACE PHOTOGRAPHS

14

Fairey Group Spring Trophy (Haydock)	*A. Russell*	105
Fairview New Homes Chesterfield Stakes	*John Crofts*	274
(Newmarket)		
Fay Richwhite Karamea Stakes (Newmarket)	*John Crofts*	209
Feilden Stakes (Newmarket)	*A. Johnson*	377
Garden Suite Racing Club Maiden Stakes (Div. 1)	*John Crofts*	589
(Newmarket)		
General Accident Jockey Club Stakes (Newmarket)	*John Crofts*	947
General Accident One Thousand Guineas	*A. Russell*	593
(Newmarket)		
General Accident Two Thousand Guineas	*George Selwyn*	606
(Newmarket)		
Geoffrey Barling Maiden Stakes (Newmarket)	*John Crofts*	686
Gilbey's Gin Sweet Solera Stakes (Newmarket)	*John Crofts*	579
Glasgow Stakes (York)	*A. Russell*	577
Goffs Irish One Thousand Guineas (the Curragh)	*Caroline Norris*	293
Gold Cup (Ascot)	*John Crofts*	774
Golden Gates Nursery (Ascot)	*A. Johnson*	226
Gold Seal Oaks (Epsom)	*John Crofts*	46
Goodwood Cup (Goodwood)	*John Crofts*	549
Gordon Stakes (Goodwood)	*John Crofts*	968
G.P.A. National Stakes (the Curragh)	*M. Ansell*	241
Grand Prix de Deauville Lancel (Deauville)	*P. Bertrand*	137
Grand Prix de Paris Louis Vuitton (Longchamp)	*P. Bertrand*	231
Grand Prix de Saint-Cloud (Saint-Cloud)	*P. Bertrand*	820
Gran Premio del Jockey Club e Coppa d'Oro (Milan)	*Perrucci*	82
Great Voltigeur Stakes (York)	*John Crofts*	996
Guardian Classic Trial (Sandown)	*George Selwyn*	641
Hanson Coronation Cup (Epsom)	*A. Johnson*	819
Hardwicke Stakes (Ascot)	*A. Russell*	81
Harry Rosebery Challenge Trophy (Ayr)	*A. Russell*	527
Harvester Graduation Stakes (Sandown)	*John Crofts*	689
Haydock Park July Trophy (Haydock)	*A. Russell*	52
Heinz '57' Phoenix Stakes (Phoenix Park)	*Caroline Norris*	682
Hewitson, Becke & Shaw Godolphin Stakes	*A. Russell*	864
(Newmarket)		
Hillsdown Cherry Hinton Stakes (Newmarket)	*John Crofts*	190
Hoover Cumberland Lodge Stakes (Ascot)	*George Selwyn*	932
Hoover Fillies' Mile (Ascot)	*John Crofts*	831
Howard Chapman Wicks Stakes (York)	*A. Russell*	170
Imry Solario Stakes (Sandown)	*John Crofts*	115
Jefferson Smurfit Memorial Irish St Leger	*Caroline Norris*	676
(the Curragh)		
Jennings The Bookmakers Zetland Stakes	*John Crofts*	751
(Newmarket)		
Jersey Stakes (Ascot)	*A. Russell*	1000
Jockey Club Cup (Newmarket)	*A. Russell*	972
John Roarty Memorial Scurry Handicap (the Curragh)	*John Crofts*	70
John Smith's Magnet Cup (York)	*A. Russell*	418
Juddmonte Farms Nell Gwyn Stakes (Newmarket)	*John Crofts*	292
Juddmonte International Stakes (York)	*A. Russell*	421
Juddmonte Lockinge Stakes (Newbury)	*John Crofts*	582
Keeneland Fred Archer Stakes (Newmarket)	*George Selwyn*	69
Kildangan Stud Irish Oaks (the Curragh)	*Caroline Norris*	59
King Edward VII Stakes (Ascot)	*A. Russell*	156
King George Stakes (Goodwood)	*John Crofts*	873
King George V Handicap (Ascot)	*John Crofts*	169
King George VI And Queen Elizabeth Diamond	*John Crofts*	610
Stakes (Ascot)		
King's Stand Stakes (Ascot)	*John Crofts*	427
Kiveton Park Stakes (Doncaster)	*John Crofts*	362
Krug Diadem Stakes (Ascot)	*A. Russell*	194
La Coupe (Maisons-Laffitte)	*P. Bertrand*	679
Ladbroke Chester Cup (Chester)	*George Selwyn*	378
Ladbrokes (Ayr) Gold Cup (Ayr)	*A. Russell*	449
Ladbroke Sprint Cup (Haydock)	*A. Russell*	236
Lambson Chemical Stakes (York)	*A. Russell*	417
Lancashire Oaks (Haydock)	*A. Russell*	754

15

Lanson Champagne Vintage Stakes (Goodwood)	*John Crofts*	114
Laphroaig March Stakes (Goodwood)	*John Crofts*	556
Main Reef Stakes (Newmarket)	*John Crofts*	773
Marley Roof Tile Oaks Trial Stakes (Lingfield)	*George Selwyn*	45
Marshall Stakes (Newmarket)	*John Crofts*	499
May Hill EBF Stakes (Doncaster)	*A. Johnson*	720
Michael Sobell Handicap (York)	*A. Russell*	84
Molecomb Stakes (Goodwood)	*A. Johnson*	391
Moorestyle Convivial Stakes (York)	*John Crofts*	432
Moyglare Stud Stakes (the Curragh)	*Caroline Norris*	60
Newcastle 'Brown Ale' Northumberland Plate (Handicap) (Newcastle)	*A. Russell*	653
Norwest Holst Trophy (Handicap) (York)	*John Crofts*	375
Old Newton Cup (Haydock)	*A. Russell*	622
Palace House Stakes (Newmarket)	*John Crofts*	833
Park Hill Stakes (Doncaster)	*John Crofts*	517
Paul Caddick And MacGay Sprint Trophy (Handicap) (York)	*A. Russell*	738
Phil Bull Memorial Trophy (Pontefract)	*A. Russell*	732
Philip Cornes Houghton Stakes (Newmarket)	*A. Russell*	276
Prince of Wales's Stakes (Ascot)	*John Crofts*	942
Princess Margaret Stakes (Ascot)	*A. Russell*	514
Princess Royal Stakes (Ascot)	*John Crofts*	847
Prix de Conde (Longchamp)	*P. Bertrand*	273
Prix de Diane Hermes (Chantilly)	*P. Bertrand*	480
Prix de Flore (Saint-Cloud)	*P. Bertrand*	120
Prix de la Foret (Longchamp)	*P. Bertrand*	337
Prix de la Nonette (Longchamp)	*P. Bertrand*	827
Prix de la Salamandre (Longchamp)	*P. Bertrand*	523
Prix de Malleret (Longchamp)	*P. Bertrand*	992
Prix de Meautry (Deauville)	*P. Bertrand*	218
Prix de Pomone (Deauville)	*P. Bertrand*	202
Prix de Psyche (Deauville)	*John Crofts*	40
Prix des Chenes (Saint-Cloud)	*P. Bertrand*	335
Prix de Seine-et-Oise (Maisons-Laffitte)	*P. Bertrand*	44
Prix d'Ispahan (Longchamp)	*John Crofts*	428
Prix du Conseil de Paris (Longchamp)	*P. Bertrand*	746
Prix du Haras de Fresnay-le-Buffard Jacques le Marois (Deauville)	*John Crofts*	694
Prix du Jockey-Club Lancia (Chantilly)	*P. Bertrand*	643
Prix du Moulin de Longchamp (Longchamp)	*John Crofts*	695
Prix du Petit Couvert (Longchamp)	*P. Bertrand*	519
Prix du Prince d'Orange (Longchamp)	*P. Bertrand*	433
Prix Eclipse (Saint-Cloud)	*P. Bertrand*	693
Prix Foy (Longchamp)	*P. Bertrand*	869
Prix Ganay (Longchamp)	*John Crofts*	779
Prix Hocquart (Longchamp)	*P. Bertrand*	230
Prix Jean de Chaudenay (Saint-Cloud)	*P. Bertrand*	138
Prix Jean Prat (Longchamp)	*P. Bertrand*	507
Prix Lupin (Longchamp)	*P. Bertrand*	341
Prix Marcel Boussac (Longchamp)	*P. Bertrand*	783
Prix Messidor (Maisons-Laffitte)	*P. Bertrand*	694
Prix Morny Agence Francaise (Deauville)	*John Crofts*	522
Prix Niel (Longchamp)	*P. Bertrand*	358
Prix Robert Papin (Maisons-Laffitte)	*P. Bertrand*	658
Prix Royal-Oak (Longchamp)	*P. Bertrand*	926
Prix Saint-Alary (Longchamp)	*P. Bertrand*	107
Prix Thomas Bryon (Saint-Cloud)	*P. Bertrand*	803
Prix Vanteaux (Longchamp)	*John Crofts*	514
Prix Vermeille (Longchamp)	*P. Bertrand*	993
Queen Alexandra Stakes (Ascot)	*A. Russell*	38
Queen Anne Stakes (Ascot)	*John Crofts*	965
Queen Elizabeth II Stakes (Ascot)	*John Crofts*	1003
Queen Mary Stakes (Ascot)	*A. Russell*	246
Queen Mother's Cup (York)	*A. Russell*	419
Racecall Gold Trophy (Redcar)	*A. Russell*	654
Racing Post Trophy (Newcastle)	*A. Russell*	116
R & V Europa-Preis (Cologne)	*George Selwyn*	415

Red Oaks Autumn Stakes (Ascot)	*George Selwyn*	627
Reference Point EBF Tyros Stakes (the Curragh)	*Caroline Norris*	351
Reference Point Strensall Stakes (York)	*A. Russell*	649
Ribblesdale Stakes (Ascot)	*John Crofts*	58
Rokeby Farms Mill Reef Stakes (Newbury)	*John Crofts*	975
Royal Hong Kong Jockey Club Trophy (Handicap) (Sandown)	*John Crofts*	949
Royal Hunt Cup (Ascot)	*A. Russell*	938
Royal Lodge EBF Stakes (Ascot)	*John Crofts*	257
Schweppes Golden Mile (Handicap) (Goodwood)	*John Crofts*	776
Scottish Equitable Gimcrack Stakes (York)	*John Crofts*	748
Scottish Equitable Richmond Stakes (Goodwood)	*John Crofts*	64
Sears Temple Stakes (Sandown)	*John Crofts*	233
Skol Lager Sandy Lane Stakes (Haydock)	*A. Russell*	466
Skol Lager Sprint Handicap (Goodwood)	*John Crofts*	791
Somerville Tattersall Stakes (Newmarket)	*John Crofts*	328
Sonic Lady Stakes (Newmarket)	*A. Johnson*	791
St James's Palace Stakes (Ascot)	*John Crofts*	809
St Leger Stakes (Ayr)	*A. Russell*	556
St Simon Stakes (Newbury)	*John Crofts*	806
Sun Life of Canada Garrowby Stakes (Limited Handicap) (York)	*A. Russell*	767
Swettenham Stud Sussex Stakes (Goodwood)	*John Crofts*	1002
Tara Sires EBF Desmond Stakes (the Curragh)	*Caroline Norris*	506
Tattersalls Cheveley Park Stakes (Newmarket)	*John Crofts*	248
Tattersalls EBF Rogers Gold Cup (the Curragh)	*Caroline Norris*	420
Tattersalls Middle Park Stakes (Newmarket)	*A. Russell*	93
Tattersalls Musidora Stakes (York)	*A. Russell*	846
'The Mallard' Handicap (Doncaster)	*John Crofts*	186
'The Pacemaker Update' Lowther Stakes (York)	*A. Russell*	247
Three Chimneys Dewhurst Stakes (Newmarket)	*John Crofts*	242
Timeform Futurity (Pontefract)	*A. Russell*	922
Timeform Race Card Stakes (Pontefract)	*A. Russell*	498
Tote Cesarewitch (Handicap) (Newmarket))	*W. Everitt*	268
Tote Ebor (Handicap) (York)	*John Crofts*	790
Tote Festival Handicap (Ascot)	*John Crofts*	140
Tote-Portland Handicap (Doncaster)	*A. Johnson*	214
Van Geest Criterion Stakes (Newmarket)	*John Crofts*	1001
Vodafone Horris Hill Stakes (Newbury)	*John Crofts*	920
Vodafone Nassau Stakes (Goodwood)	*Press Association Photos*	536
Walmac International Geoffrey Freer Stakes (Newbury)	*John Crofts*	414
Warren Stakes (Epsom)	*John Crofts*	79
Washington Singer Stakes (Newbury)	*John Crofts*	458
Whyte & Mackay Scotch Stakes (Handicap) (Ascot)	*A. Johnson*	769
William Hill Cambridgeshire (Newmarket)	*John Crofts*	724
William Hill Claiming Stakes (Lingfield)	*W. Everitt*	625
William Hill Dante Stakes (York)	*A. Russell*	928
William Hill Golden Spurs Trophy (Handicap) (York)	*A. Russell*	887
William Hill Lincoln Handicap (Doncaster)	*John Crofts*	303
William Hill November Handicap (Thirsk)	*A. Russell*	315
William Hill Sprint Championship (York)	*A. Russell*	159
Windfields Farm EBF Gallinule Stakes (the Curragh)	*Caroline Norris*	699
Windsor Castle Stakes (Ascot)	*A. Russell*	681
Wokingham Stakes (Handicap (Ascot)	*John Crofts*	526

ETALONS
1990

- **Stallion review**
- **Racing and Breeding Chronicles**
- **Statistics and Results**
  of the main sales of the year
- **Results of the 1989 Group Races**
- **Register of all stallions standing**
  in France in 1989.

NAME ....

ADDRESS ....

TOWN ....

COUNTRY ....

would like to receive (   ) copy (ies) of ETALONS 1990
at the unit price of 150 FF + 50 FF for p & p
Kindly complete and mail to :
ETALONS, 6, rond-point des Champs-Elysées, 75008 Paris, France.
Tel. : (1) 43.59.94.14. Telex : 648 665 Etalons. Fax : 42 25 44 25

☐ attached payment by check in French Francs at the order of **ETALONS**
☐ wishes to pay by charge card
☐ Visa   ☐ Mastercard

Card number _____

Expiration date _____ Signature

THE Racegoers CLUB

(The official representative of the interests of all racegoers and punters on the Horseracing Advisory Council)

★ Reduced admission to racecourses. From £1 to £3 off Tattersalls prices on more than 400 racing days. (Available also to Club Enclosure on many courses.)

★ Visits to studs, stables and other racing organisations.

★ Pioneers of Ownership Groups.

★ Racing trips at home and abroad.

★ Quarterly glossy magazine 'The Racegoer'.

★ Big money sweepstakes — prize money up to £10,000.

GET MORE FUN OUT OF RACING — JOIN THE RACEGOERS CLUB. FOR JUST £10 IT'S THE BEST VALUE IN RACING TODAY.

I wish to become a member of The Racegoers Club and, if elected, will abide by the Rules. I enclose £10* subscription which I understand will be returned in the event of non-election.
*£15 for two members resident at the same address.

NAME ....

ADDRESS ....

....

.... POST CODE ....

Send to: THE RACEGOERS CLUB, Flagstaff House, High Street, Twyford, Berks RG10 9AE.

EXPLANATORY NOTES

To assess the prospects of any horse in a race it is necessary to know two things about him: first, how good he is; and second, what sort of horse he is. In this book the merit of each horse is expressed in the form of a *rating* (printed on the right) and the *racing character* of the horse is given in the commentary.

TIMEFORM RATINGS

The Timeform Rating of a horse is simply the merit of the horse expressed in pounds. More precisely it is *the number of pounds which, in our opinion, the horse would be entitled to receive in an average Free Handicap.* Thus, a horse which we regard as worth 9st 7lb in an average Free Handicap, i.e., 133 lb, would receive a rating of 133: and one regarded as worth 8 st (112 lb) would receive a rating of 112; and so on.

This explains what the ratings are; but of course individual ratings are not actually allocated in this way, merely by "inspection". The rating of any horse is a result of careful examination of its running against other horses. We maintain a "running" handicap of all horses in training throughout the season, or, to be strictly accurate, two handicaps, one for horses aged three years and over, and one for two-year-olds.

THE LEVEL OF THE RATINGS

At the close of each season all the horses that have raced are re-handicapped from scratch, and each horse's rating is revised. It is also necessary to adjust the general level of the handicap, so that the mean of all the ratings is kept at the same standard level from year to year. Left to itself, the general level of the ratings, in each succeeding issue of Timeform, tends to rise steadily. For technical reasons it is desirable to allow it to do so during the season: but, in winter, when the complete re-handicap is done, the ratings must, of course, be put back on their proper level again.

This explains why, in this book, the ratings are in general, different from those in the final issue of the 1989 Timeform series.

RATINGS AND WEIGHT-FOR-AGE

These matters, however, are by the way. What concerns the reader is that he has, in the ratings in this book, a universal handicap embracing all the horses in training it is possible to weigh up, ranging from tip-top classic performers, with ratings from 130 to 145, down to the meanest selling platers, rated around the 30 or 40 mark. What we now have to explain is the practical use of these ratings in the business of weighing up a race.

Before doing so, it is important to mention that all ratings are at weight-for-age, so that equal ratings mean horses of equal merit: perhaps it would be clearer if we said that the universal rating handicap is really not a single handicap, but four handicaps side by side: one for 2-y-o's, one for 3-y-o's, one for 4-y-o's and one for older horses. Thus, a 3-y-o rated, for argument's sake, at 117 is deemed to be identical in point of "merit" with a 4-y-o also rated at 117: but for them to have equal chances in, say, a mile race in June, the 3-y-o would need to be receiving 13 lb from the 4-y-o, which is the weight difference specified by the Age, Weight and Distance Table on the page facing the front cover. However, let us to cases!

USING THE RATINGS

In using Timeform Ratings with a view to discovering which horses in any race have the best chances at the weights, we have two distinct cases, according to whether the horses taking part are of the same age or of different ages. Here is the procedure in each case:—

A. Horses of the Same Age

If the horses all carry the same weight there are no adjustments to be made, and the horses with the highest ratings have the best chances. If the horses carry different weights, jot down their ratings, and to the rating of each horse add one point for every pound the horse is set to carry less than 10 st, or subtract one point for every pound he has to carry more than 10 st. When the ratings have been adjusted in this way the highest resultant figure indicates the horse with the best chance at the weights.

Example (any distance: any month of the season)

2 Good Girl (9-6)	....	Rating 119	....	add 8 127
2 Paulinus (9-4)	....	Rating 113	....	add 10 123
2 Abilene (8-11)	....	Rating 107	....	add 17 124
2 Bob's Joy (8-7)	....	Rating 108	....	add 21 129
2 Time Warp (8-2)	....	Rating 100	....	add 26 126
2 Eagle Eye (7-7)	....	Rating 92	....	add 35 127

Bob's Joy (129) has the best chance; Good Girl (127) and Eagle Eye (127) are the next best.

B. Horses of Different Ages

Take no notice of the weight any horse receives from any other. Instead, consult the Age, Weight and Distance Table on the page facing the front cover. Treat each horse separately, and compare the weight it has to carry with the weight prescribed for it in the table, according to the age of the horse, the distance of the race and the month of the year. Then, add one point to the rating for each pound the horse has to carry less than the weight given in the table: or, subtract one point from the rating for every pound he has to carry more than the weight prescribed by the table. The highest resultant figure indicates the horse most favoured by the weights.

Example (1½ miles in July)

(Table Weights: 5-y-o 10-0; 4-y-o 9-13; 3-y-o 8-11)

6 Nimitz (9-12)	....	Rating 115	....	add 2.	 117
4 Red Devil (9-9)	....	Rating 114	....	add 4	 118
6 Sweet Cindy (9-5)	....	Rating 115	....	add 9	 124
3 Jailhouse (8-12)	....	Rating 120	....	subtract 1	..119
4 Haakon (8-11)	....	Rating 101	....	add 16	 117
3 Fine Strike (8-7)	....	Rating 112	....	add 4	 116

Sweet Cindy (124) has the best chance at the weights, with 5 lb in hand of Jailhouse.

JOCKEYSHIP AND APPRENTICE ALLOWANCES

There is just one further point that arises in evaluating the chances of the horse on the basis of their ratings: the question of jockeyship in general, and apprentice allowances in particular. The allowance which may be claimed by an apprentice is given to enable apprentices to obtain race-riding experience against experienced jockeys. For the purposes of rating calculations it should, in general, be assumed that the allowance the apprentice is able to claim (3 lb, 5 lb, or 7 lb) is nullified by his or her inexperience. Therefore, the *weight adjustments to the ratings should be calculated on the weight allotted by the handicapper, or determined by the conditions of the race,* and no extra addition should be made to a rating because the horse's rider claims an apprentice allowance.

The above is the general routine procedure. But of course there is no reason why the quality of jockeyship should not be taken into account in assessing the chances of horses in a race. Quite the contrary. Nobody would question that the jockeyship of a first-class rider is worth a pound or two, and occasionally an apprentice comes along who is riding quite as well as the average jockey long before losing the right to claim. There is no reason whatever why, after the age and weight adjustments have been made to the ratings, small additional allowances should not be made for these matters of jockeyship. This, however, is a matter which must be left to the discretion of the reader.

WEIGHING UP A RACE

It having been discovered, by means of the ratings, which horses in a particular race are most favoured by the weights, complete analysis demands that the racing character of each horse, as set out in the commentary upon it, shall be checked to see if there is any reason why the horse might be expected not to run up to its rating. It counts for little that a horse is thrown in at the weights if it has no pretensions whatever to staying the distance, or is unable to act on the prevailing going.

These two matters, suitability of distance and going, are no doubt the most important points to be considered. But there are others. For example, the ability of a horse to accommodate himself to the conformation of the track. Then there is the matter of pace versus stamina: as between two stayers of equal merit, racing over a distance suitable to both, firm going, or a small field with the prospect of a slowly-run race, would favour the one with the better pace and acceleration, whereas dead or soft going, or a big field with the prospect of a strong gallop throughout the race, would favour the sounder stayer. There is also the matter of temperament and behaviour at the start: nobody would be in a hurry to take a short price about a horse with whom it is always an even chance whether he will consent to race or not.

A few minutes spent checking up on these matters in the commentaries upon the horses concerned will sometimes put a very different complexion on a race from that which is put upon it by the ratings alone. We repeat, therefore, that the correct way to use Timeform, or this annual volume, in the analysis of individual races is, first to use the ratings to discover which horses are most favoured by the weights, and second, to check through the comments on the horse to discover what factors other than weight might also affect the outcome of the race.

Incidentally, in setting out the various characteristics, requirements and peculiarities of each horse in the commentary upon him, we have always expressed ourselves in as critical a manner as possible, endeavouring to say just as much, and no whit more than the facts seem to warrant. Where there are clear indications, and definite conclusions can be drawn with fair certainty, we have drawn them: if it is a matter of probability or possibility we have put it that way, being careful not to say the one when we mean the other; and where real conclusions are not to be drawn, we have been content to state the facts. Furthermore, when we say that a horse *may not* be suited by hard going, we do not expect the reader to treat it as though we had said that the horse *is not* suited by hard going. In short, both in our thinking and in the setting out of our views we have aimed at precision.

THE FORM SUMMARIES

The form summary enclosed in the brackets shows for each individual horse the distance, the state of the going and where the horse finished in each of its races on the flat during the last two seasons. Performances are in chronological sequence, the earliest being given first.

The distance of each race is given in furlongs, fractional distances being expressed in the decimal notation to the nearest tenth of a furlong. Races on an all-weather surface are prefixed by letter 'a'.

The going is symbolised as follows: h = hard or very firm; f = firm; m = fairly good, or on the firm side of good; g = good (turf) or standard (all-weather); d = dead, or on the soft side of good; s = soft, sticky or holding; v = heavy, very heavy or very holding.

Placings are indicated, up to sixth place, by the use of superior figures, an asterisk being used to denote a win.

Thus [1988 NR 1989 10s* 12f³ 11.7g a11g²] signifies that the horse was unraced in 1988. He ran four times in 1989, winning over 10 furlongs on soft going first time out, finishing third over twelve furlongs on firm going next time out, unplaced, not in the first six, over 11.7 furlongs on good going, and then second over eleven furlongs on standard going on an all-weather track.

Included in the pedigree details are the highest Timeform Annual ratings during their racing careers of the sires, dams and sires of dams of all horses, where the information is available.

Where sale prices are given F denotes the price in guineas sold as a foal, Y the price in guineas sold as a yearling. The prefix IR denotes Irish guineas.

THE RATING SYMBOLS

The following symbols, attached to the ratings, are to be interpreted as stated:-

p   the horse is likely to make more than normal progress and to improve on his rating.

P   there is convincing evidence, or, to say the least, a very strong presumption that the horse is capable of form much better than he has so far displayed.

+   the horse may be rather better than we have rated him.

d   the horse appears to have deteriorated, and might no longer be capable of running to the rating given.

§   a horse of somewhat unsatisfactory temperament; one who may give his running on occasions, but cannot be relied upon to do so.

§§ an arrant rogue or thorough jade; so temperamentally unsatisfactory as to be not worth a rating.

?   if used in conjunction with a rating this symbol implies that the rating is based upon inadequate or unsatisfactory data, upon form which it is impossible to assess with confidence. The use of a query without a rating implies that although the horse has form, his merit cannot be assessed on the data at present available.

Timeform Racing Publications

Ahead of the field

RACEHORSES OF 1989

Horse	Commentary	Rating

AAARGH 3 b.f. The Brianstan 128–Miss Binki (Great Nephew 126) [1988 8s 7g — 6g 1989 8.2m] angular filly: little worthwhile form in quite modest company. *M. W. Eckley.*

AAHSAYLAD 3 b.c. Ardross 134–Madam Slaney 92 (Prince Tenderfoot (USA) **65** 126) [1988 10d 8g 8m⁵ 1989 11f 11s 12g 12g⁴ 11g³] big, good-topped colt: quite modest form: off course 4½ months after reappearance: will stay beyond 1½m: acts on top-of-the-ground. *F. H. Lee.*

AARDVARK 3 ch.g. On Your Mark 125–Vaguely Jade (Corvaro (USA) 122) [1988 **75** 6g* 7g⁵ 6s 7f 7g 1989 7g 8.5d 8m* 8m* 8.2g³ 8h* 8g⁴ᵈⁱˢ 8m 8f⁵ 8m⁶ 8g² 7m 9g 11g⁵ 10g] lengthy gelding: good mover: fair performer: won sellers (bought in 5,400 gns then 5,000 gns) at Newmarket and Doncaster in May and handicap at Thirsk in June: below form last 4 outings: suited by 1m: acts on top-of-the-ground and possibly unsuited by a soft surface: genuine. *R. M. Whitaker.*

AARON'S ROD 3 br.c. Mansingh (USA) 120–Belinda Mede 86 (Runnymede — 123) [1988 5g 5d 1989 6s 6m 6f 8m 6g] leggy, quite good-topped colt: poor maiden: blinkered in seller on final start, first for 4 months: should stay 7f. *M. J. Charles.*

AB-ADY 3 b.g. Kafu 120–Gossip (Sharp Edge 123) [1988 5m 5d⁴ 1989 8f] sturdy — gelding: has a quick action: bit backward, well beaten in maidens and minor event: wore tongue strap at 2 yrs. *S. G. Norton.*

ABANAZAR 3 b.g. Sayf El Arab (USA) 127–Fallen Rose (Busted 134) [1988 NR — 1989 5h 6f 7f 12s] 12,000F: smallish gelding: sixth foal: half-brother to smart sprinter Sharp Reminder (by Sharpo) and 1m winner Floating Pearl (by Wollow): dam, half-sister to high-class filly First Bloom, won small 7.5f race in France: no promise in maidens and minor events: sold 1,100 gns Ascot September Sales. *G. Lewis.*

ABBERTON 3 b.f. Ile de Bourbon (USA) 133–Favoridge (USA) 122 (Riva Ridge — (USA)) [1988 6f 6m⁴ 6g⁴ 1989 8m 8g⁶ 7g 9g] small, rather unfurnished filly: easily best effort as 3-y-o in handicap on third outing: takes keen hold, stays 7f: sweating first and final starts: has carried head high and not found much under pressure: sold 66,000 gns Newmarket December Sales. *G. Wragg.*

ABBOTSLEY 3 b.f. Chief Singer 131–Abbeydale 110 (Huntercombe 133) [1988 — p NR 1989 8.2m⁶] big, very tall filly: fifth foal: half-sister to 2 winners, notably leading 1985 2-y-o and 2000 Guineas third Huntingdale (by Double Form): dam second in 1000 Guineas: 14/1, 13 lengths sixth of 17 in maiden at Haydock in September, slowly away, taking keen hold then keeping on steadily not unduly knocked about: should improve. *J. W. Watts.*

ABDERA 4 ch.f. Ahonoora 122–Gentian (Roan Rocket 128) [1988 NR 1989 10.6g] — tall, angular filly: third foal: half-sister to 3-y-o Beltalong (by Belfort), successful over 7.5f and 1½m: dam won at 10.5f in France: pulled hard when well beaten in maiden at Haydock in August: winning novice hurdler. *M. C. Pipe.*

ABEL PROSPECT (USA) 2 b.c. (Feb 8) Mr Prospector (USA)–Able Money — p
(USA) (Distinctive (USA)) [1989 7g] $750,000Y: leggy, quite attractive colt: third
foal: half-brother to a winner in North America by Secretariat: dam high class at 3
yrs in 1983, successful at up to 1¼m: 13/2, never placed to challenge or knocked
about in 28-runner maiden at Newmarket in November: should do better. *G.
Harwood.*

ABIGAIL'S DREAM 2 gr.f. (May 31) Kalaglow 132–Moss Pink (USA) **49**
(Levmoss 133) [1989 6m a8g a6g³] 3,000Y, 7,400 2-y-o: leggy, sparely-made filly:
half-sister to 2 winners, including 7f and 1¾m winner Fanny Robin (by Lucky
Wednesday): dam placed over 5f at 3 yrs in Ireland: poor maiden: 4 lengths third to
Yukosan in claimer at Southwell in December: ran in a seller on debut. *A. N. Lee.*

ABIGAILS PORTRAIT 3 ch.f. Absalom 128–Corr Lady (Lorenzaccio 130) **63**
[1988 NR 1989 7g 6f² 6h³] 14,000Y: sparely-made, angular filly: has a round action:
sixth foal: half-sister to Irish 1¼m winner Tuff Stick (by Welsh Saint), 1m and 9f
winner Miami Star (by Miami Springs) and 2 winners abroad: dam never ran: quite
modest maiden: will be suited by return to 7f: hung left final start (June) and may
prove best on less firm going: on toes, cut hind legs and withdrawn in September:
sold 3,800 gns Newmarket September Sales. *W. Jarvis.*

ABISHAG 3 b.f. Adonijah 126–Siraf 85 (Alcide 136) [1988 6m³ 6m* 6m 7f 6f⁵ 5m **46**
6d 1989 6f 5.3h 6f⁵ 7h 10.1m] workmanlike filly: has a round action: won seller as
2-y-o: worthwhile form since only when fifth in similar event in June: best efforts
over 6f: acts on firm going: has looked temperamentally unsatisfactory: sold 2,500
gns Ascot December Sales. *R. P. C. Hoad.*

A BIT OF ALRIGHT 3 b. or br.f. Lochnager 132–Bunnycraft (The Go-Between **45**
129) [1988 NR 1989 5g² 5m⁴ 5g 5f⁵ 5m 6s⁵ 6g] lengthy filly: third reported living
foal: sister to ungenuine sprint plater Bunnyloch: dam poor maiden: easily best
effort on debut: mostly poor form after, including in sellers: should stay 6f:
blinkered, slowly away and hung under pressure fifth start: sold 1,100 gns Doncaster
November Sales. *J. Etherington.*

ABLE EXPRESS (USA) 2 ch.c. (Apr 28) Miswaki (USA) 124–Ms Balding **78**
(USA) (Sir Ivor 135) [1989 5m* 5m² 5m³ 6f] $14,000Y: rangy, good-bodied colt:
half-brother to 2 minor winners in USA: dam won at up to 9f: won 6-runner maiden
at Newmarket in May: hung left and looked difficult ride final 3 starts, showing fair
form when placed in minor events but never travelling smoothly when in rear in
Coventry Stakes (taken down quietly) at Royal Ascot: should stay 6f: sold 21,000
gns Newmarket Autumn Sales. *W. A. O'Gorman.*

ABLE LEADER 3 b.g. Beldale Flutter (USA) 130–Buckham Barn (Lorenzaccio —
130) [1988 NR 1989 7g 8d 12g⁶ 12f⁵] 3,100F: slightly dipped-backed, good-quartered
gelding: half-brother to a minor winner in France: dam unraced: only sign of ability
when fifth in handicap at Edinburgh in June: unseated rider at stalls before debut:
has joined J. Gifford. *D. T. Thom.*

ABLE MABEL 3 gr.f. Absalom 128–Balidilemma 77 (Balidar 133) [1988 6v* **77** ?
1989 6s* 6d 6m 8m] strong-quartered, workmanlike filly: slowly away all starts,
winning apprentice race at Ripon in April: ran moderately after, finishing lame on
final outing: may stay 7f: goes well in the mud. *Miss S. E. Hall.*

ABLE PLAYER (USA) 2 b. or br.c. (Mar 8) Solford (USA) 127–Grecian Snow **75**
(CAN) (Snow Knight 125) [1989 6g 6f 8g⁴ a7g* a8g] $3,200Y: leggy, quite
good-topped colt: fourth reported named foal: half-brother to 3 winners in North
America: dam ran 3 times: modest performer: won maiden at Southwell in
November by 3 lengths from Sir Nick, making all: needs further than 6f. *Mrs N.
Macauley.*

ABLE ROCKET (USA) 2 b.c. (Feb 8) Shimatoree (USA)–Fast Ride (FR) **69**
(Sicambre 135) [1989 7g a7g² a6g] small, lengthy colt: half-brother to several
winners here and in North America, including Jalmood (by Blushing Groom) and
very smart Flaunter (by High Echelon), stakes winner at up to 1¼m: dam won Prix
Vanteaux: ¾-length second to Majesty's Room in maiden at Southwell in
November, easily best effort. *Mrs N. Macauley.*

ABLE SWINGER 2 b.f. (Mar 30) Jalmood (USA) 126–Cymbal 80 (Ribero 126) —
[1989 6f] small, sturdy filly: half-sister to 1¼m winner Beau Mirage (by Homing)
and a winner abroad by Moulton: dam, half-sister to smart performers Band and
Zimbalon, won 3 of her 5 starts over middle distances: carrying condition, always
behind in 15-runner Hamilton maiden in June. *Mrs N. Macauley.*

ABLE VALE 3 b.f. Formidable (USA) 125–Valeur (Val de Loir 133) [1988 6g 1989 **59**
7s 7m 7m4 8m6 10g5] close-coupled, deep-girthed filly: quite modest form in
maidens third and fourth starts: races keenly, and may well prove best at up to 1m:
sold 4,600 gns Newmarket Autumn Sales. *H. Candy.*

ABOU MINJAL (MOR) 3 ch.g. Asandre (FR)–Honeyou (MOR) (Honey Hot —
(FR)) [1988 NR 1989 8s 12f 12m 17.1f3] second living foal: half-brother to a winner in
Morocco: dam, a winner once in Morocco from 4 starts, is out of a French 1¼m and
1½m winner: third in handicap at Bath in July, only sign of ability: subsequently
gelded. *G. Lewis.*

ABOVE DISPUTE 3 b.f. Cut Above 130–Dare Me 101 (Derring-Do 131) [1988 —
8g 1989 10.1g] lengthy, sparely-made filly: never dangerous in maiden at Leicester
and minor event (hung left) at Windsor. *Major W. R. Hern.*

ABRIGO 2 b.c. (Feb 25) Aragon 118–Poshteen 86 (Royal Smoke 113) [1989 6g] **62** p
fourth reported living foal: half-brother to winning stayer/hurdler Capa (by New
Member): dam 2-y-o 5f winner: 50/1, very burly and green, around 10 lengths
seventh of 9 finishers to Tirol in minor event at Doncaster in September. *O. O'Neill.*

ABSALAMB 3 gr.f. Absalom 128–Caroline Lamb 74 (Hotfoot 126) [1988 6d5 6g4 —
6m4 1989 7f 7f 8.2g 9m] neat filly: keen walker: has a roundish action: quite modest
maiden at 2 yrs: no form in handicaps and claimer in 1989: best form at 6f: possibly
unsuited by very firm going. *Miss S. E. Hall.*

ABSENT LOVER 8 ch.m. Nearly A Hand 115–Straight Avenue 62 (Royal —
Avenue 123) [1988 10v6 12d6 10d2 10m* 10m 9g6 10g4 10m 1989 10.2g] workmanlike
mare: poor mover: quite modest handicapper as 7-y-o: not discredited when eighth
of 30 in amateurs contest at Doncaster in March, only outing in 1989: stays 1½m:
probably not ideally suited by very firm going, acts on any other: has started slowly.
F. J. Yardley.

ABSOLUTELY HUMMING 3 ch.g. Absalom 128–Hum 69 (Crooner 119) **70**
[1988 6f3 5f2 5m* 5d2 5g3 6g 6m 5d 1989 5m 6f 5g 5f4 8f2 8.3m a7g] lengthy,
good-quartered gelding: modest handicapper: set modest pace in 3-runner event at
Warwick: never dangerous otherwise: off course 4½ months before final outing:
probably stays 1m: acts on top-of-the-ground and a soft surface: has been bandaged
near-hind: bought out of G. Pritchard-Gordon's stable 10,000 gns Ascot July Sales
after fifth start. *J. Sutcliffe.*

ABSOLUTELY PERFECT 2 ch.c. (Apr 3) Absalom 128–Petalina 93 **89**
(Mummy's Pet 125) [1989 5s2 5m3 6f* 6m* 6m5 6m2 6m2 6.3g3] 13,000F, 40,000Y:
good-quartered colt: half-brother to fairly useful sprinter Ardrox Lad (by Roi Soleil):
dam 2-y-o 5f winner who failed to train on: fair performer: successful in maiden at
Brighton in May and minor event at Catterick following month: ran well final 3
starts, on final one fourth of 10, promoted, to Single Combat in pattern event at the
Curragh: better suited by 6f than 5f: visored seventh start: tends to hang left. *J. P.
Hudson.*

ABSOLUTELY TAYLOR 2 ch.f. (Apr 24) Absalom 128–Djimbaran Bay (Le **48**
Levanstell 122) [1989 7m 8m 7g6 8.2f 8f 8g] 6,400Y: leggy, angular filly: half-sister
to many winners here and abroad, including useful 1¼m winner Bettyknowes (by
Satingo) and fair 6f winner Portvasco (by Sharpo): dam won at up to 1¼m in France:
plating-class form in varied events: soundly beaten in selling nursery final start:
sold 800 gns Newmarket December Sales. *H. J. Collingridge.*

ABSOLUTE MADNESS 2 ch.g. (Feb 18) Absalom 128–Chezzy Girl (Manor **52**
Farm Boy 114) [1989 5v 5s 5m5 5m5 5f4 6m6 5f 6g] 1,000F, 10,000Y: good-bodied
gelding: first foal: dam, poor on flat, placed over hurdles: plating-class maiden: ran
moderately when sweating or blinkered on last 3 outings: sold 1,700 gns
Newmarket Autumn Sales. *M. J. Fetherston-Godley.*

ABSOLUTE STAR 2 gr.f. (Feb 28) Absalom 128–Star Display (Sparkler 130) —
[1989 5s 5d 5f 6m] 3,200Y: compact, workmanlike filly: keen walker: fourth foal:
half-sister to 3-y-o Avonmouthsecretary and 1¼m winner Gloss (both by Town And
Country): dam ran twice in Ireland: towards rear in auction events and sellers: sold
1,600 gns Doncaster June Sales. *C. Tinkler.*

ABSOLUTE STEAL 3 ro.f. Absalom 128–Thorganby Victory 82 (Burglar 128) **49**
[1988 6f4 7m* 7d5 7g6 8.2s 7m2 1989 7d 6m4 8.2f5 8m 8g* 8h4 7m 8f5] workmanlike
filly: dropped to selling company, made all at Edinburgh (bought in 6,400 gns) in
July: stays 1m: acts on hard ground. *W. J. Pearce.*

ABSOLUTION 5 gr.h. Absalom 128–Great Grey Niece 74 (Great Nephew 126) **97**
[1988 5. 1f3 5m4 5d6 5s6 5g* 6g4 6d 5m4 5m2 5g4 5d* 5d5 5s* 1989 5f* 5f3 5f2 5g4

29

6m[6] 5g[3] 5m[3] 5m[3] 6f 5g* 5g[5]] workmanlike, good-quartered horse: has shown traces of stringhalt: moderate walker and mover: fairly useful handicapper: had good season, winning at Chester in May and Haydock in August: beat stable-companion Kabcast a length in competitive £8,100 Coral Bookmakers Handicap at Haydock: unseated rider and bolted on intended reappearance: best at 5f: acts on any going: has won for apprentice: blinkered once at 4 yrs: gave bit of trouble at stalls first 2 starts: game and consistent. *D. W. Chapman.*

ABSONAL 2 gr.c. (Mar 6) Absalom 128–Aldbury Girl 79 (Galivanter 131) [1989 **45** 5s[4] 5d[3] 5g[5]] 16,000Y: strong, good-topped colt: has scope: half-brother to sprint winners by Decoy Boy and Music Boy: dam 2-y-o 5.9f winner: carrying condition, in frame in maiden at Kempton and minor event at Folkestone: not seen out after April: will probably be better suited by 6f. *R. Hannon.*

ABSTONE LAD 2 b.g. (May 26) Blazing Saddles (AUS)–Abbey Rose 84 **47** (Lorenzaccio 130) [1989 5m[4] 6g 6m[4] 7g] 1,250F, 1,700Y: leggy gelding: half-brother to 3-y-o Burtonwoods Best (by Longleat) and 2 winners by Cawston's Clown, including middle-distance plater Arclid Girl: dam second over 7f and 1m at 2 yrs: poor maiden: has run in a seller: sweating final start: has joined A. W. Jones. *W. W. Haigh.*

ABS (USA) 2 b.c. (Mar 6) Nureyev (USA) 131–Reyah 83 (Young Generation 129) **90** [1989 7g[3] 7g* 7g[5]] small, stocky colt: has a fluent, slightly round action: first foal: dam 6f and 8.2f winner: won 10-runner maiden at Leicester in September in good style by 5 lengths from Barakish: respectable fifth of 7 to Free At Last in listed race at Newmarket following month: will stay 1m. *H. Thomson Jones.*

ACAPULCO 4 b.g. May Music Boy 124–Louise 71 (Royal Palace 131) [1988 6v[5] 5g[4] **—** 7.5m 7.5f[2] 7m[3] 7f[5] 7g 7.5g[3] 7g* 7g 6g[6] 8m 8.2s 1989 8s] good-topped gelding: moderate mover: well below form since winning claimer at Ayr as 3-y-o: suited by 7f: acts on firm going: found little eighth appearance as 3-y-o: visored next 2: seems untrustworthy: sold 1,150 gns Doncaster June Sales. *Ronald Thompson.*

ACCESS CRUISE (USA) 2 ch.c. (Mar 18) Wajima (USA)–Lady of Meadowlane **78 p** (USA) (Pancho Jay (USA)) [1989 8m] 9,000Y: tall, leggy, sparely-made colt: first foal: dam won 4 times at up to 9f in USA: sire, champion 3-y-o, stayed at least 1½m: 33/1 and green, around 10 lengths seventh of 8, headed under 3f out, to Treble Eight in maiden at Newmarket in October. *R. Boss.*

ACCESS LEISURE 2 ch.f. (Apr 1) Blushing Scribe (USA) 107–Nonpareil (FR) **87** 92 (Pharly (FR) 130) [1989 5m[6] 6m[2] 5.8m* 6h[2]] 7,800Y: leggy, fair sort: poor walker and mover: second foal: sister to 3-y-o Mister Lawson, fair 5f winner at 2 yrs: dam ran well over 7f on debut at 2 yrs but poorly as 3-y-o: favourite, won temporary auction event at Bath: good second in nursery at Lingfield later in July: tends to carry head high: sent to Italy. *R. Boss.*

ACCESSOFHORNCHURCH 3 ch.g. Coquelin (USA) 121–The Saltings (FR) **78** (Morston (FR) 125) [1988 7m[5] 8.2s[6] 7s* 1989 10d[5] 7m[4] 8f 7s] tall, leggy gelding: modest handicapper: creditable fourth at Newmarket in May, easily best effort as 3-y-o: never placed to challenge after at Newbury (blinkered, got loose at start) then Ayr (carrying head awkwardly) 4 months later: races keenly and may prove suited by 6f: acts on soft going and top-of-the-ground: gelded after third start: sold to join E. H. Owen jun 4,400 gns Doncaster October Sales: not one to trust implicitly. *R. Boss.*

ACCESS SKI 2 b.c. (May 22) Bustino 136–Crimson Lake (FR) 71 (Mill Reef **72** (USA) 141) [1989 7m[3] 8f[2] 8m[3]] 6,000Y: close-coupled, robust colt: easy mover: fourth foal: brother to 3-y-o South London: dam stoutly-bred maiden placed from 1m to 1¼m: fair form in maidens: will stay 1½m. *R. Boss.*

ACCESS SUN 2 b.c. (Mar 16) Pharly (FR) 130–Princesse du Seine (FR) (Val de **96** Loir 133) [1989 8m[5] 8m* 10g[2]] 18,000Y: leggy, quite attractive colt: eighth foal: brother to French 4f to 1m winner Priene and half-brother to fair 1¼m winner Evros (by Kris) and 3-y-o Princesse du Powys (by Caerleon): dam, daughter of very useful Princess Bonita, was placed over 7f and 1m at 2 yrs: won 11-runner maiden auction race at York in October by a short head from Ambrose: always-prominent second of 14, beaten 5 lengths, to Rock Hopper in listed event at Newmarket following month: will stay 1½m. *R. Boss.*

ACCESS TRAVEL 3 b.c. Auction Ring (USA) 123–Lady Tippins (USA) 83 (Star **109 §** de Naskra (USA)) [1988 5m[4] 6s* 6g* 5g[2] 6d 6g* 6g[3] 5g 1989 6g[3] 6g[3] 5m[3] 6m[5] 5f 6m 5g[3]] small, sturdy colt: poor mover in slow paces: useful on his day but of doubtful temperament: best efforts third in 5f Palace House Stakes (always front rank) at Newmarket in May and listed event (never going that well, staying on from mid-division) at Doncaster in September: ran poorly in listed races and pattern event in between: best form at 5f on a sound surface: blinkered last 5 outings, and last 3 at 2 yrs when putting up best effort blinkered first time: carries head high: not an easy ride or one to trust. *R. Boss.*

ACHNAHUAIGH 5 ch.m. Known Fact (USA) 135–Djimbaran Bay (Le **33** Levanstell 122) [1988 9g 12f 8f* 9g 8f 8.3m⁵ 8f³ 8d⁵ 1989 11.7d 10.2h⁵ 8g] lengthy mare: poor plater: probably stays 1¼m: acts on hard going and a soft surface: on toes and took good hold last 2 starts: inconsistent. *J. M. Bradley.*

ACK VA VITE (USA) 3 b.f. Ack Ack (USA)–Fleet Arada (USA) (Fleet **85** Nasrullah) [1988 6g 8s³ 1989 8.5d 8f² 8m* 9f⁵ 8.2d] leggy filly: fair handicapper: easily best efforts when second at Newbury and comfortably justifying favouritism at Leicester in May: should be suited by 1¼m + : acts on firm going: takes keen hold. *M. R. Stoute.*

ACONITUM 8 b.g. Fair Season 120–The Yellow Girl 102 (Yellow God 129) [1988 **65** § 8d* 8g 7.6v 8.5m 8f 8f⁶ 9s 10d 1989 8s 9v² 9f 8f⁵ 8m* a8g a7g a10g⁴ a11g⁵] strong gelding: carries plenty of condition: ran well as 8-y-o when second in girl apprentices handicap at Kempton and in selling handicap (awarded race on technicality) at Yarmouth: twice refused to race in 1988 and was very reluctant to do so on first and fourth outings in 1989: best form at around 1m: probably acts on any going: usually taken quietly to post: visored twice at 7 yrs: goes well with forcing tactics: ungenuine, and thoroughly untrustworthy. *J. R. Jenkins.*

ACORN HOLLOW 4 b.g. Lomond (USA) 128–Fair Abode (Habitat 134) [1988 **—** 10m⁶ 10g⁵ 10g 1989 10. 1m] small gelding: well beaten: blinkered final appearance at 3 yrs. *N. Kernick.*

ACROSS THE BAY 2 ch.c. (Mar 2) Krayyan 117–Siofra Beag (Steel Heart 128) **87** [1989 5s² 5g⁴ 5.3m* 6f² 6g² 6m³ 5f⁵ 6f² 5m 6g 5m³ 5m⁴ 6v] IR 9,600F, IR 4,000Y, resold 6,400Y: close-coupled colt: carries condition: moderate walker: has a quick, rather round action: fourth foal: brother to moderate 1987 2-y-o 6f and 7f winner Lead On Henry and half-brother to 7.6f and 1m winner Wizzard Magic (by Ahonoora): dam ran twice in Ireland: fair colt: progressed after winning maiden at Brighton in May until running poorly, giving impression possibly something amiss, in nursery at Newbury final start: stays 6f: often on toes: got loose before fourth start. *S. Dow.*

ACROW LINE 4 b.g. Capricorn Line 111–Miss Acrow (Comedy Star (USA) 12 1) **42** [1988 12f 7m 10.2f 1989 10.2h 12m 10g³ 13.1h³ 14m* 14m 12m] stocky gelding: apprentice ridden at overweight, showed improved form when winning handicap at Salisbury in August: ran badly last 2 starts: suited by 1¾m: possibly unsuited by very firm going: has run creditably for amateur: often sweats, very much on edge on reappearance. *J. C. Fox.*

ACROW LORD 2 b.c. (Apr 25) Milford 119–Miss Acrow (Comedy Star (USA) **65** p 12 1) [1989 8m 8g] medium-sized, close-coupled, quite good-bodied colt: fourth foal: half-brother to winning stayer Acrow Line (by Capricorn Line): dam, half-sister to smart Hillandale, showed little ability: not knocked about in maidens at Newmarket (kept on steadily) in October and Leicester (ridden by 7-lb claimer) following month: will do better. *W. Jarvis.*

ACTINIUM (FR) 6 br.h. Labus (FR)–Activity (FR) (Montevideo) [1988 14d 1989 **80** § 16.2m³ 14f² 16m] big, rangy horse: moderate mover with a quick action: fairly useful handicapper at his best: lightly raced since 4 yrs: found little under pressure last 2 outings: stays extreme distances: has form on firm going, but possibly suited by an easier surface nowadays: wears bandages: has won for amateur: sometimes sweats: lazy sort: best treated with caution. *J. R. Jenkins.*

ACTRESS 3 b.f. Known Fact (USA) 135–Tin Tessa 87 (Martinmas 128) [1988 6g⁵ **73** 6m 6s 5d³ 5m 1989 6s³ 6d 8g 7f* 7m* 8f³ 7g⁵ 7m] good-bodied, angular filly: modest handicapper: successful at Thirsk in May and Leicester in June: ran creditably at Ascot (£9,200 event) and Newmarket next 2 starts: stays 1m: acts on any going: goes well with forcing tactics: game. *J. Wharton.*

ADAMLYI (USA) 3 ch.c. Sharpen Up 127–Blondy (VEN) (Lord Gayle (USA) **87** 124) [1988 6d 1989 7f 10.1m⁵ 11.7m* 10g² 12.3f⁴ 11.5g* 12m] leggy, rather unfurnished colt: fair handicapper: won at Windsor in July and Yarmouth in September: ran moderately final outing: suited by 1½m: looked unsuited by very firm ground when running poorly fifth start: sold 27,000 gns Newmarket Autumn Sales. *R. W. Armstrong.*

ADANAR (USA) 2 gr.c. (Feb 27) Irish River (FR) 13 1–Adjanada 108 (Nishapour **56** (FR) 125) [1989 5f³ 6m⁵ a8g a7g] compact, rather shallow-girthed colt: first foal:

dam, 7f winner, from family of Blushing Groom: plating-class maiden: stays 1m: sold out of L. Cumani's stable 8,000 gns Newmarket September Sales after second appearance. *R. Hannon.*

ADBASS (USA) 4 b. or br.c. Northern Dancer–Somfas (USA) (What A Pleasure **80** (USA)) [1988 7g² 8.2d² 7f* 8f³ 1989 7g⁵ 8g⁴] compact, workmanlike, attractive colt: has a quick action: won minor event at Brighton as 3-y-o when trained by H. Cecil: beaten under 6 lengths in listed race at Leopardstown and apprentice event at Ascot (kicked in stalls) in 1989: stayed 1m: acted on any going: retired at Dockenfield Stud, Surrey, fee £1,000 (Oct 1st) to winning mares or £1,500 nfnf. *G. A. Huffer.*

ADDING (USA) 2 ch.c. (Feb 6) Summing (USA)–Miss Zadig 102 (Thatch (USA) **92** 136) [1989 7m⁴ 7m 8g² 8.2d² 10g² 10g*] smallish, quite well-made colt: third reported foal: half-brother to modest 10.4f winner Timid Bride (by Blushing Groom) and a winner in North America: dam 5f and 1m winner: fairly useful performer: thrice beaten a short head before winning 18-runner minor event at Redcar in November readily by 5 lengths from Hot Rumour: will stay 1½m: strong-running sort. *G. Harwood.*

ADDISON'S BLADE 2 b.c. (Jan 31) Pas de Seul 133–Addison's Jubilee 73 **87** (Sparkler 130) [1989 5f⁵ 5m* 5f² 5g 6g⁴ 6m⁶ 6m 6g 7d⁶] compact colt: carries condition: poor mover: third reported foal: half-brother to 3-y-o 1m and 9f winner Slender Bender (by Gorytus) and 9f winner Ci Siamo (by Formidable): dam, half-sister to smart 7f to 1m winner Kashmir Love, won over 1m and 1¼m: fair performer: made all in maiden at Thirsk in May: ran very well when over 10 lengths seventh of 25 to Osario in Racecall Gold Trophy at Redcar on eighth start: suited by 6f: edgy and went very freely down fourth outing: inconsistent. *M. Johnston.*

ADJARAYN 4 b.g. Top Ville 129–Adayra (FR) (Le Haar 126) [1988 8m⁶ 12f⁵ 12f⁵ — 12f* 12.3f⁴ 12m 14m 1989 11.7d 14m 12g] sturdy, quite attractive gelding: moderate mover: well below form since making all in Edinburgh handicap as 3-y-o: tailed off in ladies handicap and seller last 2 outings: stays 1½m: acts on firm going: sometimes visored. *J. R. Jenkins.*

ADJRIYNA 3 b.f. Top Ville 129–Adjarida (Red God 128§) [1988 6g² 1989 8s³ 7m² **82** 8.5m* 8f⁵] tall, rather leggy filly: won £12,300 handicap at Epsom in June, making most: ran creditably facing stiffish task in £7,300 handicap at Goodwood 6 weeks later, leading 5f: may well stay further: acts on any going. *M. R. Stoute.*

ADMIRAL BYNG (FR) 2 ch.c. (Feb 11) Caerleon (USA) 132–Pig Tail 98 **77** (Habitat 134) [1989 7g 7d⁴] 50,000Y: workmanlike colt: second foal: dam, lightly-raced 7f winner, is sister to useful 6f and 8.5f winner Petroleuse and half-sister to outstanding middle-distance filly Pawneese: around 4 lengths fourth of 11, one pace last 2f, to Bold Performer in minor event at Thirsk in November: backward on debut: will stay 1¼m. *H. R. A. Cecil.*

ADMIRALTY WAY 3 b.g. Petorius 117–Captive Flower 99 (Manacle 123) [1988 **77** § 5d⁴ 6f 6s³ 5m³ 5g 1989 7g* 7g³ 7g⁵ 6m⁴ 7f⁵ 8.2m 9f⁴ 8.2d⁴ 8s 7f² 8g a8g* a7g³] leggy, quite attractive gelding: modest handicapper: won at Newcastle in March and Southwell in November: not discredited most outings in between but has looked reluctant: probably stays 9f: acts on firm going: visored fourth and fifth outings: pulled hard when blinkered third start (was also twice at 2 yrs) and sweating seventh: trained first 9 by J. W. Watts: one to treat with caution. *M. O'Neill.*

ADORABLE CHERUB (USA) 2 b.f. (Jan 14) Halo (USA)–Ma Petite Jolie **58** (USA) 80 (Northern Dancer) [1989 6f⁵ 6h⁴ 7m 7m⁶ 7g] small, sturdy filly: moderate mover: first foal: dam 7f winner, is half-sister to top-class North American filly Glorious Song, successful 17 times at up to 1¼m, and best 1983 American 2-y-o Devil's Bag (both by Halo): plating-class maiden: bred to stay at least 1m: ridden by 7-lb claimer first and third starts. *M. R. Stoute.*

ADORING MAN 4 b.g. Taufan (USA) 119–Adorit 76 (Habat 127) [1988 8.3m — 1989 a10g a12g] medium-sized, attractive gelding: moderate mover: fair maiden at 2 yrs: behind in handicaps, only 3 subsequent outings: stays 7f: best effort on firm going: wears bandages. *A. Bailey.*

ADVANCE TO GO 2 ch.f. (Feb 8) Horage 124–La Bellilote (Ridan (USA)) **42** [1989 5s⁵ 5d² 5g⁴ 5m] IR 2,000Y, resold 3,400Y: lengthy filly: moderate mover: third foal: half-sister to Irish 3-y-o 1½m winner Miss Cecconi (by Simply Great) and a winner in Belgium: dam fairly useful Irish 2-y-o 5f winner: poor maiden: not seen out after July: sweating final start. *J. Wharton.*

ADVIE BRIDGE 2 ch.f. (Mar 6) High Line 125–Marypark 93 (Charlottown 127) **81** [1989 8g* 8.2g³] angular filly: half-sister to several middle-distance winners, including useful pair Loch Seaforth (by Tyrnavos) and Rynechra (by Blakeney), and fairly useful stayer Halba (by Habat): dam well suited by long distances: favourite, won 15-runner maiden at Leicester in September by 1½ lengths from Lady of Persia after swerving left stalls: under 3 lengths third of 20, keeping on one pace, to Elmuraqash in minor event at Nottingham following month: will stay 1½m: strong-running sort. *H. R. A. Cecil.*

AEROBICS PLUS 3 b.c. Alzao (USA) 117–Princess Kofiyah 72 (High Line 125) **89**
[1988 6d² 6f 7m³ 7f 7d⁴ 1989 10m* 10m³ 10m² 12g 10.6d] small, sparely-made, angular colt: fairly useful handicapper: won claimer at Newbury in June: ran creditably next 2 outings, hanging left and no extra final 1f on second of them: took keen hold and below form after, tailed off final start: stays 1¼m: acts on top-of-the-ground and a soft surface: sold to race in Middle East 33,000 gns Newmarket Autumn Sales. *J. A. R. Toller.*

AFAFF (USA) 2 b.f. (Apr 9) Nijinsky (CAN) 138–Continual (USA) (Damascus **— p**
(USA)) [1989 6g] sixth foal: sister to 2000 Guineas winner Shadeed and half-sister to 9f winner Basoof (by Believe It): dam, successful at 6f and 7f, is sister to Tuerta, the dam of Kentucky Derby and Belmont Stakes winner Swale: 3/1, ran better than seventh-of-17 position suggests in maiden at Folkestone in October, eased when beaten approaching 1f out: bred to stay 1¼m. *M. R. Stoute.*

AFFIRMATION 2 b.f. (Apr 9) Tina's Pet 121–Affirmative 96 (Derring-Do 131) **72 p**
[1989 5g*] eighth reported foal: half-sister to 4 winners, including fairly useful miler Teamwork (by Workboy) and fair middle-distance winner/useful hurdler Convinced (by Busted): dam won 9 times at around 1m: 16/1, won 10-runner maiden at Sandown in September by a length from Katzakeena, running on strongly having been outpaced: should improve. *J. W. Hills.*

AFRICAN AFFAIR 4 br.g. Be My Native (USA) 122–Moment of Weakness 76 **50 §**
(Pieces of Eight 128) [1988 8.5m⁵ 8.2m⁵ 8m 10f⁴ 10m 9m* 8g² 10m⁶ 10m* 8.5f 10m² 10g 1989 10d 9f 9f⁶ 10m³ 11f⁵ 10f³ 12f² 12f³ 8.5m³ 11g³ 10.2g 10f] neat gelding: poor walker: irresolute plater: stays 1½m: acts on firm going: has often hung, and doesn't find much under pressure. *R. M. Whitaker.*

AFRICAN CHIEF 2 b.c. (Apr 27) Kafu 120–Kilfenora (Tribal Chief 125) [1989 **89**
5m³ 6m⁴ 6m* 6m⁴ 6fʷᵒ 8d⁴] 24,000Y: medium-sized, leggy colt: half-brother to a minor winner in USA: dam Irish 2-y-o 5f winner: fair performer: won 5-runner minor event at Chepstow in July by 4 lengths from Mendham: walked over in similar event at Salisbury: remote last of 4 in Country Lady Stardom Stakes at Goodwood on final start: unlikely to stay 1m: sold 28,000 gns Newmarket Autumn Sales. *R. Hannon.*

AFRICAN CHIMES 2 b.c. (Mar 4) Kampala 120–Rynville (Ballymore 123) **—**
[1989 8g] IR 10,500F, IR 27,000Y: useful-looking colt: third foal: dam unraced half-sister to dam of very useful hurdler Asir, and to Irish Derby runner-up Lombardo: 5/1, lost place soon after halfway in 15-runner maiden at Leicester in November. *P. F. I. Cole.*

AFRICAN DASH 3 b.f. African Sky 124–Nibelunga (Miami Springs 121) [1988 **69**
7m³ 1989 7f³ 8f³ 7g 6f* 7g³ 6f 6m] rather unfurnished filly: led post in maiden at Brighton in August: creditable third at Epsom, easily best effort in handicaps after: may prove ideally suited by 7f: acts on firm going: taken down early second and third starts: trained until after latter by A. Stewart. *R. Akehurst.*

AFRICAN GUEST 2 b.g. (Jan 29) What A Guest 119–Kalaya (Tanerko 134) **52**
[1989 5s² 5v 5.3m⁵ 6h 5.8h⁴] 9,000Y: quite attractive gelding: half-brother to French 3-y-o 11f winner Darroze (by Gorytus) and 3 other winners in France, including middle-distance winner Kalidjar (by Double Form): dam, French provincial 9.5f and 10.5f winner, is half-sister to Kalamoun: plating-class maiden: ran poorly in a seller last start: bred to stay quite well: probably acts on any going. *M. McCormack.*

AFRICAN LASS 5 b.m. Skyliner 117–Mallabee 92 (Pall Mall 132) [1988 5g 8.3m² **43**
6f³ 8g⁴ 8d* 6g* 8m⁵ 1989 8d⁴ 7.5g³] small mare: has a round action: poor handicapper: not seen out after May: effective at 6f and stays 1m well: acts on any going, but well suited by an easy surface: sometimes bandaged: suitable mount for inexperienced rider. *T. Casey.*

AFRICAN LIGHT 3 gr.f. Kalaglow 132–African Dancer 116 (Nijinsky (CAN) **65 §**
138) [1988 NR 1989 10f 10f⁶ 11.5m 10.6m⁶ 12.2m 9g² 10m⁵ 10m] tall, rather leggy filly: good walker and mover: half-sister to fairly useful middle-distance winners Mpani (by Habitat), Dame Ashfield (by Grundy) and On Show (by Welsh Pageant),

last-named also dam of Inchmurrin and Welney: dam won Cheshire Oaks and Park Hill Stakes: capable of modest form on her day: best at up to 1¼m: acts on firm going: led or disputed lead long way in blinkers fourth and fifth outings: awkward at stalls last 2, also on way down on final one: has flashed tail and found nothing under pressure: sold 16,000 gns Newmarket December Sales: of unsatisfactory temperament. *G. Wragg.*

AFRICAN MINSTREL   4 b.c. Longleat (USA) 109–Bewitched 63 (African Sky   —
124) [1988 8g 5f 7.6f 7f 5m 8f⁵ 8d⁴ 1989 15.3m] leggy colt: poor mover: poor maiden: stays 1m: acts on a soft surface: blinkered once at 3 yrs. *R. T. Juckes.*

AFRICAN SAFARI   5 b.g. Daring March 116–African Berry 84 (African Sky 124)   53
[1988 8d 7m 7.6m² 7m⁵ 7g* 7m 7m⁵ 7.3m 7f⁵ 8m 6m² 6g* 7g 1989 6f³ 6f² 6m 6g 6f 7g 6g a6g⁶] tall gelding: has a round action: poor handicapper: stays 7.6f: best on a sound surface: blinkered seventh start: bandaged off-hind on second: often sweats. *P. D. Cundell.*

AFRICAN SPIRIT   5 b.g. African Sky 124–Relic Spirit (Relic) [1988 6d³ 5f⁴ 6f   77
6h² 5d 6d³ 6s 8g* 8s 1989 7.6m 7f⁴ 8f⁵ 8m⁴ 8.5g⁵ 8f³ 7g³ 7g² 7m 8d 8g 10g⁴] good-topped gelding: carries plenty of condition: poor mover: modest handicapper: seems to stay 1¼m: acts on any going: blinkered once: looked none too keen under pressure fourth start: has swished tail: winning hurdler. *R. M. Whitaker.*

AFRICAN SUNSHINE   3 b.f. Kafu 120–Winter Sunshine 76 (Crisp And Even   —
116) [1988 NR 1989 8m] 8,200Y: medium-sized, lengthy filly: fourth foal: sister to 5f and 6f winner The Burden, and half-sister to 1¼m seller winner War Child (by Welsh Chanter): dam won from 6f to 12.2f and stayed 2m: gave lot of trouble at stalls and was withdrawn only appearance as 2-y-o: pulled up lame in maiden at Bath in May. *P. J. Jones.*

AFRIENDDROPPINGIN   2 b.f. (Mar 31) Taufan (USA) 119–Get Ready 91 (On   54
Your Mark 125) [1989 6g⁵ 6g⁴ 6g 6m] leggy filly: sister to fair 1982 2-y-o 6f winner Picaroon and half-sister to several other winners, including high-class sprinter Anita's Prince (by Stradavinsky): dam best at 5f: plating-class maiden: dead. *M. H. Tompkins.*

A FRIEND OF MINE   3 b.g. Noalto 120–Merency 75 (Meldrum 112) [1988 NR   —
1989 10.6g] leggy, rather narrow gelding: fifth reported foal: half-brother to fairly useful 1981 2-y-o 6f winner Tachywaun (by Tachypous), subsequently good winner in Hong Kong, and 1985 2-y-o 6f winner Carribean Time (by Tyrnavos): dam 2-y-o 5f winner: 33/1, bit backward and showed little in Haydock maiden in September. *M. H. Tompkins.*

AFRIYD   3 b.c. Darshaan 133–Afeefa (Lyphard (USA) 132) [1988 8m⁴ 1989 8.5d⁶ 103
10.1m⁵ 10m* 10g⁴ 10.5f² 14f⁴] rather leggy, good-topped colt: good walker: has a quick action: progressive handicapper: favourite, confirmed earlier promise when making all in £7,000 race at Epsom in June: in frame in £27,600 event (ran in snatches) at Sandown and in John Smith's Magnet Cup (neck second to Icona) and Tote Ebor (in superb shape, raced freely and led 4f out until 2f out) at York: gives impression will prove ideally suited by 1½m: acts on firm ground: useful. *M. R. Stoute.*

AFTER THE GLOOM   4 ch.g. Bay Express 132–Heaven And Earth   — §
(Midsummer Night II 117) [1988 8g 8.5m 8m 7.5f 10.2g 8m 10g 7f 1989 16.2m] lengthy, angular gelding: no form on flat for long time and is probably ungenuine: blinkered 3 times: winning selling hurdler. *R. Hollinshead.*

AFWAJ (USA)   3 ch.c. Caro 133–Just A Kick (USA) (Olympiad King (USA)) [1988 102
8m⁴ 8s 1989 10g 8m³ 8f³ 7f* 7m* 7.6f⁵ 7f² 6m* 6m⁶ 6g⁴] rather leggy colt: easy mover: useful handicapper: progressive form when successful at Redcar, Wolverhampton and Newcastle: not discredited in quite valuable events at Haydock and York (wandered under pressure) last 2 starts: probably suited by 6f: acts on firm going. *J. L. Dunlop.*

AGAINST THE FLOW   2 ch.f. (Apr 25) Salmon Leap (USA) 131–Tricky Tracey   —
(Formidable (USA) 125) [1989 7s] 3,400F: second foal: closely related to French 3-y-o 1m winner Trickiest (by Try My Best): dam unraced: 33/1, last of 10 in maiden at Goodwood in September. *M. J. Haynes.*

AGALEION (FR)   2 ch.c. (Feb 10) Esprit du Nord (USA) 126–Algaselle (FR)   75
(Timmy Lad 130) [1989 7g⁴ 8g⁵] 170,000 francs (approx £15,500) Y: big, rather sparely-made colt: has scope: good walker: half-brother to a winner in Italy and 2 minor winners in France, one over jumps: dam minor French 9.2f winner: 4½ lengths fourth of 15, keeping on having run green, to Karinga Bay at Newbury,

better effort in listed events: hard ridden 3f out and little response behind Spinning at Newmarket later in August. *P. A. Kelleway.*

AGENCY 3 b.f. Good Times (ITY)–Admirable 44 (Welsh Pageant 132) [1988 7g 7m 1989 12m 8.2m 6g a8g 12g] sparely-made, angular filly: no worthwhile form, including in seller: sometimes bandaged: visored final start. *K. T. Ivory.* —

AGE OF MIRACLES 2 b.c. (Apr 30) Simply Great (FR) 122–Single Gal 97 (Mansingh (USA) 120) [1989 6f⁴ 6m³ 6g⁶ 6f 6m³ 8m* 8m] leggy, rather close-coupled colt: sixth foal: half-brother to 1987 2-y-o 6f winner Step Right Up (by Beldale Flutter) and a winner in USA by Cormorant: dam best at 6f: quite useful performer: made all in 6-runner maiden at Brighton: took good hold when below par in £7,100 event at Newbury later in September: over 8 lengths sixth of 7 to Machiavellian in Prix Morny Agence Francaise at Deauville: better suited to 1m than 6f. *C. A. Cyzer.* 94 ?

AGE OF ROMANCE 2 b.f. (May 1) Chukaroo 103–Eastern Romance 73 (Sahib 114) [1989 6g] fifth foal: half-sister to 3 winners, including fair miler Miss Cuddles (by Mummy's Pet): dam won 6f seller at 2 yrs: 50/1 and backward, slowly away and always behind in 12-runner maiden at Leicester in November. *J. M. Bradley.* —

AGHANI (USA) 3 b.f. Blushing Groom (FR) 131–Moss (USA) (Round Table) [1988 NR 1989 7m 8m 10m 10g] $300,000Y: smallish, workmanlike filly: good mover: half-sister to several winners, notably Abbaye winner Polonia (by Danzig) and high-class American middle-distance stayer Peat Moss (by Herbager): dam, very useful winner at up to 7f, is half-sister to 3 good stakes winners, including Dike: little promise in minor event, maidens and a handicap: visits Danzig. *J. L. Dunlop.* —

AGNES DODD 2 b.f. (Apr 23) Homing 130–Mosso 81 (Ercolano (USA) 118) [1989 6g] 5,000Y: compact, workmanlike filly: fourth foal: half-sister to 3-y-o Mossy Rose (by King of Spain): dam 2-y-o 5.8f and 6f winner: 50/1 and backward, slowly away and always behind in 17-runner claimer at Haydock in September. *J. A. R. Toller.* —

AGRI DAGI (USA) 2 gr.f. (Jan 26) Desert Wine (USA)–Ararat 106 (Young Emperor 133) [1989 6h² 6g* 7m⁵ 6s⁶] $240,000Y: angular filly: third foal: half-sister to modest 1m winner Tafau (by Danzig) and a winner in USA: dam, useful winner over 5f at 2 yrs and fourth in Irish 1000 Guineas, is half-sister to Fabvista, smart performer at up to 7f: sire high class at 1m to 1¼m: fairly useful performer: won £7,100 event at Newmarket in July by ½ length from Rafha: good fifth of 7 to Moon Cactus in Black Bottle Scotch Whisky Prestige Stakes at Goodwood 2 months later: will stay 1m: seems unsuited by soft ground: active sort. *L. M. Cumani.* 91

AHEAD 2 b.f. (Apr 22) Shirley Heights 130–Ghislaine (USA) 71 (Icecapade (USA)) [1989 7g] tall, leggy filly: has scope: second foal: half-sister to good 3-y-o miler Markofdistinction (by Known Fact), 6f winner at 2 yrs: dam, twice-raced 1¼m winner, is half-sister to smart Pluralisme and daughter of sister to Critique: 10/1, hampered by faller after 3f and always behind in 24-runner maiden at Newmarket in November. *G. Harwood.* —

AHSANTA SANA 3 b.g. Nicholas Bill 125–Dancing Valerina 61 (Comedy Star (USA) 121) [1988 6s* 6g 5s³ 1989 7g⁴ 7g 7f 6m 6m 6m 6s³ 6s 6s*] leggy, close-coupled, unfurnished gelding: keen walker: fair at his best: easily best effort after reappearance when third in handicap at Ayr: favourite, ran as if something amiss next start then won October seller (no bid) at Hamilton 16 days later: best form at sprint distances on soft going. *Mrs J. R. Ramsden.* 69

AHWAK 3 b.c. Shareef Dancer 135–Shore Line 107 (High Line 125) [1988 8g² 1989 11.7d⁴ 12f³ 11f⁴ 14m³ 11f* 10m³ 12m² 11.5g²] useful-looking colt: moderate walker: fair handicapper: won at Redcar in August: ran creditably after: may well prove best at up to 1½m: best form on a sound surface: lacks turn of foot: sold 29,000 gns Newmarket Autumn Sales. *M. R. Stoute.* 87

AICNAL 3 b.f. Ile de Bourbon (USA) 133–Skelbrooke 77 (Mummy's Pet 125) [1988 NR 1989 16g⁴] fourth living foal: half-sister to winning hurdler Lesclacha (by Homing): dam 9.4f winner: 33/1, very green when well beaten in minor event at Carlisle in October: sold 7,400 gns Doncaster November Sales. *M. J. Camacho.* —

AILEEN'S JOY 2 b. or br.c. (Mar 10) Runnett 125–Originality (Godswalk (USA) 130) [1989 8.2d] IR 3,000F, IR 6,200Y: compact colt: first foal: dam lightly raced: well beaten in October maiden at Haydock. *R. F. Fisher.* —

AIMEE JANE (USA) 4 gr.f. Our Native (USA)–Look Out Liz (USA) (The Axe II 115) [1988 10g 14m 12m* 1989 12f] leggy, sparely-made filly: won claimer at — §

Goodwood (trained by G. Harwood) as 3-y-o: favourite, visored and bandaged, reluctant to race after 4f when tailed off in seller at Lingfield in August: suited by 1½m: acts on top-of-the-ground and seems unsuited by heavy going: sold 3,000 gns Ascot August Sales: one to leave alone. *M. C. Pipe.*

AIM TO PLEASE 5 gr. or ro.m. Gunner B 126–Declamation 93 (Town Crier 119) [1988 12g 14d 12.3v⁵ 12g* 14g⁴ 12s 12d 12m² 1989 12d 14f³ 12d⁵ 14.6g⁵ 13.3m⁶ 12m 12d] big, good-topped mare: carries plenty of condition: moderate walker: poor mover: fairly useful handicapper: ran creditably third to fifth starts: never dangerous in well-contested events at Ascot and Thirsk on last 2: stays 14.6f: acts on top-of-the-ground and heavy going: occasionally runs moderately: has joined T. Forster. *R. F. Johnson Houghton.* **90**

AIOLI 3 b.f. Tyrnavos 129–Coco de Mer (Homing 130) [1988 NR 1989 10.1g] 1,600F, 2,800 2-y-o: unfurnished filly: half-sister to a winner in Sweden (by Town And Country): dam unraced daughter of useful 6f performer Net Call: 50/1, in mid-division in minor event at Windsor in August, held up in rear then keeping on steadily not knocked about: should do better. *R. G. Brazington.* **— p**

AIR CALL 2 b.g. (Feb 2) Red Ryder (USA)–Great Land (USA) (Friend's Choice (USA)) [1989 7g 6g 8m] 6,000Y: angular gelding: has a round action: second foal: dam won 9 races at up to 9f in North America: sire unraced brother to Mr Prospector: well beaten in minor event and sellers: sold to join J. Haldane 880 gns Doncaster November Sales. *D. W. P. Arbuthnot.*

AIR COMMAND 9 ch.g. Air Trooper 115–Snotch (Current Coin 118) [1988 8d 8s⁶ 8m 7f 6s 1989 7.6m] strong, good-bodied gelding: poor mover: poor handicapper: 33/1, tailed off at Chester in September: probably stays 1m: suited by give in the ground: often apprentice ridden: sold 600 gns Newmarket Autumn Sales. *J. Mackie.*

AIRDRIE FLYER 4 ch.g. Beldale Lark 105–Rock Angel 56 (Ribero 126) [1988 NR 1989 10f] third foal: dam poor maiden, placed over 1m: 66/1 and apprentice ridden, always tailed off in maiden at Folkestone in August. *J. E. Long.* **—**

AIREDALE (USA) 2 b.c. (Mar 23) Dixieland Band (USA)–Good Hart (USA) (Creme Dela Creme) [1989 7m 8f 8g] $65,000Y: good-topped, angular colt: eighth registered foal: half-brother to prolific stakes winner at up to 9f Dr Bee Jay (by Dr Blum), a multiple minor winner by Full Pocket and a 2-y-o 7f winner by Lt Stevens: dam, third on all 3 starts, raced only at 2 yrs: plating-class form in maidens: twice gave impression capable of better: one to keep an eye on in selling or quite modest company. *W. J. Haggas.* **55 p**

AIRE VALLEY LAD 2 b.c. (Apr 13) The Brianstan 128–Rojael (Mansingh 120) [1989 5s 5d 5f 7m 6m⁵ a7g a8g] 700F, 1,500Y: lengthy, sparely-made colt: has a quick action: moderate walker: second foal: dam never ran: poor plater: broke free at stalls once in July: trained first 5 starts by J. Norton. *R. Bastiman.* **40**

AIR MUSIC (FR) 2 b.c. (Apr 25) Fabulous Dancer (USA) 126–Santa Musica (Luthier 126) [1989 7g 7m⁴ 8g² 8m³] angular, good-topped colt: fourth foal: half-brother to useful 1986 2-y-o 6f winner Rumboogie (by Sharpo): dam won over 9f and 11f in France: progressive colt: 3½ lengths third of 9, staying on strongly, to Digression in Royal Lodge EBF Stakes at Ascot: will stay at least 1¼m. *C. E. Brittain.* **107**

AIR NYMPH 2 b.f. (Feb 8) Elegant Air 119–Elfinaria 79 (Song 132) [1989 5m³ 5g⁶ 5m 6f] 16,500Y: strong, robust filly: carries condition: seventh living foal: half-sister to winners in Italy by Final Storm and Formidable: dam sprinting half-sister to smart 7f and 1m performer Fair Season: plating-class form in varied events: gave impression when blinkered on final 2 starts capable of bit better. *M. W. Easterby.* **56**

AITCH N'BEE 6 ch.g. Northfields (USA)–Hot Case 92 (Upper Case (USA)) [1988 8g 8m 7.6g³ 7.6s 8s 1989 7.5d³ a8g] small, strong gelding: modest handicapper: showed he retained ability when close third (visored) at Beverley: ran poorly in claimer at Lingfield (blinkered) over 6 months later: stays 1m well: best form with give in the ground: sometimes sweats: usually apprentice ridden nowadays: inconsistent. *Lady Herries.* **67**

AJALITA 3 ch.f. Move Off 112–Citrine 77 (Meldrum 112) [1988 5g² 6f⁶ 7m 8.2m 8g⁴ 1989 12g 10m⁴ 10g⁴ 11.5m⁶ 10m⁴ 12s³ 12g⁴ 16f⁵] leggy, lengthy filly: plating-class maiden: stays 1½m: acts on soft going, probably unsuited by top-of-the-ground. *M. J. Ryan.* **49**

AJANAC 5 br.g. Known Fact (USA) 135–Majan 67 (Brigadier Gerard 144) [1988 6m* 6g* 6f* 6m² 7g 1989 6f⁴ 6f 6m 6m² 6s³] rather angular, sparely-made gelding: **108**

good mover: useful handicapper: ran well behind Bertie Wooster in £16,300 event at York and Joveworth in £34,100 Ladbrokes (Ayr) Gold Cup (Handicap) on last 2 outings: suited by 6f: acts on any going: below form in blinkers and visor. *J. Tree.*

AJJAJ 4 b.c. Habitat 134–Cassy's Pet 89 (Sing Sing 134) [1988 6v 5g⁴ 5f* 6g* 6m 5.8f 6g 1989 5g 6f⁶] good-bodied, quite attractive colt: has a quick action: trained by J. Tree, won handicaps at Wolverhampton and Windsor (made almost all) in first half of 1988: lightly raced and no subsequent form: stays 6f: acts on firm going: sometimes blinkered, including when successful: bandaged behind final outing: sometimes sweats: takes a lot of driving and is possibly not genuine: sold 1,150 gns Doncaster November Sales. *M. Brittain.* —

AJRAAS (USA) 3 b.c. Northern Dancer–Shake A Leg (USA) 106 (Raise A Native) [1988 7g 1989 8m² 8.5f* 7.6f³ 8h³ 10m³] well-made colt: grand walker: favourite and edgy, won maiden at Beverley in May, making virtually all: better efforts in handicaps at Lingfield (wandered under pressure) and Brighton next 2 outings: took keen hold and may have proved best at around 1m: acted on hard ground: visored fourth start, blinkered previous 2: may have been somewhat temperamental: to stand at Leinster Stud, Co. Kildare; fee IR £2,500 (Oct 1st). *M. R. Stoute.* 88

AKAMANTIS 2 b.f. (Feb 19) Kris 135–Graecia Magna (USA) 109 (Private Account (USA)) [1989 8f* 7m²] big, strong filly: has plenty of scope: first foal: dam won over 7f at 2 yrs and 1½m at 3 yrs: favourite, won 19-runner maiden at Salisbury by 7 lengths: sweating and edgy, beaten length by Fearless Revival in 3-runner minor event at Ascot later in September: will be suited by middle distances: should improve further. *G. Harwood.* 87 p

AKAROA 2 ch.c. (Apr 11) Kalaglow 132–St Isadora (Lyphard (USA) 132) [1989 7g] 28,000F, IR 30,000Y: second living foal: half-brother to French 3-y-o 1m winner Sicaire (by Bustino): dam, winner twice over extended 9f in France at 4 yrs, is daughter of half-sister to smart French 1m and 10.5f winner Tintagel: 33/1 and ridden by 7-lb claimer, in mid-division in 28-runner maiden at Newmarket in November. *W. Jarvis.* — p

AKDAM (USA) 4 b.c. Arctic Tern (USA) 126–Dancers Countess (USA) (Northern Dancer) [1988 8d* 10d* 12f⁵ 10g 1989 10m 10m 10.2g5] big, strong, close-coupled colt: moderate mover: fairly useful at his best: little worthwhile form as 4-y-o: best form at 1¼m: acts on a soft surface: sold 21,000 gns Newmarket Autumn Sales. *H. Thomson Jones.* —

AKID (USA) 3 ch.c. Secreto (USA) 128–Raise The Bridge (USA) (Raise A Cup (USA)) [1988 6d⁴* 7g² 6f² 5g³ 1989 6v²] sturdy, good-topped colt: useful as 2-y-o, winning valuable maiden at Ascot and placed in listed races: 6/1 on, well below form in 4-runner minor event at Ayr in May, leading 4f: should be suited by return to 7f+: possibly unsuited by heavy going: strong-running sort: sold to join D. Topley 5,200 gns Newmarket July Sales. *H. Thomson Jones.* ?

AKII-BUA 5 b.g. Kampala 120–Bold Words (USA) (Bold Ruler) [1988 NR 1989 8g 10s 11.7d] good-topped gelding: turns fore feet in markedly: quite modest winner in 1987: well beaten in handicaps in spring: stays 9f: best form on a sound surface: blinkered twice, visored once: has hung left. *A. P. James.* —

AKIMBO 2 ch.c. (Mar 29) Bold Lad (IRE) 133–Western Gem 86 (Sheshoon 132) [1989 8v] 43,000Y: well-made colt: sixth foal: brother to useful 1m winner Bold And Beautiful and half-brother to 3-y-o 1m winner Steffi (by Precocious) and 7.6f to 9f winner Flyhome (by Home Guard): dam, half-sister to very smart performers Western Jewel and Mr Fluorocarbon, placed over 7f and 1½m: 14/1, prominent around 6f in 23-runner minor event at Newbury in October. *C. R. Nelson.* — p

AKIN TO FAME 3 ch.c. Ahonoora 122–Braneakins (Sallust 134) [1988 NR 1989 8m³ 7f² 9m²] IR 107,000F, 310,000Y: lengthy, good-quartered colt: has a rather round action: first foal: dam, Irish 1½m winner, is half-sister to Cheveley Park winner Park Appeal, very useful Irish 6f to 11f winner Nashamaa (both by Ahonoora), smart filly Desirable, and Alydaress: quite modest form in Newmarket Challenge Whip, maiden at York and minor event (running on having been driven along 4f out in late-May) at Ripon: will probably stay 1¼m. *A. A. Scott.* 70

ALACAZAM 7 gr. or ro.g. Alias Smith (USA)–Repel (Hardicanute 130) [1988 16d³ 16g 18f⁴ 14g 14.5g 14f 18g 17.1g 1989 13v 12d] poor handicapper: no form for some time: tailed off final outing (April): stays 2¼m: not at his best on firm going, acts on any other: visored 3 times, blinkered twice: difficult ride and needs strong handling: best left alone. *T. Craig.* — §

37

*Queen Alexandra Stakes, Ascot—20/1-shot Ala Hounak
beats Sergeyevich (centre) and Zero Watt (right)*

ALA HOUNAK   5 gr.h. Sexton Blake 126–Negligence 66 (Roan Rocket 128) **112** ?
[1988 12d⁶ 13.4v⁴ 13.3f⁵ 16g 16f⁴ 18.4s³ 16d⁵ 16.1m⁶ 14.6f 14f⁶ 1989 18g* 18.4m³
16f⁶ 22.2f* 16m²] close-coupled, deep-girthed horse: carries condition: 20/1, ran
easily best race in last 2 seasons when winning Queen Alexandra Stakes at Royal
Ascot by 3 lengths from Sergeyevich: stayed on strongly final 2f having been
hampered in rear before halfway when 3 lengths second to eased Orpheus in
moderately-run £43,800 handicap at Newcastle week later: successful on
reappearance (on toes) in slowly-run Doncaster Town Plate (Handicap): stays
extreme distances: unsuited by heavy going, acts on any other. *F. Durr.*

ALAMDAR (USA)   7 ch.g. Riverman (USA) 131–Anafa (FR) (Faristan 123) [1988   **52**
NR 1989 7.5d 8f 8m*dis 10f⁴ 8.2f⁵] medium-sized gelding: fair winner as 3-y-o:
showed he retains a little ability when winning selling handicap (no bid, disqualified
on technicality, slowly away) at Yarmouth in June: suited by 1m: acts on firm going:
blinkered last 2 starts: wears bandages: has got on edge: suited by strong handling.
R. W. Stubbs.

AL ANBA (USA)   2 b.f. (Jan 30) Lear Fan (USA) 130–Dacquoise (USA) (Lyphard   **64**
(USA) 132) [1989 7m² 7m² 6m²] 33,000Y: sturdy filly: has a fluent action: first foal:
dam unraced daughter of half-sister to very smart sprinter Polonia: runner-up in
maidens: 7 lengths second to Line of Thunder at Yarmouth on final start:
took keen hold and didn't handle bend well at Warwick on debut. *G. A. Huffer.*

ALAPA   2 b.g. (May 2) Alzao (USA) 117–Gay Folly (Wolver Hollow 126) [1989 7g]   **—**
IR 15,500Y: big, angular, plain gelding: third living foal: dam never ran: 10/1,
prominent 4f in 20-runner maiden at Newbury in August: subsequently gelded. *M.
Bell.*

ALA WING (USA)   2 gr.f. (Jan 12) Alla Breva (USA)–Wingless Wonder (USA)   **63**
(Naskra (USA)) [1989 6g³ 6g² 6f] small, sparely-made filly: first foal: dam never ran:
sire, stayed 13f, improved with age: quite modest form, including in a seller: will be
better suited by 7f+: sold 2,600 gns Doncaster November Sales, probably to race in
Scandinavia. *W. J. Haggas.*

AL BADETO 2 b.f. (Mar 23) Hays 120–Atedaun (Ahonoora 122) [1989 5d² 6m 6g³ 6m³ 6m 6m 5s] IR 1,500F, 2,400Y: lengthy, rather sparely-made filly: second foal: dam placed at 1m at 3 yrs in Ireland: quite modest maiden: well below form last 3 starts: better suited by 6f than 5f: possibly not suited by top-of-the-ground: visored sixth outing. *J. Norton.* **62**

ALBADR (USA) 4 ch.c. Arctic Tern (USA) 126–Spring Tour (USA) (Ack Ack (USA)) [1988 9g⁴ 12d* 1989 13.3f* 12v⁴] big, strong, workmanlike colt: suffered stress fracture of off-fore as 3-y-o, but is a winner of 3 of his 5 races, justifying favouritism in listed Aston Park Stakes at Newbury in May, quickening into lead inside final 1f and beating Ibn Bey and Green Adventure a length: modest fourth to Sesame in St Simon Stakes at same course over 5 months later: stays 13.3f: acts on firm going and a soft surface (not at his best on heavy): very useful, but clearly difficult to train: remains in training. *R. W. Armstrong.* **116**

AL BATAL (USA) 2 ch.c. (Jun 2) Blushing Groom (FR) 131–Salpinx (USA) 123 (Northern Dancer) [1989 7g] $800,000Y: fifth foal: half-brother to smart 3-y-o middle-distance performer Zalazl (by Roberto), good 6f to 1m winner at 2 yrs, very useful French 1m and 9f winner Synefos (by Irish River) and French 1½m winner Severini (by Tom Rolfe): dam, good middle-distance filly, is closely related to L'Emigrant: 50/1 and in need of race, around 14 lengths tenth of 28, shaping well from halfway, to Rami in maiden at Newmarket in November: sure to do better. *J. L. Dunlop.* **64 p**

ALBAZM 3 b.c. Caerleon (USA) 132–Sweet Marjorie (FR) (Sir Gaylord) [1988 8g⁵ 1989 12s 12h³ 14f* 14m² 14.8m⁴ 14m 14g 12f⁵] leggy, angular colt: moderate walker and mover: fair handicapper: won at Nottingham in June: good short-head second at Yarmouth, leading until post: ran moderately sixth and seventh starts: will stay 2m: best efforts on top-of-the-ground: sold 19,000 gns Newmarket Autumn Sales. *M. A. Jarvis.* **79**

ALBEDO 2 b.c. (May 15) Daring March 116–Alicia Markova 64 (Habat 127) [1989 5.8m 6m² 6h⁴ 6m 6m] 5,800F, 5,800Y: tall, useful-looking colt: has scope: moderate walker: has a round action: eighth foal: half-brother to 3-y-o Crashlock (by Tyrnavos) and 3 winners, including 1987 2-y-o 6f winner Markstyle (by Moorestyle): dam, half-sister to Music Maestro, Saulingo and Outer Circle, ran 3 **57**

Hamdan Al-Maktoum's "Albadr"

times at 2 yrs: plating-class maiden: best effort in claimer on second start: ran in a seller final one: will stay 7f. *R. Hannon.*

ALBERT 2 b.c. (Mar 11) Kings Lake (USA) 133–Darine 114 (Nonoalco (USA) 131) **71** [1989 6s* 8s] 26,000Y: good-bodied colt: has scope: shows a round action: third foal: brother to modest 1m maiden Magic Kingdom and closely related to Italian 3-y-o 1m and 1¼m winner Stua (by Caerleon): dam, middle-distance performer, improved tremendously at 5 yrs when trained in France: 25/1, won minor event at Ayr in September by ¾ length from Superenfer: ran respectably, taking keen hold and eased once beaten, in nursery there following month: bred to stay at least 1¼m. *C. W. Thornton.*

ALBERT HENRY 5 ch.h. Tickled Pink 114–Queens Pearl (Queen's Hussar 124) **—** [1988 6g 5d* 5m⁶ 6m⁶ 5d 5g⁵ 5m 5f 5s 6d 1989 6d 5s⁶ 5m⁶] small, strong, workmanlike horse: quite modest handicapper on his day: not seen out after May: best at 5f: possibly suited by an easy surface nowadays: flashed tail and looked none too keen in blinkers: inconsistent. *M. L. W. Bell.*

ALBERT PLACE 3 ch.c. Ahonoora 122–Holiday Regrets (Silly Season 127) **—** [1988 NR 1989 10m³ 8f⁵ a10g⁵] IR 18,000F, IR 50,000Y: sturdy colt: fifth foal: half-brother to fair 1½m winner Ensigne (by Master Willie): dam once-raced daughter of 1000 Guineas and Oaks second Spree: well beaten in minor event and maidens: sold 4,000 gns Doncaster November Sales. *Mrs L. Piggott.*

ALBERT'S WAY OUT 3 ch.g. Camden Town 125–Grunhilde 54 (Mountain Call 125) [1988 5s 5d* 6f² 6f⁴ 6g 1989 6s 8g 7g 10g⁶ 8f⁴ 7.6h 9m] rather leggy, short-backed gelding: quite modest as 2-y-o: showed little in handicaps and claimer in 1989: should stay 1m: best form on firm ground: visored fourth to sixth outings: has run creditably when edgy. *S. Dow.*

ALBYN GIRL 3 ch.f. Simply Great (FR) 122–Trina's Girl 78 (Nonoalco (USA) 131) [1988 6g 1989 9f⁴] angular filly: 10/1 from 4/1, 19½ lengths fourth of 16 to Torjoun in minor event at Wolverhampton in May, soon ridden along: sold 1,500 gns Newmarket September Sales. *H. R. A. Cecil.*

ALCANDANCE 2 b.f. (Mar 21) Alzao (USA) 117–Dancing Sun (Will Somers **64** 114§) [1989 5m³ 5f⁴ 5m⁴ 6g⁴ 6v⁵ 7g] IR 26,000Y: close-coupled, sturdy filly: half-sister to 1985 2-y-o 5f winner Dancing Fille (by Taufan) and 1984 2-y-o 6f winner Tricenco (by Kampala): dam never ran: quite modest maiden: best form at 6f. *C. James.*

ALCANDO 3 b.f. Alzao (USA) 117–Kaniz (Darius 129) [1988 5g² 5d* 5g* 5g⁴ 6g* **113** 6d* 1989 7m³ 8f⁴ 10m² 12g⁶ 10g* 10g] small, compact filly: very useful performer: 50/1, showed improved form when winning Group 3 Prix de Psyche at Deauville by ½ length from Shimmer, running on strongly from rear to lead inside final 1f: below form in EBF Phoenix Champion Stakes 3 weeks later: suited by 1¼m: acts on firm going and a soft surface: genuine. *C. James.*

ALCHEMISTRESS 4 gr.f. Grey Ghost 98–Pendle's Secret 73 (Le Johnstan **33** 123) [1988 7g 8m 5g 6s 1989 8d⁵ 11g 8.5d 8h 6m⁵ 6f⁵] big, workmanlike, plain filly: poor maiden: takes a keen hold, and probably best at short of 1m: acts on firm going (has tended to hang on it) and a soft surface: taken down very steadily last 2 outings: sold 1,200 gns Doncaster June Sales. *Denys Smith.*

Prix de Psyche, Deauville—a surprise winner,
British-trained Alcando beats the blinkered Shimmer

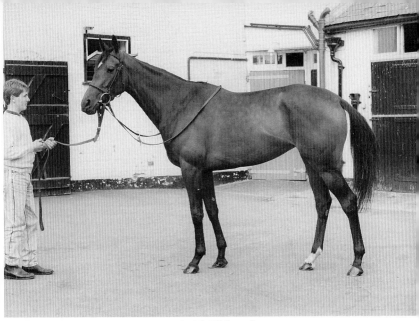

Mrs R. Smith's "Aldbourne"

ALCHIEA 2 b.f. (Apr 23) Alzao (USA) 117–Dancing Lass (King Emperor (USA)) **60**
[1989 5m⁴ 6m⁶ 6h²] IR 7,400Y: small, sturdy filly: half-sister to fair 1987 2-y-o 5f
and 6f winner Crafty Chris (by Kafu) and 3 winners in Italy, one over jumps: dam
won in Italy: ½-length second of 5, keeping on, to Simply Blue in maiden auction
event at Brighton in August, best effort. *C. James.*

ALCHI (USA) 2 b.f. (Apr 4) Alleged (USA) 138–Campechito (USA) (Olden Times **112**
(USA)) [1989 6.5d 8g* 8g³ 8.5f] second foal: dam, winner at up to 9f at 4 yrs in North
America, is out of half-sister to Bold Bikini, dam of Law Society: 2 lengths third of
15, staying on well, to Salsabil in Prix Marcel Boussac at Longchamp: earlier won
maiden at Deauville: in rear in Breeders' Cup Juvenile Fillies at Gulfstream Park in
November: should make good middle-distance 3-y-o. *F. Boutin, France.*

ALDAHE 4 ch.g. Dalsaan 125–Alanood 85 (Northfields (USA)) [1988 6m⁶ 5d³ 6g³ **59**
6m² 6m⁴ 6m 5f* 5f 6m* 1989 6g 6g 7m 6g 8g 7f 8m 5g³ 6g⁶ 5m⁶] sparely-made
gelding: usually dull in coat: has a round action: easily best efforts as 4-y-o when
third (mulish leaving paddock, slowly away) and sixth (on final outing) in handicaps
at Edinburgh: best form at sprint distances: yet to race on soft going, acts on any
other: best in blinkers: bought out of M. H. Easterby's stable 1,600 gns Doncaster
June Sales after second start. *T. Craig.*

AL DAMOUR (USA) 2 b.c. (Feb 24) Lypheor 118–Visual Effects (USA) (Silent **80 p**
Screen (USA)) [1989 7m 8g⁵] 48,000Y: sturdy colt: has a round action: fifth foal:
half-brother to 2 minor winners in USA: dam 9f winner in USA: around 11 lengths
fifth of 16, keeping on well, to Belmez in minor event at Newmarket in November,
easily better effort: will be well suited by middle distances: will improve further. *L.
M. Cumani.*

ALDBOURNE 3 b.f. Alzao (USA) 117–Steady The Buffs 62 (Balidar 133) [1988 **113**
6d* 6m* 6f* 6d² 8f⁴ 8g⁵ 8.5f⁵ 1989 7g² 8g³ 8m² 8f⁶] tall, rather angular filly:
moderate walker and mover: very useful performer: placed in Juddmonte Farms
Nell Gwyn Stakes and slowly-run General Accident 1000 Guineas (1¾ lengths

41

behind Musical Bliss) at Newmarket and in Goffs Irish 1000 Guineas (beaten 2 lengths by Ensconse) at the Curragh: reportedly pulled muscle when bit below form in Coronation Stakes at Royal Ascot: will probably stay 1¼m: acts on firm going and a soft surface: sometimes on toes: game, genuine and consistent. *R. Guest.*

ALDERHEY (USA)   2 b.c. (May 31) Blushing Groom (FR) 131–Native Nurse   — p (USA) (Graustark) [1989 8m] $700,000Y: angular colt: has scope: half-brother to Italian Oaks winner and Irish Oaks dead-heater Melodist (by The Minstrel) and several other winners, including high-class middle-distance filly Love Sign (by Spanish Riddle): dam placed at 2 yrs and 3 yrs: 12/1 from 7/1, around 11 lengths eighth of 29, keeping on well not knocked about, to Defensive Play in maiden at Newmarket in October: sure to improve. *M. R. Stoute.*

AL DIFFA (USA)   3 b.c. Star de Naskra (USA)–General Partner (USA)   67 (Understanding) [1988 7g 8m 1989 9f 10g 12h* 12.4m 14m a12g] angular, good-topped colt: carries condition: has a quick action: blinkered first time, won handicap at Thirsk in June: well beaten otherwise, tailed off in handicaps last 2 starts: stays 1½m: acts on hard ground: blinkered third to fifth outings: sold out of H. Thomson Jones's stable 17,000 gns Newmarket July Sales after fourth. *R. V. Smyth.*

ALDINGTON PRINCE   3 b.g. Creetown 123–Dear Catalpa 49 (Dear Gazelle   — 113) [1988 NR 1989 10f⁶ 8f 7g] medium-sized, good-bodied gelding: ninth reported foal: dam won over hurdles: well beaten in minor events and a maiden. *C. C. Trietline.*

ALDINO   6 ch.g. Artaius (USA) 129–Allotria 86 (Red God 128§) [1988 NR 1989   84 12s³ 14g² 12g⁵] fair handicapper: creditable second at Salisbury in May: stays 1¾m: yet to race on firm going, acts on any other: best in blinkers or visor: smart hurdler. *O. Sherwood.*

ALDRA BOND   4 ch.g. Gold Song 112–Petite Case 76 (Upper Case (USA)) [1988   66 d 8m 9g 8d³ 13.8f⁴ 14m* 16g⁴ 12g* 13g² 1989 12f 12.8m³ 13f² 12m³ 16.2g⁶ 13f² 14g 12g³ 12.3m 15s 12s] leggy gelding: moderate mover: quite modest handicapper: suited by 1½m to 1¾m and a sound surface: has hung, and needs strong handling: winning hurdler: changed hands 5,000 gns Doncaster November Sales. *G. M. Moore.*

ALDWICK COLONNADE   2 ch.f. (Apr 7) Kind of Hush 118–Money Supply   — (Brigadier Gerard 144) [1989 6g] 1,600Y: angular, sparely-made filly: half-sister to 1988 Irish 2-y-o 6.3f winner Roman Citizen (by Electric): dam never ran: 50/1, bit backward and green, prominent around 4f in 12-runner maiden at Leicester in November. *M. D. I. Usher.*

ALENTADO   2 b.c. (May 3) Alzao (USA) 117–Whichcombe 79 (Huntercombe 133)   64 [1989 5s² 5v 5h³ 5f⁴ 6v 5g] IR 4,800Y, 9,800Y: tall, leggy colt: moderate walker: fourth foal: half-brother to 3-y-o 9f seller winner Chart Cross (by Millfontaine) and a winner in Barbados: dam second over 6f at 2 yrs on only start: quite modest performer: sweating badly and on toes, creditable fourth in nursery at Warwick in July: withdrawn after reportedly coughing in parade ring next intended outing and well beaten final 2: will probably be suited by 6f: sold 2,800 gns Doncaster November Sales. *J. Berry.*

ALEXANDRA KATRINE   3 b.f. Precocious 126–Sipapu 90 (Targowice (USA)   76 d 130) [1988 5s⁴ 5d² 6g 5f⁴ 5g³ 6d 1989 5f⁵ 5f² 5h³ 6m² 6m³ 6f 5g 5f⁵ 5f³ 6f³ 6m 6g² 7g a6g³ a7g a6g⁶] strong, good-quartered filly: moderate mover: maiden handicapper: stays 6f: acts on hard going and a soft surface: not discredited in blinkers once as 2-y-o: below form in visor seventh outing: tends to hang left: has found little off bridle, and is possibly ungenuine. *R. F. Johnson Houghton.*

ALEXA'S BOY   5 b.g. African Sky 124–Regal Step 101 (Ribero 126) [1988 NR   — 1989 11.7m_11.7m] leggy gelding: poor maiden: last in handicaps at Windsor in summer: bandaged on reappearance. *T. B. Hallett.*

ALFARQAD (USA)   3 b.c. Northern Dancer–Lucky Lucky Lucky (USA)   73 § (Chieftain II) [1988 7g 7g 1989 8g 10m⁶ 10f⁴ 14f⁴ 10f² 10f⁴] compact, attractive colt: carries condition: moderate walker: modest maiden: visored, made most last 2 outings: sweating, held up, ducked left over 1f out and found little when running poorly time before: stays 1¼m: sometimes gives trouble in preliminaries: temperamental: sent to race in USA. *J. L. Dunlop.*

ALFA VITA   3 ch.f. Absalom 128–Aruba 77 (Amber Rama (USA) 133) [1988 NR   — 1989 6m 6f⁶ 7g a8g] smallish, sturdy filly: half-sister to 2 winners by Music Boy, including fair 1984 2-y-o 5f performer Carribean Song, and to 7f winner Carribean Sound (by Good Times) and a winning Irish hurdler: dam 7f winner: no worthwhile form, including in apprentice seller: changed hands 3,900 gns Newmarket July Sales after debut. *C. E. Brittain.*

ALFEREZ 2 gr.g. (Feb 11) Petong 126–Sarah's Venture 70 (Averof 123) [1989 7f 7g] 12,000Y: workmanlike gelding: first foal: dam middle-distance handicapper: well beaten in autumn maidens at Salisbury and Newmarket: subsequently gelded. *M. McCormack.* —

ALF MARHABA 5 b.g. Kris 135–Affirmative 96 (Derring-Do 131) [1988 NR 1989 10.2g 8g⁶ 12f] 105,000F, 650 4-y-o: medium-sized, rather sparely-made gelding: sixth foal: half-brother to several winners, including fairly useful miler Teamwork (by Workboy) and fair middle-distance winner and winning hurdler Convinced (by Busted): dam won 9 times at around 1m: unruly in preliminaries, poor form in seller and claimer on last 2 outings: moved badly down and slowly away on debut: sold 1,300 gns Ascot November Sales. *R. M. Whitaker.* —

ALFUJAIRAH 2 ch.c. (Apr 4) Diesis 133–Soluce 98 (Junius (USA) 124) [1989 5f² 6f³ 6f³] 260,000Y: sturdy, lengthy colt: first foal: dam Irish 7f winner, is half-sister to useful Irish middle-distance filly Cienaga: modest form in maidens: stumbled leaving stalls and found little off bridle second start: will stay 1m: may improve bit more. *J. Gosden.* **78**

ALGAIHABANE (USA) 3 b.c. Roberto (USA) 131–Sassabunda 108 (Sassafras (FR) 133) [1988 7m⁴ 8m⁴ 1989 11f³ 14g³ 14f² 13.6f³ 12.4g] close-coupled, rather finely-made colt: good mover with a light, easy action: fair maiden: stays 1¾m: acts on firm going: ran creditably when sweating, edgy and tongue tied down third start: below form in blinkers final one: sold to join Miss A. Whitfield 18,000 gns Newmarket Autumn Sales. *H. Thomson Jones.* **81**

ALGHABRAH 3 b.f. Lomond (USA) 128–Reine de Chypre (FR) (Habitat 134) [1988 7f 8s² 10g 1989 10h⁶ 10h⁶ 12f⁵] medium-sized, rather leggy filly: modest form second start as 2-y-o: well beaten since in listed race and maidens, twice looking unsuited by track at Brighton: stays 1m: best form on soft going: took good hold for apprentice: sold 5,200 gns Newmarket December Sales. *H. Thomson Jones.* —

AL HANASH (USA) 3 b.c. Green Forest (USA) 134–Prophecy (USA) (Bold Lad (USA)) [1988 7s 1989 7g² 7s 7g 8.3m* 8.2g⁴ᵈⁱˢ 8f⁵ 10g⁵] good-bodied colt: has a round action: modest handicapper: won at Windsor in July: ran fairly well next 2 starts: never able to challenge in 5-runner contest at Epsom on final one: stays 1m well: appears suited by top-of-the-ground: sold 20,000 gns Newmarket September Sales. *P. T. Walwyn.* **76**

AL HAREB (USA) 3 ch.c. El Gran Senor (USA) 136–Icing 112 (Prince Tenderfoot (USA) 126) [1988 7m* 7m⁵ 7d* 8g* 1989 8d⁵] tall, good-topped colt: good, easy mover: developed into good-class performer (rated 123) as 2-y-o, winning William Hill Futurity Stakes at Doncaster on final outing: second favourite and looking very well, poor last of 5 in Charles Heidsieck Champagne Craven Stakes at Newmarket in April, ridden along 3f out and giving impression something was amiss: should have stayed 1¼m: easily best effort on good ground: blinkered last 3 starts: to stand at Coolmore, IR 6,000 gns, in 1990. *Major W. R. Hern.* —

ALHATHAF 3 b.c. Tap On Wood 130–Aldhabyih 86 (General Assembly (USA)) [1988 6m* 6g³ 7s² 7s* 8m² 7.6s⁴ 1989 8m 9f 8.2g] quite attractive colt: moderate mover: usually looks well: fairly useful performer as 2-y-o: showed little in handicaps in 1989, not seen out after June: stays 1m: acts on top-of-the-ground but likely to prove ideally suited by a soft surface: suitable mount for a 7-lb claimer: sold 8,800 gns Newmarket Autumn Sales. *H. Thomson Jones.* —

ALHAWRAH (USA) 2 b.f. (May 12) Danzig (USA)–Khwlah (USA) 99 (Best Turn (USA)) [1989 5g⁵] rangy filly: has scope: second foal: half-sister to 3-y-o Alkariyh (by Alydar), 6f winner at 2 yrs: dam, 6f winner at 2 yrs effective at 1¼m, is half-sister to Saratoga Six and Dunbeath: 9/1, over 4 lengths fifth of 23, going on quite well, to Villeroi in maiden at Redcar in October: will be suited by further and bred to stay 1m: should improve. *H. Thomson Jones.* **66 p**

ALHISAH (USA) 3 b.f. Storm Bird (CAN) 134–Moralisme (USA) (Sir Ivor 135) [1988 NR 1989 10f] 120,000Y: medium-sized, quite good-topped filly: second foal: closely related to modest plater Fly Concorde (by Northjet): dam, who ran once in frame at 3 yrs, is half-sister to Dancing Maid: 33/1, burly and green, never placed to challenge in maiden at Sandown in May: sold 1,800 gns Newmarket December Sales. *A. C. Stewart.* —

ALIBI WARNING 2 b.c. (Apr 2) Belfort (FR) 89–Carymara (FR) (Dankaro (FR) 131) [1989 5g 5d⁴ 6m⁴ 7.5f 7f⁵ 6m⁴ 7m³ 7m² 7m⁵ 8.5f⁶ 6g] 4,400Y: tall, good-topped colt: has scope: moderate walker: half-brother to 3 winners abroad: dam never ran: **57**

Prix de Seine-et-Oise, Maisons-Laffitte—Aliocha strides clear

fairly useful plater: probably stays 8.5f, but gives impression will prove ideally suited by shorter: blinkered or visored last 2 starts. *J. Berry.*

ALICANTE 2 b.c. (Apr 10) Alzao (USA) 117–Safe And Happy (Tudor Melody 129) **62** [1989 7m⁵ 7g⁵ 7m⁶ 8m⁵ 9g⁴ 8f³ 8g] IR 3,600F, 15,000Y, 14,500 2-y-o: small, close-coupled colt: half-brother to Irish bumpers and jumps winner Night Safe (by Pollerton) and a winner in Belgium: dam never ran: quite modest maiden: ran respectably in nurseries at York and Sandown on fourth and fifth starts: never travelling well when blinkered final outing: stays 9f: has run well for 7-lb claimer *R. Guest.*

ALICE DOWNS 3 ch.f. Thatching 131–Silver Almond (Be My Guest (USA) 126) **78** [1988 8m⁶ 1989 7d² 8d³ 8f] workmanlike filly: placed in maidens at Folkestone (hampered early and unlucky) and Warwick: ran poorly in handicap at York in May: stays 1m: best efforts on a soft surface. *C. R. Nelson.*

ALIDIVA 2 b.f. (Apr 2) Chief Singer 131–Alligatrix (USA) 111 (Alleged (USA) 138) **97 p** [1989 6g*] close-coupled, sparely-made filly: third foal: dam, minor winner over 7f and third in Hoover Fillies' Mile at 2 yrs, is daughter of sister to very smart animals Cabildo and Canal: 16/1, won 28-runner maiden at Newmarket in October by ¾ length from Soy Roberto, soon prominent and running on strongly: will be suited by 7f +: sure to improve, and win more races. *H. R. A. Cecil.*

ALIJYSO 2 b. or br.c. (Apr 2) Mansingh (USA) 120–Huntergirl (Huntercombe **—** 133) [1989 5g 5g] 950Y: smallish, plain colt: poor mover: fifth reported foal: half-brother to 1988 2-y-o 5f winner Jump Dyke (by Longleat) and poor maiden Tags Clown (by Cawston's Clown): dam bad plater: tailed off in sellers at Wolverhampton (bandaged and in need of race) and Haydock (ran as though something amiss) within 5 days in July. *P. S. Felgate.*

ALIMANA 2 b.f. (Mar 27) Akarad (FR) 130–Alannya (FR) (Relko 136) [1989 9f*] **74 p** medium-sized, lengthy, rather sparely-made filly: closely related to fair stayer Altountash (by Labus) and half-sister to several winners, notably Aliysa (by Darshaan) and French 9f winner Aliyoun (by Kalamoun), subsequently useful winner at up to 1½m in USA: dam smart 1m winner in France: long odds on but very green, won 6-runner maiden at Wolverhampton in October by 2 lengths from Calabali, staying on strongly having hung left and flashed tail over 2f out: sure to improve. *M. R. Stoute.*

ALIM (CAN) 2 gr.c. (Feb 12) The Minstrel (CAN) 135–Jiving Queen (CAN) 72
(Drone) [1989 7g⁵ 8g² 8m⁴] IR 240,000Y: leggy, quite good-topped colt: first foal:
dam never ran: modest maiden: stays 1m. *B. Hanbury.*

ALI MOURAD 4 ch.g. Final Straw 127–Paper Sun 89 (Match III 135) [1988 9g⁵ —
12f⁵ 10g² 10d 1989 12m 10m 10g] compact gelding: well beaten in varied events as
4-y-o: stays 1¼m: sometimes blinkered: winning selling hurdler. *E. A. Wheeler.*

ALIOCHA (USA) 3 b.c. Miswaki (USA) 124–Chatter Box 118 (Ribot 142) [1988 122
8m⁴ 8m³ 8s² 7s² 1989 10s³ 6.5s* 7m² 7f⁶ 6d 7g 6g* 7m³ 8.5f] $410,000Y: strong,
well-made colt: half-brother to high-class middle-distance performer Bonhomie (by
What A Pleasure) and to several other winners: dam smart performer at up to 1¼m
in France: won listed race at Evry in April and Prix de Seine-et-Oise at
Maisons-Laffitte in September: very good third, beaten under 2 lengths, to Gabina
in Group 1 Prix de la Foret at Longchamp: ran moderately fourth (Jersey Stakes) to
sixth starts and in valuable handicap at Gulfstream Park on final one: effective at 6f
and 7f: acts on soft going and top-of-the-ground: very smart. *F. Boutin, France.*

ALIPURA 4 ch.f. Anfield 117–The Ranee (Royal Palace 131) [1988 7d* 8f⁵ 8g 8m² 69
10f⁴ 10d⁶ 8d⁵ 8.3m⁴ 8f* 8m⁶ 8g 1989 8s 9f 9.2f³ 8m³ 8m] plain, sparely-made filly:
often unimpressive in coat: moderate mover: quite modest handicapper: ran poorly
final outing (July): suited by 1m or 9f: acts on firm going and a soft surface. *R. F.
Johnson Houghton.*

A LITTLE PRECIOUS 3 b.c. Precocious 126–The Silver Darling 75 (John 79
Splendid 116) [1988 NR 1989 6s² 6v* 6d 7g 6g] 6,800F, 14,000Y: strong,
close-coupled, attractive colt: poor mover: half-brother to 3 winners, including very
useful sprinter Sylvan Barbarosa (by Native Bazaar) and fair sprinter Sylvan
Barnum (by Comedy Star): dam second in Britain before winning at 2 yrs in
Belgium: won maiden at Hamilton in April by 15 lengths: ran poorly after in quite
valuable handicaps at Newmarket, well-backed favourite on first occasion then off
course over 5 months: acts well on heavy going: claimer ridden first 2 and final
outings. *N. A. Callaghan.*

ALIYSA 3 b.f. Darshaan 133–Alannya (FR) (Relko 136) [1988 9g* 1989 12f* 126
12m* 12m² 12g]

The season ended with one of the classics technically still undecided. On
July 4th the story broke that Aliysa had become the first classic winner since

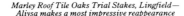

Marley Roof Tile Oaks Trial Stakes, Lingfield—
Aliysa makes a most impressive reappearance

*Gold Seal Oaks, Epsom—Aliysa is first across the line
from Snow Bride and the blinkered Roseate Tern*

Relko to react positively to a routine test. The next day it was revealed that a
derivative of the prohibited substance camphor had been detected in her urine
sample taken after the Gold Seal Oaks. Whereas most cases of this nature are
adjudicated upon by the Stewards within three or four months, a full hearing of
Aliysa's has not been held at the time of writing. When the hearing does take
place, it seems certain that her owner will argue a defence—as he did,
successfully, on behalf of the Champion Stakes winner Vayrann and the
Breeders' Cup fourth Lashkari. In December, at around the time that a copy of
the official report on the forensic evidence was belatedly forwarded to
Aliysa's trainer for perusal, the Aga Khan resigned his honorary membership
of the Jockey Club because of his strong opposition to the Club's
drugs-testing procedures. He was reported as saying: 'This is one of many
worldwide examples of camphor positives which cannot be explained. Aliysa
was in total isolation for seventy-two hours before the Oaks and, as a logical
man, I cannot, therefore, see how she could have come into contact with this
substance. If you remember in the Vayrann case, we brought the whole
subject of the nature and methods of testing into question, and this may be a
similar situation. I do not feel that I am just defending my own corner here, but
rather that I am making a stand for everyone whose horse has suffered
disqualification due to an unexplainable positive test in which camphor played
a part'.

The Oaks seemed well and truly decided on the day. The 11/10 favourite
won a fairly-run race going away by three lengths from Snow Bride, squeezing
between Snow Bride and the eventual fourth Mamaluna over a furlong out and
quickly asserting her superiority, leaving the main subjects for debate the
quality of the small field and, as a corollary, the merit of the winner. The race
is soon described. Mamaluna set a good pace and kept in front for the best part
of eleven furlongs, chased all the while by Snow Bride on her outside. Plans
for Aliysa to lie up from the start were spoilt when she stumbled out of the

46

stalls last. She eventually crept up to fourth on the rails but had to be niggled at down the hill, then ridden along more vigorously before they straightened for home, to keep her in touch in third ahead of Tessla, Musical Bliss and Roseate Tern. More work by filly and rider took Aliysa into a challenging position over two furlongs out, and after a long wait the opening came in plenty of time. Roseate Tern stayed on for third place; fifth behind Mamaluna came Knoosh; Tessla sixth, Musical Bliss seventh, Always On A Sunday eighth and Rambushka ninth and last.

The Oaks field was the smallest since 1963, when Noblesse made hacks of eight opponents. Compared to many in those intervening years it seemed lacking in quality as well as numbers, lacking an overseas challenge too. Roseate Tern, beaten only a short head for second place, was a maiden after six races: furthermore, the Guineas winner Musical Bliss, deserted by Swinburn in favour of Aliysa, ran as though she didn't stay. On the other hand Aliysa was now unbeaten in her three races. Her decisive victory at Epsom had been preceded by two of consummate ease, in a two-year-old maiden race at Wolverhampton and the Marley Roof Tile Oaks Trial at Lingfield. Wolverhampton is a most unusual place to come across a classic filly, not forgetting Indian Skimmer's three-year-old debut there, but Aliysa was so impressive that her reappearance in the Oaks Trial in May was eagerly awaited. She had the reputation of being the pick of Stoute's strong team of fillies, and she must have made up Swinburn's mind by her performance at Lingfield. She handled the track and the firm going superbly, quickening so far clear of four opponents from three furlongs out after leading from halfway that the jockey could ease right up inside the last. The winning margin over Wrapping was still eight lengths.

The Oaks field came to be seen in a better light as the season progressed—Snow Bride, Roseate Tern and Mamaluna all won pattern races, Knoosh a listed event—so that a case can be made out for regarding Aliysa as little or nothing behind the trainer's other Oaks winners Fair Salinia and Unite at her best. To regard her thus it has to be conceded that Aliysa ran slightly below her best in her two subsequent races, the Kildangan Stud Irish Oaks and the Ciga Prix de l'Arc de Triomphe. We are sure she did. She clearly suffered more than most in a rough race run in Paris and never threatened, though she was beaten no more than five lengths in tenth place behind Carroll House. She had no such excuse in running at the Curragh but was said to have returned home very sore. Alydaress proved the stronger from the turn and won comfortably by three quarters of a length, the 7/4-on shot Aliysa being pressed to hold on to second from Petite Ile. It was never the intention that Aliysa should go straight to the Arc from the Irish Oaks. She had the St Leger or the next day's Prix Vermeille as an objective first. After much deliberation she was declared to run at Doncaster; the postponement came too late for her to be re-routed to the Vermeille and she was scratched at Ayr for two connected reasons, the testing conditions and the proximity of the Arc. The postponement might well have cost Aliysa a lot more than an outing, for she seemed certain to go close at Doncaster; a mile and three quarters would have suited her, and she stood at 4/1 in the ante-post books.

Disqualification would make not a ha'porth of difference to Aliysa's stud value, nor to her sire Darshaan's though he would, admittedly, be deprived of the distinction of having a classic winner in his first crop. Aliysa descends directly from one of the century's most famous and influential mares, the flying Mumtaz Mahal, bought for the third Aga Khan by George Lambton as a yearling at Doncaster in 1922. She descends through Mah Mahal the dam of Mahmoud, Mah Iran the dam of Migoli, then as shown in the tabulated pedigree—Mah Behar, Nucciolina and Alannya, all three of them winners, the last-named also fourth in the Irish Oaks. Alannya showed smart form at a mile to a mile and a quarter in France. As a winner-producer she's equally smart and has already overtaken Nucciolina's total of five. Aliysa was her sixth and now there's a seventh, the promising Alimana (by Akarad) who followed in Aliysa's footsteps at Wolverhampton in October. And like Nucciolina (grandam of Nishapour and Nassipour) she's already the grandam of a good racehorse now at stud (the 1986 Prix du Jockey-Club second Altayan). The Aga Khan's policy of identifying families alphabetically can sometimes be

H. H. Aga Khan's "Aliysa"

confusing to others, especially when a mare has established a lengthy producing record. The names of Alannya's numerous foals tend to look alike, sound alike or both, but, confusion or not, two of the others deserve to be mentioned here—her first Aliyoun (by Kalamoun) who won in France and went on to show useful form at up to a mile and a half in the United States, and her fifth, Altiyna (by Troy), placed in the Cheshire Oaks, Lupe Stakes and Park Hill Stakes in 1986.

	Darshaan (br 1981)	Shirley Heights (b 1975)	Mill Reef
Aliysa (b.f. 1986)			Hardiemma
		Delsy (b or br 1972)	Abdos
			Kelty
	Alannya (FR) (b 1972)	Relko (b 1960)	Tanerko
			Relance III
		Nucciolina (b 1957)	Nuccio
			Mah Behar

Aliysa is very unlikely to be racing at four, though if she loses the Oaks the temptation to prove a point may be hard to resist. If the last has indeed been seen of her she'll go down as a middle-ranking Oaks winner, alongside the likes of Fair Salinia and Unite as we said, rather than Noblesse. Stamina was her strong suit, though she possessed a respectable turn of foot. A lengthy, good-topped filly with a quick action, she raced only on a sound surface. *M. R. Stoute.*

ALJANAN 2 b.c. (May 21) Pitskelly 122–Charley's Aunt 80 (Will Somers 114§) **68**
[1989 5f5 5m2 6m6 6v 6g5 6g6 6g] IR 6,400F, IR 8,000Y, 8,600 2-y-o: rather leggy, unfurnished colt: half-brother to several winners, including 5f and 1m winner Royal Revenge (by Sweet Revenge): dam won from 1m to 1½m: quite modest maiden: ran well last 3 starts: stays 6f: blinkered second outing: races freely. *M. Johnston.*

ALJARIH (USA)   3 b.c. Nijinsky (CAN) 138–Love Words (USA) (Gallant Romeo   94
(USA)) [1988 NR 1989 8m² 7f⁴ 10.6g* 11v] $575,000Y: strong, good-bodied colt: has
a rather round action: fourth foal: closely related to fairly useful 7f winner
Dwownedd (by Nureyev) and half-brother to French middle-distance winner
Fielding Grey (by Foolish Pleasure): dam lightly-raced sister to Elocutionist: 16/1
and first run for 4½ months, easily best effort when winning maiden at Haydock in
September: took keen hold and tailed off in £8,800 Newbury handicap month later:
should stay 1½m: probably unsuited by heavy ground. *H. Thomson Jones.*

ALJASUR (USA)   4 b.f. Alleged (USA) 138–Shicklah (USA) 106 (The Minstrel   —
(CAN) 135) [1988 10f⁶ 14m² 14.7m 1989 14f 16.2d] rangy filly: modest
maiden as 3-y-o: never dangerous in handicaps in autumn: stays 1¾m: sold 12,500
gns Newmarket December Sales. *H. Thomson Jones.*

ALJOOD   3 ch.f. Kris 135–Secala (USA) (Secretariat (USA)) [1988 7m² 8m⁴ 1989   —
8d 9g²] rangy, rather angular filly: has fluent, quick action: useful form as 2-y-o in
minor event at Newbury and Prix Marcel Boussac at Longchamp: ran poorly in
£8,700 contest at Ascot in April and minor event at Wolverhampton in July in 1989:
should be suited by strongly-run 1m or 1¼m. *M. R. Stoute.*

ALKARIYH (USA)   3 b.f. Alydar (USA)–Khwlah (USA) 99 (Best Turn (USA))   —
[1988 6g⁶ 6f² 6g* 1989 8f 10.6g 8f⁶ 9g] medium-sized, lengthy filly: modest winner
as 2-y-o: ran well in handicap (sweating) on reappearance but poorly afterwards:
tailed off second start then off course 4 months: suited by 1m: acted on firm going:
visits Polish Precedent. *H. Thomson Jones.*

AL KHALED   4 b.g. Lord Gayle (USA) 124–Windy Lady (Whistling Wind 123)   — §
[1988 10s 10m⁴ 10m* 11.7m⁴ 12m 10.5f³ 1989 10s] shallow-girthed, rather lightly-
made gelding: quite modest winner as 3-y-o: stays 11.7f: acts on top-of-the-ground
and soft going: blinkered final outing at 3 yrs: sold 2,000 gns Ascot 2nd June Sales:
has appeared ungenuine. *D. R. Tucker.*

AL KHOBAR (USA)   2 b.c. (Apr 19) Our Native (USA)–Blazing Grace (USA)   —
(Cannonade (USA)) [1989 8g] $150,000Y: big colt, rather unfurnished: looks weak:
fourth foal: brother to very useful 1984 American 2-y-o Crater Fire and half-brother
to another winner by Lydian: dam won at around 5f at 2 yrs: 8/1 and green, always
behind in 17-runner maiden at Leicester in November. *P. F. I. Cole.*

ALKILONG   2 b.g. (Mar 9) Longleat (USA) 109–Alkion (Fordham (USA) 117)   —
[1989 6f⁶ a6g] 6,400Y, 11,000 2-y-o: compact gelding: poor mover: first foal: dam
once-raced half-sister to very useful sprinter Oscilight: soundly beaten in maiden at
Goodwood and claimer at Lingfield. *R. Simpson.*

ALKINOR REX   4 ch.g. Welsh Pageant 132–Glebehill 76 (Northfields (USA))   81
[1988 8d* 8.2v³ 10d* 9m⁴ 1989 10d⁵ 13v 10.1m⁴ 10m⁴] useful-looking gelding:
fluent mover: fair performer: ran moderately in amateurs contest final outing: stays
1¼m: acts on a soft surface and top-of-the-ground (possibly unsuited by heavy):
ducked badly right second start at 3 yrs. *M. E. D. Francis.*

ALKIONIS   3 b.c. Dominion 123–Norfolk Gal 100 (Blakeney 126) [1988 NR 1989   —
8s 7f 10g a10g] 68,000Y: leggy colt: has a round action: fifth foal: half-brother to
smart 8.2f and 10f winner Shooting Party (by Posse) and Italian middle-distance
performer Yarmouth Pier (by Final Straw): dam 1¼m winner, is daughter of good 1m
to 1¼m winner Lucyrowe: no worthwhile form but showed signs of ability in minor
event at Nottingham third start, running wide with plenty to do on turn then staying
on steadily: bred to be better at 1¼m than 1m: has joined Mrs A. Knight. *G. Lewis.*

ALL ACTION   3 b.g. Rapid River 127–Palace Tor (Dominion 123) [1988 6g⁶ 5d   —
1989 8g 6g] sturdy gelding: backward and no form, including in seller: joined M.
Bowker after winning selling hurdle. *W. A. Stephenson.*

ALLASDALE (USA)   3 b.c. Alleged (USA) 138–Delray Dancer (USA)   85
(Chateaugay) [1988 7m⁵ 1989 10s² 12s* 12g* 15s] strong, lengthy colt: has a round
action: justified favouritism in minor events at Thirsk and Carlisle (by short head at
5/1 on) in April: tailed off in handicap final start, first for 5½ months: suited by 1½m:
acts on soft ground: edgy as 3-y-o, sweating first 2 outings: sold 20,000 gns
Newmarket Autumn Sales. *G. Harwood.*

ALLAZZAZ   3 ch.c. Mill Reef (USA) 141–Polavera (FR) (Versailles II) [1988 6f⁵   —
7d 8d 1989 6g⁶] rather leggy, sparely-made colt: no worthwhile form in maidens,
tailed off only start as 3-y-o in April. *D. T. O'Donnell.*

ALLEGED ACCOUNT (USA)   3 b.c. Alleged (USA) 138–Reckoning (USA)   76
(Olden Times) [1988 7g⁴ 1989 8v² 11.7m³] modest maiden: not seen out after early-
May: stays 1½m: acts on top-of-the-ground and heavy going. *B. Hanbury.*

49

ALLEZ AU BON 3 gr.c. Alzao (USA) 117–Love Locket (Levmoss 133) [1988 6f⁵   **96**
1989 7s⁶ 7f* 8m* 8m 8.2d] sturdy colt: won maiden at Sandown and £7,400 handicap
(well-backed favourite, ran on strongly to lead close home) at Newcastle in June: ran
poorly in quite valuable handicaps afterwards, bit backward final start: stays 1m:
acts on firm going: has turn of foot. *L. M. Cumani.*

ALLEZ-OOPS 2 ch.f. (Feb 16) Moulin 103–Ever So Cool (FR) (Never Say Die   **64**
137) [1989 7f² 8g² 8.2g⁵ 8.2g⁵] 3,000Y, 11,000 2-y-o: smallish, sturdy filly:
half-sister to French 10.5f winner Spring Breeze (by King of Macedon) and
ex-French 15f winner Laxdaela (by Sagaro): dam poor French 11f winner: quite
modest form in varied company: below form final start: will stay 1¼m. *J. G.
FitzGerald.*

ALL FIRED UP 2 b.f. (May 14) Song 132–Honey Pot 111 (Hotfoot 126) [1989 5g*   **74**
5m² 6g] rather leggy, unfurnished filly: seventh foal: sister to 3-y-o Chinese
Whispers and half-sister to 4 winners, including useful 1987 2-y-o 5f winner Ship of
Fools (by Windjammer) and fairly useful 6f to 1m winner Great Northern (by Dom
Racine): dam sprinting 2-y-o: won maiden at Catterick in August by 3 lengths from
Young India: had stiff task in Racecall Gold Trophy at Redcar final start: keen sort,
likely to prove best at 5f. *R. J. R. Williams.*

ALL GOOD FRIENDS 3 br.c. Prince Tenderfoot (USA) 126–Flash of Gold 78   **—**
(Pardao 120) [1988 6d 1989 17.6f] leggy colt: showed signs of ability in maiden as
2-y-o: pulled up in similar event in July one year later: sold 780 gns Doncaster
November Sales. *P. A. Blockley.*

ALL HONESTY 4 b. or br.g. Tyrnavos 129–Integrity 108 (Reform 128) [1988 7g⁵   **—**
6f 5f 6f 6m 6d 6d* 1989 7g 6f 6m 6m] tall, leggy gelding: has a round action: won
claimer at Nottingham (bandaged behind) at 3 yrs, only form for long time: broke
blood vessel and collapsed over 2f out final outing: stays 6f: suited by a soft surface:
blinkered 5 times. *A. Hide.*

ALLIAGE (USA) 2 b.f. (Apr 25) Alleged (USA) 138–Professional Dance (USA)   **?**
(Nijinsky (CAN) 138) [1989 8s*] $105,000Y: third foal: half-sister to a minor 7.5f
stakes winner by Forli: dam unraced half-sister to dam of good French performers
L'Emigrant and Salpinx: won 15-runner maiden at Saint-Cloud in November by 1½
lengths: will stay 1¼m. *F. Boutin, France.*

ALLIED FORCE 7 b.g. High Line 125–Summer Madness 88 (Silly Season 127)   **62**
[1988 NR 1989 8m 12f*] ex-Irish gelding: half-brother to 1½m winner Gay Appeal
(by Star Appeal), winning sprinter Favourite Girl (by Mummy's Pet) and a 1989
2-y-o winner in Italy: dam won 3 races up to 1m: made all in ladies race at Lingfield in
June, beating odds-on Carmagnole 2 lengths: stays 1½m: acts on any going. *A. W.
Denson.*

ALL NIGHT DELI 2 b.c. (Feb 19) Night Shift (USA)–Tzarina (USA) (Gallant   **67**
Romeo (USA)) [1989 6f 7m 6g⁴ 7m³] 4,000Y: compact, workmanlike colt: fourth
reported foal: closely related to fairly useful sprinter Mandub (by Topsider): dam
placed 3 times in USA: quite modest maiden: sweating, best effort when third in
selling nursery at Sandown in August: stays 7f: visored second outing. *R. Boss.*

ALL OVER THE WORLD 5 b.g. Kind of Hush 118–Bosworth Moll (Henry   **—**
The Seventh 125) [1988 8g 1989 8d 12m 10f 10f] lengthy, hollow-backed gelding:
virtually no form on flat since winning maiden early as 3-y-o: tailed off in handicaps
in 1989: stays 1½m: best form with give in the ground: blinkered once: has been
awkward in preliminaries and is a difficult ride: winning hurdler. *Denys Smith.*

ALL SAINTS DAY (USA) 3 b.f. Alydar (USA)–Christchurch (FR) 88 (So   **80**
Blessed 130) [1988 8.2m⁶ 1989 10h* 12m⁴ 11.5m⁶] leggy filly: favourite, won maiden
at Brighton in June: below form in minor events after, leading or disputing lead long
way: appears suited by 1¼m. *Major W. R. Hern.*

ALL SHOOK UP 3 b.c. All Systems Go 119–Mary of Scots 84 (Relic) [1988 7g 7s   **—**
1989 7s⁵ 7s 8f 8.5g 8m 8m⁵ 7m 10g 8g a8g a6g] workmanlike colt: quite modest at
best: well below form in varied events after reappearance: stays 7f: acts on soft
going: blinkered sixth and ninth starts: sweating eighth: bought out of G.
Pritchard-Gordon's stable 4,000 gns Ascot July Sales after sixth. *P. Howling.*

ALL WELCOME 2 b.c. (Feb 15) Be My Guest (USA) 126–Pepi Image (USA) 111   **—**
(National) [1989 8d] IR 55,000F, IR 130,000Y: half-brother to several winners,
including 1987 Irish 2-y-o 6f winner Pepelin (by Coquelin): dam third in Irish 1000
Guineas: 6/1, well-beaten tenth of 18, fading last 2f, in maiden at Thirsk in
November: has joined J. Fanshawe. *H. R. A. Cecil.*

ALMAGHRIB 2 b.c. (Feb 26) Red Sunset 120–Another Match (Sovereign Path   **72**
125) [1989 6f⁶ 6m² 6m³ 6m² 6m 6g³] IR 10,000F, 23,000Y: workmanlike colt: good

mover: fifth foal: half-brother to a winner in Italy by Be My Guest: dam, of no account, is sister to smart 1m to 1½m winner Royal Match: modest maiden: will be suited by 7f: blinkered final outing. *R. Hannon.*

AL MAHEB (USA) 3 b.c. Riverman (USA) 131–Une Amazone (USA) (Youth **100** (USA) 135) [1988 NR 1989 8g 8g 10m* 10f² 13.3m*] $185,000Y: small, quite attractive colt: third foal: half-brother to French 1987 2-y-o 1m winner Manaos (by Sharpen Up) and Le Cannibal (by Great Nephew), a winner from 9f to 1½m in France: dam unraced half-sister to Prix French Oak winner Henri Le Balafre: won maiden at Ripon in May and moderately-run £11,000 handicap at Newbury in July: odds on in 2-runner minor event in between: stays 13.3f well. *A. C. Stewart.*

ALMANAMA (USA) 2 b.f. (Mar 30) Diesis 133–Albadeeah (USA) 85 (Nashua) **58** [1989 6g⁵ 7.5f³] workmanlike, rather unfurnished filly: good walker: second reported foal: dam 2-y-o 6f winner: over 4 lengths third of 11 to very easy winner Tamahan in maiden at Beverley in August, better effort: may improve. *H. Thomson Jones.*

AL MANSOURA (USA) 3 b. or br.f. Al Nasr (FR) 126–Supper Show (USA) **64** (Knightly Manner (USA)) [1988 6f² 7g⁴ 7.5f² 1989 10s* 8.5s⁴ 12.3m⁵ 10m 12.3g 18d 10v³ 10d] close-coupled, good-bodied filly: moderate walker and mover: quite modest handicapper: won at Folkestone in April, making most: ridden by 5-lb claimer, creditable third in handicap at Navan in November: suited by 1¼m: probably needs a soft surface: likely to prove suited by forcing tactics: trained until after fifth start (tailed off as if something amiss) by N. Callaghan. *P. J. Flynn, Ireland.*

ALMETINGO 4 ch.f. Touching Wood (USA) 127–Cruise Port 73 (Homeric 133) **43** [1988 9g 10m⁶ 12.2g⁶ 12g 12s³ 14.5g⁶ 13.8f³ 10m 12g* 18d 1989 15.5s³ 15.5s⁶ 14.8d² 14f 16m] small, sturdy filly: poor handicapper: stays 2m: possibly needs an easy surface nowadays: sold 3,000 gns Ascot 2nd June Sales: has found little. *P. Mitchell.*

ALMOST BLUE 3 ch.c. Ballacashtal (CAN)–Blue Garter 70 (Targowice (USA) **103** 130) [1988 5g⁶ 5m² 5g* 6f³ 6f 5g* 5s* 5d* 5g³ 5s³ 1989 5m 5f⁶ 5m⁴ 5g² 5m⁴ 5m⁴ 5g⁵ 5g] deep-girthed, lengthy colt: moderate mover: easily best efforts as 3-y-o in listed races at Sandown and Tipperary fourth and fifth starts and Group 3 event won by Lugana Beach at Longchamp on final one: speedy: ideally suited by an easy surface: virtually bolted to post second outing: changed hands 60,000 gns Doncaster September Sales after sixth: useful. *J. Berry.*

AL MUFTI (USA) 4 b.c. Roberto (USA) 131–Lassie Dear (USA) (Buckpasser) **109** [1988 7g⁵ 10m³ 12m 10g² 12s³ 1989 12s² 14f⁵ 12g 10m⁵] big, strong, most attractive colt: good mover: very useful at his best: ran well on reappearance when beaten ½ length by Luigi in Gerling-Preis at Cologne: well beaten after in Coloroll Yorkshire Cup, Hanson Coronation Cup at Epsom and 5-runner listed event (blinkered and sweating) at Kempton: stays 1½m: acts on top-of-the-ground and soft going: sent to race in USA. *H. Thomson Jones.*

ALMUINJJID (USA) 2 ch.c. (Mar 30) Blushing Groom (FR) 131–Herb Wine **76** (USA) (Full Pocket (USA)) [1989 8.2d* 10g] $375,000Y: sturdy, attractive colt: second reported foal: half-brother to minor winner in USA by Mr Prospector: dam, half-sister to good 1979 2-y-o Romeo Romani, won at up to 9f in USA: won 11-runner maiden at Haydock in October by short head from Rubicund, good turn of foot to get up on line in slowly-run affair after showing inexperience: never in contention in 13-runner listed race at Newmarket following month: should stay further than 1m. *H. Thomson Jones.*

AL MUJIL (USA) 2 b.c. (Apr 26) Shareef Dancer (USA) 135–Ibtihaj (USA) 97 (Raja Baba **73** (USA)) [1989 5g 5g³ 6g 5m*] small, stocky colt: has a quick action: third foal: half-brother to quite useful 1986 2-y-o 5f winner Abhaaj (by Kris): dam, 5f winner at 2 yrs, is half-sister to Danzig: made all in 11-runner nursery at Redcar in September, easily best effort: should stay 6f: acts well on top-of-the-ground: wears blinkers. *H. Thomson Jones.*

AL NAJAH (USA) 3 b.f. Topsider (USA)–Personal Attention (USA) (Alydar **87** (USA)) [1988 6g² 7h² 1989 8.5m* 7m³] lengthy, workmanlike filly: favourite, comfortably made all in maiden at Epsom in June: failed to confirm that good impression in minor event at Kempton later in month: may stay 1¼m: keen, active sort. *M. R. Stoute.*

ALNASMAH (USA) 3 ch.f. General Holme (USA) 128–Talibaba (USA) (Raja **—** Baba (USA)) [1988 NR 1989 8m 7g 6g] $185,000Y: sturdy filly: second foal: dam, third on only start, out of half-sister to top-notch 2-y-o Talahasse: no promise in maidens and claimer: sold out of R. Armstrong's stable 1,800 gns Newmarket September Sales after debut. *R. W. Stubbs.*

ALNASRIC PETE (USA) 3 b.c. Al Nasr (FR) 126–Stylish Pleasure (USA) 86
(What A Pleasure (USA)) [1988 8m* 1989 8s 12f 9f2 9m6] rather leggy, good-topped
colt: carries condition: won maiden at Doncaster as 2-y-o: looking very well, fair
second of 3 at Kempton in June, only form in handicaps: front rank 7f in strongly-run
ladies race at same course 2 weeks later: should stay at least 1¼m: looks ill at ease
on very firm ground (shaped well on soft): takes keen hold. *G. Harwood.*

ALO' BABY 3 gr.g. Julio Mariner 127–Bellarina (Rugantino 97) [1988 6g 7g 8.2m —
6g 1989 8h 7m 10f] medium-sized gelding: little sign of ability, including in sellers:
blinkered last 2 outings. *J. R. Jenkins.*

ALO EZ 3 b.f. Alzao (USA) 117–Azina (USA) (Canonero II (USA)) [1988 6m 6m2 100
5d* 1989 6m* 7f 6m5 6m* 6g4] neat, good-quartered filly: showed improved form
when winning strongly-run races at Newmarket for handicap (25/1) in May and
listed race (50/1) in August, in latter running on from rear to lead inside final 1f then
holding Hafir by a head: modest fourth in £5,500 contest at Goodwood: suited by 6f:
best efforts on top-of-the-ground: sweating third start. *J. Pearce.*

ALOHA JANE (USA) 3 ch.f. Hawaii–Dorothy Gaylord (USA) (Sensitivo) [1988 57
NR 1989 12g 16f*] $69,000Y, resold $150,000Y: big, lengthy filly: sister to 2
winners, including Qualique, smart 9f stakes winner at 2 yrs, and half-sister to a
winner by Three Bagger: dam unraced half-sister to smart mile filly Island Charm
(by Hawaii): second favourite, won 5-runner maiden at Newcastle in July by short
head, setting modest pace early and rallying well: stays 2m. *G. Harwood.*

ALONG ALL 3 b.c. Mill Reef (USA) 141–All Along (FR) 135 (Targowice (USA) 113
130) [1988 8m3 8m* 8s2 1989 10.5s* 10.5m5 10g6 12d5] first foal: dam won Prix de
l'Arc de Triomphe: smart as 2-y-o, winner of Prix des Chenes and second in Grand
Criterium, both at Longchamp: won Group 2 Prix Greffulhe at same course in April:
below form after in Prix Lupin, Prix Guillaume d'Ornano and Prix Niel: stays 10.5f:
best efforts on soft ground. *A. Fabre, France.*

ALPHABEL 3 b.c. Bellypha 130–Absolute (FR) (Luthier 126) [1988 7g 1989 116
10.1m* 10.6g2 12m* 12f2 13.3g3 14.6s] big, strong colt: moderate walker and mover:
won minor event at Windsor in May and listed Haydock Park July Trophy: placed
next 2 starts behind idling Warrshan in Gordon Stakes at Goodwood, staying on and
beaten a head, and Ibn Bey in Geoffrey Freer Stakes at Newbury: soundly beaten in
St Leger at Ayr: probably stays 13f: acts on firm ground, apparently unsuited by soft:
tends to edge left: smart. *A. C. Stewart.*

Haydock Park July Trophy—
Alphabel (left) beats Relief Pitcher (rails) a shade comfortably

ALPHA HELIX 6 b.g. Double Form 130–Daidis 66 (Welsh Pageant 132) [1988 **59**
12d 12g 12m 12f⁵ 13m⁴ 12.3f⁶ 12f⁶ 15g 13s 12m 13.8g² 14.7d² 15d⁴ 1989 13.8d 12d*
13.8d* 12g* 12m⁵ 13f* 12g³ 13m³ 13g³ 12.3m 14m² 15g³ 13.6f⁶] deep-girthed
gelding: not a good walker or mover: quite modest handicapper: became
temperamentally unsatisfactory as 5-y-o, but in excellent heart for most of 1989,
winning at Edinburgh, Catterick, Hamilton and Ayr: ran poorly final outing: stays
15f: yet to show his form on very soft going, acts on any other: has worn blinkers,
visored nowadays: best held up. *J. S. Wilson.*

ALPHA LADY 3 b.f. Daring March 116–Fair Persuasion (Fair Season 120) [1988 **—**
5g⁴ 6g 5f 1989 7s 7m 6f 6f] good-topped, lengthy filly: moderate mover: poor plater:
form only on debut: should stay 6f: blinkered on reappearance. *P. D. Cundell.*

ALPHASONIC (USA) 5 b.g. Super Concorde (USA) 128–My Kinda Lady (USA) **—**
(Canadian Gil (CAN)) [1988 NR 1989 12m] tall, rather sparely-made gelding: has
quite a long stride: modest maiden as 3-y-o: always behind in minor event at
Leicester in June: should stay beyond 1½m: acts on top-of-the-ground: winning
hurdler with G. Harwood. *P. D. Cundell.*

ALQIRM (USA) 7 b.h. Drone–Joie (USA) (Speak John) [1988 8d 10f* 10f* 10f⁵ **78**
1989 8g⁴ 10f² 10m² 10.5f⁵] rangy horse: good walker and mover: modest
handicapper: not seen out after July: probably better suited by 1¼m than 1m
nowadays: best on a sound surface and goes very well on firm going: blinkered once:
has sweated and got on edge: has won 4 times at Salisbury: genuine. *R. J. Holder.*

ALQUOZ (USA) 4 bl.c. Caerleon (USA) 132–I Understand (USA) (Dr Fager) **109**
[1988 8g* 10.5g 7f⁵ 7d* 7g³ 7d³ 7g² 8g 1989 7g² 7.2g⁴ 8g⁴ 8g³ 7f* 7d*]
close-coupled colt: useful performer: successful in autumn in minor event at
Warwick decisively by 4 lengths from Admiralty Way and Group 3 Premio Chiusura
at Milan by ¾ length from Savahra Sound: ran creditably in listed races at Leicester
and Haydock on first 2 starts: stays 1m: acts on firm going and a soft surface. *J. L.
Dunlop.*

AL RAJA 3 b.f. Kings Lake (USA) 133–Rare Roberta (USA) 118 (Roberto (USA) **79**
131) [1988 NR 1989 9m² 8m³ 8g 8m 10m* 12g³] lengthy, angular filly: moderate
walker: second foal: sister to quite modest maiden Unique: dam 6f and 1m winner:
always close up when winning handicap at Newbury in September: good third in
apprentice handicap at York following month: stays 1½m: sold 22,000 gns
Newmarket December Sales. *A. C. Stewart.*

ALREEF 3 b.g. Wassl 125–Joey (FR) 110 (Salvo 129) [1988 6g 7f 7m⁵ 8s 8f⁴ 8.2m **76**
8f³ 1989 10g* 10.6m*] sparely-made, rather dipped-backed gelding: good walker
and mover: showed improved form when winning handicaps at Leicester (20/1) and
Haydock (amateurs, favourite) in September: will stay 1½m: appears unsuited by
soft ground: blinkered or visored last 4 starts at 2 yrs, once edgy. *T. Thomson Jones.*

ALRIYAAH 2 b.f. (Mar 29) Shareef Dancer (USA) 135–Sharpina (Sharpen Up **73**
127) [1989 5f² 5f* 5.8f⁵ 5m] medium-sized, lengthy filly: moderate walker and
mover: third foal: half-sister to 7f and 1¼m winner Paddy Egan (by Tap On Wood)
and 3-y-o Northern Brave (by Mill Reef): dam never ran: odds on, won 5-runner
maiden at Folkestone in August easily by 3 lengths from Marasol: well beaten in
minor event (eased considerably) at Bath and nursery at Newbury afterwards: bred
to stay much further. *A. A. Scott.*

ALRRBID 2 br.c. (Apr 16) Wassl 125–Turkish Treasure (USA) 111 (Sir Ivor 135) **—**
[1989 6f] ninth foal: closely related to smart middle-distance stayer The Miller (by
Mill Reef) and half-brother to 3 other above-average winners at 2 yrs, including
Magic Mirror (by Nureyev): dam won over 6f and 7f at 2 yrs: 10/1 and bit backward,
took keen hold and ran green when last of 7 in maiden at Goodwood in July: sold
8,000 gns Newmarket Autumn Sales. *J. L. Dunlop.*

ALSAAMER (USA) 2 ch.c. (Apr 3) Megaturn (USA)–Regal Nip (USA) (Raja **79**
Baba (USA)) [1989 7m⁴ 8g⁵ 8g a8g²] $18,000Y: lengthy, robust colt: good mover:
seventh reported foal: half-brother to winners in USA by Raise A Man and
Explodent: dam, winner at up to 9f at 4 yrs, is daughter of half-sister to 1970 Galtres
winner Pretty Puffin: sire won from 6f to 9.5f: blinkered, length second of 13, clear,
to French Bay in maiden at Southwell, best effort: will probably stay 1¼m. *S. G.
Norton.*

ALSABIHA 3 ch.f. Lord Gayle (USA) 124–Swan River 70 (Roan Rocket 128) **99**
[1988 6f⁴ 6m² 7g³ 7g² 7.3s⁴ 1989 8s* 8v 10g] well-made filly: good walker: evens,
won 3-runner listed race at Kempton in March by 2 lengths from Wrapping, ridden
along before straight then running on gamely: over 9 lengths ninth of 15 in Premio
Regina Elena at Rome: 25/1 on first run for over 6 months, prominent 1m when well

beaten in listed race at Newmarket: stayed 1m: acted on soft going: visits Lead On Time. *P. T. Walwyn.*

AL SAHIL (USA) 4 b.c. Riverman (USA) 131–Tobira Celeste (USA) (Ribot 142) — [1988 8d* 1989 10g 10.2g 10m⁵] smallish, sturdy colt: bad mover: coltish, made most when winning maiden at Newmarket, only outing as 3-y-o: shaped quite well on reappearance, but well beaten after in handicap and private sweepstakes (sweating badly): should stay 1¼m: sold J. White 11,000 gns Newmarket Autumn Sales. *H. Thomson Jones.*

ALSHAHHAD (USA) 3 b.f. Slew O' Gold (USA)–Shicklah (USA) 106 (The 70 Minstrel (CAN) 135) [1988 6m⁴ 7f³ 1989 8d 12.2m² 12.3g] big, workmanlike filly: modest maiden: blinkered, didn't get clear run and found little in handicap at Ripon final start: stays 12.2f: possibly needed top-of-the-ground: refused to enter stalls second intended start: visits Vision. *H. Thomson Jones.*

AL SHANY 3 ch.f. Burslem 123–Paradise Regained 41 (North Stoke 130) [1988 87 5d* 5s⁵ 6g 6s 7d⁵ 7s 1989 6m⁴ 7g⁵ 7m² 6m 7g] 8,600Y: close-coupled, angular filly: moderate walker: first foal: dam placed at 1½m and 15.4f: fair form at 2 yrs in Ireland when trained by L. Browne, winning maiden at the Curragh: creditable second in minor event at Catterick, best effort in 1989: tailed off in handicap final start, first for 3 months: suited by 7f: acts on top-of-the-ground and a soft surface. *W. Carter.*

ALSHEEN 2 br.f. (Mar 8) Alzao (USA) 117–Miss Olympus (Sir Gaylord) [1989 7m — 6d] 4,000Y: strong filly: second living foal: closely related to 3-y-o Love And Life (by Lyphard's Special), successful over 1m at 2 yrs: dam, placed over 1m, is daughter of very smart sprinter Merry Madcap: burly, well beaten in October maidens at Chepstow and Newbury. *K. M. Brassey.*

AL SKEET (USA) 3 b.g. L'Emigrant (USA) 129–Processional (USA) (Reviewer 80 § (USA)) [1988 7g 7s* 1989 8d⁶ 9f 9f² 10f³ 12m³ 12m] tall, lengthy, quite attractive gelding: good mover: fair handicapper: stays 1½m: acts on any going: ran poorly in blinkers final start: sold to join V. Young 11,500 gns Newmarket September Sales and subsequently gelded: carries head high under pressure and is probably irresolute. *J. L. Dunlop.*

ALTAIA (FR) 2 gr.f. (Mar 19) Sicyos (USA) 126–Haloom (Artaius (USA) 129) 73 [1989 6m⁶ 7g 7f³] 120,000 francs (approx £10,980) Y: workmanlike filly: has scope: half-sister to 5f claimer winner Mr Berkeley (by Bay Express) and a winner in Belgium: dam never ran: progressive form: closely third of 11 to Ivrea in maiden at Leicester in October: may improve further. *W. J. Haggas.*

ALTERED BEAST (USA) 2 b.c. (Feb 18) Danzig (USA)–Poz (USA) (Bold 80 Forbes (USA)) [1989 5s⁶ 5h* 6mʷᵒ 7g 6v*] $300,000Y: smallish, sturdy colt: third reported foal: dam, successful at up to 7f at 4 yrs, is half-sister to smart 1983 American 2-y-o filly Bottle Top and to dam of very smart 1981 2-y-o Lets Dont Fight: successful in maiden at Lingfield in June and 23-runner nursery at Newbury in October: walked over in minor event at Catterick: should stay 7f: acts on any going. *P. F. I. Cole.*

ALTERO 3 ch.f. Noalto 120–Lindy Ann (King's Leap 111) [1988 5m⁶ 5g⁴ 5m⁵ 5m³ — 5g⁵ 5d 1989 5d⁵ 5m] leggy, rather sparely-made filly: quite modest maiden as 2-y-o: below form in spring of 1989: sold 920 gns Doncaster August Sales. *T. D. Barron.*

ALTOBELLI 5 b.g. Northern Treat (USA)–Imagination (FR) (Dancer's Image 45 (USA)) [1988 8g 7f 8f 8s² 8g⁴ 8g 8s 7d 1989 7v 7g 8f⁶ 7m⁶ 7f 7.6f 10h 10f⁴ 12m* 12f] leggy, good-topped gelding: poor handicapper nowadays: 25/1 and apprentice ridden at overweight, won 7-runner event at Lingfield (edged right) in August: stays 1½m: acts on any going: blinkered twice: inconsistent. *P. Mitchell.*

AL-TORFANAN 5 b.g. Taufan (USA) 119–Powder Box (Faberge II 121) [1988 71 6m 7m* 7d 8g 7.6f* 7.6m⁶ 7m 7.6s³ 7m⁶ 7f⁵ 7.6f⁴ 7m 8m² 7m² 8f 9g 8g³ 6d 7g² 7m 1989 8g 7s 7g² 7m⁶ 7.6f³ 8h* 7g 8h* 8f 7.6m⁴ 8m 7.6f⁴ 8h 8f 8f] leggy gelding: has a round action: modest handicapper: won at Bath in May and Brighton (making all unchallenged) in June: below form afterwards: suited by 7f to 1m: acts on any going, but particularly well on firm: best racing up with pace: good mount for in-experienced rider. *P. Howling.*

ALTOUNTASH 5 b.h. Labus (FR)–Alannya (FR) (Relko 136) [1988 12d⁵ 19v — 16.5m 1989 19f³] fair winner over 1¾m + as 3-y-o: tailed off subsequently in varied company on flat: bandaged last 3 outings. *I. P. Wardle.*

ALUDA QUEEN 3 gr.f. Alzao (USA) 117–Ajuda Palace 62 (Royal Palace 131) — [1988 8.2s 8g 1989 7s 12.5f 12.2m 16.2g 16m] leggy, medium-sized filly: has a round action: little sign of ability, including in seller: not an easy ride: sold 3,300 gns Newmarket July Sales. *A. N. Lee.*

ALVARES 2 b.c. (Mar 8) Alzao (USA) 117–Cooliney Contessa (Furry Glen 121) **64**
[1989 5d 5g⁴ 6m⁴ 7m 7m³ 7g² 7g a7g] IR 6,000F, 26,000Y: close-coupled, sparely-made colt: moderate walker: has a round action: first reported foal: dam placed over 7f at 3 yrs in Ireland: quite modest maiden: will be suited by 1m: blinkered second and last 3 starts: has given trouble at stalls: has run creditably for 7-lb claimer: sold 9,000 gns Newmarket Autumn Sales. *A. Bailey.*

ALVECOTE LADY 4 b.f. Touching Wood (USA) 127–Sawk (Sea Hawk II 131) —
[1988 8m 8d 10f 10d 12.2f 12s 12.3g 10m⁵ 10d³ 12g* 1989 12m 12.4m 12m 12g 11s 12m 15g] close-coupled filly: winning plater as 3-y-o: well beaten in varied events in 1989: fell final outing: suited by 1½m: acts on a soft surface: visored once at 3 yrs: moved down badly third outing: sweating on fifth. *P. S. Felgate.*

ALVELEY 4 b.f. Lochnager 132–Orien (Goldhill 125) [1988 8m 7g⁴ 8g⁴ 1989 7.5d **37**
7.6m 8m⁶ 8v 7m] workmanlike filly: moderate mover: poor maiden: blinkered final outing. *J. Etherington.*

ALVIN YORK 4 b. or br.c. Known Fact (USA) 135–Aventina 83 (Averof 123) —
[1988 8.2v 12.2m⁶ 10.2g 8.5f 8m 12f 8f² 8.3m 10m⁶ 10m* 10g 10g 1989 10s⁵] leggy, rather light-bodied colt: poor mover: fair plater on his day: well beaten only outing at 4 yrs: stays 1¼m: acts on firm going and a soft surface: thoroughly inconsistent. *I. Campbell.*

ALWATHBA (USA) 2 b.f. (Jan 26) Lyphard (USA) 132–D'Arqueangel **100 P**
(USA) (Raise A Native) [1989 6g*]
  For the fourth year running, and the third in succession with a daughter of Lyphard, Luca Cumani won the Blue Seal Stakes at Ascot in September as Alwathba emulated White Mischief, New Trends and Ensconse. The Blue Seal invariably attracts some well-bred, highly regarded fillies and is usually a reliable pointer to the future; Sonic Lady and Dafayna also won it in recent times. We have no way of knowing at this stage how good Alwathba might become, but she looks very much the type to go on and she had behind her at Ascot several fillies whose subsequent form reads well. In a six-runner field, all of whom were running for the first time, Alwathba started second favourite at 5/2 behind the 15/8-chance Hasbah, the first foal of the top-class miler Al Bahathri; then came Negligent, a sister to the One Thousand Guineas third Ala Mahlik, at 100/30; Prince of Dance's half-sister Ruby Setting at 7/1; Dreamawhile, a half-sister to the Italian Derby winner My Top, at 14/1; and Lakeland Beauty at 25/1. After giving considerable trouble at the stalls (she was unruffled before that), Alwathba broke as well as any and, though running green, soon held a prominent position just behind the leaders. Approaching the final furlong she looked to be coming off second best with Hasbah, still travelling strongly in the lead, but under a firm ride stuck determinedly to her task and got her head in front in the very last stride. Alwathba wasn't seen out

Blue Seal Stakes, Ascot—three potential Guineas contenders, Alwathba (No. 1) keeps on strongly to beat Hasbah (noseband) by a short head with Negligent (near side) in third

again. However, Hasbah trotted up next time by seven lengths in a maiden at Redcar; third-placed Negligent, who'd stayed on well to finish three quarters of a length behind, took the Group 3 Chevington Stud Rockfel Stakes at Newmarket in good style by five lengths to force herself into the reckoning for the One Thousand Guineas; fourth-placed Lakeland Beauty also won a maiden (by four lengths) at Redcar before showing fairly useful form when sixth of twenty-five in the Racecall Gold Trophy; and Dreamawhile, who finished seven lengths down in last place, was touched off narrowly in a maiden at Folkestone. Alwathba, a sturdy, good sort with scope, is virtually certain to be capable of significantly better than she showed at Ascot and is an interesting prospect for the coming season.

Alwathba (USA) (b.f. Jan 26, 1987)	Lyphard (USA) (b 1969)	Northern Dancer (b 1961)	Nearctic Natalma
		Goofed (ch 1960)	Court Martial Barra II
	D'Arqueangel (USA) (ch 1975)	Raise A Native (ch 1961)	Native Dancer Raise You
		Beaver Street (b 1953)	My Babu Wood Fire

Alwathba was purchased for 500,000 dollars at Keeneland's July Selected Sale. She is the fourth foal and third winner from her dam D'Arqueangel after her full brother Dreams To Reality, a smart seven-furlong performer here and in France, and the mile-and-a-quarter winner but mainly disappointing Kuwait Team (by Graustark). D'Arqueangel won over six furlongs in the States and is closely related to the very smart fillies Native Street, who won the Kentucky Oaks, and Street Dancer. Native Street, incidentally, has foaled the good-class colts Royal And Regal, successful in the Florida Derby, and Regal And Royal, and is also the grandam of the high-class sprinter Dowsing. Alwathba's second dam Beaver Street had an excellent record as a broodmare: twelve winners from thirteen foals. She revealed no sign of merit on the racecourse herself, running eight times without winning a cent. Alwathba, who'll stay a mile, has already earned her connections nearly £10,000 and she should have little difficulty in boosting that sum at three. *L. M. Cumani.*

ALWAYS ALEX 2 b.f. (Apr 14) Final Straw 127–Two High 89 (High Top 131) **51 p** [1989 6m*] 6,000Y: smallish, workmanlike filly: third foal: half-sister to 3-y-o middle-distance stayer Diva Madonna (by Chief Singer) and 1½m winner Needle Light (by Kris): dam won 4 times over 1½m: 33/1 from 16/1 and bit backward, won 9-runner seller (bought in 12,500 gns) at Goodwood in August by length from Pinnacle Point, running green then keeping on well final 2f to lead inside last: will stay at least 1m: will improve. *Mrs Barbara Waring.*

ALWAYS FAIR (USA) 4 b.c. Danzig (USA)–Carduel (USA) (Buckpasser) **106** [1988 7d⁶ 7s² 7.3g² 8g* 8m² 1989 8s⁵ 7.2g²] good-quartered, quite attractive colt: very smart at his best: successful as 3-y-o in Prix Quincey at Deauville: good second also in 1988 to Salse in 'Federation Brewery' Beeswing Stakes at Newcastle and in Gardner Merchant Hungerford Stakes at Newbury and to In Extremis in Ciga Prix du Rond-Point at Longchamp: well-backed favourite, runner-up to Weldnaas in listed John of Gaunt Stakes at Haydock in June, better effort at 4 yrs: stayed 1m: didn't race on firm going, acted on any other: genuine: reportedly cracked cannon-bone and retired to stand at Haras de la Verrerie in Normandy. *M. R. Stoute.*

ALWAYS GREAT 3 b.g. Vaigly Great 127–Jinja 85 (St Paddy 133) [1988 5m 5m⁴ —
5f⁶ 5g⁶ 5g⁵ 1989 8d 6m 6f⁶ 8m 7m 7h] leggy, good-topped gelding: little worthwhile form, including in seller: doesn't stay 1m: visored final start at 2 yrs and 3 yrs: gave trouble in stalls and withdrawn intended second outing: sold to join W. Clay 2,700 gns Ascot 2nd June Sales. *T. M. Jones.*

ALWAYS NATIVE (USA) 8 b. or br.g. Our Native (USA)–Mountain Memory —
(USA) (Groton) [1988 6f 10m 1989 10s 8v 12m 6f 5m⁶ 12f 5f 8f] workmanlike gelding: of little account nowadays: has sweated profusely. *G. P. Kelly.*

ALWAYS ON A SUNDAY 3 b.f. Star Appeal 133–Justine (GER) (Luciano) **101** [1988 6g³ 6f⁴ 6g² 6d³ 8f³ 8g 1989 7g⁵ 10g* 12m 10d 10g⁵ 9g⁶ 10g⁶] small, narrow, sparely-made filly: has a rather round action: useful performer: awarded listed Crawley Warren Pretty Polly Stakes at Newmarket in May having been beaten neck by Rambushka: tailed off in the Oaks: not discredited in pattern and listed races after: suited by 1¼m: acts on firm going and a soft surface: retained by trainer 74,000 gns Newmarket December Sales. *P. A. Kelleway.*

ALWAYS READY 3 b.c. Tyrnavos 129–Merchantmens Girl 58 (Klairon 131) 66
[1988 5d 5f 5g² 5f³ 5d³ 5g* 5g 5m⁵ 1989 5s* 5s 5s 5g 5m 5m 5g⁵ 5d a6g] strong, good-bodied colt: carries plenty of condition: modest handicapper: won at Leicester in April: should stay 6f: acts on soft going: blinkered final outing: visored previous 4 starts and final 3 at 2 yrs. *L. J. Holt.*

ALWAYS TAKE PROFIT 3 ch.g. Noalto 120–Pour Moi 73 (Bay Express 132) —
[1988 7m 7d4 7g⁵ 1989 12s 10f⁵ 12m 8m] leggy, shallow-girthed gelding: plating-class form at best: none in 1989, including in 1m seller on final start in June: best effort over 7f on a soft surface: blinkered, sweating and edgy final start at 2 yrs: wears crossed noseband. *C. N. Allen.*

ALWAYS TREASURE 3 b.f. Lochnager 132–Rosinka 62 (Raga Navarro (ITY) 44 §
119) [1988 6g 5g 5f 5g⁴ 5d 1989 5s⁶ 5g 5m 5m 5m⁵ 5f 8f⁵ 6g⁵ 6g] lengthy, workmanlike filly: poor maiden: stays 6f: best efforts on good ground: has looked unenthusiastic and hung left: one to treat with caution. *J. Balding.*

ALWAYS VALIANT 3 b.c. Valiyar 129–Silent Pearl (USA) (Silent Screen 113
(USA)) [1988 6f 6g* 6d* 7d² 7.3s² 1989 8s³ 8v⁶ 8f⁵ 10g⁶ 10g* 10g³] strong, lengthy, useful-looking colt: 16/1 on first run for over 3 months, returned to form when winning £8,400 apprentice handicap at Newmarket in October: very good third of 9, running on in listed race there 13 days later: moved badly to post before Queen Anne Stakes at Royal Ascot third start: stays 1¼m: acts on soft going. *N. A. Callaghan.*

ALWUHUSH (USA) 4 b.c. Nureyev (USA) 131–Beaming Bride (King Emperor 121
(USA)) [1988 8g⁵ 10m* 12d³ 12f³ 11.1g³ 10g* 9d³ 1989 10s 10g* 12m* 12g² 11s³ 10f*] attractive colt: smart performer: successful in 2 Group 1 events in Italy, namely Premio Presidente della Repubblica at Rome in May by 2 lengths from Love The Groom and Gran Premio di Milano month later comfortably by 1¼ lengths from Tisserand: creditable second to Mondrian in Aral-Pokal at Gelsenkirchen: subsequently sold to race in USA, and on second run there won Grade 1 Carleton F Burke Handicap at Santa Anita by 4½ lengths: stays 1½m: acts on firm going and a soft surface: sometimes on toes: has carried head bit high: trained until after fifth outing by J. Dunlop. *A. Penna, USA.*

ALYDARESS (USA) 3 gr.f. Alydar (USA)–Balidaress (Balidar 133) [1988 124
NR 1989 7g³ 10f* 12f* 12m* 12f² 12m²]
   Firmish going, a shortage of good middle-distance fillies and the presence of a solid favourite all contributed to single-figure fields for the Oaks and the Irish Oaks—single figures for only the fifth time this century at Epsom, for the fifth time in a row at the Curragh. The late withdrawal of Snow Bride and Tursanah from the Irish Oaks left just five contesting a prize that with help of sponsorship from the Kildangan Stud had been bumped up finally to rival Epsom's. However, as in all the last five years, the quality of the field left less to be desired than its numbers: the race brought together the Oaks winner Aliysa and the Ribblesdale Stakes winner Alydaress, the latter a stable-mate of Snow Bride entered at the four-day supplementary stage at a cost of IR £20,000. Although Aliysa was unbeaten and deservedly odds on, there was plenty of support for the rapidly-improving Alydaress down to 7/4. Unlike Aliysa, Alydaress hadn't run as a two-year-old. She'd been brought along steadily to the Ribblesdale through maidens over seven furlongs at Newmarket in April and a mile and a quarter at Sandown in May; she won the Sandown race by a length in the style of one who'd be suited by further. The Ribblesdale provided an early opportunity to test the Oaks form, for Roseate Tern, around three lengths third at Epsom, was in the line-up of six. Alydaress beat her two and a half lengths after quickening clear a furlong out; when allowance was made for Roseate Tern's being unsuited by the moderate early pace at Ascot and for her having trouble obtaining a clear passage in the straight, the impression was still that Alydaress would be capable of giving Aliysa a run when they met.
   The Irish Oaks looked a virtual match on form but it didn't turn out that way, as the most promising of the home-trained trio Petite Ile also managed to get into contention in the straight. The 100/1-shot Caerless Writing made the

57

Ribblesdale Stakes, Ascot—Alydaress quickens away from a good-class field

running on sufference at a fair pace, followed by Aliysa, Alydaress, Petite Ile and Royal Climber. The order remained the same until early in the straight, less than three furlongs out, where Aliysa was ridden along into the lead on the rails, trying in vain to shake off Alydaress and Petite Ile. A hard, grinding struggle ensued between the three, Alydaress in the middle. Gradually Alydaress began to get on top under pressure, and had so clearly taken Aliysa's measure inside the last furlong that even though she never went a length up Swinburn on Alyisa put down the whip. At the line there was three quarters of a length between them, Petite Ile staying on strongly just a head further back. Defeat for Aliysa brought to an end the run of success in the race for Michael Stoute, trainer of Colorspin in 1986, Unite in 1987 and one of the dead-heaters in 1988, Melodist. But Alydaress' win continued the run of Sheikh Mohammed, owner also of Unite and Melodist (and dead-heater Diminuendo come to that). Irish stables last won with Princess Pati in 1984. They scarcely had a look-in in their other classics in the latest season either, only the Jefferson Smurfit Memorial St Leger eluding the Sheikh's British-based runners. However, the winning ride on Alydaress fell to Kinane, booked at a time when Snow Bride was the probable mount of Cauthen. Kinane was leading jockey on the flat in Ireland again in 1989, and later had the most important win of his career in the Prix de l'Arc de Triomphe.

Alydaress' own run of victories came to an end on her next outing. Her performance in the Irish Oaks had been a good, very genuine one which showed further improvement without setting her above several of her contemporaries; in all probability Aliysa ran a few pounds below her best. In the Aston Upthorpe Yorkshire Oaks at York in August Alydaress beat Petite

*Kildangan Stud Irish Oaks, the Curragh—Alydaress (centre) upsets odds-on Aliysa (left)
with third-placed Petite Ile (right) best of the home-trained challengers*

Ile by a head, but Roseate Tern came from behind both to win going away by a
length and a half. Very well in herself beforehand, Alydaress was under
pressure early in the straight and never looked to be striding out with
complete freedom; she tended to edge left as she tackled Petite Ile and took
almost to the line to wear her down for second place. Possibly she was feeling
the firm ground, as her trainer suspected. Whether or not, her run was plenty
good enough not to need excusing. Alydaress next raced in late-October,
when she finished an excellent second to Assatis on slightly easier going in
the Gran Premio del Jockey Club at San Siro in Milan; the older colt beat her
comfortably by half a length at weight-for-age, moving that bit better ahead of
her throughout the straight.

Fillies outnumber colts among the pick of Alydar's relatively few
runners in Europe so far. Alydaress joins Alydar's Best, Fatah Flare, Haiati
and Hiaam; the pick of the colts over here is Cacoethes. In the States Alydar
has gone from success to success, crop by crop, and his latest three-year-olds
included Easy Goer. Alydaress' dam Balidaress, a minor winner from seven
furlongs to a mile and a quarter and hurdles-placed in Ireland, had a producing
record by 1985 which eminently qualified her for a visit to Alydar, as by then
she'd been responsible for two Cheveley Park Stakes winners, Desirable (by
Lord Gayle) and Park Appeal (by Ahonoora), and two other winners, Salidar
and Braneakins (both by Sallust) from four foals. Her foal of 1983, Park
Appeal's brother Nashamaa, went on to prove more than useful at up to a mile
and a half, but the two others prior to Alydaress, the fillies Sacristy (by
Godswalk) and Balidarina (by Shareef Dancer) were just ordinary maidens. A
further visit to a top-class American stallion resulted in a colt foal by Nureyev

Sheikh Mohammed's "Alydaress"

in 1987, since named City Ballet. The second dam Innocence had much less chance to prove herself at stud: she died at an early age leaving Balidaress her only live foal. Twice successful over nine furlongs, she was one of four minor winners out of the two-year-old five-furlong winner Novitiate, a half-sister to the smart Lord David, the Princess Margaret Stakes winner Red Velvet and Miss Melody, dam of the Poule d'Essai des Pouliches winner Masarika.

Alydaress (USA) (gr.f. 1986)	Alydar (USA) (ch 1975)	Raise A Native (ch 1961)	Native Dancer Raise You
		Sweet Tooth (b 1965)	On-And-On Plum Cake
	Balidaress (gr 1973)	Balidar (br 1966)	Will Somers Violet Bank
		Innocence (gr 1968)	Sea Hawk II Novitiate

Naturally, the average price for a representative from this family has risen considerably more than inflation since Balidaress went for 2,400 guineas as a yearling in Ireland. Alydaress cost 650,000 dollars as a yearling, at that some way behind Desirable as a three-year-old (1,000,000 guineas) and five-year-old (1,600,000 dollars). As a racemare the close-coupled, workmanlike Alydaress differed substantially from Desirable: she had none of the precocity of her half-sister or of the other Cheveley Park winner Park Appeal. She was a late-developing, staying type, well suited by a mile and a half (she would have stayed further), a strong galloper with less of a turn of foot than some recent Irish Oaks winners. Like many of her contemporaries, she spent most of her three-year-old career racing on firm or firmish going.

60

She ran on good going only once—on her first outing, in the spring—and never on anything softer. *H. R. A. Cecil.*

ALYSARDI (USA) 2 ch.f. (Jan 27) Alydar (USA)–Passamaquoddy (USA) 69 (Drone) [1989 7f* 7g] $205,000Y: medium-sized, sparely-made filly: first foal: dam minor 7f stakes winner at 5 yrs, is sister to smart Navajo Princess, dam of Dancing Brave: favourite, won 6-runner maiden at Brighton in September very easily by 2 lengths from Peak Dancer: well beaten facing stiff task in nursery at Ascot following month. *A. C. Stewart.*

ALZAMINA 3 b.f. Alzao (USA) 117–Timinala 58 (Mansingh (USA) 120) [1988 5f — 5m⁴ 6f 5f³ 6d³ 7g 6g⁴ 6m 6m⁵ 6m 5d 1989 6m 6f⁴ 7g 7m⁶ 7m⁶ 7m] leggy, sparely-made filly: plating-class on most form: has run in sellers: suited by 6f: acts on firm going and a soft surface: tends to get on toes: to join J. White. *R. Hollinshead.*

ALZANAZ 2 b.g. (Mar 18) Alzao (USA) 117–Clonderlaw 68 (Kalamoun 129) [1989 47 5f⁴ 5m⁴ 6m 6m⁴ 6s 6f] IR 5,000F, 20,000Y: strong, lengthy gelding: has plenty of scope: has a round action: fifth foal: dam, disqualified Irish 1½m winner, half-sister to very useful sprinter Irish Love: plating-class maiden: ran poorly when blinkered in nurseries on last 2 outings, final one a seller: subsequently gelded: stays 6f: trained first 4 outings by R. Hannon. *K. M. Brassey.*

AMADORA 3 b.f. Beldale Flutter (USA) 130–Zerbinetta 96 (Henry The Seventh 71 125) [1988 6d 7m² 7s 1989 8g⁴ 8f a8g2] leggy, angular filly: poor walker: moderate mover: modest maiden: in frame at Newmarket and Southwell: ran badly in between and off course 6½ months after: should stay further: possibly unsuited by firm going: bandaged off-fore at 2 yrs. *J. L. Dunlop.*

AMANA RIVER (USA) 2 ch.f. (Feb 6) Raise A Cup (USA)–Barada (USA) 73 (Damascus (USA)) [1989 5m*] lengthy, quite attractive filly: first foal: dam lightly-raced half-sister to high-class 2-y-o filly Althea (stayed 9f) and to dam of Green Desert: favourite but bit backward and green, won 6-runner maiden at Nottingham in June in good style by 2 lengths from Dancing Breeze: looked sure to improve considerably but wasn't seen out again: will stay 6f. *J. Gosden.*

AMAREDO 3 b.c. Akarad (FR) 130–Amila 89 (Great Nephew 126) [1988 NR 1989 69 12f 10.6g 12f2] quite good-topped colt: has a round action: second foal: dam, daughter of close relative of Nishapour, won over 7.2f at 2 yrs and stayed 1½m: second in claimer (claimed £12,001) at Goodwood in June, leading until inside final 1f: coltish, well beaten in maidens: stays 1½m: winning novice hurdler for M. Pipe. *L. M. Cumani.*

AMATHUS GLORY 2 b.f. (Apr 14) Mummy's Pet 125–Copt Hall Realm 85 76 (Realm 129) [1989 5f² 5m* 5f 5g3] good-topped filly: has scope: has a round action: fifth foal: half-sister to 1988 2-y-o 6f winner Blazing Realm (by Blazing Saddles) and moderate plater Mascalls Girl (by Moorestyle): dam 2-y-o 5f winner: made all in maiden at Nottingham in June: sweating, over 3 lengths third of 4 to Shamshoon in minor event at Sandown in July, better subsequent effort. *P. J. Makin.*

AMAZAKE 2 ch.c. (Mar 10) Rousillon (USA) 133–Kesarini (USA) (Singh (USA)) 71 [1989 6g⁴ 7g 8d3] 31,000Y: close-coupled, angular colt: third foal: half-brother to 3-y-o That's The One, useful 5f winner at 2 yrs, and poor Henry William (both by Known Fact): dam, daughter of Coronation Stakes winner Kesar Queen, won over 5f at 2 yrs: modest maiden: ran poorly second start: stays 1m. *A. C. Stewart.*

AMAZING SILKS 4 b.f. Furry Glen 121–Child of Grace 100 (King's Leap 111) 41 d [1988 12.2g 12f⁵ 8.2g 10g⁵ 10g 1989 12g* 12g 13.6f⁵ 16.5g 12m 15g] small, angular filly: turns off-fore out: moderate mover: 20/1 and ridden by 5-lb claimer, won 13-runner handicap at Beverley in May: well beaten in similar events afterwards: bandaged near-hind final outing: stays 1½m: active type. *A. M. Robson.*

AMBER LIGHTNING 2 ch.f. (Feb 13) On Your Mark 125–Purple Princess 93 61 (Right Tack 131) [1989 5d² 5d² 5d⁶ 5m⁴ 5f* 5f² 5.3h⁵ 5m⁵ 5g⁴ 5m] IR 5,600F, 19,000Y: small, lengthy filly: has a quick action: sister to useful 1983 2-y-o 5f winner Running Princess, closely related to a winner in Italy by Windjammer and half-sister to modest sprinter Shades of Night (by Red Sunset): dam won 3 times at around 7f: quite modest performer: won 5-runner maiden at Edinburgh in June: ran creditably in nurseries afterwards, hanging badly when ridden once by 7-lb claimer: speedy. *M. Bell.*

AMBER LOCH 4 br.f. Lochnager 132–Amber Doll (Amber Rama (USA) 133) — [1988 6d 6g 7.5f 8g 10m 1989 10d] workmanlike filly: poor maiden: probably stays 1m. *M. W. Ellerby.*

AMBER LOCH (USA) 4 b.c. Lomond (USA) 128–Ambrellita (FR) (Misti IV 87
132) [1988 12f³ 10g* 10m² 10d* 10g³ 1989 8g 10s³ 10.4m³ 10f 10f⁴ 10m* a10g² a10g]
strong, angular colt: fair handicapper: favourite and sweating, made all in 4-runner
amateurs event at Goodwood in August: good second to My Chiara, pair clear, at
Lingfield 2 months later: suited by 1¼m: unsuited by firm going, acts on any other:
blinkered fourth outing: best racing up with pace: good mount for inexperienced
rider: game: sold 36,000 gns Newmarket December Sales. *P. F. I. Cole.*

AMBER NECTAR 3 ch.c. Sallust 134–Curtana (Sharp Edge 123) [1988 5g⁶ 5.8g 74
6s 7m 7g 1989 6f* 6m 5.8m² 6f* 6m* 6g⁵ 7g] workmanlike, deep-girthed colt:
modest handicapper: successful in summer at Chepstow (twice) and Yarmouth:
easily best effort at last-named but well beaten after: best at sprint distances: acts
on firm going: ridden by 7-lb claimer first 2 outings: tends to sweat and has looked
dull in coat. *L. J. Holt.*

AMBROSE 2 b.c. (May 8) Ile de Bourbon (USA) 133–Famous Band (USA) 77 §
(Banderilla (USA)) [1989 8m⁶ 8m² 10g³ 8g²] 6,000Y: lengthy, workmanlike colt: has
scope: fourth foal: half-brother to quite moderate 1986 2-y-o 5f winner Oriole
Dancer (by Dance In Time) and Irish 1m winner Famous Lad (by Bold Lad): dam
unraced granddaughter of good American filly Lalun, dam of Never Bend and Bold
Reason: modest maiden: stays 1¼m: hung left on last 2 starts (markedly so when
blinkered on final outing) and seems of unsatisfactory temperament. *R. F. Johnson
Houghton.*

AMELIANNE (FR) 3 b.f. Bustino 136–My Candy 81 (Lorenzaccio 130) [1988 8s 98
1989 12f³ 12m* 14f* 14f⁶ 12m] lengthy, unfurnished filly: looking very fit,
successful in July in maiden (sweating) at Kempton and £7,200 handicap (odds on) at
Goodwood: favourite, fair sixth in £12,000 handicap at York, handling turn badly:
faced stiff task in Group 3 event at Ascot final outing: stays 1¾m: acts on firm going.
D. R. C. Elsworth.

AMENABLE 4 b.g. Kampala 120–Kirin (Tyrant (USA)) [1988 7d⁵ 6g 7d 7m⁶ 8f² 75
8f 1989 7g² 8s³ 8m 7.6m 7f* 7.6f⁶] sturdy, compact gelding: modest handicapper:
ran well prior to winning at Thirsk in May: not seen out after following month: stays
1m: acts on any going: has got on toes. *T. D. Barron.*

AMERICAN CONNEXION 2 ch.c. (Jan 13) Tender King 123–Chieftain Girl 71
(USA) (Chieftain II) [1989 6m 6g² 8g³ 7g 6v] IR 18,500Y: workmanlike colt:
half-brother to several winners, including stayers Trampler (by Bustino) and Coral
Heights (by Shirley Heights) and fairly useful miler Park Street (by Runnett): dam,
daughter of sister to Sir Gaylord, won at up to 1m: modest maiden: hung markedly
left third start: never dangerous in nurseries at Newmarket and Newbury last 2:
stays 1m: twice slowly away: trained first 3 starts by Dr J. Scargill. *J. Sutcliffe.*

AMETHYSTINE (USA) 3 ch.f. Barachois (CAN)–Amathus (Song 132) [1988 57
6s³ 6g² 7f 6s 1989 6s 6v 8d 7f 8f⁵ 7m 7m³ 7m³ 9f* 8h² 10h⁴ᵈⁱˢ 8.3m 8m 7s]
sparely-made, angular filly: plating-class performer: won claimer at Wolverhampton
in July: ran very well in handicap next start: below form in similar events after,
finding little penultimate start then racing alone on final one: stays 9f: probably acts
on any going. *R. J. Hodges.*

AMIGA IRLANDE 2 ch.f. (Apr 19) Whistling Deer 117–Chive (St Chad 120) —
[1989 5g 5f] strong, sturdy filly: moderate mover: fifth foal: sister to useful sprinter
Amigo Loco and 3-y-o Amigo Menor, fairly useful 5f and 6f winner at 2 yrs, and
half-sister to one-time useful sprinter Evichstar (by Jasmine Star), since successful
at up to 1m: dam never ran: carrying condition, soon behind in autumn maidens at
Wolverhampton (slowly away) and Folkestone. *K. M. Brassey.*

AMIGO FEO 3 ch.c. Tap On Wood 130–Field Day 87 (Northfields (USA)) [1988 72
7g⁵ 1989 10g 11.7d 13.1h³ 16.2f³ 9m 15.3m* 16.5f² 16f³ 15g² 17.1f³ 17f² 13.8d a16g³]
tall, workmanlike colt: modest handicapper: won at Wolverhampton in July: will be
suited by thorough test of stamina: acts on hard ground, possibly unsuited by a soft
surface: blinkered last 11 starts: usually races up with pace. *K. M. Brassey.*

AMIGO MENOR 3 ch.c. Whistling Deer 117–Chive (St Chad 120) [1988 5m 5m² 96 d
6m 5g 6g* 5g* 6g* 5g⁶ 1989 6f4 6m⁴ 7.2g 6f⁴ 6g⁶ 6m 6f 6d 6g] leggy, lengthy colt:
fairly useful as 2-y-o: generally below form in 1989, in very useful company in spring
then mostly in handicaps: appears suited by 6f: acts on firm going: sweating fifth
outing: blinkered. *K. M. Brassey.*

AMINATA 2 b.f. (May 17) Glenstal (USA) 118–Belle Epoque 64 (Habitat 134) —
[1989 6g² 6f* 6f³ 6g* 5m* 6d⁴ 6g⁴ 8g] first reported foal: dam quite modest maiden
who stayed 7f, is sister to top-class sprinter Double Form and half-sister to smart
middle-distance filly Scimitarra: won maiden at Navan, £10,000 event at

Leopardstown and Shernazar EBF Curragh Stakes (beat Janubi 2½ lengths) at the Curragh: over a length fourth to Polar Bird in Barronstown Stud EBF Debutante Stakes at Phoenix Park, penultimate start: well beaten in Prix Marcel Boussac at Longchamp in October on final outing: stays 6f. *J. S. Bolger, Ireland.*

AMIRA T' SAHRRA 2 b.f. (Mar 27) Little Wolf 127–Mummy's Whistler — (Mummy's Pet 125) [1989 7g 6g] third reported live foal: half-sister to 7f seller winner Pokey's Pet (by Uncle Pokey): dam poor plater: plating-class form in autumn maidens at Catterick and Redcar. *W. W. Haigh.*

AMITY PET 3 b.f. Mummy's Pet 125–Rockery (FR) 101 (Roan Rocket 128) [1988 — 5m 6f 1989 7m 8.3g] smallish, angular filly: little sign of ability. *R. Akehurst.*

AMOODI (USA) 3 ch.c. Forli (ARG)–Love's Reward (Nonoalco (USA) 131)   85 [1988 7d⁶ 8f⁵ 8s³ 1989 12g⁵ 12.5f² 14f* 13.3g² 13.3m³ 19f⁶] strong, lengthy, workmanlike colt: carries condition: has a round action: fair handicapper: won at Redcar in May: ran creditably afterwards: stays 19f: probably acts on any going: likely to prove best on a galloping track: genuine. *P. F. I. Cole.*

AMOOD POINT 2 ch.g. (May 28) Jalmood (USA) 126–Nice Point (Sharpen Up — p 127) [1989 8.2g] 10,000Y: unfurnished gelding: second foal: half-brother to Italian miler Northern Alert (by Northern Tempest), fair 5f and 6f winner here at 2 yrs: dam never ran: 33/1, seventh of 14 finishers behind Golan Heights in maiden at Haydock in September: subsequently gelded. *J. Etherington.*

AMOUR DU SOIR (USA) 2 b.c. (Mar 7) L'Emigrant (USA) 129–Evening Kiss   72 (USA) (Saggy) [1989 5f² 5f³] rather leggy, useful-looking colt: has a roundish action: brother to 3-y-o 6f winner Maybe Siam and half-brother to numerous winners, including very useful 1984 2-y-o 7f and 1m winner Concorde Affair (by Super Concorde): dam second once from 9 starts: modest form in autumn maidens at Beverley and Wolverhampton (pulled hard to post). *Sir Mark Prescott.*

AMPHOTERIC VENTURE 4 ch.c. Sparkler 130–Covenant 75 (Good Bond — 122) [1988 7g 6f 6g⁴ 7m 1989 a7g] sturdy, good-topped colt: has a quick action: poor maiden: bred to stay much further than 6f. *K. A. Morgan.*

AMRON 2 b.c. (Apr 4) Bold Owl 101–Sweet Minuet (Setay 105) [1989 5v* 5g⁵ 5s⁶   62 5s⁵ a6g³] 6,200Y: brother to 6f and 7f winner Glory Bee and 3-y-o Woodland Steps, 7f winner at 2 yrs, and half-brother to several winners, including useful sprinter Tinjar (by Brittany): dam ran once on flat and once over hurdles: quite modest performer: won early-season maiden at Hamilton by 4 lengths: creditable third to Swing North in nursery at Southwell in November: stays 6f: has run respectably for 7-lb claimer. *J. Berry.*

AMRON LAD 3 ch.g. Tumble Wind (USA)–Red Nanda (Status Seeker) [1988   64 6m⁴ 6f 6f⁵ 7g 1989 8d 8g 8g⁶ 9f 12m⁵ 10m* 10g 10f⁵ 12m² 10m² 10.6s 11f³ 12.4g] small, lightly-made gelding: moderate walker: won slowly-run maiden claimer at Yarmouth in August: better efforts when placed in sellers: stays 1½m: probably best on top-of-the-ground: has run creditably for 7-lb claimer and when sweating: sold 9,400 gns Newmarket Autumn Sales. *R. J. R. Williams.*

AMWAJ 5 gr.h. Tumble Wind (USA)–Centennial Rose 109 (Runnymede 123) — [1988 NR 1989 10m 9m 12.2m⁴] robust, good-bodied horse: poor maiden: visored final start. *A. W. Denson.*

AMY'S STAR 3 b.f. Touch Boy 109–Keep Believing (Sweet Revenge 129) [1988 — 6d 7.5m 6g 1989 8g] lengthy, lightly-made filly: moderate mover: behind in maidens in the North. *P. Wigham.*

ANADAX 4 b.g. Mummy's Game 120–Adana (FR) (Green Dancer (USA) 132)   78 [1988 7g² 8g* 1989 9d 8s 8f⁴ 8.2m² 8f⁴ 8.2m² 9f² 12m 9m³ 8g] tall, useful-looking gelding: has a round action: fair handicapper: stays 9f: probably best on a sound surface: sweating eighth start: has run creditably for apprentice: winner over 1m in Italy late on in year. *M. A. Jarvis.*

ANATROCCOLO 2 b.f. (May 1) Ile de Bourbon (USA) 133–Art Deco (Artaius   63 p (USA) 129) [1989 6g a7g*] unfurnished filly: fourth foal: sister to 3-y-o Fort Dauphin and ungenuine maiden Skiary: dam unraced daughter of sister to 1000 Guineas winner Glad Rags, dam of Gorytus (by Nijinsky): won 14-runner maiden at Lingfield by a head from Dr Maccarter: will be better suited by 1m + . *C. A. Horgan.*

ANCIENT CITY 2 gr.c. (Mar 15) Persepolis (FR) 127–Fair Melys (FR) 81 — (Welsh Pageant 132) [1989 6g a7g] leggy, sparely-made colt: fifth live foal: dam, 7f and 1m winner, is half-sister to high-class middle-distance winner Pelerin: around 7 lengths seventh of 13 to Erik Odin in maiden at Lingfield: slowly away and green on debut. *G. Wragg.*

ANDBELL   3 b.f. Trojan Fen 118–Ring The Changes 72 (Auction Ring (USA) 123)   —
[1988 NR 1989 8m 8m 5.8h6] 45,000Y: leggy filly: fourth foal: half-sister to useful
Bell Tower (by Lyphard's Wish), winner over 6f and 7f, and a winner in USA by
Diamond Prospect: dam 5f winner at 3 yrs: no worthwhile form in maidens:
bandaged behind last 2 starts. *C. A. Horgan.*

ANDHRA   3 b.f. Indian King (USA) 128–Altara (GER) (Tarim) [1988 5f 5g 7f 8m   **44**
1989 7.5d2 7.5d4 6g 9f4 7m 7m] lengthy, plain filly: quite modest plater: probably
best at around 7f: acts on top-of-the-ground and a soft surface: bandaged last 4
outings and first 3 at 2 yrs: moved scratchily to post but ran creditably final start:
often apprentice ridden. *J. Wharton.*

ANDREA DAWN   8 ch.m. Run The Gantlet (USA)–Life Story 65 (Only For Life   —
126) [1988 17.1f* 16m4 17.1g4 13.1g 1989 14f5] poor handicapper: bandaged and in
need of race only outing as 8-y-o: needs further than 1¾m: blinkered nowadays.
Andrew Turnell.

ANDRELOT   2 b.c. (Mar 17) Caerleon (USA) 132–Seminar 113 (Don (ITY) 123)   **57**
[1989 6m 6m5 8.2f] IR 55,000Y: tall, close-coupled colt: half-brother to numerous
winners, 3 by The Minstrel, including useful 1981 2-y-o 6f winner Solaboy, and to
3-y-o Dance Festival (by Nureyev): dam, half-sister to Boldboy, very useful over 5f
at 2 yrs and won over 1m at 3 yrs in USA: plating-class form in maidens: blinkered
and sweating second start: should stay further than 6f. *Mrs J. Pitman.*

ANDREW'S FIRST   2 br.g. (May 23) Tender King 123–Dame Kelly (Pitskelly   **88 ?**
122) [1989 7f5 7f5 8.2f 10.6d2 8g a8g* a8g*] 3,600 2-y-o: leggy, rather sparely-made
gelding: third foal: half-brother to 3-y-o Dame Zao (by Alzao) and poor 1987 2-y-o
Gomax (by Red Sunset), later successful in Sweden: dam no worthwhile form in
Ireland: ridden by 7-lb apprentice, easily best efforts when winning claimers at
Southwell in December, first by 10 lengths: narrowly beaten over 1¼m, but best
form at 1m. *T. D. Barron.*

ANDROBOTE (FR)   3 ch.g. The Wonder (FR) 129–Andromeda (FR) (Dankaro   **80**
(FR) 131) [1988 NR 1989 8g 12.3d6 12m5 12m 16.5g5 16.2g6 19g*] 97,000 francs
(approx £9,700) Y, 650 2-y-o: rangy gelding: third foal: half-brother to a winner in
Belgium by Hand In Hand: dam, French 1¼m and 1½m winner: 100/1 and ridden by
7-lb claimer, showed much improved form when winning minor event at Goodwood
in October, edging left from over 3f out (causing interference) and leading inside
last: well suited by test of stamina: best efforts on an easy surface: trained first 6
outings by D. Smith. *R. Curtis.*

ANDY-TOM   2 b.c. (Apr 22) My Dad Tom (USA) 109–Queen of The Kop 60   —
(Queen's Hussar 124) [1989 5d6 5.3m6 6m] small colt: has a round action: fourth
foal: half-brother to 3-y-o Stage Queen (by Dawn Johnny) and 1987 2-y-o 5f winner
Hayden Court (by The Brianstan): dam stayed 1¾m: slowly away, well beaten in
varied races, including a seller: bandaged final start: sold 650 gns Ascot July Sales.
F. Jordan.

ANFIELD SALLY   3 b.f. Anfield 117–Bargain Line 68 (Porto Bello 118) [1988 NR   —
1989 8g 7d6 7m 7.5m 8s 10g a11g] rather leggy filly: fourth foal: half-sister to 1½m to
13.8f winner Nicholas Mark (by Gunner B): dam won 1m seller at 2 yrs: seems of
little account: visored sixth outing. *R. M. Whitaker.*

ANGEL BRIGHT   3 ch.f. Krayyan 117–Godhood 86 (Green God 128) [1988 NR   **84**
1989 7m2 7m3 8s3 8.2m2 9g5 10d2] IR 2,100F: leggy, angular filly: fifth foal: sister to
1987 2-y-o 5f and 7.3f winner Get The Money Down and half-sister to fair 1985 2-y-o
5.3f winner Joab (by Absalom), later successful in USA: dam 2-y-o 6f winner: fair
maiden: suited by 1¼m: yet to race on very firm going, acts on any other: sweating
last 2 outings. *E. Eldin.*

ANGELICA PARK   3 b.f. Simply Great (FR) 122–Rosana Park 83 (Music Boy   **53**
124) [1988 7g 8s6 1989 9f 8.2d4 8.2g6 10g5 a11g] stocky filly: plating-class form:
stays 1¼m: acts on a soft surface. *J. Wharton.*

ANGELIC NOTE (USA)   3 ch.f. The Minstrel (CAN) 135–Sateen (USA)   —
(Round Table) [1988 6m3 7f* 7.3s5 1989 8f5] smallish, sparely-made filly: keen
walker: fair form as 2-y-o, easily best effort when winning minor event at York: well
behind in listed race at Kempton in May: should stay 1m. *M. R. Stoute.*

ANGELS KISS   3 b.f. Taufan (USA) 119–Mexican Girl (Gala Performance (USA))   **73**
[1988 6f6 6f2 6g5 7f3 7d3 7g3 8v6 1989 8s5 8m5 8m 7m3 8s 7m 7d] good-topped filly:
has a round action: modest maiden: below form in handicaps last 3 starts: will be
suited by return to further than 7f: acts on top-of-the-ground and a soft surface:
visored fifth start: tends to hang: carried head badly left on reappearance. *Miss S. E.
Hall.*

64

ANGLOINTERNATIONAL 2 b.f. (Feb 15) Millfontaine 114–Brigadiers **51**
Nurse (Brigadier Gerard 144) [1989 5f3 5.8h6 5f 5.8h* 6f4 5m2 6g2 6g 7g] IR 7,000Y,
6,700 2-y-o: compact filly: first foal: dam never ran: fair plater: won 5-runner event
(no bid) at Bath in July: ran poorly last 2 starts: probably better suited by 6f than 5f,
and should stay 7f: blinkered and sweating third outing: sold 3,200 gns Newmarket
Autumn Sales. *R. W. Stubbs.*

ANGUS HABIT 3 ch.g. Henbit (USA) 130–Molly Malone (Bold Lad (IRE) 133) **63**
[1988 NR 1989 8d2 8.2g6 7g 7h 8m4 7g 9f] 6,400Y: neat gelding: half-brother to 2
winners, including fairly useful 1979 2-y-o 6f winner Live Ammo (by Home Guard):
dam half-sister to high-class performers Hot Spark and Bitty Girl: quite modest
form: always behind in handicap and seller (blinkered) last 2 starts: should stay
beyond 1m: acts on top-of-the-ground and a soft surface. *G. A. Huffer.*

ANIMAL ACTOR 4 b.f. Relkino 131–Matilda Cave 80 (King's Leap 111) [1988 —
10m 10.2f 10g 10m 1989 6d] strong, compact filly: little sign of ability, including in
handicaps. *W. T. Kemp.*

ANKARA'S PRINCESS (USA) 2 ch.f. (May 2) Ankara (USA) 106–Tales of **81**
Long Ago (USA) (Raise A Cup (USA)) [1989 5g* 5m* 5s6 6g] $35,000Y:
workmanlike filly: fifth reported foal: half-sister to 4 winners, including minor
stakes winner at up to 9f Ellusive Tales (by Lucy's Axe): dam unraced: successful at
Chester in maiden in June and 5-runner nursery in September: very good sixth of 7
to Mademoiselle Chloe in listed race at Ayr, much better subsequent effort: should
stay 6f. *S. G. Norton.*

ANNABELLE ROYALE 3 b.c. Anfield 117–France (Milesian 125) [1988 6m **74**
6m3 6m5 7g4 7f4 6m2 8m2 7g 8d 8g 7g 1989 8.2s4 6s2 8d2 7.5f 8m 8.2f* 10g 8.2f5 8g3
8.2m4 8m5 7g5 8.2f* 7m2 7.6f* 9g 8.2g] lengthy colt: has a quick action: won
maiden auction race at Hamilton in June and handicaps (looked really well) at
Nottingham and Lingfield (comfortably and best effort) in the autumn: effective at 7f
and 1m: acts on any going, though goes particularly well on firm: bandaged 4
occasions: seems rather inconsistent. *Mrs N. Macauley.*

ANNABRIANNA 3 ch.f. Night Shift (USA)–Aviceda 72 (Morston (FR) 125) **88**
[1988 7g 1989 10f3 12f2 10f3 10g 12g4 9g 10d*] quite good-topped filly: 25/1, won
maiden in October at Newbury gamely by 2 lengths from Angel Bright: stays 1½m:
acts on a soft surface: ran creditably on firm ground first 3 starts, hanging on second
of them. *J. A. R. Toller.*

ANNACERAMIC 4 b.f. Horage 124–Miss Redmarshall 80 (Most Secret 119) **65**
[1988 5g* 6f4 6m 6m 6g 5g 5g 5f5 6d* 5.6m6 5m6 7g2 1989 6m 8f6 7m 7s 9m3 8.2d]
workmanlike filly: poor mover: fair winner as 3-y-o: well below her best in 1989:
best effort on fifth outing: best form at up to 7f: probably acts on any going:
occasionally visored: didn't handle track at Epsom third outing at 3 yrs. *R. M.
Whitaker.*

ANNAF (USA) 3 b.c. Topsider (USA)–Kawkeb (USA) 72 (Vaguely Noble 140) **93**
[1988 7.5f* 7.3s3 1989 10.1g5 10.8m* 9f3] rather leggy, angular colt: moderate
walker and mover: fairly useful performer: won minor event at Warwick in October:
unlikely to stay beyond 10.8f: acts on any going: took good hold to post when below
form on reappearance: refused to enter stalls second intended outing. *H. Thomson
Jones.*

ANNA PETROVNA (FR) 2 b.f. (Mar 6) Wassl 125–Anna Paola (GER) (Prince **72**
Ippi (GER)) [1989 7m5 8f2] third living foal: half-sister to useful 1¼m to 1½m
winner Atlaal (by Northern Dancer): dam, leading filly at 2 yrs and 3 yrs in Germany,
won 11f Preis der Diana: length second of 9 to Madiriya in maiden at Brighton in
October, better effort: will stay 1¼m: may improve again. *J. L. Dunlop.*

ANN DU FEU 4 b.f. Tyrnavos 129–Rebecca (Quorum 126) [1988 10m 11.5m 10m **35**
10d 12m 12s6 12m3 12m 1989 12s 14.8d 10d 12m5 10.1m4 8.3g 10f] small, rather leggy
filly: poor mover: poor maiden: stays 1½m: acts on top-of-the-ground: blinkered last
3 outings: has run well for apprentice: inconsistent. *J. R. Jenkins.*

ANNIE LAURIE 2 b.f. (Mar 30) Aragon 118–Drama School 72 (Young **91**
Generation 129) [1989 5m4 6g 6m2 6g6 7m2 7m5 7g6 8d* 6g3 8d2 8s4 7d6 9s2]
4,000Y: second foal: half-sister to a winner at 2 yrs and 3 yrs in Germany by Valiyar:
dam, maiden, stayed 1m, is daughter of half-sister to Final Straw and Achieved:
quite useful filly: won minor event at Tralee in August: in frame at the Curragh in
Moyglare Stud Stakes (7½ lengths third to Chimes of Freedom), Panasonic Smurfit
EBF Futurity Stakes and Juddmonte EBF Beresford Stakes (nearly 3 lengths fourth
to Victory Piper) in the autumn: stays 9f: seems suited by soft ground: blinkered
fourth outing. *L. Browne, Ireland.*

ANNIO CHILONE 3 b.c. Touching Wood (USA) 127–Alpine Alice 94 (Abwah   73
118) [1988 7g 7g 10d⁵ 1989 10g 15.3f⁴ 14.5g² 14g 19f³] strong, good-bodied colt:
carries condition: modest form at best: beaten 2 lengths by Sierra Star in St Leger
Italiano at Turin: stays 1¾m: sold 33,000 gns Newmarket Autumn Sales. *J. L.
Dunlop.*

ANODYNE 3 b.f. Dominion 123–My Therape 112 (Jimmy Reppin 131) [1988 5g   100
6m* 6g* 7f 6d⁴ 7d 1989 6m⁶ 6g* 7g 6s] strong, deep-girthed filly: has plenty of
scope: good walker: has a slightly round action: co-favourite and looking very well,
showed improved form when winning handicap at Haydock in July, making virtually
all in good style: second and better effort after when creditable seventh of 29 in Ayr
Gold Cup, leading 4f: stays 6f well: acts on soft going and is possibly unsuited by
very firm. *J. W. Watts.*

ANOTHER ALOOF 3 b.f. Sayf El Arab (USA) 127–Lady Ever-So-Sure 80   —
(Malicious) [1988 NR 1989 6g 7m] small, plain filly: first foal: dam, out of fairly useful
sprinter Time of Hope, won sellers from 6f (at 2 yrs) to 1½m: showed signs of ability
in seller in May but tailed off in similar event 11 days later. *J. Pearce.*

ANOTHER BOY 3 br.g. Manor Farm Boy 114–Haverhill Lass 67 (Music Boy   —
124) [1988 NR 1989 7h⁵ 8g] leggy, sparely-made gelding: first live foal: dam
sprinter: well beaten in maidens at Brighton and Yarmouth. *A. Bailey.*

ANOTHER EARL (USA) 5 ch.h. Belted Earl (USA) 122–Aloran (USA) (Prince   —
John) [1988 8s 6v 6d 8d² 9f 7g** 7s 1989 8m³ 8m 8m a8g] lengthy, robust ex-Irish
horse: third foal: dam French 6f winner: won handicap at Sligo as 4-y-o: little form in
1989, but showed signs of retaining some ability: off course nearly 5 months before
final outing: stays 1m: acts on heavy going: blinkered twice at 4 yrs and on final
outing: sweating and moved poorly down third start: none too consistent. *B. Smart.*

ANOTHER LANE 2 b.f. (Mar 14) Tina's Pet 121–Spinner 59 (Blue Cashmere   73
129) [1989 5g⁴ 5m* 5m⁵] smallish, sturdy, sprint type: moderate mover: third foal:
sister to 5f winner Thorner Lane and half-sister to 3-y-o Resolute Bay (by Crofter),
5f and 6f winner: dam sprinter: won 5-runner minor event at Thirsk in September by
a neck from Lyndseylee: had difficult task when last of 5 in similar event at York 4
days later. *R. M. Whitaker.*

ANOTHER MARCH 3 b.g. Marching On 101–River Sirene (Another River 89)   66 §
[1988 5g⁵ 6f 6g** 7f² 7f 7f 7g³ 6g** 1989 6d⁴ 6m 7f 6h⁵ 6f² 7f⁵ 6m² 7f⁶ 6g 6g a7g⁶ a6g
a6g⁶] leggy gelding: has a round action: quite modest handicapper: well below best
in claimers last 4 starts, looking hard ride penultimate one: effective at 6f and 7f:
acts on firm going and a soft surface: sometimes sweating and edgy: blinkered tenth
outing: has found little off bridle: inconsistent and not one to rely on. *T. D. Barron.*

ANOTHER MARQUESSA 2 b.f. (Mar 22) Beldale Flutter (USA) 130–   51
Marquessa d'Howfen 93 (Pitcairn 126) [1989 5m⁴ 6f² 6g⁵ 7g] 2,000Y: tall, leggy,
unfurnished filly: easy mover: third foal: half-sister to 2 maidens by Ardross: dam
2-y-o 7f winner: plating-class form in maiden auction events on first 3 starts: off
course for 3 months, well beaten in nursery at Leicester on return: bred to stay
quite well but races keenly. *F. H. Lee.*

ANOTHER NICK 3 ch.g. Nicholas Bill 125–Another Move 69 (Farm Walk 111) — p
[1988 NR 1989 14d 15s⁴ 12d] 16,000Y: tall, lengthy, sparely-made gelding: moderate
walker: third foal: brother to 1½m to 14.6f winner and winning hurdler Tancred
Sand and half-brother to 5f and 7f winner Ela-Yianni-Mou (by Anfield): dam, 1½m
winner, sister to very useful middle-distance stayer Move Off: showed promise in
maiden (in need of race, moved badly down) at Haydock and minor event (good
headway 4f out then one pace) at Ayr: slipped and fell at Thirsk final start: may well
be capable of better. *J. M. Jefferson.*

ANOTHER RHYTHM 5 b.g. Music Boy 124–Just You Wait (Nonoalco (USA)   56 §
131) [1988 5g² 5.8g* 5d 5g⁶ 5f* 5g⁵ 5d⁶ 5m 1989 5f³ 5f 6g 5g 5f² 5f] big, lengthy
gelding: looked irresolute when neck second of 14 in seller at Beverley in
September: tailed off third and fourth (visored) outings and soundly beaten on last:
unlikely to stay beyond 6f: best on a sound surface: often taken down early or very
steadily: goes well with forcing tactics: highly-strung: not genuine. *J. R. Jenkins.*

ANOTHER SEASON 5 b.g. Ya Zaman (USA) 122–Another Tune (Red God   48
128§) [1988 8g⁶ 12f⁴ 10f⁴ 9g 12h 12f⁶ 1989 10g 12f⁵ 12h² 12h⁴ 10m⁵ 12h 10h*] leggy,
angular, quite attractive gelding: 20/1, won for first time in seller (no bid) at
Brighton in August: subsequently joined D. Browning and gelded: stays 1½m: acts
on hard going: has been tried in blinkers and a visor: has pulled hard. *A. Moore.*

ANOTHER WISH 3 ch.f. Horage 124–Cheerleader 90 (Floribunda 136) [1988   48
5d 6f⁵ 7m² 7.5s 7f⁵ 8m 1989 7g 10.1m 10f⁴ 10g² 10f* 8.2g³ 12g³ 10m⁴] smallish,

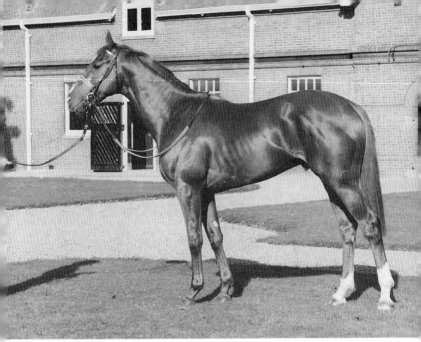

Sheikh Mohammed's "Anshan"

plain, sparely-made filly: moderate mover: favourite, won moderately-run claimer at Redcar in August: below form in seller final start: stays 1½m: acts on firm going: best ridden close to pace: wanders under pressure but has run creditably for 7-lb claimer: sold 5,000 gns Newmarket Autumn Sales. *W. J. Haggas.*

ANQUETIL 3 b. or br.g. Valiyar 129–Racemosa 70 (Town Crier 119) [1988 7d — 1989 7s 8g 8.2m 10h 10f⁵ 12s⁶ 10g 12g] neat gelding: little worthwhile form in varied company, including selling: trained until after fifth start by J. Sutcliffe. *C. Holmes.*

ANSHAN 2 ch.c. (Feb 19) Persian Bold 123–Lady Zi (Manado 130) [1989 7g⁵ 7f* **116** 8m* 7g³ 7g³] IR 100,000Y: leggy, quite good-topped colt: second foal: half-brother to Italian 3-y-o middle-distance winner Freeway of Love (by High Top): dam, minor winner at 1½m in France, is half-sister to dam of French 2000 Guineas winner No Pass No Sale: very useful colt: successful at Sandown in maiden in July and minor event in August: over 3 lengths third to The Caretaker in Cartier Million at Phoenix Park and very close third, making most and rallying well, to Dashing Blade in Three Chimneys Dewhurst Stakes at Newmarket: will stay 1¼m. *J. Gosden.*

ANSTEY BOY 4 gr.g. Decoy Boy 129–Miss Twiggy 80 (Tycoon II) [1988 7d² **33** 10.1d 7f⁶ 7m 8f 8d⁶ 8d 8d² 6d 9v 1989 10s 8s⁶ 8.3m⁵ 7g⁴ 8g⁴ a10g] small gelding: moderate mover: poor maiden: stays 1m: goes particularly well with a bit of give in the ground: visored once at 3 yrs: has run well for apprentice. *C. N. Allen.*

ANSWERS PLEASE 5 b.m. Don 128–Whichcombe 79 (Huntercombe 133) — [1988 NR 1989 16m 18f] poor maiden. *Capt. R. M. Smyly.*

ANTHONY LORETTO 4 b.g. Mummy's Game 120–Miss Silly (Silly Season **85** 127) [1988 5g² 5d* 5f 5f² 5f⁶ 5d 6g 5.6m 7g* 7g 1989 7g⁴ 7.6f⁴ 7f³ 7f 7m² 7g 6m⁵ 6d⁶ 6g* 6v*] smallish, good-quartered gelding: moderate walker: fair handicapper: successful in October in 25-runner event at Nottingham and 27-runner event at

67

Newbury, better effort when beating Joveworth on latter: effective at 6f and 7f: acts on any going: has worn crossed noseband: usually taken early or steadily to post nowadays: trained until after sixth outing by R. Casey. *Lord John FitzGerald.*

ANTHONY PASHA 3 b.c. Jalmood (USA) 126–Park Parade 94 (Monsanto (FR) — 121) [1988 NR 1989 10g 12f] short-legged, heavy-topped colt: moderate mover: first foal: dam, winner 5 times over 1½m, is out of sister to best staying 3-y-o filly of 1966 Parthian Glance: tailed off in maidens at Salisbury and Brighton in May. *J. L. Dunlop.*

ANTIGUAN STING 3 b.g. Head For Heights 125–Honey Bridge 99 (Crepello — 136) [1988 NR 1989 14g] 17,000Y: half-brother to St Leger winner Minster Son (by Niniski) and to 2 winners in Italy: dam 6f winner at 2 yrs: 20/1, tailed off in minor event at Redcar in November, chasing leaders 11f. *Mrs L. Piggott.*

ANTIQUE ANDY 2 br.c. (Mar 15) Mansingh (USA) 120–Spanish Bold 78 — (Tower Walk 130) [1989 5m] 3,600Y: neat colt: first foal: dam 7.6f and 1m winner: 33/1, beaten around 12 lengths when in mid-division in 17-runner maiden at Windsor in August. *D. J. G. Murray-Smith.*

ANTIQUE MAN 2 b.g. (May 18) Sayyaf 121–Firey Ann 80 (Firestreak 125) [1989 — 5g 5d⁶] IR 2,600F, 5,000Y: angular, sparely-made gelding: half-brother to several winners here and abroad, notably useful Irish 7f and 1m winner Kifinti (by Welsh Saint): dam won over 7f at 2 yrs: well beaten in spring sellers at Newcastle and Warwick. *J. Berry.*

ANTOINETTE JANE 2 b.f. (Mar 10) Ile de Bourbon (USA) 133–Hability 86 (Habitat 134) [1989 7g* 7m⁴ 10g] 32,000Y: lengthy, dipped-backed filly: has scope: fourth foal: sister to modest middle-distance filly Reunity: dam, unraced daughter of July Cup winner Parsimony, comes from excellent sprinting family: odds on, made all in 5-runner maiden at Sandown in July: around 7 lengths fourth to Moon Cactus at Newmarket month later, better effort in listed races: appeared not to stay 1¼m on final start, first for 3 months. *G. Harwood.*

ANURAG 3 br.g. Indian King (USA) 128–Merta (USA) (Jaipur) [1988 6d 6g 6d 52 1989 8g 8g 7m 9m 10g⁵] big, workmanlike gelding: 10/1 from 25/1, first worthwhile form when fifth in selling handicap at Nottingham in October: bit backward most other starts: evidently suited by 1¼m: retained by trainer 2,800 gns Ascot November Sales. *W. J. Musson.*

ANYTHING GOES 2 ch.f. (Mar 7) All Systems Go 119–Songful 73 (Song 132) 43 [1989 5g³ 5g⁶ 5g 5m⁴ 5m⁶] IR 1,500Y: leggy filly: poor mover: third reported foal: half-sister to disqualified 1986 2-y-o 5f seller winner Sam's Refrain (by Le Soleil): dam, out of daughter of Irish Oaks second Nile Bird, poor on flat and over hurdles: modest plater: blinkered (and on toes) fourth start: will probably be better suited by 6f. *T. D. Barron.*

ANYTIME ANYWHERE 2 b. or br.f. (Mar 17) Daring March 116–Martini Time 77 ? 90 (Ardoon 124) [1989 5g⁵ 5s³ 5d² 5d⁵ 5f⁵ 5f* 5m*] 3,600Y: sparely-made filly: sister to 1986 2-y-o 5f winner Dutch Courage and a winner in Belgium: dam raced only at 2 yrs, when tough and genuine 5f performer: smart plater: successful at Pontefract (retained 3,200 gns) and, appearing to put up much improved performance, at Edinburgh (retained 7,200 gns) in June: will prove best at 5f. *Mrs G. R. Reveley.*

AONIA 3 b.f. Mummy's Pet 125–Princely Maid 71 (King's Troop 118) [1988 6f 5m³ — 5d² 5g* 5m* 1989 6m 6g 6g] tall filly: fairly useful as 2-y-o, winning nurseries at Newmarket and Doncaster: well below that form in handicaps and minor event in 1989, running as if something amiss first 2 outings and off course 5 months after: one to be wary of. *M. A. Jarvis.*

APACHE 4 b. or br.c. Great Nephew 126–Siouan 78 (So Blessed 130) [1988 8v* 121 8g³ 10d⁵ 10.5g⁶ 10d* 10d* 12s² 11s² 12g* 12s² 1989 12g³ 12d³ 12s⁵ 12m* 13.3g² 13.5s³ 12d³] big, strong, workmanlike colt: usually looks very well: has a scratchy action: good performer: won strongly-run listed Keeneland Fred Archer Stakes at Newmarket in July by 1½ lengths from Emmson: placed also in £10,500 Doncaster Shield (first past post, demoted for interference), Lanes End John Porter EBF Stakes and Walmac International Geoffrey Freer Stakes (good second to Ibn Bey) at Newbury, Grand Prix de Deauville Lancel and Prix Foy (beaten at least 10 lengths by Star Lift and Robore) at Longchamp: better suited by 1½m than shorter, and will stay at least 1¾m: yet to race on firm going, acts on any other: has given trouble in paddock and is mounted in saddling box: best racing up with pace: tough and genuine: a credit to his trainer: sold to race in Saudi Arabia. *C. W. Thornton.*

APACHE PRINCE 2 gr.g. (Apr 14) Red Sunset 120–Maxi Girl (My Swanee 122) 66 [1989 7m 8m 8g] IR 10,000F, 50,000Y: rangy, rather attractive gelding: good walker:

half-brother to French listed 11f winner L'Effrontee (by Persian Bold), a prolific winner in Italy by Sallust and a bumpers winner in Ireland: dam, Irish 9f winner, is half-sister to Don: quite modest maiden: below form when ridden by 7-lb claimer on final start: subsequently gelded: looks sort to do better. *D. Morley.*

APACHE RYTHEM 6 b.g. Elvaston–Semi Quaver (Seminole II) [1988 NR 1989 12f] plain non-thoroughbred gelding: fourth foal: dam never ran: bandaged, tailed off after 2f in maiden at Brighton in May. *D. J. Wintle.* —

APHABEL 3 gr.f. Belfort (FR) 89–Aphaia (Prince de Galles 125) [1988 6m⁴ 6g 6m 5g 5m* 6d⁴ 7d 1989 7g⁶ 8g 8m⁶ 6g 7d a8g] lengthy, sparely-made filly: has scope: good walker: modest winner as 2-y-o: generally well below form in 1989: stays 7f: acts on top-of-the-ground and a soft surface: on toes and blinkered fourth start: visored final one: edgy on reappearance: suitable mount for a claimer. *S. G. Norton.* —

APHELINA 2 b.f. (Feb 23) Belfort (FR) 89–Aphaia (Prince de Galles 125) [1989 6m] tall, angular filly: moderate walker: third reported foal: sister to 2-y-o 5f winners Bellefire and Aphabel: dam unraced: 33/1, well beaten in 24-runner minor event at Windsor in August. *J. S. King.* —

APOLLO KING 3 b.c. Indian King (USA) 128–Mehudenna 77 (Ribero 126) [1988 6m³ 6g⁵ 6s² 7d² 8.5m 8s 1989 8d⁶ 8g 8g² 10m 10g⁴ 11m⁴ 11.7m⁴ 11f² 10g⁴ 10f² 12m⁶] leggy, rather close-coupled, angular colt: quite modest handicapper: stays 11f: acts on firm ground and a soft surface: has run creditably for 5-lb claimer and when sweating: winning novice hurdler. *P. Mitchell.* 66

APPAREL 2 ch.f. (Apr 30) Absalom 128–Anoda (FR) (Amber Rama (USA) 133) [1989 5g³ 5v 5d⁵ 5m⁵ 5f⁵ 5f⁵ 5f³ 7f⁵ 7f⁵ 5m 6g 5m 6g] 7,200Y: smallish filly: poor walker and moderate mover: sister to useful 1985 2-y-o 5f winner Sundeed, later successful in USA, and half-sister to 2 other winners, including 3-y-o Tanoda (by Tyrnavos), 5f to 1m winner at 2 yrs: dam placed in Italy: plating-class maiden: stays 7f: best form on a sound surface. *M. Brittain.* 51

Keeneland Fred Archer Stakes, Newmarket—
Apache keeps on well at the end of a strongly-run contest;
Emmson (right) and Per Quod fill the places

APPEAL FOR HELP 4 br.c. Star Appeal 133–Sovereign Help 98 (Sovereign — Lord 120) [1988 5g 5g 5d 5g 5g 1989 5s 5g] small, sturdy colt: poor maiden: blinkered, sweating and edgy on reappearance. *J. L. Spearing.*

APPELANIA 2 b.f. (Feb 3) Star Appeal 133–Penna Bianca (My Swallow 134) 63 [1989 7m 8m5 7.3v] strong, workmanlike filly: has plenty of scope: fourth foal: half-sister to 1988 2-y-o 6f winner Musiania (by Music Boy): dam won in Italy: quite modest form in Newmarket maidens on first 2 starts: soundly beaten in listed race at Newbury: stays 1m. *M. H. Tompkins.*

APPELLANT 4 b.c. Star Appeal 133–St Louis Sue (FR) 79 (Nonoalco (USA) 131) 55 [1988 10s 8g 6d 7g4 7g 7d 7g 7.5m 7g4 7m 1989 7d3 7d 6g 6g 8m* 8f 8f] tall, useful-looking colt: apprentice ridden, won for first time in seller (no bid) at Edinburgh: ran moderately in handicaps (second non-selling) later in June: needs at least 7f: acts on top-of-the-ground and a soft surface: below form in blinkers: wears bandages: sometimes on toes: trained on reappearance by W. Brooks. *D. H. Topley.*

APPETIZER 3 ch.g. Star Appeal 133–Zedative (FR) 74 (Zeddaan 130) [1988 NR 67 1989 12s5 8.2f 9m 10.6s a10g2 a11g] 12,000Y: lengthy, workmanlike gelding: second reported foal: half-brother to plating-class 4-y-o Durative (by Moorestyle): dam barely stayed 5f: 16/1 and ridden by 7-lb claimer, second to Steel Spark in maiden at Lingfield in October, apparently easily best effort: ran in seller time before: stays 1¼m. *C. E. Brittain.*

APPLE LANE (USA) 9 ch.g. Star Envoy (USA)–Queen of Diamonds (USA) — (Alcibiades 95) [1988 NR 1989 8m] ex-Irish gelding: easily justified favouritism in NH Flat race at Tralee in 1984: over 10 lengths tenth of 24 in amateurs event at Warwick in May. *B. J. Curley.*

APPLIANCEOFSCIENCE 2 b.g. (Mar 31) Bairn (USA) 126–Moonlight 69 Serenade 66 (Crooner 119) [1989 6m3 6f3 6m3 7g] 8,000Y: neat gelding: fifth foal: half-brother to 3-y-o 5f winner Stocious (by Petong) and useful 7f and 1m winner King Balladeer (by Dominion): dam, sister to smart sprinter Blackbird, stayed 1m: modest form in varied races: will be suited by 1m. *D. W. P. Arbuthnot.*

A PRAYER FOR WINGS 5 gr.g. Godswalk (USA) 130–Late Swallow (My 118 Swallow 134) [1988 NR 1989 5s* 6f2 6.3g* 6g3 7g5] tall, rather leggy gelding: won £7,600 handicap at Sandown (slowly away, first outing for 19 months) in April and IR £24,000 handicap at the Curragh (favourite) in July: put up much improved performance when third to Danehill in Ladbroke Sprint Cup at Haydock: modest fifth of 6, never a threat, to Gold Seam in Kiveton Park Stakes at Doncaster 2 weeks later: stays 6f: acts on any going: looked difficult ride when tried in blinkers. *J. Sutcliffe.*

APRES HUIT 2 b.f. (Apr 18) Day Is Done 115–Ma Minti 62 (Mummy's Pet 125) 43 p [1989 5v5] sparely-made filly: first foal: dam 5f winner: 50/1, under 4 lengths fifth of 20, one pace final 1f, to Puffy in seller at Ayr in October. *Mrs N. Macauley.*

APRIL CRACKER 2 b.f. (Apr 1) Cragador 110–Chanita (Averof 123) [1989 6f 53 7g2 8.2f] angular filly: second foal: half-sister to 3-y-o Merseyside Man (by My Dad

*John Roarty Memorial Scurry Handicap, the Curragh—
A Prayer For Wings (grey) is another successful British raider*

Tom), 6f seller winner at 2 yrs: dam unraced: running-on second in claimer at Yarmouth in September: moved down poorly and ran well below that form in seller later in month: wears bandages. *Dr J. D. Scargill.*

APTITUDE 4 gr.g. Rusticaro (FR) 124–Moonscape 87 (Ribero 126) [1988 6g 6d⁵ **89** 6f 6f 7g⁶ 7m⁴ 7d 7g 7d 1989 9d³ 10g* 12d⁴ 10.4m 10g 10m* 9m* 10m⁶ 10g] close-coupled gelding: has a quick, round action: fair performer: won apprentice event at Brighton in April and handicaps at Yarmouth (3-runner event, making all) in June and Wolverhampton in August: creditable sixth to Monastery in £24,200 handicap at Newbury, easily better subsequent effort: best at up to 1¼m: acts on firm going and a soft surface: blinkered twice in 1988: good mount for apprentice. *G. A. Huffer.*

AQUAGLOW 3 b.f. Caerleon (USA) 132–Light of Eire (USA) (Majestic Light **84** (USA)) [1988 NR 1989 7s* 8.5s² 8f* 10g 7m⁴ 8m] 65,000Y: medium-sized, sturdy, angular filly: moderate walker and mover: third foal: half-sister to useful Italian winners Spend A Penny (by Glint of Gold), winner from 7.5f to 11f, and Life On Light (by Arctic Tern), successful over middle distances: dam ran twice: fair performer: won maiden at Folkestone in April and handicap (made all) at Doncaster in June: ran badly fourth and sixth (pulled hard) starts: stays 8.5f: acts on any going: didn't handle descent well (probably green) at Epsom second outing. *Mrs L. Piggott.*

AQUAINTED 4 b.f. Known Fact (USA) 135–Gay Trinket 72 (Grey Sovereign **31** 128§) [1988 6v⁵ 8g 7.5f⁵ 8m 8f⁵ 7.5s⁶ 8d 7g⁴ 7m⁶ 8g⁴ 6m 1989 7d⁴ 7d⁶ 7f 8m 7g⁴ 6f a8g] leggy, rather sparely-made filly: moderate mover: poor performer: stays 1m: possibly unsuited by soft going, acts on any other: has run creditably for apprentice, but is not an easy ride: inconsistent. *M. Brittain.*

AQUALIS 2 b.c. (May 25) Taufan (USA) 119–Watermark 83 (Henry The Seventh **39** 125) [1989 6m 7f⁴ 7f] 9,000Y: small, close-coupled colt: fluent mover: half-brother to several winners, notably smart miler Spanish Pool (by Gay Fandango), subsequently a very good winner in South Africa: dam, 2-y-o 1m winner, is closely related to smart middle-distance performer Entanglement: fourth in maiden at Brighton in September: well beaten in Redcar seller on final start: sold 2,500 gns Newmarket Autumn Sales. *C. F. Wall.*

AQUARIAN PRINCE 4 ch.g. Mansingh (USA) 120–Princess Story 64 (Prince **42 d** de Galles 125) [1988 8f 7f 6f* 5g⁴ 6m³ 6m 6m 6h 1989 6d⁴ 7m 7.6f 6f 10.2h 6f 7h 5.3f] angular, sparely-made gelding: bad mover: poor handicapper: form as 4-y-o only in apprentice event on reappearance: virtually pulled up fifth outing: suited by 6f: acts on firm going and a soft surface: sometimes blinkered or visored: changed hands 1,300 gns Ascot July Sales after seventh outing: resold 1,150 gns Ascot October Sales: inconsistent. *P. Howling.*

AQUATIC 3 br.f. Mummy's Game 120–Pacific Polly (Mount Hagen (FR) 127) **68** [1988 5f² 6f² 6g 1989 6g³ 7f⁶ 6m³ 6f⁴ 7f⁴ 7.6m² 7g⁶ 7f² 8.2g a8g³] lengthy, shallow-girthed filly: quite modest maiden: has run in sellers: stays 7f: acts on firm going: suitable mount for apprentice: has run creditably when sweating: sold 3,400 gns Newmarket Autumn Sales. *R. J. R. Williams.*

AQUATIC (USA) 2 b.c. (Feb 10) Riverman (USA) 131–Troyanna 109 (Troy 137) **92** [1989 7m² 7m* 8m 8m] leggy, attractive colt: second foal: brother to 3-y-o 1¼m and 1¾m winner Trojan River: dam, 7f winner at 2 yrs and fourth in Irish Oaks, is daughter of half-sister to very smart 1963 American 2-y-o Traffic: fairly useful performer: won 11-runner Eagle Lane Acomb Stakes at York in August by 2 lengths from Smokey Native: ran creditably in Royal Lodge EBF Stakes and listed race at Ascot afterwards: stays 1m. *M. R. Stoute.*

ARABIAN BLUES 6 gr.h. Jellaby 124–Abercourt 89 (Abernant 142) [1988 12d — 1989 12m] tall horse: no form on flat since winning in the mud as 2-y-o. *S. Dow.*

ARABIAN NYMPH 2 ch.f. (Feb 23) Sayf El Arab (USA) 127–Connaught Nymph **49** 71 (Connaught 130) [1989 5d 5f⁴ 6f³ 5m⁶ 6g 6g] 3,000Y: small, sturdy filly: fourth foal: half-sister to 2 winners in Norway: dam stayed 1m at 2 yrs: moderate plater: probably better suited by 6f than 5f: has run creditably for 7-lb claimer. *J. Berry.*

ARABIAN SILENCE 2 ch.c. (Mar 19) Sayf El Arab (USA) 127–Silent Prayer 58 **78** (Queen's Hussar 124) [1989 6m 6m⁴ 7m⁶ 7g 7m² 8g⁴ 8g²] big, strong, useful-looking colt: has scope: turns off-fore in: fifth foal: half-brother to 3-y-o Vaigrant Wind (by Vaigly Great), a 6f winner at 2 yrs: dam won over hurdles: modest maiden: ran very well in nurseries on last 3 starts: stays 1m. *R. Hannon.*

ARABIAN STAR 2 ch.c. (Apr 10) Sayf El Arab (USA) 127–Tahoume (FR) **50** (Faristan 123) [1989 5f⁵ 6m 8f 8.2s] 105,000 francs (approx £9,700) Y, 24,000 2-y-o: strong, quite good-bodied colt: half-brother to French 1m to 1¼m winner

Tropea (by Trepan) and a winning hurdler in France: dam, placed in France, is half-sister to Prix de Diane winner Rescousse: plating-class form in maidens and a nursery: unseated rider fourth start. *J. G. FitzGerald.*

ARADU 5 b.g. Posse (USA) 130–Hollow Heart 89 (Wolver Hollow 126) [1988 7g⁵ 7m⁵ 7m⁴ 7m* 7m* 8s* 7m 7g 8d 1989 6f 7g 6f 7f 8.5g* 7.6m³ 7.6m³ 7g² 8m*] tall, rather sparely-made gelding: fairly useful handicapper: in excellent form in second half of season, winning at Epsom and Ascot: travelled strongly most of way when beating Gilderdale a length, idling, in £11,100 Brocas Stakes (Handicap) at Ascot: stays 1m well: acts on top-of-the-ground and soft going: best ridden up with pace: occasionally sweating and on toes: sold to race in Saudi Arabia 56,000 gns Newmarket Autumn Sales. *L. G. Cottrell.* 97

ARAGANT MAN 2 b.g. (Mar 21) Aragon 118–Cuillin Gael (Scottish Rifle 127) [1989 7g] 1,200Y: fourth foal: dam lightly-raced daughter of sister to high-class Italian colt Hoche: 33/1, slowly away and always behind in 20-runner maiden auction race at Goodwood in October. *B. Stevens.* —

ARAGON GIRL 3 ch.f. Aragon 118–Hi Love 83 (High Top 131) [1988 6g 6m 1989 8m⁶ 7m 8f 7.6m⁴ 8f 8.2g⁵] sparely-made, angular filly: poor form: not discredited when sweating and edgy in apprentice seller final start: will prove best at up to 1m: sold 2,000 gns Newmarket Autumn Sales. *E. Eldin.* 38

ARAMA 3 b.g. Sallust 134–Facade 99 (Double Jump 131) [1988 7m 7g 7g 1989 12d⁶ 15.5s] close-coupled gelding: soundly beaten in maidens and a handicap: sold to join R. Hoad 850 gns Ascot May Sales. *M. J. Haynes.* —

ARANY 2 b.c. (Apr 26) Precocious 126–Bellagio 68 (Busted 134) [1989 5d⁶ 6m⁵ 6g³ 6s 6g⁴ 6d*] 25,000F, 24,000Y: quite attractive colt: has a round action: second foal: half-brother to 1988 2-y-o 6f winner Slice (by Sharpo): dam 1¼m winner, stayed 1½m: showed vastly improved form when beating Dancing Party by 6 lengths in minor event at Catterick in October: will stay 7f: acts well on a soft surface. *M. H. Tompkins.* 96

ARASTOU 6 br.g. Pitskelly 122–High Lake (Quisling 117) [1988 NR 1989 11.7m²] smallish gelding: fair maiden at 2 yrs: ridden by 5-lb claimer, length second of 6, taking keen hold, in handicap at Windsor in July, only second subsequent outing on flat: will probably stay beyond 1½m: winning hurdler. *Miss B. Sanders.* 55

ARBITRAGEUR 2 ro.c. (Apr 25) Ile de Bourbon (USA) 133–Jenny Diver (USA) (Hatchet Man (USA)) [1989 6m* 7m³ 7m 6f] 2,800F: lengthy, rather unfurnished colt: fourth foal: half-brother to 3-y-o 8.5f seller winner Sukey Tawdry (by Wassl): dam won twice in USA: 33/1, won 4-runner minor event at Pontefract: hung left closing stages when last of 3 in similar event at Chester later in July: ran moderately final 2 starts: will stay 1m. *E. H. Owen jun.* 72

ARBORY STREET 4 b.g. Anfield 117–Melvin (Quiet Fling (USA) 124) [1988 6v 6g 5g⁶ 7m 8m 8v 6v⁶ 1989 8s*] lengthy, useful-looking gelding: good mover: well backed, apprentice ridden, won 19-runner selling handicap (bought in 3,200 gns) at Leicester in April: much better suited by 1m than shorter: acts on soft going. *Mrs J. R. Ramsden.* 56

ARBOUR (USA) 3 ch.f. Graustark–Vip (CHI) (Clever (ARG)) [1988 NR 1989 11.7m* 12h] $40,000F: neat filly: third foal: dam, winner at 2 yrs in Chile, is half-sister to dam of Irish St Leger winner Protection Racket: weak 7/2 and carrying condition, won maiden at Bath in July by short head from Golden Scissors, leading over 4f out and running on well: facing very stiff task, pushed along 6f out when tailed off in handicap at Brighton 4 weeks later. *G. Harwood.* 76

ARCH BIDDER 2 b.g. (Mar 6) Gabitat 119–Queen's Bidder (Auction Ring (USA) 123) [1989 5g⁵ 6d] compact gelding: fourth live foal: dam daughter of half-sister to Stanford Lad: backward, well beaten in maidens at Catterick (swerved stalls) and Goodwood. *B. Gubby.* —

ARC LAMP 3 b.g. Caerleon (USA) 132–Dazzling Light 116 (Silly Season 127) [1988 5g⁴ 6s² 6m⁵ 5g* 5f 5g* 1989 5m a6g⁴ a6g]] workmanlike, angular gelding: moderate walker: fair winner (apprentice ridden) as 2-y-o: below form in 1989: best form at 5f, though bred to stay further: seems unsuited by extremes of going: bought out of W. Jarvis' stable 1,250 gns Newmarket Autumn Sales after reappearance. *C. Spares.* —

ARCTIC CIDER (USA) 4 b.c. Arctic Tern (USA) 126–All Dance (USA) (Northern Dancer (CAN)) [1988 14s⁵ 12d⁴ 12s 1989 10.2g 10.1m] $575,000Y, 36,000 2-y-o: smallish colt: ex-Irish: first foal: dam, winner over 1m at 3 yrs in France and later placed in USA, is from good family: modest form at best as 3-y-o when trained by T. Stack: well beaten in maiden and claimer in first half of 1989. *D. L. Williams.* —

ARCTICFLOW (USA) 4 ch.g. Arctic Tern (USA) 126–Bold Flora (USA) (Bold —
Favorite (USA)) [1988 14.7m² 16m² 15s² 14m⁵ 16s 1989 a14g] rather leggy,
good-topped gelding: has a quick action: fair maiden as 3-y-o when trained by G.
Harwood: 20/1, tailed off in Southwell handicap in December: stays 2m: yet to race
on firm going, acts on any other: rather lazy first 2 starts in 1988: wore blinkers next
2, and ran badly without them final outing. *Mrs J. R. Ramsden.*

ARCTIC HEIGHTS (USA) 2 ch.c. (Apr 11) Arctic Tern (USA) 126–Dols — p
Jaminque (USA) (Kennedy Road (CAN)) [1989 6f⁶ 7m⁵] $97,000Y: half-brother to
several winners in France, including 1m and 9f winner Gazelia (by Helapade) and
middle-distance filly Sihame (by Crystal Palace): dam lightly raced: soundly beaten,
not knocked about, in maiden at Goodwood in July and minor event at Sandown in
September: may do better. *G. Lewis.*

ARCTIC HEROINE (USA) 3 ch.f. Arctic Tern (USA) 126–Proud Pattie (USA) —
(Noble Commander) [1988 NR 1989 10m 12m] $600,000Y: tall filly: moderate
walker: poor mover: half-sister to several winners, including very useful
middle-distance filly Ghaiya and high-class American 1987 3-y-o Fiesta Gal (both by
Alleged): dam, half-sister to dam of Nonoalco, won 6 times at up to 7f: well beaten in
competitive races for maiden and minor event at Leicester in the summer: sold
60,000 gns Newmarket December Sales. *H. R. A. Cecil.*

ARCTIC KEN 6 ch.g. Stanford 121§–Peggy Dell (Sovereign Gleam 117) [1988 —
8m² 8m² 9g 8f 1989 8m 8f⁶ 8m⁶ 8.5m] sturdy gelding: carries plenty of condition:
good mover: quite modest handicapper: 9/2 from 10/1, creditable eighth of 20 at
Doncaster (taken down early) in May on reappearance: no form after: suited by 7f or
1m: unsuited by soft going, acts on any other: visored final outing at 5 yrs, blinkered
second one (found very little) in 1989: good mount for inexperienced rider: joined
William Price. *Lady Herries.*

ARCTIC PLAY (USA) 3 b.f. Arctic Tern (USA) 126–Dream Play (USA) —
(Blushing Groom (FR) 131) [1988 6g² 1989 10f⁶] small, angular, unfurnished filly:
second in maiden at Leicester as 2-y-o: 20/1, well-beaten sixth of 7 in listed race at
Goodwood in May: should be suited by at least 1m: refused to enter stalls on
intended reappearance. *I. A. Balding.*

ARDELLE GREY 2 gr.f. (Mar 11) Ardross 134–Fair Eleanor (Saritamer (USA) 54
130) [1989 5g 5h³ 6m⁵ 6m² 7m* 7g⁶ 7g² 7m⁴ 7m³ 8.5f 10.6d⁴] 2,500Y: small,
good-quartered filly: moderate mover: first foal: dam poor plater (stayed 1m) from
family of Swiss Maid: fair plater: ridden by 5-lb claimer, won 6-runner event (bought
in 6,200 gns) at Brighton in June: stays 10.6f: sold 6,000 gns Newmarket Autumn
Sales. *M. H. Tompkins.*

ARDEN 5 b.g. Ardross 134–Kereolle (Riverman (USA) 131) [1988 12g* 12f² 14g⁴ 113
16f⁵ 12g 1989 16.2m* 20f] close-coupled, good-topped gelding: usually looks very
well: good mover: capable of very useful form: showed he'd retained all his ability
when winning minor event at Haydock by 4 lengths from Lauries Crusador, making
virtually all and quickening clear 3f out: on toes, made lot of running and eased
considerably final 2f when tailed-off last of 8 in Gold Cup at Royal Ascot almost
month later: effective at 1½m and stays 2m: acts on any going: seems to need a
galloping track: inconsistent: fairly useful hurdler. *C. P. E. Brooks.*

ARDLUI 2 b.c. (Apr 27) Lomond (USA) 128–Rocket Alert 110 (Red Alert 127) 71 p
[1989 8m⁴] 72,000F, 30,000Y: second foal: dam 5f to 7f winner: favourite, over 2
lengths fourth of 14, staying on steadily having run wide bend, to Daromann in
maiden at Edinburgh in October: should improve. *G. Harwood.*

ARDORAN 3 ch.g. Little Wolf 127–Smoke Creek 67 (Habitat 134) [1988 10d 1989 51 §
10.8s 10s 12.5f 13.8m 12m³ 15g² 16.5f* 14f 16.2m 15.5f⁶ 12.5f 12.5f²] lengthy,
good-bodied gelding: set very slow pace when winning handicap at Folkestone in
July: easily best effort after in Wolverhampton seller on final start: stays 2m: acts on
firm going: tailed off (pulled hard in blinkers), ninth and tenth outings: sold
9,400 gns Newmarket Autumn Sales: has appeared irresolute and is not one to trust.
M. L. W. Bell.

ARDOUR 3 b.g. Ardross 134–Evita 111 (Reform 132) [1988 7g 1989 10g 10m⁵ 58
10.2h²] angular gelding: quite modest form: claimed £12,051 to join M. Pipe when
second in claimer at Bath in June: should be suited by 1½m: winning hurdler. *W.
Jarvis.*

ARDROSS BEST 3 ch.c. Ardross 134–Do Your Best 89 (Try My Best (USA) —
130) [1988 8m 1989 10f 8.2m⁶] strong, good-topped colt: has a light, easy action: about 13
lengths sixth to Princess Accord in minor event at Nottingham in May, eased final
2f: stumbled on reappearance: should stay 1½m. *M. A. Jarvis.*

ARD T'MATCH 4 b.g. Ardross 134–Love Match (USA) (Affiliate (USA)) [1988   —
NR 1989 22.2f⁵ 14f⁵ 16.2m⁴] rangy gelding: has a long, rather round stride: first
reported foal: dam twice-raced half-sister to 2 winners in USA: 100/1, 18½ lengths
fifth of 8, weakening final 2f, to Ala Hounak in Queen Alexandra Stakes at Royal
Ascot: long way below that form when fourth in uncompetitive amateurs event at
Beverley: virtually pulled up second outing: will prove suited by thorough test of
stamina: gives strong impression will be better on easier ground (won NH Flat race
in March on good) and with stronger handling: bandaged behind last 2 starts. *R.
Simpson.*

AREA CODE 5 gr.h. Blakeney 126–Fayreela (Zeddaan 130) [1988 18d 16g 18.4v   —
18m⁴ 20f 16f 18.4s² 18.8d* 20.4d³ 16d² 16f⁶ 19v 17.4s⁵ 16s 1989 17.4s⁴ 16m a14g⁴]
leggy, sparely-made horse: fair handicapper at his best, but has deteriorated: tailed
off in £9,500 event at Ascot (had tongue tied down) in September: finished lame final
outing: suited by test of stamina and give in the ground (unsuited by heavy going):
usually blinkered nowadays: good mount for apprentice.*J. Mackie.*

ARETHUSA LEISURE 2 gr.f. (Apr 4) Homing 130–Birch Creek (Carwhite   **67** ?
127) [1989 5m³ 5m⁴] 2,000F, 10,500Y: medium-sized, lengthy filly: first foal: dam
French maiden also placed in pattern company in Italy: 4½ lengths third of 6 to La
Cabrilla in maiden at Salisbury in June: badly hampered on home turn in similar
event at Chester following month. *M. J. Fetherston-Godley.*

ARGELITH 3 b.g. Runnett 125–Miss Redmarshall 80 (Most Secret 119) [1988 6f   —
5g 5f⁶ 5f⁶ 1989 8s 9f 10f⁶ 10f] sturdy, good-quartered gelding: plating-class maiden:
little worthwhile form as 3-y-o, including in selling handicap: should stay 1¼m: sold
950 gns Doncaster October Sales. *R. M. Whitaker.*

ARGENTUM 2 br.c. (Feb 20) Aragon 118–Silver Berry (Lorenzaccio 130) **116**
[1989 5f* 6m⁵ 6f* 5m* 6g]
      Argentum's baffling display in the Racecall Gold Trophy at Redcar in
October, where he trailed in twenty-first of the twenty-five runners behind
Osorio, compels us to temper slightly our earlier enthusiasm for his prospects
as a three-year-old. Starting the well-supported favourite at 2/1 following his
highly impressive wide-margin defeat of Somethingdifferent in the Cornwallis
Stakes at Ascot earlier in month, Argentum was never travelling with the
fluency which characterised his victory at Ascot, took a bump two furlongs out
and was eased soon afterwards as the leaders went beyond recall. The
suggestions offered by Argentum's connections to the stewards at an inquiry
into his lack-lustre display—that he may have been unsuited by the loose
ground and that the race may have come too soon after the Cornwallis—are
entirely reasonable. It's quite possible, too, that Argentum just had an off day.
Whatever the reasons the fact remains that while Argentum is undoubtedly
blessed with plenty of ability and has the strength and scope to train on into a
good-class sprinter, his record of three wins and two poor efforts from five
races isn't one which instils maximum confidence in his fulfilling his potential.

Cornwallis Stakes, Ascot—Argentum shows a fine turn of foot

Argentum began his season in an auction event at Sandown in June where the unconventional conditions of the race meant that all five runners carried the same weight. It didn't matter much that Argentum, a small, good-quartered colt, needed the race for he could be named the winner shortly after halfway, and the two and a half lengths by which he disposed of India's Twist hardly reflected his superiority. Argentum was widely expected to follow up in a minor event at Windsor the following month but odds-on backers had a shock as he dropped away with two furlongs to run to finish a remote sixth of seven behind La Cabrilla. Argentum's disappointing performance was reportedly attributed to a throat infection and he wasn't seen on the racecourse again until late-September, when he lined up in a race of no great importance at Nottingham. Looking burly after his ten-week absence Argentum made short work of his ten opponents, travelling smoothly from the start, moving easily to the front when asked and having only to be pushed out in the closing stages to foil a gamble on Line of Vision by two lengths. Argentum was evidently progressing the right way again and the following month he took on the likes of Somethingdifferent, Haunting Beauty and the top Belgian two-year-old Deux Anes in the Cornwallis Stakes. There was no shortage of market confidence in Argentum's chance—he started third favourite—but even his most ardent supporters could scarcely have imagined his winning with such ease. Held up on the far side as the nine-runner field split into two groups Argentum was switched to challenge the front-running Dancing Music and Somethingdifferent running into the penultimate furlong, quickened immediately when shaken up with over a furlong to run and stormed clear in the last hundred yards to win by six lengths and three quarters (Dancing Music kept on well to third) as those runners on his part of the track dominated the finish. It was the first pattern-race victory for Argentum's trainer Holt, known principally as a trainer of sprinters, since Sweet Monday won the Mill Reef Stakes nine years previously: if Argentum progresses satisfactorily there may well be more big-race victories to savour in 1990.

		Mummy's Pet	Sing Sing
	Aragon	(b 1968)	Money For Nothing
	(b 1980)	Ica	Great Nephew
Argentum		(gr 1974)	Intent
(br.c. Feb 20, 1987)		Lorenzaccio	Klairon
	Silver Berry	(ch 1965)	Phoenissa
	(gr 1976)	Queensberry	Grey Sovereign
		(gr 1957)	Blackberry

The smart five-furlong to one-mile winner Aragon is one of several sons of Mummy's Pet available to domestic breeders and in common with his paternal half-brothers Runnett, Precocious and Petorius has made a steady rather than spectacular start to his time at stud. His name will no doubt be a familiar one to those buyers who frequent the less fashionable sales at Newmarket and Doncaster; besides his first pattern winner Argentum, who cost 13,000 guineas as a foal and 12,000 guineas as a yearling, the smart sprinter Point of Light and the listed Scherping-Rennen winner Sylvan Mistral, his best other representatives, could also have been bought for less than 16,000 guineas. Argentum's dam Silver Berry showed little in the way of ability in six attempts from five furlongs to a mile as a three-year-old but has fared much better at stud, producing four winners in all, including Argentum's stable-companion Eurodollar (by Sparkler), an honest if modest handicapper at around a mile, and the 1981 two-year-old six-furlong seller winner Strawberry Fields (by Song). Silver Berry is well related: she's a half-sister to the useful French sprinter Absalom (not to be confused with the Vernons Sprint Cup winner of the same name) and the very smart mile-and-a-quarter filly and successful broodmare Cranberry Sauce, dam of the good-class filly Sauceboat and grandam of Kind of Hush and Dusty Dollar. Argentum's grandam Queensberry also possessed more than her share of ability, figuring highly in the 1959 Free Handicap and winning the One Thousand Guineas Trial from two starts as a three-year-old. Seven furlongs was probably the limit of her stamina; her dam, Blackberry, barely stayed six. Argentum's best form is at five furlongs. He stays six, but he's very much an active type—he tended to get on edge on his last three starts and was attended on each occasion by two handlers in the paddock—and we doubt if he'll be given the opportunity to race over further. Argentum acts well on firm going. *L. J. Holt.*

ARIBIE 3 b. or br.f. Konigsstuhl (GER)–Arita (FR) (Kronzeuge) [1988 8d 8d* 1989 9f 12.2m⁵ 10m⁴ 8m 12f⁶ 9g 10v] plain filly: quite modest handicapper: below form in 1989, easily best effort on second start: should stay 1½m: acts on a soft surface: bandaged final start: found nothing under pressure fifth and is possibly unsatisfactory: sold to join P. Leach 2,300 gns Newmarket Autumn Sales. *N. A. Callaghan.* —

ARISTOCRATIC PETER (USA) 2 b.c. (Apr 5) Sir Ivor 135–Glimmer Glass (USA) (The Axe II 115) [1989 7g 7g] $75,000Y: good-topped colt: third foal: half-brother to Kohen Witha K (by Kings Lake), stakes winner from 5f to 9f: dam successful at up to 9f in USA: backward, never placed to challenge or knocked about in maiden at Sandown in July and all-aged event at Newmarket 4 months later: looks sort to do much better in time. *G. Harwood.* **66 p**

ARISTOCRAT VELVET 7 b.g. Bold Lad (IRE) 133–Majestic's Gold (Rheingold 137) [1988 NR 1989 10s 10m 8.2f 12h] leggy, good-topped gelding: quite modest handicapper in 1987: well beaten as 7-y-o, on final outing (July) tailed off in selling event at Brighton: stays 1¼m: unsuited by soft going and used to go very well on top-of-the-ground: occasionally blinkered: bandaged last 2 starts: one to leave alone. *J. Ringer.* —

ARITA 2 b.f. (Feb 10) Never So Bold 135–Exotic (Jaazeiro (USA) 127) [1989 5f* 5.3f*] second foal: dam twice-raced half-sister to 1000 Guineas winner Full Dress II: successful in September in maiden at Beverley and 4-runner minor event (by a head from Lake Mistassiu, having been outpaced to halfway) at Brighton: will be better suited by 6f. *R. W. Armstrong.* **78 p**

ARIZELOS 4 b.c. Shirley Heights 130–Swanilda (FR) (Habitat 134) [1988 12g* 12g⁶ 1989 16g* 20f*] strong, rangy colt: carries plenty of condition: winner of 3 of his 4 races, putting up a splendid performance under 10-0 to justify favouritism in **107**

Ascot Stakes—a splendid performance under 10-0,
Arizelos wins from stable-companion Santella Bobkes (blinkers)

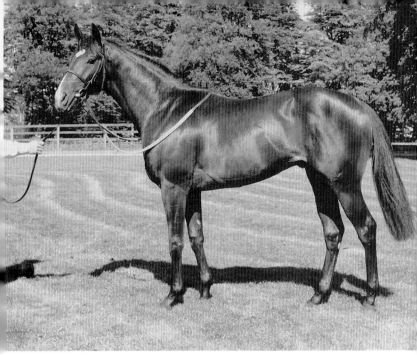

Mrs J. S. Bolger's "Armanasco"

£11,300 Ascot Stakes (Handicap) at Royal Ascot, making steady headway to lead 1f out and running on well, despite tending to hang left, to beat stable-companion Santella Bobkes 2 lengths: accounted for Nomadic Way very cleverly by a neck in Newmarket handicap 7 weeks earlier: stays 2½m well: acts on firm going: reportedly finished lame at Royal Ascot, and wasn't seen out again. *G. Harwood.*

ARMAGRET 4 b.g. Mandrake Major 122–Friendly Glen (Furry Glen 121) [1988 10m 12d 1989 13s⁴] medium-sized gelding: little sign of ability on flat: winning hurdler. *B. E. Wilkinson.*

ARMANASCO 2 br.c. (May 28) Ahonoora 122–For Going (Balidar 133) [1989 6g* 7s²] third reported foal: dam Irish 2m bumpers and hurdles winner: won Anheuser Busch EBF Railway Stakes at the Curragh in July by 1½ lengths from Neat Dish: beaten ¾ length by Victory Piper in Juddmonte EBF Beresford Stakes there over 3 months later: will stay 1m: useful 3-y-o in making. *J. S. Bolger, Ireland.*

ARMORY SHOW (FR) 2 b.c. (May 10) Mille Balles (FR) 124–Bamburi 93 (Ragusa 137) [1989 8m] workmanlike colt: half-brother to useful 6f to 1m winner Eldoret (by High Top): dam won twice at 1m: 16/1 and bit backward, always behind in 14-runner maiden at Thirsk in September. *J. G. FitzGerald.*

ARMY OF STARS 4 b.c. Posse (USA) 130–Starawak 68 (Star Appeal 133) [1988 10m⁶ 10m 10.2g⁵ 12g⁵ 14d⁴ 10g³ 10.2m* 1989 8s³ 8f³ 8f 8g 8f 8g 10.2g* 12g² 10.6s*] tall, useful-looking colt: fairly useful handicapper: in excellent heart in autumn, winning at Doncaster by 3 lengths from William Four and Haydock (looked tremendously well) in good style by 5 lengths, making virtually all and clear over 2f out, from Splashman: stays 1½m: acts on any going: blinkered once at 3 yrs: has

98 p

99

77

carried head high and found little, but did nothing wrong on last 3 starts: sold 82,000 gns Newmarket Autumn Sales. *C. E. Brittain.*

ARODSLOCH 3 br.f. Lochnager 132–Arodstown Alice (Sahib 114) [1988 6s 6m 5s 1989 5g 8.2g] leggy, plain filly: no sign of ability in varied events. *J. S. Haldane.* —

AROMATIC 2 b.c. (Apr 28) Known Fact (USA) 135–Mint 100 (Meadow Mint (USA)) [1989 7g⁶ 7m* 8f* 8g 8g] well-made, quite attractive colt: has a free, round action: fifth foal: half-brother to fair 7f to 9f winner Solo Style (by Moorestyle): dam middle-distance stayer: fairly useful colt: successful in maiden at Goodwood in August and nursery at Pontefract in September: below form last 2 starts: better suited by 1m than 7f. *G. Harwood.* **97**

AROUSAL 2 br.f. (Apr 2) Rousillon (USA) 133–Model Girl (FR) (Lyphard (USA) 132) [1989 6g³ 6f* 7s* 8m⁴] rangy, rather unfurnished filly: seventh foal: half-sister to 2 winners in France by Sharpman, including In Focus, successful at up to 1½m: dam French 1¼m and 10.5f winner: favourite, made virtually all in 5-runner maiden at Goodwood in July and Prix du Calvados at Deauville: creditable fourth of 8 to Silk Slippers in Hoover Fillies' Mile at Ascot: stays 1m. *Major W. R. Hern.* **101**

ARPERO 2 b.f. (Mar 19) Persian Bold 123–Arvel (Thatching 131) [1989 7f* 7m² 8m⁵] IR 26,000Y: strong, workmanlike filly: has scope: shows a round action: first foal: dam, out of half-sister to Oaks winner Ginevra, won 6 times in Italy, including Group 3 5f Premio Omenoni: quite useful filly: won maiden at Brighton in August: better form in Black Bottle Scotch Whisky Prestige Stakes at Goodwood (1½ lengths second to Moon Cactus) and Hoover Fillies' Mile at Ascot: stays 1m. *Sir Mark Prescott.* **95**

ARRAGUANIE 3 gr.c. Tolomeo 127–Princess Runnymede 108 (Runnymede 123) [1988 NR 1989 8m 12g] big, leggy, good-topped colt: sixth reported foal: half-brother to fairly useful staying handicapper Prince of Princes (by Bustino) and fair 1m and 11.1f winner Framlington Court (by High Top): dam stayed 6f: 33/1 and bit backward, never dangerous in maidens at Newbury in the summer: slowly away and green on debut. *P. T. Walwyn.* —

ARRANDALE 3 b.f. Tickled Pink 114–Dawn Affair 77 (Entanglement 118) [1988 5m⁵ 5f³ 6d³ 7g 5m 6g 1989 6f 8g 8g⁶ 10s] leggy, lightly-made, angular filly: poor plater: no form as 3-y-o: stays 6f: acts on firm going and a soft surface. *J. Parkes.* —

ARRAN VIEW 3 br.g. Aragon 118–Shadow Play (Busted 134) [1988 6s⁴ 7g 1989 7v⁵ 8d⁴ 8.5g³ 8g 8f 10.6g⁵ 8.2g] tall, fair sort: moderate walker: modest maiden: in frame at Ripon and Beverley: quickly eased when beaten in handicaps on 3 of last 4 starts: stays 1m, probably not 1¼m: acts on a soft surface: sold to join B. Llewellyn 4,400 gns Doncaster September Sales. *P. Calver.* **67**

ARROW DANCER 3 b.g. Gorytus (USA) 132–Rose And Honey (Amber Rama (USA) 133) [1988 6g⁵ 7g⁶ 6g 7d³ 7m⁵ 1989 8d⁴ 7m⁴ 8f⁶ 8f⁶ a8g⁵] lengthy, useful-looking gelding: comfortably best efforts in handicap and claimer (blinkered) on second and final starts: stays 1m: acts on top-of-the-ground and a soft surface: sold to join R. O'Sullivan 10,000 gns Ascot December Sales. *P. F. I. Cole.* **73**

ARSAAN (USA) 3 b. or br.f. Nureyev (USA) 131–Anne Campbell (USA) (Never Bend) [1988 7g* 1989 10g 8f* 10m³ 8g⁵] big, workmanlike filly: has scope: won listed race at Kempton in May by 2½ lengths from Rain Burst: 11/10 on, creditable third to Shyoushka in similar event at Newbury, leading over 2f: modest fifth in Child Stakes at Newmarket in July: may well prove best at around 1m: acts on firm going. *M. R. Stoute.* **106**

ARTAIUS STAR 5 b.g. Artaius (USA) 129–Godwyn (Yellow God 129) [1988 12g 12g 8g² 9g⁴ 1989 8h⁶] workmanlike, good-quartered gelding: plating-class maiden: keen-going type, suited by strongly-run race at 1m to 1¼m: acts on top-of-the-ground and a soft surface: blinkered once at 3 yrs and on only outing (found little) at 5 yrs: has run well for apprentice: inconsistent: sold to join O. Brennan 2,700 gns Doncaster August Sales: winning selling hurdler despite looking none too genuine. *J. J. O'Neill.* —

ARTHUR DEVIS 2 ch.c. (Apr 21) Superlative 118–Venetian Sky 85 (Touch Paper 113) [1989 5s² 5d 6g⁶] 20,000Y: good-topped colt: first foal: dam 7f winner is daughter of half-sister to high-class miler Hilal: 4 lengths second to Prince Jakatom in early-season maiden at Newbury: well beaten in Lingfield seller on final start, first run for over 4 months. *W. Jarvis.* **55**

ARTHURS STONE 3 ch.c. Kings Lake (USA) 133–Two Rock 70 (Mill Reef (USA) 141) [1988 7d 7.5f 1989 12.2m* 16.2g 12f 13.8g⁶ 12m 12s² 12.5f³ 10.6s*] quite modest performer: confidently ridden when winning claimer at Catterick in May: fell next outing: ran as if something badly amiss third to fifth starts: joint favourite, **67**

Warren Stakes, Epsom—Artic Envoy is a comfortable winner

easy winner of seller (sold to join J. S. Wilson 9,800 gns) at Haydock in October: effective at 1¼m to 1½m: acts on any going. *N. A. Callaghan.*

ARTIC ENVOY (USA) 3 ch.c. Arctic Tern (USA) 126–Eternity (FR) (Luthier **114** 126) [1988 7m³ 10g³ 1989 12s* 12m² 12f4 15g 12g² 12m4] big, angular colt: has plenty of scope: won listed race at Epsom in April: good staying-on second in Derby Italiano at Rome and Gran Premio d'Italia at Milan, best efforts after: fair fourth of 8 to Assatis in Group 1 event at Milan final outing: hung persistently in King Edward VII Stakes at Royal Ascot third start: suited by 1½m: acts on soft going and top-of-the-ground: very useful. *P. A. Kelleway.*

ARTILLERY FLIGHT 2 ch.c. (Mar 21) Henbit (USA) 130–Any Price (Gunner — B 126) [1989 5g 6m 7f6] IR 6,500F, 4,800Y: good-topped colt: second foal: half-brother to 3-y-o Heron's Green (by Petorius): dam half-sister to All Systems Go: poor maiden: unruly at stalls and looked a difficult ride second outing: sold 700 gns Ascot November Sales. *R. Simpson.*

ART JOY 3 b.f. Humdoleila 103–Red Squaw 61 (Tribal Chief 125) [1988 6m 1989 — 10m 10m 15.3g] small filly: of little account: sold 1,100 gns Ascot September Sales. *B. Preece.*

ARTY SCHWEPPES (USA) 3 ch.g. Super Concorde (USA) 128–Mon Solange **64** (USA) (Bold Reason) [1988 6g5 7d 10d³ 10.2m 1989 10g 10d 11.7m 14f 14f³ 14m³ 17.6f³ 16f* 16f³ 16f4dis] angular gelding: favourite, won 4-runner maiden at Lingfield in July: below form in handicaps after, moving moderately down on final start: stays 17.6f: acts on firm going and a soft surface: sold 10,000 gns Newmarket Autumn Sales. *R. J. R. Williams.*

ARYAF (CAN) 3 b.f. Vice Regent (CAN)–Fashion Front (Habitat 134) [1988 6g4 — 1989 8m 10.6g] workmanlike filly: bit backward, little worthwhile form in maidens: moved moderately down final start: should stay 1m: sold 2,100 gns Newmarket December Sales. *H. Thomson Jones.*

ASBAAB 4 b.g. Young Generation 129–The Yellow Girl 102 (Yellow God 129) **78** § [1988 8g5 8.5f* 8f6m 9m 10g 10.2g5 1989 8g 8g5 9f 7m³ 7m³ 10g³ 8.3m³ 7f 9m 9g 7g 8g a8g² a7g] good-bodied, useful-looking gelding: carries plenty of condition: moderate mover: placed as 4-y-o in handicap and claimers, but finds little off bridle: effective at 7f and probably stays 1¼m: has won on firm going, but needs an easier surface nowadays: has had tongue tied down: trained until after eighth start by D. Chapman: changed hands 7,000 gns Ascot November Sales: not one to trust. *W. J. Musson.*

ASCENDING DREAM (USA) 2 ch.f. (Feb 18) Nureyev (USA) 131–Sharp **57**
Ascent (USA) 97 (Sharpen Up 127) [1989 5m* 5m⁶ 5m] small, attractive filly: turns
off-fore out: poor mover: first foal: dam, a 2-y-o 5f performer here later Grade 3 8.5f
winner in USA, is daughter of Rivermande, a very useful winner at around 1m in
France: won maiden at Wolverhampton in August, running on well despite edging
left: behind in nurseries, facing stiff task on first occasion. *B. W. Hills.*

ASCENMOOR 10 b.g. Ascendant 96–Honeymoor 64 (Pardao 120) [1988 NR 1989 —
12g 10m] no longer of much account: blinkered and bandaged final outing. *S. R.
Bowring.*

AS D'EBOLI (FR) 2 b.c. (Apr 14) What A Guest 119–Ana d'Eboli (FR) (King of **60**
The Castle (USA)) [1989 5m⁴ 6f⁴ 6m⁶ 8m⁶ 10g] 50,000 francs (approx £4,600) Y:
sturdy colt: moderate mover: half-brother to several minor winners in France,
including 15.5f winner Acteon (by Lightning): dam twice-raced half-sister to Prix
Dollar winner Semillant: quite modest form in maidens and minor events: stays 1m:
blinkered last 2 starts. *J. G. FitzGerald.*

AS GOOD AS GOLD 3 ch.g. Oats 126–Goldyke 63 (Bustino 136) [1988 7m⁵ 7d —
8s 1989 12g⁶ 14f⁵] robust, workmanlike gelding: quite modest maiden in 1988, best
effort on debut: well below form in handicaps in July as 3-y-o: sweating and edgy,
tailed off when 32 lb out of handicap final start: should be suited by a test of stamina:
winning juvenile hurdler. *G. B. Balding.*

ASHAL 3 b.c. Touching Wood (USA) 127–Johara (USA) 92 (Exclusive Native **111** p
(USA)) [1988 7m 1989 14f² 16f* 16f* 14g*] tall, quite attractive colt: grand mover,
with a long stride: successful at Redcar in 4-runner maiden (most impressively) in
July, 2-runner minor event (25/1 on) in October and 13-runner minor contest (by 6
lengths from Sudden Victory) in November: wears tongue strap: smart stayer in the
making. *H. Thomson Jones.*

ASH AMOUR 2 gr.f. (Mar 28) Hotfoot 126–Loving Doll 72 (Godswalk (USA) 130) **54** p
[1989 7m] sparely-made filly: first foal: dam stayed 7f and would have been suited by
further: 33/1 and ridden by 7-lb claimer, never-nearer twelfth of 21 in maiden at
Newmarket in October. *R. J. R. Williams.*

ASHDREN 2 b.c. (May 12) Lochnager 132–Stellaris (Star Appeal 133) [1989 6g 6f **75**
6g*] 4,400Y, 4,000 2-y-o: angular, plain colt: second living foal: half-brother to poor
3-y-o Rapidaris (by Rapid River): dam, ran 4 times at 3 yrs, is half-sister to Rapid
Knot, a fair 7f and 1m winner: confirmed earlier promise when winning 20-runner
maiden claimer at Goodwood in October, beating Ala Wing by ½ length: may stay 7f.
A. M. Robson.

ASHTINA 4 b.g. Tina's Pet 121–Mrewa (Runnymede 123) [1988 5m⁴ 5d 6f* 5m 6f **93**
5g 5m 6m 5g 1989 5s* 5m 5f 5f 5g 6f 6f 6s 5m* 5m] leggy, good-topped gelding:
quite useful on his day: best efforts as 4-y-o when winning 17-runner handicap at
Epsom in April and £7,800 handicap at Ascot, making virtually all, by short head
from Sloe Berry, in September: well below his best most other starts: stays 6f: acts
on any going: blinkered fifth start: often gets on toes: trained first 7 starts by A.
Ingham: subsequently gelded: not one to trust implicitly. *J. Sutcliffe.*

ASHWAQ (USA) 3 b.f. Robellino (USA) 127–Vexation (USA) (Vice Regent **78**
(CAN)) [1988 6g³ 7d⁶ 1989 10s³ 8d² 8m³ 8m⁵ 10d⁶] lengthy, quite attractive filly:
moderate walker and mover, with a quick action: fair maiden: best efforts first 2
starts: sweating and edgy on final one, first for over 4 months: should prove better at
1¼m than 1m: acts on soft going, probably unsuited by top-of-the-ground: sold
25,000 gns Newmarket December Sales. *P. T. Walwyn.*

ASIAN PETE 2 br.c. (Mar 6) Persian Bold 123–Native Melody (Tudor Music 131) **100**
[1989 5f³ 7g* 7m⁵ 7m 8f* 8f*] 48,000Y: good-topped colt: has a powerful action:
fourth foal: half-brother to 5f and 1m winner Formatune (by Double Form) and a
winner in Scandinavia: dam Irish 7f winner: showed much improved form when
blinkered in nurseries on last 2 starts, making all at Brighton (won by 3 lengths,
clear) and Pontefract (won by 6 lengths) within a week in October: earlier won
maiden at Newmarket: suited by 1m: races keenly and is suited by forcing tactics:
ran poorly when sweating and edgy fourth start: sold to race in Saudi Arabia 96,000
gns Newmarket Autumn Sales. *G. Harwood.*

ASITAPPENS 3 ch.g. Music Maestro 119–Dalchroy (Hotfoot 126) [1988 6g 5m⁵ **67**
1989 7m⁵ 7m* 7.5m* 8m* 9m 7s 8.2d²] compact gelding: won sellers at Leicester
(bought in 8,500 gns) and Beverley (bought in 15,500 gns) and handicap (ridden by
5-lb claimer, holding on by a neck) at Yarmouth in space of 2 weeks in August: good
second in claimer at Haydock, easily best effort after: should prove best at up to 1m:

acts on top-of-the-ground and a soft surface: gelded after final outing. *M. H. Tompkins.*

ASLIA   3 b.f. Henbit (USA) 130–Fantasy Land (Nonoalco (USA) 131) [1988 7g² 7m —
1989 10s 12m] big, rangy filly: second in maiden at Sandown as 2-y-o: last in
moderately-run listed race at Newmarket and maidens (tailed off) at Sandown and
Newbury. *I. A. Balding.*

ASONESS   3 b.f. Laxton 105–Asicion 89 (Above Suspicion 127) [1988 6m* 6f⁵ —
1989 7g 8m a7g] lengthy, workmanlike filly: has a round, powerful action: quite
modest seller winner as 2-y-o: well beaten in handicaps in 1989, in need of race and
sweating badly when tailed off final start: should stay 7f. *M. R. Leach.*

ASQUITH (USA)   3 ch.g. Golden Act (USA)–Sweet Patina (USA) (Moonsplash   59
(USA)) [1988 7g 8d 1989 10m⁴ 8g* 7m⁶ 8.2m⁵ 8.3d⁵ 8.2g] sparely-made,
close-coupled gelding: has a fluent, rather round action: won claimer at Pontefract
in July: blinkered and not discredited, making most, in similar event fourth start:
below form after, pulling hard in apprentice handicap final outing: suited by 1m: acts
on top-of-the-ground: bought out of W. Haggas's stable 9,500 gns Doncaster August
Sales after fourth outing: resold 3,200 gns Newmarket Autumn Sales. *N. Tinkler.*

ASSATIS (USA)   4 b.c. Topsider (USA)–Secret Asset (USA) (Graustark) 125
[1988 10d* 12d² 12m* 1989 12f² 12g² 11.1m* 12m* 12f]
So impressive was Assatis in the Cumberland Lodge Stakes at Ascot on
his final outing as a three-year-old that a season which included just two
defeats—the first to the Arc winner Carroll House—was something of an
anticlimax, and had its disappointments in the doubts about his resolution and
his non-appearance in the major European races. He missed the Coronation
Cup and wasn't even entered for the King George VI and Queen Elizabeth
Diamond Stakes because, apparently, he took too long coming to himself; the
Grand Prix de Saint-Cloud was also passed over at a late stage to give him
more time. As for the Prix de l'Arc de Triomphe, to which his whole season
had supposedly been geared, speculation started a week before the race that
he had been sold and would not run. Confirmation came in the next few days
that a Japanese client of the BBA had bought the colt and that Assatis would be
retired to stud in Japan in 1991 after being kept in training as a five-year-old.
Enough of the races Assatis missed as a four-year-old; what of the ones
he didn't? The Hardwicke Stakes at Royal Ascot attracted just four runners
for the third time in the last five years. Besides Assatis, who started odds on
in all his races in Europe in the latest season, Top Class, Emmson and Glacial
Storm went to post. Assatis raced in second behind Emmson until the home
straight when, pushed along vigorously, he improved his position and took the
lead more than a furlong out. He was well on top inside the final furlong and
had only to be pushed out to beat Top Class by three lengths; he had beaten
him by eight in the Cumberland Lodge. The betting again suggested a
one-horse affair in the Princess of Wales's Stakes at Newmarket the following
month, but subsequent events were to show the nature of the task facing
Assatis in a very different light. Assatis was niggled along as early as half a

Hardwicke Stakes, Ascot—Assatis lands the odds

*Gran Premio del Jockey Club e Coppa d'Oro, Milan—British-trained challengers
Assatis and Alydaress dominate Italy's most valuable open-aged event*

mile from home and inside the last furlong he was always being held by Carroll House and went down a neck, the pair three lengths clear of Michelozzo. When coming under strong pressure Assatis swished his tail and gave the impression he was reluctant. In the BonusPrint September Stakes at Kempton his temperament was again called into question and it was only a tremendous ride from Cochrane (recently announced as Harwood's new stable jockey for 1990) that prevented Assatis from meeting the same fate as Hot Touch, Slip Anchor, Bakharoff, Bellotto and Glacial Storm—all beaten favourites in the race's short history. At halfway Assatis was being ridden along well adrift of the pace-setting Tralos and most of his supporters must have already resigned themselves to defeat. Even early in the straight his chance looked slim, particularly when he began swishing his tail again and threatening not to respond. Eventually, he started to run on and wore down Relief Pitcher in the final strides. The winning margin was a head with stable-companion Tralos, winner of the Cumberland Lodge Stakes next time out, three lengths away in third. The same weekend that Tralos was sent to Woodbine for the Rothmans International, Assatis was dispatched to Milan to contest the Gran Premio del Jockey Club e Coppa d'Oro along with two other British challengers, Alydaress and Artic Envoy. On his first run abroad, his first for his new owner and his first in a Group 1 event he put up an excellent performance: always in touch, he led over two furlongs out and held off Alydaress by half a length, the two clear of the rest. In the Japan Cup a month later he faced stiffer opposition and was unequal to the task: in a strongly-run race, he was never better than mid-division and beat just three home.

			Northern Dancer	Nearctic
	Topsider (USA)		(b 1961)	Natalma
Assatis (USA)	(b 1974)		Drumtop	Round Table
(b.c. 1985)			(b 1966)	Zonah
	Secret Asset (USA)		Graustark	Ribot
	(b 1977)		(ch 1963)	Flower Bowl
			Numbered Account	Buckpasser
			(b 1969)	Intriguing

Assatis' pedigree details were fully documented in *Racehorses of 1988*. In the latest season his three-year-old close relation Warrshan (by Northern

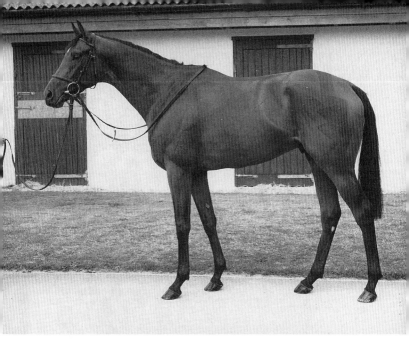

Yoshiyuki Ito's "Assatis"

Dancer) won the Predominate Stakes and Gordon Stakes at Goodwood despite finding little when in front. Assatis' trainer described him as 'a better horse sitting in behind a good pace and coming with a late burst'. Razeen, a two-year-old brother to Warrshan who was bought by Darley Stud Management for 1,175,000 dollars as a foal, is in training with Cecil but has yet to race. Secret Asset's first foal Secret Prospector (by Mr Prospector), a stakes-placed winner at up to a mile at four years, is now at stud in South Africa. The unraced Secret Asset is a daughter of Numbered Account, the best American two-year-old filly of 1971, and a half-sister to Grade 1 winners Dance Number and Private Account, the former the dam of the Breeders' Cup Juvenile winner Rhythm, the latter the sire of the top-class filly Personal Ensign and the Cherry Hinton Stakes and Moyglare Stud Stakes winner Chimes of Freedom. Assatis, a tall, good-topped colt, has a fluent, rather round action. The stiffer the test of stamina at a mile and a half the better—he will stay further given the chance. He has not been raced on very soft going and has shown his best form on top-of-the-ground. He tends to get a little worked up in the preliminaries. *G. Harwood.*

ASSIGNMENT 3 b.c. Known Fact (USA) 135–Sanctuary (Welsh Pageant 132) **78**
[1988 6d³ 6g 1989 8s⁶ 7h² 7f⁴ 8m⁵ 7h* 7m² 7d a8g³] strong, deep-girthed colt: modest performer: well backed, won claimer at Brighton in August: placed after, running creditably, in similar event at Salisbury (not finding great deal) and handicap at Lingfield: pulled hard for apprentice in between: stays 1m: acts on any going: wore severe noseband last 3 outings: bandaged behind. *P. F. I. Cole.*

ASTLEY JACK 3 gr.c. Belfort (FR) 89–Brigado 87 (Brigadier Gerard 144) [1988 **63**
5v 5d 1989 6s⁵ 6m a7g] leggy colt: 100/1 and ridden by 5-lb claimer, fifth in minor

Michael Sobell Handicap, York—
Athens Gate (right) is the only northern-trained winner on Timeform Charity Day

event at Nottingham, only sign of ability: faced very stiff task in handicap final start, first for 6 months: suited by 6f: sweating and edgy first 2 outings. *K. White.*

ASTRAKHAN LAD   2 gr.c. (Mar 18) Persian Bold 123–Mrs Mutton 89   —
(Dancer's Image (USA)) [1989 5f⁵ 5f⁵ 8m⁶] IR 2,500Y: good-bodied colt: carries condition: sixth foal: half-brother to Italian 3-y-o Jill-Vision (by Vision), French 11f winner Mutton Foot (by Prince Tenderfoot) and 5.8f and 6f winner Useful (by Thatching): dam, placed at 1½m, was disappointing: poor maiden: best effort over 1m: slowly away first 2 starts: flashed tail final one. *P. T. Walwyn.*

ASTRID GILBERTO   2 b. or br.f. (Apr 10) Runnett 125–Natasha 87 (Native   75
Prince) [1989 6h⁴ 6m* 6f² 5m* 5m⁶] 6,000Y: lengthy, quite attractive filly: sister to one-time fairly useful sprinter Gilberto and half-sister to 3-y-o Brave Heroine (by Sandhurst Prince) and several winners, including fairly useful sprinter New Express (by Bay Express): dam won 3 times over 5f at 2 yrs: modest filly: made all or most in small fields in summer for maiden at Yarmouth and nursery at Windsor: ran moderately final start (August): stays 6f: tends to flash tail: sold 7,000 gns Newmarket December Sales. *G. A. Huffer.*

ASTRONEF   5 b. or br.h. Be My Guest (USA) 126–Mill Princess (Mill Reef (USA)   112
141) [1988 6m² 7g² 6m² 6d* 6g 5s³ 6g⁵ 7s 1989 5m² 6g* 5f 6.5d⁶ 6s* 5g 6.5s⁴]
strong, lengthy horse: very useful performer: won Group 2 Premio Melton at Rome in May by 3 lengths from Cricket Ball and Group 3 Goldene Peitsche at Baden-Baden (for second year running) in August by neck from Savahra Sound: well behind in King's Stand Stakes at Royal Ascot and Ciga Prix de l'Abbaye de Longchamp on third and sixth outings: suited by 6f: acted on soft going and top-of-the-ground: retired to Knocktoran Stud, Co Limerick, fee IR £2,750 (special live foal). *R. Collet, France.*

ASTRONOMER   3 b.g. Head For Heights 125–Diamonds In The Sky (African   55
Sky 124) [1988 6d 6m⁶ 5g⁶ 6s 6f 1989 6s 5f⁴ 5f 5m⁶ 7.5f 7f⁴ 8.5f* 8m 8m⁴ 8g⁶ 8f⁴ 8f
8f⁶] workmanlike, good-topped gelding: has quick action: plating-class performer: won apprentice handicap at Beverley in July: better at around 1m than shorter: acts on firm going: sometimes slowly away: takes strong hold and is best held up: gelded after final start. *F. H. Lee.*

ASTURIAS   6 b.g. Artaius (USA) 129–Tanaka 106 (Tapalque 126) [1988 10.2s*   —
10v 10m³ 10.2m 1989 10.8s⁴ 10m] robust gelding: plating-class winner as 5-y-o: tailed off in Nottingham handicap in May, and not seen out again: best at 1¼m: acts on top-of-the-ground and soft going. *J. M. Jefferson.*

ATALL ATALL 6 b.h. Kampala 120–Bint Africa 71 (African Sky 124) [1988 5g **93**
5g² 5m⁵ 6f 6f 5g 6s 6d 1989 6v 5d³ 6.1f² 6f³ 6f³ 6f 6m³ 7.6m² 6f³ 6f² 6m⁵ 6m* 6m 6f]
rather leggy, attractive horse: not a good walker or mover: very useful at his best as
2-y-o: ridden by 7-lb claimer, won for first time since when beating Chaplins Club ¾
length in claiming event at Ayr in August: placed in handicaps earlier in season: ran
well in face of stiff task final outing: seems to stay 7.6f: acts on any going: tailed off
when blinkered, visored once at 5 yrs: often taken down quietly nowadays. *G. M.
Moore.*

ATEAMBER 2 b.g. (Mar 11) Hays 120–Princess Lamia (Home Guard (USA) 129) **—**
[1989 6m 8.2d] quite attractive gelding: second foal: brother to quite modest 1988
2-y-o Just Fun: dam unraced: soundly beaten in maidens at Nottingham (trained by
J. Norton) in May and Haydock in October. *R. Bastiman.*

ATHAUF (FR) 2 b.c. (Feb 22) Mille Balles (FR) 124–Tarsiere (FR) (Tarbes (FR) **105**
125) [1989 5g⁵ 6d⁴ 7d* 7g² 7d² 7g³ 8d⁵ 7.5g⁶] 130,000 francs (approx £11,900) Y:
workmanlike colt: third foal: half-brother to French 1½m winner Oro (by General
Holme): dam, French 1¼m to 12.5f winner, is half-sister to Ginger Brink: improved
after winning claimer at Longchamp, best effort third in valuable restricted race at
Deauville: last of 6 in Prix Thomas Bryon on final start: better suited by 1m than
shorter by end of season, and will stay 1¼m: wears blinkers. *G. Collet, France.*

ATHENE NOCTUA 4 b.f. Aragon 118–Lady Lorelei 105 (Derring-Do 131) [1988 **—**
7m 10g 10f³ 10g 10m 10.5f* 10g 1989 12f 12g⁶ 10.2f 10f] leggy, light-framed filly:
tailed off in handicaps at 4 yrs: stays 10.5f: acts on any going. *D. H. Topley.*

ATHENS GATE (USA) 5 ch.h. Lydian (FR) 120–Pago Miss (USA) (Pago Pago) **83**
[1988 8.5m 8g⁶ 8f⁵ 8m 9f 9d 10s 7m 1989 7m 7.6m² 8f⁵ 9m* 10.5f⁶ 9f 9g4] smallish,
sparely-made horse: has a quick action: fair handicapper: favourite, won £7,500
Michael Sobell Handicap at York in June: 50/1, creditable fourth of 34 to Rambo's
Hall in William Hill Cambridgeshire Handicap at Newmarket: best at short of 1¼m:
probably unsuited by soft going, acts on any other: blinkered once at 4 yrs: sold to
join N. Tinkler 16,500 gns Newmarket Autumn Sales. *J. W. Watts.*

ATHLON 2 b.c. (Mar 6) Kings Lake (USA) 133–Antilla 87 (Averof 123) [1989 8v] **— p**
46,000Y: fourth foal: half-brother to 3-y-o 7f winner Sympathy (by Precocious) and
1986 2-y-o 6f winner Uniformity (by Formidable): dam, 2-y-o 5f winner, is half-sister
to very smart John French and daughter of half-sister to Derrylin: 25/1 and green,
well-beaten eleventh of 23, fading quickly having travelled smoothly, in minor event
at Newbury in October: should improve. *M. E. D. Francis.*

ATHYKA (USA) 4 ch.f. Secretariat (USA)–Princesse Kathy (FR) (Luthier (FR) **117**
126) [1988 10.5v⁶ 9.2d³ 10.5f* 10.5d⁴ 9s* 12g³ 12m⁵ 9.2m* 1989 10.5v* 12m³ 12g*
10d³ 9.2g* 10s] French filly: smart performer: successful in Prix Corrida at
Saint-Cloud and in La Coupe and Ciga Prix de l'Opera (for second year running,
rallying to beat Sherarda a head in very close finish) at Longchamp: creditable third

Ciga Prix de l'Opera, Longchamp—a blanket finish!
Athyka (far side) just gets up from Sherarda (noseband), the dead-heaters for third
Filia Ardross (one off the rails) and J'ai Deux Amours (quartered cap),
and Ode (No. 16)

to Boyatino in Prix Jean de Chaudenay at Saint-Cloud and to In The Wings in Prix du Prince d'Orange at Longchamp: reportedly rapped herself beforehand when well-beaten last of 8 in E P Taylor Stakes at Woodbine: effective at 9f and stays 1½m: acts on any going: consistent. *Mme C. Head, France.*

ATLAAL 4 b.g. Shareef Dancer (USA) 135–Anna Paola (GER) (Prince Ippi (GER)) **110** [1988 10v* 10.5d* 12d* 12f⁴ 1989 12g² 9g] tall, good-topped, attractive gelding: has been operated on for a soft palate: has a quick action: useful winner as 3-y-o when trained by H. Cecil: kept on well until checked inside final 1f when third, promoted a place, in £10,500 event at Doncaster in April: backward, well beaten in listed race at Newmarket 6½ months later: stays 1½m: has given impression ill at ease on firm going: a winner over hurdles, but has twice run as though something amiss. *J. R. Jenkins.*

ATLANTIC CEDAR 3 b.g. Touching Wood (USA) 127–Enchanted 116 (Song — 132) [1988 7g⁴ 7g 7f⁵ 1989 11.7m 12h⁶ 12f] compact, good-bodied gelding: plating-class maiden: soundly beaten as 3-y-o: should be suited by further than 7f: best effort on firm ground: has joined P. Hayward. *R. Hannon.*

ATLANTIC CLEAR 2 b.c. (Mar 25) Starch Reduced 112–Kathy King (Space **63** King 115) [1989 5s⁶ 5f³ 7g³ 6g⁵] medium-sized, leggy, unfurnished colt: brother to useful sprinter Kathred, 2 poor animals and a winner in Sweden, and half-brother to poor 6f to 1m winner Little Newington (by Most Secret): dam well beaten: quite modest maiden: stays 7f but gives impression may prove ideally suited by 6f. *B. Palling.*

ATOLL 2 b.f. (May 26) Caerleon (USA) 132–Shirley Reef (Shirley Heights 130) **99 p** [1989 7g* 7g²] quite well-made, attractive filly: third foal: sister to 1½m winner Ahoy: dam useful 2-y-o in Italy: made most when winning 5-runner minor event at York readily by 2½ lengths from Wasnah: looking very well, beaten a short head by Duke of Paducah in £10,000 event at Newmarket later in October, rallying very strongly: will stay middle distances: sure to win more races. *B. W. Hills.*

AT PEACE 3 b.c. Habitat 134–Peace 118 (Klairon 131) [1988 NR 1989 8d³] **83** medium-sized, useful-looking colt: half-brother to numerous winners, including good middle-distance performers Quiet Fling and Peacetime (both by Nijinsky) and Cambridgeshire winner Intermission (by Stage Door Johnny), herself the dam of Interval (by Habitat), a good-class winner at up to 1m: dam won 6f Blue Seal Stakes at 2 yrs: 33/1 and bit backward, 8½ lengths third of 22 to Monsagem in maiden at Newbury in April, towards rear at halfway, quickening in good style 1½f out and running on well: looked sure to win races but wasn't seen out again. *J. Tree.*

ATTIC WIT (FR) 3 b.g. Shirley Heights 130–Laughing Matter 56 (Lochnager 132) [1989 NR] IR 60,000Y: stocky, well-made gelding: first foal: dam, sprinter, half-sister to dams of Jester and Reesh: 14/1, refused to enter stalls before maiden at Bath in July. *C. A. Austin.*

ATTILA THE HONEY 4 b.f. Connaught 130–Kimbo (Golden Dipper 119) [1988 — 7d 7d² 7.5m 8.5g⁴ 8m⁵ 7m⁵ 8.2s 6s 8d² 9v 1989 10m 11f 10f 7g] small, good-bodied filly: fair plater as 3-y-o: lightly raced and below her best in 1989: probably doesn't stay 1¼m: needs a soft surface: blinkered final start at 3 yrs: has run creditably for apprentice. *S. R. Bowring.*

AUCALE (USA) 2 gr.f. (Apr 7) Nijinsky (CAN) 138–Lady's Slipper (AUS) **81 p** (Dancer's Image (USA)) [1989 7g*] $135,000Y: third foal: closely related to a winner in USA by Solford: dam good winner in Australia: 4/1 from 5/2, won 14-runner maiden at Phoenix Park in August by ½ length, making most: will stay 1¼m: should improve. *J. Oxx, Ireland.*

AUCTION DAY 2 b.c. (Mar 9) Runnett 125–Valediction 71 (Town Crier 119) **56** [1989 5m³ 6g 6g² 6g 8f³ 8m² 8g] IR 15,000Y, 7,200 2-y-o: leggy, rather sparely-made colt: moderate mover: second foal: half-brother to 1987 Irish 2-y-o 6f winner Classic Dilemma (by Sandhurst Prince): dam ungenerous middle-distance staying maiden: plating-class maiden: caught near line, having been well clear, in seller at Warwick on sixth start: constantly hung left and ran wide entering straight when running poorly at Carlisle final outing: suited by 1m: has joined F. Jordan. *J. Berry.*

AUCTION FEVER 6 b.g. Hello Gorgeous (USA) 128–Auction Bridge 76 — § (Auction Ring (USA) 123) [1988 NR 1989 12m4] strong, deep-bodied gelding: moderate mover: fair but untrustworthy handicapper in 1987: 20/1 and very burly, stayed on well final 2f after being hampered on home turn when over 14 lengths fourth of 6 finishers at Doncaster in May, only subsequent outing: stays 1½m:

probably unsuited by soft going: best in blinkers: needs strong handling and is suited by waiting tactics. *A. P. Stringer.*

AUCTION NEWS 2 b.g. (Apr 25) Auction Ring (USA) 123–Cestrefeld 94 59 (Capistrano 120) [1989 6f 6f⁵ 6m⁴ 6g⁶ 7g] IR 26,000Y: useful-looking gelding: has scope: has a quick action: half-brother to 3-y-o 1¼m and 1½m winner First Victory (by Concorde Hero) and winners in West Indies: dam, 5f and 6f winner at 2 yrs, is half-sister to Young Generation: plating-class maiden: looked and ran very well in nursery at Leicester on final outing: subsequently gelded: better suited by 7f than 6f. *R. Hannon.*

AUDRINA 4 b.f. Young Generation 129–Patosky 94 (Skymaster 126) [1988 12s⁴ — 10d 11.7m 14.7f 16.5f⁴ 14m⁶ 16m 10d 12g 1989 12.4g] leggy filly: poor maiden: has run in sellers: barely stays 2m: acts on any going. *S. E. Kettlewell.*

AUGHFAD 3 b.c. Millfontaine 114–Saulonika 94 (Saulingo 122) [1988 5d⁶ 6m⁴ 77 6m² 5g 5g* 5g 1989 5s 6s⁶ 5f⁶ 6m³ 6m* 6f² 6m³ 5.8m⁶ 6f 6g a8g a7g] strong, workmanlike colt: usually looks well: poor mover: modest handicapper: won at Nottingham in June, quickening well to lead on line: ran creditably next 2 starts but well below form after: suited by 6f: acts on top-of-the-ground and soft going: blinkered fourth to tenth and final starts. *T. Casey.*

AUGUST (USA) 8 b.g. Sensitive Prince (USA)–Polynesian Charm (USA) (What — § A Pleasure (USA)) [1988 NR 1989 12g 15.8m⁶ 11f⁶] robust, good-bodied gelding: carries plenty of condition: quite modest performer in 1987: never dangerous in handicaps as 8-y-o: best at 1¼m or 1½m: probably unsuited by soft going, acts on any other: has started slowly: tends to pull hard and is not an easy ride: no battler. *Denys Smith.*

AUNTIE DI 3 ch.f. Shy Groom (USA)–Royal Tucson 87 (Henry The Seventh 125) — [1988 5g 5g 5v³ 5g⁶ 7.5g 7d 7g⁴ 6d² 5d* 1989 5m] strong, workmanlike filly: moderate mover with a quick action: modest winner in 1988: in need of race only outing as 3-y-o, in May: best form at 5f: apparently not suited by heavy going: blinkered last 2 starts at 2 yrs. *M. W. Easterby.*

AUNTIE GLADYS 3 ch.f. Great Nephew 126–Vitalise (Vitiges (FR) 132) [1988 49 NR 1989 8g⁵ 12s 9f 7m 7.5f 12.4m 10f⁴ 12g 12g a8g⁴ a13g] 14,000Y: rather leggy, lengthy filly: second foal: half-sister to Simon Rattle (by Tap On Wood), a fairly useful winner at around 6f: dam Irish 1¼m winner: poor on most form: doesn't stay 1½m: may well need give in the ground: blinkered fifth and sixth outings: mulish at stalls seventh. *C. E. Brittain.*

AUNT MABEL 4 b.f. Jalmood (USA) 126–Mi Tia 79 (Great Nephew 126) [1988 — 11.5m 12f* 10g² 11.7g² 10m* 10m⁶ 10.2g* 9g 10g² 1989 10g 10m³ 12m] sturdy filly: fair winner as 3-y-o: broke leg and destroyed at Doncaster in May: had useful turn of foot, and was at least as effective at 1¼m as at 1½m: acted on firm going: tended to hang and swish tail: was best produced late. *J. A. R. Toller.*

AURORA GLITZA 2 ch.f. (Feb 28) Sayf El Arab (USA) 127–Linda's Design 52 (Persian Bold 123) [1989 5g 5v 5g a6g⁵ a7g⁶ a7g³] small filly: moderate mover: second foal: half-sister to 3-y-o Madonijah (by Adonijah): dam daughter of half-sister to very smart animals Prominent and Dominion: fair plater: good third to Petite Butterfly in maiden at Lingfield in December: best form at 7f. *Dr J. D. Scargill.*

AUSTHORPE SUNSET 5 b.g. Majestic Maharaj 105–Kings Fillet (King's 44 Bench 132) [1988 10g* 12d⁴ 10f 1989 12g² 13f² 10m] small, dipped-backed gelding: poor handicapper: stays 13f: acts on firm going: winning hurdler. *Mrs R. Wharton.*

AUTHORSHIP (USA) 3 b. or br.g. Balzac (USA)–Piap (USA) (L'Aiglon (USA)) — [1988 6g 6m 1989 8.5d 8.2s 8m 11.7m 8.3g 8g] leggy, rather sparely-made, plain gelding: little worthwhile form in varied company, including selling: probably doesn't stay 11.7f: winning novice hurdler. *W. J. Musson.*

AUTO BENZ 3 b.g. Young Generation 129–Calling High (USA) 88 (Mountain 54 Call 125) [1988 5s⁴ 6d⁴ 6m 6s 7f⁶ 8.2d 1989 8g 8h⁶ 9g⁶ 10.2g⁶ 7.6m⁶] useful-looking gelding: plating-class performer: stays 1¼m, but may well prove ideally suited by around 1m: acts on firm going and a soft surface: blinkered last 2 starts. *M. H. Easterby.*

AUTOBIRD (FR) 2 b.c. (Mar 2) Procida (USA) 129–Star of The Stage (Nureyev 67 (USA) 131) [1989 6f 6f² 7.3g 7f⁴ 7m a6g³ a6g⁶] 11,500Y: first foal: dam unraced granddaughter of high-class French 1m to 1½m winner Saraca: quite modest maiden: better suited by 6f than 7f: visored final start. *C. N. Allen.*

AUTO CONNECTION 3 b.f. Blushing Scribe (USA) 107–Smitten 72 (Run The 68
Gantlet (USA)) [1988 7g 6m 1989 7f³ 8m⁶ 8f³ 10.2g⁵ 10g* 10m³ 10m⁵ 12g] leggy,
lengthy filly: has a rather round action: modest handicapper: well-backed favourite
and on toes, won at Nottingham in July, quickening really well to lead over 2f out
then hanging left: possibly unlucky after poor run next start: stays 1¼m: acts on
firm going: claimer ridden first 4 outings: has run creditably when sweating: may
need waiting tactics. *G. A. Huffer.*

AUTOMART 4 b.f. Martinmas 128–Prime Thought 69 (Primera 131) [1988 7d⁴ 34
8g² 8g 9m⁴ 8g² 8s 10f 8d⁵ 1989 8.2v² 8v 8g 8.2g 12m] leggy, sparely-made filly:
moderate mover: poor plater: suited by 1m: best form with give in the ground:
slowly away fourth start: sold 720 gns Doncaster November Sales. *W. Bentley.*

AUTONOMOUS 4 b.g. Milford 119–Mandrian 103 (Mandamus 120) [1988 12m³ 56 §
12m³ 10.5d⁵ 12g 12g 12m 14s 12m 1989 10.2g 9f 10m 12.3m³ 16.5g* 15m⁴ 16.2m³
16.5m⁴ 19f* 15.8g⁴ 16.2m⁴ 18m⁶ 15g a16g a14g³] lengthy gelding: carries condition:
quite modest handicapper nowadays: won at Doncaster in July and Redcar
(slowly-run 4-runner contest) following month: creditable fourth at Catterick, next
and best subsequent effort: twice tailed off afterwards: stays 19f, at least in
slowly-run race: acts on firm going and a soft surface: visored twice at 2 yrs:
blinkered last 2 outings: has run well for apprentice and when sweating: unreliable.
D. W. Chapman.

AUTUMN FESTIVAL (USA) 3 ch.f. Alydar (USA)–Durga (USA) (Tatan) 84
[1988 NR 1989 8m² 10m³ 9m*] $710,000Y: big, rangy filly: half-sister to numerous
winners, notably Santa Anita Derby winner An Act (by Pretense): dam unraced: won
apprentice maiden at Ripon in June by 2½ lengths, carrying head in air, quickening
clear over 2f out then having to be pushed out vigorously close home: pulled hard
then didn't look keen under pressure time before: may have proved suited to 1m:
edgy and went freely to post last 2 starts: dead. *J. Gosden.*

AUTUMN MORNING 2 b.c. (Mar 27) Elegant Air 119–Short And Sharp 88 —
(Sharpen Up 127) [1989 7m 7.6m 7m] 4,400Y: strong, rangy colt: has plenty of scope:
third reported living foal: half-brother to Italian 3-y-o 1m winner Il Grande Adriano
(by Young Generation), also successful over 6f and 7f at 2 yrs: dam placed over 6f
and 7f at 2 yrs, her only season to race: well beaten in maidens: twice bit backward.
T. M. Jones.

AVERAX 3 b.c. Taufan (USA) 119–La Primavera (Northfields (USA)) [1988 NR 76
1989 8.5d³ 8m² 8m 8.2g* 10m] leggy, unfurnished colt: fifth foal: half-brother to
very smart 1¼m to 1½m winner Highland Chieftain (by Kampala) and a winner in
Italy by Mansingh: dam won over 1½m in Ireland: won maiden at Hamilton in
September by a head: ridden by 5-lb claimer, prominent 1m in £8,000 handicap at
Newmarket 3 weeks later: appears suited by 1m and an easy surface: sold 13,000 gns
Newmarket Autumn Sales. *M. A. Jarvis.*

AVERON 9 b.g. Averof 123–Reluctant Maid 94 (Relko 136) [1988 12g³ 12g 1989 —
14.8s] tall, workmanlike gelding: poor handicapper: probably stays 1¾m: acts on
any going but used to go particularly well on heavy: blinkered once. *C. P. Wildman.*

AVIONNE 4 b.f. Derrylin 115–Concorde Lady 66 (Hotfoot 126) [1988 8d 7m³ 8m³ 59
8f 7m 10m 10g 8s* 1989 8s²] lengthy filly: plating-class performer: should stay
1¼m: possibly unsuited by firm going, acts on any other: winning hurdler. *M. C.
Pipe.*

AVOCA HOLMES 2 ch.f. (Mar 29) Be My Guest (USA) 126–Bid For Freedom 73
(Run The Gantlet (USA)) [1989 7m⁴ 7g] IR 20,000Y: leggy, sparely-made filly:
second foal: half-sister to fairly useful 1987 2-y-o 1m and 10.2f winner Night Pass (by
Pas de Seul): dam once-raced half-sister to Ragstone, Castle Keep and Castle Moon,
dam of Moon Madness and Sheriff's Star: under 5 lengths fourth of 20, keeping on
well, to Glen Kate in maiden at Lingfield in September: last of 20 in Cartier Million
at Phoenix Park: will stay 1¼m. *Lord John FitzGerald.*

AVONMOUTHSECRETARY 3 b.f. Town And Country 124–Star Display —
(Sparkler 130) [1988 6g 7g 8s 1989 12g 12.5f 15.5f⁵ 12f] strong, workmanlike filly:
poor performer: tailed off final start: may prove suited by about 1½m. *R. J. Holder.*

AVONSIDE 2 b.f. (Apr 2) Ile de Bourbon (USA) 133–Lady Abernant 90 (Abwah 39
118) [1989 5d 6g 7g 7m⁵ 8.5f 8.2s⁴ 10.6d 7d] 8,000Y: leggy, sparely-made filly: third
reported foal: dam won from 7f to 1½m: poor plater: should stay well: acts on soft
ground: visored fourth, fifth and final starts: ridden by 7-lb claimer sixth. *S. J.
Muldoon.*

AWA'WI'YE 4 b.c. Daring March 116–Gangawayhame 91 (Lochnager 132) [1988 63
5g⁴ 6d³ 7f³ 6f³ 5d⁴ 5.8d* 5.3f⁴ 6m⁵ 6m⁴ 1989 5d⁴ 6v 7.6f 5f] leggy colt: modest

winner as 3-y-o: ran creditably on reappearance, but poorly in Britain afterwards: later a winner in Belgium: ideally suited by 6f: seems to act on any going: blinkered second outing: has run well for claimer. *R. V. Smyth.*

AWAYED (USA) 3 b.f. Sir Ivor 135–Unyielding (USA) (Never Bend) [1988 6g 7g³ 7s² 9g 1989 8.5s* 12f4 9.2f* 10g 8m* 8g* 8g² 8g] good-bodied filly: good walker: has a round action: useful performer: successful in handicaps at Epsom, Goodwood and Newmarket and listed race at Leopardstown: not discredited in Group 3 event at the Curragh and listed race at Newmarket last 2 outings: stayed 9.2f, probably not 1¼m: acted on any going: visits Unfuwain. *P. T. Walwyn.* **108**

AWKAS 4 b.g. Busted 134–Moreno (Varano) [1988 12f 10.8s* 10.1m4 11.7g 1989 13.8d² 12d³ 12d³ 13m* 12m] workmanlike, good-bodied gelding: moderate mover: modest handicapper: in good form in spring, winning 17-runner event at Hamilton: soon ridden when last of 7 at Haydock later in May, and not seen out again: best form at around 1½m: acts on top-of-the-ground (has looked ill at ease on it) and soft going. *G. M. Moore.* **71**

AWKWARD HARRY 3 b.g. Glenstal (USA) 118–Roscrea (Ballymore 123) [1988 6d 6f 8.5f 1989 12g] leggy, angular gelding: well behind in maidens and maiden claimer: sold 1,600 gns Doncaster November Sales. *M. J. O'Neill.* —

AYLSHAM BOY 3 b.c. Cragador 110–Celeste 83 (Sing Sing 134) [1988 6g 6m 1989 6m 6f] close-coupled, sparely-made colt: little worthwhile form in maidens then a seller: visored final start: sold 750 gns Ascot July Sales. *R. F. Casey.* —

AYODESSA 2 b.f. (Apr 12) Lochnager 132–Melody Song 74 (Saintly Song 128) [1989 5d6 5d3 5g² 5m² 5m* 5f3 5f² 5g6 5m4 5g² 5g] 2,500F, 2,000 (privately) Y: good-topped filly: progressing well physically: fifth reported foal: half-sister to 1m winner Moon Melody (by Silly Season): dam won over 5f and 6f at 2 yrs: former plater: made all in maiden at Edinburgh in June: progressed after, in listed race eighth outing and close second, hanging left 1f out, in nursery at Wolverhampton on tenth: will prove best at 5f: usually taken steadily down. *Ronald Thompson.* **78**

AYR BAY 4 b.g. Vaigly Great 127–Hopeful Subject 82 (Mandamus 120) [1988 8g 11m 1989 8d 11g 12m] close-coupled, workmanlike gelding: well beaten in maidens and claimers. *J. S. Wilson.* —

AYR RAIDER 2 ch.c. (Apr 28) Claude Monet (USA) 121–Thimothea (FR) (Timmy My Boy 125) [1989 6f* 6v 6g] strong, workmanlike colt: seventh foal: half-brother to modest middle-distance maiden Marie Zephyr (by Treboro): dam poor half-sister to Mill On The Floss and Kashmir Lass: won 15-runner maiden at Hamilton in June readily by 4 lengths: ran creditably in Racecall Gold Trophy at Redcar, keeping on not knocked about, on final start: will stay 1m: off course 4 months after debut: sort to do better. *J. S. Wilson.* **80 p**

AZADEH (USA) 2 ch.f. (Feb 1) Compliance (USA)–Mervat (USA) (Vaguely Noble 140) [1989 8g*] angular, leggy, lengthy filly: has plenty of scope: first foal: dam unraced daughter of very useful French 2-y-o Doha: sire lightly-raced brother to El Gran Senor and Try My Best: 7/1 but green, won 15-runner maiden at Leicester in November very easily by 5 lengths from Hidden, leading on bridle 2f out and leaving impression could have doubled winning margin: will stay 1¼m: sure to improve considerably, and is a very interesting prospect. *G. Harwood.* **90 P**

AZAIYMA 3 b. or br.f. Corvaro (USA) 122–Aytana (FR) (Riverman (USA) 131) [1988 NR 1989 10m 12f 12h 10d³ 12f²] 1,600 2-y-o: good-bodied filly: turns fore-feet in markedly: first living foal: dam, French 1¼m winner, is daughter of Prix d'Astarte winner Kirmiz and granddaughter of Irish Oaks winner Amante: showed improved form in handicaps last 2 starts: stays 1½m. *J. Ffitch-Heyes.* **58**

AZEB 3 br.c. Young Generation 129–Visible Form 99 (Formidable (USA) 125) [1988 6m* 1989 8s³ 10.1g 9g 8g5 8f4 10g a8g4] small colt: good walker: fair form in varied events, including claimers: well below best second, third and last 2 outings: should stay 1¼m: probably acts on any going: has run creditably for apprentice: bought out of H. Thomson Jones's stable 6,800 gns Newmarket July Sales after reappearance. *R. W. Stubbs.* **88**

AZUBAH 2 b.f. (Apr 16) Castle Keep 121–Louisianalightning (Music Boy 124) [1989 5f³ 5m 6g] 6,000Y: lengthy, rather sparely-made filly: moderate walker: turns near-fore in: third foal: half-sister to 3-y-o Mimining (by Tower Walk), 5f winner at 2 yrs, and bad maiden Decanna (by Decoy Boy): dam ran once: ridden by 7-lb claimer, around 4 lengths last of 3 to Western Music in maiden at Ayr in June, best effort: very free to post, unruly stalls and swerved start second outing. *G. M. Moore.* **56**

AZZAAM (USA) 2 ro.c. (Mar 5) Chief's Crown (USA)–Princess Oola (USA) (Al Hattab (USA)) [1989 6m³ 7m³ 7g* 7m4 7d*] $425,000Y: tall, close-coupled colt: has **95**

a sharp action: third reported foal: half-brother to a winner in USA by Mr Prospector: dam, minor 8.5f stakes winner at 4 yrs, is half-sister to leading American filly Althea: sweating, won maiden at Leicester in September: better effort when making all in 16-runner nursery at Thirsk in November, quickening 3f out and beating Prince Jakatom easing up by 3 lengths: will stay 1m: gave impression doubtful temperamentally on fourth start. *J. L. Dunlop.*

B

BABIANA (CAN) 3 ch.f. Sharpen Up 127–Jordy's Baba (USA) (Raja Baba 85 (USA)) [1988 5m⁴ 5g³ 7d* 8f⁵ 1989 6f 7m 7h³] rather sparely-made, angular filly: moderate walker: has a slightly round action: fair performer: returned to form when running-on third in handicap at Brighton in August: may well be suited by return to 1m: yet to race on very soft ground, probably acts on any other. *B. W. Hills.*

BABIL 4 b.g. Welsh Pageant 132–Princess Eboli 108 (Brigadier Gerard 144) [1988 81 § 8g³ 10.2f⁴ 12f³ 10m² 10m* 10m* 15s³ 10m* 1989 10g 10m 11f 12m⁴ 11.5g⁶] leggy gelding: has a quick, round action: fair winner as 3-y-o: ran in snatches and looked ungenuine when fourth of 5 in handicap at Newbury in June: faced stiffish tasks earlier in season: effective at 1¼m and not discredited in moderately-run race over 15f: possibly not at best on firm going, acts on any other: blinkered third outing at 3 yrs and 4 yrs: visored last 2: a difficult ride: sold to join N. Twiston-Davies 15,000 gns Newmarket July Sales: subsequently gelded: winning hurdler: not one to trust. *P. T. Walwyn.*

BAB'S MOSS 3 b.c. Known Fact (USA) 135–Milly Moss 112 (Crepello 136) [1988 — 7g⁴ 7s⁶ 1989 10.1m 11.7m⁵ 12.3m 18g] lengthy, good-bodied colt: quite modest maiden: ran badly in handicaps last 2 outings, carrying plenty of condition on final one: stays 11.7f: possibly unsuited by soft ground: sold 3,800 gns Newmarket Autumn Sales. *B. W. Hills.*

BABY ASHLEY 3 b.f. Full of Hope 125–Nello (USA) 85 (Charles Elliott (USA)) — [1988 NR 1989 10.6g 10g 10g] big filly: fourth foal: sister to a bad maiden and half-sister to a winner in Italy and a temperamental plater: dam won over 6f at 2 yrs but became disappointing: no worthwhile form but showed signs of ability in minor event on second start, first for over 4½ months: faced stiff task in claimer final outing: worth a try over 1m. *P. J. Feilden.*

BABY BOY 8 b.h. Mummy's Pet 125–Lucent 117 (Irish Ball (FR) 127) [1988 — 10.8d⁵ 11.7f⁴ 10f 10g 12g 10.2g 1989 10s⁴ 12s] strong, good-topped horse: bad handicapper: stays 11.7f: probably acts on any going: raced keenly when blinkered in apprentice event final outing in 1988. *T. B. Hallett.*

BABY VIX (USA) 3 b.c. Northern Baby (CAN) 127–La Roussiere (FR) (Le — Fabuleux 133) [1988 8d 8g³ 1989 10s 10g] big, rangy colt: modest maiden in 1988: below form in May as 3-y-o when in mid-division at Nottingham, tending to carry head to one side, and in handicap at Leicester, staying on steadily until checked and eased considerably inside final 1f: should prove suited by at least 1¼m. *J. L. Dunlop.*

BACANDA 2 ch.f. (May 12) Mandrake Major 122–Okavamba 82 (Wollow 132) — [1989 5f⁵ 6g 6m] 1,050Y: lengthy, rather dipped-backed filly: fifth foal: dam 2-y-o 6f winner: backward, well beaten in sellers. *J. White.*

BACHELOR'S PET 3 b.g. Petorius 117–Smile For Me Diane (Sweet Revenge 59 129) [1988 5g⁵ 6d 6d 7m 1989 8g⁴ 7m² 7f a7g a10g³] sturdy, close-coupled gelding: plating-class handicapper: below form since second start but shapes as though stays 1¼m: acts on top-of-the-ground: has run creditably for claimer: visored, swerved left stalls once at 2 yrs: blinkered first 3 starts in 1989: bought out of M. McCormack's stable 2,400 gns Ascot July Sales after third. *D. Burchell.*

BACK RAISE (USA) 2 ch.c. (May 15) Raise A Man (USA)–Double Polite (USA) 58 (Nodouble (USA)) [1989 6s 7m 6g] workmanlike colt: plating-class maiden: best effort final start: bred to stay beyond 6f. *S. G. Norton.*

BACOLET 4 ch.f. Dominion 123–Blissful Evening (Blakeney 126) [1988 NR 1989 — 8.5f] fourth foal: half-sister to winning stayers Inlander (by Ile de Bourbon), top-class winner over jumps in USA, and In Dreams (by High Line), and a winner abroad: dam temperamental half-sister to high-class 1¼m performer Rarity: 50/1, tailed off in maiden at Beverley in June. *N. J. Henderson.*

BADGERS DASH 2 b.f. (Mar 21) Jalmood (USA) 126–Noire Small (USA) 69 (Elocutionist (USA)) [1989 6m² 6f²] 4,000Y: leggy filly: first foal: dam won 3 races in

Italy and has run over hurdles here: quite modest form when runner-up in maiden at Kempton and auction event at Folkestone (finished lame) in summer. *P. J. Makin.*

BAGDAD CAFE 2 b. or br.f. (Feb 21) Sayf El Arab (USA) 127–Roman River II 50 (Bonconte di Montefeltro) [1989 5v⁴ 5g 5d³ 6m] 7,800F, 9,200Y: close-coupled filly: half-sister to 1982 Irish 2-y-o 5f winner Burrow Hill (by Godswalk), later successful abroad, and a listed winner in Italy by Brigadier Gerard: dam won in Italy: in frame in maiden auction race at Kempton in April and maiden at Warwick following month: sent to race in Italy. *Lord John FitzGerald.*

BAHRAIN BRIDGE 4 b.g. Formidable (USA) 125–Hide Out (Habitat 134) 62 [1988 8f 8f* 8h 10m 8.2s 1989 10.1m 7.6f² 7f⁴ 8f 7m] strong, good-topped gelding: quite modest handicapper: stays 1m well: acts well on firm going and is possibly unsuited by soft: blinkered last 4 outings: tended to run in snatches second start: often taken down very quietly nowadays: sold to join A. Denson 6,000 gns Ascot July Sales: subsequently gelded: none too reliable. *A. P. Ingham.*

BAILEY'S SONG 2 b.c. (Apr 15) Song 132–Gay Maria (Tacitus 124) [1989 5m — 5.8h 5g 6g] 5,400Y: sparely-made colt: half-brother to useful 7f performer Jenny Splendid (by John Splendid) and 1½m to 2m winner Aniece (by Ballymoss): dam unraced: seems of little account. *G. Blum.*

BAJAN BEAUTY 3 b.f. Castle Keep 121–Dalbreac 73 (Bustino 136) [1988 6g 33 5.8d 8.2m 1989 12d 12.2d⁵ 10f 13.8m⁶ 7h⁵ 8g 10.1m] quite attractive filly: poor walker and mover: poor plater: should be suited by middle distances: acts on hard ground and a soft surface: bandaged last 2 outings. *K. O. Cunningham-Brown.*

BAJAN BREEZE 3 b.f. Tumble Wind (USA)–Cristalga 90 (High Top 131) [1988 — 6g 1989 6s] lengthy, unfurnished filly: irresolute 3f in maidens at Newmarket and Nottingham, in latter tailed off: bred to stay 1m +: sold 1,550 gns Newmarket July Sales: resold 675 gns Ascot November Sales. *C. F. Wall.*

BAKER CONTRACT 4 ch.g. Roman Warrior 132–Toe Tapper 73 (Record Run — 127) [1988 5g 7s 5f⁶ 6g 6f 6d⁶ 7f 5m 5f⁶ 5.8f 5g 1989 6f 5m 5h 6f] big, workmanlike gelding: poor maiden: suited by 5f and firm going: blinkered once at 3 yrs. *J. M. Bradley.*

BAKER'S LAMB 4 br.g. Creative Plan (USA)–Argalie (USA) (Ace of Aces — (USA) 126) [1988 8d 7.6g³ 8f 7.5f 7.6m⁵ 9g 9g⁴ 8g 7f 8g 7m 10m 1989 7d⁵] tall, good-bodied gelding: poor handicapper: stays 9f: acts on top-of-the-ground and a soft surface: blinkered 3 times at 3 yrs: has found little. *B. Richmond.*

BALANCED REALM (USA) 6 b.g. Lines of Power (USA)–Brown Hare — (USA) (Coursing) [1988 10.8d 7g⁵ 1989 a7g] workmanlike gelding: 66/1, around 5 lengths fifth of 16, outpaced, in minor event at Leicester in November, 1988, only third outing on flat: behind in December handicap at Southwell, only outing as 6-y-o: should be suited by further than 7f. *T. Casey.*

BALAO 3 ch.f. Mr Fluorocarbon 126–Bombay Duck 65 (Ballyciptic 122) [1988 5g — 7g⁶ 7s⁵ 10s 1989 7s 12.2d 10m⁶ 10f] leggy, close-coupled filly: modest plater: sign of ability as 3-y-o only on third start, having had plenty to do 3f out: stays 1¼m: best efforts on a sound surface. *R. Hollinshead.*

BALASANI (FR) 3 b.c. Labus (FR)–Baykara (Direct Flight) [1988 7s⁶ 1989 12v³ ? 12s* 8g 8m⁵] sturdy colt: second foal: half-brother to Baliysha (by Shakapour), twice successful at around 9f in French Provinces: dam, French 3-y-o 1m winner on only start, is out of half-sister to smart French middle-distance stayer Budapest: won maiden at Saint-Cloud in April when trained by A. de Royer-Dupre: burly, always behind in minor event at Leicester and 5-runner £9,200 contest at Newmarket in autumn: stays 1½m. *J. R. Jenkins.*

BALDOMERO 4 b.f. Pas de Seul 133–Clonavee (USA) (Northern Dancer) [1988 96 7d³ 7g³ 7f⁶ 8g 7g* 7g³ 7f* 1989 7d⁵ 8m⁵ 8f 7g* 7f 7m² 7g³] workmanlike filly: good mover: fairly useful handicapper: successful in £16,300 Ladbroke Bunbury Cup (Handicap) at Newmarket in July by 2½ lengths from Pinctada, sent clear from 3f out and never looking likely to be caught: ran excellent races when placed in £49,600 event at Ascot (first run for 2 months) and in 16-runner contest at York: suited by 7f: acts on firm going and a soft surface: blinkered nowadays: occasionally sweats. *W. Jarvis.*

BALIBRAY 3 b.g. Balidar 133–Our Mother 95 (Bold Lad (IRE) 133) [1988 5d 6g 61 5g⁶ 5g⁶ 5g 6g³ 8m 1989 7m 8f 7m 8f² 8m⁶ 7g³ 8m] lengthy, robust gelding: carries condition: good walker: quite modest on most form: easily best efforts as 3-y-o when placed in handicap (hung left 2f out) at Redcar and seller at Catterick: well beaten in amateurs handicap final start: stays 1m: acts on firm going: has run creditably for 7-lb claimer: takes keen hold: sold 850 gns Doncaster November Sales. *G. M. Moore.*

BALIDUCK 5 ch.m. Balidar 133–Bombay Duck 65 (Ballyciptic 122) [1988 9g⁶ 10.1d 7f 7.6s 8.3m 7m² 8g 1989 6f 8h 6m 7m] compact mare: plater: stays 9f: yet to show her form on extremes of going: inconsistent. *D. Yeoman.* —

BALIGAY 4 b.f. Balidar 133–Gaygo Lady 113 (Gay Fandango (USA) 132) [1988 7g 7m 8m³ 8h⁴ 7g* 1989 7v 7f 8f 8m 7f³ 8f 8.3m] lengthy, workmanlike filly: moderate mover: modest winner as 3-y-o when trained by B. Hills: form in 1989 only when close third in handicap at Chepstow (ridden by 7-lb claimer) in July: probably stays 1m: acts on hard going: blinkered last 3 outings. *R. J. Hodges.* 61

BALIGH 2 b.c. (Feb 17) Sadler's Wells (USA) 132–Santa's Sister (USA) 104 (Middle Brother) [1989 8m⁴ 8g* 8g²] 210,000Y: rangy, attractive colt: half-brother to numerous winners, including My Sister (by Nonoalco), successful over 7f and fourth in Irish Oaks, and 6f winner Copper Creek (by Habitat): dam, winner at up to 1m, is half-sister to Yorkshire Cup winner Noble Saint: odds on following promising debut, won 3-runner maiden at York by a neck from Alim: sweating slightly, showed much improved form when beaten 4 lengths by Be My Chief in Racing Post Trophy at Newcastle later in October, keeping on well: will be well suited by middle distances. *J. L. Dunlop.* 112

BALI LADY 2 b.f. (Apr 21) Balidar 133–Silk's Suggestion (Shantung 132) [1989 6g⁴] third foal: sister to 3-y-o Bally Knight: dam little worthwhile form on flat: 16/1, around 3 lengths fourth of 19, disputing lead to halfway and keeping on, to Reference Light in maiden at Redcar in November: will improve. *J. R. Shaw.* 73 p

BALINGO 3 b.f. Balinger 116–Natalgo (Native Admiral (USA)) [1988 5g 1989 12d 10s 12h 10f] angular, leggy filly: has stringhalt: no sign of ability, including in sellers: blinkered penultimate start: sold 1,000 gns Ascot October Sales. *W. T. Kemp.* —

BALING OUT 2 b.f. (May 16) Prince Tenderfoot (USA) 126–Quantas 91 (Roan Rocket 128) [1989 5g⁵ 5d³ 5m³ 7g a6g] 4,800Y: leggy, sparely-made filly: poor walker: moderate mover: half-sister to several winners, including sprinter Stepping Gaily and hurdler Clover Hill Lad (both by Gay Fandango): dam won over 6f at 2 yrs: moderate plater: blinkered third outing: bandaged off-fore second: sold 800 gns Ascot December Sales. *M. Bell.* 42

BALISHY 2 ch.f. (Mar 5) Shy Groom (USA)–Bally 74 (Balidar 133) [1989 5f⁵ 5h* 6m⁶ 6m* 6f⁵ 6g⁴ 6f² 6f⁴] 4,400Y: leggy, good-topped filly: shows a round action: second foal: dam best effort at 1m: won maiden auction race at Bath in June and claimer at Warwick, making virtually all, following month: ran creditably on last 3 starts: will stay 7f: sweating fifth and final outings. *R. J. Holder.* 72

BALI SUNSET 3 b.f. Balidar 133–Orange Silk 68 (Moulton 128) [1988 NR 1989 6g* 6f⁴ 6f⁴ 5g⁵ 8f⁵ 6g⁶ 6s 6m] 9,000Y: lengthy, workmanlike filly: has a rather round action: fourth foal: half-sister to 4-y-o 7f seller winner Sicilian Vespers (by Mummy's Game), useful middle-distance colt Bocatower (by Tyrnavos), 7.6f winner at 2 yrs, and a winner in Italy: dam placed over 5f and 6f at 2 yrs: gambled-on favourite, won seller (bought in record 23,000 gns) at Leicester in May: easily best other efforts in handicaps third and sixth starts: should stay beyond 6f: has given impression is unsuited by very firm ground. *G. M. Moore.* 67

BALIZARA 3 gr.f. Belfort (FR) 89–Swing Is Back (Busted 134) [1988 5f⁴ 5g* 7g² 6g² 6d³ 1989 8s⁵ 8m⁴ 8f 8m* 8f⁴ 8h² 8m⁴ 8g⁴ 10f⁵ 8g 7s⁴] leggy filly: fairly useful performer: didn't run to her best when winning minor event at Edinburgh in June: ran creditably next 2 starts but generally below form in handicaps and minor events after: stays 1m: acts on firm going and a soft surface: often mounted on track and taken down early: usually leads or races close to pace: retained by trainer 14,000 gns Doncaster November Sales. *Denys Smith.* 92

BALKAN LEADER 5 b.g. Balidar 133–Perfect Lady 85 (Sovereign Lord 120) [1988 5d 5m 6m⁵ 5f² 5m* 5f⁶ 5m² 5g 5g 5d⁶ 5m 7f 5f² 5m* 5g* 1989 5m 5m* 5f* 5f² 5m⁴ 5m 5m* 5m² 5g⁶ 5.6g 5f⁵] strong, compact gelding: fair handicapper: successful at Edinburgh (apprentice event) and Hamilton (very much on toes, idling) in June and at Edinburgh following month: best at 5f: needs a sound surface: usually blinkered: often apprentice ridden: usually races up with pace: sometimes wears a tongue strap: tough. *J. G. FitzGerald.* 78

BALLA COVE 2 b.c. (Mar 18) Ballad Rock 122–Coven (Sassafras (FR) 135) [1989 5m³ 6m² 6m⁵ 7m³ 7m* 7m³ 6m* 8.5f] 119

The decline of the Middle Park Stakes has been a recurring topic in recent years. Once the unrivalled championship event for two-year-olds the

Middle Park has lost prestige as attitudes towards racing two-year-olds have changed (arguably for the worse) and races fashioned more for the stoutly-bred youngster, such as the Three Chimneys Dewhurst Stakes and the Racing Post Trophy, have grown in importance. Small wonder, then, that Tattersalls, sponsors of the Middle Park since 1985, decided in the autumn to discontinue their sponsorship, particularly now the race has also come under threat from the newly-instituted Racecall Gold Trophy at Redcar. Paradoxically, the latest Middle Park was a more relevant contest than for many seasons, and, in terms of quality, attracted as representative a field as any assembled for a two-year-old pattern race during the year. Yet the near-£80,000 first prize money, almost a three-fold increase on 1985, went not to the connections of the Gimcrack and Coventry Stakes winner Rock City nor the highly-regarded Cordoba (already favourite at the time for the Two Thousand Guineas) as the betting suggested, but to the little-considered Balla Cove, whose previous six outings had yielded just one win in minor company.

Although he was progressing steadily with his races, nothing in Balla Cove's record suggested that he had the beating of Rock City, who was still widely accepted as the leading British-trained two-year-old despite his defeat by Machiavellian in France, over a distance which appeared more likely to suit the Gimcrack winner. Not even the fact that Balla Cove's victory, by two lengths from Digression in the seven-furlong Whitcombe Stakes at Salisbury in August, had been achieved at the expense of the subsequent Royal Lodge winner. Digression, it should be emphasised, was nothing like the force at Salisbury that he became in the autumn, and Balla Cove's five other races had seen him beaten fairly and squarely by Be My Chief on three occasions. Even though Balla Cove's last meeting with Be My Chief, in the three-runner Imry Solario Stakes at Sandown in August where he finished nearly four lengths down in last place, represented his best effort his form looked no better than

Tattersalls Middle Park Stakes, Newmarket—a much improved Balla Cove becomes the second consecutive winner of the race for his small trainer; Rock City and Cordoba fill the places

useful. Nonetheless, it was on a par with that of Cordoba, whose odds of 13/8 on owed more to his reputation than his actual achievements. The pair of them seemed to have something to find too with the thrice-successful Batzushka and the Heinz '57' Phoenix Stakes runner-up Duck And Dive among the remaining three runners. While 20/1 appeared to be a fair reflection of Balla Cove's chance (Rock City started second favourite at 9/4) the manner in which he worked at home prior to the race reportedly persuaded his trainer, who sent out Mon Tresor to win the Middle Park in 1988, that the colt had a much better chance than the form-book implied. His judgement was vindicated as Balla Cove, who took the eye beforehand, put up a thoroughly convincing performance in a race run at a blistering gallop from start to finish—the winning time of 1m 11.04 sec equalled the course record for two-year-olds set by Junius in the corresponding event eleven years earlier. Batzushka took the field along in the early stages followed by Balla Cove, sensibly ridden close to the front by Cauthen, with the stable-companions Rock City (who had begun slowly) and Duck And Dive matching strides just behind. Balla Cove took up the running two furlongs out as Batzushka began to tire and gradually established a lead of a length and a half or so. Though Rock City and Cordoba, who had taken closer order at halfway, were hard ridden in pursuit, neither threatened to reduce the deficit through the last furlong, and Balla Cove passed the post two lengths ahead of Rock City, nearly four in front of Cordoba, who ran as though he needed further, and around ten to the good over Croupier, who stayed on strongly to snatch fourth place near the line. Rock City's rider Carson again reported his colt to be below form but we're reluctant to suppose Rock City didn't reproduce his best, and are content to accept that Balla Cove showed a great amount of improvement and was the best horse on the day. Unfortunately, the pair aren't likely to clash again: Balla Cove was sold for a reported six-figure sum shortly before the Middle Park to continue his racing career in California. Balla Cove ran for his new trainer McAnally in the Breeders' Cup Juvenile at Gulfstream Park in November. He failed to earn any prize money but shaped encouragingly on the unfamiliar dirt surface, taking the field along at a brisk gallop until losing his place on the home bend and fading in the straight to finish seventh of the twelve runners.

		Bold Lad	Bold Ruler
	Ballad Rock	(b 1964)	Barn Pride
	(ch 1974)	True Rocket	Roan Rocket
Balla Cove		(gr 1967)	True Course
(b.c. Mar 18, 1987)		Sassafras	Sheshoon
	Coven	(b 1967)	Ruta
	(b 1977)	Alice Kyteler	Crepello
		(b 1971)	Belitis

Balla Cove's dam Coven has proved to be a very able broodmare since she was retired to the paddocks after winning four races in Ireland from six furlongs to a mile and a quarter. All of her three live foals before Balla Cove showed well-above-average form and each has won at least one race: Tribal Rite (by Be My Native) and Blasted Heath (by Thatching) were successful in listed company in Ireland over seven furlongs and a mile respectively while the ex-Irish Burning Issue (by Persian Bold, and so a three-parts sister to Balla Cove) won seven times to the end of 1988, including in minor stakes in North America. Since Balla Cove, a 21,000-guinea foal and 35,000-guinea yearling, Coven has produced a colt by Glow, who was sold for 90,000 guineas at the Irish National Yearling Sale in the week following the Middle Park, and a filly by Be My Native. Coven is a daughter of the Irish nine-furlong winner Alice Kyteler, a mare whose other winning progeny include the very useful French mile-and-a-quarter Interdit and the useful Irish two-year-old Rathvindon. The third dam Belitis and fourth dam Mesopotamia were also bred by the McCalmont family. Belitis was among the best of her sex at up to a mile at both two and three in Ireland yet wasn't nearly so good as Mesopotamia, who showed high-class form as a two-year-old in 1963 and went on to fill third place in the Irish One Thousand Guineas.

The Two Thousand Guineas was mooted as a possible target for Balla Cove after the Middle Park, despite his impending departure to the States, but as we've said, it's improbable he'll return to take his chance. Once he has acclimatised to conditions in California, Balla Cove's connections can look forward to a return on their investment: the hell-for-leather nature of racing there should suit Balla Cove, who's best ridden up with the pace. A leggy, sparely-made colt who has a quick action, Balla Cove has shown his best form at six furlongs but should stay a mile. *R. Boss.*

BALLAD BAY 3 ch.c. Ballad Rock 122–Swan Upping 74 (Lord Gayle (USA) 124) — [1988 NR 1989 10s 14m⁴ 11f] 30,000Y: good-bodied colt: fourth foal: half-brother to 6-y-o Belgian pattern winner Klammering (by Thatching): dam won from 7f to 9f: 12½ lengths fourth of 7 to Weld at Newmarket, only form in maidens in the spring, leaving impression might be suited by 1½m: ridden by 7-lb claimer on debut. *J. P. Hudson.*

BALLAD DANCER 4 ch.c. Ballad Rock 122–Manx Image (Dancer's Image **76** d (USA)) [1988 6d* 5g² 6v³ 5s* 8g 7d⁵ 6g⁶ 7g³ 7g* 8s 7g⁶ 6m 6s 1989 5g⁶ 6v 11.7d⁶ 7.6m 6f 6g³ 6f 6f⁶ 6m 7g 6m 6d 8v⁶ 6g] angular, lengthy colt: moderate mover: apprentice-ridden third in handicap at Haydock in July: little other form for long time, but ran bit better last 2 outings: best form at 6f or 7f: needs an easy surface: blinkered seventh outing: sometimes starts slowly: trained first 4 outings by G. Price: inconsistent. *M. O'Neill.*

BALLAD RULER 3 ch.g. Ballad Rock 122–Jessamy Hall 77 (Crowned Prince — § (USA) 128) [1988 7g 1989 12s⁶ 12f 10m⁵] big, rangy gelding: 25/1 and wearing crossed noseband, staying-on fifth of 6 in slowly-run maiden claimer at Yarmouth in August: blinkered, refused to settle and well beaten in varied company previously: awkward to post on reappearance: sold to join P. Pritchard 4,600 gns Newmarket September Sales: temperamental. *B. Hanbury.*

BALLAFA 3 b.f. Ballacashtal (CAN)–Fortune's Fancy (Workboy 123) [1988 NR — 1989 5h 7f] strong, plain filly: turns fore-feet out markedly: third foal: sister to quite modest 6f winner Ballafort: dam daughter of very smart sprinter Polly Peachum: little promise in maidens at Bath and Kempton in the summer: sold 1,000 gns Ascot December Sales. *E. A. Wheeler.*

BALLAFORT 4 b.f. Ballacashtal (CAN)–Fortune's Fancy 48 (Workboy 123) **56** [1988 8g 10.2g 10.2f 8d 7f⁴ 6f* 6m 6m⁴ 1989 6f⁶ 6f 5.8h 6f⁵ 6f⁴ 7f 6g⁵ 6m 6f² 6m⁶ 6g] big, workmanlike filly: easy mover: quite modest winner as 3-y-o: variable form in handicaps in 1989: suited by 6f: acts well on firm going: visored once at 3 yrs: often sweats: none too consistent. *J. R. Bosley.*

BALLA LAD 2 b.c. (May 7) Ballacashtal (CAN)–Limerick Lace (Pall Mall 132) — [1989 7m a8g] medium-sized, quite attractive colt: has a round action: sixth foal: dam unraced half-sister to very useful hurdler/chaser Tartan Tailor: well beaten in maidens. *J. M. Bradley.*

BALLAROCK 3 b.f. Ballacashtal (CAN)–Rockery 91 (Track Spare 125) [1988 NR — 1989 8s 7.6m 7g] fifth foal: half-sister to Irish 5f to 1m winner Rocky Domain (by Dominion): dam stayed 1¼m: backward and claimer ridden, tailed off in maidens at Goodwood and Lingfield and £5,000 apprentice race at Ascot. *J. C. Fox.*

BALLATICO 6 b. or br.g. Ballad Rock 122–Sweetham 84 (Tudenham 118) [1988 — 9m² 9m* 7.5f² 8f* 10d⁴ 9m 8.5g* 9g⁶ 9m 1989 10d 8m⁶ 10.1m 8m 8f 8m 8f 8g] medium-sized ex-Irish gelding: third foal: dam 6f winner: won handicaps at Naas, Bellewstown and Galway as 5-y-o when trained by O. Finnegan: plating-class form at best in similar company in Britain: stays 1¼m: acts on any going: good mount for apprentice: wears bandages. *J. R. Jenkins.*

BALLERINA GIRL 4 b.f. Hays 120–Dance Away (Red God 128§) [1988 7.6s — 6g* 6s 6m⁴ 6m 6g 1989 10.1m] leggy, sparely-made filly: moderate mover: quite moderate plater: stays 6f: possibly unsuited by soft going. *Miss L. Bower.*

BALLET BLISS 2 ch.f. (Apr 5) Balidar 133–Nocturnal Bliss (Pyjama Hunt 126) **47** [1989 5m² 5f² 5f² 5m 5f³ 5.3h* 5.1m⁴ 5f⁶ 5f] 2,000Y: small, strong, lengthy filly: first foal: dam twice-raced half-sister to fairly useful 1979 2-y-o 5f winner Our Mother: moderate plater: made all at Brighton (bought in 3,000 gns) in August: ran moderately final start: sold 1,400 gns Doncaster October Sales. *J. Berry.*

BALLINAGAR 2 b.c. (May 14) Hays 120–Costly Lady (Bold Lad (IRE) 133) — [1989 7g] first foal: dam lightly-raced Irish maiden: 25/1 and very edgy, last of 14 in seller at Catterick in August: took strong hold down: sold 1,600 gns Newmarket Autumn Sales. *Sir Mark Prescott.*

BALLOT 3 b.f. Final Straw 127–Rattle (FR) (Riverman (USA) 131) [1988 NR 1989 7m[6]] 16,000Y: smallish, workmanlike filly: first foal: dam won from 7.5f to 1¼m in France: bit backward, well beaten in maiden at Leicester in July, staying on having been green and well behind: sold 800 gns Newmarket December Sales. *R. F. Casey.* —

BALLYDURROW 12 ch.g. Doon 124–Even Tint (Even Money 121) [1988 12d 12m* 12m[4] 12f[2] 13f[2] 12f* 12d[4] 12d[6] 12g 12m 13.8g 12m 1989 12m* 12g 12h[6] 10.6g[5] 12.3f[3] 12.3m[2] 12m[5] 12m 12f[2] 13.6f[5] 12g a11g[2]] big, strong gelding: moderate mover: quite modest handicapper nowadays: led on line when winning at Carlisle in April: reportedly finished distressed with irregular heart-beat when virtually pulled up next outing: best at around 1½m: acts on any going: slowly away third and fourth starts: has sweated and got on toes: held up and suited by a strong pace: particularly well handled by D. Nicholls: tough. *R. F. Fisher.* 66

BALLYFEE 12 br.m. Sovereign Bill 105–Ballyarctic (Arcticeelagh 119) [1988 7f 1989 8m] plain mare: of little account: bandaged only outing at 12 yrs: banned from racing in 1983 by Stewards of Jockey Club for being very troublesome at start. *W. G. Morris.* —

BALLYHOOLY 2 ch.f. (May 17) Pas de Seul 133–Barbara Ann (Nebbiolo 125) [1989 5g[3] 5d[3] 5m[3] 6m* 7.5f[2] 6m 7.5f[2] 7f*] 6,000Y: small, close-coupled filly: keen walker: good mover: third foal: dam, stayed 1¼m, is daughter of half-sister to Providential: modest performer: successful in claimer at Leicester in June and nursery (ridden by apprentice) at Lingfield in August: stays 7.5f: acts well on firm going: sold 13,000 gns Newmarket Autumn Sales. *N. A. Callaghan.* 77

BALLY KNIGHT 3 b.g. Balidar 133–Silk's Suggestion (Shantung 132) [1988 6d 6d 1989 8.2f 10g a6g a11g] smallish, workmanlike gelding: sign of ability only when staying on in selling handicap at Nottingham second start: evidently better at 1¼m than shorter. *J. R. Shaw.* —

BALLYVAUGHAN LADY 3 ch.f. Burslem 123–Liangold (Rheingold 137) [1988 7g 7m 1989 8f 12m] leggy, sparely-made filly: well beaten in maidens. *D. Haydn Jones.* —

BALLYZAO 2 b.g. (Apr 10) Alzao (USA) 117–Ballynanty (King's Bench 132) [1989 5f 6m 6g[2] 6m[6] 7g 6v 7g] IR 8,000Y: tall, close-coupled gelding: half-brother to several winners here and abroad, including good 1972 2-y-o filly Silver Birch (by Silver Shark): dam unraced half-sister to smart 5f to 1m performer Pugnacity: quite modest performer: strongly-ridden staying-on second in claimer at Haydock, best effort: should stay further than 6f: best run on good ground: visored final start: sweating fourth and sixth. *C. Tinkler.* 61

BALTANA 4 b.f. Balidar 133–Swing Back (Great Nephew 126) [1988 5m 5g 5s 5d[6] 5f 12d 1989 10m 6f 6f] lengthy, leggy filly: made all in seller as 2-y-o: no subsequent form: has been blinkered: bandaged on reappearance. *W. G. Morris.* —

BALTHUS (USA) 6 b.g. Forli (ARG)–Keep Off 99 (Bold Lad (IRE) 133) [1988 8d 10.4s 9m[3] 10f 8f 1989 8f 10f 8f 10.2m[4] 8m[6]] good-topped gelding: carries plenty of condition: turns fore-feet in: poor walker and moderate mover: 50/1-winner of William Hill Cambridgeshire Handicap at Newmarket as 4-y-o: little subsequent worthwhile form: stays 1¼m: probably unsuited by extremes of going: blinkered at Newmarket and 4 times since: occasionally sweats: has swished tail: has reportedly suffered back trouble: inconsistent. *J. A. Glover.* —

BALUOD 2 ch.f. (Mar 4) Doulab (USA) 115–June Darling (Junius (USA) 124) [1989 5m[6]] 6,800F, 21,000Y: close-coupled filly: first foal: dam never ran: 16/1 and in need of race, slowly away, green and soon outpaced in 7-runner maiden at Windsor in July. *G. Lewis.* —

BALZAON KNIGHT 2 b.c. (May 21) Alzao (USA) 117–April Sal 65 (Sallust 134) [1989 6m 7g a6g a7g] 9,000Y: rather sparely-made, angular colt: third foal: dam placed from 5f to 1¼m: poor maiden. *P. J. Makin.* 50

BANANA CUFFLINKS (USA) 2 b.c. Peterhof (USA) 116–Heather Bee (USA) (Drone) [1988 NR 1989 7d 10.1m 14g 10m 7f[2] 7.6m 7m[6] 9g] $55,000Y: lengthy, attractive colt: has a fluent, rather round action: fifth foal: half-brother to 2 winners, notably useful 1985 2-y-o 7f winner Air Display (by Nikoli), later 9f Grade 3 winner in USA: dam 4f winner: quite modest performer: best efforts second in handicap at Lingfield and sixth in £49,600 handicap (hanging right 2f out) at Ascot: 20 lb out of handicap in Cambridgeshire at Newmarket week after Ascot: may well prove suited by 1m: acts on firm going: visored last 4 starts: sold 6,800 gns Newmarket Autumn Sales. *J. R. Shaw.* 69

BAND OF HOPE (USA) 2 ch.f. (May 11) Dixieland Band (USA)–Reflection 111 (Mill Reef (USA) 141) [1989 7m] second foal: half-sister to ungenuine 3-y-o 7f (at 2 —

yrs) and 1¼m winner Hall of Mirrors (by Clever Trick): dam, 5f to 7f winner at 2 yrs, disappointed as 3-y-o: 20/1, bit backward and very green, tailed off in £8,200 event at Newbury in September. *I. A. Balding.*

BAND ON THE RUN 2 ch.c. (May 31) Song 132–Sylvanecte (FR) 70 (Silver 60 Shark 129) [1989 5m⁵ 5d⁴ 6d⁵] 12,500Y: rather angular colt: brother to 3 winners including American 3-y-o Song Quest and Shark Song, successful here and in USA at up to 9f, and half-brother to useful 6f and 7f winner Silver Lord (by Abwah), later prolific winner in Italy: dam won over 1¼m: quite modest maiden: stays 6f: slowly away second start. *B. A. McMahon.*

BANHAM COLLEGE 3 b.c. Tower Walk 130–Baby Flo 67 (Porto Bello 118) — [1988 5g 7f 1989 10m] robust, rather dipped-backed colt: moderate mover: backward, no sign of ability in claimers and seller: bandaged at 3 yrs. *J. Ringer.*

BANKER MASON (USA) 3 b.c. Sadler's Wells (USA) 132–Alwah (USA) 61 (Damascus (USA)) [1988 7g² 8.5m³ 1989 8.2s² 7d 6m 8g a10g² a11g³ a10g* a10g⁴] smallish, sparely-made colt: quite modest performer: won maiden claimer at Lingfield in December: should stay 1½m: yet to race on firm ground, acts on any other: blinkered, spread plate and withdrawn at start fourth intended outing: changed hands 7,400 gns Newmarket Autumn Sales. *N. A. Callaghan.*

BANKROLL 2 b.g. (Apr 29) Chief Singer 131–Very Nice (FR) (Green Dancer 90 (USA) 132) [1989 7g 7m⁴ 7m⁴ 7.5f* 7g⁶ 8m] 7,000Y: leggy, unfurnished gelding: shows a round action: third foal: dam, winner from 9f to 11f in France, is out of sister to Dahlia: fair performer: won 17-runner maiden auction race at Beverley in September by a neck from Jokers Patch, pair well clear: ran well afterwards in listed races won by Free At Last at Newmarket and Noble Patriarch at Ascot: stays 1m: gelded after final start. *C. A. Cyzer.*

BANK VIEW 4 ch.c. Crofter (USA) 124–Stony Ground (Relko 136) [1988 10s⁴ — 10m⁴ 8d² 8.2s* 8f* 10d⁶ 10.2g 9g 1989 10.4m] stocky, workmanlike colt: poor mover: modest winner as 3-y-o: soon struggling in handicap at Chester in May: should prove as effective at 1¼m as 1m: has won on firm going, but possibly needs an easy surface nowadays: has been tried in blinkers and visor: tends to get on edge: usually given plenty to do: winning hurdler. *N. Tinkler.*

BANNEROL (USA) 6 b.g. Smarten (USA)–Queen's Standard (USA) (Hoist The — Flag (USA)) [1988 NR 1989 18f 12m⁵ 16.5m] big, strong gelding: fairly useful winner as 3-y-o: met with set-back afterwards: well beaten in handicaps in 1989: used to stay well: acts on firm going (yet to race on a soft surface): winning novice hurdler with Mrs S. Bramall. *M. J. Camacho.*

BANNISTER 4 b.g. Known Fact (USA) 135–Swiftfoot 119 (Run The Gantlet 52 (USA)) [1988 12d⁶ 12g 11.7m⁵ 1989 9d 10.2g 7.5g 8m 8.2g 7m⁵ 8m 12g⁵ 14f] sturdy gelding: quite useful winner as 2-y-o: little subsequent worthwhile form: probably best at short of 1½m: acts on firm going: wore net muzzle last 2 starts: takes strong hold, and often wears crossed noseband: often taken down quietly: trained until after seventh outing by M. Brittain. *C. C. Elsey.*

BANTON LOCH 2 br.g. (May 26) Lochnager 132–Balgownie 43 (Prince 67 Tenderfoot (USA) 126) [1989 6f 6g³ 7v⁴ 8g² 8d] 5,400Y: leggy, good-topped gelding: first foal: dam won twice at about 1¼m: quite modest maiden: best efforts second and fourth starts: stays 1m. *C. Tinkler.*

BARACHOIS PRINCESS (USA) 2 b.f. (Feb 9) Barachois (CAN)–Egregious 59 (USA) (Barbizon) [1989 6m⁵ 7m⁵] $8,200Y, resold $9,500Y: workmanlike filly: tenth named foal: half-sister to 4 minor winners in USA, one in stakes company: dam sprinter: sire won from 6f to 8.5f in Canada and stayed 1¼m: bit backward, plating-class form in September in minor event at Chester and maiden at Redcar: will stay 1m. *S. G. Norton.*

BARAKISH 2 b.c. (Feb 23) Mummy's Pet 125–Blissful Evening (Blakeney 126) 94 [1989 6m 6g² 7g² 7v* 8g³] lengthy, attractive colt: has a quick action: fifth foal: half-brother to winning stayers Inlander (by Ile de Bourbon), later top chaser in States, and In Dreams (by High Line), and a winner abroad: dam temperamental half-sister to high-class 1¼m performer Rarity: showed improved form when winning 17-runner maiden at Ayr by 12 lengths from Doulab's Image: not discredited when one-paced third to Karazan in nursery at Redcar later in October: will be well suited by middle distances: acts well on heavy going. *M. R. Stoute.*

BARAMUL 3 br.f. Radetzky 123–Highland Berry (Scottish Rifle 127) [1988 6f⁴ — 6m 5g⁶ 1989 6m 5m⁶ 6m 6g] leggy, sparely-made filly: poor mover: poor form, including in seller: sold 750 gns Doncaster November Sales. *M. Brittain.*

BARANYKA 2 b.f. (Mar 4) Horage 124–Sister Jinks 88 (Irish Love 117) [1989 6m **66** 7.5f³ 7f* 7m] 10,500Y: sparely-made filly: sixth foal: sister to Italian 3-y-o James Payne, fairly useful 5f and 7f winner here at 2 yrs: dam 2-y-o 9f winner in Ireland: favourite, won 11-runner maiden auction event at Redcar by short head from Rope Trick: well beaten in nursery at York later in August: stays 7.5f. *M. H. Tompkins.*

BARAOORA 7 gr.g. Bruni 132–Tory Island (Majority Blue 126) [1988 NR 1989 — 10f⁶ 8m 8h] well-made gelding: good mover: very lightly raced on flat: blinkered last 2 outings. *R. J. O'Sullivan.*

BARATIJO 4 b.g. Krayyan 117–Another Match (Sovereign Path 125) [1988 7d 10v — 1989 6s] apparently of little account: ran out second outing at 3 yrs: blinkered only one in 1989. *G. P. Kelly.*

BARAZ 4 ch.c. Busted 134–Astra Adastra (Mount Hagen (FR) 127) [1988 10m⁶ **93** 12g* 10d² 14d² 1989 12s⁶ 12g² 12g⁵ 18g² 16d 16g 12m 12m* 12f 14m⁶ 14.6g² 10m⁴] strong, lengthy colt: poor mover: fairly useful handicapper on his day: returned to form when winning £7,100 5-runner event at Newbury in June: 20/1, creditable second of 8 to Chelsea Girl in moderately-run £23,200 race at Doncaster, easily best subsequent effort: stayed 2¼m: acted on top-of-the-ground and a soft surface: sold 27,000 gns Newmarket Autumn Sales: inconsistent: dead. *R. W. Armstrong.*

BARBEZIEUX 2 b.c. (Mar 3) Petong 126–Merchantmens Girl 58 (Klairon 131) — [1989 7g 5g] half-brother to 3-y-o 5f winner Always Ready (by Tyrnavos) and 4 other winning sprinters, including fairly useful 1983 2-y-o Netsuke (by Tachypous): dam placed over 5f: soundly beaten in minor event at Kempton and maiden at Sandown in September. *D. A. Wilson.*

BARCHAM 2 b.c. (Mar 8) Blakeney 126–La Pythie (FR) 89 (Filiberto (USA) 123) **67** [1989 7g 7m* 7m] sixth foal: half-brother to 3-y-o 7f winner Mark Birley (by Night Shift): dam, granddaughter of top-class La Sega, won twice over 7f at 2 yrs: won 5-runner minor event at Leicester by a neck from Stanway: ran as if something amiss later in July and not seen out afterwards: will stay 1m. *G. A. Pritchard-Gordon.*

BARCHAM PRINCE 7 b.g. Balliol 125–Barcham Bride 70 (Henry The Seventh — 125) [1988 NR 1989 12m] apparently no longer of any account: has worn blinkers. *T. Kersey.*

BARCLAY STREET (USA) 6 b. or br.g. Nureyev (USA) 131–Avanie (USA) — (Avatar (USA)) [1988 7m³ 8f 7.6g⁶ 6g 8d² 7m² 8g 7m 7g 1989 7d] big, quite attractive gelding: quite useful but inconsistent: on toes, tailed off in Insulpak Victoria Cup (Handicap) at Ascot in April, only outing at 6 yrs: stays 1m: unsuited by soft going, acts on any other: has worn a tongue strap: bandaged behind nowadays. *I. V. Matthews.*

BARDOLPH (USA) 2 b.c. (May 1) Golden Act (USA)–Love To Barbara (USA) **83** (Stewvard) [1989 7.3g⁵ 7f⁴ 6h* a8g²] $17,000Y: compact colt: half-brother to 3 minor winners in USA: dam won 4 times at up to 7f: sire top-class middle-distance performer: won 4-runner minor event at Lingfield comfortably by 3 lengths from Glentor, making all: fine second to San Pier Niceto in nursery (bandaged behind) there in November: will probably stay 1¼m. *P. F. I. Cole.*

BAR FLY (FR) 3 ch.g. Salmon Leap (USA) 131–Breathalyser (Alcide 136) [1988 — 7g 1989 5s⁵ 6s 5g⁵ 12.3m⁶ 11s⁵] medium-sized, rather plain gelding: plating class at best: bred to stay 1¼m: joined M. Pipe. *M. W. Easterby.*

BARHOOM 2 ch.c. (May 30) Nicholas Bill 125–Strathclair (Klairon 131) [1989 — p 8g⁵] 12,000Y: strong, useful-looking colt: brother to 3-y-o Loadplan Lass, closely related to winning Irish stayer/hurdler Strathline (by High Line) and half-brother to several other minor winners: dam, placed at up to 7f, is half-sister to good sprinter Right Strath: 20/1 and better for race, around 17 lengths fifth of 16, fading from 2f out, to My Lord in maiden at Leicester in November: should improve. *S. G. Norton.*

BARKSTON SINGER 2 b.f. (Apr 7) Runnett 125–Miss Flirt (Welsh Pageant **75** 132) [1989 7f⁴ a8g² a8g*] IR 5,000Y: leggy, lightly-made filly: third foal: half-sister to 3-y-o 1m winner Evening Affair and 1½m and 2m winner Russian Affair (both by Red Sunset): dam lightly raced: won 13-runner maiden at Southwell in December by 2 lengths from Indian Fashion: better suited to 1m than 7f. *I. Campbell.*

BARLEY MOW 3 b.g. Wolverlife 115–Ellette 105 (Le Levanstell 122) [1988 NR **66** 1989 7m⁵ 10m 10.1g] IR 3,300F: half-brother to fair 1981 2-y-o 5f winner Red Ellette (by Red Alert) and 2 winners abroad: dam won over 5f and 1m at 2 yrs in Ireland: about 5½ lengths fifth of 15 in maiden at Tipperary in May: well beaten in similar event at Phoenix Park later in month and in 23-runner minor event (bandaged, tailed off) at Windsor in August: uncertain to stay 1¼m: trained first 2 starts by Ruby Walsh: has joined N. Bradley. *M. Bradstock.*

BARNABY BENZ 5 b.g. Lochnager 132–Miss Barnaby 75 (Sun Prince 128) —
[1988 8d⁴ 9m 10g³ 11m* 12g 10s* 10g 10v 1989 12.4g] big, workmanlike gelding:
quite modest handicapper as 4-y-o: 33/1, weakened and eased from 2f out at
Newcastle in October: stays 11f: acts on top-of-the-ground and soft going: visored
once: has often found little. *M. H. Easterby.*

BARNACK 3 b. or br.g. Montekin 125–Damastown's Lady (Rarity 129) [1988 6d —
1989 7m 6f⁵ 7.6m 6g] small gelding: no worthwhile form in sellers and claimers:
gives impression will prove suited by 5f: blinkered final outing: sold Horse France
3,000 gns Newmarket Autumn Sales. *A. Bailey.*

BARNBY LADY 3 br.f. Raga Navarro (ITY) 119–Jolliffe's Treble (Lochnager **65**
132) [1988 NR 1989 5d⁴ 5g⁵ 6f] 3,800Y: medium-sized, rather sparely-made filly:
second foal: sister to 1987 2-y-o Barnby Moor, disqualified 6f winner at 2 yrs: dam
never ran: quite modest maiden: easily best effort in the spring on debut: ran in
seller next time: should stay 6f: sold 1,500 gns Newmarket Autumn Sales. *A. Bailey.*

BARNDANCE 3 b.c. Nureyev (USA) 131–Strigida 120 (Habitat 134) [1988 NR —
1989 7d 8g⁵] leggy, rather angular colt: third foal: dam won Ribblesdale Stakes and
is daughter and granddaughter of winners of same race: 8/1 and better for race on
first run for 5 months, about 9 lengths fifth of 10 in moderately-run maiden at
Yarmouth in September: sold 8,000 gns Newmarket Autumn Sales. *H. R. A. Cecil.*

BARONESS GYMCRAK 2 b.f. (Feb 7) Pharly (FR) 130–My Therape 112 **53** §
(Jimmy Reppin 131) [1989 6m 6m³ 6g⁴] angular filly: moderate mover: half-sister to
several winners, including very useful 1983 2-y-o 5f and 6f winner Domynsky (by
Dominion), later successful in stakes company in USA, and smart 1¼m and 1½m
winner Petrullo (by Electric): dam won 7 times at up to 1m: plating-class maiden:
found little off bridle and showed undesirable temperament last 2 starts, final one
July: clearly one to be wary of. *M. H. Easterby.*

BARONESS JULIE 3 ch.f. Stanford 121§–Sarsenet (Saritamer (USA) 130) —
[1988 5g 5g⁵ 5m 1989 5f 5m 6h 7m 5f] sturdy, dipped-backed filly: moderate walker
and mover: plating class as 2-y-o: no form in first half of 1989, blinkered in sellers
last 2 starts: should be suited by further than 5f. *J. Etherington.*

BAROUF (FR) 2 gr.c. (Apr 11) Kenmare (FR) 125–Emmanuelle (FR) **103**
(Margouillat (FR) 133) [1989 5g* 5.5g* 6m⁴ 7g 7g* 9d³] 200,000 francs (approx
£18,300) Y: second foal: half-brother to French 3-y-o 10.5f winner Quiriquino (by
Trepan): dam multiple winner in France from 1m to 11f: successful in newcomers
race at Le Lion-d'Angers, minor event at Angers and 120,000-franc event at
Bordeaux: 6½ lengths third to Bleu de France in Prix Saint-Roman at Longchamp:
will stay 1¼m: blinkered third start. *H. Pantall, France.*

BARRICADE 2 b.g. (Apr 21) Viking (USA)–Avebury Ring (Auction Ring (USA) —
123) [1989 6m 6g] 9,000Y: second foal: half-brother to 3-y-o 1m winner Twotime Bid
(by Taufan): dam 5f winner at 3 yrs in Ireland: behind in maidens at Ripon and
Redcar: off course 4 months in between. *C. W. Thornton.*

BARRISH 3 b.c. Wassl 125–Rowa 83§ (Great Nephew 126) [1988 7g 1989 8s⁴ **80**
8.5g⁵ 10m 12f* 12.4g 12g⁶] angular colt: easily best effort when comfortable winner
of handicap at Brighton in August: may well stay beyond 1½m: acts on firm going:
sold out of A. Stewart's stable 17,000 gns Newmarket Autumn Sales after fifth start.
R. Akehurst.

BARRYS GAMBLE 3 gr.c. Nishapour (FR) 125–Scoby Lass (Prominer 125) **102**
[1988 5d² 5m 5f* 5g* 5f* 5d³ 5d⁴ 6f⁵ 5d 1989 6g 5g² 5f⁶ 5f⁵ 5m 5g 5f³ 5m⁶ 5m]
robust, good-quartered colt: carries plenty of condition: moderate mover, with a
quick action: useful performer: fifth in Temple Stakes at Sandown in May: ran
moderately after, suffering cannon bone injury fifth start then off course over 3
months: will prove best at 5f on a sound surface: sweating seventh (odds on, last of
3) and final outings: blinkered fifth and last two. *T. Fairhurst.*

BARTAT 2 b.g. (Apr 29) Habitat 134–Sephira (Luthier 126) [1989 6g 7f* 8s³] **90**
robust gelding: fourth foal: brother to 3-y-o 1m winner Tatsfield, useful 6f and 7f
winner at 2 yrs, and to a winner in Sweden, and closely related to 6f and 7f winner
Geltser (by Sir Ivor): dam, French 1m winner, is sister to Sigy and Sonoma: won
maiden at Salisbury in good style: creditable third, never travelling particularly
well, to Golden Torque in nursery at Ayr later in October: sold 14,000 gns
Newmarket Autumn Sales. *G. Harwood.*

BARTER 3 b.c. Petorius 117–Fingers (Lord Gayle (USA) 124) [1988 5g⁵ 6m² 6m⁴ —
5g² 5.8d³ 5g⁵ 5m³ 1989 5g 5g⁴ 5m] rather leggy, quite attractive colt: good mover:
modest maiden at 2 yrs: below form in the spring in 1989: may prove best at 5f: acts
on top-of-the-ground: blinkered last 7 starts. *R. F. Casey.*

BARTON DENE   2 br.c. (Apr 26) Gorytus (USA) 132–Tersiva (Song 132) [1989   **73**
5f* 5m⁴ 5m³] 12,500F, 19,000Y: compact colt: good walker and mover: half-brother
to 2 winners in Italy: dam joint-third top-rated filly in Italy at 2 yrs: won 5-runner
maiden at Goodwood in May: third of 4, squeezed over 1f out and unable to recover,
to Dream Talk at Salisbury in August, better effort in minor events: will be suited by
6f. *B. W. Hills.*

BARUT (USA)   4 b.g. Lines of Power (USA)–Brookbourn (USA) (Kennedy Road   —
(CAN)) [1988 8g 7d 9m 8m⁵ 1989 7.6m] rangy gelding: has a long, round stride: quite
useful winner as 2-y-o, but has deteriorated considerably: 33/1 and sweating, tailed
off in Lingfield handicap in September: suited by 7f: acts on soft going. *R. Champion.*

BASENITE   2 br.f. (May 12) Mansingh (USA) 120–Iridium 78 (Linacre 133) [1989   — p
6g⁶] leggy, rather sparely-made filly: sister to 4 winners here and abroad, notably
Petong, and half-sister to a winner abroad: dam stayed 1¼m: 12/1, looked and ran as
though in need of race in 12-runner maiden at Leicester in November: will improve.
M. A. Jarvis.

BASHAQ   3 b.c. Jalmood (USA) 126–Welwyn 92 (Welsh Saint 126) [1988 5f 6m 7m   **42**
8d 1989 6s 8g 5.3h⁶ 6f 7f* 6m 7m 7f⁶] medium-sized, good-bodied colt: poor
handicapper: won at Folkestone in July by short head, running on steadily to lead
inside final 1f, hanging right: creditable sixth at same course, easily best effort after:
worth another try over 1m: acts on firm going. *C. J. Benstead.*

BASHFUL BOY   4 b.g. Jalmood (USA) 126–Sesta (Artaius (USA) 129) [1988
10g* 10.1g* 10.5g* 1989 10v⁴ 8m⁴ 11.1m⁵ 10m] big, heavy-topped gelding: carries
plenty of condition: good mover: showed progressive form in 1988 (not seen out
after July), unbeaten in 3 races notably John Smith's Magnet Cup (Handicap) at
York: well below his best as 4-y-o: stays 10.5f: best efforts on good going: raced
keenly second and fourth (taken down early) starts: clearly not easy to train. *W.
Hastings-Bass.*

BASHKIROV (USA)   3 b.c. Northern Dancer–Smuggly (USA) 121 (Caro 133)   —
[1988 7s 1989 10.1m] rather unfurnished colt: showed signs of ability in maiden on
debut but pulled hard early and drifted badly left: 33/1, tailed-off last of 14 in minor
event at Windsor in June: should stay 1¼m. *P. F. I. Cole.*

BASIC FUN   3 b.f. Teenoso (USA) 135–Sirenivo (USA) 113 (Sir Ivor 135) [1988 7g   **73**
1989 10s² 10f 10m⁵ 11.7m⁶ 14g⁴ 15g] leggy, rather sparely-made filly: modest
maiden: probably stays 1¾m: unsuited by top-of-the-ground: sweating fourth start:
sold 3,800 gns Doncaster November Sales: winning hurdler for J. Spearing. *P. T.
Walwyn.*

BASIC TRUTH (USA)   4 b.c. Lyphard (USA) 132–Stark True (USA)   —
(Graustark) [1988 8d 8g³ 8f² 1989 7v 8g] big, angular colt: has been tubed: poor
walker: modest maiden at 3 yrs when trained by J. Tree: tailed off in spring
handicaps in 1989: stays 1m: seems to act on any going: blinkered final outing: has
worn tongue strap: best left alone. *R. J. Hodges.*

BASTINADO   6 ch.g. Bustino 136–Strathspey 105 (Jimmy Reppin 131) [1988 10g⁶   **55**
10m 9g⁴ 10g* 12g⁵ 10.2g² 10s 1989 10f² 10.2f 10m] big, rangy gelding: has been
hobdayed: quite modest handicapper: ran poorly last 2 starts: best at around 1¼m:
acts on firm going and probably unsuited by soft: excellent mount for inexperienced
rider: sold 5,000 gns Newmarket Autumn Sales. *I. A. Balding.*

BATCHWORTH DANCER   4 b.f. Ballacashtal (CAN)–Acca Larentia   —
(Romulus 129) [1988 5s⁵ 6v⁵ 6s² 6g* 6d* 6d* 8m 6g⁶ 7m⁴ 7g⁵ 6m 7m* 7m 7g 7g
6s⁴ 7g 1989 7s 6f 5g 6m 6g⁵ 7m 7.6m 10.6m 8f] leggy, sparely-made filly: has a round
action: quite modest winner as 3-y-o when trained by M. Brittain: very little form in
1989: suited by testing conditions at 6f and stays 7f: acts on top-of-the-ground and
heavy going: good mount for apprentice: occasionally sweats. *C. Holmes.*

BATEAU ROUGE   2 b.c. (Mar 27) Red Sunset 120–Last Gunboat 50 (Dominion   **79**
123) [1989 6m 5.8f* 6m³ 5.8f⁵ 6f³ 9g*] 38,000Y: useful-looking colt: good mover:
third foal: half-brother to French 10.5f winner James Star (by Star Appeal): dam
middle-distance maiden, is half-sister to Oaks third Suni and Oaks second Media
Luna: successful in maiden at Bath in July and 13-runner nursery at Sandown in
September: much better suited by 9f than shorter. *I. A. Balding.*

BATSHOOF   3 b.c. Sadler's Wells (USA) 132–Steel Habit (Habitat 134) [1988 7g² **114**
7f² 7g³ 1989 7s* 7d³ 7.6m* 10.5m* 10m* 10.6g³ 10.5f⁵ 9m³] leggy, quite attractive
colt: has a quick action: successful in minor events (odds on) at Leicester in April
and Chester in May and in June listed races at York and Kempton: favourite, good
third of 5 to Opening Verse in listed event at York final outing: ran fairly well in
pattern events previous 2 starts, notably when fifth to Ile de Chypre in Juddmonte

Daniel Prenn Royal Yorkshire Stakes, York — Batshoof wins a shade cleverly from Dolpour

International Stakes at York: stays 10.5f: acts on any going: usually held up in rear: smart and consistent. *B. Hanbury.*

BATU PAHAT 3 b.f. Impecunious–Dicopin (Deauville II 97) [1988 7g 8.2m 8d⁶ **63** 1989 8g⁴ 12d³ 16.2d⁴ 12f⁵] leggy, sparely-made filly: quite modest maiden: stayed 2m: acted on firm going and a soft surface: claimer ridden as 3-y-o: dead. *W. G. M. Turner.*

BATZUSHKA (USA) 2 b.c. (May 23) Danzig (USA)–Nicole Mon Amour (USA) **102** (Bold Bidder) [1989 6f² 7.3g² 6m* 6m⁶ 6g⁶ 6f* 5m* 6m⁶] good-bodied colt: half-brother to 3 winners by Conquistador Cielo, including Irish 3-y-o 9f and 11f winner Orbis and useful 7f and 1m winner Cielamour: dam, winner twice at up to 1¼m, is half-sister to Kentucky Derby and Belmont Stakes runner-up Stephan's Odyssey and Grade 1 Acorn Stakes winner Lotka (both by Danzig), best at up to 9f: useful colt: made all in maiden at Newmarket (bandaged behind) in July and in September minor events at Folkestone and Lingfield: below form in Tattersalls Middle Park Stakes at Newmarket final start: races freely and appears best at 5f: blinkered last 3 starts. *Mrs L. Piggott.*

BAWBEE 2 gr.f. (Feb 15) Dunbeath (USA) 127–Fee 111 (Mandamus 120) [1989 **77** p 8.2g⁵ 8g*] angular, unfurnished filly: has scope: fifth foal: half-sister to 3-y-o 10.2 f to 1½m winner Perk (by Jalmood) and 2 winning stayers, including fair Franchise (by Warpath): dam thoroughly genuine 1¼m handicapper from stoutly-bred family: favourite, won 16-runner maiden at Leicester in November by 2½ lengths from High Purse, tending to idle: will stay 1½m: likely to improve bit further. *R. F. Johnson Houghton.*

101

BAY BAY 3 ch.f. Bay Express 132–Lambay 88 (Lorenzaccio 130) [1988 NR 1989 **101** 6s⁵ 7.6m* 8f³ 6f 6m⁴ 6v 6d³] sturdy, lengthy filly: has scope: good walker: third foal: half-sister to useful 1m to 11f winner My Lamb (by Relkino): dam 7f winner at 2 yrs: won maiden at Chester in May: best efforts in £12,300 handicap at York and listed race at Thirsk fifth and final starts: seems suited by 6f: acts on top-of-the-ground and a soft surface. *R. F. Johnson Houghton.*

BAYBEEJAY 2 b.f. (Mar 16) Buzzards Bay 128§–Peak Condition (Mountain Call **52** 125) [1989 8g a7g⁵] leggy filly: first reported foal: dam of little account: plating-class form in maidens. *H. J. Collingridge.*

BAY BIRD (USA) 3 b.c. Storm Bird (CAN) 134–Rain Wind (USA) (Apalachee **101** (USA) 137) [1988 8.2d³ 1989 8g³ 8f³ 11m* 12m³ 12m* 12h² 12f* 12m] leggy, angular colt: moderate walker: progressed into a useful handicapper, winning at Newbury, Kempton and York: stays 1½m well: yet to race on very soft going, probably acts on any other: game: sold to race in Singapore 62,000 gns Newmarket Autumn Sales. *M. R. Stoute.*

BAY CHIMES 2 b.f. (May 11) Buzzards Bay 128§–Wrekin Belle (Dance In Time **50** (CAN) [1989 5f⁵ 7f 5f 5g 8.2s] small, sturdy filly: second foal: dam raced twice: poor maiden: best effort at 5f. *A. D. Brown.*

BAYFOOT 2 b.f. (Apr 11) Commanche Run 133–Grayfoot 87 (Grundy 137) [1989 **55** 7m⁵] sparely-made filly: first foal: dam, maiden half-sister to Irish Guinness Oaks winner Swiftfoot, looked short of pace and possibly bit temperamental: 8/1, over 6 lengths fifth of 10 to Star Child in maiden at Wolverhampton in July: will stay 1½m: sold 1,000 gns Newmarket December Sales. *Major W. R. Hern.*

BAYFORD ENERGY 3 ch.g. Milford 119–Smiling 62 (Silly Season 127) [1988 — 8m⁵ 8f 8g³ 1989 12d⁴ 12f⁵ 10m 12.4g³ 16m³ 16.2f³ 18g] rather leggy, workmanlike gelding: little worthwhile form as 3-y-o, giving impression one paced and should stay well: best efforts with some give in the ground. *R. M. Whitaker.*

BAY MOUNTAIN 3 b.c. Tyrnavos 129–Just You Wait (Nonoalco (USA) 131) — [1988 7g 8m 8g 1989 10s 10g] tall, well-made colt: good walker: shows knee action: well beaten in varied company, including handicap. *G. Lewis.*

BAY POND 7 b.g. Grundy 137–Summer Bloom 68 (Silly Season 127) [1988 NR — 1989 a10g] medium-sized gelding: no form on flat: winning selling hurdler. *J. White.*

BAY REEF 2 b.f. (Apr 20) Glenstal (USA) 118–Tableline (USA) (Round Table) **76** [1989 5g⁶ 5m* 5g⁵] 2,600F, 17,500Y: medium-sized, useful-looking filly: good walker: half-sister to 3-y-o 1½m seller winner Sherzine, Irish 2-y-o 6f winner Tickeridge (both by Gorytus) and a winner in Italy by Lydian: dam second on only start in USA: won maiden at Warwick in July by length from Dancing Breeze: ran well when slow-starting fifth of 9 to Polar Bird in listed race at Newbury following month: will be suited by 6f: sold 15,000 gns Newmarket December Sales. *D. J. G. Murray-Smith.*

BAYSHAM (USA) 3 b.c. Raise A Native–Sunny Bay (USA) (Northern Bay — (USA)) [1988 7g 1989 10.6g 10.2f⁴] tall, close-coupled colt: well beaten in maidens: sweating, very awkward in stalls and withdrawn final appearance: later sold 5,000 gns Newmarket Autumn Sales. *G. Harwood.*

BAY TERN (USA) 3 b.c. Arctic Tern (USA) 126–Unbiased (USA) 81 (Foolish **86** Pleasure (USA)) [1988 NR 1989 9g⁴ 10s³ 10f⁵] $100,000Y: rangy colt: third-named foal: half-brother to a minor winner by Key To The Mint: dam, 7f winner, is sister to very smart American sprinting filly Pleasure Cay: fair form in maidens in first half of season: worth a try over 1m: moved moderately down and below form on firm ground: sold 10,000 gns Newmarket Autumn Sales. *L. M. Cumani.*

BAY WINDOW 5 b.g. Bay Express 132–Broken Record 106 (Busted 134) [1988 **83** 10f³ 10m⁶ 9d* 10d² 8g 10f 8f 1989 8.3m 8g⁶ 10.6d 11s* 10v⁶] medium-sized gelding: bad mover: fair handicapper: successful in 19-runner event at Ayr in September, only form at 5 yrs: stays 11f: has won on top-of-the-ground, but needs plenty of give nowadays: apprentice ridden at 5 yrs. *I. Campbell.*

BEACHY GLEN 2 b.c. (Mar 29) Glenstal (USA) 118–Ampersand (USA) 86 (Stop **75** The Music (USA)) [1989 5v⁴ 5d* 5f³ 6m³ 6m² 6d 6f³ 6f] IR 4,000Y: leggy, quite good-topped colt: second foal: half-brother to winner in Denmark: dam, 7f and 1m winner, is from family of Forest Flower: won auction event at Edinburgh in April: ran very well when second in valuable seller at York in August and third in minor event at Pontefract in October: suited by 6f. *C. Tinkler.*

BEALE STREET 4 b.g. Kris 135–Dare Me 101 (Derring-Do 131) [1988 NR 1989 — 7d 6m 11f 9f⁶] smallish, angular gelding: has a round action: little worthwhile form in varied company, including selling: pulled up after saddle slipped third outing: sweating last 2: changed hands 1,000 gns Doncaster June Sales. *M. P. Naughton.*

BEAN BOY   11 ch.g. Some Hand 119–Battling 75 (Pinza 137) [1988 10.2d^6 12m   **48** 12g^6 12g 12f* 12f^6 12m^3 12f^5 12g^4 12d^5 10s^6 12m 10m^5 14f^6 12.2f 14m 10s 12f 1989 10.2g 14s 12f* 15.8m] sturdy, workmanlike gelding: carries plenty of condition: often dull in coat: won handicap at Thirsk in May: not seen out after later in month: best form nowadays at 1½m to 1¾m: acts on any going: has worn blinkers: sweating on reappearance: suitable mount for inexperienced rider. *M. H. Easterby.*

BEAN DREAMS   4 b.g. Prince Bee 128–Travelling Fair 95 (Vienna 127) [1988 7d   **45** 10g 10.2g 12.2g 13.8d* 12g^3 12g^6 12.2g^5 1989 10.2g 12d 11f 12g 15.8g^2 16m^5] leggy, lengthy gelding: winning plater as 3-y-o: poor form in 1989: collided with rail and rider unseated third outing: stays 15.8f: suited by an easy surface: blinkered once at 3 yrs: winning hurdler with W. Bissill. *H. P. Rohan.*

BEAN KING   3 gr.g. Ardross 134–Meanz Beanz (High Top 131) [1988 8m^2 1989   **96** 8s^2 9.5g^4 8g* 10.1m^3 10.1m 11.7m^6 10m^3 10m^6 a12g^2 a12g* a14g^2] robust gelding: fair performer: won at Cagnes-sur-Mer in March and handicap (by 10 lengths, showing improved form) at Lingfield in November: probably stays 1¾m: acts on top-of-the-ground. *R. W. Armstrong.*

BEAU BENZ   5 b.g. Camden Town 125–War Lass 100 (Whistler 129) [1988 10.2d^3 **67** 12.3s^4 12g^2 10m* 10m^3 12.2g^4 10d* 10g^6 10d^6 10s^4 11m 10g 12d 10s^2 8.2s^3 1989 10.2g 10d 10.8d 10d* 12g 11.7m 10.4m 10.6s] rather leggy, good-topped gelding: carries plenty of condition: quite modest handicapper: successful at Beverley in May by 6 lengths, only form at 5 yrs: unseated rider leaving stalls final outing: ideally suited by 1¼m and an easy surface: effective with or without blinkers or visor: slowly away on reappearance and seventh outing: tends to carry head high: inconsistent. *M. H. Easterby.*

BEAUCADEAU   3 b.g. Alzao (USA) 117–Pretty Gift (Realm 129) [1988 5g* 5g^6 **81** 5.3f^4 6f^5 5d^3 5g^3 6s 1989 6s^2 6s^4 5s* 6f^6 5g^3 5d 5s 5s a6g a6g] leggy, close-coupled gelding: moderate mover: won handicap at Thirsk in April: ran moderately last 5 outings: needs testing conditions at 5f and stays 6f well: acts on soft going: blinkered last 2 starts: inconsistent. *K. M. Brassey.*

BEAUCHAMP CACTUS   4 b.f. Niniski 125–Buss 102 (Busted 134) [1988 11g   **83** 11f^5 10d^4 12g^2 12g^4 12.3g^4 14.6g^2 10g^2 1989 14g^4 17.6f* 19f^3 20f^3 19f^3 17.6d^3 17.4s 18g] useful-looking filly: favourite, beat easing up Crime Passionnel by 8 lengths in handicap at Wolverhampton in May: third in similar company after, best efforts in Ascot Handicap at Royal Ascot and Pimm's Goodwood Stakes on fourth and fifth outings: 33/1, fair eighth of 21 finishers to Double Dutch in Tote Cesarewitch (Handicap) at Newmarket: suited by good test of stamina: acts on firm going and is unsuited by soft: occasionally on toes: ran poorly when forcing pace. *J. L. Dunlop.*

BEAUCHAMP CREST   4 b.f. Jalmood (USA) 126–Jubilee 101 (Reform 132)   — [1988 10g 12m^3 12d^3 12f^3 13.1f* 1989 12g 17.1h^6] angular filly: moderate mover: modest winner as 3-y-o when trained by J. Dunlop: blinkered, led until halfway and soon tailed off in handicap at Bath (reportedly sustained back injury) in June: stays 13f: yet to race on soft going, acts on any other: sold to join K. Morgan 2,500 gns Ascot 2nd June Sales. *M. C. Pipe.*

BEAUCHAMP DREAM   3 ch.f. Castle Keep 121–Buss 102 (Busted 134) [1988   **97** 7m^6 7g* 7d 1989 8.5s^6 11.5f 12f 13.3m^2 14f^2 16.1m 11.7f^4 14m*] close-coupled, medium-sized filly: fairly useful handicapper: won £6,400 contest at Newmarket in October: ran unaccountably poorly at 2m: probably acts on any going: sold 13,000 gns Newmarket Autumn Sales. *J. L. Dunlop.*

BEAUDENE   3 b.c. Song 132–Princess Tavi (Sea Hawk II 131) [1988 NR 1989 7f^5 — 8m 8m 10m] workmanlike colt: has a round action: fifth live foal: half-brother to 7f and 1m winner Vanroy (by Formidable), 1½m to 18.4f winner Tilly Tavi (by Welsh Pageant) and fairly useful 1981 2-y-o 6f and 7f winner Straeker (by Sharpen Up): dam well beaten all starts: no worthwhile form in maidens and in handicap in the North. *J. Mackie.*

BEAU ECHARPE   4 b.f. Relkino 131–Rapidus (Sharpen Up 127) [1988 12s^4 **48** 16m^4 12d 16g 14g^6 12g 16m 18g 1989 12m 14m 10.8f^3 8m 10f^2 10f* 10f^3] big, angular, plain filly: has a round action: co-favourite, won for first time when making all in seller (bought in 5,000 gns) at Folkestone in August: likely to prove best at up to 1¼m: acts on firm going and possibly unsuited by soft: blinkered sixth outing at 3 yrs, visored seventh: sold 10,000 gns Newmarket Autumn Sales. *M. F. D. Morley.*

BEAU GUEST (FR)   7 ch.g. Be My Guest (USA) 126–Belle Zed (FR) (Zeddaan   **72** 130) [1988 10g 7g^6 8f^6 7f 7.6g 7d 8f^3 12d 10m 1989 10.2g* 8.5d* 9f 10.2g 8.5f^3 10.6m] leggy gelding: modest handicapper: well ridden when winning 30-runner amateurs event at Doncaster (edgy and went freely to post) and strongly-run contest at Beverley (claimer ridden) in spring: form after only on fifth outing: effective over 1¼m and strongly-run 1m: acts on any going: usually bandaged at 6 yrs: often sweats: slowly away fourth start. *J. Parkes.*

BEAU IDEAL 4 b.c. Brigadier Gerard 144–Princess Lieven (Royal Palace 131) [1988 9g 12d² 12g³ 12g⁵ 1989 14g 11f 10f⁶ 13.3m³ 11.5g* 12g 11v³ 12g] smallish, leggy, lightly-made colt: won for first time when making all in handicap at Sandown in July: ran poorly final outing: probably best at up to 1½m: acts on top-of-the-ground and heavy going: sweating, bit edgy and hung left fourth start. *C. E. Brittain.* **82**

BEAUJOLAIS NOUVEAU 2 ch.c. (Mar 23) Aragon 118–No Halo 74 (Aureole 132) [1989 5g] 5,600F, 4,200Y: compact colt: seventh foal: brother to quite modest 1987 2-y-o maiden Mans No Angel and half-brother to a winner in Italy: dam won over 1½m: 16/1 and in need of race, prominent 3f in 15-runner maiden auction race at Salisbury in May. *K. O. Cunningham-Brown.*

BEAUMONT'S KEEP 3 b.c. Castle Keep 121–Powderhall 81 (Murrayfield 119) [1988 6g⁶ 6d⁶ 5m³ 6g⁴ 1989 5.8m 5h 6m 5f⁶ 5f³ 6f² 5m⁶] leggy colt: quite modest form: 5/4 on, unlucky second in 5-runner maiden at Folkestone in August: ran creditably in handicaps third to fifth outings, twice again not getting best of runs: will prove better at 6f than 5f, and is bred to stay further. *L. J. Holt.* **66**

BEAUMOOD 3 b.c. Jalmood (USA) 126–Falcon Berry (FR) (Bustino 136) [1988 7d⁴ 10g 1989 10g⁴ 10.6g⁵ 10m⁵ 10.6g⁶ 12g⁵ 13s* 12s² 13.3d] neat colt: modest handicapper: won at Hamilton in September: very good second of 16 (clear) at Haydock, making most and battling on well: will stay 2m: acts on soft ground. *M. A. Jarvis.* **77**

BEAU NASH 5 b.g. Prince Tenderfoot (USA) 126–Dominica (GER) (Zank) [1988 10d 10.2d³ 12g² 11.7m⁴ 12f 12d 13.8g⁶ 11s 1989 12.4g* 12d⁵ 12f 12g⁶ 14g 12.4m² 13m⁶ 12m 12.3m 13s 12.4g] compact gelding: carries plenty of condition: good mover, with a quick action: modest handicappper on his day: won at Newcastle in March: best subsequent effort when second in moderately-run race at same course: stays 1½m: best form on a sound surface: blinkered once at 4 yrs: suitable mount for inexperienced rider. *A. P. Stringer.* **67**

BEAU QUEST 2 b.c. (May 31) Rainbow Quest (USA) 134–Elegant Tern (USA) 102 (Sea Bird II 145) [1989 6m 7m⁴ 8.5f 8f³] smallish colt: ninth foal: half-brother to several winners, including 3-y-o miler Roseate Lodge (by Habitat), smart 1¼m performer Elegant Air (by Shirley Heights) and useful 5f and 7f winner Fairy Tern (by Mill Reef): dam won 3 times at around 1m and stayed 1½m: quite modest form in maidens and when blinkered in a nursery: will be suited by 1¼m: sold 10,000 gns Doncaster November Sales. *A. A. Scott.* **63**

BEAUREPAIRE BOY 5 ch.h. Thatching 131–First Sun (FR) (Margouillat (FR) 133) [1988 6v* 6g⁴ 6d⁴ 6s 1989 6d] angular horse: moderate mover: plating-class winner early as 4-y-o: bandaged, had stiff task in Thirsk handicap in April, only outing for long time: suited by 6f and plenty of give in the ground: apprentice ridden at 4 yrs. *J. Pearce.* **—**

BEAU ROLANDO 3 b.g. Teenoso (USA) 135–Fabulous Luba (Luthier 126) [1988 NR 1989 12.2d] 6,200 3-y-o: second foal: half-brother to fairly useful 7f and 1m winner Kristal Rock (by Kris): dam, second twice over 1m in France, is daughter of Altesse Royale: 50/1, not knocked about in mid-division in claimer at Catterick in October: may do better: winner over hurdles. *N. Tinkler.* **— p**

BEAU ROU 2 br.c. (Mar 17) Rousillon (USA) 133–Beautiful Dawn (USA) (Grey Dawn II 132) [1989 6d] big, useful-looking colt: has scope: third foal: half-brother to useful 7f winner Point House (by Diesis): dam won minor 6f stakes at 5 yrs: 20/1 and in need of race, in mid-division in 24-runner maiden at Newbury in October, very slowly away, close up 2f out then weakening and eased approaching final 1f: sure to improve and win a race. *D. R. C. Elsworth.* **— p**

BEAU'S DELIGHT (USA) 3 b.f. Lypheor 118–Beauvoir (Artaius (USA) 129) [1988 NR 1989 7.6m⁵ 10h 10m 12h 7g] small filly: has a round action: first reported living foal: dam, French 1m winner, is half-sister to smart French 1¼m winner Sangue (by Lyphard), later top class in USA: staying on only in maiden at Chester, only sign of ability: should stay at least 1m: visored final outing: sweating and edgy third start: trained until after then by R. Simpson. *B. Gubby.* **—**

BEAU SHER 6 b.h. Ile de Bourbon (USA) 133–Mai Pussy 91 (Realm 129) [1988 10g 8d* 9m* 8g² 10.5g⁴ 10m³ 8g 8g* 8s³ 8d² 1989 8g* 8d² 7g* 7.2s* 8g² 8.5g² 10f² 8g⁶ 12s⁶] big horse: has a rather round action: in tremendous form in first half of **119**

Fairey Group Spring Trophy, Haydock—
Beau Sher takes it up from Folly Foot close home

season, winning listed events at Doncaster, Leicester and Haydock: showed himself better than ever when length second of 8, rallying well, to Two Timing in 1¼m Prince of Wales's Stakes at Royal Ascot: reportedly badly struck into next outing, and off course over 3 months afterwards: effective at 7f to 1¼m: acts on any going: sweated when tried in blinkers (ran too freely) and on sixth start: splendidly tough, genuine and consistent: a credit to his trainer. *B. Hanbury.*

BEAUTIFUL NINA 3 ch.f. Rabdan 129–Donna Sirena 72 (Julio Mariner 127) —
[1988 6m 6m⁶ 1989 7f 8m] leggy, close-coupled, plain filly: no sign of ability when backward in maidens. *G. Blum.*

BEAUTIFUL ORCHID 3 b.f. Hays 120–Pageantry 83 (Welsh Pageant 132) —
[1988 NR 1989 10f 12f 8.5f⁵ 10.6s 12s] 5,800 2-y-o: big, angular filly: has a round action: second foal: half-sister to Just Class (by Dominion), useful 7f and 1m winner here later graded winner in USA: dam ran only at 2 yrs when placed over 5f and 6f: well beaten in maidens and handicaps: reportedly lame when tailed off final start. *S. G. Norton.*

BEBE WIND 2 b.c. (Mar 14) Tumble Wind (USA)–Bebe Diane (GER) (Days At —
Sea (USA)) [1989 7m 6m 6f] 6,000Y: workmanlike, deep-girthed colt: has a round action: half-brother to a winner in Germany: dam won in Germany: well beaten in varied races: blinkered final start. *Capt. R. M. Smyly.*

BECKINGHAM BEN 5 gr.g. Workboy 123–Pickwood Sue 74 (Right Boy 137) 49
[1988 5f² 5f⁶ 5f* 5m⁴ 5d 5f 5m* 5g⁶ 5f³ 5g⁶ 6g 1989 5m⁶ 5m 5f⁶ 5f⁴ 5m⁶ 5f⁶ 6f³ 5m⁶ 5f² 5.1g² 5f 5g³ a5g] tall gelding: poor mover: poor handicapper: suited by 5f: acts on firm going and a soft surface: often visored or blinkered nowadays: good mount for apprentice: suited by forcing tactics. *J. P. Leigh.*

BECKWITH 4 b.g. Wolver Hollow 126–La Cita (Le Levanstell 122) [1988 12g⁶ 42
12m 14.7m 1989 12.4g 14.6g 8v⁵ 11g⁵ 13m 12f³ 11s 12m] sparely-made gelding: moderate mover: poor maiden: placed in seller: needs further than 1m and stays 1½m: blinkered on reappearance, visored afterwards. *M. P. Naughton.*

BECOCIOUS 2 b.g. (Mar 27) Precocious 126–Baheejah (Northfields) (USA)) 55
[1989 5f³ 6m 6m 6m⁵ 5m⁶ 6s] 8,600Y: good-bodied gelding: has a quick action: second foal: half-brother to a winner abroad: dam lightly-raced half-sister to Irish Guinness Oaks winner Olwyn: plating-class maiden: best effort, ridden by 7-lb claimer, in nursery at Haydock on fourth start: best form at 6f: blinkered or visored last 3 outings: gelded after final start. *J. Etherington.*

Charles St George Stakes, York—Becquerel makes a winning debut

BECQUEREL (USA) 3 ch.c. Sharpen Up 127–Marie Curie 96 (Exbury 138) **96**
[1988 NR 1989 8m* 8m⁴ 8f] compact, attractive colt: half-brother to several
winners, notably very smart miler Crofter (by Habitat) and useful 5f and 7f winner
Mazilier (by Lyphard), later successful in 8.5f stakes race in USA: dam won over 6f
at 2 yrs: held up in rear when winning £5,300 maiden at York in June: well-backed
favourite, creditable fourth of 14 in £15,700 handicap (struggling in rear 4f out) at
Newmarket: pulled hard and never dangerous in £20,900 handicap at York in
August: may well stay further but needs to settle. *J. Tree.*

BEC ROUGE 3 ch.c. Ballad Rock 122–Mrs Tittlemouse (Nonoalco (USA) 131) **—**
[1988 NR 1989 8s 7f 8m³ 9m] 17,000F, 68,000Y: leggy, angular colt: first living foal:
dam unraced half-sister to high-class miler Bairn: 8 lengths third of 4 to odds-on
Santa Tecla in apprentice race at Warwick in July, first show in maidens: bit
backward in apprentice handicap at Kempton 2 months later: moved poorly down
and gave impression ill at ease on firm going. *C. R. Nelson.*

BEDE LADY 3 b.f. Montekin 125–Devine Lady (The Parson 119) [1988 6f 6g⁴ 7g **43**
1989 8g 8g⁴ 12f⁵ a11g] small, dipped-backed filly: poor maiden: stays 1m, most
probably not 1½m: keen sort: sweating and edgy first 2 starts: sold out of C.
Tinkler's stable 1,250 gns Doncaster September Sales before final one. *R. T. Juckes.*

BEDELIA 3 ch.f. Mr Fluorocarbon 126–Devadara 73 (Royal Levee (USA)) [1988 **—**
NR 1989 12g 10g] fifth foal: half-sister to 3 winners, including 5f to 7f winner Pete
Rocket (by Roan Rocket): dam showed some ability at 2 yrs: no sign of ability in
late-season seller and claimer. *M. Blanshard.*

BEECHWOOD COTTAGE 6 ch.g. Malinowski (USA) 123–Drora (Busted **70**
134) [1988 6g 6s 7f² 6m³ 6f* 7g* 8f 8f³ 6g 6g 7m 7f⁴ 7f 6s 6d² 6d 6d 6s 1989 6d 7m 8h
7h* 7m 7.6m 7m 7f² 7.6m 7m² 7m⁴ 6m 7d a7g*] small, sturdy gelding: poor walker
and mover: modest handicapper: successful at Brighton (apprentices) in June and
Lingfield (having been tailed off to halfway) in November: best at 6f or 7f: acts on
any going: effective with or without blinkers: bandaged fifth outing: has started
slowly: excellent mount for inexperienced rider: goes well with tender handling:
inconsistent. *A. Bailey.*

BEEHIVE BOY 2 b.g. (Apr 12) Longleat (USA) 109–Queensbury Star 76 **73**
(Wishing Star 117) [1989 5f² 6m² 5f 5h³ 7f² 7m³ 6f* 6g⁴ 6m* 7f* 6s] 3,300Y: strong,
workmanlike gelding: has scope: third foal: brother to 3-y-o Vuchterbacher and a
poor animal: dam won over 6f at 2 yrs but showed no form after: successful in
maiden auction race at Redcar, seller (bought in 19,000 gns) at Newcastle and a
claimer at Salisbury in summer: stays 7f: visored fourth and last 3 outings. *C.
Tinkler.*

BEEKMAN STREET 3 b.c. Jalmood (USA) 126–Plato's Retreat 73 (Brigadier **78**
Gerard 144) [1988 6m 6s⁵ 7d³ 7.5m* 8f 1989 8s 10.6s 11m* 12.4m⁴ 14m* 14m⁴ 14f

106

16m² 17.4s² 16m⁴ 18g² 15g⁴] leggy, fair sort: modest handicapper: won at Sandown in July: ran creditably next 6 starts: stays well: acts on any going: sold I. Wardle 28,000 gns Doncaster November Sales. *C. W. Thornton.*

BE FRESH 3 ch.c. Be My Guest (USA) 126–Fresh (High Top 131) [1988 NR 1989 **104** 8m⁵ 7m⁵ 6g* 6g* 6v 6d] good-topped, attractive colt: second foal: dam, good middle-distance performer in Italy, is half-sister to several winners, notably high-class middle-distance filly Free Guest (by Be My Guest): always front rank when winning 21-runner claimer at Haydock in September and 24-runner £8,900 handicap at Newmarket in October: unfavourably drawn, ran moderately in handicap and listed race after: headstrong (pulled far too hard second start) and is suited by 6f: probably needs a sound surface. *L. M. Cumani.*

BEHERA 3 b.f. Mill Reef (USA) 141–Borushka 115 (Bustino 136) [1988 8s⁵ **129** 8s* 1989 10.5d* 10m* 10g³ 12g² 12f⁴]

In a round-about way the *Thoroughbred Times* paid a handsome tribute to the Breeders' Cup Turf series so far in commenting that this year's field was not as formidable as in past runnings. For while, as was also said, there were no foreign competitors with credentials akin to those of All Along, Pebbles or Dancing Brave, or any North American representatives with the proven mettle of Manila or Theatrical, the field was still a good one, worthy of the occasion. The French in particular could be well satisfied with the strength of their challenge. Behera, Sierra Roberta and Star Lift represented top French middle-distance form and all came out with credit, even Behera who had Ciga Prix de l'Arc de Triomphe tables turned on her by the other two. The tight turns and short circuit at Gulfstream told against Behera. All Along herself would have had trouble getting up from ninth-of-fourteen position, eight lengths down, going into the last bend. The less flexible Behera, among the backmarkers from the start, improved a couple of places before the straight, then, back on an even keel, finished as well as any to take fourth behind Prized, beaten just over a length.

Behera's season, like that of some of her stable-mates, was disrupted by illness. Normally, a filly of her breeding who'd started off in the spring by winning the Prix Penelope and the Prix Saint-Alary would go on to contest the Prix de Diane, a race at Deauville maybe, the Prix Vermeille certainly, and, if considered good enough, the Prix de l'Arc de Triomphe. However, Behera had to miss almost all the summer, forfeiting what seemed a favourite's chance in the Diane following her narrow defeat of Louveterie and Lady In Silver in the Group 1 Saint-Alary. And the race chosen for her return in September was the Prix de la Nonette at Longchamp, probably because it looked easier than the Vermeille; she had, after all, been away for over three

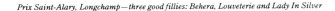

Prix Saint-Alary, Longchamp—three good fillies: Behera, Louveterie and Lady In Silver

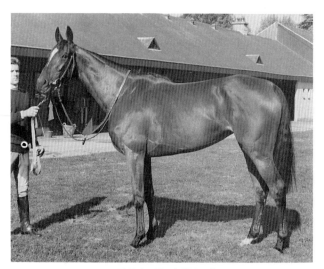

H. H. Aga Khan's "Behera"

months. Behera's performance in the Nonette was sufficiently encouraging to earn her a place in the Arc line-up though she was beaten at odds on. Sierra Roberta and Nadina ran her out of it in the last furlong or so, receiving weight as were the rest of the opposition.

Behera made one of a powerful quartet of three-year-old fillies in the Arc, along with her owner's Aliysa and the Vermeille first two, Young Mother and Sierra Roberta. In the British books, which differ from the French Tote in that they show individual odds rather than coupling owners' representatives, she was the outsider of the four. Fair enough. But she left her previous form behind, and even if you'd never seen her run you'd be able to explain why by reference to her pedigree: she is bred to be suited by a good test of stamina. Behera won over a testing mile as a two-year-old; she'd snatched both her wins in 1989 by staying on very strongly. On this first attempt at a mile and a half, she raced close up from the start in the usual strongly-run Arc and turned for home in a handy third place. Carroll House hampered her slightly when coming to challenge but clearly had the better pace and, in our opinion, would have won anyway. Once switched Behera galloped on strongly again, securing second place from Saint Andrews near the line; Carroll House beat her a length and a half.

Behera would definitely have started favourite for the Prix Royal-Oak but she could hardly go for that and the Breeders' Cup Turf, since the two races were only a week apart (the eventual choice of objective, by the way, is a reflection on the current standing of the last and longest of France's classics). The further step up in distance would have suited her, just as the step up for the 1984 Park Hill Stakes run over the St Leger course at Doncaster had suited her dam. Borushka had previously won three races, notably the Galtres Stakes at York, and she gained another in the Park Hill. On both subsequent starts over a mile and a half she ran as though by then she needed further.

This is a notable staying family. The second dam Valdavia, a half-sister to the Diane winner and King George VI and Queen Elizabeth Stakes third Crepellana, won over a mile and a half in France and is also the dam of the useful Italian stayer Walid. The third dam Astana was out of a mare whose other foals included the Prix du Jockey-Club winner Philius and Anyte II, the dam of the Irish Oaks winner Ancasta; Astana herself showed more than useful form at up to thirteen furlongs.

		Never Bend	Nasrullah
	Mill Reef (USA)	(b 1960)	Lalun
	(b 1968)	Milan Mill	Princequillo
Behera		(b 1962)	Virginia Water
(b.f. 1986)		Bustino	Busted
	Borushka	(b 1971)	Ship Yard
	(b 1981)	Valdavia	Ribot
		(b 1968)	Astana

There is an obvious case to be made out for keeping Behera in training. However, very few indeed of the two hundred or more broodmares presently in the Aga Khan's studs raced beyond three years of age. Borushka didn't. Behera, the first foal of Borushka, probably acts on any going. *A. de Royer-Dupre, France.*

BEHIND THE CLOCK 2 b.c. (Apr 22) Sula Bula 109–Hale Lane 59 (Comedy — Star (USA) 121) [1989 6f] first foal: dam poor plater: 66/1 and backward, slowly away and well behind last 2f in 11-runner minor event at Nottingham in September. *T. M. Jones.*

BEL BYOU 5 b.h. Try My Best (USA) 130–Ring Lady 98 (Thatch (USA) 136) 95 [1988 6d⁴ 6g 6g⁶ 7m* 6g 7g 6d 1989 6s⁵ 7g⁶ 7f² 7g⁵ 5g⁴ 6v] good-quartered horse: usually looks well: fairly useful performer: ran creditably in handicaps at Thirsk (apprentice ridden) and Epsom, third and fourth outings: long way below his best both starts in autumn: ideally suited by 7f: acts on any going, except possibly heavy: very slowly away when blinkered: sold 16,000 gns Newmarket Autumn Sales. *P. F. I. Cole.*

BELDALE LADY 2 b.f. (May 20) Beldale Flutter (USA) 130–Knavesmire 82 38 (Runnymede 123) [1989 6f 7g 7d a7g] 2,000Y: close-coupled filly: sixth foal: half-sister to 5f performer Bluemede (by Blue Cashmere) and a winner in Italy: dam at her best at 2 yrs: of little account: blinkered final start. *W. W. Haigh.*

BELDONAYR 2 ch.f. (Apr 11) Rabdan 129–Pearl Cove 63 (Town And Country 54 124) [1989 7m⁶ 7m 7g] 1,400Y, 3,500 2-y-o: angular filly: first foal: dam lightly raced: plating-class maiden. *E. Weymes.*

BELFIL (USA) 3 ch.f. Believe It (USA)–Filter (USA) (Sir Ivor 135) [1988 NR 47 1989 7g 10f⁵ 9g a10g a8g⁵] $20,000Y: lengthy, angular filly: fourth foal: half-sister to Land of Liberty (by Star Spangled), twice successful at around 6f, and to another winner in USA by Full Pocket: dam unplaced from 7 starts: plating-class maiden: only sign of ability when fifth at Beverley and Southwell (blinkered, driven along throughout): sold 3,200 gns Doncaster November Sales. *R. W. Armstrong.*

BELFORT GIPSY 3 b.g. Belfort (FR) 89–Tringa (GER) (Kaiseradler) [1988 5d 56 6d 6f 6g⁵ 5g⁵ 6s⁴ 6m⁴ 5d 1989 6d⁶ 7s 6m⁵ 6m⁴ 8h⁶ 6g 6f³ 6g a7g] neat gelding: quite modest maiden: suited by 6f and top-of-the-ground: blinkered once at 2 yrs: visored fourth and final outings in 1989: sold to join J. Norton 2,300 gns Newmarket Autumn Sales. *S. G. Norton.*

BELFORT PRINCESS 3 b.f. Belfort (FR) 89–Princess Scarlett (Prince 70 Regent (FR) 129) [1988 5g⁴ 5d⁵ 6m* 6h³ 6m⁵ 6g 7f 7g⁵ 8g³ 7m² 1989 10.6s 9f⁶ 10.2f 8.5g⁶ 7g² 8f⁶ 7m] smallish, angular filly: modest form at best as 3-y-o, best efforts second and fifth starts in handicap at York and claimer (first run for over 3 months) at Edinburgh: probably stays 9f: acts on firm going: visored third outing: has run creditably when sweating and on toes, and for 5-lb claimer: sold 1,100 gns Newmarket December Sales. *S. G. Norton.*

BELFORT RULER 2 b.c. (Feb 8) Belfort (FR) 89–Call Me Kate 72 (Firestreak 54 p 125) [1989 5f4] 8,800Y: workmanlike colt: sixth foal: brother to quite modest 1987 2-y-o 5f and 6f winner Defence Call, later successful from 7.5f to 1¼m in Italy, and to a winner in Denmark: dam won over 1¼m at 4 yrs: carrying condition, 5½ lengths fourth of 6, after swerving stalls, to Pippa's Dream in minor event at Chepstow in July. *B. Gubby.*

BELHAVEN BILL 3 ch.g. Windjammer (USA)–Correct Approach 77 (Right 47 Tack 131) [1988 5f⁴ 5.8g⁵ 6g 5g 8f 1989 8h 8h⁴ 5f 5.8h] workmanlike gelding: plating-class maiden: blinkered final outing: sold privately 3,000 gns Ascot December Sales. *R. J. Holder.*

BELHAVEN SPECIAL 3 b.f. Ile de Bourbon (USA) 133–Saran (Le Levanstell — 122) [1988 6g² 8m 7m 1989 8g 7f 10m 8m] close-coupled, sparely-made filly: quite modest maiden as 2-y-o: well beaten in 1989, including in seller: should stay 1¼m+: sweated third outing: sold to join A. Moore 2,000 gns Ascot July Sales. *R. J. Holder.*

BELHOMME 3 ch.c. Habitat 134–Fair Sousanne 75 (Busted 134) [1988 6g* 1989 94 8.2s⁴ 7f³ 7g³ 7f* 7f³] strong, angular colt: carries plenty of condition: has a quick, short action: won minor event at Goodwood in June: odds on, below form in similar event at Warwick almost 4 months later: should stay 1m: probably unsuited by very soft going: sold 26,000 gns Newmarket Autumn Sales, probably to Italy. *H. R. A. Cecil.*

BELINDA'S BOY 2 b.g. (Mar 9) Swing Easy (USA) 126–Queen of The Hills 72 48 (Connaught 130) [1989 5g⁴ 6m⁶ 6m⁶ 5g 5f 5g 5g⁴] 3,700Y: medium-sized, quite attractive gelding: brother to a multiple winner in Italy and half-brother to a winner by King of Spain: dam won 1m seller: plating-class maiden: best form at 5f on easy ground: gelded after final outing. *W. Carter.*

BELLAGHY BRIDGE 2 b.f. (Mar 16) Dublin Taxi–Red Solitaire 76 (Red God — 128§) [1989 5f] half-sister to several winners, including quite useful 7f to 9f winner Masubeni (by Monseigneur) and fair 7f performer Azerila (by Prince Regent): dam stayed 1¼m: 50/1, slowly away and always behind in 15-runner maiden at Beverley in September: unruly stalls. *J. Parkes.*

BELLA MAGNA 3 b.f. Mr Fluorocarbon 126–Bella Travaille 82 (Workboy 123) — [1988 NR 1989 6s 5s 5h] 1,100F: lengthy, dipped-backed filly: third foal: sister to fair 1987 2-y-o 5f winner Magna Travaille and half-sister to 5f and 6f winner On The Record (by Record Token): dam, best at 2 yrs, won 3 times at 5f: behind in minor event and maidens in the spring. *D. J. Wintle.*

BELLA NOAL 3 b.f. Noalto 120–Nimble Fingers 64 (Burglar 128) [1988 NR 1989 — 12f 10g⁶ 10f] workmanlike, plain filly: fifth living foal: half-sister to a winner in Italy by High Line: dam 1m winner: no worthwhile form, including in seller. *W. T. Kemp.*

BELLARIDA (FR) 3 br.f. Bellypha 130–Lerida (Riverman 131) [1988 7.5g⁴ 8g² 111 9s 9g² 8s* 1989 11d* 10.5m* 10.5g* 10.5d 9.2g 10.5s] third foal: half-sister to French 1¼m winner Rayon Vert (by Green Dancer) and French provincial 4-y-o 1¼m winner Darian (by Habitat): dam French 9f and 11f winner out of Prix Saint-Alary winner Lalika: won maiden at Maisons-Laffitte as 2-y-o and at Longchamp in handicap in April and listed race and Group 3 Prix de Royaumont (by 1½ lengths from Tessla who gave 4 lb) in May: below form after in pattern events at Chantilly (off course 4 months after), Longchamp and Saint-Cloud: stays 11f: has won on soft going but best form on a sound surface. *Mme C. Head, France.*

BELLA ROSSI 3 b.f. Mummy's Pet 125–Rosalka (ITY) (Relko 136) [1988 5d⁶ 83 5g* 5g³ 6g⁴ 5d* 6g⁵ 5g 5m³ 5g³ 1989 6g⁴ 5m 5f³ 5g 5g² 5m* 5m⁵ 6f 5m³] leggy filly: moderate mover, with a quick action: fair handicapper: won at Chester in July: fair fifth at Newmarket, easily best effort after: best at 5f: acts on firm going and a soft surface: below form when sweating fourth (visored, found little) and last 2 outings. *M. McCormack.*

BELLA SEVILLE 5 gr.m. King of Spain 121–Tempered Wind (Fleece 114) [1988 67 6f⁶ 5g⁵ 5m⁵ 5f³ 5g³ 5g* 5d⁴ 5g³ 5f 5m 5g* 5s 5m* 5f⁶ 5g² 5g⁵ 5s⁶ 5d³ 1989 6m 5m⁴ 5g⁶ 5f⁵ 5g⁶ 5f⁵ 5m* 5g 5m² 5d 5s² 5f* 5d⁴ 5d] lengthy mare: quite modest handicapper: won at Pontefract in August and October: best at 5f: acts on any going: best in blinkers: needs plenty of driving, and probably best with strong handling. *T. D. Barron.*

BELLA SOFIE 5 ch.m. Sallust 134–Kath (Thatch (USA) 136) [1988 7.6g 10f 8g 37 7m 10m 1989 8f⁴ 8.5f 7f² 7g⁴ 8f⁶ 8f* 7m] deep-girthed mare: poor mover: poor performer: 10/1 from 6/1, won for first time in seller (no bid) at Brighton in September: edged left 3f out and soon beaten in handicap at Redcar 3 days later: stays 1m: acts on firm going: has run creditably for apprentice: sweating second outing: sold to join I. Semple 1,900 gns Newmarket Autumn Sales. *E. Eldin.*

BELL CORD 4 b.f. Beldale Flutter (USA) 130–Cordon 89 (Morston (FR) 125) — [1988 8m² 8m 8.5m² 8d* 8g* 8g⁵ 8d⁶ 8g³ 8.2g 1989 7d] leggy filly: fifth foal: half-sister to 3 winners, including 1¼m winner Fayette (by Dom Racine) and French 1m winner Taparis (by Tap On Wood): dam won over 7f and 1½m: successful

4 times in France, including in claimers as 3-y-o: in need of race, behind in seller at Catterick in March: possibly needed further than 7f: acted on top-of-the-ground and a soft surface: usually blinkered at 3 yrs: in foal to Dunbeath. *N. Tinkler.*

BELLE-COTE 3 b.f. Coquelin (USA) 121–Lovely Clare 106 (Sing Sing 134) [1988 — 5d⁶ 6m 6m³ 6m⁴ 7f³ 7m⁶ 6m⁵ 8g⁵ 1989 7d 8.2g 6m 7.5m 8f] medium-sized, unfurnished filly: moderate mover: modest form as 2-y-o: showed little in 1989, well backed in seller fourth start: best at up to 7f: acts on firm going: blinkered last 2 starts at 2 yrs (not discredited first time) and final outing: tends to carry head awkwardly: bought out of W. O'Gorman's stable 2,500 gns Newmarket July Sales after reappearance: resold 3,000 gns Doncaster September Sales. *J. Norton.*

BELLE DE MONT 3 b.f. Montekin 125–Magic Lady (Gala Performance (USA)) — [1988 7g 7g⁴ 6s⁵ 7s 8s 1989 6m 8m 5f 6g 8.2g] medium-sized, sparely-made filly: poor walker: half-sister to fair 6f and 7f winner Goose Hill (by Don), modest 7f winner Malacca Street (by Wolverlife) and a winner in Hong Kong: dam placed over 1½m in Ireland: poor maiden: no worthwhile form (including in sellers) as 3-y-o: should stay 1m: blinkered third and fourth starts: bandaged final one: trained at 2 yrs by P. Finn in Ireland and first 4 starts in 1989 by R. Stubbs. *T. Kersey.*

BELLEPHERON 6 b.h. Bellypha 130–Une Pavane (FR) (Caro 133) [1988 8d — § 12.2g² 12g⁵ 13s⁶ 12m³ 12f⁵ 1989 13.8d] lengthy, quite attractive horse: poor handicapper: effective at 1¼m and 1½m: best form on sound surface: sometimes has tongue tied down: winning hurdler: unreliable. *W. Storey.*

BELLHOPPER 3 b.f. Sacrilege 95–Ty-With-Belle 62 (Pamroy 99) [1988 5d³ — 5m⁶ 6g³ 5g 5d⁶ 5.8d⁶ 7g 1989 6f] small, sparely-made filly: poor plater: ran too freely for 7-lb claimer once at 2 yrs: sweats up and gets on edge. *B. Palling.*

BELLINGTON 3 b.g. Beldale Flutter (USA) 130–Halba 91 (Habat 127) [1988 **72** 7m⁴ 7m 8g 10.2m 1989 12g³ 12s* 11m⁶ 13.3g 11.7m 12g 12m] strong gelding: has scope: good walker: won claimer at Kempton in May: below form in handicaps last 4 starts: stays 1½m: yet to race on every firm ground, probably acts on any other: has run creditably for 5-lb claimer: sold 17,000 gns Newmarket Autumn Sales. *M. A. Jarvis.*

BELL TOLL 3 b.f. High Line 125–Heaven Knows 113 (Yellow God 129) [1988 6f⁵ **80** 7d* 8m⁴ 8g* 7.3s 1989 8f 10m⁶ 12s] lengthy, good-quartered filly: carries condition: has a markedly round action: fair winner at 2 yrs: creditable sixth in handicap at Epsom in June: gave trouble at stalls and tailed off in similar event 4 months later: should be suited by at least 1¼m: acts well on an easy surface: has won for 7-lb claimer but likely to prove best with strong handling. *G. A. Pritchard-Gordon.*

BELL TURRET 2 b. or br.c. (Apr 22) Beldale Flutter (USA) 130–Base Camp 80 — (Derring-Do 131) [1989 7m³ 7g 8.2d] seventh foal: half-brother to 3-y-o Depot (by Sharpo) and several winners, including stayer Revisit (by Busted) and useful performer at up to 1¼m Crampon (by Shirley Heights): dam won 3 times over 1¼m: always behind in maidens: slowly away first 2 starts: sweating, edgy and pulled hard final one: sold 2,200 gns Ascot November Sales. *G. A. Pritchard-Gordon.*

BELLWICK 2 b.f. (Apr 7) Norwick (USA) 120–Dusty Bluebell (Sky Gipsy 117) **42** [1989 6f 6f⁵ 6m 6f] leggy, unfurnished filly: has a round action: half-sister to fair sprinter Alpine Rocket (by Shiny Tenth) and 2 winners abroad: dam of little account: poor maiden: best effort (ridden by 7-lb claimer) second start: tailed off in nursery final one. *J. W. Payne.*

BELMEZ (USA) 2 b.c. (Jan 11) El Gran Senor (USA) 136–Grace Note (FR) **109 p** 99 (Top Ville 129) [1989 8g*]

The reports from the Newmarket training grounds which appear regularly in the racing Press had no word of Belmez before his debut in the Carlsberg Stakes at Newmarket in November, but his presence on the gallops is unlikely to be overlooked in the future after he belied his starting price of 50/1 and ran out a most convincing winner from useful stable-companion Satin Wood. Thought by his trainer to be a lazy, late-developing type who would need the race Belmez, who was ridden by the stable's second jockey Ryan, left his home work well behind with a startling performance which, if our assessment is correct, puts him among the higher echelons of the two-year-old order. Soon travelling strongly in the first half-dozen of a sixteen-runner field which also included the previous winners Needham Hope and Long Island, the promising Chapman's Peak and the unraced but heavily-backed favourite Berillion from the Harwood stable, Belmez was shaken up three furlongs out as Satin Wood came under strong pressure in front, took up the running with a furlong to go and, after showing his inexperience, galloped on strongly in the last hundred yards to increase his advantage. By the post the quite attractive Belmez had put three lengths between himself and Satin Wood with another six (it was officially returned as five) back to third-placed Ibn Sina; the rest of the runners finished quite well strung out. It's by no means unusual that when Cecil runs two horses in a race the apparently lesser-fancied of the pair emerges on top, and there was certainly no suspicion of a fluke about the manner in which Belmez outran his opponents. While the fact that none of the principals ran again makes evaluation of the form a more difficult task, we see no reason to assume that Satin Wood ran much, if anything, below the form he showed when fourth to Digression in the Royal Lodge and so are willing to accept that Belmez is, at the very least, useful. With improvement virtually guaranteed he looks an interesting middle-distance prospect.

		Northern Dancer (b 1961)	Nearctic
Belmez (USA) (b.c. Jan 11, 1987)	El Gran Senor (USA) (b 1981)		Natalma
		Sex Appeal (ch 1970)	Buckpasser
			Best In Show
	Grace Note (FR) (b 1982)	Top Ville (b 1976)	High Top
			Sega Ville
		Val de Grace (b 1969)	Val de Loir
			Pearly Queen

Belmez is from the second crop of the 1984 Two Thousand Guineas and Irish Derby winner El Gran Senor who despite fertility problems has still managed to sire Classic Fame, Saratogan, Gran Alba, De Rivera, Cordoba and Al Hareb from only a few runners in England and Ireland. The dam Grace Note, a fairly useful racemare who was bred and raced by Sir Michael Sobell's Ballymacoll Stud, won a mile-and-a-quarter maiden at Chepstow in 1985 and ran second in the Group 3 Lingfield Oaks Trial from three attempts at a mile and a half before her acquisition by Sheikh Mohammed. Her excellent family will be a familiar one to those readers who have a particular interest in racing and breeding in France. Among her several winning half-sisters, all of whom have been successful over middle distances, are the useful filly Model Girl, third in the Prix Fille de l'Air and dam of the very useful mile to mile-and-a-half winner In Focus, and the mile-and-a-quarter winner Gracefully, whose daughter Lypharita won the 1985 Prix de Diane. Lypharita, by the way, is now also a member of Darley Stud's ever-increasing band of broodmares: she was purchased by Sheikh Mohammed for 1,200,000 dollars at the end of 1986. The second dam Val de Grace and the third dam Pearly Queen were both winners over an extended mile and a quarter; the latter is also a half-sister to the Prix de Diane winner and Prix Vermeille third Fine Pearl. Other prominent runners from this family in the last thirty years include the very smart middle-distance filly Pink Pearl, the Grand Prix d'Evry and graded-stakes winner Palace Panther and the Prix de Sandringham winner Blue Bell Pearl. *H. R. A. Cecil.*

BELMOREDEAN 4 ch.g. Be My Guest (USA) 126–Hanna Alta (FR) (Busted 134) [1988 8.5m3 10.2m2 10g3 12m2 12m* 12g4 1989 10f4 12m 12m2 12g2 12d] **92** angular, sparely-made gelding: quite useful handicapper: runner-up at Ascot (apprentices) and Newmarket (favourite, beaten ½ length by Osric) in autumn: ran moderately in William Hill November Handicap at Thirsk: stays 1½m: acts on firm going and seems not at his best on a soft surface: takes keen hold: ran in snatches third outing at 3 yrs. *A. C. Stewart.*

BELOW ZERO 6 ch.g. Northfields (USA)–Indigine (USA) 71 (Raise A Native) — [1988 8d 7g 7m 1989 7s 10.6d] small, close-coupled gelding: has a round action: fair handicapper as 3-y-o: lightly raced and well beaten last 2 seasons: used to be suited by 7f: acts on any going: best without blinkers: often sweats and gets on toes: suited by waiting tactics: has tended to hang and best with strong handling: a most difficult ride. *L. J. Codd.*

BELPENEL 3 ch.g. Pharly (FR) 130–Seldovia (Charlottown 127) [1988 7g 8m5 **73 ?** 8d 1989 8d5 10m3 10m3 8m5] quite attractive gelding: has a quick action: modest maiden: best effort in claimer at Newbury second start, keeping on despite flashing tail: favourite, ran moderately in similar events later in summer, claimed £10,150 to join B. Key on final outing: stays 1¼m: blinkered final starts at 2 yrs and 3 yrs. *B. W. Hills.*

BELTALONG   3 gr.f. Belfort (FR) 89–Gentian (Roan Rocket 128) [1988 8s⁶ 8g   **66** 1989 9d 7.5d* 10m 9f³ 10f² 12m* a12g] leggy, angular filly: won seller (no bid) at Beverley in May and claimer at Newmarket in August: ran moderately in handicap final start, first for 3 months: best form over middle distances on top-of-the-ground: ridden by 5-lb claimer first 3 outings: bandaged last three. *J. Wharton.*

BELUGA GREY   2 gr.c. (Feb 2) Bellypha 130–Lucky For Me 116 (Appiani II 128)   — [1989 8g] IR 26,000Y: close-coupled, good-bodied colt: brother to very useful 1980 Irish 2-y-o 6f and 1m winner Euclid and half-brother to several other winners, including very smart stayer Yawa (by Luthier): dam middle-distance performer: 20/1, very backward, green and bit coltish, tailed off in 17-runner maiden at Leicester in November. *C. E. Brittain.*

BE MY CHIEF (USA)   2 b.c. (Mar 7) Chief's Crown (USA)–Lady Be Mine   **123 p** (USA) 76 (Sir Ivor 135) [1989 6m* 6f* 7m* 7f* 7m* 8g*]

'If you are going to go and run in those Grade 1 races, you have to leave a little something on the racetrack, obviously. The other way is to stay here and get fresh, take one shot and swing for the fences, and if the ball goes over, you are a champion. But if we ever get that attitude I think we will hurt the racing program throughout the year, because people will say "To hell with the Frizette, I'm going to wait for the Breeders' Cup" . . . . . I think you *have* to run in the championship events'. Those words, spoken by champion American trainer Wayne Lukas after the Breeders' Cup Juvenile Fillies, in which his filly Stella Madrid, previously unbeaten in three Grade 1 races, had surrendered her grip on the divisional Eclipse Award by finishing third, reflect a spirit of competition which two-year-old racing in Europe could do with. In the States the two-year-old championship is as relevant as any other and no less important than it was twenty years ago. The principal triple crown contenders are more often than not exposed by the close of their first season, and it's not uncommon for the leading two-year-old to have started ten times. Would that our best two-year-olds were still campaigned so boldly. One has to go back to My Swallow in 1970 to discover the last youngster to head the Free Handicap which had run as many times (seven) as his American counterpart has *averaged* during the same period. The increasing tendency to save top horses for a three-year-old campaign pays off in some cases but it's sad that

Chesham Stakes, Ascot—Be My Chief wins going away from Osario

the big two-year-old races are becoming less significant than in former times. Be My Chief, rather like his stable-companion High Estate before him, is an all-too-rare example nowadays of a two-year-old near the head of the Free Handicap who has completed a full programme of races which were designated to test the best horses of each generation. He won all of his six races, which took in Royal Ascot and built up to a convincing victory in the Group 1 Racing Post Trophy, and compiled a record which was unmatched by any other home-trained two-year-old. That his form falls short of most recent champions of his age shouldn't be held against him. He did all that was necessary as connections of those that might have extended him more declined the challenge. At the very least Be My Chief is a good-class colt, one whose lazy style of running raises the possibility that he may be better than we have been able to rate him. Let's hope he is, and does his part to debunk the idea that a full campaign at two spoils the party at three.

Be My Chief looked a first-rate prospect as soon as he stepped into the paddock before the six-furlong Zetland Maiden Stakes at Doncaster in May. A good-topped, attractive colt the like of which is seldom seen out so early in the season nowadays, Be My Chief dominated his opponents in the eight-runner race as clearly as he had in the preliminaries, finding his stride in the penultimate furlong and keeping on strongly to belie his slightly backward appearance and pull three lengths clear of Balla Cove in a fast time. The Zetland Stakes has an unrivalled record of late for throwing up winners at Royal Ascot and Be My Chief followed in the footsteps of the Coventry winners High Estate (in 1988) and Always Fair (in 1987) by landing the Chesham Stakes on his next outing at odds of 5/2 on. The decision to run in the Chesham, which is confined to the progeny of stallions which won over a mile and a quarter or more, and not against the speedier types in the Coventry proved to be a wise one, as Be My Chief was made to work hard by the Salisbury maiden race winner Osario before staying on stoutly to win by a length. At Newmarket the following month, in the listed Bernard Van Cutsem Stakes, Be My Chief extended his winning sequence to three with a useful performance over seven furlongs. Benefiting from a more enterprising ride than he'd had at Ascot, as well as the extra furlong, Be My Chief brushed aside his five opponents, three of whom were winners, without much

Lanson Champagne Vintage Stakes, Goodwood—
Be My Chief beats Robellation and the course record

*Imry Solario Stakes, Sandown—Be My Chief idles in front
but still holds Robellation; Balla Cove is behind*

difficulty and galloped on enthusiastically to account for Long Island by three lengths.

The Lanson Champagne Vintage Stakes at Goodwood in July was Be My Chief's first venture into pattern company. The dual winner Dashing Blade, the Coventry Stakes disappointment Robellation and the unbeaten northern-trained colt Sheer Precocity all had their supporters in a field of five but none was able to prevent Be My Chief giving a determined display of front-running which trimmed nearly two-tenths of a second off the two-year-old course record set by Trojan Fen in the same event six years earlier. The half-length which Be My Chief had in hand over Robellation, to whom he was conceding 3 lb, could quite easily have been doubled had his rider Cauthen, who had exhibited his usual excellent judgement of pace, not taken things so easily in the last twenty yards. Be My Chief confirmed the form with Robellation in the less strongly-run Imry Solario Stakes at Sandown in August where Balla Cove was the only other participant in a dismal turn-out. Looking well as usual, if slightly on his toes, Be My Chief took up the running from Balla Cove with two furlongs to go and held Robellation at bay rather more comfortably than the three-quarter-length margin might suggest.

By the time of the Racing Post Trophy in October, run at Newcastle instead of Doncaster where parts of the track had subsided, the order of merit among the two-year-olds was no clearer than when Be My Chief had taken temporary leave. Robellation had been beaten three times, running poorly on the first two occasions; Balla Cove had caused a 20/1-upset in the Middle Park, ending Rock City's unbeaten run in Britain as well as the much-vaunted Cordoba's reign as Two Thousand Guineas favourite; Dashing Blade had scraped home in the Dewhurst; Dead Certain had done much the same in the Cheveley Park; and the other races to which one is accustomed to looking for evidence of superior merit, such as the Royal Lodge Stakes, hadn't produced an outstanding candidate for top honours. The Racing Post Trophy, run for the previous thirteen years as the William Hill Futurity, was last won by the two-year-old who went on to head the Free Handicap when Reference Point demolished his field in 1986. Three years on, the stage seemed set for Be My Chief to assume the mantle that much of the racing Press had already

*Racing Post Trophy, Newcastle—Be My Chief puts up his best performance
and retains his unbeaten record*

convinced themselves was his. Starting at 7/4 on in a field of five Be My Chief,
who towered over his rivals in the paddock, made virtually all the running,
stepping up what had been a fair gallop anyway when shaken up approaching
the last quarter of a mile and stretching out in fine style to win unchallenged
by five lengths (it was officially returned as four) and a neck. It was an
impressive performance visually but inspection of the form suggests it didn't
merit all the adulation it received in the media. The second horse home,
Baligh, whose trainer felt was still on the backward side, had struggled to land
the odds in a three-runner minor event at York on his previous outing;
third-placed Qathif, who'd looked Be My Chief's main rival on account of his
victory in a valuable maiden at Ascot earlier in the month, weakened
noticeably in the final furlong and didn't stay; Loch Fruin, three lengths back
in fourth, had been soundly trounced in the Cartier Million last time out; and
Cutting Note, half a length back in last place, had won only a fair Newmarket
maiden on his previous appearance. In short, Be My Chief achieved all that his
vastly superior form had entitled him to against second-rate opposition; and
just enough, in our opinion, to entitle him to marginal preference over the
French colts Machiavellian and Jade Robbery in a European Free Handicap. It
wasn't an outstanding performance, however, and he's not so far ahead of his
contemporaries that we know about to recommend backing him now for the
classics. Far better to wait and see what happens in the spring.

The racing career of Chief's Crown, the sire of Be My Chief, backs up the
argument that in America the dollar competed for on the racetrack is at least
as important as the dollar earned in the breeding shed. Chief's Crown was
campaigned extensively at the highest level during his two seasons in
training, winning four Grade 1 events and 920,890 dollars as a two-year-old, in
the process earning top spot in the Experimental Free Handicap, and four
more at three when he was also placed in every leg of the triple crown. All
told, Chief's Crown won twelve of his twenty-one races and more than two
million dollars for his connections. His first yearlings to be sold at public

auction averaged over 364,000 dollars, easily the highest of any first-season sire and more than that of such established stallions as Blushing Groom, Seattle Slew and Alydar. Besides Be My Chief, who was bred by his owner Peter Burrell, Chief's Crown's initial crop includes the Prix de Conde winner Dr Somerville, the promising Tanfith, and useful animals in North America in Glowing Tribute, Crowned and Crown Quest. Be My Chief is the third foal and second winner from his dam Lady Be Mine following the 1986 two-year-old five-furlong winner Run Little Lady (by J. O. Tobin); her other foal Blaze O'Gold (by Slew O'Gold) has run twice, coming second in a minor event at Newmarket and a mile-and-a-quarter maiden at Leicester. Lady Be Mine, a fair racemare whose one win came over a mile at Yarmouth, is a half-sister to several winners, among them the Irish one-mile winner Monte Rosa and the two-year-old five- and seven-furlong winner Mixed Applause, who's probably better known as the dam of the Gold Cup winner Paean and Be My Chief's promising stable-companion Shavian. The third dam My Game is, through her speedy daughter Lady Seymour, the grandam of the top-class sprinter Marwell and the very useful middle-distance colt Lord Seymour. There are plenty of other good winners in this family. Marwell, of course, is the dam of the smart Irish colt Caerwent; and another of My Game's granddaughters, Pro Patria, is the dam of the Gold Seal Oaks winner Unite.

Be My Chief (USA) (b.c. Mar 7, 1987)	Chief's Crown (USA) (b 1982)	Danzig (b 1977)	Northern Dancer Pas de Nom
		Six Crowns (ch 1976)	Secretariat Chris Evert
	Lady Be Mine (USA) (b 1978)	Sir Ivor (b 1965)	Sir Gaylord Attica
		My Advantage (b 1966)	Princely Gift My Game

A pedigree as diverse as Be My Chief's doesn't lend itself to hard and fast conclusions concerning his stamina potential, and his prospects of staying middle distances is something we should have more idea about after his three-year-old season is under way. What can be said, however, is that Chief's Crown stayed much further than the 'typical' racehorse by Danzig, whose older horse average winning distance index is approximately nine furlongs, and, on the limited evidence available, already seems to be endowing his stock with a fair amount of stamina. Also, the strong-galloping Be My Chief showed no signs of stopping at the end of the one-mile Racing Post Trophy, and it's our view that he'll stay a mile and a quarter and quite probably a mile and a half, too. So far, the powerful, round-actioned Be My Chief has raced only on a sound surface; his connections believe softer conditions, which hardly ever prevailed during the season, will show him to much better advantage. Whatever Be My Chief's fate as a three-year-old he will eventually stand at the National Stud, which acquired a twenty-five-per-cent interest in the colt shortly before his victory at Sandown and have an option to purchase another twenty-five when his racing days are over. *H. R. A. Cecil.*

BE MY RUNNER 3 b.g. Runnett 125–Ivorysguest (Be My Guest (USA) 126) **84** [1988 5m4 5g3 6m 5m6 6m3 1989 5s6 6d3 7g2 6m3 6m6 7g2 8m 7m* 7s2 8d2] quite attractive, leggy gelding: fair handicapper: won maiden at Sandown in September: good running-on second of 27 in £6,100 contest at Newbury final start: stays 1m: yet to race on very firm going, acts on any other: below form in blinkers (edgy and taking good hold) seventh start: consistent. *J. Sutcliffe.*

BEN ADHEM 7 b.g. Hotfoot 126–Heaven Chosen 91 (High Top 131) [1988 10d* **79** 10g 10m 11.7d5 11.7g2 11.7g3 12g* 12g6 12g 1989 11v 12d5 a12g4] leggy, rather lightly-built gelding: has a rather round action: fair handicapper on his day: best efforts in autumn when fifth to Firelight Fiesta in William Hill November Handicap at Thirsk and fourth to 10-length winner Bean King at Lingfield: stays 1½m: suited by give in the ground: has won for apprentice: occasionally on toes: none too consistent. *H. Candy.*

BENAZIR 2 b.f. (May 8) High Top 131–Crusader's Dream 88 (St Paddy 133) [1989 **80 p** 7g4] lengthy, good-topped filly: has plenty of scope: fifth foal: sister to 3-y-o Glasnost and half-sister to 1¼m winners Historical Fact and King's Crusade (both by Reform): dam 2-y-o 6f winner from family of high-class miler Lucyrowe: 25/1 and bit edgy, over 2 lengths fourth of 24, soon close up after slow start and no extra last 2f, to Katsina in maiden at Newmarket in November: should improve. *W. Jarvis.*

BEN LEDI 5 b.g. Strong Gale 116–Balacco 70 (Balidar 133) [1988 NR 1989 8f 8m³ 66 12g⁵ 12m⁶] workmanlike gelding: moderate mover: quite modest handicapper: likely to prove best at up to 1¼m: acts on firm going and a soft surface: ran moderately in blinkers: has run well for apprentice: winning novice chaser: sold to join Mrs J. Wonnacott 8,000 gns Ascot October Sales. *J. J. O'Neill.*

BENNY LEONARD 3 b.c. Henbit (USA) 130–Brenda (Sovereign Path 125) — [1988 5m 6f 6d 7m³ 8.2d 7g 1989 10m] big, lengthy, good-quartered colt: quite modest form as 2-y-o: 25/1 and facing stiff task, always behind in handicap in July on only start in 1989: should stay at least 1¼m: best effort on top-of-the-ground: has joined M. Tompkins. *M. J. Ryan.*

BEN ROYALE 2 b.g. (Feb 12) King of Spain 121–Fille de General (Brigadier 53 Gerard 144) [1989 6g 8.2s⁶ 8.2g] IR 6,600F, 8,000Y: fourth foal: half-brother to quite modest and seemingly ungenuine maiden Santella Jack (by Tina's Pet) and a winner in Hong Kong: dam never ran: poor form in varied races at Hamilton: best effort second start. *J. M. Jefferson.*

BENS BOY 2 ch.c. (Apr 11) Stanford 121§–Onde de Choc (USA) (L'Enjoleur 48 (CAN)) [1989 7f 7m] IR 7,200Y: angular colt: has a quick action: second foal: dam never ran: poor form in maiden auction event and claimer in August. *J. S. Wainwright.*

BENZ BEST 3 gr.g. Busted 134–Howzat (Habat 127) [1988 NR 1989 12s⁵ 16d⁶ 62 12m³ 14f⁶] sturdy, round-barrelled gelding: second foal: half-brother to plating-class maiden Boca Chimes (by Welsh Saint): dam once-raced daughter of Heaven Knows, Lingfield Oaks Trial winner but better at up to 9f: quite modest maiden: best efforts in moderately-run minor event and amateurs race at Thirsk, first and third outings: not seen out after May: worth a try over 1¼m. *M. H. Easterby.*

BENZINE (USA) 2 b.c. (Mar 16) Secreto (USA) 128–Baby Diamonds (Habitat 97 134) [1989 8m⁴ 8s³] $300,000Y: strong, stocky colt: fourth reported foal: half-brother to 2 winners in USA, including good-class miler Gem Master (by Green Dancer): dam, 6f winner at 2 yrs in USA (only season to race), sister to smart 1982 2-y-o sprinter Tatibah: 11/2 and green, under 6 lengths fourth to Treble Eight in maiden at Newmarket in September: 4 lengths third of 11 to Candy Glen in Gran Criterium at Milan following month: sure to win a maiden. *P. F. I. Cole.*

BEQUEST (USA) 3 ch.f. Sharpen Up 127–Quest (USA) 90§ (The Minstrel 108 ? (CAN) 135) [1988 7g² 1989 6g* 8g⁶ 8f] well-made filly: has a powerful, fluent action: 6/1 on, won maiden at Brighton: 10/1, on toes, about 5 lengths sixth of 7 to Musical Bliss in slowly-run 1000 Guineas, held up taking good hold, weakening approaching final 1f: tailed off as if something amiss in listed race at Sandown later in May: gives impression may prove suited by 7f or 6f. *G. Harwood.*

BERBERANA 2 b.f. (Feb 12) Never So Bold 135–Ricura 83 (Hello Gorgeous 68 (USA) 128) [1989 6m* 6s] IR 38,000Y: first foal: dam 1m winner, is daughter of Sookera: won minor event at York in June by 1½ lengths from Quite A Fighter: well-beaten last of 7 in listed race at Ayr over 3 months later: sold 15,000 gns Newmarket December Sales. *J. W. Watts.*

BERCY (USA) 2 ch.c. (Feb 15) Diesis 133–Bechamel (USA) 91 (Sauce Boat — p (USA)) [1989 6m⁵] leggy colt: has scope: first foal: dam sprinter: 5/1, sweating and coltish, over 9 lengths fifth of 8, slowly away and tending to hang around halfway, to Yaazi in minor event at Newmarket in August. *G. Harwood.*

BERILLON 2 b.c. (Feb 11) Rousillon (USA) 133–Obertura (USA) 100 (Roberto 71 p (USA) 131) [1989 8g] rangy, rather unfurnished colt: first foal: dam stayer: favourite but in need of race, around 15 lengths ninth of 16, very slowly away, to Belmez in minor event at Newmarket in November: evidently considered capable of lot better. *G. Harwood.*

BERKELEY HILL BOY 2 ch.c. (Mar 12) Castle Keep 121–Brown Velvet 68 52 (Mansingh (USA) 120) [1989 7f 6d 7g] big, angular colt: third foal: brother to French 7f and 1m winner Bartizan and half-brother to 3-y-o Sunley Sunshine (by Sunley Builds): dam, possibly short runner, is half-sister to smart Stumped, dam of Sonic Lady: poor form in maidens and a minor event. *R. Akehurst.*

BERKLEY EXPRESS 3 b.f. The Brianstan 128–Deise Girl (Stranger) [1988 5g — § 5f 5g 5f 5g⁵ 1989 6m⁶ 6m 7m] close-coupled, leggy filly: has some ability and unsatisfactory temperament: should stay 6f: bandaged behind in 1989: sweating profusely on reappearance: often mulish in paddock and/or on way down at 2 yrs and refused to enter stalls once: has re-joined J. O'Shea. *B. A. McMahon.*

BERMUDA LILY 2 br.f. (Apr 15) Dunbeath (USA) 127–Lily Bank 73 (Young 78
Generation 129) [1989 5f 5m* 6g 5f 6g⁵ 6f⁵ 6d⁵] angular, sparely-made filly:
moderate walker and mover: second foal: half-sister to 3-y-o State Bank (by
Kampala): dam 6f winner probably stayed 7f: modest performer: made most and
kept on gamely in maiden at Newbury in June: out of depth third, fourth and final
(blinkered) outings: stays 6f: thrice bandaged behind. *R. Hannon.*

BERNSTEIN BETTE 3 b.f. Petong 126–Glenfield Portion 86 (Mummy's Pet 73
125) [1988 5m 5m⁴ 5m 5s⁴ 5g³ 5g 6d* 5m² 1989 6m* 6f³ 6f⁴ 6g² 6g² 6f⁴ 7d]
good-quartered filly: modest handicapper: won at Nottingham in May: stays 6f well:
acts on top-of-the-ground and a soft surface: sweating and on edge fourth start at 2
yrs: has given trouble at stalls. *P. S. Felgate.*

BERRY'S DREAM 2 b.f. (Feb 12) Darshaan 133–Berrys Cay (USA) (The 99 p
Minstrel (CAN) 135) [1989 7.3v*] leggy filly: has scope: first foal: dam unraced close
relative of very useful 1984 French 2-y-o Envol and half-sister to very useful
middle-distance filly Egalite: well-backed 4/1-shot, won 12-runner listed race at
Newbury in October by a length, clear, from Cosmic Princess, leading 1f out and
running on well: will be suited by 1m + : sure to improve, and win more races. *R. W.
Armstrong.*

BERTIE WOOSTER 6 ch.g. Homeboy 114–Peace of Mind 81 (Midsummer 92
Night II 117) [1988 7m 6f 6m³ 6m* 6g² 6g* 6f 6s 7m 7g⁶ 6d⁴ 6g² 6s 1989 7d 6g* 6f²
6f³ 6m⁵ 6m⁶ 6m* 6s 6g 6v] strong, compact gelding: moderate mover: fairly useful
handicapper: won at Newmarket in May and £16,300 Lawrence Batley Handicap
(better effort, by ½ length from Ajanac) at York in September: never able to
challenge in well-contested events last 3 outings: suited by 6f: probably unsuited by
soft going, acts on any other: has occasionally given trouble at start: effective with
blinkers or without: sweating first 2 starts: usually gets behind, and has looked not
the easiest of rides: tough. *R. J. Holder.*

BERYL'S YOUNG MAN 3 ch.g. Young Man (FR) 73–Beryls Dream 77 —
(Garda's Revenge (USA)) [1988 NR 1989 7m 10.2g a14g⁶] leggy, medium-sized
gelding: lacks scope: first reported foal: dam, best at 2 yrs, stayed 7f: no form in
summer maidens and November claimer. *C. F. Wall.*

BESCABY BOY 3 b.g. Red Sunset 120–Charo (Mariacci (FR) 133) [1988 5g⁶ 5g³ 81
5f⁵ 5f* 5s⁶ 6m³ 5f⁵ 7g 1989 8.2s² 8g² 8.2s³ 8.2m² 10m⁵ 8g⁴ 8m* 8.2m* 8.3g⁵ 7s]
strong, angular, workmanlike gelding: fair performer: won claimers at Newmarket
in July and Nottingham in August: ran badly final start: stays 1m well: acts on any
going: blinkered on 4 of last 5 outings at 2 yrs: has worn bandages: active type, tends
to get on toes and give trouble at stalls. *J. Wharton.*

BESITO 2 b.f. (Apr 7) Wassl 125–Field Day 87 (Northfields (USA)) [1989 7g] 65 p
23,000Y: small, close-coupled filly: fourth foal: half-sister to 3-y-o 15.3f winner
Amigo Feo (by Tap On Wood), 6f to 1¼m winner Darweesh (by Cure The Blues) and
7f winner Evening Hour (by Glenstal): dam, 1¼m and 1½m winner, is daughter of
sister to Irish 2000 Guineas third Sovereign Edition: 50/1, around 10 lengths eighth
of 24, one pace last 2f, to Sardegna in maiden at Newmarket in November: should
improve. *R. Hollinshead.*

BEST EFFORT 3 ch.g. Try My Best (USA) 130–Lunaria (USA) (Twist The Axe 67
(USA)) [1988 NR 1989 10.6g 11.5g⁵ 10m³ 12g] strong, workmanlike gelding: third
live foal: half-brother to quite modest maiden Super Gunner (by Homing): dam
thrice-raced half-sister to smart sprinter Abeer: quite modest form first 3 starts:
burly, faced stiff task in £6,800 handicap on final one: stays 11.5f: sold 15,500 gns
Newmarket Autumn Sales. *M. E. D. Francis.*

BEST NIECE 4 ch.f. Vaigly Great 127–Grove Star (Upper Case (USA)) [1988 8s³ —
10m² 12m² 10g⁴ 10g* 9s³ 10f² 10d 1989 10m] leggy, sparely-made filly: moderate
mover: fair winner as 3-y-o: dropped right away final 2f in handicap at Newmarket in
May: suited by forcing tactics at 1¼m: probably acts on any going: has carried head
bit high. *H. R. A. Cecil.*

BEST OF BRITISH 4 br.f. Young Generation 129–Laisser Aller (Sagaro 133) —
[1988 10g 12m⁵ 10.2g 11.7m 12m⁴ 12m 12g² 12d* 1989 12s] rather sparely-made filly:
winning plater as 3-y-o: always behind in non-selling handicap at Folkestone in
April: stays 1½m: acts on top-of-the-ground and a soft surface: blinkered once at 3
yrs. *B. Stevens.*

BESTOW 2 br.f. (May 19) Shirley Heights 130–Clandestina (USA) 98 (Secretariat 64 p
(USA)) [1989 6m⁶ 8g⁵] quite attractive filly: good mover: third living foal: half-sister
to 3-y-o 1¼m winner Night Secret (by Nijinsky): dam Irish 1¼m winner, is
half-sister to Seattle Slew and Lomond: favourite, around 3 lengths fifth of 16,

keeping on one pace, to High Beacon in maiden at Leicester in November: backward on debut in August: should do better over 1¼m+. *B. W. Hills.*

BE TENDER   3 b.f. Prince Tenderfoot (USA) 126–The Habit of Being (Busted 134) [1988 7s 7s 8.2m⁶ 9f 1989 12.2d⁶ 12g 12.3g 10.6m 12.2d] workmanlike filly: moderate mover: poor plater: stays 1½m. *J. S. Wainwright.* —

BETETH   3 b.f. Hard Fought 125–Queen Caroline 86 (Ragusa 137) [1988 5m⁵ 5m 5d 6g 1989 7d 6g 8h 7m 8.3g] close-coupled, deep-girthed filly: poor mover: poor maiden: stays 1m: sometimes sweats. *K. O. Cunningham-Brown.* —

BETHEL ORCHARD   4 b.f. Tyrnavos 129–Skysted (Busted 134) [1988 7d 9d 10.2f 10d 10d 11.7g⁴ 10g⁵ 1989 10.1m 8.3m² 10f 14m 15.3m] leggy, angular filly: poor maiden: ridden by 7-lb claimer, runner-up in selling handicap (claimed out of D. Elsworth's stable £6,100) at Windsor in May, only form at 4 yrs: effective at 1m and stays 11.7f: bandaged first 2 starts. *C. Holmes.* 44

BETTER NOW   3 ch.g. Thatching 131–Reap The Wind 110 (Roan Rocket 128) [1988 7d 7m³ 7f² 6s⁵ 8g⁴ 7f⁴ 7g 1989 7s 6f* 6m 6g 6g³ 7m*] tall, leggy, angular gelding: has a long stride: modest handicapper: won at Nottingham in June and Warwick (ridden by 7-lb claimer and rallying splendidly) in August: stays 7f: acts on firm going: blinkered last 2 starts: probably best with forcing tactics. *J. Etherington.* 73

BETWEEN THE SHEETS   4 b.g. Crooner 119–Miss Chianti (Royben 125) [1988 8.3g 1989 12s 15.8m⁴ 15.8m 18.8f⁴ 16.2f* a16g] rangy gelding: poor handicapper: won poor 5-runner contest at Beverley in September unchallenged by 20 lengths, making all and clear from over 3f out: ran moderately at Lingfield 7 weeks later: stays 2m: acts on firm going: has taken keen hold: winning hurdler. *W. Carter.* 51

BETWEEN THE STICKS   2 gr.f. (Feb 28) Pharly (FR) 130–Sandstream 72 (Sandford Lad 133) [1989 5g* 5m* 5f² 5m⁴ 5f⁶ 6g³] 23,000Y: smallish, rather sparely-made filly: sixth foal: half-sister to 3-y-o Singing Stream (by Chief Singer) and 3 winners abroad, 2 of them by General Assembly: dam, 6f winner at 2 yrs, is half-sister to Manado: successful in maiden at Newmarket in April and minor event at Windsor following month: very good third of 9 to Star Hill in listed race at Kempton in September: will be suited by 7f: bandaged behind second to fourth starts. *R. Hannon.* 83

BETWEEN TIME   2 gr.f. (Mar 31) Elegant Air 119–Beveridge (USA) 86 (Spectacular Bid (USA)) [1989 6f³ 6f² 6h* 7f² 6m² 7m 6s] rather sparely-made filly: first foal: dam, best at 2 yrs when 7f winner, is daughter of half-sister to Formidable and Ajdal: modest performer: made virtually all in maiden at Carlisle in June: easily best subsequent efforts in nurseries when second at Thirsk and Nottingham: will stay 1m. *P. Calver.* 75

BEX (USA)   3 ch.f. Explodent (USA)–Bay Street 114 (Grundy 137) [1988 NR 1989 8m* 10f³ 10g* 10.5s*] useful-looking filly: fifth foal: half-sister to 4 winners, including fair 9f and 1¼m winner Bird Point (by Allegro) and useful 2-y-o Daarik (by Diesis): dam won over 7f and 8.5f: won maiden at Newmarket in July and listed race at Phoenix Park and Group 3 Prix de Flore, making all to beat Dimmer 4 lengths, at 116 p

Prix de Flore, Saint-Cloud—Bex makes all

120

Saint-Cloud in October: should stay 1½m: goes well on soft ground, and possibly unsuited by very firm: progressive. *R. W. Armstrong.*

BEYOND MOMBASA   2 br.f. (Feb 6) Silly Prices 110–Elitist 72 (Keren 100)   —
[1989 7m] compact filly: first foal: dam promised to stay 1¼m: 100/1 and very green, tailed off in seller at Thirsk in September. *N. Chamberlain.*

BEYOND THE LAKE   3 b.c. Kings Lake (USA) 133–Sensibility (USA) (Hail To **110**
Reason) [1988 7g⁶ 8d² 8v* 9v* 10s 1989 8v* 10s³ 10g* 12g* 12g² 12m* 14d] Irish colt: successful in minor event at the Curragh in March, £6,000 event at Gowran Park in May, listed race at Leopardstown in June and Group 3 EBF Royal Whip Stakes, always prominent and putting up best effort to hold Tyrone Bridge by a short head, at the Curragh in August: well beaten in Irish St Leger at the Curragh: stays 1½m: yet to race on very firm going, acts on any other: blinkered in 1989: very useful and consistent. *D. K. Weld, Ireland.*

B GRADE   4 b.f. Lucky Wednesday 124–Hitravelscene (Mansingh (USA) 120)   **58**
[1988 8.5m 7.5m 6m 6g³ 6g 6g³ 6d* 7m² 6d 6s* 6s⁴ 6s² 1989 7.5d 6g⁵ 6m 6g⁶ 7g 6g⁴ 6s² 6g 6g 5s] leggy, plain filly: has a round action: quite modest handicapper: easily best efforts as 4-y-o (often faced stiff task) on fifth to seventh outings: suited by 7f or stiff 6f: ideally suited by an easy surface: refused to enter stalls once at 3 yrs: sometimes starts slowly: has got on toes: mounted outside paddock sixth start. *J. Balding.*

BHARKAT   3 b.g. Beldale Flutter (USA) 130–Cienaga (Tarboosh (USA)) [1988   —
7m 7s³ 6g³ 7d 8.2m 1989 8g 10.5g⁵] leggy, rather dipped-backed gelding: has a fluent action: plating-class maiden: faced stiff tasks in claimer and seller as 3-y-o: off course over 3 months in between: should be suited by 7f+: sold to join J. Norton 4,000 gns Doncaster October Sales. *R. Boss.*

BIAS NATURE   3 b.c. Habitat 134–Virna (USA) (Coursing) [1988 NR 1989 7d   —
7m] IR 22,000Y: medium-sized, good-topped colt: brother to a poor maiden and half-brother to 4 winners, notably Drumalis (by Tumble Wind), high class at up to 11f in Europe and USA: dam won from 6f to 9f in France: backward, well beaten in Newmarket maiden in April and seller at Yarmouth in July: has joined J. Czerpak. *G. A. Huffer.*

BIBLICAL   2 b.f. (May 29) Montekin 125–Bap's Miracle (Track Spare 125) [1989   —
5d 5m⁶ 6m] IR 2,000Y: leggy, sparely-made filly: moderate walker and mover: fourth foal: half-sister to 1987 2-y-o 5f and 6f winner Master of The Roll and 1986 2-y-o 5f to 7.5f winner Team Effort (both by Stanford): dam unraced half-sister to Queen Anne winner Baptism: soundly beaten in sellers: sold 720 gns Doncaster June Sales. *K. Stone.*

BICKERMAN   6 b.h. Mummy's Pet 125–Merry Weather 69 (Will Somers 114§)   —
[1988 10g 12m⁴ 10d 10.2g 1989 10.6d 10m⁶ 10m⁶] leggy, lightly-made horse: modest handicapper as 4-y-o: no subsequent form on flat: stays 1¼m: acts on firm going: hung final outing at 5 yrs (blinkered) and second one at 6 yrs: keen sort: winning hurdler. *J. L. Spearing.*

BIDDERS CLOWN   4 b.g. Ring Bidder 88–Lucky Joker 67 (Cawston's Clown   **56**
113) [1988 NR 1989 16f²] first foal: dam middle-distance handicapper: won NH Flat race in February: 6/1, short-head second of 5, leading inside final 1f and caught on line, in maiden at Newcastle in July. *Mrs R. Wharton.*

BIDDERS LAD   4 ch.g. Ring Bidder 88–Anniversary Token 54 (Record Token   **44**
128) [1988 8d 6s³ 7d⁵ 8f 6f 1989 6v* 7.5g 8m 8g 7m⁴ 8g³ 9f⁴ 7f] leggy, workmanlike gelding: has a quick action: quite modest plater: stays 9f: appears to act on any going: visored fourth (ran too freely) and final outings: has run creditably for apprentice: bandaged near-fore and sweating seventh start. *R. M. Whitaker.*

BID LATER   3 b.f. Auction Ring (USA) 123–Twenty Two (FR) 90 (Busted 134)   **61**
[1988 NR 1989 6f²] 8,400 2-y-o: fourth foal: half-sister to modest middle-distance stayer and winning hurdler/chaser Tresidder (by Connaught): dam, closely related to very smart Mil's Bomb and Cheshire Oaks winner Milly Moss, won over 1½m from only 3 starts: 6/1, beaten 2 lengths by The Kings Daughter in minor event at Folkestone in July, keeping on steadily if not knocked about: should be suited by at least 1m: has joined R. Guest. *R. F. Casey.*

BID OF LUCK   2 ch.c. (Mar 21) Caerleon (USA) 132–Restless Lady (Sandford   —
Lad 133) [1989 5d] IR 40,000Y: compact colt: fourth foal: half-brother to 3-y-o 5f winner Kali Kopella (by Ahonoora), fairly useful 6f performer Catherines Well (by Junius) and plater Sorority (by Tap On Wood): dam showed little worthwhile form: 7/1, in need of race and very green, struggling by halfway in 8-runner minor event at Folkestone in April: sold 1,850 gns Newmarket Autumn Sales. *R. V. Smyth.*

BID ONLY 2 b.f. (Apr 14) Creetown 123–Cody (USA) (Giacometti 130) [1989 5g*] **50**
750Y: fifth foal: dam never ran: won 17-runner seller (no bid) at Beverley in May by
a head from You Sure: sold 1,600 gns Doncaster October Sales. *J. Berry.*

BIDSTON MILL 4 ch.g. Main Reef 126–Allotria 86 (Red God 128§) [1988 12m —
12f 14m 15g⁵ 10f 12.2g 1989 13.8m⁵] of little account on flat: has been blinkered and
visored: bandaged only start at 4 yrs: winner over hurdles. *R. A. Bennett.*

BIENNIAL (USA) 3 b.c. Lear Fan (USA) 130–Six Months Long (USA) **104**
(Northern Dancer) [1988 NR 1989 10f* 10.1g* 10f* 10.1d⁶ 10g4] $200,000Y:
good-topped, useful-looking colt: sixth foal: half-brother to top-class miler Half A
Year (by Riverman): dam won twice at up to 1m from 4 starts: successful in maiden
at Goodwood, minor event at Windsor and £29,000 Extel Stakes Handicap
(well-backed favourite) at Goodwood in the summer, making virtually all on last 2
occasions: ran poorly in listed race at Windsor and handicap (bit edgy and sweating)
at Yarmouth: stays 1¼m well: possibly unsuited by a soft surface: taken down early
third and fourth starts. *G. Harwood.*

BIFOCAL 2 b.g. (May 10) Vision (USA)–Night Vision 100 (Yellow God 129) [1989 **61**
6m 6f⁶ 6m 7.6m a8g4] 4,600F: tall, rangy gelding: has plenty of scope: half-brother
to several winners, including 7f (at 2 yrs) and 8.2f seller winner Sveltissima (by
Dunphy), and 7f and 1m winner Lautrec (by Wolver Hollow): dam, half-sister to
high-class Take A Reef, won over 6f at 2 yrs: quite modest form in maidens and a
valuable seller: stays 1m: formerly trained by R. Hannon. *R. Akehurst.*

BIG ALICK 3 br.c. Another Realm 118–Abercorn Flyer 63 (Silly Season 127) —
[1988 NR 1989 8h⁵ 10f 12f 10.1m] leggy, angular colt: third foal: half-brother to
novice hurdler Solo Player (by Blue Refrain): dam placed over 5f at 2 yrs probably
stayed 1m: seems of little account. *W. T. Kemp.*

BIG BASS (USA) 2 b.c. (Mar 9) Danzig (USA)–Sunny Slew (USA) (Seattle Slew **76**
(USA)) [1989 7m* 7g4] $500,000Y: medium-sized, good-topped colt: has scope:
good walker: second foal: dam, minor winner at around 6f at 4 yrs, is half-sister to
champion sprinter Gallant Bob: 5/1 on, won maiden at Yarmouth in July comfortably
by ¾ length from Broadway Star: 4½ lengths fourth of 17, keeping on one pace, to
Starstreak in minor event at Leicester 4 months later. *H. R. A. Cecil.*

BIG BEAR 3 ch.c. Tolomeo 127–Alma Ata 113 (Bustino 136) [1988 NR 1989 10.1m **97**
10m²] big, angular, unfurnished colt: fourth foal: dam, tough and genuine
middle-distance stayer, won Park Hill Stakes: 6/1, beaten ½ length by Flockton's
Own in 7-runner maiden at Newmarket in August, switched over 1f out and staying
on steadily under pressure: shaped most promisingly on debut: will probably be
suited by 1½m. *L. M. Cumani.*

Extel Handicap, Goodwood—the favourite Biennial
wins from Shamirani and Regent Light (noseband)

BIG CHIEF 4 b.g. Gorytus (USA) 132–Maybe So 90 (So Blessed 130) [1988 7g³ **56**
8g⁴ 6f 6f³ 5f 7g 1989 7.5g 8g 6.5s 5g 6v²] angular, workmanlike gelding: quite
modest maiden: caught final strides when neck second in seller at Ayr in April: little
show on 4 starts at Cagnes-sur-Mer earlier in year: stays 7f: acts on heavy going:
suited by strong handling: sold 2,500 gns Ascot May Sales. *W. Hastings-Bass.*

BIG ECK 2 b.c. (Apr 7) Precocious 126–Dora's Rocket 69 (Roan Rocket 128) —
[1989 6g] 11,000Y: third foal: dam, raced only at 2 yrs when placed at 6f, is sister to
very useful sprinter Rory's Rocket: well-beaten seventh of 9 in claimer at Haydock
in July: may improve. *M. Brittain.*

BIG FINISH 4 b.g. Persian Bold 123–Azurn (Klairon 131) [1988 10.8d* 10m —
11.7m⁶ 9g 9m 9g 1989 12.2s⁴ 15.5s 14s 16f] neat gelding: has a rather round action:
well below form in handicaps since winning maiden at Warwick early as 3-y-o: best
run at 10.8f: needs give in the ground: has joined Miss B. Sanders. *H. O'Neill.*

BIG NEPHEW 2 ch.c. (May 22) Adonijah 126–Little Niece 79 (Great Nephew **69** p
126) [1989 8f³] useful-looking colt: second foal: half-brother to 3-y-o 10.6f winner
Straw Blade (by Final Straw): dam 1¼m winner: 8/1 and bit green, 10½ lengths third
of 10, running on well final 2f, to Missionary Ridge in maiden at Leicester in
October: will stay 1¼m: sure to improve and win a race. *J. L. Dunlop.*

BIG SHUFFLE (USA) 5 b.h. Super Concorde (USA) 128–Raise Your Skirts **116**
(USA) (Elevation (USA)) [1988 6g* 6d² 6s⁴ 5m⁵ 7s³ 1989 6m² 5m 6m 6g⁴] lengthy,
good-bodied horse: has a quick action: very smart at his best: placed in Norcros July
Cup at Newmarket and Prix de la Foret at Longchamp as 4-y-o: not quite so good in
1989, best effort when second to Puissance in EBF Greenlands Stakes at the
Curragh in May: well below form in Compaq Computer EBF Ballyogan Stakes at
Leopardstown, Carroll Foundation July Cup at Newmarket and Keeneland EBF
Phoenix Sprint Stakes: best at 6f or 7f: acted on top-of-the-ground and soft going:
blinkered second and final outings: stud in Germany. *D. K. Weld, Ireland.*

BIG SURPRISE 2 b.g. (Mar 5) Comedy Star (USA) 121–Maxine's Here 52 **50**
(Copte (FR)) [1989 5s⁵ 5g 6m⁵ 6m a8g³ a7g⁵] workmanlike gelding: poor walker:
fourth foal: half-brother to a winning 1½m plater by Cawston's Clown: dam, winner
of 2-runner 5f seller at 2 yrs, stayed 1m: moderate plater: best run at 1m, and will
stay further: blinkered first 2 starts: has worn bandages. *J. Wharton.*

BILANDER 3 ch.f. High Line 125–Sea Pageant (Welsh Pageant 132) [1988 9g² **71**
8g⁶ 1989 11.5m⁴ 12.5m⁵] angular, workmanlike filly: modest form: ran creditably in
minor event at Sandown, taking keen hold and settled behind 3f out, and maiden at
Wolverhampton in August: stays 1½m: sold 5,400 gns Newmarket December Sales.
Major W. R. Hern.

BILIMBI 2 ch.f. (May 6) Nicholas Bill 125–Scrub Oak 84 (Burglar 128) [1989 6f] — p
fifth foal: half-sister to fairly useful 1983 2-y-o 6f winner Conscript (by Warpath):
dam 6f winner at 2 yrs: 20/1, around 12 lengths eighth of 10, slowly away, to
Lakeland Beauty in maiden at Redcar in October. *J. W. Watts.*

BILLET 6 ch.g. Nicholas Bill 125–Cosset 56 (Comedy Star (USA) 121) [1988 12m² **89** +
11f* 12m* 12f 14f⁴ 13.3f 1989 10.2g⁶] leggy, rather sparely-made gelding: has a long
stride: fairly useful handicapper: shaped well in May (taken down steadily and
mulish at stalls) when sixth of 18 in handicap at Doncaster, but wasn't seen out
again: suited by 1½m + : suited by top-of-the-ground: often slowly away: has a good
turn of foot and best with waiting tactics: suited by strong handling: has reportedly
had tendon trouble. *H. Candy.*

BILLHEAD 3 b.g. Nicholas Bill 125–Time-Table 66 (Mansingh (USA) 120) [1988 **75** d
8.5f³ 8m³ 1989 10f³ 10.2g 10g⁵ 10m⁴ 10.2g 10f 10s⁶] leggy gelding: modest maiden:
easily best effort as 3-y-o on reappearance: well beaten in handicap, claimer and
seller (travelling well 1m) last 3 starts: suited by 1¼m: possibly needs firm ground:
often wears severe bridle and takes good hold: sold to join B. Preece 6,200 gns
Doncaster September Sales: not one to trust implicitly. *J. W. Watts.*

BILLIE BLUE 3 b.f. Ballad Rock 122–Blue Nose 108 (Windjammer (USA)) [1988 **63**
NR 1989 7s²] 5,300F, IR 17,000Y: fifth foal: half-sister to 6f winner Blue Horizon (by
African Sky) and to a winner in Spain: dam winner at around 6f as 2-y-o in Ireland:
9/2, 4 lengths second of 15 to Ghassanah in maiden at Folkestone in April, always
close up and keeping on at one pace. *Dr J. D. Scargill.*

BILL MOON 3 ch.c. Nicholas Bill 125–Lunar Queen 96 (Queen's Hussar 124) —
[1988 NR 1989 8m] 27,000Y: leggy, quite attractive colt: brother to 9f and 1¼m
winner Mark Aizlewood and French 1¼m winner Triera and half-brother to 3 other
winners here and abroad, including sprinter Parabems (by Swing Easy): dam won
three 5f races at 2 yrs: 9/2 and very much in need of experience, slowly away when

123

tailed off in 9-runner maiden at York in September: moved badly down: sold 8,000 gns Newmarket Autumn Sales. *L. M. Cumani.*

BILLSHA 3 b.f. Ahonoora 122–Sanjana (GER) (Priamos (GER)) [1988 6f³ 6m⁴ 1989 8m⁶ 8m⁴ 8f⁴ a8g] rangy filly: modest maiden: best effort in minor event at Edinburgh second outing: off course over 4 months then ran moderately, favourite for claimer final start: stays 1m: sold 2,000 gns Newmarket December Sales. *B. Hanbury.*   67

BILLY BUBBLES 3 br.c. Tower Walk 130–Dark Mystique (USA) 39 (Fleet Allied (USA)) [1988 6m 6g 6v⁶ 1989 6m⁶ 7m³ 6f 6f] compact, quite attractive colt: poor mover: plating-class performer: best form at 7f: acted on top-of-the-ground: dead. *Mrs N. Macauley.*   47

BILLY'S DANCER 6 ch.g. Piaffer (USA) 113–Hay-Hay 62 (Hook Money 124) [1988 8s 8.2m⁴ 8.3m⁴ 1989 8d a8g a8g] close-coupled, sparely-made gelding: poor mover: quite modest handicapper at his best: well beaten in 1989: backward and slowly away final outing: stays 9.4f: probably ideally suited by give in the ground and acts on heavy: blinkered once at 2 yrs and on final outing: sometimes bandaged: formerly an excellent mount for apprentice. *W. Wilson.*   —

BILOXI BLUES 7 gr.g. Blue Refrain 121–Haunting 79 (Lord Gayle (USA) 124) [1988 NR 1989 12m*] half-brother to numerous winners, including useful 1986 5f and 6f winner Amigo Sucio (by Stanford) and Norsk St Leger winner Our Martin (by Martinmas): dam stayed 1m: 16/1, won 11-runner amateurs event at Newmarket in July: useful hurdler/chaser. *K. C. Bailey.*   77

BILSTRANO 2 b.f. (May 1) Headin' Up–Bilbao 65 (Capistrano 120) [1989 5m 5m⁴] good-quartered filly: turns fore-feet in: fifth live foal: sister to 3 poor animals: dam, temperamental plater, stayed 7f: green, well behind from halfway in maiden (backward) and claimer: not seen out after June. *L. J. Barratt.*   —

BIMBO 2 ch.f. (May 10) Bustino 136–Brazen Faced 84 (Bold And Free 118) [1989 6m² 8m² 8g⁴ 8.2f*] medium-sized, rather unfurnished filly: has scope: seventh foal: half-sister to several winners, including useful 7f and 1m winner Sheer Cliff (by Shirley Heights) and useful sprinter Wanton (by Kris): dam 2-y-o 5f winner: progressive filly: won 15-runner nursery at Nottingham in September by a length from Zammah: much better suited by 1m than 6f and will stay 1¼m: races keenly. *M. F. D. Morley.*   87

BIN DAAHIR (USA) 3 ch.c. Blushing Groom (FR) 131–Bolt From The Blue (USA) (Blue Times (USA)) [1988 6m 1989 10.1m³ 10m⁵ 12g] compact, strong-quartered colt: showed signs of ability in maidens and minor event: should be suited by at least 1¼m: sold 3,200 gns Newmarket Autumn Sales. *P. T. Walwyn.*   —

BINGDON BUILDERS 5 br.m. Derrylin 115–Forini 79 (Fortino II 120) [1988 6f 6m 6m 7m 12g⁵ 12m 10m⁵ 10g 12m* 12g 12d⁶ 12m 1989 12h] lengthy, workmanlike mare: poor handicapper: tailed off at Lingfield in July: withdrawn lame at Yarmouth over month later: suited by middle distances: acts on top-of-the-ground: suitable mount for inexperienced rider: sometimes bandaged off-fore. *D. T. Thom.*   —

BINGO BONGO 2 gr.f. (Mar 26) Petong 126–Daring Display 85§ (Daring March 116) [1989 5m 6h³ 6m⁶ 6g] 8,200Y: rangy filly: has scope: first foal: dam unreliable sprint handicapper, won twice: plating-class maiden: best effort second start: stays 6f. *R. V. Smyth.*   60

BINKLEY (FR) 3 ch.c. Bikala 134–Jinkitis 104 (Irish Love 117) [1988 7m 7g⁶ 7g 1989 10m 13.8f⁴ 12m² 12g 12g] lengthy, rather dipped-backed, angular colt: second of 4, leading over 11f, in claimer at Edinburgh in July, only worthwhile form: lacks pace and should be suited by long distances: possibly needs top-of-the-ground: gave trouble at stalls on reappearance: sold 5,600 gns Newmarket Autumn Sales. *Sir Mark Prescott.*   49

BIOTIN 5 gr.g. Star Appeal 133–Maruka 70 (Abernant 142) [1988 9g 5d² 7m 8g 1989 5f] workmanlike gelding: quite modest plater: best form at 5f: acts on top-of-the-ground and a soft surface: has worn blinkers and eyeshield twice, visor once: has given considerable trouble going to post and at stalls: temperamentally unsatisfactory. *D. Haydn Jones.*   — §

BIPHARY 3 ch.f. Pharly (FR) 130–Lady Habitat (Habitat 134) [1988 6m⁶ 6d² 7d⁶ 7g 6m 8.2m 8.2d 1989 8s 10.6m 14f⁶ 15m 12m* 12m³] sparely-made filly: won 4-runner maiden claimer at Edinburgh in July: well below form otherwise: takes keen hold and unlikely to stay 1¾m: acts on firm going: bandaged off-hind fifth outing: sweating on reappearance. *P. Calver.*   50

BIRD BATH 3 ch.f. Longleat (USA) 109–Red Lory 87 (Bay Express 132) [1988   ?
5m³ 5m³ 5m⁵ 5m² 6m 5d 1989 6s 6m] small, rather sparely-made filly: plating class
at 2 yrs: well behind in seller and handicap in spring as 3-y-o: sold 2,000 gns
Doncaster May Sales: won over 6f in Holland in August: resold 1,800 gns Doncaster
September Sales. *C. Tinkler.*

BIRDING (USA) 3 b.c. Yukon (USA)–Oriole (USA) (Buffalo Lark (USA)) [1988   —
7m* 7g* 7m⁵ 8g⁵ 10g 1989 11d⁴] useful-looking colt: fairly useful as 2-y-o,
successful in maiden at Kempton and minor event at Newmarket: 10/1, distant
fourth of 6 to Old Vic in £6,000 event at Newbury in April, only outing in 1989:
should stay at least 1m. *C. E. Brittain.*

BIRD OF LOVE 3 ch.f. Ela-Mana-Mou 132–Sea Harrier (Grundy 137) [1988 7f⁴   82
1989 10.1m³] sparely-made, plain filly: in frame in minor events at York as 2-y-o and
Windsor (moved well to post, stayed on strongly behind Roll A Dollar) in July: will
be suited by 1½m. *Major W. R. Hern.*

BIRMINGHAM'S GLORY 3 b.f. Hays 120–Exmoor Lass (FR) 86 (Exbury   —
138) [1988 5g 5m² 7m⁶ 6d 7m 6m 5d 1989 6s 5m 6g 5f 6f 6g] sparely-made filly:
little worthwhile form for some time: should stay beyond 5f: best effort on
top-of-the-ground: blinkered final outing at 2 yrs: often apprentice ridden: sold 925
gns Ascot November Sales, resold 1,700 gns Ascot December Sales. *R. Hollinshead.*

BIRMINGHAM'S PRIDE 3 br.f. Indian King (USA) 128–Cooliney Dancer   54 §
(Dancer's Image (USA)) [1988 5d³ 5g⁶ 5d 6f 6f 6m⁴ 7g 8g 6g⁶ 6g 7m 1989 8.2s 8s⁶
8.2s 8m⁴ 9f³ 10g² 9f⁴ 8h² 12f³ 10m³ 8.5m⁴ 11g⁶ 10f² 8.2f⁴ 9g⁴ 8.2f⁶ 9m 8.2d 10g³ 8g
a8g] strong, close-coupled filly: plating-class maiden: won seller at Nottingham
tenth start by short head but demoted for interference: stays 1¼m (pulled hard in
moderately-run race over 1½m): acts on firm ground, possibly unsuited by soft: may
prove best covered up and with waiting tactics: finds little under pressure and is one
to treat with caution. *R. Hollinshead.*

BIRSTWITH (USA) 4 gr.c. Valdez (USA)–La Chaumiere (Thatch (USA) 136)   81
[1988 8v⁵ 8m⁵ 10g 8m 8f⁴ 7.6m² 7.6s² 8m² 8d 8d³ 8s* 10.5f 9f 1989 8g⁴ 8d⁶ 8f 8.2g⁶
9g 8g⁴] leggy, close-coupled, angular colt: fair handicapper: ran creditably in
William Hill Lincoln Handicap at Doncaster and in quite valuable event at Newbury
on first 2 starts: best effort after on final outing: ideally suited by forcing tactics at
about 1m: best with give in the ground: bandaged off-hind third and fourth outings:
has gone freely to post. *C. W. C. Elsey.*

BIRTHDAY PARADE (USA) 2 b.f. (Feb 7) Chief's Crown (USA)–Jubilous   — p
(USA) (Sir Ivor 135) [1989 6g] $900,000Y: strong, lengthy filly: has scope: first foal:
dam graded stakes-placed winner at up to 11f, is daughter of a Grade 1 winner: 6/1
and very green, around 11 lengths ninth of 29, making eye-catching late headway not
at all knocked about, to Sure Sharp in maiden at Newmarket in November: sure to
improve good deal. *H. R. A. Cecil.*

BIRWAZ 5 b.g. Moorestyle 137–Red Madonna 84 (Red God 128§) [1988 9d⁶ 11.7m   46
10g 1989 8.3m⁶ 10.8m] close-coupled, deep-girthed gelding: has a round action: poor
maiden: best at 1m or 9f: acts on top-of-the-ground and a soft surface: ran creditably
when blinkered: sweating and bandaged final outing: winning but thoroughly
temperamental hurdler. *D. Haydn Jones.*

BISHOPSFORD 3 b.g. Henbit (USA) 130–Arena 86 (Sallust 134) [1988 NR 1989   53
10.8s⁶ 8.5g 12m⁴ 10f³ 10.8f] 6,400Y: tall, close-coupled gelding: second foal:
half-brother to poor 1987 2-y-o Sunday Sport Flyer (by Cure The Blues), later a
winner over 7f and 1¼m in Scandinavia: dam lightly-raced daughter of very useful 7f
and 9f winner Melodramatic: plating-class maiden: creditable third in seller at
Chepstow: blinkered, raced freely and ridden along 6f out when tailed off in similar
event next time: should stay 1½m: sold to join N. Waggott 5,200 gns Ascot July
Sales. *Sir Mark Prescott.*

BIT OF A LASS 3 br.f. Wassl 125–Idiot's Delight (USA) (Bold Ruler) [1988 9g 8g   59
1989 9f⁶ 10.6m⁶ 12f 10m* 10.2f² 11g³ 12f 10m 10.2f⁴ a12g³ a12g⁶] angular filly: quite
modest handicapper: won at Nottingham (moved moderately down) in June: rare
third of 14 at Lingfield penultimate start, travelling strongly long way: suited by
1¼m: acts on firm going: bandaged behind final start. *D. W. P. Arbuthnot.*

BITONE 3 gr.c. Tolomeo 127–Into Harbour (Right Tack 131) [1988 8d³ 1989 9g³   80
10g³ 11.7m] big, good-topped colt: has plenty of scope: fair form when third in
maidens at Newmarket and Salisbury: below form in handicap at Windsor in May:
races keenly and likely to prove best at 1¼m. *L. M. Cumani.*

BIT ON EDGE 3 b.f. Henbit (USA) 130–Border's Edge (Habitat 134) [1988 NR   —
1989 15s 11g] IR 16,000Y: workmanlike filly: third foal: half-sister to Inmar (by

125

Ballad Rock), fair sprint maiden here as 2-y-o in 1986 later successful in Malaysia: dam unraced half-sister to high-class miler Pitcairn: soundly beaten in minor event and claimer in the autumn. *J. S. Wilson.*

BLACK AND BLUES 3 b.g. Music Boy 124–Blackeye (Busted 134) [1988 5m 5m² 5m⁴ 5f³ 5f³ 6g⁴ 7d⁴ 7g⁶ 6s 1989 6v 8m 7m 8f] workmanlike gelding: quite modest form at best in maidens as 2-y-o: no form in 1989, including in sellers: stays 6f: best form on a sound surface: has been tried in blinkers: went keenly to post and in race final start (June). *W. J. Pearce.* —

BLACK COMEDY 6 b.h. Blakeney 126–Laughing Goddess 92 (Green God 128) [1988 10.8d⁶ 10s⁵ 10.8s 11f 11.1m⁴ 10m² 10d 10.2g⁴ 10m⁴ 10f³ 10m⁶ 10g² 12.2d 1989 10.8m⁶ 10f⁴ 10.2h 12.3m* 12.3g³ 10.6g⁴ 12m³ 12g 12m³ 12f] sturdy, compact horse: carries plenty of condition: quite modest handicapper: looking really well, won at Chester in July, responding gamely to pressure to lead virtually on line: better suited by 1½m than 1¼m nowadays: acts on any going: visored twice in 1988: sometimes sweats: has worn crossed noseband: goes particularly well on turning track: slowly away seventh outing. *J. Mackie.* 60

BLACK FIGHTER (USA) 2 br.f. (Mar 8) Secretariat (USA)–Faten (USA) (Northern Dancer) [1989 7g] quite attractive filly: third foal: half-sister to French 11f to 13f winner Forest Dreamer and French 3-y-o 11.5f and 1½m winner Forest Force (both by Green Forest): dam French 1½m winner from family of Be My Guest: 16/1, around 10 lengths seventh of 13, never dangerous, to Duke of Paducah in £10,000 event at Newmarket in October: got loose before start: sure to improve. *M. Moubarak.* 63 p

BLACKGUARD (USA) 3 ch.g. Irish River (FR) 131–Principle (USA) (Viceregal (CAN)) [1988 7d 1989 8d 8s⁵ 10f] big, strong gelding: modest maiden: ridden by 5-lb claimer, running-on fifth at Kempton, best effort: tended to carry head high on reappearance: stays 1m: evidently needs soft ground: gelded after final start (May): has joined Mrs J. Pitman. *I. A. Balding.* 73

BLACK HELMET 5 gr.g. General Ironside 121–Triple Fire (Deep Run 119) [1988 14.6d 16m⁵ 10g 16f 16f⁵ 18.8d⁴ 1989 16.2m 13f⁴ 16f³] sparely-made, angular gelding: poor maiden: stays 2m. *T. D. Barron.* 38

BLACK MARKETEER (NZ) 4 ch.g. Sir Tristram 115–Satina (NZ) (Montecello 102) [1988 8s³ 8d 12m 14m⁶ 16g 13s 1989 9v 10f 9f² 12m 10m² 8g] sparely-made, angular gelding: good mover: poor maiden: suited by 9f or 1¼m: acts on any going: blinkered once in 1988: suitable mount for apprentice: inconsistent, and possibly temperamental. *D. W. Chapman.* 40

BLACK MONDAY 3 b.c. Busted 134–Lightning Legacy (USA) 78 (Super Concorde (USA) 128) [1988 NR 1989 10.1m⁴ 10.1m* 11m* 12f² 10f* 10g² 12m⁶ 11v] angular colt: progressed well physically: unimpressive mover: first foal: dam, maiden, stayed 1m: won minor events at Windsor in June and Wolverhampton in July and apprentice race (6/1 on) at Chepstow in September: good second to Run Don't Fly in handicap at Goodwood in between: stays 1½m: acts on firm going, probably unsuited by heavy: should prove best with strong handling: useful and consistent. *L. M. Cumani.* 104

BLACKTHORN WINTER 2 b.c. (May 10) Carwhite 127–Red Sanders 71 (Red Alert 127) [1989 5g 5f³ 7m⁴ 7m 6g 7f⁶ 8g 8m 10f⁵] angular, narrow colt: has a round action: fourth foal: dam raced only at 2 yrs, placed over 5f: inconsistent plater: hung left turn and approaching final 1f in selling nursery at Ayr on last outing: should stay 1¼m: sold 2,200 gns Newmarket Autumn Sales. *M. Blanshard.* 45

BLADE OF GRASS 3 b.f. Kris 135–Clare Island 108 (Connaught 130) [1988 NR 1989 10m² 9m⁶ 7g* 8g 7g] angular filly: third foal: half-sister to disappointing 4-y-o House of Commons (by General Assembly) and 1½m winner Island Lake (by Kalaglow): dam, half-sister to very smart 1½m horse Caliban, won Princess Elizabeth Stakes: 4/1 on, easy winner of maiden at Epsom in August: ridden by 5-lb claimer, easily best other effort second in similar event at Leicester when looked sure to win over 1f out: bred to stay 1¼m. *A. C. Stewart.* 78

BLAKENEYS GIFT 3 gr.c. Blakeney 126–Teleflora 89 (Princely Gift 137) [1988 6f 7d 8f 7g 10d 1989 10.6s⁴ 10f⁵ 12m³ 12g⁴ 15g] leggy, unfurnished colt: quite modest handicapper: has run creditably in apprentice and amateur contests: stays 1½m: acts on top-of-the-ground and soft going: worth a try in blinkers. *J. P. Hudson.* 57

BLAKE'S PROGRESS 3 b.c. Blakeney 126–Patosky 94 (Skymaster 126) [1988 7m 6m⁵ 6d³ 10.2m³ 1989 8.2v⁶ 12s⁶ 12f² 12h⁴ 10f⁶ 14m*] medium-sized, quite attractive colt: won maiden claimer (claimed to join M. Pipe £12,001) at Yarmouth in 73

August: stays 1¾m well: best form on top-of-the-ground, possibly unsuited by very soft: visored third outing at 2 yrs: winning hurdler. *I. V. Matthews.*

BLAKES SON 4 b.g. Blakeney 126–Susanna (USA) 81§ (Nijinsky (CAN) 138) **89** [1988 10v² 12g³ 11f³ 10g² 8f* 8d⁴ 8d⁶ 7g 1989 12g² 12f 15.8m⁵ 12h³] big, deep-girthed gelding: usually looks well: quite useful handicapper: looked none too keen when second at Doncaster in March: well below form afterwards: effective at 1m and probably best at up to 1½m: probably acts on any going: best without blinkers: has given bit of trouble at stalls: successful hurdler. *M. W. Easterby.*

BLAKE'S TREASURE 2 b.c. (Apr 9) Mummy's Treasure–Andamooka (Rarity **75 p** 129) [1989 a8g*] half-brother to Irish 11f winner Regal Charmer (by Royal And Regal) and Irish 7f to 1m winner Sorry Ever After (by Balboa): dam, raced only at 3 yrs in Ireland, placed at 6f: ridden by 7-lb claimer, won 11-runner maiden at Lingfield in December by ¾ length from Yeoman Bid: should improve. *T. Thomson Jones.*

BLAKESWARE GOLD 3 ch.g. Vaigly Great 127–Presentable 60 (Sharpen Up **60** 127) [1988 6g 8f 8g⁵ 7v 8g⁶ 1989 10d 12m² 8m⁵ 10f* 12.2m 10f⁶ 10g* 9f³ 9f* 10.6d 10f³ 10f³] angular, plain gelding: poor walker: moderate mover: useful plater: successful at Redcar (twice) and Beverley (in between), bought out of M. Tompkins' stable 6,000 gns on first occasion and no bid subsequently: should stay beyond 1¼m: acts on firm going, probably unsuited by a soft surface: not discredited when sweating. *G. M. Moore.*

BLANDELL BEAUTY 5 b.m. Mummy's Pet 125–Maria Luiza (Stradavinsky — 121) [1988 7f⁶ 10.1g 10g 1989 8m⁵ 6f 7h 7.6f 7h⁶ 7g 7m] tall, leggy, close-coupled mare: bad maiden: blinkered twice: has broken blood vessel over hurdles. *R. P. C. Hoad.*

BLASTED HEATH 3 b.f. Thatching 131–Coven (Sassafras (FR) 135) [1988 5g* **105** 5d² 6g 6g² 7g⁴ 1989 7s² 8g* 8m 8m⁴ 7f³ 8g⁴] useful Irish filly: made all in listed race at Leopardstown in May: creditable third to Milieu in similar event there, best subsequent effort: ran moderately final start, in August: stays 1m: acts on any going. *M. Kauntze, Ireland.*

BLAZAIR 3 ch.f. Full of Hope 125–Zeldabec (Saulingo 122) [1988 8m 1989 8m 8f³ **51 d** 12f 11.7g⁶ 10g 11.7f 8f] tall, leggy filly: 33/1, on toes and ridden by 7-lb claimer, third in seller at Brighton in May, only worthwhile form: unlikely to stay beyond 1m: sometimes sweating: sold 850 gns Ascot October Sales. *Miss A. J. Whitfield.*

BLAZE OF GOLD 5 b.m. Sonnen Gold 121–Alauna 73 (Most Secret 119) [1988 **44** 8d² 9m 8g⁵ 9g 8.2g 8s⁴ 10g 8.2s⁶ 8d² 8.2s 8v⁵ 9v 8m 1989 8h⁴ 7.5f 10m 8.2d 8.2d] sparely-made mare: poor maiden: best at around 1m: seems to act on any going: ran poorly in blinkers: hooded twice at 4 yrs: sometimes on toes: usually taken down early: mounted on track last 2 outings: has tended to carry head high and is none too genuine. *E. J. Alston.*

BLAZE O'GOLD (USA) 3 b.c. Slew O' Gold (USA)–Lady Be Mine (USA) 76 **81** (Sir Ivor 135) [1988 7d² 1989 10g²] very big, strong colt: moderate walker: fair form in minor event at Newmarket as 2-y-o and maiden (weak 5/1 and carrying condition, led over 1m and not knocked about) won by Gold Pavillion at Leicester in April: should stay 1½m. *H. R. A. Cecil.*

BLAZING AWAY 3 gr.g. Blazing Saddles (AUS)–Norton Princess 76 (Wolver — Hollow 126) [1988 6f⁵ 6g 6g 5d⁶ 6g 6g 1989 6s⁶ 8.2s 7f 6m 5f 8.2g] smallish, workmanlike gelding: plating-class maiden: showed little as 3-y-o: stays 7f: best efforts on firm going: usually started slowly at 2 yrs: put head in air and didn't look keen on reappearance, and is one to be wary of. *L. J. Barratt.*

BLAZING SUNSET 2 ch.f. (Mar 20) Blazing Saddles (AUS)–Krishnagar (Kris **55** 135) [1989 5d⁴ 6m³ 6m⁶ 6m* 7g 5f³ 6f* a6g a7g a6g⁴ a8g] small, sparely-made filly: lacks scope: first foal: dam never ran: successful in sellers at Yarmouth and Lingfield, bought out of W. Jarvis' stable 4,000 gns on first occasion and R. Stubbs's stable 4,200 gns on second: creditable fourth of 13 to Corrin Hill in nursery at Lingfield in December: suited by 6f: has worn bandages. *D. A. Wilson.*

BLAZING TOUCH (USA) 3 ch.c. Critique (USA) 126–Miss Flambette (FR) **111** (Crimson Satan (USA)) [1988 9g 9.7g* 1989 9s 12m 12m* 12g³ 10.5d³ 14.6s⁵] 200,000 francs (approx £20,200) Y: tall, lightly-built colt: fifth reported foal: half-brother to French provincial 10.7f winner Reduced (by Irish River) and French 4f (as 7-y-o) to 10.5f winner Groomy (by Blushing Groom): dam, winner 3 times over 1m in France, is out of Prix Vanteux winner Flamboyante: 100/1, showed much improved form when 12½ lengths fifth of 8 to Michelozzo in St Leger Stakes at Ayr, prominent 1½m: won maiden at Argentan as 2-y-o and handicap at Saint-Cloud in

May: suited by 1¾m: best form on soft going: blinkered last 4 starts: trained until after penultimate one by J. de Chevigny. *C. P. E. Brooks.*

BLENDERS CHOICE 7 b.g. Cavo Doro 124–Harriny 94 (Floribunda 136) — [1988 12g 10d 1989 11.7m 12m⁵ 11.7m⁵ 14m⁶] rangy, good-bodied gelding: one-time fair handicapper, but has deteriorated considerably: stays 1½m: best on a sound surface: has won for amateur: winning hurdler/chaser. *J. S. King.*

BLEU DE FRANCE (FR) 2 b.c. (Feb 6) Crystal Glitters (USA) 127– **116** p Emeraldine (FR) (Tanerko 134) [1989 8d* 9d*] half-brother to several winners, notably very smart French middle-distance stayer Galant Vert (by Luthier) and smart French 10.5f and 1½m winner Iris Noir (by Pharly): dam French 1½m winner: successful in maiden at Deauville and 6-runner Prix Saint-Roman (by 1½ lengths from Horatio Luro) at Longchamp: likely to make good middle-distance 3-y-o. *J-M. Beguigne, France.*

BLINDER (USA) 3 b.f. Nijinsky's Secret (USA) 113–Winter Tour (USA) **72** (Kalamoun 129) [1988 7g 1989 10g 8.5g* 8.5m⁴ 10g 8f4 8m] rangy, quite attractive filly: has scope: modest handicapper: won maiden at Beverley in May by short head, rallying well: stays 8.5f: acts on top-of-the-ground: twice on toes: ran fairly well when sweating penultimate start: tail flasher. *H. Candy.*

BLIND FAITH 4 b.g. Known Fact (USA) 135–Rosetta Stone 89 (Guillaume Tell — (USA) 121) [1988 12f 12f 13.3g* 14f 19v 16d² 1989 18g 18.4m 13.3m] compact gelding: good mover, with a long stride: fair handicapper as 3-y-o when trained by M. Stoute: well beaten all starts in first half of 1989: stays 2m: acts on a soft surface, but is possibly unsuited by heavy going: has worn blinkers and visor: has shown a tendency to wander: sold 2,900 gns Ascot 2nd June Sales. *N. A. Gaselee.*

BLINDMANS DOUBLE 2 b.c. (Mar 23) Mansingh (USA) 120–Myriad **48** § (Sovereign Path 125) [1989 5d⁶ 5f⁴ 5g a6g] leggy, close-coupled colt: half-brother to plating-class 1986 2-y-o Gloriad (by Hittite Glory): dam Irish 1½m winner: poor maiden: ran too freely in blinkers on final outing, first for around 5 months: has twice carried head high: one to be wary of. *J. A. Glover.*

BLOCK THE DAY (ITY) 2 b.c. (Feb 16) Alzao (USA) 117–Canterbury Tale **57** (Exbury 138) [1989 7m 8.2f] fair sort: half-brother to poor 1½m handicapper Miller's Tale (by Mill Reef) and 4 winners abroad: dam, very useful in USA, won 1m stakes race: about 8 lengths seventh of 12 to Marquetry at Salisbury in June, first and better effort in maidens. *J. L. Dunlop.*

BLONDE BELLA 4 b.f. Pablond 93–Donna Bellina (Porto Bello 118) [1988 NR — 1989 5f 5f 8m] sparely-made, long-backed filly: well beaten in varied events. *N. R. Mitchell.*

BLOOD COLD (ITY) 2 b.c. (Apr 19) Private Account (USA)–Sparklet (USA) — (Sir Ivor 135) [1989 7.6m 8m 8g] quite attractive colt: shade unfurnished: has a roundish action: third named foal: dam minor winner at up to 11f: sire smart 9f and 1¼m stakes winner: soundly beaten in maidens: not at all knocked about final start: will be well suited by 1¼m + . *J. L. Dunlop.*

BLOW A KISS 2 b.f. (Mar 6) Auction Ring (USA) 123–Follow Me Follow 92 **?** (Wollow 132) [1989 6f²] 5,800Y: medium-sized, quite good-topped filly: third foal: half-sister to 3-y-o Voltz (by Electric): dam 5f winner at 2 yrs, from family of Honeyblest: 10/1 and bit backward, beaten 2½ lengths by Rafha in 2-runner maiden at Goodwood in June. *C. A. Cyzer.*

BLUE BELL RIBBONS 2 b.g. (May 11) Music Boy 124–Ribbons of Blue 60 **49** (Jimmy Reppin 131) [1989 5d⁴ 5s 5m⁴ 5f⁴ 6g 6f 6m 8.5f] 4,200F, 17,500Y: close-coupled gelding: shows a quick action: first foal: dam staying mudlark: moderate plater: races keenly, and best form at 5f: tends to get on toes: sweated and wore tongue strap sixth outing. *J. Berry.*

BLUEBIRD LADY 4 ch.f. Thatching 131–Grankie (USA) (Nashua) [1988 7g **67** 1989 9m⁶ 6f² 5m³ 5m⁴ 6m³ 5f 5f⁵ 6f² 5m³ 6m⁵ 5.1g* 5.3f 5f⁶ 5m⁴] angular, shallow-girthed filly: poor mover: showed improved form when winning handicap at Yarmouth in September: best effort in similar company when fourth to Captain's Bidd at Edinburgh: suited by 5f: yet to race on a soft surface: visored and bit awkward at stalls ninth start, blinkered eleventh to thirteenth: has worn bandages: has run creditably for apprentice. *Mrs N. Macauley.*

BLUEBLACK 2 br.g. (Mar 4) Kampala 120–Captivate 79 (Mansingh (USA) 120) **52** [1989 5d³ 6m⁶ 6m⁵ 6m 6f] 13,000Y: workmanlike, sparely-made gelding: keen walker: good mover: second foal: half-brother to 3-y-o Masirah (by Dunphy): dam, 5f winner, from speedy family: poor maiden: blinkered final start. *J. Berry.*

BLUE CHATEAU 3 ch.g. Longleat (USA) 109–La Sinope (FR) (Thatch (USA) 65
136) [1988 6f 6f 1989 9v 10d⁶ 9d² 10f* 8m² 9f³ 8f* 8g⁵ 8f 8.2g] compact gelding: won
sellers at Pontefract (bought in 4,200 gns) in May and Ayr (no bid) in June: ran
moderately in non-selling handicaps last 2 outings: at least as effective at 1m as
1¼m: acts on firm going and a soft surface: not discredited when visored. *C. Tinkler.*

BLUECHIPENTERPRISE 3 br.f. Blakeney 126–Hey Skip (USA) (Bold —
Skipper (USA)) [1988 7f 1989 10m] workmanlike filly: has a round action: bit
backward, always behind in maiden at Salisbury and claimer (in June) at
Nottingham. *P. F. I. Cole.*

BLUE DISC 4 br.g. Disc Jockey 95–Kaotesse (Djakao (FR) 124) [1988 6m 5g 8f² 47 d
6f 8.3d³ 6g² 6m 10m 1989 5d³ 7g² 7m 6f 8.3m 10g] workmanlike gelding:
plating-class handicapper on his day: well below form last 4 outings: hung left 4f out
and tended to wander under pressure fifth start: finds 5f on short side and stays 1m:
acts on any going: tends to sweat: possibly ungenuine. *J. R. Jenkins.*

BLUE GRIT 3 b.g. Thatching 131–Northern Wisdom (Northfields (USA)) [1988 —
7s 1989 10f⁵ 10f⁶ 12.5f⁶ 10g] leggy, quite attractive gelding: little worthwhile form,
including in sellers: sold to join R. Dods 5,200 gns Newmarket Autumn Sales. *R. J.
R. Williams.*

BLUE HABIT 2 b.f. (Mar 8) Cure The Blues (USA)–Miss Habitat (Habitat 134) 49
[1989 5m³ 5m⁵ 6m 5m 6g 8g] IR 5,100F, 2,600Y: leggy, light-framed filly: moderate
mover: fourth foal: half-sister to a winner in USA by General Assembly: dam won in
Italy: poor maiden: well beaten in sellers last 2 starts: should stay at least 6f:
blinkered fifth outing. *J. Mackie.*

BLUELLA 2 b.f. (Mar 16) Blue Cashmere 129–Set To Work (Workboy 123) [1989 —
5m 6g 5f 6m] lengthy, robust filly: fifth living foal: half-sister to 3-y-o Work On Air
(by Doc Marten), modest 1986 2-y-o 5f winner Upset (by Uncle Pokey) and 11.5f and
1½m winner Tour de Force (by Reliance II): dam never ran: no form in maidens and
sellers. *J. S. Wainwright.*

BLUE MALORY (USA) 3 b.f. Caro 133–Think Blue (USA) (Cornish Prince) —
[1988 NR 1989 12f⁵] $200,000Y: second foal: dam, minor winner at around 6f, is
half-sister to useful miler Fawn and to the grandam of Dancing Brave: weak 5/1, 16
lengths last of 9, weakening final 2f, in maiden at Folkestone in September: sold
13,000 gns Newmarket December Sales. *G. Harwood.*

BLUE MISCHIEF 3 ch.f. Precocious 126–Deep Blue Sea (Gulf Pearl 117) [1988 79
6m⁶ 7m³ 7d⁵ 1989 5d² 8.2g² 6f* 8m⁵ 5m 7g6 6s 6s 5m²] strong, useful-looking
filly: good walker and mover: won maiden at Hamilton in May: good second after in
handicaps at Hamilton and Edinburgh: best at sprint distances: acts on firm going.
R. Allan.

BLUE MONEY 3 br.c. Aragon 118–Salary (Faberge II 121) [1988 5d 5v6 5m* 5g —
5g 5g⁵ 5f 5g⁴ 5d 1989 5f 5f 5f] workmanlike, quite attractive colt: carries condition:
has a quick action: made all in minor event early on as 2-y-o: speed long way when
well beaten in handicaps in spring of 1989: speedy, and likely to prove suited by fast
conditions at 5f: blinkered final start. *Mrs N. Macauley.*

BLUE ORCA 3 b.c. Caerleon (USA) 132–Blue Shark (Silver Shark 129) [1988 92
6m² 6s 1989 8m⁶ 10f* 10f* 10m* 10g³ 9g] sparely-made, rather angular colt:
moderate walker: good mover: fairly useful handicapper: progressive form when
successful at Lingfield in July and Redcar and Sandown (impressively by 6 lengths
from Monastery) in August: disappointed when odds on at Epsom penultimate start
and ran poorly in Cambridgeshire Handicap (14/1) at Newmarket 6 weeks later:
stays 1¼m well: needs top-of-the-ground. *B. W. Hills.*

BLUE RHYTHM 4 b.f. Blue Cashmere 129–Abalone (Abwah 118) [1988 6d² 7g* 66
6f³ 6g 6g 6g 7f 6g⁶ 6d 1989 7s* 6m* 6m] lengthy, workmanlike filly: moderate
mover: quite modest handicapper: clearly difficult to train as 4-y-o, but won her first
2 races, narrowly beating Standing Count in April and Gorytus Star at
Salisbury in June: well beaten final outing: stays 7f: acts on any going: visored once
at 3 yrs: bandaged in 1989: game. *T. Thomson Jones.*

BLUE ROOM 2 b.f. (Mar 9) Gorytus (USA) 132–Jokers High (USA) (Vaguely 65
Noble 140) [1989 7g² 7f² 7g⁵ 7g a8g] lengthy, rather leggy filly: fifth foal: half-sister
to modest 1988 2-y-o Preben (by Known Fact): dam unraced daughter of Joking
Apart, very smart performer at up to 1m: quite modest maiden: didn't handle bend at
Sandown on debut: will stay 1¼m: reluctant to post and at stalls when running
poorly third start: sold 1,550 gns Ascot December Sales. *P. F. I. Cole.*

BLUES INDIGO 4 b.f. Music Boy 124–Blueit (FR) 101 (Bold Lad (IRE) 133) 92
[1988 6g 5g² 6f* 6m² 5f⁶ 5m 5d 1989 6g 5m 5f 6m 5m² 5m² 5f 5g] neat,

good-quartered filly: fairly useful on her day: good second to Carol's Treasure in £8,000 handicap at York in July, always close up stand side, hanging left under pressure 1f out: well below form on most other starts: speedy: best form on a sound surface: inconsistent. *J. Wharton.*

BLUE STAG 2 b.c. (Mar 2) Sadler's Wells (USA) 132–Snow Day (FR) 123 **88** p (Reliance II 137) [1989 7m5 10g*] 49,000Y: lengthy, attractive colt: second known foal: closely related to modest 1½m winner Snowkist (by The Minstrel): dam, very smart winner at 10.5f in France, stayed 1½m: well-backed favourite following promising debut, won 13-runner maiden at Nottingham in October by 1½ lengths from Snurge, making smooth progress to lead over 2f out but running green: will stay 1½m: sure to improve further. *B. W. Hills.*

BLUSHING BLOOM (USA) 2 ch.f. (Mar 25) Blushing Groom (USA) — p 131–Catherine's Bet (USA) (Grey Dawn II 132) [1989 6g5] $135,000Y, resold $95,000Y: medium-sized, rather sparely-made filly: moderate walker and mover: sister to a minor 2-y-o winner in USA and half-sister to 2 other winners: dam Grade 2 9f winner at 4 yrs in North America: weak 8/1 and bit green, around 10 lengths fifth of 12, slowly away and unable to quicken approaching final 1f, to Sally Rous in maiden at Leicester in November: will improve. *L. Cumani.*

BLUSHING BUNNY 3 b.f. Blushing Scribe (USA) 107–Blesseen 71 (So — Blessed 130) [1988 5d2 5m6 5m 5d4 1989 5.3h 5f] workmanlike, rather angular filly: quite modest maiden as 2-y-o: no worthwhile form in handicap and claimer in first half of 1989: blinkered, very mulish in paddock, taken quietly to post then gave trouble in stalls when tailed off final start: one to have reservations about. *D. J. G. Murray-Smith.*

BLUSHING RED 2 b.f. (May 29) Jalmood (USA) 126–Mother Brown 103 (Candy — Cane 125) [1989 6g] workmanlike, plain filly: moderate walker and mover: half-sister to several winners, including 1m winner Macarthurs Head (by Dom Racine): dam genuine handicapper at up to 1¼m: 50/1 and bit backward, last of 10, hampered start and always in rear, in maiden at Doncaster in July. *N. Bycroft.*

BLUSHING RIBERO 3 ch.c. Coquelin (USA) 121–Roses 103 (Ribero 126) — [1988 6d 1989 10s 9f] rather leggy, good-topped colt: soundly beaten in maiden and minor events. *J. P. Hudson.*

BLUSHING SPY 6 b.h. Great Nephew 126–Red Spider 78 (Red God 128§) [1988 — NR 1989 17.6f 12f 16f] compact horse: winning handicapper as 4-y-o: visored, soundly beaten in 1989: suited by 1½m: acts on top-of-the-ground and soft going: best form in blinkers: temperamental hurdler: sold 1,950 gns Ascot August Sales. *D. R. Tucker.*

BLYTON LAD 3 b.g. Skyliner 117–Ballinacurra (King's Troop 118) [1988 7.5m **103** 7m4 1989 8.5d 6d3 7f 6m6 7f 5g* 6f2 5f* 5m3 5m* 5g 6d2] rangy gelding: has plenty of scope: won handicaps (staying on strongly from rear) at Doncaster in July and Redcar in August and £5,700 event at Newbury in September: 10/1, 1½ lengths second of 13 to Dawn Success in listed race at Thirsk final start, always front rank but edging left: suited by 6f or stiff 5f: acts on firm going and a soft surface: sweating profusely fifth outing: has been unruly in preliminaries and was withdrawn once at 2 yrs: should win more races. *J. Balding.*

BOAMBER 2 ch.g. (Mar 30) Anfield 117–Rykneld (Warpath 113) [1989 5s 5f 6g — 5m6] 7,000Y: small gelding: has a quick action: fourth reported foal: half-brother to 3-y-o 1m winner It's Me (by Good Times) and fair 6f winner Derwent Valley (by Frimley Park): dam never ran: little worthwhile form in maidens, including auction events: gave impression on final start (August) something amiss: had tongue tied down last 2 starts: has joined L. Barratt. *J. Berry.*

BOBBY ON THE BANK 3 ch.g. Monsanto (FR) 121–Dewberry 68 (Bay **50** Express 132) [1988 5f 5m 6m 7m 7g4 8.5f 10s3 10.2m 1989 9v* 10d5 8g 9f4 11f 10.6g 8.2g5 8.2g 8g] small, rather sparely-made gelding: moderate mover: plating-class handicapper: won at Hamilton in April: stays 1¼m: goes well in the mud: claimer ridden: inconsistent. *M. J. O'Neill.*

BOB'S BALLAD 5 ch.g. Ballad Rock 122–Twice Regal (Royal Prerogative 119) — [1988 8f 10f6 8g* 1989 8d 10.1m 8m5] leggy gelding: plater: best at up to 1m: dead. *D. Burchell.*

BOCA LAD 2 b.c. (Mar 22) Pharly (FR) 130–Scented Air 92 (Derring-Do 131) **86** [1989 6m* 6g4 6m] 25,000Y: lengthy, angular colt: good walker: half-brother to several winners here and abroad, including fairly useful 1983 2-y-o 5f winer Twice Fragrant (by Double Form): dam, 2-y-o 5f winner, is daughter of very fast 1971 2-y-o filly Rose Dubarry: made most in minor event at York in June, rallying gamely:

EBF Duchess of Kent Stakes, York—Boca Lad rallies gamely to beat Tod

creditable last of 4 to Rock City in Anglia Television July Stakes at Newmarket:
gave impression something amiss in listed race at Ripon in August: will stay 1m.
Lord John FitzGerald.

BOCAS ROSE 3 ch.f. Jalmood (USA) 126–Strathoykel 94 (Aberdeen 109) [1988   **98**
5d 5d³ 5.3f* 5.3f* 5f² 6d⁴ 5d⁵ 5g* 6g⁴ 1989 8f 8g⁴ 7f⁴ 8d 7m⁴ 6m] lengthy filly: has a
rather round action: useful performer: easily best efforts as 3-y-o when fourth in
Child Stakes at Newmarket and listed races at Goodwood and York: stays 1m: acts
well on a sound surface: bandaged near-hind twice at 2 yrs: sold P. Kelleway 68,000
gns Newmarket December Sales. *R. Hannon.*

BOCAS SONG 2 b.f. (Feb 26) Song 132–La Jeunesse (Young Generation 129)   **39**
[1989 5s 6f 6h⁴ 5.3h³ 5g⁶ 6f 6g] 7,000Y: tall, lengthy filly, shade unfurnished: has
scope: second foal: dam ran twice at 2 yrs: poor form in varied races, including
sellers: sold 5,400 gns Newmarket Autumn Sales. *R. Hannon.*

BODAMIST 2 b.c. (Feb 7) Swing Easy (USA) 126–Diorina 91 (Manacle 123) [1989   **66**
6m⁶ 6m* 6m² 7m 8g a7g] 5,000Y, 6,600 2-y-o: angular colt: half-brother to 3-y-o Di
Bravura (by Noalto), fair sprinter Cheri Berry (by Air Trooper) and a winning
hurdler: dam best at 2 yrs, successful over 5.3f: quite modest performer: won seller
(bought in 7,200 gns) at Windsor in June by 5 lengths. *J. White.*

BODGE 2 b.f. (Apr 28) Horage 124–The Flying Sputnik (Touch Paper 113) [1989   **64**
6m 7m³ 7m 7m⁶ 7g² 8m⁵] IR 5,400Y: workmanlike filly: has scope: third foal:
half-sister to 3-y-o Sam's Choice (by Kampala), modest 5f winner at 2 yrs: dam Irish
2-y-o 5f winner: quite modest maiden: ran in snatches when short-head second of
20, going on strongly, to Fosse Gill in claimer at Leicester in September: very edgy
when below form in seller at Newmarket following month: stays 7f: blinkered last 2
starts. *G. A. Pritchard-Gordon.*

BOHEA DESTROYER 4 b.g. Crofter (USA) 124–Bold Kate (Bold Lad (IRE)   **38**
133) [1988 9d 8f 11d 10.8g 11.7m 11g 12m 10d 1989 10.1m 14.8m 12f⁵ 12g² 12s] leggy
gelding: moderate mover: modest winner as 2-y-o: has deteriorated: stays 1½m:
suited by an easy surface and used to go very well with plenty of give in the ground:
visored last 3 outings. *P. Burgoyne.*

BOLDABSA 3 ch.f. Persian Bold 123–Absaroka (Prince Tenderfoot (USA) 126)   **96**
[1988 NR 1989 8s⁴ 10m⁴ 10m⁵ 10f* 12f⁶ 11d 9g 9m*] strong, workmanlike filly: has a
round action: sixth reported foal: half-sister to fair 9f and 10.6f winner Pichincha (by
Pharly), also successful at 5f at 2 yrs, and Irish 1¼m winner La Calera (by Corvaro):
dam very useful French 1¼m winner: won maiden at Navan in June and handicap

under 9-13 at Clonmel in September: in rear in Ribblesdale Stakes (took keen hold and led 1¼m) at Royal Ascot and valuable handicaps at the Curragh and Leopardstown in between: suited by 1¼m: acts on firm going. *C. Collins, Ireland.*

BOLD AMBITION   2 b.c. (Feb 8) Ela-Mana-Mou 132–Queen of The Dance   **88** (Dancer's Image (USA)) [1989 7g² 8m] 78,000Y: good-bodied colt: has scope: fifth foal: brother to 3-y-o Elastic and half-brother to Irish 1¼m winner Artie Shaw (by Artaius) and a middle-distance winner in French Provinces: dam second over 7f from 2 starts at 2 yrs in France: 6/1 and carrying condition, 3 lengths second of 9, clear, to Digression in minor event at Kempton in September: last of 8 in Ciga Grand Criterium at Longchamp following month: should stay at least 1m. *B. W. Hills.*

BOLD ANGEL   2 b.c. (Mar 2) Lochnager 132–Lobela 77 (Lorenzaccio 130) [1989   **84** 5f 5d³ 6g⁴ 6g* 6d⁵ 6m³ 7m³] strong, close-coupled colt: carries plenty of condition: fourth reported foal: half-brother to 6f winner Afrabella (by African Sky) and fair 6f and 7f winner Baton Boy (by Music Boy): dam won at 1m and 1¼m: made all in 2-runner maiden at Nottingham in July: ran well in nurseries on last 3 starts: suited by 7f. *J. S. Wainwright.*

BOLD-BRI   2 gr.f. (Mar 10) Bold Owl 101–Bri-Ette 53 (Brittany) [1989 6g 7.5f]   — 1,400F, 5,600Y: workmanlike filly: third foal: sister to 1988 2-y-o 6f seller winner Miss Ellie Pea and to 5f winner Mom Sally: dam sister to useful sprinter Tinjar: well behind in maiden auction races. *Miss L. C. Siddall.*

BOLD CELT   6 b. or br.h. Brave Shot–Pearl Locket (Gulf Pearl 117) [1988 7d⁵   — 1989 7m 8.2d⁵ 8.2g 8g 7g] leggy, quite good-topped horse: poor maiden: stays 7f: has worn bandages: sweating on reappearance. *C. B. B. Booth.*

BOLD CHOICE   3 b.g. Auction Ring (USA) 123–Inner Pearl (Gulf Pearl 117)   **70** [1988 7g 1989 8s 8m 10m³ 12.2m² 10m⁵ 14m] angular, workmanlike gelding: modest handicapper: should prove suited by 1½m: acts on top-of-the-ground: blinkered (ran creditably) fourth start: visored last 2: ridden up with pace: sold to join J. Joseph 9,400 gns Newmarket Autumn Sales. *M. R. Stoute.*

BOLD CROFT   2 b.f. (Apr 7) Crofter (USA) 124–Blajina (Bold Lad (IRE) 133)   **31** [1989 5d⁴ 5f 6f⁴ 7m 7f a8g] IR 700F, IR 1,000Y: unfurnished filly: half-sister to fair 1¼m winner Diamond Flight (by Skyliner): dam ran twice at 2 yrs: bad maiden: likely to prove best at 5f. *T. D. Barron.*

BOLD DAEDALUS   3 b.c. Dalsaan 125–Excruciating (CAN) (Bold Forbes   — (USA)) [1988 6f 6s 1989 a6g] tall colt: modest at best: will be suited by 7f+: best effort on soft ground. *R. Hannon.*

BOLDDEN   7 b.h. Bold Lad (IRE) 133–Golden Keep 77 (Worden II 129) [1988   **61** 10m⁴ 10m 8f 10f⁴ 8.2s 1989 10.4m 8m 10m⁴ 8g⁶ 8h³] strong, good-quartered horse: moderate mover: quite modest handicapper nowadays: ideally suited by 1¼m: needs a sound surface: ran creditably for apprentice final outing (July). *J. Hanson.*

BOLD DIFFERENCE   5 b.m. Bold Owl 101–Subtle Queen (Stephen George   — 102) [1988 12d⁴ 10m 12f⁶ 12f 10f 12m 12m 1989 10m 12m⁵ 12m⁴ 12.3f 14f] plain, sparely-made mare: poor performer: form for some time only in handicap on third outing: stays 1½m: probably not at best on extremes of going: has seemed a difficult ride: inconsistent. *K. A. Morgan.*

BOLD ENDEAVOUR   2 b.g. (Apr 17) Try My Best (USA) 130–Explorelka   **63** (Relko 136) [1989 5s 5s 5f 6m⁴ 6m 7m⁵ 8f⁵] IR 17,500F, 8,400Y: quite attractive gelding: has a quick action: half-brother to several winners, notably smart middle-distance performer Explorer King (by Roi Dagobert): dam unraced daughter of sister to Bold Ruler: quite modest maiden: stays 1m: tends to wander. *M. J. Fetherston-Godley.*

BOLD FOX   3 b.c. Ballad Rock 122–Spadilla 59 (Javelot 124) [1988 NR 1989 10g*   **103** 9f* 10.2g⁴ 12d] 12,000F, 31,000Y: good-topped, good sort: good walker: half-brother to several winners, including useful 1¼m winner Power Bender (by Prince Tenderfoot): dam Irish 1½m winner: won maiden at Salisbury in May and minor event (odds on) at Wolverhampton in October: 9½ lengths fourth of 7 to Drum Taps in £21,100 limited handicap at Newcastle: tailed off in November Handicap at Thirsk 2 weeks later: stays 1¼m: acts on firm ground, possibly unsuited by dead: useful. *G. Harwood.*

BOLD FURY   6 ch.g. Bold Lad (IRE) 133–Falassa (Relko 136) [1988 NR 1989 12g   — 10f⁶ 8.3m] workmanlike gelding: no worthwhile form in handicaps and a claimer (bandaged) as 6-y-o: should stay 1¼m: acts on top-of-the-ground: visored once: winning hurdler. *J. D. Roberts.*

BOLD GAMBLE   3 ch.g. Bold Owl 101–Subtle Queen (Stephen George 102)   **65 d** [1988 5d 5m* 5g 7.5f⁵ 7f* 8.2m 8g 1989 7d 8s 7.5d* 8m 12f 10m 10f 9s] leggy, sparely-made gelding: poor walker and moderate mover: comfortable winner of seller (bought in 5,500 gns) at Beverley in May: ran badly in handicaps and seller afterwards, in last-named (favourite and visored) front rank over 6f on final start: suited by around 7f: best form on a soft surface: edgy sixth outing. *Ronald Thompson.*

BOLD HABIT 4 ch.g. Homing 130–Our Mother 95 (Bold Lad (IRE) 133) [1988 6g² 6m⁴ 6d 5g 7m 6g³ 8m 7f 1989 5f² 6g* 6m² 7g³ 6f 6m⁴ 7.6m 8f² 9f⁵ 10g⁴ a8g a7g*] sturdy, strong-quartered gelding: won claimer at Carlisle in June and handicap at Lingfield in December: ran at least creditably most starts in between: barely stays 1¼m: acts on firm going and a soft surface: blinkered once: slowly away fifth and seventh start. *W. J. Pearce.*   **73**

BOLD HEIGHTS 2 b.c. (Apr 27) Persian Bold 123–Great Tom 99 (Great Nephew 126) [1989 6s] 10,000Y: sixth foal: half-brother to fair 1½m and 1¾m winner Five Farthings (by Busted) and 1¼m winner Warning Bell (by Bustino): dam, 2-y-o 6f winner, is half-sister to top 1981 2-y-o filly Circus Ring: 16/1, last of 13 in minor event at Ayr in September: bred to stay 1m + . *J. Berry.*   **—**

BOLD ILLUSION 11 ch.g. Grey Mirage 128–Savette (Frigid Aire) [1988 12v 12d³ 14s* 16d⁵ 14.6g 1989 14.8s 12s] close-coupled, sparely-made gelding: a grand old servant who won early in season for fourth year running in handicap at Nottingham in 1988: well below his best in similar company in spring as 11-y-o but later won over hurdles: stays 1¾m well: suited by give in the ground and goes very well in the mud: best forcing pace: apprentice ridden nowadays: genuine. *M. W. Eckley.*   **—**

BOLD IMP 4 bl.c. Dubassoff (USA)–Woodlands Girl (Weepers Boy 124) [1988 10.2g 10.1d 12g 1989 10.8s] compact colt: little worthwhile form in modest company: sweating, edgy, bit troublesome at start and raced freely in blinkers only outing (March) at 4 yrs. *R. J. Holder.*   **—**

BOLD LEZ 2 b.c. (May 4) Never So Bold 135–Classy Nancy (USA) (Cutlass (USA)) [1989 6m 6g⁶ 6g³ 6d³] 9,800Y: leggy colt: has scope: has a round action: fourth foal: half-brother to 3-y-o Nancy Ardross (by Ardross): dam won at up to 6f in USA: progressive colt: 9 lengths third of 9, staying on having been outpaced 2f out, to Cullinan in maiden at Goodwood in September: will probably stay 7f. *M. J. Haynes.*   **69**

BOLD LILLY 3 b.f. Montekin 125–Topless Dancer (Northfields (USA)) [1988 6d 6g⁵ 6s⁴ 7m 7g 1989 8g³ 8.2m 10f⁵] quite good-topped filly: plating-class maiden: ran creditably in handicap and seller first and final starts: stays 1¼m: probably acts on any going: has joined N. Ayliffe. *C. W. C. Elsey.*   **57**

BOLD MAC 3 b.g. Comedy Star (USA) 121–Northern Empress 80 (Northfields (USA)) [1988 NR 1989 7f 7h 8.2f* 8m⁶ 7f⁶ 6m⁶] tall gelding: fourth living foal: half-brother to 6f and 7f winner Nevada Mix (by Alias Smith) and a winner in Belgium by Hotfoot: dam ran 3 times: sweating, won 4-runner minor event at Nottingham in June: little other form, including in handicaps: stays 1m: sold to join D. Gandolfo 5,700 gns Ascot October Sales. *N. A. Gaselee.*   **64**

BOLD PASSION 2 b.c. (Mar 27) Persian Bold 123–Destina (USA) 85 (Youth (USA) 135) [1989 7m⁴ 8m* 8f*] angular colt: first foal: dam 2-y-o 8.2f winner stayed 1½m, is out of half-sister to dam of Trillion, herself dam of Triptych: odds on, won maiden at Chepstow in August and minor event at Wolverhampton in October: will be well suited by 1¼m + : lazy sort: sold to race in Italy 54,000 gns Newmarket Autumn Sales. *G. Harwood.*   **89**

BOLD PATRICK 2 b.c. (Mar 17) Never So Bold 135–Baby's Smile 68 (Shirley Heights 130) [1989 6f 8.2g³ 10g] 11,000Y: tall, rather leggy, close-coupled colt: not a good walker: second foal: half-brother to 3-y-o 15.3f seller winner For A While (by Pharly): dam suited by good test of stamina: third of 14 finishers behind Golan Heights in maiden at Haydock in September: well beaten, fading final 2f, in similar event at Nottingham following month: off course 4 months after debut. *M. Bell.*   **76**

BOLD PERFORMER 2 b.c. (May 17) Bold Lad (IRE) 133–Miss St Cyr 86 (Brigadier Gerard 144) [1989 7d*] brother to smart sprinter Cyrano de Bergerac and half-brother to a winner in Switzerland: dam 2-y-o 6f winner stayed 7f: 33/1, won 11-runner minor event at Thirsk in November in close finish with Stagecraft and Lady of Vision, leading on line: should improve. *J. Wharton.*   **87 p**

BOLD PILLAGER 7 b.g. Formidable (USA) 125–Pilley Green 100 (Porto Bello 118) [1988 8d 8m 8g 8f 8g 10m⁵ 8f 1989 9.2f 8f² 8m⁴ 8f⁵ a10g] strong, deep-bodied gelding: carries plenty of condition: has been hobdayed: has a round action: fair handicapper: ran best race for some time when short-head second of 5, setting slow pace, at Bath in August: tailed off final outing: stays 9f: suited by sound surface and goes very well on firm going: often sweats. *Lady Herries.*

BOLD RAB 2 ch.c. (Mar 20) Rabdan 129–Herbary (USA) (Herbager 136) [1989   **57** 5m 6m 6f6] compact, quite attractive colt: seventh foal: half-brother to fair 1¼m winner Slix (by High Top): dam never ran: plating-class maiden: best effort final start. *P. T. Walwyn.*

BOLD REPUBLIC 3 gr.g. Nishapour (FR) 125–Gallant Believer (USA) (Gallant   **80** Romeo (USA)) [1988 6s2 6m5 1989 8f3 8g5 10f4 9m3 10g* 10s] leggy, workmanlike gelding: has scope: fair handicapper: favourite, won slowly-run 5-runner event at Ayr in July: ran fairly well previous 4 starts: stays 1¼m well: probably acts on any going: tends to take keen hold: usually held up in rear. *T. D. Barron.*

BOLD RUSSIAN 2 b.c. (Feb 27) Persian Bold 123–Russian Ribbon (USA) 86   **80** (Nijinsky (CAN) 138) [1989 5m* 6g5 6f4 6g3 8.2d6 7g4] IR 31,000Y: quite good-topped, attractive colt: first foal: dam, 1m winner from 3 starts as 3-y-o, is daughter of half-sister to several smart performers: won maiden at Haydock in June: put up good effort when over 5 lengths fourth to Dame Rousara in nursery at Ascot on final start: will stay 1¼m. *B. W. Hills.*

BOLD SINGER 3 b.g. Ballad Rock 122–Grande Maison (Crepello 136) [1988 5g   — 5m 7m 8m 7f 1989 7m 6f 6h 7.5f 7m6] leggy, quite good-topped gelding: moderate walker: poor maiden: visored third start: sold to join T. J. Etherington 2,300 gns Doncaster August Sales. *J. Etherington.*

BOLD STRANGER 4 br.c. Persian Bold 123–Lorna Doone (USA) (Tom Rolfe)   **99** ? [1988 8.2s2 12g* 16f3 1989 16.2m4 20f6 16m6 12f4 13.4m5 14.6g] angular, workmanlike colt: poor mover: won maiden at Newmarket early in 1988: turns as 4-y-o only when sixth to Orpheus in moderately-run £43,800 handicap over 2m at Newcastle in July, close up until tending to hang, flashing tail and weakening over 1f out: tailed off final outing: stays 2m: best form on a sound surface: one to treat with caution. *C. E. Brittain.*

BOLD STREET BLUES 2 b.g. (May 13) Bold Owl 101–Basin Street (Tudor   **66** Melody 129) [1989 6m 7.5f 7f6 7g5 7m4 8.2s* 8.2g4 8s2 8.2s3] 7,400Y: quite good-topped gelding: carries condition: has a markedly round action: half-brother to several minor winners: dam showed no worthwhile form: former plater: won 10-runner nursery at Hamilton in September by 4 lengths: ran very well in nurseries and a claimer afterwards: will stay 1¼m: acts on soft going: gelded after final start. *C. Tinkler.*

BOLD TRY 4 ch.g. Try My Best (USA) 130–Persian Polly 99 (Persian Bold 123)   **67** [1988 8g5 8.2d 7g6 8m 8.3m 7m 7g6 6d3 6d4 1989 7m5 8m 7.5m2 7.6h* 8m4 7f3 8.3d* 9g2 8s 9f 8g4] strong, lengthy, rather dipped-backed gelding: quite modest performer: won amateurs handicap at Lingfield in June and seller at Windsor (sold out of P. Cole's stable 4,500 gns) in August: given lot to do and did very well when second in handicap at Hamilton in September: stays 9f: acts on any going: has worn a tongue strap and a severe bridle: winning hurdler. *N. Tinkler.*

BOLLIN GORGEOUS 3 b.f. Hello Gorgeous (USA) 128–Treberth 60 (Gay   **58** Fandango (USA) 132) [1988 5g 6m3 6f2 1989 6d2 8.2s 6g3 8m4 6g5 7m4 7g* 8f 8.2g 8g5 8g3 a11g6] workmanlike filly: turns off-fore in: poor mover: favourite, won claimer (claimed out of M. H. Easterby's stable £6,776) at Edinburgh in September: saddle slipped next start: mostly not discredited in sellers and claimer after: stays 1m: possibly unsuited by soft going: blinkered last 8 starts. *C. R. Beever.*

BOLLIN PATRICK 4 b.c. Sagaro 133–Bollin Charlotte 79 (Immortality) [1988   **95** ? 8g5 12m* 10.2m* 12f4 14.8d3 12g* 12d4 10.2g4 11d4 1989 12f* 12m 12g 12m 12f] strong, workmanlike colt: has a rather quick action: developed into quite a useful handicapper in spring, justifying favouritism easily at Thirsk and York: ran as though something amiss at Epsom (virtually pulled up) and York (moved down moderately) on fourth and final outings: suited by 1½m: acts on any going: best treated with caution. *M. H. Easterby.*

BOLLIN TINO 3 ch.c. Bustino 136–Strong Light 103 (Fortino II 120) [1988 7m4   — 7d 8d 1989 12.2d 7.5f 10.4g 8g 6m 8f5] compact colt: form only on debut: should stay at least 1m: possibly unsuited by a soft surface: blinkered last 5 outings, pulling hard on first 3 of those and setting strong pace over 5f on final one. *M. H. Easterby.*

BOLLIN ZOLA 3 b.f. Alzao (USA) 117–Sauntry (Ballad Rock 122) [1988 5g* 6m2   **90** 1989 5s3 8g4 6m5 7g2 7.6g* 7.6f2 7g2 7m5] lengthy, good-quartered filly: fairly useful handicapper: on toes and looking very well, won at Chester in June by short head: ran well after at Chester, Newmarket and York: should stay 1m: acts on any going: visored last 4 outings. *M. H. Easterby.*

BOLSHOI PRINCE 2 b.c. (Apr 9) Gorytus (USA) 132–Achafalaya (USA) **78** ? (Apalachee (USA) 137) [1989 5f² 6g 5f⁶ 5g a7g*] 9,400F, 25,000Y: leggy, close-coupled, rather unfurnished colt: second foal: dam maiden probably stayed 1½m, is half-sister to smart Le Joli, stakes winner at up to 1m: 8-length winner of nursery at Southwell in December, easily best effort: much better suited by 7f than shorter. *A. Bailey.*

BOMBER BILL 3 b. or br.g. Mansingh (USA) 120–Marchuna 96 (March Past **—** 124) [1988 NR 1989 6f] angular gelding: fifth living foal: half-brother to a winner in Belgium: dam, half-sister to good miler General Vole, won 5 times at up to 1m: 33/1, moved badly down and struggling by halfway in apprentice maiden at Pontefract in June. *J. W. Payne.*

BOMMING AROUND (FR) 5 b.g. Maelstrom Lake 118–Like A Dream **§§** (Young Emperor 133) [1988 11s 8d 7.6f⁵ 8.5g 10m 8d 8f 1989 7g 8m] rangy gelding: ungenuine maiden, one to leave well alone. *M. J. Fetherston-Godley.*

BONDAID 5 b.g. Main Reef 126–Regency Gold (Prince Regent (FR) 129) [1988 **—** NR 1989 10.1m⁵ 8m] sturdy gelding: has been hobdayed: moderate mover: poor maiden. *J. White.*

BONDSTONE 2 b.c. (Feb 16) Miller's Mate 116–Doumayna 79 (Kouban (FR)) **92** [1989 7s* 8.2g2] small, close-coupled colt: second foal: dam, 2m winner, is half-sister to Darshaan and Darara: won maiden at Goodwood in September by neck from Burford: beaten a head by Elmuraqash in minor event at Nottingham following month, making most and rallying really well under strong handling: will stay well. *H. R. A. Cecil.*

BONITA KATHRYNIA 4 b.f. Starch Reduced 112–Kathanco (Panco 91) [1988 **—** NR 1989 12.5g] lengthy filly: second living foal: dam soundly beaten all starts: 25/1, backward and edgy, tailed off from halfway in claiming event at Wolverhampton in May. *B. Preece.*

BONNIE BONNIE 3 b.f. Lomond (USA) 128–Believer 112 (Blakeney 126) [1988 **—** 7g 1989 12f6] lengthy filly: moderate walker and mover: 16/1, about 12 lengths sixth of 12 to Castle Peak in maiden at Thirsk in May, held up, green on turn and running on steadily not knocked about: gave trouble at and in stalls and withdrawn following month. *A. C. Stewart.*

BONNY ROSA 2 b.f. (Apr 7) Dunbeath (USA) 127–Emmuska (USA) 68 (Roberto **—** (USA) 131) [1989 8m] tall, leggy, sparely-made filly: third foal: half-sister to a winner in Spain: dam, suited by 1½m, is daughter of May Hill and Galtres Stakes winner Tartan Pimpernel, a sister to Dunfermline: 16/1, never a factor in 29-runner maiden at Newmarket in October. *G. A. Huffer.*

BONPHARD (USA) 3 ch.f. Lyphard (USA) 132–Little Bonny 126 (Bonne Noel **—** 115) [1988 6g 6g 8m 8g6 1989 10m⁵ 13.1h⁶] leggy, close-coupled, rather plain filly: quite modest maiden in 1988: showed little, including in handicap (sweating), in May as 3-y-o: stays 1m: sometimes on toes. *J. L. Dunlop.*

BON RETOUR 4 ch.f. Sallust 134–Marphousha (FR) (Shirley Heights 130) [1988 **—** 10v 12g 9d 14s⁶ 12v 1989 12g] ex-Irish filly: first foal: dam placed at 1½m at 3 yrs in Ireland: made all in maiden at Thurles as 2-y-o: no subsequent form in varied events: blinkered last 2 outings at 3 yrs. *J. P. Hudson.*

BOOBY PRIZE 3 ch.f. Bustino 136–Killarney Belle (USA) (Irish Castle (USA)) **60** [1988 6s 8m 1989 8g* 10f* 10h⁴ 10g] small, close-coupled filly: won claimer (claimed out at H. Thomson Jones's stable £8,525) at Salisbury and strongly-run handicap at Folkestone in May: no form after: may stay 1½m: acts on firm going: apprentice ridden second and third outings: sold 2,700 gns Newmarket Autumn Sales. *G. Lewis.*

BOO HOO 3 br.f. Mummy's Pet 125–Boo 77 (Bustino 136) [1988 7s³ 8.2s³ 1989 **—** 8d 10m 12g4 16.2d 12s] lengthy, rather shallow-girthed filly: quite modest maiden: fair fourth of 18, leading 1¼m, in handicap at Hamilton in September: little other form as 3-y-o: worth another try over 1¼m: acts on soft going. *C. W. Thornton.*

BOOK THE BAND 2 ch.c. (Mar 2) Be My Guest (USA) 126–Love Land (FR) **106** (Kautokeino (FR)) [1989 6m² 6f* 6m² 7g³ 7g4] 27,000F, IR 66,000Y: strong, good-bodied, angular colt: has scope: half-brother to 3-y-o 1m to 11f winner Tenter Close (by Gorytus) and 2 winners in France, including 10.5f winner Loving Hand (by High Top): dam once-raced half-sister to Crystal Palace: useful colt: easy winner of maiden at Goodwood in July: in frame afterwards in Scottish Equitable Gimcrack

Kennet Valley Thoroughbreds Ltd's "Book The Band"

Stakes at York, GPA National Stakes at the Curragh and Cartier Million at Phoenix Park: will stay 1m. *R. W. Armstrong.*

BOOT-ON   2 b.f. (Jun 1) Welsh Captain 113–Deise Girl (Stranger) [1989 5d 5v] tall, close-coupled filly: poor walker and mover: third reported foal: half-sister to temperamental 3-y-o Berkley Express (by The Brianstan): dam ran once in Irish bumper: backward, behind in maiden at Newbury and seller at Ayr (in need of race) 6 months later: trained on debut by J. O'Shea. *B. A. McMahon.*   —

BOOT POLISH   7 gr.g. Godswalk (USA) 130–Flirting Countess 75 (Ridan (USA)) [1988 7m 7f⁵ 8f* 8h³ 8m 8d 8f⁴ 7m 1989 8s 10.2g 8f* 8f⁵ 8.2g* 8m] compact, workmanlike gelding: fair handicapper: won at Redcar in May and Haydock in August: fractured his pelvis at Ripon later in August and had to be put down: suited by 1m: acted on any going: ran poorly in blinkers. *J. W. Watts.*   83

BOOTSCRAPER   2 ch.g. (Apr 7) Doc Marten 104–Impish Ears 65 (Import 127) [1989 5g 6g 8f 8.2s⁵ 9g⁵ 8g] 5,200Y: good-bodied gelding: has scope: fourth foal: half-brother to temperamental 1987 2-y-o sprint plater Bashibazouk (by Mansingh): dam stayed 7f: poor form in varied events: best efforts fourth and fifth (sweating) starts: stays 9f: acts on soft going: sold 1,550 gns Doncaster November Sales. *C. Tinkler.*   47

BOOZY   2 b.f. (Feb 24) Absalom 128–The High Dancer (High Line 125) [1989 5g² 5d⁵ 5f⁵ 5m* 6g 5f³ 5g4] deep-girthed, workmanlike, angular filly: progressed well physically: has a fluent action: second foal: dam poor maiden: fair performer: made all in maiden (hung badly left) at Wolverhampton in May and quite well-contested minor event at Epsom following month: ran creditably in Molecomb Stakes at   87

136

Goodwood and listed event at Newbury final 2 starts: speedy, and suited by fast conditions at 5f. *J. Berry*.

BORN TO SWING (USA)   2 b.c. (Jan 26) Robellino (USA) 127–Fancy Walk 89   84
(Tower Walk 130) [1989 5s³ 6f⁴ 5f* 5g² 5m² 6f* 5m⁶ 6f⁴ 6g] compact colt: keen walker: moderate mover: first foal: dam 6f winner promised to stay 1m: fair performer: successful in maiden at Doncaster in June and minor event at Lingfield in August: below form final start: suited by 6f: bandaged behind fourth start: usually on toes, very much so on seventh outing: sold 25,000 gns Newmarket Autumn Sales. *Mrs L. Piggott*.

BORN WITH A VEIL   3 b.g. Thatching 131–Star Harbour 76 (St Paddy 133)   —
[1988 NR 1989 5m 7f⁴ 9f⁶ a7g a8g] IR 9,400Y: leggy gelding: sixth foal: dam won over 1m at 3 yrs: fourth in maiden at Lingfield in October: faced stiff tasks in minor event and handicaps after: should stay 1m. *D. Haydn Jones*.

BORROMINI   3 b.c. Henbit (USA) 130–Good To Follow 82 (Wollow 132) **124**
[1988 8d² 1989 10.5g* 10g³ 11g² 13.5s*]

At a time when Derby winner Henbit has been 'relegated' to the role of dual-purpose stallion in Ireland he has come up with several significant money-earners on the flat abroad, notably the Grand Prix de Deauville Lancel winner Borromini who, until he had a set-back, was Pat Eddery's intended Prix de l'Arc de Triomphe mount. Borromini remains in training apparently, and could develop into a good middle-distance stayer. The form of the Grand Prix is some way below Arc standard. The winner received 3 lb from the two-and-a-half-length second Norberto and 12 lb, roughly weight-for-age, from the five-length third, the British four-year-old Apache; the hot favourite Top Sunrise ran no race at all. Apache took the field of seven along at an ordinary pace in the soft going. Norberto went on two furlongs out after mounting a challenge early in the straight but soon gave way to Borromini who was well in command at the end. This represents Borromini's best form. He'd been improving through a light season prior to then, following up a win in a minor race at Evry on his reappearance with two places in better company at

Grand Prix de Deauville Lancel—Borromini wins from the blinkered Norberto

137

Longchamp, only just beaten by Louis Cyphre in a listed race in June on the second occasion.

		Hawaii	Utrillo II
	Henbit (USA)	(b 1964)	Ethane
	(b 1977)	Chateaucreek	Chateaugay
Borromini		(ch 1970)	Mooncreek
(b.c. 1986)		Wollow	Wolver Hollow
	Good To Follow	(b 1973)	Wichuraiana
	(b 1979)	Pavello	Crepello
		(ch 1972)	Piave

Borromini cost 17,500 guineas as a yearling, almost double Henbit's average in 1987. The distaff side of the family is a highly respectable one. His great-grandam was a winning half-sister to the Oaks winner Pia and produced five winners, notably the smart middle-distance horse Rymer. The grandam Pavello produced five also, including the good sprinter Sayyaf and Good To Follow, successful over seven furlongs. Good To Follow produced two foals before Borromini, the poor maiden Indiraji (by Indian King) and the middle-distance handicapper Vintage (by Noalcoholic) who enjoyed such a fine season in Britain in 1989. *A. Fabre, France.*

BORUFUS 3 b.g. Sunley Builds 102–Song of Pride (Goldhills Pride 105) [1988 7d 32 7g 7s 8m 1989 7g 7g 6m⁴ 6f 6m 6m] sparely-made gelding: poor maiden: worth a try over 5f: blinkered third outing (ran well) and final one at 2 yrs: visored and sweating last 3: wore crossed noseband last 5 outings. *R. Thompson.*

BOSTON BILL 2 ro.g. (Apr 14) Magic Mirror 105–Barrow Girl (Dike (USA)) 63 [1989 5f 6f 5m⁵ 6m 5m] 1,500F, 5,600Y: light-framed gelding: fourth foal: dam unraced: plating-class maiden: best effort on debut: ran badly final start: blinkered second outing: has worn bandages behind: sold to join B. Millman 2,400 gns Doncaster November Sales. *J. Hetherton.*

BOSTON TWO STEP (USA) 2 b.c. (Apr 7) Green Dancer (USA) 132–Baby 107 Louise (USA) (Exclusive Native (USA)) [1989 7.5d² 8g* 8g⁵] $245,000Y: half-brother to numerous winners, notably smart 1981 American 2-y-o Proud Lou (by Proud Clarion): dam minor sprint stakes winner at 2 yrs: useful colt: won minor event at Longchamp in September: under 4 lengths fifth to Funambule in Prix des Chenes at Saint-Cloud in October: stays 1m. *A. Fabre, France.*

BOTTLES (USA) 2 b.c. (Mar 29) North Pole (CAN) 96–Fooling Around — (Jaazeiro (USA) 127) [1989 7g] IR 8,500Y: useful-looking colt: third foal: dam, lightly raced in France, is half-sister to useful Irish 5f and 6f winner Late Sally: sire fairly useful Irish 7f and 1m winner later stakes placed in USA: 33/1, prominent to halfway in 29-runner maiden at Newmarket in November. *G. A. Huffer.*

BOUGAINVILLEA 2 ch.f. (Mar 11) Longleat (USA) 109–Diamante 83 (Sparkler — 130) [1989 5f] 4,000Y, 6,000 2-y-o: fourth foal: half-sister to a winner in Denmark: dam 2-y-o 7f seller winner: 4/1, around 6 lengths seventh of 14 in seller at Doncaster in May. *R. O'Leary.*

BOULES 3 gr.g. Petong 126–Placid Pet 65 (Mummy's Pet 125) [1988 6s⁵ 6d* 75 1989 6.5s² 7.5g 7s 6s*] strong, compact gelding: 9/4 from 5/4, won minor event at Hamilton in September, idling and leading well inside final 1f: visored, last in handicap previous outing nearly 5 months earlier and subsequently gelded: stays 6f well: acts on soft going: sold to join G. Cottrell 10,500 gns Newmarket Autumn Sales. *W. Hastings-Bass.*

Prix Jean de Chaudenay, Saint-Cloud—Boyatino is clear of Robore and Athyka

BOULEVARD GIRL 4 b.f. Nicholas Bill 125–Gay Stampede (Lord Gayle (USA) —
124) [1988 10g^5 12f 12.3s^4 14f 13s^6 14s* 14f* 13.3s^4 16m 1989 14g 14f^6 14g 14f 14m
16.2d] leggy filly: poor mover: modest winner as 3-y-o: no worthwhile form in 1989:
suited by 1¾m: acts on any going: occasionally sweats. *C. B. B. Booth.*

BOUNDER ROWE 2 b.g. (May 23) Henbit (USA) 130–Arita (FR) (Kronzeuge) 63
[1989 7g 7m 6f] quite attractive gelding: shows a quick, moderate action: second
foal: half-brother to 3-y-o Aribie (by Konigsstuhl), 1m winner at 2 yrs: dam, French
bred, has been in Germany: quite modest form at best in varied events: will stay
1¼m. *N. A. Callaghan.*

BOURBON ROSE 3 b.f. Ile de Bourbon (USA) 133–Tantot 65 (Charlottown — p
127) [1988 NR 1989 8s] fourth reported foal: half-sister to fair 1984 2-y-o 6f winner
Kentucky Quest (by Darby Creek Road): dam stayed 1½m and is half-sister to 2000
Guineas winner Mon Fils and very smart Son of Silver: 16/1, 10¾ lengths seventh of
14 to Double Entendre in maiden at Goodwood in September: should stay further
and improve: has joined P. Leach. *L. G. Cottrell.*

BOURBON TOPSY 4 b.f. Ile de Bourbon (USA) 133–Topsy 124 (Habitat 134) —
[1988 7d 10.5g^2 11.5m* 12.2f^2 12g^3 11.5m^5 14.6f^6 15s* 14f* 16g* 1989 16f] tall,
rather sparely-made filly: useful winner as 3-y-o, including of listed event at
Newmarket: sweating slightly, tailed-off last of 8 in Mappin & Webb Henry II EBF
Stakes at Sandown in May, only outing in 1989: stayed 2m: acted on any going: stud.
G. Wragg.

BOURBONVILLE (DEN) 2 b.f. (May 16) Ile de Bourbon (USA) 133–Indoor 64 p
Games (Habitat 134) [1989 7g] IR 26,000Y: leggy, unfurnished filly: seventh foal:
half-sister to modest 7f and 1m winner Grundy's Flame (by Grundy): dam unraced
half-sister to St Leger and Irish Sweeps Derby second Meadowville: 50/1, around 10
lengths ninth of 24, always about same place, to Sardegna in maiden at Newmarket
in November: should improve. *R. Guest.*

BOURNVILLE 3 b.f. Lochnager 132–Channing Girl 73 (Song 132) [1988 6m^6 86
1989 6s^4 7f 7m* 7g^4 7g^5 7g^3 7m^5] big, good-bodied filly: has plenty of scope: fair
handicapper: won £11,600 event at Newmarket in July: best efforts at Doncaster and
Newmarket last 2 outings: will stay 1m: acts on top-of-the-ground. *D. W. P.
Arbuthnot.*

BOUTAYNA (MOR) 3 ch.f. Happy Lord (FR)–Parmioca (MOR) (Parmel) [1988 —
NR 1989 10.2f 8m] half-sister to 2 winners in Morocco: dam won 6 times in Morocco:
sire French 1m and 9f winner, later successful at up to 1½m in Morocco: always
behind in maidens at Bath and Sandown in July: sold 920 gns Doncaster August
Sales. *G. Lewis.*

BOWMONT SWEETIE 3 b.g. Sweet Monday 122–Streets Ahead 67 (Ovid 95) —
[1988 6g 6s 1989 12m] leggy non-thoroughbred gelding: no sign of ability, including
in seller: sold 600 gns Ascot October Sales. *Capt. J. Wilson.*

BOX STAR 3 gr.g. Comedy Star (USA) 121–Starky's Pet (Mummy's Pet 125) —
[1988 6m 7m^6 7.5m^3 7g 1989 8g] big, useful-looking gelding: quite modest maiden:
carried head high and looked unenthusiastic third start at 2 yrs: tailed off in
Brighton handicap in April, only outing in 1989: should stay 1m: not discredited in
blinkers final start at 2 yrs: one to treat with caution. *A. C. Stewart.*

BOYATINO (FR) 5 b.h. Concertino (FR) 123–Boyarina (FR) (Beaugency (FR) 124
126) [1988 10v* 10v^6 12d^2 12m* 12s^5 10m^5 12v^3 12m^3 1989 12d^2 10.5s^5 12m* 12g^3]
French horse: 138/1, well ridden and showed much improved form when over length
third to Tony Bin in Ciga Prix de l'Arc de Triomphe at Longchamp on final outing
(fractured near-fore) as 4-y-o: ran well again in first half of 1989, winning Prix Jean
de Chaudenay at Saint-Cloud by 2 lengths and 1½ lengths from Robore and Athyka:
close third of 6, staying on strongly, to Sheriff's Star in Grand Prix de Saint-Cloud:
suited by 1½m: won on heavy going, but best form on a sound surface: genuine:
finished lame at Saint-Cloud, and retired to stud. *J. Lesbordes, France.*

BOY EMPEROR 2 ch.c. (Mar 12) Precocious 126–Much Too Risky 87 (Bustino 60 p
136) [1989 7g 8g4] tall, leggy, sparely-made colt: has a quick action: first foal: dam,
7.2f and 1m winner at 2 yrs, is daughter of half-sister to very smart animals He
Loves Me and Wattlefield, and closely related to smart Common Land: around 10
lengths fourth of 16, one pace final 2f not knocked about, to My Lord in maiden at
Leicester in November: slowly away and green on debut: gives impression probably
capable of better. *M. R. Stoute.*

BOY JAMIE 5 ch.g. Nicholas Bill 125–Petard 112 (Mummy's Pet 125) [1988 9d^4 46
9g^2 10m^5 10m^3 10s 8.2d 1989 12d 14m 12g^5 12g^3 10m 10f^5 8.5f 10.6m] big, plain
gelding: has a rather round action: plating-class performer nowadays: suited by

about 1¼m: has won on top-of-the-ground, but well suited by an easy surface nowadays: blinkered last 5 starts: has won for apprentice: sometimes bandaged: inconsistent. *J. W. Payne.*

BOY SANDFORD 10 br.g. Sandford Lad 133–Perldia (FR) (Diatome 132) [1988 10g 8m 8.5g 7.6s³ 8g* 9g 10.4d 1989 10.4m] compact gelding: poor handicapper: stays 11f: acts on any going: has won for apprentice: bandaged only outing at 10 yrs: has worn a tongue strap: sold 700 gns Ascot October Sales. *P. J. Bevan.* —

BRAASHEE 3 b.c. Sadler's Wells (USA) 132–Krakow 85 (Malinowski (USA) 123) [1988 NR 1989 9g 10.1m² 12f² 10.1d* 13.3m* 12m* 10g] 170,000Y: good-topped colt: has plenty of scope: second foal: half-brother to Nell Gwyn Stakes winner Ghariba (by Final Straw): dam, from good family, won twice over 7f: progressed well in the autumn, winning minor event (odds on) at Windsor, £20,400 'Coral' Autumn Cup (Handicap) at Newbury and £71,300 Tote Festival Handicap (running on strongly from off pace to beat Free Sweater 1½ lengths) at Ascot: 13/2, not discredited in Champion Stakes at Newmarket final start, chasing leader 7f: probably best at around 1½m: acts on top-of-the-ground and a soft surface: goes well with waiting tactics: smart. *A. C. Stewart.* 115

BRABAZON (USA) 4 b.g. Cresta Rider (USA) 124–Brilliant Touch (USA) (Gleaming (USA)) [1988 12s⁴ 12g³ 12g⁴ 10g⁴ 12s⁴ 12g* 12m 10.5s³ 1989 11.7m⁶ 18f⁴ 19g⁶] leggy, close-coupled ex-French gelding: poor walker and mover: half-brother to useful French middle-distance stayer Gleam Out (by Full Out): dam once-raced half-sister to dam of high-class filly Love Sign: trained by A. Fabre, won 60,000-franc event at Vichy as 3-y-o: beaten at least 12 lengths in minor events and £7,000 race in 1989: never placed to challenge nor knocked about first 2 outings: possibly doesn't stay extreme distances: acts on soft going: blinkered once at 3 yrs: should do better in handicaps. *M. H. Tompkins.* —

BRACKEN BAY 2 ro.f. (Jan 14) All Systems Go 119–War Bird (Warpath 113) [1989 7g⁶] sturdy filly: fifth foal: half-sister to poor staying maiden Silver Sleek (by Royal Palace): dam never ran: 25/1, around 7½ lengths sixth of 14, eye-catching late headway not knocked about, to Hot Performer in seller at Catterick in August: may improve. *R. M. Whitaker.* — p

BRACKEN BELLA 2 br.f. (May 10) Gorytus (USA) 132–Habella 82 (Habitat 134) [1989 5d 6f⁵ 5m⁶ 7f³ 7g⁶ 7f⁶] 5,200Y: fourth living foal: half-sister to 1m winner Shirbella (by Shirley Heights): dam ran only at 3 yrs when winner at 6f and 7f: plating-class maiden: suited by 7f. *E. Weymes.* 57

BRADMORE'S CLASSIC 2 ch.c. (Mar 2) Jalmood (USA) 126–Water Pageant 58 (Welsh Pageant 132) [1989 6f 6f 6f⁵ 6f 6m³ 8g 6f⁶ 7d³] 19,000Y: chunky, workmanlike colt: half-brother to 4 winners here and abroad, including middle-distance stayer Sanchi Steeple (by Niniski): dam middle-distance maiden: fair plater: bred to stay 1m: highly-strung and races freely: blinkered last 4 starts. *G. Lewis.* 50

Tote Festival Handicap, Ascot—the most valuable handicap in Britain is won by Braashee; Free Sweater (rails) and Run Don't Fly come next

Maktoum Al-Maktoum's "Braashee"

BRAISWICK   3 b.f. King of Spain 121–Laughing Girl 110 (Sassafras (FR) **120** 135) [1988 6g³ 1989 8s* 11.3m* 12f⁵ 12g⁴ 10.6g* 10g* 10s*]
    Horama updated. News of the imminent sale to leading owner Sheikh Mohammed of the White Lodge Stud and its bloodstock, including descendants of the mare Horama, coincided with one of the best recent performances on the racecourse by a White Lodge representative, Braiswick's win in the Sun Chariot Stakes at Newmarket in October. Two weeks later Braiswick followed up in the new colours in the E P Taylor Stakes at Woodbine, Toronto. There were few more desirable collections of broodmares in Europe not in Middle-East ownership than the one built up over forty years by the late Moller brothers at White Lodge. How desirable can be seen by reference to entries in past *Racehorses* on the numerous animals to have earned essays, working back from Percy's Lass, Most Welcome and Ashayer, to Old Country, Teenoso, Give Thanks and so on. Here briefly, so not to read too much like the Book of Genesis, is where Braiswick fits in: she's a half-sister to the good-class though somewhat untrustworthy middle-distance filly Percy's Lass and is the fourth winner from eight foals of racing age out of the Oaks fourth Laughing Girl, herself one of Cambridgeshire Handicap dead-heater Violetta III's ten winners. Also in Violetta's ten were the Irish One Thousand Guineas winner Favoletta, the Oaks second Furioso (Teenoso's dam) and the Sun Chariot third Parthica (Give Thanks's dam). Violetta's dam was Urshalim, daughter of Horama.
    The choice of King of Spain as a mate for Laughing Girl seems an odd one: she, like the rest of the mares in the Stud, is usually covered by an established stallion with top-class form over a mile or more. Percy's Lass is by

141

*Cheshire Oaks, Chester—Braiswick steps up in distance
and wins with authority from By Charter*

Blakeney; the dam's other middle-distance winner No No Girl is by Nonoalco;
her other winner, the free-running seven-furlong colt Happy House, is by
Habitat. However, a share in King of Spain was purchased when it was
decided the need had arisen to make more use of stallions likely to transmit
speed; he'd been used on three other mares without much success before
Laughing Girl. The season hadn't long begun before it became apparent that
for stamina Braiswick was going to take after her dam. She set off at a mile in
the incongruously-named 'Back A Winner By Train' Classic Trial at Thirsk in
April, and showed right away that a further step up in distance would suit her,
in gamely coming from behind to catch Terimon on the line. Because she's by
a sprinter Braiswick hadn't been entered for the Oaks, but probably that was
no great omission, for her form fell short of the top until the autumn and she
was beaten in the Ribblesdale Stakes and the Lancashire Oaks after her
decisive win from By Charter in the Cheshire Oaks had confirmed she stayed
quite well. Braiswick finished fifth at Royal Ascot and fourth at Haydock; she
might have gone closer in the former had she not been slightly hampered but
in both she seemed just to lack the pace of the opposition. There was no lack
of pace about her when brought back to ten and a half furlongs in the
Burtonwood Brewery Rose of Lancaster Stakes at Haydock in August. The
withdrawal of Two Timing and Pirate Army from the race left only five
runners, and they went a moderate gallop. Braiswick lay prominent from the
start. Having taken over in front from the long-time leader Organza around
three furlongs out, she responded to a sustained challenge from Pelorus and
held him by a head.

Despite the probability that the odds-on favourite for the Rose of
Lancaster, Batshoof, hadn't run up to his best, Braiswick's performance still
strongly suggested improvement. She wasn't seen out again until the
Cheveley Park Stud Sun Chariot Stakes nine weeks later, when she stood out
a mile in the paddock in a field of nine, mostly wintry-looking, three-year-old
fillies. What seemed an open, substandard event beforehand turned into a
procession. Braiswick went past the favourite Mamaluna at least as far out as
she'd taken it up from Organza at Haydock, and this time began to draw clear
at once. On top two out she stayed on strongly, kept up to her work, to win by

142

Cheveley Park Stud Sun Chariot Stakes, Newmarket—
Braiswick is the last big-race winner in the colours of White Lodge Stud

seven lengths from Life At The Top who never showed with a chance. Pass The Peace finished a clear third on her first outing since the French Oaks. The reader won't be in the least surprised to learn that Braiswick isn't the first of Horama's stock to win the Sun Chariot: in 1979 Topsy, first foal of Furioso, coasted in by four lengths. The Sun Chariot is much less likely now than in Topsy's day to mark the end of the campaign for any of its contestants still in form; there are plenty of big races left, particularly with today's ease of travel. And the E P Taylor Stakes, run over a mile and a quarter on turf, is well worth going for. It has fallen to a European challenger every year since 1983. The British-trained Ivor's Image won in 1986, Sudden Love in 1988 (with Braiswick's stable-companion Inchmurrin fourth); in between, Infamy finished third after running second in the Sun Chariot. In the last two years the race has been upgraded to Grade 1 and the latest renewal carried a first prize roughly equivalent to £112,000, prizes down as far as fifth. Braiswick had seven opponents, none apparently in Infamy's class or Sudden Love's; the previous season's third Arcroyal took her chance again and there was the customary challenge from France, on this occasion Athyka. Arcroyal came third again but was beaten easily by Braiswick who recovered well enough from a slowish start to allow her jockey to ride a similar race to that at Newmarket and Haydock. Braiswick won readily, by a length and a quarter from the Irish-bred three-year-old Rasant; Athyka finished last, clearly well below her best.

		Philip of Spain	Tudor Melody
	King of Spain	(b 1969)	Lerida
	(br 1976)	Sovereign Sails	Sovereign Path
Braiswick		(b 1962)	Red Sails
(b.f. 1986)		Sassafras	Sheshoon
	Laughing Girl	(b 1967)	Ruta
	(b 1973)	Violetta III	Pinza
		(b 1958)	Urshalim

So Braiswick ended her first full season on the crest of a wave. There is much to be said for keeping her in training—she's such a progressive and genuine sort that she'll surely be more successful than Percy's Lass was as a four-year-old. Alas, if she is she won't boost King of Spain's career any more—he had to be put down in November after suffering a heart attack. Braiswick, a lengthy, quite good-bodied filly with a sharp action, acts on any going. *G. Wragg.*

BRAMBER 3 b.f. Castle Keep 121–Hartnell Dream (Grundy 137) [1988 7m³ 7g⁵ 6m³ 6m⁶ 1989 7s 10f⁶ 7f³ 10g a7g⁵] workmanlike, good-quartered filly: quite modest maiden: seems suited by 7f or 1m, though bred to stay further: bought out of J. Dunlop's stable after fourth start 4,400 gns Newmarket July Sales. *M. C. Pipe.*   **60**

BRAMDEAN 3 b.f. Niniski (USA) 125–Elizabethan 89 (Tudor Melody 129) [1988 7m 1989 12g³ 12.5f⁵ 10f 12g⁴ 10m⁴ 10v a10g³ a11g⁵] useful-looking filly: has scope: has a quick action: modest maiden: should stay 1¾m: appears unsuited by extremes of going: weakened quickly 4 out when running badly third and sixth outings, in latter giving impression possibly temperamentally unsatisfactory: sold 21,000 gns Newmarket December Sales. *P. T. Walwyn.*   **68**

BRAMLEY BOY 3 ch.c. Burslem 123–Louisa Jane (Never Return (USA) 121) [1988 NR 1989 11f 13.3m 11.5g² 10m²] IR 4,200F, 15,000Y: workmanlike colt: second foal: dam won from 1m to 9.5f in Ireland: easily best efforts but ran in snatches when second in claimers at Sandown: hung right 2f out, later claimed £20,000, on final start (July): stays 11.5f: not an easy ride and worth a try in blinkers. *G. Harwood.*   **76**

BRANSTOWN SUNSET 5 b.g. Red Sunset 120–Lydja 75 (Hethersett 134) [1988 13.5g 1989 10g 10f] poor form in varied company, including selling: refused to race in amateurs event at Dundalk, only outing on flat at 4 yrs: winning selling hurdler. *P. Butler.*   **—**

BRASSY NELL 3 b.f. Dunbeath (USA) 127–Raashideah 88 (Dancer's Image (USA)) [1988 6m⁵ 6f² 6g 6f³ 6f² 7s⁴ 7f⁵ 6d 1989 7f 6h 6f² 7h⁵ 5m 7.6m² 7.6m* 6f 6g] compact filly: moderate mover: favourite, made all in seller (bought in 6,200 gns) at Lingfield in September: ran creditably at Chester previous start: stays 7.6f: probably acts on any going: below form when sweating and edgy, also when blinkered then visored fourth and fifth starts. *R. Hannon.*   **55**

BRAVE HEROINE 3 ch.f. Sandhurst Prince 128–Natasha 87 (Native Prince) [1988 5f 6f 1989 7d 7g 5g 7.5d 5f³ 5.8h 6m] good-quartered, workmanlike filly: 33/1, running-on third in seller at Chepstow in May, only worthwhile form: blinkered first 2 and last 3 outings: bandaged near-hind on sixth: hung throughout on reappearance: sold 840 gns Newmarket July Sales. *F. Durr.*   **42**

BRAVE MELODY 3 b.c. Heroic Air 96–Kaymay 76 (Maystreak 118) [1988 5g 5f 5g⁴ 6m 7f⁴ 7g⁵ 7f 5g* 5g⁴ 5m⁶ 1989 6m 6h³ 6f⁴ 5m 5m⁵ 5m² 5f⁵ 5f 6g 6s] compact colt: quite modest handicapper: saddle slipped and rider unseated when leading inside final 1f at Edinburgh on fourth start: easily best efforts after at same course and Chester next 2 outings: best at 5f: acts on hard going: inconsistent. *Capt. J. Wilson.*   **55**

BRAVE MUSCATEER 2 ch.g. (Feb 14) Muscatite 122–Amazing Gretts (Pitskelly 122) [1989 6h⁶ 6g⁶ 5f³ 5f³ 6v 5g] 14,500Y: strong, quite good-topped gelding: half-brother to leading Irish 1986/7 juvenile hurdler Full Flow (by Viking) and a winner in Hong Kong: dam little worthwhile form: quite modest maiden: ran badly (last of 23) final start: subsequently gelded: likely to prove better suited by 6f than 5f: blinkered fourth outing: of doubtful temperament. *J. Etherington.*   **65**

BRAVO STAR (USA) 4 b.g. The Minstrel (CAN) 135–Stellarette (CAN) (Tentam (USA)) [1988 12s³ 10d⁴ 10m 10.1d⁶ 11.7m 11.5d³ 12m³ 12g⁴ 12g 12g² 11d⁶ 12f⁶ 14m 12m 12f² 1989 12m 14f 12f] sturdy, close-coupled gelding: quite modest maiden as 3-y-o: well beaten in handicaps in 1989: moved down moderately, tailed off final outing: suited by 1½m: acts on firm going and a soft surface: blinkered 3 times, including final start: usually takes plenty of driving: inconsistent. *P. Mitchell.*   **—**

BRAZILIAN BOY (FR) 4 b.g. Formidable (USA) 125–Longest Day (FR) (Lyphard (USA) 132) [1988 NR 1989 10.1m 10.1g 11.7m a8g a14g] stocky, heavy-bodied gelding: moderate mover: fourth foal: half-brother to modest 7f winner Artful Day (by Artaius): dam French 1½m winner: of little account: blinkered fourth outing: sold 600 gns Ascot December Sales. *M. McCourt.*   **—**

BREAK LOOSE 3 ch.f. Krayyan 117–Free Course 80 (Sandford Lad 133) [1988 6s 6m 6f 5m⁶ 6g* 6s 1989 5s 5d⁶ 6f 7g 6m 7g 7g³ 8.2f 6g] lengthy filly: moderate mover: won seller as 2-y-o: little form in 1989, leading 6f when third in claimer at Edinburgh: probably stays 7f: possibly unsuited by soft going: blinkered last 6 starts except sixth when visored: sold 2,400 gns Newmarket Autumn Sales. *M. W. Easterby.*   **46**

BREAKOUT 5 ch.g. High Line 125–Wolverhants 79 (Wolver Hollow 126) [1988 **50**
15.5m* 14d² 17.1g² 16m⁴ 20f 1989 a14g³ a14g⁴ a14g] leggy, lightly-made gelding:
has a fluent, rather round action: fair winner early as 4-y-o: well below his best in
claimer and handicaps at Southwell in 1989: stays 17f: acts on firm going and a soft
surface: has won for amateur: used to go well with forcing tactics: wears bandages.
J. L. Harris.

BREAK THE DUCK 3 b.f. Absalom 128–Bally Tudor 75 (Henry The Seventh —
125) [1988 6f 6m 7f 1989 8s] workmanlike, plain filly: has a round action: little
worthwhile form, including in sellers: has joined Miss G. Rees. *J. Balding.*

BREAK THE MOULD 3 b.g. Burslem 123–Genzyme Gene 38 (Riboboy (USA) —
124) [1988 5g 6m⁵ 6m⁵ 7f⁵ 6f² 1989 10s 8f⁶ 10f 7h 10.8f⁶ 7g 9f 10f⁶ 12g⁶] small,
close-coupled gelding: plater: stays 1½m: acts on firm ground: blinkered second
outing at 2 yrs: visored fourth start at 2 yrs until fifth as 3-y-o: often apprentice
ridden but is suited by strong handling: often sweating: trained first 5 outings by W.
Wilson. *P. J. Feilden.*

BRECKENBROUGH LAD 2 b.c. (Mar 12) Uncle Pokey 116–Fabulous Beauty —
91 (Royal Avenue 123) [1989 6m] leggy, useful-looking colt: fourth reported foal:
brother to modest middle-distance handicapper Uncle Wilko: dam genuine 5f
winner at 2 yrs and 3 yrs: 33/1 and backward, always behind in 10-runner maiden at
York in October. *T. D. Barron.*

BREEZED WELL 3 b.c. Wolverlife 115–Precious Baby (African Sky 124) [1988 **96**
5f⁶ 6f³ 5m* 6g* 5f 6g³ 6f⁵ 1989 6m⁴ 7f⁶ 7m³ 6m 6m² 6m⁵ 6f⁶ 6m³ 8d 7g⁵ 7g* 6d
a7g² a8g²] smallish, sparely-made colt: poor mover: fairly useful handicapper:
ridden by 7-lb claimer, quickened in good style to lead close home in minor event at
Leicester in November: good second at Southwell and Lingfield last 2 starts: stays
1m: acts on top-of-the-ground: below form when blinkered seventh start. *C. N.
Allen.*

BREEZY BAY 3 b.f. The Brianstan 128–Watt Bridge (Mandamus 120) [1988 8.2s **44**
7g 7g 1989 8f 9f 8g⁴ 8f³ 10f 10f] medium-sized filly: quite modest plater: in frame at
Pontefract and Newcastle, only worthwhile form: should stay beyond 1m: sweating
and edgy fifth outing. *Miss L. C. Siddall.*

BREEZY DAY 3 ch.f. Day Is Done 115–Bedouin Dancer 79 (Lorenzaccio 130) **85**
[1988 5m 5s⁴ 6f⁴ 1989 6f² 5m² 5g* 7g⁴ 6m⁵] compact filly: fair performer: odds on,
made all in maiden at Beverley in July: best at 5f: acts on top-of-the-ground. *B. A.
McMahon.*

BREEZY MONARCH 2 b.f. (Apr 30) Tender King 123–Airy Queen (USA) — p
(Sadair) [1989 6g] 10,000Y: leggy filly: half-sister to several winners, including fairly
useful 1981 Irish 2-y-o 6f winner Okanango (by Homeric): dam won at 2 yrs and 3 yrs
in Italy: 33/1 and in need of race, ran better than position in rear suggests in
16-runner maiden at Newmarket in October, fading final 2f: should do better. *G. A.
Pritchard-Gordon.*

BREEZY SAILOR 3 ch.g. Tumble Wind (USA)–Bouganville (Gulf Pearl 117) —
[1988 5m 5d 5g⁴ 6f 5m³ 6f 5f 5m 5d 5d 6g⁴ 6m 1989 5d 5f⁴ 6m 5m 6f 5g 6f a6g] robust,
good-quartered gelding: quite modest maiden as 2-y-o: well below form in 1989,
putting up best effort in Newcastle claimer penultimate start: suited by 6f: best form
in blinkers: visored fourth start: not one to trust implicitly. *R. Thompson.*

BREGUET 6 b.m. Rouser 118–Span (Pan II 130) [1988 12g 12d 12s³ 13m⁵ 12f⁴ **29**
16m⁴ 12g² 13g³ 13d⁴ 12m 12f⁴ 16g⁴ 14.6m 1989 12d 12f 12g² 15m³ 12f⁶ 12f⁶ 13s
15.8g⁴ 14g] small mare: poor mover: bad maiden: probably doesn't stay 2m: seems
to act on any going: often bandaged: held up, usually with too much to do. *Don
Enrico Incisa.*

BRIC LANE (USA) 2 br.c. (May 1) Arctic Tern (USA) 126–Spring Is Sprung — p
(USA) (Herbager 136) [1989 8v] $52,000Y: smallish colt: half-brother to 2 winners
in France, including quite useful 7f and 1¼m winner Primevere (by Irish River), and
a minor winner in USA: dam ran once, from good family: 33/1, around 18 lengths
seventh of 23, running on well having been slowly away, to Tyburn Tree in minor
event at Newbury in October: will improve. *C. R. Nelson.*

BRIDAL RUN 3 ch.f. Shy Groom (USA)–Xanthoria (Levmoss 133) [1988 7s³ **60**
1989 7m³ 8.2f²] smallish, lengthy filly: quite modest maiden: 5/1 on and looking very
fit, second of 4 in claiming event at Hamilton in July: stays 1m: appears to act on any
going: sold 4,000 gns Newmarket Autumn Sales. *R. J. R. Williams.*

BRIDAL TOAST 2 b.c. (Apr 12) Rousillon (USA) 133–Romantic Feeling 88 **108**
(Shirley Heights 130) [1989 7m* 8m²] 105,000Y: rangy, good-topped colt: has a
quick action: first foal: dam 1½m winner, is daughter of half-sister to Malinowski

and Gielgud and to El Gran Senor's dam: won minor event at York in September comfortably by 2 lengths from Norwich: much better effort when 3 lengths second of 9 to Digression in Royal Lodge EBF Stakes at Ascot: will probably stay 1¼m. *L. M. Cumani.*

BRIERY FILLE 4 b.f. Sayyaf 121–Zeddera (FR) (Zeddaan 130) [1988 8s⁴ 7g 7m **63** 8.3m⁶ 7m² 8m 7g³ 7g⁶ 7g⁴ 1989 7v 7g 7f 7f⁵ 7m 8.2g 8m⁵ 7m³ 7g³ 7s 7g* 7m 8f* 8.2g⁵ a8g³] lengthy, angular filly: quite modest performer nowadays: ridden by 7-lb claimer, won sellers (bought in 3,800 gns each time) at Catterick in September and Warwick (handicap, gamely by head) in October: effective at 7f and 1m: acts on firm going and probably unsuited by soft: sold 5,400 gns Newmarket Autumn Sales. *R. J. R. Williams.*

BRIGADIER BILL 4 ch.g. Nicholas Bill 125–Sailing Brig (Brigadier Gerard **60** 144) [1988 12f⁴ 9f⁶ 11g³ 10m 10g² 11s⁶ 10m⁴ 1989 9f 10m³ 10f³ 10.2f² 11f 10.6d³] big, angular gelding: quite modest maiden: stays 11f: acts on firm going and a soft surface: has run creditably for apprentice: possibly needs waiting tactics. *Mrs G. R. Reveley.*

BRIGADIERS GLORY 3 ch.f. Castle Keep 121–Join The Club 67 (Dance In — Time (CAN)) [1988 6g 6f 5g 1989 8f 6g] neat filly: poor form at best: bred to stay 1¼m: swerved left leaving stalls final start at 2 yrs: twice on edge: sold 1,100 gns Doncaster October Sales. *B. A. McMahon.*

BRIGARA 2 ch.f. (Apr 18) Aragon 118–Brig of Ayr 90 (Brigadier Gerard 144) — [1989 6g a6g] sixth foal: half-sister to 3-y-o Superlassie (by Superlative) and 4 winners, including fair 5f to 7f winner Fag In Hand (by Music Boy) and 1983 2-y-o 5f winner Pageantic (by Welsh Pageant): dam won from 1m to 11f at 4 yrs: soundly beaten in maidens. *P. Howling.*

BRIGGSCARE 3 b.g. Chief Singer 131–Magonis 74 (Blakeney 126) [1988 6f⁴ 6f⁵ **81** 7g² 7m² 8m* 8g⁵ 10g 1989 8s 10g 10m⁴ 10g⁴ 14f⁴ 14m* 14m* 14m³ 14m⁴ 14g² 16m³] leggy gelding: fair handicapper: ridden by 7-lb claimer M. Tebbutt, won at Yarmouth and Sandown in August: given too much to do in ladies race next start: ran creditably after at Sandown (twice) and Newmarket: stays 2m: acts on top-of-the-ground: carries head high: looked unsatisfactory in blinkers third to fifth outings: well suited by tender handling and waiting tactics. *W. Jarvis.*

BRIGHT AISLE 4 ch.c. Don 128–Church Bay 76 (Reliance II 137) [1988 8v⁴ 8d* — 8m 8f⁵ 10.2f 8d⁵ 8v⁶ 8d 1989 10.2g] sparely-made, rather angular colt: modest handicapper: suited by 1m: best form on an easy surface: none too reliable: dead. *N. Tinkler.*

BRIGHTANDBEAUTIFUL 2 ch.f. (Apr 24) Sallust 134–Shopping (FR) **54** (Sheshoon 132) [1989 8f⁶ 5s⁶] 13,000Y: robust, lengthy filly: has scope: half-sister to several winners in France, including minor 12.2f winner Shopping Center (by Top Ville): dam French 12.5f winner: carrying condition and green, 9 lengths sixth to Hafhafah in maiden at Wolverhampton: again slowly away, outpaced from halfway in 6-runner minor event at Ayr (went keenly down) later in October: likely to prove better suited by 1m than shorter. *C. E. Brittain.*

BRIGHT FAVOR 5 b.m. Sparkler 130–Pink Garter (Henry The Seventh 125) — [1988 NR 1989 10s] leggy, sparely-made mare: has a round action: poor maiden. *A. Moore.*

BRIGHT FLOWER (USA) 2 b.f. (Feb 4) Irish River (FR) 131–Youthful Lady **85** ? (USA) (Youth (USA) 135) [1989 5f³ 6m* 6f* 6m⁴] good-bodied filly: half-sister to 3 winners in USA, including Young Flyer (by Flying Paster), stakes winner at up to 1m: dam once-raced half-sister to 1¼m Grade 1 winner Slew's Exceller: made all in June in maiden at Leicester and minor event at Ripon: odds on, ran as though something badly amiss (running subject of stewards inquiry) when last of 4 in minor event at Pontefract following month and not seen out again: should stay 1m. *L. M. Cumani.*

BRIGHT HOUR 4 ro.g. Kabour 80–Amber Vale 98 (Warpath 113) [1988 NR 1989 — 10.2g 8d 16.2d 12g 12g 12m 14f⁵ 15.8f 8m] lengthy, workmanlike gelding: first foal: dam, half-sister to very useful chaser Amber Rambler, stayed 2m: of no account: blinkered or visored sixth to eighth outings. *D. W. Chapman.*

BRIGHT-ONE 4 b.f. Electric 126–Lady Doubloon (Pieces of Eight 128) [1988 8m **56** 10d² 12d 10.2m⁶ 8s⁴ 8s 1989 10d 8f⁵ 8.5f⁶ 12m 8.5f² 10m 9m⁶] angular filly: plating-class maiden: probably best at around 1m: acts on any going: ran creditably in blinkers on reappearance: sometimes takes keen hold: trained first 2 outings by R. Whitaker: winning hurdler. *J. G. FitzGerald.*

BRIGHT RED 2 ch.c. (May 23) Kris 135–Chiltern Red (Red God 128§) [1989 6g 6d] short-backed colt: eighth foal: half-brother to several winners, including very useful 1981 2-y-o sprinter Travel On (by Tachypous) and 1¼m and 1½m winner Min Baladi (by Welsh Pageant): dam poor sister to Red Alert: burly, well beaten in maidens at Newmarket and Newbury (bandaged near-hind, moved poorly to post) within a week in October. *P. W. Harris.* —

BRIGHT SAPPHIRE 3 b.g. Mummy's Pet 125–Bright Era 79 (Artaius (USA) 129) [1988 6d⁵ 7g³ 1989 7s 8.5g⁵ 7m 8f] small, lightly-made gelding: easily best effort final start at 2 yrs: never placed to challenge or knocked about in seller final one in 1989: should be suited by 1m: blinkered third outing: sold out of J. Hills's stable 1,300 gns Ascot 2nd June Sales afterwards: resold 3,300 gns Ascot December Sales. *D. Burchell.* —

BRIGLEN 4 b.f. Swing Easy (USA) 126–Blou Hemel 47 (Virginia Boy 106) [1988 NR 1989 7.5m 10f] plain, sparely-made filly: poor walker and mover: fifth foal: half-sister to winning plater Maundy Gift (by Goldhills Pride): dam placed on flat and over hurdles: tailed off in maiden at Beverley (slowly away) and seller at Pontefract. *R. Thompson.* —

BRILLIANT BAY 4 b.g. Hello Gorgeous (USA) 128–Cala-Vadella 110 (Mummy's Pet 125) [1988 7f 10g⁴ 1989 7g] big, rangy, workmanlike gelding: extremely lightly raced since winning valuable maiden at York as 2-y-o: in need of race, soundly beaten in Newmarket handicap in October: stays 1¼m. *M. D. I. Usher.* —

BRILLIANT CHANCE 4 b.f. Young Generation 129–Brightelmstone 105 (Prince Regent (FR) 129) [1988 6g⁵ 6m 7m⁶ 6d⁴ 8h⁵ 6m 1989 6m 5f⁴ 6d 6g] rangy filly: good mover: plating-class maiden: stays 7f: acts on firm going and a soft surface: has given trouble at stalls. *J. D. Czerpak.* 54

BRILLIANT TIMING (USA) 2 ro.f. (Apr 28) The Minstrel (CAN) 135–Timely Roman (USA) (Sette Bello (USA)) [1989 6m³] $275,000Y: sister to Irish 1m to 1¼m winner Minstrel's Best and half-sister to several other winners, including Grade 1 performers Timely Assertion (by Assert) and Timely Writer (by Staff Writer): dam, unraced, from family of Indian Skimmer: long odds on but green, slow-starting 3¾ lengths last of 3, unable to quicken last 2f, to Astrid Gilberto in maiden at Yarmouth in June: can improve. *M. R. Stoute.* — p

BRINKSWAY 3 ch.c. Electric 126–Nom de Plume 70 (Aureole 132) [1988 7s⁵ 7g³ 6m⁵ 8.2s⁴ 8.2v 1989 12m] useful-looking colt: quite modest form in varied races: dead. *J. J. O'Neill.* —

BRISAS 2 ch.c. (Mar 17) Vaigly Great 127–Legal Sound 85 (Legal Eagle 126) [1989 5g³ 5v⁶ 5f* 5m² 6m² 5m⁶ 5f4 6m4 5f* 5d* 5m 5m³ 5m³ 6g 6g] 11,500F: strong-quartered, attractive colt: progressed well physically: has a quick action: second foal: half-brother to 3-y-o Reason To Laugh (by Comedy Star): dam 6f winner: fairly useful filly: successful in maiden at Redcar in May and summer nurseries at Thirsk (sweating) and Haydock: very good third, tending to hang, to Rivers Rhapsody in nursery at Newbury on thirteenth outing: suited by 5f: possibly unsuited by heavy ground: blinkered last 3 starts: has a good turn of foot: tends to be on toes nowadays. *T. Fairhurst.* 97

BRITANNIA BELL 4 br.g. Pitskelly 122–Saintly Angel 87 (So Blessed 130) [1988 7d* 8.2v² 8m 8g 8s⁵ 1989 8g 12s⁶ 10d⁶ 8.2g a11g] leggy, sparely-made gelding: moderate mover: fair winner early in 1988: well beaten in handicaps at 4 yrs: stays 1m: requires give in the ground: suitable mount for apprentice: usually races up with pace: changed hands 10,000 gns Doncaster November Sales. *M. Brittain.* —

BRITISH TOMMY 2 b.c. (Apr 1) Petorius 117–Tap Lightly (Tap On Wood 130) [1989 5d] 6,400Y, 8,000 2-y-o: first foal: dam little sign of ability: 14/1, bit backward and bandaged behind, slowly away and soon struggling in 8-runner minor event at Beverley in April. *M. W. Easterby.* —

BRITTLE (USA) 3 ch.f. Diesis 133–Ashbrittle 101 (Great Nephew 126) [1988 6d⁴ 1989 10s³ 12f⁵ 7m] rather unfurnished filly: moderate walker: in frame in £7,100 event at Ascot at 2 yrs and maiden at Sandown: showed little in listed race and minor event and not seen out after June: stays 1¼m: possibly unsuited by top-of-the-ground: sold 8,800 gns Newmarket December Sales. *C. E. Brittain.* 67

BRIZLINCOTE (USA) 4 b.f. Cawston's Clown 113–Teresa Way 66 (Great White Way (USA)) [1988 5f4 7s² 7g* 6g 7g 1989 8m 7m 8.2g 8.2g 6f⁶ 6m 7m 6f4 7g* a7g⁵] leggy, quite attractive filly: moderate mover, with a slightly round action: ran easily her best race of season when winning 26-runner handicap at Redcar in November by 4 85 lengths: suited by 7f: acts on firm going: blinkered eighth outing: suitable mount for apprentice: on toes second start. *J. Mackie.*

BROAD BRIDGE 3 b.f. Broadsword (USA) 104–Tye Bridge (Idiot's Delight 115) [1988 6m 5g* 7.3s 1989 7m² 7m 7h⁴ 9m⁴] lengthy filly: fair performer: stays 9f: acts on hard ground, possibly unsuited by soft. *J. R. Jenkins.* **79**

BROADWAY STAR 2 b.c. (Feb 21) Alzao (USA) 117–Broadway Royal (Royal Match 117) [1989 7m² 7f* 7m⁵ 7g⁵] strong, deep-girthed, attractive colt: moderate mover, with a roundish action: half-brother to Irish 3-y-o 6.3f winner Broadway Rosie (by Absalom), fair 5f and 6f winner Royal Crofter (by Crofter) and a winner in France by Jaazeiro: dam never ran: made all in 5-runner minor event at York in July, drifting right last 2f: respectable fifth in moderately-run nursery at Newmarket, next and easily better effort afterwards: will probably stay 1m. *M. Bell.* **73**

BROCKSHILL 2 gr.c. (Feb 12) Taufan (USA) 119–Aerobic Dancer (Bold Lad (IRE) 133) [1989 6f 5m2] 17,500Y: well-made colt: has scope: first foal: dam, unraced, from family of Ballad Rock: wore crossed noseband when 5 lengths second of 13, keeping on not knocked about, to Priority Paid in maiden at Windsor in June: sold 3,000 gns Newmarket Autumn Sales. *A. A. Scott.* **64**

BROCTUNE GREY 5 gr.m. Warpath 113–Hitesca 110 (Tesco Boy 121) [1988 NR 1989 14.6g 16.2d 12g² 14f⁵ 18h⁵ 16.5g² 14f² 16.1m² 17.6d⁴ 16m⁴ 18g⁴] angular, sparely-made mare: sister to modest out-and-out stayer Hydrangea and half-sister to fairly useful middle-distance colt Rodeo (by Bustino) and miler Referendum (by Reform): dam very game middle-distance performer: modest form in handicaps: 50/1, good fourth of 21 finishers, nearest at finish, to Double Dutch in Tote Cesarewitch (Handicap) at Newmarket in October on final outing: out-and-out stayer: yet to race on soft going, acts on any other except possibly hard: often claimer ridden: tended to wander seventh start: swished tail under pressure next time: winning staying hurdler. *Mrs G. R. Reveley.* **72**

BRODERIE ANGLAISE 3 b.f. Night Shift (USA)–Emblazon 91 (Wolver Hollow 126) [1988 7f 7g⁶ 1989 8g⁵ 8m³ 8m 8g 8f a8g] workmanlike filly: good third in handicap at Ripon in August, staying on well: below form after, twice not getting best of runs: will probably be suited by 1¼m: acts on top-of-the-ground: blinkered final outing: sold D. Ringer 5,600 gns Newmarket December Sales. *Lord John FitzGerald.* **69 d**

BRODIE 5 b.g. Nicholas Bill 125–Grecian Palm 78 (Royal Palm 131) [1988 10v 14s 10d 8d⁶ 8d 8m⁴ 6g³ 6v³ 1989 6s³ 6v* 7d⁶ 6g 7m] close-coupled gelding: apprentice ridden when winning handicap at Hamilton in April by 5 lengths: ran moderately in similar company afterwards: suited by 6f and plenty of give in the ground: visored once at 4 yrs: sold 2,500 gns Ascot September Sales, resold 1,500 gns Ascot December Sales. *C. B. B. Booth.* **44**

BROKEN LINE 3 br.g. Dara Monarch 128–Bustina (FR) (Busted 134) [1988 NR 1989 11.7d 11.7m⁵ 12f 10m 16.2g] IR 13,000F, IR 75,000Y: medium-sized gelding: keen walker: half-brother to 3 winners in Ireland, including useful 6f to 1m winner Miss Lilian (by Sandford Lad), later a winner in USA: dam ran once in France: quite modest form in maidens first 2 starts: well beaten after, including in claimer: stays 11.7f: sold to join W. Clay 5,600 gns Newmarket July Sales. *P. F. I. Cole.* **—**

BROKEN SILENCE 4 ch.f. Busted 134–My Lynnie 74§ (Frankincense 120) [1988 8.5m³ 8.2g⁴ 10g⁶ 10g 11s⁴ 10s 10g 1989 7d 8d 8.5d 12f 8f 10.1m⁵ 8.3g² 8m⁶ 8f 10.8m] leggy, rather angular filly: often doesn't impress in appearance: bad mover: poor maiden: probably best at 1m: best form on an easy surface: often blinkered nowadays: inconsistent: sold 1,400 gns Newmarket December Sales. *J. A. Glover.* **39**

BROMWICH BILL 4 b.g. Headin' Up–Bilbao 65 (Capistrano 120) [1988 6m 5f 8s 1989 6m] appears of little account: sweating and hung left throughout only outing at 4 yrs. *L. J. Barratt.* **—**

BRONZE CROSS 4 b.g. Rontino 109–Make Your Mark (On Your Mark 125) [1988 8g³ 10f³ 10f 7g² 8.2g² 8g² 7g 8g 7.5m⁵ 9d⁴ 8m 8v⁴ 8s 8.2d 12d⁶ 1989 7d² 7s³ 6d⁵ 6f 7m 7.5f⁴ 7f 8f⁴ 8.5g⁶ 8g* 8.5m 8m 8.5f 7m⁵ 8g a7g² a7g⁶ a6g* a6g⁵] robust gelding: moderate mover: quite modest performer on his day: won handicap at Pontefract in July and claimer at Southwell (apprentice ridden) in December: effective at 6f and stays 1m: acts on firm going, but particularly well suited by an easy surface: sometimes sweats: has carried head high and found nothing under pressure: inconsistent. *T. D. Barron.* **61 §**

BRONZE RUNNER 5 b. or ro.g. Gunner B 126–Petingalyn (Petingo 135) [1988 10.2s 12d 12m⁶ 11.1m 11.5g 11.7m 10g⁵ 10m 10m 10.2f⁴ 1989 10g 12m 10m 12g⁴ 12f⁴ 14f 10m⁶ 16.5f⁴ 13.1h⁶] leggy gelding: poor mover: fair performer in 1987: has **40**

deteriorated considerably, and tailed off final outing (July): stays 1½m: acts on any going: suitable mount for inexperienced rider: often blinkered or visored nowadays. *E. A. Wheeler.*

BROSNA (USA) 3 ch.f. Irish River (FR) 131–Proud Lou (USA) (Proud Clarion) — [1988 NR 1989 12h³] third foal: dam best at 2 yrs, winning at 6f and 1m including in Grade 1 Frizette Stakes: 5/2, 12 lengths third of 4 to Isabella Ra in maiden at Brighton in August, taking keen hold early and no extra 2f out. *J. Tree.*

BROTHER RAY 2 b.c. (May 18) Chief Singer 131–Havara 82 (African Sky 124) — [1989 6g 6g] leggy, unfurnished colt: backward: dam 6f winner: backward, always behind in late-season maidens at Newmarket. *J. Sutcliffe.*

BROUGHTINO 2 b.g. (May 7) Sandhurst Prince 128–Modest Maiden (FR) — (Bustino 136) [1989 6m 6s] IR 6,600F, 15,000Y: small, angular gelding: poor walker: first foal: dam never ran: never dangerous or knocked about in 28-runner seller (backward) at Newmarket and 15-runner claimer at Hamilton. *W. J. Musson.*

BROUGHTON BAY 2 b.c. (Apr 20) Trojan Fen 118–Rose Noir (Floribunda 136) 97 [1989 5d³ 5m* 5m* 5f⁴ 6m³ 6g] 5,400F, 17,500Y: leggy colt: has a quick action: half-brother to 3 winners, including Irish 1000 Guineas runner-up Clover Princess (by Right Tack): dam lightly-raced sister to Florescence: won maiden (by 8 lengths) and minor event at Windsor in May: ran very well when staying-on third to Night At Sea in nursery at Newmarket but poorly in Racecall Gold Trophy at Redcar later in October: probably better suited by 6f than 5f: off course 4 months after fourth start. *W. J. Musson.*

BROWN CARPET 2 b. or br.c. (Feb 21) Never So Bold 135–Geopelia 109 69 (Raffingora 130) [1989 5s⁶ 5s² 6f⁴ 5m² 6f 6f⁴ 5m⁴ 5f 6m] 27,000Y: smallish, workmanlike colt: has a quick action: half-brother to ungenuine 1m winner Flitterkiss Park (by Beldale Flutter) and 2 winners in South Africa: dam sprinter: modest maiden: best effort on sixth start: suited by 6f: blinkered fourth and fifth starts: has been slowly away. *G. Lewis.*

BROWNIE SARAH 2 b.f. (May 1) Mansingh (USA) 120–Alchemilla (Derring- 57 d Do 131) [1989 5s⁴ 5d 6m² 6f³ 7m² 7g 7m⁶ 6m* 6g³ 7g 7f 7d] 840F, 2,900Y: angular filly: has a roundish action: half-sister to winning stayer Romana (by Roman Warrior) and a winner in West Indies: dam of no account: won selling nursery at Ripon in August: ran moderately last 3 outings: best form at 6f: sold 2,000 gns Doncaster October Sales after final one. *J. Berry.*

BROWN PEPPER 3 b.g. Sharpo 132–Petrary 67 (Petingo 135) [1988 5m⁵ 5m² 73 6f⁶ 6m² 7d 7.3m⁶ 6d 1989 9s 7g 8g² 9s⁵ a8g] small, leggy gelding: modest handicapper: second at Goodwood in October on first run for 3 months: fair fifth at Hamilton, never able to challenge but only other show as 3-y-o: stays 1m: acts on top-of-the-ground. *R. Akehurst.*

BROWN RIFLE 9 bl.g. Scottish Rifle 127–Mother Brown 103 (Candy Cane 125) — [1988 NR 1989 9v⁴] winning hurdler: well-beaten fourth of 10 in maiden claiming event (favourite) at Hamilton in April, only race on flat since 1983. *D. Burchell.*

BRUNTSFIELD (USA) 2 b.c. (Feb 24) Critique (USA) 128–Rosie Rose (USA) 63 (Unconscious (USA)) [1989 8.2d 7g 8s⁶] $5,000Y: very big, lengthy colt: has a markedly round action: half-brother to 2 minor winners in USA and to useful Italian colt Rutilio Rufo (by One For All), placed in Italian St Leger: dam unraced from family of Mansingh: quite modest maiden: will stay beyond 1m. *S. J. Muldoon.*

BRUSH ASIDE (USA) 3 b.c. Alleged (USA) 138–Top Twig (High Perch 126) 100 [1988 NR 1989 9g* 10g²] $1,100,000Y: strong, lengthy colt: has plenty of scope: moderate mover: half-brother to several winners, notably good-class French middle-distance performers Tip Moss and Twig Moss (both by Luthier): dam last both starts: 3/1 on, won 22-runner maiden at Newmarket in April comfortably by 2½ lengths (clear) from Prorutori: near head of betting for the Derby until beaten 2 lengths by N C Owen in £6,200 event (again heavily backed at odds on) at same course 16 days later: will be suited by 1½m: may prove suited by more give in the ground. *H. R. A. Cecil.*

BRUSHER 4 b.c. Tap On Wood 130–Enchanted 116 (Song 132) [1988 8g 1989 — 8.5f⁴ 8h⁴ 13f⁵] sturdy, close-coupled colt: good walker: poor maiden: tailed off in June handicap at Hamilton, and not seen out again: should stay 1¼m. *A. D. Brown.*

BRUSQUE (USA) 5 b.g. Assert 134–Cecelia (USA) (Royal Levee (USA)) [1988 60 NR 1989 11v² 12g³ 10f] compact, attractive ex-Irish gelding: half-brother to numerous winners, notably useful French miler Absentia (by Raise A Cup), subsequently 9f stakes winner in USA: dam unraced daughter of half-sister to top American colts Chieftain and Tom Rolfe: quite modest form when placed in maiden and minor event (slowly away) in spring: not raced after May: should be suited by 1½m + : joined Don Enrico Incisa and gelded after final start. *N. Tinkler.*

BRUTUS 5 ch.g. Junius (USA) 124–Orangery (Realm 129) [1988 5m 6g⁶ 5f⁶ 5f* 5g³ 5f² 5g³ 5.1g⁶ 6f³ 6g² 6g³ 5m³ 5f 6f 6m³ 6g 1989 5m 5m³ 5m⁴ 5m* 5m 6g 6m² 6m 5m 6g 7m⁵ 7g 6f*] workmanlike gelding: quite modest handicapper on his day: won at Ripon (favourite) in June and Redcar (hung left) in October: worthwhile form in between only when second at Doncaster: best at up to 6f: acts on firm going and a soft surface: blinkered (unfavourably drawn) tenth outing: often gets on edge: has won for apprentice: inconsistent. *Miss L. C. Siddall.* **61**

BRYANT 3 b.f. Touching Wood (USA) 127–Bless The Match 101 (So Blessed 130) [1988 6f² 6d* 5.5d⁶ 5g 6f⁴ 1989 8m³ 10m 8m² 8m³] strong, useful-looking filly: moderate walker: has a quick action: fair performer: stays 1m: acts on top-of-the-ground and a soft surface: blinkered once at 2 yrs: sold 7,200 gns Newmarket Autumn Sales. *C. R. Nelson.* **86**

BRYDONNA 4 br.f. Good Times (ITY)–Duchy 99 (Rheingold 137) [1988 8m 8.5m 6d² 7.5f³ 6g⁴ 6m 7m 1989 7f] big, rangy filly: turns off-fore in: moderate mover: plating-class maiden: suited by 6f and give in the ground: sweating final appearance (June) at 3 yrs. *C. Tinkler.* **—**

BUBULINA 2 b.f. (Apr 22) Dunphy 124–Hi There 89 (High Top 131) [1989 7g³] 2,200Y: fourth living foal: half-sister to 1½m winner Nikitas (by Touching Wood) and 3-y-o Schweppes Time (by Formidable): dam, half-sister to Pas de Seul, won over 5f at 2 yrs: 33/1, over 3 lengths third of 20, keeping on last 2f, to Oh So Risky in maiden auction event at Goodwood in October: should improve. *Miss A. J. Whitfield.* **60 p**

BUCHANAN (USA) 14 gr.g. Dancer's Image (USA)–Fiery Diplomat (USA) (Diplomat Way) [1988 NR 1989 11.5m 8.5g 10.2m] of no account. *M. C. Chapman.* **—**

BUDAPEST 3 ch.c. Diesis 133–Salidar (Sallust 134) [1988 5f⁶ 5.8g 6m 1989 6m 6m* 6m⁴ 6m 6m 7g*] small, sturdy, quite attractive colt: modest handicapper: won at Windsor (co-favourite) in May and Kempton (20/1 and showing improved form, staying on strongly from rear to lead close home) in September: well below form in between, sweating fourth outing and twice ridden by 7-lb claimer: stays 7f well. *B. W. Hills.* **78**

BUESTA 3 b.f. Bustino 136–Quest 72 (Welsh Pageant 132) [1988 NR 1989 12f 13.3m 11.7m³ 16f² 16f² 17.6m³ 15.8g³ 15g⁵] 23,000Y: lengthy, unfurnished filly: moderate walker and mover: fourth foal: half-sister to 2-y-o 7f winners Spotter (by Beldale Flutter) and Creese (by Kris), latter fairly useful and subsequently a winner in Italy: dam ran only at 2 yrs, winning at 7f: modest maiden: suited by test of stamina: acts on firm going: hung left fifth start: visored after, running creditably first 2 occasions. *K. M. Brassey.* **73**

BUFFS EXPRESS 2 ch.f. (Apr 5) Bay Express 132–Buff Beauty 92 (Mossborough 126) [1989 6m 5.8m⁴ 6g 5m³ 6g] workmanlike filly: sister to a winner in Sweden and half-sister to winning stayer Cavalier's Blush (by King's Troop), 1¼m seller winner Banna's Retreat (by Vitiges) and a winner in Italy: dam stayer: showed much improved form when 7 lengths third to Batzushka in minor event at Lingfield in September: eased considerably once beaten final start: should stay further than 5f. *W. G. R. Wightman.* **68**

BUILDERS GOLD 3 b.c. On Your Mark 125–Linanbless (So Blessed 130) [1988 5f⁴ 1989 8d 8g 11m 7m 8h⁵ 10m] sparely-made, angular colt: poor form in varied events: seems suited by 1m: acts on hard ground. *J. J. O'Neill.* **45**

BUILDMARK 3 ch.f. Longleat (USA) 109–Crescentia (Crepello 136) [1988 NR 1989 12s⁴ 11v⁶ 7m⁶ 10.2f⁵ 10g²] 620Y: workmanlike filly: has scope: sixth foal: half-sister to Spanish 1¼m winner Malviz (by Hotfoot): dam unraced daughter of Oaks third Pouponne: 40/1, showed much improved form when second in slowly-run claimer at Goodwood in October, staying on well: stays 1¼m: moved poorly down, unruly at stalls and withdrawn intended fourth outing: trained first 2 starts by A. Hide, third by R. Guest. *W. G. M. Turner.* **59**

BULLACE 2 ch.c. (Mar 4) Bustino 136–Brush (Laser Light 118) [1989 7m] IR 6,600F, 11,000Y: third foal: half-brother to 1983 2-y-o 6f seller winner Your Choice (by Hot Grove): dam never ran: 33/1, 15½ lengths eighth of 17, staying on well from rear final 2f, to Zoman in maiden at Chepstow in October: should improve. *J. L. Dunlop.* **— p**

BULLI'S LAD 4 b.g. Bold Owl 101–Subtle Queen (Stephen George 102) [1988 NR 1989 11g] angular, deep-bodied gelding: modest form as 2-y-o: second favourite, well beaten in seller at Hamilton in August: should stay 1¼m: sold 800 gns Doncaster November Sales. *W. J. Pearce.* **—**

BULLY BOY 6 ch.g. Margouillat (FR) 133–Chere Madame (Karabas 132) [1988 — NR 1989 10.1m] lengthy, dipped-backed gelding: bad plater: stays 1¼m: acts on firm going: blinkered 3 times: winning chaser. *D. L. Hanley.*

BUNDLE OF FUN (USA) 3 ch.f. Diesis 133–Royal Bund (USA) (Royal 77 Coinage) [1988 NR 1989 7g 8m² 8m⁵ 10h³ 12.5m4] $400,000Y: workmanlike, sparely-made filly: sister to twice-raced Etheldreda and half-sister to numerous winners, including very smart 2-y-o fillies Bundler (by Raise A Native) and Picture Tube (by T V Commercial): dam minor stakes winner at 2 yrs: modest maiden: best form over 1m: possibly unsuited by hard ground: sold 30,000 gns Newmarket December Sales. *H. R. A. Cecil.*

BUNDLE OF LUCK 2 ch.f. (May 1) Touching Wood (USA) 127–Best Offer 96 58 (Crepello) [1989 8f⁵ 9f⁴ a8g] small, close-coupled filly: fifth foal: half-sister to Belgian winner Acceptable (by Tina's Pet) and a winner in Italy: dam won over 7f and 1m: quite modest maiden: ran badly final start: will stay well. *Lord John FitzGerald.*

BUNNY LADY 3 ch.f. Blushing Scribe (USA) 107–Swing The Cat (Swing Easy — (USA) 126) [1988 NR 1989 10.2h⁶ 10.4g 11.7h⁵ 10f a10g⁶] 860F: strong, angular filly: half-sister to 4 winners including fair 6f and 7f winner Tamdown Flyer (by Hotfoot), later successful in Spain, and quite useful 1984 2-y-o 5f and 6f winner Love In Spring (by Owen Dudley): dam never ran: promise in claimers and seller only on debut: may do better at around 1m. *D. J. G. Murray-Smith.*

BUNNYLOCH 5 b.m. Lochnager 132–Bunnycraft (The Go-Between 129) [1988 37 § 5f² 5g³ 5g 5f⁴ 5m⁶ 5f 5f 5m⁴ 5s⁶ 5d 1989 5f⁴ 5m 5m² 5f 5m² 5f⁶ 5f 7g⁶ 6m³ 5g² 6f] rangy, angular mare: poor maiden: best at 5f: acts on firm going and a soft surface: has worn blinkers and visor, but not for some time: not genuine. *J. Etherington.*

BURAN (USA) 2 ch.f. (Feb 18) Blushing Groom (FR) 131–Born A Lady (USA) — p (Tentam (USA)) [1989 7g] $550,000Y: small, stocky filly: lacks scope: first known foal: dam winner at up to 1m, is half-sister to Northern Dancer: 12/1, hampered start when never-nearer eighth of 17 to Starstreak in minor event at Leicester in November: has joined J. Fanshawe: may do better. *M. R. Stoute.*

BURASPUN 3 b.f. Burslem 123–Up And At It 72 (Tamerlane 128) [1988 6m 7g 7g — 1989 6m 6h 6f 7f] close-coupled, deep-girthed filly: not a good walker: little worthwhile form but showed strong signs of ability when in mid-division in handicaps last 2 starts: not seen out after July: stays 6f well. *R. Earnshaw.*

BURCROFT 5 ch.g. Crofthall 110–Two's Up (Double Jump 131) [1988 12g⁴ 12s* 50 12m³ 13m² 12m⁴ 16m 12g⁵ 12m* 12g² 12d* 12g³ 12m 12f⁶ 12s 12v 1989 12.3s 12d² 12d⁴ 12g⁵ 16m 12g 12h 12m⁶ 12g⁴ 16.2f² 13s³ 17f 15s⁴ 13.6g⁴ a14g4] leggy, sparely-made gelding: moderate mover: plating-class handicapper: stays an easy 1¾m: has form on firm going, but well suited by an easy surface nowadays: has run well for apprentice: effective with or without a visor. *R. M. Whitaker.*

BURFORD (USA) 2 ch.c. (Mar 28) Time For A Change (USA)–Windrush Lady 79 (USA) (Unconscious (USA)) [1989 7s² 7f] fifth foal: half-brother to 3-y-o Pay Corps (by Private Account), Irish 7f winner Psyched (by Hagley), later graded 7f winner in USA, and a winner in USA: dam 6f winner: sire won from 7f to 9f: favourite, beaten a neck by Bondstone in 10-runner maiden at Goodwood in September: around 8½ lengths seventh of 14 to El Paso in similar event at Salisbury following month. *I. A. Balding.*

BURGOYNE 3 b.c. Ardross 134–Love Match (USA) (Affiliate (USA)) [1988 NR 81 p 1989 12.2d* 11g*] 41,000Y: lengthy, angular colt: shade unfurnished: second foal: dam, who ran twice, is from family of top German horses Neckar and Naxos: won claimers at Catterick and Redcar (claimed to join M. H. Easterby £21,001) in October: will be suited by at least 1½m: still bit green at Redcar and can improve. *H. R. A. Cecil.*

BURKAN 4 ch.c. Star Appeal 133–Ana Gabriella (USA) (Master Derby (USA)) 91 [1988 9g 10m⁴ 8g⁵ 8f³ 8d 9f 10.1m⁴ 8m⁵ 9g 8d⁴ 1989 8s 10.4m⁴ 8.2m 8m* 10g⁶ 12m³ 8f] small colt: has a quick action: fairly useful handicapper on his day: won for first time since 2 yrs in 6-runner event (apprentice ridden) at Edinburgh in June: not seen out after Royal Ascot: possibly best at up to 1¼m: acts on firm going: blinkered final 3 appearances at 3 yrs and on third one at 4 yrs: not an easy ride. *N. A. Callaghan.*

BURKES PROGRESS 3 b. or br.f. Tyrnavos 129–Pushkar (Northfields (USA)) 58 [1988 6f 6s 7f* 8g² 8.2v 1989 7d 7m 10m 9g⁴ a11g⁶ a14g] leggy, rather sparely-made filly: poor mover: favourite, best effort in handicaps and claimer in 1989 but still well below 2-y-o form when fourth at Hamilton in September, ridden along with fair bit to do 3½f out then staying on steadily: well behind final start: should be suited by middle distances: best form on a sound surface: trained until after fourth start by R. O'Leary. *T. D. Barron.*

BURN BRIDGE (USA) 3 b.c. Linkage (USA)–Your Nuts (USA) (Creme Dela — Creme) [1988 6d 6s* 6g 1989 9f 10m 10.6m 10.6s] small, lightly-made colt: moderate mover: modest handicapper: not discredited at York and Epsom first 2 outings: off course nearly 4 months after, then twice well beaten at Haydock, in amateurs event on first of them and moving poorly down on second: stays 9f: probably acts on any going. *W. J. Haggas.*

BURNDITCH GIRL 3 ch.f. Raga Navarro (ITY) 119–Queen of The Nile (Hittite 54 Glory 125) [1988 6f 5g 6g² 7g⁶ 7d² 7m 8m 7v⁵ 1989 8.2s* 10m 7f] compact filly: moderate mover: 16/1 and sweating, won amateurs handicap at Haydock in late-April: below form after and not seen out after June: will be suited by return to 1m and should stay further: best form on an easy surface. *M. W. Eckley.*

BURNING BRIGHT 6 b.g. Star Appeal 133–Lead Me On (King's Troop 118) 33 [1988 10.8d 10g 12g 14m 11.7g 1989 16f² 16.5g] strong, compact gelding: poor performer nowadays: stays 2m: acts on firm going and probably unsuited by soft: blinkered last 2 outings in 1988: sweated badly on reappearance: often slowly away. *R. Curtis.*

BURNING FEET 3 b.g. Alzao (USA) 117–Babylon Queen (Prince Tenderfoot 62 (USA) 126) [1988 7m² 7.5s⁵ 7g⁶ 7m³ 8.2m³ 8.2s² 1989 10s⁶ 12v⁵ 9s 12m² 12g] leggy, close-coupled gelding: has a roundish action: ridden by 7-lb claimer, easily best effort as 3-y-o when second in claimer at Newmarket: off course over 5 months after: stays 1½m: acts on top-of-the-ground and soft going: may prove suited by waiting tactics. *R. J. R. Williams.*

BURNING VOLCANO 3 b.c. In Fijar (USA) 121–Diatoma (FR) (Diatome 132) 86 [1988 NR 1989 8s⁴ 10.4m⁴ 10f⁵ 12h² 12f⁶ 12m⁶ 8.5f³] leggy, quite good-topped colt: moderate walker and mover: sixth reported living foal: half-brother to 4 winners in France, including Diatomica (by Homing), successful from 1m (at 2 yrs) to 1¾m: dam, successful 3 times at around 1m in France, is half-sister to Blue Tom, Amber Rama, Timmy My Boy and the dam of Fast Topaze: fair maiden: placed at Lingfield (led 1¼m) and in allowance race at Gulfstream Park: ran badly in between: probably stays 1½m: acts on hard going: wears tongue strap: reportedly stays in USA. *M. Moubarak.*

BURNT FINGERS 5 ch.g. Busted 134–Madame's Share 115 (Major Portion 61 129) [1988 12g 9f 8f 10m 14.8d² 16g² 14g* 17.1g 16s⁴ 1989 12s⁵ 14s³ 16g⁴ 16m² 14.8m² 17.1h* 16f⁵ 18.4f* 19f⁴ 17.4s] sparely-made gelding: usually dull in coat: moderate mover: quite modest handicapper: won from small fields at Bath in June and Chester following month: tailed off final outing: lacks pace, and well suited by forcing tactics and a good test of stamina: best form on top-of-the-ground: sometimes sweating and on edge: often wears tongue strap: often apprentice ridden: sold to join J. White 9,000 gns Newmarket Autumn Sales: consistent. *J. D. Bethell.*

BURSANA 3 b.f. Burslem 123–Lady of Surana (Shirley Heights 130) [1988 6s 8v⁴ 65 8g* 1989 10g³ 10s² 9.5g³ 10g⁴ 10s² 10g⁵ 12.3m 12.2m 12.3g⁴ 12m³ 12.3m² 11s³ 14m] sparely-made filly: moderate walker: poor mover: quite modest performer: stays 1½m: acts on top-of-the-ground and soft going. *C. B. B. Booth.*

BURSLEM BEAU 2 gr.g. (Feb 12) Burslem 123–Divine Apsara (Godswalk 62 (USA) 130) [1989 5g 5v 5d 5f* 5f³ 5g⁴ 5f] IR 5,000Y: quite good-topped, leggy gelding: poor walker: second foal: dam Irish 5f to 1m winner: won maiden auction race at Redcar in May: good fourth to Nout in minor event at Ripon, best effort afterwards: ran poorly later in July and wasn't seen out again: worth a try at 6f: acts on firm ground, and seems unsuited by soft: sometimes edgy and on toes. *C. Tinkler.*

BURTONWOOD HARP 2 ch.g. (Feb 12) Mandrake Major 122–Misty Arch 56 (Starch Reduced 112) [1989 5s 5f 5g⁴ 5g² 5g* 5f 6g a6g a5g] 7,600Y: angular gelding: first foal: dam twice-raced sister to fair sprinter Little Starchy: fair plater on his day: ran poorly after winning at Windsor (sold out of J. Berry's stable 6,200 gns) in summer: headstrong, and will prove best at 5f: has looked a hard ride, and wore a severe bridle at Windsor: sold 950 gns Ascot December Sales. *M. H. Tompkins.*

BURTONWOODS BEST 3 b.g. Longleat (USA) 109–Abbey Rose 84 51 (Lorenzaccio 130) [1988 5s³ 6g 6g 6m⁴ 1989 7.5f 8.2d⁵ 10g] leggy gelding: blinkered and edgy (took keen hold to post), fifth in claimer at Haydock in August, staying on well and only form as 3-y-o: stays 8.2f: acts on top-of-the-ground and a soft surface: also blinkered final start (sweating in seller) and last at 2 yrs. *W. W. Haigh.*

BUSH HILL   4 b.g. Beldale Flutter (USA) 130–Butosky 71 (Busted 134) [1988   **82**
8m³ 8g* 8f⁴ 8f 8s 8m⁴ 10m³ 9d⁵ 11d³ 12g³ 12m³ 1989 12m 16f 14f² 13.3m 12m⁵ 12s]
leggy, rather sparely-made gelding: has a rather round action: fair handicapper: 50/1 and first outing for 2 months, returned to form when excellent second of 18, battling on well, to Sapience in Tote Ebor (Handicap) at York in August: fair fifth of 17 to Braashee in £71,300 Tote Festival Handicap at Ascot, easily best subsequent effort: should stay 2m: ideally needs a sound surface: has tended to hang: genuine: sold to join J. FitzGerald 30,000 gns Doncaster November Sales. *I. V. Matthews.*

BUSHRA   3 ch.f. Kris 135–Fly Baby 101 (African Sky 124) [1988 NR 1989 8g* 8s⁵]   **65**
workmanlike filly: third foal: half-sister to quite modest 6f winner Mazyooneh (by Bustino): dam sprinter: co-favourite, won moderately-run maiden at Newcastle in April: led 5f and weakened inside last when beaten 13 lengths in minor event at Leicester 10 days later: should be suited by 1¼m. *B. Hanbury.*

BU-SOFYAN   5 b.g. Runnett 125–London Spin 86 (Derring-Do 131) [1988 6g 1989   **74**
6v 8m⁵ 7m 8h⁴ 7.6h³ 7m* 8f* 8h³ 7f³ 8f³ 8m a10g⁴] tall, rather leggy gelding: modest handicapper: comfortable winner at Brighton in June and July: effective at 7f and 1m: acts on hard going and is possibly unsuited by soft. *M. Madgwick.*

BUSORM   9 ch.g. Bustino 136–Wrekinianne 96 (Reform 132) [1988 NR 1989 5g 5f   —
8m a11g a6g] no longer of any account. *M. C. Chapman.*

BUSTALA   2 ch.f. (May 1) Bustino 136–B A Poundstretcher 82 (Laser Light 118)   —
[1989 7g] 4,000Y: small, sparely-made filly: second foal: half-sister to 3-y-o 1¼m winer Touch Above (by Touching Wood): dam 5f and 6f winner: 50/1, soon behind in 24-runner maiden at Newmarket in November. *A. N. Lee.*

BUSTED ROCK   4 b.c. Busted 134–Mexican Two Step (Gay Fandango (USA)   **90**
132) [1988 8g² 10d⁶ 10g* 10g³ 12m³ 12g² 12s⁶ 10g⁶ 10.5f* 10.2g⁶ 1989 12h* 10.5f 10m⁶] rangy, quite attractive colt: moderate mover: quite useful performer: long odds on, won uncompetitive 4-runner minor event at Thirsk in May: well beaten in handicaps at York (£32,000 event) and Newmarket afterwards: not seen out after July: effective at 1¼m and stays 1½m: suited by a sound surface. *Mrs L. Piggott.*

BUTLERS WHARF   4 b.g. Burslem 123–Regal Promise (Pitskelly 122) [1988   **86 §**
6d⁶ 8.2d⁴ 1989 10d 8f 12f² 12g 12m³ 14f⁴ 10f] big, lengthy gelding: 50/1, appeared to run excellent race when second to Stratford Ponds in Bessborough Stakes (Handicap) at Royal Ascot: well below form after, finding little on fifth and final outings: stays 1½m well: acts on any going: has worn blinkers (not since first start at 3 yrs): visored fifth outing: occasionally on edge: has been mulish in preliminaries: has looked a difficult ride: has joined R. Hollinshead: thoroughly untrustworthy. *M. F. D. Morley.*

BUTTERLEY LAD   4 b.c. Taufan (USA) 119–Viva Amore (Red Alert 127) [1988   —
10.1m 10f⁴ 10. 1d 17g 12.2f 1989 10s 15.5s 10m] angular ex-Irish colt: behind in varied company (visored since 2 yrs): stays 7f. *J. P. Hudson.*

BUY A LITE   4 ch.c. Last Fandango 125–Beamless 73 (Hornbeam 130) [1988 12g   —
12m³ 12.2m³ 13.8f 12f³ 13.8d 16f⁵ 1989 16g 16.2m 18h 16.5g⁵ 16.2g⁴] leggy, close-coupled colt: poor maiden: has run in seller: may prove best at up to 1¾m: possibly best with give in the ground nowadays: visored 3 times at 3 yrs: sold 2,000 gns Doncaster October Sales. *R. M. Whitaker.*

BUZZARDS CREST   4 ch.g. Buzzards Bay 128§–Diamond Talk (Counsel 118)   —
[1988 8g⁶ 9f⁴ 7g 7g 7m 1989 8m 8m 10.6s 7g] lengthy gelding: won maiden as 2-y-o: lightly raced and little show in minor events and handicaps last 2 seasons: stays 7f: acts on soft going: sweating on reappearance. *H. J. Collingridge.*

BUZZARDS SON   3 b.c. Buzzards Bay 128§–Night Cap (SWE) (Hornbeam 130)   **65**
[1988 6f 6s² 7m 7f 7g 7s² 1989 8d³ 8s⁴ 8g 7s⁴ 7m³ 6h 7m 7g a8g] rangy, rather unfurnished colt: has a round action: quite modest maiden: good third in claimer at Epsom in June: behind in varied events after: stays 1m: acts on soft going and top-of-the-ground: blinkered third outing: often sweats up. *H. J. Collingridge.*

BY CHARTER   3 b.f. Shirley Heights 130–Time Charter 131 (Saritamer (USA)   **103**
130) [1988 7f* 8g⁶ 1989 11.3m²] medium-sized, rather unfurnished filly: lacks scope: has a quick action: won maiden at Yarmouth and sixth in Hoover Fillies' Mile at Ascot as 2-y-o: weak 4/1 and patchy in coat, 1½ lengths second of 8 to Braiswick in Cheshire Oaks in May, leading 2½f out then tiring inside last on only start in 1989: will stay 1½m. *M. R. Stoute.*

BY CHOICE 3 ch.g. Sallust 134–Jamie's Girl (Captain James 123) [1988 6m⁶ 8g*   **71** 8.2d 1989 8g² 10m* 11f² 10m² 12.3g 12f² 10g* 10g⁵ 10f⁵ 10s⁵] small, sparely-made gelding: moderate walker: poor mover: modest performer: favourite, won claimers at Nottingham (claimed out of R. J. R. Williams' stable £12,010) in June and Ayr in July: ran moderately last 3 starts, including in seller: stays 1½m: possibly requires sound surface: sold 4,100 gns Newmarket Autumn Sales. *N. Tinkler.*

BY FAR (USA) 3 b.f. Far North (CAN) 120–Countess Babu (USA) (Bronze Babu)   — [1988 6g⁶ 1989 7f⁵ 10.1g 8g⁵ a8g⁶] smallish, close-coupled, sparely-made filly: quite modest form: best at around 1m: acts on firm ground: races freely: sold O. O'Neill 4,500 gns Newmarket December Sales. *D. R. C. Elsworth.*

BY GEORGE 3 b.c. Valiyar 129–Georgie Girl (FR) 96 (Exbury 138) [1988 6g³ 7s⁴   — 7m³ 6d² 7g⁴ 1989 8s⁵ 10.6s 10.4m 10.2f 11f] tall, quite attractive colt: moderate mover: quite modest maiden: always behind as 3-y-o, except for reappearance: stayed 1m: acted on soft going: hadn't ideal attitude: dead. *R. Hollinshead.*

BYKER LASS 2 b.f. (Mar 12) Superlative 118–Golden Tern (FR) (Arctic Tern   — (USA) 126) [1989 5f 6f 7m 7f] 3,000F, 4,200Y: leggy filly: first foal: dam, winner of a race in Italy, is half-sister to Italian Derby winner Elgay: seems of little account: unruly stalls second outing. *J. S. Wainwright.*

BY LINE 5 b.m. High Line 125–Mount Hala 74 (Mount Hagen (FR) 127) [1988 NR   **64** 1989 10m⁴ 11.5m⁵ 10h 10f⁵ 10m²] leggy, quite good-topped mare: quite modest maiden: stays 1¼m: acts on firm going: winning hurdler with F. Walwyn. *T. Thomson Jones.*

BYRONIC (USA) 4 b.g. Storm Bird (CAN) 134–Nellie Forbes (USA)   **49** (Secretariat (USA)) [1988 8.5m 10g 1989 10.1m⁴ 7h⁴ 8m⁵ 9m] rangy gelding: ex-Irish: third foal: closely related to Irish 1m to 11f winner Ancient Times (by Nijinsky): dam, winner at 1m at 2 yrs in Ireland, is half-sister to Bold Forbes, a top-class winner from 5f to 1½m including in Kentucky Derby and Belmont Stakes: plating-class form in claimers (second one for apprentices) and maiden on first 3 starts: stayed 1¼m: sometimes on toes: dead. *R. Akehurst.*

BYWELL LAD 4 ch.g. Mandrake Major 122–Juliette (Julio Mariner 127) [1988   **65** 8d³ 8g 10m 12f 10m³ 10g⁴ 14m⁶ 12s² 12m³ 16m 12d⁶ 16d 1989 12s² 15.5s* 13.8d⁵] rangy, angular gelding: quite modest handicapper: led final strides when winning at Folkestone in April: modest fifth at Catterick 2 weeks later, and not seen out again: stays 2m well: acts on top-of-the-ground and soft going: apprentice ridden as 4-y-o: tends to carry head high: best with waiting tactics in strongly-run race: moody. *R. Curtis.*

C

CABALLINE 5 ch.g. Last Fandango 125–Rosalia (Tower Walk 130) [1988 10.2d²   — 15.5m 16d 12g 10s 12d 1989 12d 10g] big, workmanlike gelding: tubed: poor maiden: suited by 1¼m: yet to show his form on firm going, acts on any other: has run creditably for amateur. *M. J. Haynes.*

CABLELINK 2 ch.c. (May 25) Horage 124–Night of Gladness 98 (Midsummer   — Night II 117) [1989 6f4] 12,000F, IR 8,800Y: brother to Swedish 3-y-o winner Late Night, closely related to useful 1983 2-y-o 5f winner Night of Wind (by Tumble Wind) and half-brother to 2 other winners: dam won from 5f to 1m: 10/1, soundly-beaten last of 4 in maiden at Newcastle in October. *S. J. Muldoon.*

CABRA 3 ch.f. Red Sunset 120–Shangara (Credo 123) [1988 5m⁴ 6m 6d 1989 6d   — 7g] good-quartered, workmanlike filly: no form, including in sellers: burly in spring as 3-y-o when sweating final start: bred to stay at least 1m: has joined C. Horgan. *H. P. Rohan.*

CACOETHES (USA) 3 b.c. Alydar (USA)–Careless Notion (USA) **130** (Jester) [1988 8d³ 1989 10m* 12f* 12g³ 12f* 12m² 10.5f² 12g]

    Nashwan's reputation in some quarters in midsummer approached that of the finest post-war champions, but the aura of invincibility was dented when Cacoethes ran him very close in the King George VI and Queen Elizabeth Diamond Stakes. Cacoethes had been comprehensively defeated by Nashwan on both the previous occasions they had met, as two-year-olds in a listed event at Ascot and in the Ever Ready Derby in which Cacoethes came third, beaten seven lengths by Nashwan. Cacoethes surpassed himself in the

Calor Derby Trial Stakes, Lingfield—an impressive victory for Cacoethes who upsets the odds laid on Pirate Army

King George, extending the unbeaten Nashwan—who started at 9/2 on—to the limit after looking for a stride or two inside the final furlong as if he might gain the upper hand. Nashwan and Cacoethes both showed top-class finishing speed at the end of a King George which was less strongly run than usual; Cacoethes quickened in tremendous style early in the straight to tackle Nashwan from over a furlong and a half out, having been pocketed on the rails rounding the home turn. In a pulsating finish, Cacoethes went down by a neck, held by the winner close home; first and second left their rivals standing in the closing stages, Cacoethes coming home seven lengths ahead of third-placed Top Class.

The performance of Cacoethes at Ascot looked right out of the top drawer at the time and made his stable's extravagant claims about some of his home work easier to understand. Cacoethes had reportedly been described by his trainer before the Derby as 'every bit as good as Dancing Brave over a mile and a half'. Harwood said in a *Timeform Interview* (given after the King George): 'Cacoethes is as good a mile and a half horse as I've ever trained. In his early pieces of work at home I thought that he might prove a little one paced, but his speed has developed as we've gone through the season. He can really turn it on now; he's done nothing but strengthen and strengthen. I'm sure he will be a real champion as a four-year-old . . . . . he's one of the few horses I've trained that has really put on weight as a three-year-old'. The big, rangy Cacoethes' physical development was pronounced during the season—he was rather unfurnished in the early part of his three-year-old career but was the outstanding individual on looks in the field for the Ciga Prix de l'Arc de Triomphe in October. Cacoethes' stable, incidentally, is one that consistently follows the admirable maxim 'Never be afraid of one horse' and the decision to run Cacoethes in the King George, rather than take an easier option of the Gordon Stakes at Goodwood the next week, paid a handsome dividend; the horse earned considerably more prize-money and far greater prestige at Ascot than a victory in the Gordon Stakes would have brought. Cacoethes looked a far better horse in the King George than his previous form had shown him to be. He started the season with victories in a minor event at Brighton and in the Calor Derby Trial at Lingfield, where he trounced the leading Derby hope Pirate Army, setting a gallop which resulted in a new time record for the course and distance. On the strength of his performance at Lingfield—and his considerable home reputation—Cacoethes started clear second favourite to Nashwan at Epsom. Cacoethes was provided with a pacemaker, Polar Run, to ensure that the Derby was run at a blistering gallop. Cacoethes was sent for home some way out but Nashwan made mincemeat of him, moving comfortably to the front before the two-furlong marker and soon forging clear, disproving any preconceived notions that a searching end-to-end gallop would draw Nashwan's 'sting'. Rather it was Cacoethes who struggled to keep up the gallop, tiring in the closing stages and losing second to the 500/1-shot Terimon. Cacoethes recovered well from his hard race in the Derby and landed the odds in the King Edward VII Stakes at Royal Ascot thirteen days later, his rider—Eddery replaced injured stable-jockey Starkey—glancing round several times at the opposition before and after taking the lead approaching the final furlong; Cacoethes had more in hand than the three quarters of a length by which he beat the Greenham winner Zayyani.

Cacoethes' campaign after the King George VI and Queen Elizabeth Diamond Stakes was an anti-climax. He was seen out twice, in the Juddmonte International Stakes at York in August and in the Prix de l'Arc de Triomphe at Longchamp in October; he would also have contested the St Leger in between had that race not been postponed for a week. The International Stakes, formerly the Benson and Hedges Gold Cup, has proved the undoing of several top-class horses who have figured prominently in the King George but Cacoethes' defeat at the hands of his stable-companion Ile de Chypre is not to be explained away in terms of his losing battle against Nashwan at Ascot. Starkey rode an ill-judged race on Cacoethes, the 5/2-on favourite, being

King Edward VII Stakes, Ascot—Cacoethes wins from Zayyani

caught in a poor position, several lengths behind the leaders and hemmed in near the rails, when Ile de Chypre quickened clear early in the straight. Once extricated, Cacoethes made up half a dozen lengths on Ile de Chypre to reach his quarters entering the final furlong, but Ile de Chypre had something in reserve and Cacoethes could do no more inside the final furlong, going down by a length and a half, eased once pursuit was hopeless. Cacoethes finished four lengths ahead of third-placed Shady Heights, who had been awarded the race the previous year after the disqualification of first-past-the-post Persian Heights. Starkey was much criticised for his riding of Cacoethes at York and lost the mount in the Prix de l'Arc, by which time it had been announced that Cochrane was to take over as stable-jockey at Coombelands in 1990. Asked how he felt about being replaced on Cacoethes in the Arc, Starkey reportedly replied: 'I don't give a hoot, the horse hasn't won yet anyway'. Starkey announced his retirement at the end of the season after a splendid career in which he earned a reputation as one of the most formidable jockeys of his day, strong and dashing, and a shrewd tactician. Ironically, Starkey will probably be remembered longest for his near-miss on Dancing Brave in the Derby, another ride for which he came in for strong criticism, than for his many big-race victories which included a Derby victory on Shirley Heights and a Prix de l'Arc success on Star Appeal, as well as a string of important wins for Coombelands stables. Cauthen took over on Cacoethes in the Prix de l'Arc but the partnership managed only sixteenth of nineteen. Cacoethes ran way below his best, making no impression in the straight after enduring a rough passage in the middle part of the race and turning for home well down the field.

	Alydar (USA) (ch 1975)	Raise A Native (ch 1961)	Native Dancer Raise You
Cacoethes (USA)		Sweet Tooth (b 1965)	On-And-On Plum Cake
(b.c. 1986)	Careless Notion (USA) (b 1970)	Jester (b 1955)	Tom Fool Golden Apple
		Miss Uppity (b 1956)	Nasrullah Nursery School

Cacoethes and the Kildangan Stud Irish Oaks winner Alydaress gave their sire Alydar a boost in Europe in the latest season. Alydar's prolonged rivalry with Affirmed was one of the great American racing stories of the 'seventies. Alydar came off second best to Affirmed in each of the legs of the American triple crown, the Kentucky Derby, the Preakness Stakes and the Belmont Stakes. But Alydar's achievements at stud have outstripped those of his great contemporary, though his reputation has been made largely in North America where he has been responsible for a number of top performers including, most notably, that outstanding Horse of the Year Alysheba and the latest Belmont Stakes winner Easy Goer whose epic rivalry with Sunday Silence engendered almost as much interest as that between Affirmed and Alydar. Cacoethes' dam Careless Notion won only once, over six furlongs as a four-year-old, but she has done much better at stud, the best of her ten foals before Cacoethes being Fabulous Notion (by Somethingfabulous), winner of nine races including the Grade 1 Santa Susana Stakes over eight and a half furlongs; Careless Notion has bred at least five winners. Cacoethes stays a mile and a half and acts well on firm going. A good mover in all his paces, Cacoethes took the eye time and again in the paddock before his races—his condition reflecting great credit on those responsible for him—and he should make up into a most impressive individual as a four-year-old. Judged on his best form, he'll be a tough opponent for the best in the top open-aged middle-distance events, though at a mile and a quarter he'll need riding more enterprisingly than at York. *G. Harwood.*

CACOPHANY 2 b.f. (Mar 27) Music Maestro 119–Primrolla 64 (Relko 136) [1989 **63** 5m⁴ 6g 5m² 5m⁴ 5g 7m⁴ 7g] strong, sturdy filly: has scope: has a quick action: third foal: half-sister to 5f and 1m winner Primulette (by Mummy's Pet): dam won over 1¼m and was also useful young hurdler: quite modest maiden: stays 7f well: blinkered fifth outing: mulish in preliminaries fourth start: sold to race in Saudi Arabia 11,000 gns Newmarket Autumn Sales: inconsistent. *H. Candy.*

CADEAUX GENEREUX 4 ch.c. Young Generation 129–Smarten Up 119 **131** (Sharpen Up 127) [1988 5g* 6f* 6m* 7f* 6.5m² 5d⁶ 6g* 5m*dis 1989 5f³ 5f 6m* 5m* 8g³]

Cadeaux Genereux improved as a three-year-old to end the season rated behind only Soviet Star among the European sprinters; and with Soviet Star retired to stud, he looked likely to climb to the top of the tree in 1989 unless an outstanding younger horse came along. But after his first two starts Cadeaux Genereux was so struggling to hang on to the middle branches that doubts were raised as to whether he'd trained on. He was beaten into third at odds on by Dancing Dissident and Wonder Dancer in the Sears Temple Stakes at Sandown, and could never get into a challenging position in the King's Stand Stakes at Royal Ascot where he finished around six lengths eighth behind the favourite Indian Ridge. Those doubts didn't last long. He'd trained on all right, and in his next two races beat most of the best around in the Carroll Foundation July Cup at Newmarket and the William Hill Sprint Championship at York. A relaxation in training routine—he was apparently worked only once between Royal Ascot and Newmarket—was thought the most likely reason for the large turnaround in his form, and seems a more likely explanation than the slightly easier ground; perhaps he just needed time to come to himself.

The eleven-runner field for the July Cup was well up to standard despite the absence of Silver Fling, Indian Ridge, Cricket Ball, Nabeel Dancer, Dancing Dissident and Tigani. The Royal Ascot winners Danehill (evens) and Golden Opinion (11/4), the latter back from a mile and sprinting for the first time, and supplemented into the race at a cost of £10,000, had the best recent form and headed the market. Next came the One Thousand Guineas runner-up Kerrera (9/1), Cadeaux Genereux (10/1) and the King's Stand third Gallic League (12/1). Among those at 25/1 or longer were Big Shuffle and Handsome Sailor, second and third behind Soviet Star in the race the previous year, but disappointing on their latest runs. As usual Cadeaux Genereux looked really well and kept exceptionally cool in the preliminaries. When the stalls opened Gallic League showed very good speed, chased closely by Mon Tresor, Danehill and Handsome Sailor. Cadeaux Genereux tracked the quartet moving extremely well and was the only one still on the bridle two furlongs out, by which stage Mon Tresor and Handsome Sailor had started to

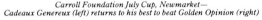

Carroll Foundation July Cup, Newmarket—
Cadeaux Genereux (left) returns to his best to beat Golden Opinion (right)

William Hill Sprint Championship, York —
Cadeaux Genereux completes a Group 1 pattern-race double

drop away. He moved into the lead shortly afterwards and going into the dip looked likely to win comfortably. Inside the final furlong he began to idle and had to be driven out firmly as Golden Opinion finished strongly having been outpaced, four lengths adrift of him at halfway. Golden Opinion closed the gap with every stride, but Cadeaux Genereux responded to pressure and held on by a head. Danehill kept on without quickening and was two and a half lengths back in third, with Kerrera another length and a half away fourth. The winning time provided confirmation of how fast Gallic League had taken them along, for it bettered by more than a second the course record set by Ajdal in the July Cup in 1987.

Record times don't necessarily translate into exceptional timefigures when ground, weight and wind direction have been taken into account. Cadeaux Genereux's timefigure of 1.25 fast was one of the best by a sprinter in the last fifteen years, however. His victory was the first for both his jockey, Paul Eddery, and trainer in Group 1 company. For his trainer it provided the highlight of an excellent first season which saw him finish among the top ten trainers in terms of prize money won in Britain. Nabeel Dancer, Great Commotion, Magic Gleam and Petillante also distinguished themselves in pattern company. Scott, who learnt his trade through spells with Calver, Thomson Jones and Hern, took over many of his horses, including Cadeaux Genereux, from Olivier Douieb, who returned to France at the end of 1988 because of ill health and died in June. Cadeaux Genereux faced an easier task in the William Hill Sprint Championship than in the July Cup, though this time Silver Fling, Tigani and Dancing Dissident were in opposition, as was Statoblest, the winner of the King George Stakes at Goodwood. None of those he defeated at Newmarket reopposed. Cadeaux Genereux, the clear favourite, was the seventh horse in the 'eighties to run in the Sprint Championship (reportedly to revert to its former title of Nunthorpe Stakes in future) after taking the July Cup. Ajdal, Never So Bold, Habibti and Sharpo all completed the double, whereas Green Desert and Marwell were both beaten. Soviet Star, Chief Singer and Moorestyle did not run in the Sprint Championship; Chief Singer did go to York, but for the Benson and Hedges Gold Cup over twice the distance. The latest Sprint Championship went as the July Cup had for Cadeaux Genereux, in that he comfortably tracked a strong pace, set on this occasion by Eloquent Minister, though his challenge was delayed slightly longer and he didn't take up the running until just inside the final furlong. Again he didn't produce much in front and he needed to be ridden out to hold on by three quarters of a length from the strong-finishing Silver Fling, who

159

Maktoum Al-Maktoum's "Cadeaux Genereux"

got up close home to deprive Statoblest and Tigani of second. The stable's other runner Petillante finished ninth; so it's now thirty-three years since a two-year-old, Ennis, won the event. Coincidentally, the first two home were the same as in the William Hill Golden Spurs Trophy Handicap at York the previous season when Cadeaux Genereux had half a length to spare over Silver Fling. On that occasion Cadeaux Genereux had been in receipt of 16 lb.

With little more to prove as far as sprinting was concerned, Cadeaux Genereux next took on some of the best milers in the Prix du Moulin de Longchamp presumably in an attempt to increase his value as a stallion. He had twice before run over seven furlongs, the second time when beating Salse on firm going in the Van Geest Criterion Stakes at Newmarket, but never over further. He had no answer to the two-length winner Polish Precedent in the final furlong but, nevertheless, ran creditably to be involved in a three-way photograph for second. Short heads separated he, Squill and Green Line Express. The Moulin turned out his last race. He was to be kept in training as a five-year-old, but while being prepared for the Prix de l'Abbaye de Longchamp and the Breeders' Cup Mile in the autumn he sustained a slight strain to his near-fore tendon and was retired.

Cadeaux Genereux retires to the Whitsbury Manor Stud, Fordingbridge, at £10,000, live foal. The good-bodied Cadeaux Genereux, a moderate mover in his slower paces, is the best produce of the high-class miler Young Generation, who died in 1986 having also stood at Whitsbury. Young Generation was also represented in the latest season by the Grade 1 Arlington Handicap winner Unknown Quantity and the Schweppes Golden Mile winner Safawan. Cadeaux Genereux's dam Smarten Up has produced all sorts. Two of

		Balidar	Will Somers
	Young Generation	(br 1966)	Violet Bank
	(b 1976)	Brig O'Doon	Shantung
Cadeaux Genereux		(ch 1967)	Tam O'Shanter
(ch.c. 1985)		Sharpen Up	Atan
	Smarten Up	(ch 1969)	Rocchetta
	(ch 1975)	L'Anguissola	Soderini
		(b 1967)	Posh

her other four winning foals were successful at around a mile in the latest season—Young Jason (by Star Appeal) three times in handicaps and the three-year-old Military Fashion (by Mill Reef) in a maiden on his debut. Her first two foals Brightner (by Sparkler) and La Tuerta (by Hot Spark) were both quite useful winners; Brightner was a stayer and won over hurdles in 1988/9, where as La Tuerta was very speedy and is the dam of the fair 1989 two-year-old La Cabrilla, third in the Princess Margaret Stakes at Ascot. Smarten Up's yearling, a colt by Be My Guest, was knocked down to ZHL Associates for 200,000 guineas at the Highflyer Sales, 10,000 guineas less than Cadeaux Genereux made at the same age. ZHL Associates also paid 700,000 guineas for the sale-topper, a colt by Nureyev. Smarten Up was herself a smart sprinter, running her best race on her final outing as a three-year-old when second to Solinus in the William Hill Sprint Championship. She is a half-sister to Solar, very useful at up to a mile and a quarter, and to the very useful sprinter Walk By. The second dam L'Anguissola, a useful winner at two years but disappointing at three, is a half-sister to the dam of the tough handicap sprinter Dawn's Delight. Cadeaux Genereux was effective at five furlongs to a mile, though he'll be remembered principally for sprinting. He showed his best form on a sound surface. Waiting tactics suited him, on account of his tendency to idle in front, but he was thoroughly genuine. He used to race with his tongue tied down, but didn't in his final season. *A. A. Scott.*

CADFORD BALARINA 2 ch.f. (Feb 19) Adonijah 126–Jarama (Amber Rama (USA) 133) [1989 5d 5d 5d⁵ 7f 6f² 7m⁵ 7f⁴ 6m] smallish, sparely-made filly: half-sister to Irish middle-distance winner Red Rose Garden (by Electric) and French 9f winner Kenoba (by Young Generation): dam unraced half-sister to top-class 1972 2-y-o Jacinth: moderate plater: best effort fifth start: will stay 1m. *W. G. M. Turner.* **47**

CAERLEON'S EDGE 3 br.f. Caerleon (USA) 132–Edge of Town 101 (Habitat 134) [1988 7f 7s 1989 10.1d⁵ 12g] sturdy, angular filly: well beaten, including in seller. *P. Mitchell.* **—**

CAERNARVON ROYAL 4 ch.g. Main Reef 126–Berserk 68 (Romulus 129) [1988 6m* 6d² 6m 6d 1989 8s 7g 8m 7f a6g] compact gelding: modest winner (for apprentice) as 3-y-o: well beaten in varied events in 1989: stays 6f: acts on top-of-the-ground and a soft surface: sweating second outing: visored fourth: has shown a tendency to edge left: trained first 4 starts by C. Hill. *R. J. Hodges.* **—**

CAFFARELLI 2 b.c. (Apr 17) Mummy's Pet 125–Klewraye (Lord Gayle (USA) 124) [1989 6f² 5m² 6g³] 31,000Y: smallish, close-coupled, sparely-made colt: good mover: fifth foal: half-brother to 3-y-o 1¼m and 11.7f winner High I Kew (by High Top), quite useful 1986 2-y-o 6f winner Pas d'Enchere (by Pas de Seul), later successful abroad, and a winner in West Indies: dam Irish 2-y-o 7f winner: modest maiden: will probably stay 7f. *R. Guest.* **73**

CAGLIARI 2 ch.c. (Apr 15) Dominion 123–Bedeni 100 (Parthia 132) [1989 8m 10g a8g] IR 21,000Y: half-brother to 3-y-o Power Boat (by Jalmood) and several winners, including very useful 1976 2-y-o 5f to 7f winner Sky Ship (by Roan Rocket) and smart 1¼m filly Upper Deck (by Sun Prince): dam disappointing half-sister to smart animals Torpid and Admiral's Launch: well beaten in maidens and a minor event. *R. J. R. Williams.* **—**

CAIMANITE 3 ch.f. Tap On Wood 130–Tanzanite (USA) (Mongo) [1988 6f³ 6d 1989 7m⁵ 7m⁶ 6f³] unfurnished filly: quite modest maiden: best effort in minor event at Salisbury on reappearance: should stay 1m: blinkered final outing. *B. W. Hills.* **62**

CAIRNCASTLE 4 b.g. Ardross 134–Brookfield Miss 73 (Welsh Pageant 132) [1988 10.1m 12g² 16m* 16g² 18d⁴ 16d 16m⁵ 1989 16.1g² 19f] close-coupled, **75**

sparely-made gelding: has a rather round action: 20/1, good second of 7 in handicap at Newmarket in July: always behind in £7,400 handicap at Goodwood 2 weeks later: suited by 2m: acts on top-of-the-ground: sold to join J. White 7,000 gns Newmarket Autumn Sales. *R. J. R. Williams.*

CAJUN DANCER 5 ch.g. Cajun 120–Gay Folly (Wolver Hollow 126) [1988 NR 1989 10.8d] strong, lengthy gelding: quite modest maiden at 2 yrs: well beaten only 2 subsequent outings on flat. *J. L. Harris.* —

CALABALI 2 b.f. (Mar 9) Persian Bold 123–Bedfellow 104 (Crepello 136) [1989 8f 9f2] 12,000Y: workmanlike filly: half-sister to 17f winner Bedfellow (by Shirley Heights), 13f winner Major Setback (by Brigadier Gerard) and useful Italian winner Blood Royal (by Silly Season): dam, half-sister to Oaks winner Polygamy and Cheshire Oaks winner One Over Parr, stayed at least 1½m: edgy, 2 lengths second of 6 to Alimana in maiden at Wolverhampton in October, much better effort: will stay well. *R. Hollinshead.* 69

CALACHUCHI 2 b.f. (Apr 12) Martinmas 128–Seleter (Hotfoot 126) [1989 6m 6m5] first foal: dam in rear, including in sellers: over 13 lengths fifth of 19, running on final 2f, to Beehive Boy in seller at Newcastle in August: slowly away on debut: should stay 7f. *M. J. Camacho.* —

CALAFURIA 3 b.f. Chief Singer 131–Cattarina Ginnasi (ITY) (Tierceron (ITY)) [1988 6m 1989 8d 10.6g 8g 8s4 a8g] tall, leggy filly: poor maiden: worth a try over 7f: possibly suited by a soft surface: refused to enter stalls intended debut: trained until after third outing by Don Enrico Incisa. *N. Tinkler.* —

CALAHONDA BAY 4 b.c. Bay Express 132–Bauhinia 70 (Sagaro 133) [1988 6g 8f 8g 6s 8s* 6f2 7g 7g 1989 6s 7s 7.5d 8.2m 6m 8g5 9g 6g] medium-sized, good-bodied colt: poor mover: plater: form as 4-y-o only on sixth outing: stays 1m: acts on any going: inconsistent: sold 1,000 gns Doncaster November Sales. *N. Bycroft.* 51

CALAHONDA DAVE 2 gr.g. (Apr 17) Song 132–Great Grey Niece 74 (Great Nephew 126) [1989 6f3 7m2 6s 6g3] 14,500F, 6,200Y: leggy, close-coupled gelding: closely related to 7f winner Petrice (by Mummy's Pet) and half-brother to winning sprinters Absolution (by Absalom) and Peckitt's Well (by Lochnager) and a winner in Belgium: dam placed over 5f at 2 yrs: useful form in sellers on first 2 starts: favourite, creditable third to Mac Kelty in nursery at Hamilton final start: gives impression may prove best at 6f: bandaged second start. *R. M. Whitaker.* 61

CALAHONDA SONG 3 ch.c. Song 132–Obergurgl 69 (Warpath 113) [1988 6f 6g 6g6 5m 6f 10d 8.2v6 1989 7m 6m 8.5f5 9f5 11f4 10g 8.5f 10.2g 10m5] rangy colt: poor maiden: should prove best at up to 9f: possibly needs firm ground: blinkered third outing: visored (wearing crossed noseband and edgy) sixth: sometimes takes strong hold. *N. Bycroft.* 47 d

CALGARY REDEYE 2 gr.c. (May 13) Kalaglow 132–River Call (FR) 103 (Riverman (USA) 131) [1989 7g4 8.2g6 a8g* a8g5] 7,000Y: small, dipped-backed colt: moderate walker: brother to modest maiden First Forum and half-brother to 3-y-o 11.7f winner Ferrystream (by Niniski), fair stayer Tiber River (by Troy) and 2 other winners abroad: dam won from 7f to 11f: modest performer: outpaced most of way when winning Lingfield maiden narrowly in November: will be suited by 1¼m. *P. J. Makin.* 73

CALGROUP LAD 2 ch.g. (Mar 31) Free State 125–At First Sight (He Loves Me 120) [1989 5f 6m 6g 8.5f4 8.2s 7f] 600F, IR 4,400Y, 6,000 2-y-o: compact gelding: good mover: first foal: dam unraced: of little account: sold 975 gns Ascot October Sales. *J. S. Wilson.* 34

CALICON 3 ch.g. Connaught 130–Calgary 63 (Run The Gantlet (USA)) [1988 NR 1989 11s4 11.7d5 13.3m4 15s* 13.3d] lengthy, angular gelding: has scope: fourth foal: half-brother to 1½m and 1¾m winner Widdicombe Fair and to a winner abroad (both by Fair Season): dam, middle-distance maiden, is half-sister to Cesarewitch winner Centurion: won minor event at Ayr in September, leading on bridle over 4f out, soon clear then weakening and edging badly right final 2f: second favourite, lost position long way out when tailed off in handicap at Newbury 5 weeks later: may prove best at bit short of 15f: best efforts on soft going, but shaped reasonably well on top-of-the-ground: winning hurdler. *I. A. Balding.* 90

CALLAGHAN 4 b.g. Cut Above 130–Super Restless (USA) (Restless Wind) [1988 10d 8g 10m 10d 8.2d 8m 1989 12.5f6 9f] compact, good-bodied gelding: poor mover: poor maiden: has run in sellers: sometimes pulls hard, and has worn severe bridle: bandaged as 4 yrs: sold to join S. Kettlewell 1,200 gns Doncaster May Sales: winning selling hurdler. *K. G. Wingrove.* —

CALL A TRUCE 4 b.g. Hard Fought 125–Celestial Star 108 (So Blessed 130) **48**
[1988 12g 12.2m 8s 10s³ 10d² 12g² 1989 10s² 10g⁵ 12s⁴ 12s 10.1m] small,
close-coupled gelding: poor mover: poor maiden: ran moderately last 2 outings:
better suited by 1¼m than 1½m, particularly when conditions are testing: acts on
soft going and possibly unsuited by top-of-the-ground: sometimes wears crossed
noseband: sold 4,100 gns Ascot July Sales: subsequently gelded: has appeared
ungenuine. *P. Mitchell.*

CALL FOR TAYLOR 5 b.m. Giacometti 130–Indian Wells (Reliance II 137) —
[1988 14s 1989 8g] tall, leggy, workmanlike mare: has a round action: form on flat
only when winning seller as 3-y-o: suited by 1m: acts on top-of-the-ground:
sweating only outing at 4 yrs: bandaged only one at 5 yrs: sold 1,000 gns Newmarket
December Sales. *H. J. Collingridge.*

CALLIPOLI (USA) 2 br.f. (Mar 7) Green Dancer (USA) 132–Minstrelete (USA) **73**
(Round Table) [1989 7f⁶ 7g] 82,000Y: fair sort, rather angular: half-sister to several
winners here and abroad, including smart Irish 7f and 9f winner Punctilio (by Forli)
and dam of Always Fair: dam, winner over 1m, is half-sister to top-class Gay
Fandango: 50/1, around 6 lengths eighth of 24 to Katsina in maiden at Newmarket in
November, much better effort: green and in need of race on debut. *Lord John
FitzGerald.*

CALL RACECALL 2 b.c. (Apr 27) Reasonable (FR) 119–Miel (Pall Mall 132) **68**
[1989 5m⁵ 5d⁵ 6g⁶ 8g³ 8m 8g] IR 5,000F, 14,000Y: smallish, sturdy colt: has a quick
action: half-brother to useful middle-distance stayer Prince of Peace (by Busted),
1986 2-y-o 6f winner Wind of Peace (by Taufan) and 1988 2-y-o 1m winner Evanna's
Pride (by Main Reef): dam never ran: quite modest maiden: ran moderately in
nursery on final start: better suited by 1m than shorter. *C. W. Thornton.*

CALL TO ARMS 2 b.c. (Mar 30) North Briton 67–Branitska (Mummy's **116**
Pet 125) [1989 6m* 5f4 7.5f* 7.3m² 7g² 6g²]
    North Briton was retired to his owner's Stetchworth Park Stud at the
end of the 1984 Flat season as the winner of two ordinary twelve-furlong
handicaps from a career total of twenty-eight starts. Even at the modest fee of
£100 he attracted just nine mares in his first year; his fertility rate was
moderate too, and by the 1986 covering season he'd been handed the
unenviable role of teaser. Under normal circumstances little more would have
been heard of North Briton, but on one occasion the three-year-old filly
Branitska refused to have anything to do with her intended mate Wolver
Heights. So, North Briton was allowed to deputise. The union provided one of
the more unusual success stories of 1989 when the resultant foal Call To
Arms came close to capturing the Group 1 Three Chimneys Dewhurst Stakes
at Newmarket in October. Call To Arms was the 66/1-outsider of seven in the
Dewhurst—on form even those odds didn't appear particularly generous. His
two wins, at Newmarket and Beverley in early-summer, had both come in
auction company, and even the form he showed to finish runner-up in a
Newbury nursery on his latest start after a fourteen-week lay-off seemed to
leave him with at least a stone to make up on the likes of Welney. Call To
Arms wasn't overshadowed in the paddock—he'd progressed well physically
since his lay-off—and he justified his presence in the line-up with a fine
performance, battling on splendidly once Dashing Blade hit the front to go
down by a neck, with Anshan a short head away in third. With the whole field
covered by little over four lengths the Dewhurst form clearly wasn't
exceptional, and that Call To Arms had occupied a prominent position from
the start in a race that wasn't run at an end-to-end gallop suggested he might
have been flattered. However, he put up another fine performance when he
turned out for the inaugural running of the Racecall Gold Trophy at Redcar
eleven days later. Instead of being found wanting for pace on his return to six
furlongs, the 8/1-shot Call To Arms had every chance throughout and stayed
on strongly under pressure to finish a clear second of twenty-five behind the
highly-regarded Osario.
    While North Briton's form hardly qualified him for a place at stud it was
still way ahead of Branitska's. Branitska showed no semblance of ability in a
career which saw her beat only two opponents in four races each of which
contained at least eleven runners. She has some breeding, in that her unraced
dam is closely related to the successful sire Dominion and is a half-sister to

Mr W. J. Gredley's "Call To Arms"

numerous other winners including that admirable old warrior Prominent. North Briton could be said to be bred well enough to win a classic. His dam Juliette Marny won two of them, the Oaks and the Irish Guinness Oaks, and was out of the same mare as two other classic winners, Julio Mariner and Scintillate. Now that Call To Arms has given him a start perhaps he'll get a better chance to prove himself as a stallion.

Call To Arms (b.c. Mar 30, 1987)	North Briton (b 1979)	Northfields (ch 1968)	Northern Dancer
			Little Hut
		Juliette Marny (b 1972)	Blakeney
			Set Free
	Branitska (b or br 1983)	Mummy's Pet (b 1968)	Sing Sing
			Money For Nothing
		Top Piece (b 1978)	High Top
			Picture Palace

Call To Arms is a leggy, quite good-topped colt who cost 7,200 guineas as a yearling. The Two Thousand Guineas is reportedly on his agenda for 1990, but we very much doubt he'll be good enough for that, although the distance of the race ought to suit him well. In fact, Call To Arms could be a difficult horse to place: he doesn't seem open to any abnormal improvement, and his form, smart though it is, falls a fair way short of what's required to beat good horses at levels. However, all that's unlikely to dissuade his trainer from pitching him in against the best. Clive Brittain is renowned not only for his optimism in placing his horses, but for the frequency with which it proves justified. We had plenty of examples in the latest season, from the likes of Terimon, Spring Hay, Air Music, Top Class, Cottenham and, of course, Call To Arms who all reached the frame at 50/1 or longer in pattern races. *C. E. Brittain.*

CALVANNE MISS 3 b.f. Martinmas 128–Blue Empress (Blue Cashmere 129) **46**
[1988 5.8f* 5g* 6g3 5g5 5.8d 1989 5s 6g 5h 5m 6m2 6m6 7m] leggy filly: modest plater: should stay 7f: possibly unsuited by a soft surface. *C. J. Hill.*

CALYPSO REEF 3 b.c. Cragador 110–Kellys Reef 92 (Pitskelly 122) [1988 NR **66**
1989 6g 6m5 8f 7f* 6m5 7m 7g 6f 5f 6g3] compact colt: has a quick action: first foal: dam sprinter: quite modest handicapper: won maiden at Edinburgh in June: well below form sixth to ninth outings: best form over 6f or sharp 7f: acts on firm going: blinkered seventh and eighth outings: sold 10,000 gns Newmarket Autumn Sales. *A. Hide.*

CAMBO (USA) 3 b.c. Roberto (USA) 131–Cameo Shore (Mill Reef (USA) 141) **94** p
[1988 NR 1989 11s3 10s2 10g*] close-coupled, good-quartered colt: has scope: fourth foal: half-brother to modest maiden Atropa (by Vaguely Noble) and 11f winner Bronte (by Bold Forbes): dam very useful winner over 7f and 10.5f in France: won minor event at Nottingham in October by ¾ length (clear) from Marcinkus, always close up and quickening well to lead over 2f out: fairly useful form in maidens in the spring: will stay 1½m: may well improve further. *J. Tree.*

CAMDEN KNIGHT 4 b.c. Camden Town 125–Motionless 109 (Midsummer **67**
Night II 117) [1988 8v3 9g4 10d 8g* 8g 10g 8g 8.2m3 8d* 8v 10g 1989 8g 8.5d4 10.2g3 12f3 11m6 14f] leggy, good-topped colt: poor mover: quite modest handicapper on his day: 66/1, always behind in Tote Ebor (Handicap) at York final outing: stays 1½m: acts on any going: inconsistent. *N. Bycroft.*

CAMDEN'S RANSOM (USA) 2 b.c. (Jan 20) Hostage (USA)–Camden Court **58**
(USA) (Inverness Drive (USA)) [1989 6m 7f] lengthy, rather angular colt: first foal: dam unraced half-sister to 9f graded-stakes winner Ironworks: around 11 lengths eighth of 14, never dangerous, to El Paso at Salisbury in October, second and better effort in maidens. *M. J. Fetherston-Godley.*

CAMEO PERFORMANCE (USA) 2 b. or br.f. (Feb 24) Be My Guest (USA) **78**
126–Nancy Chere (USA) (Gallant Man) [1989 7g3 7m2] IR 135,000Y: good-bodied filly: fifth foal: dam, stakes-placed winner at up to 1m, is half-sister to smart middle-distance filly Joli Vert, smart 1m to 1½m performer Grey Beret and smart 1984 French 2-y-o Rapide Pied: still bit backward, ½-length second of 6, travelling strongly long way, to Glazerite in minor event at Doncaster in July: will probably stay 1m. *B. W. Hills.*

CAMMY COME HOME 2 b.f. (Apr 3) Camden Town 125–Thank You Fans 67 —
(Be My Guest (USA) 126) [1989 5g 5d 5f 5f 6f 6g 5f] 720Y: leggy, rather narrow filly: poor mover: first foal: dam stayed 1m: well beaten in varied company, including selling: blinkered last 2 outings. *J. Balding.*

CAMPAI 2 b.c. (Mar 26) Try My Best (USA) 130–Musing 79 (Music Maestro 119) **72** p
[1989 7g6] neat colt: first foal: dam 2-y-o sprint winner, is granddaughter of Oaks runner-up West Side Story: 33/1 and backward, over 10 lengths sixth of 28, going on well, to Rami in maiden at Newmarket in November: sure to improve. *R. W. Armstrong.*

CAMPFIRE 3 b.f. Auction Ring (USA) 123–Ardneasken 84 (Right Royal V 135) —
[1988 7s 1989 12d5 12.3m5 15s] small, sparely-made filly: probably of little account. *C. W. Thornton.*

CAMPING OUT 4 b.f. Beldale Flutter (USA) 130–Base Camp 80 (Derring-Do —
131) [1988 10d 11.7m6 12.2d5 14.5g3 14f2 16m4 12d 16d 1989 12.5g] strong, deep-girthed filly: has a powerful, round action: quite modest maiden at best: tailed off when pulled up at halfway in claimer at Wolverhampton (moved moderately down) in May: needs at least 1¾m: acts on firm going. *R. P. C. Hoad.*

CAMSHAFT 3 b.f. Camden Town 125–Doll Acre (Linacre 133) [1988 5s4 5f3 6f3 **53**
6m 6d5 7m 6m5 5f5 5g 1989 6s5 8.2s 6m 6g 6f2 7h6 6m6] small, rather sparely-made filly: fair plater: suited by 6f: acts on any going: claimer ridden first 3 and final starts: often bandaged off-hind: has run below form when sweating: inconsistent. *E. Eldin.*

CANBRACK COTTAGE 3 ch.f. Gorytus (USA) 132–Cottage Style 65 (Thatch —
(USA) 136) [1988 NR 1989 8m] first foal: dam, winner twice at 1½m, is daughter of

half-sister to Lorenzaccio: 100/1, always behind in minor event at Edinburgh in October. *W. A. Stephenson.*

CANBRACK STYLE 2 b.f. (Apr 10) Glenstal (USA) 118–Cottage Style 65 — (Thatch (USA) 136) [1989 8m 8g] second foal: half-sister to 3-y-o Canbrack Cottage (by Gorytus): dam, winner twice at 1½m, is daughter of half-sister to Lorenzaccio: well beaten in maidens at Edinburgh. *W. A. Stephenson.*

CANDAVIA 2 b.f. (Feb 25) Ardross 134–Sly Wink (Song 132) [1989 6m 8.2g] 9,200Y: good-quartered filly: first foal: dam unraced half-sister to speedy Hawkins: soundly beaten in maiden (bit backward) at Newbury and auction event at Hamilton. *M. D. I. Usher.*

CANDESCO 3 b.f. Blushing Scribe (USA) 107–Madame Mim 57 (Artaius (USA) — 129) [1988 NR 1989 8.2m 10d] 700F: strong, close-coupled filly: second foal: closely related to a winner in Italy by Coquelin: dam, plating-class maiden, stayed 1½m: backward, no promise in maidens at Haydock and Newbury (pulled hard) in the autumn. *B. A. McMahon.*

CANDLE TIME 3 ch.f. Aragon 118–Nimbostratus (Lorenzaccio 130) [1988 7g — 1989 6f 8m] angular, sparely-made filly: little worthwhile form in maidens: sold 1,250 gns Newmarket September Sales. *M. H. Tompkins.*

CANDY GLEN 2 b.c. (Mar 25) Glenstal (USA) 118–Maiden Concert (Condorcet **106** (FR)) [1989 5d* 5m* 6f3 7m* 6m 8s*] IR 12,000Y: well-made, quite attractive colt: has scope: good mover: second foal: dam once-raced half-sister to dam of Irish 1000 Guineas winner More So: useful colt: successful in maiden at Newmarket in April, minor events at Beverley in June and Sandown in September and Gran Criterium (by 2 lengths from Naval Party) at Milan in October: ran poorly in Rokeby Farms Mill Reef Stakes at Newbury, fourth outing: suited by 1m: probably acts on any going. *C. F. Wall.*

CANNEY'S KINGDOM 3 ch.f. Noalto 120–Sand Valley (FR) 61 (Arabian) — [1988 6f 6m5 7h 7g 1989 6s 5s6 6m 6m 6f] sparely-made filly: little form for some time: not seen out after June: best form at 6f, but should be suited by further: blinkered fourth start: sometimes sweating and edgy. *E. A. Wheeler.*

CANNON'S SPIRIT 2 gr.c. (May 4) King Persian 107–Tinsel 95 (Right Boy **61** ? 137) [1989 5s4 5m 6f2] IR 8,000F, 16,500Y: workmanlike colt: half-brother to several winners here and abroad, notably very useful sprinter Sparkling Boy and quite useful sprinter Roger Bacon (both by Comedy Star): dam genuine 5f to 7f handicapper: beaten 2 lengths by sole rival Yanabee in maiden at Thirsk in August: poor form in similar events previously, hanging left in auction race on second start. *J. Berry.*

CANNON'S WAY 3 b.c. Young Generation 129–Lady of Ireland 82 (Be My **75** d Guest (USA) 126) [1988 5d* 5m* 5m* 6g2 5g5 5f4 5d4 5g3 1989 5g3 5v4 7f4 6m2 5f3 5m 6g 6m] lengthy, robust, rather dipped-backed colt: good, keen walker: fair performer at his best: well below form last 4 outings: claimed out of J. Berry's stable £10,101 sixth out: appears to stay 7f: possibly unsuited by heavy going: blinkered fifth start: one to treat with caution. *G. A. Pritchard-Gordon.*

CANONESS 8 b.m. St Paddy 133–Sea Fable 51 (Typhoon 125) [1988 11.7m2 12f3 **52** 10m 1989 11.7d* 11.7m6 10f6 13.3m4 12m 11.7m 10.2f 10.2f6 12.2f2 a12g] small mare: poor handicapper: won at Bath in April: form after third outing only when 5 lengths second in apprentice event at Warwick: probably better suited by 1½m than 1¼m: acts on firm going and a soft surface: good mount for apprentice: sweating and bit edgy sixth outing: usually races up with pace: sold 3,200 gns Ascot November Sales. *P. Hayward.*

CANON'S COURT 4 b.g. Main Reef 126–My Fawn 67 (Hugh Lupus 132) [1988 — 8f 8g 8f 8m 10.2g6 8g 6m 8g 1989 8.3m 11.7g] angular, workmanlike gelding: has a round action: bad maiden. *M. Madgwick.*

CANTDONOWTRITE 2 gr.c. (Mar 7) Belfort (FR) 89–Miss Tantan (Native **74** Admiral (USA)) [1989 5d* 5g4 6m5 5m* 5g2 5s2 5g] 7,000Y: lengthy colt: second foal: half-brother to poor 1988 2-y-o plater Pa-Ross-Ite (by Raise A Dancer): dam little worthwhile form: modest performer: won 4-runner minor event at Catterick in April and 3-runner nursery at Edinburgh in July: ran badly final start: best form at 5f: suited by an easy surface: often edgy: tends to hang, and is not an easy ride. *J. Berry.*

CANTORIS 3 b.f. Song 132–Singing Witch 71 (Sing Sing 134) [1988 NR 1989 5f3 **71** 6h2 5m2 6g4 5.3f* 5m6 a6g] leggy, close-coupled filly: half-sister to several winners, including 1987 2-y-o 5f winner Annie Sullivan (by Aragon) and 1985 2-y-o 1m winner My Ton Ton (by Good Times): dam half-sister to smart sprinter Vilgora: improved form when winning maiden at Brighton in October, hanging left and leading close home: ran creditably next start: suited by 5f: acts on firm ground: didn't look entirely satisfactory second and fourth (apprentices) outings. *R. J. R. Williams.*

CANTUS FIRMUS   3 b.c. Lyphard's Special (USA) 122–Capricious (FR) 105   **78** (Snob II 130) [1988 NR 1989 7g⁵ 7v³ 10s 10f 8.5g 7m 10.4g* 12m* 16g⁴ 18.4f³ 14f 12m] IR 5,400Y: angular, dipped-backed colt: moderate walker and mover: half-brother to Italian 4-y-o Zoc (by Posse), successful from 6f to 1¼m, Irish 1¼m winner Tapcap (by Tap On Wood) and winners abroad: dam won from 7f to 1½m: won claimers at Chester (maiden event, went badly down) and Goodwood within 3 days in late-June: gives impression may prove suited by around 1¾m: acts on firm going: well below form in blinkers fifth start: trained until after tenth by P. Kelleway. *P. Leach.*

CANTY'S GOLD   3 b.f. Sonnen Gold 121–Canty Day 87 (Canadel II 126) [1988 5d   — 6m 6f⁵ 7g² 7g³ 7m 8g 10s 1989 8m 12.2m] leggy, angular filly: has a long stride: poor maiden: well behind in claimers in spring as 3-y-o: blinkered third outing. *J. J. O'Neill.*

CAPA   9 ch.g. New Member 119–Poshteen 86 (Royal Smoke 113) [1988 17.1g³ 16f   — 17g⁴ 17.1g* 18g⁶ 16d⁶ 1989 16f³ 18g] sturdy, plain gelding: good sixth in Tote Cesarewitch at Newmarket on penultimate outing in 1988: has not reproduced that form, and tailed off in same event (burly) as 9-y-o: stays 2¼m: possibly needs a sound surface: ridden by 7-lb claimer first 3 starts in 1988: fairly useful hurdler. *O. O'Neill.*

CAPABILITY BROWN   2 b.c. (Feb 22) Dominion 123–Tomfoolery 73 (Silly   **84** Season 127) [1989 8m³ 10g⁵] good-topped, close-coupled colt: moderate walker: eighth living foal: half-brother to 3-y-o 10.4f and 12.5f winner Springs Welcome (by Blakeney) and 3 winners in Belgium: dam raced only at 2 yrs: 33/1, 4½ lengths third of 29 to Defensive Play in maiden at Newmarket in October: will stay 1½m. *D. Morley.*

CAPEABILITY POUND   6 ro.g. Balboa–Olibanum 61 (Frankincense 120)   — [1988 5m 5d 5m 5d⁴ 6g 6m 5m 5s 5m 1989 6m 5m 5m 5m 7f 8g 5m 7m 5f] lengthy, good-quartered, active sort: modest at best, but has shown virtually nothing for long time: stays 6f: best form on a sound surface: sometimes blinkered or visored: has sweated: has won for apprentice. *A. W. Jones.*

CAPE PEARL   3 ch.f. Dominion 123–Pearlesque 88 (Gulf Pearl 117) [1988 NR   **73** 1989 7f 7f³ 6f 7.6m] small, compact filly: sister to 4-y-o Dominion Pearl and half-sister to 4 winners, including Pearlescent (by My Swallow), a smart winner at up to 1m: dam won over 5f: fair maiden: third at Kempton in June: below form after: may prove best at up to 7f: sold, probably for export, 2,000 gns Newmarket Autumn Sales. *C. R. Nelson.*

CAPE PIGEON (USA)   4 ch.g. Storm Bird (CAN) 134–Someway Somehow   **81** (USA) (What Luck (USA)) [1988 8d⁶ 10g⁴ 10d 10d⁴ 10.8d 1989 7f 9.2f 7f³ 6m 6g³ 7f² 7f⁴ 7m²] big, strong, angular gelding: fair maiden: ideally needs further than 6f and stays 1¼m: acts on firm going and a soft surface: visored final start at 3 yrs. *L. G. Cottrell.*

CAPITAL BUILDER   3 b.g. Pas de Seul 133–Double Touch (FR) (Nonoalco   **54** (USA) 131) [1988 6d 5f⁴ 5d⁵ 7f³ 6s 1989 8.5d 8.5g 8g 8f 7m⁴ 8g* 9f⁶ 11g] good-topped gelding: moderate walker: fair plater: won moderately-run race (bought in 5,300 gns) at Ayr in July, making most: stays 1m, at least in moderately-run race: acts on firm going: has joined I. Semple. *G. M. Moore.*

CAPTAIN BONKERS   3 ch.g. Jasmine Star 113–Royal Tip (Mount Hagen (FR)   — § 127) [1988 5g 6g 5f 1989 5g⁶ 5g] leggy gelding: no worthwhile form and looks thoroughly ungenuine: has been tried in blinkers and hood: changed hands 2,600 gns Doncaster May Sales: sold to join M. Clutterbuck 2,200 gns Ascot August Sales: clearly one to avoid. *Capt. J. Wilson.*

CAPTAIN BROWN   2 b.g. (May 18) Welsh Captain 113–Belinda Brown 83   — (Legal Eagle 126) [1989 a6g] angular, lightly-made gelding: second live foal: dam 2-y-o 5f winner: soundly beaten in Southwell claimer in December. *T. D. Barron.*

CAPTAIN CHROME   2 b.g. (May 14) Welsh Captain 113–Chrome Mag 63   — (Prince de Galles 125) [1989 5g⁶ 8f 7g] leggy gelding: second foal: dam 1m and 1¼m winner: soundly beaten at Leicester in maidens and minor event. *K. S. Bridgwater.*

CAPTAIN CUTE   4 ro.g. Absalom 128–Cute 75 (Hardicanute 130) [1988 6g 8s   **54** 7m 8f 6m 7m³ 8.2m³ 8g 8g 8.2d³ 9v³ 1989 8d 9f⁵ 10f] workmanlike gelding: good mover: plating-class maiden: stays 9f: acts on any going: sold to join R. Barr 1,100 gns Newmarket September Sales. *D. T. Thom.*

CAPTAIN FAWLEY 2 br.g. (Jan 24) Petorius 117–Lady Fawley 86 (He Loves — p
Me 120) [1989 7g 6g 5g] IR 7,400Y, 14,500 2-y-o: strong, useful-looking gelding:
second foal: dam Irish 2-y-o 1m winner: shaped quite well, never placed to challenge
or knocked about, in October maidens at Goodwood (auction event), Newmarket
and Redcar: looks sort to do better. *W. J. Musson.*

CAPTAIN MAVERICK (USA) 3 ch.c. Nureyev (USA) 131–Little Tobago —
(USA) (Impressive (USA)) [1988 NR 1989 8v⁵ 10.2f 10f] 35,000Y: big, leggy, lengthy
colt: eighth foal: brother to 1¼m winner Monfarid and half-brother to 4 winners,
notably Preakness Stakes runner-up Play On (by Stop The Music): dam won at up to
7f and is half-sister to dam of very smart Beau's Eagle: appears of little account:
trained debut by H. O'Neill: sold 2,800 gns Doncaster November Sales. *C. E.
Brittain.*

CAPTAIN'S BIDD 9 ch.g. Captain James 123–Muffet 75 (Matador 131) [1988   69
5m 5d 6g 5f 5f³ 5. 1f 5f 5g⁴ 5m⁴ 5g⁶ 5g⁵ 6m 7f⁶ 7m 6m 5d² 5v⁶ 1989 7d 6d² 6m⁶ 6f
5m* 6m 5f² 5m² 5f⁴ 5m³ 7f⁵ 5g² 5g⁵ 5m 5f³ 5. 1g⁴ 5f* 5m 6g 5m* a6g* a5g⁶] sturdy,
workmanlike gelding: carries plenty of condition: usually dull in coat: moderate
mover: quite modest handicapper: kept his form really well, winning at Edinburgh in
June (selling event, no bid) and October, Beverley (carried 7 lb overweight) in
September and Southwell in November: best at 5f or easy 6f nowadays: acts on any
going: effective with or without blinkers or visor: ran poorly when sweating: good
mount for apprentice: tough and consistent. *R. Thompson.*

CAPTIVE HEART 3 b.f. Conquistador Cielo (USA)–Knights Beauty (USA)   74
(True Knight (USA)) [1988 NR 1989 10g 8m⁶ 7f² 8g 7g⁶] smallish, workmanlike
filly: second foal: dam won at up to 9f: modest maiden: hung left from halfway when
putting up easily best effort on fourth start: faced stiff task in handicap next time:
suited by 7f and top-of-the-ground. *H. Candy.*

CARANIYA 3 br.f. Darshaan 133–Callianire (Sir Gaylord) [1988 8g* 1989 10m⁵   94
12.3f* 14m⁶] leggy, sparely-made filly: has a quick action: won 5-runner handicap at
Ripon in August, staying on strongly to lead close home: favourite, beaten when not
much room 3f out and not given hard race in similar event next time: suited by 1½m:
acts on firm going. *M. R. Stoute.*

CARAZZA 2 b.f. (Apr 29) Norwick (USA) 120–B M Wonder (Junius (USA) 124) —
[1989 7m] small, sturdy filly: second foal: half-sister to 3-y-o Hostage (by Homing):
dam, granddaughter of Oaks winner Carrozza, well beaten on only 3 starts: 16/1 and
bit backward, ran green and always behind in 16-runner seller at Wolverhampton in
August. *J. W. Hills.*

CARBISDALE 3 ch.g. Dunbeath (USA) 127–Kind Thoughts 71 (Kashmir II 125)   73
[1988 8f⁶ 8m 1989 10m² 12.3m³ 14g] workmanlike gelding: has a round action:
modest maiden: suited by 1½m: changed hands 7,200 gns Newmarket Autumn
Sales. *E. Weymes.*

CARBONATE 4 b.g. Mr Fluorocarbon 126–Girl On A Swing 79 (High Top 131) —
[1988 10d⁴ 10s⁵ 7m 1989 8v 8m 8g] strong gelding: won maiden auction race only
start as 2-y-o: lightly raced and little subsequent form on flat: stays 1m: winner over
hurdles. *M. H. Easterby.*

CARBON TRACK 3 ch.c. Mr Fluorocarbon 126–Track Anna 73 (Track Spare —
125) [1988 5g 5m⁶ 5g⁴ 5.1g 5d 6f⁵ 5g 5f 8g 7g 1989 6f 7m 8.5m 11g 10g] smallish,
close-coupled, angular colt: plating-class maiden: well below form (mostly in
sellers) as 3-y-o, blinkered and leading 7f final start: should be suited by further
than 5f: visored fifth start at 2 yrs, blinkered seventh to ninth: sold 820 gns
Doncaster September Sales. *P. S. Felgate.*

CARDIFF ARMS 2 b.f. (Mar 4) Another Realm 118–Gemgem 54 (Lochnager   51
132) [1989 5m⁵ 6m³ 6m 6f 6m] 1,500Y: small filly: first foal: dam won 7f seller: poor
maiden: shaped quite well in nursery at Nottingham fourth start, travelling
smoothly when not getting clear run 2f out and eased: poorly drawn in similar event
at Haydock (on toes, taken quietly down) later in September: better suited by 6f
than 5f. *D. Haydn Jones.*

CAREER BAY 7 b.g. Orange Bay 131–Career (Hotfoot 126) [1988 NR 1989 12.2s] —
lengthy gelding: poor handicapper: tailed off at Warwick in March: best form at 1½m
on an easy surface: winning chaser. *D. Haydn Jones.*

CAREFUL LAD 3 b.c. Precocious 126–Arenetta (Bold Lad (IRE) 133) [1988 NR   75
1989 6s⁵ 6d² 7m* 6s³] IR 36,000Y: sturdy, good-quartered colt: closely related to
1986 2-y-o French 1m winner Arabella (by Runnett), later successful in Belgium,
and half-brother to another winner in France: dam French 1m winner: moved poorly
down and struggled to land the odds in seller (bought in 7,500 gns) at Leicester in

June: ran moderately in similar event 5 months later: stays 7f: easily best effort on a soft surface. *J. P. Hudson.*

CARELESS BOY 3 b.c. Stifelius–Dominia (Derring-Do 131) [1988 NR 1989 12d⁵ — 11f⁵ 16m] fifth foal: half-brother to 2 winners in USA: dam won at around 1m in USA: backward, only sign of ability when fifth of 6 at Redcar in May on second start, having moved very badly in rear early on: sold 3,300 gns Doncaster August Sales. *I. V. Matthews.*

CARELESS KISS 5 ch.m. Persian Bold 123–More Kisses 86 (Morston (FR) — 125) [1988 10g 12d⁴ 11m 10s⁶ 12g² 12v³ 1989 10s 14.8d³ 13m 12m 15g⁴] neat mare: moderate walker and mover: well below her best in handicaps at 5 yrs: best form at up to 1½m: has won on firm going, but possibly needs an easy surface nowadays: sometimes sweats: suitable mount for apprentice: sold 1,700 gns Newmarket Autumn Sales. *I. V. Matthews.*

CARELESS LAD 3 ch.g. Precocious 126–Mousquetade (Moulton 128) [1988 8f² **77** 8m⁴ 1989 10.6g 12.5f³ 13.3d] big, rangy gelding: has scope: modest maiden: third of 4 in slowly-run minor event at Wolverhampton, easily best effort in the autumn: probably stays 1½m: possibly unsuited by a soft surface: sold J. Frost 13,000 gns Doncaster November Sales. *I. V. Matthews.*

CARINA BELLE 3 gr.f. High Top 131–Caraquenga (USA) 72 (Cyane) [1988 6d⁴ **69** 6g³ 6f³ 7f 1989 7d 7h* 7.3m⁵ 7g⁶ 8.3m² 10f⁶ 8d² 8g⁶ a7g⁶] medium-sized, workmanlike filly: modest handicapper: won at Brighton in May: creditable second at Windsor and Goodwood: stays 1m: acts on hard going and a soft surface: slowly away final start: sold 6,600 gns Newmarket December Sales. *I. A. Balding.*

CARJUJEN 5 b.g. Tumble Wind (USA)–Baldritta (FR) (Baldric II 131) [1988 10m — 1989 10m 12g 8m 10.8f⁴ 8g 9g] close-coupled gelding: modest winner as 3-y-o: no form since: stays 9f: acts on top-of-the-ground and soft surface: gelded after final start. *B. Preece.*

CARLINGFORD (USA) 3 ch.c. Irish Castle (USA)–Delta Sal (USA) (Delta **94** Judge) [1988 7s 1989 12f* 12f*] rangy colt: made virtually all when winning maiden

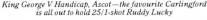

King George V Handicap, Ascot—the favourite Carlingford is all out to hold 25/1-shot Ruddy Lucky

Howard Chapman Wicks Stakes, York—Carnival Spirit makes virtually all

at Brighton in April by 25 lengths and King George V Stakes Handicap (favourite) at Royal Ascot driven out by ¾ length (clear) from Ruddy Lucky: should stay beyond 1½m: acts on firm going. *G. Harwood.*

CARLTON MOOR 2 gr.f. (Mar 15) Mandrake Major 122–Greyburn 85 (Saintly Song 128) [1989 6m 7d] quite good-topped filly: sixth foal: half-sister to 1m seller winner Cover Inn (by Tachypous) and a winner in Norway by Music Boy: dam 6f to 1m winner: not dangerous last 3f in late-season maiden (backward and green) and minor event at Thirsk. *W. W. Haigh.*   —

CARMAGNOLE (USA) 3 b.c. Lypheor 118–La Bonzo (USA) (Miracle Hill) [1988 8h³ 7g² 8d³ 1989 10.8s* 12m² 12f² 17.1h² 13.1m* 14m⁵ 12mʷᵒ 14g 12m* 12g⁵] angular, quite attractive colt: shade unfurnished: made virtually all to win maiden at Warwick in March and handicaps at Bath in July and Ascot (apprentices) in September: best at short of 2m: acts on any going: goes well with forcing tactics: winning novice hurdler. *G. Harwood.*   **93**

CARNBREA FRED 3 b.g. Montekin 125–Vote Barolo (Nebbiolo 125) [1988 5g 5d 6m⁴ 7m 7m 8f 8f 1989 10f 10.2f⁶ 14g⁵ 12g⁶ 10g 10f 12.5f] medium-sized, lengthy gelding: good walker: showed little as 3-y-o, including in sellers: bred to stay 1m: sometimes blinkered: trained on reappearance by D. Elsworth: sold out of Dr J. Scargill's stable 850 gns Newmarket September Sales after fourth start: looks a difficult ride. *J. L. Harris.*   —

CARNIVAL SPIRIT 3 ch.f. Kris 135–Fiesta Fun 105 (Welsh Pageant 132) [1988 NR 1989 10s 10m³ 8m* 8m⁵ 6v] 230,000Y: angular filly: second foal: half-sister to fairly useful 1987 2-y-o 5f and 6f winner Vivienda (by Known Fact): dam, 1m and 1¼m winner, is half-sister to smart 6f and 7f winner Derrylin: favourite, made virtually all to win £5,400 maiden at York in June: creditable fifth in £11,100 handicap at Ascot 4 months later: stays 1m: acts on top-of-the-ground, possibly unsuited by heavy. *M. R. Stoute.*   **92**

CAROLES CLOWN 3 gr.f. Another Realm 118–Show Business 72 (Auction Ring (USA) 123) [1988 5g 5m* 5m⁶ 5g⁴ 5g 6f 8f³ 8f⁴ 7d 1989 6s 6m 7f⁶ a8g⁶ a6g] leggy, lightly-made filly: has a round action: plating-class winner at 2 yrs: well beaten in handicaps and claimer as 3-y-o, moving very badly to post third start: stays 1m: visored once at 2 yrs: has run creditably for 7-lb claimer but looks a difficult ride, and hasn't ideal attitude. *M. J. Haynes.*   — §

CAROLS BELLE 6 ch.m. Ballymore 123–Love For Money 71 (Be Friendly 130) [1988 12g⁴ 11.7m⁶ 1989 5f 8m] small, angular mare: poor maiden: possibly best at short of 1½m: has worn blinkers. *C. F. C. Jackson.*   —

CAROL'S HEIGHTS 5 ch.g. Young Man (FR) 73–Virginia Heights (Virginia Boy 106) [1988 NR 1989 12.2m⁴ 15.8f⁶ 12m⁴] leggy, angular gelding: well beaten in varied events, sweating and edgy on reappearance. *E. Weymes.*   —

CAROL SINGING 3 b.c. Lyphard's Special (USA) 122–Welsh Pride 75 (Welsh Saint 126) [1988 6f 7m 1989 8m] rangy colt, bit unfurnished: always behind in maidens and claimer. *J. Ffitch-Heyes.*   —

A. F. Budge Handicap, York—Carol's Treasure puts up a smart performance under 10-0

CAROL'S TREASURE   5 b.h. Balidar 133–Really Sharp (Sharpen Up 127) **117**
[1988 5g⁴ 5f² 5m⁴ 5g⁶ 5g⁵ 5m⁵ 6m 5.7g 5g 5g⁴ 1989 5g³ 5f² 5f* 6f⁵ 5f 5g⁶ 5m* 5f³]
quite attractive, good-quartered horse: good mover: won for first time since 2 yrs
when justifying favouritism in £12,800 Weathercall Stakes (Handicap) at Goodwood
in May: put up smart performance (under 10-0) when winning £8,000 A. F. Budge
Handicap at York 2 months later by 2 lengths from Blues Indigo: good third of 13,
running on well after not having best of runs, to Statoblest in King George Stakes at
Goodwood later in July: best at 5f: needs a sound surface: reportedly ran too freely
when blinkered: best held up: has often sweated, got on edge and given trouble at
stalls. *J. W. Hills.*

CAROMISH (USA)   2 br.f. (Mar 6) Lyphard's Wish (FR) 124–Carom (USA)   **91**
(Caro 133) [1989 5s⁶ 6g 6m⁴ 7f² 6g* 6g* 7s* 6g] $20,000Y: tall, rather leggy filly:
third reported foal: dam minor winner at around 7f: fairly useful performer:
successful in nurseries at Windsor in August and Goodwood following month: ran
poorly final start: stays 7f: best form on an easy surface. *M. D.
I. Usher.*

CAROTIC (USA)   3 b.c. Caro 133–World of Suzy Wong (USA) (Full Pocket   **90**
(USA)) [1988 NR 1989 8m⁵ 10f* 12g 16m 12g] $160,000Y: angular, workmanlike colt:
second foal: favourite, made most when winning maiden at Sandown in June: well
beaten in handicaps after, taking strong hold first 2 starts and wearing net muzzle on
final one: should prove best forcing pace at up to 1¼m: sold 16,000 gns Newmarket
Autumn Sales. *G. Harwood.*

CAROUSEL CALYPSO   3 ch.c. Whistling Deer 117–Fairy Tree (Varano) [1988   **—**
7s⁶ 6d² 8d 8s⁵ 8m 8v 1989 11m 12f³ 12f⁵ 15m 15s 18g] leggy, angular colt: quite
modest form at best: showed little in handicaps as 3-y-o, best effort on second start:
stays 1½m: acts on any going: sweating final outing. *W. J. Pearce.*

CARPE DIEM   4 b.f. Good Times (ITY)–Olympic Visualise 84 (Northfields   **58**
(USA)) [1988 7m 6m 8m⁶ 8m⁶ 6m³ 7d³ 6s 1989 7s 7g⁵ 7.6f 6m 7m 7.6f⁴ 8.3m² 8m]
medium-sized filly: has a round action: quite modest maiden: stays 1m: yet to show
her form on firm going, acts on any other: inconsistent: has joined E. Wheeler. *L. J.
Holt.*

CARPET CAPERS (USA)   5 b.g. Dance Bid (USA) 114–Cofimvaba (FR)   **—**
(Verrieres 131) [1988 10s 10f³ 10.1d 12f 12m⁴ 10f⁴ 1989 10d 7h] small, close-coupled
gelding: poor plater: needs further than 7f and stays 1½m: acts on any going: seems
best without blinkers or visor: winning hurdler. *J. Ffitch-Heyes.*

CARPET SLIPPERS   3 br.f. Daring March 116–Mollified 67 (Lombard (GER)   **75**
126) [1988 NR 1989 8m 12.5m³ 10.2f² 12f⁶ 10d] tall, leggy filly: fourth living foal:
half-sister to winning hurdler Steady State (by Star Appeal): dam stayed 1¼m:
modest maiden: placed at Wolverhampton and Bath: well beaten after: may prove
best at short of 1½m. *J. D. Bethell.*

CARROLL HOUSE 4 ch.c. Lord Gayle (USA) 124–Tuna 63 (Silver Shark **132** 129) [1988 9g³ 12m³ 12s² 12d* 12s³ 11s* 12v* 12v³ 10v⁴ 1989 10s³ 10m³ 12g* 12m⁵ 10g* 12g* 12f]

> 'Where are the songs of spring? Ay, where are they?
> Think not of them, thou hasn't thy music too'

Keats's description of autumn was applicable to the latest running of Europe's richest and most prestigious race, the Ciga Prix de l'Arc de Triomphe at Longchamp in October. The Prix de l'Arc is traditionally the principal test for the top middle-distance performers; but the field for the latest edition was substandard and there wasn't the usual speculation beforehand that an open-looking race would settle the championship of Europe. Where were the Nashwans, the Old Vics and the Dancehalls? Ay, where were they?

The seven-strong group of three-year-old colts that contested the Arc lacked a known championship contender, unless the King George VI and Queen Elizabeth Diamond Stakes runner-up Cacoethes (who had lost three times to Nashwan) could be counted as one. Cacoethes, beaten seven lengths into third in the Ever Ready Derby by Nashwan, and the Michael-trained Norberto, a well-beaten fourth behind Old Vic, Dancehall and Galetto in the Prix du Jockey-Club Lancia, were the only three-year-old colts in the Arc field that had run in the Derby, the Prix du Jockey-Club or the Budweiser Irish Derby (which had provided Old Vic with a second Derby victory). No filly has won the Arc since All Along became the fifth of her sex in a row to do so, back in 1983 when fillies took five of the first six places (ten of the twenty-six runners that year were fillies). The four three-year-old fillies saddled for the race in 1989 were worthy representatives of their generation. They were: the Gold Seal Oaks winner Aliysa; the Prix Vermeille winner Young Mother and runner-up Sierra Roberta; and the Prix Saint-Alary winner Behera who had come third behind Sierra Roberta in the Prix de la Nonette on her return to the track in September after an absence of over three months. The field of nineteen was completed by eight older horses (among them one filly) including Carroll House and Saint Andrews, the only Arc runners that had won more than one Group 1 event. Saint Andrews had been successful in the last two runnings of the Prix Ganay but seemed to be on the downgrade and had run an ignominious Arc trial in the Prix Foy, being pulled up after virtually refusing to race; he was fitted with blinkers in the Arc in the hope that they might rekindle his interest. The British-trained four-year-old Carroll House had been raced mainly on the Continent as a three-year-old when his three victories included the Group 1 Grosser Preis von Baden on heavy ground. His Italian owner had bought him, reportedly for around £170,000, after his second outing principally as a Derby Italiano prospect and he had lost that race only by a short neck to the home-trained favourite Tisserand. British racegoers saw slightly more of the progressive Carroll House in the latest

EBF Phoenix Champion Stakes, Phoenix Park—
Carroll House gets up from front-running Citidancer;
Petrullo and Mamaluna complete a British clean sweep

*Ciga Prix de l'Arc de Triomphe, Longchamp—Carroll House runs on strongly
to beat Behera, Saint Andrews, Young Mother and Sierra Roberta*

season and he earned a chance against Nashwan in the King George VI and
Queen Elizabeth Diamond Stakes with a high-class performance in the
Princess of Wales's Stakes at Newmarket's July meeting where he ran on
gamely to get the better of a sustained duel with odds-on Assatis by a neck.
Carroll House had every chance when fifth in the King George but won his
only other race before the Arc, the Group 1 EBF Phoenix Champion Stakes at
Phoenix Park in September. Horses trained in Britain plundered Ireland's
pattern races almost at will in 1989 and Carroll House led home a British
1,2,3,4 in the Phoenix Champion, steadily wearing down the front-running
Citidancer under hard riding to win by three quarters of a length, with Petrullo
and Mamaluna fairly close up in third and fourth.

For all the improvement made by Carroll House—he also thrived
physically from three to four—his chances of winning the Arc looked only
average. He started at just under 19/1 on the French Tote, favouritism going
to one of the four runners from the in-form Fabre stable, the three-year-old
colt In The Wings who was the only unbeaten horse in the field; he had won
the Prix du Prince d'Orange, one of the recognised Arc trials, on his belated
reappearance.

It has become less fashionable than it used to be for the top jockeys to
seek a forward position in the Arc—the first and second the previous year
Tony Bin and Mtoto came from well behind in a big field—but being handy
certainly paid dividends in the latest running. The first four Carroll House,
Behera, Saint Andrews and Young Mother were in the first half dozen or so
practically all the way, in the best place to avoid the trouble that frequently
attends the running of the Arc when there's a sizeable field. A number of
fancied horses that were held up met with interference as the tightly-bunched
field—the early pace wasn't so strong as usual—negotiated the long,
sweeping bend on the approach to the home straight. Saint Andrews, in front
rounding the final turn, was sent for home in earnest once the straight was
reached, with Behera and Carroll House in hot pursuit. Carroll House forged
ahead about a furlong and a half out, edging to the right towards Behera as he
did so, and kept on strongly, never looking as if he would be caught, to cross
the line a length and a half in front; Behera stayed on to deprive Saint Andrews
of second near the finish by a short neck, with Young Mother a further neck

173

Mr Antonio Balzarini's "Carroll House"

behind; Sierra Roberta, Robore and Norberto (the first three-year-old colt to finish) came next, with less than half a dozen lengths separating Carroll House from tenth-placed Aliysa. Aliysa was among those who had a poor passage in a race described by several of the jockeys as 'very rough'. Legal Case, who did second-best of the six British challengers in eighth, Cacoethes, In The Wings, French Glory and the Prix Foy first and second Star Lift and Robore were others who ran into trouble. Carroll House survived an objection from Behera's rider to become only the fifth British-trained Prix de l'Arc winner in the past forty years, following Mill Reef (1971), Rheingold (1973), Rainbow Quest (1985) and Dancing Brave (1986). Carroll House's success had a truly international flavour: owned by an Italian and trained by an Englishman, he was ridden by Ireland's leading jockey Kinane, for whom he provided a second big-money victory in as many days, following his triumph on The Caretaker in the Cartier Million at Phoenix Park. Carroll House returned after the Arc with a cut hind leg, caused when he struck a rail when lashing out at an assortment of photographers and over-enthusiastic admirers as he was mobbed on his way to the winner's circle. Thankfully, no-one was hurt and the injury to Carroll House wasn't serious, but the Longchamp authorities will presumably take steps to see that there is no repeat of such riotous scenes.

The widely-travelled Carroll House had been raced in five countries—Britain, France, Ireland, Germany and Italy—and Japan was added in November when Carroll House followed in the footsteps of the previous year's Arc winner Tony Bin and was sent to Tokyo for the Japan Cup. Like Tony Bin, Carroll House was acquired by Japanese interests after the Prix de l'Arc. He was purchased by Mr Zenya Yoshida who also, incidentally, paid 2,800,000 dollars for a Northern Dancer yearling colt out of Mrs Penny, the highest-priced lot at the two-day Keeneland July Selected Sale. The Japanese racing authorities do an excellent job promoting and organising the Japan Cup and were rewarded with a very good field for the ninth running. Carroll House was one of three British-trained horses among the fifteen starters—Ibn Bey and Assatis were the others—but he managed only fourteenth on going much too firm for him. The race was won for the first time by an Australasian challenger, the six-year-old New Zealand-trained mare Horlicks who got home by a neck and three lengths from the home-trained Emperor's Cup runner-up Oguri Cap and one of the two runners from North America, the 1988 winner Pay The Butler; Ibn Bey came sixth, Assatis twelfth; French-trained Top Sunrise, the only other runner from Europe, finished tenth.

		Sir Gaylord (b 1959)	Turn-To
Carroll House (ch.c. 1985)	Lord Gayle (USA) (b 1965)		Somethingroyal
		Sticky Case (ch 1958)	Court Martial
			Run Honey
	Tuna (ch 1969)	Silver Shark (gr 1963)	Buisson Ardent
			Palsaka
		Vimelette (b 1960)	Vimy
			Sea Parrot

The good-topped, useful-looking Carroll House is a moderate mover but usually impresses in appearance. Carroll House is the best horse sired by the now-retired Irish National Stud stallion Lord Gayle, also sire of the dual Oaks winner Blue Wind. Carroll House's dam Tuna showed only poor form in five races over a mile as a three-year-old, her only season to race. Carroll House was her ninth winner at stud, and the middle-distance handicapper Northumbrian King (by Indian King) became her tenth when successful at Redcar and Beverley in the latest season. The best of Tuna's previous winners was probably the Irish Cesarewitch winner Jean-Claude (by Malinowski). Tuna is a granddaughter of the Yorkshire Oaks and Nassau Stakes winner Sea Parrot but this is not, in all honesty, a pedigree to delight the purist and Carroll House's future as a stallion almost certainly lies in Japan. But before taking up stud duties, he is to remain in training for another season, with the Prix Ganay as his first important target and a crack at the Breeders' Cup Turf in the autumn also on his programme. The overwhelming majority of Prix de l'Arc winners have to give the best performances of their careers to earn victory, a remark which applies to Carroll House more than most. Perhaps he hasn't had all the credit he deserves for a tip-top performance, one bettered during the European season over middle distances only by Old Vic and Nashwan. There will certainly be no tougher, nor more genuine top-class performer in training in 1990 than Carroll House and granted suitable underfoot conditions—he is best on an easy surface and acts on heavy going—he is sure to continue to give a good account of himself in the best company. He is effective at a mile and a quarter and stays a mile and a half well. *M. A. Jarvis.*

CARROLL PRINCESS 3 br.f. Trojan Fen 118–Juvita (Junius (USA) 124) [1988   57
NR 1989 10m 10.4g³ 11.3f 12g 12g²] IR 8,000F, IR 5,800Y: small filly: first foal: dam lightly-raced half-sister to Trevita, a smart winner from 6f to 1m here and a good winner in USA: plating-class maiden: placed in claiming events at Chester and Hamilton: best effort over 1¼m: possibly unsuited by very firm going: bandaged behind on debut: sold 3,600 gns Newmarket Autumn Sales. *W. J. Haggas.*

CARROLL QUEEN 3 b.f. Auction Ring (USA) 123–Peacehaven 71 (Home   —
Guard (USA) 129) [1988 NR 1989 7g 8m 7m⁵ 8m 8.2g a8g⁶] 16,500F, IR 50,000Y: lengthy, workmanlike filly: first foal: dam, plating-class maiden who possibly stayed 11.7f, is granddaughter of Peace: quite modest maiden at best: showed plenty of promise at Newmarket first 2 starts, but disappointed after: stays 1m: took keen hold and ran badly in blinkers fourth outing: slowly away final one. *B. Hanbury.*

CARRY ON CARY 3 b.g. Carriage Way 107–Greenhill Lass (Upper Case (USA))   79
[1988 5s² 5v² 5d* 5g⁶ 6m⁶ 7g³ 7g² 7g³ 6s⁶ 8v³ 8.2d 8.2v³ 1989 8m² 8m² 10h² 8m⁴

10f3] leggy, sparely-made gelding: moderate walker and mover: fair handicapper: stays 1¼m: acts on any going: gelded after final start: genuine and consistent. *R. W. Stubbs.*

CARTEL 2 b.c. (Mar 13) Kris 135–Meis El-Reem 124 (Auction Ring (USA) 123) **65 p**
[1989 6m2] first foal: dam 5f to 1m winner: 5/2, 7 lengths second of 7, headway 2f out and keeping on well considerably handled, to impressive Cordoba in maiden at Newmarket in August: sure to improve. *A. A. Scott.*

CARTIER BIJOUX 3 br.f. Ahonoora 122–Tremiti 84 (Sun Prince 128) [1988 5g5 —
5g2 5g* 7g 1989 5m6 5f 5g6 5d] angular, workmanlike filly: fairly useful winner as 2-y-o: below form in handicaps in 1989, tailed off final start: stays 7f: best form with some give in ground: often bandaged behind. *D. R. C. Elsworth.*

CARVER LAD 4 b.g. Balinger 116–Chevulgan (Cheval 117) [1988 NR 1989 12m] —
rather sparely-made gelding: moderate walker: fourth foal: half-brother to 1m to 1½m winner Cheerful Times (by Faraway Times): dam, plating class on flat, won over hurdles and fences: 100/1, well behind in minor event at Leicester in June. *K. T. Ivory.*

CARVICK 3 br.c. Swing Easy (USA) 126–Pas de Chat (Relko 136) [1988 5f 6m 5f —
6d 1989 6v 5s 5.8m5 7h 6m 5.3f5] leggy, workmanlike colt: plating-class form at best: blinkered, behind in seller and handicap last 2 starts: trained first 2 outings by G. Lewis: sold 1,050 gns Newmarket Autumn Sales. *R. Akehurst.*

CASAMURRAE 2 b.f. (Feb 14) Be My Guest (USA) 126–Loralane 86 (Habitat **79 p**
134) [1989 7g4 7g2] angular, useful-looking filly: has a quick action: fifth foal: closely related to 1m winner Nuryana (by Nureyev) and half-sister to useful miler Digger's Rest (by Mr Prospector) and useful 1¼m winner Cowley (by Kalaglow): dam, 7f winner, is half-sister to On The House (by Be My Guest): still bit green, stayed on strongly last 2f when beaten a head by Surpassing in maiden at Leicester in August, much better effort: will stay 1m and improve again. *G. Wragg.*

CASBATINA 3 b.f. Castle Keep 121–Balatina 85 (Balidar 133) [1988 6m* 6s 6d4 —
6d3 1989 8h] lengthy, angular, sparely-made filly: landed gamble in seller at Doncaster as 2-y-o: bit backward in handicap in June, only outing in 1989: possibly unsuited by very soft going. *J. Pearce.*

CASE LAW 2 ch.c. (Apr 28) Ahonoora 122–Travesty 63 (Reliance II 137) [1989 **83**
5g* 5s2 5m2 5s] IR 24,000Y: strong, good-bodied colt: has scope: fifth foal: half-brother to 3-y-o Fulham Trader (by Absalom) and 5f winner Munawar (by Sharpo): dam twice-raced half-sister to numerous winners, including dams of Governor General and Galunpe: won 6-runner maiden at Catterick in August: progressive form in nurseries on next 2 starts: moved badly down and ran poorly final start: will be suited by 6f. *Sir Mark Prescott.*

CASHEW KING 6 b.g. Faraway Times (USA) 118–Sinzinbra 112 (Royal Palace —
131) [1988 14s6 1989 10.2g] tall, sparely-made gelding: has a round action: useful jumper: very lightly raced on flat nowadays: probably best at around 1½m: acts on any going: has run well when sweating. *B. A. McMahon.*

CASHTAL DAZZLER 2 b.c. (May 8) Ballacashtal (CAN)–Miss Meg 68 (John **82**
Splendid 116) [1989 6m2 7m* 7f4 7m3] 7,400Y: leggy, fair sort: good walker: has a quick action: fourth reported foal: brother to 1987 2-y-o 5f winner Miss Chrissy: dam 5f performer: favourite, won 4-runner minor event at Newcastle in June, rallying gamely despite edging right: good third to Eire Leath-Sceal at same course, better subsequent effort in nurseries: will stay 1m. *J. Berry.*

CASPIAN GATES 5 b.g. Persian Bold 123–Galka 98 (Deep Diver 134) [1988 **72**
10m* 16g4 12m5 13.5g5 10s4 1989 10s6 10v 10d6 10.8d4 12m 11.5f5 12.4m* 14m2 12m 14m3 12f* 12f2 13.8d] small, sturdy ex-Irish gelding: half-brother to 3 winners, including 1m winner Guess Again (by Stradavinsky): dam won twice over 5f at 2 yrs: modest handicapper: successful at Sandown and Newcastle (hanging final 1f) in June and Beverley (favourite) in September: stays 1¾m: suited by top-of-the-ground: wore blinkers in Ireland and on fifth outing: has sweated. *A. N. Lee.*

CASPIAN MIST 4 b.f. Remainder Man 126§–Bay Foulard (Shantung 132) [1988 **85**
8g 10g 10.1m3 12g 10s 1989 10.2g2 12v* 10s4 12f4 12m6 12m2 11.5g5 12f5 11.7d5 14f4 14g2] big, good-bodied filly: moderate mover: fair handicapper: won at Kempton in April, holding on gamely by neck from Jinga: stays 1¾m: acts on any going: has run creditably when sweating and for apprentice. *G. Lewis.*

CASSANOVA LAD 3 b.c. Swing Easy (USA) 126–Sallusteno 80 (Sallust 134) —
[1988 5s4 7g 1989 10f6] soundly beaten in modest company. *S. E. Kettlewell.*

CASSIBELLA   3 b.f. Red Sunset 120–Crane Beach (High Top 131) [1988 6f 7g* 8g 10m⁵ 1989 12.2d 10m 10.2f 8g] small, leggy, lightly-made filly: useful plater as 2-y-o: ran poorly in 1989: suited by 1¼m: usually claimer ridden and blinkered. *Mrs N. Macauley.*   —

CASTEL VISCADO   2 b.c. (May 4) Castle Keep 121–Myrtlegrove (Scottish Rifle 127) [1989 a7g a8g] second foal: dam never ran: well beaten in December maidens at Lingfield. *J. L. Dunlop.*   —

CASTILLO   2 b.c. (Apr 27) Dreams To Reality (USA) 113–Belle Lutine (Relkino 131) [1989 5g 5m 10g] compact colt: fourth foal: dam never ran: held back backward, well beaten in maidens: off course over 5 months after second start: may well stay 1¼m. *J. R. Bosley.*   —

CASTING VOTE (USA)   3 ch.f. Monteverdi 129–Myra's Best 107 (Pampapaul 121) [1988 6g 1989 10h 10f⁵ 10h⁴ 12h⁴] leggy, sparely-made filly: fourth in handicaps at Brighton and Lingfield in July, only form: suited by 1¼m. *R. Hannon.*   54

CASTLEACRE   3 ch.g. Mr Fluorocarbon 126–Misfired 101 (Blast 125) [1988 7m 6f 6m 7g⁴ 7d⁶ 1989 7f 8.5g⁵ 8f 10m² 11.5g³] small, angular, sparely-made gelding: quite modest maiden: placed in claimers at Nottingham and Sandown (claimed to join J. Colston £ 10,105) in the summer: may prove ideally suited by bit shorter than 11.5f: yet to race on very soft going, appears to act on any other. *G. B. Balding.*   65

CASTLE BYTHAM   2 br.c. (Apr 6) Goldhills Pride 105–Lucy Brotherton (Pieces of Eight 128) [1989 8g] fourth foal: half-brother to a winner in Italy: dam ran twice at 2 yrs: 33/1 and backward, slowly away and soon well tailed off in 16-runner maiden at Leicester in November. *J. Dooler.*   —

CASTLE CARY   3 gr.f. Castle Keep 121–Tibouchina 75 (Runnymede 123) [1988 6g 6s⁵ 5m 5g⁴ 5s² 1989 5s² 6s 5.8m² 5f⁴ 5f 5g 5g 7.6m⁵ 6g 6g⁶ 7g] workmanlike filly: carries condition: has a quick action: quite modest maiden: stays 7.6f: acts on top-of-the-ground and soft going: inconsistent: doesn't find much off bridle. *M. Blanshard.*   65

CASTLE CLOWN   4 ch.g. Castle Keep 121–Peteona 97 (Welsh Saint 126) [1988 8m³ 8g⁵ 10f 12m⁵ 11.7g⁴ 10s² 10d* 1989 10d² 10m* 11f 12g] tall, lengthy gelding: fair handicapper: won £7,600 event at Newmarket in May by head, pair well clear, from Ile de Chypre: below form next 2 outings, and not seen out after July: suited by 1¼m: yet to show his best form on extremes of going: visored last 6 appearances. *Lady Herries.*   86

CASTLE COURAGEOUS   2 b.g. (Apr 23) Castle Keep 121–Peteona 97 (Welsh Saint 126) [1989 7s⁴ 7f³ 8g*] leggy gelding: seventh living foal: brother to fair 7f and 1¼m winners Castle Clown and Tilting Court and half-brother to a winning hurdler: dam 5f to 1m winner: 8/1, won 17-runner maiden at Leicester in November by 4 lengths from Toledo: will probably stay 1¼m. *Lady Herries.*   91

CASTLE DANCE   3 b.f. Castle Keep 121–Coming Out (Fair Season 120) [1988 6g 7d² 1989 8d 8.5m⁶ 10.1m 10g 8m 13.3d] smallish, sparely-made filly: modest form at best: never dangerous in handicaps last 3 starts: should stay beyond 1m: acts on top-of-the-ground and a soft surface. *G. B. Balding.*   —

CASTLE HEIGHTS   5 b.g. Shirley Heights 130–Good Try 92 (Good Bond 122) [1988 7.6d 12f 12f 12f* 11.5g³ 12m² 10f 12f* 12f* 12f 12g 1989 11.7d 12f 11.5f 12f² 15.3f³] short-backed, sparely-made gelding: poor walker: quite modest winner as 4-y-o: below his best in 1989, and not seen out after July: suited by 1½m: acts very well on firm going: somewhat headstrong but has won for apprentice: temperamental hurdler: sold 1,000 gns Ascot November Sales. *R. Curtis.*   53

CASTLE MOAT   4 b.g. Jalmood (USA) 126–Fotheringay 101 (Right Royal V 135) [1988 NR 1989 10.1m 10g 12m 12g] leggy gelding: half-brother to several winners, notably Ascot Gold Cup winner Ragstone (by Ragusa), very smart middle-distance stayer Castle Keep and Castle Moon (both by Kalamoun), last-named dam of Moon Madness and Sheriff's Star: dam won at 1m: well beaten in varied events, including July handicap at Salisbury (gambled on) final outing: bandaged and slowly away on debut. *Lady Herries.*   —

CASTLE PEAK   3 b.f. Darshaan 133–Edinburgh 117 (Charlottown 127) [1988 7m⁴ 1989 12f* 12.2m³ 12m⁴] rangy, angular filly: good walker: won maiden at Thirsk in May: ran well in summer minor events at Warwick and Newmarket: will stay further: sold 41,000 gns Newmarket December Sales. *M. R. Stoute.*   90

CASTLEREA FAIR   2 b.f. (Apr 11) Sweet Monday 122–La Bird 61 (Le Johnstan 123) [1989 5m⁵ 5m 5g³ 5g 5.1m⁵] angular filly: second foal: dam won at 1m and 1¼m: modest plater: best effort fourth start: bred to stay beyond 5f. *J. Berry.*   43

CASTLE SECRET 3 b.c. Castle Keep 121–Baffle 87 (Petingo 135) [1988 8s² 1989 10s 12f 12f⁴ 12g* 14m* 16g²] medium-sized, quite attractive colt: moderate mover with a quick action: successful in September handicaps at Leicester and Haydock: favourite, good second of 7, wandering under pressure, in £9,600 handicap at Ascot: stays 2m: probably acts on any going. *J. L. Dunlop.* **86**

CASTORET 3 b.c. Jalmood (USA) 126–Blaskette 99 (Blast 125) [1988 NR 1989 8s³ 8f⁶ 10.1m⁶ 8d] 41,000Y: useful-looking colt: half-brother to several winners, including useful 6f and 1m winner Sharblask (by Sharpo) and 1¼m winner Golden Capistrano (by Dominion): dam middle-distance handicapper: fair maiden: no show in handicap final start, first for over 4 months: stays 1¼m: possibly unsuited by very firm going. *R. F. Johnson Houghton.* **76**

CASUAL FLASH (USA) 2 ch.c. (Feb 14) Sharpen Up 127–Annie Edge 118 (Nebbiolo 125) [1989 7f⁵ 7g] leggy, rather sparely-made colt: first foal: dam 5f and 7f winner later successful at up to 11f in North America: under 6 lengths fifth to El Paso at Salisbury, better effort in late-season maidens. *I. A. Balding.* **70**

CASUAL PASS 6 ch.g. Formidable (USA) 125–Pitapat (Shantung 132) [1988 11v⁴ 12d 12s* 12g 1989 12d 12m² 12h⁶ 15.8m⁵ 12f² 15.8g 12.2g] sturdy, workmanlike gelding: has a round action: plating-class handicapper: stays 1½m: acts on any going, but well suited by the mud: has won for apprentice: inconsistent. *G. Richards.* **57**

CASWELL 2 ch.f. (Jan 23) Saher 115–Holy Water (Monseigneur (USA) 127) [1989 5s⁴ 5f⁶ 5f 5f] IR 2,000 (privately) Y, resold 725Y: angular, sparely-made filly: first foal: dam unraced daughter of sister to Deep Diver and half-sister to Irish 2000 Guineas winner King's Company: well beaten in varied events, including sellers: sold 900 gns Ascot November Sales. *R. J. Holder.* **—**

CATALANI 4 ch.f. Music Boy 124–Two Stroke (Malicious) [1988 6g 1989 7g 6m⁵ 5m* 6v 5d] workmanlike, angular filly: clearly difficult to train, and was having only fourth outing when winning maiden at Warwick (favourite, wore small bandage near-hind) in August: unfavourably drawn final outing: stays 6f: probably not at her best on heavy going: apprentice ridden last 4 starts. *W. Jarvis.* **80**

CATBALLOU 2 b.f. (Apr 14) Tina's Pet 121–Blue Brocade 91 (Reform 132) [1989 6g³] 16,000Y: first foal: dam, 10.6f winner, half-sister to very smart Lockton: 9/1, under 2 lengths third of 9, keeping on well final furlong, to Va Toujours in maiden at Newmarket in August: will be suited by 7f: should improve. *J. A. R. Toller.* **77 p**

CATCH TWENTY TWO 2 b.c. (Jan 30) Taufan (USA) 119–Dancing Decoy 78 (Troy 137) [1989 7g⁴ 7m⁴ 7m⁵ 7m² 8s* 9d*] IR 11,000Y: first foal: dam placed from 1m to 11f at 3 yrs, is half-sister to smart sprinter Defecting Dancer: fairly useful colt: made all in maiden at Navan and listed event (beat Annie Laurie 3 lengths) at the Curragh late in season: suited by a test of stamina: acts on soft ground: blinkered last 3 starts. *M. Kauntz, Ireland.* **98**

CATHEDRAL PEAK 5 b.g. Tyrnavos 129–Honeypot Lane 91 (Silly Season 127) [1988 11.7f⁶ 14m⁶ 13.1d 10s* 10.5f² 12.2g² 11s⁵ 1989 10f⁵ 10m 10m* 10m 12d 10f 10.6m] tall gelding: quite modest handicapper: 11/2 from 12/1, won 17-runner apprentice event at Kempton in July: below his best afterwards: probably best at around 1¼m: acts on any going: good mount for inexperienced rider: sold 7,200 gns Newmarket Autumn Sales. *C. A. Cyzer.* **65**

CATHERINE PARR (USA) 2 br.f. (Apr 22) Riverman (USA) 131–Regal Exception (USA) 126 (Ribot 142) [1989 6.5d³ 8g²] closely related to good-class middle-distance stayer Orban (by Irish River) and half-sister to several winners, including smart French 1m and 10.5f winner Twilight Hour (by Raise A Native): dam won Irish Oaks and was fourth in Arc: placed in newcomers race at Deauville in August and Prix d'Aumale (beaten a neck by Mackla) at Longchamp in September: will stay middle distances. *A. Fabre, France.* **108**

CATHOS (FR) 4 b.g. Bellman (FR) 123–Charming Doll (Don (ITY) 123) [1988 9g* 10g³ 10.5g³ 10m⁶ 10.5g² 1989 10v⁶ 10d 13.3f⁶ 10.6s a10g] leggy ex-French gelding: half-brother to several winners, notably useful winner at up to 1m Chartino (by Concertino): dam French 7f to 1m winner: won handicap at Maisons-Laffitte as 3-y-o: never dangerous in varied events in 1989: stays 10.5f: edgy and slowly away third start: blinkered last. *J. A. B. Old.* **—**

CATIMINI 4 ch.g. Coquelin (USA) 121–Espadrille 81 (Hotfoot 126) [1988 5m 9.5d 5g 6v 8s 1989 10m 6f 9f 7g a6g] small, sparely-made gelding: quite modest 2-y-o winner: well beaten and 3 yrs and 4 yrs: blinkered once: bought out of J. Hayden's stable 1,200 gns Newmarket Autumn Sales after fourth outing. *D. W. Chapman.* **—**

CATKIN (USA) 3 b.f. Sir Ivor 135–Catty (USA) (Never Bend) [1988 7s⁶ 6g 1989 7f] good-bodied, workmanlike filly: moderate mover: no worthwhile form in minor event and maidens: sweating only start as 3-y-o, in June: bred to stay 1¼m. *J. Tree.* **—**

CAUGHT UNAWARES 2 ch.g. (Feb 28) Longleat (USA) 109–Mrs Cullumbine **78**
60 (Silly Season 127) [1989 6f² 6g³] tall gelding: has scope: second foal: half-brother
to fairly useful 7f and 1½m winner Rakes Lane (by Pitskelly): dam, stayed 1½m,
half-sister to useful 6f winner Chantry Bridge: modest form in minor event at
Pontefract and maiden at Redcar in autumn: should stay 7f. *S. G. Norton.*

CAUSLEY 4 br.g. Swing Easy (USA) 126–Four Lawns 77 (Forlorn River 124) **78**
[1988 6v 8g* 8.2v⁵ 8g⁶ 9g 8f³ 8.2m² 8d⁴ 7m⁴ 8.2g* 8g⁶ 8.2f 8g⁴ 8.2m* 8g² 8s² 7g⁵
1989 8.2m 7.5m⁶ 8f⁵ 8f 8.2g² 8.5m³ 8m⁵ 8.5g⁴ 10.6m 8.2d* 8.2g³ a8g*]
good-topped, workmanlike gelding: often fails to impress in appearance: has a round
action: modest performer: won claimer at Haydock (blinkered, making virtually all)
and handicap at Southwell in latter stages of season: suited by 1m: not ideally suited
by firm going, acts on any other except possibly heavy: usually takes good hold:
suitable mount for inexperienced rider: has been mulish at stalls. *B. A. McMahon.*

CAVALCANTI (USA) 3 b.c. Sir Ivor 135–Forelie 88 (Formidable (USA) 125) —
[1988 NR 1989 10f] 80,000Y: rangy, good sort: first foal: dam, 6f winner who only
raced at 2 yrs, is half-sister to Derby Italiano winner My Top: about 6½ lengths
eighth of 12 to Shellac in maiden at Sandown in May, edging right over 2f out then
not knocked about. *H. R. A. Cecil.*

CAVALIERAVANTGARDE 7 b.g. Rarity 129–Erica (Ballyciptic 122) [1988 —
NR 1989 13s⁶] lengthy gelding: form only when winning selling handicap as 4-y-o:
stays 1m: suited by soft ground: has worn bandages. *P. Wigham.*

CAVALIER CLASSIC 2 b.g. (Apr 29) Nemorino (USA) 81–Quoro Star —
(Quorum 126) [1989 6m 6m 7f 7m] smallish gelding: half-brother to middle-distance
stayer Cavalier Servente (by Barbaro): dam never ran: little worthwhile form: will
probably stay well: broke out of stalls and was withdrawn third intended outing and
gave trouble start final run (August). *R. Earnshaw.*

CAVALIER SPIRIT 3 ch.g. Sicyos (USA) 126–Cyclamen (FR) (Luthier 126) **59**
[1988 6d 6m 5g 1989 8.2s 8m⁴ 8.5f⁶ 7m 11.3f] medium-sized, sparely-made gelding:
fourth in claimer at Warwick in May: poorish form otherwise: stays 1m well:
blinkered final outing at 2 yrs: sold 2,200 gns Ascot October Sales. *J. A. C. Edwards.*

CAVALLA 2 b.f. (Mar 19) The Brianstan 128–Bombay Duck 65 (Ballyciptic) [1989 **71**
9f² a8g³ a8g³] strong, good-topped filly: has plenty of scope: eighth foal: sister to 7f
and 1m winner Bombil and half-sister to 1½m and 1¾m winner Pinwiddie (by
Moulton) and 3-y-o Balao (by Mr Fluorocarbon): dam won over 13f: modest form in
maidens and a claimer: stays 9f: has run creditably for 7-lb claimer: got loose at
stalls and was withdrawn second intended outing. *R. Hollinshead.*

CAVENDISH DIAMOND 3 b.f. Decoy Boy 129–Tactile (Tacitus 124) [1988 6d **47**
1989 8d² 10f 10m 8.5g 10.2h] workmanlike, smallish filly: moderate mover: fair
plater at best: suited by 1m: best effort on a soft surface: edgy and tailed off final
start (June). *R. Simpson.*

CAXTON (USA) 2 b.c. (Feb 3) Halo (USA)–Printing Press (USA) (In Reality) **58**
[1989 7f⁴ 8m] $90,000Y: quite attractive, medium-sized colt: second foal: dam
placed once from 4 starts at 3 yrs in USA: sire high class at up to 1½m: around 11
lengths fourth of 13 to Bartat in maiden at Salisbury in September: well beaten in
similar event at Newmarket following month. *I. A. Balding.*

CAYMANIA 3 b.f. Wolver Hollow 126–Takachiho's Girl (Takachiho 111) [1988 6d —
6m 9g 1989 10g 8m] lengthy, workmanlike filly: moderate walker: little indication of
ability in maidens and handicaps. *P. Howling.*

CAYMAN QUEEN 4 b.f. Tina's Pet 121–Harpers Girl 74 (Crowned Prince —
(USA) 128) [1988 12d⁵ 11g⁴ 13.8f⁵ 16g² 17.1g 15.8g 13.3s⁵ 1989 12.5g] workmanlike
filly: poor mover: plating-class maiden: suited by 2m: acts on firm going: bandaged
last 2 outings: has found little. *M. H. Tompkins.*

CB SPECIAL 2 ch.f. (May 7) Absalom 128–Terre Promise (Soderini 123) [1989 5f —
5f 6g 6m 7f] IR 1,000Y, resold 2,700Y: compact filly: half-sister to ungenuine 1988
2-y-o Earthy Note (by Music Boy) and several winners, including fair 1980 2-y-o 6f
winner Miss St Mawes (by Derring-Do): dam ran once: seems of little account. *R.
Bastiman.*

CECILIANO (USA) 3 ch.c. Irish River (FR) 131–Derly (FR) (Lyphard (USA) **97**
132) [1988 7g⁶ 7g² 7f³ 1989 12d* 12m 12f⁵ 12v] big, rangy, heavy-topped colt: odds
on, won maiden at Kempton in March by 25 lengths: looking very well and on toes,
under 9 lengths last of 8 in Prix Hocquart at Longchamp: well beaten after in Group
3 events at Lingfield and Newbury, reportedly suffering knee injury and off course
5½ months in between: suited by 1½m: acts on a soft surface. *P. A. Kelleway.*

CEDAR RUN 6 b.g. Billion (USA) 113–Sapele 73 (Decoy Boy 129) [1988 NR 1989 —
10s⁵ 10g 16.2d] lengthy gelding: fifth foal: dam sprinter: winning but ungenuine

CED

selling hurdler: never dangerous in varied events in spring: not seen out after April: slowly away first 2 starts: changed hands 3,000 gns Ascot March Sales. *R. Simpson.*

CEDAR SHELL   4 b.c. Sharpo 132–Cedrella 73 (Averof 123) [1988 7g 8.2m² 9f³   51
8.5f* 8.2d 8g* 1989 8m 8.3m 7f 7g⁶ 10g] compact colt: has a quick action: modest winner as 3-y-o: well below his best in handicaps in 1989: stays 8.5f: acts on firm going: trained on reappearance by J. Glover. *Andrew Turnell.*

CEE-EN-CEE   5 b.g. Junius (USA) 124–Lady Red Rose 87 (Pitskelly 122) [1988   69
7g 6f 5m 6m² 5f³ 5d⁴ 5d⁴ 6d⁵ 6m 5m⁵ 6m⁶ 5.8f* 6d 6d 1989 7.6f⁵ 5.8h 6f 6m* 6m⁵
6g⁶ 6m* 6m² 5m² 6m 6m 6m⁴ 5d a6g⁶] workmanlike gelding: has a round action: quite modest handicapper: won at Windsor in June and at Newmarket following month: best at 5f or 6f: acts on any going, but particularly well on top-of-the-ground: best in blinkers nowadays. *M. McCourt.*

CEE-JAY-AY   2 gr.g. (Mar 1) Free State 125–Raffinrula 75 (Raffingora 130) [1989   56
6m 5h² 6h 7m⁴ 7.5f 8g⁶] 7,300 2-y-o: sturdy gelding: half-brother to a winner in Belgium: dam won twice over 5f at 2 yrs: plating-class maiden: best form at 7f: sometimes slowly away. *J. Berry.*

CELESTIAL GUEST (USA)   2 b.c. (May 4) Northjet 136–Tobira Celeste   —
(USA) (Ribot 142) [1989 8m] 46,000Y, 32,000 2-y-o: medium-sized, sturdy colt: eighth foal: half-brother to several winners, notably top-class middle-distance colt Celestial Storm (by Roberto) and to dam of River Memories: dam, winner at up to 9f in France, is half-sister to smart A Thousand Stars: 33/1, never dangerous in 29-runner maiden at Newmarket in October. *R. Guest.*

CELESTIAL MELODY (USA)   3 ch.f. The Minstrel (CAN) 135–Tobira   75
Celeste (USA) (Ribot 142) [1988 6g 6d⁵ 1989 8m 7m³ 10f⁴ 8m²] small, close-coupled filly: good mover: in frame, running well, in handicaps at Yarmouth (apprentices), Redcar and Newmarket: stays 1¼m: acts on firm going: sold 94,000 gns Newmarket December Sales. *L. M. Cumani.*

CELLATICA (USA)   2 ch.f. (May 1) Sir Ivor 135–Sweetsider (USA) (Topsider   55
(USA)) [1989 6g 7s⁵ 8m] $12,000Y: lengthy, rather angular filly: second reported foal: dam, won at about 9f at 2 yrs, out of half-sister to very useful Miss Toshiba and to dam of Committed: plating-class form in maidens: best effort at 1m: has joined D. Browne. *C. F. Wall.*

CELTIC BHOY   3 b.g. Red Sunset 120–Nighty Night (Sassafras (FR) 135) [1988   63
6m 6m 6f8d³ 1989 10v⁵ 11.5f 12f 12m³ 12f* 13f* 14f⁵ 12f* 12g² 10f³ 12f4 12f³] strong, close-coupled gelding: carries condition: quite modest handicapper: narrow winner at Hamilton (twice) in July and Folkestone in August: should stay 1¾m: acts on firm going and a soft surface. *P. Mitchell.*

CENTENARY STAR   4 b.g. Broadsword (USA) 104–Tina's Gold 66 (Goldhill   —
125) [1988 NR 1989 12.2m 12.2g 16g⁵] leggy, fair sort: third foal: dam winning sprinter: very little sign of ability. *R. Hollinshead.*

CERRO TOLOLO (USA)   3 b.g. Conquistador Cielo (USA)–Colony Club   —
(USA) (Tom Rolfe) [1988 8g 1989 12f 16.2f] big, workmanlike, plain gelding: little worthwhile form in maidens: not seen out after June. *I. A. Balding.*

CERTAIN STAR   2 b. or br.g. (Mar 7) Good Times (ITY)–Summer Fayre 64   41
(Reform 132) [1989 6m⁶ 6f4] 3,100Y, 1,000 2-y-o: first foal: dam appeared to stay 1¼m: poor form in seller and maiden: bred to stay 1m. *W. T. Kemp.*

CETAGLOW   2 b.f. (Mar 29) Kalaglow 132–Avocet 106 (Crowned Prince (USA)   —
128) [1989 6g] 2,000Y, 9,400 2-y-o: leggy, angular filly: half-sister to 1984 2-y-o 9f winner Eider (by Niniski): dam 2-y-o 5f winner: 33/1, soon behind in 19-runner auction event at Epsom in June: has joined K. Cunningham-Brown. *R. Akehurst.*

CETONG   3 gr.g. Petong 126–My Cecilia 83 (Prevailing (USA)) [1988 5.3f* 6m⁴   66
6m 5m⁵ 1989 6m⁴ 5.8m 8.2m⁴ 6f⁵ 6m³ 5.8m⁴ 6f 6m] angular, workmanlike gelding: quite modest handicapper: blinkered fourth to seventh starts, running fairly well on first 3 of them: stays 6f: yet to race on an easy surface: tends to get on toes: bandaged behind last 3 outings, sweating and below form penultimate one: has joined P. Calver. *K. M. Brassey.*

CHACEWATER   3 b.f. Electric 126–Winding River 101 (Entanglement 118)   —
[1988 5.8d⁵ 1989 7f 10.1m] angular, unfurnished filly: easily best effort in minor events and maidens on debut at 2 yrs: should stay at least 1m. *H. Candy.*

CHADENSHE   4 b.f. Taufan (USA) 119–Cookie B (USA) (Prince Taj 123) [1988   94
8d³ 8g⁶ 9g⁶ 8m⁴ 7.6s⁶ 7s* 7g* 7f4 8g³ 1989 7g³ 7f⁶] medium-sized filly: fairly useful winner as 3-y-o: appeared to run well (raced down advantageous centre of track) when third to Beau Sher in listed event at Leicester in April: last of 6, leading

180

5f, in similar contest at Goodwood 3 months later: suited by 7f to 1m: acts on any going: good mount for apprentice: game. *W. Jarvis.*

CHAFF 2 b.c. (Apr 9) Final Straw 127–Silky (USA) 112 (Nijinsky (CAN) 138) [1989 — 5m 7m] smallish, rather unfurnished, angular colt: shows a quick action: half-brother to good middle-distance horse Kirtling (by Grundy), and quite useful Abington (by Jukebox) and Crossways (by Habitat): dam, Irish 1000 Guineas second, is half-sister to Moulton and Freefoot: never dangerous in summer maidens at Windsor and Newmarket: bred to stay 1m: may do better. *G. Wragg.*

CHAGHATAI (USA) 3 ch.c. Sir Ivor 135–Clutch Hitter (USA) (Nodouble — (USA)) [1988 NR 1989 17.6m⁶ 10.2f⁵ 10f] $15,000Y, resold IR 40,000Y: rangy, angular colt: first foal: dam won at up to 7f in USA: well beaten in maidens and claimer: sold 3,000 gns Newmarket Autumn Sales. *Mrs L. Piggott.*

CHAIN SHOT 4 b.g. Pas de Seul 133–Burnished (Formidable (USA) 125) [1988 63 5g² 5g⁵ 6g 6m⁵ 5.3f* 5m⁴ 5m⁵ 5g 5.3f⁶ 5g 5m² 5g⁶ 6g⁵ 6h⁵ 5f² 5g⁴ 5s 1989 5s⁴ 5s⁶ 6f 5.8h 5f² 5f 5m 6f² 6m³ 6g⁵ 6m⁴ 5s³ 5.3f a6g a6g⁴] sturdy, workmanlike gelding: moderate mover: quite modest handicapper: effective at 5f and 6f: acts on any going: sometimes blinkered or visored: not an easy ride. *J. D. Bethell.*

CHALKHILL BLUE 4 b.f. Dunphy 124–Lady Probus 70§ (Shantung 132) [1988 — 9g 8.5m 6f⁵ 6g 8m 1989 15.5s 8f 12.5f] leggy filly: of little account. *D. C. Jermy.*

CHAMBROS 2 ch.g. (Mar 21) Krayyan 117–Chilcombe (Morston (FR) 125) [1989 69 6m 6m² 6g 8.2f³ 9g 8.2g⁵] IR 1,200F, 12,000Y: medium-sized gelding: second foal: dam ran 3 times: quite modest maiden: ran creditably for 7-lb claimer final start: suited by 1m: gelded after final start. *J. W. Hills.*

CHAMPAGNE DANCER 4 b.f. Vaigly Great 127–Elixir 99 (Hard Tack 111§) — [1988 8g 8f 6m 7f 6m 8s³ 10g 8g⁴ 8.3m² 10g 8f 8d⁶ 1989 8.2v 5g] leggy, close-coupled filly: inconsistent plater: needs further than 5f and stays 1m: acts on top-of-the-ground and soft going: visored 3 times in 1988, blinkered final outing at 4 yrs: sold 850 gns Ascot May Sales. *D. Burchell.*

CHAMPAGNE GOLD 2 ch.c. (Apr 14) Bairn (USA) 126–Halkissimo 61 **106** + (Khalkis 127) [1989 5g² 5s* 5g* 6g* 6g* 6g² 6m⁵ 8d*]

Dual-purpose trainer Denys Smith had had a lean time on the flat since he won the Flying Childers in 1976 with Mandrake Major. His fortunes took a turn for the better in 1989, when Champagne Gold and Karinga Bay, two of around only a dozen two-year-olds in the stable, proved good enough to win a listed race apiece in the South. Neither is in the same league as Mandrake Major, or Smith's 1972 Middle Park winner Tudenham; they're useful colts, though, and each contributed prominently to what was a relatively successful season for northern-trained two-year-olds.

The Country Lady Stardom Stakes at Goodwood, which was instituted as a listed event in 1987, was Champagne Gold's eighth race in a season which had started with second place in the Brocklesby Stakes at Doncaster in March. He clearly learned from his run there as he went on to win his next four races, battling on keenly in a maiden at Thirsk, a minor event at Pontefract and the Woodcote Stakes at Epsom (where he accounted for Across The Bay by a length and a half) then finding his task simpler in the Homefire Stakes at Doncaster. His winning sequence came to a halt, not surprisingly, in the Anglia Television July Stakes where he came up against the Coventry Stakes winner Rock City for the first time; Champagne Gold, who'd fly-jumped leaving the stalls, began a forward move at halfway but was readily outpaced in the last furlong and went down by five lengths. A month later, in the Scottish Equitable Gimcrack Stakes at York, Rock City confirmed the form almost to a pound: on this occasion Champagne Gold, who as in all his later races was edgy and on his toes, finished out of the money in fifth and last position having found the pace too hot from over two furlongs out. On the form-book third place looked the best that Champagne Gold's connections could fairly expect at Goodwood, for among his three opponents were the seven-length Danepak Bacon Stakes winner Spinning, an even-money favourite, and the consistent Robellation, twice second to Be My Chief in pattern company. Overnight rain turned the ground soft, however, conditions which Champagne Gold had handled comfortably enough earlier in the season and which the two principals had yet to meet. Champagne Gold, attempting a mile for the first time, clearly relished the test of stamina which ensued, closing on Robellation and Spinning with a quarter of a mile left, staying on strongly to take up the running inside the final furlong and then holding Robellation's renewed challenge gamely by a neck; Spinning was hampered slightly in the closing stages and was eased to finish four lengths behind. Champagne Gold's performance raised hopes that Karinga Bay would acquit himself well in the Vodafone Horris Hill at Newbury. Though in the event Karinga Bay ran poorly, seemingly unable to cope with the soft conditions, it may be worth bearing in mind that he is reportedly a five-length better horse than Champagne Gold at home.

	Bairn (USA) (ch 1982)	Northern Baby (b 1976)	Northern Dancer, Two Rings
Champagne Gold (ch.c. Apr 14, 1987)		Lady Mouse (ch 1970)	Sir Ivor, Vimere
	Halkissimo (ch 1968)	Khalkis (b 1960)	Vimy, Merry Xmas
		Clairvoyant (br 1954)	Dante, Claire

Champagne Gold is the best representative from the first crop of the St James's Palace winner and Two Thousand Guineas runner-up Bairn, whose several other winning produce include his highest-priced 1988 yearling Ruling Passion, who had only the one start, and the useful Belgian filly Precious Reward. Champagne Gold's dam Halkissimo has provided the stable with a continuous supply of winners under both codes in the last fourteen years; among the more familiar are Onapromise (by Sharp Edge), who won over six furlongs as a two-year-old and later became a fairly useful if moody chaser, the fair middle-distance handicapper Mac's Delight (by Scottish Rifle) and The Grey Bomber, who was unbeaten over hurdles and thought set for the top until his freak death by electrocution at exercise. Halkissimo is a half-sister to two minor winners and, like her dam, Clairvoyant, was best at around a mile. What does the future hold for the leggy, rather sparely-made Champagne Gold? Well, he hasn't the scope of his stable-companion, and will need to improve to hold his own against the late-developing three-year-olds in listed events; he's also unlikely to be shown any leniency by the handicapper. If kept to the flat, he'll stay a mile and a quarter; if he doesn't progress, we could see him over hurdles. *Denys Smith.*

CHAMPION GIRL 3 b. or br.f. Blazing Saddles (AUS)–Mercy Cure 81 (No   53
Mercy 126) [1988 5d6 5g 5g* 5s3 5g2 5g 1989 5s 5s 5f 5m3 5m 5g6 5m 5.1f 5.1g a6g]
workmanlike, sparely-made filly: plating-class performer nowadays: effective at 5f
and 6f: best form on good ground: blinkered last 2 outings: often claimer ridden and
sweating: moved badly to post penultimate start at 3 yrs: inconsistent. *A. Bailey.*

CHANCE OF STARDOM 3 b.c. Star Appeal 133–Chantal 74 (Charlottesville   89
135) [1988 10.2m 1989 17.6m* 17.6g3 13v3] rangy colt: fair performer: bit coltish,
won maiden at Wolverhampton in August: suited by thorough test of stamina:
difficult at stalls second start and edgy otherwise as 3-y-o: sold 13,000 gns
Newmarket Autumn Sales. *G. Harwood.*

CHANDANNE 2 ch.f. (Mar 22) Ballad Rock 122–Affirmation (FR) (Affirmed   49
(USA)) [1989 5d4 5s3 5f4 6f 6g3] 12,500Y: small filly: moderate mover: first foal:
dam, minor French 11f winner at 4 yrs, is from good family: poor maiden: bred to stay
1m: off course over 5 months after third outing. *R. Hannon.*

CHAN FU 4 b.g. Kafu 120–Chanrossa (High Top 131) [1988 10f 12d4 12m 1989   47
12m5 14.8f6] leggy, rather sparely-made gelding: has round action: poor maiden:
stays 1½m: acts on firm going and a soft surface: sold 1,200 gns Ascot December
Sales. *R. Curtis.*

CHANGE GUARD 3 b.f. Day Is Done 115–Mittens (Run The Gantlet (USA))   56
[1988 6g3 7.5m 7s2 6d5 7g 1989 8g4 9f 10f5] leggy, angular filly: modest maiden:
below form as 3-y-o: stays 1m: acts on soft going: tends to hang left, and is likely to
prove best with strong handling. *A. D. Brown.*

CHANGE OF MOOD 2 b.f. (Mar 28) Dominion 123–Particular Miss 70   56
(Luthier 126) [1989 6f4 6m2 6m 6g 8m 10f] 10,500Y: compact, dipped-backed filly:
has a roundish action: fourth foal: half-sister to 3-y-o 5f winner Elder Prince (by
Final Straw) and modest maiden Pigeon English (by Homing): dam, 1m winner at 3
yrs, is out of very useful middle-distance filly One Over Parr, a sister to Polygamy:

plating-class form in maidens on first 2 starts: well beaten afterwards, in selling nursery (on toes, took good hold) on final start: sold 2,000 gns Newmarket Autumn Sales. *C. A. Cyzer*.

CHANGE WEAR 3 b.g. Alzao (USA) 117–Piccadilly Lil 92 (Pall Mall 132) [1988 7g 1989 11.7h 10f4 10.2h 8m] lengthy, angular gelding: 50/1, fourth of 7 in minor event at Folkestone in June, leading over 1m and only sign of ability. *K. M. Brassey*. —

CHANNOR 2 b.f. (May 18) Norwick (USA) 120–Channing Girl 73 (Song 132) [1989 6g 8m] leggy filly: has scope: second foal: half-sister to 3-y-o 7f winner Bournville(by Lochnager): dam 1½m winner: bit backward, well beaten in August maidens at Newbury and Chepstow. *K. M. Brassey*. —

CHANTERESSE 2 b.f. (Jan 20) Chantro 104–Miss Friendly 72 (Status Seeker) [1989 5v 6s] sixth foal: sister to a poor plater on flat and over hurdles and to 2 bad animals: dam placed at up to 11f: well beaten in late-season seller at Ayr and claimer at Hamilton. *W. Bentley*. —

CHANTRY BARTLE 3 ch.g. Say Primula 107–Sallametti (USA) 69 (Giacometti 130) [1988 NR 1989 7f 8.5f 8f 10f 12g2 12.5f* 12g6] sparely-made gelding: first foal: dam, 11f winner, stayed well: won selling handicap (no bid) at Wolverhampton in October by 6 lengths: will be suited by 1¾m: acts on firm ground. *C. W. Thornton*. **48**

CHANTRY BOY 3 b.g. Balliol 125–Glebe 83 (Tacitus 124) [1988 NR 1989 10s 12d] big gelding: poor maiden: probably doesn't stay middle distances. *W. Holden*. —

CHAPEL CHIMES 3 b.f. Song 132–Lady Spey 55 (Sir Gaylord) [1988 6g 6d 1989 8s4 9d3 12m a8g 10g a8g a10g6] angular, sparely-made filly: has a round action: plating-class form at best, including in sellers: seems to stay 1¼m: visored penultimate start. *P. J. Feilden*. —

CHAPLINS CLUB (USA) 9 ch.g. Parade of Stars (USA)–Nautical Rose (USA) (Henrijan) [1988 6g 6g 6g 5g3 6g5 5g 6d* 6g* 5g* 5s5 6g* 6m* 6g2 5g* 5m* 6g 5.6m 6s2 5g 5s* 6d* 5f2 6f6 6s5 6s6 6s3 5m 1989 6.1f 6f 6f 6g2 6g4 6f 5g 6m2 6f 5m* 6s2 6m 6s5 6s3] small, strong gelding: fair performer: won 20-runner claimer at Ripon in August: 16/1, good second of 29 to Jovewerth in £34,100 Ladbrokes (Ayr) Gold Cup (Handicap) following month: odds on, poor third of 10 in Hamilton seller final outing: effective at 5f or 6f: ideally suited by an easy surface: has won for apprentice, but best with strong handling: has hung and is blinkered off-side only: best covered up: tough and genuine: a credit to his trainer. *D. W. Chapman*. **86**

CHAPMAN'S PEAK 2 b.g. (May 21) Top Ville 129–Cape Race (USA) 88 (Northern Dancer) [1989 8m2 8g a7g3] 38,000Y: medium-sized, quite attractive gelding: closely related to French 10.8f winner Brickfield Queen (by High Top) and half-brother to several winners, including useful 1m to 1¼m winner Raiwand (by Tap On Wood) and useful 1981 2-y-o 5f and 7f winner Final Strike (by Artaius): dam, half-sister to very smart colts Lord Gayle and Never Return, won over 1m: modest form: didn't confirm promise of debut (4 lengths second of 29 to Defensive Play in maiden at Newmarket) and gelded after final start: will stay 1¼m. *D. Morley*. **73**

CHARADE DANCER (USA) 2 ch.f. (Feb 20) Barachois (CAN)–Asphodel 55 (Busted 134) [1989 5m* 6f4 5f 6m6 6g 5g5 6g] smallish, sparely-made filly: half-sister to a winner in North America by Diamond Prospect: dam 1½m winner: quite modest performer: won maiden at Newcastle in July by a short head having been long way behind: fifth in minor event at Catterick, best subsequent effort: best form at 5f: has run well for 7-lb claimer: sold 4,600 gns Doncaster November Sales. *J. Etherington*. **66**

CHARBATTE (FR) 3 b.f. In Fijar (USA) 121–Evonsville (FR) (Val de Loir 133) [1988 NR 1989 8m4 7m3] big, leggy filly: half-sister to several winners in France, including 1m and 1½m winner Envie de Rire (by Trepan): dam minor 7f winner at 2 yrs in France: green, fairly useful form in minor event (taken very quietly and last to post) at Newmarket and listed race (didn't handle turn) at York: gave a lot of trouble at stalls and withdrawn at Beverley in between: bandaged all round all appearances: will be suited by return to 1m. *M. Moubarak*. **93**

CHARCOAL BURNER 4 br.g. Royal Match 117–Resist 55 (Reliance II 137) [1988 8f 11.7g 8m 7f3 7f 7f2 8g2 7g2 1989 7m3 7f 7m4 8.2g 7g 7f* 7m 10.2f2 10f6] compact gelding: won for first time (had previously appeared irresolute) in handicap at Folkestone in August: effective at 7f and stays 1¼m: acts on firm going: seems best without visor: often pulls hard, and has gone freely to post: taken down early seventh outing: untrustworthy. *L. G. Cottrell*. **49** §

CHARDEN 3 b.g. Touching Wood (USA) 127–Fighting Lady 104 (Chebs Lad 120) [1988 7g 1989 10f6 10.1m5 10f2 14m2 11.7m6 16m] close-coupled, angular gelding: fair maiden: best effort when second in handicap at Salisbury fourth outing, leading **79**

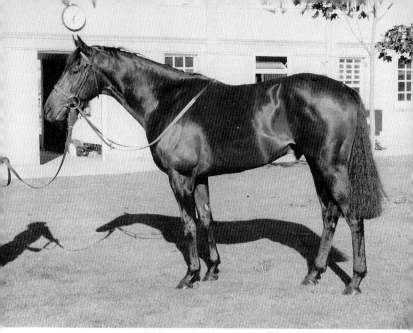

The Dowager Lady Beaverbrook's "Charmer"

2f out then hanging right, carrying head awkwardly: seems suited by 1¾m. *D. R. C. Elsworth.*

CHARIOT OF PEACE 3 b.f. Young Generation 129–Western Partner (USA) **68**
(West Coast Scout (USA)) [1988 6m³ 1989 7m⁴ 7f³ 7.6m⁵] leggy, sparely-made filly: third in Blue Seal Stakes at Ascot: below that form in minor event and maidens as 3-y-o, hanging badly left and looking unsatisfactory final start: should be suited by 7f+. *Major W. R. Hern.*

CHARLES DEVON LAD 4 br.c. Fitzwilliam (USA)–Devon Maid (Meldrum —
112) [1988 8m⁴ 10g⁵ 12m 12g 1989 9f 10f] angular colt: moderate mover: poor maiden: soundly beaten in handicaps at 4 yrs. *D. Lee.*

CHARLES THE GREAT 2 b.g. (May 20) Vaigly Great 127–Tin Tessa 87 —
(Martinmas 128) [1989 6g a8g] angular colt: fifth foal: half-brother to 7f winner Actress (by Known Fact) and 1986 2-y-o 5f winner Tiszta Sharok (by Song): dam best at 2 yrs, successful over 5.8f: well beaten in maidens. *J. Wharton.*

CHARLIE ME DARLING 5 ch.h. Sharpo 132–Hithermoor Lass 75 (Red Alert —
127) [1988 NR 1989 10.8m 8f] robust, round-barrelled horse: poor and lightly-raced maiden: visored at 5 yrs. *D. J. G. Murray-Smith.*

CHARLY O'BRIAN (USA) 3 b.g. Lypheor 118–Out of Joint (USA) (Quack —
(USA)) [1988 7m³ 7m⁴ 7m 8g 1989 10g] leggy, useful-looking gelding: has a long stride: modest form first 2 outings but has run poorly since: only start as 3-y-o in April. *R. F. Casey.*

CHARM BIRD 4 b.f. Daring March 116–Hot Bird 98 (Birdbrook 110) [1988 6m —
5m 6f⁵ 5m⁶ 5f³ 5.1m* 5f³ 5g 1989 5f 5m 5m⁶] leggy, medium-sized filly: quite modest winner as 3-y-o: below her best in 1989: mounted on track final outing (July): form only at 5f on top-of-the-ground: suitable mount for apprentice, but got loose at start when ridden by inexperienced 7-lb claimer second outing. *L. J. Holt.*

CHARMED KNAVE 4 b.g. Enchantment 115–Peerless Princess (Averof 123) — [1988 8g 7d⁶ 6g² 6f⁶ 6g 6f 7f 6h 6g⁵ 6d 1989 7.6f 6f 5.8h 6f] lengthy, medium-sized gelding: poor mover: generally well below form since third outing at 3 yrs: stays 6f: acts on firm going: sometimes blinkered. *E. A. Wheeler.*

CHARMER 4 b.c. Be My Guest (USA) 126–Take Your Mark (USA) (Round **114** Table) [1988 7g² 8g² 12m 10g 1989 9g³ 8m² 10g⁵ 8g⁴] well-made, attractive colt: poor walker: runner-up to Doyoun in General Accident 2000 Guineas at Newmarket in 1988: lightly raced and below that form subsequently: placed in slowly-run races at Newmarket as 4-y-o behind Reprimand in Earl of Sefton EBF Stakes in April and Sabotage in £9,200 event (sweating and coltish) in October: bit mulish at start, never reached leaders in Dubai Champion Stakes (stiff task, visored) and listed contest, also at Newmarket: stays 1¼m: yet to race on very firm going or a soft surface: trained until after reappearance by R. Hern. *C. E. Brittain.*

CHARMING BALLERINA 2 ch.f. (Feb 24) Caerleon (USA) 132–Sound of **89 p** Success (USA) (Successor) [1989 6m³ 6m² 7m* 7.3m*] IR 75,000Y: medium-sized, leggy filly: has scope: fluent mover: sister to Irish 1½m winner Caerleon's Success and half-sister to several winners, including Derby runner-up Hawaiian Sound (by Hawaii) and very useful 1m to 1¾m filly Rapids (by Head of The River): dam ran twice: progressive filly: successful in September in maiden at Chester and nursery (by a head from Call To Arms) at Newbury: will be well suited by 1m + : likely to improve again. *M. R. Stoute.*

CHARMING MOLLY (USA) 3 b.f. Diesis 133–Mimi J (USA) (Angle Light **86** (USA)) [1988 6d* 1989 8m 7f 7f 7.6m³ 8s] leggy filly: won £7,100 event at Ascot as 2-y-o: good third in £6,200 event at Lingfield best effort in handicaps, running on well: stays 7.6f: acts on top-of-the-ground and a soft surface: sold 35,000 gns Newmarket December Sales. *M. R. Stoute.*

CHARM TIME 2 ch.g. (Apr 2) Good Times (ITY)–Glamorous Girl (Caliban 123) **45** [1989 7m 7v 8g⁶] tall, rangy gelding: has scope: fifth living foal: half-brother to 3-y-o Steele's (by Music Boy), fair 5f and 6f winner at 2 yrs, and to 1979 2-y-o 7f winner Georgina Park (by Silly Season): dam ran over hurdles: poor form in maidens: likely to do better in sellers: gelded after final start. *T. D. Barron.*

CHAROSSA 4 b.f. Ardross 134–Charter Belle 60 (Runnymede 123) [1988 10g — 12f⁵ 10f⁴ 1989 12d a13g] workmanlike filly: moderate mover: lightly-raced maiden: cocked jaw final outing (June) at 3 yrs. *Miss B. Sanders.*

CHART CROSS 3 b.c. Millfontaine 114–Whichcombe 79 (Huntercombe 133) **59** [1988 7g 7m 7f 8d² 7d 1989 8.3m 8f⁴ 9f* 10m⁵ 10h⁵ 8.2f³ 9m 8g² a7g a7g⁶] rather leggy, angular colt: quite modest performer: favourite and ridden by 5-lb claimer, won seller (no bid) at Redcar in June: should be suited by return to 9f + : acts on firm going and a soft surface. *N. A. Callaghan.*

CHASING THE DRAGON 7 b.g. Moulton 128–Lead Me On (King's Troop **68** 118) [1988 18v* 16g* 19f³ 19g³ 18g 1989 14.8s³] big, good-bodied gelding: modest handicapper: co-favourite but in need of race, shaped well when third at Warwick in March, but wasn't seen out again: suited by a test of stamina: acts on any going: blinkered nowadays: sometimes sweats: suited by forcing tactics. *O. Sherwood.*

CHATEAUBABY (USA) 2 b.f. (Apr 13) Nureyev (USA) 131–Chateaucreek **62** (USA) (Chateaugay) [1989 5m² 7f³ 7m² 8f⁵ 8s] $350,000Y: smallish filly: keen walker: half-sister to several winners, notably Henbit (by Hawaii) and quite useful middle-distance stayer Henbane (by Alydar): dam minor stakes winner at up to 6f: quite modest maiden: below form in September nurseries at Pontefract and Ayr: best form at 7f: bandaged, reared in paddock and threw jockey at York in May. *J. W. Watts.*

CHATEAU DE BERNE (USA) 2 b.c. (Mar 19) Fit To Fight (USA)–Liberally — Laced (USA) (Silent Screen (USA)) [1989 7m 6d] $37,000Y: rangy, rather unfurnished colt: sixth foal: half-brother to minor stakes winner Lady Lush (by Nikoli), successful at up to 9f: dam won at up to 7f at 2 yrs: sire won from 6f to 1½m: well beaten in October maidens at Newmarket and Newbury. *M. A. Jarvis.*

CHATEAU DE LYONS 3 b.c. Longleat (USA) 109–French Cooking 70 (Royal — And Regal (USA)) [1988 8g 1989 10s 16.5g⁶ 17.6f⁶] strong, workmanlike colt: well beaten in maidens. *A. Bailey.*

CHATEAUNEUF 2 b.c. (May 14) Niniski (USA) 125–Valois (Lyphard (USA) — 132) [1989 7g] 65,000Y: half-brother to fairly useful 7f winner Shannon Cottage (by Shecky Greene) and 1985 2-y-o 7f winner Shannon Vale (by Irish River): dam half-sister to High Top and Camden Town: 20/1, prominent around 4f in 28-runner maiden at Newmarket in November. *B. W. Hills.*

CHATTERIS 3 b.g. Shareef Dancer (USA) 135–Fenella 91 (Thatch (USA) 136) —
[1988 NR 1989 11s⁵ 10.6g] smallish, sturdy gelding: moderate mover: sixth foal:
half-brother to 4 winners, including useful middle-distance stayer Kashi Lagoon (by
Ile de Bourbon) and Queen Anne Stakes winner Trojan Fen (by Troy): dam, from
good family, won over 7.6f: well beaten in maidens at Newbury in April and Haydock
in June: sold 3,600 gns Newmarket Autumn Sales and subsequently gelded. *P. F. I.
Cole.*

CHECKLEY 4 ch.g. Record Token 128–Land And Sea 65 (Realm 129) [1988 8d 7d —
11.7f 1989 8.3m 10m] workmanlike gelding: poor maiden: tailed off in selling
handicaps at 4 yrs: wears a crossed noseband. *R. Dickin.*

CHECKPOINT CHARLIE 4 b.g. Artaius (USA) 129–Clouded Issue (Manado 76
130) [1988 10g² 9g⁵ 12g* 10m² 10.2g 10m* 9g 1989 11f 8m⁴ 12m]
useful-looking gelding: modest handicapper: creditable fourth at Yarmouth and
Newmarket in July: probably best at 1¼m: possibly needs a sound surface: has won
for apprentice: sweating and edgy on reappearance: sold 6,400 gns Newmarket
Autumn Sales. *W. Jarvis.*

CHEEKY BABY 3 b.f. Derrylin 115–Private Benjamin (Queen's Hussar 124) —
[1988 5.8d 5f 1989 6f 7h 8m⁶ 8f] sparely-made filly: of little account. *D. W. P.
Arbuthnot.*

CHEEKY FOX 3 b.g. King of Spain 121–Diamond Talk (Counsel 118) [1988 NR —
1989 a10g 10g] lengthy gelding: half-brother to 4-y-o Buzzards Crest (by Buzzards
Bay), 7f winner at 2 yrs, and several other winners, including fairly useful miler
Corn Street (by Decoy Boy) and sprinter Pusey Street (by Native Bazaar): dam
never ran: bit backward, well behind in late-season maiden and competitive minor
event. *J. R. Bosley.*

CHEERFUL TIMES 6 b.g. Faraway Times (USA) 123–Chevulgan (Cheval 117) 83
[1988 10.2s 10s⁴ 10.8s² 9f 10m 13.3m 11.7d² 11.7m⁵ 11.7g⁵ 10g* 8m 10g⁶ 8g⁵ 10s⁴
12g 1989 10f* 12m* 12g² 10.2f* 14f] rangy gelding: usually looks well: poor walker:
fair handicapper: much improved as 6-y-o, winning at Nottingham and Carlisle in
June and Newcastle in July: never-dangerous eleventh of 18 in Tote Ebor
(Handicap) at York: needs further than 1m and stays 1½m: acts on any going: has
worn bandages: has worn a visor, but better without: often apprentice ridden:
occasionally reluctant at stalls: well suited by extreme waiting tactics. *B. A.
McMahon.*

CHELSEA GIRL 3 b.f. Pas de Seul 133–Buffy (French Beige 127) [1988 7m 8s⁶ 103
8d 1989 10m 12m* 12m* 12g² 14.8m* 14.6g* 14m 18g²] leggy filly: moderate mover:
won auction race at Edinburgh in June, amateurs event at Newmarket in July and
handicaps at Newmarket in August and Doncaster ('The Mallard' Handicap) in
September: 12/1, good neck second of 22 to Double Dutch in Tote Cesarewitch at
Newmarket, leading inside final 1f until close home: reportedly struck into when
well below form time before: stays well: acts on top-of-the-ground: ridden by
claimer D. Biggs last 5 starts: useful. *M. A. Jarvis.*

'The Mallard' Handicap, Doncaster—Chelsea Girl draws away from Baraz

CHEPSTOW HOUSE (USA) 2 b.f. (Feb 14) Northern Baby (CAN) 127– **56**
Chepstow Vale (USA) 97 (Key To The Mint (USA)) [1989 5f³ 6m] leggy, rather
unfurnished filly: first foal: dam 2-y-o 5f and 6f winner stayed 1m: very green,
eased-down third of 7 to Dead Certain in maiden at Salisbury in May: always
struggling in similar event (went very freely down) at Leicester following month:
sold 1,900 gns Newmarket December Sales. *Major W. R. Hern.*

CHEREN LADY 2 br.f. (Apr 25) Comedy Star (USA) 121–Lilly Lee Lady (USA) —
(Shecky Greene (USA)) [1989 7g 7d] workmanlike filly: first reported foal: dam,
unraced, is out of half-distance to smart middle-distance winner Salt Marsh: never
dangerous in maiden at Newmarket and minor event at Thirsk in November. *R.
Curtis.*

CHEROKEE MAID 2 b. or br.f. (May 1) Anfield 117–Hopi 68 (The Brianstan **31**
128) [1989 5d 5m² 6m 5m] smallish, lengthy filly: keen walker: moderate mover:
first foal: dam barely stayed 6f: poor plater: slowly away last 2 outings. *P. S. Felgate.*

CHERRY CHAP 4 b.g. Kabour 80–Mild Wind (Porto Bello 118) [1988 8m 8.5m **39** §
6g 6d 6f 7g 6s 6m 7g⁵ 7g 1989 6f⁵ 7m 5m 5m² 5g 5m 5f 5g⁴ 7g 7m 8f 5g² 5m 5s]
strong, compact gelding: poor maiden: effective at 5f and stays 7f: acts on firm
going: blinkered or visored nowadays: usually apprentice ridden: winning selling
hurdler: inconsistent, and probably ungenuine. *D. W. Chapman.*

CHERRY CROWN 2 gr.f. (May 9) Uncle Pokey 116–Cherry Season 62 (Silly —
Season 127) [1989 6f 8m 10g] leggy filly: third foal: dam 7f winner: well beaten in
maidens and a seller. *J. F. Bottomley.*

CHERRYWOOD SAM 5 ch.h. Dublin Taxi–Tollers Rose 53 (Some Hand 119) —
[1988 5s 5g 5m 5f 1989 5f 5f] angular horse: no form for long time: stays 6f: acts on
firm going: visored once, often blinkered. *H. O'Neill.*

CHESS PIECE 2 b.f. (May 20) Castle Keep 121–Princess Log 78 (King Log 115) **70**
[1989 5m⁴ 6f² 6g 7f³ 8m³ 8.5g³ 7s⁵] leggy, quite good-topped filly: good walker:
sister to modest maiden Flying Buttress and closely related to very useful French 9f
to 11.5f winner Ragnel (by Ragstone): dam miler and half-sister to Roi Soleil: modest
performer: best efforts on fourth to sixth starts: suited by 1m + . *P. Mitchell.*

CHESTER HOUSE 3 b.f. King of Spain 121–Storm Crest 80 (Lord Gayle (USA) **46**
124) [1988 7m 6g 1989 8m 7m 7m 6m⁴ 6f⁵] poor form in varied events, including
sellers: stayed 7f: blinkered last 3 starts: ran creditably when edgy and sweating:
dead. *M. F. D. Morley.*

CHESTER TERRACE 5 ch.g. Crofter (USA) 124–Persian Mourne (Mourne **44**
126) [1988 10s 10d 9f 12.2d 8.2s⁴ 9g 1989 10f³ 10.8m³ 10m 11.7m⁶] compact gelding:
moderate mover: poor handicapper: not seen out after July: suited by 1¼m: probably
acts on any going: has run creditably for apprentice: has joined K. Bridgwater. *R.
Dickin.*

CHEVALIER DECOUPES 2 b.c. (May 16) Krayyan 117–Crathie 66 —
(Lochnager 132) [1989 5f 8g] IR 1,800F, IR 4,100Y: leggy, close-coupled colt: second
foal: dam placed over 1m here and from 9.5f to 13f in Ireland, is granddaughter of
Irish Guinness Oaks winner Celina: well beaten in claimer (backward) at Kempton
in June when trained by P. Burgoyne and maiden at Leicester in November. *W.
Carter.*

CHEVEUX MITCHELL 2 ch.c. (Apr 30) Dunbeath (USA) 127–Hide Out **67**
(Habitat 134) [1989 7f⁵ 7m 7m⁶ 7f* 9g 8f⁴ 7g] 5,800F: sturdy colt: half-brother to
1984 2-y-o 5f winner Fair Charter (by Be My Guest) and 1m winner Bahrain Bridge
(by Formidable): dam ran once: quite modest performer: lowered in class, made all
in claimer at Salisbury in September: ran moderately in nurseries afterwards: stays
7f: bandaged behind final start. *K. O. Cunningham-Brown.*

CHEZ JARRASSE 2 b.c. (Mar 22) Pharly (FR) 130–Miss Saint-Cloud 102 **61** p
(Nonoalco (USA) 131) [1989 6g 7m] leggy, close-coupled colt: first foal: dam 7f to
1¼m winner: better effort in maidens on second outing, when eleventh of 21 at
Newmarket in October. *G. Wragg.*

CHEZ POLLY 3 ch.f. Homing 130–My Pink Parrot (Pirate King 129) [1988 NR —
1989 8g 10.1g 12.5g³ 10f⁶] tall, workmanlike filly: half-sister to several winners here
and abroad, including fair 1978 2-y-o 5f winner Leo Vert (by Ballymoss): dam never
ran: well beaten, including in seller: will be suited by return to 1½m: has joined P.
Hedger. *J. W. Payne.*

CHICA MIA 5 b.m. Camden Town 125–Backwoodsgirl (Young Emperor 133) **79**
[1988 10v 12g 8.5f² 8.5g³ 8.5d* 9.5f 8s* 8.5d² 9v 1989 10s³ 8g 6s 8m 8.5d 8.2g
7.6m* 7g* 7m⁴ 7.5m⁴ 7.6m⁶ 8s] workmanlike ex-Irish mare: carries condition:

second live foal: sister to 1m winner Camden Lad: dam never ran: won handicaps at Chester (33/1, apprentices event) and Ayr (favourite) in July: suited by 7f to 1m: acts on any going, except possibly heavy. *J. Parkes.*

CHIC-ANITA 4 b.f. Tina's Pet 121–Chiquitita 44 (Reliance II 137) [1988 7m 8f 6g 6d 8f 5f 6m 7g 7g⁴ 8.3g 7m 8g 12g 1989 8m 8g² 8h 8m⁴ 10m 8.3d 10.4m 8f 12.5f⁵ a12g] small filly: poor plater: stays 12.5f: acts on any going: has been blinkered: usually apprentice ridden nowadays: slowly away third and eighth outings: inconsistent. *T. B. Hallett.* — **27**

CHIC ANTIQUE 5 ch.m. Rarity 129–What A Picture 80 (My Swanee 122) [1988 5d⁵ 8f⁴ 7f⁴ 8g⁵ 8f³ 8g³ 6g 1989 7h⁴ 6m² 5f* 6f² 5m 6f³ 6f 6f] workmanlike mare: has a quick action: poor handicapper: won apprentice event at Sandown in July: ran moderately last 2 outings: effective at 5f and stays 1m: acts on firm going: occasionally sweats and gets on toes. *P. J. Makin.* — **44**

CHIC CAROLE 3 ch.f. Dalsaan 125–Valley of Diamonds 74 (Florescence 120) [1988 6g 7g 6g 1989 7s 8m 8.3d 10.6s⁶] leggy filly: of little account. *J. W. Payne.* —

CHICO VALDEZ (USA) 5 ch.g. Valdez (USA)–Lypatia (FR) (Lyphard (USA) 132) [1988 12.3s 12g 17.1g 12g 10m² 12f³ 10g 1989 12g] close-coupled, rather sparely-made gelding: has a round action: poor handicapper: placed in selling company: effective at 1¼m and 1½m: acts on firm going and a soft surface: visored 4 times at 4 yrs. *M. C. Chapman.* —

CHIEF DANCER 2 b.f. (Apr 11) Chief Singer 131–Palumba 100 (Derring-Do 131) [1989 5d⁴] 31,000Y: stocky filly: fourth foal: half-sister to fair 1985 2-y-o 6f winner C Jam Blues (by Milford) and plating-class miler Victoria Line (by High Line): dam won over 5f at 2 yrs and stayed 1¼m: backward, 7 lengths fourth of 7, slowly away, to Norton Challenger in minor event at Thirsk in April: unseated rider leaving paddock and was withdrawn from maiden there earlier in month. *M. W. Easterby.* —

CHIEF RUNNER 7 b.g. Arapaho 108–Waterhen (Deep Run 119) [1988 7f 8g 7f 1989 12m] sparely-made gelding: of little account: visored once: bandaged only start at 7 yrs. *P. Howling.* —

CHIEF'S CHOICE 4 b.g. Coquelin (USA) 121–Douschkina 86 (Dubassoff (USA)) [1988 NR 1989 10m⁴ 10f 10.6s] good-topped gelding: modest maiden as 2-y-o, found to have irregular pulse-rate after running poorly final outing: well beaten in varied events in 1989. *E. H. Owen jun.* —

CHIEF'S IMAGE 3 br.c. Chief Singer 131–Dance Card 69 (Be My Guest (USA) 126) [1988 6d* 6g³ 7g⁶ 1989 7s³ 7d 10.4f⁴ 10f⁶ 8m² 8m] big, good-topped, angular colt: fairly useful performer: beaten neck by Samoan in minor event at Newcastle: pulled hard and led 6f when below form in £15,700 handicap at Newmarket later in July: should prove best at around 1m: may prove best with give in the ground: carried head high third start: sometimes bit edgy and went very freely to post at Newcastle. *G. A. Huffer.* — **91**

CHILD OF THE MIST 3 b.c. Lomond (USA) 128–Lighted Lamp (USA) (Sir Gaylord) [1988 7m² 7g³ 8g⁵ 1989 10m³ 12.3m⁴ 12f* 13.3m⁴] strong, lengthy colt: has plenty of scope: moderate mover: ridden by 7-lb claimer, won maiden at Doncaster in May despite hanging left and flashing tail under pressure: good fourth in moderately-run £11,000 handicap at Newbury in July, carrying head bit high: will be suited by further: has form on firm going, but may prove best with some give: below form in blinkers second start: sold to join O. Sherwood 30,000 gns Newmarket Autumn Sales. *B. W. Hills.* — **99**

CHILDREN'S JOIE 3 b.g. Auction Ring (USA) 123–Port La Joie (Charlottown 127) [1988 NR 1989 7s 8g⁴ 10f² 10m 12m⁴ 10m 10g 12.5f 12g] 4,800Y: medium-sized, deep-girthed gelding: moderate walker: long-striding, quite good mover: sixth foal: half-brother to very useful jumper Southernair (by Derrylin): dam unraced daughter of 1000 Guineas and Oaks second Spree: plating class at best: ran moderately last 4 starts, including in sellers: stays 1½m: acts on firm going: blinkered sixth and final outings: sold 6,200 gns Newmarket Autumn Sales. *D. W. P. Arbuthnot.* — **56**

CHILDREY (USA) 2 ch.c. Chief's Crown (USA)–Batna (USA) (Cyane (USA)) [1989 6g* 7g³] 2 10,000F, $275,000Y: good-bodied, attractive colt: has scope: first foal: dam very useful winner at up to 9f: odds on, won 15-runner maiden at Folkestone in October in good style by 5 lengths from North Country: well-backed favourite, close third to Two Left Feet in all-aged event at Newmarket following month: will stay 1m: wears a net muzzle. *G. Harwood.* — **93**

CHILIBOY 2 gr.c. (Apr 2) Precocious 126–Chili Girl 112 (Skymaster 126) [1989 6f⁵ 6g] stocky colt: half-brother to 3-y-o Eccolina (by Formidable) and several winners, including smart sprinter Chilibang (by Formidable) and quite useful 6f and —

7f winner Hot Case (by Upper Case): dam sprinting half-sister to useful Steel Heart: 12/1 and green, over 7 lengths fifth of 11, headed 2f out and eased closing stages, to Robellation in minor event at Kempton in May: on toes, never placed to challenge in 28-runner maiden at Newmarket 5 months later. *J. L. Dunlop.*

CHILIPOUR 2 gr.g. (May 4) Nishapour (FR) 125–Con Carni (Blakeney 126) — [1989 6g 6g 8g] IR 12,000F, 12,000Y: leggy, close-coupled gelding: second foal: dam poor daughter of very useful sprinter Chili Girl, half-sister to Steel Heart and dam of Chilibang: well beaten in maidens. *G. Lewis.*

CHILLING BREEZE (USA) 2 ch.f. (Feb 23) It's Freezing (USA) 122–Payee 65 (USA) (For The Moment (USA)) [1989 5m* 5m 6g5 5m] $42,000F, $65,000Y: workmanlike, good-quartered filly: fifth foal: dam showed a little ability at 2 yrs in North America: odds on, won 5-runner maiden at Edinburgh in July: creditable fifth of 17 to Rose of Miami from disadvantageous draw in Haydock claimer following month, best subsequent effort: stays 6f: free to post second and third starts: sold 8,000 gns Newmarket Autumn Sales. *W. Hastings-Bass.*

CHILTERNS 2 b.f. (Mar 10) Beldale Flutter (USA) 130–Ballad Island 83 (Ballad — Rock 122) [1989 6g 6m 6m a6g a8g a7g] 2,300Y: leggy filly: second foal: half-sister to winning 3-y-o sprinter Hong Kong Girl (by Petong): dam 7f and 1m performer: of little account. *D. Marks.*

CHIMES OF FREEDOM (USA) 2 ch.f. (Jan 23) Private Account 112 (USA)–Aviance 112 (Northfields (USA)) [1989 6f* 6m* 6g* 6g* 6m3]

Third place in the Tattersalls Cheveley Park Stakes at Newmarket in October ended Chimes of Freedom's unbeaten sequence and simultaneously quashed the idea that she was very much the dominant home-trained contender for the One Thousand Guineas that her wide-margin victory in the Moyglare Stud Stakes had made her out to be. She shouldn't be dismissed from the Guineas picture, however, as a moderately-run six furlongs on good to firm ground was, by that stage of the season, almost certainly on the sharp side—the Moyglare a month earlier had been run at a strong pace on easier ground—and there was no ignominy in losing to Dead Certain, whose form entitled her to considerable respect anyway. Chimes of Freedom is essentially a strong-running filly who needs riding close to a true pace over six furlongs and, more relevantly, will be very much more at home over longer distances; she would have been an interesting participant in either the Hoover Fillies' Mile or the Prix Marcel Boussac, races which were reportedly considered as alternatives to the Cheveley Park. The distance of the One Thousand Guineas will undoubtedly suit the leggy, good-topped Chimes of Freedom ideally, and if all goes well with her over the winter—we think she's the type to train on—she must have reasonable prospects of reaching a place.

The opposition couldn't have been much further removed from classic standard when Chimes of Freedom began her career in a maiden race at Lingfield in May, and although she wasn't hard pressed to score by six lengths it wasn't until the Kingsclere Stakes at Newbury the following month, when she toyed with her two rivals, who included the previous winner Tribal Lady, and won in a canter by a length and a half that she hinted that she might be out of the ordinary. The race which confirmed that was the Hillsdown Cherry Hinton Stakes at Newmarket in July where Chimes of Freedom came up against the first three in the Queen Mary Stakes, Dead Certain, Please Believe Me and Performing Arts respectively; she all but lost her unbeaten record as Dead Certain, in spite of her 5-lb penalty, came within a short head of landing her second pattern race in under a month. Chimes of Freedom was held up several lengths off the front-running Boozy in a race which wasn't run at a noticeably good gallop to halfway, but she came under pressure over two furlongs out as Dead Certain delivered what seemed to be a perfectly-timed challenge. Chimes of Freedom, the long-odds-on favourite, still had three lengths to make up at that point but she began to eat into Dead Certain's advantage approaching the distance, inched closer with every stride in the last furlong and just got up in a thrilling finish to win with nothing to spare; the newcomer Palace Street came through to take third, three lengths behind, with Performing Arts fourth. The next stop for the improving Chimes of Freedom was the Group 1 Moyglare Stud Stakes at the Curragh in September. Seven runners went to post but none of the home-trained contingent could be

*Hillsdown Cherry Hinton Stakes, Newmarket—
only a short head between two of the season's leading two-year-old fillies,
Chimes of Freedom (second left) and Dead Certain*

seriously fancied and the IR £110,000 first prize looked a straight match
between Chimes of Freedom and her compatriot Pharoah's Delight, who had
won the Heinz '57' Phoenix Stakes since her victories in the Windsor Castle
Stakes and the Princess Margaret Stakes. In the event Pharoah's Delight ran
below her best form, but nonetheless Chimes of Freedom couldn't be faulted
in the manner in which she overwhelmed the others, sweeping into the lead
with a furlong to run and staying on strongly, as Pharoah's Delight was eased
off, to win by six lengths. Her victory completed a highly satisfactory
afternoon for her owner Niarchos, as his leading French colt Machiavellian
had won the Prix de la Salamandre at Longchamp shortly before. The winning
time in the Moyglare of 1m 10.9sec was marginally inside the accepted
standard for the course and distance and was the fastest time for the race
since its inception in 1975; Chimes of Freedom also succeeded where
Minstrella failed narrowly three years earlier and became the first to land the
Cherry Hinton-Moyglare Stud double. Chimes of Freedom was one of seven
supplementary entries at £10,000 for the Cheveley Park. On ground faster
than she'd encountered on her two previous starts Chimes of Freedom, who,
as at the Curragh, was sensibly ridden close to the front, looked unlikely to
justify her position at the head of the market from two furlongs out, and
couldn't quicken towards the finish. At the line she was nearly a length down
on Dead Certain and a head behind Line of Thunder; her efforts earned almost
£25,000, which after deducting the supplementary payment, still left a healthy
sum and so justified, in financial terms at least, the late decision to take part.

Two Group 1 or Grade 1 winners during the course of the year would
normally be considered a handsome advertisement for most stallions but even
though Silver Hello, successful in the Arlington-Washington Futurity, also
helped keep Private Account's name in the spotlight they couldn't prevent his
slipping down the General Sires List from fourth position in 1988. Most of
Private Account's top progeny—Personal Flag, Personal Ensign and Private
Terms in the States and Graecia Magna in Britain—have taken after their sire
and shown their best form over middle distances, so it's rather surprising that
Chimes of Freedom wasn't given the opportunity to race over further than six
furlongs in her first season. Her connections may well have been influenced

190

Moyglare Stud Stakes, the Curragh—Chimes of Freedom is well on top

by the racing career of her dam, Aviance, who never raced beyond a mile even though she was bred to stay a mile and a quarter. Aviance was a very useful racemare: as a two-year-old she won twice, including in the six-furlong Heinz '57' Phoenix Stakes, and kept her form the following season, although failing to win again, finishing a creditable sixth in both the One Thousand Guineas and the July Cup. Aviance's family is one of the best in the American Stud Book, and a familiar one in Britain, too. Her dam Minnie Hauk, a useful winner at seven furlongs and a mile at three in Ireland, is a daughter of the first-class broodmare Best In Show, who virtually every other year in the 'seventies produced a superior runner or a mare who went on to make a name for herself at stud. Among her progeny are Minnie Hauk's brothers Malinowski and Gielgud, winners of the Craven Stakes and the Laurent Perrier Champagne Stakes respectively, and her half-sisters Blushing With Pride, very smart at up to eleven furlongs in the States, and Sex Appeal, who never ran but is the dam of El Gran Senor, Try My Best and Solar.

		Damascus	Sword Dancer
	Private Account (USA)	(b 1964)	Kerala
	(b 1976)	Numbered Account	Buckpasser
Chimes of		(b 1969)	Intriguing
Freedom (USA)		Northfields	Northern Dancer
(ch.f. Jan 23, 1987)		(ch 1968)	Little Hut
	Aviance	Minnie Hauk	Sir Ivor
	(ch 1982)	(b 1975)	Best In Show

Unusually, perhaps, most of Chimes of Freedom's immediate family showed their best form at up to a mile, and maybe Chimes of Freedom won't be effective over so far as may be anticipated from her pedigree. Nonetheless, she'll be well suited by a step up to a mile in the immediate future; we'll know more about her prospects of staying further when she's tackled the One Thousand Guineas. Chimes of Freedom has raced only on a sound surface; interestingly, her connections are adamant that yielding conditions will suit her better. *H. R. A. Cecil.*

CHIMES OF THE DAWN 5 ch.g. Tower Walk 130–Neptia's Word (Great   —
Nephew 126) [1988 8g² 11m⁴ 12m 8d³ 8m⁶ 8g* 8f* 8f 9f 8g 8g² 8m 8m 8g 1989 10.6g 8.2d] workmanlike gelding: shows plenty of knee action: modest winner as 4-y-o when trained by S. Norton: well beaten in handicap and claimer in 1989: suited by enterprising tactics at 1m: yet to race on soft going, acts on any other: good mount for apprentice. *D. Burchell.*

CHINA CRISIS 2 b.f. (Apr 20) Tina's Pet 121–Yellatown (Carnival Night) [1989   **47**
5m 5f⁴ 6f 6m⁶ 6f⁵ 7d] small, workmanlike filly: second reported foal: half-sister to 7f seller winner Shoot The Moon (by Sparkling Boy): dam never ran: quite modest plater: ran badly final start: should stay 7f: seems unsuited by a soft surface. *P. Mitchell.*

CHINA MOON 2 ch.f. (Mar 27) Blushing Scribe (USA) 107–Derring Venture   **63**
(Camden Town 125) [1989 7g⁴ 7f⁴ 7f 5f 5f³ 5d a6g³ a5g] leggy filly: fair sort: second

foal: dam last on only start at 2 yrs: quite modest maiden: best form at sprint distances: possibly unsuited by a soft surface. *F. Durr.*

CHINA'S WAY (USA) 3 b. or br.f. Native Uproar (USA)–China Tea (USA) 95 **57** (Round Table) [1988 7g 6g 1989 8v⁶ 8g⁶ 7m⁶ 9g⁶ 12g² 10f⁴] leggy, angular filly: keen walker: ridden by 5-lb claimer, best effort when short-head second in claimer (claimed out of S. Norton's stable £8,001) at Leicester in September: suited by 1½m: possibly unsuited by extremes of going: edgy third outing: pulled hard next: has joined A. Reid. *Dr J. D. Scargill.*

CHINESE WHISPERS 3 b.f. Song 132–Honey Pot 111 (Hotfoot 126) [1988 NR **56** 1989 5h⁶ 6f⁶ 5m⁵ 7m⁴ 6m³] lengthy, sparely-made filly: sixth foal: half-sister to 4 winners, including useful 1987 2-y-o 5f winner Ship of Fools (by Windjammer), later successful in USA, and fairly useful 6f to 1m winner Great Northern (by Dom Racine): dam sprinting 2-y-o: quite modest form in varied events, including seller: hung left second start: stays 7f: sold 3,400 gns Newmarket Autumn Sales. *R. J. R. Williams.*

CHIPANDABIT 2 b.c. (Mar 29) Mummy's Pet 125–Parlais 101 (Pardao 120) **75** [1989 5g* 5m* 5f⁶ 6g³ 7g 5g] IR 95,000Y: medium-sized, lengthy, leggy colt: good walker: brother to 3 sprint winners and half-brother to several more winners: dam sprinter: odds on, made most or all in May in maiden at Hamilton and minor event at Ripon: creditable third to Daarik in nursery at Ascot: stays 6f: trained first 3 outings by J. Berry. *J. Sutcliffe.*

CHIRONE (USA) 2 b.c. (Jan 23) Lypheor 118–Distaff Magic (USA) (Fluorescent **101** Light (USA)) [1989 7m⁵ 8g* 8.2g* 8m⁵] $75,000Y: neat, quite attractive colt: first foal: dam winner at up to 11f in USA: useful colt: showed progressive form when winning maiden at Yarmouth and minor event (making all) at Haydock in September: ran well when 4½ lengths fifth to Noble Patriarch in listed race at Ascot following month, hampered badly 1f out when disputing third place and eased 3 lengths: will stay 1¼m. *L. M. Cumani.*

CHLOE'S PET 2 ch.f. (May 2) Local Suitor (USA) 128–Mischiefmaker 73 — (Calpurnius 122) [1989 6m 6m 7f⁶ 7f] 1,900Y: compact filly: poor walker: fourth living foal: half-sister to a winner in Norway by Czarist and poor animal Gunabee Royal (by Gunner B): dam won 1m seller as 2-y-o and stayed 1¼m: poor form in varied races: twice slowly away. *M. D. I. Usher.*

CHLOROPHYLL 6 b.m. Ballymore 123–Mandy Girl (Manado 130) [1988 10.2d — 14v⁴ 14s 16d⁶ 14m 1989 14m 12m] small, plain, sparely-made mare: has stringhalt: poor handicapper: tailed off last 3 outings: stays 1¾m: seems to need a soft surface: sold 700 gns Doncaster August Sales. *M. C. Chapman.*

CHOIR'S IMAGE 2 br.f. (May 30) Lochnager 132–Choir (High Top 131) [1989 **53** 8m 7g⁴] lengthy, quite good-topped filly: third foal: half-sister to 3-y-o 8.5f to 10.2f winner Choral Sundown (by Night Shift): dam behind in 4 races: plating-class form in autumn maidens at Thirsk and Catterick. *Denys Smith.*

CHORAL SUNDOWN 3 b.f. Night Shift (USA)–Choir (High Top 131) [1988 5g⁵ **81** 5m³ 5m³ 5f² 5g⁴ 5g⁵ 5d⁶ 6s 1989 8d 8.5d* 8g³ 10f² 10.2g* 8m⁶ 10f² 12m⁶ 10.6d 9g* 9g] medium-sized, stocky filly: has scope: fair handicapper: won at Beverley in May, Doncaster in June and York (£8,000 event, idled in front) in October: ran moderately ninth and final starts: at least as effective over 9f as 1¼m: has form on firm ground but probably ideally suited by an easy surface: suitable mount for apprentice. *C. W. C. Elsey.*

CHORUS BOY 4 br.g. Sonnen Gold 121–Toccata (Kythnos 126) [1988 9g 9g⁴ᵈⁱˢ **58** 10.2m² 1989 10.2g 12.4g⁵ 9m 8v 8g³] tall, useful-looking gelding: has a rather round action: one-time modest maiden: below his best as 4-y-o: stays 1¼m: acts on race on firm going, acts on any other: ideally needs strong handling. *E. Weymes.*

CHOTOMSKI 5 b.g. Busted 134–Crown Witness 95 (Crowned Prince (USA) — 128) [1988 NR 1989 9v 8.5g 10g⁵] half-brother to 3-y-o 1¼m winner Oral Evidence (by Rusticaro), successful over 9f at 2 yrs: dam miler: little sign of ability in modest company in spring: slowly away second start: placed in NH Flat races. *M. W. Easterby.*

CHOUCHOUNOVA 3 ch.f. Lomond (USA) 128–Vicomtesse 97 (Relko 136) **105** [1988 6f³ 7g* 7g 1989 8d¹² 12f³] rangy, workmanlike filly: moderate walker: has a short, sharp action: 25/1 but looking very well, won £8,700 event at Ascot in April, staying on very strongly to lead close home: second favourite, 10½ lengths third of 5 to impressive Aliysa in listed race at Lingfield following month: stays 1½m: acts on

192

firm going and a soft surface: sold 60,000 gns Newmarket December Sales. *H. R. A. Cecil.*

CHOU-CHOU ROYALE   2 b.f. (Apr 12) Petorius 117–Royal Sensation 103   75
(Prince Regent (FR) 129) [1989 5f* 6h³ 6m 6g⁶ 6f 8.2g*] 8,000F, IR 10,000Y:
close-coupled, leggy filly: has a quick action: half-sister to several winners on flat
and over hurdles, including sprinters Royal Rouser and Hello Cuddles (both by He
Loves Me): dam stayed 1¼m: modest performer: won claimer (bandaged) at
Kempton in June and 19-runner nursery at Nottingham in October: suited by 1m:
looked unenthusiastic in blinkers on fourth outing: appears suited by waiting
tactics. *A. A. Scott.*

CHRISTIAN'S GOLD   3 b.c. Electric 126–Victa 79 (Northfields (USA)) [1988   91
7m⁶ 8s 1989 16d* 15.5f* 16f 16g 16m⁴] good-topped colt: keen walker: won maiden
at Thirsk in April and moderately-run handicap at Folkestone in May: below form
after, better than position suggests penultimate start (moved poorly down) and
probably in need of race on final one: stays 2m: acts on firm going and a soft surface:
sold 9,200 gns Newmarket Autumn Sales. *G. Harwood.*

CHRISTINE MORGAN   3 b.f. Mummy's Pet 125–Goldeane (USA) (Bold   —
Native (USA)) [1988 6s 6g 1989 7f 5m] leggy filly: has a round action: little sign of
ability in maidens and apprentice handicap: edgy and backward in 1989. *Mrs Barbara Waring.*

CHRISTMAS HOLS   3 b.g. Young Generation 129–Foston Bridge 68 (Relkino   55
131) [1988 7m⁵ 6m 1989 7d 8s 10m⁶ 7h 8m 6m 11.7g³ 10f² 12g 10f*] lengthy, angular
gelding: won seller (bought in 6,800 gns) at Folkestone in September: suited by
1¼m: acts on firm going: blinkered fifth outing: inconsistent: sold to join J. Bosley
8,400 gns Newmarket Autumn Sales. *C. A. Cyzer.*

CHROEMARLIN   3 b.f. Tanfirion 110–Danova (FR) (Dan Cupid 132) [1988 NR   —
1989 8f 12g 10g a12g a16g] IR 1,300Y: workmanlike filly: half-sister to several
winners, including 1987 2-y-o 7f seller winner Saddique and good 1985 Norwegian
2-y-o Big Band Beat (by Orchestra): dam French 10.5f winner: no sign of ability,
including in seller: blinkered final start. *J. W. Payne.*

CHRONIC REMORSE   3 b.f. Tender King 123–Ile d'Amour (Sassafras (FR)   —
135) [1988 5m 5g 1989 7s 8g 6g] sparely-made, dipped-backed filly: well beaten in
varied events including seller on final start, first for 6 months. *M. J. Fetherston-Godley.*

CHRONOLOGICAL   3 b.g. Henbit (USA) 130–Forward Princess (USA)   —
(Forward Pass) [1988 5s⁵ 6d⁶ 6f 7.5f⁶ 8.2m⁴ 8d² 8.2d⁶ 1989 12.3d⁵] sparely-made,
angular gelding: moderate walker and mover: modest at 2 yrs: below form only
outing at 3 yrs (April): will be suited by forcing tactics and a test of stamina. *M. H. Tompkins.*

CHUCKLESTONE   6 b.g. Chukaroo 103–Czar's Diamond 66 (Queen's Hussar   69
124) [1988 NR 1989 16f⁵ 14m⁴ 15.3m⁴ 16m* 16m* 16.1m³ 17.6f⁵ 16m⁶ 16m⁵] neat
gelding: has a free, rather angular action: modest handicapper: successful in July in
10-runner event at Newbury and 5-runner £9,000 Brown Jack Stakes (Handicap) at
Ascot: suited by test of stamina: particularly well suited by top-of-the-ground: tailed
off when visored: game. *J. S. King.*

CHUMMY'S CHARM   4 ch.g. Bay Express 132–Alpine Damsel 46 (Mountain   80
Call 125) [1988 6f 7d 8.3m³ 7.6f⁵ 7f³ 7g 6g* 5g² 6m² 6g⁴ 5f² 6g² 6d* 1989 6s⁴ 6s⁴
6f⁴ 6m² 6m⁵ 6h² 6f* 6g* 6f* 6f 6g 5m 5.6g 6m] leggy, good-quartered gelding:
moderate mover: fair handicapper: successful in July at Lingfield, Nottingham
(£7,300 event) and Ayr: best effort at last-named in £15,400 Tote Bookmakers
Sprint Trophy (Handicap) when beating Duckington ¾ length: below form last 5
outings: suited by 6f: acts on any going: usually wears blinkers: has won for lady. *G. Lewis.*

CHUMMY'S FAVOURITE   4 b.c. Song 132–Ma Famille 90 (Welsh Saint   120
126) [1988 6f⁵ 7m² 6g⁴ 6f² 7d 6m⁵ 6f* 6m* 5m⁶ 5.6m⁴ 6g³ 5g 1989 6g 6g² 6f⁶
6f 6h* 7g 6f⁶ 7g 6m² 6f³ 6m⁴ 6s² 6m* 5g]
          Lightning doesn't strike twice in the same place, or so the saying goes.
Chummy's Favourite went some way to disproving such in the Group 3 Krug
Diadem Stakes at Ascot in September. In the same race twelve months earlier
he'd put up an astonishing effort for one considered by most as a no-hoper by
finishing within a length of Cadeaux Genereux in third place. It was a
performance so far in advance of anything previously achieved that it was
considered, if not a fluke, one of those inexplicable results sprint conditions

races have a habit of throwing up. Chummy's Favourite's only subsequent outing in 1988 and his first twelve in 1989 failed to produce form that was in any way comparable to his Ascot run. His four-year-old season prior to the Diadem Stakes comprised mainly of runs in handicaps, one of which he won under 10-0 at Brighton in May. His one run in pattern company produced a seventh of ten to Indian Ridge in the Duke of York Stakes. It was hard to foresee that a return to Ascot would bring about another much improved performance for he had already run there twice in 1989 and had shown his normal level of form in finishing sixth in the Wokingham and second in the Havelet Handicap, and though the field for the Diadem Stakes was below-average strength Chummy's Favourite started as one of the outsiders at 40/1, with only the three-year-old Hadif at longer odds. Silver Fling was a well-backed favourite, followed in the market by Dancing Dissident, Green's Canaletto and Point of Light. In the race Nabeel Dancer broke best of all from stall ten and soon left Chummy's Favourite, who was drawn right on the outside in eleven and who also raced down the centre of the track, six lengths adrift. By halfway Nabeel Dancer had begun to hang to his left, causing interference to both Silver Fling and Dancing Dissident, but he kept the lead until Silver Fling went by him passing the furlong marker. Favourite backers looked sure to collect until Chummy's Favourite staged a strong, late run, got his head in front well inside the final furlong and went on to account for Silver Fling by three quarters of a length. Nabeel Dancer finished two lengths further back in third, but was put back to fourth behind Dancing Dissident by the stewards. Chummy's Favourite's performance represented a step up of more than a stone on his form earlier in the year; it also provided Dettori with his fiftieth winner of the season, a season he started as a 5-lb claimer and ended as champion apprentice and Cumani's stable jockey.

Chummy's Favourite (b.c. 1985)	Song (b 1966)	Sing Sing (b 1957)	Tudor Minstrel / Agin The Law
		Intent (gr 1952)	Vilmorin / Under Canvas
	Ma Famille (b 1975)	Welsh Saint (b 1966)	St Paddy / Welsh Way
		May First (b 1961)	Pall Mall / Tikva

It goes almost without saying that Chummy's Favourite is suited by a stiff six furlongs. The shorter distance was much too sharp for him in the Ciga Prix de l'Abbaye de Longchamp (for which he was supplemented at a cost of approximately £7,000) on his only outing after the Diadem. He never went the pace and this time was beaten around four lengths by Silver Fling and Nabeel Dancer. A tall, attractive colt with a round action, he acts on any going. He was twice tried in blinkers in the latest season, the first occasion being when he won at Brighton. It's not unusual for him to get on his toes in the preliminaries. Chummy's Favourite, who was sold for 12,500 guineas as a yearling, nearly twice as much as he made as a foal, is the second produce of Ma Famille, a fair winner from six furlongs to a mile. Ma Famille's next two foals are both by Mummy's Game. The three-year-old Roses In May has yet to show any ability, while the two-year-old Orway Ash is still unraced. The grandam May First, a five-furlong winner on her debut as a two-year-old, is a half-sister to Killiney Hill, the dam of the outstanding novice chaser Killiney and the grandam of the smart jumper Chief Ironside. The third dam Tikva won the Cherry Hinton Stakes. *N. A. Callaghan.*

CHURCH LIGHT 3 ch.f. Caerleon (USA) 132–Highland Light 105 (Home Guard **88** (USA) 129) [1988 6g* 1989 10f⁵ 10f³ 7.6h³ 8g* 8s 7d] leggy, close-coupled filly: fair performer: made all in 4-runner minor event at Ayr in July: behind in Group 3 event at Baden-Baden and IR £11,500 event at the Curragh last 2 outings: effective at 1m and 1¼m: acts on firm ground. *M. A. Jarvis.*

CHURCH STAR 5 b.m. Cajun 120–Lady of Rathleek (Furry Glen 121) [1988 9g — § 10d 8g⁵ 8d⁵ 7f⁴ 8g⁶ 12f 12m 10m⁴ 9g 12h⁵ 1989 9v] compact, good-bodied mare: ungenuine maiden: stays 1½m: has worn blinkers: bandaged only start at 5 yrs: visored and claimer ridden nowadays. *J. J. Bridger.*

CIRCE 3 b.f. Main Reef 126–Elysian 94 (Northfields (USA)) [1988 6f 8s 8m 1989 **73** 9m³ 11m⁶ 10g⁴ 9g² 10m³ 10m² 8f* 8s³ 9g⁴] rangy filly: modest handicapper: won at Pontefract in September: stays 1¼m: acts on any going: visored fifth outing, blinkered after: often set plenty to do. *C. W. C. Elsey.*

CIRCUIT RING 3 b.g. Electric 126–Brookfield Miss 73 (Welsh Pageant 132) **76** [1988 NR 1989 12.2m³ 12.2g³ 14d 12d⁵] workmanlike gelding: fifth foal: half-brother to 3 winners, including useful 5f to 1m winner Littlefield (by Bay Express) and 2m winner Cairncastle (by Ardross): dam showed some ability at 2 yrs: modest maiden: best effort at Catterick second start: out of depth final one: stays 1½m but probably not 1¾m. *P. Calver.*

CIRCUS FEATHERS 2 ch.f. (Feb 10) Kris 135–Circus Plume 124 (High Top — 131) [1989 7m 7f] smallish, good-quartered filly: first foal: dam, 7f winner at 2 yrs, won Oaks: well beaten in maidens at Newmarket (on toes and very green) and Leicester in October: will be suited by 1¼m +: looked ill at ease on firm ground second start. *J. L. Dunlop.*

CIREN JESTER 5 b.g. Cajun 120–Miss Africa (African Sky 124) [1988 8d 8g³ **49** § 8g² 8f⁶ 7m⁴ 7.6m³ 8.3m 7m³ 7.6f² 8m 8.5f³ 8g² 8g 1989 8d⁶ 8d³ 8f 9f 10m³ 9m³ 10.4m⁴ 10g] leggy gelding: usually looks well: plating-class handicapper: in frame (without winning) numerous times since 1987, mainly in apprentice events: stays 1¼m: acts on any going: went too freely in blinkers: has worn crossed noseband: sold 3,500 gns Newmarket Autumn Sales: tends to flash tail: a difficult ride, who doesn't find much off bridle. *W. J. Musson.*

CITIDANCER 3 b.c. Lomond (USA) 128–Mrs McArdy 123 (Tribal Chief **120** 125) [1988 7d* 7m* 1989 8d³ 8d² 10g⁵ 10m* 10g² 9g* 10s]

Henry Cecil lost the trainers' championship in 1989 but led the way among British trainers abroad, campaigning with a vigour that again belied his reputation for being reluctant to travel his horses overseas. To Citidancer fell the most travelling of all the Warren Place horses: to Ireland, France and North America during the course of the season. In chasing good prizes Citidancer found himself chasing some top-notch performers, naturally, and he couldn't contribute much by way of victories to his trainer's total. His best effort came in defeat in the EBF Phoenix Champion Stakes at Phoenix Park in September, where Citidancer made most and stayed on resolutely under pressure to hold off the determined challenge of Mamaluna only to be caught close home and beaten three quarters of a length by Carroll House with Petrullo a length away in third. Citidancer also ran well in defeat on his first three starts. He was beaten three lengths behind Shaadi and Exbourne in the Charles Heidsieck Champagne Craven Stakes at Newmarket, finished two and a half lengths behind Polish Precedent in the Prix de la Jonchere at Chantilly, and was under three lengths fifth of eight to Dancehall in the Grand Prix de Paris Louis Vuitton at Longchamp. Citidancer finished in front on two occasions—starting odds on both times. He made heavy weather of winning a minor event at Newbury in July by half a length from Nemesia but took the four-runner Group 3 Hennessy EBF Ballymacmoy Stakes at Leopardstown in the style anticipated after his performance against Carroll House, by six lengths from Vestris Abu. On his final start Citidancer put up a somewhat lack-lustre performance behind Caltech in the Grade 1 Budweiser International at Laurel Park, Maryland, dropping away tamely into seventh-of-eleven place having been a close second entering the short straight.

Not even One Thousand Guineas winners are guaranteed to be successful broodmares. It's probably fair to say that the 1977 winner Mrs McArdy has exceeded expectations, for she isn't so well bred as most. Citidancer is her fifth foal to race and her fifth winner; the other four are all winners in Ireland. Due Dilligence (by General Assembly) was successful at seven furlongs and a mile, his sister Cabinet Level won at a mile and a half and is the dam of Italian listed race winner Clooncara; Scuba Diver (by Kings Lake) was a winner at about a mile and Rising Spirit (by Cure The Blues) won at seven furlongs at two years before racing successfully in America. Mrs McArdy also has a two-year-old by Chief Singer named Hot Chocolate. Her dam Hanina was a plating-class two-year-old and improved only a little at three years, whilst her grandam Blue Sash was a useful two-year-old but failed to train on.

	Lomond (USA) (b 1980)	Northern Dancer (b 1961)	Nearctic Natalma
		My Charmer (b 1969)	Poker Fair Charmer
Citidancer (b.c. 1986)			
	Mrs McArdy (b 1974)	Tribal Chief (b 1967)	Princely Gift Mwanza
		Hanina (b 1965)	Darling Boy Blue Sash

The strong, deep-bodied Citidancer cost IR 160,000 guineas as a yearling at the Cartier Million Sale. He seemed to have strong prospects in the inaugural running of the Million in 1988 but a damaged cartilage ruled him out. His yearling half-brother by Ahonoora was sold for IR 30,000 guineas at the latest sale. Citidancer is better suited by a mile and a quarter than a mile. He lacks his dam's turn of foot and is suited by a good gallop. He acts on top-of-the-ground and a yielding surface, his only outing on anything like extremes being at Laurel Park. Whether the very soft going there affected his performance is debatable; we may have more idea another season hence. *H. R. A. Cecil.*

CITY LINK PET   3 b.f. Tina's Pet 121–City Link Rose (Lochnager 132) [1988 NR 1989 5g] first foal: dam showed signs of ability on last of 3 starts: 33/1, 7 lengths eighth of 14 in claimer at Sandown in September, slowly away and never placed to challenge: should improve. *D. A. Wilson.*   — p

CITY NATIVE   3 b.c. Be My Native (USA) 124–Blue Kingsmill 69 (Roi Soleil 125) [1988 7g⁶ 6g 7m 1989 10s 12g 12.5f 12m 13.8f³ 16f³] leggy, plain colt: moderate walker: poor maiden: third in handicaps at Catterick (visored) and Chepstow (blinkered) in July: tailed off fourth outing: stays 2m: sold 3,600 gns Doncaster November Sales. *W. J. Musson.*   45

CITY TO CITY   3 b.f. Windjammer (USA)–Beamless 73 (Hornbeam 130) [1988 6f⁵ 6f 7g 8g⁶ 8d⁶ 1989 8s 10s 8m 8m 6m 6h⁶ 6f⁵ 7m 7f 8m⁴ 8f³ 6g⁶ 8g 7m 6m 7g⁵ 6f] leggy, close-coupled filly: moderate walker and mover: turns fore-feet in: poor maiden: stays 1m: acts on firm going: sometimes blinkered: hung right for 7-lb claimer penultimate start: trained first 4 by P. Feilden. *D. W. Chapman.*   40

CLANWILLIAM PRINCE   4 gr.g. Sexton Blake 126–Gentle Heiress (Prince Tenderfoot (USA) 126) [1988 12g⁶ 12m 14f³ 12s² 12g 14g³ 1989 10g 12m⁴ 12f⁶ 14f³ 15.3f 13.1h⁵] ex-Irish gelding: fourth living foal: half-brother to 2-y-o 5f winners Queen of Sahara (by Royal Match) and Ahona (by Ahonoora), and to 1½m winner Prince Newport (by Prince Regent): dam placed at 2 yrs in Ireland: poor maiden: well beaten in handicaps last 2 starts: stays 1¾m: acts on any going: sometimes blinkered, visored third outing. *B. Smart.*   38

CLARE COURT 2 ch.f. (Mar 30) Glint of Gold 128–Clare Bridge (USA) 107 **78**
(Little Current (USA)) [1989 7f³ 7f² 8m*] medium-sized, unfurnished filly: first
foal: dam 1m winner stayed 1½m: odds on, won maiden at Chepstow in August by ¾
length (value 1½) from Gliding Musician, making all and keeping on gamely: will
stay 1½m. *I. A. Balding.*

CLARENTIA 5 ch.m. Ballad Rock 122–Laharden (Mount Hagen (FR) 127) [1988 **89**
5s* 5m⁵ 1989 5s 5g 5g 5f 5g 5m 5g* 5d⁴ 5.6g 5m 5f* 5m²] leggy, lightly-made mare:
fair handicapper: won at Newmarket in August and Lingfield in October: very good
second to Joe Sugden at York final outing: suited by 5f: acts on any going: usually
bandaged nowadays: good mount for apprentice: reportedly broke blood vessel
second start at 4 yrs. *M. D. I. Usher.*

CLARE'S DELIGHT 4 b.f. Viking (USA)–Miss Inglewood 61 (Dike (USA)) **48** d
[1988 5g 5f 5f 5h⁴ 6m² 6g* 6m³ 6f* 6d² 7f 7g⁵ 6d⁶ 7g 6d 1989 5d³ 6m 6m 6m 6g 6g 6f
6m a6g a6g] small, light-framed filly: plating-class winner as 3-y-o: no form in 1989
after first outing: stays 7f: yet to race on soft going, acts on any other: sometimes
sweating and edgy: has run creditably for apprentice: has tended to drift right. *B. C.
Morgan.*

CLASS ACT 3 b.g. Shirley Heights 130–Thespian 76 (Ile de Bourbon (USA) 133) **67** §
[1988 7g 7g⁶ 7d⁵ 1989 10m⁴ 10g 13.1h⁴ 12m² 12m⁵ 14f⁵ 14m] sturdy gelding:
moderate mover: modest maiden: shapes like a stayer: acts on firm going: sweating
final start (July): subsequently gelded and joined N. Henderson: probably
ungenuine. *R. Hannon.*

CLASSIC FAME (USA) 3 b.c. Nijinsky (CAN) 138–Family Fame (USA) (Droll **111**
Role) [1988 7d* 7d* 8s* 1989 8m⁵ 12g] strong, rangy colt: successful as 2-y-o in

Classic Thoroughbreds Plc's "Classic Fame"

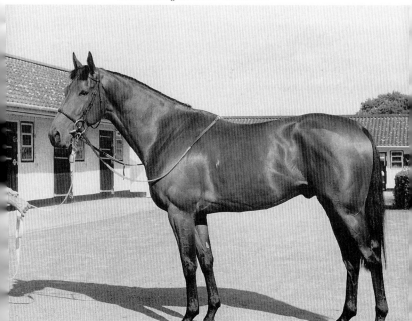

minor event at Phoenix Park and in GPA National Stakes and Juddmonte Beresford Stakes at the Curragh: operated on after bout of colic in November at 2 yrs: 6 lengths fifth of 12 to Shaadi in Irish 2000 Guineas at the Curragh, staying on from last place 2f out until hanging right and no extra inside last: 33/1 and on toes, well-beaten seventh of 12 in Ever Ready Derby at Epsom 18 days later: should be suited by at least 1¼m: acts on soft going and top-of-the-ground: sent to race in California. *M. V. O'Brien, Ireland.*

CLASSIC FEATURE 2 ch.f. (May 23) Roman Warrior 132–Harroway Jig (Doudance 99) [1989 5m³ 6f 5m 6g] rather leggy, sparely-made filly: third reported foal: half-sister to bad maiden Harry Hatler (by Buzzards Bay): dam unraced: plating-class maiden: should stay 6f: tended to hang and carry head awkwardly second start, blinkered final: sold 1,050 gns Ascot November Sales. *J. S. King.*   **50**

CLASSIC STATEMENT 3 ch.c. Mill Reef (USA) 141–Lady Graustark (USA) (Graustark) [1988 7d⁴ 7g³ 1989 10.6g a10g 10g] 500,000Y: leggy, quite attractive colt: half-brother to several winners, including Siyah Kalem (by Mr Prospector), Milieu (by Habitat) and Bel Bolide (by Bold Bidder), all at least very useful at around 1m: dam won twice at up to 6f at 2 yrs: fair form in Ireland as 2-y-o when trained by M. V. O'Brien: beaten at least 10 lengths in maidens and minor event here in 1989: should stay 1¼m. *Mrs J. Pitman.*   —

CLASSIC SUITE 3 b.g. Ya Zaman (USA) 122–Lady Bidder (Auction Ring (USA) 123) [1988 5g 6d⁴ 6m⁶ 7m² 7m 6g⁵ 8f² 8.2m⁶ 8d⁴ 8.2d 10.2m⁶ 1989 8.2s* 9f 8m 8f⁵ 7f² 8.2f4 8m* 8m 8.2d* 7s³ 8d] lengthy, rather sparely-made gelding: moderate walker and poor mover: modest performer: won claimers at Nottingham in March, Newmarket in August and Haydock in September: best form at about 1m: probably acts on any going but may well prove ideally suited by some give in the ground: gelded after final start. *R. M. Whitaker.*   **79**

CLAUDIA MISS 2 b.f. (Feb 5) Claude Monet (USA) 121–Palace Travel (High Top 131) [1989 6g³ 7m⁵] workmanlike filly: fourth foal: half-sister to fair 1988 2-y-o 6f winner Miss Bentley (by Simply Great) and a winner in Spain by High Top: dam lightly-raced daughter of half-sister to very smart performers Command Freddy and Ridaness: 25/1 and in need of race, 7 lengths third of 6, keeping on well having been outpaced, to Curved Blade in maiden at Haydock in August: pulled hard when fifth of 6 to Silk Slippers in slowly-run minor event at York following month: will be suited by 1m. *W. W. Haigh.*   **58**

CLAY COUNTY 4 b.g. Sheer Grit 117–Make-Up 69 (Bleep-Bleep 134) [1988 10g 12g⁶ 12d 1989 12g⁵] leggy, quite good-topped ex-Irish gelding: has a round action: half-brother to a winner in Holland and a winning hurdler in Ireland: dam ran 3 times: little sign of ability in modest company: pulled hard only outing (April) at 4 yrs. *R. Allan.*   —

CLAYSUUMAR 2 b.f. (Apr 8) Montekin 125–Good Court (Takawalk II 125) [1989 5.3g³ 5s⁴ 5f* 6f³ 7m] IR 1,450F, IR 3,500Y: lengthy, plain, sparely-made filly: half-sister to 1980 2-y-o 1m winner Santella Ascot (by Furry Glen), a winner in Belgium and a winner over hurdles: dam poor Irish maiden: showed much improved form when winning maiden auction event at Sandown in May: creditable third of 5 to Star Hill in nursery at Goodwood over 2 months later: not seen out after mid-August: better suited by 6f than 5f, and should stay 7f. *R. Hannon.*   **60**

CLEAN AND POLISH 2 ch.g. (Apr 30) Superlative 118–Greek Blessing 83 (So Blessed 130) [1989 6m 6g] 5,600Y: tall, rather sparely-made gelding: seventh foal: half-brother to modest 11f and 1½m winner Greek Flutter (by Beldale Flutter): dam 7f and 9f winner: always behind in minor event at Windsor (slowly away) and maiden at Epsom in August: subsequently gelded. *G. Lewis.*   —

CLEAR LIGHT 2 ch.c. (Apr 5) Exhibitioner 111–Beach Light 89 (Bustino 136) [1989 6f⁵ 6g⁴] IR 15,000Y: angular, useful-looking colt: third foal: half-brother to 1987 2-y-o 7f winner Mayohora (by Final Straw) and Irish 3-y-o 1¼m winner Magic Million (by Gorytus): dam, 1¼m winner, is daughter of smart sprinter Street Light: ridden by 7-lb claimer, 3½ lengths fourth of 10, leading briefly 2f out, to Fanellan at Yarmouth in August, better effort in maidens. *G. A. Huffer.*   **72**

CLEARWATER BAY 3 ch.c. Creetown 123–Vacation 102 (Remainder 106) [1988 5m 5g 7m 7m 5g 1989 8.5m 12f] leggy colt: good mover: poor form at best, mostly in sellers: visored final start at 2 yrs. *G. R. Oldroyd.*   —

CLEAVERS GATE 4 ch.c. Touching Wood (USA) 127–Thimblerigger 62 (Sharpen Up 127) [1988 8m 8g 13.8f* 16f² 16d4 15.8f* 18g 16f³ 1989 16.2g⁶ 15.8m* 18f 20f 15.8f² 15.8g³] rather leggy, angular colt: good mover: modest handicapper: **72**

won for third time at Catterick when beating Dalby Dancer 2 lengths in May: placed at same course last 2 outings: suited by a test of stamina: acts well on firm going: usually blinkered nowadays: finds little in front and suited by waiting tactics: sold to join N. Tinkler 14,000 gns Doncaster August Sales. *J. W. Watts.*

CLEMCO BELLE   4 b.f. Young Generation 129–Easterly Wind 94 (Windjammer (USA)) [1988 7m 8.2m 8d 1989 7f] leggy, rather unfurnished filly: little sign of ability, including in claimers: bandaged and backward only start at 4 yrs: sold 1,250 gns Ascot September Sales. *D. J. Wintle.*   —

CLEVER CLAUDE   3 b.g. Cragador 110–La Mirabelle 92 (Princely Gift 137) [1988 6m 7g⁵ 7g 1989 8g⁶ 7f 10h⁴ 11.7m 7m⁶] medium-sized, leggy, shallow-girthed gelding: modest form as 2-y-o: well below best in handicaps and maiden after reappearance: should stay 1m: seems unsuited by top-of-the-ground: sweating first (edgy) and fourth outings: blinkered and ridden by 5-lb claimer first two. *R. F. Casey.*   —

CLIFTON CHAPEL   4 b.g. High Line 125–Britannia's Rule 108 (Blakeney 126) [1988 8d² 10v* 10.4v* 12m 12g⁶ 13.3g⁴ 15m 14v 18g 1989 16f³ 14m 12g 11v⁴ᵈⁱˢ 12d a14g³ a16g³] medium-sized, rather angular gelding: keen walker: powerful mover: one-time useful performer: not seen out until August, and below his best as 4-y-o: rider failed to weigh in fourth outing: possibly doesn't stay 2¼m: goes particularly well with plenty of give in the ground: slipped when blinkered: bought out of S. Norton's stable 50,000 gns Doncaster February Sales. *H. Candy.*   —

CLIFTON GIRL   3 b.f. Van Der Linden (FR)–Wrekin Belle (Dance In Time (CAN)) [1988 NR 1989 6s 8d 6m⁶ 9m 8f 6f 8f 6f⁶] angular filly: first foal: dam twice-raced daughter of fairly useful performer at up to 1m Wrekinianne: poor form at best, including in seller: hung throughout for 7-lb claimer final start: takes keen hold and has twice run very wide on turn. *K. White.*   —

CLOCK GOLF   2 b.f. (Feb 6) Mummy's Game 120–Stuff And Nonsense 86 (Crooner 119) [1989 6d 6g a6g⁴ a7g a8g³] workmanlike, angular filly: sixth foal: half-sister to very useful 3-y-o Folly Foot (by Hotfoot), successful at around 7f at 2 yrs, 1m and 9f winner Sillitoe (by Tachypous) and a winner in Belgium: dam 1¼m winner: quite modest maiden: best effort final outing when blinkered: suited by 1m. *R. F. Johnson Houghton.*   65

CLOCKWORK ORANGE   2 ch.f. (Mar 3) Move Off 112–Citrine 77 (Meldrum 112) [1989 5f² 5f² 5m⁵ 5g⁴ 5g] leggy filly: moderate mover: sister to 3-y-o Ajalita and 1984 2-y-o 5f seller winner Lemon Grove, later successful at up to 11f in Italy: dam second over 6f at 2 yrs: modest plater: bred to stay beyond 5f. *T. D. Barron.*   47

CLONBROCK BOY   3 b.g. Stanford 121§–Kellys Risc (Pitskelly 122) [1988 5f 6g 5f 7f 6f 5g 1989 7g 6m 9f 10g 12m] strong-quartered gelding: poor form, mainly in sellers: blinkered third and final outings at 2 yrs: visored last 4 in 1989: has joined T. Laxton. *J. S. Wainwright.*   —

CLOS DU BOIS (FR)   3 b.c. High Top 131–Our Shirley 84 (Shirley Heights 130) [1988 NR 1989 10.1m⁵ 12m³ 12g³ a11g a8g] small, sparely-made colt: first foal: dam, half-sister to smart 1m and 9f winner Miner's Lamp (by High Top), won over 1¼m: fair form in Windsor minor event on debut: well beaten in varied events after: should stay 1½m: visored final start: pulled hard for apprentice third: sold out of R. J. R. Williams' stable 7,000 gns Newmarket Autumn Sales after third. *Mrs N. Macauley.*   85 d

CLOSED SHOP   2 b.f. (Apr 3) Auction Ring (USA) 123–Silent Sun 90 (Blakeney 126) [1989 5d⁶ 6m* 7m* 7m⁶ 7f³ 8g⁵ 8f*] 3,300Y, 6,000Y: neat filly: poor mover: first foal: dam won at 1¼m here and 1m in France: successful in seller (sold out of D. Morley's stable 8,000 gns) at Nottingham in June, claimer at Yarmouth following month and nursery (by 4 lengths from Sum Mede) at Warwick in October: suited by 1m: good mount for an apprentice: trained third to fifth outings by R. Stubbs: genuine. *S. Dow.*   69

CLOUD BASE   3 br.g. Another Realm 118–A-Bye 116 (Abernant 142) [1988 5v⁵ 5s⁴ 6f 1989 7m 5m] sparely-made gelding: no form, including in seller. *O. O'Neill.*   —

CLOUD CHASER   6 ch.g. Hardgreen (USA) 122–Tudor Zara 63 (Tudor Melody 129) [1988 NR 1989 10d] strong gelding: poor maiden: blinkered only start at 6 yrs. *B. Forsey.*   —

CLUZO   3 b.c. Sharpo 132–Silka (ITY) (Lypheor 118) [1988 6d 6g² 7m³ 6s 7f² 1989 6s* 6d 7.5f* 8f 7.6f 8m⁵ 7h² 7.6f⁶] small, sturdy colt: fair handicapper: successful at Warwick (minor event, making all) in March and Beverley in May: ran moderately   87

final start, in August: best at around 7f: has won on soft going, but best form on firm. *M. H. Tompkins.*

CLWYD LODGE 2 b.c. (May 2) Blakeney 126–High Caraval (High Top 131) — [1989 a7g] closely related to 3-y-o Its Coco (by Mr Fluorocarbon) and half-brother to several winners, including Irish 1¾m winner Carniski (by Nijinsky): dam unraced half-sister to Ribblesdale winner Northern Princess: soundly beaten in Southwell maiden in November. *D. T. Thom.*

COCK-A-DOODLE-DO 3 b.g. Petorius 117–Bertida 76 (Porto Bello 118) [1988 — 5g 6s 8s⁵ 1989 7s 8g 9f a8g] close-coupled, sparely-made gelding: quite modest handicapper: easily best effort as 3-y-o on reappearance: off course 6 months before final start: best form at 1m: acts on soft going. *C. W. Thornton.*

COCKED HAT GIRL 2 ch.f. (Jan 9) Ballacashtal (CAN)–Screen Goddess 65 **47** (Caliban 123) [1989 5g⁶ 5d⁶ 6f⁵ 6g⁵ 6f² 6m⁶ 7m⁶ 6g 10.6d⁵] 3,100Y: tall filly: half-sister to 1¾m winner and winning hurdler Walcisin (by Balboa): dam, placed at up to 1½m, is half-sister to Cambridgeshire winner Negus: modest plater: stays 10.6f: blinkered sixth to eighth starts: trained first 8 starts by T. Barron. *S. R. Bowring.*

COEUR DE MIEL (USA) 5 b.h. Danzig (USA)–Ignore (USA) (Buckpasser) **98** [1988 8f³ 10.1m² 10g² 9g³ 1989 8f²] rangy horse: not raced until 4 yrs: placed in varied events, on final outing in 1988 in William Hill Cambridgeshire Handicap at Newmarket: very good second to Greensmith in another valuable handicap at Sandown in May: stays 1¼m: acts on firm going: sometimes sweats: sent to race in USA. *A. C. Stewart.*

COEURETTE 3 b.f. Nicholas Bill 125–Take To Heart 72 (Steel Heart 128) [1988 — 7m 1989 a12g a10g] sparely-made filly: third foal: half-sister to poor maiden Eppiette (by Milford): dam, in frame over 5f and 6f, ran only at 2 yrs: seems to be of little account. *H. Candy.*

COGNIZANT 4 b.f. Known Fact (USA) 135–Alia 112 (Sun Prince 128) [1988 10m³ **39** 10m 1989 8m 10f⁵ 10f³] leggy filly: poor plater: stays 1¼m: winning hurdler. *J. Ffitch-Heyes.*

COINAGE 6 gr.g. Owen Dudley 121–Grisbi 96 (Grey Sovereign 128§) [1988 14g — 16f 16f 14f 16f 1989 16f⁵] big, rangy gelding: tubed: fairly useful performer in 1986: no subsequent worthwhile form on flat: suited by a test of stamina: used to go very well on top-of-the-ground. *R. F. Johnson Houghton.*

COINCIDENTAL 7 b.g. Persian Bold 123–Gentle Mulla (Sun Prince 128) [1988 **74** 8d 6g 7g 7.6v 8d 7f² 8.5m⁵ 7.6f³ 7m² 7m³ 7m³ 7f⁴ 7.6f* 7.6m² 8m⁴ 7f⁵ 7d 1989 7g 6f⁶ 7f 7m 7f² 7g 7f 8m³ 8g² 8.2m⁵ 8g⁵ 9.1f³ 8m³ 8f³ 8g 7.3m* 8g 7g 7g a7g³] close-coupled, workmanlike gelding: moderate walker: poor mover: modest handicapper: won strongly-run event at Newbury in September: ran at least creditably numerous other times: effective at 7f and stays 9.1f: acts very well on top-of-the-ground and is unsuited by heavy: has worn a tongue strap: has gone freely to post, and been taken down quietly: keen sort, usually ridden up with pace: tough: trained first 14 outings by D. Chapman. *P. J. Feilden.*

COLD BLOW 2 b.f. (Feb 21) Posse (USA) 130–Warm Wind 84 (Tumble Wind **67** (USA)) [1989 5g 6f 7m²] 32,000F: rather sparely-made filly: second reported foal: half-sister to 3-y-o Fleeting Breeze (by Mr Fluorocarbon): dam, 7f to 1¼m winner, is half-sister to Yorkshire Oaks winners Sally Brown (by Posse) and Untold and very useful performer at up to 1m Shoot Clear: 3 lengths second of 12, leading over 5f, to Pencarreg in maiden at Lingfield in September, easily best effort: will stay 1¼m. *I. V. Matthews.*

COLD KUMMEL 4 ch.c. Dublin Taxi–Mistress Meryll 61 (Tower Walk 130) — [1988 6g 7m 5m 1989 15f] of little account: possibly temperamental. *P. Monteith.*

COLD MARBLE (USA) 4 b.g. Told (USA)–Coney Dell 77 (Ercolano (USA) **88** 118) [1988 8g⁵ 12m* 12f* 12.3f* 14.8d* 14m² 14f⁵ 14.6f⁵ 1989 12d 12f² 12m⁶ 16m⁴ 16m⁴] rather leggy, workmanlike gelding: usually looks well: moderate mover: fairly useful performer: ran moderately in quite valuable handicap at Ascot in July, and wasn't seen out again: stays 2m, at least in moderately-run race: yet to race on soft going, acts on any other: has won for apprentice: badly hampered third outing. *W. Haggas.*

COLERE ROUGE (USA) 2 b.f. (Mar 19) Argument (FR) 133–Red Beauty — (ITY) (Molvedo 137) [1989 5m 7h⁶ 5g] 20,000 francs (approx £1,900) Y: good-bodied filly: carries condition: third foal: dam placed in Italy: well beaten in maidens and a seller. *M. Madgwick.*

COLFAX LADY 2 b.f. (Mar 26) Noalto 120–Imacarboncopy (USA) (Imacornish-prince (USA)) [1989 6m 6v 5g] 4,200Y: leggy filly: fifth foal: half-sister to 1986 2-y-o 5f winner Sandall Park (by Frimley Park): dam won over 5f at 2 yrs in USA: poor form in auction events: best effort over 5f: dead. *J. Parkes.* **46**

COLFAX SAM 2 b.c. (Apr 9) Norwick (USA) 120–Alwen (Blakeney 126) [1989 7.5f 7m⁵ 6m 8.2f] 6,000Y: light-framed colt: moderate mover: half-brother to 1985 2-y-o 7f winner When You're Smiling (by Comedy Star): dam never ran: poor maiden: blinkered on debut: has twice run wide into straight. *P. A. Blockley.* **—**

COLIN SELLER 2 ch.c. (Feb 21) Noalto 120–Mallow 70 (Le Dieu d'Or 119) [1989 7m⁴ 6m 6f² 8f a6g² a7g⁴ a8g⁴] 6,400Y: good-topped, workmanlike colt: half-brother to 3-y-o Songbird Miracle (by Music Maestro) and to minor 2-y-o sprint winners by Mummy's Game and Music Maestro: dam, winner over hurdles, is half-sister to smart sprinter Bream: quite modest performer: best form at 6f. *R. Boss.* **67**

COLLAGE 3 b.f. Ela-Mana-Mou 132–Cojean (USA) 86 (Prince John) [1988 6m³ 7m 6f² 6f² 7m 6g⁴ 1989 8f 8h 8m⁶ 9g a7g] lengthy, rather hollow-backed filly: has a round action: turns off-fore in: worthwhile form at 3 yrs only when sixth in handicap at Kempton in September: stays 1m (took keen hold over 9f): acts on firm ground: blinkered final start. *P. T. Walwyn.* **68**

COLLISON LANE 3 b.f. Reesh 117–Everingham Park 54 (Record Token 128) [1988 5f⁴ 5f² 6g 1989 5g 5g⁶ 6f 6g 5m 5m 6f⁴ 6g* 6f³ 6g 6g] medium-sized, sturdy filly: favourite, won handicap at Hamilton in September: below form last 2 starts, moderately drawn on final one: stays 6f: acts on firm going: visored last 6 starts: sometimes sweating and edgy. *J. G. FitzGerald.* **64**

COLNE VALLEY KID 4 ch.g. Homing 130–Pink Garter (Henry The Seventh 125) [1988 10d 6m 8g 12d 8d 1989 10.1m] of little account on flat: winning selling hurdler. *A. Moore.* **—**

COLOMBIERE 4 ch.g. Sallust 134–Shere Beauty 83 (Mummy's Pet 125) [1988 8d* 8f 11.7m 8m 8d 7m 8m 1989 7g] workmanlike gelding: modest winner on first outing at 3 yrs: no subsequent form, including in selling company, on flat: stays 1m: acts on a soft surface: has worn crossed noseband and carried head high: probably ungenuine: winning selling hurdler. *R. Simpson.* **— §**

COLONEL CHINSTRAP 4 ch.g. Milford 119–Deep Blue Sea (Gulf Pearl 117) [1988 8d 10g 10.1d 1989 12g 12.5g⁶ 12m⁶ 12h⁴ 12g 10h³ 11g 12m*] lengthy gelding: moderate mover: poor performer: won apprentice selling handicap (sold to join A. Moore 2,800 gns) at Brighton in September, staying on despite drifting left to lead close home: hung right at same course sixth start: will stay beyond 1½m: acts on hard going: blinkered seventh outing. *P. J. Makin.* **51**

COLONIAL OFFICE (USA) 3 ch.g. Assert 134–Belles Oreilles (CAN) (Nentego 119) [1988 7m 7g 1989 11.7m 14f 16.2f² 14.8m³ 17.6f⁴ 14m⁴] workmanlike gelding: quite modest maiden: never going particularly well in claiming event (claimed P. Hobbs £8,055) final start, in August: suited by 2m: acts on firm going. *B. W. Hills.* **60**

COLONIA (USA) 2 br.f. (Feb 17) Verbatim (USA)–Sail Loft 74 (Shirley Heights 130) [1989 6f³ 7m⁴ 8m⁴ 8g³ 8f] 12,000Y: small, lengthy filly: third foal: dam, placed over 1½m, is half-sister to classic winners Julio Mariner, Juliette Marny and Scintillate: modest maiden: best effort fourth start: will be suited by good test of stamina: sweating third outing: sold 11,000 gns Newmarket Autumn Sales. *M. A. Jarvis.* **73**

COLONNA (USA) 3 b.c. Run The Gantlet (USA)–Evolutionary (USA) (Silent Screen (USA)) [1988 NR 1989 12f³ 14d 12.4g²] $4,000F: close-coupled, quite good-topped colt: moderate walker and mover: first foal: dam never ran: 11/10 on, would have done fair bit better ridden with enterprise when 2 lengths second in seller (claimed C. Beever £10,898) at Newcastle in October: will stay 2m. *H. R. A. Cecil.* **65**

COLORADO DANCER 3 b.f. Shareef Dancer (USA) 135–Fall Aspen (USA) (Pretense) [1988 NR 1989 10.5g* 12g² 12g* 13.5g* 12d³ 10g³ 9f4] 200,000Y: rangy, good sort: has plenty of scope: fifth foal: closely related to smart 1m to 1¼m winner Northern Aspen (by Northern Dancer) and half-sister to 3 winners, including good French 1m to 10.5f winner Elle Seule (by Exclusive Native) and smart stayer Mazzacano (by Alleged): dam smart stakes winner at up to 7f: won maiden at Saint-Cloud in May, Prix Minerve at Evry in July and Prix de Pomone, leading close home in narrow finish with Summer Trip and Young Mother, at Deauville: in frame **122**

Prix de Pomone, Deauville—a last-stride victory for Colorado Dancer (No. 7)
over Summer Trip (noseband) and Young Mother

at Longchamp in Prix de Malleret and Prix Vermeille then in California in 2 Grade 1 events: stays 13.5f: trained final start by N. Drysdale. *A. Fabre, France.*

COLOUR CHART (USA) 2 b.f. (Mar 22) Mr Prospector (USA)–Rainbow   ?
Connection (CAN) (Halo (USA)) [1989 8d*] $675,000F: fourth foal: half-sister to disappointing Zajal (by Seattle Slew), promising 6f winner at 2 yrs in 1986, and useful middle-distance colt Dance Spectrum (by Lyphard): dam, champion filly in Canada, won at up to 1¼m: won 6-runner newcomers race at Longchamp in September by a short neck: likely to do much better. *A. Fabre, France.*

COLOURIST 2 b.c. (Apr 20) Petorius 117–Flaxen Hair (Thatch (USA) 136) [1989   70
6m³ 6g⁵] 25,000Y: well-made colt: half-brother to very useful 3-y-o miler Mirror Black (by Alzao), 1¼m seller winner Rangers Lad (by Sallust) and a winning hurdler: dam unraced: modest form in minor event at Windsor in July and maiden at Redcar over 3 months later: will stay 7f. *A. C. Stewart.*

COLSAN BOY 2 b.c. (Apr 3) Remainder Man 126§–Wimbledon's Pet (Mummy's   55
Pet 125) [1989 5m⁵ 5m 6f⁴ 6m 5f⁴ 5d⁶ 5m a6g] 1,200Y: leggy, unfurnished colt: poor walker: second reported foal: dam poor maiden: plating-class maiden: bred to stay 7f: blinkered or visored second to seventh starts, running much too freely on fourth outing. *M. D. I. Usher.*

COLVIN LAD 2 gr.g. (Mar 17) Rusticaro (FR) 124–Twice Regal (Royal   53
Prerogative 119) [1989 6m⁶ 6g] IR 3,400F, 5,000Y: sixth foal: half-brother to 1m seller winner Bob's Ballad (by Ballad Rock) and a winner in Belgium: dam poor Irish maiden: around 11 lengths ninth of 18 to Peterhouse in maiden at Redcar in November, better effort: will stay 7f. *W. W. Haigh.*

COLWAY RALLY 5 ch.h. Final Straw 127–Boswellia 109 (Frankincense 120) 105
[1988 8d³ 8g² 7.6f² 8m⁵ 8m 1989 6s⁴ 8m⁶ 8f4 8.2m* 8.2g* 8f 7g⁴ 8g³ 8m³ 8.5f²]
lengthy, attractive horse: carries condition: moderate mover: useful performer: successful in handicaps at Haydock in May and June: ran creditably after in valuable handicaps at Royal Ascot and Newmarket and Group 3 events at Cologne and the Curragh: then sold to race in USA, finishing second in valuable handicap at Gulfstream Park (trained by J. Canani) in November: effective at 7f and 1m: best on a sound surface: blinkered twice: not the easiest of rides and best with strong handling and waiting tactics: has a turn of foot: tough and consistent. *J. W. Watts.*

COMBINED EXERCISE 5 br.g. Daring March 116–Dualvi 91 (Dual 117) [1988 **52** 10d 10d 10.8s⁶ 11.1m⁵ 12g⁶ 12.2d⁴ 12g 1989 10.1m² 10f³ 10m⁴ 11.5f4] good-topped gelding: poor mover: modest performer as 3-y-o, only plating class nowadays: not seen out after June: best at up to 1¼m: acts on any going: often apprentice ridden: usually races up with pace: has looked none too enthusiastic. *R. Akehurst.*

COME AND STAY 2 ch.f. (Mar 10) Be My Guest (USA) 126–Julip 99 (Track **54** p Spare 125) [1989 6g] IR 20,000Y: sixth foal: closely related to quite modest maiden Comfrey Glen (by Glenstal) and half-sister to useful miler Patriarch (by London Bells) and Irish 1½m winner Fiestal (by Last Fandango): dam, 2-y-o 7f winner, stayed 1½m and comes from good family: 16/1, around 11 lengths seventh of 20, keeping on never able to challenge, to Nice Day in maiden at Newcastle in October: will stay 1m: should improve. *J. W. Watts.*

COMEDY FUN 5 b.g. Comedy Star (USA) 121–Get Involved 79 (Shiny Tenth — 120) [1988 NR 1989 7.5f 5m 8.2g] big, good-topped gelding: has a round action: of little account: blinkered last 2 outings. *N. Bycroft.*

COMEDY RIVER 2 br.c. (Mar 15) Comedy Star (USA) 121–Hopeful Waters 66 **67** (Forlorn River 124) [1989 5m² 6g 5f² 6g 5g] leggy, rather sparely-made colt: moderate walker: has a roundish action: first foal: dam 6f and 7f winner: quite modest maiden: seems better suited by 5f than 6f: gave trouble stalls second outing. *J. L. Spearing.*

COMEDY SAIL 5 b.h. Comedy Star (USA) 121–Set Sail 64 (Alpenkonig (GER)) **51** [1988 12.2d 12d⁵ 12f⁵ 14g 13.1g 14m 12h 12g 12g⁵ 1989 15.5s⁴ 17f* 16m 15.5f⁴ 18h³ 16f* 16m 17.1f⁵] neat horse: has a quick action: plating-class handicapper: won 7-runner events at Pontefract and Redcar (making all) in first half of year: well beaten last 2 outings, and not seen out after July: stays 2¼m: best efforts on top-of-the-ground: often wears bandages: below his best in blinkers. *S. Dow.*

COME HALLEY (FR) 3 b.g. Crystal Glitters (USA) 127–Edition Nouvelle (FR) **57** (New Chapter 106) [1988 7g 7s 8m 1989 10v* 12g 10f 9m⁵ 8m⁵ a8g] sturdy gelding: quite modest handicapper: won at Lingfield in April by short head, rallying well: easily best effort after on fourth start, leading 6f and running fairly well: stays 1¼m: acts on heavy going. *R. Boss.*

COME HOME KINGSLEY 2 ch.g. (Mar 27) Formidable (USA) 125–Pearl — Wedding 83 (Gulf Pearl 117) [1989 6g 8.2d] 8,600F, 15,000Y: lengthy, rather angular gelding: half-brother to William Hill Cambridgeshire winner Century City (by High Top) and a winner in Italy by Bustino: dam 1¼m and 1½m winner: behind in autumn claimer (backward and green) and maiden at Haydock. *J. Berry.*

COME NUH 3 ch.f. Be My Guest (USA) 126–Sandy Doll (Thatching 131) [1988 — NR 1989 11.5m] IR 20,000Y: second foal: half-sister to quite modest maiden Sheshells (by Zino): dam, never ran, from family of Riboboy: 50/1, tailed off in maiden at Yarmouth in June: sold 1,600 gns Ascot July Sales. *Mrs L. Piggott.*

COME ON CHASE ME 5 ch.h. Sharpo 132–Dragonist 82 (Dragonara Palace **85** (USA) 115) [1988 5v⁵ 5g 5m⁵ 5m⁵ 5g 5g 1989 5g 5f* 5m 5g] rather leggy, good-quartered horse: poor mover: useful at his best: form for long time only when winning claimer at Sandown in June: ran as though something amiss afterwards: best at 5f with forcing tactics: acts on any going: blinkered once at 4 yrs: wears crossed noseband. *J. Etherington.*

COME ON NORA 2 ch.f. (Feb 26) Norwick (USA) 120–Chicory (Vaigly Great **37** 127) [1989 5.8h⁵ 5f 6m 5.8m 10f] 2,800Y: lengthy, unfurnished filly: second foal: half-sister to 3-y-o Electric Dancer (by Electric): dam twice-raced half-sister to very useful middle-distance performer Baz Bombati: well beaten in quite modest company: well backed in selling nursery at Leicester on final outing: should stay 1¼m: sold 780 gns Newmarket Autumn Sales. *M. D. I. Usher.*

COME ON ROSI 2 b.f. (Apr 15) Valiyar 129–Victory Kingdom (CAN) (Viceregal **72** p (CAN)) [1989 6g 6g] strong, good sort: has scope: fifth live foal: closely related to French 1m and 9f winner Blushing All Over (by Blushing Groom) and half-sister to 2 winners, including 3-y-o Duende (by High Top), 6f winner at 2 yrs: dam (stakes placed) won 5 times in USA: about 8 lengths ninth of 28 to Alidiva, second and easily better effort in October maidens at Newmarket: looks sort to do better. *D. R. C. Elsworth.*

COME TO TERMS 3 gr.g. Welsh Term 126–Sparkling Time (USA) (Olden **76** Times) [1988 6f 7.5f 7.5s 8s 9f⁶ 1989 9d 11m² 12f³ 12f² 12f* 12.3g² 14m⁴ 12d⁶ 13s⁴ 14m] leggy gelding: modest handicapper: won at Beverley in June having had a lot to do entering straight: stays 1¾m: acts on any going: has run creditably for 7-lb claimer: usually held up: inconsistent. *T. D. Barron.*

COMHAMPTON 8 ch.g. Roi Soleil 125–Salambos (Doon 124) [1988 NR 1989 — 10d] plain gelding: poor performer: stays 1½m: acts on firm going and a soft surface. *J. R. Jenkins.*

COMIC RELIEF 2 br.f. (Apr 15) Comedy Star (USA) 121–Moberry 54 — (Mossberry 97) [1989 5f6 5m5] 2,800Y: sturdy filly: turns fore-feet in: second foal: sister to 3-y-o The Lighter Side: dam poor maiden, stayed 1m: bit backward and green, well beaten in maiden (slowly away) and claimer. *B. C. Morgan.*

COMIC TALENT 3 b.f. Pharly (FR) 130–Hysterical 68 (High Top 131) [1988 6g3 105 7m* 1989 8s* 8d* 9g* 8f* 8f] workmanlike, good-quartered filly: progressive: landed odds in minor events at Leicester, Pontefract and Wolverhampton prior to winning listed race at Sandown in May: keeping on steadily until hampered over 1f out when about 7 lengths ninth of 12 in Coronation Stakes at Royal Ascot: will stay 1¼m: acts on any going. *L. M. Cumani.*

COMINO GIRL 3 b.f. Indian King (USA) 128–Arab Art (Artaius (USA) 129) 55 [1988 NR 1989 10g 12s 12m 10h5 10m4 10f 9m 10g2 a11g2 a10g] small, sturdy filly: plating-class form: creditable second in claimers at Newmarket (ridden by 5-lb claimer) and Southwell (setting strong pace): stays 11f (backward over 1½m): blinkered fourth to ninth starts. *A. Hide.*

COMMANCHE MAGIC (FR) 2 b.c. (Apr 21) Commanche Run 133–Boissiere — (High Top 131) [1989 8g] IR 10,000Y: third foal: half-brother to 1987 French 2-y-o 6.5f and 1m winner Barbade (by Dunphy) and 3-y-o Golden Vintage (by Glint of Gold): dam French 9.2f winner, is half-sister to Bering: 50/1 and backward, soon tailed off in 15-runner maiden at Leicester in November: wore blinkers. *I. Campbell.*

COMMANCHE NATION 2 b.c. (Apr 21) Commanche Run 133–Rally 88 — p (Relko 136) [1989 10g] IR 62,000Y: seventh foal: half-brother to 5 winners on flat, including very useful 1985 2-y-o 7f winner Picatrix (by Thatch) and fairly useful 1987 2-y-o 1m winner The Domain (by Good Times): dam, sister to very smart Relay Race, won over 1½m: 20/1 and very green, never a factor in 12-runner maiden at Nottingham in October won by Rock Hopper: should do better. *Mrs L. Piggott.*

COMMANCHE SONG 2 ch.f. (May 13) Commanche Run 133–American 48 Beauty 74 (Mill Reef (USA) 141) [1989 7m 8s 8m6 8g] 15,000Y: leggy, sparely-made filly: has a quick action: sixth foal: half-sister to smart French 7f to 9f winner Stephany's Dream (by Reform) and moderate 1984 2-y-o 5f and 5.8f winner Musing (by Music Maestro): dam, second twice over 1¼m, is daughter of Oaks second West Side Story: poor maiden: best effort third start: will be suited by 1¼m +. *R. M. Whitaker.*

COMMANDER CARVER 3 b.g. Owen Anthony 102–Carvers Corah 60 45 (Easter Island 101) [1988 6g 1989 10.8s 10g 12.5f 12h4 16.5f5 10f 12.5f4] angular, workmanlike gelding: easily best efforts when fourth in sellers at Brighton and Wolverhampton: worth another try beyond 1½m: acts on hard ground: visored sixth start. *I. Campbell.*

COMMANDER MEADEN 6 b.g. Gold Song 112–Girl Commander (USA) 52 (Bold Commander (USA)) [1988 5d2 5d 5g 5m4 5g2 5m* 5m2 5g* 5.1f* 5.8g3 5m5 1989 7f 5f6 5h3] lengthy gelding: moderate mover: plating-class handicapper: not seen out after June: speedy, and best at 5f: possibly unsuited by soft going and goes particularly well on top-of-the-ground: has worn blinkers and visor, but not for some time: wears bandages: very good mount for apprentice: genuine. *J. H. Baker.*

COMMAND PERFORMER 3 b.f. Comedy Star (USA) 121–Freely Given 69 88 (Petingo 135) [1988 6g2 6g3 7d3 8m5 1989 7.6m2 8h* 8f2 10m4 8g3 9g6] tall, sparely-made filly: odds on, won maiden at Carlisle in May: ran creditably in minor events and handicap next 3 starts: sixth of 8 in listed event at Bordeaux: stays 1¼m: acts on hard going and a soft surface. *P. T. Walwyn.*

COMMON ACCORD 6 b.g. Tyrnavos 129–Carol Service 64 (Daring Display — (USA) 129) [1988 11.5g 12m4 16.5g6 1989 10s 12m] compact, attractive gelding: poor handicapper: probably stays 1½m: acts on firm going: sometimes blinkered or visored: sold 900 gns Ascot June Sales. *S. Woodman.*

COMPLEAT 6 b.h. Anax 120–Gay City 99 (Forlorn River 124) [1988 7.6g3 7m4 73 1989 7v 7d2 7s* 8m 7g 7m 7d] strong, well-made horse: modest handicapper: not seen out as 5-y-o after being struck into at Epsom in June and subsequently had carbon fibre implant operation: returned as good as ever in spring, winning at Epsom: below form last 4 outings: stays 8.5f: possibly needs plenty of give nowadays: blinkered once: has sweated: has pulled hard going down (led to post in apprentice race final start): sold only 700 gns Newmarket Autumn Sales. *R. Akehurst.*

COMPLINE 3 b.c. Night Shift (USA)–Mystic Margaret 61 (Realm 129) [1988 NR — 1989 7g 7d 8s] heavy-topped colt: second foal: dam won 1¼m seller: easily best effort in maidens at Kempton on final start in May: stayed 1m: dead. *A. Hide.*

COMPOSER 11 ch.h. Music Boy 124–Contadina (Memling) [1988 NR 1989 11d] — lengthy horse: poor mover: poor plater: best form at 1m to 1¼m: acts on any going: visored once, often blinkered. *M. B. James.*

COMPOS MENTIS 2 b.c. (Apr 21) Homeboy 114–Rhythm 64 (Bleep-Bleep 134) **69** [1989 6m 7g⁴ 6m* 6g 8s] smallish, angular colt: half-brother to useful 1979 2-y-o 5f and 6f winner Pink Blues and moderate plater Agnetha (both by Tickled Pink), and 2 winners by Crooner including Vocalist, very useful winner at up to 9f in USA: dam, non-thoroughbred, seemed to stay 1½m: quite modest performer: won claimer at Leicester in July by ½ length from Albedo: ran moderately on last 2 starts, sweating and on toes on first occasion: stays 7f: visored second and fourth starts. *R. J. Holder.*

COMSTOCK 2 ch.c. (May 4) Coquelin (USA) 121–Maura Paul (Bonne Noel 115) **76** [1989 7.5f 7f² 7m* 7m³] IR 9,000Y: fifth foal: half-brother to 3-y-o Sign People (by Sayyaf), fairly useful 6f winner at 2 yrs, 2 winners in Ireland (one in bumpers) and a winner in Hong Kong: dam placed at up to 2m on flat in Ireland, in bumpers race and over hurdles: modest performer: favourite, won maiden auction event at Edinburgh: good third to demoted Walking Saint in nursery at Newmarket later in July: will be suited by 1m. *J. G. FitzGerald.*

CONCERT PITCH 10 ch.g. Royal Match 117–Ballychord (DEN) (Ballymoss **49** 136) [1988 8d 8d⁶ 8d 7g 7m⁶ 8f 7d 8g⁶ 7m⁵ 8f 7d 8g 7d 1989 8m⁴ 7f² 7.6h 7f⁴ 6f 7g 8m³ 7m⁵ 8f⁴ a8g² a7g a6g] strong, dipped-backed, lengthy gelding: has a round action: poor performer nowadays: best at 7f or 1m: acts on any going: has won in blinkers, but wore them for only time since 1983 on final outing: good mount for inexperienced rider: tough. *B. Palling.*

CONEJITO 3 b.c. Main Reef 126–La Perricholi (FR) 80 (Targowice (USA) 130) — [1988 NR 1989 8m⁶] angular, sparely-made colt: first foal: dam won 3 times over 6f: bandaged, well beaten in seller in July. *R. J. R. Williams.*

CONE LANE 3 ch.g. On Your Mark 125–Cee Beauty 74 (Ribero 126) [1988 5d 6f⁶ **45** 5.8g 7m 8.5m⁴ 6f⁵ 1989 7s⁶ 6f⁵ 6g 7m³ 6m 6m 7h 7m 6m 12.2d] workmanlike gelding: poor maiden: suited by 6f or sharp 7f: acts on firm going: ran poorly in blinkers penultimate start at 2 yrs: tended to sweat and be on edge at 2 yrs and early as 3-y-o: winning hurdler. *B. Gubby.*

CONFIDENCE 2 ch.f. (Mar 18) Noalto 120–Orange Silk 68 (Moulton 128) [1989 **54** 5f³ 7.5f 6g⁶ 6g] 6,000Y: sturdy filly: fifth foal: half-sister to 3-y-o 6f winner Bali Sunset (by Balidar), useful middle-distance colt Bocatower (by Tyrnavos) and a winner in Italy: dam placed over 5f and 6f at 2 yrs: plating-class form in auction events (one a maiden) and claimers: stays 6f. *J. W. Watts.*

CONFUCIUS 2 b.c. (Apr 13) Stanford 121§–Carrhae (Home Guard (USA) 129) **62** [1989 5g⁵ 6d 5g] IR 4,500F, 15,000Y: tall, fair sort: first foal: dam lightly raced from family of Porto Bello: over 4 lengths fifth of 10 to Affirmation at Sandown, best effort in autumn maidens: caught eye at Redcar final start, never placed to challenge or knocked about: capable of winning a seller. *W. J. Musson.*

CONJURER 2 gr.c. (May 7) Magic Mirror 105–Morning Miss 59 (Golden Dipper **74** 119) [1989 6f³ 5.8h* 6g 6h⁵ 8m 7m³ a7g a7g³ a8g*] 2,300F, 5,400Y: medium-sized, leggy, close-coupled colt: fifth foal: half-brother to bad plater Red Rosco (by Porto Bello): dam, plater, stayed 1¼m: modest performer: won maiden auction event at Bath in May and nursery at Southwell in December: suited by 7f and 1m. *R. Hannon.*

CONJURE THE WIND 2 b.f. (Feb 10) Kala Shikari 125–Woodrush 70 — (Mummy's Pet 125) [1989 5f] small, lengthy, sparely-made filly: third reported foal: half-sister to quite modest 1987 2-y-o 5f winner Quick Or Be Damned (by Mandrake Major): dam sprint plater: carrying condition, soundly beaten in 9-runner Beverley claimer in July. *R. Earnshaw.*

CONNAUGHT BROADS 6 b.m. Connaught 130–Suffolk Broads (Moulton — 128) [1988 10g⁴ 12f⁶ 12f 10.8f⁴ 1989 10.8m 10m 12h⁶ 10f⁶] small, sparely-made mare: bad performer: stays 11f: sometimes sweats and gets on toes: often apprentice ridden. *M. J. Charles.*

CONNAUGHTS DREAM 2 gr.c. (Apr 21) Connaught 130–Precious Love — (Precipice Wood 123) [1989 6m] 1,400Y: sixth live foal: dam never ran: 50/1, tailed-off last of 7 in maiden at Newmarket. *R. W. Stubbs.*

CONNEMARA DAWN 5 ch.g. Viking (USA)–Amendola (FR) 71 (Amen (FR)) — [1988 NR 1989 14s] tall, close-coupled, workmanlike gelding: plating-class maiden as 3-y-o: edgy, tailed off in handicap at Nottingham in March: suited by 1½m: acts on any going: has worn blinkers and visor. *R. J. Holder.*

CONNIE'S GIFT (USA) 3 b.f. Nijinsky (CAN) 138–Connie Knows (USA) **95** (Buckpasser) [1988 7m* 1989 11.5m³ 10m³] tall, rangy filly: odds on and very reluctant at stalls, won maiden at Yarmouth in July as 2-y-o: good third, making most, in minor event at Yarmouth and handicap at Newmarket one year later: stays 11.5f: swished tail under pressure first and third starts: edgy and pulled hard to post on second: fairly useful. *H. R. A. Cecil.*

CONSTANT DELIGHT 2 b.f. (Apr 6) Never So Bold 135–Lady Constance 118 **70 p** (Connaught 130) [1989 6g³] IR 105,000Y: sixth foal: half-sister to fair 1m winner Zaytoon (by Formidable), fair 1984 2-y-o 6f winner Bahrain Star (by Star Appeal) and maiden sprinter Blow The Whistle (by Music Maestro): dam winner over 5f and 7f at 2 yrs: 9/2, 6½ lengths third of 15, one pace final 1½f, to Childrey in maiden at Folkestone in October: should improve. *M. R. Stoute.*

CONSULATE 3 gr.g. Absalom 128–Maiden Pool 85 (Sharpen Up 127) [1988 5f³ **71** 5g* 5f⁴ 1989 6m 5g 6g 9m 8g a8g* a8g*] small, stocky, robust gelding: worthwhile form in handicaps and claimers as 3-y-o only when winning late-season claimers (always close up) at Lingfield: stays 1m. *P. J. Makin.*

CONTACT KELVIN 7 br.g. Workboy 123–Take My Hand 49 (Precipice Wood — 123) [1988 12d* 12f 12g 11s 1989 12d 12g] big, strong gelding: no form in handicaps since first outing at 6 yrs: stays 1½m: acts on a soft surface. *N. Bycroft.*

CONTEMPLATE 2 b.c. (Apr 20) Fappiano (USA)–Good Thinking (USA) (Raja — Baba (USA)) [1989 6g 6m] well-made colt: third foal: half-brother to 3-y-o Mary Bankes (by Northern Baby): dam, 2-y-o 7f winner in Ireland, is half-sister to Treizieme: always behind in August minor events at Windsor: unseated rider in stalls second occasion. *P. W. Harris.*

CONTINENTAL CLAIRE (USA) 3 b.f. Peterhof (USA) 116–Topolly (USA) — (Turn-To) [1988 5f³ 5m* 5m⁴ 5g² 6m⁶ 5g⁴ 5d² 5g³ 1989 8.5s 8f⁵ 8.5m 7m 7m 8f⁴ 7d] small, sturdy filly: good walker: has a quick action: fair performer as 2-y-o: below form in handicaps in 1989, best efforts on first 2 outings: should be suited by 6f+: acts on top-of-the-ground and a soft surface: blinkered final start: has run well for claimer: sold 13,000 gns Newmarket December Sales. *B. W. Hills.*

CONTRACT LAW (USA) 2 b.c. (Mar 25) Lypheor 118–Permissible **108** Tender (USA) (Al Hattab (USA)) [1989 6m² 6f*]

It remains to be seen whether Contract Law will realise the abundant promise he showed when winning the Scottish Equitable Richmond Stakes at Goodwood in July. He fractured a bone in his knee while being prepared for the Heinz '57 Phoenix Stakes in Ireland the following month and underwent corrective surgery in the autumn. At the time of writing Contract Law is reported to be convalescing satisfactorily, and is expected to race again. Until

Scottish Equitable Richmond Stakes, Goodwood—Contract Law draws clear of Qui Danzig

such time as he has proved his well-being on the racecourse, however, his future will remain in doubt; in the circumstances the 16/1 offered by one leading bookmaker in October about his winning the Two Thousand Guineas is laughably short.

There was no lack of confidence behind Contract Law at Goodwood despite his narrow defeat by the northern-trained colt Karinga Bay, the pair well clear, in a maiden at York shortly before, and he started third choice at 9/2 from 7/1 in a field of five behind Qui Danzig, who'd beaten another Richmond runner Wave Master by seven lengths in a minor event at Windsor on his only start, and the Manton Rose Bowl winner Rushmore. That confidence wasn't misplaced either, as Contract Law returned as impressive a performance as we'd seen by a two-year-old at that stage of the season. Held up in last place as Rushmore took the runners along at a decent gallop, Contract Law made headway to track Qui Danzig by halfway, accelerated in great style when given the office approaching the distance and ran on more determindly than Qui Danzig to win going away by two and a half lengths with four back to Rushmore. Contract Law's connections can count themselves unfortunate to have been denied a tilt with their colt, said by his trainer Jarvis to be the best he's had, at the Phoenix Stakes: he would have needed only to reproduce his Richmond form to have gone very close to winning the IR £120,000 first prize. Group 1 races in England and Ireland don't come much easier to win than the Phoenix Stakes however, and if Contract Law is to compete successfully at the top level in 1990 he'll need to have not only recovered fully from his injury but to have improved by around a stone as well. Such a scenario is, for the time being, mere conjecture. We'll know a great deal more about him after he's run once or twice as a three-year-old.

			Lyphard	Northern Dancer
	Lypheor		(b 1969)	Goofed
	(b 1975)	Klaizia		Sing Sing
Contract Law (USA)			(b 1965)	Klainia
(b.c. Mar 25, 1987)		Al Hattab		The Axe II
	Permissible		(ro 1966)	Abyssinia
	Tender (USA)	Oh So Bold		Better Bee
	(gr 1980)		(b 1974)	Bold Bikini

Contract Law, one of twenty yearlings by the deceased Lypheor to be sold at auction in the States in 1988, was bought for 85,000 dollars at Fasig-Tipton's September Sale shortly before his dam Permissible Tender, whose second foal he is after the minor American winner Randolph (by Icecapade), was knocked down for 140,000 dollars at Keeneland's November Breeding Stock Sale. Permissible Tender was a fair racemare in the States where her three wins, including in minor stakes company, were gained at up to nine furlongs. She is one of three winners from the well-related Oh So Bold (better of the others is the fair 1988 two-year-old six-furlong winner Hope And Glory) whose half-brothers Law Society, successful in the Joe McGrath Irish Sweeps Derby, Legal Bid, a good-class middle-distance colt, and Strike Your Colors, a very smart two-year-old in the States in 1978 and one of the few horses to beat Spectacular Bid, have done much to keep the family in the spotlight over the last fifteen years. Most members of the family have stayed at least as far as their pedigrees suggested they would, but Contract Law, who could be expected to get a mile and a quarter, impresses as one who'll prove best at up to a mile. If he fails to recover from injury he's well-enough bred to command a place at stud. *W. Jarvis.*

CONVINCING 5 ch.g. Formidable (USA) 125–Star of Bagdad (USA) 95 (Bagdad) —
[1988 10.2d 12.2d 12g 8f 6m⁵ 7g⁴ 6m 7d⁴ 1989 10.2g 14s] big, strong gelding: has a round action: poor maiden: stays 1¼m: suited by a soft surface: probably best without blinkers or visor: has run creditably for apprentice: sold 3,000 gns Doncaster October Sales. *Mrs G. E. Jones.*

CONWAY FLYER 3 ch.c. Stanford 121§–Track Down 69 (Take A Reef 127) —
[1988 7d 7s 1989 11s 8g 6m 8f] plain, unfurnished colt: good mover: little worthwhile form, including in sellers. *Miss A. J. Whitfield.*

CONWAY KING 3 b.g. King of Spain 121–Conway Bay 74 (Saritamer (USA) 130) **56**
[1988 5m 5g⁶ 5m² 5f² 5m³ 5g³ 1989 6f 6f⁶ 6g 10g 5m 6f⁴ 6m* 6g 6g] strong, lengthy

gelding: moderate mover: made all (alone far side) in handicap at Lingfield in September: hung right third start: best over 6f on top-of-the-ground: blinkered last 5 outings: sold 7,200 gns Newmarket Autumn Sales. *K. M. Brassey.*

COOKS GORSE 3 br.c. Alzao (USA) 117–Hill's Realm (USA) 68 (Key To The Kingdom (USA)) [1988 6f³/7g* 7s* 7g³ 8f² 1989 8v 8f³] quite attractive colt: has a quick, fairly fluent action: fairly useful winner as 2-y-o: creditable third in handicap at Salisbury in May: well behind in Group 1 event at Rome 3 weeks earlier: suited by 1m: acts on any going: sometimes on toes. *J. W. Hills.* **89**

COOLAGOWN 2 b.g. (Apr 5) Castle Keep 121–Little Oncer (Hot Spark 126) [1989 5m⁶ 6f 8m 10f] 1,900Y: rather sparely-made gelding: first foal: dam unraced: bad plater: most unsatisfactory temperamentally: sold 1,000 gns Newmarket Autumn Sales. *N. A. Callaghan.* **30 §**

COOL DANCER 2 ch.f. (Feb 17) Fabulous Dancer (USA) 124–Sarajill (High Line 125) [1989 8g] strong, lengthy, rather plain filly: third foal: half-sister to plating-class maiden Learning Fast (by Bold Lad): dam poor sister to Nicholas Bill, Centroline and Centrocon (dam of Time Charter): weak 9/1-shot, never dangerous in 17-runner maiden at Leicester in November: will be suited by 1¼m +: should improve. *M. R. Stoute.* **— p**

COOL EMM 4 b.c. Miami Springs 121–Wise Countess (USA) (Count Amber) [1988 7d⁴ 8g 7d⁶ 9f³ 10s 12g 12g⁶ 12m⁵ 1989 5f 8m⁶ 7f 6f⁵ 8m⁵ a8g⁵] big, strong colt: poor mover: plating-class maiden: seems to stay 1½m. *D. Haydn Jones.* **46**

COOL ENOUGH 8 ch.g. Welsh Captain 113–Sundrive (Status Seeker) [1988 7d⁶ 6g 7f 7m² 8f² 7g⁴ 8g 8g² 7d* 7g² 7.6s³ 7m³ 7m 7f⁵ 8m 7g³ 1989 7d* 8d* 7m* 8h² 8.5m 8.2m⁴ 8f² 7g⁴ 8m 7.5m 7f³ 7m 7g²,7m 8.2g 8g⁶] small, sturdy gelding: quite modest handicapper: successful at Catterick (twice) and Pontefract in spring: looked certain to complete 4-timer at Carlisle, but was eased close home (jockey fined £525) and caught on line: best efforts in autumn when third at Redcar and Catterick: best at 7f or 1m nowadays: acts on any going: has been taken very quietly to post: best waited with: tough. *Mrs J. R. Ramsden.* **64**

COOL RUN 4 b.f. Deep Run 119–Loyal And Regal 51 (Royal And Regal (USA)) [1988 10.2m 8s* 8d⁶ 8g* 10g⁴ 1989 8h⁴ 8.2g 8g 10m* 8m⁴] leggy, quite good-topped filly: carries condition: moderate mover: won 4-runner handicap at Newmarket in July: fair fourth of 7 in Pontefract handicap 2 weeks later: stays 1¼m: best form with give in the ground. *B. A. McMahon.* **75**

COOLULAH 2 b.g. (Apr 23) Dominion 123–Phoebe Ann 76 (Absalom 128) [1989 5f⁵ 7m 6d 6g a7g⁶] medium-sized, quite attractive gelding: second foal: half-brother to 3-y-o Poor Phoebe (by Vaigly Great): dam lightly-raced 2-y-o 5f winner, is daughter of Molecomb winner Lowna: plating-class maiden. *H. Candy.* **53**

Skol Lager Sprint Handicap, Goodwood—
Coppermill Lad (right) pips Chummy's Favourite (centre) and Green Dollar

COPFORD   2 b.c. (Feb 23) Teenoso (USA) 135–Chalkey Road 100 (Relko 136)   **71 p**
[1989 7m[6] 8m] strong, lengthy colt: third foal: half-brother to a fair maiden by
General Assembly: dam, middle-distance stayer, is half-sister to smart middle-
distance filly Cheveley Princess out of Irish 1000 Guineas second Feather Bed:
backward, shaped promisingly in late-season maidens won by Mukddaam and
Defensive Play at Newmarket: will do much better given a stiff test of stamina. *G.
Wragg.*

COPPERBOTTOM   2 b.c. (Feb 8) Night Shift (USA)–Crimson Damask   **69**
(Windjammer (USA)) [1989 6m 6m[2] 6f[4] 7m a7g[4] 7g a7g[2] a6g[4] a7g] leggy,
good-topped colt: second foal: brother to 3-y-o Land Breeze: dam never ran: quite
modest maiden: seems suited by 7f: has been bandaged behind: active sort. *R. V.
Smyth.*

COPPERMILL LAD   6 ch.g. Ardoon 124–Felin Geri (Silly Season 127) [1988 6m   **82**
6m[2] 6m[5] 6m 6m[4] 6g 5g 6m[6] 5g 5d 6s 1989 5s[5] 6v* 5s 6f[5] 6m[4] 6m[6] 6s* 6s[4] 6v]
compact gelding: carries plenty of condition: has a round action: fair handicapper:
successful at Lingfield in April and Goodwood in September: favourite, beat
Chummy's Favourite and Green Dollar by 2 lengths in £7,800 event at Goodwood:
creditable fourth of 29, finishing strongly, to Joveworth in Ladbrokes (Ayr) Gold
Cup (Handicap), better subsequent effort: suited by 6f: acts on any going: usually
gets behind. *L. J. Holt.*

COPPER TOP   2 b.f. (Mar 10) Longleat (USA) 109–Quorn Rocket (Roan Rocket   **62**
128) [1989 5f[3] 5h[3] 5.1f* 5m 8m[6] 5m 5m] 500F, 6,000Y: angular filly: moderate
walker: first foal: dam little sign of ability: quite modest performer: won maiden
auction event at Yarmouth in July: should stay further than 5f. *H. J. Collingridge.*

COQUETA   4 ch.f. Coquelin (USA) 121–Clara Petacci (USA) (Crepello 136) [1988   **—**
8f 10g 8m 12m 10d[2] 8.3m 10s 7g 10g 1989 8.2v[5] 8d 7.6m 12h[5] 10m[6]] neat filly: has a
quick action: probably stays 1½m: acts on hard going and a soft surface: blinkered
once at 3 yrs: visored last 2 starts: winning hurdler. *E. J. Alston.*

CORAKI   3 b.g. Crofter (USA) 124–Eyry 85 (Falcon 131) [1988 6s 6m 5f[2] 6d[6] 6g   **71**
1989 6m 6m[5] 6f[5] 7h 6m[4] 6m 6f[2] 5f[5] 6m[4] 6g[4] 7s*] strong gelding: carries condition:
quite modest handicapper: 33/1 and ridden by 5-lb claimer, showed improved form
when winning £5,600 event at Ayr in September, making most and keeping on well:
suited by 7f: clearly goes very well on soft ground: ran creditably in blinkers fifth
start: inconsistent. *J. Douglas-Home.*

CORAL FLUTTER   2 b.f. (Apr 15) Beldale Flutter (USA) 130–Countess Olivia   **61**
80 (Prince Tenderfoot (USA) 126) [1989 5f 5m[4] 5f[6]] 4,100Y: lengthy, angular filly:
has a quickish action: fourth foal: half-sister to 3-y-o Donna Elvira (by Chief Singer):
dam stayed 1¼m: quite modest maiden: hung left second start: will be better suited
by further: keen sort. *J. W. Payne.*

CORAL SWORD   3 ch.c. Main Reef 126–Foil 'em (USA) 82 (Blade (USA)) [1988   **84**
5f 6d[5] 7.5f[2] 7d 8g 1989 10.6s 9f 7.5f[2] 8h* 8.2g[4] 8f 8.2g[2] 8f[3] 8.2g[5] 9f 8m]
close-coupled, sparely-made colt: fair handicapper: won at Carlisle in May: ran well
after when in frame: stays 1m: acts on hard going and possibly unsuited by a soft
surface: visored or blinkered nowadays: sold to race in Middle East 20,000 gns
Newmarket Autumn Sales. *F. H. Lee.*

CORDOBA (USA)   2 ch.c. (Feb 15) El Gran Senor (USA) 136–Gay Senorita   **112**
(USA) (Raise A Native) [1989 6m* 6m[3] 7g[5]] sturdy, attractive colt: good walker and
mover: first foal: dam, minor winner at around 1m in USA, is half-sister to good-class

*Fay Richwhite Karamea Stakes, Newmarket —
much-vaunted Cordoba wins in good style on his debut*

1975 American 4-y-o Gulls Cry (successful at up to 1¼m), dam of good Irish middle-distance stayer Nemain, and to very smart Gala Regatta, successful at up to 9f: put up very useful performances in Tattersalls Middle Park Stakes and Three Chimneys Dewhurst Stakes (around 2 lengths fifth to Dashing Blade, fading gradually last 1½f) at Newmarket in October: wide-margin winner of maiden there in August: bred to stay at least 1m: sent to race in USA. *M. R. Stoute.*

CORICK BRIDGE 3 b.c. Homing 130–Sussex Queen 82 (Music Boy 124) [1988 5g 6m 1989 8d 7m] neat colt: moderate mover: little sign of ability, including in sellers: should be suited by further than 6f: sweating final start. *D. Marks.* —

CORINTHIAN GIRL 2 b.f. (Mar 24) Welsh Captain 113–Combe Grove Lady (Simbir 130) [1989 6g a7g] leggy filly: moderate walker and mover: sixth foal: half-sister to 7f and 1¼m winner Predestine (by Bold Owl), modest 1986 2-y-o 5f winner Lawnswood Lad (by Runnymede) and a winner in Belgium: dam lightly-raced half-sister to disqualified French Gold Cup winner Tulip II: ridden by 7-lb claimer, well beaten in late-season maidens. *R. Dickin.* —

CORIO BAY 2 br.c. (May 17) Blue Cashmere 129–Rushley Bay 87 (Crooner 119) [1989 6f 7f 7m] 6,000Y: leggy colt: third live foal: dam 2-y-o 5f firm-ground winner: ridden by 5-lb claimer, about 8 lengths tenth of 17 to Mull House in maiden at Chepstow on final start, only worthwhile form in autumn events. *D. Haydn Jones.* 53

CORMAC'S 3 gr.g. Superlative 118–Tahoume (FR) (Faristan 123) [1988 NR 1989 8s 10f² 12f³ 9m a10g] 7,600F: tall, leggy, plain gelding: eighth living foal: half-brother to French 1m to 10.5f winner Tropea (by Trepan): dam, placed in France, is half-sister to Prix de Diane winner Rescousse: placed in seller and claimer: ran poorly in claimers last 2 starts, slowly away and not handling bend well at Lingfield final one: off course over 5 months after debut: stays 1½m: acts on firm ground. *A. Bailey.* 54

CORMORANT CREEK 2 b.f. (Apr 24) Gorytus (USA) 132–Quarry Wood 89 (Super Sam 124) [1989 7m⁶] big, strong, rangy filly: fourth reported foal: half-sister to top-class 1¼m filly Cormorant Wood (by Home Guard): dam won at up to 1¾m: 7/1 and on toes, shaped quite well when around 10 lengths sixth of 21 to Cutting Note in maiden at Newmarket in October, not knocked about when beaten: sure to improve. *B. W. Hills.* 64 p

CORNCHARM 8 b.g. Thatch (USA) 136–Just Larking (USA) (Sea Bird II 145) [1988 7f⁴ 7m 5d⁴ 6m 7d 6m 5.8f 1989 5f⁴ 6f 5f] robust, compact gelding: moderate mover: modest at best, but has deteriorated considerably: best at 6f: acts on any going: has worn blinkers and visor: has won for apprentice: inconsistent. *D. C. Jermy.* 43

CORNET 3 b.g. Coquelin (USA) 121–Corny Story 75 (Oats 126) [1988 5g 6d* 7f⁵ 8s² 8s 8v 1989 10.6s⁵ 12g] quite attractive gelding: modest handicapper: stays 1¼m: best efforts on soft going: needs a lot of driving: sweating final start (July): has joined D. Smith. *J. W. Watts.* —

CORNFLOWER BLUE 3 b.f. Tyrnavos 129–Late Idea 78 (Tumble Wind (USA)) [1988 6m 1989 8.2g] leggy filly: no worthwhile form in auction race (slowly away, virtually pulled up soon after) as 2-y-o and maiden in September: sweating, withdrawn lame in May: bred to stay 1m + . *R. M. Whitaker.* —

CORN LILY 3 ch.f. Aragon 118–Ixia 91 (I Say 125) [1988 8d 10d⁴ 1989 10g 14f 11.7m⁴ 12.3g 10f* 13.8g* 12.3m* 11g* 11s⁴ 10.6m 11f² 12m*] tall, leggy filly: very useful plater: won at Yarmouth (claimer), Catterick, Ripon (claimer) and Hamilton in space of 4 weeks in the summer and at Hamilton in October: claimed out of G. Pritchard-Gordon's stable £8,336 first occasion then bought in 6,200 gns, 18,000 gns and 10,500 gns on second, fourth and fifth: best efforts at up to 1½m on top-of-the-ground: sweating fourth start: suited by forcing tactics: winning novice hurdler. *N. Tinkler.* 69

CORNWALL PRINCE 2 b.c. (May 16) Taufan (USA) 119–Peach Stone (Mourne 126) [1989 7g] 30,000Y: half-brother to several winners here and abroad, including fair middle-distance handicapper Florida Son (by Busted): dam won at around 9f in France: 50/1 and backward, slowly away and always behind in 28-runner maiden at Newmarket in November. *N. A. Callaghan.* —

CORONATION MARCH (USA) 5 b.g. Blushing Groom (FR) 131–Princess Ribot (Ribot 142) [1988 8f⁵ 11m³ 10.5g 11.5g* 12.2g³ 1989 8g] ex-French gelding: half-brother to numerous winners, notably champion handicap mare Cascapedia (by Chieftain): dam won over 1m at 2 yrs in Ireland: won in French Provinces early as 4-y-o: sold out of J. Hammond's stable 3,000 gns Newmarket Autumn (1988) Sales: —

resold 1,400 gns Ascot March Sales: resold privately 1,500 gns Ascot May Sales: 66/1 and bandaged near-hind, tailed-off last of 9 in apprentice race at Ascot in October: resold 650 gns Ascot December Sales. *G. G. Gracey.*

CORPORATE MEMBER   2 ch.g. (Feb 13) Exhibitioner 111–Sciambola (Great   69
Nephew 126) [1989 5g^6 5v^3 5d^5 7g^6 8.2s^2 8m 8d] IR 8,400Y: tall, close-coupled, workmanlike gelding: has plenty of scope: second foal: half-brother to a winner in Norway: dam ran in Italy without success: quite modest maiden: easily best effort second at Hamilton in September: ran moderately afterwards: suited by 1m: acts on soft going: trained first 3 outings by S. Muldoon. *C. Tinkler.*

CORRIN HILL   2 b.c. (Apr 20) Petorius 117–Pete's Money (USA) (Caucasus   91
(USA)) [1989 5.3m^4 5s^2 6m^3 6m* 7m 6m 6g^2 6g^5 7g^6 a6g^4 a7g^3 a6g* a7g*] IR 25,000F, 7,400Y: third foal: half-brother to 3-y-o 1m winner Yuno Why (by Horage): dam unraced: useful-looking colt: fair performer: won maiden auction event at Nottingham in June and late-season nurseries at Lingfield: stays 7f: effective with or without blinkers: sometimes hangs, and flashes tail. *N. A. Callaghan.*

CORSEE   2 ch.g. (May 23) Song 132–Bundling (Petingo 135) [1989 5s 5d 5f 6m^2]   52
8,000Y: lengthy, angular gelding: has a round action: half-brother to several winners here and abroad, including fair 1m and 10.6f winner Boltingo (by Bold Lad, IRE) and modest 6f winner Clouded Vision (by So Blessed): dam, half-sister to dam of Enstone Spark, won over 5f in Ireland: 33/1, staying-on second, wandering last 2f, in seller at Ripon in June: slowly away first 3 starts: suited by 6f. *M. W. Easterby.*

CORSTON MAGIC   4 ch.f. Relkino 131–Corston Lass (Menelek 114) [1988   —
10m^6 13g^2 12.2f^3 1989 13v 13m^4] big, workmanlike filly: poor maiden: stays 13f: acts on firm going and unsuited by heavy. *Denys Smith.*

CORWYN BAY   3 gr.c. Caerleon (USA) 132–Baccalaureate 109 (Crowned Prince   115
(USA) 128) [1988 6d* 6.3d* 7d^4 7g* 1989 8m 8m^2 8g^2 7g^2 6g^2 6g* 6s^5] smart Irish colt: favourite, won listed race at the Curragh in October: ran creditably starts either side behind Point of Light in Group 3 Keeneland EBF Phoenix Sprint Stakes at Phoenix Park and Cricket Ball in Laurel Dash: suited by 6f: acts on top-of-the-ground and soft surface: reportedly to stay in USA. *T. Stack, Ireland.*

COSMIC DANCER   2 ch.c. (Apr 15) Horage 124–Royal Cloak (Hardicanute 130)   52
[1989 5m^5 6m^4 6f 6m^4 6h 7.5m 8f 7g a6g a8g] IR 12,000F, 25,000Y: good-quartered colt: moderate walker and mover: closely related to 1988 Irish 2-y-o 7f winner Coat of Arms (by Tumble Wind) and half-brother to 2 other winners in Ireland and USA: dam placed at 7f in Ireland at 2 yrs: plating-class maiden: should be better suited by 7f + than shorter: races freely. *F. Durr.*

COSMIC PRINCESS   2 b.f. (Apr 26) Fairy King (USA)–Come True (FR)   97 p
(Nasram II 125) [1989 6g 7.3v^2] IR 7,800Y: half-sister to several winners, including useful 1m to 1¼m winner Spanish Dancer (by Gay Fandango): dam won over 1½m in Ireland: 12/1, length second of 12, clear, to Berry's Dream in listed race at Newbury in October: slowly away on debut: should stay 1¼m. *M. A. Jarvis.*

COSMIC RAY   4 b.g. Comedy Star (USA) 121–Hey Skip (USA) (Bold Skipper   —
(USA)) [1989 9v^5 8g 8g 9g^6 8.2s 8f 8g 13.8f 1989 10d] leggy, workmanlike gelding: has a round action: plater: little form for long time: probably doesn't stay 1¼m: acts on heavy going: has been blinkered and visored: possibly ungenuine. *S. J. Muldoon.*

COSSACK GUARD (USA)   3 br.c. Nureyev (USA) 131–Kilijaro 126 (African   106
Sky 124) [1988 7m 8g^3 10s 1989 9d^5 10f^2 12f^3 12g^6 12g* 14f^6 13.3m^2 12m] compact, quite attractive colt: useful performer: on toes, won maiden at Newbury in August: ran well in competitive handicaps at Royal Ascot and Haydock previous 2 outings and at York and Newbury on next 2: not discredited in Tote Festival Handicap at Ascot on final one: lacks turn of foot, and should stay further than 1¾m: acts on any going. *C. E. Brittain.*

COSSACK STEPPE   3 ch.g. Pas de Seul 133–Mariakova (USA) 84 (The   —
Minstrel (CAN) 135) [1988 NR 1989 12.2g^5] IR 26,000Y: second foal: dam, placed over 6f and 1m on only starts, is sister to smart miler Zaizafon: 25/1, well-beaten fifth of 9 in apprentice race at Catterick in October: may improve. *R. J. R. Williams.*

COST EFFECTIVE   2 ch.c. (May 8) Burslem 123–Perle's Fashion (Sallust 134)   53
[1989 6f^6 6m^5 6g] IR 7,500Y: medium-sized, rather angular colt: fourth foal: half-brother to 3-y-o Wolver Gem (by Wolver Hollow), 6f seller winner Main Fashion (by Main Reef) and 1986 Irish 2-y-o 5f winner Snappy Dresser (by Nishapour): dam Irish 9f to 1½m winner: 7 lengths sixth of 12 to Wadood at York in May, best effort in maidens: off course almost 3 months before final start. *M. Brittain.*

Mrs J. L. Hislop's "Cottenham"

CO-TACK 4 ch.g. Connaught 130–Dulcidene 71 (Behistoun 131) [1988 10m⁴ 12m — 13.8f 13.8d³ 13.8f* 12d 13.8f⁶ 16m 1989 12f] smallish gelding: has a round action: winning plater as 3-y-o: sweating, soundly beaten at Thirsk in May: stays 1¾m: acts on firm going and a soft surface: winning selling hurdler with J. FitzGerald. *J. Mulhall.*

COTSWOLD COMEDY 2 b.f. (May 20) Flying Tyke 90–Comedy Spring — (Comedy Star (USA) 121) [1989 8.2g 8g] sister to 4 animals, notably modest 1m to 1¼m performer The White Lion, and half-sister to 2 poor animals: dam never ran: well behind in late-season minor event (backward, slowly away) at Nottingham and maiden at Leicester. *R. Dickin.*

COTTENHAM 3 b.c. Night Shift (USA)–Countess Walewski 85 (Brigadier **109** Gerard 144) [1988 5d³ 6g⁴ 6f² 6g 7m* 7g⁵ 1989 7g 8s 8.2m³ 7f⁴ 10m⁴ 7g⁶ 8m⁵] leggy, quite attractive colt: easily best efforts fourth and final starts when strong-finishing fourth of 12 to Zilzal in Jersey Stakes at Royal Ascot and last of 5 to same colt in Queen Elizabeth II Stakes at Ascot: stays 1m well: acts on firm going and probably unsuited by soft: sold to race in USA. *C. E. Brittain.*

COTTON ON QUICK 4 ch.g. Bold Owl 101–Silvery Moon (Lorenzaccio 130) **57** [1988 6d² 6f⁶ 6d 6m 5m⁶ 5.8g³ 5d* 5g⁵ 5.1g 5g 5f³ 5m² 5g 5g 5d 1989 5d 6g 5f⁵ 5f 5m 5m 5g 7g 5f³ 5m³ 5m 5m² 5.3f³ 5f 6g] compact gelding: has a quick action: quite modest handicapper: stays 6f: acts on any going: effective with or without blinkers: has run well for apprentice: usually bandaged near-hind and sometimes in front: has sweated: sold 3,700 gns Newmarket Autumn Sales. *A. Bailey.*

COUGAR 3 ch.g. Song 132–Flying Milly (Mill Reef (USA) 141) [1988 NR 1989 8.5d **51** 12.3m⁵ 11g 8.2g⁴] workmanlike gelding: fourth foal: dam showed little worthwhile form: quite modest plater: should stay 11f: moved badly down on debut: may improve again. *C. W. Thornton.*

212

COULD BE CLOUDY 3 b.g. Coded Scrap 90–Grecian Cloud 76 (Galivanter   —
131) [1988 6m 1989 8g 7s 8d 8m] leggy gelding: probably of little account: has been
tried in blinkers: sold 1,150 gns Doncaster September Sales. *J. R. Jenkins.*

COUNCIL ROCK 4 b.f. General Assembly (USA)–Dancing Rocks 118 (Green   —
Dancer (USA) 132) [1988 9g⁴ 8m 10m³ 10d⁶ 8m 7m 7g 1989 8g 8f 7m] medium-sized,
rather sparely-made filly: modest maiden at her best: below form in handicaps in
spring: suited by 1¼m: acted on top-of-the-ground: sometimes started slowly,
including when blinkered: sweating final start: sold 10,000 gns Newmarket
December Sales in foal to Jalmood. *C. E. Brittain.*

COUNT BERTRAND 8 b.h. Brigadier Gerard 144–Gingerale (Golden Horus   **58**
123) [1988 10f 8m* 10m 1989 10s 8.2f* 8f³ 8.2g 8m 8m⁴ 7.6m 8g] lengthy horse:
quite modest handicapper: well backed, showed improved form when winning at
Nottingham in June by 7 lengths: best efforts after when in frame: suited by 1m and
top-of-the-ground: none too easy a ride, often gets well behind and is suited by
strong gallop: goes well on a turning track: particularly well handled by J. Lowe:
inconsistent. *W. Holden.*

COUNTER TENOR 3 ch.g. Absalom 128–Divine Penny 65 (Divine Gift 127)   —
[1988 NR 1989 10.1m⁶ 10f⁶] stocky gelding: fourth reported foal: half-brother to
1¼m and 1½m winner Divine Charger (by Treboro) and 1¾m winner Pour
Encourager (by Kind of Hush): dam, placed in sellers at up to 1¼m, later won 5
times in Hong Kong: backward, slowly away and no promise in minor event and
claimer in July. *G. Lewis.*

COUNT ME OUT 4 ch.g. Vaigly Great 127–Balatina 85 (Balidar 133) [1988 6s 7d   —
5f 5d⁵ 5.1g 5g² 5m³ 5g³ 6m* 5f 7g⁴ 6d⁵ 1989 7g 6f 6f⁵ 8.3g 6g 5m a6g] lengthy, plain
gelding: has a round action: plating-class winner as 3-y-o: no worthwhile form in
1989: suited by 6f and top-of-the-ground: usually wears blinkers: on toes third
outing: slowly away last 2, edging left on first occasion: often finds little. *R. P. C.
Hoad.*

COUNT MY BLESSINGS 4 b.g. Touching Wood (USA) 127–Topaz Too 78   **68**
(Sun Prince 128) [1988 10v⁴ 12d² 14f³ 15.8m³ 16f⁶ 14.8d 14.7m³ 17g* 16g 1989 12s
18.4m 18f⁴ 17.1h³ 16.5g 16f³ 17f³] neat, quite attractive gelding: usually looks well:
moderate mover: modest handicapper: suited by a test of stamina: best on a sound
surface: blinkered twice at 3 yrs: bandaged fourth outing: not the easiest of rides. *C.
F. Wall.*

COUNT NULIN 4 b.g. Pas de Seul 133–Lost Splendour (USA) (Vaguely Noble   **91**
140) [1988 NR 1989 10g² 12s⁴ 12g* 10g* 12d² 14s 8g³ 10g] good-topped gelding: in
frame at Cagnes-sur-Mer before twice making all there in March: creditable second
in strongly-run apprentice handicap at Ascot following month: lightly raced
afterwards: headstrong, suited by forcing tactics at 1¼m to 1½m: acts on soft going:
sold 22,000 gns Newmarket Autumn Sales. *W. Hastings-Bass.*

COUNTRY COTTAGE (USA) 2 br.f. (Apr 6) Full Out (USA)–La Chaumiere   **70**
(Thatch (USA) 136) [1989 6f³ 5f* 6m] rather leggy, quite attractive filly: third foal:
half-sister to 2 winners by Valdez, including fair 4-y-o miler Birstwith: dam poor
half-sister to very useful French 1971 2-y-o 5.5f winner Tamiran: sire high class at
up to 1m: co-favourite, won minor event at Bath by 1½ lengths from Dounhurst:
always struggling in nursery at Newmarket later in October. *P. T. Walwyn.*

COUNT SEPTIMO 3 b.c. Seymour Hicks (FR) 125–Countess Decima (USA)   —
(Sir Gaylord) [1988 NR 1989 11.7m 12f 12f⁶] IR 2,200F: lengthy, unfurnished colt:
half-brother to several winners, including useful French sprinter Miliar (by Thatch)
and Irish 12.8f and 1¾m winner Ard Countess (by Ardross): dam never ran: never
dangerous in maiden at Bath and claimers at Goodwood: sold to join T. Kersey 1,600
gns Ascot July Sales. *J. L. Dunlop.*

COUNTY MEO 3 b.f. Tolomeo 127–City Sound 63 (On Your Mark 125) [1988 NR   —
1989 8m 10.1g 12.5g⁴ a10g] sparely-made, angular filly: fifth living foal: half-sister to
fair winner at up to 7f Ashley Rocket (by Roan Rocket), 5f and 6f winner Flomegas
Day (by Lucky Wednesday), successful in Sweden in 1989, and to a winner in
Holland: dam won over 6f: well beaten in claimers and minor events, once sweating:
trained debut by W. Musson. *I. V. Matthews.*

COURAGEOUS BIDDER 4 b.g. Known Fact (USA) 135–Hysterical 68 (High   —
Top 131) [1988 8g 8s⁶ 7g⁶ 10m 8f* 8.2m 7f 1989 8m] angular, deep-girthed gelding:
33/1, enterprisingly ridden when winning apprentice maiden at Yarmouth (trained
by R. J. R. Williams) as 3-y-o: quite modest judged on most other form: well beaten
in apprentice handicap at Salisbury in August: suited by 1m: acts on firm going. *M.
H. B. Robinson.*

*Tote-Portland Handicap, Doncaster—one of the season's most controversial
and eventful races ends in victory for outsider Craft Express
(three jockeys were injured in a pile-up at around the two-furlong marker,
after which the state of the course came under suspicion)*

COURT CHARMER 3 b.c. Enchantment 115–Abercourt 89 (Abernant 142) —
[1988 5g 5g 1989 6s 6g a6g] workmanlike colt: well beaten (twice coltish) in varied
events, including seller: trained until after reappearance by M. Usher. *C. C. Elsey.*

COURTESY TITLE (USA) 2 ch.c. (May 1) Golden Act (USA)–Social Registry 81
(USA) (Raise A Native) [1989 5.8h⁵ 7m² 7f* 8.2d³ 8d⁴ 8.5g] $27,000Y: good-bodied
colt: second foal: dam won at around 1m: favourite, comfortable winner of 6-runner
maiden at Brighton in July: beaten about 2½ lengths in minor event at Pimlico and
over 15 lengths behind Go And Go in Grade 2 Laurel Futurity at Laurel (dirt) on last
2 starts: stays 1m: strong-running sort. *P. F. I. Cole.*

COURT TOWN 6 gr.m. Camden Town 125–Luciennes 108 (Grey Sovereign 61
128§) [1988 10.2d 8g* 7m² 7d 8g⁵ 7.6f 8d³ 8m 8m⁴ 7f 1989 8f² 7f 8m 8m² 8m] leggy,
close-coupled mare: has a round action: quite modest handicapper: suited by 1m:
acts on any going: excellent mount for inexperienced rider: sweating second start:
often gets outpaced: has been taken down very quietly. *R. Hannon.*

COURT (USA) 3 ch.f. Devil's Bag (USA)–Queen To Conquer (USA) 112 (King's —
Bishop (USA)) [1988 6m* 6f* 1989 7.2g] rangy filly: useful winner as 2-y-o of
maiden at Yarmouth and listed race at York: 6/1 co-second favourite and taken down
early, ridden along 3f out when well-beaten tenth of 13 in listed race at Haydock in
June, only outing in 1989: bred to be better suited by 7f or 1m. *A. C. Stewart.*

COUTURE INNOVATORS 2 b.c. (May 7) Music Boy 124–Miss Couture 59 —
(Tamerlane 128) [1989 8v a7g] sturdy, lengthy colt: fourth foal: dam won over 13.8f
and 15.8f: behind in minor event and maiden late in year. *P. J. Makin.*

COVE COTTAGE 2 b.f. (Feb 14) Swing Easy (USA) 126–Blue Empress (Blue ?
Cashmere 129) [1989 5g²] 2,500Y: leggy filly: fourth foal: half-sister to 3 winners
here and abroad, including 1m and 1¼m seller winner Miami Blues (by Palm Track)
and 1988 2-y-o plating-class 5f and 5.8f winner Calvanne Miss (by Martinmas): dam
showed no ability: 9/1, ¾-length second of 15, leading inside last furlong, to
stable-companion Osario in maiden auction race at Salisbury in May: sent to race in
Italy and won 7.5f listed race at Rome in September. *R. Hannon.*

COWLEY 4 gr.c. Kalaglow 132–Loralane 86 (Habitat 134) [1988 10v³ 10m* 10.5d⁴ 94
10f* 10.5m³ 1989 14g 10g* 12f 10m⁶] big, angular, rather plain colt: carries

condition: poor walker: won minor event at Pontefract in May for second year running, staying on well to beat Polar Boy ½ length, pair well clear: below form when visored final outing: suited by good gallop at 1¼m: probably unsuited by a soft surface: sold to join J. Glover 26,000 gns Newmarket Autumn Sales: quite useful. *G. Wragg.*

COXANN 3 b.g. Connaught 130–Miss Nelski 84 (Most Secret 119) [1988 8m 1989   **54** 8f6 7m5 8.2f4] good-bodied gelding: carries condition: plating-class maiden: may well stay beyond 1m: has joined J. McConnochie. *I. V. Matthews.*

CRACKLE MOOR 4 b.f. Don 128–Carol Day (Tudor Melody 129) [1988 8d 8g*   **—** 8g3 8.2s3 9g6 11d* 12.3s* 10g3 11s 1989 11v4] lengthy, useful-looking filly: quite modest winner in first half of 1988: favourite, one-paced fourth of 6 in apprentice handicap at Hamilton in April: suited by 1½m: acts on soft going: suitable mount for inexperienced rider. *M. W. Easterby.*

CRAFT EXPRESS 3 b.c. Bay Express 132–Lydia Rose 68 (Mummy's Pet 125)   **101** [1988 5m 5g* 5m 1989 5g* 6d 5m5 5f 5m 5g3 5.6g* 5m3 6v3] compact colt: has a quick action: useful handicapper: won at Doncaster in March and September, on latter occasion showing much improved form to win £25,000 Tote-Portland Handicap by 3 lengths: good third at Ascot and Newbury last 2 outings: best over 5f or stiff 5f: acts on top-of-the-ground and heavy going. *M. Johnston.*

CRAGSIDE 7 b.h. Hot Spark 126–Amerella (Welsh Pageant 132) [1988 6d2 6m4   **—** 6g 5v3 6d 5m5 5m* 5m 5g4 5g* 5g 1989 8g] sturdy horse: smart performer at his best as 3-y-o: bandaged, pulled up badly lame (damaged near-fore tendon) in valuable handicap at Doncaster in April: suited by forcing tactics at 5f and stayed 6f: acted on any going: tried in blinkers: retired to The Hall Stud, Newmarket, fee £250 (July 1) + £500 nfnf (Oct 1). *C. R. Beever.*

CRAIL HARBOUR 3 b.g. Don 128–Broccoli (Welsh Saint 126) [1988 NR 1989   **46** 8f3 8m] IR 9,200Y, 15,000 2-y-o: angular, sparely-made gelding: sixth living foal: brother to 3 Irish 2-y-o winners, including 1984 7f winner Gobolino and 1987 5f winner Dorp, later successful over 7f and 1½m in Ireland and over hurdles: dam won over 7f and 1½m in Ireland and over hurdles: ridden by 7-lb claimer, 4 lengths third of 11, leading over 6f, in seller at Ayr in June: tailed off in claimer following month: has joined M. Johnston. *J. S. Wilson.*

CRAKAFU 3 b.g. Kafu 120–Gayles Bambina 75 (Lord Gayle (USA) 124) [1988 5d   **59** 5g4 6f6 5g* 5m 5g 1989 6s4 5g4 5f3 5m2] rather unfurnished gelding: creditable second in handicap at Catterick in May, best effort as 3-y-o: stays 6f: acts on firm going: tends to hang. *M. H. Easterby.*

CRASHLOCK 3 gr.f. Tyrnavos 129–Alicia Markova 64 (Habat 127) [1988 NR   **—** 1989 11g 12d 12f6] 7,100Y: lengthy, angular filly: sister to 1986 2-y-o 7f and 8.2f winner Trynova and half-sister to 2 winners, including 1987 2-y-o 6f winner Markstyle (by Moorestyle): dam, half-sister to Music Maestro, Saulingo and Outer Circle, ran 3 times at 2 yrs: well beaten in northern maiden events and seller in the spring. *M. Brittain.*

CRAVEN 2 b.c. (Jan 25) Thatching 131–Rustle of Silk 67 (General Assembly   **63 p** (USA)) [1989 7s 6g6] first foal: dam lightly-raced half-sister to very smart middle-distance horse Kirtling and daughter of Irish 1000 Guineas second Silky, a half-sister to Moulton and Freefoot: 6 lengths sixth of 18, no impression last 2f, to Peterhouse in maiden at Redcar in November: will stay 1m: may improve again. *Miss S. E. Hall.*

CRAWLEY 2 b.f. (Mar 27) High Top 131–Version Latine (FR) (Riverman (USA)   **62** 131) [1989 5g3 6g 6g] 290,000 francs (approx £26,500) Y: rather unfurnished filly: looks weak: first foal: dam showed some ability in France: plating-class maiden: best effort on debut: bred to be suited by much further than 5f. *C. F. Wall.*

CRAZY RIVER 2 b.g. (May 12) Vision (USA)–Etty 81 (Relko 136) [1989 8m4 8g5   **60** 8f6] IR 21,000Y: workmanlike gelding: has a round action: fifth foal: half-brother to Belgian 3-y-o winner Night Fighter (by Ela-Mana-Mou), very useful 1988 3-y-o middle-distance filly Miss Boniface (by Tap On Wood), successful at 4 yrs in America, and a winner over hurdles: dam, 1¼m winner, is half-sister to Whip It Quick, a very smart colt in Britain and Germany: quite modest maiden: bred to be suited by 1¼m +. *Mrs J. Pitman.*

CREAKE'S PET 4 b. or br.c. Mummy's Pet 125–Creake 80 (Derring-Do 131)   **—** [1988 7v 7v* 8g5 7.5f 1989 6s 7g 7.2s 6f] leggy, medium-sized ex-Irish colt: third foal: half-brother to 1984 Irish 2-y-o 6f winner Stanhoe (by Star Appeal) and 1m winner Affaire de Coeur (by Imperial Fling): dam, 1½m winner from 3 starts, is daughter of half-sister to Blakeney and Morston: won handicap at Phoenix Park as 3-y-o when trained by D. K. Weld: behind in varied events in spring: stays 7f: acts on any going: blinkered twice at 3 yrs and on final outing (went freely to post): slowly away second start. *J. P. Hudson.*

CREAM AND GREEN 5 b.g. Welsh Chanter 124–Jumana (Windjammer 56 §
(USA)) [1988 8d 8d 7.6v 7g 7f⁶ 8d 6h 10d 6d* 6g 6d³ 5g 6s 6d 6d² 7g 1989 6s 7.5d⁶ 7g
6m a7g⁶ a7g⁵ a8g⁴] leggy, close-coupled, sparely-made gelding: plating-class
handicapper on his day: best at 6f to 1m: suited by plenty of give in the ground:
visored 3 times at 4 yrs: has raced very freely and often wears severe bridle: often
slowly away: unreliable and not to be trusted. *K. White.*

CREATOR 3 ch.c. Mill Reef (USA) 141–Chalon 125 (Habitat 134) [1988 8s 126
7d² 7v* 1989 10s* 12m⁵ 10g³ 10m² 10g* 9.7m*]

Nashwan's defection from the Dubai Champion Stakes left the French
colt Creator ante-post favourite for a couple of days until he, too, went out, as
a result of knocking himself at home. Creator deserved the bookmakers'
respect. He was a very well-bred, fairly lightly-raced, improving three-year-
old, little behind the best over the distance in France on recent form, proven
on the prevailing ground. He'd won his last two races, both Group 2 events,
the Prix Guillaume d'Ornano at Deauville in August and the Ciga Prix Dollar
at Longchamp in October. The subsequent Prix de l'Arc seventh Norberto
finished second at Deauville, beaten a length and a half on merit. A penalty
incurred for winning there resulted in Creator's giving weight all round in the
Dollar; because of that, he hardly seemed an odds-on chance beforehand, but
he won like one, in good style by two lengths from the four-year-old Hello
Calder, dominating from a long way out, stretching the field shortly after
making the home turn and keeping up a strong gallop from there to the line.
There was no suggestion that Creator was flattered by the result, though his
jockey Asmussen, successful in five of the afternoon's races, rightly received
credit for a masterly demonstration of the difficult art of riding in front.

Connections seem satisfied that Creator's right distance is a mile and a
quarter. They tried him over a mile and a half—without his customary
blinkers—in the Prix Hocquart at Longchamp in May following an easy win in
a listed race over a mile and a quarter in testing conditions on the same course
on his season debut, and they've kept him to the shorter distance since.
Creator couldn't be said to have failed miserably in the Hocquart.
Considerably upgraded, he finished fifth of nine to Dancehall, beaten just
under five lengths: he raced close up, came off the bridle before the straight,
then kept on steadily. But he left that form behind next time out when third to
Dancehall in the Grand Prix de Paris Louis Vuitton and never looked back,
though he was beaten again in the Prix Eugene Adam before he went to
Deauville. The fact that Creator's stable-companion River Warden came from
behind to pip him on the post in a slowly-run Eugene Adam suggests a mile
and a quarter could be Creator's minimum. Asmussen's subsequent tactics on
the horse also suggest he at least suspects so, though he reportedly attributed
defeat at Saint-Cloud to Creator's 'failure' to handle the left-hand turns (round
which the horse had been successful in a small field as a two-year-old).

		Never Bend	Nasrullah
	Mill Reef (USA)	(b 1960)	Lalun
	(b 1968)	Milan Mill	Princequillo
Creator		(b 1962)	Virginia Water
(ch.c. 1986)		Habitat	Sir Gaylord
	Chalon	(b 1966)	Little Hut
	(ch 1979)	Areola	Kythnos
		(ch 1968)	Alive Alivo

Creator's dam was a good racemare trained by Cecil. She missed the
Guineas in favour of a seven-furlong event because of a doubt about her
stamina, but subsequently proved well suited by a mile. Her run of six wins in
1982 included the Coronation Stakes and the Child Stakes. Chalon's breeding
rather than her style of running gave rise to the doubt. Her dam Areola never
raced beyond seven furlongs and was a very speedy two-year-old, and
sprinting was also the fourth dam Fluorescent's forte. The majority of
Areola's numerous winning offspring have stayed a mile, some further; the
best of them apart from Chalon, the Irish colt Executive Perk, got a mile and a
quarter, but stable-companion Elegance In Design, Chalon's sister, seems

Ciga Prix Dollar, Longchamp — Creator makes all to win in good style from Hello Calder

best at sprint distances. Chalon produced two foals before Creator, only one of whom, the Irish hurdles winner Sam Weller (by Be My Guest), survived. She wasn't covered in 1986 as Creator is a June foal (the second-last of all Mill Reef's foals); she's since produced fillies by Danzig and Ajdal.

Despite all the pessimism, there should be enough high-class older horses still around to provide competitive middle-distance racing in 1990. The first four in the Champion Stakes remain in training, so does Creator who could have as much improvement in him as any. Granted just normal progress he should win more good races. A short-backed colt, Creator has yet to race. on very firm going but acts on any other. He is best in blinkers. *A. Fabre, France.*

CREDIT LINE (FR) 3 b.f. Young Generation 129–Truly Blest 75 (So Blessed 130) [1988 6m 6g 1989 8f 8f 6g] lengthy, angular filly: poor mover: no worthwhile form in varied events: moved badly to post and withdrawn lame on intended reappearance. *R. Boss.*   —

CREEAGER 7 b.g. Creetown 123–Teenager 71 (Never Say Die 137) [1988 10.2s⁵ 12d* 12.3v³ 12f* 10f⁴ 12m² 12s 12g 12g 1989 10d⁵ 10.2g 12f³ 12.8m a11g a14g⁵ a16g⁴ a14g⁶] lengthy, good-bodied gelding: carries plenty of condition: poor mover: quite modest handicapper: favourite, creditable third, edging left in behind winner having looked sure to get up, at Thirsk in May: virtually pulled up at Ripon 2 weeks later: subsequently off course nearly 6 months, and after only when fourth, weakening final 1f, at Southwell: barely stays 2m: unsuited by soft going, acts on any other: has worn blinkers (did so for first time in long while final outing): has occasionally sweated: best waited with. *J. Wharton.*   62

CREE BAY 10 b.g. Bay Express 132–Porsanger (USA) (Zeddaan 130) [1988 6f² 6m⁵ 5m² 6m⁶ 6m 5m 5m⁵ 5g 6m⁴ 5g 6d 6d 1989 6m³ 5m² 5f³ 5g⁵ 6g 5m 5d a6g] keen walker: quite modest handicapper on his day: effective at 5f and 6f: acts on any going: sometimes blinkered or visored: often slowly away: suited by strong gallop and needs to be produced late: very difficult to win with. *J. L. Spearing.*   57 d

CREE DANCER 2 b.f. (Mar 13) Creetown 123–Marching Dancer (Niniski (USA) 125) [1989 5g 5d⁵ 5g 5g 6g 5f] 600Y: small filly: first foal: dam of no account: bad plater: sold 740 gns Doncaster November Sales. *D. W. Chapman.*   34

CREEFLEUR 3 b.f. Creetown 123–Florence Mary 51 (Mandamus 120) [1988 5s⁵ 5s 5f 1989 6g² 6s* 6g 6f 6g⁴ 7m] workmanlike non-thoroughbred filly: plating-class handicapper: won apprentice race at Folkestone in April: should stay 7f: acts on soft going and probably unsuited by top-of-the-ground. *K. M. Brassey.*   54

CREE LEADER 4 b.g. Creetown 123–Figurehead (Seaepic (USA) 100) [1988 8g 1989 8.2g 8.2d 11s 14g] rangy gelding: little sign of ability. *N. Bycroft.*   —

CRESELLY 2 b.f. (Feb 11) Superlative 118–Gwiffina 87 (Welsh Saint 126) [1989 7m⁵ 7d⁵] rather unfurnished filly: first foal: dam 2-y-o 6f winner stayed 7f, didn't train on: modest form in autumn maiden at Newmarket won by Mukddaam and minor event at Thirsk won by Bold Performer. *I. V. Matthews.*   80

CRETAN BOY 4 b.g. Beldale Flutter (USA) 130–Haida (Astec 128) [1988 8d 8f 10m 9m 7f 7m 8g 10m 8d 1989 7d 8.2v⁶ 6d⁶ 7m⁶ 8f⁶ 8.3g] leggy gelding: poor plater: 34

stays 1m: visored once at 3 yrs: often sweating and edgy: sold to join Miss J. Blakeney 1,950 gns Newmarket Autumn Sales: probably none too genuine. *C. C. Trietline.*

CREVASSE (USA) 3 b.f. Diesis 133–Ice Wave (USA) (Icecapade (USA)) [1988 83 7g 1989 8d⁶ 9m² 10m* 10g a10g] good-topped, attractive filly: moderate walker and mover: 7/1 on, comfortably won maiden at Beverley in August having led 6f out, hung left on turn then right 2f out: off course 3 months then below form in handicaps: will probably stay further: best efforts on top-of-the-ground: sold 23,000 gns Newmarket December Sales. *H. R. A. Cecil.*

CREVE COEUR 4 b.c. Aragon 118–Friths Folly 62 (Good Bond 122) [1988 10s — 11.7m³ 11.7g² 11.7m 1989 11.7m 12f⁶ 11.5f 12m 12.2m⁵ 10.1m4] strong, quite attractive colt: good mover: poor maiden nowadays: not seen out after July: stays 11.7f: acts on top-of-the-ground and heavy going: has appeared headstrong and worn crossed noseband. *S. Dow.*

CRIBELLA (USA) 2 b.f. (Feb 21) Robellino (USA) 127–Crinoline 72 (Blakeney 70 p 126) [1989 7.3v⁵] 36,000Y: first foal: dam, 1½m winner who stayed 2m, is out of half-sister to Shiny Tenth: 33/1, backward and apprentice ridden, around 14 lengths fifth of 12, keeping on, to Berry's Dream in listed race at Newbury in October: should improve. *K. M. Brassey.*

CRICKET BALL (USA) 6 b.h. Olden Times–Caterina 124 (Princely Gift 124 137) [1988 8s 5d³ 7g 7m⁵ 6d⁴ 6.5m⁵ 6m* 6d² 6g⁵ 6g⁴ 7s 1989 5.5s* 5m⁴ 6g² 5g³ 7g⁴ 6d* 6.5d* 6g* 6g² 5g 6s*]

Top French sprinter Cricket Ball's fifth season of racing was his best. He met with considerably more success than in previous years, was out of the frame in just one of his eleven starts, nine of them in pattern races, and, in passing, laid to rest the suggestion that he was incapable of winning away from Deauville. Until 1989 Cricket Ball had done all his winning at the French seaside course's festival meeting. At two he won the Prix des Foals, in each of the next three seasons the Prix de Meautry. Cricket Ball's success in the Prix Cor de Chasse in April was therefore of more significance than might normally be accorded to a listed race at Maisons-Laffitte. When Cricket Ball beat Whippet by half a length in the Prix de Ris-Orangis at Evry in July the notion that there was something special about the Deauville air was all but forgotten; in the end he managed to win across the Atlantic. Notwithstanding,

Prix de Meautry, Deauville—a fourth consecutive win in the race for Cricket Ball who gets up in the final strides to edge out Nabeel Dancer

Cricket Ball's performances at Deauville in 1989 exceeded his previous attainments there and were as good as anything he achieved all season. He won the Prix Maurice de Gheest—his only Group 2 success—by one and a half lengths from Fieldwork and nine days later took the Prix de Meautry yet again, getting up in the final strides to beat Nabeel Dancer by a short neck, in so doing surpassing the feats of Sagaro in the Gold Cup and Sharpo in the William Hill Sprint Championship by winning the same pattern race in four successive years. He was giving Nabeel Dancer 8 lb.

Cricket Ball's trainer had reportedly considered missing the Prix de Meautry in favour of the Ladbroke Sprint Cup, and although the horse eventually took in both races a Group 1 prize remained out of reach. Cricket Ball ran near his best at Haydock but was no match for Danehill, going down by two lengths. A further attempt came to nothing in unfortunate circumstances in the Ciga Prix de l'Abbaye de Longchamp, where he was beaten over six lengths behind Silver Fling. This might seem a modest effort, but Cricket Ball had been unsettled at the stalls. His tail apparently became trapped and as the handlers attempted to force him in Cricket Ball reared and unseated his jockey. Even in a below-standard edition of the Abbaye Cricket Ball had seemed an unlikely winner though. In top company he needed further than five furlongs, though he had run creditably over the minimum distance at Longchamp and Chantilly earlier in the season. The curtain came down on Cricket Ball's long career in the Laurel Dash at Laurel Park, Maryland. The fourteen-runner field contained five European challengers, but it was the home-trained Oraibi that led inside the final furlong until caught by the strong-finishing Cricket Ball who had three quarters of a length to spare at the line. Point of Light was a length away in third. Cricket Ball's victory netted 150,000 dollars (approximately £94,300) for his connections, about £26,000 more than Silver Fling won in the Abbaye and almost £20,000 more than Danehill in the Ladbroke Sprint Cup. And this for a race that did not have graded status! Small wonder that so many were prepared to journey across the Atlantic.

		Relic	War Relic
	Olden Times	(bl 1945)	Bridal Colors
	(b 1958)	Djenne	Djebel
Cricket Ball (USA)		(b 1950)	Teza
(b.h. 1983)		Princely Gift	Nasrullah
	Caterina	(b 1951)	Blue Gem
	(gr 1963)	Radiopye	Bright News
		(gr 1954)	Silversol

French breeders should find Cricket Ball's pedigree attractive. He's a brother to Ancient Regime, the leading French two-year-old filly of 1980 who showed smart form at up to a mile at three, and to Olden, a very useful sprint stakes winner. The dam is also the dam of Mug Punter (by Warfare), a stakes winner at up to nine furlongs, and Firing Squad (by Pronto), successful at a mile and a quarter in France. Caterina's daughters Likely Split (by Little Current) and Close Comfort (by Far North) are dams of winners too, the latter being the dam of Husyan. Caterina was a good five-furlong mare. She won the Nunthorpe as a three-year-old, having finished second in the race at two. On the other hand, her half-brother, the Eclipse winner Scottish Rifle, showed sufficient stamina to win the March Stakes over a mile and three quarters. Their dam Radiopye was a useful performer at six furlongs to a mile. Cricket Ball's sire, the American Olden Times, now dead, is not so well known over here that he needn't be mentioned. He was an enormously versatile performer, winning stakes races at distances from five furlongs to a mile and three quarters; like Cricket Ball he remained in training five seasons. His progeny include numerous graded stakes winners, among them the champion American two-year-old Roving Boy and the good-class winner at up to a mile Vittoriosso, and the prolific sires of winners Full Pocket and Hagley. Olden Times has also an excellent record as a sire of broodmares. Ancient Regime and Olden have both produced winners, the former being the dam of Prix de l'Abbaye runner-up La Grande Epoque and the promising two-year-old Rami. Olden Times also sired the dams of Washington D.C. International winner Johnny D and Japan Cup winner Half Iced.

Mr R. Scully's "Cricket Ball"

Cricket Ball, a small horse, was a credit to his trainer; tough and consistent, he won nine of his forty-four races and came in the frame in another twenty. He tended to get behind in his races, a particular disadvantage at five furlongs, and was best at around six. He acted on any going. Bought for 175,000 dollars as a yearling, he has been retired to the Haras d'Ommeel at a fee of 35,000 francs (approximately £3,500). *J. Fellows, France.*

CRICKET FAN 2 br.c. (Apr 19) Gorytus (USA) 132–Nollet (High Top 131) [1989 6m* 7m 7g 7g] 11,500Y: leggy, sparely-made, angular colt: shows a quick action: first foal: dam won 3 races in Italy: beat Croupier by 3 lengths in slowly-run 2-runner maiden at Ascot in July: well beaten in £15,300 event at York and nurseries at Ascot and Newmarket. *S. Dow.*   **83 ?**

CRIME PASSIONNEL (USA) 4 b.g. Rich Cream (USA)–Fresh And Fancy (Irish Lancer) [1988 11.7g⁶ 13.3d³ 13.1f⁴ 14g⁵ 16f* 16f 18.1m⁶ 16g* 1989 14g⁶ 16g⁶ 17.6f² 19f² 20f⁵ 19f² 16.1m⁶] well-made gelding: has a long stride: modest handicapper: suited by thorough test of stamina: yet to race on soft going, acts on any other: lacks a turn of foot: sold 8,000 gns Newmarket Autumn Sales: game. *P. T. Walwyn.*   **76**

CRIMINAL LAW 2 b.c. (Apr 11) Law Society (USA) 130–Indian Maid 117 (Aztec 128) [1989 8.2d 6g⁶] IR 22,000Y: big, lengthy colt: has scope: has a long stride: half-brother to 6 winners, including very smart French stayer El Badr (by Weavers' Hall) and useful 3-y-o stayer Noble Savage (by Caerleon), 1m winner at 2 yrs: dam, lightly-raced winner at up to 1m, is daughter of half-sister to Irish Derby winner Dark Warrior: under 8 lengths sixth of 7, slowly away, to Montendre in listed race at York in October, better effort: will improve again, particularly when returned to longer. *R. Hollinshead.*   **75 p**

CRIMPSALL 4 b.f. Vaigly Great 127–Janlarmar 69 (Habat 127) [1988 6v* 6m* 51
7v⁴ 6g⁵ 5g³ 5g 6s 6m² 6g 1989 5g⁵ 7s⁶ 6d 6m 6f⁶ 7m³ 6m⁴ 6f 6m 6g] lengthy,
sparely-made filly: tubed: winning plater: stays 7f: yet to show her form on firm
going, acts on any other: has raced with tongue tied down: sometimes sweats, and
has got on edge. *M. W. Easterby.*

CRIMSON GLEN 3 br.f. Glenstal (USA) 118–Crimson Crown (Lord Gayle 43
(USA) 124) [1988 5m 5m² 6m 7f 7m 7g² 6g 1989 8h 7m 8g 12f⁴ 9f⁵ 8.5m⁵ 10.8m 7g²
8m] small filly: poor maiden: probably stays 8.5f: best form with give in the ground:
sometimes blinkered: visored last 2 outings: swishing tail and not looking too keen
on first of them. *J. G. FitzGerald.*

CRISP HEART 5 b.m. Dominion 123–Persevering 95 (Blakeney 126) [1988 30
14.8s 15.5f 13.3m 12m⁵ 12g⁴ 13.1d⁵ 14.5g 14f 1989 10f 15.3m⁵ 12h* 13.1h⁴] small
mare: moderate maiden: won for first time in selling handicap (no bid) at Brighton in
July: suited by 1½m + : acts on any going. *C. P. Wildman.*

CRISPY DUCK 2 b.c. (Mar 24) Reasonable (FR) 119–Kalakan (Kalamoun 129) 59
[1989 5g* 5d² 5d 5m² 6m⁴ 6m 6f* 6g⁶] IR 4,200Y: small, lengthy colt: moderate
mover: third foal: dam, lightly raced, placed over 7.5f at 2 yrs in Ireland: quite
modest performer: won seller (no bid) at Newcastle in March and 4-runner claimer
at Hamilton in July: sweating, ran poorly following month: suited by 6f: visored fifth,
sixth and final outings: of dubious temperament. *C. Tinkler.*

CROFTER'S CLINE 5 b. or br.g. Crofter (USA) 124–Modena (Sassafras (FR) 74
135) [1988 6g⁵ 6g⁵ 5v⁴ 6m 8d⁵ 7m 7g⁴ 7d⁶ 7f 6d⁵ 6g 6g 6m³ 6m⁵ 7g 1989 6m² 6m* 6f
6f* 6f⁶ 6g* 6m² 6m⁶ 7.5m⁵ 7f 6g] strong gelding: modest handicapper nowadays:
successful at Hamilton (twice) and Carlisle in first half of season: best at 6f: acts on
any going: usually blinkered or visored nowadays: apprentice ridden at 5 yrs: sold
11,000 gns Doncaster November Sales. *Capt. J. Wilson.*

CROFTER'S COURT 3 ch.c. Crofthall 110–Northgate Lady 54 (Fordham 46
(USA) 117) [1988 7f⁵ 8.2s⁵ 8m 1989 6s⁶ 7.5d⁵ 8d 7.5d² 8m 7m 8g 8.2d⁵ 11s⁶]
sparely-made colt: modest plater: should stay beyond 1m: seems to need plenty of
give in the ground: blinkered 5 of last 6 outings: isn't an easy ride. *M. Brittain.*

CROFTHALL BLINDER 4 ch.f. Crofthall 110–Blinder (Bing II) [1988 5m 10m —
10.2g 1989 12f a14g] tall, leggy, plain filly: has a round action: poor maiden: has run in
sellers: bandaged, tailed off in handicap at Leicester (on toes, pulled hard) and
claimer at Southwell in August. *T. Kersey.*

CROFT IMPERIAL 2 ch.c. (Mar 11) Crofthall 110–Farinara (Dragonara Palace 96
(USA) 115) [1989 5d* 5d² 5d² 5g² 5f* 5g³ 5f³ 5m³ 5g* 5s⁵] 940F, 6,200Y:
workmanlike, good-quartered colt: keen walker: has a quick action: first foal: dam
unraced daughter of useful soft-ground 5f mare Faridina: fairly useful performer:
successful in minor events at Catterick in March, Ayr in June and Ripon in
September: better efforts when third in listed races at Newmarket and York, and in
nursery at Redcar (saddle slipped) in between: likely to prove best at 5f: seems to
act on any going: blinkered fourth outing: tends to idle. *J. Berry.*

CROFT VALLEY 2 ch.c. (Mar 10) Crofthall 110–Sannavally (Sagaro 133) [1989 64
6f⁶ 6f⁴ 5g] workmanlike colt: first foal: dam ran once: quite modest form in maidens
on first 2 starts: well beaten final outing. *R. M. Whitaker.*

CRONK'S COURAGE 3 ch.g. Krayyan 117–Iresine (GER) (Frontal 122) [1988 —
5g 5g* 6f* 6f 6g⁶ 7s⁵ 1989 6s⁴ 6d⁵ 6m 6m 5f] big, strong, lengthy gelding: has a
quick action: fair winner as 2-y-o: well below form in handicaps in 1989: visored,
showed tremendous early speed third start: always struggling off pace on final one,
in July: stays 7f: acts on any going: has run well for 7-lb claimer. *G. Lewis.*

CRONK'S QUALITY 6 b.g. Main Reef 126–Ozone (Auction Ring (USA) 123) —
[1988 6g 6d* 7m 5m³ 6f 5g³ 6f 5m 6s 6s 6s 1989 5g] small, good-quartered gelding:
moderate mover: fair winner early as 5-y-o: ran only once (July) in 1989: effective at
5f and 6f: seems unsuited by firm going, acts on any other: ran poorly when
blinkered: occasionally on toes: has run well for apprentice: sometimes taken down
early nowadays. *G. Lewis.*

CROSBY 3 b.c. Music Boy 124–Yelney 65 (Blakeney 126) [1988 5g 5g 6f 5f⁴ 6g* 75
6d* 5s² 6m 6s 1989 6s 7s 5f 6m 6f⁵ 7m* 7m a6g⁶ a8g] good-bodied, quite
useful-looking colt: second favourite, showed improved form when making virtually
all to win handicap at Lingfield in September: easily best other efforts as 3-y-o on
fifth and eighth (hampered early) starts: suited by 7f: probably acts on any going:
sometimes on toes: often sweating. *J. W. Payne.*

CROSBY PLACE 3 gr.f. Crooner 119–Royal Bat 69 (Crowned Prince (USA) 128) 58
[1988 5m⁵ 5f 6d 8m 7s 1989 10v 7s⁶ 6f³ 7f⁶ 8f⁴ 7f 7g² 8.2f 7.6m] workmanlike,

221

close-coupled filly: quite modest maiden: stays 1m: easily best efforts on a sound surface: blinkered last 8 outings: bandaged near-hind third and eighth. *M. J. Haynes.*

CROSS MAGS 2 ch.f. (Apr 14) Hasty Word 84–Red Squaw 61 (Tribal Chief 125) **46** [1989 5f3 6m5] 750F: small, stocky, plain filly: sixth foal: half-sister to 3-y-o Art Joy (by Humdoleila): dam of little account: ridden by girl apprentice, poor form in Wolverhampton seller and Leicester maiden in May. *G. Price.*

CROSS RATE 2 gr.g. (Feb 17) Carwhite 127–Fuddled 74 (Malacate (USA) 131) **—** [1989 5d6 6m 8g a8g] 5,200F, 19,000Y: smallish, leggy, close-coupled gelding: second reported foal: dam 1½m winner: poor maiden: blinkered final start: sold 900 gns Ascot December Sales. *J. W. Payne.*

CROSSROAD LAD 3 b.g. Beldale Flutter (USA) 130–Croda Rossa (ITY) (Grey **—** Sovereign 128§) [1988 7g 1989 8g 9s 12s 8m] leggy gelding: moderate walker: no form in varied events: blinkered and tailed off in claimers last 2 starts: sold to join T. Thomson Jones 4,600 gns Ascot 2nd June Sales and afterwards did well over hurdles. *G. Wragg.*

CROSS THE MOAT 5 b.g. Castle Keep 121–Wayleave (Blakeney 126) [1988 **—** 10.8s 12f 10f2 12f5 19f6 12f 10.2h] workmanlike gelding: poor maiden: well beaten in handicaps as 5-y-o, last selling event (blinkered) at Bath: stays 1½m: acts on any going: has pulled hard: sold 2,500 gns Ascot July Sales. *N. R. Mitchell.*

CROUPIER 2 b.c. (Apr 3) Night Shift (USA)–Countess Walewski 85 (Brigadier **93** Gerard 144) [1989 6m2 6m4 7g*] rather leggy, attractive colt: sixth foal: brother to useful 3-y-o Cottenham, fair 7f winner at 2 yrs, and half-brother to fair 1984 2-y-o 6f winner Sparkling Wit (by Sparkler) and a winner in Holland: dam won both her starts, over 1m: put up fairly useful peformance when around 10 lengths fourth of 6 to Balla Cove in Tattersalls Middle Park Stakes at Newmarket, staying on well final furlong having been pushed along after 2f: easy winner of 3-runner private sweepstakes there later in October: will stay 1m: sure to win a maiden. *C. E. Brittain.*

CROWN BALADEE (USA) 2 b. or br.c. (Apr 4) Chief's Crown (USA)– **70** Naseem Baladee 82 (Kris 135) [1989 7.3g4 7m4 8f2] strong, close-coupled, chunky colt: first foal: dam, 6f winner at 2 yrs lightly raced afterwards, is half-sister to very smart 1982 2-y-o sprinter Kafu and smart 7f to 1½m winner Moomba Masquerade: sire champion 2-y-o colt later stayed 1½m: modest maiden: off course 3 months after second outing: stays 1m. *A. A. Scott.*

CROWN CLASS (USA) 2 b.f. (Jan 29) Chief's Crown (USA)–Club Class (USA) **53** 88 (Roberto (USA) 131) [1989 7m6 6f 7f 8.2f6] $240,000Y: sturdy filly: moderate mover: third reported foal: dam, best run at 1½m, is daughter of sister to champion 2-y-o's Bold Lad (USA) and Successor: sire champion 2-y-o later stayed 1½m: plating-class form in varied races: will stay well: blinkered final start. *P. F. I. Cole.*

CROWN CREST 3 ch.f. Mill Reef (USA) 141–Crown Treasure (USA) **91** (Graustark) [1988 NR 1989 10g4 10m2 11.5m2 10m* 11s6] rangy, workmanlike filly: sister to top-class middle-distance stayers Glint of Gold and Diamond Shoal and fair staying handicapper Emerald Point, and half-sister to a disappointing maiden by Troy: dam very useful 2-y-o 5f winner in USA: 11/8 on, won minor event at Sandown in September, leading over 6f out: last of 6 in listed race at Ayr 11 days later: also in frame in quite valuable events at Newmarket (flashing tail) and Ascot and minor event at Sandown: probably stays 11.5f: acts on top-of-the-ground, possibly unsuited by soft: bandaged off-hind. *I. A. Balding.*

CROWN EYEGLASS 3 ch.c. Niniski (USA) 125–Peaceful 92 (Crepello 136) **— §** [1988 NR 1989 12g4 12m4 11f6] 10,000Y: angular, rather unfurnished colt: half-brother to several winners, including useful 7f and 1m winner Romara (by Bold Lad, IRE), dam of Ela Romara: dam, from excellent family, won at up to 1¼m: best effort in maidens on debut: blinkered, took good hold in lead then appeared to try and pull himself up 4f out final start, in June: will be well suited by 1¾m: one to treat with caution. *B. Hanbury.*

CROWNING AMBITION (USA) 2 b.f. (Mar 27) Chief's Crown (USA)– **59** Fabulous Notion (USA) (Somethingfabulous (USA)) [1989 6g 8.2s3 6g6] $230,000Y: leggy, workmanlike filly: second foal: dam top-class stakes winner from 6f to 8.5f: plating-class maiden: wore net muzzle final start: probably stays 1m. *J. Tree.*

CROWNING GLORY 3 ch.g. Be My Guest (USA) 126–Princess Tiara 111 **58 +** (Crowned Prince (USA) 128) [1988 NR 1989 8g 8s 10.2m4 13.3g 16f3] tall, close-coupled gelding: good mover: seventh foal: brother to smart French 7f to 1¼m winner What A Guest and half-brother to 2 winners, including very smart 10.4f winner Infantry (by Northfields), later stakes winner in USA: dam 2-y-o 7f winner who appeared to stay 1¼m at 3 yrs: favourite, first form and probably unlucky when about length third of 5 in moderately-run maiden at Newcastle in July, losing deal of ground when switched 2f out: sold 12,000 gns Newmarket Autumn Sales. *B. W. Hills.*

CROWN JUSTICE 5 b.g. High Top 131–Justicia 87 (Nonoalco (USA) 131) [1988 **38** 7g³ 8d 6g⁴ 7m 8.3m⁶ 8f* 8f² 9m⁵ 8g 8.3m⁶ 8d⁶ 8d 1989 7.5d 10.1m 8m 8.2f² 7f² 8.2g 8.2f³ 8.5m⁵ 9g] small, deep-girthed gelding: moderate mover: poor handicapper: broke leg and destroyed at Wolverhampton in July: stayed 9f: acted on any going: often blinkered. *Mrs N. Macauley.*

CROWTHERS 3 gr.g. Mandrake Major 122–Milnsbridge (Dragonara Palace **69** (USA) 115) [1988 5g⁵ 5g⁵ 5d 5f* 6m* 7g⁴ 7s* 6g³ 7d⁶ 7g⁶ 7m 1989 6s⁵ 7s⁶ 7f⁵ 7f³ 8f 7m² 8f⁴ 8m² 7.6m 8.2f⁴ 6f⁵ 7d² 7g] leggy, plain gelding: moderate walker: has a quick action: modest handicapper: ran creditably when placed: stays 1m well: acts on any going: has run well for a claimer: changed hands 8,200 gns Newmarket Autumn Sales before final start. *E. Weymes.*

CROXDALE GREY 2 gr.f. (Feb 1) Alias Smith (USA)–La Fille 58 (Crooner 119) — [1989 6f 5f⁴] sparely-made filly: fifth foal: half-sister to winning sprinters Spittin Mick (by The Brianstan) and Restless Don (by Mandrake Major): dam 11f seller winner and winning selling hurdler: well beaten in minor event at Ripon in June and maiden (last of 4) at Ayr following month. *J. H. Johnson.*

CRY FOR THE CLOWN 5 b.h. Cawston's Clown 113–Bayberry 77 (Henry The — § Seventh 125) [1988 8d 10d⁵ 9g⁴ 8m 8d 8g 9g 1989 9g 8f] leggy, sparely-made horse: moderate mover: useful at his best: tailed off in Earl of Sefton EBF Stakes at Newmarket and Royal Hunt Cup (Handicap) at Royal Ascot as 5-y-o: best at around 1m: acts on a soft surface and seems unsuited by firm going: often bandaged: often blinkered, visored both starts at 5 yrs: thoroughly inconsistent. *C. Spares.*

CRYPTIC GIRL 2 b.f. (Mar 24) Tower Walk 130–Lucky Saran 72 (Lucky **32** Wednesday 124) [1989 5f 6m⁶ 6g] sparely-made filly: first foal: dam plater suited by 1m, is half-sister to useful sprinter Cyril's Choice: poor form in sellers and a claimer: off course 4 months after debut. *W. J. Pearce.*

CRYPTO 3 b.f. Bold Lad (IRE) 133–Cryptomeria 86 (Crepello 136) [1988 NR 1989 **60** 8m 12m 10.2f⁴ 10.2f] angular filly: sixth foal: half-sister to 1985 2-y-o 6f winner Stedham (by Jaazeiro) and a winner in Italy by Habat: dam middle-distance winner: quite modest form in maidens: well beaten facing stiff task in apprentice handicap final start: probably stays 1½m: sold 20,000 gns Newmarket Autumn Sales. *H. Candy.*

CRYSTAL BEAM 2 b.c. (Feb 25) Crystal Glitters (USA) 127–Jem Jen 85 (Great **85** Nephew 126) [1989 6f⁴ 7.3g* 7m⁵ 8.5g⁴ 7g] 18,000Y: quite good-topped colt: half-brother to French 3-y-o 8.2f winner Jane's Nephew (by Kings Lake), 11.5f winner Northern Moon (by Ile de Bourbon) and 2 other winners: dam 1¼m winner: fair performer: won £6,300 event at Newbury in June by 5 lengths from Batzushka: fair fourth to Toast The Host in nursery at Epsom in August, best subsequent effort: blinkered in GPA National Stakes final start: probably stays 8.5f. *P. A. Kelleway.*

CRYSTAL HEIGHTS 3 ch.g. Wolver Heights 99–Crystal's Solo (USA) — § (Crystal Water (USA)) [1988 7g⁴ 7m* 8.2m 7m 1989 7f 8f 9f 14f 12f³] quite modest form when winning claimer as 2-y-o: modest third in Salisbury claimer in August, taking keen hold and finding little: should be suited by further than 7f: seems unsuited by firm ground: sometimes sweating: blinkered, edgy and seemed to take little interest final start at 2 yrs: won listed race over hurdles on soft ground for Mrs J. Retter. *L. G. Cottrell.*

CRYSTAL PARK 3 b.f. Head For Heights 125–So Precise (FR) (Balidar 133) **64** [1988 NR 1989 9f 10.2m 11g a14g² a14g] workmanlike filly: form only when beaten neck in claimer at Southwell in November: backward previously, off course 5 months after second start. *J. Wharton.*

CRYSTAL POOL 3 b.f. Taufan (USA) 119–Watermark 83 (Henry The Seventh **53** 125) [1988 NR 1989 7g 7f 7m⁶ 7.6m⁶ 8.2g⁵ a8g* a7g] 56,000Y: small, good-quartered filly: half-sister to several winners, notably smart miler Spanish Pool (by Gay Fandango), subsequently a very good winner in South Africa: dam, 2-y-o 1m winner, is closely related to smart middle-distance performer Entanglement: won maiden at Southwell in November: faced very stiff task in handicap there 10 days later: stays 1m: needs give in the ground: blinkered second and third starts. *M. A. Jarvis.*

CRYSTAL SPIRIT 2 b.c. (Jan 28) Kris 135–Crown Treasure (USA) (Graustark) — [1989 7m⁶] tall, rangy, good-looking colt: has plenty of scope: half-brother to several winners, notably top-class middle-distance stayers Diamond Shoal and Glint of Gold (both by Mill Reef): dam very useful at 2 yrs in USA when winner over 5f: 8/1 and carrying condition, tailed off from halfway in £8,300 event at Newbury in July. *I. A. Balding.*

CRYSTAL SPRAY 3 b.f. Beldale Flutter (USA) 130–Crystal Fountain (Great **75** Nephew 126) [1988 NR 1989 10g 12g 10m⁶ 10.4m² 10g⁵ a12g² a13g³ a12g] medium-sized filly: fourth foal: half-sister to one-time quite useful 1¼m winner Flood Mark (by High Line): dam once-raced half-sister to Royal Palace: modest form in handicaps fourth to seventh starts: should prove better at 1½m than 1¼m: has run creditably for 7-lb claimer. *H. Candy.*

CRYSTAL SPRITE 3 b.f. Crystal Glitters (USA) 127–Leprechaun Act (USA) **68** (Forli (ARG)) [1988 5f 6m² 6d⁵ 1989 6h⁵ 6f⁵ 5f³ 6g⁴ 5m 5m 5f* 5s a6g] leggy, light-framed filly: modest performer: blinkered, won handicap at Wolverhampton in October, checked 1f out then leading on post: ran moderately otherwise after third start: stays 6f: acts on firm going, possibly unsuited by soft surface: sold 5,400 gns Newmarket December Sales. *Lord John FitzGerald.*

C SHARP 2 ch.g. (Apr 29) Song 132–Simply Jane (Sharpen Up 127) [1989 5g³ 5g⁶ **59** 5g³] 16,500Y: compact, rather sparely-made gelding: shows a quick action: half-brother to 2 winners, including fair sprinter Jondebe Boy (by John de Coombe): dam never ran: plating-class form in maidens and a minor event: gelded after final outing. *K. M. Brassey.*

CULLINAN (USA) 2 b.c. (Jan 27) Diamond Prospect (USA)–Meshuggenah **107** (Sharpen Up 127) [1989 7m³ 6d* 7g² 7g] $18,000F, IR 50,000Y: well-made, attractive colt: first foal: dam unraced daughter of very useful 6f to 1¼m winner Foiled Again: odds on following most promising debut, won maiden at Goodwood in September comfortably by 6 lengths: ran well when 3 lengths second of 20 to The Caretaker in Cartier Million at Phoenix Park and around 4 lengths last of 7 to Dashing Blade in Three Chimneys Dewhurst Stakes at Newmarket following month: will stay 1m. *L. M. Cumani.*

CUMBRIAN EXPRESS 4 b.g. Bay Express 132–Astral Suite 82 (On Your — Mark 125) [1988 5m⁵ 6g³ 5m² 5f 6m⁶ 6f* 6g³ 6g⁴ 5m* 6g³ 5f 5f³ 6g⁴ 5m 1989 6d 5f 5f] strong, quite attractive gelding: carries condition: usually unimpressive in coat: poor mover: fair winner as 3-y-o: below form in first half of 1989: effective at 5f and 6f: has won on firm going, but given impression ill at ease on it: usually blinkered. *M. H. Easterby.*

CUMBRIAN MELODY 3 gr.f. Petong 126–Avahra 108 (Sahib 114) [1988 5m⁴ **82** 6m² 5g* 6g² 6d* 1989 6d 6m³ 6m⁵ 5g² 6f 6f 6g 6g] lengthy, good-quartered filly: fair handicapper: may prove suited by 6f: acts on top-of-the-ground and a soft surface: sold 14,500 gns Newmarket December Sales. *M. H. Easterby.*

CUMBRIAN SINGER 2 b.g. (May 2) Chief Singer 131–Bloomsday 69 (Sparkler **70** 130) [1989 6f⁴ 6g⁴ 5g³ 7m 7v 6g] rather leggy, good-topped gelding: has scope: moderate mover: second foal: dam 9f winner: modest maiden: below form last 2 starts: subsequently gelded: stays 7f: races keenly. *M. H. Easterby.*

CUMBRIAN WALTZER 4 b.g. Stanford 121§–Mephisto Waltz 98 (Dancer's **99** Image (USA)) [1988 6m⁵ 7d 5g³ 5m 5s³ 5m⁶ 5m* 5f² 5d* 1989 5g⁵ 5m⁵ 6m⁵ 6f³ 5m² 5m⁵ 6f 5g⁵ 6m³ 6m⁵ 5m* 5g* 5m²] leggy gelding: good mover: favourite, always close up when winning claimers at Sandown in September: ran well vast majority of other starts, on last short-head second to Lugana Beach in £16,300 handicap at Ascot: ideally suited by 6f or stiff 5f: acts on any going: blinkered once at 3 yrs: has sweated: has run creditably for apprentice: game and consistent. *M. H. Easterby.*

CUM LAUDE 2 b.f. (Apr 21) Shareef Dancer (USA) 135–With Distinction (USA) **61** p (Distinctive (USA)) [1989 8g] 145,000F: big, rangy filly: has plenty of scope: seventh foal: half-sister to 3-y-o High Repute (by Shirley Heights) and to 3 winners abroad, notably high-class French 7f to 9f winner Procida (by Mr Prospector): dam won 7 times at up to 7f: 7/2 and green, 7 lengths eighth of 16, fading from 2f out and not knocked about, to High Beacon in maiden at Leicester in November: sure to improve. *H. R. A. Cecil.*

CUMLODEN 3 ch.g. Creetown 123–Melinda Jane (Compensation 127) [1988 5g — 1989 8m 8m 7m] no worthwhile form, including in seller (bandaged behind) final start: has joined C. Wildman. *R. Hannon.*

CUP OF TRICKS (USA) 2 br.f. (Feb 20) Clever Trick (USA)–Cup of Honey **83** (USA) (Raise A Cup (USA)) [1989 5m³ 6g* 7h² 7m 8g³] $72,000Y: close-coupled filly: fourth named foal: half-sister to 2 minor winners in USA: dam winner at up to 9f, including minor stakes: made all in 5-runner maiden at Ayr in July: fair form when placed in nursery at Brighton (caught on line) and listed event at Newmarket following month: stays 1m. *B. Hanbury.*

CURIA REGIS (USA)   2 b.c. (Apr 10) Deputy Minister (CAN)–Katie Cochran (USA) (Roberto (USA) 131) [1989 6m* 6f² 7m* 7g³] $95,000Y: medium-sized, attractive colt: good mover: fifth foal: half-brother to a minor winner in USA: dam, winner at around 6f, is half-sister to Oaks third Ludham, subsequently smart grass performer in USA, and very useful 1m to 1¼m winner Indus Warrior: successful in maiden at Newbury in July and nursery at Chester in September: looked and ran very well when under 3 lengths third of 7, keeping on strongly, to Free At Last in listed race at Newmarket in October: will be suited by 1m: progressing well. *Major W. R. Hern.*   **98 p**

CURIOUS FEELING   3 gr.f. Nishapour (FR) 125–Noirima 110 (Right Track 131) [1988 NR 1989 10g5 10s 10g 8.2m 10f5] 5,000Y: leggy, angular filly: half-sister to 1984 2-y-o 1m winner Asticot (by Posse), 1m and 1¼m winner Noirio (by Blakeney) and 1989 Italian middle-distance winner Neorama (by Touching Wood): dam best at up to 1m: poor maiden: easily best effort on debut: sold to join J. Bosley 2,000 gns Newmarket Autumn Sales. *C. A. Cyzer.*   **45**

CURRAGH CADET   4 ch.g. Sandhurst Prince 128–Dunstells (Saint Crespin III 132) [1988 NR 1989 9.5m³ 11.7g] workmanlike ex-Irish gelding: half-brother to several winners, including 1981 Irish 2-y-o 5f winner Red Jersey (by Red Alert): dam ran twice: never-nearer third of 11 in maiden at Dundalk in May: well tailed off final 3f in claimer at Windsor 3 months later: trained until after reappearance by K. Connelly. *D. R. Gandolfo.*   **53**

CURRANT OFFER   3 ro.f. Sayf El Arab (USA) 127–Raise The Offer 76 (Auction Ring (USA) 123) [1988 NR 1989 9m5 10m5 6f] first foal: dam stayed well: no sign of ability in minor events and maiden, hanging right throughout final start: sold 1,050 gns Ascot October Sales. *K. M. Brassey.*   **—**

CURTAIN CALL   3 ch.c. Final Straw 127–Hathaway (Connaught 130) [1988 6m 6g³ 7s⁴ 1989 10g⁴ 8f 7g³ 8f² 8m² 7m² 7h* 7f³ 8f* 8f* 8g* 9g] strong colt: has scope: progressive form in second half of season when winning maiden at Brighton and handicaps at Chepstow, Bath and York: never dangerous facing stiff task in £15,400 handicap at Newmarket final start: races keenly, and best at 7f or 1m: acts on any going: blinkered third start. *P. J. Makin.*   **93**

CURVED BLADE (FR)   2 ch.c. (May 12) Kris 135–Kaliopa (FR) (Zeddaan 130) [1989 5m² 6g² 6g* 7m²] rather leggy, attractive colt: has scope: half-brother to several winners in France, notably smart 1m to 1¼m performer Katowice (by Targowice): dam won twice at up to 1¼m: fair performer: favourite, won maiden at Haydock by a length from Kadim, making all: good second to Premiere Moon in nursery at Yarmouth later in August: will stay at least 1m: races keenly. *J. Gosden.*   **87**

CUSTARD PIE   2 b.f. (Feb 15) Castle Keep 121–Pirate Queen 77 (Pirate King 129) [1989 8f 7f] smallish, sparely-made filly: turns off-fore out: half-sister to 3 winners, notably Goodwood Cup winner Tug of War (by Reliance II): dam placed over 7f at 2 yrs: soundly beaten in October maidens at Brighton and Leicester: bred to stay well. *R. Akehurst.*   **—**

CUT A CAPER   7 b.g. Gay Fandango (USA) 132–Brilliant Gem 83 (Charlottown 127) [1988 NR 1989 10s² 12s6 10f² 10h5 10.2h² 10m*] small gelding: poor mover: poor handicapper: won slowly-run apprentice event at Lingfield in June: stays 1¼m well: probably acts on any going: ran freely in blinkers. *R. J. O'Sullivan.*   **46**

CUT AHEAD   3 b.f. Kalaglow 132–Cut Loose 118 (High Top 131) [1988 8m² 9g⁴ 1989 12g⁴ 16m6 10f* 10m² 10.2f] angular, rather unfurnished filly: considerably handled when winning strongly-run maiden at Chepstow in July, leading inside final 1f: made most both starts after, easily better effort when creditable second of 3 in minor event at Chepstow: bred to stay 1½m, but races keenly and suited by shorter: acts on firm going: very reluctant to go down final outing. *Major W. R. Hern.*   **85**

C U TECHNIMECH   3 b.f. Chukaroo 103–Karyobinga 66 (So Blessed 130) [1988 6m⁴ 7g 7g 1989 6f] lengthy, good-topped filly: form in sellers as 2-y-o only on debut: well beaten in handicap in June, only outing in 1989: will prove best at sprint distances. *M. W. Eckley.*   **—**

CUTE ENCHANTRESS   2 b.f. (May 9) Enchantment 115–Chalk Your Cue (Pals Passage 115) [1989 5d] dipped-backed, sparely-made filly: third foal: dam winning Irish hurdler: 33/1, backward and green, soon behind in 10-runner maiden at Bath in April. *T. B. Hallett.*   **—**

CUTLASS PRINCESS (USA)   2 b.f. (Apr 22) Cutlass (USA)–T N T Gal (USA) (Baldski (USA)) [1989 5g5 6f⁴ 7m 8.5f] $40,000Y: smallish, sparely-made filly: third   **41**

foal: half-sister to a winner in North America: dam, ran 5 times, is half-sister to Green's Gambados, good class at up to 1¼m: sire won from 6f to 8.5f: poor form in maidens. *S. G. Norton.*

CUTTING NOTE (USA)   2 ch.c. (Feb 22) Diesis 133–Hasty Key (USA) (Key **103** To The Mint (USA)) [1989 6g² 7m* 8g⁵] 110,000Y: quite attractive colt: second foal: half-brother to 3-y-o Hasty Vessel (by Raise A Cup), modest 7f winner at 2 yrs: dam minor winner at up to 9f in USA: won maiden at Newmarket by 2 lengths from Dara Dee: on toes, around 8 lengths last of 5 to Be My Chief in Racing Post Trophy at Newcastle later in October, hard ridden 2f out and soon beaten: stays 1m. *G. A. Huffer.*

CUT UP ROUGH   5 b.g. Mummy's Pet 125–Albany 120 (Pall Mall 132) [1988 6s   **64** 7g 6m 1989 6v 8d 6f⁴ 5.8h⁴ 6f³ 6f⁵ 6m⁴ 6g 6f* 5m 7m] leggy, quite attractive gelding: well-backed favourite: won maiden claimer at Chepstow (edgy and sweating) in July: always behind in handicaps (blinkered in first) following month: suited by 6f: acts on firm going: apprentice ridden second to fourth outings: inconsistent. *L. G. Cottrell.*

CUVA   4 b.g. Cure The Blues (USA)–Vaguely Mine 90 (Silly Season 127) [1988 10s   — 12g⁵ 10g⁵ 12m 11.7g³ 13.1f³ 12d² 14g³ 12m 12m⁴ 12g 16d 1989 15.5s³ 14g] tall, quite attractive gelding: has a round action: poor and inconsistent maiden: pulled up lame at Salisbury in May, and wasn't seen out again: possibly best at up to 1¾m: acts on top-of-the-ground and a soft surface: tends to wander, and probably needs strong handling. *S. Dow.*

CUVEE CHARLIE   5 b.h. Treboro (USA) 112–Opal Fancy 83 (Kibenka 119)   **83** [1988 8d* 8d 8m³ 10f⁶ 8f 8g 8g⁵ 8m* 9g 8d 8s⁵ 8g⁶ 1989 8g 8d⁵ 8s 8.2g 8f³ 8m 8g 8d 10g] good-topped horse: poor mover: fair handicapper on his day: 33/1, good third of 27 to True Panache in Royal Hunt Cup (Handicap) at Royal Ascot: ran poorly next outing and off course nearly 4 months afterwards: suited by stiff 1m: acts on any going: blinkered twice at 4 yrs: sometimes sweats: goes well on straight track: suited by good gallop: inconsistent. *H. J. Collingridge.*

CUVEE ROSE   2 b.f. (May 21) Lafontaine (USA) 117–Champers Club (Run The   **64** Gantlet (USA)) [1989 6m 6f² 6g³ 7m 7m* 8g* 8f] small, leggy filly: first living foal: dam placed at 10.1f on flat, winning selling hurdler: useful plater: successful at Thirsk (no bid) and Leicester (bought in 4,200 gns after beating Foreign Currency gamely by ½ length in nursery) in September: will be well suited by 1¼m. *C. E. Brittain.*

D

DAARIK   2 b.c. (Apr 26) Diesis 133–Bay Street 114 (Grundy 137) [1989 6f* 7m* **107** 6f* 6g* 6g²] 240,000Y: leggy, rather shallow-girthed colt: has a fluent, round

Golden Gates Nursery, Ascot—Daarik (noseband) keeps on strongly to win from the blinkered Corrin Hill

action: closely related to fairly useful 1987 2-y-o 7f winner Bay Shade (by Sharpen Up) and half-brother to 3-y-o 1m to 10.5f winner Bex (by Explodent) and 2 winners by Alleged, including fair 9f and 1¼m winner Bird Point: dam won at 7f and 8.5f: useful colt: successful in maiden at Redcar in June, minor events at Chester (looked ill at ease on track) and Thirsk in July and a valuable nursery (by 2 lengths from Corrin Hill, keeping on strongly) at Ascot in September: beaten 1½ lengths by Montendre in listed race at York on final outing: will prove better suited by 7f than 6f. *H. Thomson Jones.*

DAARKOM 6 b.g. Be My Guest (USA) 126–Lady Regrets (FR) (Sir Gaylord) — [1988 14d³ 20f 14v² 15.5s 1989 16f⁴ 14d] lengthy, useful-looking gelding: poor mover: very useful at his best: well below form, though shaped quite well under unsuitable conditions, when fourth to Sadeem in Mappin & Webb Henry II EBF Stakes at Sandown in May: well beaten in Jefferson Smurfit Irish St Leger at the Curragh 4 months later: suited by further than 1½m and stays 2m: gives strong impression not at ease on top-of-the-ground and very well suited by the mud: not easy to train. *A. C. Stewart.*

DAAWI 2 ch.c. (Apr 12) Doulab (USA) 115–Natural Sunshine (Manado 130) [1989 93 5.1m⁶ 6f³ 5m* 5.8f² 5m* 6g² 5d] 22,000Y: close-coupled, well-made colt: turns off-fore in: good mover: third foal: half-brother to 3-y-o Britannia Venture and Irish 1m and 9f winner Natural Lad (both by Kafu): dam Irish 7f winner at 3 yrs: fairly useful performer: successful in maiden at Windsor in July and nursery at Goodwood following month: showed further improvement when beaten 1½ lengths by Star Hill in listed race at Kempton: last of 8 in listed race in Ireland on final start: stays 6f: sold to race in Italy 41,000 gns Newmarket Autumn Sales. *A. A. Scott.*

DADDY'S DARLING 4 b.f. Mummy's Pet 125–Annie Get Your Gun 69 44 (Blakeney 126) [1988 8f 8f 8.3d⁴ 10g* 10g 12m⁴ 11.5f 10g⁴ 10m* 10g 10d⁶ 1989 12m 10f⁶ 10f 10m³ 10h² 12f⁴ 12m³ 12m³ 12g⁶ 12g⁴] small, sparely-made filly: moderate plater: stays 1½m: acts on hard going and a soft surface: effective with or without blinkers or visor: has run creditably for apprentice: trained until after third outing by G. Blum. *J. T. Gifford.*

DAFFODIL FIELDS 4 ch.f. Try My Best (USA) 130–Water Frolic (USA) 92 — (Sir Ivor 135) [1988 10m 8d 12m⁶ 12m 14f 10g³ 12g² 16v 12s⁵ 1989 10.2g] small, angular filly: half-sister to quite modest 7f winner Watered Silk (by Kris): dam, daughter of 1000 Guineas winner Waterloo, stayed 1¼m: placed 6 times in Ireland: went freely to post, well beaten in maiden at Doncaster in March: stays 1½m (out of depth over 2m): probably acts on firm going: blinkered twice: sometimes ridden by 7-lb claimer. *J. Mackie.*

DAILY SPORT SOON 4 b.c. Star Appeal 133–Pritillor 93 (Privy Councillor 88 d 125) [1988 10d* 12g 12m³ 12m⁵ 11.5g* 11.7g* 12m* 11.7m⁴ 13.3f³ 16g³ 14d* 12m 1989 14f² 16g 12.3g⁴ 16.1m 14.8m⁶ 14.6g⁶ 13.3m] small, sparely-made colt: fair handicapper: facing stiff task, very good second to Run High at Sandown in May: well below that form afterwards: effective at 1½m in strongly-run race and stays 2m: acts on firm going and a soft surface: winning hurdler. *J. R. Jenkins.*

DAIRA FORT (USA) 3 b.c. Nureyev (USA) 131–Lady B Gay (USA) (Sir 78 Gaylord) [1988 8m 1989 10g 10s 14f⁴ 14f* 14m* 14f³ 14m⁴] lengthy, medium-sized, quite attractive colt: good walker: moderate mover: modest handicapper: justified favouritism at Nottingham in June and Yarmouth (moved poorly down) in July: shapes like a thorough stayer: acts on firm going: sold 29,000 gns Newmarket Autumn Sales. *A. C. Stewart.*

DAISY GIRL 3 b.f. Main Reef 126–Mellow Girl 88 (Mountain Call 125) [1988 NR 52 + 1989 10.2g 10.4m⁵ 8m² 10.6d] sturdy, workmanlike filly: fifth foal: half-sister to staying maiden Kirsheda (by Busted) and plating-class 9.4f winner Riva Renald (by Try My Best): dam 5f and 6f winner at 2 yrs: held up in rear long way when strong-finishing second of 6 in maiden at Edinburgh in July: bred to stay 1¼m but may prove best at slightly shorter: possibly unsuited by a soft surface. *J. Mackie.*

DAISY MILLER 4 b.f. Daring March 116–Holiday Season 60 (Silly Season 127) — [1988 8g² 10g 7f 7d 8m 8m 9g⁶ 1989 8f 12.5f] tall, rather unfurnished filly: no form since first outing at 3 yrs: tailed off in selling handicaps in autumn: stays 1m: blinkered once at 3 yrs and on final outing. *M. Castell.*

DAISYS DELIGHT 3 ch.g. Sandhurst Prince 128–Dunstells (Saint Crespin III — 132) [1988 8m 1989 10.1m 14m 10.1m] small, leggy, sparely-made gelding: no sign of ability. *J. White.*

DAISY WHEEL 2 ch.f. (Apr 8) Doulab (USA) 115–Princesse Anglaise (Crepello 68 136) [1989 5f⁵ 6m⁵ 6m³ 6h⁴ 6f* 6m* 7m 6f 6g⁴ 6m⁴] 15,000F, 12,500Y: lengthy, angular filly: moderate mover: half-sister to 3-y-o Salmon Prince (by Salmon Leap) and 2 winners abroad: dam unraced half-sister to Irish Derby winner English Prince: modest performer: successful in summer in claiming race (easily) and a nursery (sweating and on toes) at Nottingham: ran well in nurseries at Newmarket on last 2 starts: suited by 6f: sold 11,500 gns Newmarket December Sales. *A. Hide.*

DAKIN BROOK 2 b.f. (Apr 5) Prince Ragusa 96–Minster Melody 73 (Highland — p Melody 112) [1989 8f] 1,500Y: second reported foal: half-sister to 3-y-o Midweek Chorus (by Lucky Wednesday): dam won 7f seller: 100/1, over 13 lengths seventh of 15, some late headway, to Karazan in maiden auction event at Redcar in October: may do better. *S. G. Norton.*

DALBY DANCER 5 b.m. Bustiki–Wensum Girl (Ballymoss 136) [1988 10g 10g 71 12m³ 10s* 10m 10m 10s 1989 14.8d* 16.2g* 15.8m² 14m* 10.6g⁶ 12g² 16.2g⁵ 14.8f* 14g⁵ 16f⁴ 14f⁴ 14g 14f³] rather leggy, workmanlike mare: modest handicapper: had good season, winning at Warwick (twice), Beverley and Nottingham: needs strong gallop over 1½m and stays 2m: acts on any going: has won for apprentice: tough and consistent. *B. A. McMahon.*

DALE PARK 3 b.c. Kampala 120–Coshlea 63 (Red Alert 127) [1988 5s 5v* 5m⁶ 79 ? 6g⁵ 7g⁵ 7g⁵ 8s 8.2s³ 8v* 7g⁵ 1989 10v³ 10.6s² 8.2g² 11m³ 10.2f 9m 11s 10s⁵ 12g 13v* a12g] leggy, sparely-made colt: has a round action: fair handicapper: easily best effort after fourth start when winning claimer at Ayr in October: stays 13f: acts on any going, with possible exception of very firm: best efforts when ridden up with pace: game: winning novice hurdler. *N. Tinkler.*

DALESIDE LADYBIRD 3 b.f. Tolomeo 127–Dawn Redwood 63 (Mummy's 66 Pet 125) [1988 5d 5m⁴ 5g 6f⁶ 7f 6s 6f* 5g 5m 1989 7f⁶ 7.5f⁶ 6f 6f² 5m⁴ 8.5g 6g⁴ 6f³ 5f 7g 6f² 7d 7g] rather leggy, good-topped filly: has a round action: quite modest handicapper: 20/1, won by short head at Redcar in October on eleventh outing but demoted for interference: generally below that form otherwise as 3-y-o: best at 6f or 7f: goes well on firm ground: suitable mount for 7-lb claimer: takes good hold: often sweating. *T. Fairhurst.*

DALLAS FAB 2 b.g. (Feb 17) Pas de Seul 133–Sun Lassie (FR) (King Emperor — (USA)) [1989 7m 8m] IR 6,000F, IR 10,000Y: stocky gelding: sixth foal: half-brother to 7f winner Tocave (by Northern Dancer) and 1m claimer winner Sonoma Mission (by Glenstal): dam of no account in Ireland: backward, well beaten in maidens at Newmarket: swerved stalls on debut. *E. Eldin.*

DALLYA 2 b.f. (Feb 3) Doulab (USA) 115–Allya (USA) 74 (Little Current (USA)) — [1989 5h⁶ 6g 5f] 4,600Y: smallish, good-quartered filly: second foal: dam stayed 7f: well beaten in maiden and sellers: trained on debut by J. Berry: blinkered second outing: sold 950 gns Ascot October Sales. *R. O'Leary.*

DALMAHOY 4 ch.g. Ela-Mana-Mou 132–Abbeydale 110 (Huntercombe 133) — [1988 10g⁵ 10f⁴ 1989 8m 9f 12.3m] good-topped, angular gelding: has a quick action: quite modest maiden: well beaten in handicaps in first half of 1989: has given impression barely stays 1¼m: takes a good hold, and has worn a severe bridle. *J. W. Watts.*

DAL MISS 2 b.f. (Apr 1) Dalsaan 125–Loyal And Regal 51 (Royal And Regal — (USA)) [1989 5m] workmanlike filly: fourth reported foal: half-sister to 4-y-o 1m and 1¼m winner Cool Run (by Deep Run) and fair sprinter Tax Roy (by Dublin Taxi): dam winning selling hurdler: 33/1 and backward, slowly away, ran green and always behind in maiden at Chester in September. *R. E. Peacock.*

DALSANNA 2 ch.f. (Mar 18) Dalsaan 125–Half Chance 65 (Sandford Lad 133) 46 [1989 6m⁵ 6f⁴ 6m 6m³ 7m⁴] IR 1,200F, IR 1,500Y: sparely-made filly: poor mover: second foal: half-sister to a winner in Belgium: dam 2-y-o 5f seller winner later successful in Belgium: modest plater: ran well for 7-lb claimer fourth start: suited by 7f: sold 2,000 gns Doncaster November Sales. *M. Brittain.*

DALSTON 2 ch.c. (Feb 12) Dalsaan 125–So Generous (Young Generation 129) 57 [1989 5f 5g⁴ 6m⁴ 5f⁴ 5.3h³ 5m⁴ 5g* 5g⁴ 5m⁵ 5f² 5g] 5,200Y, 7,400 2-y-o: small colt: poor mover: first foal: dam unraced daughter of sister to Yorkshire Oaks winner Outcrop: plating-class performer: ridden by 7-lb claimer, won nursery at Wolverhampton in September by a neck: ran well in similar events on next 3 starts: worth another try at 6f: ran moderately when blinkered: sold 9,500 gns Doncaster November Sales. *R. Guest.*

D'ALTAGNAN 3 ch.g. Dalsaan 125–Fresh As A Daisy (Stanford 121§) [1988 6f 68 6d 1989 8h³ 6m³ 7m* 7f³ 8.3m⁴ 7g² 7.6f³ a8g a7g] workmanlike gelding: quite modest handicapper: won at Sandown in July: suited by 7f: acts on firm going: ran creditably for 7-lb claimer at Folkestone fourth start, but didn't handle bends well then and has looked unsuited by track at Brighton. *R. Hannon.*

DAMANOUR (USA) 3 gr.g. Lypheor 118–Damana (FR) (Crystal Palace (FR) **65** 132) [1988 NR 1989 8m⁶ 14g] good-bodied gelding: first foal: dam won from 1m to 1¾m in France: bit backward, over 7 lengths sixth of 9, staying on well despite running green, in maiden at York in September: sold out of L. Cumani's stable 13,500 gns Newmarket September Sales then soundly beaten in competitive minor event in November. *G. Richards.*

DAMART (USA) 5 b.g. Verbatim (USA)–Ice Wave (USA) (Icecapade (USA)) **30** [1988 8g 9d 9f⁶ 12g³ 12f* 12g 13g⁵ 12g 12g 12f9s⁶ 12f 13.8g 12g 1989 10v 12m 12m³ 12.3m 12g⁴ 12f⁴ 12m 11s a11g⁴] neat gelding: moderate mover: poor handicapper nowadays: stays 1½m: acts on any going: visored 4 times, blinkered once: has won for lady: pulled hard seventh start: inconsistent. *M. P. Naughton.*

DAMASKEEN (USA) 3 b.g. Caveat (USA)–Double Damask (USA) (Damascus **67** (USA)) [1988 5m³ 6m⁴ 5m³ 5g 5g⁵ 5f⁴ 1989 6f 6m⁶ 6g⁴ 6m² 5m⁵ 6g 5m* 5f³ 6m] compact gelding: has a quick, fluent action: quite modest handicapper: won apprentice race at Goodwood in August: good third at Salisbury: speedy, and should prove suited by 5f: acts on firm going: sometimes sweats: often claimer ridden. *Mrs S. Armytage.*

DAME ELUSIVE 3 b.f. Blakeney 126–Girl On A Swing 79 (High Top 131) [1988 **78** 7s 6m³ 1989 9g 10f 10.2f⁶ 11m⁵ 13f² 14.8f³ 14f⁵ 14g* 16m²] lengthy, workmanlike filly: poor mover: modest handicapper: won at Sandown in September: ridden by 5-lb claimer, ran well starts either side in £12,000 contest at York and £7,400 race at Newmarket: stays 2m: acts on firm ground: usually held up: lacks turn of foot. *H. J. Collingridge.*

DAME LYNET 3 ch.f. Pharly (FR) 130–Noble Elaine (USA) (Vaguely Noble 140) **55** [1988 NR 1989 8g² 8m⁶ 7.5m 8m⁶ a8g⁶ a8g] neat filly: moderate walker and mover: first foal: dam unraced daughter of Tintagel, smart winner at 1m and 10.5f in France: quite modest maiden: best efforts in claimers first and fourth starts: edgy third one: bred to stay 1¼m +, but races keenly: sold 6,000 gns Newmarket December Sales. *M. A. Jarvis.*

DAME ROUSARA 2 b.f. (Apr 8) Rousillon (USA) 133–Dame Ashfield 90 **88** (Grundy 137) [1989 6f* 6g⁴ 7g*] lengthy, quite attractive filly: second foal: half-sister to 3-y-o Valiant Dash (by Valiyar), winning juvenile hurdler: dam, 1½m winner, is daughter of Cheshire Oaks and Park Hill winner African Dancer: successful in maiden at Goodwood in June and nursery (in good style by 3 lengths from Empshott when visored first time) at Ascot in October: will stay 1m: sold 84,000 gns Newmarket December Sales. *W. Hastings-Bass.*

DAM INQUISITIVE 5 br.g. Don 128–Inquisitive Girl 97 (Crepello 136) [1988 **—** NR 1989 8g⁴ 10f 8.2d⁶ 6s] big gelding: poor plater: needs further than 6f: wears bandages: apprentice ridden first 2 starts. *J. W. Payne.*

DANAX 3 b.f. Jalmood (USA) 126–Adana (FR) (Green Dancer (USA) 132) [1988 **—** NR 1989 10.6m 12.2g⁵] lengthy filly: second foal: half-sister to fair 1m winner Anadax (by Mummy's Game): dam won over 9.5f in French Provinces: well beaten in maidens at Haydock and Catterick in the summer. *M. A. Jarvis.*

DANBURY (USA) 3 b.c. Danzig (USA)–Lovin' Lass (USA) (Cutlass (USA)) **93 §** [1988 NR 1989 10.1d² 10.6g² 8f² 8m⁶] tall, leggy colt: fourth foal: half-brother to 2 winners in USA, including Irish Chili (by Graustark), successful at up to 9f: dam stakes-placed winner at 6f and 7f in USA: fairly useful form in minor events and maiden, making most third start: 5/4 favourite, blinkered and unruly at stalls, never-dangerous sixth in Edinburgh minor event, not handling turn then hanging right when ridden along in straight: best effort over 1m: takes keen hold: sold 40,000 gns Newmarket Autumn Sales: probably not one to trust. *G. Harwood.*

DANCE BUSTER 2 b.c. (Feb 28) Bustino 136–Dance In Rome 79 (Dance In **—** Time (CAN)) [1989 7g] 17,000F, 33,000Y: fifth foal: closely related to 3-y-o Dr Zeva (by Busted) and half-brother to two 2-y-o winners: dam raced only at 2 yrs, winning over 6f: 33/1, backward and green, slowly away and always behind in 29-runner maiden at Newmarket in November. *Sir Mark Prescott.*

DANCE FESTIVAL 3 b.f. Nureyev (USA) 131–Seminar 113 (Don (ITY) 123) **101** [1988 6m² 1989 7g² 8m⁶] leggy, quite good-topped filly: moderate walker: favourite, second in maidens at Nottingham at 2 yrs and Newmarket: 9/2 co-second favourite, showed much improved form when about 5 lengths sixth of 13, always close up, to Enscone in Irish 1000 Guineas at the Curragh in May but not seen out again: suited by 1m. *M. R. Stoute.*

DANCEHALL (USA) 3 b.c. Assert 134–Cancan Madame (USA) (Mr **127**
Prospector (USA)) [1988 8m* 9s* 1989 11d* 12m* 12g² 10g*]
    Turning for home in the Prix du Jockey-Club Lancia, Dancehall was
travelling smoothly towards the rear, some eight lengths off the lead, then
Asmussen pulled him to the outside two furlongs out and Dancehall produced
a fine turn of foot and ran on strongly to go eight lengths clear of ten pursuers
headed by the Prix Lupin winner and short-priced favourite Galetto. Without
Old Vic, Dancehall would have been a most impressive winner. As it was, the
French-trained colt lost little ground on Old Vic in the straight but could
never get in a blow, being beaten almost as far as he beat Galetto. It was
Dancehall's only defeat in six outings. He came to Chantilly 7/2 second
favourite after wins in a maiden at Maisons-Laffitte and the Group 3 Prix de
Conde at Longchamp as a two-year-old, and Group 2 contests, also at
Longchamp, for the Prix Noailles and Prix Hocquart. The last of those races
had demonstrated Dancehall's gameness and his effectiveness over a mile and
a half but not much to mark him out from his contempories as, having led
approaching the final furlong, Dancehall held on only narrowly from the
fast-finishing pair Norberto and Louis Cyphre who'd both been given more to
do. Reflecting on the colt's standing after the Hocquart, one French
publication went so far as to liken the race to 'une sorte de victoire a la
Pyrrhus'.
    The Prix du Jockey-Club put Dancehall's merits relative to his
compatriots in an altogether different light of course and three weeks later he
started at odds-on for the Grand Prix de Paris Louis Vuitton in what was
probably as strong a field as France could muster at that stage of the season.
Galetto and Norberto reopposed, joined by the Poulains winner Kendor and
subsequent Prix Guillaume d'Ornano winner Creator. Dancehall beat them all
comfortably, having two lengths to spare over Norberto, Creator and Kendor
who finished virtually in line with sole British challenger Citidancer another
half length back in fifth. Dancehall would have been a worthy opponent for Ile
de Chypre and Cacoethes in the International at York but nine days before the
race it was announced that he'd broken down in training and wouldn't race
again. He's to stand at the Haras d'Etreham in 1990.
    Dancehall's sire Assert went one better in the Prix du Jockey-Club,
beating Real Shadai by three lengths, before winning the Irish Derby, Benson
and Hedges Gold Cup and Joe McGrath Memorial with an authority
comparable to that of Old Vic at Chantilly. He'd also contested the King
George VI and Queen Elizabeth Diamond Stakes (beaten a neck by Kalaglow)

*Prix Hocquart, Longchamp—it's a close-run thing between Dancehall,
Norberto and Louis Cyphre*

Grand Prix de Paris Louis Vuitton, Longchamp—
Dancehall lands the odds in what was to be his last race

and Arc de Triomphe (disappointing as favourite) before being syndicated at a value of 25,000,000 dollars to stand in the USA. It's fair to say that Assert's stud career so far hasn't been so eyecatching. Dancehall is comfortably his best runner, though he's had two Grade 1 successes in the USA, including the 1987 Santa Anita Oaks with Timely Assertion. Most of his representatives in this country have shown plenty of stamina, among them the 1988 winners Zaffaran (March Stakes), Dam Busters (Lonsdale Stakes) and Nomadic Way (Cesarewitch). Dancehall is also the best for some time from the dam's American family, his female antecedents being considerably less racy than their names might suggest; the dam Cancan Madame won once at around nine furlongs from twenty-two starts and is a daughter of the unraced Wild Madame who's out of the minor American winner Madame du Barry. A half-sister to Wild Madame produced the 500,000 dollar-earner Fast Gold from a mating with Mr Prospector. Dancehall, a first foal, is half-brother to a 1987 filly by Icecapade who fetched just 7,000 dollars at the yearling sales. A strong, deep-bodied colt, Dancehall was effective at a mile and a quarter and stayed a mile and a half well. The brevity of his career meant he never raced

Mr T. Wada's "Dancehall"

		Be My Guest (ch 1974)	Northern Dancer
	Assert		What A Treat
	(b 1979)	Irish Bird	Sea Bird II
Dancehall (USA)		(b or br 1970)	Irish Lass II
(b.c. 1986)		Mr Prospector (b 1970)	Raise A Native
	Cancan Madame (USA)		Gold Digger
	(b 1981)	Wild Madame	Le Fabuleux
		(ch 1976)	Madame du Barry

on very firm ground. More importantly, it prevented Dancehall's participation in the big autumn races in which he'd have played a major role. *A. Fabre, France.*

DANCE OF A GUNNER 2 ch.f. (Apr 5) Gunner B 126–Kilttaley 74 (Tower — Walk 130) [1989 6g] first foal: dam stayed 1m: 25/1, in rear in 19-runner maiden at Redcar in November. *R. J. Holder.*

DANCE OF GOLD 2 b.c. (Apr 16) Jalmood (USA) 126–Prima Ballerina (FR) — p (Nonoalco (USA) 131) [1989 7g 7m⁵] 7,000Y: strong, useful-looking, angular colt: third foal: brother to 1988 2-y-o Pivot, successful at 7f, and half-brother to 1¼m winner Harvest Dance (by Mill Reef): dam unraced half-sister to Greenland Park (dam of Fitnah) and Red Sunset: showed signs of ability in maiden auction race at Doncaster in June (very much in need of race) and minor event at Leicester following month: probably capable of better. *M. H. Easterby.*

DANCER BY NATURE 3 b.c. Lyphard's Special (USA) 124–Miss Africa 39 (African Sky 124) [1988 5f 5m⁴ 5m⁶ 7d 1989 6g 5f 8h³ 10.2h 8.3d 8f⁵ 10g] small, deep-girthed colt: poor plater: best effort as 3-y-o on sixth outing: sweating previous 2 starts, virtually pulled up on first of them: best form short of 1m. *Miss A. J. Whitfield.*

DANCE SPECTRUM (USA) 3 b.c. Lyphard (USA) 132–Rainbow Connection 105 (CAN) (Halo (USA)) [1988 NR 1989 10g* 12d* 10.6s⁶ 12m²ᵈⁱˢ 12s⁶] strong, well-made colt: has a short, sharp action: third foal: half-brother to disappointing Zajal (by Seattle Slew), promising 6f winner at 2 yrs in 1986: dam, champion filly in Canada, won at up to 1¼m and is half-sister to very smart Canadian colt Mr Macho: successful in April in maiden at Brighton and 3-runner minor event (12/1 on) at Beverley: very good second in £14,200 limited handicap at York in September, held up, not having clear run 2f out and subsequently disqualified for interference: stays 1½m: acts on top-of-the-ground and is unsuited by very soft: very edgy third outing and off course 4 months afterwards. *G. Harwood.*

DANCING BELLE 5 ch.m. Dance In Time (CAN)–Off The Reel (USA) 81 41 (Silent Screen (USA)) [1988 6g 6g 5d⁴ 5m² 5f 5f⁵ 5m 5f³ 5m³ 5g* 5g⁴ 5g 5f 5m 5f 1989 8f 8m 6h⁴ 6m⁴ 8g⁵ 7m 10.2f 6m 5g 5f⁶ 6f] lengthy, good-quartered mare: has a round action: poor handicapper: seems to stay 1m: yet to show her form on soft going, probably acts on any other: sometimes sweats: has often worn blinkers, but didn't in 1989: wore martingale and taken down early third and fourth starts: suitable mount for inexperienced rider: sold 2,600 gns Doncaster September Sales: inconsistent. *Mrs J. R. Ramsden.*

DANCING BREEZE 2 ch.f. (Apr 7) Horage 124–Lady's Guest (Be My Guest 61 (USA) 126) [1989 5.3g 5g⁴ 5g 5f⁴ 5m² 5m² 5m⁴ 5f⁵ 5m] IR 2,200Y: lengthy, workmanlike filly: has scope: first foal: dam placed from 1m to 1¼m in Ireland: quite modest maiden: will stay 6f. *Pat Mitchell.*

DANCING CANDLE 2 b.f. (Apr 26) Mashhor Dancer (USA)–Lovers Light 55 (Grundy 137) [1989 5m 5h⁴ 5f³ 7m 8.2f] 7,600F: leggy, close-coupled filly: good walker: shows a round action: second foal: dam out of half-sister to Main Reef: plating-class maiden: best efforts second and third starts: should be suited by further than 5f: ran very freely in blinkers final outing: sold 1,000 gns Newmarket Autumn Sales. *I. A. Balding.*

DANCING DAFFODIL 2 ch.f. (Jun 2) Doulab (USA) 115–Avereen (Averof — 123) [1989 6g] 11,000Y: half-sister to 3-y-o 1m winner Evening Star (by Red Sunset) and 4 other winners, including Mac's Reef (by Main Reef), very useful at up to 1½m here and later successful in North America, and 1¼m winner Mac's Sister (by Krayyan): dam poor half-sister to Goodwood Cup winner Tug of War: 25/1, blinkered and ridden by 7-lb claimer, soundly beaten in claimer at Goodwood in October: sold 900 gns Newmarket Autumn Sales. *M. Bell.*

DANCING DAYS 3 ch.c. Glenstal (USA) 118–Royal Agnes 71 (Royal Palace 131) 66 [1988 8m 7g 6v 1989 10v⁵ 8g* 8m³ 10f⁴ 10m³ 10g* 10m⁴ 12.3g³ 11s] smallish,

Sears Temple Stakes, Sandown—Dancing Dissident is clear of Wonder Dancer

attractive colt: moderate mover: modest handicapper: won at Carlisle in April and Pontefract in July: ran fairly well final start: will prove best at up to 1½m: probably unsuited by heavy going: sometimes wanders under pressure: consistent. *J. W. Watts.*

DANCING DISSIDENT (USA)   3 b.c. Nureyev (USA) 131–Absentia (USA) **119** 108 (Raise A Cup (USA)) [1988 6f* 6f² 6d³ 1989 6g 6f* 5f* 6f⁴ 5m⁵ 6m³] smallish, leggy, quite attractive colt: good mover, with a light action: smart sprinter: successful in May in £6,100 event at Newbury and Group 2 Sears Temple Stakes at Sandown: ran creditably after in Cork and Orrery Stakes at Royal Ascot, William Hill Sprint Championship (running on well from rear) at York and Krug Diadem Stakes (bumped 2f out) at Ascot: stayed 6f: easily best efforts on top-of-the-ground: often sweating and on toes: blinkered last 5 starts: retired to Irish National Stud, fee IR £6,000 (Oct 1st). *M. R. Stoute.*

DANCING EARL   2 gr.c. (Feb 19) Lomond (USA) 128–Baccalaureate 109   — (Crowned Prince (USA) 128) [1989 8g³ 7g] 37,000F: sturdy colt: fifth foal: half-brother to smart Irish 6f and 7f performer Corwyn Bay (by Caerleon) and modest 1¼m winner Trois Vallees (by Ile de Bourbon): dam, daughter of smart sprinter Bas Bleu, won over 7f and 1m: backward, soundly beaten in autumn maidens at York (very mulish, last of 3) and Newmarket. *C. E. Brittain.*

DANCING FALCON   3 b.c. Mill Reef (USA) 141–Vielle 123 (Ribero 126) [1988   **63** NR 1989 12s²] 300,000Y: smallish, well-made colt: fourth foal: closely related to twice-raced Pyrenees (by Shirley Heights) and half-brother to fair 12.2f winner Chevrefeuille (by Ile de Bourbon): dam middle-distance filly: second favourite but carrying condition, 8 lengths second of 8 to eased Allasdale in moderately-run minor event at Thirsk in April: moved poorly down: sold 3,800 gns Newmarket Autumn Sales. *M. R. Stoute.*

DANCING MAY   2 b.f. (Apr 2) Tina's Pet 121–Breckland Lady 62 (Royalty 130)   **31** [1989 5g 6f⁶ 6h³ 7f 7m⁶ 6m 10.6d] 3,500Y: sparely-made filly: has a round action: first foal: dam 9f and 1¼m winner: poor form, including in sellers: sweating sixth start. *P. Howling.*

DANCING MONARCH   4 ch.c. Dara Monarch 128–Maiden's Dance 65   **95** (Hotfoot 126) [1988 8d³ 8g 8f* 9m³ 8g⁴ 8v⁵ 7g 9f* 1989 8m* 8f 8.2g² 8f 8m 10.6g³ 8f² 8f² 8g³ 8d 8g] strong, lengthy, quite attractive colt: moderate walker and mover: fairly useful handicapper: 25/1, showed improved form when winning £8,400 Thirsk Hunt Cup (Handicap) in May: ran well when placed over 1m afterwards: needs further than 7f and stays 9f: best on a sound surface: usually held up and suited by strong gallop: has hung. *R. Hollinshead.*

233

DANCING MUSIC   2 ch.c. (Mar 4) Music Boy 124–Miss Rossi (Artaius (USA) **103**
129) [1989 5s* 5d² 6g 6f 5g* 5f* 5m⁴ 5m² 5s* 5m³ 6g] 3,800F, 13,500Y: rather
leggy, workmanlike colt: usually dull in coat: good walker and mover: first foal: dam
unraced: successful in maiden at Leicester in April, in minor event at Windsor and
nursery at Goodwood in July and an Ayr nursery in September: ran well when under
7 lengths third to Argentum in Cornwallis Stakes at Ascot: speedy, and suited by 5f:
acts on any going: sometimes drifts left. *J. Berry.*

DANCING PARTY (USA)   2 b.f. (Apr 23) Danzig (USA)–Irish Party (USA)   **90**
(Irish Lancer) [1989 5f* 6g³ 5f 5f* 5s⁴ 6d²] strong, smallish, chunky filly: closely
related to 3-y-o Secret Favor (by Secreto) and half-sister to several winners,
notably French 2000 Guineas winner Recitation (by Elocutionist) and very useful
French miler Doyle (by Irish River): dam won 9 of her 40 starts, including 2 stakes
races at around 1m: fairly useful performer: successful in maiden at Nottingham in
June and minor event at Folkestone in September: creditable fourth to
Mademoiselle Chloe in listed race at Ayr, better subsequent effort: stays 6f: acts on
any going: inconsistent. *B. W. Hills.*

DANCING SCHOLAR   2 ch.c. (May 22) Exhibitioner 111–Mississipi Shuffle 78   **—**
(Steel Heart 128) [1989 5d] 3,500Y, 7,200 2-y-o: medium-sized, useful-looking colt:
sixth foal: half-brother to French 3-y-o 8.5f winner Dunshufflin (by Dunbeath): dam
sprinting daughter of July Cup winner Merry Madcap: 25/1, over 11 lengths tenth of
19, unable to quicken 1½f out and eased, to Pago in maiden at Haydock in
September: sold 1,300 gns Doncaster October Sales. *J. J. O'Neill.*

DANCING SENSATION (USA)   2 b.f. (Apr 10) Faliraki 125–Sweet Satina   **59**
(USA) (Crimson Satan) [1989 5m³ 6d³ 6g] $20,000Y: good-topped, attractive filly:
fluent mover: half-sister to numerous minor winners in USA, including stakes-
winning steeplechaser: dam never ran: quite modest form in minor events at
Newmarket and Goodwood on first 2 starts: not at all knocked about final start: bred
to stay 1m: off course 4 months after debut. *J. W. Hills.*

DANCING TENDER   2 b.c. (Mar 23) Tender King 123–Dance Away (Red God   **62**
128§) [1989 5s⁴ 5v 5f² 5f* 6m² 6f* 6m 6g⁵ 6f⁴ 6m³ 6f⁶] 15,000Y: neat colt:
half-brother to several winners, most at up to 7f, including useful 1981 2-y-o 6f
winner Risk Taker (by Auction Ring): dam fairly useful Irish 2-y-o 5f winner: useful
plater: won at Doncaster (bought in 8,600 gns) in May and claimer at Chepstow,
making all, in July: stays 6f: has run well for a 7-lb claimer. *M. Bell.*

DANCING TRIBUTE (USA)   3 b.f. Nureyev (USA) 131–Sophisticated Girl **115**
(USA) (Stop The Music (USA)) [1988 6m* 6f* 6g² 1989 6m⁵ 8m* 9.2g 7m²]
lengthy, good-quartered filly: good walker and mover: won £6,500 contest at
Newbury in September: again favourite, tenth of 15 in Group 2 event at Longchamp:
good 1½ lengths second of 6 to Distant Relative in Group 2 Bisquit Cognac
Challenge Stakes at Newmarket 11 days later: best at 7f or 1m: acts on firm ground:
very useful. *M. R. Stoute.*

DANCING WAY   2 b.c. (Mar 15) Sadler's Wells (USA) 132–Waterway (FR) 112   **— p**
(Riverman (USA) 131) [1989 8d] fifth live foal: brother to 3-y-o Rosebery Avenue
and half-brother to Irish Oaks winner Helen Street (by Troy): dam, from family of
Sun Prince, very useful at up to 1m in France: 7/1, slowly away and always behind in
18-runner maiden at Thirsk in November: should improve. *Major W. R. Hern.*

Arlington Stakes, Newbury—there's no catching Dancing Tribute

DANDY'S GIRL 4 ch.f. Record Token 128–Miss Rockefeller (Richboy 117) —
[1988 NR 1989 8.5g⁶ 12f³ 14m⁵] big, plain filly: third foal: dam never ran: of little
account: gets on toes. *S. R. Bowring.*

DANEHILL (USA) 3 b.c. Danzig (USA)–Razyana (USA) 69 (His Majesty **126**
(USA)) [1988 6d² 6d* 7m 1989 7g* 8m³ 8m⁴ 6f* 6m³ 6g*]
    A return to sprint distances was the making of the high-class colt
Danehill. His is by no means a unique experience, of course. Every year the
lure of the classics is compounded by a relatively weak representation of
sprint contests in the early-season pattern to such effect that the various
Guineas tend to provide a prime source of pointers to the top sprints. In 1988
there were Caerwent and Bluebook who ended the season second and fourth
highest-rated three-year-olds over sprint distances, and before them Ajdal,
Polonia and Big Shuffle in 1987; Hallgate and Green Desert in 1986; Vilikaia
and Dafayna in 1985; Chief Singer in 1984; and Habibti and Maximova in 1983,
all of whom registered leading sprint performances having earlier been beaten
in one or more classics. The Premio Certosa, Prix Saint-Georges, Palace
House Stakes, Premio Melton, Duke of York Stakes and Greenlands Stakes
have little attraction for trainers whose best three-year-olds hold the
slightest chance of staying a mile.
    Danehill was one of those given an extended run at the distance. At
Newmarket he was Pat Eddery's selected from three Abdulla colts—
Exbourne and Greensmith were the others—and was a 9/1-shot in the
fourteen-runner field. His record thus far was two wins from four starts,
having landed the odds in a maiden at York as a two-year-old then made a
winning reappearance under 9-1 in the seven-furlong Ladbroke European
Free Handicap. Danehill had pulled too hard when behind in the Prix de la
Salamandre on his final start at two years and he took a keen hold in the Free
Handicap, racing in the rear early on. He made smooth headway to join leaders
Folly Foot and Mon Tresor approaching the Dip then ran on well when ridden

*Cork And Orrery Stakes, Ascot—Danehill contributes to a fine Royal Ascot
for his trainer in his final season*

Ladbroke Sprint Cup, Haydock—a change of name for this Group 1 event, but it's the same winning connections as in 1988; Danehill (Pat Eddery) carries the Abdulla colours to a clear-cut victory over French challenger Cricket Ball

out, despite edging right, for a convincing two-length victory. The Guineas mile now seemed likely to be within his compass. Again Eddery tried to hold Danehill up but this time with rather less success; Danehill was already close behind Nashwan after three furlongs, then was his closest pursuer from over two furlongs out until inside the last where, as Nashwan stretched away, Exbourne also got the better of him. For 'failures' at Newmarket, however, there's usually the temptation of rather easier pickings at the Curragh two weeks later. Danehill took this well-trodden route and started a short-priced favourite but here the cost of attempting to settle him finally proved too great. Danehill again fought for his head, behind and between horses, and though he stayed on in the straight his effort never looked a dangerous one and petered out in the final furlong before he finished fourth to the revitalised Shaadi.

Danehill's next race saw a new trip, new tactics and a resounding success in the Cork And Orrery Stakes at Royal Ascot. He carried none of the penalties and was a well-backed favourite. Eddery being unable to do the weight, Carson took the ride and soon had Danehill close behind Nabeel Dancer before bringing him to the front over two furlongs out. Dancing Dissident flattered at the distance and that was the only threat as Danehill strode clear under hands and heels, Nabeel Dancer hanging on for second, beaten three lengths, with Savahra Sound a further length and a half back in third. Danehill broke the course record set by Posada, another Guineas graduate, in the same race twelve months earlier. The programme for leading sprinters after Royal Ascot is a fairly well-defined one, the next stop being the July Cup at Newmarket. The field was a lot stronger than at Royal Ascot and there were no allowances but such was the impression made by Danehill in the Cork And Orrery that he was again favourite and at an even shorter price of even money. However, having been checked at the stalls to get a lead from Gallic League, it wasn't long before Danehill was niggled at to hold his prominent position and when Gallic League dropped out at the distance, Cadeaux Genereux had already flown. Danehill's stride was shortening at the finish where Golden Opinion had also surged clear of him. It was a creditable effort but with fast conditions (which resulted in another course record) on a

236

slightly easier track, Danehill had found the step up in company too much for him. He'd probably have struggled in the William Hill Sprint Championship, and his fifth attempt at a Group 1 victory came in the recently upgraded Ladbroke Sprint Cup at Haydock. Racing on an easy surface for the first time since the spring, Danehill produced an impressive effort in the absence of those who had beaten him at Newmarket. Tracking Holst on the rails, he couldn't be so forcefully ridden as on his previous two outings but it didn't matter; Danehill was always travelling supremely well, Eddery switched him towards the centre two furlongs out then the horse quickened in fine style between Kerrera and Silver Fling at the furlong pole before going on to win easily by two lengths from Cricket Ball who didn't get the best of runs. That turned out to be Danehill's final appearance as a minor joint injury prevented his being got ready in time for the Abbaye.

		Danzig (USA) (b 1977)	Northern Dancer (b 1961)	Nearctic Natalma
Danehill (USA) (b.c. 1986)			Pas de Nom (b or br 1968)	Admiral's Voyage Petitioner
		Razyana (USA) (b 1981)	His Majesty (b 1968)	Ribot Flower Bowl
			Spring Adieu (b 1974)	Buckpasser Natalma

Danehill was one of three leading three-year-old colts by Danzig whose retirements were announced in the autumn, the others being Polish Precedent (valued at £7,200,000) and Shaadi (£4,500,000). Danehill was reportedly sold for £4,000,000 to a partnership between Coolmore and the Australian stud Arrowfield and he'll stand at a fee of IR 25,000 guineas before covering in Australia in the second half of 1990. Physically, the strong, good-bodied Danehill concedes little if anything to his two contemporaries; he has a quick, fluent action, and from Royal Ascot onwards his well-being was striking. Polish Precedent has the edge in ability but there's not much

Mr K. Abdulla's "Danehill"

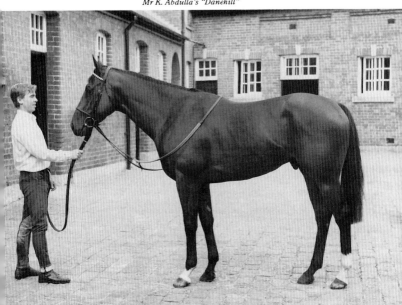

between Danehill and Shaadi and in terms of pedigree Danehill can't be far behind either of them. He's a result of inbreeding to the celebrated Natalma, purchased by E. P. Taylor for 35,000 dollars as a yearling in 1958. Natalma's brightest moment on the racetrack was a fleeting one as she made all in one of the most important American races for two-year-old fillies, the Spinaway Stakes, but only after forcing an opponent into the rails and earning a demotion. She chipped a knee bone when being trained for the Kentucky Oaks and retired with a record of three wins from seven starts and prize money of 16,015 dollars. The result of her hastily arranged mating with the same owner's Nearctic (then in his first season's stud duties) was, of course, Northern Dancer. Remarkably, Natalma's dam Almahmoud was grandam of America's champion three-year-old filly Tosmah in the same year that Northern Dancer was champion three-year-old colt. Natalma went on to foal another nine winners. The Buckpasser filly Spring Adieu—Polish Precedent's dam is also by Buckpasser, incidentally—succeeded in three small sprints as a three-year-old but has only produced one winner herself. Her third foal Razyana, a 350,000-dollar yearling, was second in a large field of maidens at Newmarket as a two-year-old but ran only twice (over a mile and a quarter) at three years. Danehill, her first offspring, is followed by the El Gran Senor filly Emerald and Razyana was reportedly mated to El Gran Senor again in 1987 and to other sons of Northern Dancer, The Minstrel and Nureyev, in 1988 and 1989. *J. Tree.*

DANE ROSE 3 b.f. Full of Hope 125–Roella (Gold Rod 129) [1988 NR 1989 9g3 10.2f6] third foal: dam of little account: 50/1, no worthwhile form in 3-runner minor event (backward) at Wolverhampton in July and maiden at Bath in September: sold 1,550 gns Ascot December Sales. *O. O'Neill.* —

DANGER SIGN 3 b.g. Ginger Brink (FR) 117–Norman Native (FR) (Bourbon (FR) 129) [1988 5s 6d 6f 7d 1989 6f 7m 6f] workmanlike, rather leggy gelding: poor form at best in varied events: trained by H. O'Neill first outing: blinkered third start at 2 yrs: sold Horse France 1,700 gns Newmarket Autumn Sales. *D. R. C. Elsworth.* —

DANNY BLANCHFLOWER 2 ch.g. (Apr 19) Rabdan 129–Caffre Lily (Hittite Glory 125) [1989 6f 5f4 5f 7g 6v 6g] 3,300Y: workmanlike gelding: moderate walker: has a round action: first foal: dam poor maiden: poor maiden: may prove best at up to 6f: gelded after final start. *P. S. Felgate.* 43

DANRAB 3 b.c. Rabdan 129–Friendly Pet (Be Friendly 130) [1988 NR 1989 7d3 7m4 8.2f2 8m3 10m 10.6g 9s] 7,200Y: compact, good-bodied colt: moderate mover: second foal: half-brother to poor maiden Sandmoor Cord (by Wattlefield): dam unraced sister to Runnett: quite modest form in varied events first 4 outings: showed nothing after: stays 1m well: ridden by 5-lb claimer: visored final start: bandaged second and third. *M. J. O'Neill.* 59 d

DANRIBO 6 b.g. Riboboy (USA) 124–Sheridans Daughter 75 (Majority Blue 126) [1988 8d 12f6 12f 13.3m 16f 14.6m 1989 11d6] big, strong gelding: has a quick action: bad maiden: probably doesn't stay 2m: edgy and slowly away only start at 6 yrs: sold to join C. Popham 4,400 gns Ascot July Sales. *J. Parkes.* —

DANSON BOATHOUSE 3 b.g. Niniski (USA) 125–Boathouse 116 (Habitat 134) [1988 NR 1989 10m] lengthy gelding: fourth foal: half-brother to smart middle-distance stayer Dry Dock (by High Line) and modest maiden Head of The River (by Shirley Heights): dam, who stayed 1¼m, is half-sister to Oaks winner Bireme and high-class middle-distance stayer Buoy: on toes, always behind in claimer at Sandown in July: sold 850 gns Ascot November Sales. *R. Simpson.* —

DAN THE MAN 3 b.c. Rabdan 129–Liberty Light 82 (Henry The Seventh 125) [1988 5d 5m 1989 12.2d2 12m 11m5 12.2m5 15g4 12g 12g] plain, angular colt: moderate mover: poor maiden: beaten short head in seller at Catterick in April: below form in varied events after: stays 1½m well: seems to need a soft surface: apprentice ridden: sold 2,300 gns Doncaster November Sales. *M. J. O'Neill.* 44

DANZA HEIGHTS 3 br.c. Head For Heights 125–Dankalia (Le Levanstell 122) [1988 NR 1989 7g 8f] 3,600F, 15,500Y: leggy, workmanlike colt: closely related to twice-raced maiden Kalia Crest (by Shirley Heights) and half-brother to several winners here and abroad, including fairly useful 1984 2-y-o 6f winner Dan Thatch (by Thatch), later winner at 3 yrs in Italy and half-sister to 3 good Italian winners: well beaten in newcomers race (edgy) at Doncaster and maiden at Pontefract in the spring. *J. A. Glover.* —

DARA DEE 2 b.f. (May 31) Dara Monarch 128–Not Mistaken (USA) (Mill Reef 87
(USA) 141) [1989 6m⁵ 7m⁵ 7m⁵ 7m² 7v⁶] IR 16,000F, 8,400Y: leggy, close-coupled
filly: sixth live foal: half-sister to Italian 3-y-o Identity Parade (by Rusticaro), 5f
winner here at 2 yrs later successful at 1¼m and 11f, and 2 other winners, including
useful Irish 1m and 1½m winner Bay Empress (by Empery): dam never ran: showed
much improved form when 2 lengths second of 21, always prominent, to Cutting
Note in maiden at Newmarket: ran poorly in similar event at Ayr later in October:
will stay 1m: possibly unsuited by heavy going. *C. E. Brittain.*

DARA DOONE 3 b.g. Dara Monarch 128–Lorna Doone (USA) (Tom Rolfe) [1988 —
7m 7f 8h 1989 12d⁵ 13.1h⁵ 10f⁶ 12g⁵] strong, good sort: good walker: poor form in
handicaps last 2 outings: stays 1½m: sweating and took good hold third start:
trained before then by R. Hannon. *P. J. Jones.*

DARAKAH 2 ch.f. (Apr 15) Doulab (USA) 115–Ladytown (English Prince 129) 69
[1989 5m² 6g 5m⁵ 5m*] 31,000F, 14,000Y: third foal: dam, Irish 1¼m winner, is
half-sister to Irish St Leger winner M-Lolshan: won maiden at Lingfield in
September by head from Number Eleven, making most: should stay at least 6f. *C. J.
Benstead.*

DARANIYDA 2 b.f. (May 21) Mouktar 129–Dramatic Lady (Lyphard (USA) 132) 52 p
[1989 a7g⁴] sixth foal: half-sister to 3-y-o Darannda (by Darshaan) and 2 winners,
includig quite useful 1984 2-y-o 7.3f winner Daniyar (by Riverman): dam, placed
over 1m and 10.5f at 2 yrs in France, is out of very smart middle-distance filly
Bubunia: 7½ lengths fourth of 14 to Persian Soldier in maiden at Lingfield in
December: will be suited by further: should improve. *M. R. Stoute.*

DARA PRINCE 2 ch.c. (Mar 14) Dara Monarch 128–Dowcester 63 (Habitat 134) 39
[1989 5g⁵ 5m⁴ 5g⁴ 5m 5f] IR 7,600F, 15,500Y: small, sturdy colt: first foal: dam
placed at 7f from 2 starts at 3 yrs, is daughter of half-sister to high-class performers
Hot Spark and Bitty Girl: poor form in maidens: blinkered final outing: sweating and
edgy third start: has joined D. Chapman. *J. Berry.*

DARAROYAL 2 ch.c. (May 6) Dara Monarch 128–Palace Guest (Be My Guest —
(USA) 126) [1989 a8g] 4,600Y: leggy colt: second foal: half-brother to a winner in
Sweden: dam, won in Sweden, is half-sister to smart 1983 2-y-o Palace Gold: bit
backward, slowly away and always behind in maiden at Southwell in December. *Mrs
N. Macauley.*

DARBY SKY (USA) 2 b.c. (Feb 15) Darby Creek Road (USA)–Wimborne Sky 83
(USA) (Sir Wimborne (USA)) [1989 6g⁴ 6g⁶] close-coupled, good-topped colt: first
foal: dam stakes winner at 1¼m: 50/1, around 2 lengths fourth of 6, keeping on, to
Qathif in minor event at Ascot: below that form in maiden at Newcastle later in
October: will be suited by 7f. *M. E. D. Francis.*

DARING DASH 3 br.f. Daring March 116–Lucky Run 101 (Runnymede 123) —
[1988 NR 1989 10f] half-sister to several winners here and abroad, including 7f to
1¼m winner High Pitched (by Crooner): dam won over 5.9f at 2 yrs: 33/1 and bit
backward, tailed off in maiden at Lingfield in May. *R. V. Smyth.*

DARING DELIGHT 4 b.f. Daring March 116–Noble Mistress 80 (Lord Gayle —
(USA) 124) [1988 6f 5g⁴ 6g⁴ 1989 6g] sparely-made filly: quite modest maiden at 2
yrs: lightly raced subsequently and well below her best in handicaps: best form at 5f.
M. Brittain.

DARING JOY 2 b.f. (Apr 27) Daring March 116–African Berry 84 (African Sky —
124) [1989 7g] 3,000Y, 4,300 2-y-o: workmanlike filly: fifth foal: sister to 1985 2-y-o
5f seller winner Parading and poor 6f and 7f winner African Safari: dam, 5f winner,
ran only at 2 yrs: 50/1 and backward, prominent to halfway in 17-runner minor event
at Leicester in November. *B. A. McMahon.*

DARING MINSTREL 2 br.c. (Apr 19) Daring March 116–Miss Twomey (Will —
Somers 114§) [1989 5s⁴ 5d 5m 7m] 4,900Y: leggy, sparely-made colt: half-brother to
several winners, including 5f performer Miss Poinciana (by Averof): dam poor Irish
maiden: poor maiden: blinkered, very edgy and keen to post first time, taken down
early and on toes final. *P. A. Blockley.*

DARING SWALLOW 3 b.f. Daring March 116–Second Swallow 55 (My —
Swallow 134) [1988 NR 1989 10m 11.5m 8m 8m 8.2d] big, lengthy filly: moderate
walker: fourth live foal: dam, in frame over sprint distances at 3 yrs, is half-sister to
high-class Gold Rod: no worthwhile form in maidens and claimers: has been
bandaged, and taken keen hold: sold W. Clay 1,200 gns Doncaster November Sales.
E. Eldin.

DARING TIMES 4 gr.g. Good Times (ITY)–She Who Dares (Bellypha 130) 79 d
[1988 10m 8g² 8d⁵ 10m* 10m³ 10g 1989 8d 10m⁶ 9f⁴ 10f³ 10g 8m² 9f 9f 9g 8m 8g 10g]

strong, rangy gelding: fair handicapper on his day: well below form last 6 outings: effective at 1m and 1¼m: acts well on top-of-the-ground: suitable mount for inexperienced rider: suited by forcing tactics: bought out of C. Brittain's stable 12,500 gns Newmarket Autumn Sales after eleventh outing: inconsistent. *Mrs J. R. Ramsden.*

DARING TO GO 4 b.f. Daring March 116–Summer Lightning 66 (Hot Spark 126)   57
[1988 NR 1989 12g⁴ 12m] rangy filly: first foal: dam placed over 1½m: 12/1, 6 lengths fourth of 9 in minor event at Carlisle in April: tailed off in amateurs race at Thirsk week later, then joined Miss J. Eaton. *J. Berry.*

DARK CITY 2 b.f. (May 16) Sweet Monday 122–City's Sister 72 (Maystreak 118)   —
[1989 5h 6h] slightly dipped-backed, sparely-made filly: third foal: sister to 1987 2-y-o 6f winner Sweet City (stays 1¼m): dam won over 6f and 7.2f at 3 yrs and over 1½m and 13f at 4 yrs: soundly beaten in maidens at Carlisle: not seen out after June. *G. Richards.*

DARK DESIRE 3 b.g. Alzao (USA) 117–Treble Cloud (Capistrano 120) [1988 NR   —
1989 10f⁶] IR 7,500F, 16,000Y: sturdy gelding: fourth reported foal: half-brother to 1981 2-y-o 5f and 7f winner Welsh Cloud (by Welsh Saint) and 6f winner Triad Treble (by Sweet Revenge): dam ran twice in Ireland: 33/1 and bit backward, not given hard race when 12 lengths sixth of 10 in maiden at Sandown in June: moved moderately to post: subsequently gelded. *M. E. D. Francis.*

DARK FLOOD (USA) 6 b.h. Noble Dancer 125–Silent Flood (USA) (Silent   98
Screen (USA)) [1988 NR 1989 12m 10g] tall, leggy horse: third foal: half-brother to a winner in USA at about 6f by Tromos: dam, placed in USA: won 7 minor races in USA from 3 yrs to 5 yrs at up to 1½m: also placed in graded stakes from 9f to 1½m: 25/1, about 6 lengths seventh of 8, leading over 9f and eased once beaten, to Spritsail, first and better effort in autumn listed events at Newmarket. *A. C. Stewart.*

DARK GISELLE 4 b.f. King of Spain 121–Giselle 104 (Pall Mall 132) [1988 5d   —
6g⁴ 7m 8.2m 7d* 6g 6g 8.3g 8d 1989 8s a6g] lengthy, sparely-made filly: poor mover: poor plater: below form since winning at Warwick as 3-y-o: suited by 7f: possibly needs an easy surface nowadays: trained on reappearance by C. Hill. *R. J. Hodges.*

DARK HERITAGE 6 b.g. Scorpio (FR) 127–Mother of The Wind 82 (Tumble   —
Wind (USA)) [1988 12d 9f 8g³ 10f* 10f³ 10m* 1989 10f] big, strong, good-bodied gelding: quite modest winner as 5-y-o: facing stiffish task, prominent until 3f out in handicap at Salisbury in September: best form at 1¼m: acts on firm going: ran moderately in blinkers: has sweated: has won for apprentice: winning jumper. *D. J. G. Murray-Smith.*

DARK JESTER 4 b.g. Jester 119–Chilcombe (Morston (FR) 125) [1988 12m 12m   —
1989 12.2m] big, good-topped gelding: poor form. *G. M. Moore.*

DARKORJON 8 ch.g. Whistling Top 107–Hildamay (Cantab 94) [1988 12g*   —
18m⁶ 1989 21.6d] big, angular ex-Irish gelding: useful chaser at his best: soundly beaten in handicap at Pontefract in April: should stay beyond 1½m: possibly unsuited by top-of-the-ground: has won for amateur. *N. Tinkler.*

DARMENT 2 b.f. (May 20) Darshaan 133–Nijinsky Sentiment (USA) (Nijinsky   —
(CAN) 138) [1989 6g] 28,000Y: second foal: dam, 7f winner, is daughter of smart 2-y-o 7f winner Harrapan Seal, a sister to Steel Heart: 50/1 and backward, never dangerous in 29-runner maiden at Newmarket in November. *R. F. Johnson Houghton.*

DAROMANN 2 b.c. (Apr 4) Caerleon (USA) 132–Dananira 98 (High Top 131)   78
[1989 8m² 8m*] small, angular colt: moderate mover: first foal: dam French 7f and 1½m winner, is half-sister to Darshaan and Darara: won maiden at Edinburgh in October by 1½ lengths from Shifting Breeze, staying on well: will stay 1½m: sold 24,000 gns Newmarket Autumn Sales. *M. R. Stoute.*

DARTING MOTH 2 br.f. (May 8) Mansingh (USA) 120–Crescent Dart 103 (Sing   67
Sing 134) [1989 6g⁶ 5g⁴] 4,800Y: lengthy, slightly dipped-backed filly: half-sister to several winners, mostly sprinters, including smart 1974 2-y-o Double Dart (by Songedor): dam sprinter: quite modest form in October maidens at Newmarket and Redcar: worth another try at 6f. *G. A. Pritchard-Gordon.*

DARUSSALAM 2 ch.f. (Mar 13) Tina's Pet 121–Chinese Falcon 81 (Skymaster   57
126) [1989 6f³ 5m³ 8f⁶ 7f 7g] 3,300Y, 7,600 2-y-o: sparely-made filly: has a poor, round action: sister to plating-class sprint maiden Tina's Song and half-sister to useful 5f performer Miss Import (by Import): dam 2-y-o 6f winner: plating-class form in maidens on first 2 starts: should be suited by at least 6f. *Denys Smith.*

G. P. A. National Stakes, the Curragh—
first of two Group 1 pattern-race victories for Dashing Blade

DASHING BLADE 2 b.c. (Mar 1) Elegant Air 119–Sharp Castan 101 **117** (Sharpen Up 127) [1989 6m* 6m* 7f³ 7g* 7g*]
  Talk about damning with faint praise! Press reaction to Dashing Blade's narrow victory in the Three Chimneys Dewhurst Stakes at Newmarket in October was lukewarm to say the least, and the vast majority of journalists elected to centre their copy around the defeat of the much-vaunted Irish colt Royal Academy and its possible effects on the share price of Classic Thoroughbreds. Such a response isn't altogether surprising, of course. It's long been the way that a high-priced failure is equally if not more newsworthy than a deserving yet unspectacular winner, and with little more than four lengths spanning the entire field it's hard to imagine that the Dewhurst form is anywhere near top class. However, when you examine Dashing Blade's record closely it's equally hard to escape the conclusion that he wasn't accorded the credit he deserved. Two Group 1 wins and only one defeat in five outings is a record most definitely not to be sneezed at, and even if his Dewhurst victory turns out to be his last, which seems unlikely, Dashing Blade owes his connections and supporters nothing whatsoever.
  Unusually for such a large stable, Ian Balding's two-year-old colts and geldings didn't manage to win a race between them during 1988 and the spring of 1989. Dashing Blade was well backed to end the losing sequence on his debut in a minor event at Newbury in June though, and he justified the support in most impressive fashion, recovering swiftly from a slow start and sprinting clear in the final furlong to beat Osario by three lengths in the style of a very useful horse in the making. The next day at Newbury saw Major Hern introduce a Danzig colt named Dayjur to make a similarly impressive winning debut, and the intended clash between him and Dashing Blade in the Veuve Clicquot Champagne Stakes at Salisbury a couple of weeks later looked likely to prove highly informative. Unfortunately for his connections Dayjur was ruled out on the morning of the race by a slight temperature. At long odds on

Dashing Blade got the better of his two remaining rivals with ease, and he then took his place in a field of five for the Lanson Champagne Vintage Stakes at Goodwood as the 5/2 second favourite. In the paddock at Goodwood Dashing Blade didn't look himself—he was sweating, a shade edgy and if anything looked to have lost condition since his debut. Nevertheless, he ran a sound race, travelling keenly to past halfway and keeping on under pressure to finish third, half a length and a length behind the odds-on Be My Chief and the 25/1-chance Robellation. Goodwood wasn't the first time Dashing Blade had shown signs of a nervous disposition—apparently, he got loose on the gallops and bolted for around three miles prior to his debut, and he also proved difficult to pull up after winning at Salisbury. Dashing Blade's enthusiasm for racing, however, is beyond question. According to his trainer he progressed really well in the weeks leading up to the G.P.A. National Stakes at the Curragh in September—a race in which his sire finished fourth behind El Gran Senor six years earlier—and in a weak-looking field by Group 1 standards he started 3/1 second favourite, a point behind his fellow English-trained challenger, the Gimcrack runner-up Book The Band. The race, quite a rough one, saw Dashing Blade put up an admirable strong-galloping performance. Well ridden by Matthias, he was never far away and after squeezing through a narrow gap to lead just under two furlongs out he stayed on most determinedly despite edging left to win by three quarters of a length. The filly Wedding Bouquet, bidding to become Vincent O'Brien's fourteenth winner of the National Stakes, ran a highly creditable race for second, and so did Book The Band, who finished just a neck away in third and would have done even better had he not been slightly short of room as the race began in earnest.

And so to the Dewhurst. Royal Academy, at 3,500,000 dollars the highest-priced yearling of his generation, had stormed home by ten lengths in a maiden race at the Curragh on the day after the National Stakes and was all the rage in the betting, eventually being sent off at evens after a welter of four-figure bets; Welney, who'd looked potentially high class when successful in the Rokeby Farms Mill Reef Stakes, came next on 7/2, followed by the Middle Park third Cordoba and Dashing Blade on 5/1 and 8/1 respectively; Cullinan (14/1) and Anshan (12/1), who'd been separated by a head when second and third behind The Caretaker in the Cartier Million thirteen days previously, and the 66/1-outsider Call To Arms, beaten in a Newbury nursery on his previous start and seemingly fully exposed, completed the field. In the

Three Chimneys Dewhurst Stakes, Newmarket—almost as close as in 1988, with Dashing Blade, Call To Arms (striped sleeves) and Anshan fighting out the finish

Mr J. C. Smith's "Dashing Blade"

preliminaries Dashing Blade again looked to be carrying little surplus flesh. He remained calm this time, and once again his willingness to knuckle down in a driving finish stood him in excellent stead. The early pace set by Anshan wasn't particularly searching, and the time for the race was just over a second slower than that recorded by Negligent in the Rockfel Stakes half an hour or so earlier. Even so, it was clear passing halfway that Welney's rider wasn't happy. Dashing Blade, on the other hand, travelled fairly comfortably under restraint for the first four furlongs. Asked to quicken soon after, he made good headway to take a slight lead running into the Dip and battled on tenaciously under forceful driving to prevail by a neck; Call To Arms, who raced prominently throughout and stayed on strongly, excelled himself in second, in doing so becoming the longest-priced runner to reach a place in the Dewhurst since Tough Commander finished a remote third of four at 200/1 behind Diesis in 1982; Anshan rallied in fine style once headed and was only a short head behind in third, while Royal Academy failed by some way to live up to his pre-race billing, travelling smoothly in behind for most of the trip only to find little off the bridle, eventually finishing sixth.

When injury forced Elegant Air into retirement in the spring of 1985 there was little doubt he had plenty to recommend him as a stallion prospect. He was a big, strong, good-looking horse with an excellent pedigree, and though short of the top bracket he had a fine career behind him, being the winner of the Horris Hill Stakes at two, the Andy Capp Handicap under 9-6 at three and both the Westbury Stakes and the Tattersalls Rogers Gold Cup at four. Elegant Air's first crop of yearlings weren't particularly well received at the sales. Many of them were sold at a loss to their breeders, and Dashing Blade himself was reportedly only kept away from the sale-ring because connections considered his physical appearance would prevent his fetching a decent price. The colt isn't so bad now: he's tall, rather leggy but quite attractive. Dashing Blade's achievements enabled Elegant Air to fend off strong challenges from Chief's Crown and Fairy King for champion first-season sire. The dam Sharp Castan, bought by her present owner for 50,000 guineas while carrying Dashing Blade at the December Sales, showed useful form as a two-year-old when she won over five furlongs at Newmarket and finished third of nine behind Quick As Lightning in the Hoover Fillies' Mile. Sharp Castan's record as a broodmare is a good one, too. All her foals prior to Dashing Blade were winners. The Dominion colt Navarzato, a useful performer at up to a mile both here and in France, was probably the best of them, but she's also produced the Ayr Gold Cup runner-up Fairways Girl (by Young Generation) who went on to win in the States, and the fair mile-and-a-half winner Belle Enfant (by Beldale Flutter). Her two-year-old for 1990 is a colt by Chief Singer. Sharp Castan's dam Sultry One had training problems and made only two appearances, unplaced both times, in two seasons. She comes from a good family and she's also produced a number of winners at stud, notably General Vole, who wasn't far behind the best over a mile back in 1974.

			Shirley Heights	Mill Reef
	Elegant Air		(b 1975)	Hardiemma
	(br 1981)		Elegant Tern	Sea Bird II
Dashing Blade			(b 1971)	Prides Profile
(b.c. Mar 1, 1987)			Sharpen Up	Atan
	Sharp Castan		(ch 1969)	Rocchetta
	(ch 1977)		Sultry One	Tropique
			(ch 1961)	Sweet Heart V

At the time of writing it seems Dashing Blade will be prepared with the Two Thousand Guineas as his first major objective for 1990. Undoubtedly the distance of that race will suit him, and he'll almost certainly stay further in due course. Whether Dashing Blade, who should train on, will be good enough to make his presence felt at classic level is another matter, though. We rather doubt it. To begin with the likes of Be My Chief, Machiavellian and Jade Robbery all look to have better Guineas credentials at this stage, and there's plenty of room for more lightly-raced colts to stake their claim in the trials. However, if Dashing Blade doesn't prove quite up to beating the best it's most unlikely to be for lack of trying. *I. A. Balding.*

DASHING SENOR 2 b.c. (Mar 19) El Gran Senor (USA) 136–Zillionaire (USA) 85 (Vaguely Noble 140) [1989 6m2 7g3 7g6] IR 240,000Y: strong, good-bodied colt: fifth reported foal: dam, winner at around 6f at 4 yrs in USA, is daughter of Cheveley Park and Flying Childers winner Gentle Thoughts: fair form in maidens won by In The Groove at York in August and Tanfith at Yarmouth following month: creditable sixth to The Caretaker in Cartier Million at Phoenix Park: will be suited by 1m. *A. C. Stewart.*

DATELINE AVALON 3 ch.g. Caerleon (USA) 132–Bottom Line 90 (Double 84 Jump 131) [1988 7g 7s3 1989 10.6g 10g2 10g5] useful-looking gelding: edgy, given too much to do when beaten short head in £8,400 apprentice handicap at Newmarket in October: again favourite, fair fifth in £8,900 handicap at Redcar 10 days later, no extra and hanging left final 1f: moved poorly down but shaped well on reappearance, off course 4½ months after: should stay 1½m: bit coltish first 2 starts: gelded after final start. *W. Jarvis.*

DAUNOU (FR) 3 b.c. Fabulous Dancer (USA) 124–Dourdan (Prudent (USA)) 60 [1988 7.5g4 1989 10m2 12.2m5 10f4 10f5 12.2d] rangy colt: turns fore feet in: good mover: closely related to smart French 8.5f to 10.5f winner Devalois (by Nureyev) and half-brother to numerous winners, notably good 1m to 1¼m colt Dunphy (by Riverman) and very useful middle-distance performer Doux Lord (by Sir Gaylord): dam won Prix Cleopatre and is daughter of Arc second Denisy: second in maiden at Longchamp when trained by Mme C. Head: quite modest form in similar events here: tailed off (soon eased) in claimer final outing: stays 1¼m: possibly unsuited by a soft surface: bandaged behind last 3 starts: has joined S. Christian. *D. Morley.*

DAUNTESS 2 ch.f. (Apr 13) Formidable (USA) 125–Cantico 58 (Green Dancer **67** (USA) 132) [1989 6g 6g²] sparely-made, angular filly: first foal: dam staying maiden, is half-sister to very smart 1m to 1½m filly Calderina: 2 lengths second of 12 to Himmah in maiden at Leicester in November: will be better suited by 7f: slowly away both starts. *D. R. C. Elsworth.*

DAUNTING PROSPECT 5 b.g. Formidable (USA) 125–Acquire 105 (Burglar — 128) [1988 NR 1989 16.2g 16.5g 16.5m] small, strong gelding: poor mover: of little account: visored first 2 starts. *M. C. Chapman.*

DAURICUM 5 ch.m. Mandrake Major 122–Rhododendron 50 (Warpath 113) — [1988 9v³ 8d 12d* 1989 11d] sparely-made, angular mare: winning plater as 4-y-o: stays 1½m: acts on heavy going: sold 2,200 gns Doncaster May Sales: unreliable. *C. W. Thornton.*

DAWES OF NELSON 4 b. or br.g. Krayyan 117–Killyhevlin (Green God 128) — [1988 6d 6f 6d² 6m 6g⁴ 7m 6g² 7m 1989 7.6f 6m 7m⁴ 6g 6m 7d] workmanlike gelding: poor maiden: probably stays 7f: best form with give in the ground. *M. J. Bolton.*

DAWN BELL 4 b.f. Belfort (FR) 89–Dobrina (FR) (Our Mirage 123) [1988 NR — 1989 10d 7d 5g 5f] good-bodied filly: no longer of much account: has worn blinkers. *J. M. Bradley.*

DAWN LOVE 6 b.m. He Loves Me 120–Fog 87 (English Prince 129) [1988 10.2s **59** 10.2d⁵ 10.8m⁵ 9f* 10f³ 9m 11m 10f 10m³ 9d 10.2f 11m³ 10m⁶ 12g⁶ 12m 12g 1989 10.2g 9f⁶ 12f* 12h² 12.3m⁵ 12m² 11f⁴ 12m³ 12.3f⁴ 12.3m 12f² 13.6g³ a13g⁵] narrow, sparely-made mare: quite modest handicapper: led final strides when winning at Beverley in May: ran at least creditably most starts afterwards: stays 13.6f: probably unsuited by soft going, acts on any other: goes very well for A. Culhane: held up: winning hurdler. *R. Hollinshead.*

DAWN'S DELIGHT 11 b.g. Dawn Review 105–Bird of Passage (Falcon 131) **84** [1988 6d* 6d² 6m⁶ 6g 6d 6g 6m 6g³ 6m 6f 6d⁶ 6s 6d 6s 1989 6d⁴ 6v³ 6v⁴ 6s* 6m 6m 5.6g 6s 6m 6d* 6s⁶ 6v] leggy, workmanlike gelding: moderate mover: fairly useful handicapper: successful at Haydock in April and October: 8/1 from 14/1 and apprentice ridden, gained his nineteenth victory when beating Sharp Times 1½ lengths in 24-runner event on latter occasion: best at 6f: suited by plenty of give in the ground: has worn blinkers and a visor: sometimes bandaged: often on toes: held up and is suited by strong gallop: tough: a credit to his trainer. *K. T. Ivory.*

DAWN STORM 3 b.g. Runnett 125–Dawn Star 94 (High Line 125) [1988 7g 7g² **81** 1989 8f² 8m 7.6m 7s 6f* 7g] rather leggy, close-coupled gelding: fluent mover: won minor event at Lingfield in October: pulled hard and swerved left 2f out on reappearance: probably stays 1m: acts on firm going: inconsistent: sold 10,000 gns Newmarket Autumn Sales, gelded afterwards. *J. L. Dunlop.*

DAWN SUCCESS 3 br.c. Caerleon (USA) 132–Dawn Echo (Don (ITY) 123) **101** [1988 6d* 6m⁴ 6f 6m⁶ 7f* 7g 8v³ 7g 1989 8s² 7d 8.5s² 10f 8f 10g 8m² 8m⁵ 9g² 8m 6d*] medium-sized, leggy, close-coupled colt: useful performer: won listed race (well drawn) at Thirsk in November by 1½ lengths from Blyton Lad: beaten 6 lengths by Rambo's Hall in William Hill Cambridgeshire Handicap at Newmarket ninth start: effective at 6f, and stays 9f: acts on heavy going and top-of-the-ground: often sets pace: rather inconsistent. *C. E. Brittain.*

DAWSON CITY 2 ch.g. (Jan 28) Glint of Gold 128–Lola Sharp (Sharpen Up 127) **82** [1989 6f² 6f* 7f²] IR 24,000Y: sturdy gelding: third foal: half-brother to 3-y-o 6f winner Rocquaine (by Ballad Rock): dam won in Italy at 3 yrs: won maiden at Catterick in July: again odds on but facing stiff task, 5 lengths second to comfortable winner Trojan Excel in nursery at Redcar following month: better suited by 7f than 6f. *M. H. Easterby.*

DAYJUR (USA) 2 br.c. (Feb 6) Danzig (USA)–Gold Beauty (USA) (Mr **103 p** Prospector (USA)) [1989 6m* 6m²] $1,650,000Y: robust, good-quartered, attractive colt: second foal: closely related to American 4-y-o Maplejinsky (by Nijinsky), Grade 1 winner at 9f and 1¼m in 1988: dam champion sprinter in USA in 1982: odds on, won maiden at Newbury in June comfortably by 2 lengths from Almaghrib, quickening really well 1f out: sweating and edgy, ½-length second of 5, clear, to Rushmore in listed race there following month, short of room over 1f out then no extra last 100 yds: should stay 7f: should improve further, and win another race or two. *Major W. R. Hern.*

DAZZLING HEIGHTS 3 b.f. Shirley Heights 130–Cape Chestnut 87 (Bustino **99** 136) [1988 7m* 1989 10g* 12m⁵ 12m] sparely-made, useful-looking filly: keen walker: won apprentice event at Leicester in September, always front rank (pulling hard early) and rallying well: good fifth to Spritsail in listed race at Newmarket: sweating, weakened over 3f out in Group 3 event at Ascot 9 days later: stays 1½m: sold 50,000 gns Newmarket December Sales. *A. C. Stewart.*

DAZZLINGLY RADIANT 2 gr.f. (Mar 2) Try My Best (USA) 130–Elvina (FR) **52 p**
(Dancer's Image (USA)) [1989 5m³ 8m 8g] 15,500Y: sturdy, workmanlike filly: has scope: fifth living foal: closely related to moderate 1984 2-y-o 7f winner Dance By Night (by Northfields) and half-sister to 2 winners, including stayer Dominate (by Pitskelly): dam Irish 6f and 1¼m winner: plating-class form in maidens: stays 1m: likely to do better in modest handicap company. *R. Hannon.*

DEAD CERTAIN 2 b.f. (Mar 19) Absalom 128–Sirnelta (FR) (Sir Tor) **114**
[1989 5m² 5f* 5f* 6g² 6m* 6m*]
The unremitting expansion of the Al-Maktoum family's racing and breeding empire in Britain has caused understandable concern in some quarters, but a study of the twenty-four pattern races confined to two-year-olds which were run in 1989 doesn't substantiate the widely-held belief that their dominance has reached an unhealthy level: only one of the thirty or so pattern races the Al-Maktoums won during the year in Britain went to a two-year-old. Even if 1989 was an unusually barren year in that department the message remains clear that it doesn't necessarily require a Sheikh's ransom to pick up a good two-year-old at the sales. The pattern winners Argentum, Tirol, Haunting Beauty (who was purchased in the States) and Dead Certain were all obtained as foals or yearlings for the equivalent of a few months' training fees; and the newly-instituted Racecall Gold Trophy winner Osario, who was one of the very best two-year-olds around, cost virtually next to nothing. Few two-year-olds exemplified the point better than Dead Certain who cost 5,800 guineas as a foal yet has won three pattern races, including the Group 1 Tattersalls Cheveley Park Stakes, and earned in excess of £200,000 altogether.

The Cheveley Park was the highlight of Dead Certain's season which had lacked nothing in sustained improvement and spirited endeavour since it began five months earlier in a minor event at Windsor in May. Dead Certain went down that day by two lengths to the fitter and more-experienced Between The Sticks, who was conceding 8 lb, but made much the greater progress so that when they met again, in the Queen Mary Stakes at Royal Ascot, Dead Certain reversed the form in unequivocal fashion. In the interim

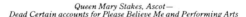

Queen Mary Stakes, Ascot—
Dead Certain accounts for Please Believe Me and Performing Arts

'The Pacemaker Update' Lowther Stakes, York—Dead Certain is always out in front

Dead Certain had made all the running in a maiden race at Salisbury, beating Love Returned readily by a length and a half, and lined up at Ascot as one of ten winners in a thirteen-runner field which was a representative collection of the best fillies around at the time, even if the standard didn't match up to some years. The race provided Dead Certain with the first of her three pattern victories after it had appeared for much of the penultimate furlong that the prize would be heading North with Please Believe Me. Dead Certain, who was bandaged in front, didn't respond immediately as Please Believe Me took a narrow advantage but drew level with a furlong to run and, despite edging to her right on the firm ground, ran on the stronger, as no late challenges materialised, to win by a length and a half. Winning the Queen Mary in recent years has, as often as not, been a ticket to obscurity. Only Forest Flower and Gwydion among its previous winners in the 'eighties did much to enhance their reputations, but Dead Certain, a robust, round-barrelled filly, had always looked the type who'd train on satisfactorily, and she all but carried a 3-lb penalty to success in the Hillsdown Cherry Hinton Stakes at Newmarket (where she was bandaged on her off-hind) in July. The race seemed to be hers as she took a three-length advantage over the odds-on favourite Chimes of Freedom into the last two-hundred-and-fifty yards, but though she saw her race out well Chimes of Freedom pipped her on the line. The following month saw Dead Certain conceding weight all round again, in 'The Pacemaker Update' Lowther Stakes at York. The race, which has Group 2 status, disappointingly went by without Chimes of Freedom, the Heinz '57' Phoenix winner Pharoah's Delight and the Prix Robert-Papin winner Ozone Friendly; and Dead Certain, who was bursting with well-being beforehand, took full advantage, dominating proceedings from the outset and drawing clear in the last furlong to beat Routillante by two and a half lengths.

The Cheveley Park Stakes at Newmarket in October is Britain's top race for two-year-old fillies and regularly decides their order of merit. Its value was increased considerably in 1989 when, for the first time, the initial entry stage was brought forward from mid-August to mid-April whilst giving owners the option to pay £10,000 (nearly forty times the fee in April) to enter at a supplementary stage nine days before the race. Several owners took advantage of the supplementary clause, so boosting significantly the total prize-money for the race, the basic intention of the new conditions, to over £200,000. Besides Dead Certain, whose trainer reportedly had little idea of her ability in April, the progressive Yarmouth and Goodwood winner Line of Thunder, Chimes of Freedom, the Prix d'Arenberg winner Repercutionist and the unbeaten northern fillies Haunting Beauty and Mademoiselle Chloe, who filled the first six places respectively, all came in at the late stage. The eleven-runner line-up also included the six-length Firth of Clyde winner Tabdea as well as Ozone Friendly (but not Pharaoh's Delight, who was injured) and looked to be a thoroughly informative affair. After leading for a furlong or so Dead Certain, who started second favourite behind Chimes of Freedom, was passed by the hard-pulling In The Papers who settled in front until Dead Certain took up the running again two furlongs out attended closely by Chimes of Freedom and the maiden winner Kissogram Girl. Entering the final furlong, where Line of Thunder joined the battle for the lead, Dead Certain looked to be travelling more comfortably than the others and she responded when asked to quicken again a hundred and fifty yards out, reaching the post three quarters of a length ahead of Line of Thunder; the next three home, of whom only Chimes of Freedom had been in serious contention in the last furlong, were separated by a head, the same and half a length. That less than three lengths covered the first six, however, seemed only to confirm what had been suspected earlier in the season, that the leading two-year-old fillies were not a top-notch bunch. Nevertheless that shouldn't detract from the performance of Dead Certain, who was skilfully brought back from a bout of flu, and looked in splendid shape in the paddock. In fact, it was noticeable how well Dead Certain progressed physically with her races during the season, and by the end she'd made up into a really grand filly.

The question invariably asked about the Cheveley Park winner is whether or not she'll stay the extra two furlongs of the One Thousand Guineas. Certainly, most recent winners (Forest Flower, for these purposes, being regarded as the winner in 1986) have got a mile the following season but the racing Press was by no means unanimous that Dead Certain, a daughter of the high-class sprinter Absalom, will continue the trend. Our opinion is that she will. Absalom is best remembered for winning the Vernons Sprint Cup and the Diadem Stakes over six furlongs, but he was pretty good over seven furlongs too, as he showed when landing the Premio Chiusura in Italy shortly before his retirement. His own pedigree is a mix of speed and stamina which is reflected to some extent in the multiplicity of winning distances, from five to seventeen furlongs, of his older progeny in England and Ireland. Even more encouraging is the distaff side of Dead Certain's pedigree. Dead Certain is the best of a long line of foals produced by her dam Sirnelta, whose seven other produce to have run include five that stayed at least a mile and a quarter,

Tattersalls Cheveley Park Stakes, Newmarket —
the season's most valuable prize in Britain for two-year-olds goes to Dead Certain

among them Fire Top (by Hotfoot), who has also won over hurdles, and Lady Gerard (by Brigadier Gerard) and another, Jigs And Reels (by Comedy Star), who stays a mile; the seventh saw a racecourse only twice. Sirnelta stayed as far as most of her winning offspring, gaining one of her three wins in France over a mile and a quarter, and further perhaps than a mating between the French five-and-a-half- and seven-and-a-half-furlong winner Sir Tor and the good French two-year-old Finelta may have suggested. Finelta never won beyond seven furlongs but she is a full sister to the French Derby winner Sanctus II and the Prix Penelope winner Straight On; she is also a half-sister to the grandam of the top-class French middle-distance colt Le Marmot.

		Abwah	Abernant
		(gr 1969)	The Creditor
	Absalom	Shadow Queen	Darius
	(gr 1975)	(ch 1965)	Shadow
Dead Certain		Sir Tor	Round Table
(b.f. Mar 19, 1987)		(b 1963)	Never Too Late
	Sirnelta (FR)	Finelta	Fine Top
	(b or br 1971)	(b or br 1959)	Sanelta

Although we expect Dead Certain, who's an excellent walker and has a powerful, fluent action, to stay a mile it's questionable whether she'll derive so much benefit from the additional distance as will both Line of Thunder and Chimes of Freedom, and she may be hard pressed to confirm the form of the Cheveley Park. She also has something to find with Salsabil, who's already won over a mile. Whatever happens in the future, however, Dead Certain will still be remembered for her feats as a two-year-old. Like most of the other top fillies, Dead Certain's racing has so far been confined to a sound surface. *D. R. C. Elsworth.*

DEADLOCK 2 ch.c. (Feb 1) The Minstrel (CAN) 135–Roses To Rachel (Artaius — (USA) 129) [1988 8v] 50,000Y: well-made colt: first foal: dam, placed twice in USA at 3 yrs, is half-sister to top-class 1985 2-y-o Huntingdale: 16/1 and carrying condition, slowly away and always behind in 23-runner minor event at Newbury in October. *D. R. C. Elsworth.*

DEADLY CHARM (USA) 3 b. or br.f. Bates Motel (USA)–Certain Something 73 102 (Solinus 130) [1988 8v 9v6 1989 10.1m5 10f2 12m5] $125,000Y: rangy filly: first reported foal: dam Irish 2-y-o 6f winner: sire high-class 1m to 1¼m performer: modest maiden: gives impression may prove ideally suited by 1¼m: trained at 2 yrs by J. Oxx in Ireland: has joined D. Nicholson. *J. Gosden.*

DEAR MIFF 4 ch.f. Alias Smith (USA)–Dear Jem 78 (Dragonara Palace (USA) 44 115) [1988 8f* 10g2 11.7m 8f4 10.2f 10.4d 1989 12.3s5 11.7d4 14g 10f 12m 8.5g 10m2 9m a12g5] plain filly: winning plater as 3-y-o: runner-up in ladies handicap at Pontefract in August: weakened from around 2f out majority of other starts, quickly so on several occasions as though something amiss: best at short of 1½m: acts on any going: blinkered last 3 outings: sometimes sweats: has run well for apprentice. *A. Bailey.*

DEAR OLD GIRL 2 gr.f. (Apr 5) Carwhite 127–Curfew 76 (Midsummer Night II — 117) [1989 5.3g 5d 6m 8m] 2,600Y: smallish filly: half-sister to 1980 2-y-o 5f winner Goodbye Starter (by Owen Dudley), later 1m winner in USA, and 2 winners in Italy: dam placed over 6f at 2 yrs: well beaten, including a seller: should stay 1m. *D. T. Thom.*

DEBACH DAISY 2 b.f. (Mar 5) Ahonoora 122–Princess Seal 108 (Prince 72 Tenderfoot (USA) 126) [1989 6m2] 40,000Y: workmanlike filly: second live foal: half-sister to 1987 2-y-o 5f winner Waitingformargaret (by Kris): dam sprinter: 8/1 and backward, 2 lengths second of 5 to Naval Party in maiden at Newmarket in May: looked sure to win a race but wasn't seen out again. *C. E. Brittain.*

DEBACH DARKNESS 3 b.f. Dara Monarch 128–Lenticular 42 (Warpath 113) — [1988 NR 1989 12g 12f] IR 10,000F, 37,000Y: rangy filly: first foal: dam third in 1¼m seller from 3 starts at 3 yrs: raced keenly and prominent 1m when behind in minor event (backward and green) and maiden (sweating) at Salisbury in May: sold T. Cunningham 1,500 gns Newmarket July Sales. *C. E. Brittain.*

DEBBIE'S NEXT (USA) 3 b.f. Arctic Tern (USA) 126–Babes Sis (USA) (Raise 82 ? A Native) [1988 NR 1989 7d4 10f4 8m3 7.5m3 9g a8g3] rather sparely-made filly: good walker: third foal: half-sister to 1986 2-y-o Born To Race (by Dr Blum), a fairly useful winner at around 5f: dam, minor winner at up to 7f in USA at 3 yrs, is half-sister to Monmouth Oaks winner Sharp Belle: fair maiden: sweating, best effort in £5,400 event at York third start: ran moderately after, looking really well first 2 occasions then soon driven along (blinkered) final one: stays 1m (took keen hold over 1¼m): gives impression will prove suited by an easy surface. *B. W. Hills.*

DEBONAIR   4 b.g. Taufan (USA) 119–Just Gorgeous (Home Guard (USA) 129) —
[1988 12g² 14g 12d 14m 1989 14.6g] tall gelding: first foal: dam plating-class maiden at up to 6f at 2 yrs: second in maiden at Laytown in 1988 when trained by M. O'Toole: always behind in similar event at Doncaster in April: stayed 1½m: dead. *P. A. Blockley.*

DEB'S BALL   3 b.f. Glenstal (USA) 118–De'b Old Fruit (Levmoss 133) [1988 NR   70
1989 7m⁶ 8.2m⁵ 7g³] IR 16,000F, 11,000Y: quite good-topped filly: half-sister to a winner in Norway and a winner over jumps: dam won over 1½m in Ireland: quite modest maiden: bit backward first 2 starts: should stay further. *D. Moffatt.*

DECANNA   4 ch.f. Decoy Boy 129–Louisianalightning (Music Boy 124) [1988 8g⁵   —
10g 8f 1989 8g] seems of little account: has been blinkered: sold 1,100 gns Doncaster June Sales. *G. M. Moore.*

DECEIT   2 b.c. (May 10) On Your Mark 125–Second Movement (Music Boy 124)   66
[1989 5s 5s⁴ 5.3m² 5f 5f⁵ 5g⁴] IR 2,800F, 10,500Y: small, compact colt: half-brother to 2 winners abroad by Faraway Times: dam sister to Ayr Gold Cup winner First Movement: quite modest maiden: ran very well in nurseries final 2 starts. *G. Lewis.*

DECIDING BID   3 ch.c. Valiyar 129–Final Call 79 (Town Crier 119) [1988 6g 6g³
6m 1989 6m 8f 7g 6f 7h 10f a10g] smallish, good-bodied colt: quite modest form at 2 yrs: well beaten in 1989, including in sellers: probably doesn't stay 7f: bought out of A. Ingham's stable 2,400 gns Ascot July Sales after fifth outing. *J. E. Long.*

DEE AND EM   4 ch.g. Crofter (USA) 124–Cousin Clare (Pontifex (USA)) [1988   61
6m⁵ 5f 5g³ 6g 6f³ 5m⁴ 6d⁵ 7g 1989 5m 5m 6f 6f³ 6m 6f* 6m 5m 5.3f⁴ 6g 6m 6g] compact, workmanlike gelding: quite modest handicapper: won for first time, at Thirsk in August, soon leading on advantageous stand rail and staying on despite carrying head high and looking little reluctant: stays 6f: acts on firm going and a soft surface: blinkered last 7 outings: very slowly away eighth start: has seemed unsuited by course at Catterick: usually taken steadily to post: sold 1,750 gns Newmarket Autumn Sales: inconsistent, and none too genuine. *W. J. Pearce.*

DEE JAY PEE   3 ch.g. Electric 126–Lady Gaston 76 (Pall Mall 132) [1988 6f 7s 5g
1989 8g 7g 8.5f 9m] angular gelding: moderate walker: has a round action: no worthwhile form in varied company, final start in June: may be suited by further. *B. Preece.*

DEEMSTER WILLOW   3 b.f. Ballacashtal (CAN)–Sprightly Willow 45 (Native   —
Bazaar 122) [1988 6g 6d 6d 1989 8g 12g] lengthy, rather angular filly: soundly beaten in maidens and handicaps: trained on reappearance by B. Stevens and off course 5½ months after. *G. B. Balding.*

DEEP REEF   3 ch.c. Main Reef 126–Kareela (FR) (Deep Diver 134) [1988 5m⁴ 6g   80
6d⁵ 6g⁵ 6d* 7d 1989 6f³ 8d 6v 7g] lengthy, rather angular colt: fair handicapper: made all in maiden as 2-y-o: easily best effort in 1989 on reappearance, off course nearly 4 months after: showed signs of retaining his ability at Redcar final start, staying on from rear: should stay 1m: acts on firm going and a soft surface. *L. G. Cottrell.*

DEEP TAW   5 br.m. Kala Shikari 125–Florence Mary 51 (Mandamus 120) [1988 8f   32
8f 1989 5f 5m⁴ 5h 5f⁴ 5f⁴ 5f⁶ 8m] small non-thoroughbred mare: carries plenty of condition: poor mover: poor handicapper: doesn't stay 1m: acts on firm going: has run well for apprentice. *C. J. Hill.*

DEEPWOOD NANUSKET   3 b.f. Sayf El Arab (USA) 127–Nanushka 53   47
(Lochnager 132) [1988 NR 1989 6s 6m⁶ 7.6m] workmanlike filly: second foal: half-sister to 1¼m winner Not So Shy (by Star Appeal): dam, out of half-sister to Altesse Royale, best at 5f: showed quite modest form in minor event at Kempton in May: didn't reproduce that in claimer and sellers: possibly unsuited by top-of-the-ground. *P. F. I. Cole.*

DEERCAL DANCER   3 ch.g. Ballacashtal (CAN)–Lookslike Reindeer (Bonne   58
Noel 115) [1988 NR 1989 7d⁶ 7.5d² 7g³ 6f⁴ 7m³ 7m 7m⁶ a6g] small gelding: third foal (first 2 by Chinese Kung Fu): dam won over 5f at 2 yrs in Ireland and stayed 1½m: modest form in varied events, including sellers: below form last 3 outings, off course 4 months and gelded before final one (edgy): stays 7.5f: acts on firm going and a soft surface: blinkered sixth outing. *R. Simpson.*

DEERNESS LAD 2 b.g. (Apr 26) Kala Shikari 125–Il Regalo (Meadow Mint **44**
(USA) 120) [1989 5g 6f⁵ 7.5f 7f 8.5f] 2,600Y, 6,000 2-y-o: leggy, sparely-made
gelding: sixth foal: half-brother to a winner in Italy by Frimley Park: dam placed
over 1m and 1¼m: poor form in varied events, including a seller. *D. H. Topley.*

DEFENCE POLICY 4 ch.c. Kings Lake (USA) 133–Frivolous Relation (USA) **92**
59 (Buckpasser) [1988 8g² 8g 7d⁶ 7g² 8g* 8g* 7f² 7g² 7m⁵ 1989 8g 10g⁶ 10.4m²
10.6d³ 10m 9g] medium-sized colt: has a quick action: beaten only narrowly when
placed in handicaps (off course nearly 4 months in between) at Chester (not finding
much off bridle) and Haydock: creditable seventh in £24,200 handicap at Newbury
and William Hill Cambridgeshire Handicap at Newmarket last 2 outings: stays 10.6f:
seems to act on any going: needs holding up until last moment. *B. W. Hills.*

DEFENSIVE PLAY (USA) 2 b.c. (Mar 10) Fappiano (USA)–Safe Play (USA) **87 p**
(Sham (USA)) [1989 7m³ 8m*] big, strong, lengthy colt: has plenty of scope: second
foal: half-brother to French 11f winner Livry (by Lyphard): dam, winner from 5.5f to
9f in USA including in Grade 1 company, is half-sister to 1000 Guineas winner
Musical Bliss: sire won stakes from 6f to 9f: favourite, won maiden at Newmarket in
October by 4 lengths (actually 5½) from Chapman's Peak, making most and drawing
clear last 1½f: tended to hang at Lingfield on debut: will be suited by 1¼m: likely to
improve further. *G. Harwood.*

DEFICIT (USA) 2 ch.c. (May 2) Deputy Minister (CAN)–Go Leasing 121 (Star **66 p**
Appeal 133) [1989 6m 8m³] robust, medium-sized colt: has plenty of scope: has a
quick action: second foal: dam 6f to 1m winner and third in 1000 Guineas, later won
at 9f in USA: shaped with considerable promise when around 9 lengths third of 9 to
Primacy in maiden at Warwick in October, running on strongly from rear without
being knocked about: sure to win a race. *B. W. Hills.*

DEGANNWY 2 br.f. (Apr 27) Caerleon (USA) 132–Delagoa (FR) (Targowice —
(USA) 130) [1989 7f⁴] 28,000Y: half-sister to 5 winners abroad, including French
9.2f winner Le Coureur (by Nureyev), later successful over hurdles, and half-sister
to 2 other winners abroad: dam, French 10.5f winner, is half-sister to Durtal (dam of
Gildoran) and Detroit: weak 12/1, 12½ lengths fourth of 6, slowly away and always in
rear, to Courtesy Title in maiden at Brighton in July. *Dr J. D. Scargill.*

DEHAR BOY 3 b.g. Buzzards Bay 128§–Nahawand 51 (High Top 131) [1988 7g **54**
7.5f 8.2s 1989 10s 9f³ 10.2f⁵ 11m 10m⁶ 10g⁴ 8f⁵ 9f⁵] strong, lengthy gelding:
moderate mover: plating-class form in varied events, including seller: suited by
1¼m: acts on firm going. *P. J. Feilden.*

DEINOPUS 5 b.g. Hittite Glory 125–Flying Fire 78 (Sparkler 130) [1988 8.2m 8g §§
5f⁶ 1989 6v 7d 6g 8.2f 8h³ 7f 7.6m 10.8m 8.2d 6m⁴ 8g] neat gelding: most
unsatisfactory temperamentally and should be left alone: bought out of D. Moffatt's
stable 1,800 gns Doncaster September Sales after ninth start. *S. E. Kettlewell.*

DELAMERE ROSE 2 b.f. (Apr 18) Lyphard's Special (USA) 122–Royal Rosette —
66 (Pardao 120) [1989 6m] 5,000Y: half-sister to several winners here and abroad,
including 6f winner Hot Ember (by Hot Spark) and 7f and 1¼m winner Dragon's
Head (by Star Appeal): dam stayed 1¼m: slowly away and always behind in
20-runner maiden auction race at Leicester in July: dead. *W. G. A. Brooks.*

DELIGHTFUL DIANE 2 b.f. (May 19) Kalaglow 132–Whip Finish 77 (Be **49**
Friendly 130) [1989 5.8m⁵ 6g] 10,000Y: leggy, unfurnished filly: half-sister to three
5f winners, notably very useful Whipper In (by Bay Express) and Molecomb winner
Hotbee (by Hotfoot): dam won twice over 5f at 2 yrs: poor form in summer maiden
auction events. *R. J. Holder.*

DELIORMAN 3 ch.c. Pharly (FR) 130–Dedra (FR) (Faunus (FR)) [1988 NR 1989 **121**
10.5d⁴ 10.5d* 10d⁶ 12.5g² 12g* 12m⁴] second foal: dam, 8.5f winner on first of 2
starts in France, is half-sister to 1986 Grand Criterium winner Danishkada: won
maiden at Longchamp in July and listed race at Saint-Cloud in September: good
fourth to Robore in Prix du Conseil de Paris at Longchamp in October: stays 12.5f:
acts on top-of-the-ground and a soft surface. *A. de Royer-Dupre, France.*

DELLWOOD RENOWN 7 b.g. Connaught 130–Erstung 83 (Shantung 132) —
[1988 12g 12m 12v 1989 10.2g 12g 10f] strong, workmanlike gelding: poor
handicapper: best form at 1½m: unsuited by soft going and used to act well on
top-of-the-ground: has worn a crossed noseband: sometimes bandaged: has given
trouble for an amateur. *W. Holden.*

DELORAINE 3 b.f. Pharly (FR) 130–Fruition 89 (Rheingold 137) [1988 7g⁶ 7g³
7.5f 1989 10.6g] angular, workmanlike filly: half-sister to good stayer Kneller (by
Lomond): dam suited by 1½m: modest form when third of 5 in slowly-run minor

H. H. Aga Khan's "Demawend"

event in July as 2-y-o: badly hampered next start and on only one in 1989 (June): should be suited by at least 1¼m. *M. H. Easterby.*

DEMAWEND 3 b.c. Mill Reef (USA) 141–Demia (FR) (Abdos 134) [1988 8m³ **113** 1989 10d² 12m* 16f² 16f² 14m² 15m²] rangy, deep-girthed colt with plenty of scope: good walker and mover, with a fluent, quick action: odds on, won maiden at Haydock in May, making most: good second after to Weld in Queen's Vase at Royal Ascot and Lonsdale Stakes at York, Michelozzo in March Stakes (sweating, 4 days after York) at Goodwood and to Mardonius in Group 3 Prix de Lutece, beaten a neck, at Longchamp: stays 2m: acts on firm going and a soft surface: game and smart. *M. R. Stoute.*

DEMESNE FLYER 2 ch.g. (Apr 26) Tower Walk 130–Covenant 75 (Good Bond   — 122) [1989 6g] 4,200Y: fourth foal: brother to 7f and 1¼m seller winner Royal Treaty: dam won over 7f at 2 yrs and stayed 1½m: 25/1, slowly away and always behind in 18-runner maiden at Redcar in November. *R. Hollinshead.*

DEMILINGA 3 gr.f. Nishapour (FR) 125–Senane 86 (Vitiges (FR) 132) [1988 NR   — 1989 7g 6g 6g] 11,000F, 17,000Y: leggy, close-coupled filly: first foal: dam, daughter of top staying 2-y-o filly of 1978 Formulate, won over 1m at 2 yrs and stayed 1½m but didn't look entirely genuine: well behind in minor event and claimers: bit backward first 2 starts: bandaged off-hind final one: bred to need much further than 6f. *P. J. Feilden.*

DEMOKOS (FR) 4 ch.g. Dom Racine (FR) 121–Eagletown (FR) (Dictus (FR)   **66** 126) [1988 10v³ 1989 12.2m⁴ 12.4g⁶ 12m* 13s⁵ 12g* 13.6g* 12g³ a14g⁶ a14g* a14g] lengthy gelding: successful in handicaps at Thirsk (gambled on), Carlisle, Redcar and Southwell in second half of season: close up when stumbling and falling 3f out at Southwell final outing: stays 1¾m: seems unsuited by soft going: apprentice ridden

252

fifth to seventh starts: sweated first 2: has appeared lazy: winning hurdler. *J. G. FitzGerald.*

DENBERDAR   6 b.g. Julio Mariner 127–Penumbra 99 (Wolver Hollow 126) [1988   —
NR 1989 10.8s⁵ 12s 10.6g 10f] sparely-made gelding: turns near-fore in: poor
maiden: needs further than 1½m and stays 2m well: probably unsuited by firm
going, acts on any other: has run in snatches: winning hurdler. *A. P. James.*

DENCAST   2 b.c. (Apr 14) Battle Hymn 103–Ishiyama 62 (Owen Anthony 102)   —
[1989 7d a6g a6g] rather sparely-made colt: second live foal: dam plating class at 2
yrs: seems of little account. *S. G. Norton.*

DENHAM GREEN   3 b.g. Dominion 123–Ariadne 79 (Bustino 136) [1988 5s*   82
5m2 5g5 6m3 7m* 6g6 7m5 6g4 6s* 6s2 6m6 6s2 1989 7g3 6v6 6d 9f 5m3 5g2 5g 6m
5s 5m] lengthy, good-quartered gelding: has a roundish action: trained first
3-y-o: ran moderately after sixth outing: best form over 6f (as 2-y-o): acts on
top-of-the-ground, but ideally suited by soft: has run well for a claimer: trained first
4 outings by S. Muldoon. *M. H. Easterby.*

DENHAM HOUSE   2 ch.g. (Jan 21) Jalmood (USA) 126–Ariadne 79 (Bustino   49 d
136) [1989 5v3 5s5 5g 7g 10.6d] 7,000Y: workmanlike, good-quartered gelding:
carries condition: keen walker: fourth foal: half-brother to 3-y-o Denham Green (by
Dominion), fairly useful 5f and 6f winner at 2 yrs, and 1½m winner Cas-En-Bas (by
Good Times): dam 2m winner: poor maiden: off course all summer, and well beaten
in claimer and selling nursery on return: bred to stay well: trained first 3 outings by
S. Muldoon: sold to join T. Kersey 2,000 gns Doncaster November Sales. *C. Tinkler.*

DENISE SIMIANE (ITY)   4 ch.f. Maffei (ITY)–Daralda (FR) (Mannsfeld   —
(ITY)) [1988 10g6 12.3g 1989 12g] seems of little account. *Don Enrico Incisa.*

DENITZ (FR)   7 ch.g. Sharpman 124–Djerba (My Swallow 134) [1988 11.7g 9g 8g   —
8g 7g 1989 8f 8f 7d5] good-bodied gelding: has been hobdayed: won handicap early in
1986: well beaten majority of subsequent starts, but showed he retains a little ability
when fifth of 27 in apprentice handicap at Newbury in October: best form at 1m:
needs give in the ground and acts on heavy. *C. Holmes.*

DENSBEN   5 b.g. Silly Prices 110–Eliza de Rich 57 (Spanish Gold 101) [1988 5g   76
6g3 6f3 5m4 5f 6f 5g* 5g3 6g2 5d* 5g 6f 6g 5s 5f 5g3 6s* 5v2 1989 5g4 5g* 6v* 6.1f3
6f 6m 6m3 5m 6m 6m2 6f 6m 5s4 6s 6m 6d5 6g2 5s 5d6] smallish, sparely-made
gelding: modest handicapper: in good form early in season, winning at Doncaster
and Ayr: effective at 5f ridden up with pace and stays 6f well: acts on any going: good
mount for inexperienced rider: has started slowly: none too consistent. *Denys Smith.*

DEN'S SONG   3 ch.g. Sallust 134–Princess Ru (Princely Gift 137) [1988 6f 7m   58
7g4 1989 7s 8m 7f5 7m4 7m5 7m3 8.2f 7m6 7d] compact gelding: has a long
stride: 50/1 and ridden by 7-lb claimer, won handicap at Redcar in September: suited
by 7f: acts on top-of-the-ground. *W. Carter.*

DEPLOY   2 b.c. (May 15) Shirley Heights 130–Slightly Dangerous (USA) 122   88 p
(Roberto (USA) 131) [1989 8v3] fourth foal: half-brother to Warning (by Known
Fact) and useful 7f to 12.3f winner Timefighter (by Star Appeal): dam, from
excellent family, won at 6f and 7f and second in Oaks: 20/1, staying-on 4½ lengths
third of 23 to Tyburn Tree in minor event at Newbury in October: will be well suited
by 1¼m +: sure to improve, and win a maiden at least. *J. Tree.*

DEPOT   3 b.c. Sharpo 132–Base Camp 80 (Derring-Do 131) [1988 7g6 6d 6g4 1989   —
6m] strong, short-backed colt: quite modest maiden as 2-y-o: bit backward and on
toes, tailed off as if something amiss at Newmarket in May, only start in 1989:
should be suited by 7f. *G. A. Pritchard-Gordon.*

DEPUTY TIM   6 ch.g. Crofter (USA) 124–Kindle (Firestreak 125) [1988 8.2v*   67
7d4 8g4 7m3 8f* 8g* 8.2s2 8.2g3 10g 7m 8m 1989 8.2v* 9f* 8m2 8.2g 7.6h 7m* 8m
7.5m 7f 8s5 9f 7m] neat gelding: carries plenty of condition: has a quick action:
modest handicapper: successful at Hamilton (winning same race for second year
running) and York (ladies event) in spring, making all on both occasions, and at Ayr
in July: effective at 7f to 9f: acts on any going: best without blinkers: sometimes
apprentice ridden, but has hung left (did so at Hamilton) and is not the easiest of
rides. *R. Bastiman.*

DERAB (USA)   3 b.c. Alleged (USA) 138–Island Charm (USA) (Hawaii) [1988 NR   93
1989 12m³ 12m3 12g* 14f 12s] workmanlike, angular colt: has a sharp, rather round
action: third foal: half-brother to 7f winner Musical Charm (by The Minstrel): dam
champion older female sprinter in USA: won maiden at Newmarket in May and
slowly-run minor event (9/4 on, very easily) at Pontefract in July: below form facing

stiff tasks in handicaps final 2 starts: stays 1½m: acts on top-of-the-ground: sold to race in France 25,000 gns Newmarket Autumn Sales. *J. Tree.*

DERECHEF 2 ch.f. (Apr 18) Derrylin 115–Songe d'Inde (Sheshoon 132) [1989 — 7.3v] leggy, unfurnished filly: sister to a minor winner in France: dam French 10.5f winner: 33/1, always behind in 12-runner listed race at Newbury in October. *T. Thomson Jones.*

DE RIVERA (USA) 3 b. or br.c. El Gran Senor (USA) 136–Vive La Reine **92** (Vienna 127) [1988 7g⁴ 7.6s² 1989 12g³ 12m* 12g 12m⁴ 12m² 12m*] medium-sized, well-made, attractive colt: fairly useful performer: won maiden (odds on) at Lingfield in June and handicap at Chepstow in October: may well stay beyond 1½m: probably acts on any going: ran creditably when edgy fifth start: sold 54,000 gns Newmarket Autumn Sales. *G. Harwood.*

DERRALEENA 4 b.f. Derrylin 115–Diorina 91 (Manacle 123) [1988 7g 7.3m 7f 6f **36** 6m⁵ 6g⁶ 7m 7f 6g² 1989 5f 5f 5f 6f⁴ 7f 6f³ 7f 6m] strong, lengthy filly: carries condition: poor mover: poor maiden: tailed off virtually throughout final outing: stays 6f: acts on any going: effective with or without blinkers: has swished tail. *W. G. R. Wightman.*

DERRY REEF 2 b.f. (Apr 22) Derrylin 115–Ballyreef (Ballymore 123) [1989 7d — 6s] 3,600Y: first foal: dam poor granddaughter of Prix de Diane winner Belle Sicambre: well beaten in late-season seller (slowly away) at Catterick and claimer at Hamilton. *Mrs J. R. Ramsden.*

DERRY RHYTHM 4 b. or br.g. Derrylin 115–French Music (French Beige 127) **39** [1988 8f³ 1989 7m 8h 10m 10.1m 10f³ 12.2f a14g] workmanlike gelding: carries plenty of condition: poor handicapper: worthwhile form as 4-y-o: won third in pattern selling event at Folkestone in August: tailed off in apprentice race 2 months later: stays 1¼m: acts on firm going and a soft surface: tends to get on toes. *P. Burgoyne.*

DERWENT VALLEY 5 gr.h. Frimley Park 109–Rykneld (Warpath 113) [1988 6g 6g⁴ 6f 6m³ 6f 6m* 6m² 6g⁶ 5.8d⁴ 5m⁶ 5.6m 6s 5g 5f⁵ 5s³ 5m² 1989 5s] small, sparely-made horse: modest winner as 4-y-o: weakened quickly over 1f out on only outing (April) in 1989: finds 5f on short side and stays 6f well: acts on any going: has won when sweating and edgy and for apprentice: none too consistent. *R. Hannon.*

DESERT BLUEBELL 3 gr.f. Kalaglow 132–Idle Waters 116 (Mill Reef (USA) **83** 141) [1988 NR 1989 10f² 12.2m² 10f² 13.6g⁵] 58,000Y: rangy filly: has long stride: sister to very useful stayer Shining Water and half-sister to winning staying handicapper Ancient Mariner (by Wollow): dam thoroughly genuine stayer: second in maidens at Beverley, Catterick and Chepstow: flashed tail and looked none too keen at Catterick but battled on well (leading 9f) at Chepstow: not discredited in handicap final start, first for over 3 months: probably stays 13.6f: may prove suited by a galloping track: sold 7,000 gns Newmarket December Sales. *M. R. Stoute.*

DESERT DANCER 3 ch.g. Enchantment 115–Crimson Queen 49 (Crimson — Beau 124) [1988 7m 7g 8g 7s 1989 12f⁶ 14f 12f⁴] workmanlike gelding: well beaten in varied company, including selling: sold 1,500 gns Doncaster August Sales. *J. J. O'Neill.*

DESERT DAWN 3 b.f. Belfort (FR) 89–Cast Pearls (USA) 83 (Cutlass (USA)) **108** [1988 5d² 5g* 5s⁵ 6m⁴ 5f² 5f² 5g³ 5d* 1989 5f³ 6f 5f⁵ 5g* 5m 5g 5m] small, sparely-made filly: useful performer: 100/1, very good fifth in King's Stand Stakes at Royal Ascot: won listed race at Sandown 15 days later: behind after in pattern races at York and Phoenix Park and listed race (badly hampered early on) at Newmarket: suited by 5f: acts on any going, with possible exception of very soft: sold 43,000 gns Newmarket December Sales. *Lord John FitzGerald.*

DESTINY DANCE (USA) 3 b.f. Nijinsky (CAN) 138–Althea (USA) (Alydar **100** (USA)) [1988 NR 1989 10s 10m² 12g* 11.5m* 12m⁵] tall, lengthy, rather unfurnished filly: first foal: dam, high-class American 2-y-o, won Grade 1 races over 8.5f and 9f at 3 yrs: useful performer: second favourite, successful in August in maiden at Haydock and minor event at Sandown: fair fifth of 10 to Snow Bride in Princess Royal Stakes at Ascot: will stay beyond 1½m. *M. R. Stoute.*

DEUX ANES 2 b.f. (Feb 19) Longleat (USA) 109–Song God 96 (Red God 128§) **92** [1989 5g* 5g* 5g* 5g* 7g* 6g² 7g* 5m⁵] 4,800F: good-quartered, sprint type: half-sister to several winners, including French 1m to 9f winner Rebecca's Song (by Artaius): dam 2-y-o 5f winner: the leading 2-y-o filly in Belgium, successful 6 times, including in 4 listed events: beaten short head by Somethingdifferent in Moet et Chandon-Rennen at Baden-Baden in September: creditable fifth to Argentum in Cornwallis Stakes at Ascot following month, making most on unfavoured side: stays 6f: has joined N. Graham. *J. Naylor, Belgium.*

DEVILS DIRGE 3 b.f. Song 132–Devils Alternative 67 (Hotfoot 126) [1988 5d6 **68** 5.3f2 5m6 6m3 6g2 6m2 6m4 5m5 5d 1989 6s 5m4 5f3 5g2 5f2 5.3h2 5m5 6m2 5.3f3] lengthy, sparely-made, angular filly: has a round action: modest handicapper: ran well at Brighton last 2 outings: should prove better over 6f than 5f: acts on hard ground: has run well for 7-lb claimer. *G. A. Pritchard-Gordon.*

DE WINTER 2 b.c. (Apr 8) Formidable (USA) 125–Mrs Danvers 87 (Balidar 133) **65** [1989 5m3 5m3 6s5] lengthy, deep-girthed colt: moderate mover: first foal: dam, winner at 2 yrs, was best at 5f: quite modest form in maidens on first 2 starts: possibly best at 5f. *C. R. Nelson.*

DHABIHA 2 b.f. (Mar 23) Dunbeath (USA) 127–Walladah (USA) 71 (Northern **69** Dancer) [1989 6g 9f5 7g3] useful-looking filly: has scope: second foal: half-sister to 3-y-o Jalees (by Precocious): dam, second 3 times at 1¼m, is closely related to very smart performer at up to 7f Beaudelaire and a daughter of very smart winner at up to 1m Bitty Girl: 2½ lengths third of 17, keeping on, to Starstreak in minor event at Leicester in November, first worthwhile form: virtually pulled up previous start, 3 weeks earlier: sold 11,500 gns Newmarket December Sales. *P. T. Walwyn.*

DHAKRAH 3 b.f. Touching Wood (USA) 127–Petrol 73 (Troy 137) [1988 7g 1989 **79** 10f3 12g2 14m2 14m3 19f2 16g*] angular, sparely-made filly: modest performer: odds on, easy winner of minor event at Carlisle in October: stays 2m: acts on top-of-the-ground: sold 15,500 gns Newmarket Autumn Sales. *H. Thomson Jones.*

DIACO 4 b.g. Indian King (USA) 128–Coral Cave 79 (Ashmore (FR) 125) [1988 8v **73** § 6m 6g5 6f4 7.6m3 8.5g5 7m 7.6d 9g 1989 8f 7.6m 8h6 8h4 7m3 7m2 7.6f2 8h4 7m2 7.6m6] leggy, quite attractive gelding: often in frame in handicaps, but generally disappointing: stays 7.6f: suited by a sound surface: blinkered once at 3 yrs: has given trouble at start (withdrawn once) and is highly-strung: not genuine. *M. A. Jarvis.*

DIADAD 2 ch.g. (Mar 30) Doulab (USA) 115–Numidia (Sallust 134) [1989 5f4 5m6 **58** 5m4 5m4 5g5 5m] IR 35,000F, IR 24,000Y: sturdy gelding: carries condition: first foal: dam, stayed 9f, is half-sister to very useful French middle-distance winner Dieter: plating-class performer: had stiff task in nursery final start: subsequently gelded: likely to prove best at 5f: has given trouble stalls. *F. H. Lee.*

DIADEM DANCER 3 b.g. Solford (USA) 127–Pure Music (FR) (Pure Flight — (USA)) [1988 5g 6g* 6f5 8f 8.2m 1989 10s 10g 8m 7m 7m5 10.1m 8.3g 10.1m 10f] small, compact gelding: poor walker and mover: plating-class winner at 2 yrs: little sign of ability in sellers in 1989: blinkered last 5 outings, twice sweating. *J. E. Long.*

DIAMOND APPEAL 3 b.f. Star Appeal 133–Ivoronica 89 (Targowice (USA) **88** 130) [1988 5g2 5g* 6m 8f5 6d* 6g2 1989 6m 8f5 7f 7f4 8f 6m* 7s] rangy filly: has plenty of scope: good walker: won handicap at Chester in September, leading inside final 1f: suited by 6f: acts on top-of-the-ground and a soft surface: active type, tends to be on toes and pull hard: sold 15,000 gns Newmarket December Sales. *M. H. Easterby.*

DIAMOND BAY 2 b.f. (Apr 21) Buzzards Bay 128§–Czar's Diamond 66 (Queen's — Hussar 124) [1989 5m 8m 8f] sister to poor maiden Rhum Bay and half-sister to several winners, including stayer Chucklestone (by Chukaroo): dam plater: soundly beaten in maidens and a minor event. *J. R. Bosley.*

DIAMOND PATH 3 ch.c. Morston (FR) 125–Glide Path 91 (Sovereign Path 125) **98** [1988 NR 1989 10g2 12f4 12m2 12m3 12g 10g3] strong colt: has a quick action: third foal: half-brother to fair 1987 2-y-o 8.5f winner Stryder (by Jalmood): dam, most genuine, won 7 times over middle distances: fairly useful on his day: may prove best over 1¼m: ran badly in visor fifth outing: doesn't find much and sometimes edges under pressure. *R. Boss.*

DIAMOND PRINCESS 3 ch.f. Horage 124–Finesse 87 (Miralgo 130) [1988 6f **69** 7g3 6f 8f6 1989 12d* 12s2 16.2g6 12m3 a13g4 a14g] workmanlike filly: moderate mover: modest handicapper: won at Folkestone in April: good fourth at Lingfield in November, first outing for 5 months: stays 13f: may prove suited by an easy surface, and acts on soft ground. *P. F. I. Cole.*

DIAMONDSAREFOREVER 4 b.g. Sparkling Boy 110–Flying Glory (Flying — Mercury) [1988 10v 8.5f 7g 1989 8m] tall gelding: poor maiden judged on most form. *C. W. Thornton.*

DIAMONDS HIGH 8 ch.g. Diamonds Are Trump (USA) 108–Easy Path (Swing — Easy (USA) 126) [1988 NR 1989 10.2g] well-made gelding: fair at best: never dangerous in amateurs handicap at Doncaster (sweating) in March, only race on flat after 1985: stayed 1½m: dead. *B. Forsey.*

DIAMOND SHOES (USA) 2 b.f. (May 12) Diamond Shoal 130–Raise A Baby **85** p
(USA) (Raise A Native) [1989 7g²] 16,000Y: strong, good-bodied filly: good walker:
seventh foal: half-sister to 3 winners abroad, including French 1m winner Summer
Review (by Graustark), the dam of smart middle-distance filly Summer Trip: dam
useful winner at up to 1¼m in France: 6/1 and very green, neck second of 24,
disputing lead 2f out and running on strongly, to Katsina in maiden at Newmarket in
November: will be suited by 1m+: sure to improve, and win a race. *G. Harwood.*

DIAMOND SINGH 2 b.c. (Apr 15) Mansingh (USA) 120–Prime Thought 69 **43**
(Primera 131) [1989 5d 5d⁴ 5g 6g 8.2g] IR 2,000Y: rather unfurnished colt:
half-brother to 3 winners, including useful sprinter Chantry Bridge (by Porto Bello):
dam from good family: poor form in varied races: best run at 5f, but should stay
further. *J. S. Wainwright.*

DIAMOND SPRITE (USA) 2 b.g. (Apr 27) Diamond Prospect (USA)–Implicit **70**
(Grundy 137) [1989 7m² 7m³ 8m⁶ 8.2f] IR 16,000Y, 14,000 2-y-o: dipped-backed,
good-quartered gelding: has scope: moderate walker: good mover: brother to fair
1m winner Magic At Dawn and a winner in USA and half-brother to 2 winners: dam
showed little ability in varied events: modest form in varied events: stays 1m: has twice sweated:
gelded after final outing. *J. Etherington.*

DIANABELLE 3 b.f. Vision (USA)–Grande Madame 64 (Monseigneur (USA) —
127) [1988 5g 5d 5f* 6f² 5.1m 5g³ 5m² 5.1f 5m 5g⁵ 6m 6g 1989 5s] smallish, sturdy
filly: moderate walker: moderate winning plater at 2 yrs: struggling at halfway in
non-selling handicap in April, only start in 1989: stays 6f: suitable mount for a
claimer: sometimes on toes: inconsistent. *Pat Mitchell.*

DIANA DEE 3 b.f. Blakeney 126–Deep River (FR) (Val de Loir 133) [1988 8d⁶ **70**
8g³ 1989 10f⁴ 12.2m³ 14g 12f⁴ 12.4g a13g] quite attractive filly: modest maiden:
tailed off at Lingfield final start: stays 1½m: acts on firm going: sold to join P. Bailey
8,600 gns Newmarket December Sales. *B. W. Hills.*

DIASKING 3 b.g. King of Spain 121–Diascia (Dike (USA)) [1988 5m 6m⁵ 1989 —
13.3m 12m³ 10.5g⁶ 10g] compact, workmanlike gelding: not of much account: sold
1,900 gns Newmarket Autumn Sales. *J. W. Hills.*

DI BRAVURA 3 b.g. Noalto 120–Diorina 91 (Manacle 123) [1988 6f 5.8g³ 6g **37**
5.8d⁶ 7.3m 7g 1989 6f 8f 12h 8m⁵] tall, leggy gelding: poor maiden: fifth in seller in
July: stays 1m: seemed unsuited by track at Lingfield third start. *W. G. R. Wightman.*

DICTATORS SONG (USA) 2 b.c. (Feb 25) Seattle Song (USA) 130–Buck's **106**
Dame (USA) (Damascus (USA)) [1989 6d 8g⁴ 8g* 8g⁵ 8g² 7g* 6.5s²] $32,000Y:
third foal: dam showed a little ability in France: won minor event at Clairefontaine in
August and nursery at Saint-Cloud in October: 5 lengths second to Pole Position in
Prix Eclipse there in November: stays 1m, but best form at shorter. *R. Collet,
France.*

DIDICOY (USA) 3 b.f. Danzig (USA)–Monroe (USA) 102 (Sir Ivor 135) [1988 **104**
6d⁴ 6f* 7m³ 1989 6m⁶ 6m² 6g²] rather leggy, useful-looking filly: has scope: useful
performer: won £21,600 Coral Bookmakers Handicap at Newmarket in May: good
second in William Hill Golden Spurs Trophy (on toes) at York in June and listed race
at Phoenix Park in September: may prove ideally suited by stiff 6f: yet to race on
very soft going, appears to act on any other. *J. Tree.*

DIEGO RIVERA 5 b.g. Shirley Heights 130–Brazen Faced 84 (Bold And Free **70**
118) [1988 NR 1989 8.5d 10d⁴ 12d 11s] tall, angular gelding: fair winner as 3-y-o when
trained by M. Stoute: 20/1 and ridden by 7-lb claimer, about 8 lengths fourth of 16 in
handicap at Beverley in May, only form in 1989: backward next outing 3½ months
later: one paced, and should be suited by further than 1¼m: probably needs an easy
surface nowadays. *M. W. Easterby.*

DIET 3 b.g. Starch Reduced 112–Highland Rossie 67 (Pablond 93) [1988 NR 1989 **74**
8.2v 8g 8.2g 11m 8.2f3 7m* 6f* 6f⁶ 7m² 6f 7g⁶ 7m 6g* 6m 6s 6s³ 6s] 2,200Y: angular
gelding: second foal: half-brother to ungenuine plater The Overnight Man (by
Smackover): dam won sellers over 7f and 1m: modest performer: made all in
handicaps at Edinburgh (wandering under pressure) and Hamilton in June and
claimer at Hamilton in August: below form 6 times at Ayr and once at Chester: best
over 6f and sharp 7f: probably acts on any going: usually visored, but wasn't final
start: goes well with forcing tactics and on a sharp track. *J. S. Wilson.*

DIGRESSION (USA) 2 b.c. (Feb 2) Seattle Slew (USA)–Double Axle **116** p
(USA) (The Axe II 115) [1989 7m² 7g* 8m*]
   With the exception of the 1985 winner Bonhomie, who went on to win the
King Edward VII Stakes and finish runner-up in three other pattern races, the

Royal Lodge EBF Stakes, Ascot—
Digression leaves his rivals toiling

record of recent winners of the Royal Lodge Stakes makes uninspiring reading. The 1984 winner Reach ran just twice as a three-year-old, finishing soundly beaten on each occasion; Bengal Fire, who touched off Deputy Governor in 1986, failed to win in fifteen attempts over the next two seasons and left for stud in Australia with his enthusiasm for racing seeming a thing of the past; then came Sanquirico and High Estate, winners in 1987 and 1988 respectively. This pair were undoubtedly high class as two-year-olds, both winning five times from as many attempts. However, Sanquirico showed nothing like that form in his second season, eventually being sold to stand in Japan, while High Estate, possibly hindered by the effects of surgery for a split pastern, had only a win in a three-runner minor event at Newcastle to show for his efforts in 1989. So, what of the prospects for the latest Royal Lodge winner Digression? In short, we reckon they're bright—he's an imposing individual, and with further improvement on the cards he ought to make his presence felt in good company in 1990.

Digression was being touted as one of the best two-year-olds in the Harwood stable well before he made his debut in a minor event at Salisbury in August. A combination of inexperience and lack of peak fitness saw him unable to cope with the subsequent Middle Park winner Balla Cove that day, but Digression landed the odds in very smooth fashion in modest company at Kempton three weeks later; and in a field of nine at Ascot he was sent off a well-backed 4/1 joint-favourite. Truth to tell, the opposition didn't seem strong by Group 2 standards. Digression's stable-companion Robellation— the only runner who'd contested a pattern race previously—was a 15/2 chance, but most backers seemed keener on more lightly-raced types like the other joint-favourite Satin Wood, Bridal Toast (9/2), Marienski (5/1), Spinning (6/1) and Aquatic (7/1). The betting pointed towards a close race, then, but we didn't get one. Digression ran out a very decisive winner, travelling close up from the start, leading early in the straight and, despite flashing his tail, forging clear in the final furlong to beat Bridal Toast officially by three lengths—it was actually slightly further—with Air Music, a 66/1-chance beaten on all his three previous starts, half a length away in third. Robellation turned in a rare below-par effort in fifth, and Spinning produced an extremely wayward performance, hanging severely left from halfway and being virtually pulled up in the final two furlongs.

Digression's sire Seattle Slew was a brilliant racehorse, one who, in 1977, became the first horse to complete the American triple crown while still undefeated. He made a similar impact on retiring to stud, too, but not, initially at least, in Europe. True, Seattle Song—a member of Seattle Slew's second crop—proved himself a high-class colt both at two years and at three; but there were also several expensive and well-publicised failures in the next few years, notably Amjaad, Alchaasibeyeh and Zajal, a trio who cost nigh-on thirteen million dollars collectively as yearlings yet managed to win only a single race between them. As a result of these and other disappointing animals it seemed possible that Seattle Slew's progeny were unsuited to racing under European conditions. However, in the last few seasons he has had several run well in big races, the Coronation Stakes winner Magic of Life

257

and the Criterium de Maisons-Laffitte winner Bitooh for instance. Besides Digression there were two other interesting two-year-olds by Seattle Slew seen on the racecourse over here in 1989, namely Vincent O'Brien's Tributary, who made a successful debut in a maiden race at Phoenix Park in September, and the French-trained Septieme Ciel, a highly-regarded colt who really thrived during the autumn, when he ran out the impressive winner of the Prix Thomas Bryon at Saint-Cloud and the Criterium de Maisons-Laffitte. Digression's dam Double Axle was bought on behalf of Juddmonte Farms for 500,000 dollars at the Keeneland November Sales in 1984. Double Axle, the winner of four moderate races at up to a mile, has a pedigree that would attract just about any breeder. At the time of her purchase Double Axle's close relation, the stakes-winning Swinging Lizzie, was in the news as the dam of the high-class mile-and-a-quarter performer Swing Till Dawn; in the latest season the same dam had the smart Halo colt Lively One running. Double Axle's record as a broodmare is a good one, too. Digression is her eighth foal and fourth winner from four starters; the others include Parfaitement, another son of Halo, who put up arguably his best effort when going down narrowly to Seattle Slew's son Slew O'Gold in the Grade 1 Wood Memorial in 1983, and the Irish River filly Double River, a winner over six and seven furlongs in France during 1988.

		Bold Reasoning	Boldnesian
	Seattle Slew (USA)	(b or br 1968)	Reason To Earn
	(b or br 1974)	My Charmer	Poker
Digression (USA)		(b 1969)	Fair Charmer
(b.c. Feb 2, 1987)		The Axe II	Mahmoud
	Double Axle (USA)	(gr 1958)	Blackball
	(ch 1974)	Snow Bower	Nearctic
		(b 1969)	Sulenan

As we said earlier, Digression is an imposing colt—big, good-bodied and powerful—with plenty of scope for improvement over the winter, and like many of his sire's stock he's a good walker and a fluent mover. If early reports prove accurate he'll be trained more with the Derby in mind than the Guineas. Digression needs to progress a fair bit to be regarded as a strong Derby contender, and on pedigree there has to be a doubt as to whether he'll prove fully effective over a mile and a half. However, to write down a horse of such obvious ability and potential would be wrong. He was clearly one of the best of his generation at two. *G. Harwood.*

DIMENSION 7 b.g. Dominion 123–Airy Queen (USA) (Sadair) [1988 9d 8g 8d6 — § 11.7m 10m 1989 10f 10f] lengthy gelding: carries plenty of condition: poor mover: won 3 handicaps in 1987, but has since lost his form and enthusiasm: suited by 1m or 1¼m: acts on any going: best form in blinkers: suited by waiting tactics: one to leave alone. *D. M. Grissell.*

DIMMER 3 gr.f. Kalaglow 132–Vaguely 92 (Bold Lad (IRE) 133) [1988 NR 1989 **108** 8m5 8m2 10f* 8m* 10g 8g5 10.5s2] good-topped filly: fifth foal: half-sister to useful 1985 2-y-o 6f winner Top Ruler (by High Top) and top-class winner at up to 10.5f Shady Heights (by Shirley Heights): dam 1m and 1¼m winner: made all at Sandown in maiden in July and listed race in August: not discredited in smart company after, best effort when beaten 4 lengths by Bex in Group 3 event at Saint-Cloud final start: effective at 1m and 1¼m: acts on any going: suited by forcing tactics. *R. W. Armstrong.*

DIMPLE STAR 2 b.c. (May 6) The Brianstan 128–Hanovia Gold 72 (Yellow — River 114) [1989 5h6 7m] leggy colt: second reported foal: dam sprinter: soundly beaten in summer in maiden (awkward stalls) at Lingfield and seller at Wolverhampton. *S. Dow.*

DINNINGTON BUMBLE 2 ch.f. (Feb 11) Miramar Reef 100§–Sandra's Secret — 88 (Most Secret 119) [1989 7f] 1,000F, 2,000Y: third reported foal: dam best at 5f: 25/1, soundly beaten in 28-runner seller at Redcar in October. *R. M. Whitaker.*

DINSDALE LAD 3 ch.g. Sweet Monday 122–Forgets Image 87 (Florescence — 120) [1988 5g 6f 5f 5g2 5g3 1989 9d 6m 6m6] leggy, rather unfurnished gelding: has a round action: form only when placed in sellers (blinkered) as 2-y-o: bit backward all outings in 1989, sweating and edgy on reappearance: should stay 6f: sold to join M. Barnes 900 gns Doncaster June Sales. *G. M. Moore.*

DIRECTLY   6 b.g. Bay Express 132–Veracious 86 (Astec 128) [1988 NR 1989   67
15.5s 12d* 12d⁴] lengthy gelding: has been hobdayed: has a rather round action: won
minor event at Pontefract in April by 5 lengths: good fourth of 15 in handicap at
Haydock over week later: much better suited by 1½m than 2m: acts on a soft
surface: winning hurdler. *G. B. Balding.*

DIRECTORS' CHOICE   4 b.g. Skyliner 117–Hazel Gig (Captain's Gig (USA))   — §
[1988 8s 6d 8g³ 9g 8g³ 9m³ 12m 10m 9f⁶ 9g 1989 10f⁵ 10f 10g] tall, leggy gelding: has
a long stride: quite useful at 2 yrs: has deteriorated since finishing third in handicaps
as 3-y-o: stays 9f: acts on any going: blinkered 3 times, visored once: winning
hurdler: ungenuine. *W. Carter.*

DISCORD   3 b.g. Niniski (USA) 125–Apple Peel 109 (Pall Mall 132) [1988 7g² 7g   75
1989   8s⁵   6d   11m*   11m   13.3g*] tall, rather unfurnished, fair sort: modest
handicapper: won at Hamilton in May and Newbury in June: stays 13.3f well: best
efforts on a sound surface: gelded after final outing. *W. Hastings-Bass.*

DISCREET AFFAIR   2 ch.g. (May 11) Beldale Lark 105–Moonsail (Wind-   —
jammer (USA)) [1989 6m 7m] 1,000Y: angular gelding: moderate mover: sixth foal:
brother to 3-y-o Return Fair and half-brother to 12.3f winner Mazeltov Linda (by
Remainder Man): dam unraced half-sister to smart sprinter Communication: no sign
of promise in sellers at Warwick in May and Wolverhampton in August. *J. Mackie.*

DISMISS   4 b.f. Daring March 116–Sweet Jane 59 (Furry Glen 121) [1988 7g² 7g   95
7f² 7m 8m* 8m* 8g* 10m⁶ 8g³ 1989 9v³ 10s* 8s⁵ 12m 10m² 10f 10g²] tall, leggy
filly: showed much improved form when winning 7-runner £19,500 City and
Suburban Stakes (Handicap) at Epsom in April decisively by 3 lengths from
Hauwmal: creditable second of 5 to Summer Fashion at Goodwood and Fire Top at
Epsom, best subsequent efforts: suited by 1¼m: acts on top-of-the-ground and soft
going: has won for apprentice: well below form when sweating and edgy. *R. V.
Smyth.*

DISNEYLAND (POL)   5 ch.g. Dixieland (POL)–Dzungaria (POL) (Antiquarian   —
102) [1988 NR 1989 12m⁶ 8g 9g⁶ 7g 9m] sturdy, lengthy Polish-bred gelding: well
beaten in varied events on flat as 5-y-o: winning hurdler: keen sort. *Mrs J. Pitman.*

DISPORT   7 b.g. Import 127–Diorina 91 (Manacle 123) [1988 NR 1989 12m 10g]   —
tall, quite attractive gelding: poor maiden: stays 1m: blinkered twice: has often
sweated. *W. G. R. Wightman.*

DISSOLUTION   4 b.f. Henbit (USA) 130–Persian Case (Upper Case (USA))   —
[1988 10d 10g 1989 16g] sparely-made filly: modest winner at 2 yrs: lightly raced and
well beaten in last 2 seasons: should stay beyond 7.5f: acts on soft going. *R. J. R.
Williams.*

*BBA Atalanta Stakes, Sandown—
Dimmer crosses the line with ears pricked*

DISSONANT (USA) 3 ch.c. Diesis 133–Nashualee (USA) (Nashua) [1988 7g* **96**
1989 8d² 10.6s² 10f⁴ 10m² 10g⁶] rather unfurnished colt: good mover: fairly useful
performer: good second in minor events (sweating) at Pontefract and Haydock and
£8,000 handicap at Newmarket: set plenty to do and bit below best final start: stays
1¼m: possibly unsuited by very firm ground, acts on any other: may prove suited by
more enterprising tactics. *H. R. A. Cecil.*

DISTANT RELATION 4 b.f. Great Nephew 126–Perchance 77 (Connaught   —
130) [1988 11g* 1989 12g 19g 16g a13g] lengthy filly: second foal: half-sister to 3-y-o
1½m winner Highland Park (by Simply Great) and to Irish 9f winner American Lady
(by Ile de Bourbon): dam, 7f and 1½m winner, is out of half-sister to smart Albany
and Magna Carta: won in French Provinces as 3-y-o when trained by A. Fabre: well
beaten in varied events on flat in 1989: stays 11f: blinkered on reappearance and last
2 starts: a winner in Jersey and over hurdles. *K. O. Cunningham-Brown.*

DISTANT RELATIVE 3 b.c. Habitat 134–Royal Sister II (Claude) [1988 **127**
7d⁵ 6s² 6f* 1989 7g* 8m³ 7f³ 8g* 7.3g* 8m* 8m³ 7m*]
    Encouraging though they were, Distant Relative's wins in a Newbury
maiden as a two-year-old, when he reportedly finished lame, and in a
Newmarket handicap on his reappearance, were scarcely an indication of the
fine season he would have. He developed into a high-class miler. His
participation in the Airlie/Coolmore Irish Two Thousand Guineas on his
second outing seemed optimistic—he started at 25/1—and his two-and-a-half-
length and half-length third behind Shaadi and Great Commotion represented
considerable improvement, especially as he was checked briefly two furlongs
out and would have troubled the runner-up with a clear run. Distant Relative
met Great Commotion on two more occasions and came out top in both
events. The first was the Gardner Merchant Hungerford Stakes at Newbury
in August. Both had raced twice in the interim. Distant Relative, after
finishing third behind Zilzal and Russian Royal in the Jersey Stakes at Royal
Ascot, won the EBF Phoenix International Stakes at Phoenix Park by two
lengths from Sagamore with Executive Perk, who finished lame, a head away
in third. Great Commotion had taken the Beeswing Stakes at Newcastle on
his latest outing, with Russian Royal among those behind him. Great
Commotion was sent off the even-money favourite at Newbury. Kerita,
winner of a listed race at Goodwood, was also preferred in the betting to
Distant Relative who started at 5/1 in a seven-runner field. Characteristically
Distant Relative had to be niggled along some way out, but he came back on
the bridle soon after halfway, kicked for home two furlongs out and
maintained a length-and-a-half advantage to the line. This time it was Great
Commotion who suffered a slightly obstructed run, though the pair were
three lengths clear of Moviegoer in third.
    If there was a suspicion that Distant Relative had been a slightly
fortunate winner at Newbury his success in the Beefeater Gin Celebration
Mile (formerly the Waterford Crystal Mile) at Goodwood in August was
emphatic. Apart from Great Commotion the field comprised of the Trusthouse

Beefeater Gin Celebration Mile Stakes, Goodwood—
Distant Relative has come from last to first

Bisquit Cognac Challenge Stakes, Newmarket—fifth win of the season for Distant Relative

Forte Mile winner Reprimand, the 6/4 favourite, and the outsiders Samoan and Point House. Great Commotion led, setting a muddling pace, whilst Distant Relative was held up last of the five runners. Switched to deliver his challenge when the leader quickened for home three out, Distant Relative was checked at first, showed his customary turn of foot to lead on the outside well over a furlong out, and kept on quickening to go three and a half to four lengths clear before being eased; in the end he had two and a half lengths to spare over Great Commotion. Reprimand was a length behind in third.

Distant Relative continued to run well, though his best wasn't good enough to bring him more than third place in the Queen Elizabeth II Stakes at Ascot, where Zilzal beat him five lengths and Polish Precedent two. He had a much easier task in the Bisquit Cognac Challenge Stakes at Newmarket in October where he won ridden out by a length and a half from Dancing Tribute after taking time to find his full stride. The Challenge Stakes was Distant Relative's third Group 2 prize of the season. In earlier years he might well have attempted the Group 1 Prix de la Foret as Salse had done the previous season. In 1989, however, the French race was brought forward two weeks, resulting in two of Europe's best seven-furlong races being run within four days of each other—a ridiculous state of affairs.

		Sir Gaylord	Turn-To
	Habitat	(b 1959)	Somethingroyal
	(b 1966)	Little Hut	Occupy
Distant Relative		(b 1952)	Savage Beauty
(b.c. 1986)		Claude	Hornbeam
	Royal Sister II	(b 1964)	Aigue-Vive
	(b 1977)	Ribasha	Ribot
		(b 1967)	Natasha

Distant Relative, bought for IR 210,000 guineas at the inaugural Cartier Million Sale, has proved to be the most successful of Habitat's penultimate crop to date. His sire's record is a most impressive one and it has continued to improve since his death in 1987. Among Habitat's winning progeny in 1989 were Steinlen, winner of the Breeders' Cup Mile and Arlington Million, and Mill Reef Stakes winner Welney. The maternal side of Distant Relative's pedigree is a good one and shows more stamina than Distant Relative seems to possess. His dam Royal Sister II won eight races from three to five years, seven in Italy and a mile-and-a-quarter apprentice handicap in Ireland. Her

261

Mr Wafic Said's "Distant Relative"

half-sister Ribarbo was second in the Chester Cup and won races from a mile and a half to two miles. Natasha's granddaughter Arkadina (by Ribot and hence closely related to Ribasha) is the dam of Irish St Leger winner Dark Lomond, whilst Arkadina's brother Blood Royal won the Jockey Club Cup and has proved to be a strong influence for stamina as a stallion. Distant Relative is the second foal of Royal Sister II. She has a two-year-old by Dara Monarch named Lightning Thunder and a yearling colt by Glow, sold for 120,000 guineas at Newmarket's Highflyer Sales having fetched just IR 18,500 guineas as a foal. Distant Relative is as attractive as his pedigree. A strong, lengthy, useful-looking colt, he carries condition and usually looks very well. His action is much less imposing. Distant Relative is equally effective at seven furlongs and a mile and seems best on a sound surface. He's a genuine and consistent colt and a credit to his trainer who'll no doubt be looking to find a Group 1 race for him as a four-year-old. Should that prove too much, there will still be more good prizes to be won. *B. W. Hills.*

DISTANT RULER 5 b.h. Indian King (USA) 128–Faraway Places (Flair Path 122) [1988 5d³ 5d 5m² 5f² 5g* 5g 5m* 5f 5d 1989 5s 5f 5f⁵ 5g³ 5g* 5f⁴ 5g 5m 5f 5g⁶] 80 lengthy, good-topped horse: has a quick action: fair handicapper: won at Sandown (for third time) when beating Frimley Parkson a head in very close finish in July: well below his best last 2 outings: suited by forcing tactics at 5f: acts on firm going and a soft surface: occasionally blinkered: hung right sixth outing: takes plenty of driving. *C. R. Nelson.*

DISTINCT NATIVE 2 ch.c. (Feb 4) Be My Native (USA) 122–Miami Life (Miami Springs 121) [1989 8g] IR 14,000Y: strong, good sort: first foal: dam daughter 71 p of half-sister to Wolverlife: 50/1, very green and burly, never dangerous in 16-runner minor event at Newmarket in November, keeping on not unduly knocked about: should do better. *R. W. Armstrong.*

DIVA MADONNA 3 b.f. Chief Singer 131–Two High 89 (High Top 131) [1988 7d⁴ 7f⁵ 7m 8f 1989 10.6m⁴ 12m* 12g² 14f⁴ 14f 14m⁴ 14m²] lengthy, angular, 85 good-topped filly: moderate mover: fair handicapper: won apprentice event at York in June: stays 1¾m: acts on firm going: blinkered (ran creditably) final start: usually apprentice ridden but is a difficult ride and may prove best with strong handling. *C. W. C. Elsey.*

DIVIDIA 2 b.f. (Apr 14) Pas de Seul 133–Divina (GER) (Alpenkonig (GER)) [1989 5m⁶ 6m³ 5f² 6m 6m 8.2s5] IR 1,000Y: smallish, sparely-made filly: poor mover: half-sister to 2 winners in USA and Italian 3-y-o 1¼m winner Demades (by Solford), 1m winner at 2 yrs: dam won at 3 yrs in Germany: poor form in varied events: stays 1m: probably acts on any going. *M. Brittain.* **47**

DIVILMINT 2 b.g. (Apr 11) Absalom 128–Miss Diaward 82 (Supreme Sovereign 119) [1989 6m⁴ 7v] 6,000Y: rangy gelding: second foal: brother to a poor plater: dam won from 11f to 1¾m: showed signs of ability in maidens: almost certainly capable of better. *Miss S. E. Hall.* **43 p**

DIVINE PET 4 br.g. Tina's Pet 121–Davinia 92 (Gold Form 108) [1988 5g 6g 5f³ 5m³ 6m 5g³ 5g² 6f* 6h³ 5f⁴ 6g 1989 6v 5s 6f* 5.8h⁴ 6m⁵ 6g 6f² 6h* 5g* 6m 5.8f6] strong, good-topped gelding: has been hobdayed: has a quick action: fair handicapper: won at Salisbury in May and Brighton and Newbury in August: long way below his best last 2 outings: effective at 5f and 6f: suited by a sound surface: ran well when on toes seventh outing. *W. G. R. Wightman.* **82**

DIZZY GEE 3 br.g. Gorytus (USA) 132–Tizzy 79 (Formidable (USA) 125) [1988 6m 1989 8d 7s 10g 6m⁴ 6m 7g⁶ 6f] well-made gelding: moderate walker: plating-class maiden: stayed 7f: blinkered fifth start: dead. *J. Sutcliffe.* **56**

DJANILA 2 ch.f. (Apr 1) Fabulous Dancer (USA) 124–Happy River (Riverman (USA) 131) [1989 7m⁵ 7f* a7g] 150,000 francs (approx £13,700) Y: small, strong filly: third reported foal: half-sister to 3-y-o 14.8f winner World Party (by Esprit du Nord): dam French maiden out of 13f Prix de Pomone winner Felicite: won minor event at Ostend in July by 2½ lengths: well beaten here, sweating and on toes final start: sold out of M. Jarvis's stable 1,000 gns Ascot November Sales. *G. G. Gracey.* **45 ?**

DOC LODGE 3 b.f. Doc Marten 104–Cooling 89 (Tycoon II) [1988 NR 1989 8.2g 9s² 8.2d³ 7g⁴ a8g³] third foal: half-sister to 1983 2-y-o 5f winner Airling (by Import) and a poor plater by Sonnen Gold: dam won over 1¼m and 13f: quite modest maiden: has run in seller: appears suited by 7f. *R. D. E. Woodhouse.* **68**

DOCTOR FELL (USA) 3 ch.c. Miswaki (USA) 124–Leixable (USA) (Crimson Satan) [1988 7g⁵ 7d⁴ 8g 1989 8s 8g² 8v³ 8d] strong, sturdy colt: fair form when placed in handicaps at Salisbury and Ayr, off course over 5 months in between: suited by 1m: acts on heavy going: possibly best on a galloping track: sold to race in Saudi Arabia 19,000 gns Newmarket Autumn Sales. *I. A. Balding.* **79**

DOCTOR RHYTHM 4 ch.g. Cure The Blues (USA)–Mombones (Lord Gayle (USA) 124) [1988 10m⁴ 10m³ 12f³ 13m⁵ 12.3s* 1989 12g] neat gelding: quite modest winner as 3-y-o when trained by G. Pritchard-Gordon: 33/1 and bandaged, always behind in handicap at Leicester in November: acted on any going: blinkered twice, including when successful: dead. *F. Jordan.* **—**

DOCTOR'S REMEDY 3 br.c. Doc Marten 104–Champagne Party (Amber Rama (USA) 133) [1988 5g 5g 7m 5g⁴ 6f 5g 6d³ 5d⁶ 1989 7d 5f 8m⁶ 10f⁵ 10g⁴ 12f a8g] sturdy, rather dipped-backed colt: carries condition: has a round action: inconsistent and quite modest maiden as 2-y-o: little worthwhile form in varied events in 1989: stays 6f: probably doesn't act on firm ground. *M. Tate.* **—**

DODGER DICKINS 2 gr.c. (Mar 8) Godswalk (USA) 130–Sronica (Midsummer Night II 117) [1989 6m⁵ 5d 5d a6g⁶ a7g] IR 11,000Y: workmanlike colt: first foal: dam placed once over 1m at 2 yrs in Ireland: plating-class maiden: stays 6f: gave trouble stalls second start. *R. Hollinshead.* **49**

DODGY 2 b.c. (May 16) Homing 130–Beryl's Jewel 86 (Siliconn 121) [1989 6f 7m] fifth foal: brother to 5f winner Tylers Wood and half-brother to 3-y-o Murmuring (by Kind of Hush) and two 5f winners, by Kind of Hush and Saritamer: dam best at 5f: about 7 lengths eighth of 17 to Mull House at Chepstow, second and easily better effort in October maidens. *W. J. Haggas.* **56**

DO-I-KNOW-YOU 3 b.f. Kafu 120–Galaxy Scorpio (Saritamer (USA) 130) [1988 5g⁴ 5s³ 5d* 5f⁴ 6f 5g 5g⁶ 5g 5m⁴ 5d⁵ 5m 7m 1989 5f 5.1m⁶ 5f⁵ 6h³ 5g⁴ 5m 6g 6g 6g a6g a6g⁵] lengthy, good-quartered filly: moderate mover: plating-class at best as 3-y-o: stays 6f: seems to act on any going: blinkered sixth and first 2 starts, also hooded on second: often apprentice ridden and wears a severe bridle: inconsistent, and seems temperamental. *C. N. Williams.* **52 d**

DOLLAR'S SISTER   3 b.f. Mandrake Belle 78–Burglars Girl 63 (Burglar 128)   —
[1988 6m 1989 6g] lengthy, workmanlike filly: well beaten in maiden and seller: sold
1,000 gns Ascot October Sales. *B. Gubby.*

DOLLY BEVAN   3 b.f. Another Realm 118–Elkie Brooks 82 (Relkino 131) [1988   **46**
6m 6m2 6m 6s2 6s* 6m2 7m 6m 1989 8d4 10s 10.2h 10g a6g] lengthy, robust filly:
turns off-fore in: carries condition: fair plater: ran creditably on reappearance, below
form after: stays 1m: acts on top-of-the-ground and soft going. *D. Haydn Jones.*

DOLPOUR   3 b.c. Sadler's Wells (USA) 132–Dumka (FR) 117 (Kashmir II **128**
125) [1988 7g4 1989 10m2 10m* 10.5m2 10.1d* 10g2]
Dolpour's three-year-old campaign was one of humble origins compared
to that of his half-brother Doyoun as, almost one year to the day after Doyoun
won the Two Thousand Guineas, Dolpour was beaten seven lengths in a
Brighton minor event. However, it's not often that one reads a tale of humble
origins that has a humble ending as well, and Dolpour's is no exception. By the
end of the season he'd shown a higher level of form than Doyoun with the
distinct possibility of further improvement to come as a four-year-old. For
racehorses related and of such comparable merit, Doyoun and Dolpour
provide an interesting contrast. Doyoun won at the first time of asking at two
years then put up as good a performance as any in his career in beating
Warning four lengths in the Craven Stakes on his reappearance. Progress
dramatically as he did, Dolpour's early appearances certainly weren't bereft of
merit—he'd shown considerable promise in a Newmarket maiden and it was
Cacoethes who beat him so comprehensively at Brighton—but his first
success came at the same stage that Stoute had finalised Doyoun's
preparation for the Derby. Dolpour gained that victory at odds of 11/8 on in a
maiden race at Leicester—but only after he'd received a big scare from the
newcomer Blade of Grass.
More strongly-run races undoubtedly contributed to Dolpour's marked
improvement from that point on. He put up a very useful performance when
beaten three quarters of a length by Batshoof in the Daniel Prenn Royal
Yorkshire Stakes at York in June but it was his victory in the listed Winter Hill
Stakes at Windsor ten weeks later which proved the revelation. In a
seven-runner field, Dolpour was a 9/1-chance behind Opening Verse, who
appeared after very smart efforts in the Eclipse and Sussex Stakes, the tough
four-year-old Per Quod, Extel winner Biennial and the lightly-raced but
well-touted Legal Case who started favourite. A competitive contest on paper
then but when Dolpour took up the running three furlongs out only Legal
Case could make a race of it and Dolpour beat him three lengths, running on
strongly. With Per Quod fully seven lengths back in third, this was an
eye-catching performance which became even more taking when Legal Case
first coasted in in the Select Stakes at Goodwood then ran so well in the Arc de
Triomphe. Dolpour, meanwhile, was saved for the Champion Stakes and was
backed down to favouritism. Kept within about two lengths of the pace-setting
Ile de Chypre early on, Dolpour was one of the first to be pushed along and
conceded what looked a decisive advantage as the leader quickened over two
furlongs out. He began to stay on strongly as they met the rising ground
though and, together with Legal Case, had reduced Ile de Chypre's lead to half
a length with a hundred yards to go where Dolpour caught a slight bump
before the three of them passed the post virtually in line. Dolpour had come
within a head of succeeding where Doyoun had failed by seven lengths as
Legal Case got the decision.

		Northern Dancer	Nearctic
	Sadler's Wells (USA)	(b 1961)	Natalma
	(b 1981)	Fairy Bridge	Bold Reason
Dolpour		(b 1975)	Special
(b.c. 1986)		Kashmir II	Tudor Melody
	Dumka (FR)	(b or br 1963)	Queen of Speed
	(br 1971)	Faizebad	Prince Taj
		(br 1962)	Floralie

Dumka must be one of an elite half-dozen amongst the Aga Khan's two
hundred-plus broodmares but she's not from one of those families with which
the Aga Khan has such long-standing associations. He acquired her at

H. H. Aga Khan's "Dolpour" (W. Swinburn)

Tattersalls for 60,000 guineas at the end of her three-year-old season. That season was one of rather mixed fortunes for Dumka, the highlight being her win in the Poule d'Essai des Pouliches, the low-points her four other races, and she had the unusual distinction for a Pouliches winner of starting complete outsider for both that race (30/1) and the Prix de Diane (59/1) only seven weeks later. Dumka's standing as a broodmare, however, is based on consistent success. All of her six foals before Dolpour have won and they include the Hungerford Stakes winner Dalsaan and the Cork and Orrery winner Dafayna (both by Habitat), as well as Doyoun who's by Mill Reef. Her eighth foal is the unraced Shernazar filly Dumalya. Further back in the pedigree, the family's most notable representative of recent years is the grandam Faizebad's half-sister Flossy who provided another shock result when winning the 1969 Champion Stakes from Park Top. Dolpour's running in the Champion (and, indeed, his previous races) suggest that he's well worth trying over a mile and a half. Doyoun's stamina was a matter of some popular controversy but there's no doubt that, in coming third to Kahyasi at Epsom, he stayed the trip. Over whatever distance Dolpour is campaigned, there's a strong likelihood that he'll prove best on the easy surface he encountered at Windsor and Newmarket when recording comfortably his best efforts. A leggy, attractive colt, Dolpour has rather less substance to him than his half-brother and, for that matter, Ile de Chypre and Legal Case, both of whom should be renewing rivalries in 1990. As thrilling an encounter as that we saw at Newmarket may be too much to ask for but all three should figure prominently in pattern events in 1990, in which Dolpour will carry no penalty—initially, at least. *M. R. Stoute.*

DOM EDINO   6 b.g. Dominion 123–Edna 92 (Shiny Tenth 120) [1988 2 1.6g² 20.4d   —
16d* 16f³ 18g 1989 16m⁶] rangy gelding: has been hobdayed: poor winner

(apprentice ridden) as 5-y-o: soundly-beaten sixth of 7 in handicap at Newcastle in August: suited by good test of stamina: acts on firm going, but well suited by an easy surface: smart form over hurdles: winning novice chaser. *M. Avison.*

DOMINICUS 3 b.g. Dominion 123–Pulcinella 95 (Shantung 132) [1988 7d³ 8m 8d⁵ 10g 10.2m⁵ 1989 12g 12s⁵ 12.3m⁶ 12f 10.5g 8s a11g a16g] lengthy, rather sparely-made gelding: fair form at best but showed little last 5 outings, off course 4½ months after first of them: stays 1½m: visored seventh start: ran creditably in blinkers once at 2 yrs: bought out of C. Brittain's stable 8,400 gns Doncaster August Sales after fourth start. *M. P. Naughton.* —

DOMINION FAYRE 3 b.f. Dominion 123–Pasty 122 (Raffingora 130) [1988 5m⁵ 5g⁴ 6m 6s⁵ 1989 7.3m 10m] smallish, workmanlike filly: has a quick action: plating-class maiden: behind facing very stiff tasks in handicaps in summer as 3-y-o: should be suited by further than 6f: bandaged off-hind final start. *M. H. Tompkins.* —

DOMINUET 4 b.f. Dominion 123–Stepping Gaily 79 (Gay Fandango (USA) 132) [1988 8d 6m 5.3f² 1989 5m 6h⁶ 6f 5m³ 6m 5m⁴] lengthy, quite attractive filly: poor maiden: form only at 5f: sometimes gives trouble in preliminaries, and is temperamentally unsatisfactory. *J. L. Spearing.* 47 §

DOMRUN 2 b.f. (May 10) Runnett 125–Dominion Blue 66 (Dominion 123) [1989 5g⁵ 5m³ 5f⁶ 5m⁴ 6f² 6g 5g⁶ 5m² 6f⁶ 5v² 5m⁵ a8g] 2,900Y: leggy, close-coupled filly: has a roundish action: first foal: dam 1¼m winner: fair plater: stays 6f: appears suited by plenty of give in the ground. *N. Tinkler.* 53

DOMUS 5 gr.h. Kalaglow 132–On The House (FR) 125 (Be My Guest (USA) 126) [1988 10g⁴ 8d⁴ 7.6f 1989 8m 8g 7m⁴ 7.6m* 7m] leggy, quite attractive horse: moderate mover: fair handicapper nowadays: made all at Chester in September: stays 7.6f: acts on top-of-the-ground: often takes very keen hold to post: sold 10,000 gns Newmarket Autumn Sales. *H. Candy.* 78

DONA KRISTA 3 br.f. King of Spain 121–Kristallina 84 (Homeric 133) [1988 6f⁴ 5m 6g² 6d⁶ 6g* 7m⁴ 7d⁶ 1989 7.3s 6f 7f⁴ 7m] workmanlike filly: fair winner as 2-y-o: creditable fourth in minor event at Goodwood: faced stiff tasks earlier in season and ran poorly in visor final start (June): may well stay beyond 7f: acts on firm going and a soft surface: usually makes running: sold 6,000 gns Newmarket Autumn Sales, resold 8,000 gns Ascot December Sales. *R. Hannon.* —

DONATIST 3 b.c. Dominion 123–Kaftan 68 (Kashmir II 125) [1988 6g 6s 1989 8v³ 8d⁴ 8g⁴ 9.2m*] rather angular, quite attractive colt: has a quick action: first run for nearly 4 months, won 5-runner claimer (claimed to join Miss L. Bower £9,060) at Goodwood in August, making virtually all: should stay 1¼m: acts on top-of-the-ground and a soft surface. *H. Candy.* 72

DONE BETTER 3 b.f. Dunphy 124–Have A Flutter (Auction Ring (USA) 123) [1988 5d² 5g* 5g 5m³ 5m⁵ 1989 5f 7g 5.8m] small filly: modest winner as 2-y-o: behind in handicaps in 1989, flashing tail on second start: suited by 5f: visored final start at 2 yrs: blinkered (sweating slightly) last one in 1989: sold 3,900 gns Newmarket July Sales. *C. F. Wall.* —

DONFIL 4 ch.g. Don 128–Philanderess (Philemon 119) [1988 8f 8f³ 10.1g³ 10g 10g 8m⁵ 7f 1989 10m 9f⁶ 7m 8f] compact gelding: poor plater: stays 1¼m: acts on firm going: blinkered once: trained until after third outing by J. Jenkins. *P. D. Evans.* —

DON MARTINO 8 br. or gr.g. Martinmas 128–Silbadora 67 (Don (ITY) 123) [1988 6d⁶ 6f 6f⁵ 7d⁴ 7d* 6g 7f² 7s⁶ 1989 7g⁶ 7m⁶] lengthy, workmanlike gelding: good walker and mover: fair handicapper: sixth at Newmarket to Baldomero (ran on strongly after not getting clear run) and Mango Manila (co-favourite, raced on unfavoured stand side) in July: best at 7f: probably not ideally suited by soft going nowadays, acts on any other. *G. B. Balding.* 88

DONNA BOLD 2 b.f. (Mar 15) Never So Bold 135–Domynga 85 (Dominion 123) [1989 6f 6m] IR 66,000Y: sturdy, good-quartered filly: has a quick action: first foal: dam 7f winner, is sister to Fair Dominion, useful at up to 1¼m, and daughter of half-sister to good sprinter Daring Boy and smart Daring March: around 9 lengths ninth of 22, fading final furlong, to Hebba in maiden at Newbury in September: slowly away and swerved right stalls on debut. *J. D. Bethell.* 51

DONNA DEL LAGO 3 b.f. Kings Lake (USA) 133–Cannon Boy (USA) (Canonero II (USA)) [1988 6f 1989 10s 12f⁶ 12h] big, leggy, good-topped filly: has scope: no sign of ability in maidens and a handicap: sold to join T. Casey 5,400 gns Newmarket July Sales: winning novice hurdler. *R. Hannon.* —

DONNA ELVIRA 3 b.f. Chief Singer 131–Countess Olivia (Prince Tenderfoot (USA) 126) [1988 6m² 1989 8m³ 8.5m⁴ 7g²] rather unfurnished, quite attractive 88 filly: has a quick action: fair maiden: 33/1 on first run for 5 months, very good neck second of 21 in all-aged event at Newmarket in November, always prominent and clear far side: possibly best at 7f with some give in the ground: trained first 2 starts by L. Cumani. *C. F. Wall.*

DONNA LORENZA 2 br.f. (May 14) Ahonoora 122–Lockwood Girl 81 (Prince 66 Tenderfoot (USA) 126) [1989 5d 5f² 6f³ 6h³ 6h 8m⁵ 7g a7g⁵ a8g⁶] IR 8,800Y: small, lengthy filly: fourth living foal: half-sister to fairly useful 11.7f winner Dunphy's Special and a winner in Italy (both by Dunphy): dam winning sprinter: quite modest maiden: lost form towards end of year: best form at 6f: has run respectably for 7-lb claimer. *R. Hannon.*

DONOSA 4 ch.f. Posse (USA) 130–Love Supreme 84 (Sallust 134) [1988 6m 6m — 7m 7g 10g 1989 10f 6f 5f] of little account: visored once. *R. Voorspuy.*

DONOSTI 5 b.g. Rusticaro (FR) 124–Blue Flame (USA) (Crimson Satan) [1988 — NR 1989 10v] close-coupled, good-topped ex-Irish gelding: fifth live foal: half-brother to good winner in Spain: dam won over 1m in France: won minor event at Phoenix Park as 2-y-o: in need of race, well behind in similar contest at Kempton in April, only second subsequent outing on flat. *Miss L. Bower.*

DONOVAN ROSE 4 b.c. Song 132–Piccadilly Rose 63 (Reform 132) [1988 5v³ 76 5g 5m 6g⁵ 5m⁵ 5m² 6m² 5f⁴ 6g* 5g⁴ 6g* 6s* 6d⁴ 6d* 6s⁴ 6s 1989 6v² 6v³ 6m 6g⁴ 6m* 6f⁶ 6h* 7m 6g⁴ 6m³ 7g² 7s⁴ 6s 6s] good-quartered, quite attractive colt: modest handicapper: favourite, won at Hamilton (apprentices, moved moderately down) and Carlisle in July: good second of 18, making all on stand side, to Superoo at Doncaster in September: suited by 6f or 7f: acts on any going: often blinkered or visored nowadays: tough and genuine. *J. Berry.*

DONTWORRYABOUTIT 2 ch.g. (Apr 2) Aragon 118–Spanish Chestnut 44 (Philip of Spain 126) [1989 5m⁵ 6m³ 7m⁶ 5f⁴ 5.3h⁶ 6g 7f a8g a8g a6g] 4,200F, 11,000Y: shallow-girthed, angular gelding: eighth foal: closely related to 2 plating-class animals by Tina's Pet, including 3-y-o Lana's Pet, and half-sister to 1982 2-y-o 5f winner Loddon Music (by Music Boy) and a winner in Trinidad: dam poor plater: modest plater: stays 7f: has twice bolted to post, withdrawn on first occasion and when blinkered fifth start: sold out of G. Lewis's stable 1,250 gns Ascot August Sales. *Mrs N. Macauley.*

DOODLE DANDY 3 b.g. Prince Tenderfoot (USA) 126–Peggy Dell (Sovereign — Gleam 117) [1988 NR 1989 12f 13f⁵ 12.2f⁵ 12f] 3,100Y, 8,200 2-y-o: workmanlike, sparely-made gelding: half-brother to 2 winners, including 7f and 1m winner Arctic Ken (by Stanford): dam won over 7f at 2 yrs in Ireland: poor form in varied events, including seller on trial start (July): has joined R. Juckes. *Ronald Thompson.*

DOODLIN 5 ch.g. Matsadoon (USA)–Grankie (USA) (Nashua) [1988 NR 1989 — 8m] workmanlike, plain gelding: good mover: modest maiden at 3 yrs: 20/1, over 7 lengths seventh of 12 in apprentice handicap at Newbury in June, only subsequent outing on flat: barely stays 9f: acts on top-of-the-ground: has run creditably when sweating: sold 2,900 gns Ascot August Sales. *S. Christian.*

DOOLAR (USA) 2 b.c. (Feb 20) Spend A Buck (USA)–Surera (ARG) (Sheet 82 Anchor) [1989 7g² 7m³] $150,000Y: strong, good-bodied colt: has scope: shows a powerful, round action: half-brother to 3-y-o Zarrara (by Desert Wine), 6f winner at 2 yrs, and a stakes winner by Raja Baba: dam won 11f Argentinian Oaks: sire Kentucky Derby winner and Horse of the Year: fair form when placed in August behind Southern Beau in maiden at Newbury and Aquatic (USA) in £15,300 event at York: will be suited by 1m: sure to win a race. *P. F. I. Cole.*

DORADO LLAVE (USA) 2 br.f. (Apr 3) Well Decorated (USA)–Turn The Key — 85 (Home Guard (USA) 129) [1989 6g 6m⁵] IR 37,000Y: first foal: dam 6f and 8.5f winner later successful in USA, is sister to useful 1¼m winner Double Lock, dam of Sure Blade, and daughter of half-sister to Irish Guinness Oaks winner Celina: sire 6f and 7f winner: backward, behind in August maidens at Newbury (green) and Yarmouth. *B. W. Hills.*

DORIMAR 2 b.g. (May 3) Wolverlife 115–Ahoy Dolly (Windjammer (USA)) [1989 — 7.5f 9g] IR 2,000 (privately) Y, 2,800 2-y-o: half-brother to a winner in USA: dam placed at 5f and 9f in Ireland: soundly beaten in autumn maiden auction race (slowly away) at Beverley and claimer (led 6f) at York. *M. H. Tompkins.*

DORIS GIRL 2 gr.f. (Jan 22) Absalom 128–Targos Delight (Targowice (USA) 55 130) [1989 5g 5d 5f 5m² 5m 6g³ 6m] good-bodied, workmanlike filly: seventh foal: half-sister to 3-y-o Squirsky (by Tina's Pet), Irish 1m winner Tatra (by Niniski) and 2 other winners: dam unraced half-sister to top 1974 Irish 2-y-o Sea

Break: plating-class maiden: best efforts fourth and sixth starts: not seen out after early-August: stays 6f. *W. J. Pearce.*

DORKING LAD 7 b.g. Cawston's Clown 113–High Voltage 82 (Electrify) [1988 **85** 6g* 7f6 6f 6s3 6g2 6g6 6f 6s4 6s 6d2 6g 6s2 1989 6g 6f 6f5 7g 6f 6m2 6m5 6s5 6m 6g3 6g 6v] lengthy, dipped-backed gelding: has a round action: fair handicapper: placed at York in £12,300 event won by Sully's Choice in August and £11,900 contest won by Khaydara in October: also ran well when moderately drawn in Ladbrokes (Ayr) Gold Cup on eighth outing: suited by 6f: not at his best on firm going, acts on any other: blinkered twice, sweating and edgy second time: sometimes apprentice ridden nowadays: suited by waiting tactics and strongly-run race. *M. H. Tompkins.*

DORSET DELIGHT 2 gr.f. (Mar 29) Red Sunset 120–Tippity Top 56 (High **—** Top 131) [1989 7f a7g a6g] 13,000Y: half-sister to modest 1987 2-y-o 5f winner Sharp Pip (by Pitskelly) and 1983 2-y-o 5f winner Rizla Blue (by Persian Bold), later winner in South Africa: dam won 5f seller at 2 yrs: no form in maidens. *T. Thomson Jones.*

DORSET DUKE 2 b.c. (Feb 23) Beldale Flutter (USA) 130–Youthful (FR) **106 p** (Green Dancer (USA) 132) [1989 6m* 6m*] smallish, quite attractive colt: first foal: dam, French 1½m winner, is daughter of high-class French staying 2-y-o First Bloom: successful in July in maiden and nursery (ran on strongly, having had poor run, when beating Absolutely Perfect 2 lengths) at Newmarket: wasn't seen out again: will stay at least 1m: likely to progress further if all is well with him. *G. Wragg.*

DOSTOYEVSKY (USA) 2 b.c. (May 13) Nureyev (USA) 131–Mairzy Doates **— p** (USA) (Nodouble (USA)) [1989 7g] rather leggy colt: fourth foal: closely related to a winner in North America by Lyphard: dam won Japan Cup: 12/1, never dangerous in 28-runner maiden at Newmarket in November: should do better. *M. R. Stoute.*

DOUBLE BLUSH (USA) 3 ch.c. Blushing Groom (FR) 131–Double Delta **80** (USA) (Delta Judge) [1988 7m5 8m3 8f 1989 10.1m 10h* 10f 11.7m] angular, leggy colt: moderate mover: won maiden at Brighton in June: ran poorly in Britain after but won 3 times at Aqueduct, USA, late in year: should stay beyond 1¼m: yet to race on an easy surface. *J. L. Dunlop.*

DOUBLE-DOO 3 b.f. Daring March 116–Ozra 63 (Red Alert 127) [1988 7f 6m 8m **—** 1989 8m 15.3m 12m] sturdy filly: soundly beaten in maidens and sellers: sweating second start: sold 1,250 gns Newmarket September Sales. *D. T. Thom.*

DOUBLE DUTCH 5 b.m. Nicholas Bill 125–Dutch Princess 70 (Royalty 130) **98** [1988 12s4 14g* 14g* 16f2 16g 16d2 18g2 16d3 1989 16s* 16s2 14s* 14f6 16f4 16g3

Tote Cesarewitch (Handicap), Newmarket—mares fill three of the first four places, Double Dutch (white cap) goes one better than in 1988 and beats Chelsea Girl, the gelding Travelling Light (almost hidden) and Broctune Grey

16m* 18g* 16g⁴] lengthy, sparely-made mare: usually fails to impress in paddock: turns fore feet out: fairly useful performer: progressed considerably again in 1989, winning Queen's Vase (Handicap) at Kempton, £7,400 Forte Hotels Stakes (Handicap) at Sandown, £9,500 Gordon Carter Stakes (Handicap) at Ascot and £49,400 Tote Cesarewitch (Handicap) at Newmarket, in last-named (third favourite) beating Chelsea Girl and Travelling Light 2 necks: co-favourite, good fourth to Upper Strata in listed race at Newmarket 2 weeks later: suited by testing conditions at 1¾m and stays 2¼m: probably acts on any going: often sweats: has a turn of foot and best in strongly-run race: splendidly tough, genuine and consistent: a credit to her trainer. *Miss B. Sanders.*

DOUBLE ENCORE (USA) 3 ch.c. Nodouble (USA)–Flo Russell (USA) **99** (Round Table) [1988 7g³ 7g 1989 8.2m* 8m⁴] rather leggy, good-topped colt with scope: has a quick action: won 3-runner minor event at Haydock in May by 2 lengths from Scarron: 5/1, about 2 lengths fourth of 5 to Sabotage in moderately-run £9,200 contest at Newmarket over 4 months later: should stay further: takes keen hold. *C. R. Nelson.*

DOUBLE ENTENDRE 3 br.f. Dominion 123–Triumphant 90 (Track Spare **67** 125) [1988 NR 1989 7d 7g 7f⁶ 7g 6m 8s* 8m 8g] leggy filly: fourth foal: half-sister to 5-y-o 1¼m seller winner Fresh From Victory (by Hotfoot): dam, winner over 7.6f at 3 yrs, is daughter of smart 5f to 1¼m filly Pugnacity: 25/1, won maiden at Goodwood in September: little worthwhile form in varied events otherwise: stays 1m well: evidently needs soft going: sold to join R. Curtis 4,600 gns Newmarket Autumn Sales. *J. D. Bethell.*

DOUBLE HANDFULL 3 gr.f. Pas de Seul 133–Love Tangle 77 (Wollow 132) **51** [1988 5d⁵ 5m³ 5g⁶ 5f 5f 8d 7d⁶ 6s 7.6s 1989 8s³ 8s⁶ 8g 7g] leggy filly: has a round action: good third in handicap at Warwick, running on having been outpaced: well below that form after, bit backward and first run for over 4 months final start: suited by 1m: acts on soft going. *P. J. Arthur.*

DOUBLE TALK 5 b.m. Dublin Taxi–Half Truth (Straight Lad 110) [1988 6s 6m **—** 1989 8m 5m] leggy, workmanlike mare: no longer of much account: has worn bandages: tends to sweat: sold 3,600 gns Ascot September Sales. *K. G. Wingrove.*

DOUBTFIRE 3 br.f. Jalmood (USA) 126–Wollingo 71 (Wollow 132) [1988 5d³ 5d³ **—** 5s³ 6m² 6f* 7f 6g⁵ 6g⁶ 7f 7f² 8g 1989 10.2g³] smallish, angular filly: moderate walker and mover with a quick action: won seller as 2-y-o: not discredited in handicap at Newcastle in March, only outing in 1989: probably stays 1¼m: probably acts on any going: ran very well in visor penultimate outing at 2 yrs: sold 1,200 gns Doncaster September Sales. *R. M. Whitaker.*

DOULAB'S IMAGE 2 ch.c. (Apr 2) Doulab (USA) 115–Haneena 118 (Habitat **69 +** 134) [1989 6m⁴ 7v² 6g⁴ 6g⁵] smallish, good-bodied colt: eighth foal: half-brother to 3-y-o Simply Perfect (by Wassl), very useful French miler North Haneena (by Far North) and fair 1985 2-y-o 5.1f and 7f winner Light Bee (by Majestic Light): dam sprinter, later raced in USA: quite modest maiden: stays 7f: blinkered final start. *H. Thomson Jones.*

DOULALLY 2 ch.f. (Mar 13) Doulab (USA) 115–June Maid 56 (Junius (USA) 124) **59** [1989 5f⁵ 5m⁵ 6m³ 5f³ 5f⁵ 6g⁵ 6g⁴ 6f 6f* 6g] IR 6,400Y: small, lengthy filly: first foal: dam second over 7f at 3 yrs, is half-sister to very useful 6f and 1m winner Magnetic Field: fairly useful plater: won nursery (no bid) at Lingfield in October by ¾ length: suited by 6f: blinkered last 4 starts: sold 2,200 gns Newmarket Autumn Sales: none too consistent. *E. Eldin.*

DOUNHURST 2 b.f. (Apr 18) Saher 115–Wernlas (Prince Tenderfoot (USA) 126) **65** [1989 6g⁵ 5f² 5f⁶ 6g a7g⁴] small, lengthy, well-made filly: has a quick action: first foal: dam Irish 7f winner at 2 yrs: quite modest maiden: best efforts on second and final outings: stays 7f. *R. Hannon.*

DOVEDON LADY 3 ch.f. Castle Keep 121–Copt Hall Princess 70 (Crowned **52** Prince (USA) 128) [1988 7g 1989 12s⁴ 10g 10s⁶ 10f* 12m* 12m² 14g² 12g³ 14f 12f] big, leggy filly: won sellers at Ripon (no bid) in June and Newmarket (slowly-run race, bought in 4,600 gns) in July: ran creditably in claimer and handicap next 2 starts: stays 1¾m: acts on any going: genuine. *M. H. Tompkins.*

DOVE GREY 4 gr.g. Belfort (FR) 89–Turtle Dove (Gyr (USA) 131) [1988 8m⁵ **53** 8g⁴ 10g 12.3s 1989 13.8d³ 12g⁴ 15.8m⁵ 16.2m⁵ 15f² 15m 13.8d] leggy gelding: plating-class maiden: tailed off in handicap sixth outing, and off course 3½ months afterwards: stays 2m: acts on firm going and a soft surface: sold 12,000 gns Doncaster November Sales. *C. W. Thornton.*

DOVE HOUSE HOSPICE 5 gr.m. Whistlefield 118–Dumbella 80 (Dumbarnie — 125) [1988 NR 1989 16.2d] rather plain mare: half-sister to winning hurdler Celtic Bell (by Celtic Cone): dam 2-y-o 5f winner, later successful over hurdles: 33/1, tailed off in maiden at Beverley in April: dead. *A. D. Brown.*

DOVEKIE 2 b.c. (May 14) Ela-Mana-Mou 132–Sacred Ibis (Red God 128§) [1989 105 p 7m*] 72,000Y: good sort: has plenty of scope: half-brother to 3-y-o Excelsis (by Shirley Heights) and several winners, including useful 5f to 1m winner Cremation (by Ashmore) and fairly useful 1980 2-y-o 5f winner Sybaris (by Crowned Prince): dam, sister to very useful 1969 2-y-o Red Velvet, looked a short runner: weak 3/1 and carrying condition, won 3-runner minor event at Ascot in October by 8 lengths from Valira, leading 2f out: will stay 1¼m: sure to improve. *G. Harwood.*

DOVENBY (USA) 3 b.c. Fit To Fight (USA)–Dovie Lee (USA) (Drone) [1988 — 6m⁵ 6m 1989 8g 6m⁶ 8f 8m 6g] leggy, angular, lightly-made colt: good walker: quite modest as 2-y-o: well beaten in handicaps in 1989: visored second start: blinkered, sweating and edgy final one (July). *M. Brittain.*

DOWN THE VALLEY 3 b.f. Kampala 120–Abertywi 87 (Bounteous 125) [1988 63 5g 5f 5g⁴ 7f* 7s² 7.3m⁵ 1989 8f 8m³ a8g³ a8g a8g⁵ a11g a11g²] strong, heavy-topped filly: carries condition: quite modest performer: creditable second in December claimer at Southwell: stays 11f: acts on any going: blinkered fifth and final outings: hung badly left for apprentice once at 2 yrs. *R. Hannon.*

DRAG ARTIST 4 br.g. Artaius (USA) 129–Drag Line (Track Spare 125) [1988 62 6v* 8v⁶ 7g 7v 7m 8f⁴ 8g 10g 10s 8d⁶ 12d² 12v 1989 12d 12d 12g⁵ 12g⁵ 12m⁵ 12g a11g² a11g² a14g² a14g⁵] small, plain, dipped-backed gelding: moderate mover: quite modest performer: stays 1¾m: particularly well suited by give in the ground: seems effective with or without blinkers: has run well for apprentice: usually held up: tends to wander: changed hands 1,550 gns Doncaster September Sales: inconsistent. *M. Brittain.*

DRAGONS LAIR 3 b. or br.g. Homing 130–Dragonist 82 (Dragonara Palace 68 (USA) 115) [1988 NR 1989 8f 8f 8g⁶ 12m* 13.8g³ 12.3m⁵ 10m* 10f⁵] heavy-topped gelding: carries condition: third foal: half-brother to useful sprinter Come On Chase Me (by Sharpo) and fair 1¾m winner Arsonist (by Ardross): dam winning sprinter: won handicaps at Pontefract (33/1) in July and Redcar (apprentices, on toes) in September, in latter making all and running very wide far turn: stays 1½m: acts on top-of-the-ground: gave trouble at stalls and withdrawn intended fourth outing. *M. J. Camacho.*

DRAGONS NEST 2 b.c. (May 18) Welsh Term 126–Laxmi 108 (Palestine 133) — [1989 7f] 15,500F, 10,000Y: half-brother to 1000 Guineas winner Enstone Spark (by Sparkler) and 3 other winners: dam best at 5f: 33/1, last of 14 in maiden at Salisbury in October. *Miss A. J. Whitfield.*

DRAKE'S DRUM 4 b.g. Palm Track 122–Pim (Game Warden) [1988 NR 1989 — 10.2g] workmanlike gelding: fourth foal: dam behind in NH Flat race: 25/1 and apprentice ridden, slowly into stride and always well behind in maiden at Doncaster in March. *D. Moffatt.*

DRAMATIC EVENT 4 b.g. Kind of Hush 118–Welsh Jane 71 (Bold Lad (IRE) 88 133) [1988 6m² 6g* 7g* 7g* 7g 7g⁴ 7f 1989 7.6m 7f 7m⁶ 8m* 8m⁴ 7.3m 8f] strong, close-coupled gelding: has a round action: fair handicapper: won £7,700 event at Ripon in August: well below form most other starts: stays 1m: acts on top-of-the-ground: often on toes: apprentice ridden last 4 outings: inconsistent. *J. Etherington.*

DRAYTON SPECIAL 2 b.g. (Apr 12) Lyphard's Special (USA) 122–Paradise 97 Bird 94 (Sallust 134) [1989 5.1m³ 5f* 5f²] IR 17,500Y: strong, lengthy, good-quartered gelding: has scope: fourth foal: half-brother to Irish 3-y-o 6f and 7f winner Sandhurst Goddess and Irish 7.9f to 9f Paradise Princess (both by Sandhurst Prince): dam 2-y-o 6f winner: odds on, made all in maiden at Pontefract in June: 1½ lengths second of 6 to Petillante in Norfolk Stakes at Royal Ascot: subsequently gelded and not seen out again. *B. Hanbury.*

DREAMAWHILE 2 b.f. (May 20) Known Fact (USA) 135–Forgotten Dreams 67 (FR) 82 (Shoemaker 121) [1989 6g⁶ 5f²] useful-looking filly: half-sister to several winners, including Derby Italiano winner My Top and smart 1986 2-y-o 6f winner Mountain Memory (both by High Top), later successful over 1m: dam won 3 times over 2m: beaten a neck by Nazakat in maiden at Folkestone in October, keeping on well: last of 6 when backward in Blue Seal Stakes at Ascot on debut: bred to stay 1m. *P. T. Walwyn.*

DREAMING SPIRES 2 b.f. (Feb 18) Sadler's Wells (USA) 132–Impossibility 64 (Posse (USA) 130) [1989 6m⁴ 8f] 15,000F, IR 40,000Y: first foal: dam twice-raced half-sister to smart 1979 2-y-o 6f and 7f winner Marathon Gold and useful middle-distance performer Honeybeta, and daughter of Attica Meli: backward, around 10 lengths fourth of 5, weakening quickly 1f out, to Gharam in maiden at Ascot in July: soundly beaten in similar event at Salisbury 7 weeks later: bred to stay 1m. *C. E. Brittain.*

DREAM MERCHANT 7 ch.g. Welsh Pageant 132–Waladah (Thatch (USA) — 136) [1988 NR 1989 12m 10.2f⁵ 12m] strong, close-coupled gelding: quite modest performer in 1985: well beaten in handicaps (last selling event) as 7-y-o: stays 1½m: possibly unsuited by heavy going, acts on any other: has worn blinkers and visor: has sweated: sold privately 2,500 gns Ascot November Sales. *R. J. O'Sullivan.*

DREAM OF FAME 3 b.c. Petorius 117–Snoozy Time 65 (Cavo Doro 124) [1988 92 6g³ 6g 1989 8d* 8m* 8.2m 8f² 10g⁴ 8.2d 9g 9g] compact, useful-looking colt: carries plenty of condition: has a long, roundish stride: fairly useful handicapper: won at Edinburgh (maiden) and Newmarket (£7,700 event) in the spring: very good second in Britannia Stakes at Royal Ascot, running on strongly from rear: showed little at Newmarket (Cambridgeshire) and York last 2 outings: stays 1m well: acts on firm going and a soft surface: often sweating and edgy. *J. W. Watts.*

DREAM OF JENNY 2 b.f. (Apr 21) Caerleon (USA) 132–Summer Dreams 73 (CAN) (Victoria Park) [1989 6f 6m⁴ 6g 7.5m² 8f³] 78,000Y: lengthy filly: has scope: half-sister to several winners in France and North America, including 1983 2-y-o 5.5f stakes winner Deputy General (by Vice Regent): dam lightly-raced 2-y-o winner at around 5f from good family: modest performer: ran well in nurseries final 2 starts: suited by 7f+: best form in blinkers. *M. H. Easterby.*

DREAMS TO RICHES 3 b.f. Busted 134–Divine Thought 102 (Javelot 124) — [1988 NR 1989 10d 14g] tall, leggy, lengthy filly: sister to fair 1¾m winner Field Conqueror and half-sister to very useful stayer Inde Pulse (by Troy) and Dee Stakes winner Great Idea (by Great Nephew): dam, half-sister to high-class 1969 2-y-o Divine Gift, won from 1¼m to 12.5f: behind in maiden (in need of race and very green) at Newbury and competitive minor event at Redcar in late-autumn: went down well at Newbury, showing a round action: may do better. *L. M. Cumani.*

DREAM TALK 2 b.c. (Apr 29) Dreams To Reality (USA) 113–Lala 91 (Welsh 81 Saint 126) [1989 6m⁵ 5m* 5m* 5m²] leggy colt: second foal: dam, 2-y-o 6f winner stayed 7f, is daughter of half-sister to Cajun: fair performer: made all in small fields in maiden at Catterick in July and minor event at Salisbury following month: creditable second to In The Papers in nursery at Sandown in September: should stay 6f. *J. Berry.*

DREAMTIME DANCER 3 b.f. Town And Country 124–Aleda Rose 56 — (Charlottown 127) [1988 NR 1989 8d 8f 7m 6f 7m 8.2m 8f 7g⁶] lengthy filly: has a round action: third living foal: sister to a winner in USA: dam winning plater from 7f to 1¼m: sixth of 13 in maiden at Catterick in October, first sign of ability: may do better over middle distances: evidently suited by some give in the ground. *J. Balding.*

DRESS PERFORMANCE (USA) 2 b.f. (Mar 4) Nureyev (USA) 131– — p Hortensia (FR) 119 (Luthier 126) [1989 6g] leggy, workmanlike filly: fifth foal: half-sister to 3-y-o Helen's Song and Derby second Glacial Storm (both by Arctic Tern) and 2 middle-distance winners: dam smart at around 1¼m in France: 12/1 and on toes, slowly away and always in rear in 13-runner maiden at Newmarket in July: should improve. *B. W. Hills.*

DRINNY'S DOUBLE 2 ch.g. (Feb 10) Connaught 130–Caramel 93 (Crepello — 136) [1989 6g 8s 8.2s] 2,000F, 1,000Y, 3,500 2-y-o: small, sturdy gelding: half-brother to numerous winners, including very useful middle-distance performer Northern Princess (by Sir Ivor) and fairly useful 1983 2-y-o 5f winner Carabineer (by Formidable): dam won at 1½m: well beaten in varied events in Scotland. *J. S. Wilson.*

DR MACCARTER (USA) 2 gr.c. (May 27) Dr Carter (USA)–Now Voyager 76 (USA) (Naskra (USA)) [1989 a7g² a8g⁴ a7g²] $42,000Y: sturdy colt: half-brother to 3 minor winners in USA: dam once-raced half-sister to Florida Derby winner Croeso: sire high class from 1m to 1¼m: modest maiden: beaten a neck by Petite Butterfly at Lingfield on final start: will probably stay 1¼m: wears blinkers. *W. A. O'Gorman.*

DR SOCK IT TO ME 4 b.g. Stanford 121§–Dr Shadad (Reform 132) [1988 5d 6g⁵ 52 d 6m⁶ 6g⁵ 7g³ 7f³ 10m 1989 10.8d 7.6f 7f 7m³ 7f 7m 7g 6f] leggy, lengthy gelding: poor maiden: worthwhile form as 4-y-o only on fourth outing: fell second start: stays 7f:

271

acts on any going: has worn blinkers, visored final start: trained until after third outing by J. Long: inconsistent. *S. Dow.*

DR SOMERVILLE (USA) 2 b.c. (Apr 18) Chief's Crown (USA)–Icing 112 **112** (Prince Tenderfoot (USA) 126) [1989 7d⁵ 7g² 9g* 9m* 10v] $450,000Y: half-brother to several winners, notably very smart 1988 2-y-o Al Hareb (by El Gran Senor), successful at 7f and 1m, and Ulster Harp Derby winner Rising (by Relkino): dam won from 5f to 1m at 2 yrs: won minor event at Evry by 1½ lengths and 4-runner Prix de Conde at Longchamp, making all, by 5 lengths: behind in Criterium de Saint-Cloud won by subsequently-demoted Snurge in November: should stay 1¼m: seems unsuited by heavy ground. *Mme C. Head, France.*

DRUMHEAD 3 ch.g. High Line 125–Wig And Gown (Mandamus 120) [1988 7g⁶ **93** 8g⁴ 1989 12g² 12m 12f⁶ 14d² 15s* 19g⁴ 14m⁴] workmanlike gelding: moderate walker: easily landed odds in amateurs race at Ayr in September: second and easily better effort after in £6,400 handicap at Newmarket, rallying well and not given hard race: may prove suited by 2m: acts on soft going, unsuited by very firm: sweating and on toes third and fourth starts: lacks turn of foot. *P. T. Walwyn.*

DRUMLEY DAWN 4 b.f. Red Sunset 120–Bamstar 70 (Relko 136) [1988 10f **58** 8.5f³ 8f² 8.2g⁵ 1989 8v⁴ 8d² 8m⁶ 12m² 13f⁴ 10m⁵ 11m 9f⁴ 10.6d 12g*] sturdy filly: quite modest handicapper: won at Hamilton in September: stays 1½m: acts on firm going and a soft surface: good mount for apprentice: visored sixth and seventh starts: twice very mulish leaving paddock. *J. S. Wilson.*

DRUM SERGEANT 2 b.c. (Jan 31) Elegant Air 119–Cala-Vadella 110 (Mummy's **79** p Pet 125) [1989 6d⁴] 22,000F, IR 65,000Y: strong, sturdy colt: has plenty of scope: fifth foal: half-brother to 1987 2-y-o 6f winner Brilliant Bay (by Hello Gorgeous) and 6f winner Hokusan (by Reform): dam, sister to Runnett, won 4 times over 5f at 2 yrs: 33/1, 4½ lengths fourth of 24, always prominent, to Notley in maiden at Newbury in October: should improve. *W. Jarvis.*

DRUMSTICK 3 ch.g. Henbit (USA) 130–Salustrina (Sallust 134) [1988 7m 7g⁵ **67** 1989 8.5f² 10h⁴ 8m⁵ 7.5f⁵ 7g⁶ 7f] angular gelding: quite modest maiden: blinkered, raced freely when below form final outing: stays 8.5f well: acts on firm going: has tended to hang right: possibly unsatisfactory, and gelded after final start. *Capt. R. M. Smyly.*

DRUM TAPS (USA) 3 b.c. Dixieland Band (USA)–Lavendula Rose 108 (Le **118** Levanstell 122) [1988 NR 1989 10.1m² 10m⁴ 10g* 10m* 10.2g*] good-topped, quite attractive colt: half-brother to numerous winners, including Miss Mars (by Red God), a very useful stakes winner at up to 9f in USA, and useful 1980 2-y-o 5f and 7f winner Stats Emmar (by Steel Heart): dam, third in Irish Oaks, is half-sister to Wrekin Rambler: progressed extremely well, winning maiden (odds on) at Ripon and £9,300 handicap at Ascot in September and £21,000 Doncaster EBF Limited Handicap at Newcastle in October: beat Firelight Fiesta 1½ lengths, pair clear, in last-named: also first past post on second outing but edged right and demoted for

Doncaster EBF Handicap, Newcastle—an excellent performance from Drum Taps to get the better of Firelight Fiesta

Prix de Conde, Longchamp—Dr Somerville is in no danger

interference: will be suited by 1½m: won for Neil Howard at Calder, USA, in December. *Major W. R. Hern.*

DRU RI'S BRU RI   3 b.g. Kafu 120–Bru Ri (FR) (Sir Gaylord) [1988 6d 5f 7m 8m   —
1989 12.2d 10d 12.2d 7.5d 12.2m 8m⁶ 12m] rather leggy gelding: moderate walker: poor mover: little worthwhile form in varied events, including sellers: likely to prove best at around 1m: blinkered third and fourth starts. *W. Bentley.*

DRY GIN   6 ch.g. Grundy 137–Karajinska (USA) (Nijinsky (CAN) 138) [1988 NR   —
1989 17f] leggy, angular gelding: no longer of any account on flat: winning chaser. *M. C. Chapman.*

DRY POINT   3 ch.c. Sharpo 132–X-Data 93 (On Your Mark 125) [1988 NR 1989   72
6g* 5m³ 6g⁶ 6m⁴] 44,000Y: strong, angular, workmanlike colt: has a round action: fifth foal: half-brother to 3 winners, including fairly useful 1984 2-y-o 5f winner Show Home (by Music Boy) and fair 1m winner Local Hero (by Tina's Pet): dam 5f and 6f winner: made virtually all when dead-heating in apprentice maiden at Pontefract in July: best efforts in handicaps when in frame twice at Newmarket: stays 6f: acts on top-of-the-ground: wears crossed noseband. *J. A. R. Toller.*

DR ZEVA   3 b.c. Busted 134–Dance In Rome 79 (Dance In Time (CAN)) [1988 7g   51
8d 7s 1989 10v⁶ 12s 8.5g 10m⁶ 9g⁴ 10g⁶ 11.7f⁶ 8.2g⁴ a8g⁶ a10g² a11g] big, deep-girthed colt: plating-class maiden: stays 1¼m. *J. R. Jenkins.*

DUAL CAPACITY (USA)   5 b.g. Coastal (USA)–Fenney Mill 99 (Levmoss 133)   56
[1988 16g 16g⁴ 12v 1989 14s 14s 12m⁵ 11.5f⁶ 12g* 12f² 10m* 12g 12g] tall gelding: poor mover: plating-class handicapper: won at Beverley (bandaged) in July and Pontefract (ladies event) in August: ran poorly last 2 outings: suited by good gallop at 1¼m and stays 1½m: appears to act on any going: usually has tongue tied down nowadays: winning hurdler. *W. J. Musson.*

DUAL VENTURE   7 ch.g. Brigadier Gerard 144–Selham 71 (Derring-Do 131)   —
[1988 NR 1989 12.3s 12.4g] strong, workmanlike gelding: has a markedly round action: fair handicapper in 1986: well beaten both outings (off course 6½ months in between) as 7-y-o: stays 1¾m: possibly not at his best on soft going, acts on any other: bandaged on reappearance: possibly best with strong handling. *J. G. FitzGerald.*

DUBAI LADY   3 ch.f. Kris 135–Amata (USA) (Nodouble (USA)) [1988 NR 1989   78
12.5m² 12m³ 10d³] 165,000Y: sparely-made, angular, plain filly: half-sister to several winners abroad, including useful French 1m and 9.5f winner Grammene (by Grey Dawn II): dam, French middle-distance winner later successful in USA, is half-sister to Princess Royal Stakes winner Trillionaire: modest maiden: will stay beyond 1½m: bandaged first 2 starts: sweating final one. *B. Hanbury.*

DUBAI VIEW   2 b.c. (Apr 19) Doulab (USA) 115–Anglo Irish (Busted 134) [1989   —
6d] 38,000 2-y-o: first foal: dam never ran: 50/1, soon outpaced in 24-runner maiden at Newbury in October. *D. Morley.*

DUBLIN BREEZE 2 b.g. (Apr 17) Dublin Taxi–Dusty Foot (Simbir 130) [1989   **57**
5m 7m 6g 10.6d* 8g²] IR 2,800Y, 5,000 2-y-o: compact, rather sparely-made
gelding: third foal: dam last on 3 starts at 4 yrs in Ireland, only season to race:
plating-class performer: won selling nursery (no bid) at Haydock by 1½ lengths
from Andrew's First: good second in similar event at Carlisle later in October: stays
10.6f well. *M. H. Tompkins.*

DUBLIN DRAGON 3 ch.c. Dublin Taxi–Casbar Lady 79 (Native Bazaar 122)   **—**
[1988 5m² 5f² 5f* 5.1m* 5g⁴ 1989 5g 5f 8m] good-quartered, close-coupled colt:
modest winner of sellers as 2-y-o: well below form in 1989: edgy and taken very
quietly down second start: pulled hard final one (May): likely to prove best at 5f: acts
on firm going: sold 5,400 gns Ascot June Sales. *Sir Mark Prescott.*

DUCHY OF CORNWALL (USA) 3 b.f. The Minstrel (CAN) 135–Queen of   **83**
Cornwall (USA) 109 (Cornish Prince) [1988 NR 1989 7s² 7.6m³ 7m* 8f 7.6f]
medium-sized, sturdy, angular filly: shows knee action: third foal: closely related to
1986 2-y-o 5f winner Veryan Bay (by Storm Bird): dam sprinting half-sister to smart
1975 American 2-y-o Favourite Beau: favourite, won minor event at Catterick in
June: ran moderately in handicaps, and not seen out after July: stays 7f well:
possibly unsuited by firm ground. *B. W. Hills.*

DUCK AND DIVE 2 ch.c. (Apr 30) Lomond (USA) 128–Avec L'Amour 75 **107**
(Realm 129) [1989 5g³ 5m* 6f 5g* 6d² 6m⁵ 6m⁵] 19,000F, 36,000Y: small,
well-made colt: has a quick, short action: fifth foal: dam disappointing daughter of
half-sister to very useful animals Harken and High Powered: useful colt: successful
in maiden at Epsom in June and listed race (sweating, beat Somethingdifferent by ½
length) at Newmarket following month: very good second, beaten a length, to
Pharaoh's Delight in Heinz '57' Phoenix Stakes at Phoenix Park: below form in
pattern events last 2 starts: effective at 5f and 6f. *R. Hannon.*

*Fairview New Homes Chesterfield Stakes, Newmarket—Duck And Dive gamely keeps
Somethingdifferent (hooped sleeves) and Croft Imperial at bay*

Mr Jim Horgan's "Duck And Dive"

DUCK FLIGHT 7 b.g. Decoy Boy 129–Chinafield 52 (Northfields (USA)) [1988 —
5d 5v* 5m 5g 5g⁶ 5g³ 5s* 5g⁴ 6s⁶ 5s⁴ 5d⁶ 5s⁵ 6s* 1989 5s⁵ 6m 6g 6m 6s 6g] small
gelding: has a round action: fair winner as 6-y-o: shaped well on reappearance but
lightly raced and below form afterwards: effective at 5f and 6f: well suited by plenty
of give in the ground: usually comes from behind: sold only 600 gns Newmarket
Autumn Sales. *J. Douglas-Home.*

DUCKINGTON 5 b.h. Bustino 136–Cribyn 96 (Brigadier Gerard 144) [1988 7d² **92**
7m⁴ 7g* 7.5m² 8f* 7m² 7f* 6g² 6m⁴ 7f* 7d⁴ 1989 6.1f* 6f² 6m 7m* 6f²] leggy,
close-coupled horse: fairly useful handicapper: improved throughout 1988 (had
operation for soft palate before season started) and better than ever as 5-y-o,
winning 11-runner race at Redcar and £7,700 event at Newcastle: good second to
Chummy's Charm in £15,400 event at Ayr in July, but wasn't seen out again: ideally
suited by strong gallop at 6f and has won over 1m: yet to race on soft going and
particularly well suited by firm: probably unsuited by track at Epsom: has found
little and best waited with: consistent. *M. H. Easterby.*

DUE DILLIGENCE 7 ch.h. General Assembly (USA)–Mrs McArdy 123 (Tribal **54**
Chief 125) [1988 8d 11.7f 11.7d4 10f 11.7m 1989 10.8d a8g a11g⁵] tall, workmanlike
horse: lightly raced nowadays: gave indications of retaining a little ability in
Southwell claimer final outing: probably stays 11.7f: acts on any going: wears
bandages. *K. White.*

DUENDE 3 b.f. High Top 131–Victory Kingdom (CAN) (Viceregal (CAN)) [1988 **70**
6f⁴ 6m* 1989 8m 8g⁴ 7s⁵ 9f 7d 7d] tall, leggy filly: good mover: modest
handicapper: ran moderately last 3 starts: stays 1m: acts on top-of-the-ground and
soft going: blinkered fifth start: ran creditably when on toes on second. *M. F. D.
Morley.*

275

DUFFER'S DANCER 7 ch.g. Miami Springs 121–Evening Chorus (Mountain 40 Call 125) [1988 5m⁶ 6f⁵ 6m 5g 1989 6h⁵ 5f⁴ 6g⁵ 6h⁶ 6m 7g 6g] small, angular gelding: poor handicapper: better suited by 6f than 5f: goes well on top-of-the-ground: sometimes blinkered: ran poorly when visored: has won for apprentice: sold 750 gns Doncaster September Sales: resold 800 gns Doncaster November Sales: inconsistent. *W. J. Pearce.*

DUGGAN 2 b.c. (Feb 5) Dunbeath (USA) 127–Silka (ITY) (Lypheor 118) [1989 7m — 7g 7d] 17,000F, 25,000Y: useful-looking colt: has scope: second reported foal: half-brother to 3-y-o 6f and 7.5f winner Cluzo (by Sharpo): dam won in Italy: well beaten in late-season maidens at Newmarket and minor event at Thirsk. *R. J. R. Williams.*

DUKE OF IMPNEY 2 b.c. (Apr 3) Roscoe Blake 120–Top Secret 90 (Manacle — 123) [1989 a8g] workmanlike colt: has scope: half-brother to 1m seller winner Star Issue 8 by Comedy Star): dam won over 5f and 1m: bit backward and green, well beaten, slowly away, in maiden at Southwell in December. *F. Jordan.*

DUKE OF PADUCAH (USA) 2 gr.c. (Mar 14) Green Dancer (USA) 97 p 132–Flordelisada (USA) (Drone) [1989 7g*]

Half an hour after Ray Cochrane had given Legal Case a powerful ride to land the Dubai Champion Stakes and so end a fruitful association as first jockey to Cumani he was back in the winners' enclosure again, this time for his new retaining stable, after working just as hard on Harwood's promising newcomer Duke of Paducah in the Philip Cornes Houghton Stakes. Both trainer and jockey must have been pleased with the spirited manner in which the colt, who was very green beforehand and in running, responded after coming off the bridle with more than half the race to run, and he looks an interesting prospect. A tall, attractive colt, if rather on the leg, Duke of Paducah wasn't strongly fancied for his debut—he attracted only four recorded bets—and started third favourite in a field of thirteen behind the Cumani-trained Rudy's Fantasy, who'd shown plenty of ability when fourth to Mukkdaam in a maiden over the course and distance earlier in the month, and the impressive York winner Atoll. Duke of Paducah didn't start to pick up the leaders until after halfway, by which time he was already being niggled along, and began to come seriously into the reckoning only when switched to the far rail with two furlongs to run. Staying on strongly to reach the front with a hundred yards to go Duke of Paducah almost immediately started to flag and he held on by inches as Atoll and Rudy's Fantasy, a length and a half further behind, edged closer again. The Houghton Stakes has not always been a reliable guide to the future despite being won by such as One In A Million and

Philip Cornes Houghton Stakes, Newmarket—
Duke of Paducah (nearest camera) makes a winning debut

Shadeed in recent times. Duke of Paducah doesn't strike us as quite their equal, but he's got plenty of improvement in him and he should develop into a good three-year-old over middle distances.

			Nijinsky	Northern Dancer
		Green Dancer (USA)	(b 1967)	Flaming Page
		(b 1972)	Green Valley	Val de Loir
Duke of Paducah (USA)			(br 1967)	Sly Pola
(gr.c. Mar 14, 1987)			Drone	Sir Gaylord
		Flordelisada (USA)	(gr 1966)	Cap And Bells
		(gr 1977)	Lava Creek	Jacinto
			(b 1968)	Island Creek

At 170,000 dollars Duke of Paducah was one of the most expensive of Green Dancer's numerous yearlings sold at public auction in 1988. The 1975 French Two Thousand Guineas winner has yet to make much of an impact in the statistics in Britain but the likes of Aryenne, Maximova, Lovely Dancer and Greinton have kept his name to the fore in France where, of course, he did most of his racing. Duke of Paducah is the fourth foal and fourth winner from his dam Flordelisada, and second to win in Britain following the smart miler Dallas (by Blushing Groom) who equalled the weight-carrying record for a three-year-old when winning a shortened Cambridgeshire in 1986. Flordelisada, a winner twice over sprint distances at three and once over a mile at four, is out of a half-sister to the Dewhurst winner Ribofilio, who started favourite for four classics and was beaten each time, as well as the fairly useful mile-and-a-half winner Bella Sorella, dam of the useful French stayer Bel Sorel and the useful middle-distance colt My Volga Boatman. *G. Harwood.*

DUKE'S DUET (USA) 2 b.c. (May 21) Seattle Song (USA) 130–Haute Sanga (Guillaume Tell (USA) 121) [1989 8v5] \$100,000Y: leggy, unfurnished colt: has scope: third foal: dam sister to Stanerra: 20/1 and on toes, under 13 lengths fifth of 23, keeping on not knocked about from rear 2f out, to Tyburn Tree in minor event at Newbury in October: should improve. *G. Lewis.*   **63 p**

DUKHAN 2 ch.c. (May 11) Doulab (USA) 115–Barbara Zapolia (ITY) (Great Nephew 126) [1989 5m2 6f5] IR 100,000Y: smallish, sparely-made colt: half-brother to useful 1987 2-y-o 5f winner Babita (by Habitat) and 3 winners in France and Italy: dam won at 2 yrs in Italy: staying-on 2½ lengths second of 6 to Able Express in maiden at Newmarket: never travelling well after slow start in similar event at York later in May: sold 8,000 gns Newmarket Autumn Sales, probably for export to Italy. *R. W. Armstrong.*   **68**

DUMBRECK 2 b.f. (Mar 26) Another Realm 118–Eagle's Quest 62 (Legal Eagle 126) [1989 6f4 6m4 7m5 6f4 6m 6s* 6v4 7g4] 3,000F, 6,600Y, 7,400 2-y-o: workmanlike filly: fourth foal: half-sister to 1985 2-y-o 5f seller winner Legalize (by Fair Season) and 1986 2-y-o 6f winner Tez Shikari (by Kala Shikari): dam 5f winner at 3 yrs: modest performer: won nursery at Ayr in September: ran well in similar events there and at Newcastle afterwards: stays 7f: acts well on soft ground. *A. P. Stringer.*   **72**

DUMDUMSKI 2 b.c. (Feb 8) Niniski (USA) 125–Live Ammo 94 (Home Guard (USA) 129) [1989 6m3 7m4] smallish, sparely-made colt: fourth foal: half-brother to 3-y-o Powder Lass, 5f winner at 2 yrs, and smart sprinter Powder Keg (both by Tap On Wood): dam 2-y-o 6f winner: over 5 lengths fourth of 21, leading around 5f, to Cutting Note in maiden at Newmarket in October, better effort: will stay 1m. *Lord John FitzGerald.*   **82 p**

DUNCTON HILL 3 ch.f. Formidable (USA) 125–Hazel Bush 71 (Sassafras (FR) 135) [1988 7f 8m 8d2 8d 1989 10.6s6 11m 12m4 10f 11s3 10g6] sturdy filly: quite modest at best: deteriorated at 3 yrs and ended up in sellers: should prove best at up to 11f: suited by an easy surface: sold to join J. White 4,600 gns Newmarket Autumn Sales. *Sir Mark Prescott.*   **49**

DUNDEE VIOLET 3 ch.f. Ballacashtal (CAN)–Treatise (Bold Lad (IRE) 133) [1988 6m 5f 8.2s 1989 6f] seems of little account: slowly away all starts. *Miss Z. A. Green.*   **—**

DUNMAGLASS 2 b.c. (May 16) Sayf El Arab (USA) 127–Stubble 93 (Balidar 133) [1989 5f5 6f 6d] 14,000F, IR 26,000Y: leggy colt: first foal: dam, best at 2 yrs when successful over 5f and 7f, is daughter of fairly useful 2-y-o sprinter Caught In   **58**

The Rye: plating-class maiden, best effort final start: sort to do better in handicap company. *Sir Mark Prescott.*

DUNMOUNIN 2 ro.f. (Feb 21) Alias Smith (USA)–Poly Negative (Polyfoto 124) **35** [1989 6g⁶ 7g 6m 6m 7f 6g⁴ 6s a8g] plain filly: moderate mover: fifth reported foal: dam never ran: poor plater: appeared to run well sixth start: should stay 1m. *W. Bentley.*

DUN SHINING 2 b.g. (Feb 18) Lochnager 132–Miss Barnaby 75 (Sun Prince **55** 128) [1989 5g 5d² 5m³ 6m 6m² 6g] angular, deep-girthed gelding: easy mover: brother to 1¼m and 11f winner Barnaby Benz, 5f and 6f winner Roper Row and 1984 2-y-o 5f winner Belle Marina, and half-brother to modest 1987 2-y-o Cat-Arrowed (by Sonnen Gold): dam won at 1½m and stayed 13f: plating-class maiden: best effort fourth start: has run in sellers: stays 6f: gelded after final start. *M. H. Easterby.*

DUNSTAR 2 b.c. (Apr 25) Dunphy 124–Starlit Way 92 (Pall Mall 132) [1989 5v⁴ **49** 5d² 5g⁶ 6m 6m 6v 6s⁴ a8g] IR 850F, 1,000Y: sparely-made colt: poor mover: half-brother to 2 winners in Ireland by Monseigneur, including 6f and 7f winner Afef John, and Irish 9.5f winner Neville Ring (by Auction Ring): dam 5f winner: fair plater: stays 6f: best form on soft ground. *M. Brittain.*

DURASINGH 7 b.g. Mansingh (USA) 120–Mildura 98 (Vilmorin) [1988 5d 5g — 5m* 5g 5m² 5g 5f² 5g* 5d³ 1989 5m 5m⁵ 6m 6m 5g 5m⁴ 5g 5g] strong gelding: has been hobdayed: fair winner in 1988: below form as 7-y-o: ran as though something amiss third to fifth outings, and tubed on sixth: best at 5f: acts on firm going and a soft surface: blinkered once: best treated with caution. *M. A. Jarvis.*

DURBO 5 b.g. Bustino 136–Durun 89 (Run The Gantlet (USA)) [1988 16s⁶ 16g — 14m³ 14.6g 1989 15.5s⁵] neat, attractive gelding: moderate mover: modest at his best: blinkered, led until under 2f out when fifth of 16 in handicap at Folkestone in April: stays 2m: acts on soft going and top-of-the-ground: occasionally sweats: apprentice ridden last 2 outings as 4-y-o: possibly needs to dominate. *R. Akehurst.*

DURGAM (USA) 3 b.c. Nureyev (USA) 131–Famed Princess (USA) (Nashua) — [1988 NR 1989 10g 10.1m 8m] $1,100,000Y: well-made colt with scope: half-brother to 3 winners, notably Grade 1 1¼m winner Clear Choice (by Raise A Native): dam won at up to 9f, including in stakes company: well beaten in maidens and minor event in first half of season, though showed signs of ability first 2 outings: twice bit coltish: sold 17,000 gns Newmarket Autumn Sales. *A. C. Stewart.*

DURLEY SONG 3 gr.c. Cree Song 99–Donrae 106 (Don (ITY) 123) [1988 NR **52** 1989 7f⁶ 7.5m 6m³] leggy, angular colt: sixth foal: half-brother to moderate 6f winner Brampton Grace (by Tachypous) and 7.2f and 12.2f winner Lyn Rae (by Derrylin): dam best at 2 yrs when winning twice over 5f: progressive form in maiden (moved poorly down), seller and minor event in the North. *M. H. Easterby.*

DURZI 4 b.g. High Line 125–Sookera (USA) 117 (Roberto (USA) 131) [1988 8g⁵ 7f — 7m⁴ 7.3m² 7g⁴ 1989 11.7m 8f] well-made gelding: modest maiden as 3-y-o: needed race both outings in first half of 1989: keen sort, suited by 7f (had stiff task when tailed off over 11.7f): acts on top-of-the-ground and soft going: bandaged behind at 4 yrs. *D. R. C. Elsworth.*

DUSHENKA 2 b.f. (Mar 9) Jalmood (USA) 126–Ideal Home 104 (Home Guard — (USA) 129) [1989 5s⁶] 19,000Y: tall, leggy filly: second foal: dam 2-y-o 5f winner: 5/1, bit backward and green, slow-starting 13½ lengths sixth of 8, some headway from 2f out, to Raschester in maiden at Haydock in April. *M. W. Easterby.*

DUSKY DAI 3 gr.g. Day Is Done 115–El Diana (Tarboosh (USA)) [1988 7g 6d 6s **48** 1989 8.3m 8m 6m³ 6m⁴ 6m 7m 10g] big, good-topped gelding: has a round action: plating-class form when in frame in handicaps: below form in sellers after, tailed off final outing: probably doesn't stay 1m: blinkered last 5 starts: broke out of stalls intended reappearance: trained until after sixth outing by M. Usher. *C. C. Elsey.*

DUSTBOWL 2 br.c. (May 9) Sharpo 132–Duboff 120 (So Blessed 130) [1989 5f⁵ **59** 5m⁵ 6g 6f] 36,000Y: rather unfurnished colt: has scope: seventh foal: half-brother to 3-y-o 5f and 6f winner Elegant Rainbow (by Formidable) and several other winners, including fair middle-distance winner Durun (by Run The Gantlet): dam won 11 races, including Sun Chariot Stakes and Child Stakes: plating-class maiden: should be better suited by 6f than 5f: sold 7,000 gns Newmarket Autumn Sales. *P. T. Walwyn.*

DUST DEVIL 4 b.c. Horage 124–Witch of Endor 80 (Matador 131) [1988 8m² 8d⁴ **110** 8d 10g⁵ 10v³ 10g* 10d⁶ 10.2g* 10s³ 1989 8d 10m 10g⁵ 10m² 10g² 12g⁴ 11s⁴ 12d] strong, lengthy colt: very useful performer: returned to its best when second of 5 to Light of Morn in £10,100 handicap at Ascot in July: poor fourth of 6 to Shellac in listed event at Ayr in September: in frame in similar contests in between at

Deauville and Bordeaux: probably stays 1½m: yet to race on firm going, acts on any other: usually blinkered nowadays. *J. L. Dunlop.*

DUSTY EMERALD (USA) 3 ch.g. Green Forest (USA) 134–Grey Reliance 85 (USA) (Cloudy Dawn (USA)) [1988 NR 1989 8g 8g 10f⁵ 10f 11f* 13.3m 14f³] big, useful-looking gelding: first reported foal: dam very useful winner at up to 9f, including in stakes company: won handicap at Redcar in June: not discredited in similar event final start, in July: took keen hold and saddle slipped in between: should be suited by further than 11f: acts on firm going: has joined K. Morgan. *L. M. Cumani.*

DUTCH MAJESTY 3 b.f. Homing 130–Dutch Princess 70 (Royalty 130) [1988 6f — 1989 10s 10g] compact filly: burly, no promise in maidens. *Miss B. Sanders.*

DUTEST 2 b.c. (Apr 7) Aragon 118–Indian Call 72 (Warpath 113) [1989 6g⁵ 6g 60 8m⁵] 31,000Y: leggy, angular colt: first foal: dam winning plater at 7f and 1m on flat: quite modest form in maidens and a minor event: probably stays 1m. *A. C. Stewart.*

DUTYFUL 3 b.f. Bold Owl 101–My Duty 70 (Sea Hawk II 131) [1988 5g 6m³ 7m² 78 7m 7g⁴ 7g⁴ 8m⁶ 8.5m⁶ 7m⁵ 1989 7s⁶ 9f 12f⁵ 16m 12m² 12f* 10m⁵ 13.3d] sturdy, workmanlike filly: comfortable winner of maiden at Folkestone in September: stays 1½m, not 2m: acts on firm going, possibly unsuited by a soft surface: visored seventh outing at 2 yrs. *M. J. Haynes.*

DUXFORD LODGE 2 b.f. (May 15) Dara Monarch 128–Simmay (Simbir 130) 33 [1989 6m 7g⁴ 6m 8.5f] IR 2,400F, IR 2,000Y: close-coupled, sparely-made filly: third foal: dam placed at up to 1¼m in Ireland: poor plater. *J. F. Bottomley.*

DWADME 4 b.g. High Top 131–Durun 89 (Run The Gantlet (USA)) [1988 11.7f⁵ 90 11.7g³ 12f⁴ 12g* 14f³ 14.6f⁶ 1989 14g* 14m 14f⁴ 15f³ 14f 16m²] tall, rather sparely-made gelding: fair handicapper: won at Salisbury in May: placed after, running creditably, in 4-runner £14,800 event at Ayr and 10-runner contest at Chester: stays 2m: yet to race on a soft surface: has got on toes: wandered final start at 3 yrs: sold to join O. Sherwood 29,000 gns Newmarket Autumn Sales. *H. Candy.*

DWELLING 3 b.g. Habitat 134–Lady Oriana 91 (Tudor Melody 129) [1988 NR — 1989 7g 8d 7m⁶] 56,000Y: leggy, rather angular gelding: sixth foal: half-brother to 1¼m and 1½m winner Coulee Queen (by Bustino) and a winning plater: dam, daughter of very smart sprinter Merry Madcap, won over 7f at 2 yrs: soundly beaten in maidens: tailed off final start (July) and subsequently gelded: visored second outing. *P. T. Walwyn.*

DWELL (USA) 4 ch.f. Habitat 134–Wink (USA) 101 (Forli (ARG)) [1988 8g⁵ 8m* 96 8m² 8m⁵ 7g² 6m³ 1989 6g 7g³ 7g 6v] smallish, useful-looking filly: moderate mover: fairly useful handicapper: ran very well when third to Southern Sky in £8,700 event at Epsom in June, poorly in competitive events after: at least as effective at 6f as at 1m: seems unsuited by heavy going: often sweating and on edge: sold 145,000 gns Newmarket December Sales. *A. C. Stewart.*

DYFED 4 b.c. Daring March 116–Regency Brighton (Royal Palace 131) [1988 6d 8f — 6m 5.8f 7d⁶ 10.8s 1989 10.8s 9f] sparely-made colt: poor plater: stays 7f. *M. Tate.*

D'YQUEM 3 b.f. Formidable (USA) 125–Bargouzine 67 (Hotfoot 126) [1988 5g 6d §§ 1989 12v 10s 8d 12m] no form, and has looked singularly reluctant: visored third start: one to avoid. *M. D. I. Usher.*

DZET (USA) 2 b.c. (May 7) Caerleon (USA) 132–Tendresse (USA) (Secretariat — (USA)) [1989 8.2d 8m] medium-sized colt: first foal: dam unraced from family of Majestic Prince and Crowned Prince: well beaten in October maidens at Haydock (green) and Newmarket. *Mrs L. Piggott.*

E

EAGER DEVA 2 b.c. (Mar 14) Lochnager 132–Deva Rose 80 (Chestergate 111) 72 [1989 5f* 5m 6v] robust, good-quartered, sprint type: has plenty of scope: good walker and easy mover: brother to 1987 2-y-o 5f winner Ashlar Boy and half-brother to 3 winners, including fair sprinter Rosie Dickens (by Blue Cashmere): dam won 4 times over 5f: won maiden at Nottingham in September: ran well facing stiff task in all-aged event at Chepstow on next outing, easily better subsequent effort. *R. Hollinshead.*

EAGLES LAIR 3 b.c. Head For Heights 125–Just A Shadow (Laser Light 118) 89 d [1988 NR 1989 10g⁴ 12d3 9m⁴ 11f³] 51,000F, 17,000Y: rather sparely-made, attractive colt: third living foal: half-brother to modest miler Overpower (by Try My Best): dam fair Irish 5f performer: made most promising debut in £6,200 event at

Newmarket but disappointed after: hung left and gave impression will prove best with strong handling in apprentice handicap final start, in early-July: stays 1¼m: sold to join D. Marks 5,000 gns Newmarket September Sales: may not be 100% genuine. *L. M. Cumani.*

EARLY BREEZE 3 b.g. Tumble Wind (USA)–Dawn Hail 74 (Derring-Do 131) **78**
[1988 6g 5g⁴ 6g³ 7m³ 7d 7.3m 7d² 7d³ 1989 6s⁶ 6s* 6m² 6m⁶ 7g⁴ 7m 7g 6m 7d] compact gelding: modest handicapper: won maiden at Nottingham in April: ran moderately last 4 outings (subsequently gelded): stays 7f: has run creditably on top-of-the-ground but may be ideally suited by some give: has run well for 7-lb claimer. *M. McCourt.*

EARLY SOUND 3 ch.f. Baptism 119–Ribero's Overture 72 (Ribero 126) [1988 —
5m 7m 7g⁴ 8.5f² 1989 12.4f³ 16f 13.8g] leggy filly: has a round action: poor maiden: below form in varied events in 1989, running as though something amiss in seller final start: may prove best at around 1¼m with forcing tactics. *H. P. Rohan.*

EARTHLY PLEASURE 3 b.f. Music Boy 124–May Fox 67 (Healaugh Fox) **50**
[1988 7g 7m 1989 10.1g 12m 12m³ 12g⁴ 15.3g⁵ 10g 10.6s] good-topped, useful-looking filly: plating class at best: blinkered, in frame at Newmarket in slowly-run seller and a claimer: stays 1½m, at least in slowly-run race: best efforts on top-of-the-ground: also blinkered final outing. *P. J. Makin.*

EARTH SPACER 5 b.m. Mandalus 110–Geisha Dancer (Hul A Hul 124) [1988 —
NR 1989 13.8m⁶] half-sister to Irish 2m winner Whistling Dancer (by Whistling Deer): dam poor Irish maiden: won maiden at Downpatrick (apprentice ridden) as 3-y-o: 12/1 and bandaged, tailed off (finished lame) in 6-runner apprentice claiming event at Catterick in July: stayed 1½m: dead. *J. H. Johnson.*

EASTBROOK 9 b. or br.g. Lochnager 132–Lush Gold 91 (Goldhill 125) [1988 6v⁴
6g⁵ 6d 6g 7g⁶ 6s 6m 1989 6f] strong, compact gelding: usually dull in coat: carries plenty of condition: poor handicapper: below form since second outing in 1988: suited by 6f: possibly unsuited by firm going, acts on any other: twice blinkered: has run well for apprentice: suited by forcing tactics. *Miss S. E. Hall.*

EASTDENE MAGIC 2 ch.f. (Mar 22) Nicholas Bill 125–Step Softly 81 (St Chad **66**
120) [1989 6f⁶ 7f² 7f³ 7.5m⁵ 7f* 7m 7m²] 1,300Y: leggy, sparely-made filly: good mover: sixth living foal: half-sister to 1985 2-y-o 1m winner Kerry May Sing and 3-y-o One Lady Owner (both by Mansingh), 6f seller winner Walk Softly (by Tower Walk) and a winning hurdler: dam 2-y-o 5f winner: ridden by 5-lb claimer, won seller at Redcar in July by a head: second to Eire Leath-Sceal in nursery at Newcastle following month, better effort: will be suited by 1m: sold 6,500 gns Doncaster October Sales. *Mrs G. R. Reveley.*

EASTER BABY 3 ch.f. Derrylin 115–Saintly Miss 63 (St Paddy 133) [1988 NR —
1989 a6g] sister to modest maiden Saintly Lad and half-sister to useful 1m to 1½m performer Holy Spark (by Sparkler), fair 1¼m winner Virgin Soldier (by Queen's Hussar) and a winning sprint plater: dam stayed 1½m: always behind in claimer at Lingfield in December. *P. D. Cundell.*

EASTER GLORY 3 b.f. Dalsaan 125–Precious Egg (Home Guard (USA) 129) **60**
[1988 5g⁴ 5g⁴ 6f³ 6m³ 8g 8g² 1989 8.2s³ 8s² 8d³ 6g* 6f 7.3m⁴ 7m 7m 8m 7g 6f* 7m] leggy, rather sparely-made filly: poor mover: quite modest performer: twice successful in handicaps at Salisbury, in apprentice event in May then returning to form in October: best at up to 7f: acts on any going: best in blinkers: sold to race in Middle East 6,400 gns Newmarket Autumn Sales. *A. N. Lee.*

EASTERN DIAMOND (USA) 3 b.f. Diamond Shoal 130–Liturgism (USA) **92**
(Native Charger) [1988 7d⁵ 8s² 9g³ 1989 14m³ 12.2m² 14f* 12g* 12s* 13.3d] leggy, sparely-made filly: progressive form when winning maiden (odds on) at Redcar in August and handicaps at Haydock in September and October: favourite, ran poorly in Newbury handicap final start: effective at 1½m ridden close up and stays 1¾m well: acts on any going: sold 46,000 gns Newmarket December Sales. *H. R. A. Cecil.*

EASTERN EMBER 3 br.f. Indian King (USA) 128–Pithead 70 (High Top 131) **80**
[1988 5g 5f 7d 6g 1989 8.2s 8s 6s* 5m* 5m 6m⁶ 5g⁵ 5g* 5f³ 6f³ 6f 5m³ 6m 6m 5f 6s 5m] leggy, lengthy filly: fair handicapper: won seller (making all, bought in 2,400 gns) at Thirsk in April and strongly-run races at Chester in May and Beverley in July: moved poorly down when below form fifth (trained until after then by M. W. Easterby) and final (unimpressive in appearance) outings: should prove suited by stiff 5f: acts on any going: blinkered nowadays: has run creditably for 5-lb claimer. *C. C. Elsey.*

EASTERN MELODY 4 b.f. Tudor Rhythm 112–Casbar Lady 79 (Native Bazaar —
122) [1988 7d⁶ 5s⁴ 5m⁴ 6d 7.6m 5s⁶ 6s⁶ 6d⁵ 6d 6d⁴ 5g 6s⁵ 6m 1989 7s 6g⁵ 5f 5f 6f

10f] small, rather lightly-made filly: moderate mover: poor handicapper: suited by 6f and an easy surface: sometimes blinkered or visored: has wandered and carried head high: sold 1,700 gns Doncaster September Sales. *E. J. Alston.*

EASTER RAMBLER 7 b.g. Scott Joplyn 108–Victory Corner 68 (Sit In The — Corner (USA)) [1988 NR 1989 10g] workmanlike gelding: no longer of much account: has worn blinkers and visor. *P. Butler.*

EASTFIELD BOY 2 b.c. (Mar 11) Sayf El Arab (USA) 127–Dog's Bay (Tumble — Wind (USA)) [1989 5g⁶ 5v] 7,000F: leggy, fair sort: moderate walker: second living foal: brother to 3-y-o Sandmoor Corner, 5f winner at 2 yrs: dam good winner in Belgium: poor form in maidens at Doncaster and Ayr in April. *J. Etherington.*

EASY LENDER 2 b.f. (Apr 10) Sandhurst Prince 128–Nest Builder 85 (Home — Guard (USA) 129) [1989 6m 6m 6f⁶] 3,000Y: sister to bad animal Babe In Arms and half-sister to fairly useful 1984 2-y-o 6f and 7f winner Nesting Time (by Dance In Time): dam won over 5f at 3 yrs: soundly beaten in sellers: slowly away first 2 starts: sold 700 gns Ascot August Sales. *P. Mitchell.*

EASY LINE 6 ch.g. Swing Easy (USA) 126–Impromptu 88 (My Swanee 122) **86** [1988 6d 6m² 6s⁶ 5m* 6f* 7d 6g 5g⁶ 5g 6s⁵ 6v⁵ 1989 6f 6f² 6f² 6f 6m* 6f³ 6f³ 6m⁴ 6f⁴] tall, lengthy gelding: moderate mover: fair handicapper: successful at Kempton in June comfortably by 4 lengths: ran well last 3 outings: suited by 6f: has form on soft going, but possibly needs a sound surface nowadays: visored once: has hung, and is suited by waiting tactics. *P. J. Feilden.*

EASY MAN 2 b.g. (Mar 5) Mansingh (USA) 120–Easy Gal (Swing Easy (USA) **50 §** 126) [1989 5f⁴ 6g 6f 8.5f] 4,100Y: neat gelding: first foal: dam unplaced in 4 starts at 3 yrs: moderate plater: best effort on debut in non-seller: blinkered, unruly at start, slowly away and ran badly final start. *M. W. Ellerby.*

EASY OVER (USA) 3 ch.c. Transworld (USA) 121–Love Bunny (USA) **84 ?** (Exclusive Native (USA)) [1988 7s² 7s² 8s⁴ 1989 8g* 10v² 10.2g 10.5m a10g] big, workmanlike colt: won slowly-run apprentice maiden at Newcastle in March: beaten short head in handicap at Ayr following month: below form in similar events after, twice sweating, and running as if something amiss third start: suited by 1¼m: acts on heavy going: sold 11,000 gns Newmarket Autumn Sales. *S. G. Norton.*

EASY PREP 2 b.g. (Feb 20) Reasonable (FR) 119–Professor's Choice 86 (Mount **84** Hagen (FR) 127) [1989 6m⁶ 6m* 5g⁴ 6s³] IR 9,000F, 8,000Y: angular gelding: third foal: half-brother to 1½m winner Professional Touch (by Touching Wood): dam 2-y-o 7f winner: made virtually all in maiden at Yarmouth in August: good third to Dumbreck in nursery at Ayr following month: will stay 7f: hung continually right third outing. *G. A. Pritchard-Gordon.*

EASY PURCHASE 2 br.c. (Mar 9) Swing Easy (USA) 126–Dauphiness 76 — (Supreme Sovereign 119) [1989 7f] 3,000Y: brother to a winner in Scandinavia and plating-class sprinter Parade Girl, and half-brother to a winner here and abroad: dam 2-y-o 7f winner: 33/1, always towards rear in 14-runner maiden at Salisbury in October. *D. Haydn Jones.*

EASY TIME (GER) 4 b.g. High Line 125–Easily (Swing Easy (USA) 126) [1988 **55** 11.7f 11.7g 12m 14g⁴ 1989 15.5s 11.7d 10.1m 12m 12h* 12f* 16m⁵ 12f²] rangy, workmanlike gelding: won uncompetitive handicaps at Lingfield in June and Folkestone in July: seems best at 1½m: acts on hard going: took good hold when blinkered third and fourth outings. *P. F. I. Cole.*

EBOR NOVA 3 b.g. Krayyan 117–Turbo Lady (Tumble Wind (USA)) [1988 5d 5v⁶ — 5m 5d⁴ 6f 6m⁶ 6f 6f 6g 5f 5f 1989 7g 5m] close-coupled, angular gelding: poor mover: poor plater: blinkered 5 times, including final start (May): active type, tends to be on toes: possibly ungenuine. *J. S. Wainwright.*

EBRO 3 ch.g. Aragon 118–Caribbean Blue (Blue Cashmere 129) [1988 8d 10d 1989 **67** 8g³ 10f² 10m 8.2f 10f⁶ 10f³ 12f 10g] big, workmanlike gelding: turns fore-feet out: quite modest form: placed in claimers and a maiden: may prove best short of 1¼m: acts on firm going. *Mrs L. Piggott.*

ECCOLINA 3 ch.f. Formidable (USA) 125–Chili Girl 112 (Skymaster 126) [1988 6f **65** 6d⁵ 6m³ 7.3m 1989 6s⁶ 8g⁵ 8.5f 8m a7g³] medium-sized, rather angular filly: poor walker: moderate mover: quite modest maiden: strong-finishing third in handicap at Southwell in December: stays 7f: acts on top-of-the-ground: unruly in paddock and slowly away fourth start: not one to trust implicitly. *J. L. Dunlop.*

ECHO CHAMBER 3 ch.f. Music Boy 124–Abalone (Abwah 118) [1988 5m⁴ 5g⁵ **72** 5m 6f* 6d² 6s⁶ 1989 6m 6m 6m⁵ 6f³ 6m 6m⁴ 6s 6g⁶ 6g] small, lightly-made filly:

moderate mover: modest handicapper: may stay 7f: acts on top-of-the-ground, possibly unsuited by very soft. *M. H. Tompkins.*

ECHO PRINCESS 2 b.f. (Apr 28) Crofter (USA) 124–What A Breeze (Whistling **75** Wind 123) [1989 5m 5m3 5g2 5g2 5f2 5d6 5m3 5m2 5g2 5f2 5f* 5s3] 9,000 2-y-o: lengthy, good-quartered filly: half-sister to several winners, including useful Irish 6f and 7f winner Mistral Man (by Sweet Revenge) and 1987 2-y-o 6f winner Lauries Treasure (by Don): dam ran 3 times: modest performer: won maiden auction event at Warwick by ½ length from Quinta Royale: very good third of 6 to odds-on Tatwij in minor event at Ayr later in October: worth a try at 6f: has given trouble stalls. *J. Berry.*

ECONOLOFT 3 ch.g. Aragon 118–Hussy 82 (Queen's Hussar 124) [1988 6m5 7g — 7g 1989 10.6g 12.3m 15.8m3 12.3f] strong, workmanlike gelding: no form in varied events: unlikely to stay 1½m: edgy and sweating on reappearance: sold 920 gns Doncaster September Sales. *G. M. Moore.*

ECOSSAIS DANSEUR (USA) 3 ch.c. Arctic Tern (USA) 126–Northern **82** Blossom (CAN) (Snow Knight 125) [1988 7m4 7.3s 1989 10.2d2 12f6 10m4 9.1f* 10.5m5 9g2] lengthy, rather angular colt: has a rather round action: made all in maiden at Newcastle in July: easily best other efforts as 3-y-o when second in minor event at Bath and £15,400 handicap (first of main group on far side, behind Secretary of State) at Newmarket: stays 1¼m: has won on firm going, and goes well on a soft surface. *B. W. Hills.*

ECRAN 3 b.f. Kings Lake (USA) 133–High Finale 100 (High Line 125) [1988 NR **81** 1989 13.3m6 16m3 17.6f* 17.6m* 16m6 18g3 19g3] rangy, workmanlike filly: has a rather round action: fifth foal: half-sister to very useful 7f and 9f winner My Generation and useful 6f to 1m winner Que Sympatica (both by Young Generation): dam, winner over 1¼m, is sister to Park Hill winner Quay Line: won maiden and handicap at Wolverhampton in summer: out of depth, appeared to run very well in 3-runner Doncaster Cup: hampered when running creditably in minor event at Goodwood 3 weeks later: suited by test of stamina: may prove best on an easy surface. *J. L. Dunlop.*

EDENLAD 4 b.g. Hotfoot 126–Apple of My Eye 83 (Silver Cloud 122) [1988 11g **49** 11.7f 14.8s 1989 12f5 12m] medium-sized, quite attractive gelding: poor mover: poor maiden: probably stays 1½m: acts on firm going, tailed off on soft: sweating final outing: sold 3,400 gns Ascot August Sales. *R. F. Johnson Houghton.*

EDEN'S DAWN 2 ch.c. (Apr 18) Godswalk (USA) 130–Fresh As A Daisy **44** (Stanford 121§) [1989 6f6 5h3 6f 6f 6m 8.2f 6g3 8g] 7,000Y: leggy, quite good-topped colt: good walker: second foal: half-brother to 3-y-o 7f winner D'Altagnan (by Dalsaan): dam lightly raced: poor maiden: tailed off in Carlisle selling nursery final start: best form at 6f: sold 2,600 gns Newmarket Autumn Sales. *R. Hollinshead.*

EDGEWISE 6 b. or br.g. Tanfirion 110–Regency Girl 89 (Right Boy 137) [1988 7d — 7g 7g 6m 7m 7m3 8g 1989 8.2g] compact gelding: good mover: poor handicapper: 33/1 and bandaged, always behind at Nottingham in July: free runner, best at up to 7f: acts on any going: occasionally visored: sometimes sweats: sometimes taken down early: inconsistent. *W. Wilson.*

EDUCATED RITA 2 b.f. (Apr 29) The Brianstan 128–Sobriquet (Roan Rocket **47** 128) [1989 6g 6m 7d] angular filly: first foal: dam poor half-sister to very useful 1976 2-y-o 5f performer The Andrestan (by The Brianstan): plater, only form on debut. *Miss L. C. Siddall.*

EDWARD LEAR (USA) 3 b.c. Lear Fan (USA) 128–Coed (USA) (Ribot 142) **74** [1988 8g 1989 9m4 11g2] workmanlike colt: in frame in claimers at Newmarket and Redcar (went down well, claimed to join J. FitzGerald £18,300) in the autumn: may prove best at up to 11f. *L. M. Cumani.*

EECEE TREE 7 ch.g. Young Generation 129–Golden Treasure 106 (Crepello — 136) [1988 5m* 5m6 1989 5f6 5f 5m5 5m] good-topped gelding: moderate mover: quite modest performer: below form in handicaps last 3 outings, not seen out after July: best at 5f: acts on any going: often sweating and on edge: has worn blinkers and a crossed noseband: races up with pace: often taken down early: has won for apprentice, but is not an easy ride. *J. Sutcliffe.*

EEZEPEEZE 3 b.f. Alzao (USA) 117–Tacama 64 (Daring Display (USA) 129) **83** [1988 6m5 6f 6m2 6g2 6g2 6g* 6m* 6m* 6m* 7s3 6s5 6m 1989 7g 6d 8f 6m 7f4 7g 7g5] compact filly: carries condition: moderate walker and mover: easily best efforts as 3-y-o in handicaps at Redcar fifth and final (got poor run) starts: stays 7f well: acts on any going: sometimes wanders: edgy, ran poorly fourth (visored) start and final one at 2 yrs: sold out of D. Thom's stable 14,500 gns Newmarket July Sales after fourth start. *J. Etherington.*

EFFERVESCENT 4 ch.c. Sharpo 132–Never So Lovely 87 (Realm 129) [1988   **60**
6s⁵ 6m³ 7g* 7g⁴ 7.6s⁶ 7f 7d 7.6d² 7g 1989 7g 7f 6f⁶ 7.5m 7f⁶ 7.6h⁴ 7f⁵ 8f* 8m³ 9f³
8.3m² 8f* 8.5g] rather leggy, useful-looking colt: poor walker and mover: quite
modest handicapper: won by short head at Bath in July and August: ran poorly at
Epsom final outing: suited by around 1m: acts on firm going and a soft surface:
blinkered nowadays. *G. Lewis.*

EINSTEIN 5 b.g. Mummy's Pet 125–Piccadilly Etta 76 (Floribunda 136) [1988 8g   **— §**
7f 7g 10s 1989 6s 8d 10m 7f] strong, compact gelding: moderate mover: fair winner at
2 yrs: little show in subsequent handicaps: stays 6f: acts on firm going and a soft
surface: has been tried in blinkers: often on toes: has tended to carry head high and
look temperamental: sold 3,100 gns Ascot June Sales. *D. W. P. Arbuthnot.*

EIRE LEATH-SCEAL 2 b.c. (Mar 13) Legend of France (USA) 124–Killarney   **80**
Belle (USA) (Irish Castle (USA)) [1989 5d³ 6m⁵ 6f² 6m² 7m* 7.5m* 7m² 7m* 8m²
8g³ 7g 7m⁵ 7g³ 8g⁵] 2,100Y: compact, attractive colt: poor mover: second foal:
half-brother to 3-y-o 1m to 1¼m winner Booby Prize (by Bustino): dam never ran:
progressive colt: successful in nurseries in August at Leicester, Beverley and
Newcastle: mostly ran very well afterwards: will stay 1¼m: tough and genuine. *M.
Brittain.*

EJAY HAITCH 4 b.c. Be My Native (USA) 122–Miss Spencer (Imperial Fling   **—**
(USA) 116) [1988 11v* 12m⁵ 12.3s 14m 16m 18d* 1989 21.6d 18s⁴] good-topped colt:
quite modest winner as 3-y-o: fair fourth of 12 in Nottingham handicap in May, but
wasn't seen out again: suited by a good test of stamina and plenty of give in the
ground: has run creditably when sweating and on toes. *Mrs R. Wharton.*

EJREE 4 b.c. Runnett 125–Carntino (Bustino 136) [1988 6m 6g⁶ 8g 10g 10.2g 8g   **—**
1989 a14g] attractive, rather leggy colt: poor maiden. *R. G. Brazington.*

ELA-AYABI-MOU 3 ch.f. Absalom 128–Fairfields 73 (Sharpen Up 127) [1988   **—**
5v⁵ 6m 6f⁵ 7m⁵ 7f* 7f³ 7g 1989 7g⁶ 8f 8m 7g 7m 7f⁶ 6f 7d⁵] workmanlike filly: quite
modest handicapper on her day: suited by 7f: acts on firm going and a soft surface:
often apprentice ridden: sold to join A. Reid 3,200 gns Newmarket Autumn Sales. *J.
W. Payne.*

ELADHAM 3 b. or br.c. Lyphard's Special (USA) 122–Derrede (Derring-Do 131)   **67**
[1988 7g 7g⁵ 1989 8m⁶ 10f 12g 12.5f⁵ 10.5g*] sparely-made, angular colt: easily best
effort as 3-y-o when winning selling handicap at York in October by a neck, soon
long way clear and battling on gamely despite tending to drift: stays 1¼m: seems
best on an easy surface: bandaged behind third and fourth outings: bought out of R.
Armstrong's stable 8,600 gns Newmarket July Sales after reappearance. *D. Morley.*

ELA MEEM (USA) 3 ch.f. Kris 135–La Dolce 108 (Connaught 130) [1988 NR   **—**
1989 7s⁴ 10s⁴ 10.6g⁴ 14g⁶] rather sparely-made, attractive filly: keen walker: sixth
foal: closely related to top-class 1m to 1½m filly Pebbles (by Sharpen Up) and
half-sister to fair 1¼m winner Petradia (by Relkino): dam won twice over 1m and
finished fifth in Oaks: modest form at best: off course over 3 months before and after
third start: probably stays 1¼m. *C. E. Brittain.*

ELAPSE (USA) 2 gr.c. (Mar 24) Sharpen Up 127–Bygones (USA) (Lyphard   **92**
(USA) 132) [1989 5s³ 6f² 5m* 5f³] big, strong, close-coupled colt: has plenty of
scope: first foal: dam, winner at up to 9f in USA, is half-sister to useful 1986 2-y-o 6f
and 7f winner At Risk: odds on, made all in maiden at Leicester, beating Green's
Stubbs in good style by 4 lengths: never travelled particularly smoothly and tended
to hang when 3 lengths third to Petillante in Norfolk Stakes at Royal Ascot later in
June: withdrawn (reportedly cut off-hind) at York in August and wasn't seen out
again: best form at 5f. *B. W. Hills.*

EL ARAB 2 b.g. (Mar 28) Sayf El Arab (USA) 127–Sally Conkers (Roi Lear (FR)   **70**
126) [1989 5s 5s 6f 6f³ 6f² 6f* 6m⁴ 7m 6v² 7g⁵] 1,700Y: leggy, good-topped gelding:
moderate mover: seventh foal: half-brother to 1982 2-y-o 6f winner Judy Conkers
(by Swing Easy), later successful in West Indies, and to winning hurdler
Trebonkers (by Treboro): dam well beaten: quite modest performer: made all in
maiden auction race at Newcastle in July, beating Eire Leath-Sceal by 4 lengths:
good second to Scorpio Lady in auction event at Ayr in October, best subsequent
effort: stays 7f: acts on any going: visored fourth to eighth outings. *E. J. Alston.*

ELARQAM 3 b.c. Shareef Dancer (USA) 135–Noble Treasure (USA) (Vaguely   **87**
Noble 140) [1988 7d 8g² 1989 11.7d* 12.3m³ 11.5f² 13.3g 13.1m³ 13.1f⁶ 14m] smallish,
lengthy colt: won maiden at Bath in April: placed, running well, in handicaps at
Chester, Sandown and Bath: should stay 1¾m: acts on firm going and a soft surface:

wears tongue strap: visored last 5 outings: sold 17,500 gns Newmarket Autumn Sales. *J. Tree.*

ELASTIC 3 b.f. Ela-Mana-Mou 132–Queen of The Dance (Dancer's Image (USA)) — [1988 5m 6m4 6m6 6g 1989 10f5] leggy filly: plating-class maiden: bred to stay middle distances but may not do so: reared stalls second start: ridden by apprentice first 3 at 2 yrs. *J. S. Wilson.*

ELA-YEMOU 2 ch.g. (May 2) Dara Monarch 128–Micro Mover (Artaius (USA) 77 129) [1989 5g 6m5 6m* 6m2 6m3 5d4] 4,200Y: tall gelding: has scope: has a fluent, rather round action: fourth foal: half-brother to Irish 3-y-o 9f winner Rockwell (by Glenstal) and winners in Spain and Italy: dam won at 10.5f in France: modest performer: won maiden auction event at Leicester in July: ran respectably in nurseries next 2 starts but moderately in auction race (edgy) following month and wasn't seen out again: better suited by 6f than 5f, and is bred to stay at least 7f: tends to hang left, and possibly ungenerous: trained on debut by K. Brassey. *C. N. Allen.*

ELA-YIANNI-MOU 4 br.f. Anfield 117–Another Move 69 (Farm Walk 111) — [1988 7d3 6s3 7d* 7m 7m 7.3m 1989 6v 7f] small, lengthy filly: poor mover: quite modest winner early as 3-y-o: below her best both outings (off course 7 weeks in between) in first half of 1989: suited by 7f: probably acts on any going: good mount for apprentice. *C. N. Allen.*

EL DALSAD 3 b.c. Dalsaan 125–Safidar 83 (Roan Rocket 128) [1988 6d4 6f 6m 7g6 7m 8.2s* 8v 1989 13m 12g 10.2g] lengthy, good-quartered colt: keen walker: poor mover: quite modest nursery winner as 2-y-o: well beaten in handicaps in 1989, blinkered final start: stays 1m well, unlikely to stay 1½m: acts on soft ground: visored last 4 starts as 2-y-o. *T. Craig.*

ELDER PRINCE 3 ch.g. Final Straw 127–Particular Miss 70 (Luthier 126) [1988 76 5g2 5g* 5f3 1989 7g 5d* 7f 6m4 5f 8f4 6m3 8m 8g] workmanlike gelding: won strongly-run minor event at Pontefract in April: sweating, creditable third in claimer at Haydock, again staying on having been outpaced: below form in handicaps after, and is worth another try over 7f: acts on top-of-the-ground and a soft surface. *M. H. Easterby.*

ELECTED LADY 2 b.f. (Feb 28) Homing 130–Electo (Julio Mariner 127) [1989 5f 6g] leggy, sparely-made filly: second foal: half-sister to 3-y-o Optaria (by Song), 5f winner at 2 yrs: dam well beaten in varied races: well beaten in quite valuable event at Beverley in June and maiden at Goodwood 4 months later: sold 2,200 gns Newmarket Autumn Sales. *I. A. Balding.*

ELECTRIC DANCER 3 br.g. Electric 126–Chicory (Vaigly Great 127) [1988 61 NR 1989 10g 12f6 10.1m 11.7m 12g2 12s4 16f] 4,000Y: medium-sized, rather leggy gelding: first foal: dam twice-raced half-sister to very useful animals Macmillion, winner at 1m and 1½m, and Baz Bombati, middle-distance performer: first worthwhile form (had previously shown signs of ability) when second in claimer at Newmarket in August: below that form in similar event and a handicap after: stays 1½m: best effort on good ground. *C. A. Horgan.*

ELECTRIC LADY 4 b.f. Electric 126–Eulalie 85 (Queen's Hussar 124) [1988 105 7g4 7m* 7d4 10f3 8m4 10g4 1989 8d 8s* 8g 7g 8g] lengthy, good-quartered filly: 14/1, showed improved form when winning £20,200 Evening Standard Jubilee Handicap at Kempton in May: lightly raced and little show subsequently: stays 1¼m: acts on any going: sold 18,000 gns Newmarket December Sales. *M. R. Stoute.*

ELECTRIC MONEY 3 b.c. Kafu 120–Silver Bullion (Silver Shark 129) [1988 58 6d5 6m* 7g3 6d 1989 6m5 6m 6f] rather leggy, workmanlike colt: quite modest winner as 2-y-o: ran creditably facing stiff tasks in handicaps first 2 outings: well beaten in claimer on final one, in June: sold to join W. Turner 2,700 gns Ascot September Sales. *G. A. Pritchard-Gordon.*

ELECTRIC ROSE 4 ch.f. Electric 126–Rose And The Ring (Welsh Pageant 132) 39 [1988 6f5 5g* 6m3 6m 6f 6g 6m 1989 6g 7f 8m2 7m 12.3m 12m 10f] leggy, good-topped filly: bad mover: modest winner as 3-y-o: long way below her best in 1989: stays 1m: acts on top-of-the-ground: usually wears severe bridle or crossed noseband. *C. N. Allen.*

ELEGANCE IN DESIGN 3 ch.f. Habitat 134–Areola 114 (Kythnos 126) [1988 105 6d4 6s5 1989 8g2 8m5 7g3 6g* 6g2] useful Irish filly: won maiden at the Curragh as 2-y-o and listed race (by 2½ lengths from Didicoy) at Phoenix Park in September: best other efforts when about 4 lengths fifth to Ensconse in Irish 1000 Guineas and 1½ lengths second to Corwyn Bay in listed race in October, both at the Curragh:

possibly best at 6f: yet to race on very firm ground, probably acts on any other: blinkered after first start. *D. K. Weld, Ireland.*

ELEGANT LASS 3 ch.f. Adonijah 126–Elegante 105 (Frankincense 120) [1988 — 5m 6f 7f 6m 1989 10m 10f⁶ 8.2m 8f 10f⁵ 8.3d 9f] compact filly: poor maiden: twice visored. *M. D. I. Usher.*

ELEGANT MONARCH 3 ch.c. Ardross 134–Supremely Royal (Crowned 73 Prince (USA) 128) [1988 7d⁵ 8s⁴ 7g 8m⁶ 1989 12.5f³ 14f 11f 12f⁴ 10.6d 12.3m 16m* 17.4s 16.2d] big, rangy colt: has plenty of scope: has a markedly round action: won handicap at Chester in September, under pressure 4f out but quickening well inside last to lead close home: well beaten in similar events after: stays 2m: acts on firm going, probably unsuited by soft: has run well when edgy. *F. H. Lee.*

ELEGANT RAINBOW 3 b. or br.f. Formidable (USA) 125–Duboff 120 (So 99 Blessed 130) [1988 7m³ 1989 5h* 6h* 6g 6m* 5m⁴ 7m³ 8g² 8g] lengthy, attractive filly: good walker: won maiden at Bath in May and handicaps at Lingfield (odds on) in June and Doncaster in July: ran creditably next 3 outings, putting up best effort when beaten ½ length by Princess Accord in listed race at Ascot having been short of room until inside final 1f: stays 1m: acts on hard going: visored fourth and fifth starts. *A. C. Stewart.*

ELEGANT ROSE 3 ch.f. Noalto 120–Shapina 105 (Sharp Edge 123) [1988 6d 63 7m² 6m 7.3m² 8.2m² 7f 8.2v 1989 10.2g 7m³ 8m⁵ 7.6m³ a10g⁵ a8g² a8g²] sturdy filly: quite modest maiden: stays 1m: possibly needs sound surface: blinkered last 3 starts. *O. O'Neill.*

ELEGANT STRANGER 4 b.g. Krayyan 117–Tumvella (Tumble Wind (USA)) 63 [1988 7g 8g² 8.2m² 8g² 8h² 10d⁶ 8.2g 8.2s⁵ 9s 8g 1989 7g 8f² 8g] good-quartered, attractive gelding: quite modest performer: form on flat for some time only when second of 19 in handicap at Leicester in October: suited by 1m: acts on any going: winning hurdler. *M. H. Tompkins.*

ELEMENTARY 6 b.g. Busted 134–Santa Vittoria 100 (Ragusa 137) [1988 12s* 112 11g⁴ 12s⁴ 10s* 1989 10s³ 12g² 12g* 10m³ 9f* 12m³ 9g² 9g] strong, quite attractive gelding: put up very useful performances in July when winning IR £17,700 handicap at the Curragh under 10-0 and IR £16,300 handicap at Leopardstown under 10-4: in frame in varied events most other starts, on seventh one unlucky ½-length second of 10 under 10-10 in IR £17,300 handicap at Leopardstown: apprentice ridden, moved moderately to post and ran rare poor race in William Hill Cambridgeshire Handicap at Newmarket 6 weeks later: effective from 9f to 1½m: acts on any going: blinkered last 4 outings as 4-y-o: good hurdler: tough, genuine and consistent. *J. S. Bolger, Ireland.*

ELEMIS (USA) 2 ch.f. (Jan 21) Sir Ivor 135–'tis A Kitten (USA) (Tisab (USA)) — [1989 7g 8g] sparely-made filly: has a quick action: third foal: half-sister to a winner in USA: dam winner at up to 9f, from good family: carrying condition, well beaten in late-season £8,000 event at Newmarket and maiden at Leicester: to join J. Fanshawe. *B. W. Hills.*

ELENOS 3 b.c. Trojan Fen 118–Strapless 84 (Bustino 136) [1988 7g² 7g² 7f² 9m 86 § 8s⁵ 1989 8f 10f² 12f² 12m⁵ 10f³ 10f⁴ 10g] lengthy, quite atttractive colt: good mover: fair maiden on his day but thoroughly irresolute: stays 1½m: acts on firm going: takes keen hold: blinkered fourth outing: sold 11,000 gns Newmarket Autumn Sales: one to leave alone. *G. Harwood.*

ELEVEN LIGHTS (USA) 5 ch.g. Lyphard (USA) 132–Eleven Pelicans (USA) 44 (Grey Dawn II 132) [1988 8g 7.5m 8f 8g⁴ 8g⁶ 8d⁶ 10m³ 10m⁵ 10g⁶ 12m³ 12m⁶ 12m² 1989 12d 12g 12f² 12g⁶ 12h² 13.6f⁴ 12g 12h³ 12m⁴ 12g⁴ 15g⁶] small gelding: active type: moderate walker and mover: poor maiden: stays 1½m: acts on hard going: has sweated: has run creditably for apprentice: usually held up and often given plenty to do: winning hurdler: often finds little off bridle. *Mrs G. R. Reveley.*

ELFING 2 b.f. (Apr 27) Fairy King (USA)–Near The End (Shirley Heights 130) — [1989 5m] IR 17,500Y: neat, well-made filly: third foal: half-sister to Irish 3-y-o Dash of Red (by Red Sunset), fairly useful 7f winner at 2 yrs, and a winner in Spain: dam unraced: 5/1 and backward, last of 8, hanging badly left from 2f out, in maiden at Newbury in July. *R. Hannon.*

ELLA MON AMOUR 3 ch.f. Ela-Mana-Mou 132–Impudent Miss 105 (Persian 65 Bold 123) [1988 7g³ 6g 1989 7h⁴ 7f⁵ 8m³ 9m 9g³ 8f⁴] lengthy filly: keen walker: quite modest maiden: in frame in handicaps at Yarmouth (ridden by 7-lb claimer), Wolverhampton and Brighton: stays 9f: acts on firm going. *W. Jarvis.*

ELLA STREET 2 b.f. (Apr 1) King of Spain 121–More Fun (Malicious) [1989 — 7m⁶] 9,400Y: third foal: half-sister to 3-y-o Like Amber (by Aragon), 5f winner at 2 yrs, and 1½m winner Magic Tower (by Tower Walk): dam never ran: backward, soundly-beaten last of 6 in minor event at Doncaster in July. *N. Tinkler.*

ELLIE MINXY MOU 2 b.f. (Mar 28) Enchantment 115–Correct Approach 77 — (Right Tack 131) [1989 6m] 6,400Y: half-sister to 3-y-o Belhaven Bill (by Windjammer), 1¼m and 1¾m winner Rostherne (by Crimson Beau) and 2 winning 2-y-o platers: dam best at 2 yrs: well beaten in 14-runner Windsor seller in June. *R. J. Hodges.*

ELMAAMUL (USA) 2 ch.c. (Feb 8) Diesis 133–Modena (USA) (Roberto **117** p (USA) 131) [1989 7m* 8g*]

A crystal ball would have been a handy companion to the form-book for those looking forward to the big three-year-old races of 1989. Zilzal, Michelozzo and Legal Case didn't run once between them as two-year-olds; Cacoethes, Polish Precedent and Dolpour ran once each; Old Vic, Nashwan and Behera twice. Where, among the less exposed animals, do 1990's good horses lie? As usual, there are plenty of lightly-raced youngsters around with bags of potential, particularly so among the colts. Cecil's stable, for example, houses among others the highly promising Belmez and Shavian, while in Raj Waki and Duke of Paducah Harwood has a couple of interesting prospects under his care. Those involved with Major Hern's yard also seem to have plenty to look forward to. Nashwan's half-brother Mukddaam received rave reviews when making a successful debut at Newmarket in October. However, Mukddaam is far from the only interesting three-year-old colt in his stable. Elmaamul won both his starts in impressive fashion, and had he not been put out of action by a bout of coughing this essay might well have centred around him as the winner of the Cartier Million at Phoenix Park—his form gave him a definite favourite's chance in that race.

Although he started second-favourite Elmaamul seemed not particularly fancied on his debut in a thirteen-runner maiden race at Newmarket in July. He did look fit and well, though, and he put up a most encouraging first effort, making virtually all and striding clear in fine style up the hill to beat the heavily-backed Satin Wood by three lengths with the rest well strung out. Several of those who finished behind Elmaamul at Newmarket that evening won during the next few weeks, and Elmaamul himself was sent off at 5/2-on for the Reference Pointer Stakes at Sandown in September. As the title suggests Reference Point features among the previous winners of the Sandown race, and under its previous title of the Dorking Stakes this was also the contest in which Dancing Brave began a winning sequence which wasn't to end until the Derby. Elmaamul emulated those two fine horses with plenty to spare, being sent for home early in the straight and galloping on relentlessly to win by seven lengths. Admittedly, the seven who chased him home are no world-beaters, and most of them were handled with an eye to the future once the winner had gone clear. Nevertheless, the runner-up Air Music

EBF J. M. Ratcliffe Maiden Stakes, Newmarket—newcomer Elmaamul catches the eye

did the form no harm by finishing third, beaten around four lengths behind Digression, in the Royal Lodge Stakes on his only subsequent start. Elmaamul recorded a good time at Sandown too, and he should make a good three-year-old over a mile, or a mile and a quarter.

			Sharpen Up	Atan
	Diesis		(ch 1969)	Rocchetta
	(ch 1980)		Doubly Sure	Reliance II
Elmaamul (USA)			(b 1971)	Soft Angels
(ch.c. Feb 8, 1987)			Roberto	Hail To Reason
	Modena (USA)		(b 1969)	Bramalea
	(b 1983)		Mofida	Right Tack
			(ch 1974)	Wold Lass

With Diminuendo retired, Diesis didn't figure so prominently in the latest season. He was responsible for the amusingly-named Rooten-tootenwooten, who won the Grade 1 Demoiselle Stakes on dirt in November, and plenty of winners at a lower level; besides Elmaamul his third crop also included Cutting Note, Swordsmith, Daarik, and the unbeaten filly Ra'a. Elmaamul is the first foal produced by his dam. Modena never made the racecourse, but a couple of her relatives were well above average. Her dam Mofida was an admirable filly; she earned a reputation as one of the toughest and gamest horses around in the late-'seventies, when her eight wins at up to seven furlongs included the William Hill Trophy at York on Timeform Charity Day. Mofida's stud record is rather mixed so far. A couple of her foals have failed to win on the flat, but Badihar went on to show fairly useful form over hurdles, while Zaizafon ran some excellent races in good company as a three-year-old in 1985, notably when third behind Shadeed and Teleprompter in the Queen Elizabeth II Stakes. A rather finely-made, attractive colt with a fluent action, Elmaamul cost IR 320,000 guineas at the Cartier Million Sale in 1988; his half-brother by Al Nasr fell to a bid of IR 220,000 guineas at the same sale in 1989. *Major W. R. Hern.*

ELMAYER (USA) 3 ch.c. Sharpen Up 127–Dancing Lesson (USA) (Nijinsky **106** (CAN) 138) [1988 6d³ 7g⁵ 6f³ 1989 10.5m² 12g 8m 10m 12d³] tall, lengthy colt: placed in Prix Lupin (beaten 5 lengths by Galetto) at Longchamp in May and minor event (first run for 4 months) won by Per Quod at Thirsk in November: well beaten in Prix du Jockey-Club (raced keenly and close up 9f) at Chantilly, maiden (sweating and edgy) at York and Prix Eugene Adam at Saint-Cloud: should prove suited by 1¼m: acts on top-of-the-ground and a soft surface. *P. A. Kelleway.*

ELMDON PRINCE 2 b.c. (May 9) Ela-Mana-Mou 132–Be My Queen 84 (Be My **51** Guest (USA) 126) [1989 8s 8.2g] tall, leggy colt: second foal: half-brother to 3-y-o Miss Butterfield (by Cure The Blues): dam, 1m winner, is daughter of half-sister to Derby runner-up Cavo Doro: plating-class form, never dangerous, in autumn maiden at Ayr and minor event at Nottingham. *M. Bell.*

ELMSALL LAD 2 ch.c. (Apr 19) Bay Express 132–Miss Natalie 62 (African Sky — 124) [1989 5s 7.5f] 2,100F, 6,000Y: sparely-made colt: first foal: dam 2-y-o 5f winner: well beaten in auction races at Ripon (trained by C. Beever) in April and Beverley in September: sold 700 gns Doncaster October Sales. *Ronald Thompson.*

ELMURAQASH 2 gr.c. (Apr 18) Ela-Mana-Mou 132–Queen's Counsellor 92 **87 p** (Kalamoun 129) [1989 8m⁵ 8.2g*] leggy, workmanlike colt: fifth foal: half-brother to 3-y-o Iraja (by Kris) and 3 winners, including winning stayer/fairly useful jumper Assaglawi (by Troy) and quite useful but ungenuine 7f and 1m winner Jurran (by Formidable): dam won over 6f at 2 yrs and stayed 1m at 3 yrs: 5/1, won minor event at Nottingham in October by a head from Bondstone, running on strongly to lead near finish: will be suited by 1¼m +: sure to improve and make a useful performer. *P. T. Walwyn.*

ELOFAHABIT 3 b.g. Headin' Up–Eleonora 70 (Falcon 131) [1988 5g⁶ 5g* 6s 7f — 1989 7s⁶ 6m 6g 8g] sturdy gelding: moderate walker: won maiden in April as 2-y-o: little worthwhile form since: should stay 7f. *L. J. Barratt.*

ELOQUENT MINISTER (USA) 3 b.f. Deputy Minister (CAN)–Art Talk **109** (USA) (Speak John) [1988 5g* 5.5g* 7g⁵ 5g* 8.5g 1989 5m³ 5f5m* 6g² 5m⁶ 5g⁴ 6s] rangy, angular filly: made all in listed race at York: ran creditably last 3 starts, in William Hill Sprint Championship at York, showing fine early speed, Waterford Foods EBF Phoenix Flying Five at Phoenix Park and the Laurel Dash:

best at 5f: acts on any going: slowly away at Royal Ascot second start and blinkered next 4: often unruly at stalls and refused to enter them on intended reappearance: reportedly to stay in USA (won three twice at 2 yrs). *T. Stack, Ireland.*

EL PADRINO   4 ch.g. Good Times (ITY)–Kirsova (Absalom 128) [1988 8.2v 9d   **33**
8f⁵ 7.5f³ 8m⁵ 10s 8m 8m 12g 8g 6g 1989 10f⁴ 8m 8m⁴ 8.3g 8m³ 14f⁵ 8f 8g] lengthy, angular gelding: poor walker: poor plater: stays 1¼m: acts on firm going: sometimes sweats: has joined J. Bostock. *C. E. Brittain.*

EL PASO   2 b.c. (Mar 7) Alzao (USA) 117–Invery Lady 65 (Sharpen Up 127) [1989   **85** p
6g³ 7f*] IR 6,800F, 39,000Y: leggy colt: has scope: half-brother to quite modest 1m winner Reggae Beat (by Be My Native) and a winner in Sweden: dam, placed over 5f at 2 yrs, is daughter of half-sister to Irish Guineas Oaks winner Aurabella: odds on, won maiden at Salisbury in October readily by 1½ lengths from Syrtos: will stay 1m: likely to improve again, and win more races. *L. M. Cumani.*

EL-PAYASO   3 b.c. Cure The Blues (USA)–Baroness (FR) (Captain's Gig (USA))   **—**
[1988 6g 7m 8g 6d 6m 1989 7s 6f 10m 7m 11.7g 10g] leggy, shallow-girthed colt: poor mover: ridden by 7-lb claimer final outing as 2-y-o, only form in varied events: should stay 7f: visored fourth outing: trained until after fifth by Pat Mitchell: sold 550 gns Ascot November Sales. *A. Moore.*

EL REY   5 b.h. King of Spain 121–Powderhall 81 (Murrayfield 119) [1988 8s² 8g*   **90**
10m² 10g² 8d* 8d⁵ 6d³ 8d* 1989 8g⁴ 6g] tall horse: moderate mover: fairly useful winner as 4-y-o: shaped well when fourth of 9, no extra final 1f, to Wood Dancer in £27,100 handicap at Sandown in July: never near to challenge when eleventh of 24 at Newmarket 3½ months later: best form at up to 1m, but needs testing conditions at 6f: acts very well on a soft surface: good mount for apprentice. *W. Hastings-Bass.*

EL SOBERANO   3 br.c. King of Spain 121–Wheatley (Town Crier 119) [1988 5m²   **—**
5m² 5m⁴ 6m 1989 6g 6g 6m] strong, good-bodied colt: has a quick action: quite modest maiden in 1988: well beaten in apprentice handicaps and seller (blinkered and coltish) as 3-y-o: should be better at 6f than 5f. *R. Hannon.*

ELUSIVE LADY   2 b.f. (Mar 15) Blakeney 126–Bewitched 63 (African Sky 124)   **—**
[1989 6f] third living foal: half-sister to fair 3-y-o sprinter Martinosky (by Martinmas): dam half-sister to Lucky Wednesday, high-class winner at up to 1¼m: 33/1, slowly away and always behind in 10-runner maiden at Lingfield in October. *W. G. R. Wightman.*

ELVOL   2 ch.f. (Apr 12) Whistling Deer 117–Haleys Mark (On Your Mark 125)   **—**
[1989 5f 5m⁵ 5m a6g] IR 1,400Y: leggy, unfurnished filly: first foal: dam never ran: well beaten in maidens: usually slowly away. *P. J. Arthur.*

EL VOLADOR   2 br.c. (Apr 27) Beldale Flutter (USA) 130–Pharjoy (FR) 85   **65**
(Pharly (FR) 130) [1989 5s⁵ 5d 5.8h³ 7.5f³] 8,000Y: medium-sized colt: first foal: dam, beaten at 2 yrs when successful over 6f, is daughter of Prix Robert Papin second Promise of Joy: quite modest maiden: will stay 1m +: acts on hard going. *K. O. Cunningham-Brown.*

ELWADI   2 b.c. (Jan 29) Vaigly Great 127–Final Act 64 (Decoy Boy 129) [1989 6m   **—**
6d 7g] 15,500F, 40,000Y: rangy, attractive colt: carries condition: has a round action: brother to very useful 1984 2-y-o sprinter Vaigly Oh and half-brother to a winner in Belgium: dam won three 1m sellers: well beaten in maidens: off course over 3 months after debut. *C. J. Benstead.*

ELYSIAN WARRIOR   4 b.g. Full of Hope 125–Paddock Princess 80 (Dragonara   **—**
Palace (USA) 115) [1988 10v 11.7f 10g 11.7f⁶ 10m 9f 7.6m 7m 8g 1989 a10g] big, leggy gelding: poor maiden: slowly away and always tailed off at Lingfield in October. *E. A. Wheeler.*

ELZAEEM (USA)   3 b.c. Secreto (USA) 128–Billy Sue's Rib (USA) (Al Hattab   **—**
(USA)) [1988 6f³ 7.3d* 7f² 8g³ 7.3s 1989 8.5s⁵ 10g] smallish, robust colt: has a quick, rather round action: fairly useful winner as 2-y-o: well beaten in quite valuable events at Epsom (carrying plenty of condition) and Newmarket in the spring: lacks turn of foot, and likely to prove suited by a strongly-run race at 1m +: remains in training. *J. L. Dunlop.*

EMARATI (USA)   3 b.c. Danzig (USA)–Bold Example (USA) (Bold Lad (USA))   **74**
[1988 NR 1989 8f² 8m⁶ 8m³ 8s⁵] $400,000Y: medium-sized, slightly dipped-backed, attractive colt: has a quick action: twelfth reported foal: closely related to a winner in USA by Northern Baby and half-brother to several winners, including very smart stakes winner at up to 9f French Charmer (by Le Fabuleux), herself dam of Zilzal, and to the dam of Polish Precedent (by Danzig): dam minor stakes-placed winner at up to 7f: modest maiden: best effort third outing: possibly unsuited by soft ground:

visored and made most last 2 starts: at Britton House Stud, Somerset, fee £2,000 (Oct 1st). *J. H. M. Gosden.*

EMBARKATION 3 ch.g. Main Reef 126–Pointe de Grace (FR) (Dapper Dan (USA)) [1988 NR 1989 11f⁶ 14f* 13.6f* 12m 14g³] IR 10,000F: medium-sized gelding: sixth reported living foal (fifth to northern hemisphere time): half-brother to 1983 Irish 2-y-o 6f winner Park Lady and French 9f winner Grace de Bois (both by Tap On Wood): dam, French 9f winner, is half-sister to smart American horse Point du Jour: odds on, won maiden and handicap at Redcar in June: very good third of 6 in handicap at Kempton in early-September: below form for 7-lb claimer in between: may well stay 2m: gelded after joining F. Jordan. *L. M. Cumani.* **90**

EMERALD BOW 3 ch.f. Mr Fluorocarbon 126–Moorgreen 68 (Green God 128) [1988 5g⁴ 5s⁴ 1989 6m 6g⁶ 6f³ 6f⁶] sparely-made, angular filly: moderate mover: quite modest maiden: wearing tongue strap, creditable third in apprentice claimer at Nottingham in June: below form in claimer there 5 days later: stays 6f: acts on firm going: sold 1,150 gns Newmarket September Sales. *B. Hanbury.* **58**

EMERALD EDGE 2 b.g. (Feb 22) All Systems Go 119–Dream Again 88 (Blue Cashmere 129) [1989 5g⁶ 5m] angular gelding: second foal: dam 2-y-o 5f winner: last in August maidens at Catterick and Newcastle (ridden by 7-lb claimer, hung left throughout). *J. H. Johnson.* **—**

EMERALD MOON 2 b.c. (Apr 3) Auction Ring (USA) 123–Skyway 76 (Skymaster 126) [1989 6f 6f 6g⁴ 6g] IR 17,000Y: strong colt: brother to Prix Robert Papin winner Maelstrom Lake and Irish 1¼m winner Flying Bid, latter dam of useful Irish 1987 2-y-o 5f and 6f winner Flutter Away, and half-brother to several minor winners: dam 1¼m winner: modest maiden: best effort eighth of 16 in Coventry Stakes at Royal Ascot on second start: will be better suited by 7f. *R. Hollinshead.* **70**

EMERALD RING 3 b.f. Auction Ring (USA) 123–Nephrite 106 (Godswalk (USA) 130) [1988 5m⁵ 5s⁵ 5g³ 1989 6g* 6s 6f⁵ a6g] good-topped filly: has a roundish action: modest handicapper: bit edgy, easily best effort when winning apprentice event at Newbury in August, running on strongly despite drifting left to lead close home: stays 6f. *P. J. Makin.* **74**

EMERALD SUNSET 4 b.g. Red Sunset 120–Kelly's Curl (Pitskelly 122) [1988 8f 8g⁴ 9f² 10m² 10g² 8g⁵ 8.5s² 10g⁵ 1989 10g 8m] ex-Irish gelding: fourth foal: closely related to 5-y-o Parklands Belle (by Standard) and half-brother to Irish 1m winner Secundus (by Junius): dam won twice over 5f in Ireland: modest maiden as 3-y-o when trained by M. Grassick: 33/1, always behind in apprentice race and maiden at Brighton in spring: stays 1¼m: acts on any going: blinkered once at 3 yrs: has run well for apprentice. *A. R. Davison.* **—**

EMLYN'S DREAM 2 ch.f. (May 10) Dreams To Reality (USA) 113–Emlyn Princess (Julio Mariner 127) [1989 6m 7m⁶ 7m] 2,100Y, 3,000 2-y-o: smallish, workmanlike filly: first foal: dam useful hurdler and winning chaser: well beaten in varied events in summer, including listed event at Newmarket: sold 620 gns Newmarket Autumn Sales. *R. Guest.* **47**

EMMA MAY 2 b.f. (Jun 10) Nicholas Bill 125–Nonsensical 99 (Silly Season 127) [1989 8.2g 8g] 2,800Y: half-sister to several winners, including useful 1975 2-y-o Drop of A Hat (by Midsummer Night II), successful up to 7.2f, and fair but unreliable 1½m to 13f winner Haggs Tavern (by Tower Walk): dam won at up to 1¼m: always behind in late-season auction events at Hamilton (slowly away) and Edinburgh. *N. Bycroft.* **—**

EMMA'S SPIRIT 3 b.f. Thatching 131–Emma Royale 69 (Royal And Regal (USA)) [1988 NR 1989 7f 10.6m] second foal: half-sister to poor maiden Emma's Treasure (by Pas de Seul): dam 1½m winner: always behind in maidens at Kempton (backward) and Haydock (sweating, tended to hang) in the summer. *M. E. D. Francis.* **—**

EMMA'S TREASURE 4 br.f. Pas de Seul 133–Emma Royale 69 (Royal And Regal (USA)) [1988 9d 10.2g 10m 13.1f 1989 12.5f] smallish, sparely-made filly: moderate mover: poor maiden: best form in blinkers: bandaged near-fore only start at 4 yrs: sold 1,500 gns Ascot August Sales. *Mrs A. Knight.* **—**

EMMA TOM BAY 4 b.g. Bay Express 132–Counsel's Verdict (Firestreak 125) [1988 8d 7d² 6m 6f⁶ 6g 6m 6f⁶ 1989 7g 9f 7g 8.3d] good-bodied gelding: poor mover: runner-up in maiden at Folkestone early as 3-y-o: very little other form. *Mrs Barbara Waring.* **—**

EMMSON 4 b.c. Ela-Mana-Mou 132–Happy Kin (USA) (Bold Hitter (USA)) [1988 10.5g⁴ 12d³ 12m 12s 1989 10s⁶ 12f³ 12m² 10d*] well-made, quite attractive colt: good mover: smart performer: blinkered, led well inside final 1f when winning **116**

289

8-runner Prix Gontaut-Biron at Deauville by ¾ length from Sweet Chesne: placed, running creditably, behind odds-on Assatis in Hardwicke Stakes at Royal Ascot and Apache in strongly-run listed event at Newmarket previous 2 outings: stays 1½m well: unsuited by soft going, acts on any other: lacks a turn of foot and is best racing up with pace: game: reportedly operated on after suffering a bout of colic before start of season and again after Deauville: to be trained in France. *Major W. R. Hern.*

EMPERORS WARRIOR 3 ch.g. High Line 125–Cocoban (Targowice (USA) 72
130) [1988 NR 1989 10g⁵ 12f 11.3f² 13.1f⁵ 18g] 5,800Y: lengthy, rather sparely-made gelding: third foal: half-brother to Irish 1987 2-y-o 6f winner Daroban (by Formidable), and to a winner abroad: dam won in Italy: modest maiden: probably stays 13f: didn't enter stalls intended second start: bandaged behind then and fifth. *P. F. I. Cole.*

EMPIRE BLUE 6 b.g. Dominion 123–Bold Blue 82 (Targowice (USA) 130) [1988 93
12s* 12g* 12f² 12m⁵ 16f⁶ 14g³ 12f 12s⁶ 12m 1989 12s* 12m 11v* 12d4] workmanlike gelding: fairly useful handicapper: changed hands 16,000 gns Doncaster February Sales: won Great Metropolitan Stakes (Handicap) at Epsom first time out for second year running in April and £8,900 event at Newbury in October: creditable fourth of 19, staying on without reaching leaders, to Firelight Fiesta in William Hill November Handicap at Thirsk: stays 1¾m: acts on any going, but particularly well on very soft: has worn blinkers, but not for long time: has gone freely to post: goes very well fresh. *P. F. I. Cole.*

EMPIRE JOY 4 ch.g. Sallust 134–Vivchar 80 (Huntercombe 133) [1988 6g² 7g⁶ 60
6g 6g 7g⁵ 8m² 7g⁵ 7d 1989 9d 7g 7f 10f 8m³ 7m⁶ 8m] good-bodied gelding: carries condition: poor mover: quite modest maiden on his day: stays 1m: acts on top-of-the-ground: found little under pressure fourth outing: raced freely on sixth. *C. A. Horgan.*

EMPRESS LINE 3 b.f. Equal Opportunity 91–Damsel II (Chamier 128) [1988 —
NR 1989 10.1g 10.8f⁵] sparely-made filly: sister to quite modest maiden First Opportunity and half-sister to several winners abroad: dam won 7 races in Italy: scant promise in minor event (unseated rider before start) at Windsor and maiden (led 5f) at Warwick in July: sold 950 gns Ascot November Sales. *P. J. Arthur.*

EMPRESS NICKI 3 ch.f. Nicholas Bill 125–Tzu-Hsi 66 (Songedor 116) [1988 —
6g⁶ 6m 1989 6s⁶ 5g 7.5m] robust filly: poor maiden: bit backward, wore crossed noseband in seller final start (August): tongue tied down on reappearance: seems suited by 5f. *W. W. Haigh.*

EMPRESS WU 2 b.f. (Apr 10) High Line 125–Elm Park (Aberdeen 109) [1989 62 p
8f4] 27,000Y: medium-sized, leggy, quite good-topped filly: keen walker: sister to 4 winners, including French 8.5f and 1¼m winner Becontree and modest 1½m winner Two Minutes, later successful over 7f in Ireland, and half-sister to winners by Take A Reef and Quadratic: dam never ran: 7/2, over 5 lengths fourth of 9 to Hafhafah in maiden at Wolverhampton in October: should improve. *H. R. A. Cecil.*

EMPSHOTT (USA) 2 b.c. (Feb 28) Graustark–Call The Queen (USA) (Hail To 78 §
Reason) [1989 6h³ 6m² 7f² 7f² 7f4 8f³ 7g² 7g] $57,000Y, resold 61,000Y: good-bodied, medium-sized colt: has scope: good walker: closely related to a winner at up to 9f in USA by Key To The Mint and half-brother to several other winners, including 1985 2-y-o 9f winner Shekana (by The Minstrel): dam won over 6f at 3 yrs and is daughter of champion 2-y-o filly Queen Empress: modest maiden: second of 15, held up taking strong hold then staying on steadily, to Dame Rousara in £9,600 nursery at Ascot on penultimate start: ran poorly in similar event at Newmarket on final outing: stays 1m: blinkered last 2 outings: has tended to hang and carry head awkwardly: possibly none too genuine, and is one to be wary of. *G. Harwood.*

EMSALCLA 4 ch.g. Ballacashtal (CAN)–Miss Times 78 (Major Portion 129) 35
[1988 5d⁶ 7d4 5g⁵ 6m⁶ 7m 8v⁶ 6d 1989 6m 6f 8.2g 7m 8.2d⁶ a8g4] angular, sparely-made gelding: poor maiden: probably stays 1m: ran badly in visor: has joined R. O'Leary. *M. Brittain.*

EMSLEYS CHOICE 3 ch.g. Windjammer (USA)–Derrygold (Derrylin 115) 67 d
[1988 5s 5g 6d 6f⁶ 5g 8m³ 8m4 7.5f² 8m³ 9f4 8g 1989 10f⁵ 8.5g 9f 8.2f² 8h* 9f 8m4 12g⁶ 9f⁵ 8f 8.5f⁶ 10m 9f] leggy, good-topped colt: carries condition: quite modest handicapper: made all at Carlisle in June: below form after: stays 1¼m: acts on hard going: sold 3,200 gns Ascot November Sales. *T. Fairhurst.*

EMTYAAZ (USA) 3 b.c. Danzig (USA)–The Wheel Turns (USA) (Big Burn 83
(USA)) [1988 NR 1989 6m³] $725,000Y: robust, good sort: third foal: half-brother to minor winners at up to 1m in USA by Alydar and Wavering Monarch: dam stakes winner at 6f and 7f: 11/8 favourite though carrying plenty of condition, over 2 lengths

third of 18 to Silca Supreme in maiden at Newmarket in May, slowly away, making smooth headway after halfway until over 1f out. *L. M. Cumani.*

EMVEN 2 b.f. (Apr 12) Dara Monarch 128–La Vosgienne (Ashmore (FR) 125) **44** [1989 7m 8f⁴ 10g] IR 3,100Y: lengthy, workmanlike filly: third foal: half-sister to 3-y-o Shelbourne Lady (by Coquelin), 7f seller winner at 2 yrs, and 1¾m winner Ya Muna (by Vitiges): dam, showed some ability in France, is half-sister to Royal Lodge winner Bengal Fire: poor form in maidens, first 2 auction events: sweating, took keen hold and ran wide bend at Nottingham final start. *C. E. Brittain.*

EMY'S WAY (USA) 2 ch.f. (May 13) Super Concorde (USA) 128–Armada Way **57** (USA) (Sadair) [1989 5f⁴ 5m³ 6h² 6g⁵ a7g] $110,000Y: sixth foal: half-sister to disappointing Irish 3-y-o Flamenco Wave (by Desert Wine), useful 6f winner at 2 yrs, and to a minor winner in USA by Somethingfabulous: dam stakes winner at up to 9f: plating-class maiden: should stay 7f. *P. F. I. Cole.*

ENAAM 3 b.f. Shirley Heights 130–Elzaahirah (Irish Ball (FR) 127) [1988 NR 1989 **65 §** 10f 10.2g 10.1m⁶ 10f⁴ 8.2f 9g² 8f³ 8f 8f] lengthy, angular filly: turns off-fore in: fifth foal: closely related to fair 1½m winner Habub (by Mill Reef), later successful in South Africa: dam, winner at up to 1m in Cyprus, is half-sister to Give Thanks and from family of Teenoso: quite modest maiden: in frame in handicaps: ran moderately last 2 outings: should stay beyond 1¼m: acts on firm ground: has worn tongue strap: flashes tail, looks difficult ride and none too keen: sold 5,500 gns Newmarket December Sales. *J. L. Dunlop.*

ENCHANTED COURT 5 b.g. Enchantment 115–Abercourt 89 (Abernant 142) — [1988 5d 5m 6g 12f³ 9m³ 12g⁶ 10f 10m 1989 10f] compact, workmanlike gelding: poor judged on most form: probably best at short of 1½m: acts on firm going: often blinkered or visored: occasionally on toes. *G. R. Oldroyd.*

ENCHANTED GODDESS 3 ch.f. Enchantment 115–Song God 96 (Red God — § 128§) [1988 6f⁵ 6m⁶ 5d 1989 5s 5h 7f 5m 10m] good-quartered, workmanlike filly: quite modest maiden: ran poorly as 3-y-o, including in seller: stays 6f: blinkered second and third outings: sold out of C. Nelson's stable 2,100 gns Ascot 2nd June Sales after third: unsatisfactory. *M. Castell.*

ENCHANTED MAN 5 b.g. Enchantment 115–Queen's Treasure 69 (Queen's **66** Hussar 124) [1988 NR 1989 11v* 12s] leggy, close-coupled gelding: fourth foal: dam winning stayer: co-favourite, first race on flat when winning April maiden at Hamilton: always behind in handicap at Epsom 3 weeks later: winner over hurdles. *D. Burchell.*

ENCHANTED SPEED 3 b.f. Enchantment 115–Speed Up 44 (Mount Hagen **57** (FR) 127] [1988 NR 1989 7f³ 8m] lengthy, quite attractive filly: first foal: dam placed once over 1¼m and of little account over hurdles: green, staying-on third of 6 in maiden at Chepstow in July: always struggling in similar event at Warwick following month. *R. Simpson.*

ENCHANTED TALE (USA) 4 b.f. Told (USA)–Fairest Forest (USA) (Big **59** Spruce (USA)) [1988 6s⁶ 6m⁵ 1989 7.5m 6f 7g⁶ 8g] leggy, quite attractive filly: quite modest maiden: tailed off in handicap final outing: stays 7f: raced too freely on reappearance, and has worn crossed noseband. *W. Jarvis.*

ENCHANTED WOOD 3 ch.f. Enchantment 115–Perang's Niece 82 (High — Award 119) [1988 6m 1989 7m] sturdy filly: no worthwhile form in maiden and seller: sold 1,250 gns Ascot August Sales. *W. Hastings-Bass.*

ENCHANTING HABIT 2 b.c. (Feb 16) Enchantment 115–Miss Worth 73 **66** (Streak 119) [1989 6m⁵ 6f⁴ 7m² 6f 6s⁵ 6v⁶] 500F, 5,000Y: medium-sized, useful-looking colt: has scope: fourth foal: half-brother to 3-y-o Thornylee (by Ballacashtal) and winning 1m plater Inner Calm (by Jellaby): dam 5f winner: quite modest maiden: ran creditably in nurseries at Ayr on last 2 starts: stays 7f: probably acts on any going. *W. J. Pearce.*

ENCHANTING MELODY 3 ch.f. Chief Singer 131–Pagan Deity 88 (Brigadier — Gerard 144) [1988 5g⁴ 6d⁶ 6m² 8s 8.5f⁴ 1989 8f 12.2m 8g⁴ 8f 12g] big, lengthy filly: has a rather round action: modest maiden at best: easily best effort third start as 2-y-o: should stay 1m: blinkered third outing: visored final one at 2 yrs. *M. W. Easterby.*

ENDLESS JOY 2 b.f. (Mar 19) Law Society (USA) 130–La Joyeuse (USA) 95 **90** (Northern Dancer) [1989 5f³ 6m* 6f³ 6g⁵ 7m³ 7g³ 8g* 7g] 45,000Y: small, lengthy, robust filly: sort to carry condition: has a quick action: first foal: dam Irish 2-y-o 6f winner stayed 7f, is granddaughter of Coronation Stakes winner Lisadell: fairly useful performer: successful in maiden at Leicester in May and Hennessy X O EBF Killavullan Stakes (by ½ length from Front Line Romance) at Leopardstown in

September: below-form eighth in Bottisham Heath Stud Rockfel Stakes at Newmarket: suited by 1m. *R. J. R. Williams.*

ENDOLI (USA) 2 b.c. (Mar 7) Assert 134–Grabelst (USA) (Graustark) [1989 7g] **64** p 280,000Y: strong, lengthy colt: second foal: half-brother to French 10.5f winner Gotsum (by Green Dancer): dam, winner in Italy, is half-sister to Alysheba: weak 12/1-shot and green, around 10 lengths eighth of 29, keeping on under hand riding, to Lord of The Field in maiden at Newmarket in November: sure to improve, particularly over middle distances. *Major W. R. Hern.*

ENERGIA 3 gr.f. Alias Smith (USA)–Ermione (Surumu (GER)) [1988 NR 1989 **68** 12.3d² 12d 16.2m² 16f⁵ 12g⁶] IR 2,000Y: smallish, angular filly: first reported foal: dam won in Germany: modest form when second in maiden (finishing strongly) at Ripon and moderately-run amateurs event (backward on first run for 3 months) at Beverley: tailed-off fifth in listed race and below-form sixth in handicap: should prove suited by further than 1½m: claimer ridden 3 times. *P. A. Blockley.*

ENGLISH RIVER (USA) 5 b.g. Irish River (FR) 131–Belle Sorella (USA) 99 §§ (Ribot 142) [1988 NR 1989 10s 6m 12.2g] thoroughly ungenuine, and must be left well alone. *R. J. Weaver.*

ENHARMONIC (USA) 2 ch.c. (Apr 13) Diesis 133–Contralto 100 (Busted 134) **79** P [1989 6f*] good-topped colt: sixth foal: half-brother to 4 winners, including very useful miler Soprano (by Kris) and fairly useful 1¾m winner Musical Box (by Grundy): dam, closely related to smart Rhyme Royal, won over 6f and 7f at 2 yrs: favourite but bit backward, won 9-runner minor event at Pontefract in October in good style by 2 lengths from Caught Unawares, always travelling strongly and not at all hard pressed: will stay at least 1m: sure to improve considerably, and win more races. *W. Hastings-Bass.*

ENIGMA (CAN) 3 b.c. Miswaki (USA) 124–Lasting Secret (USA) (Lyphard **83** (USA) 132) [1988 7m⁵ 8g 1989 8.5f² 10m*] strong, rangy, good sort: odds on, won maiden at Brighton in June by ¾ length, disputing lead from 3f out and keeping on steadily: beaten ¾ length by Legal Case in similar event at Beverley 2 weeks earlier, having quickened clear over 2f out: stays 1¼m: acts on firm going. *G. Harwood.*

ENOUSSIAN BREEZE 3 b.c. Formidable (USA) 125–Egnoussa 76 (Swing **72** Easy (USA) 126) [1988 7m³ 1989 10f² 12f⁶ 12m 11.7f] compact colt: bad mover: modest form when second in minor event at Nottingham in June: behind in £7,700 event (facing stiff task, swishing tail in paddock) at Ascot, minor event (again tailed off) at Newmarket and maiden claimer at Bath: probably doesn't stay 1½m: sold 6,000 gns Newmarket Autumn Sales. *C. E. Brittain.*

ENSCONSE (USA) 3 b.f. Lyphard (USA) 132–Carefully Hidden (USA) **117** (Caro 133) [1988 6m* 6m* 1989 7g* 8g⁴ 8m* 10.5d⁶ 8g²]

Fly-jumping once, flashing her tail half a dozen times, putting her head in the air and generally looking less than enthusiastic, Ensconse was still

Juddmonte Farms Nell Gwyn Stakes, Newmarket—Ensconse retains her unbeaten record

Goffs Irish One Thousand Guineas, the Curragh—tail-swishing Ensconse is driven out

a decisive winner of the Goffs Irish One Thousand Guineas. It was a characterful performance. Connections must have wished that her challenge could be delayed longer but Ensconse was simply pulling double over the rest before quickening clear in impressive style then leaving Cochrane with the task of persuading her to complete the job over the last two furlongs. The loss of her near-fore shoe during the race may partly explain Ensconse's apparent reluctance. Aldbourne was left to finish her usual honest race two lengths back in second, but in hindsight it's clear that of the eleven other runners at the Curragh, only Pirouette and Tursanah were capable of giving Ensconse much of a race and neither had conditions to suit in a substandard running.

That said, however, Ensconse was probably as good as any filly seen out in the early-spring. She'd completed her two-year-old season unbeaten, leading two furlongs out then having to be firmly driven to hold on in both a maiden race at Nottingham and the Blue Seal Stakes at Ascot. Cumani's winners of the two previous editions of the Blue Seal, White Mischief and New Trends, failed to improve at three and hadn't reappeared by the time the Guineas came round but with Ensconse things were very different and confidence behind her was such that she was made co-favourite for the Juddmonte Farms Nell Gwyn Stakes at Newmarket in April. Clearly mindful of Ensconse's outings as a two-year-old, her jockey was intent on waiting tactics, and in a strongly-run race she won in convincing style; Cochrane produced her with a good turn of foot between horses a hundred and fifty yards out to win by one and a half lengths, Ensconse doing little once she'd passed the eventual second Aldbourne. Sixteen days later Ensconse started favourite for the General Accident One Thousand Guineas, still a bit backward in her coat but in excellent physical condition. If everything had gone according to plan in her Guineas preparation, the same certainly couldn't be said of the race itself. The field began seemingly determined to take longer coming back than going down and, again held up, Ensconse was last of the seven runners entering the Dip. She ran on strongly but never threatened in finishing two lengths behind Musical Bliss. At that stage we were keen on Ensconse's prospects for the remainder of the season—she's a tall, good sort with scope—but after justifying favouritism at the Curragh she raced only twice and never again got to the front. Ensconse finished well in the Prix de Diane-Hermes at Longchamp, but only after losing all chance with a rough passage at halfway, and then chased home Magic Gleam (who received 6 lb) at a distance of four lengths in the Child Stakes at Newmarket in July.

293

Sheikh Mohammed's "Ensconse"

			Northern Dancer	Nearctic
	Lyphard (USA)		(b 1961)	Natalma
	(b 1969)		Goofed	Court Martial
Ensconse (USA)			(ch 1960)	Barra II
(b.f. 1986)			Caro	Fortino II
	Carefully Hidden (USA)		(gr 1967)	Chambord
	(b 1979)		Treasure Chest	Rough'n Tumble
			(b 1962)	Iltis

Ensconse's family is regularly referred to in *Racehorses*, Treasure Chest being the grandam of Glint of Gold, Diamond Shoal, I Want To Be and Media Starguest as well as Ensconse. Treasure Chest produced thirteen foals and before that was kept pretty busy on the racecourse as well, running forty-nine times in four seasons and winning ten races, including two minor stakes. Carefully Hidden is one of her nine winners, the winner of a maiden and an allowance race at three years in the USA, both over seven furlongs, from only four starts. She too has begun well at stud. Her first foal ran just twice but was followed by the fairly useful 1987 two-year-old seven-furlong winner Rimsh (by Storm Bird), Ensconse, then the Nureyev filly Jathibiyah who dead-heated in a Redcar maiden in September. After a fine start to the season, with Pearl Bracelet winning the French One Thousand Guineas two weeks before Ensconse's success in the Irish version, the Gainesway stallion Lyphard didn't attract much attention until Funambule won the Prix des Chenes. He could be a Guineas contender in 1990 and seems similar to Ensconse in that he's got a good turn of foot. *L. M. Cumani.*

ENSHARP (USA) 3 b.c. Sharpen Up 127–Lulworth Cove 114 (Averof 123) [1988 **81** 7f4 1989 7s3 7s3 7f2 7m2 9m] sturdy, good-bodied, attractive colt: has long stride:

294

fair maiden: second in handicaps at Sandown and Leicester: ran moderately in similar event final start, in August: should be suited by further than 7f: acts on any going: likely to be suited by a galloping course: sold 11,000 gns Newmarket Autumn Sales. *M. R. Stoute.*

ENTERPRISE LADY (FR)   2 ch.f. (Apr 10) Gorytus (USA) 132–Calder Hall (Grundy 137) [1989 6f² 6f³ 7g 6f² 6g] 15,500Y: unfurnished filly: first foal: dam, French maiden, is daughter of good-class French 7f to 1½m performer Calderina: quite modest maiden: should be better suited by 7f than 6f and bred to stay 1m: sometimes sweating and edgy. *P. J. Makin.*   69

ENTERPRISE PRINCE   3 b.g. Lucky Wednesday 124–Avona (My Swallow 134) [1988 7f* 8g 1989 7g⁶ 10.6m 10g] leggy, angular gelding: moderate walker and mover: turns fore feet out: won seller as 2-y-o, tending to hang right: staying-on sixth in similar event at Doncaster, easily best effort after: tailed off in handicap final start (May) and subsequently gelded: stays 7f. *Ronald Thompson.*   51

EPHOR   3 ch.f. Battle Hymn 103–Spartan Doll (Country Retreat 91) [1988 6m 5g 6m 1989 8g] smallish, sparely-made filly: of little account. *T. Kersey.*   —

EQUALLY ELECTRIC   3 b.f. Electric 126–Equal Chance 95 (Hitting Away) [1988 NR 1989 10d] workmanlike filly: half-sister to several winners, including 1983 Irish 2-y-o 6f winner A Flame, later 5f winner in South Africa, and speedy 1979 Irish 2-y-o Jay Bird (both by Hot Spark): dam sprinter: 33/1, bit backward and never dangerous in maiden at Newbury in October: sold 3,000 gns Newmarket Autumn Sales. *C. C. Elsey.*   —

EQUATOR   6 ch.g. Nijinsky (CAN) 138–Sound of Success (USA) (Successor) [1988 15s⁶ 11v³ 12d³ 1989 14.6g] leggy, lengthy, plain ex-Irish gelding: second in Group 3 event at the Curragh on debut at 3 yrs: lightly raced subsequently: well behind in maiden at Doncaster in April: suited by further than 1¼m: has run creditably for amateur and apprentice: winning hurdler. *J. S. Haldane.*   —

EQUINOR   2 b.c. (May 21) Norwick (USA) 120–Cithern 91 (Canisbay 120) [1989 5s 5f 5.8h 6m⁶ 7m⁶ 7f 8f⁶ 10g a8g⁶] 3,200Y: workmanlike colt: moderate walker and mover: half-brother to fair 1981 2-y-o 5f and 6f winner Ten-Traco (by Forlorn River), later successful in USA, and a winner abroad and a winner over hurdles: dam, 2-y-o 7f winner, half-sister to smart performers Zimbalon and Band: plating-class maiden: stays 1¼m: best form on good. *R. A. Bennett.*   56

ERADICATE   4 b.c. Tender King 123–Pushkar (Northfields (USA)) [1988 7d² 7d³ 7d 7g* 8d⁵ 8d* 8d⁴ 8d³ 9g³ 1989 8g³ 8s 8f 9g² 8g⁶ 8m⁵ 8s 10.5m 10g² 10g] lengthy, well-made colt: usually looks well: has a long, round stride: useful winner as 3-y-o: ran well when third in William Hill Lincoln Handicap at Doncaster in April: generally well below his best afterwards: stays 1¼m: suited by an easy surface (possibly not at his best on very soft going): blinkered sixth outing, visored last 2: has hung and is suited by strong handling: none too consistent nowadays. *P. Calver.*   97 d

EREVNON   2 b.c. (Apr 30) Rainbow Quest (USA) 134–Embryo (Busted 134) [1989 8g⁶] 520,000Y: medium-sized, rather unfurnished colt: half-brother to fair 1986 Irish 2-y-o 7f winner Strath Farrar (by Nijinsky) and 2 winners by Sir Ivor, notably Oaks d'Italia and E P Taylor Stakes winner Ivor's Image: dam, sister to smart Irish middle-distance performer Bog Road, won 3 times at around 1m in Ireland: 15/2 and green, around 9 lengths sixth of 17, from rank over 6f, to Lover's Moon in maiden at Leicester in November: will be suited by 1¼m: should improve. *Major W. R. Hern.*   67 p

ERIC'S PET   2 gr.c. (May 28) Petong 126–When I Dream (Sparkler 130) [1989 6m 6f 7.6m 6g] rangy colt: has scope: second foal: dam poor maiden out of very useful 5f winner Grey Home: poor form in maidens: tailed off final start: better suited by 6f than 7f. *M. D. I. Usher.*   42

ERIK ODIN   2 b.c. (Apr 26) Nordico (USA)–Assurance (FR) (Timmy Lad 130) [1989 7g 6g 6g³ a7g* a7g4] IR 11,500Y: sturdy colt: fourth foal: half-brother to French 1¼m winner Courdimanche (by Junius): dam won in Germany: modest performer: won maiden at Lingfield in November by ½ length: fair fourth in nursery final start: stays 7f. *Mrs L. Piggott.*   74

ERIN'S TOWN   3 b.g. Town And Country 124–Erin's Hospitality (Go-Tobann) [1988 NR 1989 10g⁴ 10f³] workmanlike gelding: first reported living foal: dam never ran: 33/1, 12½ lengths fourth of 9 to Drum Taps in maiden at Ripon, held up and keeping on steadily not knocked about: soundly beaten in minor event at Brighton later in September, outpaced 3f out: should stay 1½m. *W. Carter.*   —

ERIVAN   3 ch.c. Shakapour 125–Eurissia (FR) (Sir Gaylord) [1988 8d 1989 7m* 8.5m 10.1m4] sparely-made colt: ridden by 7-lb claimer, won maiden at Catterick in   86

May: good fourth at Windsor, making most 7f and easily better effort in handicaps in June: stays 1¼m: acts on top-of-the-ground: sold to join I. Semple 11,000 gns Doncaster August Sales. *M. R. Stoute.*

ERMO EXPRESS   2 b.f. (Apr 30) Bay Express 132–Dalchroy (Hotfoot 126)   **64**
[1989 5m⁴ 5m*] 3,600Y: workmanlike filly: moderate mover: half-sister to 3-y-o 7f to 1m winner Asitappens and poor 1986 2-y-o Trafford Way (both by Music Maestro): dam, poor maiden, ran only at 2 yrs: won maiden at Catterick in June by 2½ lengths from Tender Trail: sent to Italy and won over 6f at Milan in October. *E. Eldin.*

ERNANI   2 b.c. (Mar 30) Sadler's Wells (USA) 132–Godzilla 106 (Gyr (USA) 131)   **112**
[1989 5g² 6g* 7g² 7g³ 8g²] 1,500,000 francs (approx £137,200) Y: closely related to high-class French miler Phydilla (by Lyphard) and half-brother to several winners, including 3-y-o Observation Post (by Shirley Heights), 7f and 8.2f winner at 2 yrs now suited by 1½m: dam won 5 times at up to 7.5f at 2 yrs in Italy and showed form over 6f at 3 yrs here: very useful colt: successful in minor event at Evry: placed subsequently in valuable restricted event at Deauville, Prix de la Salamandre (2½ lengths third to Machiavellian) at Longchamp and Prix des Chenes (beaten 1½ lengths by Funambule) at Saint-Cloud: will stay 1¼m: has raced only on good ground. *R. Collet, France.*

ERREMA   4 b.f. Workboy 123–Piethorne 86 (Fine Blade (USA) 121) [1988 7g 8d²   **62**
8.5g⁶ 8d 8.2g² 9g* 10g² 8g² 10g 9f⁴ 8m⁴ 1989 8g 10.8f³ 10f² 8g 8.5m⁴ 9f 10.2g⁴ 12m⁶] close-coupled filly: quite modest handicapper: stays 1¼m well: acts on firm going and a soft surface: visored sixth outing: has started slowly and carried head high: has run well for apprentice. *R. M. Whitaker.*

ERRIS EXPRESS   4 b.g. Bay Express 132–Royal Home 69 (Royal Palace 131)   **88**
[1988 5.8g 6m 5.3f³ 5m 5m² 6f⁶ 5m 6m 1989 7d⁶ 7d 8m 8.3g⁶ 6f* 6m 5m* 6f² 6m* 6s⁶ 6s 5m] medium-sized, attractive gelding: poor mover: well backed, won seller (bought in 7,600 gns) at Ayr in July and handicaps at Beverley and Ripon (much improved form) following month: well beaten last 3 outings: suited by 6f or stiff 5f: suited by top-of-the-ground: wears bandages: has tended to edge: ran well for apprentice eighth start: best racing up with pace. *F. Durr.*

ESCAPE HATCH   3 b.g. Thatching 131–La Troublerie (Will Somers 114§) [1988   **64**
NR 1989 7g³ 7m⁴ a8g* a7g⁴] 50,000F, 20,000Y: workmanlike gelding: half-brother to 1m winner Nobody's Perfect (by Vitiges) and 2 minor middle-distance winners in France: dam won 7 times at up to 1¼m, including Prix d'Ispahan: won maiden at Southwell in November: creditable fourth in handicap there 10 days later: green first 2 outings: stays 1m. *R. Hannon.*

ESCAPE PATH   4 b.f. Wolver Hollow 126–Keep Right (Klairon 131) [1988 9g   **—**
7m⁵ 10g⁵ 8f⁶ 1989 12g 12g] leggy, sparely-made filly: good mover: quite modest maiden at best: well beaten in handicaps at Leicester (slowly away) and Beverley (too keen) in 1989: sold 1,700 gns Ascot November Sales. *K. A. Morgan.*

ESCAPE TALK   2 gr.f. (Mar 2) Gabitat 119–Getaway Girl 63 (Capistrano 120)   **63**
[1989 5g 5s 5m* 5f³ 6m³ 5f* 5f* 6f³ 7f* 8.2g 7g] 5,800Y: smallish, close-coupled filly: moderate mover: third reported foal: half-sister to poor 1985 2-y-o Mousseline (by Gunner B), later winner in Eastern Europe: dam stayed 13f: useful plater: successful at Beverley (bought in 3,100 gns) in June, Catterick (no bid) and Beverley (claimer) in July and Wolverhampton (nursery) in October: best form at 7f: often edgy. *Mrs J. R. Ramsden.*

ESCRIBANA   4 b.f. Main Reef 126–Amorak 85 (Wolver Hollow 126) [1988 NR   **—**
1989 12.5g 10.1m 14f 14m 11.5m] good-topped filly: no sign of ability on flat: winning hurdler. *J. R. Jenkins.*

ESCRIME (USA)   2 b.f. (Feb 18) Sharpen Up 127–Doubly Sure 59 (Reliance II   **79 P**
137) [1989 7g⁵] big, angular filly: sister to top-class colts Kris and Diesis and smart 6f and 1m winner Keen and half-sister to very smart 1984 2-y-o Presidium (by General Assembly) and dam of Lockinge winner Prismatic: dam, placed over 1½m, is daughter of high-class staying 2-y-o Soft Angels: 8/1 and very green, shaped promisingly when under 3 lengths fifth of 24, running on strongly towards finish, to Katsina in maiden at Newmarket in November, giving impression would have won with clearer run at halfway: will be well suited by 1m: sure to improve considerably, and is an interesting prospect. *H. R. A. Cecil.*

ESPECIALLY BOLD   3 b.f. Lyphard's Special (USA) 124–Bold Design (Bold   **—**
Lad (IRE) 133) [1988 NR 1989 6f 6g 7m 7m] IR 2,300Y: smallish, good-quartered filly: fourth foal: half-sister to 2 poor animals: dam ran twice: well beaten in minor

event and sellers: should be suited by further than 6f: bandaged off-hind last 2 starts: has joined Miss H. Knight. *W. Holden.*

ESPRIT DE FEMME (FR) 3 b.f. Esprit du Nord (USA) 126–Bustelda (FR) **68**
(Busted 134) [1988 7.5f³ 8f 8.2m 1989 10g 8.5s⁵ 12f² 14m⁴ 11.7h* 12h⁴ 12m⁴] leggy, rather angular filly: keen walker: 2/1 on, made all in maiden claimer at Bath in July: fair fourth at Pontefract, second and easily better effort in handicaps early following month: may prove best at up to 1½m: probably acts on any going: has joined V. Young. *P. A. Kelleway.*

ESTEFAN 2 b.f. (Feb 7) Taufan (USA) 119–Benita 94 (Roan Rocket 128) [1989 **58**
5g³ 5s4] 11,500F, 31,000Y: tall, good-topped filly: sister to poor maiden Invisible Touch and half-sister to several winners, including fairly useful sprinter Red Rosie (by Red Alert) and 1984 2-y-o 7f winner Maid of Arosa (by Baptism): dam sprinter: backward, plating-class form in Scotland in October: will stay 6f. *P. S. Felgate.*

ETEREA LEAP 2 ch.f. (May 15) Salmon Leap (USA) 131–Eterea Salt (Sallust —
134) [1989 7g] half-sister to winners in Italy: dam won in Italy: 66/1, in mid-division, slowly away, in 13-runner minor event at Carlisle in October. *Dr J. D. Scargill.*

ETERNAL TRIANGLE (USA) 3 b.f. Barachois (USA)–Clover Lady (USA) **69**
(Iron Constitution (USA)) [1988 5m⁴ 5f² 5f² 5h* 6g* 6g³ 6s 6m 1989 8g⁵ 8h 8g⁴ 7m⁶ 10g] close-coupled, workmanlike filly: moderate walker: modest handicapper: stays 1m: best efforts on good ground: very much on toes when well below form on soft. *S. G. Norton.*

ETOIT 3 b.g. Kala Shikari 125–Paddyswitch (St Paddy 133) [1988 6g⁶ 6m 6g⁴ 6m⁵ **77**
5m³ 5g⁴ 5d 5m 1989 7v⁴ 7f* 7f⁵ 7f³ 8.2g⁵ 7.6g⁴ 7.6m⁴ 7s⁴ 7g] sturdy gelding: moderate mover: modest handicapper: won at Chester in May: ran creditably most other starts but poorly at York on final one: at least as effective over 7f as 1m: acts on any going: has run creditably for 5-lb claimer, poorly when blinkered once at 2 yrs: sold A. Ingham 21,000 gns Newmarket Autumn Sales. *S. G. Norton.*

ETON LAD 2 b.c. (Mar 22) Never So Bold 135–Carolside 108 (Music Maestro **97** p
119) [1989 8m²] 84,000Y: tall, rather sparely-made colt: good mover: third foal: half-brother to rather unsatisfactory 3-y-o 6f winner Sure Gold (by Glint of Gold): dam 2-y-o 5f winner didn't progress: 7/1, 1½ lengths second of 8, leading soon after halfway until 100 yds out, to Treble Eight in maiden at Newmarket in October: sure to improve, and win a similar event. *N. A. Callaghan.*

EUCHAN GLEN 2 b.c. (Feb 16) Wolverlife 115–Down The Line 74 (Brigadier **76**
Gerard 144) [1989 6f* 6m 6s4 6m 6g⁴ 7g*] 15,000Y: leggy colt: second foal: half-brother to 1988 plating-class 2-y-o Be Forum (by Coquelin): dam, winner at 1½m in Ireland at 4 yrs, is daughter of close relation to More Light and half-sister to Shoot A Line: modest performer: won 4-runner maiden at Ayr in July and nursery at Edinburgh by a short head from Orchard Court in November: should stay 1m: probably acts on any going: has run well for 7-lb claimer. *R. M. Whitaker.*

EUROBLAKE 2 b.g. (Mar 7) Roscoe Blake 120–Pie Eye 88 (Exbury 138) [1989 **62**
5f⁴ 6m 5f⁵ 7f⁴ 7.5m* 7f⁶ 7f⁶ 7.5m³ 8m⁴ 7g 8f⁶ 7d⁶ 8g] 480Y: compact, good-quartered gelding: turns off-fore in: has scope: brother to 2 maidens and half-brother to several winners, including very useful 5f and 7f winner Sharpen Your Eye (by Sharpen Up): dam 9f winner: quite modest performer: won nursery at Beverley in July: below form in sellers last 2 outings: will stay 1¼m: sometimes takes keen hold: tends to be on toes: has sweated up. *T. D. Barron.*

EUROCON 5 b.g. Ile de Bourbon (USA) 133–Consistent 90 (Connaught 130) **61**
[1988 13.8g* 13.8g² 17.1g³ 12.2g⁵ 15.8m⁴ 16g² 16f³ 14g⁶ 16d⁶ 15.8f⁵ 16g* 15m⁵ 1989 13.8d* 13.8d² 17f⁵ 15.8m 15.8m² 16f⁶ 16g³ 15.8f³ 15.8g⁵ 16.2f⁴ 17f 15.8g* 15g] small gelding: good mover: quite modest handicapper on his day: goes very well at Catterick and justified favouritism there in March and October: apprentice ridden, gambled on on latter occasion: best at 1¾m to 2m: acts on firm going and a soft surface: best ridden up with pace: slowly away when tried in visor: has run moderately when sweating: inconsistent. *T. D. Barron.*

EURO GALAXY 2 ch.c. (Mar 28) Crofthall 110–Patent Pending (Goldhill 125) **48**
[1989 6f4] 6,400Y: leggy, lengthy, sparely-made colt: turns fore-feet out: second foal: dam minor 9f winner at 4 yrs in France: 7/2, over 6 lengths fourth of 7, weakening final furlong having recovered well after slow start, to El Arab in maiden auction race at Newcastle in July: may do better. *R. M. Whitaker.*

EUROLADY 3 b.f. Kafu 120–Miss Portal (St Paddy 133) [1988 7g 6g 6d 1989 8m **41**
7f⁵ 8g 10g⁶ 10m 9g 10.6s³] leggy, angular filly: moderate mover: poor maiden on most form: stays 10.6f: probably acts on any going: sold 750 gns Ascot December Sales. *E. Eldin.*

EUROLINK THE LAD 2 b.g. (Apr 23) Burslem 123–Shoshoni Princess **84** (Prince Tenderfoot (USA) 126) [1989 6f⁶ 6m⁴ 7g 6f² 7m³ 6d⁴ 6f² 6f* 6v⁴ 7d] IR 10,000F, 11,500Y: medium-sized, rather unfurnished gelding: first foal: dam unraced daughter of half-sister to high-class stayer Mr Bigmore: fair performer: won maiden at Folkestone readily by 2 lengths from Jagged Edge: on toes, very good fourth of 23 to Altered Beast in nursery at Newbury later in October: better suited to 6f than 7f: acts on any going. *G. B. Balding.*

EVENING AFFAIR 3 b.f. Red Sunset 120–Miss Flirt (Welsh Pageant 132) **77** [1988 6g⁶ 6d⁴ 6m² 1989 11.3m⁶ 12f⁴ 11.5m⁶ 16m 12.5m⁶ 11.7f² 8f* 9f² 8g² 7g] sparely-made, lengthy filly: won handicap at Wolverhampton in October in good style: ran creditably after in handicaps at Redcar and Newmarket and all-aged contest at Newmarket: stays 9f: acts on firm going: blinkered sixth to ninth outings. *R. Boss.*

EVENING HOUR 4 ch.f. Glenstal (USA) 118–Field Lady 71 (Habitat 134) [1988 **43** 8g 8s 7f 6m 7g⁶ 1989 6d 7m 7h⁵ 7g* 7f] good-quartered filly: 20/1-winner of 12-runner handicap at Yarmouth: ran moderately in apprentice handicap at Folkestone later in July: form only at 7f: sometimes sweats: sold to join P. Felgate 2,400 gns Newmarket Autumn Sales. *W. Holden.*

EVENING RAIN 3 b.c. Hays 120–Fine Form (USA) (Fachendon) [1988 7m 8d 7s **65** 1989 8s 8g* 8.2g* 10m⁵ 9m] big, workmanlike colt: quite modest handicapper: well backed, won at Leicester and Hamilton in the spring: well beaten after, but backward penultimate outing (first for 3½ months, moved moderately down) and sweating slightly final one: stays 1m well: trained until after third outing by Sir Mark Prescott. *R. J. Hodges.*

EVENING STAR 3 b.f. Red Sunset 120–Avereen (Averof 123) [1988 NR 1989 **63** 8m⁵ 8m⁵ 10f 7.6f 8g a8g³ a8g³ a8g³] 10,500Y: leggy filly: half-sister to 4 winners, including plating-class 1¼m winner Mac's Sister (by Krayyan) and Mac's Reef (by Main Reef), very useful performer here at up to 1½m later successful in North America: dam poor half-sister to Goodwood Cup winner Tug of War: modest maiden: should stay beyond 1m: possibly unsuited by firm ground: visored last 3 starts. *A. Hide.*

EVENING SUNSET 3 b.c. Red Sunset 120–Princess Elinor (Captain James — 123) [1988 NR 1989 8m 10.1g 10.1d⁴ 10.2f] IR 5,600F, 14,000Y: sturdy colt: first foal: dam Irish 2-y-o 6f winner: well beaten in maiden (soon ridden along and carrying head high), minor events and a handicap. *C. R. Nelson.*

EVENTIDE 3 ch.f. Red Sunset 120–Tagik (Targowice (USA) 130) [1988 NR 1989 **47** 7m³ 8g 8m⁴ 8m⁴ 8m 7m⁵ 7g] 6,200Y: sparely-made filly: has no scope: half-sister to winners in Italy and Malaysia: dam, winner in Italy, is half-sister to high-class sprinter Green God: poor form, including in sellers: sweating and carried head high when running creditably sixth start: suited by 1m: blinkered fourth and fifth outings: below form in visor final one: sold to join D. Burchell 2,000 gns Ascot September Sales. *D. Burchell.*

EVERALDO (FR) 5 b.g. Top Ville 129–Floressa (FR) 120 (Sassafras (FR) 135) — [1988 14.6d³ 10v⁴ 12g⁴ 19f* 19m⁶ 16f⁶ 16d* 1989 18g⁶ 16d 16f⁶] tall, quite good-topped gelding: modest winner (including for amateur) as 4-y-o: finished very lame (had run as though something amiss previous outing) when sixth of 11 in handicap at Kempton in May, and wasn't seen out again: suited by extreme test of stamina: has won on firm going, but given impression ideally suited by an easy surface: has run well when sweating: bandaged at 5 yrs. *P. F. I. Cole.*

EVERDENE 2 b.f. (Mar 19) Bustino 136–Deed 86 (Derring-Do 131) [1989 6g] — 8,000Y: sister to smart 7f and 1¼m winner Busaco and half-sister to several other winners, including 1m winner Prohibited (by Formidable): dam 2-y-o 5f winner: 16/1, never better than mid-division in 17-runner Folkestone maiden in October won by Les Amis: bred to stay at least 1m. *D. R. C. Elsworth.*

EVER RECKLESS 3 ch.f. Crever 94–Gold Spangle 97 (Klondyke Bill 125) **58** § [1988 5g⁴ 5d² 6m³ 5.3f² 5m 5m 5f⁴ 5g⁵ 1989 5s⁴ 5s 5g 5f⁴ 5f⁶ 5m 5m 5.8h* 5g 5f 5m⁴ 5m⁶ 5m* 5g 5f 5.1g 5m] leggy, lengthy, unfurnished filly: poor walker: made all in seller (bought in 2,800 gns) at Bath in June and apprentice handicap (swerving left final 2f) at Windsor in August: very speedy: probably best on top-of-the-ground: not discredited in visor final start: blinkered previous 9: bandaged seventh: tends to sweat: sometimes taken down early: trained until after eleventh start by F. Durr: thoroughly inconsistent. *R. W. Stubbs.*

EVER SHARP 5 b.g. Sharpo 132–Blue Jane 81 (Blue Cashmere 129) [1988 5v 6g — 5g⁵ 5g* 5m⁵ 5f³ 6g⁵ 5m² 5d⁴ 5m³ 5g 5d³ 1989 5g⁵ 5f 5g 5m 5m] big, lengthy, workmanlike gelding: poor mover: smart performer at one time in 1988 but below his best towards end of season and no worthwhile form in 1989: suited by 5f: acts on any going: blinkered once at 4 yrs, visored final outing: bandaged near-fore coronet and swished tail under pressure on reappearance: has found little off bridle and is suited by waiting tactics: best left alone for time being. *L. G. Cottrell.*

EVER SO SHARP 6 br.h. Caruso 112–Sealed Contract 76 (Runnymede 123) [1988 5g 6m 5m 6m 7f 5d⁵ 6d 5g⁴ 5f 5m 5g 5f 5g 1989 6f 5f 7m 5f 5m a7g a6g] small, workmanlike horse: poor mover: no form in 1989: suited by 5f: acts on top-of-the-ground: blinkered fourth to sixth outings: has run well for apprentice: has carried head high. *J. P. Smith.* —

EVER WELCOME 4 ch.f. Be My Guest (USA) 126–Ghaiya (USA) 110 (Alleged (USA) 138) [1988 7d 10g 10m 10g 10m 10s⁶ 9f³ 10d⁴ 1989 8g⁶ 8f 10d² 10f* 10m⁵ 10m] rangy, sparely-made filly: won for first time in handicap at Salisbury in May: stayed 1¼m: acted on firm going and a soft surface: a difficult ride: in foal to Hadeer. *Lord John FitzGerald.* — 58

EVERY ONE A GEM 2 ch.g. (Mar 6) Nicholas Bill 125–Lady Bequick 81 (Sharpen Up 127) [1989 7m 8.2g 8g⁵] 12,500Y: big, good-bodied gelding: seventh foal: half-brother to useful sprinter Joytotheworld (by Young Generation) and sprint winner Kept Waiting (by Tanfirion): dam ran only at 2 yrs when successful twice at about 5f: shaped with promise in big fields of maidens, particularly catching eye final start: looks sort to do better, and is one to keep an eye on in modest company. *M. J. Ryan.* — 66 p

EVICHSTAR 5 ch.g. Jasmine Star 113–Chive (St Chad 120) [1988 5v 6m* 6g² 7f⁴ 6m⁶ 7d 6d 6d 6f 6g⁶ 6m 1989 6m.6f 8.2m 7m⁴ 8m⁵ 8g³ 10g⁴ 10.2g 10.6m⁶ 10f³ 8.2d² 8g² 8g* a7g* a7g³] close-coupled, good-quartered gelding: useful at his best early as 4-y-o, only modest nowadays: made all or most in seller (bought in 9,000 gns, wandering under pressure) at Edinburgh and claimer at Southwell in November: best form at up to 1m: acts on any going: has been tried in blinkers, including on last 4 starts: has worn bandages: has often sweated and got on edge: twice withdrawn after bolting, including ninth intended outing: has proved difficult to settle, and has been tried in severe bridle, net muzzle and tongue strap: has been taken down early or very quietly: has not pleased with attitude, but became more reliable in autumn. *J. G. FitzGerald.* — 75

EVOCATRICE 2 b.f. (Feb 27) Persepolis (FR) 127–Northern Trick (USA) 131 (Northern Dancer (CAN)) [1989 9m² 7s*] first foal: dam, high-class middle-distance performer who won Prix de Diane Hermes and Prix Vermeille and was second in Prix de l'Arc de Triomphe: won maiden race at Saint-Cloud in November by 5 lengths: will stay 1¼m. *F. Boutin, France.* — 91 p

EXACT ANALYSIS (USA) 3 b. or br.c. Verbatim (USA)–Mity Nice Girl (USA) (Handsome Boy) [1988 7s⁴ 1989 8g² 10f⁶ 14f² 14m⁴] lengthy, rather dipped-backed colt: has a long, rather round stride: seventh reported foal: half-brother to 2 winning sprinters in USA by Nashua and Mr Prospector: dam, 5f stakes winnner at 2 yrs and successful at up to 7f in USA, is half-sister to prolific stakes winner Dainty Dotsie: sire fair influence for stamina: modest maiden: ran poorly final start (June): stays 1¾m: wearing crossed noseband and bandaged behind, took good hold second start: trained by J. Oxx in Ireland on debut: sold 2,900 gns Newmarket Autumn Sales. *J. Gosden.* — 77

EXBOURNE (USA) 3 br.c. Explodent (USA)–Social Lesson (USA) (Forum (USA)) [1988 7s* 1989 8d² 8m²] — 125

In two seasons Exbourne has been seen on the racecourse only three times, but limited opportunity hasn't prevented his showing himself a high-class colt. He was obviously something out of the ordinary when on his only start at two years he landed the odds in a back-end maiden at Lingfield by eight lengths; and he made his reappearance in what's usually the best of the Guineas trials, the Charles Heidsieck Champagne Craven Stakes at Newmarket, starting 3/1 in a five-runner field. A good-topped individual with scope, he ran well. He led at a sound pace until joined by Shaadi three furlongs out, battled on, and gave way only inside the last, eventually going down by two and a half lengths. For what turned out to be his only subsequent start Exbourne was returned to Newmarket for the General Accident Two Thousand Guineas. Eddery chose Free Handicap winner Danehill in preference to Exbourne, who drifted from 7/1 to 10/1. There was little between them in the race. Exbourne was always travelling strongly. He made headway three furlongs out and, driven along, stayed on well to take second from Danehill close to home without ever threatening Nashwan, who was a length clear at the line. Exbourne reportedly pulled a muscle during his preparation for the Derby; nothing more was heard of him.

Exbourne (USA) (br.c. 1986)	Explodent (USA) (b 1969)	Nearctic (br 1954)	Nearco
			Lady Angela
		Venomous (b 1953)	Mel Hash
			Spiteful Sue
	Social Lesson (USA) (b 1974)	Forum (b or br 1967)	Jaipur
			Decor
		Cherry Red (b 1968)	Eurasian
			Cherie Rose

Exbourne, who cost 140,000 dollars at the Saratoga Select Yearling Sale, is the fifth reported foal out of sprint claimer winner Social Lesson. All the previous four are winners, notably Top Socialite (by Topsider), a smart filly at up to a mile. Social Lesson was bought in foal to Secreto for 390,000 dollars by Juddmonte Farms at the 1989 Keeneland January Mixed Sale. She's a half-sister to the stakes winner Cherry Pop out of a winner at up to a mile. The sire Explodent, a winner at up to eight and a half furlongs, has had relatively few representatives in Europe; two others that did represent him in the latest season were the sprinter Holst and the middle-distance performer Bex.

Exbourne featured prominently in the Derby betting at the time of his withdrawal but isn't sure to stay a mile and a half; a mile and a quarter should be no problem, though. He will be an interesting horse if he comes back to the course as a four-year-old. In his three races so far he has been beaten only by two Guineas winners, so there should be some good prizes to be won with him. *G. Harwood.*

EXCELSIS 3 b.c. Shirley Heights 130–Sacred Ibis (Red God 128§) [1988 7g 7m **75** 8m³ 8g⁶ 7g 1989 8f⁵ 10m² 12m 11.7m⁴ 10h³ 10m a10g a10g⁶] neat colt: modest maiden: ran badly third and last 3 starts: suited by 1¼m: acts on hard ground. *J. L. Dunlop.*

EXCEPTIONAL BID (USA) 4 b.c. Spectacular Bid (USA)–Gulls Cry (USA) **85** (Sea-Bird II 145) [1988 10m² 1989 10f² 13.3f⁵ 10m² 11.5m* 12m⁵ 12g] angular, useful-looking colt: poor mover: made all when landing the odds in poorly-contested amateurs maiden at Yarmouth in July: tailed off in Newmarket handicap final outing: stays 1½m. *H. R. A. Cecil.*

EXCHANGE FAYRE 2 ch.c. (Mar 25) Burslem 123–Sanibel (Ahonoora 122) — [1989 6m a6g] close-coupled, sparely-made colt: poor form in seller and a claimer: blinkered debut. *R. O'Leary.*

EXECUTIVE PERK 4 b.c. Lord Gayle (USA) 124–Areola 114 (Kythnos 126) **120** [1988 8v* 8g* 8g⁴ 9m* 8m⁴ 8d⁵ 1989 10s* 10m² 8m* 8g³] tall, leggy, sparely-made colt: justified favouritism in listed contest at the Curragh in April by length from Pylon Sparks and in Kilfrush EBF Concorde Stakes at Phoenix Park (odds on) in June comfortably by 2 lengths from Corwyn Bay: creditable second to Ile de Chypre in Tattersalls EBF Rogers Gold Cup Stakes at former course in between: damaged tendon on off-fore and finished lame when third to Distant Relative in EBF Phoenix International Stakes: didn't race on firm going, acted on any other: very smart: retired to Kilsheelan Stud, Co Tipperary. *D. K. Weld, Ireland.*

EXECUTIVE STAR 3 b.f. Raga Navarro (ITY) 119–Belligerent 74 (Roan — Rocket 128) [1988 7d 7s 1989 8f] neat filly: has a quick action: well beaten in minor events and maiden. *Miss A. J. Whitfield.*

EXHAUST LADY 4 b.f. Blue Refrain 121–Silk Fashion 61 (Breeders Dream 116) **36** [1988 10m 8f* 8f³ 7m⁵ 10f 8g³ 8.3g³ 8.3g² 10f³ 7m³ 10m 8g⁵ 6g 1989 6d 10m 8m⁵ 8.3m 8.5m 7m⁴ 10.1m 7h⁴ 8f⁵ 10f 12g] neat filly: quite modest plater: claimed out of J. Jenkins's stable £9,115 tenth outing: suited by 7f or 1m: acts on hard going: inconsistent. *R. P. C. Hoad.*

EXHAUST MAN 5 b.g. Crooner 119–Silk Fashion 61 (Breeders Dream 116) — [1988 10s* 12d⁴ 15.5f³ 12m² 12f⁶ 16m* 9m⁶ 14g 16f² 1989 12g 12s⁵ 16m⁵] small, compact gelding: plating-class handicapper: not seen out after May: needs further than 9f and stays 2m: acts on any going, but well suited by top-of-the-ground: suitable mount for inexperienced rider: ran moderately in blinkers. *Miss B. Sanders.*

EXHIBITION ROAD   2 ch.c. (Apr 17) Exhibitioner 111–The Way She Moves   **45**
(North Stoke 130) [1989 5d 5g 6d 7m⁵] IR 16,500F, 14,000Y: strong, compact, sprint
type: third foal: half-brother to 3-y-o Welsh Governor (by Welsh Term) and a winner
in Scandinavia: dam, little worthwhile form, from family of Master Willie: poor form
in varied company. *L. G. Cottrell.*

EXPRESS ACCOUNT   2 b.f. (Apr 15) Carr de Naskra (USA)–Miss Audimar   **75**
(USA) (Mr Leader (USA)) [1989 7m³ 6f³] IR 10,000Y, 10,000 2-y-o: leggy filly:
second reported foal: dam graded stakes-placed winner at up to 11f in USA: sire won
from 6f to 1¼m: 25/1 and ridden by 7-lb claimer, third to Go Holimarine in maiden
auction event at Yarmouth and to Native Twine in 3-runner minor event at
Leicester: should stay 1m: may improve further. *R. J. R. Williams.*

EXPRESS EDITION   2 b.f. (May 8) Comedy Star (USA) 121–June Fayre   **58**
(Sagaro 133) [1989 5s 6f 7m⁶ 7m³ 7m⁶ 7g⁵ 6g 6g* 6g] compact filly: moderate
walker: fourth foal: half-sister to Norwegian 3-y-o winner Imperial Boy (by Raga
Navarro) and modest 1987 2-y-o 5f winner Very Special Lady (by Mummy's Game):
dam twice-raced daughter of Pasty, best British 2-y-o filly of 1975: blinkered,
showed improved form when winning 12-runner claimer at Catterick in October by a
length, clear, from Phoenix Jule: soundly beaten in claiming nursery at Newmarket
final outing: seems suited by 6f. *M. H. Tompkins.*

EYE BEE AITCH   4 b.f. Move Off 112–River Petterill 89 (Another River 89)   **—**
[1988 8.2g 8g⁶ 6d 6s 5m 1989 7f 8f 11g 11s] bad plater: winning hurdler. *W. Storey.*

EYE IN THE SKY   4 ch.f. Red Sunset 120–Holernzaye 93 (Sallust 134) [1988 6m   **69**
7f⁴ 7.5f* 7.9m² 6g 7g³ 7g² 8d 1989 9f 12m³ 10g⁴ 10f 9m* 11f³ 9f 10f³ 8.5f⁵ 9m 10f]
lengthy filly: confirmed promise shown earlier in season when justifying
favouritism in 5-runner handicap at Hamilton in July: ran poorly last 2 outings:
probably best at 1m to 1¼m: acts on firm going: moved moderately to post final
outing: sold 3,000 gns Doncaster October Sales. *C. Tinkler.*

EYE OF THE TIGER   2 ch.c. (Apr 3) Vaigly Great 127–Ritruda (USA) 95 (Roi   **86** ?
Dagobert 128) [1989 6g² 6m] 11,000Y: close-coupled colt: brother to 1m seller

Moyglare Stud Farm's "Executive Perk"

winner Line of Succession and half-brother to 3 other winners, including 1½m winner Saturn Moon (by Monsanto): dam stayed 7f: length second of 4 to Tidemark in maiden at Ascot in September: broke leg at York following month: dead. *M. E. D. Francis.*

EYES ON THE PRIZE   2 ch.f. (Feb 16) Lomond (USA) 128–Girl Friday (USA)   — 106 (Secretariat (USA)) [1989 8m 10g] strong, good-bodied filly: has plenty of scope: second foal: dam 2-y-o 1m winner stayed 1½m, is daughter of very useful sprint stakes winner Patience Worth: never a factor in late-season maiden (green) at Newmarket and minor event at Redcar. *W. Hastings-Bass.*

EYLAK (USA)   3 b.c. Devil's Bag (USA)–Dame Mysterieuse (USA) (Bold   **65** Forbes) [1988 NR 1989 7d 8g 8m 8f⁴] strong, good sort: has scope: fourth foal: half-brother to 1½m winner Barn Five South (by The Minstrel), 5f pattern race winner in Italy: dam, smart sprinter, is half-sister to good French middle-distance performer Paint The Town: modest maiden at best: probably stays 1m: may prove best with more forcing tactics. *H. R. A. Cecil.*

F

FABLED ORATOR   4 b.g. Lafontaine (USA) 117–Brompton Rose 98 (Sun   **74** Prince 128) [1988 8g 7m³ 6m² 7m 6g* 6g 6g 6g³ 7g 6s 7m 1989 6s⁵ 6v 7d 7.6f 6f² 7f* 6f a10g] tall, angular gelding: modest handicapper on his day: won at Chepstow in May by 5 lengths, making all and clear 2f out: ran poorly final outing, first for 5 months: stays 7f: acts well on firm going: has worn blinkers, including at Chepstow: apprentice ridden last 3 outings: suited by forcing tactics and seems best racing away from others: bought out of R. Hannon's stable 6,400 gns Newmarket September Sales after seventh start: subsequently gelded. *G. G. Gracey.*

FABULOUS DEED (USA)   2 ch.f. (May 15) Shadeed (USA) 135–Fabulous Salt   — p (USA) 88 (Le Fabuleux 133) [1989 7g] rather unfurnished filly: fourth foal: half-sister to 3-y-o Knoosh (by Storm Bird), successful at 7f (at 2 yrs) to 1½m, and 14.8f winner Lypheoric (by Lypheor): dam won at 1m here and in USA: 14/1, never dangerous or knocked about in 24-runner maiden at Newmarket in November. *M. R. Stoute.*

FABULOUS SHAUN   3 b.g. Petong 126–High State 72 (Free State 125) [1988   — 5d⁵ 6d⁴ 6m 5d 6s 1989 7d 8m⁶ 6f 9m 8m 6m 6g 6s] workmanlike gelding: first foal: dam 9f seller winner: plating-class maiden at best: probably best at up to 6f: blinkered twice at 2 yrs and first 6 starts in 1989: trained until after then by B. Kelly in Ireland. *P. S. Felgate.*

FACE THE TRUTH   3 gr.g. Neltino 97–Cry of Truth 129 (Town Crier 119) [1988   — NR 1989 10.1m 10.1m 10.2m⁵ 8m] 14,000F: tall gelding with scope: half-brother to 3 winners, including useful sprinter Integrity (by Reform): dam best 2-y-o filly of 1974: plating-class form at best in minor events and handicap: bit backward first 3 starts: pulled hard final one (July). *R. Boss.*

FACILITY LETTER   2 gr.g. (Mar 16) Superlative 118–Facetious 88 (Malicious)   **83** [1989 5f⁴ 6g² 6m³ 6g* 7f 6m⁴ 6g² 5m⁶ 7g² 6v² 7d] 8,000F, 7,000Y: sturdy gelding: good walker: half-brother to two 2-y-o 5f winners, better of them fairly useful Bottesford Boy (by Record Token), and 2 winners abroad: dam disappointing maiden: won maiden auction event at Pontefract in July: ran very well in nurseries ninth and tenth starts: stays 7f: acts on any going: has been tried in blinkers, better form without. *W. J. Haggas.*

FACT FINDER   5 br.h. Known Fact (USA) 135–Idealist (Busted 134) [1988 6s²   **83** 6d 10g⁶ 8g⁵ 8g* 8g³ 8d* 8.3m⁵ 8g² 8v² 8m³ 8d* 1989 8g* 8d] good-topped horse: bad mover: successful in £49,500 William Hill Lincoln Handicap at Doncaster in April by neck from fast-finishing Ottergayle: never a threat in quite valuable handicap at Newbury 2 weeks later: best at around 1m: acts on top-of-the-ground, but well suited by an easy surface. *R. Akehurst.*

FACT OR FICTION   3 br.g. Known Fact (USA) 135–Noble Wac (USA) (Vaguely   **47** Noble 140) [1988 6m 7m 8d 1989 8.2m 11.7m 16m 10.2f³ 8s 10g a11g³ a10g⁴] angular gelding: sign of ability only when in frame in apprentice maiden at Bath in July and claimers at Southwell and Lingfield in December: stays 11f. *H. Candy.*

FACTOTUM   6 b.g. Known Fact (USA) 135–Blue Shark (Silver Shark 129) [1988   **56** 10m 10m⁴ 10g 12g 1989 10h⁴ 10f 10f] small, good-bodied gelding: carries plenty of condition: good mover: quite modest handicapper: stays 1¼m: acts on hard going: has run creditably for apprentice: winning hurdler: inconsistent. *R. Akehurst.*

FACTUELLE 2 ch.f. (May 3) Known Fact (USA) 135–Cayla (Tumble Wind 69
(USA)) [1989 5s* 6f² 6g³ 5f] 5,000Y: small, stocky filly: third foal: half-sister to
3-y-o 5f winner Touch of White (by Song) and poor maiden Akaylaah (by Valiyar):
dam, from good family, showed signs of ability: quite modest performer: won
maiden at Kempton in May: not seen out after late-June: should stay 1m. *M. J.
Fetherston-Godley.*

FAG IN HAND 4 ch.g. Music Boy 124–Brig of Ayr 90 (Brigadier Gerard 144) 82
[1988 7d⁴ 6g³ 6d⁴ 7d² 6m⁴ 7d 7d* 7g⁴ 7g 1989 8g 7d 7.6m⁴ 7f⁶ 6m 6d 6g] strong,
workmanlike gelding: poor mover: capable of fair form: creditable fourth to Young
Jason, hanging left under pressure, in handicap at Chester in May: off course over 4
months after next outing and well below form last 3: probably finds 6f on sharp side
and seems to stay 1m: acts on top-of-the-ground and a soft surface: often sweats
slightly: difficult ride. *W. Haggas.*

FAILAND 2 b.f. (Apr 24) Kala Shikari 125–What A Mint (Meadow Mint (USA) 64
120) [1989 5m³ 6h⁵ 6f 5m⁴ 6g 7f⁴ 6g⁶ 7f² 8.2g] useful-looking filly: poor walker: has
a quick action: third reported foal: dam won at 1½m in Ireland at 3 yrs and several
times at up to 2½m over hurdles here: quite modest performer: carried 2 lb
overweight when beaten short head by Escape Talk in nursery at Wolverhampton in
October: ran well in similar time before: better suited by 7f than shorter, and
probably stays 1m. *R. J. Holder.*

FAILSAFE 4 ch.g. No Lute (FR) 129–Judeah 69 (Great Nephew 126) [1988 8m 61 §
12d* 10.2m 13g⁶ 1989 14m 12h 12h 8m² 10.1m] leggy, angular gelding: 25/1 and
apprentice ridden, creditable second of 14 in selling handicap at Bath in July: tailed
off all other outings as 4-y-o, in seller on final one: effective at 1m and stays 1½m:
acts on a soft surface and top-of-the-ground: sold 1,400 gns Newmarket Autumn
Sales: unreliable. *C. A. Cyzer.*

FAIRFAX LAD 3 b.g. Ballacashtal (CAN)–Just Janie 84 (John Splendid 116) —
[1988 NR 1989 10m] 900F, 2,400Y, 1,200 2-y-o: half-brother to a winner in Belgium:
dam sprinter: blinkered, mulish and got loose leaving paddock when tailed off in
Newmarket claimer in July: sold 875 gns Ascot September Sales: resold 1,000 gns
Ascot October Sales. *C. N. Allen.*

FAIRFIELD LAD 4 b.g. Krayyan 117–Mock Auction 55 (Auction Ring (USA) 58 d
123) [1988 5s³ 6g³ 6d³ 6d³ 5m* 5g 5m⁴ 5f⁶ 6m 7g 6s 5s 1989 6.1f 6f 6g⁵ 6m 6m 5s
6g⁵ 6m] quite attractive gelding: moderate mover: quite modest handicapper as
3-y-o: well below his best in 1989 after third outing: suited by 6f or stiff 5f: acts on
any going: has worn blinkers, but best form without. *M. H. Tompkins.*

FAIR MINSTREL 5 ch.m. Longleat (USA) 109–Western Vale (Milesian 125) —
[1988 NR 1989 12m 8f] smallish, sparely-made mare: little sign of ability in modest
company: bandaged and on toes as 5-y-o: blinkered final outing: sold 525 gns Ascot
November Sales. *R. Dickin.*

FAIR PORT 4 gr.g. Belfort (FR) 89–Shamsha (FR) (Bold Lad (USA)) [1988 6m 5g —
5f 5g 6g 1989 7m 10h] stocky gelding: fairly useful on his day at 2 yrs: has
deteriorated markedly: tailed off in seller final outing: best at 5f: somewhat
highly-strung and is taken down early. *A. Bailey.*

FAIR PROSPECT 3 b.c. Shirley Heights 130–Sans Blague (USA) 108 (The 95
Minstrel (CAN) 135) [1988 NR 1989 11s² 12s³] good sort, with plenty of scope: third
foal: half-brother to very useful 1986 2-y-o 6f and 7.3f winner Nettle (by Kris), who

*William Hill Lincoln Handicap, Doncaster—Fact Finder stretches out to hold off Ottergayle
(light colours, challenging on outside)*

appeared to stay 1½m: dam, suited by 1½m, is half-sister to very useful middle-distance filly Deadly Serious: favourite, placed in April in maiden won by Golden Pheasant at Newbury and listed race won by Artic Envoy at Epsom, in latter (on toes) leading 1m, not handling turn at all well then battling on gamely despite edging right: will prove suited by 1½m+: sold to join Miss H. Knight 21,000 gns Newmarket Autumn Sales. *Major W. R. Hern.*

FAIR SEAS 3 b.f. General Assembly (USA)–Seven Seas (FR) 78 (Riverman (USA) 131) [1988 6g 1989 8m⁶ 8m 10.1m²] angular, sturdy filly: 2½ lengths second of 4 to Nesaah in minor event at Windsor in July, first worthwhile form: shaped promisingly in maidens: suited by 1¼m: sold 5,000 gns Newmarket December Sales. *G. Wragg.* **72**

FAIR SENTENCE 2 b.f. (Apr 19) Montekin 125–Quartette Royale 65 (Jukebox 120) [1989 5g³ 6f 7f 7d] IR 800F, IR 1,500Y: lengthy filly: half-sister to unreliable sprinters Kelly's Royale and Brotherton Castle (both by Pitskelly): dam placed over 5f at 2 yrs: bad maiden: trained first 2 starts by M. Brittain. *Miss L. C. Siddall.* **37**

FAIR TITANIA 2 b.f. (May 2) Fairy King (USA)–Miss Robust (Busted 134) [1989 6m⁵ 5.8h² 5f* 5m⁶ 5f⁵ 6m* 7h* 7m⁴ 8g³ 7g⁵] IR 8,400Y: lengthy, workmanlike filly: moderate walker: ninth reported foal: half-sister to several winners, including fair 1m and 9f winner London Bus (by London Bells) and 1¼m winner Bonny Quiver (by Gorytus): dam never ran: successful in maiden auction event at Chepstow in May and in summer nurseries at Windsor and Brighton: fairly useful form on last 3 starts in Black Bottle Scotch Whisky Prestige Stakes at Goodwood, May Hill EBF Stakes (sweating) at Doncaster and Oh So Sharp Stakes at Newmarket: stays 1m: suitable mount for a 7-lb claimer: on toes last 2 starts. *M. Bell.* **90**

FAIRWAY ROYALE 4 b.g. Runnett 125–Lady Salinia (Sovereign Path 125) [1988 6v 8f² 7m⁵ 8f³ 7d 7g 1989 8.2m 8.2g 10g² a12g] lengthy, quite attractive gelding: has a quick action: modest maiden: tailed off in Lingfield handicap final outing: stays 1¼m: acts on firm going: ran creditably for apprentice third start. *P. J. Makin.* **75**

FAIR WICKET 2 ch.g. (Apr 1) Norwick (USA) 120–Fairford Lass (Sandford Lad 133) [1989 8.2g 8.2d] big, rangy gelding: has scope: fourth reported foal: dam never ran: well beaten in autumn maidens at Haydock, showing signs of a little ability final start. *J. Berry.* **—**

FAIRY FEET 3 b.f. Sadler's Wells (USA) 132–Glass Slipper 100 (Relko 136) [1988 NR 1989 11f²] tall, rather unfurnished filly: half-sister to numerous winners, including 1000 Guineas winner Fairy Footsteps (by Mill Reef) and St Leger winner Light Cavalry (by Brigadier Gerard): dam staying half-sister to Royal Palace: 7/2 and very green, beaten 3 lengths by Ruddy Lucky in 6-runner maiden at Redcar in May: should be suited by 1½m+: sold 185,000 gns Newmarket December Sales. *H. R. A. Cecil.* **78**

FAIRY FORTUNE 2 ch.f. (May 2) Rainbow Quest (USA) 134–Fairy Tern 109 (Mill Reef (USA) 141) [1989 6d] leggy, unfurnished filly: good mover with a light action: fourth foal: half-sister to very useful 6f (at 2 yrs) and 1m winner Hoy (by Habitat) and 1986 2-y-o 6f winner Greencastle Hill (by High Top): dam, winner at 5f and 7f, is closely related to smart 1¼m colt Elegant Air: 20/1 and green, slowly away and not knocked about in 24-runner maiden at Newbury in October. *I. A. Balding.* **— p**

FAIRY GROOM 2 ch.c. (Apr 4) Shy Groom (USA)–Arafy 80 (Sharpen Up 127) [1989 6m 6f³ 8.2d 8.2s a6g⁶] IR 3,400Y: leggy colt: first foal: dam, 1m winner, is half-sister to useful 1½m and 1¾m winner Rowlandson out of Fred Darling Stakes winner Rotisserie: plating-class maiden: should stay further than 6f: sold 5,400 gns Doncaster November Sales. *R. Hollinshead.* **55 ?**

FALCON BLUE 2 ch.g. (May 3) Blue Cashmere 129–Tralee Falcon 82 (Falcon 131) [1989 5f 5f² 5m⁵ 6m³ 5g] 7,200Y: lengthy gelding: fifth foal: half-brother to 1984 2-y-o winner Kenton's Girl and 1¼m winner Kenton's Lad (both by Record Token): dam stayed 7f: fairly useful plater: better suited by 6f than 5f: has run well for 7-lb claimer. *J. G. FitzGerald.* **61**

FALCON FLIGHT 3 ch.g. Tampero (FR) 115–Kemoening 78 (Falcon 131) [1988 6d² 6d 7m³ 7g* 7g* 1989 8g⁴ 7f² 8.5g² 8h⁴ 6m² 7f⁵ 6g² 7m] smallish, rather sparely-made gelding: modest performer: possibly best at up to 7f: acts on firm going: sold to join J. Mackie 13,000 gns Doncaster September Sales. *J. Berry.* **76**

FALCONS DAWN 2 b.c. (Mar 24) Exhibitioner 111–African Bloom (African Sky 124) [1989 5s* 5d⁵ 5f² 5f 5d 6d] IR 9,000Y: leggy, quite good-topped colt: has scope: has a round action: second foal: half-brother to 3-y-o Hogans Hero (by Krayyan), 5f **71**

seller winner at 2 yrs: dam won twice over 7f in Ireland: modest performer: won auction event at Ripon in April: best effort, staying-on second to Croft Imperial in minor event at Ayr in June: best form at 5f: acts on any going. *M. O'Neill.*

FALCONWOOD 3 b.c. Sharpo 132–Treeline 59 (High Top 131) [1988 NR 1989 — 6s 5f 6g 10.6s] close-coupled colt: moderate walker: third foal: brother to winning Norwegian sprinter Sharp Echo and half-brother to fair 1985 2-y-o 7f winner Wryneck (by Niniski): dam showed some ability over sprint distances at 3 yrs: no form in varied events, including seller: gave trouble in stalls and withdrawn under starters orders second appearance: bought out of J. Tree's stable 1,100 gns Ascot July Sales at four-year-old debut. *M. B. James.*

FALL ABOUT 4 b.f. Comedy Star (USA) 121–Ultra Vires 87 (High Line 125) **68** [1988 8.5m⁵ 1989 10f⁶ 12f² 14m³ 12f* 12m] tall, leggy filly: modest handicapper: favourite and apprentice ridden, won 4-runner event at Folkestone in August very easily by 6 lengths: looking tremendously well, ran badly at Leicester (moved down poorly) 6 days later: suited by 1½m: acted on firm going: sweated on reappearance: sold 13,000 gns Newmarket December Sales: in foal to Music Boy. *W. Jarvis.*

FALLING FOSS 5 br.g. Workboy 123–Lorna Dell 54 (Forlorn River 124) [1988 — 8f 8f 1989 10.2g 8.5f 12.3m 8f] plain, workmanlike gelding: of little account. *P. Beaumont.*

FALLING SHADOW 5 b.m. Red Sunset 120–Oileann Carrig 80 (Pitcairn 126) **28** [1988 10f4 12h4 12d4 1989 12s³ 18s 12f³] sparely-made mare: poor performer: stayed 1½m: probably acted on any going: blinkered once: dead. *R. Akehurst.*

FALLOPOLIS (FR) 4 b.g. Persepolis (FR) 127–Fancy's Child (USA) (Nijinsky — (CAN) 138) [1988 12g 11d³ 11g⁵ 10s 11g 11.5g⁵ 9d⁵ 10s 15s 1989 12.2g] ex-French gelding: fourth foal: half-brother to French 9f to 1½m winner Gay Francois (by Gay Mecene): dam unraced: modest maiden at his best as 3-y-o when trained by F. Boutin: 33/1, tailed off in apprentice race at Catterick in October. *J. A. C. Edwards.*

FALLOW DEER 2 ch.f. (Feb 28) Jalmood (USA) 126–Regent's Fawn (CAN) 72 **62** (Vice Regent (CAN)) [1989 6f⁵ 5f5dis] small, good-quartered filly: first foal: dam, maiden suited by 1½m, is sister to Bounding Away, a top-class Canadian middle-distance filly, and close relation to high-class 1¼m winner Ascot Knight: quite modest form in maidens at Nottingham (green, ridden by 7-lb claimer) and Bath: bred to stay 1¼m: sold 9,000 gns Newmarket Autumn Sales. *B. W. Hills.*

FALSE START (USA) 3 gr.f. Robellino (USA) 127–Tiger Trap (USA) 80 (Al **85** Hattab (USA)) [1988 6d² 1989 6s 7s4 8m² 9.2f² 9m* 10m* 10g* 10g4 10g4] lengthy, good-topped filly: fair handicapper: won at Wolverhampton in June, Newbury (keen in paddock and race) in July and Goodwood (apprentices, in good style) in October: ran fairly well in quite valuable events after: stays 1¼m: probably acts on firm going, though best form with some give: suitable mount for apprentice: sold 30,000 gns Newmarket December Sales. *W. Hastings-Bass.*

FALSE TENET (USA) 3 b.f. Alleged (USA) 138–Percipient (USA) (Topsider **80** (USA)) [1988 NR 1989 7s³ 12g* 10g³ 12g 11.7m4] small, compact filly: first foal: dam, winner 5 times, placed in Grade 1 events over 8.5f at 2 yrs and 9f at 4 yrs: won minor event at Salisbury in May: edgy and below form last 2 outings: stays 1½m well. *B. Hanbury.*

FAME AND FORUM 2 b.g. (Apr 24) Balidar 133–Davinia 92 (Gold Form 108) — [1989 6h4 6h⁵ 6g 6g] good-quartered gelding: has a round action: fifth foal: half-brother to quite useful sprinter Paparelli (by King of Spain) and to 5f and 6f winner Divine Pet (by Tina's Pet): dam 2-y-o 5f performer: well beaten in varied events: ran as if something amiss final start. *J. Sutcliffe.*

FAME AND GLORY 4 b.c. Shareef Dancer (USA) 135–Oh So Fair (USA) — (Graustark) [1988 12d³ 12f² 16g³ 14g* 14f 17g 1989 14.8s 16s 12s 12g 12s] lengthy, quite attractive colt: put up quite a useful performance when making all in handicap at Sandown (trained by M. Stoute) as 3-y-o: no subsequent form: suited by 1¾m. *J. P. Hudson.*

FAME 'N FORTUNE 2 ch.f. (Mar 6) Exhibitioner 111–Rags To Riches (High **43** Hat 131) [1989 6m 5f² 5.3h⁵ 5.1m] IR 5,000Y: leggy filly: half-sister to 1979 Irish 2-y-o 6f winner Horatio Alger (by Karabas): dam 7f to 9f winner in Ireland: quite modest plater: looked unsatisfactory in blinkers final start. *Dr J. D. Scargill.*

FAMILIAR SPIRIT 3 b.c. Pitskelly 122–Witch of Endor 80 (Matador 131) [1988 **82 ?** 7m4 7m⁵ 7m⁵ 1989 9g 8m 10.2f² 10.1m⁵ 10g 12g 9f] sparely-made, quite attractive colt: good walker: best efforts in handicaps third and fourth outings: off course 3 months and soundly beaten afterwards: suited by 1¼m: acts on firm going:

blinkered final start: sold to join N. Tinkler 9,000 gns Newmarket Autumn Sales: carries head high under pressure: one to be wary of. *J. L. Dunlop.*

FAMILIAR (USA) 3 ch.f. Diesis 133–Lost Virtue (USA) (Cloudy Dawn (USA))   **96**
[1988 NR 1989 7g⁶ 8m⁵ 8m* 8m³ 10m⁴ 10m²] sparely-made, quite attractive filly: has a fluent action: fifth foal: half-sister to smart 7f and 1m winner Over The Ocean (by Super Concorde) and 3 winners in North America: dam unraced daughter of half-sister to Damascus: bit edgy, won maiden at Yarmouth in June: ran creditably in minor events and £6,800 contest after: stays 1¼m. *H. R. A. Cecil.*

FAMOUS BEAUTY 2 br.f. (Feb 25) Vision (USA)–Relfo 124 (Relko 136) [1989   **72**
6g² 6g* 6f² 6m 8g] IR 13,500Y: leggy, sparely-made filly: keen walker: eighth foal: half-sister to 3 winners, including fair 1988 2-y-o 7.5f winner Pericot (by Persian Bold) and fair 1984 2-y-o 7f winner Artarel (by Artaius): dam won Ribblesdale Stakes and second in Prix Vermeille: modest performer: won maiden at Haydock in July: sweating, 2 lengths second of 5, staying on strongly, to easy winner Hana Marie in minor event at Thirsk later in month: never dangerous in late-season nurseries: should stay 1¼m. *R. Hollinshead.*

FANATICAL (USA) 3 b.c. Lear Fan (USA) 130–Gal A Tic (USA) (Assagai)   **80**
[1988 7.5f 7g 1989 8.5f 12.4m* 14.8m³ 12m³ 12g 12.4g5] rather good-topped colt: good mover: fair handicapper: first worthwhile form when winning at Newcastle in July by 6 lengths: below form penultimate outing: uncertain to stay beyond 15f: acts on top-of-the-ground: ran creditably in blinkers final start. *J. W. Watts.*

FANDANGO KISS 6 ch.m. Gay Fandango (USA) 132–Bridewell Belle   **—**
(Saulingo 122) [1988 NR 1989 12.2g³] leggy, sparely-made mare: of little account: bandaged only outing at 6 yrs. *T. Kersey.*

FANELLAN 2 b.f. (Feb 8) Try My Best (USA) 130–Scotia Rose (Tap On Wood   **76**
130) [1989 6g* 6g5] quite attractive, rather unfurnished filly: first foal: dam, Irish middle-distance winner, is half-sister to dam of Greenland Park (dam of Fitnah) and Red Sunset: won maiden at Yarmouth in August by ½ length: still green, never-dangerous fifth of 12 to Daarik in nursery at Ascot following month: will be better suited by 7f + . *M. R. Stoute.*

FANILLE 3 b.c. Top Ville 129–Flying Fantasy (Habitat 134) [1988 NR 1989 9g   **—**
10s] smallish, lengthy colt: second foal: dam disappointing sister to Flying Water: in need of experience, always behind in maidens at Newmarket and Nottingham in the spring: sold to join D. J. Bell 1,400 gns Newmarket July Sales. *P. T. Walwyn.*

FANMAN 4 b.c. Taufan (USA) 119–Courreges 75 (Manado 130) [1988 7d³ 1989   **—**
12g 11g 8m] leggy, rather angular colt: poor walker: in frame in maidens when beaten in modest company, including selling, in first half of 1989: stays 7f: blinkered final outing. *C. Parker.*

FANNY DILLON 5 b.m. Orchestra 118–Sunshot (Candy Cane 125) [1988 NR   **—**
1989 16d] useful-looking ex-Irish mare: half-sister to Irish 1m and 1¼m winner All Grey (by Yankee Gold): dam 1½m winner: won 2 handicaps at Leopardstown in 1987 when trained by J. Oxx: 33/1 and bandaged, well beaten in Insulpak Sagaro EBF Stakes at Ascot in April: suited by test of stamina: acts on any going: has won for apprentice: winning hurdler. *D. R. C. Elsworth.*

FANSHAW GOLDBERG 3 ch.f. Ballad Rock 122–Fair Chance (Young   **58**
Emperor 133) [1988 5m⁵ 5m⁶ 5s³ 5.1g² 5g 6m 5d² 1989 5s⁶ 5f 5f 5m⁴ 5f 5m 5m 6g⁶] leggy filly: modest maiden in 1988: below form as 3-y-o: likely to prove best at 5f: best form on an easy surface: has run moderately when sweating and edgy: very slowly away third start: sold 1,250 gns Newmarket Autumn Sales. *M. J. Fetherston-Godley.*

FANTASIE IMPROMPTU 4 gr.f. Ballad Rock 122–Gay Nocturne 63 (Lord   **43** +
Gayle (USA) 124) [1988 6f5 6f5 7m⁴ 8f 8f² 8.2m⁴ 8m 1989 8g 9f²] tall, leggy filly: good mover: plating-class maiden: runner-up in seller at Hamilton in July: stays 9f: acts on any going: winning hurdler. *K. A. Morgan.*

FARA 2 gr.f. (May 3) Castle Keep 121–Faridetta 107 (Good Bond 122) [1989 6m³   **66**
6f³ 6m⁶ 8s⁴ 7g⁵ 8g] 1,800Y: leggy, angular filly: closely related to 3-y-o 19f winner Far Glow and modest and ungenuine 2m winner Mighty Glow (both by Kalaglow) and half-sister to two 2-y-o 5f winners: dam won four 5f races at 2 yrs: quite modest performer: ran well in nurseries fourth and fifth starts: will stay 1½m. *Miss S. E. Hall.*

FARAWAY BLUES 2 b.f. (Apr 3) Pharly (FR) 130–Belmont Blue 75 (Kashmir   **50**
II 125) [1989 7f³ 6g⁴ 6f⁴ 6g⁵ 7m⁴ 7m³ 6f 7d²] IR 5,000Y: sturdy filly: fifth foal: half-sister to 7f winner Blue Brilliant (by Thatching) and a winner in Italy by

Rusticaro: dam won over 1¼m: fair plater: will stay 1¼m: sold 2,000 gns Doncaster October Sales. *Mrs J. R. Ramsden.*

FARAYAR (USA)   4 b.g. Alleged (USA) 138–Felix Culpa (Kashmir II 125) [1988   — 10.1d² 12g⁴ 10f⁵ 8g³ 10.1g² 10s⁵ 10.8d⁵ 8m³ 1989 12m⁴ 16m] big, strong, rangy gelding: has a round action: fair maiden as 3-y-o when trained by F. J. Houghton: well beaten at 4 yrs: stays 10.8f: acts on top-of-the-ground and a soft surface: has run creditably when sweating and on edge: tends to carry head high. *R. J. O'Sullivan.*

FAR DARA   3 ch.f. Pharly (FR) 130–Sardara 106 (Alcide 136) [1988 7s 7g 1989 8g³   **52** d 8d 12.5f 10.6m 16.2g 10m 16.2m 10.2g 8f 15s 13s] small, close-coupled filly: has a round action: plating class at best: appears suited by 1m, though bred to stay further: has pulled hard for 7-lb claimer. *N. Bycroft.*

FARFELU   2 b.c. (Apr 24) Lyphard's Special (USA) 122–Spring Azure 98   **77** (Mountain Call 125) [1989 5d⁴ 5d² 5g³ 5f* 6m² 6f* 5g⁴ 7m⁵] IR 10,000Y: robust, good-quartered, sprint type: has plenty of scope: half-brother to several winners, including useful 7f winner Thug (by Persian Bold), later successful in USA: dam 2-y-o 5f winner: modest performer: won hands auction event at Lingfield in May and minor event at Folkestone following month: below form last 2 outings: will be suited by return to 6f. *K. M. Brassey.*

FAR GLOW   3 gr.c. Kalaglow 132–Faridetta 107 (Good Bond 122) [1988 NR 1989   **86** 10.1m⁴ 12m⁶ 12.2g² 19f*] 41,000Y: big, strong, close-coupled colt: moderate walker: fifth reported foal: brother to ungenuine 2m winner Mighty Glow and half-brother to 2-y-o 5f winners Farida Fair (by Cawston's Clown) and Dramatic (by Dragonara Palace): dam won four 5f races at 2 yrs: won 4-runner maiden at Redcar in October: best other effort in minor event at Windsor on debut: seems to stay 19f: sold to join A. Stringer 25,000 gns Newmarket Autumn Sales. *G. Harwood.*

FARMER JOCK   7 ch.h. Crofter (USA) 124–Some Dame 72 (Will Somers 114§)   **72** [1988 5m 6m 6m⁴ 6s³ 5g 5.1g³ 5g 7f⁵ 5m³ 5g 1989 6s 5f³ 5.1m 6f³ 5f³ 5m* 6m⁶ 5g² 5m* 5f² 5f³ 5g³ 6f 5m 5g 5m 5.6g² 5.1g⁶ 5m 5f⁵ 5m] strong, good-bodied horse: carries condition: modest handicapper: successful at Wolverhampton, Leicester and Yarmouth in summer: placed after, running well, at Thirsk, Wolverhampton and in Tote-Portland Handicap (40/1, beaten 3 lengths by Craft Express) at Doncaster: better suited by 5f than 6f: not at his best on soft going, acts on any other: effective with or without blinkers or visor: has worn bandages: has worn severe bridle: tends to hang: needs strong handling and to be held up. *Mrs N. Macauley.*

FARMIN   2 b. or br.c. (Feb 7) Rousillon (USA) 133–Jendeal (Troy 137) [1989 8g⁴]   **70** p rather sparely-made, quite attractive colt: first foal: dam unraced half-sister to useful sprinter Tarib and daughter of Australian graded race winner Red Coral: weak 6/1 and green, under 5 lengths fourth of 16, staying on not knocked about unduly, to Bawbee in maiden at Leicester in November: sure to improve. *A. C. Stewart.*

FAR MORE   3 ch.g. Gorytus (USA) 132–Demare (Pardao 120) [1988 7m³ 8d 1989   **65** 7d 8f⁴ 10m⁴ 13.3m 16m⁵ 12h³ 12m 10m⁵ 8.5m⁵ 8m 8s 8f⁴ 8f a10g⁵] workmanlike colt: quite modest maiden on most form: stays 1½m: acts on hard ground, probably unsuited by a soft surface: below form in blinkers seventh and eighth outings: carried head high and hung left for apprentice tenth one: sometimes has tongue tied down: has worn crossed noseband: usually bandaged. *F. Durr.*

FARNDALE   2 gr.c. (Apr 27) Vaigly Great 127–Beloved Mistress 84 (Rarity 129)   **53** [1989 5d³ 5g² 5g⁶ 5m⁵ 6g⁵ 6m] 15,000Y: small colt: moderate mover: fifth foal: brother to 3 winners, notably high-class sprinter Hallgate: dam 5f winner at 2 yrs: plating-class form early in season: blinkered, below that level in sellers last 2 starts: sold to join Miss S. Wilton 6,500 gns Newmarket Autumn Sales. *A. Bailey.*

FARNLEY HEY (USA)   2 b.f. (Feb 17) Full Extent (USA) 113–Belle Biz (USA)   **35** (Crimson Satan) [1989 5f³ 5f³ 6m 6m] $5,200Y: rather leggy, unfurnished filly: moderate walker and mover: half-sister to several winners in North America: dam won at up to 1m at 2 yrs: poor plater: ran too freely in visor final start (July): likely to prove best at 5f. *C. Tinkler.*

FAR OASIS (USA)   3 b.f. Key To Content (USA)–Arabia (USA) (Damascus   — (USA)) [1988 7g⁶ 7f 8g⁶ 1989 8g 6m 10g⁶] tall, lengthy filly: moderate walker: plating-class maiden: well beaten in 1989: should stay beyond 1m. *B. A. McMahon.*

FAR OUT   3 b.g. Raga Navarro (ITY) 119–Spaced Out (Space King 115) [1988 NR   — 1989 11m⁴] leggy, sparely-made gelding: first foal: dam winning jumper: moved poorly down when tailed-off fourth of 5 to Black Monday in minor event at Wolverhampton in July: has joined K. Bailey. *J. A. C. Edwards.*

FAR TOO LOUD 2 b.c. (Apr 8) Taufan (USA) 119–Octet (Octavo (USA) 115) — [1989 8v] IR 8,500Y: workmanlike colt: third foal: dam daughter of Lancashire Oaks winner Red Chorus: 33/1, bit backward and very green, behind last 3f in 23-runner minor event at Newbury in October. *Capt. R. M. Smyly.*

FAR TOO RISKY 4 b.g. Prince Tenderfoot (USA) 126–Red For Go (Tanfirion 56 110) [1988 8g 11d 1989 8m⁵ 8g⁴ 12m 10g] lengthy, workmanlike gelding: moderate mover: lightly-raced maiden: below form in handicaps last 2 outings: should stay beyond 1m: on toes on reappearance: visored final outing. *Capt. R. M. Smyly.*

FAR TOO SMART 2 br.f. (Apr 12) Trojan Fen 118–Bonnie Bess 95 (Ardoon 124) — [1989 6d] IR 8,500Y: second foal: dam Irish 1m to 1¼m winner, is half-sister to Italian 1000 Guineas winner Grande Nube: 50/1 and wintry in coat, always behind in 24-runner maiden at Newbury in October. *Capt. R. M. Smyly.*

FASCINATE 3 b.f. Fabulous Dancer (USA) 126–Enthralment (USA) (Sir Ivor — 135) [1988 6f 1989 7m⁶] leggy, fair sort: turns off-fore in: shaped very well in maiden at Newbury as 2-y-o: never going particularly well only start in 1989: bred to stay around 1¼m: sold 3,000 gns Newmarket December Sales. *R. V. Smyth.*

FASCINATION WALTZ 2 b.f. (Apr 28) Shy Groom (USA)–Cuckoo Weir 69 (Double Jump 131) [1989 6g³ 5m 6m²] IR 600F, 3,000Y: angular, sparely-made filly: half-sister to 1¼m winner Queen's Eyot (by Grundy) and a winner in Malaysia: dam lightly-raced granddaughter of excellent broodmare Kyak: quite modest form when placed in August maiden auction events won by Stylish Gent at Haydock and Young India at Ripon: well below form in between: will be suited by 7f. *J. Mackie.*

FASHION PRINCESS 3 gr.f. Van Der Linden (FR)–Pendle's Secret 73 (Le — Johnstan 123) [1988 5d 5m 5f⁶ 1989 8m 10.2h] small filly: poor plater: should be well suited by further than 5f. *Mrs A. Knight.*

FASHION SCENE (USA) 3 ch.f. London Bells (CAN) 109–Yes Please 108 — (Mount Hagen (FR) 127) [1988 NR 1989 8d 8m⁴ 10g a10g] rangy, sparely-made filly: third foal: half-sister to 2 maidens by Monteverdi: dam useful 2-y-o 6f winner: form only when fourth in maiden at Edinburgh in June, not handling turn well: off course 5 months then tailed off facing stiff task in claimer and handicap: sold 2,200 gns Ascot December Sales. *J. W. Hills.*

FAST AND FREE 3 b.g. Kafu 120–Santa Maria (GER) (Literat) [1988 6g 6m⁵ 7f 55 1989 7s* 7d 8m 8m] leggy, lightly-made gelding: poor walker: has a round action: easily best effort when winning seller (retained 2,800 gns) at Warwick in March: not seen out after July: stays 7f: evidently needs very soft going: sweating penultimate outing. *P. J. Feilden.*

FAST APPROACH 3 br.f. Daring March 116–Honest Opinion 68 (Free State 51 125) [1988 5d5 5g 5g6 5d 7g 1989 10f* 8f 10f⁴ 10f5 10g] leggy filly: moderate mover: fair plater: 33/1 and ridden by 5-lb claimer, won at Pontefract (no bid) in May: suited by 1¼m: acts on firm going: didn't look keen fourth start: tends to hang and pull hard, and is not an easy ride. *A. M. Robson.*

FASTAUFAN 2 b.g. (Apr 30) Taufan (USA) 119–Maggie Mine 85 (Native Prince) — [1989 6g 7.5f] IR 10,000F, IR 5,200Y: quite good-topped gelding: half-brother to several winners, including fair 1988 2-y-o 5f winner Cherokee Brave (by Horage) and smart 5f filly Storm Warning (by Tumble Wind): dam 2-y-o 5f winner: always behind in claimer (slowly away) at Haydock and maiden auction race at Beverley in September. *R. M. Whitaker.*

FAST CHICK 4 ch.f. Henbit (USA) 130–Hasten (Northfields (USA)) [1988 12g² 93 12f4 10m 10.8g² 10.2f* 10g² 10f* 10m 10m² 9g 1989 10g 9f* 10g 10m³ 9m³ 10f² 9m 10f² 10.6m² 10.5m³ a12g* a12g] angular, sparely-made filly: moderate mover: fairly useful handicapper: won at Wolverhampton in May and Southwell in November: ran poorly final outing: effective at 1¼m and 1½m: acts well on firm going: has got on toes: has won for apprentice: swished tail ninth outing (amateurs), unlucky on next: best with waiting tactics. *J. L. Dunlop.*

FAST IMAGE 3 ch.f. Crofthall 110–Diamante 83 (Sparkler 130) [1988 6m⁴ 7f4 7.5g6 6g6 1989 8f 8.5m 10f] workmanlike filly: modest plater: probably stays 1m: best efforts on firm going. *G. M. Moore.*

FAST MARKET 3 gr.f. Petong 126–Sweet Candice 71 (African Sky 124) [1988 54 6f5 6m 7m 1989 10m 10g 10m 10.1m 10f* 10m⁶] tall, close-coupled filly: 20/1, made all and kept on well despite flashing tail under pressure when winning seller (bought in 7,800 gns) at Chepstow in July: well beaten in varied company otherwise as 3-y-o:

stays 1¼m: acts on firm going: blinkered fourth outing: sold to join J. Baker 4,000 gns Newmarket July Sales. *M. Blanshard.*

FAST OPERATIVE 2 ch.c. (Apr 14) Absalom 128–Thorganby Victory 82   54
(Burglar 128) [1989 6f³ 7m³ 6f 7d 6s⁴] 2,800F, 3,000Y: angular colt: has a roundish action: sixth foal: brother to 3-y-o 7f and 1m winner Absolute Steal and half-brother to 6f and 7f winner Taskforce Victory (by Record Token): dam 5f winner at 2 yrs: fair plater: stays 7f: acts on any going: visored last outing. *J. P. Hudson.*

FATHER TIME 5 ch.g. Longleat (USA) 109–Noddy Time 97 (Gratitude 130)   74
[1988 6g 6g 6g 6m 6m 6f 7.6g² 7.6s⁵ 7f 7s 10s⁵ 1989 8f 7.6f 8.3m* 8m 8.3m 7s 8s] strong, workmanlike gelding: carries plenty of condition: modest handicapper nowadays: returned to form when winning at Windsor in July: ran poorly last 2 outings: suited by 1m nowadays: unsuited by firm going, acts on any other: effective with or without blinkers: goes well with forcing tactics: inconsistent. *M. H. Tompkins.*

FAULTLESS SPEECH 2 ch.c. (Feb 11) Good Times (ITY)–Fine Asset (Hot   62 p
Spark 126) [1989 6m 6d⁶] 7,400Y: strong, stocky colt: second living foal: dam poor half-sister to smart 7f performer Tudor Mill and useful Lyric Dance, successful at 6f and 7f: off course almost 4 months, caught eye, staying on well not at all knocked about, when 10½ lengths sixth of 24 to Notley in maiden at Newbury in October: should stay 7f: can improve further and win a race. *G. Lewis.*

FAUX PAVILLON 5 ch.g. Alias Smith (USA)–Beech Tree 67 (Fighting Ship   69 §
121) [1988 16s 16g 14d* 20f⁶ 16g² 19g⁵ 17.4s⁴ 18g³ 16m* 1989 18g 14g 14g 20f 16. 1m⁵ 16m² 17f 18g 16g] big, workmanlike gelding: often fails to impress in coat: modest handicapper on his day: mostly below form in 1989: stays well: probably acts on any going: blinkered twice, usually visored nowadays: has raced with head high, wandered under pressure and looked a difficult ride: not one to trust: sold 8,600 gns Ascot November Sales. *A. Hide.*

FAVOSKI 3 b.c. Niniski (USA) 125–Favoletta 115 (Baldric II 131) [1988 7m 7m 7g   —
1989 8s 10m⁴ 11.7m] small, quite attractive colt: has a quick action: fourth in maiden at Leicester in May, easily best effort: never placed to challenge in handicap month later: suited by 1¼m: sold 11,500 gns Newmarket Autumn Sales. *G. Wragg.*

FAVOURITE GUEST 5 b. or br.g. Be My Guest (USA) 126–Favoletta 115   54
(Baldric II 131) [1988 NR 1989 11f² 8.3m 12f] sparely-made gelding: poor mover: turns near-fore out markedly: useful performer early as 3-y-o when trained by G. Wragg: has deteriorated considerably: probably stays 11f: acts on firm going and a soft surface. *Miss S. J. Wilton.*

FAWLEY'S GIRL 7 b.m. He Loves Me 120–Princess Biddy 86 (Sun Prince 128)   50
[1988 6v 6d 6g 6s 6m⁶ 6d 7m⁵ 6m⁶ 7g 1989 8g 6d⁴ 6g⁶ 7f 6h* 6f⁵ 6g 6g* 6m 7.5m] sparely-made mare: plating-class handicapper: won at Carlisle in May and Pontefract in July: pulled up after 3f final outing: suited by stiff 6f: didn't show her form on soft going, acted on any other: often taken down steadily: often slowly away: held up: inconsistent: dead. *R. Hollinshead.*

FAYAFI 2 b. or br.f. (Feb 4) Top Ville 129–Muznah 92 (Royal And Regal (USA))   72
[1989 8m³ 10g⁴] third foal: dam 7f and 1m winner seemed to stay 1½m: modest form, staying on, behind Daromann in late-season maiden at Edinburgh and Adding in minor event at Redcar: will stay 1½m. *H. Thomson Jones.*

FAYGATE 3 ch.f. Vaigly Great 127–Fayette 80 (Dom Racine (FR) 121) [1988 6g   79
7g² 7f4 9g³ 1989 8.5m² 8m⁶ 7g] sparely-made filly: modest maiden: good second at Epsom, best effort in 1989: may prove best at 1m: hung violently left once at 2 yrs, and isn't the easiest of rides. *P. T. Walwyn.*

FAYNAZ 3 ch.c. Tumble Wind (USA)–Ceduna (FR) (Right Tack 131) [1988 6f*   80
6m* 1989 7f 8.3m³ 7g] well-made colt: won maiden and nursery as 2-y-o: weak favourite, fair third at Windsor, best effort in handicaps: sweating slightly, ran poorly final outing: stays 1m. *A. C. Stewart.*

FEARLESS FIGHTER 4 b.g. Formidable (USA) 125–Wild Asset (Welsh   — §
Pageant 132) [1988 8g 8f 8m⁵ 7g⁶ 7f 1989 9m 10f⁴ 8m] workmanlike, angular gelding: poor maiden: visored final start at 3 yrs: appears ungenuine and is best left alone. *G. P. Enright.*

FEARLESS NATIVE 3 br.c. Final Straw 127–Nativity (USA) 91 (Native   58
Royalty (USA) [1988 6m 6g 8d 1989 8g⁶ 8.2f⁴ 10f* 11m⁴ 10g 9.2m⁵ 10f 10g⁵ 10s²] leggy, close-coupled colt: won maiden claimer (went down well) at Ayr in June: ran poorly in claimers and sellers after next outing: suited by 1¼m: goes well on firm ground: blinkered seventh (reluctant to race) and eighth starts: sold to join R. Manning 10,000 gns Doncaster September Sales. *J. Berry.*

*EBF Kensington Palace Graduation Stakes, Ascot—
Fearless Revival gets the better of Aramantis*

FEARLESS REVIVAL 2 ch.f. (Mar 3) Cozzene (USA)–Stufida (Bustino 136) **102**
[1989 6g³ 6g* 7m* 7g²] medium-sized, useful-looking filly: good mover, with a
quick action: first reported foal: dam very good Italian filly, winner of Premio Lydia
Tesio (1¼m) at 3 yrs: successful in maiden (by 10 lengths) at Epsom in August and
3-runner minor event (showing good turn of foot) at Ascot following month: ran very
well when staying-on 5 lengths second to Negligent in Bottisham Heath Stud
Rockfel Stakes at Newmarket: will be suited by 1m: progressing well. *M. R. Stoute.*

FEARLESS STAND 3 ch.c. Import 127–Glendyne 58 (Precipice Wood 123) **47**
[1988 NR 1989 8g⁴ 8.2v 8d⁵ 12f⁶ 10f 5m⁶ 12.2g² 12g] leggy, sparely-made colt: first
foal: dam best at 1½m on flat, won over hurdles and fences: poor maiden: should
prove best at up to 1¼m: possibly unsuited by extremes of going: sold 4,000 gns
Doncaster October Sales. *S. E. Kettlewell.*

FEARSOME 3 gr.g. Formidable (USA) 125–Seriema 72 (Petingo 135) [1988 7s 6s **67**
7g* 7m 1989 7g 8s 7d 7m 8.5d⁶ 7.5f 8m⁶ 7m 8g² 10g⁴ 10g² 10f] strong, compact
gelding: quite modest performer: in frame, running well, in handicap (made most)
and claimers, on last occasion claimed out of Mrs J. Ramsden's stable £10,550:
blinkered, prominent 7f in handicap final start: suited by 1¼m: acts on top-
of-the-ground. *K. M. Brassey.*

FECAMP (USA) 3 b.c. Nureyev (USA) 131–Fallacieuse (Habitat 134) [1988 6d **92**
6g³ 7g³ 7g² 8d* 1989 7g⁴ 9f 8f⁶ 8g* 8m⁵ 8g² 8m 8g⁴ 8g] robust, attractive colt:
carries condition: has a fluent, slightly round action: fairly useful handicapper: won
at Salisbury in July: ran moderately (leading 6½f then eased) at York final start:
suited by 1m: goes well on an easy surface: sometimes moves keenly to post: ran
creditably when sweating: sold 38,000 gns Newmarket Autumn Sales. *B. W. Hills.*

FEDORIA 3 b.c. Formidable (USA) 125–Zepha 88 (Great Nephew 126) [1988 6g **80**
1989 7s*] leggy colt: 3/1 co-favourite from 12/1, won 16-runner maiden at Leicester
in April shade comfortably by 1½ lengths from Guidobaldo: looked likely to improve
but not seen out again: bred to stay 1m. *M. A. Jarvis.*

FELLOWS DREAM 2 b.f. (Apr 9) Milk of The Barley 115–Stonebow Lady 52 **—**
(Windjammer (USA)) [1989 5f 6f] 1,000F: leggy, compact filly: half-sister to some
poor animals: dam runner-up over 1m and 9f is half-sister to dam of Petong: slowly
away and always behind in summer maiden at Warwick and seller at Nottingham. *L.
J. Codd.*

FEMME FORMIDABLE 3 b.f. Formidable (USA) 125–Saint Osyth 105 **—**
(Blakeney 126) [1988 NR 1989 8.2m 8f a10g⁴ a8g⁶] workmanlike filly: poor mover:
fifth foal: half-sister to useful middle-distance stayer King of Mercia (by Great
Nephew): dam won over 1½m: poor maiden: stays 1m: hung left on debut. *C. F. Wall.*

FENAMICA 2 b.f. (Apr 10) Trojan Fen 118–My Tootsie 88 (Tap On Wood 130) **—**
[1989 7m 7g] 13,000F, 10,500Y: close-coupled filly: second foal: half-sister to 3-y-o
1¼m winner My Chiara (by Ardross), 6f winner at 2 yrs: dam won from 7.2f to 1¼m:
backward, behind in late-season maidens at Newmarket. *M. J. Ryan.*

310

FENFIRE 3 b.f. Trojan Fen 118–Upanishad 85 (Amber Rama (USA) 133) [1988   74
NR 1989 8d 7f⁶ 7f 8m⁵ 8m* 8m* 9m⁶ 8m 9g² 9g a10g] close-coupled, useful-looking
filly: moderate mover: half-sister to 2 winners, including useful 1¼m winner Goody
Blake (by Blakeney): dam, 1¼m winner, is half-sister to smart sprinter Bas Bleu:
modest performer: won claimer at Leicester and handicap (claimer ridden, running
on strongly from rear) at Newmarket in July: good staying-on second in £8,000
event at York, easily best effort in handicaps after: suited by 9f: yet to race on very
soft going, appears to act on any other: 3 times edgy: sold N. Tinkler 12,000 gns
Newmarket December Sales: not entirely reliable. *G. Wragg.*

FENJAAN 3 b.c. Trojan Fen 118–Joma Kaanem (Double Form 130) [1988 NR 1989   77
10.6g 8m² 8.2m* 8.2f* 8f* 8.3m* 7.3m⁵ 9g 8g⁵] 32,000Y: leggy, rather
sparely-made filly: moderate walker and mover: first foal: dam, ran once at 3 yrs in
Ireland, is daughter of sister to smart Selhurst and half-sister to Royal Palace:
progressive form in summer when justifying favouritism in maiden (odds on) at
Hamilton and handicaps at Nottingham, Redcar and Windsor in under 4 weeks: good
fifth of 27 in Newmarket handicap final start: should stay beyond 1m: acts on firm
going: tends to idle in front. *M. A. Jarvis.*

FENLASS 3 b.f. Trojan Fen 118–Pitiless Panther 97 (No Mercy 126) [1988 5d   71
1989 7f⁵ 7f³] leggy filly: first run for over 4 months, 4½ lengths third of 10 to
odds-on Sappho Comet in maiden at Lingfield in October, making most and first
worthwhile form: sold to Horse France 2,400 gns Newmarket Autumn Sales. *R. J. R.
Williams.*

FEROX 3 b.g. Formidable (USA) 125–La Grange 79 (Habitat 134) [1988 NR 1989   75
6g⁴ 6m⁴ 6f³] 30,000F: strong, good-bodied gelding: half-brother to useful Irish 9f
and 1¼m winner Jazz Me Blues (by Jaazeiro) and French 7f to 10.5f winner
Grundyssime (by Grundy): dam, formerly known as Bygone, won from 7f to 2m:
modest maiden: 11/10 favourite and looking very well, below-form third in
apprentice event at Pontefract in June: will stay further: may prove suited by some give in the ground. *H. R. A. Cecil.*

FERRYMAN 13 b.g. Forlorn River 124–La Miranda 80 (Miralgo 130) [1988 5m⁶   68
6m⁵ 6f* 5d* 5g⁴ 5g 1989 5f 6m³ 6g² 5f⁶ 5f 5m⁶] small gelding: modest handicapper:
stays 6f: acts on any going: has worn blinkers, but not for long time: apprentice
ridden nowadays: suited by forcing tactics: a grand old servant. *D. R. C. Elsworth.*

FERRYSTREAM 3 b.c. Niniski (USA) 125–River Call (FR) (Riverman (USA)   82
131) [1988 8d² 1989 11.7m* 14.8m⁶] rangy, quite attractive colt: favourite, won
maiden at Bath in May: odds on, never going well in handicap at Warwick later in
month: should stay beyond 1½m: sold 10,500 gns Newmarket Autumn Sales. *G.
Harwood.*

FESTIVE FALCON 3 ch.c. Sandhurst Prince 128–Caelidh 98 (Silly Season 127)   57
[1988 7g 1989 8d 8s 10m⁶ 8s 10g a12g²] tall, close-coupled colt: form only in claimers
at Nottingham (hanging badly left, off course 4½ months after) and Lingfield third
and final starts: will stay further. *P. J. Makin.*

FESTIVE FLING 4 b.g. Last Fandango 125–Pandomyne 71 (Pandofell 132)   —
[1988 10g 8m 8g 8g⁵ 8m⁴ 10g⁴ 8g⁶ 8.2s* 10s 10g 1989 10.2g 8f] workmanlike
gelding: bad mover: plating-class winner as 3-y-o: no subsequent form on flat:
slowly away as 4-y-o: stays 1¼m: acts on top-of-the-ground and heavy going:
suitable mount for apprentice: winning hurdler. *Denys Smith.*

FETTLE FLAME 3 b.f. Gorytus (USA) 132–Fettle (Relkino 131) [1988 NR 1989   95
8m² 7f* 7g* 9.2g³] 37,000F, 32,000Y: sparely-made, quite attractive filly: poor
mover: third foal: half-sister to 1986 2-y-o 6f winner Khakis Love (by Dominion):
dam unraced half-sister to Circus Plume: won poor maiden at Yarmouth very
easily and minor event (favourite, quickening well to lead 1f out) at Yarmouth in
September by 1½ lengths from Shieling: beaten 3½ lengths in listed race at Le
Croise-Laroche in November: may well prove best at up to 1m, though bred to stay
further: sold 50,000 gns Newmarket December Sales. *A. C. Stewart.*

FIEFDOM 9 ch.g. Home Guard (USA) 129–Eastwood Bounty 87 (Bounteous 125)   —
[1988 13.8g 1989 10.2g 15s 13s 13.8d] big, strong gelding: quite modest handicapper
in 1986: lightly raced and no form on flat nowadays: stays 1½m when conditions
aren't testing: acts on any going: sweating on reappearance: sometimes bandaged
behind: has worn tongue strap: fair winning hurdler. *W. Storey.*

FIELD GLASS (USA) 2 b.c. (May 2) Mr Prospector (USA)–Stellarette (CAN)   83 p
(Tentam (USA)) [1989 7g*] $400,000F: fourth foal: brother to fair 9f winner
Graphite and half-brother to winning hurdler Bravo Star (by The Minstrel): dam,
smart sprinter at 5 yrs, is half-sister to champion Canadian filly Kamar and daughter

of champion Canadian filly Square Angel: 11/2, won 16-runner maiden at Folkestone in October by ½ length, clear, from Halston Prince, making good progress from 2f out to lead inside last: sure to improve. *M. R. Stoute.*

FIELDS OF FORTUNE 2 ch.f. (Mar 26) Anfield 117–Suffolk Broads (Moulton 128) [1989 7m 7m 10g] leggy, lightly-made filly: fourth foal: dam never ran: well beaten in maidens. *J. L. Spearing.* —

FIELDWORK (USA) 3 b.g. Riverman (USA) 131–Lorelei's Lead (USA) (Raise **117** A Native) [1988 NR 1989 8s⁵ 8.5g* 7g² 6.5d² 8d⁵ 6g] $510,000Y: ninth reported foal: half-brother to several winners, notably Pennsylvania Derby third Intention (by Believe It) and very useful 1980 2-y-o Circle of Steel (by Noholme), later successful at up to 9f: dam won 7 minor races at up to 9f: won maiden at Longchamp in June: second in listed race there and Prix Maurice de Gheest at Deauville (beaten 1½ lengths by Cricket Ball, easily best effort): suited by about 6f and a soft surface. *A. Fabre, France.*

FIERY SUN 4 b.g. Sexton Blake 126–Melanie Jane (Lord Gayle (USA) 124) [1988 **43** 7d 8f 9f 8.5f⁶ 8.5m⁴ 12f⁵ 12.2g⁴ 1989 11d³ 12.3g] smallish gelding: quite moderate plater: will stay beyond 1½m: acts on firm going and a soft surface: sometimes visored: winning hurdler. *G. R. Oldroyd.*

FIESOLE 3 ch.f. Sharpo 132–Flaming Peace 104 (Queen's Hussar 124) [1988 5m **43** 6s 6m 7g 1989 8s 8g 8m 10g⁶ 8m⁴ 8m 8f 9m 8f 10f⁶] leggy filly: poor maiden: best form at 1m: acts on firm going. *Don Enrico Incisa.*

FIFTY NOT OUT 3 ch.g. Tender King 123–Our Sarah (Pampapaul 121) [1988 5g — 1989 8s 7g 10f] sturdy gelding: apparently of little account: has been tried in blinkers. *A. W. Potts.*

FIGHTING DAYS (USA) 3 ch.g. Fit To Fight (USA)–August Days (USA) (In — Reality) [1988 NR 1989 11.7m 10f⁶] $48,000F, $110,000Y: well-made gelding: second foal: dam won at up to 7f: sire high-class middle-distance performer: well beaten in maiden (chasing leaders 1¼m) at Bath and minor event (tailed off) at Brighton: off course nearly 5 months in between: sold out of I. Balding's stable 3,000 gns Newmarket July Sales and subsequently gelded. *A. Moore.*

FIGHTING SUN 2 ch.c. (Apr 4) Hard Fought 125–Sunny Waters (High Top 131) — [1989 a7g a8g] first foal: dam never ran: towards rear in December maidens at Lingfield. *H. J. Collingridge.*

FIGMENT 2 b.f. (May 11) Posse (USA) 130–Honey Thief 77 (Burglar 128) [1989 **46** 5v 6s⁵ a6g⁴] 4,000F, IR 10,500Y: leggy filly: ninth living foal: half-sister to 3-y-o Queen's Beeches (by Reesh) and 3 winners, including smart sprinter Prince Reymo (by Jimmy Reppin) and very speedy Silks Venture (by Lochnager): dam won over 5f at 2 yrs: poor maiden: slowly away when favourite for seller on debut. *Sir Mark Prescott.*

FIGURE OUT (USA) 3 b.c. Alleged (USA) 138–Preceptress (USA) (Grey **101** Dawn II 132) [1988 8g⁴ 1989 10.2g⁴ 10.1m* 12m⁴ 12f² 12m⁴] lengthy, useful-looking colt: has scope: moderate walker: favourite and sweating, won maiden at Windsor in July: useful form when narrowly beaten in strongly-run £19,100 handicap at Newmarket and £8,100 handicap (co-favourite) at York: sweating slightly, below form in £14,200 limited handicap at York on final outing: will probably stay further: acts on firm going. *B. Hanbury.*

FIJAR TANGO (FR) 4 br.c. In Fijar (USA) 121–Last Tango (FR) (Luthier 126) **120** [1988 9.2d² 10m* 10.5f4 12m* 12m 1989 10s³ 8s⁴ 10f 12g] close-coupled, angular colt: high-class performer as 3-y-o when trained by G. Mikhalides, winner at Longchamp of Grand Prix de Paris Louis Vuitton and moderately-run Prix Niel: in frame in spring as 4-y-o in Prix d'Harcourt (beaten 2½ lengths and ¾ length by Star Lift and Saint Andrews) at same course and Prix du Muguet at Saint-Cloud: beaten fair way in Arlington Million (blinkered) at Chicago and Turf Classic at Belmont Park in autumn: stayed 1½m in moderately-run race, but ideally suited by shorter: acts on any going: sometimes wore tongue strap: retired to Haras de Clairfeuille at 70,000 francs, nfnf. *R. Wojtowiez, France.*

FILAGO (USA) 2 b.c. (May 19) Foolish Pleasure (USA)–Derly (USA) 113 **108** p (Lyphard (USA) 132) [1989 7d⁷ 7d* 7g* 8m⁵] 2,400,000 francs (approx £219,600) Y: third foal: half-brother to 3-y-o winner Ceciliano and French 1m winner Derring (both by Irish River): dam won over 1m in France, and is half-sister to Detroit: successful in newcomers event at Evry and listed race and valuable restricted event (by a length from Ernani) at Deauville: had poor run when over 6 lengths fifth of 8 to Jade Robbery in Ciga Grand Criterium at Longchamp in October: stays 1m: improving. *Mme C. Head, France.*

FILIA ARDROSS 3 b.f. Ardross 134–Sari Habit (Saritamer (USA) 130) [1988 **121**
8g* 8g* 1989 8g* 8g* 11d* 11g* 12g² 8s² 11g⁵ 9.2g³] 6,600F: strong, good-topped
filly: second living foal: dam won in Italy: won twice in Germany in October at 2 yrs,
including listed race: successful in first half of 1989 season in listed event at
Dusseldorf and Group 2 contests at Dusseldorf (German 1000 Guineas), Mulheim
(German Oaks) and Hamburg: beaten 1½ lengths by Mondrian in Grosser Preis der
Berliner Bank at Dusseldorf next start: always prominent and battled on gamely
when narrowly-beaten third to Athyka in Prix de l'Opera at Longchamp in October:
best form at 9f to 1½m: acts on a soft surface: very smart. *B. Schutz, Germany.*

FILICAIA 3 ro.f. Sallust 134–Fine Flame (Le Prince 98) [1988 5g⁶ 5g⁴ 5g* 5f* **65**
5g⁴ 5d⁴ 5g⁴ 5d⁴ 6s 1989 5d 5m 5m 6f 6f⁴ 6f⁵ 6g] compact filly: modest performer:
should stay 7f: acts on firm and dead going: slowly away fourth start: ran badly final
one. *Don Enrico Incisa.*

FILLE DE FRAISE 3 b.f. Mr Fluorocarbon 126–Strawberry Fields 66 (Song **52**
132) [1988 NR 1989 8d* 10f 8m 8.2g⁶] leggy, angular filly: second foal: sister to 1987
2-y-o 7f winner Lynsdale Boy: dam ran only at 2 yrs, when 6f seller winner: 12/1,
won seller (retained 3,200 gns) at Bath in April, running on strongly from towards
rear to lead inside final 1f: below form after in handicap and claimers: should stay
beyond 1m: acts on a soft surface: slowly away first 2 starts. *Dr J. D. Scargill.*

FILL THE JUG 8 br.m. Derrylin 115–Fleur d'Amour (Murrayfield 119) [1988 NR —
1989 10.8m] plating-class mare: has been tried in blinkers. *D. C. Tucker.*

FINAL ACE 2 ch.c. (Feb 10) Sharpo 132–Palmella (USA) 89 (Grundy 137) [1989 **69** p
7m²] 40,000Y: robust, sprint type: fifth foal: half-brother to 1¼m winner Tino-Ella
(by Bustino) and fairly useful middle-distance winner Norpella (by Northfields):
dam, 1¼m winner stayed 1½m, is half-sister to Teenoso and Topsy: 6/1 and carrying
condition, 5 lengths second of 8, running on strongly after slow start, to very easy
winner Kadim in maiden at Redcar in September: should improve, and win a race. *W.
A. O'Gorman.*

FINAL ENIGMA 2 ch.c. (Feb 23) Final Straw 127–Mystery Ship 105 (Decoy **60**
Boy 129) [1989 5d 6m 5v] 9,000F, IR 15,500Y: neat, good-quartered colt: first foal:
dam 2-y-o 5f and 7f winner ideally suited by latter distance: plating-class maiden:
best form in listed event at Fairyhouse, second outing: blinkered in seller final start.
P. J. Makin.

FINAL FLUTTER 4 b.f. Beldale Flutter (USA) 130–Star Story 117 (Red God —
128§) [1988 8d⁶ 10.1m⁴ 8m⁵ 9g 8g⁶ 1989 12f] leggy, sparely-made filly: quite modest
maiden at her best: blinkered, well beaten in amateurs handicap at Goodwood in
June: stays 1m. *R. F. Johnson Houghton.*

FINAL HARVEST 2 ch.f. (Mar 5) Final Straw 127–Gas Only 63 (Northfields **61**
(USA)) [1989 6f³ 6m² 6f⁵ a5g] small filly: has a sharp action: second foal: half-sister
to 1987 2-y-o 6f winner Glowing Report (by Kalaglow): dam 9f and 1¼m winner:
quite modest maiden: best form on first 2 starts: sold out of R. J. R. Williams' stable
7,100 gns Newmarket Autumn Sales after third outing. *D. W. Chapman.*

FINALLY 2 ch.f. (Mar 4) Final Straw 127–Boswellia 109 (Frankincense 120) —
[1989 5f⁵ 5m⁵ 7f] leggy, lightly-made filly: sister to useful 6f to 8.2f winner Colway
Rally and half-sister to several other winners, including fairly useful 1983 2-y-o 7f
winner Topple (by High Top): dam won 1m William Hill Gold Cup: well beaten in
maidens and a seller: slowly away and swerved stalls first 2 starts. *Mrs R. Wharton.*

FINAL MADNESS 3 ch.f. Final Straw 127–Summer Madness 88 (Silly Season **48**
127) [1988 5g 7m 6g 1989 8d⁵ 7f 7f 8m 11.7f³ 12.5f] workmanlike filly: has run in
sellers, including when blinkered, wearing severe bridle and taken early to post
fourth outing: worth a try over 1¼m: yet to race on very soft going, appears to act on
any other: bandaged final start: bought out of K. Brassey's stable 1,250 gns Ascot
July Sales after fourth. *C. L. Popham.*

FINAL PASS 4 b.g. Anfield 117–Gimima 54 (Narrator 127) [1988 5g² 6g 5m⁵ 6m —
5f 6g² 5g 5m 6m⁴ 8v 1989 6d⁵ 5f] compact gelding: poor maiden: has run in seller:
suited by 6f and give in the ground: sold 1,300 gns Doncaster June Sales. *Ronald
Thompson.*

FINAL PLAYER 3 gr.c. Absalom 128–Oakwoodhill (Habat 127) [1988 6f 6g³ 7.5f —
7g 1989 9d 7g 10f 8g 12m⁶] lengthy, workmanlike colt: has rather a round action:
quite modest at best: below form as 3-y-o, mostly in sellers: should stay further than
7.5f: sweating and on toes fourth start: sold 4,200 gns Newmarket Autumn Sales. *M.
W. Easterby.*

FINAL SHOT 2 br.f. (Apr 21) Dalsaan 125–Isadora Duncan (Primera 131) [1989 **69**
5d 5m* 5f² 7f² 5d³ 6m³] IR 2,000Y: small, workmanlike filly: half-sister to 1¼m

seller winner Holdenby (by Henbit) and to a minor winner at up to 9f in USA by Lorenzaccio: dam, placed in minor 7.5f race in France, is half-sister to very useful Fisherman's Bridge: won maiden auction race at Thirsk in May: ran well in varied events afterwards, on final start narrowly-beaten third of 20 to Super One in valuable seller (claimed £11,101) at York in August: stay 7f. *M. H. Easterby.*

FINAL SOUND 4 b.g. Final Straw 127–Sound Type 92 (Upper Case (USA)) 52
[1988 9v* 12g 9g 9s 9s* 10g⁴ 8.2s 1989 10.2g 10v⁴ 10d* 10.1m⁵ 9f 8.2g⁴ 9g 12g⁵ 12s a11g] leggy, angular gelding: plating-class performer: battled on gamely when winning selling handicap at Pontefract (bought in 3,600 gns) in April: ran poorly last 2 starts: stays 1¼m: well suited by an easy surface: has worn blinkers and visor (did so at Pontefract): has run well for apprentice: inconsistent. *P. J. Feilden.*

FINE A LEAU (USA) 4 b.f. Youth (USA) 135–What A Candy (USA) (Key To 51
The Mint (USA)) [1988 8.2v⁶ 8d 7g 5m³ 6m³ 5f⁶ 5g⁴ 5g⁶ 5d 5m 5d 1989 6s 6d⁴ 6v⁶ 6d 5m* 5f² 5m* 5m⁴ 5f³ 5m³ 5f² 5m 5m⁵ 5m* 5g 5m² 5m³ 5f⁵ 5f] small, stocky filly: poor mover: improved considerably once running at 5f on top-of-the-ground, making all in handicaps (last 2 apprentice events) at Thirsk (mulish at stalls), Edinburgh and Goodwood in first half of year: tailed off when visored: bandaged 4 starts prior to last one: apprentice ridden: tough: in foal to Indian Forest. *M. Brittain.*

FINEST 4 bl.f. Final Straw 127–Finest View 66 (Bold Lad (IRE) 133) [1988 7m 8g 59
8m² 8g 8m³ 8g⁶ 1989 9f³ 10f 10m⁴ 11f³ 10m a8g⁶] leggy, quite good-topped filly: moderate mover: plating-class maiden: bandaged and wearing crossed noseband, creditable sixth in handicap at Southwell in December, first outing for over 5 months: possibly best at up to 1¼m: acts on firm going. *P. Calver.*

FINETTE (USA) 2 b.f. (Jan 29) Northern Baby (CAN) 127–Karelia (USA) 111 70 §
(Sir Ivor 135) [1989 7g⁶ 7g⁶ 7m² 8.2f 7g³] leggy, workmanlike filly: has a roundish action: sixth foal: closely related to 1¼m winner Gopak (by Nureyev) and half-sister to untrustworthy 1¼m 2-y-o 5f winner Dubrovnik (by L'Emigrant) and French 1¼m winner Kia Real (by Irish River): dam, daughter of half-sister to high-class American sprinter Full Out, won twice at 1m and stayed 1½m: modest maiden: easily best effort third start: ran poorly in nursery at Nottingham and maiden (visored) at Catterick on last 2 starts: should stay 1m: sold 12,000 gns Newmarket Autumn Sales: looks ungenuine, and is one to be wary of. *M. R. Stoute.*

FINE TUDOR 3 b.g. Jimsun 121–Mill Haven (Mannion 95) [1988 6m⁶ 7d* 7m⁶ —
8f² 8g⁵ 8s⁵ 8.2s 1989 12g 10f⁵ 10.2f] small, sturdy gelding: good walker: won seller as 2-y-o: below form in handicap and claimers in 1989: should be suited by 1¼m +: probably acts on any going: ran poorly in blinkers final start at 2 yrs: sold 6,000 gns Newmarket July Sales. *M. H. Tompkins.*

FINE WARRIOR 2 b.c. (May 4) Anita's Prince 126–Thistle Grove (Sagaro 133) 33
[1989 5f³ 5f³ 6f⁴] first reported foal: dam second over 2m at 4 yrs in Ireland also in frame over hurdles: bad plater: best effort on final outing. *J. Berry.*

FINGEST 6 b.g. Imperial Fling (USA) 116–Derry Daughter (Derring-Do 131) 44
[1988 14.5g 16m⁴ 1989 14.8s⁴ 17.1m⁵ 16m] close-coupled, lightly-made gelding: poor maiden: stays 2m: acts on any going: usually blinkered nowadays: bandaged as 6-y-o: winning hurdler/chaser. *P. D. Evans.*

FINJAN 2 b.c. (Feb 1) Thatching 131–Capriconia (Try My Best (USA) 130) [1989 70
7f³ 6d⁵] 51,000F: strong, sturdy colt: first foal: dam unraced: quite modest form in maidens won by Sasaki at Leicester and Heart of Joy at Newbury: will probably stay 1m. *P. T. Walwyn.*

FINLUX SKY DESIGN 2 b.c. (May 15) Ballad Rock 122–Slip The Ferret 109 47
(Klairon 131) [1989 8g⁵ 8s 6f] 10,500Y: leggy, angular colt: has scope: fourth living foal: half-brother to Irish middle-distance winner Fly The Coop (by Kris) and a winner in Italy: dam very useful at up to 1m: poor form in maidens: backward first 2 starts. *E. Weymes.*

FINNAIR FINESSE 3 b.f. Camden Town 125–Shady Glade (Sun Prince 128) —
[1988 5d⁵ 5d* 5s⁴ 6f³ 5f 5d 7d 6s 1989 6m 7g] leggy, close-coupled filly: modest winner as 2-y-o: behind in pattern company and handicaps last 6 outings: not seen out after early-May in 1989: should stay 7f: visored as 3-y-o: tends to sweat. *M. J. Haynes.*

FIRE AND SHADE (USA) 2 ch.f. (Mar 8) Shadeed (USA) 135–Fatah Flare 91
(USA) 121 (Alydar (USA)) [1989 6m² 6m* 6m⁶] angular, workmanlike filly: good walker: first foal: dam, successful over 6f at 2 yrs and in 10.5f Musidora Stakes as 3-y-o, is half-sister to outstanding filly Sabin and daughter of half-sister to dam of Miss Oceana (by Alydar) and Larida, latter dam of Magic of Life: fair performer: odds

314

on, ¾-length second of 5 to Gharam in maiden at Ascot in July: landed odds easily in
similar event at Nottingham following month: ran as though something very much
amiss in 'The Pacemaker Update' Lowther Stakes at York, tending to hang
throughout and virtually pulled up final 1f: will be suited by 7f. *M. R. Stoute.*

FIRE GOLD 2 b.f. (Mar 28) Never So Bold 135–Seein Is Believin (USA) (Native **48**
Charger) [1989 6g 7g⁵ 6f] 90,000 francs (approx £8,200) Y: angular, dipped-backed,
sparely-made filly: moderate walker and mover: half-sister to several winners,
including very useful 1½m winner Believer and French 1¼m winner Prince
Blakeney (both by Blakeney), latter successful in USA: dam daughter of Prix Morny
winner Princeline: poor form in July maidens at Doncaster (hampered start) and
Yarmouth: on toes, moved poorly down and always behind in claimer at Leicester 3
months later. *P. A. Kelleway.*

FIRE LADY 3 ch.f. Hotfoot 126–Hindu Flame 83 (Shiny Tenth 120) [1988 NR **52**
1989 6s 6f³ 5m 6f] big, lengthy filly, rather dipped-backed: sixth foal: closely related
to 1983 2-y-o 5f winner Dellwood Iris (by Firestreak): dam 5f winner at 2 yrs: third
in seller at Folkestone in June, no extra inside final 1f, easily best effort in modest
company. *W. Holden.*

FIRELIGHT FIESTA 4 ch.g. Sallust 134–Caithness 78 (Connaught 130) [1988 **115**
10s 10d 10g³ 9f² 9g* 10s* 8g³ 8m⁴ 9m 10m² 9s⁵ 10g 9g 1989 11f² 10f* 10m* 12f³
10.5f⁴ 10.6d⁴ 12m* 12g* 10.2g² 12d*] workmanlike, good-bodied gelding: good
mover: had a tremendous season and developed into a smart handicappper, winning
at Chepstow, Yarmouth (trained first 5 outings by M. Tompkins), Newmarket, York
(apprentices) and Thirsk: favourite, always travelling well, led 2f out and steadily
drew clear when beating Re-Release easily by 7 lengths in 19-runner £23,800
William Hill November Handicap at Thirsk: stays 1½m: acts on any going:
splendidly genuine and consistent. *B. Hanbury.*

FIRESTREAM 3 br.f. Blazing Saddles (AUS)–Dovey (Welsh Pageant 132) [1988 **66**
NR 1989 7m⁴ 8g³ 7f² 8f⁴ 7s 7g] angular filly: second foal: dam never ran: quite
modest maiden: faced stiff tasks last 2 outings: stays 1m: acts on firm going. *G. M.
Moore.*

FIRE THE GROOM (USA) 2 b.f. (Apr 13) Blushing Groom (FR) 131– **67 p**
Prospector's Fire (USA) (Mr Prospector (USA)) [1989 7g] $185,000Y: sixth foal:
half-sister to 2 winners, notably very smart sprinter Dowsing (by Riverman): dam,
placed twice at 3 yrs, is half-sister to Florida Derby winner Royal And Regal: 20/1,
shaped very well when 9 lengths seventh of 24 to Sardegna in maiden at Newmarket
in November, keeping on strongly last 2f under considerate handling: sure to
improve, and win a race. *L. M. Cumani.*

FIRE TOP 4 br.c. Hotfoot 126–Sirnelta (FR) (Sir Tor) [1988 8g* 8m 8m 8f⁵ 10g⁶ **98**
8d 8.3m⁶ 8s⁶ 1989 9d² 8s⁴ 8f 10g² 10f* 10f⁶ 10g* 10f⁵ 10g* 10g*] sparely-made colt:
fairly useful handicapper: had an excellent season, winning at Sandown in June,
Epsom in August and Ascot (accounting for Green Emperor by a length in 7-runner
£10,300 event) and Redcar (making virtually all, rallying splendidly) in October:
stays 1¼m well: best form on a sound surface: visored once at 3 yrs: well suited by
enterprising tactics: tremendously game and genuine. *R. Akehurst.*

FIRM MIST (USA) 3 b.f. Affirmed (USA)–Swoonmist (USA) (Never Bend) —
[1988 6m⁵ 6g³ 1989 10.1g 12f⁶ 7.6m] compact filly: moderate walker: has a round
action: quite modest maiden at 2 yrs: showed little in 1989, blinkered final outing:
should be suited by at least 1m: sold 4,300 gns Newmarket December Sales. *P. F. I.
Cole.*

*William Hill November Handicap, Thirsk—last big handicap of the season,
Firelight Fiesta rounds off a marvellous campaign*

FIR

FIRM POLICY 3 ch.f. Miami Springs 121–Matin 64 (Rheingold 137) [1988 6d 6s — 8m 8v 6m 1989 8v⁵ 12.3d] medium-sized, leggy filly: plating-class maiden: well behind in spring as 3-y-o: best run at 1m on top-of-the-ground: has joined J. C. Haynes. *R. F. Fisher.*

FIRST ADMIRAL 3 b.c. Lord Gayle (USA) 124–Grecian Blue 68 (Majority Blue — 126) [1988 6m 8.2m 1989 8.2m 10m 10.8m 8.2g⁶ 10m] rather finely-made, workmanlike colt: has a short, quick action: plating-class form at best: should be suited by 1¼m +: possibly suited by some give in the ground: blinkered third start: has joined D. Wintle. *G. A. Huffer.*

FIRST AVENUE 5 b.g. Tina's Pet 121–Olympus Girl 65 (Zeus Boy 121) [1988   55 7f* 8g⁵ 10f* 8g 1989 8m 11.7m⁵ 10f* 10f* 10.2f4 10f*] compact gelding: plating-class handicapper: successful at Folkestone (has now won there 3 times) in August and September and at Brighton (for second successive year) in October: suited by 1¼m: acts very well on firm going: has worn blinkers and visor: good mount for apprentice. *Andrew Turnell.*

FIRST BID 2 ch.c. (Mar 9) Crofthall 110–Redgrave Design 77 (Nebbiolo 125) — [1989 6v] 8,000Y: workmanlike colt: has scope: second foal: brother to 1987 2-y-o 5f seller winner Arroganza: dam 2-y-o 5f winner: slowly away and tailed off in 15-runner auction event at Ayr in October. *R. M. Whitaker.*

FIRST BILL 6 ch.g. Nicholas Bill 125–Angelica (SWE) (Hornbeam 130) [1988   72 14d³ 12m* 12.2d* 12g 12g4 12m 12g 12m 1989 12d 11.7g³ 12d 11.7m³ 12g] smallish, well-made gelding: moderate mover: modest handicapper: favourite, won 15-runner event at Pontefract in July, making virtually all and holding on gamely: below form final outing, first for 3 months: well suited by 1½m: goes particularly well on an easy surface: sometimes sweats: suitable mount for apprentice. *H. Candy.*

FIRST BLESSED 2 b.f. (May 29) Music Boy 124–Blessit 79 (So Blessed 130)   51 p [1989 5g 6g] neat filly: first reported foal: dam sprinter: still bit backward, 10 lengths ninth of 22, prominent around 4f, to Lip Sing in maiden at Leicester in November: will improve again. *W. J. Pearce.*

FIRST BORN 2 br.f. (Feb 4) Be My Native (USA) 122–Feat of Arms (Jaazeiro   42 (USA) 127) [1989 5d⁶ 5f⁵ 7g 6m 7g] IR 900F: leggy, light-framed filly: has a round action: first foal: dam never ran: quite moderate plater: should stay 7f: trained first 4 starts by A. Potts: blinkered final one. *G. P. Kelly.*

FIRST CHOICE 2 b.g. (May 24) Marching On 101–Carrula (Palm Track 122)   65 [1989 6m 5f⁵ 5h² 5f² 5f* 5f4 5f2] 800Y: rather angular gelding: fourth foal: half-brother to winning Swedish 3-y-o Errol Duprey (by Dublin Taxi): dam unraced: quite modest performer: made all in maiden auction event at Redcar in June: ran creditably in nurseries afterwards: not seen out after July: will prove best at 5f: often hangs left. *M. W. Ellerby.*

FIRST DREAM 2 b.f. (Mar 22) Dreams To Reality (USA) 113–Khloud 76   69 (Pitskelly 122) [1989 5g² 5f³ 5v4 6s*] 7,400F: leggy, sparely-made filly: second foal: dam, placed over 7f at 3 yrs, is half-sister to Young Generation: won claimer at Hamilton in November (claimed to join M. Johnston £11,375) readily by 4 lengths from Phoenix Jule: better suited by 6f than 5f. *S. G. Norton.*

FIRST EXHIBITION 2 b.f. (Mar 12) Claude Monet (USA) 121–All Hail 112   58 p (Alcide 136) [1989 7m³] leggy, sparely-made filly: half-sister to several winners, including middle-distance winners Geminiani (by Lorenzaccio) and Bunce Boy (by King Emperor): dam staying daughter of St Leger second None Nicer: 14/1, over 4 lengths third of 10, bumped over 1f out and then running green, to Star Child in maiden at Wolverhampton in July: withdrawn in paddock at Haydock in September and not seen out again: will stay 1m: should improve: to join J. Fanshawe. *R. F. Casey.*

FIRST FASTNET 4 b.f. Ahonoora 122–Jolie Brise (Tumble Wind (USA)) [1988   57 7g 10f5 8h² 8d5 6g 1989 5d* 6g 5m 5f³ 5m4 5m* 5g 5g 6f 5m4 5.3f 5m a5g] workmanlike filly: quite modest handicapper: won apprentice event at Catterick in April and 10-runner race at Windsor in July: below form afterwards: seems suited by 5f nowadays: yet to race on soft going, acts on any other: blinkered eleventh and twelfth outings: taken down late seventh start: changed hands 4,200 gns Newmarket December Sales: inconsistent: sold 4,200 gns Newmarket December Sales. *F. Durr.*

FIRST FLUSH 3 b.g. Precocious 126–Rosananti 107 (Blushing Groom (FR) 131) — [1988 6s⁵ 7s4 8.5v⁶ 1989 7d 6f 6f4 6f 6m 5m 6g 8.2d a8g 6g] sturdy ex-Irish gelding: bought out of J. Oxx's stable 3,000 gns Newmarket Autumn (1988) Sales: poor walker: third foal: half-brother to 1m winner Persian Emperor (by Persepolis): dam, half-sister to good English and German performer Claddagh, won from 6f to 1m and

316

stayed 1½m: showed quite modest form in Ireland at 2 yrs but little (including in seller) here, putting up best effort on third start: probably suited by 6f: acts on firm ground: visored last 2 outings: gelded after final one. *K. T. Ivory.*

FIRST FORUM   4 b.g. Kalaglow 132–River Call (FR) 103 (Riverman (USA) 131)   —
[1988 8d³ 10f⁵ 10g⁴ 10g⁴ 10g⁵ 10g² 12f 12d 1989 10.2g 10g] rather unfurnished gelding: tubed: modest maiden as 3-y-o: 33/1, always behind in apprentice event at Brighton in April, and wasn't seen out again: suited by 1¼m: best efforts on good going: blinkered once at 3 yrs: has appeared a difficult ride. *J. E. Long.*

FIRST HOME   2 b.g. (Apr 15) Homing 130–Mill Wind 68 (Blakeney 126) [1989   51
5d⁶ 5f 6m 5.1m⁶ 5f² 6m⁴ 6f² 6f³ 6f⁵ 6m 7g 6g a7g a8g] 3,000Y: rather leggy gelding: has a quick action: sixth foal: half-brother to 3-y-o Honour The Wind (by Ahonoora) and fair 1½m winner Starwind (by Star Appeal): dam stayed 1½m: inconsistent plater: stays 7f. *Pat Mitchell.*

FIRST INNINGS (USA)   3 b.c. Verbatim (USA)–Double's Nell (USA)   —
(Nodouble (USA)) [1988 7g⁴ 6d² 1989 8f³ 10f³] $100,000Y: sparely-made, angular colt: eighth foal: half-brother to several winners, notably good-class winner at up to 1m Nell's Briquette (by Lanyon): dam unraced: fair form as 2-y-o when trained by J. Oxx in Ireland: 6 lengths last of 3 to impressive Go On Smile in maiden at Thirsk in August, readily outpaced: always well behind in similar event at Brighton later in month: should stay at least 1m: sold 800 gns Newmarket Autumn Sales. *J. Gosden.*

FIRST MISTAKE   2 b.f. (May 5) Posse (USA) 130–Gentle Star 77 (Comedy Star   57
(USA) 121) [1989 5f 6g⁴ 6g⁶ 6m⁴] 2,200F: big, rangy filly: has plenty of scope: second foal: half-sister to 1988 2-y-o 5f seller winner Tell Me This (by Goldhills Pride): dam 6f winner: quite modest maiden: not seen out after early-August: worth another try at 5f. *M. W. Easterby.*

FIRST TERM   3 b.f. Welsh Term 126–Cresta (FR) 84 (Ribero 126) [1988 NR 1989   —
8m] 2 1,100Y: unfurnished, round-actioned filly: fourth foal: half-sister to 3 winners, including 1m winner Pendori (by Junius), later successful in South Africa, and quite modest 1985 2-y-o Oh So Vague (by Vaigly Great), later successful in USA: dam, half-sister to high-class middle-distance colt Electric, won over 7f on only start: no promise in maiden at Brighton in May: sold 1,150 gns Newmarket July Sales. *Mrs L. Piggott.*

FIRST TOWER   3 ch.f. Tower Walk 130–Gluhwein (Ballymoss 136) [1988 NR   —
1989 10f 12.2m 7.5m⁶] 2,800Y: smallish, sparely-made filly: third foal: half-sister to 1987 2-y-o 5f winner Lusty Lad (by Decoy Boy): dam unraced: claimer ridden, always behind in seller (gave trouble at stalls) and claimers in the North. *A. M. Robson.*

FIRST TRADITION   4 ch.f. Sayyaf 121–Traditional Miss 90 (Traditionalist   38
(USA)) [1988 9d 8g 7d 7d 6m* 5m 7f 6h 6m 1989 5f 7m 8m 6m⁵ 7f³ 7m 6m³ 6f⁵] lengthy, good-bodied filly: poor performer: best form at 6f and 7f: acts on firm going: blinkered and sweating third outing: trained until after then by C. Hill: has won for apprentice. *R. J. Hodges.*

FIRST VICTORY   3 gr.c. Concorde Hero (USA) 101–Cestrefeld 94 (Capistrano   87 p
120) [1988 8s 1989 7s 7fʷᵒ 9m⁵ 10.2g 10g* 12g*] tall colt: has scope: half-brother to winners in West Indies: dam, 5f and 6f winner at 2 yrs, is half-sister to Young Generation: walked over in minor event at Brighton in July: ridden by 7-lb claimer, stayed on well to lead inside final 1f when winning late-season handicaps at Folkestone (by short head) and Leicester: better at 1½m than 1¼m and should stay further: fairly useful handicapper in the making. *R. Hannon.*

FIRST VINTAGE (USA)   2 b.c. (Apr 28) Ruthie's Native (USA)–Champagne-   71
andlace (USA) (Champagne Charlie (USA)) [1989 6f 6d³] good-quartered colt: has scope: sixth foal: half-brother to 3 minor winners in North America: dam unraced: sire won 9f Florida Derby: 10/1, 3 lengths third of 11 to Reasonable Kid in maiden at Catterick in October, much better effort. *S. G. Norton.*

FIRST WHIP   3 ch.g. Dublin Taxi–Whip Finish 77 (Be Friendly 130) [1988 NR   —
1989 8h³ 8g] eighth foal: half-brother to 3 winners, including very useful 5f performer Whipper In (by Bay Express): dam won twice over 5f at 2 yrs: bit backward, poor form in maiden (hanging right) at Carlisle and claimer (wearing crossed noseband) at Doncaster in the summer: takes keen hold: sprint bred, and worth a chance over shorter: sold to join J. Thomas 4,200 gns Doncaster August Sales. *J. Etherington.*

FIRTHLANDS   7 ch.g. Czarist 89–Fair Ellender (Sailing Light 119) [1988 NR   —
1989 12.3f] sparely-made gelding: fifth living foal: dam well beaten: 50/1 and wearing tongue strap, tailed off after 4f in maiden at Ripon in June. *S. J. Muldoon.*

FISHERMAN'S CROFT 3 b.c. Dunbeath (USA) 127–Russeting 76 (Mummy's **61**
Pet 125) [1988 6m² 6d⁴ 7m⁶ 8s 8f² 8f² 1989 7f 8.2m 6g 8f⁴ 8g* 8g⁵ 8g⁵]
sparely-made, medium-sized colt: has a markedly round action: 10/1 from 16/1, won
claimer at Doncaster in June: easily best other effort as 3-y-o next time: may well
stay beyond 1m: seems suited by a sound surface: retained 3,500 gns Newmarket
Autumn Sales: prolific winning selling hurdler. *N. Tinkler.*

FISHERMAN'S YARN (USA) 2 b.c. (Mar 29) Foolish Pleasure (USA)– —
Perliere (FR) (Rheingold 137) [1989 8.2g] 35,000Y: half-brother to 1¼m winner
Pearl Fisher (by Ile de Bourbon): dam, French 2-y-o 9f winner, is half-sister to
Persepolis: 33/1, ran wide bend and never dangerous in 20-runner minor event at
Nottingham in October: sold 10,000 gns Newmarket Autumn Sales. *R. J. R.
Williams.*

FISHKI 3 b.f. Niniski (USA) 125–Ladyfish 79 (Pampapaul 121) [1988 NR 1989 **77 ?**
10.5f⁶ a8g4] workmanlike, angular filly: modest form in £5,600 event at York
(bandaged off-hind) in May: soon outpaced in maiden at Southwell 6½ months later:
needs further than 1m. *B. Hanbury.*

FISHY BUSINESS 5 gr.g. Morston (FR) 125–No Cards 109 (No Mercy 126) —
[1988 16g* 1989 16f4] workmanlike ex-Irish gelding: fifth foal: half-brother to 3
winners, including useful 7f and 1m winner Dabdoub (by Habat): dam won at up to
1m: easy winner of maiden at Ballinrobe as 4-y-o: runner-up in 2 point-to-points
earlier in year: 33/1, soundly-beaten last of 4 in minor event at Redcar in August. *T.
H. Caldwell.*

FISTFUL OF BUCKS 3 b.g. Lochnager 132–Crimson Ring (Persian Bold 123) **52**
[1988 5g 6d⁵ 6f 7m 1989 8g 10.6m 10m³ 11.7m 10m 12g 8m³ 7m 8.2d* 8m 8.2d⁶]
angular, plain gelding: won claimer at Haydock in August, leading close home but
tending to edge left and not look keen: took good hold and ran moderately next start:
stays 1¼m: acts on top-of-the-ground and a soft surface: blinkered last 6 starts: has
run well when sweating: winning claiming hurdler with C. Weedon. *E. Eldin.*

FIT FOR A QUEEN (USA) 3 ch.f. Fit To Fight (USA)–Titled (CAN) **81**
(Impressive) [1988 5g³ 6f* 6f² 7g 5g 1989 6m⁶ 6f³ 5m² 6g² 6g⁶] tall, short-looking
filly: very good walker: fair handicapper: should prove at least as effective returned
to 5f: acts on firm going: visored last 4 starts. *J. Gosden.*

FIT FOR COUNSEL 3 b.f. Hotfoot 126–Rose of Shenfield 86 (Upper Case **58**
(USA)) [1988 6f 6g³ 6m⁶ 6g⁴ 7g* 8g⁴ 7d³ 1989 8s 8.2s² 10.6g 10.6g4] useful-looking
filly: moderate mover: plating-class performer: creditable second in amateurs
handicap at Haydock in April: below form in similar event and claimer (claimed
£6,000) at same course in the summer: should be well suited by 1¼m +: acts on soft
going: lacks turn of foot. *C. W. Thornton.*

FITZROY BELL 2 ch.g. (Apr 16) Red Sunset 120–Gaychimes (Steel Heart 128) —
[1989 8g a8g⁶ a7g] IR 9,000F, IR 7,500Y: workmanlike gelding: fifth foal:
half-brother to 1m and 1¼m winner Gibbot (by Taufan): dam unraced half-sister to
useful Irish 6f to 1¼m winner Gaily Gaily, later successful in USA: well beaten in
maidens and a claimer: blinkered last 2 starts. *M. Bell.*

FIVE STAR AFFAIR 4 b.f. Mummy's Game 120–Deux Etoiles 86 (Bay **49**
Express 132) [1988 7s⁶ 8f 7f 5.8f 6f⁴ 6g³ 1989 7g4 8.3m⁶ 8h 10m* 10m 10.2h 8f 8f]
rather leggy, workmanlike filly: has a quick action: modest plater: won handicap at
Leicester (no bid) in May: below form afterwards: stays 1¼m well: acts on any
going, except possibly hard: visored once: blinkered 3 times, including first 2 starts:
bandaged seventh outing, first for 3 months. *Miss J. Thorne.*

FIVE TOWNS 4 b.c. Burslem 123–Sarafri (African Sky 124) [1988 NR 1989 10m] —
good-topped, quite attractive colt: modest winner as 2-y-o: bandaged, soundly
beaten in handicap at Yarmouth in June: stays 1m: best form on a sound surface:
showed nothing in blinkers: sold 3,000 gns Newmarket Autumn Sales. *C. N.
Williams.*

FIXERS DILEMMA 2 ch.g. (Apr 14) Tender King 123–Stormy Princess 76 — §
(Ballymoss 136) [1989 5d 5g 5f] IR 5,800F, 6,400Y: sparely-made gelding: seventh
foal: dam won at up to 13f: no form in Ripon maiden and Beverley sellers: ducked
badly left leaving stalls last 2 starts, and seemed reluctant to race on final one
(blinkered): bred to stay at least 1m. *M. W. Easterby.*

FLAIR PARK 5 b.m. Frimley Park 109–Follow The Brave 68 (Owen Anthony —
102) [1988 NR 1989 8d 8.5d 10f] tall, workmanlike mare: plating-class handicapper in
1987: well below his best, including in apprentice events, in spring as 5-y-o: stays 7f:
acts on firm going and a soft surface: has sweated. *D. T. Thom.*

FLAMBERGE 2 ch.f. (Mar 20) Kris 135–Valkyrie 87 (Bold Lad (IRE) 133) [1989 **63** 6m* 6g⁶] workmanlike filly: second foal: half-sister to 1987 2-y-o 6f to 1¼m winner Valentine (by Cure The Blues): dam, half-sister to smart middle-distance performer Sabre Dance, ran only at 2 yrs, winning over 5f: odds on but green, won moderately-run 4-runner maiden at Yarmouth in June by 2½ lengths from Change of Mood: ran as though something amiss, leading 4f then virtually pulled up, in minor event at Windsor month later: sold 11,000 gns Newmarket Autumn Sales. *H. R. A. Cecil.*

FLAMBOYANCE 2 b.f. (Apr 1) Exhibitioner 111–Mock Auction 55 (Auction — Ring (USA) 123) [1989 a6g] 5,600Y: small filly: fifth foal: half-sister to sprint winners (one at 2 yrs) by Krayyan and Taufan: dam out of half-sister to good stayer New Brig, ran only at 2 yrs: bit backward, well beaten in 13-runner maiden at Lingfield in November. *J. Ringer.*

FLAME OF ARAGON 3 ch.f. Aragon 118–Enlighten (Twilight Alley 133) [1988 — 6f 6f⁴ 6g⁶ 6m 7g 7m² 7f² 7m⁵ 1989 9d⁵ 12m⁴] close-coupled, angular filly: fairly useful plater at her best: well below form in spring as 3-y-o, held up and struggling (tending to hang) over 2f out then running on strongly inside last when fourth at Thirsk: evidently stays 1½m: acts on firm going and probably unsuited by a soft surface: ran freely in blinkers third start at 2 yrs: sold to join M. Naughton 2,600 gns Doncaster October Sales. *R. M. Whitaker.*

FLAMING GLORY 2 b.c. (May 21) Alzao (USA) 117–Engage (Whistling Wind **78** 123) [1989 6m⁵ 6m³ 7g* 8m² 9g] 31,000Y: stocky colt: seventh foal: half-brother to 4 winners, including quite useful sprinter African Lady (by African Sky) and Irish 9f winner Cluster of Diamond (by Ballad Rock): dam won from 5f to 1m in Ireland: won maiden at Sandown in July by 1½ lengths from Jebali: good second to Green's Leader in nursery there following month, much better effort: suited by 1m. *M. Bell.*

FLAMING GORGE 3 ch.c. Electric 126–Glory Isle 60 (Hittite Glory 125) [1988 — 7g 1989 12f 12f] leggy colt: towards rear in maidens and a claimer. *D. R. C. Elsworth.*

FLAMINGO POND 3 b.f. Sadler's Wells (USA) 132–Anegada 79 (Welsh **110** Pageant 132) [1988 7g³ 7.3s² 1989 10.5f⁴ 10.1m* 10m⁵ 10m* 10.2m³ 11s⁵] angular, sparely-made filly: successful in 22-runner minor event (making all) at Windsor in June and 4-runner £6,800 contest (sweating) at Newbury in August: third in moderately-run race at Newcastle, easily better effort in listed races after: saddle slipped third start: should be suited by further than 1¼m: best efforts on top-of-the-ground, though has fairly useful form on soft. *J. Tree.*

FLAMING TORCH 2 ch.f. (Mar 10) Rousillon (USA) 133–Flaming Peace (USA) **92 p** 64 (Lyphard (USA) 132) [1989 8g⁵ 8d*] second foal: half-sister to 3-y-o Peace King (by Adonijah): dam disappointing close relation to very smart middle-distance performers Quiet Fling and Peacetime and half-sister to Cambridgeshire winner Intermission: won maiden race at Maisons-Laffitte in September by ¾ length: will stay 1¼m. *A. Fabre, France.*

FLANAGAN 2 br.c. (Mar 16) Comedy Star (USA) 121–Bold Blue 82 (Targowice — (USA) 130) [1989 7m] 15,000Y: sixth foal: half-brother to useful 1¾m winner Cadmium (by Niniski) and 5.8f to 1½m winner Empire Blue (by Dominion): dam, half-sister to smart 1974 2-y-o Brer Rabbit, won over 1¼m: 33/1 and ridden by 7-lb claimer, soundly beaten in 17-runner maiden at Chepstow in October. *P. F. I. Cole.*

FLASHING SILKS 4 b.f. Kind of Hush 118–Hit The Line 71 (Saulingo 122) — [1988 12f 12g 8g 1989 15.5f 8f] workmanlike filly: has stringhalt: has a round action: of little account. *A. Moore.*

FLASH OF GENIUS 2 b.c. (Apr 17) Formidable (USA) 125–Lucent 117 (Irish — Ball (FR) 127) [1989 6m] 10,000Y: heavy-topped colt: half-brother to 1¼m winner Sonic Lord (by Final Straw) and winning hurdler Taxodium (by Sharpen Up): dam, daughter of good sprinter Cuslasland, smart winner at 1m to 1½m from 2 yrs to 4 yrs: very backward and green, slowly away and soon tailed off in maiden at Pontefract in August. *W. J. Pearce.*

FLEET FOOTED 6 b.h. Tachypous 128–More Or Less 64 (Morston (FR) 125) **46** [1988 9g 10f⁵ 11.5g 10.8g⁶ 9g* 1989 12f 8m 10m 10m* 8.5f³ 10g⁴ 10f³ 10g] close-coupled, quite attractive horse: moderate mover: poor handicapper: first form as 6-y-o when winning at Pontefract (apprentice ridden) in July: ideally suited by around 1¼m: suited by a sound surface: blinkered 3 times: sweating second outing: seems to need plenty of driving: winning selling hurdler. *Mrs G. R. Reveley.*

FLEETING BREEZE 3 b.f. Mr Fluorocarbon 126–Warm Wind 84 (Tumble — Wind (USA)) [1988 NR 1989 8s 10g 10f 8g] 37,000Y: sturdy, quite attractive filly: first reported foal: dam, half-sister to Yorkshire Oaks winners Sally Brown and

Untold and very useful performer at up to 1m Shoot Clear, won from 7f to 1¼m: no worthwhile form in maidens and a claimer but showed signs of ability second (swerved stalls) and third starts: tailed off on debut and after course 5 months after: bred to stay 1¼m. *M. J. Camacho.*

FLEET SPECIAL 7 gr.g. High Top 131–Rockney 84 (Roan Rocket 128) [1988   **68**
12f 10g 10f* 8.2g* 10f⁶ 10f 9f⁵ 10.5f⁵ 10m 10d 1989 10f 10h² 12h⁵ 8h² 10f³] lengthy, sparely-made gelding: modest handicapper: finds easy 1m on sharp side and stays 1¼m: suited by a sound surface: good mount for apprentice: usually wears a tongue strap: genuine: sold to join P. Monteith 4,800 gns Doncaster November Sales. *I. V. Matthews.*

FLIGHT HOSTESS 3 b.f. Seymour Hicks (FR) 125–No Flight (Nonoalco (USA))   **—**
131) [1988 5g 5g⁶ 6g⁶ 5g⁶ 1989 6f 5m 11f⁴ 8.2f³ 8g] sparely-made filly: poor walker and mover: poor maiden: has run in seller: will be suited by bit shorter than 11f: sold to join S. Dow 720 gns Doncaster August Sales. *J. S. Wilson.*

FLIGHTING MOON 4 gr.g. Moorestyle 137–Perlesse 88 (Bold Lad (USA))   **59**
[1988 6m 7f⁵ 7g 5m⁴ 6g 7.9d 10s 1989 8m² 6f⁵ 6g⁴ 6f* 7h² 7m⁶ 6g] tall, leggy ex-Irish gelding: has a quick action: third foal: half-brother to ungenuine sprinter Samleon (by Kind of Hush): dam 6f winner at 2 yrs: gambled-on co-favourite, won maiden claimer at Chepstow in July, quickening well to lead close home: best effort after when second, travelling well long way, in claimer at Brighton: will probably prove best at sprint distances: acts on hard going: blinkered second to fifth outings at 3 yrs: has carried head high and not found much under pressure: probably suited by extreme waiting tactics: not entirely reliable. *F. Jordan.*

FLIRTING 5 b.m. Free State 125–Mrs Palmer 88 (Martinmas 128) [1988 9g   **33**
10.1d⁵ 10d⁵ 10f⁴ 10g 8f* 8g⁵ 8.2d 1989 10m 8g 10m 10.8m⁴ 12m⁵ 12f⁴ 10f⁶ a11g] rather plain mare: poor plater: stays 1½m: acts on any going: blinkered once: has worn severe bridle: slowly away second and final starts. *J. Mulhall.*

FLITCHAM 2 b.f. (Jun 11) Elegant Air 119–Seldom (Rarity 129) [1989 6m]   **—**
4,000Y: small, close-coupled, angular filly: fifth foal: half-sister to Irish 1½m winner Great Alexandra (by Runnett) and 2 winners abroad: dam, poor Irish maiden, is half-sister to useful Irish 1983 2-y-o King Persian: 20/1, well beaten in maiden auction race at Newmarket in May. *W. J. Musson.*

FLOATING NOTE 4 ch.f. Music Boy 124–Red Crest 64 (Red God 128§) [1988   **— §**
6v⁵ 5m 5d 6g⁵ 6m⁶ 5f⁵ 6h⁶ 6m² 6g 6g 1989 6d 6m 5f 6f 7f 6m 8.5m 6m] leggy, close-coupled filly: poor maiden: virtually no form as 4-y-o: stays 6f: acts on top-of-the-ground and soft going: blinkered once, visored 4 times: has sweated, and often got on edge: unreliable. *J. S. Wainwright.*

FLOCKTON'S OWN 3 b.c. Electric 126–Tree Mallow 71 (Malicious) [1988 7s²   **98**
1989 8s² 10.5f⁶ 12g 12m³ 10m*] neat, quite attractive colt: useful performer: second favourite and visored, won Newmarket maiden in early-August: outpaced then stayed on well when 8 lengths sixth of 7 in William Hill Dante Stakes at York: looking very well, well beaten in Ever Ready Derby (visored) and below form in minor event at Newmarket in between: should be very well suited by 1½m: probably acts on any going. *J. R. Shaw.*

FLOOD MARK 5 ch.g. High Line 125–Crystal Fountain (Great Nephew 126)   **—**
[1988 10g 14d 8g 12f⁵ 14g 1989 10g 10m 10f 8h] big, deep-girthed gelding: no form in minor event or handicaps (last selling) since winning maiden as 3-y-o: stays 1½m: bandaged off-hind in 1988. *R. J. Hodges.*

FLOOSE 5 b.h. Ballad Rock 122–Carnival Dance 69 (Welsh Pageant 132) [1988   **—**
NR 1989 8g 8m] lengthy, quite attractive horse: quite useful winner as 3-y-o: ran as if something amiss both races at 5 yrs, first one a seller: suited by 7f: has won on a soft surface, but best form on top-of-the-ground: bandaged at 5 yrs. *M. L. W. Bell.*

FLORAFORD 3 b.g. Stanford 121§–Floraventure 89 (Floribunda 136) [1988 NR   **—**
1989 10s] 7,000F, 7,000Y: half-brother to several winners, including useful Irish 5f performer Solo Venture (by Sing Sing): dam sprinting half-sister to Italian Oaks winner Claire Valentine: 33/1, backward and green, soon well behind in maiden at Leicester in April. *Ronald Thompson.*

FLORA MAY 5 ch.m. Connaught 130–China Girl 76 (Shantung 132) [1988 NR   **47**
1989 8.2g⁵ 6m⁶ 6g 7d] big, lengthy, plain mare: gave indications of a little ability on first 2 outings in autumn: sweating badly and taken early to post second start. *P. D. Cundell.*

FLORET 5 b.m. Monsanto (FR) 121–Royal Declaration 78 (Breeders Dream 116)   **—**
[1988 7f⁶ 9g² 10d 8d 10f⁴ 10g 10g³ 8f² 10d 12d² 8m 1989 10d⁵ 10s⁶ 10f 8f 12.2f]

smallish, angular, leggy mare: poor maiden: no worthwhile form as 5-y-o: stays
1½m: acts on any going: trained first 3 outings by Pat Mitchell. *I. Campbell.*

FLORIDA GOLD   2 b.c. (Feb 11) Hard Fought 125–Klairelle (Klairon 131) [1989   **51**
6m⁵ 7f⁵ 7m⁴ 7m² 7f³ 8g 8g 6m 8.2s] IR 1,500Y, 3,000 2-y-o, resold 7,000 2-y-o:
compact colt: moderate mover: third foal: brother to Belgian 3-y-o winner Hardiela,
and half-brother to 15.5f and 2m winner Lurex Girl (by Camden Town): dam, placed
at 5f to 1m in Ireland, is sister to Baudelaire, smart performer at up to 1m: fair plater:
ran moderately last 4 starts: should be suited by 1m: bandaged behind seventh start:
has run creditably for 7-lb claimer: trained first 7 outings by R. Simpson. *D. A.
Wilson.*

FLORIDA SECRET   2 b.c. (May 7) Miami Springs 121–Close Secret 80   **57**
(Reliance II 137) [1989 6m 6m² 7g*] 3,000F, 800Y: sparely-made colt: half-brother
to winners in Hungary and Canada, latter stakes placed: dam late-developing stayer:
favourite and bandaged, made all in 3-runner seller (bought in 5,000 gns) at
Yarmouth in July: will stay at least 1m: has swished tail under pressure: slowly away
second start. *J. Pearce.*

FLOWER DEW LANE   3 gr.f. Kalaglow 132–Temple Wood 105 (Sweet   —
Revenge 129) [1988 7g 10.2m 1989 12.5f⁴ 14f⁶ 17.6f⁵] big, long-backed filly: quite
modest maiden: not seen out after running poorly (flashing tail under pressure) in
July: probably stays 1¾m: swished tail repeatedly in paddock and gave trouble at
stalls on reappearance. *R. Hollinshead.*

FLOWER GIRL   2 ch.f. (Jan 30) Pharly (FR) 130–Dancing Meg (USA) 113   **85**
(Marshua's Dancer (USA)) [1989 6f* 7g³ 6g] 41,000Y: good-topped, robust filly: has
plenty of scope: third foal: half-sister to 3-y-o Jahzeen (by Shareef Dancer) and fair
12.3f winner Please Kenneh (by Golden Fleece): dam won at 6f and 1m at 2 yrs and
later stayed 1½m: odds on, won maiden at Redcar in August by 4 lengths: good
staying-on third of 8 to Va Toujours in Oh So Sharp Stakes at Newmarket in
October, better subsequent effort: will be better suited by 1m. *H. Thomson Jones.*

FLOWER GODDESS   3 b.f. Gorytus (USA) 132–Star of Andros (FR) (Habitat   —
134) [1988 NR 1989 8.5f 8m 12g 7g] leggy, quite good-topped filly: moderate walker:
poor mover: second foal: closely related to fair middle-distance maiden Galactic
Hero (by Ile de Bourbon): dam lightly-raced daughter of half-sister to Malinowski,
Gielgud and dam of El Gran Senor: probably of little account: visored second start
(subsequently sold out of J. W. Watts's stable 2,000 gns Newmarket July Sales) and
blinkered final one. *I. Campbell.*

FLOWERY   3 gr.f. Kind of Hush 118–Red Rose Bowl (Dragonara Palace (USA)   —
115) [1988 5g⁴ 1989 6s⁴ 6f] quite good-topped filly: fourth in maidens at Newmarket
(in April 1988) and Nottingham: unruly in preliminaries and ran poorly in similar
event at Hamilton in May: stays 6f: possibly unsuited by firm going: split pastern
after debut. *B. W. Hills.*

FLUTE ROYALE   3 b.f. Horage 124–Royal Nell (King's Leap 111) [1988 5g³ 5g²   **61**
5f* 6s⁴ 5d³ 6d 7m⁶ 1989 5d⁴ 7m 6m³] workmanlike filly: carries condition:
moderate walker and mover: third of 23 at Nottingham in May, easily best effort in
handicaps: speedy, and likely to prove best at sprint distances: acts on a firm surface
and unsuited by very soft going: has reportedly suffered hairline fracture. *R. M.
Whitaker.*

FLYAWAY (FR)   4 ch.c. Touching Wood (USA) 127–Flying Sauce 107 (Sauce   **67**
Boat (USA)) [1988 8g 10.1d³ 10m* 11g 10g³ 10g⁶ 12m⁶ 12g⁴ 12g² 10d 11s 1989 12g⁵
12s³ 12f⁴ 18f⁵ 12.3m⁶ 16.5m⁶ 12s 14g⁵ 12.4g⁵ a12g³] lengthy colt: carries condition:
poor walker and mover: modest handicapper on his day: should stay 1¾m: not at his
best on firm going and well suited by an easy surface: blinkered final 4 outings as
3-y-o: bought out of N. Tinkler's stable 3,400 gns Newmarket Autumn Sales after
ninth outing: a difficult ride: winning hurdler. *J. L. Harris.*

FLY BY KNIFE   3 ch.f. Kris 135–Daring Lass 87 (Bold Lad (IRE) 133) [1988 6m*   **96**
8f 7d* 1989 8s⁶ 10f⁵ 10f³ 12g⁴ 12m² 13.3m 12s⁵] tall, rather angular filly, bit
unfurnished: good mover: fairly useful handicapper: ran well first 5 starts, keeping
on well when second in £7,300 event at Kempton: took keen hold and below form
last 2 outings, sweating and on toes before £20,400 contest on first of them: stays
1½m: acts on any going. *M. R. Stoute.*

FLYING   3 b.f. Head For Heights 125–Pine (Supreme Sovereign 119) [1988 8m²   **73**
1989 10s⁶ 12.5f³ 12f³ 13.1m⁴ 16f⁶ 12g³ 10.6g] leggy, close-coupled filly: poor mover,
with a markedly round action: modest maiden: stays 13f: possibly unsuited by soft
ground: sold to join R. Manning 7,000 gns Newmarket Autumn Sales. *Major W. R.
Hern.*

FLYING BRIGADIER 3 b.c. Brigadier Gerard 144–Farsound 79 (Wolver —
Hollow 126) [1988 7m⁴ 7g 8.2m 1989 10.6g 16.2m] sparely-made colt: turns fore feet
out: well beaten in varied events, appearing to finish lame in handicap final start:
bred to stay 1½m: takes keen hold: sold 675 gns Ascot November Sales. *B. A.
McMahon.*

FLYING DIVA 2 b.f. (Feb 6) Chief Singer 131–Flying Fantasy (Habitat 134) 89 p
[1989 6g* 7g*] 54,000Y: medium-sized, good-quartered filly: has scope: third foal:
half-sister to 3-y-o Fanille (by Top Ville): dam sister to Flying Water: won minor
events at York (by length from Miss Java) and Carlisle (by head from Minimize) in
October: may well stay 1m and improve again. *B. W. Hills.*

FLYING JUNCTION 3 ch.g. Burslem 123–Windy City (Windjammer (USA)) —
[1988 5g 5g³ 7d⁶ 6m 6m⁴ 7m⁵ 8f 6d 1989 7s 7f 11.7f⁶ 10.8m] leggy, workmanlike
gelding: modest maiden at best: little form for some time: best form over 6f on
top-of-the-ground: blinkered final start at 2 yrs: trained until after second as 3-y-o
by R. Hannon. *J. S. King.*

FLYING MONARCH 2 b.c. (Apr 24) Tender King 123–Flying Melody (Auction 59
Ring (USA) 123) [1989 5d³ 5g²] IR 8,000F, IR 4,000Y: leggy, angular colt: fourth
foal: half-brother to fair 1987 2-y-o 5f and 6f winner Mere Melody (by Dunphy):
dam, Irish 5.5f and 6.5f winner, is half-sister to several useful performers: placed in minor
event at Catterick and seller (retained 12,000 gns) at Doncaster in March: will be
better suited by 6f: sold privately to race in Italy. *M. Brittain.*

FLYING PHEASANT 3 b.f. Balliol 125–Partridge 65 (Mossborough 126) [1988 —
5d⁶ 1989 7.5d 8f 11.5m 15.3m] small, sturdy filly: no form in sellers and a maiden:
sold 1,000 gns Newmarket September Sales. *D. T. Thom.*

FLYING ROOFER 3 b.f. Jester 119–Forest Glen (Tarqogan 125) [1988 5m⁵ — §
1989 8m⁴ 6g 6m 7m 10f] smallish, quite well-made filly: has shown more temperament than ability. *D. Haydn Jones.*

FLYING STEEL 4 b.g. Skyliner 117–Trusian (Milesian 125) [1988 7s 8m 45
8h 1989 10.8m⁵ 11f*] small gelding: apprentice ridden, won 6-runner handicap
at Redcar (reportedly finished lame) in June: stays 11f: acts on firm going. *R.
Hollinshead.*

FOLK DANCE 7 b.g. Alias Smith (USA)–Enchanting Dancer (FR) (Nijinsky 76
(CAN) 138) [1988 12m³ 16m* 20f 16f⁵ 14g² 16g⁴ 12f⁵ 16f⁵ 1989 16s³ 16s* 14s³ 14g⁴
14g 12f³ 18g⁶] big, strong, quite attractive gelding: modest handicapper: won
moderately-run event at Newbury in April: 28/1 and facing stiffish task, good sixth
of 21 finishers, running on well final 3f, to Double Dutch in Tote Cesarewitch
(Handicap) at Newmarket: stays well: acts on any going: usually visored nowadays:
has won for apprentice: none too enthusiastic and best covered up: has a turn of
foot: winning jumper. *G. B. Balding.*

FOLLIDAYS (FR) 2 b.c. (Mar 20) Gay Mecene (USA) 128–Elezinha (FR) 110
(Tourangeau (FR) 99) [1989 7d³ 7.5d* 8g* 8g⁴] half-brother to very smart French
7f to 1¼m winner Mille Balles (by Mill Reef) and 2 minor middle-distance winners:
dam, half-sister to very smart French 1m to 1½m performer Solicitor, was smart
winner from 4f to 7.5f: very useful colt: successful in maiden race at Deauville and
listed Prix Herod at Evry: best effort over 2 lengths fourth of 8 to Funambule in Prix
des Chenes at Saint-Cloud: will stay 1¼m. *J-M. Beguigne, France.*

FOLLOW THAT TAXI 3 b.f. Dublin Taxi–Arkengarthdale (Sweet Story 122) 32
[1988 6d⁵ 6g 5g 1989 5g⁶ 6f 6m 7f 9m³ 8h 8f³ᵈⁱˢ 12f⁶ 12f 10f 7g 9s] close-coupled,
leggy filly: moderate walker and mover: poor form at best, including in sellers:
should prove best at up to 1m: pulls hard. *N. Bycroft.*

FOLLOW THE DRUM 4 b.g. Daring March 116–Pretty Miss (So Blessed 130) 54
[1988 8f 8f 7.5f² 7f* 7.5s⁴ 8f⁴ 7f 7f 8m 8.5f⁵ 8g 1989 10m 10.8m² 10m* 10h⁶ 10f³ 10f
10g a12g⁴] tall, leggy gelding: has a long, rather round action: plating-class
handicapper: won at Leicester in June: best subsequent effort when third in
uncompetitive race at Chepstow: likely to prove best at up to 1¼m: probably acts on
any going: visored twice at 3 yrs: suitable mount for apprentice: hung left at
Lingfield fourth outing: sold 10,000 gns Newmarket Autumn Sales. *J. D. Bethell.*

FOLLOW THE SEA 3 b.c. Tumble Wind (USA)–Seapoint (Major Point) [1988 73
6f 8d³ 9g³ 8d⁴ 1989 6v³ 5v 10f 8g 8m⁶ 8m 9m 8.2g] sturdy, lengthy colt: first
reported living foal: dam Irish 7f and 1m winner: modest maiden: trained until after
second outing by R. Connolly in Ireland: best effort in Britain when sixth at
Newbury: ran poorly in handicaps after: stays 1m: acts on top-of-the-ground and
heavy going: hung right fourth start. *R. Akehurst.*

322

FOLLY FOOT   3 b.c. Hotfoot 126–Stuff And Nonsense 86 (Crooner 119) [1988 **111**
6g³ 7m² 7g* 7d* 7.6s* 1989 7g² 7.2s² 8d⁶ 10.8m² 8g³] lengthy, workmanlike colt:
moderate mover with a rather round action: very useful performer: second in
Ladbroke European Free Handicap at Newmarket (to Danehill) and listed race at
Haydock (to Beau Sher) in April: best effort after when fair staying-on third of 6 to
Rain Burst in £7,100 event at Kempton early in September: should stay at least 1m:
gives impression ill at ease on top-of-the-ground: races with plenty of enthusiasm:
sold 66,000 gns Newmarket Autumn Sales to race in Singapore, but reportedly
failed by vet. *R. F. Johnson Houghton.*

FOND KISS   4 b.f. Young Generation 129–Firente 85 (Firestreak 125) [1988   —
8.2v² 8d* 9m⁶ 8g⁵ 9g⁵ 8.2g⁴ 8d³ 9g* 8d² 10g⁴ 9f 1989 9d 10s 10s⁶ 9f 10m 8m 8.2d
9.2d⁵ 7.6m] workmanlike, rather angular filly: modest winner (including for
apprentice) as 3-y-o when trained by S. Norton: little show in handicaps and claimer
in 1989: stays 1¼m: best with a bit of give in the ground (possibly unsuited by very
soft going): sold 3,200 gns Newmarket Autumn Sales. *C. A. Cyzer.*

FONTAINE LADY   2 b.f. (Mar 14) Millfontaine 114–Lady Begorra (Roi Soleil   —
125) [1989 5f⁶ 5.8f⁶] IR 1,000Y: leggy filly: good walker: fourth reported foal: dam
unraced: well beaten in summer minor events: bred to be suited by further. *E. A.
Wheeler.*

FOOLISH BEHAVIOUR   3 b.f. Dominion 123–Indulgence 83 (Prominer 125)   **85**
[1988 5m 5f* 6f 7s³ 7g* 7f⁶ 8v² 8.2d* 7m 1989 10.4f 10.6g 8.5g⁶ 9g⁶ 8d 10g]
close-coupled, workmanlike filly: fair performer: ridden by 5-lb claimer, easily best
effort as 3-y-o in £8,000 handicap at York on fourth start, first for 3 months: should
be suited by 1¼m: acts on any going but is most effective with some give: tends to
get behind early: sold 13,000 gns Newmarket December Sales. *S. G. Norton.*

FOOLISH TOUCH   7 b.g. Hot Spark 126–Nushka (Tom Fool) [1988 6g⁶ 6g* 6f²   **78**
6f 7d 6g 6m 6g² 6s³ 6s 6d 6g* 7m 1989 6v 7d⁶ 6g⁵ 7m* 6m 7m⁵ 7m³ 6m³ 6m 7m 6v⁴
7g] lengthy gelding: poor walker: fair handicapper: won for fifth time at Newmarket
when beating Vanroy a neck in May: ideally suited by strong gallop at 6f and stays 7f:
acts on any going: ran freely when blinkered: often visored, but wasn't after third
outing: sometimes sweats: has run well for apprentice: has started very slowly:
tends to wander under pressure and is suited by exaggerated waiting tactics. *W. J.
Musson.*

FOOTPATH   2 ch.g. (Mar 22) Final Straw 127–Troyenne 81 (Troy 137) [1989 6s   —
6d] 6,400Y: first foal: dam 1¾m winner, is half-sister to Knockando: well beaten in
autumn maidens at Ayr and Catterick. *J. Berry.*

FOOT PATROL   8 br.g. Daring March 116–Molly Polly (Molvedo 137) [1988 8d   —
8.5m* 8g² 10f⁶ 9m* 10g² 8g⁴ 10.2g² 9f⁴ 9d 1989 8g] shallow-girthed gelding:
modest winner as 7-y-o: always behind on only outing (March) in 1989: effective at
1m and stays 1½m: acts well on top-of-the-ground: has worn blinkers, but not for
some time: suitable mount for apprentice: usually held up. *N. Tinkler.*

FOOT SOLDIER   2 b.c. (Feb 7) Hotfoot 126–Gunnard 62 (Gunner B 126) [1989   **52**
5m⁴ 6m 6m 7g⁵ 8f 8g⁶] 10,500Y: workmanlike, sparely-made colt: third foal:
half-brother to 3-y-o 1½m seller winner Innovator (by Relkino): dam won 1m and
1¼m sellers: fair plater: looked of unsatisfactory temperament on fifth start,
flashing tail and seeming none too keen: should stay 1¼m: one to be bit wary of. *Mrs
J. R. Ramsden.*

FOOTSTOOL   6 b.m. Artaius (USA) 129–Footway 97 (Sovereign Path 125) [1988   **45**
10g³ 8d³ 10g 10g 8g 8m 8.2s³ 10g⁶ 12.2d⁴ 12d⁵ 12v⁵ 1989 10.2g⁵ 10d* 10s* 12s 10m
10f* 10g⁴ 10g⁵ 10g⁵ 10m 10f 10f⁶ 11s⁴ 10.6m⁶] close-coupled mare: carries plenty of
condition: poor mover: successful in 3 handicaps at Folkestone, in selling events
(bought in 2,000 gns and 3,600 gns) in April and amateurs contest in July: better
suited by 1¼m than 1½m: acted on any going: tried in blinkers, a visor and a hood,
but not as 6-y-o: occasionally sweated: occasionally wore bandages: good mount for
inexperienced rider: in foal to Aragon. *D. A. Wilson.*

FOOT THE BILL   4 b.g. Tachypous 128–Currency (Crepello 136) [1988 10m²   **73**
10g* 10.1m⁵ 16f 16d³ 16.1m 1989 12.2s* 12.3s 14g⁶ 14g⁶] tall, workmanlike gelding:
had operation on knee as 3-y-o: won handicap at Warwick in March: below form
afterwards: best efforts at up to 1½m: acts on top-of-the-ground and soft going:
slowly away final start: usually forces pace: has given trouble at stalls. *R. F. Johnson
Houghton.*

FOR ACTION (USA)   4 ch.f. Assert 134–Battlewind (USA) 113 (Restless Wind)   **93**
[1988 10d⁵ 11f² 12m* 13.3g⁶ 12m⁶ 14f 18.1m² 16m⁴ 19g² 1989 17.1m* 19f* 20f⁴ 16g⁶
16m² 19f⁴ 18f² 16m² 16g⁶] strong, deep-girthed filly: fairly useful handicapper:

always close up when winning at Bath and Goodwood in spring: ran well after when in frame in competitive events, on final occasion second of 10 to Double Dutch in £9,500 race at Ascot: suited by thorough test of stamina: acts well on firm going: visored final outing at 3 yrs: usually gets on toes and sweats: genuine and consistent. *J. W. Hills.*

FOR A WHILE 3 ch.f. Pharly (FR) 130–Baby's Smile 68 (Shirley Heights 130) **51 §** [1988 NR 1989 8.5m 11.3f4 16f4 12m2 15.3g* 12g 15.3f] 2,000Y: leggy, sparely-made filly: has a markedly round action: first foal: dam suited by good test of stamina: favourite and reluctant to go down, won seller (bought in 4,250 gns) at Wolverhampton in September easing down by 8 lengths: behind in handicaps after, sweating and edgy facing stiff task final start: stays well: possibly suited by an easy surface: sold 2,200 gns Newmarket Autumn Sales: not one to trust implicitly. *C. A. Cyzer.*

FORBES SPIRIT (USA) 4 b.f. Bold Forbes (USA)–Hasty Viento (USA) — (Gallant Man) [1988 8g4 8f 8g 12.2g4 11s2 12.2m4 10.2g* 10g5 10m 10m 9s 1989 12.5f] lengthy, good-bodied filly: tubed: quite modest winner as 3-y-o: no subsequent form: suited by about 1¼m: acted on soft going: visored twice at 2 yrs: dead. *P. Howling.*

FORBIDDEN CITY (NZ) 2 b.c. (Jan 22) Babaroom (USA)–The Empress (NZ) **52** (Imperialist (USA)) [1989 7g a7g] angular colt: New Zealand bred: over 7 lengths eighth of 13 to Erik Odin in maiden at Lingfield in November: needed race on debut. *J. R. Jenkins.*

FOR BILLY 6 b.g. Lord Ha Ha 116–Rare Blue (Rarity 129) [1988 NR 1989 11.5m] — 2,400 6-y-o: small ex-Irish gelding: third foal: dam behind on only outing: 66/1, tailed off from halfway in amateurs maiden at Yarmouth in July. *R. Curtis.*

FORCELLO (USA) 6 b.g. Forli (ARG)–Heavenly Bow (USA) (Gun Bow) [1988 **37** 10.4s6 10d 11.5g6 10f 9m4 10m 9g 8.2d2 9g2 8g 10s3 1989 10s3 8d] strong, good-bodied gelding: has a quick action: poor handicapper: well-backed favourite for selling event on reappearance: best at 1m to 1¼m: probably not at his best on firm going, acts on any other: visored once at 5 yrs: well served by forcing tactics: occasionally sweats: has run creditably for apprentice: inconsistent. *D. Burchell.*

FORD KING 2 b.f. (Apr 24) Sandhurst Prince 128–Douala (GER) (Pentathlon) **50** [1989 5g 7m 6g 7d4 7g3] sparely-made, leggy filly: fifth foal: half-sister to Irish 1½m and 13f winner Priscillian (by Runnett) and a winner over jumps in France: dam won at 3 yrs in Germany: ran well in seller at Catterick and non-selling nursery at Edinburgh on last 2 starts: will stay 1m. *M. O'Neill.*

FOREIGN ASSET (USA) 3 b.c. Nijinsky (CAN) 138–Bon Debarras (CAN) **98** (Ruritania (USA)) [1988 7g2 1989 12f* 14g 14f2 16m2 16f* 14f* 14g6] well-made, good sort: carries condition: moderate walker and mover: won maiden at Salisbury in May then slowly-run 4-runner handicap (odds on) at Thirsk and £12,000 handicap (by ¾ length from Out of Funds) at York in August: favourite, not discredited facing stiffish task final start: stays 2m: possibly best on top-of-the-ground: sold 38,000 gns Newmarket Autumn Sales. *G. Harwood.*

FOREIGN CURRENCY 2 b.g. (Mar 31) Electric 126–Tekatrack 81 (Track **57** Spare 125) [1989 5v4 5d2 6m5 6g 7.5g4 8g2 8s3] workmanlike, angular gelding: half-brother to Irish 1¼m winner Emma's Double (by Double Form): dam lightly-raced 2-y-o 5f winner: quite useful plater: ran well in blinkers last 2 starts: suited by 1m: sometimes edgy, and once got loose from stalls: dead. *M. H. Easterby.*

FORESHADOWING (USA) 3 ch.f. Linkage (USA)–Old Gypsy (USA) (Olden **81 ?** Times) [1988 NR 1989 12f2 11f4 12.2g4] good-topped, quite attractive filly: half-sister to smart 6f and 1¼m winner Zinzara (by Stage Door Johnny), and to 3 minor winners in USA: dam stakes winner at up to 1m: sire won at up to 9f: in frame in northern maidens, on first 2 starts hanging and giving strong impression unsuited by firm going: however, soundly beaten (weakening quickly 3f out) final outing: one to treat with caution. *J. W. Watts.*

FOREST BLAZE (USA) 3 ch.f. Green Forest (USA) 134–Akita (USA) — (Restless Native) [1988 5g6 5d 6g* 1989 8f 7m 8f4] small, lengthy filly: modest winner as 2-y-o: ridden by 5-lb claimer, well beaten in handicaps and minor event in 1989: tailed off second start and off course 4 months after: should stay beyond 6f: seems unsuited by top-of-the-ground: sold 19,000 gns Newmarket December Sales. *I. A. Balding.*

FOREST FAWN (FR) 4 b. or br.f. Top Ville 129–Red Deer (FR) (Kirkland **51** Lake) [1988 NR 1989 10.1m2 12f2 12h5 11.5f 13.4m6 10.2f5 10g6 a10g6] medium-sized, rather sparely-made filly: half-sister to several winners in France, including 9f to 10.5f winner My Moose (by Carmarthen): dam French 11f winner: plating-class maiden: stays 1¼m. *C. P. Wildman.*

FOREST MONARCH (USA)   3 b.g. Green Forest (USA) 134–Uncommitted   — (USA) 101 (Buckpasser) [1988 NR 1989 8m 8m 8m 8m] lengthy, tall, good-topped gelding: has scope: sixth foal: half-brother to useful 1983 French 2-y-o 6f winner Ruby Green (by J O Tobin), useful French 1¼m winner Florenza (by Wajima) and very smart American horse Wavering Monarch (by Majestic Light): dam, 2-y-o 7f winner in France, is half-sister to dam of Posse: modest maiden: ran moderately last 2 starts: will stay beyond 1m: tongue tied down first 3 starts. *M. Moubarak.*

FOREVER DIAMONDS   2 ch.c. (Apr 20) Good Times (ITY)–Mel Mira 68 (Roi   **58** Soleil 125) [1989 5v 5d* 5f6] leggy, rather sparely-made colt: second foal: dam won 7f and 8.2f sellers: won seller (retained 11,200 gns) at Beverley in April by 2 lengths from Dunstar: creditable sixth to Croft Imperial in Ayr minor event 2 months later: will be suited by 6f. *J. S. Wilson.*

FOREVER MORE   2 gr.c. (May 22) Magic Mirror 105–Silette 84 (Siliconn 121)   **53** [1989 5m3 5h5 6m 6g] 4,000Y, 7,800 2-y-o: angular, sparely-made colt: seventh foal: half-brother to 3 winners, including 1983 2-y-o 7f winner Anything Else (by Absalom): dam top-of-the-ground 1¼m performer: plating-class form: best effort on debut: sold 2,600 gns Doncaster October Sales. *J. J. O'Neill.*

FOREVER TINGO   7 ch.g. Evertingo 84–September Sal (Ritudyr 113) [1988 NR   — 1989 8.5g 7f] big, rather sparely-made gelding: poor mover: poor maiden: stays 11f: acts on top-of-the-ground: has run creditably for apprentice: sold 1,300 gns Doncaster October Sales. *C. R. Beever.*

FORGE BEAU   4 b.g. Swing Easy (USA) 126–Korresia (Derring-Do 131) [1988   **34** NR 1989 8m 5f 7m5 8f 7g 7g3 8f] lengthy, angular gelding: poor plater: didn't look keen under pressure sixth outing. *G. Blum.*

FORLIANN   2 ch.f. (Feb 14) Posse (USA) 130–Smurfiusa (USA) (Sharpen Up 127)   — [1989 5g] 5,400Y: first foal: dam won in Italy, including in listed company: well beaten in 17-runner seller at Beverley in May: sold 720 gns Doncaster June Sales. *N. Tinkler.*

FORMATION   3 b.g. Tanfirion 110–Imagination (FR) (Dancer's Image (USA))   **65** [1988 6d5 6g 7f 8m 8s 1989 8s 12.2m3 13.8m* 11f3 16.2g 13.8g2 18m3 16m5 13.8g5 13.8d] workmanlike gelding: moderate walker and mover: quite modest handicapper: won at Catterick in June: stays 2¼m: suited by a sound surface: has run creditably for apprentice. *E. Weymes.*

FORMIDABLE TASK   2 ch.f. (May 2) Formidable (USA) 125–Light O'Battle   **61** 97 (Queen's Hussar 124) [1989 5f 6f5] 18,000Y: half-sister to 3-y-o 10.2f winner Height O'Battle (by Shirley Heights), fairly useful sprinter Lobbit (by Habitat) and winning hurdler Lobric (by Electric): dam, winner over 7f from 2 starts at 2 yrs, is sister to 1000 Guineas and Prix de Diane winner Highclere: around 2½ lengths fifth of 10 to In Excess in maiden at Lingfield in October, better effort: should stay further: sold to join Miss S. Hall 17,500 gns Doncaster November Sales. *I. V. Matthews.*

FORMIDARE   3 b.c. Formidable (USA) 125–Vadrouille (USA) 111 (Foolish   — Pleasure (USA)) [1988 5d4 5d5 5g 6g 6m6 7.3m4 8g5 7d5 8d 1989 10s] leggy, useful-looking colt: has a round action: quite modest maiden: well beaten in handicap in March on only outing in 1989, set plenty to do in moderately-run race: stays 1m: likely to prove suited by an easy surface: has run moderately for an apprentice: sold 760 gns Newmarket Autumn Sales. *S. Dow.*

FOR NOTHING   4 gr.c. Bay Express 132–Flitterdale 81 (Abwah 118) [1988 8d   **52** 8.5m5 8g 7d3 7.5s5 7m3 7f 8s3 8g6 8m2 1989 10d4 10d 9g 8.2g 8.5f] good-bodied, workmanlike colt: modest maiden at his best: little worthwhile form in 1989: probably stays 1¼m: acts on top-of-the-ground and soft going: blinkered once at 3 yrs: sold 6,200 gns Doncaster October Sales. *J. A. Glover.*

FOR REAL   2 ch.f. (Apr 7) Tina's Pet 121–Golden Decoy 73 (Decoy Boy 129)   **62** [1989 5g3 5f4 5f* 5m* 5m* 5m2dis 5m 5f3 6g2 6f4 6m* 6f5 5m] 4,000Y: small, good-quartered filly: first reported foal: dam 7f winner: quite modest performer: successful in sellers (no bid) at Thirsk in May and Redcar in September and claimers in between: ran creditably most other starts: stays 6f: usually wanders around: has sweated up: sold 3,200 gns Doncaster October Sales. *J. Berry.*

FORTAN PRINCE   2 b.c. (Apr 21) Burslem 123–Hark Hark 75 (Sing Sing 134)   **62** [1989 5f4 5f4 5h4 5f3 5f6 5g a5g] IR 8,700F, 17,000Y: lengthy colt: half-brother to 4 winners, including 1986 2-y-o 5f winner Sparsholt (by Miner's Lamp) and 7.6f and

1m winner Bounty Bay (by Pitcairn): dam disappointing: quite modest maiden: best effort fourth outing: will stay 6f: blinkered third start. *S. T. Harris.*

FORT DAUPHIN 3 b.c. Ile de Bourbon (USA) 133–Art Deco (Artaius (USA) 73 129) [1988 7m 7g⁴ 1989 12d² 12f] leggy, attractive colt: modest maiden: hung badly when claimer ridden first outing: worth a try over 1¼m: acts on a soft surface: not an easy ride: sold, probably to race in Singapore, 9,000 gns Newmarket Autumn Sales. *I. A. Balding.*

FORTETO 2 b.g. (Jan 24) Seymour Hicks (FR) 125–Finlandaise (FR) (Arctic 60 Tern (USA) 126) [1989 6g³ 7g² 7m⁴ 6g 7v³] IR 2,900F: sturdy gelding: moderate mover: second foal: brother to 1988 Irish 2-y-o 6f winner Ingmar: dam French 9f and 1m winner: quite modest form in maidens: will be suited by 1m: sold 6,000 gns Newmarket Autumn Sales. *N. Tinkler.*

FORT FLUTTER 3 b.f. Beldale Flutter (USA) 130–Shindella 104 (Furry Glen — 121) [1988 6g⁵ 1989 7f] tall, rather leggy, quite attractive filly: well beaten in valuable maiden at Ascot and July maiden at Kempton nearly 12 months later: sold 2,100 gns Newmarket December Sales. *I. A. Balding.*

FORTUNE'S KOP 2 b.f. (May 23) Anfield 117–Fortune's Fancy (Workboy 123) — [1989 7f⁵ 6d 6g] close-coupled, deep-girthed filly: fourth foal: half-sister to 3-y-o Ballafa and quite modest 6f winner Ballafort (both by Ballacashtal): dam daughter of very smart sprinter Polly Peachum: soundly beaten in maidens: blinkered and edgy final outing: sold 950 gns Ascot December Sales. *J. R. Bosley.*

FORULI 4 b.f. Last Fandango 125–Unbeknown 62 (Most Secret 119) [1988 10g 43 6m⁶ 8g 6g 1989 7g 6f 5f⁵ 5f⁵ 5f 5f 6f] lengthy filly: has a quick action: poor maiden: probably best at sprint distances: acts on firm going: blinkered & 4-y-o except on second outing: sweating fifth: has given trouble in preliminaries. *R. Voorspuy.*

FORVOLA (USA) 3 ch.f. Forli (ARG)–Frivole (FR) (Val de Loir 133) [1988 NR — 1989 7f] big, angular filly: half-sister to French 7.5f and 8.5f winner Mille Vols (by Mill Reef) and good 1977 French 2-y-o 6.5f winner Bilal (by King of The Castle), later successful at 1½m: dam unraced daughter of half-sister to the dam of Bustino: 33/1 and backward, no promise in maiden at Goodwood in May: wore tongue strap. *M. Moubarak.*

FOSSE GILL 2 b.f. (Feb 10) Night Shift (USA)–Gold Market (Hotfoot 126) [1989 64 5m 6m⁴ 6m⁴ 6g 6g⁶ 7g* 7g] 8,800Y: lengthy filly: has scope: fourth foal: half-sister to a winner in Sweden: dam ran once: quite modest performer: won claimer at Leicester in September by a short head from Bodge, leading at halfway and clear 2f out: stays 7f: visored last 2 starts: sold 2,100 gns Newmarket Autumn Sales: inconsistent: has refused to enter stalls, tends to flash tail and looks a hard ride. *A. N. Lee.*

FOSTERS FOLLY 3 gr.g. Petong 126–Dastina 80 (Derring-Do 131) [1988 6f 5m 57 5m 6f⁴ 6d 8m 1989 8s 8d 7f³ 8h⁴ 9f⁴ 10.6g 10f 10f⁴ 10.6s² 11g⁴] smallish, workmanlike gelding: moderate mover: plating-class maiden: worth a try over 1½m: suited by a sound surface: blinkered second (edgy, raced too freely in apprentice event) and eighth outings: visored in between and once at 2 yrs: sold to join J. Walmsley 9,600 gns Newmarket Autumn Sales. *S. G. Norton.*

FOUJITA (USA) 4 b.c. Tap Shoes (USA)–Ivory Smooth (USA) (Sir Ivor 135) — [1988 10.1m⁶ 10g 1989 12g 12s] lengthy, angular colt: modest winner at 2 yrs: lightly raced on flat nowadays: 33/1, soundly beaten in handicaps at Haydock in autumn: stays 1¼m: winning hurdler. *Miss S. J. Wilton.*

FOUNTAIN LOCH 2 b.f. (Mar 24) Lochnager 132–Fountain 90 (Reform 132) — [1989 6m 5g] 11,000Y: half-sister to 3 winners, notably very smart middle-distance performer Royal Fountain (by Royalty), and a winner over hurdles: dam, 2-y-o 5f winner, is half-sister to high-class French sprinter King of Macedon: well beaten in late-season seller (backward, very green) at Newmarket and maiden at Redcar. *R. M. Whitaker.*

FOUR ALLS LADY 3 b.f. Broadsword (USA) 104–Hazeldean 90 (St Paddy 133) — [1988 NR 1989 10f 9f] 820 2-y-o: lengthy, angular filly: second foal: half-sister to a poor hurdler: dam 1m and 1¼m winner also successful over hurdles: 100/1, tailed off in maiden (went down poorly) at Beverley and seller at Redcar in the summer. *J. S. Wainwright.*

FOUR AWAY 2 br.c. (Apr 9) Valiyar 129–Edwins' Princess 75 (Owen Dudley — 121) [1989 7g 7f 8m] 3,800F, 28,000Y: leggy, rather close-coupled colt: good walker: first foal: dam disappointing 2-y-o 5f winner who stayed 1m: no worthwhile form in maidens. *N. A. Callaghan.*

FOUR-LEGGED FRIEND 3 b.f. Aragon 118–Marista (Mansingh (USA) 120) **101**
[1988 5m² 5m* 5d* 1989 5f² 6f] small filly: successful in summer of 1988 in maiden
auction event at Goodwood and listed race at Newmarket: favourite, good second to
Tigani in minor event at Kempton, easily better effort in early-summer as 3-y-o:
likely to have proved best at sprint distances: acted on firm going and a soft surface:
refused to enter stalls intended debut: retired. *Dr J. D. Scargill.*

FOURSHOON 3 b.g. Stanford 121§–Haunting 79 (Lord Gayle (USA) 124) [1988 **56** d
5m⁶ 6m⁴ 6g⁵ 7g⁶ 1989 8.2s³ 10g 8g 9m 16m 10g] leggy gelding: quite modest
maiden: well below form after reappearance and not seen out after early-August:
stays 1m: acts on soft going: bandaged 4 times: sold 4,000 gns Ascot October Sales.
Mrs N. Macauley.

FOUR STAR THRUST 7 ch.m. Derrylin 115–Smiling 62 (Silly Season 127) **88** d
[1988 12m⁴diss 12m⁴ 12g* 12m³ 12f 12h* 12d 12m² 14f 14.8m⁵ 12m 1989 12.3f* 14m
12m 12m⁶ 12m⁵ 12f⁵ 12.3g⁶ 12m 12g⁵ 12d] workmanlike mare: poor mover: fair
handicapper: below her best after winning 5-runner event at Chester in May: suited
by 1½m: well suited by sound surface: occasionally sweats: not an easy ride, and
needs exaggerated waiting tactics: sold 10,500 gns Newmarket December Sales. *R.
M. Whitaker.*

FOURTH PROTOCOL 5 ch.g. Gay Fandango (USA) 132–Miss Golightly 83 —
(Jimmy Reppin 131) [1988 5s 10.8d 11.7f 8s 5.8f⁶ 7d 5.8g⁴ 6m 5.8d 1989 7g 7d]
workmanlike gelding: poor maiden judged on most form: saddle slipped and rider
unseated on reappearance: ideally needs further than 6f: blinkered or visored final 3
appearances in 1987: has worn a tongue strap. *L. G. Cottrell.*

FOURWALK 5 br.h. Godswalk (USA) 130–Vaunt (USA) (Hill Rise 127) [1988 5d⁶ **77**
5v⁴ 6m 5d 6f 5.6m 6s 6s 5s 5m 1989 5g 6f⁵ 6m⁴diss 6m 7f⁵ 6m* 6f² 6g² 6f 6m⁵
6m³ 5.6g] strong, close-coupled, plain horse: poor walker and bad mover: fair
handicapper nowadays: won for first time since early 1987 when making all at
Nottingham in June: stays 6f: acts on any going: visored twice, blinkered final outing
(not discredited): has worn tongue strap. *Mrs N. Macauley.*

FOX CHAPEL 2 b.g. (May 11) Formidable (USA) 125–Hollow Heart 89 (Wolver **70**
Hollow 126) [1989 6m 6m* 7g] 38,000Y: good-bodied gelding: has scope: fourth foal:
closely related to fairly useful 7f to 8.5f winner Aradu (by Posse) and half-brother to
3-y-o 7f winner Take Heart (by Tender King): dam, 5f winner at 2 yrs, is closely
related to smart middle-distance handicapper Royal Match: 2/1 on, made virtually all
in 3-runner maiden at Salisbury in June: ran well in 7f nursery at Newmarket nearly
4 months later: subsequently gelded. *R. Hannon.*

FOX PATH 5 b.g. Godswalk (USA) 130–Precious Egg (Home Guard (USA) 129) —
[1988 8.2v³ 8d 7g 5m 8f 8.3g 8.3m 6s* 6g 1989 5s 6d 8f a6g] small, sparely-made
gelding: successful in same October selling handicap at Hamilton at 3 yrs and 4 yrs:
very little other form: suited by 6f and plenty of give in the ground: sweating final
outing: inconsistent: winning selling hurdler. *F. Jordan.*

FOXTROT OSCAR 2 b.c. (May 22) Mummy's Game 120–Glint of Silver 69 **73**
(Sallust 134) [1989 5f* 6d³ 5g] 6,200Y, 15,500 2-y-o: robust colt: second foal:
half-brother to 1988 2-y-o 5f winner (including sellers) Petongs Weeyin (by
Petong): dam placed at 6f: won maiden auction event at Beverley in August: over 3
lengths third, hanging left and no extra last furlong having taken keen hold, to
Platonique in nursery at Haydock following month: wore brush pricker when
running as if something amiss final outing: stays 6f: on toes last 2 starts. *J. A. R.
Toller.*

FOXTROTTER 3 ch.f. Mansingh (USA) 120–Pipul 82 (Pitskelly 122) [1988 8m —
7g⁶ 1989 10.8f⁴ 15.3g 12.5f] tall, leggy, sparely-made filly: poor form, including in
sellers: may prove best short of 1¼m: mulish in paddock last 2 starts, blinkered and
mounted on track final one: bandaged behind second: sold 600 gns Ascot November
Sales. *D. W. P. Arbuthnot.*

FRAGRANT PARK 2 ch.f. (Mar 14) Gorytus (USA) 132–Park Lady 82 (Tap On **77** p
Wood 130) [1989 7m 8m³] 20,000Y: close-coupled, sparely-made, angular filly:
second foal: half-sister to 3-y-o Lady Tap (by Red Sunset), fairly useful 5f winner at
2 yrs: dam, 6f winner at 2 yrs, is daughter of half-sister to smart American horse
Point du Jour: backward, always-prominent third of 11, keeping on well, to Access
Sun in maiden auction race at York in October: changed hands 19,000 gns
Newmarket December Sales: will improve again. *J. W. Hills.*

FRANCIS FURNESS 2 b.f. (Mar 25) Burslem 123–Sodium's Niece **58**
(Northfields (USA)) [1989 6f⁴ 6m 7.5f 7m a7g⁴ a8g⁵] IR 1,200Y: leggy, rather
sparely-made filly: has a round action: second foal: dam, lightly raced, placed over

8.5f at 2 yrs in Ireland: quite modest maiden: easily best effort on fifth start: beaten in a seller previously when trained by J. H. Johnson. *Denys Smith.*

FRANK HARRIS 3 ch.g. Star Appeal 133–Sociable (Be Friendly 130) [1988 7g **70** 1989 10.4g² 10.6g³ 10m* 10m* 10m] strong, deep-girthed gelding: successful in summer in claimer (claimed out of H. Cecil's stable £21,550) at Newmarket and handicap (made most) at Yarmouth 12 days later: blinkered, edgy and sweating, ran poorly in handicap final start: stays 1¼m well: acts on top-of-the-ground: usually coltish, and was gelded after final start: game in the finish though clearly has mind of his own, needs a lot of driving and is hard ride. *R. Champion.*

FREDDIE'S STAR 2 b.c. (Mar 18) Tina's Pet 121–Wellington Bear (Dragonara **67** Palace (USA) 115) [1989 5s³ 5g⁴ 6f 6m 6f³ 7m² 7m⁶ 7m* 6g a8g] 3,000Y: leggy colt: third foal: half-brother to 3-y-o Suniram (by Marching On): dam never ran: quite modest performer: given good ride by 7-lb claimer D. Biggs when winning summer nursery at Newmarket: stays 7f: active sort, takes a keen hold: ran poorly once at Catterick. *R. A. Bennett.*

FREE AT LAST 2 b.f. (Feb 13) Shirley Heights 130–Brocade 121 (Habitat **101** p 134) [1989 5m² 6f² 7f* 7m* 7g*]

Unremitting improvement was the hallmark of Free At Last's first season which culminated in her going one better than her owner's Bequest the year before in the listed Somerville Tattersall Stakes at Newmarket. Unlike Bequest, whose first experience of racing it was, Free At Last lined up at Newmarket with four races and two wins behind her, having won her maiden at Salisbury the previous month. It was no real surprise that Free At Last had lost her first two races, which were over five and six furlongs: winners over sprint distances by Shirley Heights are exceedingly rare, and Free At Last was outpaced in the closing stages each time. The extra furlong at Salisbury was clearly to Free At Last's advantage: kept close to the pace by Clark, who partnered her in all her races, she took up the running two furlongs out and wasn't pressed unduly to hold Sajjaya by a length and a half. Later in September Free At Last took on Salsabil, who'd hardly had a race when successful in a maiden at Nottingham on her only previous start, in the Jock Collier Memorial Graduation Stakes at Newbury. The pair dominated the race as completely as they did the market, with Free At Last getting the better of an exciting tussle by a short head after they had drawn five lengths clear. The opposition facing Free At Last at Newmarket looked more exacting still (Salsabil, of course, hadn't been the force at Newbury that she was in the Marcel Boussac) and included Teleprompter's half-brother Message Pad, of

Somerville Tattersall Stakes, Newmarket—Free At Last wins narrowly from Qui Danzig

whom high hopes were held after his smooth defeat of Shavian in a minor event at Doncaster, and the Scottish Equitable Richmond runner-up Qui Danzig. Free At Last, who looked in excellent condition, maintained her improvement and was well up to the task. Soon close up in a race which was run in a moderate time as well as heavy drizzle, Free At Last was driven into the lead two furlongs out, went a length or so up emerging from the Dip and held on tenaciously as Qui Danzig whittled her advantage down to a neck at the line. The Somerville Tattersall Stakes is nearly always won by a useful horse (Salse and Opening Verse were its last two winners) and the neat, good-quartered Free At Last looks sure to progress and boost her winning tally as a three-year-old. Whether that tally will include the One Thousand Guineas, her immediate target and for which she was generally quoted at 25/1 at the time of writing, must be doubted: her form falls well short of the standard usually required and there are several fillies around with better credentials.

		Mill Reef	Never Bend
	Shirley Heights	(b 1968)	Milan Mill
	(b 1975)	Hardiemma	Hardicanute
Free At Last		(b 1969)	Grand Cross
(b.f. Feb 13, 1987)		Habitat	Sir Gaylord
	Brocade	(b 1966)	Little Hut
	(b 1981)	Canton Silk	Runnymede
		(gr 1970)	Clouded Lamp

Free At Last was bred by her owner Gerald Leigh at his Eydon Hall Farm Stud in Northamptonshire. She's the first foal of her dam Brocade, who showed smart form in the mid-'eighties over seven furlongs and a mile, winning five races over two seasons, including the Bisquit Cognac Challenge Stakes and the Prix de la Foret. Brocade is a daughter of the useful five-furlong performer Canton Silk. The latter has repaid her owner handsomely since he acquired her in 1973, and has bred seven winners in all. Three of them besides Brocade are at least useful; her full brother Cause Celebre, a winner over five furlongs at two and over a mile in the States at four, where he was sent after a disappointing second season here; the mile-and-a-quarter winner Organza; and the 1979 two-year-old sprinter Royal Pinnacle, who continued his racing career in France where he won at up to eight and a half furlongs. The third dam Clouded Lamp won four times at up to seven furlongs and produced several winners at stud, including the very useful sprint handicapper Irma Flintstone. Most of the family have stamina limitations, but with Shirley Heights as her sire Free At Last can be expected to stay a mile and a quarter. So far she's raced only on a sound surface; her trainer has been reported as saying that he doubts she'll be suited by very soft ground. *G. Harwood.*

FREEDOM 2 b.f. (May 9) Free State 125–Pied A Terre (Ribocco 129) [1989 5g 6m] 3,600Y: smallish, sparely-made filly: sister to French 1m and 1¼m winner Live With Me and half-sister to three 2-y-o winners here, including fair 1980 2-y-o 7f winner Salon Privee (by Dragonara Palace): dam lightly-raced daughter of sister to Reform: well beaten in maiden auction races at Salisbury and Newmarket in May. *J. Pearce.* —

FREE MINX 3 b.g. Free State 125–Musical Minx 75 (Jukebox 120) [1988 6s 6m⁶ 6s³ 1989 8g³ 8s 7m 11m 8g] sturdy, useful-looking gelding: quite modest maiden: ran moderately in handicaps and claimer after reappearance: not seen out after July: may prove best at 7f: needs an easy surface: blinkered final start at 2 yrs. *M. J. Camacho.* 60

FREE SKIP 5 b.m. Free State 125–Economy Pep 69 (Jimmy Reppin 131) [1988 18v 16g 16m⁵ 16g⁵ 16f 16g* 16g 16m⁶ 1989 14s 18s* 16.2g³ 17.6m³ 18m²] leggy mare: quite modest handicapper: 11/2 from 10/1, won at Nottingham in May by 5 lengths: good second of 10, keeping on gamely, at Ripon (appeared to be walking feelingly afterwards) in August: suited by a thorough test of stamina: unsuited by firm going, acts on any other: sweating and swished tail in paddock third start: genuine. *P. S. Felgate.* 58

FREE STYLE 3 b.f. Liberated 85–Coquet Lass (Bing II) [1988 NR 1989 8.2g 7s] first reported foal: dam non-thoroughbred: well behind in maiden (50/1) at Hamilton and minor event (150/1) at Ayr in September. *M. P. Naughton.* —

FREE SWEATER (USA) 3 br.c. Summing (USA)–Chichibam (USA) **116**
(Chichester (USA)) [1988 7m⁴ 7g³ 8s³ 1989 10.4f* 12m 16f⁴ 12m⁴ 12m² 12v]
good-topped, quite attractive colt: moderate mover, with a rather round action:
smart performer: won listed Dee Stakes at Chester in May, making virtually all:
25/1, showed improved form when 1½ lengths second of 17 to Braashee in Tote
Festival Handicap at Ascot in September: 7/1, tailed off in Group 3 event at Newbury
4 weeks later: suited by strong gallop over 1½m and may prove suited by 1¾m:
seems unsuited by heavy going, probably acts on any other: sold 120,000 gns
Newmarket Autumn Sales, reportedly to race in Middle East. *B. W. Hills.*

FREE THINKER (USA) 2 b.f. (Apr 14) Shadeed (USA) 135–Top Hope 115 **77 p**
(High Top 131) [1989 6m²] lengthy, useful-looking filly: third foal: dam 7f winner at
2 yrs stayed 1m: 8/1, 1½ lengths second of 3 to easy winner Chimes of Freedom in
minor event at Newbury in June, running on well not unduly knocked about: looked
sure to improve but reportedly went lame shortly afterwards and wasn't seen out
again. *I. A. Balding.*

FREMONT BOY 7 b.h. Ahonoora 122–Shoshoni Girl (USA) (Winning Hit) [1988 **58**
6d* 6f² 6m* 6m 6m² 6m² 5.8d⁵ 6m 6m 6s 1989 6v 6d² 6f 6m⁴ 6f 6m⁴ 6g* 6m⁶ 6g]
small, strong, lengthy horse: carries condition: quite modest handicapper:
favourite, won at Lingfield (for third time) in August: suited by 6f: acts on any going:
effective with or without blinkers. *C. James.*

FRENCH BAY 2 ch.c. (Feb 12) Pharly (FR) 130–Finbay (ITY) 82 (Canisbay 120) **81**
[1989 8g a7g³ a8g*] stocky colt: sixth living foal: half-brother to middle-distance
winners by Nebbiolo and Mummy's Pet: dam 1¼m winner: progressive colt: won
13-runner maiden at Southwell late in year by a length: will stay 1¼m: may improve
further. *D. Haydn Jones.*

FRENCH COTTAGE 3 ch.g. Don 128–Lady Hanora (Ahonoora 122) [1988 5g —
5g 6m 1989 8s 6s⁶ 5g 6f] small, compact gelding: little sign of ability, including in
sellers: not seen out after June: blinkered last 2 outings: apprentice ridden. *R.
Curtis.*

FRENCH GLORY 3 b.c. Sadler's Wells (USA) 132–Dunette (FR) 127 (Hard To **116**
Beat 132) [1988 NR 1989 10m⁶ 10m* 12d⁴ 12.5g* 12d² 12g] IR 150,000Y: third foal:
half-brother to one-time useful Irish winner at up to 1½m Golden Isle (by Golden
Fleece) and modest middle-distance maiden Donya (by Mill Reef): dam won French
Oaks: won maiden at Saint-Cloud in May and listed race at Deauville: beaten 1½
lengths by Golden Pheasant in Group 2 Prix Niel at Longchamp, rallying splendidly:
behind in Prix de l'Arc de Triomphe there 3 weeks later: suited by 1½m: acts on
top-of-the-ground and a soft surface. *A. Fabre, France.*

FRENCH GONDOLIER (USA) 5 b.h. Riverman (USA) 131–Miss Gallivant **69**
(USA) (Gallant Man) [1988 NR 1989 12.4g 8.2v³ 12d² 10.4m] compact horse:
moderate mover: won maiden at Leicester as 2-y-o: best effort in 5 subsequent
handicaps on flat when second at Edinburgh in April: needs further than 1m
nowadays and stays 1½m: acts on heavy going: winner over hurdles. *R. Allan.*

FRENCH RIVIERA 3 b.c. Teenoso (USA) 135–Miss Beaulieu 106 (Northfields **90 d**
(USA)) [1988 NR 1989 10f⁶ 10.1m⁴ 10g³ 12m³ 10g³ 10m] smallish, robust, attractive
colt: has a quick action: capable of fair form: didn't impress last 2 outings, hanging
and looking none too keen in Ripon maiden then pulling hard in blinkers when
behind in £8,000 handicap (sweating) at Newmarket: probably stays 1½m: acts on
top-of-the-ground: sold 7,200 gns Newmarket Autumn Sales: one to avoid. *G.
Wragg.*

FRENCH SCARLET 3 b.f. Legend of France (USA) 124–Dame Scarlet —
(Blakeney 126) [1988 6f 6g 5f 1989 10m 11.7m] rather unfurnished filly: poor maiden:
should be suited by further than 6f. *W. G. A. Brooks.*

FRENCH STRESS (USA) 4 b.c. Sham (USA)–Stresa (Mill Reef (USA) **125**
141) [1988 9g* 8m² 9.2d⁵ 8g* 8d* 1989 8v* 8s² 9.2g³ 8d* 8f⁴ 8g² 8g⁵]
Fabre had such an embarrassment of riches with his milers that French
Stress, a high-class colt in his own right, was his stable's third string and
spent much of the season in the shadow of the three-year-olds Polish
Precedent and Golden Opinion. He lacked the turn of foot of his stable-
companions and was just found wanting in the top flight, but could always be
relied upon to give his running with some give in the ground. He ran his best
race when chasing home Polish Precedent in the Prix du Haras de Fresnay-
le-Buffard Jacques le Marois at Deauville on his first run for almost two
months. All the better for his break, he raced close up from the outset and

Mr Paul de Moussac's "French Stress"

stayed on right to the line, but was unable to cope with Polish Precedent's impressive finishing burst and went down by two lengths, the distance by which he kept long-time leader Magic Gleam out of second. In the Prix du Moulin de Longchamp three weeks later Polish Precedent doubled his advantage over French Stress in a truer-run race. French Stress was slightly impeded by the weakening pacemaker Nursery Slope when going for a gap on the rails two furlongs out, but he had plenty of time in which to recover and his fifth placing was a fair reflection of his merit.

French Stress had returned after fracturing a cannon bone to win his last two races as a three-year-old and added to those successes in the first half of the latest season in the Prix Edmond Blanc at Saint-Cloud and the Prix du Chemin de Fer du Nord at Chantilly, both Group 3 events. On his reappearance in March (nearly a month before either Polish Precedent or Golden Opinion first appeared on a racecourse) he pulled hard in the heavy ground at Saint-Cloud and struggled to land the odds from Nice That, three lengths covering the seven runners. At Chantilly things were almost as tight, but French Stress always looked in control and in a slowly-run affair accounted for Super Arianne, third in a claimer the time before, by three quarters of a length. In between Saint-Cloud and Chantilly, French Stress reached a place in the Trusthouse Forte Mile at Sandown and the Prix d'Ispahan at Longchamp. At Sandown on the first of two trips to Britain as a four-year-old (he found the ground too firm in the Queen Anne Stakes on the other) he could never peg back Reprimand who got first run, and went down by a length; whilst at Longchamp Indian Skimmer proved too strong for him in the closing stages, as did Gabina who twice finished behind him later in the year.

It is somewhat surprising that French Stress has never been tried over a mile and a quarter in view of his style of running and his pedigree. He's a half-brother to Mill Native, who showed improved form when put back to a

331

			Pretense	Endeavour II
	Sham (USA)		(b or br 1963)	Imitation
	(b 1970)	Sequoia	Princequillo
French Stress (USA)			(b 1955)	The Squaw
(b.c. 1985)		Mill Reef	Never Bend
	Stresa		(b 1968)	Milan Mill
	(gr 1975)	Ileana	Abernant
			(gr 1965)	Romantica

mile and a quarter from a mile in the Arlington Million in 1988. Mill Native's sire Exclusive Native is slightly less of an influence for stamina than French Stress's sire Sham, who won the Santa Anita Derby over nine furlongs and was runner-up in the Kentucky Derby and the Preakness Stakes. French Stress's dam Stresa also won over a mile and a quarter. Her first foal American Stress (also by Sham) won the five-furlong Prix du Bois as a two-year-old, but ran only twice at three, while her sixth Private Talk (by Private Account) won an 80,000-franc event over a mile and a quarter at Deauville as a three-year-old in the latest season. Stresa, a half-sister to the very smart Antrona and Terreno, is a daughter of Ileana, the winner of three races as a three-year-old, including the Ascot One Thousand Guineas Trial. Ileana's dam Romantica won the Galtres Stakes and Princess Royal Stakes and was a daughter of Vertige, a half-sister to My Babu and Sayani. The genuine and consistent French Stress, a rangy, attractive colt and a moderate mover, normally takes the eye in the paddock. He is usually taken quietly to post. *A. Fabre, France.*

FREQUENT FLYER   3 b.c. Night Shift (USA)–Porto Alegre (Habitat 134) [1988 **103** 5f* 6f* 6d2 6g4 6f6 8g3 8g3 1989 8d4 10.4f 8.5g 9f3 7g* 7m 9g] smallish, rather angular colt: good walker: has a quick action: won £6,200 handicap at Sandown in July, always prominent: shaped promisingly in £49,600 handicap at Ascot next outing, first for nearly 3 months: 33/1, hampered start and never dangerous in Cambridgeshire Handicap at Newmarket week later: stays 1m: best form with some give in the ground: looked very well last 3 outings. *R. V. Smyth.*

FRESCO   3 b.f. Shirley Heights 130–Free Dance (FR) (Green Dancer (USA) 132)   **87** [1988 7m4 1989 10.2f2 10f2 14f* 14m4 11v] quite attractive filly: good mover: won handicap at Nottingham in September: suited by 1¾m: acts on firm ground, probably unsuited by heavy: sold 25,000 gns Newmarket December Sales. *Major W. R. Hern.*

FRESCOBALDO (USA)   3 b.c. Run The Gantlet (USA)–Voice of The River   **81** (USA) (Speak John) [1988 NR 1989 10g3 12m2 14g4] medium-sized, rather leggy colt: has scope: moderate walker: has a rather round action: second foal: dam lightly-raced sister to Breeders' Cup Steeplechase winner Census: fair maiden: favourite but carrying condition, placed at Leicester and Newmarket: 11/10 on, driven along before halfway when running poorly at Nottingham: lacks turn of foot, and should be suited by further than 1½m: sold 10,000 gns Newmarket Autumn Sales. *H. R. A. Cecil.*

FRESH FROM VICTORY   5 b.g. Hotfoot 126–Triumphant 90 (Track Spare   **41** 125) [1988 8.5m 6f 7m 8f5 10d 10d 1989 10s 10s* 10.1m 10f5 12h 10f 12m] workmanlike, angular gelding: 25/1, won selling handicap (no bid) at Folkestone in April: soundly beaten in handicaps last 3 outings: stays 1¼m: possibly needs a soft surface nowadays: probably best with strong handling. *A. Moore.*

FRESH LINE   3 b.f. High Line 125–Snow Tribe 94 (Great Nephew 126) [1988 NR   **60** 1989 12.2d2 12.3d4 12f 12g] leggy, sparely-made filly: sixth foal: sister to Yorkshire Cup winner Line Slinger and half-sister to several other winners, including fair 11f and 1½m winner and useful hurdler Past Glories (by Hittite Glory): dam, daughter of St Leger third Close Dorstrage, stayed well: quite modest form, running in snatches, when in frame in maidens at Catterick and Ripon: blinkered, ran badly in handicap final start, first for nearly 4 months: should be suited by good test of stamina: probably unsuited by firm going: usually edgy and gives trouble at stalls. *J. Hetherton.*

FRIARS HILL   2 b.g. (Apr 20) Doc Marten 104–Dancing Amber (Broxted 120)   **—** [1989 5f 5g 6g] angular gelding: rather unfurnished: third reported foal: half-brother to a poor maiden by Sagaro: dam tailed off in novice hurdle: always behind in maidens at Redcar: off course 6 months after debut. *M. W. Ellerby.*

FRIDAY SPORT   2 ch.g. (Jun 23) Bairn (USA) 126–Dutch Gold 117 (Goldhill 125)   **58** [1989 5g 5g2 5m 5g] small, close-coupled gelding: turns fore-feet out: moderate mover: fourth living foal: half-brother to 3 winning sprinters, 2 by Sonnen Gold, including quite modest filly Golden Guilder: dam sprinter: plating-class maiden: 3 lengths second of 6, good speed 4f, to Case Law at Catterick, best effort: well beaten in nursery at Edinburgh final outing. *M. W. Easterby.*

FRIENDLY COAST 3 b.g. Blakeney 126–Noreena (Nonoalco (USA) 131) [1988   **58** 7g 6m5 6m 6m 1989 7d 8g5 8m 7f 11.7m 10m4 12m5 15.3g3 14g6 14m 12g5 8f2 10d5 9m 10f] leggy gelding: plating-class handicapper: easily best efforts when in frame: stays 15f, at least in moderately-run race: acts on firm going: visored fourth and final outings: seems unreliable. *D. T. Thom.*

FRIENDSHIP RENEWED 2 b.f. (Feb 13) Vaigly Great 127–Polly Oligant   **62** (Prince Tenderfoot (USA) 126) [1989 5f3 5h4 6m4dis 6m 6g 6f* 5m6 6g6 7d6] 7,200Y: good-quartered, workmanlike filly: fourth foal: half-sister to 3-y-o Golden Ann (by Absalom) and fair 5f to 1m winner Swift's Pal (by Record Token): dam fair 5f winner at 2 yrs in Ireland: showed improved form when winning nursery at Nottingham in September by a length from Hot Tootsie: ran moderately in Catterick seller final start: should stay 7f: inconsistent: sold 3,600 gns Doncaster November Sales. *C. W. Thornton.*

FRIMLEY PARKSON 5 br.g. Frimley Park 109–Frimley Grove (Tower Walk   **64** 130) [1988 6d 5.8f3 5g4 5f 5f4 5g 6f3 5m 5f 5d 1989 5s2 5.8h 5f6 6f 5g2 5m5 5f3 5f4 5g3 5m 5d3 5m2 6m5 5d2 a6g a6g] sturdy, compact gelding: carries plenty of condition: bad mover: quite modest handicapper: ideally suited by stiff 5f: acts on any going: has worn a visor and blinkers: has carried head bit high, and is not the easiest of rides: bought out of G. Cottrell's stable 7,200 gns Newmarket Autumn Sales after fourteenth outing. *P. J. Arthur.*

FRISKY HOPE 7 gr.g. Full of Hope 125–Sharavogue (Silly Season 127) [1988   **—** NR 1989 9g] leggy, short-coupled gelding: fair plater in 1985: extremely lightly raced on flat subsequently: stays 1½m: acts on top-of-the-ground and soft surface. *B. R. Cambidge.*

FRIVOLOUS 2 ch.f. (Apr 13) Bairn (USA) 126–Wild Asset (Welsh Pageant 132)   **—** [1989 6g 6m 7s] 6,800Y: half-sister to smart 7f and 1m winner Attempt (by Try My Best) and Irish middle-distance winner Gentle Stream (by Sandy Creek): dam poor maiden: well beaten in maidens. *R. M. Whitaker.*

FROGS FIRST 3 b.f. Beldale Flutter (USA) 130–Lareyna 98 (Welsh Pageant   **55** 132) [1988 5d 5m 1989 8d 8.2g 10m6 7m 7m 5m 7.6m4 8m4 8g] workmanlike filly: fourth in maiden at Lingfield and claimer at Chepstow: little other worthwhile form: suited by 1m: sweating sixth and seventh starts, edgy first of them. *Mrs Barbara Waring.*

FROME LASS 3 br.f. Oats 126–Groundsel 72 (Reform 132) [1988 NR 1989 12f]   **—** fifth foal: half-sister to winning selling hurdler Frome Girl (by Balinger): dam placed at 9f at 2 yrs: 33/1, tailed-off last of 13 in maiden at Chepstow in May. *R. J. Holder.*

FRONT LINE ROMANCE 2 ch.f. (Feb 19) Caerleon (USA) 132–Bottom Line   **89** 90 (Double Jump 131) [1989 6g6 7f* 7m3 8g2] workmanlike filly: has scope: sixth foal: sister to 3-y-o Dateline Avalon and fairly useful 1½m winner Knight Line Dancer, later smart middle-distance winner in Italy, and half-sister to fairly useful 1983 2-y-o 5f winner Red Line Fever (by Bay Express) and a winner in Malaysia: dam won from 1m to 1½m: won moderately-run minor event at Redcar in July by ¾ length from Tears of Happiness: ½-length second to Endless Joy in Hennessy X O EBF Killavullan Stakes at Leopardstown in September: will stay 1¼m. *M. A. Jarvis.*

FRONT PAGE 2 ch.c. (Apr 5) Adonijah 126–Recent Events (Stanford 121§)   **78** [1989 7g 6m4 6f5 7s4 6g 7g3] heavy-topped colt: carries condition: has plenty of scope: second foal: half-brother to 3-y-o Never In (by Aragon): dam Irish 5f winner: modest maiden: ran creditably in nurseries at Goodwood (sweating) and Ascot on fourth and fifth starts: stays 7f. *Mrs L. Piggott.*

FUGLER'S FOLLY 2 b.g. (Apr 6) King of Spain 121–Djellaba 74 (Decoy Boy   **—** 129) [1989 7m 7g] 900Y, 6,600 2-y-o: half-brother to modest 1985 2-y-o 6f winner Stay Lucky (by Lucky Seventeen): dam won over 5f: well beaten in large-field late-season maidens at Chepstow and Newmarket. *W. J. Haggas.*

FUJAIYRAH 2 b.f. (Feb 24) In Fijar (USA) 121–Ananiyya (FR) (Faristan 123)   **98 ?** [1989 6f* 7m2 8m3 7g] strong, close-coupled filly: ninth foal: half-sister to 1½m winner Malek (by Be My Guest) and winners in USA and Belgium: dam French 2-y-o 1m winner: won maiden at Ascot in June: appeared to put up much improved performance when staying-on third of 8 to Silk Slippers in moderately-run Hoover Fillies' Mile there in September: last of 12 in Bottisham Heath Stud Rockfel Stakes at Newmarket following month: better suited by 1m than shorter and will stay 1¼m. *R. Boss.*

FULHAM TRADER 3 gr.g. Absalom 128–Travesty 63 (Reliance II 137) [1988   **50**
5d 5.1f3 6g5 5d2 5s2 5g 6s 1989 6v3 5s4 5g3 5m] good-topped gelding: carries
condition: plating-class maiden: ran well in minor event and seller second and third
starts: virtually bolted to post when well beaten final one (May): should be suited by
6f: acts on soft going: blinkered first 2 outings: sold out of J. Berry's stable 6,500 gns
Doncaster May Sales before final outing. *Mrs N. Macauley.*

FULL BELT (USA) 2 b.f. (Mar 19) Full Extent (USA) 113–Snow Ridge (USA)   **—**
(King Pellinore (USA) 127) [1989 5s 5s 5g] $100Y: lengthy filly: first foal: dam minor
winner at up to 9f in North America: last in early-season sellers in the Midlands:
blinkered final start. *C. Tinkler.*

FULL BLAST 4 ch.f. Sayyaf 121–Fahrenheit 69 (Mount Hagen (FR) 127) [1988   **43** §
5m 6g3 7g 7.3m6 6m 7m 8m2 6g2 7g5 7m 7g 6f5 8.2m 8.2m 8g 6d 1989 8s 10.1m 9f
8m3 7g 10m5 11.5m2 12m6 10f6 10.2g 9m] angular, sparely-made filly: good mover:
poor handicapper: stayed 11.5f: suited by a sound surface: ran moderately in
blinkers: sometimes wore bandages: unreliable: in foal to Clantime. *Mrs N.
MaCauley.*

FULL MONTY 3 ch.g. Raga Navarro (ITY) 119–Miss Quay (Quayside 124) [1988   **51**
6h5 6g 7.5m 1989 8d 7f 12m4 12h5] tall, plain gelding: good walker: plating-class
form, including in handicaps: not seen out after June: best form over 1m on a soft
surface (ran fairly well in slowly-run race over 1½m). *Denys Smith.*

FULL OF DREAMS 8 ch.g. Maystreak 118–Panda's Gambol 66 (Richboy 117)   **—**
[1988 12f 14m 11.7m] lightly-made, short-coupled gelding: no longer of any account:
has worn blinkers and visor. *G. G. Gracey.*

FULL OF LIFE 6 b.m. Wolverlife 115–Sea Kale 94 (Sea Hawk II 131) [1988 NR   **—**
1989 7m 8h5 7f 8m 10m5] rather sparely-made mare: quite modest handicapper
when trained by M. Pipe in 1987: well below her best as 6-y-o: reluctant to go down
and took keen hold final outing: stays 1m: possibly not at her best on soft going, acts
on any other: sold 850 gns Ascot October Sales. *R. J. Holder.*

FULL OF OATS 3 b.c. Oats 126–Miss Melita (Paveh 126) [1988 NR 1989 10.8s   **—**
14m] sparely-made colt: turns near-fore out: third foal: dam, slow maiden on flat
later winning hurdler/modest chaser, is out of half-sister to very smart stayer Raise
You Ten: bit backward, no sign of ability in maidens at Warwick and Newmarket in
the spring. *H. O'Neill.*

FULL OF PORT 3 ch.f. Krayyan 117–Galva (Gulf Pearl 117) [1988 5d 5s4 6m5   **—**
7.9g4 7f4 7m 6m 1989 7.5d6 12h 12f4] leggy, workmanlike filly: in frame in maidens
in Ireland as 2-y-o when trained by P. Finn: poor form in Britain in seller (favourite)
and handicaps in first half of 1989: probably stays 1½m: best efforts in blinkers: has
joined T. Donnelly. *R. J. R. Williams.*

FULL ORCHESTRA 2 b.f. (Apr 8) Shirley Heights 130–Harp Strings (FR) 109   **76**
(Luthier 126) [1989 6f2 7g3] close-coupled, angular filly: not a good walker: fourth
living foal: half-sister to 3-y-o Lilac Time (by Town And Country), fairly useful 1986
2-y-o 6f winner Gentle Persuasion (by Bustino) and a winner abroad: dam useful at
up to 9f: made most when beaten under 2 lengths in summer maidens won by
Fujairyah at Ascot and Surpassing at Leicester: will stay 1m + . *Major W. R. Hern.*

FULL QUIVER 4 br.g. Gorytus (USA) 132–Much Pleasure (Morston (FR) 125)   **69**
[1988 10g6 10.4s 10g3 10g 1989 7g 7f2 7f6 8f5 8m5 8m2 8m2 8m2 8m6 8m3 11v] leggy
gelding: modest maiden: finds easy 7f on sharp side and stays 1¼m: acts on firm
going: blinkered once at 3 yrs, visored ninth and final outings in 1989: sometimes
sweats: has worn tongue strap: best waited with and is a difficult ride. *Mrs Barbara
Waring.*

FULL SPEED AHEAD 6 gr.g. Hotfoot 126–Here We Go (Hallez (FR) 131)   **40**
[1988 16d2 1989 15.5s* 18s2] tall, leggy gelding: has a markedly round action: poor
handicapper: well ridden when winning slowly-run event at Folkestone in April:
ideally suited by 2m: acts well on soft going and probably unsuited by top-
of-the-ground. *Capt. R. M. Smyly.*

FULL VOLUME 2 b.f. (May 25) Kind of Hush 118–Polonaise (Takawalk II 125)   **64**
[1989 5s* 5m4 6d] 5,000Y: rather leggy, lengthy filly: half-sister to several winners,
including fairly useful 7f and 1m winner Wibis Range (by Wolver Hollow): dam won
over 9f at 2 yrs in Ireland: won maiden auction event at Epsom in April by 2½
lengths from Across The Bay: always-prominent fourth to Shunt in auction event at
Newmarket (bit unruly start) much better subsequent effort: off course 4 months

Prix des Chenes, Saint-Cloud—Funambule from Ernani and Slew The Slewor

afterwards: trained first 2 outings by J. Berry: sold 4,400 gns Newmarket Autumn Sales. *K. M. Brassey.*

FUNAMBULE (USA) 2 b.c. (Apr 25) Lyphard (USA) 132–Sonoma (USA) 121 **115** p (Habitat 134) [1989 8g* 8g*] 2,000,000 francs (approx £186,400) Y: third foal: closely related to Bal du Seigneur (by Nureyev), French 5f winner at 2 yrs, and half-brother to Bahiram (by Irish River), successful at up to 7f in France: dam, sister to top-class Sigy, very smart sprinter: won newcomers race at Longchamp and Group 3 Prix des Chenes (by 1½ lengths from Ernani) at Saint-Cloud in the autumn: good-class performer in the making. *Mme C. Head, France.*

FUNNY SARAH 5 b.m. Cawston's Clown 113–Nimbostratus (Lorenzaccio 130) — [1988 8d⁴ 8g 8g 9g 11.5m³ 11s 12f⁶ 12m 1989 10.2g 15.5s] leggy mare: poor handicapper: stays 11.5f: acts on top-of-the-ground and heavy going: has won for apprentice: usually blinkered nowadays. *M. H. Tompkins.*

FUNUN (USA) 2 b.f. (Apr 1) Fappiano (USA)–Toutski (USA) (Baldski (USA)) **71** [1989 6f⁴ 7m] $600,000Y: lengthy, unfurnished filly: has a quick action: first foal: dam, winner at up to 1m, is half-sister to Tasso (by Fappiano), joint-best 2-y-o colt in America in 1985: shaped quite well when around 3 lengths fourth of 5 to May Hinton in £8,500 event at Salisbury, headway 2f out having started slowly but no extra final furlong: well below that form in similar contest at Newbury later in September. *P. T. Walwyn.*

FURNACEMAN 3 b.c. Battle Hymn 103–Killala Too (Hot Brandy 119) [1988 NR — 1989 5h 6g 6f 10.8f] leggy, sparely-made colt: fifth live foal: of little account: sold 1,000 gns Ascot August Sales: resold 875 gns Ascot November Sales. *K. S. Bridgwater.*

FURNACE MILL 4 b. or br.g. Tumble Wind (USA)–Jane Bond 59 (Good Bond — 122) [1988 8.5m⁶ 10g⁶ 8m⁴ 7m 8g 10g³ 10d* 12g 12d 1989 10.2g 12s] strong, compact gelding: has a round action: winning plater as 3-y-o: well beaten in non-selling handicaps at Doncaster (bandaged, trained by R. Allan) and Hamilton in 1989, off course 7 months in between: stays 1¼m: acts on top-of-the-ground and a soft surface. *A. P. Stringer.*

FURRY PATH 4 b.g. Furry Glen 121–Troubled Heart (Prefairy 99) [1988 NR — 1989 12g] compact gelding: first foal: dam behind both outings in Irish NH Flat races: 33/1, led 6f when well-beaten eighth of 9 in minor event at Carlisle in April: then joined J. S. Wilson. *T. Craig.*

FURRY QUEEN 3 b.f. Furry Glen 121–Release Record (Jukebox 120) [1988 5m⁶ **36** 7.5g⁴ 7d⁶ 6g 8.5f 10s⁴ 1989 13.8m²] lengthy, plain filly: plater: creditable second of 6 in poor apprentice claimer at Catterick in July having been behind entering straight: stays 1¾m: acts on top-of-the-ground and soft going: visored once at 2 yrs: tends to race freely. *M. H. Easterby.*

FURTHER FLIGHT 3 gr.g. Pharly (FR) 130–Flying Nelly 107 (Nelcius 133) **72** [1988 7d 1989 8d 7s 10m* 11.7m] leggy, angular gelding: favourite, first worthwhile form (confirming promise of previous start 3 months earlier) when winning handicap at Ayr in August, keeping on well: co-favourite, moved moderately down

335

and never going particularly well in moderately-run handicap 2 weeks later: stays 1¼m. *B. W. Hills.*

FUSILIER 7 b.g. Habitat 134–Formentera (FR) (Ribot 142) [1988 8m⁴ 8g 7.6f³ 67 §
10g 7d 7.6f 7f 7g 1989 7m² a7g] big, strong, good-topped gelding: carries plenty of condition: not a good walker or mover in slower paces: quite modest handicapper on his day: best form at 7f or 1m: suited by a sound surface: usually wears blinkers, but didn't at 7 yrs: unreliable. *T. Thomson Jones.*

FUSION 5 b.g. Mill Reef (USA) 141–Wolf Wrapped 116 (Wolver Hollow 126) [1988 61
8.3m 10m 10d 1989 10f* 11.5f² 11.5g 11f 12.3f 12f] rangy gelding: landed gamble (5/2 from 16/1) in selling handicap (bought in 6,200 gns) at Lingfield in May: ran poorly last 4 outings: should stay 1½m: acts on firm going: bandaged at 5 yrs: was taken down early. *R. Earnshaw.*

FUTURE GAMBLE 4 b.g. Auction Ring (USA) 123–Silja (FR) (Masetto) [1988 47
12d 10v⁶ 8f 12s 13s 1989 8s³ 10m 8.2f² 8h 8m² 8f² 8f*] sturdy gelding: modest plater: won handicap (no bid) at Thirsk in August, despite wandering under pressure: stays 1m well: acts on any going: visored last 2 starts: has worn bandages: ran moderately when sweating fourth outing. *P. J. Feilden.*

FUTURE GLORY 3 b.c. Ile de Bourbon (USA) 133–Bombshell 76 (Le —
Levanstell 122) [1988 8s* 8g 1989 12.3m⁵ 10.2m] leggy, lengthy colt: moderate mover: won maiden at Ayr as 2-y-o: well beaten in William Hill Futurity at Doncaster, Dalham Chester Vase and graduation race at Doncaster since: not seen out after May in 1989: likely to stay well: best effort on soft going. *J. Hanson.*

FUTURE SUCCESS 3 b.c. Wassl 125–Favorite Prospect (USA) (Mr Prospector 91
(USA)) [1988 NR 1989 8d 12h² 12.3f* 12f* 13.1m² 12g⁶ 12s⁴ 12g⁵] leggy, lightly-made colt: fourth foal: half-brother to 1½m winner Island Aspect (by Ile de Bourbon) and 6f to 1m winner Verdant Boy (by Green Dancer): dam won 6f stakes at 3 yrs: successful in poor maiden at Ripon and handicap (odds on) at Lingfield in summer: best effort in handicaps after when second at Bath but appeared not to respond to pressure: stays 13f: acts on firm going: sold 28,000 gns Newmarket Autumn Sales. *J. L. Dunlop.*

FUTURE TREASURE 3 b.f. Habitat 134–Canton Lightning 102 (Rheingold 88
137) [1988 NR 1989 7d*] 130,000Y: close-coupled, sparely-made filly: fourth foal: half-sister to Irish 4-y-o 1½m and 2m winner Lightning Bug (by Prince Bee) and to a winner in Norway by Cut Above: dam best at up to 1½m: favourite, won 17-runner newcomers race at Newbury in April on only outing comfortably by 3 lengths from Summa Cum Laude, held up and quickening well to lead over 1f out: should stay 1m. *B. Hanbury.*

FYFIELD HOUSE 2 b.c. (Feb 2) Gorytus (USA) 132–Pirate Lass (USA) 90 70
(Cutlass (USA)) [1989 5s⁶ 6m³ 7h² 6f⁵ 8m 7m 8f⁴ 8.2f⁶ 10f* a7g⁵] quite attractive, well-made colt: good walker: first foal: dam, 6f and 7f winner at 2 yrs, is out of half-sister to both smart Father Hogan and dam of Salieri: modest performer: won 13-runner selling nursery (bought in 4,250 gns) at Leicester by ¾ length: stays 1¼m: sweating and ran poorly when visored: sold 18,000 gns Newmarket Autumn Sales. *G. B. Balding.*

G

GAASID 4 ch.c. Kings Lake (USA) 133–Le Melody 102 (Levmoss 133) [1988 12g* 85
13.3d⁶ 10.2f 10s⁶ 12g* 12d* 1989 14s² 18.4m⁵ 12m* 12f 16g 13.3m⁵ 12m 12m² 11v 12d] lengthy, quite attractive colt: carries plenty of condition: fair handicapper: successful in £23,100 Northern Dancer Stakes (Handicap) at Epsom in June by ¾ length, hanging left, from Staten Island: well below his best after except when fifth to Braashee in £20,400 event at Newbury and second to De Rivera at Chepstow: probably best at up to 1¾m: not at his best on firm going, acts on any other. *R. Akehurst.*

GABARDOON 2 b.g. (Mar 7) Gabitat 119–Its For Sure 63 (Ardoon 124) [1989 —
6m] second foal: dam lightly-raced 5f performer: bit backward, tailed off in 18-runner maiden at Windsor in July. *B. Gubby.*

GABBIADINI 2 b.g. (Apr 14) Taufan (USA) 119–Galerida (Silver Shark 129) 73
[1989 5f 6m⁵ 6f* 6m 6f* 6m⁵ 7m* 7m 7s 7g⁵ 6m²] IR 8,000Y: close-coupled, angular gelding: has shown a smooth action: half-brother to 2 winners in Ireland, including 1984 2-y-o 6f winner Silver Lark (by Sexton Blake): dam Irish 6f and 1m winner, is half-sister to Meadowville and Nuthatch: modest performer: successful

in summer in seller (bought in 12,200 gns) at York and nurseries at Folkestone and Thirsk: stays 7f: best form on a sound surface. *M. H. Tompkins.*

GABINA (USA) 4 gr.f. Caro 133–Gold Bird (FR) 115 (Rheingold 137) [1988 **121** 10d* 10.5g6 10.5m 8g* 8m3 8s3 9.2m 7s2 1989 8s* 9.2g2 8d4 7g* 8d2 8g4 7m*]

The American breeding industry was dealt a double blow in the first week of October with the deaths of Secretariat and Caro. The latter, twenty-two years old, suffered a heart attack at Spendthrift Farm while covering a southern hemisphere mare in an out-of-season mating. Caro showed top-class form at up to a mile and a half, winning the Poule d'Essai des Poulains on the disqualification of Faraway Son and the Prix d'Ispahan as a three-year-old and the Prix Ganay as a four-year-old when he also finished in the frame behind Mill Reef in the Eclipse and Prix de l'Arc. He proved equally successful at stud, beginning stallion duties in France where he was leading first-season sire in 1975, and then being bought by Spendthrift after being champion sire in France in 1977 and having the classic winners Crystal Palace and Madelia amongst his second crop. The more recent of Caro's near-seventy stakes winners have included Siberian Express, Cozzene and Winning Colors; and in the latest season, his best in terms of results since crossing the Atlantic, the Canadian triple crown winner With Approval, the Prix Niel winner Golden Pheasant, the Prix de l'Esperance winner Turgeon, the Prix Lupin winner Galetto and Galetto's sister Gabina, successful in the Prix de la Foret on her final outing before being retired.

The decision to keep Gabina in training as a four-year-old was soon rewarded with wins over In Extremis in the Prix du Muguet at Saint-Cloud and Dom Valory in the Prix de la Porte Maillot at Longchamp and a second place behind Indian Skimmer in the Prix d'Ispahan at Longchamp. Her run in the Ispahan was a particularly fine effort for she finished strongly and went down by only half a length, two lengths clear of French Stress in third. She was apparently in season when a moderate fourth to French Stress in the Prix du Chemin de Fer du Nord at Chantilly. In the second half of the year she was campaigned much the same way as she had been as a three-year-old. That season, she won the Prix d'Astarte at Deauville and finished third in the Prix du Haras de Fresnay-le-Buffard Jacques le Marois at Deauville. In the same races at four she finished second to Navratilovna and fourth to Polish Precedent, respectively. In 1988 she finished third in the Prix du Moulin de Longchamp before disappointing in the Prix de l'Opera. In the latest season she missed both races, the Moulin by design, the Opera after giving a mulish display at the stalls and twice unseating her rider. As a consequence of her misbehaviour, she was returned to Longchamp for the Prix de la Foret a week

Prix de la Foret, Longchamp—Gabina crowns her career with a short-head victory from Royal Touch in this Group 1 event; British-trained Shaadi is only fifth

Dr J. D. Schiefelbein's "Gabina"

later a fresh horse. Runner-up to Salse in the race the previous year, she rounded off her career with her first Group 1 victory. Required to pass a stalls test in the intervening week, she proved much more amenable than in the Opera and, fitted with blinkers for the first time, raced close up from the start behind Ocean Falls and Royal Touch. Ocean Falls dropped away two furlongs from home, and inside the last furlong Royal Touch and Gabina had the race between them. On the line Gabina got the better of a tremendous duel by a short head and had a length-and-a-half advantage over the third, Aliocha. Shaadi and Gold Seam, the two British challengers, could manage only fifth and seventh, with Ocean Falls last of the eight runners.

Gabina (USA) (gr.f. 1985)	Caro (gr 1967)	Fortino II (gr 1959)	Grey Sovereign
			Ranavalo III
		Chambord (ch 1955)	Chamossaire
			Life Hill
	Gold Bird (FR) (b 1979)	Rheingold (br 1969)	Faberge II
			Athene
		Orange Bird (ch 1970)	Sea Bird II
			Mock Orange

Gabina and Galetto are the first two foals out of Gold Bird, the winner of a valuable handicap over a mile and a quarter at Longchamp as a three-year-old. The grandam, the one-mile winner Orange Bird, is a half-sister to the very smart performers Duke of Marmalade and Aladancer and to Naval Orange, the dam of the good American horse Cryptoclearance. From a study of her pedigree, Gabina would have been expected to stay middle distances, but although she won over a mile and a quarter her best form was over shorter;

she was never tried over less than seven furlongs. A big, rangy, angular filly, she was unraced on firm going but acted on any other. She visits Kris. *J.-C. Cunnington, France.*

GABISH 4 b.g. Try My Best (USA) 130–Crannog (Habitat 134) [1988 6d³ 6g⁵ — 7.5f* 8f³ 8s⁵ 8.2f 7g 8g 7.6d 10d 1989 7g 10m 8m 10f 12h 12m 8f] compact gelding: modest winner early as 3-y-o: virtually no subsequent form, including in sellers: tailed off fifth outing: trained until after then by R. Hoad: stays 1m: acts on firm going and a soft surface: blinkered 3 times. *J. Ffitch-Heyes.*

GABRIELLA MIA 4 b.f. Ranksborough 117–Gin And Lime 75 (Warpath 113) [1988 NR 1989 13.3f 9m] strong filly: first reported foal: dam 14.6f to 2m winner: tailed off in listed event at Newbury and ladies race at Kempton. *P. J. Arthur.*

GABRIELLE'S ANGEL 2 br.f. (Mar 29) Another Realm 118–Leaplet (Alcide — 136) [1989 5f] 680Y: sixth foal: sister to 3-y-o Suburbia and half-sister to 2 winning platers, including 1984 2-y-o 6f winner Full of Ale (by Full of Hope): dam unraced: 25/1 and backward, slowly away and soon tailed off in maiden auction event at Lingfield in May. *P. Butler.*

GAELGOIR 5 gr.g. Godswalk (USA) 130–Sagosha (Irish Love 117) [1988 8m 16g 54 1989 10s 14s²] medium-sized ex-Irish gelding: plating-class form when second in 19-runner handicap at Nottingham in April: stays 1¾m: seems to act on any going: blinkered once. *C. F. C. Jackson.*

GAELIC AIR 3 b.f. Ballad Rock 122–Gaelic Jewel 89 (Scottish Rifle 127) [1988 6s 65 1989 6g⁶ 7g] small, leggy filly: quite modest form, stiff task final start: should be suited by 7f at least: sold 1,000 gns Newmarket December Sales. *G. Wragg.*

GAICK FOREST 3 b.f. Known Fact (USA) 135–Jolly Bay 108 (Mill Reef (USA) — 141) [1988 NR 1989 7.6m 8.2m a10g] strong filly, sparely-made filly: second foal: half-sister to a winner in Austria: dam, Pretty Polly Stakes winner, is out of dual Oaks winner Juliette Marny, herself sister to Julio Mariner and half-sister to Scintillate: prominent to halfway when well beaten in late-season maidens at Lingfield (twice) and Haydock. *C. F. Wall.*

GAIJIN 3 b.f. Caerleon (USA) 132–Resooka (Godswalk (USA) 130) [1988 6g* 7m⁶ 81 7g 1989 7f³ 7.3m 7g 7g⁴ 11.7f⁵ 12.2g⁴ a10g] well-made filly: has scope: easy mover: fair handicapper: best efforts at Newbury and Epsom third and fourth starts: well beaten early, including in apprentice race: best form at 7f with some give in the ground: ran well in blinkers final start at 2 yrs. *B. W. Hills.*

GAILAN'S MAGIC 3 b.g. Montekin 125–Densidal (Tanfirion 110) [1988 7g 8m 40 1989 8s³ 10v 8g 7d 8m 8f 7h⁴ 8g 7m² 8m 7m 7g 7f] strong, lengthy gelding: carries condition: poor mover: poor maiden: easily best effort after reappearance when second, swishing tail and carrying head awkwardly, in seller at Warwick: may prove best at 7f: acts on top-of-the-ground and soft going: blinkered fourth, fifth and final starts: inconsistent. *C. N. Williams.*

GALACTIC SCHEME (USA) 2 b.c. (Feb 16) Exclusive Era (USA)–Cosmic 76 Time (USA) (Jig Time (USA)) [1989 6f* 6g 6m²] $27,000Y, resold $63,000Y, $185,000 2-y-o: good-bodied, useful-looking colt: brother to 2 winners in North America, one minor stakes placed, and half-brother to a minor winner: dam minor winner in USA: well-backed favourite, won maiden at Salisbury in August: wearing tongue strap, ½-length second, keeping on well, to Thehool in minor event at Chester: best subsequent effort. *R. Hannon.*

GALAGAMES (USA) 2 ch.c. (Apr 24) Lyphard (USA) 132–Morning Games — p (USA) (Grey Dawn II 132) [1989 8v] round-barrelled colt: eighth foal: closely related to 3-y-o 1¼m winner Gran Alba (by El Gran Senor) and half-brother to several winners, notably high-class 1m to 1½m winner and St Leger third Alphabatim (by Verbatim), later successful in USA: dam unplaced only start: 13/2 and in need of race, faded quickly last 2f in 23-runner event at Newbury in October: should do better. *G. Harwood.*

GALATEA PEARL 2 b.f. (May 12) Rabdan 129–Bridal Wave (Julio Mariner 127) — [1989 5g⁶] 3,500Y: first foal: dam unraced half-sister to Cambridgeshire winner Century City: 20/1, backward and green, sixth of 10 in maiden auction event at Wolverhampton in May: will be better suited by 6f +. *B. A. McMahon.*

GALATRIX 3 b.f. Be My Guest (USA) 126–Alligatrix (USA) 111 (Alleged (USA) 72 138) [1988 NR 1989 6m⁶ 8f⁴ 7d³ 7g² 8g³ 6s² 8s³ 7d a8g*] leggy filly: second foal: dam, 2-y-o 7f winner and third in Hoover Fillies' Mile, is out of sister to very smart animals Cabildo and Canal: favourite and bandaged, won maiden at Southwell in December by ½ length from Amadora, a lot to do entering straight then staying on well under severe pressure: placed in varied events in Ireland: should stay beyond 1m: acts on soft ground: has joined J. Gosden. *T. Stack, Ireland.*

GALETTO (FR)   3 ch.c. Caro 133–Gold Bird (FR) 115 (Rheingold 137) [1988 8s² **118** 10s² 1989 10s* 10.5s* 10.5m* 12g³ 10g⁶] second foal: brother to very smart French 7f to 1¼m winner Gabina: dam middle-distance performer: successful at Longchamp in the spring in maiden, listed race and Prix Lupin, last-named impressively by 5 lengths from Elmayer: 17/10 favourite and looking tremendously well, 15 lengths third to Old Vic in Prix du Jockey-Club Lancia at Chantilly: sixth in Grand Prix de Paris at Longchamp later in June: should have proved suited by around 1¼m: acted on top-of-the-ground and soft going: will stand at the Haras du Bois-Roussel (at a fee of 60,000 francs) in 1990. *J-C. Cunnington, France.*

GALE YAKA   3 b.c. Habitat 134–Dancing Rocks 118 (Green Dancer (USA) 132)   **87** [1988 NR 1989 7g 8m 8g* 8f] medium-sized, useful-looking colt: moderate mover: third foal: half-brother to modest maiden Council Rock (by General Assembly) and 10.4f winner Kirpan (by Kris): dam won Nassau Stakes: showed improved form when making all in maiden at Ripon in July: 7/1, set strong pace 6½f when in mid-division in £20,900 handicap at York following month: stays 1m well. *G. Wragg.*

GALITZIN   4 b.c. Hotfoot 126–Midnight Music (Midsummer Night II 117) [1988   — 8g³ 10g* 10.5g⁶ 10f⁴ 10g⁵ 10g* 12f⁴ 10d 1989 10s 10f] tall, lengthy colt: moderate mover: smart 3-y-o, winner of Guardian Classic Trial at Sandown and listed Burtonwood Brewery Summer Trophy at Haydock: soundly beaten in Gordon Richards EBF Stakes at Sandown and Prince of Wales's Stakes at Royal Ascot (bandaged and carrying plenty of condition) in 1989: stayed 1¼m well: gave strong impression not at best on firm going: sold only 3,600 gns Newmarket Autumn Sales: retired to Foxley Farm Stud, Warwick, fee £500 + £1,000 (Oct 1st). *C. E. Brittain.*

GALLANT HOPE   7 ch.g. Ahonoora 122–Amiga Mia 71 (Be Friendly 130) [1988   **90** 6m 6f* 5f 6m² 6f⁵ 6m⁴ 6g³ 6g³ 6g⁶ 6f* 5.6m 5f 5g² 5d² 6g 5m⁶ 1989 5s 6f 5f⁴ 5g* 6m* 6f⁴ 6f 6m⁵ 5g 6m 5.6g³ 6s 7m 5m] small, stocky gelding: carries plenty of condition: has been hobdayed: fairly useful handicapper: successful at Epsom in June in £13,800 Night Rider Stakes (Handicap), making all, and in £10,600 Tokyo Trophy (Handicap): creditable third to Craft Express in £24,800 Tote-Portland Handicap at Doncaster in September: effective at 5f to 6f: unsuited by soft going, acts on any other: usually blinkered nowadays: best with strong handling: has got behind on occasions: splendidly tough and genuine: a credit to his trainer. *L. G. Cottrell.*

GALLERATE   3 b.c. Lucky Wednesday 124–Lady Sangara (Sagaro 133) [1988 NR   — 1989 16d 12m] sparely-made, angular colt: has a roundish action: first foal: dam, lightly raced, showed little worthwhile form: no sign of ability in maiden and seller at Thirsk in the spring. *W. J. Pearce.*

GALLIARI (USA)   3 b.c. Lypheor 118–Hail To Boldness (USA) (Bold Reason   — (USA)) [1988 7g⁴ 7m* 8g 1989 10m⁵ 8f 7m] close-coupled, quite attractive colt: fair winner as 2-y-o: well-beaten fifth to Cacoethes in minor event at Brighton, easily best subsequent effort: well-backed favourite in handicap next time: not seen out after June: will be suited by return to 1¼m: best form on top-of-the-ground: very edgy on debut. *H. R. A. Cecil.*

GALLIC LEAGUE   4 br.c. Welsh Saint 126–Red Rose Bowl (Dragonara Palace   **117** (USA) 115) [1988 7d³ 6f* 5f⁵ 6d 5d 1989 5m⁴ 6f² 5m* 5f³ 6m 6.5d 6g⁶] well-made, good-quartered colt: good mover: returned to near his best as 4-y-o, making all in Group 3 Compaq Computer EBF Ballyogan Stakes at Leopardstown in June, beating Shuttlecock Corner in very good style by 5 lengths: in frame also in Palace House Stakes at Newmarket, Duke of York Stakes and King's Stand Stakes at Royal Ascot: creditable seventh, setting strong pace, in Carroll Foundation July Cup at Newmarket: below form when blinkered final outing: best at sprint distances on top-of-the-ground: almost bolted to post final outing at 3 yrs, taken down steadily subsequently: often sweated, got on edge and gave trouble at stalls: highly-strung: retired to Castle Hyde Stud, Fermoy, expected fee IR £3,500. *B. W. Hills.*

GALWAY ANNIE   2 ch.f. (Apr 25) Chukaroo 103–Moonvein (New Member 119)   — [1989 7f] small, plain filly: third reported foal: half-sister to winning hurdler Martinsmoon (by Homeboy): dam poor plater: 50/1 and fractious at stalls, soon tailed off in maiden at Leicester in October. *K. G. Wingrove.*

GALWEX LADY   3 gr.f. Mendez (FR) 128–Shadiliya 90 (Red Alert 127) [1988 5g   **43** 5d 6d⁶ 6f 6m 6d 1989 8d⁶ 8m⁵ 10m⁴ 10.2h³ 12m 11.7m] lengthy filly: modest plater: should stay 1½m: acts on hard ground: blinkered final outing and once (keen, tended to wander) as 2-y-o: visored, virtually bolted to post final one at 2 yrs: has joined M. Pipe and is a winning juvenile hurdler. *R. J. Holder.*

340

Prix Lupin, Longchamp — Galetto draws clear impressively

GAMEFISHER 2 br.c. (May 3) Claude Monet (USA) 121–Resurgence —
(Runnymede 123) [1989 7g] 1,200F, IR 3,700Y: half-brother to several winners,
including useful Reside (by Quayside), successful at up to 1½m: dam lightly raced
and no sign of ability: 33/1, tailed off in Folkestone maiden in October. *E. A. Wheeler.*

GAME OF DOMINOES 3 b.f. Dominion 123–Honeybuzzard (FR) (Sea Hawk —
II 131) [1988 8d 8g 1989 12.2f 10f] tall, dipped-backed filly: no worthwhile form in
claimers in July as 3-y-o: pulled hard and travelled strongly long way on
reappearance: tailed off (lame) final start: may prove best at up to 1¼m. *M. F. D.
Morley.*

Mr R. E. Sangster's "Gallic League"

341

GAMEOVER LADY 4 br.f. Aragon 118–Panalogue (King Log 115) [1988 6m — 1989 12f 7.6h 9m 10g 6f] compact filly: of no account: blinkered fourth outing. *M. H. B. Robinson.*

GAME TRY 4 gr.g. Mummy's Game 120–Pariscene 86 (Dragonara Palace (USA) — 115) [1988 7g 7f⁵ 12g⁶ 1989 8.5g] little form in varied events. *M. C. Chapman.*

GANGER CAMP 3 bl.f. Derrylin 115–Way of Life 61 (Homeric 133) [1988 6f 6g² 65 1989 7f 7f 7f 7m⁴ 8s² 8.2m⁴ 7d 8g⁴ a8g⁴ a10g] sturdy, good-bodied filly: poor mover: quite modest maiden: only show as 3-y-o when in frame, in claimer at Lingfield penultimate start: should stay further than 1m: acts on soft going, possibly unsuited by very firm: visored last 2 starts. *L. J. Holt.*

GANT BLEU (FR) 2 ch.c. (Apr 22) Crystal Glitters (USA) 127–Gold Honey 65 (Artaius (USA) 129) [1989 6g³ 5d⁵ 5g⁶] leggy, rather sparely-made colt: first foal: dam ran twice in France: quite modest form in maidens and a minor event in the North: will stay 7f. *R. M. Whitaker.*

GARDA'S GOLD 6 b.g. Garda's Revenge (USA) 119–Mielee (Le Levanstell 122) — [1988 10s² 8s 10d6 1989 12s6] leggy, narrow gelding: moderate mover: poor handicapper: stays 1½m: suited by soft going: has worn crossed noseband: suitable mount for apprentice: has run well when sweating. *R. Dickin.*

GARDEN CENTRE BOY 5 ch.g. Riboboy (USA) 124–Miss Topaz 64 (Pitcairn — 126) [1988 NR 1989 8.2g 15s] fourth foal: dam suited by 1½m: soundly beaten in maiden and amateurs race in Scotland: winning but ungenuine hurdler: sold 1,700 gns Ascot October Sales. *J. S. Wilson.*

GARDIEN DU JOUR (USA) 3 gr.f. Grey Dawn II 132–Bridge Master (USA) 59 (Iron Ruler (USA)) [1988 7g⁵ 6m 1989 10f 10g 7h² 7g 6m 7g] close-coupled filly: quite modest maiden: best effort second in Brighton handicap: ran poorly last 2 starts, off course 4 months in between: should stay 1m: acts on hard going. *M. E. D. Francis.*

GARGOOR 3 ch.c. Kris 135–Icena 117 (Jimmy Reppin 131) [1988 NR 1989 13v⁵ — 12d] IR 85,000Y: big, strong colt: sixth foal: half-brother to 2¼m winner Teevano (by Blakeney): dam won Lowther Stakes: well beaten in late-season claimer (edgy) at Ayr and minor event at Thirsk: withdrawn at start on veterinary advice before Newmarket claimer in between. *N. A. Callaghan.*

GARISSA (FR) 2 b.f. (Mar 3) Gorytus (USA) 132–Reasonable Mona (USA) (Bold — Reason) [1989 6f⁴ 7m] 42,000 francs (approx £3,800) Y: sturdy filly: moderate mover: fifth foal: dam, winner at around 6f at 2 yrs, only season to race, is half-sister to Prima Voce: bit backward, showed signs of a little ability in summer sellers at Lingfield and Wolverhampton. *D. Haydn Jones.*

GARSCUBE 2 gr.g. (Apr 13) Petong 126–Brigado 87 (Brigadier Gerard 144) 84 [1989 5g⁴ 7f* 7m⁴ 7m⁵ 7m³ 7m⁵ 8m³ 8g⁵] tall, leggy, unfurnished gelding: good walker: third foal: half-brother to 3-y-o Astley Jack (by Belfort) and a modest maiden by Dublin Taxi: dam won over 1m at 2 yrs: fair performer: made all in Kempton maiden in July: stays 1m: best form on top-of-the-ground. *S. J. Muldoon.*

GARTH LADY 3 ch.f. Jalmood (USA) 126–Lady Capilano 87 (Nebbiolo 125) 75 [1988 7f⁴ 7d² 8f 1989 7m³] rather unfurnished filly: modest form as 2-y-o: creditable third in handicap (bandaged) at Wolverhampton in July, only outing in 1989: bred to stay further. *D. Haydn Jones.*

GATHERING SPEED 3 b.c. Formidable (USA) 125–Arthur's Daughter 77 84 (Artaius (USA) 129) [1988 6s 6m* 7g 1989 6s⁵ 6h 8.5f* 8.5g² 9m 7f* 7g 7m 7g 7m⁵] lengthy, powerfully-built colt: has a quick action: fair handicapper: won at Beverley in June and Newcastle in July: keen sort, unlikely to stay beyond 8.5f and at least as effective over 7f: acts on firm going: visored penultimate start: sold to race in Middle East 20,000 gns Newmarket Autumn Sales. *F. H. Lee.*

GAY FINALE 3 ch.f. Final Straw 127–Mistress Gay 76 (Lord Gayle (USA) 124) — [1988 6m 6m 6f 7g 1989 10f6] leggy, good-topped filly: appears of little account, and somewhat temperamental to boot: sold 950 gns Ascot August Sales. *J. D. J. Davies.*

GAY RUFFIAN 3 b.g. Welsh Term 126–Alcinea (FR) 93 (Sweet Revenge 129) 61 [1988 6g 6m⁵ 5g³ 6d⁴ 7g³ 6m⁴ 7g² 7m 8.2m 1989 10.2h 12m² 12g] lengthy, sparely-made gelding: has a round action: fairly useful plater on his day: 20/1 and sweating, best effort when beaten short head at Pontefract in July, running on strongly: stays 1½m well: acts on top-of-the-ground: has run well for apprentice: winning hurdler: inconsistent. *D. Burchell.*

GAZETTALONG 3 b.f. Taufan (USA) 119–Albeni 84 (Great Nephew 126) [1988 78 6f⁴ 6g³ 7m* 7g⁴ 7m³ 7f² 7g* 1989 6d 7f 10.2f³ 10m² 10.1m⁶ 12m⁵ 10.2m 10.6d

8.2g*] sparely-made filly: moderate mover: modest handicapper: won claimer (claimed to join J. Gillen £8,300) at Hamilton in September by 4 lengths, travelling strongly 6f and leading 1½f out: effective at 1m and 1¼m: acts on firm going: below form when blinkered and edgy penultimate outing. *M. H. Tompkins.*

GAZZYMAZ   3 ch.g. Longleat (USA) 109–Vaguely Hopeful 65 (Fortino II 120)   —
[1988 NR 1989 12h⁵ 14f⁴ 15s⁶ 15g] workmanlike gelding: half-brother to several winners, including fair 1983 2-y-o 6f winner Manerly, later winner in USA, and quite useful 1m to 1¼m winner Doubly Hopeful (by Double Jump): dam ran 3 times: showed signs of ability (very green) on debut but well beaten in varied events after. *S. G. Norton.*

GEBLITZT   5 b.h. Tumble Wind (USA)–Tatty Kay (Tarqogan 125) [1988 8g 8f³   **41**
7f² 9m³ 7g 8m 9g 1989 10.1m³] sparely-made horse: poor maiden: placed in selling and claiming company: stays 1¼m: acts on firm going and a soft surface. *J. E. Long.*

GEE DOUBLE YOU   3 ch.g. Tap On Wood 130–Repicado Rose (USA)   **62**
(Repicado (CHI)) [1988 7s³ 7m* 8.2m⁴ 8.2m⁵ 1989 12g 10m⁴ 11.7m a12g] rangy, angular gelding: has scope: won maiden auction race as 2-y-o: fair fourth in handicap at Leicester in July: should face facing stiff tasks in similar events after: should stay 1½m: acts on top-of-the-ground. *D. Haydn Jones.*

GEE SHARP   3 ch.c. Sharpo 132–Rahesh 111 (Raffingora 130) [1988 5g 5m 6d 6g   —
7m 5g⁵ 1989 6m 6m 6f 10g⁶ 13f] tall, strong colt: poor form in varied company, including selling: not seen out after July: sold 1,050 gns Doncaster November Sales. *T. Fairhurst.*

GEM BRACELET (USA)   3 b.f. Sir Ivor 135–Chain Bracelet (USA) (Lyphard   **68**
(USA) 132) [1988 NR 1989 10.6m 12g⁶ 10.4m⁴ a10g³ a13g²] leggy, angular filly: fourth foal: half-sister to Irish 1m winner Division (by In Reality) and French 1¼m winner Zahy (by Alleged): dam, from good family, good-class winner at up to 1¼m, best at 4 yrs: form only when placed in maiden and handicap at Lingfield in late-season: stays 13f: pulled hard third start: sold 60,000 gns Newmarket December Sales. *J. H. M. Gosden.*

GEMINI BLUE   2 gr.f. (Mar 26) Blue Cashmere 129–Olibanum 61 (Frank-   —
incense 120) [1989 5f 5h⁵ 6f⁶ 6m] 4,800Y: leggy, angular filly: half-sister to winning sprinters Capeability Pound (by Balboa) and Blochairn Skolar (by Most Secret) and a winner in Belgium: dam plater: of little account. *N. Tinkler.*

GEMINI FIRE   5 b.g. Mansingh (USA) 120–Sealady (Seaepic (USA) 100) [1988   **91**
5d³ 5f 5m* 5m 6f* 5f⁴ 5g⁵ 5g 5f 5m 5g 1989 5g 6v 5g 5f 5m⁴ 5m² 5f⁵ 6f⁴ 5m³ 6m 5g 5d³ 5d*] sparely-made gelding: well backed, ran easily best race for some time when winning 21-runner £6,900 handicap at Thirsk in November by 4 lengths, making all on stand rail, from Royal Fan: stays 6f: acts on firm going and a soft surface (probably unsuited by heavy): visored 6 times, including on fourth to eighth starts: sometimes edgy: inconsistent. *M. P. Naughton.*

GENAIR (FR)   4 ch.c. General Assembly (USA)–Metair 118 (Laser Light 118)   **70**
[1988 8g³ 8d 8.5g⁴ 10f³ 10m³ 10g 12m 7g⁵ 1989 7.6m⁶ 8.5d³ 8f² 9f² 8f³ 8m* 8g³ 8f⁵ 9f³ 8.2g 8.2d 8g* 8m⁶ 8m 8g] big, rather dipped-backed colt: has had soft palate operation: won handicaps at Ripon in June and Newcastle in August: worth another try over 1¼m: acts on any going: visored twice as 3-y-o: tends to get behind early: suited by strong gallop: has found little, and is not an easy ride: winning hurdler. *G. M. Moore.*

GENERAL GREGORY   4 ch.g. Moor House 84–Harveys' Pride VII (Tudor   —
Cliff) [1988 10m 12g 12f 8.5g 8d 1989 10m⁶] of little account: sometimes blinkered. *R. Earnshaw.*

GENERAL PERSHING   3 br.c. Persian Bold 123–St Colette (So Blessed 130)   **67**
[1988 7m 7m 1989 12.2d* 12s³ 12.5f⁵ 16.2g 14m⁶ 13.8f⁵] good-topped, workmanlike colt: quite modest performer: won maiden at Catterick in March, not handling turn well: ran fairly well last 2 outings but well below form after: should be suited by further than 1½m: acts on a soft surface: bandaged behind last 2 outings: sweating, raced too freely in visor final one: winning hurdler with F. Jordan. *M. F. D. Morley.*

GENERALS DAUGHTER (USA)   2 ch.f. (Apr 22) General Holme (USA)   **92 ?**
128–Evelle (USA) (Gentlemans Game) [1989 6g² 6m³ 7m⁵ 8m] $57,000Y: leggy, narrow, light-framed filly: sister to French 3-y-o 7.5f and 1m winner My Genelle and half-sister to graded stakes winner at 2 yrs Don't Hold Back (by Big Spruce) and 2 winners in USA by Lt Stevens: dam unplaced in 5 starts: quite useful third to Green's Belle in listed race at Ripon in August: below form after, possibly unsuited by track at Brighton third start: should stay further than 6f: trained first 3 starts by A. Stewart. *N. A. Callaghan.*

GENERAL SILKY   4 ch.g. General Assembly (USA)–Silky (USA) 112 (Nijinsky — (CAN) 138) [1988 7d 8.3m 7g 7m⁴ 6s⁴ 6s 1989 11.7m] big, rangy, well-made gelding: modest maiden as 3-y-o when trained by G. Wragg: best form at 6f (took keen hold and finished well tailed off over 11.7f): acts on soft going: has given trouble at stalls. *N. A. Callaghan.*

GENERAL SIPPERS   3 ch.g. Tap On Wood 130–Gaygo Lady 113 (Gay   62 Fandango (USA) 132) [1988 5m⁴ 6g⁶ 7g⁴ 1989 8.2s⁴ 8s 9f 10g⁶ 12f⁴ 12h²] medium-sized, quite useful-looking gelding: has a round action: quite modest maiden: beaten head in handicap at Thirsk in June: suited by strongly-run race over 1½m: acts on hard going: lacks turn of foot. *R. Hollinshead.*

GENOTIN   6 b.g. Pitskelly 122–Bazaar Goddess (USA) (Bazaar) [1988 10.2d 10v³   69 12g³ 8.5m* 10d 7.6f 8.5g* 10m⁵ 8d 8m³ 8g⁶ 8m 7f 1989 10.2g 8m⁵ 9.2f² 8f⁴ 10m² 10.6d 8m* 8m*] leggy, good-topped gelding: quite modest performer: won handicaps at Salisbury (apprentices) in August and Kempton early following month: stays 1½m, but at least as effective at 1m: acts on any going: has worn bandages: has sometimes tended to hang: excellent mount for inexperienced rider: tough. *S. Mellor.*

GENTLE GAIN   2 ch.f. (Mar 23) Final Straw 127–Regain 86 (Relko 136) [1989   44 5f⁶ 6g] 11,000F: deep-girthed filly: fourth foal: half-sister to 3-y-o White River (by Pharly), 1986 2-y-o 7f winner Counter Attack (by Nishapour) and Italian 1m winner Sharp Gain (by Sharpo): dam, 1½m winner, is daughter of half-sister to very smart Double-U-Jay and Riverside, latter dam of Riverqueen: carrying condition, poor form in summer maidens at Wolverhampton and Newbury. *K. White.*

GENTLE HERO (USA)   3 ch.g. Hero's Honor (USA)–Tender Camilla 115   92 p (Prince Tenderfoot (USA) 126) [1988 NR 1989 5s³ 5m* 6g* 6m* 6s*] $65,000Y, 3,800 2-y-o: sturdy gelding: blind in right eye: half-brother to 4 winners, notably Noble Damsel (by Vaguely Noble), successful in graded company in USA: dam, seemed to stay 1¼m and is half-sister to smart stayer Bonne Noel: successful in apprentice maiden at Edinburgh in July and handicaps at Ripon in July, Newmarket in August and Ayr in September: suited by 6f: yet to race on very firm going, acts on any other: sometimes hangs under pressure: progressive. *M. P. Naughton.*

GENTLEMAN'S JIG (CAN)   4 gr.g. Jig Time (USA)–Sunny Season (USA)   82 (Haveago (USA)) [1988 8g⁶ 10.2f⁴ 10.1m 10g² 1989 10.4m⁵ 12m² 12m 10f⁶] big, rangy gelding: moderate mover: fair handicapper: sweating badly and dull in coat, good second of 7 to Rashtoun at Haydock in May: ran moderately last 2 outings, and not seen out after July: stays 1½m: yet to race on soft going, acts on any other: probably best on a galloping track: has joined J. Edwards. *J. W. Hills.*

GENTLE SATIN   2 b.c. (May 9) Anita's Prince 126–Drora (Busted 134) [1989   70 5m a7g a8g³] 7,200Y: useful-looking colt: fifth foal: half-brother to 3-y-o Tender Dealer (by Tender King) and to 6f and 7f winners Dunenny (by Dunphy) and Beechwood Cottage (by Malinowski): dam ran once: 2¼ lengths third of 11 to Blake's Treasure at Lingfield in December, first worthwhile form in maidens. *P. Mitchell.*

GENTLESHAW   3 b.c. Try My Best (USA) 130–Rings 104 (Realm 129) [1988 NR   64 1989 8g⁵ 7f³ 8h⁴] IR 4,400F, IR 21,000Y: rangy colt: brother to Irish 6f winner Sunday Chimes and half-brother to fair 7f winner Aulait (by Gay Fandango), later successful in Italy: dam 6f performer: quite modest maiden: in frame at York (edging left) and Carlisle (pushed along some way out) in May: likely to prove suited by around 1m. *R. Hollinshead.*

GENUINE GIFT (CAN)   4 ch.c. Blushing Groom (FR) 131–Barb's Bold (USA)   71 112 (Bold Forbes (USA)) [1988 8f⁵ 10s⁴ 1989 11.5m² 12m³ 12g⁶] workmanlike colt: has been hobdayed: 14/1, 2 lengths second of 8 to odds-on Exceptional Bid at Yarmouth, best effort in amateur events in summer: soundly beaten at Epsom final outing: stays 1½m: sold 850 gns Ascot December Sales. *C. P. E. Brooks.*

GEORGE WILLIAM   8 b.h. Import 127–Bloomsbury Girl 63 (Weepers Boy — 124) [1988 5s 5g⁵ 6m⁵ 5m 5m 5f 5f 1989 6m 5m] strong, good-bodied horse: carries plenty of condition: moderate mover: modest handicapper on his day: well below form since third outing in 1988: ideally suited by 6f or stiff 5f: probably needs give in the ground nowadays: has been tried in blinkers and visor: has often worn bandages: inconsistent. *M. O'Neill.*

GEORGIA STEPHENS (USA)   3 b.f. The Minstrel (CAN) 135–Ancient   64 Fables (USA) (Pronto) [1988 7g 1989 7.5m⁶ 7g⁴ 8m² a8g] good-topped filly: has scope: has stringhalt and turns off-fore in: modest maiden: may well be suited by further: sold 21,000 gns Newmarket December Sales. *W. Hastings-Bass.*

GERRAWAY   2 b.f. (Mar 8) Song 132–Sister Racine 58 (Dom Racine (FR) 121)   —
[1989 5d] sturdy, workmanlike filly: first foal: dam, maiden plater, is daughter of useful miler Geoffrey's Sister, also the dam of useful 6f and 7f winner Mac's Fighter: 50/1 and ridden by 7-lb claimer, over 10 lengths seventh of 13 to Lyndseylee in maiden at Ripon in April: dead. *T. Fairhurst.*

GERSHWIN   6 b.g. Gold Song 112–Firey Kim (CAN) (Cannonade (USA)) [1988   **61**
7d 7g 6g* 7f³ 6f² 6f² 6g 6g 6g⁶ 6g* 6s 6f 6s 7m 1989 6v 5s 6f 7h³ 6h* 6m⁶ 6m⁵ 6h
7.6f 5m 6f 7m] tall, leggy gelding: quite modest handicapper: won at Brighton in June: below form after next outing: effective at 6f and 7f: probably unsuited by soft going, acts on any other: effective with or without visor: has won for apprentice: has been taken very quietly to post. *P. Howling.*

GET GOING   2 b.f. (Apr 5) Petorius 117–Regal Promise (Pitskelly 122) [1989 6m⁴   **81**
6m* 6v² 7d] IR 3,200Y: smallish filly: second living foal: half-sister to fairly useful 1987 2-y-o 6f winner Butlers Wharf (by Burslem), now ungenuine middle-distance performer: dam, Irish 11f winner,is out of half-sister to very useful 1983 Irish 2-y-o Gala Event: well-backed favourite, won maiden at Thirsk in September by 4 lengths from Regal North: ½-length second of 15, leading briefly inside final 1f, to Silverdale Fox in nursery at Ayr following month: should stay 7f. *C. W. C. Elsey.*

GET ON GERAGHTY   5 ch.g. Main Reef 126–Gold Cypher 76 (Pardao 120)   —
[1988 6m 7g 8m 8.5g 8d² 8f 7.5m 10m 8.5f 10v 1989 8d 8f] rather lengthy, angular gelding: form since 2 yrs only when second in poor seller at Ayr in 1988: stays 1m: probably best on an easy surface nowadays (yet to show his form on very soft going): often slowly away: sold 1,000 gns Doncaster May Sales. *S. J. Muldoon.*

GHADBBAAN   5 b.h. Kalaglow 132–Firework Party (USA) 115 (Roan Rocket   **88**
128) [1988 9m* 8f² 10g 8m 1989 12d a7g²] lengthy, leggy horse: scratchy mover: fairly useful performer: favourite, gave impression would have won with stronger handling when ½-length second, slowly away, in claimer at Southwell in November: acted as pacemaker on reappearance 7 months earlier: stays 1¼m: acts on firm going and a soft surface: bought out of R. Hern's stable 17,500 gns Newmarket September Sales: winning hurdler. *N. Tinkler.*

GHARAH (USA)   2 b.f. (Apr 30) Shadeed (USA) 135–Bolt From The Blue (USA)   **64**
(Blue Times (USA)) [1989 7g⁵ 7s⁴] rangy, quite attractive filly: second foal: half-sister to 3-y-o Bin Daahir (by Blushing Groom): dam, half-sister to Alydar's Best, won from 9f to 1½m in USA and third in E P Taylor Stakes: 11 lengths fourth of 10, no impression last 2f, to Sajjaya in maiden at Ayr in September: needed race on debut: will be better suited by 1m. *P. T. Walwyn.*

GHARAM (USA)   2 ch.f. (Apr 10) Green Dancer (USA) 132–Water Lily   **107** p
(FR) 116 (Riverman (USA) 131) [1989 6m* 7m²]

For one reason or another trainer Alec Stewart failed to enjoy quite so successful a season in 1989. The retirement of Mtoto meant he went largely unrepresented in the top races, and a higher-than-average proportion of the stable's horses seemed to suffer from training problems. Even so, the year wasn't without encouragement. The three-year-olds Alphabel and Braashee both developed well, and among the two-year-olds the filly Gharam did enough from limited opportunities to suggest she'll be an asset to the stable in 1990. Gharam's debut came in the Virginia Water Stakes, a valuable newcomers' race at Ascot in July. Musical Bliss had won the race twelve months earlier, and the market suggested that Stoute had another strong candidate in Fire And Shade, a Shadeed filly who was backed down to 7/4-on. Fire And Shade ran well too, but not quite well enough to beat the 4/1 second-favourite Gharam, who got the better of a good tussle by three quarters of a length with the three other runners a long way back. Gharam was also second favourite on her only subsequent start in the Gilbey's Gin Sweet Solera Stakes at Newmarket the following month. This time she was beaten, but only just, staying on really strongly having been outpaced when the winner first quickened, to go down by half a length, clear of the remainder again, to Moon Cactus who was receiving 6 lb. Gharam sustained a knee injury at Newmarket. Surgery wasn't necessary, though, and her trainer reported her fit and well by the end of the season.

The way Gharam sustained her effort up the hill at Newmarket suggested a longer trip would be very much in her favour; her pedigree backs

		Nijinsky (b 1967)	Northern Dancer Flaming Page
	Green Dancer (USA) (b 1972)	Green Valley (br 1967)	Val de Loir Sly Pola
Gharam (USA) (ch.f. Apr 10, 1987)		Riverman (b 1969)	Never Bend River Lady
	Water Lily (FR) (b 1976)	First Bloom (b 1969)	Primera Flower Dance

that up. Her sire Green Dancer had another successful season, his sons Icona, Green Adventure and Torjoun all showing smart form over middle distances; Green Dancer was also responsible for several good performers in the States too, and besides Gharam he has another good prospect in the Houghton Stakes winner Duke of Paducah. Gharam is the fifth foal out of her dam Water Lily, who showed very useful form in France as a two-year-old and went on to win the Grade 3 Next Move Handicap at Aqueduct as a four-year-old. The fourth foal Noble Lily (by Vaguely Noble) failed to win for Fabre in the latest season, but the previous three were all successful, particularly the Alydar colt Talinum, who emulated his sire by winning the Grade 1 Flamingo Stakes over nine furlongs. Gharam's grandam First Bloom was also a good horse. She was the best two-year-old filly in Europe in 1971, and besides Water Lily she also produced the smart French middle-distance performer First Prayer. A leggy, sparely-made filly, Gharam cost 410,000 dollars as a yearling at the Nelson Bunker Hunt Dispersal sale. Both her outings at two were on good to firm ground. *A. C. Stewart.*

GHASSANAH   3 ch.f. Pas de Seul 133–Debutante 78 (Silly Season 127) [1988 7g   73
7s 1989 7s* 7s*] sparely-made filly: co-favourite, won maiden at Folkestone in April and handicap at Kempton in May: stays 7f: acts on soft going: takes strong hold. *G. A. Pritchard-Gordon.*

GHATHANFAR (USA)   4 b.c. Riverman (USA) 131–Hartebeest (USA) 120   83
(Vaguely Noble 140) [1988 8m3 10.5d6 1989 10m6 8m2] close-coupled, well-made colt: has a quick action: impressive winner on only start at 2 yrs: lightly raced subsequently, but showed he retained ability when 2 lengths second of 14 in minor event at Edinburgh in October: possibly doesn't stay 1¼m: sold 12,500 gns Newmarket December Sales. *H. Thomson Jones.*

GHAYAAT (USA)   2 ch.f. (Feb 28) Lyphard (USA) 132–Goodbye Shelley (FR)   —
116 (Home Guard (USA) 129) [1989 6f] small, angular filly: third foal: half-sister to a winner in USA by Halo: dam won from 7f to 1m, and is half-sister to Heighlin: 16/1 and better for race, ridden along at halfway and soon dropped out in 10-runner maiden at Lingfield in October. *P. T. Walwyn.*

GHILLIE (USA)   3 b.f. Forli (ARG)–Thong (Nantallah) [1988 NR 1989 7d 8m4   —
6f4] close-coupled, unfurnished filly: sister to top-class sprinter Thatch, good filly Lisadell and dam of Nureyev and Fairy Bridge, and half-sister to several winners, including St Leger and Irish Derby runner-up King Pellinore (by Round Table): dam stakes-placed sister to Ridan and Lt Stevens, and dam of Apalachee: easily best effort in maidens, at Edinburgh in July on second start: better at 1m than shorter. *A. C. Stewart.*

GIBBOT   4 b.g. Taufan (USA) 119–Gaychimes (Steel Heart 128) [1988 8.2v6 8.2s4   43
8f 8.5g3 8m* 10d* 10f* 10.2f4 10m5 10s 1989 10.2g5 10g 10.8d 10f 10f 10m 10m6 12g 10.6d2 11v] close-coupled, workmanlike gelding: carries plenty of condition: has a round action: modest winner as 3-y-o: showed he retains a little ability when second of 19 in apprentice handicap at Haydock in October: wearing tongue strap, had very stiff task final outing: better suited by 1¼m than 1m: acts on any going: hung right and put head in air penultimate start at 3 yrs: slowly away when blinkered seventh one in 1989. *P. Howling.*

GIDGEGANNUP   3 b.c. Magnolia Lad 102–Vulrory's Lass (Saucy Kit 76) [1988   —
7.5m 7m 1989 10.1m 12g 12g] leggy, close-coupled colt: poor form, including in seller: may well be suited by return to shorter. *J. A. Glover.*

GIFTED NEPHEW   5 b.g. Great Nephew 126–Sakeena 76 (Moulton 128) [1988   —
NR 1989 18g 17.1m] quite modest maiden at his best: stayed 1½m: probably unsuited by top-of-the-ground and went well on heavy: visored twice: dead. *N. R. Mitchell.*

GIFT OF LIFE   2 b.c. (Apr 30) Formidable (USA) 125–Mattagirl 78 (Music Boy   —
124) [1989 a8g a7g] smallish, sparely-made colt: second foal: half-brother to 3-y-o Lord of Gymcrak (by Absalom): dam, placed over 5f at 2 yrs, is sister to Middle Park

winner and 2000 Guineas runner-up Mattaboy: soundly beaten in late-season maidens at Southwell and Lingfield. *W. Wilson.*

GILBERTO 5 b.g. Runnett 125–Natasha 87 (Native Prince) [1988 6g 6f 6f 5m 1989 6f 6f4 6f2 7f 6g 6g 7m4 6m6 7f] rather finely-made, attractive gelding: useful winner as 3-y-o: showed he'd retained some ability when in frame in handicaps at Thirsk and Redcar (amateurs) in May: also ran as though something amiss on several occasions in 1989: best form at 6f: seemed to act on any going: blinkered sixth to eighth starts: dead. *M. H. Easterby.* **62**

GILBERT'S GIRL 2 b.f. (Apr 23) Castle Keep 121–Traditional Miss 90 (Traditionalist (USA)) [1989 7m] third foal: half-sister to 6f seller winner First Tradition (by Sayyaf): dam, extremely tough and genuine, won 13 races from 7f to 1½m from 4 yrs to 7 yrs: tailed off in 17-runner maiden at Chepstow in October. *R. J. Hodges.* **—**

GILDED PAST 2 ch.c. (Mar 11) Glint of Gold 128–Historia 71 (Northfields (USA)) [1989 7m 6m6 8f4 7.5f5] 3,200Y: first foal: dam, ran once at 2 yrs, is daughter of half-sister to high-class Moulton and Derby third Freefoot: plating-class maiden: best efforts last 2 starts: will be suited by 1½m: unruly stalls second start. *A. N. Lee.* **53**

GILDED YOUTH 4 ch.g. Young Generation 129–Woodwind (FR) 103 (Whistling Wind 123) [1988 8g2 8d3 8m6 10f 8h* 10f 1989 8m 9m 8.3m3 8.5g6] close-coupled, rather lightly-made gelding: quite modest winner as 3-y-o: 33/1, easily best effort in 1989 when third of 15 in handicap at Windsor: slowly away final outing: suited by 1m: acts on hard going and a soft surface: blinkered once: trained first 2 starts by J. White: heavily bandaged on reappearance: bolted to post when tailed off in ladies race second outing: has appeared not keen: winning hurdler. *T. Thomson Jones.* **—**

GILDERDALE 7 ch.g. Gunner B 126–Mertola (Tribal Chief 125) [1988 7m6 7.6g4 7m2 8f 8f4 7f* 7f6 7.3m6 8g 1989 7g6 7f* 7g4 8f4 8m2 7f5 8f3 8.5g 7m 8m2 8g5] close-coupled gelding: fairly useful handicapper: won 20-runner event at Kempton in May: ran well when in frame after, on last occasion beaten length by Aradu in 16-runner £11,100 race at Ascot: best at 7f or 1m: acts on any going, but particularly well on firm. *J. W. Hills.* **92**

GILD THE LILY 4 b.f. Ile de Bourbon (USA) 133–Meliora 73 (Crowned Prince (USA) 128) [1988 9d* 10f2 11.7g5 1989 10g 12m5 16g6] leggy, quite attractive filly: fair winner as 3-y-o when trained by H. Cecil: not entirely discredited in autumn in handicaps at Goodwood (apprentices, first run for nearly 15 months) and Chepstow and in listed event (stiff task) at Newmarket: seems to stay 2m. *M. Madgwick.* **—**

GILLIES EXPRESS 3 b.f. Bay Express 132–Miss Moss Bros 69 (Sparkler 130) [1988 6g 5g 1989 6s] sparely-made filly: little sign of ability in maidens and minor event: sold 1,000 gns Ascot October Sales. *P. D. Cundell.* **—**

GILT NOTE 2 b.c. (May 22) Nordico (USA)–Coneenford (Ballymore 123) [1989 6s2 6g* 6f* 6d6 5g* 8d] IR 14,000Y: half-brother to 4 winners in Ireland, including 1½m winner Guest House (by What A Guest): dam Irish 1m winner out of useful 1968 2-y-o Hot Penny: fairly useful performer: successful in maiden at Leopardstown, listed race at Phoenix Park and a nursery (by ¾ length) at the Curragh: around 8 lengths sixth to Pharaoh's Delight in Heinz '57' Phoenix Stakes: not discredited when ninth of 11 to Teach Dha Mhile in Panasonic Smurfit EBF Futurity Stakes at the Curragh in September: stays 1m. *C. Collins, Ireland.* **86**

GIN AND ORANGE 3 b.c. Mummy's Pet 125–Amberetta 72 (Supreme Sovereign 119) [1988 7g 1989 7d* 8m3 7f 8m5 8m 8s a7g] rangy, quite attractive colt: modest handicapper at his best: well-backed favourite, won maiden at Folkestone in April: on toes, creditable third at Newmarket following month, finding less than seemed likely and edging left, best other effort: moved poorly down fifth start: should prove suited by 7f: acts on a soft surface and top-of-the-ground: may prove best with waiting tactics. *C. R. Nelson.* **77 d**

GINA'S CHOICE 3 b.f. Ile de Bourbon (USA) 133–Modern Romance (Dance In Time (CAN)) [1988 6m 6g 1989 10g 8.5f 7m 6m 7m] big, rather plain filly: has a round action: well beaten, including in handicaps and sellers: bandaged second (sweating) and final starts: bred to stay further than 6f. *J. Wharton.* **—**

GINATA 3 gr.f. Petong 126–Raffinata (Raffingora 130) [1988 5f3 5m 1989 6s 6s 6m6 5m 8.2f 6g] leggy, angular filly: poor maiden: unlikely to stay 1m: acts on firm going and possibly unsuited by soft: on toes first 2 outings: bandaged behind final one at 2 yrs. *Mrs N. Macauley.* **—**

GINGERNUT (USA) 2 ch.c. (May 27) Timeless Moment (USA)–United Appeal (USA) (Valid Appeal (USA)) [1989 5m4 6f5 5f4 5.8h2 5h2 5.8f3 6m3 6g3 7g6 a7g a6g] **65**

$60,000Y: smallish, good-quatered colt: good mover: fifth reported foal: brother to a minor winner in USA and half-brother to 2 other minor winners: dam won at up to 7f: sire smart sprinter: quite modest maiden: stays 6f: sometimes hangs left: unseated rider and bolted on debut: shade temperamental. *M. D. I. Usher.*

GINGER'S GONE 2 b.f. (Feb 23) Ginger Brink (FR) 117–Away And Gone (Comedy Star (USA) 121) [1989 5m 6f 6g] 300F: angular, plain filly: first reported foal: dam unraced, has been in Belgium: poor form in maidens and a claimer. *E. H. Owen jun.* **42**

GIPPESWYCK LADY 2 b.f. (Apr 25) Pas de Seul 133–Estivalia (Persian Bold 123) [1989 6m 6g5 8.2g3 8d6] IR 5,000Y: medium-sized, rather leggy filly: has scope: third foal: dam, from family of Pampapaul, never ran: plating-class maiden: best effort third start: will be suited by 1¼m. *M. H. Tompkins.* **57**

GIPPING 3 br.f. Vision (USA)–Narration (USA) (Sham (USA)) [1988 9g6 10.2m 1989 9g4] rather sparely-made filly: 20/1 and wearing dropped noseband, fourth of 11 in minor event at Wolverhampton in May, ridden 3f out and tending to edge left: takes hold and not certain to stay beyond 1¼m. *R. F. Casey.* **72**

GIPSY RAMBLER 4 gr.g. Move Off 112–Gipsy Silver (Pongee 106) [1988 7d 8g 8d6 9m 9f 12.2g 12.3s 10g 10g 11s 10s 8.2s 1989 7d 6v5] rather sparely-made gelding: form only when winning nursery in 1987: stays 6f: acts on heavy going: blinkered once at 3 yrs: often races freely. *N. Chamberlain.* **—**

GIRTON LADY 3 b.f. Uncle Pokey 116–Gay Twenties 70 (Lord Gayle (USA) 124) [1988 NR 1989 10f a11g] leggy filly: turns off-fore in: second foal: half-sister to poor maiden Kind of Magic (by Record Token): dam, half-sister to very useful 6f and 7f performer Step Ahead, won several times over hurdles: bit backward and ridden by 5-lb claimer, very slowly away and always behind in claimer at Redcar in August. *R. M. Whitaker.* **—**

GIVE IN 2 gr.c. (Apr 21) Harlow (USA) 111–Moment of Weakness 76 (Pieces of Eight 128) [1989 5s* 5s6 6m3 6f4 7m2 6m4 7f4 7m5 6f2 6g 6g 6g 6m4 6f a6g a8g*] 2,000Y: leggy, narrow, sparely-made colt: third reported foal: half-brother to modest 9f and 1¼m winner African Affair (by Be My Native): dam won from 6f to 10.2f, including a seller: quite useful plater: won maiden auction event at Leicester in April and claimer at Southwell in December: stays 1m: usually visored nowadays, but wasn't at Southwell: inconsistent. *Mrs N. Macauley.* **62**

GIVE ME A DAY 3 b.f. Lucky Wednesday 124–Dutch May 109 (Maystreak 118) [1988 5m6 6m 7g 7g 1989 7d 6s 7.5d4 8d 10f] small, unfurnished filly: moderate plater: blinkered, sweating and bit edgy, always behind on final start (May): stays 1m: acts on a soft surface. *M. W. Easterby.* **—**

GLACIAL STORM (USA) 4 b.c. Arctic Tern (USA) 126–Hortensia (FR) 119 (Luthier 126) [1988 10g2 10.5g3 12m2 12m3 12d 11.1g2 12m 12s6 1989 12m2 12g4 12f4 12m5 13.3g4] lengthy, heavy-topped, most attractive colt: usually looks very well: has rather a round action: placed in Ever Ready Derby and Budweiser Irish Derby: subsequently generally disappointing, running best race in 1989 when staying-on length second to eased Unfuwain in General Accident Jockey Club Stakes at Newmarket in May: well beaten in 4-runner Hardwicke Stakes at Royal Ascot and listed event at Newmarket (finding little) on third and fourth outings: should stay 1¾m: probably unsuited by firm going, acts on any other: blinkered last 7 appearances: has joined J. Hammond in France: best treated with caution. *B. W. Hills.* **114 §**

GLADYS PUGH 3 b.f. Comedy Star (USA) 121–Nylon Pirate 80 (Derring-Do 131) [1988 6g 7d 6g5 1989 8g 7.3m 8g 6m 7m] strong, workmanlike filly: keen walker: plating-class maiden: little worthwhile form as 3-y-o: not seen out after July: should stay beyond 6f: changed hands 2,000 gns Ascot March Sales. *G. B. Balding.* **—**

GLASNOST 3 b.f. High Top 131–Crusader's Dream 88 (St Paddy 133) [1988 NR 1989 5m] fourth foal: half-sister to 1989 Italian 1m winner White Crusader (by Final Straw) and 1¼m winners Historical Fact and Kings Crusade (both by Reform): dam 2-y-o 6f winner from family of high-class miler Lucyrowe: 7/1 and looking very well, never able to challenge and tended to hang in 23-runner maiden at Thirsk in May: bred to be suited by further. *W. Jarvis.* **—**

GLASS CASTLE (FR) 5 b.h. Crystal Palace (FR) 132–Halliana (USA) (Bold Reason) [1988 NR 1989 10g3 10.6m4 12g3 12g] plating-class maiden: in frame in apprentice and amateur events in autumn: barely stays 1½m: acts on top-of-the-ground and a soft surface, but possibly unsuited by very soft going: has hung and raced with head high. *A. Hide.* **—**

GLASTONDALE 3 b.g. Beldale Flutter (USA) 130–Glastonbury 73 (Grundy 59
137) [1988 5s 6d 7m 7g 8.5f 7g 1989 12m³ 12.2m⁶ 12m* 12m⁶ 12.3g* 12.2m² 10f*
10m⁶ 10.2g² 10.4m⁶ 12f³ 12.2m] compact gelding: carries condition: quite modest
handicapper: in good form in the summer, successful at Edinburgh, Ripon and
Redcar: stays 1½m well: acts on firm going: visored final 2 outings at 2 yrs:
bandaged first 2 in 1989: has run well when sweating and for apprentice: goes well
with forcing tactics: game: sold to join T. Barron 14,000 gns Newmarket Autumn
Sales. *F. H. Lee.*

GLAZERITE 2 b.c. (Feb 2) Dunphy 124–Rust Free 58 (Free State 125) [1989 7g⁶ 84
7m* 8m 8g* 8m] 5,600Y: strong, useful-looking colt: second foal: half-brother to a
winner in Hong Kong by Mansingh: dam, maiden who stayed 1¼m, is half-sister to
high-class sprinter Petong: fair performer: won minor event at Doncaster in July
and nursery at Yarmouth in September: good eighth of 9 to Digression in Royal
Lodge EBF Stakes at Ascot: much better suited by 1m than 7f. *R. Guest.*

GLEBELANDS GIRL 2 b.f. (Apr 20) Burslem 123–Genzyme Gene 38 38
(Riboboy (USA) 124) [1989 5g 5s⁶ 5m⁴ 6f 5f⁶ 7m³ 7f⁵ 7m⁶ 7f 8g 8m] 4,600Y: small,
sparely-made filly: has a round action: second foal: sister to plating-class 3-y-o
Break The Mould: dam, plater, stayed 1¼m: poor plater: stays 1m. *R. A. Bennett.*

GLEEFUL 3 b.f. Sayf El Arab (USA) 127–School Road 88 (Great Nephew 126) —
[1988 5g⁴ 5m³ 5f* 1989 5m] neat, good-quartered filly: progressive as 2-y-o, making
all in maiden at Folkestone: virtually pulled up (lame) in handicap in August, only
start in 1989: speedy. *R. Boss.*

GLENBEIGH SUMMER 3 gr.f. General Assembly (USA)–What A Summer 94
(USA) (What Luck (USA)) [1988 5g* 1989 7.6f* 8m 6m 7g⁶ 7d] leggy filly: fairly
useful form when winning handicap (hung left) at Lingfield and about 8 lengths
eighth of 13 in Irish 1000 Guineas at the Curragh in May: not entirely discredited
when sixth in Leicester minor event in November on first run for nearly 5 months:
behind in listed race at Leopardstown 12 days later: should stay beyond 1m: acts on
firm going: on toes first and third (also sweating) starts. *D. J. G. Murray-Smith.*

GLENCOE LADY 2 b.f. (Apr 20) Thatching 131–Borgia (GER) (Orsini 124) —
[1989 7m 7f] IR 2,000Y: angular filly: has a round action: half-sister to poor 1987
2-y-o Summit Accord (by Meinberg) and several winners in Germany, 3 by
Meinberg: dam won in Germany: faded last 2f when well-beaten eighth of 10 to
Native Tribe in July maiden at Chester: slowly away and badly hampered after 1f on
debut. *D. Haydn Jones.*

GLENCROFT 5 b.g. Crofter (USA) 124–Native Fleet (FR) (Fleet Nasrullah) 103 d
[1988 7m* 7f³ 8f 8f² 8.2m 7g⁴ 7m* 8g* 8g* 6g² 7d³ 6f* 6s³ 6m* 6d* 5.6m² 6s 7g³
5g* 5f* 5d 6g³ 5s 6m 1989 5f 6f⁶ 6m 5m⁵ 5g 5m 5g 6m 6m 5d] big, strong gelding:
successful in 9 handicaps (having been hobdayed) in 1988, showing around 4½
stones improvement (rated 110 at his best) during the year: showed signs of
retaining his ability as 5-y-o, but also ran on numerous occasions as though
something again badly amiss: tubed after third outing: best at 5f: not at best on soft
going and well suited by firm: hangs left and is not an easy ride: usually wears
blinkers: changed hands 10,000 gns Ascot December Sales. *D. W. Chapman.*

GLENDERRY 7 br.g. Derrylin 115–Summer Mist 57 (Midsummer Night II 117) — §
[1988 8v² 8g 10g³ 1989 8v⁴ 8.2d] neat, strong gelding: poor mover: bad and
ungenuine plater: stays 1¼m: possibly needs give in the ground nowadays: wears
blinkers or visor: occasionally sweats. *S. J. Muldoon.*

GLEN KATE 2 b.f. (Apr 13) Glenstal (USA) 118–Miss Kate (FR) (Nonoalco 85 p
(USA) 131) [1989 7m*] 8,400F: angular filly: third foal: half-sister to 3-y-o 1½m
winner Ktolo (by Tolomeo) and 1987 2-y-o 5f and 6f winner Tamarindo (by Touching
Wood): dam, 1¼m winner in France, is half-sister to very smart stayer Midshipman:
25/1 and bit backward, won 20-runner maiden at Lingfield in September by 2½
lengths from Sahara Baladee, making all and quickening 2f out: will improve. *I. V.
Matthews.*

GLEN MADDIE 2 b.f. (Mar 10) Reasonable (FR) 119–Iresine (GER) (Frontal 45
122) [1989 5d 5d4] IR 2,800F, 7,000Y: strong, dipped-backed filly: has plenty of
scope: half-sister to 3-y-o Cronk's Courage (by Krayyan), 5f and 6f winner at 2 yrs,
and to winners in Belgium and USA: dam lightly raced: still backward, over 7
lengths fourth of 13, fading final furlong, to Lyndseylee in maiden at Ripon in April.
R. M. Whitaker.

GLENMERE PRINCE 3 b.c. Prince Tenderfoot (USA) 126–Ashbourne Lass 47
(Ashmore (FR) 125) [1988 5g 7m 7g 1989 11v 12.2d 6f⁴ 7f⁴ 7m³ 8.2f 8m 8f] leggy,
unfurnished colt: poor form, including in sellers: not discredited in amateurs

349

handicap penultimate outing: beaten when hampered and fell in handicap on final one: may prove suited by 1m: acts on firm going: blinkered twice. *P. J. Feilden.*

GLEN NOVA 3 ch.f. Glenstal (USA) 118–Geppina Umbra (Sheshoon 132) [1988 **42** 6f 6m 1989 7f4 8f 6f4 6f 12f6] lengthy, workmanlike filly: poor maiden: form only at 6f: blinkered, sweated up penultimate start: has carried head high: sold 1,250 gns Ascot August Sales. *M. J. Fetherston-Godley.*

GLENSANDA 4 b.f. Shareef Dancer (USA) 135–Pluvia (USA) (Raise A Native) **— §** [1988 NR 1989 6d6 8m 8m 5f] heavy-topped filly: carries condition: second foal: sister to 3-y-o French 1½m winner Plus Mark: dam unraced daughter of Singing Rain, stakes winner in USA: poor and temperamental maiden. *J. Ffitch-Heyes.*

GLENSCAR 3 gr.c. Glenstal (USA) 118–Caranina (USA) (Caro 133) [1988 NR **57** 1989 6m 5m 7m6 6m* 6g2 6f5 6g] IR 2,000Y: sparely-made, angular colt: poor walker and mover: first foal: dam Irish 6f winner: fairly useful plater: 20/1 and ridden by 7-lb claimer, won at Windsor (no bid) in August, slowly away and running on well to lead inside final 1f: good second at Newcastle (made most), best effort after: worth another try over 7f: has joined M. Charles. *M. Brittain.*

GLENSTAL PRINCESS 2 ch.f. (Apr 30) Glenstal (USA) 118–Jessamy Hall 77 **65 p** (Crowned Prince (USA) 128) [1989 5f5 6f*] IR 26,000Y: sixth foal: half-sister to 3-y-o Ballad Ruler (by Ballad Rock) and 3 winners, including Italian Group 3 1¼m winner Cunizza da Romano (by Milford) and Irish 1¾m winner Aussie Dream (by Pas de Seul): dam 1m winner: won 4-runner maiden at Newcastle in October by 3 lengths from Nice Day, making all. *S. G. Norton.*

GLENSTAL PRIORY 2 b.f. (Mar 5) Glenstal (USA) 118–Jumbolia (Wolver **— p** Hollow 126) [1989 6m5 7m 8g] IR 18,000Y: leggy, quite attractive filly: third dam, placed over 6f and 7f in Ireland, is half-sister to Cajun and Ubedizzy: showed signs of ability in maidens at Chester and Leicester on last 2 starts: sort to do better in handicaps. *G. B. Balding.*

GLENTOR 2 b.c. (Mar 26) Glenstal (USA) 118–More Reliable (Morston (FR) 125) **65** [1989 5f3 5h2 6f2 6h2 7g5 8.2f 6m] sparely-made, angular colt: has a round action: third foal: half-brother to very useful 1984 2-y-o 5f and 6f winner Star Video (by Hittite Glory): dam never ran: quite modest maiden: blinkered in seller final start: should stay 1m. *G. Lewis.*

GLENVALE 3 b.g. Hays 120–Deira (Bold Lad (IRE) 133) [1988 6g 7m 6m 1989 **—** 10.1m 8.5g 11.7g] angular gelding: poor maiden: no form as 3-y-o: visored, tailed off in Epsom claimer second start: should be suited by further than 7f. *P. Burgoyne.*

GLIDING MUSICIAN (USA) 2 ch.f. (May 12) The Minstrel (CAN) 135–Easy **67** Step (USA) (Overskate (CAN)) [1989 8m2 9f6] IR 110,000Y: smallish, angular filly: first foal: dam won at up to 9f at 2 yrs in USA: ¾-length second to Clare Court in maiden at Chepstow in August, soon disputing lead and keeping on well: odds on and on toes, pulled very hard and hung badly right when last of 6 in similar event at Wolverhampton nearly 2 months later: headstrong. *D. J. G. Murray-Smith.*

GLINETTE 3 br.f. Chief Singer 131–Florita 86 (Lord Gayle (USA) 124) [1988 5f6 **48** 6m6 6f 1989 8m 7f5 8m3 10f5] neat filly: poor maiden: stays 1m: bandaged behind last 3 outings: pulled hard second and final (sweating) starts: somewhat temperamental. *C. F. Wall.*

GLITTERBIRD 2 br.f. (May 15) Glint of Gold 128–Dovetail 80 (Brigadier **58 p** Gerard 144) [1989 7g6 7m] 11,500Y: big, workmanlike filly: has scope: half-sister to French 3-y-o Persicaria (by Persian Bold), 7f winner at 2 yrs, French 1m and 1¼m winner Diamond Dove (by Bellypha) and a winner in Italy: dam, 1¼m winner, is daughter of Sun Chariot and Child Stakes winner Duboff: around 12 lengths ninth of 21, not knocked about, to Cutting Note in maiden at Newmarket in October: bit backward on debut: sort to do better. *G. A. Pritchard-Gordon.*

GLOBE HABIT 3 ch.c. Sayyaf 121–Samkhya (Crocket 130) [1988 7m 1989 8f] **—** close-coupled, dipped-backed colt: bit backward, well beaten in maidens. *C. R. Nelson.*

GLORIOLE 5 b.g. Indian King (USA) 128–Escorial 110 (Royal Palace 131) [1988 **—** NR 1989 12g 13m 12g 18h6 13m 20.4g5] strong, lengthy gelding: plating-class maiden as 3-y-o: well beaten in handicaps in 1989: swished tail and didn't look keen fourth and final outings: best effort at 1½m. *R. Allan.*

GLORY GOLD 5 b.m. Hittite Glory 125–Flowering (Reform 132) [1988 6v2 8d6 **55** 8g 7g4 6d* 6s2 7g* 7.5m3 8f3 7m6 7f6 7.5g5 7.6s 8g6 8g 8.2s5 7d4 8s 8g5 8s5 8m 8v 8g 8.2d2 1989 8g5 6v 8d 7m* 7.5m6 8.2g6 8g 8m] close-coupled mare: carries condition: poor mover: plating-class handicapper: 25/1, returned to form when winning at Ayr in August, first run for over 3 months: below her best after: better at 7f than 6f and stayed 1m: not at her best on firm going, acted on any other: suitable mount for apprentice: tough: in foal to Grey Desire. *M. Brittain.*

GLOSS 4 b.g. Town And Country 124–Star Display (Sparkler 130) [1988 11.7m 12.2g³ 8.5f³ 10m⁴ 8.2s⁵ 8.2m 10g* 1989 10m 10f 8g] workmanlike, good-bodied gelding: modest winner as 3-y-o when trained by R. J. R. Williams: well beaten in sellers and handicap (pulled hard) in 1989: stays 1¼m: probably acts on any going: visored final outing: sometimes sweats: usually taken early to post: often hangs and finds little: bought 2,500 gns Ascot June Sales: sold 1,000 gns Ascot November Sales: untrustworthy. *M. B. James.* — §

GLOWING PICTURE 4 b.g. Kalaglow 132–Perfect Picture (FR) 78 (Hopeful Venture 125) [1988 11.7m⁴ 12m⁴ 14g 10.1g 12f 14m* 18.1m³ 16m 16.5g 1989 14s 11.7m 16f* 16f⁶ 17.1f] rather sparely-made gelding: quite modest handicapper: form as 4-y-o only when winning at Doncaster in June: stays 2m: acts on firm going: has won for apprentice: inconsistent. *A. P. Ingham.* 58

GOADBY VENTURE 2 ch.f. (Apr 16) Saxon Farm 75–Pixie's Party (Celtic Cone 116) [1989 5f 7g] fair sort: first foal: dam poor over jumps: green, no sign of ability in maidens at Warwick (backward, slowly away) and Leicester. *Miss S. J. Wilton.* —

GO ALL NIGHT 2 b.g. (Mar 2) All Systems Go 119–Flash O' Night (Patch 129) [1989 5.3g 5f⁵] 2,500Y: small gelding: half-brother to a winner abroad: dam never ran: poor form in maiden auction event at Brighton and June seller (blinkered) at Pontefract: sold 1,450 gns Ascot November Sales. *C. N. Allen.* —

GO AND GO 2 ch.g. (Mar 2) Be My Guest (USA) 126–Irish Edition (USA) (Alleged (USA) 138) [1989 6g⁶ 7g* 7m* 7g 8.5g* 8.5f] second foal: half-brother to a winner in the States by Kris: dam Irish 9f winner: useful colt: successful in maiden at Galway in July, Reference Point EBF Tyros Stakes at the Curragh in August and Laurel Futurity (by a head, pair clear) on dirt at Laurel in October: eighth of 12 in Breeders' Cup Juvenile at Gulfstream Park in November: should stay 1¼m: useful. *D. K. Weld, Ireland.* ?

GO BOY GO 2 b.g. (Apr 13) All Systems Go 119–Chubby Ears (Burglar 128) [1989 5s⁵ 5s² 5m] 4,000Y: rather leggy, useful-looking gelding: half-brother to ungenuine 3-y-o Print Finisher (by Mandrake Major) and a winner in Spain: dam ran twice: plating-class maiden: will be better suited by 6f: on toes final start (May). *K. M. Brassey.* 55

GO BUY BAILEY'S 2 b.c. (Apr 26) Rousillon (USA) 133–Geoffrey's Sister 102 (Sparkler 130) [1989 8.2g² 8m 8g* 7d⁴] 11,000F, 11,000Y: small, close-coupled colt: half-brother to 3-y-o Yesican (by Kalaglow), very useful 6f and 7f performer Mac's Fighter (by Hard Fought) and poor 12.2f winner Keep Hoping (by Busted), later winner in USA: dam genuine and consistent miler: well-backed 7/1, won maiden at Edinburgh by 4 lengths from Haitham, quickening ahead home turn and running on strongly: respectable fourth to Azzaam in nursery at Thirsk later in November: will probably stay 1¼m: best form on an easy surface. *M. Johnston.* 80

GOD BLESS YOU 2 b.c. (May 10) Vision (USA)–Maestrette 77 (Manado 130) [1989 7g] 27,000Y: third foal: half-brother to 3-y-o Thimbalina (by Salmon Leap): dam 1m winner: 66/1, around 12 lengths seventh of 13, never dangerous, to Flying Diva in minor event at Carlisle in October: should improve. *S. G. Norton.* 57 p

Reference Point EBF Tyros Stakes, the Curragh—Go And Go has gone!

GODDARD'S GIRL 3 b.f. Martinmas 128–Ready Steady Go 87 (On Your Mark 125) [1988 NR 1989 11m⁵ 12d⁶ 8m 10.6d] unfurnished, rather dipped-backed filly: fourth reported foal: dam placed at 6f and 1m: little promise in varied events: pulled hard first 2 starts: wore severe bridle third. *M. W. Eckley.* —

GODLORD 9 gr.g. Godswalk (USA) 130–Gay Pariso 82 (Sir Gaylord) [1988 9f⁴ 10.8m 12m⁶ 10s 10m 10m 10m 8m 10m 10.8m⁴ 16.5g 11f 12m] strong, good-bodied gelding: carries condition: poor performer: stays 10.8f well: acts on any going: has been tried in blinkers: often bandaged nowadays: often apprentice ridden: finds very little off bridle and needs to be produced late: best left alone. *P. J. Bevan.* 34 §

GODSALL 2 gr.f. (May 13) Godswalk (USA) 130–Sallail (Sallust 134) [1989 5f 5m² 5m⁴ 6m 5f³ 7m⁶ 7m 5.1m³ 6f] IR 4,000F, 4,200Y: leggy, sparely-made filly: eighth foal: half-sister to several winners, including Irish 1½m winner Innate (by Be My Native) and 1m to 15.5f winner Mailman (by Malacate): dam Irish 7f winner: poor form in varied races: effective at 5f and seems to stay 7f: ducked badly right 2f out on second start, and left 1f out on third: seems bit temperamental. *Mrs N. Macauley.* 46

GODS LAW 8 gr.g. Godswalk (USA) 130–Fluently (Ragusa 137) [1988 10m 8.5m³ 8f 12f* 10g 11m³ 11g² 12m² 12m⁴ 11m² 12f* 13s 12f* 1989 12f⁵ 12m 12m⁴ 12.3m⁶ 12m* 15m³ 12g² 12m² 12m⁶ 12m² 12.3m] leggy, good-topped gelding: quite modest handicapper: returned to form when winning same race at Edinburgh in June for second year running: suited by 1½m: suited by a sound surface: blinkered twice: good mount for apprentice: held up and ideally suited by strong gallop: slowly away third (pulled hard and found little) and fourth outings: often takes keen hold to post, and has been taken down early. *Mrs G. R. Reveley.* 59

GODS SOLUTION 8 gr.h. Godswalk (USA) 130–Campitello (Hornbeam 130) [1988 6g* 6d 6g² 7m³ 6f 6s 6d 6s 7f⁵ 6g 5g⁶ 7f⁴ 1989 6d* 7d 7m⁴ 6f⁴ 7m⁴ 6f* 6f² 6f² 6f³ 6g 7m⁵ 6g 6f] rangy horse: poor mover: quite modest handicapper: goes very well with forcing tactics on a turning track, and won first time out at Catterick (has now won there 7 times) in March for fifth time in succession: again ideal conditions when comfortable winner at Pontefract in June: stays 7f: not at his best on soft going, acts on any other: has worn blinkers: occasionally sweats: tough. *T. D. Barron.* 65

GO DUTCH (USA) 2 ch.c. (Apr 1) Lyphard's Wish (FR) 124–Parema (USA) (Explodent (USA)) [1989 6m 6g 7g² 6g³ 6m⁵] $12,500Y: leggy, sparely-made colt: third foal: half-brother to a minor winner in USA by Muttering: dam unraced half-sister to very useful French 1¼m winner La Pompadour: modest performer: ran creditably in Newmarket nurseries on last 2 starts: should stay 1m: to join C. Nelson. *Capt. R. M. Smyly.* 73

GO FOR GLORY 2 b. or br.c. (May 29) My Dad Tom (USA) 109–Ardtully Lass 64 (Cavo Doro 124) [1989 6g⁶ 6m 7g a6g a7g⁵] 4,000Y, 6,000 2-y-o: leggy, quite attractive colt: good walker: fifth foal: sister to 3-y-o My Sporting Lady and 1987 2-y-o plater Glucinium: dam won over 1m and 1¼m: plating-class maiden: showed plenty of promise (including for 7-lb claimer) first 2 starts: well beaten after: should stay 7f. *J. J. O'Neill.* 58

GO FORUM 4 ch.g. Tumble Wind (USA)–Devine Lady (The Parson 119) [1988 11.7f⁵ 12m* 11.1m* 12m³ 14m* 12m 12g⁵ 16m 1989 12s 12m 12f 12m 11.5g³ 14m³ 12f³ 12h⁵ 14f⁵ 14g² 14m² 13.3m a12g² a12g] sturdy, good-bodied gelding: fair handicapper: stays 1¾m: acts on firm going: has run creditably for apprentice: taken down early second outing: blinkered next time: winning hurdler. *J. Sutcliffe.* 81

GO GO BOY 2 b.g. (Apr 15) All Systems Go 119–Sandra's Sovereign (Workboy 123) [1989 5g 5f a6g] first reported foal: dam of little account on flat, pulled up in hurdle race: probably of little account. *S. R. Bowring.* —

GO HOLIMARINE 2 gr.f. (Apr 13) Taufan (USA) 119–Standing Ovation (Godswalk (USA) 130) [1989 6g⁵ 6g 5.1f⁵ 7m* 7m⁵ 8g⁴ 7.3m 7g⁴ 7g] 2,000F, 3,800Y: leggy, quite good-topped filly: moderate walker and mover: third foal: dam Irish 1½m winner: quite modest performer: won maiden auction event at Yarmouth in August: ran moderately and looked bit ungenerous on final outing: stays 1m: blinkered last 2 starts. *C. N. Williams.* 65

GOING GOING GONE 2 b.c. (Apr 27) Final Straw 127–Coins And Art (USA) (Mississipian (USA)) [1989 5v 5f⁴ 5f⁶ 6g 8m] rather leggy, close-coupled colt: moderate mover: fourth foal: closely related to a winner in Norway by Thatch and half-brother to 1987 2-y-o 7f seller winner Valued Collection (by Valiyar): dam never ran: poor form in varied races, including a seller: bred to stay at least 1m. *R. Hannon.* 50

GOLAN HEIGHTS 2 b.c. (Jan 30) Shirley Heights 130–Grimpola (GER) 93
(Windwurf (GER)) [1989 7g² 8.2g* 8m] good-bodied colt: first foal: dam won at 6f
and 1m (Group 2 event) in Germany and stayed 1½m: 7/4 on, won maiden at
Haydock in September by 7 lengths: odds on, pulled hard and tended to hang when
well beaten in listed race at Ascot following month: will be suited by 1¼m+:
created a very favourable impression at Haydock. *H. R. A. Cecil.*

GOLD COLLAR 4 ch.f. Sayyaf 121–Colonial Line (USA) 75 (Plenty Old (USA)) —
[1988 7f⁵ 8.5m 7f 7g 7f 1989 10d 10m 12f³ 12h] tall, workmanlike filly: moderate
mover: bad maiden. *A. Moore.*

GOLD DIVER 2 ch.g. (Feb 18) Main Reef 126–Ice Baby (Grundy 137) [1989 7g 60
7m 8f⁵ 8.2s] IR 3,800Y: lengthy, dipped-backed gelding: third foal:
half-brother to 1987 2-y-o 6f seller winner Winter House (by Viking): dam, placed at
3 yrs in Ireland, is half-sister to useful Hollywood Party: quite modest maiden: best
effort fourth start: blinkered, well beaten in Hamilton nursery on final outing: will
stay well. *M. W. Easterby.*

GOLD DUCAT 3 b.f. Young Generation 129–Sagar 74 (Habitat 134) [1988 5f 6g³ 52
6m² 6g 5d* 5f⁴ 5f³ 5s⁵ 1989 7s 5f 5.3h 5m 5g 5f 5.3h³ 5f⁶ 5g³ 5f 5m 5f³] compact
filly: moderate walker and mover: plating class nowadays: best form at 5f: seems to
act on any going: has run creditably for apprentice: ran creditably in blinkers final
start: very mulish on way down when below form time before. *G. Lewis.*

GOLD DUST 4 b.c. Golden Fleece (USA) 133–Soba 127 (Most Secret 119) [1988 84
7m² 7g² 7g* 1989 12m* 12g] ex-Irish colt: first foal: dam tough and consistent
sprinter: won amateurs event at Thirsk in May in good style by 5 lengths: tailed off
in £24,300 handicap at Haydock 2 months later: suited by 1½m: acts on top-
of-the-ground: blinkered last 2 outings at 3 yrs. *R. Akehurst.*

GOLDEN ALCHEMIST 2 ch.g. (Mar 6) Ballacashtal (CAN)–Pts Fairway —
(Runnymede 123) [1989 5d 6m 8m] 8,400Y: lengthy, dipped-backed gelding: fifth
foal: half-brother to 1988 2-y-o 5.8f winner Roheryn, 1986 2-y-o 5f seller winner
Real Rustle (both by Enchantment) and 1m seller winner On Impulse (by Jellaby):
dam well behind both starts at 2 yrs: of little account. *J. S. Wilson.*

GOLDEN ANCONA 6 ch.h. London Bells (CAN) 109–Golden Darling 86 93
(Darling Boy 124) [1988 7m 6g³ 5f 6g* 6s² 6g 6f 6s* 6d² 6s 6d 6f 6g² 1989 6v² 7d 6g
6m³ 6m⁴ 6m 6m⁵ 5.6g⁴ 6s 6g⁵ 6v⁶ 6d⁴] close-coupled, lightly-made horse: poor
mover: fairly useful performer: retains all his ability, on eighth outing fourth of 19
finishers to Craft Express in £24,800 Tote-Portland Handicap at Doncaster:
finished strongly when fourth to Dawn Success in Thirsk listed event in November:
stays 7f: particularly well suited by give in the ground: has worn blinkers and a
visor, but better without: has shown a tendency to edge: tough: sold 8,800 gns
Newmarket December Sales. *M. H. Easterby.*

GOLDEN ANN 3 b.f. Absalom 128–Polly Oligant (Prince Tenderfoot (USA) 126) 62 +
[1988 6m 6f 1989 6s 8g 8g 9m 10g³] compact filly: showed improved form in
handicaps at Sandown and Folkestone (8/1 from 14/1, looking unlucky after poor run)
last 2 outings: sometimes takes good hold. *G. B. Balding.*

GOLDEN BEAU 7 b.g. Crimson Beau 124–Kantado 93 (Saulingo 122) [1988 8d 68
7g⁵ 8g² 8g* 8.5m 9f⁴ 9f⁵ 8f² 8.5g³ 8d⁴ 8g* 8g³ 8s² 1989 8g 8d* 8m 9f⁶ 8f 9f 8m²
8m⁶ 8.2m 8f* 8m 7m³ 8g² 8m 8s 8m⁵ 8.2d] sparely-made, rather hollow-backed
gelding: good mover: quite modest handicapper: successful in apprentice event at
Thirsk in April for second year running and in moderately-run 4-runner race at Ayr
in July: suited by about 1m: acts on any going, except possibly hard: excellent mount
for inexperienced rider: blinkered once: visored 5 times at 7-y-o, including at
Thirsk: often sweats profusely and gets on edge: sold 4,400 gns Ascot December
Sales. *M. P. Naughton.*

GOLDEN BOREEN 6 b.g. Boreen (FR) 123–Golden Track (Track Spare 125) —
[1988 NR 1989 10m] leggy, workmanlike gelding: fifth foal: half-brother to fair 5f
winner Schula (by Kala Shikari) and Irish 9f winner Just Touch (by Touch Paper):
dam ran once: 66/1, bandaged and on toes, well-beaten last of 7 in maiden at
Beverley in August: dead. *O. Brennan.*

GOLDEN CAJUN 5 ch.h. Cajun 120–Miscellaneous (Lord Gayle (USA) 124) —
[1988 NR 1989 8.2g 7m 5f] lengthy horse: plating-class maiden in 1987: well beaten
in handicaps as 5-y-o: stays 7f: acts on top-of-the-ground and a soft surface: visored
second start (saddle appeared to slip), blinkered on last: has found little. *Mrs G. E.
Jones.*

GOLDEN CLOGS 2 b.c. (Apr 20) Lochnager 132–Dutch Girl 78 (Workboy 123) —
[1989 6g 6m 8.5f] neat colt: fourth foal: brother to quite modest maiden Sendim On

Sam and half-brother to modest 5f and 6f winner Golden Flats (by Sonnen Gold): dam, daughter of smart sprinter Dutch Gold, won 5 times over 5f: of little account. *M. W. Easterby.*

GOLDEN DELLA 2 b.f. (Mar 6) Glint of Gold 128–Shindella 104 (Furry Glen 65 p 121) [1989 7g] leggy filly: second foal: half-sister to 3-y-o Fort Flutter: dam 5f and 1m winner at 2 yrs, disappointed as 3-y-o: 16/1, in mid-division, keeping on towards finish, in 24-runner maiden at Newmarket in November: should do better. *I. A. Balding.*

GOLDEN ERA (USA) 2 ch.f. (Feb 28) Hero's Honor (USA)–Golden 113 Secretariat (USA) (Secretariat (USA)) [1989 8g* 8m*] third foal: dam ran 5 times: sire won from 7f to 11f: successful in newcomers race at Saint-Cloud in September and Prix des Reservoirs (by ½ length from Miss Afrique) at Longchamp in October: will probably stay 1¼m. *P. Bary, France.*

GOLDEN FLATS 4 br.f. Sonnen Gold 121–Dutch Girl 78 (Workboy 123) [1988 79 5m 5s 5g 6f⁶ 5s 5g 8.5f 5g 5f 6m 1989 6m 5m 6g 5m 5f² 6m* 6f² 6m² 5m⁴ 6g³ 5m* 6f* 5d² 6m² 6g² 5f³ 6f* 5g* 6m⁶ 5m⁴ 6f⁶] workmanlike filly: modest handicapper: in tremendous form for much of second half of season, winning at Pontefract, Ripon, Redcar, Nottingham and Haydock: effective at 5f and 6f: acted on firm going and a soft surface: visored once: effective with or without blinkers: sometimes wore bandages: often looked none too keen and was suited by waiting tactics: tough: in foal to Risk Me. *M. W. Easterby.*

GOLDEN FLIGHT 2 ch.f. (Apr 26) Remainder Man 126§–Wigeon 80 (Divine 48 Gift 127) [1989 5d⁶ 5f⁶ 5m² 7m³ 6g 8.2d 7.5f⁶ 8.2g] 880Y: leggy, plain filly: has a round action: seventh foal: half-sister to 6f winner Premier Lad (by Tower Walk) and 5f to 1¼m winner Ma Pierrette (by Cawston's Clown): dam won 5 times at up to 1¼m: poor maiden: will stay 1¼m: sometimes hangs: often edgy. *E. J. Alston.*

GOLDEN GARTER 4 ch.g. Ballacashtal (CAN)–Blue Garter 70 (Targowice 73 (USA) 130) [1988 6d⁶ 6d² 6d 6f 7d⁵ 6m 6g 7s³ 6m 6f⁴ 6s 1989 6s³ 5g 6g 6f³ 5f 6m] medium-sized gelding: moderate mover: useful 2-y-o, only modest nowadays: not seen out after May: subsequently gelded: suited by 6f: probably ideally suited by plenty of give nowadays: visored last 3 outings: has run creditably for apprentice: has shown a tendency to hang: has got on edge. *M. Brittain.*

GOLDEN GENERATION 3 b.c. Young Generation 129–Song of Gold 85 63 (Song 132) [1988 NR 1989 10g 8m⁶ 7h² 6f 7.6f] 25,000F, 25,000Y: big, strong, good-topped colt: fifth foal: half-brother to 6f and 7f winner Postorage (by Pyjama Hunt) and a winning plater: dam sprinter: easily best effort in maidens when second at Brighton in August, making most: behind facing stiff task in handicap final start: coltish on debut: sold 7,400 gns Newmarket Autumn Sales. *G. Harwood.*

GOLDEN IMAGE 3 ch.f. Bustino 136–Kingston Rose (Tudor Music 131) [1988 48 6g 1989 8s⁴ 10g 8.2g⁴ 10m 12g] sturdy filly: plating-class form: stays 1m: possibly needs some give in the ground: sold to join R. Dods 5,000 gns Newmarket Autumn Sales. *Capt. R. M. Smyly.*

GOLDEN ISLE 5 b.h. Golden Fleece (USA) 133–Dunette (FR) 127 (Hard To — Beat 132) [1988 10g 10g⁶ 13.3f 16m⁶ 1989 10f] strong, useful-looking horse: carries plenty of condition: poor mover, with a rather round action: won minor events at Phoenix Park and the Curragh in 1987: lightly raced and well beaten last 2 seasons: gambled-on favourite on first run for over 16 months and bandaged on Pontefract seller in October: stays 1½m: suited by an easy surface (probably not at best on very soft going): has gone freely to post and pulled hard. *B. J. Curley.*

GOLDEN LOFT 2 b.f. (Feb 26) Thatching 131–Often (Ballymore 123) [1989 7g⁴] 66 p IR 30,000Y: unfurnished filly: second foal: half-sister to Irish 3-y-o 7f winner Outeniqua (by Bold Lad (IRE)): dam unraced half-sister to very useful Foiled Again: 8/1 and green, 3 lengths fourth of 8, staying on well, to Kerama in minor event at Kempton in September: will improve. *D. J. G. Murray-Smith.*

GOLDEN MACHINE 4 ch.f. Glint of Gold 128–Adrana 86 (Bold Lad (IRE) 133) — [1988 6v² 7s² 10f 8f 1989 16.2d 16g] tall, lengthy, sparely-made filly: modest maiden at her best: tailed off in spring as 4-y-o: stays 7f: acts on heavy going: has carried head high: best left alone. *M. W. Easterby.*

GOLDEN MADJAMBO 3 ch.c. Northern Tempest (USA) 120–Shercol 74 — (Monseigneur (USA) 127) [1988 5g 6g 7.5f 1989 10.2g 12s 8.2m 12g] leggy, angular colt: well beaten in varied events, including seller on final start, first for 6 months: probably doesn't stay 1¼m: trained until after third start by M. Brittain. *B. A. McMahon.*

GOLDEN MAIN 3 b.c. Glint of Gold 128–Sea Venture (FR) 98 (Diatome 132) **70**
[1988 NR 1989 11.5m⁴ 12m⁵ 12m⁴ 14g⁶ 16m 12f⁶] medium-sized, well-made colt:
closely related to very useful 1½m winner Sailor's Mate (by Shirley Heights) and
half-brother to several winners, including useful 1980 French 2-y-o 6f winner
Grecian Sea (by Homeric): dam, from family of Reform, won over 6f at 2 yrs and
stayed 1m: modest maiden: below form in handicaps last 2 outings, taking keen hold
on first of them: stays 1¾m: sold 14,500 gns Newmarket Autumn Sales. *C. E.
Brittain.*

GOLDEN OPINION (USA) 3 ch.f. Slew O'Gold (USA)–Optimistic Lass **127**
(USA) 117 (Mr Prospector) [1988 NR 1989 8d* 8m³ 8g* 8f* 6m² 8g*]
    Trainer Fabre's marvellous season could have sparkled even more but
for set-backs to a number of the stable's best horses; Dancehall, Creator and
Golden Opinion to name three. Dancehall ran his last race in June. The other
two were still winning in the autumn, until injury intervened when Creator
was favourite for the Dubai Champion Stakes and Golden Opinion second
favourite for the Breeders' Cup Mile. Golden Opinion's injury—to a
tendon—was more serious than Creator's and she has been retired. It's a pity
Golden Opinion couldn't run in the Breeders' Cup. Not only was she in
tremendous form, having just returned from a break to give weight and a
drubbing to the Ciga Prix du Rond-Point field, she also looked the right type
for Gulfstream Park, quick enough to take on top sprinters (she very nearly
won the Carroll Foundation July Cup) yet better suited by the extra two
furlongs.
    Golden Opinion didn't race as a two-year-old and she made only six
appearances in all, tackling the July Cup on her fifth. Before Newmarket she'd
been kept to mile races for three-year-old fillies, and by the fourth of them, the
Coronation Stakes at Royal Ascot, had established herself among the best
over the distance. All France seemed to know of her ability in the spring.
Along with the same owner's Russian Royal and a pacemaker, she started 5/4
favourite for the Poule d'Essai des Pouliches on the sole public evidence of a
listed-race success at Maisons-Laffitte three weeks earlier. Confidence in
Golden Opinion proved misplaced on the day, but not before she'd come

*Coronation Stakes, Ascot—the contrasting styles of Asmussen
on Golden Opinion (nearest camera) and Pat Eddery on Magic Gleam*

through very smoothly to show ahead approaching the distance; Pearl Bracelet and Pass The Peace just ran her out of it towards the end. Inexperience might have cost Golden Opinion the classic though that's not to take anything away from the winner, a once-raced maiden going into it. The Prix de Sandringham, a weakly-contested, moderately-run Group 3 race at Chantilly in June, saw the odds-on Golden Opinion gain more experience and a second win. She was badly bumped when denied an opening full of running approaching the final furlong but got through in plenty of time to settle the issue with a turn of foot.

Not all the portents were favourable for Golden Opinion at Royal Ascot, though she started favourite again in a field of twelve. She scratched down on ground much firmer than she'd encountered before, bandaged in front as at Chantilly where her jockey had given the impression he'd been keen to nurse her along. However, she turned in a fine performance. She was held up well in touch with Magic Gleam who set a steady pace, and when the leader showed no sign of stopping into the turn Golden Opinion was sent in pursuit, getting a lovely run on the rails, quickening well. Magic Gleam quickened too, so that she still held a narrow lead over Golden Opinion approaching the last furlong; a close struggle ensued, with Golden Opinion, possibly feeling the ground, needing to be ridden once in front to hold on by half a length. The others were put firmly in their place, Guest Artiste, who hampered Comic Talent and Kerita as she made her run in the straight, finishing four lengths down in just beating Tessla and Rain Burst for third.

The three previous July Cups had been won by a horse brought back in distance, Green Desert from a mile in 1986, Ajdal from a mile and a half in 1987 and Soviet Star from a mile in 1988. Perhaps it was the example of Soviet Star that inspired owner and trainer to look for a repeat from Golden Opinion, helped, no doubt, by the fact that they'd another string to their bow at a mile in Polish Precedent. The bid failed by a head. On the firmish going Golden Opinion ran much more like one who'd been brought back to sprinting than Soviet Star did on the soft. Initially things went smoothly. She looked very well beforehand, and whereas she could sometimes be really keen she remained calm and relaxed, taken down quietly to the start (mercifully the traditional parade has been dispensed with). But the race hadn't been under way long before she began to find the pace hot; in the circumstances on this occasion she could ill afford forfeiting position as a result of the usual tactic of steadying her leaving the stalls. As she came off the bridle she began to lose ground gradually on the leaders, so that by halfway her cause seemed virtually hopeless. Cadeaux Genereux up ahead was moving well within himself still. From there until near the finish the longer the race went on the stronger Golden Opinion got, and though she hung left inside Cadeaux Genereux after making good progress up the rise, she put in a sustained challenge.

As Polish Precedent's winning run continued nothing was seen of Golden Opinion. After the Prix du Moulin the plan apparently was for one of the pair to tackle Zilzal at Ascot, the other to run in the Prix de la Foret in mid-October; only then would a decision be made on the Breeders' Cup. The decision came to be made rather earlier in the end. Golden Opinion would be the one to go to Gulfstream Park and would be supplemented to have her preparatory race in the Rond-Point, a Group 3 event for three-year-olds and upwards on the Prix de l'Arc de Triomphe card. The need for the right kind of preparation seems to have been the motivation behind the very unusual step of running a Group 1 winner in a Group 3 event; she was penalized 7 lb. There would normally be little or no prestige to be gained, plenty to be lost, but Golden Opinion made the most of her opportunity to leave all who saw her with the memory of a good filly winning in style. She won by six lengths. Asmussen rode her supremely confidently, and waited until around a furlong and a half out before taking the lead. Golden Opinion sailed clear on the bridle and was just pushed along at the finish to keep well on top of Good Example and Star Touch.

Golden Opinion is from the first crop of her sire and is the first foal of her dam. Like an increasing number of her owner's better horses, she's home bred. The dam Optimistic Lass was acquired for 700,000 dollars as a yearling and sent on to Stoute to be trained. She won over six furlongs on her only start

Ciga Prix du Rond-Point, Longchamp—Golden Opinion makes it look so easy

as a two-year-old; the following season she developed into one of the best fillies in Britain at around a mile and a quarter, winning the Musidora Stakes and the Nassau Stakes. She found the distance of the Oaks a shade too far and was weakening when badly baulked inside the last furlong by Out of Shot—an incident which led to Optimistic Lass's promotion to fourth. Golden Opinion's sire Slew O'Gold, champion three-year-old colt and champion handicap male

Golden Opinion (USA) (ch.f. 1986)	Slew O' Gold (USA) (b 1980)	Seattle Slew (b or br 1974)	Bold Reasoning My Charmer
		Alluvial (ch 1969)	Buckpasser Bayou
	Optimistic Lass (USA) (b 1981)	Mr Prospector (b 1970)	Raise A Native Gold Digger
		Loveliest (ch 1973)	Tibaldo Lovely Ann

Sheikh Mohammed's "Golden Opinion"

at four, stayed a mile and a half really well though he was equally effective over three furlongs less. With the other good fillies Gorgeous and Tactile in his first crop in the States he looks highly promising. Optimistic Lass's dam Loveliest, a half-sister to the Grade 1 Stakes winner Arbees Boy, showed very useful form at up to ten and a half furlongs in France and later won at up to nine furlongs across the Atlantic. The stakes winner Indian Romance is the best of her several successful foals apart from Optimistic Lass.

On breeding Golden Opinion might well have stayed further than a mile, but the fact that she was given a crack at the sprint championship suggests connections saw her very differently. And who's to say they were wrong? It's unlikely that her premature retirement robbed us of the chance to find out. What may well have been lost was the opportunity of watching her at her peak, for she was definitely on the upgrade when she left. Golden Opinion, a lengthy filly, ran well on all the types of surface she encountered—good to soft, good, good to firm, and firm—though she was never impressive in her slower paces, sometimes wore bandages and eventually broke down. *A. Fabre, France.*

GOLDEN PHEASANT (USA)   3 gr.c. Caro 133–Perfect Pigeon (USA) **119**
(Round Table) [1988 NR 1989 11s* 12.3m² 12d² 12g² 12d* 12g]

For the winner of the race, Golden Pheasant didn't have much space devoted to him after the Prix Niel. The Group 2 contest attracted plenty of comment from the Press but that was mainly about the race Nashwan lost, leaving Golden Pheasant and French Glory who beat him to become the stuff of racing quizzes rather than racing legend. Golden Pheasant is a smart and consistent racehorse but some way off the best. That much was evident to the French backers who had him disputing second favouritism for the Prix Niel at 7/1 and Nashwan dominating the eight-strong field at 5/1 on. Hopes of a Golden Pheasant victory rested on the receipt of 7 lb and the possibility of improvement with experience and the fitting of blinkers. He'd had only four previous outings, winning a maiden at Newbury on the first of them, then being put straight into pattern company where he was beaten two and a half lengths by Old Vic in the Dalham Chester Vase, driven along to stay in touch from five furlongs out. Following his sale and transfer from Brittain's stable to race in France, Golden Pheasant was touched off by both Harvest Time in the Prix du Lys at Chantilly and Sheriff's Star in the Grand Prix de Saint-Cloud. His performance in the latter—finishing strongly in a very slowly-run race—prompted his trainer to contemplate a try in blinkers and an impressive piece of work in them just before the Prix Niel apparently convinced him. Golden Pheasant was settled in mid-division at Longchamp as the field first virtually ignored Nashwan's pacemaker then swallowed him up as they straightened for home where French Glory went on, closely attended by

Prix Niel, Longchamp—Golden Pheasant springs a surprise as Nashwan, only third, suffers his first defeat

Mr B. McNall's "Golden Pheasant"

Nashwan. The favourite looked to have French Glory's measure shortly after, but far from going clear, Nashwan couldn't extend his advantage to more than a neck and was soon labouring as Golden Pheasant, who tended to hang when first asked for his effort, ran on strongest in the final furlong to win by a length and a half, French Glory regaining second close home.

Golden Pheasant (USA) (gr.c. 1986)	Caro (gr 1967)	Fortino II (gr 1959)	Grey Sovereign
			Ranavalo III
		Chambord (ch 1955)	Chamossaire
			Life Hill
	Perfect Pigeon (USA) (b 1971)	Round Table (b 1954)	Princequillo
			Knight's Daughter
		Pink Pigeon (ro 1964)	T V Lark
			Ruwenzori

Clive Brittain is reported to have told Golden Pheasant's owners that he was 'the most grossly undersold horse they would ever have' when Golden Pheasant had left for France. Whatever the truth of that, he was a gift at the 44,000 dollars which Pin Oak Stud paid for him at the Keeneland September Yearling Sales. The reason for that initial figure is very probably his unimposing physique: he's a workmanlike, angular, sparely-made colt. It can have little to do with the dam Perfect Pigeon's producing record. She's had nine winners from ten runners before Golden Pheasant, the best of them being Golden Pheasant's brother Trial By Error who won a maiden at

359

Yarmouth and the Dee Stakes at Chester from six outings for Cumani before being sent to the USA where he ran once, unplaced, as a four-year-old. Among the dam's other progeny are minor stakes winners by Best Turn and Providential. Perfect Pigeon's racing record also has a consistency of sorts; she ran unplaced in all of her thirteen starts. There are plenty of winners elsewhere in the pedigree, however, notably the grandam Pink Pigeon who won twelve of her forty-six races, including the Santa Barbara, American and Beverly Hills Handicaps on turf, all of which now carry Grade 1 status. A daughter of the Hollywood Oaks third Ruwenzori, Pink Pigeon produced only three foals but her unraced sister Gray Dove has had a far more fruitful spell in the paddocks, having a dozen foals to date, including the Prix du Moulin winner Gravelines and the d'Harcourt and King George V Handicap winner Grand Pavois. Golden Pheasant was made a 10/1-chance to further boost the family's French pattern-race tally in the Arc de Triomphe but neither he nor French Glory did anything to advertise the Prix Niel form; and having travelled to Florida in the hope of contesting the Breeder's Cup Turf then failed to secure a place in the field it was reported that Golden Pheasant would undergo another change of stable and be trained by Whittingham. A share in him has reportedly been bought by Sylvester Stallone. A moderate walker with a rather round action in his faster paces, Golden Pheasant should stay a mile and three quarters and may well prove best on an easy surface. He wore blinkers in the Arc as well as the Niel. *J. E. Pease, France.*

GOLDEN SABRE 3 b.c. Sayf El Arab (USA) 127–Bohemian Rhapsody 86 (On   **59** Your Mark 125) [1988 5g⁴ 5f⁴ 6m 1989 6s 6g⁴ 5.8m³ 6m⁶ 7f 7f 7f⁶ 7m 6f³ 7m³ 6g] small colt: has a quick action: quite modest handicapper: suited by 6f: acts on firm going: visored last 3 starts: sold 2,300 gns Ascot December Sales. *D. W. P. Arbuthnot.*

GOLDEN SAMPHIRE 4 b.f. Hays 120–Sea Shrub (Ballymore 123) [1988 6d 7f   **— §** 8d 1989 12d 12h 12h] good-quartered filly: plating-class maiden at 2 yrs: no subsequent form on flat: refused to race final outing: should stay beyond 6f: one to leave alone. *M. C. Chapman.*

GOLDEN SCISSORS 3 gr.f. Kalaglow 132–Hide Out (Habitat 134) [1988 NR   **76** 1989 12.2m⁵ 12h⁵ 11.7m²] leggy filly: seventh living foal: half-sister to 1m winner Bahrain Bridge (by Formidable) and 1984 2-y-o 5f winner Fair Charter (by Be My Guest): dam ran once: sweating slightly, short-head second of 6 to Arbour at Bath in July, running on well after slow start and best effort in maidens. *K. O. Cunningham-Brown.*

GOLDEN TORQUE 2 br.g. (Apr 7) Taufan (USA) 119–Brightelmstone 105   **84** (Prince Regent (FR) 129) [1989 5m³ 6m⁵ 6g* 6d⁴ 6s 8s* 7g⁶ 7d⁶] 11,500Y: strong, close-coupled gelding: good walker: seventh reported foal: half-brother to 3 winners, including 1981 2-y-o 5f winner Debian (by Relko) and 1¼m to 11.5f winner Boon Point (by Shirley Heights): dam useful at up to 7f: fair performer: won claimer at Haydock in August and nursery at Ayr in October: suited by 1m: effective with or without a visor: has looked an awkward ride: bandaged off-fore fourth outing: gelded after final one. *Mrs J. R. Ramsden.*

GOLDEN TREASURY (USA) 2 b.f. (Apr 7) Lyphard (USA) 132–Belle   **75 p** Pensee (USA) (Ribot 142) [1989 7g] $650,000Y: strong, sturdy filly: closely related to high-class 1983 French 2-y-o Treizieme and 9f and 1¼m winner Quest (both by The Minstrel), latter dam of Bequest, and half-sister to several other winners, including Gold Cup runner-up Eastern Mystic (by Elocutionist): dam, French 1¼m winner, is half-sister to Junius and Gentle Thoughts: 7/1 and very green, around 4½ lengths seventh of 24, keeping on well, to Katsina in maiden at Newmarket in November: will stay 1¼m: sure to improve, and win a race. *H. R. A. Cecil.*

GOLDEN VEST 5 b.g. Sonnen Gold 121–Key Harvest (Deep Diver 134) [1988   **66 §** 12g⁴ 10f 10g⁵ 11g³ 1989 12g³ 17.6m⁶ 12d] tall, rather leggy gelding: has been hobdayed: quite modest handicapper: pulled hard when tailed-off last on final 2 starts: probably stays 1½m: acts on any going: blinkered once at 4 yrs and on last 2 starts: often used to sweat and get very much on edge: winning hurdler: wanders under pressure: ungenuine, and best left alone. *J. Mackie.*

GOLDEN VINTAGE 3 ch.c. Glint of Gold 128–Boissiere (High Top 131) [1988   **67** NR 1989 8d 10g⁵ 10g 11.7m³ 12g] 5,000Y: second foal: half-brother to French 1987 2-y-o 6.5f and 1m winner Barbade (by Dunphy): dam, French 9f winner at 4 yrs, is half-sister to Bering: modest maiden: good third in handicap at Windsor in June: off course 3 months after: stays 11.7f. *S. Dow.*

GOLD FLAIR   3 ch.f. Tap On Wood 130–Suemette (Danseur 134) [1988 8s³ 8g 7g   **68** 1989 10s⁵ 16.5g4] big, leggy filly: showed fairly useful form last 2 outings as 2-y-o: well below best in 1989, pulling hard and wandering under pressure when fourth in ladies maiden event (sweating and edgy) at Doncaster in June: should be suited by at least 1¾m: best form on good going: blinkered final start at 2 yrs: doesn't look ideal mount for amateur. *P. F. I. Cole.*

GOLDIE OF PARIS   4 ch.f. Tickled Pink 114–Bernina (FR) (Prudent II 133)   — [1988 8f⁶ 10d 10g 1989 10.1m 13.1h] plain, sparely-made filly: seems of little account. *J. Douglas-Home.*

GOLD MINORIES   5 b.h. Baptism 119–Viva La Weavers (Weavers' Hall 122)   **91** [1988 7.6g 7f² 7m⁵ 7f² 7f* 6m 7m* 1989 7f 6f 6f 7f* 7.6f* 7m⁵] rather lightly-made, close-coupled horse: moderate mover: fair handicapper: twice made all at Lingfield (has now won there 5 times) in August: best at around 7f: suited by top-of-the-ground: ran well for apprentice and when sweating fourth outing at 4 yrs: taken down early third one in 1989: well served by forcing tactics: sold 16,500 gns Newmarket Autumn Sales. *P. J. Makin.*

GOLDNEYEV (USA)   3 b. or br.c. Nureyev (USA) 131–Gold River (FR) 132 **114** (Riverman (USA) 131) [1988 6g* 8m³ 8m³ 1989 8d³ 8m² 8d] big, strong colt: fourth foal: closely related to very smart French 1m to 1¼m winner Riviere d'Or (by Lyphard), smart French middle-distance colt Chercheur d'Or (by Northern Dancer) and French 1½m winner Riviere d'Argent (by Nijinsky): dam won Arc de Triomphe and stayed very well: won Prix Yacowlef at Deauville at 2 yrs: placed as 3-y-o behind Kendor in Prix de Fontainebleau and Poule d'Essai des Poulains (beaten 2 lengths) at Longchamp: behind in Prix de la Jonchere there in June: should be suited by further: acts on top-of-the-ground and a soft surface. *Mme C. Head, France.*

GOLD NOSTALGIA   2 ch.f. (Feb 4) Glint of Gold 128–Crepellora (Crepello 136)   **84** [1989 7g³ 7m* 8g⁵ 8m⁶] 50,000Y: good-bodied filly: sister to useful 1½m winner Reflect, closely related to a winner in Spain by Milford and half-sister to 2 winners in Spain: dam, winner in France and Spain as a 3-y-o, is half-sister to smart Italian filly Dudinka: made most in maiden at Newmarket in July: good sixth of 8, leading over 6f, to Silk Slippers in Hoover Fillies' Mile at Ascot: will stay 1½m: sweating third outing. *P. A. Kelleway.*

GOLD 'N SOFT   5 br.m. Whistling Deer 117–Wine Lake (Guillaume Tell (USA)   — 121) [1988 NR 1989 12d] ex-Irish mare: first reported foal: dam Irish 1m winner: poor maiden: stays 1½m: acts on firm going. *J. G. O'Shea.*

GOLD OF HONOUR   2 ch.c. (Apr 12) Vaigly Great 127–Golden Treasure 106   **60** (Crepello 136) [1989 6f 6m³] 13,000Y: angular colt: half-brother to 4 winners, including fairly useful 1½m winner Fair of Face (by Grundy) and useful sprinter Precious Metal (by Mummy's Pet): dam, unbeaten in 3 races over 5f and 6f at 2 yrs, stayed 1¼m: blinkered, staying-on 3½ lengths third of 9, not knocked about, to Ballyhooly in claimer at Leicester in June: will be suited by 7f: sent to Italy. *I. A. Balding.*

GOLD PAINT   5 b.m. Glint of Gold 128–Depict 84 (Derring-Do 131) [1988 NR   — 1989 12d⁵] rather leggy, angular mare: modest maiden as 3-y-o when trained by I. Balding: bandaged and carrying condition, prominent until 2f out when 13 lengths fifth of 11 in minor event at Pontefract in April: stays 2m: acts on top-of-the-ground. *C. C. Elsey.*

GOLD PAVILION (USA)   3 ch.f. Lemhi Gold (USA) 123–Santa Linda (USA)   **93** (Sir Ivor 135) [1988 NR 1989 10g* 12.5f*] $75,000Y: good-topped, attractive filly: has plenty of scope: first foal: dam, unraced half-sister to smart middle-distance colt Noble Saint, is daughter of half-sister to Tom Rolfe and Chieftain: odds on, successful in 18-runner maiden at Leicester in April by 2½ lengths from Blaze O'Gold and 5-runner minor event (made all, still bit green) at Wolverhampton in May by 2 lengths from Zia: will stay further. *M. R. Stoute.*

GOLD PROSPECT   7 b.g. Wolverlife 115–Golden Darling 86 (Darling Boy 124)   **93** [1988 8d⁵ 8m² 8f 7.6g³ 8m 8g* 7g 8d 6s 1989 7d 8s 8.2g³] lengthy, sparely-made gelding: often impresses in appearance: moderate mover: fairly useful handi-capper: best effort in first half of 1989 when third to Colway Rally, running on strongly final 2f, at Haydock in June: best at 7f to 1m: ideally suited by an easy surface: has a good turn of foot and is held up: ran moderately when edgy: genuine. *G. B. Balding.*

GOLD SEAM (USA) 3 b.c. Mr Prospector (USA)–Ballare (USA) **124**
(Nijinsky (CAN) 138) [1988 NR 1989 7d⁵ 8m³ 6m* 7g* 7g* 7m]

The old racing adage 'no foot, no horse' has been illustrated on a number
of occasions in recent years, most notably by the career of the leading
middle-distance horse of 1988 Mtoto, whose fragile hooves made him difficult
to train at three. In the latest season the feet of the good three-year-old Gold
Seam attracted some publicity. Gold Seam has very thin walls to his hooves, a
condition which resulted in his losing a shoe during his second race, a maiden
at Newbury in July. A novel remedy was found. Subsequently Gold Seam was
equipped with stick-on plastic shoes, and, significantly or otherwise, he
improved by leaps and bounds, winning three of his remaining four races. Gold
Seam's rise from relative obscurity in the second half of the season was really
quite meteoric. The last of those three wins was gained in the Group 3
Kiveton Park Stakes at Doncaster in September. So much did Gold Seam
improve in so short a space of time that, just three months after his third place
in that ordinary Newbury maiden, it came as a major disappointment that he
finished only seventh of eight behind Gabina in the Group 1 Prix de la Foret at
Longchamp. We would rather judge him on his performance at Doncaster,
where he accounted for the General Accident Two Thousand Guineas fourth
Markofdistinction in decisive style. Gold Seam started second favourite to
that horse in a field of six. On form he clearly had a lot to find, but his wins in
August in a minor event at Leicester and a handicap at Newmarket showed he
was going the right way. In the latter contest he carried 9-7 and beat Bollin
Zola (who received 19 lb) by two and a half lengths. Another point to impress
itself before the Doncaster race was what a grand sort on looks Gold Seam is.
A big, rangy colt with plenty of scope, Gold Seam continually took the eye,
both in his athletic physique and his general well-being. In comparison
Markofdistinction, a rangy individual, no longer looked imposing. On this
occasion paddock impressions were borne out on the racecourse. In a race run
at a moderate pace Gold Seam tracked his main rival as the early running was
cut out by the outsider Cottenham. The principals were asked for their efforts
at about the same place, just over two furlongs out, and, for a while, it looked
like being a close thing. But at the distance Gold Seam really got into his
stride, quickening much the better and striding out well to the line, which he
reached with two lengths to spare. The very useful filly Kerita, who never got
in a blow, was the same margin back in third. All in all, Gold Seam gave the
impression he takes time to hit top pace, but he is undeniably impressive
when he does. If he is to be returned to six furlongs then he will probably
require a stiff track and a strong gallop to be seen to best advantage, and he's
worth another try at a mile. For a while Gold Seam was spoken of as a possible
for the Whyte & Mackay Scotch Handicap at Ascot and William Hill
Cambridgeshire Handicap at Newmarket, but connections opted instead for
the Foret. His moderate showing in France, where he never really looked a
danger, has a number of possible explanations. His jockey, Carson, felt that
the horse failed to handle the home turn; there's also the chance that the

Kiveton Park Stakes, Doncaster—Gold Seam is too good for Markofdistinction and Kerita

Mr Peter M. Brant's "Gold Seam"

ground (more 'on top' than at Doncaster) was against him; he was clearly at a disadvantage in terms of experience; also his stable was under something of a cloud at the time. Whatever, it's pretty certain that Gold Seam will show himself to better effect in such company in the future.

Gold Seam (USA) (b.c. 1986)	Mr Prospector (USA) (b 1970)	Raise A Native (ch 1961)	Native Dancer
			Raise You
		Gold Digger (b 1962)	Nashua
			Sequence
	Ballare (USA) (b 1977)	Nijinsky (b 1967)	Northern Dancer
			Flaming Page
		Morgaise (b 1965)	Round Table
			Nanka

To say that Gold Seam 'looks a million dollars' is almost damning with faint praise, for he's probably worth a good deal more than that already; and he'll certainly be worth a princely sum if he can find success in Group 2 or Group 1 company as a four-year-old. He is a son of the tremendously successful Mr Prospector, perhaps the most sought after sire in the world since Northern Dancer's retirement, and he comes from a choicely-bred and largely successful female line. Gold Seam's dam, Ballare, won four races at up to a mile, including the quite valuable Senorita Stakes. She is a daughter of the Hollywood Oaks second Morgaise and a half-sister to two winners, including Fabulous Salt, winner of the Masaka Stakes and third in the Pretty Polly Stakes in 1981. Fabulous Salt is also the dam of the very useful three-year-old of the latest season Knoosh. Gold Seam is a fourth foal, following the stakes-placed sprint winner Balladry (by In Reality) and colts by Spectacular Bid and Conquistador Cielo. He also has a year younger full brother called Yellow Metal.

The prospects for Gold Seam in 1990 look bright. His rate of progress was so rapid prior to his defeat at Longchamp that, particularly considering his physical scope, there must be a good chance he'll improve further. He seems sure to win more good races. *Major W. R. Hern.*

GOLD STRATA 3 b.g. Gold Song 112–French Strata (USA) 76 (Permian (USA)) — [1988 6g 6s 7g 1989 12d⁵] strong, sturdy gelding: no sign of ability in maidens and handicap: visored, pulled hard for 7-lb claimer only start as 3-y-o, in April. *P. Howling.*

GOLDUST (FR) 4 ch.f. Dublin Taxi–Aberklair 72 (Klairon 131) [1988 6m⁴ 7d 6f 6f 1989 6f 5d 6d] lengthy, sparely-made filly: modest maiden at best: no form since first outing in 1988: stays 6f: acts on top-of-the-ground and a soft surface: sweating on reappearance. *Miss A. J. Whitfield.*

GOLFE DU LION 4 b.c. Longleat (USA) 109–Welsh Jewel 72 (Welsh Pageant 64 132) [1988 8g 7d 8m 7f 10g³ 10g 10d 8m* 1989 8d* 8f⁵ 10m⁵ 8.2g*] medium-sized, quite attractive colt: quite modest handicapper: won apprentice event at Warwick in May and 18-runner contest at Hamilton (making virtually all) in August: suited by 1m: acts on firm going and a soft surface: blinkered nowadays. *P. J. Makin.*

GOLFER'S SUNRISE 4 b.g. Red Sunset 120–Miss Stradavinsky (Auction 35 Ring (USA) 123) [1988 5f 10m 8d 10d 1989 12.5g² 9f⁴ 14m⁶ 8f 12.5f] workmanlike gelding: bad maiden: stays 12.5f: acts on firm going: has worn blinkers: apprentice ridden as 4-y-o: has carried head high. *K. White.*

GOMARLOW 2 gr.c. (Mar 20) Belfort (FR) 89–Tringa (GER) (Kaiseradler) 95 [1989 6g 7g²] 3,200F, 8,800Y: strong, lengthy, angular colt: brother to 3-y-o Belfort Gipsy and half-brother to a winner abroad: dam won in Germany: 1½ lengths second of 28, clear, to Rami in maiden at Newmarket in November: backward and green on debut: should win a similar event. *D. Morley.*

GO MAROCK 3 ch.f. All Systems Go 119–Marock Morley 59 (Most Secret 119) — [1988 5g 5g 5s 1989 5m 7.5d 6m] sturdy filly: moderate mover, with a quick action: poor maiden: no show in spring as 3-y-o, including in sellers: should be suited by further than 5f. *W. W. Haigh.*

GO MILORD (FR) 3 b.c. Solicitor (FR)–Go Mila (FR) (Go Marching (USA)) 112 [1988 5.5m⁵ 6s* 7g* 7.5g² 8d 6.5d² 6.5s³ 1989 8s 9.2m* 8d³ 8.5d* 9g³ 8d* 8g⁴ 9g] first reported foal: dam French provincial 9f to 11f winner: much improved colt: won handicap at Longchamp in May, listed race at Longchamp in July and Group 3 Prix Quincey at Deauville: in frame in pattern events at Longchamp (twice) and Evry (fifth start): trained by D. Wayne Lukas, in mid-division in Hollywood Derby final outing: stays 9f: acts on top-of-the-ground and a soft surface: ran well when sweating penultimate start. *M. Rolland, France.*

GONDO 2 br.g. (Apr 24) Mansingh (USA) 120–Secret Valentine 71 (Wollow 132) 63 [1989 5m 7g 5.1f 8g 6s² a6g⁴] 4,200Y: good-quartered gelding: has scope: has a quick action: first foal: dam 6f to 1m winner: quite modest maiden: suited by 6f: acts on soft going. *M. J. Ryan.*

GONNENSOLD 3 b.f. Sonnen Gold 121–Good Form 54 (Deep Diver 134) [1988 — NR 1989 9d 10f] half-sister to winning sprinter Loch Form and quite modest 1983 maiden 2-y-o Rookaburgh (both by Lochnager): dam stayed 1¼m: well beaten in sellers at Ripon and Pontefract (blinkered): sold 1,050 gns Ascot June Sales. *M. H. Easterby.*

GO NOBLEY 3 b.g. Gorytus (USA) 132–Noblanna (USA) 85 (Vaguely Noble 140) — [1988 NR 1989 10f 12m 10.1g] medium-sized, lengthy gelding: fourth foal: half-brother to Irish 9f winner Roblanna (by Roberto): dam, middle-distance winner, is half-sister to good middle-distance horse Anne's Pretender and daughter of Prix Vermeille winner Anne La Douce: well beaten in maidens (bit backward) at Kempton and Newbury (tailed off) and minor event (sweating, keeping on steadily not knocked about) at Windsor in the summer. *T. Thomson Jones.*

GOOD EGG 3 ch.f. Tachypous 128–Get Involved 79 (Shiny Tenth 120) [1988 6d — 8.2d 8g 1989 6m 6f 7m 6m 6f a6g] deep-girthed filly: has a free, rather round action: no worthwhile form, including in handicap and claimers: blinkered final start. *D. Marks.*

GOODFELLOWS LOT 2 br.g. (May 26) Blazing Saddles (AUS)–Just Kidding **68**
(USA) (Jester) [1989 6g⁴ 5d³] 4,100F, 4,400Y: good-quartered gelding: half-brother
to 1m winner Trompe d'Oeil (by Longleat) and several winners in USA: dam very
smart stakes winner at up to 1m in USA: 12/1, over a length third of 12, one pace last
furlong, to Jagged Edge in maiden at Catterick in October: very much in need of race
on debut. *W. W. Haigh.*

GOOD FOR THE ROSES 3 b.c. Kampala 120–Alleyn (Alcide 136) [1988 7m **66**
7m 1989 10g 8.2f 7m 7m² 7m 8.2f³ a8g²] workmanlike rather unfurnished colt: has a
round action: quite modest maiden: placed in handicap at Leicester and claimers at
Nottingham and Lingfield: stays 1m: acts on firm ground. *G. A. Pritchard-Gordon.*

GOOD HAND (USA) 3 ch.g. Northjet 136–Ribonette (USA) (Ribot 142) [1988 **81**
7g 7d 8.5f⁴ 1989 10.2f 12f³ 13.6f² 16.2g* 16f² 17.6d² 16m⁵] close-coupled,
sparely-made gelding: fair handicapper: won at Haydock in July: ran well
afterwards: lacks turn of foot and shapes like a thorough stayer: acts on firm going
and a soft surface: tends to edge left: blinkered first 3 starts. *J. W. Watts.*

GOOD HOLIDAYS 3 b.f. Good Times (ITY)–Mistress Bowen (Owen Anthony —
102) [1988 5.3f³ 6m² 7g⁴ 6s 7f 1989 7.6m 5m 5m 5m 5m 7.6m 6g] rather
sparely-made filly: has a long stride: plating class at best: has run poorly since third
start at 2 yrs: visored last 2 outings: reluctant to go down final one: bought
out of Lord Jion FitzGerald's stable 1,900 gns Doncaster April Sales before
reappearance: resold 1,050 gns Ascot October Sales. *M. B. James.*

GOOD MEDICINE 4 b.g. Star Appeal 133–Jacoletta 74 (Artaius (USA) 129) **45**
[1988 8g⁴ 8d 8.2s 6g⁶ 6g² 10m⁶ 10s 10g⁵ 12d² 1989 12m 14m 11g 12g³ a14g³ a12g³
a16g] workmanlike gelding: poor performer: best at up to 1½m: possibly unsuited by
soft going, acts on any other: blinkered once, often visored: has run creditably for
apprentice: inconsistent. *P. J. Feilden.*

GOOD MOOD 4 b.g. Jalmood (USA) 126–Key of The Kingdom 111 (Grey —
Sovereign 128§) [1988 12g³ 11m 12g* 12.3f³ 12.3s⁶ 13.8f³ 12d³ 13.8g³ 1989 12d]
close-coupled gelding: quite modest winner as 3-y-o: looked unco-operative
seventh outing: tailed off in Edinburgh handicap in April: stays 1¾m: unsuited by
soft going, probably acts on any other: blinkered twice, running badly on second
occasion: winning hurdler with I. Semple. *J. S. Wilson.*

GOODNIGHT MOON 3 ch.f. Ela-Mana-Mou 132–Her Grace 101 (Great **95**
Nephew 126) [1988 6f³ 7m* 8m³ 1989 8f² 8f³ 8m⁶] strong, good-quartered filly:
fairly useful form when placed in listed race at Sandown and minor event at
Goodwood: never placed to challenge (long way off pace 2f out) in £22,000 handicap
at Newmarket in July: will be suited by 1¼m. *I. A. Balding.*

GOOD N SHARP 8 br.g. Mummy's Pet 125–Sharp Lady 70 (Sharpen Up 127) **51**
[1988 8f 8g 8m* 8m² 8.3m⁵ 8g 8.5f 8m² 1989 8m⁵ 8m 8h* 8h 8f 8g 8m] rather leggy,
sparely-made gelding: plating-class handicapper: well ridden by J. Lowe when
fortunate winner at Carlisle in June, quickening to catch eased Cool Enough on line:
never a threat all starts afterwards: suited by 1m and top-of-the-ground: has been
tried in blinkers: often hangs badly and not an easy ride: best held up. *Mrs G. R.
Reveley.*

GOOD PARTNERS 3 b.f. Belfort (FR) 89–Sharpenella 72 (Sharpen Up 127) **93**
[1988 6m² 6f² 5f* 6g* 6d 6g⁴ 7g² 7d 1989 8s³ 8g³ 8m⁴ 7.6f² 8.2m⁵] rangy,
workmanlike filly: moderate mover, with a quick action: fairly useful handicapper:
not seen out after good fifth in £19,300 event at Haydock in May: may prove as
effective over 7f as 1m: acts on any going: has run well for apprentice. *M. J. Ryan.*

GOODREDA 2 b.f. (Apr 24) Good Times (ITY)–Gundreda 93 (Gunner B 126) **58**
[1989 6m⁶ 8g 5d⁴ 7d⁴ a7g] rather unfurnished filly: first foal: dam 8.2f and 1¼m
winner: plating-class maiden: really needs further than 5f, and should stay 1m. *C. E.
Brittain.*

GOOD SKILLS 2 b.f. (Mar 30) Bustino 136–Gunner's Belle 67 (Gunner B 126) **57**
[1989 7m 7m⁶] 31,000Y: leggy filly: second foal: half-sister to 1988 2-y-o 5f winner
Gunmaster (by Precocious): dam won from 7f to 1¼m: plating-class form in maiden
(better effort) at Newmarket and minor event (pulled hard) at York: bred to stay
1½m. *G. A. Pritchard-Gordon.*

GO ON SMILE (USA) 3 ch.c. Diesis 133–Key Tothe Minstrel (USA) 108 (The **88**
Minstrel (CAN) 135) [1988 7f³ 6d⁴ 1989 8m⁴ 8f 10f⁴ 8f* 8f⁶ 8g] small, strong,
good-topped colt: poor mover: fair performer: easily made all in 3-runner maiden at
Thirsk in August: ran creditably in valuable handicaps at Royal Ascot and Goodwood
previous 2 outings and York penultimate one: led 5½f when below form at Ascot
final start: may well prove best at around 1m: acts on firm going. *A. A. Scott.*

GO ON THE GRAIN 2 ch.g. (May 13) Remainder Man 126§–Femme Fatale 67   **48**
(King's Leap 111) [1989 7m 8.2d 8s 8.2g] IR 8,000Y, 35,000 2-y-o: lengthy,
workmanlike gelding: carries condition: seventh living foal: half-brother to 3-y-o
Raven's Affair (by Tower Walk) and 3 minor winners: dam placed over 5f at 2 yrs, is
half-sister to Middle Park winner Spanish Express: poor form in varied races. *J. S.
Wilson.*

GO PATHFINDER 2 b.g. (May 21) Swing Easy (USA) 126–Pollinella 108   **53**
(Charlottown 127) [1989 6g a8g] 5,000F, 6,400Y: leggy, workmanlike gelding:
brother to modest 1½m winner Mansfield House and half-brother to several other
winners, notably useful 5f to 1m winner Castle Tweed (by Daring March), later
successful in USA: dam stayed 1½m: plating-class form in late-season maidens at
Folkestone (slowly away) and Lingfield. *J. Sutcliffe.*

GO RABALL GO 3 br.g. All Systems Go 119–Rabeeb 64 (Home Guard (USA)   **—**
129) [1988 5m 6g 5.8f² 6m² 6m* 6g⁴ 7d 7g³ 7g² 7m⁴ 7m⁴ 6g⁵ 7f⁵ 7m 8g 7d⁵ 7d 7g*
7m 1989 10g 7g a7g] small, leggy gelding: modest winner at 2 yrs: well beaten in
late-season claimers and handicap as 3-y-o: suited by 7f: acts on firm going and a soft
surface: bandaged on reappearance: suitable mount for apprentice: tends to flash
tail: inconsistent. *C. N. Allen.*

GORDANO 2 ch.g. (Mar 10) Muscatite 122–Coral Star (Tarboosh (USA)) [1989   **35**
7m 6m 8m 7f⁵ 7g a6g] 480Y: first foal: dam never ran: bad maiden. *R. J. Holder.*

GORGEOUS STYLE 3 b.f. Sharpo 132–Westgate Sovereign 89 (Sovereign   **66**
Path 125) [1988 NR 1989 8s³ 7g² 6g² 7g⁵ a6g] 35,000Y: sparely-made filly:
half-sister to 3 winners, including fairly useful 1986 Irish 2-y-o 5f winner Harry
Quinn (by Jaazeiro): dam 5f winner at 2 yrs: quite modest form in varied events:
stays 7f: below form for 7-lb claimer final start: moved very poorly to post on debut.
G. A. Huffer.

GORYTUS PRINCESS 2 b.f. (Apr 18) Gorytus (USA) 132–Latin Verses   **37**
(Appiani II 128) [1989 5h⁵ 6f 7g 8.2f⁶ 7f 6g] 4,600F, 9,000 2-y-o: sturdy filly: closely
related to winners by Ile de Bourbon and Kings Lake (modest stayer Queen's Lake)
and half-sister to 2 other winners, including useful 6f winner Blessed Soandso (by
So Blessed): dam Irish 1½m winner: poor form in varied races, including a seller:
bred to be suited by further than 6f: blinkered or visored last 2 starts. *S. G. Norton.*

GORYTUS STAR 3 ch.c. Gorytus (USA) 132–Bean Siamsa (Solinus 130) [1988   **84**
5g² 5s* 7m 5m 1989 6m²] close-coupled colt: ridden by 5-lb claimer, won maiden at
Haydock as 2-y-o by 8 lengths: 13/2 from 14/1, good neck second of 9, staying on, in
handicap at Salisbury in June, only start in 1989: stays 6f well: acts on top-
of-the-ground and soft going. *J. P. Hudson.*

GOSCAR 4 b.g. Vaigly Great 127–More Or Less 64 (Morston (FR) 125) [1988 10g   **81**
8.5m⁴ 8m* 8s⁶ 10m² 8g 8.2m* 10m* 8f⁵ 10d 9g 1989 10f² 10g 8f 9m⁵ 9m 10m 8m]
dipped-backed gelding: moderate walker and mover: fair handicapper: good second
to Inaad in valuable event at Redcar in May: below form after except on fourth
outing: needs strongly-run race at 1m and stays 1¼m well: well suited by top-
of-the-ground: blinkered final outing at 3 yrs, visored last one in 1989: sometimes sweats: has hung right: sold 7,400 gns Newmarket Autumn Sales: none
too consistent nowadays. *I. V. Matthews.*

GO SOUTH 5 b.g. Thatching 131–Run To The Sun (Run The Gantlet (USA))   **73** §
[1988 10m 10f⁶ 12f⁴ 1989 12.2s² 12g* 12m 16m* 14m² 19f⁶ 14f⁶ 14g³ 18g a13g* a14g
a16g* a16g²] sturdy gelding: moderate mover: modest handicapper on his day:
successful at Brighton and Nottingham in spring and at Lingfield (twice) late in
season: stays 2m: probably acts on any going: blinkered nowadays: has won for
apprentice, but is not an easy ride: soon pushed along in rear fifth outing, and took
little interest when tailed off next one: winning hurdler: unreliable. *J. R. Jenkins.*

GOT AWAY 3 b.c. Final Straw 127–Miss Thames 105 (Tower Walk 130) [1988   **94**
6g⁴ 6f² 6g* 6g⁶ 6g* 1989 6m* 6m 6m⁶] robust, good-bodied colt: has a quick action:
fairly useful handicapper: best effort when dead-heating at Doncaster in May,
running on strongly from towards rear: got poor run next start: not seen out after
early-July: will stay 7f: acts on top-of-the-ground: sold 20,000 gns Newmarket
Autumn Sales. *M. R. Stoute.*

GOTCHER 2 b.f. (Apr 27) Jalmood (USA) 126–Sipapu 90 (Targowice (USA) 130)   **74**
[1989 6f* 7m⁵ 6m³ 6g⁵ 5g⁴ 6d³] 3,800Y: lengthy, useful-looking filly: fifth foal:
half-sister to 3-y-o Alexandra Katrine (by Precocious) and a winner in Norway by
Tap On Wood: dam won at 6f and 7f: won maiden at Lingfield in July: ran well in
minor events on next 2 starts: has shown signs of unsatisfactory temperament:
needs further than 5f, and stays 7f: blinkered fifth start: keen-going type. *W. Carter.*

GOTHIC FORD 5 b.g. Stanford 121§–Gothic Lady (Godswalk (USA) 130) [1988 **62**
7g³ 6g 6g 5s⁵ 6s 7f 7m 7f 8m² 7d⁶ 8d³ 8m 1989 7d³ 7d³ 7d² 6m⁵ 8m* 7m 7m² 7f*
7m 7m 7g 7f⁵ 7g⁵ 7m a7g⁵ a6g² a8g² a7g²] short-legged, rather dipped-backed
gelding: moderate mover: led on bridle over 1f out when winning handicaps at
Edinburgh (selling event, no bid, hung left) and Ayr in first half of season: ideally
suited by 7f or 1m: acts on any going: has been tried in visor and severe bridle: often
apprentice ridden as 5-y-o, but not when successful: goes well on turning track:
none too keen. *C. Tinkler.*

GOTT'S DESIRE 3 ch.g. Sweet Monday 122–Steel Lady 60 (Continuation 120) **63**
[1988 6s⁵ 7v⁴ 7g 1989 7.5d³ 8.2f 8m² 7m* 7m⁶ 7f 8.2d³ 7m* 7.6m 7g² 7d³ a7g³]
angular gelding: won sellers at Catterick (no bid) in June and Newmarket (bought in
7,000 gns) in August: ran creditably last 4 outings, including in non-selling
handicaps at Chester and Catterick and claimer at Southwell: keen sort, suited by
7f: probably unsuited by very firm going. *J. Berry.*

GOURIEV 3 b.c. Gorytus (USA) 132–Balilla 94 (Balidar 133) [1988 6f⁴ 7g² 7.3s* **91**
1989 7d 8.5s⁶ 5m³] robust, good sort: won Horris Hill Stakes at Newbury as 2-y-o:
edgy and well below form first half of 1989 in Group 3 event (pulled hard) at
Newbury, £10,300 contest (sweating) at Epsom and minor event (ridden by 7-lb
claimer) at Chepstow: should stay 1m: acts on soft ground: sold 23,000 gns
Newmarket July Sales: one to be wary of. *P. J. Makin.*

GOVERNOR'S HARBOUR 4 b.g. Lomond (USA) 128–Inchmarlo (USA) 99 **—**
(Nashua) [1988 8d⁴ 10d 10m⁴ 10f* 10d 12d* 12m 12d* 12s 1989 12m 12g] strong,
lengthy gelding: moderate mover: quite useful winner as 3-y-o: soundly beaten in
handicaps at Ascot (apprentices) and Newmarket (still backward) in autumn: stays
1½m: seems to act on any going: goes well ridden up with pace: sold 10,000 gns
Newmarket Autumn Sales. *R. W. Armstrong.*

GOVERNORSHIP 5 ch.g. Dominion 123–Angel Beam (SWE) 115 (Hornbeam **95** §
130) [1988 7m⁴ 8g 7d 8f* 8g 8d⁴ 8d 1989 7d 8f⁵ 8f 8f³ 8m⁶ 8f] lengthy, good-topped
gelding: poor walker: has a quick action: fairly useful handicapper on his day: best
effort as 5-y-o when third to Still Surprised at York in July: unsuited by 1m: acts on firm
going and a soft surface: usually blinkered nowadays: edgy last 2 starts in 1988: sold
to join J. Hills 18,000 gns Newmarket Autumn Sales: thoroughly inconsistent. *C. R.
Nelson.*

GO WITH THE FLO 3 br.f. Indian King (USA) 128–Doon Belle (Ardoon 124) **67 p**
[1988 NR 1989 11.7d 8m 8m 6g 6g² 6f*] 22,000Y, 26,000Y: workmanlike filly: third
foal: half-sister to Irish 1985 2-y-o 7f winner La Belle Princesse (by Royal Match):
dam, half-sister to smart 7f to 1¾m performer Rocamadour, won over 5f and 7f in
Ireland: 5/4 favourite and ridden by 5-lb claimer, won maiden at Nottingham in
September: best other efforts in handicaps previous 2 starts: wore crossed
noseband last 5: may well improve again over 5f. *J. Mackie.*

GOZONE 2 ro.g. (Apr 15) Carwhite 127–Perlesse 88 (Bold Lad (USA) 133) [1989 **62**
7d⁵ a7g⁵ a8g] 900Y: leggy gelding: fifth foal: half-brother to 4-y-o 6f winner
Flighting Moon (by Moorestyle) and ungenuine sprinter Samleon (by Kind of
Hush): dam 2-y-o 6f winner: quite modest maiden: best effort second start: should
stay 1¼m. *S. G. Norton.*

GRABEL 6 b.m. Bold Owl 101–Gay Dawn (Gay Fandango 132) [1988 8d 12m 12m⁶ **96**
13f* 13.5g* 14s 16s 1989 14g* 16g³ 13m⁶ 22.2f⁴ 14m 14v*] Irish mare: first foal: dam
unraced daughter of useful middle-distance filly Slap Up: successful at Gowran Park
in handicap in May and minor event in November: in frame in between in listed
event at Leopardstown and Queen Alexandra Stakes (sweating, beaten 8½ lengths
by Ala Hounak) at Royal Ascot: stays extremely well: acts on any going: good mount
for inexperienced rider: good hurdler. *P. Mullins, Ireland.*

GRAB THE LAUGHS 2 b.f. (Feb 18) Comedy Star (USA) 121–Miss Serlby 65 **37**
(Runnett 125) [1989 5s 5g 5g⁵ 5f 5m³ 5f⁴ 5g 6g⁶ 6m 5v 5m] 3,200Y: small filly: first
foal: dam, maiden, best at 5f: poor plater: best efforts over 5f on stiff tracks:
sweating fourth outing: sold 1,750 gns Doncaster November Sales. *W. Bentley.*

GRAMINIE (USA) 3 gr.g. Graustark–Etoile d'Orient (Targowice (USA) 130) **80 d**
[1988 8d 1989 8m⁴ 14g⁵ 10m⁵ 10g⁵ 8g] lengthy, angular gelding: modest maiden: fourth in
apprentice race at Yarmouth in August: ran moderately after, including in
handicaps: should stay further than 1m: blinkered final outing: sold 20,000 gns
Newmarket Autumn Sales. *R. Guest.*

GRAN ALBA (USA) 3 gr.c. El Gran Senor (USA) 136–Morning Games (USA) **107**
(Grey Dawn II 132) [1988 7m³ 7.3s⁵ 7.6s³ 1989 10f* 10f⁴ 12g⁶ 12f² 10d* 11s⁴ 12m
9g⁴ 10g⁵] heavy-topped colt: moderate walker: has a roundish action: won maiden at

Lingfield in May and listed event at Phoenix Park in August: blinkered, easily best efforts after when running creditably in listed races at Newmarket last 2 outings, edgy on first of them: 11½ lengths sixth in Ever Ready Derby at Epsom: stays 1½m: appears to act on any going. *R. Hannon.*

GRAND BLUSH (USA)   3 gr.f. Blushing Groom (FR) 131–Versatile (FR)   76
(Versailles II) [1988 6d⁴ 7m⁵ 7f 7g⁶ 1989 7s 7g³ 7g] rather leggy, close-coupled filly: modest form: reluctant to go down, staying-on third in minor event at Yarmouth, easily best effort as 3-y-o: worth a try over 1m: possibly unsuited by soft ground: tended to pull hard at 2 yrs, once sweating: has tongue tied down. *M. Moubarak.*

GRAND FRERE   3 br.c. Gorytus (USA) 132–Balista 86 (Baldric II 131) [1988 5g⁵   87
5g³ 6f⁵ 6m³ 7f⁴ 8f* 1989 8s 8f 8f⁴ 8m* 10m² 8f² 8g] sparely-made, quite attractive colt: moderate walker: fair handicapper: justified favouritism at Goodwood in June: ran well when placed afterwards: worth another try over 1¼m: best form on top-of-the-ground: sweating sixth outing. *R. Hannon.*

GRAND PARTY   4 ch.f. Revlow 108–Grand Melody (Song 132) [1988 8d 1989 5f   —
a10g] lengthy, workmanlike filly: no sign of ability. *J. M. Bradley.*

GRAND PRIX   4 b.c. Formidable (USA) 125–Mumruffin 101 (Mummy's Pet 125)   84
[1988 5d 5m² 5f* 5f⁶ 5g⁵ 5.3f² 5m³ 5f⁴ 5f 1989 5.8h 5g⁵ 5.8h* 6m² 6f² 6f 6h 6m 5g] neat, good-bodied colt: moderate mover: fair handicapper: goes well at Bath, and won there in June: below his best last 4 outings: speedy: acts very well on top-of-the-ground: has run creditably for apprentice: often sweating and on edge: sometimes starts slowly. *R. Akehurst.*

GRAND TOUR   5 b.h. Troy 137–Peculiar One (USA) (Quack (USA)) [1988 10d⁵   95
12m 12f⁴ 13.4s² 12s³ 10.8d* 1989 12g* 12g⁵] big, strong, good-bodied horse: has a long, rather round stride: useful performer: short-head winner of 8-runner event on first of 2 outings at Cagnes-sur-Mer early in year: then sold to race in Switzerland, and won over 1½m in May: finds 1¼m on short side and stays 15f: acts on top-of-the-ground and soft going: raced too freely when visored. *W. Hastings-Bass.*

GRANEMORE   3 br.c. Millfontaine 114–Polyxo (Polyfoto 124) [1988 5g 7g 6d⁶   —
1989 7m 7.5d 6m 7m 8f⁶ 7.5m] sparely-made colt: poor form: show only in seller on fourth start, given a lot to do and finishing well: stays 7f: drifted right in blinkers third start. *P. A. Blockley.*

GRANITOBI   2 br.f. (Feb 8) Noalto 120–Love Unspoken 54 (No Mercy 126) [1989   —
5d 5f 5f] 1,550F, 2,300Y: sister to 3-y-o Lovistone and half-sister to winners in Italy and Scandinavia by Absalom: dam showed form only at 5f: soundly beaten in maidens and seller: blinkered final start (May). *T. D. Barron.*

GRANITTON BAY   2 b.c. (May 12) Prince Tenderfoot (USA) 126–Miss   65
Redmarshall 80 (Most Secret 119) [1989 5m³ 5g* 5f 5f⁴ 5m* 5m² 5g6] 9,200Y: lengthy, rather dipped-backed colt: moderate walker and mover: fourth living foal: half-brother to 3-y-o Argelith (by Runnett), 5f and 6f winner Annaceramic (by Horage) and 7f winner Sequestrator (by African Sky): dam best at 5f: quite modest performer: 4-length winner at Beverley of a minor event in July and claimer following month: ran respectably in nurseries on fourth and sixth starts. *R. M. Whitaker.*

GRATCLO   3 gr.f. Belfort (FR) 89–Shagra (Sallust 134) [1988 5s 5g 5f² 5m 6m²   63
6m* 7f³ 6f⁴ 6g 5g 1989 5s 6m 6g 6f 6m 7m 8f 8f 7f* 6f⁴ 6g*] strong, workmanlike filly: has a quick action: won sellers at Brighton (bought in 3,300 gns) in October and Leicester (apprentices, bought in 4,100 gns) in November, both in good style: well behind most other starts: stays 7f: acts on firm ground: tends to hang left: very slowly away sixth and seventh (reluctant to race for 7-lb claimer) outings: trained first 8 by C. Hill: not one to trust implicitly. *R. J. Hodges.*

GREAT AIM   3 b.f. Great Nephew 126–Perfect Aim 97 (Busted 134) [1988 7m   —
1989 8f³ 16g a10g a14g] leggy, angular filly: 66/1, 11½ lengths third of 5 to odds-on Guest Artiste in minor event at Leicester in November, leading 6f: behind in listed race and handicaps after: should be suited by further than 1m: bandaged behind on debut. *C. James.*

GREAT ASPECT   5 b. or br.g. Great Nephew 126–Broad Horizon 89 (Blakeney   —
126) [1988 8s⁶ 1989 12.2s 10d] good-bodied gelding: moderate mover: one-time useful performer: bandaged in last 2 seasons: stays 1½m: acts on firm going and a soft surface. *K. White.*

GREAT BIRCHAM   3 b.g. Show-A-Leg 107–Galignani (FR) 82 (Trepan (FR)   55 §
133) [1988 6g 6g⁶ 6g 7g 1989 8g 8.3g⁵ 8m³ 7.6m⁶ a8g⁴] lengthy, sparely-made gelding: fair plater: ran on strongly under tender handling second start: didn't impress with attitude after, appearing not to go through with effort third outing then

Maktoum Al-Maktoum's "Great Commotion"

constantly flashing tail under pressure on fourth: bred to stay 1¼m: sold 3,500 gns Newmarket Autumn Sales: not one to trust. *W. J. Musson.*

GREAT CHADDINGTON 4 b.g. Crofter (USA) 124–Mainly Dry (The Brianstan 128) [1988 5s 5v³ 6d 6f³ 5m⁴ 6f 6g 6g 5g² 5.5g⁴ 5m⁶ 1989 5g³ 5s 5m 5f² 5f⁴ 5m² 5m⁶ 5d] tall, leggy, close-coupled gelding: moderate mover: fair handicapper: best at 5f: acts on any going: blinkered twice at 3 yrs and on final outing (ran poorly): suitable mount for apprentice. *J. Berry.* **90 d**

GREAT COMMOTION (USA) 3 b.c. Nureyev (USA) 131–Alathea (Lorenzaccio 130) [1988 NR 1989 7d* 8m⁵ 8m² 8f⁴ 7f* 7.3g² 8m²] medium-sized, quite good-topped, attractive colt: has a fluent, quick action: sixth live foal: brother to good 6f to 7f winner Lead On Time and a French provincial 8.7f winner and half-brother to 3 winners, notably very useful French miler Keyala (by Key To The Mint), later winner in USA: dam lightly-raced half-sister to R B Chesne out of sister to Vaguely Noble: won Newmarket maiden in April and Group 3 'Federation Brewery' Beeswing Stakes (making all) at Newcastle in July: ran creditably in pattern company all other starts, second to Shaadi in Airlie/Coolmore Irish 2000 Guineas at the Curragh, and to Distant Relative in Gardner Merchant Hungerford Stakes at Newbury and Beefeater Gin Celebration Mile at Goodwood: capable of smart form over 1m, but gives impression may well prove ideally suited by 7f: yet to race on very soft going, acts on any other. *A. A. Scott.* **118**

GREAT DILEMMA 6 b.m. Vaigly Great 127–Solo Reign 84 (Space King 115) [1988 7.6m⁴ 8g* 8g* 8g⁶ 8g 1989 8f³ 7f³ 8f³] lengthy mare: modest handicapper: not seen out after June: best at around 1m: suited by sound surface: sometimes **70**

369

sweats: has won for apprentice, but has tended to hang and appeared not an easy ride. *P. J. Makin.*

GREAT GUSTO 3 b.g. Windjammer (USA)–My Music 68 (Sole Mio (USA)) 63
[1988 6f⁴ 6g⁶ 7g 7m 7m 7m⁴ 8m 7m³ 6d 8g* 6g 1989 10.1m 10m 10.6m 12.3m* 14m 10f³ 10g 10m 8m* 8m 8.2f³ 8g* 8.5f] leggy, good-topped gelding: quite modest handicapper: won ladies race (given enterprising ride) at Ripon in June, apprentice event (sweating) at Salisbury in August and 8-runner contest at Yarmouth in September: probably best at around 1m: acts on firm going: seems to go well when on toes: sold 18,000 gns Doncaster September Sales: rather inconsistent. *D. T. Thom.*

GREAT HAND 3 b.c. Tumble Wind (USA)–Great Aunt 74 (Great Nephew 126) 68
[1988 7m⁶ 6m 1989 6d⁵ 8.5d 7.5f 8h 8f³ 9m³ᵈⁱˢ 9f] leggy colt: quite modest maiden: worth a try over 1¼m: acts on firm going: ran poorly when edgy third start: swerved left and disqualified penultimate one: sold to join D. Wilson 10,500 gns Newmarket Autumn Sales. *J. W. Watts.*

GREAT HEIGHTS 2 b.c. (Mar 28) Shirley Heights 130–As You Desire Me 112 86 p
(Kalamoun 129) [1989 7g⁴] fifth foal: half-brother to 3 winners, including useful but untrustworthy 6f to 1m winner Intimate Guest (by Be My Guest) and fairly useful 7f and 1m winner Prince Lyph (by Bellypha): dam, from very good family, won 3 times at around 1m in France: 8/1 and green, around 2 lengths fourth of 29, keeping on well despite tending to wander, to Lord of The Field in maiden at Newmarket in November: sure to improve, particularly over middle distances, and win races. *H. R. A. Cecil.*

GREAT LEGEND 3 ch.c. Vaigly Great 127–Chinese Legend (Shantung 132) 75
[1988 NR 1989 7f⁵ 7m³] half-brother to several winners abroad, including British 1984 2-y-o 7f winner Rushad (by Crofter) and 1989 Belgian 1½m winner Geoffrey's Choice (by Moorestyle): dam unraced: modest form in maidens at Sandown and Kempton in the summer. *J. R. Shaw.*

GREAT MILL 2 b.c. (Apr 12) Simply Great (FR) 124–Milly Lass (FR) 85 (Bold 76
Lad (USA)) [1989 6m⁶ 7f² 7g 9g² 8m⁴ 10g⁴ 8g³] IR 11,500Y: rather leggy, close-coupled colt: has a quick action: half-brother to 7.6f winner Azyaa (by Kris), out-and-out stayer Otabari (by Welsh Pageant) and a winner in Hong Kong: dam 2-y-o 7f winner, is half-sister to smart Kashmir Lass: modest performer: will be suited by 1½m: blinkered final outing: sweating sixth: has looked a hard ride. *M. E. D. Francis.*

GREAT RELATIONS (USA) 3 b.c. Caro 133–Northern Oasis (USA) 90
(Damascus (USA)) [1988 8.2m² 8g 1989 12h* 14m⁴ 13.3m 12.2g² a12g] big, close-coupled colt: has a round action: won maiden at Lingfield in June: ran very well when last of 4 to Michelozzo in listed race at Goodwood: below form after in £20,400 handicap at Newbury, apprentice race at Catterick and handicap (faced stiff task) at Lingfield, making most first 2 occasions: suited by 1¾m, and possibly by top-of-the-ground: sold 34,000 gns Newmarket December Sales. *P. F. I. Cole.*

GREAT SERVICE 2 ch.c. (Mar 2) Vaigly Great 127–Janlarmar 69 (Habat 127) 62
[1989 5g⁵ 5v* 6f⁵ 7f 7g a8g] 11,000F, 20,000Y: angular, plain colt: has a rather round action: fourth foal: brother to 3-y-o Sea Siesta and 6f seller winner Crimpsall and half-brother to a poor animal by Monsanto: dam won 6f seller: quite modest maiden: won early-season maiden at Ayr: had interrupted season after: should be suited by further than 5f: acts on heavy ground, and seems unsuited by firm. *Ronald Thompson.*

GREAT SONG 2 ch.f. (Mar 10) Vaigly Great 127–Suzannah's Song (Song 132) 45
[1989 5g 7f 7m 5g³ 5f 5.1m 6g 5g 6m⁴ 6g a7g a6g⁴ a5g⁵] 560F, 500Y: small, lengthy filly: second foal: quite modest plater: stays 6f: blinkered nowadays. *T. Fairhurst.*

GRECIAN HILL 3 b.f. Ela-Mana-Mou 132–Hill Moss 87 (Priamos (GER)) [1988 84
7f⁵ 1989 12.2f* 14f] leggy filly: won 5-runner maiden at Catterick in July: pulled very hard to post and took keen hold in race (leading 6f) when tailed off in £12,000 handicap at York 7 weeks later: stays 1½m well: sold 7,000 gns Newmarket December Sales. *C. E. Brittain.*

GREEK DESIRE 2 b.c. (Mar 12) Lyphard's Special (USA) 122–Mountain 34
Heather (Daring Display (USA) 129) [1989 6f 5.1m⁴ 5f⁶ 5f] IR 6,800F, 4,900Y: lengthy, heavy-topped colt: fourth reported foal: dam unraced: poor plater. *J. W. Payne.*

GREEK FLUTTER 4 b.g. Beldale Flutter (USA) 130–Greek Blessing 83 (So —
Blessed 130) [1988 8d⁴ 12m² 12f² 12g* 11m* 12d 11m* 10.5f³ 10g 1989 12g] rather

leggy, workmanlike gelding: carries condition: has a scratchy action: fair winner as 3-y-o: soundly beaten in handicap at Haydock in September: suited by further than 1¼m and stays 1½m: suited by a sound surface: often hangs: goes well for K. Fallon. *J. G. FitzGerald.*

GREEK GODDESS 3 b.f. Young Generation 129–Cassandra 99 (Troy 137) [1988 6g 6s³ 1989 7m⁵ 6m 6m] small, sturdy, lengthy filly: fair maiden at best: well below form in 1989, easily best effort on reappearance: bred to stay beyond 6f: best form on soft ground. *Major W. R. Hern.*

GREEN ADVENTURE (USA) 4 b.c. Green Dancer (USA) 132–Simply **119** Furious (USA) (Delta Judge) [1988 12m* 16f* 14g² 13.3f* 1989 13.3f³ 12g³ 20f⁵ 12.5m⁵] rangy, good sort: smart performer: ran very well when third to Sheriff's Star in Hanson Coronation Cup at Epsom in June: looking very well, weakened final 2f when fifth of 8 to stable-companion Sadeem in moderately-run Gold Cup at Royal Ascot: not seen out again after finishing about 4 lengths fifth to Ibn Bey in Prix Maurice de Nieuil at Saint-Cloud month later: effective from 1½m to 2m: acts on firm going. *G. Harwood.*

GREEN ARCHER 6 b.g. Hardgreen (USA) 122–Mittens (Run The Gantlet **39** (USA)) [1988 14v 17.1g² 16g 18f² 14m³ 20.4d* 14g 16g⁶ 17.1g² 1989 14s 21.6d⁵ 18s 16.5g⁶ 20.4g* 17f⁵] close-coupled gelding: poor handicapper: won at Ayr in July: suited by extreme test of stamina: appears to act on any going: has run creditably for apprentice. *Mrs J. R. Ramsden.*

GREEN DOLLAR 6 b.g. Tickled Pink 114–Burglars Girl 63 (Burglar 128) [1988 **78** 6v 6m² 6d⁵ 6m 6m* 6f⁵ 6m 6m 6m* 6g 5.8d² 6f 6d 6g 6m 5.8f⁶ 1989 5s 5f³ 7m 5.8h 6f⁴ 5f⁵ 6m² 6m* 6f² 5g³ 6m 6m² 7f 6g 6f* 6m⁵ 6s³ 6m³ 5m⁶ 6g] smallish gelding: modest handicapper: in good form for much of summer, winning at Brighton in June and Folkestone in September: best at 6f: acts on any going: has worn blinkers and visor, but not for some time: sometimes sweats: good mount for apprentice, but hung badly right penultimate outing. *E. A. Wheeler.*

GREEN EMPEROR 3 b. or br.c. Head For Heights 125–La Padma (Sassafras **86** (FR) 135) [1988 7s⁵ 8m⁵ 1989 8m⁶ 10f⁴ 13.3m² 16f 13.3m 14m⁶ 10g* 10g²] 15,000Y: leggy, close-coupled colt: has a round action: fifth foal: half-brother to Irish 1½m winner Shrewd Lady (by Sharpman) and Irish 2m winner Glen of Ealy (by Glenstal): dam unraced half-sister to Poule d'Essai des Pouliches winner Ukraine Girl: made all in handicap at Sandown in September, holding on by short head: on toes and sweating, good second in £10,300 handicap at Ascot following month, making most: best form at 1¼m on good ground: pulled hard first start: trained at 2 yrs by E. O'Grady in Ireland. *R. W. Armstrong.*

GREEN FLAG (USA) 3 ch.c. Green Dancer (USA) 132–Coy Maid (FR) **100** (Habitat 134) [1988 6d* 6m² 7.5g* 7f⁴ 1989 9m* 10.8m* 11.1m⁴ 9g] lengthy, attractive colt: has a rather round action: won minor events at Ripon in May and Warwick (making all) in July: well beaten in September Stakes (sweating, gave trouble at stalls and took keen hold) at Kempton and listed race at Newmarket: stays 10.8f: acts on top-of-the-ground and a soft surface. *H. R. A. Cecil.*

GREENHILLS JOY 6 b.m. Radetzky 123–Soheir 74 (Track Spare 125) [1988 **71 +** 12v* 12g⁵ 12g 13s 12s 12s⁴ 12m 1989 12g⁴] deep-bodied mare: poor mover: fair winner early as 5-y-o: stayed on strongly final 2f after struggling to quicken and to find room for much of straight when fourth of 7 to Positive Way in handicap at Doncaster in March: best at around 1½m: well suited by plenty of give in the ground. *M. J. Ryan.*

GREENHILLS PRIDE 5 b.g. Sparkling Boy 110–Soheir 74 (Track Spare 125) **65** [1988 12.2d 12d 10.8g 10m 12m 10m 8.2s³ 8m³ 8g² 9v² 1989 10.2g³ 10s³ 8f 10v* 12.4g 12s] tall, close-coupled gelding: quite modest handicapper: 16/1 and first outing for over 5 months, won 19-runner event at Ayr in October: well beaten at Newcastle over week later: stumbled and unseated rider after 1f final outing: stays 1¼m well: possibly unsuited by firm going, acts on any other: blinkered seventh outing at 4 yrs, visored final three. *H. J. Collingridge.*

GREEN LINE EXPRESS (USA) 3 ch.c. Green Forest (USA) 134– **126** Laylitna (USA) (Key To The Mint (USA)) [1988 7m² 1989 8.2g* 8f² 8g⁴ 8m⁴ 8f]

   Green Line Express must be the epitome of the stable star. Winner of a maiden at Haydock then second in the Swettenham Stud Sussex Stakes nineteen days later, he is almost the sole contributor to trainer Moubarak's somewhat bizarre 1989 season statistics of races won—one; win prize

Ecurie Fustok's "Green Line Express"

money—£2,979; win and place prize money—£90,293. Moubarak must be glad that Green Line Express remains in training and the colt's performances in only six outings to date suggest he should win a good race.

Green Line Express' one success came on his reappearance in early-July. His length-and-a-half second to Tessla in a Newmarket maiden the previous August had been full of promise but he'd then split a pastern, and the much more recent debutant Rah Wan started odds on at Haydock despite Green Line Express' looking very well and the rare British appearance of M. Fustok's retained jockey Cruz to ride him. In a moderately-run race, Green Line Express was travelling much the best once the pace quickened and, after a few reminders approaching the final furlong, finished well on top in beating Rah Wan two and a half lengths. That said, however, a step up to what looked to be a particularly hotly-contested Sussex Stakes at Goodwood, seemed over-ambitious. Only the pacemaker Hilton Brown started at longer odds but 100/1-chance Green Line Express more than vindicated his trainer's judgement. Again he travelled strongly for a long way, this time with never more than three in front of him behind a very strong pace set by Shaadi and Opening Verse. At the three-furlong pole Cruz had still to ask Green Line Express for his effort and the rest were being pushed along; all, that is, except the colt next to him, Zilzal. Green Line Express had come under full pressure two furlongs out, Cruz having to change his whip hand, and he couldn't match Zilzal who drew away to win by three lengths with another length and a half back to the remainder headed by Markofdistinction. A high-class performance after which Green Line Express was kept to the very best company. In the

372

Prix du Moulin de Longchamp, Green Line Express led the main contenders chasing two pacemakers, one of which, Good Example, carried the Fustok second colours. He'd got to Good Example about one furlong out but had already been swamped by Polish Precedent and then lost out more narrowly to Squill and Cadeaux Genereux. A rematch with both Zilzal and Polish Precedent in the Queen Elizabeth II Stakes at Ascot nearly four weeks later resulted in another honourable fourth but Green Line Express brought up the rear in the Breeders' Cup Mile having encountered none of the difficulties Zilzal and Most Welcome had in assuming a prominent position early on; he dropped away rapidly on the last turn.

		Green Forest (USA) (ch 1979)	Shecky Greene (b 1970)	Noholme II
Green Line				Lester's Pride
Express (USA)			Tell Meno Lies (gr 1971)	The Axe II
(ch.c. 1986)				Filatonga
		Laylitna (USA) (b 1978)	Key To The Mint (b 1969)	Graustark
				Key Bridge
			Furl Sail (b 1964)	Revoked
				Windsail

Green Line Express' sire Green Forest and dam Laylitna both raced for Fustok out of the Mitri Saliba stable. Green Forest's achievements will be familiar—he won three of the four French Group 1 races for two-year-old colts and the Prix du Moulin de Longchamp at three—Laylitna's less so as she recouped only 4,900 francs of her 230,000-dollar yearling purchase price in gaining one fourth place from three starts in France as a two-year-old. Green Line Express is the best colt in Green Forest's first three crops; the fourth includes the Moet et Chandon-Rennen winner Somethingdifferent and the filly Ozone Friendly who went one better than her sire in winning the Prix Robert Papin. Green Forest's best filly by some way is Forest Flower. He had serious problems in the 1987 covering season, getting only five live foals from thirty-one mares covered. Green Line Express is Laylitna's fourth living foal after the modest lightly-raced seven-furlong winner Evening Blush (by Blushing Groom) and two by Silver Hawk, the first only twice-raced and the second a minor winner in the USA. An unraced Green Forest two-year-old of 1989 out of Laylitna called Sonic Music was listed among Moubarak's charges in *Horses In Training*. Laylitna is out of Furl Sail, the champion American three-year-old filly in 1967 when she ran seventeen times in a campaign spanning nine and a half months, winning ten races, six of them stakes from six furlongs to eight and a half furlongs, including the Grade 1 Acorn Stakes and Mother Goose Stakes. Furl Sail's owner/breeders also bred the previous four dams in this pedigree but Furl Sail must have rather disappointed them in the paddocks because, despite breeding winners, she hasn't produced anything approaching her own merit. One of her offspring, the Sir Ivor filly Wedgewood Blue, won for Vincent O'Brien as a two-year-old and has foaled the fairly useful fillies Bashayer and Minstrel Guest. Furl Sail hasn't foaled to a top stallion in the 'eighties and her progeny no longer fetch the sort of price commanded by Laylitna. In fact her 1984 yearling by Recitation (one of her five winners) fetched just 1,500 dollars.

Report had it that Green Line Express would be tried over a mile and a quarter in 1990 to avoid Zilzal, but as Zilzal won't be around after all perhaps that plan will be amended. It's not certain that Green Line Express will be so effective over the extra two furlongs anyway. Neither parent was tried over the trip and their American pedigrees are, as is so often the case, distinctly equivocal on the subject. Put against the very best in four of his six races, it's difficult to draw firm conclusions from Green Line Express's racecourse appearances either. The going was firm for the Sussex Stakes and he has yet to race on anything softer than the good ground he encountered at Haydock and Longchamp. A good-quartered, quite attractive colt, Green Line Express wore a tongue strap in 1989; that's a precaution usually taken with his stable's runners. *M. Moubarak.*

GREEN'S BELLE   2 ch.f. (Apr 22) Night Shift (USA)–Ribellina (Ribero 126)   **92**
[1989 6m2 6f* 6m* 6g] 26,000Y: medium-sized, close-coupled filly: good mover: half-sister to 1988 2-y-o 5f seller winner Sunnyside John (by Monsanto) and 2

winners abroad: dam won in Italy and is half-sister to top-class Italian stayer Weimar: fairly useful performer: successful in minor event and a listed race (by short head from Tod) at Ripon in August: not discredited when in mid-division in Racecall Gold Trophy at Redcar: will stay 7f: withdrawn after unseating rider on way down second intended outing: sold 56,000 gns Newmarket December Sales. *W. Jarvis.*

GREEN'S CANALETTO (USA) 3 b.c. Hagley (USA)–Gaucherie (USA) 108 (Sharpen Up 127) [1988 6f³ 6d* 1989 6f² 6m³ 6f 6m* 6m³ 5g² 6m⁵ 5g] tall, leggy, lengthy colt: really good mover with a long stride: won listed race at Newbury in July by 6 lengths, drifting right: not discredited in similar events at Newmarket and Doncaster and Group 3 contest at Ascot next 3 starts: chased leaders 3f in Prix de l'Abbaye de Longchamp final one: effective at 5f and 6f: yet to race on very soft going, appears to act on any other: useful. *W. Jarvis.*

GREEN'S COLLECTION 3 b.f. High Top 131–Gauloise 93 (Welsh Pageant 65 132) [1988 7g 7f⁶ 8m 1989 10f⁴ 12f³ 13.1m⁵ 16f* 16f* 15.3m⁴ 14f 16f³ a16g] leggy, sparely-made filly: has a slightly round action: quite modest handicapper: bandaged near-hind and ridden by 5-lb claimer, won in small fields at Chepstow in July and Nottingham in August: ran creditably after when in frame: suited by 2m: acts on firm going: genuine. *P. F. I. Cole.*

GREEN'S COROT 2 b.g. (Apr 17) Prince Tenderfoot (USA) 126–Song Beam 84 72 p (Song 132) [1989 a6g*] IR 28,000F, IR 26,000Y: workmanlike gelding: half-brother to 3 winners, including miler Hooray Lady (by Ahonoora) and fairly useful 1987 2-y-o 5f winner Fast As Light (by On Your Mark): dam won twice over 6f: weak 10/1-shot, bit backward and bandaged, won 14-runner maiden at Lingfield in November by ¾ length from Sockem: will stay 7f: sure to improve. *P. F. I. Cole.*

GREEN'S FINE ART 3 ch.g. Kind of Hush 118–L'Hawaienne (USA) (Hawaii) 73 [1988 NR 1989 10g³ 12f² 12f⁶ 13f³ 12m²] 3,000Y, 20,000 2-y-o: angular, workmanlike gelding: third foal: half-brother to fair 1½m winner How Very Touching (by Touching Wood), successful in USA in 1989: dam never ran: quite

Richard Green's "Green's Canaletto"

modest maiden: best effort over 1¼m: blinkered, pulled hard in moderately-run race
final start: taken down early on debut: winning novice hurdler with M. Pipe. *W. J.
Haggas.*

GREEN'S LEADER (USA)   2 b.g. (Feb 21) Fatih (USA) 85–Amberina (FR) **102**
(Amber Rama (USA) 133) [1989 6m³ 7g* 7f* 8m* 8g⁵ 7g* 8m³] $11,000Y, resold
4,200Y: rather unfurnished gelding: third known named foal: half-brother to 2 minor
winners in USA: dam French 2-y-o 5f winner: progressive sort: successful in
maiden auction race at Doncaster, auction event at Thirsk and nurseries at Sandown
and Newmarket: good third of 10 to Noble Patriarch in listed race at Ascot: stays 1m:
suited by forcing tactics. *W. J. Haggas.*

GREENSMITH   3 b.c. Known Fact (USA) 135–Infra Green 121 (Laser **121**
Light 118) [1988 7m³ 7g* 7g* 7g* 1989 7g 8m 7f* 8f* 8.5g³ 8f² 10g⁶]
    When Greensmith went into Timeform's *Horses to Follow* for 1989 it
wasn't envisaged that the St James's Palace Stakes would be one of his
engagements, but the improvement he showed prior to Royal Ascot entitled
him to take his chance. Successful on his last three outings as a two-year-old,
he'd resumed winning ways at York in May where he took the Norwest Holst
Handicap by a length and a half from Rose Glen, driven out having tended to
idle in front; and another valuable handicap victory followed in the Selfridges
Whitsun Cup at Sandown, a shade cleverly by a neck from Coeur de Miel.
Opportunities limited, a step up to pattern company was almost inevitable and
Greensmith was sent to Epsom for the Diomed Stakes on Derby Day. He
started favourite in an eight-runner field, but having made good headway in
the straight he began to edge left inside the final furlong and finished just a
creditable third, beaten two necks behind Shining Steel and Beau Sher. It was
a similar story in the St James's Palace Stakes. Greensmith—on his toes and
sweating freely beforehand—was held up last of the five runners. He made a
strong run from early in the straight but found no extra inside the last and

Norwest Holst Trophy (Handicap), York—Greensmith returns to winning ways

went down by two lengths to Shaadi: a smart performance nevertheless. On what turned out to be his final start, in the Coral-Eclipse Stakes at Sandown, Greensmith was given the pacemaking role he had played on behalf of Danehill and Exbourne in the Two Thousand Guineas on his second start, this time for Warning. Greensmith was an unusual choice for pacemaker, for he isn't a natural front-runner. On this occasion he was never travelling with any great freedom in front and dropped away quickly after the home turn to finish last of the six runners. Shortly after, Greensmith was sent to continue his racing career with E. Gregson in America, where suitable opportunities should be easier to find.

		In Reality	Intentionally
	Known Fact (USA)	(b 1964)	My Dear Girl
	(b 1977)	Tamerett	Tim Tam
Greensmith		(b or br 1962)	Mixed Marriage
(b.c. 1986)		Laser Light	Aureole
	Infra Green	(ch 1966)	Ruby Laser
	(ch 1972)	Greenback II	Fric
		(b 1967)	Mrs Green

Greensmith is the seventh living foal and fifth winner out of Infra Green. The best of the previous ones are the smart Prix de Psyche winner Green Reef (by Mill Reef) and the useful middle-distance stayer Verdance (by Green Dancer). Infra Green improved with age, winning at six furlongs at two years and from a mile to a mile and a half at three and four, notably in the Prix Ganay and the Gran Premio del Jockey Club. Her dam, the lightly-raced (not unraced as reported in some previous editions of *Racehorses*) Greenback II, was quite stoutly bred, by the very good middle-distance performer Fric out of Mrs Green, a winner at up to thirteen furlongs. Greensmith is a strong, deep-girthed colt, a moderate walker and mover with a quick action. He stays a mile and acts on firm going. *G. Harwood.*

GREEN'S SEASCAPE 3 b. or br.f. Mummy's Pet 125–Empress Catherine 73 **85**
(Welsh Pageant 132) [1988 5m³ 5f⁶ 5m⁴ 6g⁵ 6d 1989 6m² 6g² 8m* 7g* 7m² 8f⁴ 8m³ 8m] useful-looking filly: has a round action: favourite, idled in front when successful in June in maiden at Edinburgh and handicap at Doncaster: ran creditably after in handicaps and a listed race: effective at 7f and 1m: acts on firm ground: ran moderately in blinkers second start, creditably when sweating penultimate one: should prove best with waiting tactics. *W. Jarvis.*

GREEN'S SISLEY (USA) 2 gr.c. (Mar 31) Dr Carter (USA)–Romeo's **?**
Coquette (USA) (Gallant Romeo (USA)) [1989 5m⁶ 5m* 5m⁵] $52,000Y: workmanlike colt: turns off-fore in: half-brother to 2 winners in North America, notably very useful Billy Sue's Rib (by Al Hattab), stakes winner at up to 9f: dam, winner at up to 7f, is half-sister to My Bupers, dam of champion sprinter My Juliet and Lyphard's Special: sire high-class 1m to 1¼m performer: made most when beating Able Express by ½ length in 5-runner minor event at Windsor in May: bit on toes, 10 lengths fifth of 9 to Candy Glen in quite well-contested minor event at Beverley following month (worth rating of 71 on British form): sent to Italy and won 7.5f events at Leghorn and Rome. *P. F. I. Cole.*

GREEN'S STILL LIFE 3 ch.f. Valiyar 129–Clicquot 101 (Bold Lad (IRE) 133) **—**
[1988 6g⁶ 6f⁴ 7m 8.5f³ 1989 8g 8f] smallish, sturdy filly: quite modest maiden at 2 yrs: hit rail 4f out and unable to recover on reappearance: blinkered, never dangerous in seller in May: suited by 1m: acts on firm ground. *P. F. I. Cole.*

GREEN'S STUBBS 2 b.c. (Mar 18) Ballad Rock 122–Aventina 83 (Averof 123) **73**
[1989 5g⁴ 5m² 5m³ 6m* 6m⁴] 19,500F, 34,000Y: close-coupled, strong colt: has a sharp action: fifth foal: half-brother to winning 7f to 1¼m plater Alvin York (by Known Fact) and 2 other winners also successful at 2 yrs, including 1986 6f and 7f winner Monterana (by Sallust): dam, half-sister to Italian Derby winner Ruysdael II, won over 7f at 2 yrs: made all in maiden at Brighton in June, drawing clear under 2f out to beat Empshott easing up by 5 lengths: weakened quickly in 5-runner minor event at Chepstow 4 days later: should stay 7f. *P. F. I. Cole.*

GREEN TIN HUT (USA) 2 b.g. (Apr 2) Strike Gold (USA)–Cazeez (USA) **— p**
(Cannonade (USA)) [1989 8d] $15,000F, 2,100Y: fifth foal: dam unraced half-sister to Obraztsovy: 14/1, slow-starting eighth of 18 in maiden at Thirsk in November: should improve. *M. H. Tompkins.*

*Feilden Stakes, Newmarket—33/1-chance Greenwich Papillon
proves too strong for odds-on Opening Verse*

GREENWICH PAPILLON 3 b.c. Glenstal (USA) 118–Coca (Levmoss 133) **114**
[1988 7m 6g 8s 7g* 7d 7g² 1989 8s⁴ 9d* 10f² 10m² 12f⁴ 10.6g⁴ 9m² 10d² 9g] rangy,
angular colt: has scope: usually impresses in appearance: very useful performer:
33/1, won listed Feilden Stakes at Newmarket in April: ran solely in listed and
pattern races after, beaten 4 lengths by Legal Case in Select Stakes at Goodwood
penultimate outing: ran moderately at Newmarket final one: probably stays 1½m:
acts on any going: game, genuine and consistent. *W. Carter.*

GREETLAND GRIT 2 ch.f. (Apr 26) Ballacashtal (CAN)–Tempered Wind **—**
(Fleece 114) [1989 5g⁵ 7m 6v 6s] 750F, 5,000Y: sturdy, workmanlike filly: poor
mover: half-sister to sprint handicapper Bella Seville (by King of Spain) and 1m
winner Blow My Top (by Some Hand): dam never ran: little worthwhile form in
varied races. *J. Berry.*

GREY AREA 2 gr.c. (Mar 26) Petong 126–Little Mercy 90 (No Mercy 126) [1989 **—**
6d] 5,400Y: good-topped colt: has plenty of scope: third foal: half-brother to quite
useful 3-y-o sprinter Knight of Mercy (by Aragon) and 1987 2-y-o 6f winner Silent
Sister (by Kind of Hush): dam 7f and 1m winner, best at 5 yrs: 20/1 and green, never
dangerous in 24-runner maiden at Newbury in October. *R. Hannon.*

GREY DUSTER (USA) 2 b.c. (Mar 12) L'Emigrant (USA) 129–Dry Fly (FR) **94**
(Mill Reef (USA) 141) [1989 6f* 6f² 7g* 7m*] 145,000Y: close-coupled, quite
attractive colt: good walker and mover: half-brother to smart 1986 French 2-y-o 5.5f
and 1m winner Fotitieng (by Nureyev): dam French 1¼m winner, is half-sister to
Gay Mecene and Gallanta (by Nureyev): progressive colt: successful in maiden at
Redcar in May and minor events at Chester and Newmarket (edged right) later in
summer: suited by 7f: visored third start, blinkered fourth: sold privately to race in
Hong Kong. *H. R. A. Cecil.*

GREY FELLOW 3 gr.c. Absalom 128–Follow The Brave 68 (Owen Anthony **48**
102) [1988 6f 6m 6s 1989 7d² 8g 8m 6g⁵ 7m 8g 8f² 8m 8f*] workmanlike colt:
moderate mover: plater: won (bought to join J. Ffitch-Heyes 6,400 gns) at Brighton
in August, making most: should stay further than 1m: acts on firm going, possibly
unsuited by very soft: blinkered fourth, fifth and last 3 starts: winning novice
hurdler: inconsistent. *Sir Mark Prescott.*

GREYFRIARS BOBBY 3 ch.g. Hard Fought 125–Victorian Pageant 95 (Welsh **49**
Pageant 132) [1988 NR 1989 8d 7f 8h⁶ 10.1m 8m 8m³ 7h 7m] IR 9,500F: leggy,
workmanlike gelding: poor walker and mover: fifth foal: brother to 1¼m winner
Merchants Dream and fair 7f and 1m winner Heavy Brigade and half-brother to a
winner in Italy by Blushing Groom: dam lightly-raced 1¼m winner: 25/1-third in
seller at Leicester in August, always close up and hanging right from 3f out, only
form: didn't handle bend at Brighton third start: suited by 1m: sold 2,400 gns Ascot
November Sales. *L. J. Holt.*

Ladbroke Chester Cup—Grey Salute (Pat Eddery) just holds on from Travel Mystery

GREY GYPSY 3 gr.f. Absalom 128–Nyeri 104 (Saint Crespin III 132) [1988 6m 1989 6s² 6v 6m 6f⁵ a6g] good-bodied filly: has a quick action: quite modest maiden: favourite, form only when second in minor event at Warwick in March: blinkered and bit backward, found nothing off bridle fourth outing: should be suited by 7f+: sold 8,200 gns Newmarket December Sales: one to leave alone. *P. T. Walwyn.*   56 d

GREY MERLIN 2 gr.c. (May 4) Derrylin 115–Sea Kestrel 82 (Sea Hawk II 131) [1989 6g⁵ 6m⁵ 6m 7m³ 7m 8.2g 8d⁴] 23,000Y: sturdy colt: has a markedly round action: fifth reported foal: brother to useful Derry Kestrel, successful over 7f and 1m at 2 yrs in 1987, and half-brother to a winning hurdler/chaser: dam genuine stayer: plating-class form in varied races: will stay 1¼m: has run well for 7-lb claimer. *Miss L. C. Siddall.*   59

GREY OWL (USA) 2 gr.c. (Apr 25) Caro 133–Demure (USA) (Dr Fager) [1989 7g⁵] $100,000F: good-topped colt: brother to a minor winner in North America and half-brother to 2 others: dam, winner twice at up to 9f at 2 yrs, is half-sister to 2 graded-stakes winners: 25/1, around 9 lengths fifth of 28, running on well last 2f, to Rami in maiden at Newmarket in November: sure to improve. *J. Gosden.*   74 p

GREY POWER 2 gr.f. (Mar 8) Wolf Power (SAF)–Periquito (USA) (Olden Times) [1989 6g 7d⁶] good-topped filly: sixth foal: half-sister to 3-y-o Sayyure (by Lydian) and 4 winners on flat, notably very useful 7f (at 2 yrs) to 2m winner Primitive Rising (by Raise A Man): dam ran 4 times: around 10 lengths sixth of 11, fading final 2f, to Himmah in minor event at Thirsk in November: backward on debut. *W. Hastings-Bass.*   52

GREY RUM 4 gr.g. Absalom 128–Cuba Libre (Rum (USA)) [1988 7g 7g⁶ 7.5m 8f* 8m⁴ 7f* 7d³ 7.5f² 7.5m 7m⁶ 8m 7f 1989 6g 8m 8h⁵ 7.5m 8.2g⁵ 8g² 7f² 8f⁵ 8.3d² 7s² 7g* 7m* 7m⁶ a8g⁶] leggy, close-coupled gelding: quite modest handicapper: successful in September at Catterick and Redcar: effective at 7f and 1m: acts on any   60

378

going: effective with or without blinkers: good mount for inexperienced rider. *W. J. Pearce.*

GREY SALUTE (CAN)   6 gr.g. Vice Regent (CAN)–Night Out (USA) (Bustino 136) [1988 16s³ 16g* 16g⁶ 16g⁴ 1989 16s 18.4m* 20f] big, heavy-topped gelding: has a round action: fair handicapper: showed improved form when given a good ride to win £22,000 Ladbroke Chester Cup (Handicap) by neck from Travel Mystery: bandaged, well beaten in Ascot Stakes (Handicap) at Royal Ascot 6 weeks later: stays 2¼m: best form on a sound surface: smart hurdler in 1988/9. *J. R. Jenkins.*   83

GREY SHIMMER (USA)   2 gr.c. (Apr 9) Caro 133–Beauty's Image (USA) (Wajima (USA)) [1989 7g 8g] 48,000Y: big, lengthy colt: has plenty of scope: has a quick action: second foal: dam closely related to high-class 2-y-o Whatsyourpleasure and Five Star Flight, very smart at around 9f: well beaten, never placed to challenge, in late-season £10,000 event won by Duke of Paducah and minor race won by Belmez at Newmarket: withdrawn from maiden there on intended debut after getting very edgy then proving troublesome at stalls: should stay 1m: looks sort to do better. *L. Cumani.*   63 p

GREY SONATA   2 gr.f. (Mar 24) Horage 124–The Grey (GER) (Pentathlon) [1989 6f³ 5m 5f 7g⁴ 7.3m a7g 7g] IR 4,000F, IR 9,500Y: well-grown, good-bodied filly: poor walker and mover: first known foal: dam reportedly placed in Germany: quite modest maiden: hung right throughout in Queen Mary Stakes at Royal Ascot on third start, and has looked unsatisfactory elsewhere: sold 1,400 gns Ascot December Sales. *M. E. D. Francis.*   62

GREY TUDOR   2 gr.g. (Apr 30) Import 127–Grey Morley 78 (Pongee 106) [1989 6f⁴ 6s a6g* a6g] 2,700Y: sparely-made gelding: second reported foal: dam, placed at 5f at 2 yrs, winning hurdler: looked very well when winning 12-runner claimer at Lingfield in November: ran poorly at Southwell final start. *C. N. Allen.*   65

GREY WOLF   2 gr.g. (Mar 15) Bellypha 130–Matinee 119 (Zeddaan 130) [1989 7g² 6d] tall, rather leggy gelding: half-brother to several winners, including useful performers Celebrity (by Troy), successful over 10.2f, Melodrama (by Busted), winner over 6f and 1m, and 1981 2-y-o 7f winner Candide (by Bustino): dam sprinter: beaten 3 lengths by easy winner Croupier in 3-runner private sweepstakes at Newmarket: weakened 2f out in 24-runner maiden at Newbury later in October. *R. J. R. Williams.*   ?

GRIMSTON AGAIN   3 b.f. Lochnager 132–Lush Gold 91 (Goldhill 125) [1988 5f² 6g* 1989 5g⁶ 7f 6m 7m⁵ 8h⁶ 6g 7g⁵ 6g] workmanlike, good-quartered filly: capable of quite modest form but deteriorated: ran in sellers last 2 outings, pulling hard final one: will probably be suited by 6f: acts on firm going: bandaged near-hind at 2 yrs: sweating profusely, bolted when taken down early and withdrawn sixth intended outing: sold 2,400 gns Doncaster November Sales: one to be wary of. *M. H. Easterby.*   71 d

GROBYA (USA)   3 b.f. Gregorian (USA) 115–Northern Lullaby (USA) (Northern Dancer) [1988 NR 1989 11.5m 16.5g] $65,000Y: big, sparely-made filly: fifth foal: sister to useful 1984 Irish 2-y-o 7f winner Rodrigue, later successful at up to 1¼m in USA, and half-sister to 2 winners, including useful 1986 2-y-o 7f winner Orne (by Val de L'Orne), later a minor stakes winner in USA: dam 5f and 6f winner: well beaten in maidens at Yarmouth and Doncaster, pulling hard in ladies event (edgy and green) in latter: sold 2,800 gns Ascot July Sales. *Mrs L. Piggott.*   —

GRONDOLA   2 b.f. (Apr 3) Indian King (USA) 128–Trysting Place (He Loves Me 120) [1989 7.5f 8f³ 7g a8g] 4,000F, 7,800Y: leggy, close-coupled filly: first live foal: dam unraced: staying-on third of 15 in late-season maiden auction event at Redcar, best effort: may stay 1¼m. *P. A. Kelleway.*   65

GROOM PORTER (USA)   3 ch.c. Blushing Groom (FR) 131–Maurita (NZ) (Harbor Prince (USA)) [1988 NR 1989 15.3f⁵ 14f² 14f*] good-topped colt: moderate walker: fluent mover: second foal: half-brother to once-raced Maurist (by Sir Ivor): dam won from 1¼m to 1½m in New Zealand, including New Zealand Oaks: odds on, won maiden at Redcar in July by short head, battling on well: blinkered, well beaten in moderately-run race on debut: will be suited by 2m: sold to join S. Cole 30,000 gns Newmarket July Sales. *G. Harwood.*   85

GROOM STAR (USA)   3 ch.c. Blushing Groom (FR) 131–Guiding Star (SWE) 70 (Reliance II 137) [1988 7g³ 1989 12.3d³ 10f4 12f 12m⁵ 11.7f² 13.6f* 12f* 14m] leggy colt: good mover: fairly useful handicapper: won at Redcar and Leicester within 6 days in October: favourite, ran poorly at Newmarket 3 days after Leicester: stays 13.6f: gives impression should prove best on a sound surface: takes keen hold   95 and carries head high: wore net muzzle last 3 outings: sold 15,500 gns Newmarket Autumn Sales: winning novice hurdler with N. Tinkler. *G. Harwood.*

GROWN AT ROWAN 2 b.f. (Apr 7) Gabitat 119–Hallo Rosie 67 (Swing Easy (USA) 126) [1989 6f 6f 6m 6f³] first reported foal: dam won 5f seller: showed vastly improved form from favourable draw when around length third to Doulally in selling nursery at Lingfield in October. *M. Madgwick.*   60

GRUMBLE 7 b.g. Skyliner 117–Chantry Pearl (Gulf Pearl 117) [1988 8d 8m 8g 9m 8.3m 1989 9d 14g] leggy, medium-sized gelding: quite modest on his day, but has become thoroughly temperamental: one to leave well alone. *K. O. Cunningham-Brown.*   §§

GRUNDY LANE 7 b.g. Grundy 137–Tamilian 89 (Tamerlane 128) [1988 8d 8m 7g 7.6v 8g² 7.6s⁵ 8m 10g 9s³ 8s⁶ 8.2d⁶ 8d² 1989 8d 12d 10d a7g] small, dipped-backed gelding: quite modest on his day: no form in 1989: off course over 6 months before final outing: best at around 1m on an easy surface: good mount for apprentice: sometimes on toes and occasionally sweats: inconsistent. *B. C. Morgan.*   —

GUALDO (USA) 3 b. or br.c. Play Fellow (USA)–Shall Return (USA) (Fair Ruler) [1988 6m 6m³ 8.2m 8.2d 1989 8g 10g² 11.5f* 12m⁴ 12.3m³ 10m³ 10.6d] rangy, useful-looking colt: fairly useful handicapper: made all, at modest pace initially, when comfortable winner at Sandown in May: creditable third at Chester and Sandown, best other efforts: stays 1½m: acts on firm going. *M. R. Stoute.*   92

GUARANTEE 2 b.c. (Mar 18) Persian Bold 123–Kendie Blue (FR) (Kenmare (FR) 125) [1989 6m⁶ 6f 7g 6m³ 5f² 5d 8f 8s⁶ 5g a5g² a6g⁵ a5g] neat colt: good walker: first foal: dam, maiden, stayed 9f, is daughter of half-sister to Dewhurst winner King's Lane: quite modest maiden: bred to stay at least 7f: blinkered sixth start: has run well for 7-lb claimer: has hung left: inconsistent. *C. E. Brittain.*   61

GUEST ARTISTE 3 ch.f. Be My Guest (USA) 126–On Show 92 (Welsh Pageant 132) [1988 6m² 1989 7g⁴ 8f³ 8g³ 8m* 10g 8m³ 8f* 8g] rangy, rather unfurnished filly: moderate walker and mover with a quick action: useful performer: short-priced favourite, won minor events at Newmarket in July and Leicester in October: best efforts first 3 outings in Nell Gwyn Stakes at Newmarket, Coronation Stakes (ducking right over 1f out) at Royal Ascot and Child Stakes at Newmarket: ran poorly in listed race final start: best form at 1m: acts on firm going: sometimes mulish at stalls. *G. Wragg.*   110

GUIDOBALDO (USA) 3 b.c. Sir Ivor 135–Hankow Willow (USA) (No Robbery) [1988 NR 1989 7s² 8s 8f 8g] $50,000Y, 3,000 2-y-o: leggy, rather unfurnished colt: has scope: fourth foal: half-brother to 2 winners in North America: dam stakes-placed winner at up to 7f: second in maiden (moved poorly down) at Leicester in April, easily best effort: off course 5 months before tailed off in handicap final start: should stay 1m. *S. Dow.*   75

GUILTY GUEST (USA) 4 b.f. Be My Guest (USA)–Innocent Victim (USA) (No Robbery) [1988 9g 8f² 10m⁶ 9f² 10.2g⁴ 8h⁴ 8g⁴ 9g 1989 8.2f⁵ 8f 8m² 8g 9g 8m] lengthy, sparely-made filly: ungenuine maiden: stays 9f: acts on hard going: blinkered debut: visored final start at 3 yrs (most reluctant to race) and last one in 1989: has pulled hard: trained until after fourth outing by J. Glover. *C. Tinkler.*   59 d

GUIZA (USA) 2 b.f. (Mar 3) Golden Act (USA)–Cairene (Artaius (USA) 129) [1989 8m³ 10v³] first foal: dam 1m winner in States, is half-sister to useful 1985 French 2-y-o Al Joharak: third in maiden at Longchamp in October and Criterium de Saint-Cloud (over 3 lengths behind demoted Snurge) following month: will stay 1½m: sure to win a race. *J-C. Cunnington, France.*   109 ?

GULFLAND 8 ch.g. Gulf Pearl 117–Sunland Park (Baragoi 115) [1988 12.2d³ 12m 12.3v* 12m² 12.3s⁴ 11.7g⁵ 12g⁴ 12g 12g* 1989 12.2s⁵ 12s 12f² 12.4m 11s 12.2f⁴ 12g⁶ a12g⁵] workmanlike, good-bodied gelding: carries condition: moderate mover: fair winner in 1988: below his best as 8-y-o: best effort when second in amateurs event at Hamilton in June: suited by 1½m: ideally suited by an easy surface: slowly away at Hamilton and on seventh outing: held up and is suited by strong gallop. *G. A. Pritchard-Gordon.*   64

GULF PALACE (USA) 4 ch.c. Green Dancer (USA) 132–Sanctum Sanctorum (USA) (Secretariat (USA)) [1988 10g 10.1g 10m³ 10d* 12m 10f 10m 10m⁵ 12d 1989 12s⁴ 12d² 11.7m⁴ 10f* 12f⁵ 12m³ 12m* 10g² 12f² 12m² 10m 12m] rangy, well-made colt: moderate mover, with a quick action: quite useful handicapper: had fine season, winning at Lingfield in May and Kempton following month: better efforts after when second to Unknown Quantity in £27,600 event at Sandown, Pokey's Pride in 6-runner contest at Goodwood and Timothy's Toy in strongly-run £19,000   92 race at Newmarket: effective at 1¼m and stays 1½m well: acts on any going: usually held up and suited by strong gallop. *R. Akehurst.*

GULLANE 3 b.g. Valiyar 129–Olivian 79 (Hotfoot 126) [1988 8g 8m 1989 12s² 11v⁴ 12.2d 12f 10m⁵ 12m 15g³ a16g³] sturdy, heavy-bodied gelding: moderate mover: poor maiden: stays 2m: acts on soft going: blinkered second and fourth starts: visored fifth: often pulls hard: sold out of Sir Mark Prescott's stable 3,000 gns Newmarket July Sales: ungenuine and one to leave alone. *A. Smith, Belgium.*   **40** §

GULMARG 2 b.c. (Mar 9) Gorytus (USA) 132–Kashmiri Snow 83 (Shirley Heights 130) [1988 6m³ 8m 6d⁴ 6g⁴] rangy, attractive colt: has scope: first foal: dam 1m winner: modest maiden: best effort final start: bred to stay at least 1m. *H. Candy.*   **73**

GULSHA 3 b.f. Glint of Gold 128–Mai Pussy 91 (Realm 129) [1988 NR 1989 7g⁵] fifth foal: half-sister to 3 winners, including smart 7f to 9f winner Beau Sher (by Ile de Bourbon) and fair 1m to 1¼m winner Samhaan (by Niniski): dam stayed 6f: 7/1 from 2/1, about 3 lengths fifth of 11 to La Grande Affaire in maiden at Lingfield in August, ridden along over 4f out and staying on steadily: should improve. *B. Hanbury.*   **64** p

GUNBOAT 3 ch.g. Relaunch (USA)–Ferjima's Gem (USA) (Wajima (USA)) [1988 7s 1989 6m² 6f² 6m 6f³ 7g] good-topped gelding: runner-up in maiden (edging right) at Newmarket and minor event at Folkestone in May, easily best efforts: stays 6f: acts on firm going: gelded after final start. *K. M. Brassey.*   **84**

GUN HAPPY 5 b.g. Formidable (USA) 125–Naughty One Gerard (Brigadier Gerard 144) [1988 7g 7m⁵ 7m 8f⁵ 9m² 9d⁶ 9g³ 10d⁴ 12m 1989 9s⁶] lengthy, workmanlike gelding: poor maiden: stays 9f: acts on firm going and possibly not at best on soft: blinkered once at 4 yrs. *R. J. Holder.*   **—**

GUNNER'S HILL 4 b.g. Dara Monarch 128–West Bank (Martinmas 128) [1988 7d⁴ 8d³ 10m⁵ 10f 7m 8g 1989 12.4g] rather unfurnished gelding: has a round action: modest handicapper at his best: well below form since second outing in 1988: stays 1m: acts on any going: bandaged near-hind first 3 starts at 3 yrs: not an easy ride. *K. Stone.*   **—**

GUN RULE 5 ch.g. Posse (USA) 130–Brave Lass 114 (Ridan (USA)) [1988 NR 1989 8g 7m⁴ 7f* 7g 8m] big, workmanlike gelding: carries plenty of condition: has scar on near quarter: bad mover: has run only 7 times on flat: won 15-runner handicap at Doncaster in June, battling on well to get up on post: well beaten in £16,300 handicap at Newmarket and £5,000 ladies event (leading over 5f) at Ascot within next 5 weeks: should stay 1m: possibly unsuited by soft going: sweating last 3 outings. *Andrew Turnell.*   **78**

GUNRUNNER GIRL 2 ch.f. (May 9) Longleat (USA) 109–Witchingham Lass 83 (Sweet Revenge 129) [1989 6g 7g] rangy, rather unfurnished filly: sister to a winner in Scandinavia and half-sister to 3-y-o 6f winner Koko Queen (by Noalto): dam stayed 7f: soundly beaten in late-season maiden at Goodwood and (still in need of race) minor event at Leicester. *R. Voorspuy.*   **—**

GURTEEN BOY 7 ch.g. Tickled Pink 114–Joie d'Or (FR) (Kashmir II 125) [1988 8g 8d 9d⁵ 7.6d 8g⁶ 10d 8g 1989 11v²] strong, sturdy, plain gelding: moderate mover: shows signs of stringhalt: poor handicapper nowadays: stays 11f: acts on any going: blinkered once, visored once, hooded once: ran creditably for apprentice only outing at 7 yrs. *J. J. O'Neill.*   **41**

GUSHY 3 ch.c. Hard Fought 125–Be Gustful (Ballymore 123) [1988 6g 7.5g 6g 7m* 8.2m* 8s⁴ 8v 1989 8.2m* 9f⁴ 8g 8.2g² 10s³ 9s³] smallish, workmanlike colt: moderate walker and mover: won claimer at Hamilton in May: good second in similar event at same course: suited by 1m: acts on top-of-the-ground and soft going: usually blinkered or visored: has worn bandages. *M. W. Easterby.*   **70**

GUSTY LADY 2 ch.f. (Apr 2) Montekin 125–Windy City (Windjammer (USA)) [1989 7f 6g 6m] IR 2,200Y: half-sister to 3-y-o Flying Junction (by Burslem) and 1984 2-y-o 6f seller winner Ras-El-Tin-Palace (by Hardgreen): dam quite useful 2-y-o 5f winner in Ireland: poor form in sellers and a claimer: sold 2,000 gns Newmarket Autumn Sales. *R. W. Stubbs.*   **32**

GUTHRIE COURT 2 b.f. (May 7) Daring March 116–Gangawayhame 91 (Lochnager 132) [1989 5m* 6f² 5f*] 4,400Y: stocky filly: third foal: sister to 3-y-o Robbie Burns and 5.8f winner Awa'wi'ye: dam won over 6f at 2 yrs and stayed 7f: fair plater: successful at Bath (comfortably, retained 7,200 gns) in May and Hamilton (not impressive in slowly-run event, retained 7,400 gns) following month: has given impression will prove better suited by 5f than 6f. *M. H. Easterby.*   **54**

GWENNI   3 gr.f. Gwynfi Ni–Tanwen 74 (Firestreak 125) [1988 NR 1989 10f] plain   —
filly: second reported foal: sister to winning hurdler and temperamental flat
performer Gwynras: dam suited by a test of stamina: 50/1, tailed off in maiden at
Chepstow in July. *J. M. Bradley.*

GYDAROS   4 b.c. Ardross 134–Handy Dancer 87 (Green God 128) [1988 12d⁴   —
12m² 14g* 16g⁵ 14f 1989 13s] strong, lengthy colt: has a rather round action: modest
winner as 3-y-o: 50/1, well tailed off in handicap at Ayr in September: should stay
2m + . *Denys Smith.*

GYMCRAK GOLD   2 ch.g. (Mar 19) Vaigly Great 127–Sweet Louise 67 (Sweet   —
Revenge 129) [1989 5g 5d] 3,800F, 8,000Y: smallish, workmanlike gelding: good
walker and mover: half-brother to 3-y-o Nordcraft (by Kind of Hush) and 2 poor
animals, one a winner over hurdles: dam placed over 5f at 2 yrs: backward, well
beaten in early-season maiden at Doncaster and seller (blinkered) at Beverley. *M.
H. Easterby.*

GYMCRAK LOVEBIRD   2 b.f. (Apr 5) Taufan (USA) 119–Waadi Hatta (USA)   **71**
47 (Upper Nile (USA)) [1989 5g 5h* 6m* 7f* 7f² 7m] IR 13,000Y: leggy, lengthy
filly: moderate mover: second reported foal: dam won at 1½m at 4 yrs in Ireland:
modest performer: successful in sellers at Carlisle (no bid) in May and Leicester
(bought in 5,000 gns) and slowly-run nursery (made all) at Thirsk in July: sweating,
head second (clear) to Trojan Excel at Thirsk, battling on splendidly, easily better
effort in nurseries following month: will be suited by 1m: on toes last 3 starts. *M. H.
Easterby.*

GYPSY'S BARN RAT   5 br.m. Balliol 125–Chebs Lass 84 (Chebs Lad 120) [1988   —
7f⁵ 7g 9f 7f* 8m* 8m 9f 7f 1989 8d 6f 7f 8f] leggy, quite good-topped mare: has
stringhalt: successful twice in poor company as 4-y-o: no form in 1989, including in
seller (favourite) final outing: suited by 7f or 1m: acts on firm going and a soft
surface: sometimes sweats: has worn bandages: has won for apprentice, but not the
easiest of rides and suited by waiting tactics: sold 1,300 gns Ascot November Sales.
W. Holden.

H

HABETA (USA)   3 ch.c. Habitat 134–Prise (Busted 134) [1988 NR 1989 8d 8f   **72**
10m⁶ 8g 7s 8.2d² 8.2g* a8g³ a10g* a11g] $11,000F: quite good-topped colt: has
scope: second known foal: half-brother to modest 1¼m winner Innes House (by
Great Nephew), later winner in USA: dam once-raced half-sister to very speedy
fillies Rose Dubarry, Hecla and Mange Tout: modest handicapper: led close home
when winning at Nottingham in October and Lingfield in November: facing stiff
task, ran badly final outing: should stay 1½m: best form on an easy surface (below
form on very soft). *J. W. Watts.*

HABIOLA   4 b.c. Hays 120–Warbiola (Nebbiolo 125) [1988 NR 1989 5m⁶ 6f 6f⁵]   —
poor plater. *P. Monteith.*

HABITANCY   3 b.f. Habitat 134–Bright Landing 78 (Sun Prince 128) [1988 NR   **95**
1989 7g 5m² 5s² 5g³ 6d] lengthy, good-quartered filly: has scope: moderate walker:
moderate mover, with a quick action: fourth foal: half-sister to useful 4-y-o
middle-distance stayer Upper Strata (by Shirley Heights): dam, placed over 5f at 2
yrs, is granddaughter of very smart sprinter Lucasland: placed, showing fairly
useful form, in £5,700 event at Newbury, minor event at Haydock and listed race
(hanging left then running on strongly) at Newmarket: co-favourite, ran moderately
in listed race at Thirsk final start: should stay 6f: acts on top-of-the-ground and soft
going. *R. F. Johnson Houghton.*

HACKFORTH   3 ch.c. Hard Fought 125–Sweet And Sour 96 (Sharpen Up 127)   **65**
[1988 5m³ 5d⁵ 6d 5g⁴ 5m⁵ 1989 6s 6m 10f⁶ 7m* 8m² 7g 7g 6f⁶ 8f⁶ a8g* a10g a8g]
neat colt: quite modest handicapper: won at Warwick in June and Lingfield (claimer)
in October: ran poorly last 2 outings: probably stays 1¼m: acts on firm going,
possibly unsuited by soft: keen sort: retained 11,500 gns Newmarket Autumn Sales
before penultimate outing: not particularly consistent. *J. D. Bethell.*

HADIF (USA)   3 b.c. Clever Trick (USA)–Ciao (USA) (Silent Screen (USA))   **111**
[1988 5m* 5d 6f³ 5m² 5d* 5d* 1989 5m⁶ 6f⁵ 6f⁵ 5m⁵ 5m² 5g⁴ 6v] close-coupled,
well-made colt: moderate walker and mover: ran creditably in pattern events at
York and Royal Ascot second and thirds starts and when second in listed contest at
Newmarket: below form, showing early speed, in listed race and handicap last 2
starts: likely to prove best at 5f: acts on firm going and a soft surface: blinkered last
4 outings: sent to race in USA. *R. W. Armstrong.*

HADLEIGHS CHOICE 2 b.c. (May 13) Fairy King (USA)–Jillette (Fine Blade 57 (USA) 121) [1989 6g 7.6m⁴ 7.5f 8f 7g] 7,000Y: close-coupled colt: eighth foal: half-brother to 1¼m winner Egidia and a winner in Belgium (both by Welsh Saint), and 2 other winners: dam Irish 1½m winner: plating-class maiden: very slowly away last 2 starts: will probably prove suited by 1m+: blinkered final outing. *H. J. Collingridge.*

HAEBEH (USA) 3 ch.f. Alydar (USA)–Foresight Princess (USA) (Reviewer 88 (USA)) [1988 7s 1989 12.2f² 10f* 10f³] rather unfurnished filly: favourite, made all unchallenged in maiden at Folkestone in August: will be suited by return to 1½m: blinkered last 2 starts. *M. R. Stoute.*

HAFHAFAH 2 b.f. (Apr 29) Shirley Heights 130–Shurooq (USA) 94 (Affirmed 74 (USA)) [1989 8f⁵ 8.2g] medium-sized filly: first foal: dam 6f and 7f winner at 2 yrs stayed 1½m: won maiden at Wolverhampton by 2½ lengths from Kitty Russe, headway to lead over 1f out and quickening well: favourite, under 12 lengths seventh of 20 to Elmuraqash in minor event at Nottingham later in October: will stay 1¼m. *H. Thomson Jones.*

HAFIR 3 b.c. Tender King 123–Spring Bride 57 (Auction Ring (USA) 123) [1988 103 5m³ 5f² 6g² 5f³ 5d² 6m³ 5m* 5f* 1989 6d* 6m² 6f 6m 6m² 6s 6m 7m⁶] big, good-topped colt: carries condition: has a quick action: won handicap at Newmarket in April: narrowly-beaten second at same course in £21,600 handicap and very strongly-run listed race: ran creditably last 2 outings, well below form otherwise: probably stays 7f: acts on firm going and a soft surface: sometimes on toes: sold 66,000 gns Newmarket Autumn Sales. *C. J. Benstead.*

HAGGS TAVERN 4 b.c. Tower Walk 130–Nonsensical 99 (Silly Season 127) 77 d [1988 10g² 12m⁴ 12m* 12g² 10.2m⁶ 12g 12g* 14s⁶ 10v⁶ 1989 13v 12f⁶ 12m 13f* 13f⁴ 13m 14g 12g⁵ 13s 13s] tall, leggy colt: moderate mover: modest handicapper on his day: won 5-runner event at Hamilton in June easily by 6 lengths: didn't find great deal next outing and ran moderately after: suited by about 1½m: acts on firm going and is unsuited by soft nowadays: blinkered 6 of last 7 outings: often hangs, but has run well for apprentice: has worn crossed noseband: withdrawn after refusing to enter stalls sixth intended start: unreliable. *W. J. Pearce.*

HAITHAM 2 b.c. (Jan 26) Wassl 125–Balqis (USA) 93 (Advocator) [1989 8g² 8d⁵] 70 first foal: dam 5f and 6f winner at 2 yrs, is half-sister to dam of Hollywood Derby winner Slew The Dragon: 4 lengths second, clear, to Go Buy Bailey's at Edinburgh, better effort in November maidens. *H. Thomson Jones.*

HAKEDMA 3 ch.c. Van Der Linden (FR)–Duty Watch 40 (Import 127) [1988 7g — 7g 6s 6d 1989 8g 6m 6f 7f 7h 10.1m 16f³ 10f 15.3g] lightly-made colt: keen walker: plating-class form at best: soundly beaten in sellers last 2 starts: probably stays 2m: sometimes pulls hard, and did so when taken last and quietly to post final outing: trained first 7 outings by W. Brooks. *Ronald Thompson.*

HALA 2 b.f. (May 7) Persian Bold 123–True Respect (USA) (Baldski (USA)) [1989 57 5d⁴ 5f 5g⁴ 6g³ 7f 7m³ 7g 8g] 4,800Y: leggy, sparely-made filly: moderate walker: has a fluent, round action: first foal: dam, winner in Norway, is out of half-sister to good sprinter Shoolerville: plating-class maiden: ran poorly last 4 starts: should stay beyond 6f: pulled hard fifth start. *C. W. C. Elsey.*

HALEIM 2 ch.c. (Mar 15) Formidable (USA) 125–Miss Reasoning (USA) (Bold 64 Reasoning (USA)) [1989 5f³ 6g* 6m] 20,000F, 34,000Y: lengthy, sturdy colt: seventh foal: half-brother to 3-y-o 1½m winner Knowlton and 1987 2-y-o 6f winner Realism (both by Known Fact) and to modest stayer Guessing (by Be My Guest): dam French sprint winner out of Poule d'Essai des Pouliches winner Pampered Miss: odds on, won maiden at Pontefract by 1½ lengths from Sandmoor Denim: ran moderately in nursery at Newmarket later in July and wasn't seen out again. *Dr J. D. Scargill.*

HALF A LEAGUE 3 b.g. Reesh 117–En Famille (Alcide 136) [1988 6m 6m 1989 — 12s 8d 8m] compact, workmanlike gelding: quite modest plater: only sign of ability at 1m on a soft surface when also edgy: blinkered (tailed off) final start: sold 2,100 gns Ascot 2nd June Sales. *G. A. Pritchard-Gordon.*

HALF A PINK JO 2 ch.c. (Feb 20) Absalom 128–Habitual Beauty (Habat 127) — [1989 5g⁵] 13,500Y: compact, good-quartered colt: third foal: half-brother to bad sprint maiden Vagara (by Vaigly Great): dam never ran: 17 lengths last of 5, fading final 2f and finishing very tired, to Champagne Gold in slowly-run minor event at Pontefract in May. *M. McCormack.*

HALHOLAH (USA) 3 b.f. Secreto (USA) 128–Sugar And Spice (USA) (Key To — The Mint (USA)) [1988 6f⁵ 8g 1989 10g⁶ 11m 9s] well-made, attractive filly: modest maiden at best: ran poorly last 2 outings, off course nearly 5 months in between: stayed 1¼m: visits Silver Hawk. *P. T. Walwyn.*

HALIGI (USA)   3 b.f. Assert 134–Noble Mark 120 (On Your Mark 125) [1988 7m⁵   **98**
1989 12g] medium-sized filly: fifth in £8,500 event at Newbury as 2-y-o: finished
lame when about 5½ lengths seventh of 15 to Nydrion in Oaks d'Italia at Milan in
May: probably stayed 1½m: dead. *B. W. Hills.*

HALIMAH   3 ch.f. Be My Guest (USA) 126–Crannog (Habitat 134) [1988 NR 1989   **56**
8m⁵ 8.5m² 8m] rather unfurnished filly: sixth foal: closely related to 7.5f winner
Gabish (by Try My Best) and half-sister to Shujun (by Shergar), disappointing here
later successful in Australia: dam, Irish 6f winner, is sister to very smart sprinters
Bitty Girl and Hot Spark: plating-class maiden: may be worth a try over shorter: sold
2,600 gns Newmarket September Sales. *H. Thomson Jones.*

HALKOPOUS   3 b.c. Beldale Flutter (USA) 130–Salamina 106 (Welsh Pageant   **87**
132) [1988 7m 8m 7g³ 1989 10.6s* 9f⁴ 12f⁵ 12g⁶ 12m* 12g⁴ 10.5m* 10g] compact
colt: fair handicapper: won at Haydock in April, Kempton (£7,300 event) in
September and York (quickening to lead 2f out and just holding on despite drifting
left) in October: stays 1½m: acts on any going. *M. H. Tompkins.*

HALL OF MIRRORS (USA)   3 b.c. Clever Trick (USA)–Reflection 111 (Mill   **90** §
Reef (USA) 141) [1988 6g² 7g* 7g* 1989 8s⁴ 8s 8f 10m⁵ 12m⁴ 10m* 10f³ 10m]
good-topped, attractive colt: moderate mover: fairly useful handicapper: favourite,
clearly best effort when winning at Newmarket in July: often failed to impress with
attitude otherwise: should stay 1½m: acts on top-of-the-ground and soft going:
blinkered last 3 outings: sold to race in France 42,000 gns Newmarket Autumn
Sales: ungenuine. *Major W. R. Hern.*

HALLOWED   7 br.m. Wolver Hollow 126–Saintly Angel 87 (So Blessed 130)   **—**
[1988 10.8f³ 10d⁶ 1989 10.8m 12.2m⁶ 10.8m] leggy, lightly-made mare: poor maiden:
bolted and withdrawn second intended outing: visored then and on next 2
appearances: stays 1½m: acts on firm going and a soft surface: blinkered once. *P. A.
Pritchard.*

HALLOW FAIR   4 b.c. Wolver Hollow 126–Fingers 124 (Lord Gayle (USA) 124)   **59**
[1988 10m 10.1m 12m⁶ 10d 1989 10f 11.1f³ 10f³ 12m⁶ 10g⁵ 8m⁴ 10f* 12f⁶ 12.2m⁴]
leggy, attractive colt: hung left when winning handicap at Nottingham in August:
seems best at 1¼m: acts on firm going. *C. A. Horgan.*

HALOX (USA)   3 b.g. Little Current (USA)–Noble Legion (CAN) (Vaguely Noble   **—**
140) [1988 NR 1989 10g 8m] $13,000Y: third foal: half-brother to a minor winner in
USA by Overskate: dam Irish 1½m and 13f winner, later placed in USA: modest form
in maidens at Brighton in April and Newbury in July: may be capable of better. *J.
Sutcliffe.*

HALSTEAD   3 b.f. Bustino 136–Romara 105 (Bold Lad (IRE) 133) [1988 6g⁶ 6g⁵   **76**
7s⁴ 1989 11.3m 10f 10m⁴ 9g 10m⁴ 10f* 8g* 8m⁶] leggy, quite attractive filly: has a
quick, fluent action: fair performer: successful in September handicaps at Salisbury
(making all) and Sandown: stays 1¼m: acts on firm going: has run creditably for a
7-lb claimer: acted as pacemaker first 2 outings. *G. Wragg.*

HALSTON PRINCE   2 b.c. (Apr 13) Petorius 117–Repicado Rose (USA)   **82**
(Repicado (CHI)) [1989 6f² 7g²] 8,400F, 26,000Y: fifth foal: half-brother to 3-y-o
Gee Double You (by Tap On Wood), 7f winner at 2 yrs, and a winner on flat and over
jumps in France: dam placed in USA: favourite, beaten ½ length in October maidens
won by In Excess at Lingfield and Field Glass at Folkestone: better suited by 7f than
6f: can win a maiden. *H. R. A. Cecil.*

HALVOYA   4 gr.f. Bay Express 132–Porsanger (USA) (Zeddaan 130) [1988 6d³   **51**
5f⁴ 5g 5h² 6g⁴ 5.8d⁴ 6m 5f 1989 5d 5f 6f² 6m 5f³ 6f* 5f² 6f 5g⁵ 5g³ 5m 5f] leggy,
rather angular filly: plating-class handicapper: won for first time when making all in
apprentice event at Ayr in June: ran creditably in similar contests last 3 outings:
stays 6f: acts on hard going and a soft surface: blinkered 3 times: best handled
tenderly. *J. L. Spearing.*

HAMMY   3 b. or br.f. Henbit (USA) 130–Sumintra 82 (El Gallo 122) [1988 6f 1989   **—**
7.6m 8m] leggy, good-topped filly: little worthwhile form in maidens and claimer:
edgy on reappearance: sold 2,400 gns Newmarket September Sales. *J. W. Hills.*

HAMPER   6 ch.g. Final Straw 127–Great Care 66 (Home Guard (USA) 129) [1988   **—**
NR 1989 14s] compact, workmanlike gelding: modest winner in 1986: never
dangerous in handicap at Sandown in April, only subsequent outing on flat: stays
1¼m: acts on soft going and top-of-the-ground: has won for apprentice: sold to join
N. Mitchell 13,200 gns Ascot June Sales: winner over hurdles. *J. T. Gifford.*

HANA MARIE   2 b. or br.f. (Apr 6) Formidable (USA) 125–Milk And Honey 102   **81** p
(So Blessed 130) [1989 6m² 5f* 5g 6f*] 22,000Y: medium-sized, workmanlike filly:
has scope: good walker: seventh foal: closely related to 1983 2-y-o 5f winner Ideal

Home (by Home Guard) and half-sister to 3-y-o 1m winner You Missed Me (by Known Fact) and 2 other winners: dam won over 5f and 6f at 2 yrs but didn't train on: successful maiden at Sandown in June and minor event (beat Famous Beauty very easily by 2 lengths) at Thirsk following month: ran creditably in listed race at Newmarket in between: better suited by 6f than 5f: may improve further. *G. A. Huffer.*

HANDANLEE 2 ro.f. (Apr 22) Battle Hymn 103–Wedding Guest (Sanbal) [1989 5.8h⁵] fourth foal (previous 3 by Ivotino): dam ran once: tailed off in 5-runner seller at Bath in July. *J. M. Bradley.* —

HAND IN GLOVE 3 b.g. Star Appeal 133–Cash Limit 62 (High Top 131) [1988 NR 1989 10.1m 12g² 14g⁶ 14m⁶] 4,700F, 11,000Y: deep-girthed, angular gelding: half-brother to Italian 1988 7.5f and 1m winner Big Sandy (by Hotfoot) and 1984 2-y-o 7f and 1m winner Double Limit (by Roan Rocket): dam lightly raced: quite modest maiden: takes keen hold, and may be suited by return to 1½m. *W. J. Haggas.* **61**

HANDSOME CHARLIE 4 ch.f. Some Hand 119–Allied Cardiff 60 (Import 127) [1988 NR 1989 11v 10f 8m] sparely-made filly: second living foal: dam won 6f seller at 2 yrs and later over hurdles: soundly beaten, including in sellers: blinkered final outing: sold 1,350 gns Ascot August Sales. *F. Watson.* —

HANDSOME JINKO 4 ch.c. Some Hand 119–Nelodor 69 (Nelcius 133) [1988 6m 7d 8d 1989 8d 8.5g 7f 10f⁵ 11.7m 11.7m 10f*] angular, dipped-backed colt: moderate mover: dropped in class, landed gamble in selling handicap (no bid) at Folkestone in August: stays 1¼m: acts on firm going: bandaged last 2 starts: trained until after fourth outing by J. Edwards. *B. Stevens.* **34**

HANDSOME LEADER (USA) 3 b.g. Green Forest (USA) 134–Mazyoun (USA) 57 (Blushing Groom (FR) 131) [1988 NR 1989 9f 10f] 1,150 2-y-o: small, sturdy gelding: first foal: dam, placed at 6f and 7f, is from family of Mysterious and J O Tobin: bandaged near-hind, no sign of ability in sellers at Wolverhampton and Leicester in October. *A. Hide.* —

HANDSOME SAILOR 6 ch.h. Some Hand 119–Found At Sea (USA) (Pieces of Eight 128) [1988 6d³ 6d* 5m* 6f⁶ 6d³ 5d* 6s⁵ 5m* 6f⁵ 1989 6g⁴ 6f 5f 6m 5g*] lengthy horse: poor mover: improved into one of the best sprinters as 5-y-o, **113**

winning Duke of York Stakes, Sears Temple Stakes at Sandown and William Hill Sprint Championship at York, and awarded Ciga Prix de l'Abbaye de Longchamp: below his best in 1989, but ran considerably better than on previous 3 outings when beating Teeming Shore a head in Waterford Foods EBF Phoenix Flying Five in September: effective at 5f and 6f: not at his best on extremes of going: best ridden up with pace: sometimes sweated and got on edge: retired to Emral Stud, Cheshire, fee £1,300 nfnf. *B. W. Hills.*

HANDY MO 3 b.g. Rolfe (USA) 77–Stephouette 47 (Stephen George 102) [1988 65 NR 1989 8s 7m⁶ 10.1m⁵ 12m² 12g⁴] useful-looking gelding: second reported foal: half-brother to NH Flat race winner Tee Qu (by Jimsun): dam plater who showed best form at 1m, later running novice hurdler: in frame in autumn handicaps at Chepstow (apprentices) and Leicester: should be suited by return to 1¼m. *H. Candy.*

HANNAH'S CHOICE 2 b. or br.f. (Apr 14) Kampala 120–Cape of Storms — (Fordham (USA) 117) [1989 a6g] first foal: dam, raced only at 2 yrs, out of staying half-sister to top-class sprinter Sandford Lad: behind in late-year claimer at Southwell. *P. A. Blockley.*

HANNAH'S SECRET 3 ch.f. Starch Reduced 112–Lana's Secret 79 (Most 47 Secret 119) [1988 5g 1989 5f⁴ 5h 5f 5f⁵ 5f⁴ 5g 6m 5m 5f⁵ 5m 5g⁶] medium-sized filly: poor performer: should be suited by further than 5f: acts on firm going: blinkered last 3 starts: has run well for 7-lb claimer: has been slowly away. *B. Palling.*

HANOVER STREET 2 b.c. (Mar 26) Doc Marten 104–Carnation 64 (Runny- 39 mede 123) [1989 5d 5g⁶] 5,800Y: third reported live foal: half-brother to 3-y-o Virginia's Bay (by Uncle Pokey), 6f winner at 2 yrs: dam best at 5f: over 6 lengths sixth of 17 in seller at Beverley in May, better effort. *S. J. Muldoon.*

HANSEATIC 5 b.g. Free State 125–Marista (Mansingh (USA) 120) [1988 8g² — 10m 8d⁶ 8m⁵ 8.3m⁵ 7.6f⁶ 8.3m* 8.5m⁵ 8f⁴ 8d 1989 8s 8.5d 10.2g] attractive gelding: fair winner as 4-y-o when trained by P. Makin: well beaten in 1989 (not seen out after May): suited by 1m: acts on top-of-the-ground and probably unsuited by soft going: blinkered last 4 outings in 1888 and on reappearance: winning selling hurdler in 1988/9. *N. Tinkler.*

HANSOM LAD 6 b.g. Dublin Taxi–Trackalady 96 (Track Spare 125) [1988 5d 61 5d³ 5m 6g⁵ 5d² 6f 1989 6s 5m 5g 5m 5g 6m 6g a6g* a6g⁴] big, good-topped gelding: carries plenty of condition: first form as 6-y-o and won for first time in claimer at Southwell in December: suited by sprint distances: acts on any going: wore blinkers and crossed noseband third outing: none too genuine. *W. W. Haigh.*

HAPPY CAVALIER 4 b.g. King of Spain 121–Happy Donna 106 (Huntercombe — § 133) [1988 5m 5d 7g 6m⁴ 6m⁵ 6f 6g⁵ 5f 6f 6s 6s 6m⁶ 5g 1989 7d 6d 5d 5m 5m 6m] compact gelding: has a round action: bad maiden: suited by 6f: acts on top-of-the-ground and soft going: usually blinkered: sold to join R. Barr 1,700 gns Don-caster June Sales. *D. Yeoman.*

HAPPY HARRINGTON 3 br.c. Dara Monarch 128–Forlorn Chance (Fighting — Don) [1988 5m 7d 7m 1989 8g 10m 10g 8m] smallish, angular colt: plating-class form at best: keen sort, should prove best at up to 1m: sold 1,850 gns Ascot August Sales. *J. A. C. Edwards.*

HAPPY HUNTING 4 b.f. Good Times (ITY)–Deer Forest (Huntercombe 133) — [1988 NR 1989 12.3f] sparely-made filly: well beaten in modest company: blinkered only start at 4 yrs. *C. N. Allen.*

HAPPY POLLYANNA 3 br.f. Caerleon (USA) 132–Mortefontaine (FR) (Polic — 126) [1988 7d⁵ 1989 7h⁶] pulled hard when well beaten in valuable race at Ascot as 2-y-o and maiden at Brighton (stumbling leaving stalls, prominent 5f then eased right down) in August: has scope and looked capable of better. *C. E. Brittain.*

HAPPY VISION 2 br.c. (Apr 17) Kala Shikari 125–Rainbow Vision 73 (Prince 32 Tenderfoot (USA) 126) [1989 5s 5f⁶ 5h⁴ 6f⁵ 7m 7.5g] neat colt: keen walker: moderate mover: first foal: dam 2-y-o 7f winner: poor plater. *N. Tinkler.*

HARBOUR BAR (USA) 2 b.c. (Feb 12) Cure The Blues (USA)–Little Deep 103 Water 98 (General Assembly (USA)) [1989 6f² 6m* 5f⁵ 7m³ 8m² 10v³] $25,000Y: tall, quite attractive colt: has scope: first foal: dam 7f and 1¼m winner, is half-sister to stayer Van Dyke Brown and 2 other useful winners: made most when winning 16-runner maiden at Haydock in June: useful form on last 2 starts in listed race at Ascot in October and Group 2 event at Rome in November: stays 1¼m. *M. A. Jarvis.*

HARDALE 2 b.f. (Jun 15) Beldale Lark 105–Jachar (Lighter 111) [1989 8m] — angular filly: second foal: dam unraced: 25/1 and backward, soon well behind in 17-runner seller at Warwick in October: has joined C. Holmes. *J. D. Czerpak.*

Andy Capp Handicap, York—Hard As Iron (rails) continues his excellent run, just holding unlucky-in-running top-weight Light of Morn who puts up one of the best performances seen in a handicap all season

HARD AS IRON 6 b.g. Ardoon 124–Prancer 70 (Santa Claus 133) [1988 8d 10g⁵ **104** 9m⁴ 8f 10f³ 10m³ 8g⁵ 10g⁵ 8.2s⁴ 9g 10g 1989 10f* 8f* 8f 9f* 8m* 9f* 9m* 9g] tall gelding: poor walker: useful handicapper: vastly improved and a winner of 6 of his 8 races as 6-y-o, one at Sandown, Chepstow, Redcar, Pontefract and 2 at York: beat unlucky Light of Morn a head in £12,200 Andy Capp Handicap and Monastery 2 lengths in 9-runner event at York for last 2 successes: never dangerous in William Hill Cambridgeshire Handicap at Newmarket: best at 1m to 1¼m: best form on top-of-the-ground: blinkered twice in 1988: tends to idle, and suited by waiting tactics: splendidly genuine and consistent: a credit to his trainer. *M. H. Tompkins.*

HARDIHERO 3 b.g. Henbit (USA) 130–Hardirondo 93 (Hardicanute 130) [1988 **53** 7m 8g 10d 1989 12s² 16d⁴ 12.5f] leggy, quite attractive gelding: plating-class maiden: will prove suited by thorough test of stamina: probably acts on any going: ran creditably in blinkers final start (May). *K. O. Cunningham-Brown.*

HARDIHEROINE 2 b.f. (May 16) Sandhurst Prince 128–Hardirondo 93 **76** (Hardicanute 130) [1989 7m⁴ 7h* 7m 8.2f² 8f² 8.2f⁵] smallish, sparely-made filly: good walker: has a quick, moderate action: seventh foal: half-sister to 3-y-o Hardihero (by Henbit) and several winners, including smart 1¼m performer Belle Poitrine (by Dominion) and 1½m winner Cataclysmic (by Ela-Mana-Mou): dam game stayer: modest performer: won maiden at Brighton in August by 1½ lengths: stayed on strongly in nurseries on last 3 starts: will be suited by 1¼m+. *J. L. Dunlop.*

HARD SELL 2 ch.g. (May 28) Hard Fought 125–Misoptimist 111 (Blakeney 126) **53** [1989 6f⁵ 6m 8g] 1,000Y: half-brother to 3 winners abroad: dam won over 6f and 1¼m: plating-class maiden: best effort second start: gelded after final one. *R. Hannon.*

HARD TO COME BY 4 br.c. Ile de Bourbon (USA) 133–Callianire (Sir Gaylord) **70** [1988 10v 12m⁴ 12f⁴ 12.2g 10m⁶ 10m² 13.8f² 14f* 14m* 14m⁴ 13.8g 1989 16m⁴ 14m 14m* 14f²] neat colt: moderate walker: has a rather round action: quite modest handicapper: favourite, held on by short head from Needwood Nymph at Yarmouth in June: good second in 5-runner event at Nottingham over week later: probably stays 2m: acts on firm going: has twice got loose and been withdrawn, but races gamely. *M. F. D. Morley.*

HARD TO FIGURE 3 gr.c. Telsmoss 91–Count On Me 77 (No Mercy 126) **74** [1988 5m³ 5.8g* 6g 5g³ 5g 5m 1989 8d 6g 5.8m 6m 6f³ 6m* 5.8m* 5f* 8h³] compact colt: modest handicapper: successful at Chepstow then Bath (twice, slowly away

387

second occasion) within 12 days in July: never-dangerous third of 4 later in month: may prove ideally suited by 6f: acts on firm ground. *R. J. Hodges.*

HARD TO GET 2 b.c. (May 10) Rousillon (USA) 133–Elusive 94 (Little Current 65 (USA)) [1989 6m⁵ 7m⁶ 6m² 6g³ 7f⁵ 7g³ 9g³ 10g⁵] close-coupled, finely-made colt: good walker: second foal: half-brother to Danish 3-y-o winner Skipper (by Niniski): dam, daughter of May Hill and Galtres Stakes winner Tartan Pimpernel, won over 7f at 2 yrs and ran well over 1½m only start at 3 yrs: quite modest form in maidens and claimers: claimed out of I. Balding's stable £7,275 sixth outing: stays 9f: blinkered fourth start: tends to carry head high, has twice hung right, and looks a difficult ride. *J. Wharton.*

HARD TO NAME 2 b.c. (Feb 6) Connaught 130–Printafoil (Habat 127) [1989 7m 74 7m 8.5f*] strong, workmanlike colt: second living foal: dam poor half-sister to smart middle-distance stayer Major Green and Irish Guineas fourth Miss Connaught (by Connaught): showed improved form when winning maiden at Beverley in September by a short head from Longshoreman, making all: will stay 1¼m. *E. Eldin.*

HARKEN PREMIER 4 gr.g. Hard Fought 125–Maraquiba (FR) (Kenmare (FR) 54 125) [1988 8d 9m 9f 5f 8g* 7g⁶ 8g³ 8.2s 8m* 10g 1989 7.5g 7m 7m 8f⁴ 10f⁶ 10m 11f* 8.2g⁵ 8.2d 9g⁶ 8.5f 12f*] strong, lengthy gelding: plating-class handicapper: won at Hamilton in July and Brighton in September: stays 1½m: acts on firm going: blinkered as 4-y-o except when successful: has seemed temperamental, and is inconsistent: has joined J. Jenkins. *W. J. Pearce.*

HARMONY PARK 4 b.f. Music Boy 124–Georgina Park 88 (Silly Season 127) 55 [1988 8m⁴ 7g 6m³ 6m³ 6m 5g³ 6d 6g 1989 7m 7m* 7g 7m 7g* 8.2g 7m 7m² 8f⁴ 7d 8g] leggy, close-coupled filly: led close home when winning seller (no bid) at Yarmouth in July and handicap at Leicester in August: suited by 7f: probably needs a sound surface: sweating last 2 starts: suited by waiting tactics: inconsistent. *M. J. Ryan.*

HARREEK 4 ch.g. Tap On Wood 130–Footway 97 (Sovereign Path 125) [1988 74 12d² 16m* 14g² 14.8m 13s 1989 16s⁶ 13v⁶ 17.1m³ 20f] useful-looking gelding: carries condition: moderate mover: fair winner as 3-y-o: easily best effort in first half of 1989 on third outing: suited by a test of stamina: acts on top-of-the-ground and a soft surface (unsuited by very soft going): visored as 4-y-o, except second start: sweating and ran in snatches third start at 3 yrs: sold 8,000 gns Newmarket Autumn Sales: inconsistent. *P. F. I. Cole.*

HARRY'S COMING 5 b.g. Marching On 101–Elegant Star 86 (Star Moss 122) 47 [1988 6f6 6m* 5f6 5d² 6d³ 1989 5f* 7f² 6f* 6f* 5f6 6f6] leggy, good-topped gelding: plating-class performer: won claimer at Wolverhampton in May and handicaps at Lingfield and Nottingham following month: below his best last 2 outings: seems ideally suited by 6f: probably acts on any going, but goes very well on firm: has run creditably for apprentice: blinkered or visored final 3 appearances at 3 yrs. *R. J. Hodges.*

HARTLEY 2 gr.g. (Feb 10) Final Straw 127–She Who Dares (Bellypha 130) [1989 66 6f 6m⁵ 5g* 5f 5g⁶] 4,600F: angular, rather leggy gelding: poor mover: third foal: half-brother to smart 3-y-o sprinter Tigani and to quite useful 1¼m winner Daring Times (both by Good Times): dam never ran: won maiden at Edinburgh in July: should stay 6f: slowly away fourth start. *T. Fairhurst.*

HARVEST MINSTREL 2 ch.g. (Apr 28) Final Straw 127–Smagiada (Young 70 Generation 129) [1989 5m² 8m 6d] 9,400Y: strong, angular gelding: second foal: half-brother to 3-y-o Sweet 'N' Sharp (by Sharpo), 5f winner at 2 yrs: dam, winner in Italy, is half-sister to leading 1982 Italian 2-y-o filly Stemegna: short-head second of 8, losing 1f out to line, to Charade Dancer in maiden at Newcastle in July: off course 3 months afterwards and never placed to challenge or knocked about in maiden auction race at York and maiden at Catterick on return. *M. H. Easterby.*

HARVEST SPLENDOUR (USA) 2 b.f. (Mar 2) Solford (USA) 127–Autumn — p Splendour (AUS) (Luskin Star (AUS)) [1989 7m] $27,000Y: compact filly: first foal: dam won from 5.5f to 1m in Australia: 16/1, never dangerous or knocked about unduly in 21-runner maiden at Newmarket in October. *J. W. Watts.*

HARVEST TIME (FR) 3 b.c. Noir Et Or 125–First Crop (BRZ) (Lunard) [1988 119 8.2g* 10g* 1989 10g* 10g* 12g* 12g* 12d* 12.5m 12g 12g²] third foal: half-brother to a 1¼m to 11.5f winner in French Provinces by Nodouble: dam Brazilian bred: won first 6 races in French Provinces, last of them listed Derby de l'Ouest at Nantes in May: won Group 3 Prix du Lys at Chantilly in June by nose from Golden Pheasant next start: behind in Group 2 event at Saint-Cloud, reportedly suffering blood disorder, and Prix de l'Arc de Triomphe at Longchamp: fair second in listed race at

Hamdan Al-Maktoum's "Hasbah"

Nantes in November: stays 1½m: acts on a soft surface: usually blinkered. *H. Pantall, France.*

HASAIF 3 b.f. Niniski (USA) 125–Karissima 90 (Kalamoun 129) [1988 6g⁶ 1989 — 10m] 10,000Y: leggy, sparely-made filly: third foal: dam 2-y-o 7f winner in Ireland: behind in maiden at Tipperary (trained by D. K. Weld) in June as 2-y-o and claimer (raced keenly and weakened final 3f) at Nottingham year later: has joined N. Callaghan. *A. Hide.*

HASBAH 2 ch.f. (Feb 10) Kris 135–Al Bahathri (USA) 123 (Blushing Groom (FR) **100 p** 131) [1989 6g² 7f*] lengthy, good-topped filly: first foal: dam won Lowther Stakes and Irish 1000 Guineas: long odds on, won maiden at Redcar in October very easily by 7 lengths from Tarazed: short-head second to Alwathba in Blue Seal Stakes at Ascot: will stay 1m: likely to go on to better things. *H. Thomson Jones.*

HASLAND 2 b.f. (Mar 5) Aragon 118–Pop Gun 85 (King's Troop 118) [1989 5s* **40** 5s⁴ 6m⁴ 7f⁶ 6f 7f⁴ 6g³ 7g] 7,400Y: neat filly: poor mover: half-sister to 2 winning platers, a winner abroad, a winner over hurdles and temperamental 1987 2-y-o Gunner's Moon (by Relkino): dam best at 5f: poor plater: narrow winner at Warwick (bought in 3,200 gns) in March: stays 7f: sweating fifth outing: sometimes slowly away: sold 720 gns Doncaster October Sales. *N. Tinkler.*

HASLINGDEN BOY 2 b.c. (Feb 28) Another Realm 118–Sharp Celeste 81 **52** (Sharpen Up 127) [1989 5g 5v³ 5f⁶ 5g 7.5f⁶ 7f⁴ 7.5g* 7.5m⁴ 7f⁵ 7.5m⁵ 8f 8.2s] 5,200F, 4,200Y: smallish, sparely-made colt: second reported foal: half-brother to 7f seller and 1m winner Bleu Celeste (by Rabdan): dam 5f and 7f winner: gambled-on 6/1-shot, won strongly-run seller (no bid) at Beverley in July by 6 lengths: below form afterwards, on final start never travelling well when blinkered: should stay 1m: best form on good ground. *A. M. Robson.*

HASTY THRILL (USA) 2 b.c. (Apr 5) Lines of Power (USA)–Ashbud (Ashmore (FR) 125) [1989 6f a8g] third foal: dam poor maiden half-sister to smart 1972 2-y-o Perdu: well behind in maidens at Goodwood and Lingfield 6 months apart. *R. Hannon.*   —

HASTY VESSEL (USA) 3 b.f. Raise A Cup (USA)–Hasty Key (USA) (Key To The Mint (USA)) [1988 5g² 6d 6g⁵ 7g* 1989 7.3s 8f³ 7m] lengthy, rather unfurnished filly: modest winner as 2-y-o, making most despite tending to carry head high: good third in handicap at Kempton, leading over 6f: last in Group 3 event and £11,600 handicap other starts in 1989, not seen out after July: stays 1m: acts on firm going: keen sort. *C. E. Brittain.*   **80**

HATARI (CAN) 2 b.c. (May 24) Assert 134–Lady Roberta (USA) (Roberto (USA) 131) [1989 6f³ 7m] 14,500Y: leggy, quite attractive colt: half-brother to North American 3-y-o King Roberto (by Spectacular Bid), listed placed at 2 yrs, and a minor winner at up to 9f in USA by Key To The Mint: dam leading 3-y-o filly in Canada in 1980 when successful at up to 9f: over 2 lengths third of 7, staying on well, to Absolutely Perfect in maiden at Brighton in May: broke hind leg and destroyed at Kempton following month. *W. Jarvis.*   **62**

HATAY 4 ro.f. Alias Smith (USA)–Panay 77 (Arch Sculptor 123) [1988 5m⁵ 5d² 5d² 5g⁴ 5m 7g 5s 5d⁶ 1989 6f 5g² 5g 5g 6m 6f 5m] strong, good-bodied filly: quite modest handicapper on her day: neck second of 7, making running and rallying well, at Chester in June, only worthwhile form as 4-y-o: suited by 5f and give in the ground: occasionally blinkered, including when on toes final outing: probably needs strong handling: sold 2,100 gns Doncaster October Sales: inconsistent. *T. T. Bill.*   **60 d**

HATEEL 3 b.c. Kalaglow 132–Oatfield 69 (Great Nephew 126) [1988 NR 1989 8g 10s⁵ 15.3f² 12f² 14m* 13.3g⁵ 13.3m⁶ 14m* 14.6g 10m³ 12g*] 190,000Y: strong, well-made colt: fourth foal: half-brother to very useful winner at around 1m Barley Bill and a winner in Malaysia (both by Nicholas Bill) and to 2m winner High Plains (by High Line): dam, out of half-sister to High Line, ran 3 times: won maiden (easily) at York in June, ladies handicap at Yarmouth in August and amateurs handicap at Ascot in October: stays 1¾m: acts on firm going: inconsistent. *P. T. Walwyn.*   **85**

HATS HIGH 4 b.g. High Top 131–Peculiar One (USA) (Quack (USA)) [1988 10.1m 10.1g 12d 12s* 12d* 1989 15.5s⁶ 14g] lengthy, angular gelding: poor mover: won claimers as 3-y-o: 33/1 and apprentice ridden, tailed off in 1¾m handicap at Sandown in September, first outing for 5 months: best form at 1½m: goes well with plenty of give in the ground: visored last 2 starts in 1988 on reappearance: winning but untrustworthy hurdler. *J. R. Jenkins.*   —

HAUNTING BEAUTY (USA) 2 ch.f. (Jan 25) Barachois (CAN)–Vitale (Vitiges (FR) 132) [1989 5f* 5f* 5f* 6m⁵ 5m]   **110**

In Haunting Beauty and Mademoiselle Chloe the North had, unusually, two of the season's best two-year-old fillies. There was little to choose between them on their form in the Tattersalls Cheveley Park Stakes at Newmarket in October, where they finished a close fifth and sixth respectively, and there would have been less still had Mademoiselle Chloe been ridden with equal enterprise. Nevertheless, pride of place goes to Haunting Beauty, whose victory in the Group 3 Molecomb Stakes at Goodwood's summer festival was the only time during the year that a northern-trained two-year-old won a pattern race. The Molecomb Stakes, let alone the Cheveley Park, was a far cry from the maiden race in which Haunting Beauty made her debut at Ripon in June. Looking well, though a trifle backward, Haunting Beauty travelled comfortably from the off and quickened readily to account for the Newmarket-trained challenger Super Deb by half a length in a fast time. On the basis of that run, with improvement expected, Haunting Beauty looked favourably treated in the Foster's Nursery at York in July. Considering she missed the break and met frequent trouble in running Haunting Beauty did exceptionally well to maintain her unbeaten record, making up four lengths or so in the final furlong to catch Final Shot and win by half a length. Later in the month Haunting Beauty continued her progress with a three-quarter-length defeat of Red Henry and eight others in the Molecomb Stakes. Slowly away again, though not so markedly as at York,

Molecomb Stakes, Goodwood—four in line abreast,
Haunting Beauty (near side) is about to get up from Red Henry (No. 3),
Boozy (noseband) and the blinkered Shamshoon

Haunting Beauty made her effort from the rear two furlongs out and ran on strongly to win going away. Haunting Beauty wasn't seen out again until the Cheveley Park, for which she was supplemented at a cost of £10,000, although her name wasn't forgotten altogether as the Press regularly highlighted her unfortunate ineligibility for the newly-instituted Racecall Gold Trophy at Redcar on account of her sire Barachois' being omitted from the qualifying list of stallions. Had a fit and well Haunting Beauty been allowed to take part at Redcar she must have played a part in the finish on the form she displayed in the Cheveley Park: just over a length down on Dead Certain at the line, she'd stayed on well from two furlongs out without really threatening to reach the winner. At the end of October, though, when the Racecall Gold Trophy was run, Haunting Beauty was past her best for the season and said to be coughing. Two weeks earlier she'd run in the Cornwallis Stakes at Ascot, had the best form of the nine runners, but didn't take the eye in the preliminaries and finished tailed off having come under the whip by halfway. It was an uncharacteristic performance which is probably best forgotten: clearly, on her day, Haunting Beauty is a very useful filly.

Haunting Beauty, who cost 17,000 dollars at the Ocala Breeders' Sales Company Yearling Sale in Florida, is by a Northern Dancer stallion who's a winner from six furlongs to eight and a half furlongs in Canada and a full brother to Night Shift as well as the Champion North American filly Fanfreluche. Barachois is also the sire of the high-class middle-distance gelding Win and around twenty other stakes winners. Haunting Beauty's once-raced dam Vitale, by the Champion Stakes winner Vitiges, has bred two other minor winners by Barachois in her short time at stud. Vitale, who was

391

exported to the States in 1982, is a half-sister to the Wildenstein-bred 1980 two-year-old five-furlong winner Disco Dancing, who later showed quite useful form in Italy.

		Northern Dancer	Nearctic
	Barachois (CAN)	(b 1961)	Natalma
	(b 1969)	Ciboulette	Chop Chop
Haunting Beauty (USA)		(b 1961)	Windy Answer
(ch.f. Jan 25, 1987)		Vitiges	Phaeton
	Vitale	(ch 1973)	Vale
	(ch 1979)	Fire Dance	Habitat
		(b 1973)	Faucille d'Or

Barachois' several winning older progeny in Britain and Ireland have an average winning distance of nearly a mile. It's likely though that the compact Haunting Beauty, very much a sprint type, will prove best at around six furlongs. So far she's raced only on top-of-the-ground. *J. Etherington.*

HAUWMAL   6 ch.h. Troy 137–Sovereign Rose 116 (Sharpen Up 127) [1988 10d **70** §
10d⁶ 12m⁵ 12m³ 11f⁵ 14g⁵ 11g⁵ 11.7g⁶ 12m⁶ 13.3f 10s⁶ 1989 10s² 18.4m⁴ 12m⁴ 12f 12g
14f 12g² 12m² 13.3m 11v a10g⁶] compact horse: carries plenty of condition: one-time useful performer, but has not won since 1986: stays 2m: acts on any going, except heavy: ran moderately when sweating fourth and sixth (also on toes) outings: has worn a crossed noseband: takes a strong hold and is a difficult ride: disappointing. *D. A. Wilson.*

HAVE A BREEZE   3 ch.f. Coquelin (USA) 121–Courreges 75 (Manado 130)   **—**
[1988 6g 1989 7f 8.2m 10m 12g] small, lightly-made filly: no sign of ability, including in sellers: ducked left under pressure third start. *C. Spares.*

HAVERTON   2 b.g. (Feb 16) Carwhite 127–Rosie Pug (Mummy's Pet 125) [1989   **48**
6f⁵ 6m 7m⁶ 6v] 12,000Y: strong, useful-looking gelding: first foal: dam lightly-raced sister to smart sprinter The Pug and useful sprinter The Dinmont and closely related to Music Boy: poor form in varied races: best effort, ridden by 7-lb claimer, third outing. *R. Hannon.*

HAVON AIRCO   3 b.g. Lafontaine (USA) 117–Sunland Park (Baragoi 115) [1988   **—**
7m⁵ 7g* 7g³ 8g⁶ 8s 1989 12.3m 10.2f 7.6h 8m] robust, deep-girthed gelding: carries condition: fair winner as 2-y-o: well beaten in handicaps in 1989, blinkered final start in July: should be suited by further than 7f: probably unsuited by top-of-the-ground: often ridden by 5-lb claimer at 2 yrs: has joined G. Yardley. *M. F. D. Morley.*

HAWAIIAN REEF   2 b.c. (Mar 6) Henbit (USA) 130–Raffmarie 78 (Raffingora   **60** p
130) [1989 7m] IR 8,400Y: rather leggy, attractive colt: half-brother to 6f and 1½m winner No-U-Turn (by Nonoalco) and modest 7f winner Northern Love (by Northern Baby): dam, sister to good 1975 2-y-o Pasty, stayed 6f: 33/1 and green, about 11 lengths last of 18, slowly into stride then keeping on steadily, to Marienski in maiden at Newmarket in August: likely to improve. *J. P. Hudson.*

HAWAIIAN ROMANCE (USA)   3 ch.f. Hawaii–Chateau Princess (USA)   **—**
(Majestic Prince) [1988 NR 1989 7g 8m 10f 12f 10f] 55,000Y: big, lengthy filly: first foal: dam, Irish 1¼m winner, is half-sister to Henbit (by Hawaii): modest maiden: stays 1¼m: trained first 2 outings (pulled hard second) by G. Lewis: sweating final one (July). *R. Curtis.*

HAWAIIAN SONG   3 b.f. Henbit (USA) 130–Sea Music 108 (Atan) [1988 7m 6g   **63**
7m 1989 8g 6f⁴ 7f* 7m 7g² 7.6f] leggy, angular, workmanlike filly: quite modest handicapper: won at Lingfield in July: good second at Epsom, easily best effort after: should stay 1m: acts on firm going: sometimes on edge and swishes tail in preliminaries: sold 16,000 gns Newmarket December Sales. *H. Candy.*

HAWWAM   3 b.c. Glenstal (USA) 118–Hone 79 (Sharpen Up 127) [1988 5g 5g² 5d³   **98**
7m* 7.3d³ 7d* 7m² 9m 7d³ 7d² 1989 8s* 8m² 10m 8f 8m² 8m³ 8g⁴ 9g] good-topped, quite attractive colt: usually takes the eye: useful handicapper: won at Newbury in May: wearing severe bridle, very good second in £15,600 event at Newmarket in July, having had a lot to do: suited by 1m (bit backward over 9f): acts on any going, except perhaps very firm: tends to wander and idle in front, and is best with waiting tactics and strong handling: tough. *C. J. Benstead.*

HAYYA YA SHAREEF   2 b.c. (Mar 17) Shareef Dancer (USA) 135–Hayya (FR)   **—**
(Shergar 140) [1989 7.6m] first foal: dam unraced half-sister to Luderic, a smart French performer at up to 9f: around 11 lengths seventh of 12 in maiden at Lingfield in September: sold 6,400 gns Newmarket Autumn Sales. *M. R. Stoute.*

HAZY DANCER 3 b.c. Hays 120–Miami Dancer 55 (Miami Springs 121) [1988   **52**
6g⁶ 7m 5f⁶ 6f 1989 7d 7.5d 8d 7.5d 8.2f⁴ 10g³ 8g* 11m² 12.4f⁴ 9g* 10.6d 10f 8m 8.2f
10g] angular, sparely-made, dipped-backed colt: moderate walker: has a round
action: plating-class performer: made all at Ripon in July in seller (no bid) and
handicap: below form after in handicaps and seller, sweating final start: probably
stays 11f: acts on firm going and a soft surface: bandaged off-hind third outing: tends
to hang, and has looked a hard ride: sold G. Thorner 4,000 gns Doncaster November
Sales. *M. Brittain.*

HAZY HEATH 2 b.f. (Mar 21) Wolver Heights 99–Bumfuzzle (USA) (Fleet   **—**
Nasrullah) [1989 7g 6f] 920Y: workmanlike filly: fifth foal: dam won in USA: bit
backward, never dangerous in minor event at Doncaster and auction race at
Nottingham in September. *E. J. Alston.*

HEADBEE 3 b.f. Head For Heights 125–Plaits 93 (Thatching 131) [1988 6g 8m⁵   **46**
1989 10f⁶ 10g 11.7m 8.3d³ 10f⁴ 9m 12g² 12g⁵] leggy filly: poor maiden: good second
in seller at Folkestone: stays 1½m: acts on firm going: sweating fourth start: has
joined M. Castell. *R. Hannon.*

HEAD GROOM 2 ch.c. (Apr 21) Shy Groom (USA)–Solarina (Solinus 130) [1989   **49**
6m⁵ 7g⁶ 5f 6g] IR 4,600F, IR 3,300Y, resold 10,000Y: compact colt: second living
foal: half-brother to 3-y-o 5f and 6f winner Zeboim (by Stanford): dam placed over 7f
on first of only 2 starts in Ireland as 3-y-o: poor maiden: needs further than 5f. *J. D.
Bethell.*

HEAD OF DEFENCE 4 ch.c. Tachypous 128–Headliner (Pampered King 121)   **—**
[1988 NR 1989 14m 12m] leggy, angular colt: moderate mover: poor form in varied
company, including selling: visored once. *B. Palling.*

HEADQUARTERS 3 b.c. Habitat 134–Guillotina 118 (Busted 134) [1988 6m²   **85**
7m* 1989 8m 8f⁵ 8d] good-quartered, quite attractive colt: made all in maiden as
2-y-o: not discredited first 2 starts in 1989, off course over 5 months in between:
front rank 5f when tailed off in handicap 10 days after second of them: will be suited
by further than 1m: sold A. Falourd 14,000 gns Newmarket Autumn Sales. *H. R. A.
Cecil.*

HEADSTRONG 3 ch.c. Precocious 126–Catherine Howard 68 (Tower Walk   **74**
130) [1988 6m² 6m⁴ 6s⁶ 7d 7d² 1989 8g 8m 8m 6g³ 6f³] leggy, angular colt: modest
maiden: blinkered, form as 3-y-o only when creditable third in smallish fields for
handicap at Yarmouth, making most and not looking keen, and minor event at
Lingfield, checked 1f out and running on: stays 7f: acts on firm going and a soft
surface: has worn crossed noseband: sold 5,200 gns Newmarket Autumn Sales: one
to be wary of. *R. W. Armstrong.*

HEAR A NIGHTINGALE 2 br.c. (Mar 27) Pitskelly 122–Calarette 85   **75**
(Caliban 123) [1989 5m⁴ 6f⁴ 5f⁴ 7s⁶ 8.2s*] IR 13,000F, IR 8,700Y: smallish colt:
half-brother to two 2-y-o winners, including 1986 5f and 6f winner Jay Gee Ell (by
Vaigly Great): dam won from 8.2f to 12.3f: showed much improved form when
winning nursery at Hamilton in November by a length, clear, from Mr Optimistic:
clearly suited by 1m +: acts on soft ground: blinkered third outing. *T. Thomson
Jones.*

HEARD IT BEFORE (FR) 4 b.c. Pharly (FR) 130–Lilac Charm 87 (Bustino   **52**
136) [1988 9d⁶ 8d* 8.2m* 10m* 8.5f⁴ 10m³ 12g⁶ 10g 12d 10m⁵ 12m⁶ 10s 10s 1989
10.2g 12d 10f⁴ 9f* 8h³ 10m⁵ 10m⁵ 8g⁴ 9g³ 8m* 10f 8f 8f3] smallish, attractive colt:
poor mover: won claimer at Wolverhampton in May and apprentice handicap at
Pontefract (making virtually all and battling on really well) in August: stays 1¼m:
acts on any going: good mount for apprentice: genuine. *R. Hollinshead.*

HEARTHRUG 2 br.f. (Apr 24) Persian Bold 123–Chauffeuse 76 (Gay Fandango   **—**
(USA) 132] smallish, rather leggy filly: second foal: dam, winner over 5f at
2 yrs on only start, is out of half-sister to high-class sprinters Home Guard and
Boone's Cabin: 10/1, last of 12, weakening quickly 2f out, in maiden at Nottingham in
September. *P. T. Walwyn.*

HEART OF ARABIA 3 b.c. Habitat 134–Ramiana (USA) 68 (Blushing Groom   **—**
(FR) 131) [1988 6m* 6g³ 6g* 7g 1989 7g] rangy, good-topped colt: has a long,
powerful stride: successful twice at Goodwood in summer as 2-y-o, notably in
Scottish Equitable Richmond Stakes: ran moderately in Ladbroke European Free
Handicap (taken very quietly to post) at Newmarket in April, only start in 1989:
should stay 1m. *C. E. Brittain.*

HEART OF FIRE 3 b.c. Kalaglow 132–Snub (Steel Heart 128) [1988 NR 1989   **77**
8s⁶ 7v* 8s⁴ 7f 10m³ 11.7m* 12g³ 12g⁵] 62,000Y: lengthy, good-topped colt: good
walker: second foal: half-brother to poor plater Jolly Vic (by Mr Fluorocarbon): dam

won over 7f and 9f in Ireland and later in USA: modest handicapper: won maiden at Ayr in April and slowly-run race at Windsor in June: ran creditably when in frame in quite valuable contests at Sandown, Epsom and Newbury: claimer ridden, hung left in last-named then carried head high when well below form final start (August): suited by 1½m: acts on any going, except perhaps very firm. *P. F. I. Cole.*

HEART OF GROOM (USA) 3 b.c. Blushing Groom (FR) 131–Polar Bear **107** (USA) (Hoist The Flag (USA)) [1988 7g 8h 8g 1989 12g 12.5f 12h⁵ 12f⁶ 10g* 9g* 12s* 14s*] good-topped colt: moderate walker: appeared only quite modest handicapper in 4 outings here as 3-y-o for J. Dunlop: unbeaten in 4 outings in Italy in the autumn, notably Group 3 Premio Roma Vecchia on final one, in November: stays 1¾m: probably suited by plenty of give in the ground: blinkered fourth start. *O. Pessi, Italy.*

HEART OF JOY (USA) 2 b.f. (Mar 1) Lypheor 118–Mythographer (USA) **92 p** (Secretariat (USA)) [1989 6d*] $63,000F: useful-looking filly, shade unfurnished: fourth foal: half-sister to 2 minor stakes winners by Hold Your Peace and a minor winner by Fappiano: dam half-sister to 1987 Grade 3 winning 2-y-o White Mischief: well-backed favourite, won 24-runner maiden at Newbury in October by 3 lengths from Zanoni, running on strongly to lead just inside final 1f: will stay 1m: sure to improve and win more races. *M. R. Stoute.*

HEAVENLY CAROL 6 br.m. King of Spain 121–Heavenly Chorus 87 (Green **—** God 128) [1988 10.2d 7g 6m 5d 7g⁶ 5d 6d⁴ 7m 1989 6s 5f 6f] small, workmanlike mare: moderate mover: poor handicapper: stays 1m: best form with plenty of give in the ground: sweating first 2 starts: occasionally blinkered. *P. D. Cundell.*

HEAVENLY HOOFER 6 b.g. Dance In Time (CAN)–Heavenly Chord 89 **38** (Hittite Glory 125) [1988 7g⁴ 8g 7.5m 9m² 8f 8f⁵ 8h⁴ 8.5g³ 8m 8g 8m⁵ 8.5f 8g 7g 1989 7d⁵ 8m³ 8.2f⁶ 8f] lengthy gelding: poor handicapper: stays 9f: ideally suited by top-of-the-ground: well beaten when blinkered final outing: suitable mount for inexperienced rider: has edged left: inconsistent: sold to join W. Storey 2,200 gns Doncaster June Sales: winning hurdler. *Denys Smith.*

HEAVENLY NOTE 3 b.f. Chief Singer 131–Glebehill 76 (Northfields (USA)) **80** [1988 7.5m* 8g⁴ 7f⁴ 1989 8f² 8f² 8.5g⁵ 8.2d 8g⁶ 10.2g⁵ 12.2g⁵] good-topped, angular filly: carries condition: fair handicapper: probably stays 1½m: acts on firm going: blinkered last 3 starts: has tended to edge: probably best tenderly handled. *J. W. Watts.*

HEAVEN'S GATE 2 ch.f. (May 23) Godswalk (USA) 130–Algonkin (USA) (Tom **44** Rolfe) [1989 6g 6m⁵ 5f⁴ 6g³ 6g a6g] IR 2,900Y, 5,400 2-y-o: smallish, close-coupled filly: half-sister to 1987 2-y-o 5f winner Northern Scene (by Habitat) and 2 winners abroad: dam winner over 1m and 9f at 6 yrs in Ireland: quite modest plater: sold 625 gns Ascot November Sales. *R. Hannon.*

HEAVEN'S HIGHWAY 2 gr.c. (Apr 17) Godswalk (USA) 130–Sweet Sharlie **53** 77 (Fighting Charlie 127) [1989 5s³] IR 3,700Y: close-coupled colt: half-brother to several winners, including 5f to 7f winner Sharlie's Wimpy (by Tumble Wind): dam won over 1m at 3 yrs: 16/1, 3½ lengths third of 11, disputing lead 4f, to Full Volume in maiden auction event at Epsom in April. *M. Brittain.*

HEAVY BRIGADE (FR) 6 ch.h. Hard Fought 125–Victorian Pageant 95 **—** (Welsh Pageant 132) [1988 NR 1989 8f] well-made horse: winner of his only races on flat prior to 1989, 1m maiden at Thirsk and 7f handicap at Newmarket as 3-y-o: soundly beaten in handicap at Salisbury in October: clearly very difficult to train. *A. Barrow.*

HEBBA (USA) 2 b.f. (Mar 19) Nureyev (USA) 131–Likely Exchange (USA) **76 p** (Terrible Tiger (USA)) [1989 6m*] $875,000Y: rather sparely-made filly: half-sister to top-class middle-distance colt Creme Fraiche (by Rich Cream) and a winner by Sharpen Up: dam won 23 races, including Grade 1 1¼m Delaware Handicap: 4/1 and on toes, won 22-runner maiden at Newbury in September by ¾ length from Languedoc, keeping on strongly to lead near line: will be better suited by 7f +: sure to improve. *M. R. Stoute.*

HEEMEE 3 br.f. On Your Mark 125–Beyond The Rainbow (Royal Palace 131) **66** [1988 5g³ 5f* 5g² 5g² 5d⁵ 5f* 5g⁵ 5m 1989 5f³ 5m 5f³ 5f 6g 6f 5m⁶] sparely-made filly: moderate walker and poor mover: fair winner as 2-y-o but only quite modest at best in 1989: ran creditably in claimer (blinkered) and handicap last 2 starts: likely to prove best at 5f: probably unsuited by a soft surface: sometimes sweating and on toes. *P. A. Blockley.*

HEIDI'S PAL 2 ch.f. (Jan 25) Superlative 118–Marsroyal (Royal Orbit (USA)) **—** [1989 6m 7f] 880F: small, stocky filly: half-sister to 9f winner Long View (by Persian

Bold) and winners in France and Italy: dam of no account in Ireland: no sign of ability in seller and claimer. *J. S. Wainwright.*

HEIGH-HO   2 b.c. (Mar 6) Jalmood (USA) 126–African Setting 69 (African Sky   **60**
124) [1989 6m⁵ 7f 7m 9g⁶ 8f⁴] 26,000Y: small, sparely-made colt: first foal: dam,
best at 2 yrs, is daughter of half-sister to top sprinter Double Form: quite modest
maiden: wandered and looked of unsatisfactory temperament in nursery at
Pontefract final start: stays 9f: sold 7,200 gns Newmarket Autumn Sales. *W. J.
Haggas.*

HEIGHT O'BATTLE   3 b.c. Shirley Heights 130–Light O'Battle 97 (Queen's   **74 +**
Hussar 124) [1988 NR 1989 8s 12.3d 10.2f* 8f] 33,000Y: angular colt: sixth foal:
half-brother to fairly useful sprinter Lobbit (by Habitat), subsequently a winner in
USA, and to Lobric (by Electric), a modest maiden on flat successful over hurdles:
dam, 7f winner from 2 starts at 2 yrs, is sister to Highclere: very easy winner of
claimer (claimed out of P. Calver's stable 13,050) at Doncaster in June: no other
worthwhile form, never placed to challenge or knocked about in apprentice claimer
final start, in July: stays 1¼m. *Mrs S. Oliver.*

HEIR OF EXCITEMENT   4 b.g. Krayyan 117–Merry Choice (Yankee Gold   **55 §**
115) [1988 8m⁵ 8.2s² 8g⁵ 8m² 8m² 8d² 1989 10.2g⁶ 7d 8f 8m² 9f 8g⁵ 12f³ 11f² 10f³
10.6d 10m 10.2g] lengthy, rather angular gelding: carries plenty of condition: usually
looks well: plating-class maiden: probably stays 11f: acts on any going: visored
second to fifth outings, blinkered ninth: has run creditably for apprentice: has worn
a tongue strap: finds little. *A. P. Stringer.*

HEISMAN (USA)   2 b.c. (Feb 26) Halo (USA)–Sophisticate (USA) (Vaguely   **69 p**
Noble 140) [1989 8f*] $200,000Y: half-brother to high-class Uptown Swell (by
Master Derby), graded-stakes winner at 9f to 1½m: dam French 10.5f winner, later
placed in USA: odds on, won 5-runner maiden at Redcar in October by ½ length
from Night-Shirt, keeping on well to lead near line: should improve. *J. H. M. Gosden.*

HEJAZ   2 b.c. (Mar 20) Electric 126–Daisy Warwick (USA) 91 (Ribot 142) [1989 7g]   **—**
12,000Y: sixth living foal: half-brother to 5 winners, including 1982 2-y-o 5.8f winner
No Fluke (by Averof), French 10.5f and 11f winner Paganelli (by Ile de Bourbon) and
13.8f winner Tranby Croft (by Final Straw), later successful in Belgium: dam placed
twice over 5f at 2 yrs: 16/1, slowly away and always in rear in 16-runner maiden at
Folkestone in October. *D. R. C. Elsworth.*

HELAWE   6 ch.g. Last Fandango 125–Pigmy (Assagai) [1988 6f⁴ 6f⁵ 6m 1989 6m⁶   **63**
6f 6g² 6f² 6m⁴ 5.3f⁵ 6g] big, lengthy, angular gelding: good walker: quite modest
handicapper nowadays: stays 6f: best on sound surface: lazy sort, who needs
blinkers. *R. Hannon.*

HELEN HOTEL   4 ch.g. High Line 125–Orange Sensation 69 (Floribunda 136)   **—**
[1988 7g 8f⁶ 7m⁵ 6m⁵ 8m 7g 1989 10m 7m 7.6h 7m 14.8m⁴ 12h⁶ 8m⁵] close-coupled
gelding: has a quick action: bad maiden: probably stays 1m: blinkered twice: visored
4 times at 4 yrs: reluctant to go down fifth start: has raced freely. *D. T. Thom.*

HELEN RED   3 b.f. Trojan Fen 118–Spindle Berry 92 (Dance In Time (CAN))   **— §**
[1988 6m* 1989 8g 13.1h 9m 11.5g 8m 8.2d 10f⁶ 15.3g⁶ 12.5f 11f⁴] lengthy,
dipped-backed, plain filly: has a round action: plater: well beaten in 1989: bred to
stay 1m +: has been unruly at stalls, including when visored and looking a difficult
ride sixth start: blinkered after, sweating and edgy on first occasion: ungenuine. *A.
Hide.*

HELENS DREAMGIRL   3 ch.f. Caerleon (USA) 132–Helen's Dream (Troy   **95**
137) [1988 6g⁴ 1989 10s² 10m* 10f² 12.2m⁴ 10g* 8g⁴] leggy, light-bodied filly: fairly
useful performer: made all in maiden (odds on) at Brighton in May and £6,900 event
(at modest pace early) at Yarmouth in September: ran well in listed event at Ascot
final outing: stays 1¼m: best form on a sound surface. *H. R. A. Cecil.*

HELEN'S GUEST   2 ch.f. (Jan 30) Be My Guest (USA) 126–Helenetta 97 (Troy   **74**
137) [1989 7g⁴ 7g⁵] unfurnished filly: first foal: dam, suited by 1½m, is daughter of
very useful middle-distance performer Lauretta: modest form in late-season minor
event at York won by Atoll and maiden at Newmarket won by Sardegna: will be well
suited by middle distances. *G. Wragg.*

HELEN'S SONG (USA)   3 ch.f. Arctic Tern (USA) 126–Hortensia (FR) 119   **75**
(Luthier 126) [1988 NR 1989 8.5s⁶ 10g 12g 14d] workmanlike filly: fourth foal: sister
to disappointing Derby second Glacial Storm, smart 7.3f winner at 2 yrs, and
half-sister to fairly useful 12.3f winner Chaudennay (by Assert) and 1¼m to 12.3f
winner Albert Hall (by Monteverdi): dam smart at around 1¼m in France: modest
form in listed event at Epsom (didn't handle descent) then maidens: stays 1¾m. *B.
W. Hills.*

HELLBRUNN 3 ch.c. Hotfoot 126–Midnight Music (Midsummer Night II 117) **66**
[1988 7m 8s 1989 14m⁶ 12f⁵ 16.2f⁴ 16f 17.6g* 17.4s⁶] strong, lengthy colt: has scar
on near-hind knee: has a powerful action: 16/1, won slowly-run 6-runner handicap at
Wolverhampton in September, getting poor run and leading on post: little
worthwhile form otherwise in maidens, listed race and handicap: stays 2¼m:
possibly best on an easy surface: has joined W. Clay. *C. E. Brittain.*

HELLENIC 2 b.f. (Apr 25) Darshaan 133–Grecian Sea (FR) 107 (Homeric 133) **74 p**
[1989 8g4] sturdy filly: fifth foal: half-sister to 3 winners, including useful 6f to 1½m
winner Golden Wave (by Glint of Gold): dam won over 6f at 2 yrs in France: 11/4,
green and better for race, around 4 lengths fourth of 17, going on well last 2f, to
Lover's Moon in maiden at Leicester in November: sure to improve, and win a race
over middle distances. *M. R. Stoute.*

HELLENIC PRINCE 3 b.c. Ela-Mana-Mou 132–Pipina (USA) 81 (Sir Gaylord) **75**
[1988 6m 6f 1989 10s⁵ 10d⁴ 10.4m 12f] close-coupled, workmanlike colt: modest
maiden: not seen out after May: stays 1¼m: acts on soft going, probably unsuited by
top-of-the-ground: sold to join J. Pearce 4,200 gns Newmarket Autumn Sales. *G.
Wragg.*

HELLO AVONDALE 3 b.g. Bay Express 132–Chiparia 82 (Song 132) [1988 NR **—**
1989 8m⁵ 8s⁶ 7f⁶] good-topped gelding: sixth foal: half-brother to 3 winners,
including 6f winner Young Tearaway (by Young Generation) and 1985 2-y-o 6f
winner Our Tilly (by Grundy): dam best at 5f: modest form in maidens: dead. *M. J.
Ryan.*

HELLO CALDER 4 b.c. Hello Gorgeous (USA) 128–Calderina (ITY) 121 **116**
(Lyphard (USA) 132) [1988 10.5v* 11d² 12m 12.5m 12g* 11s⁵ 12g⁴ 1989 10.5v² 12d⁶
9m² 11g* 10d⁶ 10s* 10d³ 9.7m² 12f⁵] French colt: third foal: half-brother to French
11f and 1½m winner Place des Ternes (by Arctic Tern): dam very smart 7f to 1½m
filly in France, later graded-stakes winner in USA: smart performer: successful in
listed events at Lyon and Deauville: placed afterwards in La Coupe de
Maisons-Laffitte (beaten under 2 lengths by Petrullo) and Ciga Prix Dollar (2
lengths second to stable-companion Creator) at Longchamp: 6 lengths fifth to
Frankly Perfect in Hollywood Turf Cup at Hollywood Park: effective at 9f and stays
1½m: acts on any going. *A. Fabre, France.*

HELLO PET 2 b.f. (Apr 13) Tina's Pet 121–Kuwait Night 67 (Morston (FR) 125) **—**
[1989 5.3g 5f] IR 1,150Y: sparely-made filly: first foal: dam, 1½m winner, is sister to
useful middle-distance stayer Mubarak of Kuwait: well beaten in maiden auction
race (slowly away) at Brighton in April and seller at Pontefract in June. *D. T.
O'Donnell.*

HELLO SPARKLER 4 b.c. Hello Gorgeous (USA) 128–Rheinsparkle 102 **—**
(Rheingold 137) [1988 8.2s* 10.4v⁴ 10.1m 9m 1989 10.4m 7f 10.6g 8.2f 8g 9g] big,
rather angular colt: carries condition: has a round action: fair winner early as 3-y-o
when trained by J. Hills: no form in 1989: doesn't quite stay 1¼m in testing
conditions: seems to need plenty of give in the ground: sweating on reappearance:
slowly away fourth outing. *R. D. E. Woodhouse.*

HELLO SWEETIE 3 ch.f. Hello Gorgeous (USA) 128–My Sweetie (Bleep- **44**
Bleep 134) [1988 5g 1989 7.5d 8d 7.5d³ 10f 8.2d] smallish, sparely-made, angular
filly: lacks scope: quite modest plater: suited by 1m: off course over 4 months and
sold out of M. H. Easterby's stable 1,900 gns Doncaster June Sales before final start.
Mrs A. Knight.

HELLO TROUBLE 5 ch.h. Hello Gorgeous (USA) 128–La Troublerie (Will **—**
Somers 114) [1988 14g 10m 10f 1989 11.7d 10f] rather leggy horse: poor walker:
lightly raced on flat: little sign of ability since only outing at 2 yrs. *E. A. Wheeler.*

HELLO VAIGLY 4 b.c. Hello Gorgeous (USA) 128–Dervaig 90 (Derring-Do **110**
131) [1988 8g4 7g 7g* 7g* 8d* 8m⁵ 8d² 7g⁵ 1989 8g² 8f 8m³ 8v 10s] leggy,
lightly-made colt: moderate mover: useful performer: placed, running well, behind
Wood Dancer in £27,100 handicap at Sandown in July and Sabotage in slowly-run
£9,200 contest at Newmarket in October: behind in Premio Ribot at Rome and in
Premio Roma last 2 outings: suited by 1m: unsuited by firm going and goes
particularly well with a bit of give in the ground: trained until after third start by M.
Stoute. *O. Pessi, Italy.*

HELLUVA TIME 3 b.f. Young Generation 129–Sometime Lucky 89 (Levmoss **—**
133) [1988 NR 1989 12f³] fifth foal: half-sister to 1m to 1½m winner and smart
hurdler Pike's Peak (by High Top), 4-y-o stayer Late Cut (by Tap On Wood) and
modest 1½m winner Step In Time (by Bellypha): dam lightly raced: 11/2, showed

signs of ability when 11 lengths third of 5 to Lovely Fairy in maiden at Lingfield in August: has joined O. Sherwood. *L. M. Cumani.*

HENRIETTA PLACE 5 b.m. Sayyaf 121–Gilana (Averof 123) [1988 8s 8f 9m⁴ **39** 7m⁴ 9g 9g⁶ 1989 10m 9m 8f³] smallish mare: poor handicapper: probably suited by 1m: acts on any going: usually apprentice ridden. *G. A. Pritchard-Gordon.*

HENRYK 5 ch.g. Gay Fandango (USA) 132–Clouds 70 (Relko 136) [1988 12f⁶ **—** 11.1m 10f* 12f² 10g 14f 1989 12m⁶ 12f 11.7m 11.7m 12f] angular gelding: fair winner as 4-y-o: no worthwhile form in 1989: stays 1½m: requires top-of-the-ground: occasionally bandaged: sometimes sweating and on toes: well suited by forcing tactics: excellent mount for apprentice: bought out of R. Simpson's stable 6,200 gns Doncaster May Sales. *B. J. Curley.*

HENRY'S WOLFE 4 b.g. Coquelin (USA) 121–Grangemore (Prominer 125) **—** [1988 10m 6s 6m² 6m³ 5h* 6d⁵ 6s 6s 1989 5f 5f 5f 6f⁵ a6g a6g] lengthy, good-quartered gelding: has a round action: quite modest winner as 3-y-o: well below his best subsequently, including in selling contests: suited by sprint distances: possibly unsuited by soft going, acts on any other: blinkered or visored nowadays: sweating second outing. *P. J. Feilden.*

HENRY WILL 5 b.g. Nicholas Bill 125–Silver Cygnet 71 (My Swanee 122) [1988 **61** 7d 8g 7g 6d 6f⁴ 6f 8h⁶ 6d³ 6g 1989 6d⁴ 6d 6f 7m 6f⁵ 7m⁵ 7f⁵ 6f² 6g* 7.6m 6f⁶ 6f⁴ 6g 6m⁶ 6f⁶ 6g³ 7g 7g³ 6d 6f 6g 7m] workmanlike, angular gelding: moderate mover: quite modest handicapper: apprentice ridden at overweight, won at Ripon in July: best at 6f or 7f: particularly well suited by a bit of give in the ground nowadays: blinkered 7 outings prior to final one: has run creditably for amateur and apprentice: chipped bone in knee at 4 yrs: inconsistent. *T. Fairhurst.*

HENRY WILLIAM 4 b.g. Known Fact (USA) 135–Kesarini (USA) 87 (Singh **50** (USA)) [1988 6d⁵ 7f 6m 6g 5g 6m⁶ 7f 6m 1989 5d 5f 5g³ 5m 5f² 5.1f⁴] small, short-backed gelding: poor maiden: best efforts at sprint distances: acts on firm going. *Pat Mitchell.*

HEPHZIVAH 2 b.f. (Mar 21) Dreams To Reality (USA) 113–Grey Twig 68 **—** (Godswalk (USA) 130) [1989 6m⁴] lengthy filly: third living foal: half-sister to 1986 2-y-o 5.8f and 6f winner Grey Wolfe Tiger (by Rolfe) and 7f seller winner Kachina Maid (by Anfield): dam ran only at 2 yrs: backward and green, 14 lengths fourth of 6 to Silver Ore in minor event at Windsor in July. *R. Hannon.*

HERCLE (FR) 3 b.c. Fabulous Dancer (USA) 124–L'Exception (FR) (Margouil- **68** lat (FR) 133) [1988 6f 7.5m 9g 6g 9.2g 8g 1989 8v* 9.6s 8g* 8s 8m³ 8g² 10g* 11m 8.2d⁴ 8.2d 8g⁵ 8.2d⁴ 8v] compact, rather sparely-made colt: moderate mover: half-brother to 3 winners in France, including 9f to 1½m winner Scapio (by Belgio) and Executive (by Don Roberto), successful at around 1m: dam French 1m and 9f winner: won handicaps at Maisons-Laffitte in March and Evry in April and claimer at Longchamp in June when trained by R. Collet: modest form at best in 6 outings here: found little in claimer penultimate start: sweating and tended to hang on tenth one: effective at 1m to 1¼m: acts on heavy going. *N. Tinkler.*

HERCULES 2 gr.g. (Apr 6) Bay Express 132–Firdale Rosie 78 (Town Crier 119) **—** [1989 5f 6m 6s] 6,200Y: close-coupled gelding: good walker: half-brother to plating-class 2-y-o's Rosie's Glory (by Hittite Glory) and Decoy Express (by Decoy Boy): dam 2-y-o 5f winner, appeared not to train on: well beaten in varied races, including a Newmarket seller. *P. Burgoyne.*

HERE HE COMES 3 b.g. Alzao (USA) 117–Nanette 100 (Worden II 129) [1988 **82** 5g⁴ 6d 5g 5m 6g 7d² 8g 8v⁴ 7g 10g⁴ 10s⁵ 1989 6v⁶ 7s⁵ 7f² 7f⁴ 8m 8.3g] IR 6,000Y: small gelding: half-brother to 6 winners, notably useful sprinter Tanella (by Habitat) and Ribblesdale Stakes winner Nanticious and useful 6f to 1m winner Repetitious (both by Northfields): dam stayed 1¼m: fair maiden: appears suited by 7f (faced stiff tasks over 1m at 3 yrs): acts on firm going: blinkered final start and ninth at 2 yrs: trained until after reappearance by P. Matthews in Ireland. *R. Akehurst.*

HERESHEIS 3 b.f. Free State 125–Gambela (USA) 88 (Diplomat Way) [1988 8m **—** 7g 1989 10m] angular, workmanlike filly: quite modest maiden: moved badly to post, never placed to challenge or knocked about in Newmarket claimer in July, only start in 1989: should stay at least 1m. *J. Pearce.*

HERMITAGE ROCK 2 ch.c. (Feb 28) Ballad Rock 122–Verde Dimora (Sir Ivor **77** 135) [1989 6m⁵ 6h* 6m⁵ 6h 7f⁵ 7m⁵ 7m* 7s³ 8g³] 29,000Y, IR 70,000Y: angular, good-bodied colt: has scope: seventh foal: half-brother to useful 1982 2-y-o 5f winner Sir Alco (by Nonoalco): dam useful winner in Italy: modest performer: successful in maiden at Brighton in May and nursery (by a length from Logical Lady)

397

at Chepstow in August: ran well over 1m after: blinkered or visored last 3 starts. *G. Lewis.*

HEROES SASH (USA) 4 b.c. Lypheor 118–Salish (USA) (Olden Times) [1988   **88**
7g³ 7g⁶ 1989 6d² 6g 8m 6f 8h⁶ 9m² 8g 8f⁶ 7.6f⁵ 7m⁴] useful-looking colt: poor
mover: fair performer nowadays: runner-up as 4-y-o in minor contest at Folkestone
(first run for almost a year) and strongly-run ladies event at Kempton: ran well after
when sixth to Safawan in £57,400 Schweppes Golden Mile at Goodwood and fourth
to Runun in £49,600 Whyte & Mackay Scotch Stakes (Handicap) at Ascot: stays 9f:
acts on firm going and a soft surface: blinkered (on toes) fourth outing: often sweats
nowadays. *R. Guest.*

HERON'S GREEN 3 b.c. Petorius 117–Any Price (Gunner B 126) [1988 7g 1989   **66** d
8.2d⁴ 7m² 7m 6m⁶ 7m 9f] sturdy colt: quite modest maiden: hung right when ridden
along at halfway fourth start: well beaten in seller final one, setting strong pace 7f:
best effort over 7f: took good hold in blinkers fifth start: sold 2,800 gns Newmarket
Autumn Sales. *J. W. Hills.*

HERON'S ROCK 5 gr.g. Kalaglow 132–Zantedeschia 91 (Zimone) [1988 NR   **64**
1989 11.5m³ 12m⁴] big, rangy gelding: half-brother to several winners, including
2000 Guineas fourth Cut Throat (by Sharpen Up): dam miler: in frame in amateur
events at Yarmouth (carrying condition) and Newmarket in summer. *H. Candy.*

HERO'S WELCOME 2 br.c. (Mar 5) Simply Great (FR) 124–Airport (Warpath   **94**
113) [1989 6f⁴ 6f³ 7m* 7m* 8d³ 8s³] IR 12,000Y: first foal: dam poor sister to Derby
fourth Shotgun: progressive colt: won maiden at Limerick and EBF Orby Stakes (on
demotion of Neat Dish) at Leopardstown in July: third at the Curragh in Panasonic
Smurfit EBF Futurity Stakes and Juddmonte EBF Beresford Stakes (over 2 lengths
behind Victory Piper) in the autumn: suited by 1m: acts on top-of-the-ground and
soft going. *N. McGrath, Ireland.*

HIBERNIAN GOLD (USA) 4 ch.c. Golden Act (USA)–Irish Wave (USA) **117**
(Raise A Native) [1988 7f³ 8d* 8d² 10.1m* 10.1m* 10m² 10g* 10g⁴ 1989 10s 10f²
10f* 10f 10m⁴] strong, deep-bodied, useful-looking colt: smart performer: very well
ridden by G. Starkey when making all in Brigadier Gerard Stakes at Sandown in

*Brigadier Gerard Stakes, Sandown—a first pattern-race success for Hibernian Gold,
after an excellent ride by G. Starkey*

May, setting slow early gallop, quickening over 3f out and running on well to hold off Highland Chieftain and Reprimand by 2 necks: didn't dominate when well below form in Prince of Wales's Stakes at Royal Ascot and in 5-runner listed event at Kempton following month: suited by front-running tactics over 1¼m: best form on top-of-the-ground and unsuited by soft going: headstrong at 2 yrs but has settled down considerably: has sweated and got on toes, but looked in tremendous shape in 1989: often taken early to post: wears a net muzzle: sent to race in USA. *G. Harwood.*

HICKLAM MILLIE 2 ch.f. (May 2) Absalom 128–Embarrased 81 (Busted 134) **49**
[1989 5d 6m6 8f] 2,500F, 3,200Y: medium-sized filly: half-sister to 3-y-o Rhapsody In Red (by Song), 6f winner Don't Annoy Me (by Manado) and a winning hurdler by Henbit: dam won twice at around 2m: poor maiden: pulled hard final start. *P. Calver.*

HICKORY RUN 3 b.g. Seymour Hicks (FR) 125–Ardent Runner 94 **–**
(Runnymede 123) [1988 5f5 6d3 1989 8g5 6m] good-bodied, workmanlike gelding: modest form at best: not seen out after July: suited by 1m: best efforts on an easy surface. *G. B. Balding.*

HICKORY WIND 2 ch.c. (Apr 30) Dalsaan 125–Derrain (Prince Tenderfoot **74**
(USA) 126) [1989 5v5 6m3 7f* 7f2 8.2d] IR 4,800F, 7,000Y: big, lengthy, workmanlike colt: looks weak: turns off-fore in fourth known foal: half-brother to 3-y-o Prince Rob (by Robellino): dam, Irish 2-y-o 1m winner, is half-sister to very useful 8.5f winner Long Pond: made most in moderately-run minor event at Ayr in July, winning by short head from Comstock: good second at York, easily best effort in minor events after: stays 7f. *Denys Smith.*

HIDDEN BEAUTY 3 ch.f. Vaigly Great 127–Phoebe Ann 76 (Absalom 128) **51**
[1988 NR 1989 7g 9g 7d5 7f 7f 10f6 8f2 7m4 7.6m 8s] workmanlike, sparely-made filly: first foal: dam, 2-y-o 5f winner who raced twice at 3 yrs, is out of Molecomb Stakes winner Lowna: in frame in sellers at Brighton and Newmarket (bandaged): little other sign of ability: stays 1m: acts on firm going: bandaged and edgy final start: sold D. Burchell 1,450 gns Ascot November Sales. *K. T. Ivory.*

HIDDEN CREEK 4 ch.c. Mummy's Game 120–Brandon Creek 79 (Be My **60**
Guest (USA) 126) [1988 5s4 6g 7.5s 9f5 6v5 5g 1989 5m4 5g 6s* a6g a6g a6g3] medium-sized colt: successful in seller (no bid) at Hamilton in November: below form afterwards: suited by sprint distances: acts on soft going: winner in Italy, including of listed event. *N. A. Callaghan.*

HIDDEN PLANET 4 ch.g. Star Appeal 133–Neptune's Treasure 65 (Gulf Pearl **47**
117) [1988 10v 12f 12f* 12d2 1989 10.2g 13.8d 12m 10m 15.5f4 15s5 12g] sparely-made gelding: quite modest winner of amateurs race at Brighton as 3-y-o: well below his best in 1989: best form at 1½m: acts on firm going and a soft surface: trained first 2 starts by J. Berry: inconsistent. *G. A. Pritchard-Gordon.*

HIDDEN QUIVER (USA) 3 b.g. Secreto (USA) 128–Feather Bow (USA) (Gun **–**
Bow) [1988 NR 1989 12.3d] $100,000F: heavy-topped gelding: half-brother to 2 winners in North America, including a prolific minor winner at up to 7f by Transworld: dam won 8 times at up to 9f in USA, including in minor 6.5f stakes event at 5 yrs: weak 7/2 and green, over 14 lengths seventh of 11 to Norinski in maiden at Ripon in April, leading 4½f out until approaching last 2f, eased once beaten: sold K. Morgan 6,000 gns Newmarket Autumn Sales and subsequently gelded. *H. R. A. Cecil.*

HIDDEN (USA) 2 ch.f. (Jan 20) Secreto (USA) 128–Shark Song 103 (Song 132) **69**
[1989 10g5 8g2] $100,000Y: small, close-coupled filly: has a quick action: fourth foal: closely related to Yugoslavian 3-y-o winner Echo of The Deep (by Shareef Dancer) and half-sister to 1¼m and 1½m winner Magsood (by Mill Reef) and 5f winner Bundukeya (by Beldale Flutter): dam, winner from 5f to 9f including in USA, is sister to very smart sprinter Prince Sabo: second favourite, 5 lengths second of 15, keeping on well never dangerous, to Azadeh in maiden at Leicester in November: bandaged both starts. *H. Thomson Jones.*

HIGH ALOFT 5 b.h. Cut Above 130–Think Ahead 104 (Sharpen Up 127) [1988 **54**
16g 14g 15.8m 16d2 16g 1989 12s 16s 16.2g4 18h4] leggy, workmanlike horse: has a quick action: plating-class handicapper: suited by a test of stamina: acts on any going: usually blinkered nowadays: inconsistent: winning but irresolute hurdler. *T. Casey.*

HIGH BEACON 2 ch.c. (Feb 26) High Line 125–Flaming Peace 104 (Queen's **78**
Hussar 124) [1989 7g 7g3 8m 8g*] sturdy, workmanlike colt: keen walker: brother to winning middle-distance stayer Fair And Wise and half-brother to 3-y-o Fiesole (by Sharpo) and several winners here and abroad: dam won twice over 7f at 2 yrs:

33/1, won maiden at Leicester in November by ½ length from Ambrose, leading inside final furlong and battling on gamely: will be suited by middle distances. *H. Candy.*

HIGH CAIRN (FR) 3 ch.f. Ela-Mana-Mou 132–Parmesh 105 (Home Guard 73 d (USA) 129) [1988 7h⁴ 6m* 7d 1989 7h⁴ 7g⁵ 7m 8f 7h] leggy, sparely-made filly: modest handicapper: ran well first 2 starts, moderately after: blinkered, hung left in Brighton claimer final start: suited by 7f: acts on hard going, and is possibly unsuited by a soft surface: often bandaged behind: sold 4,400 gns Ascot August Sales. *K. M. Brassey.*

HIGH CASTE 2 ch.c. (May 24) Carwhite 127–Brazen 83 (Cash And Courage 116) — [1989 8.2g 8g] close-coupled colt: half-brother to several winners here and abroad, including 1¼m and 17.1f winner Sir Crusty (by Gunner B): dam won from 6f to 11f: backward, well beaten in late-season minor event at Nottingham and maiden at Leicester: bred to stay quite well. *R. J. Holder.*

HIGHCOMBE LAD 3 b.g. Class Distinction–Liana Louise (Silly Season 127) — [1988 5g 6f⁶ 6m 7g 1989 8g 7f 6m] tall, workmanlike gelding: little worthwhile form in varied company: moved badly down final start (July). *J. J. Bridger.*

HIGH ELEGANCE 2 b.f. (Apr 7) Elegant Air 119–Tula Singh 66 (Mansingh — p (USA) 120) [1989 6g] 7,200F: well-grown, workmanlike filly: poor walker: half-sister to 1984 2-y-o 5f winner Green Spirit (by Dragonara Palace): dam, best at sprint distances, is sister to high-class sprinter Petong: 33/1, around 11 lengths twelfth of 22, weakening approaching final 1f and hanging badly left, to Lip Sing in maiden at Leicester in November: sure to improve. *M. Johnston.*

HIGHER HAMILL 2 b.c. (Apr 27) Taufan (USA) 119–Judy's Pinch (Ballymore 89 123) [1989 5g⁵ 5v² 5d* 5m⁴ 6s 6m 6g* 7g*] IR 4,400Y, resold 6,600Y: leggy, close-coupled colt: moderate walker: fourth foal: half-brother to Irish 3-y-o 1m and 1¼m winner Fuchsia Belle (by Vision) and a winner in Malaysia: dam never ran: improved colt: successful in early-season maiden auction race at Beverley and nurseries at York and Newcastle (beat Puffy by a neck, having made all) in October: better suited by 7f than shorter: best form on good ground: easily best form when ridden by M. Birch. *N. Tinkler.*

HIGH ESTATE 3 b.c. Shirley Heights 130–Regal Beauty (USA) (Princely 116 Native (USA)) [1988 6f* 6f* 7m* 7m* 8g* 1989 10f⁵ 10.2m* 10m³ 10g] rangy, attractive colt: moderate mover: unbeaten and one of best 2-y-o's of 1988, but was found to have split a pastern after Royal Lodge Stakes at Ascot: odds on, made all in 3-runner minor event at Newcastle in July: 3½ lengths last of 3 to Scenic in moderately-run William Hill Classic at Ayr: 9/1 and in superb shape, about 12 lengths eighth of 11 in Champion Stakes at Newmarket 3 months later: stayed 1¼m: acted on firm going: purchased by Coolmore Stud and will stand at fee of IR 10,000 gns (n.f.n.f) in 1990 (will also stand in Australia later). *H. R. A. Cecil.*

HIGHEST PRAISE (USA) 6 ch.g. Topsider (USA)–Prides Promise (USA) 80 (Crozier (USA)) [1988 6f⁴ 7d⁴ 7m⁵ 7f³ 7s* 7g 7f 7d 1989 7v⁶ 7d 7g 7g⁶ 7g 7f⁴ 7m³ 7s⁶ 7d] strong, good-bodied gelding: moderate mover: fair handicapper: stays 7f well: acts on any going: good mount for apprentice: hung left seventh and final outings: sold 8,800 gns Newmarket Autumn Sales. *I. A. Balding.*

HIGH FAITH 3 ch.c. Adonijah 126–Faith Lift (USA) (Nearctic) [1988 5g 7m 7m — 8m 10m 1989 11.7m 12m 10g⁵ 12.4f 8.2g] small, sparely-made colt: plater: suited by 1¼m: trained until after penultimate outing by P. Rohan: winning novice selling hurdler with W. Bissill. *O. Brennan.*

HIGHFIELD PRINCE 3 b.g. Prince Tenderfoot (USA) 126–Parler Mink 57 (Party Mink) [1988 7m 7g 1989 7d⁴ 8m⁵ 12m³ 8g 9f* 12f⁵] rather lengthy, sparely-made gelding: moderate mover: fairly useful plater: won at Hamilton (no bid) in July: pulled hard and given too much to do at Thirsk 9 days later: effective at 9f and 1½m: easily best efforts on top-of-the-ground: winning hurdler. *R. O'Leary.*

HIGH FINANCE 4 ch.g. Billion (USA) 113–Miss Plumes 62 (Prince de Galles — 125) [1988 NR 1989 12m 12f²] workmanlike gelding: moderate mover: fourth live foal: dam plater, won from 1m to 1¼m: 20/1 and bandaged, no chance with long-odds-on Konigsberg in 3-runner minor event at Beverley in July: slowly away and never dangerous in minor contest at Leicester (swished tail in paddock) over month earlier. *R. J. Weaver.*

HIGHFLYING 3 br.g. Shirley Heights 130–Nomadic Pleasure 91 (Habitat 134) — [1988 NR 1989 9f] third foal: half-brother to Park Hill Stakes winner Trampship (by High Line): dam, 9f winner, is half-sister to Prix Vermeille winner Paulista: in need of race, always well behind in 21-runner maiden at Kempton in May: sold to join S. Muldoon 6,200 gns Newmarket Autumn Sales and later gelded. *B. W. Hills.*

HIGH HOLBORN 3 b.c. Electric 126–Beira's Gift (Dominion 123) [1988 7g — 1989 8f⁵ 8m 8f] good-quartered colt: modest maiden at best: easily best effort in minor event at Sandown on reappearance: worth a try over further: sold to join J. Joseph 5,600 gns Ascot July Sales. *P. T. Walwyn.*

HIGH I KEW 3 b.c. High Top 131–Klewraye (Lord Gayle (USA) 124) [1988 7g **81** 8d³ 1989 8s⁶ 11.7m² 10m* 10g³ 11.7m* 11.7d² 11s²] medium-sized, useful-looking colt: good mover: fair handicapper: successful at Yarmouth in July and Windsor in August: good second after at Windsor (beaten neck after modest run) and Ayr: stays 1½m: acts on top-of-the-ground and soft going: consistent. *C. F. Wall.*

HIGHLAND BIDDER 2 b.f. (Apr 1) Ring Bidder 88–Highland Rossie 67 **48** (Pablond 93) [1989 7m 7g³ 7.5f 8m 8g] 1,100Y: third foal: half-sister to 3-y-o 6f and 7f winner Diet (by Starch Reduced) and ungenuine plater The Overnight Man (by Smackover): dam won sellers over 7f and 1m: modest plater: form only on second start: blinkered last 3 starts. *I. Campbell.*

HIGHLAND BOUNTY 5 b.g. High Line 125–Segos 81 (Runnymede 123) [1988 — NR 1989 17.6f⁵ 19f⁵] good-bodied gelding: has a markedly round action: poor maiden on flat: stays 1¾m: fair hurdler. *S. Dow.*

HIGHLAND CHIEFTAIN 6 b.h. Kampala 120–La Primavera (Northfields **121** (USA)) [1988 12s² 12d 10d* 10f³ 10s* 11g* 12s³ 10s² 1989 10d 10.5f⁶ 10g 10f² 11g³ 11f* 11s* 10s*] finely-made, quite attractive horse: keen walker: has a quick action: good-class performer: won listed Grand Prix Prince Rose at Ostend in July, Group 3 Preis der Spielbanken des Landes Nordrhein Westfalen at Dusseldorf (odds on) in October and Group 1 Premio Roma (beating Yellow King a nose) in November: neck second to Hibernian Gold in slowly-run Brigadier Gerard Stakes at Sandown in May: out of frame in 3 Group 1 events in Australasia in spring: stays 1½m: acts on any going: has reportedly suffered back trouble: tough and genuine: remains in training. *J. L. Dunlop.*

HIGHLAND MADNESS 2 b.c. (May 7) Monsanto (FR) 121–Contessa (HUN) — (Peleid 125) [1989 6m 6m 6g] seventh foal: half-brother to 3-y-o 6f winner Sarum (by Tina's Pet) and 5f seller winner Tiarum (by Tiran): dam of no account: tailed off in sellers and a claimer. *P. Burgoyne.*

HIGHLAND PARK 3 ch.g. Simply Great (FR) 124–Perchance 77 (Connaught **60** 130) [1988 6d³ 6f⁶ 6g⁵ 6f⁴ 7.5g 8g 7f 1989 11m 12m³ 11f⁵ 12m⁵ 12.2f* 12.4f² 12.3m⁶ 12m 12m⁵] deep-girthed, workmanlike gelding: plating-class performer: won claimer at Catterick in July: stays 1½m well: acts on firm going: visored 3 occasions: tends to hang, and looks difficult ride. *F. Watson.*

HIGHLAND ROWENA 4 ch.f. Royben 125–Highland Lassie 62 (Highland **59** Melody 112) [1988 5f 5m 5g⁶ 6d 5m² 5m 5f 5g⁴ 6m⁵ 5g⁶ 5v 1989 5f* 6m³ 5f* 5m⁴ 5g* 5m⁴ 5g⁴ 5m 5m⁴ 5f⁵ 5f] good-quartered filly: poor mover: made all or virtually all when winning claimer at Wolverhampton in May and handicaps at Beverley and Newbury (holding on gamely) following month: speedy: acts well on firm going: withdrawn second intended outing after breaking out of stalls: consistent. *B. A. McMahon.*

HIGH LIVING 2 b.g. (Mar 16) Good Times (ITY)–Visible Asset (Vitiges (FR) **48** 132) [1989 6m 6g 5m 6g] 3,100F, 2,500Y: sturdy gelding: fourth foal: half-brother to 3-y-o Final Asset (by Final Straw) and a winner in Spain: dam poor maiden from family of high-class stayer Raise You Ten: poor form (though has thrice given impression capable of lot better) in varied events, sellers included: will be much better suited by 7f+. *Mrs J. R. Ramsden.*

HIGHLY SECURE 2 b.c. (Mar 9) Shirley Heights 130–Caring (Crowned Prince **66** p (USA) 128) [1989 7g] 10,000Y: medium-sized, quite attractive colt: good walker: half-brother to useful 1¼m and 1½m winner Bishop's Ring (by Northfields), later successful in USA: dam unraced half-sister to good Italian filly Godzilla and Grease's dam Greedy of Gain: 16/1, around 10 lengths eighth of 13, in touch 5f and not knocked about, to Duke of Paducah in £10,000 event at Newmarket in October: sure to improve. *J. L. Dunlop.*

HIGH MARINER 3 ch.f. Julio Mariner 127–High Lee 71 (Will Hays (USA)) — [1988 NR 1989 9m] second reported foal: dam, form on flat at 2 yrs, later won over hurdles: bit backward and taken down early, soon well behind in minor event at Wolverhampton in June: refused to enter stalls at Chepstow 3 weeks earlier. *C. L. Popham.*

HIGH POKEY   3 b.f. Uncle Pokey 116–High Seeker 54 (Hotfoot 126) [1988 NR   —
1989 10g⁶ 10f 10g 7g] sparely-made filly: seventh living foal: half-sister to a winner
in Malaysia and some poor animals: dam poor maiden: always behind in maidens and
minor events. *J. L. Spearing.*

HIGH PURSE   2 ch.c. (Feb 1) High Line 125–Petty Purse 115 (Petingo 135) [1989   **76**
7g 8.2g⁴ 8g²] 21,000Y: workmanlike colt: fifth foal: half-brother to winners abroad
by Ile de Bourbon and Final Straw: dam, daughter of very smart sprinter Parsimony,
won from 5f to 7f: modest maiden: will stay 1¼m: carries head high. *G. A. Huffer.*

HIGH QUINTA   3 ch.f. High Line 125–Jacquinta 95 (Habitat 134) [1988 7m 1989   **51**
10g 12m a8g² a8g] deep-girthed, workmanlike filly: third foal: closely related to 7f
winner Toohami (by Nicholas Bill): dam, 6f winner, is daughter of Jacinth, leading
2-y-o of 1972 and high-class miler at 3 yrs: first run for 4 months, would probably
have won with clear run when second in maiden at Southwell in November: well
beaten in similar events otherwise: takes keen hold, and will prove best at up to
1¼m: sold 3,700 gns Newmarket December Sales. *H. Candy.*

HIGH REPUTE   3 b.c. Shirley Heights 130–With Distinction (USA) (Distinctive   —
(USA)) [1988 NR 1989 11f 12m] 520,000Y: big, strong colt: sixth foal: half-brother to
3 winners, notably high-class French 7f to 9f winner Procida (by Mr Prospector):
dam won 7 times at up to 7f in USA: always behind in summer maidens at Newbury:
carrying plenty of condition, swerved right 2f out then eased final start: may do
better in time and over 1¾m + . *Major W. R. Hern.*

HIGH RODING   2 b.c. (Feb 27) High Top 131–Ryoanji 100 (Lyphard (USA) 132)   —
[1989 7g 10g] 13,000Y: heavy-bodied colt: seventh foal: half-brother to unreliable 7f
and 1¾m winner Miss Annie (by Scottish Rifle) and 1983 2-y-o 6f winner Ritsurin
(by Mount Hagen): dam ran only at 2 yrs when winner twice over 7f: around 16
lengths eighth of 18 to Adding in minor event at Redcar in November, second and
better effort. *C. E. Brittain.*

HIGH SPIRITED   2 b.f. (Apr 18) Shirley Heights 130–Sunbittern 112 (Sea Hawk   —
II 131) [1989 7g³] sister to 2 winners, notably high-class middle-distance stayer
High Hawk, and half-sister to several other winners, including dam of Infamy: dam
6f and 7f winner at 2 yrs became temperamental: 6/4, soundly-beaten last of 3 in
private sweepstakes at Newmarket in October. *J. L. Dunlop.*

HIGH TENSION   7 ch.g. Vitiges (FR) 132–Montania 68 (Mourne 126) [1988 12d   —
12g⁵ 12d* 12m⁵ 12g 1989 10.6s 12g] strong, deep-girthed gelding: carries plenty of
condition: has a round, powerful action: fair handicapper at his best: apprentice
ridden, soundly beaten at Haydock and Leicester in autumn: suited by middle
distances: acts on any going: has won when sweating: usually held up. *D. L.
Williams.*

HIGH TILT   3 b.f. My Dad Tom (USA) 109–Torlonia 63§ (Royal Palace 131) [1988   —
NR 1989 7g 10f 10g] fifth reported foal: dam, placed at up to 2m, was most
unsatisfactory temperamentally: well beaten in maiden, seller and claimer (pro-
inent 1m) in the autumn. *C. James.*

HIGH WATER   2 ch.g. (Mar 8) High Line 125–Sextant 98 (Star Appeal 133)   **68**
[1989 8m 8s⁴ 8f⁴] 10,500 2-y-o: workmanlike gelding: has a round action: fifth foal:
half-brother to 3-y-o 7f winner Pilot (by Kris), a winner in Italy by Brigadier Gerard
and quite modest maiden Jib (by Welsh Pageant): dam won twice at around 1¼m and
is daughter of smart Fluke, a half-sister to Oaks winner Bireme and high-class
Buoy: quite modest maiden: will stay well: acts on soft going. *T. Fairhurst.*

HI JERICHO   2 b.g. (Apr 27) Joshua 129–Cynelva View 62 (Sahib 114) [1989 6m   —
7.5f] 1,500F, 8,600Y: second reported foal: dam well beaten over further than 5f, is
half-sister to Buzzard's Bay (by Joshua): slowly away and tailed off in auction events
at Hamilton (maiden) and Beverley. *M. W. Easterby.*

HI LASS   4 b.f. Shirley Heights 130–Good Lass (FR) (Reform 132) [1988 12g 12g⁶   **106**
17g² 1989 12g* 12g⁵ 12g³ 10.5g⁶ 12g⁶ 15g² 20m*] leggy, quite attractive filly: 14/1
and wearing eyeshield, appeared to show improved form when winning 5-runner
Ciga Prix Gladiateur at Longchamp in October by 2 lengths, travelling strongly long
way, from Rachmaninov (gave 12 lb): ran mainly in Provinces earlier in season,
winning minor event (blinkered) in May and runner-up in handicap in September:
suited by extreme test of stamina: acts on top-of-the-ground: trained by J. Dunlop at
3 yrs. *J. E. Pease, France.*

HILLDYKE MAC   3 b.g. Lochnager 132–Gold Pension 76 (Compensation 127)   —
[1988 NR 1989 6s 5d 6g⁵ 5m 5s 5s 6g] 400Y: compact gelding: poor walker and

mover: half-brother to 3 minor winners: dam best at 5f: no worthwhile form: tailed off in seller final outing. *N. Bycroft.*

HILLMOOR BELLA 2 ch.f. (May 9) Creetown 123–Confleur 81 (Compensation 127) [1989 7m 6g 5v] 420F, 300Y: workmanlike, plain filly: sixth foal: half-sister to a winner in Norway by Manor Farm Boy: dam 6f winner: soundly beaten in varied company, including selling. *J. Norton.*   —

HILL'S HALO 3 b.g. Kampala 120–Clanjingle (Tumble Wind (USA)) [1988 6g 7g 7d 1989 10s 12f³ 12f³ 16m⁵] good-topped, quite attractive gelding: good walker: has a round action: form only when third in maiden (staying on from rear) at Chepstow and handicap at Beverley in the summer: suited by 1½m: sweating badly on reappearance. *J. A. C. Edwards.*   70

HILTON BROWN 8 br.h. Daring March 116–Holiday Season 60 (Silly Season 127) [1988 6g 1989 8f⁴ 8f⁶ 8f] small, well-made horse: has a round action: fairly useful winner as 6-y-o: subsequently very lightly raced, acting as pacemaker for Warning all outings (wearing net muzzle) in 1989: stays 7f: acts on any going: has worn blinkers, but hasn't won in them. *G. Harwood.*   —

HIMLAJ (USA) 4 b.g. Far North (CAN) 120–Lusaka (USA) (Tom Rolfe) [1988 10s 11g 14m⁵ 10g⁵ 12d³ 12g³ 14v⁵ 1989 10s] ex-Irish gelding: half-brother to 3 winners, notably very useful French middle-distance colt Trokhos (by Tromos): dam unraced sister to Tanagra, very smart at around 1m: won maiden at Tralee and apprentice nursery at the Curragh as 2-y-o: placed in handicaps in 1988: never placed to challenge in ladies race at Nottingham in March: stays 1½m: acts on firm going and a soft surface: blinkered last 3 outings at 3 yrs. *S. Mellor.*   —

HIMMAH (USA) 2 b.f. (Apr 30) Habitat 134–Charmie Carmie (USA) (Lyphard (USA) 132) [1989 6g* 7d*] 170,000Y: smallish, workmanlike filly: has a quick action: third foal: dam, placed in USA, from excellent family: favourite, successful in maiden (in good style) at Leicester and minor event (readily by a neck from I Perceive) at Thirsk in autumn: will stay 1m: may improve again. *H. Thomson Jones.*   78 p

HINARI DISK DECK 3 b.f. Indian King (USA) 128–Little Cynthia 76 (Wolver Hollow 126) [1988 5d 5g 5f* 5m⁴ 6h⁴ 6g 6g 5f³ 5g 5g⁶ 5m 1989 6g a6g a5g] leggy, sparely-made filly: modest winner as 2-y-o: well beaten in claimer and handicaps in winter at 3 yrs: best at 5f on firm ground: has twice tended to hang: inconsistent. *M. Johnston.*   —

HINARI HI FI 4 b.f. Song 132–Sarah Siddons (Reform 132) [1988 6m³ 5d⁴ 6g² 5f* 6f* 5s⁵ 5g 5m 1989 5m 6m 6f³ 5g 5m⁶ 6h 6m⁴ 5d 6f 6g⁵ 6m³ 6g] sparely-made filly: quite modest handicapper: effective at 5f and 6f: acts on any going: inconsistent. *B. A. McMahon.*   56

HINARI SOUND 3 b.g. Song 132–Sarah Siddons (Reform 132) [1988 NR 1989 6m 7m⁵] 2,700F, 5,000Y: workmanlike gelding: poor walker: eighth foal: brother to 5f and 6f winner Hinari Hi Fi and half-brother to 2 winners, including 1986 2-y-o 6f seller winner Sands of Time (by Dance In Time): dam, French 8.5f winner, is sister to top 1982 Italian 2-y-o Anguillo: 14/1, about 5 lengths fifth of 18 in seller at Leicester in August, leading over 3f and running on steadily: sold 1,000 gns Newmarket Autumn Sales. *M. Johnston.*   57

HINARI SUNRISE 3 ch.c. Tap On Wood 130–Miss Markey 98 (Gay Fandango (USA) 132) [1988 6m 1989 8g⁴ 10f⁵ 12f* 13.8m² 12m* 12m⁵ 13.3d 12g] leggy, sparely-made colt: won maiden auction race (made virtually all) at Hamilton in May and handicap at Salisbury in June: well beaten in listed race at Down Royal sixth start: off course 3½ months and ran moderately (taking keen hold) after: suited by 1½m: acts on firm going. *M. Johnston.*   78

Ciga Prix Gladiateur, Longchamp—the vastly improved Hi Lass wins from Rachmaninov

HINARI TELEVIDEO 3 b.f. Caerleon (USA) 132–Red Jade 82 (Red God 128§)   97
[1988 6m⁵ 5g* 6f⁶ 6g³ 5s⁶ 6d 1989 6s⁵ 5f³ 5m³ 5f* 5f 5m 5g] lengthy filly: has a
quick action: fairly useful handicapper: won £12,500 event at Ascot in June in good
style: ran well at Epsom previous outing: last after in pattern events at Goodwood
(saddle slipped) and York and listed race at Doncaster: suited by 5f: best form on a
sound surface: refused to enter stalls once: found little off bridle second start and
goes well with waiting tactics. *M. S. Johnston.*

HINARI VIDEO 4 b.g. Sallust 134–Little Cynthia 76 (Wolver Hollow 126) [1988   59
7d 6s 5m² 5g⁵ 5f⁵ 5m⁶ 1989 5g 5d 5g* 5f 5m 5f⁶ 5g² 5m 5f 5f⁴ 5d⁶ 5s⁶ a5g³]
smallish, workmanlike gelding: plating-class performer: made all in seller (bought
in 3,000 gns) at Hamilton in May: suited by 5f: seems best on an easy surface
nowadays: ran creditably in blinkers: suitable mount for apprentice: has run well
when sweating: suited by forcing tactics. *M. S. Johnston.*

HINTIKKA 2 gr.g. (Apr 16) Magic Mirror 105–Margaret's Ruby (Tesco Boy 121)   80
[1989 5f⁵ 5d³ 5m² 6m²] 9,200Y: leggy, angular gelding: half-brother to numerous
winners here and abroad, including fairly useful 1976 2-y-o 5f performer Yes Love
(by On Your Mark) and 3-y-o Midnight's Reward (by Night Shift), fair 5f winner at 2
yrs: dam Irish 2-y-o 5f winner: won claimer at Redcar in May: placed in claimers
afterwards, on final outing (July) excellent second, rallying gamely under vigorous
ride (jockey suspended for misuse of whip), to Sharp Anne at Newcastle: suited by
6f: wears blinkers: sold 6,200 gns Newmarket Autumn Sales. *M. H. Easterby.*

HINTLESHAM HARRY 2 b.g. (May 7) Pas de Seul 133–Silver Glimpse 108   72 ?
(Petingo 135) [1989 7m 7.5f³ 8m⁵ 8g] IR 6,500Y: lengthy gelding: half-brother to
3-y-o Rare Vision (by Salmon Leap) and 3 winners in France, including 1m claimer
winner Coffee Song (by What A Guest): dam 7f winner at 2 yrs in France:
progressive form in maidens on first 3 starts then soundly beaten at Leicester on
final one: should stay 1¼m: gelded after final start. *G. A. Pritchard-Gordon.*

HINT OF SPRING 4 b.g. Pitskelly 122–Rare Find (Rarity 129) [1988 12m 8s   —
1989 12m⁵ 12f 18f] long-backed gelding: poor maiden: has run in seller: trained on
reappearance by J. Mackie. *P. A. Blockley.*

HIRSEL LAW 3 ch.g. Blue Cashmere 129–Worthy Venture 76 (Northfields   —
(USA)) [1988 7g 6m 6m 1989 6m 5g 8m 7m 8.2f 10.6s] small, sparely-made gelding:
poor mover: of no account: sold 800 gns Newmarket Autumn Sales. *J.
Douglas-Home.*

HISPANIC (USA) 3 b.c. Conquistador Cielo (USA)–English Legend (USA)   90 p
(Carlemont 132) [1988 NR 1989 8.5d⁵ 12d⁴] $110,000F: compact, attractive colt:
seventh foal: half-brother to 2 minor winners in USA by Akureyri and Private
Account: dam, unraced, is from excellent family: 11/1, about 8 lengths fourth of 10 to
Per Quod in minor event at Thirsk in November: favourite but very much in need of
experience in Beverley maiden nearly 7 months earlier, running on well: may
improve. *H. R. A. Cecil.*

HITCHENSTOWN 6 b.g. Town And Country 124–Veinarde (Derring-Do 131)   37
[1988 12.3s⁶ 8g 6s⁴ 6m 6f⁵ 7.6s² 8d* 8m 10.4d* 8.2s⁵ 10s 1989 8d³ 8.5d 8f⁶ 8.2g⁶
7.6m 8f² 8m²] strong, lengthy gelding: carries plenty of condition: poor
handicapper: stays 1¼m: acts on any going: occasionally blinkered: has sweated. *M.
J. O'Neill.*

HI-TECH BOY 7 ch.g. Tickled Pink 114–Jetwitch 56 (Lear Jet 123) [1988 NR   —
1989 10s] workmanlike gelding: plater: stays 1¼m: probably acts on any going:
blinkered once. *T. B. Hallett.*

HIT THE HIGH SPOTS 3 b.f. High Top 131–Criminelle (Crepello 136) [1988   92
7m 7m³ 7g 1989 10f 11m a12g* a14g*] rangy filly: bandaged off-fore, won handicaps
at Lingfield and Southwell in December: off course 6 months after shaping well
second start: will stay 2m. *J. L. Dunlop.*

HIZEEM 3 b.c. Alzao (USA) 117–Good Member (Mansingh (USA) 120) [1988 6d 7f   50 §
1989 7d 7.5d 8d 8.2g³ 10f 8.2f³ 10f² 10f⁵ 12f⁶ 8m⁶ 7.5f⁶ 7m² 8m 7g* 7m 8.2g⁶ 8.2g]
small, angular, well-made colt: won seller (bought in 4,500 gns) at Yarmouth in
September: effective at 7f and 1¼m: acts on firm going: blinkered last 6 outings:
inconsistent and probably ungenuine. *D. W. Chapman.*

HOBOURNES KATIE 6 b.m. Starch Reduced 112–Kathy King (Space King   —
115) [1988 5g⁴ 5m⁶ 5f⁴ 5f⁴ 5m⁴ 5g⁶ 5g 5g⁶ 1989 5f 5m] sparely-made mare: poor
maiden: best at 5f: acts on any going: blinkered once: suitable mount for apprentice.
R. M. Whitaker.

HOCUS 3 b.f. High Top 131–Hazy Idea 118 (Hethersett 134) [1988 6g 6m 8g³ 7m³   88
1989 8f 7f* 8m⁴ 10m² 10m³ 8d⁴] workmanlike, good-quartered filly: won minor

event at Folkestone in August, making most: ran well after in handicaps at Kempton, Newbury (twice) and Newmarket: well worth a try over 9f: acts on firm and dead going: sweating, very mulish on way down and never going well on reappearance: blinkered second and third outings: sold 62,000 gns Newmarket December Sales. *H. Candy.*

HODAKA (FR)   12 b.h. Sir Gaylord–Chigusa 89 (Skymaster 126) [1988 8g⁶ 9g   —
1989 8g] small, strong horse: poor plater: stays 9f: acts on any going: sometimes blinkered: has run creditably for apprentice. *B. R. Cambidge.*

HOGAN'S RUN   4 br.c. Tender King 123–Moment To Remember (USA)   66
(Assagai) [1988 8.2v² 6s⁶ 7g 6g 6d 8.2m* 7m 8.5g 8m* 7g² 8.2f⁵ 8d 10m³ 8.2m⁶ 8g 1989 8f 7.5g 8m 8.3m*] smallish, sparely-made colt: moderate mover: confirmed promise of previous outing when justifying favouritism in seller (bought in 9,600 gns) at Windsor in July by 8 lengths: ideally suited by about 1m and a sound surface: sometimes wanders: winning hurdler. *C. Tinkler.*

HOLDENBY   4 b.c. Henbit (USA) 130–Isadora Duncan (Primera 131) [1988 8m 8g   —
7g 7.5f4 8.5g² 7.5f⁵ 9f³ 8m 7g 8.5f⁵ 6f 13.8f4 10f* 8.2m 1989 10.2g 8f 12f] close-coupled colt: bad mover: winning plater as 3-y-o: below form in non-selling handicaps in first half of 1989: effective at 1¼m and probably stays 1¾m: acts on firm going: usually makes running, but went too fast when blinkered in apprentice event (sweating) on reappearance: winning hurdler. *T. Fairhurst.*

HOLDFORTH   2 b.c. (Mar 27) Sayyaf 121–Chief Dilke 82 (Saulingo 122) [1989 7g   —
8g] IR 3,500F, 6,200Y: third reported foal: half-brother to winner in Belgium: dam 6f winner at 2 yrs, later successful on flat and over jumps in Belgium: poor form in late-season minor event at Carlisle and maiden at Edinburgh. *Denys Smith.*

HOLLIA   4 ch.f. Touch Boy 109–Starproof 46 (Comedy Star (USA) 121) [1988 5g   —
5m 5s² 5g⁶ 5g³ 5g⁵ 6d 6m² 1989 5g 5m⁶ 6h] lengthy filly: modest at her best as 3-y-o: well below form in handicaps in 1989 (not seen out after July): best form at 5f: acts on any going: blinkered second outing. *J. Berry.*

HOLLY BUOY   9 b.h. Blind Harbour 96–Holly Doon (Doon 124) [1988 16g 15f*   — §
16.5f 15g 15.8g² 16d⁵ 15.8f⁶ 1989 13.8d 15.8m 15g] sturdy horse: moderate mover: poor handicapper: always behind all starts in 1989, on first reluctant to race and on last 2 off bridle throughout: probably best at around 2m: acts on any going, but used to be well suited by easy surface: temperamentally unsatisfactory and one to leave alone. *Mrs G. R. Reveley.*

HOLLY HERB (USA)   3 b.f. Clever Trick (USA)–Pollcam (USA) (Pollux) [1988   —
NR 1989 8d] sturdy filly: fifth foal: sister to useful sprinter Polly Daniels: dam, winner at up to 1m including in claiming company, is half-sister to Canadian Oaks winner Par Excellance, dam of Royal Lodge runner-up Khozaam: sire high-class sprinter/miler: 33/1, slowly away and never placed to challenge in 22-runner maiden at Warwick in May. *C. R. Nelson.*

HOLME HALE (USA)   3 b.c. General Holme (USA) 128–Fleet Moment (USA)   74
(Turn And Count (USA)) [1988 8d⁵ 8s⁵ 1989 8.5d² 10g] rather leggy, lengthy colt: has a short, quick action: modest maiden: beaten 5 lengths at Beverley in April: favourite, ran poorly in handicap 2 weeks later: should stay beyond 1m: sold 1,800 gns Newmarket Autumn Sales. *J. Tree.*

HOLSTER   3 b.g. Gorytus (USA) 132–Action Belle (Auction Ring (USA) 123)   52
[1988 5s* 5g² 5m² 6f 7g 7f4 6m* 7f⁶ 6d 1989 8d 6v 8g 8g⁶ 7m4 7m4 8f 12g] compact, good-quartered gelding: moderate mover: plating-class performer: fourth in sellers within 5 days at Leicester in June, only worthwhile form as 3-y-o: best form at 6f: probably acts on any going: often blinkered: tends to hang and is a difficult ride: sold 1,250 gns Ascot October Sales. *Miss A. J. Whitfield.*

HOLST (USA)   5 b. or br.h. Explodent (USA)–Angel Rouge (USA) (Crimson   119
Satan) [1988 6v* 6v³ 5.5g4 5d² 5d² 6s 6.5m 6d 1989 5.5s² 5m* 5g² 6d⁶ 6g 6g] big, workmanlike horse: won Prix de Saint-Georges at Longchamp in May by 2 lengths and neck from Astronef and Viva Zapata: runner-up in Prix du Gros Chene at Chantilly for second year running month later, beaten neck by Viva Zapata: well below form in Prix de Ris-Orangis at Evry, Prix de Meautry at Deauville and Ladbroke Sprint Cup (led over 3f, last of 9) at Haydock last 3 outings: suited by 5f: yet to race on firm going, acts on any other: smart on his day. *A. Fabre, France.*

HOLTERMANN (USA)   5 b.g. Mr Prospector (USA)–Royal Graustark (USA)   79
(Graustark) [1988 8s4 10.2m³ 1989 8g 8g⁶ 7.6f² 7f⁵ 7g⁶] rangy gelding: fair performer: effective at 7.6f and stays 1¼m: acts on any going: blinkered second outing: sometimes sweats: slowly away on reappearance and on fourth start: rather

headstrong and has tended to hang: a difficult ride: sold to join M. Haynes 4,000 gns Newmarket Autumn Sales. *D. R. C. Elsworth.*

HOLY GAIT 2 ro.f. (Mar 19) Godswalk (USA) 130–Deverell's Lady (Sterling Bay (SWE)) IR 4,800F, 11,000Y: neat, angular filly: moderate walker: has a round action: sixth foal: half-sister to quite modest 5f and 6f winner Dancing Sarah (by Malinowski) and 3 other winners here and abroad: dam never ran: still bit backward, over 11 lengths seventh of 24 to Heart of Joy in maiden at Newbury in October. *L. G. Cottrell.* **59**

HOLYPORT VICTORY 7 br.g. Free State 125–Snow Goose (Santa Claus 133) [1988 NR 1989 12s] lengthy, workmanlike gelding: has a round action: winning handicapper in 1986: well behind at Folkestone in April, only subsequent outing on flat: stays 1½m: acts on top-of-the-ground and heavy going: winning hurdler. *M. D. I. Usher.* **—**

HOLYROOD 5 gr.m. Royal Palace 131–Lizzie Eustace 64 (Firestreak 125) [1988 12f4 1989 11d] lengthy, dipped-backed, sparely-made mare: poor maiden: blinkered once. *V. Thompson.* **—**

HOLY ZEAL 3 b.g. Alzao (USA) 117–Crystal Halo 78 (St Chad 120) [1988 7g3 8.2d6 1989 11.7d6 11.7m 14f5 13f* 14f* 14g2 14.8m 14m* 13.3m 16.2d4] medium-sized, useful-looking gelding: successful in smallish fields for maiden auction race at Ayr in June and handicaps at Nottingham in July and Sandown in September: suited by 1¾m: acts on firm going: had tongue tied down last 6 outings: gelded after final one: genuine. *D. W. P. Arbuthnot.* **87**

HOME JOHN 2 b.c. (Apr 29) Homeboy 114–Fantasy Royale 84 (Breeders Dream 116) [1989 5m 5m 6f6 6g] 1,200F, 3,200Y: sturdy colt: poor mover: third living foal: half-brother to quite modest 10.1f winner Electropet (by Remainder Man): dam, winner over 5f at 4 yrs, is half-sister to very smart Hillandale: soundly beaten in sellers and a claimer. *R. J. Hodges.* **—**

HOMELY TOUCH 3 b.f. Touching Wood (USA) 127–Home Address 83 (Habitat 134) [1988 6m3 6m6 7m3 1989 7s3 8s2 8.5s3 8f3 8m2 8m4 8m4 8m2 7s3 8f2] small filly: moderate mover: fair but rather disappointing maiden: will stay 1¼m: acts on any going. *G. Wragg.* **79**

HOME POOL 4 ch.c. Habitat 134–Rossitor 78 (Pall Mall 132) [1988 8g6 7d3 10m6 12.3g 1989 12.4g 13.8d5 12s 13v 14s] leggy colt: poor mover: little sign of ability in varied events: visored fourth outing: sold to join D. Wintle 1,400 gns Doncaster May Sales. *M. Brittain.* **—**

HOME STRAIGHT 3 b.c. Homing 130–Fast Asleep (Hotfoot 126) [1988 NR 1989 5g4 6g6 6g 8s5 10g 9s] 2,900Y: leggy, rather dipped-backed colt: moderate mover: brother to modest 7f and 1m winner Thomas Leng and half-brother to fair 6f winner Kip (by Cawston's Clown): dam showed no ability: plating-class form on first and fourth starts: stays 1m well: sold 1,600 gns Doncaster November Sales. *M. Brittain.* **—**

HO MI CHINH 7 ch.g. Homing 130–Fiordiligi 109 (Tudor Melody 129) [1988 6m 6f 6m6 5.8d 6m 6m 6d 1989 5s 5d 5d 6g3 5.8h 5m5 7f 6f 8m 7m5 a8g5 8g3 a7g] big, strong, lengthy gelding: moderate mover: fairly useful handicapper at his best, but has deteriorated considerably: seems to stay 1m: best with give in the ground: has been tried in blinkers, visored nowadays: bandaged in front. *J. M. Bradley.* **45**

HOMME D'AFFAIRE 6 br.g. Lord Gayle (USA) 124–French Cracker (Klairon 131) [1988 10d2 10g4 12m6 1989 10d 12g2 12g] well-made, quite attractive gelding: modest handicapper: good second of 20 at Brighton in April, rallying gamely: well-backed favourite, weakened from 3f out in amateurs event at Folkestone over 6 months later: stays 1½m: not at his best on firm going, acts on any other: good mount for apprentice. *R. J. O'Sullivan.* **74**

HOMO SAPIEN 7 b.h. Lord Gayle (USA) 124–Bold Caress 104 (Bold Lad (IRE) 133) [1988 NR 1989 6d5 8g4 6s2 7g4 7.2s5 8m 6f 8f 9m3 7g 8g 8f6 8f 8m3 8s] well-made horse: moderate walker and mover: good-class performer at his best at 5 yrs: showed useful form in varied events in 1989, on penultimate outing (apprentice ridden) third to Dramatic Event in £7,700 handicap at Ripon: effective at 6f given testing conditions and stayed 1m: acted on any going: slowly away tenth start: retired to Ballee House Stud, Downpatrick, fee £750 nfnf. *D. W. Chapman.* **97**

HOMOSASSA 2 ch.f. (Mar 14) Burslem 123–Salt 90 (Sallust 134) [1989 6f2 6m3 6m 5d4 5g2 5s5] IR 7,800Y: small, workmanlike filly: fourth foal: half-sister to winning Irish sprinter Two Seats (by Hays) and a winner in Norway: dam, 2-y-o 5f and 6f winner, is half-sister to useful sprinter Bold Tack: put up fair performance when about 2 lengths fourth of 8 to Wedding Bouquet in listed race at **82 ?**

the Curragh in September: beaten at least 7 lengths by Tatwij in maiden at Hamilton and minor event at Ayr (on toes, looked ill at ease on ground) on last 2 starts: best form at 5f. *Noel T. Chance, Ireland.*

HONEST GLORY (USA) 3 b.f. Al Nasr (FR) 126–Mistress Lea (USA) —
(Reverse (USA)) [1988 NR 1989 7d 7m⁶ 8.5f] $90,000Y: workmanlike, sparely-made filly: fifth foal: half-sister to 2 winners in North America: dam never ran: always behind in maidens in first half of season: moved poorly down on debut: wears tongue strap: sold 800 gns Newmarket Autumn Sales. *M. Moubarak.*

HONEY BOY SIMBA 3 ch.g. Mansingh (USA) 120–Continental Divide 50 **66** d
(Sharp Edge 123) [1988 5s 5g 5f* 6m⁵ 6d² 6m² 5g² 5d 5g 6s⁴ 7f* 6s² 6s² 7d² 1989 7s 7m³ 7m³ 7h² 8f² 8f² 8.2m 9m 10.2f⁶ 8m 8f 6g 7g 8.2g 7d⁴ 7d⁶] smallish, lengthy gelding: carries condition: moderate mover: quite modest handicapper: placed in first half of season but deteriorated: stays 1m: below form on hard ground but probably acts on any other: suitable mount for a claimer: visored third, fourth and last 2 outings. *M. J. O'Neill.*

HONEY DANCER 5 b.g. Tyrnavos 129–Hello Honey 105 (Crepello 136) [1988 —
12g 14d*] 1989 14g] well-made gelding: moderate mover: fair winner (flashed tail) early as 4-y-o: 33/1, never dangerous in Sandown handicap in September: needs further than 1½m and stays 2¼m: acts on any going: pulled too hard in blinkers. *Miss A. J. Whitfield.*

HONEY MILL 3 b.f. Milford 119–Sharp Venita 84 (Sharp Edge 123) [1988 6g 7d **63**
6g⁴ 1989 10f 8g 7f 6f³ 7m² 6g a7g] rangy filly: quite modest maiden: placed in handicaps at Salisbury and Warwick in August: suited by 7f: acts on top-of-the-ground: usually blinkered nowadays. *O. O'Neill.*

HONEY PLUM 5 b.m. Kind of Hush 118–Rosaceae 101 (Sagaro 133) [1988 7.6d —
12f 11.7d 11.1m 12f 9m 9m 12m 16.5g 12f 10d 12d 1989 10f 8m 12f⁶ 12g] smallish, sparely-made mare: no longer of much account. *J. O'Donoghue.*

HONEY REEF 3 b.f. Mill Reef (USA) 141–Attica Meli 125 (Primera 131) [1988 **66**
NR 1989 10f⁵ 12f² 12.2g³] small, lightly-made, angular filly: half-sister to several winners here and abroad, including useful middle-distance performer Honeybeta (by Habitat) and smart 1979 2-y-o 6f and 7f winner Marathon Gold (by Derring-Do): dam won Yorkshire Oaks and Park Hill Stakes: quite modest maiden: badly hampered final start: stays 1½m: very slowly away first outing: got loose on way down then refused to enter stalls on intended debut. *H. R. A. Cecil.*

HONEY'S FORTUNE 2 gr.c. (Feb 19) Magic Mirror 105–Close To You 44 —
(Nebbiolo 125) [1989 8.2s] 5,000Y: second foal: half-brother to plating-class 1988 2-y-o Solar Reef (by Simply Great): dam 7f winner: 8/1, soundly-beaten seventh of 11 in Hamilton maiden in September. *I. Semple.*

HONG KONG GIRL 3 br.f. Petong 126–Ballad Island 83 (Ballad Rock 122) **94**
[1988 5d³ 5f⁶ 5f* 5m 5d² 5g² 5s⁶ 1989 5m 5h⁵ 5f* 5g 5g⁴ 5s* 5g² 5g 5m⁵ 5d] rather leggy filly: fairly useful handicapper: won at Goodwood in July and Ayr (making all) in September: below form last 3 outings: speedy: acts on any going: twice below form when slowly away: bandaged near-hind last 4 outings at 2 yrs: changed hands 24,000 gns Doncaster September Sales after sixth start. *J. Berry.*

HONKS 7 b.g. Ballymore 123–Katie Cecil 120 (Princely Gift 137) [1988 NR 1989 —
15.5f 12h⁶ 19f⁴] strong, good-bodied gelding: quite modest maiden as 3-y-o: well beaten in handicaps in first half of 1989: blinkered 3 times. *R. P. C. Hoad.*

HONORIA (USA) 3 b.f. Danzig (USA)–Royal Honoree (USA) (Round Table) **103**
[1988 5m* 5f³ 6m* 6d³ 6g 6s² 8m 1989 6s⁵ 7v³ 6m⁴ 8m⁴ 8f 8g⁴ 10d⁶] strong, rangy filly: has a round action: ran well when in frame, including when fourth to Ensconse in Irish 1000 Guineas at the Curragh and Distant Relative in Group 2 EBF Phoenix International Stakes at Phoenix Park: ran poorly in Coronation Stakes at Royal Ascot in between and listed event at Phoenix Park in August: stays 1m: probably not suited by very firm going, but acts on any other: blinkered twice at 2 yrs and on first and last 2 outings in 1989. *J. S. Bolger, Ireland.*

HONOR RAJANA (USA) 2 b.c. (Mar 17) Hero's Honor (USA)–Rajana (USA) **112**
(Rajab (USA)) [1989 7d* 7g² 8d³ 8m³] $70,000Y: good-looking colt: second foal: dam graded winner in Puerto Rico: very useful colt: improved after winning maiden at Longchamp, on last 2 starts third to Linamix in Prix La Rochette and to Jade Robbery in Ciga Grand Criterium (blinkered) there in autumn: stays 1m. *P. Bary, France.*

HONOUR'S DEGREE 4 b.c. Balliol 125–Cheb's Honour 70 (Chebs Lad 120) **61** d
[1988 7g 1989 6d⁵ 6g 5f 6f⁴ 5f⁶ 5m⁵ 5m³ 5m⁶ 6m 7g 7m⁶ 6f⁶ 5f] lengthy, angular colt: bad mover: plating-class maiden: often gets outpaced, and finds 5f on sharp

side: trained until after second outing by C. Williams: blinkered last 4: slowly away final one. *D. W. Chapman.*

HONOUR THE WIND 3 ch.c. Ahonoora 122–Mill Wind 68 (Blakeney 126) **68** [1988 6g³ 7d 7m⁵ 7f 7d⁶ 1989 7g 10g 9s³ 10f 8m 8f² 7g⁵ 8m² 8m] strong, lengthy colt: carries condition: modest maiden: stays 9f: probably acts on any going: blinkered last 4 starts: has given trouble at stalls: sold 2,600 gns Newmarket Autumn Sales. *R. Hannon.*

HOOP LA 3 b.f. Final Straw 127–Out of Shot 116§ (Shirley Heights 130) [1988 6g — 8.2m 1989 10g 10m] sparely-made filly: no form in maidens and minor event: sold 920 gns Newmarket July Sales. *J. L. Dunlop.*

HOORAY LADY 5 ch.m. Ahonoora 122–Song Beam 84 (Song 132) [1988 8d 8m **92** 8f³ 10m 8f⁵ 8d⁵ 8f* 10f² 8g³ 8g³ 8f² 8g* 9g 8d⁵ 8s 1989 8g 8f 8.2m⁴ 8h* 8.5m⁵ 10f⁴ 8h* 10g 8m³ 8f 12h³ 8m² 10m³ 8m] strong, lengthy mare: good mover: fairly useful handicapper: a course specialist at Brighton, and has gained 5 of her 6 wins there, comfortably beating Sierra Snow 2 lengths and Fleet Special 3 lengths in June: ran creditably when placed afterwards: seems to stay 1½m: unsuited by soft going and goes very well on firm: blinkered once at 4 yrs: suited by strong pace and waiting tactics. *G. B. Balding.*

HOPEA (USA) 3 ro.f. Drone–Hope So (USA) (Tudor Grey 119) [1988 7f 1989 — 10.1g] rather leggy, good-topped filly: well beaten in minor events at York and Windsor: sold D. Thom 2,000 gns Newmarket December Sales. *B. W. Hills.*

HOPEFUL HEART 2 br.f. (May 11) Derrylin 115–Take To Heart 72 (Steel — Heart 128) [1989 6m 7f] angular filly: fourth foal: dam, in frame at 5f and 6f, ran only at 2 yrs: soundly beaten in minor event and claimer. *M. D. I. Usher.*

HOPEFULL CHARMER 3 br.f. Full of Hope 125–Targow Girl (Targowice **45** (USA) 130) [1988 7g⁵ 6m 1989 6s³ 7s 7d 6m] leggy, lightly-made filly: third in minor event at Warwick, only form: faced stiff tasks in handicaps later in spring on last 2 starts: should stay 1m: acts on soft ground: sometimes sweating. *P. J. Arthur.*

HOPEFULL LADY 3 ch.f. Full of Hope 125–Frimley's One Oak (Pieces of — Eight 128) [1988 NR 1989 7s 10g 7f⁵ 7f] workmanlike filly: second reported living foal: dam poor maiden: probably of little account. *P. J. Arthur.*

HOPING FOR GLORY (USA) 3 b.c. L'Emigrant (USA) 129–Hope For All **73** (USA) (Secretariat (USA)) [1988 NR 1989 6g² 6s³] sturdy, attractive colt: has a quick action: fourth foal: half-brother to French Oaks winner Lacovia (by Majestic Light) and a claiming race winner in USA: dam, placed from 6f to 8.3f in USA, is half-sister to Miswaki: beaten about 2 lengths, running on, in maiden (well-backed second favourite) at Newmarket and minor event (pulled hard early) at Nottingham in the spring: will be suited by 7f: sold to join D. Nicholson 16,000 gns Newmarket Autumn Sales. *H. R. A. Cecil.*

HOPPING AROUND 5 b.g. Prince Tenderfoot (USA) 126–Wurli 70 (Wolver **62** Hollow 126) [1988 12s⁴ 12v 12g⁴ 12m 12g⁴ 12g 12d³ 13g⁴ 12d 12d² 13s² 12s⁴ 12d² 12g* 12g⁶ 12m 1989 12.4g³ 13v⁵ 12d² 12f4 12g⁵ 12m⁴ 12d 15g* 16m⁴ 15s² 15g³ a13g⁶] neat gelding: poor mover: quite modest handicapper: won at Edinburgh in September in good style by 5 lengths: ran creditably next 3 outings: stays 2m: acts on firm going, but well suited by an easy surface: has won for apprentice: tends to carry head high: often doesn't find great deal under pressure. *C. W. Thornton.*

HOPSCOTCH 2 b.f. (Mar 24) Dominion 123–Tartan Pimpernel 109 (Blakeney **68** 126) [1989 7f³ 8m² 9g² a8g⁶] lightly-made filly: moderate mover: seventh foal: half-sister to 3 winners, including fairly useful 1983 2-y-o 7f winner Elusive (by Little Current), and winning hurdler Red Hackle (by Beldale Flutter): dam, half-sister to Dunfermline, won May Hill and Galtres Stakes: quite modest maiden: will stay 1¼m. *W. Hastings-Bass.*

HOPTONS CHANCE 7 b.g. Kala Shikari 125–Ariel 59 (The Go-Between 129) — [1988 10.2d 8g 8.5m 8m* 8.2m 8f³ 8f³ 8g 8g 7m 8g 7f 6m 7d 1989 8v 7h⁶ 8.5g] leggy gelding: winning plater at 6-y-o: has lost his form completely: suited by 1m: used to act well on top-of-the-ground: usually blinkered or visored: often apprentice ridden, but wasn't when successful: wears bandages: races freely. *J. Norton.*

HORALDO 2 ch.g. (Apr 4) Horage 124–Nebanna 74 (Nebbiolo 125) [1989 7f 8g **42** 10g] IR 8,800Y: second foal: brother to 3-y-o Miss Willow: dam 1½m winner from family of Providential and Play It Safe: never dangerous in varied races, including a seller. *R. M. Whitaker.*

HORATIAN 4 b.g. Horage 124–Assurance (FR) (Timmy Lad 130) [1988 7g³ 7m⁴ **69** 7.6m⁶ 7g 8g⁶ 1989 8f 10h⁴] close-coupled gelding: has a rather short, quick action:

modest maiden: stays 1¼m well: best form on top-of-the-ground: has looked difficult ride: sold to join J. Wonnacott 2,100 gns Ascot 2nd June Sales: inconsistent. *R. V. Smyth.*

HORATIO LURO (USA)   2 b.c. (Mar 9) El Gran Senor (USA) 136–Solo Haina   **113**
(USA) (Solo Landing (USA)) [1989 8g² 9d²] fourth foal: dam won at up to 9f in USA, including in stakes company: runner-up in newcomers race and Prix Saint-Roman (beaten 1½ lengths by Bleu de France) at Longchamp in September: will stay 1¼m: sure to win races. *A. Fabre, France.*

HORNBLOWER LASS   3 ch.f. Sayyaf 121–Ambient 68 (Amber Rama (USA)   —
133) [1988 5f 7m 6g 8m 1989 8.2s 10f⁶ 12.4f 16f⁵ 10f] workmanlike filly: has a round action: little worthwhile form, including in sellers and handicap: twice sweating: pulled hard in blinkers final outing: sold 1,250 gns Ascot August Sales. *H. P. Rohan.*

HORN DANCE (USA)   3 b.c. Green Dancer (USA) 132–Fair Salinia 125   **109** ?
(Petingo 135) [1988 8d* 1989 14f³ 17.6d⁶ 16m] close-coupled, finely-made colt: won Newmarket maiden as 2-y-o: heavily-backed favourite, 2½ lengths third of 18 to Sapience in Tote Ebor (Handicap) at York in August, always close up, soon under pressure in straight then keeping on well despite edging left: ran as though something amiss in quite valuable handicaps at Haydock and Ascot (sweating and edgy) following month: stays 1¾m: one to be wary of. *G. Harwood.*

HORN PLAYER (USA)   2 ch.c. (May 26) The Minstrel (CAN) 135–Qualique   **62** p
(USA) (Hawaii) [1989 8g] 62,000Y: big, lengthy colt: has scope: second foal: dam smart 2-y-o in USA, winner of 9f Demoiselle Stakes: 7/1 and on toes, around 11 lengths eighth of 17, running green 2f out and eased closing stages, to Lover's Moon in maiden at Leicester in November: sure to improve. *B. W. Hills.*

HORSESHOE REEF   3 ro.f. Mill Reef (USA) 141–Miss Toshiba (USA) 113 (Sir   **88**
Ivor (USA) 135) [1988 NR 1989 8f⁵ 10f*] angular filly: seventh foal: half-sister to 2 winners, including Irish 1988 9f winner Tobolsk (by Storm Bird) and Irish 7f winner North Eastern (by Northern Dancer), subsequently a stakes winner in USA: dam won from 7f to 1½m before showing very smart form at up to 9f in USA: 10/3, won 6-runner maiden at Folkestone in July by ½ length from Lovely Fairy, leading inside final 1f: may well stay 1½m. *L. M. Cumani.*

HORSEY PIE   2 br.g. (Apr 30) King of Spain 121–Velvet Pigeon 70 (Homing 130)   —
[1989 5g 5g 5f] 1,600F, 15,000Y: neat, attractive gelding: first foal: dam lightly-raced half-sister to useful middle-distance performer Heighten and daughter of half-sister to Final Straw and Achieved: well beaten in early-season maidens: slowly away second start. *N. Tinkler.*

HORTONDALE   4 ch.g. Tickled Pink 114–Jamaya 71 (Double-U-Jay 120) [1988   —
NR 1989 10.2g 7.5d] compact gelding: little sign of ability on flat: sweating on reappearance: visored and wore pricker on near-side second outing. *R. J. Holder.*

HOSKINS (USA)   3 b.g. Hostage (USA)–Shalimar Gardens (USA) (Raise A   — §
Native) [1988 7g 8g² 8d³ 1989 12d⁴ 8d 7.6f 10f] tall, quite attractive gelding: turns fore-feet in: fair maiden at 2 yrs: well below form in 1989, looking reluctant to race on final start: wearing dropped noseband, sweating and edgy, ran wide on turn at Bath second time: stays 1m: sold to join J. Harris 7,600 gns Ascot June Sales and subsequently gelded: one to have strong reservations about. *R. V. Smyth.*

HOSTAGE   3 b.g. Homing 130–B M Wonder (Junius (USA) 124) [1988 NR 1989   —
8.3m 7m 6m] rather sparely-made gelding: first foal: dam, granddaughter of Oaks winner Carrozza, well beaten on only 3 starts: bandaged, no promise in sellers, sweating and moving badly to post final start: sold 1,300 gns Ascot September Sales. *K. T. Ivory.*

HOSTESS QUICKLY   2 b.f. (Mar 8) Hotfoot 126–Linda Dudley 81 (Owen   **47**
Dudley 121) [1989 7f 8.2f⁵] IR 4,200F, 6,800Y: second living foal: half-sister to 3-y-o Shinnel Water (by Rolfe): dam lightly-raced half-sister to William Hill Futurity winner Count Pahlen: bandaged near-hind, around 8 lengths fifth of 20 in seller at Nottingham in September, better effort. *Dr J. D. Scargill.*

HOT COMPANY   4 ch.g. Hotfoot 126–Campagna (Romulus 129) [1988 10d⁵ 9g   **58** §
10f² 10m³ 12m* 12f⁵ 12m⁴ 1989 12g 14m³ 13.6f⁶ 12m⁴ a14g⁴] sparely-made, angular gelding: quite modest handicapper: possibly better suited by 1½m than 1¾m: yet to race on soft going, acts on any other: usually blinkered nowadays (wasn't final outing): bought out of G. Pritchard-Gordon's stable 7,000 gns Ascot August Sales after fourth start: winning hurdler: ungenuine. *D. Burchell.*

HOTFOOT HENRY   2 ch.g. (Apr 22) Hotfoot 126–Courting Day 90 (Right Boy   **42**
137) [1989 5d⁶ 5d 6m 5f 6g a6g a7g] 5,100Y: leggy, angular gelding: sixth living foal: half-brother to 3-y-o Lockhart (by Lochnager), successful over 5f at 2 yrs, and to 2

other winners, including useful 7f and 1m winner Courting Season (by Silly Season): dam won twice over 1m: poor form in varied races: got loose from stalls when blinkered at Beverley in May and was withdrawn. *A. Smith.*

HOT GIRL 7 b.m. Hot Grove 128–Gloria Maremmana (King Emperor (USA)) [1988 12f³ 10.8m 12.2d⁶ 1989 10m⁴] lengthy mare: poor handicapper: facing stiff task, soundly-beaten last of 4 in amateurs event at Goodwood in August: stays 1½m: probably acts on any going: has worn blinkers: slowly away final outing at 6 yrs and at Goodwood. *K. Bishop.*

HOT HOPE 2 b.f. (May 25) Blazing Saddles (AUS)–Return Home (Nonoalco (USA) 131) [1989 5v 5g⁶ 5f 6g a6g a6g] 400Y: plain filly: third foal: dam once-raced granddaughter of Oaks winner Long Look: poor maiden: sweating final start. *J. J. Bridger.*   **41**

HOT PERFORMER 2 ch.f. (May 11) Hotfoot 126–Show Business 72 (Auction Ring (USA) 123) [1989 6h 5f⁴ 6g⁶ 7.5g² 7m* 7f³ 7g* 7m 7g* 7g] 500F: tall, lengthy filly: moderate walker: second foal: half-sister to 3-y-o Caroles Clown (by Another Realm), temperamental 5f winner at 2 yrs: dam 12.2f winner at 5 yrs: favourite, successful in summer sellers at Catterick (bought in 5,000 gns on first occasion, no bid on second) and in claimer (comfortably by 2 lengths from April Cracker) at Yarmouth in September: virtually refused to race for 7-lb claimer eighth start and ran poorly for one final start: will stay 1m. *T. Fairhurst.*   **55 ?**

HOT RUMOUR 2 ch.g. (Mar 8) Hotfoot 126–Clear As Crystal 80 (Whitstead 125) [1989 6h 8.2s⁵ 8m 10g²] 8,800Y, 2,600 2-y-o: lengthy, angular gelding: first foal: dam 11.7f winner on only start: showed much improved form when 5 lengths second of 18, always prominent, to Adding in minor event at Redcar in November: suited by 1¼m: blinkered last 2 starts: gelded after final one. *S. G. Norton.*   **81**

HOT SHOE SHUFFLE (USA) 2 ch.c. (Mar 20) Fire Dancer (USA)–Best Impression (USA) (Iron Ruler (USA)) [1989 7f 7.5f 8.5f⁵ 8m 7d] $14,000Y: robust colt: sixth reported foal: brother to minor winner in USA, and half-brother to 2 other winners: dam unplaced in 6 starts in USA: plating-class maiden: best effort third outing: ran moderately in sellers last 2: stays 8.5f: blinkered third and fourth starts: races keenly: sold 3,800 gns Doncaster October Sales. *J. Etherington.*   **61 d**

HOT STAR 3 b.g. Hotfoot 126–La Camargue (Wollow 132) [1988 6f 6h⁶ 1989 8s 8.2m 10f 9.1f⁵ 12.3f 13s² 15s* 12.4g⁴] leggy, unfurnished gelding: has a markedly round action: in good form in handicaps last 3 starts, winning at Ayr in October by 8 lengths: will prove better at 15f than shorter: goes well on soft ground: trained until after third outing by K. Stone: has run creditably for 7-lb claimer: sweats and gets on toes. *J. F. Bottomley.*   **71**

HOT TAN 3 ch.f. Hotfoot 126–Tanara 93 (Romulus 129) [1988 5m 5m 1989 7g 10f 8f 7g⁵] small, quite good-topped filly: moderate mover: little sign of ability, including in sellers: should be suited by further than 7f: possibly needs give in the ground. *Ronald Thompson.*   **—**

HOT TOOTSIE 2 b.f. (May 15) Hotfoot 126–Lady of The Isle 72 (Pitskelly 122) [1989 5f⁴ 5f 5m 5f⁵ 5g* 5f⁴ 6m* 6m 6f² 5s 6v⁵ 6g] 1,750Y: small, good-bodied filly: fourth live foal: half-sister to 8.2f seller winner Nasdarovye (by Balidar): dam won over 6f here and 7f in Belgium: very useful plater: successful in July at Pontefract (bought in 3,600 gns) and Doncaster (no bid): very good second to Friendship Renewed in nursery (on toes) at Nottingham in September, running on strongly after poor run: suited by 6f: seems to act on any going: sometimes hangs, and is a difficult ride: inconsistent. *J. Balding.*   **68**

HOT WIRE 3 b.f. Belfort (FR) 89–Girl Commander (USA) (Bold Commander (USA)) [1988 5d 5m 5m 5m³ 5g 5d 1989 5f 5m 5.3h] leggy, close-coupled filly: no form since third in maiden as 2-y-o: faced stiff tasks in handicaps in 1989, weakening rapidly 2f out when last of 14, blinkered, at Brighton final start: should be suited by 6f: sold 720 gns Doncaster June Sales: temperamentally suspect. *R. W. Stubbs.*   **—**

HOUGHTON 3 b.g. Horage 124–Deirdre Oge (Pontifex (USA)) [1988 NR 1989 8s⁶ 8d² 12d⁶ 8m 8.5g⁴ 9g 12.3f³ 12.3g 14g³ 13.6g] big, rangy gelding: moderate mover: second foal: dam second over 5f at 2 yrs in Ireland: modest maiden: winning 1½m (ran creditably in moderately-run race over 1¾m): acts on firm ground and a soft surface: winning novice hurdler. *M. W. Easterby.*   **72**

HOULIHAN 3 ch.f. Stanford 121§–Arodstown Tan (Atan) [1988 5s 5f⁴ 6m⁴ 7d 1989 8g 11f³ 12m⁶ 12f⁴ 8g 9f* 10f 8.2g] smallish, lengthy filly: won strongly-run seller (no bid) at Wolverhampton in October: ran moderately in similar events after: stays 11f (hung right and found little third start): acts on firm ground. *M. H. Tompkins.*   **55**

HOUSE OF COMMONS 4 b.c. General Assembly (USA)–Clare Island 108   83
(Connaught 130) [1988 8d³ 9g² 10g³ 7d⁴ 8d 1989 10.2g² 10g 7.6m⁵ 7m 8f⁴ 9m⁴ 10f²
10.5f] rangy colt: good mover: in frame in varied events, but is still a maiden: stays
1¼m: yet to race on soft going, acts on any other: ran creditably when blinkered fifth
start: occasionally sweats, and has got on edge: sold 13,000 gns Newmarket Autumn
Sales: disappointing. *C. E. Brittain.*

HOUSE OF FRUIT 2 b.g. (Feb 2) Mansingh (USA) 120–Rheinbloom 66   65
(Rheingold 137) [1989 7g⁵ 7m³ 7m 8.2g 8.2g] 8,500 2-y-o: tall, rather unfurnished
gelding: has scope: half-brother to fairly useful middle-distance stayer Rhusted (by
Busted) and a winner in USA: dam, 1½m winner, is half-sister to high-class Gold
Rod: quite modest maiden: soundly beaten last 3 starts: stays 7f. *C. N. Allen.*

HOUSEPROUD (USA) 2 br.f. (Apr 25) Riverman (USA) 131–Proud Lou (USA) 112
(Proud Clarion (USA)) [1989 5g³ 5.5g* 8g²] fourth foal: closely related to 3-y-o
Brosna (by Irish River): dam best at 2 yrs in USA, winning at 6f and 1m: 2 lengths
second of 15, going on strongly, to Salsabil in Prix Marcel Boussac at Longchamp in
October: won minor event at Évry previous month, first run for over 3 months: will
probably stay 1¼m. *A. Fabre, France.*

HOUSEWORK 3 b. or br.f. Homing 130–Asnoura (MOR) (Asandre (FR)) [1988   —
7f⁶ 8.5f* 8s⁴ 1989 8s⁶ 8g 11.7m] workmanlike, good-quartered filly: has a powerful,
rather round action: modest winner at 2 yrs: below form since and not seen out after
June in 1989: should stay 1¼m: possibly unsuited by soft going. *I. A. Balding.*

HOVINGHAM 2 ch.g. (Mar 15) Krayyan 117–Free Course 80 (Sandford Lad 133)   51
[1989 5d 5m 5m⁴ 5m 5g 6m⁵ 7m 8.5f] IR 17,500Y: sixth foal: brother to 3-y-o Break
Loose, 6f seller winner at 2 yrs, and half-brother to 2 modest 2-y-o 6f winners by On
Your Mark: dam 2-y-o 5f winner: moderate plater: easily best effort in non-seller
third start: blinkered seventh outing. *M. W. Easterby.*

HOW 3 b.c. Horage 124–Rathcoffey Dodo 108 (Jukebox 120) [1988 NR 1989 8m   75
10.2f⁴ 10m 11.7f* 13.8d⁶] IR 5,200F, 10,500Y: useful-looking colt: good walker: sixth
foal: half-brother to a French 2-y-o 5f winner by Pampapaul, later successful in Italy,
and to a winner in the USA by Miami Springs: dam Irish sprinter: won maiden
claimer at Bath in September: well beaten in Catterick handicap month later: suited
by 1½m: acts on firm going: moved badly to post third start. *Mrs L. Piggott.*

HOWGILL 3 b.g. Tower Walk 130–In Form 76 (Formidable (USA) 125) [1988 6d   67
7d 6g⁵ 1989 8s³ 8g 7f⁴ 8h² 8m⁵ 6g³] strong, lengthy gelding: quite modest maiden:
in frame in handicaps: probably suited by 1m and acts on any going: blinkered, took
good hold to post and below form final start: hung left on third: sold 16,500 gns
Doncaster August Sales. *J. W. Watts.*

HOWLING GAEL (USA) 3 b.g. Peterhof (USA) 115–Night of Wind 101   —
(Tumble Wind (USA)) [1988 5d⁵ 5s* 5s⁶ 5g 5m⁶ 5m⁵ 6g 5g 5d 1989 5f 5f 5m 6f 5g 6s]
small, good-quartered gelding: moderate mover: quite modest winner early as 2-y-o
but failed to progress, showing little in handicaps in 1989: best at 5f: blinkered twice
at 2 yrs, on first occasion slowly away: has sweated up: sold 2,800 gns Doncaster
September Sales. *D. W. Chapman.*

HOW'S YER FATHER 3 b.g. Daring March 116–Dawn Ditty 100 (Song 132)   61
[1988 6d³ 5g⁵ 6d⁴ 1989 6s 6s 7m⁶ 6m⁴ 6f² 5m⁵ 5m³ 6m⁵] leggy, sparely-made
gelding: quite modest maiden: in frame in claimers and apprentice handicap: suited
by 5f: acts on any going with possible exception of very soft: blinkered last 4 starts:
edgy fifth and final outings: ran creditably when sweating penultimate one:
bandaged fourth. *P. D. Cundell.*

HOY 4 b.c. Habitat 134–Fairy Tern 109 (Mill Reef (USA) 141) [1988 7g 9g³ 8f* 8f 109
8g* 8m³ 8s² 9s² 9m³ 1989 8g² 9g⁵ 7.2s⁴ 8f²] small colt: has a quick action: very
useful performer: successful in good style in handicaps at Salisbury and Sandown in
1988: in frame in varied events afterwards, in listed contests at Doncaster, Haydock
and Kempton in spring as 4-y-o: stayed 9f well: acted on any going: ran well for 7-lb
claimer: invariably held up and well served by strongly-run race: consistent: sold
66,000 gns Newmarket December Sales to stand at stud in Turkey. *I. A. Balding.*

HUANG TUAH 4 ch.c. Crofthall 110–Dizzy Heights 68 (Daring Display (USA)   50
129) [1988 6m 6s 6d 5.6m 1989 5f² 6f⁶ 6g] workmanlike colt: moderate mover:
½-length second of 14 in claimer at Wolverhampton in May: has faced stiff tasks in
handicaps otherwise since 2 yrs: finds easy 5f on sharp side: acts on firm going and a
soft surface: blinkered once at 3 yrs. *R. Guest.*

HUD 2 b.g. (Apr 17) Prince Tenderfoot (USA) 126–Kingston Rose (Tudor Music   61
131) [1989 5f⁵ 5g* 5m⁶ 5m] 11,000Y: leggy, rather shallow-girthed gelding:
moderate walker and mover: fifth foal: half-brother to 3-y-o Golden Image (by

Bustino) and 2 winners, including fair 1985 2-y-o 5f winner King's Reef (by Main Reef): dam Irish 5f winner: plating-class performer: made all in 2-runner maiden at Salisbury in July: sold 8,200 gns Newmarket Autumn Sales: subsequently gelded. *R. Hannon.*

HUDSON BAY TRADER (USA)   2 b.c. (Feb 7) Sir Ivor 135–Yukon Baby   — p (USA) (Northern Dancer) [1989 7g] $35,000Y: good-topped, attractive colt: has plenty of scope: first foal: dam, unraced close relation of Beaudelaire and daughter of Bitty Girl: 33/1 and in need of race, never dangerous in 29-runner maiden at Newmarket in November. *C. F. Wall.*

HUFOOF   3 b.f. Known Fact (USA) 135–Al Washl (USA) 79 (The Minstrel (CAN)   87 135) [1988 6g* 6f* 6f³ 5d 1989 5f* 5f 5g 5m 6m 5s⁴] angular filly: poor walker: won 4-runner minor event at Beverley in June: ran well at Haydock in £8,100 handicap and minor event third and final outings: effective over 6f and stiff 5f: acted on any going: visits Persian Heights. *H. Thomson Jones.*

HUG   4 ch.f. Ahonoora 122–Nectareous (Tutankhamen) [1988 6v* 8g⁶ 10d⁵ 10d⁶   — 1989 8h 15.8m] big, strong filly: won maiden at Nottingham early as 3-y-o: always behind in handicaps at Carlisle and Catterick in June: stays 1¼m: acts on heavy going and probably unsuited by hard: often flashes tail: a difficult ride: winning hurdler. *G. Richards.*

HUGLI   2 ch.g. (May 12) Relkino 131–Hors Serie (USA) 103 (Vaguely Noble 140)   68 [1989 7f 8m³] well-grown, workmanlike gelding: brother to fairly useful 1½m and 1¾m winner and winning hurdler Bespoke and half-brother to 3-y-o 12.2f winner Wick Pound and ungenuine middle-distance maiden Cock Sparrow (both by Niniski), disqualified 1¼m winner, and 2 other winners: dam stayed 1½m: still bit backward, over 4 lengths third of 5 to Tory Conquest in maiden at Warwick in October: will be well suited by 1¼m+: sold 12,000 gns Newmarket Autumn Sales. *Major W. R. Hern.*

HUJUM   4 b.c. Glenstal (USA) 118–Sea Queen (FR) (Le Fabuleux 133) [1988 8d   — 10g³ 1989 10.1m⁶ 8g] quite an attractive colt: lightly-raced maiden: looked headstrong on reappearance: sold 6,000 gns Newmarket Autumn Sales. *C. J. Benstead.*

HUMALONG   4 b.f. Bay Express 132–Hum 69 (Crooner 119) [1988 7f³ 7g² 7m³   61 7d 8g 1989 10f 7f⁶ 7g² 7f 7m² 7.6m⁵ 6m² 6g] rangy, workmanlike filly: quite modest maiden nowadays: stays 7f well: acts on firm going: has run creditably for lady: trained first 5 starts by S. Christian. *W. G. A. Brooks.*

HUMBER COOPER   4 b.g. Lochnager 132–September Fire (Firestreak 125)   — [1988 NR 1989 9s 12f] strong gelding: no form in modest company: bandaged and sweating final outing. *P. A. Blockley.*

HUNG OVER   3 b.f. Smackover 107–Passionate 57 (Dragonara Palace (USA) 115)   50 [1988 5m 5g³ 5g 1989 6f 5m 6f⁴ 5f 6g⁴ a8g a6g³] leggy, lengthy filly: easily best efforts as 3-y-o in apprentice seller and claimer fifth and final starts: stays 6f: best on an easy surface. *B. A. McMahon.*

HUNKY DORIUS   2 b.f. (Apr 28) Petorius 117–Always Smiling (Prominer 125)   52 § [1989 5f 5m 5m³ 5h³ 5f² 5f³ 6g 5d⁴ 6g 5f⁵] IR 2,600Y: leggy, sparely-made filly: half-sister to winning Irish hurdler Welsh Laughter (by Welsh Saint): dam winning Irish middle-distance stayer: plating-class maiden: will be suited by 7f: blinkered last 5 starts: tends to carry head high, often gets edgy and hasn't ideal attitude. *Capt. J. Wilson.*

HUNSINGLORY   2 b.f. (Apr 20) Prince Ragusa 96–Doyles Folly (Rheingold   — 137) [1989 5f 8m] leggy filly: third reported foal: dam poor daughter of half-sister to Prix de l'Arc de Triomphe winner Bon Mot III: soundly beaten in sellers at Catterick (very slowly away) and Warwick. *D. W. Chapman.*

HUNTER VALLEY   3 b.g. Valiyar 129–Taken By Force (Persian Bold 123)   78 [1988 6g 6m 7f* 1989 7g² 8s 8g 10g* 12f⁵ 10.2g² 12m² 12m* 12m² 12d 13s⁵ 14m 12g⁴] leggy gelding: moderate walker and mover: fair handicapper: won at Salisbury in May and Doncaster (apprentices) in June: held up towards rear last 3 starts, soundly beaten in amateurs event on final one: should stay beyond 13f: probably acts on any going: below best when sweating fifth start: usually on toes after: sometimes wanders under pressure: often claimer ridden: lacks turn of foot. *Mrs J. R. Ramsden.*

HUNTING HORN (USA)   2 b.c. (Mar 1) Northern Dancer–Buzz My Bell   — p (USA) (Drone) [1989 6g] angular, unfurnished colt: good mover: second foal: half-brother to a minor winner by Secretariat: dam one of leading 2-y-o fillies in USA in 1983: 16/1, in mid-division, slowly away and not knocked about, in 28-runner maiden at Newmarket in October: should improve. *M. R. Stoute.*

HUNZA'S CHOICE 2 b.c. (Mar 9) Exhibitioner 111–Romantic Air 62 (He Loves **48** Me 120) [1989 5m⁴ 5m 6m 6m⁵ 6f⁵ 6m 6g⁶ 7f 8f a6g³ a7g] small, rather sparely-made colt: poor maiden: stays 6f: blinkered sixth outing: sold 725 gns Ascot October Sales. *P. Mitchell.*

HURRICANE POWER 2 br.c. (Apr 19) Wolverlife 115–Libby Jayne 67 **— p** (Tumble Wind (USA)) [1989 6f⁵] IR 4,200F, IR 17,500Y: rangy, quite attractive colt: first foal: dam winning sprinter in Ireland at 4 yrs: 4/1, 13 lengths fifth of 11, running green from halfway and not knocked about, to Argentum in minor event at Nottingham in September: sure to improve. *J. P. Hudson.*

HUSYAN (USA) 3 b.c. Alleged (USA) 138–Close Comfort (USA) (Far North **115 p** (CAN)) [1988 NR 1989 7.5g 12g* 10.1g* 12m²] strong, rangy, good sort: second foal: half-brother to 1987 2-y-o 7f winner Gazayil (by Irish River): dam unraced half-sister to very smart French sprinter Cricket Ball and Ancient Regime, leading French 2-y-o filly of 1980 who showed smart form at up to 1m at 3 yrs: won maiden (very green) at Leicester and 23-runner minor event (making all to beat If Memory Serves 2 lengths) at Windsor in August: 7/1, excellent 2 lengths second of 4 to Tralos in Hoover Cumberland Lodge Stakes at Ascot, taking keen hold, driven along over 2f out and battling on splendidly: well suited by 1½m: acts on top-of-the-ground: grand sort, sure to win another race or two. *P. T. Walwyn.*

HYDEONIAN 2 ch.g. (Mar 18) Viking (USA)–Precious Lady (Home Guard **—** (USA) 129) [1989 6f⁵ 7.5f 6m] IR 3,400F, 5,000Y: sparely-made gelding: second foal: dam placed at 6f and 7f in Ireland: well behind in varied races: slowly away first 2 starts: on toes final one. *C. Tinkler.*

HYDEONIUS 4 b.g. Crystal Palace (FR) 132–Razannda (FR) (Labus (FR)) [1988 **46** 8m⁴ 8g 8f⁴ 11m⁵ 1989 10f 8f 10m⁶ 9m⁴ 10m] workmanlike gelding: keen walker: moderate mover: poor maiden: should stay beyond 1¼m: acts on firm going: sometimes sweats: below form for apprentice last start in 1988 and for lady on

Hamdan Al-Maktoum's "Husyan"

second and final ones in 1989: changed hands 2,400 gns Doncaster September Sales: winning hurdler. *J. A. Glover.*

HYDE PRINCESS 4 ch.f. Touch Paper 113–Wild Elk Inn (CAN) (Briartic (CAN)) [1988 5m 5s 5f 6f⁶ 5m⁴ 5d 5m 5f 6m 5f 5g 1989 5d 5m 7m 5f⁵ 5g] smallish, close-coupled filly: has a quick action: successful 3 times as 2-y-o, including in seller: little subsequent worthwhile form: best at 5f: best efforts on good going: visored last 2 outings: suitable mount for apprentice. *R. M. Whitaker.* **41**

HYDRO-ELECTRIC 4 b.f. Electric 126–Lady Spey 55 (Sir Gaylord) [1988 11.5g 1989 10f] no sign of ability. *K. G. Wingrove.* **–**

HYDROPIC 2 b.g. (Apr 22) Kabour 80–Hydrangea 73 (Warpath 113) [1989 7f 8m a8g a7g] second foal: brother to 3-y-o Snydale: dam won from 1½m to 16.5f: quite modest plater: best run at 7f. *D. W. Chapman.* **46**

HYMN OF HARLECH 6 b.g. Welsh Chanter 124–Church Bay 76 (Reliance II 137) [1988 9g* 8g 9m⁵ 8.3m* 8g 8.3m³ 8m³ 7.3m 7m³ 8d 1989 7.6m 8m* 9m 8g² 8m⁵ 8g³ 8m⁵] smallish gelding: has a quick action: fair handicapper: raced alone virtually throughout when winning apprentice event at Newbury in June: bandaged, went too fast early final outing: stays 9f: ideally suited by top-of-the-ground: wears blinkers: occasionally on edge: races up with pace: has looked none too enthusiastic and best handled tenderly. *D. R. C. Elsworth.* **81**

I

I AM ONLY DREAMING 2 b.g. (Feb 21) Dreams To Reality (USA) 113–Safidar 83 (Roan Rocket 128) [1989 8s 8.2s 7v] 5,600F: small, sturdy gelding: fourth reported living foal: half-brother to 3-y-o El Dalsaan (by Dalsaan), 8.2f winner at 2 yrs: dam 1m winner: soundly beaten in maidens. *T. Craig.* **–**

IBN BEY 5 ch.h. Mill Reef (USA) 141–Rosia Bay 102 (High Top 131) [1988 13.3f³ 12f⁴ 12d⁴ 13.3g⁴ 13.5g* 1989 13.3f² 16f⁵ 14f* 12.5m* 13.3g* 12s* 12f⁶] **126**
Three years after his death Mill Reef topped the list of sires of pattern-race winners in Europe. In all, he was responsible for the winners of thirteen pattern races in 1989, two more than Danzig and Nureyev and five more than Blushing Groom and Caerleon. Almost half his wins were provided by Star Lift and Ibn Bey between them, both of whom showed themselves to be better than ever at the age of five. Star Lift's improvement was the easier to foresee, even if his best performances did come over distances much shorter than his eight-length win in the Prix Royal-Oak on his final outing in 1988 suggested they would. Ibn Bey's only attempt over further than a mile and three quarters, in the Mappin & Webb Henry II EBF Stakes at Sandown in May, resulted in his only disappointing effort of the season; he weakened from

Walmac International Geoffrey Freer Stakes, Newbury—
a tremendous duel the length of the straight as Ibn Bey (near side) wears down Apache

*R & V Europa-Preis, Cologne—Ibn Bey, blinkered for the first time,
emphatically denies home-trained Mondrian a clean sweep of the
five Group 1 events in Germany; the grey Sheriff's Star fills the minor place*

two furlongs out and finished over thirteen lengths behind Sadeem in fifth. Ibn
Bey was unbeaten in Europe throughout the remainder of the year, recording
victories in Britain, France and Germany, and it wasn't until his sixth placing
in the Japan Cup in November that he suffered defeat.

After beating the odds-on Mountain Kingdom two lengths in the
three-runner listed Leisure Investments Silver Cup at Lingfield, Ibn Bey was
dispatched along with the Gold Cup fifth Green Adventure to Saint-Cloud to
contest the Prix Maurice de Nieuil. Just as at Lingfield, he went to the front a
quarter of a mile from home, but this time Quinn took matters almost too
easily, eased him up and had his blushes spared by only a short neck, with the
fast-finishing Mardonius pulling three lengths clear of the others. Ibn Bey was
penalized for his Group 1 win in Italy as a three-year-old in the Walmac
International Geoffrey Freer Stakes at Newbury and looked up against it
having to give 6 lb to Apache, who last time had beaten Emmson in a listed
event at Newmarket. The three-year-old Alphabel, runner-up to Warrshan in
the Gordon Stakes at Goodwood, divided the two in the market, but could
never divide them in the race and for the length of the straight Ibn Bey and
Apache were locked in a tremendous battle for the lead. Apache nearly always
looked to be travelling the better, but Ibn Bey refused to accept defeat,
responded to Quinn's persistent driving and inside the last fifty yards edged
his way to the front. He prevailed by a head, with Alphabel three lengths
down. It was third time lucky, as they say, for Ibn Bey in the Geoffrey Freer,
for he'd finished third to Moon Madness and fourth to Top Class in the
previous two years. While Mill Reef topped the pattern-race sires in Europe
this proved, remarkably, his only one of the season in Britain, the majority of
the others being in France.

Ibn Bey, a good mover with a powerful action, had shown his best form
on a sound surface prior to the R & V Europa-Preis at Cologne, in which
Mondrian was seeking to complete a clean-sweep of the five Group 1 races in
Germany. Blinkered for the first time, Ibn Bey coped admirably with the
rain-softened ground and made every post a winning one. Soon four lengths
clear, he was never challenged and had drawn six lengths in front of Mondrian
by the line, with Sheriff's Star another length and a half away in third. This
performance gave Ibn Bey a good chance in the Japan Cup in November, the
race chosen instead of the Prix de l'Arc, and he seemed to be on the upgrade.
In the event he did much better than the other European challengers without
doing enough to impress the locals with the standard of European
middle-distance racing. Blinkered again, he raced very freely and led until
weakening two furlongs out. Apparently he'd lost a fair amount of weight on
his journey.

Ibn Bey cost 210,000 guineas as a yearling. He's the third foal of Rosia
Bay, twice a winner at around a mile and a half-sister to Teleprompter. Rosia

Mr Fahd Salman's "Ibn Bey"

		Never Bend	Nasrullah
	Mill Reef (USA)	(b 1960)	Lalun
	(b 1968)	Milan Mill	Princequillo
Ibn Bey		(b 1962)	Virginia Water
(ch.h. 1984)		High Top	Derring-Do
	Rosia Bay	(b 1969)	Camenae
	(b 1977)	Ouija	Silly Season
		(b or br 1971)	Samanda

Bay, whose first foal Cerise Bouquet (by Mummy's Pet) won over five furlongs as a two-year-old, was also represented in the latest season by the Lancashire Oaks and Yorkshire Oaks winner Roseate Tern (by Blakeney) in whose essay further details of the family can be found. There are definite similarities between Teleprompter, Roseate Tern and Ibn Bey. All are well-built individuals—Ibn Bey is a big, strong horse—and they have all at one time or another looked not the easiest of rides, needing strong handling to bring out the best in them. Teleprompter showed his best form in a visor, Roseate Tern hers in blinkers. It will be interesting to see if the blinkers are persevered with on Ibn Bey. Ibn Bey is effective at a mile and a half to a mile and three quarters; he acts on any going except possibly heavy. He is best ridden up with the leaders and, as he showed in Germany, can be at least as effective making the pace as he is tracking it. Tremendously tough and genuine, he has sweated up on occasions. *P. F. I. Cole.*

IBN NAAS (USA) 3 ch.c. Diesis 133–La Vie (USA) (Le Fabuleux 133) [1988 7d 8m³ 1989 12s⁴ 9f] rather sparely-made, attractive colt: quite modest form: should be suited by middle distances: possibly unsuited by track at Chester on debut: sold 2,100 gns Newmarket Autumn Sales: of doubtful temperament. *B. Hanbury.*   **62**

IBN SINA (USA) 2 b.c. (Feb 20) Dr Blum (USA)–Two On One (CAN) (Lord **88**
Durham (CAN)) [1989 6f 7m² 8g³] $50,000Y: lengthy, well-made colt: has a rather
round action: fourth foal: half-brother to winners in North America, one in minor
stakes: dam minor winner at up to 9f: progressive form: 8 lengths third of 16 to
Belmez in minor event at Newmarket in November: will stay 1¼m. *P. F. I. Cole.*

IBN ZAMAN (USA) 3 b.c. Graustark–Wake Robin (Summer Tan) [1988 NR —
1989 10.1m 12m⁵ 14m⁶] $210,000F: sturdy, useful-looking colt: tenth foal: brother to
1986 Breeders' Cup Classic and Florida Derby winner Proud Truth, American 9f
winner The Real Truth and half-brother to winners by Bold Lad (USA) and Arts And
Letters: dam won twice at up to 1m: slow maiden: 9/1 from 20/1, lost place on turn
when sixth at Yarmouth in June: likely to need forcing tactics over 1¾m +: sold
2,400 gns Newmarket Autumn Sales. *A. A. Scott.*

ICARNAFORDIT 2 b.f. (May 19) The Dissident 85–Italian Summer 83 (Silly —
Season 127) [1989 7f 8.2f] second foal: dam's best form over 5f at 2 yrs: well beaten
in claimer at Salisbury and seller at Nottingham in September. *W. G. M. Turner.*

ICARUS (USA) 3 b.g. Wind And Wuthering (USA) 132–Cedar Waxwing (USA) **66**
(Tom Fool) [1988 6s⁶ 7.5f 6s⁵ 9f⁵ 10d² 1989 12.3m 10.2f 10.6g³ 11.7m⁶ 12.4g] sturdy
gelding: modest performer: third in amateurs handicap at Haydock, best effort as
3-y-o: off course over 4 months before final start: stays 10.6f: acts on a soft surface:
lacks a turn of foot: trained until after penultimate start by S. Norton. *M. H.
Easterby.*

ICE BREAKER (FR) 6 b.h. Arctic Tern (USA) 126–Figure de Proue (FR) —
(Petingo 135) [1988 10g 12.2g⁶ 12.2f⁶ 11d* 10m 10g 12m 1989 8g 12d] rather leggy,
good-topped horse: moderate mover: poor handicapper: stays 11f: seems to need a
soft surface nowadays. *J. S. Haldane.*

ICELANDER 3 b.c. Kris 135–Oh So Fair (USA) (Graustark) [1988 NR 1989 12g* **99**
14f*] big, strong, lengthy, fine stamp of colt: brother to fillies triple crown winner
Oh So Sharp and half-brother to numerous other winners, including very smart 5f to
1¼m winner Roussalka, 1000 Guineas second Our Home (both by Habitat) and 1¾m
winner Fame And Glory (by Shareef Dancer): dam won over 1¼m in Ireland:
favourite though green and better for race, impressive winner of maiden at
Doncaster, held up: 7/4 on, made all when beating shade unlucky stable-companion
Knifeboard ¾ length in minor event at York later in May: stays well: has plenty of
scope. *H. R. A. Cecil.*

Lambson Chemical Stakes, York — Icelander looks a good prospect but isn't seen out again

ICE MAGIC   2 ch.c. (Mar 8) Red Sunset 120–Free Rein (Sagaro 133) [1989 6m^3 **58**
6m^4 6f^6] 11,000Y: lengthy, useful-looking colt: second reported foal: brother to
modest 1m winner Sunset Reins Free who stays 1½m: dam, unraced, from family of
Troy: quite modest maiden: best effort second start: not at all knocked about final
one: bred to stay at least 1m. *P. Calver.*

ICE QUEEN   3 ro.f. Kings Lake (USA) 133–Ica (Great Nephew 126) [1988 6g^6 **85**
1989 7.3s^5 10s^4] useful-looking filly: 10/1 and bit backward, over 11 lengths fifth of 10
to Pass The Peace in Group 3 event at Newbury, unable to quicken and tending to
wander over 2f out: below form in maiden at Sandown in April having joined leaders
on bridle 3f out: may prove suited by 1m. *B. W. Hills.*

ICONA (USA)   3 ch.c. Green Dancer (USA) 132–Flyingtrip (USA) (Vaguely **119**
Noble 140) [1988 8d^6 8.2d^2 1989 10s* 11d^2 12f^3 12m* 12m^5 10.5f* 10g*]
sparely-made colt: usually looks well: has a quick action: easy winner of maiden at
Leicester in April and £7,400 ladies race at York in June: continued to progress,
putting up smart performances when winning John Smith's Magnet Cup (Handicap)
at York by neck from Afriyd and listed James Seymour Stakes, making most and
quickening clear 2f out, at Newmarket nearly 4 months later by ½ length from
Rambo's Hall: stays 1½m: acts on any going: game and consistent: reportedly sold
to race abroad. *M. R. Stoute.*

IDLE CHAT (USA)   2 ch.f. (Feb 15) Assert 134–Gossiping (USA) (Chati (USA)) **82** p
[1989 8.2f* 7g] workmanlike filly: has scope: second foal: dam, 6f winner in USA, is
half-sister to Committed: made all in 6-runner minor event at Nottingham in
September, beating Liffey Lace comfortably by 2 lengths: carrying condition, never
dangerous in Bottisham Heath Stud Rockfel Stakes at Newmarket following month:
will stay 1¼m: looks sort to do better at 3 yrs. *B. W. Hills.*

IF MEMORY SERVES (USA)   3 b.c. Youth (USA) 135–Royal Recall (USA) **106** p
(Native Royalty (USA)) [1988 NR 1989 7m* 10.1g^2 10m 10g*] leggy colt: second
foal: half-brother to 1987 USA stakes-placed 2-y-o winner Phantom Knight (by
Fairway Phantom): dam won once at about 6f at 3 yrs in USA: won maiden at York in
July and competitive minor event at Leicester in November, in latter short of room

John Smith's Magnet Cup, York—stable-companions Icona and Afriyd have it between them

*Queen Mother's Cup, York—Icona lands the odds
in the season's most valuable race for lady riders*

over 1f out and rather idling in front when beating Marcinkus ½ length: ran moderately third start: stays 1¼m well: can progress further. *J. H. M. Gosden.*

IJAZAH 5 b.m. Touching Wood (USA) 127–Soubrette (Habat 127) [1988 12f 14m 12h 1989 16.5f] small, sparely-made mare: lightly raced and little sign of ability: wore net muzzle and pulled hard only outing at 5 yrs: has worn a crossed noseband. *R. Curtis.*   —

IJTIHAAD (USA) 2 b.c. (Feb 18) Arctic Tern (USA) 126–Corita (Satingo 129) [1989 8m³] 140,000F, 270,000Y: rangy, attractive colt: has plenty of scope: brother to French 1¼m winner Tortosa: dam won 1¼m Premio Legnano: favourite, under 2 lengths third of 8, staying on well after running green, to Treble Eight in maiden at Newmarket in October: will stay 1¼m: sure to improve, and win a race. *Major W. R. Hern.*   **96 p**

IKDAM 4 b.c. Glint of Gold 128–Run To The Sun (Run The Gantlet (USA)) [1988 11g 11.7g 11.7m⁵ 14.7f* 12g* 11f* 12f⁴ 14.6g 1989 18g⁴ 16s³ 17.6d 17.4s⁵ 16m 18g] quite attractive, good-bodied colt: usually looks really well: fluent mover: modest winner as 3-y-o when trained by P. Walwyn: in frame, running creditably, in handicaps at Doncaster and Newbury in spring: off course 4½ months afterwards and well beaten last 4 outings: needs extreme test of stamina nowadays: acts on any going: blinkered last 2 outings: won Daily Express Triumph Hurdle at Cheltenham in March. *R. J. Holder.*   **74**

IKRAAJ 2 b.c. (Mar 18) Auction Ring (USA) 123–Crepe de Paille (Final Straw 127) [1989 7m³ 6f³ 6m³ 7m⁵ 5g] 22,000F, 30,000Y: good-bodied, useful-looking colt: first foal: dam should have stayed 1m+: plating-class maiden: visored in nurseries last 2 starts, running freely on final outing: stays 7f. *D. Morley.*   **59**

ILCHESTER (USA) 3 b.c. Seattle Song (USA) 130–Tahiche (USA) 81 (Topsider (USA)) [1988 8d 1989 8m 10.1m 14m 12m³ 16f²] lengthy, rather sparely-made colt: has a quick action: led 13f when second in maiden claimer at Redcar in August: suited by 2m. *W. A. O'Gorman.*   **58**

ILDERTON ROAD 2 br.f. (Jan 23) Noalto 120–Mac's Melody (Wollow 132) [1989 8v] lengthy filly: fourth foal: half-sister to 3-y-o Mean To Me (by Homing): dam ran once at 2 yrs: 33/1 and backward, prominent to halfway in 23-runner minor event at Newbury in October. *Mrs Barbara Waring.*   —

419

ILE DE CHYPRE   4 b.c. Ile de Bourbon (USA) 133–Salamina 106 (Welsh **128** Pageant 132) [1988 12g² 12f 12g² 10.5g³ 12g* 12s 10f* 9g² 1989 8g 10m² 10m* 12g² 10m² 10.5f* 10g³ 12f]

Ile de Chypre's fame had already spread to North America before his arrival for the Breeders' Cup Turf at Gulfstream Park in November. But it wasn't Ile de Chypre's racing record that was the principal interest. The horse was figuring at the time in a sensational court case in London in which it was claimed that he had been 'nobbled' by an ultrasonic device in the King George V Handicap at Royal Ascot in 1988. The jury in the case—which involved an alleged conspiracy to supply cocaine—watched a video of the race which showed Ile de Chypre, in a clear lead, veering badly left and unseating his rider close home. One of the defendants in the case, denying the serious drugs charges, claimed his only involvement with the so-called 'mastermind' of a £15m cocaine ring was in a plot to win money gambling. It was claimed that a 'sonic gun' concealed in a pair of binoculars had been used to send Ile de Chypre out of control (the gun allegedly worked by emitting a high frequency sound undetectable to the human ear). During the case the device was tested for the benefit of the court on three ponies—provided by Ile de Chypre's jockey Starkey—and two were said to have behaved erratically. The jury had to decide whether the story they heard was just a smokescreen to divert attention from involvement in a drugs ring—in the case of one defendant they decided it was—but there were serious implications for racing. Was the gun actually used at Royal Ascot, and did it change the course of the King George V Handicap? Informed opinion within racing was sceptical of the claims made during the court hearing. The defendants changed their evidence about the position from which the device was allegedly used (originally said to be one hundred and seventy feet from where Ile de Chypre's rider fell). The Ascot course is seventy-six feet wide at the point where Ile de Chypre swerved, and the defendant who claimed to be the inventor of the 'sonic gun' had said it had a range of only fifty feet. How could the gang have been sure of hitting the selected animal? How, in any case, could they have profited greatly by 'nobbling' Ile de Chypre, the second favourite in a very open eighteen-runner handicap? At the time of writing the Jockey Club was hoping it would be possible to test the equipment at the Animal Health Trust.

Tattersalls EBF Rogers Gold Cup, the Curragh—Ile de Chypre makes virtually all to win from Executive Perk, Carroll House and Per Quod

Juddmonte International Stakes, York—
Ile de Chypre floors the odds laid on his stable companion Cacoethes

Ile de Chypre showed plenty of temperament as a three-year-old when, at one time, he seemed to have his own ideas about the game. He carried his head high and failed to go through with his effort on at least two occasions. But Ile de Chypre showed ability as well as temperament, winning twice and finishing a good second in the William Hill Cambridgeshire. He began the latest season a very useful handicapper, starting favourite under top weight for the William Hill Lincoln Handicap on his reappearance. By the end of an eight-race campaign—he came a creditable ninth, leading for a long way, in the Breeders' Cup Turf—he was established among the leading middle-distance horses in Europe. With his temperament problems behind him, Ile de Chypre made a successful transition to pattern-race company, winning the Tattersalls EBF Rogers Gold Cup at the Curragh in May and the Juddmonte International at York in August, and gaining a place in the Hanson Coronation Cup at Epsom (half a length second to Sheriff's Star), the William Hill Classic at Ayr (beaten a length by Scenic) and the Dubai Champion Stakes at Newmarket (third, a head and a short head behind Legal Case and Dolpour). Ile de Chypre does best when allowed to stride along and he was enterprisingly ridden in the Rogers Gold Cup and the International. He made virtually all and galloped on very strongly to beat Executive Perk by three lengths at the Curragh and had a length and a half to spare over his injudiciously-ridden, odds-on stable-companion Cacoethes at York where Clark (who was also in the saddle at the Curragh) rode a well-judged race on the 16/1-shot, stretching the field from early in the straight after Two Timing had set a good gallop, and keeping enough in reserve to respond when challenged by Cacoethes.

The strong, rangy, attractive Ile de Chypre carries plenty of condition. His sire Ile de Bourbon, now in Japan, finished sixth in the list of sires of winners in Britain and Ireland in 1989 when his winners also included Petite Ile, successful in the Jefferson Smurfit Memorial Irish St Leger, and the splendidly genuine and consistent Beau Sher. Ile de Chypre's dam Salamina, a

Mr Athos Christodoulou's "Ile de Chypre"

Ile de Chypre (b.c. 1985)	Ile de Bourbon (USA) (br 1975)	Nijinsky (b 1967)	Northern Dancer Flaming Page
		Roseliere (br 1965)	Misti IV Peace Rose
	Salamina (ch 1978)	Welsh Pageant (b 1966)	Tudor Melody Picture Light
		Femme Elite (ro 1969)	Young Emperor Fairy Flax

granddaughter of the high-class sprinter Fairy Flax, won at five and six furlongs as a two-year-old and at a mile at three, when she gave the impression she would have stayed further. Ile de Chypre is Salamina's third foal, following the modest middle-distance winners King Tefkros (by Star Appeal) and Tamassos (by Dance In Time); Salamina's fourth foal Halkopous (by Beldale Flutter) showed fair form in handicaps at middle distances in the latest season, winning at Haydock, Kempton and York. King Tefkros, Tamassos and Halkopous acted on any going, but Ile de Chypre needs a sound surface and acts very well on firm going. The thoroughly tough, genuine and consistent Ile de Chypre stays in training. He should continue to do well in good company at a mile and a quarter, at which distance his connections have announced he'll be campaigned. *G. Harwood.*

ILE DE NISKY 3 b.c. Ile de Bourbon (USA) 133–Good Lass (FR) (Reform 132) **116**
[1988 8d* 1989 10.2m* 12g⁴ 12g³ 10g² 10g⁶] big, rather sparely-made colt: has a very powerful, round action: won minor event at Doncaster in May: in frame in

strongly-run Ever Ready Derby at Epsom (7½ lengths behind Nashwan) and Budweiser Irish Derby at the Curragh (6½ lengths behind Old Vic): off course 3 months then bit below best in listed race (length behind Monastery) at Goodwood and Champion Stakes (beaten about 8 lengths) at Newmarket: better at 1½m than 1¼m, and should stay further: acts on top-of-the-ground and a soft surface: smart. *G. A. Huffer.*

ILE DE REINE 3 b.f. Ile de Bourbon (USA) 133–Fair Fight 84 (Fine Blade (USA) 121) [1988 7m 1989 11.7d 12f⁴ 14f] big, rangy filly: 7½ lengths fourth in maiden at Chepstow in May, leading over 1m: favourite, tailed off in handicap 2 weeks later, pulling hard, leading 1m out, soon ridden and finding nothing: should stay middle distances: has ability but is temperamental and not one to trust. *H. Candy.* — §

ILE DE ROI 6 b.h. Ile de Bourbon (USA) 133–Regal Lady (FR) 93 (Relko 136) [1988 14f* 14d² 16.1d² 14f 18f⁴ 1989 12.2s 17.1m² 18f* 16f²] big, rather angular horse: carries plenty of condition: powerful mover: fair handicapper: led on bridle over 2f out when winning at Doncaster in May: never looked likely to catch sole opponent Princess Sobieska at Ripon over 3 weeks later: stays 2¼m: probably not at his best on soft going, acts on any other: apprentice ridden last 2 starts. *F. J. Yardley.* — 87

ILE DE ROMA 2 b.c. (Apr 18) Ile de Bourbon (USA) 133–Romara 105 (Bold Lad (IRE) 133) [1989 7g² 7m³ 8s*] good-bodied colt: has scope: sixth living foal: half-brother to 3-y-o 1m and 1¼m winner Halstead (by Bustino) and 4 other winners, including smart 6f and 1¼m winner Ela Romara (by Ela-Mana-Mou): dam won over 7f and 1m: fair performer: won maiden at Ayr in September by 2 lengths from King's Shilling, staying on well last 2f: will stay 1¼m: tends to carry head high. *G. Wragg.* — 78

ILE NOIRE 3 b.f. Ile de Bourbon (USA) 133–Noirmont Girl 95 (Skymaster 126) [1988 7f 7m 1989 10s 10m 8.5m⁴ 7g 9g] sparely-made, workmanlike filly: —

H. H. Prince Yazid Saud's "Ile de Nisky"

plating-class maiden: sign of ability only on third start: apprentice ridden otherwise, edgy and pulling hard when tailed off time before: appears suited by 1m. *M. J. Ryan.*

ILEWIN 2 br.c. (May 8) Ile de Bourbon (USA) 133–City Swinger (Derrylin 115) — [1989 a7g a8g a8g] sturdy colt: second foal: dam, of little account, is half-sister to smart 5f sprinter Bold And Free and good sprinter Watergate: well behind in Southwell maidens and claimer late in season. *J. Wharton.*

I'LL SOON KNOW 2 ch.f. (Jan 30) Known Fact (USA) 135–Soolyn (Dominion 48 123) [1989 5m⁴ 6g 6d] smallish, angular filly: third foal: dam ran 4 times at 2 yrs: plating-class maiden: unfavourably drawn last 2 starts: bred to stay beyond 6f. *R. J. Holder.*

ILLUSORY 2 b.f. (Feb 8) Kings Lake (USA) 133–Bold Fantasy 115 (Bold Lad 81 p (IRE) 133) [1989 5m³ 6d²] strong, good-bodied filly: has plenty of scope: sister to Lowther Stakes winner Kingscote and half-sister to Irish 5f winner Fantasy Land (by Nonoalco) and French 9f winner Esna (by Troy): dam Irish 7f winner second in Irish 1000 Guineas: 2 lengths second of 24 to Notley in October, better effort in maidens at Newbury: very green on debut over 4 months earlier: will stay 1m: can improve further. *J. Tree.*

IMHOTEP 2 gr.c. (May 8) Claude Monet (USA) 121–Miss Melmore (Nishapour 73 (FR) 125) [1989 5s⁴ 6m 6m⁵ 6g² 8g 6f³ 6m 7g] tall, workmanlike colt: has scope: first living foal: dam placed over 6f in Ireland: modest maiden: best effort in nursery fourth start: should stay further than 6f: best form on good ground: trained first 2 starts by W. Kemp. *A. M. Robson.*

IMMORTAL IRISH 4 b.g. Lord Gayle (USA) 124–Royal Meath 83 (Realm 129) — [1988 10m⁶ 1989 9f 12m 8.3m⁴ 10m 9m] rather sparely-made ex-Irish gelding: fourth foal: dam, 6f winner at 2 yrs in Ireland, is out of half-sister to very smart middle-distance performer Knockroe: fourth of 15 in seller at Windsor in July: never a threat in handicaps at Beverley (stiff task, didn't have clear run) and Kempton (apprentices) afterwards: stays 1m: keen sort: winning hurdler. *D. R. Gandolfo.*

IMMOTIVE 4 ch.c. Great Nephew 126–Affirmative 96 (Derring-Do 131) [1988 66 10s³ 8d* 10.2m⁴ 1989 12s⁴] medium-sized colt: moderate mover: modest winner at 3 yrs: never able to challenge in handicap at Thirsk in April: probably stays 1½m: yet to race on firm going, acts on any other. *B. A. McMahon.*

IMPALA LASS 6 b.m. Kampala 120–Sheil-Na-Gig 63 (Ridan (USA)) [1988 5g⁵ 81 + 5s² 5v⁶ 5f* 5m² 5m 5d² 5g* 5d⁵ 5g 5m² 5g⁶ 5s 5m⁴ 1989 5m⁶ 5g 5g* 5g⁵ 5m 5d 5d] good-bodied mare: carries condition: showed improved form when winning £8,500 handicap at Epsom in August: facing stiff task, appeared to run very well when fifth to Statoblest in listed event at Doncaster: below that form after in listed race and handicaps: very speedy and races only at 5f nowadays: acts on any going, but soft going taxes her stamina: sometimes edges right, but has won for apprentice. *B. A. McMahon.*

IMPERIAL FLAME 3 b.f. Imperial Lantern–Three Terns (Seaepic (USA) 100) — [1988 NR 1989 6s 8d 8m 5m 6f⁶ 5m⁶] compact, rather sparely-made filly: second foal: dam never ran: behind in sellers and handicaps: pulls hard and looks difficult ride. *D. W. Chapman.*

IMPERIAL FLIGHT 4 b.g. Pampabird 124–Queen of Time (Charlottown 127) — [1988 7g⁴ 8d² 8f⁵ 7g⁶ 10g⁵ 1989 10f] strong, good-topped gelding: modest maiden at his best: 20/1, always behind in Salisbury handicap in September: stays 1m. *P. G. Bailey.*

IMPERIAL FRIEND 5 b.m. Imperial Fling (USA) 116–Happy Donna 106 43 (Huntercombe 133) [1988 7g* 7m³ 7d 8g* 8f⁴ 7f 8s 1989 6v 8d 6f 7.6f 7g⁴ 8.3m 8m³ 8f 7d] deep-bodied mare: poor handicapper: better suited by 1m than 7f: best form on a sound surface, but not on very firm going: has won for apprentice: trained until after seventh outing by C. Hill. *R. J. Hodges.*

IMPERIAL GLORY 4 b.g. Ahonoora 122–Sovereign Bloom (Florescence 120) — [1988 8m⁵ 7g³ 1989 6d] rather leggy gelding: extremely lightly raced but has shown a little ability in maidens and minor event: pulled hard second start at 3 yrs. *S. Mellor.*

IMPERIAL TORTE 3 b.g. Bold Lad (IRE) 133–Borshch (Bonne Noel 115) [1988 — NR 1989 11f⁵] IR 12,000F, 16,500Y: second foal: dam, lightly raced in Ireland, is from family of Arctique Royal and Ardross: weak 10/1, 13¾ lengths fifth of 17, close up over 9f, to Val Recit in maiden at Newbury in May: subsequently gelded: sold 1,500 gns Ascot September Sales. *G. Harwood.*

IMPETULENCE   3 ch.f. Kind of Hush 118–Longgoe 70 (Lorenzaccio 130) [1988   —
NR 1989 8.2m 10m 10f 7m] rather sparely-made filly: has a slightly round action:
third foal: dam showed some ability at 2 yrs but little at 3 yrs: no worthwhile form
though has shown signs of ability: may prove best at short of 1¼m: appears
somewhat temperamental. *R. Dickin.*

IMPORTANT GUEST   2 b.f. (Feb 9) Be My Guest (USA) 126–Riboule 69   53
(Ribero 126) [1989 8f 7f⁶] 20,000F: medium-sized, unfurnished filly: moderate
walker and mover: closely related to fairly useful 1985 2-y-o 6f winner North King
(by Northfields): dam won over 1½m and is half-sister to good middle-distance filly
Shebeen: better effort in Midlands maidens on debut: bred to stay middle distances.
I. V. Matthews.

IMPUNITY   4 b.g. Blakeney 126–Lantern Light 86 (Le Levanstell 122) [1988 10v   42
11.7f⁶ 12m 11d 8m⁶ 10d⁴ 12.3s 1989 12d⁴ 12g 12f⁴ 12h³ 18h² 15f⁴ 12f⁵ 15.8m² 16f⁵ 14f]
neat gelding: moderate mover: poor maiden: stays 2¼m: acts on hard going and a
soft surface: visored seventh outing (hung right under pressure and didn't look
keen) and final 2 starts at 3 yrs: reluctant at stalls on reappearance: often apprentice
ridden nowadays. *R. M. Whitaker.*

INAAD   5 b.h. Mill Reef (USA) 141–Rambling Rose 118 (Silly Season 127) [1988 9g   93
9d³ 8g* 8f 10d⁶ 10m* 10g* 1989 9f³ 10f* 10g⁵ 12f 10m³ 10.5m²] rather leggy, quite
attractive horse: usually looks very well: good mover: fairly useful handicapper:
well-backed favourite, won £20,100 Zetland Gold Cup (Handicap) at Redcar in May:
off course 3 months after fourth outing and returned in good form: neck second of
10, staying on well, to Halkopous at York: much better suited by 1¼m than shorter,
and should stay 1½m: best form on a sound surface: has run creditably for
inexperienced rider: suited by strong gallop. *H. Thomson Jones.*

INBIHAR   2 br.f. (May 15) Doulab (USA) 115–Silojoka 95 (Home Guard (USA)   —
129) [1989 6g] fourth foal: half-sister to 3-y-o Sakkbah (by Wassl) and quite
moderate middle-distance winner Yamrah (by Milford): dam sprinting daughter of
half-sister to very smart Golden Horus: 33/1, well-beaten seventh of 15 to Childrey
in maiden at Folkestone in October: sold 1,000 gns Newmarket Autumn Sales. *C. J.
Benstead.*

INCOLA   3 b.g. Liboi (USA) 76–Sdenka (FR) 79 (Habitat 134) [1988 NR 1989 7f⁵   —
a 10g] small, angular gelding: ninth foal: brother to quite modest 1m winner Mansio:
dam placed over 7f: showed promise in maiden at Lingfield in October, running on
steadily: ridden by 7-lb claimer, soundly beaten in maiden claimer there 2 months
later. *H. Candy.*

INCREDIBLE LADY   4 gr.f. Rusticaro (FR) 124–Lady d'Arbanville (FR)   —
(Luthier 126) [1988 7s⁴ 7g 10f 1989 12.5f 10f 8f] leggy, close-coupled filly: moderate
mover: fair plater at 2 yrs: lightly raced and very little subsequent form: stays 1m:
best form on top-of-the-ground: occasionally on toes: trained until after second
outing by H. O'Neill: has found little. *J. D. Czerpak.*

INDELIBLE MARK   3 b.c. Bustino 136–Current Pattie (USA) 102 (Little   — p
Current (USA)) [1988 NR 1989 10g⁵ 10g] lengthy, attractive colt: third foal:
half-brother to fairly useful 1¼m and 1½m winner Timothy's Toy (by High Top):
dam, out of half-sister to dam of Nonoalco, fourth in Cheveley Park Stakes on
second of 2 starts at 2 yrs, well beaten as 3-y-o: 12/1, stayed on steadily after slow
start when in mid-division in maiden at Epsom in June: pulled hard and saddle
slipped in £5,700 maiden at Newmarket following month: may be capable of better.
C. E. Brittain.

INDIANA SCARLETT   2 ch.f. (Apr 14) Blazing Saddles (AUS)–Littleton Song   —
73 (Song 132) [1989 6g] compact filly: moderate walker: third foal: dam, 6f winner at
2 yrs, is closely related to quite useful sprinter Chin-Chin: 33/1 and in need of race,
slowly away and behind in 22-runner maiden at Leicester in November. *C. A.
Horgan.*

INDIAN CHIEF   2 b.c. (Apr 11) Indian King (USA) 128–Gay Broad 78 (Gay   75
Fandango (USA) 132) [1989 5d⁵ 6g 6m⁴ 6h* 6v] IR 8,400Y: strong, useful-looking
colt: has plenty of scope: good walker: moderate mover: third foal: half-brother to
winners in Hong Kong and France: dam won over 7f at 3 yrs: modest performer:
made all in 3-runner maiden at Brighton in August: carrying condition, well beaten
in nursery at Newbury nearly 3 months later. *R. Hannon.*

INDIAN FASHION (USA)   2 ch.f. (May 14) General Holme (USA) 128–Your   71
Place Or Mine (USA) (Pass Catcher (USA)) [1989 6g a8g⁴ a8g²] $16,000Y:
sparely-made filly: half-sister to minor winners in USA: dam very useful at 3 yrs,

when successful at up to 9f: progressive filly: 2 lengths second of 13 to Barkston Singer in late-year maiden at Southwell: stays 1m. *M. A. Jarvis.*

INDIAN MAESTRO 3 b.g. Music Maestro 119–Indian Wells (Reliance II 137) **74**
[1988 7g⁴ 7g 7g⁵ 6g³ 1989 6m* 7m 6h² 8h⁵ 6m* 7g 6g⁴ 7m⁴ 7g⁵] leggy, angular gelding: modest handicapper: won at Carlisle (making all) in May and Yarmouth (apprentices, hanging right) in July: ridden by 7-lb claimer and below form after, running on never placed to challenge last 2 starts: suited by 6f: acts on hard going: retained 25,000 gns Doncaster May Sales after reappearance. *R. Guest.*

INDIAN PLUME 2 b.g. (Mar 8) Commanche Run 133–Fettle (Relkino 131) **65 p**
[1989 7m³] 31,000F, 21,000Y: fourth foal: half-brother to 3-y-o 7f winner Fettle Flame (by Gorytus) and 1986 2-y-o 6f winner Khakis Love (by Dominion): dam unraced half-sister to Circus Plume: 9/4 and green, over 5 lengths third of 4, outpaced final 3f, to Cashtal Dazzler in minor event at Newcastle in June: may improve. *M. H. Easterby.*

INDIAN QUEEN 4 ch.f. Electric 126–Taj Princess 88 (Taj Dewan 128) [1988 **111**
8s* 8.5d⁴ 10g⁴ 10m² 8.3m 10d* 10g* 9g* 12g* 1989 8g 12s 10f⁴ 10g* 10d⁴ 10d³ 9.2g 12s*] leggy, quite good-topped filly: very useful performer: won Group 3 Premio Legnano at Milan in June and Group 2 EBF Blandford Stakes at the Curragh (making most to beat Tursanah ½ length) in October: on toes, creditable third of 5, never a threat, to Legal Case in Select Stakes at Goodwood, best effort in between: needs further than 1m and stays 1½m: well suited by give in the ground: usually blinkered or visored: has run creditably when sweating: has won for apprentice. *W. Hastings-Bass.*

INDIAN RIDGE 4 ch.c. Ahonoora 122–Hillbrow 100 (Swing Easy (USA) **123**
126) [1988 7f* 6d 7.3g⁶ 8g⁶ 1989 6f* 5f* 6.5d⁵]
Shortly after Ahonoora died in September it was announced that Indian Ridge would be his first son to stand at stud in England. It was hoped that Ahonoora could be saved after he fractured his near-hind pastern in a paddock accident while at the Segenhoe Stud in New South Wales, but complications developed and he had to be put down. Ahonoora showed his best form as a four-year-old, when he won the King George Stakes at Goodwood and was awarded the William Hill Sprint Championship at York on the disqualification of Thatching. His qualifications weren't the best and he began his stallion duties at the Irish National Stud at a fee of just IR £2,250 in 1980. Mainly as a result of the performances of Don't Forget Me, Park Express and Park Appeal, he was bought by Coolmore in 1987 for IR £7 million and by the time of what turned out to be his final season in Ireland his fee had shot up to IR 40,000 guineas. He was a good stallion and in the latest season he was also represented by Statoblest, Negligent, Armanasco and old Noora Abu. Indian Ridge is to begin his new career at the Campbell Stud at Elmswell Park on the outskirts of Bury St Edmunds, at a fee of 5,000 guineas with the October 1st concession.

Indian Ridge, at his best, showed form at least as good as Ahonoora's and he goes to stud with the distinction of being a pattern-race winner at five, six and seven furlongs and a winner at Royal Ascot two years in succession. As a three-year-old Indian Ridge took the Jersey Stakes on his reappearance, after which he disappointed and failed to make the frame in three outings. Next time round Indian Ridge went to Royal Ascot already the winner of the Duke of York Stakes in which he gave weight to all nine rivals except Handsome Sailor—the winner of the race the two previous years— and had behind him, amongst others, Gallic League, Point of Light, Chummy's Favourite and Nabeel Dancer. Always in the first three, Indian Ridge quickened to lead a furlong out and stayed on well, despite edging left, to beat Gallic League and Nabeel Dancer a shade comfortably by a length and a half.

With Kerrera, Cadeaux Genereux and Handsome Sailor all a long way below form, Indian Ridge, a heavily-backed favourite, didn't have to be at his best to win a substandard running of the King's Stand Stakes. Brought back to five furlongs for the first time since finishing runner-up to Warning on his debut as a two-year-old, Indian Ridge looked in splendid shape at Royal Ascot, just as at York. He was again ridden up with the pace, took a narrow advantage with a quarter of a mile to run and held off a succession of challenges before accounting for Tigani and Gallic League by a neck and a head. In winning the

King's Stand Stakes, Ascot—Indian Ridge narrowly holds Tigani (noseband) and Gallic League to win for the second year in succession at the Royal meeting

King's Stand he emulated his grandsire Swing Easy, who beat Mummy's Pet in the mud in 1971, and went one better than his sire, who was beaten by Double Form in 1979. Indian Ridge's season again petered out after Royal Ascot. He ran just once more, finishing fifth to Cricket Ball when odds on in the Prix Maurice de Gheest at Deauville.

Indian Ridge (ch.c. 1985)	⎧ Ahonoora ⎪ (ch 1975)	⎧ Lorenzaccio ⎪ (ch 1965)	⎧ Klairon ⎨ Phoenissa
	⎨	⎨ Helen Nichols ⎪ (ch 1966)	⎧ Martial ⎨ Quaker Girl
	⎪ Hillbrow ⎩ (ch 1975)	⎧ Swing Easy ⎪ (b 1968)	⎧ Delta Judge ⎨ Free Flowing
		⎩ Golden City (ch 1970)	⎧ Skymaster ⎨ West Shaw

Indian Ridge is the third foal out of Hillbrow, who failed to train on after winning twice over six furlongs as a two-year-old. Hillbrow's only other winner to date is the 1986 two-year-old six-furlong winner Plague O'Rats (by Pitskelly). Her latest foal to reach the course is Lady Ellen, a filly by Horage, who has shown modest form in maiden company. Hillbrow has a yearling filly by Petorius. Indian Ridge's grandam Golden City is a winning half-sister to Marisela, runner-up in the Cheveley Park Stakes and the One Thousand Guineas. Indian Ridge, a good walker and quick-actioned galloper, was effective from five to seven furlongs. Although he won on soft ground as a two-year-old, he ran easily his best races on firm; he was best allowed to stride on. His trainer, to whom sprinters and staying chasers come alike, was quoted as saying that Indian Ridge would have made a top-class miler had he learnt to settle. A lengthy, good-quartered colt, Indian Ridge ran particularly well when fresh. *D. R. C. Elsworth.*

INDIAN SET 5 b.m. Windjammer (USA)–Bourges (FR) (Luthier 126) [1988 6d   42 d
7f⁵ 6f 6m 7m 8g 8f 5f 6g⁴ 1989 6v⁴ 7.5d² 8d 7g 8.2d 7d a8g a14g] lengthy, leggy mare: has stringhalt: has a round action: poor handicapper: failed to get up by short head at Beverley in April after being slowly away and pushed along early: off course 5 months after next outing: well beaten in second half of season, usually facing stiff task: stays 7.5f well: best form with give in the ground: visored once at 4 yrs: has run creditably when sweating: usually apprentice ridden nowadays. *P. Howling.*

INDIAN SKIMMER (USA)   5 gr.m. Storm Bird (CAN) 134–Nobiliare **121**
(USA) (Vaguely Noble 140) [1988 10d³ 10g⁴ 10.5f² 10d* 10g* 10g* 12g³ 1989
10s* 9.2g* 10g³]

Another year on, at least one more comparison can be drawn between
the two outstanding Warren Place greys Petite Etoile and Indian Skimmer: as
with the former at five the decision to keep Indian Skimmer in training for
another season did not meet with the success that had been anticipated. The
prolonged dry spell made training Indian Skimmer difficult and kept her off
the course after the Coral-Eclipse, for connections had always maintained
that she wouldn't be risked on firm going again. She made only three
appearances in 1989 and though she won twice she was never seen as
anywhere near her brilliant best.

Conditions were very much in her favour when Indian Skimmer made
her reappearance in the Gordon Richards EBF Stakes at Sandown at the end
of April. Her form entitled her to start odds on, but she didn't have the
advantage of fitness. She was carrying plenty of condition and gave the
impression the race would bring her on, whereas her closest market rival Per
Quod had already run twice, finishing second to Unfuwain in the John Porter
Stakes at Newbury. As sometimes with her, Indian Skimmer pulled very hard
in the early stages but had no trouble holding her position when the pace
quickened and challenged for the lead on the outside two furlongs out. No
sooner had she got there than she started to struggle, but inside the final
furlong she got her second wind and rallied bravely to get up in the final
strides and touch off Per Quod and Carroll House by two heads.

Shortly before Sandown, Cecil was quoted as saying 'So far this year
Indian Skimmer's a totally different animal, being sound, moving well and
eating up. If I can keep her like this she'll be unbelievable; at the moment
she's definitely better than she's ever been in her life'. A month after her first
run Indian Skimmer took on five opponents in the Prix d'Ispahan at
Longchamp. Saint Andrews and Mansonnien were returned to the track
where they'd finished first and third, respectively, in the Prix Ganay four
weeks earlier, while Gabina and In Extremis were others to renew rivalry,
having filled the first two places in the Prix du Muguet at Saint-Cloud on their
reappearances. French Stress, runner-up to Indian Skimmer's stable-
companion Reprimand in the Trusthouse Forte Mile at Sandown, completed
the line-up. Indian Skimmer steadily wore down In Extremis in the straight,
having raced three to four lengths adrift of him for much of the way, and once
in front in the final furlong ran on strongly without coming under strong
pressure to hold off the challenge of Gabina by half a length. French Stress
could keep on at only one pace and finished two lengths further back, while
Saint Andrews ran well below his best in last place and was off the track for a

Prix d'Ispahan, Longchamp—a final win for Indian Skimmer

long time afterwards. From then on things didn't go as planned. Indian Skimmer became increasingly difficult to train and because of the firm ground was forced to miss the Prince of Wales's Stakes at Royal Ascot. It wasn't until the morning of the Coral-Eclipse Stakes that the decision was made to allow her to take her chance alongside Nashwan, Warning and the rest. Her performance reflected the indecision behind running plans. She was held up along with Nashwan and Warning, but was in trouble the moment Nashwan began his forward move early in the straight, and eventually she failed by a short head to catch her 200/1-stable-mate Opening Verse for second place, the pair five lengths adrift of Nashwan.

		Storm Bird (CAN) (b 1978)	Northern Dancer (b 1961)	Nearctic Natalma
Indian Skimmer (USA) (gr.m. 1984)			South Ocean (b 1967)	New Providence Shining Sun
		Nobiliare (USA) (gr 1976)	Vaguely Noble (b 1965)	Vienna Noble Lassie
			Gray Mirage (gr 1969)	Bold Bidder Home By Dark

Indian Skimmer is the third foal of the unraced Nobiliare, whose first foal Lordship (by Tentam) was successful in North America at up to a mile. Nobiliare's dam Gray Mirage, an above-average performer at up to a mile in the States, is a half-sister to Dark Mirage, the American fillies' triple crown winner of 1968. The third dam Home By Dark is also the third dam of the King's Stand Stakes winner Bluebird, like Indian Skimmer from the second crop of Storm Bird. Indian Skimmer, a tall, deep-girthed mare with a short, rather round action, was ideally suited by a mile and a quarter and an easy surface, though she was capable of high-class form at a mile and a half and on firm going. She was splendidly tough and genuine, but sometimes gave a little trouble in the preliminaries, either on the canter down or at the stalls. Indian Skimmer was retired the winner of ten of her sixteen races, unbeaten in five as a three-year-old including the Prix de Diane in which she defeated Miesque. An excellent record and pedigree, not that that guarantees success at stud. In fifteen years at stud Petite Etoile produced just three foals to reach the track, only one of which won. *H. R. A. Cecil.*

INDIAN SNAKE 2 br.f. (Feb 27) Mansingh (USA) 120–Boa (Mandrake Major 122) [1989 5m⁵ 5m* 5g 6d] sturdy filly: carries condition: keen walker: second foal: sister to winning 3-y-o sprinter Snake Song: dam lightly-raced half-sister to useful stayers Frog and Ophite: 20/1, won maiden at Pontefract in July by head from Romantic Saga: well beaten after in listed event at Newbury and minor event at Catterick: refused to enter stalls fifth intended outing: best form at 5f. *J. Wharton.* **69**

INDIAN SOVEREIGN 5 br.h. Indian King (USA) 128–Sovereign Dona 117 (Sovereign Path 125) [1988 NR 1989 6f³ 7.5m 6m² 6g⁶ 7m] workmanlike horse: quite modest maiden: probably best at 6f: has run creditably for apprentice: sold 3,200 gns Ascot October Sales. *B. Preece.* **58**

INDIAN SPIRIT 3 ch.g. Mansingh (USA) 120–Funny-Do (Derring-Do 131) [1988 5g 5f 5m 5m 1989 5d 5m] good-topped gelding: poor form: tailed off in spring as 3-y-o: tends to wander: bandaged near-hind at 2 yrs when blinkered once: changed hands 580 gns Doncaster February Sales. *M. W. Ellerby.* **—**

INDIAN STAR 2 b.f. (Mar 12) Indian King (USA) 128–Salique (Sallust 134) [1989 5g³ 5g* 5d⁵ 6f⁵ 5m⁶ 5m³ 6m⁴ 6f⁵ 5f 6m 6d⁶ 6g] leggy, light-framed filly: moderate walker: fourth foal: half-sister to 3-y-o Simply Henry (by Simply Great), successful at 6f (at 2 yrs) and 7f, and to 5f winner Ridgiduct (by Ahonoora): dam second over 7f in Ireland: plating-class performer: won maiden auction event at Wolverhampton in May: ran creditably in valuable seller at York and nursery at Haydock on tenth and eleventh starts: better suited by 6f than 5f: yet to race on very soft ground but acts on any other: bandaged on debut. *M. Brittain.* **54**

INDIAN UPRISING 3 b.c. Indian King (USA) 128–Infanta (USA) (Intrepid Hero (USA)) [1988 7m 7d 1989 6g 6f³ 7f 6f 7f] sturdy, good-bodied colt: third in minor event at Goodwood, only worthwhile form: blinkered, went very freely to post and virtually bolted in race for amateurs handicap final start (June): suited by 6f. *R. Hannon.* **61**

INDIA'S TWIST 2 ch.c. (Apr 5) Exhibitioner 111–West Bank (Martinmas 128) [1989 5s 5f² 6f⁴ 5m² 5m* 5g⁶] IR 5,800F, 10,500Y: workmanlike colt: third foal: **80**

half-brother to 1987 2-y-o 7f winner Gunner's Hill (by Dara Monarch), also successful over hurdles: dam winning Irish hurdler: modest performer: given very strong ride when beating Case Law a short head in nursery at Newmarket in October: best form at 5f. *J. D. Bethell.*

INDIVISIBLE   3 ch.f. Remainder Man 126§–Red Ragusa 62 (Homeric 133) [1988   56
7m 1989 8g³ 12f 12f 12.2g 8f 8f] leggy filly: plating-class maiden: should stay 1¼m:
best effort with some give in the ground. *R. Hollinshead.*

INDOMITABLE REB (USA)   4 ch.c. Nijinsky (CAN) 138–Spectacular Gift   75
(USA) (Alleged (USA) 138) [1988 NR 1989 12f² 22.2f] lengthy colt: second foal: dam
unraced half-sister to Spectacular Bid: won NH Flat races at Naas in May and Navan
(long odds on) following month: runner-up in amateurs event at Fairyhouse in
between: 33/1, weakened from under 4f out when last of 8 in Queen Alexandra
Stakes at Royal Ascot. *C. Collins, Ireland.*

IN DREAMS   6 b.g. High Line 125–Blissful Evening (Blakeney 126) [1988 16g⁵   —
14f² 14d* 16f⁵ 14g* 16.1m⁴ 13.3f 1989 14m 16f⁴ 14g] narrow, rather leggy gelding:
has a slightly round action: fair winner as 5-y-o: no form in 1989: ran as though
something amiss final outing: effective at 1¾m to 2m: probably unsuited by soft
going, acts on any other: suited by forcing tactics: has run well for apprentice:
trained until after second outing by W. Haggas. *T. Kersey.*

INDUBITABLE   4 ch.f. Sharpo 132–Veracious 86 (Astec 128) [1988 10d³ 10d*   82 +
10m⁵ 10d 1989 11.7m⁵ 13.3m⁴] workmanlike filly: fair winner as 3-y-o: shaped well,
running on under tender handling, in handicaps at Windsor and Newbury (under 4
lengths fourth of 16 to Braashee in £20,600 event) in second half of 1989: stays 13.3f:
acts on top-of-the-ground and a soft surface. *G. B. Balding.*

IN EXCESS   2 b.c. (Apr 8) Siberian Express (USA) 125–Kantado 93 (Saulingo   105 p
122) [1989 6f* 6g⁴] big, useful-looking colt: has plenty of scope: sixth living foal:
half-brother to fairly useful 1988 2-y-o 5f winner Konbola (by Superlative), 1¼m
winner Beau Fils and 7f and 1m winner Golden Beau (both by Crimson Beau): dam
raced mainly at 5f: won maiden at Lingfield by ¾ length from Halston Prince: ran
very well when 7 lengths fourth of 25 to Osario in Racecall Gold Trophy at Redcar
later in October, finishing strongly after slow start: sure to win more races, and is
one to follow. *W. A. O'Gorman.*

IN GLORY   5 b.m. Dalsaan 125–Indigine (USA) 71 (Raise A Native) [1988 8m⁴   —
7.6f⁴ 7g² 7d² 7m 7g 7g 7m 1989 7f 8.2m 7m⁶ 7f 7s 7m 6m] strong, lengthy mare: has
a round action: well below form since finishing runner-up in Ladbroke Bunbury Cup
at Newmarket as 4-y-o: visored, slowly away and never dangerous in York seller
final outing: better suited by 7f than 1m: probably not at best on soft going, acts on
any other: sometimes bandaged behind nowadays: doesn't find great deal off bridle:
sold 950 gns Doncaster October Sales. *Miss S. E. Hall.*

INHIBITION   2 ch.g. (May 4) Gorytus (USA) 132–Gothic Lady (Godswalk (USA)   50 d
130) [1989 5m⁵ 6m 7f 7f] IR 7,500Y: well-grown, angular gelding: has a round action:
fourth foal: half-brother to 5f to 1m winner Gothic Ford and inconsistent plater
Stanford Boy (both by Stanford) and a winner in Norway: dam won over 9f and 9.5f at
3 yrs in Ireland: poor form in varied events, including a seller: should stay 7f:
visored final outing. *S. J. Muldoon.*

INISHPOUR   7 b.h. Nishapour (FR) 125–Miss Britain (Tudor Melody 129) [1988   85
8s⁴ 7d⁶ 8d⁴ 8g* 8.5m* 7d 8m 8g 10.2f 8v 10s 1989 8s* 8m 10f⁶ 8.2g⁴ 9m² 8m⁵
10.2m⁶ 8m³ 8f 8.2d] tall, leggy, lengthy horse: usually looks very well: moderate
mover: fair handicapper: led final strides when winning strongly-run event at Thirsk
in April: best efforts after when placed at York and Pontefract: suited by around 1m:
acts on any going: ran moderately when blinkered: good mount for apprentice:
usually held up. *Mrs R. Wharton.*

INNOCENT GUY (USA)   3 b.g. Ginistrelli (USA) 117–Casaro Doll (USA)   —
(Brazen Brother (USA)) [1988 NR 1989 8.2s 10s 10.2h] leggy, sparely-made gelding:
third foal: brother to a minor winner in North America: dam winner at around 6f at 2
yrs: scant promise in claimers and a seller: blinkered, edgy and sweating final outing
(June). *Mrs L. Piggott.*

INNOVATOR   3 ch.g. Relkino 131–Gunnard 62 (Gunner B 126) [1988 6m³ 7d 7g   60
7f 8.2v⁴ 1989 10.2g⁶ 10d³ 11f 11m 12.2m⁶ 12m* 12.4f*dis 11f⁵ 12.3f 12.3m 14f 16f³
13.8d] small, sparely-made gelding: won seller (bought in 5,400 gns) at Pontefract
and handicap (disqualified for interference) at Newcastle in July: below form in
handicaps after: needs stiff 1½m and should stay further: best efforts on
top-of-the-ground: below form when sweating: apprentice ridden seventh to tenth
and final starts: has joined F. Jordan. *Mrs J. R. Ramsden.*

IN PURSUIT 2 ch.c. (Apr 27) Rainbow Quest (USA) 134–Silk Stocking 109 — (Pardao 120) [1989 8v] half-brother to several winners, including useful 1983 2-y-o 7f and 1m winner Satinette (by Shirley Heights) and useful 1982 2-y-o 7f winner Silk Pyjamas (by Queen's Hussar), later minor stakes winner in USA: dam stayed 1½m and is half-sister to good sprinter Shiny Tenth: 20/1 and better for race, always behind in 23-runner minor event at Newbury in October. *W. Hastings-Bass.*

INSAN (USA) 4 b.c. Our Native (USA)–Artania (USA) (Ruritania (USA)) [1988 **109** 12g2 12m2 12f2 12m4 12m5 1989 10f3] tall, leggy colt: has a free, rather round action: smart 3-y-o, short-headed by Kahyasi in Budweiser Irish Derby at the Curragh: in frame in Great Voltigeur Stakes at York and Prix Niel at Longchamp later in 1988: favourite, finished lame (reportedly suffered hairline fracture of foreleg cannon bone) when 3 lengths third of 6 to Sweet Chesne in listed event at Goodwood in May, only outing in 1989: ideally needed strongly-run race at 1½m: probably acted on any going: blinkered once at 2 yrs: retired to Sledmere Stud, Yorkshire, fee £2,000 (Oct 1st). *P. F. I. Cole.*

IN SEPTEMBER 3 b.f. Head For Heights 125–Maylands (Windjammer (USA)) **48** [1988 6g 1989 8.5d 8.2g3 8m3 12m6 8.5f 10d 8g] angular filly: plating-class maiden: stays 1m: acts on top-of-the-ground: blinkered final start. *J. L. Spearing.*

IN SHARP FOCUS 2 ch.f. (Apr 11) Final Straw 127–Little Change 70 (Grundy **63** 137) [1989 5m3 5m3 7g 5f2 7f3 6m4 5g 7g] 10,000Y: small, lengthy filly: keen walker: moderate mover: third foal: half-sister to 3-y-o 8.2f winner Mr Wishing Well (by Dunbeath) and 1m to 1½m winner Forfun (by Jalmood): dam, from good family, best at 2 yrs when placed over 5f: quite modest performer: very good fourth of 20 to Super One in valuable seller at York in August: suited by 6f. *J. S. Wilson.*

INSIDER'S VIEW 2 ch.f. (Jun 6) Caerleon (USA) 132–Sweet Mint 116 (Meadow **86** Mint (USA) 120) [1989 6g* 8g4] half-sister to several winners in Ireland and USA, most at 2 yrs: winner over 9.5f at 2 yrs, developed into smart 6f and 7f performer: won maiden at Phoenix Park in August by a length: under 2 lengths fourth of 7 to Endless Joy in Hennessy XO Killavullen Stakes at Leopardstown the following month: will probably stay 1¼m. *D. K. Weld, Ireland.*

INSPIRATION 4 b.g. Dominion 123–Placid Pet 65 (Mummy's Pet 125) [1988 8f4 — 7g 1989 8f 7g 6g] sturdy, good-bodied gelding: has a round action: fair maiden at 2 yrs: very lightly raced subsequently: well beaten in handicaps in 1989: stays 6f: best form with give in the ground: blinkered final outing: sold 1,750 gns Newmarket Autumn Sales. *R. J. R. Williams.*

INSPIRED LOVE 4 gr.f. Dalsaan 125–Inspiring (Home Guard (USA) 129) [1988 **56** 7g 8d5 6m2 7g6 6g2 7g2 7m2 7g 7g 1989 7g 8.5g 8.5f2 10.2m2 10.6d 8.2g 13.6g] strong, lengthy filly: plating-class maiden: runner-up in apprentice handicap at Beverley and amateurs event at Doncaster in summer: ran moderately last 3 outings: stays 10.2f: acts on firm going: ran well 3 times at 3 yrs. *F. J. Yardley.*

INSTANT DESIRE (USA) 2 ch.f. (Feb 24) Northern Dancer–Pink Topaze **86** (FR) (Djakao (FR)) [1989 6g3 7m3] strong, lengthy, good-quartered filly: fifth foal: half-sister to 2 winners in France, notably French 2000 Guineas and Prix Lupin winner Fast Topaze (by Far North): dam, unplaced in France but showed ability, is half-sister to Blue Tom, Amber Rama and Timmy My Boy: third in autumn maidens won by Walkern Witch at Yarmouth and Cutting Note at Newmarket: will stay 1m: wears a tongue strap: sure to win a maiden. *M. Moubarak.*

INSULAR 9 b.g. Moulton 128–Pas de Deux 80 (Nijinsky (CAN) 138) [1988 16g3 — 14d6 16m 12m* 16g* 16d3 14.7m4 1989 16m 16.1m 14m 14m 17f] big, good-topped gelding: good walker: fair winner as 8-y-o: well below his best in 1989: stays well: used to be particularly well suited by a sound surface: excellent mount for an inexperienced rider. *I. A. Balding.*

INSWINGER 3 br.g. Swing Easy (USA) 126–Cheri Berry 87 (Air Trooper 115) — [1988 5g 5m6 6f 5f 6m4 5m3 5g 5f5 5d5 6s 1989 6g5 5h 6f 6m 5.3h a6g5] small, lengthy, slightly dipped-backed gelding: carries condition: quite modest maiden at best: ran moderately after reappearance: probably suited by 6f: acts on firm going: ran well in blinkers once at 2 yrs. *W. G. R. Wightman.*

INTEBAH (USA) 3 ch.f. The Bart (USA) 108–Dance Empress (USA) (Empery — (USA) 128) [1988 7g* 1989 8.5s] leggy, unfurnished filly: won maiden at Sandown in July as 2-y-o: second favourite but edgy, pulled hard early when well-beaten eighth of 9 in listed race at Epsom in April, only outing in 1989: bred to be suited by middle distances: sold 4,000 gns Newmarket December Sales. *P. F. I. Cole.*

INTEGRITY BOY 2 b.c. (Feb 27) Touching Wood (USA) 127–Powderhall 81 **70** (Murrayfield) 119) [1989 6f 6g 6m 8.5f2 10.6d3 8g* 10g] 5,800F, IR 3,000Y:

medium-sized colt: eighth living foal: half-brother to 3-y-o Beaumont's Keep (by Castle Keep) and 5 winners, including quite useful 6f and 1m winner El Rey (by King of Spain) and fair 1m winner Clarandal (by Young Generation): dam won 4 times at up to 10.6f: modest performer: won selling nursery (no bid) at Carlisle in October by 4 lengths from Dublin Breeze: will stay well: blinkered last 4 outings: trained first 4 starts by P. Rohan. *R. O'Leary.*

IN THE GROOVE 2 b.f. (Feb 25) Night Shift (USA)–Pine Ridge 80 (High 92 p Top 131) [1989 5m² 6g² 6m* 7g³]

With victories in the Queen Mary, Lowther and Cheveley Park Stakes, Dead Certain proved herself one of the toughest and best two-year-olds around. And her trainer is adamant that in In The Groove he has another filly capable of doing well in good company, although her form at two was a long way removed from the best. In The Groove shaped promisingly in maiden company at Newbury on her debut in June only to be beaten when odds on for a Windsor minor event the following month when she reportedly jarred herself up. A seven-week lay-off followed, and on her return In The Groove gave her first public indication that she was potentially useful. The race in question was the Moorestyle Convivial Maiden Stakes at York, an eight-runner, open-looking contest which In The Groove won easily, travelling supremely well throughout and striding powerfully clear from the distance to beat the newcomer Dashing Senor by six lengths in a time only a fraction slower than that recorded by Dead Certain in the Lowther later in the afternoon. The Hoover Fillies' Mile was spoken of as In The Groove's next race; as it turned out she was sent for what seemed a slightly easier objective, the Group 3 C. L. Weld EBF Park Stakes at Phoenix Park on Cartier Million day. One of three British-trained runners in a field of fifteen, In The Groove started even-money favourite; all seemed to be going to plan as she led comfortably early in the straight, but it was clear two out that Cauthen was becoming uneasy; losing his whip soon after didn't help matters, and after being eased once clearly held In The Groove finished third behind Wedding Bouquet and Remthat Naser. That wasn't a bad effort, but In The Groove's connections were again of the opinion she hadn't been at her best, this time suggesting that lack of suitable ground on which to work her had left her just short of peak fitness.

So, despite having had four outings In The Groove ended her first season as something of an unknown quantity, and it could pay to reserve judgement on her until she's had another chance to take on the better fillies. In The Groove is very much the sort to progress physically from two to three. She's a strong, deep-girthed filly with plenty of scope, very well bought as a yearling for 20,000 guineas. Her sire Night Shift, the winner of a six-furlong minor event from seven attempts in the States, owes his position at stud mainly to his pedigree. Being a son of Northern Dancer is always a selling point to breeders, and there's much of interest on the female side of his pedigree. His dam Ciboulette, herself a smart performer, produced Fanfreluche from an earlier visit to Northern Dancer. Fanfreluche was an outstanding filly in Canada and the United States, winning eleven races from seven furlongs to a mile and a half, and she's also excelled at stud as the dam of horses like L'Enjoleur, twice Canadian Horse of The Year, and La Voyageuse, whose twenty-six wins included the Canadian Oaks in 1978. Night Shift himself has made a promising start to his stud career; he's finished among the top twenty

Moorestyle Convivial Stakes, York—
In The Groove is the easiest winner at the Ebor meeting

sires of two-year-olds twice running, and besides In The Groove his second crop also included Green's Belle, Night At Sea, the useful northern filly Mademoiselle Chloe and the Middle Park fourth Croupier. In The Groove's dam Pine Ridge, who won a couple of races over a mile and a half when trained by Stoute, has produced two previous foals; the minor American winner Stripped Pine (by Sharpo) and the King of Spain colt Spanish Pine, who won three times at up to a mile. The second dam Wounded Knee also stayed quite well, while the third dam La Lidia has produced numerous winners including Sinzinbra, the dam of the well-known jumpers Cashew King, Young Snugfit and Mr Snugfit.

In The Groove (b.f. Feb 25, 1987)	Night Shift (USA) (b 1980)	Northern Dancer (b 1961)	Nearctic Natalma
		Ciboulette (b 1961)	Chop Chop Windy Answer
	Pine Ridge (b 1980)	High Top (b 1969)	Derring-Do Camenae
		Wounded Knee (ch 1973)	Busted La Lidia

In The Groove doesn't run like one who'll stay as well as her dam: she appears to have plenty of speed and she may well prove best at up to a mile. It's unlikely she'll be risked much on very firm ground, although she's a good mover. She was withdrawn from her intended debut at Goodwood because her trainer considered the firm going unsuitable. *D. R. C. Elsworth.*

IN THE PAPERS 2 b.f. (Apr 18) Aragon 118–Mistress Gay 76 (Lord Gayle (USA) 124) [1989 5f² 5m* 5m* 6m] strong, compact filly: half-sister to 3-y-o Gay Finale (by Final Straw) and a winner in Italy by High Top: dam 9f and 1¼m winner: fair performer: successful in maiden at Wolverhampton in August and nursery (by 2½ lengths from Dream Talk, going on strongly) at Sandown following month: ran much too freely when last of 11 in Tattersalls Cheveley Park Stakes at Newmarket. *J. Sutcliffe.*   87

IN THE WINGS 3 b.c. Sadler's Wells (USA) 132–High Hawk 124 (Shirley Heights 130) [1988 6m* 7d* 1989 10d* 12g] small colt: second foal: half-brother to   124

Prix du Prince d'Orange, Longchamp—In The Wings enters the Arc picture

Sheikh Mohammed's "In The Wings"

poor maiden Swooping (by Kings Lake): dam, high-class middle-distance stayer, is half-sister to dam of Infamy: won 5-runner Group 3 Prix du Prince d'Orange at Longchamp in September by ½ length from Mansonnien, quickening well from rear to lead inside final 1f: favourite, never able to challenge in Prix de l'Arc de Triomphe 2 weeks later, beaten about 6 lengths: won maiden at Chantilly in June and listed race at Deauville as 2-y-o: subsequently chipped knee-bone: probably stays 1½m: very smart and may be capable of better. *A. Fabre, France.*

INTIMIDATE 4 b.g. Formidable (USA) 125–Zoomie 78 (Pinza 137) [1988 7d² **106** §
8g⁶ 8g³ 8.5m⁶ 7f 8m⁵ 8m⁶ 7d 1989 6d* 6g 7.2s⁶ 5m² 6v] small, deep-girthed gelding: moderate mover: smart at his best, third in Airlie/Coolmore Irish 2000 Guineas at the Curragh early in 1988: long way below his best in spring, though justified favouritism in £6,000 Quail Stakes at Kempton: 1½ lengths second to Or Acier in Premio Omenoni at Milan in October, first run for nearly 6 months: effective at 5f and stays 1m: probably unsuited by firm going, acts on any other: found little when blinkered: trained until after fourth start by J. Gosden: a difficult ride and not one to trust. *B. Agriformi, Italy.*

INTIMISTE (USA) 2 ch.c. (Mar 20) Arctic Tern (USA) 126–Bubble Company **113** ?
(Lyphard (USA) 132) [1989 6d* 10g² 10v*] $175,000Y: brother to French middle-distance winner Basiluzzo and half-brother to 2 other winners, notably French 2000 Guineas runner-up Candy Stripes (by Blushing Groom): dam, placed at 3 yrs, is daughter of French Oaks second Prodice and sister to good French and American middle-distance filly Sangue: won newcomers race at Saint-Cloud in October and Criterium de Saint-Cloud (fortunately, on demotion of 3-length winner Snurge) following month: will stay 1½m. *F. Boutin, France.*

INTO MY STRIDE (USA) 3 b.f. Assert 134–Cellist (USA) (Bagdad) [1988 NR —
1989 14m 16m⁴ 14g] 35,000Y: rangy filly: closely related to 1987 2-y-o 6f winner

Glockenspiel (by Peterhof), and half-sister to several other winners, including useful 1984 2-y-o 7f winner Concert Hall (by Monteverdi): dam, smart stakes winner at up to 1m, is half-sister to top-class Gay Fandango: fourth at Nottingham, only sign of ability in summer maidens. *Mrs L. Piggott.*

INTRANSIT 2 ch.c. (Apr 17) Night Shift (USA)–Valpolicella 63 (Lorenzaccio 130) [1989 5.8h⁴ 7g 6m 6g 7g 8f⁵ 6g²] 7,000Y, 25,000 2-y-o: compact, good-quartered colt: half-brother to some poor animals: dam plater: plating-class maiden: appears suited by 6f: ran respectably when visored sixth outing: has run moderately for 7-lb claimer: sold to race in Saudi Arabia 9,200 gns Newmarket Autumn Sales. *R. Hollinshead.*   **58**

INTREPID LASS 2 b.f. (Apr 18) Wassl 125–Risk All 90 (Run The Gantlet (USA)) [1989 7g 7m 8g⁵] 5,200Y: quite attractive filly: has scope: moderate mover: second foal: dam, winner over 7.6f and 1¼m, is out of half-sister to Castle Keep and Ragstone: plating-class form in maidens: fell second start: will be well suited by 1¼m + . *H. Candy.*   **58**

INTREPID WORLD (USA) 3 b.g. Transworld (USA) 121–Intrepid Mary Ann (USA) (His Majesty (USA)) [1988 7s⁴ 6s 8d 1989 10.2g⁵ 12.3d 12.5f⁴ 13m³ 13.8m³ 12g 13.8g⁶ 15.3f⁴ 17f 18g] leggy gelding: keen walker: plating-class maiden: probably stays 15f: best form on top-of-the-ground: tailed off in blinkers on reappearance: often ridden by 5-lb claimer: sold to join J. Walmsley 4,800 gns Newmarket Autumn Sales. *S. G. Norton.*   **49**

INTRIGUE 2 b.c. (Feb 21) Mummy's Pet 125–Subtlety (Grundy 137) [1989 5f] lengthy, rather finely-made colt: first foal: dam is half-sister to smart stayer Buttress and smart middle-distance performer Dukedom: 12/1, slowly away and soon struggling in 7-runner maiden (visored) at Lingfield in May: sold to join M. Murphy 2,000 gns Ascot July Sales. *I. A. Balding.*   **—**

INTROVERT 5 b.h. Niniski (USA) 125–Consister 89 (Burglar 128) [1988 NR 1989 14s] leggy, sparely-made horse: of little account: blinkered twice. *A. Smith.*   **—**

INTUITIVE JOE 2 b.g. (May 14) Petorius 117–Super Girl (Super Sam 124) [1989 5s 5g⁵ 5.1f⁴ 5m⁴ 6g⁴ 5f² 5f⁴ 6g⁴ 6f* 6g] IR 2,200Y, 15,000 2-y-o: quite attractive gelding: half-brother to good Italian sprinter Super Sky and 6f winner Today And Tomorrow (both by African Sky) and a useful winner in Italy by Malinowski: dam   **67**

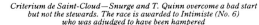

Criterium de Saint-Cloud—Snurge and T. Quinn overcome a bad start but not the stewards. The race is awarded to Intimiste (No. 6) who was adjudged to have been hampered

435

unraced half-sister to Quisling: quite modest performer: 16/1, won claimer at Leicester in October: worth a try at 7f: looks a hard ride. *G. Lewis.*

INVASION 5 b.g. Kings Lake (USA) 133–St Padina 91 (St Paddy 133) [1988 NR 1989 14g 16m] rangy gelding: carries plenty of condition: fair winner as 3-y-o when trained by B. Hills: well beaten in handicaps in 1989: acts on a soft surface and is possibly not at his best on firm going: has shown a tendency to hang and looked none too keen when blinkered: winning hurdler. *J. A. Glover.* —

INVERTIEL 5 b.g. Sparkling Boy 110–Phyl's Pet (Aberdeen 109) [1988 8g³ 7f* 1989 9f² 7h* 8f6] quite good-topped gelding: has run only 7 times: showed improved form when hacking up by 10 lengths in 7-runner handicap at Carlisle in June: creditable sixth, no extra final 1f, of 7 in similar contest at Pontefract 2 weeks later: possibly better suited by 7f than 1m: acts on hard going: has won for apprentice. *P. Monteith.* 82

INVISIBLE HALO (USA) 2 b.f. (Mar 11) Halo (USA)–Placer Queen (Habitat 134) [1989 5f 6g* 7m4 8m6 7g] leggy filly: first known foal: dam ran 3 times before later won at up to 1¼m in Canada: won maiden at Doncaster by 2 lengths from Famous Beauty: better effort over a length fourth to Mogul Prince in nursery at Newmarket later in July: well beaten last 2 starts: suited by 7f. *P. W. Harris.* 75

INVITE 3 b.f. Be My Guest (USA) 126–Burghclere 86 (Busted 134) [1988 7m 7g 1989 10g6 11.7m4 14f5 14f2 16m 16m2 16f* 15.3f*] well-made filly: led inside final 1f when winning autumn handicaps at Nottingham and Wolverhampton: often reluctant previously (and also at Nottingham) and swished tail under pressure: stays 2m: acts on firm going: well beaten in blinkers fifth start. *J. L. Dunlop.* 79

I PERCEIVE 2 b.c. (May 9) Vision (USA)–Wavetree (Realm 129) [1989 6f 6g5 7d2] IR 50,000Y: tall, useful-looking colt: half-brother to several winners, including useful Irish 6f and 7f winner Southern Music (by Music Boy): dam unraced half-sister to smart Imperial Dancer, successful at up to 1¼m: showed much improved form (first run for 3 months) when beaten a neck by Himmah in minor event at Thirsk in November: better suited by 7f than 6f: may improve again. *F. H. Lee.* 78 p

IRAJA 3 gr.f. Kris 135–Queen's Counsellor 92 (Kalamoun 129) [1988 NR 1989 7d6] lengthy, angular, dipped-backed filly: fourth foal: half-sister to fairly useful but probably ungenuine 7f and 1m winner Jurran (by Formidable), 1985 2-y-o 6f winner Akaaleel (by Tyrnavos) and winning stayer Assaglawi (by Troy): dam won over 6f at 2 yrs and stayed 1m as 3-y-o: 14/1, 6 lengths sixth of 17 in newcomers race at Newbury in April, travelling well over 2f out but no extra inside last, carrying head bit high: sold 3,300 gns Newmarket December Sales. *J. Tree.* 74

IRENE'S CHARTER 4 b. or br.f. Persian Bold 123–Crestia (Prince Tenderfoot (USA) 126) [1988 7f* 10g 7f 7m6 8m3 7g5 1989 9f4 9f5 10f2 10f4 8m3 a12g3 a10g* a10g] leggy, workmanlike filly: moderate mover: modest handicapper: dull in coat, won at Lingfield in November: ran creditably all starts earlier in season, well beaten final outing: probably ideally suited by 1¼m: acts on firm going: sweating and on toes second start: has run creditably for lady: changed hands 4,600 gns Newmarket Autumn Sales. *D. J. G. Murray-Smith.* 72

IRISCAR 3 b.f. Valiyar 129–Dellwood Iris 71 (Firestreak 125) [1988 5g 6m 5f 1989 6g] sturdy filly: probably of little account. *W. Holden.* —

IRISH DITTY 3 ch.f. Derrylin 115–Falcrello 51 (Falcon 131) [1988 6f4 5.8g4 6m5 6m 7m2 7g 1989 10f 11m 10h3 10h6 8m6] smallish, rather dipped-backed filly: plating-class maiden: third at Lingfield in June, easily best effort in handicaps: stays 1¼m: acts on hard ground: winning novice hurdler. *R. V. Smyth.* 52

IRISH EMERALD 2 b.c. (Apr 14) Taufan (USA) 119–Gaelic Jewel 89 (Scottish Rifle 127) [1989 5s* 5d3 6g 6g6 6v 5g] 31,000Y: close-coupled, workmanlike colt: moderate mover: second foal: half-brother to 3-y-o Gaelic Air (by Ballad Rock): dam, winner at 1¼m, is daughter of very useful miler Red Ruby, a half-sister to smart sprinter Laser Light: modest performer: won maiden at Kempton in March: best effort under 7 lengths sixth of 9 to Star Hill in listed event at Kempton in September: suited by 6f. *C. V. Bravery.* 72

IRISH FLASHER 2 b.g. (Apr 12) Exhibitioner 111–Miss Portal (St Paddy 133) [1989 8.2g 6v4 6s] IR 7,200F, IR 3,600Y, resold 5,200Y: tall, rather plain gelding: sixth living foal: half-brother to 3-y-o Eurolady (by Kafu) and useful 7f and 1m winner Vianora (by Ahonoora): dam poor maiden: about 3 lengths fourth of 15, staying on well final 2f, to Scorpio Lady in auction event at Ayr in October: well beaten in claimer at Hamilton (unruly stalls) following month. *M. O'Neill.* ?

IRISH GROOM 2 b.c. (May 7) Shy Groom (USA)–Romany Pageant (Welsh —
Pageant 132) [1989 8.2g 7g] 6,000Y, 5,800 2-y-o: smallish, workmanlike colt: fourth
foal: half-brother to useful 7f and 8.5f winner Laurie's Warrior (by Viking) and 7.5f
seller winner Naseeb (by Red Sunset): dam never ran: tailed off in maiden and minor
event. *J. P. Smith.*

IRISH PASSAGE 6 gr.g. Welsh Captain 113–Honey's Queen (Pals Passage 115) 71
[1988 8s 8m 1989 8d 8f² 7.5g² 8f 8f⁵ 8f 7.5m 8g 8m³ 8g³] workmanlike gelding:
carries plenty of condition: good mover: quite modest handicapper on his day:
virtually pulled up (running subject to stewards inquiry, jockey reported horse had
history of breathing problems) on fourth outing, and again ran as though something
amiss on sixth: stays 9f: possibly unsuited by soft going, acts on any other:
blinkered once: has looked a difficult ride and goes very well for D. Nicholls: none
too reliable. *T. D. Barron.*

IRISH SUNSET 2 b.f. (Mar 14) Red Sunset 120–Meisha (On Your Mark 125) —
[1989 6m 8.5f 7m] IR 2,900Y: compact, workmanlike filly: second foal: half-sister to
a winner in Hong Kong: dam Irish 1½m winner, also successful over hurdles: little
worthwhile form in maidens: has joined D. Smith. *J. H. Johnson.*

IRISH VELVET 3 b.g. Ballacashtal (CAN)–Normandy Velvet (Normandy 103) —
[1988 NR 1989 12v 11.7d 10f 8h] rangy gelding: second reported foal: dam unraced:
appears of little account: sold 1,550 gns Ascot July Sales. *P. Howling.*

IRON KING 3 gr.c. Tender King 123–Zanskar (Godswalk (USA) 130) [1988 5s⁶ 73
5s⁶ 5.3f* 5d⁴ 6f³ 5m² 5f⁶ 5f 5g⁶ 6g* 6s³ 1989 6s 5s 6f³ 7h³ 7m⁵ 6f² 6m⁴ 6m 5f* 6f
a6g⁵ a6g⁴ a7g⁴] sturdy, useful-looking colt: modest handicapper: led on line at
Salisbury in September: creditable fourth at Lingfield last 2 outings, visored first of
them and bandaged on second: stays 7f: best form on a sound surface: has run
creditably for an apprentice: reportedly had heart murmur: rather inconsistent. *R.
Hannon.*

I RUN I WIN 2 b.c. (Feb 4) Bairn (USA) 126–Historical Fact 78 (Reform 132) —
[1989 a7g] 11,500Y: fifth foal: dam 1¼m winner: 20/1, slowly away and always behind
in late-season maiden at Lingfield. *R. Boss.*

ISABELLA RA (USA) 3 ch.f. Roberto (USA) 131–My Maravilla (USA) 94 92
(Blushing Groom (FR) 131) [1988 6g⁵ 1989 9f³ 10h² 10.5m⁶ 12h* 12g³ 12f*]
short-backed, leggy, light-framed filly: made all in maiden at Brighton in August and
handicap (showing improved form) at Salisbury in September: stays 1½m well: acts
on hard ground: sweating second and third starts: wore net muzzle then and in
preliminaries at Brighton: sold 60,000 gns Newmarket December Sales. *G.
Harwood.*

I SEE ICE 2 b.f. (Feb 26) High Top 131–Climb The Heights (USA) (Majestic Light —
(USA)) [1989 7m 7f⁵] medium-sized filly: first foal: dam minor winner at around 9f in
USA: little sign of ability in maidens at Newmarket and Leicester. *B. W. Hills.*

ISHAPOUR 2 b.g. (May 5) Nishapour (FR) 125–Ganna (ITY) (Molvedo 137) —
[1989 5d⁵ 5d⁶ 6f] 20,000 francs (approx £1,900) Y: tall, leggy, lengthy gelding: poor
mover: second foal: dam unraced sister to Italian St Leger winner Gallio and John
Porter winner Salado: well beaten in minor events and a seller: not seen out after
May. *W. T. Kemp.*

ISHTIHAAR (USA) 2 b. or br.c. (Feb 15) Alydar (USA)–Ambassador of Luck 89
(USA) (What Luck (USA)) [1989 7.3g³ 7m² 7m⁶] $500,000Y: rangy colt: has scope:
easy mover: second foal: half-brother to 3-y-o Zakhir (by Topsider), fairly useful 6f
winner at 2 yrs: dam, stayed 1m, was champion mare in USA: fair maiden:
keeping-on length second of 6, clear, to Sober Mind in £8,300 event at Newbury in
July, best effort: staying on when hampered over 1f out and not knocked about in
minor event at Salisbury following month: will be suited by 1m: sure to win a race.
Major W. R. Hern.

ISIPINGO 2 b.c. (Apr 14) Pitskelly 122–Nemoralis (Great White Way (USA)) —
[1989 7f⁶] IR 1,900Y, 4,300 2-y-o: seventh foal: half-brother to winner in Italy by On
Your Mark: dam won 5 races at 5f and 6f in Ireland: 33/1, last of 6, slowly away, to
Garscube in maiden at Kempton in July. *D. A. Wilson.*

ISLAND ADVENTURE 3 b. or br.f. Touching Wood (USA) 127–Acquire 105 —
(Burglar 128) [1988 5d 7g 10d 1989 10s 8.2f 8h] good-topped, useful-looking filly:
sign of ability in maidens and sellers only on reappearance: not seen out after June.
Sir Mark Prescott.

ISLAND FOREST (USA) 3 ch.g. Green Forest (USA) 132–Bonnie Isle 115 66
(Pitcairn 126) [1988 NR 1989 8g⁶ 9g 11f 8m⁴ 7.5f⁵ 8.3m] medium-sized, attractive
gelding: fourth foal: half-brother to French 10.5f winner Wave The Banner (by Irish

River): dam won from 6f to 1m and second in Oaks: quite modest maiden: blinkered, ran creditably in handicaps at Edinburgh and Beverley fourth and fifth starts, making most: suited by 1m: usually wears tongue strap (didn't do so last time): takes keen hold. *M. Moubarak.*

ISLAND JETSETTER 3 ch.g. Tolomeo 127–Baridi 82 (Ribero 126) [1988 NR 1989 10.2g³ 12.3d 8f⁶ 8.2g³ 8.2g 10m 8s⁶] 20,000Y: workmanlike, angular gelding: has a rather round action: third foal: half-brother to poor maiden Raintree Tonic (by Noalcoholic): dam placed over 6f and 1½m: modest maiden: third at Haydock in July: below form in handicaps after, taking very strong hold on first of them: best at around 1m: suited by some give in the ground. *M. H. Easterby.* **82 d**

ISLAND MEAD 3 ch.f. Pharly (FR) 130–Aunt Judy (Great Nephew 126) [1988 6f⁶ 7d⁴ 7g* 7f⁴ 8f⁶ 1989 8s 8f⁴ 8f⁵ 8f³ 7g 7.3m] small, good-topped filly: fair performer: ran creditably in listed race at Kempton and quite valuable handicaps at Ascot and Goodwood second to fourth outings: below form in £6,000 handicaps at Newbury after, tailed off first occasion then travelling well long way on second: stays 1m: acts on firm going and a soft surface: bandaged off-hind. *I. A. Balding.* **86**

ISLAND RULER 2 b. or br.f. (Apr 29) Ile de Bourbon (USA) 133–Dominant 86 (Behistoun 131) [1989 7m⁴] 21,000Y: leggy, rather sparely-made filly: half-sister to several winners, including useful middle-distance stayer Mubarak of Kuwait (by Morston) and winning stayer Sabatash (by Blakeney): dam, winner at 1½m, is half-sister to very smart Dominion: 20/1, green and in need of race, under 6 lengths fourth of 10, staying on strongly under considerate handling, to Free At Last in £8,200 event at Newbury in September: sure to improve and win races. *A. C. Stewart.* **69 p**

ISLAND SPIRIT 2 b.c. (Apr 4) Ile de Bourbon (USA) 133–Zeyneb 65 (Habitat 134) [1989 8v 8g] rangy, useful-looking colt: has plenty of scope: second foal: half-brother to 1988 2-y-o 6f winner Known Lady (by Known Fact): dam, in frame at 1m and 1¼m, is half-sister to very smart stayer General Ironside and useful 7f to 1½m winner Welsh Dancer: backward, soundly beaten in late-season minor event at Newbury (sweating) and maiden at Leicester. *B. W. Hills.* **—**

ISLAND WEDDING (USA) 2 b.f. (Mar 8) Blushing Groom (FR) 131–South Sea Dancer (USA) (Northern Dancer) [1989 7f³ 7m³] $1,000,000Y: sparely-made, rather shallow-girthed filly: first foal: dam, winner at up to 9f at 3 yrs and 5 yrs, is sister to Storm Bird and Northernette, dam of Gold Crest: under 5 lengths third of 13, no extra last furlong and eased, to Free At Last in maiden at Salisbury: odds on, below that form in similar event at Redcar later in September. *M. R. Stoute.* **71**

ISLE OF ARRAN 2 b.c. (May 7) Ile de Bourbon (USA) 133–Marzooga 84 (Bold Lad (IRE) 133) [1989 8m 9g* 8g 10g] 15,500Y: strong, close-coupled colt: third foal: half-brother to moderate plater Space Lab (by Tanfirion): dam 2-y-o 6f winner: 16/1, won 11-runner claimer at York in October by 2½ lengths after slow start: creditable seventh to Adding in minor event at Redcar following month: ran poorly in between: stays 1¼m. *R. Hollinshead.* **74**

ISOBAR 3 b.g. Another Realm 118–Lady Eton 106 (Le Dieu d'Or 119) [1988 5g 6d⁶ 5m⁶ 5m² 6g* 7g³ 7g* 7g⁶ 7m 7d 7f 7m⁴ 1989 10.2g 7.5d 8d 12m⁵ 8g] close-coupled, leggy gelding: moderate mover: won sellers in summer as 2-y-o: below form in 1989: best efforts at 7f: likely to prove best on an easy surface: blinkered or visored nowadays: winning selling hurdler. *S. J. Muldoon.* **—**

ISOM DART (USA) 10 b.g. Bold Forbes (USA)–Shellshock 110 (Salvo 129) [1988 10d 10.2g 16f² 17.1g 12d 1989 15.5s 17.1m] neat, well-made, attractive gelding: bad mover: poor handicapper: tailed off both starts in spring: stays 2m: acts on firm going: ran badly in blinkers: has run creditably for apprentice: inconsistent. *T. B. Hallett.* **—**

ITCHEL LEGEND 3 ch.f. Longleat (USA) 109–Ladyswood 61 (Great Nephew 126) [1988 NR 1989 7m 8.3m 12g] lengthy, sparely-made filly: second foal: half-sister to poor plater Lady Columbine (by Cawston's Clown): dam best at 2 yrs on flat later won over hurdles: behind in minor event (moved poorly down) and claimers. *M. J. Fetherston-Godley.* **—**

ITMA 6 b.g. Nicholas Bill 125–Civic Duty (Averof 123) [1988 16g 14g 15.5f 16m² 16g* 19g 16f³ 16f⁴ 14f³ 17.1g 1989 12v 14f⁵ 16m⁵ 17.1f² 16f⁴ 15s 15g] big, plain gelding: moderate mover: poor handicapper: seems best at around 2m: acts on firm going and possibly unsuited by soft: often given lot to do: trained until after fifth outing by J. Benstead. *R. Allan.* **50**

IT'S ME 3 gr.f. Good Times (ITY)–Rykneld (Warpath 113) [1988 6m² 1989 8g* 8h* 8m 8m⁵ 10m³ 8s 10.6d] lengthy, workmanlike filly: good walker: successful at **71**

Carlisle in maiden in June and 2-runner minor event (14/1 on) in July: ran creditably in handicaps fourth and fifth outings but poorly after, in apprentice event final start: stays 1¼m: acts on top-of-the-ground. *J. Hanson.*

IT'S RABALA 3 b.g. High Top 131–Pearl Wedding 83 (Gulf Pearl 117) [1988 NR 1989 11g⁴ 12m 12f 11m 12g] workmanlike gelding: eighth foal: brother to Cambridgeshire winner Century City and half-brother to a winner in Italy by Bustino: dam won over 1¼m and 1½m: plating-class maiden: should have stayed 1½m: possibly unsuited by top-of-the-ground: possibly ungenuine: dead. *J. S. Wilson.* **49**

ITS SMITHY 3 b.g. Red Sunset 120–Kelly's Curl (Pitskelly 122) [1988 5m⁵ 5d⁶ 1989 6m 6f⁵] small gelding: has a quick action: plating-class maiden in 1988: no form in August as 3-y-o, badly hampered at stalls in claimer on reappearance. *R. Akehurst.* **—**

IT'S VARADAN 5 ch.h. Rabdan 129–Miss Casanova 84 (Galivanter 131) [1988 10d 11.5g* 10f³ 11.5g⁴ 10m 1989 12g⁶ 11.7d* 10f* 10g] leggy, close-coupled horse: modest handicapper: won at Windsor (8/1 from 14/1, first outing for new trainer, formerly with H. O'Neill) in August and Chepstow (strongly-run race) following month: suited by 1¼m to 1½m: probably acts on any going: has won for apprentice. *P. Mitchell.* **72**

ITTIHAAD 6 gr.g. Rusticaro (FR) 124–Perfect Bid (USA) (Baldric II 131) [1988 12f* 12f³ 12f² 12f² 12m 12m 1989 14m⁶ 14g] lengthy gelding: good mover: quite modest handicapper: below best in 1989: best at up to 1¾m: well suited by top-of-the-ground: sometimes sweats: has run well for apprentice: goes very well fresh. *R. Akehurst.* **—**

ITTISAAL 2 b. or br.f. (Apr 13) Caerleon (USA) 132–House Tie (Be Friendly 130) [1989 5f⁴] 100,000Y: rather leggy, close-coupled filly: seventh foal: half-sister to 5 winners, including 3-y-o 7f winner Nahilah (by Habitat), fairly useful sprinter Bag O'Rhythm (by Be My Guest) and French 1m and 1¼m winner Academic (by Mill Reef): dam, Irish 1m winner, is daughter of high-class 2-y-o Mesopotamia: 5/2, over 6 lengths fourth of 7, edging left and eased final furlong, to Please Believe Me in maiden at York in May: bred to stay at least 1m: may improve. *H. Thomson Jones.* **64**

IVEAGH HOUSE 3 b.c. Be My Guest (USA) 126–Waffles 100 (Wollow 132) [1988 NR 1989 10g] IR 220,000Y: tall colt: third foal: closely related to Irish 6f winner Great Shearwater (by Storm Bird): dam Irish 6f winner, is out of 1000 Guineas winner Night Off: 100/1, well beaten in 17-runner minor event at Leicester in November. *Mrs J. Pitman.* **—**

I'VE GOTTA TELL YA 3 b.g. Petong 126–Super Jennie 80 (Stephen George 102) [1988 7m 7g⁶ 7g 8m 1989 8g 12.5f 10.6m 16.2g 13f⁴ 11f⁴ 11m⁵ 14d] big, rather leggy gelding: moderate mover: plating-class form at best: stays 13f, at least in moderately-run race: acts on firm going: edgy final start. *Capt. J. Wilson.* **49**

IVORDALE 4 b.g. Beldale Flutter (USA) 130–Ivoronica 89 (Targowice (USA) 130) [1988 8.5m 8.5m⁴ 8.5f⁵ 7.5f* 6g⁶ 7.5s² 7m 7s 7f 1989 7s 8f 7.5g 7f³ 7.5m³ 7f 8.5f⁴ 8m 7.5f 7.5m 8m] big, rangy gelding: bad mover: quite modest handicapper: easily best efforts as 4-y-o when third at Thirsk and Beverley: slowly away, reluctant to race early and hung right ninth outing: suited by around 7f: acts on any going: best form in blinkers: visored sixth (sweating badly) and seventh outings: goes well with forcing tactics (sometimes goes too fast): unreliable. *M. H. Easterby.* **60 d**

IVORDOLL 4 ch.f. Ivotino (USA)–Come On Doll (True Song 95) [1988 7d 8s 10g 12f 10g* 10.2g 12f 10g 10.8s² 10m 8.2s⁶ 9s² 10d 1989 8s 10d 10f] small filly: moderate mover: ungenuine plater: stays 10.8f: suited by easy surface: usually blinkered: sold 1,300 gns Doncaster June Sales: one to leave alone. *K. S. Bridgwater.* **— §**

IVOROSKI 7 b.g. Malinowski (USA)–Fado (Ribero 126) [1988 12g 12g⁵ 12.2g 12f³ 12f³ 12.3f² 12g⁴ 11m⁵ 10g³ 12.2f 12m 12m³ 13.8g 1989 12.4g⁵ 10v 12g³ 12g⁵ 12h⁵ 12.3m⁴ 12m³ 15m 12g⁴ 12h² 11f³ 10f² 10.6d4 10m³ 10.2g* 12.3m⁴ 10.6m a12g⁵ a14g⁵] workmanlike gelding: poor handicapper: often reaches frame, but won for only time in almost 2 years at Newcastle in August: stays 1½m: probably not at his best on soft going nowadays, acts on any other: blinkered sixth outing: sometimes sweats: suitable mount for inexperienced rider: consistent. *Denys Smith.* **42**

IVORS GUEST 3 b.c. Be My Guest (USA) 126–Ivor's Date (USA) (Sir Ivor 135) [1988 NR 1989 8m 10g] 50,000Y: leggy, quite good-topped colt: fourth foal: brother to Irish 1¾m winner Jaiyaash: dam French maiden: second favourite, about 10 lengths seventh of 10 in maiden at the Curragh in May when trained by M. V. O'Brien: 100/1, always behind in minor event at Leicester over 5 months later. *Mrs J. Pitman.* **—**

IVORY'S OF RADLETT 2 b.g. (May 17) Alzao (USA) 117–La Croisette 54 (Nishapour (FR) 125) [1989 6m 6m 5f⁵ 5f* 5f⁵ 5.3h² 5.8f⁶ 5.1m² a6g a5g a6g⁵ a7g⁶ a8g] IR 1,000F: small gelding: third foal: dam ran once at 2 yrs in Ireland: won seller (no bid) at Warwick in July: ran moderately in nurseries: best form at 5f: sometimes bandaged: inconsistent. *K. T. Ivory.*

IVORY WAY (USA) 3 b.c. Sir Ivor 135–Frederick Street (Traffic Judge) [1988 90 NR 1989 9f 10f³ 10.4m* 12g] $55,000Y: compact, attractive colt: half-brother to numerous winners in USA: dam prolific winner at up to 1m: impressive winner of maiden at Chester in July: never dangerous facing stiff task in £8,000 handicap at Newbury 4 weeks later: stays 1¼m well. *J. H. M. Gosden.*

IVREA 2 b.f. (May 14) Sadler's Wells (USA) 132–Ivy (USA) (Sir Ivor 135) [1989 88 P 7f*] 160,000Y: well-grown, angular filly: third foal: half-sister to Irish 7f (at 2 yrs) and 13f winner Royal Climber (by Kings Lake): dam, placed twice at 2 yrs in USA, is half-sister to An Act, high-class 3-y-o in USA when successful in 9f Santa Anita Derby: odds on, won 11-runner maiden at Leicester in October easily by 3 lengths from Katsina, leading 2f out then quickening clear inside last: will be well suited by middle distances: sure to improve considerably: a useful filly in the making. *M. R. Stoute.*

IVYCHURCH (USA) 3 ch.c. Sir Ivor 135–Sunday Purchase (USA) (T V Lark) 81 [1988 NR 1989 11.7d² 16.5g* 14.8m] heavy-topped colt: carries condition: brother to 1979 Horris Hill winner Super Asset and high-class 8.5f to 1¼m winner Bates Motel and half-brother to several winners, including very smart middle-distance winner Hatim (by Exclusive Native), later Grade 1 winner in USA: dam, 1m winner, is half-sister to high-class 1971 USA 2-y-o Rest Your Case: favourite, won ladies maiden race at Doncaster in June: second favourite but facing stiff task, driven long way out when last of 7 in £7,200 handicap at Newmarket 2 weeks later: looks very much a stayer: possibly unsuited by top-of-the-ground: sold to join J. Joseph 17,000 gns Newmarket September Sales. *G. Harwood.*

IVY ROSS 3 ch.f. Sandhurst Prince 128–Light Diamond (Florescence 120) [1988 — 6d⁶ 6f 6f⁴ 7.5g 1989 8s 8g] angular, sparely-made, plain filly: poor walker: well beaten, in sellers in spring as 3-y-o: reportedly in foal to Grey Desire. *M. Brittain.*

I WANNA DANCE 2 b.c. (Mar 20) Music Boy 124–Magic Formula 70 (St Paddy — 133) [1989 6m] 19,000Y: third foal: half-brother to Italian 3-y-o 1¼m winner Optimist (by Blakeney), fairly useful stayer at 2 yrs, and 1987 2-y-o 7f seller winner Caesar's Palace (by Mr Fluorocarbon): dam showed some ability on flat and won 2m selling hurdle: 25/1 and in need of race, well-beaten seventh of 8 in maiden at Pontefract in August: gave trouble stalls: sold 2,500 gns Newmarket Autumn Sales. *N. Tinkler.*

IZYORZAHALF 4 b.f. Vaigly Great 127–Quick Half (Quorum 126) [1988 8g⁵ — 1989 12.5g 10.6g 10.8f⁵ 10f⁶ 8h²] leggy, angular filly: poor maiden: unlikely to stay 1½m: bandaged off-fore at 4 yrs: sold 900 gns Doncaster October Sales. *D. McCain.*

J

JABARABA (USA) 8 b.g. Raja Baba (USA)–Time To Step (USA) (Time Tested — (USA)) [1988 11.7f 12g⁴ 13.3m 12f⁵ 12f* 12m⁵ 12d⁵ 12f* 12f³ 12m³ 12m 1989 14s 12s 12f] tall gelding: plating-class winner as 7-y-o: well beaten in 1989: stays 1½m: suited by top-of-the-ground: showed nothing in blinkers or visor: good mount for apprentice: has won 4 times at Folkestone. *J. A. Bennett.*

JACAMAR 3 b.c. Jalmood (USA) 126–Streamertail 81 (Shirley Heights 130) [1988 84 § 6f³ 6f* 7d³ 1989 12s⁵ 8m 8f⁴ 7m 7m 7.6g 8f* 8g 8.3g 8g 9g 9g a7g⁴ a10g⁵ a8g* a10g²] good-topped, lengthy colt: keen walker: has a quick action: fair handicapper on his day: in good form on the all-weather, winning at Lingfield in December, but little other form as 3-y-o besides making all at Newcastle in July: stays 1¼m: goes well on firm going and unsuited by a soft surface: wearing tongue strap, virtually pulled up sixth start: can't be relied upon. *B. Hanbury.*

JACKANDORA 4 b.f. Workboy 123–Betrothed (Aglojo 119) [1988 8v⁶ 7m⁴ 8m⁵ — 7.5g 7d 1989 6d 8.2v⁴ 10d] medium-sized, rather unfurnished filly: moderate mover: poor plater: stays 1m: acts on top-of-the-ground: blinkered 4 times, including all starts as 4-y-o: sweating on reappearance: has looked ungenerous: sold 950 gns Ascot June Sales. *A. D. Brown.*

JACK BOY 4 b.g. Sparkling Boy 110–Miss Deed 83 (David Jack 125) [1988 8f 5d⁶ — 6m⁴ 6m* 6h 7g 6m³ 5d² 5g² 1989 5g 6f 5m 5f 5d 5m 5g] small, sturdy gelding:

winning plater as 3-y-o when trained by M. Tompkins: well beaten in handicaps in 1989: suited by sprint distances: acts on top-of-the-ground and a soft surface: blinkered sixth outing. *J. Balding.*

JACK TULLY 2 b.c. (Apr 9) Mouktar 129–Fabulous Luba (Luthier 126) [1989 7g] — 7,400Y: leggy, angular colt: third foal: half-brother to 3-y-o winning hurdler Beau Rolando (by Teenoso) and fairly useful 7f and 1m winner Kristal Rock (by Kris): dam, second twice over 1m in France, is daughter of Altesse Royale: 50/1 and burly, never in contention in 28-runner maiden at Newmarket in November. *G. A. Huffer.*

JACOMINO 2 gr.c. (Apr 10) Petong 126–Balearica 90 (Bustino 136) [1989 5s 6f³ 77 6g*] 22,000Y: compact, quite well-made colt: second foal: half-brother to 3-y-o Where's The Money (by Lochnager), fair 5f winner at 2 yrs: dam, placed from 6f to 1m, is daughter of sister to Runnett: made all and kept on strongly in maiden at Goodwood in October, beating Usaylah by a length: off course over 5 months after debut: will probably stay 7f: sold to race in Macau 15,000 gns Doncaster November Sales. *I. V. Matthews.*

JADEBELLE 3 b.f. Beldale Flutter (USA) 130–Precious Jade 72 (Northfields 62 (USA)) [1988 6f 7m³ 6g* 1989 7s 8f 8m² 8f4 8g³ 10m⁵ 12f²] small, strong, lengthy filly: carries condition: quite modest performer: good second in claimer at Salisbury (claimed to join W. G. M. Turner £12,000) in August on final start: stays 1½m: acts on firm going. *M. A. Jarvis.*

JADEITE (FR) 3 b.c. Crystal Glitters (USA) 127–Jawhara 93 (Upper Case 85 (USA)) [1988 6d 7m 7s 1989 8g4 10m* 10.6m* 10.6g4 12f 10m³ 8.2g* 8f 10f4 10g6] tall, lengthy colt: carries condition: has a rather round action: fair handicapper: successful at Nottingham in May then Haydock in May and August: below form last 3 starts: at least as effective over 1m as 1¼m: acts on top-of-the-ground: wears crossed noseband: best when able to set pace. *R. Boss.*

JADE 'N AMBER 4 b.f. Sonnen Gold 121–Madame Quickly 80 (Saint Crespin III — 132) [1988 NR 1989 10f 10.1m] leggy, rather angular filly: half-sister to several winners, including useful French 6f and 1m winner Kisty (by Kashmir II): dam won at up to 7f: well beaten in sellers at Chepstow (slowly away) and Windsor in July. *C. P. Wildman.*

JADE ROBBERY (USA) 2 br.c. (Mar 14) Mr Prospector (USA)–Number 121 p (USA) (Nijinsky (USA) 138) [1989 6d² 7g* 8d² 8m*]

If most reports are to be believed the relationship between Andre Fabre and his retained jockey Cash Asmussen is occasionally somewhat strained. That's as maybe, as they say, but there's no denying that the two combine to make one of the most potent forces French racing has ever seen. Fabre and Asmussen won their respective trainers' and jockeys' championships by a street's length in 1989, in the course of doing so achieving some remarkable statistics, with Fabre himself winning almost a third of all French pattern races. The opening day of the Ciga Prix de l'Arc de Triomphe meeting at Longchamp in October was exceptional for the partnership even by their standards. Asmussen rode four of the day's five pattern-race winners, three of them for Fabre, notably the Grand Criterium winner Jade Robbery who is probably a top-class colt in the making.

Jade Robbery made his first appearance in the Prix Yacowlef at Deauville in August, a newcomers race that traditionally attracts some of the better French two-year-olds. Although he proved no match for Machiavellian he shaped with plenty of promise, and an impressive defeat of Honor Rajana and four others in a listed race on the same course later in the month indicated he was likely to make a name for himself in good company before the end of the year. Jade Robbery's first chance to tackle a pattern race came in the Group 3 Prix La Rochette at Longchamp in September. In a seven-runner field Honor Rajana was again among the opposition; so was Linamix, an impressive course and distance winner on his debut, and also the highly-regarded Septieme Ciel. The race was straightforward. Linamix was sent off in front until challenged, possibly headed, by Jade Robbery a furlong and a half out. However, Linamix rallied splendidly to regain the initiative inside the last and ran on strongly to win by three quarters of a length with Honor Rajana the same distance back in third. Doubtless those who'd supported Jade Robbery at odds on were a shade disappointed, but considering he was conceding 4 lb to the winner—a colt said to be rated only just behind the Prix Morny and Prix de la Salamandre winner Machiavellian by the Boutin stable—it was a very good effort indeed.

The Grand Criterium has long been regarded as the most significant French two-year-old race of the season, and even without Machiavellian, who was withdrawn coughing, the line-up for the latest renewal looked a strong one. The first three from the Rochette renewed rivalry, this time on level terms; they were joined by five others, including Filago, unbeaten in three starts and stepping up to a mile after winning France's richest two-year-old race the Challenge d'Or Piaget at Deauville, and also the British challenger Bold Ambition, who'd shaped promisingly to chase home the subsequent Royal Lodge winner Digression in a minor race at Kempton on his debut. There was particularly strong support for Filago, the unbeaten Linamix and Jade Robbery: the last-named started at 22/10, just behind the two others at 2/1. It was clear early in the straight, by which point the front-running Linamix was being asked to stretch for home, that Filago's supporters were unlikely to be collecting. Honor Rajana, equipped with blinkers for the first time, was also prominent, but Jade Robbery was the biggest danger of all. Eased left to challenge approaching the final furlong, Jade Robbery quickened really well to take the lead, and despite veering noticeably right in front he continued to run on strongly, eventually winning by three quarters of a length from Linamix; Honor Rajana, unable to quicken with the principals, was four lengths away in third with Filago and Bold Ambition fifth and last respectively. Fabre announced after the Criterium that he didn't consider Longchamp the ideal track for Jade Robbery and that he was more likely to send the colt for the General Accident Two Thousand Guineas than its French equivalent. With that statement in mind it's hard to understand why Jade Robbery is still quoted at 25/1 or thereabouts at the time of writing for the Guineas while Machiavellian is favourite in all lists. Admittedly, Machiavellian came out clearly the better in the Yacowlef, and he'd almost certainly have started a hot favourite had he been fit enough to contest the Criterium. However, in pulling four lengths clear of the very useful and consistent Honor Rajana at Longchamp Jade Robbery and Linamix proved themselves colts with genuine classic potential. Moreover, Jade Robbery gave the impression he could have doubled his winning margin had he kept straight, and if he does arrive at Newmarket fit and well on Guineas day he will have to be considered very seriously indeed.

If Jade Robbery wins a good race in 1990 he'll be a valuable stallion commodity. There are few, if any, shortcomings in his pedigree. Like Gold Seam he's the product of a mating between the outstanding stallion Mr Prospector and a Nijinsky mare, in his case Number. Number was a very smart performer both at three and four, winning eight races including the Grade 2 Firenze and Hempstead Handicaps over nine furlongs. Her two foals prior to Jade Robbery, a filly by Spectacular Bid and a colt by Devil's Bag, are

Ciga Grand Criterium, Longchamp—Jade Robbery turns the tables on Linamix and provides jockey Asmussen with the third of four pattern-race victories during the afternoon

both minor winners in the States, and her credentials as a broodmare are hard to fault. A daughter of Special, herself a sister to Thatch and a half-sister to King Pellinore and Marinsky, Number is a sister to another good stakes-winning filly in Bound and a close relation to Nureyev; if that's not enough she's also a half-sister to the smart Irish two-year-old Fairy Bridge, who's earned a reputation as one of the most successful broodmares of the last decade through the exploits of, among others, Sadler's Wells, Tate Gallery and the successful first-season sire Fairy King.

			Raise A Native (ch 1961)	Native Dancer
				Raise You
	Mr Prospector (USA) (b 1970)		Gold Digger (b 1962)	Nashua
Jade Robbery (USA) (br.c. Mar 14, 1987)				Sequence
			Nijinsky (b 1967)	Northern Dancer
				Flaming Page
	Number (USA) (b 1979)		Special (b 1969)	Forli
				Thong

As can be seen, this family has produced horses who stay beyond a mile, but Fabre has expressed doubts whether Jade Robbery will; they could prove well founded. Jade Robbery is a free-running colt who can also produce a sharp turn of foot that might well mean he could eventually prove best suited to waiting tactics. He cost 800,000 dollars at the Keeneland July Sale as a yearling, and his owner returned to the same venue in the latest season to pay 2,800,000 dollars for the sale-topping son of Northern Dancer out of Mrs Penny. *A. Fabre, France.*

JAGGED EDGE 2 ch.c. (Apr 18) Sharpo 132–Tura (Northfields (USA)) [1989 6m 6f² 5d* 6v] 29,000Y: neat colt: second foal: half-brother to 3-y-o Young Turpin (by Young Generation), fair performer at up to 1m: dam 7f winner in Ireland: favourite, won maiden at Catterick by ½ length from Madeley's Pet, having been outpaced: favourite, respectable tenth of 23 (having been bumped in early stages) in nursery at Newbury later in October: likely to prove suited by further than 5f: sold to join R. Holder 9,000 gns Newmarket Autumn Sales. *A. C. Stewart.* **72**

JAGJET 2 ch.c. (Apr 16) Vayrann 133–Ritsurin 79 (Mount Hagen (FR) 127) [1989 5v 5.3g* 5m 7m² 7m⁶ 9g⁵ 7g⁵ 8g 7d] 5,000Y: smallish, good-topped colt: poor mover: third foal: half-brother to fair 1987 2-y-o 6f winner Reformando (by Formidable): dam 6f winner at 2 yrs, only season to race: modest performer: won maiden auction race at Brighton in April: showed better form later in season: best form at 7f. *W. Carter.* **72**

JAHZEEN 3 b.c. Shareef Dancer (USA) 135–Dancing Meg (USA) 113 (Marshua's Dancer (USA)) [1988 NR 1989 10.8s² 10g] 180,000Y: medium-sized, useful-looking colt: moderate mover: second foal: half-brother to 12.3f winner Please Kenneh (by Golden Fleece): dam won over 6f and 1m at 2 yrs and stayed 1½m at 3 yrs: 11/2, 3 lengths second of 10 to Carmagnole in maiden at Warwick in March, always close up but green on home turn: well beaten in similar event at Leicester following month: should be suited by 1½m: possibly needs plenty of give in the ground: sold to join J. Mackie 8,200 gns Newmarket July Sales. *P. F. I. Cole.* **67**

JAILBREAKER 2 ch.g. (May 19) Prince of Peace 109–Last Farewell (Palm Track 122) [1989 7f] second foal: dam never ran: 33/1, well beaten in 14-runner maiden at Salisbury in October. *R. J. Holder.* **—**

JALEES 3 b.c. Precocious 126–Walladah (USA) 71 (Northern Dancer) [1988 6f 7g 1989 6v⁵ 7s 7s 7f 6m] compact, good-bodied colt: little worthwhile form in varied events, off course 5 months before final start: blinkered time before. *G. G. Gracey.* **—**

JALJULI 3 b.f. Jalmood (USA) 126–Anjuli (Northfields (USA)) [1988 5m* 6d⁴ 6d⁴ 6f* 6g³ 7d² 1989 7m⁵ 7m] compact, attractive filly: has a rather round action: useful at 2 yrs, successful twice and in frame in 4 pattern events: early speed when tailed off as 3-y-o in £10,500 event at Newmarket in June and £49,600 handicap at Ascot in September: should stay 1m: best efforts on an easy surface. *R. W. Armstrong.* **—**

JALMUSIQUE 3 ch.g. Jalmood (USA) 126–Rose Music 86 (Luthier 126) [1988 6m³ 7m* 6g⁴ 8s 7.5f* 7g 1989 10v 9f* 8.2m 10.6g³ 8f² 8g] strong, good-bodied gelding: fairly useful handicapper: won at York in May, always prominent and rallying well: placed, running creditably, at Haydock and Newcastle: needs forcing tactics over 1m, uncertain to stay beyond 1¼m: acts on firm going and possibly unsuited by soft. *M. H. Easterby.* **89**

JALOPY 3 b.f. Jalmood (USA) 126–Starry Way (Star Appeal 133) [1988 6g 5s³ 6g 71 1989 5d* 6h²] useful-looking filly: won maiden at Edinburgh in April: again favourite, good head second in handicap at Carlisle following month: suited by 6f: acts on any going. *Sir Mark Prescott.*

JAMALEY 3 b.g. Relkino 131–Clatter 67 (Songedor (116) [1988 NR 1989 10f] big, — good-topped gelding: eighth foal: closely related to 9f and 1¼m winner Breckland Lady (by Royalty) and half-brother to 5f winner Burglar Tip (by Burglar): dam placed over 5f at 2 yrs: green, slowly away and always behind in claimer at Folkestone in May: sold to join S. Davis 1,650 gns Ascot July Sales. *P. Howling.*

JAMARJ 4 br.f. Tyrnavos 129–Veneziana 91 (Tiger 125) [1988 9g* 8m* 8d⁴ 8m 102 10g⁵ 9s³ 8g* 7g 8d* 1989 6s⁶ 7g 8f 9m⁴ 8m 8m² 9m³ 8g 7g] medium-sized, good-quartered filly: has a quick action: developed into a very useful performer as 3-y-o, winning handicaps at York and Haydock and listed events at Doncaster and Ascot: not so good in 1989: easily best efforts when placed in handicaps at Ripon and York: suited by 1m or 9f: acts on any going: usually taken down early nowadays: sometimes hangs: tail swisher. *M. H. Easterby.*

JAMESIE 2 ch.g. (Jan 28) Noalto 120–Ann Wilson (Tumble Wind (USA)) [1989 7f — 7m 6g] fourth foal: brother to 3-y-o Miss Kilpatrick: dam never ran: ridden by 7-lb claimer, tailed off in maidens. *D. C. Jermy.*

JAMES RIVER 3 ch.c. Star Appeal 133–Yorktown (Charlottown 127) [1988 7g 7g 53 1989 10m⁴ 11.5f 16f⁶ 12f a12g a16g⁵ a12g⁴] leggy, light-framed colt: virtually only signs of ability in handicap and claimer (blinkered) at Lingfield last 2 outings: should stay beyond 1½m. *J. L. Dunlop.*

JAMES'S PET 2 gr.c. (Mar 2) Petong 126–Conway Bay 74 (Saritamer (USA) 54 130) [1989 6m 6f³ 5f⁴ 6f* 6m⁵] 12,000Y: quite good-topped colt: moderate mover: half-brother to 3-y-o 6f winner Conway King (by King of Spain) and 8.2f seller winner Light The Way (by Nicholas Bill): dam, placed over 5f at 2 yrs, appeared not to train on: fair plater: won at Yarmouth (no bid) in July: ridden by 7-lb claimer, modest fifth in nursery at Nottingham following month: suited by 6f: retained 3,400 gns Newmarket Autumn Sales. *N. A. Callaghan.*

JAMIE LOCH 2 br.f. (Mar 6) Daring March 116–Daisy Loch (Lochnager 132) 43 [1989 5m 6f⁶ 5.3h³ 5f 5g 6f] compact filly: carries condition: has a markedly round action: first reported foal: dam poor plater: quite modest plater. *L. J. Holt.*

JAMIN 2 b.c. (Mar 17) Teenoso (USA) 135–Miss Longchamp 94 (Northfields 67 p (USA)) [1989 6m] strong, lengthy colt: fourth foal: half-brother to 3-y-o Pharamineux (by Pharly), Irish 6f winner Miss Bagatelle and fair 1986 2-y-o 6f winner Le Favori (both by Mummy's Pet): dam won at 7.2f and 1m at 3 yrs: 11/2, around 9 lengths seventh of 11, bit slowly away and never dangerous, to stable-companion Dorset Duke in maiden at Newmarket in July: should improve. *G. Wragg.*

JANE'S BRAVE BOY 7 b.g. Brave Shot–Jane Merryn (Above Suspicion 127) 41 [1988 7g 7d* 8g 7g 7.5m 7f* 7.5f 7g* 7d 7d³ 7f 7m 7f 8m 1989 8g 7m⁶ 7m 7f 7.5f³ 7g* 7.5m 7s 7g 7m⁶] workmanlike gelding: carries plenty of condition: poor handicapper: justified favouritism at Catterick in August, second outing in 2 days: suited by 7f and a turning track: possibly unsuited by soft going, acts on any other: goes well with forcing tactics: ran poorly when sweating third start: often apprentice ridden. *D. W. Chapman.*

JANIE-O 6 ch.m. Hittite Glory 125–Tweezer (Songedor 116) [1988 7d³ 7.6d⁶ — 7.6g² 7.6f 7.6f 8.5g⁴ 10m 1989 7m 10m 8.2d] compact, good-bodied mare: quite modest handicapper at her best: lightly raced and below form as 6-y-o: best at 7f to 1m with forcing tactics: ideally suited by an easy surface: blinkered twice, usually visored: often wears crossed noseband: has sweated and got on toes: good mount for inexperienced rider: winning selling hurdler. *M. H. Tompkins.*

JANISKI 6 b.g. Niniski (USA) 125–Seasurf 106 (Seaepic (USA) 100) [1988 12g⁵ 79 16m⁵ 14g⁵ 14d 16.5g³ 16m² 16m* 18g 16m* 18g⁶ 1989 16f⁶ 16m⁴ 16.1m⁴] strong gelding: has a quick action: fair handicapper: suited by 2m and top-of-the-ground: has run well in blinkers, usually visored nowadays: a difficult ride who's best covered up. *Mrs Barbara Waring.*

JANUARY DON 4 b.c. Hold Your Peace (USA)–Meg's Pride (Sparkler 130) — [1988 7d 12f 10g 10f* 10g⁶ 12m 1989 12s 10.1m] angular, lengthy colt: plating-class winner as 3-y-o: well behind both outings in first half of 1989: suited by 1¼m and forcing tactics: acts on any going: often blinkered. *G. A. Pritchard-Gordon.*

JARPEE 3 ch.g. Bay Express 132–Romancing 82 (Romulus 129) [1988 5g 6m⁶ — 1989 6s 5f 7.5f⁵ 8h⁶ 8g] lengthy, sparely-made gelding: moderate mover: quite

444

modest maiden: little form as 3-y-o, soon struggling in claimer on final start (June) when claimed to join N. Ayliffe £6,100: probably stays 1m. *R. M. Whitaker.*

JASCHA 3 b.f. Music Boy 124–Ardmay 57 (Roan Rocket 128) [1988 NR 1989 7f 7.6m³ 5g 6f 6d a8g4] 10,000Y: strong, sturdy filly: third foal: half-sister to Irgaim (by Valiyar), fairly useful 6f and 7f winner: dam sister to Gairloch and Whistlefield: quite modest form when in frame in claimer at Chester and maiden (better for race) at Southwell: stays 1m: acts on top-of-the-ground: sweating last 2 starts, edgy on first of them. *R. F. Johnson Houghton.* **61**

JASGALORE 3 ch.g. Simply Great (FR) 122–Caithness 78 (Connaught 130) [1988 7.5s 6g 6m 1989 11f 12g²] lengthy gelding: carries condition: 16/1, showed improved form when beaten length in 18-runner handicap at Hamilton in September, always close up and keeping on well: may well stay further: possibly unsuited by very firm going. *J. G. FitzGerald.* **62**

JATHIBIYAH (USA) 2 b.f. (Apr 2) Nureyev (USA) 131–Carefully Hidden (USA) (Caro 133) [1989 7m* 8.2s²] $850,000Y: leggy, quite attractive filly: good walker: fourth foal: closely related to Irish 1000 Guineas winner Enscorse (by Lyphard) and fairly useful 1987 2-y-o 6f winner Rimsh (by Storm Bird): dam, minor 7f winner at 3 yrs, is half-sister to dam of Glint of Gold and Diamond Shoal: 9/4, dead-heated with Mermaid's Purse in maiden at Redcar in September, disputing lead 2f out and rallying strongly final ½f: beaten a head by Liffey Lace in 4-runner minor event at Haydock following month, unable to quicken having travelled strongly: stays 1m: likely to improve further. *H. Thomson Jones.* **85 p**

JAUNTY SLAVE 5 ch.m. Le Johnstan 123–May Slave (Arctic Slave 116) [1988 NR 1989 12d³ 8.5g 8.5f 7.5f 7f³ 7m⁶ 6f 6m] lengthy, workmanlike mare: half-sister to winning point-to-pointer Rastasemefaich (by Goldhill): dam lightly-raced novice hurdler: poor maiden: should stay 1m: acts on firm going: sold 8,800 gns Doncaster August Sales. *J. P. Leigh.* **27**

JAVERT 4 ch.c. Kings Lake (USA) 133–Red Berry 115 (Great Nephew 126) [1988 NR 1989 10d 8.5g4] strong, sturdy, medium-sized colt: runner-up in maiden at Leicester only outing as 2-y-o: sold out of L. Cumani's stable 6,200 gns Newmarket September (1988) Sales: shaped well in minor event (took keen hold) at Pontefract and maiden at Beverley in spring, but wasn't seen out again: should stay beyond 8.5f. *M. Brittain.* **63**

JAWBREAKER 3 b.c. Bustino 136–Miss Candine 66 (King Emperor (USA)) [1988 6m⁶ 8s 10d⁵ 1989 12m⁶] sturdy, lengthy colt: modest form: 20/1 and bit backward, about 4 lengths sixth of 8 to Derab in maiden event at Newmarket in May, given plenty to do and staying on strongly: will stay beyond 1½m. *R. W. Armstrong.* **72**

JAYDEEGLEN 2 b.f. (May 17) Bay Express 132–Friendly Glen (Furry Glen 121) [1989 5f² 5g4] leggy, sparely-made filly: second foal: dam, winning chaser, ran 3 times on flat: lengths second of 6, keeping on, to Night At Sea at Wolverhampton in October, much better effort in maidens: poorly drawn next time. *M. Johnston.* **73**

JAY-DEE-JAY 6 b.m. Mljet–Tagliatelle (Straight Lad 110) [1988 NR 1989 12m] third foal: dam novice hurdler/chaser: tailed off in amateurs event at Newmarket in July: winning hurdler. *J. D. J. Davies.* **—**

JAYIZ (USA) 2 ch.c. (Apr 7) The Minstrel (CAN) 135–Celebrity Guest (USA) (Gallant Man) [1989 8g*] $55,000Y: fourth foal: half-brother to winners in USA by Icecapade and Tom Rolfe: dam, winner twice at up to 7f in USA, is half-sister to very smart 1978 American 2-y-o filly Fall Aspen, the dam of Northern Aspen and Mazzacano: awarded 5-runner maiden at Leopardstown in September after being beaten a neck: will probably stay 1¼m. *K. Prendergast, Ireland.* **86 p**

JAYLAND 3 ch.c. Kings Lake (USA) 133–Santarelle 78 (Jim French (USA)) [1988 6d 8s 8g 1989 10s4 8g 10f³ 12f4 10g 14g² 12m⁶] smallish, rather dipped-backed colt: moderate walker: quite modest maiden: well-backed favourite, best effort when second in claimer at Yarmouth, leading well over 3f out but outstayed: blinkered, not discredited in seller later in July: should prove suited by 1½m: probably acts on any going: has joined P. Jones. *R. Hannon.* **59**

JAZAF (USA) 2 b.g. (Mar 12) Hero's Honor (USA)–Fleeing Partner (USA) (Fleet Nasrullah) [1989 8g³] $30,000Y: half-brother to numerous winners in USA, notably 7f and 8.5f stakes winner Varick (by Mr Prospector): dam, 2-y-o 6f winner, is half-sister to Santa Anita Derby winner Jim French and to dam of good performers Formidable, Fabuleux Jane and Ajdal: weak 12/1 and green, over 4 lengths third of 16, clear, to My Lord in maiden at Leicester in November: sure to improve. *P. F. I. Cole.* **73 p**

J BRAND 2 b.c. (Mar 1) Persian Bold 123–Napa Valley 89 (Wolver Hollow 126) —
[1989 7m 7g 6f⁵ a7g] 10,500Y: sparely-made colt: has a short, sharp action: third
foal: dam 1m winner at 2 yrs, is half-sister to good continental stayer Duky and
daughter of half-sister to Gold Cup winner Shangamuzo: poor form in maidens and a
nursery: will probably be better suited by 1¼m + . *P. F. I. Cole.*

J CHEEVER LOOPHOLE 4 gr.g. King of Spain 121–Sally's Silver 62 (No **89**
Mercy 126) [1988 6d 5v 5g 5m 5f 5g⁶ 5f² 5f³ 5g 5f 6g 5m 1989 5g⁵ 5g 5f 5f² 5.8f⁵ 5d
5d a6g² a6g* a5g⁵ a6g²] lengthy gelding: fair handicapper nowadays: made all at
Lingfield in November: best at 5f or easy 6f: probably acts on any going: has
appeared unsuited by track at Epsom: blinkered twice at 3 yrs, visored third outing:
has not found great deal under pressure. *C. Tinkler.*

JEALOUS LOVER 5 gr.m. Alias Smith (USA)–Drawing Room Car **49**
(Chingacgook 128) [1988 10f* 10.1g⁵ 10.1g⁶ 10g 12h⁶ 10d³ 1989 10s² 10f 15.3m 12h²
10f⁵ 12f* 12.2f³ a11g] small mare: modest plater: won moderately-run
event at Lingfield (bought in 4,200 gns) in August: better suited by 1½m than 1¼m,
and should stay further: acts on any going: usually blinkered nowadays: has also
worn a hood. *P. J. Makin.*

JEAN DUKE'S LAD 3 ch.g. Bay Express 132–Pounakha (USA) (Shecky —
Greene (USA)) [1988 5v⁴ 5s 5.1f 5g* 1989 6m 10m⁴ 10f 10g 10.2m⁶ 8m 9f] smallish,
strong gelding: blinkered, won seller in July as 2-y-o: bandaged, showed little in
1989, including in handicaps. *T. Kersey.*

JEBALI 2 ch.c. (Jan 31) Good Times (ITY)–Penitent 85 (Sing Sing 134) [1989 6m⁴ **74**
7m² 7g² 7f] 8,200F, 9,000Y: big, lengthy colt: has plenty of scope: half-brother to
several winners, including useful Irish middle-distance colt March Song (by
Blakeney) and quite useful sprinter Penumbra (by Wolver Hollow): dam closely
related to top sprinter Song: modest maiden: best effort third start: not seen out
after July. *R. Hannon.*

JEEDAMAYA 3 b.f. Taufan (USA) 119–Rosie O'Grady (Barrons Court) [1988 6g —
7m³ 7.5s⁶ 7f³ 8.2m 1989 10.2m 12h 12f⁵] leggy, sparely-made filly: plating-class
maiden at 2 yrs: well beaten in handicaps and claimer (claimed £5,000) in first half of
1989: stays 1m: possibly unsuited by very firm going: tailed off when blinkered:
races keenly. *D. W. P. Arbuthnot.*

JEHOL 3 b.c. Teenoso (USA) 135–Buz Kashi 123 (Bold Lad (IRE) 133) [1988 7g **101**
8d⁵ 1989 10m³ 12m* 12m⁶] lengthy, useful-looking colt: sweating slightly,
comfortably landed the odds in slowly-run maiden at York in September: 6/1, about 5
lengths sixth of 8 to Spritsail in listed race at Newmarket 4 weeks later: stays 1½m:
took good hold last 2 outings: useful. *G. Wragg.*

JENDRA 3 b.f. Horage 124–Mother White (Jukebox 120) [1988 5.1g⁴ 6f 6g 8g 8d —
1989 6v 6s 8h 6f 7h] workmanlike filly: plating-class maiden at best: no worthwhile
form as 3-y-o, in sellers last 3 outings: not seen out after June: doesn't stay 1m. *P.
Howling.*

JENNY B QUICK 2 ch.f. (Mar 1) Mandrake Major 122–Clairwood (Final Straw —
127) [1989 5s 5f] lengthy, workmanlike filly: moderate walker: first foal: dam lightly
raced: backward, well beaten in early-season maiden at Thirsk and claimer at
Redcar. *E. Weymes.*

JEROZA (USA) 3 b.f. Shareef Dancer (USA) 135–Tarpoon (USA) (Vaguely —
Noble 140) [1988 NR 1989 8g 8.2m] good-bodied, attractive filly: poor
mover: second foal: dam, Irish 9f winner, half-sister to Irish 1000 Guineas winner
Gaily and high-class American 6f to 9f winner King's Bishop: well beaten in maidens
at Yarmouth (ridden by 7-lb claimer, edgy and very green) and Haydock (pushed
along over 4f out) in September: will stay further: sold 2,600 gns Newmarket
December Sales. *L. Cumani.*

JESSAMINE 4 ch.f. Jalmood (USA) 126–Broad Horizon 89 (Blakeney 126) [1988 —
8m⁶ 10.2m 1989 10m] sturdy filly: little worthwhile form in fair company: slowly
away only outing at 4 yrs. *C. F. Wall.*

JESTMENOT 3 gr.g. Jester 119–Petite Ville (Ballymore 123) [1988 5f 5g 1989 6s —
6m 8g 7f 11s] leggy gelding: no form in varied events in the North, including sellers.
J. S. Wainwright.

JIGGER 2 ch.c. (Apr 20) Miramar Reef 100§–Visiting 77 (Vitiges (FR) 132) [1989 —
5m 6m] leggy, unfurnished colt: first foal: dam 11.7f winner, always backward, always
behind in maidens at Bath (slowly away) and Haydock (June). *L. G. Cottrell.*

JIGGERY POKERY 3 ch.f. Final Straw 127–Well Off (Welsh Pageant 132) **94**
[1988 NR 1989 8m 8m³ 9g* 10.2m⁶] lengthy, rather unfurnished filly: good walker:

half-sister to French 9f winner Miss Moneybags (by Dominion), useful 6f and 7f winner Royal Loft (by Homing) and winners in Belgium and Malaysia: dam, of little account, is half-sister to useful sprinter Doc Marten: bit green, won 3-runner minor event at Wolverhampton in July by 10 lengths from eased Aljood, leading on bridle 1f out: 8/1, never dangerous when about 4½ lengths sixth of 7 to Rambushka in moderately-run listed race at Newcastle 4 weeks later: stays 1¼m: quite useful. *W. Jarvis.*

JIGS AND REELS   3 b.f. Comedy Star (USA) 121–Sirnelta (FR) (Sir Tor) [1988   **63** 5m³ 7g⁶ 7g 7m 7m* 7g* 1989 8s 8f 8.5g³ 7.6h 8m³ 7f² 8.2m 7g³ 8g 8f] leggy, sparely-made filly: moderate mover: quite modest performer: stays 8.5f: acts on firm going: sometimes blinkered or visored: has pulled hard: ran well when edgy but badly when sweating. *R. F. Johnson Houghton.*

JIM BRIDGER   4 ch.g. Little Wolf 127–Candid Queen 80 (Good Bond 122) [1988   **51** d 12m⁶ 14m⁴ 15g* 12m³ 14g 12g² 12g* 15m 17g⁴ 12g⁴ 12d⁵ 1989 12d 12.5g³ 12h 15.3m² 18.8f 14m 12.5f] sparely-made gelding: would have won selling handicap at Wolverhampton in June (beaten ¾ length) had he not been hampered: ran moderately in handicaps afterwards: stays 15f: acts on top-of-the-ground (possibly unsuited by very firm going): sweating and edgy sixth start: has won for apprentice: often takes strong hold, and has worn crossed noseband: trained until after fifth outing by W. Wilson. *P. J. Feilden.*

JIMMY JUDGE   3 ch.g. Longleat (USA) 109–Immatation (FR) 67 (Polyfoto 124)   — [1988 6f 1989 11.7g² 8.3d] good-topped gelding: poor mover: soundly beaten in sellers and a claimer. *P. Burgoyne.*

JINDABYNE   3 b.f. Good Times (ITY)–Wayleave (Blakeney 126) [1988 NR 1989   — 8m] 1,500Y: fourth living foal: half-sister to 1½m seller winner S S Santo (by Monsanto): dam ran once: backward, always behind in Newmarket maiden in July: sold 1,200 gns Newmarket Autumn Sales. *M. J. Ryan.*

JINGA   4 b.c. Castle Keep 121–Eldoret 100 (High Top 131) [1988 11.7g² 14m² 16f*   **88** 18d³ 16m² 1989 12v² 12d* 14s⁴ 14m⁶ 16m 16.2m* 16.5m³ 13.1f⁴ 14.8m²] lengthy, quite attractive colt: fair handicapper: won at Newmarket in April and Beverley (odds on) in July: ran creditably last 2 outings: effective at 1½m and stays well: acts on any going: inconsistent. *Lady Herries.*

JIVE MUSIC   3 b.f. Music Boy 124–Swift To Conquer 87 (Solinus 130) [1988 5g   **43** 5m 5g 5f³ 5d² 5f⁶ 5g² 5m⁵ 5d² 6g 5d⁶ 6f 6s 6s 1989 5s⁵ 5d 6m⁴ 5m⁴ 6g⁴ 5f 5m 5g 5m⁵] smallish, workmanlike, good-quartered filly: poor mover: poor maiden: should prove best at 5f: acts on top-of-the-ground and a soft surface: sometimes sweating and on edge: has run well for apprentice: occasionally blinkered at 2 yrs. *N. Bycroft.*

J M OWEN (USA)   3 ch.c. Plugged Nickle (USA)–Charmina (FR) (Nonoalco   — § (USA) 131) [1988 NR 1989 9s⁵ 8s 10d 9f 10g 16f³ 15.3g] 14,500Y: big, angular colt: moderate walker and mover: third foal: brother to maiden Charme The Nickle and half-brother to 6f winner Floral Charms (by Shecky Greene): dam, 8.2f winner in France, is from family of Dahlia: of little account and probably ungenuine: visored final start: trained first 4 by M. Brittain. *C. Spares.*

JOBISKA   3 b.f. Dunbeath (USA) 127–Jolisu 110 (Welsh Abbot 131) [1988 6g 1989   — 8d 8f 8g 10.1m] strong, good-bodied filly: quite modest maiden: not seen out after July: probably stays 1¼m: acts on top-of-the-ground and a soft surface. *Lord John FitzGerald.*

JODEES LUCK (USA)   3 b.c. Storm Bird (CAN) 134–Heathers Surprise (USA)   — (Best Turn (USA)) [1988 NR 1989 8m] leggy, close-coupled, angular colt: third foal: brother to 1986 2-y-o 7f winner Wuzo: dam twice-raced half-sister to dam of top-class performers Glorious Song, successful 17 times at up to 1¼m for over $1,000,000, and Devil's Bag, best American 2-y-o of 1983: 33/1, led 5f when well-beaten last of 12 in maiden at Newmarket in May: showed a round action. *R. W. Armstrong.*

JOE BUMPAS   3 b.c. Noalto 120–Montana Moss (Levmoss 133) [1988 8m 8m³   **54** 8.2s² 8f³ 1989 12.2d⁵ 10v⁶ 11f 13m 10g 12.2g 17f 10v 13.8d⁵ 9s³ 12g²] sturdy colt: shows plenty of knee action: plating-class maiden: well backed last 3 starts (5/1 favourite from 50/1 on first of them), best effort when beaten neck in seller at Leicester after quickening clear 3f out: stays 1½m: may prove best with some give in the ground: twice sweating, including when edgy third start: winning novice hurdler. *T. D. Barron.*

JOE SUGDEN   5 b.g. Music Boy 124–Sum Star 67 (Comedy Star (USA) 121)   **93** [1988 5s³ 5g 5f 5m 5g⁵ 5g² 5g⁴ 5d² 5g³ 6s⁶ 5m⁴ 1989 5f² 5f* 5m³ 5f² 5g⁵ 5m 5m⁴ 5f⁴ 5g³ 5g² 5m³ 5g² 5d⁵ 5s 6s 5m* 5d 5d³] tall gelding: moderate mover: fairly useful handicapper: successful at York in May (£11,600 Homeowners Sprint Handicap) and October: much better effort on latter occasion when beating Clarentia decisively by 2 lengths: suited by 5f: not at his best on soft going nowadays, acts very well on top-of-the-ground: has been tried in visor: has won for apprentice: tough and consistent. *R. M. Whitaker.*

JOHANNA THYME 2 b.f. (Apr 13) Reesh 117–Sea Thyme (Persian Bold 123) — [1989 6g 6g] 700F, 3,000Y, 5,600 2-y-o: poor mover: half-sister to a winner in Hong Kong by Balidar: dam never ran: well beaten in summer maidens at Redcar and Haydock (auction event, slowly away). *R. Bastiman.*

JOHN BOWLES (USA) 3 ch.c. Riverman (USA) 131–Exactly So (Caro 133) **90** [1988 NR 1989 8s² 8d* 9m²] $100,000Y: sparely-made, rather plain colt: moderate walker: third foal: half-brother to very smart French 7f (at 2 yrs) to 10.5f winner Exactly Sharp (by Sharpen Up) and a winner in USA by Blushing Groom: dam won at 10.5f at 3 yrs in France and later successful in USA: favourite, won maiden at Ripon in April: ridden by 7-lb claimer, creditable second in minor event at Wolverhampton 3½ months later, outpaced 2f out then staying on well: will stay 1¼m: sold 24,000 gns Newmarket Autumn Sales. *H. R. A. Cecil.*

JOHN NICK 4 b.g. Silly Prices 110–Unique Lady 69 (Lord David 121) [1988 NR — 1989 8m 8f 12g] workmanlike, close-coupled gelding: well beaten in maidens and handicaps. *F. Watson.*

JOHNS JOY 3 b.g. Martin John–Saybya (Sallust 134) [1988 10m⁵ 10d³ 8g² 8g² 8f* **89** 8g⁵ 1989 8f 8f 8g⁵] medium-sized, angular gelding: has a round action: fairly useful winner as 3-y-o: creditable fifth to Wood Dancer in valuable handicap at Sandown in July, but wasn't seen out again: had run disappointingly (hung right) at same course second outing: best form at 1m: acts on firm going and showed promise on a soft surface. *D. R. C. Elsworth.*

JOHNSTED 3 ch.g. Red Johnnie 100–Busted Love (Busted 134) [1988 6g⁴ 6f 7m⁴ **71** § 7m⁴ 8m³ 8f⁴ 8f³ 9m³ 1989 10s⁴ 11f⁴ 13.1h 16.2g 14m* 16g 14m 14g³] rangy gelding, shade unfurnished: good walker: modest handicapper: led on post in moderately-run race at Yarmouth in June having hung left 1f out: stays 1¾m: acts on any going: takes keen hold: sold 11,000 gns Newmarket Autumn Sales: inconsistent, ran out on third outing and is not one to trust. *C. E. Brittain.*

JOIE DE ROSE 4 b.f. Tickled Pink 114–Joie d'Or (FR) (Kashmir II 125) [1988 8d **73** 7g 6g 8m² 8.2g³ 9g 8g* 7m* 7g 7.3m 7g² 7g 8g⁴ 1989 6d 7g 7.6f 7f³ 7f* 7m² 6f 7m 7f 7f³ 7f 7m⁴ 8m 7.6m⁴ 8f⁶ 7g] plain filly: usually unimpressive in coat: has a round action: modest handicapper: made all in apprentice event at Doncaster in May: ran creditably when in frame at Yarmouth (apprentices), Lingfield (twice) and Chepstow afterwards: suited by 7f: acts on any going: blinkered once at 3 yrs: often apprentice ridden: inconsistent. *M. Blanshard.*

JOKERS PATCH 2 ch.g. (Apr 11) Hotfoot 126–Rhythmical 69 (Swing Easy **68** (USA) 126) [1989 7f² 7.5f² 8f² a8g⁵] 1,850Y: medium-sized, rather angular gelding: has a quick action: second foal: half-brother to 3-y-o Milton Girl (by Netherkelly): dam maiden plater, stayed 7f: quite modest form in varied races: stays 1m. *P. J. Makin.*

JOKIST 6 ro.g. Orchestra 118–What A Picture 80 (My Swanee 122) [1988 8d 7g **62** 6g* 6f 6f 6g 7d 6g⁵ 6m 6g² 6d⁵ 6s⁶ 6s³ 6s 1989 6s 6v⁶ 6s⁶ 6f 6g 6m² 6m* 6d 6g] workmanlike gelding: quite modest handicapper on his day: won at Lingfield in September: best at 6f: unsuited by firm going, acts on any other: blinkered once: trained until after fourth outing by P. Cundell: inconsistent. *P. S. Felgate.*

JOLEJESTER 4 b.f. Relkino 131–Mirthful 73 (Will Somers 114§) [1988 NR 1989 — 14g] first foal: dam successful at around 1¼m: won NH Flat race at Edinburgh early in year: 20/1, well beaten in minor event at Redcar in November. *C. W. C. Elsey.*

JOLESIAN 3 b.g. Le Johnstan 123–Levandale 102 (Le Levanstell 122) [1988 5v 5f — 7.5s 6g 5f 1989 10d 10f] workmanlike gelding: has a round action: no worthwhile form in sellers in first half of 1989: sold to join T. Walford 1,250 gns Doncaster September Sales. *Ronald Thompson.*

JOLIES EAUX 3 b. or br.f. Shirley Heights 130–Joking Apart 120 (Jimmy Reppin **73** 131) [1988 NR 1989 7d 10f⁵ 12f] rangy, quite attractive filly: has plenty of scope: ninth foal: closely related to fair 1m winner Sleeping Beauty and very useful 1983 2-y-o 5f and 7f winner Reflection (both by Mill Reef) and half-sister to several winners, including Galtres Stakes winners Deadly Serious (by Queen's Hussar) and Sans Blague (by The Minstrel): dam very smart at up to 1m: quite modest maiden: ran poorly final start (May): probably stays 1¼m. *Major W. R. Hern.*

JOLLIENNE 5 ch.m. Absalom 128–Bourienne 58 (Bolkonski 134) [1988 10m 11.7g 14f 10g⁶ 1989 15.5s] sparely-made, angular mare: bad maiden: winning hurdler. *S. Woodman.* —

JOMANA 3 ch.f. Roman Warrior 132–Tina's Magic (Carnival Night) [1988 5f 5g⁴ 5f* 6m 5g 1989 5f³ 6f⁶ 6g⁵ 5m 5m 6f 8g⁶ 6g a6g] tall filly: modest winner as 2-y-o: below best in 1989: seems suited by 5f and top-of-the-ground: refused to enter stalls on intended reappearance: ran poorly in blinkers final start. *J. C. Fox.* 61 d

JONITE 5 gr.g. Neltino 97–Early Morning 81 (Dual 117) [1988 NR 1989 10f] workmanlike gelding: poor maiden: sold 650 gns Ascot July Sales. *J. J. Bridger.* —

JONJO'S SON 3 b.g. Song 132–Speed The Plough (Grundy 137) [1988 5g 7d 8m⁶ 8s 7g 1989 8f 8m 7g 5m 6m] tall, workmanlike gelding: plating-class maiden at 2 yrs: no form in 1989, virtually bolting to post and quickly tailed off in blinkers third start: needs further than 5f but appears not to stay 1m: best effort on a soft surface: takes good hold: trained until after second outing by M. McCormack. *W. Carter.* —

JOPANINI 4 b.g. Homing 130–Honeybuzzard (FR) (Sea Hawk II 131) [1988 8f 12f⁶ 12f⁶ 14m² 14g⁴ 14.6g² 14m⁴ 16m⁶ 15.8g⁴ 18d² 1989 16f² 17f 18g] big, workmanlike gelding: moderate mover: quite modest maiden: ran out after 4f in Tote Cesarewitch (Handicap) at Newmarket final outing: stays 2¼m: acts on firm going and a soft surface: best kept up with pace and with strong handling: dull in coat as 4-y-o: winning hurdler. *D. T. Thom.* 59

JOSHYKIN 3 b.g. Montekin 125–Miss Annie 73 (Scottish Rifle 127) [1988 6m 7d 7g 1989 7s⁵ 8d³ 6m 7m⁶] leggy gelding: has a round action: moderate plater: not seen out after June: suited by 1m: acts on a soft surface: bandaged last 3 starts: gelded after final one. *K. T. Ivory.* 47

JOSIE SMITH 5 gr.m. Alias Smith (USA)–Josilu (Caliban 123) [1988 13.8g⁴ 18v⁴ 1989 14s⁵ 18s] workmanlike mare: shows traces of stringhalt: poor handicapper: probably stays 1¾m: suited by give in the ground: blinkered once: soundly beaten when visored final outing (May): has joined O. O'Neill. *R. J. Holder.* —

JOVEWORTH 6 gr.g. Monsanto (FR) 121–Flitterdale 81 (Abwah 118) [1988 5d⁴ 6v⁶ 7g* 8m* 7g* 7.6v² 8g⁴ 7g³ 8.5m² 9m⁴ 8g⁴ 8m 9f 8g⁶ 6g 7d³ 9g 1989 7g⁵ 8d³ 7s⁶ 8m 10.4m 8.2m 8.5m⁴ 9m 7m² 7m² 8.2d* 8f⁴ 8.2d⁵ 7g 6s* 9g 7g² 7m* 6v²] 104

In general, the better the horse the less often it's seen out. Of the twenty horses who put in more than eighteen appearances on the racecourse in 1989, only three could be regarded as being within 50 lb of the likes of Zilzal, Old Vic

Ladbrokes (Ayr) Gold Cup—Joveworth completes a 50/1-success for his new stable; blinkered Chaplins Club is second in the race again

and Nashwan. The best of the three, and by a clear margin, was the splendidly tough and genuine Joveworth, who raced nineteen times, all in handicap company. He was transferred from J. Glover to M. O'Neill after his eighth outing and was much improved for his change of surroundings, winning at Haydock, Ayr and Newmarket, the highlight being his 50/1-success in the Ladbrokes (Ayr) Gold Cup in September.

Back to six furlongs for the first time in over a year he was clearly helped by the very testing ground. Always prominent, he led under pressure from a furlong out and forged clear inside the last, beating Chaplins Club by a length. Joveworth faded out of contention two furlongs out in the William Hill Cambridgeshire the following month but, returned to a shorter trip on his last three outings, he put up the best performances of his life. A three-quarter-length win at Newmarket owed much to Joveworth's fighting qualities as he appeared held by the runner-up, Ned's Aura, going into the Dip. At Newbury on his final start, Joveworth was one of only two of the twenty-seven runners to stay close to the far rail. Leading two furlongs out and keeping on strongly, he went down by three quarters of a length to Anthony Loretto.

		Breton	Relko
	Monsanto (FR)	(b or br 1967)	La Melba
	(b 1972)	Moonmadness	Tom Fool
Joveworth		(ch 1963)	Sunset
(gr.g. 1983)		Abwah	Abernant
	Flitterdale	(gr 1969)	The Creditor
	(gr 1976)	Love Seat	King's Bench
		(b 1968)	Criterion Maid

Joveworth's dam Flitterdale, who won twice over five furlongs as a two-year-old, died in 1986. Of her four other foals Playtex (by Be Friendly) won over a mile as a three-year-old and was returned to win at six furlongs in both the following seasons. Vanishing Trick (by Silly Season) won three times over sprint distances. Joveworth acts on any going and is effective from six furlongs to a mile. After his stable transfer, he was ridden in all his races except the Cambridgeshire by the 5-lb claimer J. Fortune. *M. O'Neill.*

JOVIAL 2 b.c. (Mar 29) Northern Jove (CAN)–Rensaler (USA) (Stop The Music (USA)) [1989 6m* 8g4 7g5] IR 105,000Y: well-grown, attractive colt: good walker: third foal: half-brother to 1987 2-y-o 8.5f stakes winner Never Force (by Full Out): dam, winner at around 1m in USA, is half-sister to smart 1982 American 3-y-o Rose Bouquet and very useful 7f and 1m winner Shmaireekh: odds on, won 3-runner minor event at Nottingham comfortably by 5 lengths from Metal Boys in June: put up useful performance when over 5 lengths fifth of 20, not much room over 1f out, to The Caretaker in Cartier Million at Phoenix Park in October: reportedly ill after second start: best form at 7f. *M. R. Stoute.* **101**

JOVIAL KATE (USA) 2 gr.f. (Apr 30) Northern Jove (CAN)–Flashy Feet (USA) (Pretense) [1989 6g 7f 5f5 6g5 6f a6g2 a6g2 a6g2] $14,000Y: workmanlike filly: has scope: half-sister to 3 winners in North America: dam unraced: modest maiden: good second in Lingfield nursery in December on final outing: stays 6f: wears bandages behind. *M. D. I. Usher.* **71**

JOYCE'S BEST 3 ch.f. Tolomeo 127–Zither 72 (Vienna 127) [1988 NR 1989 7g 7f 6f 12f4 12f 10g4] 52,000Y: sparely-made filly: has a sharp action: half-sister to numerous winners, including high-class middle-distance performer Zimbalon (by Ragusa): dam won at 1¼m: form only when fourth in maiden at Folkestone and claimer at Newmarket, in latter taking keen hold in blinkers and leading 1m: sold 7,200 gns Doncaster November Sales. *I. V. Matthews.* **58**

JOYCE'S CARE (USA) 3 gr.f. Green Dancer (USA) 132–Imminent (USA) (Secretariat (USA)) [1988 6d5 7f6 1989 12d2 16d2 14f2 16.2g5 15s3 18g] leggy, sparely-made filly: modest maiden: 100/1 and ridden by 5-lb claimer, creditable seventh of 22 to Double Dutch in Cesarewitch Handicap at Newmarket: stays 2¼m: acts on firm ground, possibly unsuited by a soft surface: sold Miss S. Hall 8,800 gns Doncaster November Sales. *I. V. Matthews.* **79**

JOYFULNESS (FR) 4 b.f. Cure The Blues (USA)–Jermaric 105 (Great Nephew 126) [1988 10g2 8m3 1989 10.2g 9f 10.8m 10m 10f5] leggy, rather angular filly: moderate walker: poor maiden: probably stays 1¼m: winning hurdler. *P. J. Bevan.* **—**

JOY'S TOY 3 ch.f. Wolverlife 115–Tanzanite (Marino) [1988 5g 5d6 5d 5g 7m 6d 6g 1989 8d* 8g 8m 8m 8g 7m a8g] leggy, shallow-girthed, sparely-made filly: poor **50**

mover: 33/1, won seller (bought in 2,600 gns) at Thirsk in April: easily best effort after in Newmarket claimer fourth start, making most: unlikely to stay much beyond 1m: may well prove suited by some give in the ground: usually apprentice ridden: inconsistent. *Pat Mitchell.*

JOYTOTHEWORLD 4 b.g. Young Generation 129–Lady Bequick 81 (Sharpen Up 127) [1988 7g 5m 5g* 6g² 5g* 5g* 1989 6d 6g 5f²] stocky, plain gelding: progressive form as 3-y-o, winning minor contest at Beverley and handicaps at Sandown and Haydock: chipped bone in knee after final outing: best effort 1989 when second to Come On Chase Me in claimer at Sandown (favourite but didn't take eye in paddock) in June: suited by 5f: usually sweating: sweating on reappearance. *W. A. O'Gorman.* **94**

J R JONES 2 b.c. (Jan 21) Blakeney 126–Bonne Baiser 88 (Most Secret 119) [1989 6g 6h* 6g⁴ 8m 7g* 7g 7.3d] 6,400F, 7,000Y: small, good-quartered colt: second foal: dam sprinter: successful in 4-runner maiden at Carlisle in July and nursery (by 1½ lengths from Kaapstad) at Catterick in September: better suited by 7f than 6f, and should stay 1m. *J. Berry.* **66**

JR'S PET 2 b.f. (Apr 22) Auction Ring (USA) 123–What A Pet (Mummy's Pet 125) [1989 7g] 7,400F, 21,000Y: close-coupled, unfurnished filly: second foal: half-sister to French 3-y-o 9.5f winner Bourrasque (by What A Guest): dam, French 1m winner, is sister to very useful filly Teacher's Pet and from family of high-class stayer Grey Baron: 33/1, never dangerous in 24-runner maiden at Newmarket in November: constantly swished tail beforehand. *R. J. R. Williams.* **—**

J-TEC BOY 3 gr.g. Orange Reef 90–Fotostar (Polyfoto 124) [1988 6f 6g 6g 8.2s 6d 1989 8.2s 12f] leggy, sparely-made gelding: of little account: has joined J. Gillen. *P. J. Feilden.* **—**

JUBILEE MONDAY 3 b.c. Sweet Monday 122–Jubilee Joy 69 (Burglar 128) [1988 NR 1989 9f 6g] leggy, lengthy colt: second reported foal: half-brother to a temperamental maiden plater by Owen Anthony: dam lightly raced: well behind in minor event at Wolverhampton and seller (hung left at halfway) at Leicester in the spring: sweating, edgy and mulish on way down at Leicester: sold 1,300 gns Ascot September Sales. *B. Preece.* **—**

JUBILEE TRAIL 2 b.f. (Feb 9) Shareef Dancer (USA) 135–Miss Petard 113 (Petingo 135) [1989 7g⁴] eighth living foal: half-sister to 6 winners, including Musidora and Park Hill Stakes winner Rejuvenate (by Ile de Bourbon) and useful miler Cracking Form (by Habitat): dam won at up to 1½m: 11/4, 4 lengths fourth of 24, one pace last 1½f, to Sardegna in maiden at Newmarket in November: will be well suited by 1¼m +: sure to improve. *B. W. Hills.* **79 p**

JUBRAN 3 b.g. Vaguely Noble 140–La Vue (USA) (Reviewer (USA)) [1988 8g 1989 11.7m⁶ 12g³] quite attractive, close-coupled gelding: ridden by 7-lb claimer, 12 lengths third of 6 to Husyan in maiden at Leicester in August: sold 20,000 gns Newmarket Autumn Sales. *P. F. I. Cole.* **75**

JUDGED LUCKY (FR) 2 br.g. (Apr 3) Vayrann 133–Friluck (USA) (Judger (USA)) [1989 7g] 35,000 francs (approx £3,300) Y, resold 1,100Y: leggy gelding: second foal: half-brother to French 9f winner Nice And Lucky (by Nice Havrais): dam French 1¼m winner: 50/1, always towards rear in 28-runner maiden at Newmarket in November. *R. Curtis.* **—**

JUDGEMENT CALL 2 b.c. (Apr 23) Alzao (USA) 117–Syllabub (Silly Season 127) [1989 5g² 5m² 6f* 5m² 5f5 5m² 5f* 5f* 5f* 5m³ 6g* 5g²] IR 7,800F, 15,500Y: close-coupled, good-quartered colt: half-brother to a winner in Spain: dam never ran: fairly useful colt: successful in June maiden and July minor event at Hamilton, 3 nurseries at Redcar in August and a claimer at Catterick in October: stays 6f: visored fifth start. *M. H. Easterby.* **91**

JUMBY BAY 3 b.g. Thatching 131–Ridge The Times (USA) 78 (Riva Ridge (USA)) [1988 6d⁵ 1989 7f⁴ 10m⁵ 8f 8f* 8m²] big, rangy gelding: won maiden at Pontefract in October, plenty to do 3f out then staying on well to lead close home: hung markedly left then and again, taking strong hold early and looking unsatisfactory, when beaten 2 lengths (clear) by Secretary of State in Chepstow claimer week later: stays 1m: sold 14,500 gns Newmarket Autumn Sales and subsequently gelded: not one to trust. *G. Harwood.* **88 §**

JUNE'S FANCY 3 ch.f. Mr Fluorocarbon 126–Havaneza 65 (Simbir 130) [1988 7m⁶ 7f 7m⁶ 9g 1989 8m 7m 11.7f⁴ 15.5f 11.7f] sparely-made filly: 50/1, only show when fourth in maiden claimer at Bath: has run in sellers: suited by 1½m: sweating on reappearance: bought out of E. Eldin's stable 950 gns Ascot July Sales after second outing. *D. R. Tucker.* **46**

JUNES STAR 2 b.f. (Apr 29) Taufan (USA) 119–Stapelea (FR) (Faraway Son — (USA) 130) [1989 7g 6m] IR 6,500Y: leggy filly: sister to 1987 Irish 2-y-o 7f winner Not A Lite and half-sister to 2 winners: dam from family of Erin's Isle and Erin's Hope: always behind in maiden (backward and green) at Leicester and valuable seller (stumbled after start, tailed off) at York in August. *N. Tinkler.*

JUNGLE KNIFE 3 b.c. Kris 135–Jungle Queen (Twilight Alley 133) [1988 NR **81** d 1989 8g6 8g2 7.5m5 10d 10m 9f] 74,000Y: tall, workmanlike colt: moderate walker and mover: closely related to 1983 Lowther Stakes winner Prickle (by Sharpen Up) and half-brother to 3 winners: dam showed little worthwhile form: fair maiden: second at Newmarket in May: off course 3½ months and well below form after, unruly at start before handicap final outing: stays 1m: probably needs an easy surface: sold K. Morgan 13,000 gns Doncaster October Sales. *C. E. Brittain.*

JUNGLE PIONEER (USA) 3 b.c. Conquistador Cielo (USA)–Untitled 98 **106** (Vaguely Noble 140) [1988 7m2 7g2 7m* 1989 8s4 10.1m4 10f* 10f* 12g] tall, leggy colt: has a quick action: has scope: made all in minor events at Pontefract (by 7 lengths from Marine Diver) in June and Nottingham in September: unplaced for J. Hammond in listed event at Toulouse in November: should be suited by 1½m: acts on firm going: suited by forcing tactics. *H. R. A. Cecil.*

JUNGLE ROSE 3 b.f. Shirley Heights 130–Prickle 114 (Sharpen Up 127) [1988 **90** 7g5 1989 10f* 10f* 12f6] tall, lengthy, rather unfurnished filly: successful in small fields for maiden at Nottingham in July and minor event (25/1 on, making all) at Lingfield in August: virtually pulled up in listed race at York later August: should stay 1½m. *H. R. A. Cecil.*

JUNUH 3 br.f. Jalmood (USA) 126–Adeebah (USA) 94 (Damascus (USA)) [1988 — 7s4 6m6 7f* 8.2m 1989 8g 8f] smallish, lightly-made filly: moderate walker: easy mover: fair winner of maiden at Brighton as 2-y-o: behind in handicaps in summer at 3 yrs: suited by 7f: acts on firm ground: possibly held up: slowly away final start: sold to join W. Fairgrieve 4,000 gns Newmarket Autumn Sales. *H. Thomson Jones.*

JURRAN 4 ro.c. Formidable (USA) 125–Queen's Counsellor 92 (Kalamoun 129) — § [1988 8g6 8f* 8g 9s 1989 8h4 8.5m6] strong, lengthy colt: has a free action: fairly useful at his best: well below form as 4-y-o: tended to hang and found little when sixth in handicap at Beverley in July: stays 1m: acts on firm going and a soft surface: ran moderately in blinkers: usually wanders: ungenuine. *H. Thomson Jones.*

JUSSOLI 5 b.m. Don 128–Torino (Firestreak 125) [1988 8f5 11m 9.5g6 12g3 11s4 9.5d 10g3 12g2 11d2 10s* 9s3 1989 16.2m6 9m5 12m 10m 12m 10v5] strong, compact, attractive ex-Irish mare: fourth foal: sister to useful Irish 6f to 1¼m performer Don Justice and half-sister to unreliable miler Moores Metal (by Wolverlife) and Irish 1m and 9f winner Dream Machine (by Oats), later successful in USA: dam won over 9.5f in Ireland: won handicap at Leopardstown as 4-y-o when trained by K. Prendergast: no worthwhile form in 1989: stays 1½m: seems best with plenty of give in the ground: blinkered twice, visored final outing: good mount for apprentice: slipped up third start. *Miss S. E. Hall.*

JUST A FLUTTER 5 b.h. Beldale Flutter (USA) 130–Precious Jade 72 **115** (Northfields 130) [1988 8d 8d2 7m 8m* 8g3 8m2 8g2 8g* 8g2 8s2 8m2 1989 8s4 8g3 8s4 8g*] robust, good-topped horse: moderate mover: very useful performer: successful in Group 1 Premio Vittorio di Capua at Milan in October by 2 lengths from Miss Secreto: in frame in Trusthouse Forte Mile at Sandown and Badener Meile in spring when trained by M. Jarvis: suited by 1m: acts on any going: tough and consistent. *H. Jentzsch, Germany.*

JUST A GLIMPSE 3 b.f. Pas de Seul 133–Reveal (Pitskelly 122) [1988 6f3 6m4 6f4 7g2 1989 7f 7m 8.2m] leggy, quite attractive filly: good walker: modest maiden at 2 yrs: in mid-division as 3-y-o, not discredited facing stiff task in handicap second outing: best form at 6f: tongue tied down in 1989: sold 1,150 gns Newmarket Autumn Sales. *M. Moubarak.*

JUSTAGLOW 3 b.f. Kalaglow 132–Justicia 87 (Nonoalco (USA) 131) [1988 7g4 **82** 8s4 1989 8f*] useful-looking, shallow-girthed filly: made all in 3-runner maiden at Ayr in July by 1½ lengths, never challenged, swishing tail and idling inside final 1f: should stay beyond 1m: acts on any going. *B. W. Hills.*

JUST A SONG 3 br.f. Song 132–Atoka 97 (March Past 124) [1988 6m 9g 1989 6f — 8m 10f 12.3f] big, lengthy filly: no sign of ability, including in handicaps: visored final start: often sweating: trained on reappearance by P. Felgate. *C. Tinkler.*

JUST A STEP 3 br.c. Lochnager 132–My Louise 54 (Manado 130) [1988 6f 6g6 **76** 6m 1989 6v6 7s3 6g2 7f* 7m5 7g] modest handicapper: best effort when making all at Folkestone in June by 6 lengths: moved moderately down next start and not seen out after mid-August: suited by 7f: acts on firm going. *M. McCormack.*

JUST CRUISE   3 ch.c. Milford 119–Glenside Lady 79 (So Blessed 130) [1988 6s 6m 1989 10s⁶ 12v⁴ 12.5f 13.8m⁵ 10.1m a10g] small, leggy, dipped-backed colt: has a round action: little worthwhile form, tailed off in seller (visored) and maiden claimer (blinkered, 6 months later) on last 2 starts: stays 1½m. *K. T. Ivory.*

JUST DAVID   6 b.g. Blakeney 126–Reltop 72 (High Top 131) [1988 NR 1989 14g]   — big, good-topped, quite attractive gelding: has a long, rather round stride: put up quite useful performance under 9-8 to win Ladbroke Chester Cup (Handicap) in 1987 but reportedly damaged tendons: never-nearer seventh of 17 in handicap at Haydock in June, only subsequent outing: suited by test of stamina: acts on firm going and a soft surface. *A. C. Stewart.*

JUST DIZZY   4 br.c. Noalcoholic (FR) 128–Cadasi 68 (Persian Bold 123) [1988 7f 7m⁶ 6m 10m⁴ 10g⁶ 1989 12.5f] leggy, sparely-made filly: plater: pulled hard, saddle slipped and rider unseated on only outing at 4 yrs: stayed 1¾m: sold 1,400 gns Doncaster November Sales in foal to Vaigly Great. *R. Curtis.*

JUST GO   2 ch.f. (Mar 8) All Systems Go 119–Argostone (Rockavon 120) [1989 5s² 56 5g⁶ 6m⁶ 5g³ 6m² 6g* 6m] small filly: poor mover: half-sister to 1m winner and winning hurdler Little Miss Horner (by Sit In The Corner): dam well beaten, including in a seller: favourite, won seller (no bid) at Ripon in July by 8 lengths from Si Sawat: ran moderately in similar event there final start: will stay 7f. *M. H. Easterby.*

JUST GREAT   3 br.g. Simply Great (FR) 122–Bourton Downs 74 (Philip of Spain 50 126) [1988 5g 5d 6f 6m 8g 1989 8s⁵ 10m² 8.2s⁵ 8m⁶ 12f 12m 10g⁴ 11s 10g 10g 12g] leggy, sparely-made gelding: fair plater: stays 1¼m: acts on soft going and top-of-the-ground: visored final outing: blinkered twice at 2 yrs: below form when sweating. *D. T. Thom.*

JUSTIFICATION   3 b.c. Millfontaine 114–Gybe (Captain's Gig (USA)) [1988 8s   — 8.2s 8v³ 1989 12.3g] rather leggy colt: quite modest form when third in maiden as 2-y-o: slowly away, tailed off in handicap in July, only start in 1989: sold to join S. Avery 420 gns Doncaster September Sales. *M. Brittain.*

JUST IMAGINE   2 b.f. (Apr 5) Head For Heights 125–Lochboisdale (Saritamer 49 (USA) 130) [1989 5f⁶ 5m⁵ 6g 6f 8.5f 8.2f 6m² 7f⁶ 7d] 6,200F, 5,000Y: compact filly: poor mover: fourth foal: half-sister to 7.5f and 1¼m seller winner Basirah (by Persian Bold) and 2 bad animals: dam, who showed a little ability at 2 yrs, is daughter of smart Hecla: moderate plater: best form at 6f though bred to stay further: seems suited by a sound surface: sometimes slowly away: has looked a difficult ride. *T. Fairhurst.*

JUST JEAN   2 b.f. (Feb 6) Kala Shikari 125–Curzon House 73 (Green God 128) 59 [1989 5d 7s³ 8g⁴] workmanlike, good-quartered filly: has scope: third reported foal: dam sprint plater: plating-class form, keeping on well, in autumn maidens won by Sajjaya at Ayr and Shifting Breeze at Edinburgh: off course over 4 months after debut. *S. G. Norton.*

JUST JENNINGS   4 ch.g. Horage 124–Sally St Clair (Sallust 134) [1988 5s 5d 69 5m⁴ 5g 6m* 6f³ 1989 6f⁶ 5.8h 5f⁵ a6g³] close-coupled gelding: quite modest performer: creditable sixth of 10 in £9,200 handicap at Lingfield in May: below form after, on final outing (first for 6 months) slowly away: better suited by 6f than 5f: possibly best on a sound surface: usually blinkered nowadays (wasn't final start): apprentice ridden as 4-y-o except on third start: sometimes sweats and gets on toes: sold out of G. Lewis's stable only 1,000 gns Ascot September Sales. *D. Haydn Jones.*

JUST LIKE YOU   2 ch.f. (May 4) Sandhurst Prince 128–Gentle Heiress (Prince   — Tenderfoot (USA) 126) [1989 8f 8.2s 6f⁶ 7d] IR 2,000Y: angular, sparely-made filly: sixth living foal: half-sister 3 winners, including 1985 2-y-o 5f winner Queen of Sahara (by Royal Match) and 1½m winner Prince Newport (by Prince Regent): dam placed at 2 yrs in Ireland: well beaten in maidens, one an auction event, and a seller: ridden by 7-lb claimer first 3 starts: sold 680 gns Doncaster October Sales. *J. J. O'Neill.*

JUST LYNN   2 b.f. (May 31) Legend of France (USA) 124–Ardent Runner 94   — (Runnymede 123) [1989 5m 5m] rather unfurnished filly: poor mover: sixth foal: half-sister to 3-y-o Hickory Run (by Seymour Hicks) and two 2-y-o winners, including 1987 7f winner Passion King (by Dara Monarch): dam sprinting 2-y-o: backward, well beaten in August in maiden at Windsor and minor event (repeatedly swished tail) at Warwick. *L. J. Holt.*

JUST MY BILL   3 ch.g. Nicholas Bill 125–Misnomer 85 (Milesian 125) [1988 6m   **84**
7d² 7d⁵ 8d³ 8s³ 1989 8v* 10g⁶ 10.5f³ 12m⁴ 12g 10.5f 10s³ 10.6s] leggy, rather
sparely-made gelding: fair form in varied events: won maiden at Ayr in April: ran
poorly sixth start and as though something amiss final one: subsequently gelded:
may well prove suited by 1½m and some give in the ground. *C. W. C. Elsey.*

JUST ONE KISS   4 ch.f. Tower Walk 130–Mistress Royal 74 (Royalty 130) [1988   —
10g 1989 a8g] rather sparely-made filly: always behind in maidens at Newmarket
and Southwell: reluctant at stalls on latter. *W. Wilson.*

JUST PRECIOUS   4 b.f. Ela-Mana-Mou 132–Border Squaw 84 (Warpath 113)   —
[1988 9d 10g 12m 10m 7.5m* 8.2m 8m* 8g 9f³ 8g 10.2m 1989 7g 8g⁴] leggy,
sparely-made filly: modest winner as 3-y-o: given tremendous amount to do when
never-nearer fourth of 17 at Doncaster in March: not seen out again: stays 9f well:
acts on firm going: sweating as 4-y-o: usually held up and suited by strong gallop. *M.
Johnston.*

JUST PULHAM   4 b.g. Electric 126–Lady Acquiesce 67 (Galivanter 131) [1988   —
NR 1989 12m 11.5m⁶ 11g 8f a12g⁶] smallish gelding: well beaten in varied events as
4-y-o: moved down poorly second start. *G. A. Huffer.*

JUST SEYMOUR   3 ch.g. Seymour Hicks (FR) 125–Pennycress 99 (Florescence   —
120) [1988 5d⁴ 5m 6m² 6s⁴ 6g² 1989 7d 7g a8g] leggy gelding: quite modest form at 2
yrs: behind in varied events in winter as 3-y-o, facing stiffish tasks first 2 outings:
best form at 6f: visored (sweating) once at 2 yrs. *B. Gubby.*

JUST SUSANNA (USA)   3 b.f. Master Willie 129–Whose Broad (USA) (Hoist   **75**
The Flag (USA)) [1988 NR 1989 8m 8m³ 8m] workmanlike, angular filly: moderate
walker: poor mover: sister to useful 1987 2-y-o 5f and 7f winner William's Bird and
half-sister to minor winner in USA: dam never ran: in need of race, third at Warwick
in September, best effort in maidens: favourite, took keen hold at York 9 days later:
sold 2,000 gns Newmarket December Sales. *H. Candy.*

JUST THE TICKET   6 gr.m. Faraway Times (USA) 118–Rum Year (Quorum   —
126) [1988 NR 1989 8g 10v⁵] workmanlike mare: has a round action: poor
handicapper: effective at 7f to 1¼m: acts on any going: occasionally sweats: won for
apprentice in 1987: sold to join J. Baker 2,700 gns Ascot July Sales. *C. B. B. Booth.*

JUSTTHEWAYYOUARE (CAN)   6 ch.g. Ziad (USA)–Helen Dickerman (Joe   —
Price) [1988 NR 1989 13.8d] workmanlike gelding: no worthwhile form on flat:
blinkered twice at 3 yrs. *R. Curtis.*

JUST THREE   3 b.c. Tina's Pet 121–Mio Mementa 61 (Streak 119) [1988 5m⁶ 6f   **116**
6d⁶ 6g 6g⁴ 6m³ 6d 1989 8g 7s² 7s* 7g* 7.6f 7f* 7f 7g³ 7.6f* 7g* 7g⁶ 7m⁴ 8g² 7d³]
lengthy, useful-looking colt: usually impresses in appearance: had fine season,

EBF Hardwicke Cup, Phoenix Park—
the admirable Just Three makes all to win from Corwyn Bay

making all or virtually all in handicaps at Epsom, Salisbury, Sandown and Chester and listed race at Phoenix Park: 25/1, very good 3 lengths second of 12 to Light of Morn (rec 6 lb) in listed race at Newmarket in November: suited by 1m: acts on any going: suited by forcing tactics: genuine and consistent: a credit to his trainer. *M. McCormack.*

JUST TOO BRAVE 6 b.g. Beldale Flutter (USA) 130–Georgina Park 88 (Silly Season 127) [1988 11.7d 10f 12m 12g⁴ 11.7m 11.7g 10m⁴ 10.2g⁴ 10d² 1989 a10g] big, strong gelding: poor mover: plating-class maiden: effective at 1¼m to 1½m: well suited by a bit of give in the ground (unsuited by heavy): blinkered last 2 outings in 1988: has run creditably for inexperienced rider: usually races up with pace: winning novice hurdler. *M. McCourt.* —

JUVENARA 3 b.g. Young Generation 129–Sharrara (CAN) 61 (Blushing Groom (FR) 131) [1988 5f⁵ 5g⁴ 6m⁴ 6m⁵ 7m 1989 8m 7m 5m⁵ 6f⁶ 6f³ 8f⁴ 7m⁴ 8f⁴ 7s 9f³ 8m* a8g² a10g] small, workmanlike gelding: lacks scope: poor walker: quite modest performer: won claimer at Chepstow in October: suited by 1m: acts on firm going: has run well when edgy: often claimer ridden: below form for amateur: trained first 7 outings by C. Hill: inconsistent. *R. J. Hodges.* **69**

K

KAAPSTAD 2 b.g. (May 10) Kafu 120–Daring Choice (Daring Display (USA) 129) [1989 6m⁶ 6f² 7m* 7m* 7m⁶ 7g² 8f⁵ 6g] IR 13,000Y: leggy gelding: brother to winning 3-y-o Italian sprinter Lord Kafu, also successful at 2 yrs, and half-brother to fairly useful sprinter Bonny Light (by Welsh Saint) and a winning jumper: dam second twice in Ireland at 3 yrs: modest performer: won sellers (bought in 5,000 gns and 4,750 gns) at Wolverhampton in August: good second of 15 in nursery at Catterick following month: suited by 7f and forcing tactics: sold 11,500 gns Newmarket Autumn Sales. *D. Morley.* **68**

KABCAST 4 b.g. Kabour 80–Final Cast 50 (Saulingo 122) [1988 5v 6m 5m⁶ 5s 5g* 5f 6m 5g* 5g 6f 5m 5g 5m 5g 1989 5d 5m⁵ 5.1m² 5m² 5f* 5g* 5f* 5m* 5m* 5m² 5g² 5g 5g² 5.6g 5f 5g⁵ 5g³ 5m⁵ 5d a5g4] good-bodied gelding: vastly improved, showing tremendous pace and soon clear when justifying favouritism in handicaps at Catterick (twice), Edinburgh (amateurs), Hamilton and Ayr within 14 days in July: ran excellent races off much higher mark when placed at Pontefract, Haydock, Epsom and Goodwood afterwards: best at 5f on a sound surface: usually blinkered nowadays: has run well for apprentice: often sweats: edgy and hung left twelfth start: tough and genuine: very speedy. *D. W. Chapman.* **82**

KABELLA 3 ch.f. Kabour 80–Right Abella 74 (Right Boy 137) [1988 NR 1989 6g 6g] 1,200Y: sixth foal: half-sister to a winner in Denmark: dam sprinter: 33/1, backward when behind in claimers at Haydock and Nottingham (good early speed) in the autumn. *D. W. Chapman.* —

KACHINA MAID 4 b.f. Anfield 117–Grey Twig 68 (Godswalk (USA) 130) [1988 6g 6f 5.8d 6m 6m³ 5.8f 7f* 8d³ 1989 8d 7f 8f 7m² 7f² 6f³ 7h³ 7f⁶ 7f⁴ 7m³] sturdy, workmanlike filly: plating-class performer: finds easy 6f on sharp side and stays 1m: yet to race on soft going, acts on any other: blinkered once: slowly away fourth outing: consistent. *L. G. Cottrell.* **51**

KADAN (GER) 5 b.g. Horst-Herbert–Ling Lady (GER) (Marduk (GER)) [1988 10g⁶ 10d⁵ 12m⁶ 10f 10g 8v 8g 1989 8f* 8g³] rather sparely-made gelding: moderate mover: 12/1 from 33/1, won 19-runner handicap at Wolverhampton in October, leading well inside final 1f: slowly into stride and never reached leaders when creditable third of 15 in similar company at Carlisle under week later: effective at 1m and best at short of 1½m: possibly unsuited by soft going, acts on any other: winning hurdler. *M. H. Tompkins.* **64**

KADIM (USA) 2 ch.c. (Apr 19) Diesis 133–Alghuzaylah 90 (Habitat 134) [1989 6g² 7m* 8m⁶ 7.3d⁶] sturdy, quite attractive colt: shows some knee action: second foal: dam 2-y-o 5f winner stayed 1m, is half-sister to very smart French 5.5f to 10.5f winner Pitasia: odds on, impressive 5-length winner of maiden at Redcar in September, making all: creditable sixth to Noble Patriarch in listed event at Ascot but ran moderately in Horris Hill Stakes at Newbury: stays 1m. *H. Thomson Jones.* **93**

KADIR 4 b.g. Kris 135–Upanishad 85 (Amber Rama (USA) 133) [1988 10g 12g 12d 14.6m 1989 12g] strong gelding: little sign of ability in modest company: dead. *R. A. Bennett.* —

KAFARMO 6 b.h. High Line 125–Fashion Club 95 (Tribal Chief 125) [1988 12g — 12.2d 1989 14.8s⁵] strong, medium-sized, angular horse: has a round action: modest winner in 1986: very lightly raced on flat subsequently: stays well: best form on top-of-the-ground: visored only start at 6 yrs. *J. R. Jenkins.*

KAFKIN 3 b.g. Kafu 120–Miskin 58 (Star Appeal 133) [1988 5g⁴ 5m² 6g³ 5m⁶ 70 § 5m* 5g 1989 6s 5f² 5m 5f 5m 5f⁶ 5f² 6g³ 6m 5f 5.1g³ 5.3f 6f] sturdy, good-topped gelding: carries condition: has a quick action: modest handicapper: easily best efforts when placed: stays 6f: acts on firm going, probably unsuited by soft: usually blinkered: sold 5,200 gns Newmarket Autumn Sales: inconsistent, moody and not easiest of rides. *Mrs L. Piggott.*

KAFU D'AMOUR 2 b.f. (May 9) Kafu 120–Ile d'Amour (Sassafras (FR) 135) 45 [1989 5f 6f⁴ 6f³ 6f] IR 500F: close-coupled filly: has a quick action: third foal: dam ran twice: modest plater: ran badly final outing: sold 980 gns Newmarket Autumn Sales. *M. H. Tompkins.*

KAFU LADY 3 b.f. Kafu 120–Susie's Baby (Balidar 133) [1988 5v* 5g³ 5s 5m* 5g² 5d² 5m³ 5m² 6g⁴ 6g 5f⁵ 6m 5d² 1989 6s 5m 5m⁶ 7h⁶ 6m] small, sparely-made filly: keen walker: turns fore-feet out: modest performer at best: stays 6f: has won on heavy, but best form on top-of-the-ground: has run creditably for 7-lb claimer: sold 6,000 gns Newmarket Autumn Sales. *A. Bailey.*

KAHEEL (USA) 2 ch.c. (Mar 14) Caro 133–Escaline (FR) 123 (Arctic Tern 94 p (USA) 126) [1989 7m²] 1,750,000 francs (approx £180,000) Y: medium-sized, lengthy colt, rather unfurnished: second foal: dam won from 1m to 10.5f in France, including French Oaks: 9/1, 3 lengths second of 5 to easy odds-on winner Shavian in minor event at Ascot in September: will stay at least 1m: sure to win a race. *A. C. Stewart.*

KAHER (USA) 2 b.c. (Mar 1) Our Native (USA)–June Bride (USA) (Riverman 74 p (USA) 131) [1989 7g³] $45,000Y: close-coupled colt: second foal: dam, minor 1½m winner, is daughter of Deesse du Val, smart stakes winner at up to 9f in USA as 5-y-o: 6/1, 6 lengths third of 10, going on strongly, to Abs in maiden at Leicester in September: will stay at least 1m: sure to improve, and win a similar event. *A. C. Stewart.*

KAHSHED 2 ch.g. (Mar 28) Wolverlife 115–Lady Margaret (Yellow God 129) 54 [1989 6f 6m⁵ 7m 7g] IR 3,000Y: medium-sized gelding: fifth foal: dam Irish sprinter: plating-class maiden: best effort second start: better suited by 6f than 7f. *M. H. Tompkins.*

KALA EAGLE 3 gr.g. Kalaglow 132–Mamzelle 85 (King's Troop 118) [1988 8s 87 1989 10d⁴ 12g³ 10m 8s⁴ 10.6s⁴ a10g²] medium-sized, leggy, quite good-topped colt: moderate walker: has a fluent, slightly round action: fair form when in frame in varied events, including handicap at Haydock and maiden (blinkered, making most) at Lingfield last 2 outings: stays 1¼m: acts on a soft surface and probably unsuited by top-of-the-ground: twice unruly at stalls: sold to join J. McConnochie 25,000 gns Newmarket Autumn Sales. *P. T. Walwyn.*

KALAHARI 3 gr.f. Kalaglow 132–Hot Case 92 (Upper Case (USA)) [1988 NR — 1989 10.6g] 22,000Y: lengthy, unfurnished filly: fourth foal: half-sister to quite useful 1m winner Aitch N' Bee (by Northfields): dam best at 7f: backward, slowly away and always behind in maiden at Haydock in June: has joined L. Codd. *J. W. Hills.*

KALALEE 2 ch.g. (Apr 19) Doulab (USA) 115–Silk Empress (Young Emperor — 133) [1989 7g 8m] leggy, workmanlike gelding: half-brother to 12.2f winner Desert Emperor (by Ahonoora): dam, unplaced in 4 races, is closely related to disqualified 1978 Italian 1000 Guineas winner Romantic Love: backward, well beaten in maidens at Newmarket (bandaged) and Warwick: off course over 3 months in between. *F. Durr.*

KALANSKI 3 ro.c. Niniski (USA) 125–Kalazero 96 (Kalamoun 129) [1988 7m* 92 8m² 7d² 1989 9m³ 11.7m³ 10.8m² 10g] rangy colt: has scope: good walker: favourite, placed in minor events at Wolverhampton, Windsor and Warwick, in last-named carrying head high and tending to hang right: visored, pulled very hard and ran poorly final start: will prove best at around 1¼m: acts on top-of-the-ground and a soft surface: fairly useful but of suspect temperament. *J. L. Dunlop.*

KALAPARTY 3 gr.f. Kalaglow 132–Firework Party (USA) 115 (Roan Rocket 128) 54 § [1988 6g 6m 6d⁴ 1989 7g 10g 8f⁶ 11m 10g⁵ 11.7m 10m 8m⁴ 10d a12g] workmanlike filly: maiden, plating class on most form: stays 1¼m: best effort on a soft surface: blinkered and sweating eighth outing: unsatisfactory (has been reluctant to race) and not one to rely on. *C. J. Benstead.*

KALA ROSA 3 gr.f. Kalaglow 132–Golden Palermo 70 (Dumbarnie 125) [1988 — 6m² 1989 10f⁴ 8f⁵ a10g] rather leggy, lengthy, useful-looking filly: showed modest form in Yarmouth maiden on debut but little in autumn as 3-y-o: possibly unsatisfactory. *A. C. Stewart.*

KALA'S PRINCESS 2 b.f. (Mar 23) Kampala 120–Dasa Girl (Prince de Galles — 125) [1989 5f 6m 6m⁶] IR 1,500F, resold IR 1,600F, IR 2,000Y, 2,800 2-y-o: medium-sized filly: shows a round action: half-sister to Irish 1½m winner Terrific Chance (by Corvaro): dam French 1m winner: well beaten in auction events and a seller. *D. A. Wilson.*

KALAURA 3 b. or br.f. Kala Shikari 125–Il Regalo (Meadow Mint (USA) 120) — [1988 5d⁵ 5m 5g 7m 8m 10m 1989 12.2d 8g 15.8m⁴] big, leggy, angular filly: moderate mover: plater: best efforts final 2 starts as 2-y-o: stays 1¼m. *A. Smith.*

KALIBERTO (FR) 5 b.g. Don Roberto (USA)–Lady Bella (FR) (Bold Lad — (USA)) [1988 NR 1989 12f⁵] lengthy, angular gelding: poor mover: useful form as 3-y-o: never dangerous in handicap at Goodwood in May, only subsequent outing: effective at 1¼m and stayed 1½m: acts on firm going and seemed unsuited by soft: sometimes sweated: dead. *Miss B. Sanders.*

KALI KOPELLA 3 ch.f. Ahonoora 122–Restless Lady (Sandford Lad 133) [1988 65 6g 5d² 1989 6s 5d³ 5m 5m² 5m* 5f 5.3h⁴ 5m 5g 5d] big, lengthy filly: poor walker and mover: quite modest handicapper: won at Edinburgh in June, leading well inside final 1f: below form last 3 outings: form only at 5f: acts on top-of-the-ground and a soft surface: sold 1,700 gns Newmarket Autumn Sales. *J. W. Payne.*

KALVEE DANCER 2 b.f. (Feb 25) Kalaglow 132–Clonavee (USA) (Northern — Dancer) [1989 5g] 5,200F, 13,500Y: third foal: half-sister to 3-y-o Moharabuiee and 7f winner Baldomero (both by Pas de Seul): dam unraced daughter of very smart stakes winner Molly Ballantine: 25/1, slowly away and always behind in 10-runner minor event at Catterick in September: bred to need much further. *E. Weymes.*

KALZAO 3 b.f. Alzao (USA) 117–Kilcurley Lass (Huntercombe 133) [1988 8.2m 61 d 7m 7s 1989 10.2g 11d⁵ 12.5f* 13f³ 13.8m⁴ 12h³ 12f³ 11.5m 12m³ 12f 12f] good-bodied filly: won seller (bought in 4,400 gns) at Wolverhampton in May: below form after, tailed off on 3 of last 4 starts: stays 1½m well: acts on firm going: has worn severe bridle and a martingale: sold 8,000 gns Newmarket Autumn Sales: headstrong and is one to be wary of. *Sir Mark Prescott.*

KAMAKAZE GIRL 3 b.f. Kampala 120–Glencara 104 (Sallust 134) [1988 6d⁵ 7m 67 1989 6s⁵ 8g⁶ 7f 7m³ a8g] big filly: moderate walker: quite modest maiden: 11/1 from 25/1, good third in handicap at Redcar on first run for almost 4 months: best form at 7f on top-of-the-ground: edgy on reappearance. *M. J. Ryan.*

KAMUR 3 b.f. Kafu 120–Namur (Amber Rama (USA) 133) [1988 5f⁴ 5f 5m 1989 6g] — small, lightly-made filly: little sign of ability, mostly in sellers. *W. G. Morris.*

KARAKA 3 ch.f. Good Times (ITY)–Buff Beauty 92 (Mossborough 126) [1988 8m — 1989 12f⁴] sparely-made filly: well beaten in maidens. *J. Pearce.*

KARAZAN 2 gr.c. (Mar 23) Nishapour (FR) 125–Celestial Path 101 (Godswalk 97 p (USA) 130) [1989 8.5f⁴ 8f* 8g*] IR 3,500Y: big, strong colt: has scope: third foal: half-brother to 3-y-o 7f winner Miss Pisces (by Salmon Leap) and a winner in Belgium: dam Irish 5f to 7f winner: successful in maiden auction race (by 4 lengths) and nursery (by 2½ lengths from Arabian Silence, running on strongly) at Redcar in October: will stay 1¼m: sure to make useful performer. *J. G. FitzGerald.*

KARBAJ 5 ch.g. Arctic Tern (USA) 126–Jadhringa (Petingo 135) [1988 11.1m⁶ 14d 61 10m 10m 11.5m² 12g⁶ 10d 14.6g 1989 12g⁴ 16g⁵ 12m³ 16f* 18h* 20f] close-coupled gelding: comfortable winner of handicaps at Kempton and Pontefract (favourite) in first half of season: suited by test of stamina: acts well on very firm going: occasionally bandaged. *C. A. Horgan.*

KARENS PRINCE 2 b.c. (Apr 17) Ampney Prince 96–Karen's Girl (Joshua 129) — [1989 5g⁵ 6s a7g a5g] third foal: brother to 2 poor platers: dam never ran: leggy colt: has a round action: poor maiden. *Mrs R. Wharton.*

KARENS STARLET 3 b.f. Ampney Prince 96–Karen's Girl (Joshua 129) [1988 — 5g 5d⁴ 6d⁴ 6g 5g⁵ 1989 5m 6f 5m⁵ 9f⁵ 10g⁴] lengthy, dipped-backed filly: has a rather round action: poor maiden: best form over 5f on top-of-the-ground: has tended to wander (including in blinkers once at 2 yrs), and pulled hard and didn't look keen final start. *Mrs R. Wharton.*

KARFIA 3 b.f. Royal Match 117–Kasarose § (Owen Dudley 121) [1988 NR 1989 10f — 10.2f 10.2f 14g] sparely-made filly: second reported foal: half-sister to poor maiden

Washington Singer Stakes, Newbury—Karinga Bay leads inside the final furlong

Brave Setanta (by Hillandale): dam lightly raced at 2 yrs and temperamental: no sign of ability in maidens and claimers: sold to join W. Price 1,000 gns Ascot July Sales. *A. P. Ingham.*

KARINGA BAY 2 ch.c. (Mar 12) Ardross 134–Handy Dancer 87 (Green God 128) [1989 5f⁶ 6m* 7g* 7.3d] big, strong, close-coupled colt: did well physically: good walker: fifth foal: brother to modest 1¾m winner Gydaros and half-brother to 3-y-o 10.1f and 11.7f winner Roll A Dollar (by Spin of A Coin) and 1986 2-y-o 5f and 6f winner Mr Grumpy (by The Brianstan): dam won 3 times over 1¼m: successful in maiden at York in July, running on strongly to beat Contract Law a neck, and slowly-run listed race (by a length from Marquetry) at Newbury following month: never going well in Vodafone Horris Hill Stakes at Newbury: will be well suited by 1m + : gives impression will prove much better than we are able to rate him: one to keep on right side. *Denys Smith.* **97 p**

KARRI 4 gr.f. On Your Mark 125–Grey Fleck (Sing Sing 134) [1988 6m 5f 1989 5s 5f] of little account: sold 900 gns Ascot July Sales. *M. Castell.* **—**

KASSIYDA 3 b.f. Mill Reef (USA) 141–Kadissya (USA) (Blushing Groom (FR) 131) [1988 NR 1989 10.2f³ 10f* 10.1g³ 10m* 10g⁴] leggy, sparely-made filly: second foal: half-sister to dual Derby winner Kahyasi (by Ile de Bourbon): dam French 1¼m winner: successful in small fields for maiden at Redcar in July and minor event at Chepstow in August: evens, fair fourth after slow start in moderately-run £6,900 event at Yarmouth in September: will be suited by 1½m. *L. M. Cumani.* **98**

KATAHDIN 2 b.c. (Apr 15) Sandhurst Prince 128–Grand Teton 64 (Bustino 136) [1989 6g 7g⁶ 6f⁵ 6f⁴ 6g] 5,400F, 6,200Y: neat colt: second foal: half-brother to 3-y-o Peak District (by Beldale Flutter): dam placed over 1¼m: plating-class maiden: will be suited by return to 7f. *G. Wragg.* **59**

KATALANTA 3 b.f. Kafu 120–Miss Atalanta 83 (Hethersett 134) [1988 6g 7m² 6s* 6g 6g 6d 1989 6m 6m⁵ 5s] workmanlike, rather sparely-made filly: moderate mover: modest winner as 2-y-o: below form in claimer and handicaps in 1989: best form at 6f: acted on soft going: dead. *B. W. Hills.* **—**

KATANGO BEAT 2 b.f. (Feb 28) Dunbeath (USA) 127–Kittycatoo Katango (USA) (Verbatim (USA)) [1989 7m 8.2f a8g] angular filly: moderate walker: first foal: dam winner in Italy: little worthwhile form in maiden and claimer: blinkered third outing: trained first 2 starts by Sir Mark Prescott. *W. Wilson.* **—**

KATHERINES EMERALD 3 b.f. Aragon 118–Emerin 85 (King Emperor (USA)) [1988 5g* 5m² 5g² 5m² 5f³ 6g 1989 5v³ 5d³ 7m⁵ 6m³ 5g³ 6f⁶ 5f⁴ 6g 5f² 5f² **62 §**

458

5m⁵ 5g] leggy, rather angular filly: moderate mover: quite modest handicapper: probably stays 7f: acts on any going: ran moderately in blinkers sixth outing (edgy) and once at 2 yrs: has run creditably when sweating: often finds little off bridle. *C. W. Thornton.*

KATHTEEN 3 b.g. Teenoso (USA) 135–Kath (Thatch (USA) 136) [1988 NR 1989 **58** d
10g 8d 8m³ 7m 7h 8m] lengthy gelding: third live foal: half-brother to 1m seller winner Bella Sofie (by Sallust): dam lightly-raced daughter of half-sister to high-class miler Saintly Song: sweating, always-prominent third in well-contested seller at Doncaster, only form: should stay beyond 1m: trained first 5 starts by Mrs L. Piggott, off course 4 months after last of them. *D. H. Topley.*

KATHY COOK 4 b.f. Glenstal (USA) 118–Belmont Blue 75 (Kashmir II 125) **41** §
[1988 12g 10.5g 11f4 10m 14s⁶ 16.5g⁶ 12.2f⁶ 12g⁶ 10g 14.5g² 13.8f 16.5f² 17g² 1989 16f 12m 16.2m³ 17f⁶ a16g] good-topped filly: moderate mover: unreliable maiden: has run in seller: stays 17f: acts on firm going: tail swisher: difficult ride: not genuine. *R. Hollinshead.*

KATICA 3 b.f. Jester 119–Gwen Somers (Will Somers 114§) [1988 NR 1989 6m —
8.2d 9f 14d 8f] IR 3,000Y: leggy, quite good-topped filly: sixth reported living foal: half-sister to fairly useful 6f winner Transflash (by Auction Ring): dam unraced half-sister to smart animals Cyprus and Right of The Line: well beaten in varied events, including claimers. *D. McCain.*

KATIE JO 3 b.f. Taufan (USA) 119–Wyn Mipet (Welsh Saint 126) [1988 NR 1989 **80**
8m 8m⁶ 8g³ 7.6m² 9m²] 21,000Y: stocky, quite attractive filly: second foal: half-sister to modest 1986 2-y-o 5.1f and 6f winner Victory Ballard (by Ballad Rock): dam placed over 5f as 2-y-o in Ireland: fair maiden: kept on strongly when second at Lingfield (beaten head) and Redcar (handicap) in September: will be suited by further. *M. J. Ryan.*

KATIE SCARLETT 3 b.f. Lochnager 132–Final Request 63 (Sharp Edge 123) **63**
[1988 5m⁵ 5m⁵ 5f³ 5d⁴ 5g² 5d 6m⁵ 1989 7d⁴ 7g 6s⁶ 7f 5f 6f⁶ 6f 6m a8g a12g] big, short-backed, workmanlike filly: has scope: good mover with a long stride: quite modest maiden: stays 7f: acts on any going: has run well when sweating and on edge, and when ridden by claimer: inconsistent. *J. J. Bridger.*

KATSINA (USA) 2 b.f. (Feb 26) Cox's Ridge (USA)–Katsura (USA) (Northern **86** p
Dancer) [1989 7f² 7g*] compact, good-quartered filly: fifth foal: half-sister to 3-y-o 7f (at 2 yrs) and 10.2f winner Rambushka (by Roberto): dam, Irish 7f and 1½m winner, is daughter of sister to very smart middle-distance filly Trillionaire: 7/1, won 24-runner maiden at Leicester in November by a neck from Diamond Shoes, soon prominent and running on strongly to lead towards finish: will be well suited by 1m +: sure to improve again. *B. W. Hills.*

KATSUE 2 ch.g. (Jun 2) Noalto 120–Gamma (GER) (Zank) [1989 7f 10g] 5,800Y: —
neat gelding: half-brother to several winners, including Royal Whip (by Pitskelly), winner at 8.5f at 2 yrs in Ireland later successful in Norwegian St Leger: dam placed over 1½m at 3 yrs in Ireland: bit backward, well beaten in seller at Redcar and maiden at Nottingham. *Miss L. C. Siddall.*

KATY LOU 3 gr.f. Nishapour (FR) 125–Emmylou (Arctic Tern (USA) 126) [1988 —
7g 7m⁵ 7.5f⁶ 1989 10f 8h⁴ 12f⁵ 10.1m 10.1m⁶ 10f⁴ 12h⁶] small, lengthy filly: poor form: probably stays 1¼m: tends to race freely: blinkered fourth and fifth outings: visored last 2, carrying head high on last: winning selling hurdler. *Miss B. Sanders.*

KATY'S LAD 2 b.c. (Feb 28) Camden Town 125–Cathryn's Song (Prince **65**
Tenderfoot (USA) 126) [1989 5s* 5s³ 5m⁶ 7.5f⁴ 7g⁴ 7m⁴ 8.2g²] IR 1,400F, 2,400Y: rather leggy colt: has a quick action: first foal: dam never ran: quite modest performer: won maiden at Warwick in March: ran well in Chester minor event on fifth start and Nottingham nursery on last: stays 1m: acts on any going: effective with or without blinkers. *B. A. McMahon.*

KATZAKEENA 2 b.f. (Apr 25) Gorytus (USA) 132–Current Bay (Tyrant (USA)) **77**
[1989 5g² 5g² 6g²] 9,800F, 15,000Y: fifth foal: closely related to 1985 French 2-y-o 7f winner Lac Aux Dames (by Kings Lake): dam won from 6.5f to 1m in Italy and France: modest maiden: beaten a length by Reference Light at Redcar on final start: better suited by 6f than 5f and bred to stay at least 1m. *P. J. Makin.*

KAWARAU QUEEN 2 b.f. (Jan 25) Taufan (USA) 119–Hasty Goddess 72 **67**
(Nebbiolo 125) [1989 5g 5m³ 5m² 5g²] 5,200F, 6,200Y: workmanlike, deep-girthed filly: second foal: dam middle-distance winner stayed well: quite modest form in maiden auction races on last 3 starts: will be better suited by 6f + . *S. G. Norton.*

KAWTUBAN 2 b.c. (Apr 7) Law Society (USA) 130–Thunderflash (FR) — p (Northfields (USA)) [1989 6m] 90,000F: second foal: dam, winner at around 1m in USA, is daughter of Catherine Wheel, also dam of Cheshire Oaks winner Hunston: 9/1, coltish and green, over 12 lengths tenth of 24, slowly away then staying on well final 3f, to Royal Fi Fi in minor event at Windsor in August: will be suited by 7f+: sure to improve. *J. Tree.*

KAWWAS 4 b.c. Persian Bold 123–Tifrums 77 (Thatch (USA) 136) [1988 5f⁵ 7g³ 63 7f⁶ 6m⁵ 6g 7.6d 6d 1989 8g 8d 6f³ 7m⁵ 6f* 7f 7f⁵ 6g³ 7m⁶ 7g 6m] smallish, sparely-made colt: won (for first time) handicap at Brighton in July: stays 7f: seems to need a soft surface: blinkered once at 3 yrs: sometimes gets on toes, and has sweated: has given trouble at stalls (refused to enter them third intended start) and tended to hang: inconsistent. *W. Holden.*

KAYCEN 2 b.g. (Apr 5) Kind of Hush 118–Tomard (Thatching 131) [1989 7m⁶ 6f⁴ 63 6g⁶ 6g 8.2g] 9,000F, 12,500Y: good-topped gelding: carries condition: second foal: half-brother to 3-y-o 15f winner Tophard (by Lyphard's Special): dam ran only at 2 yrs when 5f winner in Ireland: quite modest maiden: stays 1m: has joined C. Brittain. *Mrs L. Piggott.*

KAYRAWAN 2 ch.c. (Mar 14) Nishapour (FR) 125–Karkiya (USA) (Riverman 71 (USA) 131) [1989 6m 6f² 6g] medium-sized colt: has scope: first foal: dam, 13f winner in France, half-sister to dam of Kahyasi: 50/1 and ridden by girl apprentice, equal-second of 6, head behind Born To Swing, in minor event at Lingfield in August, hanging left and no extra close home: ran poorly in minor event at Hamilton following month: will be better suited by 7f+. *M. R. Stoute.*

K-BRIDGE DOMINION 3 b.c. Dominion 123–Mariko (Dancer's Image — (USA)) [1988 NR 1989 10g 12f⁵ 10.1m 10g 12m] leggy, good-topped colt: moderate mover: fifth reported foal: dam Irish 5f winner: plating-class form at best: virtually tailed off in seller final start, July: should be suited by 1½m. *C. A. Horgan.*

K-BRIGADE 4 b.c. Brigadier Gerard 144–Kajetana (FR) (Caro 133) [1988 8s 8s* 78 10m* 9f 10g* 10.2g 10g 1989 8g² 10g⁴ 12d⁶ 10f 12.4g 10g⁶ a16g³] big colt: modest handicapper: apprentice ridden, stayed on well after being held up when third at Southwell in December: stays 2m: possibly not at his best on firm going, acts on any other: visored fourth start: lacks a turn of foot and is normally ridden up with pace: game. *C. W. C. Elsey.*

KEEN AS MUSTARD 3 ch.f. Precocious 126–Sharp Lady 70 (Sharpen Up 127) 61 [1988 NR 1989 8g 8m 8m² 8f 8s³] 22,000Y: tall, leggy filly: closely related to 1¼m winner Spoiled Brat and 5f and 1m winner Good N' Sharp (both by Mummy's Pet): dam won five 6f races: quite modest form when placed in seller and claimer, latter first run for 4 months: should stay further: gives impression will prove best on an easy surface: sold 6,000 gns Newmarket Autumn Sales. *M. F. D. Morley.*

KEEN BREEZE 2 b.f. (Mar 30) Chabrias (FR) 103–Ginger Tart 87 (Swing Easy — (USA) 126) [1989 6f 5m⁶ 7m⁶] third reported foal: sister to 6f winner Sister Chabrias: dam second over 1m from 2 starts at 2 yrs: tailed off in maidens and a seller in Scotland: slowly away first 2 starts. *T. Craig.*

KEEN EDGE 5 b.h. Good Times (ITY)–Razor Blade 65 (Sharp Edge 123) [1988 75 6d² 6d² 6g² 7m 6m* 6g³ 6g 6d 7m 1989 5s 5s⁴ 6f* 6m⁵ 6f³ 6m 6f 6f 6f⁵ 6f⁴ 6m⁵ 5m] small, compact horse: modest handicapper: favourite, made virtually all, racing almost alone, in quite valuable event at Lingfield in May: ran creditably on next 2 and on ninth and tenth (beaten around 3 lengths in Chicago) outings: speedy, and best at sprint distances: probably acts on any going: has worn blinkers, but not since 1987: genuine. *P. Mitchell.*

KEEN HUNTER (USA) 2 ch.c. (Mar 29) Diesis 133–Love's Reward (Nonoalco 73 p (USA) 131) [1989 6g⁵] tall, quite attractive colt: second foal: half-brother to 3-y-o 1¾m Amoodi (by Forli): dam lightly-raced half-sister to high-class 1984 2-y-o Bassenthwaite and very useful 1981 2-y-o sprinter Glancing: co-favourite, green and coltish, under 8 lengths fifth of 29, keeping on having tended to hang, to Sure Sharp in maiden at Newmarket in November: will be better suited by 7f+: sure to improve. *J. Gosden.*

KEEN MELODY (USA) 2 b.f. (May 5) Sharpen Up 127–Sweet Abandon (USA) 53 (Lyphard (USA) 132) [1989 6g 6f⁶ 8f⁶] first foal: dam, placed at 1¼m in Ireland and later successful at about 1m in USA, is half-sister to top-class middle-distance performer Mac Diarmida: plating-class maiden: ran moderately final start, fading quickly under 2f out: should stay 1m. *R. Hannon.*

KEEP BIDDING 3 br.g. Hays 120–Keep Chanting (Auction Ring (USA) 123) 55 [1988 6f 6s 7m 7f 1989 8g 8m 8m³ 6m 10s] big, lengthy gelding: has a round action:

plating-class maiden: worthwhile form in handicaps as 3-y-o only when third at Thirsk, hampered and staying on well: stays 1m: acts on top-of-the-ground: blinkered third and fourth starts and final one at 2 yrs. *M. W. Easterby.*

KEEP MUM 4 b.f. Mummy's Pet 125–Someone Talked (USA) (Barbizon 110) — [1988 6m 5g 10m 5m 5v 1989 5m 6f 5f 5m 5f 6f 7f] small filly: no longer of any account: sometimes blinkered or visored. *G. P. Kelly.*

KEEP ON RUNNIN' 2 b.g. (Apr 30) Ballacashtal (CAN)–Lake Victoria 94 **65** (Stupendous) [1989 5g* 5s⁴ 5f² 6g 5s³ 5v] 13,500Y: leggy, medium-sized gelding: half-brother to 1979 2-y-o 6f winner Stubbington Green (by Swing Easy): dam winning sprinter: quite modest performer: won maiden at Newcastle in March: well beaten in seller final start: stays 6f: acts on any going except possibly heavy: blinkered last 3 outings. *J. Berry.*

KEEP STRAIGHT 3 b.g. Castle Keep 121–Straight To Bed (Dominion 123) — § [1988 5g 6f 7m 7f⁶ 8m³ 8.2m³ 8d³ 1989 8h 8m⁵ 8m] leggy gelding: carries condition: quite modest form at best as 2-y-o: well beaten in sellers in 1989: best form at 1m: blinkered second outing and twice at 2 yrs: changed hands 1,000 gns Ascot August Sales: winning selling hurdler: probably ungenuine. *W. Carter.*

KEEP YOUR WORD 3 ch.f. Castle Keep 121–So True 116 (So Blessed 130) **69** [1988 7g 8s⁶ 1989 10f 9m³ 10m] sparely-made filly: poor walker: has a rather round action: modest maiden: may prove suited by 9f. *G. B. Balding.*

KEFAAH (USA) 4 ch.c. Blushing Groom (FR) 131–Tertiary (USA) (Vaguely **120** Noble 140) [1988 9g* 10.5g² 12m⁵ 8m* 10g* 10.5f⁵ 8g⁵ 1989 8h* 10f⁵ 8g⁶] well-made colt: fluent mover: good-class performer: successful in Feilden Stakes at Newmarket, 3-runner minor event at Kempton and Mecca Bookmakers' Classic at

Ayr as 3-y-o: long odds on, made all in canter in 2-runner minor contest at Brighton in August: creditable fifth of 13, always tracking leaders, no extra final 1f, to Steinlen in Arlington Million at Chicago month later: raced too freely in Ciga Prix du Rond-Point at Longchamp: best at about 1¼m: acted on hard going, didn't race on soft surface: often sweated slightly and got bit on edge: reportedly fractured tibia in off-hind in February: retired to Tara Stud, Co. Meath, fee IR £5,000 (Oct 1st). *L. M. Cumani.*

KELLY'S BID 3 b.f. Pitskelly 122–Galetzky 86 (Radetzky 123) [1988 NR 1989 10f 10.6m 14f⁴ 14m] medium-sized, rather unfurnished filly: has a quick action: first foal: dam won twice at 1m and stayed 1¼m: little worthwhile form in maidens and in ladies handicap. *J. W. Hills.* —

KELLY'S DARLING 3 b.g. Pitskelly 122–Fair Darling 93 (Darling Boy 124) [1988 6d 6m⁵ 1989 7m⁴ 7m⁴ 8g⁵ 10g⁵ 12.2m³ 12m³ 12m⁵ 10f² 10f 10g³ 10f⁵ 10f⁵] lengthy, angular gelding: carries little condition: moderate walker: quite modest maiden: ran moderately in claimer and sellers last 4 starts, refusing to go through with his effort on final one: stays 1½m: acts on top-of-the-ground: takes keen hold: sold 2,700 gns Newmarket Autumn Sales: ungenuine. *R. J. R. Williams.* 64 d

KEMOSABE 3 b.c. Caerleon (USA) 132–Spirit In The Sky 106 (Tudor Melody 129) [1988 6s 7s² 1989 9g 10.4m⁵ 12.2m* 12m² 12m² 12f] compact, attractive colt: has a rather round action: won maiden at Catterick in June: creditable second in amateurs events at Newmarket: always behind in £8,100 handicap at York in August: should stay beyond 1½m: acts on top-of-the-ground and soft going: sold 18,000 gns Newmarket Autumn Sales. *B. W. Hills.* 85

KENDOR (FR) 3 gr.c. Kenmare (FR) 125–Belle Mecene (FR) (Gay Mecene (USA) 128) [1988 6d* 6m* 6d⁵ 7m² 8s* 1989 8d* 8m* 9.2g² 10g⁴] 121

Kendor's season ended prematurely, in anticlimax. He'd begun the year rated the best of his generation seen out in France, second overall to High Estate in the International Classification, mainly as a result of an easy win in the Grand Criterium; and he picked up in the spring where he'd left off the previous autumn, winning two races at Longchamp, the classic trial Prix de Fontainebleau followed by the Dubai Poule d'Essai des Poulains. He took the Poulains in the manner of a very good horse, but by the end of June, two defeats later, his career was at an end. Proposed attempts to re-establish him among the European milers came to nothing when reportedly a low blood count stopped his running in the Prix Jacques le Marois at Deauville and when a chipped bone in a knee, sustained in his final preparation for the Prix du Moulin de Longchamp, put him out for good. Kendor, a close-coupled colt, is set to stand as a stallion in France and Australia, six months about. He has been bought by the Arrowfield Stud, owners of his sire Kenmare.

While Kendor looked a very good horse in the Poulains the form of the race is nothing out of the ordinary by classic standards: Stone Flake finished only six lengths behind in eighth place in a strongly-run affair. So whether excuses are necessary for Kendor's subsequent defeats is problematical. He has an obvious one, of course, in the longer distance of both races, and in addition he might have been inconvenienced by having to make his own

Dubai Poule d'Essai des Poulains, Longchamp—
Kendor impresses in beating Goldneyev and Ocean Falls

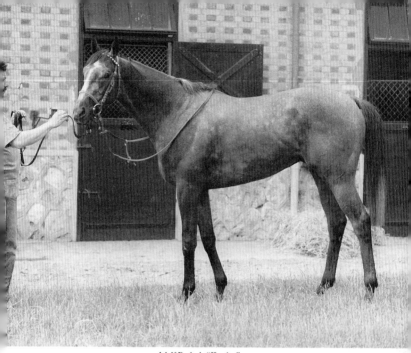

Adolf Bader's "Kendor"

running in the Jean Prat, in which Local Talent, just over four lengths behind in the Grand Criterium, quickened the better in the closing stages and beat him half a length. Kendor went down by two lengths, a neck and a short neck in the Grand Prix de Paris, finishing less strongly than the first two after being held up pulling hard. The first two, Dancehall and Norberto, turned out to be high-class animals; so did the third Creator, and maybe this was a fair reflection of Kendor's merit. All the same, it might well have been more informative if connections had taken up another of their options and run him in the St James's Palace Stakes instead.

Having shown his well-being by beating the much-fancied Prix Djebel winner Ocean Falls convincingly by half a length in the Fontainebleau, Kendor started a short-priced favourite for the Poulains, reopposed by Ocean Falls and the Fontainebleau third Goldneyev (out of Gold River). This trio, plus Tagel who'd reportedly had set-backs, appeared the backbone of the home defence against the challenge of Stone Flake, the second favourite Great Commotion and Sylvan Tempest. The ground had come up too firm for late-entry Sylvan Tempest during the week, and apparently doubts were entertained whether Kendor would handle it well enough—he'd won the Grand Criterium on soft. In the conditions the course record, previously set by Soviet Star in the 1987 Poulains, went by a tenth of a second. Asmussen on Ocean Falls set such a gallop that they had all bar Kendor and Great Commotion off the bridle after about three furlongs. Kendor was still full of running turning for home in around fifth-of-ten place. Halfway up the straight

463

he'd quickened past Corviglia, Great Commotion and Goldneyev to challenge the leader, and it was all over. Once in front Kendor needed no more than vigorous pushing along to make sure by two lengths from Goldneyev and Ocean Falls virtually together, three quarters of a length in front of Star Touch then double that to the inexperienced Great Commotion who'd had every chance. The first four did little racing afterwards, and the season ended without any of Kendor's nine opponents winning a top-class event.

Kendor (FR) (gr.c. 1986)	Kenmare (FR) (gr 1975)	Kalamoun (gr 1970)	Zeddaan Khairunissa
		Belle of Ireland (ch 1964)	Milesian Belle of The Ball
	Belle Mecene (FR) (b 1982)	Gay Mecene (b or br 1975)	Vaguely Noble Gay Missile
		Djaka Belle (b 1975)	Djakao Orleans Belle

That Kendor took such a keen hold early on in his races raised serious doubts about his effectiveness over middle distances. On breeding the probabilities were that he'd get at least a mile and a quarter, the average distance of races won at three years and upwards by the stock of the 1978 Marois winner, Kenmare. The dam Belle Mecene, the offspring of two middle-distance winners but a half-sister to the useful sprinter Zinbeau, never ran; Kendor is her first foal. Djaka Belle's dam Orleans Belle, who showed modest form at up to a mile in Britain, was a half-sister to the Preakness Stakes and Kentucky Derby winner Canonero. *R. Touflan, France.*

KENIANT (FR) 3 ch.f. Noir Et Or 125–Zana (FR) (Trepan (FR) 133) [1988 8g* **113** 8s* 8s³ 1989 10.5g⁶ 8s* 8m⁴] second foal: half-sister to French 11f and 1½m winner

H. H. Aga Khan's "Kerita"

Vizan (by Vitiges): dam, who ran 4 times, is half-sister to good French stayer Yelpana and very useful French middle-distance performer Zamp: successful 3 times at Longchamp, in maiden and listed race at 2 yrs and in Group 3 Prix de la Grotte in April: 2¼ lengths fourth to Pearl Bracelet in Poule d'Essai des Pouliches there in May: best form at 1m though bred to be well suited by 1¼m: yet to race on very firm ground, acts on any other. *P.-L. Biancone, France.*

KENILWORTH CASTLE 3 b.c. Dunbeath (USA) 127–Ravenshead **66** (Charlottown 127) [1988 6m 1989 14f⁶ 14f³ 15.3f 18g⁶] leggy, quite good-topped colt: quite modest maiden: form only on second start: backward most other outings: worth a try over 1½m: winning selling hurdler. *R. Hollinshead.*

KENTRA 3 ch.f. Grey Ghost 98–La Raine 93 (Majority Blue 126) [1988 5g² 5f² **58** 5g⁴ 6g 5m 6f⁶ 5g³ 5d³ 1989 5s² 5f 5m⁶ 5m] lengthy, angular filly: keen walker: has a quick action: quite modest maiden: second at Thirsk in April, best effort in handicaps in 1989: speedy, and best at 5f: easily best form on an easy surface: blinkered final start (June): keen sort: broke out of stall and was withdrawn once at 2 yrs. *T. D. Barron.*

KERAMA 2 b.f. (Feb 23) Glenstal (USA) 118–Timid Bride (USA) 76 (Blushing **86** Groom (FR) 131) [1989 6f³ 6f* 7g* 8g²] rather unfurnished, quite attractive filly: first foal: dam 10.4f winner, is daughter of useful 5f and 1m winner Miss Zadig: fair performer: successful in maiden at Folkestone in August and minor event (by a length from Razzberry, making most) at Kempton following month: 2½ lengths second of 11 to Ruby Tiger in Premio Dormello at Milan in October: stays 1m: tends to flash tail. *J. L. Dunlop.*

KERITA 3 b.f. Formidable (USA) 125–Kermiya (FR) (Vienna 127) [1988 NR 1989 **111** 7g² 7g² 7f* 7m* 8f 7f* 7.3g⁴ 7g³ 7g* 7m³] sturdy, lengthy filly: good walker: sixth foal: half-sister to 2 winners, including smart miler Kareena (by Riverman): dam won over 9f and 1¼m in France: led close home to beat Mirror Black a head in Group 3 Supreme Stakes at Goodwood then good third to Distant Relative in Group 2 contest at Newmarket last 2 starts: earlier easy winner of maiden at Goodwood, minor event (bandaged off-hind) at Leicester and listed race at Goodwood: best over 7f: acts on firm going: consistent and very useful. *R. F. Johnson Houghton.*

KERRERA 3 b.f. Diesis 133–Rimosa's Pet 109 (Petingo 135) [1988 6m* **115** 6d* 6d² 6d⁵ 5g² 1989 8g² 6m* 5f 6m⁴ 6g]

Having gone the wrong way as a two-year-old, Kerrera returned to be beaten only three quarters of a length in the General Accident One Thousand Guineas. She looked relaxed and well beforehand but pulled hard behind the farcically slow pace and was settled at the back of the seven-runner field before being switched over two furlongs out. Despite stumbling entering the Dip, she produced the most dangerous challenge to stable-companion Musical Bliss on whom Swinburn had dictated matters from the front; Kerrera quickened in fine style but couldn't make much ground in the final furlong. This classic was full of 'ifs and buts', not least surrounding Kerrera. She'd have settled better in a strongly-run race but would she have stayed? Connections clearly had their reservations on the latter point as it was quickly announced that Kerrera would be put back to sprint distances. The listed Skol Lager Sandy Lane Stakes at Haydock offered a straightforward opportunity with only four opponents, the best of whom were apparently Thorn Dance, side-lined since August, and the ungenuine Access Travel. The race developed into a match between Kerrera and Thorn Dance with Kerrera prevailing by three quarters of a length having hung left across to the far rail. Despite her course record—clocked by our race-reader as the official timing system had broken down—Kerrera hadn't looked entirely at ease on the going. On even firmer ground in the King's Stand Stakes at Royal Ascot four weeks later she never got into contention. By the end of the Royal meeting the value of her form at Newmarket and Haydock was looking even more questionable than it had at the time and, in retrospect, Kerrera's performance in the Carroll Foundation July Cup at Newmarket seemed the most reliable guide to her merit. Starting 9/1 third favourite of eleven and getting quite warm in the preliminaries, Kerrera was beaten about four lengths into fourth behind Cadeaux Genereux having had every chance. She couldn't follow that good effort with another one in the Ladbroke Sprint Cup at Haydock in

Skol Lager Sandy Lane Stakes, Haydock—Kerrera (right) and Thorn Dance have pulled clear

September when, from the number-one stall, she bowled along keenly up front in the centre of the course before dropping out approaching the final furlong.

	Diesis (ch 1980)	Sharpen Up (ch 1969)	Atan
			Rocchetta
		Doubly Sure (b 1971)	Reliance II
Kerrera (b.f. 1986)			Soft Angels
	Rimosa's Pet (b 1976)	Petingo (b 1965)	Petition
			Alcazar
		Rimosa (br 1960)	Mossborough
			Rosy Dolly

Kerrera's family is discussed at length in her entry in *Racehorses of 1988* and in that of her half-brother Rock City in this volume. It soon became apparent that her headstrong nature wouldn't allow Kerrera to prove best at the distances suggested by her pedigree. A compact, workmanlike filly, she was a good walker and mover who acted on top-of-the-ground but gave the impression that a bit more give would suit her ideally. The temperament which seemed to get the better of her as a two-year-old didn't affect her too adversely in 1989. As for Kerrera's form, well, by most standards that can't be worth the reputed seven-figure sum which Sheikh Mohammed paid for her ten days before her racecourse debut. But there's still her career in the paddocks to come. *M. R. Stoute.*

KERRY CALLUNA 5 b.m. Celtic Cone 116–Erica Alba (Yukon Eric (CAN)) — [1988 NR 1989 10s 9s 12m 10m 14.8m] lengthy, workmanlike mare: sister to winning staying hurdler/chaser Celtic Fleet: dam never ran: well beaten in modest company: wore blinkers or visor first 4 outings: taken down early on debut. *J. L. Spearing.*

KESWA 3 b.f. Kings Lake (USA) 133–Reves Celestes (USA) 82 (Lyphard (USA) 94 132) [1988 8g* 1989 10.2m⁴ 12f* 12m³ 12f⁴ 10g⁴ 10s 12v³] leggy filly: fairly useful handicapper here: won £6,000 event at Newbury in May: below form in listed races and Group 3 event in Italy last 3 outings: will probably stay further: acts on firm going, possibly unsuited by heavy: trained until after fourth start by M. Stoute. *V. Valiani, Italy.*

KETTI 4 br.f. Hotfoot 126–Nigrel (Sovereign Path 125) [1988 7f 12m 12m³ 10g 12f 52 1989 7v⁴ 8f] smallish, sparely-made filly: won 2 sellers at 2 yrs: form on flat since (out of handicap and carrying overweight) only when around 2 lengths fourth of 17 at Lingfield in April: should stay beyond 7f: has won on top-of-the-ground, but well suited by plenty of give nowadays: blinkered 3 times, including both starts in spring: winning hurdler. *D. M. Grissell.*

KEVIN'S PET 3 b.f. Petorius 117–Ruby Relic (Monseigneur (USA) 127) [1988 7g 1989 7d] small, narrow, close-coupled filly: no sign of ability in minor event and seller. *K. Stone.* —

KEY ROYAL (USA) 8 br.m. Key To The Kingdom (USA)–Cool Value (USA) (Cool Moon (USA)) [1988 12g 15.8g 12.2f4 1989 13.8d6 11d* 12g] narrow, rather leggy mare: bad mover: won selling handicap at Edinburgh (no bid) in April: ran poorly in non-selling handicap at Hamilton over 2 weeks later: stays 2m: probably needs a soft surface nowadays: visored at 8 yrs. *M. P. Naughton.* **36**

KEY SHIFT 2 b.c. (Apr 22) Night Shift (USA)–Quaver 86 (Song 132) [1989 6g 5g3 5f* 6d5] compact, quite attractive colt: good mover: first foal: dam sprinter: modest performer: won maiden at Wolverhampton by a length: well beaten in Catterick minor event later in October: best form at 5f: has run well for 7-lb claimer: sold 11,500 gns Newmarket Autumn Sales. *L. M. Cumani.* **77**

KEY TO THE MUSIC (USA) 3 b.g. Key To The Kingdom (USA)–Lilting Lily (King Emperor (USA)) [1988 6g 6g3 6m2 7g 1989 7g3 7s4 6f4 6m* 6f* 6f* 6m3 6m 6g6] good-quartered gelding: has a round action: fairly useful handicapper: won at Haydock (claimer) in May and Redcar and Ripon in June: ran creditably next start: best at 6f: suited by top-of-the-ground: blinkered last 6 starts: has turn of foot: gelded after final start. *M. F. D. Morley.* **92**

KHADINO 3 b.f. Relkino 131–Khadine 79 (Astec 128) [1988 7m 1989 9g 12f 10m 7m 8m] leggy, angular filly: no form: blinkered last 2 outings. *P. J. Feilden.* —

KHAIRULLAH 2 b.c. (Mar 29) Adonijah 126–Naamullah (Reform 132) [1989 7f] stocky colt: first foal: dam unraced: 50/1, green and burly, well beaten in 10-runner maiden at Leicester in October. *J. D. Czerpak.* —

KHARIF 5 b.g. Formidable (USA) 125–Pass The Rulla (USA) (Buckpasser) [1988 12m 8g6 12f6 12g3 12g4 13g* 13d3 12d5 14.7d 15d 1989 12d 12g2 13m5 15s] quite attractive, well-made gelding: poor handicapper: suited by around 1½m: acts on a soft surface: best form without blinkers or visor: has run well for apprentice: has looked none too keen: winning hurdler. *R. Allan.* **36**

KHAYAMOUR 3 gr.c. Habitat 134–Khayra (FR) (Zeddaan 130) [1988 NR 1989 8m3] third living foal: half-brother to good middle-distance stayer Khairpour (by Arctic Tern): dam unraced sister to high-class miler Kalamoun: 7/4 second favourite from 7/2, 4 lengths third of 14 to Salman in minor event at Edinburgh in October, losing position on turn then staying on steadily: should improve, probably over further: sold 22,000 gns Newmarket Autumn Sales. *R. F. Johnson Houghton.* **71** p

KHAYDARA 3 b.f. Indian King (USA) 128–Khatima (Relko 136) [1988 NR 1989 7g5 7g3 6m* 6m3 6m2 6g* 5g] big, strong, good-bodied filly: has plenty of scope: has a quick action: second living foal: dam French 12.5f winner: progressive: won £6,800 contest at Newmarket in May and £11,900 handicap (by short head) at York in October: second favourite, always outpaced in listed race at Newmarket final start: hung continually left at Epsom fifth start, off course 4 months after: suited by 6f: acts on top-of-the-ground. *L. M. Cumani.* **103**

KHETA KING 6 b.g. Hittite Glory 125–Matala (FR) 65 (Misti IV 132) [1988 11s2 12d3 12m* 14g6 12m 10m 12.2d 16d 1989 10g 12g3 16s5] angular, sparely-made gelding: moderate mover: successful at Cagnes-sur-Mer as 5-y-o for second year in succession: well-beaten third of 6 on second of 2 outings there in spring: blinkered, modest fifth of 11, off bridle virtually throughout, in handicap at Kempton 2 weeks later: stays 2m: acts on any going: has joined D. Elsworth. *W. Hastings-Bass.* —

KHIOS (USA) 2 b.c. (May 6) Lord Gaylord (USA)–Monelia (USA) (Mongo) [1989 8m5 6d] $95,000Y: medium-sized, good-topped colt: half-brother to numerous winners in USA, including stakes winner at up to 1m Command Control (by Rambunctious): dam ran 4 times: made running to 2f out in October maidens at Warwick (backward, and eased considerably) and Catterick. *F. Durr.* —

KHOREVO 4 b.g. Tyrnavos 129–Amina 80 (Brigadier Gerard 144) [1988 10s 12.2g6 1989 8s 10s 8d 5f a11g] quite attractive gelding: moderate mover: very little form, and reluctant to race fourth outing: one to leave alone. *I. Campbell.* — §

KHULM 2 b.c. (Apr 25) Kafu 120–Little Wild Duck 78 (Great Heron (USA)) [1989 6m 6g] 8,800Y: leggy, close-coupled colt: half-brother to 3-y-o Wild Abandon (by Sallust), fair 6f winner at 2 yrs, Irish 5f winner Sallywell (by Manado) and winners in France and Belgium: dam, placed at up to 1½m, is half-sister to smart miler Sin Timon: shaped quite well when around 10 lengths eleventh of 22 to Hebba in maiden at Newbury in September: favourite, well beaten in similar event at Goodwood following month. *L. J. Holt.* **53**

KID LEWIS 2 b.c. (Apr 15) Thatching 131–Mirkan Honey 83 (Ballymore 123)   **56**
[1989 7m 7m] medium-sized, quite attractive colt: good walker: third foal:
half-brother to 3-y-o Norwegian listed winner Tiger Bill, useful winner at 2 yrs, and
to modest middle-distance maiden Adanus (both by General Assembly): dam Irish
2m winner as 4-y-o: about 7 lengths seventh of 17, weakening final 2f, to Mull House
in maiden at Chepstow in October: very green on debut. *J. L. Dunlop.*

KIDWAH 2 b.f. (Feb 28) Shareef Dancer (USA) 135–Aldhabyih 86 (General   **—**
Assembly (USA)) [1989 8f] second foal: half-sister to 3-y-o Alhathaf (by Tap On
Wood), fairly useful 6f and 7f winner at 2 yrs: dam, half-sister to very smart 1982
2-y-o sprinter Kafu and smart 7f to 1¼m winner Moomba Masquerade, won over 5f
at 2 yrs and stayed 7f: broke a leg in maiden at Redcar: dead. *H. Thomson Jones.*

KIKALA 3 gr.f. Kalaglow 132–Jhansi Ki Rani (USA) 94 (Far North (CAN) 120)   **83**
[1988 8s 7f* 8g⁴ 1989 8g⁴ 8.5s⁴ 7.6f⁴ 8h³ 9.2f³ 8f* 8g⁴] leggy, lengthy filly: fair
handicapper: 13/8 on, won 4-runner auction race at Redcar in June: not seen out
after early-August: should be suited by return to 9f: probably acts on any going:
visored last 3 starts: consistent. *K. M. Brassey.*

KILBARRY LAD 4 b.g. Mr Fluorocarbon 126–Gosforth Lady 73 (Linacre 133)   **—**
[1988 7d 12m 10.1m 12m 8f 1989 12g] of no account: visored final start at 3 yrs. *P.
Butler.*

KILDONAN 2 b.g. (May 14) Welsh Captain 113–Madam Import 63 (Import 127)   **58**
[1989 6h² 7f 7m 8.2f⁴ 8.5f* 8.2f⁴ 8f⁵] 300Y: big, good-topped gelding: carries
condition: has a long stride: second foal: dam sprint maiden: fairly useful plater: no
bid after beating Integrity Boy a short head at Beverley in September: creditable
fourth to Bimbo in non-selling nursery at Nottingham, better subsequent effort:
strong-running type, better suited by 1m + than shorter: looked none too easy a ride
fourth outing. *T. D. Barron.*

KILIFI (USA) 2 b.f. (May 10) Topsider (USA)–Dare To Be Bare (USA) (Grey   **—**
Dawn II 132) [1989 6g 6m] $40,000F: workmanlike filly: sixth foal: closely related to
fairly useful 1¼m winner Mawzoon (by Danzig) and half-sister to 2 minor winners in
USA: dam won at up to 9f: well beaten in big fields in claimer at Goodwood and seller
at Newmarket: sold 1,700 gns Doncaster November Sales. *A. A. Scott.*

KILLIMOR LAD 2 b.c. (Apr 11) Tina's Pet 121–Jeldi 58 (Tribal Chief 125) [1989   **—**
7s 7m] 6,800Y: brother to 7f winner Pretty Soon and half-brother to 4 other winners,
including Jeldaire (by Radetzky), successful from 5f to 8.3f: dam ran only at 2 yrs:
poor form in autumn maidens at Goodwood and Chepstow. *M. McCormack.*

KILRONAN 5 gr.h. Rusticaro (FR) 124–Firdosa (Relic) [1988 6v 7v 7g 7g⁴ 5m   **—**
6g* 6g 8g 7v² 6m 6v 5g 11d 1989 6f³ 10f³ 7f 7.6m a6g] small ex-Irish horse: fourth
reported living foal: half-brother to Irish 7f winner Legal Expertise (by Royal And
Regal) and a winner in Italy: dam closely related to high-class milers Buisson
Ardent and Venture VII: won handicap at Tipperary as 4-y-o: little form in minor
contests and a handicap in 1989: stays 7f: appears to act on any going: blinkered
twice: sweating and on toes third outing: often ridden by apprentice in Ireland: sold
1,700 gns Ascot November Sales: inconsistent. *R. Curtis.*

KIMBLE BLUE 6 b.m. Blue Refrain 121–Cratloe (African Sky 124) [1988 NR   **—**
1989 6m 7m 6g 7m] neat, robust mare: moderate walker: plating-class handicapper:
missed break final outing (July): suited by stiff 6f: best form with give in the ground:
often blinkered: usually has tongue tied down: usually taken down quietly. *W. J.
Musson.*

KIMBOLTON KATIE 3 ch.f. Aragon 118–One Sharper (Dublin Taxi) [1988 5g²   **79** d
6f⁴ 5d⁵ 5g* 6m³ 1989 6m³ 6g⁶ 6m 6g⁶ 5g 6g] sturdy filly: has a rather round action:
fair performer at her best: creditable third in £6,800 event at Newmarket in May,
easily best effort as 3-y-o: well behind last 3 starts, twice blinkered: stays 6f:
bandaged off-hind. *J. W. Payne.*

KIND A LUCKY 2 br.c. (Apr 29) Kind of Hush 118–Joker's Luck (Bold Lad (IRE)   **—**
133) [1989 7g 8g] 2,600Y, 6,200 2-y-o: first foal: dam never ran, is granddaughter of
Joking Apart: of no account. *N. R. Mitchell.*

KIND OF SHY 3 ch.f. Kind of Hush 118–Peta 93 (Petingo 135) [1988 6g⁵ 6g 6f   **61**
1989 8.5f 9f 8g 8m² 8.2f² 8.2g 7.5m² a8g a11g] leggy, sparely-made filly:
plating-class performer: second in handicap and sellers: should stay beyond 1m:
suited by top-of-the-ground: blinkered once at 2 yrs: has taken keen hold. *R.
Hollinshead.*

KIND OF USEFUL 3 b.c. Kind of Hush 118–Klaire 85 (Klairon 131) [1988 NR   **63**
1989 10m⁶ 7m*] 11,000F: workmanlike colt: half-brother to very useful sprinter
Young Hal (by Young Generation) and 2 other winners: dam, 7f winner at 2 yrs, is

half-sister to high-class stayer Proverb: 11/1 and looking very well, won 18-runner seller (sold to join Mrs J. Ramsden 10,500 gns) at Leicester in August by 3 lengths from Koko Queen, soon pushed along, leading 1f out and driven clear: edgy and green, led early when tailed off in maiden: will stay 1m. *Mrs L. Piggott.*

KING AL   2 b.c. (Apr 1) Indian King (USA) 128–Impudent Miss 105 (Persian Bold   **96** 123) [1989 6g³ 6m* 6f² 6g] IR 9,200Y: medium-sized colt: second foal: half-brother to 3-y-o Ella Mon Amour (by Ela-Mana-Mou): dam, 5f to 1m winner at 2 yrs in Ireland, is half-sister to very smart sprinter Sayyaf: well-backed favourite, won maiden auction race at Pontefract in August by over 10 lengths (officially 8) from Eire Leath-Sceal: ran very well when beaten a neck by Tod in minor event there following month, rallying well despite tending to wander: never in contention in Racecall Gold Trophy at Redcar nearly 2 months later: will stay 7f. *Dr J. D. Scargill.*

KING CHARLEMAGNE   10 gr.g. Habat 127–Calibina 103 (Caliban 123) [1988   **57** 5g 5g 5d 5f 5m 5g 5m 5f⁶ 1989 5f⁵ 5m³ 5m* 5f² 5m⁴ 5m] strong gelding: usually looks well: moderate mover: quite modest handicapper: won for sixth time at Edinburgh when beating Kabcast a neck in July: suited by 5f: acts on any going, but particularly well on top-of-the-ground: blinkered once: suitable mount for inexperienced rider. *Mrs G. R. Reveley.*

KING CRACKER   2 ch.c. (May 6) King of Clubs 124–Brenda (Sovereign Path   **73 p** 125) [1989 6m⁴] 5,000F, 12,500Y: neat colt: seventh foal: half-brother to 3-y-o Benny Leonard (by Henbit), very useful 1m to 11.7f winner Brady (by Pitcairn), later successful in USA, and a winner in Belgium: dam unplaced 5 times in Ireland: 7/1, over 3 lengths fourth of 8, running on never able to challenge, to Yaazi in minor event at Newmarket in August: likely to improve. *L. M. Cumani.*

KING HIGH   2 b.c. (Jun 1) Shirley Heights 130–Regal Twin (USA) 77 (Majestic   **78 p** Prince) [1989 8m⁶] 14,000Y: rather leggy, unfurnished colt: looks weak: closely related to fair 1983 2-y-o Refill (by Mill Reef), later successful in USA, and half-brother to several winners, including useful 1981 2-y-o sprinter Corley Moor (by Habitat) and fairly useful stayer Split Image (by Star Appeal): dam won at 8.2f: 16/1 and in need of race, around 10 lengths sixth of 8, always behind, to Treble Eight in maiden at Newmarket in October: should improve. *J. L. Dunlop.*

KING MENELAOS   4 b.g. Ile de Bourbon (USA) 133–Be Sweet 117 (Reform   **—** 132) [1988 12g⁵ 12m⁵ 12g⁵ 15.5g 16d⁴ 13.3s* 1989 13.3m 16f⁶] close-coupled, workmanlike gelding: modest winner as 3-y-o: poor sixth of 10 in amateurs handicap at Chepstow in July, and wasn't seen out again: possibly doesn't quite stay 2m: suited by soft going: hung right fifth outing at 3 yrs: sold to join J. Pearce 8,000 gns Newmarket Autumn Sales. *P. F. I. Cole.*

KING OF MILEEN   3 b.c. Castle Keep 121–Port Meadow 83 (Runnymede 123)   **81** [1988 7g² 8.2d⁴ 1989 10.1m 8f³ 10.1m 10.6s 10g⁴ 10g] lengthy, quite attractive colt: ran creditably when in frame in handicaps at Goodwood and Newmarket: worth a try over 1½m: acts on firm ground (shaped well on soft). *Lady Herries.*

KING OF SAILORS   5 br.g. King of Spain 121–Found At Sea (USA) (Pieces of   **31** Eight 128) [1988 8.5m 10m 8m 1989 5g 10s 8f a8g a14g a16g⁵] rangy, angular gelding: 33/1 and apprentice ridden, showed signs of a little ability when fifth in handicap at Southwell in December: blinkered first 3 starts. *R. Thompson.*

KING OF SPEED   10 b.h. Blue Cashmere 129–Celeste 83 (Sing Sing 134) [1988   **42** NR 1989 7g⁶ 7m a8g] lengthy, quite attractive horse: moderate mover: poor performer: effective at 7f to 1¼m: acts on any going: good mount for inexperienced rider: blinkered once: bandaged second outing. *B. J. Wise.*

KING OF THE RING   4 b.g. Rusticaro (FR) 124–Coumfea (Gulf Pearl 117)   **57** [1988 10g 11.7f 12f 12d 10m⁵ 12m⁴ 13.1f² 1989 12.5g³ 10.1m³] modest maiden at his best: third in claimers at Wolverhampton (tended to run in snatches) and Windsor (claimed to join J. Thomas £12,000) in spring: will stay beyond 13f: acts on firm going: sometimes sweats. *J. Sutcliffe.*

KING OF THE SEA   6 b.g. Tachypous 128–Cooralie 71 (Connaught 130) [1988   **—** NR 1989 18s⁵ 17.1m 12g 14m] compact, workmanlike gelding: moderate mover: plating-class staying handicapper as 4-y-o: well beaten in first half of 1989: winner over hurdles. *Mrs S. Oliver.*

KING ORPHEUS   2 b.c. (Mar 6) King of Spain 121–Nanushka 53 (Lochnager   **78** 132) [1989 6g⁵] 11,000Y: stocky, lengthy colt: third foal: half-brother to 1¼m winner Not So Shy (by Star Appeal): dam, out of half-sister to Altesse Royale, best at 5f: 33/1, around 5 lengths fifth of 9 finishers to Tirol in minor event at Doncaster in September: dead. *Miss L. C. Siddall.*

KING PHILIP 2 b.c. (Apr 29) King of Spain 121–Midnight Music (Midsummer 51
Night II 117) [1989 5g 5d 6m 6s⁶ 6g] small, stocky, attractive colt: good walker:
moderate mover: sixth foal: half-brother to 3-y-o 17.6f winner Hellbrunn and
one-time very useful 7f and 1¼m winner Galitzin (both by Hotfoot) and a winner in
Scandinavia by Radetzky: dam of little account: plating-class maiden: last of 11 in
nursery at York final start. *J. S. Wainwright.*

KINGS ALDERMAN 2 b.c. (Mar 4) Kings Lake (USA) 133–Keep The Thought 72
(USA) 84 (Valdez (USA)) [1989 8.2f⁶ 8.5f³ 10g³ 10g] 35,000F: rather leggy, quite
attractive colt: shade unfurnished: first foal: dam 1m winner, is daughter of sister to
dam of Seattle Slew and Lomond: modest maiden: probably better suited by 1¼m
than 1m: wore tongue strap on debut: sold 11,000 gns Doncaster November Sales. *I.
V. Matthews.*

KINGS ASH 3 gr.f. Hill Farmer–Mentone-Lillie (Saunter) [1988 7g 8m 7f³ 1989 —
12.2d] workmanlike filly: poor walker: third in seller as 2-y-o, only form. *R. M.
Whitaker.*

KING'S BEECHES 3 b.g. Welsh Saint 126–Vynz Girl 82 (Tower Walk 130) 64
[1988 6g⁵ 6m 1989 9f 7f² 7m⁵ 7.6m 8.2g] good-topped gelding: first worthwhile form
when beaten short head in handicap at Folkestone in July: ran fairly well in similar
event next start but moderately after when favourite at Chester and Hamilton:
should stay 1m: acts on firm going. *B. W. Hills.*

KINGSFOLD FLAME 6 ch.m. No Loiterer 90–Kingsfold Flash 50 (Warpath 99
113) [1988 9d* 10d 8m⁵ 8g⁴ 9m² 8g⁶ 8d* 8d* 9s* 9m⁴ 1989 10v⁵ 10m⁴ 10g⁴ 9m
10.1d⁴ 12.5m] sparely-made, workmanlike mare: moderate mover: much improved
as 5-y-o, winning handicaps at Kempton, Ascot and York and listed contest at York:
stayed on strongly having got long way behind when in frame in handicaps at
Newmarket and Epsom in first half of 1989: facing stiff tasks, never dangerous last 2
outings: effective at 1m and 1¼m: best form with plenty of give in the ground: well
served by waiting tactics: often taken down quietly: tough and genuine. *M. J.
Haynes.*

KINGS FOLLY 7 b.g. Hillandale 125–Sovereign's Folly (Sovereign Bill 105) 53
[1988 NR 1989 12d²] second foal: dam never ran: winning hurdler: first race on flat, 5
lengths second of 11 in minor event at Pontefract in April. *D. Burchell.*

KINGSIZE 4 ch.c. Burslem 123–Vesper Bell (Larkspur 128) [1988 8.5f² 12g⁶ 64 d
12g⁵ 12m³ 1989 10.2g 12d³ 14m 18.1g³ 16f] leggy, close-coupled colt: modest maiden
at his best: sweating, creditable third in strongly-run apprentice handicap at Ascot
in April: off course over 4 months afterwards, and well beaten last 3 outings: dull in
coat, ran as though something amiss final one: stays 1½m well: yet to race on soft
going, acts on any other: has run creditably for amateur: sold 5,000 gns Doncaster
November Sales: best treated with caution. *C. E. Brittain.*

KINGS MEETING 2 b.c. (Jan 23) Kings Lake (USA) 133–Meeting Adjourned 49
94 (General Assembly (USA)) [1989 7.5f 7f 7m⁵ 8f] IR 3,600Y: leggy, lightly-made
colt: moderate mover: first foal: dam Irish 1m and 11f winner: poor form, including in
a seller: should be well suited by 1m +. *M. Brittain.*

KINGSMERE 2 ch.c. (Apr 19) Kings Lake (USA) 133–Mrs Hippy (Tudor Music 42
131) [1989 5f⁵ 6m 6m 6g a6g a7g] 6,000Y, 11,500Y: smallish, good-quartered colt:
fourth live foal: dam, winner from 9f to 11f in France, is half-sister to good filly
Sanedtki: poor form in claimers and a seller. *R. Hannon.*

KING'S SHILLING (USA) 2 b.c. (Apr 22) Fit To Fight (USA)–Pride's 77
Crossing (USA) (Riva Ridge (USA)) [1989 6m⁵ 7g³ 8.2d⁴ 8s²] leggy, sparely-made
colt: second foal: dam winner at up to 9f, is half-sister to very useful 1977 2-y-o 5f
winner Deed of Gift, from an excellent family: sire won from 6f to 1½m: modest form
in maidens and a minor event: will be suited by 1¼m. *I. A. Balding.*

KINGSTONE AISLE 2 ch.f. (Mar 17) Godswalk (USA) 130–Touch My Heart 61 55 §
(Steel Heart 128) [1989 5g 5f 6d] 9,000Y: smallish, angular filly: fourth foal: sister to
fair 1986 2-y-o 5f winner Flaxley and half-sister to Irish 3-y-o So Tenderly (by
Prince Tenderfoot), 5f winner at 2 yrs, and Irish 12.8f winner Bally James Duff (by
Ballymore): dam placed over 5f at 3 yrs: 9 lengths ninth of 12 to Duck And Dive in
listed race at Newmarket in July, only form: refused to race for 7-lb claimer final
start: best left alone: sold 1,000 gns Newmarket Autumn Sales. *M. Bell.*

KINGSTRACK 3 b.f. King's Ride 88–Cinder Belle (Track Spare 125) [1988 NR —
1989 7f 7.6m] medium-sized, leggy filly: fourth foal: dam never ran: tailed off in
maidens: very slowly away on debut. *W. G. R. Wightman.*

KING'S VALE 3 gr.c. Absalom 128–Belmont View (Roan Rocket 128) [1988 NR —
1989 6f 5m⁵ 5g 5f 7m] 9,200F, 10,000Y: sturdy, plain colt: second foal: dam poor

maiden: plating-class form at best: always struggling in seller final start: should be suited by further than 5f: sold 1,150 gns Ascot December Sales. *J. W. Payne.*

KINGSWICK (USA) 9 br.g. King's Bishop (USA)–Caught In The Act (USA) 57 (Nijinsky (CAN) 138) [1988 NR 1989 16f2 20f] strong, lengthy gelding: has a round action: 33/1, first race on flat since 1986 when 2 lengths second of 11 in handicap at Kempton: sweating freely, never dangerous in Apprentice Stakes (Handicap) at Royal Ascot over 3 weeks later: stays 2m: acts on any going: bandaged at 9 yrs: has reportedly had operation for soft palate and been hobdayed. *S. Christian.*

KING'S WISH 3 b.c. Reesh 117–Masandra 100 (Whistling Wind 123) [1988 6s 5m4 5d 1989 6m 7m 8f6 7f4 10g6] leggy, quite good-topped colt: quite modest maiden at 2 yrs: below form in handicaps and claimer in 1989: sprint bred: visored final start: slowly away when blinkered once at 2 yrs. *J. S. Wilson.*

KING TOH-TOH 3 b.c. Simply Great (FR) 122–Chrisanthy 81 (So Blessed 130) — [1988 6f 6f5 7g5 7m 7m 8.2m2 8g 10s5 1989 8m 10s6 8m 8m a8g] sparely-made, angular colt: plating-class maiden: well beaten in 1989, including in sellers: probably stayed 1¼m: dead. *P. Howling.*

KING TREVISIO 3 b.c. King of Spain 121–Gundi 57 (Mummy's Pet 125) [1988 — 6s6 6m6 6m 1989 7s] workmanlike colt: good walker: poor mover: quite modest maiden: bit backward, always behind in handicap in April, only outing in 1989: may stay 7f: sold 2,200 gns Doncaster October Sales. *R. M. Whitaker.*

KING WILLIAM 4 b.g. Dara Monarch 128–Norman Delight (USA) (Val de 59 L'Orne (FR) 130) [1988 10f6 10g4 10f3 11m6 12f3 9g 1989 10m 8f5 8f6 10g6 10f2 12m2 10.2g 12g* 10.6m 13.6f a11g6] robust gelding: carries condition: favourite and sweating, well ridden by D. McKeown when making all in handicap at Edinburgh in September: well below his best in similar company afterwards: best at 1¼m to 1½m: acts on firm going and ran badly on soft: blinkered once at 3 yrs and on third outing: trained first 4 starts by N. Callaghan: takes keen hold, and suited by strong handling. *Denys Smith.*

KINKAJOO 2 b.f. (May 19) Precocious 126–Skyey 70 (Skymaster 126) [1989 6g] 53 p leggy, angular filly: half-sister to several winners, including very useful 1978 2-y-o Eyelet (by Sharpen Up) and 1986 2-y-o 1¼m winner Amadeus Rock (by Touching Wood), later successful in Italy: dam 6f winner: 33/1, 9 lengths eighth of 22, chasing leaders 4f, to Lip Sing in maiden at Leicester in November: should improve. *M. A. Jarvis.*

KINLACEY 2 b.f. (Mar 30) Aragon 118–Mimika 85 (Lorenzaccio 130) [1989 5m6 74 ? 6m4 8m6 8m 8.2s4] 1,500F: workmanlike filly: good walker: has a long stride: half-sister to moderate stayer San Carlos Bay (by Julio Mariner) and 1984 2-y-o 5f winner Boardmans Glory (by Hittite Glory), later successful abroad: dam 2-y-o 5f winner: appeared to put up improved effort when last of 8 in slowly-run Hoover Fillies' Mile at Ascot in September: didn't confirm form when last of 4 behind Liffey Lace in minor event at Haydock following month: will be suited by return to shorter than 1m. *B. A. McMahon.*

KINO 2 b.c. (Mar 11) Niniski (USA) 125–Relkina (FR) 85 (Relkino 131) [1989 7m 65 8m3 7g5] leggy, unfurnished colt: looks weak: third foal: half-brother to 3-y-o Rubinka (by Bustino) and poor maiden Omyword (by Bustomi): dam, daughter of Queen Mary winner Grizel, won over 1m: 4 lengths third of 8, staying on, to Bold Passion in maiden at Chepstow in August, best effort: sweating final start: will be well suited by stiffer test of stamina: sent to C. Brittain. *Major W. R. Hern.*

KINTAIL 4 ch.f. Kris 135–Sleat 112 (Santa Claus 133) [1988 10m2 1989 12.4g2 69 10.2f3 14g a10g] workmanlike, angular filly: has a round action: modest form in minor event and maidens: ran poorly last 2 outings: stays 12.4f. *H. R. A. Cecil.*

KIRAM (USA) 4 b.c. Gold Stage (USA)–Alight (FR) (Habitat 134) [1988 6f 7.5f4 — 7m5 8g 1989 6d 6d 10v 8d 7.6f6 7m 7.6f 7.6h 8.2g 10.2f 7g 10f 10f] small, quite attractive ex-Irish colt: poor mover: second reported foal: dam unraced half-sister to Noalcoholic: won maiden at Dundalk as 2-y-o: has lost his form completely: should stay beyond 1m: acts on firm going: often blinkered nowadays: saddle slipped and rider unseated fourth appearance: sold 1,000 gns Ascot December Sales. *W. G. A. Brooks.*

KIRBY'S BEST 2 ch.f. (Apr 29) Sayf El Arab (USA) 127–Betty's Bid (Auction 33 Ring (USA) 123) [1989 5d 5f5 5g 5.1m 6g 6f] 1,600Y: small, close-coupled filly: has a round action: third foal: half-sister to 1986 2-y-o 6f seller winner The Chippenham Man and poor plater Mad Milly (both by Young Man): dam poor daughter of half-sister to Royal Hunt Cup winner Picture Boy: poor plater: blinkered last 2 outings. *G. Blum.*

KIRBY'S PRINCESS 4 b.f. Indian King (USA) 128–Caerinion 76 (Royal Palace —
131) [1988 7f 10d 10.2f 1989 10s 12d 12g 12g6 9f 10m] angular filly: poor maiden:
blinkered fourth outing. *K. Stone.*

KIRKBY FLYER 5 b.m. Gay Pilot 92–Impatience (Kibenka 119) [1988 9f* 10g2 39
10f4 10g3 11d6 8g 8m3 10m5 8m2 1989 11d2 8h2 11f5 8f5 8g3 8.2f2 8m 8.5f3 8g5 9m5]
smallish mare: has a quick action: poor performer: effective at 1m and stays 11f: acts
on hard going and a soft surface: has worn a visor, but better without: has run
creditably for apprentice: didn't find great deal under pressure eighth start: winning
selling hurdler. *R. M. Whitaker.*

KIRKLEES ROCK 2 br.f. (Mar 13) Kala Shikari 125–Lady Farrier (Sheshoon 50
132) [1989 6h3 6f6 7m 7s 8f] 2,400F: good-topped filly: second foal: dam never ran:
plating-class maiden: best effort on debut: very stiff task final outing. *Denys Smith.*

KIRKMAN'S KAMP 4 b.g. Royal Palace 131–The Guzzler 69 (Behistoun 131) 66
[1988 15s6 1989 14.6g 16.2d3 16.2g2 16.2m6 16.5g] angular, workmanlike gelding:
has a rather round action: improved form when placed in maiden and handicap at
Beverley: ran poorly final outing (July): stays 2m: put head in air and wandered
under pressure fourth start. *P. Calver.*

KIRPAN 5 b.g. Kris 135–Dancing Rocks 118 (Green Dancer (USA) 132) [1988 NR —
1989 10f] strong, angular gelding: has a round action: fairly useful winner as 3-y-o:
33/1 and in need of race, always well behind in handicap at Sandown in May: stays
1¼m: best on a sound surface: blinkered twice in 1987: pulled up only 2 outings over
hurdles. *T. M. Jones.*

KIRSHEDA 4 b.f. Busted 134–Mellow Girl 88 (Mountain Call 125) [1988 12.2g2 —
14s3 14.7m5 1989 12.3s 16g 15m2 12m 18m] angular, sparely-made filly: modest
maiden at her best: no worthwhile form in handicaps in 1989: stays 1¾m: best with
give in the ground. *J. Mackie.*

KIRSTENBOSCH 2 b.c. (Mar 23) Caerleon (USA) 132–Flower Petals (Busted 68
134) [1989 6g5 7f4 8g3] IR 140,000Y: leggy, rather sparely-made colt: has a fluent,
slightly round action: half-brother to 1¼m and 11.7f winner Arnaldo (by Upper
Case), also successful over hurdles: dam, Irish 1¼m winner, is sister to smart
middle-distance performer Bog Road: favourite, quite modest form in autumn
maidens at Yarmouth and Leicester (tending to hang 2f out) on first 2 starts: poor
third at Edinburgh final outing: will stay 1¼m: appears one paced: sold to join T.
Barron 20,000 gns Doncaster November Sales. *H. R. A. Cecil.*

KIRTLINGTON 4 b.g. Gay Mecene (USA) 128–Cley 85 (Exbury 138) [1988 11.7f —
1989 12m3] leggy, angular gelding: well beaten in maidens at Bath and Lingfield: off
course 14 months in between: sold to join K. Morgan 1,800 gns Ascot July Sales. *R.
F. Johnson Houghton.*

KISSAVOS 3 ch.c. Cure The Blues (USA)–Hairbrush (USA) (Sir Gaylord) [1988 75 ?
6g4 6f3 8h 7d 1989 5v2 6s 6m5 6m5 6g5 6g* a6g] small, angular colt: favourably
drawn, appeared to show improved form when winning claimer at Nottingham in
October by 5 lengths, making all: always struggling in Lingfield handicap following
month: stays 6f: possibly best on an easy surface: ran creditably for 7-lb claimer and
when tending to carry head high fifth start. *N. A. Callaghan.*

KISSOGRAM GIRL (USA) 2 b. or br.f. (Feb 3) Danzig (USA)–Foreign 100
Courier (USA) (Sir Ivor 135) [1989 5f* 6m 5m] leggy, good-topped filly: fourth foal:
sister to high-class sprinter Green Desert: dam unraced half-sister to top-class filly
Althea: odds on but bit green, won maiden at Sandown in May by 2 lengths from In
The Papers: around 5 lengths eighth of 11 to Dead Certain in Tattersalls Cheveley
Park Stakes at Newmarket, front rank until weakening inside final furlong and
eased: ran poorly in Cornwallis Stakes at Ascot later in October: better suited by 6f
than 5f. *M. R. Stoute.*

KITTY CRISP 2 b.f. (May 10) Music Maestro 119–Makinlau 88 (Lauso) [1989 7g] —
fourth foal: closely related to a winner abroad by Song: dam won from 1m to 1½m:
12/1 and backward, always behind in 20-runner claimer at Leicester in September.
M. H. Tompkins.

KITTY RUSSE 2 b.f. (Apr 12) Nureyev (USA) 131–Kittyhawk 113 (Bustino 136) 68 p
[1989 8f2] medium-sized, quite attractive filly, rather unfurnished: fifth foal: closely
related to 3-y-o Musical Interval (by The Minstrel) and 1¼m winner Storm
Force (by Storm Bird) and half-sister to Cesarewitch winner Nomadic Way (by
Assert) and smart 1985 French 2-y-o maiden With Hope (by Irish River): dam won
Lowther Stakes and showed very useful form at up to 1m: co-favourite and on toes,
2½ lengths second of 9 to Hafhafah in maiden at Wolverhampton in October,
keeping on well having run green 2f out: sure to improve. *B. W. Hills.*

KIVETON KOMET 2 ch.f. (Apr 26) Precocious 126–Beaufort Star 95 (Great **71** Nephew 126) [1989 6g 6g² 5g] 20,000Y: angular, plain filly: third living foal: half-sister to modest 1m and 10.6f winner Touching Star (by Touching Wood) and a winner in Italy by Julio Mariner: dam sprinting sister to Uncle Pokey: favourite, 2 lengths second of 15, keeping on, to Ra'a in maiden at Goodwood: odds on, ran poorly in similar event at Redcar later in October: will be better suited by 7f. *L. M. Cumani.*

KIWAYU (USA) 3 br.c. Nureyev (USA) 131–Kuja Happa (USA) (Tell (USA)) **93** [1988 6f 6g 1989 7h³ 7f³ 8h² 8f⁵ 8h* 8m² 8.5g²] small colt: has a long stride: won handicap at Brighton in August: favourite, good second in similar events at Wolverhampton and Epsom (leading over 1f out until post) later in month: stays 1m: acts on hard ground: has worn net muzzle. *J. Tree.*

KIYA (USA) 3 b.f. Dominion 123–Melodrama 102 (Busted 134) [1988 7g 8m 1989 **85** 8g* 10m⁴ 8g* 8m* 8m* 8m 9g⁴] leggy, lengthy filly: sometimes unimpressive in appearance: won claimers at Salisbury (dead-heated) in May and Newmarket (changed hands 20,000 gns) in July then handicaps at Ascot in July and September: easily better effort after, good fourth of 17 to Secretary of State in £15,400 handicap at Newmarket, staying on well: should stay 1¼m: acts on top-of-the-ground. *W. Hastings-Bass.*

KLAIROVER 2 b.f. (Feb 21) Smackover 107–Klairove 74 (Averof 123) [1989 6m — 5g] 1,000Y: first foal: dam, won 1m seller on flat and also won over hurdles, is daughter of half-sister to high-class stayer Proverb: poor form in autumn seller (slowly away) at Lingfield and maiden at Hamilton: trained on debut by C. Hill. *R. J. Hodges.*

KLAMMERING 6 ch.g. Thatching 131–Swan Upping 74 (Lord Gayle (USA) 124) **105** [1988 7g* 8g* 10g* 8m 1989 8g* 7.2g⁵ 11f³ 7g 11d⁴] good-topped gelding: bad mover: runner-up in seller on second of 2 outings in Britain as 3-y-o: a winner 8 times in Belgium, including £8,900 Grade 1 event at Groenendael in May: 100/1, appeared to run very well when never-nearer fifth to Weldnaas in listed contest at Haydock following month: 16/1, never a threat under 10-0 in £16,300 handicap at Newmarket fourth outing: stays 11f. *Allan Smith, Belgium.*

KLEMZIG 3 gr.f. Buzzards Bay 128§–Mary Crooner 57 (Crooner 119) [1988 NR — 1989 10.1g 10.1d⁶ 7.6m] strong, lengthy filly: sixth reported foal: half-sister to 5f seller winner Hallo Rosie (by Swing Easy) and winning hurdler The Grifter (by Treboro): dam sprint plater: tailed off in minor events at Windsor and maiden at Lingfield. *M. Madgwick.*

KNAVE OF CLUBS 2 ch.g. (Mar 20) King of Clubs 124–La Calera (GER) **66** (Caracol (FR)) [1989 6m⁶ 6f 8g³] 15,000F: workmanlike gelding: has plenty of scope: third foal: half-brother to 3-y-o Sandswallow (by Sandhurst Prince): dam, winning 2-y-o in Germany, is half-sister to leading 1983 German 2-y-o filly La Colorada: 2 lengths third of 11 to Shifting Breeze in maiden at Edinburgh in November, easily best effort: much better suited by 1m than shorter: sold 6,400 gns Doncaster November Sales. *M. J. Camacho.*

KNIFEBOARD 3 b.c. Kris 135–Catalpa 115 (Reform 132) [1988 NR 1989 12g* **101** 14f² 15g⁵] big, round-barrelled colt: has a round action: brother to useful middle-distance winner Kenanga and half-brother to 3 other winners, including Ribblesdale Stakes winner Strigida (by Habitat) and 10.5f winner Catawba (by Mill Reef): dam and grandam won Ribblesdale Stakes: weak 10/1, burly and green when winning maiden at Newmarket in April: may well have won with clear run when beaten ¾ length by stable-companion Icelander in minor event at York: 9/10, beaten just over a length when fifth of 6 to Sharnfold in moderately-run Group 3 event at Chantilly in June: will be suited by test of stamina: usually lethargic in preliminaries: sold to join T. Hallett 12,500 gns Newmarket Autumn Sales. *H. R. A. Cecil.*

KNIGHT OF KIRKTON 2 b.g. (May 17) State Trooper 96–Musical Piece 91 — (Song 132) [1989 6d 7f] good-topped gelding: half-brother to 1983 2-y-o 6f seller winner Dancing Orange (by Orange Bay) and a winner in Norway: dam best at sprint distances: ridden by 7-lb claimer, showed signs of ability in autumn maidens at Goodwood (bit backward) and Salisbury (not knocked about): subsequently gelded. *R. Hannon.*

KNIGHT OF MERCY 3 b.g. Aragon 118–Little Mercy 90 (No Mercy 126) [1988 **103** 5m³ 5m* 6m² 6g 1989 6d⁶ 6d² 6f* 6f⁴ 6m³ 6m⁴ 7g³ 6f 6m⁴ 7.3m 6g⁶ 6v 6d] strong, good-bodied gelding: carries condition: usually looks well: useful performer: won minor event at Folkestone in May: ran well in listed race (unlucky) and handicaps next 4 starts and fairly well in £8,900 handicap at Newmarket eleventh one: may well prove ideally suited by 6f: acts on firm going and a soft surface: slowly away in blinkers twelfth start: gelded after final one: game. *R. Hannon.*

KNIGHT'S BARONESS 2 b.f. (Apr 16) Rainbow Quest (USA) 134–Knights **106** Beauty (USA) (True Knight (USA)) [1989 7m² 7m* 8g²] leggy, rather unfurnished filly: moderate walker: third foal: half-sister to 3-y-o Captive Heart (by Conquistador Cielo): dam won at up to 9f: won 4-runner maiden at Yarmouth in August by 4 lengths, easing up, from Zarna: much better effort, length second of 5, making most, to Rafha in May Hill EBF Stakes at Doncaster following month: will stay 1¼m. *P. F. I. Cole.*

KNIGHTS SECRET 8 ch.g. Immortal Knight 103–Lush Secret 50 (Most Secret **65** 119) [1988 8m 8.5m⁴ 7.6v 7g⁵ 8m⁴ 8.5g⁶ 7.5f 8g⁶ 7m² 7f³ 8m⁵ 7g* 7m³ 1989 7.5d 7g 7m⁶ 8m² 8.5g⁴ 7.6m³ 8m⁵ 7m 8m⁵ 7s⁴ 8m* 7m 8g² 7g⁴] workmanlike gelding: moderate mover: quite modest handicapper: won for only second time since early-1986 when making all in amateurs event at Redcar in September: best around 1m: acts on any going except heavy: usually blinkered nowadays: usually ridden up with pace: suitable mount for inexperienced rider: tough. *M. H. Easterby.*

KNOCK KNOCK 4 ch.g. Tap On Wood 130–Ruby River (Red God 128§) [1988 **77** 10m³ 12g⁵ 10m⁴ 11d⁵ 10.4m* 10.1m³ 10g 10.2f 1989 10s⁶ 10.8d⁶ 10f³ 10f³ 10f 9m* 10g² 9f² 8m* 10m* 9.2d³ 10g⁴ 10g⁵] good-quartered gelding: fair performer: won strongly-run ladies event at Kempton in June and invitation handicap at Newmarket and amateurs contest at Sandown in August: stays 1¼m: best efforts on a sound surface: blinkered twice at 2 yrs: too keen in visor fifth outing: finds little in front, and is suited by good gallop, waiting tactics and tender handling. *I. A. Balding.*

KNOOSH (USA) 3 ch.f. Storm Bird (CAN) 134–Fabulous Salt (USA) 98 (Le **113** Fabuleux 133) [1988 7d* 1989 10f* 12m⁵ 12g⁵ 12f* 12f*] rangy, good sort: has plenty of scope: has a quick action: very useful performer: successful in listed races at Newbury in May, Goodwood in July and York (below form, rallying gamely to beat Nesaah a head) in August: fifth in Gold Seal Oaks at Epsom and Lancashire Oaks (below form) at Haydock: will be suited by 1¾m: has won on a soft surface, but best efforts on top-of-the-ground. *M. R. Stoute.*

Maktoum Al-Maktoum's "Knoosh"

Bradford & Bingley Handicap, York—
Known Ranger completes his unbeaten season, holding off Dancing Monarch

KNOWETOP 3 ch.f. Sayyaf 121–Heirline 60 (Great Nephew 126) [1988 5m 5m⁶ — 5g⁵ 6m² 6g 7f 1989 7g⁵ 6v⁶ 6s 6m 10f 6m] dipped-backed filly: modest plater as 2-y-o: well beaten in 1989: suited by 6f: best form on top-of-the-ground: visored final outing (July): sold to join F. Barton 650 gns Doncaster November Sales. *S. J. Muldoon.*

KNOWLTON 3 br.c. Known Fact (USA) 135–Miss Reasoning (USA) (Bold **84** Reasoning (USA)) [1988 7m 8g³ 7g⁴ 1989 10m² 12h* 12m² 12.3f⁵ 10m] good-topped colt: turns off-fore in: has a quick action: won maiden at Brighton in June: ran poorly in handicap final start: stays 1½m: acts on hard going: swished tail on reappearance: tends to carry head high: makes the running: sold 40,000 gns Newmarket Autumn Sales. *G. Harwood.*

KNOWN RANGER 3 br.g. Known Fact (USA) 135–Home On The Range 124 **109** (Habitat 134) [1988 6g⁴ 7g² 1989 7m* 7fʷᵒ 8f* 8f*] well-made gelding: has a quick action: successful in the summer in maiden (made all) and minor event (walked over) at Warwick, £7,300 handicap at Goodwood and Bradford & Bingley Handicap (beat Dancing Monarch a neck) at York: may stay further: acts on firm going: gelded and operated on for wind infirmity after final start at 2 yrs: progressive: reportedly to join Bill Badgett in New York. *H. R. A. Cecil.*

KOKA-BRONZE 2 ch.c. (May 31) Never So Bold 135–Temple Wood 105 (Sweet — Revenge 129) [1989 5s⁶ 6f] 3,100Y: dipped-backed, lengthy colt: poor mover: half-brother to 3-y-o Flower Dew Lane (by Kalaglow) and 3 winners, including 9f to 15.8f winner Temple Walk (by Bustino): dam, winner from 5f to 1m, is half-sister to very smart Town And Country: well beaten in spring sellers at Warwick (bandaged off-hind) and Lingfield. *R. W. Stubbs.*

KOKO QUEEN 3 ch.f. Noalto 120–Witchingham Lass 83 (Sweet Revenge 129) **53** [1988 6f 6m 6d 1989 6d 9d 8g 6m* 6f 7m²] leggy, rather sparely-made filly: poor walker: 50/1, won claimer at Catterick in July after slow start: creditable staying-on second of 18 in seller at Leicester, only other worthwhile form: stays 7f (pulled hard over 1m): suited by top-of-the-ground: sometimes sweating: sold to join W. Price 1,900 gns Ascot August Sales. *H. P. Rohan.*

KOKOSCHKA 7 gr. or ro.g. Alias Smith (USA)–Opinion 71 (Great Nephew 126) — [1988 6f 10f 8m 17.1f⁶ 16m 12h 14m 14m 1989 14.8s] strong gelding: no form in varied company for long time: blinkered once at 6 yrs: sometimes bandaged. *G. Roe.*

KOLINSKY 3 ch.g. Dunbeath (USA) 127–Kolomelskoy Palace 77 (Royal Palace **70** 131) [1988 7m 7d 10d 8d⁵ 1989 12g 11m 16.2g 12f² 11m* 12g² 11g² 11f* 12.3f 12m⁴

12.2g[6] 10.6m 10v] tall, leggy, good-topped gelding: carries condition: moderate mover: quite modest handicapper: in good form in July, winning at Edinburgh and Redcar: below form last 3 starts: stays 1½m (tailed off over 2m): acts on firm going: has run creditably when edgy and sweating badly: hung badly left ninth start: suited by forcing tactics: gelded after final start. *F. H. Lee.*

KOLONAKI 2 b.c. (Feb 28) Busted 134–Nuppence 79 (Reform 132) [1989 6m 7g[5] **68** 6g[4]] 56,000Y: big, good-bodied colt: has a quick, shortish action: fourth foal: half-brother to very useful sprinter Posada (by Homing) and fairly useful 1985 2-y-o winner Mihaarb (by Formidable), successful 3 times at up to 1m in France in 1986: dam, second twice over 5f, is half-sister to Mummy's Pet: carrying condition, staying-on 4½ lengths fifth of 9, not handling home turn, to Flaming Glory in Sandown maiden in July, best effort: burly, well-beaten last of 4 in similar event at Ascot nearly 3 months later. *G. Lewis.*

KONIG 3 ch.c. Jalmood (USA) 126–Spring Lane 85 (Forlorn River 124) [1988 5g[6] **81 d** 5m 7m 7g[3] 8s* 9f[2] 1989 11v* 12s[3] 12m 11m[2] 13.3g[6] 11.5g* 10m[2] 10.6m[5] 10f[3] 11v 12g[3] a11g] leggy, rather angular colt: blind in off-side eye: moderate mover: won claimers at Ayr in April and Sandown in July: ran fairly well despite running in snatches eighth start but moderately after: stays 1½m: acts on any going: sometimes hangs left: equipped with eyeshield first 3 starts: claimed out of M. H. Easterby's on third: has joined A. S. Reid. *R. Akehurst.*

KONIGSBERG 3 b.c. Shirley Heights 130–Konigsalpen (GER) (Priamos **104** (GER)) [1988 7f[3] 8g* 1989 10.5f[2] 12m[2] 16f[5] 12f* 12f[3]] tall, deep-girthed colt: good walker: useful performer: 20/1 on, facile winner of 3-runner minor event at Beverley in July: looking extremely well, led 1¼m when creditable last of 3 to Knoosh in listed race at Goodwood 11 days later: should prove best over 1¾m: acts on firm going: lacks turn of foot, and makes the running: sold 25,000 gns Newmarket Autumn Sales to go to Saudi Arabia. *H. R. A. Cecil.*

KOO 3 b.f. Crofter (USA) 124–Sue's Dolly (Quorum 126) [1988 6s 1989 6v[4] 6v[3] 6m **—** 8f 6m 6f 6g[5] 6f] sturdy filly: moderate walker: plating-class maiden: worth a try over 7f: acts on heavy going: blinkered penultimate start: sometimes sweating: twice successful in selling hurdles, sold to join R. Hartop after second of them. *N. Tinkler.*

KORACLE BAY 2 b.f. (Apr 1) Kind of Hush 118–Sea Aura 89 (Roi Soleil 125) **81** [1989 6m* 7g[3]] 5,000Y: lengthy filly: has scope: moderate mover: fourth foal: half-sister to Norwegian 3-y-o winner Shantyman (by Song): dam probably best at 7f: won maiden at Yarmouth in July by ½ length from Final Harvest, running green 2f out then staying on to lead final 1½f: favourite, showed lot of improvement (though looked bit ungenerous) when third of 8 to Satis Dancer in nursery there 2 months later: should stay 1m. *C. F. Wall.*

KOSCIOSKO (USA) 3 b.c. Arctic Tern (USA) 126–Ancient Jewel (USA) (Hail **72** To Reason) [1988 NR 1989 14f[3] 16f[2] 14f[3] 11.5g[3] 10f] tall, lengthy colt: poor walker: has a rather scratchy action: sixth foal: half-brother to useful 1¼m and 1½m winner Tertiary Zone (by The Minstrel), later graded winner in USA, Irish 8.5f winner Law Lord (by Blushing Groom) and 3 other winners in USA: dam winning sister to dams of Crystal Glitters and Danzatore: modest maiden: ran moderately in handicap final start: may prove ideally suited by forcing tactics at around 1½m (hung left under pressure over 1¾m): twice edgy: sold 8,000 gns Newmarket Autumn Sales: winning selling hurdler for N. Tinkler. *L. M. Cumani.*

KOUKLA 2 b.f. (Jan 29) Precocious 126–Thessaloniki 94 (Julio Mariner 127) **—** [1989 6f[5]] 9,200Y: second foal: half-sister to 6f winner Tolo (by Bold Lad, IRE): dam won 3 races over 1¼m and stayed 1½m: 10/1, soundly-beaten last of 5, losing touch 2f out, in maiden at Ascot in June. *G. Lewis.*

KOVALEVSKIA 4 ch.f. Ardross 134–Fiordiligi 109 (Tudor Melody 129) [1988 **71** 12g* 11m[4] 11.7m 12f[6] 14s[5] 12m[5] 14.7m 1989 10s[3] 12d 12m* 14g[5] 15.5f 13s 12g* a12g 12g a10g*] small, sparely-made filly: modest handicapper: easy winner of uncompetitive event at Edinburgh, amateurs race at Folkestone and 7-runner contest at Lingfield: stays 1½m well: possibly unsuited by firm going, acts on any other: best ridden up with pace: bought out of C. Wall's stable 13,500 gns Newmarket July Sales after third outing: inconsistent. *D. A. Wilson.*

KOWZA 3 ch.f. Young Generation 129–Follow The Stars 86 (Sparkler 130) [1988 **—** NR 1989 8m 8g[6] 8.2d] 36,000Y: leggy, lengthy filly: first foal: dam, 8.5f and 1¼m winner, is half-sister to smart sprinter Florestan and very useful French 9f to 1¼m winner Schoeller: well beaten in maidens and a claimer: sold out of M. Jarvis' stable 2,400 gns Newmarket July Sales after second outing. *Mrs A. Knight.*

KRAMERIA 3 b.f. Kris 135–Sookera (USA) 117 (Roberto (USA) 131) [1988 5g3 — 5m* 5m5 1989 5g] well-made filly: has a long stride: modest winner of Windsor maiden as 2-y-o: edgy, behind facing very stiff task in handicap in June, only start in 1989: bred to stay further. *J. Tree.*

KRAYMARK 3 ch.g. Krayyan 117–Caroline's Mark (On Your Mark 125) [1988 48 5.8g6 6f 1989 10.1m 8g6 7m5 8.3m6 a6g] lengthy, sparely-made gelding: plating-class form at best: appears suited by 7f. *R. Curtis.*

KREMLIN GUARD 4 ch.f. Home Guard (USA) 129–Laurel Wreath (Sassafras 72 (FR) 135) [1988 7g 7m5 7m 7.6s 7g3 7.6d3 8g6 1989 7g3 7f5 7m2 7g3 8g5 8g a10g5] leggy filly: has a rather round action: modest handicapper: probably best at short of 1¼m: acts on firm going and a soft surface: has got on toes. *J. A. R. Toller.*

KRIBENSIS 5 gr.g. Henbit (USA) 130–Aquaria (Double-U-Jay 120) [1988 10g5 101 1989 12g4 13.3f4] tall, lengthy gelding: moderate mover: useful handicapper as 3-y-o: subsequently very lightly raced on flat: fourth in £10,500 event at Doncaster (better effort) and listed contest at Newbury in spring: stays 1½m: acts on any going: top-class hurdler. *M. R. Stoute.*

KRISALYA 3 b.f. Kris 135–Sassalya (Sassafras (FR) 135) [1988 6g6 1989 10g6 98 10.5f3 10m6 10.4m* 10f 12m] leggy, sparely-made, angular filly: has a round action: fairly useful performer: won 4-runner maiden at Chester in September: easily best other effort third in £5,600 contest (bit edgy) at York in May: always behind in Group 3 event at Ascot final start: may prove as effective over 1m as 1¼m: acts on firm going: sometimes sweating. *G. Wragg.*

KRISFIELD 4 b. or br.c. Anfield 117–Kristallina 84 (Homeric 133) [1988 6d3 7g 69 6f5 6g 8m 9m 7d4 7d 6g 1989 7g6 7s3 6m 6g 10g5] lengthy colt: poor mover: modest handicapper on his day: 20/1 and apprentice ridden, good third of 17 at Epsom in April: off course almost 5 months after next outing: stays 7f well: needs plenty of give in the ground. *M. Brittain.*

KRISTA KALA 2 b.f. (May 2) Kala Shikari 125–Kristallina 84 (Homeric 133) 43 [1989 5f6 5m5 6m5] good-quartered filly: third reported foal: half-sister 3-y-o Dona Krista (by King of Spain), fair 6f winner at 2 yrs, and fairly useful 1987 2-y-o 5f winner Krisfield (by Anfield): dam won over 13.8f: poor form in maidens and a seller: sold 880 gns Newmarket Autumn Sales. *R. Hannon.*

KRISTIN'S LIGHT 2 b.f. (Mar 30) Noalto 120–Parez 67 (Pardao 120) [1989 44 5.3h4 6m2 6f2 6h3 7m* 7g 6f6 7m 7g] 3,600Y: leggy, sparely-made filly: poor mover: half-sister to numerous winners, including fairly useful 1982 2-y-o 6f winner Sparkling Moment (by Hot Spark) and 7f and 1m winner Persian Dynasty (Persian Bold): dam seemed not to stay 1m: modest plater: no bid after winning at Lingfield in June: showed nothing afterwards: suited by 6f: visored seventh start: sold 2,300 gns Newmarket Autumn Sales. *R. W. Stubbs.*

KRISTIS GIRL 2 ch.f. (Mar 10) Ballacashtal (CAN)–Fleur d'Amour 85 66 (Murrayfield 119) [1989 5d* 5m3 5.8h3 6m5 6m2] 550F, 1,100Y: plain, angular filly: moderate mover: half-sister to 1983 2-y-o 6f winner Fill The Jug (by Derrylin): dam 6f and 7f winner: quite modest performer: won maiden auction race at Pontefract in April by 4 lengths: good second of 3 to Mountview in minor event at Chester final start (July): suited by 6f: yet to race on very soft going, but acts on any other. *D. Haydn Jones.*

KRUSAVITCH 3 ch.f. Sunley Builds 102–Dipsicato (Music Maestro 119) [1988 — § 6s 6m 7d 1989 8s 10g 11.7m] sparely-made, plain filly: plating-class at best but looks temperamental and one to leave alone. *R. Curtis.*

KRYPTON KNIGHT 4 ch.g. Star Appeal 133–Bold Pioneer (Wolver Hollow — 126) [1988 8g 10g* 10m 1989 10.6g 15.3m 12m 17.6f] medium-sized gelding: won apprentice handicap at Haydock in May, 1988: soundly beaten (tailed off 3 times) in handicaps as 4-y-o: stays 1¼m: probably needs give in the ground: on toes second start: bought 1,300 gns Ascot May Sales: best left alone. *D. R. Tucker.*

KTOLO 3 b.f. Tolomeo 127–Miss Kate (FR) (Nonoalco (USA) 131) [1988 7m 1989 80 7g 8m3 11.5f4 10g4 12f3 12m 14m 12f* 12f3 12s*] leggy, unfurnished filly: has a round action: showed improved form when winning handicaps at Folkestone in October and Hamilton (by ½ length, travelling very strongly to lead approaching final 1f then driven out) in November: stays 1½m well: acts on any going: sometimes takes keen hold: trained first 3 starts by A. Stewart. *R. Akehurst.*

KUMADA 2 b.g. (Apr 3) Vision (USA)–Fan The Flame 69 (Grundy 137) [1989 5s5 61 § 5m2 6m4 5f2 5f2 5f2 7m5 6f3 6g6] 7,000Y: slightly dipped-backed gelding: easy mover: third foal: dam Irish 1½m winner: quite modest maiden: best form at 5f: blinkered or visored on 5 occasions: often hangs left: ungenuine. *F. H. Lee.*

KURDISH PRINCE 5 b.g. Dunphy 124–Lea Landing 81 (Meadow Court 129) — [1988 12g 14s 1989 16m 18.1g5] small gelding: moderate mover: of little account: blinkered final outing. *R. Thompson.*

KWACHA 3 b.c. Reesh 117–Madame Quickly 80 (Saint Crespin III 132) [1988 6g 6s 7d 1989 12g 11f 8m 7m 10.2h 15.3g] rather leggy, workmanlike colt: poor form, including in handicaps and a seller: blinkered fourth start: sold to join T. Craig 5,200 gns Doncaster October Sales. *J. Mackie.*

KWI 3 b.g. Krayyan 117–Angevin 61 (English Prince 129) [1988 6m 6g5 7m 6g2 — 1989 8g 6m 10m 8m 8f] leggy, workmanlike gelding: has a markedly round action: easily best effort final start as 2-y-o: plating-class form at best otherwise, including in sellers: unseated rider leaving stalls penultimate start: probably doesn't stay 1¼m: possibly requires give in the ground: sometimes blinkered: sold to join F. Gray 4,000 gns Newmarket July Sales: sometimes wanders under pressure and looks difficult ride. *M. H. Tompkins.*

KYRA 3 b.f. Sadler's Wells (USA) 132–Aunty (FR) (Riverman (USA)) [1988 **101** 5m* 5d6 7d3 6d* 1989 7d4 8g6 8m 8m6] 120,000Y: first foal: dam French 1¼m winner: justified favouritism as 2-y-o in maiden at the Curragh and nursery at Naas: 25/1, ran well when about 5 lengths seventh of 13 to Ensconse in Irish 1000 Guineas at the Curragh, staying on steadily from rear: ran moderately starts either side (reportedly in season on first occasion) and not seen out after June: will be suited by 1¼m: acts on top-of-the-ground and soft going. *M. V. O'Brien, Ireland.*

L

LA BALLERINE 3 b.f. Lafontaine (USA) 117–Kirsova (Absalom 128) [1988 NR **62** 1989 8m3 8m5 10g3 9g* 11s 10.5g3 a11g6] medium-sized filly: second foal: half-sister to poor maiden El Padrino (by Good Times): dam lightly raced: led post in handicap at Wolverhampton in September: good third of 7, running on steadily having had plenty to do 4f out, in selling handicap at York in October: stays 1¼m: hung left third start: best with waiting tactics. *C. E. Brittain.*

LABEKA LAO (USA) 2 ch.f. (Feb 20) Laomedonte (USA) 116–Pitty Pal (USA) **40** (Caracolero (USA) 131) [1989 7f 7m* 7g 7m 8.5f 10.6d] lengthy, angular filly: first foal: dam, 5f stakes winner at 2 yrs, half-sister to Lao Pal (by Laomedonte), minor winner at up to 1m: won poor 4-runner seller (no bid) at Edinburgh in July by ½ length, only form. *J. Berry.*

LA BELLE VIE 3 b.f. Indian King (USA) 128–Engage (Whistling Wind 123) **65** [1988 7m 1989 7s 10.1m 9.2f 7f 6f* 7m4 6g 6g* 7g 6g* 7g5 6f* 6g6] strong filly: moderate mover: quite modest handicapper: successful 3 times at Yarmouth in second half of season then awarded race at Redcar in October: stays 7f: acts on firm going. *D. A. Wilson.*

LABELON LADY 3 ch.f. Touching Wood (USA) 127–Princess Dina 87 **87** (Huntercombe 133) [1988 7m* 1989 10m 10f 11.5m5 8g2 8f] sparely-made, angular filly: fair handicapper: appears suited by 1m (bit backward over 1¼m) and forcing tactics: acts on firm ground. *H. R. A. Cecil.*

LA BIENVENIDA 3 b.f. Ahonoora 122–Lady Bennington (Hot Grove 128) [1988 — NR 1989 10.6g] medium-sized, unfurnished filly: first foal: dam, granddaughter of Italian 1000 Guineas and Oaks winner Dolina, well behind in 3 races on flat and failed to complete over hurdles: always behind in maiden at Haydock in June. *Lord John FitzGerald.*

LA CABRILLA 2 b.f. (Mar 21) Carwhite 127–La Tuerta 96 (Hot Spark 126) [1989 **89** 5m4 5m* 6m* 6m3 7s6] good-bodied, quite attractive filly: good walker: first foal: dam sprinting half-sister to high-class 5f to 7f winner Cadeaux Genereux and quite useful stayer and successful hurdler Brightner: successful in maiden at Salisbury in June and minor event (beat Potter's Dream 2 lengths) at Windsor following month: on toes, 4 lengths third of 6, keeping on, to Pharaoh's Delight in Princess Margaret Stakes at Ascot: well beaten in pattern race at Deauville final start (August): should stay at least 7f. *P. T. Walwyn.*

LA CASTANA 3 ch.f. Dunbeath (USA) 127–Din Brown (USA) (Tom Rolfe) [1988 **61** 6f5 7h 1989 7g 12f5 10f 8.2f3 8.2m3 8m6 8.2f2 10f3 12f 12g*] sparely-made filly: won seller (sold 4,400 gns) at Leicester in November after slow start: sweating slightly, tailed off in handicap time before: stays 1½m: acts on firm going: below form in blinkers (led 9f) third start: often comes from well off pace: winning selling hurdler for C. Beever. *Lord John FitzGerald.*

LA CHIQUITA 5 b.m. African Sky 124–La Cita (Le Levanstell 122) [1988 7.9f3 **84**
8m* 8m6 9m 7g 1989 5m* 5f3 5f* 5m* 6f4 5f] lengthy, good-topped ex-Irish mare:
third foal: half-sister to fairly useful stayer Special Vintage (by Nebbiolo): dam won
from 1½m to 1¾m in Ireland: in fine form in first half of season, winning minor event
at Edinburgh (66/1, making all) and handicaps at Ayr and Haydock: probably best at
5f: acts well on top-of-the-ground: bought out of B. Kelly's stable IR 2,000 gns Goffs
February Sales. *T. Craig.*

LACIDAR 9 b. or br.g. Radical 104–No Dice (No Argument 107) [1988 NR 1989 —
16f5] first foal: dam poor Irish maiden hurdler/point-to-pointer: last of 5 in maiden at
Newcastle in July: fair handicap chaser. *J. H. Johnson.*

LACK OF PEARLS 5 ch.m. Laxton 105–Double Pearl 76 (Gulf Pearl 117) [1988 —
NR 1989 10.2g 11v5 8v] compact mare: poor maiden: visored, soundly beaten in
selling handicap final outing: blinkered twice: has sweated. *R. D. E. Woodhouse.*

LADDERMAN 3 ch.g. Salmon Leap (USA) 131–Joanne's Joy (Ballymore 123) **88** d
[1988 7g 1989 8.2s2 8f3 10g 7m 8f] good-bodied, useful-looking gelding: carries
condition: has a light action: awkward in preliminaries, second in minor event at
Nottingham in April, hanging right under pressure but easily best effort: stays 1m:
best form on soft going: trained until after second outing by B. Hills: gelded after
final one: difficult ride and seems unreliable. *R. V. Smyth.*

LA DOMAINE 2 b.f. (May 20) Dominion 123–La Galette 76 (Double Form 130) **89**
[1989 5f5 5f5 6g5 6g* 6g3 6s2 6g] IR 38,000Y: medium-sized, lengthy,
good-quartered filly: good walker: has a fluent, roundish action: second foal:
half-sister to 3-y-o 6f winner Quiche (by Formidable): dam, lightly-raced maiden, is
daughter of Cambridgeshire and Irish 1000 Guineas winner Lacquer and half-sister
to good middle-distance colt Shining Finish and very smart stayer Bright Finish: fair
performer: won minor event at Windsor in August by 4 lengths: excellent second of
18 to Dumbreck in nursery at Ayr following month: suited by 6f: best form on an
easy surface. *C. R. Nelson.*

LADY ALONE 2 ch.f. (Mar 14) Mr Fluorocarbon 126–Empress Corina 74 (Free **59**
State 125) [1989 5d2 5m2 5f3 6m6 5.1f2 6g a5g] 800F, 4,600Y: leggy, sparely-made
filly: moderate mover: first foal: dam 7f winner: plating-class maiden: stays 6f:
trained first 5 starts by J. Pearce. *W. Wilson.*

LADY BAY 3 b.f. Balidar 133–Dingle Belle 72 (Dominion 123) [1988 6m 5g 6m —
1989 5s 7.5d] dipped-backed, sparely-made filly: moderate mover: of little account:
blinkered in 1989: sold 1,300 gns Ascot 2nd June Sales. *J. Wharton.*

LADY BAZAAR 4 b.f. Crofthall 110–Fidget (Workboy 123) [1988 NR 1989 10m —
12h4 7f5 7f] sparely-made filly: second foal: dam never ran: appears of little account:
gave trouble at stalls third outing. *C. R. Beever.*

LADY BEHAVE 5 b.m. Crofter (USA) 124–In Motion 91 (Monsanto (FR) 121) —
[1988 NR 1989 5d 5f 6m] small, light-framed mare: no longer of much account:
visored twice, blinkered once. *K. O. Cunningham-Brown.*

LADY BLUES SINGER 3 ch.f. Chief Singer 131–Moaning Low 85 (Burglar **47**
128) [1988 5d5 5s6 7d 6m 6m5 1989 6s4 5f 5.8h3 8.2f 6g3 a8g a6g4 a6g] close-coupled
filly: poor performer: stays 6f: acts on any going: blinkered twice at 2 yrs. *J. Perrett.*

LADY BOWLER 2 ch.f. (Mar 13) Relkino 123–Grade Well 78 (Derring-Do 131) **43**
[1989 5s2 5v2 5g* 6m 8.2f] 3,100Y: leggy, quite good-topped filly: fourth foal:
half-sister to poor staying handicapper Queen of Swords (by Reform) and a winner
in Italy by Hand of Hush: dam won from 9f to 1½m: made all in seller (sold out of J.
Berry's stable 4,300 gns) at Leicester in April: well beaten in similar events over 4
months later: bred to stay middle distances: sold 950 gns Doncaster October Sales.
Mrs J. R. Ramsden.

LADY BUNTING 2 b.f. (Mar 6) Well Decorated (USA)–Lady's Flag (USA) **63**
(Fifth Marine (USA)) [1989 7m 8v 8g4] leggy, useful-looking filly: third foal:
half-sister to minor winner in USA by Lyphard's Wish: dam won twice at up to 9f in
USA: around 9 lengths fourth of 17, one pace last 2f, to Castle Courageous in maiden
at Leicester in November, best effort: will stay 1¼m. *R. F. Casey.*

LADY CARROLL 3 ch.f. Horage 124–Moortown Lady (No Mercy 126) [1988 6d **68**
7g 1989 8m2 7m2 6h* 7f4 7h2 7m3 7f4 7g] small, angular filly: modest performer:
won maiden at Carlisle in June: in frame in varied events after, below form last 3
outings: suited by stiff 6f or easy 7f: acts on hard going: sold 12,000 gns Newmarket
Autumn Sales. *M. A. Jarvis.*

LADY COLUMBINE 4 b.f. Cawston's Clown 113–Ladyswood 61 (Great —
Nephew 126) [1988 8m 8f 10.8s⁶ 10g 1989 10f] lengthy, sparely-made filly: moderate
mover: poor and unreliable plater. *J. Douglas-Home.*

LADY ELECTRIC 3 b.f. Electric 126–Romping (Sir Gaylord) [1988 NR 1989 9f 52
7m 8f 11.7f 12g* 18g⁴] workmanlike filly: half-sister to smart middle-distance
winner Romper (by Ribero) and useful middle-distance winner Mallard Song (by
Tudor Melody): dam won at up to 1½m in Ireland: 33/1 and ridden by 5-lb claimer,
first form when winning maiden claimer at Hamilton in October: not discredited in
handicap 2 weeks later but gave impression should prove best at up to 2m: evidently
needs give in the ground: trained first 4 starts by C. Hill. *R. J. Hodges.*

LADY ELLEN 2 b.f. (Apr 9) Horage 124–Hillbrow 100 (Swing Easy (USA) 126) 67
[1989 5f² 5m² 5g⁴ 5m²] IR 12,500Y: leggy, quite attractive filly: has a quick action:
fifth foal: half-sister to good-class 5f to 7f winner Indian Ridge (by Ahonoora) and
1986 2-y-o 6f winner Plague O' Rats (by Pitskelly): dam 2-y-o 6f winner: quite
modest maiden: best effort ½-length second to Nazela at Beverley final start: will
stay 6f: has got on toes. *J. S. Wainwright.*

LADY EMMA 2 b.f. (May 10) Kafu 120–Nadja 77 (Dancer's Image (USA)) [1989 39
5m 5f 5m 5m⁵ 5f⁵] IR 2,800Y, 4,600 2-y-o: moderate filly: moderate mover: fifth
foal: half-sister to 1988 2-y-o 5f winner Leg Before (by Runnett) and a winner
abroad: dam won over 1m at 2 yrs: poor form in maidens (one an auction event) and a
seller: not raced after July. *S. E. Kettlewell.*

LADY GHISLAINE (FR) 2 b.f. (Apr 7) Lydian (FR) 120–Planeze (FR) —
(Faraway Son (USA) 130) [1989 6g] workmanlike, plain filly: moderate walker: fifth
foal: sister to French 3-y-o Philycia, successful from 9.1f to 1¼m, and half-sister to a
winning hurdler in France: dam French 9f winner: 33/1 and bit backward, prominent
to halfway in 12-runner maiden at Leicester in November: gave trouble stalls. *T.
Casey.*

LADY GRENVILLE 2 b.f. (Apr 9) Aragon 118–Tri'as (Tyrant (USA)) [1989 6f 68
6g 7m 6g⁴ a7g⁴] medium-sized filly: first foal: dam lightly-raced daughter of
half-sister to smart 1977 2-y-o Bolak: quite modest maiden: best effort fourth
outing: better suited by 6f than 7f. *M. D. I. Usher.*

LADY HENRIETTA 2 b.f. (Feb 15) Aragon 118–Bold Apple (Bold Lad (IRE) 35
133) [1989 5s⁵ 5m⁴ 5f 5m] 9,000F: sturdy, workmanlike filly: first foal: dam
half-sister to smart 6f and 1¼m winner Sarania and to dam of Pennine Walk: well
beaten in spring maidens: sold 2,000 gns Newmarket July Sales. *D. T. Thom.*

LADY IN SILVER (USA) 3 ch.f. Silver Hawk (USA) 127–Lorn Lady 127
(Lorenzaccio 130) [1988 6d* 8m² 8s² 1989 9s* 9.2s⁴ 10m³ 10.5d* 10f² 12f]
The finish of the Prix de Diane Hermes was much more closely
contested than that of its counterpart, the Gold Seal Oaks. The post came just
in time for Lady In Silver in a very rough race in which she avoided trouble
while the runner-up Louveterie did not. The worst of the trouble occurred at
around halfway, scrimmaging involving the favourite Ensconse, and the
outsiders Akadya, Belle Tempete and Sudaka as well as Louveterie. Exactly
how it started was difficult to make out—the stewards apportioned no
blame—but seemingly one of the fourteen runners stumbled, possibly Belle

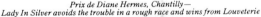

Prix de Diane Hermes, Chantilly—
Lady In Silver avoids the trouble in a rough race and wins from Louveterie

Tempete or Akadya, and started a chain reaction in the middle of the field. Of those involved only Louveterie was on the premises at the finish, though Ensconse made some late headway into sixth. When the scrimmaging occurred Lady In Silver held second place on the heels of Sentimental Side, as she'd done virtually from settling down, and the order was maintained into the straight, Sentimental Side going well about a length and a half clear with the same between Lady In Silver and the chasing group of Bellarida, Pass The Peace and Rose de Crystal. Lady In Silver overtook the leader running into the last two furlongs and for a while looked like winning comfortably; then Louveterie, seventh some way adrift into the straight, managed to sustain a strong run all the way home that took her to within a short neck. Premier Amour finished almost as strongly for third but she'd been held up at the back so long—she was next to last when the winner went on—that she still had two and a half lengths to find on Louveterie at the end.

Lady In Silver's victory caused much less of a surprise than stable-companion Pearl Bracelet's in the Dubai Poule des Pouliches. Apart from one disappointment in the Prix Vanteaux on her second start she'd been running well in the fillies' trials; she'd won the Prix Finlande at Evry in April by a length and a half from Navratilovna and finished a close third to Behera and Louveterie in the Prix Saint-Alary at Longchamp in May. Her disappointing fourth to Louveterie in the Vanteaux was explained by her swallowing her tongue, so afterwards she was fitted with a tongue strap as a precaution. And Lady In Silver went on to show that while the field she beat in the Diane was substandard she could stand comparison with absentees like Behera, Young Mother, Sierra Roberta and Colorado Dancer. She showed it not in France but in the United States, having been sent there to be trained following her sale out of Wojtowiez's stable towards the end of the summer. Instead of the Prix Vermeille and the Prix de l'Arc de Triomphe, Lady In Silver tackled the Arlington Million then the Breeders' Cup Turf. For some reason she failed to give her running over the longer distance at Gulfstream Park, dropping back from a prominent position on the inside after a mile to finish third last. However, she very nearly won the Million. She handled the track well, kept well in contention down the far side, and put in a strong effort on the outer round the last turn which took her past the long-time leader Frosty The Snowman into a narrow, momentary lead less than two furlongs out, just as Steinlen found room to make his challenge on the rails. When Steinlen went on, Lady In Silver stuck stoutly to him so that there was only half a length between them at the finish.

Lady In Silver (USA) (ch.f. 1986)	Silver Hawk (USA) (b 1979)	Roberto (b 1969)	Hail To Reason Bramalea
		Gris Vitesse (gr 1966)	Amerigo Matchiche II
	Lorn Lady (ch 1976)	Lorenzaccio (ch 1965)	Klairon Phoenissa
		Renounce (b 1957)	Big Game Refreshed

There's an outside chance that Lady In Silver finds a mile and a half too far; she stays ten and a half furlongs really well, though. Her sire definitely got the trip—he was third in Golden Fleece's Derby, staying on having been hampered—so does his best-known colt, the Oak Tree Invitational winner Hawkster, and so did Lady In Silver's sister Yarzah. Silver Hawk, who started favourite for the Guineas, was retired through injury to the Airdrie Stud in Kentucky after finishing second in the Irish Sweeps Derby. Lady In Silver's dam, Lorn Lady, was retired after winning a maiden race at Galway over a mile and a hundred yards, almost as far as she ever tackled. At the end of that year she went for 56,000 guineas at the Newmarket Sales, and has proved much more valuable as a broodmare than on the track. Her first foal Bright Ivor (by Sir Ivor) showed quite useful winning form in the States; the next three, Gracious Girl (by Forli), Ancient Tradition (by Raja Baba) and Yarzah also won in either the States or in France; the fifth let the side down although he made the races; then along came Lady In Silver. The second dam Renounce made her own mark in the paddocks as the dam of Double-U-Jay, a good horse at a mile and a mile and a quarter in Britain, and of the high-class French middle-distance mare Riverside, herself the dam of the French classic winner Riverqueen. Renounce's dam Refreshed, third in the One Thousand Guineas, was a half-sister to the Guineas winner Festoon. If Lady In Silver can be brought back to the form she showed at Arlington Park she should have a bright future in North America; it's unlikely we'll see her in Europe again. She acts on any going. *F. S. Schulhofer, USA.*

LADY IN THE LAKE 2 b.f. (Feb 13) Kings Lake (USA) 133–Trouble Me Not (USA) (Nodouble (USA)) [1989 6f 7g 10g] 3,900 2-y-o: workmanlike, plain filly: second foal: dam stakes-placed winner at up to 1m as 3-y-o in USA: tailed off in minor events and a maiden: unseated rider at start on debut. *R. O'Leary.* —

LADY IN WHITE 3 b.f. Shareef Dancer (USA) 135–Fremanche (FR) (Jim **93** French (USA)) [1988 7g4 1989 8g* 10.6g6 10g5] rangy, quite attractive filly: won maiden at Carlisle in April: good sixth in £7,800 handicap at Haydock in June, edging left and tending to carry head high: in need of race 3 months later: better over 1¼m than 1m. *M. R. Stoute.*

LADY KATHY 4 ch.f. Day Is Done 115–Jukella (Jukebox 120) [1988 5g 5g 6h2 — 7.5g5 6g4 7g 1989 6d 8g] workmanlike filly: plater: not seen out after May: suited by 6f: acts on any going: sometimes blinkered: below form when sweating: sold 1,850 gns Ascot November Sales. *J. L. Harris.*

LADY KEYSER 3 b.f. Le Johnstan 123–Fanny Keyser (Majority Blue 126) [1988 **55** 5d3 5.3f* 5m4 5g 5m2 5g2 5g 5d2 1989 6d 5.8m 5m 5.3h 5f6 5m 5f* 5.1f6 5f 5m4] angular, workmanlike filly: has a sharpish action: plating-class handicapper nowadays: made virtually all to win at Wolverhampton in July: suited by 5f: yet to race on very soft going, acts on any other: has run well for 7-lb claimer: blinkered penultimate start: trained until after fifth by P. Feilden. *D. W. Chapman.*

LADY KHADIJA 3 b.f. Nicholas Bill 125–Chenkynowa 48 (Connaught 130) — [1988 NR 1989 6f 10.2f5 14g] second foal: dam, only form when second in 5f seller at 2 yrs, ran 6 times: ridden by 5-lb claimer, little sign of ability in maidens and a competitive minor event. *G. P. Kelly.*

LADY LITA 2 b.f. (May 4) Jalmood (USA) 126–Lady of The Manor 78 (Astec 128) **54** p [1989 8.5f5 7f4] 500F: half-sister to a winner in Belgium: dam placed at around 1¼m at 3 yrs, is half-sister to Ragstone, Castle Keep and dam of Moon Madness and Sheriff's Star: over 9 lengths fourth of 8, not knocked about, to Oblist at Leicester, better effort in autumn maidens: bred to stay at least 1¼m. *R. Guest.*

LADY LLANFAIR 3 b.f. Prince Tenderfoot (USA) 126–Picnic Time (Silly **61** Season 127) [1988 5m6 6f 7d2 7f3 8s 8g 7d 1989 12f6 10m6 10f 11.7f* 10.2f 12.2m3 a12g] leggy, workmanlike filly: won maiden claimer at Bath in August: good staying-on third in handicap (moved freely to post) at Warwick, easily best other effort: suited by 1½m: acts on firm going and a soft surface: unruly when blinkered final start at 2 yrs: active type. *R. Hannon.*

LADY LONGLEAT 2 ch.f. (Feb 26) Longleat (USA) 109–Kip's Sister **36** (Cawston's Clown 73) [1989 6g5 5f2 6g 5g 5s] 6,000Y: small, angular filly: first foal: dam unraced from family of Grey Desire: poor maiden: seems best at 5f: blinkered penultimate outing. *M. Brittain.*

LADY MADINA 2 b.f. (May 11) Legend of France (USA) 124–Double Touch — (FR) (Nonoalco (USA) 131) [1989 7g 6g 6m] 6,000Y: workmanlike filly: second foal: half-sister to 3-y-o 1m seller winner Capital Builder (by Pas de Seul): dam never ran: little worthwhile form, including in sellers. *M. J. Ryan.*

LADY MIAMI 2 ch.f. (Mar 31) Mansingh (USA) 120–Miami Star 80 (Miami — Springs 121) [1989 6m 6g] 540F: sparely-made filly: first foal: dam, 1m and 9f winner, is half-sister to winners in Ireland, Norway and Morocco: well beaten in summer claimer at Warwick and minor event (went freely down, slowly away) at Windsor. *T. Casey.*

LADY MIDAS (USA) 3 ch.f. Golden Act (USA)–Lady Inyala (USA) (Apalachee **66** (USA) 137) [1988 7m6 1989 10.1m 10.1m 12.3g 12h2 12f5] angular filly: quite modest maiden: not seen out after August: stays 1½m: acts on hard ground: blinkered last 2 starts: one paced. *M. R. Stoute.*

LADY OF PERSIA (USA) 2 ch.f. (Apr 5) Persian Bold 123–Tants 111 (Vitiges **82** (FR) 132) [1989 7g6 8g2 8f5 7g] $27,000Y: rather unfurnished filly: third foal: dam 7f and 1½m winner: fair performer, best effort staying-on seventh of 12 to Negligent in Bottisham Heath Stud Rockfel Stakes at Newmarket in October: should be suited by 1m +: possibly unsuited by firm ground. *M. A. Jarvis.*

LADY OF THE LODGE   3 gr.f. Absalom 128–Hotazur 52 (Hotfoot 126) [1988   —
5s² 6s⁶ 6m 6m 1989 7g 8m 10.2f] lengthy, angular filly: no form since debut but gave
impression retains ability in sellers first 2 outings in 1989 (not seen out after June):
doesn't stay 1¼m. *J. Wharton.*

LADY OF THE SEA   3 ch.f. Mill Reef (USA) 141–La Mer (NZ) (Copenhagen   86
107) [1988 NR 1989 12g 11.5m⁵ 10.6m² 8g 8.2g² 10f² 8.2m*] 335,000Y: lengthy,
rather sparely-made filly: fourth foal to Northern Hemisphere Time: half-sister to
fairly useful performer at up to 1m Cipriani, a winner in Australia and a moderate
animal (all by Habitat), and to a winner in New Zealand by Artaius: dam best of sex in
New Zealand at 2 yrs and 3 yrs when 10 wins from 14 starts included 1½m New
Zealand Oaks: favourite, won maiden at Haydock in September by 8 lengths: beaten
head in similar events previous 2 starts: probably stays 1¼m: acts on firm going:
sweating and edgy fourth (well beaten in handicap) and sixth starts. *M. R. Stoute.*

LADY OF VISION   2 b.f. (Apr 9) Vision (USA)–Lady of The House 98 (Habitat   85
134) [1989 6m 7m* 7d³] IR 19,000F, 22,000Y: second foal: dam Irish 7.9f winner at 2
yrs but better as 3-y-o, is daughter of Ribblesdale Stakes winner and Prix Vermeille
runner-up Relfo: 20/1, made most when winning 23-runner maiden at Fairyhouse in
October by 2 lengths, pair well clear: caught near line when third of 11 to Bold
Performer in minor event at Thirsk: will stay 1m. *J. C. Hayden, Ireland.*

LADY OMEGA   3 b.f. Precocious 126–Zoomie 78 (Pinza 137) [1988 NR 1989 7g   —
7g] half-sister to useful but untrustworthy sprinter/miler Intimidate (by
Formidable) and several other winners, including very useful Irish and American
middle-distance filly Countess Tully (by Hotfoot): dam, 1m and 9f winner, is
half-sister to smart Irish 2-y-o Pithivers and smart 1m to 1¼m performer Blinis:
backward, well beaten in late-season maiden at Catterick and all-aged contest at
Newmarket: may do better. *W. Jarvis.*

LADY PENNINGTON   2 b.f. (May 22) Blue Cashmere 129–Lady Carol 42   51
(Lord Gayle (USA) 124) [1989 5s⁵ 5d³ 5d⁶ 8.5f⁶ 7f 6f] lengthy, lightly-made filly:
moderate mover: second foal: dam 1m winner: plating-class maiden: probably stays
7f. *J. P. Leigh.*

LADY ROSANNA   4 b.f. Kind of Hush 118–Rosaceae 99 (Sagaro 133) [1988 9d⁵   89
12g⁴ 11.7f³ 16d⁴ 14f² 13.1g* 19v⁴ 16m⁶ 14d⁵ 1989 12v 14.8d⁵ 12f² 14f* 14g⁶ 14f³
14m* 13.1f² 12g³] quite attractive filly: moderate mover: fair handicapper: won at
Sandown in May (making all in moderately-run contest) and July: suited by about
1¾m: acts on any going, except possibly heavy: good mount for claimer: best racing
up with pace: game: winning hurdler. *I. A. Balding.*

LADY ROSEMARY   2 b.f. (Apr 30) Burslem 123–Sweet Foot (Prince   40
Tenderfoot (USA) 126) [1989 5f⁵ a6g a6g] IR 2,800F, IR 1,450Y, 4,000 2-y-o: small
filly: dam unraced half-sister to Brightelmstone: poor maiden: off course 6 months
after debut, and bit backward on return: blinkered final start: bandaged penultimate.
I. Campbell.

LADY SHIPLEY   3 b.f. Shirley Heights 130–Circus Ring 122 (High Top 131) 111
[1988 7m* 7g⁶ 1989 10f* 12g⁵ 10f² 12f⁴ 12m³ 12f] tall, rangy filly: progressed well
physically: good walker: has a quick, fluent, light action: impressive winner of listed
race at Goodwood in May: ran creditably in Prix de Malleret at Longchamp, Nassau
Stakes at Goodwood and Yorkshire Oaks (making most) at York next 3 starts: below
form in Princess Royal Stakes at Ascot and St Simon Stakes at Newbury: stays
1½m: acts on firm going, possibly unsuited by heavy: sometimes gives trouble at
stalls: very useful. *M. R. Stoute.*

LADY'S MANTLE (USA)   5 ch.m. Sunny Clime (USA)–Alchemilla (USA)   47
(Quadrangle) [1988 6f 5f 5f 5g 5f 5f⁵ 5m⁵ 1989 6d 5f 5m⁵ 5m² 5.1m* 5f* 5m⁵ 5h⁴ 5f²
5f⁴ 5m² 5.1f³ 5g 5m⁵ 5.1g] compact, good-bodied mare: carries plenty of condition:
moderate mover: poor handicapper: successful at Yarmouth and Goodwood
(apprentices) in June: ran well when placed afterwards: suited by 5f: acts on hard
going and a soft surface: has been tried in blinkers: sometimes sweats and gets on
edge: has worn a crossed noseband. *R. Bastiman.*

LADY SNOOBLE   2 b.f. (Feb 21) King of Clubs 124–Ides of March 87 (Mummy's   —
Pet 125) [1989 8.2f5] 8,000Y: small, sturdy filly: first foal: dam sprinting half-sister
to very useful 1981 2-y-o 6f winner Foam Bath and middle-distance stayer/jumper
Cima: 16/1 and carrying condition, slowly away, ran wide bend and soon well behind
in 6-runner minor event at Nottingham in September. *R. Boss.*

LADY SPEED STICK   3 b.f. Tender King 123–Tetrazzini 70 (Sovereign Path   50
125) [1988 5g 5f 5f³ 5m⁶ 6g 6s 7m² 7f⁶ 8m⁴ 7d 1989 6d 6m 8m 8.5f 7g⁵ 7m 6g⁶ 6f 7f
6f⁴ 7m] smallish, lengthy filly: moderate walker and mover: plating-class maiden:

probably stays 1m: best on a sound surface: blinkered sixth, eighth and tenth outings, edgy and below form first 2 of them: has run well when sweating: retained by trainer 660 gns Doncaster November Sales: inconsistent. *W. Bentley.*

LADY'S SEAL 3 ch.f. Ahonoora 122–Lady North 103 (Northfields (USA)) [1988 NR 1989 8.5m 7f⁴ 7f³] IR 34,000Y: leggy filly: half-sister to 5 winners, including fairly useful Irish 1¼m winner Elite (by Lord Gayle) and Irish 6f and 9f winner North Telstar (by Sallust): dam Irish 1m winner: quite modest maiden: best effort fourth at Chepstow in July: hung left at Epsom on debut: bred to stay 1m: sold 13,000 gns Newmarket December Sales. *B. W. Hills.* **66**

LADY STOCK 3 ch.f. Crofter (USA) 124–Millingdale 65 (Tumble Wind (USA)) [1988 5m 6f 6g 5d 1989 6g 5h 6f 7m 7f* 7h 7g 8d 6f] smallish, close-coupled filly: form as 3-y-o only when dead-heating in maiden at Chepstow in July, soon pushed along and hard driven to join Petriece on post: better at 7f than shorter: acts on firm going: sweating badly on reappearance: twice bandaged near-hind. *L. G. Cottrell.* **63**

LADY TAP 3 ch.f. Red Sunset 120–Park Lady 82 (Tap On Wood 130) [1988 5m³ 6f⁵ 5m* 5f² 6g⁴ 5d⁴ 5g⁵ 1989 5m 6m² 5m 5d] compact filly: fairly useful and progressive at 2 yrs: easily best effort in 1989 when fair second in minor event at Leicester: best form at 5f: yet to race on very soft ground, acts on any other: visored final outing. *W. Hastings-Bass.* **82**

LADY TELLER (USA) 2 b.f. (Apr 29) Buckfinder (USA)–Bistort (USA) (High Echelon) [1989 6m 6m⁴ 6m 7.3m] $13,000Y: leggy filly: has a round action: seventh foal: half-sister to 3 minor winners in USA: dam stakes winner at 1m: plating-class maiden: tailed off in nursery at Newbury final start. *Capt. R. M. Smyly.* **57**

LADY TOPAZ 2 b.f. (May 8) Jalmood (USA) 126–Town Lady 93 (Town Crier 119) [1989 6g 5m³ 6g⁴ 7m 7g] small, sturdy filly: half-sister to several winners, including Italian 3-y-o 7.5f winner Clive (by Rabdan) and 1¼m and 1½m winner The Freshes (by Good Times): dam won over 5f at 2 yrs: quite modest maiden: will be suited by 1m. *T. Thomson Jones.* **62**

LADY VERDI (USA) 4 ch.f. Monteverdi 129–My Kinda Lady (USA) (Canadian Gil (CAN)) [1988 10g⁴ 12m⁴ 12g⁵ 12f 12f⁵ 11g⁶ 14f 13.8f² 12g* 12g² 1989 12m⁶ 12f² 14g] smallish, angular filly: plating-class handicapper: best form at 1½m: acted on firm going: blinkered twice, visored once: looked a difficult ride, needing plenty of driving: in foal to Farajullah. *G. A. Huffer.* **53**

LADY WESTMINSTER (USA) 3 ch.f. Key To Content (USA)–Pamlisa (USA) (What A Pleasure (USA)) [1988 6g⁵ 6f 6f 6d 6d 8m 1989 8.2f 10f⁶ 12.5f 16f] rather leggy, quite attractive filly: little worthwhile form, including in sellers and handicap: sold 900 gns Newmarket Autumn Sales. *M. D. I. Usher.* **—**

LADY WESTOWN 5 b.m. Town And Country 124–Hay-Hay (Hook Money 124) [1988 12m 1989 12g 16m³ 16.2m* 16.2m³ 16.5m⁵] small mare: favourite, game winner of handicap at Beverley in June: suited by test of stamina: acts on top-of-the-ground: has run creditably for apprentice: has sweated: winning hurdler. *R. J. Holder.* **45**

LADY WINNER (FR) 3 ch.f. Fabulous Dancer (USA) 124–Ameridienne (FR) 79 (Targowice (USA) 130) [1988 6.5d* 7.5g⁴ 7m⁴ 1989 8s⁶ 8g* 8g⁵ 8g² 8g* 9.2g⁶ 9s*] 450,000 francs (approx £45,400) Y: third foal: dam unraced half-sister to high-class French filly Aryenne and to the dam of very useful French 1m to 10.5f winner Alexandrie: won minor events at Evry as 2-y-o and Compiegne in July and listed races at Saint-Cloud and Laurel Park (All Along Stakes, by 7 lengths) in October: suited by 9f: acts on top-of-the-ground and soft going: trained until after reappearance by J. de Roualle. *M. Zilber, France.* **115**

LADY WISHING WELL (USA) 2 gr.f. (Mar 16) Hero's Honor (USA)– **71** Ispahan 85 (Rusticaro (FR) 124) [1989 7g³ 7g⁴ 7m⁵ 6g a8g³ a8g⁵] $50,000Y: sturdy, useful-looking filly: has a quick action: second foal: half-sister to fairly useful 1988 Irish 2-y-o 6f winner Lem's Peace (by L'Emigrant): dam, 2-y-o 6f winner successful at 1m in France, is daughter of Irish 1000 Guineas winner Royal Danseuse, also dam of very useful Irish sprinter Royal Hobbit and smart middle-distance performer Bog Road: sire won from 7f to 11f: modest maiden: staying-on third at Lingfield penultimate start: slowly away and had poor run final outing: will stay 1¼m. *B. Hanbury.*

LAFKADIO 2 b.g. (Apr 5) Gay Mecene (USA) 128–Lakonia (Kris 135) [1989 5f] **—** 12,000Y: good-bodied gelding: first foal: dam, unplaced in 3 races in France, is half-sister to Japan Cup winner Le Glorieux out of a sister to Oaks third La Manille: never dangerous in 11-runner maiden auction race at Lingfield in May. *J. H. M. Gosden.*

LA GALERIE 2 b.c. (Feb 28) Glenstal (USA) 118–Tizzy 79 (Formidable (USA) **96**
125) [1989 5s 5d² 5g* 5g* 5f⁶ 5f³ 6m⁵ 5m² 6g² 6f³ 5s³ 6g⁴] 13,000F, 22,000Y:
lengthy colt: has a quick action: second foal: half-brother to 3-y-o Dizzy Gee (by
Gorytus): dam 9f and 1¼m winner from family of Mummy's Pet: fairly useful
performer: successful in spring in maiden at Leicester and minor event at Salisbury:
progressed afterwards, running well in listed races won by Mademoiselle Chloe at
Ayr and Montendre at York on last 2 starts: stays 6f: acts on any going. *W. Carter.*

LA GLORIOSA 3 ch.f. Ardross 134–Skiboule (BEL) (Boulou) [1988 NR 1989 **56**
12.2g⁴ 12g³ 16g² a16g] 5,000Y: angular, sparely-made filly: eighth foal in Britain:
half-sister to several winners, including useful middle-distance fillies Rollrights and
Rollfast (both by Ragstone): dam won in Belgium: plating-class maiden: faced very
stiff task and always struggling in handicap at Lingfield: stays 2m. *A. C. Stewart.*

LA GRACILE (USA) 3 b. or br.f. Nijinsky (CAN) 138–Pagan Queen 83 **89**
(Vaguely Noble 140) [1988 NR 1989 10.1g⁵ 12m* 14m 16g] leggy, lengthy, angular
filly: fourth reported foal: closely related to 1½m winner Green Steps (by Green
Dancer): dam won at 1½m and 1¾m: hard driven 4f out and led close home in minor
event at Newmarket in July: wintry in coat and facing stiff tasks, well beaten in
handicap and listed race at same course after: should stay beyond 1½m: sold 20,000
gns Newmarket December Sales. *G. Wragg.*

LA GRACIOSA 4 b.f. Comedy Star (USA) 121–Grey Charter 58 (Runnymede **—**
123) [1988 NR 1989 6d 7g 12.5g 8h 7.6h 6f 7s] compact, workmanlike filly: first foal:
dam, poor sprint maiden, is half-sister to Starfen, useful winner at 1m to 1¼m
subsequently high-class hurdler: winner twice over sprint distances in Scandinavia
as 2-y-o: ran 7 times there without success in 1988: well behind in varied events in
Britain at 4 yrs: unlikely to stay 1½m. *G. B. Balding.*

LA GRANDE AFFAIRE 3 b.f. Lomond (USA) 128–Summer Affair (USA) **81**
(Cornish Prince) [1988 7f³ 1989 8d⁶ 10.5f⁵ 10m⁶ 7g* 7s a10g³ a10g³] lengthy,
angular filly: has a round action: won maiden at Lingfield last August: good third in
handicaps there last 2 starts, blinkered on final one: suited by 1¼m: acts on firm
ground and a soft surface. *P. F. I. Cole.*

LAIRD OF BALMORAL 2 b.c. (May 2) Lochnager 132–Baggin Time 91 **84**
(Pinsun 108) [1989 6m⁴ 6m⁶ 6m 6g* 8.2d* 8g 6v³] 7,600Y: compact, useful-looking
colt: good walker: fifth foal: half-brother to moderate handicappers Brewin Time
and Mashin Time (both by Palm Track), winners from 6f to 1m: dam won from 5f to
1½m: showed much improved form when winning maiden (backed from 14/1 to 4/1)
at Hamilton in August: followed up in minor event at Haydock in September: good
third in auction event at Ayr on final outing: stays 1m: possibly best with some give
in the ground. *M. H. Easterby.*

LA KARADIA 3 b.f. Akarad (FR) 130–Gnulia (Margouillat (FR) 130) [1988 7m³ **—**
1989 8d 10m] leggy, sparely-made filly: quite modest form at best in maidens and
£8,700 contest: took keen hold on final start, May: should stay middle distances. *P.
T. Walwyn.*

LAKE DANCER 3 b.c. Kings Lake (USA) 133–Windy Cheyenne (USA) (Tumble **66**
Wind (USA)) [1988 6g 6m⁶ 7g 1989 7d³ 7m² 8m⁶ 8g a6g a7g] tall colt: moderate
walker and mover: favourite, second in handicap at Thirsk in May, edging left and
easily best effort: off course nearly 5 months after fourth: should stay beyond 7f:
gives impression may prove best with some give in the ground: didn't handle track
at Edinburgh: has often had tongue tied down: taken down early final start. *J. W.
Payne.*

LAKELAND BEAUTY 2 b.f. (Mar 2) Mummy's Pet 125–Skiddaw (USA) (Grey **95**
Dawn II 132) [1989 6g⁴ 6f* 6g⁶] 7,600Y: lengthy, angular filly: has plenty of scope:
has a roundish action: first foal: dam unraced: favourite, won maiden at Redcar
comfortably by 4 lengths from Platoon, quickening clear 1f out: stayed on strongly
when over 9 lengths sixth of 25 to Osario in Racecall Gold Trophy there later in
October: will be suited by 7f. *W. G. A. Brooks.*

LAKE MAHWA 2 b.f. (Apr 25) Ya Zaman (USA) 122–Another Tune (Red God **56**
128§) [1989 5f 6f⁶ 5g⁵ 6m³ 6f³ 7g⁵ a8g] 1,150Y: leggy, sparely-made filly: fifth foal:
sister to poor animal Another Season and half-sister to a winner in Belgium by
Private Walk: dam of little account: plating-class maiden: ran moderately last 4
starts: best form at 5f: sold 500 gns Ascot December Sales. *M. J. Haynes.*

LAKE MISTASSIU 2 b.f. (May 18) Tina's Pet 121–Kakisa 81 (Forlorn River **86**
124) [1989 6m⁵ 6f⁴ 5f* 5.3f² 5s* 5g] medium-sized filly: first foal: dam 5f and 6f
winner: fair performer: won maiden at Bath in September readily by 3 lengths from

Sharp N' Easy and nursery at Haydock following month by 2½ lengths from Cantdonowtrite: best form at 5f: acts on any going. *G. A. Pritchard-Gordon.*

LAKE ORMOND 3 b.f. Kings Lake (USA) 133–Roof (Thatch (USA) 136) [1988   — NR 1989 10d 14g⁶] workmanlike, sturdy filly: second foal: half-sister to 4-y-o maiden Vison Gris (by Lord Gayle): dam Irish 2-y-o 6f winner: well beaten in late-season maiden at Newbury and minor event at Redcar. *J. W. Hills.*

LAKESIDE LASS 3 b.f. Import 127–Celtic Love (Irish Love 117) [1988 NR 1989   — 12g 9f 12f] workmanlike filly: second reported foal: sister to a once-raced maiden: dam won 2m novice hurdle: behind in maiden and minor events in the spring: has joined G. Gracey. *K. M. Brassey.*

LAKE TAUPO 2 b.c. (Apr 29) Taufan (USA) 119–Merriment (USA) (Go   **51** Marching (USA)) [1989 5f⁶ 6f⁵ 6g⁴ 6f⁴ 7m 5s] IR 7,500Y: small, close-coupled, quite attractive colt: moderate mover: half-brother to 2 winners in France and Belgium: dam sister to high-class French miler Brinkmanship: plating-class form in varied events: likely to prove best at around 6f. *R. Hollinshead.*

LAKE VALENTINA 8 br.g. Blakeney 126–La Levantina (Le Levanstell 122)   **56** [1988 NR 1989 18g 16g² 16.2g⁵ 18f⁶] small, quite attractive gelding: plating-class handicapper nowadays: stays well: used to act well on top-of-the-ground: bandaged at 8 yrs. *M. W. Easterby.*

LALITPOUR 5 b.g. Top Ville 129–Labusfille (FR) (Labus (FR)) [1988 12m 12f²   — 14g⁶ 14.5g² 14f³ 16m² 16d³ 1989 14g] lengthy, rather dipped-backed gelding: moderate walker: placed in minor event and handicaps as 4-y-o: ran poorly in Newmarket handicap in April, only outing on flat in 1989: possibly best in strongly-run race over 1¾m: acts on firm going and a soft surface. *J. R. Jenkins.*

LAMBOURN CITIZEN (USA) 3 ch.c. L'Emigrant (USA) 129–Journey (USA)   **71** (What A Pleasure (USA)) [1988 5g 5g³ 5g⁴ 6f 5m⁵ 6m⁵ 5m² 6m⁴ 5g 6f³ 6s 5g⁶ 1989 7d⁵ 8g⁶ 9s⁵ 8f³ 10h³ 8f*] 8.3m⁴ 8m⁶] close-coupled colt: has a long, rather round action: won apprentice claimer at Warwick in July: ran poorly in handicap final start (August) but consistently otherwise: stays 1¼m: acts on hard going and a soft surface: ran too freely when blinkered once at 2 yrs. *J. P. Hudson.*

LAMBOURN RAJA 3 b.c. Indian King (USA) 128–Take A Chance (FR) (Baldric   — II 131) [1988 6s⁵ 5d 5m 7d 7g⁶ 6g 6g 1989 8.2g] lengthy, workmanlike, rather angular colt: modest form in varied races as 2-y-o, including Molecomb Stakes at Goodwood and GPA National Stakes at the Curragh: burly, outpaced and never dangerous facing stiff task in handicap in October, only start in 1989: stays 7f: visored penultimate start at 2 yrs. *J. P. Hudson.*

LAMBTON LAD 2 b.g. (May 2) Saher 115–Illaqua (USA) (Empery (USA) 128)   — [1989 a8g] IR 5,200Y: lengthy gelding: second foal: dam never ran: bit backward, very green and soon well behind in late-season maiden at Lingfield. *E. Eldin.*

LA MINOR (USA) 3 ch.c. The Minstrel (CAN) 135–Lady Norcliffe (USA)   **72** (Norcliffe (CAN)) [1988 7d 7s⁵ 1989 10g 12f⁴ 12m² 11.7m⁴] stocky colt: modest maiden: best effort fourth in handicap at Windsor final outing: stays 1½m: often sweats: sold 9,600 gns Newmarket July Sales. *P. T. Walwyn.*

LANA'S PET 3 b.f. Tina's Pet 121–Spanish Chestnut (Philip of Spain 126) [1988   — 5g³ 7g² 7m⁶ 5d 6g 1989 8.2f⁶ 5.8h] leggy, sparely-made filly: failed to progress: blinkered final outing at 2 yrs. *W. G. M. Turner.*

LANCE'S LASSIE 2 b.f. (Apr 11) King of Spain 121–Charlotte's Image (Towern   **50** ? 96) [1989 6f 6g* 6f⁵ 6m⁶ 6m 7g 6g] 1,000F, 2,900Y: compact, quite attractive filly: fifth reported foal: dam never ran: won 2-runner seller (bought in 3,400 gns) at Nottingham in July. *C. Tinkler.*

LANCHESTER (USA) 3 b.c. Linkage (USA)–Bank The Turns (USA) (Shecky **104** d Greene (USA)) [1988 5m² 5m³ 5f⁶ 7s⁴ 6m² 6g⁵ 6m* 6f³ 6m* 6g³ 1989 6m 6f⁵ 6f 5m 6f* 6f 6m 5m⁶ 5m 6g] lengthy colt: moderate walker and mover: made all in minor event at Lingfield in August: not discredited when sixth in listed race at Newmarket: well below form otherwise as 3-y-o: best form at 6f: acts on firm going: goes well with forcing tactics: sold to race in Saudi Arabia 27,000 gns Newmarket Autumn Sales. *R. J. R. Williams.*

LAND AFAR 2 b.c. (Mar 22) Dominion 123–Jouvencelle 68 (Rusticaro (FR) 124)   **84** [1989 6m* 6g⁵] 38,000Y: good-quartered colt: first foal: dam plating-class maiden at up to 14.7f: 40/1, won 6-runner maiden at Newmarket in July by head from stable-companion Green's Belle: bandaged behind, over 5 lengths fifth of 9, staying on having been outpaced at halfway, to Star Hill in listed race at Kempton 5 weeks later: will be suited by 1m. *W. Jarvis.*

LANDMARK 6 b.h. Mill Reef (USA) 141–Christchurch (FR) 88 (So Blessed 130) [1988 12g⁶ 12d² 12s⁶ 11.7d 12g 1989 12v 12s 8f 12f⁴ 12f⁴] medium-sized, good-bodied horse: has been hobdayed: poor handicapper: well beaten in 1989: stays 1½m: easily best efforts with a bit of give in the ground: sold 1,400 gns Newmarket Autumn Sales. *P. Howling.* —

LAND OF GOLD 3 b.f. Glint of Gold 128–Docklands 91 (On Your Mark 125) [1988 7s⁵ 8g⁵ 1989 13.3m] medium-sized, rather sparely-made filly: modest form in minor events as 2-y-o: collapsed and died on first outing at 3 yrs. *Major W. R. Hern.* —

LAND OF HOPE 2 b.f. (Jan 20) Dominion 123–Vielle 123 (Ribero 126) [1989 6m⁵] lengthy, quite good-topped filly: has scope: fifth foal: half-sister to 3-y-o Dancing Falcon (by Mill Reef) and fair 12.2f winner Chevrefeuille (by Ile de Bourbon): dam very smart middle-distance filly: 14/1 and bit backward, shaped promisingly when over 6 lengths fifth of 22, keeping on not knocked about, to Hebba in maiden at Newbury in September: sure to improve, particularly over further. *P. T. Walwyn.* 59 p

LAND OF WONDER (USA) 2 b.g. (Apr 8) Wind And Wuthering (USA) 132–Heat Haze (USA) 66 (Jungle Savage (USA)) [1989 5d⁵ 5s⁴ 7m] leggy, rather unfurnished gelding: has scope: has a round action: first known foal: dam lightly raced here and in USA: poor maiden: better suited by 7f than 5f: gelded after final outing: seems of dubious temperament. *C. A. Cyzer.* 46

LANDSKI 6 b.g. Niniski (USA) 125–Misacre 66 (St Alphage 119) [1988 10f⁴ 12m⁴ 10g³ 10f⁵ 12m⁴ 1989 10g 11.7m 12f⁴ 15.5f⁶] rangy, quite well-made gelding: keen walker and mover: fair winner at his best: well below form in first half of 1989: ideally suited by 1¼m: acts on any going: blinkered once at 5 yrs: has run creditably for inexperienced rider: winning hurdler. *J. R. Jenkins.* —

LANGHAM LADY 3 b.f. Dunbeath (USA) 127–Rosinante (FR) 65 (Busted 134) [1988 6m⁴ 6d⁴ 6d² 5.8d* 6g² 7m 5.8d* 5g² 5g⁶ 1989 5.8m 7m³ 7m 6g a7g a6g⁵] leggy, close-coupled filly: modest winner as 2-y-o: generally well below form in handicaps and claimers in 1989: should be suited by further than 6f: suited by an easy surface. *D. Haydn Jones.* —

LANGTON STREET 3 ch.f. Jalmood (USA) 126–Gold Rupee 86 (Native Prince) [1988 6f³ 6m* 7g 8d 1989 7g 7f 7m⁶ 6g 8.3m] sturdy filly: quite modest winner as 2-y-o: below form in handicaps in 1989: probably needs further than 6f and should stay 1m: acts on firm going: visored and edgy final start: sold 3,700 gns Newmarket Autumn Sales. *Capt. R. M. Smyly.* —

LANGTRY LADY 3 b.f. Pas de Seul 133–Arianna Aldini (Habitat 134) [1988 5m³ 6m³ 1989 6s* 7g² 7s⁴ 7m⁶ 8g 7g⁴] leggy, sparely-made filly: modest handicapper: won maiden at Nottingham in March: stays 7f (faced stiff task on first run for over 5 months at 1m): acts on soft going, possibly unsuited by top-of-the-ground: tends to carry head high: ridden by claimer except for fourth start: changed hands 9,000 gns Newmarket Autumn Sales. *M. J. Ryan.* 75

LANGTRY LASS 2 b.f. (Feb 26) Tina's Pet 121–Nimble Star (Space King 115) [1989 6m⁴ 6g⁴] 8,000Y, 9,000 2-y-o: lengthy, good-topped filly: has a round action: sister to an animal of little account and half-sister to useful 1984 2-y-o 6f winner Meadow Star and prolific 1m to 1¼m winner Oratavo (both by The Brianstan): dam unraced: bit backward, over 4 lengths fourth of 12, staying on well, to Himmah in maiden at Leicester in November: last on debut in June: will be better suited by 7f: sure to improve again. *M. J. Ryan.* 60 p

LANGUEDOC 2 b.c. (Feb 23) Rousillon (USA) 133–Can Can Girl 69 (Gay Fandango (USA) 132) [1989 6m² 6m⁴] 60,000Y: rangy colt: has plenty of scope: second reported foal: dam lightly-raced half-sister to speedy Noiritza, the dam of Al Sylah: favourite but backward, ¾-length second of 22 to Hebba in maiden at Newbury in September, travelling strongly in lead much of way but weakening and headed near line: failed to fulfil that promise in similar event at York following month, held up pulling very hard and unable to quicken: very headstrong. *Major W. R. Hern.* 79

LANZAROTE 2 b.f. (Feb 26) Longleat (USA) 109–Bel Esprit (Sagaro 133) [1989 5s² 5g⁵ 5m⁵ 7g⁴ 8s 6g⁵ 7g 7g] IR 5,000Y: workmanlike filly: third foal: half-sister to 6f and 7.3f winner Fille d'Esprit (by Cragador) and a winner in Germany: dam showed no form on flat or over jumps: quite modest maiden: fell final outing: stays 7f: ran poorly fifth start: has run well for 7-lb claimer. *A. Bailey.* 61

LAPIERRE 4 b.c. Lafontaine (USA) 117–Lucky Omen 99 (Queen's Hussar 124) [1988 8s² 7g* 8g 9.2d* 8g 10.5f6 1989 10.5f 7.5s 10f⁵ 10f⁵ 10.2m² 10.5f 10d⁵ 10.2g³] rangy, quite attractive colt: bad mover: smart at his best, winning Ladbroke 108

European Free Handicap at Newmarket and Prix Jean Prat Ecurie Fustok at Longchamp in first half of 1988: generally well below form subsequently, but showed he retains some ability when 9½ lengths third of 7 to Drum Taps in £21,100 handicap at Newcastle in October: probably stays 1¼m: acts on soft going and is unsuited by firm: hung left in 3-runner race fifth start. *C. E. Brittain.*

LA PLACE 2 ch.f. (Apr 1) Mansingh (USA) 120–Pegs Promise (Tumble Wind 45 (USA)) [1989 5g 5m 6g] 5,200Y: angular, sparely-made filly: sister to a winner in Belgium and a poor animal, and half-sister to 2 winning 2-y-o platers: dam well beaten in 2 starts at 2 yrs: poor form in varied company, including selling. *R. M. Whitaker.*

LAP OF THE GODS (FR) 3 ch.f. Tap On Wood 130–Nip In The Air (USA) 114 — (Northern Dancer) [1988 6s 1989 8m 11.7h 12f⁵ 8f 8f 6f⁵] sturdy filly: little sign of ability: pulls hard. *P. J. Arthur.*

LA POMME DE PIN 2 b.f. (May 8) Ile de Bourbon (USA) 133–Sweep Up (FR) — 82 (Relko 136) [1989 5m 8f] half-sister to fairly useful 1984 2-y-o Thalestria (by Mill Reef), later a winner in France at 11f: dam suited by a test of stamina: well beaten in autumn maidens: ran wide 3f out at Brighton final start: bred to stay well. *C. E. Brittain.*

L'AQUINO 4 ch.f. Kings Lake (USA) 133–Willowy (Mourne 126) [1988 10s³ 12d 63 1989 12d⁶ 12.5g² 16m 12h⁵ 13.6g a14g] leggy, medium-sized filly: moderate walker and mover: quite modest maiden: well beaten last 4 outings: stays 1½m: unsuited by top-of-the-ground: sweating and on toes second start. *M. A. Jarvis.*

LA RAPTOTTE 2 b.f. (Feb 28) Alzao (USA) 117–Maypole Hie (Bold Lad (IRE) 50 133) [1989 5f⁶ 6m 5m⁵ 5.1f⁶ 7m³ 7m⁵] IR 6,500Y: angular, narrow filly: second foal: dam never ran: plating-class maiden: ran respectably when visored final outing: stays 7f: usually ridden by 7-lb claimer: sold 3,100 gns Newmarket Autumn Sales. *G. A. Huffer.*

LARA'S ELEGANT 2 b.c. (Feb 3) Elegant Air 119–Lara's Song (USA) 69 — (Russian Bank (USA) 110) [1989 7m] 42,000 2-y-o: third foal: half-brother to 13.1f winner and successful hurdler Russian Lullaby (by Sparkler): dam winning stayer: 33/1, tailed off in 17-runner maiden at Chepstow in October. *K. White.*

LARISTON GALE 3 b.f. Pas de Seul 133–Gigiolina (King Emperor (USA)) 76 [1988 6f 6g² 7f 6s* 7d² 7g 1989 7m 11.7m⁶ 10m⁴ 11.7m⁵ 11s⁴ 15s⁵ 13.3d⁵] compact, workmanlike filly: modest handicapper: should be suited by 1½m+: acts on top-of-the-ground and soft going: blinkered final start. *M. H. Tompkins.*

LA ROSETTE 3 b.f. Lomond (USA) 128–Sairshea (Simbir 130) [1988 7g⁴ 1989 95 10g⁴ 10.5f 12d* 12m] lengthy, angular filly: moderate mover, with a quick action: odds on, won maiden at Haydock in August: in need of race, faced stiff task in £71,300 handicap at Ascot 7 weeks later: should be suited by 1½m: probably best with give in the ground. *J. W. Watts.*

LARS PORSENA 2 b. or br.g. (Feb 12) Trojan Fen 118–Apocalypse (Auction 66 Ring (USA) 123) [1989 5s 6m³ 5g² 5f² 5m* 5m 5m 5s] IR 27,000F, 20,000Y: good-quartered gelding: fourth foal (previous 3 by Dunphy): dam, winner over 1m in French Provinces, is half-sister to King's Company and Deep Diver: won 5-runner maiden at Newcastle in June by ½ length from Vintage Type: equally effective at 5f and 6f: has looked bit irresolute and none too easy a ride: gelded after final start. *P. S. Felgate.*

LASER CONTACT (ITY) 2 ch.c. (Mar 28) Riverman (USA) 131–Inward Bound 86 ? (USA) (Grey Dawn II 132) [1989 8g 7m 8s] fifth known foal: half-brother to French 3-y-o 10.5f winner Bounden Duty (by His Majesty) and 2 other winners, including fair 1984 2-y-o 8.2f winner Destina (by Youth): dam half-sister to dam of Trillion, herself dam of Triptych: under 9 lengths seventh of 11 to Candy Glen in Gran Criterium at Milan in October: well beaten in minor event at Sandown and maiden at Chepstow previously. *J. L. Dunlop.*

LASERS LULABY 3 ch.f. Kind of Hush 118–Laser Song 69 (Laser Light 118) — [1988 NR 1989 12m 12f] half-sister to 1978 2-y-o 5f winner Lisa Laser, fairly useful 1985 2-y-o 6f and 7f winner St Sepulchre, later successful in USA, and winners in Malaysia and Italy (all by Comedy Star): dam won over 1¼m at 2 yrs: no form in claimers at Thirsk (fractious in stalls, pulled up as bit reportedly slipped) and Beverley (tailed off) in September. *D. H. Topley.*

LASSIA 2 b.f. (May 4) Teenoso (USA) 135–Tolmi 122 (Great Nephew 126) [1989 77 p 6g³] rangy, good-bodied filly: fifth foal: half-sister to a winner abroad by Niniski: dam, second in 1000 Guineas is daughter of outstanding broodmare Stilvi: 5/1 and carrying condition, under a length third of 16 to Roman Walk in maiden at

Newmarket in October: will be better suited by 7f + : sure to win a maiden. *H. R. A. Cecil.*

LASSIE'S HOLME (USA) 2 ch.f. (Feb 6) General Holme (USA) 128–Rich   59
Irish Lassie (USA) (Irish Ruler (USA)) [1989 6f³ 6g⁵ 8m] $50,000Y: sparely-made, shallow-girthed filly: half-sister to 4 minor winners in USA, one in minor stakes: dam poor maiden: quite modest form in maidens: stays 1m. *J. W. Watts.*

LAST DETAIL 3 b.f. Dara Monarch 128–Smash (Busted 134) [1988 NR 1989 8m   73
12h³ 12.2m⁶ 10f⁵ 16f² 17.6m⁵] 24,000F: good-bodied filly: sister to good 1m and 1¼m winner Broken Hearted and half-sister to 1¼m winner Smashing Mille (by Mill Reef): dam once-raced daughter of sister to Selhurst and half-sister to Royal Palace: neck second in handicap at Lingfield in August, hanging left over 2f out then running on well: well beaten in maidens previous 2 and final outings: suited by test of stamina: mulish before fourth start: one to have reservations about. *P. F. I. Cole.*

LAST EMPEROR (USA) 2 b.c. (Jan 16) Forli (ARG)–Image Intensifier (USA)   85
(Dancer's Image (USA)) [1989 5v⁶ 6m³ 6m* 6f⁵ 7g⁴] $21,000Y: useful-looking colt: half-brother to 3 winners in USA, including very smart Alabama Nana (by Thatching), successful at up to 9f: dam 7.1f winner at 3 yrs in Ireland: fair performer: won maiden race at Phoenix Park by a neck from Janubi: weakened quickly 2f out and tended to hang in Chesham Stakes (moved badly down) at Royal Ascot: off course 3 months afterwards, running well on return: stays 7f. *D. Cordell-Lavarack, Ireland.*

LASTING MEMORY 3 b.f. Ardross 134–Irreprochable (Mount Hagen (FR)   —
127) [1988 NR 1989 12.2d 8m 8m 10.2f] 2,100 2-y-o: workmanlike filly: moderate mover: first reported foal: dam Irish 3-y-o 9f winner on only start: no sign of ability, including in seller: sold to join R. Frost 1,800 gns Doncaster June Sales. *D. W. Chapman.*

LATE CUT 4 b.g. Tap On Wood 130–Sometime Lucky 89 (Levmoss 133) [1988   71
10g⁴ 12f² 12m³ 12g 14g² 14m⁴ 12f⁴ 19m4 14.6g⁵ 14f 10m 12f 16m 15.3f² 19f* 20f*] angular, useful-looking gelding: moderate mover, with a markedly round action: modest performer: 2-length winner of £7,400 Pimm's Goodwood Stakes (Handicap) in July and Gladiateur d'Ostende (Handicap) following month: suited by an extreme test of stamina: acts on firm going: lacks a turn of foot. *H. J. Collingridge.*

LATERAL THINKING (USA) 3 gr.f. Caro 133–Calpoppy 90 (Be My Guest   —
(USA) 126) [1988 NR 1989 7f] $55,000F, 56,000Y: medium-sized, workmanlike filly: first foal: dam, awarded 1m race, is half-sister to smart French middle-distance performer Mazus: 33/1 and burly, well-beaten ninth of 10 in maiden at Goodwood in May: sold 4,600 gns Newmarket December Sales. *W. J. Haggas.*

LATIN LEEP 2 b.c. (Jan 19) Castle Keep 121–Balatina 85 (Balidar 133) [1989   53
a6g⁶ a6g⁵ a7g⁶] smallish colt: third foal: brother to 3-y-o Casbatina, 6f seller winner at 2 yrs, and half-brother to 6f winner Count Me Out (by Vaigly Great): dam sprint handicapper: plating-class maiden: probably stays 7f. *J. Pearce.*

LATVIAN 2 gr.c. (Mar 8) Rousillon (USA) 133–Lorelene (FR) 97 (Lorenzaccio   74 P
130) [1989 8g] strong, leggy colt: seventh foal: half-brother to fairly useful 1m winner Ladrone (by High Top) and quite modest 1½m winner Leon (by Niniski) also successful over jumps: dam won 4 times from 1¼m to 1½m and was second in Ebor: 33/1, very backward and green, most promising 14 lengths seventh of 16 to Belmez in minor event at Newmarket in November, running on strongly under very considerate handling having been well behind after very slow start: sure to improve considerably, and win races. *L. Cumani.*

LAUGHING HOME 4 gr.f. Tickled Pink 114–Grey Home 110 (Habitat 134)   —
[1988 7m⁶ 7.6m⁵ 7g³ 7g⁶ 6g² 7m² 7m 7.3m 6m⁴ 1989 6h⁵ 7f 6m⁶ 6f] small filly: quite modest maiden as 3-y-o: little worthwhile form in 1989: stays 7f: acts on top-of-the-ground. *R. Akehurst.*

LAURA DEAR (USA) 3 b.f. Lypheor 118–Laura's Jet (USA) (Wajima (USA))   79 d
[1988 NR 1989 10f³ 12f 10m³ 10f³] rangy filly: third foal: dam won 4 races at up to 9f, including in stakes company: modest maiden: ran poorly second (ridden by 7-lb claimer) and final (visored and found little, in July) starts: stays 1¼m well: seems one to be wary of. *M. R. Stoute.*

LAURIES CRUSADOR 4 b.c. Welsh Pageant 132–Square Note 85 (High Top   106 ?
131) [1988 12f³ 13m² 17g*¹ 16f* 19v 16m 1989 16d 16g 14m⁴ 16.2m² 20f³ 21f⁵] big, rangy colt: has a roundish action: 66/1, appeared to show much improved form when third of 8 in moderately-run Gold Cup at Royal Ascot, staying on strongly without having any chance with very easy winner Sadeem: reportedly suffered stress fracture of near-fore cannon-bone when well-beaten last of 5 in Goodwood Cup

489

month later: suited by extreme test of stamina: acts well on firm going and is unsuited by heavy: equipped with severe noseband third to fifth outings: taken down early first occasion. *R. Boss.*

LAVA FALLS (USA) 3 b. or br.c. Riverman (USA) 131–In Triumph (USA) 79 (Hoist The Flag (USA)) [1988 6g2 1989 8.2g* 10m3 9g 7g] close-coupled, rather leggy colt: has a short, roundish action: easily landed odds in maiden at Hamilton in September: ran well in quite valuable handicaps at Ascot (ridden by 5-lb claimer) and York (found little off bridle) next 2 starts: may well prove best at about 1m: sold 17,000 gns Newmarket December Sales. *W. Hastings-Bass.*

LA VIE EN PRIMROSE 4 br.f. Henbit (USA) 130–Skhiza 63 (Targowice — (USA) 130) [1988 10s4 10g* 10.5g6 12f 1989 10s 10f5 7g 10m5 10.5m 10g] leggy, lengthy filly: 33/1-winner of slowly-run Crawley Warren Pretty Polly Stakes at Newmarket as 3-y-o: behind in varied events subsequently: stays 1¼m. *C. E. Brittain.*

LA VISIR (USA) 3 b.f. Sir Ivor 135–Vireo (USA) (True Knight (USA)) [1988 NR 97 1989 10g 12g3 12m4 10s 18g* 14s4] $120,000F: big, leggy filly: has a round action: fifth reported foal: half-sister to useful 15.5f to 19f winner Careo (by Caro) and winners in USA by Master Derby and Quack: dam, 1m winner, is half-sister to high-class middle-distance performer Native Courier: favourite, set fair bit to do when winning handicap at Nottingham in October: very good fourth to Heart of Groom in Group 3 event at Rome following month: suited by test of stamina: acts on soft ground. *J. L. Dunlop.*

LAVROSKY (USA) 5 b.g. Nijinsky (CAN) 138–Just A Game 108 (Tarboosh 62 (USA)) [1988 10.2s 11.7d4 11.7g3 11.7m2 12d 1989 8.3m 8.3m 10g 12g4] lengthy, rather finely-made gelding: has been pin-fired: moderate mover: quite modest maiden on flat: backed at long odds, form as 5-y-o only in Leicester handicap (wandered under pressure) on final outing: suited by enterprising tactics and strong pace at 1½m and will stay further: acts on top-of-the-ground and heavy going: usually bandaged nowadays: lacks a turn of foot: has joined B. Stevens: winning novice hurdler/chaser. *G. Lewis.*

LAWHILL 3 b.c. Lomond (USA) 128–Fair Abode (Habitat 134) [1988 7m3 7m4 — 1989 10.6g] strong, lengthy, good-topped colt: modest form in maidens as 2-y-o: edgy and moved moderately down when shaping quite well at Haydock in June, only start in 1989: stays 10.6f: sold 6,000 gns Newmarket Autumn Sales. *A. C. Stewart.*

LAWNSWOOD JUNIOR 2 gr.c. (May 6) Bairn (USA) 126–Easymede 85 76 (Runnymede 123) [1989 5f 5.8m2 5m3 7m* 7m 8g 7g4] 5,200Y: workmanlike colt: moderate mover: half-brother to 3-y-o 1¼m seller winner Trip The Daisey (by Touching Wood), 1m winner Windmede (by Windjammer) and 2 other winning platers: dam 6f winner: well-backed 5/2, won maiden auction race at Doncaster in July by 4 lengths from Puligny: suited by 7f. *R. Hollinshead.*

LAW STUDENT 2 ch.f. (May 4) Precocious 126–Star Court 102 (Aureole 132) — p [1989 7g] useful-looking filly: seventh foal: half-sister to 5 winners, including Ribblesdale Stakes winner Queen Midas (by Glint of Gold) and useful 1978 2-y-o 7f winner Etoile des Indes (by Kashmir II): dam, half-sister to Abwah and Owen Dudley, won over 7f at 3 yrs: 16/1, prominent to halfway in 24-runner maiden at Newmarket in November. *P. T. Walwyn.*

LAXEY BAY 2 b.c. (Mar 1) Caerleon (USA) 132–Franconia (AUS) (Rheingold 90 137) [1989 7.3g6 7g3 7m2 8f* 10g3] compact, workmanlike colt: moderate walker: good mover: fourth foal: closely related to winner in Italy by Golden Fleece and half-brother to Irish 3-y-o 9f winner Spanish Head (by Sadler's Wells): dam, winner 3 times in Australia, is half-sister to No Lute and River Lady: odds on, won 5-runner maiden at Newcastle in October by 6 lengths from Tory Conquest, making all and quickening well approaching final furlong: creditable third of 13 to Rock Hopper in listed race at Newmarket following month: will stay 1½m. *B. W. Hills.*

LAZAZ (USA) 4 ch.c. Blushing Groom (FR) 131–Lodeve (Shoemaker 121) [1988 113 8g2 10.4s* 10.2f* 12f4 11.1g4 11s3 1989 10d* 13.4f2 12g 10m3 13.4m2 14d3 12v5] leggy, close-coupled colt: has a long, quite powerful action: smart at his best: landed the odds in minor event at Pontefract in April: close second at Chester to Mountain Kingdom in slowly-run 3-runner Ormonde EBF Stakes (tried to bite winner 1f out) and to Nemesia in listed contest: creditable third to Petite Ile in Jefferson Smurfit Memorial Irish St Leger at the Curragh, easily best other effort in 1989: stays 1¾m: acts on any going, except heavy: visored once at 3 yrs and when running poorly third outing: well below form for amateur next one: occasionally sweats and gets on edge. *M. R. Stoute.*

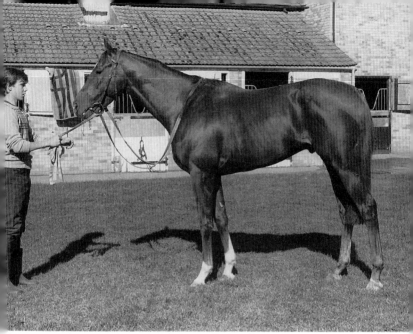

Sheikh Mohammed's "Lazaz"

LAZY RHYTHM (USA) 3 gr.c. Drone–Ritual Dance 84 (Godswalk (USA) 130) **77**
[1988 6m 7m 8g 1989 8g⁶ 8.2s* 8f³ 10m 8.3g³ 10s⁶ 8.2d*] lengthy, rather
sparely-made colt: won handicap at Nottingham in May and claimer at Haydock in
October: best form at about 1m but should stay further: acts on soft going, possibly
unsuited by firm: sold to join R. Akehurst 27,000 gns Newmarket Autumn Sales. *J.
L. Dunlop.*

LEACROFT 5 b.g. Domitor (USA) 98–Whitmarsh 56 (Hessonite 88) [1988 7.5f **52**
7.5m³ 7m 8.5f⁶ 1989 7.5g⁶ 7m 7h³ 8g⁴ 10f* 10.2f⁴ 10f³ 9m⁶ 9f] good-bodied gelding:
carries plenty of condition: moderate mover: 16/1, well ridden by 5-lb claimer when
winning 12-runner handicap at Redcar in July: ran well in similar events next 3
outings: stays 1¼m: acts on firm going: probably best with tender handling. *W. W.
Haigh.*

LEADING GUEST 4 b.g. What A Guest 119–Light House (Primera 131) [1988 **54**
10.8d³ 11.7g 10f³ 8f³ 8h³ 8.2g² 10f² 10m⁴ 1989 10.8s 11.7d 10.8d 9f 8f 10f²] big,
lengthy gelding: has a round action: modest maiden as 3-y-o: easily best effort in
1989 in seller on final outing: suited by 1m to 1¼m and forcing tactics: acts on hard
going: bandaged and taken down very quietly fourth start: trained until after then by
C. Hill: has run creditably for amateur: occasionally on toes. *R. J. Hodges.*

LEAH JAY 2 ch.c. (May 15) Sayyaf 121–Patriots Day (Red Regent 123) [1989 6g] **—**
IR 4,000F, 8,000Y: second foal: dam Irish 1¾m winner at 4 yrs: 50/1, soundly beaten
in 15-runner maiden at Folkestone in October. *E. A. Wheeler.*

LEARYCAL (USA) 2 br.f. (Apr 24) Lear Fan (USA) 130–Gracious Lassie
(Kalamoun 129) [1989 8g⁴ 8m] fifth foal: half-sister to 3 winners, notably useful
French 3-y-o Oczy Czarnie (by Lomond), successful at 6f (at 2 yrs) and 7f: dam
French 2-y-o 5f winner, is daughter of half-sister to Gold River: in frame in
newcomers race at Saint-Cloud in September and Prix des Reservoirs (2 lengths

491

third to Golden Era) at Longchamp in October: may stay 1¼m. *J. E. Hammond, France.*

LEAVE IT TO LIB   2 b.f. (Mar 3) Tender King 123–Nuit de Vin (Nebbiolo 125) [1989 6g² 6f² 5m³ 6f⁵ 6g⁶] 6,600F: medium-sized, sparely-made filly: second reported foal: dam, ran only at 3 yrs when placed at 7f, is half-sister to useful 1975 2-y-o 6f winner Night Vision and high-class 1¼m performer Take A Reef: quite modest maiden: will probably stay 7f. *P. Calver.*   62

LE CHIC   3 b.g. Kabour 80–Boom Shanty 66 (Dragonara Palace (USA) 115) [1988 5g 5g 1989 5m 5m 5.1g⁵ 5g 5f] strong, workmanlike gelding: plating-class maiden: mainly faced stiff tasks in 1989: speedy, and will prove best over 5f: got loose from stalls and withdrawn third intended outing: blinkered final start. *D. W. Chapman.*   56

LEDSHAM   4 b.g. Gorytus (USA) 132–Concert (Appiani II 128) [1988 11f⁵ 12f 1989 12g 12g] quite good-topped gelding: plating-class maiden: not seen out as 3-y-o after June: backward, held up and never a threat in handicaps at Pontefract in 1989. *M. J. Camacho.*   —

LEENAN BAY   2 b.g. (Apr 25) Mummy's Treasure 84–Ottavia Abu (Octavo (USA) 115) [1989 5m⁴ 6m 6d⁶ 6m 8m⁵] IR 8,800Y: leggy, unfurnished gelding: first reported foal: dam poor maiden on flat and over hurdles in Ireland: fair plater: stays 1m: has twice hung right. *R. Hannon.*   51

LEFT RIGHT   6 b.m. Marching On 101–Beryl's Gift 80 (Sayfar 116) [1988 6v⁴ 6g* 6g⁶ 6m 6m³ 5f⁵ 6s² 6d 6m 5g 6d 5v* 1989 6s 6d 5f⁶ 6m⁵ 6f 5g⁴ 5m 7.5f² 7.5m 6f 5g 5m 5s³ a6g] leggy, good-topped mare: poor handicapper: stays 7.5f: acts on any going: has worn blinkers, but probably best without: often sweats and gets on toes: sometimes bandaged nowadays: inconsistent and not genuine. *P. S. Felgate.*   49 §

LEGAL CASE   3 b.c. Alleged (USA) 138–Maryinsky (USA) (Northern Dancer) [1988 NR 1989 8.5f* 10.1m* 10.1d² 10d* 12g 10g*]   128

With Nashwan and Michelozzo both absentees the Dubai Champion Stakes at Newmarket in October might have been remembered more for those who didn't take part than for those who did. But, in the event, if the race lacked in quality—Michelozzo's late defection left it the first Champion Stakes since 1983 without a classic winner in the line-up—it wanted for nothing in terms of excitement and went to a very interesting prospect. The contest seemed wide-open beforehand. The market was headed by the well-bred Dolpour, winner of a listed race at Windsor on his previous outing. The equally lightly-raced Legal Case, beaten three lengths by Dolpour at Windsor, started at 5/1 along with the International Stakes winner Ile de Chypre who would have been shorter had the ground been firm. Scenic,

Dubai Champion Stakes, Newmarket—a great finish: from right to left, Legal Case, Dolpour and Ile de Chypre

Sir Gordon White's "Legal Case"

winner of the William Hill Classic, the well-backed Tote Festival Handicap winner Braashee and High Estate also started at under 10/1 in an eleven-runner field. In the race Ile de Chypre led at a good pace, whilst Legal Case was held up in the rear, tracking the favourite. Cochrane was hard at work on Legal Case some way out, and when Ile de Chypre quickened clear passing the Bushes he looked to have stolen the race. But as they came up the hill Dolpour, Scenic and Legal Case began to wear down his lead, battle was joined entering the final furlong and all four kept on splendidly. Scenic gave way close home but the others passed the post together. Legal Case, keeping pretty straight under pressure, got the verdict by a head from Dolpour who had been slightly impeded as the short-head third Ile de Chypre drifted left. Scenic was a length and a half behind, well clear of the remainder. In a year when retirements received so much adverse publicity the news that the first four home in the Champion Stakes remain in training was welcome indeed, particularly so with regard to Legal Case whose racing career was just four months old. Legal Case was entered for the Champion Stakes ten weeks before he was seen on the racecourse, a series of minor set-backs contributing to his delayed debut. It was a typically low-key start by a good horse from this stable, at Beverley where he landed the odds in a fourteen-runner maiden. Victory in a graduation race at Windsor in July was another of abundant promise rather than achievement, and it was in expectation of considerable improvement that he was made favourite for the listed Winter Hill Stakes when he was returned there the following month. Although Legal Case went down to Dolpour he had Per Quod and Opening Verse seven lengths or more behind. Legal Case continued to step up in class when he contested the Select Stakes at Goodwood in September, though arguably it was a less competitive event than the one at Windsor. Once again Legal Case was sent off favourite, and after a brief moment of concern when short of room early in the straight, won comfortably by four lengths from Greenwich Papillon, with Indian Queen a further three lengths behind.

Although his trainer had had the foresight to enter Legal Case for the Champion Stakes, the horse was not among Bedford House's eight original Ciga Prix de l'Arc de Triomphe entries. None of those made the race but after Legal Case's impressive performance at Goodwood the decision was made to supplement him at a cost of 300,000 francs (£29,200 approximately). Once again Legal Case was held up, but it barely needs saying that there is a world of difference between being last of five in a race at Goodwood and last of nineteen in a Prix de l'Arc at Longchamp. At Goodwood Legal Case had found it relatively easy to extricate himself from an awkward position on the rails. At Longchamp he was obstructed on each bend, badly checked two or three times on the home turn, and by the time a way through appeared on the rails his chance had gone. Legal Case ran on to finish under five lengths eighth to Carroll House; with a clear run he would almost certainly have been involved in the battle for the places.

Legal Case (b.c. 1986)	Alleged (USA) (b 1974)	Hoist The Flag (b 1968)	Tom Rolfe
			Wavy Navy
		Princess Pout (b 1966)	Prince John
			Determined Lady
	Maryinsky (USA) (b 1977)	Northern Dancer (b 1961)	Nearctic
			Natalma
		Extra Place (b 1963)	Round Table
			Rich Relation

The well-made, attractive Legal Case was purchased as a yearling at the inaugural Cartier Million Sale for IR 180,000 guineas. The way he's bred it's unlikely that he was acquired with the main object of winning the Million. He's the third foal out of Maryinsky, a winner in America of two races at up to nine furlongs as a three-year-old. The dam's previous foals were fillies by To The Quick: Giselle, who was placed once from eight starts, and To The Dancer who won four races at up to nine furlongs. Since being imported to Ireland in 1986 Maryinsky has three times visited Law Society—a son of Alleged. She was barren in 1987 but has since produced a filly—sold for 260,000 guineas at the latest Newmarket Highflyer Sale before Legal Case's Champion Stakes win—and a colt. The grandam Extra Place, twice a winner at up to a mile, has been an excellent broodmare, producing eleven winners, including the graded stakes winner Bold Place, herself the dam of smart French sprinter Gem Diamond. The third dam Rich Relation also won a couple of times. Although Legal Case is clearly effective at a mile and a quarter, a mile and a half should suit him ideally. The top middle-distance races promise to be particularly competitive in the next season, but this is a cracking good four-year-old in the making who'll be a force to be reckoned with in any company and he's sure to win more top races. *L. M. Cumani.*

LEGAL STREAK 2 b.c. (Mar 13) Mr Fluorocarbon 126–Streakella 79 (Firestreak 125) [1989 5m⁵ a8g] 800F, 5,400Y: leggy, sparely-made colt: third living foal: brother to 1988 2-y-o 5f winner Princess Way: dam 5f winner at 2 yrs: well beaten in maiden at Haydock in May and claimer at Southwell in December. *B. A. McMahon.* —

LEGAL TINA 4 ch.f. Ballacashtal (CAN)–Pitapat (Shantung 132) [1988 7g 10f⁴ 10.1m⁵ 1989 12.5g⁶ 10.1m] poor mover: plating-class form in modest company: bandaged twice. *S. Dow.* —

LEGIN 2 b.c. (Feb 19) Tender King 123–Burren Star (Hardgreen (USA) 122) [1989 5v⁵ 5d 7.5g 7f 7m⁴] IR 4,600Y: leggy colt: has a round action: first foal: dam lightly raced in Ireland: poor plater. *N. Tinkler.* 35

LEG SLIP 4 b.f. Dominion 123–Leg Glance 87 (Home Guard (USA) 129) [1988 NR 1989 8.5f] compact filly: tailed off in maiden at Beverley in June, only second outing: sold 1,100 gns Doncaster November Sales in foal to Jester. *J. G. FitzGerald.* —

LEIA MECENE (FR) 3 b.g. Gay Mecene (USA) 128–Dekeleia (Exbury 138) —
[1988 NR 1989 8g 10f 10.1m] 90,000 francs (approx £8,600) 2-y-o: sparely-made,
angular gelding: moderate mover: half-brother to French 1m winners by Margouillat
and Irish River and to a winning jumper in France: dam useful winner in France,
notably at 9.5f: well beaten in maidens and minor event in first half of season: has
joined Miss P. O'Connor. *R. Guest.*

LEIGH BOY (USA) 3 b.c. Bates Motel (USA)–Afasheen (Sheshoon 132) [1988 77
NR 1989 11.7d 10g 12d* 12m⁶ 15.3m² 14.8m⁶ 16.2d 14m] $30,000F, 17,000Y:
workmanlike colt: half-brother to Irish 1¼m winner On The Tiles (by Thatch), a
winner in USA by Be My Guest and 3 French middle-distance winners: dam, placed
in France, is half-sister to dam of Blushing Groom: 100/1, made all in maiden auction
race at Beverley in May: good second at Wolverhampton, easily best effort in
handicaps: should prove suited by further than 1½m: acts on a soft surface and
top-of-the-ground: sold G. Moore 22,000 gns Newmarket Autumn Sales: winning
hurdler. *R. J. R. Williams.*

LEMHILL 7 b.g. He Loves Me 120–Moonscape 87 (Ribero 126) [1988 13.4v⁶ 1989 87
13m³ 22.2f⁶ 14m] big, strong gelding: good walker: has rather a round action: very
useful at his best: lightly raced on flat in last 2 seasons, only placing third of 8 in
minor contest at the Curragh in May: well beaten in Queen Alexandra Stakes at
Royal Ascot (raced freely) and listed event at the Curragh later in summer: stays
2m, except in very testing conditions: acts on any going: has won when sweating:
has reportedly broken blood vessel over hurdles (winner at Newton Abbot in
August when trained by M. Pipe). *K. Connolly, Ireland.*

LEMON BALM 3 b.f. High Top 131–Applemint (USA) 100 (Sir Ivor 135) [1988 —
NR 1989 10d 14g] 11,500F: big filly: third foal: half-sister to a poor maiden by
Kalaglow: dam stayed 1m well: soundly beaten in late-season maiden at Newbury
and minor event (bumped and virtually fell entering straight) at Redcar: has joined J.
McConnochie. *W. Hastings-Bass.*

LENZERHEIDE 3 b.f. Tumble Wind (USA)–Centennial Rose 109 (Runnymede — p
123) [1988 NR 1989 7g 7.6m] 7,000Y: tall, lengthy filly: sister to poor maiden Amwaj
and half-sister to 3 winners, including Irish 7.5f to 9f winner Pinch Hitter (by
Auction Ring): dam 5f performer: ridden by 7-lb claimer, over 10 lengths eighth of
15, prominent 5f, in slowly-run maiden at Newmarket in April: eased considerably in
similar event at Lingfield 5 months later: may improve. *R. J. R. Williams.*

LE SAINT GERAN (FR) 3 b.c. Margouillat (FR) 133–Rain Later (USA) (Rainy —
Lake) [1988 NR 1989 a12g] leggy colt: first foal: dam, little sign of ability in 3 starts
at 3 yrs in French Provinces, is granddaughter of useful 1967 2-y-o 5f performer
Canteen: 16/1, carrying condition and moved badly to post when well beaten in
claimer at Lingfield in November. *H. J. Collingridge.*

LES AMIS 2 b.f. (Apr 4) Alzao (USA) 117–Les-Sylphides (FR) (Kashmir II 125) 70
[1989 6h⁵ 5f⁴ 6g* a6g] 12,500Y: workmanlike filly: half-sister to 3-y-o 1m winner Na
La Giri (by Nishapour), French provincial 1m winner Nadezhka (by Gay Mecene)
and useful 1986 2-y-o sprinter Quel Esprit (by What A Guest): dam, minor 1m
winner in France, is sister to Moulines: won maiden at Folkestone in October by 2
lengths: better suited by 6f than 5f. *M. J. Ryan.*

LE SAULE D'OR 2 br.f. (Mar 22) Sonnen Gold 121–Richesse (FR) (Faraway 70
Son (USA) 130) [1989 6f⁶ 8m* 7g⁶ 7d] 5,800F: leggy, sparely-made filly: fifth foal:
sister to winner in Belgium and half-sister to 9.4f winner Rabirius (by Mandrake
Major): dam ran once: 20/1, won maiden at Thirsk in September by ½ length despite
veering badly left and right: ran creditably in nursery there on final start: suited by
1m. *J. W. Watts.*

LESBET 4 b.f. Hotfoot 126–Remeta 67 (Reform 132) [1988 12s² 12d² 12m 12m —
12m 16s* 16f⁶ 1989 15.5s 19f⁶ 19f⁵] plating-class winner as 3-y-o: soundly beaten in
handicaps in first half of 1989: suited by test of stamina: form on flat only with plenty
of give in the ground, though has won on firm over hurdles. *C. P. Wildman.*

LES MAINS DOUCES 3 b.f. Free State 125–Bella Abzug (Karabas 132) [1988 —
5f⁶ 5f 6m⁶ 5.1g⁵ 7m² 8m* 7f 1989 8.2m 8m 10g 7f 8.2g] small, sparely-made filly:
quite modest winner at 2 yrs: ran poorly in varied company (including selling) in
1989: should stay 1¼m: takes keen hold: sold 1,600 gns Newmarket Autumn Sales.
E. Eldin.

LES SYLPHIDES 2 b.c. (Mar 15) Top Ville 129–Nadia Nerina (CAN) 82 60 p
(Northern Dancer) [1989 7g] good-topped, attractive colt: second foal: half-brother
to French 3-y-o 10.5f winner Nadina (by Shirley Heights): dam, 6f winner, is sister
to Danzatore and closely related to useful but disappointing London Bells: 5/1,

carrying condition and in need of race, over 8 lengths seventh of 17, not knocked about, to Starstreak in minor event at Leicester in November: should improve. *H. R. A. Cecil.*

LES TAMARIS 3 b.f. Red Sunset 120–Countess Eileen 111 (Sassafras (FR) 135) 69
[1988 8m 7f 8g 1989 12d² 12g 12.5f 12h 12m* 11m³ 12h* 13.8g⁵ 12m* 15.3f³ 18g]
workmanlike, angular filly: moderate mover: modest handicapper: won at Lingfield
(heavily backed) in June and Brighton in August and September: goes well with
forcing tactics over 1½m, and stays 15f: yet to race on very soft going, probably acts
on any other: sold 17,000 gns Newmarket Autumn Sales. *Sir Mark Prescott.*

LES YEUX D'AMOUR 3 br.f. Vision (USA)–Adorit 76 (Habat 127) [1988 5s² —
5g³ 5g* 6g 6s⁴ 5d 1989 6m 6f 5g 5f 5.3h 6f 7f] small, sparely-made filly: quite modest
winner as 2-y-o: well beaten in handicaps and seller in 1989: stays 6f: acts on soft
going, possibly unsuited by top-of-the-ground. *W. Holden.*

LET FLY 2 ch.c. (Feb 12) Kris 135–Cut Loose 118 (High Top 131) [1989 7g] — p
good-topped colt: third foal: half-brother to 3-y-o 1¼m winner Cut Ahead (by
Kalaglow) and modest middle-distance maiden Big Red (by Final Straw), latter a
winner over hurdles: dam, smart winner over 1¼m and 10.5f, is sister to St Leger
winner Cut Above and half-sister to Irish 2000 Guineas winner Sharp Edge: 25/1,
never dangerous in 13-runner £10,000 event at Newmarket in October: sort to do
better. *G. Wragg.*

LETSBEONESTABOUTIT 3 b.c. Petong 126–My Bushbaby 100 (Hul A Hul 73 §
124) [1988 5m 5m⁴ 5g 5.3f⁶ 6f* 6f* 6s 1989 8.2s 6s 5.8m* 6m 6m² 7g 6f* 6f 7g⁵ 5f⁵
7h⁵ 6g 6g³ 6f² 6f³ 6f³ 6g⁴ 5d a6g] tall, strong colt: has a quick action: modest
performer: led close home when winning handicap at Bath in May and claimer at
Nottingham in June: inconsistent but mostly ran creditably last 7 outings: stays 7f:
acts well on firm ground and probably unsuited by soft: has been tried in visor, and is
usually blinkered nowadays: trained first 12 starts by G. Lewis: ungenerous (clear
then turned it in close home fourteenth outing). *Mrs N. Macauley.*

LETS GO ALLEGRO 4 b.f. Le Johnstan 123–Fanny Keyser (Majority Blue —
126) [1988 5g 5m 6g³ 5f 6s⁴ 6g² 8.2s 1989 7d 6g 8.2f 8f 6f⁶ 8f] workmanlike filly: fair
plater as 3-y-o: no worthwhile form in 1989: stays 6f: acts on top-of-the-ground: has
run well for lady: sold out of J. S. Wilson's stable 1,600 gns Ascot June Sales after
third start. *B. Palling.*

LET'S GO BABY 3 b.f. Kafu 120–Sarah Pipellini (French Beige 127) [1988 6g —
1989 8.2s 12.2d] sparely-made filly: no sign of ability in sellers and claimer:
blinkered final start. *K. T. Ivory.*

LET'S MOVE 3 ch.f. Move Off 112–Let's Dance 83 (Mansingh (USA) 120) [1988 —
NR 1989 8m 8g 10f⁴] plain, angular filly: third living foal: dam won from 7f to 1½m:
no sign of ability in maidens (sweating) and claimer. *Mrs G. R. Reveley.*

LETTEREWE 3 b.f. Alias Smith (USA)–Princess Nefertiti (Tutankhamen) —
[1988 NR 1989 12m⁵ 15s⁵] leggy, sparely-made filly: sister to plating-class staying
maiden Letteressie and half-sister to several winners here and abroad, including
quite useful 6f to 7.6f winner Global Lady (by Balliol) and useful 1983 2-y-o 5f and 6f
Any Business (by Music Maestro), also successful at 1¼m: dam ran twice: 33/1,
about 11 lengths fifth of 7, slowly away and never dangerous, to Jehol in slowly-run
1½m maiden at York in September: winning novice hurdler. *G. A. Pritchard-Gordon.*

LETTERKENNY TOWN 2 b.f. (Mar 20) Andy Rew 103–Sudden Light (Royal —
Match 117) [1989 5g] small, good-bodied filly: first foal (a twin): dam plater: 50/1 and
burly, slowly away and always behind in 9-runner maiden at Wolverhampton in
September. *E. J. Alston.*

LEVEN BABY 2 br.f. (Jun 10) Blazing Saddles (AUS)–Farababy (FR) (Faraway 60
Son (USA) 130) [1989 5m⁴ 6m 7g⁴] 3,500Y: leggy filly: half-sister to a winner in
South America by Vitiges: dam, French 7f winner, is half-sister to very useful stayer
Spruce Baby: still bit backward, over 2 lengths fourth of 20, staying on strongly, to
Fosse Gill in claimer at Leicester in September: ridden by 7-lb apprentice
previously: better suited by 7f than shorter: can win a seller. *Mrs G. R. Reveley.*

LEVISHAM 4 ch.r. Valiyar 129–Bridesmans 92 (Jan Ekels 122) [1988 8g 10.2m —
14g⁵ 14.5g⁴ 16.5m 16m 1989 13.8d] moderate mover: poor maiden: stays 1¾m:
suited by give in the ground: sold 1,550 gns Ascot September Sales: resold 800 gns
Ascot November Sales. *Mrs D. Haine.*

LEVITT LADY 3 gr.f. Another Realm 118–My Cervantes (Hill Clown (USA)) —
[1988 5g 5g³ 5g⁴ 6f² 7m⁶ 6m 1989 7d⁵] lengthy, angular filly: good mover: quite
modest form at best as 2-y-o: bit backward, slowly away only start in 1989: suited by
6f: acts on firm going. *D. Haydn Jones.*

LE VOYAGEUR (USA) 3 b.c. Seattle Slew (USA)–Davona Dale (USA) (Best **122** ?
Turn (USA)) [1988 6g⁵ 8d* 9s⁴ 1989 8v⁵ 12s⁶ 9.2s⁴ 12f³ 9g⁵ 10g⁵ 10g] $1,500,000Y:
fifth reported foal: half-brother to minor winners in USA by Mr Prospector and
Alydar: dam champion 3-y-o filly of 1979 in USA when successful from 7f to 1½m:
won maiden at Deauville as 2-y-o: 9 lengths third of 10 to Easy Goer in Belmont
Stakes in June: other form bears little resemblance, in listed race at Saint-Cloud and
Group 3 event at Longchamp (last both times) previous 2 starts and in 3 other Grade
1 races in USA after: appears suited by 1½m. *P.-L. Biancone, France.*

LEXDEN 3 b.c. Blakeney 126–Annabella 88 (Habitat 134) [1988 7g 1989 10s² 12g **79**
12g⁵ 11.7m2] well-made colt: modest maiden: ran well in Windsor handicap final
start (May): stays 1½m: acts on top-of-the-ground and soft going: sold to join W.
Perrin 13,000 gns Newmarket Autumn Sales. *G. Wragg.*

LIANE BEAUTY 3 b.f. Castle Keep 121–Princess Fair (Crowned Prince (USA) **—**
128) [1988 6f 5g 5.8d 1989 7f 7f 10h 10.1m 8.3m⁵ 8f⁶ 8.3d] leggy filly: poor form,
including in sellers: visored sixth start: has joined Mrs S. Armytage. *L. J. Holt.*

LIBERAL LADY 3 ch.f. Be My Guest (USA) 126–Amenity (FR) 76 (Luthier 126) **76**
[1988 NR 1989 10g⁶ 12.2m* 13.3g] 24,000Y: rangy, rather unfurnished filly: second
living foal: closely related to useful 1986 2-y-o 7f winner I Try (by Try My Best),
later successful in South Africa: dam 10.4f winner from excellent family: won
maiden at Catterick in June, staying on strongly: took keen hold other starts, tailed
off in handicap later in June: stays 12.2f. *M. R. Stoute.*

LIBERTO 2 b.g. (Mar 19) Seymour Hicks (FR) 125–Countess Decima (USA) (Sir **—**
Gaylord) [1989 6f 8.2g 6g] IR 4,000F, 5,200Y: brother to 3-y-o Count Septimo and
half-brother to several winners, including useful French sprinter Miliar (by Thatch)
and useful 1¼m winner Kuwait Sun (by Bruni): dam never ran: well beaten in
maidens and an auction event. *T. Fairhurst.*

LIEUTENANT GENERAL 3 gr.g. Sandhurst Prince 128–Miscellaneous **—**
(Lord Gayle (USA) 124) [1988 5m⁵ 6f 8m 1989 10f 10f 12m] small, sparely-made
gelding: well beaten in sellers as 3-y-o: sold 1,500 gns Doncaster August Sales:
dead. *C. W. Thornton.*

LIFE AT THE TOP 3 b.f. Habitat 134–Bold Flawless (USA) (Bold Bidder) [1988 **107**
6m² 6m* 7m* 7m* 1989 7.3s⁴ 8m⁶ 10g² 10g] leggy, quite good-topped filly: useful
performer: 14/1, staying-on 7 lengths second to Braiswick in Cheveley Park Stud
Sun Chariot Stakes at Newmarket in October, best effort as 3-y-o: 25/1, well behind
in Champion Stakes there 2 weeks later: off course over 5 months after
reappearance: stays 1¼m: acts on top-of-the-ground: sold 480,000 gns Newmarket
December Sales. *A. C. Stewart.*

LIFE PEERAGE (USA) 4 b.g. Roberto (USA) 131–Countess Tully 112 **—**
(Hotfoot 126) [1988 10d 12g 1989 14.6g 14s 10.8d 10f 14.8m³ 14g] rangy,
heavy-topped gelding: virtually only form on flat when 10 lengths third of 12 in
handicap at Warwick in May: almost pulled up in seller previous outing: has broken
blood vessels. *J. Mackie.*

LIFESONG 3 b.f. Song 132–Blakesware Saint 74 (Welsh Saint 126) [1988 5g 5f **—**
1989 7g 6s⁶ 5g 5m 6m 5m⁵] rangy filly: no form (including in sellers): barely stays
5f: sold 2,400 gns Doncaster June Sales. *J. Norton.*

LIFEWATCH CHECK 2 b.c. (Mar 2) Tumble Wind (USA)–Habilite 94 (Habitat **57**
134) [1989 5h⁴ 7f⁴ 7.5f⁵ 6m 7f⁴ 7d a7g⁴ a8g⁵] IR 5,200Y, 7,200 2-y-o: leggy, rather
sparely-made colt: half-brother to several winners, including 1979 2-y-o 5f winner
Primula Girl (by Mount Hagen): dam best at up to 6f: fair plater: suited by 7f+:
possibly unsuited by a soft surface: swished tail and carried head high on second
appearance. *M. Johnston.*

LIFEWATCH VISION 2 b.c. (Apr 16) Vision (USA)–Maellen (River Beauty **90**
105) [1989 6f3 6m* 6m* 6g* 7f⁵ 6.3g⁵ 7.3d⁵ 6g] IR 5,000Y, 11,000 2-y-o: stocky colt:
third foal: half-brother to ungenuine plater Uncle Bucky (by Nishapour): dam Irish
1½m winner: successful in summer in maiden at Ripon, auction event at Salisbury
and listed race (wandered when beating Megyaas by ½ length) at Haydock: ran well
in pattern races at Goodwood, the Curragh (demoted after finishing close third) and
Newbury (beaten over 9 lengths by Tirol in Vodafone Horris Hill Stakes) on next 3
outings, moderately in Racecall Gold Trophy at Redcar: stays 7f. *M. Johnston.*

LIFFEY LACE (USA) 2 b.f. (May 11) Sagace (FR) 135–Liffey (FR) (Irish River **85 p**
(FR) 131) [1989 7m* 8.2f² 8.2s* 9s*] $23,000F, $75,000Y: smallish, leggy filly:
third reported foal: dam unraced half-sister to Godswalk: progressive performer:
successful in maiden at Brighton in September, and 4-runner minor event (by a head
from Jathibiyah, keeping on really well having made most) at Haydock and listed

Timeform Race Card Stakes, Pontefract—Light Hand lands the odds

race (by 2 lengths) at Milan following month: will be well suited by 1¼m: acts on any going. *J. L. Dunlop.*

LIFFEY REEF   3 ch.f. Main Reef 126–Sloane Ranger 84 (Sharpen Up 127) [1988   **67**
6g 6m* 5g² 6m 1989 7g 7m 8g³ 8h* 10g⁴ 7m* 8.2d² 8g4] rather sparely-made filly: moderate walker: has a quick action: won claimers at Carlisle in July and Salisbury (in good style) in August: ran well last 2 starts: effective at 7f and 1m: acts on hard ground and a soft surface: blinkered sixth and seventh outings. *C. R. Nelson.*

LIFT AND LOAD (USA)   2 b.c. (Feb 3) Lyphard's Wish (FR) 124–Dorit (USA)   **86**
(Damascus (USA)) [1989 7m³ 7g² 7m² 7f² 7m⁵ 8d*] IR 26,000Y: useful-looking colt: shows some knee action: half-brother to several winners in USA: dam never ran: fair performer: favourite, won 18-runner maiden at Thirsk in November by 4 lengths from Linpac Light, leading 3f out and running on strongly: will probably stay 1¼m: races keenly: sometimes wanders. *R. Hannon.*

LIGHT DANCER   3 ch.g. Niniski (USA) 125–Foudre 76 (Petingo 135) [1988 NR   —
1989 12m⁴ 10.8f⁴ 10f⁶ 12g 12.4g] sparely-made, compact gelding: fifth living foal: half-brother to a temperamental maiden by Thatch: dam, half-sister to smart animals Lighted Glory and Torius, won over 1¼m: no worthwhile form, including in handicaps: bred to stay at least 1¼m. *L. J. Codd.*

LIGHT HAND   3 br.f. Star Appeal 133–No Cards 109 (No Mercy 126) [1988 8m   **66**
9g⁵ 10d⁶ 1989 10m 12g⁵ 8m² 8m⁴ 10f* 10s 10f* 11g] leggy, workmanlike filly: moderate mover: quite modest performer: dropped to selling company, won twice at Pontefract in the autumn (bought in 11,000 gns both times): stays 1¼m (blinkered and raced freely over 11f): acts on firm ground and a soft surface. *M. H. Tompkins.*

LIGHTNING BYTE   6 ch.g. Ahonoora 122–Robusta (Saint Crespin III 132)   —
[1988 NR 1989 10h 7h 12h³ 16m 12h] leggy, plain gelding: bad maiden: blinkered twice. *R. Curtis.*

LIGHTNING THUNDER   2 b.g. (Mar 6) Dara Monarch 128–Royal Sister II   **52**
(Claude) [1989 7g 7d a8g4] IR 15,000F, IR 18,000Y: third foal: half-brother to high-class 3-y-o miler Distant Relative (by Habitat): dam, from good family, won over 1¼m at 4 yrs in Ireland: plating-class maiden: best effort final start. *D. Morley.*

LIGHT OF MORN (USA)   3 b.c. Alleged (USA) 138–Flaming Leaves 117
(USA) 108 (Olden Times) [1988 7d³ 1989 10.6g* 12f 10g* 10m* 10m* 9f² 9.7m
9g³ 8g*]
The five-day entry system has given the handicapper means to a much tighter hold than before, but some horses still improve too quickly for him at times. Here's one of them, Light of Morn, a strong, good-topped colt with lots of scope who was improving so quickly at one stage of the season that he managed to win three handicaps inside four weeks; he also improved so much overall that he graduated to listed and pattern company in the autumn, and though unable to do himself justice at the first two attempts he made amends at the third. Light of Morn remains in training, either in Britain or the United States. On the face of it he'll be considerably harder to place in future in Europe but there may well be more improvement to come: he's always looked the sort who'd make an even better four-year-old.

Light of Morn's winning run began in quite a competitive handicap at Newmarket in July. Not a lot was known about his ability beforehand. He'd had two outings in maiden company, beating a big field at Haydock on the

498

second; next he'd run as if failing to stay in the King George V Handicap at Royal Ascot. After he'd just held on from Marcinkus off a reduced mark at Newmarket it was reported that he'd swallowed his tongue in the King George, and for most of the rest of the season he wore a tongue strap. Wins in the Sandringham Handicap at Ascot (from Dust Devil) and at Newmarket again in an eight-runner event (from Miss Garuda), the one achieved very easily, the other with something in hand, brought Light of Morn to the York August meeting in search of a four-timer in the Andy Capp Handicap, an intriguing, strongly-contested event with a number of improving types in the field. He was unlucky not to obtain it as the remarkable Hard As Iron's own winning run continued. He found himself with nowhere to go when attempting to follow the winner through two furlongs out, and didn't get free until inside the last furlong. How unlucky he was may be judged from the fact that once in the clear he made up two lengths on Hard As Iron to go down by only a head. By now Light of Morn was beginning to look a likely Cambridgeshire type. The handicapper paid him a compliment by awarding him 9-6, as high a weight as any of the three-year-olds. Light of Morn eventually missed the race in favour of the Ciga Prix Dollar at Longchamp, where he never got in a blow in finishing seventh to Creator. Reportedly he'd been coughing since York. A modest third place to Princess Accord in the Baring International Darley Stakes at Newmarket later in October suggested to some that maybe he'd been flattered by his performances in handicaps; he started favourite and looked in magnificent condition but found little of his usual acceleration. However, instead of putting him away for the season connections chose to run him again at Newmarket in a similar race to the Darley, the Marshall Stakes in November, and experimented by fitting him with a hackamore, a bitless bridle which has been found of help to tongue-swallowers and which he reportedly wears in all his work. Light of Morn produced his best form in winning by three lengths from Just Three.

		Hoist The Flag	Tom Rolfe
	Alleged (USA)	(b 1968)	Wavy Navy
	(b 1974)	Princess Pout	Prince John
Light of Morn (USA)		(b 1966)	Determined Lady
(b.c. 1986)		Olden Times	Relic
	Flaming Leaves (USA)	(b 1958)	Djenne
	(ch 1975)	Distaff Decider	Khaled
		(ch 1967)	Lady O'War

Light of Morn would probably do well in the States. A very keen sort with plenty of pace, suited by truly-run races, effective at a mile to a mile and a quarter, proven on firm going, he'd be certain of plenty of opportunities. Light of Morn is clearly at least as effective at a mile. One might not have anticipated it on breeding, since he's by Alleged and his dam's previous foals, both by the same sire, showed more stamina than speed. The first Twenty Five Grand broke a leg while running over a mile and three quarters in Ireland on his second outing, having won over a mile and a half on his debut; the second, the maiden Ancient Flame trained by Hanbury, needed at least a mile

Marshall Stakes, Newmarket—fifth win of the season for Light of Morn

Mr R. E. Hibbert's "Light of Morn"

and a quarter. However, the dam Flaming Leaves was an eight-length winner over six furlongs at Newbury as a two-year-old and later won five races at up to nine furlongs in the States; she was also stakes placed over there. Flaming Leaves is out of an unraced mare and is a granddaughter of Lady O'War who ran three times without winning. Lady O'War's half-sister Providence was the dam of two top-class runners in France in the 'sixties, the two-year-old Prudent II and the middle-distance stayer Timmy Lad. *B. Hanbury.*

LIGHT ON HER TOES 2 b.f. (Apr 30) Cragador 110–Oscilight 112 (Swing Easy —
(USA) 126) [1989 5g 6g 7m] 775Y: lengthy filly: half-sister to modest 7f and 1m winner Norfolk Breeze (by Blakeney): dam sprinter: well beaten in varied races. *M. J. Bolton.*

LIGHT ROMANCE 4 ch.f. Be My Guest (USA) 126–Admit (Welsh Pageant 76
132) [1988 7d 10.2g 8f4 9g* 10m* 10.5f 1989 9d 12v6 11.7m2 14m* 16f4 12f 14f 12m3 12m4 16g5] close-coupled filly: usually dull in coat: modest handicapper: successful in slowly-run event at Newmarket in May: possibly best at up to 1¾m: suited by top-of-the-ground. *C. E. Brittain.*

LIGHT YOUR FIRE 4 b.f. Bay Express 132–Alumia (Great Nephew 126) [1988 62
7m4 6d2 6s3 7g 1989 6g 6g 6m 6g3 a6g a7g6] workmanlike filly: quite modest maiden: best efforts at 6f on an easy surface: has run creditably for apprentice. *W. Hastings-Bass.*

500

LIHAR 3 ch.g. Lomond (USA) 128–Mpani 97 (Habitat 134) [1988 NR 1989 10.1g — 12m] lengthy, workmanlike gelding: good walker: first foal: dam, 1¼m winner, is daughter of Cheshire Oaks and Park Hill winner African Dancer and half-sister to the dam of Inchmurrin (by Lomond): lethargic in paddock and soon some way behind in minor event and maiden in July: sold to join R. Dods 3,400 gns Newmarket Autumn Sales. *G. Wragg.*

LIHBAB 6 ch.g. Ballad Rock 122–Sovereign Bloom (Florescence 120) [1988 8s 47 1989 8f³] rangy gelding: very lightly raced: well backed when winning seller as 4-y-o: bandaged and again gambled on in similar events only 2 subsequent outings on flat: never able to challenge when third of 21 at Chepstow in September: stays 9f: acts on any going with possible exception of very soft. *J. M. Bradley.*

LIKE AMBER 3 ch.f. Aragon 118–More Fun (Malicious) [1988 5s* 5f² 6d 1989 79 5s 5s⁴ 5m 5m⁴ 5g] useful-looking filly: modest handicapper: ran badly final start (early-July): probably stays 6f: acts on any going. *Lord John FitzGerald.*

LILAC TIME 3 b.f. Town And Country 124–Harp Strings (FR) 109 (Luthier 126) — [1988 5m⁵ 7m⁶ 7m⁶ 1989 10m 12f 10.6d 12g] workmanlike filly: plating-class form at best: should stay at least 1¼m: visored second outing. *R. Hollinshead.*

LILLIEMAS 2 b.f. (Apr 6) Martinmas 128–Espiritu Santo (Pitcairn 126) [1989 5m — 6g 5.8f⁶] leggy filly: good walker: fourth foal: sister to 1988 2-y-o 5f winner Dancing Daza: dam unraced: no worthwhile form in maidens and a minor event: blinkered final start. *M. Madgwick.*

LILLY CAMILLY 2 ch.f. (Feb 13) Electric 126–Be Sharp 85 (Sharpen Up 127) 41 [1989 5g 5f] 3,000F, 4,800Y: lengthy, sturdy filly: second living foal: half-sister to a bad animal: dam 5f winner: poor form in maidens: burly and slowly away on debut: will be better suited by 6f. *Miss L. C. Siddall.*

LILY'S LOVER (USA) 3 b.g. Sensitive Prince (USA)–Rushing Stream (USA) 89 (Delta Judge) [1988 7f⁵ 7s² 7.5m² 8m² 7g* 10g⁴ 1989 8g 7g 9f⁵ 11f² 12f⁴ 12m 10f⁴ 12g 12d] tall, sparely-made gelding: moderate walker and mover: fair handicapper: best efforts fourth and fifth outings: suited by 1½m: best form on sound surface: pulled hard and ran poorly for amateur sixth start: retained by trainer 12,500 gns Ascot November Sales. *G. A. Pritchard-Gordon.*

LILY'S SUN 2 gr.c. (Mar 27) Kala Shikari 125–Lily of France 81 (Monsanto (FR) — 121) [1989 5f⁶ 6d] leggy, unfurnished colt: first foal: dam, sprinter, won twice at 2 yrs: bandaged behind, well beaten in maidens at Lingfield (sixth of 7) in May and Newbury over 5 months later. *W. G. R. Wightman.*

LIMEBURN 3 b.c. Young Generation 129–Brickfield Queen (High Top 131) 90 [1988 NR 1989 11f³ 10.1m 12d² 10m² 12g² 10g] 170,000Y: robust colt: has scope: first foal: dam French provincial 10.8f winner from family of very smart colts Lord Gayle and Never Return: second in maiden at Haydock, and £9,300 handicap and apprentice event (leading until close home) at Ascot: stays 1½m: acts on top-of-the-ground and a soft surface: blinkered last 3 starts, running moderately final one: blind in right eye. *G. Harwood.*

LINAMIX (FR) 2 gr.c. (Feb 5) Mendez (FR) 128–Lunadix (FR) (Breton 130) 119 p [1989 8g* 8d* 8m²] ninth foal: half-brother to 3 winners in France, notably good-class 1983 staying 2-y-o Long Mick (by Gay Mecene), later very useful over middle distances: dam French 6f and 1m winner: successful in newcomers race and Prix La Rochette (by ¾ length from Jade Robbery, rallying splendidly after pulling hard) at Longchamp: ¾-length second to Jade Robbery in Ciga Grand Criterium there in October: will stay 1¼m: sure to win more races. *F. Boutin, France.*

LINAVOS 6 b.h. Tyrnavos 129–Linmill 74 (Amber Rama (USA) 133) [1988 5d³ 32 5m³ 5f⁴ 5f⁵ 5d 5d⁵ 5g 1989 5f⁴ 5f] compact horse: poor performer: stays 6f: acts on firm going and a soft surface: suitable mount for apprentice: occasionally sweats. *W. G. A. Brooks.*

LINDA'S FIRST 2 b.f. (Apr 14) Welsh Captain 113–Teenager 71 (Never Say Die 42 137) [1989 5s 5d 6f 8f 9f⁵ a8g] 4,000Y: small, close-coupled filly: half-sister to good hurdler Creeager (by Creetown), also successful from 7.6f to 1½m on the flat, 1¼m winner Standon Rock (by Mansingh) and a winner in Hong Kong by Crofthall: dam second over 6f at 2 yrs: poor form in varied events: sold 900 gns Ascot December Sales. *J. Wharton.*

LINE OF THUNDER (USA) 2 b.f. (May 27) Storm Bird (CAN) 112 p 134–Shoot A Line 127 (High Line 125) [1989 6g³ 6m* 6d* 6m²]
Much has been written about the fine record of Cheveley Park winners in the One Thousand Guineas—eight fillies since the War have won

both—while the subsequent achievements of its runners-up have been largely ignored. In recent years On The House and the Breeders' Cup Turf winner Pebbles both went one better in the Guineas, while Favoridge, Fair Salinia (who later won the Oaks) and Marisela have all come second; and such as the Oaks winner Pia, the smart sprinter Kilijaro and the milers Delmora and Lucyrowe all enhanced their reputations at three having either missed the Guineas or failed to reach a place. There have been disappointments, of course, as the connections of Canadian Mill, Kingscote, Red Berry and First Waltz will be well aware. Line of Thunder, the latest Cheveley Park runner-up, has sound enough credentials to support hopes of a bright future: she showed progressive form at two, has the physique to train on, and will be much better suited by longer distances than she's had so far. We're not saying she'll win the Guineas, but we'll be surprised if she doesn't at least maintain her standing amongst the fillies.

Line of Thunder was brought along steadily, and had her first race the day after some of her rivals in the Cheveley Park had fought out the finish of the Hillsdown Cherry Hinton Stakes at Newmarket's July meeting. Considering the event chosen for her debut was only a maiden race, she was rather unfortunate to come up against the subsequent pattern-race winners Ozone Friendly and Moon Cactus, and it was no disgrace to go down in a triple photo with the fourth horse five lengths away. Line of Thunder met nothing of their calibre in a similar event at Yarmouth the following month or a minor contest at Goodwood in September, and was able to land the odds comfortably on each occasion. She was particularly impressive at Yarmouth, where she won by seven lengths despite being eased considerably, and was let down only by her appearance—she was sweating, and generally didn't take the eye—at Goodwood where she had two and a half lengths to spare over Native Twine. Line of Thunder took her place at Newmarket in October after being supplemented nine days before the race at a cost of £10,000. The subject of several large bets, she started at 10/1 in a market headed by the Cherry Hinton winner Chimes of Freedom and the Cherry Hinton runner-up and Lowther Stakes winner Dead Certain, who together with the absent Pharaoh's Delight had dominated the top fillies' races. The relatively modest early pace soon made it evident, however, that the Cheveley Park wasn't going to be a two-horse affair, and approaching the Bushes two furlongs out, where Line of Thunder was poised behind the leaders, several horses were still in with a

Beauchamp Stakes, Yarmouth—hot favourite Line of Thunder is impressive

realistic chance. As the eventual winner Dead Certain struck for home over a furlong out Line of Thunder was switched to the far rail. Her inability to find an immediate turn of foot counted against her, and though she stuck on willingly to get second virtually on the line, Dead Certain was still three quarters of a length to the good. Third-placed Chimes of Freedom as well as Line of Thunder will be seen to much better advantage over a mile or more, and the pair of them must have reasonable prospects of turning the tables on Dead Certain in the Guineas, the distance of which isn't likely to benefit the winner as greatly.

		Northern Dancer	Nearctic
Line of Thunder (USA) (b.f. May 27, 1987)	Storm Bird (CAN) (b 1978)	(b 1961)	Natalma
		South Ocean (b 1967)	New Providence
			Shining Sun
	Shoot A Line (b 1977)	High Line (ch 1966)	High Hat
			Time Call
		Death Ray (b 1959)	Tamerlane
			Luminant

Line of Thunder wasn't the only good filly to carry Peter Brant's colours in 1989; in the States his two-year-old Stella Madrid won three Grade 1 events and came third in the Breeders' Cup Juvenile Fillies. Whereas Stella Madrid was purchased as a yearling from the Saratoga Sales, Line of Thunder was bred by her owner, who acquired the dam Shoot A Line after her best racing days were over. In her heyday Shoot A Line was a top-class filly. She won the Irish Guinness Oaks, the Yorkshire Oaks, the Ribblesdale Stakes and the Park Hill Stakes as a three-year-old, and, though not so good at four, still finished second in the Gold Cup. Rather than being retired to stud Shoot A Line was campaigned in the States as a five-year-old, but deteriorated markedly and sadly ended her career a shadow of her former self. Line of Thunder is her fourth foal following two fillies by Mr Prospector, one of them the disappointing 1987 two-year-old seven-furlong winner Pamusi, and the unraced Shooting Line (by Roberto). Many of Shoot A Line's immediate relatives were in their element over middle distances. Several were at least quite useful, too, notably her half-brother More Light, a very smart colt who also stayed two miles well enough to run second to Ardross in the Jockey Club Cup. Their dam Death Ray was useful at around a mile; she is a half-sister to some much speedier animals in the July Cup winner Daylight Robbery and the very useful sprinting two-year-olds Hell's Angels and Winkie.

So far the lengthy, good-quartered Line of Thunder hasn't raced on very soft going; she showed a moderate action in her final two races, though, suggesting that she won't be inconvenienced by soft (which suited Shoot A Line ideally) if she encounters it. Whatever her fate in the Guineas it's a fair bet she'll win a good race. *L. M. Cumani.*

LINE OF VISION (USA) 2 gr.c. (Mar 30) Liloy (FR)–Invision (USA) (Grey Dawn II 132) [1989 6g6 5f4 6f2 7g] $22,000Y: rangy, rather unfurnished colt: fifth foal: half-brother to 3 minor winners in North America, one stakes placed: dam won at up to 1¼m: modest performer: well-backed favourite on last 2 starts, running well on first occasion: should stay 7f: carries head high and looks an awkward ride. *Mrs J. R. Ramsden.*   75

LINGER LONGER 2 b.f. (May 5) Auction Ring (USA) 123–Gelignite 84 (St Paddy 133) [1989 6d 6g] fourth living foal: dam won over 1¼m from 2 starts: in mid-division in late-season maidens at Newbury and Leicester. *H. Candy.*   —

LINGFIELD LASS (USA) 2 b.f. (Feb 6) Advocator–Royal Caprice (USA) (Swaps) [1989 6g 6f6 8g6 7m] 20,000F, 17,500Y: sparely-made filly: half-sister to 5 winners, notably high-class 1986 2-y-o 6f and 7f winner Genghiz (by Sir Ivor), a useful 1¼m winner at 3 yrs: dam won 3 times at up to 1m: sire very smart stakes winner from 6f to 1½m: plating-class maiden: stays 1m. *W. J. Musson.*   59

LINK MARKET (USA) 3 b.f. Linkage (USA)–Motor Mouse (USA) (Outing Class) [1988 7m 1989 8s3 10g 8.2m 9m] rangy filly: has a round action: little worthwhile form though has shown signs of ability: should be suited by further than 1m. *M. J. Ryan.*   —

LINORIS 3 b.f. Derrylin 115–Naturally Oris 52 (Lypheor 118) [1988 5g 1989 10.1m 7f6 7m 7f 8.3m] medium-sized filly: quite modest maiden: edgy, easily best effort when running-on sixth at Kempton in June: should stay beyond 7f: sold 3,600 gns Newmarket Autumn Sales. *P. T. Walwyn.*

LINPAC LIGHT 2 gr.f. (Apr 16) Kalaglow 132–North Page (FR) 81 (Northfields (USA)) [1989 5m⁴ 8d²] unfurnished filly: has scope: sixth foal: half-sister to 3-y-o 8.2f and 10.6f winner Linpac West (by Posse) and 2 other winners, including 6f to 1m winner Linpac Leaf (by Tower Walk): dam placed at up to 10.6f: 20/1, 4 lengths second of 18, keeping on well last 2f, to Lift And Load in maiden at Thirsk in November: made debut in May: likely to win a staying maiden. *C. W. C. Elsey.*   72 p

LINPAC WEST 3 b.c. Posse (USA) 130–North Page (FR) 81 (Northfields (USA)) [1988 6g⁶ 7g⁵ 1989 8.2v* 9s² 10.6s* 9f 10g³] lengthy, angular colt: poor mover: successful in maiden (easily) at Hamilton and minor event at Haydock in the spring: 20/1 and ridden by 5-lb claimer, creditable third in handicap at Redcar on first run for 6 months: should stay further: probably unsuited by very firm ground, and goes well in the mud. *C. W. C. Elsey.*   97

LION'S PRIDE 3 ch.g. Longleat (USA) 109–Stylogram 75 (Record Token 128) [1988 5m 5g⁵ 5m 6s 1989 6f] workmanlike gelding: poor mover: plating-class maiden: best effort second start at 2 yrs: blinkered, 9/1 from 16/1 but in need of race in Brighton handicap in May, only start in 1989. *P. G. Bailey.*   —

LIP SING (USA) 2 b.f. (Feb 27) Clever Trick (USA)–Spanish Tune (USA) (Drone) [1989 6g 5g³ 6g*] $40,000Y: useful-looking filly: fourth foal: half-sister to 2 winners in USA: dam stakes placed winner at up to 9f: favourite, won 22-runner maiden at Leicester in November by 2½ lengths from Vote In Favour, quickening over 1f out and staying on strongly: will improve again. *B. Hanbury.*   80 p

LIQUID ASSET 3 ro.f. Alzao (USA) 117–Golden Dividend (Golden Years 94) [1988 5g² 5m 6m⁵ 7d⁶ 7f 7g³ 7g 1989 10f 7f 7m* 8.2g² 8m⁴ 10.2m⁴ 10g³ 14m²] neat filly: good walker: has a short, choppy action: led close home in strongly-run handicap at Doncaster in July: ran well last 3 starts in listed event at Newcastle, £6,900 event at Yarmouth and minor event at York: stays 1¾m: acts on top-of-the-ground: sold 45,000 gns Newmarket Autumn Sales. *E. Weymes.*   95

LIRCHUR 3 b.f. Lir 82–Amberush 41 (No Rush) [1988 8g 1989 10g 8m 10f⁵ 12f⁵] sparely-made filly: poor form at best: probably doesn't stay 1½m: winning hurdler. *A. Moore.*   35

LISA'S FAVOURITE 3 ch.f. Gorytus (USA) 132–Milveagh 92 (Milesian 125) [1988 NR 1989 7g 8.2g⁴ 10.6g 10d] workmanlike filly: half-sister to several winners here and abroad, including useful 1987 2-y-o 6f winner Madam de Seul (by Pas de Seul) and 5f winner Coming About (by Right Tack): dam won at up to 1m: fourth in maiden at Hamilton, close up 6f and only form: off course over 5 months after debut. *A. Bailey.*   —

LISLE'S LASS 3 b.f. Magnolia Lad 102–Lisle's Filly (Burglar 128) [1988 7g⁵ 6g 1989 8h 10.2h] leggy, angular filly: poor form, including in seller. *D. W. P. Arbuthnot.*   —

LISSAHANE LASS 3 b. or br.f. Daring March 116–The Suestan 71 (Ballyciptic 122) [1988 5f 1989 10g 9f 10f] leggy, unfurnished filly: has a round action: signs of ability though well beaten in modest company: should stay 1¼m: has joined P. Hedger. *R. Simpson.*   —

LITTLE BESSIE 2 gr.f. (May 6) Carwhite 127–Top Love (USA) (Topsider (USA)) [1989 7g 6m 6f⁶ 7g] IR 3,400Y: rather leggy filly: poor walker and mover: first foal: dam ran twice at 2 yrs: well beaten in auction events and a claimer: bandaged penultimate start. *R. F. Casey.*   —

LITTLE BIG 2 b.c. (Apr 1) Indian King (USA) 128–Route Royale (Roi Soleil 125) [1989 6g⁴ 7g] IR 4,200F, 9,600Y: close-coupled, useful-looking colt: half-brother to 4 winners, including 1983 2-y-o 6f winner Iran Flyer and Irish 1¾m winner Persian Caprice (both by Persian Bold): dam never ran: quite modest form in late-season maidens won by Childrey at Folkestone and Rami at Newmarket: will stay 1m. *R. Boss.*   68

LITTLE CORPORAL 2 b.c. (Feb 15) Music Boy 124–Amina 80 (Brigadier Gerard 144) [1989 6g⁴ 6d² 6g³] 6,600Y: workmanlike, deep-girthed colt: fourth foal: half-brother to a winner in Italy by Dance In Time and disappointing Khorevo (by Tyrnavos): dam, 1¼m winner, is sister to Cheshire Oaks and Lancashire Oaks winner Princess Eboli: modest form in maidens and a claimer: will be better suited by 7f: sold 13,000 gns Newmarket Autumn Sales. *L. Cumani.*   75

LITTLEDALE (USA) 3 b.c. Lypheor 118–Smeralda 105 (Grey Sovereign 128§) [1988 NR 1989 8g³] $50,000Y, resold 84,000Y: lengthy, rather sparely-made colt: half-brother to several winners, including fairly useful 1982 2-y-o 7f winner Toveris   81

(by Homing) and fair middle-distance performer Jorgue Miguel (by Welsh Pageant), and to the dam of Royal Heroine (by Lypheor), a good 6f to 9.2f winner here later top class in USA: dam sprinter: 5/1 but bit backward, about 2 lengths third of 17 to Phountzi in maiden at Newmarket in May, staying on strongly: moved moderately down: sold 15,000 gns Newmarket Autumn Sales. *L. M. Cumani.*

LITTLE DOUGLAS 4 b.c. Lochnager 132–Mary of Scots 84 (Relic) [1988 6v 7d⁵ 7g⁴ 7m⁴ 6f 8g* 8s³ 8.2f⁴ 7f* 8g 7g 1989 7m⁶ 7.6f⁵ 8g 8g 8g⁶ 7g] strong, workmanlike colt: moderate mover: modest handicapper: facing stiffish task, creditable fifth in £9,200 event at Lingfield in June: below form afterwards: effective at 7f and 1m: acts on any going: has hung right: possibly needs to be covered up. *M. L. W. Bell.*   76 d

LITTLE GOOSE GIRL 3 ch.f. Alias Smith (USA)–Mother Goose (Absalom 128) [1988 NR 1989 10f⁶ 8.3m 11.7f 8f] 800 2-y-o: lengthy filly: first reported foal: dam never ran: no sign of ability in sellers and claimers. *C. P. Wildman.*   —

LITTLE KRAKER 2 b.f. (Apr 11) Godswalk (USA) 130–Wyn Mipet (Welsh Saint 126) [1989 6g⁵ 6m⁶ 6g] 6,400Y: smallish, shallow-girthed filly: third foal: half-sister to 3-y-o Katie Jo (by Taufan) and 1986 2-y-o 5.1f and 6f winner Victory Ballard (by Ballad Rock): dam placed over 5f as a 2-y-o in Ireland: quite modest maiden: best effort on debut: will be better suited by 7f. *R. Hannon.*   66

LITTLE POCKTHORPE 3 ch.f. Morston (FR) 125–Pink Streamer (Birdbrook 110) [1988 NR 1989 12.3m 14m] 300 2-y-o: sparely-made filly: fifth foal: half-sister to 2 poor animals by Dublin Taxi: dam of little account: no promise in claiming events. *P. A. Blockley.*   —

LITTLE RED FLOWER 3 b.f. Blakeney 126–Roda Haxan 67 (Huntercombe 133) [1988 NR 1989 10g 11f] 7,200Y: sturdy filly: seventh foal: half-sister to useful sprinter Novello (by Double Form): dam sister to high-class Pyjama Hunt: always behind in maidens: sold 1,150 gns Newmarket July Sales: resold 950 gns Doncaster October Sales. *J. L. Dunlop.*   —

LITTLE RIPPER 2 br.f. (Jan 5) Belfort (FR) 89–Harem Queen 66 (Prince Regent (FR) 129) [1989 6m* 7m⁴ 6f⁴ 7.5f 6f⁵ 7m* 6g 7m a7g a8g] 3,100Y: small, sparely-made filly: seventh foal: sister to 3-y-o Fort Regent, quite modest here at 2 yrs later successful in Italy, and a winner in Holland: dam half-sister to very smart 1976 2-y-o Avgerinos: quite useful plater at best: bought in 6,200 gns then 4,600 gns when successful at Warwick and Yarmouth respectively: ran poorly afterwards: much better suited by 7f+ than by 6f: effective with or without blinkers: trained first 8 outings by A. Bailey: tends to flash tail. *M. D. I. Usher.*   59 d

LITTLE RIVER GOLD (USA) 3 b.f. Buckfinder (USA)–Dancing North (USA) (Northern Dancer) [1988 6f 1989 8d 9f 8.2m⁶] workmanlike, angular filly: little worthwhile form, including an apprentice handicap: sold 6,400 gns Newmarket July Sales. *M. A. Jarvis.*   —

LITTLE SACY 5 b. or br.g. Sacrilege 95–Saucy Walk (Saucy Kit 76) [1988 7g 5d 6d 1989 5f 5f] leggy, lightly-made gelding: quite modest maiden at 3 yrs: no subsequent form: dead. *B. Palling.*   —

LITTLE SAFFRONS 2 b.c. (Mar 2) Hard Fought 125–Miss Pinkerton (Above Suspicion 127) [1989 5v⁶ 5m 5m³ 5f⁶ 7m⁵ 7f⁵ 6m 7f] 8,400F, 5,200Y: lengthy, workmanlike colt: brother to 1987 2-y-o 5f winner Hard To Stop and half-brother to several winners, including Tumbledownwind (by Tumble Wind), smart performer at up to 1m: dam won over 1½m in Ireland: plating-class form: best efforts at Catterick on third and fifth outings: ran poorly when blinkered or visored last 2 starts, first a seller: stays 7f: carries head bit high. *W. J. Pearce.*   54 ?

LITTLE TINKER 2 b.f. (Apr 17) Prince Tenderfoot (USA) 126–Thorganby Bella (Porto Bello 118) [1989 6f 5f 6m 5f a6g] IR 1,400Y, resold 1,000Y: compact filly: moderate mover: half-sister to several winners here and abroad, including sprint handicapper Bella Travaile (by Workboy): dam ran twice: well beaten in maiden auction races and a claimer: sweating fourth start. *S. G. Norton.*   —

LITTLETON LULLABY 4 ch.f. Milford 119–Littleton Song 73 (Song 132) [1988 7f 7f⁵ 1989 6d³ 10s 8f 10f 10m⁶ 10.1m³ 10m⁵ 14m⁵] smallish, good-quartered filly: moderate mover: poor maiden: stays 1¾m: bandaged off-hind at 3 yrs: slowly away first 2 starts in 1989: inconsistent. *C. A. Horgan.*   41

LIVELY COCKNEY (USA) 3 ch.g. Our Native (USA)–Pert Lassie (USA) (Torsion (USA)) [1988 NR 1989 7s* 7d² 8f 8d] $52,000: third foal: half-brother to a minor winner at up to 1m in USA by Proctor: dam never ran: easy winner of maiden at Folkestone in April: ran moderately in Newbury handicaps last 2 starts, ridden by 7-lb claimer and tongue tied down on first of them then off course 5 months: should   88

Tara Sires EBF Desmond Stakes, the Curragh—Llyn Gwynant contributes to a prize money total of over £850,000 won by her stable's runners abroad in 1989

be suited by 1m: possibly unsuited by firm going: sold 15,500 gns Newmarket Autumn Sales. *J. Gosden.*

LIVELY MEASURE 4 b.g. Nearly A Hand 115–Way of Life 61 (Homeric 133) [1988 7d 8m 8g⁶ 8d 8m⁵ 7g 8g 8.2d 1989 9.2f] strong, lengthy gelding: quite modest maiden at best: in need of race, always behind in Goodwood handicap in June: stays 1m: acts on top-of-the-ground and a soft surface: sometimes starts slowly: has joined N. Gaselee. *L. J. Holt.* —

LIVING PROOF 5 ch.g. Known Fact (USA) 135–Lady Esmeralda 79 (Karabas 132) [1988 8f 8s 7g 5f 1989 5f² 5m⁶ 5m] strong, angular gelding: carries condition: 50/1, first form when 1½ lengths second of 19 in claimer at Chepstow in June: not seen out after later in month: best at 5f: acts on firm going: sweating final outing: often taken down early. *J. P. Smith.* 54 ?

LIZZY CANTLE 2 b.f. (May 20) Homing 130–Muninga 108 (St Alphage 119) [1989 5f 5f⁵ 6m a6g³] small, good-bodied filly: sister to 1m winner Mr Kewmill and half-sister to 3-y-o Burning Breeches (by Blazing Saddles): dam 5f sprinter: poor form in varied races, including a seller: better suited by 6f than 5f. *C. P. Wildman.* 48

LLANDOVERY 2 br.c. (Feb 2) Caerleon (USA) 132–Copy Conforme (FR) (Top Ville 129) [1989 7m] medium-sized, quite attractive colt: second foal: half-brother to Irish 3-y-o 9f winner Frock (by Lomond): dam French 11f and 1½m winner: 20/1, prominent over 4f then eased in 19-runner maiden at Newmarket in October. *B. W. Hills.* — p

LLANGWARREN 3 br.g. Penmarric (USA) 111–Young Mistress (Young Emperor 133) [1988 5s 5.3f 5f⁵ 6d 1989 7f 5.8h] lengthy, shallow-girthed gelding: of little account: has been tried in blinkers and in a hood. *D. Burchell.* —

506

LLANTRISANT (USA) 2 b.c. (Apr 18) Private Account (USA)–Ambry (USA) —
(Gallant Man) [1989 6m] $125,000Y: sixth foal: half-brother to 5 winners, including
1987 2-y-o 1m winner Church Lyric (by Stop The Music), later successful in USA,
and American 3-y-o Wonders Delight (by Icecapade), good filly at 2 yrs: dam won
small race at around 6f and is half-sister to Hollywood Derby winner Poleax: 11/2,
over 11 lengths seventh of 9, bit slowly away and no headway final 2f, to Batzushka
in maiden at Newmarket in July. *J. Gosden.*

LLENNODO 2 ch.f. (Feb 15) Castle Keep 121–Incarnadine 67 (Hot Spark 126) 53
[1989 5m⁵ 6f⁵ 5g³ 6g³ 8.2f 6f] small, sparely-made filly: third foal: half-sister to
modest 1987 2-y-o 5f and 6f winner Roedean Honey (by Good Times): dam won over
7f and 1m: fair plater: below form last 2 starts: bred to stay further than 6f: usually
sweating and edgy. *T. Casey.*

LLYN GWYNANT 4 b.f. Persian Bold 123–Etoile des Galles (Busted 134) [1988 112
8d* 7d² 8f⁶ 7d* 8g² 8g* 8s* 9.2m⁴ 1989 9g 10g⁴ 8m* 8g³ 8.5s] lengthy, quite
attractive filly: very useful performer: won Group 3 Tara Sires EBF Desmond
Stakes at the Curragh in August by 1½ lengths from Upward Trend, first outing for
over 2 months: odds on, 4 lengths third of 5 to same filly in Mount Coote Stud EBF
Matron Stakes at same course 3 weeks later: well-beaten last of 7 in Grosser Preis
Von Dusseldorf final outing: stays 9f: possibly unsuited by firm going, acts on any
other. *J. L. Dunlop.*

LOADPLAN LASS 3 b.f. Nicholas Bill 125–Strathclair (Klairon 131) [1988 6g² —
6g⁴ 6g 1989 8g 6m 8.2d 10g 12g] leggy, narrow filly: quite modest as 2-y-o: well
beaten in 1989, including in sellers: bred to stay middle distances: blinkered and
edgy final start: twice reluctant at stalls. *C. B. B. Booth.*

LOADSAMONEY 3 b.g. Gypsy Castle 96–Ladyville (Lord Nelson (FR) 107) —
[1988 8g 7d 6d 1989 a10g] good-topped gelding: has a round action: no worthwhile
form in varied events. *D. J. G. Murray-Smith.*

LOBRIC 4 b.g. Electric 126–Light O'Battle 97 (Queen's Hussar 124) [1988 10f² 76
12f⁴ 12f⁵ 10.2m⁴ 7f 1989 14.6g³] workmanlike gelding: quite modest maiden: stays
1¾m: acts on any going: looked none too keen only outing at 4 yrs: active type. *J. R.
Jenkins.*

LOCAL COUNCIL 2 ch.c. (Feb 27) Local Suitor (USA) 128–Hants 111 (Exbury 56
138) [1989 7m 10g] rangy colt: has scope: half-brother to several winners, including
very useful 6f to 1m winner Potemkin (by Sir Gaylord), later winner in USA, and
very useful 7f and 1½m winner Tants (by Vitiges): dam won 4 times at about 1¼m:
plating-class form in maiden (favourite) at Newmarket and minor event (never
travelling well after slow start) at Nottingham: sold 6,400 gns Doncaster November
Sales. *W. Jarvis.*

LOCALITY 4 b.f. Lochnager 132–Declamation 93 (Town Crier 119) [1988 8g 8g 52
8g³ 7m 8g² 8d³ 9s⁵ 9s² 8.2s² 9f 1989 10f⁶ 12f⁵ 12.8m⁶ 12.4m⁵ 11f³ 10m⁵ 12.3m 12d
12g 11s³ 10v 12d] close-coupled, heavy-topped filly: plating-class maiden: brought
down final outing: probably stays 1½m: acts on any going: has run creditably for
apprentice. *Don Enrico Incisa.*

LOCAL TALENT (USA) 3 b.c. Northern Dancer–Home Love (USA) (Vaguely 122
Noble 140) [1988 6s* 6m⁴ 6d⁴ 8m* 8s⁴ 1989 9.2s² 9.2g*] sixth foal: half-brother to

Prix Jean Prat, Longchamp—biggest success in the short-lived career of Local Talent

Sheikh Mohammed's "Local Talent"

4 winners, most notably high-class 1984 2-y-o Local Suitor (by Blushing Groom): dam unraced half-sister to very smart Sportin' Life and good filly Folk Art (both by Nijinsky): won moderately-run Group 1 Prix Jean Prat at Longchamp in May by ½ length from odds-on Kendor, leading close home: odds on, beaten 1½ lengths (well clear) by Val des Bois in 4-runner Group 3 Prix de Guiche at same course 5 weeks earlier: should have stayed 1¼m: acted on top-of-the-ground and soft going: progressive but reportedly suffered joint injury: to stand at Gainesway Farm in 1990 at $20,000 (guaranteed live foal). *A. Fabre, France.*

LOCHCROSS   3 b.f. Lochnager 132–Cross Your Heart (Busted 134) [1988 NR   65 d
1989 7d 7s 5s 7f 7.3m 6f⁴ 7f 7.6m 6f] 5,000Y, 750 2-y-o: lengthy, good-topped filly: poor mover: fifth foal: dam unraced: 50/1 and burly, form only when fourth in maiden at Lingfield in July: should stay 7f. *W. T. Kemp.*

LOCH DUICH   3 ch.c. Kris 135–Sleat 112 (Santa Claus 133) [1988 NR 1989 10.6g   81
10g³ 14g] leggy colt: brother to useful 1¼m winner Kristana and 4-y-o Kintail, closely related to 1m winner Reuval (by Sharpen Up), and half-brother to 2 other winners, including fairly useful stayer Sligo Bay (by Sassafras): dam, half-sister to St Leger winner Athens Wood, won over 6f and 1¼m: 33/1 and sweating, 6¾ lengths third of 14 to Cambo in minor event at Nottingham in October, smooth headway, not getting clear run over 1f out then running on strongly: will be suited by return to shorter than 1¾m: ridden by 7-lb claimer first 2 outings. *W. Jarvis.*

LOCH FRUIN   2 b.c. (Apr 28) Lomond (USA) 128–Miralove 91 (Mount Hagen 104
(FR) 127) [1989 7m² 7g 8g⁴] IR 300,000Y: good sort: second foal: half-brother to a winner in Germany by Henbit: dam, half-sister to Irish 1000 Guineas winner Miralla and daughter of half-sister to top-class Dickens Hill, stayed 1m but became

508

disappointing: put up useful performance when over 7 lengths fourth of 5 to Be My Chief in Racing Post Trophy at Newcastle in October, no impression last 2f: runner-up to Marienski in Newmarket maiden on debut: well beaten in Cartier Million in between: may well stay further. *B. W. Hills.*

LOCH KNOWE (USA) 3 b.c. Lomond (USA) 128–Never Regret (USA) — (Nashua) [1988 NR 1989 10g] 270,000Y: leggy colt: fourth foal: closely related to French 6-y-o 1¼m winner Straight N' Narrow (by Try My Best) and half-brother to 2 winners, including useful 1986 Irish 2-y-o 6f and 1m winner Kharshuf (by Known Fact): dam showed modest form in Ireland at 2 yrs: weak 16/1, prominent 1m when well beaten in minor event at Nottingham in October: moved poorly down and bit mulish at stalls: sold 3,800 gns Newmarket Autumn Sales. *G. Harwood.*

LOCH SPEY 2 ch.f. (Feb 23) Formidable (USA) 125–River Spey 96 (Mill Reef — (USA) 141) [1989 6g 8g] 40,000Y: medium-sized, strong, sturdy filly: first foal: dam, 7.3f winner at 2 yrs later stayed middle distances, is out of a sister to very smart Joking Apart: never near to challenge in large-field maidens at Newmarket (backward) and Leicester late in season. *G. A. Pritchard-Gordon.*

LOCHTILLUM 10 b.h. Song 132–Spring Storm 74 (March Past 124) [1988 5d 5d 52 6f 5.8f 5m 5g 5f 5d⁶ 5m⁵ 5g² 5g⁶ 5g 5.8d* 6g 5m 5m 5f 5f⁵ 5g 5d 6d 5v 1989 5.8h 5f 6m 5m⁵ 5g 5g 5f 5f² 6m 5m 5m] good-quartered horse: poor walker: bad mover: fair handicapper at his best in 1985 when winner of Portland Handicap at Doncaster: broke leg in Sandown claimer in September: suited by 6f or stiff 5f: capable of form on firm going, but very well suited by an easy surface: usually got well behind: inconsistent: dead. *J. Douglas-Home.*

LOCKHART 3 b.f. Lochnager 132–Courting Day 90 (Right Boy 137) [1988 5g³ — 5m² 5m* 5g⁴ 5f³ 5g⁵ 7g⁴ 7g 1989 8.5d 5m 5g 5f] workmanlike, close-coupled filly: moderate mover: quite modest maiden: winner at 2 yrs: no form in handicaps in first half of 1989: speedy, and doesn't stay 7f: blinkered final start. *A. Smith.*

LOCK KEEPER (USA) 3 b.c. Riverman (USA) 131–Jamila (Sir Gaylord) [1988 73 6m² 1989 8d 8.2d²] stocky, attractive colt: moderate walker: modest maiden: second of 4 at Haydock in May, leading 1½f out and edging left inside last: stays 1m: sold 4,000 gns Newmarket Autumn Sales. *J. Tree.*

LOFT BOY 6 b.g. Cawston's Clown 113–Burglar Tip 73 (Burglar 128) [1988 6g 5d 70 6m 5g 5.8g⁶ 6m⁵ 6d⁶ 5g* 6m³ 5m² 5m³ 5f* 5s 5g³ 5g 5d 5s 1989 5m² 6f³ 6f³ 6f 5f³ 5m³ 5.6g⁶ 5m⁴ 5g⁴ 5d⁵ 5d a6g6] sturdy gelding: modest handicapper: effective at 5f to 6f: acts on any going: sometimes blinkered or visored: occasionally bandaged off-hind: tough. *J. D. Bethell.*

LOGAMIMO 3 br.c. Lord Gayle (USA) 124–Miss Morgan (Native Prince) [1988 82 7g⁴ 6d 7s⁵ 7f 8g* 8m³ 9m⁴ 1989 8d 10v 10.6s 11f² 8g 11f⁶ 10.2g 12g⁶ 11m* 11f* 12.2m* 11g* 12.2g* 10.2f³ 10f⁴ 12g] rather leggy, quite good-bodied colt: good mover: fair handicapper: successful at Hamilton, Ayr (twice) and Catterick in space of 8 days in July, mostly in small fields: facile winner of trainers invitation race at Catterick in August: took little interest (tailed off) in apprentice handicap at York final outing: better at 1½m than 1¼m: acts on firm going: blinkered last 8 outings except in invitation race: retained by trainer 19,000 gns Doncaster November Sales. *N. Tinkler.*

LOGICAL LADY 2 b.f. (Feb 17) Tina's Pet 121–Lady Andrea (Andrea 78 Mantegna) [1989 5d 5d 5d³ 6f* 7f 7m² 8f⁶ 7.3v⁶] good-topped, close-coupled filly: third foal: half-sister to Likeable Lady (by Piaffer), successful at 9f and 11f: dam never ran: modest performer: won nursery at Chepstow in July: length second to Hermitage Rock in similar event there following month: out of depth final start: stays 1m: acts on firm ground. *R. J. Holder.*

LOMAX 3 b.c. Lomond (USA) 128–Cornish Heroine (USA) 101 (Cornish Prince) — [1988 7g⁶ 7m² 7g* 7f* 7m* 1989 8f⁶ 7f 7g] lengthy, attractive colt, rather dipped-backed: progressed into fairly useful performer as 2-y-o: below form in handicaps in 1989: burly and well behind on last of them: should stay 1m: acts well on firm ground: blinkered last 6 outings. *G. Harwood.*

LOMBARD FLYER 2 b.c. (Jun 4) Exhibitioner 111–Quirina (GER) (Marduk 56 (GER)) [1989 7g 8.2g 8m⁴ 8.2s] tall, leggy colt: third foal: dam, winner at 3 yrs in Germany, is half-sister to smart miler Quebracho and granddaughter of 1000 Guineas runner-up Catchit: plating-class form: best effort third start: well beaten on soft ground. *M. O'Neill.*

LOMBARD THATCH 2 ch.f. (May 29) Thatching 131–Molly Malone (Bold Lad 45 (IRE) 133) [1989 5m⁶ 5d 7g] IR 2,200Y: small, dipped-backed filly: half-sister to 3-y-o Angus Habit (by Henbit) and 2 winners, including fairly useful 1979 2-y-o 6f winner Live Ammo (by Home Guard): dam half-sister to high-class performers Hot Spark and Bitty Girl: poor maiden: best effort on debut: well beaten final start. *M. O'Neill.*

LOMBOK 2 ch.c. (Mar 16) Lomond (USA) 128–Enthralment (USA) 78 (Sir Ivor 135) [1989 7g] fourth foal: half-brother to a winner in Belgium by Kings Lake: dam, winner over 6f on 2-y-o debut but well beaten otherwise, is daughter of sister to Forli: 7/1, soundly-beaten ninth of 16, weakening 2f out, in maiden at Folkestone in October: sold 3,600 gns Newmarket Autumn Sales. *G. Harwood.* —

LOMOND LADY 2 b.f. (Mar 13) Lomond (USA) 128–Miellita 98 (King Emperor (USA)) [1989 6g] angular filly: sixth foal: half-sister to middle-distance winner In The Shade (by Bustino): dam won over 6f at 2 yrs and stayed at least 1¼m: 14/1, never better than mid-division in 23-runner maiden at Newbury in August. *I. A. Balding.* — p

LOMPOA 3 b.f. Lomond (USA) 128–Whampoa (FR) (Wittgenstein (USA) 123) [1988 NR 1989 7m 6s6] 350,000 francs (approx £33,400) 2-y-o: fourth foal: half-sister to French 1m and 9f winner Lucky Wampoa (by Nice Havrais): dam unplaced at 3 yrs and 4 yrs in France: behind in maiden (headstrong and tailed off) and minor event in September. *J. Berry.* —

LONDON LOUISE 3 b.f. Ile de Bourbon (USA) 133–Miss St James's 92 (Sovereign Path 125) [1988 NR 1989 10f3 12m a12g2 a10g] 2,500Y: leggy, lightly-made filly: moderate walker: second foal: dam 2-y-o 6f and 7f winner, once-raced at 3 yrs: placed in maiden (very green) at Nottingham and claimer at Lingfield: showed nothing otherwise: bandaged behind final start: probably stays 1½m. *R. J. R. Williams.* 58

LONDON SOCIETY 2 b.f. (Mar 2) Law Society (USA) 130–Tenea (Reform 132) [1989 6f4] 27,000Y: lengthy, quite attractive filly: half-sister to 2 winners in Ireland by Golden Fleece, notably fairly useful 1987 2-y-o 1m winner Gold Discovery: dam once-raced half-sister to numerous winners, including Tolmi, Tachypous, Tromos and Tyrnavos: favourite but better for race and green, around 13 lengths fourth of 5, soon pushed along, to Star Hill in maiden at Goodwood in June. *R. Hannon.* —

LONDON STANDARD 4 b.g. Shack (USA) 118–Red Realm (Realm 129) [1988 6g2 6d6 6m6 6g5 7m4 8.2g5 7d6 7f2 7f 7g 7.6d 6d2 1989 6d6 6f 7f] leggy, narrow gelding: irresolute maiden: suited by 6f to 7f: acts on any going: usually blinkered nowadays. *P. Mitchell.* — §

LONDON WINDOWS 7 b.g. Balliol 125–Chebs Lass 84 (Chebs Lad 120) [1988 NR 1989 8m 10.1m 10f 10h6 10m6 10f 8f 11f2 12g* 12f3 10m 12f4 11.7m] tall gelding: poor handicapper: won slowly-run event at Doncaster in June: below that form afterwards: seems to stay 1½m: acts on firm going: blinkered or visored 4 times: sold 2,300 gns Newmarket September Sales: resold 4,200 gns Doncaster November Sales: winning chaser with D. Williams. *D. T. Thom.* 34

LONELY LASS 3 b.f. Headin' Up–Lonely Dawn (USA) 63 (Plenty Old (USA)) [1988 5g6 6v 1989 6m 5m2 6g] lengthy, rather sparely-made filly: form only in maiden at Warwick and handicap at Hamilton last 2 starts: stays 6f. *L. J. Barratt.* 53

LONELY STREET 8 b.m. Frimley Park 109–Abalone (Abwah 118) [1988 5s* 6d* 6g5 5d4 5g 6g5 6f 5g 5s 1989 6v2 6g5 5s3 6f4 6f 6f6 6f 5g6 5g5 6s 6d 6v] plain, close-coupled mare: usually dull in coat: fair performer: in frame in handicaps in spring: generally well below form afterwards: better suited by 6f than 5f: well suited by plenty of give in the ground: has sweated: has worn blinkers and a visor, but not for some time: excellent mount for apprentice. *P. J. Arthur.* 87

LONE RUNNER 3 br.c. Chief Singer 131–Helpless Haze (USA) 87 (Vaguely Noble 140) [1988 6g 6g3 7g3 7g* 6.3d2 7g 7d* 1989 7v2 7v3 8d5 10m4 10m2 12m* 9m2 10d3 14g*] useful Irish colt: won listed Ulster Harp Derby (making most) at Down Royal in July and minor event (odds on) at Phoenix Park in August: about 1½ lengths third to Gran Alba in listed race at Phoenix Park in between: probably best at 1½m+: yet to race on very firm going, acts on any other: blinkered third start. *D. K. Weld, Ireland.* 109

LONG ARM OF TH'LAW 3 ch.g. Longleat (USA) 109–Burglar Tip 73 (Burglar 128) [1988 5d6 5m4 5g6 5f4 5h6 6g2 5g* 6f 5m6 1989 5m2 5m 6m 6g3 6s 5s a7g] rather leggy, close-coupled gelding: modest performer: easily best efforts as 3-y-o when placed in minor event (ruining chance by hanging right) at Edinburgh and claimer and minor event at Hamilton: stays 6f: acts on top-of-the-ground and soft going: best in blinkers. *W. J. Pearce.* 61

LONG ARROW 3 ch.f. Longleat (USA) 109–Western Vale (Milesian 125) [1988 5m 5g 6g5 1989 8d] neat filly: of little account. *D. C. Tucker.* —

LONG BAY 7 b.h. Song 132–Sundream (Petingo 135) [1988 7m² 8d 1989 10.2g 33 8.2f⁵ 8m 7.6h⁵ 10m³ 10g⁶ 10h⁵ 7g* 7g 8f⁵] sturdy, workmanlike horse: carries condition: moderate mover: poor performer: led close home when winning apprentice handicap at Lingfield in August: effective at 7f and stays 1¼m: acts on firm going: has worn blinkers. *H. J. Collingridge.*

LONGDRUM 2 ch.c. (Apr 1) Sayf El Arab (USA) 127–Geppina Umbra (Sheshoon 46 132) [1989 6m³ 6f⁶] tall, strong, rangy colt: half-brother to 3-y-o Glen Nova (by Glenstal) and 3 winners abroad: dam, half-sister to good Italian performers Guido Lord and Giadolino, won twice at 3 yrs in Italy: poor form in summer maidens at Salisbury (needed race, last of 3) and Lingfield. *M. J. Fetherston-Godley.*

LONG ISLAND 2 b.f. (Mar 13) Law Society (USA) 130–Palm Dove (USA) 86 (Storm Bird (CAN) 134) [1989 5v⁵ 6m* 6g⁴ 6f⁴ 7m* 7m² 7m³ 7g 8g⁶] leggy, unfurnished filly: first foal: dam twice-raced daughter of good 2-y-o 6f and 7f stakes winner Prayers 'n Promises, a half-sister to Little Current: ridden by apprentice, won minor events at Catterick in May and Warwick in July: improved afterwards, running very well when 12 lengths sixth of 16 to Belmez in minor event at Newmarket in November: may well stay further than 1m. *N. A. Callaghan.*

LONG ISLAND BOY 5 ch.g. Assert 134–Lady of Cornwall (USA) 85 (Cornish —
Prince) [1988 NR 1989 10s] lengthy gelding: first foal: dam, winner at up to 10.4f, is daughter of very smart stakes winner Molly Ballantine: 50/1, unseated rider in stalls when tailed off in ladies race at Nottingham in March. *C. Holmes.*

LONGLYN 2 b.f. (Mar 10) Longleat (USA) 109–Quenlyn (Welsh Pageant 132) —
[1989 5m 5m] 4,100Y: half-sister to modest 5f winner Roxby Melody (by Song) and a winner in Belgium by Absalom: dam ran 3 times at 2 yrs: backward, well beaten in maiden at Lingfield and auction event at Redcar in September. *W. Carter.*

LONGSHOREMAN 2 gr.g. (Feb 26) Longleat (USA) 109–Cabotage 54 (Sea 74 Hawk II 131) [1989 6m 7m³ 8.5f² 7g 7d] sturdy gelding: eighth foal: half-brother to 6f and 15f winner Curricle (by Hotfoot) and 1¼m winner Cabalistic (by Gunner B): dam poor maiden: modest maiden: below form in nurseries last 2 starts: stays 8.5f: blinkered first start: subsequently gelded. *R. F. Johnson Houghton.*

LONGSLEEVES 3 b.c. Move Off 112–Red Jeans 73 (Manacle 123) [1988 8g 1989 66 10s 8.5g⁴] smallish, sparely-made colt: quite modest maiden: fourth at Beverley in May: may prove best over 1m. *W. A. O'Gorman.*

LONG TALL SALLY 3 b.f. Adonijah 126–Double Shuffle 103 (Tachypous 128) 51 [1988 6g⁴ 1989 10.1m⁵ 10m⁴ 10g⁵ 12g] tall, leggy filly: plating-class maiden: worthwhile form only when staying on in slowly-run claimer at Goodwood third start: unseated rider before start second outing: stays 1¼m (led long way in amateurs handicap over 1½m): possibly unsuited by top-of-the-ground. *R. Curtis.*

LOOK AT ME NOW 3 b.f. Blushing Scribe (USA) 107–Shortigal (Galivanter —
131) [1988 7m 1989 7d 5m 7.5d 6m 9f 6f 8g] leggy, sparely-made filly: little sign of ability, including in sellers. *B. Richmond.*

LOOTING (USA) 3 b. or br.g. Pirate's Bounty (USA)–Bank Examiner (USA) 76 (Buckfinder (USA)) [1988 6f⁵ 6f* 6g⁴ 1989 7m 6m 7.6f a8g⁶ a6g*] strong, good-looking gelding: form at 3 yrs only when winning claimer (well-backed favourite) at Lingfield in December: best form at 6f: bought out of W. Jarvis' stable 16,500 gns Newmarket September Sales after second start. *R. J. O'Sullivan.*

LORD BALMERINO (USA) 3 ch.c. The Minstrel (CAN) 135–Exit Smiling 88 p (USA) (Stage Door Johnny) [1988 7m² 1989 12m² 10f* 12.5f*] well-made colt: good mover: odds on, successful in small fields for Brighton maiden in September and slowly-run minor event (pulling very hard early and leading 7f out) at Wolverhampton in October: carried head to one side and didn't find great deal off bridle on reappearance: will be suited by stronger pace over 1½m: acts on firm going: sometimes on toes. *G. Harwood.*

LORD BERTIE (USA) 2 b.c. (Mar 8) Roberto (USA) 131–Honorine (USA) 78 p (Blushing Groom (FR) 131) [1989 6f 6m⁴ 8.2d²] $60,000F, IR 105,000Y: close-coupled, quite attractive colt: moderate walker: second foal: dam placed at 1m in France: 12/1, ¾-length second of 11, running on strongly final furlong, to Laird of Balmoral in minor event at Haydock in September: will stay 1¼m: likely to improve bit further, and win a race. *J. Sutcliffe.*

LORD DAVID S (USA) 3 b.c. Nijinsky (CAN) 138–Mirthful Flirt (USA) 107 96 (Raise A Native) [1988 NR 1989 8g 8m² 10m* 10m* 10.2g 8.1g] big, strong, rangy colt: has plenty of scope: eighth foal: half-brother to several winners, including smart 1982 USA 2-y-o What's Dat (by Believe It): dam sprinting half-sister to Gorytus (by Nijinsky): narrow winner of moderately-run 4-runner minor event (odds on, pulling hard early) at Ripon in August and £8,000 handicap at Newmarket in October: well-beaten sixth of 7 in £21,000 limited handicap at Newcastle: stays 1¼m well: game. *B. W. Hills.*

LORD FLOREY (USA) 2 b.c. (Mar 15) Blushing Groom (FR) 131–Remedia (USA) (Dr Fager) [1989 7m³ 7g²] $625,000Y: angular, good sort: brother to Grade 1 1m winner Too Chic and half-brother to 2 minor winners in USA: dam, winner at up to 1m, is daughter of Oaks winner Monade, grandam of Prima Voce and Sadeem: favourite, beaten a neck by Lord of The Field in maiden at Newmarket in November, pulling hard close up and leading 1f out until line: very green when third to Shavian in Ascot minor event on debut: will stay at least 1m: sure to win a race. *L. M. Cumani.* **90 p**

LORD GLEN 2 gr.c. (Feb 18) Rabdan 129–Rage Glen 67 (Grey Mirage 128) [1989 5g* 5d³ 5d⁴ 5f³ 6g 5f* 5g⁵ 6f* 5f⁵ 5m² 5s] leggy, quite good-topped colt: progressed well physically: has a sharp action: first reported foal: dam headstrong 8.2f and 1¼m winner also successful over jumps: useful colt: successful in maiden at Doncaster in April and minor events at Catterick in July: showed improved form when short-head second of 9, always close up and running on gamely, to Old Alliance in listed event at York in August: best form at 5f: unsuited by soft ground: usually keen in preliminaries and to post. *R. Boss.* **102**

LORD IT OVER (USA) 6 b.g. Best Turn (USA)–Idle Hour Princess (USA) (Ribot 142) [1988 10m 1989 10s 12h⁵ 13.8m⁴] compact, attractive gelding: poor plater: best form at 1m: acts on top-of-the-ground and a soft surface: blinkered once: visored last 2 outings: bandaged final start: has sweated: has won for apprentice. *J. R. Jenkins.* **—**

LORD MAGESTER (FR) 2 ch.c. (Mar 30) Magesterial (USA) 116–Lady Zia (FR) (Sir Tor (FR)) [1989 7m 7g⁵] 350,000 francs (approx £32,000) Y: strong, chunky colt: closely related to French 7f and 1m winner Chinguetti (by Green Dancer), later successful in USA, and half-brother to 2 other winners: dam French 5.5f to 9f winner: around 8 lengths fifth to Duke of Paducah in £10,000 event at Newmarket in October, one pace after pulling hard: shaped well, not knocked about, on debut: likely to win an ordinary race at 7f or 1m. *L. Cumani.* **73 p**

LORD OF GYMCRAK 3 gr.c. Absalom 128–Mattagirl 78 (Music Boy 124) [1988 5g 5m³ 6s 6s 1989 6d 5f] workmanlike, rather plain colt: form only on second outing as 2-y-o: should stay beyond 5f: blinkered final outings at 2 yrs and 3 yrs: sold 950 gns Ascot June Sales. *M. H. Easterby.* **—**

LORD OF THE FIELD 2 b.c. (Mar 21) Jalmood (USA) 126–Star Face (African Sky 124) [1989 7g*] 54,000Y: sixth foal: half-brother to 3-y-o Zode (by Simply Great) and 2 winners, including 6f and 1m winner Torquemada (by Try My Best): dam won over 10.5f in French Provinces: 33/1 and bit green, won 29-runner maiden at Newmarket in November by a neck from Lord Florey, running on strongly to lead line: has scope, and will improve. *J. A. R. Toller.* **91 p**

LORD OF TUSMORE 2 b.c. (Jan 29) Al Nasr (FR) 126–Princess Toy (Prince Tenderfoot (USA) 126) [1989 6g⁶] 36,000F, IR 195,000Y: third reported foal: dam won at up to 9f in USA: weak 14/1, sixth of 19, one pace last 2f, to Reference Light in maiden at Redcar in November: will be better suited for 7f or 1m: should improve. *B. W. Hills.* **— p**

LORD PATRICK 5 b.g. Formidable (USA) 125–Boldie 81 (Bold Lad (IRE) 133) [1988 7d 7m³ 7d 1989 6m 7m 8.3m⁵ 7m 7d] strong, good-bodied gelding: keen walker: modest handicapper at his best: below form as 5-y-o: ridden by 7-lb claimer, bolted and withdrawn on intended reappearance: off course 3 months before final outing (sweating): effective at 7f and 1m: acts on any going: bandaged twice at 4 yrs: usually taken quietly to post nowadays: well served by waiting tactics. *J. A. R. Toller.* **—**

LORD RINUS 2 b.c. (Apr 15) Strong Gale 116–Jamie's Girl (Captain James 123) [1989 5d 6g 10g] 15,000, 2-y-o: second foal: half-brother to 3-y-o By Choice (by Sallust), successful at 1m (at 2 yrs) and 1¼m: dam unraced: plating-class form in maidens and a minor event: easily best effort final start: will stay 1½m. *G. Richards.* **57**

LORD ROLFE 3 ch.c. Rolfe (USA) 77–Stepout 78 (Sagaro 133) [1988 10d⁶ 10.2m 1989 12.2d⁴ 16d³ 12.5f] lengthy, rather plain, medium-sized colt: quite modest maiden: blinkered, sweating and edgy when running poorly final start: stays 2m: possibly unsuited by top-of-the-ground: has joined J. Davies. *W. G. A. Brooks.* **57**

LORDSHIP 4 b.g. Lord Gayle (USA) 124–All Gold Rose (Rheingold 137) [1988 9v* 7m* 10f 8d 7g⁴ 7m⁴ 7g 9g 1989 8g] close-coupled gelding: moderate mover: fair winner as 3-y-o: 33/1, behind in 27-runner handicap at Newmarket in October: stays **—**

9f: acts on top-of-the-ground and heavy going: has run well for apprentice: sold to join M. Barnes 5,100 gns Doncaster November Sales. *I. V. Matthews.*

LORD WINDERMERE 4 b.g. Taufan (USA) 119–Repercussion 90 (Roan Rocket 128) [1988 NR 1989 10.1m] leggy, lengthy gelding: very lightly raced and no sign of ability. *J. M. Bradley.* —

LOREN'S COURAGE (USA) 4 ch.g. Solford (USA) 127–Roman Luster (USA) (Proudest Roman (USA)) [1988 12f5 12m* 1989 12m5 12f6 12m* 12g* 12.3g2 14f 12d] strong, good-topped gelding: fairly useful handicapper: justified favouritism in summer in good style in amateurs event at Salisbury and strongly-run contest at Haydock: good second to Solo Act in slowly-run £7,600 race at Ripon: should stay beyond 1½m: best on a sound surface: pulled hard second outing: suited by enterprising tactics. *G. Harwood.* 97

LORENTEGGIO (USA) 4 b.g. Al Nasr (FR) 126–Clairvoyance (USA) (Round Table) [1988 8.2s3 10g3 10m4 1989 12g 9v 12s 8g 8g5 8g3 9f 12f* 8.5m 11g5 10f6 16m3 17.6f* 17f* 16.2d 15.8g a16g] compact gelding: moderate walker and mover: plating-class performer nowadays: won selling handicap (no bid) at Beverley in August and claimer at Wolverhampton and handicap at Pontefract in October, making all in last 2: soundly beaten in handicaps last 3 outings: suited by test of stamina: best on top-of-the-ground: bought out of D. Chapman's stable 5,800 gns Doncaster October Sales after sixteenth outing. *T. B. Hallett.* 52

LORETTO COLLECTION (USA) 3 ch.c. Raise A Cup (USA)–Indian Queen (USA) (Nashua) [1988 NR 1989 8g 8g6 9f 10f 9m 9m] IR 31,000Y: angular colt: bad mover: half-brother to several winners in USA, including very smart 6f and 9.5f stakes winner Screen King (by Silent Screen): dam, placed twice in USA, is half-sister to dam of Palace Music: sire raced only at 2 yrs when high-class winner at around 5f: easily best effort sixth in Newmarket maiden in May: coltish in paddock and very awkward at stalls fourth start: trained until after fifth by R. Casey: sold to join M. Castell 1,300 gns Ascot September Sales. *R. Guest.* —

LORICA D'OR 2 ch.c. (Mar 17) Hotfoot 126–Dayana (Burglar 128) [1989 8g] leggy, angular colt: sixth foal: half-brother to a winner in Belgium: dam ran once: 14/1, well-beaten ninth of 16, never dangerous, in maiden at Leicester in November. *N. A. Callaghan.* —

LOST EMPIRE 2 b.c. (Mar 29) Lomond (USA) 128–Fantasy Land (Nonoalco (USA) 131) [1989 6g] fourth foal: dam, Irish 5f winner, is half-sister to Kingscote: weak 9/1, around 12 lengths tenth of 20, never dangerous, to Nice Day in maiden at Newcastle in October: should improve. *B. W. Hills.* — p

LOST INNOCENCE (USA) 2 ch.c. (Mar 27) Blushing Groom (FR) 131–Olamic (USA) (Nijinsky (CAN) 138) [1989 7g] third foal: dam won from 7f to 9f in USA, and is from family of Swale and Forty Niner: 8/1, slowly away and never dangerous or knocked about in 29-runner maiden at Newmarket in November: sure to do better. *M. R. Stoute.* — p

LOTHIAN 2 b.c. (Feb 18) Top Ville 129–Cojean (USA) 86 (Prince John) [1989 7g] 40,000Y: well-made, attractive colt: fifth foal: brother to useful 1986 2-y-o 7f winner Iosifa and half-brother to 3-y-o Collage (by Ela-Mana-Mou) and a winner in Italy: dam ran only at 2 yrs when successful over 5f: backward 20/1-shot, about 11 lengths seventh of 9 in maiden at Salisbury in July: looked sure to improve but wasn't seen out again. *B. W. Hills.* —

LOTS OF LUCK 6 gr.m. Neltino 97–Safe Passage (Charlottown 127) [1988 10f4 8m5 8f4 8d6 8g6 8g6 8s2 1989 8s 10.8d2 9f6 12m6 8.2f 12g4 8.2g* 8m 9f5 8.2d4 8m6 9.2d2 9g a10g] sparely-made mare: has a quick action: modest form in varied company in Britain: won 18-runner handicap at Nottingham in July: ran well when in frame in similar company after at Haydock and Goodwood: stays 11f, but at least as effective at 1m: particularly well suited by an easy surface: blinkered first 2 and last 3 starts in 1988: suitable mount for apprentice. *J. Pearce.* 73

LOTUS ISLAND 5 gr.h. Ile de Bourbon (USA) 133–Be Easy 110 (Be Friendly 130) [1988 12s2 12g 12m 12g 12m 10g2 12m 10v2 1989 12s 12m6 12g6 10f 10g] neat horse: has a quick action: modest form at best, but has looked irresolute: stays 1½m: acts on top-of-the-ground and heavy going: usually wears blinkers: sometimes sweats: usually held up: prolific winning hurdler. *N. Tinkler.* — §

LOUIS CYPHRE 3 b.c. Niniski (USA) 125–Princesse Timide (USA) (Blushing Groom (FR) 131) [1988 9s2 10s2 10g 12m3 12g5 11g* 10m 10d4 12m2] medium-sized, attractive colt: second foal: dam French 7.5f and 1¼m winner: won listed race at Longchamp in June by short neck from Borromini: ran creditably last 2 starts in Prix du Prince d'Orange and Prix du Conseil de Paris (beaten length by 122

Prix Vanteaux, Longchamp—Louveterie beats Lightning Fire (striped sleeves),
Be Exclusive and Lady In Silver

Robore, staying on from rear) at Longchamp: stays 1½m well: acts on soft going and top-of-the-ground: consistent. *F. Boutin, France.*

LOUVETERIE (USA) 3 ch.f. Nureyev (USA) 131–Lupe 123 (Primera 131) **123** [1988 8d* 1989 9.2s* 10m² 10.5d²] closely related to very smart 1m and 9f winner Legend of France (by Lyphard) and half-sister to several winners, including smart Leonardo da Vinci (by Brigadier Gerard), winner at up to 11f here and in USA, and French 10.5f and 1½m winner Lascaux (by Irish River): dam won Oaks and Coronation Cup: won minor event at Saint-Cloud as 2-y-o and Group 3 Prix Vanteaux at Longchamp in April: narrowly beaten by Behera in Prix Saint-Alary at Longchamp in May and Lady In Silver in Prix de Diane Hermes (badly hampered at halfway) at Chantilly in June: stays 10.5f: yet to race on very firm ground, acts on any other. *A. Fabre, France.*

LOVE AND LIFE 3 b. or br.f. Lyphard's Special (USA) 122–Miss Olympus (Sir **53** Gaylord) [1988 6d⁴ 6f⁴ 6m⁶ 7g⁴ 7g⁶ 8f⁴ 8.2s 8m* 1989 10m⁶ 10.2m 8f 7m 10.2h⁴] angular, dipped-backed filly: quite modest winner as 2-y-o: fair fourth in seller (claimed to join W. Turner £6,010) at Bath in June: stays 1¼m: yet to show her form on very soft going, acts on any other. *C. A. Cyzer.*

LOVELACE PARTY (USA) 2 b.c. (Apr 16) Sir Ivor 135–Unyielding (USA) **— p** (Never Bend) [1989 7m³] fifth foal: brother to 3-y-o 1m to 9.2f winner Awayed and half-brother to fair 11.5f winner False Front (by Bustino) and a winner in Italy: dam thrice-raced daughter of Irish 1000 Guineas winner Lacquer and half-sister to Bright Finish and Shining Finish: weak 14/1-shot, remote third of 6 to Candy Glen in minor event at Sandown in September, not at all knocked about last 2f: will improve. *R. Hannon.*

LOVE LEGEND 4 ch.c. Glint of Gold 128–Sweet Emma 108 (Welsh Saint 126) **75** [1988 6v⁶ 8.2v 7s 6g 6m* 6g 6g⁴ 1989 5m* 5f³ 6m² 6f 5g 5.6g 5g 6d³] smallish, sparely-made colt: poor walker: has a quick action: fair handicapper: improved form when making all at Newmarket in May: ran well in valuable events at Goodwood and Epsom next 2 outings: form after only on final start: effective at 5f and 6f: acts on firm going and a soft surface: blinkered nowadays. *D. W. P. Arbuthnot.*

LOVELY EARS 3 b.f. Auction Ring (USA) 123–Baldritta (FR) (Baldric II 131) **—** [1988 5d 5m² 5g² 5f⁶ 5m* 5.8g⁶ 6f⁴ 5g² 5g³ 6m⁴ 5m 5d 5g 5d 1989 7m] workmanlike filly: quite modest winner as 2-y-o: no form last 5 outings: stays 6f: suited by a sound surface: has run well for apprentice: blinkered once at 2 yrs. *J. P. Hudson.*

LOVELY FAIRY 3 b.f. Beldale Flutter (USA) 130–Fairy Footsteps 123 (Mill **87** Reef (USA) 141) [1988 7m 1989 11.5m³ 10.2h² 10f² 12f* 11.7f* 12m] lengthy filly: won 5-runner races for maiden (odds on) at Lingfield in August and handicap at Bath in October: on toes, faced stiff task in Group 3 event at Ascot final outing: suited by 1½m: sold 150,000 gns Newmarket December Sales. *W. Jarvis.*

LOVELY FLOWER 3 ch.f. Hello Gorgeous (USA) 128–Apricot Rose (Mill Reef **65** (USA) 141) [1988 6m³ 6f⁶ 7f⁴ 1989 7g³ 7.6m 7m] lengthy, angular filly: has a rather round action: quite modest maiden: well below form after reappearance in late-August: will be suited by 1m + : possibly best with some give in the ground: sold 4,200 gns Newmarket December Sales. *W. Jarvis.*

LOVELY WONGA 3 b.g. Tanfirion 110–Teala (Troy 137) [1988 5f 6m 6m 7f 8.2m⁵ 6d 8m⁶ 10m⁶ 1989 7s 7f 7m 10.1m 12m⁶ 12g] plain gelding: moderate mover: plater: showed little in 1989: probably stays 1½m: best form on top-of-the-ground: visored third and fourth outings: blinkered once at 2 yrs: winning juvenile hurdler. *D. A. Wilson.* —

LOVENKO 5 b.g. Relkino 131–Malicious Love 79 (Malicious) [1988 14v⁶ 16g 16.5g 16m 16f² 1989 14s 16g 15.8m 16.2m⁵] rather sparely-made gelding: has a markedly round action: poor maiden: blinkered once: sold 2,200 gns Doncaster October Sales. *R. M. Whitaker.* —

LOVE PRINCE 3 b.g. Indian King (USA) 128–Chanrossa (High Top 131) [1988 6d 1989 6v 6g⁶ 5f* 6f 5f⁶ 5g 5d] leggy, quite good-topped gelding: won handicap at Sandown in May, running on strongly to lead inside final 1f after slow start: not discredited second and fifth outings: appears suited by 5f: acts on firm going: blinkered sixth start: gave trouble at stalls at Sandown. *W. Carter.* 68

LOVE RETURNED 2 b.f. (Feb 15) Taufan (USA) 119–Miss Loving 89 (Northfields (USA)) [1989 5f² 5m² 5m⁶ 6g²] 4,500F, 6,000Y: rather unfurnished filly: moderate mover: first foal: dam, won at 5f and 7f at 2 yrs, is half-sister to several winners including useful 5f to 1m winner Cremation: fair maiden: best effort over 11 lengths sixth of 9 from unfavourable draw to Argentum in Cornwallis Stakes at Ascot: stays 6f: found very little off bridle second start. *W. Jarvis.* 80

LOVER'S MOON 2 b.c. (Apr 18) Ela-Mana-Mou 132–Ce Soir (Northern Baby (CAN) 127) [1989 7m⁵ 8g*] IR 28,000Y: lengthy colt: second foal: dam won over 11f at 3 yrs in Ireland: well-backed favourite, won 17-runner maiden at Leicester in November by 3 lengths from Sanglamore, disputing lead and running on strongly final furlong: will stay 1½m: sure to make useful colt. *G. Harwood.* 89 p

LOVERS' PARLOUR 3 b.f. Beldale Flutter (USA) 130–Ready And Willing 82 (Reliance II 137) [1988 NR 1989 7g⁴] lengthy, quite good-topped filly: ninth foal: sister to quite modest 1½m winner Butterfly Kiss and half-sister to 5 winners, including smart 1m to 1¼m performer Kufuma (by Habitat) and high-class 6f (at 2 yrs), 1m and disqualified 10.5f winner Persian Heights (by Persian Bold): dam from good family, won over 12.2f: 6/4 favourite, looking very well but carrying bit of condition, 4½ lengths fourth of 15 to Pilot in slowly-run maiden at Newmarket in April: should stay at least 1m. *G. Wragg.* 83

LOVER'S SECRET 4 b.g. Skyliner 117–Nistona (Will Somers 114§) [1988 8.2v 9m 8.2m⁶ 9g² 12m⁶ 10f⁴ 1989 9f⁴ 10f] close-coupled, workmanlike gelding: moderate mover: poor plater nowadays: barely stays 1¼m: probably acts on any going: ran poorly in blinkers. *D. R. Tucker.* —

LOVE STREET 2 b.f. (May 28) Mummy's Pet 125–Crime of Passion 115 (Dragonara Palace (USA) 115) [1989 5f⁴ 5m 5m⁴ 5m⁵] leggy, sparely-made filly: third foal: half-sister to fair 1988 2-y-o 5f winner Cardinal Sin (by Pharly): dam smart sprinting 2-y-o didn't train on: quite modest maiden: gave trouble stalls on debut. *P. F. I. Cole.* 62

LOVE TO DANCE 4 b.c. Dominion 123–Atoka 97 (March Past 124) [1988 12f⁴ 10.2m⁴ 8f* 10d* 10.1g² 12f 1989 10d] leggy, sparely-made colt: winner plater as 3-y-o when trained by N. Tinkler: bandaged, mulish in paddock and mounted on track, never dangerous in handicap at Folkestone in April: suited by 1m to 1¼m: yet to race on soft going, acts on any other: tends to get on toes: of doubtful temperament. *R. Hoad.* —

LOVING 4 b.g. Good Times (ITY)–Exquisite 80 (Exbury 138) [1988 12m² 12m² 14m 12f⁵ 12m 12m⁵ 11.5f 12g 1989 12.5f² 12f⁵ 14m⁵ 15.3m⁴ 14m 12.5f] smallish, workmanlike filly: poor mover: unreliable plater: stays 15f: acts on firm going: has been blinkered. *G. Blum.* 36 §

LOVING BROTHER SID 3 b.g. Prince Tenderfoot (USA) 126–Full of Flavour (Romulus 129) [1988 NR 1989 9d⁶ 9s 12g 11s] leggy gelding: brother to useful 1978 2-y-o sprinter Sweet And Lovely and half-brother to smart 1977 French 2-y-o Royal Flavour (by Hardicanute): dam, half-sister to high-class 7f to 1¼m performer Full of Hope, won over 9f in France: well beaten in sellers and maiden claimer, showing signs of ability first 2 starts: sweating final one: off course 5 months after debut. *C. W. Thornton.* —

LOVING OMEN 2 ch.c. (Feb 9) Touching Wood (USA) 127–Etoile d'Amore (USA) 81 (The Minstrel (CAN) 135) [1989 7g 6m 8m³ 8f 8m⁵] big colt: first foal: dam twice-raced 7f winner, is daughter of high-class sprinter Gurkhas Band: modest 72

maiden: best effort third start: shapes like a thorough stayer: sold 11,500 gns Newmarket Autumn Sales. *B. Hanbury.*

LOVISTONE 3 b.c. Noalto 120–Love Unspoken 54 (No Mercy 126) [1988 5g3 — 5m5 6f5 7g 8f 1989 6d 6m6 6m] leggy colt, rather unfurnished: quite modest maiden at 2 yrs: no form in handicaps, breaking blood vessel final start: dead. *A. Bailey.*

LOW DALBY 3 ch.f. Longleat (USA) 109–Bridestones 92 (Jan Ekels 122) [1988 **64** 7m 7m 1989 8d3 8f5 11m5 11.7m3 11.5m 10.6d5 10v4 12s3] strong filly: quite modest maiden: suited by 1½m: best efforts on top-of-the-ground: has run well for apprentice.*J. A. R. Toller.*

LOWELL (USA) 3 ch.c. General Holme (USA) 128–Lady Sharp (FR) (Sharpman **114** (FR) 124) [1988 7.5m* 8m2 8m5 1989 10s 10g4 8g 9g* 8g4 11g* 9g4] first foal: dam French 1¼m winner: won listed race at Evry in September and Group 3 event (by 2 lengths from Tartas) at Lyon in October: fourth in Hollywood Derby in November: stays 11f: acts on top-of-the-ground: trained at 2 yrs by J. Cunnington and first 3 starts in 1989 by O. Douieb. *A. de Royer-Dupre, France.*

LUAGA 3 b.f. Tyrnavos 129–Lady Rushen (Dancer's Image (USA)) [1988 5g 6d **49** 6m 1989 8m 6m 7m 9g 8f3 10.8m5] tall, leggy filly: moderate walker and mover: poor form: should be suited by bit further than 1m: acts on firm going: often sweating and edgy. *M. Blanshard.*

LUCEDEO 5 ro.g. Godswalk (USA) 130–Lucy Limelight 98 (Hot Spark 126) [1988 **68** 5g 5f3 5g3 6m 1989 6m6 5f4 5m4 5f4 6f2 5m2 5m6 5h6 5g* 5m2 5m2 5f5 5m5 5m5 6f 5f3 5m6 6f* 6m3 7m3 5g* 6g] sturdy, compact gelding: carries condition: quite modest handicapper: had very good season, winning at Wolverhampton in July and Folkestone (apprentices) and Catterick in October: effective at 5f and 6f: best on a sound surface: excellent mount for inexperienced rider: has been taken down quietly: tough and consistent.*J. L. Spearing.*

LUCK O' THE IRISH 2 ch.g. (Apr 1) Sallust 134–Sweet Hostess (Candy Cane **48** 125) [1989 7g 8.2d 8g] IR 8,000Y: big, workmanlike gelding: half-brother to several winners, including fairly useful 1980 2-y-o 5f winner Katysue (by King's Leap) and 1m and 1½m winner Mrs Pistol (by Camden Town): dam never ran: poor maiden: best effort on debut: will be better off in sellers. *N. Tinkler.*

LUCKY BARNES 2 b.c. (Jan 10) Lucky Wednesday 124–Hutton Barns 92 **75** (Saintly Song 128) [1989 5f* 6m2 6g 6g6 6g4 6g4 5m2 a6g] workmanlike colt: moderate mover: brother to 6f seller winner Wednesday Boy, a winner in Belgium and plating-class maiden Card Party: dam at her best at 2 yrs, when winner over 5f: modest performer: won 5-runner claimer at Hamilton in June by 4 lengths: very good second in nursery at Edinburgh on penultimate start: best form at 5f: effective with or without blinkers. *W. J. Pearce.*

LUCKY BLUE 2 b.g. (May 12) Blue Cashmere 129–Cooling 89 (Tycoon II) [1989 **63** 5f 5m2] unfurnished gelding: fourth foal: half-brother to 1983 2-y-o 5f winner Airling (by Import): dam won at 1¼m and 13f: always-prominent length second of 10 to Addison's Blade in maiden at Thirsk in May: hampered by faller on debut: will be much better suited by 6f. *M. H. Easterby.*

LUCKY CONQUEROR 3 ch.c. On Your Mark 125–Rekolette (Relko 136) [1988 — 5g* 6m 1989 6d 8.2m] IR 4,800Y: neat ex-Irish colt: poor walker: moderate mover: fourth foal: brother to 1984 2-y-o 5f seller winner Winning Mark: dam never ran: trained by C. Collins, won maiden at Phoenix Park in April as 2-y-o: second favourite, about 8 lengths eighth of 9 to Tantum Ergo in restricted IR £14,600 event at same course nearly 3 months later: behind in minor event and claimer in the North in spring at 3 yrs.*J. Parkes.*

LUCKY CRYSTAL 3 ch.f. Main Reef 126–Please Oblige (Le Levanstell 122) **73** [1988 6f3 6m3 7m* 6m2 7d 7d 1989 6d3 7f 8f 8f4] lengthy, fair sort: modest handicapper: good third at Pontefract in April, best effort in 1989: has won over 7f, but best efforts over 6f: acts on top-of-the-ground and a soft surface. *H. P. Rohan.*

LUCKY FLINDERS 3 ch.f. Free State 125–Lucky Kim (Whistling Wind 123) **77** [1988 6g 7d5 6g3 1989 7f 8m 7g 7.6m* 8g*] strong filly: carries condition: modest performer: won handicaps at Lingfield in September, probably making all stand side and running on strongly, and Goodwood in October, apprentice ridden and leading over 1f out: stays 1m: acts on top-of-the-ground. *P. J. Makin.*

LUCKY FROSTY (USA) 2 br.c. (Apr 19) What Luck (USA)–Frosty Stare **67** (Targowice (USA) 130) [1989 5f2 6m5 6m4 6m5 5m3 5f 6m] $12,000Y, $21,000Y: compact, quite attractive colt: shows a quick, moderate action: fifth foal: half-brother to 3-y-o 1m winner Musical Look (by Diesis) and winners abroad by

Rusticaro and Main Reef: dam Irish listed 7f winner: quite modest maiden: good third in Redcar nursery in September: stays 6f. *P. A. Kelleway.*

LUCKY GROVE 4 b. or br.f. Lucky Wednesday 124–Saran (Le Levanstell 122) [1988 5m 7.5m3 9f 10f 8g3 8s2 8g4 10m 8.5m* 10g 1989 8s 10f4 8g5 10m 8f 8g] angular, medium-sized filly: carries condition: moderate mover: poor plater: stays 1¼m: acts on firm going: has run creditably for apprentice: sometimes mounted on track and taken down early. *S. Bowring.* 32

LUCKY HUMBUG 6 ch.g. Lucky Wednesday 124–Be My Sweet 78 (Galivanter 131) [1988 NR 1989 14.6g 16.2d 16f5] sparely-made gelding: has a round action: poor maiden: stays 2m: acts on top-of-the-ground and a soft surface: occasionally sweating (profusely final outing) and on toes: sometimes has tongue tied down: unruly at start on reappearance and unseated rider going down final appearance (June). *W. J. Pearce.* —

LUCKY LYPHARD (USA) 2 b.f. (Mar 27) Lyphard's Wish (FR) 124–Klaizia (FR) (Sing Sing 134) [1989 6g6 6g] $50,000Y: tall, useful-looking filly: has scope: closely related to 2 winners by Lyphard, notably smart French miler Lypheor, and half-sister to 2 other winners: dam smart sprinter: quite modest form, beaten at least 6 lengths, in maidens at Newbury and Goodwood: will be better suited by 7f. *P. F. I. Cole.* 64

LUCKY MOON 2 b.c. (Apr 24) Touching Wood (USA) 127–Castle Moon 79 (Kalamoun 129) [1989 8.2d] lengthy, quite attractive colt: half-brother to 3-y-o Moon Mystery and 5 winners, including 4-y-o Sheriff's Star (by Posse), smart stayer at 2 yrs and good-class winner at 1½m, and St Leger winner Moon Madness (by Vitiges): dam, winner at 1m to 13f, is sister to good middle-distance stayer Castle Keep and half-sister to Gold Cup winner Ragstone: 5/1 and in need of experience, around 5 lengths seventh of 15, staying on not unduly knocked about, to Ridgepoint in maiden at Haydock in October: should improve. *J. L. Dunlop.* — p

LUCKY NATIVE 3 br.c. Be My Native 122–Change of Luck (Track Spare 125) [1988 5m6 5m5 6g5 6m 8f 6g 1989 8.2s4 6f 12g*] good-topped colt: has a round action: won seller (bought in 9,000 gns) at Folkestone in October: off course 2½ months between outings: well suited by 1½m. *D. Marks.* 53

LUCKY OAK 3 ch.g. Tap On Wood 130–Zalinndia (FR) (Brigadier Gerard 144) [1988 7f4 8d 7m 8d 1989 10f5 8.2m 10h3 12h4 9m 12g 12g] medium-sized, close-coupled gelding: plating-class maiden: good third in handicap at Brighton in July, leading over 9f: well beaten afterwards, in amateurs handicap final outing: suited by 1¼m: form only on top-of-the-ground: bought out of P. Cole's stable 10,000 gns Newmarket July Sales after third start. *R. P. C. Hoad.* 59 d

LUCKY ROUND 3 b.f. Auction Ring (USA) 123–La Fortune (Le Haar 126) [1988 6g3 1989 10f 10.2h4 10m3 10.6g2 10f2 10.4m2 10f*] rangy, attractive filly: favourite, won minor event at Brighton in September by 7 lengths: best efforts in minor events at Brighton and Chester previous 2 starts: may prove as effective with forcing tactics short of 1¼m: acts on firm going. *Major W. R. Hern.* 82

LUCKY SONG (USA) 3 b.f. Seattle Song (USA) 130–Lucky Us (USA) (Nijinsky (CAN) 138) [1988 6g4 7s* 8.2m* 7.3s* 1989 10.5f4 10f3 12g2 13.5g 12m* 14.6g* 117

Park Hill Stakes, Doncaster—odds-on Lucky Song (left) catches Princess Sobieska close home

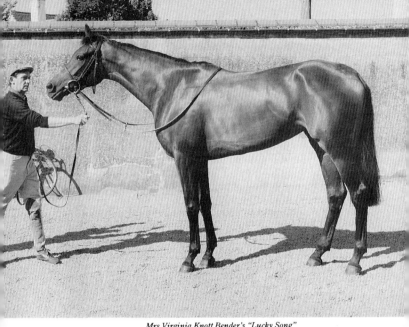

Mrs Virginia Knott Bender's "Lucky Song"

12.5m 12f4] lengthy, shallow-girthed filly: smart performer: successful in small fields for £7,300 event (making all) at Kempton and Group 2 Park Hill Stakes (1¼ on) at Doncaster in September, in latter given fair bit to do and hard ridden to lead close home and beat Princess Sobieska a neck: ran moderately in Group 2 event at Longchamp penultimate start: beaten about 2 lengths in £66,700 handicap at Gulfstream Park on final one: stays 14.6f: probably acts on any going: reportedly to remain in USA. *L. M. Cumani.*

LUCKY STRAW 4 b.f. Tumble Wind (USA)–Hi Little Gal (Garda's Revenge 45 (USA) 119) [1988 6s* 6d 6f 6g 7g³ 7.6m⁴ 7.6s 8m⁵ 8m 6s 7g 7g 9g 1989 7.5d 6g* 6m⁴ 7f 6m 6g 6m] small, sturdy filly: moderate mover: poor handicapper: won at Hamilton in May: stays 7f: unsuited by firm going, acts on any other: blinkered twice at 3 yrs, on first occasion giving trouble in preliminaries and not looking keen: trained until after fifth outing in 1989 by K. Stone: taken down early next time: inconsistent. *J. F. Bottomley.*

LUCKY SUNDAY 3 b.f. Lucky Wednesday 124–Liscannor Lass 83 (Burglar 128) — [1988 5m 7f 8m 8g 1989 7.5d 8m 7m 7s 8s 6s] leggy filly: quite modest plater at 2 yrs: well beaten 1989, visored first 2 outings and blinkered final one: stays 1m. *J. S. Wainwright.*

LUCKY VERDICT 3 b.g. Touching Wood (USA) 127–Noor 76 (Mill Reef (USA) 81 141) [1988 7g 8s 8.2m 9f³ 1989 8d 8.5d 10.8m³ 12.2m⁴ 16g⁵ 16f* 14m³ 16m* 17.6g² 16m* 16g³] smallish, sturdy gelding: has rather round action: fair handicapper: successful in autumn in maiden claimer (easily, blinkered first time as 3-y-o) at Redcar and moderately-run races at Warwick and Redcar: stays 2m: goes well on top-of-the-ground: best in blinkers: soundly beaten in visor at Chester fifth outing: seems best held up: sold to join M. Pipe 29,000 gns Newmarket Autumn Sales. *J. W. Hills.*

LUCY'S DAY 3 ch.f. Anfield 117–April Days 75 (Silly Season 127) [1988 5m 7g* — 7d³ 7f² 7s 1989 7g 10.2m] workmanlike filly: modest winner as 2-y-o: behind in handicaps in spring of 1989: should be suited by 1m + : possibly unsuited by very soft going. *P. T. Walwyn.*

LUCY'S LUCK 4 ch.f. Jester 119–Our Bernie (Continuation 120) [1988 6s 6m 6m 43 5m⁶ 6m² 6s⁶ 5d⁴ 1989 5s 5s 5f⁶ 5f⁴ 5f] workmanlike filly: moderate mover: poor maiden: stays 6f: probably not at her best on firm going, acts on any other: blinkered last 4 outings: sometimes apprentice ridden: has sweated and got on edge: has not found much off bridle: sold 940 gns Newmarket Autumn Sales. *G. Lewis.*

LUGANA BEACH 3 br.c. Tumble Wind (USA)–Safe Haven (Blakeney 126) **115** [1988 5m* 5g⁴ 5f 5d⁵ 5g² 1989 5m 6f⁵ 5m* 5m* 5g* 5g*] compact, useful-looking colt: moderate mover: in excellent form in second half of season: won handicaps at York (£9,200 event) and Ascot (£16,300 Bovis Handicap), then strongly-run listed race by ¾ length from Ski Captain at Newmarket and Group 3 Prix du Petit Couvert by nose from Pont Aven, leading close home, at Longchamp 8 days later: best at 5f: acts on firm going and a soft surface: blinkered last 8 outings: sometimes slowly away: very useful. *D. R. C. Elsworth.*

LUIGI'S STAR 6 b.g. Import 127–Luigi's Girl (The Brianstan 128) [1988 10f 1989 — 5f 7m] tall gelding: of little account. *W. Carter.*

LULWH (USA) 3 b.f. Secreto (USA) 128–Yellow Serenade (USA) (Graustark) — [1988 NR 1989 10d] $320,000F: lengthy, angular filly: sixth foal: half-sister to high-class 1m to 1¼m performer Dontstopthemusic and fairly useful 6f winner Stop Day (both by Stop The Music): dam never ran: 16/1 and very green, headway from rear to be in touch 2f out when well beaten in 22-runner maiden at Newbury in October: sold 25,000 gns Newmarket December Sales. *A. C. Stewart.*

LUMBERJACK (USA) 5 b.g. Big Spruce (USA)–Snip (Shantung 132) [1988 NR 83 + 1989 13s* 18g] close-coupled gelding: odds on, very easy winner of poorly-contested minor event at Ayr in September: second favourite, eased from 2f out when well beaten in Tote Cesarewitch (Handicap) at Newmarket month later: doesn't stay 2¼m: acts on any going: useful hurdler. *J. G. FitzGerald.*

LUNA BID 6 b.g. Auction Ring (USA) 123–Moonscape 87 (Ribero 126) [1988 6g⁵ 93 6g⁶ 6m⁵ 6f² 6m³ 6f 6g 6g 6g³ 6g 7.6s 7m 7s⁵ 6s 1989 6v* 6d* 6g 6f⁵ 6m² 6f³ 6m 6m³ 6m² 6m* 6m⁵ 6m⁶ 6s⁵ 6m* 6g⁶ 6g 6v 6d] good-topped gelding: carries condition:

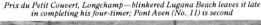

Prix du Petit Couvert, Longchamp—blinkered Lugana Beach leaves it late in completing his four-timer; Pont Aven (No. 11) is second

turns fore-feet in markedly: poor mover: fairly useful handicapper: successful at Kempton and Thirsk in spring, Newmarket in July and Haydock (£9,000 Bucklow Hill Handicap, by ¾ length from Profilic) in September: best at 6f: acts on any going: best held up: has reportedly broken blood vessels. *M. Blanshard.*

LUNA PROBE   2 b.f. (Feb 22) Pas de Seul 133–Dancing Song 87 (Ridan (USA))   53
[1989 5d⁵ 5s 5d 5f 6f⁶ 5g 5g² 5m 7m 6f 5g] 5,200Y: sparely-made filly: keen walker: has a round action: fifth reported foal: half-sister to 3 winners in Belgium: dam 5f and 6f winner at 3 yrs later successful in Belgium: plating-class maiden: best form at 5f on easy ground: has run well for 7-lb claimer: once appeared reluctant to race. *S. J. Muldoon.*

LUNAR MOVER (USA)   3 b.c. Sharpen Up 127–Intentional Move (USA)   114
(Tentam (USA)) [1988 7m* 7g³ 1989 8s* 7d² 8m⁶] useful-looking colt: has scope: good mover: won listed race at Kempton in March: on toes, 2½ lengths second to Zayyani in Singer & Friedlander Greenham Stakes at Newbury: 50/1, reportedly fractured cannon bone when running his best race in General Accident 2000 Guineas at Newmarket in May, quickening well 3f out but no extra approaching last and beaten under 6 lengths: will prove best at up to 1m: acts on soft going and top-of-the-ground: carries head high under pressure: reportedly remains in training. *C. R. Nelson.*

LUNCH BOX   4 ch.f. Great Nephew 126–Supper Time 71 (Shantung 132) [1988   65
10.1g⁴ 12g 10g³ 10s³ 8d⁴ 9v* 1989 10.2g 10m 12.3m² 11.7g² 10.6d 12g³ 13.6g a14g*] workmanlike, rather angular filly: moderate mover: quite modest performer: evens, won claimer at Southwell in November: stays 1¾m: acts on top-of-the-ground and heavy going: effective with or without visor: on toes and slowly away second start: suitable mount for inexperienced rider. *W. Hastings-Bass.*

LUNGUNIA   3 b. or br.f. Prince Bee 128–Stipa (Silver Shark 129) [1988 NR 1989   —
9m 11g] IR 6,000F: angular filly: half-sister to several winners here and abroad, including a listed winner in Belgium by Welsh Saint: dam won at up to 6.5f in France: claimer ridden, never dangerous in claimers at Newmarket (in need of race) and Redcar in October. *A. N. Lee.*

L'UOMO CLASSICS   2 b.g. (May 9) Indian King (USA) 128–Sperrin Mist 83   79
(Camden Town 125) [1989 5m* 5g⁴ 6g 6g³ 6m] IR 11,000Y: medium-sized, good-quartered gelding: has scope: keen walker: second foal: half-brother to 3-y-o Pastoral Jem (by Horage), 5f winner at 2 yrs: dam 2-y-o 5f winner: modest performer: won minor event at Windsor in June by 2½ lengths from The Irish Sheikh: very good third of 11 to Higher Hamill in nursery at York in October: ran poorly in similar event at Newmarket final start: stays 6f: looked irresolute third outing. *Mrs J. Pitman.*

LUREX STAR   3 b.g. Thatching 131–Stellarevagh (Le Levanstell 122) [1988 6g   —
6f⁶ 6g⁵ 1989 10f4 12h 10m 8.3g 8m] workmanlike gelding: plating-class form: probably stays 1¼m: blinkered last 3 starts, with tongue tied down on first 2: gelded after final start (July): has joined Miss P. O'Connor. *K. M. Brassey.*

LURKING   2 b.f. (May 4) Formidable (USA) 125–Hiding 84 (So Blessed 130)   69
[1989 6m 5f4 7g² 6v a7g³] 10,000Y: workmanlike filly: half-sister to 3-y-o Fading (by Pharly) and fair 1986 2-y-o 5f winner Aid And Abet (by Pas de Seul): dam lightly-raced 2-y-o 5f winner from same family as Bassenthwaite: quite modest maiden: creditable third in nursery at Lingfield in October: better suited by 7f than shorter: seems unsuited by heavy ground. *W. Hastings-Bass.*

LUST OF LOVE   3 b.f. Sallust 134–Aridje 79 (Mummy's Pet 125) [1988 NR 1989   74
6s 5g⁵ 7m² 7m* 6g 6m⁵ 5m] 26,000Y: leggy, rather sparely-made filly: third foal: sister to useful 1987 2-y-o 5f and 6f winner Lust of Power and half-sister to Irish 1½m winner/winning hurdler Fragrant Dawn (by Strong Gale): dam, out of half-sister to very speedy Singing Bede, won over 5f at 2 yrs: won maiden at Thirsk in September: creditable fifth in £7,900 event at Newmarket, easily best effort in handicaps: stays 7f: acts on top-of-the-ground: sold 7,600 gns Doncaster November Sales. *A. Bailey.*

LUSTREMAN   2 ch.c. (Jun 5) Sallust 134–Miss Speak Easy (USA) (Sea Bird II   —
145) [1989 7m 8v 8g] IR 6,000Y: workmanlike, close-coupled colt: half-brother to several winners, including 3-y-o 1¼m to 1½m winner Sabarab (by Sayf El Arab) and very useful French middle-distance winner Natchitoches (by Pontifex): dam minor French 9f winner: soundly beaten in minor events and a maiden. *B. Stevens.*

LUSTY LAD   4 b.g. Decoy Boy 129–Gluhwein (Ballymoss 136) [1988 6g 6g 5m⁵   —
5g 5g 7g² 7g³ 7g 7.6m⁶ 1989 7f 6f4 6m 9m 8h⁵] rather sparely-made gelding: modest

handicapper as 3-y-o: long way below his best in 1989: stays 7f: acts on firm going: hooded fourth outing: winning hurdler. *M. J. Haynes.*

LUTINE ROYAL 3 b.f. Formidable (USA) 125–State Ball 61 (Dance In Time **46** (CAN)) [1988 NR 1989 7f⁵ 8g 7g 10d] small, sparely-made: second foal: dam, placed 5 times at around 1½m, is half-sister to Royal Palace, Prince Consort, Selhurst and Glass Slipper, last-named dam of Fairy Footsteps and Light Cavalry: sign of ability only on debut in May: should stay 1m. *R. F. Johnson Houghton.*

LUZUM 5 ch.h. Touching Wood (USA) 127–Velvet Habit 89 (Habitat 134) [1988 **112** 8f² 8.5m² 8f* 7s* 8g² 8d² 7g³ 1989 8m*] small, sturdy horse: moderate mover: very useful performer: odds on, comfortable winner of uncompetitive minor event at Brighton in April by 5 lengths from Shabanaz: not seen out again but remains in training: suited by 7f or 1m: acts on any going: edged markedly right in front final outing at 4 yrs: races up with pace: wears blinkers. *H. Thomson Jones.*

LYDNEY (USA) 3 b.f. Lyphard (USA) 132–Condessa 121 (Condorcet (FR)) [1988 **66** NR 1989 7f⁴ 7m 10.2f⁴ 10m] $360,000Y: rather lightly-made, attractive filly: third foal: dam won Yorkshire Oaks: fourth of 20 to Magic Gleam in maiden at Kempton: refused to settle when disappointing in varied events after: should be suited by further than 7f: sold 28,000 gns Newmarket December Sales. *J. Tree.*

LYNDSEYLEE 2 b.f. (Mar 14) Swing Easy (USA) 126–Miss Merlin 79 (Manacle **91** 123) [1989 5d* 5m* 5m* 5f 5f* 5f³ 5m² 5m³ 5m 5m² 6g] 1,900F, 8,200Y: workmanlike, good-quartered filly: has scope: has a quick action: half-sister to 2-y-o 5f seller winners Meralto (by Noalto) and Sister Cheryl (by Vaigly Great) and a winning hurdler: dam won twice over 6f: fairly useful performer: successful in spring in maiden at Ripon and minor events at Chester and Newmarket and in July nursery (ridden by 7-b claimer) at Hamilton: ran creditably most subsequent starts: best form at 5f: occasionally sweating and edgy: sometimes taken down quietly. *J. Berry.*

LYNKIMGEM 3 ch.g. Royal Match 117–Sweet Millie (Methane 93) [1988 NR **—** 1989 8f] second reported foal: dam winning hurdler: 50/1, very backward and tailed off in maiden at Pontefract in October. *M. C. Chapman.*

LYNSEYS LAD 2 ch.g. (Apr 29) Blue Cashmere 129–Lynsey-Louise (Three **—** Sevens 103) [1989 6f] leggy, plain gelding: third reported foal: half-brother to bad 3-y-o Sarah's Fantasy (by Uncle Pokey): dam unraced: 20/1 and backward, tailed off in 7-runner seller at Thirsk in June: hung left throughout. *M. W. Ellerby.*

LYPHARD'S STAR 2 b.f. (Mar 15) Lyphard's Special (USA) 122–Nigel's Star **—** (Ashmore (FR)) [1989 6f] IR 1,000Y, resold 2,500Y: first foal: dam ran twice: broke leg in maiden at Chepstow. *B. Palling.*

LYPHAROS 2 b.g. (Apr 19) Lyphard's Special (USA) 122–Cocarde (Red God **—** 128§) [1989 6g 6d⁶ 6d] IR 6,500Y: half-brother to several winners, including French 1¼m and 1½m winner Edward French (by Jim French) and fair 1m winner Woodcarver (by Tap On Wood): dam, French 1¼m winner, is half-sister to Caro: poor maiden: sweating and taken quietly to post, tailed off at Newbury final start: green, tailed badly left and ran out at halfway at Windsor on debut. *P. Mitchell.*

LYPHENTO (USA) 5 b.h. Lyphard's Wish (FR) 124–Hasty Viento (USA) **83** (Gallant Man) [1988 NR 1989 15.5f³] tall horse: has a round action: useful 3-y-o when trained by G. Harwood: 16/1, 3½ lengths third of 11 under 13-0 in amateurs handicap at Folkestone in September, only subsequent outing on flat: best form at up to 1½m with give in the ground: useful but inconsistent handicap hurdler: stud. *J. T. Gifford.*

LYPHEOR'S HONOUR (CAN) 3 b.c. Lypheor 118–Intriguing Honor (USA) **101 d** (Sham (USA)) [1988 NR 1989 11.7h* 10f* 10.5m³ 12f4 12f⁶ 9f 10g] $23,000Y: rather leggy colt: good mover: second reported foal: dam minor stakes winner in USA at 1m: useful at best: won maiden at Bath in May and minor event at Folkestone in June: in frame in listed race at York and £7,700 event at Ascot: below form in quite valuable handicaps after, tailed off in apprentice contest final start: stays 1½m: acts on hard going: trained first 5 starts by F. J. Houghton: sold 48,000 gns Newmarket Autumn Sales. *R. F. Casey.*

LYPH (USA) 3 b.c. Lypheor 118–Scottish Lass (Scotland) [1988 NR 1989 8g 10g] **—** $50,000Y: good-quartered colt: half-brother to several winners in USA, including stakes winners Scottish Time (by Li'l Fella) and Silverbatim (by Verbatim): dam unplaced from 8 starts: well beaten in £8,300 newcomers race at Newmarket and maiden at Salisbury in the spring: sold 4,700 gns Newmarket Autumn Sales. *J. Gosden.*

LYREEN RIVER 5 b.g. Rusticaro (FR) 124–Mehudenna 77 (Ribero 126) [1988 **70**
10g* 1989 11.5f 10f 12f⁶ 12f² 10m³ 10f²] leggy gelding: stayed 1½m: probably acted
on any going: usually wore blinkers: also tried in hood: occasionally sweated: suited
by forcing tactics: winning hurdler: trained until after fifth start by B. Curley: dead.
C. R. Beever.

M

MABROVA 2 gr.f. (Mar 9) Prince Mab (FR) 124–Makarova (USA) (Nijinsky **108**
(CAN) 138) [1989 7d* 7g² 8m4] half-sister to minor middle-distance winners in
France by Secretariat and Arctic Tern: dam French 1¼m and 10.5f winner:
successful in 7-runner newcomers event at Saint-Cloud in July: over 2 lengths
fourth to Golden Era in Prix des Reservoirs at Longchamp in October, better
subsequent effort: will stay 1¼m: useful. *Mme C. Head, France.*

MACARI MAN 2 ch.c. (Apr 22) Coquelin (USA) 121–Final Game 83 (Pardao 120) —
[1989 5d 5g] IR 6,000Y: close-coupled colt: half-brother to 2 winners, including very
smart sprinter Mummy's Game (by Mummy's Pet): dam 1¼m winner: well beaten
in maiden at Catterick and seller at Leicester in April. *N. Tinkler.*

MACHIAVELLIAN (USA) 2 b.c. (Apr 25) Mr Prospector (USA)–Coup **122 p**
de Folie (USA) (Halo (USA)) [1989 6d* 6g* 7g*]
    The Two Thousand Guineas has long been regarded as more prestigious
than its French counterpart, the Poule d'Essai des Poulains, yet unlike its
sister event the One Thousand Guineas it seldom lures the top colts from
across the Channel. Indeed, the French have won only three of the last
twenty-five Guineas though they have provided at least one challenger nearly
every year, and haven't done better than fourth in the last seven runnings.
However, one man who has been a persistent thorn in the home trainers' side
at Newmarket, and has long supported British racing, is Francois Boutin, who
sent out Zino in 1982 and Nonoalco in 1974, the last two French-trained
winners of the Guineas, as well as the disqualified Nureyev in 1980. Boutin,
who had a runner every year between 1974 and 1983, has been less in
evidence of late—Common Grounds in 1988 was his last raider—but most
likely he will be back in 1990 with the currently-unbeaten Machiavellian,
already a clear favourite in most lists. Although Machiavellian's form, which is
highlighted by victories in the Prix Morny Agence Francaise and the Prix de la
Salamandre, two of France's Group 1 races, doesn't measure up to the
standard usually required to win the Guineas, there's not many around with
better, and if he comes across he looks sure to be thereabouts. The Guineas is
not the one-horse affair that the betting suggests, however, and Machiavellian
doesn't really represent value at 6/1 with the race still months off at the time
of writing.

Prix Morny Agence Francaise, Deauville—Machiavellian beats Qirmazi

Prix de la Salamandre, Longchamp—Machiavellian comes out on top again

Machiavellian made his bow in the six-furlong Prix Yacowlef for newcomers at Deauville in August. The Yacowlef has a long-established reputation as a pointer to the future, and racegoers at Deauville had the good fortune, though they wouldn't have realized it at the time, of course, of seeing the subsequent Ciga Grand Criterium winner Jade Robbery and the dual pattern winner Septieme Ciel in opposition as well. Starting at 5/1, Machiavellian was held up at the rear of the eight runners, came through approaching the final furlong and went away to beat Jade Robbery by two lengths with Septieme Ciel well back in fifth. Later in the month Machiavellian took his chance in the Prix Morny over the same course and distance. Since the Prix Robert Papin's demotion to Group 2 status in 1987 the Morny has become the first Group 1 race of the season for two-year-olds in France. Run three weeks after the five-and-a-half-furlong Robert Papin it's ideally placed to attract that race's protagonists, and the latest renewal drew its British-trained winner Ozone Friendly as well as third-placed Mill Lady; completing the seven-runner field were the Prix de Cabourg winner Qirmazi and second Spendomania, and the British challengers Waki Gold and Age of Miracles. Machiavellian, who was sweating slightly on his neck on what was a sunny day, landed the odds in impressive fashion, settling the issue with an excellent turn of foot in the penultimate furlong. Racing alone on the stand side, Machiavellian drifted off a true line and changed his stride at halfway, but steered a straight course after quickening clear, and kept on strongly to account for Qirmazi by two lengths with another four back to Mill Lady, who denied Ozone Friendly of third spot close home. Machiavellian was his trainer's fourth winner of the Morny following Nonoalco in 1973, Super Concorde in 1977 and Tersa in 1988; more surprisingly he was also the first colt to win the race since Siberian Express in 1983.

The latter-day fillies' monopoly of the Morny is the main reason why the Morny-Salamandre double, achieved five times in the 'seventies, hadn't been completed since Deep Roots dead-heated with Maximova at Longchamp in 1982. Machiavellian's chief rival in a field of six looked to be the unbeaten Rock City, successful in the Anglia Television July Stakes and the Scottish Equitable Gimcrack Stakes on his last two outings and seeking his fourth win in pattern company. Machiavellian faced useful opposition too in the form of the Challenge d'Or Piaget runner-up Ernani, the Prix du Calvados third El Quahirah and his old adversary Qirmazi, who was re-opposing on identical terms; Machiavellian's stable-companion and pacemaker Tulsa Time, with whom he was coupled at 10/7-on for betting purposes, completed the sextet.

Mr S. S. Niarchos' "Machiavellian"

Tulsa Time filled his role admirably for five furlongs, setting a strong, consistent pace several lengths ahead of Rock City and Machiavellian with the others following in Indian file. Running into the last three hundred yards Machiavellian, who'd pulled quite hard early on and looked to have difficulty negotiating one of the turns, was switched outside the hard-ridden Rock City, quickened a length or so ahead, then tended to idle as Qirmazi came with a late rally to get within half a length at the line. Rock City, two and a half lengths back in fourth, half a length down on Ernani, found little in the final furlong and was afterwards said to have been running a temperature. Rock City's defeat did nothing to detract from the winner's performance though, and Machiavellian was swiftly installed as favourite for the Guineas. It was Boutin's intention to run the colt in the Grand Criterium at Longchamp on Arc weekend, but Machiavellian started coughing in the run-up to the race and was withdrawn several days before. In the event his stable was prominently represented by Linamix, reportedly slightly Machiavellian's inferior at home, who beat all except the progressive Jade Robbery and finished four lengths clear of the third. Should Machiavellian and Jade Robbery meet again in the coming season, a distinct possibility as Jade Robbery is also said to be an intended runner at Newmarket, there shouldn't be much to choose between them on their form at two.

Machiavellian is a son of the highly fashionable American sire Mr Prospector. Jade Robbery, Gold Seam and the smart American two-year-olds

Carson City and Golden Reef also helped keep Mr Prospector's name to the fore in 1989 though he finished the year down in sixth place in the General Sires List over two years in top position. The demand for his yearlings, however, shows no sign of abating: in 1988 he had the second highest sale average after Northern Dancer (whose sons and grandsons occupied the next five places) and at Keeneland's most recent July Selected Sale he had three sell for in excess of 1,000,000 dollars each, more than any other stallion. Machiavellian's dam Coup de Folie, whose first foal he is, was acquired by Niarchos for 825,000 dollars as a yearling in 1983. She went on to show very useful form in two seasons in training, beating Triptych when winning the Prix d'Aumale at two and returning from injury at three to win over a mile and a mile and a quarter before ending her career in the States. Coup de Folie is also a first foal: her unraced dam Raise The Standard, who was born as recently as 1978 and has also produced a full sister to Coup de Folie of little account as well as a minor winner in North America, was one of the last foals from the famous broodmare Natalma. Natalma, of course, is the dam of Northern Dancer, whose grandam Almahmoud appears elsewhere in Machiavellian's pedigree as the second dam of Coup de Folie's sir e Halo. Natalma is also the grandam of the champion 1972 American two-year- ld filly La Prevoyante as well as the great grandam of the high-class s rinter Danehill.

		Raise A Native	Native Dancer
	Mr Prospector (USA)	(ch 1961)	Raise You
	(b 1970)	Gold Digger	Nashua
Machiavellian (USA)		(b 1962)	Sequence
(b.c. Apr 25, 1987)		Halo	Hail To Reason
	Coup de Folie (USA)	(b or br 1969)	Cosmah
	(b 1982)	Raise The Standard	Hoist The Flag
		(b 1978)	Natalma

The quick-actioned Machiavellian has raced so far only on good or good to soft ground. He stayed seven furlongs well as a two-year-old but is a keen, headstrong sort not particularly amenable to restraint and he's not sure to be so effective at much beyond a mile. We await his reappearance in the Prix Djebel at Maisons-Laffitte with interest. *F. Boutin, France.*

MACHO MAN 4 br.g. Mummy's Game 120–Shoshoni 72 (Ballymoss 136) [1988 11.7m 8.5m6 7g4 10m 8.3m* 8.2m6 8.2s* 1989 11s 8.2g 10v] smallish gelding: trained by B. Hanbury, made all in seller at Windsor and claimer at Hamilton as 3-y-o: well below form otherwise in 1988 and in handicaps in Scotland (apprentice ridden) as 4-y-o: suited by 1m: acts on top-of-the-ground and soft going: has often worn blinkers, but didn't at 4 yrs: bought 7,200 gns Doncaster May Sales: inconsistent. *J. J. O'Neill.* —

MAC KELTY 2 b.c. (Apr 30) Wattlefield 117–Thevetia 65 (Mummy's Pet 125) 64 [1989 5g 6m 6g 6m 6g* 6v3 5m4 7g5 7d a5g] stocky colt: first foal: dam should have stayed 7f: quite modest performer: won 18-runner nursery at Hamilton by 4 lengths from Rainbow Bridge: ran well most starts after: really needs further than 5f, and stays 7f. *N. Bycroft.*

MACKENZIES 4 ch.f. Homing 130–Miss Henry 78 (Blue Cashmere 129) [1988 32 9f5 8m 7m 6m3 7f 7g 8g5 8.2d 6g4 1989 7g 10m 8g 8m 7.6h 7m 7f6 8m 8g3 12g a11g a10g2] lengthy, workmanlike filly: poor mover: poor maiden: stays 1¼m: visored fourth to eighth outings. *M. J. Ryan.*

MACKLA 2 ch.f. (Mar 14) Caerleon (USA) 132–Mariella 123 (Sir Gaylord (USA)) 109 [1989 8g2 8g* 8g] attractive filly: good walker: fourth foal: half-sister to French 3-y-o Marcure (by Cure The Blues), winner at 1m (at 2 yrs) and 9f: dam French 1½m to 1¾m winner, is sister to very smart 1½m performer Scorpio and half-sister to Sagaro: won Prix d'Aumale at Longchamp by a neck from Catherine Parr, late run to lead line: never able to challenge in Prix Marcel Boussac in October, though stayed on well towards finish: will be well suited by middle distances. *F. Boutin, France.*

MAC RAMBLER 2 b.c. (Mar 28) Hotfoot 126–Arkengarthdale (Sweet Story 122) [1989 7m] second living foal: half-brother to 3-y-o Follow That Taxi (by Dublin Taxi): dam, ran once at 2 yrs on flat, won over jumps: 100/1, soundly beaten (slowly away) in maiden at Ayr in August. *N. Bycroft.* —

MACREE 2 b.f. (Mar 18) Another Realm 118–Mrs Willie (St Paddy 133) [1989 6f 7f5 7h5] workmanlike filly: third foal: half-sister to 2 poor maidens by Record Run: dam of little account: well beaten in maidens. *A. Moore.* —

525

Wokingham Stakes (Handicap), Ascot—Mac's Fighter defies top weight;
A Prayer For Wings comes second

MACROBIAN 5 b.g. Bay Express 132–White Domino 67 (Sharpen Up 127) [1988 **104** 6m⁶ 6f 6f⁶ 6d 6g⁵ 6s 6f³ 5g 1989 6m* 6m⁵ 6m* 6m* 6g 6m³ 6g 6g² 6g*] good-bodied gelding: good mover: better than ever in 1989 (having had operation for soft palate) and won handicaps at Thirsk, Haydock, York and Newcastle: best effort at Newcastle (favourite) when making all on stand side to beat Densben 2½ lengths: suited by 6f: best on a sound surface: suited by forcing tactics: visored twice, blinkered once. *M. H. Easterby.*

MAC'S FIGHTER 4 ch.c. Hard Fought 125–Geoffrey's Sister 102 (Sparkler **116** 130) [1988 6g² 6d² 6f 6m 6f* 7d³ 6m* 7m⁴ 6g* 7g 6d³ 5f^wo 7g* 5g 6f² 6m² 1989 6g² 6g 6m⁴ 7.2g³ 6f* 8f] compact colt: moderate mover: put up improved performance when winning £28,100 Wokingham Stakes (Handicap) at Royal Ascot under top weight in good style by 2 lengths from A Prayer For Wings: in frame earlier in season in listed events at Doncaster and Haydock and in EBF Greenlands Stakes at the Curragh: fair seventh of 14, taking keen hold, to Safawan in £57,400 handicap at Goodwood in July, final outing: best at 6f or 7f: possibly unsuited by soft going, acts on any other: suitable mount for apprentice: usually wears blinkers or visor: usually taken very quietly to post: waited with and is suited by strong gallop. *W. A. O'Gorman.*

MACS IDEA 2 b.c. (Feb 3) Noalto 120–Rising Star (St Paddy 133) [1989 6m³] **47** 17,000F, 5,800Y: half-brother to several winners abroad: dam temperamental half-sister to very useful animals Riot Act and Laurentian Hills: 7 lengths third of 14 to Bodamist in seller at Windsor in June: sent to race in Italy. *W. A. O'Gorman.*

MACS MAHARANEE 2 b.f. (Mar 23) Indian King (USA) 128–High State 72 **72** (Free State 125) [1989 5m⁴ 5f⁴ 5g³ 6g² 6f⁶ 6g²] leggy, rather unfurnished filly: moderate mover: second foal: half-sister to 3-y-o Fabulous Shaun (by Petong): dam 9f seller winner: modest maiden: runner-up in nurseries fourth and (unfavourably drawn) final starts: much better form at 6f than 5f. *P. S. Felgate.*

MAC'S SISTER 4 ch.f. Krayyan 117–Avereen (Averof 123) [1988 8s² 9d³ 10m 8d **55** 10m² 10m* 10g 8.2m⁴ 8s⁵ 8d³ 8g³ 1989 10.1m 9f² 10h 10.6g 12m 10h⁴ 10m² 12f²] smallish, rather sparely-made filly: poor mover: fair plater: finds 1m on short side and stays 1½m: probably acts on any going: often blinkered or visored nowadays: inconsistent: has joined C. Brooks. *M. H. Tompkins.*

MADAME BOVARY 3 br.f. Ile de Bourbon (USA) 133–Coppice (Pardao 120) **82** [1988 7f⁴ 8g⁵ 7d 1989 8g 10.2m* 11.5f³ 9f* 10g² 9m* 8h* 9f 10g 8f] small filly: fair handicapper: progressed well, winning at Bath in May, Kempton in June and York and Bath in July: ran poorly at Bath final start: stays 1¼m, possibly not 11.5f: acts on firm going: genuine and consistent. *B. W. Hills.*

MADAME DUBOIS 2 ch.f. (Mar 4) Legend of France (USA) 124–Shadywood 96 **68** p (Habitat 134) [1989 7g] big, useful-looking filly: has plenty of scope: third foal: dam, 1¼m winner stayed 1½m, is half-sister to smart 6f to 1m winner Kashmir Lass and daughter of Cheshire Oaks winner Milly Moss: 16/1, very green and ridden by 7-lb claimer, tenth of 24, losing place at halfway then running on near finish, to Katsina in maiden at Newmarket in November: sure to improve. *H. R. A. Cecil.*

526

MADAME MINT 4 b.f. Raga Navarro (ITY) 119–What A Mint (Meadow Mint — (USA) 120) [1988 8d² 5d⁵ 5.8g⁴ 8.5m 7g³ 8g⁶ 7m 8.2m 1989 11.7d 8.3m 5.8h 7f 6s⁶] small, lengthy filly: poor maiden: suited by 7f or 1m and give in the ground: blinkered third start: trained until after next one by C. Popham. *R. J. Holder.*

MADAM HOTFOOT 2 br.f. (Apr 18) Hotfoot 126–Gloria Maremmana (King 47 Emperor (USA)) [1989 5f⁵ 6m] workmanlike, sparely-made filly: sister to Swedish 3-y-o winner Glorious Hotfoot and modest 7f to 1¼m performer Emperor Hotfoot and closely related to 2 winners by Hot Grove, including 1½m winner Hot Girl: dam won at 2 yrs in Italy: poor form in maidens at Chester (slowly away, green) and Brighton in first half of season. *R. F. Johnson Houghton.*

MADAM MELODY (FR) 3 b. or br.f. Big John (FR)–Infanta (FR) (Prince — Regent (FR) 129) [1988 5g 6m 5f⁴ 5m⁵ 8g 1989 7m 6f] lengthy, leggy ex-Irish filly: fourth foal: sister to 2 winners in France, including 6.5f (at 2 yrs) and 9.5f winner Jacinta John: dam ran twice at 3 yrs: poor maiden: behind in summer as 3-y-o, drifting badly right in seller final outing: sold to join R. Williams 1,100 gns Doncaster August Sales. *T. D. Barron.*

MADAM MILLIE 3 b.f. Milford 119–Proper Madam 93 (Mummy's Pet 125) — [1988 6f⁴ 6g² 6g² 5f* 5d* 5d* 5s 1989 5m 5f] leggy, unfurnished filly: fairly useful winner in August as 2-y-o: last in quite valuable handicaps at Epsom and Ascot in June, 1989: best form at 5f: best form on a soft surface: has won when sweating. *R. Boss.*

MADAM TAYLOR 4 b.f. Free State 125–Hourglass (Mansingh (USA) 120) 55 [1988 6d⁴ 5m 5g 8m 7g 9g² 10g⁴ 10.4d⁶ 10m 10m⁴ 9g⁴ 10d* 10g* 10.2m 1989 10.2g⁴ 12d 10m 9f 10m³ 10m 10.6d* 9m² 10g⁶ 11s³ 10.6m 8g] dipped-backed filly: moderate mover: plating-class handicapper: won apprentice event at Haydock in August: stays 11f: has won on firm going, but suited by an easier surface nowadays: not discredited in blinkers, but didn't wear them when successful: sometimes bandaged behind nowadays: occasionally sweats. *H. J. Collingridge.*

MADAM TUDOR 2 b.f. (Feb 17) Blue Cashmere 129–Proper Madam 93 68 (Mummy's Pet 125) [1989 5m 5m* 6m⁵ 5m² 5m] leggy filly: has a quick, roundish action: third living foal: half-sister to 3-y-o Madam Millie, fairly useful 5f winner at 2 yrs, and useful but inconsistent sprinter Naive Charm (both by Milford): dam sprinter: modest performer: won claimer at Bath in July: easily best subsequent effort penultimate start: likely to prove suited by 5f: wore tongue strap and severe bridle last 2 starts: sweating and on edge final one: sold 1,600 gns Newmarket Autumn Sales. *R. Boss.*

MADELEY'S PET 2 ch.f. (Apr 13) Tina's Pet 121–Thorganby 75 (Decoy Boy 67 129) [1989 5d³ 5f³ 5g² 5d² 5d²] 14,000Y: sturdy, good-quartered filly, slightly dipped backed: moderate mover: sixth reported foal: half-sister to Irish 7.9f to 13f winner Dazzlem (by Monsanto): dam won 8 times over 5f: quite modest maiden: may stay 6f: has run creditably for 7-lb claimer: sometimes on toes. *Denys Smith.*

MADEMOISELLE CHLOE 2 b.f. (Mar 21) Night Shift (USA)–Emerald 106 p Rocket 69 (Green God 128) [1989 5m* 5m* 5s* 6m⁶] 10,500Y: lengthy, good-quartered filly: has plenty of scope: fifth foal: half-sister to 3 winners, including fair 1985 2-y-o Mandrake Madam and quite modest 9f winner Donnysnookercentre (both by Mandrake Major): dam 1m winner: progressive filly:

Harry Rosebery Challenge Trophy, Ayr—
the progressive Mademoiselle Chloe goes clear of Tadwin

successful in maiden at Newcastle in August and in minor event at York and Harry Rosebery Challenge Trophy (by 2 lengths from Tadwin) at Ayr following month: ran better than sixth-of-11 position, around 3 lengths behind Dead Certain, suggests in Tattersalls Cheveley Park Stakes, going on in good style having been held up and given lot to do: stays 6f: likely to improve further, and win more races. *C. B. B. Booth.*

MADFA 4 b.g. Prince Tenderfoot (USA) 126–Vectis 75 (Quorum 126) [1988 12f6 12.8d4 12g* 14s4 11s 1989 8m4] ex-Irish gelding: brother to Irish 9f to 1½m winner Prince of Rondo and half-brother to 2 other winners in Ireland: dam 13f winner: won maiden at Tramore as 3-y-o when trained by K. Prendergast: 33/1 from 10/1, well-beaten fourth of 8 in minor event at Brighton in April: needs further than 1m and stays 1¾m well: acts on soft going: blinkered final start at 3 yrs: winning hurdler in 1988/9. *R. Akehurst.*   —

MAD HOUSE 4 b.f. Kabour 80–Open House 91 (Road House II) [1988 NR 1989 8m 6f 8g] sturdy filly: half-sister to 5f and 6f winner Mendick Adventure (by Mandrake Major) and 6f winner Pentoff (by Dubassoff): dam best at up to 7f: of no account. *D. W. Chapman.*   —

MADIRIYA 2 ch.f. (May 17) Diesis 133–Majanada (Tap On Wood 130) [1989 6g4 8f*] lengthy, rather sparely-made filly: has scope: first foal: dam French 1m winner: favourite, won 9-runner maiden at Brighton in October by a length from Anna Petrovna, running on well final furlong: will stay 1¼m: may improve again. *L. M. Cumani.*   74 p

MADONIJAH 3 ch.f. Adonijah 126–Linda's Design (Persian Bold 123) [1988 6s4 6s 6g 6s3 7.5m6 7s6 6s5 6s2 6d4 7g6 6d 1989 6s 8s6 8g 8m6 10f 8f 9f3 9f6 10f4 10m] smallish, lengthy filly: has a roundish action: fair plater at best nowadays: stays 1¼m: probably acts on any going: tends to race freely: mulish in preliminaries last 2 appearances, unseating rider and withdrawn final one: inconsistent and of questionable attitude. *M. Brittain.*   50

MADONNINA 3 b.f. King of Spain 121–My Haven 77 (Godswalk (USA) 130) [1988 5f 7.5f 1989 6s5 7g5 6m 8g 9f] small filly: plater: sweating, only sign of ability over 6f on soft going: pulled up lame third outing: sold 750 gns Doncaster September Sales. *Don Enrico Incisa.*   —

MADRACO 6 b.h. Hot Spark 126–Aberdeen Lassie 102 (Aberdeen 109) [1988 5g 6m5 6f 6g 6m 6g 6g 5f3 6m 5f2 6d 6m 5m 1989 5.8h* 6m4 6f 6f3 6g 6f 6f* 5g4 6m* 6f 6m6 6m2 6m 5.6g] close-coupled horse: moderate mover: fairly useful handicapper: won at Bath (making all) in May, Goodwood in July and Nottingham in August: easily best effort when beating Densben by 5 lengths in £8,000 Nottingham Stewards Cup (Handicap): fell 2f out and broke off-hind fetlock in Tote-Portland Handicap at Doncaster: stays 6f: suited by a sound surface: sweated when tried in blinkers: visored twice as 5-y-o: has won for apprentice: tough. *L. J. Codd.*   94

MAE PLOI 3 b.f. Mummy's Pet 125–Ring Rose 86 (Relko 136) [1988 NR 1989 7f] leggy, close-coupled, rather unfurnished filly: fifth foal: half-sister to French 4-y-o 6.5f and 1m winner Tangle Thorn (by Thatching) and useful middle-distance performer Balladier (by Busted): dam, winner of 3 middle-distance races, is out of very smart Heath Rose: 33/1, tailed off in maiden at Chepstow in July: sold 1,300 gns Ascot September Sales. *J. D. Bethell.*   —

MAFAZA 3 b.c. Mummy's Pet 125–Woodwind (FR) 103 (Whistling Wind 123) [1988 6d 7g5 7m5 5g2 6m5 5g5 5g2 6v3 1989 6g5 6m3 7.5f3 7m5 7f2 8m4 7g5 10m3 10g 8.2g3 9s4 9f4 8s] strong, close-coupled colt: carries condition: good mover: modest maiden: below form in claimers and sellers last 6 starts: appears best at up to 1m: acts on any going: sometimes visored or blinkered: trained until after ninth outing by G. Huffer: quite possibly ungenuine. *J. Berry.*   70 d

MAGIA (USA) 2 b.f. (Apr 19) Vaguely Noble 140–My Sister 101 (Nonoalco (USA) 131) [1989 7g] $75,000Y: third reported foal: dam Irish 7f winner stayed 1½m, is out of half-sister to Yorkshire Cup winner Noble Saint: 33/1 and in need of race, never a factor in 24-runner maiden at Newmarket in November. *C. F. Wall.*   —

MAGICAL STRIKE (USA) 3 b.c. Danzig (USA)–Egyptian Rose (USA) (Sir Ivor 135) [1988 7m* 1989 8s3 7m* 8f* 8.5g4 6m 7m* 7m5] medium-sized, good-bodied, attractive colt: has a quick, fluent action: successful in smallish fields for £10,500 event at Newmarket and listed races at Kempton (odds on) in May and York (making all to beat Tatsfield 4 lengths) in August: modest fifth of 6 in Distant Relative in Group 2 event at Newmarket: soon off bridle when last of 11 in July Cup at same course: stays 1m: best on top-of-the-ground. *M. R. Stoute.*   114

Maktoum Al-Maktoum's "Magical Strike"

MAGIC ANA 2 b.f. (Jan 24) Magic Mirror 105–Ana Gabriella (USA) (Master ?
Derby (USA)) [1989 6d 7g* 7g² 8g³ 7g 7g³ 8.9s 7.5d⁴ a8g4] ex-French filly: third
foal: half-sister to quite useful 7f and 1m winner Burkan (by Star Appeal): dam ran
once: claimed out of J. Dubois' stable 70,050 francs (approx £7,060) after finishing
fourth at Evry in November: had earlier won seller at Clairefontaine: respectable
fourth of 13 to Andrew's First in claimer at Southwell in December: stays 1m. *M. C.
Pipe.*

MAGIC AT DAWN (USA) 4 ch.g. Diamond Prospect (USA) 126–Implicit 70
(Grundy 137) [1988 8.5m 8g³ 8m⁶ 7g 8f* 8h* 10g 8m⁶ 8g 8m⁶ 1989 8h⁵ 9f⁵ 8f⁵]
sturdy, deep-girthed gelding: has been operated on for a soft palate: fair winner as
3-y-o when trained by S. Norton: best effort in 1989 on reappearance: suited by 1m,
front-running tactics and firm going: winning hurdler: inconsistent. *G. M. Moore.*

MAGIC BULLET (USA) 2 b.f. (Mar 28) Northern Baby (CAN) 127–Probation 50
(USA) (Bold Ruler) [1989 5g 5d 6m] 46,000Y: leggy, rather unfurnished filly: sister
to fair 1¼m winner Young Offender and half-sister to minor winners in USA by
Buckpasser and Graustark: dam, winner at up to 1m, is from family of Posse and
leading American 4-y-o filly Goodbye Halo: poor form in maidens: slowly away final
start (July): wears a severe bridle. *W. A. O'Gorman.*

MAGIC CRYSTAL 2 b.f. (Feb 1) Ahonoora 122–Carntino (Bustino 136) [1989 — p
7g] 34,000Y: third foal: dam ran once in Ireland at 2 yrs: 25/1, prominent around 4f in
24-runner maiden at Newmarket in November. *Lord John FitzGerald.*

MAGIC EXPRESS (USA) 2 ch.c. (Mar 23) Green Forest (USA) 134–
Secretariat Flag (USA) (Secretariat (USA)) [1989 7g] stocky colt: first foal: dam ran
once at 2 yrs: 20/1 and carrying condition, prominent to halfway in 29-runner maiden
at Newmarket in November. *M. Moubarak.*

MAGIC FLUKE   2 b.c. (Mar 13) Kafu 120–Rareitess (Rarity 129) [1989 5d² 5v²]   **61**
IR 5,200F, 4,000Y: rangy colt: fourth foal: dam, lightly-raced Irish maiden, is
half-sister to useful 1979 Irish 2-y-o Daness: runner-up early in season in minor
event (backward and green) at Catterick and maiden at Hamilton: sent to race in
Italy. *W. Bentley.*

MAGIC GLEAM (USA)   3 b.f. Danzig (USA)–All Agleam (USA) **122**
(Gleaming (USA)) [1988 7m² 7g⁶ 1989 8d 7f* 8f² 8g* 8g³ 10.5f⁴]
Few seasons began so inauspiciously and revived so rapidly as Magic
Gleam's in 1989. With the preparation of classic contenders what it is these
days perhaps we shouldn't be surprised when a high-class horse suddenly
emerges from comparative obscurity. Even so, Magic Gleam's reappearance
effort in a valuable graduation race at Ascot in April was disconcerting,
particularly so for those who'd backed her down from 8/1 to 7/2 and
second-favouritism. She'd apparently always revealed plenty of talent in her
home work—so much so that she'd been preferred to Shaadi in the betting for
a Doncaster maiden on her debut—but at Ascot she took a keen hold early and
was left floundering at the back of the nine-runner field. Her trainer told us
later that he'd hoped to get another run into Magic Gleam before a crack at the
Poule d'Essai des Pouliches but she returned lame from Ascot. To give her a
race before her next target, Royal Ascot, proved a close-run thing even; a
week before the meeting Magic Gleam stripped a lot fitter than on her
reappearance and made all in a twenty-runner maiden race at Kempton,
running rather lazily in beating Zeffirella two lengths. The choice of
engagements the following week was between the Coronation Stakes, the last
fillies' Group 1 event over a mile run in Britain, for which nine of the twelve
runners had already been tried in pattern company, and the Fern Hill
Handicap on the Saturday for which Magic Gleam would race off a mark in the
eighties. A bold decision to go for the former nearly received the perfect
reward. Magic Gleam was the only one to test the French-trained favourite
Golden Opinion; she led after a furlong and though never able to shake off

Child Stakes, Newmarket—Magic Gleam makes all

Maktoum Al-Maktoum's "Magic Gleam"

Golden Opinion who beat her half a length, Magic Gleam finished at least four lengths up on the rest.

That effort gave Magic Gleam an excellent chance against Ensconse (who gave her 6 lb) in the Child Stakes at Newmarket three weeks later and this time she was never headed, going clear into the dip and galloping on strongly under hands and heels to beat the Irish Guineas winner comfortably by four lengths. It was a second pattern-race success for her first-season trainer who followed up with Cadeaux Genereux in the Carroll Foundation July Cup twenty-four hours later and ended the year in tenth place in the trainers' table in terms of prize money won having sent out just a hundred-and-thirty-two runners. Magic Gleam couldn't add to that win but she was pitched against the best on her two remaining starts. The milers were a strong bunch in 1989 and in the Jacques-le-Marois at Deauville she took on one of the division's best in Polish Precedent and was beaten two lengths and the same by him and French Stress, having set the pace. Only nine days later Magic Gleam was stepped up in distance for the Juddmonte International at York but ran a bit below her best in fourth, pulling quite hard early and finding only one pace when Ile de Chypre went on early in the straight.

Magic Gleam (USA) (b.f. 1986)	Danzig (USA) (b 1977)	Northern Dancer (b 1961)	Nearctic
			Natalma
		Pas de Nom (b or br 1968)	Admiral's Voyage
			Petitioner
	All Agleam (USA) (b 1975)	Gleaming (b or br 1968)	Herbager
			A Gleam
		Royal Entrance (b 1965)	Tim Tam
			Prince's Gate

Magic Gleam, a 570,000-dollar foal and 650,000-dollar yearling, is the best of All Agleam's first five foals. Perhaps that should be very probably the

531

best as her half-sister Flying Snowdrop (by Soy Numero Uno) is a winner of eight races in South Africa, including the Grade 1 Stuttafords Fillies Guineas, and was placed in four other pattern events. All Agleam also produced two winners by Full Out, the better of them Shining Out who showed fairly useful form in winning twice over six furlongs for Guy Harwood as a three-year-old and later won four races in North America. All Agleam never raced but it's easy to see how she merited a meeting with Danzig. Her year-younger half-sister is the Eclipse Award-winning three-year-old of 1979 Davona Dale. Of thirteen starts that season Davona Dale won eight in a row and was second twice, her wins including two versions of the fillies' triple crown—the more established series comprising the Kentucky Oaks, Black-Eyed Susan Stakes and Coaching Club American Oaks and the New York rendering that also includes the mile-and-a-half CCA Oaks, the most prestigious race for three-year-old fillies, which Davona Dale won by eight lengths. Her dam Royal Entrance won seven races (none in better than allowance company) at up to one mile from two to four years and is bred on very similar lines to the dam of Preakness winner Gate Dancer.

Magic Gleam is likely to stay in training and has the physical scope to do at least as well at four years; a big, strong, lengthy filly, she usually impresses in appearance. She takes the eye in all her paces, as well. Forcing tactics over a mile may well suit Magic Gleam best and she goes well on firm ground. *A. A. Scott.*

MAGIC IMAGE 2 gr.g. (May 4) Magic Mirror 105–Starela (Starch Reduced 112) [1989 5d 5g 7f 5f4] 800F, 920Y: compact gelding: first live foal: dam no form: appears of little account: blinkered final outing (July). *M. W. Ellerby.* —

MAGIC MILLY 3 b.f. Simply Great (FR) 122–Supreme Fjord 92 (Targowice (USA) 130) [1988 5d2 5g5 7d2 7m6 8.2s 8d* 7g5 1989 10s 9f 6g a8g] small, sparely-made filly: lacks scope: quite modest winner as 2-y-o: well beaten (including in sellers) in 1989, off course 6 months after reappearance: suited by 1m: best form with give in the ground: trained until after reappearance by Dr J. Scargill: sold to join B. Millman 1,050 gns Doncaster November Sales. *M. Johnston.* —

MAGIC QUEST 3 ch.f. Posse (USA) 130–Satina 83 (Pall Mall 132) [1988 NR 1989 10f 9m 10g] lightly-made, leggy filly: bad mover: ninth foal: half-sister to several winners, including quite useful 1980 2-y-o 5f winner Jiva (by Mummy's Pet) and quite modest 1¾m winner Chetinkaya (by Ragstone): dam, placed at up to 1m, is daughter of Irish 1000 Guineas winner Black Satin: no sign of ability in claimers: trained debut by Dr J. Scargill. *R. Hollinshead.* —

MAGNA TRAVAILLE 4 br.c. Mr Fluorocarbon 126–Bella Travaille 82 (Workboy 123) [1988 6v4 8g5 8f 6f5 6d 10f6 10s 10m 7g 1989 10g] angular, workmanlike colt: moderate mover: fair winner at 2 yrs: little subsequent worthwhile form: probably doesn't stay 1m: possibly unsuited by extremes of going: blinkered once at 3 yrs. *S. R. Bowring.* —

MAGNETISM 2 b.c. (Mar 6) Magnolia Lad 102–Mystrique (Streak 119) [1989 6f 7f] fifth reported foal (third by Magnolia Lad): dam poor half-sister to smart sprinter Blue Courtier: tailed off in summer sellers: very slowly away on debut. *D. L. Williams.* —

MAGNETIZE 2 b.f. (Feb 14) Electric 126–Silver Birch 122 (Silver Shark 129) [1989 5m 6m2 6f3 6m4 5m5 6g] sturdy, lengthy filly: carries condition: half-sister to 2 winners by High Top, 6f to 1m winner Golden Elder and 7f and 1m winner Silver Tips: dam, unbeaten at 2 yrs, stayed 1m: quite modest maiden: should be suited by 6f +. *W. G. R. Wightman.* 60

MAGNOLIA EXPRESS 5 b.h. Magnolia Lad 102–Wasdale 97 (Psidium 130) [1988 NR 1989 15.3m] leggy, close-coupled horse: seems no longer of much account: often used to wear blinkers: sold 2,100 gns Ascot August Sales. *R. T. Juckes.* —

MAGNUS PYM 4 b.c. Al Nasr (FR) 126–Full of Reason (USA) 105 (Bold Reason) [1988 11g3 11f* 12g4 10g2 12m5 12s4 10g4 10d 1989 16s6 12d* 12g] big, close-coupled, good-bodied colt: carries condition: rather scratchy mover: favourite, won handicap at Haydock in May: probably in need of race, soundly beaten in similar company at Newmarket 5½ months later: likely to prove best at 1½m to 1¾m: acts on any going. *D. R. C. Elsworth.* 92

MAGSOOD 4 ch.g. Mill Reef (USA) 141–Shark Song 103 (Song 132) [1988 10g3 12f* 12f6 12m2 12g 12m* 13s 12g 1989 10s 12v 12d] lengthy, good-looking gelding: —

532

moderate mover: fair winner as 3-y-o when trained by M. Jarvis: subsequently lost his form, and not seen out in 1989 after April: stays 1½m: acts on firm going and probably unsuited by soft: blinkered twice, including when winning for second time (wandered) in 1988: sweating on reappearance: best left alone. *S. Mellor.*

MAHRAH (USA) 2 b.f. (May 7) Vaguely Noble 140–Montage (USA) (Alydar (USA)) [1989 7m² 7g⁶] $235,000Y: medium-sized, rather unfurnished filly: has scope: shows knee action: second foal: dam winner at around 1m in USA: 11/4, short-head second of 6 to Silk Slippers in minor event at York in September, running green 2f out then finishing well considerably handled: co-favourite, dropped away 2f out in £8,000 event at Newmarket following month. *A. C. Stewart.* — 78

MAHRAJAN 5 b.h. Dominion 123–Dame Julian 84 (Blakeney 126) [1988 8d 8g³ 10f⁴ 8f³ 9d³ 8d 10m* 10m* 9f 8m 10d 11s 1989 9d* 10g³ 8m 10m 9g 8d] rangy horse: moderate mover: fair handicapper: successful at Kempton in March: ran creditably next outing: off course nearly 5 months afterwards and well beaten last 4 starts: effective at 1m to 1¼m: acts on any going: none too consistent. *C. J. Benstead.* — 83

MAIDEN BIDDER 7 b.m. Shack (USA) 118–Wolveriana 78 (Wolver Hollow 126) [1988 5g⁵ 7g³ 6f³ 5f² 6f⁴ 5d* 5d² 5g² 5g³ 6m⁴ 5m 5g 6g⁶ 5f 6m⁵ 5d 6d 1989 6f 5.1m³ 6m³ 7f* 6f* 6m 6f⁵ 6f⁵ 5g 7f 7.6f 5m 6g² 6f 6m 5m 7g 6m 6g] lengthy mare: justified favouritism comfortably in handicaps at Chepstow (amateurs) and Goodwood on successive days in June: form in second half of season only when second in similar company at Epsom: effective at 5f and stays 7f: probably unsuited by soft going, acts on any other: blinkered 3 times: has won for apprentice: has found little in front and best with waiting tactics. *D. A. Wilson.* — 57

MAID OF ESSEX 3 b.f. Bustino 136–Magelka 77 (Relkino 131) [1988 NR 1989 7d 9g] medium-sized, attractive filly: second foal: dam, lightly-raced half-sister to Coronation Cup winner Easter Sun (by Bustino), ran best race over 1m: 7 lengths eighth of 17 in newcomers race at Newbury in April: again bit backward, led briefly over 3f out when well beaten in York maiden 6 months later: should stay at least 9f. *C. E. Brittain.* — —

MAID WELCOME 2 br.f. (Mar 16) Mummy's Pet 125–Carolynchristensen 58 (Sweet Revenge 129) [1989 5d 5s 5.8f 6f] sturdy filly: has a round action: first foal: dam won from 5f to 9.4f, including in sellers: well beaten in maidens and a minor event. *G. Lewis.* — —

MAILMAN 10 ch.g. Malacate (USA) 131–Sallail (Sallust 134) [1988 10f 10g⁴ 10.8s 10g 9m* 10m² 10s* 8m⁶ 10g³ 10s⁵ 1989 10s⁵ 10v² 11.7d 9f 10m 11.7m 12f⁴ 12m* 15.5f* 12m³] tall gelding: quite modest handicapper: an excellent mount for inexperienced rider, and won apprentice event at Chepstow and amateurs contest at Folkestone (carrying 10 lb overweight, very easily by 1½ lengths) within 9 days in late-summer: stays 15.5f: acts on any going. *I. A. Balding.* — 58

MAINLY SUNSET 3 b.f. Red Sunset 120–Mainly Dry (The Brianstan 128) [1988 NR 1989 a8g] 30,000Y: sparely-made filly: second foal: brother to quite useful sprinter Great Chaddington (by Crofter): dam never ran: 33/1, bit backward and tongue tied down, slowly away then chased leaders 6f when well beaten in maiden at Southwell in December. *A. Bailey.* — —

MAIN OBJECTIVE 4 ch.g. Main Reef 126–Winter Queen 60 (Welsh Pageant 132) [1988 8m* 8g⁴ 10m³ 8m² 10g* 10g² 1989 8f6 10g* 10g³] smallish, lengthy gelding: useful handicapper: shaped very well on reappearance and 3 weeks later justified favouritism in £19,900 Silver Seal Stakes (Handicap) at Epsom: good third to Unknown Quantity in £27,600 event at Sandown: stays 1¼m well: acts on any going: has won for apprentice: sent to race in USA. *L. M. Cumani.* — 110

MAINWARING 4 br.g. Comedy Star (USA) 121–Major Barbara 90 (Tambourine II 133) [1988 10v 8.5m* 10m 10m⁶ 10f⁴ 11.5m⁶ 1989 12m⁶] leggy, close-coupled, angular gelding: quite modest winner as 3-y-o: faced stiff task in Brighton handicap in May: stays 1¼m in moderately-run race: acts on firm going and is unsuited by heavy: has run in snatches: sold 6,000 gns Ascot 2nd June Sales. *G. A. Pritchard-Gordon.* — —

MAISON DES FRUITS 2 b.f. (Apr 15) Balidar 133–Thorganby Tina 72 (Averof 123) [1989 5f⁵ 5m³ 5g⁶ a6g² a5g] workmanlike filly: shade unfurnished: fifth foal: dam stayed 1m: quite modest maiden: better suited by 6f than 5f: bandaged off-hind last 3 starts. *C. N. Allen.* — 60

MAJESTIC ACE (USA) 3 b.c. Majestic Light (USA)–Kesar Queen (USA) 117 (Nashua) [1988 NR 1989 8f² 10f⁴ 8m* 8f³ 7f⁴ 8g] strong, quite good-bodied colt: sixth foal: half-brother to fair 1981 2-y-o 5f winner Kesarini (by Singh): dam won Coronation Stakes and third in 1000 Guineas: sire top-class middle-distance — 83 performer: favourite, won maiden at Pontefract in July: good third in minor event at Thirsk, travelling really well long way, easily best effort after: stays 1m: possibly needs top-of-the-ground: sold 9,600 gns Newmarket Autumn Sales. *H. Thomson Jones.*

MAJESTIC GROOM (USA) 6 ch. or br.h. Blushing Groom (FR) 131– — Sweetbidder (USA) (Bold Bidder) [1988 NR 1989 10s 10.2g 11.7m 8f 10f] moderate mover: little sign of ability in modest company: blinkered last 2 outings. *J. P. Hudson.*

MAJESTICIAN (GER) 6 b.g. Honduras (GER)–Marlova (FR) (Salvo 129) — [1988 14.8d⁶ 14d 16f 18g⁵ 17g* 16m³ 18g 1989 14g 20f 16g] big, rangy gelding: carries plenty of condition: moderate mover: fair handicapper at his best: below form as 6-y-o, but shaped as though he'd retained some ability on first 2 starts: out-and-out stayer: yet to race on soft going, acts on any other: best on a galloping track: lazy type: sold 9,500 gns Ascot August Sales. *G. A. Pritchard-Gordon.*

MAJESTIC IMAGE 3 ch.f. Niniski (USA) 125–Regal Twin (USA) 77 (Majestic 64 Prince) [1988 8d² 1989 6g 7f 11m 10.5g² 10g] medium-sized, rather angular filly: has a rather round action: quite modest maiden: will be suited by a return to further: possibly needs an easy surface: visored final start: sweating second outing: changed hands 6,400 gns Newmarket Autumn Sales. *W. Hastings-Bass.*

MAJESTIC JEM 3 b.f. Majestic Maharaj 105–Mia Samira (Allangrange 126) — [1988 NR 1989 8d 8.2m] workmanlike filly: third foal: dam pulled up over hurdles both outings: well beaten in seller and minor event in the spring. *R. J. Hodges.*

MAJESTIC RING (CAN) 7 b.g. Majestic Prince–Savage Call (USA) (Jungle — Savage (USA)) [1988 NR 1989 10.2g 10d] lengthy gelding: modest winner as 3-y-o: below form in spring in 1989: stays 1½m: possibly unsuited by soft going: blinkered twice: faint-hearted novice hurdler/chaser: sold privately to join P. Monteith 6,000 gns Doncaster August Sales. *P. A. Kelleway.*

MAJESTY'S ROOM (USA) 2 br.g. (Apr 4) Majestic Light (USA)–My Room 74 (USA) (Bold Lad (USA)) [1989 5m² 6m³ 8g⁴ 7f³ 8g⁶ a7g*] $30,000Y: sturdy gelding: has scope: half-brother to several winners, including useful Italian 1m to 1¼m performer Malevic (by Hawaiian Sound) and fair middle-distance stayer Zaubarr (by Hawaii): dam closely related to stakes winners: won 13-runner maiden at Southwell by ¾ length from Able Rocket: should stay 1m: bandaged behind last 2 starts: has been reluctant stalls. *A. Bailey.*

MAJHOUL 3 b.c. Glint of Gold 128–Ophrys 90 (Nonoalco (USA) 131) [1988 NR — 1989 10g] 26,000Y: attractive colt: first foal: dam won over 7f at 2 yrs and ran only 4 times: 14/1 from 5/1, bandaged near-hind and carrying condition, over 15½ lengths seventh of 18 in maiden at Leicester in April, prominent 7f and not knocked about. *B. Hanbury.*

MAJOR DON 9 ch.g. Mandrake Major 122–Kindling (Psidium 130) [1988 10g 8g 42 8m⁴ 8g 7m 7f⁶ 8m 1989 7m 6g² 6f⁴ 7f 7g 6f² 6g⁵ 7g 8m] big, strong, good-bodied gelding: good mover: one-time useful performer: effective at 6f to 1m: acted well on top-of-the-ground: dead. *E. Weymes.*

MAJOR FREDIE 3 ch.g. Major Petingo (FR)–Piber 53 (Saintly Song 128) [1988 54 7m 7.5f 1989 8g 11m 10f³ 10f³ 9f⁶ 10.4m 12f⁶] compact, plain gelding: has a quick action: plating-class form: stays 1¼m: acts on firm going: blinkered third, fourth and last 2 outings: keen sort: winning selling hurdler for K. Ryan. *A. D. Brown.*

MAJORITY HOLDING 4 b.c. Mandrake Major 122–Kirkby 85 (Midsummer 58 Night II 117) [1988 6v* 6d⁴ 7g 8m 7g⁵ 8g² 8s 9g 1989 9d 7v 8.3m 8g 10.1m 10.1m 8m* 8.3m 9m⁴ 8s 10.6d* a10g² a12g⁵ a12g⁵] lengthy, rather dipped-backed colt: landed gamble in selling handicap (no bid) at Yarmouth in August and apprentice handicap at Haydock in October: stays 10.6f: acts on top-of-the-ground and heavy going: usually bandaged nowadays: slowly away third and fifth starts: inconsistent. *K. T. Ivory.*

MAJOR IVOR 4 ch.c. Mandrake Major 122–Double Birthday (Cavo Doro 124) 84 [1988 6f 5m 6g⁴ 6g³ 7m⁴ 6g⁵ 6f⁵ 6s 6m 7g 1989 7f³ 8.2g 7f³ 8f* 8f² 8f* 9f³ 8.2d³] big, workmanlike colt: carries condition: fair handicapper: won at Redcar in July and August: good third, tending to edge left, to Hard As Iron in £12,200 event at York and to demoted Turbo Speed in £8,300 contest at Haydock last 2 outings: suited by around 1m: acts on firm going and a soft surface: well suited by strong handling. *Mrs G. R. Reveley.*

MAJOR JACKO 6 b.h. Mandrake Major 122–Toreadora 103 (Matador 131) [1988 77 ? 7g 6f 6f⁴ 6m 6m³ 6f⁶ 6g⁴ 6m 6d* 6d⁴ 1989 5d⁵ 6d² 6f 6m 6g 6m a7g*] big, lengthy horse: moderate mover: appeared to show vast improvement when winning claimer at Southwell in November: successful on only 2 of his previous 41 outings: effective at 6f and 7f: best on an easy surface: blinkered twice: often apprentice ridden: inconsistent. *R. Hannon.*

MAKARIM (FR)   4 b.c. Shareef Dancer (USA) 135–Chappelle Blanche (USA) 96   77 §
(Olden Times) [1988 NR 1989 10f3 12f 12.3f4 10f* 11f6 10m] 470,000F: strong, stocky colt: carries plenty of condition: fifth foal: half-brother to 3 winners, including fair 1m winner Chantry (by Habitat): dam, half-sister to Beldale Flutter, won at 6f and stayed 1m: won uncompetitive handicap at Chepstow in July, looking unenthusiastic in front: probably better suited by 1¼m than 1½m: acts on firm going: blinkered first 3 starts: started slowly and carried head high last occasion: has pulled hard: sold 14,000 gns Newmarket Autumn Sales: suspect temperamentally. *H. Thomson Jones.*

MAKBUL   2 b.c. (Feb 18) Fairy King (USA)–Royaltess (Royal And Regal (USA))   104 p
[1989 6f* 6f*] IR 18,000F, 23,000Y: compact, good-quartered colt: first foal: dam unraced sister to useful Irish sprint winner Regaltess and half-sister to useful Irish 1979 2-y-o Daness: green, successful in June in minor event at Pontefract and £7,700 race (stayed on strongly having looked held 1f out when beating Somethingdifferent by a neck) at Ascot: wasn't seen out again: will be suited by 7f: may well improve further. *D. Morley.*

MAKE AND MEND   2 gr.f. (May 13) Godswalk (USA) 130–Social Partner   —
(Sparkler 130) [1989 6m 5m] 3,200Y: good-topped filly: fourth foal: sister to 1986 Irish 2-y-o 5f winner With Gods Help: dam of little account: bit backward, little worthwhile form in auction events at Ripon (maiden) and Redcar. *J. Wharton.*

MAKE CONTACT (USA)   3 b.c. Fappiano (USA)–Touch (USA) (Herbager 136)   81
[1988 6f6 7m5 7g2 1989 11.7m 12m6 12h2 15.3m* 16m2 14g] rangy, quite attractive colt: has a long stride: on toes, made all in handicap at Wolverhampton in August: appears suited by 15f+: acts on hard ground: blinkered on reappearance: sold R. Akehurst 29,000 gns Newmarket Autumn Sales. *Major W. R. Hern.*

MAKE OR MAR   5 b. or br.m. Daring March 116–Martelli 70 (Pitskelly 122)   81
[1988 5s4 5f2 5m6 6f 5d 5m 1989 5s 5f4 5m3 6f* 6m 6f] sparely-made mare: fair performer: made virtually all and rallied splendidly when winning handicap at Newbury in May: stayed 6f: well suited by firm going: in foal to Sayf El Arab. *J. R. Jenkins.*

MAKE SAIL   3 ch.f. Main Reef 126–Banda Sea (Balidar 133) [1988 NR 1989 7d 8g   43
8.2f 8f5 8.2g a8g] lengthy, angular filly: second foal: dam unraced daughter of half-sister to Bireme, Buoy and Fluke: poor form, including in sellers: may well stay 1¼m: off course 5 months and bought out of L. Cumani's stable 1,900 gns Newmarket July Sales after debut: slowly away final start. *W. Wilson.*

MAKE THE WEIGHT   2 b.c. (Apr 3) State Trooper 96–Aucuba Queen   —
(Spanish Jet) [1989 6m] first reported foal: dam unraced: 25/1 and bit backward, always behind in 18-runner seller at Lingfield in September. *J. R. Jenkins.*

MAKE YOUR PLANS (USA)   3 ch.f. Runaway Groom (CAN)–Lay Your   —
Course (USA) (Sir Ivor 135) [1988 5m* 5s4 7d 1989 6s 6f] neat filly: moderate walker: well below form since winning debut, in sellers in first half of 1989: probably unsuited by soft going: sold 1,350 gns Doncaster June Sales. *N. Tinkler.*

MALAMUTE SALOON (USA)   3 ch.c. Arctic Tern (USA) 126–Square   83
Generation (USA) (Olden Times) [1988 7g5 1989 9f4 10.6g6 12g4 10.6g3 8f3 12g2] leggy, rather unfurnished colt: fair maiden: stays 1½m: sold to join M. Pipe 30,000 gns Newmarket Autumn Sales. *H. R. A. Cecil.*

MALASPINA   5 b. or br.h. Bellypha 130–Mondovision (FR) (Luthier 126) [1988   118
7s* 8s* 8g4 8d3 10g3 1989 8s*dis 7s3 8d2 7d* 7m4 8v5 8s*] French horse: smart performer: first past the post in 90,000-franc event (rider weighed in at incorrect weight) at Saint-Cloud in April and in listed races at Longchamp in September and Maisons-Laffitte in November: best effort when over 2 lengths fourth to Gabina in Prix de la Foret at Longchamp: best at 7f or 1m: acted on any going: retired to Cronkwell Grange Stud, Bath, fee £200 + £800 (Oct 1st). *Mme C. Head, France.*

MALEVICH (USA)   3 b.c. Lear Fan (USA) 130–Icy Time (USA) (Icecapade   102
(USA)) [1988 7m4 7g3 1989 7d4 8s* 7f3 8f4 8g 8g* 9g 8g] well-made colt: won maiden at Kempton in May and minor event at Leicester in September: ran quite well most other starts: stays 1m: acts on any going: wore crossed noseband at 2 yrs, on final start pulling very hard: suited by waiting tactics in strongly-run race. *H. R. A. Cecil.*

MALHAMDALE (USA)   3 ch.c. Dixieland Band (USA)–Golden Rhyme 87   81
(Dom Racine (FR) 121) [1988 6m5 1989 8g 7s6 7m* 7f4 8f4 7.6f3 8f* 7m* 8.3g2 8g5

8m² 10m] compact colt: good mover: fair handicapper: won at Thirsk in May and July (apprentices) and Yarmouth in August: stays 1m well: acts on firm going, probably unsuited by soft: sold 17,500 gns Newmarket Autumn Sales. *W. J. Haggas.*

MALIBASTA   3 b.f. Auction Ring (USA) 123–Basta 72 (Busted 134) [1988 5f 6m* 1989 8f² 8f²] quite attractive filly: won maiden at Goodwood as 2-y-o: ran well in handicaps there in summer 1989: will be suited by 1¼m. *D. R. C. Elsworth.*   **82**

MALLAU   3 b.c. Runnett 125–Brierley Lodge 67 (Lorenzaccio 130) [1988 5g 5g 6f4 5.8g 6g 6f4 7m⁵ 7f⁶ 1989 6s 6s 8d⁵ 6f 5.8h 6m² 6m 6f* 7f² 5.3h⁶ 7f* 7m⁵ 7m] good-topped colt: made virtually all to win apprentice seller (bought in 3,600 gns) at Nottingham in July and handicap at Lingfield in August: effective at 6f and easy 7f: seems to need firm ground: blinkered fifth outing: slowly away penultimate one: good mount for apprentice. *L. J. Holt.*   **63**

MALLYAN   2 b.f. (May 10) Miramar Reef 100§–Charlie's Sunshine 77 (Jimsun 121) [1989 8d] second reported foal: dam 7.6f winner at 3 yrs also won over jumps: 50/1, always behind in 18-runner maiden at Thirsk in November. *G. R. Oldroyd.*   **—**

MALMESBURY   2 ch.g. (Apr 15) Burslem 123–Malmsey (Jukebox 120) [1989 6m 7g 7g⁴ 8g] workmanlike gelding: has scope: has a long stride: half-brother to 3-y-o Moon Reef (by Main Reef), 8.2f winner at 2 yrs, and 2 other winners, including 1981 2-y-o 5f winner Lockwood Girl (by Prince Tenderfoot): dam won over 1¼m and 1¾m in Ireland: quite modest form in maidens: ran moderately in nursery at Goodwood final start: subsequently gelded. *G. B. Balding.*   **62**

MALPAS   2 br.g. (May 11) Camden Town 125–Pollixena (Sexton Blake 126) [1989 5d⁵ 5d⁶ 6g 7m⁶ 7f] IR 6,600Y: useful-looking gelding: good walker: has roundish action: second foal: dam fourth over 9f and 1½m in Ireland: poor form in varied races: blinkered and on edge, dropped out from halfway and looked ungenerous in seller at Redcar final start (July): one to avoid. *M. H. Easterby.*   **42 §**

MALUNAR   4 gr.g. Mummy's Pet 125–Tranquility Base 112 (Roan Rocket 128) [1988 6g⁴ 8g⁶ 6m⁶ 7m 7d 8g 1989 6s 6d* 7s 6g⁴ 5.8h 6m] small, close-coupled, lightly-made gelding: well backed, returned to his best when winning minor event at Folkestone in April: 25/1, good fourth in handicap at Newmarket following month: badly hampered next outing: best at 6f: acts on a soft surface: blinkered 3 times, visored last 5 outings: has looked a difficult ride and suited by strong handling. *J. R. Shaw.*   **77**

MAMALUNA (USA)   3 ch.f. Roberto (USA) 131–Kadesh (USA) (Lucky Mel) [1988 8s* 8g 10g* 1989 10f² 12m⁴ 10d² 10f* 10g⁴ 10g] rangy filly: smart performer: made all in Vodafone Nassau Stakes at Goodwood in July to beat Lady Shipley 1½ lengths: in frame in listed race at Newbury, Gold Seal Oaks at Epsom (5½ lengths fourth to Aliysa), Budweiser Pretty Polly Stakes at the Curragh (beaten ½ length by Noora Abu) and EBF Phoenix Champion Stakes at Phoenix Park (2½ lengths fourth to Carroll House): favourite, ran poorly in Sun Chariot Stakes at Newmarket: stays 1½m: probably acts on any going: suited by forcing tactics: game and consistent. *G. Harwood.*   **114**

MANABEL   7 br.m. Manado 130–Fire Bell 93 (Firestreak 125) [1988 6g⁶ 6g 5m 5g* 8g* 6g 8f 6m⁴ 12m 7m 8g³ 7m 5f 8.2s² 7g 7d⁴ 5v 1989 8d 6m 7m 8f] lengthy, sparely-made mare: poor mover: poor winner (including for apprentice) as 6-y-o: below form in first half of 1989: effective at 5f to 9f: suited by give in the ground: effective with or without blinkers: inconsistent. *S. R. Bowring.*   **—**

Vodafone Nassau Stakes, Goodwood—Mamaluna holds on well from Lady Shipley

MANCHESTERSKYTRAIN 10 b.g. Home Guard (USA) 129–Aswellas 93 (Le — Levanstell 122) [1988 NR 1989 8h 6f 7f] workmanlike gelding: quite modest handicapper as 8-y-o: well behind all starts in first half of 1989: stays 1m: acts on any going: blinkered once: sometimes sweats: has gone freely to post (taken down early final outing) and often gives bit of trouble at stalls. *K. Bishop.*

MANDALAY PRINCE 5 b.g. Nishapour (FR) 125–Ops (Welsh Saint 126) [1988 54 §
16g 16m 15.5f4 18m 16f5 20.4d6 16m 18g 18g6 1989 16m 18f3 20f] lengthy, well-made gelding: has a round action: long way out of handicap, form on flat for some time only when 5 lengths third of 11 at Doncaster: tailed off in Ascot Stakes (Handicap) at Royal Ascot 3 weeks later: out-and-out stayer: acts on firm going and is unsuited by a soft surface: has sweated and got on toes: tried in blinkers and visor as 4-y-o: bandaged last 2 starts: ran out once at 4 yrs. *T. Kersey.*

MANDERLEY BOY 3 b.g. Absalom 128–Phlox 101 (Floriana 106) [1988 5v5 6f — 5f 5m 7g 6m 1989 7s4 7.5d 8d 6m 6m6 7g6] small, sparely-made gelding: plating-class maiden at best: below form as 3-y-o in sellers and apprentice handicap: probably stays 7f: claimer ridden last 4 starts: sold 1,000 gns Newmarket Autumn Sales. *A. Bailey.*

MANDRAKE MAGIC 3 br.f. Mandrake Major 122–Veruschka (USA) — (Turn-To) [1988 5g 5d 5f 10d 1989 10g] leggy, plain filly: moderate walker: has a roundish action: no form in varied company, including selling. *Pat Mitchell.*

MANDY'S LOVE 4 b.f. Tower Walk 130–Our Mandy (Mansingh (USA) 120) — [1988 6d 5f 5d* 6g 6f 5d6 1989 5f] lengthy, rather dipped-backed filly: winning plater as 3-y-o: little other form, mainly in better company: very much in need of race on only outing (May) in 1989: suited by 5f and a soft surface. *C. J. Hill.*

MAN FOR ALL SEASON (USA) 3 b.c. Sir Ivor 135–Val de Val (FR) (Val de 76 Loir 133) [1988 NR 1989 11.7d3 11.7m6 11g] rather leggy, plain colt: has plenty of scope: moderate mover: half-brother to several winners in France, including 1m and 1¼m winner Valamine (by Melyno), and winner at up to 10.5f Vallee de la Cour (by Pharly): dam, poor maiden, is daughter of high-class staying filly Valya: well below form after promising debut: in need of race and didn't handle bend in Redcar claimer final start, first for nearly 6 months: should stay further: sold 16,000 gns Newmarket Autumn Sales. *R. J. R. Williams.*

MANGO MANILA 4 b.c. Martinmas 128–Trigamy 112 (Tribal Chief 125) [1988 77 8g 8f 10m6 6g6 8d3 7m* 1989 8g 8m5 7m* 8.2g 7m 8g] robust colt: bad mover: co-favourite, showed improved form when winning handicap at Newmarket (second course victory) in July: not discredited final outing: suited by 7f: acts on top-of-the-ground and a soft surface: slowly away fourth start: sometimes wears crossed noseband nowadays. *C. A. Horgan.*

MANHATTAN RIVER 3 ch.g. Gorytus (USA) 132–East River (FR) (Arctic 60 Tern (USA) 126) [1988 6g5 1989 8.2m2 8f3 a7g] compact, workmanlike gelding: quite modest maiden: second of 4 at Hamilton in July: well beaten at Ayr 4 days later and in Southwell handicap (had stiff task) 5 months after that: may prove suited by 9f or 1m: trained until after second outing by A. Bailey. *E. Weymes.*

MANHUNT 3 b.f. Posse (USA) 130–Macarte (FR) (Gift Card (FR) 124) [1988 6m3 51 1989 7s 7.6m6 6f 6f3 a6g a7g] angular, unfurnished filly: quite modest maiden: form as 3-y-o only on second and fourth starts: probably stays 7f: form only on top-of-the-ground. *J. L. Dunlop.*

MAN IN THE MOON 6 b.g. Mansingh (USA) 120–Lady Antonia 66 (Owen — Anthony 102) [1988 NR 1989 10g] compact gelding: of little account: often blinkered: has worn bandages. *Miss L. Bower.*

MANIPUR 2 b.g. (May 24) Mansingh (USA) 120–Edna Lawn (USA) 63 (Mr Redoy 40 (USA)) [1989 5f 5g 5m 5m] leggy gelding: first foal: dam 5f winner: poor form in varied events, including a seller. *J. Wharton.*

MANIX 8 b.g. Manado 130–Ixee (FR) (Breton 130) [1988 7d 6m 1989 12m 8.2f4 — 7m] lengthy gelding: no longer of much account: blinkered 3 times: trained on reappearance by T. Craig. *P. Monteith.*

MANJANIQ 5 b.g. Kings Lake (USA) 133–Ivory Home (FR) (Home Guard (USA) — 129) [1988 14d 1989 12d5 17.6f 12f] medium-sized, attractive gelding: moderate mover: fair winner as 3-y-o: very lightly raced and little subsequent worthwhile form on flat: stays 13.3f: acts on heavy going. *D. W. Chapman.*

MANNA FROM HEAVEN 4 b.f. Ela-Mana-Mou 132–Saintly Game (Welsh 68 Saint 126) [1988 9g* 8d6 1989 8h* 12f3 12m4 11f3] rather sparely-made ex-Irish filly: poor mover: second living foal: dam won twice over 5f in Ireland: won poor

537

apprentice event at Carlisle in June: beaten fair way in varied events afterwards, finishing badly lame final outing: stays at least 9f: acts on hard going and is unsuited by heavy: changed hands 5,100 gns Doncaster June Sales. *Denys Smith.*

MAN OF MAUM 4 ch.c. Stanford 121§–Kitty Ellis (Le Levanstell 122) [1988 8g 7d 7f 8m 7g 1989 12.2g⁶] poor maiden. *R. Earnshaw.* —

MANOFTHEYEAR 2 b.c. (Feb 10) Sayf El Arab (USA) 127–Vexed Voter (Pontifex (USA)) [1989 5d⁵ 5m] 12,500F, 16,000Y: compact colt: not a good walker: fifth foal: half-brother to 3-y-o Super Bid (by Superlative) and 5f winner Silent Majority (by General Assembly): dam useful 5f winner in Ireland: good speed 3f in maiden and auction event (blinkered) at Newmarket when trained by W. O'Gorman: sent to Italy to be trained by B. Agriformi and won listed races at 5f and 6f and 6f Group 3 event at Milan. *W. A. O'Gorman.* ?

MANOR HOUSE (USA) 2 b.c. (Jun 6) El Gran Senor (USA) 136–Rose Cream (USA) (Rich Cream (USA)) [1989 6g] medium-sized, angular colt: first foal: dam stakes winner at up to 1¼m: 25/1 and backward, never dangerous in 29-runner maiden at Newmarket in November. *L. Cumani.* —

MANOSA MILL 4 b.g. Red Sunset 120–Egyptian Moon 78 (Kalamoun 129) [1988 NR 1989 8m] lengthy, angular gelding: second reported foal: dam, second over 1m on only start at 2 yrs, is half-sister to Circus Plume: 50/1, backward and green, well-beaten last of 10 in minor event at Carlisle in June. *Roy Robinson.* —

MANOUSHKA 4 b.f. Ile de Bourbon (USA) 133–Gilwanigan (Captain's Gig (USA)) [1988 8s 8f⁵ 9f⁶ 10g 8g² 7m⁶ 7f⁶ 8.2m⁵ 8g 1989 8m 8.3m 10.1m⁵ 8.3m⁶ 8m a10g a16g⁴] close-coupled filly: poor mover: poor maiden: probably stays 1¼m: acts on top-of-the-ground: blinkered 3 times as 3-y-o: visored twice in 1989: occasionally sweats: inconsistent. *P. Butler.* —

MANSE KEY GOLD 2 ch.f. (May 6) Vaigly Great 127–Carafran (Stanford 121§) [1989 5d⁵ 5g² 6m³ 6f 7f⁴ 6m 6g⁵ 5g⁶ 6s*] 420Y: unfurnished filly: first foal: dam lightly-raced daughter of half-sister to Yorkshire Cup winner Pragmatic: 16/1, won 15-runner claimer at Hamilton in November: ran creditably most other starts: suited by 6f: probably acts on any going: changed hands 2,500 gns Doncaster October Sales. *R. Earnshaw.* 58

MANSFIELD HOUSE 4 ch.g. Swing Easy 126–Pollinella 108 (Charlottown 127) [1988 12d 10m 11.7m 1989 14f 16.5g 12h*] good-topped gelding: 33/1, form since 2 yrs only when winning 10-runner handicap at Lingfield (set slow pace) in July: seems suited by 1½m: acts on hard going: has started very slowly. *J. L. Dunlop.* 47

MANSICK 3 b.f. Mansingh (USA) 120–Siconda 66 (Record Token 128) [1988 5d 7f⁶ 1989 8d⁶ 7g⁴ 8m 8g 7m] small, lengthy filly: maiden plater: fourth at Doncaster, easily best effort: stays 7f: blinkered third, sweating and edgy fourth starts: tends to wander under pressure, and is hard ride: sold 775 gns Ascot 2nd June Sales. *M. McCormack.* 53

MANSIO 5 b.g. Liboi (USA) 76–Sdenka (FR) 79 (Habitat 134) [1988 12g 10.8s 8f* 8g³ 9m 8g² 8s⁴ 9g 1989 8g 7f 10f⁴ 10m⁶ 11.5g 10f²] workmanlike, good-bodied gelding: moderate walker and mover: plating-class handicapper: form as 5-y-o only when in frame at Sandown and Folkestone: stays 1¼m: seems to act on any going: blinkered once: sweating second outing. *H. Candy.* 55

MANSION HOUSE 3 b.c. Thatching 131–El Pina (Be My Guest (USA) 126) [1988 6d 5v 6s* 7s⁶ 1989 7s⁵ 7m* 6m⁶ 7g* 7g⁴ 6g⁶ 6g⁴] IR 16,000F, IR 35,000Y: strong, good-bodied colt: has a round action: first foal: dam unraced daughter of Princess Royal Stakes winner Aloft: won minor events at Punchestown as 2-y-o and Phoenix Park in May and July: below-form fourth in listed races at Phoenix Park and the Curragh: 100/1, not discredited behind Danehill in Ladbroke Sprint Cup at Haydock in between: stays 7f: acts on soft going and top-of-the-ground: blinkered last 5 outings. *M. A. O'Toole, Ireland.* 103

MANS NO ANGEL 4 b.g. Aragon 118–No Halo 74 (Aureole 132) [1988 8d⁶ 8.2m 8m 8.2g⁶ 8.2g⁵ 8.2s 12m 9s⁴ 10v³ 12d⁴ 1989 8v 7d 7f⁵ 7m²ᵈⁱˢ 8.2f⁶ 9.1f⁴ 8g] smallish, workmanlike gelding: poor plater: 20/1, ¾-length second (disqualified on technicality) of 15 in handicap at Edinburgh in July: effective at 7f and stays 1¼m: acts on any going. *T. Craig.* 33

MANSONNIEN (FR) 5 ch.h. Tip Moss (FR)–Association (FR) (Margouillat (FR) 133) [1988 12d⁶ 12d* 12m³ 12m⁶ 12m³ 11g² 10m⁴ 11g³ 10g² 1989 10v³ 10.5s³ 9.2g⁴ 11d* 11f² 10d² 12g] French horse: smart performer: won listed race at Chantilly in June: in frame in Prix Exbury at Saint-Cloud, Prix Ganay, Prix d'Ispahan and Prix du Prince d'Orange (½-length second to In The Wings) at Longchamp and 119 in listed event (on fifth outing) at Ostend: well beaten in Ciga Prix de l'Arc de Triomphe: stays 1½m: probably acts on any going: consistent. *N. Pelat, France.*

MANTINIK 4 b.g. Sayyaf 121–Bonny Rand (USA) (Hillary) [1988 10.8d⁵ 12g 11.7m 10d⁴ 10s⁶ 10g 10.2g* 1989 8f 10g] rather sparely-made gelding: plating-class winner of apprentice event as 3-y-o: soundly beaten both outings in 1989, off course 5 months in between: suited by 1¼m: acts on heavy going: blinkered 3 times at 3 yrs. *J. D. J. Davies.* —

MANTRAKI 2 ch.c. (Jan 21) Good Times (ITY)–Tota Tora (Home Guard (USA) 129) [1989 7m³ 8.2g³] 13,000Y: leggy, workmanlike colt: first foal: dam, ran 3 times, is daughter of sister to Derby fourth Great Wall: placed in minor events at Newmarket (better effort) and Haydock. *C. E. Brittain.* 75

MANX PRINCESS 2 b.f. (Mar 12) Roscoe Blake 120–Princess Scarlett (Prince Regent (FR) 129) [1989 6g⁶ 6m 7g⁵] rather sparely-made filly: fourth foal: half-sister to 3-y-o Belfort Princess (by Belfort), 6f winner at 2 yrs: dam twice: poor maiden: best effort final start: bred to stay quite well. *Mrs J. R. Ramsden.* 47

MA PETITE CHOU 2 gr.f. (Mar 25) Known Fact (USA) 135–Boule de Suif 88 (Major Portion 129) [1989 6f] smallish, workmanlike filly: half-sister to several winners here and abroad, including 1m to 1½m winner Dumplino (by Bustino): dam, who stayed 1m, is half-sister to 3 good performers: 12/1, slowly away and always behind in 9-runner minor event at Pontefract in October. *G. Wragg.* —

MAPLE HAYES 3 b.f. Pas de Seul 133–Sweet Eliane (Birdbrook 110) [1988 6d 6s 10.2m 1989 8g 10.2f⁵ 8g 12.5f] leggy, angular, close-coupled filly: fifth in claimer at Doncaster in June, only sign of ability: sweating and edgy before seller final start: suited by 1¼m: bought out of R. Hollinshead's stable 3,000 gns Doncaster September Sales after third outing. *Mrs A. Knight.*

MAPLELINE 2 ch.f. (Feb 7) Shy Groom (USA)–Skimmer 86 (Skymaster 126) [1989 5.1f 6m] IR 1,300Y, 1,900 2-y-o: small, lightly-made filly: half-sister to several winners: dam 2-y-o 5.9f winner: slowly away and always behind in summer maiden auction events at Yarmouth and Pontefract. *M. H. Tompkins.* —

MAPPA MUNDI 2 b.c. (May 15) Formidable (USA) 125–Rosni 66 (Blakeney 126) [1989 7g 7g a8g⁵] robust, lengthy colt: has a round action: third foal: half-brother to 3-y-o 6f to 10.2f winner Perosini (by Persian Bold) and a winning hurdler by Song: dam twice-raced half-sister to smart miler Alert: quite modest maiden: looked ungenerous final start: will stay 1½m. *L. J. Holt.* 61

MARADIT 3 b.c. Glenstal (USA) 118–Shirley's Joy (Shirley Heights 130) [1988 5m² 1989 8.5g³ 8m 6m³] rather leggy, angular colt: fair maiden: may well prove ideally suited by 7f: bandaged as 3-y-o. *B. Hanbury.* 80

MARASOL 2 gr.f. (May 2) Siberian Express (USA) 125–Macarte (FR) (Gift Card (FR)) [1989 5.8f² 6f² 5f² 8m* 7s² 8f a8g] angular, sparely-made filly: moderate walker: fourth foal: half-sister to 3-y-o Manhunt (by Posse) and 6f winner Mariano (by Aragon): dam minor French 1m and 9f winner: modest performer: won nursery at Warwick by a length: will stay 1¼m: races keenly. *J. L. Dunlop.* 71

MARAZION 2 b.c. (Apr 21) Undulate (USA)–Tavaro (Gustav 121) [1989 5f⁶ 6m⁵ 7f] workmanlike colt: brother to 1m winner Solent Steel and half-brother to a winning hurdler: dam won in Norway: blinkered, ran very wide home bend in seller at Wolverhampton, crashed through rails and was destroyed. *K. M. Brassey.* —

MARBELLA SILKS 4 b.g. Balidar 133–Worthy Venture 76 (Northfields (USA)) [1988 6v 6g* 5d² 6f* 6m* 6m³ 6f* 5g³ 6g* 6g⁵ 7d² 7m² 7g 6f 6g⁵ 6g 1989 6d³ 6g⁴ 6g³ 6g³ 6f³ 7.2g⁶ 6m² 6g⁵ 7f⁴ 6h] lengthy gelding: often unimpressive in appearance: poor mover: had a fine season as 3-y-o, winning 5 handicaps (unimpressively when blinkered): gave good account of himself in useful company in 1989 but ran rare modest race on final one (early-August): effective at 6f and 7f: acts on firm going (probably unsuited by hard) and a soft surface: sweating on reappearance: bandaged off-hind sixth start: suited by waiting tactics: tough and genuine. *M. J. Ryan.* 101

MARCELLINA 7 ch.m. Welsh Pageant 132–Connarca (Connaught 130) [1988 NR 1989 12g⁶] compact mare: poor maiden on flat: winning hurdler. *E. J. Alston.* —

MARCHINELLA 3 br.f. Daring March 116–Pollinella 108 (Charlottown 127) [1988 6m⁴ 6f* 6d 1989 7m 7f⁴ 8m⁵ 7g⁶ 6f] close-coupled, deep-girthed filly: quite modest handicapper: stays 1m: acts on firm going: bandaged near-hind fourth start. *W. Jarvis.* 66

MARCHING STAR 3 ch.f. Marching On 101–Elegant Star 86 (Star Moss 122) [1988 5v* 5g² 5m³ 7.5f³ 6m³ 5g⁶ 5m 1989 6v⁶ 7.5d 6m 7m 8f⁶ 8g 6f 7m 7g a6g⁶ a6g] —

Mr C. d'Alessio's "Marcinkus"

neat filly: good mover: quite modest winner at 2 yrs: little form as 3-y-o, including in sellers: showed signs of retaining her ability last 2 outings: should be suited by return to 1m: acts on any going: blinkered last 3 starts. *T. Fairhurst.*

MARCHMAN 4 b.g. Daring March 116–Saltation 111 (Sallust 134) [1988 10.1d 12.2g² 13.8g² 12g² 12g 1989 12m 10f⁵ 10f 10m* 11.7m⁶ 10f² 12g] good-topped gelding: quite modest handicapper: (won for first time) at Chepstow in July: good second at Salisbury in September: well beaten in amateurs event final outing: effective at 1¼m and stays 1¾m: acts on firm going: bandaged on reappearance. *J. S. King.*   **62**

MARCH ON 3 b.g. Daring March 116–Dualvi 91 (Dual 117) [1988 NR 1989 a10g] 2,000Y: fifth foal: brother to fairly useful 1983 2-y-o 1m winner Double Quick Time, later stakes-placed winner in USA, and 1¼m winner Combined Exercise: dam won over 7f at 2 yrs: 20/1 and ridden by 7-lb claimer, well beaten in maiden at Lingfield in October, slowly away: winning juvenile hurdler. *R. V. Smyth.*   **—**

MARCIANA 2 b.f. (Mar 4) Valiyar 129–Sari Habit (Saritamer (USA) 130) [1989 6g⁴ 6g⁴] leggy filly: third live foal: half-sister to good German 3-y-o Filia Ardross (by Ardross): dam won in Italy: around 5 lengths fourth of 15, slowly away, to Ra'a in maiden at Goodwood in October: well-backed favourite, hung right and looked temperamentally unsatisfactory in similar event at Leicester following month. *J. H. M. Gosden.*   **63**

MARCINKUS 3 br.c. Tolomeo 127–Magic Spell (FR) (Dancer's Image (USA)) **113** §
[1988 NR 1989 10m² 10.2g* 10g² 10f² 10m⁵ 10g² 10g²] 50,000Y: tall, rather leggy
colt: moderate walker: has a quick action: half-brother to very smart
French 7.5f to 10.5f winner Metal Precieux (by High Line) and a winner over jumps
in France by Crimson Beau: dam, second over 6f from 2 starts, is half-sister to very
smart middle-distance performer Maitland: won maiden at Doncaster in July by
short head: narrowly beaten in £7,200 handicap at Newmarket and Chesterfield Cup
(favourite) at Goodwood next 2 outings: didn't impress with attitude after, hanging
right once ridden along final start: should stay 1½m: acts on firm going: should
prove best with waiting tactics in strongly-run race: has twice given trouble at
stalls, withdrawn intended second start: very useful but not one to trust. *L. M.
Cumani.*

MARCROFT 3 ch.f. Crofthall 110–Squires Girl (Spanish Gold 101) [1988 5g 5f* **90**
5g³ 5g² 6g² 6g* 6d⁶ 6d 1989 6g 7g³ 7m⁵ 6m 7s² 6m 6f⁶] sparely-made,
close-coupled filly: fairly useful performer: placed in minor events at Catterick and
Ayr: better at 7f than 6f: best form on an easy surface: tends to carry head high. *R.
M. Whitaker.*

MARDONIUS 3 b.c. Persian Bold 123–Dominica (GER) (Zank) [1988 NR 1989 **118**
10m* 10.5d³ 12.5m² 12g² 15m* 15.5g⁵] IR 16,000F, 58,000Y: seventh foal: brother
to 1983 French 2-y-o 7f winner Perdomi, closely related to a maiden by Bold Lad,
and half-brother to 3 winners, including fair 1m and 1½m winner Beau Nash (by
Prince Tenderfoot): dam 9f and 1½m winner in Ireland: won newcomers race at
Longchamp in June and Ciga Prix de Lutece (leading close home to beat Demawend
a neck) at Longchamp in October: good fifth in Prix Royal-Oak later: suited by test
of stamina: acts on top-of-the-ground: blinkered last 4 starts. *A. Fabre, France.*

MARDOOD 4 b.c. Ela-Mana-Mou 132–Tigeen (Habitat 134) [1988 5f 7d* 10g **83**
10d* 8s⁵ 10s 1989 12.2s³ 8d 12d] lengthy colt: moderate mover: fair performer: not
seen out after May: probably needs further than 1m and stays 12.2f: acts on soft
going. *G. Price.*

MARGS GIRL 2 b.f. (Apr 11) Claude Monet (USA) 121–Aquarian Star (Cavo Doro **57**
124) [1989 5f 5f² 6m 7m* 6m⁴ 7m³ 7m³ 7m³ 7m² 8.2s³ 8m⁶ 6g⁵ 6g²] leggy,
sparely-made filly: poor mover: second living foal: dam temperamental half-sister to
smart 1¼m performer The Dunce: 20/1, won seller (no bid) at Carlisle in June by 3
lengths from Brownie Sarah: ran creditably, including for 7-lb claimer, most
subsequent starts: stays 1m: acts on any going: game and genuine. *T. Fairhurst.*

MARGUB (USA) 4 b. or br.c. Topsider (USA)–Kissapotamus (USA) —
(Illustrious) [1988 5m² 5g 6g 7m 1989 6.5s⁵ 8g⁵ 8f 7f] big, strong, good sort: fairly
useful winner as 2-y-o: ran creditably on first outing (September) in 1988, but little
subsequent worthwhile form: probably best at short of 1m: acts on firm going and a
soft surface: sold 7,400 gns Newmarket Autumn Sales. *R. W. Armstrong.*

MARIAN EVANS 2 b.f. (Apr 8) Dominion 123–Kindjal 84 (Kris 135) [1989 6g] —
first foal: dam, 1m winner from 3 starts at 3 yrs, is daughter of Yorkshire Oaks and
Nassau Stakes winner Connaught Bridge: 12/1, backward and green, over 11 lengths
seventh of 8 in maiden at Haydock in July. *P. W. Harris.*

MARIANO 4 b.g. Aragon 118–Macarte (FR) (Gift Card (FR) 124) [1988 6g 8m 7g³ —
7g 8f⁶ 6m* 6f³ 6m 6s 1989 6m 6f 6f] leggy, close-coupled gelding: moderate winner as
3-y-o: well beaten in summer handicaps in 1989: suited by 6f to 7f: acts on firm going
and a soft surface: never going well in blinkers: difficult ride, who finds little in
front. *T. Thomson Jones.*

MARIDANA (USA) 3 b.f. Nijinsky (CAN) 138–Mabira (Habitat 134) [1988 7g **86**
1989 8s* 9g³ 10m] lengthy, workmanlike filly: favourite, won maiden at Thirsk in
April: good third in minor event at Wolverhampton, again edging left, 2 weeks later:
last of 11 in handicap at Newbury in July: stays 9f: acts on soft going. *M. R. Stoute.*

MARIENSKI (USA) 2 b.c. (Apr 11) Nureyev (USA) 131–Highclere 129 **89**
(Queen's Hussar 124) [1989 6m³ 7m* 8m⁶] rangy, good sort: has a fluent action:
half-brother to 4 winners, including smart middle-distance performer Milford (by
Mill Reef) and very smart 7f to 1½m winner Height of Fashion (by Bustino), the dam
of Unfuwain (by Northern Dancer) and Nashwan: dam won 1000 Guineas and French
Oaks: odds on, won 18-runner maiden at Newmarket in August by 1½ lengths from
Loch Fruin, keeping on well despite tending to run green: didn't make anticipated
improvement when sixth of 9, fading tamely 2f out, to Digression in Royal Lodge
EBF Stakes at Ascot: should stay at least 1m. *Major W. R. Hern.*

MARINE DIVER 3 b.c. Pas de Seul 133–Marine Life (Deep Diver 134) [1988 **101** ?
7g³ 8g* 1989 10d³ 10.4f² 12m 10f² 10g] quite attractive colt: good walker: has a

slightly round action: useful performer: placed in £8,500 event at Ascot and Dee Stakes (beaten head) at Chester, in both travelling really well long way and not finding great deal: appeared to run creditably in Derby Italiano at Rome next start but below form after, running as if something amiss on final outing, first for 5 months: probably stays 1½m: acts on firm going and a soft surface. *P. F. I. Cole.*

MARINER'S LAD 7 ch.g. Julio Mariner 127–Sorebelle 95 (Prince Tenderfoot — (USA) 126) [1988 16m 1989 14s] tall, narrow gelding: lightly-raced maiden on flat: stays long distances: bandaged only outing at 6 yrs. *P. J. Bevan.*

MARINERS SECRET 3 b.f. Julio Mariner 127–Midnight Pansy (Deadly — Nightshade 107) [1988 NR 1989 10g] close-coupled filly: fourth reported foal: half-sister to winning hurdlers Jimsintime (by Jimsun) and Taxi Lad (by Dublin Taxi): dam placed over hurdles: 50/1, bit backward and always behind in minor event at Nottingham in October. *R. G. Brazington.*

MARIOLINO 2 b.c. (Feb 9) Buzzards Bay 128§–Banking Coyne 76 (Deep Diver **48** 134) [1989 5v⁴ 5s⁴ 5s⁵ 7m⁶ a7g] rather leggy colt: fourth foal: half-brother to 3-y-o 5f performer Miami Banker (by Miami Springs), 1m seller winner Greek Banker (by Avgerignos) and a poor animal by Roman Warrior: dam best at 5f: poor maiden: has sweated up. *P. J. Arthur.*

MARJONS BOY 2 ch.c. (Feb 17) Enchantment 115–Nevilles Cross (USA) 67 **74** (Nodouble (USA)) [1989 7m⁶ 7m 8.2f³ 8f² 8g⁴] big, angular colt: closely related to 1½m to 14.5f winner Windbound Lass (by Crofter) and half-brother to 1981 2-y-o 6f winner Marilena (by Rolfe): dam stayed 1m: modest performer: ran creditably in nurseries on last 2 starts: much better suited by 1m than 7f. *M. Bell.*

MARK AIZLEWOOD 4 b.c. Nicholas Bill 125–Lunar Queen 96 (Queen's **67** Hussar 124) [1988 8m 8.2s² 8m³ 8f² 9f* 8m⁴ 9g⁴ 10g³ 9m² 10m³ 9f 10g* 10.2f 10s 9g⁵ 1989 12f 12g 12m⁵ 11f⁴ 11m⁵ 10m⁴ 12.3m 11s⁶ 11s²] good-topped colt: turns fore feet in: poor mover: quite modest performer: best at up to 11f: has won on firm going, but seems best on an easy surface nowadays: occasionally visored (was at Ayr): wanders in front and has to be produced late. *R. M. Whitaker.*

MARK BIRLEY 3 ch.g. Night Shift (USA)–La Pythie (FR) 89 (Filiberto (USA) **65** 124) [1988 6m³ 6s⁴ 6d³ 1989 7d 7f* 7g 7h⁴ 7f⁴ 7m³ 7f 6g] small, good-quartered gelding: quite modest handicapper: won at Salisbury in May: unlikely to stay beyond 7f: acts on firm going and a soft surface: suited by strong handling: sold 2,000 gns Newmarket Autumn Sales to race in Italy. *P. T. Walwyn.*

MARKET MAKER 3 b.c. Kafu 120–One Rose (Pall Mall 132) [1988 6d⁴ 6g⁵ 1989 **63** d 6m 6f² 6m 5g 8m 8.3m 8f⁴ 8f⁴ 10f] lengthy, rather dipped-backed colt: poor mover: form as 3-y-o only when in frame in minor event and sellers, easily best effort on second outing: stays 1m: acts on firm going: usually blinkered but wasn't second start: sold 4,200 gns Ascot September Sales: resold 1,500 gns Doncaster November Sales. *R. F. Johnson Houghton.*

MARKHAM 2 b.c. (Mar 8) Wattlefield 117–Vynz Girl 82 (Tower Walk 130) [1989 **48** 7g⁶ 7f 7m 8m 8s 6g] 7,200Y: smallish, workmanlike colt: third reported foal: half-brother to 3-y-o King's Beeches (by Welsh Saint): dam 1½m winner: plating-class maiden: best effort third outing: ran creditably in blinkers final start: stays 7f: sold 2,200 gns Doncaster November Sales. *C. B. B. Booth.*

MARKOFDISTINCTION 3 b. or br.c. Known Fact (USA) 135–Ghislaine **123** (USA) 71 (Icecapade (USA)) [1988 6g* 1989 8m⁴ 7.6h* 8f³ 7g² 7g³]

Racing experience was limited among the fourteen who went to post for the General Accident Two Thousand Guineas at Newmarket in May. Eight in the field had raced a maximum of three times, three of those only twice—Exbourne, Monsagem and Nashwan—whilst Markofdistinction had just a promising victory in a Newmarket maiden as a two-year-old to his name. Markofdistinction had been an intended runner in the Charles Heidsieck Champagne Craven Stakes sixteen days earlier but was withdrawn reportedly due to a high temperature, one of a number of set-backs incurred through the season. In the circumstances Markofdistinction, who started 14/1 for the Guineas, did very well to finish fourth, under two lengths behind Nashwan. Indeed he had looked likely to play a more prominent role in the finish but having made steady headway from three furlongs out was unable to sustain his run inside the last. Markofdistinction put up another very smart performance in the Swettenham Stud Sussex Stakes at Goodwood, though never dangerous finishing third of eight behind Zilzal and Green Line

Mr Gerald Leigh's "Markofdistinction"

Express. In between he'd been a very easy winner of a three-runner listed event at Lingfield just ten days before the Sussex Stakes (a pulled muscle had prevented his being prepared for Royal Ascot), beating Tatsfield by six lengths; but he disappointed in his two subsequent races. Starting odds on he was outpaced by Gold Seam in the moderately-run Kiveton Park Stakes at Doncaster in September and was a well-below-form third to Kerita in the Supreme Stakes at Goodwood the following month.

		In Reality	Intentionally
	Known Fact (USA)	(b 1964)	My Dear Girl
	(b 1977)	Tamerett	Tim Tam
Markofdistinction		(b or br 1962)	Mixed Marriage
(b. or br.c. 1986)		Icecapade	Nearctic
	Ghislaine (USA)	(gr 1969)	Shenanigans
	(b 1981)	Cambretta	Roberto
		(b or br 1975)	Cambrienne

Details of Markofdistinction's pedigree can be found in *Racehorses of 1988*, to which there is little to add. He is the first foal out of the mile-and-a-quarter winner Ghislaine. Her two-year-old Ahead (by Shirley Heights) has raced once. Ghislaine also has a yearling filly by Shirley Heights but was barren to Sure Blade the following year. Markofdistinction is a rangy colt. There are no clear-cut explanations for his last two performances but it seems likely that he'll be well suited by a return to a mile; his best form is on a firm surface. *L. M. Cumani.*

MARLBOROUGH LADY 3 gr.f. Rusticaro (FR) 124–Noir Afrique (African **38** Sky 124) [1988 7g 6m 1989 8d 6m 7m 6f⁵ 8g 7m 10f⁶ 8f⁴] small filly: poor form at best: probably stays 1¼m: twice sweating: took keen hold and didn't look easy ride third start: sold to join Mrs A. Knight 1,800 gns Doncaster September Sales. *D. T. Thom.*

MARLEY MONARCH 5 ch.g. Dara Monarch 128–Sea Dog (Sea Hawk II 131) — [1988 12s 1989 12m] sturdy, good-bodied gelding: quite modest maiden as 3-y-o: well beaten only 2 subsequent outings: stays 1¾m: probably best with give in the ground: visored once. *D. M. Grissell.*

MARLINGFORD 2 ch.c. (Apr 24) Be My Guest (USA) 126–Inchmarlo (USA) — p (Nashua) [1989 7f⁶] IR 120,000Y: good-topped colt: has plenty of scope: eighth foal: closely related to useful 1¼m to 1½m winner Governor's Harbour (by Lomond) and half-brother to 4 more winners, notably very useful Australian winner Joy (by Habitat) and fair Irish 2-y-o 7.9f winner Reveal (by Pitskelly): dam won over 6f at 2 yrs: weak 10/1, 16 lengths sixth of 10, not knocked about, to Sasaki in maiden at Leicester in October: type to do better. *G. Harwood.*

MARLION 8 b.g. Julio Mariner 127–Rose Mullion 82 (Tudor Melody 129) [1988 **72** NR 1989 12.3s 16d⁵ 12.8m² 14g 12.3m 15m⁵ 14s* 16g*] deep-girthed, quite attractive gelding: successful in handicaps at Listowel and the Curragh on first 2 starts in Ireland, at latter (favourite and apprentice ridden) beating Suren 6 lengths in IR £13,000 Irish Cesarewitch EBF Handicap: stays well: acts on any going: effective with or without blinkers: trained until after sixth outing by Miss S. Hall. *Miss S. B. Duffy, Ireland.*

MARQUETRY (USA) 2 ch.c. (Jan 30) Conquistador Cielo (USA)–Regent's **83** Walk (USA) (Vice Regent (CAN)) [1989 7m³ 7g²] $110,000Y: big, strong colt: has an easy, fluent action: first foal: dam won at up to 7f in North America: well-backed favourite and carrying condition, won maiden at Salisbury in June by length from Courtesy Title, leading 2f out and running on well: length second of 5, unable to quicken after setting slow pace, to Karinga Bay in listed race at Newbury in August: will stay 1m. *G. Harwood.*

MARSH HARRIER (USA) 8 b.g. Raise A Cup (USA)–Belle de Jour (USA) 74 **49** (Speak John) [1988 8f 8g 10f 10f³ 12m 1989 11.7m 11.7g 10g² 10f⁴ 12m⁴ 10f] big, strong, rangy gelding: 33/1, appeared to run very well when second of 8 in claimer at Epsom in August: below that form in handicaps afterwards: stays 1¼m: suited by a sound surface: ran creditably when blinkered: bandaged second outing: best with strong handling: has run well when sweating: has worn a tongue strap. *A. Moore.*

MARSH'S LAW 2 br.c. (Mar 29) Kala Shikari 125–My Music 68 (Sole Mio **56** (USA)) [1989 5m 7m 7m⁵ 6m 6s⁵] 2,800F, 4,000Y, 5,000 2-y-o: sturdy colt: third foal: half-brother to 3-y-o 1m to 12.3f winner Great Gusto (by Windjammer): dam stayed 1m: fairly useful plater: should stay 7f: acts on soft going: often bandaged. *J. Wharton.*

MARTINI'S COURIER 2 br.c. (Apr 4) Lucky Wednesday 124–Be My Sweet 78 **55** (Galivanter 131) [1989 5d 6m⁶ 5m 7m³ 6g⁵ 6s³ a6g²] leggy good-topped colt: turns off-fore in: fifth foal: brother to poor stayer Lucky Humbug and half-brother to 3-y-o Sola Mia (by Tolomeo), 6f winner at 2 yrs, and 6f and 7f winner Sugar Token (by Record Token): dam, 1m and 1¼m winner, is half-sister to Gunner B: fair plater: stays 7f: races freely: has looked ungenerous. *W. J. Pearce.*

MARTIN-LAVELL ECHO 3 gr.f. Song 132–Noble Company (USA) (Young **58 d** Emperor 133) [1988 6g⁶ 1989 8g⁵ 7s⁴ 7g³ 6m² 7m² 7m⁵ 6f⁶ 7g 7f] tall, leggy filly: quite modest maiden: below form in sellers (edgy) and claimer last 5 outings and looks ungenuine: will prove best at up to 7f: acts on soft going, possibly unsuited by very firm: blinkered fourth, seventh and final outings: sold 2,400 gns Newmarket Autumn Sales: one to avoid. *Sir Mark Prescott.*

MARTIN-LAVELL POST 2 b.f. (Mar 22) Tina's Pet 121–Stradey Park 103 **54** (Murrayfield 119) [1989 5m⁵ 5m*] 2,200Y: half-sister to poor maiden Stradey Lynn (by Derrylin) and bad hurdler Right Formula (by Monseigneur): dam won over 5f and stayed 1¼m: 8/1, won 12-runner maiden auction race at Edinburgh in October by a neck from Kawarau Queen, leading line: made debut late-May: will stay 6f. *Sir Mark Prescott.*

MARTINOSKY 3 b.c. Martinmas 128–Bewitched 63 (African Sky 124) [1988 6g⁵ **74** 5f* 6g⁶ 6f⁶ 5m⁴ 6g 5f 1989 6s⁵ 8s 5s³ 6f² 6m* 6m 6h² 8m 8f 7m⁶ 6f 6m] big colt: good walker: modest handicapper: won at Windsor in May: good second at Lingfield: below form after: best at sprint distances: acts on any going: blinkered 3 times, first time at Windsor: sometimes takes strong hold and has run poorly for 7-lb claimer. *W. G. R. Wightman.*

MARTINS RAY   3 b.g. Red Sunset 120–Hariota 73 (Hook Money 124) [1988 NR   —
1989 10g 10g] IR 15,500Y: compact, good-bodied gelding: brother to a bad maiden,
closely related to Irish 7f to 9.5f winner Red Hari (by Red God), later successful in
Malaysia, and half-brother to 4 minor winners: dam middle-distance winner: ridden
by 5-lb claimer, always behind in maidens at Brighton and Leicester in April. *G. A.
Huffer.*

MARTINSTAR   2 b.f. (Apr 11) Norwick (USA) 120–Martin Place (Martinmas   —
128) [1989 6g 6g a6g] IR 3,000F: first foal: dam showed little worthwhile form on 3
outings: poor form in claimers and a seller. *M. J. Fetherston-Godley.*

MARTI'S SONG   4 b.g. Martinmas 128–Top Soprano 89 (High Top 131) [1988   —
11.7d 1989 7h 10f] angular, good-bodied gelding: well beaten in sellers and claimers.
R. J. Hodges.

MARY BANKES (USA)   3 ch.f. Northern Baby (CAN) 127–Good Thinking   —
(USA) (Raja Baba (USA)) [1988 5.8d 6g 1989 5h 7h 7f6] angular filly: little sign of
ability: should be suited by further than 5f: sold to join W. Jarvis 6,000 gns
Newmarket September Sales. *P. W. Harris.*

MARY GEE   3 b.f. Darshaan 133–Shamra (FR) (Zeddaan 130) [1988 NR 1989 10f3   85
10.2h* 12g 8m5 10g] 15,000Y: rangy filly: fourth reported foal: dam, French 2-y-o 1m
winner, is half-sister to French Oaks winner Reine de Saba: won maiden at Bath in
June: creditable fifth in minor event at Newmarket: tailed off in Lancashire Oaks
(pulled hard) at Haydock and Sun Chariot Stakes (as if something amiss) at
Newmarket: should prove suited by 1¼m. *C. E. Brittain.*

MARYLAND WILLIE   2 b.c. (Feb 21) Master Willie 129–Maryland Cookie   65 p
(USA) 101 (Bold Hour) [1989 7g6] fourth foal (all by Master Willie): brother to
Amber Cookie, fairly useful 7f winner at 2 yrs in 1986: dam useful sprinter: 16/1,
around 9 lengths sixth of 29, running on strongly towards finish, to Lord of The
Field in maiden at Newmarket in November: should improve. *D. R. C. Elsworth.*

MARY MILLER   3 ch.f. Sharpo 132–Alteza Real 84 (Mansingh (USA) 120) [1988   71
NR 1989 5m5 6f2 7m5 6m] leggy, rather shallow-girthed filly: has a quick action:
fourth foal: half-sister to useful 1987 2-y-o sprinter Infanta Real (by Formidable) and
8.5f winner Maksoud (by High Top): dam, 5f winner, is half-sister to Forzando and
smart filly Lady Constance: modest maiden: ran moderately in handicap final outing:
may well stay further than 7f: looked well all starts. *M. R. Stoute.*

MASAI'S MAGIC   4 b.f. Krayyan 117–Masai Princess (USA) 83 (Assagai) [1988   —
8v5 8d6 10.1d 10.1m6 1989 10v 8f] rangy filly: poor mover: poor maiden. *M.
Madgwick.*

MASCALLS GIRL   4 ch.f. Moorestyle 137–Copt Hall Realm 85 (Realm 129)   —
[1988 8g4 7f2 8m6 8f5 8m 1989 8s 8s 6f] dipped-backed filly: plater: soundly beaten
as 4-y-o: stays 1m: acts on firm going: blinkered once at 3 yrs: difficult ride. *J.
Perrett.*

MASELLA   2 ch.f. (May 2) Aragon 118–Winter Resort (Miami Springs 121) [1989   46
5m4 5f6 6g3 7f a8g5] first reported foal: dam unraced half-sister to useful 1¼m
winner Power Bender: quite modest plater: best effort third start: should be suited
by further than 6f. *J. W. Hills.*

MASHOBRA   3 br.f. Vision (USA)–Queen of The Brush (Averof 123) [1988 8m6   75
1989 8.3m* 8.3g] sparely-made filly: won claimer at Windsor in July by 5 lengths,
leading inside final 1f: co-favourite, well below that form in handicap 3 weeks later:
sold 8,000 gns Newmarket December Sales: to be covered by Glint of Gold. *D. R. C.
Elsworth.*

MASIRAH   3 b.f. Dunphy 124–Captivate 79 (Mansingh (USA) 120) [1988 6f6 5g4   —
6d 1989 6f 6f4 8.2m] smallish, deep-girthed filly: quite modest maiden as 2-y-o:
behind in 1989, appearing not to stay 1m in claimer (sweating) in August. *M. A.
Jarvis.*

MASKED BALL   9 b.h. Thatch (USA) 136–Miss Mahal (Taj Dewan 128) [1988   76
12f3 12m6 12m2 12g* 12g* 12d 11d6 12f4 12g3 1989 12.3s6 12d* 12m3 12m4 12g4
12m3 12m3 11s 12g a12g4] lengthy, good-topped horse: modest handicapper: won at
Thirsk in April: best efforts after on fifth and seventh outings: best at 1¼m to 1½m:
acts on any going: usually bandaged: excellent mount for apprentice: held up: tough.
P. Calver.

MASKEEN   7 ch.g. Morston (FR) 125–Parmesh 105 (Home Guard (USA) 129)   —
[1988 NR 1989 12f 12f 10m] no longer of much account: blinkered once: bandaged at
7 yrs. *D. A. Wilson.*

MASNUN (USA) 4 gr.g. Nureyev (USA) 131–Careless Kitten (USA) (Caro 133) **97**
[1988 7f 7d 1989 6d* 6s 5s 6f⁶ 6f* 6f² 6f⁶ 6m 6f 6h² 6m* 6v⁵] strong, sturdy gelding:
fairly useful performer: won minor event at Folkestone in April and handicaps at
Lingfield in May and Goodwood in August: showed improved form when beating
Madraco a length in £14,800 Sport On 2 Stakes (Handicap) at Goodwood: suited by
6f: seems to act on any going, but goes very well on top-of-the-ground: sometimes
on toes: has taken keen hold: has hung right. *R. J. O'Sullivan.*

MASONS AVENUE 4 b. or br.c. Taufan (USA) 119–Line of Reason (High Line **57**
125) [1988 9d² 8g* 8f 10m³ 9g* 10m² 10f² 8.2m⁵ 8g 8.2d 1989 10.2g 8d 8.5d 8m³ 7h³
8.3m²] tall, leggy colt: poor mover: quite modest winner (including for amateur) as
3-y-o: stayed 1¼m: didn't race on soft going, acted on any other: winning hurdler
with N. Tinkler: occasionally found little: dead. *R. Boss.*

MASTER DANCER 2 b.c. (Apr 24) Mashhor Dancer (USA)–Silent Dancer 76 **65**
(Quiet Fling (USA) 124) [1989 8f³ 9g⁶] 8,000Y: leggy colt: has a round action:
second foal: half-brother to 3-y-o Silent Princess (by King of Spain): dam won twice
over 13f: quite modest form, staying on never dangerous, in maiden at Newcastle
and claimer at York: gives impression will stay well. *R. M. Whitaker.*

MASTER ENGINEER 4 ch.g. Music Boy 124–Penny Pincher 95 (Constable **55**
119) [1988 5m 1989 5f 6f 5f 5f⁵ 5f 6f² 7m] rather sparely-made gelding: plating-class
maiden: runner-up in seller: suited by sprint distances: acts on firm going: changed
hands 6,100 gns Doncaster June Sales: resold 2,050 gns Ascot November Sales. *R.
M. Whitaker.*

MASTER LINE 8 ch.h. High Line 125–Fair Winter 111 (Set Fair 129) [1988 11.7m **69**
13.1d² 11.7m⁶ 12f⁵ 14f 12g 1989 11.7m³ 11f⁴ 12m² 12.2m* 11.7m⁴ 12m⁴ 11.7d³ 12f 12m
12.2m⁵] small, sparely-made horse: has a sharp action: modest handicapper: easy
winner of uncompetitive event at Warwick in July: stays 13f: probably not at best on
extremes of going: excellent mount for apprentice: occasionally sweats: genuine. *H.
Candy.*

MASTER OF THE HOUSE 3 b.g. Kind of Hush 118–Miss Racine (Dom Racine **72**
(FR) 121) [1988 NR 1989 6s 6v² 6d⁴ 5m⁴ 5m⁵ 6g⁴ 6f⁶ 6g a6g] sturdy
gelding: moderate mover: first foal: dam won over 1m at 3 yrs in Ireland: modest
maiden: best efforts seventh (handicap, visored and hung left) and eighth outings:
well below form after: worth a try over further: acts on any going: blinkered last 4
starts: sold 5,600 gns Doncaster November Sales. *I. V. Matthews.*

MASTER PIERRE 2 b. or br.c. (Mar 5) Gabitat 119–Emerglen (Furry Glen 121) **70**
[1989 5m⁵ 5m 6m 6m² 6g 5g³] 3,200Y, 5,000 2-y-o: lengthy, good-topped colt: has a
round action: half-brother to a winning selling hurdler and a winner in Trinidad: dam
showed little worthwhile form: modest maiden: stays 6f: sweating fourth and fifth
starts. *L. J. Holt.*

MASTER PLAN (FR) 3 b.g. Carwhite 127–Manene (FR) (Tapioca (FR) 123) **71**
[1988 7m 7g⁵ 8g 1989 10s⁴ 11.7m⁶ 10f 8f⁴ 9m*] compact gelding: has a quick action:
20/1, won 25-runner claimer (claimed to join J. S. Wilson £20,500) at Newmarket in
October: stays 1¼m well: acts on top-of-the-ground and soft: bit coltish second
outing and subsequently gelded. *J. S. Wilson.*

MASTER POKEY 5 b.g. Uncle Pokey 116–September Fire (Firestreak 125) **88**
[1988 6v³ 6g² 6g* 7f* 5f² 6g⁴ 5.6m 6f 1989 6m 5f⁶ 5.6g⁵ 6s] sturdy, good-quartered
gelding: fairly useful winner as 4-y-o: heavily bandaged in front, never-nearer fifth
of 19 finishers to Craft Express in Tote-Portland Handicap at Doncaster in
September: favourite, no extra from over 1f out when ninth of 29 to Joveworth in
Ladbrokes (Ayr) Gold Cup (Handicap) over week later: effective at 5f and better
suited by 6f than 7f: probably not at his best on soft going, acts on any other. *M. W.
Easterby.*

MASTER TYKE 4 gr.g. Flying Tyke 90–Habatashie 62 (Habat 127) [1988 7g⁵ 7d **49**
7.5m 7d 6m 6f 8m⁶ 10m 10m 10g 7m⁶ 6f 6m 10g 6g 6g* 1989 8m 8.3m a8g⁵ a6g³]
sturdy gelding: moderate mover: modest plater: stays 1m: acts on top-of-the-ground
and a soft surface: blinkered 4 times, including when winning apprentice race at 3
yrs. *R. P. C. Hoad.*

MASTER VINCE 11 b.g. Menelek 114–Oh Babe (Javelot 124) [1988 14v* 18v² **—**
13.8g⁵ 16m 14m 1989 18s] workmanlike gelding: plating-class winner early in 1988:
apprentice ridden, ran poorly in Nottingham handicap in May, only outing as 11-y-o:
possibly doesn't stay 2¼m: well suited by the mud: visored once at 10 yrs: winning
chaser. *J. White.*

MATASIETE (USA) 2 b.g. (Feb 5) Diamond Shoal 130–Babalowa (USA) (Raja **59**
Baba (USA)) [1989 6f 8.2g⁶ 6m] 30,000Y: lengthy, quite attractive gelding: has

scope: first foal: dam winner at around 7f in USA: 33/1, sixth of 14 finishers behind very easy winner Golan Heights in maiden at Haydock in September: tailed off in similar event at York following month. *J. G. FitzGerald.*

MATCHING LINES 2 ch.f. (Mar 22) Thatching 131–Irish Limerick 89 (Try My Best (USA) 130) [1989 5g5 5g* 5m] 10,500Y: workmanlike filly: first foal: dam 2-y-o 6f winner: 10/1, won minor event at Catterick in September by 2½ lengths from Echo Princess, leading inside final furlong: ran moderately in nursery at Newmarket following month. *Mrs J. R. Ramsden.*   72

MATCHING SPELL 3 ch.c. Tumble Wind (USA)–Lady Mary (Sallust 134) [1988 5f6 5g3 5d5 5g 5s 5d 1989 6m 5m 5m 6f] small, workmanlike colt: poor maiden: bred to stay beyond 5f: sold 750 gns Doncaster September Sales. *M. Brittain.*   —

MATERIAL GIRL 3 b.f. Busted 134–First Huntress 64 (Primera 131) [1988 NR 1989 11.7m4] lengthy, attractive filly: sister to very useful stayer Broken Rail and half-sister to several winners, including very smart middle-distance colt Town And Country (by Town Crier): dam of little account: 20/1, shaped promisingly when 5½ lengths fourth of 8 to Roll A Dollar in minor event at Windsor in August: has joined N. Gaselee. *Major W. R. Hern.*   73 p

MATERIAL GOLD 2 b.g. (May 24) Sonnen Gold 121–Miss Whitley (Hot Spark 126) [1989 5d 5f4 7m6 7.5g 7f3 6g 7d] leggy gelding: moderate walker: has a round action: third foal: half-brother to 2 animals by Lochnager: dam unraced: modest plater: stays 7f: blinkered last 3 starts, running creditably when sweating first time but poorly afterwards: pulls hard: sold 1,400 gns Doncaster November Sales. *M. H. Easterby.*   47

MATOU 9 b.h. Mummy's Pet 125–Great Optimist 55 (Great Nephew 126) [1988 6g 6g4 6f6 6g3 6f4 6s4 6g4 6m 7.6s 7g 6g 1989 7m 7m 6g2 6m3 7m5] strong, well-made horse: moderate mover: quite modest handicapper nowadays: slowly away in apprentice event second outing: best form at 6f: possibly not at best on extremes of going nowadays: blinkered once: usually bandaged behind: usually held up. *G. A. Pritchard-Gordon.*   65

MATRACE 4 ch.f. Mummy's Game 120–Sospirae 90 (Sandford Lad 133) [1988 NR 1989 9v6 11g6 12m5 12f 13f3 12g 13.8d] leggy filly: poor maiden: has sweated and got on edge. *J. S. Haldane.*   36

MATSONG 4 b.g. Song 132–Mathilde 84 (Whistler 129) [1988 6v3 6m 6g 6g 6m 6d 6g 1989 5m] leggy, sparely-made gelding: sprint plater: well below form since second start in 1988: sold 1,500 gns Ascot September Sales. *T. W. Cunningham.*   —

MATTIE'S PRIDE 2 ch.f. (Mar 20) Doulab (USA) 115–November (Firestreak 125) [1989 5f 5f 6g] IR 500Y: half-sister to 3 winners, including fairly useful 7f and 9f winner Brands Hatch (by Track Spare): dam of no account: little worthwhile form in maidens, including auction races: burly first 2 starts: sold 1,600 gns Newmarket Autumn Sales. *L. J. Holt.*   —

MATWAPA (USA) 4 ch.f. Valdez (USA)–Mattan (USA) (Tentam (USA)) [1988 10.5s6 11g5 9.5g2 10.7g4 1989 14.6g6 12.2m3 12m6 11.7m2 11.5m a10g* a11g4] leggy, good-topped ex-French filly: poor walker and mover: second foal: half-sister to a winner in USA by Flying Paster: dam half-sister to high-class middle-distance performer Mrs Penny: won maiden at Lingfield in October: favourite, modest fourth in handicap at Southwell over 2 weeks later: stays 1½m: has worn bandages: sweating third outing. *Mrs D. Haine.*   74

MAUREEN'S CAVALIER 5 ch.g. Saher 115–Aethelflaed 61 (Realm 129) [1988 7d 7m 6f 6d 7f 7f 8g 6f 1989 a6g] small gelding: winning plater as 3-y-o: no subsequent form: used to be suited by 6f and top-of-the-ground: sometimes sweats: often apprentice ridden at overweight. *P. Burgoyne.*   —

MAUVE REEF (USA) 3 b.c. Shareef Dancer (USA) 135–Avum (USA) (Umbrella Fella (USA)) [1988 NR 1989 11f 10m 8m3 11.7m5 12f3 8m3 10f3 10.6m] sturdy colt: has a moderate, quick action: eighth foal: closely related to very useful French 6f to 1m performer Lyphard's Princess (by Lyphard), later winner in USA, and half-brother to 2 winners in USA: dam won 10 races at up to 1m, including stakes, and is half-sister to Lord Avie: fair maiden: stays 1¼m: sold BBA (Italia) 15,000 gns Newmarket Autumn Sales. *A. A. Scott.*   84

MAWATHIK (USA) 2 b.c. (Apr 8) Topsider (USA)–Betsy Be Good (USA) (Pretendre 126) [1989 6m3 6f2 6f4 8g] $240,000Y: angular, lengthy colt: good walker: half-brother to several winners in North America, including Grade 2 9f winner Catherine's Bet (by Grey Dawn): dam won at up to 1¼m: modest maiden: should be suited by further than 6f: tended to wander third start: looks a hard ride: sold 8,000 gns Newmarket Autumn Sales. *R. W. Armstrong.*   73

MAXIMUM MAN 3 b.g. Sweet Monday 122–Wyn-Bank 82 (Green God 128) —
[1988 5g⁴ 5m³ 6g⁵ 6g⁵ 1989 6d 5m 5g⁶ 7.5f 9.1f 8f 5m 8.2g] strong, sturdy gelding:
quite modest form at best: never dangerous in handicaps and a claimer after third
start: should be suited by further than 6f: appears best with some give in the ground:
has run well for 5-lb claimer. *M. W. Easterby.*

MAYBE SIAM (USA) 3 b.g. L'Emigrant (USA) 129–Evening Kiss (USA) 61 p
(Saggy) [1988 NR 1989 8s 7f 6m 7m⁶ 6m*] $65,000Y: strong, good-bodied gelding:
moderate walker and mover: tenth reported foal: half-brother to 9 winners,
including useful Irish 6f winner Molly (by Christopher R) and very useful 1984 2-y-o
7f and 1m winner Concorde Affair (by Super Concorde): dam second once from 9
starts: odds on, made virtually all to win 4-runner minor event at Thirsk in
September shade comfortably by a neck: should stay beyond 6f: can improve again.
H. Candy.

MAYDAY MIRACLE 3 b.f. Superlative 118–Mayday Melody 117 (Highland 72
Melody 112) [1988 5g⁴ 6s* 1989 6m⁶ 6m 6s 6m⁴ a7g a5g a6g⁵] robust filly: has a long
stride: modest handicapper: 33/1, fourth of 24 in £9,000 event at Haydock in
September, best effort as 3-y-o: stays 6f well: acts on soft going and top-of-the-
ground: blinkered last 2 outings. *J. W. Watts.*

MAY HINTON 2 ch.f. (Jan 25) Main Reef 126–Jeanne Avril 99 (Music Boy 124) 82
[1989 6g² 6g* 6m⁴ 6f* 6s³] small, angular filly: hasn't much scope: first foal: dam, 6f
winner at 2 yrs and 3 yrs, is sister to Middle Park winner and 2000 Guineas second
Mattaboy: fair performer: made all or most in maiden at Ripon in July and £8,500
event (beat Nazela a head) at Salisbury in September: ran creditably in listed races
at Ripon and Ayr on third and final starts: will stay 7f: acts on any going. *J. L. Dunlop.*

MAYOR 6 ch.m. Laxton 105–Mayab 100 (Maystreak 118) [1988 6g 6m⁴ 6s* 1989 74
6v 6d³ 5m] lengthy, workmanlike mare: has a quick action: modest handicapper:
well suited by 6f: best form on a soft surface: has joined D. Dutton. *N. Tinkler.*

MAY OVER 4 ch.g. Smackover 107–May Bond 69 (Good Bond 122) [1988 6v⁵ 7d³ —
7.5m² 9g* 8.5m* 10.2m 8m⁶ 8.5g³ 10g⁴ 8d 8g⁵ 8g 8.5f 10s 12d⁵ 1989 10.6d 12s 12d⁶
a14g a16g] rather leggy, good-topped gelding: sometimes starey in coat: quite
modest winner (including of seller) in first half of 1988: generally below form
(mostly in handicaps) subsequently: best form at about 9f: acts on top-of-the-ground
and a soft surface: often sweats: suitable mount for apprentice: gave trouble at stalls
on reappearance. *B. A. McMahon.*

MAY QUEEN 2 b.f. (May 1) Dara Monarch 128–Markon (On Your Mark 125) —
[1989 8g] IR 7,000F, IR 5,000Y: fifth foal: half-sister to useful 1984 Irish 2-y-o 7f
winner Stramar (by Orchestra) and 7f to 1m winner One To Mark (by He Loves Me),
also successful over hurdles: dam unraced daughter of half-sister to Humble Duty:
66/1, slowly away and always behind in 11-runner maiden at Edinburgh in
November. *S. E. Kettlewell.*

MAY THE FOURTEENTH 3 br.f. Thatching 131–Nana's Girl 109 (Tin 53
Whistle 128) [1988 NR 1989 7f 7.6m⁴ 8.2d⁴ a8g] closely related to a winner in USA
by Thatch and half-sister to numerous winners, including good 1977 2-y-o Aythorpe
(by Ridan) and Royal Boy (by Realm), smart performer at up to 7f: dam, useful at up
to 1m, is sister to very smart Tin King: plating-class form when in frame in claimers
at Chester and Haydock: stays 1m. *J. W. Hills.*

MAZAG (USA) 2 b.c. (Apr 24) Mr Prospector (USA)–Rose O'Riley (USA) 94 p
(Nijinsky (CAN)) [1989 7g³ 7m³] $700,000Y: attractive, rather leggy colt: has a
sharp action: first foal: dam, 1m winner in France at 2 yrs, is sister to the best
American 3-y-o filly on turf in 1981, De La Rose, and very smart 1¼m performer
Upper Nile: fairly useful form, travelling strongly long way, behind Message Pad in
minor event at Doncaster in September and Mukddaam in maiden at Newmarket
(hampered closing stages) following month: sure to win ordinary event at 7f or 1m.
M. R. Stoute.

MAZZACANO 4 b.c. Alleged (USA) 138–Fall Aspen (USA) (Pretense) 117
[1988 12f* 12g* 14m² 14.6g⁵ 1989 16d² 14f³ 20f² 21f* 20m⁵]
The future of the Cup races again came in for plenty of discussion in the
latest season. In a *Timeform Interview* in August, trainer Harwood gave his
thoughts on the Gold Cup: 'I really don't see the point of having Group 1 races
over two and a half miles. I think if the distance of the Gold Cup at Royal Ascot
was reduced to two miles you would get a more competitive race. By all means
leave the Queen Alexandra. In fact, promote it to Group 3, then you've got a
choice: a Group 3 event for horses who need long distances and a race for

*Goodwood Cup—Mazzacano (rails) regains the lead from Sadeem,
with Princess Sobieska running on*

top-class horses who stay two miles'. Harwood himself, who's supported
long-distance racing better than most in his time, would have been affected
more than most had his suggestions been implemented in the latest season.
He supplied three of the eight runners in the Gold Cup, as well as the odds-on
favourite for the Queen Alexandra. His Sadeem and Mazzacano filled the first
two places in the Gold Cup, with Green Adventure failing to stay and fading
into fifth in the home straight, while Zero Watt ran well below expectations in
the Queen Alexandra Stakes and wasn't seen out again. Mazzacano, the
outsider of the trio in the Gold Cup, was running over more than two miles for
the first time. He had raced twice before as a four-year-old and been placed
twice—in the Insulpak Sagaro EBF Stakes at Ascot, where he was beaten half
a length by Travel Mystery, and in the Coloroll Yorkshire Cup, in which he
was outpaced a long way from home, hung left in behind the leaders inside the
final two furlongs and was beaten seven lengths by Mountain Kingdom and
Zaffaran, the latter of whom, on identical terms, finished four lengths behind
him at Ascot. The extra half a mile proved no problem to Mazzacano in the
Gold Cup; in fact, he ran as though he needed it, battling on well without
having any chance of catching Sadeem who, despite being eased, crossed the
line eight lengths to the good.

The pair met again five weeks later in the Goodwood Cup. Sadeem was
penalized 7 lb, but was still thought certain to come out on top and started
100/30 on, with Mazzacano at 15/2. The Gold Cup third Lauries Crusador was
again in opposition, while the three-year-olds Princess Sobieska (a sister to
the 1987 Goodwood Cup winner Sergeyevich) and Scotch Double (a
100/1-chance) made up the field. Mazzacano handled Goodwood's undulations
much better than Sadeem, though Sadeem was travelling very well running
downhill into the home straight and looked set to land the odds comfortably
when taking up the lead three furlongs out. Mazzacano, under a fine ride, had
set much of the early pace; he regained the initiative under forceful driving a
furlong from home and gamely repelled the challenges of Sadeem and
Princess Sobieska by a neck. The two others finished well beaten. Sadeem
and Mazzacano were due to meet for a third time in the Doncaster Cup. As it
turned out, both missed the race and when Mazzacano did reappear he ran
unaccountably badly. Odds on for the Ciga Prix Gladiateur at Longchamp on
Arc weekend, he was virtually pulled up and trailed in last of the five runners.

Mazzacano is the fourth foal of Fall Aspen, a stakes winner at up to seven
furlongs, including of the Grade 1 Matron Stakes as a two-year-old. Her first
two foals Northern Aspen (by Northern Dancer) and Elle Seule (by Exclusive
Native) were good-class winners in Europe, the former later successful in the
States, including in the Grade 1 Gamely Handicap at Hollywood Park. Native
Aspen (by Raise A Native), the dam's third foal, won four times in North

549

Mr A. P. Ward's "Mazzacano"

		Hoist The Flag	Tom Rolfe
	Alleged (USA)	(b 1968)	Wavy Navy
	(b 1974)	Princess Pout	Prince John
Mazzacano		(b 1966)	Determined Lady
(b.c. 1985)		Pretense	Endeavour II
	Fall Aspen (USA)	(b or br 1963)	Imitation
	(ch 1976)	Change Water	Swaps
		(ch 1969)	Portage

America; the three-year-old Colorado Dancer (by Shareef Dancer), the dam's latest foal to reach the racecourse, developed into one of the best middle-distance fillies in France. Fall Aspen has a two-year-old filly by Sadler's Wells called Dance of Leaves and a yearling filly by Shareef Dancer who was bought by Darley Stud Management for 240,000 guineas at the Highflyer Sales. Mazzacano's second dam Change Water won a maiden race at around seven furlongs as a three-year-old. Portage, another minor winner in the States, produced eight other winners besides Change Water, the first of which, Blue Canoe, is the great-grandam of the Breeders' Cup Mile winner Cozzene. Mazzacano, a big, lengthy, dipped-backed colt with a round action, probably does need a thorough test of stamina nowadays. He has yet to race on soft going, but acts on any other. He sweated and got on his toes at Royal Ascot and Goodwood. *G. Harwood.*

MBULWA 3 ch.c. Be My Guest (USA) 126–Bundu (FR) 88 (Habitat 134) [1988 6g **88** 6m3 1989 8.5d4 8f* 7g2 8f 7.6f4 7g] smallish, sturdy colt: won maiden at Pontefract in May: well-backed co-favourite, looked in magnificent shape but ran moderately in minor event final start, first for nearly 4 months: should prove best at up to 1m: acts on firm going: has run creditably for 7-lb claimer. *G. Wragg.*

MCA LUCKY KIST 2 b.f. (Jan 16) Lucky Wednesday 124–Starkist 81 (So **—** Blessed 130) [1989 6g 6g] sister to 3-y-o Mca Lucky Star, 5f winner at 2 yrs, and 6f and 7f winner Lucky Starkist and half-sister to fair miler Star of A Gunner (by Gunner B): dam 2-y-o 5f winner: slowly away and always in rear in minor event at Windsor and seller (reluctant to go down) at Ripon: sold 950 gns Doncaster November Sales. *W. J. Pearce.*

MCA LUCKY STAR 3 gr.f. Lucky Wednesday 124–Starkist 81 (So Blessed 130) **66 d** [1988 5g6 5g5 5m 6g2 6m2 5s* 6f6 6s5 1989 5v4 7g4 6f 8.3g 7.5m5 6g] compact, good-bodied filly: has a rather round action: modest winner at 2 yrs: showed little after reappearance, well behind in seller final start: suited by 6f: acts on soft going, probably unsuited by firm: sweating and edgy second to fifth outings, giving trouble at stalls on first occasion. *W. J. Pearce.*

MEADS BROW 3 b.c. Petong 126–Pams Gleam 89 (Sovereign Gleam 117) [1988 — 6d 6d 1989 6f4 7f 6h 6f6 6g 7d] strong colt: carries condition: has a quick action: quite modest at best: well beaten in handicaps and minor event last 4 outings, hanging under strong pressure first of them: stays 6f: best form on firm ground: blinkered final start. *R. Voorspuy.*

MEANIE MINNA 3 b.f. Derrylin 115–Pirate Maid (Auction Ring (USA) 123) **68** [1988 NR 1989 7d 7f4 6f3 5.8h5] workmanlike, angular filly: first foal: dam once-raced half-sister to fairly useful sprinter Mr Minstrel: quite modest maiden: ran poorly at Bath final start (July): stays 7f: sold to join J. Norton 1,900 gns Doncaster November Sales. *P. T. Walwyn.*

MEAN TO ME 3 b.f. Homing 130–Mac's Melody (Wollow 132) [1988 7g 1989 — 10.6m] tall, leggy, sparely-made filly: always behind in maidens at Warwick and Haydock (sweating profusely). *Mrs Barbara Waring.*

MECADO 2 b.g. (Mar 24) Ballacashtal (CAN)–Parma Nova 58 (Dominion 123) — [1989 6g a6g] 7,000 2-y-o: compact gelding: first foal: dam poor maiden: showed signs of ability (having started slowly and swerved left after 1f) in maiden auction event at Haydock in August: tailed off in Southwell claimer in November. *F. J. Yardley.*

MEDEENA (USA) 3 b.f. Foolish Pleasure (USA)–Pensamiento (USA) **42** (Damascus (USA)) [1988 7f 6f5 1989 7d 6s3 7d 7g 10f2 8m5 12f 10f6 10f2 9f 10m5 9s] sparely-made filly: moderate plater at her best: best at up to 1¼m: acted on any going: tended to wander under pressure: trained first 10 starts by Mrs J. Ramsden: dead. *W. Storey.*

MEDIA FLOW (DEN) 2 b.f. (Mar 25) Mas Media–Seaflow (USA) 60 (Little — Current (USA)) [1989 5g 6m 5m] leggy, sparely-made filly: third living foal: half-sister to 7f winner Flotena (by Bustino): dam runner-up over 6f only outing: poor form in maidens, including an auction event: ran as if something amiss final start (June). *R. Guest.*

MEDIA STAR 4 ch.f. Star Appeal 133–Linduna (Derring-Do 131) [1988 10.2m **41** 13.8d 10m 1989 12g 12f3 12f 8f 16.5g 12g 12f* 10m 14f3 12f 14g] leggy, angular filly: has a round action: 33/1-winner of 8-runner seller (no bid) at Thirsk in May: stays 1¾m well: acts on firm going: usually bandaged nowadays: inconsistent. *T. Kersey.*

MEDICOSMA (USA) 3 ch.f. The Minstrel (CAN) 135–Media Luna 119§ (Star **80** Appeal 133) [1988 6g 7f3 7h6 1989 10f5 8m 8h 12.3f* 16m* 13.8d4] small, well-made filly: good mover: showed improved form when hard driven to win August handicaps at Ripon (bandaged near-hind) and Newcastle: stays 2m: acts on firm going: sold 16,000 gns Newmarket December Sales. *B. W. Hills.*

MEESON KAMP 3 b.g. Kampala 120–Turin Rose (Martinmas 128) [1988 5g 5s* **80** 6g 5f 5g* 5s* 5m 1989 5v* 5d2 5m6 5m* 5m6 5f2 5g2 5s6 5d5 a6g3 a5g] leggy, lengthy gelding: has a roundish action: fair handicapper: won at Hamilton in April and Warwick in July: very good second at Goodwood seventh start: twice below form at Chester and Southwell: should prove best at 5f: acts on any going. *J. Berry.*

MEESON KING 8 br.g. Space King 115–Meeson Girl (Tyrant (USA)) [1988 6d2 — 6d 1989 6s a6g a6g5 a6g] small, lengthy, workmanlike gelding: plating-class handicapper on his day: stays 6f: acts on any going: blinkered once: has run well for inexperienced rider: often goes freely to post: inconsistent. *B. A. McMahon.*

MEESON SCRAP 3 b.g. Coded Scrap 90–Meeson Secret (Most Secret 119) **49** [1988 7g6 7g2 7f6 6g 1989 5f 6m 5.8h6 5f6 5m 6g 6g3 a6g] tall, leggy gelding: fair plater: will be suited by return to 7f: best form with some give in the ground: has worn bandages: has run creditably for apprentice. *F. Jordan.*

MEGAN BLAZE 2 b.f. (Feb 8) Sayf El Arab (USA) 127–Marton Maid 74 (Silly **66** Season 127) [1989 5f* 6m3 6g5 6m3 6f3 5d5 7m 5f 6m 7g 9g 8.2g6 8.2s4 7d] medium-sized, rather sparely-made filly: turns off-fore in: second foal: dam, inconsistent maiden, is half-sister to good-class sprinter Haveroid: quite modest performer: won maiden auction race at Thirsk in June: probably stays 1m: has run moderately when blinkered: inconsistent: sold to race in Norway 2,200 gns Doncaster November Sales. *J. Hetherton.*

MEGAN'S FLIGHT   4 ch.f. Welsh Pageant 132–Escape Me Never 75 (Run The   **74**
Gantlet (USA)) [1988 10g 12d4 14.7m2 1989 12s4 12s2 14.8d4 12m2 12d3 14g a14g* a16g* a14g4] leggy, workmanlike filly: favourite, successful (easing up) at Southwell in claimer in November and handicap in December: stays 2m: yet to race on firm going, acts on any other: reluctant at stalls second to fourth starts: best racing up with pace. *Lady Herries.*

MEGAN'S MOVE   6 ch.m. Move Off 112–River Petterill 89 (Another River 89)   **36**
[1988 12f 12h5 7g 9s 10m 10f 1989 15s3] lengthy, sparely-made mare: poor performer: needs further than 7f: acts on a soft surface: often has tongue tied down: has worn crossed noseband: winning hurdler. *W. Storey.*

MEGA SPORT (USA)   3 b.g. Sportin' Life (USA)–Midou (Saint Crespin III 132)   **79**
[1988 NR 1989 10g 16m* 16m3] $35,000F, 1,200,000 francs (£121,200 approx) Y: well-made gelding: moderate mover: closely related to Makarova (by Nijinsky), a winner in France at about 1¼m, and half-brother to 2 minor winners in France and USA: dam useful 7f to 1m performer in France: won slowly-run 5-runner maiden at Nottingham: creditable third of 4 in handicap at Lingfield later in August: stays 2m: sold to join T. McGovern 11,000 gns Newmarket Autumn Sales. *G. Harwood.*

MEGATHRUST   2 br.c. (Mar 10) Gorytus (USA) 132–Genuflect (Busted 134)   **52**
[1989 6m 6f4 7g4 8f] 24,000F, IR 38,000Y: quite attractive colt: first reported foal: dam, winner in Italy, is daughter of smart 2-y-o 5f performer Piney Ridge: plating-class maiden: ran moderately in blinkers (pulled hard) final start: bred to stay 1m: trained on debut by J. Berry: sold 4,300 gns Newmarket Autumn Sales. *K. M. Brassey.*

MEGYAAS (CAN)   2 br.c. (Apr 17) Shadeed (USA) 135–Wind Spray 69 (Mill   **80**
Reef (USA) 141) [1989 5g* 6g2 7m2 6f4] 140,000Y: smallish, rather sparely-made, attractive colt: good walker: has a quick action: fourth living foal: closely related to a fair maiden by Czaravich and half-brother to 3-y-o Brighton Pier (by Vice Regent): dam, second over 1½m at 3 yrs in Ireland, is half-sister to Bright Finish and Shining Finish and from family of Teenoso: fair performer: placed in listed race at Haydock and minor event at Newmarket after landing odds in maiden at Leicester in May: not seen out after below-form fourth in minor event at Lingfield in August: probably finds 6f too sharp and will stay 1m. *M. R. Stoute.*

MEHTAB   3 b.f. Touching Wood (USA) 127–Zaheen (Silver Shark 129) [1988 NR   **68 §**
1989 8d 7m3 11.5m 8g2 8m* 7m6 8g6 7g 8f] lengthy, workmanlike filly: sixth live foal: half-sister to 3 winners, including very useful 7f to 1m winner Zaheendar (by Welsh Saint) and fairly useful 5f and 6f winner Zanata (by African Sky): dam, half-sister to top-class Zeddaan, won over 5f at 2 yrs in France: ridden by 5-lb claimer, won poor minor event at Carlisle in June: suited by 1m: acts on top-of-the-ground: blinkered last 6 outings, edgy and setting too strong a pace on first occasion: sold 5,400 gns Newmarket Autumn Sales: unreliable and probably ungenuine. *B. Hanbury.*

MEINE VONNE LADY   4 br.f. Jalmood (USA) 126–Gold Rupee 86 (Native   **45**
Prince (USA)) [1988 7v2 8s5 11s6 10g 8g5 8s* 8f3 8g* 8.2d5 1989 8.2v 8d 8.2m 8g4 8f 8.2d 8f4 8f2 8f 8v] leggy, medium-sized filly: carries plenty of condition: moderate mover: winning plater: suited by about 1m: acted on any going: slowly away second start: in foal to Roaring Riva. *J. Berry.*

MELANCOLIA   3 b.f. Legend of France (USA) 124–Fardella (ITY) (Molvedo   **77 p**
137) [1988 NR 1989 8f3 10g*] 780Y: unfurnished filly: second foal: dam minor 11f winner in France: 15/8 co-favourite, won 26-runner Newmarket claimer in November (claimed to join R. Whitaker £14,001) by 4 lengths from Comino Girl, always in touch, leading 1f out then running on really well: will be suited by 1½m: acts on firm ground: may well improve again. *H. R. A. Cecil.*

MELBURY (USA)   2 ch.f. (Mar 19) Forli (ARG)–Her World (USA) (Transworld   **85**
(USA) 121) [1989 5m* 5m5 6m2 5g2 5f6 5g] $37,000Y: medium-sized, rather unfurnished filly: shows a short, quick action: third reported foal: dam won 3 races at up to 7f: fair performer: won maiden at Haydock in May: best subsequent efforts second in minor events at Bath and Sandown: ran poorly in listed race at Newbury final start: stays 6f: sweating and on toes penultimate outing. *C. R. Nelson.*

MELFA   4 b.f. Auction Ring (USA) 123–Nejwah (Morston (FR) 125) [1988 7v 6m   **—**
9f* 8m3 9g 9g 8g3 1989 10m 6f a8g a14g a12g a8g] sparely-made ex-Irish filly:

second foal: dam never ran: won handicap at Mallow as 3-y-o: well beaten in similar company and claimers in 1989: stays 9f: acts on firm going: has worn blinkers, including on reappearance: trained until after second outing by N. Meade. *J. D. J. Davies.*

MELKONO 5 br.g. Meldrum 112–Ivory Coast 90 (Poaching 115) [1988 7g 10f⁴ 10m 1989 13.8d] workmanlike gelding: 66/1, showed a little ability on second of 3 outings as 4-y-o: well behind in handicap at Catterick in March. *E. Weymes.* —

MELODY 3 b.f. Music Boy 124–Heavenly Chord 89 (Hittite Glory 125) [1988 5g⁴ 6d² 5f⁶ 7d* 7f 7m 1989 6s 7m 7f 6m⁶ 6f⁶ 9f] close-coupled, sturdy filly: modest winner as 2-y-o: well below form since, best effort in 1989 in ladies seller (sweating and edgy) fifth start: suited by 7f: acts well on a soft surface: hangs, and best with strong handling: blinkered last 2 outings: one to be wary of. *M. H. Easterby.* —

MELODY LANE 4 b. or br.f. Horage 124–Melody Ryde 90 (Shooting Chant) [1988 7d 7.6g 7m³ᵈⁱˢ 8f* 7g⁵ 7m⁵ 8d⁶ 8.2f 7m 8d 1989 7g 10m 8m 7m 8m 7.6f 9g 8m a7g] compact filly: moderate mover: quite modest winner as 3-y-o: well below form in 1989: stays 1m: suited by a sound surface: often visored, blinkered final outing: has hung, but has run creditably for apprentice: trained first 8 starts by C. Hill. *R. J. Hodges.* —

MEL'S ROSE 4 ch.g. Anfield 117–Ragtime Rose (Ragstone 128) [1988 8g 8g⁶ 8g 8d 8g⁶ 1989 8d² 9f⁵ 7m* 7f³ 7m* 7g 8m 7m 7g 7m 8g a8g²] tall gelding: has a quick action: modest handicapper: won twice at Yarmouth (first time apprentice event) in June: easily best effort after when fast-finishing second at Southwell: suited by 7f or 1m: acts on firm going and a soft surface: blinkered final outing in 1988: edgy first 2 starts at 4 yrs: good mount for apprentice. *G. A. Huffer.* 78

MEND 3 b.c. Busted 134–Sound Type 92 (Upper Case (USA)) [1988 NR 1989 14m⁴] medium-sized colt: fifth foal: brother to Curvaceous, a fair maiden here later successful in Belgium, and half-brother to 9f and 1¼m seller winner Final Sound (by Final Straw): dam won over 7f and 1¼m: weak 7/1, very lethargic in paddock and green to post, soundly-beaten fourth of 5 to Royal Vote in maiden at Yarmouth in August, slowly away. *M. R. Stoute.* —

MERALTO 3 ch.f. Noalto 120–Miss Merlin 79 (Manacle 123) [1988 5g 5f* 6g⁶ 6g 6g 1989 5s 7g⁵ 8m 7m] workmanlike filly: has a quick action: fair plater: creditable fifth at Doncaster, giving impression would have gone close had run started sooner: well beaten otherwise as 3-y-o: should stay 1m: probably unsuited by soft going: blinkered final start: sold to join H. Willis 1,450 gns Ascot July Sales. *H. P. Rohan.* 49

MERANDIS GIRL 3 ro.f. Burslem 123–A La Creme (Young Emperor 133) [1988 5m 6f⁶ 1989 12v] little worthwhile form in maidens and claimer: tailed off only start as 3-y-o: bred to stay 1m + . *K. M. Brassey.* —

MERANDI SPECIAL 2 b.g. (Mar 21) Coquelin (USA) 121–Mountain Chase (Mount Hagen (FR) 127) [1989 8g] IR 6,600F, 7,200Y: neat gelding: second foal: half-brother to 3-y-o Silk Dynasty (by Prince Tenderfoot): dam never ran: 33/1, around 17 lengths ninth of 15 in maiden at Leicester in November. *M. E. D. Francis.* —

MERBAYEH GIRL 2 b.f. (Jan 17) Wassl Merbayeh (USA) 104–Dippy Girl 104 (Sandford Lad 133) [1989 5m⁶ 5f⁴ 7f 8m⁶ 7d] quite attractive filly: shade unfurnished: third foal: half-sister to Irish 3-y-o Amiga Clara (by Whistling Deer): dam placed in Ireland at 6f and 7f: poor maiden: will stay long distances: possibly unsuited by soft surface: sold 600 gns Ascot November Sales. *K. M. Brassey.* 42

MERCURY MOON 4 gr.g. Belfort (FR) 89–Tringa (GER) (Kaiseradler) [1988 8d 8g 6m 10.1m 1989 8m 8f 7f] strong, plain gelding: carries condition: has been hobdayed: little sign of ability. *M. McCourt.* —

MERE MELODY 4 b.f. Dunphy 124–Flying Melody (Auction Ring (USA) 123) [1988 5s⁶ 5m 5d 5m 5g² 5f 5g 5s 5g 5m 5f 5g 5m 6m 1989 6d 6m⁵ 5m 6f 5f 6f] smallish, good-quartered filly: poor mover: runner-up in handicap at York in June, 1988, virtually only form since 2 yrs: stays 6f: suited by an easy surface: visored twice: has worn bandages: sweating on reappearance: has given trouble at stalls and often starts slowly: unreliable. *M. Brittain.* — §

MERMAID'S PURSE (CAN) 2 ch.f. (Apr 23) Devil's Bag (USA)–Oceana (USA) (Northern Dancer) [1989 7m* 7.3v] $324,120Y: sparely-made, plain filly: poor walker: first foal: dam unraced sister to Storm Bird and Northernette: dead-heated with Jathibiyah in 14-runner maiden at Redcar in September, quickening well to lead inside final furlong then rallying strongly: looked unsuited by heavy ground when tailed off in listed race at Newbury following month. *J. Gosden.* 79

MERRYFALL 2 ch.f. (May 9) Anfield 117–Lifestyle 80 (Jimmy Reppin 131) [1989   **73**
5d3 5f4 6f* 6m3 7.5f* 7f3 7.5m 8g] 3,800Y: angular, workmanlike filly: has scope:
quite good mover: third foal (previous 2 by Bold Owl): dam won twice at 2 yrs, and
was also successful over hurdles: modest performer: stayed on strongly when
successful in auction events at Pontefract in June and Beverley, better effort
beating Ballyhooly by 2½ lengths, following month: well beaten in Premio Dormello
at Milan final one: should stay 1m. *J. Etherington.*

MERRY MARIGOLD 3 b.f. Sonnen Gold 121–Manna Green (Bustino 136)   —
[1988 6g* 7f6 6s3 7d* 7g4 1989 10s 7s5] lengthy, workmanlike filly: has a rather
round action: modest winner as 2-y-o: well beaten in moderately-run handicap and
minor event in spring of 1989: best form at 7f: acts on a soft surface and ran poorly
(hanging badly left) on firm going. *R. W. Stubbs.*

MERRY NUTKIN 3 ch.g. Jalmood (USA) 126–Merry Cindy 63 (Sea Hawk II 131)   **89**
[1988 7g6 8m 1989 10.4m6 13f* 16.2g*] strong, workmanlike gelding: moderate
walker: has a long stride: easily best efforts when winning handicaps at Hamilton
and Haydock (comfortably) in space of a week in June: subsequently gelded:
sweating, looked unsuited by track at Chester on reappearance: stays 2m: acts on
firm going. *W. J. Haggas.*

MERSEYSIDE MAN 3 b.g. My Dad Tom (USA) 109–Chanita (Averof 123)   **55**
[1988 6g5 6m* 6g 7m 7m6 6g 1989 7f 7f4 8m3 8f3 8f3 7g 8f] lengthy, workmanlike
gelding: plating-class handicapper: has run in sellers: stays 1m: best efforts on
top-of-the-ground: visored 3 times: sometimes slowly away. *Dr J. D. Scargill.*

MERTOLA'S PET 3 b.f. Tickled Pink 114–Mertola (Tribal Chief 125) [1988 5f   **63**
5g4 5f2 1989 5h4 5.8h4 5.3f4 a6g5] small, quite good-quartered filly: quite modest
maiden: best effort as 3-y-o on reappearance: not entirely discredited last 2 outings:
may prove best at 5f: acts on hard ground. *L. G. Cottrell.*

MERTON MILL 2 b.f. (Apr 6) Dominion 123–Brookfield Miss 73 (Welsh   —
Pageant 132) [1989 7g] 34,000Y: sixth foal: half-sister to 4 winners, including useful
7f and 1m filly Littlefield (by Bay Express): dam showed a little ability at 2 yrs: 33/1,
always behind in 24-runner maiden at Newmarket in November. *D. Morley.*

MESHRARF 3 gr.g. Rusticaro (FR) 124–Lady Wise (Lord Gayle (USA) 124)   —
[1988 NR 1989 10g 10h6] IR 14,000Y: good-bodied gelding: sixth foal: half-brother to
1985 Irish 2-y-o 5f winner Before The Storm (by Thatching), subsequently a winner
in Norway: dam, placed over 8.6f at 2 yrs in Ireland, is half-sister to Middle Park
winner Spanish Express: behind in maidens at Leicester in April and Brighton in
June: has joined C. Beever. *G. A. Huffer.*

MESSAGE PAD 2 ch.c. (May 18) Rousillon (USA) 133–Ouija 104 (Silly Season   **101** ?
127) [1989 7g* 7g] rangy, useful-looking colt: has plenty of scope: good walker: has
a long stride: half-brother to several winners, notably high-class 1m to 1¼m
performer Teleprompter (by Welsh Pageant): dam best at 1m: 25/1, bit backward
and green, won minor event at Doncaster in September shade cleverly by a neck
from Shavian, soon travelling smoothly and quickening well under hand riding to
lead last 50 yds: wearing special noseband, very free to post and took strong hold in
listed race at Newmarket following month, dropping out over 1f out to finish last of
7: looked a bright prospect at Doncaster, but seems rather headstrong. *J. W. Watts.*

METAL BOYS 2 b.c. (Mar 17) Krayyan 117–Idle Gossip (Runnett 125) [1989 5m5   **82**
5f5 5h* 5m 6m2 5f3 6f3 6f4 6v 5g*] IR 8,200Y: medium-sized colt: has a quick
action: first foal: dam never ran: fair performer: successful in maiden at Carlisle in
June and nursery (well handicapped, beating Willbutwhen 2 lengths) at Newmarket
in November: stays 6f: inconsistent. *R. Hollinshead.*

METANNEE 5 b. or br.m. The Brianstan 128–Lyaaric (Privy Seal 108) [1988   **58**
10.2s 10g5 10g 10d4 8g5 9m 8g6 1989 14g5 14f6 16m] big, lengthy, slightly
hollow-backed mare: has a long stride: quite modest maiden: close up when slipping
and falling before halfway in £43,800 handicap at Newcastle in July: stays 1¾m:
winning hurdler. *M. E. D. Francis.*

METHANO 3 b.c.c. Alzao (USA) 117–Gulf Bird 71 (Gulf Pearl 117) [1988 6d3 7m   **78**
7.6s5 1989 12g 15.3f* 12m6 13.3g 14m6 16m 18g] strong, compact, quite attractive
colt: won maiden at Wolverhampton in May, setting modest pace early: no
worthwhile form in handicaps after: stayed 15.3f: acted on firm going: sold to join R.
Akehurst 13,000 gns Newmarket Autumn Sales: dead. *C. E. Brittain.*

MEXICAN VISION 2 b.c. (Feb 19) Vision (USA)–Mexican Two Step (Gay   **74** p
Fandango (USA) 132) [1989 7g 10g 7g] IR 4,000Y: strong, lengthy colt: has plenty of
scope: fifth foal: half-brother to Irish 3-y-o 7f and 9f winner Hear Me (by Simply
Great), useful 1¼m to 1½m winner Busted Rock (by Busted) and a winner in USA by

Captain James: dam fairly useful Irish 2-y-o 6f winner: still carrying condition, around 6 lengths seventh of 21, keeping on steadily, to Two Left Feet in all-aged event at Newmarket in November, third and easily best effort: looks sort to make fair handicapper as 3-y-o. *Mrs L. Piggott.*

MEY MADAM 2 b.f. (Mar 25) Song 132–Sea Chant (Julio Mariner 127) [1989 5s — 5m 6f] 2,500F, 4,300Y: rather leggy, workmanlike filly: has a round action: third foal: half-sister to 3-y-o Pansong (by Absalom), 7.5f and 8.5f seller winner at 2 yrs: dam unraced daughter of half-sister to dam of Pitcairn: soundly beaten in early-season maidens: twice slowly away: sold 1,100 gns Ascot November Sales. *J. J. Bridger.*

MEZHIROV (USA) 2 b.c. (Mar 23) Lemhi Gold (USA) 123–Santa Moira (USA) — p (Exclusive Native (USA)) [1989 7g] $6,500Y: second foal: dam twice-raced half-sister to very smart 11f to 1¾m winner Noble Saint and from family of Chieftain and Tom Rolfe: 25/1, soundly-beaten seventh of 8 in maiden at Yarmouth in August. *J. H. M. Gosden.*

MEZZARA 3 ch.g. Hard Fought 125–Serendip (Sing Sing 134) [1988 NR 1989 6g — 6s 6f 6m] IR 9,000F: heavy-topped gelding: moderate walker: poor mover: eighth living foal: closely related to fair 1984 2-y-o 5f winner Master Crofter (by Crofter), subsequently successful in USA, and half-brother to 2 other winners on flat, including very useful miler Serencia (by Great Heron), and a winning hurdler: dam never ran: little sign of ability, including in claimers: sold 1,100 gns Ascot September Sales. *L. J. Holt.*

MIA FILLIA 2 b.f. (Apr 21) Formidable (USA) 125–As Blessed 101 (So Blessed **65** 130) [1989 7m 5m 8.5f⁴ 7g a6g a7g⁴] compact filly: has a quick action: sister to 1984 2-y-o 5f and 6f winner Glory of Hera and half-sister to 2 other winners, including 1¼m and 2m winner Have Blessed (by Averof): dam, 2-y-o 5f winner, stayed 1m: quite modest maiden: better suited by 7f+ than by shorter. *C. E. Brittain.*

MIAMI BANKER 3 ch.c. Miami Springs 121–Banking Coyne 76 (Deep Diver **95** 134) [1988 5s³ 5g*dis 5m 5m⁶ 5d³ 6g 6g⁶ 5d 6s⁵ 5m⁴ 1989 5s* 6v 5s* 5s* 5m 5f⁵ 5m² 5g* 5f² 5g 5m] rangy colt: moderate mover: fairly useful handicapper: had excellent season, winning at Warwick, Newbury and Sandown (twice): creditable second at Epsom and Goodwood: burly and facing stiff task, never placed to challenge or knocked about in listed race final start: 5f performer: acts on any going: tends to idle in front, and is suited by strong handling and waiting tactics: game and consistent. *P. J. Arthur.*

MIAMI BEAR 3 b.g. Miami Springs 121–Belinda Bear (Ragstone 128) [1988 7m⁶ **52** 7.5s 7s³ 1989 8.2v⁵ 11m 9m 10.4g⁴ 12.2f⁴ 11s 12m³] strong, good-bodied gelding: has a round action: plating-class maiden: probably stays 1½m: best effort on soft ground: keen sort. *J. Berry.*

MIAMI PRIDE 3 b.f. Miami Springs 121–Gwynpride (Val de L'Orne (FR) 130) — [1988 5m⁴ 5f 5s² 5m⁴ 5g² 6m² 6m⁵ 5g⁵ 6s 5g³ 7g⁵ 5d 7g 7g⁶ 6g 5s 1989 5d 5m 6g 5f] sparely-made filly: moderate mover: plater: well behind last 3 outings: best form at 5f: blinkered 4 times, including second and third outings in 1989: twice visored: has worn bandages. *M. B. James.*

MIAMI STAR 8 b.m. Miami Springs 121–Corr Lady (Lorenzaccio 130) [1988 NR — 1989 13m 13m 12f 8f] leggy, lengthy mare: no form as 8-y-o: has worn blinkers: visored in 1989 except on third start: has been to stud. *P. Monteith.*

MICDAN 2 gr.c. (May 10) Exhibitioner 111–Galaxy Scorpio (Saritamer (USA) 130) **56** [1989 5d 5d* 7g 6m 6g a7g⁵] IR 3,000F, IR 7,400Y: close-coupled, rather unfurnished colt: moderate mover: half-brother to several winners, including 1988 2-y-o 5f winner Do I Know You (by Kafu): dam unraced daughter of sister to Abergwaun: fair plater: won at Warwick (no bid) in May: ran creditably fourth and final starts: stays 7f: best form in blinkers. *C. N. Williams.*

MICHELLE CLARE 3 b.f. Good Times (ITY)–Paradise Island (Artaius (USA) — 129) [1988 NR 1989 10d] first foal: dam, granddaughter of Prix de la Foret winner Democratie, showed little worthwhile form: 33/1, tailed off in Newbury maiden in October. *M. J. Bolton.*

MICHELOZZO (USA) 3 b.c. Northern Baby (CAN) 127–Tres Agreable **127** p (FR) (Luthier 126) [1988 NR 1989 8.2s* 12g³ 14m* 14.6s*]

The St Leger, England's oldest classic, has been lost only once since its inauguration in 1776. The 1939 edition—which would have provided Blue Peter with the chance of landing the triple crown—was cancelled because of the outbreak of war. Fifty years on, the St Leger had to be postponed when the

Laphroaig March Stakes, Goodwood—Michelozzo is pushed clear of Demawend

Doncaster meeting was abandoned after the opening event on the third of the four days. The fall of a two-year-old in that race had been preceded by three horses coming down, and their jockeys being injured, at around the same point in the Tote-Portland Handicap on the first day. The course was passed fit after the Portland, but following the second incident the stewards inspected it again and discovered subsidence which in their view made the course unfit for further racing (later meetings were transferred to Newcastle and Thirsk while repair work took place). Provisional plans to postpone, rather than abandon, major races had been drawn up by the Jockey Club following strong criticism when the Dewhurst Stakes was lost in 1987. A transfer to Ayr a week later was the choice in the event of the St Leger's postponement and the 213th St Leger became the first classic to be run in Scotland; Holsten withdrew its sponsorship when Doncaster was lost, the prize money being maintained under an insurance scheme.

The fifteen horses left in the St Leger at the original five-day stage were officially reinstated, but the later running resulted in the Gold Seal Oaks winner Aliysa and the King George VI and Queen Elizabeth Diamond Stakes runner-up Cacoethes, both intended runners at Doncaster, going straight for the Ciga Prix de l'Arc de Triomphe. But it's an ill wind that blows nobody good. Michelozzo would have been doubtful for Doncaster after pricking a foot when spreading a plate travelling to the course. He had become a leading St Leger fancy after a clear-cut victory in the Laphroaig March Stakes over the St Leger trip at Goodwood in August; the March Stakes was only his third outing and had been preceded by a ten-length victory in a minor race at Nottingham in April and a creditable third to Carroll House in the Princess of Wales's Stakes at Newmarket in July. Michelozzo started 6/4 favourite at Ayr where, after a week of rain, the going was soft (it would have been good at

St Leger Stakes, Ayr—a most impressive winner of the first classic staged in Scotland

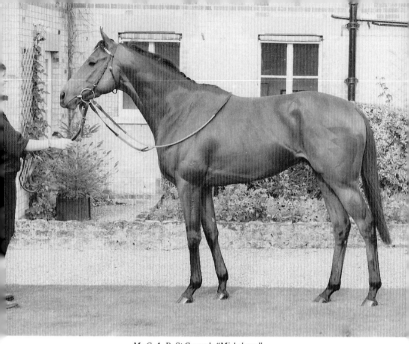

Mr C. A. B. St George's "Michelozzo"

Doncaster). Michelozzo's seven rivals included the Yorkshire Oaks winner Roseate Tern and the Derby runner-up Terimon, the latter the first horse to be supplemented for an English classic (his connections paid £25,000 at the second entry stage in September). The Gordon Stakes second and third Alphabel and N C Owen and the Tote-Ebor Handicap winner Sapience were the only other runners to start at odds shorter than 100/1. The depleted field was short of runners with form suggesting they might be up to classic-winning standard but Michelozzo's performance—he beat Sapience by a long-looking eight lengths, a very wide margin of victory for a classic—left no room to doubt that he would have been a difficult horse to beat whatever the strength of the opposition on the day. Michelozzo passed the severe test of stamina with flying colours, responding to the whip in the straight and galloping on in great style after taking the lead two furlongs from the finish; Cauthen eased him near the line but for which his victory would have been even more overwhelming. Roseate Tern, racing on soft for the first time, and Terimon ran some way below their best in third and fourth. Michelozzo gave his trainer his fourth victory in the St Leger which was the only one of the five classics won by a British-based owner. Mr St George finished eighth in the owners' list which, as usual nowadays, was dominated by members of the Al-Maktoum family who, along with Khalid Abdulla and the Aga Khan, occupied the first six places. Back in 1939, incidentally, the winning owners were headed by Lord Rosebery (who had Blue Peter), Lord Derby and Lord Glanely. How the old order changeth!

Michelozzo is a finely-made, attractive colt, but a poor mover. He was bought by his owner and a partner for 90,000 dollars as a foal; Mr St George

		Northern Dancer	Nearctic
	Northern Baby (CAN)	(b 1961)	Natalma
	(b 1976)	Two Rings	Round Table
Michelozzo (USA)		(b 1970)	Allofthem
(b.c. 1986)		Luthier	Klairon
	Tres Agreable (FR)	(b or br 1965)	Flute Enchantee
	(b 1980)	Assez Cuite	Graustark
		(b 1974)	Clinkers

bought him outright for 180,000 dollars as a yearling when he went through the sale-ring to dissolve the partnership. Michelozzo is the first classic winner sired by the Champion Stakes winner Northern Baby, who stands in Kentucky, and is Tres Agreable's first foal. Tres Agreable won over ten and a half furlongs in France as a four-year-old. There is plenty of stamina in her family. Tres Agreable's half-brother El Cuite won the Prix Royal-Oak (French St Leger) and their dam the very useful Assez Cuite, winner of the Prix Yacowlef and second in the Prix de la Salamandre, is out of a half-sister to the dam of the Gold Cup winner Ragstone and another good-class animal who stayed at least a mile and three quarters in Castle Keep. This is also the family of St Leger winner Moon Madness and Sheriff's Star. Michelozzo's strong suit is stamina and he'd be an outstanding contender for the Cup races. However, a middle-distance programme has been mapped out for him as a four-year-old when his main target will be the Prix de l'Arc de Triomphe (he was a day-of-race withdrawal for the 1989 Champion Stakes because the ground wasn't considered soft enough). He has won on good to firm but will almost certainly need soft ground and a strong gallop in good company over a mile and a half. He is just the lightly-raced progressive type one would expect to train on. *H. R. A. Cecil.*

MICROLINE 3 b.c. Henbit (USA) 130–Rosolini 109 (Ragusa 137) [1988 NR 1989 — 11f] 16,000F, 15,000Y: tall colt: half-brother to 4 winners, including Irish 7f (at 2 yrs) to 1¼m winner Modica (by Persian Bold) and useful Irish 6f and 1¼m winner Coryana (by Sassafras), dam of Waajib: dam, winner at up to 1¼m, is half-sister to very smart Knockroe: soundly beaten in maiden at Newbury in May: dead. *H. Candy.*

MICRO LOVE 5 ch.h. Vaigly Great 127–Minne Love 67 (Homeric 133) [1988 85 5m⁵ 5f 5m 5g⁴ 6g 5g⁶ 5m 5m* 5f⁴ 5g 5g 1989 5m⁴ 5f⁶ 5g⁶ 5h* 5m² 5.8h² 5g 5m* 5g⁴ 5m] small, strong, workmanlike horse: good mover: fair handicapper: won at Bath in July (first outing for new trainer, formerly with H. O'Neill) and Sandown in August: best at 5f on top-of-the-ground: slowly away third outing: has won when sweating: tends to be a little on edge. *L. G. Cottrell.*

MICRONOVA 3 ch.g. Homing 130–Tula Music 62 (Patch 129) [1988 8.2d 1989 — 10.2h 10.1m⁴ 18g] leggy, sparely-made gelding: little sign of ability. *E. A. Wheeler.*

MIDDLE KINGDOM (USA) 2 b.c. (Apr 14) Northern Dancer–Puget Sound — 95 (High Top 131) [1989 6g] IR 1,300,000Y: good-topped colt: second foal: closely related to Irish 3-y-o Sound Out (by Nijinsky): dam 7f winner, is out of half-sister to Nureyev (by Northern Dancer): 33/1, always behind in 29-runner maiden at Newmarket in November. *B. W. Hills.*

MIDFIELDER 3 ch.g. Formidable (USA) 125–Pampas Flower 80 (Pampered 89 King 121) [1988 6f⁴ 7m⁶ 8.2s⁴ 8.2d³ 1989 7g 9s² 8f* 8f 8m] deep-girthed, workmanlike gelding: quite useful handicapper: won at Newbury in May: ran moderately (very much on toes) in £15,700 event at Newmarket in July on final start: stays 9f: acts on any going: has joined P. Hobbs and is a winning juvenile hurdler. *P. T. Walwyn.*

MIDNIGHT FLAME 3 gr.g. Kalaglow 132–Midnight Flit 89 (Bold Lad (IRE) — 133) [1988 NR 1989 10.1m a8g⁶ a12g] 7,200Y: rangy gelding: second foal: dam, 7f winner, is out of very smart French performer at up to 1m Tawny Owl, also dam of useful 1m winner Bold Owl: little sign of ability in Windsor minor event (swishing tail repeatedly in paddock, off course 5 months after) and Lingfield claimers. *M. J. Fetherston-Godley.*

MIDNIGHT IMPERIAL 3 b.f. Night Shift (USA)–Tsar's Bride 69 (Song 132) — [1988 6m 5s⁵ 6v 1989 8f 8m 8g 6f 7s 7g] workmanlike, deep-girthed filly: moderate mover: no form, including in handicaps. *N. Bycroft.*

MIDNIGHT MOVES 2 ch.f. (Feb 20) Coquelin (USA) 121–Puss Moth (Hotfoot 55 126) [1989 5.3g² 5s 5m⁵ 5m 5m 5f⁴ 5g a5g] 4,600Y: smallish, sparely-made filly: has a quick action: half-sister to poor 1982 2-y-o Mollison (by Anax): dam poor half-sister to Lowther winner Kittyhawk, dam of Cesarewitch winner Nomadic Way: plating-class maiden: bred to stay much further than 5f: has twice hung badly left. *R. J. Holder.*

MIDNIGHT'S REWARD 3 b.f. Night Shift (USA)–Margaret's Ruby (Tesco — Boy 121) [1988 5g² 5g³ 5m* 5d⁴ 6g³ 5f 1989 6d 6m] workmanlike filly: fair winner as 2-y-o: below form in Newmarket handicaps in spring of 1989: best form at 6f: acted on firm going and a soft surface: reportedly cracked bone and retired. *R. M. Whitaker.*

MIDSUMMER BREEZE 2 b.f. (Mar 25) Tumble Wind (USA)–Pam Story 65 (Sallust 134) [1989 5f* 5f] 4,000F, 20,000Y: sparely-made filly: second foal: dam second over 5f at 4 yrs in Ireland: odds on, won 8-runner maiden at Wolverhampton comfortably by 2½ lengths from Echo Princess, leading 1f out: always behind in 10-runner Molecomb Stakes at Goodwood later in July. *J. P. Hudson.*

MIDWEEK CHORUS 3 b. or br.f. Lucky Wednesday 124–Minster Melody 73 — (Highland Melody 112) [1988 NR 1989 10.2h] 500Y: angular, sparely-made filly: first reported foal: dam 7f seller winner: 33/1 and ridden by 7-lb claimer, slowly away and tailed off in claimer at Bath in June. *D. Burchell.*

MIDWEST 2 ch.g. (Feb 28) Kabour 80–Boom Shanty 66 (Dragonara Palace — (USA) 115) [1989 5g] sturdy gelding: second foal: brother to 3-y-o Le Chic: dam 2-y-o 5f seller winner: 33/1, backward and ridden by 7-lb claimer, slowly away and tailed off in 10-runner seller at Wolverhampton in July. *D. W. Chapman.*

MIEKA 2 ch.c. (Mar 14) Longleat (USA) 109–Secret Pearl (Gulf Pearl 117) [1989 73 8g⁶ 7g 5g*] 9,200Y: fourth reported foal: dam unraced: 5/1, showed much improved form when winning 10-runner maiden at Edinburgh in November by a neck from Kawarau Queen, making all: bred to stay beyond 5f. *R. Boss.*

MIG 4 b.f. Sagaro 133–Lady Gaylord (Double Jump 131) [1988 NR 1989 14f 12.3f³ 58 14f⁵ 16f³ 18m 16m] workmanlike filly: good mover: half-sister to several winners, including fair middle-distance performer Sage King (by Shantung) and quite useful in 1986 2-y-o Naturally Fresh (by Thatching): dam unraced half-sister to smart colt Romper: 50/1, never-nearer third to very easy winner Future Success in maiden at Ripon in June: well beaten in similar contest and handicaps (harshly treated) afterwards: blinkered, tailed off final outing: should be suited by 2m + . *A. D. Brown.*

MIGHTY GLOW 5 gr.g. Kalaglow 132–Faridetta 107 (Good Bond 122) [1988 8d 57 § 8m 11s 12f 12h 10m 9d³ 12g 10m 1989 10s 10.2g 12m 13m² 12f 13f⁴ 12f⁶ 12g³ 16f* 12m 15.3g⁵ 10m 15.5f⁵ 15s] leggy, workmanlike gelding: moderate mover: won for first time on flat in slowly-run amateurs handicap at Chepstow in July: little other worthwhile form since 1987: carried considerable overweight last 2 outings: stays 2m: acts on firm going: sometimes visored, and was at Chepstow: ungenuine. *C. Tinkler.*

MILADY-SAL 2 ch.f. (Apr 22) Milford 119–Bralanta 71 (Green God 128) [1989 — 5m 5m⁶ 6g a7g a8g] sparely-made, angular filly: poor mover: first reported foal: dam, should have stayed 1m, is out of lightly-raced daughter of 2000 Guineas winner Garden Path: well beaten in maidens and a claimer: slowly away first 3 starts. *R. T. Juckes.*

MILAN FAIR 5 b.h. Mill Reef (USA) 141–Fairweather Friend (USA) 69 (Forli 46 (ARG)) [1988 8d³ 9d 7g 7f 6f 8g 7.6m 7m 12g 12d 12d 1989 6d 8m 10.1m* 10m 11.7m² 12f⁶ 12m⁵] lengthy horse: claimed out of C. Austin's stable £6,100 after winning 23-runner claimer at Windsor (apprentice ridden) in May: stays 11.7f: acts on top-of-the-ground and a soft surface: blinkered or visored on 4 of last 5 appearances in 1988: trained fourth start by J. White: inconsistent. *T. Thomson Jones.*

MILBURN LEISURE 2 br.g. (Apr 6) Kala Shikari 125–Paperwork (Brigadier — Gerard 144) [1989 7m] 3,600F, 5,100Y: eighth foal: half-brother to 3-y-o Wheatsheaf, 1m seller winner City Final (both by Final Straw) and quite a good winner in Germany: dam won over 8.5f in France and over hurdles here: 20/1, tailed off in 14-runner maiden auction race at Doncaster in July. *A. Smith.*

MILCLERE 3 ch.f. Milford 119–Great Lass (Vaigly Great 127) [1988 NR 1989 7f 47 10f 8f a12g⁵] leggy filly: first foal: dam never ran: first show in varied events when fifth in claimer (on toes) at Lingfield in November, staying on steadily despite edging left: suited by 1½m: trained on debut by J. Wharton. *W. G. R. Wightman.*

MILDAME 2 br.f. (Apr 25) Milford 119–Mandrian 103 (Mandamus 120) [1989 7m — 7.5f] leggy filly: moderate mover: fifth foal: sister to 1m to 19f winner Autonomous: dam won over 8.2f and 12.2f: poor form in summer maidens at Wolverhampton and Beverley. *J. Wharton.*

MILEEHA (USA)　3 ch.f. Blushing Groom (FR) 131–Melody Tree (USA) (High　**81** Tribute) [1988 7g⁵ 1989 8g 9f* 10g³ 10f] sparely-made, angular filly: won maiden at Kempton in May, drifting left: well-backed second favourite, chased leaders 1m when last of 8 in Extel Stakes at Goodwood in July: stayed 1¼m: acted on firm going: visits Shirley Heights. *R. W. Armstrong.*

MILHOLM　2 ch.c. (Mar 27) Milford 119–Hagen's Bargain 62§ (Mount Hagen　— (FR) 127) [1989 7f 6f] small colt: first foal: dam 2-y-o 5f seller winner probably stayed 9f: bit backward, always behind in October maidens at Salisbury (slowly away) and Folkestone. *J. C. Fox.*

MILIEU　4 b.c. Habitat 134–Lady Graustark (USA) (Graustark) [1988 8g 9g* 8s*　**111** 7g* 8v² 7s* 1989 8d⁶ 9g 8f⁶ 7f* 8m⁴ 8g* 7m⁴ 7d*] big, strong colt: won listed events at Leopardstown in July and November, and at the Curragh, by ¾ length from Top-Boot, in October: ran creditably when sixth to True Panache in Royal Hunt Cup (Handicap) at Royal Ascot and when fourth of 6, facing stiffish task, to Distant Relative in Bisquit Cognac Challenge Stakes at Newmarket on third and seventh outings: stays 9f: acts on any going: very useful. *D. K. Weld, Ireland.*

MILINETTA　4 b.f. Milford 119–Golden Linnet 96 (Sing Sing 134) [1988 10f 1989　— 14.8d 17f 10h 9.1f] leggy, narrow filly: moderate mover: of little account. *W. G. A. Brooks.*

MILITARY BLUE　4 ch.c. Sandhurst Prince 128–Blue Persian 112 (Majority　— Blue 126) [1988 NR 1989 6d] leggy, sparely-made colt: fair winner over 5f as 2-y-o: in need of race, well beaten in minor contest at Folkestone in April, only subsequent outing. *B. Hanbury.*

MILITARY FASHION　3 ch.c. Mill Reef (USA) 141–Smarten Up 119 (Sharpen　**102** p Up 127) [1988 NR 1989 8g* 10mʷᵒ 10g³] 210,000Y: tall, good-topped colt: moderate walker: has a quick action: sixth foal: half-brother to high-class 5f to 7f winner Cadeaux Genereux (by Young Generation) and 3 other winners, including sprinter/miler Young Jason (by Star Appeal) and middle-distance stayer Brightner (by Sparkler): dam sprinting half-sister to smart fillies Walk By and Solar: won moderately-run maiden at Yarmouth and walked over in Redcar minor event in September: 4/1 and still green to post, good third in £8,900 handicap at Redcar: will stay 1½m and improve again. *L. M. Cumani.*

MILITARY MEDIUM (USA)　2 br.c. (Jan 29) Hawaii–Giostra (AUS) (Imperial　**78** Prince 125) [1989 6m⁵ 6m*] $65,000Y: good-topped colt: moderate mover: first foal: dam quite useful sprinter in Australia, won twice at 2 yrs: won 18-runner maiden at Windsor in July by 3 lengths from Master Pierre, eased 2 lengths: dead. *W. J. Haggas.*

MILITARY SALUTE　4 b.c. Sandhurst Prince 128–Wavetree (Realm 129) [1988　**49** § 8m 1989 8g 10g⁴ 12d⁶ 12m 12f³ 14f⁴ 13s 17.6f⁶] tall, leggy colt: poor and ungenerous maiden: seems to stay 1½m: acts on firm going: trained first 6 outings by H. O'Neill. *W. J. Pearce.*

MILITARY SHOT (USA)　2 b.c. (Mar 21) Lyphard's Wish (FR) 124–Pavahra 93　**80** (Mummy's Pet 125) [1989 6m³ 6m⁶ 6f* 7m⁵] $20,000Y: leggy, workmanlike colt: half-brother to a winner in USA by Vigors: dam sprinter: modest performer: won maiden at Nottingham in August going away by 2½ lengths from Mawathik: creditable fifth to Bridal Toast in minor event at York following month: stays 7f. *G. A. Pritchard-Gordon.*

MILLBECK LAD　3 b.g. Millfontaine 114–Miss Damus 66 (Mandamus 120)　— [1988 NR 1989 7g⁴ 8m⁶ 6g 9f 8.2g⁶ 10.6s] IR 3,000Y: smallish, workmanlike gelding: sixth foal: half-brother to winners in Italy by African Sky and Northfields: dam won twice over 1m: poor form in claimers and sellers: stays 1m: mounted outside paddock first 2 outings: wore hood final one: sold out of G. Pritchard-Gordon's stable 1,500 gns Ascot 2nd June Sales after third. *D. Burchell.*

MILL DE LEASE　4 b.c. Milford 119–Melting Snows 88 (High Top 131) [1988 7s⁴　**45** 8g 7f 8f* 10.1g 8m⁴ 12m³ 10g⁵ 1989 8.5f4 12.3f⁵ 10f⁵ 17f a11g] leggy, workmanlike, angular colt: winning plater: probably needs further than 1m nowadays and stays 1½m: probably acts on any going: winning hurdler. *J. Dooler.*

MILLER'S GAIT　3 b.f. Mill Reef (USA) 141–High Gait 90 (High Top 131) [1988　— § 8m³ 9g² 10d⁴ 1989 11.7h⁵ 16.2g⁵ 14m 12g⁵ 12s a11g] smallish, close-coupled, quite attractive filly: has a quick action: modest form in 1988: best efforts as 3-y-o on first 2 outings when trained by M. Stoute: should be best at bit short of 2m: probably unsuited by soft going: showed plenty of temperament as 2-y-o and is one to have reservations about. *Mrs J. R. Ramsden.*

MILLER'S GILT 4 b.c. Glint of Gold 128–Hecalene (FR) (Sir Gaylord) [1988 —
10m 10.2g 10m 7m 8m⁴ 10g⁴ 8f 8s 8d 10d 12g⁶ 1989 8f] small, stocky colt: poor
plater: stays 1¼m: sometimes visored or blinkered: possibly ungenuine. *W. G. M.
Turner.*

MILLER'S MELODY 3 br.f. Chief Singer 131–Miller's Lass (Mill Reef (USA) 72 ?
141) [1988 6d² 6d⁶ 1989 7m³ 7m⁶ 7f⁵] angular, close-coupled filly: good walker:
modest form at best since debut: blinkered, ran poorly in maiden final start (July):
should be suited by further than 6f: possibly unsuited by top-of-the-ground: pulled
very hard second start at 2 yrs: disappointing: sold 23,000 gns Newmarket
December Sales. *D. R. C. Elsworth.*

MILLFIELDS LADY 2 b.f. (Feb 15) Sayf El Arab (USA) 127–Ma Pierrette 77 64
(Cawston's Clown 113) [1989 6h* 7f⁴ 7h³ 6g³ 6g 8m² 10f⁴ 8.2g³] 1,900Y: leggy filly:
moderate mover: third foal: half-sister to plating-class 1987 2-y-o 5f winner My
Home (by Homing): dam won from 5f to 1¼m: won 3-runner seller (retained 4,000
gns) at Brighton in June: mostly ran creditably afterwards: seems to stay 1¼m. *R.
Simpson.*

MILLIE BELLE 3 ch.f. Milford 119–Charter Belle 60 (Runnymede 123) [1988 55
7g 1989 10g 16f² 12f⁴] leggy, sparely-made filly: plating-class form in Lingfield
maidens last 2 outings: will be suited by return to further: visored final start:
winning novice hurdler. *Miss B. Sanders.*

MILLIE WATERS (USA) 4 ch.f. Master Willie 129–Miss Anagram (USA) 108 —
(Hurok (USA)) [1988 8.5s 10d 1989 10s 7h⁶] lengthy, sparely-made filly: quite
modest maiden at 2 yrs: lightly raced and no subsequent form: appears not to stay
1¼m: form only on good going: bandaged off-hind on reappearance: sold 1,100 gns
Newmarket Autumn Sales. *H. Candy.*

MILLIGAN 4 ch.c. Tap On Wood 130–Rose Music 86 (Luthier 126) [1988 8m* 90
7g⁵ 9g 7m⁴ 1989 8g* 8g 9.2f* 8f⁵ 8.2g⁴ 8m⁶ 8g] strong, compact colt: fairly useful
handicapper: successful at Newcastle in March and Goodwood in June: ran fairly
well fourth to sixth outings: suited by 9f: acts on firm going: occasionally sweats:
has worn a tongue strap: goes well fresh. *Sir Mark Prescott.*

MILLIJEST 4 b. or br.f. Jester 119–Modern Millie 95 (Milesian 125) [1988 5g⁴ —
5s⁵ 5f² 6m⁴ 5f 6m 1989 5f 5f 6f 5g] leggy, angular filly: turns fore feet in: quite
modest maiden as 3-y-o: no form in 1989: best form at 5f: acts on any going:
blinkered final outing: sold 980 gns Doncaster October Sales. *D. McCain.*

MILLION HEIRESS 2 b.f. (May 23) Auction Ring (USA) 123–Irish Isle 67 —
(Realm 129) [1989 6m 7g 6g] 17,500F, IR 18,000Y: medium-sized filly: half-sister to
useful 6f and 7f winner Benz (by Free State) and winners in Spain and France: dam
won over 1m: well beaten in minor events and a maiden: bit backward first 2 starts:
slowly away second. *G. B. Balding.*

MILL LADY (FR) 2 ch.f. (Mar 17) Moulin 103–Lutecia (FR) (Luthier 126) [1989 100
5.5g* 6g* 5.5g³ 6d4 6g³ 8g⁶ 8g 6.5s] 38,000 francs (approx £3,500) Y: small,
light-framed filly: sister to French 1m winner Light Mill and half-sister to 2 other
winners: dam French 1¼m to 12.5f winner: much improved after winning summer
claimers at Evry and Saint-Cloud: in frame in 3 pattern events, putting up useful
performances in Prix Robert Papin at Maisons-Laffitte and Prix Morny Agence
Francaise (6 lengths third to Machiavellian) at Deauville: behind last 3 starts,
including in Prix Marcel Boussac at Longchamp: best form short of 1m. *C. Lerner,
France.*

MILLPOND BOY 5 ch.g. Connaught 130–Nonsensical 99 (Silly Season 127) —
[1988 8d 10.8s⁵ 10d* 13.3m⁴ 12f² 10f⁵ 12g 10d4 14m 10d 1989 10.2g] workmanlike
gelding: has a quick action: plating-class winner (apprentice ridden) in May, 1988:
generally well below form since: stays 13f: acts on any going: sweating only start at
5 yrs. *R. J. Hodges.*

MILL POND (FR) 3 ro.c. Mill Reef (USA) 141–Royal Way (FR) (Sicambre 135) 113
[1988 NR 1989 11m² 12m* 12g⁵ 12g⁵ 12d 15m] 800,000 francs (approx £76,300)
2-y-o: close-coupled, good-topped, plain colt: moderate walker: brother to good
French 1½m winner Garde Royale and French 10.5f and 1½m winner Royal Charter
and half-brother to 3 winners, all at least very useful, including Prix Noailles winner
High Sierra (by Chaparral): dam useful French 1¼m winner out of French 1000
Guineas winner Right Away: 2/1 on, won maiden at Saint-Cloud in May: 16/1 and
edgy, 9½ lengths fifth in very strongly-run Ever Ready Derby at Epsom, staying on
strongly: easily best effort after when fourth to Sheriff's Star in slowly-run Grand
Prix de Saint-Cloud, beaten about a length but hanging and demoted: led about 13f

final start: suited by 1½m: has joined J. FitzGerald: very useful but seems somewhat unreliable. *P.-L. Biancone, France.*

MILL RUN 2 b.f. (Apr 11) Commanche Run 133–Gay Milly (FR) 74 (Mill Reef **63** (USA) 141) [1989 7m⁴ 7m⁴] rangy, angular filly: has plenty of scope: fourth foal: half-sister to very useful 1¼m winner Cocotte (by Troy) and fairly useful 1984 2-y-o 6f winner Gay Captain (by Ela-Mana-Mou), later listed winner in Italy: dam, daughter of Irish 1000 Guineas winner Gaily, won over 1m: bandaged off-hind, around 2 lengths fourth of 7 to Gold Nostalgia in moderately-run maiden at Newmarket in July: sweating slightly, poor last of 4 in similar event at Yarmouth following month. *L. M. Cumani.*

MILL TERN 7 ch.g. Milford 119–Mitsuki 79 (Crowned Prince (USA) 128) [1988 **36** NR 1989 12d⁴ 12g a14g⁵] tall, quite attractive gelding: poor handicapper: should stay beyond 1½m: yet to race on firm going, acts on any other: blinkered last 6 starts: has worn bandages: apprentice ridden first 2 outings: winning selling hurdler. *A. W. Potts.*

MILLYSPEED 3 b.f. Monsanto (FR) 121–Firbeck 78 (Veiled Wonder (USA)) — [1988 NR 1989 7g 8.2g⁴ 8.2m⁵ 8f⁵ 8.2g] sparely-made filly: has a roundish action: third foal: dam 5f performer: plating-class form, including in claimer: stays 1m: acts on firm going: sold to join J. Balding 700 gns Doncaster November Sales. *R. M. Whitaker.*

MILNE'S WAY 2 ch.f. (Feb 11) The Noble Player (USA) 126–Daring Way (USA) **83** 78 (Alydar (USA)) [1989 6f⁵ 6f³ 6g 6m 6m* 5.8f* 6g² 7g³] IR 5,200F, 4,600Y: workmanlike filly: has scope: has a round action: first foal: dam won over 7f at 3 yrs: fair performer: successful in August nurseries at Windsor, by 2 lengths from Rouski, and Bath, by 1½ lengths from Daawi: ran creditably in similar events at Newmarket and Ascot on last 2 starts: best form at 6f: has flashed tail. *G. Lewis.*

MILO 3 b.g. Lochnager 132–Mild Wind (Porto Bello 118) [1988 5s⁶ 5m 1989 5m 6g — 6f 7d] good-topped gelding: little sign of ability, backward most outings. *D. W. Chapman.*

MILS MIJ 4 br.g. Slim Jim 112–Katie Grey 60 (Pongee 106) [1988 11m 12g 12s* **67** 13s³ 12v² 1989 13v³ 18.4m⁶] smallish, sturdy gelding: quite modest handicapper: ran well when sixth (apprentice ridden) to Grey Salute in Ladbroke Chester Cup (Handicap) in May, but wasn't seen out again: stays 2¼m: acts on top-of-the-ground and heavy going: game: winning hurdler. *J. J. O'Neill.*

MILSTOCK 4 b.c. Last Fandango 125–Millingdale 65 (Tumble Wind (USA)) — [1988 8d 11.7f 8g 8f 8m 10f⁵ 8m² 10m 10f 1989 10.2g 11.5f 12m 8m] tall colt: has a round action: form only when second, edging left, in handicap at Goodwood as 3-y-o: stays 1m: acts on top-of-the-ground: blinkered final 3 appearances in 1988: occasionally on toes. *J. White.*

MILTIADES 2 gr.c. (Feb 24) Magic Mirror 105–Milva 56 (Jellaby 124) [1989 5s³ **73** 5.3m⁶ 5f³ 7m² 6f² 7m 6g 7g*] 11,500Y: compact colt: has scope: has a quick action: first foal: dam 6f winner: 16/1, made virtually all and stayed on strongly in 20-runner nursery at Leicester in November: will stay 1m: visored second outing. *G. A. Huffer.*

MILTON BURN 8 b.h. Sexton Blake 126–Neasden Belle 66 (Sovereign Path **60** 125) [1988 16s² 12g* 12s³ 12g⁵ 13.3f 14d⁵ 20f 14m 14.5g 12m² 12m⁶ 16s 16g⁵ 1989 16s² 12v³ 12s² 14f 12m 12f 14g⁴ 13.3m 18g] narrow, leggy horse: poor walker: has rather a round action: quite modest handicapper on his day: usually at his best in the spring: effective at 1½m and stays very well: ideally suited by an easy surface: has worn blinkers and a visor: often on toes: trained until after sixth outing by H. O'Neill: none too consistent. *C. A. Austin.*

MIMINING 3 ch.f. Tower Walk 130–Louisianalightning (Music Boy 124) [1988 **71** d 5g³ 5v* 5g* 5s* 5g⁶ 6g⁵ 6g³ 6g⁴ 6d³ 7g⁵ 1989 7g 7.3s 6d 6s² 5m 6m 5d 5s 6s 7d] lengthy, good-quartered filly: turns near-fore in: modest at best: creditable second in minor event at Nottingham in early-May, only worthwhile form as 3-y-o: stays 7f: acts on heavy going: tends to sweat up or be on toes: blinkered penultimate start: trained until after then by G. Moore. *P. S. Felgate.*

MIMZAR 2 b.f. (Mar 10) Dara Monarch 128–Cassina 91 (Habitat 134) [1989 5d⁶ — 5d⁶] 21,000Y: sparely-made, leggy filly: fifth foal: half-sister to 4-y-o Top Class (by High Top), 7f winner at 2 yrs and 1½m and 13.3f winner at 3 yrs, and 1986 2-y-o 7f and 1m winner State Ballet (by Pas de Seul): dam 7f winner: with leaders 3f or so in maiden at Kempton and minor event (very on edge at stalls) at Folkestone early in season. *M. Bell.*

MINE'S A DOUBLE 4 b.g. Crofter (USA) 124–Modena (Sassafras (FR) 135) **58** [1988 6d 5f 6s⁶ 6m 1989 7d 6s 5f 5m 6f 6m* 6f 5m 5f⁵ 7g 7m³ 8f* 7g⁴ a7g] strong, compact gelding: fair plater: won at Catterick (handicap, apprentice ridden, no bid) in June and Chepstow (bought in 6,000 gns, made virtually all) in September: very good fourth at Catterick, better subsequent effort: stays 1m: acts on firm going: occasionally sweats: inconsistent. *Capt. J. Wilson.*

MING HO GOLD 4 b.f. Homing 130–Pandoras Gold 68 (Wishing Star 117) [1988 NR 1989 8m 10.8m⁶ 10f⁶ 10.4m] leggy, narrow filly: poor walker and mover: plater: probably stays 1¼m: well beaten when visored final outing: has sweated and got on edge. *J. D. Czerpak.* —

MINGUS (USA) 2 b.c. (Apr 28) The Minstrel (CAN) 135–Sylph (USA) 110 (Alleged (USA) 138) [1989 8m2] compact, heavy-topped colt: third foal: closely related to 3-y-o Nesaah (by Topsider), winner at about 1¼m but of doubtful temperament: dam, 1¼m and 1½m winner, is sister to Leading Counsel and closely related to very useful stakes winner at up to 11f Present The Colors: 6/1, 8 lengths second to Primacy in maiden at Warwick in October, no impression final 1½f and not knocked about unduly: sure to improve, and win a race. *G. Harwood.* **68** p

MINIFAH (USA) 3 b.f. Nureyev (USA) 131–All Rainbows (USA) (Bold Hour) [1988 NR 1989 7g 8m4 11.5m 12.5f2 14m3] $500,000Y: lengthy, angular filly: sister to a modest French maiden, closely related to French 1m winner All Dance (by Northern Dancer) and half-sister to several winners: dam, half-sister to champion filly Chris Evert, was smart winner of three 8.5f stakes races: modest maiden: stayed 1½m: visits Kris. *H. Thomson Jones.* **69**

MINI MAID 6 b.m. Fair Hunter–Hethermai 57 (Pee Mai 107) [1988 NR 1989 10m 6f] sturdy, lengthy mare: first foal: dam winning plater over 1m: tailed off in maidens at Brighton and Chepstow (claimer, bolted going down). *N. Kernick.* —

MINIMIZE 2 b.c. (May 1) Alzao (USA) 117–Timinala 58 (Mansingh (USA) 120) [1989 7m 7f2 7g2] 31,000Y: strong, close-coupled colt: has plenty of scope: second foal: brother to 3-y-o Alzamina: dam, lightly-raced 5f performer, is half-sister to smart miler Pasticcio: runner-up in October maiden at Salisbury won by Bartat and minor event (better effort, caught line having been clear) at Carlisle won by Flying Diva: sold 58,000 gns Newmarket Autumn Sales. *L. M. Cumani.* **84**

MINIZEN LEADER 2 ch.f. (Feb 8) Salmon Leap (USA) 131–Red Line Fever 94 (Bay Express 132) [1989 5g4 6m 8f5] IR 6,800F, 3,000Y: second foal: dam 2-y-o 5f winner: well beaten in maidens: trained by M. Brittain on debut. *C. Spares.* —

MINIZEN MAGIC 4 ch.c. Don 128–Mayfield Girl (Le Prince 98) [1988 7g 8.5m 1989 14s] leggy colt: poor mover: plating-class maiden at 2 yrs: no form in subsequent handicaps: bandaged, tailed off only outing in 1989: stays 6f: sold 850 gns Doncaster May Sales. *M. Brittain.* —

MINNIE RA (USA) 3 b.f. Raise A Native–Regal Exception (USA) 126 (Ribot 142) [1988 NR 1989 7d 8m 5h] $250,000Y: sparely-made, quite attractive filly: sister to smart French 1m and 10.5f winner Twilight Hour and half-sister to several winners, notably good-class middle-distance stayer Orban (by Irish River): dam won Irish Oaks and fourth in Arc: little worthwhile form in maidens in the spring, easily best effort on debut. *R. V. Smyth.* —

MINSK 3 ch.f. Kabour 80–Wedded Bliss 76 (Relko 136) [1988 NR 1989 8m6 8.2m4 8m5 8f] workmanlike filly: second foal: dam won from 1½m to 2m at 5 yrs and 6 yrs: little worthwhile form: broke out of stalls and withdrawn once. *D. W. Chapman.* —

MINSKIP MISS 2 ch.f. (May 4) Lucky Wednesday 124–Sofica 56 (Martinmas 128) [1989 5f4 5m6 6m 5g] small, leggy filly: third foal: dam sprint plater: little worthwhile form in maidens: slowly away first 2 starts: pulled hard third. *Don Enrico Incisa.* —

MINSTREL DANCER (USA) 2 b.c. (May 20) The Minstrel (CAN) 135–Belle Gallante (USA) (Gallant Man) [1989 6g] rather unfurnished colt: seventh reported foal: half-brother to several winners in North America, including 6f stakes winner Boom And Bust (by Mr Prospector) and Bellefella (by Diesis), third here in 2000 Guineas: dam, winner twice at up to 1m as 4-y-o in USA, is half-sister to champion 2-y-o Silent Screen: 12/1, around 11 lengths eighth of 29, running green at halfway then keeping on, to Sure Sharp in maiden at Newmarket in November: should improve. *L. M. Cumani.* **63** p

MINSTREL GUEST 3 b.f. Be My Guest (USA) 126–Wedgewood Blue (USA) 87 (Sir Ivor 135) [1988 7g 1989 7g6 8d5 7f* 7.3m* 7m 8m4 12m2 8m4] leggy filly: has a quick action: fairly useful handicapper: favourite, led well inside final 1f when successful at Goodwood (maiden) in May and Newbury and Ascot in June: best efforts in 3-runner £7,300 event at Kempton and £11,700 handicap at Ascot last 2 **91**

outings: may prove ideally suited by 1¼m: acts on firm going and a soft surface: sold 76,000 gns Newmarket December Sales. *P. T. Walwyn.*

MINUS MAN 11 br.g. Firestreak 125–Cheb's Honour 70 (Chebs Lad 120) [1988 — 8.5m 10g⁵ 12m* 12h³ 1989 8s 12f⁶ 11.7d 12m] lengthy gelding: poor mover: won selling handicap at Brighton (fourth course victory) as 10-y-o: well beaten in 1989: stays 1½m: acts on any going: good mount for apprentice. *W. Holden.*

MIRA ADONDE (USA) 3 b. or br.f. Sharpen Up 127–Lettre d'Amour (Caro — 133) [1988 NR 1989 7g] third living foal: half-sister to temperamental maiden Encore L'Amour (by Monteverdi): dam unraced daughter of top-class 4.5f to 1m winner Lianga: 16/1 and backward, about 9 lengths seventh of 15 to Pilot in slowly-run maiden at Newmarket in April. *A. C. Stewart.*

MIRACLE WORKER 3 b.g. Saher 115–Divine Dilly (Divine Gift 127) [1988 8s — 8.2d 8g 1989 8g] medium-sized, good-topped gelding: little sign of ability. *G. B. Balding.*

MIRAMAC 8 b.g. Relkino 131–Magical 95 (Aggressor 130) [1988 18f 16m 1989 — 21.6d] strong, medium-sized, lengthy gelding: poor staying maiden: often apprentice ridden: sold to join R. Frost 5,300 gns Doncaster June Sales. *F. H. Lee.*

MIRED 3 b.c. Mill Reef (USA) 141–Princess Matilda 110 (Habitat 134) [1988 7m² — 7d³ 8m* 10g 1989 10g] compact, useful-looking colt: fluent mover: fairly useful winner as 2-y-o: ran moderately in listed race next start and badly when bit backward in October, only start in 1989: suited by 1m: tended to hang first 2 outings: sold 6,600 gns Newmarket Autumn Sales. *J. L. Dunlop.*

MIRGLIP (USA) 3 b.c. Pilgrim (USA) 108–Irish Rocket (USA) (Irish Ruler — (USA)) [1988 NR 1989 8d] IR 31,000Y: quite good-topped colt: moderate walker: ninth foal: half-brother to a listed winner in Italy by Val de L'Orne and 3 minor winners in USA: dam minor winner at up to 7f at 3 yrs in USA: 33/1, backward and green, slowly away and tailed off in maiden at Newbury in April. *M. E. D. Francis.*

MIRPUR 7 b.g. Leander 119–Malina 94 (Astec 128) [1988 NR 1989 16.2m] — workmanlike gelding: winning hurdler: lightly raced and little worthwhile form on flat: tends to sweat: edgy only outing at 7 yrs. *Mrs G. R. Reveley.*

MIRROR BLACK 3 b.c. Alzao (USA) 117–Flaxen Hair (Thatch'(USA) 136) [1988 **113** 6f 1989 8.2g* 8f* 8f* 8f³ᵈⁱˢ 8m³ 8f³ 7g² 8v³] close-coupled, good-bodied colt: very useful performer: won apprentice maiden at Hamilton and handicaps at Goodwood in space of 4 weeks in early-summer, all in good style: also first past post (beat Tibullo a length) in Group 2 Premio Ribot at Rome final start, but hung right and demoted for interference: placed in valuable handicaps at Royal Ascot (wandering and disqualified), Newmarket and Goodwood and in Group 3 event (beaten head by Kerita) at Goodwood: stays 1m: acts on any going: sweating and bit edgy second start: has turn of foot. *P. J. Makin.*

MISBAH (USA) 4 b.c. Lypheor 118–Tournelle (USA) (Empery (USA) 128) [1988 — 10.1m* 12m* 12g 1989 12m⁶] rangy, useful-looking colt: won minor events at Windsor and Leicester as 3-y-o when trained by A. Stewart: pacemaker for Unfuwain on only outing in 1989: stayed 1½m: acted on top-of-the-ground: dead. *Major W. R. Hern.*

MISCHIEVOUS TYKE 3 ch.f. Flying Tyke 90–Habatashie 62 (Habat 127) **50** [1988 5g 5m⁴ 5m⁴ 6g* 7d 7.5g⁵ 6f² 6g 6d 1989 7d⁶ 8.2s 7.5f 6m* 6f³ 7m 7m⁵ 6g 6g 8f⁵ 8m] leggy, good-topped filly: carries condition: won seller (no bid) at Ripon in May: below form in amateurs handicap final start: stays 7f: acts on firm going and a soft surface. *A. Smith.*

MISLEAT 4 b.f. Longleat (USA) 109–Palace Pet (Dragonara Palace (USA) 115) — [1988 6v 6m 7m 5m 5m³ 6m 5.1m² 5f⁵ 6d 6g 1989 6d 5f 6f 6m 6m 6f] sparely-made filly: no longer of much account: visored second outing: sold 1,100 gns Doncaster October Sales. *C. R. Beever.*

MISRULE 7 b.g. Dominion 123–Miss McLairon 96 (Klairon 131) [1988 NR 1989 **77** 16f 14g⁴ 16m³ 14g] strong gelding: has been hobdayed: modest handicapper: very lightly raced nowadays: 20/1, ran excellent race facing stiff task when third of 10 finishers to eased Orpheus in moderately-run £43,800 event at Newcastle in July: always behind at Sandown 2½ months later: out-and-out stayer: probably unsuited by firm going, acts on any other: wears bandages. *D. W. P. Arbuthnot.*

MISS ABBI 2 b.f. (May 21) Jalmood (USA) 126–The Shrew 92 (Relko 136) [1989 — 6m] 900F: fifth foal: half-sister to winners in Italy by Shirley Heights and Final Straw: dam best at around 1m: 25/1, always behind in 18-runner seller at Ripon in August. *C. Tinkler.*

MISS ABOYNE 4 b.f. Lochnager 132–Mia Cosa (USA) 78 (Ragusa 137) [1988 7f 56
7f⁴ 9f⁵ 7g² 7d⁵ 7m⁵ 6d⁴ 6g 7m⁴ 6s⁴ 1989 7d 8.2v⁴ 8f 6f 12f⁴ 8f* 8.5g² 10g³ 7f⁶]
lengthy, workmanlike filly: won for first time in ladies handicap at Redcar in June,
leading 3f out and soon clear: good second at Beverley, best subsequent effort in
amateur handicaps: best at 1m: acts on firm going and a soft surface: blinkered once
at 3 yrs: has hung right. *J. S. Wilson.*

MISS ADVENTURE 2 b.f. (Apr 30) Adonijah 126–Sunset Ray 74 (Hotfoot 126) 58
[1989 6m 7m² 7m⁴ 8m⁵ 8g³ 8m³ 10f²] 420Y: close-coupled filly: fourth foal: dam
won from 1m to 2m: fairly useful plater: best effort final start: better suited by 1¼m
than shorter. *M. H. Tompkins.*

MISS AFRIQUE (FR) 2 b.f. (Feb 25) African Song 124–Dictumisas (FR) 112
(Dictus (FR) 126) [1989 7.5d² 8g² 7g* 6.5m³ 8m² 6.5s³] half-sister to minor French
1m winner La Bottine (by High Line), later placed over jumps: dam French 1½m
winner also successful over hurdles: won maiden at Deauville in August: put up
very useful performance when beaten ½ length by Golden Era in Prix des
Reservoirs at Longchamp in October: suited by 1m: acts on top-of-the-ground. *D.
Smaga, France.*

MISS ALCAZAR 2 b.f. (May 9) Aragon 118–Permutation 79 (Pinza 137) [1989 —
5d⁵ 5m 7g⁵ 8g] 2,800F: leggy, sparely-made filly: half-sister to several winners here
and abroad, including modest 6f and 7f winner Helexian (by Song): dam won over
2m: soundly beaten in a minor event and maidens: blinkered final start. *Denys
Smith.*

MISS BATCHWORTH 3 ch.f. Ballacashtal (CAN)–Soft Secret (Most Secret —
119) [1988 5g 5s⁴ 5s³ 1989 6m 6m 5.1m 6g 5m 5m 7m] small, workmanlike filly:
moderate mover: only show in handicaps and claimer as 3-y-o in apprentice event at
Windsor penultimate start: gave impression barely stays 5f when conditions are
testing. *C. Holmes.*

MISS BELUGA 2 gr.f. (Mar 3) Persian Bold 123–Julia Flyte 91 (Drone) [1989 —
5g⁶ a6g] small, close-coupled filly: third foal: half-sister to 2 animals in Italy, one a
winner: dam 2-y-o 6f winner, is half-sister to very useful filly Miss Petard, dam of
Rejuvenate: well beaten in maiden (slowly away) at Wolverhampton and claimer
(sweating and edgy) at Southwell: sold 800 gns Newmarket December Sales. *A. C.
Stewart.*

MISS BLITZ 3 b.f. Formidable (USA) 125–Eightpenny 90 (Pieces of Eight 128) 83
[1988 6g 7m⁴ 6g* 1989 6s* 7g 6m⁴ 7m³ 7m] lengthy, good-bodied filly: moderate
mover: won minor event at Leicester in April: in frame, running well, in Newmarket
handicaps: well beaten in similar event there final start (July): stays 7f: acts on
top-of-the-ground and soft going: successful as 2-y-o for 5-lb claimer. *W. A.
O'Gorman.*

MISS BLOMFONTEIN 3 b.f. Homing 130–Aunt Peggy (Royal Palm 131) [1988 —
5g 6m 1989 8f] small, sturdy filly: moderate walker: no promise in maidens and
seller. *H. O'Neill.*

MISS BUTTERFIELD 3 b.f. Cure The Blues (USA)–Be My Queen 84 (Be My —
Guest (USA) 126) [1988 NR 1989 6m 5f⁵ 6m 6f 7f 7g⁴ 5g a6g] lengthy, angular filly:
first foal: dam, 1m winner, is daughter of half-sister to Derby runner-up Cavo Doro:
no form, including in handicaps. *P. Mitchell.*

MISS CAMELLIA 4 b.f. Sonnen Gold 121–Miss Cindy 95 (Mansingh (USA) 120) —
[1988 8.2v 8d* 11m* 12f⁶ 12.3f² 13.8g* 12g² 11g⁴ 1989 12.3s 12d 13.8d⁶ 12g⁶ 13m⁶
10.6g] dipped-backed, close-coupled filly: moderate mover: modest handicapper as
3-y-o, winning 3 times in North: well below her best as 4-y-o: stays 1¾m: acts on
firm going and a soft surface: visored fourth and fifth starts: sold 2,200 gns
Doncaster November Sales. *M. H. Easterby.*

MISS CELEBRITY 3 b.f. Skyliner 117–Lady O'Grady (Paddy's Stream 80) 43 §
[1988 5g 5m 6d 1989 10f* 10f 10f] neat filly: won seller (bought in 4,000 gns) at
Chepstow, making smooth headway to lead over 1f out but having to be ridden out:
last in handicaps later in July: uncertain to stay much beyond 1¼m: blinkered at 3
yrs: clearly not one to trust. *D. J. G. Murray-Smith.*

MISS CHALK 3 ch.f. Dominion 123–Stoney 73 (Balidar 133) [1988 6f⁵ 6g 6f 5.8d 42
7m 1989 7d 8m 7m⁵ 7h² 5.8h⁴ 6m 7m 7m 6m 6f 7f⁴ 10f⁴] sparely-made filly: plater:
stays 7f: acts on hard ground: sold to join M. Pipe 3,000 gns Newmarket Autumn
Sales and is a winning selling hurdler. *M. Blanshard.*

MISS CHRISSY 4 b.f. Ballacashtal (CAN)–Miss Meg 68 (John Splendid 116) 57
[1988 7.3g 6d 6f 5f 6m 5g⁶ 6f⁶ 6g 1989 5g⁵ 6f 5g] strong, workmanlike filly: has a
quick action: modest form at best since 2 yrs: best form at 5f with give in the ground:

visored final 4 appearances in 1988, blinkered as 4-y-o: sometimes sweats: sold 1,450 gns Doncaster November Sales. *W. J. Pearce.*

MISS CLAUDIA 2 ch.f. (Mar 23) Noalto 120–Perchance 77 (Connaught 130) — [1989 5g 5f⁵ 8.2d 6g a6g] €,000F: leggy, unfurnished filly: moderate walker: has a round action: fourth foal: half-sister to 3-y-o 12.2f winner Highland Park (by Simply Great) and 2 winners, including Irish 9f winner American Lady (by Ile de Bourbon): dam, 7f and 1½m winner, is out of half-sister to smart Albany and Magna Carta: well beaten in maidens and a claimer: hung left on second start: usually on toes and edgy. *K. T. Ivory.*

MISS COLENCA 3 gr.f. Petong 126–Superb Lady 106 (Marcus Superbus 100) — [1988 5g⁵ 5g 5d⁴ 7s 1989 6f 6f 5m 5f] close-coupled filly: well beaten in varied events: sprint bred: blinkered once at 2 yrs (looked none too keen) and twice in 1989: mulish in preliminaries third outing. *G. M. Moore.*

MISS CREESONG 3 ch.f. Cree Song 99–Miss Lollypop (St Paddy 133) [1988 — 5m 5g 7f⁴ 8g 1989 7g 6g 9s] deep-girthed filly: moderate plater: behind in varied events as 3-y-o: best run at 7f: sweating final start at 2 yrs and on reappearance: sold 980 gns Doncaster October Sales. *J. S. Haldane.*

MISS CUDDLES 5 b.m. Mummy's Game 120–Eastern Romance 73 (Sahib 114) — [1988 8d³ 7m 8f 7g² 8d 8g 7g 7d⁵ 8.2d* 7g² 1989 8g 8s 7f 8v 8m 8g] lengthy mare: fair winner as 4-y-o: no worthwhile form in handicaps and minor event in 1989: best at around 1m: suited by give in the ground: blinkered last 4 starts: sold 3,300 gns Doncaster November Sales in foal to Absalom. *W. J. Pearce.*

MISS DAISY 5 b.m. Final Straw 127–Petite Hester 85 (Wollow 132) [1988 7g 6g 44 6m 6f 1989 6d⁵ 8f 6f* 6h 6f⁵] small mare: good mover: poor handicapper: 20/1, advantageously drawn when winning 23-runner event at Thirsk in May: stays 7f: acts on any going except possibly hard: inconsistent. *Miss S. E. Hall.*

MISS DELILAH 3 b.f. Humdoleila 103–Pem Pem (Blakeney 126) [1988 NR 1989 — 9g 8m] third foal: half-sister to a poor plater by Starch Reduced: dam placed at 1m and winning selling hurdler: always behind in minor event and claimer 5½ months later. *K. White.*

MISS DEMURE 3 b.f. Shy Groom (USA)–Larosterna (Busted 134) [1988 6g² 94 6d* 7g² 1989 7g⁶ 8g⁶ 9s] lengthy, robust filly: useful at 2 yrs, winning 'The Update' Lowther Stakes at York and second, tending to carry head high, in Cartier Million at Phoenix Park: fair sixth of 10, disputing lead 7f, in listed event at Ascot in October on first run for 6 months, easily best run as 3-y-o: tailed off in valuable event at Laurel Park, USA, 9 days later: takes keen hold: should stay 1m: acts on a soft surface. *R. W. Armstrong.*

MISS DIRECT 4 b.f. Kabour 80–Deal Direct (Pamroy 99) [1988 7.5m 8f 7m 10g — § 8s⁶ 8.5m 10d 1989 6f 7.5f 10.8m 16.5g] workmanlike non-thoroughbred filly: of no account and temperamentally unsatisfactory: sold 1,100 gns Doncaster August Sales. *D. W. Chapman.*

MISS EMILY 5 b.m. Kampala 120–Hey Dolly (Saint Crespin III 132) [1988 8.2v³ 51 8s⁵ 8m 7.6v⁴ 8d 8f 8.2g³ 8.2g⁵ 8s³ 8g⁶ 8m 8.2d³ 8g* 8s 8.2s 8m 8v 8g 1989 7g 6d 8d 8f⁶ 7m 8.2d⁶ 8.2g³ 8.2g 8g] small, angular mare: moderate mover: quite modest winner as 4-y-o: worthwhile form in 1989 only on seventh outing: ran poorly when blinkered final one: best at 1m: suited by an easy surface and goes very well in the mud: good mount for inexperienced rider. *D. W. Chapman.*

MISS EUROLINK 2 br.f. (Mar 4) Touching Wood (USA) 127–Sule Skerry 78 50 (Scottish Rifle 127) [1989 5v* 5d⁴ 8g] 2,000Y: leggy, sparely-made filly: fifth foal: half-sister to 3-y-o Vantifantay (by Castle Keep) and 3 winners, all at 1m or more, including 1½m winner and useful hurdler Sea Island (by Windjammer): dam, half-sister to smart fillies Flighting and Bonnie Isle, won twice over 1½m: 20/1, won 15-runner maiden auction event at Kempton: not disgraced in minor event at Newmarket in November, first outing since April: bred to stay well. *G. B. Balding.*

MISS EXAMINER 3 ch.f. Absalom 128–Buttermilk Sky (Midsummer Night II 59 117) [1988 5g⁴ 5f 7s⁵ 7g 7g 8.2s² 10s 10m² 1989 10s* 10f² 10.1m⁶ 10f⁴] small filly: moderate mover: fairly useful plater: ridden by 5-lb claimer: won strongly-run race (bought in 3,800 gns) at Nottingham in May: ran moderately final start: stays 1¼m: acts on any going: sold to join W. Bissill 4,600 gns Newmarket July Sales. *M. H. Tompkins.*

MISS FANCY THAT (USA) 3 b.f. The Minstrel (CAN) 135–Splendid Girl 99 ? (USA) (Golden Eagle (FR)) [1988 7g* 7d³ 1989 10f² 11m⁵ 8m⁵ 11m²] big, deep-girthed filly: carries condition: good mover: useful performer: ran well in listed race at Goodwood and IR £9,000 event at Phoenix Park first 2 outings but moderately in Sandown listed race on third: sweating, beaten 2½ lengths by sole rival Musaahim in minor event at Redcar, leading 1m and battling on well: needs further than 1m, but may not stay 1½m: acts on firm going. *M. R. Stoute.*

MISS FEE FEE 2 b.f. (Mar 20) Red Johnnie 100–Miss Macfee (Forlorn River 124) [1989 5m⁴ 6f² 6m⁴ 5f³ 5m⁵ 6f⁴ 5g⁶ 5s⁶ 7g³] 5,000Y: leggy, sparely-made filly: shows a round action: half-sister to 3 winners, including sprinters Draidoir (by Furry Glen) and James' Pal (by Pal's Passage): dam won over 5f in Ireland: showed much improved form when equal-third of 20 to Miltiades in nursery at Leicester on final start, staying on strongly: better suited by 7f than shorter: has run respectably for a 7-lb claimer. *C. E. Brittain.*   **65**

MISS GARUDA 3 b.f. Persian Bold 123–Miss Bali 95 (Crepello 136) [1988 6f² 7d⁴ 7m* 8g⁶ 1989 8.5m⁵ 10m² 10m⁶ 10g² 10g] rangy, rather sparely-made filly: has a rather round action: fairly useful performer: second in handicap at Newmarket, leading 9f, and moderately-run £6,900 event at Yarmouth, not looking entirely enthusiastic: ran moderately in handicap at Ripon (heavily-backed favourite) and listed event at Phoenix Park third and final outings: stays 1¼m: acts on top-of-the-ground. *W. Hastings-Bass.*   **90**

MISS GOLDIE LOCKS 2 ch.f. (Mar 13) Dara Monarch 128–Really Sharp (Sharpen Up 127) [1989 5g] 14,000Y: lengthy filly: third foal: half-sister to smart sprinter Carol's Treasure (by Balidar) and Irish 7f winner Be Nimble (by Wattlefield): dam never ran: 33/1, backward, green and on toes, last of 13 in maiden at Newmarket in April: has joined Dr J. Scargill. *G. Blum.*   **—**

MISS HONEYDEW 4 b.f. Red Sunset 120–Mellifont (Hook Money 124) [1988 7d 6m 9g 7m 5.1m⁶ 7f 10g⁶ 10d 1989 10m 12.5g 16m 14m 15.3f 9g⁵ 10f⁶ 8g] leggy filly: of little account: has been blinkered and bandaged. *Mrs N. Macauley.*   **—**

MISS HOSTESS 2 gr.f. (May 26) Petong 126–Rosalina 71 (Porto Bello 118) [1989 5m 5f⁵ 5m⁵ 7m⁵ 7m³ 7m 7m 8g] 3,400F: leggy, quite good-topped filly: sister to 3-y-o Sps Creative and half-sister to several winners on flat and over hurdles, including rare 1980 2-y-o sprinter Fire Mountain (by Dragonara Palace): dam won over 7f and 1m: third of 4 in seller at Edinburgh in July, only sign of ability: stays 7f: blinkered sixth (pulled hard) and final outings: sold 1,600 gns Doncaster November Sales. *T. Craig.*   **35**

MISSING LINK 3 b.f. Workboy 123–Betrothed (Aglojo 119) [1988 NR 1989 8m 10.4m⁶] lengthy filly: turns fore-feet in: second reported foal: sister to poor plater Jackandora: dam won over hurdles: well beaten in minor event at Carlisle and maiden at Chester in the summer. *A. D. Brown.*   **—**

MISSING YOU 2 br.f. (Mar 25) Ahonoora 122–Saving Mercy 101 (Lord Gayle (USA) 124) [1989 7g² 7g] IR 82,000Y: second reported foal: dam won Lincoln Handicap and stayed 1¼m: 4/1, length second of 14 to The Caretaker in EBF Silver Flash Stakes at Phoenix Park: never dangerous behind same horse in Cartier Million there following month: should win a maiden. *T. Stack, Ireland.*   **89**

MISSIONARY RIDGE 2 ch.c. (May 8) Caerleon (USA) 132–Shellshock 110 (Salvo 129) [1989 7g 7m³ 7g⁶ 8f* 7.3d³] sturdy, workmanlike colt: keen walker: has a fluent, round action: closely related to fair 13.4f winner Bell Rammer (by Nijinsky) and half-brother to several winners, including good middle-distance stayer Seismic Wave (by Youth): dam, 1000 Guineas third who stayed 13f, is half-sister to top-class Dibidale and to dam of Tony Bin: won maiden at Leicester in very good style by 10 lengths from Crown Baladee: very good third of 8 to Tirol in Vodafone Horris Hill Stakes at Newbury later in October: will stay 1½m: a very useful colt in the making. *B. W. Hills.*   **106 p**

MISSISSIPPI BEAT (USA) 2 b.g. (May 19) Dixieland Band (USA)–Jungle Dance (USA) (Graustark) [1989 6g⁵ 6g] $85,000Y: lengthy, dipped-backed gelding: half-brother to several winners, one in minor stakes, one graded-stakes placed: dam minor winner around 6f: well beaten in autumn minor event (bit backward) at York and maiden at Newcastle. *M. P. Naughton.*   **—**

MISS JAVA 2 ch.f. (Mar 13) Persian Bold 123–Miss Bali 95 (Crepello 136) [1989 6d² 6g² 7g⁵] deep-girthed filly: sister to 3-y-o Miss Garuda, fairly useful 7f winner at 2 yrs, and several other winners, including Bali Magic, very useful 6f and 7.5f winner, and very useful 1m and 9f winner Bali Dancer (both by Habitat): dam, half-sister to good 2-y-o's Welsh Harmony and Sovereign Crest, won over 1½m: modest form when second in autumn maiden at Newmarket and minor event at York: below that form, tending to hang under pressure, in minor event at Leicester: bred to stay 1¼m. *W. Hastings-Bass.*   **72**

MISS KELLYBELL 2 ch.f. (Apr 18) Kirchner 110–California Split (Sweet 44 Revenge 129) [1989 6f 5f 6g4] 1,500Y: small, angular filly: poor walker and bad mover: fourth foal: half-sister to 6f to 7f winner By Chance (by Le Johnstan): dam of no account: poor maiden: best effort in seller on final start: better suited by 6f than 5f: slowly away and hung badly left on debut. *R. Thompson.*

MISS KENMARE (FR) 4 ro.f. Kenmare (FR) 125–Miss Lyndah (FR) (Rheffic 116 (FR) 129) [1988 8m4 8v6 8v* 7d4 8g3 8g2 8g3 7d4 8g3 6.5s2 8d2 8m 8g 8g4 7s* 1989 8v3 8d3 7m4 7g 8g4 9.7g* 9.2g 8v*] French filly: first foal: dam won twice over 1¼m as 2-y-o: showed improved form when winning Prix Perth at Saint-Cloud in November by 2 lengths: ran mostly in handicaps earlier in season, winning one at Longchamp: stays 9.7f: acts very well in the mud: trained first 4 starts by P.-L. Biancone: tough. *M. Rolland, France.*

MISS KILPATRICK 3 ch.f. Noalto 120–Ann Wilson (Tumble Wind (USA)) — [1988 6d 9g 7d 1989 10g 8f] sturdy filly: has a round action: no form, including in sellers. *D. C. Jermy.*

MISS KIVE 3 b.f. Kabour 80–Final Cast 50 (Saulingo 122) [1988 6g 8m 1989 5d 50 5m 5f6 6m5 6f 5m6 5g6 6s 5m] compact filly: plating-class maiden: form only at 5f: visored debut: blinkered otherwise: has sweated and has looked irresolute. *D. W. Chapman.*

MISS KNIGHT 2 ch.f. (May 30) Longleat (USA) 109–Ethel Knight (Thatch 50 (USA) 136) [1989 5d 5g4 6g 5s5 5m 5v3 5md] smallish, compact filly: moderate walker: first live foal: dam lightly raced: plating-class maiden: acts on heavy going. *R. Bastiman.*

MISS LAMB 5 ch.m. Relkino 131–Young Lamb (Sea Hawk II 131) [1988 12m2 53 12g5 12m5 13f5 12g3 11g2 10m 12g4 12m4 12v* 1989 13v3 12d 12d5] big, close-coupled mare: poor mover: plating-class handicapper: ran creditably in April at Ayr and Thirsk: stumbled and rider unseated after 1f at Pontefract in between: suited by 1½m: ideally suited by the mud: ran poorly when visored: often apprentice ridden. *J. J. O'Neill.*

MISS MAC 2 ch.f. (Apr 3) Smackover 107–Stewart's Rise 52 (Good Bond 122) — [1989 5s5 5g 6m 6g4 7f] small, lightly-made filly: good walker: first foal: dam, plater, won from 1m to 1½m: little worthwhile form, mostly in sellers: sweating final start. *B. A. McMahon.*

MISS MAREVA 3 b.f. Skyliner 117–Tinterne (Tin King 126) [1988 5f 6g 7.5m 7g — 6g6 1989 8g 6f] leggy, workmanlike filly: little worthwhile form, including in handicap and claimer. *J. Mackie.*

MISS MARJORIE 5 ch.m. Swing Easy (USA) 126–Flying Molly (Shiny Tenth 38 § 120) [1988 6m 7m 7f 7m6 6d 7f6 1989 5f 5f2 7h 7.6h 6f 5f3 5m2 6f* 5m 6m] angular, deep-bodied mare: carries plenty of condition: poor handicapper: won at Lingfield in August: looked none too keen previous and next outings: effective at 5f and stays 7f: acts on firm going and a soft surface: visored at Lingfield and on final start: often slowly away: reluctant to leave paddock fifth outing: unreliable. *L. J. Holt.*

MISS MATTERS 2 b.f. (Apr 25) Strong Gale 116–Miss Filbert 95 42 (Compensation 127) [1989 5.3m 6f5 6d] 3,100Y: medium-sized, leggy filly: half-sister to several winners, including sprinter Thatchville (by Thatch): dam miler: poor form in maidens and a claimer: bred to stay further. *M. McCourt.*

MISS MCKINLEY 2 b. or br.f. (Mar 4) Kind of Hush 118–Keeps Bay (Orange — Bay 131) [1989 6m] 850Y: third foal: dam unraced daughter of half-sister to very smart miler Buz Kashi: 33/1, always in rear in valuable 20-runner seller at York in August. *Miss S. E. Hall.*

MISS MICROCHIP 2 b.f. (May 1) Dreams To Reality (USA) 113–Strawberry — Ice (Arctic Storm 134) [1989 8g] small, rather leggy filly: half-sister to several winners, including 1½m to 1¾m winner Jowoody (by Tudor Rhythm) and winning stayer Pokey's Pride (by Uncle Pokey): dam Irish 1m winner: 50/1, always behind in 17-runner maiden at Leicester in November. *J. White.*

MISS MOODY 3 ch.f. Jalmood (USA) 126–Ice Galaxie (USA) (Icecapade (USA)) 45 [1988 5g 6m5 6g 5d 7.5f5 8g 1989 5f 6f 5.8h 6f 6s4] workmanlike, good-quartered filly: moderate walker: poor on most form: fourth in seller at Hamilton, only show as 3-y-o: should stay further than 6f, but tends to pull hard and appears not to do so: often on toes: sweating fourth start. *J. M. Bradley.*

MISS NANNA 3 br.f. Vayrann 133–Thereon (Nonoalco (USA) 131) [1988 5d 5s2 48 § 6m 5g2 5g5 7d6 1989 6f4 6f] close-coupled filly: plating-class maiden: stays 6f:

probably acts on any going: ran poorly in blinkers final start: looked irresolute when runner-up at 2 yrs and is temperamental. *J. Mackie.*

MISS PATDONNA 3 b.f. Starch Reduced 112–Karousa Girl (Rouser 118) [1988 — 5f⁵ 5m 6g 5m 5g⁵ 7g* 8g⁵ 8.2d 7g 1989 8d 8.2s 8m 6m 9f 10g 10f⁴ 12.5f 12g] neat filly: quite modest performer as 2-y-o, winning seller: well beaten in varied events in 1989: stays 1m well: best efforts on an easy surface. *B. Palling.*

MISS PELOTA 2 ch.f. (May 9) Mummy's Game 120–Mrs Palmer 88 (Martinmas **72** 128) [1989 6g 7g² 6f⁴ 7m* 7m* 8m⁶] 15,000Y: medium-sized, rather unfurnished filly: has a quick action: third foal: sister to sprint handicapper Mummy's Charmer and half-sister to 1m seller winner Flirting (by Free State): dam won 3 times at up to 6f at 2 yrs: successful in August in seller at Newmarket and claimer at Leicester: suited by 7f: best form in blinkers: bandaged behind last 3 outings: has given trouble stalls: not the easiest of rides: sent to Italy. *A. A. Scott.*

MISS PETELLA 4 b.f. Dunphy 124–Tavella (FR) 98 (Petingo 135) [1988 8m 12g — 11s 12s 8s 1989 10g 11v⁶ 16.2d 12m 12f 16.2m] small, angular ex-Irish filly: moderate mover: half-sister to 3 winners, including good miler Meis-El-Reem (by Auction Ring): dam at her best at 2 yrs when 5f winner: seems of little account: sold 1,000 gns Newmarket December Sales. *C. B. B. Booth.*

MISS PINOCCHIO 2 b.f. (Mar 17) Noalto 120–Floral 82 (Floribunda 136) [1989 **54** 5d⁴ 5d 5h² 5f* 6m 5g⁵ 5f⁶ 5s 5f³] 4,800Y: angular filly: half-sister to several winners, including 3-y-o Tyrnippy (by Tyrnavos), winner at 5f (at 2 yrs) to 1m: dam 2-y-o 7f winner: made all in seller (retained 2,400 gns) at Beverley in June, beating Virkon 2½ lengths: on toes, very good third to Starchy Cove in nursery at Wolverhampton in October: likely to prove best at 5f: best form on firm ground. *J. Berry.*

MISS PISCES 3 ro.f. Salmon Leap (USA) 131–Celestial Path 101 (Godswalk **86** d (USA) 130) [1988 NR 1989 7s* 8f 8m 8f⁶ 12m⁶ a10g³ a11g] IR 34,000Y: lengthy, attractive filly: has a long, rather round stride: half-sister to a winner in Belgium: dam Irish 5f to 7f winner: won maiden at Epsom in April, running on from rear: got no sort of run next start: easily best effort in handicaps after but still below form when third at Lingfield: stays 1m: appears unsuited by top-of-the-ground: sold 17,000 gns Newmarket December Sales. *B. W. Hills.*

MISS POKEY 3 b.f. Uncle Pokey 116–Silken Swift 83 (Saulingo 122) [1988 5f 5g **62** 6m 6s 7m 6g* 5.8d² 6m² 7g 1989 8d 10.2m 10f 12f² 12g* 16f⁴] leggy filly: poor mover: quite modest handicapper: won at Salisbury in July, leading inside final 1f: ran creditably at Chepstow starts either side, blinkered first occasion: probably best at distances short of 2m: acts on firm going and a soft surface: also blinkered last 4 starts at 2 yrs: winning hurdler. *R. J. Holder.*

MISS QUICK 3 ch.f. Longleat (USA) 109–Forlorn Leap (Forlorn River 124) — [1988 NR 1989 7g 8d 8m 7.6m 10f 6g a8g] angular, plain filly: half-sister to sprint winners High Voltage (by Electrify) and Mindblowing (by Pongee), 1¼m seller winner Another Angus and inconsistent 1985 2-y-o 5f to 7f winner Parkies Bar (both by Comedy Star): dam never ran: little sign of ability, including in sellers: has been bandaged. *K. T. Ivory.*

MISS QUIZZIE 6 b.m. Quizair 103–Bluebottle II (Happy Monarch 109) [1988 NR — 1989 8f] sturdy, workmanlike non-thoroughbred mare: dam won 2 point-to-points: 33/1, tailed off in seller at Chepstow in September. *R. Champion.*

MISS RELSUN 5 ch.m. Le Soleil 96–Relax 73 (Seminole II) [1988 12g 11m⁶ 12m **51** 1989 11f² 10f* 9.1f* 9f⁴ 10m* 10.2g³] big, workmanlike mare: comfortable winner of handicaps at Beverley in July and August and at Newcastle (apprentice event) in between: effective at 9f and 1¼m: acts on firm going: winning hurdler. *Mrs G. R. Reveley.*

MISS SARAHSUE 3 br.f. Van Der Linden (FR)–Blakesware Dancer 68 (Dance — In Time (CAN)) [1988 5d⁴ 7m⁴ 7g 7f 7f² 7s 7f 1989 9f 7m⁵ 7f 7m 7m⁵ 7h⁵] leggy, rather sparely-made filly: plating-class maiden: ran poorly third to fifth starts: stays 7f: acts on firm going: blinkered third start: sweating final one (July): broke blood vessel and withdrawn at start following month: trained before then by P. Feilden. *R. Akehurst.*

MISS SARAJANE 5 b.m. Skyliner 117–Taffeta 72 (Shantung 132) [1988 8d 8d **72** 8f³ 8f 8g⁴ 10g⁵ 8m³ 9f⁶ 8g⁴ 10v 9g 7d 8g 1989 10.4m 9f² 8.2m 9f³ 10f² 8g 8.2m³ 8m⁶ 8.2g 9m² 10.4m 10.2g 8g* 10g a8g] leggy, workmanlike mare: good mover: modest handicapper: probably unsuited by heavy going nowadays, acts on any going: won 27-runner event at Newmarket in October: below form last 2 starts: stays 1¼m: probably unsuited by heavy going nowadays, acts on any going: has run well for lady, but usually ridden by A. Culhane: best racing up with pace. *R. Hollinshead.*

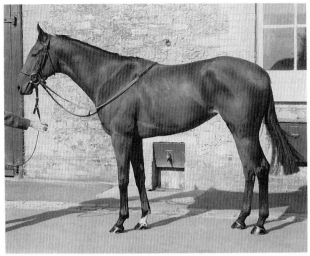

Mrs V. Gaucci del Bono's "Miss Secreto"

MISS SECRETO (USA)   3 b.f. Secreto (USA) 128–My First Fling (USA) (Olden **111**
Times) [1988 6f* 6d³ 7m² 6g³ 8m 8m* 1989 7.3s⁶ 8v* 12g⁶ 10s* 8g² 8v⁴ 10s³]
angular, sparely-made filly: moderate walker: good mover, with a long stride: won
Group 2 events at Rome for Premio Regina Elena in April and Premio Lydia
Tesio-Trofeo Saima in October: in frame in pattern events at Milan and Rome last 3
starts, demoted for interference penultimate one then good third to Highland
Chieftain in Group 1 Premio Roma: suited by 1¼m: acts on top-of-the-ground and
heavy going: tended to pull hard at 2 yrs: very useful. *J. L. Dunlop.*

MISS SIMONE   3 b.f. Ile de Bourbon (USA) 133–Nanga Parbat (Mill Reef (USA)   —
141) [1988 6g 6g 7m⁴ 8f² 1989 9f 9f⁶ 8.2g 10f] small, leggy filly: moderate mover:
modest maiden at 2 yrs: showed nothing in handicaps in 1989: should be well suited
by middle distances: blinkered last 2 starts: sold 1,550 gns Doncaster November
Sales. *W. J. Pearce.*

MISS SKINDLES   3 b.f. Taufan (USA) 119–Trapani (Ragusa 137) [1988 5s⁵ 6g⁵   **52**
7g⁵ 8f 8.2m 1989 6m⁴ 5.3h 6f 7f³ 7f* 7m⁶ 7m 6m⁵] leggy filly: plating-class
handicapper: won at Folkestone in July: well below form after: suited by 7f: acts on
firm going: blinkered final start. *P. F. I. Cole.*

MISS SPINNEY   3 b. or br.f. Uncle Pokey 116–Strath of Orchy 96 (Lochnager   —
132) [1988 NR 1989 8g] leggy, fair sort: first foal: dam 2-y-o 6f winner: 33/1, bit
backward and moved moderately down when always behind in maiden at Carlisle in
June. *Miss L. C. Siddall.*

MISS SWANSONG   3 b.f. Young Generation 129–Jubilee Song 71 (Song 132)   **61**
[1988 6g 1989 7f⁴ 7f⁵ 7m] angular, sparely-made filly: quite modest maiden:
blinkered, ran poorly in minor event final start (June): may well be suited by 1m. *D.
R. C. Elsworth.*

MISS TENAVILLE   2 b.f. (Feb 15) Kala Shikari 125–La Bambola 95 (Be   **54**
Friendly 130) [1989 5s² 5m² 5f] 6,200Y: sturdy, workmanlike filly: turns fore-feet
out: half-sister to 2 poor animals: dam won from 7f to 14.7f: plating-class maiden:

second to Sharp Mover at Sandown and Performing Arts at Newmarket: not seen out after May. *S. Dow.*

MISS TOOT   4 b. or ro.f. Ardross 134–Blue Stack (USA) (Roberto (USA) 131) **72** [1988 10s* 1989 15m*] leggy, workmanlike filly: winner of both her races, a seller at Haydock (bandaged, very slowly away and very green in front) as 3-y-o and handicap at Edinburgh in July: much better suited by 15f than 1¼m: clearly most difficult to train. *Sir Mark Prescott.*

MISS TRISTRAM (NZ)   4 b.f. Sir Tristram 115–Coole Park (Wolver Hollow —
126) [1988 8m 12.2g⁴ 12d⁶ 1989 8.5f⁵ 9f] leggy, sparely-made filly: plating-class maiden at best: stays 1½m: winning selling hurdler. *J. Parkes.*

MISS VAL   3 gr.f. Nishapour (FR) 125–Light Opera (FR) 101 (Vienna 127) [1988 —
NR 1989 15g] 6,600F, 21,000Y: half-sister to several winners, including useful 1980 2-y-o 5f winner Vienna Miss (by Thatch) and modest sprinter Godstruth (by Godswalk): dam, closely related to smart sprinter Laser Light, stayed 7f: 50/1, soon tailed off in claimer at Edinburgh in July: sold 2,500 gns Doncaster September Sales. *W. J. Pearce.*

MISS WASSL   2 b.f. (Feb 27) Wassl 125–Arena 86 (Sallust 134) [1989 7m⁴] IR **68** p
16,000Y: sparely-made filly: third foal: half-sister to winner in Scandinavia by Cure The Blues: dam lightly-raced daughter of very useful 7f and 9f winner Melodramatic: 15/2, under 4 lengths fourth of 6, leading after 2f until 2f out, to Silk Slippers in slowly-run minor event at York in September: should improve. *P. A. Kelleway.*

MISS WESLEY   4 b.f. Raga Navarro (ITY) 119–Balcanoona 87 (Cawston's Clown **34**
113) [1988 5f 5d 5d³ 5.3f 5m 5m 5.8f 5g 1989 5f⁵ 5m 5m 6f 5f 5f³ 6f] small, sparely-made filly: poor mover: poor plater: best at 5f: yet to race on soft going, acts on any other: slowly away when visored fifth start: usually apprentice ridden nowadays: inconsistent. *P. A. Pritchard.*

MISS WILLOW   3 b.f. Horage 124–Nebanna 74 (Nebbiolo 125) [1988 6g 1989 8m **60**
8m 10g² 10m⁶ 12m 10m⁵ 14g 10.6g] leggy filly: has a round action: easily best efforts in handicaps at Ripon third and sixth outings: stays 1¼m well: acts on top-of-the-ground. *H. J. Collingridge.*

MISTER BLISTER   3 b.g. Blazing Saddles (AUS)–Val Brilliant (USA) (Val de —
L'Orne (FR) 130) [1988 7m 6g 6d 1989 10.1m 11.7m] lengthy, angular gelding: poor form at best: well beaten as 3-y-o, including in handicap: sold Mrs G. Jones 3,200 gns Ascot November Sales. *Miss B. Sanders.*

MISTER BOBBINS   6 b.h. Thatching 131–Bobbins (FR) 70 (Bold Lad (IRE) **68**
133) [1988 6v⁶ 5s⁵ 7.5v² 7.5g² 7v² 7.5g⁵ 7g² 8g² 7.5g⁴ 7.5g* 8v 1989 5f² 7.2g 5f⁶ 5m⁴ 6g⁴ 6m 5m 6s 6g a6g] neat, strong ex-Italian horse: poor walker: brother to 7f winner The Rotter and half-brother to winners in Belgium and Italy: dam, half-sister to top 1977 2-y-o filly Cherry Hinton, won over 1¼m: winner of 6 races in Italy, including 4 listed events as 2-y-o: in frame in 1989 in claimer and handicaps: lost his form last 5 outings: should prove best at sprint distances: acts on any going: visored eighth and ninth outings: tends to get on edge, and has sweated: usually ridden by inexperienced apprentice in Britain. *R. Dickin.*

MISTER LAWSON   3 ch.g. Blushing Scribe (USA) 107–Nonpareil (FR) 92 —
(Pharly (FR) 130) [1988 5m* 5m* 6g² 5g 5m* 5f⁵ 5m⁶ 5f⁶ 5f³ 1989 6s 7m 6v] close-coupled, rather unfurnished gelding: fairly useful winner as 2-y-o: behind facing stiff tasks in quite valuable handicaps in 1989: best form at 5f on top-of-the-ground: has run creditably when sweating. *Mrs J. Pitman.*

MISTER MARCH   6 b.g. Marching On 101–Jetwitch 56 (Lear Jet 123) [1988 6g 6f **35**
6m 6m⁶ 6m⁴ 5.8f 1989 6m 5m³ 5m² 5m⁶ 5f 5m 5m 5m⁶ 7f 6m 7f⁶ 5.1g 7m 8f 5g 5m] leggy, sparely-made gelding: has a quick action: poor handicapper: effective at 5f and stays 7f: suited by a sound surface: tailed off in blinkers: has run creditably for apprentice: inconsistent. *D. W. Chapman.*

MISTER ODDY   3 b.g. Dubassoff (USA)–Somerford Glory 44 (Hittite Glory 125) —
[1988 5g⁵ 5f⁶ 6g 6v⁴ 1989 7s⁴ 7s 8f 6m] leggy, workmanlike gelding: modest maiden at best: ran poorly after reappearance, edgy penultimate start then tailed off facing stiff task in ladies handicap 5 months later: stays 7f: acts on heavy going. *J. S. King.*

MISTER'S SISTER   2 ch.f. (Apr 22) Tumble Wind (USA)–Joanelle (Brigadier —
Gerard 144) [1989 6m 5m⁶ 5d] IR 5,200Y: fourth reported foal: half-sister to 1987 Irish 2-y-o 6f winner Naas Lad (by Dalsaan): dam poor Irish maiden: poor form in maidens. *M. Johnston.*

MISTRAL'S COLLETTE   2 b.f. (Jan 14) Simply Great (FR) 122–Kitty's Sister   87
(Bustino 136) [1989 7g² 6g* 6g⁶ 7m² 8g³] IR 20,000Y: second foal: dam sister to
Lowther Stakes winner Kittyhawk (dam of Nomadic Way), later very useful at up to
1m: fairly useful performer: won 4-runner maiden at Phoenix Park: placed in
valuable restricted race at Fairyhouse and Hennessy XO EBF Killavullen Stakes
(1½ lengths third to Endless Joy) at Leopardstown in autumn: will stay 1¼m:
sold 57,000 gns Newmarket December Sales, probably for export to Italy. *K.
Prendergast, Ireland.*

MISTRESS CARROLL   2 ch.f. (May 13) Simply Great (FR) 122–Cariole 84   —
(Pardao 120) [1989 6g] IR 6,000F, IR 10,000Y: leggy, quite good-topped filly:
half-sister to several winners, including 3-y-o 1¼m winner New Arrangement (by
Trojan Fen), very useful 1983 2-y-o 7f winner Knoxville (by Pitskelly) and fairly
useful 5f to 7f winner Marking Time (by On Your Mark): dam won over 7.6f: 33/1,
backward and green, always behind in 13-runner maiden at Newmarket in July. *G. A.
Pritchard-Gordon.*

MISTRESS CHARLEY   6 ch.m. Bay Express 132–Mistress Maude (Welsh   — §
Pageant 132) [1988 NR 1989 6s 5f 5m 7f] big mare: of little account and
temperamental to boot: blinkered once. *C. Holmes.*

MISTRESS MONET   2 b.f. (Apr 1) Claude Monet (USA) 121–Skysted (Busted   59
134) [1989 6f⁶ 6m 6f⁵ 7g] strong, good-bodied filly: fifth foal: half-sister to 3-y-o 6f
winner Songstead (by Song): dam unraced half-sister to smart sprinter Crews Hill:
plating-class maiden: should be better suited by 7f+ than 6f: sold to join D.
Chapman 920 gns Doncaster November Sales. *M. J. Camacho.*

MISTRESS WILL (USA)   3 ch.f. Master Willie 129–Crumpets (USA) (Barrera   —
(USA)) [1988 NR 1989 8m⁵] $60,000Y: lengthy, angular filly: first foal: dam won 3
times at up to 11f: 8/1, backward and green, 11 lengths fifth of 9 to Majestic Ace in
maiden at Pontefract in July, soon towards rear, staying on steadily under hands and
heels final 2f: should be suited by 1¼m. *H. Candy.*

MISTROMA   2 gr.f. (Apr 9) Absalom 128–Conrara 82 (Balidar 133) [1989 5m 5f   37
5m 6f⁶ 7m] 5,000Y: smallish, workmanlike filly: second foal: dam sprinter: poor
form in maiden auction events and sellers. *R. M. Whitaker.*

MISTY EYES   2 b.f. (May 4) High Top 131–Ringed Aureole 77 (Aureole 132)   54
[1989 7m 8m 7m 8.2s² 8.2s⁶] tall, lengthy, unfurnished filly: has scope: sister to
prolific 1m to 2m winner Misty Halo and half-sister to 2 other minor winners: dam
won from 1½m to 2m: plating-class maiden: ran creditably in late-season nurseries
at Hamilton final 2 starts: will stay 1¼m. *Sir Mark Prescott.*

MITAKI (USA)   2 ch.c. (Feb 18) Miswaki (USA) 124–Koketka (USA) (Nashua)   76 p
[1989 6m³] $70,000Y: tall, useful-looking colt: has scope: third foal: dam sister to 2
very useful animals in France and half-sister to Taufan: favourite but on edge,
½-length third of 16 to Harbour Bar in maiden at Haydock in June, ridden along at
halfway and staying on well: looked sure to improve but wasn't seen out again. *H. R.
A. Cecil.*

MIZAJ   5 ch.g. Thatching 131–Stickpin 74 (Gulf Pearl 117) [1988 8v² 10g⁶ 1989   69
10.2g* 10g 10d³ 9f 10m² 10.8f² 10f 10.2m² 10v] rangy, deep-girthed gelding: has a
rather round action: won maiden at Doncaster in March: ran well when placed after,
but found little eighth outing: tailed off in Ayr handicap nearly 3 months later: stays
10.8f: acts on any going: hung left third outing: best with waiting tactics: winning
hurdler. *G. M. Moore.*

MIZUWARI   3 ch.f. Blazing Saddles (AUS)–River Aire 82 (Klairon 131) [1988   73
5.8d³ 6g 6g² 1989 7.3m⁶ 6m⁶ 6g* 6f* 7g³ 7.3m⁶] lengthy filly: favourite, successful
in July in apprentice maiden (given too much to do, dead-heating) at Pontefract and
uncompetitive minor event (making virtually all) at Folkestone: ran creditably after
in £6,000 handicaps at Newbury: stays 7f: acts on top-of-the-ground: sweating first
and third starts. *G. B. Balding.*

MO CERI   5 b.m. Kampala 120–Thiella 61 (Busted 134) [1988 12m⁵ 10m⁶ 12d⁴   63
14m² 12s* 12m 1989 12s* 14s] robust mare: won handicap at Folkestone in April
unchallenged by 8 lengths: ran poorly later in month: stays 1¾m: acts on
top-of-the-ground, but goes very well on soft going: good mount for inexperienced
rider. *D. R. C. Elsworth.*

MODEST HOPE (USA)   2 b.c. (Feb 4) Blushing Groom (FR) 131–Key Dancer   63 p
(USA) (Nijinsky (CAN) 138) [1989 7g] $175,000Y: angular colt: has scope: first foal:
dam, good-class stakes winner at 9.5f and 11f, out of half-sister to Ajdal, Formidable
and Flying Partner: 33/1 and backward, around 14 lengths twelfth of 28, chasing

leaders 5f and not knocked about, to Rami in maiden at Newmarket in November: should improve. *A. A. Scott.*

MODESTINO (USA) 3 b. or br.c. Fappiano (USA)–Demitasse (USA) (Young 72 Emperor 133) [1988 NR 1989 10f³ 12d³] $140,000Y: tall colt: turns fore feet in: brother to a quite modest maiden and half-brother to 2 winners, including minor 1m stakes winner Pavarotti (by What A Pleasure): dam, out of outstanding broodmare Juliets Nurse, placed once from 15 starts: third in small fields for maidens at Sandown and Haydock (still in need of experience) in the summer: sold 6,200 gns Newmarket Autumn Sales. *J. H. M. Gosden.*

MOFADOR (GER) 5 br.h. Esclavo (FR)–Mantilla (GER) (Frontal 122) [1988 — NR 1989 7.2s 8m⁴ 8m 7.6m 8v 7m] lengthy, round-barrelled horse: moderate walker: successful 6 times on flat in Germany: led fair way when beaten at least 8 lengths by odds-on Samoan and Sudden Love in minor events at Newcastle (flashed tail) and Ripon on second and third outings: no subsequent form in handicaps. *F. H. Lee.*

MOGUL PRINCE 2 b.c. (Jan 18) Mansingh (USA) 120–Valadon 72 (High Line 78 125) [1989 5s 6f³ 6m 6m² 5.8m³ 7m* 7f 7m 7.3m 7g] 3,500F, IR 4,200Y: leggy colt: good walker: first foal: dam, 12.2f winner, is half-sister to smart 6f to 1½m winner Duke of Normandy: modest performer: awarded nursery at Newmarket in July on demotion of head-winner Walking Saint: suited by 7f: blinkered sixth and seventh starts, visored final: inconsistent. *M. D. I. Usher.*

MOHAMMED EL-SAHN 3 b.g. Trojan Fen 118–Hoonah (FR) (Luthier 126) 65 § [1988 7m⁴ 7f⁵ 7.5m 8m⁶ 7f² 7v 7d⁶ 1989 10d 10s⁴ 8m⁶ 10m 10f⁵ 10f³ 12m 8f* 8f 8.5m 9m 10g* 10f 10f*] leggy, lightly-made gelding: useful plater on his day: bought in 5,600 gns, 5,500 gns and 4,800 gns when winning at Newcastle in July and twice for 7-lb claimer at Leicester in the autumn: suited by 1¼m: seems unsuited by very soft ground, acts on any other: blinkered third outing: sold 6,000 gns Newmarket Autumn Sales: unreliable and has often looked ungenerous. *M. F. D. Morley.*

MOHARABUIEE 3 b.f. Pas de Seul 133–Clonavee (USA) (Northern Dancer) 50 [1988 5f 6m⁵ 6s³ 7g 6s 8g³ 8m 6m 8g 7g⁵ 1989 7.6m 8.5f 10.2h⁵ 10m 10f² 10f⁶ 7.6m 9f 9g a8g³ a8g a8g⁵ a7g] workmanlike filly: poor form as 3-y-o: placed in seller at Chepstow and Southwell maiden: stays 1¼m well: best form on an easy surface: inconsistent and has found little off bridle. *R. Hollinshead.*

MOHINI 2 ch.f. (Feb 19) Sharpo 132–Girl's Brigade (Brigadier Gerard 144) [1989 46 5m 5g 7f⁵ 7f 8.2f 7f⁵ 7d] 6,400Y: leggy filly: moderate walker: first foal: dam, lightly raced, dead-heated over 7f at 2 yrs in Ireland and stayed 1¼m, is from family of Connaught: quite moderate plater: stays 1m: best form on firm ground: didn't handle Chester track second outing: has joined M. Usher. *E. Weymes.*

MOHSSEN (FR) 8 ch.g. Sharpen Up 127–Showery Summer (FR) (Tanerko 134) — [1988 10d⁵ 10d⁶ 12m² 10m* 10g² 11d⁵ 10s 1989 10.6g] leggy gelding: plating-class winner of ladies event as 7-y-o: backward only outing (June) in 1989: better suited by 1¼m than 1½m: suited by a sound surface: wears bandages: excellent mount for inexperienced rider. *L. J. Barratt.*

MO ICHI DO 3 b.g. Lomond (USA) 128–Engageante (FR) (Beaugency (FR) 126) 76 [1988 8m 1989 8.5g³ 10f⁵ 10.2g 10g² 10m³] big, angular gelding: has a rather round action: modest maiden: stays 1¼m: possibly unsuited by top-of-the-ground: sold to join Miss S. Wilton 11,500 gns Newmarket Autumn Sales. *B. W. Hills.*

MOLLY PARTRIDGE 6 gr.m. Sexton Blake 126–Coquette (St Paddy 133) — [1988 8g⁵ 8g 10m⁵ 10m 1989 8v³] leggy, workmanlike mare: has a round action: poor performer: suited by 1m: acts on top-of-the-ground and a soft surface: blinkered twice: thoroughly inconsistent. *R. M. Whitaker.*

MOLLY'S MOVE 2 ch.f. (May 24) Kabour 80–Sallyanda 65 (Marcus Superbus 41 100) [1989 6m 7d 6s] sparely-made, plain filly: sixth foal: dam won 6f seller at 2 yrs: poor form in sellers and a claimer: slowly stages over first 2 starts. *W. Storey.*

MOLLY SPLASH 2 b.f. (Feb 20) Dunbeath (USA) 127–Nelly Do Da 78 — p (Derring-Do 131) [1989 8g] 7,800Y: small, compact filly: sixth foal: half-sister to 7f (at 2 yrs) to 1¼m winner Retouch (by Touching Wood), fair 9f and 11.7f winner Cashmere N Caviar (by Bustino) and a winner in Italy: dam 2-y-o 5.8f winner: 25/1 and in need of race, over 12 lengths seventh of 15, prominent 5f, to Advie Bridge in maiden at Leicester in September: will improve. *C. A. Cyzer.*

MOLO 2 b.g. (May 6) Castle Keep 121–Eldoret 100 (High Top 131) [1989 6f 7f⁶ 8g] 49 leggy gelding: seventh foal: brother to fair 1½m and 2m winner Jinga and half-brother to 3-y-o 1¼m and 12.3f winner Murango (by Shirley Heights), very smart 6f to 1m winner Efisio (by Formidable) and fairly useful 1m winner Mountain

Courage Stakes (Limited Handicap), Newbury—
Monastery (left) begins to wear down Splendid Career

Bear (by Welsh Pageant), later good stakes winner in USA: dam won over 6f and 1m: poor form in maidens: pulled hard final start: may do better. *Lady Herries.*

MOMENTS JOY 3 ch.f. Adonijah 126–My Own II 96 (El Relicario 124) [1988 NR 1989 10f 12.2f⁴ 11.7h² 14m⁴ 16m⁴ 14f] workmanlike filly: half-sister to several winners, including good middle-distance performer Haul Knight (by Firestreak) and fairly useful middle-distance stayer Fleeting Affair (by Hotfoot): dam won from 1m to 11f: plating-class maiden: below form in handicaps last 3 starts: visored, sweating and edgy when tailed off final one: probably stays 1½m. *J. W. Hills.* **56 d**

MOM SALLY 4 b.f. Bold Owl 101–Bri-Ette 53 (Brittany) [1988 6m² 5m* 6d⁵ 6m 5g 5f 5g² 7.5s³ 7g 6f 6m 6m³ 7g 1989 6m³ 6f 7h⁴ 6f 7f 6g 5f] small, workmanlike filly: carries condition: poor handicapper: easily best effort as 4-y-o on reappearance: well beaten in sellers on fifth and final outings: suited by sprint distances: possibly unsuited by firm going, seems to act on any other: blinkered sixth start: inconsistent. *Miss L. C. Siddall.* **42**

MOMSER 3 ch.g. Mr Fluorocarbon 126–Jolimo 92 (Fortissimo 111) [1988 7m² 6s⁶ 7f 8g² 7d 1989 10.6m 10m³ 10.6d⁶ 10m² 12f 13.6g² a12g] leggy gelding: moderate walker: modest performer: second in Redcar handicaps, on second occasion travelling strongly long way: disappointed fifth and final starts: stays 13.6f: acts on top-of-the-ground and a soft surface: claimer ridden first 5 outings. *M. J. Ryan.* **73**

MOMTAAZ 3 ch.c. Diesis 133–Cheerful Heart (Petingo 135) [1988 7m³ 8m* 8s² 1989 10f* 8g²] well-made colt: 7/2 on, won apprentice race at Chepstow by 7 lengths, losing position entering straight, leading 2½f out and running on well: 11/10 favourite, ½-length second to Malevich in minor event at Leicester later in September, leading (at strong pace) until 100 yds out: stays 1¼m well: acts on any going. *L. M. Cumani.* **96**

MONACO GLITTERS (FR) 3 b.f. Crystal Glitters (USA) 127–Miss Monaco 107 (Crepello 136) [1988 7m⁴ 1989 10f⁵] medium-sized filly: half-sister to several winners, including useful 6f and 1¼m winner Miss Beaulieu (by Northfields): dam sprinter best at 2 yrs: quite modest form when fourth in maiden in July as 2-y-o: well-beaten last of 5 in similar event at Sandown year later. *A. C. Stewart.* **—**

MONARCH O TH GLEN 3 b.g. Glenstal (USA) 118–Abbe's Realm (Realm 129) [1988 8.2s⁶ 8v* 1989 10.6s 9f* 10.6g* 12g⁵] lengthy, rather sparely-made gelding: showed improved form when winning handicaps at Hamilton (well backed) in May and Haydock (£7,800 event) in June: second favourite, bit below best and never travelling so well when fifth of 16 in Old Newton Cup at Haydock, quick headway to lead 2f out then no extra: subsequently gelded: may prove suited by **100**

return to about 1¼m: has won on heavy going, and clearly goes very well on firm. *W. J. Pearce.*

MONARDA   2 ch.g. (Mar 14) Pharly (FR) 130–Emaline (FR) 105 (Empery (USA)   **65**
128) [1989 7m 8g⁶] second foal: half-brother to 3-y-o Oasis (by Valiyar): dam French
2-y-o 7f winner: ridden by 7-lb claimer, around 7 lengths sixth of 16, fading steadily
last 2f, to Bawbee in maiden at Leicester in November, better effort. *P. F. I. Cole.*

MONARU   3 b.g. Montekin 125–Raubritter (Levmoss 133) [1988 7m 7m 1989 7f   **57**
10f 12h⁶ 14g 16f⁴ 16f⁵ 14g] small gelding: 14/1 from 33/1, about 1½ lengths fourth of 5
in moderately-run maiden at Newcastle in July, only worthwhile form: bandaged
behind last 4 starts: visored last 3: winning novice hurdler for M. Pipe. *W. G. A. Brooks.*

MONA'S PRINCE   2 b. or br.g. (Apr 6) Class Distinction–Princess Mona 56   **—**
(Prince Regent (FR) 129) [1989 a7g] first foal: dam won over 1m at 5 yrs: backward,
slowly away and always behind in late-year maiden at Lingfield. *C. J. Benstead.*

MONASTERY   3 b.g. General Assembly (USA)–Sweet Habit (Habitat 134) [1988   **115**
NR 1989 8f* 9m 10m* 10f⁴ 10m² 9m² 10m* 10g* 10g] leggy gelding: has a rather
round action: half-brother to Chester Vase winner Nomrood and smart 1m to 1¼m
winner Alleging (both by Alleged): dam unraced daughter of Prix de Diane winner
Sweet Mimosa: won maiden at Pontefract in June, handicap at Kempton in July,
£24,200 Courage Stakes (limited handicap) at Newbury in September and listed
Foundation Stakes (by a length from Ile de Nisky) at Goodwood in October: 25/1,
soundly beaten in Champion Stakes at Newmarket: goes well with strong pace over
1¼m: acts on firm going: has run creditably when sweating and unimpressive in
appearance: game and consistent. *Mrs L. Piggott.*

MON BILL   3 ch.g. Nicholas Bill 125–Fair Madame 88 (Monseigneur (USA) 127)   **—**
[1988 6f 6m 6g⁴ 7f 6s 8v 1989 6s 7m 6m 5g] good-quartered gelding: carries
condition: moderate mover: little worthwhile form: finished lame second start: bred
to be suited by further than 6f: best effort with some give in the ground: sold 1,300
gns Doncaster November Sales. *C. B. B. Booth.*

MONDRIAN (GER)   3 ch.c. Surumu (GER)–Mole (GER) (Espresso 122)   **125**
[1988 8g⁴ 7d² 6g³ 9d² 7d² 8d* 1989 9g* 10.5g³ 11g* 11g* 12s* 12g* 12g* 12g*
12s²]
      The pursuit of that elusive artistic ideal by Dutch artist Piet Mondrian
through his black grid systems with occasional primary-coloured rectangles
must have aroused some of the art world's most diverse appraisals. He clearly
made an impression on at least three owners who had horses running under
his name in Europe in 1989, much the best of them being Mondrian (GER)
who came tantalisingly close to his own, rather less aesthetic, brand of
perfection in the form of a clean sweep of Germany's five Group 1 races. The
first of those contests, the Holsten-Cup-120th Deutsches Derby at Hamburg
in early-July, is the easiest to win, for German horses at least, as the only
qualifications by which an Italian, French, British or Irish horse can compete
are by being imported to Germany as a foal or yearling or owned and trained by
members of the armed forces stationed in Germany. However, Mondrian's
sequence very nearly didn't get under way at all as he was beaten one and
three quarter lengths in the Derby and won only in the stewards room. It was
the second consecutive year that the race had been dogged by controversy
following the 'German sausage scandal' of 1988 in which Walter Swinburn
received a late call-up for the winning ride on outsider Luigi after the original
jockey was caught pilfering a hospitality tent. The latest running escaped
such pre-race drama until almost the last possible moment when the starter
let them go before one of the eighteen runners had been installed. Taishan
went on shortly after the turn three furlongs out but hung in front of
second-favourite Mondrian at the distance before going on to pass the post
first. Mondrian's jockey, criticised in some quarters for making too much of
the incident, for this and the colt's other Group 1 victories was Kevin
Woodburn who rode without success here as an apprentice to Budgett and
Bethell in the early-'seventies.
      The partnership quickly proceeded to put their reputation on a much
firmer footing. Three weeks later Mondrian showed that, restrictions or not,
the German Derby form was worth considerably more than the Italian version
by putting Prorutori firmly in his place in the Grosser Preis der Berliner Bank

at Dusseldorf; he comfortably beat the dual German fillies' classic winner Filia Ardross by one and a half lengths, leading inside the final furlong and again coming out best in a stewards inquiry, with the smart French filly Summer Trip a further three lengths back in third and Prorutori fourth. In the Aral-Pokal at Gelsenkirchen-Horst, Mondrian settled his score with Taishan to the tune of seven lengths with Alwuhush giving him more to do but still being beaten a length and a half without much fuss. Per Quod was the only British challenger to oppose Mondrian in the Grosser Preis von Baden at Dusseldorf, won by Carroll House and Acatenango on its two previous runnings. Per Quod disputed the lead into the straight but Mondrian soon took his measure, leading earlier than usual at around the two-furlong mark, and wasn't hard pressed to win by a length with three other leading German horses in Britannia, Twist King and Turfkonig all further back. Only the R & V Europa-Preis at Cologne remained between Mondrian and an unprecedented record. Along with the Grosser Preis von Baden, the Europa Preis is Germany's richest race with 235,000 Deutschmarks (approximately £76,500) to the winner and though it tempted only three German-trained horses to take on Mondrian again, it attracted his most formidable foreign challenge in the shape of Ibn Bey and Sheriff's Star. On very soft ground for the first time since the German Derby, Mondrian got the better of a sustained battle with Sheriff's Star but never looked like getting to Ibn Bey who made all and drew away again approaching the final furlong to beat him six lengths. It appears that Mondrian is ideally suited by a sounder surface.

			Literat	Birkhahn
		Surumu (GER)	(b 1965)	Lis
		(ch 1974)	Surama	Reliance II
Mondrian (GER)			(bl 1970)	Suncourt
(ch.c. 1986)			Espresso	Acropolis
		Mole (GER)	(ch 1958)	Babylon
		(ch 1974)	Maas	Darius
			(b 1963)	Myrthe II

The Arc and Breeder's Cup were both mentioned as late-season targets for Mondrian but a bout of coughing early in October put paid to that. From what we've seen of him so far, Mondrian doesn't look good enough to have figured in either of those finishes but maybe he'll improve at four years like his sire Surumu's best known offspring Acatenango. Mondrian certainly improved markedly from two to three years; he won only the last of his six starts as a two-year-old before gaining three listed successes on his run-up to the German Derby. He's apparently the fourth consecutive German Derby winner to be offered at the Baden-Baden yearling auctions but didn't, in fact, find a buyer so raced for his breeders. His half-sister Molto Allegra (by Nebos) failed to reach her reserve at the same sale in 1989. Surumu, like Mondrian, improved as he stepped up in distance but after winning the German Derby easily he had only one more race, failing at odds on in the Aral-Pokal. Mole's five foals prior to Mondrian all won races and two of them are by Surumu; the listed-placed Masolino and filly Molto Bene were both successful on the Flat and over jumps, the latter winning over jumps in the latest season. The best of Mole's other offspring is Marcotte (by Nebos) who won five times in Belgium and was third in the Belgian Guineas. Mole won three Flat races in Germany, including a six-furlong listed race as a two-year-old, and once over hurdles. The second dam Maas won five races at two and three years, including a listed race, and her dam was also a winner. *U. Stoltefuss, Germany.*

MONDRIAN (USA) 3 ch.g. Sir Ivor 135–Turban (USA) (Bagdad) [1988 NR 1989 —
12m 14m5] $57,000Y: sparely-made, angular gelding: moderate walker and mover: tenth foal: brother to very useful 1977 2-y-o 6f and 7f winner Turkish Treasure and half-brother to several other winners: dam, minor 6f winner, is half-sister to smart Sir Wimbourne and Irish 1000 Guineas winner Lady Capulet: little show in Newmarket maidens: sold to join K. Morgan 4,000 gns Newmarket July Sales: subsequently gelded: dead. *H. R. A. Cecil.*

MONETARY FUND 5 br.g. Red Sunset 120–Msida (Majority Blue 126) [1988 63
12s 10d 8d 11.5g2 12m 12d2 11.7m 12f3 12m 12g3 12.2d2 12d 1989 14.8s* 15.5s5 14g3
16f3] tall, close-coupled gelding: quite modest handicapper: won at Warwick in

March: creditable third at Salisbury and Kempton later in spring: stays 2m: acts on any going: held up and suited by strong gallop: has run in snatches: ran poorly in blinkers: sometimes sweats. *R. Akehurst.*

MONEYRAH 3 b.f. Niniski (USA) 125–Dame Foolish 121 (Silly Season 127) [1988 NR 1989 8g⁶ 8.2v²] 15,000Y, 31,000Y: ninth foal: half-sister to modest 6f winner Strapless (by Bustino): dam best at 2 yrs when second in Cheveley Park Stakes: plating-class form in early-season maidens at Newcastle (blinkered) and Hamilton. *B. Hanbury.* —

MONIGA 3 b.f. Blazing Saddles (AUS)–Misuumi (Artaius (USA) 129) [1988 NR 1989 7d 7m² 7f² 7m* 6m 6g³ 6m³ 6m 6v] 7,000Y, 7,000Y: plain filly: shows traces of stringhalt: first foal: dam ran 3 times in Ireland: won minor event at Salisbury in June and handicap (improved form and making all) at Kempton in July: below form last 2 outings: unlikely to stay beyond 7f: possibly suited by top-of-the-ground: has run creditably for 5-lb claimer. *I. A. Balding.* 93

MONKEY LOVE 2 gr.c. (Mar 5) Carwhite 127–Minne Love 67 (Homeric 133) [1989 5f 6f⁶ 6d 5g²] 4,400Y: good-topped, workmanlike colt: third foal: half-brother to modest sprint handicapper Micro Love (by Vaigly Great): dam 2-y-o 6f winner: quite modest maiden: easily best effort final start: should stay at least 6f: trained by H. O'Neill first 2 starts. *L. G. Cottrell.* 61

MONKS FOLIE 3 b.f. Glenstal (USA) 118–Ballet Francais 118 (Faberge II 121) [1988 6g³ 7g² 7g 8d⁵ 1989 8.5d 10f 11m] lengthy, workmanlike filly: moderate mover: easily best effort second outing at 2 yrs: well backed when in mid-division in handicaps first 2 in summer as 3-y-o: should stay beyond 7f. *B. W. Hills.* —

MONKWELL LAD 2 br.c. (May 24) Town And Country 124–Brush's Choice (Robson's Choice 105) [1989 7g 6g] 4,000Y: sparely-made, plain colt: moderate mover: half-brother to several winners, including fairly useful miler Town Farm (by Tycoon II): dam of little account: slowly away and always behind in summer maiden at Sandown and minor event at Windsor. *R. Akehurst.* —

MONSAGEM (USA) 3 b.c. Nureyev (USA) 131–Meringue Pie (USA) (Silent Screen (USA)) [1988 7g² 1989 8d* 8m⁵ 10.5f* 9.2g³ 8g* 8g⁶] lengthy, round-barrelled colt: has scope: moderate walker: poor mover: smart performer: under 5 lengths fifth of 14 to Nashwan in General Accident 2000 Guineas at Newmarket: justified favouritism in maiden at Newbury and minor events at York and Newbury: good third of 6 to Local Talent in Group 1 event at Longchamp: poor sixth in Phoenix International Stakes in July: best form at up to 9.2f: acts on firm going and a soft surface. *H. R. A. Cecil.* 117

MONSIEUR TOURBIERE 3 ch.g. Le Moss 135–Miss Nelly (Saulingo 122) [1988 5f 1989 8m 10.1m 8.2d a8g] smallish gelding: no sign of ability in maidens and claimers. *M. Castell.* —

MONTE BRE 3 ch.c. Henbit (USA) 130–Madame du Barry (FR) (Wollow 132) [1988 7d⁶ 7g 8v² 1989 10g* 11d² 14m⁵ 10f⁶] 5,000Y: lengthy, workmanlike colt: 84

Glasgow Stakes, York—Monsagem justifies favouritism

moderate walker and mover: first living foal: dam, lightly-raced French maiden best at 1m, is half-sister to Prix Royal-Oak winner Mersey and from good family: favourite, won apprentice maiden at the Curragh in June: well beaten in listed Curragh Cup and Nottingham minor event (stiff task, not knocked about) last 2 outings: stays 11f: acts on heavy going: trained until after third start by J. Oxx. *R. Akehurst.*

MONTECATINI 3 b.c. Tyrnavos 129–Gunnera (Royal Gunner (USA)) [1988 7.5f — 7m 1989 8.2m 12h] close-coupled colt: little promise in varied events: sold 2,700 gns Ascot June Sales. *J. J. O'Neill.*

MONTEKIN'S LADY 3 br.f. Montekin 125–Advocada (FR) (Advocator) [1988 — § 5g6 5m3 5m4 6m 6m 6d 5.1g 8g 7s 1989 10g 7.5d 8m 6g] small, workmanlike filly: no form for some time: very slowly away, looked reluctant and hung right in May seller on final start: should be suited by further than 5f: blinkered last 2 starts and twice at 2 yrs: one to avoid. *H. J. Collingridge.*

MONTENDRE 2 b.c. (May 22) Longleat (USA) 109–La Lutine 95 (My Swallow **108** p 134) [1989 6g2 6f* 6g*] compact, workmanlike colt: second foal: brother to 3-y-o Mon Tresor, very smart sprinter at 2 yrs: dam 5f and 7f winner at 2 yrs later successful at up to 10.2f: useful performer: successful in October in maiden (very easily) at Brighton and Dewhirst Rockingham Stakes (by 1½ lengths from Daarik, edging left having travelled strongly) at York: likely to make a very useful sprinter and sure to win more races. *L. M. Cumani.*

MONTEROS BOY 4 ch.g. Crofter (USA) 124–Prima Bella 76 (High Hat 131) **66** [1988 7.6g 8f5 8.5m* 8f* 9d2 8d 8g2 8.5m2 8g6 8g 8g3 1989 8h 10f 8.5m 8m4 8h4 10f3 9m* 8.3m5 9f5 12g 10f3 10g] good-topped gelding: quite modest handicapper: won at Kempton in July, making most and clear of trouble: creditable third of 9 at Brighton, best subsequent effort: stays 1¼m: probably acts on any going: effective with blinkers or without: has run creditably for apprentice: has looked difficult ride, and best racing up with pace: sold to join B. Hills 13,000 gns Newmarket Autumn Sales. *R. Akehurst.*

MON TRESOR 3 b.c. Longleat (USA) 109–La Lutine 95 (My Swallow 134) [1988 **111** 6f2 6g* 6m* 7m2 6s* 6g* 8g 1989 7g3 8m 8.5g5 6m 6.5d 5g] close-coupled, good-quartered colt: very useful performer: successful 4 times as 2-y-o, notably in Tattersalls Middle Park Stakes at Newmarket: best efforts in 1989 an same course in European Free Handicap and July Cup first and fourth starts: behind in pattern events at Deauville and Phoenix Park on last 2: raced freely, and was best at up to 7f: best efforts on a sound surface: wore severe noseband: game: retired to Burgage Stud, Co. Carlow, fee IR 1,500 gns (Oct 1st). *R. Boss.*

MONTYKOSKY 2 b.g. (May 26) Montekin 125–Reliable Rosie (Relko 136) [1989 — 7m 6g 8m 7d] IR 5,400F, 10,000Y: sturdy gelding: half-brother to several winners here and abroad, including Irish 3-y-o Try My Rosie, successful at 6f at 2 yrs, and 1½m winner Camden Loch (by Camden Town): dam won from 8.5f to 11.5f in Ireland: soundly beaten in maidens and sellers. *E. Eldin.*

MOOD NOIR 3 b.c. Jalmood (USA) 126–Noirianna 71 (Morston (FR) 125) [1988 — NR 1989 12v6] first foal: dam, out of very useful performer at up to 1m Noirima, ran twice at 2 yrs: well beaten in claimer at Lingfield in April: dead. *Dr J. D. Scargill.*

MOOD OF THE MOMENT 2 ch.f. (Feb 15) Jalmood (USA) 126–Liberty Tree **45** 96 (Dominion 123) [1989 8f 9f4] second foal: half-sister to 1m claimer winner Take A Liberty (by Aragon): dam 6f to 1m winner: poor form in October maidens at Wolverhampton: sold 2,200 gns Newmarket Autumn Sales. *Sir Mark Prescott.*

MOODY MAN 4 b.g. Ela-Mana-Mou 132–Princess Redowa 100 (Prince Regent — (FR) 129) [1988 8d 8.2v6 6m4 7.5m* 8g* 8.2s5 1989 10.6d 12g] lengthy, workmanlike gelding: has a quick action: winning plater as 3-y-o when trained by M. H. Easterby: never dangerous in handicaps at Haydock (apprentices, needed race) and Folkestone (amateurs) in 1989: stays 1m: best form on a sound surface: winning hurdler. *P. J. Hobbs.*

MOON CACTUS 2 b.f. (Jan 21) Kris 135–Lady Moon 101 (Mill Reef (USA) **107** p 141) [1989 6g2 7m* 7m* 8m2]
Here's a filly who started a heavily-backed favourite for all her four starts as a two-year-old, winning twice and being beaten very narrowly—and arguably a shade unfortunately—in the other two. Moon Cactus made her debut in a six-furlong maiden event for fillies at the Newmarket July meeting. Considering she forfeited three or four lengths as the stalls opened she shaped with a deal of promise, finishing with a flourish to go down by a short

head to the more-experienced Ozone Friendly with another newcomer Line of Thunder a neck away in third, the trio well clear. That turned out to be a very hotly-contested maiden indeed. By the time Moon Cactus lined up for the Gilbey's Gin Sweet Solera Stakes over an extra furlong on the same course the following month Ozone Friendly had gone on to win the Group 2 Prix Robert Papin, while Line of Thunder had sauntered home in a Yarmouth maiden event; a couple of those who finished in the ruck at Newmarket had won too, and in a field of six Moon Cactus was sent off at 6/4 on. She justified the confidence, and her manner of victory set a pattern for the rest of her season. The early pace wasn't particularly strong, and Moon Cactus proved difficult to settle until halfway. She then showed a smart turn of speed to lead and draw clear passing the two-furlong pole, but she tended to idle thereafter and needed to be kept up to her work in the final hundred yards to beat Gharam, who was conceding 6 lb for having won a valuable maiden race at Ascot on her debut, by half a length. The next objective for Moon Cactus was the Group 3 Black Bottle Scotch Whisky Prestige Stakes at Goodwood in August, a race formerly known as the Waterford Candelabra Stakes. Cecil had saddled four of the previous five favourites for the race under its old title, and all four were beaten. That didn't deter backers, naturally, and those who'd supported Moon Cactus from 5/4 on to 7/4 on must have been happy as she quickened impressively to lead a furlong out. Once in front, however, Moon Cactus seemed inclined to idle again, so much so that after looking likely to win impressively she had to be pushed along quite vigorously close home to get the better of the Brighton winner Arpero by a length and a half with Native Guile the same distance away in third. The Cheveley Park and the Hoover Fillies' Mile were both mentioned as possible autumn targets for Moon Cactus after Goodwood. Her style of running suggested the step down to six furlongs at Newmarket wouldn't have troubled her, but in the event Ascot was preferred. Once more she was supported as if defeat was out of the question, and again she looked assured of victory on quickening into a lead of a couple of lengths over a furlong out. However, by this stage Silk Slippers had also begun to make significant headway, and in the final strides the concession of 3 lb proved just too much for Moon Cactus; at the line Silk Slippers held the call by a head with Fujairyah two and a half lengths away in third and Arpero back in fifth of eight. After the race Moon Cactus' trainer suggested that the filly's restricted vision in her left eye—she was equipped with an eyeshield on her debut—might have left her unaware of the winner's late challenge on her outside. The view wasn't offered as an excuse, however, and no excuse was needed. Make no mistake, Silk Slippers is potentially a very smart filly; so is Moon Cactus, and it wouldn't be at all surprising to see her improve if her finishing effort can be delayed a little longer.

			Atan
		Sharpen Up	Rocchetta
	Kris	(ch 1969)	Reliance II
	(ch 1976)	Doubly Sure	Soft Angels
Moon Cactus		(b 1971)	
(b.f. Jan 21, 1987)		Mill Reef	Never Bend
	Lady Moon	(b 1968)	Milan Mill
	(b 1980)	Moonlight Night	Levmoss
		(ch 1972)	Lovely Light

As a stallion Kris has proved quite a strong influence for stamina, and in Unite and Oh So Sharp he's already provided two Oaks winners for Sheikh Mohammed. There's also plenty of stamina on the female side of Moon Cactus' pedigree. The dam Lady Moon, who was carrying Moon Cactus when bought for 600,000 guineas at the December Sales, won three times at around a mile and a half; she gave the impression she'd have been at home over further given the chance, and so did her dam Moonlight Night, a half-sister to Main Reef who won the Musidora Stakes and finished third when favourite for Juliette Marny's Oaks. Nevertheless the odds are against Moon Cactus' proving effective over the Oaks trip, and she's not even certain to stay a mile and a quarter. Neither of Lady Moon's foals prior to Moon Cactus raced over middle distances. The first, a Mummy's Pet colt called Pharoah's Pride, showed useful form to win over six and seven furlongs at two only to disappoint the following year, while Moon Cactus' brother, the very smart and genuine Shining Steel, did all his racing at around a mile prior to being sold to continue his career in America. Furthermore Moon Cactus is a keen and active type who takes a strong hold in her races. Her first objective will probably be the Guineas. Unless she makes abnormal improvement, gaining that will be beyond her, but there are more races to be won. Moon Cactus is a leggy, workmanlike filly with a rather round action; she clearly acts on top-of-the-ground, and like so many of the best two-year-olds of 1989 she starts her second season never having raced on a soft surface. *H. R. A. Cecil.*

MOONLIGHT BLUES 3 b.g. Swing Easy (USA) 126–Moonlight Fling (Imperial Fling (USA) 116) [1988 NR 1989 8d 10f 10f 10f 10f5 8g] strong, workmanlike gelding: moderate mover: first foal: dam never ran: fifth of 18 in seller at Ripon in June, making most and only form: visored in similar event 8 weeks later: sold 1,650 gns Ascot October Sales. *Sir Mark Prescott.* **33**

MOONLIGHT SHIFT 3 ch.g. Night Shift (USA)–Rana (Welsh Pageant 132) [1988 NR 1989 10.5f5 10f2 12.3f2 12.3g 10g2] leggy, quite good-topped gelding: has plenty of scope: half-brother to useful 1982 2-y-o 5f performer Misty For Me (by Roan Rocket): dam, unraced, from family of Raffingora: maiden: should prove suited by 1¼m: acts on firm going: hung under pressure last 2 outings, not seen out after July. *R. M. Whitaker.* **75**

MOON MYSTERY 3 b.c. Mummy's Pet 125–Castle Moon 79 (Kalamoun 129) [1988 7m 7s 1989 10m5 10f 10d 8f] workmanlike colt: modest form in maiden on reappearance then always behind in handicaps: blinkered, tailed off final start: stays 1¼m: probably unsuited by a soft surface: sold 10,000 gns Newmarket Autumn Sales. *J. L. Dunlop.* **—**

MOON REEF 3 ch.f. Main Reef 126–Malmsey (Jukebox 120) [1988 6g3 8m 8.2s* 7d 8.2v 1989 9g6 10.5f 12.3g6 12.3f2 12.3g5 17.4s] big, rangy filly: modest handicapper: easily best efforts as 3-y-o at Ripon on fourth (beaten head) and fifth starts: stays 1½m well: acts on any going: lacks turn of foot: sold 9,200 gns Newmarket December Sales. *C. W. C. Elsey.* **76**

MOONTALK 3 br.f. Dubassoff (USA)–Gay Picture 62 (Linacre 133) [1988 NR 1989 7f 8f] fourth reported foal: half-sister to winning sprinter Small Fee (by Blue Cashmere): dam plater: no promise in maiden and minor event. *N. R. Mitchell.* **—**

MOON TIGER 3 b.g. High Top 131–Rivers Maid 83 (Rarity 129) [1988 7g 8s 1989 10g4 11.7h4 10.1d3 10s] strong, heavy-bodied gelding: fair maiden: best effort on reappearance: suited by 1¼m: sold 17,000 gns Newmarket Autumn Sales. *P. T. Walwyn.* **72**

MOON WALKING (USA) 2 b. or br.f. (Mar 12) Clever Trick (USA)–Sly Moon 72
(USA) (On The Sly (USA)) [1989 7m³] $20,000Y: workmanlike filly: second foal:
dam leading 2-y-o filly in Italy: 2 lengths third of 6 to Silk Slippers in minor event at
York in September: dead. *B. Hanbury.*

MOON WARRIOR 4 b.c. The Brianstan 128–Brigannie Moon (Brigadier
Gerard 144) [1988 8g 7g 8f 8f⁴ 7m 8.3g 8.3m 6m² 6h² 6g 6m⁴ 6d 1989 7m 7f 6f 6f 7f 7f
6f 8f 8f 7d 9s] short-backed colt: moderate mover: poor maiden: no form in 1989:
stays 6f: best form on top-of-the-ground: sweating and edgy tenth outing. *D. A.
Wilson.*

MOORES METAL 9 b.h. Wolverlife 115–Torino (Firestreak 125) [1988 8g 8g² 49 §
7.6v³ 9d² 8f 8d³ 8m⁵ 8g 8m 1989 8d 7g 7.6m 8.2f⁶ 10m a8g a7g⁵] rather
lightly-made, quite attractive horse: moderate mover: quite modest handicapper on
his day, but has won only 4 of his 106 races on flat: best at around 1m on an easy
surface: best without blinkers or visor: often apprentice ridden and best when
considerably handled: suited by a strong pace and needs holding up until last
moment: very mulish in preliminaries on reappearance: bought 4,200 gns
Doncaster February Sales: thoroughly untrustworthy. *J. L. Spearing.*

MOORE STYLISH 6 b. or br.m. Moorestyle 137–Coralivia (Le Levanstell 122) 39
[1988 NR 1989 12g² 11.5f 11.7m] leggy, sparely-made mare: moderate mover: poor
maiden: not seen out after July: stays 1½m: acts on firm going: bandaged on
reappearance and final outing. *J. Ringer.*

MOOR FROLICKING 3 ch.f. Morston (FR) 125–Woodland Frolic (Hittite 59 d
Glory 125) [1988 5s⁵ 5.8f⁵ 5m³ 6m* 6m 6g 5g² 7m 6m³ 5f 6d* 1989 6s 6v² 6s² 6m 6f
6f 7g 10m 10m] small, sturdy filly: keen walker: has a round action: quite modest
handicapper at her best: creditable second at Lingfield and Folkestone (apprentices)
in April: suited by 6f and a soft surface: inconsistent. *T. M. Jones.*

MOORISH IDOL 3 b.f. Aragon 118–Abergrove 103 (Abernant 142) [1988 7f⁶ 6s⁴ 86
6m³ 6m* 7d⁵ 1989 6g³ 8f⁵ 6m] rangy, useful-looking filly: good walker: fair
performer: ran creditably in minor events first 2 starts: always outpaced facing stiff
task in £8,000 handicap in August: probably stays 1m: acts on firm going and a soft
surface. *W. Jarvis.*

MORCINDA 3 ch.g. Ballacashtal (CAN)–Montelimar 108 (Wolver Hollow 126) —
[1988 NR 1989 10f⁵] fifth living foal: half-brother to 1m seller winner Saffron Poser
(by Sagaro): dam 5f and 6f winner at 2 yrs who didn't train on: 40/1, tailed off in
5-runner maiden at Brighton in August. *N. A. Gaselee.*

MORE BY LUCK 3 ch.g. Miami Springs 121–La Miranda 80 (Miralgo 130) [1988 54
6g 6m 7g 1989 7m 10f² 10.8f²] medium-sized, angular gelding: worthwhile form only
when second in sellers at Chepstow and Warwick (sweating) in the summer: worth a
try over 1½m: blinkered final start at 2 yrs. *R. J. Holder.*

MOREIRWEN 2 b. or br.f. (May 30) Bold Owl 101–Neophyte II (Never Say Die —
137) [1989 a7g a7g] sister to 3-y-o Neologist and half-sister to some winners over
jumps: dam never ran: soundly beaten in Lingfield maidens. *J. O'Donoghue.*

MORGAN THE MOON 3 b.c. Petorius 117–Uranus (Manacle 123) [1988 NR 55
1989 6v³ 8.5d 7f 6f 6g] 27,000Y: rather sparely-made colt: half-brother to several
winners, including smart 7f and 1m winner Tellurano (by Guillaume Tell) and
Bruiser (by Persian Bold), very useful at up to 9f here and in USA: dam won twice
over 5f at 2 yrs in Ireland: form only on debut: blinkered, swerved left stalls in
apprentice handicap final outing: should have been suited by further than 6f: dead.
M. Bell.

MORNING JOY 2 b.f. (Mar 7) Mummy's Pet 125–Satellite (Busted 134) [1989 5d 50
5f⁴ 5m³ 5f⁴ 5g] 16,500F, 9,400Y: workmanlike filly: has scope: moderate mover:
first foal: dam lightly-raced half-sister to very smart sprinter Street Light: poor
maiden: slowly away in nursery final start: will be better suited by 6f. *W. J. Pearce.*

MORPICK 2 ro.c. (Apr 27) Morston (FR) 125–Pickwood Sue 74 (Right Boy 137) —
[1989 5d⁴] close-coupled colt: sixth living foal: half-brother to 2 sprint winners by
Workboy: dam 5f winner: 25/1 and green, under 10 lengths fourth of 7 in minor event
at Beverley in April: will be better suited by 6f. *J. P. Leigh.*

MOSAIC LAW 3 b.f. Trojan Fen 118–Yellow Plume (Home Guard (USA) 129) —
[1988 NR 1989 8s 8.5s 8m⁵ 6f 7m 7f 10g] IR 39,000Y: leggy filly: half-sister to dam,
daughter of Prix de Diane winner Sweet Mimosa, won over 7.9f at 2 yrs in Ireland:
plating class at best: well beaten in handicap and seller last 2 starts: stays 1m well:
possibly needs top-of-the-ground. *P. A. Kelleway.*

MOSCOW DYNAMO 2 br.c. (Feb 7) Siberian Express (USA) 125–County Line   86 p
75 (High Line 125) [1989 6g³] 12,000F, 62,000Y: rather sparely-made colt: first foal:
dam middle-distance maiden: 2/1, 2 lengths third of 10 to Tirol in minor event at
Doncaster in September, disputing lead when hampered 2f out and keeping on well
when not clear run final furlong: sure to improve and win a maiden. *M. R. Stoute.*

MOSSY ROSE 3 b.f. King of Spain 121–Mosso 81 (Ercolano (USA) 118) [1988 6g   67
7f 8m 7m 7d⁶ 6m³ 1989 6d³ 6d 6m 7.3m 7f³ 6m⁴ 7g 7g] strong, good-bodied filly: has
a markedly round action: quite modest maiden: stays 7f: acts on firm going and a soft
surface. *Pat Mitchell.*

MOST OF ALL 3 gr.f. Absalom 128–Beech Tree 67 (Fighting Ship 121) [1988 7m   —
8g 1989 7m⁵ 7m] workmanlike filly: plating-class form: travelled well long way in
maiden and handicap (checked slightly and eased right down) in summer as 3-y-o,
giving impression capable of better: bred to stay 1m + . *J. A. R. Toller.*

MOST WELCOME 5 ch.h. Be My Guest (USA) 126–Topsy 124 (Habitat 124
134) [1988 10g² 8g³ 10f⁶ 12s³ 10f 1989 8s³ 8f* 10f³ 8f⁴ 8g 8f³]
      Most Welcome's fourth and final season had its ups and downs, reaching
its highest points in the Juddmonte Lockinge Stakes and Breeders' Cup Mile;
its lowest in the Prince of Wales's Stakes and Prix du Haras de
Fresnay-le-Buffard Jacques le Marois. Most Welcome went to Newbury for
the Lockinge three weeks after making his reappearance at Sandown in
late-April (just as he had as a four-year-old) when third to Reprimand and
French Stress on ground softer than ideal in the Trusthouse Forte Mile. He
was held up last of five in a moderately-run race at Sandown and was in a poor
position when Reprimand quickened from the front two furlongs out. Given
more favourable conditions, better terms and the likelihood of a more
enterprising ride at Newbury, it was reasonable to expect that Most Welcome
would improve on his Sandown running, but the race was still regarded
as principally between Warning and Reprimand. Most Welcome and Warning
had run against each other once before, when respectively third and first in
the Sussex Stakes at Goodwood in 1988; that day Most Welcome, who'd been
returning from a three-month absence, was beaten two and a half lengths.
Warning's pacemaker Hilton Brown completed the four-runner field at
Newbury. Most Welcome, impressive in the paddock as usual, was held up in
third and from some way out was travelling better than Warning who brought
up the rear. He also quickened the better, took the lead off Reprimand a
furlong from home and ran on well to beat Warning, who ran as though the
race would do him good, comfortably by two lengths for his first victory since
1987. Reprimand was another three parts of a length away third.
      Both Most Welcome and Warning started odds on for their respective
races at Royal Ascot next time out. Warning, as expected, improved on his
Newbury run but Most Welcome could manage only third in the Prince of
Wales's Stakes, keeping on at one pace after a poor run in the early part of the

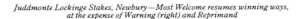

*Juddmonte Lockinge Stakes, Newbury—Most Welcome resumes winning ways,
at the expense of Warning (right) and Reprimand*

straight. The two next crossed swords in the Swettenham Stud Sussex Stakes for the second year running, for which Warning went off favourite at 7/4 and Most Welcome at 20/1. Neither made the first three, Most Welcome giving a good account of himself against a top-class field to finish fourth. Why he should have run so poorly against Polish Precedent in the Prix Jacques le Marois after this is a mystery. He did give the impression his enthusiasm might have waned, which was definitely not so when he returned after a near three-month break to run in the Breeders' Cup. Perhaps he had something wrong with him at Deauville, or maybe the break, or different surroundings, or a different jockey (he was ridden for the first time by Gary Carter, Wragg's retained jockey in 1990) brought his return to form. At any rate he ended his career on a high note in the Mile at Gulfstream Park. He defied his odds of 93/1 by leading home the European contingent completed by Royal Touch (fourth), Zilzal (sixth) and Green Line Express (last of eleven), the last two of whom had finished in front of him at Goodwood. Most Welcome didn't have the best of runs, although Royal Touch, for one, was hampered to a greater degree early in the home straight as the winner Steinlen barged his way through. Most Welcome was outpaced early on and was last going into the first bend. He made up his ground on the inside and, switched wide in the stretch, finished strongest of all, snatching third in the final stride with two lengths covering the first seven across the line.

	Be My Guest (USA) (ch 1974)	Northern Dancer (b 1961)	Nearctic
			Natalma
		What A Treat (b 1962)	Tudor Minstrel
Most Welcome			Rare Treat
(ch.h. 1984)	Topsy (ch 1976)	Habitat (b 1966)	Sir Gaylord
			Little Hut
		Furioso (b 1971)	Ballymoss
			Violetta III

Most Welcome is to stand at the Meddler Stud in Newmarket at a fee of £6,000, with an October 1st concession. His shares were soon in demand and more than the original thirty available changed hands at £20,000 each. Most Welcome's dam Topsy, whose first five foals have all been winners, is again in foal (to Shareef Dancer) having failed to produce a live foal since 1985. Topsy, a half-sister to Teenoso, won three pattern races at up to a mile and a quarter including the Sun Chariot Stakes, won in the latest season by Braiswick, a half-sister to Percy's Lass and a daughter of Laughing Girl, herself a half-sister to Oaks runner-up Furioso, the dam of Topsy and Teenoso. Another half-sister to Furioso is Nicoletta, the dam of the latest Old Newton Cup winner Nickle Plated. Violetta III won the Cambridgeshire and is also the grandam of Favoridge, Give Thanks, Old Country and Ashayer. Most Welcome's sire Be My Guest, champion sire in 1982 when his first crop included Assert and On The House, had another good year in 1989 and amongst his other winners were the Laurel Futurity winner Go And Go, the Prix Chloe winner Be Exclusive, the Premio Melton winner Astronef and the Golden Poppy Handicap winner Invited Guest.

Most Welcome ran in twenty-one races, only four of which he won, but he reached the frame in another eleven, notably, in previous seasons, the Two Thousand Guineas, the Derby, the Champion Stakes and the Turf Classic. After his two-year-old days he earned nearly £370,000 in prize money, of which only £50,000 came from his wins. A sturdy, angular, good-bodied horse with a quick action, he was effective from a mile to a mile and a half. He was capable of form on soft going, but needed sounder conditions to be seen at his best. His pedigree, looks and racing record assured him at the outset of good patronage at stud. He will be the only high-class son of Be My Guest standing in Britain, with Assert now in the States, What A Guest in Australia and Anfield in Japan. *G. Wragg.*

MOTCOMBS 2 gr.f. (Feb 22) Glenstal (USA) 118–Roof (Thatch (USA) 136) [1989 **63** 6g⁵ 6d] 16,000F, 25,000Y: plain filly: third foal: half-sister to 3-y-o Lake Ormond (by Kings Lake) and quite modest maiden Vison Gris (by Lord Gayle): dam won over 6f at 2 yrs in Ireland: bit backward, around 5 lengths fifth of 15 to Ra'a in maiden at Goodwood: weakened 2f out in similar event at Newbury later in October. *M. McCormack.*

MOTHER COUNTRY 5 b.m. Moorestyle 137–Mother Earth 100 (Jukebox 120) **41**
[1988 6s 8d⁵ 8d 6f³ 7m 7m 7f³ 7f² 7m 7m* 8s 8m 1989 7d 7m 8m 6m 8.2f⁴ 6g⁶ 7m 7m 7f] lengthy mare: poor mover: winning plater as 4-y-o: 33/1, over 7 lengths fourth of 16 in handicap at Nottingham in June, only subsequent form: needs further than 6f nowadays and seems to stay 1m: acts on top-of-the-ground: suitable mount for apprentice: inconsistent. *D. W. Chapman.*

MOTHERUBBADSCUBBAD 2 ch.f. (Feb 26) Blushing Scribe (USA) —
107–Lady of Primrose (He Loves Me 120) [1989 5f⁶ 5f⁶ a6g] leggy filly: second reported foal: half-sister to 1987 2-y-o 1m seller winner Mile End (by Camden Town): dam never ran: seems of little account: trained by Ronald Thompson on debut. *J. P. Smith.*

MOTTRAM'S GOLD 4 ch.g. Good Times (ITY)–Speed The Plough (Grundy —
137) [1988 10.2g 15.8m 10g³ 11g 12g 9m³ 8.5f⁴ 10.4d 8g 8g 9s* 10s 8g⁴ 1989 11s] leggy, sparely-made gelding: moderate mover: edged left when winning handicap at Hamilton as 3-y-o: tailed-off last of 11 in similar event at same course in September: stays 9f: acts on any going: has been visored and blinkered: a difficult ride: inconsistent. *R. Dickin.*

MOUNTAIN BLUEBIRD (USA) 3 b.f. Clever Trick (USA)–Bluebell 103 **79**
(Town Crier 119) [1988 6f 1989 9m⁵ 8.2g⁴ 8m² 8g² 8m* 10m³ 8g³ 8f] robust, deep-girthed filly: has a fluent action: made all in maiden at Warwick in August: favourite and blinkered, in touch but one pace when hampered over 1f out in Brighton handicap final start: stays 1¼m: acts on top-of-the-ground: genuine. *Major W. R. Hern.*

MOUNTAIN KINGDOM (USA) 5 b.h. Exceller (USA) 129–Star In The **116**
North (USA) 94 (Northern Dancer) [1988 8.5g 12g 11g* 1989 9g⁴ 12g* 12d⁴ 13.4f* 14f* 12g⁶ 14f²] lengthy, quite attractive horse: ran best race as 3-y-o when second to Reference Point in Holsten Pils St Leger at Doncaster: then ran 5 times in USA (trained by A. Penna jnr) winning allowance races at Aqueduct and Gulfstream Park: returned in very good heart, justifying favouritism in slowly-run 3-runner Ormonde EBF Stakes at Chester (making all) and strongly-run Coloroll Yorkshire Cup (beating Zaffaran a neck, pair clear) in May: odds on, led until final 1f when 2 lengths second of 3 to Ibn Bey in listed event at Lingfield in July: moved down poorly, and wasn't seen out again: suited by 1¾m: has won on heavy going, but best form in Britain on top-of-the-ground. *C. E. Brittain.*

MOUNTAIN MAJIC 2 b.c. (Mar 3) High Top 131–Majica 73 (Morston (FR) 125) **55**
[1989 6m 8m⁴ 6m] 10,000Y: smallish, lengthy colt: poor walker: first foal: dam, minor 11f winner in France at 4 yrs, is closely related to Princess Royal Stakes

Coloroll Yorkshire Cup, York—Mountain Kingdom (left) and Zaffaran

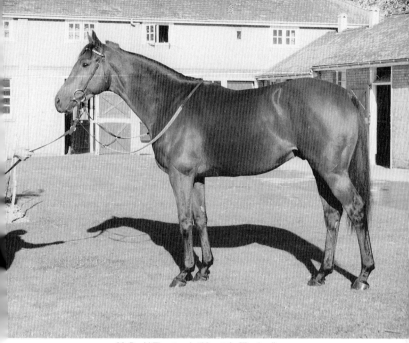

Mr David Thompson's "Mountain Kingdom"

winner Believer: fourth in seller at Warwick in October, easily best effort: will stay 1¼m + : trained by M. Usher on debut. *C. C. Elsey.*

MOUNTAIN RETREAT 3 br.g. Top Ville 129–Tarrystone (So Blessed 130) [1988 NR 1989 8g 9f⁶ 10f⁴ 14f*] 50,000Y: rather leggy, useful-looking gelding: has scope: third foal: dam thrice-raced daughter of half-sister to smart Pugnacity: 11/8 on, won 4-runner maiden at Redcar in June by a neck: stays 1¾m: didn't find much off bridle last 2 outings (subsequently gelded) and may well prove best with waiting tactics. *L. M. Cumani.* **69**

MOUNTAIN SHADOW 4 b.c. Tyrnavos 129–Follow Me Follow 92 (Wollow 132) [1988 8g 11.7g⁵ 8f² 10f⁵ 10.8s⁵ 10.1m⁵ 12m 1989 11.7d 12.5g 9f] robust, workmanlike colt: modest maiden at his best: soundly beaten in handicaps and claiming event (second outing, blinkered) in spring: stays 1¼m: acts on firm going: best left alone. *M. Scudamore.* **—**

MOUNT NELSON 3 ch.g. Morston (FR) 125–Doogali 93 (Doon 124) [1988 NR 1989 14m⁴ 16m² 15.8m* 16f* 16m*] tall, sparely-made gelding: has a roundish, fluent action: third foal: half-brother to quite useful 1m winner Daring Doone (by Daring March), subsequently successful in USA: dam won 9 times from 1m to 1¼m: successful in maiden (25/1 on) at Catterick and in small fields for handicaps at Lingfield in August, on final occasion quickening to lead 1f out and unextended: suited by a test of stamina: sold to join D. Arbuthnot 10,000 gns Doncaster November Sales. *A. C. Stewart.* **87**

MOUNTVIEW 2 b.c. (Feb 6) Montekin 125–Piney Pass (Persian Bold 123) [1989 5g⁴ 5s⁶ 5d* 5f⁴ 6f 7g² 6g* 6m* 7m 6g 6s] IR 10,500Y: small, sturdy colt: carries condition: shows a quick action: second foal: brother to 3-y-o Woosie, fair 7f winner **77**

at 2 yrs: dam Irish 2-y-o 8.5f winner: modest performer: made all or most in minor events at Beverley and Chester and a claimer at Haydock: well beaten in nurseries on last 3 starts: acts on firm going and a soft surface: hung badly second start: mostly ridden by girl apprentice afterwards. *N. Tinkler.*

MOVIEGOER 3 b.f. Pharly (FR) 130–Odeon 114 (Royal And Regal (USA)) [1988 **104** 6g² 7g⁵ 1989 7m* 8m² 7.3g³ 8g⁵] medium-sized, lengthy filly: moderate mover: 6/5 on, won maiden at Leicester in July: put up useful performances when 4½ lengths third of 7 to Distant Relative in Hungerford Stakes at Newbury and about 5 lengths fifth of 12 to Light of Morn in listed race at Newmarket nearly 3 months later: will be suited by 1¼m. *L. M. Cumani.*

MOVIE MARKET 3 b.f. Dom Racine (FR) 121–Tanimara (Sassafras (FR) 135) **49** [1988 7v 1989 10s³ 12m⁴ 13f⁶ 10.6s 11g] sparely-made filly: form only when in frame in seller and claimer in May: probably stays 1½m: sold 1,250 gns Ascot November Sales. *C. B. B. Booth.*

MOVING FORCE 2 b.g. (Mar 2) Muscatite 122–Saint Simbir 82 (Simbir 130) **44 p** [1989 6m 6m] IR 2,600Y: rather leggy, unfurnished gelding: second foal: dam Irish 9f winner at 2 yrs: beaten over 10 lengths in August in maiden auction event at Salisbury and valuable seller at York: sort to do better in time. *D. R. C. Elsworth.*

MOVING TIME 4 ch.g. Move Off 112–Ribera (Ribston 104) [1988 7d 7g 7g 8d 8g — 8g 7f 1989 6d 8d 8.2f] smallish, plain gelding: of no account. *N. Chamberlain.*

MR ACACIA 3 b.g. Enchantment 115–Lightening Blue (Roan Rocket 128) [1988 — 6m 8d 10d 1989 13.3m 12s] strong, workmanlike gelding: no worthwhile form, though showed signs of ability (staying on from rear) in handicap final start. *R. J. Holder.*

MR BROOKS 2 b.c. (Apr 7) Blazing Saddles (AUS)–Double Finesse 97 (Double **99 p** Jump 131) [1989 7d*] 21,000Y: half-brother to 3-y-o 8.2f winner Our Music and 1986 2-y-o 5f winner Marimba (both by Music Boy) and smart 6f to 1m winner Larionov (by Balidar): dam won at up to 1m: favourite, won 16-runner maiden at Leopardstown in October by 6 lengths. *K. Connolly, Ireland.*

MR CHEEKYCHOPS 2 ch.c. (May 13) Blue Cashmere 129–Tzu-Hsi 66 **38** (Songedor 116) [1989 5s 5m⁶ 7f] 5,200Y: well-grown, angular colt: half-brother to 3-y-o Empress Nicki (by Nicholas Bill) and several winners here and abroad, including sprinters Dragonist (by Dragonara Palace) and Tzutin (by Tina's Pet): dam 6f winner: poor form in maidens at Warwick and Hamilton (hung right throughout) early in season: rider lost irons at start in seller at Redcar in October, and run should be ignored. *M. Brittain.*

MR CHRIS CAKEMAKER 5 ch.m. Hotfoot 126–Polonaise (Takawalk II 125) **58** [1988 12g 10m 10g 12f⁶ 9s² 10v* 10s* 9v⁵ 1989 10d 10.2g 10.6g 11m² 11s 11s²] lengthy mare: moderate mover: form as 5-y-o only when second in claimer at Ayr and handicap at Hamilton: best at about 1¼m: acts very well in the mud: visored once at 4 yrs: has won for apprentice, but difficult ride: often sweating and on edge: injured in paddock and withdrawn seventh intended outing. *M. P. Naughton.*

MR COFFEY 6 b.g. Sallust 134–Golden Stockings (Home Guard (USA) 129) — [1988 NR 1989 11d] robust, close-coupled gelding: winning plater as 3-y-o: in need of race, very slowly away and tailed off in handicap at Edinburgh in April, only subsequent outing on flat: best form at 1½m: acts on firm going: visored twice: sold 2,000 gns Doncaster June Sales. *S. G. Norton.*

MR DORMOUSE 3 b.g. Comedy Star (USA) 121–Tea-Pot 77 (Ragstone 128) — [1988 8s 8f 1989 12m³ 12f⁵ 16.2g 14d 16.2d 18g] close-coupled gelding: moderate mover: little worthwhile form after reappearance: should stay well: probably needs top-of-the-ground: blinkered last 2 outings. *C. W. C. Elsey.*

MR KEWMILL 6 b.g. Homing 130–Muninga 108 (St Alphage 119) [1988 6d 7f 8g **32 §** 6f 8s 1989 5f 6f⁵ 6f 6f⁵ 10g 8.3m 7f 10m 10.8m³ 10f 8m a8g] close-coupled gelding: has a round action: poor handicapper: probably best at short of 1¼m: blinkered 3 times, usually visored nowadays: sometimes bandaged: not one to rely on. *J. A. Bennett.*

MR LEIF 2 b.c. (May 6) Adonijah 126–Ptarmigan 75 (Hill Clown (USA)) [1989 5v⁶ **63** 5s⁵ 5f⁵ 7f³ 7f⁶ 8.2g] 8,400Y: rather unfurnished colt: sixth foal: half-brother to 1985 2-y-o 5f winner Haverhill Girl (by Cawston's Clown) and moderate 7f and 1m winner Danish Express (by Music Boy): dam stayed 1½m: quite modest maiden: best effort fourth start: ran moderately in nurseries afterwards, blinkered on first occasion: stays 7f: sold 5,600 gns Newmarket Autumn Sales. *R. Hannon.*

MR MCGREGOR 7 b.g. Formidable (USA) 125–Mrs Tiggywinkle 109 (Silly — Season 127) [1988 6v 6m 1989 5d 7g] strong, good-bodied gelding: very lightly raced and no form since first outing in 1987: best form at short of 1m: acts on any going: blinkered 4 times, visored once: not an easy ride. *R. P. C. Hoad.*

MR MOSS 6 ch.h. Grundy 137–Bally's Mil 98 (Ballymoss 136) [1988 14v 15.5d 16d — 16g 14g 1989 14g] well-made horse: poor handicapper: stayed long distances: best form on good ground: dead. *H. O'Neill.*

MR OPTIMISTIC 2 ch.c. (Jun 2) King Persian 107–Saybya (Sallust 134) [1989 76 8s⁵ 8.2d 7v 8.2s² 10g⁶] IR 5,600Y: leggy colt: fourth foal: half-brother to Irish 3-y-o 1¼m and 1½m winner Saygoodbye (by Tampero) and useful 1m winner Johns Joy (by Martin John): dam never ran: modest maiden: easily best effort always-prominent length second of 18, clear, to Hear A Nightingale in nursery at Hamilton in November. *J. J. O'Neill.*

MR PINTIPS 5 b.h. Kris 135–Bempton 57 (Blakeney 126) [1988 10g² 12g⁴ 10v 102 10d³ 13.4v* 16g³ 15.5s 1989 16d⁵ 16m] rather leggy, quite attractive horse: poor mover: useful performer: 20/1, runaway winner of Ormonde EBF Stakes at Chester as 4-y-o: carrying condition, showed he'd retained plenty of ability when fifth to Travel Mystery in Insulpak Sagaro EBF Stakes at Ascot in April: behind when brought down before halfway in £43,800 handicap at Newcastle over 2 months later: suited by test of stamina: well suited by the mud. *W. Hastings-Bass.*

MR PRESLEY 3 b.g. Tender King 123–Theda 61 (Mummy's Pet 125) [1988 NR — 1989 10s 12g⁴ 14m⁶ 10f] 6,000Y: workmanlike gelding: first foal: dam stayed 7f: no sign of ability, including in seller: not bred to be suited by middle distances: bandaged final start. *W. Wilson.*

MR PUNCH 3 ch.g. Chaparly (FR)–Guilty Party 51 (Gold Rod 129) [1988 6s 6f — 1989 8f 10f] sparely-made, rather plain gelding: no form in maidens and sellers. *R. Simpson.*

MRS GATES 3 b.f. Good Times (ITY)–Bold Gift 61 (Persian Bold 123) [1988 5m 59 6d 6g⁶ 5m 5m⁴ 7f* 7m⁴ 8g³ 1989 10s 8g³ 8m⁴ 8h* 7h⁶ 10h] leggy, sparely-made filly: quite modest performer: won seller (bought in 1,950 gns) at Brighton in May: never dangerous when below form in handicaps there afterwards: suited by 1m: best form on a sound surface, and acts on hard going. *R. Akehurst.*

MRS GRAY 2 gr.f. (May 8) Red Sunset 120–Haunting 79 (Lord Gayle (USA) 124) 61 [1989 5d³ 5f⁵ 5m* 5f⁶ 5f⁴ 5f⁴ 5s 5m⁵] 7,000Y: smallish, sparely-made filly: closely related to 3-y-o Fourshoon and useful 1986 2-y-o 5f and 6f winner Amigo Sucio (both by Stanford) as well as fairly useful 6f and 7f winner Valley Mills (by Red Alert) and half-sister to several other winners: dam stayed 1m: quite modest performer: won maiden at Chester in July: speedy: blinkered penultimate outing: has run well for 7-lb claimer: sometimes sweats: sold 4,100 gns Doncaster October Sales: inconsistent. *A. Bailey.*

MRS HENNY PENNY 2 ch.f. (Feb 1) Absalom 128–Flopsy (Welsh Pageant 70 132) [1989 6f⁵ 6f⁴ 6f⁶ 7.3m⁴ 7g] small, sturdy filly: fourth foal: sister to useful 7f performer Captain Holly: dam unraced daughter of 1000 Guineas third Mrs Tiggywinkle, also dam of Gordian, smart winner at up to 1¼m here and in USA: modest maiden: best effort in nursery at Newbury fourth start: better suited by 7f than 6f, and will stay 1m: usually bandaged behind. *D. W. P. Arbuthnot.*

MRS MEYRICK 8 b.m. Owen Dudley 121–Social Bee 108 (Galivanter 131) [1988 42 7m 19mm 12m 8.2f 8h⁶ 10f 13f* 13.8m* 15m* 15.8g⁶ 12.3f] leggy, lengthy mare: showed first worthwhile form in July, winning claimers at Ayr (50/1, apprentice suspended for overuse of whip) and Catterick (apprentices) and 3-runner handicap (odds on) at Edinburgh: faced stiff tasks last 2 outings: better suited by 13f than shorter and seems to stay 2m: acts on firm going. *R. M. Whitaker.*

MRS MILLS 3 ch.f. Ballad Rock 122–Mill's Girl (Le Levanstell 122) [1988 7g⁴ 7s — 1989 5g 6g 7m⁵ 8g 5f 6g 8s 12g] leggy, close-coupled, sparely-made filly: quite modest maiden at best: little form after third start (edgy), mostly facing stiff tasks: kicked at start and withdrawn intended eighth outing: active type, probably best at up to 7f though bred to stay further. *P. S. Felgate.*

MRS PEOPLEATER 6 b.m. Ancient Monro 89–Flea Pit (Sir Lark 101) [1988 — NR 1989 19g] ex-Irish mare: first foal: dam never ran: won maiden at Sligo at 4 yrs: 100/1, well tailed off in minor event at Goodwood in October: stays 1½m: yet to race on top-of-the-ground and used to act well on heavy: winning hurdler with D. Wintle: bought 8,400 gns Ascot June Sales. *P. Howling.*

MRS PISTOL 5 ch.m. Sayyaf 121–Sweet Hostess (Candy Cane 125) [1988 7.6d 70 9m⁴ 8g² 8g* 8f⁶ 8g² 8g⁶ 10g⁵ 12g⁴ 1989 8m² 9m⁶ 11.7m⁴ 12d* 12g⁵] lengthy, sparely-made mare: moderate mover: modest handicapper: won at Haydock in September: stays 1½m well: acts on top-of-the-ground and a soft surface: has won for apprentice. *C. F. Wall.*

MRS SKINNER 2 ch.f. (May 26) Electric 126–Equal Chance 95 (Hitting Away) [1989 7m 6m] 1,800Y: half-sister to several winners, including speedy 1979 Irish 2-y-o Jay Bird (by Hot Spark): dam sprinter: 50/1, around 9 lengths seventh of 12, prominent 5f, to Pencarreg in maiden at Lingfield in September: sweating and edgy, no show in 28-runner seller at Newmarket following month. *C. James.*   **53**

MRS WING COMMANDER 3 b.c. Mummy's Pet 125–Empress of Russia 79 (Royal Palace 131) [1988 6d 6v² 1989 6m 6m 6f⁵ 6g 8s⁶] leggy, close-coupled colt: blinkered, first show as 3-y-o when sixth in claimer at Ayr in October: should stay further: best efforts on very soft going: sold 1,200 gns Newmarket Autumn Sales. *N. A. Callaghan.*   **—**

MR TAYLOR 4 b.g. Martinmas 128–Miss Reliant 65 (Reliance II 137) [1988 10d 12d 12m* 14.7f 12m⁵ 12g⁶ 12m 14g⁵ 15.8f³ 14m 16m 17.1g 14.7d⁵ 14.6m 1989 12d⁴ 12g³ 12f 12g* 12h² 12.4m 12m⁶ 15.3g⁴ 14m⁶ 12g 15g 14g⁵] leggy gelding: poor mover: plating-class handicapper: won at Leicester in May: likely to prove best at up to 1¾m: suited by an easy surface nowadays: slowly away ninth outing. *H. J. Collingridge.*   **53**

MR WADDILOVE 3 b.c. Bold Lad (IRE) 133–Friendly Sound 82 (Be Friendly 130) [1988 NR 1989 7g 6d 5g 5f³ 6f 5m* 5f⁶ 6m 5f⁵ 5d* 5g] 8,400Y: half-brother to 4 winners here and abroad, including fairly useful 5f to 1m winner Lady Lorelei (by Derring-Do): dam, won 3 times over 7f, is half-sister to good sprinter The Blues: modest handicapper: won at Carlisle (edgy, in good style) in June and Haydock (33/1 and favourably drawn, best effort) in September: suited by 5f: acts on firm going and a soft surface: blinkered last 6 outings: slowly away final one. *W. J. Pearce.*   **78**

MR WISHING WELL 3 ch.g. Dunbeath (USA) 127–Little Change 70 (Grundy 137) [1988 7m 1989 8.2d* 10m² 10m⁶] good-quartered gelding: fair performer: won maiden at Haydock in May: sweating, never-dangerous below-form sixth in £6,000 handicap at Newmarket in July: stays 1¼m: acts on top-of-the-ground and on soft surface. *R. J. R. Williams.*   **92**

M TWENTY FIVE 3 ch.f. Jalmood (USA) 126–New Way 103 (Klairon 131) [1988 6g 1989 6d⁵ 8d 6m] lengthy, sparely-made filly: fifth in maiden at Pontefract in April, only form: blinkered in handicap in July: should be well suited by at least 1m. *R. F. Johnson Houghton.*   **54**

MUARIJ 2 ch.f. (May 10) Star Appeal 133–Ivoronica 89 (Targowice (USA) 130) [1989 6m] 42,000Y: leggy filly: good mover: sixth foal: sister to 3-y-o sprint winner Diamond Appeal, and half-sister to 3 other winners, including formerly useful 5f and 6f winner Lochonica (by Lochnager): dam 5f winner at 2 yrs: 16/1 and very much in need of race, slowly away and always behind in 24-runner minor event at Windsor in August. *C. J. Benstead.*   **—**

MUESTA 2 b.f. (Mar 26) Bustino 136–Misguided 106 (Homing 130) [1989 5f³ 6f] 21,000Y: third foal: half-sister to 3-y-o Prime Warden (by Blakeney) and fairly useful 1987 2-y-o 5f and 7f winner Kajar (by Persian Bold): dam sprinting half-sister to smart 6f and 1m winner Missed Blessing: slow-starting 7 lengths third of 5 to Alriyaah, better effort in maidens at Folkestone in August. *K. M. Brassey.*   **47**

MUHBUBH (USA) 3 b.f. Blushing Groom (FR) 131–Manal (FR) 74 (Luthier 126) [1988 6f* 6d* 6d² 1989 7g³ 8g 10f⁵ 10g³] robust, good-topped, good sort: carries condition: useful at her best: ran creditably at Newmarket first 2 starts in Nell Gwyn Stakes and slowly-run 1000 Guineas: below form after in listed races at Goodwood, off course 4½ months in between: lacked turn of foot and should have stayed 1¼m: seemed to act on any going (didn't race on very soft): visits Unfuwain. *H. Thomson Jones.*   **108**

MUIRFIELD VILLAGE 3 b.c. Lomond (USA) 128–Ukelele (USA) (Riva Ridge (USA)) [1988 NR 1989 8g⁵] IR 88,000Y: big, lengthy, good-bodied colt: second foal: dam, from family of Golden Fleece, never ran: split a pastern at 2 yrs: 20/1 and backward, under 5 lengths fifth of 17 to Phountzi in maiden at Newmarket in May, no extra having quickened in good style over 1f out: showed a quick action: sold to join S. Dow 3,600 gns Newmarket Autumn Sales and has won over hurdles. *B. W. Hills.*   **74**

MUJAWIZ (USA) 3 b.c. Danzig (USA)–Now Voyager (USA) (Naskra (USA)) [1988 NR 1989 7d 7m] $300,000Y: sparely-made, quite attractive colt: fifth foal: half-brother to 2 winners in USA: dam ran once: over 11 lengths seventh of 20 in maiden at Newmarket in April: odds on, finished lame in similar event at Carlisle 3 weeks later: dead. *A. C. Stewart.*   **—**

MUKDDAAM (USA)   2 b.c. (Mar 20) Danzig (USA)–Height of Fashion **101** P
(FR) 124 (Bustino 136) [1989 7m*]

When Hamdan Al-Maktoum bought Height of Fashion from the Queen
for a sum reportedly between £1.4 million and £1.8 million in 1982 it seemed
that any judgement on the wisdom of the purchase was best reserved until the
end of her productive career at the least. However, it's already become clear
that the Sheikh will be hard pressed to make a better investment. In a
relatively short space of time Height of Fashion has firmly established herself
as one of the most valuable broodmares in the world. In the latest season she
accomplished the extremely rare feat of having all her four foals of racing age
win at least once. Naturally, the achievements of Nashwan and to a lesser
extent Unfuwain did most to keep their dam in the public eye, but Height of
Fashion's first foal Alwasmi added to his smart British record with a win in the
States, and judged on his one run in 1989 her fourth son Mukddaam looks a
colt with an extremely bright future. With his family so much in the news
Mukddaam's racecourse debut was bound to attract plenty of attention,
particularly as reports of his prowess on the gallops had been circulating for
several weeks. A plan to introduce him in a valuable minor event at Doncaster
in September had to be shelved when he sustained a minor cut in his box; firm
ground caused him to be pulled out of another engagement at Ascot later in
the month; and the race finally selected for his first appearance was a maiden
at Newmarket in early-October, a race which had attracted Pirate Army, Old
Vic, Dolpour, Observation Post and Two Timing the previous year. In a field
of nineteen Mukddaam proved very easy to back. He drifted from 6/4 to 7/2 in
fact, and anyone who went to inspect the runners in the paddock would have
understood why: Mukddaam was very green, constantly stopping to look
around. And his lack of experience almost cost him the race. Blindfolded and
led up to the stalls last, Mukddaam ducked sharply right as they opened. But
he was soon travelling strongly up with the leaders, though despite Carson's
strenuous efforts he began to edge noticeably right from around halfway and
with just over a furlong to run the highly-regarded newcomer Soy Roberto and
the heavily-backed favourite Mazag both looked capable of making a close
race of it. However, in the next hundred yards the complexion of the race
altered quite quickly. Mukddaam's powerful, slightly round stride became
more effective on the rising ground; he did continue to drift away from the
stands rail, but under vigorous driving he began to run on very strongly
indeed, so much so that on passing the line he was going away two lengths in
front of Soy Roberto with Mazag, who'd been squeezed out by the winner
inside the final furlong, half a length away in third. A lengthy stewards' inquiry

*Garden Suite Racing Club Maiden Stakes (Div. 1), Newmarket —
Mukddaam makes a winning debut*

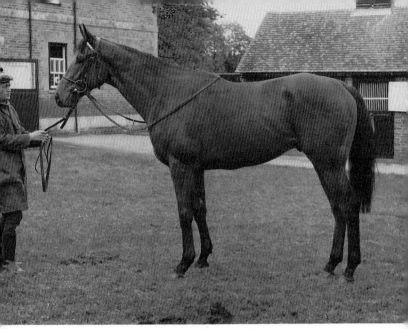

Hamdan Al-Maktoum's "Mukddaam"

followed. Its verdict—that the winner's deviation from a true line hadn't affected the positions of the placed horses—seemed a shade charitable. The form of the race didn't work out particularly well over the next few weeks. Nevertheless, the promise of Mukddaam's performance was undeniable; he'll improve vastly for the run, and with a little more experience he should prove a force to be reckoned with in good company.

Mukddaam (USA) (b.c. Mar 20, 1987)	Danzig (USA) (b 1977)	Northern Dancer (b 1961)	Nearctic Natalma
		Pas de Nom (b or br 1968)	Admiral's Voyage Petitioner
	Height of Fashion (FR) (b 1979)	Bustino (b 1971)	Busted Ship Yard
		Highclere (b 1971)	Queen's Hussar Highlight

Along with several other lightly-raced colts Mukddaam has already come in for strong support in the Two Thousand Guineas market. There's no doubt whatsoever he'll be suited by a mile; the odds are he'll stay a mile and a quarter too, but whether Mukddaam's stamina will stretch to a mile and a half is slightly open to question. Admittedly, Nashwan, Unfuwain and Alwasmi were all well suited by the trip, while Height of Fashion gave the impression a mile and three quarters would have posed her no problem. However, although Danzig has sired good middle-distance winners, notably Ascot Knight, Chief's Crown and the Belmont Stakes winner Danzig Connection, he's mainly known as an influence for speed. With this in mind it may pay to hold Derby bets for the moment, particularly as Mukddaam gives the impression that

590

Epsom's gradients and turns might not suit him. More detailed analysis of the dam's side of Mukddaam's pedigree can be found in the essay on Nashwan. Height of Fashion's winners are all imposing individuals. Mukddaam is a big, strong, rangy colt with a deal of scope, very much in the mould of Unfuwain. He looks sure to train on well and add to his family's fine record. Incidentally, Height of Fashion's two-year-old representative for 1990 is her first filly, Manwah by Lyphard; Height of Fashion was barren on a return visit to Danzig in 1988 but is reportedly now in foal to Mr Prospector. *Major W. R. Hern.*

MUKHABBR 5 b.h. Taufan (USA) 119–Ribotingo 78 (Petingo 135) [1988 6g 6f³   **70** d
6f² 5m⁴ 6f 6m 6g 6m 5g 6g 7m⁵ 1989 6v 7g* 7m 7f 6g 7m 7f³ 8.5g] quite well-made horse: moderate mover: 8/1 from 14/1, very well treated on his form in first half of 1988 when winning 19-runner handicap at Salisbury in May: form after only on seventh outing: stays 7f: probably unsuited by soft going and acts well on firm: sometimes sweats: usually wears a crossed noseband: inconsistent. *C. J. Benstead.*

MUKIR 3 ch.c. Kris 135–Velvet Habit 89 (Habitat 134) [1988 7d 1989 8m 8.2g³   **70**
8m⁴ a8g] big, strong, workmanlike colt: in frame in maiden and minor event in Scotland: will be suited by further: best effort with some give in the ground. *P. T. Walwyn.*

MULL HOUSE 2 b.c. (Mar 28) Local Suitor (USA) 128–Foudre 76 (Petingo 135)   **72** p
[1989 6m⁶ 7m*] 9,600Y, 25,000 2-y-o: strong, rangy colt: seventh foal: dam half-sister to smart animals Lighted Glory, Torus and King Luthier and to dam of Mountain Kingdom: 3/1, won 17-runner maiden at Chepstow in October by neck from Pusey Street Boy, staying on well to lead close home: will stay 1¼m: should improve further. *J. Sutcliffe.*

MULTIHANDS 4 b.g. Dara Monarch 128–Suits Me Best (Try My Best (USA)   **34**
130) [1988 10v 16g² 12m³ 14.7f³ 16g⁴ 16f⁶ 17g 16.5f³ 16d 1989 14.6g 12d 14.8m⁵ 16f⁵ 15.8f⁵ 18.8f³ 16f⁴] lengthy gelding: has a quick action: poor maiden: seems to stay 2¼m: acts on firm going: blinkered twice, including sixth outing: visored fifth: has run well for apprentice. *J. Wharton.*

MUMMY'S CHANCE 5 b.g. Mummy's Game 120–Kalopia 80 (Kalydon 122)   **48**
[1988 5g⁶ 5g 6g 5f* 5m 1989 5d 5f 5m⁴ 5f* 7m 5g³ 5.8h³ 5m 5m 5f] good-topped gelding: carries condition: led final strides when winning selling handicap (no bid) at Edinburgh in June: best at 5f: acts on hard going: usually blinkered nowadays: has given trouble at stalls (refused to enter them second intended outing): sold to join R. Manning 5,800 gns Doncaster September Sales. *J. Berry.*

MUMMY'S FOX 2 b.c. (Apr 17) Mummy's Game 120–May Fox 67 (Healaugh   **52**
Fox) [1989 5s⁵ 5d⁵ 7m⁵ 7g 7f² 7m 7g² 7m 8f 6g a7g] 6,000Y: small, close-coupled colt: sixth reported foal: half-brother to 3-y-o Earthly Pleasure (by Music Boy), 10.6f winner Moorland Lady (by Swing Easy) and a winner in South Africa: dam 2-y-o 5f winner, is half-sister to Oaks runner-up Mabel: fair plater: should stay 1m: sometimes sweating and edgy: sold 1,200 gns Ascot November Sales: inconsistent. *C. N. Allen.*

MUMMYS LAD 3 b.c. Mummy's Game 120–Piccadilly Rose 63 (Reform 132)   **—**
[1988 5v² 5g 5g⁵ 6m 1989 7g⁶ 8.2v⁴ 11v] small colt: plating-class maiden: should stay 1m: best effort on heavy going: blinkered last 2 starts. *N. Tinkler.*

MUMMY'S SONG 4 b.g. Mummy's Pet 125–Welsh Miniature 85 (Owen   **—**
Anthony 102) [1988 5f 5f⁴ 6g³ 6m 6m 7m⁴ 7f³ 1989 8s 7g 7g] leggy gelding: plater: needed race final outing, first for 5 months: stays 7f: acts on firm going: blinkered second start: trained until after then by D. Arbuthnot: sold to join J. Harriman 1,600 gns Ascot September Sales. *J. White.*

MUNJARID 4 ch.c. Habitat 134–Connaught Bridge 124 (Connaught 130) [1988   **—**
10.5g 10m* 10d⁵ 9g* 9g³ 1989 6d 10v 10d⁵ 11.7m 13.3m⁶] sturdy ex-French colt: fourth living foal: half-brother to smart French winner Conmaiche (by Kings Lake) and 2 other winners, including 1½m to 1¾m winner Wassl Reef (by Mill Reef): dam won Yorkshire Oaks and Nassau Stakes: won minor event at Saint-Cloud and in French Provinces as 3-y-o when trained by A. Fabre: beaten at least 9 lengths in minor events and handicaps in first half of 1989: needs further than 6f and stays 1¼m: acts on top-of-the-ground and a soft surface: blinkered once at 3 yrs. *G. B. Balding.*

MURANGO 3 b.c. Shirley Heights 130–Eldoret 100 (High Top 131) [1988 7g 8s⁴   **91**
8h⁶ 8d⁵ 8.2d² 1989 10g* 12.3m* 12m⁵ 13.3m 12m⁶] strong, compact colt: fairly useful handicapper: ran on strongly to lead close home when winning at Leicester (maiden) and Chester (pulled very hard early) in the spring: off course almost 4

months and below form after, not given hard race final start: stays 1½m: acts on top-of-the-ground and a soft surface: sweating and on toes fourth outing. *J. L. Dunlop.*

MURJAAN 4 b.f. No Lute (FR) 129–Grevonika (USA) (Explodent (USA)) [1988 9d⁴ 12g³ 12m⁵ 1989 9v⁵] good-topped filly: moderate mover: modest maiden at best: well-beaten fifth of 10 in maiden claiming event at Hamilton in April: stays 1½m: sold 1,000 gns Doncaster August Sales. *G. M. Moore.* —

MURMURING 3 b.f. Kind of Hush 118–Beryl's Jewel 86 (Siliconn 121) [1988 5m² 6g 5d 1989 6f 6m³ 6f² 6f² 6f² 6m a6g²] workmanlike, angular filly: good walker: has a quick action: quite modest maiden: stays 6f: acts on firm ground: bought out of W. Haggas's stable 2,400 gns Newmarket Autumn Sales after sixth outing. *S. Dow.* 66

MUSAAHIM 3 ch.c. Pharly (FR) 130–Little Loch Broom 60 (Reform 132) [1988 7m² 1989 13.3m* 12f⁵ 12f³ 12g 11m*] strong, lengthy colt: fairly useful performer: won maiden at Newbury in June by 7 lengths and minor event (looking extremely well) at Redcar in September by 2½ lengths from sole rival Miss Fancy That: will stay 1¾m: seems to need top-of-the-ground: sold 32,000 gns Newmarket Autumn Sales. *H. Thomson Jones.* 92

MUSAFIRIE 3 b.c. What A Guest 119–Perbury 88 (Grisaille 115) [1988 7g⁵ 8d⁴ 10d* 1989 8v⁴ 10g 11f⁵ 14.8m⁵ 12m⁵ 16.2d⁵ 14m⁶] lengthy, fair sort: has a long, round action: modest handicapper: seems best at around 1½m: acts on firm going and a soft surface: trained first 4 starts by R. Casey: sold 10,000 gns Newmarket Autumn Sales. *Lord John FitzGerald.* 71

MUSCA MYTH 2 b.f. (Mar 1) Muscatite 122–Persian Myth (Persian Bold 123) [1989 5d 5g] IR 400F, IR 2,000Y: neat filly: second foal: dam ran once at 2 yrs in Ireland: bit backward, behind in early-season sellers at Beverley (slowly away) and Wolverhampton: sold to race in the Netherlands 900 gns Doncaster June Sales and won twice there at 9f. *M. H. Easterby.* —

MUSCAT 2 b.c. (Mar 28) Muscatite 122–Gay Barbarella (Gay Fandango (USA) 132) [1989 6m 7m⁵ 7m⁵ 8.2s 7g 6g] IR 5,600Y: small, good-bodied colt: first foal: dam poor maiden here at 2 yrs won 3 times in Denmark as 3-y-o: quite modest maiden: best effort second outing: stays 7f: blinkered fifth start: sold to German International BA 5,600 gns Newmarket Autumn Sales. *M. A. Jarvis.* 60

MUSHTAAG 5 b.g. Posse (USA) 130–Unsuspected 95 (Above Suspicion 127) [1988 12m 12d⁵ 12m 14f 14.6f 1989 16s] lengthy, angular gelding: bad mover: useful at his best, but has deteriorated considerably: very slowly away and always tailed off in handicap at Kempton in March: stays 1½m: used to be suited by a soft surface: best left alone. *I. P. Wardle.* —

MUSICAL BLISS (USA) 3 b.f. The Minstrel (CAN) 135–Bori (USA) 117 (Quadrangle) [1988 6g* 7d* 1989 8g* 12m 8g]

The General Accident One Thousand Guineas had its smallest turn-out since 1904 when only six took on Pretty Polly. Small fields needn't be weak any more than big ones are necessarily strong (only six ran in Brigadier Gerard's Guineas, for instance, while twenty-six ran in Zino's). All the same, the latest One Thousand Guineas field was one of the weakest in living memory. On top of that, the race was run at a most unsatisfactory pace, beginning funereally and ending in a sprint out of the Dip. In the circumstances the classic seems likely to be remembered longest for Swinburn's astute tactics on Musical Bliss and for the fact that their success gave Stoute his first in the One Thousand after so many near misses.

Overnight the size of the field was more a source of disappointment than its quality. After all, five of those declared—Pass The Peace, Oczy Czarnie, Muhbubh, Musical Bliss and Kerrera—had made the International Classification as two-year-olds; another—Ensconse—the Free Handicap. Both the Tattersalls Cheveley Park Stakes winner Pass The Peace and unbeaten Ensconse had already come out and run well in the spring, the former justifying favouritism comfortably in the Gainsborough Stud Fred Darling Stakes at Newbury, the latter beating another Guineas runner Aldbourne and Muhbubh almost as comfortably in what's often the best trial, the Juddmonte Farms Nell Gwyn Stakes at Newmarket. The other runner Bequest had also been out, winning a Brighton maiden with ease, and on her breeding might have been anything. However, more disappointment arose when Oczy Czarnie's non-arrival from France became known—she took

*General Accident One Thousand Guineas, Newmarket—a close finish to a slowly-run race;
right to left, Ensconse, Aldbourne, Musical Bliss, Kerrera and Pass The Peace*

fright when being loaded onto the plane—leaving the seven home-based
runners, two of whom were trained by Stoute. Swinburn has been faced with
many a difficult choice between mounts in his association with the stable.
Almost certainly the choice between Musical Bliss and Kerrera was much
less difficult to make than some, since one filly seemed more progressive than
the other, more likely to be suited by the distance and blessed with the more
satisfactory temperament. Musical Bliss had shown considerable promise and
very useful form as a two-year-old, winning a valuable maiden race at Ascot
and the Bottisham Heath Stud Rockfel Stakes at Newmarket three months
later. The gallops reports all suggested she'd trained on and even without a
run she started joint-second favourite at 7/2 with Pass The Peace behind the
heavily-backed Ensconse. Kerrera came next in the betting at 9/1.
Unexpectedly, Musical Bliss took the preliminaries much less calmly than
Kerrera. She got on edge right away, and when she began to sweat up and then
required two attendants in the parade there couldn't be maximum confidence
in her being able to run up to her capabilities. But she responded fully to that
memorable ride. As soon as the stalls opened it became clear that no-one had
orders to make the pace; some of the runners ambled along while others
flyjumped under heavy restraint. Musical Bliss, by no means first out, was
allowed to stride on by Swinburn after half a furlong and though she set just an
ordinary gallop there was no general effort to stick close. They set off up the
Rowley Mile virtually strung out in Indian file, Pass The Peace second
followed by Aldbourne, Muhbubh, Ensconse, Bequest and Kerrera. Musical
Bliss always had the lead after that, Swinburn gradually quickening the pace
so that around three furlongs from home, where the rest had closed up, Pass
The Peace only half a length down, with less than a length to the in-line
Aldbourne, Bequest and Muhbubh, then two more back to Ensconse and
Kerrera, the race had at last begun in earnest. Going into the Dip, Swinburn
asked Musical Bliss to quicken again, giving her a couple of cracks; the
advantage of a length and a half poached turned out decisive as she ran on
strongly up the hill, ridden out vigorously to win by three quarters of a length
from Kerrera. She returned minus her off-fore shoe.

So, first two places in the race for the trainer, following seconds with
Fair Salinia, Our Home, Maysoon, Milligram and Dabaweyaa, a disqualified
second with Royal Heroine, and thirds with Bella Colora and Sonic Lady. Four

Sheikh Mohammed's "Musical Bliss"

of those fillies had been sent on for the Oaks; Musical Bliss became the fifth while Kerrera went back to sprinting. The Guineas provided no solid clue as to Musical Bliss's prospects of staying a mile and a half: the thing most in her favour was that she'd raced in a very relaxed manner. Her breeding gave her more than an outside chance. As to her prospects if she did stay—well, the way the race had been run automatically cast doubts on the Guineas form, but in the meantime Kerrera, and more relevantly Ensconse and Aldbourne in the Goffs Irish Guineas and Pass The Peace in the French equivalent, hadn't let it down. However, Swinburn switched to Aliysa who started 11/10 favourite and won, while Musical Bliss drifted to 4/1 second favourite and was well beaten. She didn't stay, and was eased over the last two furlongs having been held up to get the trip. When Musical Bliss did no better back at a mile in the Prix du Haras de Fresnay-le-Buffard Jacques le Marois at Deauville in August she was retired. She looked well, went down well and took the preliminaries in her stride there, so she had no apparent excuse. She kept up without any difficulty for over five furlongs but was in trouble straight away when they quickened.

Musical Bliss's great-grandam Arietta was among the best mares bred by Phil Bull. She came third to Honeylight in the One Thousand Guineas and to the Guineas runner-up Midget II in the Coronation Stakes in 1956. Before being sold out of Bull's Hollins Stud to North America she produced two good horses in the cleverly-named Ebor winner Sostenuto (by Never Say Die) and the top miler Romulus. Far and away the best she produced in the States was Musical Bliss's grandam Lucretia Bori, third in the Arlington-Washington Lassie Stakes as a two-year-old and winner of the less important Jasmine

Stakes over six furlongs at three. Five of Lucretia Bori's foals were sent to race in England. One broke down irreparably at Folkestone, the others—Draw The Line, Glissando, Night Watch and Settimino—all won races of some description at up to fifteen furlongs, and Draw The Line finished second in the Dewhurst. Musical Bliss's dam Bori is not among Lucretia Bori's numerous winners, but no matter. She'd already produced a high-class filly before Musical Bliss, the Grade 1 nine-furlong La Canada Stakes winner Safe Play (by Sham).

			Northern Dancer	Nearctic
Musical Bliss (USA) (b.f. 1986)	The Minstrel (CAN) (ch 1974)		(b 1961)	Natalma
		Fleur	Victoria Park
		(b 1964)	Flaming Page
	Bori (USA) (b 1972)	Quadrangle	Cohoes
		(b 1961)	Tap Day
		Lucretia Bori	Bold Ruler
		(b 1965)	Arietta

Looking at the pedigree again, running Musical Bliss in the Oaks seemed a risk well worth taking. As we learned once more though, her sire The Minstrel is no sure influence for stamina: he gets all types, Prix de l'Abbaye winners (Silver Fling) as well as Guineas winners, dual Oaks winners (Melodist) and Northumberland Plate winners (Orpheus). It will be interesting to see what mates are chosen for Musical Bliss and what types she produces. To sum her up, as far as it's possible to do from such a short, truncated career: the workmanlike, angular Musical Bliss was best at up to a mile; a good mover, she showed form only on an easy surface. *M. R. Stoute.*

MUSICAL ENCORE 3 ch.f. Chief Singer 131–Still More (Ballymore 123) [1988 6d 1989 7s] bandaged off-hind, showed signs of ability in maidens: sold 1,000 gns Newmarket December Sales. *I. A. Balding.* —

MUSICAL FLASH 2 ch.c. (Apr 24) Music Boy 124–Martin-Lavell News 90 (Song 132) [1989 5m³ 5m 5f⁵ 5f³ 5m² a6g] 13,000 2-y-o: neat, strong colt: second foal: half-brother to 3-y-o Bermuda Gold (by What A Guest): dam won twice over 5f from 4 starts at 2 yrs: plating-class maiden: changed hands 17,000 gns Newmarket Autumn Sales. *R. Hannon.* 59

MUSICAL GEM 2 br.f. (Mar 3) Sparkling Boy 110–Symphonie (Tambourine II 133) [1989 6m⁶ 7.5f⁵ 8m 7d 8g] workmanlike, sparely-made filly: turns off-fore in: moderate mover: half-sister to 2 winners: dam never ran: plating-class maiden: behind in sellers last 2 starts: stays 1m: best effort for 7-lb claimer. *Denys Smith.* 55

MUSICAL INTERVAL (USA) 3 b.f. The Minstrel (CAN) 135–Kittyhawk 113 (Bustino 136) [1988 NR 1989 7m] workmanlike, rather sparely-made filly: fourth foal: closely related to 7f and 1¼m winner Storm Force (by Storm Bird) and half-sister to smart 1985 French 2-y-o maiden With Hope (by Irish River) and useful stayer/hurdler Nomadic Way (by Assert): dam won Lowther Stakes and best up to 1m: bit backward, headstrong when well-beaten eighth of 9 in maiden at Leicester in July. *B. W. Hills.*

MUSICAL IVY 2 b.f. (Mar 25) Aragon 118–Park Parade 94 (Monsanto (FR) 121) [1989 5v⁵ 5g 5f 5f] 960F: narrow, leggy, sparely-made filly: has a round action: second foal: dam won 5 times over 1½m and is daughter of sister to Parthian Glance, best 3-y-o staying filly of 1966: poor form in maidens. *J. R. Bosley.* 43

MUSICAL LEADER 3 b.c. Music Boy 124–The Dupecat 75 (Javelot 124) [1988 6g⁵ 6g 1989 7f 8m 10m² 10m² 12m⁵ 12.2g³ 12.4g²] sturdy colt: fair maiden: probably suited by 1½m and an easy surface: visored last 4 starts: consistent: sold 16,000 gns Newmarket Autumn Sales. *J. W. Hills.* 80

MUSICAL LOOK (USA) 3 b.c. Diesis 133–Frosty Stare (Targowice (USA) 130) [1988 6g⁶ 7d 1989 8s* 8v* 10.4f⁶ 8.2m 7m³ 7.6g³ 8m 7g 8d⁶] tall, rather finely-made, quite attractive colt: moderate mover: fairly useful performer: odds on, won early-season maiden at Warwick and minor event at Kempton: ran poorly seventh and eighth outings, sweating and edgy in £5,000 ladies race (visored) at Ascot on first of them: stays 1m: acts on top-of-the-ground and heavy going. *P. T. Walwyn.* 92

MUSICAL MAJOR 2 ch.c. (Mar 23) Sharpo 132–Land of Song 82 (Sing Sing 134) [1989 5m³ 5g² 5d² 5g³] 17,000Y: smallish, good-topped colt: poor mover: half-brother to several winners, including 1¼m winner Strawberry Song and fairly 66 useful 7f winner Fintry Hills (both by Final Straw): dam, half-sister to smart stayer Celtic Cone, won over 5f: quite modest maiden: third to Stoneythorpewonder in nursery at Hamilton in September: hung badly left in seller second start: will stay 6f: sold 3,200 gns Newmarket Autumn Sales. *A. A. Scott.*

MUSICAL MOMENTS 3 b.f. Vision (USA)–Miami Melody (Miami Springs 121) [1988 6m 6g 6d 1989 8g 6f 7m4] useful-looking filly: little form: slowly away, raced very freely in blinkers in seller final start: seems unlikely to stay 1m, though bred to do so: sold to join J. Roberts 1,250 gns Newmarket September Sales. *Sir Mark Prescott.* **39**

MUSICAL NOTE 2 ch.f. (Mar 20) Sharpo 132–Fair And Wise 75 (High Line 125) [1989 6m 7g 8m 6m] 3,600Y: first foal: dam suited by 1¾m: poor maiden: should stay further than 6f. *M. Blanshard.* **44**

MUSIC IN MY HEART 3 ch.f. Music Boy 124–Canoodle 66 (Warpath 113) [1988 7s 8s 8v6 1989 8d 12f 7m 10f 10g 15.8m5 6f 9f 7.5m] small filly: no form, including in sellers: blinkered, edgy and looked temperamental final start. *N. Bycroft.* **—**

MUSIC REVIEW 6 ch.g. Music Boy 124–Right View 75 (Right Tack 131) [1988 5g 5f 5f 5.1f5 6m6 5g* 5s 6g 5m 6g4 5g 5f 5s2 5f 6s 6d 5v3 1989 5m 6f 5g 6m 6f5 6m] small, workmanlike gelding: poor mover: quite modest winner as 5-y-o: below form in 1989: suited by 6f or stiff 5f: has won on firm going, but best nowadays on any surface: sometimes sweats: blinkered once: sometimes unruly at start: often slowly away and gets behind: inconsistent. *M. H. Tompkins.* **—**

MUSIL 3 b.c. Mummy's Pet 125–Amalee 57 (Troy 137) [1988 6g* 6m6 1989 8.2s5 7g] leggy, rather angular colt: won newcomers race at Goodwood as 2-y-o: facing stiff tasks, well beaten in minor event and handicap (still carrying condition) in spring of 1989: should be suited by further than 6f: swished tail under pressure second start at 2 yrs: sold 3,000 gns Newmarket Autumn Sales. *J. L. Dunlop.* **—**

MUST BE MAGIC 5 b.m. Comedy Star (USA) 121–Jinja 85 (St Paddy 133) [1988 6d 6g 8.3m5 7m 8.3d2 8g 12.2f 10d* 9v4 1989 8.2f* 9f 8.2f2 8g4 9.1f2 8m5 10m 11s5 8g] close-coupled, deep-girthed mare: poor handicapper: won selling event at Hamilton (bought in 5,100 gns) in May: stays 1¼m: acts on any going: has won for apprentice: wears bandages: has worn a crossed noseband: withdrawn after bolting fourth intended start: inconsistent. *M. J. O'Neill.* **45**

MUTAH (USA) 2 ch.c. (Apr 20) Topsider (USA)–Bank On Love (USA) (Gallant Romeo (USA)) [1989 6m* 6g*] $180,000Y: workmanlike, good-quartered colt: moderate mover, with a quick action: fifth foal: closely related to Irish 9f winner Bank Step (by Lyphard), later winner in USA, and half-brother to 3-y-o Weldnaas (by Diesis), successful at 6f (at 2 yrs) and 7.2f, and a winner in USA: dam unraced sister to very useful 1982 2-y-o Gallant Special: odds on, won maiden at Doncaster in July most impressively by 6 lengths and 4-runner minor event at Haydock following month by 5 lengths from eased Number One Son: still bit green at Haydock and capable of better. *H. R. A. Cecil.* **89 p**

MUTLIQ 4 b.g. Moorestyle 137–Girton 68 (Balidar 133) [1988 5f2 5g2 5.8d3 5f 1989 8.3m] sparely-made gelding: modest maiden at his best: found nothing final 2 starts in 1988: tailed off in Windsor handicap in July. *W. J. Haggas.* **— §**

MUTTASIL 2 gr.c. (May 3) Mendez (FR) 128–My Candy 81 (Lorenzaccio 130) [1989 7m 7v] 30,000Y: strong, medium-sized colt: has scope: half-brother to several winners, including 3-y-o 1½m and 1¾m winner Amelianne (by Bustino), 1m and 1¼m winner Summer Fashion (by Moorestyle) and fair 1981 2-y-o 6f winner Annesley (by Relkino): dam placed over 7f at 2 yrs: well beaten in maidens: dead. *M. F. D. Morley.* **—**

MUWFIQ 2 b.c. (Feb 27) Formidable (USA) 125–Triple First 117 (High Top 131) [1989 6m6 6m*] 80,000Y: robust, good sort: brother to useful 6f and 1m winner Triagonal and half-brother to 3-y-o Triplicate (by Mill Reef) and 4 winners, including 1000 Guineas and Oaks-placed Maysoon (by Shergar) and Oaks third Three Tails (by Blakeney): dam thoroughly game winner at 5f to 1¼m: 12/1 and having first run since late-July, won 10-runner maiden at York in October by a length from Zanoni, leading 1f out and running on strongly: will stay 7f. *P. T. Walwyn.* **91 p**

MY BROTHER JAKE 3 b.c. My Dad Tom (USA) 109–Silken Sheba 70 (Royalty 130) [1988 6m 6m3 6m4 6m4 7m6 7g 8m4 8d4 1989 8.2s 9f2 12f2 12f4 12m 9f 10g a14g] smallish, plain colt: has a round action: plating-class maiden: no form (including in seller) since fourth start: stays 1½m: acts on firm going: blinkered sixth outing: tends to hang, but has run well for apprentice: sometimes reluctant at stalls: trained until after sixth start by J. Mackie. *J. M. Bradley.* **52**

MY CHIARA 3 b.f. Ardross 134–My Tootsie 98 (Tap On Wood 130) [1988 6m* 6f   **87**
6m 7m4 8m2 1989 11.3m 8f4 9m5 10g6 14m6 12g5 14.8m4 10m6 12g3 12g2 12g a10g*
12d3 a10g2 a10g] leggy, quite good-topped filly: has a fluent, slightly round action:
keen walker: fair handicapper: made all at Lingfield in October: made most and ran
well after in William Hill November Handicap at Thirsk and when short-headed at
Lingfield: stays 1¾m: acts on top-of-the-ground and dead. *M. D. I. Usher.*

MY CONCORDIA 3 b.f. Belfort (FR) 89–Princess Sharpenup 63 (Lochnager   **52 d**
132) [1988 6s 5d5 1989 6s 6f 8g3 7h6 5f6 5g 6m 6f 8f 8.3d] leggy, lengthy filly:
plating-class maiden: below form after fifth start in handicap and sellers: stays 1m:
acts on firm going and a soft surface: keen sort: trained until after fifth start by D.
O'Donnell. *P. Burgoyne.*

MY COQUETTE 2 ch.f. (Apr 24) Coquelin (USA) 121–River Lane (Riverman   **—**
(USA) 131) [1989 6g] third foal: half-sister to 3-y-o 5f winner Shalfleet (by Sharpo):
dam French 1½m winner: 25/1, slowly away and always behind in 17-runner maiden
at Folkestone in October: bred to stay much further. *C. E. Brittain.*

MY CROFT 2 b.f. (Apr 6) Crofter (USA) 124–Randolina (Wolver Hollow 126)   **64**
[1989 5d*] IR 4,200F, IR 17,000Y: first reported foal: dam half-sister to useful Irish
7f and 1m winner Final Moment: 5/1, won 10-runner maiden at Kempton in March:
has joined J. Sutcliffe. *J. Berry.*

MY DARK ROSALEEN 3 br.f. King of Spain 121–Irish Holiday 73 (Simbir 130)   **—**
[1988 6m4 5f2 6s2 6s3 6s4 1989 6g 6f 6d] workmanlike, attractive filly: modest
maiden at 2 yrs: well beaten in handicaps as 3-y-o: very edgy first (found nothing)
and final starts: unlikely to stay beyond 6f: appears to act on any going: blinkered
once at 2 yrs: bought out of J. W. Watts's stable 1,650 gns Ascot July Sales before
final outing. *Mrs A. Knight.*

MY DIAMOND RING 4 b.f. Sparkling Boy 110–Bells of St Martin 89   **46**
(Martinmas 128) [1988 6s 6d4 7s 6m 6g6 6m 6f 7g 6m5 6g 6d 1989 6v 6d 8m4 9f5 8g*
8h5 8.2f5 10.8m 8.3g* 8.5m 8.3m4 8.3m2] light-framed filly: moderate mover: won
selling handicaps at Pontefract (bought in 3,600 gns) in May and Windsor (bought in
5,400 gns) in July: stays 1m well: probably acts on any going: sometimes sweats:
suitable mount for apprentice. *M. D. I. Usher.*

MYFOR 3 ch.c. Be My Guest (USA) 126–Forliana 75 (Forli (ARG)) [1988 7g3 1989   **82 §**
8g3 8m2 8m4 10.2f2 8g] close-coupled colt: fair maiden: raced alone and ran
creditably in handicap at Newmarket final start: stays 1¼m: acts on firm ground:
sold to join M. Pipe 25,000 gns Newmarket Autumn Sales: irresolute and one to
treat with caution. *B. W. Hills.*

MY GREATEST STAR 4 ch.f. Great Nephew 126–Western Star 107 (Alcide   **—**
136) [1988 8f4 10.2m3 10f4 10m4 1989 7g 8h5] strong, good-bodied filly: modest
maiden as 3-y-o when trained by H. Cecil: well below form both outings in first half
of 1989: barely stays 1¼m: yet to race on a soft surface. *C. F. Wall.*

MYHAMET 2 b.c. (May 14) Gorytus (USA) 132–Honey Bridge 99 (Crepello 136)   **80 p**
[1989 7m4 8m2 8.2f2 8f*] rangy colt: has scope: good mover: closely related to St
Leger winner Minster Son and a winner in Italy (both by Niniski) and half-brother to
3-y-o Antiguan Sting (by Head For Heights) and another winner in Italy: dam 6f
winner at 2 yrs: progressive sort: favourite, won minor event at Bath in October by
½ length from Trying Days, leading over 2f out: suited by enterprising tactics at 1m,
and will stay 1¼m +. *Major W. R. Hern.*

MY HOME 4 ch.f. Homing 130–Ma Pierrette 77 (Cawston's Clown 113) [1988 8f   **—**
7f4 8.2m 7m3 8m 7g4 1989 7g 7m 7f 7f 7m6 8f] leggy, shallow-girthed filly: quite
modest at best: well beaten in handicaps in 1989: stays 7f: acts on firm going:
occasionally sweats: often apprentice ridden: has given trouble in preliminaries:
very slowly away third outing. *I. Campbell.*

MY LADY MINSTREL 3 ch.f. Brotherly (USA) 80–Lady Peggy (Young Nelson   **48**
106) [1988 6f 5g 7d 5.1f3 5m 6m 5g5 1989 5m 6f 5.8h5 6m 5f2 5f 5.8h2 6f 5.3h5 6g 6g
5m 6m 7g] small filly: moderate walker and mover: poor maiden: generally below
form after seventh start, including in sellers: stays 6f: acts on hard ground:
occasionally blinkered: below form when sweating: inconsistent. *J. L. Spearing.*

MY LADYS TEARS 2 gr.f. (Apr 7) Godswalk (USA) 130–Vital Spirit 65   **49**
(Tachypous 128) [1989 5f2 6g 6f 5g] IR 3,200F, IR 3,800Y, 4,600 2-y-o: leggy filly:
fourth foal: half-sister to 6f and 7f (seller) winner Roof Ghost (by Thatching) and a
winner in Spain: dam best at 2 yrs, stayed 7f: 10 lengths second of 7 to
Somethingdifferent in maiden at Nottingham in June: little worthwhile form
afterwards: pulls hard. *F. J. Yardley.*

MY LAMB 4 b.c. Relkino 131–Lambay 88 (Lorenzaccio 130) [1988 8.2v* 8g* 109
10.4s³ 8m 9g* 9m² 8d 10.2f* 10f 10.2g 1989 8d 10.2g* 11f* 12m² 12f] big,
useful-looking colt: usually looks very well: has very long stride: useful
handicapper: better than ever in first half of 1989, winning at Doncaster (rallying
splendidly) and Newbury, at latter making all, gradually increasing pace, and
running on strongly to beat Firelight Fiesta ½ length: not seen out after Royal
Ascot: stays 1½m: acts on any going: suited by forcing tactics: splendidly genuine
and consistent. *R. F. Johnson Houghton.*

MY LITTLE BIRD 2 ch.f. (Feb 28) Glenstal (USA) 118–Myna 85 (Ela-Mana- 62
Mou 132) [1989 5f* 6f4 5m a7g] 8,000Y: sparely-made filly: good mover: first foal:
dam, 11.5f winner, is half-sister to very useful 6f and 1m winner Naar: quite modest
performer: won maiden at Goodwood in June, best effort: bred to stay at least 6f:
sold 3,000 gns Newmarket Autumn Sales. *D. J. G. Murray-Smith.*

MYLORDMAYOR 2 ch.g. (Apr 17) Move Off 112–Sharenka (Sharpen Up 127) 58
[1989 5d 5f 5f 7f 7m² 7m² 7g 8.5f a6g a6g³ a7g⁵] 2,600Y: sparely-made gelding: first
reported living foal: dam won in Norway, reportedly from 6f to 1¼m: fair plater: best
efforts last 2 starts: stays 7f: suited by some give in the ground: inconsistent.
Ronald Thompson.

MY LORD (USA) 2 b.c. (May 2) Nijinsky (CAN) 138–Euphrosyne (USA) (Judger 83 p
(USA)) [1989 7g⁶ 8m⁶ 8g*] $180,000Y: lengthy, good-topped colt: carries condition:
has plenty of scope: half-brother to Orpheus Island (by Blushing Groom), winner at
up to 11f: dam graded stakes winner at up to 13f: 5/2, won 16-runner maiden at
Leicester in November by ½ length, clear, from Stereo, making most and keeping
on gamely: will be suited by 1¼m + . *J. H. M. Gosden.*

MY LUCKY STAR 3 gr.f. Ballacashtal (CAN)–La Comedienne (Comedy Star 46
(USA) 121) [1988 5m 5g 6m 5.8d 1989 6g 6f 8h⁶ 7m 7h* 7f⁶ 7f³ 7h 8f⁵ 7.6m]
sparely-made, dipped-backed filly: won seller (bought in 2,500 gns) at Brighton in
May: suited by 7f: acts on hard going: inconsistent. *G. B. Balding.*

MY MALLET (FR) 4 ch.c. Tap On Wood 130–Salma (Welsh Pageant 132) [1988 71
12d³ 12d⁵ 14g 12m⁴ 9m² 8f 7f² 7g 1989 7g 8f⁶ 10f² 10f] rangy, workmanlike colt:
modest handicapper: not seen out after running moderately at Kempton in July:
stays 1½m, but effective at much shorter: acts on any going: apprentice ridden last 3
starts: has swished tail. *Miss B. Sanders.*

MY MAVOURNIN (USA) 2 b.f. (Feb 7) L'Emigrant (USA) 129–Maid of Erin 66 p
(USA) (Irish River (USA) 131) [1989 7m 6m 7m] $55,000Y: close-coupled,
good-topped filly: first foal: dam, ran once in France, is sister to good-class River
Dancer, from family of Sun Princess: quite modest form in maidens, twice shaping
better than finishing position suggests: may do better. *A. A. Scott.*

MY MAZIONAH 4 b.f. Moorestyle 137–In My Image (Dancer's Image (USA)) —
[1988 7d⁵ 7d 7f 6d 1989 7g 10m] angular filly: little sign of ability. *D. Marks.*

MY MOTHER'S EYES (FR) 4 b.f. Saint Cyrien (FR) 128–Pollenka (FR) —
(Reliance II 137) [1988 8s 1989 9.7g 10.1m 8m 11.7m 6g⁵ a8g a7g] big, angular
ex-French filly: turns off-fore in: has a free, round action: half-sister to several
winners in France, including 1m and 9f winner Children's Corner (by Top Ville):
dam French 1m to 10.5f winner: behind in varied events: bandaged fifth and sixth
appearances, withdrawn after refusing to enter stalls on latter: trained until after
reappearance by A. Fabre. *C. A. Austin.*

MY NEW BEST FRIEND 5 b.g. Prince Bee 128–Tender Song (Pretendre 126) —
[1988 10v 16d4 1989 10f] ex-Irish gelding: half-brother to 1m winner Mr Juicy (by
The Brianstan): dam unraced half-sister to high-class Noble Dancer: lightly-raced
maiden: 50/1, tailed off at Folkestone in August: blinkered twice. *R. Lee.*

MY PAL POPEYE 4 br.g. Runnett 125–Staderas (Windjammer (USA)) [1988 6g 74 §
7m⁵ 7f³ 7g 6s⁵ 6m² 7f 6m⁶ 7m⁴ 6g⁵ 5f* 6g 5g 5s 1989 5.8h² 6f⁵ 5f 5g 5f* 5m⁵ 5f³ 5f³
5.8f 5.3f a6g⁶ a6g* a7g⁵] tall, leggy, lengthy gelding: quite modest handicapper:
won at Chepstow in July and Lingfield in December: effective at 5f and 6f: unsuited
by soft going and goes well on firm: sometimes sweats and gets on toes: has given
trouble at stalls: often taken down early nowadays: often hangs: not genuine. *P.
Mitchell.*

MY PATRICIA 4 b.f. My Dad Tom (USA) 109–Sallachy (Hot Spark 126) [1988 6f —
6g 6g⁶ 7m⁵ 6f⁵ 6g 1989 6h⁶ 8.3g] leggy, sparely-made filly: little form, including in
sellers, since 2 yrs: stays 6f: acts on any going: blinkered once: wore small bandages
final outing. *A. R. Davison.*

MY PRETTY NIECE 3 b.f. Great Nephew 126–Melbourne Miss (Chaparral —
(FR) 128) [1988 NR 1989 12m 10.6g 10g] workmanlike filly: fifth foal: half-sister to
French 1983 2-y-o 1m winner Danse du Norde (by Northfields): dam unraced close

598

relation of Grand Prix de Paris winner Tennyson: backward, no form in maidens and competitive minor event though has shown signs of ability: sold 800 gns Ascot December Sales. *N. A. Gaselee.*

MY RUBY RING   2 b.f. (Apr 15) Blushing Scribe (USA) 107–Bells of St Martin 89   — (Martinmas 128) [1989 6d 6g] leggy filly: third foal: half-sister to 1m and 8.3f seller winner My Diamond Ring (by Sparkling Boy): dam 5f winner at 2 yrs: behind in late-season maidens at Newbury (backward, 24 ran) and Leicester. *M. D. I. Usher.*

MY SERENADE (USA)   5 b.m. Sensitive Prince (USA)–Mau Mae (USA)   — (Hawaii) [1988 6g 6s 7g 7f 8f 6f 1989 5f⁶ 8m 6m 6f 5f 7f 8.5f⁵ 7f 9g 12f⁵] small, lengthy, light-framed mare: poor mover: poor performer: probably best at short of 1½m: best on top-of-the-ground: blinkered fifth outing. *P. J. Bevan.*

MY SISTER ELLEN   2 ch.f. (Mar 23) Lyphard (USA) 132–Cat Girl (USA) (Grey   **81 p** Dawn II 132) [1989 7g³] good-bodied filly: has scope: fourth foal: closely related to 1¼m winner Morasco (by The Minstrel): dam good-class winner at up to 1m in USA: long odds on but better for race, 5½ lengths third of 5 to Atoll in minor event at York in October, flashing tail, carrying head awkwardly then one pace last 1½f: should improve. *H. R. A. Cecil.*

MY SPARKLING RING   3 b.c. Sparkling Boy 110–Bells of St Martin 89   — (Martinmas 128) [1988 6g 7f 1989 10s 11.7m 10.1m 8.3m 8.3m³ 8.3d 8f 9f 10f] good-bodied colt: third in seller in July: showed little otherwise: should prove best at up to 1m: visored last 5 starts: has sometimes looked none too keen. *M. D. I. Usher.*

MY SPORTING LADY   3 b.f. My Dad Tom (USA) 109–Ardtully Lass 64 (Cavo   **51** Doro 124) [1988 5d⁴ 5g 1989 5s³ 6m 5h 8f 7h] small, leggy filly: plating-class maiden: easily best effort on reappearance: ran in sellers last 2 starts, final one in June: should stay beyond 5f: possibly needs a soft surface: has joined Miss E. Sneyd. *R. Simpson.*

MYSTERIES (USA)   3 b.f. Seattle Slew (USA)–Phydilla (FR) 126 (Lyphard **111** (USA) 132) [1988 7s 1989 8s² 10.5f³ 10d] lengthy, good-quartered filly: useful form in May in maiden (beaten head) at Kempton and Musidora Stakes (3½ lengths behind Snow Bride, not striding out with much freedom) at York: second favourite, took strong hold and led 7f in Newbury maiden over 5 months later: a keen, active filly who will be suited by return to shorter. *B. W. Hills.*

MYSTERIOUS GENT   2 ch.c. (May 6) Superlative 118–Lady Ever-So-Sure 80   **46** (Malicious) [1989 5m 6f⁶ 6g 6m 8.5f³] sturdy, close-coupled colt: first foal: dam won from 6f to 1½m, mostly in sellers: moderate plater: better suited by 8.5f than shorter: has run well for 7-lb claimer: sold 2,600 gns Doncaster October Sales. *J. Etherington.*

MYSTERY BAND (USA)   3 b.c. Dixieland Band (USA)–Lindaria (USA) (Sea   **74** Bird II 145) [1988 7m 7g 7g³ 1989 8g³ 12g 8g² 10f⁵ 10m 8g] big, angular colt: modest maiden: below form at Newmarket last 2 outings: suited by 1¼m: acts on firm ground: lost near-eye after third start and wore eyeshield afterwards. *G. A. Huffer.*

MYSTERY MUSIC   3 b.f. Bustino 136–Secret Song 83 (Tudor Melody 129)   **87** [1988 NR 1989 8m⁶ 12.2f³ 10f⁴ 8m* 8m* 8s] lengthy, sparely-made, medium-sized filly: sister to useful 1¼m winner Humming and half-sister to 3 winners, including very useful but temperamental 1977 2-y-o 6f winner Royal Harmony (by Sun Prince): dam sprinter: won handicap at Kempton and minor event (11/10 on, ridden by 7-lb claimer) at Brighton in September: saddle slipped second outing: best form at 1m: acts on top-of-the-ground, possibly unsuited by soft: sold 28,000 gns Newmarket December Sales. *L. M. Cumani.*

MYSTICAL GUEST   3 b.g. Be My Guest (USA) 126–Saygood (USA) (Royal   **78** Ascot) [1988 NR 1989 10.1g⁶ 14d⁴ 12.5g² 10m 10.6s 12.2g³ a10g²] 750,000 francs (approx £75,260) Y: lengthy, angular gelding: half-brother to smart French 1¼m winner Loyal Double (by Nodouble) and US Grade 2 9.5f winner Scythian Gold (by Selari): dam minor 6f winner: fair maiden: stays 1¾m: acts on a soft surface: took keen hold in blinkers and well beaten fourth outing: has run creditably for apprentice but hung left second and third starts: trained until after then by A. Stewart: possibly not genuine: gelded after final start. *N. A. Callaghan.*

MYSTICAL LADY   2 ch.f. (Mar 5) Sagaro 133–L'Angelo di Carlo 46 (Record   **37** Token 128) [1989 5g 5.3g⁴ 5g⁴ 5m⁶ 6f] 980Y: leggy filly: second foal: half-sister to an animal of little account: dam stayed 7f: little worthwhile form, including in sellers: trained first 4 starts by W. Turner. *Miss L. Bower.*

MYSTIC BID   2 br.c. (May 6) Auction Ring (USA) 123–Relic Spirit (Relic) [1989   **38** 6f 5f⁴ 6g] 20,000F, 18,500Y: brother to fairly useful 1983 Irish 2-y-o 5f winner

Malang-Lou and half-brother to several other winners, including fair 6f to 1m performer African Spirit (by African Sky): dam second 4 times over sprint distances in Ireland: poor form in maidens. *J. Etherington.*

MYSTIC MONKEY 4 ch.g. Royal Match 117–Thorganby Melody (Highland Melody 112) [1988 8m 1989 12h 10.1m a10g] workmanlike gelding: of little account and seems temperamental: pulled up after ducking out second outing: trained until after then by A. Barrow. *T. B. Hallett.* — §

MY STYLE 2 ch.c. (Feb 19) Kings Lake (USA) 133–Miss Mulaz (FR) 114 (Luthier 126) [1989 8d⁶ 8g² 9g² 9m²] third foal: half-brother to French 1¼m and 10.5f winner Morning Moon (by Hello Gorgeous) and French 3-y-o maiden Persiflage (by Persepolis): dam French 1½m winner, is half-sister to very useful French middle-distance winner Mulaz Palace: useful maiden: runner-up to Dr Somerville on last 2 starts, on final one beaten 5 lengths in 4-runner Prix de Conde at Longchamp in October: will stay 1½m: best form on a sound surface. *J. de Roualle, France.* 98

MY SWAN SONG 4 b.g. Soul Singer 97–Palmaria (Be Friendly 130) [1988 6v⁶ 7d 7d 8.2m 6g 10m 10m 10s 10d 12g³ 1989 10d² 12.5g* 12g 10f 12f⁵ 12.5f 12m a11g⁶] close-coupled gelding: poor mover: won claiming event at Wolverhampton in May: best effort after on fifth outing, first for over 3 months: stays 12.5f: seems to act on any going: inconsistent. *J. P. Smith.* 52

MY SWEET 2 ch.f. (Apr 5) Sweet Monday 122–Endango (Gay Fandango (USA) 132) [1989 6m] fourth foal: dam never ran: 20/1, well beaten in 19-runner seller at Newcastle in August: sold 680 gns Doncaster November Sales. *Miss L. C. Siddall.* —

MY TAI-PAN 2 b.c. (May 26) King of Clubs 124–Orchestration 116 (Welsh Pageant 132) [1989 6g² 7m⁶ 8m 7g] 7,000F: finely-made, angular colt: third foal: half-brother to a winner in Norway: dam won Coronation Stakes: plating-class maiden: best effort first 2 starts: bred to stay at least 1m. *R. Hollinshead.* 61

MYTASKI 3 b.c. Niniski (USA) 125–Mytinia 94 (Bustino 136) [1988 7g 7m⁴ 8d² 1989 10m³ 12f² 12g 14m³] lengthy colt: fair maiden: stays 13⁄4m: acts on firm going: took keen hold and found little third outing: lacks turn of foot. *Major W. R. Hern.* 87

MYTHYAAR (USA) 3 b.f. Nureyev (USA) 131–Elect (USA) 113 (Vaguely Noble 140) [1988 6g* 1989 7g 8f⁶ 7f³] tall, rather sparely-made, lengthy filly: long odds on, impressive winner of maiden at Doncaster as 2-y-o: prominent in betting for 1000 Guineas over the winter but didn't fulfil promise in Nell Gwyn Stakes (co-favourite, pulled hard) at Newmarket, listed race (set strong pace 5f) at Sandown and minor event at Kempton: bred to stay 1m but has looked very keen. *M. R. Stoute.* —

MY TOPIC 3 br.f. Mansingh (USA) 120–Well Connected (Bold And Free 118) [1988 5d* 6g⁴ 5m³ 5m⁶ 5d⁶ 5f² 5f³ 5g³ 6s⁴ 5g* 6f⁴ 1989 6v* 5d 6g 6g 6g 6g³ 6s] leggy filly: useful plater: won at Ayr (no bid) in April, rallying well: returned to selling company, easily best other effort when fair third at Hamilton: suited by 6f: probably acts on any going: blinkered 5 times as 2-y-o. *J. Berry.* 58

MY-UGLY-DUCKLING 2 ch.g. (Mar 25) Longleat (USA) 109–Snow Goose (Santa Claus 133) [1989 7m 8m 9g 8g] 3,200Y: leggy, rather sparely-made gelding: half-brother to 3-y-o Old Mother Goose (by Jalmood) and several winners, including quite useful 1983 2-y-o 7f winner Scaldante (by Hotfoot): dam never ran: plating-class form in varied events, including a Newmarket seller: seems to stay 9f: gelded after final start. *C. N. Allen.* 55

MY VALENTINE CARD (USA) 3 ch.f. Forli (ARG)–Super Valentine (USA) (Super Concorde (USA) 128) [1988 6d 7g⁵ 7m⁵ 1989 8g 10f⁶ 8h 8f⁶ 8m] leggy, rather angular filly: moderate mover: poor maiden: blinkered, reluctant to race early final outing: probably stays 1¼m: acts on firm going: sweating badly fourth start (not discredited): pulls hard: changed hands 3,000 gns Doncaster September Sales: one to treat with caution. *S. G. Norton.* — §

MYVERYGOODFRIEND 2 b.g. (Mar 25) Swing Easy (USA) 126–Darymoss 79 (Ballymoss 136) [1989 5f³ 5m⁴ 6m 7m⁴ 6m²] angular, close-coupled gelding: carries condition: third foal: dam maiden, best at up to 1m: modest maiden: stays 7f. *Andrew Turnell.* 71

MZEFF 3 br.g. Ahonoora 122–Silk Lady 97 (Tribal Chief 125) [1988 5f³ 6s 6d 1989 6d⁴ 5s 6g⁴ᵈⁱˢ 6f⁴ 5h² 5f* 6m* 5f* 5f² 6h⁶ 5g 5m⁴ 5m³] sturdy gelding: moderate mover: fair performer: won claimers at Lingfield and Haydock and handicap at Hamilton in the summer: speedy and probably suited by 5f: acts on hard ground: blinkered: sold to race in Saudi Arabia 25,000 gns Newmarket Autumn Sales. *D. R. C. Elsworth.* 84

N

NAATELL (USA) 6 b. or br.g. Cox's Ridge (USA)–Lisanninga (Whodunit) [1988 **66**
10d 10g* 10.2d* 10m* 10.5g 10m⁴ 10m⁶ 10m 10g 1989 10s⁶ 10.2g 10f* 10h³ 10f⁶ 10h
10f a10g] tall, angular, sparely-made gelding: has been hobdayed: quite modest
handicapper: won at Brighton in May: ran as though something amiss sixth outing,
and ran moderately last 2: suited by 1¼m: acts on hard going and a soft surface: has
won when sweating: trained until after seventh outing by S. Dow: none too
consistent. *N. R. Mitchell.*

NABEEL DANCER (USA) 4 b.c. Northern Dancer–Prayers'n Promises **120**
(USA) (Foolish Pleasure (USA)) [1988 NR 1989 6s* 7.2s 6f³ 5g⁴ 6f² 5f⁶ 6g²
6g³ 6m⁴ 5g³ 6s]
   Nabeel Dancer joined the ranks of the season's leading sprinters almost
out of the blue. Before mid-April he'd been restricted to just one race, a minor
event at Nottingham in September 1987 when he finished fifth of nineteen, a
well-backed favourite. His absence from the track as a three-year-old had
been due to an injury to a stifle. If he retained any ability he was favoured by
the conditions of the Thirsk Hall EBF Stakes on his reappearance, for he
received weight from all bar two of his twelve opponents. He set a modest
gallop and ran on strongly despite hanging left to beat Homo Sapien (gave 19
lb) by three lengths. A resounding defeat in a seven-furlong listed event at
Haydock two weeks later brought a swift end to attempts to make a miler of
him, and thereafter, from May through to October, he ran in pattern sprints,
consistently giving a good account of himself save for one below-par effort in
Ireland. Nabeel Dancer first served notice that he was a force to be reckoned
with in the best company when close up behind Indian Ridge and Gallic
League in the Duke of York Stakes having shown excellent speed, racing
alone, down the centre of the course. After proving himself equally effective
at the minimum trip when fourth to Viva Zapata in the Prix du Gros-Chene at
Chantilly, he took on Danehill—brought back to six furlongs after reaching
the frame in the Two Thousand Guineas and Irish Two Thousand Guineas
—in the Cork And Orrery Stakes at Royal Ascot. He was soon able to take up
his customary front-running role and only Danehill threw down an effective
challenge, drawing clear in the final furlong for a comfortable three-length
success. In the second half of the year Nabeel Dancer came up against Silver
Fling on three occasions. Each time he finished behind her; in the King
George Stakes at Goodwood (for which Nabeel Dancer went off a well-
supported favourite) they were fourth and sixth, whilst in the Krug Diadem
Stakes at Ascot they filled the minor placings behind Chummy's Favourite,
only for Nabeel Dancer to be demoted a place for causing interference to both
Silver Fling and Dancing Dissident when hanging left two furlongs out. In the
Ciga Prix de l'Abbaye de Longchamp two lengths covered the first seven
home, with Silver Fling getting up in the last strides to beat Zadracarta by a
short head and Nabeel Dancer a head. Though defeated, Nabeel Dancer came
out the best horse in the race at the weights and, in handicapping terms, put
up his best performance of the year. Nabeel Dancer ran once more, in the
Laurel Dash won by Cricket Ball. Racing on soft ground for the first time since
the spring, he faded out of contention in the last furlong and beat only three of
the fourteen runners across the line.
   While most of Northern Dancer's good horses have possessed a turn of
speed he's not renowned as a sire of sprinters. The average distance of races
won in Britain and Ireland at three years and upwards by his progeny in the
last fifteen years is just over nine furlongs. In the same period only six of his
progeny aged three and above have won at five or six furlongs but among them
is Ajdal, brought back to sprinting after being beaten in the Guineas and the
Derby; Music And Dance and Pilgrim were useful winners in Ireland, while
Golden Oriole and Nadia Nerina were successful in lesser company. Nabeel
Dancer is a natural sprinter, free running but by no means so headstrong as
his five-year-old close relation Stormy Praise (by Storm Bird), still a maiden
after nineteen attempts. Their dam's first foal (also by Storm Bird) ran only
twice in Ireland. Prayers 'n Promises won two Grade 1 events as a two-
year-old, the six-furlong Spinaway Stakes at Saratoga and seven-furlong

Matron Stakes at Belmont Park. She's a daughter of the unraced Luiana and a half-sister to Little Current, champion three-year-old colt of 1974 when he won the Preakness Stakes and Belmont Stakes. Luiana is a half-sister to Chateaugay, champion three-year-old of 1963 when the winner of the Kentucky Derby and the Belmont Stakes, and to champion handicap mare Primonetta, dam of the major stakes winner Cum Laude Laurie.

Nabeel Dancer (USA) (b.c. 1985)	Northern Dancer (b 1961)	Nearctic (br 1954)	Nearco	Lady Angela
		Natalma (b 1957)	Native Dancer	Almahmoud
	Prayers'n Promises (USA) (b 1978)	Foolish Pleasure (b 1972)	What A Pleasure	Fool-Me-Not
		Luiana (ch 1963)	My Babu	Banquet Bell

Nabeel Dancer, a lengthy, good sort who shows plenty of knee action, has won on soft ground, but has shown easily his best form on a sound surface. For much of the season he was green and often coltish in the paddock; he should mature further as a five-year-old and there must be a good chance that he'll win a pattern race over sprint distances. It almost goes without saying that he's tough, genuine and consistent. *A. A. Scott.*

NABEEL (USA) 3 ch.c. Nodouble (USA)–Abeer (USA) 115 (Dewan (USA)) **75** [1988 NR 1989 6g 7f⁵ 7h*] big, lengthy colt: half-brother to 3 winners, including 1½m winner Armourer (by Busted) and winning sprinter In Fact (by Known Fact):

dam won 3 races over 5f at 2 yrs, including Queen Mary and Flying Childers Stakes: won minor event at Brighton in June, leading 2f out and holding on by a head: unlikely to stay beyond 7f: sold 20,000 gns Newmarket July Sales. *J. Tree.*

NACONA 3 b.c. Noalto 120–Party Girl 96 (Pardao 120) [1988 8m 8m 1989 9f 10m 7m 6m⁴ 7g] big, rather leggy colt: has a round action: staying-on fourth in apprentice seller at Windsor in July, only form: should be suited by 7f or 1m. *R. Hannon.* **50**

NAD ELSHIBA (USA) 3 b.c. Nijinsky's Secret (USA) 113–Terska (USA) (Vaguely Noble 140) [1988 8m³ 1989 12g² 12d 14g⁴] rangy colt: fair maiden: second to Icelander at Doncaster in May, leading until 1½f out: off course 4½ months then set pace in Prix Niel at Longchamp and again made most in minor event at Redcar: appears suited by 1½m. *Major W. R. Hern.* **87**

NADIAD 3 b.c. Darshaan 133–Naveen (Sir Gaylord) [1988 NR 1989 10g⁶ 11fʷᵒ 10m² 12m 10g⁴] big, workmanlike colt: sixth living foal: half-brother to smart 1¼m to 1½m winner Nayrizi (by Riverman), 1½m winner Narnawa (by Blushing Groom) and a winner in USA: dam won over 12.5f in France: walked over in maiden at Redcar in August: easily best effort after when beaten short head in minor event at Ripon, not handling bends: should stay 1½m: acts on top-of-the-ground: sold 12,500 gns Newmarket Autumn Sales. *L. M. Cumani.* **99 ?**

NADINA 3 b.f. Shirley Heights 130–Nadia Nerina (CAN) 82 (Northern Dancer) [1988 8d⁴ 1989 10d³ 10.5s* 10.5m² 10.5g⁵ 10g² 10d 10.5s] first foal: dam, 3-y-o 6f winner, is sister to top 1982 Irish 2-y-o Danzatore and closely related to useful but disappointing London Bells: won maiden at Saint-Cloud in May: ran in pattern company after, beaten nose by Sudaka in Prix Cleopatre at Saint-Cloud and 1½ lengths by Sierra Roberta in Prix de la Nonette at Longchamp: below form at Maisons-Laffitte and Saint-Cloud last 2 outings: stays 10.5f: yet to race on very firm going, probably acts on any other. *A. Fabre, France.* **116**

NAFHAAT (USA) 2 ch.f. (May 21) Roberto (USA) 131–Distant Horizon (USA) (Exclusive Native (USA)) [1989 7s²] $550,000Y: second foal: dam lightly-raced sister to Sisterhood, a good winner at up to 1¼m, and half-sister to very smart French middle-distance filly Sweet Rhapsody: 7/1, 3 lengths second of 11, clear, to Sajjaya in maiden at Ayr in September, keeping on well: should improve. *H. Thomson Jones.* **77 p**

NAFPLION 4 b.f. Young Generation 129–Time For Thought 75 (Crooner 119) [1988 7g³ 8d³ 7g 8d 1989 8d 8m 10.6g 8.5g 12.2m⁶ a11g] rather leggy, workmanlike filly: poor maiden: soundly beaten in varied events in 1989: blinkered fifth outing. *R. E. Peacock.* **—**

NAFUAT 5 b.g. Taufan (USA) 119–Jerusalem (Palestine 133) [1988 8m 6g 7g⁶ 7g² 7f⁴ 7s⁴ 7d 1989 7d 6m⁴ 7g a7g a7g a6g⁶] rather leggy, sparely-made gelding: moderate mover: fairly useful handicapper at his best, but has deteriorated: hung right and didn't look keen third outing: stays 7f: ideally suited by an easy surface: sometimes blinkered: unenthusiastic. *J. W. Watts.* **71 §**

NAFZAWA (USA) 2 ch.f. (Apr 29) Green Dancer (USA) 132–Nawazish (Run The Gantlet (USA)) [1989 7f² 7.3v³] leggy, rather angular filly: has scope: fourth foal: half-sister to 3-y-o 1¼m winner Nangarar (by Topsider), 1¼m winner Najidiya (by Riverman) and temperamental Nazirzad (by Blushing Groom): dam, useful French 6f to 1½m winner, from family of Shergar: modest form in maiden at Leicester (not handling descent) and listed race at Newbury (hard ridden 3f out) in October: will stay 1¼m. *M. R. Stoute.* **75**

NAGEM 6 b.m. Headin' Up–Eleonora 70 (Falcon 131) [1988 5g 5v² 6m* 6f* 6d 5m⁵ 6s⁶ 6d 6g 5f⁶ 6m 1989 6s 5f 6f⁶ 6m⁴ 5d 6m³ 7g] strong, lengthy mare: poor mover: quite modest handicapper: generally well below her best since winning twice early as 5-y-o: taken down early and unruly leaving paddock, ran easily best race in 1989 when third at Chester in September: suited by 6f or stiff 5f: acts on any going: blinkered last 2 outings: suitable mount for apprentice: often edgy: has run tubed, but not last 3 starts. *L. J. Barratt.* **55**

NAHAR 4 b. or br.c. Known Fact (USA) 135–Muznah 92 (Royal And Regal (USA)) [1988 7d 7g³ 8f³ 8m⁶ 10s 1989 10g 12s] robust, good-bodied colt: fair maiden at his best: well beaten in spring handicaps as 4-y-o: stays 1m: acts on firm going: fairly useful over hurdles, but has looked ungenuine. *S. Dow.* **—**

NAHILAH 3 b.f. Habitat 134–House Tie (Be Friendly 130) [1988 NR 1989 7f 7m* 8m] 92,000Y: strong, lengthy filly: sixth foal: half-sister to 4 winners, including fairly useful sprinter Bag O'Rhythm (by Be My Guest) and useful Irish 6f and 1m winner Tea House (by Sassafras): dam, Irish 1m winner, is daughter of high-class **78**

2-y-o Mesopotamia: led close home in minor event at Kempton in June: not discredited facing stiff task in similar contest month later: stayed 1m: visits Darshaan. *P. T. Walwyn.*

NAIL DON 4 b.g. Don 128–Vivungi (USA) (Exbury 138) [1988 8g 9g* 8m³ 8.5m 8m³ 10d⁴ 10g³ 8g² 8g 10g 10d 1989 8d⁴] compact gelding: fairly useful winner as 3-y-o: creditable fourth of 21, staying on strongly, in quite valuable handicap at Newbury in April: should prove as effective at 1¼m as at 1m: acts on top-of-the-ground and soft going: suited by forcing tactics. *N. Henderson.*   **89**

NAILEM 2 b.c. (Jan 19) Absalom 128–La Reine de France (Queen's Hussar 124) [1989 5s⁵ 5m⁵ 5m⁴ 5f* 5m⁴ 5f⁵ 6m³] 15,000Y: sturdy colt: carries condition: has a roundish action: third foal: half-brother to modest 1988 2-y-o 5f winner Yuno When (by Sayf El Arab) and 1987 2-y-o 6f winner Rectory Maid (by Tina's Pet): dam never ran: modest performer: won 5-runner nursery at Folkestone in July by ½ length: well below best in seller final start: best form at 5f: acts on firm going. *J. W. Payne.*   **71**

NAJAT 2 b.f. (Mar 7) Tender King 123–Brave Ivy 68 (Decoy Boy 129) [1989 5f⁴ 5f* 5f⁶ 5g 5m] 24,000F, IR 17,000Y: sparely-made filly: good walker: second foal: dam placed here over 5f at 2 yrs later won in Italy: long odds on, very easy winner of 2-runner maiden event at Redcar in July: never able to challenge off modest mark in nurseries afterwards. *Dr J. D. Scargill.*   **49**

NAKORA BISTRAYA (USA) 2 b.f. (Feb 22) Robellino (USA) 127–Calypsa (USA) 83 (The Minstrel (CAN) 135) [1989 6m 8g⁵] 10,500Y: close-coupled filly: has a markedly round action: first foal: dam, 2-y-o 7f winner from 3 starts, is closely related to 2 more-than-useful winners: still backward, under 7 lengths fifth of 16, one pace last 2f, to Bawbee in maiden at Leicester in November, better effort: will be suited by 1¼m. *G. A. Pritchard-Gordon.*   **61**

NA LA GIRI 3 b.c. Nishapour (FR) 125–Les Sylphides (FR) (Kashmir II 125) [1988 5d⁶ 5m 7d 1989 10d³ 10s 10m 8f* 8m 8h² 7m 9f² 10g 8f⁵ 10h 11.7g 8g] leggy colt: moderate mover: useful plater: well backed, won at Brighton (no bid) in May: stays 1¼m: acts on firm going and a soft surface: tends to pull, and has worn severe bridle: rather inconsistent: winning selling hurdler. *R. Simpson.*   **60**

NAMASAL (FR) 3 b.f. Gay Mecene (USA) 128–Salmana (FR) (Manado 130) [1988 6g 1989 8s 11.3f 12g 12.5f⁴ 16f] sparely-made filly: little worthwhile form: stays 1½m: trained on reappearance by W. Jarvis. *Dr J. D. Scargill.*   **—**

NAMEDAY 2 gr.c. (Apr 7) Nicholas Bill 125–Workaday 85 (Workboy 123) [1989 6g 5g a6g] rather leggy colt: has a very round action: first foal: dam 5f to 7f winner: backward, well beaten in maidens and a claimer. *A. Smith.*   **—**

NANARCH (USA) 5 ch.g. Dara Monarch 128–Natuschka (Authi 123) [1988 9g⁶ 16d 10m³ 16d* 12m* 11g² 16s 16s² 1989 14g* 12f* 22.2f 12g³ 16g⁵ 16s* 16d⁵] workmanlike Irish gelding: moderate walker: second foal: half-brother to Irish 3-y-o 1¾m winner Newton John (by Head For Heights): dam won from 9f to 2m in Ireland: won handicaps at Leopardstown in May and Navan (odds on) in June and listed EBF Giolla Mear Race at the Curragh in October: well-beaten seventh of 8 in Queen Alexandra Stakes at Royal Ascot: stays 2m: acts on any going: has won for apprentice. *K. Prendergast, Ireland.*   **91**

NANCY ARDROSS 3 b.f. Ardross 134–Classy Nancy (USA) (Cutlass (USA)) [1988 7f 8m 1989 12g 16.2m⁶ 15g] lengthy, sparely-made filly: has a free, rather round action: little worthwhile form in maidens and handicaps: should prove best at short of 2m. *J. Hetherton.*   **—**

NANGARAR (USA) 3 b.c. Topsider (USA)–Nawazish (Run The Gantlet (USA)) [1988 NR 1989 8m² 10f* 10f*] rangy, angular colt: third foal: half-brother to temperamental Nazirzad (by Blushing Groom) and 1¼m winner Najidiya (by Riverman): dam, useful French 6f to 1½m winner, from family of Shergar: odds on, won maiden at Redcar and minor event at Nottingham in the summer: will stay 1½m: fairly useful. *M. R. Stoute.*   **87**

NANNY MOORE 2 b.f. (Jan 11) Mansingh (USA) 120–Irish Corn (Oats 126) [1989 5f⁵ 6f 5h⁶] small, workmanlike filly: moderate mover: first foal: dam of little account on flat also poor selling handicapper over jumps: well beaten in maidens. *L. G. Cottrell.*   **—**

NAP MAJESTICA 6 ch.g. Captain James 123–Semper Fi (Above Suspicion 127) [1988 8d 8d 8m⁵ 10m 10g* 10f 10m 10m 12m 1989 10g] neat gelding: poor mover: no form on flat since winning handicap at Sandown in May, 1988: best at 1m to 1¼m: suited by a sound surface: usually wears bandages: inconsistent. *Mrs N. Macauley.*   **—**

NARWALA   2 b.f. (Mar 24) Darshaan 133–Noufiyla 68 (Top Ville 129) [1989 7g²]   **88 p**
quite attractive filly: first foal: dam middle-distance maiden: 15/2, ½-length second
of 24, keeping on strongly, to Sardegna in maiden at Newmarket in November,
flashing tail in closing stages: will be suited by 1m + : sure to improve, and win a
race. *L. M. Cumani.*

NASHID   4 b.g. Be My Guest (USA) 126–Whispering Sands (Kalamoun 129) [1988   **99**
10g² 11.7f* 14m⁵ 13s³ 1989 11.7m* 13.3m* 14m* 12m 16g⁵] good-topped, quite
attractive gelding: won handicaps at Windsor in May, Newbury in June and York
(took keen hold) in September: below form in £71,300 handicap at Ascot (on toes,
badly hampered early) and listed event at Newmarket (co-favourite, weakened final
2f) last 2 outings: suited by 1¾m: acts on any going: has given trouble in preliminaries: quite useful. *A. C. Stewart.*

NASHMI   3 ch.c. Persian Bold 123–Nothing On (St Chad 120) [1988 NR 1989 8g   **68**
9f² 8m³ 7m] 14,000Y: big, workmanlike colt: sixth foal: half-brother to useful
middle-distance performer Rivellino and fairly useful 1½m winner Amal Naji (both
by Rheingold), later a winner in USA: dam unraced half-sister to 1000 Guineas
winner Nocturnal Spree: quite modest form when placed in minor event (well
beaten behind Torjoun) and claimer (setting good pace) in the spring: favourite, ran
poorly in Epsom claimer final start: stays 9f. *G. A. Huffer.*

NASHWAN (USA)   3 ch.c. Blushing Groom (FR) 131–Height of Fashion **135**
(FR) 124 (Bustino 136) [1988 7g* 8d* 1989 8m* 12g* 10g* 12m* 12d³]
    In the spring and summer the name Nashwan blazed like a comet
through the British racing scene in a glorious undefeated run that took in the
Two Thousand Guineas, the Derby, the Eclipse and the King George VI and
Queen Elizabeth Stakes. But on its return in the autumn it shone only briefly
before disappearing, no doubt leaving some of those observers who in the
summer had praised Nashwan to the skies with a sense of let down. But to
begin at the beginning . . .
    Before he ran in the General Accident Two Thousand Guineas Nashwan
had never contested a pattern race. As a two-year-old he had beaten a big field
of maidens at Newbury on his debut and followed up with a comfortable
four-length success in the Red Oaks Autumn Stakes, a listed event at Ascot in
October; he showed he had the makings of a good horse and looked set for a
rewarding second season, but his stable appeared to have more realistic
classic prospects in the Three Chimneys Dewhurst dead-heater Prince of
Dance and the William Hill Futurity winner Al Hareb. Odds of 40/1 were
available about Nashwan for the Guineas a month before the race, a slight
training set-back in January having ruled out any chance of his being ready to
reappear in one of the Guineas trials. However, Nashwan's form in home
gallops in the spring decided his connections to make a Two Thousand
Guineas challenge without a previous run—at one time it had been on the
cards that Nashwan would miss Newmarket and wait for one of the recognised
Derby trials. After news of Nashwan's sparkling work was divulged he
became all the rage for the Guineas and virtually monopolised the ante-post
betting in the week before the race, being backed down to 3/1 favourite on the
day. The horses with the best public form in the fourteen-strong Guineas field
were the O'Brien-trained Saratogan, a close third in the Dewhurst and winner
of both his races in Ireland during the current season, and the unbeaten
Shaadi who had won the Charles Heidsieck Champagne Craven Stakes at
Newmarket on his reappearance. Saratogan had been deposed as ante-post
favourite by Shaadi after his victory in the Craven, a race which had attracted
the Two Thousand Guineas winner in each of the previous four years—and in
which, incidentally, Al Hareb trailed in last (he wasn't seen out again).
Saratogan and Shaadi (easy in the market in the week of the race) started
second and third favourite, at 7/2 and 5/1 respectively, with the Ladbroke
European Free Handicap winner Danehill and the Singer and Friedlander
Greenham winner Zayyani (both 9/1) and the Craven runner-up Exbourne
(10/1) next in the betting. Nashwan had by this time displaced his stable-
companion Prince of Dance—successful in the Newmarket Stakes on his
reappearance the day before the Guineas—at the head of the ante-post
market on the Ever Ready Derby, disputing favouritism with Pirate Army who
had been impressive when landing the odds in the same graduation event at

Sandown won by his stable's 1988 Derby winner Kahyasi. Nashwan was down to 2/1 clear favourite for the Epsom classic after a decisive victory at Newmarket; close up from the start in a strongly-run race he took command over two furlongs out and kept on up the hill to win by a length and a half and a length from Exbourne and Danehill, with Markofdistinction a neck away in fourth; Saratogan and Shaadi—with whom there seemed something amiss—finished well down the field. The prevailing firm surface and the end-to-end gallop resulted in Nashwan's recording the fastest time— 1m 36.44sec—in a Two Thousand Guineas since electrical timing was introduced in the 'fifties; however, the *time value* of Nashwan's performance—he recorded a timefigure of 1.10 fast—suggested that Nashwan was nothing out of the ordinary as Guineas winners go. The fastest timefigure recorded in the Two Thousand Guineas in the 'eighties was 1.54 fast by El Gran Senor in 1984, a performance—translated into time ratings— 11 lb better than Nashwan's.

No winner of the Two Thousand Guineas had gone on to take the Derby since Nijinsky, but few in the interim had looked so well equipped for success at Epsom. The oft-stated view that the Derby has been won 'by horses that never truly stayed a mile and a half' is a myth, and no horse can win it, even when the going is firm, unless it is able to stay a mile and a half at racing pace. One of the first things, therefore, to check about any Derby candidate is: will it stay the trip? The Derby is run fairly early in the season and for most of the runners it is their first test over a mile and a half. For example, none of the five post-war Two Thousand Guineas successful in the Derby before Nashwan ran between Newmarket and Epsom. It is to the pedigree that one usually has to look for evidence of stamina in Derby candidates. Twenty-one of the thirty Derby winners before Nashwan were sired by a stallion who had won over at least a mile and a half or were out of a dam who had been successful at the Derby trip or further. There was a good measure of certainty on pedigree that Nashwan would possess the necessary stamina. His sire the top-class miler Blushing Groom was found out by the trip when favourite for the Derby in 1977 but he finished clear third to The Minstrel and Hot Grove and at stud has been more of an influence for stamina than might have been predicted after his racing career; the average distance of races won at three years and upwards by his progeny in Britain and Ireland is ten furlongs. Nashwan's dam the stoutly-bred Height of Fashion was a good-class racemare who stayed a mile and a half well and would have been seen to advantage over longer distances. Nashwan's older half-brothers Alwasmi and Unfuwain—

General Accident Two Thousand Guineas, Newmarket—Nashwan lives up to his reputation; behind, right to left, come Exbourne, Danehill and Markofdistinction

Ever Ready Derby, Epsom—a most decisive winner. Terimon runs on strongly for second, ahead of Cacoethes (rails) and Ile de Nisky (left)

both by Northern Dancer, less of an influence for stamina than Blushing Groom—had proved to be suited by a mile and a half. Nashwan's trainer and rider expressed full confidence after the Two Thousand Guineas that Nashwan would stay the Derby distance—and would handle Epsom's bends and pronounced downhill gradients. The Epsom course tends to favour the handy, medium-sized, quicker-actioned horse and there were some who thought the big, rangy, long-striding Nashwan might be inconvenienced. But the important consideration with a Derby horse is not size, but action. Plenty of horses of size and substance have won the Derby: Pinza, Crepello, Nijinsky, Morston, Snow Knight, Henbit, Golden Fleece, Teenoso and Slip Anchor found being of above-average size no bar to Derby success. Nashwan's freedom of action and elasticity of stride betokened a horse likely to act well at Epsom and his trainer, asked after the Guineas about whether Nashwan would handle Epsom, had no reservations: 'I would think you could ride him down the side of a house'.

There wasn't the customary large field for the Ever Ready Derby—Nashwan had only eleven opponents—and with the Chester Vase winner Old Vic tackling the Prix du Jockey-Club Lancia the main danger to Nashwan appeared to be Cacoethes who had trounced Pirate Army in the Calor Derby Trial over the full Derby distance at Lingfield. Nashwan started at 5/4, Cacoethes at 3/1, with Prince of Dance next at 11/2. None of the other contenders had produced a top-class performance in the trials. The William Hill Dante winner Torjoun started at 11/1, the NM Financial Predominate winner Warrshan at 13/1. Cacoethes' pacemaker Polar Run took the field along at a searching gallop until the top of the hill where Torjoun went on from Cacoethes. Nashwan, who had been settled in the middle of the field, improved on the outside when pushed along down the hill and was a close fourth rounding Tattenham Corner behind Torjoun, Cacoethes and Ile de Nisky. Switched towards the inside once straightened out for home Nashwan surged between Torjoun and Ile de Nisky and ranged alongside Cacoethes, who had passed Torjoun easily early in the straight. After a short struggle Nashwan forged ahead entering the final two furlongs and soon had the race in safe keeping. Given three or four backhanders Nashwan opened out in breathtaking style, drawing further and further away inside the final furlong to win by an official margin of five lengths (it was more like six). The 500/1-outsider Terimon, last but one at the top of the hill, came from well behind in the home straight to beat the tiring Cacoethes by two lengths for second place, with Ile de Nisky half a length further away fourth; Torjoun came eighth, Prince of Dance (found shortly afterwards to be suffering from cancer of the spine) tenth, and the disappointing Warrshan eleventh.

Nashwan's victories at Newmarket and Epsom took his trainer's total of English classic wins to fifteen. Dick Hern has now won the Derby three times (Nashwan's victory followed those of Troy and Henbit, all three ridden by Carson), the Oaks three times (Dunfermline, Bireme and Sun Princess), the Two Thousand Guineas twice (Brigadier Gerard was also successful in the race on his reappearance) and the One Thousand Guineas (with Highclere). Hern's finest record is in the St Leger in which he has saddled Hethersett, Provoke, Bustino, Dunfermline, Cut Above and Sun Princess; his St Leger score would have been seven but, in his absence, his assistant Neil Graham was officially credited with Minster Son's victory in 1988. Hern's West Ilsley stables are owned by the Queen and the news in March that Hern had been told that he would have to leave when his lease expired in November provoked a welter of criticism. Hern has been confined to a wheelchair since a hunting accident in 1984 and he underwent major heart surgery in the summer of 1988 which resulted in his assistant taking temporary control for the last part of that season. Few trainers have been so loudly cheered in the winner's circle after a big-race victory than 'The Major' after the Two Thousand Guineas and the Derby. Hern will train in 1991 from a new yard near Lambourn purchased by a company associated with the Al-Maktoum family; in the meantime he has been given a year's extension at West Ilsley where he will share with the new incumbent Hastings-Bass, which will result in Hern's string being halved in 1990. Hern's long-serving stable-jockey Willie Carson is the only jockey still riding with three Derby victories to his name; he was as consistent as ever in the latest season in which he rode one hundred and thirty-seven winners, finishing third in the table. Nashwan's Derby victory continued the highly successful recent run for owner-breeders in the race. Nine of the past twelve winners have carried the colours of their breeders, Nashwan following in the footsteps of Shirley Heights, Troy, Shergar, Teenoso, Slip Anchor, Shahrastani, Reference Point and Kahyasi. The three other winners in the period—Henbit, Golden Fleece and Secreto—were all purchased as yearlings in Kentucky. Nashwan's victory was a milestone for the Al-Maktoum family. The closest any member of the family had previously come to winning England's premier classic was in 1982 when Maktoum Al-Maktoum's Touching Wood came second to Golden Fleece (no other Maktoum-owned horse had made the first three in the Derby). The Al-Maktoums were responsible for forty-nine of the one hundred and sixty-nine original entries for the 1989 Derby.

Recent years have produced an unusual number of wide-margin winners of the Derby. Shergar's ten-length success in 1981 was the most prodigious in the long history of the race (surpassing Manna's official eight-length winning margin in 1925). Troy and Slip Anchor were both seven-length winners in the ten-year period before Nashwan. Nashwan's winning margin and the style of his victory earned widespread praise, partly influenced by his trainer's post-race comment that 'Nashwan could turn out even better than Brigadier Gerard or Troy'. Hern expanded on his remark by explaining that Troy would not have had the speed to win a Guineas and that he wasn't sure how Brigadier Gerard would have fared had he tackled the Derby after winning the Guineas. Hern has a reputation for never saying anything he doesn't mean and he reaffirmed his very high opinion of Nashwan after the end of the season. 'Although he had a shorter career than many of the other top horses I have been fortunate to train, I still regard Nashwan as the best', was Hern's tribute. Old Vic's most impressive seven-length victory in the Prix du Jockey-Club on the Sunday before Epsom seemed almost to be overlooked in the euphoria surrounding Nashwan's triumph. Old Vic's performance was outstanding even by classic standards and we rated the French Derby form more highly than the Epsom Derby form at the time—an assessment regarded in some quarters as outrageous (rather than merely controversial). Truth to tell, the subsequent performances of the beaten horses in both races served only to confirm that the original reaction was the right one. Apart from the winner, only Cacoethes, sixth-placed Gran Alba, ninth-placed Flockton's Own and

Warrshan among the Derby runners won a race of any description afterwards. The two Derby winners were expected to clash in the King George VI and Queen Elizabeth Diamond Stakes at Ascot in July, though Old Vic's connections stressed that their horse would run at Ascot only if they considered the ground soft enough. Old Vic outclassed the opposition in the Budweiser Irish Derby on his next outing, bringing his record for the season to five victories from five races. Nashwan meanwhile headed for his first confrontation with older horses in the Coral-Eclipse Stakes at Sandown, a week after the Irish Derby.

Nashwan's appearance in the six-runner Coral-Eclipse field was a considerable bonus for Sandown and the sponsors. The Irish Derby is a strong counter-attraction for the leaders of the classic generation of middle-distance horses; since prize money for the Irish Derby was boosted in 1962 to make it a race of international importance, the trend has been for the Epsom Derby winner to go on to the Curragh (sixteen have done so). Sir Ivor, Mill Reef and Reference Point were the only previous Derby winners in the same period to have contested the Eclipse in the same season. Sir Ivor and Reference Point failed narrowly, but Nashwan enhanced his record by joining Mill Reef in completing the double. With the opposition including the Dubai Champion Stakes winner Indian Skimmer (unbeaten in her two races in the current season) and the top miler Warning (most impressive in the Queen Anne Stakes at Royal Ascot on his previous outing) the Eclipse was presented as one of the most dramatic and momentous races seen on a British racecourse for a long time. The race was hyped on an embarrassing scale and was widely billed in the Press as 'the race of the century'. Needless to say, that particular billing proved wildly optimistic. Nashwan's main rivals ran below form. Warning was never a factor and Indian Skimmer, running under the handicap of a preparation restricted by the dry conditions, managed only third, running on steadily in the home straight. It was Indian Skimmer's 200/1 stable-companion Opening Verse who provided the only anxious moments for Nashwan's supporters. The front-running Opening Verse turned for home with a good lead—he had an advantage of at least six lengths over Nashwan—and kept on splendidly most of the way up the straight. Nashwan showed a tremendous burst of speed when set alight and wiped out Opening Verse's lead in the space of a furlong to strike the front just under two furlongs out; Carson kept Nashwan right up to the mark all the way to the post for a decisive five-length victory, the tiring Opening Verse holding off Indian Skimmer by a short head, with Warning fifteen lengths back in fourth. In retrospect, the run Nashwan was asked to make early in the straight almost certainly took more out him than if he had been able to make his challenge from a position closer to the leader on the home turn. Nashwan was almost at the end of his tether as he reached the winning post and it's arguable that he'd have been a smoother and more impressive winner had he not been given

Coral-Eclipse Stakes, Sandown—
Nashwan forges clear of Opening Verse and the grey Indian Skimmer

King George VI And Queen Elizabeth Diamond Stakes, Ascot—
Nashwan just holds Cacoethes

such a lot to do. Carson himself said afterwards that he wondered for a moment in the straight 'Oh dear, have I overdone this?'. And reflecting on the Eclipse at the end of the season he added 'I gave that horse (Opening Verse) too far a lead and I asked my horse to make it up in too short a time . . . and he did it but it was a hell of an effort to do so'.

Nashwan had only a fortnight to recover from his race at Sandown before tackling the King George VI and Queen Elizabeth Diamond Stakes at Ascot (the gap between the two races most years is three weeks). Nashwan reportedly lost only 4 lb after the Eclipse and there were no outward signs on King George day that his exertions in the Eclipse had left any mark. He was, perhaps, a little on edge in the preliminaries—he was usually most relaxed before his races—but he strode out majestically on the way to post and, in the absence of the injured Old Vic, started at 9/2 on in a field of seven, in which only Cacoethes—who had won the King Edward VII Stakes at Royal Ascot since running in the Derby—started at odds shorter than 10/1. The other runners were all older horses: the Hanson Coronation Cup and Grand Prix de Saint-Cloud winner Sheriff's Star, the Princess of Wales's Stakes winner Carroll House, the Hardwicke runner-up Top Class, the 1988 Derby Italiano winner Tisserand, and the 500/1-shot Polemos, in the field to make the pace for Nashwan. Polemos set a very steady gallop by King George standards, which connections thought was the best way to ensure that Nashwan had as easy a race as possible, bearing in mind that a full autumn campaign was being planned at this time (it had already been announced that Nashwan was unlikely to stay in training as a four-year-old). Nashwan had a close shave, being pressed by Cacoethes throughout the last two furlongs—and headed for a stride or two—after taking the lead two furlongs out. The two three-year-olds drew clear of the rest as they fought a battle-royal which Nashwan won by a neck; Top Class, who had stepped up the pace when sent to the front approaching the final straight, came third, seven lengths adrift, with Sheriff's Star fourth and Carroll House fifth. Nashwan's cause hadn't been helped by taking a bump from Top Class while challenging for the lead. But any effect on Nashwan's performance was marginal. In extending his unbeaten record to six races Nashwan became the first horse to make a clean sweep of the Two Thousand Guineas, Derby, Eclipse and King George in the same season, an achievement which captured the racing public's imagination and made Nashwan's election as Horse of the Year a virtual certainty. In the end-of-season poll of a panel of journalists, Nashwan received twenty-one of the twenty-nine votes cast, with Old Vic and Carroll House each receiving three and the others going to Zilzal and that grand old handicapper Rapid Lad.

The impression remained after the King George that Nashwan could still be on course to end his career with a record that might better those of some of the best horses of recent times. With Old Vic on the side-lines, Nashwan looked an obvious favourite for the Ciga Prix de l'Arc de Triomphe at

Longchamp in October and there was also talk of his contesting the St Leger in which victory would have made him the first triple crown winner since Nijinsky (excluding Oh So Sharp who landed the fillies' equivalent). Nashwan's trainer was reported after the King George as saying 'As far as I'm concerned the St Leger is the race I want to win. The Arc is only a bonus'. But the owner's support for a St Leger challenge was less enthusiastic and the horse was eventually trained specifically for the Prix de l'Arc, the Prix Niel over the Arc course and distance being chosen as a preliminary race. The decision to by-pass the Leger saddened many of the traditionalists, and even angered some. Tony Morris wrote in the *Racing Post* 'The Arc has a winner every year; the achievement of a Triple Crown is a once-every-thirty-years event . . . the sport, the public, and not least Nashwan himself, are all losers as a result of this unadventurous decision'; Monty Court, editor of *The Sporting Life*, said 'The decision to chicken out of running in the St Leger to try to complete the treasured Triple Crown defies any sporting explanation . . . The Maktoums have proved that in spite of their colossal wealth a sporting challenge has no price against their fear of slightly damaging the market value of a stallion. It's a shame Nashwan's brave heart is not matched by that of his owner'; *The Observer's* correspondent Richard Baerlein commented 'That Nashwan is not being given the chance to complete his Triple Crown, a rarely presented opportunity, is one of the tragedies of the modern approach to racing'. No matter how strong the criticism, however, there could be no argument that it was the right of Nashwan's owner to make his own choice. His motives can only be guessed at, though sources close to the Al-Maktoum family say that the most cynical interpretations of the decision were unwarranted; Sheikh Hamdan, it is said, formed a great sentimental attachment to Nashwan and didn't want to risk defeat in the St Leger, the distance of which in his opinion might have stretched Nashwan's stamina. If the owner was indeed terrified at the thought of Nashwan's being beaten, then the saga which followed Nashwan's flop in the Prix Niel—he managed only third behind Golden Pheasant—was comprehensible. Nashwan looked before the Prix Niel as though he was beginning to lose his summer coat, but blood tests after his mystifying defeat proved satisfactory and he pleased connections in a racecourse gallop at Newbury ten days before the Arc ('His work was super', reported Sheikh Hamdan's racing manager). Regrettably, however, the announcement was made shortly afterwards that Nashwan would not run in the Prix de l'Arc. He would be aimed instead at the Dubai Champion Stakes at Newmarket towards the end of October. Nashwan remained on course for the Champion Stakes until the Tuesday before the race when the stable issued the following statement: 'At stable time tonight Nashwan was found to have a temperature of 102. He will therefore be unable to run in the Champion Stakes at Newmarket on Saturday'. Trainer Hern refused to elaborate on the statement. Nashwan's racing career was over.

For all that his career ended on a low note, Nashwan will be remembered as the horse that did more than any other to make the 1989 flat-racing season for the British racegoer. A big, rangy, deep-girthed colt, he was a giant in stature as well as performance, and a most spectacular mover with a magnificent, ground-devouring, graceful action. As for greatness? Well, Carson described him as 'a great horse to ride, he had a terrific stride and he could turn it on . . . he was the best horse I've ever ridden, without question'. However, it could not be said of Nashwan—as it could possibly be argued for one of Carson's other Derby winners Troy—that he rose above all his contemporaries (which the great champions do—with few exceptions). Judged on racing merit alone, Old Vic had claims to being the best middle-distance horse of the year in Europe. None of Nashwan's four splendid performances matched that of Old Vic in the Prix du Jockey-Club, not the way we read the form at any rate. But it can be said of Nashwan that, although he possibly needed a sound surface to be seen to best advantage, he displayed a degree of versatility all too rare in the modern thoroughbred, winning championship events at a mile, a mile and a quarter and a mile and a half. Perhaps the fact that Nashwan didn't prove himself the mighty performer some of the Press prematurely took him to be will result in less inclination in future to report top-class performances in melodramatic, hyperbolic terms.

Hamdan Al-Maktoum's "Nashwan"

We hope so. Some of the exaggerated claims made for Nashwan in print during the season were an insult to the sense of perspective of the audiences to which they were addressed. Nashwan was a very good horse, but, in our view, it was stretching comparisons to bracket him with the best trained in Britain since the war.

		Red God		Nasrullah
	Blushing Groom (FR)	(ch 1954)		Spring Run
	(ch 1974)	Runaway Bride		Wild Risk
Nashwan (USA)		(b 1962)		Aimee
(ch.c. 1986)		Bustino		Busted
	Height of Fashion (FR)	(b 1971)		Ship Yard
	(b 1979)	Highclere		Queen's Hussar
		(b 1971)		Highlight

Nashwan's pedigree has already been touched on and was extensively covered in the essays on him and Unfuwain in *Racehorses of 1988*. Nashwan's sire is one of the most fashionable stallions around and has been responsible for a stream of good-class performers during his time at Gainesway Farm in Kentucky where he has spent all his stud career. The large majority of Blushing Groom's good horses, for obvious reasons, have been out of American mares, including his Prix de l'Arc winner Rainbow Quest. Height of Fashion, Nashwan's dam, has a thoroughly British background, being a product of the Royal Studs and a daughter of the Queen's One Thousand Guineas and Prix de Diane winner Highclere. Highclere has bred four other winners, the 1989 two-year-old Marienski and three who stayed a mile and a

612

half; Nashwan's great grandam Highlight produced nine winners; and the fourth dam Hypericum won the One Thousand Guineas, was closely-related to Aureole and a half-sister to Knight's Daughter, dam of the outstanding American racehorse and sire Round Table, and to Above Board, the dam of Doutelle and Above Suspicion. Height of Fashion won the Princess of Wales's Stakes, the Lupe Stakes, the May Hill Stakes, the Hoover Fillies' Mile and the Acomb Stakes before being purchased for between £1.4 and £1.8 million (reports varied). Sheikh Hamdan has obtained for Height of Fashion the finest nominations and she was also represented in the latest season by the potentially smart Danzig colt Mukddaam, successful on his only racecourse appearance to date. Nashwan and Unfuwain will both be standing at their owner's Nunnery Stud in Norfolk when it comes into operation for the first time in 1990; Green Desert also joins the stallions there. The terms of Nashwan's syndication valued him at £18,000,000, making him the most valuable stallion to stand in Britain: the syndicate comprised forty-five shares (with Shadwell retaining twenty-three) at £400,000 each, payable in five instalments of £80,000 over four years. *Major W. R. Hern.*

NASTURTIUM 3 ch.f. Music Boy 124–Arckaringa 79 (Persian Bold 123) [1988 5d³ 5m 5g⁵ 5.1f* 5g 5f⁵ 5g 1989 7m 5.8f] small, workmanlike filly: won seller as 2-y-o: ridden by 7-lb claimer, well behind in handicaps in 1989: acts on firm going and a soft surface: tends to hang and go keenly to post: sold 950 gns Ascot October Sales. *N. R. Mitchell.*   —

NATASHA NADINE 2 b.f. (May 14) Bay Express 132–Sweet Candice 71 (African Sky 124) [1989 5g] 2,000Y, resold 7,600Y: fifth foal: half-sister to 3-y-o 1¼m seller winner Fast Market (by Petong) and 1987 2-y-o 5.8f seller winner Almetise (by Mummy's Game): dam, 5f winner at 3 yrs, is half-sister to good French 1½m performer Odisea: 20/1 and ridden by 7-lb claimer, slowly away and always rear in minor event at Catterick in September. *R. M. Whitaker.*   —

NATHIR (USA) 3 b.c. Diesis 133–As You Would (USA) (Fleet Nasrullah) [1988 6d 6s 1989 8s 8f 8m⁶ 10m⁵ 12h⁵] lengthy, good-topped colt: has a quick action: plating-class maiden: stays 1¼m: sold to join P. Butler 4,100 gns Newmarket September Sales. *C. J. Benstead.*   **50**

NATIONAL SERVICE (USA) 4 ch.c. Master Willie 129–For The Flag (USA) 66 (Forli (ARG)) [1988 10.5d² 10g² 10s* 10.2g 10g³ 1989 10d 10g⁴] lengthy, useful-looking colt: has a quick action: useful winner as 3-y-o: not seen out in 1989 after finishing 7¼ lengths fourth of 14 in Group 3 Grosser Preis der Gelsenkirchener Wirtschaft in April: stays 1¼m: yet to race on firm going, probably acts on any other: sweating final 2 appearances at 3 yrs. *W. Hastings-Bass.*   **93**

NATIVE BREEZE 3 b.f. Windjammer (USA)–Indy 77 (Indigenous 121) [1988 6m 5g 6f 5f 1989 6d 5s 6m] neat filly: moderate walker: has a quick action: little worthwhile form in varied events, once blinkered. *K. M. Brassey.*   —

NATIVE FLAIR 4 b.f. Be My Native (USA) 122–Tuyenu 77 (Welsh Pageant 132) [1988 8g² 8.5m⁴ 10d² 9g² 10d⁵ 8m⁴ 10.2m⁵ 10m* 10s³ 10g² 1989 12d 10m⁶] tall, rather sparely-made filly: fair winner as 3-y-o: well beaten both outings in 1989: stays 1¼m: yet to race on firm going, acts on any other. *R. W. Armstrong.*   —

NATIVE FRIEND 3 b.g. Be My Native (USA) 122–Wet Powder (Above 56 Suspicion 127) [1988 7.5m 8.5f* 10.2m 1989 10.2f 12f 12.4m 8g 10m⁶ 14f 18g³] leggy, rather sparely-made gelding: has a rather round action: plating-class handicapper: form as 3-y-o only on fifth and final starts: appears to stay 2¼m: acts on firm going: blinkered fourth start: sometimes takes keen hold: winning juvenile hurdler. *J. G. FitzGerald.*   **56**

NATIVE GEM 2 b.f. (Apr 22) Be My Native (USA) 122–Diamond Gig (Pitskelly 60 122) [1989 6f* 6g² 7f⁴ 7m 8m³ 8m⁴ 8.2f³ 10.6d⁶] 7,800F, 5,200Y: leggy filly: shows a round action: first foal: dam, placed over hurdles in Ireland, is half-sister to smart 10.5f and 1½m winner Amyndas: apprentice ridden, quite modest form in nurseries: earlier won seller (bought in 4,800 gns) at Doncaster: better suited by 1m than shorter, and ran creditably over 10.6f though faded inside final furlong: sold 4,200 gns Doncaster October Sales. *Mrs J. R. Ramsden.*   **60**

NATIVE GUILE 2 b.f. (Feb 11) Lomond (USA) 128–Merlins Charm (USA) 113 91 (Bold Bidder) [1989 6m 7m* 7m³ 8g] lengthy filly: fourth foal: closely related to Black Sabbath (by Be My Guest), once raced here later 1989 7f and 1m winner in Belgium, and half-sister to 8.5f winner Island Charm (by Golden Fleece): dam won

Jersey Stakes: fairly useful filly: won slowly-run maiden at Newmarket in August by 1½ lengths from Aquatic (USA): never travelling well in Black Bottle Scotch Whisky Prestige Stakes (third to Moon Cactus) at Goodwood and Prix Marcel Boussac (tailed off) at Longchamp afterwards: should stay 1m. *B. W. Hills.*

NATIVE KNIGHT 4 b.g. Be My Native (USA) 122–Lady Pitt (Pitskelly 122) 62 [1988 8.2v³ 10m⁶ 10f⁵ 11.7m⁵ 12f² 10m⁵ 10f 10m 1989 12m² 12m⁴ 12f²] leggy, lengthy gelding: quite modest maiden: not seen out after May: suited by 1½m: acts well on top-of-the-ground: ran moderately when blinkered: occasionally sweats: lacks a turn of foot. *R. Akehurst.*

NATIVE MAGIC 3 ch.f. Be My Native (USA) 122–Tuyenu 77 (Welsh Pageant 97 132) [1988 7g⁵ 1989 10.1m⁴ 8m³ 10.2f* 10f³ 13.3d*] sparely-made, angular filly: won maiden at Newcastle and £5,300 handicap at Newbury (taken wide, by 10 lengths) in October: much better at 13f than 1¼m: acts on firm ground and a soft surface: useful. *R. W. Armstrong.*

NATIVE RIVER 4 ch.g. Deep River 103–Native Love 77 (Native Prince) [1988 38 7d 5g³ 6f 5f 5m 6s 6f⁶ 5g 1989 6v³ 6v⁵ 5d 5g 6f 5m 6s⁶] rather sparely-made gelding: moderate mover: poor maiden: effective at 5f and 6f: acts on heavy going: visored once at 3 yrs: blinkered final outing. *W. Bentley.*

NATIVE SCOT 3 ch.f. Be My Native (USA) 122–Bunduq 67 (Scottish Rifle 127) 43 [1988 7g 1989 10g 9f⁵ 10.6m 12f 9f 10m 9g 10.6d 9s²] tall filly: poor form at best: appears to stay 9f and act on any going: edgy second start: visored sixth: took good hold for apprentice: has shown signs of temperament. *F. H. Lee.*

NATIVE SUITOR 2 b.g. (Mar 30) Local Suitor (USA) 128–Bronte (USA) 88 49 (Bold Forbes (USA)) [1989 5s 5m⁴ 6m] 7,400Y: first foal: dam, 11f winner, is daughter of very useful French 7f and 10.5f winner Cameo Shore: poor maiden: should be suited by 6f. *R. Hollinshead.*

NATIVE TRIBE 2 b.g. (Apr 2) Be My Native (USA) 122–More Fuss (Ballymore 92 123) [1989 6m⁴ 6m⁴ 7f* 7f* 8g²] IR 20,000Y: leggy, close-coupled gelding: eighth foal: half-brother to a winner in Italy by Busted: dam, 9f winner in Ireland, is half-sister to high-class Little Bonny and smart Noelino: much improved on last 3 starts, winning maiden at Chester easing up by 7 lengths and nursery at Goodwood in July and finishing second to wide-margin winner Spinning in listed race at Newmarket following month: will stay 1¼m. *B. Hanbury.*

NATIVE TWINE 2 b.f. (Mar 19) Be My Native (USA) 122–Twine (Thatching 91 131) [1989 6m² 6f* 6d² 6f*] leggy, rather sparely-made filly: shows a round action: second foal: half-sister to a winner in Spain: dam unraced granddaughter of high-class Mesopotamia: won maiden at Lingfield in August and 3-runner minor event at Leicester in October, hanging right and looking ill at ease on ground on latter: good second to Line of Thunder in minor event at Goodwood in between: will stay 1m. *H. R. A. Cecil.*

NATTER PATTER 4 br.f. Undulate (USA)–Smokey's Sister (Forlorn River — 124) [1988 7d 1989 10s 10m 7m] of little account and somewhat temperamental. *B. Stevens.*

NATTFARI 3 b.f. Tyrnavos 129–Bounty Bay 74 (Pitcairn 126) [1988 7.5g 1989 — 7.5d⁶ 12.2d] moderate mover: well beaten in sellers: should be suited by further than 7.5f. *P. A. Blockley.*

NAUGHTS N' CROSSES 4 b. or br.f. Connaught 130–Criss Cross (Clever — Fella 117) [1988 8d 8.2s⁴ 11m 10d 10g 8g⁴ 8m 10s 8g 1989 16g 9f 10m³ 10f 12.3f 10f] lengthy, good-topped filly: poor mover: bad maiden: probably stays 1¼m: sometimes on toes: sold 3,000 gns Doncaster November Sales. *Capt. J. Wilson.*

NAUTY VICKI OYSTON 2 b.f. (Feb 28) Music Boy 124–I Don't Mind 97 68 (Swing Easy (USA) 126) [1989 5m³ 5m* 5m³ 5.3h⁴ 5d⁶ 5m⁴ 5m⁴ 5m] quite attractive filly: has a quick action: seventh foal: half-sister to fair middle-distance stayer and good hurdler Swingit Gunner (by Gunner B) and 2-y-o sprint winners by Dublin Taxi and Decoy Boy: dam won 10 races over 5f and 6f: made all in 3-runner minor event at Edinburgh in June: ran well in nurseries on sixth (sweating) and seventh starts: will prove best at 5f: best form on top-of-the-ground: sold 7,000 gns Doncaster November Sales. *J. Berry.*

NAVAL FAN 3 b.g. Taufan (USA) 119–Naval Artiste (Captain's Gig (USA)) [1988 80 5m⁵ 5g² 5g³ 1989 5v* 5.8m⁶ 5m² 5m² 5g⁵ 5m* 5g 5s²] leggy, rather angular gelding: has a round action: modest handicapper: successful at Ayr (well-backed favourite, easily) in April and in claimer at Pontefract in August: should stay 6f: acts on top-of-the-ground and heavy going. *M. H. Easterby.*

NAVAL PAGEANT 2 gr.c. (Apr 4) Kalaglow 132–Sea Pageant (Welsh Pageant **64** p
132) [1989 8.2d⁴] seventh foal: half-brother to 3-y-o Bilander (by High Line) and 2
winners over middle distances, including useful Ocean Ballad (by Grundy): dam
unraced half-sister to high-class Sea Anchor: 8/1, 8 lengths fourth of 15, headed 2f
out and not knocked about, to Ridgepoint in maiden at Haydock in October: should
improve. *Major W. R. Hern.*

NAVAL PARTY 2 b.c. (Apr 19) Bellypha 130–Sea Venture (FR) 98 (Diatome **102**
132) [1989 6m* 6g⁴ 7.3g] leggy, sparely-made colt: half-brother to several winners,
including useful 1980 French 2-y-o 6f winner Grecian Sea (by Homeric) and smart
middle-distance performer Sailor's Mate (by Shirley Heights): dam, from family of
Reform, won over 6f at 2 yrs and stayed 1m: odds on, won moderately-run 5-runner
maiden at Newmarket in May: sent to Italy after third outing: won 7.5f event at
Milan in September: very good second to Candy Glen in Gran Criterium there
following month. *M. R. Stoute.*

NAVARESQUE 4 b.f. Raga Navarro (ITY) 119–Esquinade 84 (Silly Season 127) —
[1988 8g 7d 10.1g 6m 7g 8m⁴ 8m³ 8m 9g* 8.2d² 1989 10.2f 8f] leggy, angular filly: has
a round action: winning plater as 3-y-o: well beaten in non-selling handicaps in
September: stays 9f: acts on top-of-the-ground and a soft surface: has run creditably
for apprentice. *R. J. Hodges.*

NAVRATILOVNA (USA) 3 b.f. Nureyev (USA) 131–Baracala (USA) (Swaps **119**
(USA)) [1988 7s* 1989 9s² 8g* 8g 8d* 8g⁴ 8g⁶ 5g 7m⁶] fifth registered foal: sister to
high-class 5f to 1m winner Vilikaia and half-sister to 1½m winner Disco Girl and 6f
and 7f winner Maximova (both by Green Dancer) and 6.5f winner Doights des Fee
(by L'Emigrant): dam, useful at around 1m in USA, is half-sister to Nonoalco: won
newcomers race at Maisons-Laffitte at 2 yrs, listed event at Chantilly in June and
Prix d'Astarte, by length from Gabina, at Deauville in August: ran creditably in
Group 1 events at Deauville and Longchamp (twice) on next 2 and final starts:
blinkered, never travelling well in Prix de l'Abbaye de Longchamp: stays 9f: yet to
race on very firm ground, probably acts on any other. *D. Smaga, France.*

NAWASSI (USA) 2 b.f. (Mar 17) Shadeed (USA) 135–Scintillate 119 (Sparkler **67** p
130) [1989 5m²] medium-sized, strong-quartered, attractive filly: sixth foal:
half-sister to useful 1985 2-y-o Alshinfarah (by Great Nephew): dam, Oaks winner,
is half-sister to Juliette Marny and Julio Mariner: travelled strongly long way when
beaten short head by Shattered Dreams in 22-runner maiden at Windsor in July:
looked sure to improve but wasn't seen out again. *J. Tree.*

NAWWAR 5 ch.h. Thatching 131–Priceless Pin (Saint Crespin III 132) [1988 6g 6f **75**
6m⁵ 6m² 7d* 6g⁶ 7.6s 6m* 7m* 7d 1989 6f⁶ 6g* 6m⁴ 6m³] strong, close-coupled
horse: modest handicapper: won at Salisbury in July, finishing very strongly to lead
close home: ran well after: best at 6f or 7f: acts on top-of-the-ground and a soft
surface (probably unsuited by very soft going): sweating and slowly away on
reappearance. *C. J. Benstead.*

NAYLAND 3 ch.c. Be My Guest (USA) 126–Troytops 66 (Troy 137) [1988 NR **86**
1989 8m⁶ 10.6g⁵ 8f²] medium-sized, angular colt: first foal: dam, 1¼m winner, is
half-sister to Most Welcome (by Be My Guest) and daughter of Topsy, a very smart
performer at up to 1¼m and half-sister to Teenoso: fair maiden: ¾-length second to
Jumby Bay at Pontefract in October: unruly stalls on debut: should stay 1¼m. *G.
Wragg.*

NAZAKAT 2 ch.f. (Feb 22) Known Fact (USA) 135–Royal Home 69 (Royal Palace **68**
131) [1989 5m⁶ 5f³ 5f* 6g] 7,200Y: small, sturdy filly: has a quick action: fourth foal:
half-sister to 3-y-o 11.7f winner Sweet N' Twenty (by High Top) and 5f and 6f
(seller) winner Erris Express (by Bay Express): dam 9f winner: quite modest
performer: won maiden at Folkestone by a neck from Dreamawhile: ran poorly in
nursery at Nottingham later in October: should stay at least 6f. *L. J. Holt.*

NAZANIN 3 ch.f. Sharpo 132–Maiden Eileen (Stradavinsky 121) [1988 6f* 1989 **88**
8d³ 8g⁴] leggy, close-coupled filly: chipped bone in knee when winning maiden at
Goodwood in 1988: in frame in £8,700 event at Ascot, still appearing very green
(behind and tending to hang early on) but running on well, and listed race at
Leopardstown in spring as 3-y-o: may well stay 1¼m: acts on firm going and a soft
surface. *J. L. Dunlop.*

NAZARE BLUE 2 b.g. (Mar 19) Absalom 128–Top Stream 87 (Highland Melody **61** ?
112) [1989 5v² 5g 5m³ 5f² 6f⁵ 6f⁴ 6m⁵] 5,200F, 11,500Y: angular, workmanlike
gelding: quite good mover: fifth foal: brother to plating-class 1m to 1¼m performer
Act of Treason and useful 6f and 7f winner Kedron and half-brother to 1m winner
Cosconi (by Tachypous): dam won 3 times over 1m at 2 yrs and seemed to stay 1½m:

Mrs Angie Silver's "N C Owen"

quite modest maiden: ran badly in seller final outing: stays 6f: acts on any going: drifted badly left first start: has joined Mrs B. Waring. *J. Berry.*

NAZELA 2 gr.f. (Mar 17) Another Realm 118–Alezan Dore 82 (Mountain Call 125) **82** [1989 5m⁴ 5m² 5m* 6f² 6g] 10,000Y: medium-sized, sturdy filly: carries condition: good walker: poor mover: half-sister to two 2-y-o winners, including 1979 5f performer Deux Etoiles (by Bay Express), and 2 other winners here and abroad: dam, half-sister to smart middle-distance filly Aloft, stayed 7f: won maiden at Beverley in August by ½ length: beaten a head in £8,500 event at Salisbury following month, best effort: badly hampered by faller final start: better suited by 6f than 5f. *J. W. Payne.*

NAZMIAH 3 b.f. Free State 125–Irish Ballad 65 (Irish Ball (FR) 127) [1988 NR **73** 1989 11.5m⁴ 12m 12m⁴ 11f⁶ 10d* 10m⁶] leggy filly: third foal: dam placed at up to 1¼m: won handicap at Goodwood in September, leading 4f out, quickening clear then holding on by a length: not entirely discredited in £8,000 handicap following month: should prove best at around 1¼m: acts on a soft surface: sweating third start. *A. Hide.*

N C OWEN 3 b.c. Bustino 136–Neenah 107 (Bold Lad (IRE) 133) [1988 NR 1989 **115** 10g* 11.5m* 12f³ 14.6s⁶] 60,000Y: strong, good-topped colt: has plenty of scope: fourth reported foal: half-brother to 1987 2-y-o 5f winner Amenaide (by Known Fact): dam, half-sister to Irish Oaks winner Swiftfoot, won over 6f at 2 yrs and stayed 1½m: won £6,200 event at Newmarket in May and minor event at Yarmouth in July: heavily-backed favourite, beaten about a length when third of 4 to Warrshan in Gordon Stakes at Goodwood, leading until 1f out: 12/1, ran moderately in St Leger Stakes at Ayr: should stay beyond 1½m: acts on firm going, possibly unsuited by soft: looked very well last 2 starts. *L. M. Cumani.*

NDITA 3 b.f. Be My Native (USA) 122–Orangery (Realm 129) [1988 6s 1989 8s* **75**
8g* 7.6f 8m 8m 8m] tall, leggy filly: moderate walker: has a quick action: won minor
event at Warwick in March and handicap at Wolverhampton (making all) in May: ran
poorly after in handicaps and claimer: stays 1m: probably unsuited by top-of-the-
ground. *M. H. Tompkins.*

NEARCTIC BAY (USA) 3 b.c. Explodent (USA)–Golferette (USA) (Mr Randy) **—**
[1988 NR 1989 10f 10g] $110,000 2-y-o: robust colt: third foal: dam 1m stakes winner
at 2 yrs: bit backward and well beaten in summer maidens at Sandown and
Newmarket: sold to join Mrs P. Barker 3,000 gns Doncaster September Sales. *R. F.
Casey.*

NEARCTIC FLAME 3 b.f. Sadler's Wells (USA) 132–Flame of Tara 124 **111**
(Artaius (USA) 129) [1988 NR 1989 10s* 10.5f* 12f3 10f5 10.2m5] 360,000Y: lengthy,
good-bodied filly: has scope: first foal: dam best at 3 yrs, winning Coronation Stakes
and Pretty Polly Stakes: won minor event at Nottingham and £5,600 event at York in
the spring: ran creditably in moderately-run Ribblesdale Stakes (weakening final 1f)
at Royal Ascot and listed race (making most 1m) at Newcastle third and final starts:
should prove suited by 1¼m: best efforts on firm ground. *M. R. Stoute.*

NEARLY RED 3 b.f. Pitskelly 122–Amber Breeze (Arctic Storm 134) [1988 6m **—**
6d 1989 7h 7h5 7f a7g] neat filly: poor form in varied events: should stay 1m. *S. Dow.*

NEARROE 3 ch.g. Noalto 120–Incarnadine 67 (Hot Spark 126) [1988 6m 7g 7d 7s **66**
1989 10.1g6 11.7m6 12g] compact, good-bodied gelding: poor walker: quite modest
form: easily best effort in Windsor handicap second start: gambled on in minor event
there week earlier: stays 1½m: possibly best on top-of-the-ground: has given
trouble at stalls. *R. Akehurst.*

NEAT DISH (CAN) 2 b.f. (Mar 12) Stalwart (USA)–Chilly Hostess (CAN) (Vice **90**
Regent (CAN)) [1989 5v 5v6 5s3 6d* 6g2 7m2 7g5 7g 5d6 7d3] $27,000Y: first foal:
dam 2-y-o sprint winner: fairly useful filly: first past post in maiden at Phoenix Park
in May and listed event (demoted for interference) at Leopardstown in July: good
second in Group 3 Anheuser Busch EBF Railway Stakes at the Curragh in between:
ran respectably final outing: stays 7f: acts on top-of-the-ground and a soft surface.
John J. McLoughlin, Ireland.

NEATFOOT 3 ch.f. Anfield 117–Whitefoot 108 (Relko 136) [1988 7g3 7f2 7m 1989 **90** §
11.3m5 10g6 12m3 10m4 10f* 10m2 10f3 10f2 10g5] rangy filly: has a rather round
action: capable of fairly useful form: given fine ride by W. Carson when winning
maiden at Nottingham in August, tenderly handled to lead close home: blinkered,
ran creditably in minor events last 3 outings: best form over 1¼m: acts on firm
going: sometimes sweating and edgy, including when successful: looked faint-
hearted on majority of starts and can't be trusted. *Major W. R. Hern.*

BBA Middleton Stakes, York—
Nearctic Flame quickens away from Shayraz (left) and Krisalya

NEAT STYLE 4 b.f. Sweet Monday 122–Octavia (Sallust 134) [1988 5g 5f³ 6f⁴ **69**
6h* 6g³ 7m* 7.5m* 8.2m 1989 7s 9f* 8h³ 10.8f* 11f² 8.5f* 8.2d] smallish, sparely-
made filly: quite modest performer: successful in claimer at Wolverhampton, seller
at Warwick (bought in 9,200 gns) and claimer at Beverley, last 2 very easily: stayed
11f: suited by top-of-the-ground: sometimes gave trouble in preliminaries and often
started slowly: consistent: dead. *R. Hollinshead.*

NEBULATIS (USA) 3 b.c. Diesis 133–Galaxy Virgo 106 (Blakeney 126) [1988 **90**
NR 1989 8g 10g⁴ 14m² 14m* 16f²] $75,000Y: useful-looking colt: moderate walker:
has a sharp action: fourth reported foal: closely related to Irish 1¾m winner/
winning hurdler Galaxy Kris (by Kris): dam useful at up to 1m: made all and idled
final 1f in maiden at Yarmouth in June: favourite, good second in £9,200 handicap at
Ascot later in month: stays 2m: acts on a firm going: looked reluctant third start: tail
flasher: sold only 1,400 gns Newmarket Autumn Sales. *J. Gosden.*

NED'S AURA 4 br.g. Dalsaan 125–My Natalie 64 (Rheingold 137) [1988 10s⁴ 8m **83**
7.5m* 8f³ 7m² 7g⁵ 7g⁴ 6d² 6m⁴ 6d⁶ 6s² 7f³ 1989 7.5d 6d⁶ 7f 6m 7f² 7f² 8f² 7f 6g
6m³ 6f² 7m² 7s³ 7g* 7m²] good-topped gelding: moderate mover: placed in
handicaps numerous times prior to winning £8,600 event at Newmarket in October:
best form at 7f: acts on any going: has worn blinkers, usually visored nowadays:
occasionally on edge: ran moderately for amateur eighth start: has hung and carried
head high: suited by extreme waiting tactics: consistent. *M. P. Naughton.*

NEEDHAM HOPE 2 b.c. (Feb 28) Full of Hope 125–Seven Year Itch 65 (Jimsun **91**
121) [1989 7m 7m² 8.2f* 8g⁵ 8g⁴] good-topped colt: has a round action: fourth
reported foal: half-brother to 1985 2-y-o 6f seller winner Young Lucy (by Young
Man): dam won sellers at 5f and 1¼m: made all in maiden at Nottingham in
September: ran very well when around 9 lengths fourth of 16 to Belmez in minor
event at Newmarket in November: will probably stay 1¼m. *P. A. Kelleway.*

NEEDS MUST 2 gr.g. (Feb 12) Another Realm 118–Miss Monte Carlo 75 **63**
(Reform 132) [1989 6m 6f³ 6g* 6g 8s⁴ 6v] 3,800Y, 8,000 2-y-o: workmanlike,
angular gelding: shows a rather round action: half-brother to a winner in Belgium:
dam sprinting 2-y-o later successful in Italy, is half-sister to Lupe winner Miss
Beaulieu: won seller (no bid) at Doncaster in July by neck: showed improved form
when under 4 lengths fourth to Puligny in nursery at Ayr in September: ran poorly
in similar event there following month: suited by 1m: acts on soft going: suited by
forcing tactics. *C. Tinkler.*

NEEDWOOD IMP 3 ch.g. Joshua 129–The Doe 82 (Alcide 136) [1988 6m 1989 **54**
8g 8.2g 8f⁵ 7m² 7m⁵ 7m 6s 7d] lengthy, rather sparely-made gelding: plating-class
maiden: suited by 7f: acts on top-of-the-ground. *B. C. Morgan.*

NEEDWOOD NIGHTLIFE 2 b.f. (May 16) Decoy Boy 129–Johnny's Pride **—**
(Frimley Park 109) [1989 5g 5.1m 5g 5f] 400Y: small, lengthy filly: shows a quick
action: second foal: dam never ran: no form in sellers or maidens: wore tongue strap
on last 3 starts, severe bridle on second and third. *B. C. Morgan.*

NEEDWOOD NUT 5 b.m. Royben 125–Needwood Nap (Some Hand 119) [1988 **53**
6d⁵ 6s 5m³ 6g 6s⁵ 6m 6g² 6m² 6d 1989 6g³ 6g 6m 6m⁶ 6m 6g] smallish,
short-backed mare: moderate mover: plating-class handicapper: refused to enter
stalls seventh intended start: better suited by 6f than 5f: best efforts on a sound
surface (yet to show her form on very firm going): has run well when sweating:
usually apprentice ridden nowadays. *B. C. Morgan.*

NEEDWOOD NYMPH 5 b.m. Bold Owl 101–Oceania (Aureole 132) [1988 10v **45**
8.5m 12f 12g 12g* 14g⁴ 13d* 12d⁴ 12s³ 15m² 15.8g⁶ 16g⁶ 15d⁶ 1989 12d* 12g⁴ 13m
12m⁴ 14m² 15f³ 15m⁶ 12g 15.3m² 16m] workmanlike mare: poor handicapper:
20/1-winner at Pontefract in April: probably stays 2m: acts on any going: good
mount for apprentice. *B. C. Morgan.*

NEEDWOOD SPRITE 3 ch.f. Joshua 129–Sea Dart 55 (Air Trooper 115) [1988 **58**
5m 5g 6s 1989 7.5d⁵ 8.2g⁵ 7m* 8g² 10m³ 8m² 9g] plain filly: won seller (bought in
4,800 gns) at Leicester in June: placed in claimers after: stays 1¼m: acts on
top-of-the-ground: ridden by 7-lb claimer first 2 outings. *B. C. Morgan.*

NEEHA 3 b.g. Nishapour (FR) 125–Acantha 77 (Prince Tenderfoot (USA) 126) **67**
[1988 6g 6f⁶ 6m⁵ 6f⁵ 6g³ 6g⁵ 5d 6s 6m 7s⁵ 8s 6d³ 1989 10m 8f 6f⁶ 5m⁴ 5f 5f⁴ 6h³ 6m
7m⁴ 7f a8g³] IR 4,600Y: workmanlike gelding: first foal: dam, out of fairly useful 1m
winner Catherine's Sister, ran 3 times early at 2 yrs, winning once over 5f: modest
form at best: easily best efforts as 3-y-o when in frame in handicaps and claimer:
seems to stay 1m: acts on any going: blinkered last 4 outings at 2 yrs when trained
by P. Matthews in Ireland: trained until after tenth as 3-y-o by R. Akehurst. *I. V.
Matthews.*

NEGLIGENT   2 gr.f. (Apr 10) Ahonoora 122–Negligence 66 (Roan Rocket 118 p
128) [1989 6g³ 7g*]

There are many factors to be taken into account when buying a
racehorse, but the colour of its coat is seldom considered of major importance.
It is, however, when Mrs Catherine Corbett makes a purchase. It seems Mrs
Corbett has a penchant for grey fillies, so much so that she's had at least one
in training for several seasons. She's had plenty of success with them, too.
The Cheveley Park winner and One Thousand Guineas third Desirable is the
best so far, and Negligent may well be another who'll be capable of making her
presence felt at a high level. Negligent's first public appearance came against
five other debutantes in the Blue Seal Stakes at Ascot in September. She was
well supported on the strength of encouraging home reports, and considering
she lost a couple of lengths through a sluggish start she ran a fine race, staying
on strongly to finish just under a length third behind Alwathba, who was
providing Cumani with his fourth consecutive winner of the race. Races
contested solely by newcomers are by their nature difficult to assess, but the
events of the next few weeks suggested the Blue Seal form was at least
useful, with second and fourth Hasbah and Lakeland Beauty both running on
wide-margin winners of maiden events at Redcar on their next start.
Negligent was asked to take on a much stiffer assignment, namely the Group 3
Bottisham Heath Stud Rockfel Stakes at Newmarket in October. The twelve
runners for the Rockfel had already won fifteen races between them, and the
15/8 favourite was the unbeaten Va Toujours, who'd won the Oh So Sharp
Stakes by seven lengths in a fast time over course and distance two weeks
earlier; Negligent was a well-backed second choice on 100/30, followed by the
impressive Ayr winner Sajjaya, the Hoover Fillies' Mile third Fujaiyrah and
the Epsom and Ascot winner Fearless Revival on 5/1, 9/1 and 11/1
respectively; Remthat Naser figured on 12/1 after finishing runner-up behind
Wedding Bouquet in a Group 3 race at Phoenix Park on her latest outing, as
did Negligent's stable-companion Idle Chat, the winner of a Nottingham
minor event on her sole previous start. The manner of Negligent's victory
must have surprised even her staunchest supporters. Held up in a
strongly-run race, she burst through to join the leaders entering the Dip and
drew clear in fine style in the final furlong to beat Fearless Revival by an
official five lengths—it was just under seven—with Va Toujours, who'd
disputed the lead for much of the way, a length and a half further back in third.
Even if Va Toujours and Fujaiyrah weren't at their best, Negligent must be
seen as a very promising filly. Her winning margin was by far the widest since
the Rockfel Stakes was first run in 1981, and the timefigure she recorded (0.65
fast), though not top class, was as good as any by a two-year-old filly all
season.

Negligent's sire Ahonoora is now dead. He was due to cover seventy-five
mares at the Segenhoe Stud in New South Wales in 1989, but after serving
seven he fractured a pastern in a paddock accident and had to be put down. His
loss to the stallion ranks is a significant one. He sired a string of good horses
over a variety of distances, including the likes of Don't Forget Me, Park
Appeal and Park Express; and besides Negligent in the latest season he was

Bottisham Heath Stud Rockfel Stakes, Newmarket—Negligent bursts onto the classic scene

also represented by two of the leading sprinters in Indian Ridge and Statoblest. Negligence has made a much better broodmare than she was a racehorse. She finished placed just once from six attempts on the flat, but at stud she's already produced Ala Mahlik, a sister to Negligent who reached the frame in the One Thousand Guineas, and also the March Stakes and Queen Alexandra Stakes winner Ala Hounak (by Sexton Blake). Negligent's grandam Malpractice wore blinkers and refused to enter the stalls on her only appearance. She comes from a successful family. Her dam Miss Justice has produced numerous winners; she's also earned a reputation as a good producer of broodmares, with the likes of Governor General, Sudden Love and Galunpe all figuring among her direct descendants.

		Ahonoora (ch 1975)	Lorenzaccio (ch 1965)	Klairon Phoenissa
Negligent (gr.f. Apr 10, 1987)			Helen Nichols (ch 1966)	Martial Quaker Girl
		Negligence (gr 1975)	Roan Rocket (gr 1961)	Buisson Ardent Farandole II
			Malpractice (ch 1971)	Pall Mall Miss Justice

Negligent was bought at the Highflyer Sale for 38,000 guineas, slightly under the average for yearlings by Ahonoora in 1988. She wasn't the most imposing filly around as a two-year-old—being angular and rather unfurnished—but there's plenty of time for her to strengthen and fill out over the winter. Indeed, it says a great deal for Negligent that she could win a race like the Rockfel so impressively when still apparently not the finished article. She looks to have sound each-way credentials for the One Thousand Guineas and is already favourite; and at this stage her staying a mile and a quarter or even a mile and a half can't be ruled out. *B. W. Hills.*

NELSON RIVER (USA)   4 br.g. Green Forest (USA) 134–Maple River (USA)   **79** (Clandestine) [1988 10g⁴ 1989 10.2g 9s⁴ 10d⁵ 10f⁶ 8f* 8h⁶ 8m* 9m] lengthy gelding: fair handicapper: won at Pontefract in June and August: ran poorly at Brighton (looked ill at ease on track) in between and at Wolverhampton (bandaged off-hind, apprentice ridden, wearing severe noseband) final outing: keen sort, well suited by 1m: acts on firm going: has sweated and got on edge: taken down early fourth to eighth starts: sold 10,500 gns Newmarket Autumn Sales: inconsistent. *I. A. Balding.*

NEMESIA   4 b.f. Mill Reef (USA) 141–Elegant Tern (USA) 102 (Sea Bird II 145)   **111** [1988 7g⁶ 10g 10g 10.2m* 10g² 1989 8m³ 10m³ 10m² 13.4m* 12m⁴] neat filly: has a quick action: very useful performer: won 6-runner listed Berry Magicoal Surefire Chester Stakes in September by ¾ length from Lazaz: creditable fourth of 8, outpaced about 2f out then staying on well, to Spritsail in similar event at Newmarket following month: suited by 1½m+: acts on top-of-the-ground: keen to post and in race on reappearance: often sweats, and has got on edge. *Major W. R. Hern.*

NESAAH (USA)   3 b.f. Topsider (USA)–Sylph (USA) 110 (Alleged (USA) 138)   **95** [1988 NR 1989 10.6m* 10.1m* 12f² 12m⁶] quite attractive filly: second foal: dam, 1¼m and 1½m winner, is closely related to Irish St Leger winner Leading Counsel: won maiden at Haydock and minor event (making all) at Windsor in July: bit edgy, beaten head by Knoosh in listed event (moved moderately down) at York, soon struggling in rear then leading 2f out until close home: visored, soon pushed along and looked unenthusiastic in Princess Royal Stakes at Ascot: suited by 1½m: hung left at Windsor and York: fairly useful but of doubtful temperament. *J. Tree.*

NESSFIELD   3 b.f. Tumble Wind (USA)–Ceiling (Thatch (USA) 136) [1988 7g   **57** 1989 10f 10f²] useful-looking filly: wearing tongue strap, second in claimer at Nottingham in September, only worthwhile form: sold 1,100 gns Newmarket Autumn Sales. *W. Haggas.*

NESSIE   3 b.f. Mansingh (USA) 120–Danaka (FR) (Val de Loir 133) [1988 5f 6d 5m   — 5s⁶ 6m 1989 6f 6m⁶ 5f 6m] sturdy, good-bodied filly: no show in claimer and handicaps as 3-y-o: should prove suited by 6f: seems unsuited by soft ground: visored final outing. *M. J. Camacho.*

NET CALL (USA)   3 b.f. Quack (USA)–Sarcenet (USA) (Inverness Drive (USA))   — [1988 6f 5m 5f⁵ 6g⁶ 7s 7d³ 7m 7m 8.2v 1989 8s 9d 11g 14f] neat filly: plater: behind in spring as 3-y-o: moved poorly down on reappearance: suited by 7f: blinkered third outing: visored once at 2 yrs. *K. Stone.*

NEVADA MIX   5 gr.h. Alias Smith (USA)–Northern Empress 80 (Northfields   **69** (USA)) [1988 6m* 6m⁶ 6f* 6g 6m² 7f 7m 7m* 6d 6s 1989 7m 7f 7f 6f³ 6f⁴ 6f⁵ 6g* 7g a6g a7g⁵] strong, stocky horse: modest handicapper judged on most form: made all at Epsom in August: best efforts earlier in season when in frame at Brighton and Goodwood: effective at 6f and 7f: acts on any going: sweated when tried in blinkers: good mount for apprentice: inconsistent. *N. A. Gaselee.*

NEVERDOWN   2 ch.f. (Mar 6) Never So Bold 135–Bourton Downs 74 (Philip of Spain 126) [1989 7g] seventh foal: half-sister to 3-y-o Just Great (by Simply Great) and a winner in Italy by Blakeney: dam 2-y-o 5f winner didn't train on: 33/1, never dangerous in 24-runner maiden at Newmarket in November. *M. Bell.*   —

NEVER IN   3 b.g. Aragon 118–Recent Events (Stanford 121§) [1988 5g⁵ 5m³ 5f⁴   52   6g⁴ 6g⁴ 6g⁵ 6m⁶ 1989 6m 6m² 7m² 7m 6f² 6f⁴ 6f 7g] big, angular gelding: fair plater: keen sort, likely to prove best at up to 7f: acts on firm going: visored seventh outing: ran creditably when sweating on fifth: sold to join T. Caldwell 3,000 gns Doncaster September Sales. *C. Tinkler.*

NEVER SO HIGH   2 b.c. (Feb 26) Never So Bold 135–High Gait 90 (High Top   64 P   131) [1989 7g] 46,000Y: quite attractive colt: fourth foal: half-brother to top-class stayer Royal Gait (by Gunner B) and ungenuine 3-y-o Miller's Gait (by Mill Reef): dam middle-distance winner: 16/1, in need of race and green, shaped most promisingly when around 10 lengths ninth of 29, steady headway last 2f under considerate handling, to Lord of The Field in maiden at Newmarket in November: sure to improve considerably, and win a similar event. *R. W. Armstrong.*

NEVER WRONG   2 b.c. (Apr 8) Kafu 120–Wolver Rose (Wolver Hollow 126)   86   [1989 5v⁴ 5v² 5v³ 5s⁶ 5g* 6f³ 5f] 750Y: good-quartered, attractive colt: good walker: first reported foal: dam ran twice: showed improved form when winning 11-runner minor event at Naas by ½ length: bumped at start when tailed off in Molecomb Stakes at Goodwood in July, and wasn't seen out again: stays 6f. *J. G. Coogan, Ireland.*

NEVIS   3 ch.f. Connaught 130–Foudroyer (Artaius (USA) 129) [1988 6g 1989 10f]   —   close-coupled, sparely-made filly: has a round action: quite modest form in maiden in August at 2 yrs: raced freely in lead 7f and eased considerably in similar event 10 months later: should stay at least 1m: sold 1,150 gns Ascot August Sales. *J. L. Dunlop.*

NEW ARRANGEMENT   3 b.g. Trojan Fen 118–Cariole 84 (Pardao 120) [1988   90   NR 1989 12g⁵ 12.3m² a10g*] 11,000Y, 5,000 2-y-o: workmanlike gelding: half-brother to several winners, including very useful 1983 2-y-o 7f winner Knoxville (by Pitskelly) and fairly useful 5f to 7f winner Marking Time (by On Your Mark): dam won over 7.6f: favourite, won maiden at Lingfield in October, pushed along long way out and leading well inside final 1f: stays 1½m: has joined J. Jenkins. *B. Hanbury.*

NEW BABY   5 b.g. Sallust 134–Lagolette (Green God 128) [1988 NR 1989 12.4g]   —   close-coupled gelding: moderate mover: quite modest plater as 3-y-o: 33/1, tailed off at Newcastle in October: stays 1½m: acts on firm going: bought 1,400 gns Doncaster February Sales. *D. Yeoman.*

NEW CHANDELIER   3 b.g. Alzao (USA) 117–New Light 78 (Reform 132) [1988   75   NR 1989 7f⁵ 7m 7f²] 9,600Y: angular gelding: half-brother to several winners here and abroad, notably high-class 6f to 1¼m winner Then Again (by Jaazeiro): dam, from excellent family, won over 1¼m: 33/1, 4 lengths second of 10 to Sappho Comet at Lingfield in October, first worthwhile form in maidens: may stay further. *P. W. Harris.*

NEW HALEN   8 br.g. Dikusa 94–Miss Pear (Breakspear II) [1988 NR 1989 12f⁴]   —   rather leggy, close-coupled gelding: 100/1, bandaged and on toes, soundly-beaten last of 4 in apprentice event at Chepstow in July, first outing on flat: winning chaser. *A. P. James.*

NEW KRISS   3 b.c. Kris 135–Vwonica (FR) (Val de Loir 133) [1988 NR 1989 8g   —   16d] 130,000 francs (approx £12,400) Y: leggy, quite good-topped colt: sixth foal: brother to Perfect Match, a useful performer here at up to 1¼m later successful in USA, and half-brother to 2 winners, including useful sprinter Kirchner (by Kashmir II): dam won over 8.5f in France: bit backward, well behind in early-season maidens: sold 2,200 gns Ascot June Sales. *A. N. Lee.*

NEW MEXICO   5 br.g. Free State 125–Trigamy 112 (Tribal Chief 125) [1988 10d   73   10s³ 11.7m³ 10m* 10m* 10d 12g 1989 10d 10f 10m 10.6d 10g³ 10.6m³ 8v* 8g* 7g³] strong, sturdy gelding: carries plenty of condition: moderate mover: modest handicapper: successful in October in 18-runner event at Ayr in good style and 24-runner contest (co-favourite) at Redcar: creditable third of 26 at Redcar following month: best at short of 1¼m nowadays: acts on any going: ran creditably for amateur sixth start. *M. F. D. Morley.*

NEW ROMANTIC (USA) 2 b.c. (Feb 18) Miswaki (USA) 124–La Romance 80
(USA) (Lyphard (USA) 132) [1989 6g⁵ 6f* 7m⁶ 6m⁶] well-made, attractive colt: has
a sharp action: first foal: dam, French 1¼m winner, is daughter of half-sister to
Green Dancer: odds on, won maiden at Nottingham in July by 2 lengths from
Caffarelli: good sixth to Petipa in nursery at York month later, next and better
subsequent effort: will stay 1m. *M. R. Stoute.*

NEWSHAM BRIDGE 2 b.f. (Apr 10) Formidable (USA) 125–Foston Bridge 68 42
(Relkino 131) [1989 5g⁴ 5f⁵] small, workmanlike filly: second foal: half-sister to
3-y-o 1¼m winner Christmas Hols (by Young Generation): dam, placed at 7f from 4
starts at 2 yrs, from family of Lancashire Oaks winner Rhein Bridge and very smart
Connaught Bridge: moderate form in Beverley sellers: dead. *M. H. Easterby.*

NEW START 3 b.g. Absalom 128–Pook's Hill (High Top 131) [1988 5g 6m⁴diˢ 6g —
7g⁶ 7g⁴ 8.5f⁴ 8d 1989 8g 9f] workmanlike, deep-bodied, plain gelding: moderate
walker and poor mover: plater: well beaten facing stiff tasks as 3-y-o: best form at
7f: sold 840 gns Doncaster October Sales. *S. J. Muldoon.*

NEW STREET (USA) 3 b.f. Our Native (USA)–Ten Strike (USA) (Tentam —
(USA)) [1988 5g 6m⁶ 6g* 1989 7f 7m] sparely-made filly: shows knee action:
blinkered, won seller in July as 2-y-o: off course over 12 months then well behind
facing stiff tasks in handicap and claimer: should stay further than 6f: sweating as
3-y-o: edgy and took good hold final start. *C. V. Bravery.*

NIARBYL BAY 2 b.g. (May 12) The Noble Player (USA) 126–Rings 104 (Realm 45
129) [1989 5m⁵ 6m 6g 7d⁵] rangy, workmanlike gelding: has scope: turns fore-feet
in: half-brother to 3-y-o Gentleshaw, Irish 6f winner Sunday Chimes (both by Try
My Best) and fair 7f winner Aulait (by Gay Fandango): dam 6f performer: moderate
plater: stays 7f. *Mrs J. R. Ramsden.*

NICE AND SHARP 2 b.c. (Apr 20) Sharpo 132–Lune de Miel 80 (Kalamoun 60
129) [1989 7f 8g⁶] 8,200Y: sparely-made colt: half-brother to a winner in Belgium by
Hittite Glory, a winner in USA by Dance In Time and a winning hurdler: dam 2-y-o 6f
winner: weakened from 2f out in late-season maidens at Leicester, better effort on
final start. *R. Hollinshead.*

NICE DAY 2 br.f. (Mar 21) Shirley Heights 130–Keyboard 88 (High Top 131) 83
[1989 6f² 6g* 7d⁵] second foal: dam, half-sister to very useful middle-distance
winner Galveston, won over 7.6f at 2 yrs but disappointed at 3 yrs: 12/1, won maiden
at Newcastle in October by 2½ lengths from Love Returned: fair fifth to Azzaam in
nursery at Thirsk following month: will stay 1¼m. *J. Etherington.*

NICE WORK 3 b.f. Workboy 123–Pandorana (Pandofell 132) [1988 NR 1989 7v⁶] —
half-sister to fair staying hurdler Crammond Brig (by New Brig): dam won at up to
3m over hurdles: 50/1 and very slowly away, tailed off in maiden at Ayr in April: has
joined C. Alexander. *J. S. Wilson.*

NICHOLAS MARK 5 ch.g. Gunner B 126–Bargain Line 68 (Porto Bello 118) 73
[1988 10g⁴ 12.2g* 12m⁴ 11m³ 12g 12d⁶ 12g 14m 12.2f* 14m 12m* 13.8g* 12m 1989
12f 12m 15.8m⁴ 12m³ 13f² 12g 13m² 13g² 11f⁴ 12f 12m* 12m² 12.2g* 12m 12.2m²
14g⁴ 13.8d a12g] close-coupled, useful-looking gelding: poor walker: modest
handicapper: won moderately-run events in September at Thirsk and Catterick:
below form last 3 outings: suited by 1½m to 1¾m: best on a sound surface: has run
creditably for lady and apprentice: wore crossed noseband sixth outing: saddle
slipped on fourteenth. *R. M. Whitaker.*

NICKLE PLATED 4 b.c. Auction Ring (USA) 123–Nicoletta 81 (Busted 134) 100
[1988 8d* 11d² 10.4v² 1989 10d 10g² 10.2g² 10f 9m³ 12g* 12m⁵ 12m⁴ 12m 11v] tall
colt: poor mover: useful performer: won strongly-run £24,300 Old Newton Cup

Old Newton Cup, Haydock—Nickle Plated lands this valuable handicap

(Handicap) at Haydock in July by 1½ lengths from Cheerful Times: ran creditably in £19,100 handicap at Newmarket and Group 3 EBF Royal Whip Stakes at the Curragh next 2 starts, poorly after: suited by 1½m: unsuited by firm going, acts on any other: ridden by 7-lb claimer third outing: sold 48,000 gns Newmarket Autumn Sales. *G. Wragg.*

NICKNAVAR 4 ch.g. Raga Navarro (ITY) 119–Bay Girl (Persian Bold 123) [1988 12f⁵ 12.2m² 14m 12.2g 1989 15.3m⁶ 12g 17.6f] rather sparely-made gelding: no longer of any account: sold 5,200 gns Ascot October Sales. *J. Wharton.* —

NICNATLOU 2 ch.f. (May 10) Van Der Linden (FR)–Double Pebble 48 (Double-U-Jay 120) [1989 7f 8m 8g 8f⁵ 10.6d 10f a8g] workmanlike filly: third reported foal: dam probably of little account: little account: blinkered fifth outing. *R. Thompson.* —

NICOLAKI 4 gr.g. Busted 134–Nicholas Grey 100 (Track Spare 125) [1988 10g 12f³ 13.3d⁵ 12g³ 10m⁵ 12m* 12m 12g⁵ 12m⁶ 1989 12d 12g] good-topped gelding: won handicap at Goodwood in September, 1988: finished lame next outing: soundly beaten in handicaps as 4-y-o: suited by 1½m: acts on top-of-the-ground. *T. M. Jones.* —

NICOLA NICKLEBY 3 b.f. Homeboy 114–Time of Your Life (Mount Hagen (FR) 127) [1988 7g 8g 1989 12f 10.6m 10f⁵ 12.5m] close-coupled, good-bodied filly: mostly burly, no form in maidens and minor event: edgy and sweating, gave trouble in stalls and withdrawn on intended reappearance. *R. Hollinshead.* —

NICOLESCO 5 b.g. Thatching 131–Blyth's Folly 93 (Prince Tenderfoot (USA) 126) [1988 10v 9g 7g⁶ 6m* 7m* 6h⁶ 7d 1989 7g 6f⁵ 8f 6m] leggy, good-topped gelding: quite modest handicapper: form in first half of 1989 only on second outing: effective at 6f and 7f: acts on firm going: has won for apprentice. *Miss B. Sanders.* 59

NICQUITA 2 ch.f. (Feb 18) Nicholas Bill 125–Jacquinta 95 (Habitat 134) [1989 5m² 6m⁴ 5g⁴ 5f³ 6v] 6,200Y, resold 7,200Y: leggy, quite good-topped filly: fourth foal: sister to 2 animals, including 7f winner Toohami, and closely related to 3-y-o High Quinta (by High Line): dam, 2-y-o 6f winner, is daughter of Jacinth, leading 2-y-o of 1972 and high-class miler at 3 yrs: quite modest maiden: will stay 1m: trained first 3 outings by M. Usher. *C. C. Elsey.* 63

NIDOMI 2 ch.c. (Apr 19) Dominion 123–Nicholas Grey 100 (Track Spare 125) [1989 6f⁵] 24,000Y: sixth foal: half-brother to 3-y-o Terimon (by Bustino), winner at 1¼m and runner-up in Derby, and 4 other winners, including 1½m winner Nicolaki (by Busted) and quite useful but unreliable 6f winner Butsova (by Formidable): dam, winner from 5f to 7f here at 2 yrs, second in Oaks d'Italia: 10/1, around 11 lengths fifth of 10 to Lakeland Beauty in maiden at Redcar in October, fading last 2f: should do better. *Sir Mark Prescott.* 55 p

NIGHT AT SEA 2 gr.f. (Apr 18) Night Shift (USA)–Into Harbour (Right Tack 131) [1989 6g⁵ 5f* 26,000Y: workmanlike, good-quartered filly: half-sister to 3-y-o Bitone (by Tolomeo) and several winners, including useful 6f winner Jack Tar (by Stanford) and middle-distance plater Manhattan Boy (by Oats): dam ran 3 times: favourite, made all or most in October in maiden at Wolverhampton and nursery (beat Shout Fore by ½ length, having quickened 4 lengths clear 2f out) at Newmarket: withdrawn at start (spread a plate) from Racecall Gold Trophy at Redcar on last day of month: stays 6f: flashed tail final outing: likely to improve further, and win more races. *L. M. Cumani.* 94 p

NIGHTBOURNE 3 ch.g. Night Shift (USA)–Catulle (Roan Rocket 128) [1988 NR 1989 8g 7g 8m⁴ 8.2d⁶ 11s⁶ 10m⁶] 2,900Y: smallish, workmanlike gelding: second living foal: half-brother to temperamental novice selling hurdler Peace Keeper (by Wolver Hollow): dam unraced half-sister to Gold Cup winner Shangamuzo: plating-class form in sellers and claimers: should stay beyond 1m: acts on top-of-the-ground and a soft surface: claimed out of R. Guest's stable £7,655 on third outing: sold to join S. Dow 1,400 gns Newmarket Autumn Sales. *M. H. Tompkins.* 52

NIGHT CHARMER 3 b.f. Burslem 123–Wind Shadow (Windjammer (USA)) [1988 NR 1989 9f⁵ 11f 10f⁴ 11g 8.2g] 5,000Y: lengthy filly: fourth foal: half-sister to a winner in Hong Kong by Don: dam unplaced on flat and over hurdles in Ireland: poor form at best, including in seller: should stay 1¼m: visored penultimate start, blinkered last. *J. S. Wilson.* —

NIGHT CLUB (GER) 5 ch.g. Esclavo (FR)–Nightlife (GER) (Priamos (GER) 123) [1988 NR 1989 12.2g⁵ 10f a8g] tall, lengthy, sparely-made gelding: appears no longer of much account: unruly in preliminaries on reappearance. *J. P. Smith.* —

NIGHT DUCHESS 2 gr.f. (Apr 15) Night Shift (USA)–Nostro Amore (GER) (Pentathlon) [1989 5g⁵ 5m 5g⁵ 6g 7g³ 7g] smallish filly: moderate walker: half- 73

sister to 3 winners abroad: dam champion 2-y-o filly in Germany: ridden by 7-lb claimer, showed improved form when around a length third of 17, leading far side long way, to Higher Hamill in nursery at Newcastle in October: best form at 7f: easily best form on good ground: sold 2,500 gns Doncaster November Sales. *M. Brittain.*

NIGHTFALL 3 b.g. Night Shift (USA)–Empress Victoria (Brave Invader (USA)) —
[1988 NR 1989 10f 17.6f 14d 12m 15.8g] 2,800Y: big, workmanlike gelding: third foal: half-brother to 1½m winner Vickstown (by Town And Country) and temperamental and unreliable plater Victoria Star (by Comedy Star): dam winning point-to-pointer and hunter chaser: little sign of ability, including in seller: sold to join G. Ham 6,400 gns Newmarket Autumn Sales. *C. A. Cyzer.*

NIGHT FERRY 2 br.g. (Mar 19) Dreams To Reality (USA) 113–Southern Aire —
(USA) (Caro 133) [1989 5d] IR 2,200Y: well-grown, rather leggy gelding: first foal: dam Irish staying maiden: 16/1, green and on edge, slowly away and soon tailed off in 10-runner maiden at Catterick in March: sold 450 gns Doncaster November Sales. *S. J. Muldoon.*

NIGHT FOLLOWS DAY (USA) 2 gr.f. (May 23) Marfa (USA)–Triggs'z 37
(USA) (Successor) [1989 5.3g 5g³ 5.8h³ 6m 7m⁵ 7m 10f] $5,000Y: small, wiry filly: moderate mover: half-sister to several winners, 3 at least useful, including 1980 2-y-o 6f to 7.6f winner Admiral's Heir (by Crafty Admiral) and 1984 2-y-o 7f winner Prince Georgetown (by Laomedonte): dam won over 6f: sire very smart winner at up to 9f: poor plater: should stay 7f: blinkered fifth and last outings: trained by P. Cole first 2 starts: sold 2,700 gns Newmarket Autumn Sales. *D. W. P. Arbuthnot.*

NIGHT JAR 2 b.f. (May 18) Night Shift (USA)–Fodens Eve 80 (Dike (USA)) 54
[1989 6m 7d] half-sister to several winners here and abroad, including 1m claimer winner Lopski (by Niniski): dam 5f winner at 2 yrs: better effort in late-season events 8 lengths seventh to Hebba in maiden at Newbury on debut. *W. Hastings-Bass.*

NIGHT LADY 3 b.f. Night Shift (USA)–Lady Donaro 76 (Ardoon 124) [1988 5s* 70
5m* 5f 5g⁴ 5g 1989 5f 7m 6g³ 6s 6g 6s 6g] strong, sturdy filly: carries condition: modest handicapper: staying-on third at Hamilton in September, easily best effort as 3-y-o: unfavourably drawn last 2 starts, blinkered final one: stays 6f: acts on top-of-the-ground and soft going: very edgy on reappearance: sold 4,400 gns Doncaster October Sales. *J. Berry.*

NIGHTMARE KNAVE 2 ch.c. (Jun 4) King of Clubs 124–Mary's Dream 80 p
(Midsummer Night II 117) [1989 6g a6g*] small, lengthy colt: half-brother to several winners, including useful Irish sprinter Pitmarie (by Pitskelly) and fairly useful 1984 2-y-o 6f winner Try Nordan (by Miami Springs): dam, Irish 1m winner, is out of half-sister to Bolkonski: won late-year maiden at Lingfield by 5 lengths: will be suited by 7f: sure to improve. *W. Carter.*

NIGHT PRINCESS 2 b.f. (Mar 24) Night Shift (USA)–Khadine 79 (Astec 128) 72 ?
[1989 6m 6f³ 6g⁶] 6,800Y: close-coupled filly: second reported living foal: half-sister to 3-y-o Khadino (by Relkino): dam required good test of stamina: close third to Purity at Brighton in October, easily best effort in maidens. *C. F. Wall.*

NIGHT SECRET 3 b.f. Nijinsky (CAN) 138–Clandestina (USA) 98 (Secretariat 86
(USA)) [1988 NR 1989 8m⁴ 10f*] 670,000Y: lengthy, angular filly: second living foal: dam, Irish 1¼m winner, is half-sister to Seattle Slew and Lomond (by Northern Dancer): evens, won maiden at Beverley in September by a head, always close up and rallying gamely: didn't handle turn in similar event (went down well) at Warwick: stays 1¼m well. *H. R. A. Cecil.*

NIGHT-SHIRT 2 b.g. (May 25) Night Shift (USA)–Vestina 85 (Run The Gantlet 65
(USA)) [1989 7m 8f 8f² a7g³] 7,600Y: workmanlike, deep-girthed gelding: half-brother to prolific Italian winner Mister Great (by Great Nephew) and a hurdles winner: dam, 7f and 1¼m winner, is daughter of Irish 1000 Guineas winner Cloonagh: quite modest maiden: will stay 1¼m. *Sir Mark Prescott.*

NIGHT TRADER (USA) 3 br.f. Melyno 130–Disco Girl (FR) (Green Dancer —
(USA) 132) [1988 NR 1989 8.5m⁶ 8.2g⁶] 4,200 2-y-o: big, workmanlike filly: fourth foal: half-sister to French winners at up to 1m by Riverman and Mr Prospector and to very useful 1985 2-y-o 6.5f winner Femme de Nuit (by Cresta Rider): dam, French 1½m winner, is half-sister to Vilikaia: well beaten in maidens in the North. *J. Berry.*

NIGHT TRANSACTION 2 ch.f. (Mar 25) Tina's Pet 121–Beech Tree 67 — p
(Fighting Ship 121) [1989 8m 8g] 15,500Y: stocky filly: half-sister to 3-y-o Most of All (by Absalom) and several winners, including middle-distance stayers Owen's

Pride (by Owen Dudley) and Faux Pavillon (by Alias Smith): dam stayer: 33/1, never dangerous in large-field maidens at Newmarket and Leicester (caught eye keeping on steadily under very considerate handling) late in season: sort to do better in time. *A. Hide.*

NIKATINO 3 b.f. Bustino 136–Latakia 80 (Morston (FR) 125) [1988 6f 7d 7m⁶ **63** 1989 8.5s 12h⁶ 11.7m* 12m² 11.7m* 12f³ 12f⁵] leggy, rather sparely-made filly: has a round action: quite modest handicapper: showed improved form when winning twice at Windsor in the summer: will stay 1¾m +: acts on firm going. *R. Akehurst.*

NIKITAS 4 b.g. Touching Wood (USA) 127–Hi There 89 (High Top 131) [1988 8g⁴ **77** § 8g⁴ 12f² 11.5d² 12f² 12g* 12m² 11.1g⁵ 13.3f⁵ 12g 11s 1989 11f 12f³ 12f 10f⁵ 11.7m] good-topped gelding: 20/1, creditable third of 6 at Lingfield, best effort in handicaps in 1989: on toes and pulled hard early next outing: gelded after final one: stays 1½m: acts on any going: a difficult ride (dropped bit tenth outing at 3 yrs) and needs strong handling: untrustworthy. *Miss A. J. Whitfield.*

NIKKI DOW 3 b.g. Tanfirion 110–Amboselli 73 (Raga Navarro (ITY) 119) [1988 **68** 5h² 5g⁴ 5d* 6g³ 1989 6m* 5m² 5m² 5m² 5g³ 5g a6g] small, angular gelding: quite modest handicapper: won claimer at Windsor in July: likely to prove suited by 6f or stiff 5f: acts on hard going and a soft surface: sold out of Sir Mark Prescott's stable 10,500 gns Newmarket Autumn Sales after sixth start. *P. Howling.*

NIKKRIS 2 ch.f. (Apr 21) Song 132–Java Jive 63 (Hotfoot 126) [1989 5m⁶ 5m⁶ **53** 5.1m⁶ 5m⁵ 5g⁴] 6,000Y: smallish, angular filly: turns fore-feet in: moderate mover: first foal: dam suited by sprint distances: plating-class form: will stay 6f: has run well for 7-lb claimer. *R. W. Stubbs.*

NIKLAS ANGEL 3 b.c. Petorius 117–The Woodbird (Tudor Melody 129) [1988 **69** 5d⁶ 5s⁵ 5g 5m 7m 7.5g³ 7g* 7m⁴ 8s 7g 1989 8.2s⁵ 10v 8.3m* 7f 8h* 8.5g 8f 10f⁶ 7.5m⁴ 7g 8f² a8g* a8g² a7g² a8g³] leggy, close-coupled, lightly-made colt: moderate mover: won sellers (bought in 1,750 gns then 5,600 gns) at Windsor and Brighton in May and claimer (returned to form) at Lingfield in October: effective at 7f and 1m: suited by a sound surface: has run well in blinkers and for an apprentice: below form when sweating: bandaged reappearance. *C. N. Allen.*

NIKOLAISE 2 b.c. (Apr 27) Niniski (USA) 125–Black Crow 72 (Sea Hawk II 131) **62** [1989 7g 8.2f 8m⁵] IR 40,000Y: close-coupled colt: poor mover: seventh living foal: closely related to useful 7f and 1m winner Ghaaer (by Gorytus) and half-brother to 3 winners, including Irish 1¼m winner and hurdler Dark Raven (by Formidable): dam won over 9f and 1¼m: quite modest maiden: will stay well: sweating second start: sold 11,500 gns Newmarket Autumn Sales. *M. A. Jarvis.*

NIMUE 4 b.f. Kris 135–Tintagel 118 (Blakeney 126) [1988 10.5m⁶ 10.7g⁶ 11g⁵ 9g³ **49** 1989 8m⁴ 10.1m 10f⁶] sparely-made ex-French filly: fifth foal: half-sister to 10.5f winner Yabis (by Bold Bidder), later useful winner over hurdles/fences: dam won over 1m and 10.5f in France: unruly in preliminaries, 6 lengths fourth of 10 in minor

William Hill Claiming Stakes, Lingfield—Niklas Angel beats Good For The Roses in the first race in Britain on an all-weather track

event at Carlisle in June: never dangerous after in similar contest at Windsor and maiden at Folkestone: blinkered once at 3 yrs: sold 4,000 gns Newmarket December Sales. *M. A. Jarvis.*

NINETEENTH OF MAY 3 b.f. Homing 130–Trigamy 112 (Tribal Chief 125) 62 [1988 6d6 6g 6m 1989 8g 11.7m5 8m* 8.2m2 9g 8f2 8f] rather leggy filly: co-favourite, much improved form when winning handicap at Doncaster in July: good second in claimer (again needing plenty of driving) and handicap: should stay beyond 1m: acts on firm ground. *C. A. Horgan.*

NINJA 3 ch.g. Niniski (USA) 125–Buckhurst 85 (Gulf Pearl 117) [1988 6g 7m6 7d3 7.3m 1989 8g 12.3m 10g] close-coupled, angular gelding: modest maiden in 1988: below form in handicaps in spring as 3-y-o, racing very freely penultimate start: lacks pace: should be suited by 1½m: best form on a soft surface: joined D. Nicholson and subsequently gelded. *G. A. Pritchard-Gordon.*

NIPOTINA 3 b.f. Simply Great (FR) 122–Mothers Girl (Huntercombe 133) [1988 53 5.8g6 6g6 6s 1989 7d4 8f 8g 8.2m5 8f 7m6 10.4m4 11g6 a11g] small filly: moderate mover: plating-class maiden: should stay at least 11f: acts on firm going and a soft surface: has run well when sweating and edgy. *R. Hollinshead.*

NIP THROUGH 3 ch.f. Move Off 112–Chomolonga (High Top 131) [1988 NR — 1989 10f 11s] small, angular filly: first foal: dam unraced: bit backward, behind in claimer and seller in the North. *Miss S. E. Hall.*

NIYIL REEF 3 b.g. Main Reef 126–Niyil (FR) (Djakao (FR) 124) [1988 8m 7m 7g 52 1989 8s 12.2d 12m* 12m4 12.2m 9f6 11f6] good-bodied gelding: has a roundish action: 33/1 and on toes, set modest pace when winning seller (no bid) at Thirsk in May: good fourth week later, making most and easily best effort in claimers and handicap after: suited by 1½m and top-of-the-ground: visored final outing, blinkered previous 4: sold 7,000 gns Doncaster August Sales. *J. S. Wainwright.*

NIZAMIYA 3 b.f. Darshaan 133–Noureen (Astec 128) [1988 NR 1989 8m5 11f6] — eighth foal: half-sister to 4 winners, including very useful 5f to 1m winner Nasseem (by Zeddaan): dam unraced half-sister to very smart Tajubena, a winner at up to 1½m: easily better effort in maidens in the spring at Bath on debut: edgy and sweating next time: should stay beyond 1m. *R. F. Johnson Houghton.*

NOALTINA 3 b.f. Noalto 120–Tantra 72 (Song 132) [1988 NR 1989 7f 6f] 4,800F, — 5,800Y: medium-sized, good-bodied filly: fifth foal: half-sister to 2 seller winners, including 1¼m winner Bewitching Wind (by Windjammer), and to 5f winner Braemar Road (by John de Coombe): dam won 3 sprints at 2 yrs: always behind in summer maidens: sold 1,100 gns Doncaster November Sales. *H. J. Collingridge.*

NOBBY 3 b.c. Dalsaan 125–Parkeen Princess (He Loves Me 120) [1988 7m 7.5f 6g 76 1989 8.2s2 8.2f* 8f* 8m* 8f4 10.2m*] workmanlike colt: has a round action: modest handicapper: successful at Hamilton, Edinburgh and Carlisle (edging right) in June and in amateurs event (7/2 on, bit below best) at Doncaster in July: best efforts over 1m: acts on any going: has joined J. Ffitch-Heyes. *Sir Mark Prescott.*

NO BEATING HARTS 6 b.g. London Bells (CAN) 109–Movement 79 (Daring 76 Display (USA) 129) [1988 5d* 5d5 5d 6f4 5g6 5m4 5g2 5g2 5s2 5g 5m4 5f6 6m 5f4 5d 5s 6s 1989 5g 5s2dis 5g* 5m 6f2 5f3 6f 5g5 5g5 6g3 5.6g 5g6 5d] rangy, good-bodied gelding: carries plenty of condition: moderate mover: modest handicapper: apprentice ridden at overweight, won decisively at Doncaster in May: second past post at Epsom week earlier, but disqualified for serious interference 1f out: suited by 5f and an easy surface: best form without blinkers or visor: has got on toes and often sweats: has looked none too keen and best with waiting tactics: consistent, but has won only 4 of his 61 races. *M. McCormack.*

NOBLE BID 5 b.h. Kings Lake (USA) 133–First Round 97 (Primera 131) [1988 — 10g 10m3 10g2 10g 1989 8g6] lengthy, attractive horse: has a short, scratchy action: fairly useful handicapper at his best: 50/1, well-beaten sixth of 8 in minor event at Leicester in September: suited by 1¼m: acts on any going: winning hurdler. *Miss S. J. Wilton.*

NOBLE BRAVE 2 b.g. (Apr 28) Indian King (USA) 128–Windy Lady (Whistling — Wind 123) [1989 6f] IR 2,000Y: rather leggy, long-backed gelding: half-brother to several winners, including 1¼m winner Al Khaled (by Lord Gayle) and 1985 2-y-o 5f winner Virgin Prince (by Prince Tenderfoot), later useful winner in Italy: dam lightly-raced Irish maiden: 33/1, backward and green, soon tailed off in 16-runner maiden at Salisbury in August: subsequently gelded. *R. Hannon.*

NOBLE LUSTRE (USA) 3 b.f. Lyphard's Wish (FR) 122–Crowned (Royal And 70 Regal (USA)) [1988 6g 6m 1989 8f 7m3 8g2 7m3 10m] medium-sized filly: modest form when placed in handicaps: appears best at up to 1m: acts on top-of-the-ground. *C. F. Wall.*

NOBLELY (USA) 2 b.c. (Feb 18) Lyphard (USA) 132–Nonoalca (FR) 120 **94** p
(Nonoalco (USA) 131) [1989 8d² 8g*] fifth foal: half-brother to French 3-y-o maiden
Nucleon (by Mr Prospector), French 10.5f winner Narmada (by Blushing Groom)
and French 7.5f (at 2 yrs) to 1½m winner Narghile (by Foolish Pleasure), later
successful in USA: dam second in Poule d'Essai des Pouliches: beaten ½ length by
Intimiste, pair 8 lengths clear, in newcomers race at Saint-Cloud in October: won
maiden at Longchamp later in month by 4 lengths: will stay 1¼m: sure to win more
races. *Mme C. Head, France.*

NOBLE MATCH 2 ch.f. (May 7) The Noble Player (USA) 126–Marylove **78**
(Kalydon 122) [1989 5d* 5m* 5f³ 5m⁵] 3,500F, 4,600Y: leggy filly: half-sister to
3-y-o 1½m winner Sam Cocktail (by Be My Guest) and several other winners here
and abroad, including 1985 2-y-o 5f winner Blessed Aisle (by Godswalk): dam, Irish
middle-distance winner, is closely related to very smart Ksar: successful in maiden
at Newbury in April and nursery (disputed lead on bridle 1f out when beating Born
To Swing by 1½ lengths) at Leicester in July: good fifth of 6 to In The Papers in
nursery at Sandown in September: bred to stay beyond 5f. *I. A. Balding.*

NOBLE PARTNER 2 b.c. (Jan 26) Blushing Scribe (USA) 107–Super Fortune —
(USA) (Super Concorde (USA) 128) [1989 7g 8g] 760F: angular, useful-looking colt:
first foal: dam unraced: well beaten in maidens at Sandown and Leicester: off course
4 months in between. *D. J. G. Murray-Smith.*

NOBLE PATRIARCH 2 b.c. (Apr 12) Alzao (USA) 117–Pampala (Bold Lad **105** p
(IRE) 133) [1989 7g 7m⁴ 8g* 8g* 8m*] IR 13,000F, 35,000Y: quite attractive colt:
half-brother to Irish 6f and 1m winner Fletcher Christian (by Ahonoora): dam Irish
maiden: progressive colt: won maiden at Wolverhampton, nursery at Goodwood and
listed Red Oaks Autumn Stakes (by ¾ length from Harbour Bar, running on well
despite poor run) at Ascot in autumn: will be suited by 1¼m. *J. L. Dunlop.*

NOBLE SAVAGE 3 ch.c. Caerleon (USA) 132–Indian Maid 117 (Astec 128) **103**
[1988 8m* 7g⁵ 1989 10f³ 16f⁶ 15g³ 14f³ 14m³ 16m* 19g² 15.5g] strong,
medium-sized colt: 6/1 on, easily made all in 4-runner minor event at Thirsk in
September: useful form second to fifth and final outings, making all and narrowly
first past post in Group 2 Prix de l'Esperance at Longchamp on third but hanging left
and demoted for interference: stays 2m: acts on firm going: useful. *G. Harwood.*

NOBLE SON 3 b.g. Thatching 131–Eden Quay (King's Bench 132) [1988 NR 1989 —
10m⁴ 8.2f 8f] 7,800Y: medium-sized gelding: half-brother to numerous winners here

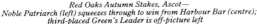

Red Oaks Autumn Stakes, Ascot—
Noble Patriarch (left) squeezes through to win from Harbour Bar (centre);
third-placed Green's Leader is off-picture left

and abroad, including fair 7f and 1m winner Alpine Meadow (by Home Guard) and fairly useful 1½m winner Santa Quay (by Santa Claus): dam lightly-raced sister to speedy Victoria Quay: well beaten, though showed signs of ability staying on steadily in claimer and maiden last 2 outings: has joined M. Naughton. *J. Hanson.*

NOBLE SOUL 2 ch.f. (May 1) Sayf El Arab (USA) 127–Fleet Noble (USA) — p (Vaguely Noble 140) [1989 a7g⁵] half-sister to several winners, including Irish 9f to 1½m winner Fleet Girl (by Habitat), dam of Oaks second Bourbon Girl: dam won over 8.5f and 9f at 2 yrs: around 10 lengths fifth of 14 to Persian Soldier in maiden at Lingfield in December: should improve. *P. T. Walwyn.*

NOBODYS SWEETHEART 2 b.f. (Mar 18) Pharly (FR) 130–Favorable 80 Exchange (USA) (Exceller (USA) 129) [1989 5f* 5f* 5.8f⁴ 6g*] 22,000Y: small, lengthy filly: second foal: dam, French winner from around 1¼m to 1½m, is closely related to Waterford Crystal Supreme Novices' Hurdle winner Vagador: modest performer: successful in maiden at Warwick in July and nurseries at Lingfield in August and Nottingham (sweating, made most) in October: stays 6f: sold 18,000 gns Newmarket December Sales. *P. F. I. Cole.*

NODFORMS DILEMMA (USA) 6 ch.g. State Dinner (USA)–Princess Jo Jo 47 (Prince John) [1988 12s³ 10m³ 14.7m 1989 16g³] workmanlike, rather leggy gelding: moderate walker and mover: modest maiden at best: favourite and blinkered, passed post second, beaten length, but was demoted a place in handicap at Doncaster in May, idling and hanging after being pushed into lead over 3f out: stays 2m: not an easy ride, and gives impression will prove best with exaggerated waiting tactics: sold to join O. Sherwood 30,000 gns Doncaster August Sales. *D. Eddy.*

NODOLYA 2 b.f. (May 4) Niniski (USA) 125–Press Corps 93 (Realm 129) [1989 — 6f⁵] leggy, medium-sized filly: half-sister to several winners, including fair 6f and 1m winner View (by Shirley Heights) and modest 1¼m winner Later Edition (by Great Nephew): dam 6f winner at 2 yrs: 6/1, soundly-beaten last of 5 in maiden at Goodwood in July. *B. Hanbury.*

NOD'S LAW 2 b.g. (Mar 27) Homing 130–Nadron 59 (Thatching 131) [1989 7m — 8d] first foal: dam, seemed to stay 7f, is out of sister to high-class miler Hilal: poor form in seller (backward, sweating, on toes) and a maiden late in season at Thirsk. *M. J. Camacho.*

NO-LOVE-LOST 2 b.f. (Apr 24) Noalto 120–Hi Love 83 (High Top 131) [1989 — 6m 7f 8m] angular, plain filly: has a quick action: second foal: half-sister to 3-y-o Aragon Girl (by Aragon): dam 1½m and 2m winner: soundly beaten in sellers and a claimer. *J. D. Czerpak.*

NOMADIC WAY (USA) 4 b.c. Assert 134–Kittyhawk 113 (Bustino 136) [1988 104 11.7f⁴ 11.7g⁴ 16f* 15.8m* 13.3d* 16d⁶ 19g³ 15.8d³ 19v* 18g* 1989 14g* 16g² 20f⁴ 16.1g⁶ 16g³] small, lengthy colt: usually looks well: moderate mover: useful performer: successful in handicap at Newmarket in April: better efforts after when in frame in another Newmarket handicap, moderately-run Gold Cup at Royal Ascot (never a threat) and listed event (first outing for nearly 4 months) at Newmarket: stays extreme distances: acts on any going: lazy, and usually blinkered nowadays: suited by strong handling: tough and consistent: smart hurdler. *B. W. Hills.*

NOMLAS 3 b.c. Salmon Leap (USA) 131–Julip 99 (Track Spare 125) [1988 NR — 1989 9f] IR 94,000Y: tall colt: fifth foal: closely related to quite modest maiden Comfrey Glen (by Glenstal) and half-brother to useful miler Patriarch (by London Bells) and Irish 1½m winner Fiestal (by Last Fandango): dam, 2-y-o 7f winner, stayed 1½m and comes from good family: green, always behind in maiden at Kempton in May: sold 3,800 gns Newmarket Autumn Sales. *G. Harwood.*

NO MORE MAS 3 br.f. Reesh 117–Ro (Absalom 128) [1988 5.1m⁵ 5g² 5m* 5g⁵ — 5.3f⁵ 1989 5v⁵ 6s 5m] small filly: made all in seller as 2-y-o: ran moderately in 1989: probably unsuited by soft going: dead. *C. Tinkler.*

NO MORE THE FOOL 3 ch.g. Jester 119–Prima Bella 76 (High Hat 131) [1988 80 5m³ 5s* 5m⁵ 7f³ 7m² 7f 1989 10.6s⁵ 10.4f 12g 12f* 12m* 11m* 12d 12.2g 12.2d] tall, leggy, lengthy gelding: has a long stride: fair performer: won claimers at Hamilton, Pontefract and Ayr in space of 3 weeks in summer: ran poorly last 2 outings and subsequently gelded: stays 1½m: acts well on firm going: sweated up and ran moderately final start at 2 yrs. *J. Berry.*

NON CONSTAT (USA) 5 b.h. Vaguely Noble 140–Jamila (Sir Gaylord) [1988 — § 14.6d² 14v 12h² 12m⁴ 12g* 13.8f² 16m³ 15s⁴ 1989 a16g] tall, attractive horse: very slowly away and hung under pressure when winning amateurs event at Redcar as 4-y-o: 33/1 and bandaged, tailed off final 6f in handicap at Southwell in December: stays 2m: acts on hard going and a soft surface: blinkered once, visored 4 times finds

Budweiser EBF Pretty Polly Stakes, the Curragh—Noora Abu (right) won't be denied; British challenger Mamaluna is second

very little off bridle and possibly best when handled tenderly: not one to trust. *T. Kersey.*

NONE SO WISE (USA) 3 ch.g. Believe It (USA)–Nonesuch Bay 103 (Mill Reef (USA) 141) [1988 7f⁶ 8g 1989 11.5g⁴ 14f² 12.2m 13.6g] big, rangy gelding: best effort second in handicap at Sandown in July: bit unruly at stalls, well beaten in similar events after, leading 11f final start: should prove as effective at 1½m as 1¾m: acts on firm ground: claimed out of I. Balding's stable £12,000 on reappearance. *R. Akehurst.* **64**

NO-NO NADIA 2 b.f. (Apr 13) Noalto 120–Blue Breeze (USA) 70 (Blue Times (USA)) [1989 8g] 2,200Y: workmanlike filly: second foal: dam middle-distance performer: 33/1 and burly, always behind in 17-runner maiden at Leicester in November. *C. N. Allen.* **—**

NON PERMANENT 3 b.g. Niniski (USA) 125–Perma Fina 69 (Nonoalco (USA) 131) [1988 NR 1989 10.1m 10f 8g 10m 9m⁵ 10g*] 30,000Y: lengthy, useful-looking gelding: fourth foal: half-brother to fairly useful 5f winner Champion Joker (by Moorestyle): dam lightly raced: co-favourite, given fine ride by Pat Eddery to win selling handicap (bought in 5,500 gns) at Nottingham in October, leading 2f out and strongly ridden to hold on by ¾ length: easily best other effort time before: stays 1¼m: possibly best with give in the ground: bandaged and moved moderately down third start: sold to join P. Blockley 16,000 gns Newmarket Autumn Sales. *A. A. Scott.* **66**

NOORA ABU 7 b.m. Ahonoora 122–Ishtar Abu (St Chad 120) [1988 9d⁴ 6g³ 7m 8s⁵ 6m 8g³ 7m³ 5g 8g⁶ 6g⁵ 1989 7m⁵ 9g² 8m³ 10g² 10d* 12g² 10g] lengthy, narrow mare: successful 7 times in 1987: won for only time afterwards and showed **113**

629

improved form when beating Mamaluna by ½ length in Group 2 Budweiser EBF Pretty Polly Stakes at the Curragh in July: creditable second of 5 to Slender Style in EBF Meld Stakes at same course 8 weeks later, weakening final 1f: ran poorly in EBF Phoenix Champion Stakes final outing: probably best at up to 1¼m: acted on any going: blinkered once: won for apprentice: splendidly tough and genuine: in foal to Nordico. *J. S. Bolger, Ireland.*

NO QUARTER GIVEN 4 b.g. Don 128–Maggie Mine 85 (Native Prince) [1988   **72** 8m 8g 7g⁶ 6g 6s⁶ 6d⁶ 1989 6s⁶ 5d 6d* 6g⁴ 6m* 5d 6g³ 5g³ 6g² 6s⁴ 5d 5s*] rangy, well-made gelding: carries plenty of condition: quite modest handicapper: made virtually all when winning at Folkestone (apprentices) in April, Doncaster (dead-heating with Got Away) in May and Hamilton (easily best effort) in November: effective at 5f and 6f: acts on top-of-the-ground and soft going: races up with pace: consistent. *P. S. Felgate.*

NORABLASSIE 2 b.f. (May 14) Norwick (USA) 120–Aberdeen Lassie 102   — (Aberdeen 109) [1989 7m 5f 8g] 4,400Y: leggy filly: half-sister to 3 winners, notably Stewards' Cup winner Madraco (by Hot Spark): dam won from 5f to 7f at 2 yrs: always behind in maidens: backward first 2 starts. *H. J. Collingridge.*

NORBERTO (CAN) 3 b.c. Roberto (USA) 131–Northern Sunset (Northfields **123** (USA)) [1988 8g² 8s* 10s⁶ 1989 11d⁵ 12m² 12g⁴ 10g² 10g² 13.5s² 12g] smallish, strong colt: won maiden at Longchamp as 2-y-o: second in 1989 in Prix Hocquart (getting much run and beaten short neck) and Grand Prix de Paris Louis Vuitton at same course, Prix Guillaume d'Ornano at Deauville and Grand Prix de Deauville Lancel: good seventh, beaten about 4 lengths, in Prix de l'Arc de Triomphe at Longchamp final start: possibly best at up to 1½m: acts on top-of-the-ground and soft going: blinkered last 4 starts: very smart and consistent. *P.-L. Biancone, France.*

NORDIC BRAVE 3 b.c. Indian King (USA) 128–Belle Viking (FR) (Riverman **67** (USA) 131) [1988 5d* 5g⁴ 5g⁵ 6g⁶ 5g⁶ 7f 6s 7g 1989 9v⁴ 6d* 7s⁵ 7g⁶ 6g⁵] leggy, lightly-made, angular colt: quite modest handicapper: ridden by 5-lb claimer, made all at Pontefract in April: 25/1 on first run for 4½ months, best effort after on final start: suited by 6f: acts on a soft surface: changed hands 1,200 gns Doncaster February Sales. *M. Brittain.*

NORFOLKIEV (FR) 3 b.c. In Fijar (USA) 121–Touraille (FR) (Jim French   — (USA)) [1988 6g³ 6d 1989 6g a6g] good-bodied colt: moderate mover: has scope: little sign of ability in maidens and a handicap: off course 7 months before final start: should stay at least 1m: tongue tied down first 3 starts. *M. Moubarak.*

NORFOLK THATCH 3 b.g. Thatching 131–Pellarosa (Crepello 136) [1988 7f   — 6g 7g 6d 7d 1989 9g 6g 6m] plating class as 2-y-o: well beaten (including in handicaps) in 1989, backward first 2 starts then facing very stiff task: bred to stay 7f. *N. A. Callaghan.*

NORINSKI 3 ch.c. Niniski (USA) 125–Never A Lady 112 (Pontifex (USA)) [1988 **91** 7g⁶ 1989 12g⁴ 12.3d* 14f³ 16f 14m⁵] lengthy colt: has a quick action: won maiden at Ripon in April: creditable fifth in handicap at Haydock: well behind in Queen's Vase at Royal Ascot: should stay beyond 1¾m: acts on firm going and a soft surface. *Lord John FitzGerald.*

NORMHURST 3 ch.g. Lucky Wednesday 124–Bronze Princess 72 (Hul A Hul **64** 124) [1988 6d 6g 7m⁴ 7.5m⁴ 8d⁶ 8.2s⁶ 8.2s* 1989 10d 10.6s 10.6m 12 12.3m 9g⁵ 11s* 12s] lengthy gelding: poor mover: quite modest handicapper: won at Hamilton by neck in September, always close up: easily best other effort as 3-y-o time before: not given hard race final start: stays 11f: acts well on soft going: sweating on reappearance and when visored fourth start. *C. Tinkler.*

NORQUAY (USA) 4 ch.g. Arctic Tern (USA) 126–Godetia (USA) 119 (Sir Ivor **76** 135) [1988 8d² 8d² 10.1m³ 8m⁴ 8g⁴ 1989 10.2g⁶ 8g⁵ 9f 9.2f⁶ 8m 8.5g* 8m⁵ 7f⁵ 10.6m⁴ 8.2d*] close-coupled, workmanlike gelding: moderate mover: modest performer: successful in amateurs handicap at Beverley in July and in claimer (well-backed favourite, claimed to join N. Tinkler £10,411) at Haydock in October: stays 10.6f: goes particularly well with a bit of give in ground: often bandaged behind nowadays: visored fifth start: winning selling hurdler. *I. A. Balding.*

NORSE COUNTRY 2 b.f. (Apr 30) Town And Country 124–Norsemen's Lady   — (Habat 127) [1989 7f 7m] angular, plain filly: fifth foal: sister to middle-distance stayers Time Warp and Norstown, latter 6f winner at 2 yrs: dam poor maiden: bit backward and ridden by 7-lb claimer, well beaten in summer sellers at Wolverhampton. *W. G. M. Turner.*

NORSTOCK 2 b.f. (May 14) Norwick (USA) 120–Millingdale 65 (Tumble Wind **52** (USA)) [1989 6g 7f 8f] workmanlike filly: fourth foal: half-sister to 3-y-o 7f winner

Lady Stock (by Crofter): dam, ran only at 2 yrs, second over 5f and 6f: best effort in maidens second start: ran poorly final one: should stay 1m. *J. White.*

NORSTOWN 7 ch.g. Town And Country 124–Norsemen's Lady (Habat 127) **58** [1988 NR 1989 14f² 16g⁴ 16f² 15.3g*] medium-sized gelding: plating-class handicapper: won at Wolverhampton in July: suited by a test of stamina: acts on any going: has often worn blinkers or a visor, but didn't in 1989: has run well for amateur: probably unsuited by track at Chester. *R. J. Holder.*

NORTHANTS 3 b.g. Northern Baby (CAN) 127–Astania (GER) (Arratos (FR)) **89 §** 127 [1988 NR 1989 12d* 14f⁵ 10.2f* 12m* 12f 12.5f³ 11d² 10f 10g² 12g* 13.3d³ 12d] 22,000Y: medium-sized, sturdy gelding: brother to modest maiden Eskimo Mite, a winner over hurdles, and half-brother to 11f and 12.3f winner Transcendence and a graded stakes winner (both by Naskra): dam, Irish 13f winner, is half-sister to dam of leading German middle-distance colt Alpenkonig: won maiden at Folkestone in April, handicap at Doncaster in May, minor event at Beverley in June and handicap at Goodwood in October: detached last for long way in November Handicap at Thirsk final start: stays 1½m well: acts on firm going and a soft surface: bandaged second outing: blinkered after: has been reluctant to race and is temperamental. *Mrs L. Piggott.*

NORTH COUNTRY 2 b.c. (Apr 9) Nordico (USA)–Loren (Crocket 130) [1989 **79** 6g⁵ 6g²] IR 90,000Y: neat, good-quartered colt: half-brother to several winners, including useful Irish 1982 2-y-o 7f winner Red Rose Bowl (by Dragonara Palace), dam of smart sprinter Gallic League, and Cesarewitch winner and useful hurdler Private Audition (by Crimson Beau): dam won 2 races in Italy at 2 yrs: sire 1m and 9f winner: around 3 lengths fifth of 6, headed under 2f out and eased last 50 yds, to Qathif in minor event at Ascot: 5 lengths second of 15, unable to quicken last 1f, to Childrey in maiden at Folkestone later in October: will stay 1m. *H. R. A. Cecil.*

NORTHENER 2 ch.c. (Apr 11) Reasonable (FR) 119–Northampton (Northfields **34** (USA)) [1989 7.5f 6m 7f] 8,000F: small, angular, plain colt: fourth foal: half-brother to 2 winners, including quite useful 1985 2-y-o 7f and 1m winner Delapre (by He Loves Me), later successful in USA: dam ran once: poor form in maiden auction event and sellers: wears a visor. *C. R. Beever.*

NORTHERN ALLIANCE 5 ch.g. Northfields (USA)–Plight (Pieces of Eight **57 d** 128) [1988 10f 14g⁴ 10m 16m 18g 16d⁵ 1989 12.2s⁶ 15.5s² 14s 14s 17f³ 15.5f 12h⁵ 17.1h⁵] tall, lengthy, sparely-made gelding: has a round action: quite modest handicapper on his day: favourite, caught final strides when neck second at Folkestone in April: well below form afterwards: stays 2m: probably acts on any going: visored sixth outing, blinkered last 2: occasionally sweats: has looked rather a difficult ride and probably best with strong handling: sold to join A. Moore 2,700 gns Newmarket September Sales: inconsistent. *G. Lewis.*

NORTHERN BRAVE 3 ch.c. Mill Reef (USA) 141–Sharpina (Sharpen Up 127) **78** [1988 7m³ 8d⁴ 1989 10f³ 12f⁴ 12h⁴ 12s³ 12g³ 10g] short-backed colt: modest maiden: possibly suited by 1½m: acts on any going with possible exception of hard: often sweats slightly: sold out of H. Thomson Jones's stable 15,000 gns Newmarket Autumn Sales after fifth start. *N. Tinkler.*

NORTHERN COMMANDER 3 ch.g. Music Boy 124–Dawn's Dream 82 **82** (Sandford Lad 133) [1988 5v³ 5g 5m³ 5h³ 7s³ 6g² 6s 6m⁵ 1989 7g* 6v* 7d] sparely-made, dipped-backed gelding: won maiden at Newcastle in March, running on well despite edging left, and 4-runner minor event at Ayr in April: tailed off in £17,000 handicap at Ascot later in April: stays 7f well: acts on top-of-the-ground and heavy going. *J. Berry.*

NORTHERN CREST 3 ch.g. Anfield 117–Contadina (Memling) [1988 7m 8m **63** 1989 8d 11.7m 14g⁵ 16f³ 16m³ 14d] tall, angular gelding: easy mover: modest maiden: soundly beaten at Nottingham (blinkered, eased considerably) and Haydock (pulled hard and tended to wander) last 2 starts: shapes like a stayer: acts on firm ground: sweating first 3 outings: looks difficult ride: sold 3,200 gns Newmarket Autumn Sales. *P. W. Harris.*

NORTHERN FIELDS 2 ch.c. (Mar 20) Gabitat 119–Hadera 74 (Northfields **51** (USA)) [1989 5s⁵ 6f⁶ 6m 7m⁵ 7.6m 6f 7d] close-coupled colt: moderate mover: second reported foal: dam won over 5f at 2 yrs and 6 times at around 1m from 3 yrs to 7 yrs: plating-class maiden: below form in sellers last 2 starts: seems to stay 7f: sweating fourth outing. *B. Gubby.*

NORTHERN FLAGSHIP (USA) 3 b.c. Northern Dancer–Native Partner **96** (USA) (Raise A Native) [1988 NR 1989 8m⁶ 8m⁴ 10m³ 10m²] strong, good-looking colt: brother to top-class 5f to 1m winner Ajdal, closely related to 3 winners by

Nijinsky, and half-brother to several more, including Formidable (by Forli) and very smart French middle-distance stayer Fabuleux Jane (by Le Fabuleux): dam, 1m stakes winner, is half-sister to Kentucky Derby second Jim French: fairly useful form in maidens at York (£5,300 event), Newbury, Newmarket and Sandown: stayed 1¼m: lacked turn of foot: retired to Saxony Farm, Kentucky, fee 2,000 dollars. *M. R. Stoute.*

NORTHERN GODDESS 2 b.f. (Mar 22) Night Shift (USA)–Hearten (Hittite Glory 125) [1989 5d⁵ 5f* 5m² 5.8f³] 21,000Y: compact, attractive filly: third foal: half-sister to 2 winners by King of Spain, including 3-y-o Spanish Oak, 5f winner at 2 yrs: dam unraced daughter of smart middle-distance mare Nortia: made most in maiden at Newbury in May, beating Amathus Glory 2 lengths: never-dangerous second to Boozy in quite well-contested minor event at Epsom following month, better subsequent effort: should stay 6f. *I. A. Balding.* **80**

NORTHERN GUNNER 6 b.g. Northern Guest (USA)–Jukella (Jukebox 120) [1988 NR 1989 10.8m] close-coupled, quite attractive gelding: no form in handicaps since 1986: bandaged, sweating and carrying condition, tailed off at Warwick (went freely to post) in June: stays 1¼m: probably acts on any going: blinkered once: ungenuine hurdler. *M. H. B. Robinson.* **—**

NORTHERN HABIT 3 ch.c. Salmon Leap (USA) 131–Manx Millenium 66 (Habitat 134) [1988 6m² 6g³ 1989 7m² 8f²] leggy, quite good-topped colt: has scope: fair maiden: led over 5f and beaten head at Kempton: eased considerably when 10 lengths behind sole opponent odds-on Sabotage in minor event at Goodwood later in July: stays 7f well. *I. A. Balding.* **82**

NORTHERN HAL 2 b.c. (Mar 28) Sadler's Wells (USA) 132–Northern Script (USA) 95 (Arts And Letters) [1989 6g³] IR 490,000Y: good-topped, attractive colt: has a quick action: third foal: half-brother to 3-y-o Caerless Writing (by Caerleon), successful from 1m (at 2 yrs) to 1¼m: dam miler: 11/8 but green, 6 lengths third of 4, eased final furlong, to Tidemark in maiden at Ascot in September: sure to improve. *P. T. Walwyn.* **70 p**

NORTHERN HEIGHTS 2 b.c. (Apr 9) Pharly (FR) 130–Ardmay 57 (Roan Rocket 128) [1989 7m* 7.5f4 7m4 8m³ 8g] 15,000Y: medium-sized, rather sparely-made colt: fourth foal: half-brother to 3-y-o Jascha (by Music Boy), fair 6f and 1m winner Irgaim (by Valiyar) and a winner in Belgium: dam sister to Gairloch and Whistlefield: won maiden at Wolverhampton in June by 3 lengths from Jebali: ran creditably when around 9 lengths last of 8 in Prix des Chenes at Saint-Cloud final start: stays 1m. *R. Boss.* **77 +**

NORTHERN LACE 2 gr.c. (Mar 6) Northern Tempest (USA) 120–Dragon Lace (Dragonara Palace (USA) 115) [1989 5f 6m 6g a6g] 580Y: close-coupled, sparely-made colt: first foal: dam never ran: seems of little account. *M. Brittain.* **—**

NORTHERN LINE 3 br.f. Camden Town 125–War Lass 100 (Whistler 129) [1988 5g 5m* 5g* 5f 5g³ 1989 6s 5g] rangy, good-topped filly: quite useful winner at 2 yrs: well beaten in £8,300 event and handicap (blinkered) in spring as 3-y-o: should stay 6f: best run on good ground: retained by trainer 4,900 gns Newmarket December Sales, in foal to Risk Me. *M. W. Easterby.* **—**

NORTHERN NIKKI 2 ch.f. (Apr 13) Nicholas Bill 125–Northern Venture 80 (St Alphage 119) [1989 6m] half-sister to 1985 2-y-o 5f winner Security Pacific (by Sonnen Gold): dam, 5f winner at 2 yrs, stayed 7f: 12/1, bit backward and green, soon behind in 21-runner 6f seller at Redcar in September: sold 2,100 gns Doncaster October Sales. *C. Tinkler.* **—**

NORTHERN PRINTER 4 ch.g. Baptism 119–Stradey Lynn 57 (Derrylin 115) [1988 5m 5g 5m 6g³ 5g 5m 5m⁵ 5s⁵ 6g⁵ 6d³ 7f* 7f* 7g² 7g³ 7g⁴ 7g* 1989 8g 7s 8m³ 7f⁵ 8.2m³ 8.2g 7m³ 8f²dis 7f⁶ 8.2d 7.6m⁵ 7g 8g² 9g 10.6s⁶ 7m 8d] strong, sturdy gelding: poor mover: fair handicapper: ran creditably numerous times in 1989: stays 1m: possibly not at his best on soft going, acts on any other: has carried head high: usually claimer ridden. *M. J. O'Neill.* **83**

NORTHERN RAIN 3 ch.g. Ballacashtal (CAN)–Summer Rain (Palestine 133) [1988 5d 5g* 5g 5d³ 5g 6g 1989 5s 7g a8g a8g³] compact gelding: plating-class performer: best effort for long time when third in claimer at Lingfield in November: off course 6 months after second start: appears to stay 1m. *C. N. Allen.* **51**

NORTHERN ROCKET 2 b.c. (Mar 17) Northern Tempest (USA) 120–Scotch Rocket 60 (Roan Rocket 128) [1989 5d 5s 6m 6g 8.5f 6g⁵ a5g⁵ a6g* a7g4] 9,800Y: close-coupled, leggy colt: first foal: dam 7f winner: quite modest performer: won late-season claimer at Southwell by a head: suited by 6f: blinkered last 5 starts: races freely. *J. P. Leigh.* **69**

NORTHERN RULER 7 br.g. Rolfe (USA) 77–Sanandrea (Upper Case (USA)) — [1988 14v⁵ 21.6g³ 16m² 16g⁵ 16g⁵ 1989 12s] neat gelding: good mover: bad handicapper: possibly doesn't stay extreme distances: acts on any going: blinkered once: has won for apprentice. *R. Thompson.*

NORTHERN STREET 2 ch.c. (Jan 26) Glenstal (USA) 118–Moaning Low 85 **57** (Burglar 128) [1989 5m 6g⁴ 6d] 31,000Y: smallish, quite attractive colt: half-brother to 3-y-o Lady Blues Singer (by Chief Singer) and to 6 winners here and abroad: dam 6f winner: around 15 lengths fourth of 12, fading final furlong, to Fearless Revival at Epsom in August, easily best effort in maidens. *J. P. Hudson.*

NORTHERN SURVEYOR 3 ch.c. Northern Tempest (USA) 120–Sadberge — Wonder 65 (Golden Mallard 103) [1988 5v⁵ 5m 6m 7f 7g 7g 1989 6f 5g 8.2g 9s⁶] smallish, sparely-made colt: moderate mover: poor form, including in seller: seems suited by 9f and soft going: blinkered final outing at 2 yrs. *A. M. Robson.*

NORTHERN TELLER (USA) 3 b.c. Majesty's Prince (USA)–Growing **65** Regard (USA) (Shecky Greene (USA)) [1988 6f³ 7f⁴ 8d 8.2m 1989 10.2g⁵ 8g² 8.5d³ 9f⁴ 11f² 11f* 12m⁴ 10s 12m 12.4g⁶ a13g] good-topped, quite attractive colt: has a round action: visored, won maiden at Hamilton in June: below form in handicaps after: suited by 11f: best efforts on a sound surface: blinkered fifth outing: also visored eighth and ninth. *S. G. Norton.*

NORTHERN TRYST (USA) 3 ch.c. Northern Baby (CAN) 127–Grand **104** d Bonheur (USA) (Blushing Groom (FR) 131) [1988 6g* 6g³ 1989 7g⁴ 10g 7f³ 7f] lengthy, useful-looking colt: put up useful performances when in frame in Middle Park Stakes and European Free Handicap at Newmarket: disappointing in 3 outings after: wearing net muzzle, taken quietly to post and never going well in Jersey Stakes at Royal Ascot final one: should prove suited by around 1m (pulled hard in lead over 1¼m): possibly not at his best on firm going: tends to carry head high: reportedly sent to race in USA. *G. Harwood.*

NORTHERN VALKYRIE 3 b.f. Glenstal (USA) 118–Katie Koo 82 (Persian — Bold 123) [1988 5g 1989 10.2h] no form in maidens at Bath: sold 800 gns Newmarket December Sales. *D. J. G. Murray-Smith.*

NORTHERN VILLAGE 2 ch.c. (Apr 3) Norwick (USA) 120–Merokette 83 — (Blast 125) [1989 8.2g] 9,200Y: close-coupled colt: fourth foal: half-brother to 3-y-o Parakeet (by Petong) and 1987 2-y-o 5f winner Straight Gold (by Vaigly Great): dam won 3 races at up to 1¾m: 25/1 and backward, well beaten in 20-runner minor event at Nottingham in October. *R. Boss.*

NORTHERN WARRIOR 3 b.c. Tender King 123–Dance Away (Red God 128§) **66** [1988 5f⁶ 7m 8g 1989 6s⁴ 7d³ 7s⁵ 7s 8.3m] close-coupled, quite attractive colt: quite modest maiden: stayed 7f: acted on soft ground: dead. *Capt. R. M. Smyly.*

NORTHERN ZENITH 2 ch.g. (Feb 19) Battle Hymn 103–Rose Bridges 63 **85** (Calpurnius 122) [1989 5m* 5f⁴ 5m⁵ 5f² 5m²] 1,100Y, 11,000 2-y-o: workmanlike gelding: half-brother to a prolific winner in Italy: dam, plater, stayed 1¼m: made all in maiden auction race at Warwick in May: sometimes gave trouble at start, and was withdrawn once: dead. *J. Berry.*

NORTHGATE KING 2 b.c. (Feb 10) Fairy King (USA)–Dollyful (Track Spare **51** 125) [1989 5v 5d⁵ 5g 5m²] IR 5,000F, IR 2,600Y: neat colt: fourth foal: dam poor maiden: staying-on second in seller at Beverley in June, only form: will stay 6f. *M. Brittain.*

NORTH OF PARADISE (USA) 3 gr.f. Northern Jove (CAN)–Rock Garden — 86 (Roan Rocket 128) [1988 7f 6f³ 1989 7s 6g] neat filly: plating-class maiden: best effort final start at 2 yrs: should stay at least 1m. *P. F. I. Cole.*

NORTH OF WATFORD 4 ch.c. Jasmine Star 113–Wallie Girl (Right Tack 131) **58** § [1988 5s 6v 5s 5s 5g 5m³ 5g 5f* 6m 5.8f⁵ 5g⁴ 5f⁴ 5g 1989 5g⁶ 5f 5f 5m⁶ 5m 5m⁵ 5g 5m³ 5g⁶ 6f 5.8f³ 5f⁶ 5g⁴ 8f³ 8f 7d] lengthy, good-quartered colt: poor walker: moderate mover: quite modest handicapper on his day: effective at 5f and stays 1m: suited by a sound surface: has won when sweating: sometimes bandaged near-hind: suitable mount for apprentice, but has hung left: probably unsuited by track at Chester: unreliable. *Capt. J. Wilson.*

NORTHUMBRIAN KING 3 b.g. Indian King (USA) 128–Tuna 63 (Silver **68** § Shark 129) [1988 6g⁵ 6s 8s 1989 10.2g⁴ 11f* 12f* 12.4m⁶ 12h⁴ 12.3g 12f⁴ 14f⁶ 13.6g⁶] tall, close-coupled gelding: moderate walker: quite modest handicapper: won at Redcar (not handling bends well) in May and Beverley in June: ran fairly well fifth, seventh and final starts but hasn't looked keen: stays 1½m: acts on firm going: blinkered fifth and final starts: gelded after latter: carries head high and probably ungenuine. *C. W. Thornton.*

633

NORTHWOLD STAR (USA) 3 br.f. Monteverdi 129–Its A Romp (Hotfoot 70
126) [1988 5m⁴ 6d 5g⁶ 6g⁴ 7g⁴ 7m⁴ 6s⁶ 7f 8m⁴ 9m⁵ 8.2s² 8g* 8g⁶ 8.2d⁴ 1989 10.5f
12f 10m 12h 16.2g² 16f⁵ 14m³ 17.6m² 16m³ 18.1g*] smallish, close-coupled filly:
turns off-fore in: modest handicapper: evens and visored, won 5-runner race at
Yarmouth in September by 15 lengths, leading 7f out: suited by good test of stamina:
unsuited by firm going, acts on any other: blinkered once at 2 yrs: has run creditably
for apprentice and when on toes: often makes running. *D. T. Thom.*

NORTON CHALLENGER 2 gr.c. (Apr 11) Absalom 128–Klaire 85 (Klairon 76
131) [1989 5s* 5d*] 9,000Y: rangy, good-topped colt: has plenty of scope: good
walker: half-brother to 4 winners, including smart sprinter Young Hal (by Young
Generation): dam, 7f winner at 2 yrs, is half-sister to high-class stayer Proverb:
successful in minor events at Thirsk: likely to be better suited by 6f: looked type to
win more races but wasn't seen out after late-April. *M. H. Easterby.*

NORWICH 2 b.c. (Apr 17) Top Ville 129–Dame Julian 84 (Blakeney 126) [1989 86
7m² 7m⁴] 76,000Y: big, useful-looking colt: has plenty of scope: brother to 3-y-o 2m
winner St Ville and half-brother to 4 winners, including useful 1m to 1¼m performer
Fair Dominion and fair 7f winner Domynga (both by Dominion): dam, half-sister to
good sprinter Daring Boy and very smart Daring March, won over 1m: fair form in
September minor events (appeared not to find much off bridle on either occasion) at
York (favourite) and Ascot. *B. W. Hills.*

NO SHARPS OR FLATS (USA) 2 ch.f. (Jan 21) Sharpen Up 127–Orientate 67
(Hotfoot 126) [1989 6f² 7m] $90,000Y: third reported foal: half-sister to minor
winner at about 6f in USA by Smarten: dam, behind in varied events and refused to
race once, is half-sister to dam of Pebbles: 2 lengths second of 5, running on, to very
easy winner Montendre in maiden at Brighton in October: second favourite,
weakened quickly 2f out in similar event at Chepstow 13 days later: has joined J.
Fanshawe. *M. R. Stoute.*

NO SUBMISSION (USA) 3 b.c. Melyno 130–Creeping Kate (USA) (Stop The 85
Music (USA)) [1988 8h² 1989 8.5d* 8f⁴ 8.2m 8f⁵] tall, leggy, quite attractive colt:
went keenly to post and in race when winning maiden at Beverley in April: not
discredited in minor event and handicaps in the summer: should be suited by
further: acts on firm going and a soft surface. *C. R. Nelson.*

NOTHALTO 2 b.g. (Apr 17) Noalto 120–Giri Lake 96 (Tap On Wood 130) [1989 45
5g⁵ 5m³ 6f] 500F: small, close-coupled gelding: has a round action: first foal: dam
2-y-o 6f winner, only season to race, is daughter of useful middle-distance performer Rheinsparkle: poor form, including in a seller: slowly away first 2 starts:
should be suited by further than 5f. *R. Curtis.*

NOTHING'S FREE 2 b.f. (Mar 29) Free State 125–Wayward Polly 63 58
(Lochnager 132) [1989 5d² 5f² 6g 7m 8s⁶ 6s] rather leggy, useful-looking filly: has
plenty of scope: second foal: half-sister to an animal of little account: dam won 5f
seller at 2 yrs: plating-class maiden: stays 1m. *M. W. Easterby.*

NOTLEY 2 b.c. (Apr 13) Formidable (USA) 125–Riviere Bleue (Riverman (USA) 91 p
131) [1989 6g² 6d*] 45,000Y: strong, sturdy colt: half-brother to Italian 3-y-o 7.5f
winner Prince Pupi (by Temperance Hill) and 2 winners in USA: dam, French 11f
winner, is half-sister to Star Pastures: favourite, won 24-runner maiden at Newbury
in October by 2 lengths from Illusory, making virtually all and running on strongly
despite tending to drift left inside final 1f: should stay further and improve again. *R.
Hannon.*

NOT SO SHY 4 b.f. Star Appeal 133–Nanushka 53 (Lochnager 132) [1988 10m⁵ —
10g³ 11s² 10g* 1989 10.2g 10g⁶ 12.3m 10.6m 10.6s 10g] workmanlike filly: poor
mover: modest winner as 3-y-o: below her best in 1989: stays 11f: probably suited by
give in the ground. *Miss L. C. Siddall.*

NOTTAGE (USA) 3 b.c. Northern Baby (CAN) 127–Salinidad (CHI) (Mr Long 70
(USA)) [1988 8m³ 8d³ 1989 11.7d 10g⁶ 12h⁴ 10.2h³] compact colt: modest maiden:
favourite and wearing tongue strap, below-form third in claimer (moved moderately
down, claimed to join M. Pipe £15,000) in June: suited by 1½m: acts on hard ground.
P. F. I. Cole.

NOTTA POPSI 8 ch.g. Nearly A Hand 115–Swaynes Lady 76 (St Alphage 119) —
[1988 18f 16d⁵ 1989 16.2m 15.3m] heavy-topped gelding: little form in modest
company on flat: winning hurdler/chaser. *J. L. Spearing.*

NOT YET 5 b.g. Connaught 130–Ritratto (Pinturischio 116) [1988 8g⁵ 10g* 8m* 63
10g⁵ 10s* 10m* 8g² 8.5f⁴ 8g⁴ 1989 8d 8.5d⁵ 9f* 9f⁵ 10f 10f⁵ 10.6d² 8g* 9f 8.2g⁴]
small, compact gelding: often doesn't take the eye: bad mover: quite modest
handicapper: successful at Redcar in May and Newcastle (dead-heating in

apprentice event) in August: effective at 1m and 1¼m: acts on any going: excellent mount for apprentice: occasionally sweats and gets on toes. *E. Weymes.*

NOUT 2 b.f. (Mar 31) Mashhor Dancer (USA)–Candide 109 (Bustino 136) [1989 5f* 5f 5g* 5f² 5m³] 38,000Y: rangy, rather unfurnished filly: has scope: good walker and quite good mover: half-sister to 1m winner Love Train (by Camden Town): dam, winner twice at around 7f at 2 yrs, is out of speedy half-sister to smart Kittyhawk: won maidens at Thirsk in May and minor event at Ripon in July: fair form in nurseries afterwards: should stay further than 5f. *J. Berry.*   **87**

NUCLEAR EXPRESS 2 b.g. (May 11) Martinmas 128–Halka (Daring March 116) [1989 5g* 5d* 5d² 6g 5f⁴ 5d³ 5g] 4,200Y: leggy, workmanlike gelding: turns fore-feet in: second foal: brother to 3-y-o plater Rose of High Legh, successful at 6f and 7f: dam, unraced, from family of Zimbalon and Band: made all in seller (retained 17,000 gns) at Doncaster and minor event at Pontefract early in season: best effort in nurseries on last 3 starts when fourth of 5 to Brisas at Thirsk in July: should be suited by 6f: tends to hang, and flashed tail closing stages on debut. *J. Berry.*   **75**

NUGOLA 7 ch.m. Derrylin 115–Nell Trent (Queen's Hussar 124) [1988 12g 11s 1989 12d 12g 12g] sturdy, slightly dipped-backed mare: bad mover: poor handicapper: lightly raced and no worthwhile form last 2 seasons: stays 1½m: acts on any going: visored twice. *Don Enrico Incisa.*

NUIT DE LUNE (GER) 3 b.f. Lagunas–Nagaika (GER) (Chief III 130) [1988 7m 1989 16d 8.2m 10f] leggy, angular filly: has a round action: no form in maidens and a seller. *P. J. Feilden.*   **—**

NUJOOM (USA) 2 b.f. (Feb 23) Halo (USA)–Bird of Dawning (USA) (Sea Bird II 145) [1989 7m⁵] $55,000Y: lengthy, unfurnished filly: half-sister to several winners, including fairly useful 1m to 1¼m performer Monongelia (by Welsh Pageant) and quite useful Irish 7.5f to 1½m winner Mice Bird (by Busted): dam, 6f winner at 3 yrs in USA, is daughter of Argentinian 1000 Guineas and Oaks winner Sweet Sue: 12/1, ridden by 7-lb claimer and very green, under 10 lengths fifth of 18, held up when running on well not knocked about, to Marienski in maiden at Newmarket in August: likely to improve. *W. Jarvis.*   **61 p**

NUMBER ELEVEN 2 b.f. (Jan 29) Local Suitor (USA) 128–Babycham Sparkle 80 (So Blessed 130) [1989 5m² 5g⁴ 6g³] 22,000Y: rather sparely-made filly: second foal: dam, 5f and 6f winner from 4 starts at 2 yrs, is half-sister to smart French middle-distance colt El Famoso: quite modest form when placed in maidens at Lingfield and Leicester (had to be checked 2f out, and is bit better than result suggests) late in season: hung left when below form in between: gave trouble stalls and withdrawn on intended debut: stays 6f. *Sir Mark Prescott.*   **69**

NUMBER ONE SON 2 b.c. (Feb 15) Kafu 120–Susie's Baby (Balidar 133) [1989 6g² 6f⁶ 6s 5m* 5s 5m] 14,000Y: angular colt: second foal: brother to 3-y-o Kafu Lady, fair 5f winner at 2 yrs: dam lightly raced: easily best effort when winning nursery at Warwick in October, staying on despite looking bit reluctant: below form in similar events afterwards: evidently better suited by 5f than 6f: seems unsuited by soft ground: blinkered third and final starts: sold 20,000 gns Newmarket Autumn Sales. *A. Bailey.*   **75**

NUMERATOR 3 b.c. Pharly (FR) 130–American Beauty 74 (Mill Reef (USA) 141) [1988 7s³ 1989 10s³ 10g³ 10d] quite attractive colt: modest form when third in maiden and minor events, tending to wander first 2 occasions and flashing tail on third: should have stayed 1½m: dead. *P. F. I. Cole.*   **75**

NUSAKAN (ITY) 2 ch.c. (Jan 3) Spring Heights–Present Arms (Artaius (USA) 129) [1989 8.2d⁶] second known foal: half-brother to a winner in Italy: dam Irish 2-y-o 7f winner: 50/1 and backward, around 8 lengths sixth of 11 to Almuinjjid in slowly-run maiden at Haydock in October, staying on from 2f out after being held up and left with plenty to do: should improve. *J. L. Dunlop.*   **58 p**

NUTWOOD EMMA 4 br.f. Henbit (USA) 130–Jubilant 60 (Welsh Pageant 132) [1988 10v 10d 9g 6d 1989 6d 15g] leggy filly: poor maiden: visored on reappearance: trained until after then by H. O'Neill: possibly temperamental. *W. J. Pearce.*   **—**

NYDRION (USA) 3 b.f. Critique (USA) 126–Nabila (USA) 58 (Foolish Pleasure (USA)) [1988 8g² 8.5s* 9v* 1989 9g* 10.5v* 12g* 12f⁵ 10s² 10s⁶] 33,000Y: rather leggy, close-coupled filly: has a rather scratchy action: second reported foal: half-sister to a maiden in Italy by Nodouble: dam, 8.2f winner at 3 yrs, is out of very useful winner at up to 1m Opec: won twice at Rome in April and Group 1 Oaks d'Italia (by head from Wrapping) at Milan in May: best effort after beaten 1½ lengths by Miss Secreto in Group 2 event at Rome: 14/1, chased leader 9f when well-beaten last   **108**

of 5 in Yorkshire Oaks: stays 1½m: acts on soft ground, probably unsuited by firm. *L. Brogi, Italy.*

NYONYA BESAR   2 b.f. (Apr 8) Ballad Rock 122–Nekhbet 74 (Artaius (USA)   **72 p** 129) [1989 6g] useful-looking filly: second foal: half-sister to 1988 2-y-o 8.2f seller winner Hillside Rose (by Beldale Flutter): dam, in frame from 5f to 7f, is half-sister to Irish St Leger winner M-Lolshan and useful sprinter Chemin: 100/1, around 8 lengths eighth of 28, keeping on steadily, to Alidiva in maiden at Newmarket in October: should improve. *C. F. Wall.*

NY OVER   4 ch.g. Smackover 107–Nyota 97 (Reform 132) [1988 10v⁴ 7d 10g² 10f   **54** 10.4m⁴ 8d* 10d⁵ 8g⁴ 10m⁴ 8g 10g 1989 10.2g 10m⁶] leggy, angular gelding: poor walker: plating-class winner of apprentice event at 3-y-o: did well after having poor run in Beverley handicap in June, but wasn't seen out again: effective at 1m and 1¼m: acts on top-of-the-ground and a soft surface: sweated when tried in blinkers: tends to get on edge: has found little. *B. A. McMahon.*

O

OAKES DAY   4 ch.f. Derrylin 115–Persian Breakfast 50 (Deep Diver 134) [1988   **29** 5f 5g⁴ 5h³ 5d 6g⁵ 6g 7g 1989 7.5d 6m 6f⁵ 7h⁵ 6f 6g 5g 5m³ 5g 5m 5f 5f 6f 5m] good-bodied filly: poor mover: bad maiden: stays 6f: acts on firm going. *Don Enrico Incisa.*

OASIS   3 ch.f. Valiyar 129–Emaline (FR) 105 (Empery (USA) 128) [1988 NR 1989 7f   — 10h] rather unfurnished filly: first foal: dam French 2-y-o 7f winner: well beaten in maidens: bought to join J. Baker's stable 2,100 gns Ascot July Sales. *R. V. Smyth.*

OBELISKI   3 b.g. Aragon 118–Pasha's Dream (Tarboosh (USA)) [1988 7m 8m   **67** 8d* 1989 8d³ 8m 8f 10g² 10s* 12s²] leggy, angular gelding: has a round action: useful maiden: won at Ayr (no bid) in September by 5 lengths, leading well over 2f out and hanging left: good second in non-selling handicap 6 weeks later, always prominent: suited by 1½m: goes well on soft going: trained until after third outing by W. Wilson. *M. H. Tompkins.*

OBERONS BUTTERFLY   2 b.g. (Jan 21) Full of Hope 125–Y I Oyston 73   — (Dublin Taxi) [1989 8g] first foal: dam 5f winner at 2 yrs, is half-sister to Swingit Gunner: soundly beaten in 16-runner maiden at Leicester. *C. F. Wall.*

OBLIST (CAN)   2 gr.f. (Mar 16) Exceller (USA) 129–Grey Sister (USA) (Iron   **77** Ruler (USA)) [1989 7f* 7g] 16,000Y: medium-sized, quite attractive filly: half-sister to 4 winners, one in a graded-stakes sprint: dam won 6 times in USA: favourite, won maiden at Leicester in August by ½ length from Oogie Poogie: never dangerous under 9-7 in nursery at Newcastle later in month: will stay at least 1m. *B. W. Hills.*

OBOLOV   2 ch.c. (Mar 12) Vaigly Great 127–Dortia (Martinmas 128) [1989 5m² 6g   **59** 5d 5g³] 11,500Y: small, shallow-girthed colt: turns off-fore in: third foal: half-brother to quite modest 1988 2-y-o Miss Mischievous (by Star Appeal): dam, half-sister to very smart 1979 2-y-o Sonnen Gold, unplaced at 2 yrs on only outing: plating-class maiden: form only at 5f: ran badly on dead ground. *P. Calver.*

OBSERVATION POST   3 b.c. Shirley Heights 130–Godzilla 106 (Gyr   **121** (USA) 131) [1988 7g* 8.2d* 1989 10m² 10.5f² 12g²]

In a *Timeform Interview* in May Barry Hills called Observation Post 'the apple of my eye'. Unfortunately the apple hasn't yet turned out to be golden, for though he showed good-class form Observation Post was unable to add to his victories in a well-contested maiden at Newmarket and a minor event at Nottingham as a two-year-old. Observation Post made his reappearance in the listed Newmarket Stakes shortly after the interview and went down by only half a length, in receipt of 4 lb, to the odds-on favourite Prince of Dance having travelled strongly for a long way and moved up smoothly to lead briefly a furlong out. On the strength of this very encouraging performance Observation Post was sent off 11/10 favourite for the seven-runner William Hill Dante Stakes at York later in May. This time he was pushed along three furlongs out and, staying on steadily, couldn't trouble the two-length winner Torjoun. For what proved to be his only subsequent appearance Observation Post missed Epsom in favour of the Budweiser Irish Derby, in which he came as close as any all season apart from Golden Pheasant to beating Old Vic. Held up towards the rear of the field, he made steady headway to get on the heels of

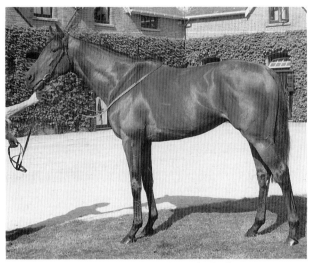

Mr R. E. Sangster's "Observation Post"

the long odds-on Old Vic entering the straight, but as the leader lengthened his stride approaching the final furlong Observation Post couldn't; he just kept on steadily for second place, four lengths down with Ile de Nisky two and a half lengths away in third.

Observation Post (b.c. 1986)	Shirley Heights (b 1975)	Mill Reef (b 1968)	Never Bend Milan Mill
		Hardiemma (b 1969)	Hardicanute Grand Cross
	Godzilla (ch 1972)	Gyr (ch 1967)	Sea Bird II Feria II
		Gently (gr 1962)	Grey Sovereign Be Careful

A run of three second places could be a sign of a professional loser, but not so with Observation Post who has none of the unsatisfactory characteristics of his half-brother Colchis (by Golden Fleece), a very useful but ungenuine middle-distance performer. Observation Post and Colchis are among numerous winners out of Godzilla, the best being the high-class French miler Phydilla (by Lyphard) and the most recent being the very useful French two-year-old Ernani (by Sadler's Wells). Godzilla won at up to about a mile in Italy at two years, but put up her best performance in Britain the following season at six furlongs. Observation Post is a tall, rather leggy, attractive colt with a quick action. His improved form in the Irish Derby suggests a mile and a half suits him better than a mile and a quarter, and that if he remains in training he'll prove best on an easy surface. Apparently the main reason for his missing Epsom was the firm ground. *B. W. Hills.*

OCCAMIST (USA) 4 ch.g. Diesis 133–Solo Naskra (USA) (Naskra (USA)) [1988 8g⁵ 7.6s⁴ 10g 1989 a10g] leggy, sparely-made, angular gelding: plating-class maiden at best: winning selling hurdler. *C. C. Elsey.* —

OCEAN FALLS   3 b.c. Wassl 125–Homing Pigeon (FR) (Habitat 134) [1988 8s* **113**
1989 7v* 8d² 8m³ 7m] 17,500F, 62,000Y: sixth foal: half-brother to Irish 11f winner
Le Soir (by Northern Baby) and 2 winners abroad, notably 1989 Belgian winner
Vanvitelli (by Ela-Mana-Mou) earlier fourth in Irish Derby: dam, granddaughter of
Oaks winner Long Look, won at 1m in Ireland and in frame in 1m listed event: won
newcomers race at Longchamp as 2-y-o and listed Prix Djebel at Maisons-Laffitte in
April: placed behind Kendor at Longchamp in Prix de Fontainebleau and Poule
d'Essai des Poulains, in latter difficult at stalls, setting strong pace and beaten just
over 2 lengths: behind in Prix de la Foret on first run for over 5 months: should
prove best at around 1m: acts on top-of-the-ground and heavy going. *A. Fabre,
France.*

OCEAN LAD   6 b.g. Windjammer (USA)–Elixir 99 (Hard Tack 111§) [1988 10.8d   —
12d³ 12g⁵ 10.8m³ 11.5g 12m³ 14.8s 1989 10.8s 10.1m 16m 12f³ 12f 10.8m 16m⁶] plain,
good-bodied gelding: poor mover: poor maiden: stays 1½m: acts on top-of-the-
ground and a soft surface: occasionally bandaged: inconsistent. *J. Perrett.*

OCKLEY   3 ch.g. Tolomeo 127–Santita 69 (Charlottown 127) [1988 6g⁶ 8s⁵ 7m   —
1989 10.8d 12f] leggy, quite attractive gelding: quite modest maiden at 2 yrs: burly,
sweating and edgy when below form in handicaps in first half of 1989: subsequently
gelded: should stay at least 1¼m: winning novice hurdler. *N. A. Graham.*

OCKY'S FLIER   5 bl.g. Aban 80–Ceile (Galivanter 131) [1988 8g³ 12m 10g 8d 16d   —
1989 16.2m 12m] leggy, close-coupled gelding: form only in seller (hung left) on first
outing in 1988: saddle slipped and rider unseated on reappearance as 5-y-o: stays
1m: often blinkered or visored, but wasn't in 1989. *N. Kernick.*

ODE (USA)   3 ch.f. Lord Avie (USA)–Ouro Verde (USA) (Cool Moon) [1988 8s² **118**
1989 10d⁵ 9g² 8g⁶ 11g* 10.5g* 9.2g⁵ 12m³] fourth reported foal: sister to a
lightly-raced French maiden: dam, French 2-y-o 7.5f winner later 1m stakes winner
in USA, is half-sister to Prix du Jockey-Club and Grand Prix de Paris winner
Sanctus: won minor event at Dieppe in August and listed race at Evry in September:
best efforts in Prix de l'Opera and Prix du Conseil de Paris at Longchamp last 2
outings: stays 1½m: acts on top-of-the-ground: trained until after second start by A.
Fabre. *E. Lellouche, France.*

ODILESE   4 b.f. Mummy's Pet 125–Odile (Green Dancer (USA) 132) [1988 6g*   —
7m⁴ 6d⁴ 6f⁴ 6m⁶ 6s* 6f 1989 6d 6m 6m 7g 8g] big, workmanlike filly: has a round
action: fair winner as 3-y-o: below form in 1989: best form at 6f: acts on any going:
sweating and on toes third outing, first for 4 months: has given trouble in
preliminaries and appeared difficult ride. *M. A. Jarvis.*

ODILEX   2 b.g. (May 11) Mummy's Pet 125–Odile (Green Dancer (USA) 132)   **64**
[1989 6m⁵ 8.2s⁴ 6g] second foal: brother to fair 6f winner Odilese: dam once-raced
granddaughter of 1000 Guineas winner Waterloo: quite modest maiden: stays 1m.
M. A. Jarvis.

ODYN PRINCE   3 br.g. Andy Rew 103–Silver Water (Wolver Hollow 126) [1988   **35**
5m⁴ 6m 7f⁴ 7m⁵ 8d 6g 1989 8.2s 10s³ 12f⁵ 12h 10f⁵ 10.1m 8.3m] leggy, angular
gelding: poor maiden: stays 1¼m: acts on top-of-the-ground and soft going:
bandaged third start: carried head awkwardly fifth: has joined B. Stevens. *M. D. I.
Usher.*

OFF AND ON   3 b.f. Touching Wood (USA) 127–Off The Reel (USA) (Silent   —
Screen (USA)) [1988 7g 1989 12f 16.2f⁶] appears of little account: sold 950 gns
Newmarket Autumn Sales. *W. Jarvis.*

OFF CHANCE   4 br.f. Magnolia Lad 102–Nicola Jane 80 (River Chanter 121)   — §
[1988 NR 1989 5f 8.3m 8m] sparely-made filly: of no account and is ungenuine: ran
out second outing: blinkered once: taken down early last 2 starts: trained until after
second outing by C. Spares. *I. Campbell.*

OFFICER CADET   2 b.g. (May 20) Shernazar 131–Selection Board 75 (Welsh   **43**
Pageant 132) [1989 7m⁶ 6f⁵ 6f] close-coupled gelding: first foal: dam twice-raced
sister to Teleprompter: poor maiden: best effort first start. *J. W. Watts.*

OFF THE RECORD (FR)   4 ch.g. Don Roberto (USA)–Farce (FR) (Bon Mot   **81** §
III 132) [1988 10.2f⁵ 9f⁴ 10.5g 10m⁶ 10g³ 9f² 9d 9g 1989 8d 10.2g 12f² 12m] leggy,
good-topped gelding: fair on his day: brought down on home turn at Doncaster in
May and wasn't seen out again: stays 1½m: suited by a sound surface: blinkered
once at 3 yrs: refused to run on twice in 1988: not one to rely on. *C. W. Thornton.*

OFF THE WALL   2 b.g. (Apr 23) Auction Ring (USA) 123–Fraudulent (Sexton   —
Blake 126) [1989 7m] IR 30,000Y: strong gelding: has scope: second foal: dam,
unraced, from family of Saintly Song and Cavo Doro: last of 13 in maiden at
Newmarket in July: gelded afterwards. *W. Hastings-Bass.*

OH DANNY BOY 5 br.g. Rabdan 129–Musical Princess 66 (Cavo Doro 124) **62**
[1988 8g 8g 12m 10f 10s 12g 10m² 11m⁶ 10f* 12m* 10m⁶ 1989 12d 12f 12.8m⁴ 10f
12m² 10m² 10.2g 12.3g² 10f* 10.6d] lengthy gelding: moderate mover: quite modest
handicapper: favourite, won same race at Beverley in September for second
successive season: ran moderately final outing: effective at 1¼m and 1½m: possibly
needs a sound surface nowadays: has run very well for apprentice. *E. Weymes.*

OH NORAH 3 ch.f. Ahonoora 122–Dianina (Bold Lad (IRE) 133) [1988 NR 1989 **—**
12m 10m 10m] 9,000Y: lengthy, dipped-backed filly: fifth foal: half-sister to a winner
in Trinidad: dam second over 6f and 1m in Ireland: well beaten in claimers: sold to
join J. L. Harris 1,050 gns Doncaster August Sales. *P. A. Kelleway.*

OH SO RISKY 2 b.c. (Mar 19) Kris 135–Expediency (USA) (Vaguely Noble 140) **78 p**
[1989 6g³ 7g*] 8,000Y: half-brother to 3-y-o Social Secret (by Secreto) and 4
winners, including 7f and 1m winner Bin Shaddad (by Riverman): dam lightly-raced
sister to Mississipian and Gonzales and half-sister to Youth: favourite, won
20-runner maiden auction at Goodwood in October by 2½ lengths from Lurking: will
stay 1m: may improve again. *D. R. C. Elsworth.*

O I OYSTON 13 b.g. Martinmas 128–Last Lap 75 (Immortality) [1988 8v* 7g² **61**
8d² 8g 7.6v* 8g 7.6s 8s 8m⁵ 7.6s⁴ 8g 8d³ 10s 8s⁴ 1989 8v* 8d⁵ 7.6m 8.2d 8.2d] big
gelding: carries plenty of condition: a grand old servant who has won 22 times on
flat, on reappearance winning Ravenspark Selling Handicap (no bid) at Ayr for third
year in succession: best at up to 9f: very well suited by plenty of give in the ground:
excellent mount for claimer: has worn blinkers, but is better without: suited by
forcing tactics: goes particularly well on a turning track: tough and genuine: a credit
to his trainer. *J. Berry.*

OKAKU 2 b.c. (Feb 13) Be My Guest (USA) 126–Be My Darling 82 (Windjammer **—**
(USA)) [1989 7m] 5,200Y: strong, good-topped colt: has plenty of scope: third foal:
brother to French 3-y-o 9f and 9.5f winner Tony's Guest: dam, 6f winner suited by
1¼m, is daughter of half-sister to high-class 1969 2-y-o Divine Gift: 33/1, slowly
away, hung left and always behind in 20-runner maiden at Lingfield in September.
Mrs L. Piggott.

OK CORRAL (USA) 2 gr.g. (Feb 26) Malinowski (USA) 123–Tiger Trap (USA) **73 p**
80 (Al Hattab (USA)) [1989 7g⁴] big, rather leggy gelding: fourth foal: brother to 1m
and 9f winner Wood Dancer and half-brother to 3-y-o 9f and 1¼m winner False Start
and highly-strung maiden Hungry Griebel (both by Robellino): dam 2-y-o 6f winner:
25/1 and bit edgy, promising 2 lengths fourth of 9, staying on strongly not knocked
about, to Flaming Glory in maiden at Sandown in July: will stay 1¼m: looked sure to
improve good deal, and win similar event, but wasn't seen out again. *W. Hastings-Bass.*

O K NURSE 5 gr.m. Mandrake Major 122–Grisma (Grisaille 115) [1988 NR 1989 **—**
10m⁵ 12f] fourth foal: dam never ran: well beaten in maiden and claimer (slowly
away) at Beverley. *J. Mulhall.*

OK RECORDS 2 b.c. (Mar 3) Cure The Blues (USA)–Last Clear Chance (USA) **— p**
(Alleged (USA) 138) [1989 a8g5] angular, lightly-made colt: second foal: half-brother
to Italian 3-y-o Mule Train (by General Assembly), second over 6f here at 2 yrs: dam
ran once: bit backward and green, around 12 lengths fifth of 13, slowly away, in
late-season maiden at Southwell: sure to improve. *W. Hastings-Bass.*

O-LA-LE 5 ch.h. Virginia Boy 106–Winning Wave (USA) (Victory Morn) [1988 7f **48**
7.6f 8m 7m 6d 1989 7d⁴ 7.5d* 8d 7.5g* 7.5m 6g 8f] rather sparely-made horse: poor
mover: won handicaps at Beverley in spring: off course over 3 months after fifth
outing: well beaten last 2: stays 7.5f: needs give in the ground. *W. G. A. Brooks.*

OLD ALLIANCE (USA) 2 b.g. (Mar 5) Danzig (USA)–Nimble Folly (USA) **103**
(Cyane) [1989 5f² 5m* 5m* 6m³] well-made, deep-girthed gelding: has plenty of
scope: very good mover: sixth foal: brother to 1987 2-y-o 5f winner Nimblefeet and
good 1984 American 2-y-o Contredance, latter successful at up to 9f, and closely
related to 3-y-o 1¼m winner Shotiche (by Northern Dancer): dam unraced sister to
useful Misgivings: successful in August in maiden at Windsor and listed race (by a
short head from Lord Glen) at York: good third, taking strong hold and no extra last
furlong, to Welney in Rokeby Farms Mill Reef Stakes at Newbury following month:
may prove best at 5f: twice unseated rider and bolted second intended start (at
Royal Ascot): gelded afterwards. *J. Tree.*

OLD COMRADES 2 ch.g. (Mar 10) Music Boy 124–Miss Candine 66 (King **65**
Emperor (USA)) [1989 5s⁵ 5m 5d³ 5f³] 5,600Y: workmanlike, good-quartered
gelding: eighth reported foal: brother to fair sprinter Puccini and half-brother to
3-y-o Jawbreaker (by Bustino) and a winner in Holland: dam, placed over 1¼m and

2m, is half-sister to very useful sprinters Canteen and Staincross: quite modest maiden: best efforts at Haydock (first run for nearly 4 months) and Bath on last 2 starts: sold 950 gns Ascot October Sales. *L. G. Cottrell.*

OLD DEER PARK 3 b.c. Blakeney 126–Hurry On Honey 76 (Be Friendly 130) **47** [1988 NR 1989 10.1m 8m 10.2h⁴] 7,400Y: useful-looking colt: second reported foal: dam, placed here at 2 yrs, later won 6 races in Jersey: poor form in summer claimers last 2 starts: stays 1¼m: has joined D. Barons. *I. A. Balding.*

OLD DUTCH HOLBORN 4 ch.g. Derrylin 115–Gay Voltage (Forlorn River — 124) [1988 6v 8g 8g 7f* 8m 7d⁵ 7m⁶ 8m² 7m³ 1989 8f] workmanlike, good-topped gelding: winning plater as 3-y-o: 25/1 and bandaged, tailed off in handicap at Bath in September: acts on firm going: usually forces pace: winning hurdler. *K. O. Cunningham-Brown.*

OLD MALTON 7 ch.g. Whitstead 125–Bridestones 92 (Jan Ekels 122) [1988 **36** 14s³ 13.8g³ 16d 17.1g³ 17.1g⁴ 1989 14s³ 21.6d] close-coupled, workmanlike gelding: poor handicapper: probably didn't stay extreme distances: acted on any going: bought 12,000 gns Doncaster May Sales: dead. *J. Mackie.*

OLD MOTHER GOOSE 3 b.f. Jalmood (USA) 126–Snow Goose (Santa Claus — 133) [1988 NR 1989 9s 9f 12d] lengthy, angular filly: poor walker and mover: half-sister to several winners, including quite useful 1983 2-y-o 7f winner Scaldante (by Hotfoot) and middle-distance stayer Wild Goose Chase (by Warpath): dam never ran: scant promise in minor events, off course 6 months before final (well out of depth) start. *N. Bycroft.*

OLD PARK LANE 5 ch.m. Longleat (USA) 109–High Voltage 82 (Electrify) — [1988 6f 7g 10d 8m² 8m 9g 8f⁴ 10d⁶ 1989 8s 5f] sturdy, angular mare: form only when in frame in sellers as 4-y-o: withdrawn after giving trouble at stalls on intended third outing in 1989: stays 1m: acts on firm going: has worn bandages. *K. T. Ivory.*

OLD VIC 3 b.c. Sadler's Wells (USA) 132–Cockade 104 (Derring-Do 131) **136** [1988 7g⁶ 8s* 1989 11d* 10s* 12.3m* 12g* 12g*]

A pulled muscle followed by a bout of coughing kept Old Vic off the course after he had taken his seasonal record to five wins from as many starts by landing the Derby double at Chantilly and the Curragh. His performances in the Prix du Jockey-Club Lancia and the Budweiser Irish Derby were outstanding—he won the first-named by seven lengths and the second by four—and whetted the appetite for his first encounter with the unbeaten Two Thousand Guineas and Epsom Derby winner Nashwan, which had widely been expected to take place in the King George VI and Queen Elizabeth Diamond Stakes at Ascot towards the end of July. Old Vic remains in training but, alas, with Nashwan now retired, these two tip-top middle-distance horses can never meet in racecourse competition. The North American racing scene was also graced by two magnificent middle-distance three-year-olds, Sunday Silence and Easy Goer, and the racing public was fortunate to see them clash on no fewer than four occasions; neither horse has yet finished out of the first two in his career and both are to be raced as four-year-olds. Sunday Silence won seven of his nine starts as a three-year-old and defeated Easy Goer in the Kentucky Derby, the Preakness Stakes and the Breeders' Cup Classic, while Easy Goer, who won his eight other races, beat his rival on their third meeting, depriving him of triple crown honours with an eight-length victory in the Belmont Stakes. Vastly greater prize money is on offer for the top horses in the States and more opportunities exist for them to meet, but it is also true that the prospect of defeat appears much less of a deterrent to champions meeting there than it sometimes seems on this side of the Atlantic. Some of the leading European owners set much greater store on preserving the reputations of their top horses than do their North American counterparts who seem, on the whole, to be less afraid of losing and, as a consequence, much more adventurous. Previewing the Breeders' Cup Classic, the climax of the magnificent Breeders' Cup day programme in November, Steven Crist of the *New York Times* summed up what was at stake for the connections of Easy Goer, the 2/1-on favourite: 'If he wins he will justly be proclaimed the Horse of the Year, the three-year-old of the decade and the best American racehorse since Spectacular Bid. If he loses, he will only be voted the second-best three-year-old of 1989'. But there were no thoughts of either horse bowing out after Sunday Silence held the strong-finishing Easy Goer by a neck in an

Guardian Classic Trial, Sandown—Old Vic stays on

event which had the American racing public on the edge of their seats. With the score standing at three-one in Sunday Silence's favour it might have been thought that his connections had everything to lose and nothing to gain by keeping him in training to take on Easy Goer again as a four-year-old. But the owner of Sunday Silence, Arthur Hancock, put the racing philosophy of the majority of North American owners in a nutshell when he said after the Breeders' Cup: 'I'll never have another one as good as this, and I want to see him race. Besides, racing needs its heroes'.

Having the stars do battle on a regular basis is the best formula for drawing the crowds, whatever the sport, and it is always to be applauded when a top-class three-year-old remains in training the next year in Europe. Old Vic could have earned a significantly greater sum for his owner through being syndicated as a stallion than he could ever make on the racecourse even in a brilliant season; and if Old Vic is not successful as a four-year-old his eventual syndication might well be at a lower sum than if he had been retired when his two spectacular classic victories were fresher in the memory. Old Vic's rapid development as a three-year-old surprised even those who worked closely with him. He could almost be described as the champion who rose without trace. His trainer described him in an early-season *Timeform Interview* (after Old Vic had won his first two races) as 'an improving horse with quite a good future . . . at home he's difficult to assess but the Italian Derby may be a possibility for him'; his regular jockey Cauthen said in an end-of-season interview on *Racing World* that after Old Vic's first two races he had thought

641

Dalham Chester Vase—Old Vic breaks the course record

him 'a very nice horse though he never gave me the feel he was going to be the horse he turned out to be'. It was the likes of Thorn Dance, Citidancer, Brush Aside, Monsagem and High Estate that were talked of as the Warren Place classic hopefuls at the start of the season. Old Vic had won a twelve-runner maiden race at Haydock in the autumn on the second of his two outings as a two-year-old, and he was out early as a three-year-old. He lost no time in extending his winning sequence, looking a smart performer when slamming a fair field by ten lengths in a minor event at Newbury in April and following up later in the month by landing the odds in the Guardian Classic Trial. He won by four lengths on very soft going at Sandown where he was opposed only by the maidens Spring Hay and Pride of Araby after the late withdrawal of Warrshan and Old Vic's stable-companion Porter Rhodes because of the state of the ground. The result of the Guardian Classic Trial has often proved significant but Old Vic's victory caused barely a ripple at the time. Even after his comfortable victory in the Dalham Chester Vase in May his connections still seemed at first inclined towards the Italian Derby rather than its much more prestigious counterparts at Epsom or Chantilly. The Chester Vase was run at a cracking gallop—which helped to produce a time record for the course and distance—and after leading at halfway on the bridle Old Vic ran on strongly, sent for home in earnest half a mile out and kept going with hands and heels, to beat Golden Pheasant by two and a half lengths with Warrshan, who started favourite ahead of Old Vic, twelve lengths further back in third. Plans for Old Vic were revised after further consideration and it was announced that he might run in the Ever Ready Derby if there was some give in the ground (he was reportedly slightly jarred after the Chester Vase which was run on good to firm).

With continuing dry weather lessening the prospects of a yielding surface at Epsom, Old Vic was supplemented—at a cost equivalent to around £18,500—for the Prix du Jockey-Club Lancia run on the Sunday before the Derby. The Prix du Jockey-Club was thought at one time to be under threat from a stable lads' demonstration and two of the eventual runners, the Prix Hocquart runner-up Norberto and the outsider Edimbourg, were left in the Ever Ready Derby, run four days later, as a precaution. The threat of disruption receded and the best of the French middle-distance three-year-old colts around at the time contested the Prix du Jockey-Club; Mill Pond was the

642

Prix du Jockey-Club Lancia, Chantilly—a spectacular front-running performance . . . . .

only French-trained challenger for the Epsom Derby. The impressive five-length Prix Lupin winner Galetto started a short-priced favourite in a field of twelve in which Old Vic and the British-trained Prix Lupin runner-up Elmayer were the only overseas challengers. The Prix Hocquart, another of the traditional trials for the Prix du Jockey-Club, had resulted in a three-horse blanket finish in which the unbeaten Dancehall, successful earlier in the Prix Noailles, came out on top, with Louis Cyphre third. Because of its proximity to the Epsom Derby, the Prix du Jockey-Club has traditionally attracted very few runners from British or Irish stables but Old Vic became the third foreign-trained winner of the race in the 'eighties, following Irish-trained Assert and Caerleon in 1982 and 1983. No British-trained horse had won the Prix du Jockey-Club this century. Old Vic routed the opposition, his rider dictating a good pace before making an enterprising break for home rounding the home turn. Cauthen's move seemed to take some of the other jockeys by surprise. Showing fine acceleration, Old Vic swept into a four- or five-length lead and soon had his closest rivals toiling. Only Dancehall and Galetto briefly threatened to mount a challenge in the straight as they drew out from the rest,

. . . . . and more of the same in the Budweiser Irish Derby at the Curragh

but Old Vic never showed the slightest sign of stopping. Dancehall stayed on strongly, pulling eight lengths clear of third-placed Galetto, but Old Vic beat him hollow and was stretching out with a will in the closing stages, the manner of his seven-length victory evoking memories in the 'eighties of Shergar's and Slip Anchor's Derby victories at Epsom and of Assert's and Shahrastani's eight-length successes at the Curragh. For the record, Norberto and Louis Cyphre came fourth and fifth, beaten sixteen and a half lengths and eighteen lengths respectively by Old Vic; Elmayer came ninth. Old Vic's performance seemed to be overshadowed in the public mind by Nashwan's resounding victory at Epsom but there was no doubt that, in this form, Old Vic was going to take some beating over middle distances in any race he contested. We rated his performance more highly than Nashwan's, and Dancehall franked the form when winning the Grand Prix de Paris Louis Vuitton from Norberto later in the month.

Old Vic's preparation for the Budweiser Irish Derby at the Curragh in early-July caused his trainer some headaches, by all accounts. The drought-like conditions kept Old Vic off the grass gallops at Newmarket throughout June and he was reportedly trained largely on artificial all-weather surfaces and in the swimming pool. There was a last-minute scare for connections when Old Vic developed a boil on his back the day before the race. The decision to let him take his chance—with the affected area under the saddle protected by sponge—was said to have been 'touch and go'. Old Vic faced only seven opponents and started at 11/4-on in the absence of Nashwan who waited for the Coral-Eclipse the following week. It was left to Ile de Nisky, beaten seven and a half lengths into fourth place by Nashwan at Epsom, to represent the Derby form and he started second favourite at 5/1. Third favourite at 10/1 was Zayyani who had run the Derby third Cacoethes to three quarters of a length in the King Edward VII Stakes at Royal Ascot on his latest outing; the William Hill Dante runner-up Observation Post was next at 12/1, with 20/1-shot Phantom Breeze shortest-priced of the home-trained runners. Old Vic won in similar manner to Chantilly, making most of the running and being virtually unchallenged in the home straight; in the closing stages Observation Post passed Ile de Nisky, who had stayed in touch with Old Vic for a long way, but never posed a serious threat to the winner. Old Vic won by four lengths and two and a half, Ile de Nisky finishing a length closer to Old Vic than he had to Nashwan at Epsom; Phantom Breeze came five lengths behind Ile de Nisky in fourth, with Zayyani only sixth. The Irish have had considerable difficulty mounting a good defence of the big Irish Derby prize in recent years; Old Vic was the fourth British-trained winner in a row, during which period only one home-trained horse—Entitled in 1987—has managed a place. Old Vic's success was a landmark for his rider Cauthen who now has winners of the Derby, the Irish Derby, the French Derby and the Kentucky Derby to his name. A pulled muscle, incurred at home, made Old Vic a definite non-runner for the King George VI and Queen Elizabeth Diamond Stakes later in July, though, according to his connections, he wouldn't have run in any case on the prevailing firm ground. Old Vic wasn't able to fulfil his Prix de l'Arc de Triomphe engagement either, because of coughing, and further revised plans to send him to Canada for the Rothman's International at the end of October came to nothing.

		Northern Dancer (b 1961)	Nearctic
Old Vic (b.c. 1986)	Sadler's Wells (USA) (b 1981)		Natalma
		Fairy Bridge (b 1975)	Bold Reason
			Special
	Cockade (b 1973)	Derring-Do (b 1961)	Darius
			Sipsey Bridge
		Camenae (b 1961)	Vimy
			Madrilene

Old Vic was bred by Bob McCreery at the Stowell Hill Stud, Somerset, and was bought for 230,000 guineas at the Highflyer Yearling Sales on behalf of Sheikh Mohammed. Old Vic gave his sire, the Irish Two Thousand Guineas and Eclipse winner Sadler's Wells, the distinction of a dual classic winner from his first crop. Old Vic's dam Cockade is a full sister to another Two

Sheikh Mohammed's "Old Vic"

Thousand Guineas winner High Top, who had a fine record at both two and three, even though he lost all his four races after beating Roberto at Newmarket. High Top, who was also bred by McCreery, died in 1988 after a successful career at stud in which many of his best progeny, including the classic winners Top Ville, Cut Above, Circus Plume and Colorspin, were effective at a mile and a half or further. High Top himself was never raced beyond a mile and Cockade's only victory came in a one-mile maiden event at Salisbury as a three-year-old. Old Vic is Cockade's fifth living foal and her fourth winner on the flat, all of them endowed with a fair measure of stamina. Cockade's first winner was the Green Dancer filly Green Lucia who finished second to Sun Princess in the Yorkshire Oaks and third to Give Thanks in the Irish Guinness Oaks; she was followed by the modest Bustino colt Jameel, successful over two miles, and the fair Glint of Gold filly Turban who was effective at a mile and a quarter and stayed a mile and a half. Cockade's sixth living foal the two-year-old Splash of Colour (by Rainbow Quest) was in training in the latest season with Vincent O'Brien but wasn't seen out. Old Vic's grandam Camenae, a moderate stayer, bred six winners who also included the Jersey Stakes winner Camden Town; Camenae is a half-sister to Petite Marmite, the dam of the Prix Vermeille winner Paulista, and to Fran, the dam of the top-class sprinter Tudor Music. Old Vic is a rangy, good-bodied colt with plenty of scope and he should make a fine-looking four-year-old. He is a powerful and impressive galloper with a slightly round action which is often taken as a sign that a horse is best served by some give in the ground. Old Vic acts on soft going and has won on a firm surface; the going was good at Chantilly and the Curragh where he put up easily his best performances. Old

Vic stays a mile and a half well—he'd get a mile and three quarters—and has first-rate prospects in the top open-aged middle-distance races in 1990. With ground conditions in his favour, out in front setting a strong gallop, he'll take some catching. *H. R. A. Cecil.*

OLEAN 3 b.f. Sadler's Wells (USA) 132–Osmunda (Mill Reef (USA) 141) [1988 7m — 1989 10h⁵] plain, leggy, sparely-made filly: always behind in maidens. *P. F. I. Cole.*

OLGA'S PET 2 br.g. (Mar 28) Tina's Pet 121–Aunt Winnie (Wolver Hollow 126) — [1989 6g 6g] 5,000Y: half-brother to 6f seller winner Sing Galvo Sing (by Music Boy) and a winner in Belgium: dam poor maiden: soundly beaten in late-season maidens at Newcastle and Redcar: gelded afterwards. *J. Balding.*

OLLIE-P 4 ch.g. Red Sunset 120–Rosemary's Rhythm (Gala Performance (USA)) — [1988 7g 6m 1989 6f] leggy, plain gelding: little sign of ability. *M. J. Haynes.*

OLYMPIAN 2 ch.c. (Mar 30) High Line 125–Elysian 94 (Northfields (USA)) 62 [1989 8f⁶ 8g] second foal: half-brother to 3-y-o 1m winner Circe (by Main Reef): dam, from excellent family, won over 6f at 2 yrs and seemed to stay 1½m: beaten at least 11 lengths in late-season maidens at Leicester: will be better suited by 1¼m + . *P. T. Walwyn.*

OLYMPIC CHALLENGER 5 b.g. Anfield 117–Calibina 101 (Caliban 123) 56 [1988 6g² 6g² 6g* 6s* 6g 6d 6g 6s³ 6s³ 1989 12g 8m 6s 6g a6g⁵] has a rather round action: quite modest handicapper: probably stays 7f: best with give in the ground: usually wears blinkers or visor: suitable mount for inexperienced rider: trained by W. Rock in Ireland on reappearance: winning hurdler. *J. Mackie.*

OLYMPIC HERO 2 b.c. (May 1) Dreams To Reality (USA) 113–Gallant Believer 97 (USA) (Gallant Romeo (USA)) [1989 5d⁴ 5g* 6f* 6g⁵ 6m⁴ 5m⁴ 6g] 14,000Y: well-made, medium-sized, attractive colt: fluent mover: fifth foal: half-brother to 3-y-o 1¼m winner Bold Republic (by Nishapour), fairly useful sprinter Norgabie (by Northfields) and a winner in Norway: dam never ran: quite useful performer: successful early season in fair company at Salisbury and Goodwood: good fourth, first home on unfavoured side, in Cornwallis Stakes at Ascot on penultimate appearance: stays 6f: sold 64,000 gns Newmarket Autumn Sales. *D. R. C. Elsworth.*

OLYMPIC TIMES (USA) 7 ch.h. Olden Times–Lady Pax (USA) (New Policy) 60 [1988 6d 10g 8f 12m 11s 12m 1989 16s 12s³ 12g] medium-sized horse: moderate mover: won handicaps at Leopardstown and the Curragh as 5-y-o: easily best effort in similar company in Britain when staying-on third at Leicester in April: weakened quickly final 3f at Brighton over week later: stays well: acts on top-of-the-ground and heavy going. *R. Akehurst.*

OMORSI 2 b.f. (Feb 24) Prince Tenderfoot (USA) 126–Her Name Was Lola — (Pitskelly 122) [1989 7g] 5,600Y: second foal: dam lightly raced at 2 yrs in Ireland: well beaten in 20-runner maiden auction at Goodwood in October. *M. J. Fetherston-Godley.*

ONCE UPON A TIME 2 b.f. (May 12) Teenoso (USA) 135–Pas de Deux 80 67 p (Nijinsky (CAN) 138) [1989 6g 7f⁵ 8.5f*] small, lightly-made filly: seventh foal: sister to Starlet, 7f and 1m winner at 2 yrs in 1988, and half-sister to several winners, including 6f to 1¼m winner Unknown Quantity (by Young Generation) and middle-distance stayer Insular (by Moulton): dam, daughter of very smart Example, won over 1¼m: progressive sort: second favourite, won 9-runner maiden at Beverley in September by a short head: will be well suited by 1¼m + . *I. A. Balding.*

ON CUE 2 br.g. (May 7) Magic Mirror 105–Tug Along (Posse (USA) 130) [1989 6f⁵ — 7f] 1,800Y: first foal: dam ran 3 times as 3-y-o: apparently of little account: wears a visor. *S. J. Muldoon.*

ONE AT A TIME 2 b.g. (Mar 21) Music Boy 124–Single Bid 68 (Auction Ring 53 (USA) 123) [1989 5d² 5f³ 5m⁴ 5f³ 6f⁴ 6f³] 13,000F, 20,000Y: big gelding: has a round action: first foal: dam ran only at sprint distances: plating-class maiden: best effort on debut: blinkered third start, ran poorly last two. *J. Berry.*

ONE A TIME 2 b.f. (Mar 13) Good Times (ITY)–Stolen Love 85 (Alcide 136) 32 [1989 5m 6m 6m 10.6d a7g] medium-sized filly: good walker: sister to 3-y-o Stolon Time, fair 6f winner at 2 yrs, 6f winner What Heaven (by So Blessed) and a winner abroad: dam placed at up to 1½m: poor form in sellers and a maiden: probably needs further than 6f. *J. A. Glover.*

ONE DEVONSHIRE 3 b.g. Sandhurst Prince 128–Raregirl (Rarity 129) [1988 58 7m³ 1989 10s 8f 12.3f² 12m⁴ 12g³] medium-sized, angular gelding: in frame in handicaps in the North: stays 1½m: acts on firm going. *M. H. Tompkins.*

ONE FOR IRENE   2 gr.f. (Mar 25) Hotfoot 126–Vila Real 76 (Town Crier 119)   —
[1989 6g 5m⁶] 1,500F, 3,200Y: small, light-framed filly: has a free, roundish action:
half-sister to 3 winners, including fair 6f and 7f winner Real Silver (by Silly Season):
dam won 4 sellers over 7f and 1m: poor form in September in claimer (slowly away)
at Haydock and auction event at Redcar: bred to need further. *R. M. Whitaker.*

ONE FOR THE BOYS   2 ch.g. (Mar 20) Superlative 118–Contenance (GER)   —
(Luciano) [1989 5m 6m 6f 6m 6g] 6,800F, 14,000Y, resold 18,000Y: sturdy,
good-topped gelding: carries condition: half-brother to French 1¼m winner Son
Tino (by Artaius): dam useful winner in Germany: well beaten in varied events,
including a seller: twice ridden by lad in paddock. *F. Durr.*

ONE FOR THE POT   4 ch.g. Nicholas Bill 125–Tea-Pot 77 (Ragstone 128)   44 §
[1988 10v⁵ 16g⁴ 12m⁵ 13m³ 16g 15g³ 16.5m⁶ 15m 1989 21.6d 15.8m 16.2m³ 15f⁶
16.2g² 20.4g⁴ 17f4] strong, short-backed gelding: irresolute maiden: probably stays
2½m: acts on firm going: often sweats and gets on edge: keen sort, usually held up:
trained until after sixth outing by W. Pearce: winning hurdler: not one to trust. *Mrs
J. R. Ramsden.*

ONE GOOD TURN   3 b.g. Tyrnavos 129–Musical Princess 66 (Cavo Doro 124)   47
[1988 NR 1989 11g² 8.2g 13v] 8,000Y: second foal: half-brother to 1m to 1½m winner
Oh Danny Boy (by Rabdan): dam won 4 times at 1½m and 2m at 5 yrs: second in
seller (claimed out of Mrs J. Ramsden's stable £8,400) at Hamilton in August, only
form: very stiff task when tailed off in claimer final start: better at 11f than 1m: dead.
D. Moffatt.

ONE HEART   4 ch.g. Seven Hearts 98–Taryn 76 (Crooner 119) [1988 6d 7s 8f⁴   31
8.3m 8.3m⁵ 10m² 12.2g 12g 1989 10m⁶ 12.5f⁴ 10.2h 8f 8f⁴ 8f] compact, workmanlike
gelding: poor plater: virtually pulled up third start: stays 12.5f: acts on firm going:
often blinkered or visored: has run creditably for apprentice: usually sweats: bought
out of E. Wheeler's stable 1,500 gns Ascot 2nd June Sales after third outing. *R. J.
Hodges.*

ONE LINER   5 b.g. Skyliner 117–Our Duck (The Go-Between 129) [1988 6g* 7m   81
6m³ 6f 6m 6s⁵ 6d⁶ 6s 6s 6s⁶ 1989 6s* 6v⁴ 6d² 6f2] lengthy, good-quartered gelding:
fair handicapper: comfortable winner at Nottingham in March: good second at
Thirsk and Pontefract later in spring: subsequently raced in Italy: suited by 6f: acts
on any going: good mount for apprentice: tended to hang under pressure when tried
in blinkers. *N. A. Callaghan.*

ONE MAN BAND   5 b.g. Formidable (USA) 125–Sideshow 103 (Welsh Pageant   64
132) [1988 6g 7g⁵ 5g² 6m* 5g² 6m 5g 7g³ 6s 6d 5s³ 1989 6g 6m 6f⁴ 6m² 7f* 6g] big,
lengthy gelding: carries plenty of condition: has been hobdayed: has a round action:
quite modest handicapper: well-backed favourite, won at Chepstow in July: effective
at 5f and stays 7f: acts on any going: often bandaged nowadays: excellent mount for
inexperienced rider: has got on edge and occasionally sweated: has been slowly
away. *Mrs S. Oliver.*

ONE MISSING   2 gr.f. (Mar 6) Comedy Star (USA) 121–Final Call 79 (Town   46
Crier 119) [1989 5s 5g 6m⁴ 6h* 5g* 6m⁴ 6f² 6m⁴ 5f6] 1,800Y: angular filly: has no
near-eye: half-sister to 3-y-o Deciding Bid (by Valiyar) and 2 winners, including
quite useful 1985 2-y-o 7f winner Stage Hand (by Sagaro): dam, 5f winner who ran
only at 2 yrs, is half-sister to good sprinter On Stage: successful early-summer in
claimer at Brighton and seller (bought in 4,750 gns) at Wolverhampton: stays 6f: ran
well when sweating and edgy: suitable mount for a 7-lb claimer: sometimes
bandaged near-hind. *M. Bell.*

ON IMPULSE   6 gr.m. Jellaby 124–Pts Fairway (Runnymede 123) [1988 10g 9f⁵   —
8f⁶ 8g 7f 1989 10h] leggy, lightly-made mare: poor performer: best at around 1m:
acts on firm going and possibly unsuited by heavy: blinkered twice: has run
creditably for apprentice: wears bandages. *R. Simpson.*

ONLY A TEMPEST   2 ch.f. (Apr 17) Northern Tempest (USA) 120–Only For   —
Fun 66 (Relic) [1989 6g a6g] sixth living foal: half-sister to fairly useful 8.2f to 1¼m
winner Gundreda (by Gunner B): dam placed over 7f: poor form in maiden at
Folkestone and claimer (slowly away) at Southwell. *Lord John FitzGerald.*

ONLY ROSES   3 b.f. Dominion 123–Ramsar (Young Emperor 133) [1988 NR 1989   —
7g 11g] third foal: half-sister to Jules Favre (by Rusticaro), a prolific middle-distance
winner in Holland: dam, 1½m winner in Ireland, is sister to Irish 1000 Guineas
fourth Ararat: never dangerous in maiden and claimer in the North. *C. W. C. Elsey.*

ONLY THE LONELY   2 b.g. (Apr 18) Mummy's Game 120–Izobia (Mansingh   —
(USA) 120) [1989 5d 7g 7f 7g] 5,600Y: workmanlike gelding: has scope: good walker
and mover: third live foal: closely related to unreliable winning sprint plater Firmly

Attached (by Tina's Pet) and half-brother to a poor maiden by Free State: dam ran 4 times: poor maiden: gelded after final outing. *R. Hannon.*

ON MY MERIT 3 ch.c. Bold Lad (IRE) 133–Borehard (Bonne Noel 115) [1988   **86** 6m⁴ 6g 1989 8.5d 6m⁶ 7g⁴ 8m* 8g* 8f* 8f³ 8m* 8g] big, lengthy colt: fair handicapper: won at Warwick (twice), Edinburgh and Ripon in the summer: ran moderately final start (August): suited by 1m: acts on firm going: tends to hang: often makes the running. *F. H. Lee.*

ON THE BEND (USA) 3 b. or br.c. Exceller (USA) 129–Belle Sorella (USA) 99   **58** (Ribot 142) [1988 7.6s⁶ 1989 12s* 11d⁶ 12s⁴ 12m³ 12.2m] small colt: apprentice ridden, won claimer at Leicester in April: should have stayed further: acted on top-of-the-ground and soft going: dead. *R. Simpson.*

ON THE BLUE 4 b. or br.g. Blue Cashmere 129–Key Wind 81 (On Your Mark   **—** 125) [1988 5m 6f 5m 6f 5.8g⁵ 5d⁴ 5g 1989 5g 5f 5f] lengthy, good-topped gelding: poor mover: poor maiden: best at 5f. *D. C. Tucker.*

ON THE WIRE 2 ch.c. (Mar 16) Kind of Hush 118–Lilli Parkin 90 (Crowned   **—** Prince (USA) 128) [1989 6f⁶ 8g 8.2f] 3,700F, 2,000Y: leggy, lengthy, angular colt: third foal: half-brother to 1984 2-y-o 6f winner Classic Capistrano (by Song): dam won over 1m at 2 yrs: little worthwhile form, including in a seller: sold 420 gns Doncaster October Sales. *C. Spares.*

ON Y VA (USA) 2 ch.f. (Jan 30) Victorious (USA)–Golden Moony (Northfields   **65** (USA)) [1989 6m² 7f⁴ 7m⁴ 6f³ 6g] $21,000Y: sparely-made, angular filly: half-sister to a winner by Star de Naskra and a winner in Italy: dam French 1¼m winner: quite modest maiden: stays 7f. *R. J. R. Williams.*

OOGIE POOGIE (USA) 2 b.f. (Mar 14) Storm Bird (CAN) 134–Cascapedia   **76** p (USA) (Chieftain II) [1989 7f²] $135,000Y: rangy, angular filly: half-sister to 5 winners in North America, notably Grade 2 7f winner Glacial Stream (by Crystal Water): dam champion older mare in 1977: 3/1 and on toes, ½-length second of 8, staying on strongly having been outpaced 2f out, to Oblist in maiden at Leicester in October: will be suited by 1m +: sure to improve and win races. *M. R. Stoute.*

OPALKINO 4 ch.f. Relkino 131–Opalescent 71 (Gulf Pearl 117) [1988 9d 8d 6m 8f   **—** 7g⁴ 7g⁶ 6s 6s 8d⁵ 1989 8d 9f 7m 5g] sparely-made filly: poor maiden: best effort at 7f: on toes when blinkered (pulled hard) second outing. *A. W. Jones.*

OPEN CHAMPION (USA) 2 b.c. (Mar 26) To-Agori-Mou 133–Lightning   **—** p Record 96 (Le Johnstan 123) [1989 6s⁶] $2,700Y: half-brother to minor winners in USA by Eleven Stitches: dam 7.6f winner later successful in USA: 12/1, around 9 lengths sixth of 13, staying on well, to Albert in minor event at Ayr in September: afterwards sent to D. Browne: should improve. *C. F. Wall.*

OPENING DEPOSIT 3 b.f. Windy Hill (FR) 94–Deposit 73 (Thatch (USA) 136)   **—** [1988 6g³ 6m 6g 1989 7g 8m⁶] smallish, workmanlike filly: moderate mover: plating-class form at best: tailed off in handicap (sweating) and maiden in 1989: should stay beyond 6f. *R. F. Casey.*

OPENING OVERTURE (USA) 3 b.f. At The Threshold (USA)–Rhine Queen   **76** (FR) (Rheingold 137) [1988 7m⁵ 1989 10f⁵ 9g² 10d⁵ 10g³ a11g³] big, angular, unfurnished filly: has a long stride: modest maiden: best efforts second and third outings: claimed out of W. Jarvis' stable £8,568 on fourth: will be suited by 1½m +: acts on firm ground: should prove best on a galloping track. *C. R. Beever.*

OPENING VERSE (USA) 3 ch.c. The Minstrel (CAN) 135–Shy Dawn 122 (USA) (Grey Dawn II 132) [1988 6g* 7g* 7d⁵ 6g* 1989 9d² 10.4f⁵ 10f⁴ 10g² 8f⁵ 10.1d⁵ 9m*]

It was probably frustrating for connections of Opening Verse to come away with just a listed win from their colt in 1989. When put against the best in the Coral-Eclipse Stakes and Swettenham Stud Sussex Stakes, Opening Verse produced the performances of his life, beaten about five lengths behind Nashwan then Zilzal, but in lesser company he largely disappointed. His two best runs came within eighteen days of each other in July and in very different circumstances. Opening Verse's presence in a six-runner field for the Eclipse was as pacemaker for stable-companion Indian Skimmer and he started at 200/1. Turning for home, however, a monumental upset wasn't beyond the realms of possibility as he'd established an advantage of at least six lengths over the principals. It wasn't to be, of course, as Nashwan got to him just after the two-furlong pole but Opening Verse ran on splendidly and held Indian Skimmer by a short head, tiring near the finish. In the Sussex Stakes he ran on

Reference Point Strensall Stakes, York—Opening Verse makes the most of the opportunity

his own merits and cut out the lead with the same owner's Shaadi; he never looked like getting away this time, though, and was headed by Zilzal well over a furlong out before keeping on well to finish fifth at 40/1. Opening Verse's other appearances as a three-year-old weren't really in the same league, though he ran a fair race in coming fourth to Two Timing in the Prince of Wales's Stakes at Royal Ascot. He was made an odds-on shot for his reappearance in the Feilden Stakes but didn't impress with his demeanour then, in going down by three quarters of a length to Greenwich Papillon, or when fifth in the Dee Stakes at Chester on his next start. In both races he'd been held up then wandered and carried his head rather awkwardly when put under pressure. His trainer explained that Opening Verse suffered 'a nervous problem which results in him holding his breath and then letting it all out at once'. He was fitted with an unorthodox bridle at Chester but, from what we saw in public anyway, it appeared that forcing tactics were what finally did the trick. Ground conditions, combined with being taken on for the lead, were probably his undoing in the Winter Hill Stakes at Windsor in August and it was September before Opening Verse won his first race of the season. He had a clear-cut chance on form in the Reference Point Strensall Stakes at York and made all, taken to the centre of the track by Cauthen as the ground by the far rail had cut up after watering, and holding Greenwich Papillon and Batshoof by a length and a half.

At 880,000 dollars, Opening Verse was easily the most expensive yearling of his year by The Minstrel. Small wonder when one reflects on the family's record and more particularly on that of his grandam Shy Dancer. Though no great shakes herself on the racetrack—she ran forty-six times for five wins and one placing in a stakes race—and by no means bred in the purple, Shy Dancer went on to become an outstanding broodmare. Every one of her sixteen living foals got to the racecourse and fourteen of them were winners. Even more remarkable was her offspring's durability; they averaged over forty-five runs each. The most frequently tried and quite possibly the best of those sixteen was Opening Verse's dam Shy Dawn. In five seasons she

649

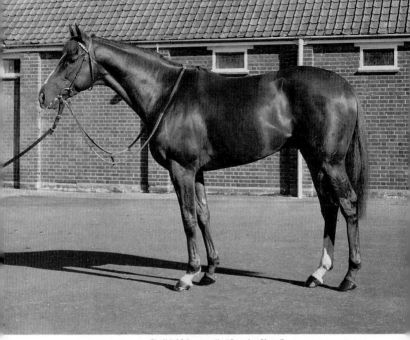

Sheikh Mohammed's "Opening Verse"

had ninety-five races, winning nineteen of them including six Grade 3 Handicaps from six furlongs to eight and a half furlongs and she was better than ever in her final season when rated 11 lb below the best of her age and sex. The most noteworthy of Shy Dancer's other foals were Petite Rouge, one of the best two-year-old fillies of 1963 in the USA, and the dams of 1988 Prix de Diane third Raintree Renegade and Heavenly Cause (by Grey Dawn and therefore a close relation to Shy Dawn) who was the top-rated American two-year-old filly of 1980 and only one pound below the best in 1981. Shy Dawn produced four living foals prior to Opening Verse; Dawn Raid (by Hail The Pirates) was a disappointing maiden here before being despatched to Trinidad but the other three all won. Two were by Seattle Slew, including the eight-and-a-half-furlong Grade 3 Columbiana Handicap winner So She Sleeps, and Shy Princess (by Irish River) was a smart French two-year-old seven-furlong winner in 1986, also successful over six furlongs as a three-year-old.

Opening Verse (USA) (b.c. 1986)	The Minstrel (CAN) (ch 1974)	Northern Dancer (b 1961)	Nearctic Natalma
		Fleur (b 1964)	Victoria Park Flaming Page
	Shy Dawn (USA) (ch 1971)	Grey Dawn II (gr 1962)	Herbager Polamia
		Shy Dancer (b 1955)	Bolero Shy Bim

Opening Verse is a rather leggy, attractive colt, clearly effective from a mile to a mile and a quarter. He acts on firm going but is probably not at his best on a soft surface; his well-beaten fifth in the Dewhurst was the only blemish of his two-year-old season. Both Opening Verse and Samoan have been bought by Allen Paulson from Sheikh Mohammed to race in the USA. Interestingly, a transaction in the opposite direction was reported in the *Thoroughbred Times* in December; having been outbid by Paulson at 1,400,000 guineas at the December Sales one year earlier, Sheikh Mohammed has completed a private purchase of the One Thousand Guineas winner Ravinella. *H. R. A. Cecil.*

OPERA GHOST 3 b.c. Caerleon (USA) 132–Premier Rose 117 (Sharp Edge 123)   **82**
[1988 NR 1989 10.1m6 10m3 8f* 10.1m3 8.3m5 9m4 10.6s] close-coupled, quite good-topped colt: third foal: half-brother to 1987 2-y-o 6f winner Rose Bouquet (by General Assembly): dam, sister to useful 7f or 1m filly Shapina, stayed 1m: fair performer: won maiden at Chepstow in July: will prove best at up to 1¼m: acts on firm going (bit burly on soft): worth a try in blinkers or a visor. *P. W. Harris.*

OPERATIC SCORE 5 ch.g. Kind of Hush 118–Grand Opera 92 (Great Nephew   **—** §
126) [1988 12g 10g6 10g3 11.5m 10m3 10.8d6 1989 12v 17.1m 11.7g5] strong gelding: poor mover: modest performer as 4-y-o: tailed off in handicaps in 1989: suited by 1¼m: acts on any going, except possibly heavy: visored twice: ran too freely when blinkered: winning hurdler: moody. *J. R. Jenkins.*

OPERATION WOLF 3 ch.c. Adonijah 126–Sesta (Artaius (USA) 129) [1988 NR   **97**
1989 10.2g2 10m4 10m* 10g2 11s3 8f* 10g] IR 3,700Y: lengthy, quite good-topped colt: third foal: half-brother to Bashful Boy (by Jalmood), useful winner at around 1¼m: dam unraced daughter of Coronation Stakes winner Calve, sister to Bold Minstrel, a very useful performer at up to 1¼m: awarded maiden at Sandown in August and won moderately-run minor event at Leicester in October: never dangerous and below form in Newmarket listed race final start: should prove best at 1m or 1¼m: acts on any going. *C. E. Brittain.*

OPTARIA 3 b.f. Song 132–Electo (Julio Mariner 127) [1988 5d* 5g3 1989 6f3 5f2   **77**
5f6 7m 6f5 5m6 6m] light-framed filly: fair performer: very good sixth in £12,500 handicap at Ascot final start: below form after, apprentice ridden at overweight and hampered early on when blinkered final start: should stay 6f: acts on firm going and a soft surface: sometimes taken down early. *I. A. Balding.*

OR ACIER (USA) 3 b.c. Lypheor 118–Secorissa (USA) (Secretariat (USA)) **118**
[1988 6.5m* 7d2 5d3 7m5 5d3 7s5 1989 7v4 5m5 6g* 6d3 6g6 5g* 5g5 5m*] neat colt: moderate mover: won listed races at Evry in June and Deauville (by short head from Whippet) in August and Group 3 Premio Omenoni (by 1½ lengths from Intimidate) at Milan in October: under 2 lengths fifth of 16 to Silver Fling in Ciga Prix de l'Abbaye de Longchamp penultimate start: best at up to 6f: acts on top-of-the-ground and a soft surface: smart. *R. Collet, France.*

ORAL EVIDENCE 3 gr.f. Rusticaro (FR) 124–Crown Witness 95 (Crowned   **74**
Prince (USA) 128) [1988 9f* 1989 9f 8.2d 8.2d3 8g 10.6m* 10.6s3 10g] leggy, angular filly: ridden by 5-lb claimer, sweating and on toes, won claimer at Haydock in September: wintry in appearance, ran moderately in £8,400 apprentice handicap final start: suited by 1¼m: acts on any going: gave trouble at stalls second outing: blinkered third (tended to hang left) and fourth. *J. Etherington.*

ORANGE GROVE (USA) 3 b.f. Sharpen Up 127–Pomegranate (USA) 96   **—**
(Damascus (USA)) [1988 6g5 5.8d* 7d3 1989 7h6 7f4 7m 7g] small, angular, sparely-made filly: moderate walker: has a quick action: fairly useful winner as 2-y-o when third in Rockfel Stakes at Newmarket: below form in 1989, best effort in mid-division in £8,800 handicap at Newmarket third outing: should stay 1m: best efforts on a soft surface: sold 33,000 gns Newmarket December Sales. *B. W. Hills.*

ORANGE KING 5 ch.g. Kings Lake (USA) 133–Jaffa 103 (Right Royal V 135)   **—**
[1988 16g 1989 12.2g4 13s5] ex-Irish gelding: half-brother to several winners, notably top-class 2-y-o and miler Jacinth (by Red God): dam stayer: no sign of ability: blinkered only outing at 4 yrs: sold out of J. Hassett's stable 5,000 gns Doncaster May Sales: resold 2,100 gns Doncaster November Sales. *M. P. Naughton.*

ORATEL FLYER 2 gr.c. (May 14) Kirchner 110–Hyperion Princess (Dragonara   **52**
Palace (USA) 115) [1989 6m 6g 6g a5g a5g6] sparely-made colt: third foal: dam well beaten in 3 starts: fair plater: best effort penultimate outing: seems a suitable mount for a 7-lb claimer. *R. Thompson.*

ORBIT (USA) 2 ch.f. (Mar 31) Sunny's Halo (CAN)–Female Star (USA) (Johnny   **68** p
Appleseed (USA)) [1989 6g4] $19,000Y: second reported foal: dam minor winner in USA: sire won Kentucky Derby: 11/2 from 3/1, around 4 lengths fourth of 18, keeping

on never able to challenge, to Peterhouse in maiden at Redcar in November: will be better suited by 7f + : should improve. *B. W. Hills.*

ORCHARD COURT (USA) 2 ch.c. (May 1) Believe It (USA)–Quilting Bee (USA) (Tom Rolfe) [1989 7m⁴ 6m⁶ 7m* 7g³ 7f* 7g 7g² 7g² a7g* a7g*] 10,000Y: quite attractive colt: moderate mover: half-brother to 2 winners in USA: dam unraced sister to Run The Gantlet: fair performer: successful in sellers (bought out of N. Callaghan's stable 6,000 gns) at Thirsk and Redcar (no bid) and in non-selling nursery and a claimer at Southwell: will be suited by 1m: best form on good ground: suitable mount for a 7-lb claimer. *T. D. Barron.* **83**

ORCHARD'S PET 3 gr.c. Petong 126–Toccata (USA) 64 (Mr Leader (USA)) [1988 5v² 5g 5m² 5g² 5m⁵ 5f⁵ 7g* 7d⁶ 7m⁵ 1989 8s 6d⁵ 7.5d 6m 7g 5f* 5m 6m² 6m⁶ 6f⁴ 7f⁵ 7f 6f⁵ 6m*] leggy, good-topped colt: has a roundish action: quite modest handicapper: won at Folkestone in June and Brighton in September: stays 7f: acts on firm going: best in blinkers or a visor: suitable mount for apprentice: very edgy when tailed off seventh start: rather inconsistent. *W. G. M. Turner.* **65**

ORCHARD STREET 4 ch.g. Glint of Gold 128–Miss Filbert 95 (Compensation 127) [1988 12d 10s 14.7m 1989 16f³] poor maiden: stays 2m: sold 850 gns Ascot December Sales. *R. Hollinshead.* **33**

ORCHESTRION 4 b.f. Song 132–Flying Milly (Mill Reef (USA) 141) [1988 7g 7.5f 8g 7f 7.5s 9g⁴ 12d 12s 1989 7d] bad maiden. *J. M. Bradley.* **—**

ORDELIA 4 b.f. Enchantment 115–Legal Fiddle 81 (Canisbay 120) [1988 8m 10g 10s 1989 8s] chunky filly: little sign of ability, including in claimer. *G. Kindersley.* **—**

ORDER OF MERIT 4 b.c. Cut Above 130–Lady Habitat (Habitat 134) [1988 10m 12g⁶ 1989 9f 12f 14f³ 12m 10.1m* 12f 10m 10f 11.7d 8.5f] small, sturdy colt: dropped in class, won 23-runner seller (sold out of D. Elsworth's stable 6,400 gns) at Windsor in July, making virtually all: behind in handicaps (first ladies event) and amateurs event afterwards: suited by 1¼m: keen sort and a difficult ride. *D. A. Wilson.* **52**

ORDER PAPER 4 b.g. Taufan (USA) 119–Lady of Surana (Shirley Heights 130) [1988 7v⁴ 8s* 7m 7v⁶ 8f 7f 8g 10g⁵ 11d* 13s⁵ 11s* 8.2s⁶ 1989 8g 12g 12d 13s² 10v² 13.6g] narrow, leggy, close-coupled gelding: has a quick action: quite modest handicapper: best at 1¼m to 13f: suited by plenty of give in the ground: visored once at 3 yrs: has won for apprentice: genuine. *J. S. Wilson.* **66**

ORGANZA 4 b.f. High Top 131–Canton Silk 108 (Runnymede 123) [1988 8g⁴ 10.4s⁴ 10f* 9d² 1989 10.1m² 10.6g⁵ 10.2m 10m 14g] sturdy, lengthy filly: has a fluent, round action: useful winner as 3-y-o: below her best in 1989: odds on, ¾-length second of 13 in minor contest at Windsor in July: well beaten in handicaps last 2 outings: stays 1¼m: unsuited by soft going, acts on any other: sold 94,000 gns Newmarket December Sales. *J. W. Hills.* **92**

ORIENTAL CHARM 4 ch.c. Krayyan 117–Little Angle (Gulf Pearl 117) [1988 6g⁶ 7s 8f 9f⁵ 8d³ 8d³ 9g⁵ 1989 10.2g 8v] strong, angular colt: moderate mover: poor maiden: stays 1m: acts on a soft surface: blinkered final 2 appearances in 1988: visored last outing: bought out of E. Eldin's stable 5,000 gns Newmarket Autumn Sales. *D. Moffatt.* **—**

ORIENTAL MYSTIQUE 2 ch.f. (Apr 14) Kris 135–Miss Toshiba (USA) 113 (Sir Ivor 135) [1989 6d⁶] rangy, good-bodied filly: has scope: eighth foal: half-sister to several winners, including 3-y-o 1¼m winner Horseshoe Reef (by Mill Reef) and Irish 7f winner North Eastern (by Northern Dancer), stakes winner in USA: dam won from 7f to 1½m, including in USA where showing very smart form: 7/1 and green, about 10 lengths sixth of 24, keeping on steadily, to Heart of Joy in maiden at Newbury in October: sure to do better over further. *B. W. Hills.* **63 p**

ORIENTAL NATIVE (USA) 2 ch.g. (Feb 21) Raise A Native–Etoile d'Orient (Targowice (USA) 130) [1989 5g] 44,000Y: half-brother to 3-y-o Graminie (by Graustark) and 2 winners in USA: dam, minor French 7f winner, is daughter of half-sister to French Oaks winner Reine de Saba: backward, never dangerous in 18-runner maiden at Ripon in July. *W. J. Pearce.* **—**

ORIENTAL SPLENDOUR 3 b.f. Runnett 125–My Fair Orchid 71 (Roan Rocket 128) [1988 5g 5d⁴ 5m⁶ 7g³ 7m* 9m 8.2m 7d 7g* 7m⁴ 1989 8.5s 7f⁴ 7g 8f 7f* 7.6m⁵ 7s⁵ 7.6f⁵] compact, workmanlike filly: fair handicapper: led well inside final 1f at Brighton in August: below form after, in quite valuable events first 2 occasions and getting poor run on first of them: appears suited by 7f: acts on firm going: blinkered twice at 2 yrs. *I. V. Matthews.* **85**

ORIENTAL TREASURE (USA) 4 ch.g. Irish River (FR) 131–Etoile d'Orient —
(Targowice (USA) 130) [1988 7d² 8g 8d 8.2g² 8f⁶ 8m 8d 1989 8s⁴ 7d 8m 10f 8.3m
a11g⁵ a10g] strong, medium-sized gelding: second in newcomers event at Doncaster
and maiden at Hamilton as 3-y-o: poor form otherwise: stays 1m: acts on a soft
surface: blinkered 4 times: trained first 4 starts in 1989 by E. Wheeler. *J. W. Hills.*

ORIENTESSA 4 b.f. Don Roberto (USA)–Green Bay (FR) (Great Nephew 126) 32 d
[1988 10m⁵ 12m 10d 10f 1989 10m⁵ 8m 10m 10.1m 12h³ 12h 12f⁵ 10f 12m⁵] tall,
sparely-made filly: bad maiden: should stay beyond 1½m: acts on hard going:
blinkered eighth outing: sweating sixth: has run creditably for apprentice: sold 875
gns Ascot February Sales. *J. E. Long.*

ORIENT LINE 5 gr.g. Capricorn Line 111–Rue Talma § (Vigo 130) [1988 10d —
10g² 12g⁶ 10m² 12d 10.5g 11g⁶ 12m 14f⁵ 12g⁴ 13.3f 1989 16s] stocky gelding:
moderate mover: fairly useful handicapper: stayed 1¾m: probably unsuited by soft
going, acted on any other: lazy sort who took a deal of driving: often got behind and
suited by strong gallop: dead. *R. Hannon.*

ORLEANS GIRL 2 b.f. (Jun 5) Dixieland Band (USA)–Philassa (USA) (Forli 59
(ARG)) [1989 6m⁵ 6m⁵ 5f² 7g] 1,800F, 3,500Y: unfurnished filly: fifth foal: closely
related to modest 1987 2-y-o Having A Blast and a minor sprint winner in USA (both
by Topsider): dam once-raced half-sister to Jockey Club Gold Cup winner Group
Plan: sire won from 5.5f to 9f: plating-class maiden: should stay 7f. *R. V. Smyth.*

ORLEANS SOUND 5 b.g. Duc d'Orleans 76–What A Performance (Gala —
Performance (USA)) [1988 NR 1989 11.7g] smallish gelding: fifth foal (all by Duc
d'Orleans): dam probably of little account: 16/1 and apprentice ridden, well beaten in
claimer at Windsor in August, slowly into stride then pulling hard. *S. Mellor.*

OR NOR 2 b.f. (Feb 23) Cure The Blues (USA)–Barely Hot (Bold Lad (IRE) 133) 47 §
[1989 5v 5s 5g 5f⁵ 5m 5m 5f* 5f² 5g⁵ 5g 5.3f4] 6,000Y: lengthy filly: has a roundish
action: second foal: half-sister to a winner in Italy by Mendez: dam, half-sister to
Trojan Fen and Kashi Lagoon, placed over 5f in Ireland: moderate plater: made all in
7-runner event (no bid) at Folkestone in July: will stay 6f: blinkered fourth outing:
has looked ungenerous. *W. Carter.*

ORPHEUS (USA) 3 ch.c. The Minstrel (CAN) 135–Mystical Mood (USA) 110
(Roberto (USA) 131) [1988 8g 8d* 8s 1989 13.1h* 16m* 15f* 15d⁶ 18f3] strong,

Newcastle 'Brown Ale' Northumberland Plate (Handicap), Newcastle—
Orpheus wins easing up, the first three-year-old successful in this historic race since 1900

close-coupled, attractive colt: good mover: successful in handicap at Bath, Newcastle 'Brown Ale' Northumberland Plate at Newcastle (from Ala Hounak) and 4-runner Tennent Trophy at Ayr (making all and keeping on gamely) in the summer: below form in Prix Kergorlay at Deauville and in £7,000 event at Pontefract (weakening quickly over 1f out) after: stays 2m but not 2¼m: has won on a soft surface but easily best efforts on top-of-the-ground: keen-going type. *G. Harwood.*

ORSETT (USA) 3 ch.g. Our Native (USA)–Ornamental (USA) (Triple Crown — (USA)) [1988 6g³ 1989 7m⁴ 10g⁶] lengthy, rather angular, useful-looking gelding: quite modest form: may be suited by around 1m: possibly unsuited by top-of-the-ground· sold to join Dr J. Scargill 10,500 gns Newmarket Autumn Sales and subsequently gelded. *B. W. Hills.*

ORVIETTO 2 ch.c. (Mar 12) Try My Best (USA) 130–Ventimiglia (Bruni 132) **76** [1989 7v 10g⁶ 10g⁵] IR 22,000Y: tall, leggy colt: second foal: dam, raced only at 2 yrs, out of half-sister to Music Boy: modest maiden: best effort second start: will stay well. *N. A. Callaghan.*

OSARIO 2 b.c. (Feb 12) Kind of Hush 118–Welsh Jane 71 (Bold Lad (IRE) **119** 133) [1989 5g* 6m² 6f² 6m³ 6g*]
As we last pointed out in our essay on the Cartier Million winner Corwyn Bay in *Racehorses of 1988*, the obstinacy with which the Jockey Club, unlike the Irish Turf authorities, protects its pattern of 'major' races has tended to thwart initiative and enterprise in race planning in Britain. In the circumstances it's refreshing to report that the executive at Redcar, led by Lord Zetland, came up trumps in 1989 with the Racecall Gold Trophy, which drew its inspiration from the massive interest stimulated in the Cartier Million, overcame official intransigence towards valuable 'restricted' races by its innovative conditions and, despite being run on a traditionally unappealing mid-week day at the end of October, proved such a success that it's hoped the fixture will become a permanent addition to the Calendar. Unlike the Cartier Million, which is confined solely to graduates of specially-designated sections of the Irish National Yearling Sale, the Racecall Gold Trophy is open to the produce of any stallion which had a yearling sold at any of the main public auctions in Europe and North America during the previous year. The weight each horse would carry was determined by the unconventional and not easily calculated median (middle) sale price of its sire's yearlings, and could have ranged from 7-12, if the sire's median was 2,000 guineas or less, to 9-0, if it exceeded 26,000 guineas. The conditions were deliberately biased towards the smaller owner and trainer to the extent that a bonus, up to a maximum £60,000, could also be won if the winning horse hailed from a poorly-patronized stable. These well-meaning intentions back-fired somewhat when it was discovered that the cheaply-bought Haunting Beauty, winner of the Molecomb Stakes and arguably the top two-year-old in the North, was one of several entries who weren't qualified to run, as her Florida-based sire Barachois hadn't had any of his produce sold at the major Keeneland and Fasig-Tipton Sales covered by *Nelsons Sales Digest*, who had the onerous task of collating the information and calculating the weights on behalf of the Redcar executive. This oversight, which resulted in Barachois and hundreds more American-based sires being omitted from the qualifying list, should be partly rectified in 1990 as more American sales will be covered. More

Racecall Gold Trophy, Redcar—a smart winner of a fascinating inaugural running

adequate data should also reduce the incidence of incorrect weights being alloted, as happened to Country Pine's progeny, for example, who were awarded 8-10 yet should rightly have been given 8-1. These shortcomings notwithstanding, the inaugural running went more smoothly than could have been anticipated, and took its place as the centrepiece of a good card which was partly televised by the BBC. The twenty-six-strong field (reduced to twenty-five when Night At Sea was withdrawn at the start) was the maximum permitted and, significantly, wouldn't have been out of place in the two-year-old pattern. The result was the right one, too, as far as the Redcar executive was concerned: the winner Osario, who earned over £100,000 for his connections, was the cheapest purchase in the line-up, having been bought for just 3,100 guineas at Doncaster's September Sales.

Osario's prospects against such as Argentum, the six-length winner of the Cornwallis Stakes on his previous start and a well-backed favourite as a consequence, the Dewhurst runner-up Call To Arms, and Olympic Hero and Remthat Naser, who'd both run creditably in pattern company, weren't outstanding on the form-book and were made less predictable by his absence since the Manton Rose Bowl Stakes at Newbury three and a half months earlier. He'd started a 5/2-shot that day following victory in a maiden auction race at Salisbury in May, where he came through strongly after a very slow start to account for his stable-companion Cove Cottage by three quarters of a length, and second places behind Dashing Blade and Be My Chief in the Berkshire Stakes at Newbury and the Chesham Stakes at Royal Ascot respectively. Osario, a big, robust, angular colt, held the lead running into the last furlong on the last two occasions, and though readily outpaced by Dashing Blade gave Be My Chief a fright before going down by a length. His performance in the Rose Bowl was in stark contrast to those quite useful efforts: he didn't move with his usual fluency to post and was beaten with a quarter of a mile to run, eventually finishing a remote third of five behind Rushmore and Dayjur. Osario was turned out at Redcar looking in excellent condition, better than we'd seen him all year, and put his troubles behind him with a much-improved display which, by our assessment, was as good as any by a two-year-old in Britain with the exception of Be My Chief's Racing Post Trophy success. Taken straight across to the stand rail, the favourable side over the straight six furlongs at Redcar, Osario took up the running after a furlong, was still travelling strongly two furlongs out as Argentum lost any chance he had with a bump, and kept on staunchly to belie his lack of a recent run and beat Call To Arms by two and a half lengths, with Sheer Precocity, In Excess and Shamshoon coming next three lengths or more away. The remaining twenty runners, who had won thirty-seven races between them, finished well strung out.

Osario (b.c. Feb 12, 1987)	Kind of Hush (b 1978)	Welsh Pageant (b 1966)	Tudor Melody
			Picture Light
		Sauceboat (b 1972)	Connaught
			Cranberry Sauce
	Welsh Jane (b or br 1975)	Bold Lad (b 1964)	Bold Ruler
			Barn Pride
		Abbot's Isle (b 1967)	Welsh Abbot
			Too Cute

The smart middle-distance performer Kind of Hush may not have set the domestic racing and breeding worlds alight since his retirement at the end of 1982, but he was the rage in Scandinavia in 1989 where his sons Itsabrahma and Togo collected the Norsk Two Thousand Guineas, the Merrill Lynch Two Thousand Guineas and the Dansk Derby between them. Among his best winners here from four crops of racing age are the useful middle-distance filly Early Call and Osario's brother Dramatic Event, a fair handicapper who won over six furlongs early in his career but is probably most effective at around a mile nowadays. Osario is the third winner his dam Welsh Jane, a modest maiden at up to mile, has produced; the first, Miss Plasi (by Free State), was a fair winner over five and six furlongs as a two-year-old in 1983. Welsh Jane's dam Abbot's Isle was an altogether better filly who won five races over five furlongs before producing two winners at stud, one of whom won over a mile and a half. Few of Osario's recent family have been at their best over middle distances, however, and as Kind of Hush hasn't proved to be a strong influence one way or the other as a stallion it could well be that Osario will be most effective at up to a mile. A genuine colt with the scope to train on, Osario should win his fair share of races in future. He is on a very favourable mark in the Free Handicap for a start. *R. Hannon.*

OSGATHORPE 2 ch.c. (Feb 9) Dunbeath (USA) 127–Darlingka 77 (Darling Boy 124) [1989 6m 6d4] half-brother to 1987 2-y-o 6f winner Stylish Darling (by Moorestyle), very useful 6f and 1m winner Idolized (by Mummy's Pet) and 2 winners abroad: dam won twice over 1½m: 7 lengths fourth of 11, keeping on never dangerous, to Reasonable Kid in maiden at Catterick in October, much better effort: slowly away on debut: will be better suited by 7f + . *E. Weymes.* **61**

OSRIC 6 b.g. Radetzky 123–Jolimo 92 (Fortissimo 111) [1988 12d4 1989 12g* 12d] **84** workmanlike gelding: fair handicapper: 40/1 and burly, won 16-runner event at Newmarket (cut leg badly in same race at 5 yrs) in October by ½ length from Belmoredean, making virtually all and battling on splendidly: prominent until under 3f out when well beaten in William Hill November Handicap at Thirsk: stays 1¾m: acts on any going: takes a good hold and has on occasions raced too freely: occasionally on toes: genuine and consistent: very smart hurdler. *M. J. Ryan.*

OSTORA (USA) 3 ch.f. Blushing Groom (FR) 131–My Darling One (USA) **83** (Exclusive Native (USA)) [1988 7g2 1989 10g4 10m5 8g2] smallish, angular filly: fair maiden: probably stayed 1¼m: visits Sure Blade. *R. W. Armstrong.*

OSTURA 4 b.c. Sir Ivor 135–Casual (USA) (Caro 133) [1988 8g 11.7m2 11.5d5 11d* **89** 10.1m* 12f2 10g 12g3 10.2g6 11s2 1989 11f3 10f2 10g 10.6d2] good-topped, quite attractive colt: carries plenty of condition: has a round action: fair handicapper: suited by testing conditions at 1¼m and stays 1½m: acts on any going: game. *P. F. I. Cole.*

OTTERBURN (USA) 3 b.c. Raise A Man (USA)–Summertime Lady (USA) (No **74** § Robbery) [1988 NR 1989 10m4 7.5m2 10f2 8f] angular colt: fifth foal: half-brother to useful 1986 2-y-o 8.2f winner Santella Sam (by Balzac) and useful 7f and 10.5f winner Darby Lady (by Darby Creek Road): dam lightly-raced half-sister to Bohemian Grove, a good winner in Europe, Australia and USA: sire stakes winner from 6f to 8.5f: modest maiden: has looked unsatisfactory, swerving right at start then finding little 3f out when well beaten final outing: should prove best at short of 1¼m: sold to join R. O'Sullivan 7,600 gns Newmarket Autumn Sales: one to treat with caution. *W. J. Haggas.*

OTTERGAYLE 4 br.c. Lord Gayle (USA) 124–Otterhill 67 (Brigadier Gerard **102** 144) [1988 7g 6m2 6m5 6d6 6m3 6m2 7g* 8d3 7d 1989 8g2 8d* 7d 8s 8f 10m4 9g 8d] small, finely-made colt: good mover: useful handicapper: improved in spring, winning £7,900 Old Road Securities Spring Cup (Handicap) at Newbury in good style: fast-finishing second to Fact Finder in William Hill Lincoln Handicap at Doncaster: always behind in well-contested races last 2 starts: suited by 1m: best with give in the ground: has run creditably when sweating: has won for lady: has a good turn of foot. *P. T. Walwyn.*

OUBLIER L'ENNUI (FR) 4 b.f. Bellman (FR) 123–Cassowary 82 (Kashmir II **—** 125) [1988 8g6 7f 8.5m4 10g3 12m4 10d3 10f5 1989 11.5g 14m 11.7m] good-topped filly: moderate mover: modest maiden at best: well beaten in handicaps in 1989: probably stays 1½m: seems unsuited by firm going: visored final outing: apprentice ridden first two. *Miss B. Sanders.*

OUR FAN 3 b.c. Taufan (USA) 119–Crufty Wood (Sweet Revenge 129) [1988 5g4 **79** 5d* 5m5 5g* 6f6 5g3 5m4 1989 5f* 5f5 6g3 6h* 6f3 5m3 6f2 6f* 5f* 5m4 6m 5s] neat, good-quartered colt: easily best efforts when justifying favouritism in ladies seller (no bid) at Thirsk in July by 7 lengths, making virtually all, and handicap at Nottingham in August: earlier successful in handicaps at Pontefract in May and Carlisle in June: stays 6f: acts on any going with possible exception of very soft: suitable mount for apprentice. *J. Berry.*

OUR FREDDIE 5 br.g. Cajun 120–So Valiant 80 (So Blessed 130) [1988 6g 5s 5f **72** 5m 5d3 5d* 5g2 5g 5m2 5m 5f* 5g5 5d5 1989 5s2 5m 5f* 5f4 5g 5m3 5g* 5g 5m2 5f3dis 6m] well-made, quite attractive gelding: poor mover: modest handicapper: won at Redcar in May and Catterick (apprentices, making all) in August: best at 5f: acts on any going: refused to go to post seventh intended start: usually hooded and blinkered nowadays (wasn't when well beaten final outing): finds little under pressure and suited by front-running tactics and tender handling. *W. Carter.*

OUR GINGER 5 ch.m. Le Johnstan 123–Summersoon 89 (Sheshoon 132) [1988 —
8.5m[5] 8f 8.2m 8g* 8g[4] 8m 8s* 8d 1989 8f 8g[4] 8g] leggy, plain mare: moderate
mover: winning plater as 4-y-o: well below her best in 1989: best form at around 1m
on an easy surface nowadays: inconsistent. *Ronald Thompson.*

OUR JOCK 7 br.h. Daring March 116–Sweet Jane 59 (Furry Glen 121) [1988 6m[6] 77
6m[2] 6g 6f 6m 7m[4] 5f 8g 8g[2] 7d[6] 6s[5] 6g[5] 1989 6v 7s 7m[3] 8f 7f[5] 10g* 7.6m[6] 10f[2] 7d[3]]
lengthy horse: good mover: modest performer nowadays: won claimer at Epsom in
August: best efforts in handicaps after when placed at Brighton and Newbury
(apprentices): stays 1¼m: acts on any going: has won for apprentice: has gone freely
to post: reluctant to race seventh start (visored) at 6 yrs: occasionally slowly away.
R. V. Smyth.

OUR KRYSTLE 4 ch.f. Tender King 123–Ackabarrow 97 (Laser Light 118) [1988 —
6v 8g 6d[5] 6m[6] 6m 6f 5s 6d 5m 6m 1989 10d 8m] leggy filly: quite modest winner at 2
yrs: little subsequent form, including in seller: stays 7f: yet to show her form on firm
going, acts on any other: usually visored or blinkered: has hung and appeared
ungenuine. *D. Moffatt.*

OUR MUSIC 3 ch.f. Music Boy 124–Double Finesse 97 (Double Jump 131) [1988 63
5g 6g 6m 6d 1989 6s[4] 6m 8m[3] 8.2m* 10.2f[2] 8f 11m[2] 10g 10.6s 11s[4] 10g] smallish,
angular filly: quite modest performer: won apprentice handicap at Nottingham in
June: off course 3 months then below form in sellers last 3 starts: effective at 1m and
11f: acts on firm going: races keenly: claimed out of W. Haggas' stable fifth outing:
sold 5,800 gns Newmarket Autumn Sales. *N. Tinkler.*

OUR RON 2 b.g. (Apr 21) Daring March 116–Sweet Jane 59 (Furry Glen 121) [1989 68
6f[3] 6m[2] 5m 5m 8.5g[5] 7.3m[6]] 7,000Y: leggy, quite attractive gelding: has scope:
turns off-fore in: sixth foal: brother to 1m and 1¼m winner Dismiss and Our Jock,
fairly useful winner at up to 1¼m: dam best at 5f: quite modest maiden: best efforts
second and final outings: stays 7.3f: sometimes taken down early. *R. V. Smyth.*

OUR VISION 2 b.c. (Mar 15) Vision (USA)–Faiblesse (Welsh Saint 126) [1989 67
7g[4] 7m 7m[5] 10g] IR 22,000F, 27,000Y: rangy colt: has plenty of scope: second foal:
dam showed a little ability in France: quite modest maiden: best efforts first and
third outings: out of depth final one: should stay beyond 7f. *C. E. Brittain.*

OUT OF FUNDS 3 b.c. Ela-Mana-Mou 132–Overspent 85 (Busted 134) [1988 87
6g[2] 8s[3] 1989 12g[6] 12.3m[2] 14f[2] 16m] useful-looking colt: moderate walker:
progressive form when second in handicaps at Chester and York (£12,000 event) 3
months later: pulled hard to post then tailed off in £7,400 handicap at Newmarket in
October: should stay 2m: acts on firm going. *R. Hollinshead.*

OUT ON A FLYER 5 b.m. Comedy Star (USA) 121–Listen To Me 46 (He Loves —
Me 120) [1988 6g 6m 6d 6d 6d 1989 6h] sturdy mare: winning handicapper in 1987: no
subsequent form on flat: suited by 6f: probably unsuited by soft going, acts on any
other: has run well for apprentice: winning selling hurdler. *J. J. O'Neill.*

OUT ON ALLEGE (USA) 3 b.f. Alleged (USA) 138–Musique Royale (USA) 59
(Northern Dancer) [1988 7m 1989 8m 10h[4] 10g[3] 13.8g[4] 11.5m[3] 12g[5] 10.2f] leggy filly:
moderate mover: quite modest maiden: below form in handicaps at Leicester (off
bridle throughout) and Bath (apprentices, prominent 1m in strongly-run race) last 2
outings: may well prove suited by 1½m: acts on top-of-the-ground: sold 4,800 gns
Newmarket December Sales. *P. F. I. Cole.*

OUT RUN 3 gr.g. Nishapour (FR) 125–Shalara (Dancer's Image (USA)) [1988 — §
5m[4] 6f* 6m 6g 6g 8.5m 8.2m[5] 8m* 7d 8.2d 1989 12s 12m 10m] medium-sized
gelding: carries condition: modest winner as 2-y-o: well below form in 1989:
probably doesn't stay 1½m: suited by top-of-the-ground: best blinkered: edgy last 2
outings, sweating first of them: doubtful temperamentally: winning juvenile hurdler
with M. Pipe. *R. Hannon.*

OUTSTANDING BILL 3 ch.g. Nicholas Bill 125–Hardwick Amber 58 55
(Tanfirion 110) [1988 5s[3] 5m[5] 5g 8d 7f 7f[5] 7g 1989 8f 7h 7.5m 5m 6s[4] 12g[6]] leggy,
close-coupled gelding: only show as 3-y-o in minor event and maiden claimer
(staying on rear) at Hamilton last 2 starts: gives impression may well stay
middle distances: seems to act on any going: winning hurdler. *J. M. Jefferson.*

OVERPOWER 5 b.g. Try My Best (USA) 130–Just A Shadow (Laser Light 118) 72
[1988 8d 8g[2] 8d* 8.5m[6] 8m[2] 8m[3] 8.2d[4] 8s[6] 8g 1989 8d[4] 8f 8m[6] 8g* 8g[3] 8.2g 8f[4] 8g[4]
a8g[4] a8g[5]] sparely-made gelding: modest handicapper: won at Carlisle (for second
time) in June, quickening on bridle to lead final 1f having soon been ridden and lost
his place: suited by 1m: probably not at his best on soft going, acts on any other:
blinkered twice in 1988: has sweated and got on edge: a difficult ride and suited by
waiting tactics. *J. W. Watts.*

OWEN FALLS 3 b.c. Mill Reef (USA) 141–Allegedly Blue (USA) 106 (Alleged   **88 +**
(USA) 138) [1988 NR 1989 10.1m 14g⁶ 14fʷᵒ 13.8g* 14g* 16f²] 285,000Y: leggy,
angular, narrow colt: easy mover: first foal: dam, 1½m winner suited by 1¾m, is
daughter of sister to Crowned Prince and Kentucky Derby winner Majestic Prince:
walked over in maiden at Yarmouth: most impressive when making all in handicaps
at Catterick (ridden by 5-lb claimer) and Yarmouth 6 days later: 11/8 on, led over
1½m when appearing to run creditably behind Royal Square in 4-runner minor event
at Redcar later in August, both eased from 1f out: probably stays 2m: well suited by
forcing tactics: sold 17,000 gns Newmarket Autumn Sales. *J. Gosden.*

OWN FREE WILL   4 ch.f. Nicholas Bill 125–Falcrello 51 (Falcon 131) [1988 8v²   **81 d**
8.2v* 10g* 10g5 12m 10v² 10s* 11d* 10g5 11s 1989 10d 12.3s4 12f 10.6g6 10m5 10.6d]
leggy, angular filly: poor mover: fair winner as 3-y-o: best effort in 1989 when
fourth, no extra close home, of 13 in handicap at Ripon in April: off course 2½
months after next outing: ran poorly final one: probably ideally suited by slightly
shorter than 1½m: suited by plenty of give in the ground: suitable mount for
apprentice. *Mrs J. R. Ramsden.*

OWT ON   2 ch.g. (May 6) Sweet Monday 122–Young April 46 (Young Man (FR) 73)   **51**
[1989 6m 5f 6g 6g] big, angular gelding: first foal: dam, plater, needed at least 1½m:
plating-class maiden: best effort second start: should stay beyond 5f. *Mrs J. R.
Ramsden.*

OXALIS   5 b.m. Connaught 130–Phlox 101 (Floriana 106) [1988 14.6g4 10g 10.1m3   **—**
12d6 13s² 12g 1989 12d] big, heavy-topped mare: carries plenty of condition: poor
mover: quite modest maiden as 4-y-o: ridden by 5-lb claimer, last of 15 in handicap at
Thirsk in April: probably needs further than 1¼m: acts on soft going: usually wears
bandages: sold to join R. Dods 1,300 gns Newmarket September Sales. *G. A. Huffer.*

OXBOW   2 b.c. (Feb 26) Trojan Fen 118–Shannon Princess (Connaught 130) [1989   **71 p**
8g5] 60,000Y: compact colt: seventh living foal: half-brother to 3 winners here and
abroad, notably very useful middle-distance stayer Waterfield (by Le Moss) and
fairly useful 1½m to 19f winner Fitzpatrick (by Oats): dam won over 1m and 1¼m in
Ireland: 16/1, burly and green, around 7 lengths fifth of 17 to Lover's Moon in maiden
at Leicester in November: sure to do better over further. *P. T. Walwyn.*

OXBRIDGE (FR)   4 b.c. Top Ville 129–Glitter (FR) 70 (Reliance II 137) [1988   **—**
10g 1989 12.5g 10.1m 10f] big, dipped-backed, lengthy colt: no form in modest
company. *H. O'Neill.*

OXFORD PADDY   2 b.c. (Mar 3) Taufan (USA) 119–Spyglass (Double Form   **—**
130) [1989 7m] leggy colt: moderate walker: first foal: dam second over 5f at 2 yrs in
Ireland: 33/1, bit backward and very green, slowly away and always behind in
8-runner maiden at Redcar in September. *R. O'Leary.*

Prix Robert Papin, Maisons-Laffitte—a British-trained winner in Ozone Friendly

Mr W. J. Gredley's "Ozone Friendly"

OYSTON'S WORLD 2 br.f. (Apr 22) Reesh 117–Abrasive 53 (Absalom 128) **60**
[1989 6f* 5m 6m² 6m³ 6f⁴ 6m] 3,000F: leggy filly: turns fore-feet out: shows a
roundish action: first foal: dam, stayed 6f, ran only at 2 yrs: plating-class performer:
made all in 5-runner maiden at Hamilton in May: ran badly in seller at Newmarket in
October on final outing: suited by 6f: sweating and edgy last 2 starts. *J. Berry.*

OZAL (USA) 2 ch.c. (Apr 29) Lyphard (USA) 132–L'Attrayante (USA) 127 **96 p**
(Tyrant (USA)) [1989 8v² 8v² 8s*] first foal: dam won French and Irish 1000
Guineas, and is half-sister to Prix Gladiateur winner Campo Moro: won maiden at
Saint-Cloud in December by a head: will stay 1¼m: well bred, and should go on to
better things. *F. Boutin, France.*

OZONE FRIENDLY (USA) 2 ch.f. (May 7) Green Forest (USA) 134–Kristana **107**
96 (Kris 135) [1989 5f² 5f⁴ 6g* 5.5g* 6g⁴ 6m] 41,000Y: leggy, unfurnished filly: first
foal: dam, 1¼m winner, is daughter of half-sister to St Leger winner Athens Wood:
useful performer: made all in 13-runner maiden at Newmarket in July and Prix
Robert Papin at Maisons-Laffitte over 2 weeks later: beaten about 5 lengths in
Tattersalls Cheveley Park Stakes at Newmarket in October, final outing and best
other effort: should stay 1m: best form on good ground. *B. W. Hills.*

P

PACIFIC GEM 2 br.g. (Mar 6) Valiyar 129–Mary Martin (Be My Guest (USA) **83**
126) [1989 5g⁶ 6f* 6m 7g 7d] quite good-topped gelding: first foal: dam unraced
half-sister to very smart sprinter Greenland Park (dam of Fitnah) and Coventry
Stakes winner Red Sunset: won 10-runner maiden at Ripon in August: showed
nothing in nurseries last 2 starts: suited by 6f. *P. Calver.*

PACIFIC WAVE 3 b.f. Blushing Scribe (USA) 107–Manageress 74 (Mandamus **48**
120) [1988 5g 5m⁵ 5f⁴ 5m 5f³ 6m* 5f³ 7.5g² 7g² 6m² 6f² 6f⁵ 6g 7f 1989 6m 8m⁵ 6f

6m5 6f4 7m 6m 6g] compact, workmanlike filly: modest plater: lost form last 3 outings, hanging left throughout in apprentice event on first of them: ideally suited by stiffish 6f: acts on firm going: visored: keen sort: tends to sweat and get on toes: sometimes finds little under pressure: sold 1,250 gns Doncaster November Sales. *Ronald Thompson.*

PADDY CASH 2 b.g. (Mar 28) Pas de Seul 133–Kachela (Kalamoun 129) [1989 5m] third reported foal: half-brother to winner in Sweden by Bold Lad: dam half-sister to smart French 7f to 10.5f winner Hether: last of 7 in maiden at Hamilton in May. *J. S. Wilson.* —

PADDY CHALK 3 gr.c. Tina's Pet 121–Guiletta 63 (Runnymede 123) [1988 5f* 92 6m* 6g* 5d2 6f2 1989 6s3 6f3 6f 6m2] leggy, workmanlike colt: fairly useful performer: easily best efforts as 3-y-o in £6,100 event and in listed race (not getting clear run and beaten 6 lengths by Green's Canaletto in July) at Newbury second and final starts: faced stiff task in between: ideally suited by 6f: acts on firm going and a soft surface: genuine. *L. J. Holt.*

PADYKIN 9 b.m. Bustino 136–Expadeo 82 (St Paddy 133) [1988 14.6d 12m 1989 — 10.2g 16m] workmanlike mare: of little account: wore small bandage on near-fore final outing: sold 2,400 gns Doncaster November Sales. *M. C. Chapman.*

PAGO 2 ch.c. (Mar 17) Sallust 134–Fire Dance (FR) (Habitat 134) [1989 5g5 6m 67 5d* 6v 6g] IR 7,000Y: close-coupled, workmanlike colt: has scope: turns fore-feet in and is a moderate walker and mover: half-brother to fair 1¼m winner Staravia (by Star Appeal), 1980 2-y-o 5f winner Disco Dancer (by Record Token) and a winner in Italy: dam never ran: won 19-runner maiden at Haydock in September at 20/1: good seventh, considerately handled, in 30-runner claiming nursery at Newmarket final outing: should stay 1m. *C. Tinkler.*

PALABORA (USA) 2 gr.c. (Apr 25) Wolf Power (SAF)–Peeping (USA) 66 (Buckfinder (USA)) [1989 5g 6f* 5f4 6g 5.8h4 6m4 7m 7g3 6f5 6v a7g6 7g] $5,000Y: plain, angular colt: third foal: dam unraced: sire, champion 2-y-o and older horse in South Africa, won at up to 1¼m: quite modest performer: bought out of W. O'Gorman's stable 10,500 gns after winning seller at Lingfield: inconsistent afterwards: stays 7f: appears unsuited by heavy ground. *P. J. Arthur.*

PALACE COURT 2 b.c. (May 5) Anita's Prince 126–Court Hussar (Queen's — Hussar 124) [1989 6m 8.2g 8g] IR 4,200Y: first foal: dam thrice-raced daughter of a stayer: well beaten, including in a seller. *P. Burgoyne.*

PALACE JESTER 4 ch.c. Music Boy 124–Sandray's Palace (Royal Palace 131) — [1988 8m 12g 12m4 12g 12m 12d5 1989 12d6 13m 15.8g] lengthy, rather sparely-made colt: poor maiden: barely stays 1½m. *J. S. Haldane.*

PALACE LADY 3 b.f. Ballacashtal (CAN)–Belle (DEN) (Comedy Star (USA) — 121) [1988 NR 1989 8g 5f 10f] 9,100Y: tall, workmanlike filly: fourth foal: half-sister to fairly useful 6f and 1m winner Touch of Grey (by Blakeney) and 1984 Italian 2-y-o 7f winner Ela Mana Bel (by Ela-Mana-Mou): dam won 3 times in Scandinavia: no sign of ability in claimers and a seller: sold to join T. Craig 3,200 gns Doncaster August Sales. *R. J. Hodges.*

PALACE MILL 3 b.c. Simply Great (FR) 122–Ballet Violet (Stradavinsky 121) — [1988 6m6 5g4 7m6 7d6 1989 10v 11.7d 12.5f6] big, workmanlike colt: moderate walker and mover, with a round action: plating-class maiden at best: well beaten in spring as 3-y-o, including in handicaps: probably doesn't stay 1½m: best run on top-of-the-ground. *R. J. Hodges.*

PALACE REBEL 3 gr.c. Absalom 128–Wharton Manor 86 (Galivanter 131) 76 [1988 6m6 6f2 6f 5f 7d2 7m 1989 8d 7d 8g5 8h5 7m4 10f2 10h*] lengthy colt: won handicap at Brighton in July: stays 1¼m: acts on hard going and a soft surface: sold, reportedly to race in Middle East, 16,500 gns Newmarket July Sales. *M. A. Jarvis.*

PALACE STREET (USA) 2 ch.f. (Apr 2) Secreto (USA) 128–Majestic Street 91 (USA) (Majestic Prince) [1989 6g3 6m5 6g* 8g] close-coupled, wiry filly: keen walker: half-sister to useful 1m to 1¼m winner Indian Trail (by Apalachee) and 3 winners in USA: dam, closely related to stakes winner Raise A Dancer and half-sister to 3 stakes winners, was stakes-placed winner of 2 races from 21 starts: fairly useful filly: won 23-runner maiden at Newbury in August: ran well previously in Hillsdown Cherry Hinton Stakes at Newmarket and afterwards in Prix Marcel Boussac at Longchamp: will stay beyond 1m: sold 145,000 gns Newmarket December Sales. *A. A. Scott.*

PALAIS DE DANSE 5 ch.h. Dance In Time (CAN)–Dunfermline 133 (Royal — Palace 131) [1988 12g 10g 10d5 1989 8.5d6 10m 10.4m 9s] tall, deep-girthed, rather

short-backed horse: poor maiden: stays 1¼m: acts on top-of-the-ground and soft
going: bandaged on reappearance. *A. W. Potts.*

PALATIAL STYLE 2 b.g. (Apr 18) Kampala 120–Stylish Princess (Prince   **67**
Tenderfoot (USA) 126) [1989 5m⁴ 5f⁶ 5d 5g⁴] IR 4,000Y, 6,000 2-y-o: first foal: dam
never ran: quite modest maiden: will be better suited by 6f. *M. Avison.*

PALE GLOW 3 gr.f. Kalaglow 132–Opale 117 (Busted 134) [1988 NR 1989 12g⁵]   —
lengthy, dipped-backed, angular filly: has scope: first foal: dam won Irish St Leger at
4 yrs: green and little promise in 6-runner maiden at Leicester in August: showed a
quick action. *A. C. Stewart.*

PALE STAR 7 b.m. Kampala 120–Kimstar 61 (Aureole 132) [1988 10d⁵ 10.2g 10f   —
10m 12f 12f 1989 8.3m] sparely-made mare: no form since first outing in 1988. *J.
White.*

PALE WINE 2 b.c. (Feb 17) Rousillon (USA) 133–Opale 117 (Busted 134) [1989   **63** P
7m] 125,000Y: rangy colt: shade unfurnished: has plenty of scope: second foal:
half-brother to 3-y-o Pale Glow (by Kalaglow): dam won Irish St Leger at 4 yrs: 9/1
but very green, highly-promising tenth of 21 in maiden at Newmarket in October,
last (slowly away) early on and not at all knocked about final 2f: will be better suited
by 1m +: sure to improve good deal. *A. C. Stewart.*

PALEY PRINCE (USA) 3 b.c. Tilt Up (USA)–Apalachee Princess (USA)   **110**
(Apalachee (USA) 137) [1988 5m² 5f⁵ 5g* 5d² 5d 5f² 5m* 5m* 5g⁶ 5d 1989 5m 5m 5f
5g⁴ 6f 5m* 5m² 5g 5f* 5m⁵ 5m³ 5m³ 5m*] strong-quartered, good-topped, slightly
dipped-backed colt: good mover: won handicap (return to form) at Newmarket in
July, minor event at Beverley in September and all-aged contest at Chepstow in
October: ran well in handicaps and listed race tenth to twelfth outings: not certain to
stay 6f: well suited by top-of-the-ground: very useful. *M. D. I. Usher.*

PALMAS PRIDE 2 b.g. (Mar 9) Dalsaan 125–Sabirone (FR) (Iron Duke (FR)   **64**
122) [1989 6g⁵ 7m 6m³ 6g² 6m² 7d²] 14,000Y: sturdy gelding: has scope: moderate
walker: third foal: half-brother to a winner in Australia and a poor animal: dam, 1m
and 1¼m winner in France, from family of Saint Cyrien: useful plater: runner-up to
Rainbow Bridge at Lingfield and Passed Pawn at Catterick on last 2 starts: stays 7f:
blinkered or visored last 3 outings. *D. Morley.*

PALM HOUSE 4 ch.g. Coquelin (USA) 121–Kew Gift (Faraway Son (USA) 130)   —
[1988 8f 10m⁴ 1989 11v³ 15s] lengthy, angular gelding: good mover: has shown signs
of ability in maidens: should be suited by further than 11f: winner over hurdles. *G.
Richards.*

PALMILLA 3 ch.f. Tender King 123–Silver Bonnet (Sun Prince 128) [1988 NR   —
1989 7s] 1,200Y: fifth foal: half-sister to Belgian 6f winner Jester To Glory (by
Jester) and 2 platers, one very temperamental: dam, of no account, is closely related
to Another Realm: last of 15 in maiden at Folkestone in April: sold 550 gns Ascot
June Sales. *M. J. Fetherston-Godley.*

PALM REEF 5 b.g. Main Reef 126–Fingers (Lord Gayle (USA) 124) [1988 NR   —
1989 12s 7.9m 6f 8m 8g 7s 12f a12g] well-made gelding: modest maiden as 3-y-o: no
form in 1989: occasionally blinkered: trained first 5 outings by R. Donoghue in
Ireland. *M. Madgwick.*

PALM SWIFT 3 b.f. Rabdan 129–Swiftsand 65 (Sharpen Up 127) [1988 NR 1989   —
7m 7f a8g] leggy filly: first foal: dam, raced only at 3 yrs, half-sister to St Leger
second Zilos: no worthwhile form in minor event and maidens, showing signs of
ability on debut: off course 4½ months before final start. *T. Thomson Jones.*

PAMELA PEACH 3 gr.f. Habitat 134–Casual (USA) (Caro 133) [1988 5f² 1989   **81**
7s 6s² 7.6m⁴ 6m 6m² 6v a6g⁴] tall, close-coupled filly: has scope: has a round action:
fair maiden: effective at 6f and 7f: acts on top-of-the-ground and soft: may prove
suited by a galloping track: ran creditably when sweating and on toes. *J. Tree.*

PAMPERED DREAM 4 b.g. Kafu 120–Muna (Thatch (USA) 136) [1988 5v*   — §
5v⁵ 5s 5g 5m 7m 10m 8.2d⁵ 1989 7d 12.5f 9f 6f 6g] workmanlike gelding: moderate
mover: won handicap at Ayr early in 1988: has deteriorated markedly and is probably
temperamental: best form at 5f: blinkered once at 3 yrs, visored on reappearance:
edgy and wore net muzzle fourth appearance: bandaged and trained by K. Wingrove
first 3 starts (tailed off). *M. J. O'Neill.*

PANALO 2 gr.g. (Apr 15) Magic Mirror 105–Radinka (Connaught 130) [1989 6m 7f   **67**
7m⁴ 6f 5g⁴ 5m⁶ 6m 6g 5g 6f⁶ 5f² 5m³ 5g⁵ 6s³ a6g*] 5,400Y: smallish, sparely-made
gelding: first foal: dam never ran: quite modest performer: in good form towards end
of year, and won claimer at Southwell: needs further than 5f: acts on any going: best

form in blinkers or a visor: has worn bandages: trained until after tenth outing by C. C. Elsey. *J. Hetherton.*

PANAMA PRINCESS 3 b.f. Indian King (USA) 128–Straw Bonnet (Thatch (USA) 136) [1988 6g 6g 6m 5m* 5f 6g 5g⁴ 6m 6d 1989 5.8m 6f⁵ 6f 5.3h* 5f* 5f 5m² 5f⁴ 5f³ 5f 6f³ 5m 5m⁵ 5g⁶ 5.8f] lengthy filly: quite modest handicapper: successful in June at Brighton and Sandown: suited by 5f: best form on top-of-the-ground: blinkered last 3 starts at 2 yrs: has run creditably for apprentice. *K. O. Cunningham-Brown.* **64**

PANDESSA 2 b.f. (Mar 3) Blue Cashmere 129–Jeanne du Barry 74 (Dubassoff (USA)) [1989 6f⁵ 5m⁵] 3,000Y: lengthy, unfurnished, plain filly: fourth reported foal: dam 1m winner, also successful over hurdles: poor form in quite modest company at Newcastle in the summer. *J. H. Johnson.* **—**

PANDY 3 b.g. Thatching 131–Hot Stone (Hotfoot 126) [1988 7g 1989 8.2g⁵ 8m* 8g 10g] lengthy, useful-looking gelding: won maiden at York in September: ran creditably in handicap next start: should stay beyond 1m: has taken keen hold. *J. W. Hills.* **83**

PANEL GAME 5 ch.m. Lepanto (GER)–Silly Games 62 (Siliconn 121) [1988 8g 8g⁵ 1989 10g] leggy, sparely-made mare: poor maiden: 33/1, tailed off in apprentice handicap at Goodwood in October: best efforts at 1m: yet to race on firm going, probably acts on any other: winning selling hurdler. *P. Butler.* **—**

PANICO 2 b.c. (Mar 14) Superlative 118–Ex Dancer (USA) (Executioner (USA)) [1989 6f 7g] 13,000F, 42,000Y: quite attractive colt: fourth foal: half-brother to modest 1988 2-y-o 5f winner Dancing Blade (by Sayf El Arab) and 1½m winner Disciple (by Hello Gorgeous): dam Irish 6f winner at 4 yrs: poor form in autumn maidens at Folkestone and Newmarket: sold to join Miss S. Hall 15,000 gns Doncaster November Sales. *I. V. Matthews.* **—**

PANOPLY 2 br.f. (Feb 17) Sparkling Boy 110–Petploy 82 (Faberge II 121) [1989 5v⁶ 5f 6f⁶ 6m 7m⁶ 8g] small, sparely-made filly: half-sister to several minor winners: dam won over 6f and 7f: quite modest plater: suited by 7f: sold 1,050 gns Ascot October Sales. *T. Fairhurst.* **42**

PANSONG 3 b.c. Absalom 128–Sea Chant (Julio Mariner 127) [1988 5g 5d 5g³ 5f⁵ 7f² 6f⁵ 7.5g* 7.5g⁴ 7m⁶ 8.2m 8s 8.5f* 8.2s⁵ 1989 10.2g 9v² 8.2s 8.2m 12.2m 8h⁵ 9f⁵ 7m 9f⁵ 8f 8.5m 10s⁴ 9s] leggy, angular colt: moderate walker: poor mover, with a round action: quite modest plater: stays 1¼m: probably acts on any going: blinkered or visored eighth to eleventh outings: goes well with forcing tactics. *T. Fairhurst.* **56 d**

PANT LLIN 3 b.c. Mummy's Pet 125–Goosie-Gantlet 63 (Run The Gantlet (USA)) [1988 5d 5.8g* 6g² 7s⁵ 6s 6d⁵ 7g² 1989 7f 10f 10.6g] good-quartered colt: good walker: fair winner at 2 yrs: below form in handicaps in 1989, not seen out after June: will be suited by return to shorter: best form on an easy surface (below best on very soft going): sold 7,000 gns Newmarket Autumn Sales. *B. W. Hills.* **—**

PANTO LADY 3 br.f. Lepanto (GER)–Dusky Damsel 68 (Sahib 114) [1988 NR 1989 6f 6h⁴] leggy, compact filly: sixth foal: dam won over 6f at 3 yrs: early speed when behind in maidens in the summer. *J. H. Johnson.* **—**

PANTOSCOPE 3 b.f. Lepanto (GER)–Surfacing (Worden II 129) [1988 NR 1989 10.6g 12g] unfurnished filly: half-sister to fair sprinter Master-Blow (by Roi Soleil), modest 1¼m winner Rough-Cast (by Blast) and winners abroad: dam never ran: tailed off in maiden (hung badly) and seller. *C. C. Elsey.* **—**

PANTUN 2 b.f. (Apr 19) Absalom 128–Pakpao 77 (Mansingh (USA) 120) [1989 5f⁶ 5m 5f 6g 8.5f] small, sparely-made filly: fifth foal: half-sister to poor 1987 2-y-o Plumage (by Blue Refrain) and modest 2-y-o 5f winners by Sparkling Boy and Blue Cashmere: dam 2-y-o 5f winner: of little account: blinkered fourth start: sold 650 gns Ascot October Sales. *T. Fairhurst.* **—**

PAPER BISHOP 3 b.g. Balidar 133–Ramo's Lady (Malinowski (USA) 123) [1988 5m⁵ 5g 5m 1989 11.7f] neat, good-quartered colt: has a round action: well beaten in maidens. *J. J. Bridger.* **—**

PAPER BOY 3 b.c. Montekin 125–Another Deb 78 (African Sky 124) [1988 5g 5.3f⁴ 7g 6m 8.2m 1989 7m 8m] angular colt: good walker and mover: poor maiden. *A. P. James.* **—**

PAPER SHOES 3 b.f. Workboy 123–Two Friendly 54 (Be Friendly 130) [1988 5f² 5g³ 5f⁴ 5m⁶ 1989 5d⁶ 5f 5m 5f⁴ 5f 5g* 5f 5g 5s⁴] leggy filly, rather unfurnished: 25/1 and blinkered, held on by neck in handicap at Edinburgh in September: speedy, and will prove best at 5f: seems best on an easy surface nowadays: also blinkered **54**

seventh start: often apprentice ridden: sometimes bit slowly away: inconsistent and possibly best when fresh. *R. Earnshaw.*

PAPHIDIA 4 b.f. Mansingh (USA) 120–Dust Sheet (Silly Season 127) [1988 6g⁵ 6m⁵ 9m⁵ 8g⁶ 7m 1989 7h 7m 10.1m 8.3m] sturdy filly: has a quick action: poor maiden: soundly beaten in handicaps and sellers as 4-y-o: has been blinkered and visored: possibly temperamental. *P. Howling.* —

PARADISE BEACH 4 b.g. Skyliner 117–Looks A Million (Wollow 132) [1988 8s⁵ 8.2d 12g 11v² 13.3s 14.6m³ 1989 14s⁵ 12s 12d] big, leggy, workmanlike gelding: quite modest maiden at best: not raced after spring: stays 14.6f: yet to race on firm going, acts on any other: sold 6,800 gns Ascot November Sales. *B. A. McMahon.* 53

PARADISE CLUB 2 b.f. (Apr 14) Bold Owl 101–Blotweth Girl (Blue Cashmere 129) [1989 5.1m 5f⁶] small filly: first foal: dam unraced: ridden by 7-lb claimer, well beaten in mid-season sellers at Yarmouth and Warwick. *I. Campbell.* —

PARADOR 3 ch.c. Be My Guest (USA) 126–Keep Shining (USA) 77 (Stage Door Johnny) [1988 NR 1989 5h 7h⁴ 6f⁴ 10.2f* 10m* 10f³ 9m* 9g 10g] angular, unfurnished colt: second foal: dam won over 1¼m from only 2 starts: fair handicapper: successful in apprentice events (favourite) at Bath (gambled on, very easily) and Sandown (odds on, edging markedly right) in July and at Sandown in August: below form in Cambridgeshire Handicap (travelling well) at Newmarket and £8,900 event at Redcar last 2 starts: suited by 1¼m and top-of-the-ground: carries head bit high. *G. Harwood.* 88

PAR AVION 4 b.g. Beldale Flutter (USA) 130–Pitroyal 74 (Pitskelly 122) [1988 12.3g⁵ 15.8f³ 14.7m³ 1989 16s⁵ 16.2d* 16g] rangy gelding: has a round action: modest performer: apprentice ridden, rallied gamely when winning moderately-run maiden at Beverley in April: well beaten in handicap at Newmarket 2 weeks later: suited by a good test of stamina: acts on any going: lacks a turn of foot and best ridden up with pace. *C. A. Cyzer.* 74

PAR DE LUXE 2 b.f. (Apr 19) Superlative 118–Parbold 54 (Sassafras (FR) 135) [1989 7g⁵] 4,000 2-y-o: strong, workmanlike filly: half-sister to good 1982 Austrian 2-y-o Perky Parrot (by Hotfoot) and a winning jumper: dam plater: well-beaten last of 5 in minor event at York in October: should do better. *C. W. C. Elsey.* — p

PARESSE 4 ch.c. Sallust 134–Parez 67 (Pardao 120) [1988 7d 8g 8d 8m 10m 8m³ 8d⁴ 9g 1989 10.4m] compact, sturdy colt: usually dull in coat: moderate mover: inconsistent plater: tailed off from 6f out in non-selling handicap at Chester in May: stays 1m: acts on top-of-the-ground and a soft surface: sometimes blinkered or visored at 2 yrs. *G. M. Moore.* —

PARIS FRANCE 3 ch.f. High Line 125–Adaraya (FR) (Zeddaan 130) [1988 NR 1989 12f] IR 42,000Y: medium-sized, unfurnished filly: has scope: half-sister to 4 winners in France, including 1¼m and 10.5f winner Adjlann (by Vayraan): dam, French 1m winner, is half-sister to high-class French 1¼m performer Sharapour: green, tailed off in maiden at Brighton in May. *P. F. I. Cole.* —

PARISIAN GIRL 6 br.m. Blue Cashmere 129–Confleur 81 (Compensation 127) [1988 6g⁴ 6s⁴ 6m 6d⁶ 6d 6s 6s 7g 6v 1989 7f 6m⁵ 6s] lengthy mare: poor maiden: ideally suited by 6f and give in the ground: well beaten in seller when visored final outing: often apprentice ridden. *E. J. Alston.* —

PARIS MATCH 7 b. or br.g. Bold Lad (IRE) 133–Miss Paris 111 (Sovereign Path 125) [1988 NR 1989 15.8m] big, lengthy gelding: poor mover: tailed off in handicap at Catterick in June, only race on flat since 1986: best form at 1m: acts on firm going: blinkered twice: winning selling hurdler. *G. M. Moore.* —

PARKBHRIDE 3 b.g. Wolver Hollow 126–Gulistan (Sharpen Up 127) [1988 6d 8m 8g 10.2m 1989 16m⁴] compact, quite attractive gelding: good walker: well beaten in varied events: visored only start in 1989. *C. A. Horgan.* —

PARKBORO LAD 2 b.c. (Apr 5) Kala Shikari 125–Great Lass (Vaigly Great 127) [1989 5s 5f⁶] sturdy, lengthy, workmanlike colt: second foal: half-brother to 3-y-o Milclere (by Milford): dam never ran: probably of little account. *J. Wharton.* —

PARK FORUM 2 ch.c. (Feb 18) Dunbeath (USA) 127–Heavenly Gaze (FR) (Gay Mecene (USA) 128) [1989 5m] 7,600Y: first foal: dam never ran: last of 7 in minor event at Windsor in June. *J. Sutcliffe.* —

PARKING BAY 2 b.g. (Feb 22) Bay Express 132–Sophie Avenue (Guillaume Tell (USA) 121) [1989 6f⁶ 8m 8g³] 2,400F, 11,500Y: tall, good-topped gelding: has scope: second foal: half-brother to moderate plater Thoroughfare (by Dublin Taxi): dam French 2-y-o 7f winner: over 5 lengths third of 15, staying on well having been 73 outpaced, to Azadeh in maiden at Leicester in November, easily best effort. *G. A. Pritchard-Gordon.*

PARKLAND 2 ch.f. (May 10) Highlands–Liberty Light 82 (Henry The Seventh 125) [1989 5f 5g] half-sister to 1982 2-y-o 7f seller winner Freedom Glory (by Hittite Glory) and 3-y-o Dan The Man (by Rabdan): dam won at up to 1m: always behind in seller (slowly away) at Beverley and maiden at Hamilton in the autumn. *J. H. Johnson.* —

PARKLANDS BELLE 5 b.m. Stanford 121§–Kelly's Curl (Pitskelly 122) [1988 8d 7.6d³ 7.6v 8m⁶ 9d 7m⁴ 7f 8m* 7m 8g 1989 8s 6v 7g⁵ 8d 8m 7f 8.2g³ a8g² a7g] smallish mare: poor performer: best at around 1m: acts on any going: has won when sweating and for amateur: trained until after sixth outing by C. Hill: inconsistent. *R. J. Hodges.* 41

PARLIAMENT PIECE 3 ch.c. Burslem 123–Sallywell (Manado 130) [1988 NR 1989 8f⁴ 7f* 10g 7m² 7.6g⁶ 6g 7f² 7g⁴ 7g² 7g⁴ 7g⁶] IR 16,000Y: big, lengthy colt: has plenty of scope: second foal: half-brother to Irish 5f winner Dotrecuig (by Welsh Saint): dam won over 5f at 4 yrs in Ireland: made most to win maiden at York in May: ran well in £5,000 apprentice race at Ascot and £6,400 handicap at York ninth and final outings: suited by 7f: acts on firm ground: unsuited by Chester track fifth start. *R. M. Whitaker.* 92

PARTING MOMENT (USA) 2 ch.c. (Mar 9) The Minstrel (CAN) 135– Farewell Letter (USA) (Arts And Letters) [1989 7m 7g* 7f 8.5g² 8g² 10g4] rather leggy, attractive colt: good walker: fifth foal: brother to fair 1m winner Farewell Song and half-brother to quite useful 1¼m winner Farewell To Love (by Key To Content): dam very smart over middle distances: fair performer: won 9-runner maiden at Salisbury in July: good fourth of 13 to Rock Hopper in listed race at Newmarket in November on final appearance: will stay 1½m: appears suited by some give in the ground. *I. A. Balding.* 85

PARTON EXPRESS 3 gr.f. Bay Express 132–Assembly Day 66 (General Assembly (USA)) [1988 5d 5g⁶ 5g* 6m 6m 5g³ 5g² 6d 1989 5.8m] neat filly: quite modest winner at 2 yrs: speed nearly 4f in handicap in May, only start in 1989: suited by 5f: form only on good ground: sold 1,200 gns Ascot December Sales. *L. G. Cottrell.* —

PARTY BLUES 2 gr.f. (Mar 24) Ballacashtal (CAN)–Party Cloak 68 (New Member 119) [1989 6m⁶ 7f 8.2f 9f⁶] 1,500Y, 3,000 2-y-o: leggy filly: first foal: dam, thrice raced, placed at 1¼m: of little account and temperamental. *F. J. Yardley.* — §

PAS DE REEF 2 ch.f. (Feb 27) Pas de Seul 133–La Paille 113 (Thatch (USA) 136) [1989 7.5g 7f⁵] IR 5,000F, IR 300Y: workmanlike filly: fourth foal: half-sister to 2 poor animals: dam very useful at 1m in France: poor form in summer sellers at Beverley (slowly away) and Newcastle. *M. Brittain.* 32

PASSAGE EAST 3 b.f. Indian King (USA) 128–Raise A Princess (USA) (Raise A Native) [1988 5f 5d⁶ 6m⁶ 6d² 6g 5g² 5m⁵ 5s⁵ 5g* 1989 8d 5m] sparely-made, dipped-backed filly: has a roundish action: made all in seller at 2 yrs: behind in similar events in first half of 1989: best form at 5f: best form on an easy surface: blinkered last 5 outings at 2 yrs. *Ronald Thompson.* —

PASSED PAWN 2 b.g. (Apr 24) Blakeney 126–Miss Millicent (Milesian 125) [1989 8m 7d* 8.2s] 4,700Y: half-brother to several winners, including Irish 1m and 1¼m winner Finsbury (by Levmoss): dam won at around 9f in modest company: won 18-runner seller (no bid) at Catterick in October: should stay well. *M. H. Tompkins.* 65

PASSELANDE 3 b.c. Caerleon (USA) 132–Frivolous Relation (USA) 59 (Buckpasser) [1988 7g⁵ 1989 10.1m 12f*] good-bodied colt: unimpressive to post, won claimer (claimed £11,500) at Goodwood in June, racing keenly chasing leader, leading inside final 1f and keeping on well: suited by 1½m. *J. W. Hills.* 74

PASSHOT 2 ch.f. (Apr 15) Hotfoot 126–Pass-A-Deaney 72 (Connaught 130) [1989 5g 5.3h⁵ 7m⁶] angular, plain filly: poor walker and mover: fifth living foal: half-sister to 2 bad animals: dam showed form only at 2 yrs: of little account. *R. P. C. Hoad.* —

PASSION AND MIRTH 2 b.f. (Apr 20) Known Fact (USA) 135–Bustling Nelly 94 (Bustino 136) [1989 8g] 5,600Y: compact, quite attractive filly: second foal: half-sister to 3-y-o 2m winner Silk Degrees (by Dunbeath): dam middle-distance winner, is daughter of Cambridgeshire winner Flying Nelly: always towards rear in 15-runner maiden at Leicester in September. *C. A. Cyzer.* —

PASSIONARIA (FR) 3 b.f. Beldale Flutter (USA) 130–Djallybrook (FR) 119 (Djakao (FR) 124) [1988 9d⁴ 8g* 1989 9s⁵ 10.5m³ 12.5g⁴ 10d⁴ 12g* 12.5m* 12g²] 320,000 francs (approx £32,300) Y: sixth foal: half-sister to 1982 2-y-o 7f winner Acadie (by Caracolero) and 4 winners in France, notably smart 1985 2-y-o Kanmary

Ciga Prix de Royallieu, Longchamp—Passionaria continues to improve

(by Kenmare) who later stayed 9f: dam French provincial 11f winner: much improved in the autumn, successful at Longchamp in listed race in September and Group 2 Ciga Prix de Royallieu (beat Robertet in good style by 2 lengths) in October: good second in valuable event at Gulfstream Park: stays 12.5f: acts on top-of-the-ground: blinkered fourth start: trained until after then by F. Bellenger. *J. E. Hammond, France.*

PASS THE PEACE 3 b.f. Alzao (USA) 117–Lover's Rose (King Emperor (USA)) **116** [1988 5f* 5m² 6g* 6g* 6g* 1989 7.3s* 8g⁵ 8m² 10.5d 10g³ 8g²] lengthy,

Capt B. W. Bell's "Pass The Peace"

good-quartered, attractive filly: has a quick action: leading 2-y-o filly of 1988, winning Cheveley Park Stakes final start: won Gainsborough Stud Fred Darling Stakes at Newbury in April: ran creditably in 1000 Guineas at Newmarket and Poule d'Essai des Pouliches (beaten ¾ length by Pearl Bracelet) at Longchamp but poorly in Prix de Diane Hermes at Chantilly next 3 outings: off course 4 months then beaten 8½ lengths by Braiswick in Sun Chariot Stakes at Newmarket and 1¼ lengths by Rosa de Caerleon in Group 3 event at Milan: probably stayed 1¼m: acted on soft going and top-of-the-ground: reportedly purchased by Sheikh Mohammed and retired. *M. L. W. Bell.*

PAST MIDNIGHT 3 ch.f. Longleat (USA) 109–Fearless Felon (USA) (Bail- — jumper (USA)) [1988 5g³ 6g³ 6g 1989 5g 8g] sturdy, good-quartered, workman-like filly: has a sharp action: quite modest maiden: best effort on debut: twice out of first 6 at Cagnes-sur-Mer in February: sold 1,500 gns Newmarket July Sales. *C. A. Cyzer.*

PASTORAL JEM 3 ch.c. Horage 124–Sperrin Mist 83 (Camden Town 125) 84 [1988 5g⁴ 5m² 5f* 5.3f² 5f² 5f⁵ 6g⁴ 5g³ 5d⁶ 5g 1989 7s² 7d 7f⁵ 6f⁶ 6m 8.2m 7m³ 6f⁴ 7m] sparely-made colt: moderate walker: fairly useful at his best: usually forces pace but held up and ran best race after second outing when third in handicap at Sandown: ran very wide into straight at Haydock sixth start: probably suited by 7f: acts on any going: equipped with severe bridle first 7 outings and has worn brush pricker: sometimes on toes: sold 12,000 gns Newmarket Autumn Sales: inconsistent and isn't an easy ride. *M. E. D. Francis.*

PATCHOULI'S PET 6 b.m. Mummy's Pet 125–Primage 99 (Primera 131) [1988 — 8g 1989 9m 18.8f⁶] small, leggy, sparely-made mare: has a long stride: modest maiden at 2 yrs: little subsequent form on flat. *W. G. Morris.*

PATCON 4 b.g. Kafu 120–Duchess of Howfen 66 (Steel Heart 128) [1988 6v 7d 6f⁵ 70 d 5g⁶ 5f² 5g⁴ 5s 5m⁴ 5f⁴ 6s⁵ 6d² 1989 5d* 5s 5f* 5f* 5f² 5f 5m 5m 5m 6g 5g⁵] big, strong, good-topped gelding: carries plenty of condition: bad mover: made all or virtually all in handicap at Folkestone and claimers at Wolverhampton and Redcar (claimed out of C. Nelson's stable £11,850) in first half of season: well below his best after next outing: well backed, didn't get clear run final one: suited by 5f: probably unsuited by soft going, acts on any other: blinkered twice at 3 yrs and on final start. *T. D. Barron.*

PATHERO 5 ch.g. Godswalk (USA) 130–Canoodle 66 (Warpath 113) [1988 10v³ — 12g* 12d* 12g* 12g 12m³ 16.5f⁵ 16f⁴ 15g² 15g³ 13s* 12d 15.8d 1989 14s 13v 13v 12d 16g] smallish, sturdy gelding: carries plenty of condition: moderate mover: quite modest winner as 4-y-o: well below form in 1989, though showed signs of retaining ability last 2 outings: stays 2m: probably not suited by firm going and used to go extremely well with plenty of give: blinkered once: occasionally sweats: has won for apprentice: invariably held up. *N. Bycroft.*

PATH OF CONDIE 2 b.c. (Apr 24) Vaigly Great 127–Goosie-Gantlet 63 (Run 63 The Gantlet (USA)) [1989 7g 7f⁵] 9,000Y: rather leggy, angular colt: ninth foal: brother to 1¼m winner Great Saling and 1m winner Great Leighs and half-brother to several winners, including useful 1984 2-y-o 5f and 6f winner Ulla Laing and 3-y-o Pant Llin (both by Mummy's Pet), fair 5.8f winner at 2 yrs: dam staying daughter of very useful Goosie: 9 lengths fifth of 10, keeping on steadily, to Sasaki in maiden at Leicester in October, easily better effort: will be better suited by 1m + . *B. W. Hills.*

PATIENCE CAMP 3 b.f. Bustino 136–Short Rations (Lorenzaccio 130) [1988 105 8d 1989 12g² 14m² 16g² 16m⁵ 14g* 16f* 16g²] tall, lengthy, plain filly: has a long stride: short-priced favourite, made virtually all to win maiden at Yarmouth in September and 3-runner handicap at Newcastle in October: 8/1 and wintry in coat, very good 4 lengths second of 10 to Upper Strata in listed race at Newmarket in November, battling on well: visored, raced far too freely in lead 1¼m then dropped herself out when tailed off fourth start: stays well: acts on firm ground and a soft surface: has had tongue tied down. *M. R. Stoute.*

PATIENCE CREEK 3 ch.f. Mummy's Game 120–Brandon Creek 79 (Be My 68 Guest (USA) 126) [1988 6f³ 7f 7d³ 1989 7g⁵ 8f 8f⁵ 8m 8f² 8d* 8g] workmanlike filly: has a round action: won handicap at Goodwood in September, leading inside final 1f: ridden by 7-lb claimer, creditable second at Chepstow, easily better effort in similar events either side: stays 1m: acts on firm and dead going. *C. P. Wildman.*

PATRICK JOHN LYONS 8 b.h. Cavo Doro 124–Latin Spice (Frankincense — 120) [1988 10.8d 1989 12.2s 10s 15.5s 10.1m 12.2m 11.7m 11.7m 11.7m] robust, compact horse: retains little ability nowadays. *P. J. Arthur.*

PATROCLUS 4 b.g. Tyrnavos 129–Athenia Princess 80 (Athens Wood 126) —
[1988 12d* 12m⁴ 13. If 14g² 14g² 14g⁶ 14m 16d 13.3s³ 1989 16m⁶ 19f 12f 19g⁵]
workmanlike gelding: has a round action: quite modest winner early as 3-y-o: 100/1,
best effort in 1989 when 9½ lengths fifth of 9 in minor event at Goodwood in
October: suited by test of stamina: seems to need an easy surface nowadays:
blinkered once at 3 yrs: takes a lot of driving. *R. Voorspuy.*

PATSBERIC 2 b.g. (Jan 24) Blushing Scribe (USA) 107–Manageress 74 —
(Mandamus 120) [1989 7f 7m] 2,200F, 6,200Y: third foal: brother to 3-y-o Pacific
Wave, 6f seller winner to 2 yrs, and half-brother to 1m winner Dealer's Delight (by
Ballacashtal): dam 6f winner as 2-y-o: soundly beaten in autumn maidens at
Salisbury and Chepstow. *R. J. Holder.*

PATSY WESTERN 3 ch.f. Precocious 126–Western Air 101 (Sound Track 132) 81
[1988 NR 1989 6g⁵ 6m⁶] smallish, angular filly: half-sister to 7 winners, including
Queen Anne Stakes winner Mr Fluorocarbon (by Morston) and good 1975 2-y-o 5f
performer Western Jewel (by Tower Walk): dam, from speedy family, was best at 5f:
5/1 from 12/1, won minor event at Kempton by short head, leading inside final 1f and
holding on well: co-favourite, last of 6 in £6,800 event at Newmarket 12 days later in
May: possibly unsuited by top-of-the-ground. *W. Jarvis.*

PATTAYA GIRL 4 b.f. Comedy Star (USA) 121–Mertola (Tribal Chief 125) [1988 44
5g⁵ 7m 7d 7.6s 7m 1989 7.5d 6f 9f 8m 7m⁶ 6f⁴ 7m⁵] strong, rather dipped-backed
filly: moderate mover: poor maiden: probably suited by 6f: blinkered last 4 outings.
B. C. Morgan.

PATTIE'S GREY 3 gr.f. Valiyar 129–Katysue 98 (King's Leap 111) [1988 6g⁶ 67
1989 7.5m⁴] workmanlike, good-quartered filly: moderate walker and mover: quite
modest form in maidens at Newmarket and Beverley (edging right) year later. *I. V.
Matthews.*

PAY CORPS (USA) 3 b.c. Private Account (USA)–Windrush Lady (USA) 77
(Unconscious (USA)) [1988 7m 1989 10.1m 10.1m 10m² 12f⁴ 10.2g³] rangy colt: bit
unfurnished: in frame in handicaps at Leicester, Goodwood (£11,800 event,
well-backed second favourite and making most 1¼m) and Doncaster: stays 1½m:
acts on firm going. *Major W. R. Hern.*

PAY THE BANK 2 b.f. (May 27) High Top 131–Zebra Grass 85 (Run The 69 p
Gantlet (USA)) [1989 7g⁵ 7m³ 8f*] 62,000Y: rather leggy, close-coupled filly:
half-sister to stayer Fedra (by Grundy) and a winner in West Indies: dam 2-y-o 6f
and 7f winner from family of Royal Palace: favourite, won 6-runner maiden at Redcar
in October, running on well final 2f: will stay 1¼m: probably capable of further
improvement. *B. W. Hills.*

PAYVASHOOZ 4 b.f. Ballacashtal (CAN)–Abercourt 89 (Abernant 142) [1988 7d 64
6g 7d 6f 5g 6f⁴ 5.8g* 6g⁴ 6s⁴ 7s² 7g 6f 6g 6d 5v 1989 6v 6d 6.1f 7m 7m 6d 6s* 7m³
a8g⁵ a7g*] good-topped filly: quite modest handicapper: successful at Ayr (25/1,
first form for long time) and Southwell in later stages of season: probably stays 1m:
acts on any going: blinkered once: suitable mount for apprentice. *M. Brittain.*

PEACE TALK 2 br.f. (May 18) Warpath 113–War Talk (USA) 90 (Assagai) [1989 —
7f⁶ 8g] smallish, sparely-made filly: half-sister to 6f and 1m seller winner Tufty Lady
(by Riboboy) and a prolific winner abroad: dam stayed 1m: well beaten in autumn
maidens at Leicester. *I. Campbell.*

PEACEWORK 5 br.m. Workboy 123–Flower Child (Brother 116) [1988 NR 1989 46
7f⁶ 6f⁵ 6f⁴ 7f⁵ 6m] deep-girthed mare: poor maiden: seems to stay 7f: acts on firm
going: sweating first 2 starts, edgy second occasion: has pulled hard: often slowly
away. *C. V. Bravery.*

PEACONPALA 4 br.f. Kampala 120–Kilpeacon (Florescence 120) [1988 5d 6m —
6d 9g⁶ 9g³ 1989 10.8s⁶ 8s 8m] sparely-made filly: poor walker: moderate mover:
poor performer: stays 9f: acts on any going: ran poorly in blinkers: has run well for
apprentice. *P. D. Evans.*

PEAK DANCER 2 b.c. (Apr 8) High Top 131–Verchinina 99 (Star Appeal 133) 61
[1989 6m 7m⁶ 7f² 8.2g] sturdy, well-made colt: second foal: dam 1m winner: 2
lengths second to easy winner Alysardi in maiden at Brighton, easily best effort:
virtually pulled up in nursery at Nottingham: sold 20,000 gns Newmarket Autumn
Sales. *B. W. Hills.*

PEAK DISTRICT 3 b.c. Beldale Flutter (USA) 130–Grand Teton 64 (Bustino 78
136) [1988 6m 1989 8m² 10m² 11.7d⁶ 10.5m⁴ 8g] lengthy, sparely-made colt: modest
form: good running-on fourth in handicap at York in October: tailed off in
Newmarket handicap 10 days later: should stay 1½m: possibly needs top-of-the-
ground: sold to join K. Bridgwater 13,000 gns Newmarket Autumn Sales. *G. Wragg.*

PEALLA 4 b.g. Dara Monarch 128–Nofertiti (FR) (Exbury 138) [1988 10m 11s — 12.2m 1989 10s] leggy, sparely-made gelding: poor maiden: should stay 1¼m: sometimes bandaged. *R. J. O'Sullivan.*

PEANDAY 8 b.g. Swing Easy (USA) 126–Parradell 104 (Pandofell 132) [1988 NR — 1989 12f 10f 10g] tall, good-topped gelding: carries plenty of condition: poor mover: well beaten in amateur events as 8-y-o, on 2 occasions tailed off: stays 1¼m: probably needs plenty of give nowadays: has worn blinkers, but not for long time. *J. B. Sayers.*

PEAR DROP 3 b.f. Bustino 136–Fai La Bella (USA) 85 (Fifth Marine (USA)) — [1988 8.2m³ 1989 10s 10f 10.6m] medium-sized, rather sparely-made filly: modest maiden: seemed not to train on. *L. M. Cumani.*

PEARL BRACELET (USA) 3 ch.f. Lyphard (USA) 132–Perlee (FR) 122 **118** (Margouillat (FR) 133) [1988 8d³ 1989 8m*]
The latest running of the Dubai Poule d'Essai des Pouliches brought a rare turn-up, the once-raced maiden Pearl Bracelet, bandaged in front, proving too good for her fifteen opponents. She started at 50/1, except for the Irish filly Tantum Ergo the complete outsider in a bigger-than-average field for the event which included Pass The Peace, Mary Linoa, Oczy Czarnie and Tersa, all Group 1 winners as two-year-olds. Pearl Bracelet's sole appearance had been in a contest confined to unraced two-year-old fillies over a mile at Saint-Cloud in November, and resulted in third place behind Glenbelle. Leg trouble was mainly responsible for keeping her off the course, though she lost a couple of chances to run before the Pouliches in the spring through no fault of her own, one time when a race failed to fill, another when she was eliminated overnight from a race which attracted too many entries. As was to be expected, Pearl Bracelet was reportedly highly regarded by connections. Another in the field of equally limited experience, the Prix Montenica winner Golden Opinion, was so highly regarded that she started 5/4 favourite coupled with her owner's Russian Royal and pacemaker Miss Manila, ahead of Pass The Peace (9/2) who'd also started second favourite for the General Accident One Thousand Guineas. Both Oczy Czarnie (9/1) and Mary Linoa (10/1) had been prevented by set-backs from having a preparatory run, while Tersa (20/1) had been well beaten in hers. Thanks to Miss Manila and Lakila, the latter acting on behalf of the Prix de la Grotte winner Keniant (29/4), the Pouliches was run at a much more satisfactory pace than the One Thousand Guineas, though it still resulted in a bunched finish. Pearl Bracelet, held up initially, showed no sign of inexperience: she sustained a strong run on the outside up the straight which took her to the front in the last hundred yards after first Golden Opinion and then Pass The Peace had promised to win.

Dubai Poule d'Essai des Pouliches, Longchamp—50/1-shot Pearl Bracelet runs Pass The Peace and Golden Opinion out of it

Neither Tersa, Oczy Czarnie nor Mary Linoa got into serious contention though the first two finished seventh and eighth respectively, just over five lengths down on Pearl Bracelet who won by three quarters of a length and the same, Keniant in fourth.

Pearl Bracelet failed to stand training afterwards and had to be retired without another race; she is due to be covered by In Fijar in 1990. Of those opponents who continued to run, few played much of a part in the rest of the season and only Golden Opinion showed herself top class. Clearly, Golden Opinion was nowhere near her best on Pouliches day; equally clearly, the field as a whole was not a good one by classic standards. Given that, the main virtue in Pearl Bracelet's performance lies in her having made light of inexperience and lack of a recent outing. She could have been another Golden Opinion in the making but we shall never know.

Pearl Bracelet (USA) (ch.f. 1986)	Lyphard (USA) (b 1969)	Northern Dancer (b 1961)	Nearctic Natalma
		Goofed (ch 1960)	Court Martial Barra II
	Perlee (FR) (b 1979)	Margouillat (b 1970)	Diatome Tita
		Zirconia (b 1970)	Charlottesville Zilette

Pearl Bracelet would have taken her chance in the Prix de Diane Hermes had she been able (the stable, run by Roger Wojtowiez since the suspension of George Mikhalides at the turn of the year, won with Lady In Silver). Pearl Bracelet had sound prospects of staying beyond a mile, on the manner in which she finished the course at Longchamp and on her pedigree. Her sire's previous Pouliches winners were Dancing Maid and Three Troikas; and her dam, by the Prix de l'Arc third Margouillat, was suited by a mile and a half or more. The dam Perlee had good form in France. She won three races, including the Prix de Minerve at Evry, came third in the Prix Saint-Alary and was beaten only three lengths into fifth behind All Along in the Prix Vermeille on her final start. Her previous foals were both winners in France, Million Stories (by Exclusive Native) over seven and a half furlongs as a three-year-old and Sugar Walls, a sister to Pearl Bracelet, over six furlongs as a two-year-old. Sugar Walls had the makings of a more-than-useful animal on her second place in the one-mile Prix d'Aumale in 1987 but lameness struck her down also, and she had to be retired after fracturing a sesamoid in the Prix Marcel Boussac next time out. Perlee's fourth foal Turkish Star (USA), a colt by Blushing Groom, is in training with Moubarak at Newmarket. Perlee's dam and grandam also won in France, though neither had her stamina. Zirconia was a miler and finished fifth in the One Thousand Guineas in 1973; Zilette stayed nine furlongs. *R. Wojtowiez, France.*

PEARL DOVE   2 b.f. (May 10) Oats 126–Nimble Dove 62 (Starch Reduced 112) [1989 5s⁶ 5g] small, light-framed non-thoroughbred filly: has no scope: second foal: dam soft-ground stayer also won over hurdles: well beaten in spring maidens at Leicester. *G. Price.*   —

PEARL RUN   8 ch.g. Gulf Pearl 117–Deep Down (Deep Run 119) [1988 18d* 14.8d* 18.4v 16m⁵ 17.1g⁵ 16s 1989 14.8s⁶ 16d⁴ 17.1m⁴] good-bodied gelding: moderate mover: modest handicapper: won Heart of England Handicap at Warwick for fourth consecutive season in 1988: still carrying condition, fourth in slowly-run event at Ripon in April, best effort in spring as 8-y-o: suited by a test of stamina: best on an easy surface (probably unsuited by very soft going nowadays): often bandaged: good mount for apprentice. *G. Price.*   —

PEARLS A RUNNER   4 b.f. Record Run 127–Wild Jewel (Great Heron (USA) 127) [1988 12d 1989 14.6g 12m⁵ 16f] leggy, sparely-made filly: little sign of ability. *R. Curtis.*   —

PEARL WHITE   3 ch.f. Star Appeal 133–Pearling 72 (Ribero 126) [1988 6m⁶ 6f 5g² 5g 1989 7d 8f⁴ 6g 7m 7g 6m 10f³ 11.7f⁵ 14m⁵ 9g] smallish, workmanlike filly: poor on most form, including in sellers: stays 1¼m: blinkered third outing: sold to join K. Ryan 1,600 gns Newmarket Autumn Sales. *M. L. W. Bell.*   37

PEATSWOOD SHOOTER   5 gr.h. Windjammer (USA)–Raffinata (Raffingora 130) [1988 6d 5v⁶ 6g 6d 6s 6d 6g 1989 6v] tall, angular, plain horse: poor mover: —

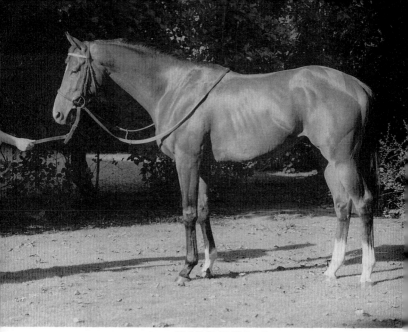

Mr J. H. Slade's "Pelorus"

one-time useful performer: has shown virtually nothing since winning listed event early as 3-y-o: suited by sprint distances: best with plenty of give in the ground: suited by forcing tactics: sold 1,000 gns Newmarket December Sales. *M. Brittain.*

PECKING ORDER 5 b.m. Henbit (USA) 130–Daring Lass 87 (Bold Lad (IRE) 133) [1988 NR 1989 6d 5f⁵] lengthy mare: fourth in Blue Seal Stakes at Ascot at 2 yrs: retains little ability: edgy and taken down early final outing. *F. J. Yardley.* **27**

PEDESTAL 3 ch.f. High Line 125–Mrs Moss 81 (Reform 132) [1988 NR 1989 8f⁶] twelfth foal: half-sister to numerous winners, including high-class 1983 2-y-o sprinter Precocious (by Mummy's Pet), very smart middle-distance winner Jupiter Island (by St Paddy) and smart 1982 2-y-o 5f winner Krayyan (by Tower Walk): dam won over 5f at 2 yrs: weak 16/1, well-beaten last of 6 to Rain Burst in minor event at Goodwood in June, pushed along and losing touch 3f out. *C. E. Brittain.* —

PEERGLOW 5 br.m. Raga Navarro (ITY) 119–Go Perrys 66 (High Hat 131) [1988 10g 10.1d 10g⁵ 8f 10.8s⁴ 11d⁴ 10.8f⁵ 10g 10m⁵ 10d⁵ 1989 10.8m] leggy, shallow-girthed mare: moderate mover: ungenuine plater: sometimes wears blinkers. *C. N. Williams.* — §

PEER PRINCE (USA) 4 br.c. Vaguely Noble 140–Sweet Maid (USA) (Proud Clarion) [1988 12s 12d 12g⁶ 10m* 10g² 10f² 10g³ 1989 10.2g] medium-sized, quite attractive colt: has a round action: won claimer at 3 yrs: suited by 1¼m: probably acts on any going: blinkered third to sixth outings as 3-y-o: below form in visor final one: needs to be produced very late: winning hurdler. *G. A. Pritchard-Gordon.* —

PEGASUS HEIGHTS 3 ch.g. Air Trooper 115–Confetti Copse 71 (Town And Country 124) [1988 NR 1989 9f] 5,200Y: lengthy, plain gelding: first foal: dam ran only at around 7f: bit backward and very green, tailed off in minor event at Wolverhampton in May. *R. J. Hodges.* —

670

PELEUS (USA) 4 b.c. Irish River (FR) 131–Pellinora (USA) (King Pellinore 96
(USA) 127) [1988 11g² 14f² 12d* 1989 14g 16g⁵] heavy-topped colt: carries plenty of
condition: poor walker and mover: fairly useful winner as 3-y-o: faced stiff tasks in
spring handicaps at Newmarket in 1989: probably stays 2m. *H. R. A. Cecil.*

PELIGROSO 3 ch.g. Star Appeal 133–Sarah Gillian (USA) (Zen (USA)) [1988 7g⁶ —
1989 8m 14g⁶ 10m⁶ a10g⁵] neat gelding: little sign of ability: not bred to stay much
beyond 1¼m. *P. A. Kelleway.*

PELORUS 4 b.c. High Top 131–St Isabel (Saint Crespin III 132) [1988 6g⁴ 8f* 116
10d* 10g² 10.5g² 12g 1989 10d 10v³ 10f* 10.6g²] leggy colt: usually looks well: smart
performer: first outing for almost 4 months, won £22,000 Racal Chesterfield Cup
(Handicap) at Goodwood in July by ½ length from Marcinkus: showed further
improvement when head second of 5, pulling hard early, to Braiswick in
moderately-run Burtonwood Brewery Rose of Lancaster Stakes at Haydock week
later: suited by about 1¼m: probably acts on any going: slowly into stride on
reappearance and at Goodwood. *W. Jarvis.*

PELOTA 3 gr.f. Petong 126–Lucky Deal 93 (Floribunda 136) [1988 7g 7g 1989 12s —
8f 8m 7m] angular filly: no sign of ability, including when blinkered and in sellers:
sold 1,400 gns Newmarket July Sales: resold 1,150 gns Newmarket September
Sales. *A. N. Lee.*

PELUMICA 5 ch.g. Young Generation 129–Sharondor 84 (Matador 131) [1988 —
10f⁶ 10m 12m 1989 10.2g 11v⁶ 12.4g] leggy gelding: has a round action: quite modest
maiden at best: has lost his form completely: blinkered, slowly away and tailed off in
seller at Newcastle final outing, first for nearly 7 months: stays 1½m: acts on any
going, except possibly heavy: often on toes: has looked none too keen. *J. Parkes.*

PENCARREG 2 b.f. (Apr 13) Caerleon (USA) 132–Mary Arden 95 (Mill Reef 87
(USA) 141) [1988 6g 7m* 7m² 7g² 8g] IR 185,000Y: angular, medium-sized, quite
attractive filly: has a quick action: half-sister to Irish 3-y-o 1¼m winner Emerald
Gem (by Henbit) and 2 other winners, including useful French sprinter Tranchard
(by Sharpen Up): dam, half-sister to Irish 1000 Guineas and Yorkshire Oaks winner
Sarah Siddons, won over 1¼m: fair performer: won 12-runner maiden at Lingfield in
September: good second following month in nurseries at York and Newmarket:
should stay 1¼m: visored last 2 appearances. *M. R. Stoute.*

PENDINE SANDS 4 ch.f. Rolfe (USA) 77–Llanmilo (Realm 129) [1988 5g³ 5g⁶ 46
5g² 5f⁴ 6m 6m² 5f* 5d⁶ 5g⁴ 5g 5m⁶ 5f 5.8f 5g 1989 7v 5f³ 5f 5.8h 5m 5.3f⁶ 6g⁴]
leggy, sparely-made filly: poor handicapper nowadays: stays 6f: acts on any going:
blinkered once: usually visored nowadays: bandaged behind second start: has run
well for apprentice: trained first 4 outings by C. Hill. *R. J. Hodges.*

PENDOR DANCER 6 b.g. Piaffer (USA) 113–Bounding (Forlorn River 124) 83
[1988 5g 5s 5g 5s 5f² 5g5 5m⁶ 5m5 5f⁶ 5s 5g⁴ 5s 1989 5d 5s⁴ 6m 6m 5m* 5m*
5m* 5g* 5g 5g³ 5.6g 5m⁴ 5d] lengthy gelding: fair handicapper: successful in only 2
of his first 49 races, but in tremendous form in summer and won at Warwick (twice),
Kempton and Wolverhampton: withdrawn third (bolted) and sixth (spread plate)
intended starts: brought down eleventh outing: best over 5f: acts on any going:
effective with or without blinkers or visor: has worn bandages behind: usually
sweating and on toes: has run well for apprentice: has shown a tendency to hang. *W.
Carter.*

PENGO 4 b.f. Bay Express 132–Penybont 81 (Welsh Pageant 132) [1988 6v⁴ 6m —
6g² 7f 7m⁶ 8d² 8.2f 8.2m 10s 1989 7f] small, light-framed filly: turns near-fore out:
moderate mover: plating-class maiden: 66/1, slowly away and always behind at
Catterick in July: suited by 1m: unsuited by firm going: usually blinkered: inconsistent. *J. Mulhall.*

PENHILL FLAME 3 ch.f. Main Reef 126–Debian 71 (Relko 136) [1988 5.8d² 7g —
1989 5m⁴ 7f a7g] close-coupled filly: well beaten in varied events in 1989: should
stay 7f. *D. Haydn Jones.*

PENLLYNE'S PRIDE 8 ch.g. Tachypous 128–Fodens Eve 80 (Dike (USA)) —
[1988 NR 1989 11.7d] lengthy, workmanlike gelding: winner in Italy in 1986: tailed
off in apprentice event on only outing in Britain that season: blinkered, well beaten
in handicap at Bath in April, only subsequent race on flat: stays 1¼m: acts on any
going: winning chaser: has looked none too resolute. *R. T. Juckes.*

PENNY CANDLE 3 b.f. Be My Guest (USA) 126–Pennyweight (Troy 137) [1988 103
NR 1989 8s³ 7s² 7m* 7m³ 6m* 6g³ 5m 5m⁴ 5g] sparely-made filly: first foal: dam
poor half-sister to Irish 2000 Guineas winner Wassl: won maiden (very edgy) at
Carlisle in May and handicap (making all) at Lingfield in June: ran well after at
Newmarket when in frame in handicap and listed race but moderately in listed event

final start: possibly suited by 5f: acts on top-of-the-ground and soft going: blinkered third and fourth starts: tends to veer markedly left: keen filly, best allowed to stride on. *W. Jarvis.*

PENNY FORUM 5 b.g. Pas de Seul 133–Kind Thoughts 71 (Kashmir II 125) 76 [1988 12f³ 16g 14g³ 14d² 14g² 16m* 14g* 19g² 16f² 17g² 12g 18g⁴ 1989 14g³ 16g³ 14m² 14f] compact gelding: has a fluent, slightly round action: modest handicapper: not seen out after May: suited by test of stamina: acts on any going, except possibly heavy: usually blinkered nowadays: suitable mount for apprentice: bandaged near-fore: suited by waiting tactics: consistent. *J. Sutcliffe.*

PENTAGON ROSE 3 b.f. Kafu 120–All Gold Rose (Rheingold 137) [1988 5m 5m 60 § 5m 5g 1989 6d 5s⁴ 6m 5m 5.3h⁴ 5m* 5g 5f⁵ 5m 5m 5f 5.1g 5m* 5.3f 5f⁶ 6f² 5g] leggy filly: has a quick action: quite modest handicapper: won at Catterick in June and Lingfield (apprentices, making all and showing improved form) in September: stays 6f: probably acts on any going: blinkered fourth start and once at 2 yrs: tends to hang left and carry head high: inconsistent and none too genuine. *W. Carter.*

PENULTIMATION 4 b.c. Young Generation 129–Maiden Pool 85 (Sharpen Up 75 127) [1988 8g⁴ 7g* 6m⁵ 6d 7g³ 7f 1989 6d² 7d 6f 6m] strong, good-bodied colt: moderate mover: fairly useful winner as 3-y-o: odds on, length second of 12, travelling strongly long way, in minor contest at Folkestone in April: ran poorly in handicaps afterwards, and not seen out after June: best form at 6f or 7f: probably unsuited by firm going: blinkered final outing. *G. Harwood.*

PERCEIVE (USA) 4 gr.f. Nureyev (USA) 131–Preceptress (USA) (Grey Dawn — II 132) [1988 7d 9f⁴ 7g 8d⁵ 1989 12f⁴ 8g] smallish, lengthy filly: modest maiden at best: best run at 9f: showed nothing in blinkers: in foal to Hadeer. *C. E. Brittain.*

PERCY'S PET 3 b.f. Blakeney 126–Oula-Ka Fu-Fu 67 (Run The Gantlet (USA)) 49 [1988 7g 1989 12.4g 12f 10.5g⁴ 12g⁴ a8g⁴] rather angular filly: fourth in seller, claimer and maiden: in last-named soon tailed off then running on really well at Southwell: will be suited by return to middle distances: blinkered last 4 starts. *C. B. B. Booth.*

PERFECT CHANCE 3 b. or br.f. Petorius 117–Perfect Line 102 (Rarity 129) 83 [1988 NR 1989 7m* 8f⁴ 6g 6g² 7g* 7m] lengthy, good-quartered filly: fifth foal: dam, useful Irish 7f winner at 2 yrs, is half-sister to Deep Run and to dam of One In A Million: won maiden at Edinburgh in June and again at Epsom in August: wearing tongue strap, tailed off in £8,800 Newmarket handicap final start: stays 7f: acts on top-of-the-ground: below form for claimer third outing. *B. Hanbury.*

PERFORMING ARTS 2 ch.f. (May 19) The Minstrel (CAN) 135–Noble Mark 90 120 (On Your Mark 125) [1989 5m* 6f* 5f³ 6g⁴ 6s² 7g⁴] small, good-topped filly: sister to good miler The Noble Player, closely related to useful 1987 2-y-o 5f and 7f winner Border Guard (by Nureyev) and half-sister to 3-y-o Haligi (by Assert) and several winners, 3 over middle distances: dam very smart sprinter: fairly useful filly: won maiden at Newmarket and minor event at Goodwood in the spring: ran well next 2 starts in Queen Mary Stakes at Royal Ascot and Hillsdown Cherry Hinton Stakes at Newmarket: will probably stay 1m: best form on a sound surface. *B. W. Hills.*

PERION 7 ch.g. Northfields (USA)–Relanca (Relic) [1988 5v* 5g* 5m² 5m⁴ 5d³ 101 5d² 5g² 6f 1989 6s³ 5m⁵ 5g 5f 5g³ 5m 5g 5g⁵ 5g⁶ 5m] lengthy, angular gelding: twice hobdayed: poor mover: smart at his best in 1988: not so good as 7-y-o, running best race when third to Desert Dawn in listed contest at Sandown: ran moderately in Ascot handicap final start: suited by 5f: acts on any going, but particularly well suited by an easy surface: blinkered ninth outing: needs strong handling: suited by strong gallop: sent to join M. Bell. *G. Lewis.*

PERISTYLE 3 b.f. Tolomeo 127–Persevering 95 (Blakeney 126) [1988 6g 7m 7g 55 1989 12h⁶ 11f 12.2f5 16f³ 13.8g³ 13.8g 12.5f6 12.2d⁴ 12m²] leggy, sparely-made filly: plating-class maiden: claimer ridden, second in seller at Edinburgh in October, best effort: apparently suited by 1½m: acts on top-of-the-ground: one paced: sold to join M. Pipe 5,200 gns Newmarket Autumn Sales. *R. Hollinshead.*

PERK 3 b.f. Jalmood (USA) 126–Fee 111 (Mandamus 120) [1988 6m⁶ 6g 7g⁶ 1989 67 7d 10f 12f6 11.7m³ 10g* 11.7g* 10m² 12s* 10f² 12.2d5] lengthy, workmanlike filly: has plenty of scope: won claimers at Leicester and Windsor in August, both moderately run, and at Goodwood in September: ran poorly final start: stays 1½m: acts on any going: blinkered last 8 outings: found little on fourth: tail swisher: sold 11,000 gns Newmarket Autumn Sales. *R. F. Johnson Houghton.*

PERMANENT LODGER 2 b.g. (Mar 31) Kala Shikari 125–Boarding House 73 40 (Shack (USA) 118) [1989 5g⁵ 5.1f] 5,400Y: first foal: dam best at 5f: poor form in quite moderate company at Edinburgh and Yarmouth in July. *J. H. M. Gosden.*

Mr H. Turney McKnight's "Per Quod"

PERMANENTLY PINK   3 b.c. Auction Ring (USA) 123–Hawaiian Joss (USA)   —
(Hawaii) [1988 6m 7g* 6m 1989 6s⁶ 6f 8h 10.2f] lengthy, angular colt: moderate
mover: won seller at 2 yrs: only sign of retaining ability in varied events in 1989 on
reappearance: should stay 1m: evidently unsuited by top-of-the-ground: trained
until after third start by H. O'Neill. *R. J. Hodges.*

PEROSINI   3 b.c. Persian Bold 123–Rosni 66 (Blakeney 126) [1988 6g 6g 6m 1989   **90**
6m* 6f³ 7m⁴ 7.6g² 8.2m⁶ 7.5f³ 9f* 10.2m* 8g⁵ 10m² 10.6d 10.2g⁴ 12g] leggy,
good-topped colt: fairly useful handicapper: successful at Haydock (claimer) in May
and Redcar and Doncaster (2 days later) at end of July: ran in snatches and no extra
final 1f when below form final outing: appears suited by 1¼m: acts on firm going,
tailed off on a soft surface: usually blinkered: often on toes: sold to race in Middle
East 25,000 gns Newmarket Autumn Sales. *F. H. Lee.*

PER QUOD (USA)   4 b.g. Lyllos (FR)–Allegedly (USA) (Sir Ivor 135) [1988 10v* **119**
12g² 12f⁵ 10d² 10d* 10g* 12g² 10g* 14f 10v* 11s* 12g² 12f 1989 10v* 12d² 10s² 10m⁴
12d³ 12m³ 10.1d³ 12g² 12s⁴ 12d*] leggy, workmanlike gelding: usually looks very
well: has a quick, round action: smart performer: won minor events at Kempton (in
very good style) in April and Thirsk (odds on) in November: generally ran well in
good-class company in between, runner-up to Unfuwain in Lanes End John Porter
EBF Stakes at Newbury, Indian Skimmer in Gordon Richards EBF Stakes at
Sandown and Mondrian in Grosser Preis Von Baden at Baden-Baden: suited by
testing conditions at 1¼m and stays 1½m well: not at his best on firm going, acts on
any other: splendidly tough, genuine and consistent: a credit to his trainer. *B.
Hanbury.*

PERSHING   8 ch.g. Gunner B 126–New Way 103 (Klairon 131) [1988 10.2s³ 10f   **34**
1989 10.2g 12d³ 21.6d] leggy, narrow gelding: often dull in coat: poor mover: poor

673

handicapper: tailed off at Pontefract in April, final outing and second in 2 days: stays 1½m: well suited by soft surface nowadays: has worn blinkers and a visor: often loses plenty of ground at start: needs holding up as long as possible and finds little off bridle: sold 2,500 gns Doncaster November Sales. *D. L. Williams.*

PERSIAN DYNASTY 5 br.h. Persian Bold 123–Parez 67 (Pardao 120) [1988 8d 10g 7g 8f³ 7d 7f* 8f² 8f⁶ 7f 8m 1989 7f 7m⁶ 8m⁵ 7f 10.2f⁶ 8f⁵ 10.2f* 12.2f⁵] small horse: poor handicapper: won apprentice event at Bath in October: stays 10.2f: acts well on firm going. *J. M. Bradley.* **46**

PERSIAN EMPEROR 4 ro.c. Persepolis (FR) 127–Rosananti 107 (Blushing Groom (FR) 131) [1988 7g 7d³ 8m³ 10d⁴ 8f⁴ 8d 8g⁵ 8f⁴ 7g² 8d 8f* 9g 1989 7f⁶ 9m 10m 8g 8g⁴ 9f 8g⁶ a10g⁴] compact colt: has a quick action: creditable fourth in minor event (facing stiff task) at Leicester and handicap at Lingfield: well below form in handicaps most other starts as 4-y-o: effective at 7f and stays 1¼m: best form on a sound surface: tailed off when visored fourth start: has shown a tendency to hang and is probably best covered up: unreliable. *R. Hollinshead.* **61**

PERSIAN LUCK 3 br.c. Persian Bold 123–Ansedonia (Captain's Gig (USA)) [1988 7m 6s 1989 7s 7f² 8f 7h 10.2g⁶ a7g³] attractive colt: easily best efforts when placed in handicaps at Chester (leading 6f and beaten head) in May and Lingfield (bandaged and first run for 5 months) in November: seems suited by 7f: acts on firm going. *P. F. I. Cole.* **68**

PERSIAN MONARCH 3 gr.c. Persepolis (FR) 127–Aristata (Habitat 134) [1988 5v⁶ 5s⁶ 6f 7g 1989 8g 8m 8h³ 10f 6m 10.6m] dipped-backed, angular colt: has a smooth action: edgy, third in seller at Carlisle in June, only worthwhile form: found little then and on next start: suited by 1m: may be temperamentally unsatisfactory. *R. Hollinshead.* **43**

PERSIAN MOON 3 ch.f. Persian Bold 123–Vital Match 113 (Match III 135) [1988 5m* 6f⁵ 6g³ 5.8d 6g 1989 10f⁴ 10m 11.5m³ 10m⁵ a10g] tall, quite attractive filly: fair performer: in frame in Lupe Stakes at Goodwood and minor event at Sandown: 20/1 and in need of race, good staying-on fifth in £8,000 handicap at Newmarket, easily better of last 2 starts: should be better at 1½m than 1¼m: acts on firm going: sold 16,000 gns Newmarket December Sales. *D. R. C. Elsworth.* **88**

PERSIAN SOLDIER 2 b.c. (Mar 10) Sandhurst Prince 128–Persian Case (Upper Case (USA)) [1989 a7g*] 19,000F, 9,200Y: fifth living foal: half-brother to 3-y-o Young Aspiration (by Coquelin) and 4-y-o Dissolution (by Henbit), 7.5f winner at 2 yrs: dam won over 7.8f at 2 yrs in France: won 14-runner maiden at Lingfield in December by 3 lengths from Transcriber: should improve. *P. T. Walwyn.* **75 p**

PERSIAN SPRING 2 ch.f. (Mar 29) King Persian 107–Northern Amber (Shack (USA) 118) [1989 6m⁶ 6m 5m 5g 5g] good-bodied, workmanlike filly: moderate mover: first foal: dam ran several times: of little account. *B. Stevens.* **—**

PERSIAN SULTAN 2 br.c. (Mar 5) Persian Bold 123–Florita 86 (Lord Gayle (USA) 124) [1989 5v 5d 6m 6m³ 6h² 7m² 7g⁴ 7m⁴] 7,000Y: small, quite attractive colt: third foal: half-brother to 3-y-o Glinette (by Chief Singer): dam 1¼m winner: fair plater: stays 7f: visored third to sixth starts: often taken down very early: races freely. *W. Wilson.* **53**

PERSIAN TAPESTRY 5 ch.m. Tap On Wood 130–Persian Polly 99 (Persian Bold 123) [1988 11f 11.1m 8f 10f 10.2f 10f⁴ 10.2g 8g 6g⁶ 1989 7f 10m⁵ 12.2m³ 10f² 10m⁴ 8m⁴ 8m 10g⁵ 10g] sparely-made, workmanlike mare: plating-class handicapper: won at Leicester in August: stayed 1¼m well: acted on firm going: ran creditably in blinkers: occasionally started slowly, and usually held up: often taken quietly to post: sold 9,000 gns Newmarket December Sales in foal to King of Spain. *P. D. Cundell.* **52**

PERSIAN VEIL 3 ch.f. Persian Bold 123–Wolverhants 79 (Wolver Hollow 126) [1988 6s³ 8m⁶ 1989 7f4 7f⁶ 7.3m² 7f⁶ 8m 7.5m³ 10.4m 8g 8f 8g⁵] small, sparely-made filly: quite modest maiden: best efforts as 3-y-o when in frame, twice in handicaps: seemed unsuited by track at Chester seventh outing: stays 1m: acts on top-of-the-ground: sold 2,300 gns Newmarket Autumn Sales. *C. E. Brittain.* **64**

PERSILLANT 5 b.h. Persian Bold 123–Gauloise 93 (Welsh Pageant 132) [1988 10d 12g³ 11f⁵ 10g* 10m² 10v⁴ 10f 10d 1989 14g* 12m* 12f⁴ 13s] good-topped horse: moderate mover: fairly useful handicapper: won at Haydock (leading on line after hanging left) in June and York in July: stays 1¾m well: probably acts on any going: tends to get on edge: winning hurdler: tough. *N. Tinkler.* **91**

PERT 3 br.f. Sayf El Arab (USA) 127–Petsy 84 (Mummy's Pet 125) [1988 NR 1989 6s 8d 7.5d⁶ 8.2f 8g] sparely-made filly: first foal: dam 2-y-o 6f winner: plater: stays **—**

7.5f: possibly unsuited by firm going: sold 700 gns Doncaster August Sales. *Ronald Thompson.*

PERUZZI 3 ch.g. Simply Great (FR) 122–Okavamba 82 (Wollow 132) [1988 7d⁴ 57 8f⁴ 1989 12d 10.6g 14m⁵ a12g³ a16g] workmanlike gelding: bit unfurnished: first run for 5½ months, sign of ability in 1989 only when third in claimer at Lingfield in November: stays 1½m: bandaged behind final start: trained first 3 by E. Weymes. *M. D. I. Usher.*

PETAMO 3 b.c. Coquelin (USA) 121–Kissing 98 (Sing Sing 134) [1988 8d⁵ 7g 1989 53 8g 10f 10.6g 12m 12h³ 12f 14m 15.5f² 15.3f⁵ 12g] close-coupled, quite attractive colt: plating class on most form: stays 15f: acts on firm ground: carried head high and flashed tail under pressure when blinkered fifth outing: sold 6,400 gns Newmarket Autumn Sales. *G. Harwood.*

PETAVIOUS 4 b.c. Mummy's Pet 125–Pencuik Jewel (Petingo 135) [1988 NR 74 1989 10g³ 8g 10m⁶ 8.3m⁴ 8f a10g⁴ a12g a11g*] medium-sized colt: well-backed favourite, won claimer at Southwell in December very easily by 6 lengths: stays 11f: acts on top-of-the-ground: hung left second start: moved down poorly on fourth. *Lady Herries.*

PETERHOUSE 2 b.c. (Apr 8) Habitat 134–Kanz (USA) 115 (The Minstrel (CAN) 86 p 135) [1989 6g 6g*] small, close-coupled colt: second foal: dam, winner at about 1m and stayed 1½m, half-sister to Crown Treasure, dam of Glint of Gold and Diamond Shoal: co-favourite, won 18-runner maiden at Redcar in November by 3 lengths, soon prominent and running on well: will stay 1m. *G. Harwood.*

PETERLEE 3 ch.g. Nicholas Bill 125–Nonasalome (Absalom 128) [1988 6f 5f 8g — 1989 8m 13.8g⁵] angular, plain gelding: has a long, round stride: no worthwhile form. *W. Wilson.*

PETER MARTIN 8 ch.g. Monsanto (FR) 121–Bouboulina (Hornbeam 130) [1988 51 § 16m 16g 18f⁵ 16g³ 14g 16g 15m* 17.1g⁵ 15.8g³ 15d² 1989 14s⁴ 17f² 16m⁶ 15.8m⁶ 16.2m⁴ 16f³ 15m² 16.2m⁴ 14.8f² 14g⁴ 16.2m² 18m⁴] workmanlike gelding: moderate mover: plating-class handicapper: stays well: acts on any going: often blinkered or visored: usually held up and is suited by strong gallop: finds nothing off bridle. *F. H. Lee.*

PETILLANTE 2 gr.f. (Apr 9) Petong 126–French Bugle 71 (Bleep-Bleep 134) 101 [1989 5m² 5f³ 5f* 5g 5g² 5m 6m⁶] 21,000Y: leggy, useful-looking filly: good mover,

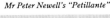

Mr Peter Newell's "Petillante"

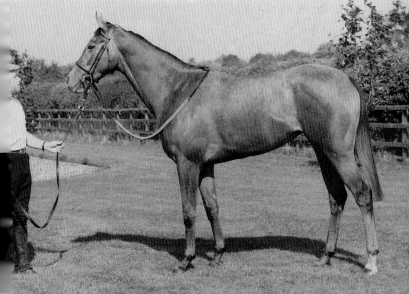

with a light action: closely related to ungenuine 7f winner Cor de Chasse (by Mansingh) and 3 other winners, and half-sister to several other winners, including useful sprinter Piencourt (by Averof): dam won over 1m: useful filly: made all in Norfolk Stakes at Royal Ascot: short-head second of 9 to Polar Bird in listed race at Newbury in August: will prove best at 5f: sold 86,000 gns Newmarket December Sales. *A. A. Scott.*

PETIPA (USA) 2 gr.c. (Feb 28) Encino (USA)–Connie O (USA) (Oxford Flight (USA)) [1989 5.3m* 5g² 5m⁴ 7m* 7g] $1,500F, IR 18,000Y: useful-looking colt: good walker: has a fluent, quick action: half-brother to a winner in USA by North Pole: dam lightly raced: sire stakes-placed winning sprinter: won 7-runner maiden at Brighton in April and 16-runner nursery (showing much improved form) at York in August: stays 7f: genuine. *R. Hannon.* **86**

PETITE ANGEL 4 ro.f. Burslem 123–Lavinia (Habitat 134) [1988 8d 8.2m 6m 8h⁶ 6g 8g 5f⁵ 6d 6g 1989 8.5f 7f 8h 5f 6f⁶ 8h⁴ 8f 8m 8f 5f⁴ 8f a8g] small, sturdy filly: poor plater. *R. Hollinshead.* **30**

PETITE BUTTERFLY 2 b.f. (Mar 6) Absalom 128–Girl of Shiraz 84 (Hotfoot 126) [1989 5m 6m a7g*] 3,800Y: smallish, lengthy filly: keen walker: won maiden at Lingfield in December by neck from Dr Maccarter: stays 7f. *W. Carter.* **67**

PETITE ILE 3 b.f. Ile de Bourbon (USA) 133–Aces Full (USA) (Round Table) [1988 7d² 8s* 1989 8g³ 10m³ 11m* 12m³ 12f³ 14d*] **121**

There was a shock result in the Jefferson Smurfit Memorial Irish St Leger—Sheikh Mohammed didn't win it. After the successes of his Enscone, Shaadi, Old Vic and Alydaress both Lazaz and Upper Strata were supplemented for the final Irish classic but to no avail. Fittingly, the horse who prevented this unprecedented clean sweep for an owner and denied British

*Jefferson Smurfit Memorial Irish St Leger, the Curragh—
Petite Ile (right) just gets home from Tyrone Bridge*

trainers victory in all of Ireland's nine Group 1 events was Petite Ile—virtually the only Irish-trained horse of three or more years who created more than a slight ripple in European competition in 1989. Prior to the Irish St Leger only two of the fifteen places available in Irish Group 1 races for three-year-olds and up had been filled by home-based animals; Petite Ile was third in the Oaks and Run To Jenny third in the One Thousand Guineas, and besides Petite Ile's third in the Yorkshire Oaks the only other Irish-trained older horses to finish in the frame in a European pattern event outside their own country were Milieu and Sagamore who were fourth in the Challenge Stakes and Östermann-Pokal.

For a Group 1 race, the opposition to Petite Ile for the Irish St Leger was substandard. The previous year's runner-up Daarkom was back again, but hadn't raced for four months, and Petite Ile excepted, only two in the ten-runner field had contested a Group 1 event earlier in the season; Sesame had been put in her place in the Coronation Cup and Phantom Breeze had stayed on to be a never-dangerous fourth in the Irish Derby. The two Sheikh Mohammed runners led into the straight but his grand-slam hopes must have been pretty fleeting, as Petite Ile could be named the winner shortly after. Anyone who'd stopped watching the race at that stage, however, would have had quite a shock on learning that Petite Ile had gone on to win only very narrowly. The Curragh Cup winner and prospective hurdler Tyrone Bridge ran the favourite to a short head. Petite Ile ranged alongside him well over a furlong out and her jockey Quinton—who thought afterwards, incidentally, that he'd been beaten—went for his whip fully a furlong later than Parnell on Tyrone Bridge before the two of them fought it out, virtually inseparable, to the post. The description 'on the nod' was never more appropriate.

It wasn't the first time that Petite Ile would have attracted all the money in running. In both the Irish and Yorkshire Oaks she'd looked to be travelling best at the distance only to finish third. In the first of those races Petite Ile was the most fancied Irish runner at 14/1 behind the British pair Aliysa and Alydaress after a third to Porter Rhodes in the Gallinule Stakes at the Curragh, where she'd been hampered twice, and a win in the listed Irish Merchants EBF Phoenix Oaks Trial in which she'd scraped home by a head from the useful Kostroma after more problems getting a clear run. Petite Ile's emergence on the classic stage in the Irish Oaks, beaten under a length behind Alydaress, gave plenty of encouragement for her prospects at York where victory came even more tantalisingly within her grasp. She was the only one of the five runners not being pushed along two furlongs out but having been switched to challenge at the furlong pole Petite Ile held the lead only narrowly and fairly briefly before Roseate Tern went by and then Alydaress also got the better of her close home.

Following Dark Lomond in 1988, Petite Ile became the second consecutive Irish St Leger winner to be sent to the Newmarket December Sales. She made 540,000 guineas, all in all quite a step up on the IR 14,000 guineas paid for her at the Goffs Invitational Foal and Breeding Stock Sale in 1986. The dam Aces Full, a winner of a maiden at around one mile from nine starts as a three-year-old, was purchased from the USA for 485,000 dollars as a five-year-old, then five years later she too went to the December Sales, fetching 34,000 guineas while carrying Petite Ile, her first runner of note. All her previous five foals made it to the racecourse but only one of them, the mile-and-a-quarter claimer winner Running Steps (by Nijinsky), won on the flat. Blackwell Boy (by Vigors) has gone on to win over hurdles and fences. Petite Ile is followed by a filly named Random Chance and a colt, both by Glenstal. Aces Full's purchase price in America is easily explained as she's a sister to the Florida Derby and Wood Memorial Stakes winner Upper Case, a very smart three-year-old colt of 1972 but very much in the shadow of his stable-companion Riva Ridge. Upper Case stood for five seasons in Britain before being returned Stateside, siring little of distinction. Petite Ile's grandam Bold Experience was the second top-rated two-year-old filly in Trotter's Experimental Handicap after victories in the five-furlong Rancocas Stakes and six-furlong Sorority Stakes.

Mr Malle has retained a share in Petite Ile and she's reportedly to go to the USA where, of course, she's likely to step down in distance. We have no

Mr J. F. Malle's "Petite Ile"

Petite Ile (b.f. 1986)	Ile de Bourbon (USA) (br 1975)	Nijinsky (b 1967)	Northern Dancer Flaming Page
		Roseliere (br 1965)	Misti IV Peace Rose
	Aces Full (USA) (b 1975)	Round Table (b 1954)	Princequillo Knight's Daughter
		Bold Experience (ch 1962)	Bold Ruler First Flush

doubts that she's effective at a mile and three quarters and prefer to put her scrambled Irish St Leger victory down to her tendency not to find much more than the one pace when off the bridle. A rather sparely-made, quite attractive filly, Petite Ile acts on any going. *J. Oxx, Ireland.*

PETITE MOU 2 b.f. (Feb 17) Ela-Mana-Mou 132–Petite Bourguoise (Crowned Prince (USA) 128) [1989 6m* 7g 8v] IR 18,000Y: tall, leggy, unfurnished filly: fifth foal: half-sister to useful Italian performer Sweet Mas (by Acamas): dam placed from 7f to 1m in Ireland: won 7-runner maiden at Kempton in July: appeared to run well in Premio Guido Berardelli at Rome in November on final outing: should stay 1¼m. *J. L. Dunlop.* **84** ?

PETITE ROSANNA 3 b.f. Ile de Bourbon (USA) 133–Let Slip 77 (Busted 134) [1988 6g⁴ 7g² 8m⁵ 8s 7f⁴ 7m 1989 9f⁵ 10g* 10f* 12g 10m⁴ 10f 10f⁵ 9.2d⁴ 10m 12m⁵] smallish, good-quartered filly: won maiden at Epsom and 2-runner minor event at Sandown in June: led 1m and best effort in £10,000 handicap at Ascot fifth start: tailed off in £24,200 handicap penultimate one: stays 1¼m: acts on firm going, and apparently unsuited by soft surface: blinkered (raced keenly) final start: sometimes wears tongue strap. *W. Carter.* **85**

PETIVARA 2 b.f. (May 17) Petong 126–Avahra 108 (Sahib 114) [1989 6g⁶ 6g⁶] 11,000Y: workmanlike filly: sister to fair 3-y-o sprinter Cumbrian Melody and half-sister to several winners here and abroad, including quite useful sprinters Mavahra and Pavahra (both by Mummy's Pet): dam stayed 6f: plating-class form in autumn maidens at Goodwood and Folkestone. *S. Dow.* **56**

PETLOVA 2 b.f. (Apr 22) Petorius 117–Vlassova (FR) 69 (Green Dancer (USA) 132) [1989 6g] 7,200F, IR 20,000Y: first foal: dam French 11.5f to 15f winner: 12/1, around 8 lengths eighth of 18, unable to challenge, to Peterhouse in maiden at Redcar in November: should improve. *S. G. Norton.*   **56** p

PETMER 2 b.c. (Apr 19) Tina's Pet 121–Merency 75 (Meldrum 112) [1989 6g] 7,800Y: tall, leggy colt: sixth reported foal: half-brother to fairly useful 1981 2-y-o 6f winner Tachywaun (by Tachypous) and 1985 2-y-o 6f winner Carriban Tyme (by Tyrnavos): dam 2-y-o 5f winner: 50/1, tailed off from halfway in well-contested minor event at Epsom in June: taken quietly down. *N. R. Mitchell.*   —

PETORINO 3 b.c. Petorius 117–Torino (Firestreak 125) [1988 5s 5v⁴ 5g⁵ 5f⁴ 5m² 5d 5m⁴ 5g⁵ 5g 6g 7g 1989 7g 8h] small, compact colt: moderate walker: has a quick action: quite modest maiden in 1988: always behind in handicaps as 3-y-o: appears to stay 6f: best form on a sound surface: trained until after reappearance by R. Hollinshead: sold 2,000 gns Doncaster June Sales. *R. O'Leary.*   —

PETRADARE 2 ch.f. (Feb 6) Wolver Heights 99–Petlady 81 (Petingo 135) [1989 6g] 540Y: angular, plain filly: half-sister to winners in Norway by Blakeney and Belgium by Northfields and to winning hurdler Vitingo (by Vitiges): dam won over 6f at 2 yrs: prominent around 3f in 22-runner maiden at Leicester in November: moved poorly down. *B. A. McMahon.*   —

PETRIECE 3 b.f. Mummy's Pet 125–Great Grey Niece 74 (Great Nephew 126) [1988 6g³ 6f 7f 7g⁴ 1989 8f⁶ 7f 8m⁵ 7f* 6m 7m 5m⁵ 6f⁵ 6g] leggy, angular filly: has a slightly round action: dead-heated in maiden at Chepstow in July: best efforts after in handicaps seventh (apprentices) and eighth starts: stays 1m: acts on firm going: sold 5,000 gns Newmarket December Sales. *R. J. R. Williams.*   **64**

PETRILLIA 3 b.f. Petorius 117–Mythical Lady 86 (Track Spare 125) [1988 5d² 5g² 6f² 5f 6s² 5g* 5g* 5s* 5f² 1989 6f 5f 6m] leggy, medium-sized filly: good walker: moderate mover: fairly useful performer as 2-y-o: well beaten in Group 3 event and valuable handicaps as 3-y-o: best form at 5f: acts on any going: suitable mount for apprentice: best in blinkers (blinkered only second start in 1989). *B. W. Hills.*   —

PETRISSA 3 b.f. Petorius 117–Sarasingh 93 (Mansingh (USA) 120) [1988 5f 5f 5m 5m 1989 6m 8m 8f 6g 5f 6s] lightly-made, leggy filly: has round action: probably of little account and temperamental: has been visored. *J. S. Wainwright.*   — §

PETROL BLUE 2 b.g. (Mar 7) Tumble Wind (USA)–Petrina 87 (Petingo 135) [1989 6g] 15,500F, 25,000Y: angular gelding: has scope: fifth reported foal: dam won twice at 1m, and daughter of Irish 1000 Guineas winner Shandon Belle: well beaten in 10-runner minor event at Doncaster in September: subsequently gelded. *M. H. Easterby.*   — p

PETRULLO 4 b.c. Electric 126–My Therape 112 (Jimmy Reppin 131) [1988 8g³ 10m 10.1m⁴ 10d² 12d³ 12g* 12s³ 12m³ 10d³ 10g* 1989 9g² 10s⁴ 11g 10f⁶ 12m⁶ 10g³   **117**

La Coupe de Maisons-Laffitte—Petrullo (right) hangs on to win from Silver Lane

10d* 12g 10g] strong, rangy colt: usually looks well: has a quick action: much improved, winning Group 3 La Coupe de Maisons-Laffitte in September by neck from Silver Lane, and in frame earlier in slowly-run Earl of Sefton EBF Stakes at Newmarket, Gordon Richards EBF Stakes at Sandown and EBF Phoenix Champion Stakes: well beaten in Ciga Prix de l'Arc de Triomphe at Longchamp and Dubai Champion Stakes at Newmarket last 2 outings: suited by 1¼m and give in the ground: tends to hang, and is suited by strong handling and waiting tactics: has joined J. Fanshawe. *R. F. Casey.*

PETTICOAT POWER   3 b.f. Petorius 117–Red Realm (Realm 129) [1988 6m⁶ **71** 6f* 7d⁴ 7d 1989 7g 6g 6m 7g 6g 6m 6d 6m⁴ 6g*] unfurnished, workmanlike filly: modest handicapper: stayed on to lead line at Folkestone in October: creditable fourth in ladies event at Chepstow: worth another try at 7f: acts on firm going and a soft surface: sold 4,200 gns Newmarket Autumn Sales. *G. B. Balding.*

PHANAN   3 ch.g. Pharly (FR) 130–L'Ecossaise (Dancer's Image (USA)) [1988 6m **83** 7d 6m⁵ 8f 1989 8f 8f⁵ 14m³ 16.5g³ 17.6f² 10.1m² 12.2g* 11.7m* 14m⁴ 12g a10g] leggy, workmanlike gelding: fair at his best: made virtually all to win maiden (best effort) at Catterick and handicap at Windsor in August: well beaten after: best efforts over middle distances: may well be suited by an easy surface: lacks turn of foot, and is suited by forcing tactics: genuine: gelded after final start. *F. Durr.*

PHANTOM AFFAIR   3 b.f. Caerleon (USA) 132–Misdevious (USA) (Alleged   — (USA) 138) [1988 7d⁵ 8g⁴ 1989 10.1g 12.2m] rangy, useful-looking filly: quite modest form in fair company at back-end of 1988: well beaten in minor event at Windsor and maiden at Catterick in July: should be well suited by 1½m + . *B. W. Hills.*

PHANTOM BREEZE   3 b.c. Vision (USA)–Ask The Wind 106 (Run The **114** Gantlet (USA)) [1988 7g* 8v* 1989 7s³ 10g* 10m² 12g⁴ 14d⁶ 12s⁴] very useful Irish colt: favourite, won Group 2 Derrinstown Stud EBF Derby Trial Stakes at Leopardstown in May: in frame after at the Curragh in Gallinule Stakes, Irish Derby

Mr Bertram R. Firestone's "Phantom Breeze"

(staying-on never-dangerous 11½ lengths fourth behind Old Vic) and Blandford Stakes: blinkered, ran moderately in Irish St Leger at same course: seems suited by 1½m: yet to race on firm going, acts on any other. *D. K. Weld, Ireland.*

PHANTOM ROW 2 b.f. (Apr 23) Adonijah 126–Front Row 111 (Epaulette 125) **37** [1989 5m 5h⁵ 5f] smallish, well-made, quite attractive filly: half-sister to several winners, including very useful 1987 2-y-o 5f winner Colmore Row (by Mummy's Pet) and smart miler Long Row (by Linacre): dam won Irish 1000 Guineas: poor form in early-summer maidens: sold 26,000 gns Newmarket December Sales. *W. Jarvis.*

PHANTOM SINGER 3 ch.f. Relkino 131–Grace Note 104 (Parthia 132) [1988 **58** 8.2d 8g⁶ 1989 11g* 12m² 12.3m³ 10m 11s⁶ 13.6g] rangy, workmanlike filly: won maiden claimer at Hamilton in May: ran creditably when third in claimer, poorly in handicaps after: probably stays 1½m: acts on top-of-the-ground (hung left on soft): sold 15,000 gns Newmarket Autumn Sales. *Sir Mark Prescott.*

PHARAMINEUX 3 ch.g. Pharly (FR) 130–Miss Longchamp 94 (Northfields **51** (USA)) [1988 NR 1989 7s 8m 10f 8m⁴ 8m 10m³ 10m 8f a10g] strong, workmanlike gelding: third foal: half-brother to Irish 6f winner Miss Bagatelle, somewhat temperamental maiden here at 2 yrs, and fair 1986 2-y-o 6f winner Le Favori (both by Mummy's Pet): dam won at 7.2f and 1m at 3 yrs: plating-class maiden: well beaten (including in handicap) last 3 outings, prominent early when blinkered final one: stays 1m: claimed out of W. Hastings-Bass's stable £7,700 in seller third start. *W. Wilson.*

PHARAOH'S DELIGHT 2 b.f. (Apr 2) Fairy King (USA)–Ridge The **108** Times (USA) 78 (Riva Ridge (USA)) [1989 6m⁶ 5f* 6m* 6d* 6g²]

Until Dashing Blade's victory in the Three Chimneys Dewhurst Stakes took Elegant Air to top spot in the first-season sires table, a position he then held for the rest of the season, the 'title' had looked set to go to a horse who in his racing days was beset by training difficulties and didn't run again after trailing in almost nineteen lengths last of eleven in a listed race at Phoenix Park on his debut. Top-class form is not a requisite for success at stud, however, and Fairy King, the horse in question, had much better credentials for making the grade as a stallion than many of his more highly-rated contemporaries: a son of Northern Dancer, he is a full brother to Sadler's Wells, a three-parts brother to Nureyev and out of a sister to Thatch. Fairy King, a former stable-companion of Sadler's Wells, was retired to Bally-sheehan Stud in County Tipperary in 1986 at a fee of IR 6,000 guineas, which had been halved by the time his first runners reached the racecourse. It's a measure of the achievements of his first crop, which contained eight individual winners of thirteen races, and the resulting clamour for his services, and for his yearlings at the sales, that his fee for the 1990 covering season has bucked recent trends and risen sharply to IR 20,000 guineas. Fairy King hasn't yet sired anything so good as the best progeny of Sadler's Wells, who has received much better mares, but he has the fairly useful filly Fair Titania, the unbeaten colt Makbul and, best of all, the very useful Pharaoh's Delight who won the richly-endowed Heinz '57' Phoenix Stakes before injury in the Moyglare Stud Stakes cut short her season.

According to the betting at the Curragh, Pharaoh's Delight held an excellent chance of adding the Moyglare Stud Stakes to a run of three

Windsor Castle Stakes, Ascot—Pharaoh's Delight wins by six lengths

Princess Margaret Stakes, Ascot—Pharaoh's Delight comfortably holds Routilante

successes which had followed a pipeopener in a maiden at Leicester, where she shaped encouragingly after a slow start to finish sixth of the ten runners behind Bright Flower. Pharaoh's Delight clearly reaped the benefit of that considerate introduction as nearly two weeks later she showed a clean pair of heels to eight previous winners in the ten-runner Windsor Castle Stakes at Royal Ascot. Starting third favourite at 11/2, Pharaoh's Delight, who had also been heavily backed on her debut, soon held a prominent pitch, took up the running two furlongs out and sprinted clear nearing the distance to put six lengths between herself and a tightly-bunched trio headed by Addison's Blade. Pharaoh's Delight was returned to Ascot in July for the Group 3 Princess Margaret Stakes over six furlongs. Making the running on this occasion she confirmed she was going very much the right way with a smooth performance, travelling comfortably from the off and quickening readily when shaken up a furlong out to account for Routilante and La Cabrilla by a length and a half and two and a half lengths.

The next stop for the progressive Pharaoh's Delight was the Group 1 Heinz '57' Phoenix Stakes at Phoenix Park in August. Various attempts have been made over the last ten years to upgrade the quality of the race, including improving its status and prize money, but apart from 1986, when Minstrella

Heinz '57' Phoenix Stakes, Phoenix Park—
much harder for Pharaoh's Delight(left); Duck And Dive (striped cap) came second,
Wedding Bouquet (noseband) third

defeated Forest Flower, it has remained largely a second-class event. The latest renewal, worth in excess of IR £120,000 to the winner, attracted ten runners, of whom only the Irish-trained Aminata, successful in the Shernazar EBF Curragh Stakes, besides Pharaoh's Delight, had won in pattern company before. Aminata wasn't greatly fancied in the market, though, and greater dangers to Pharaoh's Delight, the 2/1 favourite, were presumed to be the Curragh maiden winner Wedding Bouquet, the useful early-season filly Princess Taufan and the Molecomb runner-up Red Henry, whose stable had taken the prize with Superpower twelve months earlier. There was never any likelihood of a repeat, however, as Red Henry trailed throughout in a strongly-run race which Pharaoh's Delight dominated from halfway. Allowed to drift to her right, Pharaoh's Delight was ridden along when she reached the stand rail a furlong out and responded gamely to hold the fast-finishing Duck And Dive by a length with Wedding Bouquet, the best of the home defence, the same distance away in third.

In the seven-runner Moyglare Stud Stakes at the Curragh in September only the Hillsdown Cherry Hinton winner Chimes of Freedom looked to stand between Pharaoh's Delight and the IR £110,000 first prize. Pharaoh's Delight set out to make every post a winning one, but as she was passed by Chimes of Freedom, the eventual six-length winner, with a furlong to go her rider Eddery stopped riding as if something was amiss. Subsequent examination of the filly revealed she'd sustained a shoulder injury and was lame on her near fore. Pharaoh's Delight didn't recover in time for the Tattersalls Cheveley Park Stakes at Newmarket in October, her final intended objective for the season, in which Chimes of Freedom finished around a length third to Dead Certain. Had Pharaoh's Delight gone to post fit, well and in top form, she would probably have gone very close indeed.

Pharaoh's Delight (b.f. Apr 2, 1987)	Fairy King (USA) (b 1982)	Northern Dancer (b 1961)	Nearctic
			Natalma
		Fairy Bridge (b 1975)	Bold Reason
			Special
	Ridge The Times (USA) (ch 1981)	Riva Ridge (b 1969)	First Landing
			Iberia
		Oath of Allegiance (ch 1975)	Olden Times
			Take A Stand

The quite attractive Pharaoh's Delight was purchased for IR 14,000 guineas at the Tattersalls Ireland Yearling Sale at Fairyhouse. She is the second foal of her dam Ridge The Times following the year-older Jumby Bay (by Thatching), who made the headlines for altogether different reasons in 1989 when his reappearance at Lingfield in May resulted in his trainer and rider being fined £500 each for not running the horse on its merits. Jumby Bay showed quite useful form, and temperament too, in his subsequent races, winning over a mile. Most of Pharaoh's Delight's family have done their racing at shorter distances. Ridge The Times won a five-furlong nursery at Hamilton Park before her export to Ireland and none of her three winning half-sisters or half-brothers from the unraced Oath of Allegiance, herself a half-sister to the smart French 1975 staying two-year-old French Friend and the dam of the top American filly Open Mind, won beyond nine furlongs. Pharaoh's Delight, who has yet to race on very soft going but acts on any other, may stay a mile but strikes us first and foremost as a sprinter. *J. P. Hudson.*

PHIL-BLAKE   2 br.c. (Apr 13) Blakeney 126–Philogyny 94 (Philip of Spain 126)   **69**
[1989 6m⁴ 6g 6d] leggy, workmanlike colt: fifth foal: half-brother to 7f winner Sporting Wednesday (by Martinmas) and 1¼m winner The Footman (by Hotfoot): dam won 5 sprints: quite modest maiden: best effort on debut: will be better suited by further. *C. A. Horgan.*

PHILIP   7 b.g. Kala Shikari 125–Canteen Katie (King's Troop 118) [1988 6g 5d 5g⁴   **55**
5f 5m⁴ 5m⁵ 5m 5f 5g⁴ 6f⁵ 6g 6s 5s 1989 6d 6m 5f 5m 5f 6h 6f³ 6m 5m³ 5m³ 5m⁴ 6s 6f] strong, compact gelding: carries plenty of condition: poor mover: fairly useful handicapper as 5-y-o: has deteriorated, but showed he retained some ability when third at Thirsk, Edinburgh and Ayr in summer: stays 6f: not suited by soft going, appears to act on any other: effective with or without blinkers or visor: bandaged third outing: usually gets outpaced. *N. Tinkler.*

PHILIPPA'S HEIR 2 b.f. (Apr 23) Elegant Air 119–Ebb And Flo 82 (Forlorn   40
River 124) [1989 6m 7m³ 7g 8.2s] leggy, shallow-girthed filly: half-sister to 3
winners, including useful 6f to 1m winner Miss Thames (by Tower Walk) and fairly
useful 1981 2-y-o 7f winner Connaught River (by Connaught), later quite good
jumper: dam, 6f winner at 2 yrs, stayed 1½m: poor maiden: blinkered final start. *R.
W. Stubbs.*

PHILIPPONNAT (USA) 3 b.g. Sensitive Prince (USA)–August Bride (USA)   —
(Chieftain II) [1988 7g 8g 8m 1989 12g 15.3f 16f] well beaten in varied company:
blinkered final start: sold to join A. Leighton 2,900 gns Newmarket Autumn Sales.
M. D. I. Usher.

PHILIP'S DREAM 3 ch.g. Salmon Leap (USA) 131–Spring In Rome (USA)   56
(Forli (ARG)) [1988 6m 7f 7m 1989 10.8s⁴ 7d 11.7m 8m² 8g² 7m] lengthy, sturdy
gelding: good mover with a long stride: easily best efforts when second in Yarmouth
sellers in the summer: should prove as effective over 7f as 1m: may well prove best
on a sound surface: visored and wore tongue strap third start: sweating final one:
sold 2,000 gns Newmarket Autumn Sales. *G. A. Huffer.*

PHILJOY 3 b.f. Bustino 136–Formana (Reform 132) [1988 NR 1989 12d⁴ 12.3m⁴   73
12m⁶ 16f²] 17,000Y: workmanlike filly: poor mover: fourth foal: half-sister to a listed
winner in Scandinavia by Alias Smith: dam, winner over 13f in France, is half-sister
to smart French filly Ranimer: modest form in maidens: best effort in 3-runner
handicap (claimer ridden) final start: probably suited by 2m: acts on firm going. *C.
W. C. Elsey.*

PHILOSOPHOS 3 b.g. High Top 131–Pacificus (USA) 65 (Northern Dancer)   70
[1988 7m 7d 1989 10g⁶ 11.7m² 12g 13.3d²] smallish, angular gelding: poor walker:
form only when second in handicaps at Windsor (moderately run) and Newbury
(leading 6f out until 2f out and beaten 10 lengths): stays 13f: acts on top-of-
the-ground and a soft surface: sold to join J. Baker 6,500 gns Newmarket Autumn
Sales: winning novice hurdler. *P. T. Walwyn.*

PHILOTAS 5 b.g. Pitskelly 122–Damaring (USA) (Saidam) [1988 8d 12m 12g 11m   — §
10g 10g 10.4d³ 10m 10.2f 11m 10.5f 1989 10m 12m 10.8m] leggy gelding: moderate
mover: quite modest handicapper in 1987: little form since: stays 1¼m: seemingly
needs give in the ground nowadays: visored twice in 1988: bandaged at 5 yrs:
sometimes sweats: not genuine. *J. Balding.*

PHIL'S FOLLY 2 b.f. (Apr 14) Glasgow Central 91–Katebird 89 (Birdbrook 110)   42
[1989 5.8f⁴ 5m] smallish, deep-girthed filly: seventh live foal: half-sister to modest
1m winner Fenchurch Colony (by Tachypous), a winning plater and a winner in
Hong Kong, both by Lucky Wednesday: dam, beat at sprint distances on Flat, won
over hurdles: poor form in minor events at Bath in August and Lingfield in
September. *W. Carter.*

PHILSTAY 2 b.f. (Apr 14) Bustino 136–Magelka 77 (Relkino 131) [1989 6f 6m 8g⁶   —
10.6d] 2,100F, 5,000Y: smallish, workmanlike filly: third foal (all by Bustino): dam,
half-sister to very smart Easter Sun (by Bustino), best race at 1m: apparently of
little account. *T. Fairhurst.*

PHISUS 2 b.f. (Jan 24) Henbit (USA) 130–Daring Lass 87 (Bold Lad (IRE) 133)   48
[1989 5d³ 5s⁴ 5s⁵ 5f 6m 6g 8g] 9,200Y: leggy, narrow filly: eighth foal: sister to a
once-raced animal and a winner in Norway, and half-sister to 3-y-o Fly By Knife (by
Kris), fairly useful 6f and 7f winner at 2 yrs: dam, half-sister to top-class
middle-distance stayer Homeric, was second over 5f and 7f at 2 yrs: poor maiden:
stays 1m: acts on any going: sometimes on toes. *M. Brittain.*

PHOEBE MERYLL 3 br.f. Marching On 101–Mistress Meryll 61 (Tower Walk   55
130) [1988 6m⁴ 6s⁶ 5s⁴ 6m 1989 7g⁴ 7s 7d] lightly-made filly: has a quick action:
plating-class maiden: good fourth in handicap at Doncaster, front rank 6f: off course
3 months and below form after: may prove ideally suited by 6f: apparently not suited
by soft ground: sold 1,550 gns Doncaster November Sales. *J. W. Watts.*

PHOENIX JULE 2 b.g. (Apr 27) Coquelin (USA) 121–Ariel Sands (USA) (Super   62
Concorde (USA) 128) [1989 6f⁶ 6m 6g² 6s² a8g³ a7g⁶ a8g] IR 3,000, resold 4,400Y,
11,000 2-y-o: quite attractive gelding: first foal: dam, unplaced in 3 starts in Ireland:
quite modest maiden: stays 1m: blinkered last 2 outings. *J. G. FitzGerald.*

PHOTO CALL 2 b.f. (Apr 30) Chief Singer 131–Photo 83 (Blakeney 126) [1989   73
7s⁶ 8.2g⁵ 9f*] 32,000Y: sturdy, angular filly: moderate walker and mover: fourth
foal: half-sister to useful sprinter Quick Snap (by Try My Best): dam, 1m and 9f
winner, is daughter of 1000 Guineas second Photo Flash, a half-sister to Welsh

Pageant: won 6-runner maiden at Wolverhampton in October by ¾ length, staying on gamely final 2f: will stay 1¼m: acts well on firm going. *M. A. Jarvis.*

PHOUNTZI (USA) 3 ch.c. Raise A Cup (USA)–Pushy 112 (Sharpen Up 127) **90 p**
[1988 NR 1989 7d³ 8g*] leggy, quite attractive colt: good mover: fourth foal: half-brother to 3 winners, including smart 6f and 7.3f winner Bluebook (by Secretariat) and fairly useful 1984 2-y-o 6f winner Eye Drop (by Irish River): dam, who raced only at 2 yrs when winner of 4 races, including Queen Mary Stakes and Cornwallis Stakes, is daughter of outstanding broodmare Mrs Moss: sire raced only at 2 yrs when high-class winner at around 5f: well-backed favourite, won maiden at Newmarket in May by 2 lengths from Jungle Knife, running on strongly: reportedly split a pastern: should improve again if recovering from his injury. *M. R. Stoute.*

PHYLAE 3 b.f. Habitat 134–Hyroglyph (USA) (Northern Dancer) [1988 6s 1989 **—**
6g 8m] rangy, deep-girthed filly: no sign of ability in maidens. *I. A. Balding.*

PICADILLY PRINCE 9 b.g. Prince Tenderfoot (USA) 126–Piccadilly Belle **—**
(Pall Mall 132) [1988 NR 1989 14s] workmanlike gelding: modest at best: appears not to retain much ability: wears bandages. *A. P. James.*

PICEA 6 b.h. Mummy's Pet 125–May Hill 124 (Hill Clown (USA)) [1988 12d 11.7f³ **—**
12f² 12d* 12g⁴ 12d² 12m* 12f² 12g 1989 11.7m 11f⁶] strong, good-bodied horse: moderate mover: fairly useful handicapper at his best: favourite following promising reappearance, bit better than position (sixth of 12) suggests at Newbury in May, eased close home after quickening well when still having plenty to do over 1f out: stayed 13f: acted on firm going and a soft surface: visored twice: didn't find great deal off bridle and suited by extreme waiting tactics: retired to Upperwood Farm Stud, Hemel Hempstead, fee £1,000 (Oct 1st). *M. A. Jarvis.*

PICHON 4 b.f. Formidable (USA) 125–Sheer Bliss 76 (St Paddy 133) [1988 8v 6g **—**
5g 5m 8.5g⁵ 10m 8g⁶ 8g⁶ 8g 8f 9s 1989 10.2g 8.2g 8g 5m] good-topped, rather plain filly: poor maiden: well beaten in handicaps as 4-y-o: stays 8.5f: possibly unsuited by soft going: sometimes sweats and gets on edge. *M. O'Neill.*

PICK OF THE POPS 3 b.f. High Top 131–Rappa Tap Tap (FR) 111 (Tap On **105**
Wood 130) [1988 6f² 7s* 8g² 1989 10.5f⁶ 8f] sturdy, good-quartered filly: second in Hoover Fillies' Mile at Ascot final start in 1988: ran creditably as 3-y-o in Musidora Stakes at York and Coronation Stakes (staying on gamely, never dangerous) at Royal Ascot: should prove better suited by 1¼m than 1m: has won on soft going, but easily best efforts on a sound surface. *M. R. Stoute.*

PIC NEGRE 2 b.g. (Mar 2) Lochnager 132–Sallusteno 80 (Sallust 134) [1989 6m **60**
6g⁶ 6g 5g a5g] 2,800F: fifth foal: dam stayed 1m: plating-class maiden: blinkered final start. *S. G. Norton.*

PICTORIAL (USA) 2 b.c. (Mar 11) Aloma's Ruler (USA)–Art Talk (USA) **105 ?**
(Speak John) [1989 8f² 7g³ 7m² 7g⁴ 8d 8.5g⁵] $17,000Y: half-brother to several winners, notably 9f stakes winner Luxuriant Man (by Circle Home) and useful Irish 3-y-o sprinter Eloquent Minister (by Deputy Minister): dam 2-y-o winner in USA: sire won Preakness Stakes: put up useful performance when around a length fourth of 10 to Dashing Blade in GPA National Stakes at the Curragh in September: below form afterwards in Panasonic EBF Futurity Stakes there later in month and in Laurel Futurity (beaten around 12 lengths) at Laurel: should stay 1m: blinkered fourth and fifth starts. *T. Stack, Ireland.*

PIELD HEATH 4 b.g. Sallust 134–Lady Westleigh 76 (St Paddy 133) [1988 10s **—**
10d 12m 14m 11g 9s 1989 10d] small, workmanlike gelding: no form since 2 yrs: visored once: sometimes sweats: sold 800 gns Ascot June Sales. *P. J. Feilden.*

PIER DAMIANI (USA) 2 b.c. (Apr 25) Shareef Dancer (USA) 135–All A Lark **67 p**
(General Assembly (USA)) [1989 7s⁵ 7g] $70,000Y: deep-girthed colt: has scope: second foal: half-brother to American 3-y-o Lively Lark (by Caerleon), winner at 2 yrs: dam, Irish 1m to 9f winner, is half-sister to 3 good winners and to dam of Irish 2000 Guineas winner Flash of Steel: backward, quite modest form in autumn maidens at Goodwood and Newmarket: will be well suited by 1m +: sort to do better. *J. L. Dunlop.*

PILGRIM'S PATH 2 gr.c. (Mar 27) Godswalk (USA) 130–Lassalia (Sallust 134) **66**
[1989 5m⁶ 6m⁴ 6d] 18,500F, 37,000Y: good-topped, workmanlike colt: third foal: half-brother to French 3-y-o 1½m winner Ebene Wood (by Touching Wood), 7.5f winner at 2 yrs, and modest 8.5f winner My Reef (by Main Reef): dam placed from 6f to 9.5f in Ireland: quite modest maiden: best effort second start: will stay 7f. *G. B. Balding.*

PILGRIM'S REVENGE (USA) 3 b.g. Pilgrim (USA)–Bold Lou (USA) (Irish **59**
Castle (USA)) [1988 6g⁵ 8.2m 8m⁵ 1989 8.2g⁵ 10.6m³ 12g⁵ 12.2g] useful-looking

Geoffrey Barling Maiden Stakes, Newmarket—Pilot impresses

gelding: wearing crossed noseband and unruly in preliminaries, about 12 lengths third of 19 in apprentice handicap at Haydock, best effort in 1989: stays 10.6f: best efforts on top-of-the-ground: takes good hold: also gave trouble at stalls once at 2 yrs. *S. G. Norton.*

PILLAR OF FIRE (USA)   4 b.g. Master Willie 129–As You Would (USA) (Fleet   §§
Nasrullah) [1988 12g² 13m* 12g² 10d 1989 9f 16g] big, angular gelding: has a long,
rather round stride: fairly useful winner as 3-y-o when trained by S. Norton: refused
to enter stalls once later in 1988 and became thoroughly temperamental as 4-y-o:
reluctant to enter stalls and to race on reappearance, and refused to race from flag
start second outing: stays 13f: often pulls hard: sold to join M. Usher 4,000 gns
Newmarket Autumn Sales: one to leave alone. *C. A. Cyzer.*

PILOT   3 ch.f. Kris 135–Sextant 98 (Star Appeal 133) [1988 NR 1989 7g* 10.5f²] **117**
medium-sized, angular filly: keen, active type, takes a good hold: fourth foal:
half-sister to Italian middle-distance winner Brigadier Arrow (by Brigadier Gerard):
dam won twice at around 1¼m and is daughter of smart Fluke, herself half-sister to
Oaks winner Bireme and high-class Buoy: won slowly-run maiden at Newmarket in
April in good style by 2½ lengths from Kerita: evens, ½-length second of 6 to Snow
Bride in Tattersalls Musidora Stakes at York in May, seemingly just outstayed after
looking to be going best 2f out: afterwards found to have cracked pastern but
reportedly to remain in training in 1990. *Major W. R. Hern.*

PIMSBOY   2 b.g. (Apr 4) Tender King 123–Hitopah (Bustino 136) [1989 5m 7m*]   **71**
IR 8,000Y, 13,500 2-y-o: second foal: dam never ran: 12/1, won 9-runner maiden
auction race at Catterick in July by ¾ length: will stay at least 1m: may improve
further. *W. J. Haggas.*

PINCTADA   7 b.g. Mummy's Pet 125–Pinaka 69 (Pitcairn 126) [1988 7g³ 7g 7f⁴   **89**
7f² 7d* 8.5m³ 7g* 7d* 7d² 7.6s² 8m 7.3m⁴ 8g⁵ 7d⁵ 8s³ 7m 1989 7g* 8g 7d 7s 7g
7m⁴ 7g² 8.3m 7g⁶ 7.3m³ 7g 7g* 7m 7g] strong, compact gelding: carries plenty of
condition: poor mover: fair handicapper: successful in moderately-run contest at
Newcastle in March and in 16-runner event at York, beating Joveworth a head, in
October: better suited by 7f than 1m: well suited by an easy surface: usually held up:
excellent mount for inexperienced rider: tough. *R. Simpson.*

PINECONE PETER   2 ch.g. (Apr 16) Kings Lake (USA) 133–Cornish Heroine   —
(USA) 101 (Cornish Prince) [1989 8.2g] IR 25,000Y: third foal: half-brother to 3-y-o
Lomax (by Lomond), fairly useful 7f winner at 2 yrs: dam stayed 1½m: 20/1,
appeared to shape promisingly in 20-runner minor event at Nottingham in October:
sold to join W. Fairgrieve 4,800 gns Newmarket Autumn Sales. *Sir Mark Prescott.*

PINISI   4 ch.g. Final Straw 127–Bireme 127 (Grundy 137) [1988 NR 1989 12m⁵   —
12m⁵] strong gelding: good walker: fourth foal: half-brother to winning hurdler
Dhoni (by Bustino) and to 1989 2-y-o 7f winner Trireme (by Rainbow Quest): dam,
half-sister to high-class middle-distance stayer Buoy, won Oaks: beaten at least 13
lengths in minor event at Leicester and in slowly-run apprentice maiden (pulling

686

hard early and losing his place 7f out) at Newmarket: will be suited by 1¾m: sold to join G. Moore 18,000 gns Ascot August Sales. *Major W. R. Hern.*

PINKATAURIOUS 4 b.c. Starch Reduced 112–Mrs Dumbfounded (Adropejo 114) [1988 6f 5s 5.8d⁵ 1989 6d 8m] angular, workmanlike colt: shows knee action: poor maiden: blinkered, tailed off in selling handicap final outing: visored once at 3 yrs: sold 750 gns Ascot September Sales. *C. Holmes.* —

PINK GIN 2 ch.g. (Apr 11) Tickled Pink 114–Carrapateira (Gunner B 126) [1989 6s³ 7v] 1,100F, 7,800Y: good-topped gelding: first foal: dam unraced half-sister to very useful 6f and 7f winner Scarrowmanwick (by Tickled Pink): quite modest form first outing: tailed off second: should stay 7f. *Miss S. E. Hall.* 61

PINK HOPE (FR) 2 b.c. (Feb 4) Pink (FR) 123–Acclaimed 81 (Luthier 126) [1989 8g⁶] 1,500,000 francs (approx £137,200) Y: well-grown, angular colt: closely related to useful French 11f winner Kruguy (by Try My Best) and half-brother to French 1½m winner Money Can't Buy (by Thatching): dam 1¾m winner, is daughter to very smart 1¼m and 1½m winner Acoma, a half-sister to the high-class middle-distance stayer Ashmore: 6/1 but bit backward and green, soon well behind in 7-runner maiden at Yarmouth in September. *P. A. Kelleway.* —

PINK PUMPKIN 5 b.m. Tickled Pink 114–Wild Pumpkin (Auction Ring (USA) 123) [1988 5d⁵ 5g 6f 5g 5g 5d⁴ 5s 5g 1989 5s 5f² 5f* 5f⁴ 5m 5h 5m⁶ 5g 5m 5f⁵ 5m⁶ 5.3f 5m*] small, lightly-made mare: poor handicapper: won selling event (bought in 3,400 gns) at Chepstow in May and 18-runner contest (20/1, leading close home) at Warwick in October: best at 5f: acts on firm going and a soft surface: has sweated: ran badly in blinkers: apprentice ridden nowadays: often faces stiff task: inconsistent. *J. C. Fox.* 45

PINNACLE POINT 2 b.c. (Apr 5) Lochnager 132–Wollow Maid 73 (Wollow 132) [1989 5g 5m³ 6m⁴ 6m* 6h⁶ 7m⁶ 6m² 5f] angular colt: has a rather round action: second foal: dam, 1¼m winner, refused to race once: won 13-runner seller (retained 10,500 gns) at Ripon in June: good second in similar event at Goodwood in August: best form at 6f: blinkered last 2 starts: not particularly consistent. *J. Pearce.* 59

PINTAIL BAY 3 b.c. Buzzards Bay 128§–Pin Hole 83 (Parthia 132) [1988 8d 8g³ 1989 9f³] big, strong colt: has a round action: modest form: bit backward, creditable third in minor event at Wolverhampton in May, only start in 1989: will stay 1½m. *H. J. Collingridge.* —

PIPERS ENTERPRISE 5 b.g. Blue Cashmere 129–Erstung 83 (Shantung 132) [1988 7m 8m 1989 7f 10f⁶] angular, sparely-made gelding: poor mover: bad plater. *W. Holden.* —

PIPERS HILL 2 ch.c. (Apr 30) Creative Plan (USA)–Kindle (Firestreak 125) [1989 6m 8m⁶ 8m⁴ 10f³] small, sparely-made colt: half-brother to several winners, including 1984 2-y-o 5f winner Eagle Crest (by Crofter), later winner abroad: dam placed twice over 1½m in Ireland: quite modest maiden: best form in selling nursery at Leicester in October: evidentally suited by 1¼m. *K. O. Cunningham-Brown.* 60

PIPISTRELLE 2 b.f. (Mar 12) Shareef Dancer (USA) 135–Latin Melody 109 (Tudor Melody 129) [1989 8g] 48,000F, IR 24,000Y: smallish filly: half-sister to 4 winners, including fairly useful 7f and 1¼m winner Little Deep Water (by General Assembly) and useful stayer Van Dyke Brown (by Gay Mecene): dam best at sprint distances: soundly beaten in 15-runner maiden at Leicester in November. *Dr J. D. Scargill.* —

PIPITINA 2 b.f. (Mar 19) Bustino 136–Pipina (USA) 81 (Sir Gaylord) [1989 7g⁶] lengthy filly: fifth foal: closely related to very useful 1¼m and 1½m winner Pipsted (by Busted), also successful in Italy, and half-sister to useful 7f to 1m winner Night Out Perhaps (by Cure The Blues): dam, 10.5f winner, is half-sister to smart 5f performer Amaranda and 1000 Guineas runner-up Favoridge, and daughter of Irish 1000 Guineas winner Favoletta: 20/1, around 4 lengths sixth of 24, keeping on well hand ridden, to Katsina in maiden at Newmarket in November: will be well suited by 1¼m + : sure to improve. *G. Wragg.* 76 p

PIPPA'S DREAM 2 b.f. (Jan 22) Doulab (USA) 115–Chaldea (Tamerlane 128) [1989 5f* 7h⁴ 6g² 6f 6g⁴ 6g⁴] IR 19,000Y: workmanlike filly: moderate mover: half-sister to Kahaila (by Pitcairn), useful 1m winner who stayed 1½m: dam unraced: won 6-runner minor event at Chepstow in July: ran creditably in nurseries, one a claimer, afterwards: stays 7f. *P. F. I. Cole.* 77

PIQUANT 2 b. or br.g. (Mar 11) Sharpo 132–Asnoura (MOR) (Asandre (FR)) [1989 5s³ 5m* 6m⁵ 6m* 6m 6v³ 7d] medium-sized, stocky gelding: fifth foal: half-brother to 3-y-o Housework (by Homing), 8.5f winner at 2 yrs, and 2 winners here and abroad by Balidar, including 1½m winner Bracelet: dam Moroccan bred: 89

fair performer: won maiden at Hamilton in May and nursery (well-backed favourite) at Ayr in August: suited by 6f: acts on top-of-the-ground and heavy going: visored final start: subsequently gelded. *W. Hastings-Bass.*

PIRATE ARMY (USA) 3 br.c. Roberto (USA) 131–Wac (USA) (Lt **118** Stevens (USA)) [1988 7g* 1989 8s* 12f²]

Pirate Army was one of the more notable among the many victims of the exceptionally dry spring, summer and autumn. He became stumped up after the Calor Derby Trial, couldn't be prepared for the Derby and, in fact, wasn't seen out again. So far he has had only three races, but started odds on to beat Cacoethes at Lingfield and at the time was second favourite behind Nashwan for the Derby following impressive wins in a twenty-six-runner maiden at Newmarket at two and a five-runner graduation race at Sandown in April. Pirate Army won by twelve lengths from Flockton's Own over a mile on soft going at Sandown; more to the point, perhaps, he'd got so much on top of his only market rival Magical Strike in the straight that the latter's jockey felt obliged to accept the situation a furlong out and was fined for losing second. Cacoethes on firm going at Lingfield proved a different kettle of fish. Pirate Army, who looked keen and particularly well, quickened with the winner on the home turn though clearly travelling less smoothly (he looked ill at ease on the ground). He couldn't hold Cacoethes in the last two furlongs and went down by a flattering four lengths, giving a smart performance nonetheless which was disappointing only in that he'd been such a strong fancy for Epsom. The third horse Spitfire was well beaten off.

Pirate Army (USA) (b.c. 1986)	Roberto (USA) (b 1969)	Hail To Reason (br 1958)	Turn-To
			Nothirdchance
		Bramalea (b or br 1959)	Nashua
			Rarelea
	Wac (USA) (b 1969)	Lt Stevens (b 1961)	Nantallah
			Rough Shod
		Belthazar (br 1960)	War Admiral
			Blinking Owl

Given Pirate Army's lengthy absence, caution would seem the best advice if and when he returns to the track. Basically he's an inexperienced horse about whom comparatively little is known. He might be top-class, he might not. He clearly stays a mile and a half. Presumably the time of his return will be governed largely by the weather. A big, rather leggy colt, a good walker with a powerful, slightly round action in his faster paces, Pirate Army is a very well-bred individual, a brother to the good miler Lear Fan out of a winning sister to the dam of Alysheba. *L. M. Cumani.*

PIROUETTE 3 b.f. Sadler's Wells (USA) 132–True Rocket 116 (Roan Rocket **114** 128) [1988 7s² 1989 7s* 8m 6g⁴ 7d* 9s⁶] IR 180,000Y: closely related to Irish 1½m winner Strike Home (by Be My Guest) and half-sister to several winners, notably very smart sprinter Ballad Rock (by Bold Lad, IRE): dam very speedy 2-y-o: won listed EBF Athasi Stakes in April and another listed event (by 4 lengths from Careafolie) in September, both at the Curragh: ran moderately in Irish 1000 Guineas at the Curragh and valuable event at Laurel Park, USA, second and final outings: should stay 1m: goes well on a soft surface. *T. Stack, Ireland.*

PIT PONY 5 b.g. Hittite Glory 125–Watch Lady (Home Guard (USA) 129) [1988 — 13v⁴ 15s 1989 13v⁴] neat gelding: moderate mover: poor maiden: should stay beyond 1m: acts on top-of-the-ground and a soft surface: has been tried in blinkers and visor: winner over hurdles. *J. S. Wilson.*

PITSEA 3 b.c. Tina's Pet 121–Here's Sue 76 (Three Legs 128) [1988 5f⁴ 6d⁵ 6g **75** 5m² 5m³ 1989 5s⁵ 6m² 6f⁴ 6f* 7g 7g 6v 6g] tall, rather leggy colt: has a round action: modest handicapper: justified favouritism at Chepstow in May: well beaten facing stiff tasks last 2 outings: stays 6f: acts on firm going and a soft surface. *R. Hannon.*

PITY'S PET 4 b.f. Stanford 121§–Irish Kick (Windjammer (USA)) [1988 6g 6f³ **55** 6d³ 5f 6g 5.8f 1989 6f 5.8f² 7m 5m 6m] leggy, workmanlike filly: plating-class maiden: form as 4-y-o only on second outing: suited by 6f: yet to race on soft going, acts on any other: sweating and reluctant to post third outing: blinkered, taken down early and slowly away on fourth: somewhat temperamental. *O. O'Neill.*

Harvester Graduation Stakes, Sandown—Pirate Army enhances his glowing reputation

PLAIN FACT   4 b.g. Known Fact (USA) 135–Plain Tree 71 (Wolver Hollow 126)   **103**
[1988 7d² 7m⁵ 6m² 5.6m 5s* 5m³ 1989 5s 6f⁴ 5m⁴ 5f* 6f² 6f² 6m 6m 6m⁵ 5s³]
compact, workmanlike gelding: useful performer: won claimer at Sandown in May:
better effort on next outing when short-head second of 22 to Very Adjacent in
£52,400 William Hill Stewards' Cup at Goodwood: favourite, would have won with
clear run when third of 7 in minor event at Haydock in October: needs a stiff 5f and
probably stays 7f: acts on any going: sweating and reportedly injured off-fore sixth
start. *Sir Mark Prescott.*

PLANTERS POINT   2 b.c. (Apr 15) Ela-Mana-Mou 132–Chilblains 83 (Hotfoot   —
126) [1989 8.2g 8.2d] 54,000Y: lengthy colt, rather unfurnished: brother to bad
maiden Anhaar and half-brother to Irish 3-y-o 7f winner Chilly Rajah (by Indian
King), 6f winner at 2 yrs, and very speedy 1985 2-y-o Nashia (by Northern Guest):
dam, winner at 6f and 1m at 2 yrs, later won in Italy: well beaten in autumn maidens
at Haydock. *Lord John FitzGerald.*

PLATINUM DANCER   2 b.f. (Feb 1) Petorius 117–National Dress 64 (Welsh   **87**
Pageant 132) [1989 6g⁵ 7f² 6m* 7m] 11,000Y: workmanlike, good-quartered filly:
first foal: dam, 12.2f winner, is daughter of half-sister to Connaught: favourite, won
14-runner maiden at Salisbury in August by 6 lengths, leading 1f out: weakened 1½f
out when last of 7 in Black Bottle Scotch Whisky Prestige Stakes at Goodwood 2
weeks later: best form at 6f: sold 21,000 gns Newmarket Autumn Sales. *P. A.
Kelleway.*

PLATINUM DISC   2 b.g. (Feb 12) Song 132–Pennies To Pounds 80 (Ile de   **62**
Bourbon (USA) 133) [1989 5d 5g] 20,000Y: first foal: dam, 8.5f winner, is half-sister
to very useful 1978 2-y-o 5f winner Penny Blessing and daughter of sprinting
half-sister to Mummy's Pet, Arch Sculptor and Parsimony: showed up in second of 2
late-season outings in northern maiden events: subsequently gelded. *W. Hastings-
Bass.*

PLATINUM RANGER   2 b.g. (Mar 29) Comedy Star (USA) 121–Howzat (Habat   —
127) [1989 7s 9g] 17,000Y: third foal: half-brother to 3-y-o Benz Best (by Busted)

and quite modest maiden Boca Chimes (by Welsh Saint): dam once-raced daughter of Heaven Knows, Lingfield Oaks Trial winner better at shorter distances: in rear in maiden at Goodwood and claimer at York in the autumn: sold 2,100 gns Newmarket Autumn Sales. *G. A. Pritchard-Gordon.*

PLATONIQUE 2 b.f. (Mar 22) Dunbeath (USA) 127–Plato's Retreat 73 **97** (Brigadier Gerard 144) [1989 6m* 6m6 6d* 8g* 7g4 8m4] 5,400Y: leggy, workmanlike filly: has scope: third foal: half-sister to 3-y-o 1¾m winner Beekman Street (by Jalmood), 7.5f winner at 2 yrs, and 1987 2-y-o 5f winner Marentia (by Dominion), later successful in Italy: dam, 1½m winner, is sister to very useful French middle-distance winner Exact: progressive filly: successful in maiden auction race at Hamilton in May and nurseries at Haydock (despite poor run) and Doncaster (despite bit slipping through mouth at start) in September: beaten 1½ lengths in listed race at Ascot in October on final appearance: will stay beyond 1m. *Mrs J. R. Ramsden.*

PLATOON 2 gr.c. (Apr 11) Petong 126–Shelton Girl 64 (Mummy's Pet 125) [1989 **80** 6m 7g5 6f2 6v6] 35,000Y: leggy colt: easy mover: second reported living foal: half-brother to Italian 3-y-o My Frensis (by Good Times), successful 3 times at 3 yrs: dam lightly raced: fair maiden: stays 7f: acts on any going: sold 22,000 gns Newmarket Autumn Sales. *L. M. Cumani.*

PLAUSIBLE 4 b.c. Neltino 97–False Evidence 53 (Counsel 118) [1988 8d5 10m **67** 10m2 10s2 10m5 12s* 14m 10d3 1989 12d 12.3m2 11.7g4 14m 12m2 12m 12g6 12g* a12g] leggy colt: quite modest performer: won claimer at Leicester (claimed out of A. Hide's stable £9,350) in September, running on despite looking reluctant to lead close home: suited by 1½m: yet to race on firm going, acts on any other: blinkered or visored last 6 outings: suited by exaggerated waiting tactics: not an easy ride and not one to trust implicitly. *K. M. Brassey.*

PLAX 2 ch.c. (Apr 12) The Noble Player (USA) 126–Seapoint (Major Point) [1989 **69** 6m6 7f6 6d] 13,000Y: big, workmanlike colt: has scope: good walker: second reported living foal: half-brother to 3-y-o Follow The Sea (by Tumble Wind): dam Irish 7f and 1m winner: quite modest maiden: easily best effort second start: will stay 1m. *R. Akehurst.*

PLAYFUL POET 2 ch.g. (Apr 9) The Noble Player (USA) 126–Phamond 61 **71** (Pharly (FR) 130) [1989 5s 5d* 5s2 5d] IR 8,000Y: deep-girthed, strong-quartered gelding: moderate mover: first foal: dam, 6f winner, is daughter of Queen Mary winner Cramond: won maiden at Folkestone by 5 lengths: not raced after April. *K. M. Brassey.*

PLAYING WITH FIRE 3 ch.f. Mr Fluorocarbon 126–Cinderwench 95 **—** (Crooner 119) [1988 NR 1989 8d 7m 7f] smallish, workmanlike filly: keen walker: second foal: half-sister to 8.5f to 1½m winner Planet Ash (by Star Appeal): dam won from 1m to 1½m: no worthwhile form: 5/2 co-favourite from 50/1, never placed to challenge and not unduly knocked about when in mid-division in Chepstow maiden in July final outing: bred to stay 1m: may do better. *P. W. Harris.*

PLAY THE BLUES 2 gr.f. (Mar 4) Cure The Blues (USA)–Casual Pleasure **47** (USA) (What A Pleasure (USA)) [1989 6g 5d] IR 6,600Y: leggy, sparely-made filly: has a round action: first foal: dam unraced: poor form, backward, in maidens at Newbury in August and Haydock in September. *B. Hanbury.*

PLAY THE GAME 2 br.f. (Feb 4) Mummy's Game 120–Christine 102 (Crocket **70** 130) [1989 5f2 5f3 5g3 6g2 5f* 6m6 6f] small filly: half-sister to several winners here and abroad, including stayer Blues Player (by Jaazeiro) and Premio Parioli winner Svelt (by African Sky): dam won from 7f to 1¼m: modest performer: won 4-runner maiden at Ayr in July: probably stays 6f: unruly stalls, slowly away and looked temperamentally unsatisfactory penultimate outing: blinkered final one. *J. Berry.*

PLAYTHING 2 b.f. (Mar 16) High Top 131–Round Dance 73 (Auction Ring (USA) **61** p 123) [1989 7g5] 6,200Y: fourth foal: half-sister to a winner in Italy by Shirley Heights: dam 7f winner: 25/1, around 4 lengths fifth of 20, going on well, to Oh So Risky in maiden auction race at Goodwood in October: should improve. *A. C. Stewart.*

PLAZA GIZON (USA) 4 ch.g. Little Current (USA)–Regal Endeavour (USA) **—** (Roberto (USA) 131) [1988 11g* 10d3 12g2 12m3 13s* 12d3 12v 1989 16.2m 9g] ex-French gelding: second foal: half-brother to very useful French 1985 2-y-o 7f winner Rayonnante (by Tilt Up), later successful over 1m, and to Irish 3-y-o 1¼m winner Arctic Terrain (by Arctic Tern): dam, half-sister to high-class middle-distance stayer Esprit du Nord and Irish Oaks winner Regal Exception, won 5 times at around 1¼m in France: won maiden in French Provinces and amateurs event at

Maisons-Laffitte as 3-y-o: sweating and backward, soundly beaten in minor event at Haydock (bandaged) in May and listed race at Newmarket in October: stays 13f: acts on soft going: winning hurdler. *J. R. Jenkins.*

PLEA INNOCENCE (USA) 3 b.f. Alleged (USA) 138–Lovelight 112 (Bleep-Bleep 134) [1988 NR 1989 7g 7f⁶] compact, workmanlike filly: has a quick action: half-sister to very useful 1m and 9f winner Literati (by Nureyev) and several other winners, including very smart 6f to 1m winner Motavato (by Apalachee), later successful in USA: dam very game sprinter: shaped well when about 7 lengths eighth of 13 in maiden at Newmarket: co-second favourite but sweating, failed to confirm that promise in similar event at York in May: possibly unsuited by firm going. *B. W. Hills.*   —

PLEASE BELIEVE ME 2 b.f. (Mar 26) Try My Best (USA) 130–Believer 112 (Blakeney 126) [1989 5f* 5f* 5f² 6g⁶ 6m⁴] 39,000Y: well-grown, useful-looking filly: has plenty of scope: good walker: third foal: closely related to 3-y-o Bonnie Bonnie (by Lomond): dam won Princess Royal Stakes: fairly useful performer: successful early-season in maiden at York and quite valuable event at Beverley: ran well afterwards in Queen Mary Stakes at Royal Ascot and creditably in Hillsdown Cherry Hinton Stakes at Newmarket and 'The Pacemaker Update' Lowther Stakes (blinkered, and tended to hang) at York: should stay beyond 6f: tends to get on toes. *M. H. Easterby.*   **93**

PLEASURE AHEAD 2 b.c. (Apr 12) Taufan (USA) 119–Nan's Mill (Milford 119) [1989 5s 5d⁵ 5.3m² 5m² 6m⁶ 5m³ 6f 6g] 5,400Y: leggy, close-coupled colt: poor mover: first foal: dam seemingly of little account: quite modest maiden: form only at 5f on top-of-the-ground. *M. J. Haynes.*   **63**

PLEASURE DANCER 4 b.g. Monsanto (FR) 121–Moment's Pleasure (USA) 72 (What A Pleasure (USA)) [1988 10s² 10d² 10m 12m⁴ 10f 10.1m⁵ 11.7d 10d³ 10s 1989 10.8s 10f] leggy, close-coupled gelding: quite modest maiden at his best: 25/1, sweating and on toes, tailed off in handicap at Nottingham in August, second outing and first for over 4 months: probably stays 1½m: unsuited by firm going, acts on any other. *Miss A. J. Whitfield.*   —

PLEASURE FLIGHT 2 b.f. (Mar 2) Jalmood (USA) 126–Third Movement 75 (Music Boy 124) [1989 5m³] angular, sparely-made filly: second foal: half-sister to 1988 2-y-o Shine Again (by Longleat): dam, inconsistent maiden, stayed 7f: 7/1 and bit backward, 5 lengths third of 6, ridden along 2f out and unable to quicken, to Royal Fi Fi in maiden at Pontefract in August: went freely down: will be suited by 6f+: should improve. *W. J. Haggas.*   **52 p**

PLIE 2 ch.f. (Feb 17) Superlative 118–La Pirouette (USA) 73 (Kennedy Road (CAN)) [1989 5f² 5.8f* 6g⁴ 5m⁶ 6m] good-quartered, sprint type: third foal: half-sister to poor 1987 2-y-o Twirl (by Music Boy), later successful in Germany: dam 7f winner: won 7-runner minor event at Bath in August: ran moderately in nurseries: better suited by 6f than 5f. *D. W. P. Arbuthnot.*   **75**

POCKETED (USA) 3 b.c. Full Pocket (USA)–Duchess of Malfi (USA) (Prince John) [1988 NR 1989 7g 7s 10m⁴ 8g⁴ 7m 7m⁶ 8m³ 10f⁶] $15,000Y, resold 20,000Y: leggy, rather angular colt: half-brother to several winners, including useful jumpers in France and America: dam, winner over 9f, is sister to dam of Alleged: sire smart winner at up to 1¼m: plating-class maiden: best effort in claimers third and penultimate outings, in latter claimed out of Mrs L. Piggott's stable £7,056: stays 1¼m: possibly unsuited by extremes of going: sweating third and fourth starts: winning novice hurdler. *J. R. Jenkins.*   **55**

PODRA 2 b.f. (May 18) Sharpo 132–Dragonist 82 (Dragonara Palace (USA) 115) [1989 5m⁵ 5m⁵ 5g 5g 5v] leggy, close-coupled filly: moderate mover: fourth foal: sister to useful sprinter Come On Chase Me and half-sister to 1¾m winner Arsonist (by Ardross) and 3-y-o 1¼m and 1½m winner Dragons Lair (by Homing): dam winning sprinter: plating-class maiden: ducked badly right home bend at Chester on second outing: ran in seller final appearance: sold 1,600 gns Doncaster November Sales. *M. J. Camacho.*   **52**

PODRIDA 3 gr.f. Persepolis (FR) 127–Pot Pourri 97 (Busted 134) [1988 7g 1989 12g⁵ 14m⁵ 13.8f* 14.8m* 14g³] good-bodied filly: carries condition: showed improved form when winning handicaps at Catterick and Newmarket (sweating badly) in July: good third in similar event at Haydock, losing position over 3f out then running on well again inside last: lacks turn of foot, and will be extemely well suited by 2m+. *W. Jarvis.*   **81**

POINTE OF LAW (FR) 2 b.f. (Feb 17) Law Society (USA) 130–Ninoushka (USA) (Nijinsky (CAN) 138) [1989 6m⁵ 6m³ 8f³ 9g] 14,500Y: tall filly: moderate   **62**

walker and mover: first reported living foal: dam, who showed a little ability in France, from family of Exceller and champion American 1986 2-y-o Capote: quite modest maiden: should stay 1¼m. *P. A. Kelleway.*

POINT HOUSE 4 ch.c. Diesis 133–Beautiful Dawn (USA) (Grey Dawn II 132) **107** [1988 7g* 7g² 1989 8g² 8m⁵ 8g² 8m² 7m⁶ 7g³ 7d] big, strong, good-bodied colt: has a quick action: won maiden at Newmarket early as 3-y-o: reportedly fractured a pastern after next outing: runner-up in 1989 minor events at Newbury (twice) and Kempton: well below his best last 2 outings: stays 1m: possibly unsuited by soft surface: blinkered final start: takes keen hold: sold 21,000 gns Newmarket December Sales. *P. T. Walwyn.*

POINT OF LIGHT 4 ch.c. Aragon 118–Starry Way (Star Appeal 133) [1988 6d⁵ **117** 6g* 6m⁶ 6f³ 6s 6g* 6.5m³ 6m* 6g² 5m 7d 1989 6g⁶ 6g* 6f⁴ 6f⁶ 6d⁴ 6m⁵ 6g* 6m 5g⁴ 6s³] good-topped colt: has a quick action: smart performer: won listed Abernant Stakes at Newmarket in April going away by 1½ lengths from Sharp Reminder and Group 3 Keeneland EBF Phoenix Sprint Stakes in August by neck from Corwyn Bay: nearest at finish in Carroll Foundation July Cup at Newmarket and Ciga Prix de l'Abbaye de Longchamp on sixth and ninth outings: 1¾ lengths third to Cricket Ball in Laurel Dash 2 weeks later: finds 5f on short side and stays 6f: acts on any going: wears visor or blinkers: usually held up and suited by strong gallop: sold privately to race in Saudi Arabia. *G. Lewis.*

POINT TAKEN (USA) 2 b.c. (Mar 28) Sharpen Up 127–Furry Friend (USA) **76** (Bold Bidder) [1989 7m 6g 6g²] well-made, attractive colt: first foal: dam thrice-raced daughter of Funny Cat, smart winner at up to 9f: co-favourite, always-prominent second of 18, beaten 3 lengths, to Peterhouse in maiden at Redcar in November: should stay 1m. *L. M. Cumani.*

POKEREE 6 gr.g. Uncle Pokey 116–Border Squaw 84 (Warpath 113) [1988 15f² **30** 15g⁶ 1989 21.6d 12m³ 15s⁴ 13s 16g⁶] big, lengthy gelding: moderate mover: bad maiden: seems to stay 15f, but not extreme distances: visored first 2 and final starts: has looked none too keen under pressure: winning hurdler. *D. Moffatt.*

POKE THE FIRE 2 ch.c. (May 25) Never So Bold 135–Home Fire 99 **88** (Firestreak 125) [1989 6f³ 6f⁶ 5f* 6f⁴ 6d 6g⁴ 5m] smallish, robust colt: good walker: has a quick action: half-brother to several winners, including 3-y-o Spitfire (by Shirley Heights), useful winner at 7f (at 2 yrs) and 1¼m, and fair middle-distance stayer By The Fireside (by Ardross): dam sprinter: fairly useful on his day: wide-margin winner of 3-runner maiden at Sandown in July: fourth of 5 to Contract Law in Scottish Equitable Richmond Stakes at Goodwood later in month, best subsequent effort: ran poorly in blinkers final outing: will stay 7f: tends to sweat. *C. R. Nelson.*

POKEY'S PRIDE 6 b.g. Uncle Pokey 116–Strawberry Ice (Arctic Storm 134) **79** [1988 12f⁴ 14d⁴ 12m 13.3f 14m 14f⁵ 1989 12d² 18.4m 14m⁵ 12h* 12f³ 12m³ 12f* 12m⁶ 14f 14m³ 13s³ 12m⁶ 14g* 12g⁴ 12d] leggy, quite attractive gelding: moderate mover: fair handicapper: had fine season, winning at Carlisle in May, Goodwood in July and York in October: tailed-off last of 19 in William Hill November Handicap at Thirsk: effective at 1½m and stays 2m: acts on any going: ideally suited by strong handling: usually held up: consistent. *M. H. Tompkins.*

POLAR BIRD 2 b.f. (Feb 10) Thatching 131–Arctic Winter (CAN) (Briartic **95** (CAN)) [1989 5m* 5f* 5g* 6g* 7.3v] strong, attractive filly: has a quick action: first foal: dam unraced sister to very smart Son of Briartic, successful in 1¼m Queen's Plate: fairly useful performer: won listed race at Newbury in August by a short head from Pettilante and Group 3 event at Phoenix Park later in month by a length from Remthat Naser: earlier successful in maiden at Newbury and nursery at Warwick: well beaten in listed race at Newbury in October: should stay 7f: evidently unsuited by heavy ground. *B. W. Hills.*

POLAR BOY (USA) 3 ch.c. Northern Baby (CAN) 127–Padelia (Thatching 131) **103** [1988 7s⁶ 1989 8f* 10g² 8f* 8m*] workmanlike colt: has a long, rather round stride: progressed into a useful performer: made all or virtually all when successful in maiden at Pontefract, Britannia Stakes (Handicap) at Royal Ascot and Foodbrokers Trophy (limited handicap) at Newmarket in the summer: probably stays 1¼m, though best form over 1m: acts on firm going: sold to join Richard Mandella in USA. *H. R. A. Cecil.*

POLAR LICHEN 2 b.f. (Apr 25) Lichine (USA) 117–Polaregina (FR) (Rex **—** Magna (FR) 129) [1989 7d] 7,400F, 34,000Y: third foal: sister to minor French 11f winner In Conclusion and half-sister to French 3-y-o miler Morgause (by Mendez): dam unraced daughter of Sly Pola, from family of Green Dancer and Ercolano: 14/1, always behind in 11-runner minor event at Thirsk in November. *B. W. Hills.*

Prix Eclipse, Saint-Cloud—Pole Position has plenty to spare

POLAR REGION   3 br.c. Alzao (USA) 117–Bonny Hollow (Wolver Hollow 126)   —
[1988 6d³ 6d* 7f⁵ 7g³ 7f 8f 8s 8v 1989 8d 10d] leggy, workmanlike colt: won maiden
in June as 2-y-o: little form after: should stay 1m. *S. J. Muldoon.*

POLAR RUN (USA)   3 b.c. Arctic Tern (USA) 126–Melodina 118 (Tudor Melody **108**
129) [1988 7g* 7m² 8g⁴ 1989 12s² 12f² 12g 16f³ 12f²] good-topped, quite attractive
colt: useful performer: placed, running creditably, in Queen's Vase at Royal Ascot
(staying on well from towards rear) and £10,800 event at Chepstow in July on last 2
starts: lacks turn of foot: will prove suited by further than 1½m and stays 2m: best
form on top-of-the-ground: sometimes takes keen hold early. *G. Harwood.*

POLAR VISION   3 b.g. Lyphard's Special (USA) 122–Arctic Drama (Northern   **76**
Baby (CAN) 127) [1988 NR 1989 9g 10f 11m³ 10m³ 12g 12d² 10m⁴ 12m] IR 55,000Y:
leggy, useful-looking gelding: first foal: dam never ran: modest maiden: stays 1½m:
acts on top-of-the-ground and a soft surface: blinkered last 2 outings, running well
first of them and moderately on second: sold 15,500 gns Newmarket Autumn Sales.
C. E. Brittain.

POLEMOS   5 ch.h. Formidable (USA) 125–Polemia (USA) (Roi Dagobert 128)   **94**
[1988 12m² 14d 16m 12g 12m 12s⁵ 1989 12s 14f⁶ 12m⁶ 10m²] angular, medium-sized
horse: good mover: fair performer: stays 1½m: acts on any going: blinkered once:
bandaged second outing: usually acts as pacemaker. *H. Thomson Jones.*

POLE POSITION   2 b.c. (Jan 29) Sharpo 132–Putupon 89 (Mummy's Pet 125) **118**
[1989 5g* 7.5g³ 6.5s*] 100,000Y: first foal: dam, 2-y-o 5f winner, is sister to
high-class 1983 2-y-o sprinter Precocious and half-sister to some smart winners,
including middle-distance stayer Jupiter Island: successful in minor event at Vichy
in August and Prix Eclipse (by 5 lengths from Dictator's Song) at Saint-Cloud in
November: best form at sprint distances: smart. *A. Fabre, France.*

POLISH PRECEDENT (USA)   3 b.c. Danzig (USA)–Past Example **131**
(USA) (Buckpasser) [1988 8m 1989 7d* 7m* 7m* 8d* 8g* 8g* 8g* 8m²]
  The irresistible force met the immovable object in the showpiece of the
Festival of British Racing at Ascot in September, the Queen Elizabeth II
Stakes, an event of significance well beyond these shores since it decided the
European milers' championship. Something had to give, and that turned out to
be Polish Precedent. No excuses. Looking tremendously well beforehand, he
had every chance in a race run to suit him, but try as he might he couldn't
quite get to Zilzal in the straight after tracking him, and was held in the
final furlong. Three lengths was probably a fair reflection of the difference
between them, though Asmussen spared the runner-up when defeat became
inevitable.

Prix Messidor, Maisons-Laffitte — Polish Precedent wins comfortably
but has to survive an objection on behalf of third-placed Dom Valory (No. 3);
Sweet Chesne finishes second

Polish Precedent came to Ascot as best French miler. In the course of putting together seven successive victories as a three-year-old he'd beaten most of those competing to fill the yawning gap left by the retirement of Miesque and Soviet Star—stable-companion Golden Opinion a notable exception. At the start of the season little more was known about him than was known about Zilzal. He'd had an outing as a two-year-old in a maiden race at Maisons-Laffitte in the autumn, but had been prevented by injury from doing himself justice and had finished unplaced behind lesser-fancied Dancehall. The very powerful Fabre stable was represented in the Dubai Poule d'Essai des Poulains by Ocean Falls and went unrepresented in the General Accident Two Thousand Guineas, while Polish Precedent was returned to action in another maiden at Maisons-Laffitte in April. He made his first Group 1 appearance in the Prix du Haras de Fresnay-le-Buffard Jacques le Marois at Deauville in August, five outings later, preferred to the good

Prix du Haras de Fresnay-le-Buffard Jacques le Marois, Deauville —
Polish Precedent surges clear of French Stress and Magic Gleam

four-year-old French Stress by Asmussen. In between Polish Precedent had
been looking, as they say nowadays, 'Group-1 material', particularly in the
second of his two races at Longchamp in May, the Prix du Palais Royal; in his
next, the Prix de la Jonchere at Chantilly in June on his return to a mile after a
spell over seven furlongs, and in the Prix Messidor at Maisons-Laffitte in July;
all contested by fields of single figures. Not only did Polish Precedent have a
commanding physical presence, he was beginning to dominate the opposition
on the track, impressing with the way he could quicken inside the distance.
Some of his form was high class: in the Jonchere he gave Citidancer 3 lb and a
two-and-a-half-length beating, while in the Messidor he met second and third,
Sweet Chesne and Dom Valory, on terms 11 lb worse than weight for age.
There was a close finish to the Messidor but Polish Precedent won
comfortably, afterwards surviving an objection for interference from the
third's jockey.

The Prix Jacques le Marois is usually France's most important mile race;
whenever it's not, it comes second to the Prix du Moulin de Longchamp. The
latest field for the race seemed almost as strong as that for the Sussex Stakes
won by Zilzal, though not so strong as in 1988 when Miesque beat Warning,
Gabina and Soviet Star, and it had an open look with perhaps only Hibouni and
Tersa out of place on form. Gabina took her chance again, one of five older
horses, along with Hibouni, Squill, French Stress and Most Welcome,
opposing the three-year-olds Polish Precedent, Musical Bliss, Magic Gleam,
Navratilovna and Tersa. No horse impressed more in the paddock all season
than Polish Precedent at Deauville (though another by Danzig, Magic Gleam,
came close in this very race), and he went out to win in most emphatic style by
two lengths from his stable-companion French Stress. They made their
challenge, pushed along, to the front-running Magic Gleam on either side of
the filly over two furlongs out, having tracked her easily in a moderately-
paced race. French Stress possibly got past her first, but he had no answer to
Polish Precedent who struck the front around a furlong out and, despite
hanging right, surged clear under no pressure. The tiring Magic Gleam, two
lengths further back, just held on to third place from Gabina and Navratilovna
both of whom had been set stiff tasks by being waited with.

Despite the authority of Polish Precedent's victory he had no shortage of
opponents in the Moulin three weeks later. Nine were turned out against him
and his pacemaker Nursery Slope, and they made up a field of similar quality
to the Marois. Polish Precedent started at 5/2 on. It was difficult to see how
French Stress, Navratilovna, Squill or Sweet Chesne could turn the tables;
and of the British challengers Cadeaux Genereux would need to be every bit
as good over the longer trip to have a chance of winning while Green Line
Express would almost certainly need to improve on his three-length second to
Zilzal at Goodwood. Squill did best in the end, covering the winner's every
move until quite unable to match his finishing speed. Polish Precedent was
handled very confidently, positioned in mid-field so that he could strike at the

Prix du Moulin de Longchamp—the winning run continues; Cadeaux Genereux (rails),
Green Line Express and Squill (No. 3) dispute the minor placings ahead of French Stress

Sheikh Mohammed's "Polish Precedent"

leaders whenever the jockey chose. The time for that came inside the final two furlongs where, given backhanders, he quickened into the lead on the outside past Good Example, who'd deprived Nursery Slope of the pacemaking role, and Green Line Express, with Cadeaux Genereux on the rails appearing the biggest threat. But there was no threat to Polish Precedent in the last furlong. He won by two lengths again and in winning was, if anything, even more impressive than at Deauville, setting up the meeting with Zilzal in which, on foreign soil, he started at 11/8 against the home runner's even money. French Stress, incidentally, was slightly hampered a third of the way up the straight in the Moulin before staying on for fifth behind Cadeaux Genereux and Green Line Express. Both Polish Precedent and Golden Opinion were announced as probables for the Breeders' Cup at around this time. However, the filly couldn't go because of injury and Polish Precedent didn't go once Zilzal had beaten him. Polish Precedent has been retired to the Dalham Hall Stud in Newmarket, valued at over £7 million by the terms of his syndication.

Polish Precedent (USA) (b.c. 1986)	Danzig (USA) (b 1977)	Northern Dancer (b 1961)	Nearctic
			Natalma
		Pas de Nom (b or br 1968)	Admiral's Voyage
			Petitioner
	Past Example (USA) (ch 1976)	Buckpasser (b 1963)	Tom Fool
			Busanda
		Bold Example (b 1969)	Bold Lad
			Lady Be Good

No horse is guaranteed to make a successful stallion but with his looks, racing record and pedigree Polish Precedent is nearer a certainty than most.

Good horses are generally good looking, sprinter/milers the more so. Nearly all Danzig's leading progeny seen in Europe have come into that category on both counts, witness the likes of Danehill, Magical Strike and Shaadi, as well as Magic Gleam in the latest season. But Polish Precedent is an exceptional individual even for a Danzig. His racecourse performances were in keeping. His pedigree on the female side brings him close to Zilzal, for his unraced dam is a half-sister to the Del Mar Oaks winner French Charmer, dam of Zilzal as well as the very useful Irish filly Charmante. The stakes-placed Bold Example also produced the stakes-winning Highest Regard (dam of the good American three-year-old Awe Inspiring), and the next dam, Lady Be Good, is the grandam of Posse. Though unraced, Past Example reached six years of age before she produced her first foal, a filly by Gallant Romeo who cost 175,000 dollars as a yearling but, like her, never raced. The second foal, a filly by Danzig, never raced either, but two years later came Jasmina (by Forli), a stakes winner at just over a mile who trained on well.

We almost forgot! Polish Precedent is a big, lengthy individual; and handsome wouldn't be taking things too far. He has that quick, rather short action usually associated with top-of-the-ground horses, but while he undoubtedly acted well in those conditions he also ran well on an easy surface. He was a top-class miler and, like almost all the rest of the stable, a credit to his outstanding trainer. *A. Fabre, France.*

POLISH PRINCESS (USA) 3 b.f. Danzig (USA)–Maria Waleska (Filiberto (USA) 123) [1988 NR 1989 9g³ 7g²] $350,000Y: workmanlike, rather sparely-made filly: fifth foal: half-sister to 2 winners: dam won Italian Oaks and Gran Premio d'Italia: modest form in late-season maiden at York and minor event (bandaged off-fore) at Leicester. *L. M. Cumani.* 75

POLISTATIC 2 br.f. (May 24) Free State 125–Polyandrist 92 (Polic 126) [1989 6m 6f4] smallish filly: sister to very useful 11f and 1½m winner Mango Express and Tote Ebor winner Western Dancer, and half-sister to several winners, including very useful 5f performer Trigamy (by Tribal Chief): poor form in modest company at Newmarket (slowly away) in August and Brighton in October. *R. W. Stubbs.* 42

POLLY MULDOWNEY 2 ch.f. (May 5) Precocious 126–Follow The Stars 86 (Sparkler 130) [1989 6g] 14,000Y: second foal: half-sister to poor 3-y-o Kowza (by Young Generation): dam, 8.5f and 1¼m winner, is half-sister to smart sprinter Florestan and very useful French 9f to 1¼m winner Schoeller: slowly away and never dangerous in 29-runner maiden at Newmarket in November: has scope, and looks sort to do better. *D. R. C. Elsworth.* — p

POLONEZ PRIMA 2 ch.c. (Jan 27) Thatching 131–Taiga 69 (Northfields (USA)) [1989 6g] IR 10,500Y: first foal: dam 1¼m winner: well beaten in maiden at Newmarket in August. *G. A. Huffer.* —

POLYKRATIS 7 b.h. He Loves Me 120–Blue Persian 112 (Majority Blue 126) [1988 6d4 5v² 5m4 5d6 5m 5m³ 5g 6g 6g 6s 5g 5d 5s² 5m 1989 6v 5s 6f 6f³ 6m³ 6m5 6f 6m* 6m³ 6h4 6g 6g a6g6] rather leggy horse: good mover with a slightly round action: generally disappointing since 1986, and won for only time since in strongly-run handicap at Pontefract in July: best at sprint distances: acts on any going: usually finds little under pressure and tends to get behind: not to be trusted. *M. E. D. Francis.* 92 §

POLYNIXOS 3 b.g. Raga Navarro (ITY) 119–Whistler's Princess (King Emperor (USA)) [1988 7m 1989 7.5d 7g 8m 8f] leggy gelding: sign of ability only in seller (edgy) second start: moved poorly down and ran as if something amiss on final one, in July. *R. Thompson.* —

POLYROLL 3 b.c. Kampala 120–Hail To Feathers (USA) (Hail To All) [1988 5s³ 5g³ 6f 8m 7m 7s* 1989 8d* 8s³ 7s² 8.5m³ 9m 7.3m 7g5 8m] big, lengthy colt: moderate mover: fairly useful handicapper: won at Kempton in March by 10 lengths: placed at Newbury and Epsom (twice): best up to 8.5f: acts on top-of-the-ground and soft going: ridden up with pace: apprentice ridden as 3-y-o, except for fourth start. *Miss B. Sanders.* 95

POMATUM 4 b.g. General Assembly (USA)–Pomade 79 (Luthier 126) [1988 12f5 12g² 14m³ 16m² 1989 14s] close-coupled, workmanlike gelding: moderate mover: modest maiden at best: virtually pulled up in handicap in April: stays 2m: winning hurdler. *J. R. Bosley.* —

POMERANIA (USA) 2 b.f. (Jan 14) Danzig (USA)–Smuggly (USA) 121 (Caro — p
133) [1989 6g] strong, useful-looking filly: has a round action: second foal: closely
related to 3-y-o Bashkirov (by Northern Dancer): dam won Prix Saint-Alary and
from excellent family: 12/1 and very in need of race, slowly away and beaten soon
after halfway in 22-runner maiden at Leicester in November: looks sort to do better.
J. Gosden.

POMME D'AMOUR 2 gr.f. (Feb 11) Niniski (USA) 125–Amourette (Crowned 58
Prince (USA) 128) [1989 6m⁴ 7f⁴ 7m 6g] lengthy filly: fifth reported foal: sister to
Jasujiro, successful in Italy, and half-sister to Italian 3-y-o 1m winner Sawadee (by
Looking For), 5f winner at 2 yrs: dam never ran: plating-class maiden: bred to be
suited by further than 7f: withdrawn after refusing to be mounted on intended
debut: visored and ridden by lad in paddock final outing.*J. H. M. Gosden.*

POMPUSE LORD 3 ch.g. Posse (USA) 130–Laxay 69 (Laxton 105) [1988 NR —
1989 7m a8g] compact gelding: first foal: dam won 7f seller: 33/1, about 6 lengths
eighth of 12, never dangerous, in maiden at Southwell in November: slowly away on
debut. *M. R. Leach.*

PONIARD 4 b.g. Kris 135–Labista 116 (Crowned Prince (USA) 128) [1988 8g 7g 66
8g 8d⁴ 8g⁴ 8g⁴ 8g* 1989 10.2g 8f² 8f³ 7f 7f⁴ 8m⁴ 8m³ 6m] tall gelding, rather
sparely-made: quite modest handicapper: placed in apprentice contests at Sandown
(edgy) and Kempton in May and in amateurs event at Redcar in September: finds
easy 7f on sharp side, but not certain to stay beyond 1m: acts on firm going and a soft
surface: often wears crossed noseband nowadays: tends to hang: swerved leaving
stalls fourth outing: sold 10,000 gns Newmarket Autumn Sales. *G. Harwood.*

PONT-AVEN 2 b.f. (Mar 16) Try My Best (USA) 130–Basilea (FR) (Frere Basile 113
(FR) 129) [1989 6d³ 5d* 5g³ 5g²] second foal: half-sister to French 3-y-o 1¼m
winner Bigouden (by What A Guest), 1m winner at 2 yrs: dam, seemingly suited by
1½m in France, is half-sister to smart French sprinter Bold Apparel and daughter of
very useful Canadian 2-y-o Gay Apparel: progressive filly: won listed race at
Deauville in August by 5 lengths: beaten a nose by Lugana Beach in Prix du
Petit-Couvert at Longchamp in October: best form at 5f: very useful. *R. Collet,
France.*

PONTENUOVO 4 b.g. Kafu 120–Black Gnat (Typhoon 125) [1988 8g³ 7g² 7g³ —
6m⁵ 1989 a8g a7g] rangy gelding: fair maiden at best: never dangerous in December
handicaps at Lingfield: stays 1m: bandaged on reappearance, first outing for about 18
months, and also next time. *D. R. C. Elsworth.*

PONTEVECCHIO BELLA 3 ch.f. Main Reef 126–Linguist 90 (Mossborough 56
126) [1988 6m 6g 8g⁴ 1989 10s² 11f 11.7m 12g 12g] close-coupled filly: has a round
action: second in handicap at Folkestone in April: ran moderately in similar events
after: should stay beyond 1¼m: probably needs some give in the ground: has joined
R. Juckes. *G. A. Pritchard-Gordon.*

PONTEVECCHIO NOTTE 4 b.c. Blakeney 126–Oula-Ka Fu-Fu 67 (Run The 96
Gantlet (USA)) [1988 10f³ 12f 12g⁵ 12m 9d² 10m² 9g 1989 10g² 10.2g⁵ 12f* 12f⁵]
quite attractive colt: good walker and mover: fairly useful handicapper: won at
Goodwood in good style by length from Lady Rosanna: favourite, good fifth of 17 to
Stratford Ponds in Bessborough Stakes (Handicap) at Royal Ascot month later, after
poor run from rear: stays 1½m well: acts on firm going and a soft surface: sold to join
W. G. Turner 5,600 gns Ascot September Sales. *G. A. Pritchard-Gordon.*

POOKA 3 b.f. Dominion 123–Land of Song 82 (Sing Sing 134) [1988 5g⁴ 5g⁶ 5m² —
5g³ 5m² 5f 5m 5g 1989 5m 5f 5m] smallish, workmanlike filly: moderate walker:
quite modest at best but has run poorly since fifth outing as 2-y-o: should prove best
at 5f: possibly unsuited by very firm ground: suitable mount for apprentice:
blinkered on reappearance: bandaged and very edgy final start: sold 2,600 gns Ascot
October Sales.*J. Wharton.*

POPPETS PET 2 b.g. (May 4) Native Bazaar 122–Imperial Miss 75 (Philip of 37
Spain 126) [1989 6m 7m 7f 6f] unfurnished gelding: brother to 3 platers, one a
winner: dam 2-y-o 5f winner: poor plater: blinkered last 2 starts. *P. F. I. Cole.*

POP PICKER 8 ch.g. Record Token 128–La Brigitte 87 (Gulf Pearl 117) [1988 —
NR 1989 8s⁵ 18s] well-made gelding: first race on flat since 1984 when well-beaten
fifth of 23 in handicap at Warwick in March: always behind in similar event at
Nottingham over month later. *G. Price.*

POPPY CHARM 2 b.f. (Apr 8) Star Appeal 133–Pop Music (FR) (Val de Loir 133) 63
[1989 6g* 7m² 7m⁶ 8s² 8m 8g] sparely-made, unfurnished filly: half-sister to 2
winners abroad by Crowned Prince: dam unraced daughter of smart 2-y-o Runnello:
quite modest performer: won seller (bought in 5,500 gns) at Leicester in August:

Windfields Farm EBF Gallinule Stakes, the Curragh—Porter Rhodes improves again

good second in nursery at Ayr almost 2 months later: will probably stay 1¼m: best form on soft ground. *M. H. Tompkins.*

PORTER RHODES (USA) 3 b.c. Hawaii–Stella Matutina (FR) 103 (Bolkonski **115** 134) [1988 NR 1989 8g² 8m* 10m*] $42,000Y: strong, good-bodied colt: has a quick action: fourth foal: half-brother to 2 minor winners in North America: dam, winner from 5f to 7f at 2 yrs, is daughter of half-sister to high-class stayer Samos III: won Newmarket maiden in tremendous style: again odds on, won Group 2 Windfields Farm EBF Gallinule Stakes at the Curragh later in May by 1½ lengths from Phantom Breeze (gave 3 lb), leading over 1f out and hanging left: stays 1¼m: remains in training. *H. R. A. Cecil.*

PORTFIELD LADY 4 b.f. Sayyaf 121–Cambrian Angel (Welsh Saint 126) [1988 **30** 5.8g 5f 5.3f 5m⁵ 6h⁴ 7f 6g 1989 6d 5f 5f 5m 5f] leggy, sparely-made filly: has a round action: poor sprint maiden: acts on hard going: ran poorly in blinkers: sold 800 gns Newmarket Autumn Sales. *W. Carter.*

PORTOFINO 3 ch.g. Coquelin (USA) 121–Decoy Duck 67 (Decoy Boy 129) [1988 **—** NR 1989 8m 8m 9m 8v 12g] 14,500Y: rangy, useful-looking gelding: second foal: half-brother to poor maiden Whistling Gemma (by Ahonoora): dam 2-y-o 6f winner, only season to race: quite modest maiden at best: should stay 1½m: on toes when running poorly on heavy going: gelded after final start. *P. J. Makin.*

PORTO HELI 2 b.c. (May 18) Precocious 126–Coral Heights 86 (Shirley Heights **69** p 130) [1989 7m³] 50,000Y: second foal: half-brother to 3-y-o Supreme Heights (by Valiyar): dam, granddaughter of sister to Sir Gaylord, suited by a test of stamina: 14/1, over length third of 17, leading 2f out until close home, to Mull House in maiden at Chepstow in October: will stay further: sure to improve. *C. E. Brittain.*

PORT SODERICK (USA) 2 b.c. (Feb 14) Affirmed (USA)–Queen of Cornwall **58** p (USA) 109 (Cornish Prince) [1989 6m] lengthy colt: fourth foal: half-brother to 3-y-o 7f winner Duchy of Cornwall (by The Minstrel) and 1986 2-y-o 5f winner Veryan Bay (by Storm Bird): dam sprinting half-sister to smart 1975 American 2-y-o Favorite Beau: 14/1 and bit backward, around 9 lengths eighth of 22, keeping on steadily, to Hebba in maiden at Newbury in September: sure to improve. *B. W. Hills.*

POSEIDONIA 3 ch.g. Red Sunset 120–Late Swallow (My Swallow 134) [1988 **52** NR 1989 6d⁵ 7s 10g 6f⁴ 6f] 16,000Y: sturdy, workmanlike gelding: half-brother to 3 winners, including very useful sprinter A Prayer For Wings (by Godswalk) and fair 1m winner March Bird (by Dalsaan): dam never ran: ridden by 5-lb claimer, staying-on fourth in handicap at Goodwood in June: well beaten in varied company otherwise, on final outing weak co-favourite, sweating, slowly away and tailed off in handicap at Nottingham: mulish in stalls and withdrawn final appearance, in early-July: may prove suited by 7f: somewhat temperamental. *J. Sutcliffe.*

PO SHAN 2 ch.f. (Apr 10) Blushing Scribe (USA) 107–Tender Moon 77 (Vitiges — (FR)) [1989 5f4] second foal: dam 2-y-o 6f winner, stayed middle distances: 10/1, 10 lengths last of 4 in maiden at Ayr in July. *F. Durr.*

POSITIVE ATTITUDE 4 br.f. Red Sunset 120–Wilderness 88 (Martinmas 82 128) [1988 8m 7f6 7m3 8d2 8g3 7g2 7g6 1989 7f 7f4 6f 8.3m2 8m* 9f4 8g* 8f5 8.2d* 8s 9g] workmanlike filly: fair handicapper: won at Sandown in July, Newbury in August and Haydock (hampered and awarded race) in September: well below her best last 2 outings: suited by 1m: possibly unsuited by soft going, acts on any other: blinkered nowadays: occasionally sweats, very edgy eighth start: suited by waiting tactics. *M. Bell.*

POSITIVELY GREAT (USA) 3 ch.g. Achieved 125–Sable Linda (USA) 67 (Graustark) [1988 5m 1989 6v3 6h3 8m 8f3 9m 9g3 10m 11g] big, lengthy gelding: modest maiden: stays 9f: acts on firm going: ran moderately for 7-lb claimer seventh outing: often edgy and taken down early. *M. P. Naughton.*

POSITIVE WAY 5 b.g. Ardross 134–Abbe's Realm (Realm 129) [1988 12s 12d 62 12m 12.3v2 14d5 12g 12.3s6 10g 12m 12g 1989 12.4g6 12g* 11v* 13v 12d 13m 12.4m 12g 15.8m4 12f 10.6d 12.4g 12s a12g] big, rangy gelding: turns fore-feet in: quite modest handicapper on his day: well ridden when winning at Doncaster and Hamilton (apprentices) in first weeks of season, setting moderate gallop and staying on gamely: well beaten vast majority of subsequent starts: suited by around 1½m and an easy surface: has been tried in visor: occasionally on toes: sweating seventh outing: moved down badly ninth one: inconsistent. *S. J. Muldoon.*

POSSEBELLE 2 ch.f. (Mar 11) Posse (USA) 130–Belle Origine (USA) (Exclu- — sive Native (USA)) [1989 7m] 3,000Y: leggy, rather angular filly: first foal: dam, French 9.5f winner, is daughter of sister to Ribofilio: well beaten in 20-runner maiden at Lingfield in September. *M. J. Haynes.*

POSSESSIVE LADY 2 ch.f. (May 12) Dara Monarch 128–Possessive (Posse — (USA) 130) [1989 6g] first foal: dam unraced half-sister to smart miler Long Row and daughter of Irish 1000 Guineas winner and good broodmare Front Row: never a factor in 28-runner maiden at Newmarket in October. *A. A. Scott.*

POSSETIVE PLANT 4 ch.g. Posse (USA) 130–Sakeena 76 (Moulton 128) 64 [1988 9g 8f6 12s4 1989 13s3 15s] big, rangy gelding: 33/1, 8 lengths third of 6 to very easy winner Lumberjack in minor event at Ayr in September: 25/1, tailed off final 3f in handicap at same course over 3 weeks later. *J. M. Jefferson.*

POSSIBLE AMBITION (USA) 4 ch.g. Perrault 130–Its Possible (USA) — (Bold Ambition) [1988 NR 1989 10.2m5 8.5f 5f] lengthy ex-Irish gelding: half-brother to minor winner in USA by Exceller: dam successful at up to 7f in USA: lightly raced, and little sign of ability: blinkered final outing: sweating second. *J. W. Blundell.*

POSTAGE STAMP 2 ch.c. (Mar 16) The Noble Player (USA) 126–Takealetter — (Wolver Hollow 126) [1989 7g] IR 13,500F: third foal: dam placed over middle distances in Ireland: soundly beaten in 29-runner maiden at Newmarket in November. *J. W. Hills.*

POTTER'S DREAM 2 ch.g. (Mar 18) Horage 124–Sally St Clair (Sallust 134) 84 [1989 5g5 6m2 6g2 6g 7g] IR 15,000Y: workmanlike gelding: second foal: brother to 6f winner Just Jennings: dam, winner in Canada, is half-sister to Superlative, smart at up to 7f: fair performer: second in minor event at Windsor in July and maiden at Hamilton in August: stays 7f: tends to wander: gelded after final appearance. *G. B. Balding.*

POUR ENCOURAGER 4 ch.g. Kind of Hush 118–Divine Penny 65 (Divine Gift 63 127) [1988 8d5 10.1m 10m6 10f 11.5g3 11.7m4 14.5g* 14m* 13s 14m2 16d2 1989 10.8s 14g 14m 16.2m 16m 19f 16f3 16m 13.8d2 13.6g a16g] angular, workmanlike gelding: moderate mover: quite modest handicapper nowadays: virtually pulled up and finished lame final outing: stays 2m: acts on firm going and a soft surface: blinkered last 3 outings: ran in snatches eighth start: inconsistent. *G. Lewis.*

POWDER LASS 3 ch.f. Tap On Wood 130–Live Ammo 94 (Home Guard (USA) — 129) [1988 5g* 1989 7m 8m] leggy, light-framed filly: turns fore feet out: modest form when justifying favouritism in maiden at Sandown in July as 2-y-o: always behind in handicaps in summer of 1989, tailed off facing stiff task in £15,700 event final start: should stay at least 6f: sold 4,400 gns Newmarket December Sales. *Lord John FitzGerald.*

POWER BOAT 3 ch.g. Jalmood (USA) 126–Bedeni 100 (Parthia 132) [1988 NR — 1989 10s 10.1m 12.2d 15g a14g6] sturdy gelding: half-brother to several winners, including very useful 1976 2-y-o 5f to 7f winner Sky Ship (by Roan Rocket) and smart 1¼m filly Upper Deck (by Sun Prince): dam disappointing half-sister to smart Admirals Launch and Torpid, and to dam of Cut Above: well beaten, including in claimer and handicap: bred to stay 1½m: off course 4 months and bought out of R. Hern's stable 6,000 gns Ascot August Sales after second start. *M. Avison.*

POWER CRAZY 4 b.g. Electric 126–Divetta 72 (Ribero 126) [1988 10v⁶ 11.7g 14m⁴ 12d 14g 12m³ 12.2d 12s² 12d 1989 12f 12f 14f 12f⁵ 14g⁴ 14f] moderate mover: modest maiden at best: well beaten in handicaps and ladies event as 4-y-o: stays 1½m: acts on top-of-the-ground and soft going: often blinkered nowadays: sweating third outing: difficult ride, and one to leave alone. *P. Howling.* — §

POWER OF PRAYER 2 ch.f. (Mar 9) The Noble Player (USA) 126–Sandra's Choice (Sandy Creek 123) [1989 7m 8g 7f] IR 5,500F, IR 7,800Y: angular filly: first foal: dam placed over long distances in Ireland: always behind in maidens. *C. N. Williams.* —

POWER REIGNS 4 ch.c. Star Appeal 133–All Risks 90 (Pitcairn 126) [1988 12d 1989 10s 10m 10m 16f] workmanlike colt: of little account: visored second outing. *P. Butler.*

POWER SHIFT 2 b.g. (Feb 7) Night Shift (USA)–Red Laser 95 (Red God 128§) [1989 5g 5h⁶ 6m* 6m 6g³ 6m⁵ 5g⁴ 5.1m* 5g 5m⁵ 5m 5f* 5f 6v] compact, good-bodied gelding: has a quick action: closely related to 1983 2-y-o 5f winner Be My Valentine (by Be My Guest) and several other winners here and abroad, including fairly useful miler Regent Lad (by Prince Regent): dam 5f sprinter closely related to very speedy Ruby Laser: quite modest performer: successful in sellers at Yarmouth (bought out of M. Jarvis's stable 7,500 gns first occasion and bought in 6,000 gns on second) and in nursery at Folkestone: ran poorly final start: stays 6f: effective with or without blinkers: looks an awkward ride: sold 8,000 gns Newmarket Autumn Sales: inconsistent. *A. N. Lee.* 61

POWER'S MONET 2 b.f. (Feb 19) Claude Monet (USA) 121–Mummy's Glory 82 (Mummy's Pet 125) [1989 6m 5g⁵ 8m] 1,000Y: light-framed filly: third foal: half-sister to untrustworthy maiden Tambuli (by Mr Fluorocarbon): dam, best at 2 yrs, raced only at 5f: poor plater: form only at 5f: trained on debut by W. G. M. Turner. *K. G. Wingrove.* 38

POWER TAKE OFF 3 b.f. Aragon 118–Law And Impulse 104 (Roan Rocket 128) [1988 NR 1989 7m³ 8m² 8m* 10m³] big, angular, rather sparely-made filly: good mover: half-sister to several winners, including very useful sprinter Governor General (by Dominion) and 10.2f winner Cross-Bencher (by Sharpo): dam 2-y-o 5f winner: 11/10 favourite, won maiden at Sandown in July: much better effort 4 lengths third of 4 to Flamingo Pond in £6,800 event at Salisbury 3 weeks later: didn't handle turn at Kempton second start: better at 1¼m than 1m. *D. R. C. Elsworth.* 109

POWYS PRINCE 6 b.g. Roscoe Blake 120–Darling Eve 70 (Darling Boy 124) [1988 12.3g³ 10m 12.2g 1989 12s 12d³ 18s⁶ 12g 12m] strong gelding: quite modest maiden at best: stays 1½m: edgy on reappearance: tends to sweat: a difficult ride. *J. A. Glover.*

POYLE GEORGE 4 br.c. Sharpo 132–Hithermoor Lass 75 (Red Alert 127) [1988 5g³ 5g³ 6g⁶ 1989 5g⁴ 6m 5m*] smallish, quite attractive colt: has a quick action: put up very useful performance when winning listed Rous Stakes at Newmarket in October, leading over 1f out and battling on well, by ¾ length from Hadif: best at 5f: acts on top-of-the-ground and a soft surface. *D. R. C. Elsworth.* 113

PRAIRIE AGENT 4 b.f. Main Reef 126–Regal Guard 60 (Realm 129) [1988 9d 9g 9f⁴ 8m² 8f⁵ 8s 10g 10d 8g 1989 10s 10f 10m 15.3m⁶ 16.2g 12f 15.3g² 17.6f⁵ 12g] workmanlike filly: moderate mover: bad plater: seems to stay 15f: acts on firm going: has given trouble in preliminaries and started slowly. *P. S. Felgate.* 24

PRAIRIE ROSE 2 ch.f. (Apr 2) Blazing Saddles (AUS)–Linpac Gold 62 (Rheingold 137) [1989 6m] 500F, 850Y: compact filly: first foal: dam, one-paced maiden, stayed 1½m: tailed off in 7-runner seller at Yarmouth in June: sold 750 gns Ascot November Sales. *B. C. Morgan.* —

PRAYER FLAG (USA) 2 ch.f. (Apr 8) Forli (ARG)–Forever Waving (USA) (Hoist The Flag (USA)) [1989 5m⁶ 6f 5f] second reported foal: dam, winner at up to 9f, is half-sister to top 1976 American 3-y-o filly Revidere: plating-class maiden: best effort final start: should stay beyond 5f. *P. W. Harris.* 53

PRAYER WHEEL 2 b.f. (Mar 8) High Line 125–Heaven Knows 113 (Yellow God 129) [1989 7g] strong, sturdy filly: has plenty of scope: eighth foal: sister to 3-y-o Bell Toll, fair 7f and 1m winner at 2 yrs, and half-sister to 2 other winners, including modest 2¼m winner Relekto (by Relko), later smart novice hurdler: dam won —

Lingfield Oaks Trial but better at up to 9f: well beaten in 24-runner maiden at Newmarket in November. *G. A. Pritchard-Gordon.*

PRAY FOR RAIN 2 b.f. (Apr 11) Import 127–Sun Lamp 76 (Pall Mall 132) [1989 6m 6m 5.1m 5f 7f⁶ 7f⁶] fifth living foal: half-sister to 3-y-o Tophams (by Good Times) and sprint winner Velocidad (by Balidar): dam 7f winner: of little account: has been tried in blinkers. *F. Durr.*

PRECELLA THE HUN 2 b.f. (Mar 28) Precocious 126–Amerella (Welsh Pageant 132) [1989 5d 5s⁴ 5f⁵ 6g 6f³ 7m⁵ 6g 6g] 13,500Y: smallish, angular filly: moderate walker: seventh foal: half-sister to several winners, including smart sprinter Cragside (by Hot Spark) and fair 6f and 1m winner Mudrik (by Sparkler): dam, daughter of Molecomb winner Lowna, won over 1¼m in Ireland: plating-class maiden: best run at 7f: probably acts on any going: blinkered final start (ran poorly previous one): sometimes on toes. *G. Lewis.* **50**

PRECENTOR 3 ro.c. Music Boy 124–La Magna 104 (Runnymede 123) [1988 NR 1989 6s³ 5m* 5f 5f² 5g 5g 6d 6g a6g] 12,500Y: strong, close-coupled colt: moderate mover: brother to 4 sprint winners, including high-class French colt Kind Music and very useful Boy Trumpeter, and half-brother to 1983 2-y-o 5f winner Blanche Neige (by Forlorn River): dam won twice over 5f at 2 yrs: won maiden at Thirsk in May: easily best effort in handicaps when good running-on second at Sandown: should stay 6f: acts on firm going. *J. D. Bethell.* **65**

PRECIOUS BALLERINA 4 ch.f. Ballacashtal (CAN)–Jenny's Rocket 90 (Roan Rocket 128) [1988 8g 10m² 10m 8f 8g 1989 9m 9f] tall filly: quite modest maiden at best: well beaten in autumn handicaps at Redcar: suited by 1¼m: sometimes sweating and on edge: often finds little. *J. Hetherton.*

PRECIOUS BOY 3 b.g. Taufan (USA) 119–Carrigeen Moss (Red God 128§) [1988 5g 6f* 7g 1989 8.2s* 8s 9f³ 10m⁴ 12f 12g] compact, workmanlike gelding: moderate walker: good mover with a rather round action: fairly useful handicapper: won minor event at Nottingham in March: easily best efforts after when in frame at York and Yarmouth: sweating and bit edgy next outing, off course 4 months after: stays 1¼m: acts on any going: sold G. Moore 22,000 gns Doncaster November Sales: winning hurdler. *I. V. Matthews.* **90**

PRECIOUS GEM 2 b.f. (Apr 11) Minmax 91–Miss Hamilton (Quiet Fling (USA) 124) [1989 5f⁶ 7g 6g 7m 6f] IR 950Y: plain, sparely-made filly: first foal: dam well beaten: of little account: sold 825 gns Ascot October Sales. *B. Gubby.*

PRECIOUS MEMORIES 4 br.g. Kabour 80–Kings Fillet (King's Bench 132) [1988 8.2m 10f² 8.5g 7.5f 10g⁴ 10d³ 8g⁵ 10g⁶ 10m 10g 12m⁶ 16.5f⁴ 10m⁶ 12.2g³ 10d* 1989 12.4g 12f 10f 10.2g 8m] leggy, sparely-made gelding: poor mover: winning plater as 3-y-o: well beaten in non-selling handicaps (last for amateurs) in 1989: sweated and raced freely third outing: best form at 1¼m to 1½m: acts on firm going and a soft surface: sometimes blinkered nowadays: often races with head up and wanders. *D. W. Chapman.* §

PRECIOUS PATH 4 gr.g. Warpath 113–So Precious 100 (Tamerlane 128) [1988 12m 12.3s⁵ 1989 10.2g 10d 10f 11f] leggy, sparely-made gelding: poor maiden: broke leg and was destroyed at Redcar in July. *H. P. Rohan.*

PRECIOUS SPIRIT 2 b.f. (May 11) Simply Great (FR) 122–Arctic Drama (Northern Baby (CAN) 127) [1989 5g³ 5m⁶ 5m 5g² 5m* 7f⁴ 6m] IR 3,100Y: sparely-made, angular filly: second foal: half-sister to 3-y-o Polar Vision (by Lyphard's Special): dam never ran: won 14-runner maiden auction at Beverley in July: not raced after August: should stay at least 1m: acts on firm going. *M. Brittain.* **64**

PRECISION MACHINE 3 b.f. Dara Monarch 128–Black Fire 92 (Firestreak 125) [1988 NR 1989 8g 12.3m] small filly: ninth foal: half-sister to several winners here and abroad, including useful 1982 2-y-o sprinter Navarino Bay (by Averof) and 1½m winner Auchinlea (by High Line) later successful in Denmark: dam middle-distance handicapper: behind in maiden at Ripon: broke leg and destroyed in claimer at same course. *N. Bycroft.*

PRECOCIOUSLY 3 ch.f. Precocious 126–Grankie (USA) (Nashua) [1988 5m 6f 7s 1989 7s 10s² 10f⁶ 9f 10f* 8m 12g] close-coupled, useful-looking filly: has a slightly round action: won seller (bought in 3,300 gns) at Folkestone in October: facing very stiff task, appeared to run very well in Chepstow claimer next start: stays 1¼m well: acts on any going: visored last 3 starts. *S. Dow.* **52**

PREDICTABLE 3 ch.g. Music Boy 124–Piccadilly Etta 76 (Floribunda 136) [1988 5f⁴ 6s 1989 6s⁴ 6d⁶ 5m² 5g³ 5m³ 5m⁴ 6g 6s⁵ 6g⁴ 6f⁶ 5g 7g] lengthy, angular gelding: moderate walker: modest maiden: best form at 5f: acts on top-of-the-ground. *R. M. Whitaker.* **67**

PREFABRICATE (FR)   3 b.g. Kings Lake (USA) 133–Celtic Assembly (USA)   **73**
95 (Secretariat (USA)) [1988 NR 1989 7g 10d⁶ 8m⁶ 8m² 8f⁶ 10d⁴ 9f⁶] medium-sized,
useful-looking gelding: first foal: dam, 10.6f winner, is daughter of Welsh Garden,
top 2-y-o filly in Ireland in 1975: modest maiden: should be suited by further than
1m: possibly best on top-of-the-ground: often ridden by 7-lb claimer: gelded after
final start. *J. Gosden.*

PREMIER AMOUR   3 b.f. Salmon Leap (USA) 131–Flamme d'Amour (Gift Card   **111**
124) [1988 8s 9g* 10v 1989 10g* 8.5g² 8s² 10v4 9s* 10.5g* 10.5d³ 12g⁴ 10m 10g 11s*
9.2g 9s] fourth foal: closely related to French 6f and 1¼m winner Fleur d'Oranger
(by Northfields) and a maiden by Glenstal and half-sister to 2 other French winners
at around 1¼m by Noir Et Or and Auction Ring: dam, out of smart winner at up to
13.5f Gazolina, ran 4 times at 2 yrs and won once over jumps at 3 yrs in France: won
maiden at Compiegne as 2-y-o: progressed well in 1989, winning minor events at
Cagnes-sur-Mer in February, Evry in March and Maisons-Laffitte in June and
Group 3 contest at Baden-Baden in August: ran well in Prix de Diane Hermes at
Chantilly and Prix de Malleret at Longchamp seventh and eighth outings: stays
1½m: acts on soft ground: very useful. *R. Collet, France.*

PREMIER DANCE   2 ch.g. (May 4) Bairn (USA) 126–Gigiolina (King Emperor   **61**
(USA)) [1989 5m³ 7f³] 16,000Y: compact gelding: half-brother to 3-y-o Lariston
Gale (by Pas de Seul), 6f winner at 2 yrs, and 2 winners in Italy, including 1982 2-y-o
5f winner Fire-Thatch (by Thatch): dam, placed in Italy, is out of half-sister to
French Derby winner Hard To Beat: placed in maidens at Windsor (hung badly last
2f) in June at Chester in July: better suited by 7f than 5f, and will stay further. *D.
Haydn Jones.*

PREMIER DEVELOPER   2 b.c. (Apr 20) Precocious 126–Arderelle (FR) 80   **73**
(Pharly (FR) 130) [1989 5g⁵ 5s⁵ 5m*] 7,000Y: leggy colt: second foal: half-brother to
French 10.5f winner Ellerton (by Sharpo): dam, 1¼m winner, is daughter of smart
miler Arosa, also dam of Arokar: well backed, showed much improved form when
winning maiden at Edinburgh in May by 6 lengths: appeared leniently treated in
autumn nurseries, but wasn't seen out again: will stay 6f: acts on top-of-the-ground.
W. J. Pearce.

PREMIERE   2 b. or br.f. (May 4) Horage 124–Ballinavail (Rarity 129) [1989 5f²   **71**
5f² 5g³ 5f³ 6f* 5.8f³ 6g a7g³] IR 5,000F, IR 3,000Y: small filly: moderate walker:
sister to Irish 1m winner Tremmin and half-sister to 2 other winners: dam, Irish 1m
winner, is half-sister to high-class miler Hilal: made all in maiden auction event at
Folkestone in July: good third of 8 to Corrin Hill in December nursery at Lingfield
final start: stayed 7f: dead. *B. Stevens.*

PREMIERE MOON   2 ch.f. (Mar 10) Bold Owl 101–Silvery Moon (Lorenzaccio   **80**
130) [1989 5g 5f⁵ 6g⁴ 5f³ 7m³ 7m* 7g³ 7g] 2,300F, 8,800Y: sparely-made filly: poor
mover: fifth foal: sister to modest sprinter Cotton On Quick and quite modest 1¼m
performer The Mague, and half-sister to a winner abroad: dam of little account: fair
performer: bandaged behind, won nursery at Yarmouth in August by ½ length from
Curved Blade: good third of 20, keeping on well, to Green's Leader in similar event
at Newmarket in October: will stay 1m. *H. J. Collingridge.*

PREMIER GIRL   2 b.f. (May 2) Petong 126–Rest 70 (Dance In Time (CAN))   **46**
[1989 5f 5m* 5f⁴ 5.1m² 5f³] 2,400Y: sturdy filly: poor mover: first foal: dam 1½m
winner: modest plater: won 7-runner event (retained 7,000 gns) at Nottingham in
May by 5 lengths: not raced after July: broke loose in paddock and bolted before
start at Windsor in August: usually bandaged: sold 3,000 gns Newmarket Autumn
Sales. *R. W. Stubbs.*

PREMIER LADY   2 b.f. (Mar 16) Red Sunset 120–Be A Dancer (Be Friendly   **—**
130) [1989 5f 6m 7g] 1,600Y, 2,000Y: close-coupled, sturdy filly: fourth foal: dam
Irish 7f and 9f winner: backward, well beaten in maiden auctions: not raced after
June. *D. T. Thom.*

PREMIER PRINCE   3 b.c. King of Spain 121–Domicile (Dominion 123) [1988   **67**
5m⁴ 5f³ 5g² 6g* 6d* 7m⁴ 7f 7f 7g 1989 6d 7f⁶ 7f 9m 8f⁵ 8.2g⁵ 6g² 8m³ 6g⁵ 6s⁶ 6m]
strong, workmanlike colt: modest handicapper: hampered stalls in seller final
outing: stays 7f: acts on top-of-the-ground and a soft surface: suited by waiting
tactics: sold to join G. Cottrell 1,200 gns Newmarket Autumn Sales. *W. J. Pearce.*

PREMIER PRINCESS   3 b.f. Hard Fought 125–Manntika 77 (Kalamoun 129)   **40**
[1988 NR 1989 15g⁵ 15.8m² 16f⁴ 13.8g⁴ 16m⁴ 12g 18g] first reported foal: dam 1¼m
winner: poor maiden: finished distressed fifth start: has form at 1½m and 2m. *W.
Bentley.*

PREMIER TOUCH 2 b.c. (Apr 10) Petorius 117–Fingers (Lord Gayle (USA) **79**
124) [1989 5m3 5f* 5f3] IR 8,400F, 15,000Y: tall, sparely-made colt: has scope:
moderate walker and mover: brother to 3-y-o Barter and half-brother to useful
middle-distance stayer Hollow Hand (by Wolver Hollow) and several other winners
abroad: dam, Irish 1½m winner, is daughter of sister to very smart sprinter Forlorn
River: odds on, won 4-runner maiden at Redcar in July by 3 lengths easing up:
continually hung right when over a length third of 4 to Judgement Call in minor
event at Hamilton 2 weeks later: should stay 6f. *W. J. Pearce.*

PREPOLLO 3 gr.c. Precocious 126–Rosie Black 80 (Roan Rocket 128) [1988 6d —
6f2 6f4 6f 6m3 7g6 6m 6d 1989 8g 6m5 6f 6g 6g 6m 7g] strong, heavy-topped colt: has
rather a round action: modest maiden at best: showed little as 3-y-o, including in
handicaps and sellers: should be suited by further than 6f: possibly suited by
top-of-the-ground: tailed off in blinkers final start. *E. Weymes.*

PRESAGE 3 b.c. Petong 126–Discreet 104 (Jukebox 120) [1988 8m 7g 8g 1989 7s —
7.5d 9d4 9m6 5g 7.5m] leggy, close-coupled colt: moderate mover: little worthwhile
form, including in sellers: probably doesn't stay 9f: visored penultimate start:
mostly apprentice ridden. *J. P. Leigh.*

PRESENTE (FR) 4 br.f. Home Guard (USA) 129–Barratt Oak 59 (Daring —
Display (USA) 129) [1988 10f 10.2g 7g 7f 7m4 10m 12.2g 1989 8f a8g] leggy, rather
sparely-made filly: poor plater: blinkered, tailed off in Lingfield claimer final outing.
J. D. Roberts.

PRESENT TIMES 3 b.g. Sayf El Arab (USA) 127–Coins And Art (USA) —
(Mississippian (USA) 131) [1988 6g 6m6 7m4 1989 a11g] close-coupled, deep-girthed
gelding: good walker: quite modest maiden as 2-y-o when trained by S. Norton: bit
backward, behind in claimer at Southwell in December, 1989: stays 7f: sold 1,300
gns Ascot March Sales. *K. G. Wingrove.*

PRESET 2 ch.c. (Feb 9) Homing 130–Constanza 94 (Sun Prince 128) [1989 6g] **54 p**
7,800Y: half-brother to 10.6f and 1½m winner Toscana (by Town And Country) and a
winner in Trinidad by Sallust: dam won over 1½m from 2 starts: never-dangerous
tenth in 20-runner maiden at Newcastle in October: should improve. *P. Calver.*

PRESIDENT GEORGE 2 b.c. (May 20) Be My Native (USA) 122–Mother **50**
White (Jukebox 120) [1989 5f5 6m 8m] IR 4,700Y: leggy colt: moderate mover: sixth
living foal: brother to 1987 2-y-o 5f and 6f winner Be My Bride and half-brother to
3-y-o Jendra (by Horage) and 1985 Irish 2-y-o 5f winner Sing Song Girl (by
Pitskelly): dam, winner twice over 5f in Ireland, is half-sister to very smart
middle-distance filly Persian Tiara: plating-class maiden: should stay beyond 5f. *M.
Brittain.*

PRESIDENTIAL STAR (USA) 3 b.f. President (FR)–Out of This World 76 —
(High Top 131) [1988 6g 1989 8g 9s 8.2s5 8m 8.2m 8h4 10.4g5 8g 10f 8f] angular filly:
carries condition: poor walker: moderate mover: poor on most form, including in
sellers: best effort at 1m (may prove as effective over bit shorter) on soft ground:
blinkered fifth, seventh and eighth outings: takes good hold: bought out of S.
Norton's stable 1,300 gns Newmarket July Sales after eighth start. *P. Butler.*

PRESIDIO 3 ro.g. Beldale Flutter (USA) 130–Danielle Delight (Song 132) [1988 —
6d 8g 8d 1989 8d 11.7m 10f4 10m 10m] lengthy, shallow-girthed gelding: plating-
class maiden: showed little after reappearance: should stay beyond 1m: best form on
an easy surface: sold 1,800 gns Ascot October Sales. *Miss A. J. Whitfield.*

PRESSED FOR TIME 2 b.f. (Feb 28) Buzzards Bay 128§–Sweet Paper (Jellaby —
124) [1989 8g] big, workmanlike filly: first foal: dam unraced: very backward and
green, always behind in 16-runner maiden at Leicester in November. *H. J. Collingridge.*

PRETENTIOUS 3 ro.f. Precocious 126–Rectitude 99 (Runnymede 123) [1988 —
6m3 6m 5d* 5g 1989 7f 8g 10.2m 10.2g6 8m6 8g] leggy, quite good-topped filly: fair
winner as 2-y-o, little form at 3 yrs: worth another try over 7f: best effort on a soft
surface: blinkered last 2 starts: bandaged third: sold 2,800 gns Newmarket
December Sales. *A. Bailey.*

PRETTY COOL 2 b.f. (Mar 31) Taufan (USA) 119–Lohunda Lady (Ballymore **74**
123) [1989 5g6 5d* 5f2 5f6 6m6 6v6 6g6 6d4] IR 9,500Y, 7,000Y: small, close-coupled
filly: poor walker: half-sister to 1985 Irish 2-y-o 7f winner She's An Angel and a
winning hurdler (both by Welsh Saint): dam Irish 7.9f and 1½m winner also
successful over hurdles: modest performer: won 10-runner maiden at Bath in April:
off course 4 months after fifth outing: best form at 5f: acts on firm going and a soft
surface: visored penultimate appearance: sold 3,200 gns Newmarket Autumn Sales.
Dr J. D. Scargill.

PRETTY DUET 2 b.f. (Apr 8) Song 132–Liberation 63 (Native Prince) [1989 5g — 5f] IR 1,500Y: leggy filly: half-sister to several winners, most at 2 yrs, including 1986 2-y-o 5f winner Bastillia (by Derrylin): dam twice-raced half-sister to good sprinter Tudor Grey: poor form in maiden auction races at Salisbury (trained by K. Ivory) in May and Warwick in October. *M. J. Charles.*

PRETTY EYES 3 b.f. Habitat 134–For Your Eyes 85 (Gay Fandango (USA) 132) — [1988 NR 1989 8.2g6] second foal: half-sister to a poor maiden: dam, 6f winner, from family of Washington DC International winner Providential and smart 1981 French 2-y-o filly Play It Safe: 8/1 from 4/1, well behind long way when 11 lengths sixth of 11 in maiden at Hamilton in September. *A. C. Stewart.*

PRETTY LUCKY 3 b.f. Shirley Heights 130–The Dancer (FR) 122 (Green **68** Dancer (USA) 132) [1988 8m 9g 1989 12m6 12.2g6] sparely-made filly: 50/1 and bit backward, form only in maiden at Salisbury on reappearance, chasing leaders until inside final 1f. *Major W. R. Hern.*

PRETTY PRECOCIOUS 3 b.f. Precocious 126–Siouxsie 90 (Warpath 113) **61** § [1988 5f 6m 5m4 6s 1989 6m 7m 6m 5m 6m6 9s* 9f 10.6s 10f 8g6] tall, leggy, narrow filly: has rather a round action: easily best effort when winning seller (no bid) at Hamilton in September: stays 9f: goes well on soft going: sold out of F. Lee's stable 3,500 gns Doncaster October Sales after ninth outing: hung left final one: seems unreliable and difficult ride. *J. L. Spearing.*

PRETTY THING 4 b.f. Star Appeal 133–Monkey Tricks 85 (Saint Crespin III **83** 132) [1988 8f4 10m* 11.7g* 12g* 12g4 12.2g* 11.5f2 12s 12g3 11.7g 12g5 1989 12h* 12f3 12h* 12m2 11f* 12.3m4 14f2 12f3] leggy filly: good mover: fair handicapper: had good season, justifying favouritism in uncompetitive apprentice event and 11-runner contest at Brighton and apprentice race at Redcar: 33/1 and facing stiffish task, creditable third of 6, never a threat, to Knoosh in listed Galtres Stakes at York final outing: suited by around 1½m: acted on hard going and unsuited by soft: usually ridden by 7-lb claimer D. Biggs: game and consistent: covered by Celestial Storm. *R. J. R. Williams.*

PREVAILING WIND 3 b.c. Night Shift (USA)–Windy Sea 105 (Sea Hawk II **62** 131) [1988 5s 5s5 5f4 6g 5g 5d 1989 5s 5v3 5s2 5m4 5f6 5m3 5g4 5m3 5g4 5g 5f2 5m 5m2 5d 5f4] sturdy colt: quite modest handicapper: headstrong, unlikely to stay beyond 5f: probably acts on any going: has run creditably for apprentice: sometimes slowly away. *M. Brittain.*

PRICELESS CITIZEN 4 b.g. Skyliner 117–London Spin 86 (Derring-Do 131) — [1988 10m 10.2f 1989 17.6f] seems of little account: pulled up 3f out only outing at 4 yrs. *R. J. Hodges.*

PRICELESS FANTASY 2 ch.f. (Feb 23) Dunbeath (USA) 127–Linda's Fantasy **61** 108 (Raga Navarro (ITY) 119) [1989 6g5 5m3 7m6] smallish, lengthy filly: good walker: second foal: half-sister to winning stayer Lindross (by Ardross): dam won from 6f to 1m: quite modest maiden: will stay 1¼m. *R. W. Armstrong.*

PRICEOFLOVE 9 b.g. Blue Cashmere 129–Gay Donna (Tudor Jinks 121) [1988 — 8d 1989 6f 8.2g 10g] strong, quite attractive gelding: moderate mover: poor handicapper: needs further than 6f and stays 9f: acts on any going: has worn blinkers, but not for long time: has won for apprentice: inconsistent. *D. Moffatt.*

PRIDE OF ARABY (USA) 3 b.c. Sovereign Dancer (USA)–Miss Manon (FR) **102** (Bon Mot III 132) [1988 7g2 1989 10s3 10.6g2 10m*] tall, rather finely-made colt: not best of walkers: good mover: 6/4 favourite, made all in 4-runner £8,500 maiden at Ascot in July, quickening entering straight and drawing clear (despite wandering under pressure) to beat Crown Crest 4 lengths: keen sort, may prove as effective over 1m: acts on top-of-the-ground: useful. *J. Tree.*

PRIDE OF KIRBY 4 ch.f. Pas de Seul 133–Norme (FR) (Dark Tiger) [1988 8g — 7s 8f5 10d4 10g3 10m 8m* 8m 8.3m 7m 10d 1989 8.3m 8g 8m 7m5 7m6] poor plater: barely stayed 1m: acted on firm going and a soft surface: sometimes blinkered or visored: dead. *G. Blum.*

PRIESTGATE 4 ch.g. Stanford 121§–Change of Luck (Track Spare 125) [1988 **75** 5f5 5m6 5g 6m 7g 6f* 5m 1989 5g4 5f3 6m 6m 5g2 6m 6m* 6g4 7g] lengthy, workmanlike gelding: modest performer: won same seller (no bid) at York in October for second successive season: best at sprint distances on a sound surface: blinkered last 3 outings: good mount for apprentice: sometimes sweats: sometimes bandaged. *J. Wharton.*

PRIMACY 2 b.c. (Feb 13) Shareef Dancer (USA) 135–Primatie (FR) (Vaguely **87** Noble 140) [1989 8g2 8.2g2 8m* 10g] close-coupled, good-bodied colt: fourth living foal: half-brother to smart 1m winner Miller's Mate (by Mill Reef) and fair 1¼m winner First Kiss (by Kris): dam, French 9f winner, is daughter of top-class middle-distance filly Pistol Packer: favourite, won 9-runner maiden at Warwick in October easing up by 8 lengths after making all: favourite, headed 3f out and soon beaten in listed race at Newmarket following month: should stay 1¼m: tended to carry head high second start. *H. R. A. Cecil.*

PRIME CANDIDATE 2 gr.c. (Apr 5) Dominion 123–Bold Maneuver (USA) 75 — (Par Excellent (USA)) [1989 6d] 10,500Y: angular, unfurnished colt: third foal: dam, 1¼m winner, is daughter of French 1000 Guineas winner Bold Fascinator: slowly away and always behind in 24-runner maiden at Newbury in October: sold 1,450 gns Ascot November Sales. *D. R. C. Elsworth.*

PRIME DISPLAY (USA) 3 ch.g. Golden Act (USA)–Great Display (FR) 95 (Great Nephew 126) [1988 7g 8.2m 7m² 8s* 10g² 1989 12s⁴ 12f⁴ 14g²] big, strong, rangy gelding: has a round action: fairly useful performer: ran creditably in listed race at Epsom and minor events at Lingfield and Redcar: off course 6 months before final start: probably stays 1¾m: acts on any going: gelded after final outing. *P. F. I. Cole.*

PRIME WARDEN 3 b.c. Blakeney 126–Misguided 106 (Homing 130) [1988 NR 70 1989 10.1m 10g 8g⁴ 7g a12g] 82,000Y: strong, compact colt: has a free, rather round action: second foal: half-brother to fairly useful 1987 2-y-o 5f and 7f winner Kajar (by Persian Bold): dam, raced only at 5f and 6f, is half-sister to smart 6f and 1m winner Missed Blessing: modest maiden: fourth at Ripon in July, always prominent and under pressure long way out: should be suited by further than 1m. *J. A. R. Toller.*

PRINCE HANNIBAL 2 b.c. (May 23) High Top 131–Fluctuate 87 (Sharpen Up 62 p 127) [1989 7g] 52,000Y: rangy colt: has scope: second foal: half-brother to 3-y-o Suhail Dancer (by Shareef Dancer), strong-pulling 6f winner at 2 yrs: dam, 5f winner at 2 yrs no form as 3-y-o, is out of close relation to Irish 2000 Guineas winner Wassl: 33/1, prominent nearly 5f in 28-runner maiden at Newmarket in November: should improve. *J. L. Dunlop.*

PRINCE IBRAHIM 3 b.c. Be My Guest (USA) 126–Fanny's Cove 89 (Mill Reef 98 (USA) 141) [1988 7g² 7g* 8.5m² 8f* 8s² 10v⁶ 1989 10.2d³ 10m³ 11s⁶ 8m] lengthy, angular, rather unfurnished colt: has a long stride: fair third of 4, leading 1m, to Prince of Dance in listed race at Newmarket in May: well beaten after in Group 2 event at Cologne and £6,500 contest (soon ridden along in straight, edging left) at Newbury over 3 months later: stays 1¼m: probably acts on any going: likely to prove best on a galloping track: lacks turn of foot and requires enterprising tactics: game and genuine. *J. L. Dunlop.*

PRINCE JAKATOM 2 ch.c. (Mar 31) Ballad Rock 122–Ballysnip (Ballymore 89 123) [1989 5s* 6f⁵ 7m³ 7d²] 26,000Y: lengthy, good-quartered colt: has scope: fifth foal: closely related to 7f and 1m winner Persian Delight (by Persian Bold) and half-brother to Italian 3-y-o Lyuba (by Taufan): dam ran once in Ireland: fair performer: won 14-runner maiden at Newbury in April: progressive form afterwards in Coventry Stakes at Royal Ascot and £8,300 event at Newbury in July and nursery (3 lengths second to easy winner Azzaam) at Thirsk in November: will stay further: probably acts on any going. *P. F. I. Cole.*

PRINCE LIVERMORE (USA) 2 ch.c. (Apr 22) Mt Livermore (USA)–Abbey — Leix (USA) (Banquet Circuit (USA)) [1989 6g 6g] $75,000Y: tall, angular colt: fourth foal: half-brother to 2 winners in USA: dam, winner of 7 races at up to 9f, from family of Roberto: sire won over 1m but better at shorter: well beaten in large-field maidens at Newmarket in the autumn. *N. A. Callaghan.*

PRINCELY HEIGHTS 2 b. or br.c. (Mar 2) Shirley Heights 130–Princess — Matilda 110 (Habitat 134) [1989 5g] 40,000Y: compact, good-bodied colt: moderate walker and mover: sixth foal: closely related to Mired (by Mill Reef), 1m winner at 2 yrs in 1988, and modest performer Kalgoorlie (by Glint of Gold), successful at 1m and 9f in Italy, and half-brother to 2 other winners: dam, 7f winner at 2 yrs, is half-sister to St Leger winner Bruni and smart middle-distance winner Royal Blend: 9/1 but very backward, slowly away, green and soon well behind in 9-runner maiden at Carlisle in April. *P. S. Felgate.*

PRINCE MERANDI 6 b.g. Blakeney 126–Copt Hall Princess 70 (Crowned — Prince (USA) 128) [1988 8d* 9d³ 8m³ 8.5m 9d⁴ 8.5m 8g³ 1989 10s 8g] quite attractive gelding: quite modest winner as 5-y-o: well below form in spring: best at around 1m: acts on soft going and top-of-the-ground: inconsistent. *M. E. D. Francis.*

PRINCE OF CLUBS 2 b.c. (Apr 26) King Of Clubs 124–Dream Trader (Auction — Ring (USA) 123) [1989 5g 7f 7m] IR 6,000Y: small colt: poor mover: first foal: dam sister to useful 1983 2-y-o Grey Dream: well beaten in sellers: sold 520 gns Doncaster November Sales. *M. Brittain.*

PRINCE OF DANCE 3 b.c. Sadler's Wells (USA) 132–Sun Princess 130 **123** (English Prince 129) [1988 7g* 7g*dis 7g* 7d* 1989 10m* 12g] strong, lengthy colt: fluent, powerful mover: one of best 2-y-o's of 1988, unbeaten in 4 races, notably Laurent Perrier Champagne Stakes at Doncaster and Three Chimneys Dewhurst Stakes (dead-heated with Scenic) at Newmarket: 6/4 on, again rallied gamely when winning 4-runner listed Newmarket Stakes in May by ½ length from Observation Post (rec 4 lb): 11/2 and looking tremendously well, behind in Ever Ready Derby at Epsom following month: subsequently found to be suffering from cancer of the spine and had to be put down: should have been well suited by 1½m: acted on top-of-the-ground and a soft surface. *Major W. R. Hern.*

PRINCE OF DREAMS 2 ch.c. (Apr 23) Gabitat 119–Icacos Bay 58 (Martinmas — 128) [1989 6g] first foal: dam, placed once at 1¼m, seemed temperamental: in rear in 19-runner maiden at Redcar in November. *J. G. M. O'Shea.*

PRINCE OF TIDES 3 b.c. Welsh Saint 126–Ascalon (Levmoss 133) [1988 5m3 **61** § 5m2 1989 6g4 6m 5h5 5.3h5 5f 5m 5f3 6m 5g5 6f3 7f 6g5] strong, compact colt: quite modest maiden: stays 6f: acts on hard ground: blinkered fourth and fifth starts: sweating final one: has run well for 7-lb claimer: unreliable. *R. Hannon.*

PRINCE ROB 3 b.c. Robellino (USA) 127–Derrain (Prince Tenderfoot (USA) **53** 126) [1988 8.2d 8g 1989 10s 12g 15.3f6 12.2m4 16.2f5 12.2f2 11.3f5 12m5] strong, sturdy colt: carries condition: turns fore-feet in: poor mover: plating-class maiden: stays 1½m, not 2m: acts on firm ground: has run creditably for 5-lb claimer: sold to join Miss L. Bower 6,600 gns Ascot August Sales. *R. Hollinshead.*

PRINCE SATIRE (USA) 6 b.h. Sensitive Prince (USA)–No Comedy (USA) — (Droll Role) [1988 13.3m2 12f3 16m2 14g4 16g5 12d* 1989 16s 12g] quite attractive horse: moderate mover: won same amateurs event at Folkestone as 5-y-o for second year running: well beaten in same event in 1989, first outing for 6 months: seems to stay 2m: well suited by an easy surface: good mount for inexperienced rider: often used to wear blinkers, but hasn't since 1987. *R. Akehurst.*

PRINCE SOBUR 3 b.g. Jalmood (USA) 126–Ultra Vires 87 (High Line 125) **68** [1988 7m 8s 8g3 8.2d 1989 10v2 11m 13.3g 14m2 16.1m] rangy gelding: moderate mover: modest handicapper: 33/1, very good second at Sandown in July, soon struggling (looked ill at ease on top-of-the-ground) then staying on well having been last 3f out: ran badly at Newmarket 2 weeks later: should be suited by 2m: acts on heavy going. *M. Blanshard.*

PRINCESS ACCORD (USA) 3 b.f. D'Accord (USA)–Cohutta Princess (USA) **115** (Groton) [1988 5m3 6m* 1989 7d* 8.2m* 7g* 8g* 9g* 10g4] sparely-made filly: moderate walker and mover: trained by S. Norton, won minor events at Catterick and Nottingham in the spring: off course 4½ months then successful in £5,000 apprentice contest at Ascot and listed races at Ascot (idled in front) and Newmarket, in last-named leading virtually on line to beat Sabotage a head: favourite and on toes, below-form fourth of 9 to Icona in listed event at Newmarket, weakening final 1f: suited by 9f: acts on top-of-the-ground and a soft surface: changed hands after second start: bandaged off-hind afterwards: tough. *L. M. Cumani.*

PRINCESS ATHENA 4 b.f. Ahonoora 122–Shopping Wise (Floribunda 136) **119** [1988 5m* 5m 5f2 5g2 5m3 6g4 5m2 5m5 5g3 1989 5f2] leggy, good-quartered filly: has a quick action: smart sprinter: very good second of 13, beaten ¾ length, leading until well inside final 1f, to Statoblest in King George Stakes at Goodwood in July, only outing as 4-y-o: best at 5f: acts on any going: usually bandaged behind (near-hind only at Goodwood): game and genuine. *D. R. C. Elsworth.*

PRINCESS CAERLEON 3 ch.f. Caerleon (USA) 132–Tigeen (Habitat 134) **75** [1988 5f3 5g3 5d 6m3 7m5 6f 5d* 5g2 5m 1989 5s 5m 5m6 5f4 5f 5g 5f 5d] lengthy, rather dipped-backed filly: moderate walker and mover: modest handicapper: largely below form in 1989: best at 5f on an easy surface. *M. A. Jarvis.*

PRINCESS DANCER 2 b.f. (May 17) Alzao (USA) 117–Singing In The Sun — (Jukebox 120) [1989 7g] IR 8,800Y: small, sturdy filly: half-sister to a winner in Italy by Welsh Saint: dam never ran: 9/1, well beaten, slowly away, in 20-runner maiden auction at Doncaster in June. *Mrs L. Piggott.*

PRINCESS DIVINE 2 ch.f. (May 3) Tender King 123–Divine Fleece (Status — Seeker) [1989 6g 8m] 1,200F: seventh foal: half-sister to Divine Guest (by What A Guest), fairly useful 7f winner at 2 yrs in 1988, and 3 other winners, including Irish 5f winner Runaway Lover (by He Loves Me): dam second over 7f and 7.9f in Ireland: well beaten in sellers. *I. Campbell.*

PRINCESSE DU POWYS   3 b.f. Caerleon (USA) 132–Princesse du Seine (FR)   **66**
85 (Val de Loir 133) [1988 NR 1989 7m⁵ 8m 8.2m³] lengthy filly: seventh foal:
half-sister to fair 1¼m winner Evros (by Kris) and French 4f to 1m winner Priene
(by Pharly): dam, daughter of very useful Princess Bonita, was placed over 7f and 1m
at 2 yrs: quite modest maiden: will stay 1¼m: twice slowly away. *I. A. Balding.*

PRINCESS JESSICA   2 ch.f. (May 17) Anfield 117–Maid of Warwick 96   **42**
(Warwick 110) [1989 5d 5.3g 5d² 6f⁵ 5m⁵ 5g 6f⁶] 800Y: small, sturdy filly: half-sister
to fair 1982 2-y-o 5f winner Warwick Star (by Comedy Star): dam sprinter: modest
plater: ran respectably ridden by 7-lb claimer fifth and sixth starts: probably stays
6f. *B. Smart.*

PRINCESS LUCY   2 b.f. (Mar 12) Local Suitor (USA) 128–Jalapa (FR) 117   **42**
(Luthier 126) [1989 7g 6m] 6,000Y: big, plain filly: closely related to a winner in USA
by Blushing Groom and half-sister to several winners here and abroad, including
useful 1¼m and 1½m winner Bahoor (by L'Enjoleur) and fair 9f winner Cairo Bay
(by Lyphard): dam smart at around 1¼m in France: poor form in October in maiden
auction at Goodwood and 28-runner seller at Newmarket. *P. F. I. Cole.*

PRINCESS MARIELLA   2 b.f. (Apr 2) No Pass No Sale 120–Maria Isabella   **59**
(FR) (Young Generation 129) [1989 6m⁴ 6f² 7f³] 10,000Y: close-coupled filly: lacks
scope: poor walker and mover: first reported foal: dam, ran 3 times in France, is
half-sister to useful 1986 French 2-y-o 6.5f winner Microcosme and granddaughter
of very smart Mia Pola: plating-class maiden: best effort final outing: should stay
1m. *M. R. Stoute.*

PRINCESS OF BASRA   2 ch.f. (Apr 30) Bairn (USA) 126–Miss Nelski 84   **—**
(Most Secret 119) [1989 5g] 10,000Y: lengthy filly: fourth foal: half-sister to 5f
sprinter Ski Captain (by Welsh Captain) and 3-y-o Coxann (by Connaught): dam 5f
winner stayed 7f: last of 17, slowly away, in maiden at Leicester in April: sent to W.
Haigh. *K. Stone.*

PRINCESS SOBIESKA   3 b.f. Niniski (USA) 125–Rexana (Relko 136) [1988   **115**
7m 1989 12g 11.7h³ 16.2f* 16f* 17.1h* 21f³ 14.6g² 12m²] workmanlike filly: has a
slightly round action: successful in June in maiden at Beverley and very small fields

Mrs Douglas Riley-Smith's "Princess Sobieska"

for handicaps at Ripon and Bath: 2 lb overweight, showed much improved form when narrowly-beaten third to Mazzacano in Goodwood Cup, leading 9f out until 3f out then rallying well: good second, leading until inside final 1f, to Lucky Song in Park Hill Stakes at Doncaster and to Snow Bride in Princess Royal Stakes at Ascot: effective with forcing tactics at 1½m and stays extreme distances: acts on hard ground: game. *J. L. Dunlop.*

PRINCESS SONATA 2 b.f. (Mar 8) Music Boy 124–Jovenita (High Top 131) **40**
[1989 5d 5f⁶ 5m 5g] 7,200Y: angular filly: third foal: half-sister to plating-class sprint maiden Tough Cookie (by Lochnager) and a winner in Belgium: dam ran twice: poor form in varied company, including selling: not raced after July. *D. W. P. Arbuthnot.*

PRINCESS TANIMARA 2 b. or br.f. (Feb 20) Vision (USA)–Tanimara **46**
(Sassafras (FR) 135) [1989 7.5f 7f 7f 6g] IR 12,500Y: leggy filly: half-sister to a winner in Italy by Nadjar: dam won in Italy: poor maiden: should stay 1¼m. *Dr J. D. Scargill.*

PRINCESS TAUFAN 2 b.f. (Feb 24) Taufan (USA) 119–Guindilla (Artaius **93**
(USA) 129) [1989 5d* 5d* 5f* 5f⁵ 6d⁵ 6m³ 6m⁴] IR 17,000Y: close-coupled filly, rather unfurnished: second foal: half-sister to a poor animal by Crofter: dam unraced half-sister to useful Irish 6f to 1¼m winner Gaily Gaily, later successful in USA: fairly useful performer: successful early in the season in minor events at Folkestone and Ascot and £7,000 race (beating Old Alliance 2½ lengths) at Sandown: third to Dead Certain in 'The Pacemaker Update' Lowther Stakes at York in August, best subsequent effort in very useful company here and in Ireland: bred to be suited by further: acts on firm going and a soft surface. *Dr J. D. Scargill.*

PRINCESS WU 3 b.f. Sandhurst Prince 128–Hsian (Shantung 132) [1988 NR **59**
1989 8d 10m 10m⁶ 11.3f³ 10g a13g] sparely-made filly: second foal: dam lightly-raced half-sister to smart 6f to 1m winner Bas Bleu and very useful middle-distance performer Primerello: quite modest maiden: staying-on third in claiming event at Chester in July: off course 4 months and showed little in claimer and handicap after: should be suited by 1½m: acts on firm going: sweating third start: sold R. Stubbs 2,500 gns Newmarket December Sales. *G. Wragg.*

PRINCE VALIYAR 2 b.c. (Apr 17) Valiyar 129–Lusitanica 89 (Pieces of Eight **55**
128) [1989 8m 10g] leggy colt: third foal: half-brother to a poor maiden: dam genuine middle-distance stayer: around 15 lengths eighth of 12, staying on never dangerous, to Rock Hopper in maiden at Nottingham, second and better effort: will stay 1½m. *M. A. Jarvis.*

PRINCE ZAMARO 5 ch.g. Sagaro 133–Hazelsha (Romulus 129) [1988 12v 12g **—**
12d⁴ 12f 12f⁵ 12d 11m 11m 12f 1989 12g 10.1m 10.2f] lengthy, workmanlike gelding: poor mover: has shown very little since third outing in 1988: best form at 1½m with give in the ground: blinkered once at 4 yrs. *M. Madgwick.*

PRINGIPOULA 3 b.f. Dominion 123–Another Princess 83 (King Emperor **84**
(USA)) [1988 NR 1989 6s² 5s² 6s 6g* 6m⁴ 5f³ 6g⁴ 7m 6m] sturdy, good-bodied filly: moderate mover: sister to plating-class maiden Domineering and half-sister to 3 winners, including useful 1983 2-y-o 6f winner Throne of Glory (by Hittite Glory), later successful in Italy: dam 1m winner: fair handicapper: won maiden at Pontefract in May: ran well next 3 starts, but moderately after, moving badly to post final outing: stays 6f: probably suited by a sound surface. *C. E. Brittain.*

PRINSEPIA (USA) 3 b.f. Fappiano (USA)–Princesse Bea (FR) (Misti IV 132) **56**
[1988 NR 1989 7h³] $150,000Y: third foal: sister to minor winner in USA Whangee and half-sister to a 2-y-o winner at up to 9f in USA by Northern Jove: dam French 13f winner also successful over 1¼m at 2 yrs: second favourite, 5½ lengths third of 7 to Curtain Call in maiden at Brighton in August, close up 6f: sold 7,400 gns Newmarket December Sales. *J. Tree.*

PRINT FINISHER 3 ch.f. Mandrake Major 122–Chubby Ears (Burglar 128) **— §**
[1988 5f⁶ 5m³ 5.8g³ 5m² 5m³ 5m⁴ 5g² 5g⁴ 5m⁴ 6g 6m 5d³ 1989 6s 5s 5f 5.3h] workmanlike filly: moderate walker: has rather a round action: quite modest maiden as 2-y-o: no form in 1989, swerving badly left at stalls first 2 starts and virtually refusing to race on second of them: stays 6f: acts on top-of-the-ground and a soft surface: one to avoid. *S. Dow.*

PRIOLO (USA) 2 b.c. (Mar 17) Sovereign Dancer (USA)–Primevere (USA) 91 **98 p**
(Irish River (FR) 131) [1989 7d*] first foal: dam French 7f (at 2 yrs) and 1¼m winner: won 9-runner maiden at Deauville in August by a short head from Theatre Critic: will stay 1m. *F. Boutin, France.*

PRIORITY PAID 2 ch.f. (Feb 23) Try My Best (USA) 130–Anna Carla (GER) **74 p**
(Windwurf (GER)) [1989 5m*] lengthy, useful-looking, angular filly: first foal: dam

German bred: 7/2 but burly, won 13-runner maiden at Windsor in June (after slow start) by 5 lengths, quickening well to lead 1f out: bred to be better suited by 6f + . *W. Hastings-Bass.*

PRIORY BAY 3 b.f. Petong 126–Salt of The Earth 85 (Sterling Bay (SWE)) [1988 **46** 7g 7s4 1989 8g 10m4 7m4 10f 8f 8m5 10g] leggy filly: plating-class form at best: should prove best at up to 1m: acts on soft ground, unsuited by very firm: blinkered third and final (tailed off) starts: visored fourth (didn't handle descent at Lingfield) and fifth: claimed out of G. Pritchard-Gordon's stable on second. *J. R. Jenkins.*

PRIORY CLOUD 2 b.f. (May 4) Castle Keep 121–Misfired 101 (Blast 125) [1989 — 8m] half-sister to 3-y-o Castleacre (by Mr Fluorocarbon) and several winners, including 1978 2-y-o 6f winner Speedy Pet (by Mummy's Pet): dam won 4 races over 5f at 2 yrs: always behind in 14-runner maiden at Edinburgh in October. *A. P. Stringer.*

PRIX DU NORD (USA) 3 b.g. Northern Prospect (USA)–Bisouloun (FR) — § (Sharpman 124) [1988 7f 8.2m 8s 1989 8.2m 12h 10.2f 10f 8.5m] well-made gelding: little worthwhile form, including in sellers: blinkered last 4 starts and didn't impress with attitude, tailed off final one: probably stays 1¼m: trained first 4 starts by M. Jarvis: sold to join K. Wingrove 950 gns Doncaster September Sales: one to be wary of. *B. Preece.*

PROCENO 2 b.f. (Apr 9) Procida (USA) 129–Les Biches (CAN) (Northern — Dancer) [1989 a7g a8g] 1,000Y, 2,000 2-y-o: leggy, light-framed filly: fourth foal: half-sister to 1987 French 2-y-o 8.5f winner Simple Minds (by Top Ville) and French 9f winner Tea Beach (by Ti King): dam lightly raced: behind in late-season maidens at Lingfield and Southwell. *R. Guest.*

PROCURATOR (USA) 3 b.c. Alleged (USA) 138–Northeastern (USA) **83** (Northern Dancer) [1988 NR 1989 10.5f4 13.3m3 12m3 14m2 14m2 12g] IR 240,000Y: rather leggy, good-topped, attractive colt: has a sharp action: first foal: dam, Irish 7f winner later successful at up to 1¼m in USA, is from family of Committed: fair maiden: good second in handicaps at Sandown (beaten short head) and Newmarket: well-backed favourite, ran poorly at Carlisle final start: suited by 1¾m: sold 20,000 gns Newmarket Autumn Sales. *B. W. Hills.*

PRODEO 2 br.c. (Mar 28) Local Suitor (USA) 128–Fantasia (Town Crier 119) **35** [1989 6m 7m3 6g 7f3] 1,800Y: sparely-made colt: shows a round action: second foal: dam unraced half-sister to smart sprinter Matinee: poor plater: beaten over 5 lengths by Djanila in minor event at Ostend in July on final appearance: stays 7f. *F. Durr.*

PROFESSIONAL TOUCH 4 b.g. Touching Wood (USA) 127–Professor's **54** Choice 86 (Mount Hagen (FR) 127) [1988 8m 10.2m 12m* 12d6 14g2 16m3 14s 16m4 14.6g 14.7d 1989 10m 15f5 16.5g 13m4 12m 12g* 14f2 12g6] good-topped gelding: moderate mover: made virtually all when winning handicap at Hamilton in August, holding on by ½ length despite saddle slipping and jockey riding without irons inside final 1f: claimed £6,600 final outing: stays 2m: best on a sound surface: visored fourth and fifth (raced too freely) starts. *Mrs J. R. Ramsden.*

PROFILIC 4 b.c. Ballacashtal (CAN)–Sea Charm 70 (Julio Mariner 127) [1988 **80** 7v6 8d 6d 6g* 6f4 6g* 6g2 6m3 6f2 7m2 8g 6d 5.6m 6s 6s 6s* 1989 6m 6m 6m4 6f 6g4 6f* 6f 8.2g 6m 6f 6m6 6m5 7g5 6s 6m2 6g2 6f2 6g5 6d5] big, strong, lengthy colt: usually looks well: has a long, round stride: fair handicapper: won strongly-run event at Chester in July: ran well when second afterwards: needs strongly-run race at 6f and stays 7f: acts on any going: blinkered eleventh to thirteenth starts: tends to get behind, and ideally needs strong handling. *Capt. J. Wilson.*

PROFIT A PRENDRE 5 b.g. Tina's Pet 121–Brave Ballard (Derring-Do 131) **76** [1988 5d2 6g 6d4 6g4 6d5 6f2 6m3 7d6 7m6 5f 7f* 6d 6d5 6s4 6s5 1989 6v 7.6f 7f6 7.6f 6f 7.6h 5f 7m 7f* 8g5 7s* 8s4 8g3 8m 7m] big, lengthy gelding: modest handicapper: won amateur events at Redcar (for second successive season, hung left) in August and Goodwood (easily better effort) in September: ran moderately last 2 outings: stays 1m: acts on any going: has carried head bit high and looked none too genuine: suited by waiting tactics. *D. A. Wilson.*

PROHIBITION 2 b.c. (Apr 23) Music Boy 124–Green Chartreuse 91 (French **73** Beige 127) [1989 5g2 5g3 5m 6m2 6m* 6m* 6m3 7m 6d 6s 6m 6g3 a6g3] 10,000Y: strong, good-quartered colt: has scope: brother to Middle Park winner and 2000 Guineas second Mattaboy, useful 6f winner Jeanne Avril and an animal of little account, and half-brother to 3 other winners: dam won at 5f and 7f at 2 yrs: successful in seller (bought in 12,500 gns) at Goodwood and claimer at Kempton: best form at 6f: blinkered third start, visored eleventh: tends to hang left. *J. Berry.*

710

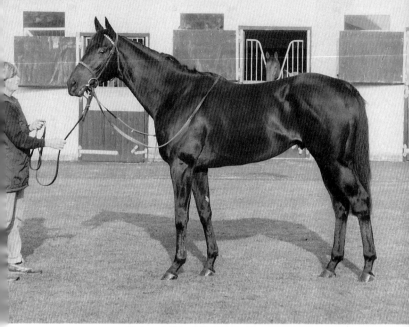

Mr Antonio Balzarini's "Prorutori"

PROMEGG 3 ch.c. Music Boy 124–Rosy Lee (FR) (Le Haar 126) [1988 7m 7m **65**
7g6 8f 1989 8m 10s2 10g5] rather sparely-made colt: quite modest maiden: stays
1¼m: acts on soft going and top-of-the-ground. *G. A. Pritchard-Gordon.*

PROPERS 3 ch.f. Noalto 120–Budget Queen 101 (Good Bond 122) [1988 7m6 7s4 **71**
1989 7s 7f2 8.5m 8m4 7g 7g] modest maiden: easily best efforts as 3-y-o when in
frame in handicaps: soon ridden along last 2 starts: should prove best over 7f or 1m:
acts on any going: went freely down fifth outing. *P. Mitchell.*

PRORUTORI (USA) 3 b.c. Providential 118–Miss Flower Belle (USA) (Torsion **111**
(USA)) [1988 7g6 8s2 8g4 1989 9g2 10f* 12m* 12g4 13.3g6 12g3 10s] tall, rather
leggy colt: successful in May in maiden (odds on) at Redcar and Group 1 Derby
Italiano by ¾ length from Artic Envoy at Rome: ran creditably in Grosser Preis der
Berliner Bank at Dusseldorf, Geoffrey Freer Stakes (moved moderately down) at
Newbury and Gran Premio d'Italia at Milan next 3 starts: suited by 1½m: acts on
firm going: very useful: sent to be trained by T. Skiffington in USA. *M. A. Jarvis.*

PROSPECTORS MOON (USA) 2 ch.f. (Jan 30) Miswaki (USA) 124–Moon **57**
Min (USA) (First Landing) [1989 6g3 7m4 6f4] $20,000Y: leggy, lengthy filly: has
scope: moderate walker: eighth reported foal: half-sister to 3 winners, notably 1983
2-y-o 7f winner Troyanna (by Troy), useful 3-y-o suited to very smart 1963 American 2-y-o
half-sister to very smart 1963 American 2-y-o Traffic: plating-class form in maidens
and a £5,600 event: should stay 1¼m. *C. F. Wall.*

PROST (USA) 2 b.c. (Mar 13) Raise A Cup (USA)–Wrap It Up (Mount Hagen **—**
(FR) 127) [1989 8m] 30,000Y: medium-sized, quite attractive colt: moderate walker:
third foal: half-brother to 3-y-o Pure Genius (by Diesis), very useful 6f winner at 2
yrs: dam thrice-raced half-sister to Gift Wrapped, smart winner at up to 1½m and

dam of Royal Lodge winner Reach: 7/2 but very backward, last of 9 in maiden at Warwick in October: went freely to post. *W. A. O'Gorman.*

PROUD AND KEEN 4 ch.c. Proud Appeal (USA)–Shiny Sneakers (USA) — (Vitriolic (USA)) [1988 5s⁴ 6s 5d⁶ 5f* 5f⁵ 5f* 5g 5g³ 5f⁶ 1989 6f 5m 5f 5.8h⁴ 6s] big, angular colt: poor walker and mover: quite useful winner as 3-y-o: well below his best in 1989, but showed signs of retaining some ability on final outing (first for nearly 3 months) when ninth of 20, poorly drawn, at Ayr: suited by 5f: best form on a sound surface: usually wears blinkers and not discredited in visor final outing at 3 yrs: bandaged behind as 4-y-o: on toes first and third starts: sold 12,000 gns Newmarket Autumn Sales. *N. A. Callaghan.*

PROUD JAK 2 gr.c. (Apr 14) Goldhills Pride 105–Armalou 54 (Ardoon 124) [1989 **49** 5f 5m 5m 5m 6g] heavy-topped, round-barrelled colt: poor walker: third foal: half-brother to 1987 2-y-o 6f seller winner Annacando (by Derrylin), suited by 1½m at 3 yrs: dam, plater, won at 1¼m: plating-class maiden: best effort third start: likely to prove best at 5f. *K. M. Brassey.*

PROUD PATRIOT 4 ch.g. Kalaglow 132–Sandforinia 86 (Sandford Lad 133) **61** [1988 8d 10v 8f 10m⁵ 12f⁶ 12m* 1989 12f 12.2f a12g*] workmanlike gelding: well-backed favourite, form as 4-y-o only when making all in claimer at Lingfield in November: suited by 1½m: acts on top-of-the-ground: winner over hurdles, but has broken blood vessels. *R. Akehurst.*

PRUSSIAN GUARD 3 b.g. Lomond (USA) 128–Friedrichsruh (FR) (Dschingis — Khan) [1988 NR 1989 8g 8g] strong, stocky gelding: seventh foal: closely related to Irish bumpers winner Baltic Sea (by Northfields) and half-brother to smart 1¼m winner Blessed Event (by Kings Lake) and 1½m winner Rhine Wine (by Home Guard): dam won 11f German Oaks and was second in German 1000 Guineas: well beaten in maidens at Newmarket in the spring: sold to join J. J. O'Neill 2,300 gns Newmarket September Sales. *B. W. Hills.*

PSYCHO SONNY 2 b.g. (May 22) Aragon 118–Sunny Reproach (High Top 131) **47 p** [1989 a6g⁶] 4,800Y: small, sparely-made gelding: poor walker: first foal: dam lightly raced and little worthwhile form: around 2 lengths sixth of 12, keeping on, to Tadeus in late-year claimer at Lingfield: should improve. *C. N. Allen.*

PUFF PUFF 3 b.f. All Systems Go 119–Harmonious Sound (Auction Ring (USA) **54** 123) [1988 5g 5d 5m⁵ 6g 5m 5m⁶ 1989 6g 6m⁶ 7f³ 8.5m 8.3m⁵ 7g 6m] rather leggy filly: plating-class maiden: suited by 1m: best efforts on top-of-the-ground. *M. J. Haynes.*

PUFFY 2 ch.g. (Feb 24) Wolverlife 115–Eskaroon (Artaius (USA) 129) [1989 5d⁴ **88** 5m* 5f³ 7f⁵ 6g⁶ 8f 6g* 7g⁴ 5v* 7g²] 9,600F, 14,000Y: leggy, rather sparely-made gelding: shows a quick action: second foal: dam unraced half-sister to Oaks and Irish Oaks runner-up Bourbon Girl: fair performer: successful in 5-runner maiden at Catterick and large-field sellers at Doncaster (bought in 3,600 gns) and Ayr (no bid): very good second to Higher Hamill in nursery at Newcastle: stays 7f: blinkered last 4 starts. *M. W. Easterby.*

PUISSANCE 3 b.c. Thatching 131–Girton 68 (Balidar 133) [1988 6d* 1989 6m* **110 p** 6m*] 34,000F, 110,000Y: fifth foal: half-brother to modest and irresolute maiden

EBF Greenlands Stakes, the Curragh—the favourite Puissance makes his effort on the outside of Young Hal and Big Shuffle (rails)

Mutliq and 5f winner Moorestyle Girl (both by Moorestyle) and a winner in Denmark: dam won over 5f and 6f: progressive form when justifying favouritism in maiden and listed race at Phoenix Park then Group 3 EBF Greenlands Stakes at the Curragh: beat Big Shuffle ¾ length at the Curragh in May, making smooth headway 2f out and driven out to lead inside last: later found to have fractured near-fore knee: will prove best at sprint distances: acts on top-of-the-ground and a soft surface: reportedly remains in training and should improve again if recovering from his injury. *M. V. O'Brien, Ireland.*

PULIGNY 2 b.g. (Mar 11) Glenstal (USA) 118–No Distractions 78 (Tap On Wood 130) [1989 5m⁶ 5f⁶ 6g² 7m² 8s*] IR 2,000Y: medium-sized, quite attractive gelding: first foal: dam won at 1½m from 2 starts: won 11-runner nursery at Ayr in September, showing much improved form: gelded afterwards: will stay 1¼m: acts well on soft going. *Mrs J. R. Ramsden.*   **71**

PULLOVER 4 ch.f. Windjammer (USA)–Woolcana 71 (Some Hand 119) [1988 6f² 7m* 7d 1989 5g 6d 6.1f 6f 7f⁶ 7.5m 7f] strong, workmanlike filly: carries plenty of condition: moderate mover: plating-class handicapper: ran poorly final outing: stays 7f: possibly needs a sound surface: sweating and slowly away on reappearance: sold 2,300 gns Doncaster September Sales. *T. D. Barron.*

PULPIT ROCK 2 ch.f. (May 7) Lomond (USA) 128–Piney Ridge 116 (Native Prince) [1989 5m⁶] IR 30,000Y: eighth foal (seventh to Northern Hemisphere time): half-sister to 4 winners, including 1984 2-y-o 5f winner Woodland Pines (by London Bells): dam smart 5f performer at 2 yrs: well-backed favourite, around 8 lengths sixth of 13, staying on, to Priority Paid in maiden at Windsor in June: will be suited by 6f. *R. F. Johnson Houghton.*   **—**

PULSINGH 7 br.h. Mansingh (USA) 120–Pulcini 61 (Quartette 106) [1988 10f⁵ 10g⁶ 10f 11.5g 11.7m* 11.7g 12f³ 14f⁶ 1989 12m⁶ 12f* 12f⁶ 11.7d 12m⁴ 12.2m 12fa12g] strong, good-topped horse: carries plenty of condition: poor handicapper: won strongly-run event at Lingfield in May: ran poorly last 2 outings: suited by around 1½m: acts well on firm going and probably unsuited by soft: always behind when tried in blinkers. *C. J. Benstead.*   **47**

PUMPKIN 2 b.f. (Apr 13) Top Ville 129–Bumpkin 108 (Free State 125) [1989 7g] 28,000Y: angular filly: third foal: closely related to Italian 4-y-o Toplofty (by High Top), modest staying maiden here at 2 yrs: dam sprinter: 33/1, over 12 lengths tenth of 24, prominent over 4f, to Sardegna in maiden at Newmarket in November: should do better. *T. Thomson Jones.*   **59 p**

PUNCHBAG (USA) 3 b.c. Glint of Gold 128–Cassy's Pet 89 (Sing Sing 134) [1988 7g⁵ 1989 10.8s³ 11s 9s⁶ 12f 12.5g⁵] good-topped, quite attractive colt: modest maiden: ran moderately after reappearance: stays 10.8f: acts on soft ground: sold to join G. Ham 4,600 gns Newmarket Autumn Sales. *C. A. Cyzer.*   **64**

PUNDLES PET 2 b.c. (Mar 29) Petong 126–Goody Goody 84 (Mummy's Pet 125) [1989 5d 5f 5m* 5f² 5f⁵ 6g⁵ 5g 5v⁶] 7,200Y: medium-sized, good-quartered colt: moderate walker: third foal: closely related to poor 1987 2-y-o Dream of Hannah (by Mansingh) and half-brother to a modest sprinting 2-y-o who didn't train on: dam 2-y-o 5f winner also didn't train on: won 6-runner seller at Carlisle (no bid) in May: likely to prove best at 5f: acts on any going: often blinkered (wasn't when successful): sometimes edgy: sometimes slowly away: doubtful temperamentally. *W. J. Pearce.*   **56**

PUNKIE 3 b.f. Kinglet 98–Nelodor 69 (Nelcius 133) [1988 NR 1989 8f 10f⁶] leggy, plain filly: fifth living foal: half-sister to 4-y-o 1¼m seller winner Handsome Jinko (by Some Hand): dam winning hurdler: always behind in maidens at Chepstow in July. *J. A. C. Edwards.*   **—**

PUPPET SHOW 5 b.g. Mummy's Pet 125–Contralto 100 (Busted 134) [1988 8m* 8m 8.5m⁴ 8f⁶ 8f 1989 8g 8f] rather leggy, good-topped gelding: modest winner as 4-y-o: well beaten in spring: stays 1m: acts on hard going: has won when sweating. *S. T. Harris.*   **—**

PURBECK MINSTREL 2 ch.g. (May 26) Lepanto (GER)–Singing Trooper (Air Trooper 115) [1989 5m 8.2f] rather sparely-made gelding: first reported foal: dam plater best run at 1½m: well beaten in maidens. *J. White.*   **—**

PURE GENIUS (USA) 3 ch.c. Diesis 133–Wrap It Up (Mount Hagen (FR) 127) [1988 6f⁴ 6g* 6g² 1989 8m 8.2m³ 7f] rangy, attractive colt: good mover with a long stride: 20/1, under 6 lengths seventh of 14, travelling well long way, to Nashwan in 2000 Guineas at Newmarket: ran moderately after in 3-runner minor event (odds on, making most over 6f) at Haydock and Jersey Stakes at Royal Ascot: may prove as effective at 7f as 1m: yet to race on a soft surface. *M. R. Stoute.*   **114 d**

Hamdan Al-Maktoum's "Qathif"

PURELIC 3 ch.g. Mummy's Game 120–Spring Maiden 90 (Silly Season 127) [1988 8g 1989 12.2f³] leggy, sparely-made gelding: third in claimer at Catterick in July: dead. *R. M. Whitaker.* — 53

PURE-LITE 4 b.f. Imperial Fling (USA) 116–The Huyton Girls 67 (Master Sing 109) [1988 NR 1989 5f 7.5m] small, sturdy filly: first foal: dam winning sprinter: tailed off in claimer at Wolverhampton (hung left throughout) and maiden at Beverley. *M. B. James.* — —

PURITY 2 br.c. (Feb 16) Petong 126–Integrity 108 (Reform 132) [1989 5f⁵ 6f*] 14,000F, 25,000Y: neat, attractive colt: good walker: fourth foal: half-brother to 6f claimer winner All Honesty (by Tyrnavos) and a minor winner in France by Welsh Pageant: dam won 3 times at 6f and is daughter of top 1974 2-y-o filly Cry of Truth: odds on, won 6-runner maiden at Brighton in October by a head: better suited by 6f than 5f: sold 19,000 gns Newmarket Autumn Sales. *L. M. Cumani.* — 78

PUSEY STREET BOY 2 ch.c. (May 12) Vaigly Great 127–Pusey Street 96 (Native Bazaar 122) [1989 7f⁴ 7m² 7g] leggy, lengthy, dipped-backed colt: second foal: dam sprinter: modest maiden: beaten neck in 17-runner event at Chepstow in October: stays 7f: acts on firm going. *R. Hannon.* — 71

PUSHY LOVER 2 ch.g. (Mar 20) Never So Bold 135–Princess Biddy 86 (Sun Prince 128) [1989 6g] IR 27,000Y: half-brother to several winners, including 1986 2-y-o 6f winner Hydraulic Power (by Northfields) and 3-y-o 7f winner Tender Bid (by Tender King): dam, half-sister to Royalty, Double Jump and Sunyboy, stayed 7f: soundly beaten in 17-runner maiden at Folkestone in October: sold to join D. Jermy 775 gns Ascot November Sales. *G. A. Pritchard-Gordon.* — —

PUSSY FOOT 3 b.f. Red Sunset 120–Cats 85 (Dance In Time (CAN)) [1988 5s² 5d⁶ 1989 6v² 6s⁴ 6f² 5m* 5.3h² 5g* 6m⁴ 5.3f* 5d] workmanlike filly: fair handicapper: successful at Catterick in May, Epsom (claimer) in August and Brighton (best effort) in September: suited by 5f and top-of-the-ground. *Sir Mark Prescott.* — 83

PYJAMA TOP 3 ch.g. Night Shift (USA)–Laisser Aller (Sagaro 133) [1988 8g 1989 8m] small, sturdy gelding: no form in maidens. *J. A. R. Toller.* — —

714

PYTCHLEY NIGHT   2 b.c. (Mar 7) Red Sunset 120–Lili Bengam (Welsh Saint   **72**
126) [1989 6m² 6m³] IR 9,000Y, 6,000 2-y-o: lengthy, quite good-topped colt: has
plenty of scope: second reported foal: dam Irish 5f winner: modest form, staying on
strongly, in summer maidens at Doncaster and York: will probably be better suited
by 7f. *R. Hollinshead.*

Q

QANNAAS   5 br.h. Kris 135–Red Berry 115 (Great Nephew 126) [1988 8v* 10d³   **82**
10g 12f² 12m* 12f⁵ 14m³ 14g² 12g⁴ 12d⁵ 12d⁴ 1989 12g⁴] strong, sturdy horse: fair
performer: 40/1 and burly, creditable fourth of 16, clear, in handicap at Newmarket in
October: stays 1¾m: acts on any going: occasionally sweats and gets on toes: races
up with pace: probably ran too keenly for amateur ninth outing in 1988: consistent:
winning hurdler. *Mrs D. Haine.*

QASWARAH   2 b.f. (Apr 6) Commanche Run 133–Donna Sabina (Nonoalco (USA)   **73**
131) [1989 7m⁶ 7f³] 62,000F: close-coupled, angular filly: lacks scope: fourth foal:
half-sister to Irish 3-y-o 11f winner Northern Descent (by Salmon Leap) and useful
1987 2-y-o 7f winner Jungle Jezebel (by Thatching): dam unraced daughter of Irish
1000 Guineas winner Lady Capulet: 1¼ lengths third 8, taking keen hold and no
extra final 1f, to Oblist in maiden at Leicester in October: can win a race. *A. C.
Stewart.*

QATHIF (USA)   2 b.c. (Mar 29) Riverman (USA) 131–Al Bayan (USA) 82 **111**
(Northern Dancer) [1989 6g* 8g³] robust, deep-girthed, attractive colt: good
mover: second foal: dam, 7f winner, is daughter of half-sister to Prix Morny winner
Broadway Dancer: favourite, won minor event at Ascot by a length from Notley,
leading 2f out but running green: second favourite, over 4 lengths third of 5 to Be
My Chief in Racing Post Trophy at Newcastle later in October, finding little having
made good headway on bridle over 2f out: likely to prove best short of 1m. *H.
Thomson Jones.*

QIRMAZI (USA)   2 ch.f. (Feb 7) Riverman (USA) 131–Cream'N Crimson (USA) **113**
(Vaguely Noble 140) [1989 6g* 6d* 6g² 7g² 8g⁵] $160,000Y: attractive filly: has a
round action: second foal: dam twice-raced half-sister to high-class filly T V Vixen,

Sheikh Mohammed's "Qirmazi"

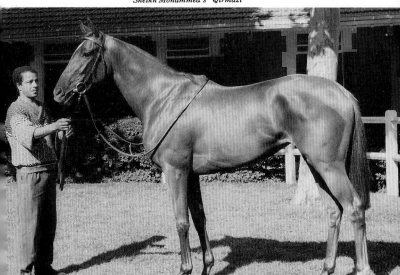

successful at up to 9f, and to useful French 1¼m performer Eastland: successful in newcomers race at Saint-Cloud and Prix de Cabourg (by ½ length from Spendomania) at Deauville: runner-up behind Machiavellian in Prix Morny Agence Francaise at Deauville and Prix de la Salamandre (beaten ½ length) at Longchamp: only fifth behind Salsabil in Prix Marcel Boussac at Longchamp in October: should stay 1m. *A. Fabre, France.*

QISMAT   2 b.c. (Feb 15) Doulab (USA) 115–Borshch (Bonne Noel 115) [1989 5d] 8,400F, 16,000Y: leggy colt: third foal: half-brother to 3-y-o Imperial Torte (by Bold Lad, IRE): dam lightly raced in Ireland, is from family of Arctique Royale and Ardross: 20/1, always outpaced in 12-runner maiden at Newmarket in April. *I. V. Matthews.*   —

QUALITAIR AVIATOR   3 b.g. Valiyar 129–Comtec Princess 73 (Gulf Pearl 117) [1988 6f 7m 8s 8.5f⁶ 8v 1989 12g⁶ 11f 12m* 16.2g⁴ 12.4m 12g⁴ 12.3m³ 12f⁵ 14m 14m 12s⁶ a14g* a11g* a14g] close-coupled, workmanlike gelding: moderate mover: won claimer at Newmarket in May and in very good form in handicaps at Southwell in December, making virtually all to win by 10 lengths then 3 lengths: stays 1¾m: possibly unsuited by extremes of going: often takes keen hold: suited by good gallop and forcing tactics: trained until after fourth outing by K. Stone. *J. F. Bottomley.*   76

QUALITAIR BLAZER   2 ch.f. (Feb 22) Blazing Saddles (AUS)–Midfirna (Midsummer Night II 117) [1989 5s 5g² 6m⁶ 6g 8g] 1,500Y: compact filly: first foal: dam unraced: poor maiden: best effort when blinkered in seller second start: trained first 3 outings by K. Stone. *J. F. Bottomley.*   39

QUALITAIR DREAM   2 b.f. (Feb 20) Dreams To Reality (USA) 113–Maputo Princess (Raga Navarro (ITY) 119) [1989 5g⁴ 5f⁶ 7g⁴ 7m² 6g* 6d² 6g* 6m 7d] small, workmanlike, good-quartered filly: third foal: half-sister to platers by Rabdan and Wattlefield: dam behind in varied company: former plater: successful in nurseries at Newmarket in August and October, putting up improved performance when beating Milne's Way 2½ lengths on seventh start: stays 7f: trained first 2 outings by K. Stone. *J. F. Bottomley.*   80

QUALITAIR SWEETIE   2 ch.g. (May 11) Sweet Monday 122–Right Abella 74 (Right Boy 137) [1989 6m 7m⁶ 8m] 2,800Y: workmanlike gelding: seventh foal: half-brother to a winner in Scandinavia by Class Distinction: dam panicer: plating-class maiden: trained by K. Stone on debut: off course over 2 months between starts. *J. F. Bottomley.*   56

QUAVERING   2 b.c. (Apr 29) The Minstrel (CAN) 135–Flicker Toa Flame (USA) 85 (Empery (USA) 128) [1989 7m 7g³] IR 360,000Y: good-bodied colt: second foal: dam, stayed 1m, is half-sister to Motavato, smart at up to 1m: always-prominent third of 29, beaten under ½ length, to Lord of The Field in maiden at Newmarket in November: very green on debut: rather headstrong, and wears a crossed noseband. *J. Gosden.*   90

QUEEN ANGEL   3 b.f. Anfield 117–More Or Less 64 (Morston (FR) 125) [1988 5f 6g⁴ 6f³ 5g⁴ 7f⁵ 6m 1989 10.2m⁶ 11.7m* 11.1f* 12m³] lengthy, good-bodied filly: moderate mover: fair handicapper: comfortable winner at Windsor and Kempton (odds on) in May: fair third at Epsom following month: stays 1½m: acts on firm going: consistent. *Miss B. Sanders.*   88

QUEEN OF ATHENS   3 b.f. Ela-Mana-Mou 132–Salote (USA) 109 (Forli (ARG)) [1988 7f 1989 10.2f³ 10f⁵] lightly-made filly: good mover: third in maiden at Bath in September, only form: should stay 1½m: sold 2,100 gns Newmarket Autumn Sales. *I. A. Balding.*   60

QUEENS MAN   7 ch.g. Remainder Man 126§–Dior Queen 92 (Manacle 123) [1988 12g⁴ 17.1g⁵ 16m 1989 21.6d⁶] tall, plain gelding: bad handicapper: probably doesn't stay extreme distances: ungenuine. *T. Fairhurst.*   — §

QUEENS TOUR   4 b.c. Sweet Monday 122–On Tour 60 (Queen's Hussar 124) [1988 9v³ 8.2v* 9d⁴ 8d⁴ 8.2s⁶ 8.2m³ 9f⁶ 9g³ 9g 8d² 8.2g⁶ 10g* 10f 10g 8.2s² 10s² 9s⁵ 8.2s* 10g⁵ 1989 10d* 12v 10g⁵ 12s 12f 10.6d a10g⁵ 10g] small, lightly-made colt: poor walker and mover: 20/1-winner of £10,800 Rosebery Handicap at Kempton in March: well below his best last 5 outings: suited by 1¼m: best with give in the ground: suitable mount for apprentice. *M. Brittain.*   81

QUELLE CHEMISE   3 b.f. Night Shift (USA)–Quaranta 83 (Hotfoot 126) [1988 6m 6m 1989 8.5g⁶ 9f⁵] rangy filly: good mover, with a quick action: quite modest maiden: not seen out after May: will be suited by 1¼m + : acts on firm ground. *W. Jarvis.*   65

QUESSARD   5 ch.g. Ardross 134–Marquessa d'Howfen 93 (Pitcairn 126) [1988 12f⁶ 12g 10d 10g 10m 14m 17.4s 1989 12d⁵ 16g 17.6f⁴ 15g 17f 15g²] strong, lengthy   47 gelding: has shown traces of stringhalt: powerful galloper with a round action: fair maiden at best, but has deteriorated considerably: stays 15f: best with give in the ground: visored once at 4 yrs: winning hurdler. *F. H. Lee.*

QUEST FOR FAME 2 b.c. (Feb 15) Rainbow Quest (USA) 134–Aryenne (FR) 89 p 125 (Green Dancer (USA) 132) [1989 8v²] rangy, good sort: third foal: half-brother to fair maidens Vestris and In Orbit (both by Habitat): dam, from fine family, won Criterium des Pouliches and Poule d'Essai des Pouliches: favourite, 4 lengths second of 23, green 2f out then running on strongly, to Tyburn Tree in minor event at Newbury in October: will stay 1¼m: sure to improve, and win a maiden at least. *J. Tree.*

QUESTION OF DEGREE 3 b.c. Known Fact (USA) 135–Bernice Clare 68 **68** (Skymaster 126) [1988 NR 1989 9s⁶ 8d 8g 8.2g² 9g 8.2f*] small colt: moderate walker: sixth live foal: half-brother to 1982 2-y-o 1m winner Mister Valentino (by Wollow) and winners in Yugoslavia and Belgium: dam won over 1m at 4 yrs: modest form: 7/1 from 16/1, won claimer at Nottingham in September: stays 1m well: acts on firm going: trained first 2 starts by J. Hanson: has joined N. Tinkler. *Miss S. E. Hall.*

QUICHE 3 b.f. Formidable (USA) 125–La Galette 76 (Double Form 130) [1988 **83** 5m⁴ 5.8d⁶ 1989 5s 6m 6m 6m⁶ 6m* 6f* 7f 6m³ 6m 6g³] small, attractive filly: fair handicapper: successful in good style at Windsor and Folkestone (odds on) in July: good third at Newmarket after: taken last and quietly to post in between: keen sort, unlikely to stay beyond 6f: acts on firm going: sold 50,000 gns Newmarket December Sales. *J. Tree.*

QUICK PROFIT 2 b.f. (Apr 9) Formidable (USA) 125–Penny Blessing 112 (So — p Blessed 130) [1989 5m] sixth foal: sister to quite moderate 9f and 1¼m winner Tizzy and half-sister to 4 winners, including 3-y-o Song of Hope (by Chief Singer), useful 5f winner in 1988: dam, at best at 2 yrs when 5f winner, is from family of Mummy's Pet, Parsimony and Arch Sculptor: well-backed 5/2, around 10 lengths seventh of 10, never able to challenge, to Darakah in maiden at Lingfield in September: evidently thought capable of better. *R. F. Johnson Houghton.*

QUICK STICKS 5 ch.m. Red Regent 123–Ahadoon (Gulf Pearl 117) [1988 5m 6g 6g 5m⁵ 6f⁵ 6f³ 5f 7g 6g 6g⁴ 7m 8f 8.5m² 12.2f 9f³ 5m² 13.8g 6s³ 1989 5g⁶ 6m 6m 5m 6f 6f 5m⁵ 5f] sturdy, lengthy mare: poor maiden: effective at 5f and stays 9f: probably acts on any going: blinkered once at 4 yrs: has run creditably for apprentice: sold 2,100 gns Doncaster June Sales. *D. W. Chapman.*

QUICK TEMPO 2 b.c. (Mar 26) Shareef Dancer (USA) 135–Mineown 85 (Roan **63** Rocket 128) [1989 6m 5.8f⁴ 6h³] smallish, stocky colt: half-brother to several winners by Bustino, including useful Italian middle-distance winner Valtino and good-class Bustomi: dam, placed over 5f and 6f, is half-sister to top-class Italian Weimar: quite modest maiden: will be better suited by 7f: has joined C. Brittain. *Major W. R. Hern.*

QUI DANZIG (USA) 2 b.c. (Feb 27) Danzig (USA)–Qui Royalty (USA) (Native **102** Royalty (USA)) [1989 6m* 6f² 7g²] $825,000Y: rather leggy, quite attractive colt: fifth foal: closely related to Bakharoff (by The Minstrel) and half-brother to 2 other winners, notably Sum (by Spectacular Bid), successful at up to 1¼m, including in graded stakes: dam very useful stakes-placed winner at up to 1m: useful colt: impressive 7-length debut winner of minor event at Windsor in June: placed in Scottish Equitable Richmond Stakes (beaten 2½ lengths by Contract Law, having travelled strongly over 4f) at Goodwood following month and listed race (beaten a neck by Free At Last) at Newmarket in October: likely to stay 1m: keen sort. *M. R. Stoute.*

QUIET ACHIEVER (CAN) 4 ch.g. Overskate (CAN)–From Nine To Five **44** (USA) (Secretariat (USA)) [1988 10.8d 8f 7m 10g 8m 10.2g 1989 10.2g 8.5f⁶ 10f⁶ 10m 10m⁵ 5f 8f*] rangy gelding: has a round action: 12/1 and wearing tongue strap, showed improved form when winning 15-runner apprentice handicap at Pontefract in October by 6 lengths: best at 1m: acts on firm going: sweating fourth outing. *C. E. Brittain.*

QUIET AMERICAN (USA) 3 b.c. Fappiano (USA)–Demure (Dr Fager) **78** [1988 7m² 1989 9s³ 10g] rangy, useful-looking colt: has an easy, long-striding action: fair form in maidens and minor event: not seen out after May: should be suited by further than 9f and by forcing tactics. *M. R. Stoute.*

QUIET ARROGANCE (USA) 3 b.f. Greek Sky (USA)–Figurative (USA) — (Bolinas Boy (USA)) [1988 6g⁶ 7g⁵ 1989 10.2m⁶ 11m] workmanlike, angular filly: quite modest form in minor events in 1988: faced stiff tasks in summer as 3-y-o: better at 7f than 6f, and should stay further. *S. G. Norton.*

QUIET AWAKENING (USA) 3 b.f. Secreto (USA) 128–Soft Morning (USA) **101** (Talc (USA)) [1988 NR 1989 12m* 10.1m* 12m⁴] $135,000Y: angular filly: first foal: dam won 11 races, including stakes events over 7f and 1m: comfortable winner of apprentice maiden at Newmarket in July and minor event (odds on) at Windsor in August: creditable fourth to Snow Bride in Princess Royal Stakes at Ascot: stays 1½m. *J. Gosden.*

QUIET RIOT 7 b.g. Hotfoot 126–Tuyenu 77 (Welsh Pageant 132) [1988 12m **58** 12.2d⁶ 12g⁴ 12m 1989 10.8s 10.2g 14m⁴ 14f* 12m⁴ 14.8m² 18.8f⁵ a13g] strong, good-topped gelding: has a round action: quite modest handicapper: won 4-runner event at Kempton in June decisively by 8 lengths: well beaten final outing, first for over 4 months: stays 1¾m: acts on any going: blinkered once, visored once: slowly away seventh start: good mount for apprentice. *J. White.*

QUINLAN TERRY 4 b.c. Welsh Pageant 132–Quaranta 83 (Hotfoot 126) [1988 **84** 8.5m² 8.2s* 8m² 10m* 9g⁴ 10f² 9g* 1989 10d⁴ 10m 12m 12f* 12.3g 12m³ 12m 12s 11v⁵] big, strong colt: has shown traces of stringhalt: carries plenty of condition: progressed throughout 1988, winning William Hill Cambridgeshire Handicap at Newmarket on final start: generally well below his best as 4-y-o: best effort when third of 6 to Halkopous in £7,300 handicap at Kempton in September: earlier justified favouritism in amateurs event at Hamilton: stays 1½m: acts on any going: raced freely in blinkers seventh outing: sold reportedly to race in Singapore 82,000 gns Newmarket Autumn Sales. *Sir Mark Prescott.*

QUINTA ROYALE 2 b.c. (Apr 15) Sayyaf 121–Royal Holly (Royal Buck) [1989 **70** 5f² 6g² 5g³] 4,800 2-y-o: strong, lengthy colt: fourth foal: half-brother to a winning hurdler: dam ran twice at 5 yrs in Ireland: quite modest form in maidens: likely to prove suited by further than 6f. *R. Akehurst.*

QUINTO 3 b.g. Tumble Wind (USA)–Con Carni (Blakeney 126) [1988 5m⁶ 6f 8d **46** 1989 8g 8f 10.1m 10f² 12f³ 10f³ 9f⁶ 10f³ 10f³] close-coupled gelding: moderate walker: moderate plater: probably stays 1½m: acts on firm going: often blinkered and claimer ridden: takes good hold: has twice tended to hang: sold to join Miss P. Hall 5,200 gns Newmarket Autumn Sales. *P. J. Makin.*

QUIP 4 ch.g. High Line 125–Sans Blague (USA) 108 (The Minstrel (CAN) 135) **46** [1988 11f⁶ 12f⁴ 13.3d 1989 13.8d 10f 12g⁴ 16f 12.3f⁶ 12m 10g 10m 11g⁴ 12g⁵ 13s⁴ 12.2f* 12s⁵] leggy gelding: has a long stride: won for first time when making all in apprentice handicap at Warwick in October: stays 1½m: acts on firm going and probably not at best on soft: visored second to sixth outings: often sweats: headstrong (saddle slipped fourth outing) and is a difficult ride: usually taken down early or very steadily. *M. P. Naughton.*

QUITE A FIGHTER 2 b.f. (May 11) Hard Fought 125–Snow Tribe 94 (Great **64** Nephew 126) [1989 6m² 7f³ 6g⁵ 8m 8.2s] rangy, angular filly: moderate mover: seventh foal: half-sister to several winners, including fair middle-distance winner and useful hurdler Past Glories (by Hittite Glory) and Yorkshire Cup winner Line Slinger (by High Line): dam staying daughter of St Leger third Cold Storage: quite modest form in minor events on first 3 starts: ran moderately in maiden and nursery afterwards: should be suited by 1m + . *J. Hetherton.*

QUITE SO 5 br.m. Mansingh (USA) 120–Chiquitita 44 (Reliance II 137) [1988 NR — § 1989 5f 5f 5m 7m] small mare: modest winner early as 2-y-o: no subsequent form and seems ungenuine. *J. Pearce.*

QUORN DONA 3 b.f. Monsanto (FR) 121–Miramichi (Artaius (USA) 129) [1988 **47** 5f³ 7g 7g 7m 7f³ 1989 6g³ 7.6m 7g⁶ 6g 6g] lengthy, workmanlike filly: moderate mover: poor maiden: ran well in seller (ridden by 5-lb claimer) and claimer first 2 outings, poorly last 2 starts: stays 7.6f: acts on top-of-the-ground: sold 1,500 gns Doncaster November Sales. *C. R. Beever.*

R

RAAHIN (USA) 4 ch.c. Super Concorde (USA) 128–Bonnie Hope (USA) **72** (Nijinsky (CAN) 138) [1988 12s* 10m² 12d 10.2m⁵ 12m² 12f³ 12f² 10g 12.2d 1989 14f³ 14f³ 14f* 16f³ 14m⁵ 16f² 14m] lengthy colt: moderate mover: modest handicapper: co-favourite, very well ridden when making all at Sandown in June: placed after, running creditably, in £9,200 contest at Ascot and 5-runner event at Lingfield: stays 2m: acts on any going: visored once at 3 yrs: goes well with forcing tactics: sold to join N. Tinkler 16,000 gns Newmarket Autumn Sales: winning hurdler. *R. Akehurst.*

RA'A (USA) 2 ch.f. (Feb 27) Diesis 133–Shicklah (USA) 106 (The Minstrel (CAN) **101** p
135) [1989 6g* 5g*] compact filly: third foal: half-sister to 3-y-o Alshahhad (by Slew
O'Gold) and 1¾m-placed Aljasur (by Alleged): dam, useful 5f and 6f winner at 2 yrs,
from family of Habitat: successful in October in maiden at Goodwood and minor
event (made all, beating Judgement Call easily by 5 lengths) at Carlisle: bred to stay
at least 7f: sure to win more races. *H. Thomson Jones.*

RACECALL GOLD CARD 2 ch.g. (Mar 5) Camden Town 125–Polly Royal 75 —
(Music Boy 124) [1989 7g] IR 3,000F, 16,000Y: good-topped gelding: third foal: dam
6f and 7f winner: 25/1 and backward, tailed-off last of 20 in maiden at Newbury in
August: subsequently gelded. *M. McCormack.*

RACEY NASKRA (USA) 3 b.f. Star de Naskra (USA)–Langness (USA) 97 **75**
(Roberto (USA) 131) [1988 NR 1989 7f⁵ 7.5m* 7g⁵ 7.6f⁴] 40,000Y: medium-sized,
rather angular filly: sixth foal: half-sister to 2 minor winners in USA: dam 1m and
1½m winner: won maiden at Beverley in August: good fourth in handicap at
Lingfield, better subsequent effort: will stay further: sold to join N. Tinkler 10,000
gns Newmarket December Sales. *H. R. A. Cecil.*

RACHEL'S DREAM 3 b.f. Grey Ghost 98–Ellaron 60 (Abwah 118) [1988 NR —
1989 8g 8m 6h⁵] smallish, lengthy filly: second reported foal: half-sister to poor
maiden Abacometti (by Giacometti): dam 1¼m winner: bit backward and ridden by
7-lb claimer, well-beaten last in maidens and claimer (pulling hard) in the North.
Denys Smith.

RACHMANINOV (FR) 4 ch.c. Brustolon 117–Rivoltade (USA) (Sir Ivor 135) **116** §
[1988 10.5v 11g* 12m⁴ 12d 12m⁴ 15m 12.5d 12.5m³ 13.5g 10m 15m² 12f 1989 12v*
15.5s³ 15.5s* 12m⁶ 12d 15d⁴ 13.5s⁴ 20m² 15.5g⁴ 11v³] French colt: bad mover:
successful in 70,000-franc event at Saint-Cloud in March and in Prix Vicomtesse
Vigier at Longchamp (beating Trebrook 1½ lengths) in April: in frame after in
pattern events at Deauville (twice), Longchamp (twice, including Prix Royal-Oak)
and Milan: ran badly fifth outing: stays extreme distances: acts on top-of-the-ground
and heavy going: has often worn blinkers, but didn't in 1989: sometimes gets well
behind: smart, but is of doubtful temperament. *E. Lellouche, France.*

RACING HOME (FR) 3 b.f. Dom Racine (FR) 121–Waulkmill (Grundy 137) **85**
[1988 7g³ 6g* 6d⁵ 7.3m 7d⁴ 7d* 1989 8s 8.5m 8f² 8g⁶] lengthy filly: has a free, round
action: fair performer: 33/1, good second in £9,200 event at Ascot in June, easily
best effort in handicaps: well out of depth in Child Stakes at Newmarket 18 days
later: will stay 1¼m: acts on firm going and a soft surface: tends to be on toes:
sweating last 3 outings: genuine: sold 15,000 gns Newmarket December Sales. *C. E.
Brittain.*

RADISH 'N' LEMON 3 b.c. Young Generation 129–Lady of Chalon (USA) **60**
(Young Emperor 133) [1988 6g 1989 8h*dis 8g 8f] leggy, lengthy, rather
sparely-made colt: won seller (bought in 5,800 gns) at Carlisle in June by 6 lengths
but disqualified after testing positive: ran poorly in handicaps after, off course
nearly 4 months before final (visored) start: stays 1m: acts on hard ground. *J. P.
Hudson.*

R A EXPRESS 4 b.g. Bay Express 132–Pinaka 69 (Pitcairn 126) [1988 5g 5m 7g **46**
6m 5g⁵ 5m 5f 1989 7.6m 5m 6g⁴ 5s⁵ 5s] rather leggy, good-topped gelding: sprint
maiden: seems to need give in the ground. *B. A. McMahon.*

RAFHA 2 b.f. (Feb 19) Kris 135–Eljazzi 92 (Artaius (USA) 129) [1989 6f* **108**
6g² 7g² 8g*]
    Seldom has a trainer dominated a pattern race in recent years as Henry
Cecil has the May Hill EBF Stakes at Doncaster. His latest winner Rafha was
his sixth since Bright Crocus started the ball rolling in 1982, a prodigious
record in a race inaugurated only as recently as 1981 and one which was
rivalled in the 'eighties only by Vincent O'Brien's seven victories in the
G.P.A. National Stakes. The small, sturdy Rafha lined up as 11/8 favourite at
Doncaster having won an uncompetitive two-runner maiden at Goodwood and
come second in minor events at Newmarket and Epsom. On each occasion
Rafha ran as if longer distances wouldn't come amiss, particularly at Epsom in
August when she couldn't quicken to hold the subsequent Premio Dormello
winner Ruby Tiger, having looked an assured winner two furlongs out, and
went down by a neck conceding 10 lb. The five-runner field that assembled for
the May Hill was one of the weakest of any pattern event during the
season—the fairly useful Fair Titania, fourth to Rafha's stable-companion
Moon Cactus in the Black Bottle Scotch Whisky Prestige Stakes at Goodwood

*May Hill EBF Stakes, Doncaster—Rafha hangs,
but is too good for the hard-ridden Knight's Baroness*

on her previous outing, and the fair maiden winner Varnish seemed the best of Rafha's opponents—but Doncaster's galloping mile brought about considerable improvement from the stoutly-bred Knight's Baroness, and Rafha had to be forcefully ridden to uphold her trainer's fine record. Dropped out at the back early on, Rafha made headway two furlongs out as Knight's Baroness kicked for home, wore down the leader under sustained pressure and stayed on gamely to win by a length. In the final furlong Rafha and Knight's Baroness drew nearly eight lengths (it was officially returned as six) clear of Fair Titania, who was eased slightly when her chance had gone, and left Varnish and Gold Nostalgia well behind. The one disconcerting aspect of Rafha's performance was her tendency to hang left as she was making her challenge, but it came to light later that her bit had slipped through her mouth causing problems for her rider. Although the distances in the May Hill read more like a three-mile chase Rafha, while undoubtedly a useful filly, didn't do enough to convince us that she's a serious contender for the classics, and she'll probably have to settle for lesser honours at three.

			Sharpen Up	Atan
		Kris	(ch 1969)	Rocchetta
		(ch 1976)	Doubly Sure	Reliance II
Rafha			(b 1971)	Soft Angels
(b.f. Feb 19, 1987)			Artaius	Round Table
		Eljazzi	(b 1974)	Stylish Pattern
		(b 1981)	Border Bounty	Bounteous
			(b 1965)	B Flat

The home-bred Rafha is the second foal and first runner from the former Cecil-trained Eljazzi, whose three other offspring are colts by Bellypha, Slip Anchor and Ardross. The lightly-raced Eljazzi looked set for a money-spinning career as a three-year-old after winning her only race (over seven furlongs) impressively at two, but she failed to make the anticipated improvement when put over middle distances and didn't add to her tally. Even if she had never made the racecourse Eljazzi always had a future at stud, for she's a half-sister to the high-class miler Pitcairn and the very smart middle-distance stayer Valley Forge out of the Yorkshire Oaks and Park Hill runner-up Border Bounty. There's plenty of stamina on this side of Rafha's family—her third dam B Flat also needed at least a mile and a half and has bred the Yorkshire Oaks third Brief Chorus besides Border Bounty—and the round-actioned Rafha will have no trouble staying a mile and a half. She has raced only on good or firm going. *H. R. A. Cecil.*

RAGLAN STREET (USA) 3 b.c. Sassafras (FR) 135–Welsh Maiden (Welsh — Pageant 132) [1988 10d 1989 8g 11v⁵ 12m⁶ 10f 11f 12h⁶ 12m] compact colt: moderate mover: poor form, including in sellers: may prove suited by 1¼m: sweating final start: sold 2,000 gns Doncaster August Sales. *T. D. Barron.*

RAGTIME 2 b.c. (Feb 25) Pas de Seul 133–Boldella (Bold Lad (IRE) 133) [1989 59 6m⁴ 7m] 10,500F, 10,000Y: neat, strong colt: good walker: fourth foal: half-brother to fairly useful Irish hurdler Lunulae (by Tumble Wind), 7f winner at 2 yrs: dam won over 11f at 3 yrs in Ireland: around 9 lengths fourth of 8, running on well from rear 2f out, to Karinga Bay in maiden at York in July: well beaten in £15,300 event there following month: should stay 1m. *C. W. C. Elsey.*

RAG TIME BELLE 3 ch.f. Raga Navarro (ITY) 119–Betbellof 65 (Averof 123) — [1988 5g 7m 1989 8s⁵ 10.2m] close-coupled filly: little form in quite modest company: pulled very hard final start: sweating on reappearance: sold to join M. Eckley 1,450 gns Ascot 2nd June Sales. *P. J. Jones.*

RAGTIME COWBOY 2 b.g. (Mar 23) Indian King (USA) 128–F Sharp 83 — (Formidable (USA) 125) [1989 6m] 10,000Y: first foal: dam, 1¼m winner stayed 1½m, is daughter of sister to Lancashire Oaks winner Rhein Bridge and half-sister to very smart Connaught Bridge: 50/1, always behind in 20-runner maiden at Ripon in August: subsequently gelded. *C. W. Thornton.*

RAGTIME SOLO 5 b.g. Raga Navarro (ITY) 119–Solentown 72 (Town Crier — 119) [1988 NR 1989 15.5s⁴] leggy, close-coupled gelding: poor mover: poor maiden: probably stays 1½m: acts on firm going and a soft surface: has shown a tendency to wander: winning selling hurdler. *R. J. Hodges.*

RAHAAM (USA) 2 gr.f. (Mar 4) Secreto (USA) 128–Fager's Glory (USA) (Mr 84 p Prospector (USA)) [1989 6g²] useful-looking filly: has scope: sixth foal: half-sister to very useful 1986 2-y-o 7f and 7.5f winner Glory Forever (by Forever Casting), later third in French 2000 Guineas, and 2 winners in USA: dam never ran: 20/1, most promising 2½ lengths second of 29, staying on in excellent style at 2f, to Sure Sharp in maiden at Newmarket in November: will be suited by 7f + : sure to improve and win races. *H. R. A. Cecil.*

RAHIK 3 b.f. Wassl 125–Rambling Rose 118 (Silly Season 127) [1988 5d* 6g² 7g² 92 1989 7g³ 8g] lightly-made filly: moderate walker and mover: fairly useful performer: creditable third, battling on well, in £5,000 apprentice race at Ascot in September: tailed off in listed event there 15 days later: best form over 7f: visits Persian Bold. *R. W. Armstrong.*

RAH WAN (USA) 3 ch.c. Riverman (USA) 131–Thorough 115 (Thatch (USA) 91 136) [1988 NR 1989 8m⁴ 8.2g² 7g*] quite attractive colt: third foal: dam French 1m to 1½m winner: weak second favourite on first run for over 3½ months, won maiden at Catterick in October: fairly useful form in similar events at York and Haydock when trained by A. Stewart: will probably stay 1¼m. *N. A. Callaghan.*

RAIL D'OR (FR) 2 ch.c. (May 7) Brustolon 117–Rain Or Shine (FR) (Nonoalco 84 (USA) 131) [1989 7m⁴ 6f² 7g* 7g 7.3m 8g] 150,000 francs (approx £13,700) Y, 25,000 2-y-o: good-quartered colt: moderate walker: poor mover: fourth foal: brother to Brin d'Or, winner in France at about 1¼m, and half-brother to French 3-y-o 7f winner Rain Or Zino (by Zino): dam unraced half-sister to smart sprinter Reasonable: fair performer: won maiden at Ayr in July: better efforts ½-length second to Lord Glen in minor event there (hung left) and seventh of 11 to Charming Ballerina in nursery (sweating) at Newbury on penultimate start: stays 7f. *P. Mitchell.*

RAINBOW BRIDGE 2 br.g. (Apr 28) Godswalk (USA) 130–Regal Entrance **67** §
(Be My Guest (USA) 126) [1989 5d⁴ 5f⁵ 5m⁶ 7f 6f 7m 6g* 6m* 6m 6g² 6v] 27,000Y:
strong, close-coupled gelding: carries condition: second foal: dam won at 7f in
Ireland: very useful plater: successful at Yarmouth (bought in 4,600 gns) and
Lingfield (bought in 8,200 gns) in September: very good second to Mac Kelty in
nursery at Hamilton: suited by 6f: often edgy: has carried head high, and looked
ungenerous: gelded after final start: thoroughly inconsistent. *P. S. Felgate.*

RAINBOW DANCER 3 ch.c. Pharly (FR) 130–Splashing 123 (Petingo 135) —
[1988 6g 5f⁶ 8g 1989 7g a6g] small, stocky, dipped-backed colt: not a good walker: no
worthwhile form, including in 1m listed race and 7f seller: off course 7 months after
reappearance: sold 675 gns Ascot November Sales. *R. Simpson.*

RAINBOW STRIPES 2 ch.c. (Feb 22) Rainbow Quest (USA) 134–Pampas Miss — p
(USA) (Pronto) [1989 7g] 18,000Y: big, useful-looking colt: rather unfurnished:
sixth foal: half-brother to 3 winners in Ireland and abroad, including very useful
French 9f and 11f winner Samalex (by Ela-Mana-Mou): dam lightly-raced daughter
of top-class American filly Bayou: 33/1 and backward, showed signs of ability when
tenth of 13, keeping on steadily, to Duke of Paducah in £10,000 event at Newmarket
in October: should improve. *R. Guest.*

RAIN BURST 3 ch.f. Tolomeo 127–Pluvial 90 (Habat 127) [1988 7f³ 7h* 8g³ **116**
1989 7f* 8f² 8f* 8f⁵ 8g³ 8g* 7d³ 8f²] well-made filly: has a quick action: won minor
events at Lingfield (well below best) in May and Goodwood in June and £7,100 event
at Kempton (by 3 lengths from Point House) in September: ran on well from off pace
and beaten neck in £50,000 event at Gulfstream Park, USA, in November: will prove
best at up to 1m: acts on hard going: smart: to be trained by Scotty Schulhofer in
USA in 1990. *L. M. Cumani.*

RAIN-N-SUN 3 gr.c. Warpath 113–Sun Noddy (Tom Noddy 104) [1988 6m 8d 6m —
1989 8m] lengthy, angular, plain colt: well beaten in quite modest company. *J. L.
Harris.*

RAISE A STAR 4 b.g. Red Sunset 120–Hill's Realm (USA) 68 (Key To The **44**
Kingdom (USA)) [1988 10d 10.1m⁵ 10m 6m 8s 1989 12f 10m⁴ 10h⁶ 8f² 8.3d⁴ 10f²
10.2f³ a10g] quite attractive gelding: poor maiden: stays 1¼m: acts on firm going and
a soft surface: has been reluctant at stalls: wandered under pressure third start. *R.
Akehurst.*

RAJA KHAN (USA) 8 br.g. Raja Baba (USA)–Whole Wheat (USA) (Prince —
Mito) [1988 NR 1989 16f] close-coupled gelding: extremely lightly raced on flat
nowadays: 33/1, tailed off in amateurs handicap at Chepstow in July: has given
trouble at start: has won for amateur. *K. G. Wingrove.*

RAJANPOUR (USA) 4 ch.c. Riverman (USA) 131–Rajpoura 118 (Kashmir II —
125) [1988 NR 1989 10v 12.5g⁵ 12m⁵] angular, sturdy colt: first foal: dam won at 1¼m
and 1½m in France and stayed 13.5f: has shown signs of a little ability: slowly away
first 2 starts: trained until after then by H. O'Neill. *R. Curtis.*

RAJ WAKI (USA) 2 b.c. (Feb 27) Miswaki (USA) 124–Script Approval **107** p
(USA) (Silent Screen (USA)) [1989 7f*]
    It's hardly making a controversial statement to say that the British- and
Irish-trained two-year-olds of 1989 weren't an outstanding bunch. That
doesn't necessarily mean high-class three-year-olds will be thin on the
ground in 1990, however, and this colt is just one of several lightly-raced
unbeaten colts who could be anything. Raj Waki made his sole appearance as a
two-year-old in the five-runner Chichester City Maiden Stakes on Extel
Handicap day at Goodwood in July. His stable had already captured the day's
feature event with Biennial, and Raj Waki, a well-backed favourite, put up a
performance of undeniable promise. Admittedly, the opposition didn't amount
to much, but Raj Waki proved himself in a different league, making smooth
headway early in the straight then quickening clear most impressively from
two out to beat Lift And Load by eight lengths, both horses being eased inside
the final furlong. The winner is apparently very highly regarded in his stable,
and it was suggested that the Imry Solario Stakes at Sandown or the Laurent
Perrier Champagne Stakes at Doncaster could be suitable targets for him
later in the season. The Granby Stakes at Sandown in September was
definitely on the agenda for he was declared overnight, only to be withdrawn a
few hours prior to the race with some reports suggesting he'd been coughing.

Mr Roy Taiano's "Raj Waki"

Raj Waki isn't the most fashionably-bred horse in his stable, but there's no shortage of winners in his family. His dam Script Approval, who ran just once, has produced several, including Agitated Lady (by the good American middle-distance horse Agitate), who showed useful form at up to nine furlongs, while his grandam Script Girl won seven times from thirty-six outings and is also responsible for a number of run-of-the-mill winners. Raj Waki's third dam is Solid Thought, a stakes winner of ten races and the dam of the Middle Park winner Junius and Gentle Thoughts, who won both the Flying Childers and the Cheveley Park Stakes back in 1973; she's also the dam of Belle Pensee, who won over a mile and a quarter in France and has since produced both the Yorkshire Cup winner Eastern Mystic and Treizieme, who showed very smart form from a mile to a mile and a half in France and subsequently did well in the States.

Raj Waki (USA) (b.c. Feb 27, 1987)	Miswaki (USA) (ch 1978)	Mr Prospector (b 1970)	Raise A Native Gold Digger	
		Hopespringseternal (ch 1971)	Buckpasser Rose Bower	
	Script Approval (USA) (b 1972)	Silent Screen (ch 1967)	Prince John Prayer Bell	
		Script Girl (b 1966)	Pappa Fourway Solid Thought	

Whether Raj Waki will stay middle distances is difficult to assess. Miswaki has sired horses who stay quite well—among them the Criterium de Saint-Cloud winner Waki River—but most of his stock so far have shown their best form at a mile or thereabouts. What isn't in doubt, though, is that Raj Waki has the potential to make his presence felt in good company during 1990. A well-made colt with plenty of scope, he cost his connections 90,000 dollars at the Keeneland September Sale as a yearling. *G. Harwood.*

RAKAN (USA) 3 b.c. Danzig (USA)–Over Your Shoulder (USA) 77 (Graustark) **79** [1988 7d⁶ 1989 8g 10m⁵ 10.8f² 12m] strong, sturdy colt: has a round action: modest maiden: should stay 1½m: acts on firm ground: sold 11,000 gns Newmarket Autumn Sales. *H. Thomson Jones.*

RAMBADALE 2 ch.f. (Feb 28) Vaigly Great 127–Corinthia (USA) (Empery **68** (USA) 128) [1989 6m² 6f² 6m* 7m⁶ 6g] small, workmanlike filly: good walker: first foal: dam, lightly raced in France, is half-sister to smart miler Nino Bibbia: favourite, made all in minor event at Carlisle in June: below form in Newmarket nurseries afterwards: should stay 7f. *M. H. Tompkins.*

RAMBO CASTLE 3 b.g. Castle Keep 121–Rampage 93 (Busted 134) [1988 7m **87** 7g 1989 10s 10m² 12h* 12g 12g² a12g³] sparely-made, angular gelding: won maiden at Carlisle in June: creditable second in apprentice handicap at York, best effort after: will stay 1¾m: acts on hard ground: genuine: winning novice hurdler. *S. G. Norton.*

RAMBO EXPRESS 2 b. or br.c. (Apr 8) New Express 95–Saul Flower (Saulingo **68** p 122) [1989 6g 6g] smallish, workmanlike colt: fifth foal: half-brother to poor plater Soul Dancer (by Niels): dam never ran: around 10 lengths seventh of 29, keeping on steadily, to Sure Sharp in maiden at Newmarket in November: backward on debut: can improve further. *G. A. Huffer.*

RAMBO'S HALL 4 b.g. Crofthall 110–Murton Crags 81 (No Argument 107) **116** [1988 7d* 8.2v² 8m⁶ 7g 1989 8.5d³ 8.2g⁵ 8.2m* 10.6g* 7s² 9g* 10g²] angular, sparely-made gelding: moderate walker: progressed really well, winning £61,900 34-runner William Hill Cambridgeshire Handicap at Newmarket (sweating) in October in excellent style by 6 lengths from Dawn Success: showed further improvement when ½-length second to Icona in listed event at same course 4 weeks later: successful earlier in truly-run handicaps at Haydock: stays 10.6f: acts on top-of-the-ground and heavy going: often gives trouble at stalls: tough and genuine: sold to race in USA. *J. A. Glover.*

RAMBUSHKA (USA) 3 b.f. Roberto (USA) 131–Katsura (USA) 104 (Northern **111** Dancer) [1988 7m² 7g* 1989 10g² 12m 10.2m* 10g] small, good-topped filly: has a rather round action: first past post in listed races for Pretty Polly Stakes at Newmarket in May, beating Always On A Sunday a neck but demoted for edging right, and moderately-run Virginia Stakes at Newcastle in August, leading inside

William Hill Cambridgeshire, Newmarket—
tough and genuine Rambo's Hall is a runaway winner

last and holding on by ½ length from Sesame: tailed off in Epsom Oaks and Sun Chariot Stakes at Newmarket: should be well suited by 1½m: acts on top-of-the-ground: very useful at her best. *B. W. Hills.*

RAMIFICATION 2 b.c. (Apr 8) Vision (USA)–Free Reserve (USA) (Tom Rolfe) [1989 5s 5g 7m 6f⁶ 6g⁵ 7m⁶] IR 16,000F, 20,000Y: leggy, close-coupled colt: first foal: dam placed from 8.5f to 1¾m in Ireland: poor maiden: bred to need a test of stamina: blinkered fourth start: looked ungenerous final outing: sold 1,950 gns Ascot August Sales. *G. Lewis.*   50

RAMI (USA) 2 br.c. (Apr 15) Riverman (USA) 131–Ancient Regime (USA) 123 (Olden Times) [1989 6g³ 7g*] $750,000Y: quite attractive colt: has scope: fourth foal: half-brother to very smart sprinter La Grande Epoque (by Lyphard): dam, French sprinter, sister to Cricket Ball: well-backed favourite, won 28-runner maiden in November by 1½ lengths, clear, from Gomarlow, leading 1f out: will prove best at up to 1m: sure to improve, and win more races. *P. T. Walwyn.*   99 p

RAMROD 4 ch.g. Giacometti 130–Come On Girl (Sheshoon 132) [1988 10.1g⁵ 7m⁶ 13.1f³ 10g⁴ 1989 10f] sparely-made gelding: poor maiden: stays 13f: acts on firm going: tends to wander: winning hurdler. *R. J. Hodges.*   —

RAMSEY STREET 2 b.f. (Apr 5) Mummy's Game 120–Green Jinks (Hardgreen (USA) 122) [1989 5f³] 4,200Y: good-topped, rather leggy filly: first foal: dam little worthwhile form: 10/1, carrying condition and green, keeping-on third of 12 to Foxtrot Oscar in maiden auction race at Beverley in August: can improve. *M. H. Tompkins.*   52 p

RANA PRATAP (USA) 9 b.h. Faliraki 125–Dodo S (USA) (Nagea) [1988 10.2s 9d 10d 10f³ 10m* 10g 10f 10g⁶ 8d³ 10d⁴ 10f⁵ 10m⁶ 12m⁵ 12g² 12g 1989 8g 9f 10f 12f³ 12g⁴ 10.6m³ 12f] lengthy horse: usually impresses in paddock: good walker: has a round action: one-time fairly useful performer: well below his best as 9-y-o: stays 1½m: acts on any going: has occasionally worn blinkers: has worn bandages: suited by good gallop: sold 4,000 gns Newmarket Autumn Sales: unreliable. *G. Lewis.*   63

R AND B UPDATE 3 b.g. Longleat (USA) 109–Neringulla (African Sky 124) [1988 6d⁶ 6f 1989 6g³ 6d 6m 7m 8m 6g⁶] leggy, good-topped gelding: quite modest maiden at best: ran in a seller first outing: may well stay beyond 6f: possibly unsuited by top-of-the-ground. *G. A. Huffer.*   72 d

RANGERS LAD 4 b.g. Sallust 134–Flaxen Hair (Thatch (USA) 136) [1988 7v 8g 8.2s⁶ 8f 7m 10.1g* 10d 10m² 8.5m 10g⁵ 1989 10.8s 10m* 9f 10m 8f⁵ 10.1m³ 10f⁶ 10.6d⁴ a14g⁵] compact gelding: carries condition: poor mover: fair plater: won 22-runner handicap (bought in 3,800 gns) at Brighton in April: should stay beyond 1¼m: possibly unsuited by soft going, acts on any other: blinkered once at 3 yrs: none too genuine. *E. Eldin.*   50

RANGOON PRINCE 3 br.g. Nishapour (FR) 125–Juhayna (USA) 78 (Diplomat Way) [1988 10d 1989 8f 6f] workmanlike gelding: no sign of ability in maiden and sellers: blinkered final start. *M. F. D. Morley.*   —

RANNOCH HOUSE 2 ch.c. (Jun 1) Final Straw 127–Stoney 73 (Balidar 133) [1989 5d 6m 5f 5m* 5m] 1,000Y: strong, angular colt: moderate walker: third foal: half-brother to 3-y-o Miss Chalk (by Dominion) and 1987 2-y-o 5f winner here Imperial King (by Imperial Fling), later 7f winner in Italy: dam, half-sister to Italian 1000 Guineas winner Sinthesis, stayed 7f: 33/1, won maiden auction race at Haydock in June: burly only subsequent start: should be suited by 6f: ridden by 7-lb claimer: sold 1,200 gns Ascot November Sales. *T. Fairhurst.*   54

RANWELI REEF 3 b.c. Superlative 118–Grace Poole (Sallust 134) [1988 5.1g* 7g³ 1989 8m 7m 6m 7m 6g] good-topped colt: modest winner as 2-y-o: well beaten in handicaps in 1989, blinkered and edgy final start: should stay 1m: sold to join D. R. Tucker 5,400 gns Newmarket Autumn Sales. *G. A. Huffer.*   —

RAPIDARIS 3 b.c. Rapid River 127–Stellaris (Star Appeal 133) [1988 5g 5m 6m 6f 6f 1989 9f 9f 11g 10f] smallish, lengthy colt: poor plater: should stay 9f: sold 1,150 gns Ascot December Sales. *T. Fairhurst.*   —

RAPID LAD 11 b.g. Rapid River 127–Seacona (Espresso 122) [1988 10m 10m⁴dis 10d⁶ 10g 10f² 10g⁴ 10m 10f* 10m 10m⁵ 10g 10f² 10f³ 8g 1989 10d 10.8d 10d⁶ 10f⁴ 10f² 10m* 10.8m⁵ 10m 10f² 10m³ 10f* 10m 10m³ 10f⁴ 10f] compact gelding: good mover: quite modest handicapper: successful at Beverley in June and August, winning there for twelfth time (has not won elsewhere since 1982) on latter occasion when beating King William comfortably by 2 lengths: best at 1¼m: needs top-of-the-ground: has worn blinkers: held up and is suited by strong gallop: not the easiest of rides and particularly well handled by D. Nicholls: tough. *J. L. Spearing.*   64

RAPID MOVER 2 ch.g. (Feb 26) Final Straw 127–Larive 80 (Blakeney 126) —
[1989 6m 6f 7g 7.5g⁵ 8g] 10,000Y: leggy gelding: first foal: dam 1½m winner stayed
2m: poor maiden: visored in a seller fourth start: sold out of C. Tinkler's stable 1,700
gns Doncaster October Sales after fourth outing. *T. Craig.*

RAPPORTEUR (USA) 3 b.g. His Majesty (USA)–Sweet Rapport (USA) 57
(Round Table) [1988 NR 1989 10g⁵ 12f 10m⁵ a10g⁵ a10g*] leggy, angular gelding:
second favourite, won maiden claimer at Lingfield in December: only previous sign
of ability time before: stays 1¼m: trained first 3 starts in 1989 by R. Hannon. *C. C.
Elsey.*

RAPSIMAS 3 b.f. Martinmas 128–Hillset (Hill Clown (USA)) [1988 NR 1989 8.2m —
8f 11g] small, leggy, unfurnished filly: half-sister to three 2-y-o 5f winners, including
fair 1978 winner Pompously (by Pompous): dam of no account: always behind in
maidens and claimer. *S. G. Norton.*

RARE VISION 3 ch.f. Salmon Leap (USA) 131–Silver Glimpse 108 (Petingo 135) —
[1988 5f⁴ 5f² 6g 5m 1989 8m 7f 11f⁵ 9f] angular filly: plating-class maiden in 1988:
below form as 3-y-o, including in seller: takes good hold, and may prove best at up to
7f: sold 920 gns Doncaster September Sales. *W. J. Pearce.*

RASAN 2 ch.c. (Mar 9) Dominion 123–Raffle 82 (Balidar 133) [1989 6g⁶ 6f⁴ 6f⁴] 70
54,000Y: good-bodied, angular colt: first foal: dam, 5.8f winner, is half-sister to
high-class sprinters Mummy's Pet and Parsimony, and very smart Arch Sculptor:
quite modest form in maidens and a minor event: may stay 7f. *R. W. Armstrong.*

RASCHESTER 2 ch.g. (Mar 22) Good Times (ITY)–Killifreth 87 (Jimmy Reppin 71
131) [1989 5s* 5f⁵ 7g] 5,800Y: workmanlike gelding: has a roundish action: third
foal: dam 1½m winner: won maiden at Haydock in April by 4 lengths from Tadeus:
well beaten in minor events at Pontefract and Chester (June) afterwards: should
stay 7f: gives impression requires soft ground. *M. H. Easterby.*

RASHEED 2 b.c. (Apr 4) Chief Singer 131–Enchanting Dancer (FR) (Nijinsky 54
(CAN) 138) [1989 6m 7g] leggy, close-coupled colt: fifth foal: half-brother to 1½m
winner Nahash and winning middle-distance stayer/jumper Folk Dance (both by
Alias Smith) and a winner in Scandinavia by Tap On Wood: dam never ran: never
dangerous in maiden at Newbury (green) in June and minor event at Leicester (in
need of race) almost 5 months later: should stay 1m. *M. Blanshard.*

RASHEEK (USA) 3 b.c. Topsider (USA)–Princess Sucree (USA) (Roberto 101
(USA) 131) [1988 6g* 6g* 6g² 7f* 1989 7g⁴ 7m⁵ 9g⁵] good-topped colt: has a quick,
fluent action: useful performer: ran creditably as 3-y-o in Group 3 event at
Doncaster, £49,600 handicap (favourite, not getting best of runs) at Ascot and listed
race (running on) at Newmarket: stays 9f: acts on firm going: to join C. Hayes in
Australia. *R. W. Armstrong.*

RASHTOUN 3 b.c. Shareef Dancer (USA) 135–Ramanouche (FR) 112 (Riverman 94
(USA) 131) [1988 8d 8g³ 1989 10.1m⁵ 12m* 12g 10f⁵ 12m] strong, angular colt: won
handicap at Haydock in May, setting modest pace early: creditable fifth at
Goodwood in July, best effort in valuable handicaps after: suited by 1½m: goes well
on top-of-the-ground: sold 28,000 gns Newmarket Autumn Sales. *M. R. Stoute.*

RATHAGE 3 b.f. Horage 124–Rathcoffey Duchy (Faberge II 121) [1988 6m⁶ 5m 61
5d 6g 1989 8g⁵ 12v² 12g* 12g 10.6m⁵ 12g 13v⁶ 12.6g⁶] lengthy, shallow-girthed filly:
quite modest handicapper: won at Leicester in April: creditable fifth in apprentice
race (off course 4 months after) at Haydock, easily best effort after: should prove
suited by 1½m: acts on heavy going and top-of-the-ground. *R. Guest.*

RATHBRIDES JOY 2 gr.c. (Mar 24) Kafu 120–Great Meadow (Northfields 64
(USA)) [1989 5d⁶ 6m 7f⁸ 7m 8.2f² 8g] IR 4,000Y: tall, sparely-made colt: has a round
action: fourth foal: half-brother to fair 1988 2-y-o 7f winner Seldom Blue (by Welsh
Saint) and winning hurdler Travel In Style (by Pitskelly): dam never ran: useful
plater: won 13-runner event (no bid) at Newcastle in July: good second at
Nottingham in September: suited by 1m: not particularly consistent. *J. S. Wainwright.*

RATHER TOUCHING 4 b.g. Touching Wood (USA) 127–Rather Warm 103 — §
(Tribal Chief 125) [1988 8.3g 10f 12.2g 10d 1989 7.6f 7f 7m⁶ 7g 7g] neat, strong
gelding: modest winner at 2 yrs, but has deteriorated: stays 7f: blinkered last 3
outings: has flashed tail under pressure, and is probably ungenuine. *C. F. Wall.*

RATHVINDEN HOUSE (USA) 2 b.c. (May 18) Hostage (USA)–Great 57 p
Verdict (USA) 110 (Le Fabuleux 133) [1989 10g⁶] $17,000F, 2,900Y: closely related
to Nijinova (by Nijinsky), winner at about 6f in USA, and half-brother to Weight In
Gold (by Alydar), winner at up to 7f in USA, and French 11.7f to 15.5f winner Popular
Decision (by Riverman): dam French 1½m winner: 10/1, sweating and green, around

14 lengths sixth of 12, slowly away and not knocked about unduly, to Rock Hopper in maiden at Nottingham in October: should do better. *R. Boss.*

RATION OF PASSION 4 b.f. Camden Town 125–Bellagold (Rheingold 137) 52
[1988 6s³ 5d⁴ 5m 6f⁶ 7.3m 5d³ 6g³ 5m² 5g⁴ 6f 5m 6g⁴ 5f 5.3f⁴ 5s 1989 5d² 6d³ 5s 5m 5m 5s a6g⁶] big, angular filly: plating-class maiden: best at sprint distances: probably acts on any going: sweating fifth outing: has run creditably for apprentice. *J. J. Bridger.*

RAVEN'S AFFAIR 3 b.g. Tower Walk 130–Femme Fatale 67 (King's Leap 111) —
[1988 5g 1989 9f 6m⁵ 8.2d] medium-sized gelding: fifth in claimer at Haydock in May, soon pushed along and only sign of ability: off course 4½ months after: should be suited by further than 6f. *M. Tate.*

RAYMONDS STAR 5 ch.g. Tickled Pink 114–Canty Day 87 (Canadel II 126) —
[1988 NR 1989 12d 6m] lengthy, sparely-made gelding: of little account: sweating and visored final outing. *M. P. Naughton.*

RAYS HONOR 4 ch.f. Ahonoora 122–Gamma (GER) (Zank) [1988 8m 7g³ 6f —
7.6s³ 7f 7f 8m 7g 1989 7f 6m 6h] smallish, sparely-made filly: bad mover: poor maiden: stays 7f: unsuited by firm going, acts on any other: sometimes blinkered or visored: sold 1,450 gns Ascot July Sales: resold 2,100 gns Goffs December Sales. *M. J. Fetherston-Godley.*

RAZEEN 4 ch.g. Be My Guest (USA) 126–Fast Motion 86 (Midsummer Night II ?
117) [1988 8g⁶ 8g² 7g⁵ 8m⁵ 10m 1989 10.2g⁵ 9v⁶ 8m] tall, rather leggy, workmanlike gelding: moderate mover: fair maiden as 3-y-o: well below his best in 1989: stays 1m: probably unsuited by heavy going: blinkered once at 3 yrs and on final start: slowly away on reappearance: wore severe bridle, pulled hard and found little second outing: trained until after then by W. O'Gorman. *J. G. FitzGerald.*

RAZZBERRY (FR) 2 br.f. (Feb 16) Be My Guest (USA) 126–Wool Princess 71
(FR) (Direct Flight) [1989 6g⁴ 7g² 6g² 7f⁴] $85,000Y: sturdy, useful-looking filly: first foal: dam, unplaced in 2 starts in France, half-sister to very smart French middle-distance performer Marie de Litz: modest maiden: will stay at least 1m. *M. A. Jarvis.*

READY WIT 8 br.g. Bay Express 132–Brevity 76 (Pindari 124) [1988 8g 1989 7g 47
a8g⁶ a7g⁴] lengthy, workmanlike gelding: modest handicapper in 1986: very lightly raced nowadays, but showed he retained some ability when fourth, slowly away, in claimer at Southwell in November: effective at 7f or 1m: used to go very well in the mud: has worn a visor. *R. Hannon.*

REALISM 4 b.g. Known Fact (USA) 135–Miss Reasoning (USA) 108 (Bold 65
Reasoning (USA)) [1988 7d² 7m² 7g 8s* 1989 8g 8d 7s 9.2f a10g⁶ a8g] lengthy, angular gelding: has a quick action: fair winner as 3-y-o: only show in 1989 on fifth outing: stays 1¼m: best efforts on soft going: bandaged near-hind on reappearance: trained until after fourth outing by R. Akehurst. *K. O. Cunningham-Brown.*

REALLY BRILLIANT (USA) 3 ch.c. Riverman 131–Waterlot (USA) 109
(Buckpasser) [1988 7f* 7g* 1989 7d 10f³ 12f⁶] rangy, good sort: has a slightly round action: about 2 lengths third of 8 to Warrshan in Predominate Stakes at Goodwood, appearing held approaching last then staying on strongly: pulled hard early, driven along to make progress on turn then weakened over 1f out when beaten about 10 lengths in moderately-run King Edward VII Stakes at Royal Ascot: ran as if something amiss on reappearance: possibly suited by 1¼m and sound surface: useful. *L. M. Cumani.*

REALLY GORGEOUS 4 ch.c. Hello Gorgeous (USA) 128–Klaxonette 88 —
(Klairon 131) [1988 8f 7g 9g 9m⁶ 8d⁴ 11s⁵ 10s* 10v⁵ 8g 1989 10v] leggy, close-coupled, sparely-made colt: bad mover: quite modest winner as 3-y-o: ran badly only outing (April) in 1989: stays 1¼m: needs plenty of give in the ground: bandaged behind final 2 appearances at 3 yrs: sold 950 gns Doncaster November Sales. *M. Brittain.*

REALLY NEAT 3 gr.f. Alias Smith (USA)–Tiddley 66 (Filiberto (USA) 123) —
[1988 NR 1989 8.2d] third foal: dam, lightly raced, best effort over 11f: 20/1, tailed off in claimer at Haydock in October. *D. R. Gandolfo.*

REALLY SQUIDGELY 2 b.f. (Mar 31) King of Spain 121–Duck Soup 55 (Decoy 52
Boy 129) [1989 5f⁶ 5m⁴ 5f³ 6f* 6f⁴ 5m⁶ 5m] 9,000Y: small, sturdy filly: moderate mover: fifth foal: sister to 3-y-o Soupcon, 6f winner at 2 yrs, and fairly useful 1985 2-y-o 5f winner Crete Cargo, and half-sister to 2 winners, including 1½m winner Joseph (by Rolfe): dam won over 7f from 3 starts: plating-class performer: won seller (bought in 5,000 gns) at Folkestone in July: better suited by 6f than 5f: on toes final start: sold 3,500 gns Newmarket Autumn Sales. *K. M. Brassey.*

REALM (USA) 2 b.f. (Apr 6) Mr Prospector (USA)–State (USA) (Nijinsky (CAN) **63** p
138) [1989 8g⁶] medium-sized, leggy, angular filly: half-sister to several winners in USA, notably Narrate (by Honest Pleasure), smart winner at up to 9f, and Hollywood Derby runner-up Double Feint (by Spectacular Bid): dam successful at up to 1¼m: 12/1, around 4 lengths sixth of 16, keeping on not knocked about, to High Beacon in maiden at Leicester in November: sure to improve. *A. C. Stewart.*

REASONABLE KID 2 ch.c. (May 9) Reasonable (FR) 119–Trust Sally 65 **79**
(Sallust 134) [1989 5m⁵ 6g⁵ 6d* 5g⁵] IR 3,000F, 11,000Y: angular colt: fourth foal: half-brother to modest 1987 2-y-o 5f winner Marley Supalite (by Jester) and a winner over jumps in Belgium: dam 5f seller winner: showed much improved form when winning maiden at Catterick in October: ran moderately in Redcar nursery following month: better suited by 6f than 5f. *R. Boss.*

REASON TO LAUGH 3 b.g. Comedy Star (USA) 121–Legal Sound 85 (Legal —
Eagle 126) [1988 6g 5f 5f 1989 6s 5f 12f 7m] compact gelding: has a rather round action: little worthwhile form, including in sellers: often edgy. *J. Balding.*

REBECCA'S PET 7 br.m. Court Circus 97–French Secret (Most Secret 119) —
[1988 NR 1989 9m 10f 8f] small, close-coupled mare: no longer of any account: sweating and wore tongue strap final outing. *G. P. Kelly.*

REBEL RAISER (USA) 5 ch.g. Raise A Native–Lady Oakley 94 (Gulf Pearl **60** d
117) [1988 9d 6m 5g 6g 7m 5g 6g 8m 1989 7g³ 7m* 6h² 7m 7h⁶ 7m 7.6m 7m 6f a7g] compact, good-quartered gelding: moderate mover: useful 2-y-o: only quite modest at best nowadays: apprentice ridden, won 18-runner handicap at Brighton in May: little form after next outing: needs further than 5f and stays 7f: acts on hard going: visored once: often sweats and gets on edge: inconsistent. *M. J. Ryan.*

RECHARGEABLE 3 b.g. Music Boy 124–Ciliata (So Blessed 130) [1988 6m⁵ —
6f⁴ 7m⁵ 1989 8m 8.2f⁵] rangy gelding: quite modest maiden at best: should stay beyond 7f: bandaged on reappearance: winning selling hurdler for A. Reid. *Dr J. D. Scargill.*

RECIDIVIST 3 b.f. Royben 125–On Remand 83 (Reform 132) [1988 6g 8m 6s⁶ **51**
8m 8g³ 1989 7s 6s 8d² 8f 8m 10f⁵ 8m] leggy filly: poor walker: moderate mover: plating-class maiden: second in seller at Bath in April: should stay 1¼m: possibly requires an easy surface: trained until after sixth start by C. Hill: winning juvenile selling hurdler. *R. J. Hodges.*

RECIPE 2 ch.f. (Apr 3) Bustino 136–Rosetta Stone 89 (Guillaume Tell (USA) 121) **66** p
[1989 9f³] useful-looking filly: has scope: fourth foal: half-sister to 3-y-o 1½m to 17.6f winner Teamster and 9f and 13.3f winner Blind Faith (both by Known Fact) and to a winner in Austria by Final Straw: dam, half-sister to very useful Irish 6f and 7f winner Columbanus, won at 1¾m: 5/1, very green and edgy, over 3 lengths third of 6, leading 3f out until 2f out and not knocked about, to Photo Call in maiden at Wolverhampton in October: will improve, particularly over 1½m +, and win a race. *M. R. Stoute.*

RECORD PRICE 3 b.g. Simply Great (FR) 122–Silk Trade (Auction Ring (USA) **76**
123) [1988 5m 5f⁶ 5m² 6g² 6g⁶ 6m 1989 10s 10d³ 8.5g² 10f² 8.2g] sparely-made, angular gelding: moderate walker and mover: modest maiden: ran poorly final start: stays 1¼m: acts on firm going and a soft surface. *J. P. Leigh.*

RECORD ROSE 4 ch.f. Record Token 128–Carline Rose (Most Secret 119) —
[1988 NR 1989 12.3f] smallish, plain filly: third foal: dam unraced: 20/1 and bandaged, reluctant to race when tailed off in maiden at Ripon in June. *J. Pearce.*

RECTILLON 2 b.c. (Mar 28) Rousillon (USA) 133–Rectitude 99 (Runnymede **70** p
123) [1989 6m⁶] 36,000Y: useful-looking colt: bit unfurnished: has scope: fifth foal: half-brother to 3-y-o Pretentious (by Precocious), 5f winner at 2 yrs, and 7f winner Mallihouana and useful 1985 2-y-o 7f winner Normanby Lass (both by Bustino): dam, daughter of smart Attitude, won at up to 8.5f: 14/1, 8 lengths sixth of 10, keeping on never dangerous, to Muwfiq in maiden at York in October: will improve. *B. W. Hills.*

RED BEACON 2 b.g. (Apr 4) Red Sunset 120–Mount of Light 61 (Sparkler 130) **41**
[1989 5f 5f⁶ 6f⁵ 7m] fair sort: fourth living foal: half-brother to 1987 2-y-o 5f and 6f seller winner Rustic Dawn (by Rusticaro): dam, half-sister to smart miler Richboy, stayed 1½m: poor form, including in sellers: bandaged twice: blinkered final outing (June). *S. G. Norton.*

RED BOLT 7 ch.g. Stanford 121§–Amy Jane (Guillaume Tell (USA) 121) [1988 NR —
1989 18h 12g⁴ 12h 15.3f⁵ 15.3g] sturdy gelding: poor mover: well beaten in modest company on flat: blinkered, tailed off in selling handicap third outing: wears bandages: sold privately 1,500 gns Ascot September Sales. *P. D. Evans.*

RED BREWSTER 3 b.g. Burslem 123–Red Magic (Red God 128§) [1988 7m 6d 6f⁵ 7d 1989 10s⁵ 10v 7m 7m] tall, angular gelding: has a round action: plating-class form: sign of retaining his ability in first half of 3-y-o season only in moderately-run handicap (on toes) on reappearance: stays 1¼m: acts on soft going: blinkered penultimate start. *G. Lewis.*   —

RED DOLLAR 4 ch.g. Tachypous 128–Burglars Girl 63 (Burglar 128) [1988 8d⁴ 7d⁶ 7s* 8m 8s 8f 7m 7g 1989 8s 7f] rangy, workmanlike gelding: good mover: won maiden at Epsom early as 3-y-o: well behind subsequently in handicaps and a Group 3 event: virtually pulled up (as though something amiss) final outing: gelded afterwards: suited by 7f and forcing tactics: acts on top-of-the-ground and soft going: possibly best in visor: sweated at 4 yrs: sometimes on edge: inconsistent. *B. Gubby.*   —

RED FESCUE 7 gr.g. Warpath 113–Jasmin (Frankincense 120) [1988 NR 1989 10g 9m] winning chaser: soundly beaten in apprentice event at Brighton and ladies race (visored) only outings on flat. *J. J. Bridger.*   —

RED GALE 2 b.c. (Feb 21) Blushing Scribe (USA) 107–Moraine (Morston (FR) 125) [1989 6g⁵ 6f³ 6g² 7f 8g] 1,400Y, 6,100 2-y-o: angular colt: first foal: dam never ran: fairly useful plater: best efforts second and third starts: ran moderately afterwards: should stay 7f: sweating final outing: trained first 2 by A. Robson. *C. Tinkler.*   59

RED GLOW 4 b.c. Kalaglow 132–Cherry Hinton (USA) 125 (Nijinsky (CAN) 138) [1988 10d² 10.5g* 12m⁴ 10m 1989 9g⁴ 12m⁵] big, most attractive colt: good walker and very good mover: high-class middle-distance 3-y-o when winning Mecca-Dante Stakes at York (quickened in excellent style) and fourth in Ever Ready Derby at Epsom: ran moderately final outing (late-June, reportedly injuring his back) in 1988 and when fifth of 6 to Unfuwain in General Accident Jockey Club Stakes at Newmarket in May: favourite, respectable fourth to Reprimand in Earl of Sefton EBF Stakes at last-named course on reappearance 2 weeks earlier: best form on a sound surface (didn't race on very firm going): sometimes didn't find much off bridle and best waited with: sold to stand at stud in New Zealand. *G. Wragg.*   118

RED HENRY (USA) 2 ch.c. (Feb 4) Red Ryder (USA)–Bay Line Girl (USA) (Sailing Along (USA)) [1989 5g* 5d² 5m² 5f* 5f² 6d] $32,000Y: leggy, good-topped colt: has plenty of scope: half-brother to Penalty Shot (by Air Forbes Won), successful at up to 7f: dam won at up to 1¼m: sire unraced brother to Mr Prospector: fairly useful performer: showed good turn of foot when winning minor events at Doncaster in March and Folkestone in May: very good second to Haunting Beauty in Molecomb Stakes at Goodwood in July: ran moderately final start: best at 5f: effective with or without blinkers. *W. A. O'Gorman.*   93

RED HOT LADY 3 b.f. Red Sunset 120–Breezy Answer (On Your Mark 125) [1988 5m 6g⁵ 7f 7s 1989 7s 8.3m 12f 12f 12f] leggy, sparely-made filly: little sign of ability: dead. *R. Voorspuy.*   —

RED INDIAN 3 ch.c. Be My Native (USA) 122–Martialette (Welsh Saint 126) [1988 6m 6m 5g² 7m 1989 6s 7g³ 8m⁴ 8.2m³ 7m² 6f 7m 7m² 7m⁶ 6g 8.2f 7m 10f² 10g² 10g] tall, lengthy, leggy colt: moderate mover: plating-class maiden: worth a try over 1½m: acts on firm ground: sometimes wears bandages: visored seventh start: has worn crossed noseband: suitable mount for apprentice: has joined W. Haigh. *Mrs N. Macauley.*   59

RED JAM JAR 4 ch.g. Windjammer (USA)–Macaw 85 (Narrator 127) [1988 8d 10d³ 9g² 10m² 10m² 10g 10g⁶ 1989 10.8m² 10m² 10f² 12.3m* 12.3g 12.2g] good-bodied gelding: moderate mover: won for first time in 19-runner handicap at Ripon in August, quickening well to lead over 1f out: well below that form in similar company following month: suited by 1½m: acts on firm going and a soft surface: sweating second start: has worn tongue strap, crossed noseband and been taken down early: withdrawn after bolting on fourth intended outing: tends to carry head high: resolution under suspicion. *J. Mackie.*   60

REDNET 2 b.f. (Apr 3) Tender King 123–Red For Go (Tanfirion 110) [1989 5m⁴ 5g 5d 5m] IR 2,000Y: third foal: closely related to poor maiden Far Too Risky (by Prince Tenderfoot) and half-sister to 3-y-o 1m and 1¼m winner Tuppenny Red (by Sallust): dam never ran: bit backward, poor form in varied races. *D. W. Chapman.*   43

RED PADDY 4 ch.g. Red Sunset 120–Irish Bride (Track Spare 125) [1988 7g 7m* 7.3m* 8g* 1989 7m 8f³ 8m* 9g⁶] sparely-made gelding: fairly useful handicapper: favourite, won £7,400 9-runner event at Sandown in September by neck from Dawn Success, quickening impressively to lead well inside final 1f: creditable sixth of 34 to Rambo's Hall in William Hill Cambridgeshire Handicap at   99

Newmarket month later: stays 9f: acts on firm going: withdrawn lame third intended appearance: tended to hang final outing at 3 yrs and on second start in 1989: probably best with waiting tactics: changed hands 31,000 gns Newmarket Autumn Sales. *P. J. Makin.*

RED PIPPIN 2 b.c. (Apr 25) Blushing Scribe (USA) 107–Orchard Road 74   **63** (Camden Town 125) [1989 6f³ 5m⁴] 400F, 3,600Y: leggy colt: third foal: dam placed at up to 7f at 2 yrs, only season to race: beaten around 2 lengths behind Intuitive Joe in claimer at Leicester and Martin-Lavell Post in maiden auction event at Edinburgh in October: wears blinkers. *Mrs N. Macauley.*

RED PLANET 4 b.g. Sir Ivor 135–Miss Mars 95 (Red God 128§) [1988 7d⁶ 10f⁴   **— §** 10g 8d 8f⁵ 8g 8g 1989 10.2g⁶ 12m⁶] sturdy gelding: bad mover: poor maiden: blinkered twice. *Denys Smith.*

RED RING 2 br.g. (Mar 2) Auction Ring (USA) 123–Rosalie II 66 (Molvedo 137)   **68** [1989 7g⁶ 7m⁵ 8g⁶] tall, rangy gelding: has plenty of scope: half-brother to several winners, including very smart 6f to 1m winner Cistus (by Sun Prince) and high-class French middle-distance performer Lancastrian (by Reform): dam won at 1¼m: quite modest maiden: ran poorly final outing and subsequently gelded: should stay 1m: sweating and edgy 2 starts, and may be unsatisfactory temperamentally: sold 12,000 gns Newmarket Autumn Sales. *Major W. R. Hern.*

RED RIVER BOY 6 b.g. Latest Model 115–Count On Me 77 (No Mercy 126)   **71** [1988 8d² 8.5m³ 8g⁴ 7.5m* 7d⁶ 6m⁶ 8f⁴ 8m* 8g³ 8d⁴ 8f⁵ 7.3m 8g 1989 8.5d 7g 8h³ 8.5m 7f⁶ 8f² 5.8h* 6h⁵ 7f 7f⁶ 5m³ 6g⁴ 5.8f* 6m 5g⁵ 6g] lengthy gelding: carries plenty of condition: has a round action: modest handicapper: successful at Bath in July (4-runner event) and September: below his best last 3 outings: finds easy 5f on sharp side and stays 1m: acts on any going: has been tried in blinkers: has won for apprentice, but has looked difficult ride. *R. J. Hodges.*

RED ROSEIN 3 b.f. Red Sunset 120–Vain Deb 66 (Gay Fandango (USA) 132)   **74** [1988 5m* 5g³ 5g² 5g² 5g² 1989 6s 5d 6d 5m 5m 6f³ 6f⁶ 6f³ 6g⁵ 6m³ 6m² 6g⁵ 7s 6g² 6f 6g³] leggy filly: has a quick action: modest handicapper: below form until eighth outing: stays 6f: best form on a sound surface: sometimes slowly away. *N. Tinkler.*

RED TOTO 2 ch.c. (May 17) Habitat 134–Soumana (FR) (Pharly (FR) 130) [1989   **80 p** 6g⁴ 7v] 69,000Y: medium-sized colt: has scope: fourth foal: half-brother to Irish 3-y-o 1¼m winner Sharakou (by Tap on Wood) and 7.5f winner Tuxedo (by Persian Bold): dam unraced half-sister to Poule d'Essai des Pouliches winner Dumka, dam of Doyoun, Dolpour and Dafayna (by Habitat): favourite but green, 4 lengths fourth of 9 finishers, keeping on well having been hampered 2f out, to Tirol in minor event at Doncaster in September: looked ill at ease on ground in maiden at Ayr following month: should stay 1m: may do better. *A. C. Stewart.*

RED VICTOR 2 b.c. (Apr 12) Bellman (FR) 123–Red Sharp (FR) (Sharpman 124)   **65** [1989 6d 7g] 3,100F, IR 2,000Y: close-coupled colt: good walker: third foal: dam ran twice in France at 2 yrs: always behind in late-season maidens at Newbury (backward) and Newmarket (ninth of 28). *R. F. Johnson Houghton.*

REEDLING (USA) 4 b.g. Riverman (USA) 131–Mary Biz (USA) (T V Lark)   **—** [1988 NR 1989 10.1m 11.7m 16f⁴ a10g] big, rangy gelding: showed promise on debut as 2-y-o, but little on other 5 outings on flat: blinkered final start: winning hurdler. *G. P. Enright.*

REEF GALLES 3 b.g. Pas de Seul 133–Etoile des Galles (Busted 134) [1988 6f⁴   **77** 7d 1989 7f³ 8f² 8m 8d⁶] angular gelding: moderate walker: modest maiden: placed at Sandown and Chepstow: below form subsequently: stays 1m: acts on firm going. *M. McCourt.*

REEF LARK 4 b.g. Mill Reef (USA) 141–Calandra (USA) 114 (Sir Ivor 135) [1988   **—** 10d² 14g* 14m⁵ 1989 18g 16d 16m] rather leggy gelding: fair winner as 3-y-o when trained by C. Brittain: sustained back injury final outing: well beaten in handicaps in spring: should stay beyond 1¾m: blinkered on reappearance, visored last 2 outings. *J. Norton.*

REEF NATIVE 2 b.f. (Mar 14) Miramar Reef 100§–Norman Native (FR)   **36** (Bourbon (FR) 129) [1989 6f⁴ 6m⁵ 6s a7g] sparely-made filly: eighth foal: closely related to 3 winners in France by Moulin, including 1¼m winner Mill of The North, and half-sister to 3-y-o Danger Sign (by Ginger Brink): dam ran once at 2 yrs in France: poor plater: hung left at halfway, and flashed tail, on debut: will stay 1m. *M. Johnston.*

REEF PATRICK 4 b.g. Main Reef 126–Dooneena (Welsh Pageant 132) [1988   **—** 12m 15s⁴ 16m⁵ 18d 1989 12m] lengthy, workmanlike gelding: poor judged on most form: probably not an out-and-out stayer: winning selling hurdler. *M. H. Tompkins.*

REEF WIND 2 b.c. (May 11) Tumble Wind (USA)–Hollow Reef (Wollow 132) **58**
[1989 5g 5s 5m6 6m 7f 7m 5f a6g4 a7g] 19,000Y: sparely-made, close-coupled, rather leggy colt: moderate walker: second foal: dam never ran: plating-class maiden: has twice contested sellers: suited by 7f: blinkered seventh outing: has been bandaged. *C. C. Elsey.*

REEL FOYLE (USA) 2 ch.f. (Jan 27) Irish River (FR) 131–Abergwaun 128 **77**
(Bounteous 125) [1989 6m3 5g* 5m4 5m6] $75,000Y, resold 34,000Y: strong, deep-girthed filly: has plenty of scope: half-sister to several winners here and abroad, including useful 1981 2-y-o 5f and 6f winner Algardi (by Avatar), later stakes winner over 7.5f in USA, and quite useful 1982 2-y-o 7f winner Mandelstam (by Vaguely Noble): dam sprinter: odds on, won modest maiden at Wolverhampton in September easily by 3 lengths from First Dream, making all: ran creditably, leading much of way, in nurseries at Newbury and Newmarket afterwards: speedy, and will be suited by sharp 5f. *Mrs L. Piggott.*

REELING 3 br.f. Relkino 131–Mother Brown 103 (Candy Cane 125) [1988 6g 7m — §
6d4 1989 6m 12f4 12h6 16f 8f] big, lengthy, plain filly: plating-class maiden: faced stiff tasks in handicaps as 3-y-o, looking most temperamentally unsatisfactory penultimate outing: should be suited by 1m+: sold 3,200 gns Ascot August Sales: one to leave alone. *R. V. Smyth.*

REFERENCE LIGHT (USA) 2 b.c. (Apr 18) Diesis 133–Lulworth Cove 114 **85 p**
(Averof 123) [1989 6g3 6g*] $250,000Y: unfurnished colt: fourth foal: closely related to 3-y-o Ensharp (by Sharpen Up) and half-brother to 2 winners abroad, including Italian 1000 Guineas third Lyme Bay (by Pharly): dam, sprinting 2-y-o, is half-sister to Supreme Leader and from family of Pebbles: odds on, won 19-runner maiden at Redcar in November by a length from Katzakeena, soon with leaders and keeping on well: third of 6 to Qathif in minor event at Ascot on debut: will stay at least 7f. *M. R. Stoute.*

REFLECTIVE 2 br.c. (Jun 1) Magic Mirror 105–Thanks Edith (Gratitude 130) **52**
[1989 6g 7.5f 8f 8f3 8.2s] 3,500Y, 6,000Y: leggy, sparely-made colt: half-brother to 3 winners, including 10.6f winner Saxon Fort (by Manado): dam, unplaced 6 times in USA, is half-sister to top-class Aunt Edith: third of 5 to Heisman in maiden at Redcar in October, easily best effort: stays 1m: twice slowly away. *Mrs R. Wharton.*

REGAL BRASS 5 gr.h. Royal Palace 131–Two Friendly 54 (Be Friendly 130) **32**
[1988 10g 6d 8m 6f 8.5s* 6d5 10m 1989 8m4 6m 12.4g] workmanlike horse: poor mover: poor handicapper: needs further than 6f and stays 8.5f: probably acts on any going: usually ridden by claimer: often races freely: inconsistent. *P. A. Blockley.*

REGALCROFT 5 b.h. Crofter (USA) 124–Regal Ray 107 (Prince Regent (FR) — §
129) [1988 10.2d 8d5 8s 10.8g 8.2m2 8.2s3 8m 1989 10m a11g] leggy, rather angular horse: poor maiden: soundly beaten both outings at 5 yrs: suited by 1m: probably acts on any going: tends to hang and is probably not genuine. *D. Haydn Jones.*

REGAL LAKE 3 b. or br.c. Kings Lake (USA) 133–Thistlewood (Kalamoun 129) **86**
[1988 NR 1989 10d2 11.7h2 12h2] IR 240,000Y: rather sparely-made, medium-sized colt: good mover, with a quick action: third foal: half-brother to 1986 Irish 2-y-o 6f winner Sylvatica (by Thatching): dam unraced half-sister to Ardross: fair maiden: ridden by 7-lb claimer, would have won with clear run on debut: again favourite, narrowly beaten at Bath in May, held up and struggling some way out, and at Carlisle, making most: may well stay beyond 1½m: sold to join Mrs J. Pitman 22,000 gns Newmarket Autumn Sales: genuine: winning hurdler. *M. R. Stoute.*

REGAL NORTH 2 b.c. (May 25) Regalberto (USA)–Nell of the North (USA) **62**
(Canadian Gil (CAN)) [1989 6m6 6f5 6m2 7g 8f5] 7,200Y: third reported foal: half-brother to a winner in USA by Drum Fire: dam successful at up to 9f in USA: sire miler: quite modest maiden: easily best effort third start: ran wide into straight at Catterick next time: should stay further than 6f. *J. Etherington.*

REGAL REFORM 6 b.g. Prince Tenderfoot (USA) 126–Polly Packer 81 **101**
(Reform 132) [1988 12m2 12m2 12g 12d3 14d2 13s3 12s2 1989 12d 12g* 14g2 12m3 12g6 14f* 16.1m* 14.8m3 18f*] workmanlike, good-bodied gelding: had excellent season and showed himself better than ever, winning handicaps in good style at Pontefract, Redcar and Newmarket (strongly-run event) and £7,000 Phil Bull Memorial Trophy at Pontefract: looking tremendously well, showed further improvement in last-named when beating For Action 2½ lengths, leading over 1f out

731

*Phil Bull Memorial Trophy, Pontefract—the richest race ever run on the course,
staged in memory of Timeform's founder who died in June,
falls to Regal Reform from For Action and Orpheus*

and running on strongly: well suited by test of stamina: acts on any going, but goes
very well on top-of-the-ground: has run creditably for apprentice: probably best
ridden close to the pace: tough and consistent. *G. M. Moore.*

REGAL SALUTE 3 br.f. Dara Monarch 128–Forelock (Condorcet (FR)) [1988   **68**
NR 1989 8f 8f² 8m⁶ 9f² 10g³ 10.6g² 10m⁵ 10f³ 10.6m 8s²] IR 31,000Y: lengthy filly:
third foal: dam, won at 1m and placed at up to 1¼m in Ireland, is half-sister to
Gladness Stakes winner Rocked: quite modest form in varied events: suited by
1¼m: probably acts on any going: bandaged third to fifth outings: ran moderately for
7-lb claimer: usually sets pace: sold to join P. Bevan 9,000 gns Newmarket Autumn
Sales. *W. J. Haggas.*

REGAL STING (USA) 2 b.c. (Apr 5) Drone–Momma Taj (USA) (Bupers) [1989   **— p**
7g] $65,000Y: heavy-topped colt: half-brother to 3 winners in North America, best
of them Colonel Stevens (by Lt Stevens), minor stakes winner at up to 9f: dam ran 3
times: 13/2, green and very in need of race, never dangerous or knocked about when
in mid-division in 15-runner maiden at Newmarket in July: needs time. *G. Harwood.*

REGAL THATCH 2 ch.c. (Jan 31) Thatching 131–Kolomelskoy Palace 77 (Royal   **84**
Palace 131) [1989 6f² 6f² 6f 7g³ 7m⁴ 8m⁴ 8g 7m* 6v 7d³] 35,000F, IR 46,000Y:
workmanlike, rather angular colt: second foal: half-brother to 3-y-o 11f winner
Kolinsky (by Dunbeath): dam, 12.2f winner from family of Connaught, is half-sister
to good French middle-distance stayer Paddy's Princess, herself the dam of
Knockando: fair performer: won nursery at York in October by ¾ length from
Pencarreg, staying on well to lead near line: stays 1m: acts on any going. *C. E.
Brittain.*

REGAL VINE 3 b. or br.f. Prince Tenderfoot (USA) 126–Calvino (Relkino 131)   **— §**
[1988 5g 6m 5f 5g 7m² 6g⁴ 8g 8m² 7g⁴ 8g 1989 7m 6m 7m] smallish, plain filly: quite
modest form at 2 yrs, including in sellers: below form in first half of 1989: suited by
7f or 1m: sweating, seemed reluctant to race and found little off bridle once at 2 yrs:
one to have reservations about (often pulls hard). *Miss S. E. Hall.*

REGENT LAD 5 b.g. Prince Regent (FR) 129–Red Laser 95 (Red God 128§)   **91**
[1988 10g⁴ 10f 10.2m⁶ 10s³ 11m⁴ 12m⁵ 12g 10m 8.5f* 8m⁴ 8g² 1989 8g* 8.5d² 8f*
8m* 8f³ 8f 8f⁴ 8f² 7.5m* 8f³ 7f* 7m 8f⁵ 8g⁶] leggy gelding: good walker: fairly
useful handicapper: had tremendous season, winning at Doncaster (twice), Redcar
(twice) and Beverley: suited by 7f to 1m: best form on top-of-the-ground: best
without blinkers: has swished tail and looked none too resolute: suited by good
gallop and exaggerated waiting tactics: consistent: a credit to his trainer. *Miss L. C.
Siddall.*

REGENT LIGHT (USA) 3 b.c. Vice Regent (CAN)–I Like To Watch (USA)   **96**
(Mickey Mcguire (USA)) [1988 5d² 6f4 7d* 8m⁴ 8s 8d⁵ 8.5m² 8f³ 9m⁴ 10f³
9f 8m] quite attractive colt: has a quick action: fairly useful handicapper: in frame,
running creditably, at Epsom, Royal Ascot, Kempton and Goodwood, staying on
strongly first 3 occasions then no extra close home in Extel Stakes: stays 1¼m: acts
on firm going and a soft surface. *G. Lewis.*

REGGAE BEAT 4 b.g. Be My Native (USA) 122–Invery Lady 65 (Sharpen Up   **66**
127) [1988 10s³ 12g⁵ 12m⁶ 10f 10m 10.1g 8m* 8g 1989 10g 8f* 9m² 10m³ 12m] leggy,
lightly-made, angular gelding: has a light action: quite modest handicapper: 5/1 from
10/1, won 14-runner apprentice event at Sandown in May: ran well when placed at
Kempton and Newmarket (pulled hard) afterwards: burly and on toes final outing:
stays 1¼m: acts on top-of-the-ground and heavy going: ridden by 7-lb claimer as
4-y-o: winning hurdler. *I. Campbell.*

REGIMENTAL MARCH (USA) 3 b.c. Diamond Shoal 130–Slow March 105   **—**
(Queen's Hussar 124) [1988 7m⁴ 7g 1989 10.6s 7g] small colt: has a roundish action:
form only on debut: blinkered, tailed off in seller final outing: should stay at least
1¼m: sold 1,100 gns Ascot June Sales: resold 600 gns Doncaster October Sales. *D.
Yeoman.*

REGINA ROYALE (USA) 2 b.f. (Mar 7) Eternal Prince (USA)–Lizzie's Light   **53**
(USA) (Icecapade (USA)) [1989 6m 6g] $20,000Y: leggy filly: has a round action:
second reported foal: dam, half-sister to smart French 1m to 1¼m filly Relasure,
won 5 times at up to 11f, including 9f stakes event: sire 6f to 9f winner: plating-class
form in autumn maidens at Newbury (bit backward) and Newmarket. *Capt. R. M.
Smyly.*

REJIM 3 br.c. Mummy's Pet 125–Lidmoor (Caerdeon 98) [1988 6m⁴ 7m³ 7g⁵ 1989   **91**
8f* 7.2g 8m⁶ 7m] rangy, useful-looking colt: has a smooth, quick action: won
maiden at Thirsk in May: under 7 lengths seventh of 13 to Weldnaas in listed race at
Haydock: on toes, ran moderately at Ascot after in £5,000 ladies race and £49,600
handicap: stays 1m: acts on firm going. *B. W. Hills.*

REJONEO (USA) 2 b.c. (Apr 27) El Gran Senor (USA) 136–Chateau Dancer   **85 p**
(USA) 104 (Giacometti 130) [1989 7m³ 6g⁶] 130,000Y: close-coupled colt: good
mover: fourth foal: closely related to modest maiden Officer Krupke (by Nureyev):
dam won twice at 6f and third in May Hill Stakes at 2 yrs, and later placed in stakes
company in USA: shaped well in maidens at Newmarket won by Elmaamul and
Alidiva: off course nearly 3 months in between: will be well suited by return to 7f +:
sure to do better, and win a race or two. *J. Gosden.*

REKLAW 2 b.g. (Apr 30) Hard Fought 125–Rubina Park 64 (Ashmore (FR) 125)   **—**
[1989 8s] 6,200F, 6,400 2-y-o: angular gelding: fourth foal: half-brother to useful 7f
to 9f winner Montfort (by Red Sunset): dam, 1½m winner, is half-sister to smart 6f
and 7f winner Skyliner: 50/1 and backward, always behind in 15-runner maiden at
Ayr in September. *Mrs R. Wharton.*

RELATIVE STRANGER 3 b.f. Cragador 110–No Relation 94 (Klairon 131)   **—**
[1988 NR 1989 8m] lengthy filly: half-sister to several winners, including fairly
useful middle-distance handicapper Warbeck (by Royal Palace): dam stayed 1m: in
need of race, soon tailed off in apprentice maiden at Yarmouth in August: sold to join
R. Hollinshead 3,000 gns Newmarket December Sales. *G. Wragg.*

RELIANT 2 b.c. (Feb 6) Shirley Heights 130–Swift And Sure (USA) 98 (Valdez   **74**
(USA)) [1989 8.2d³ 8v] smallish, lengthy colt: moderate walker and mover: first
foal: dam 5f and 10.5f winner: 8/1 and in need of race, 4 lengths third of 15, no extra
final furlong, to Ridgepoint in maiden at Haydock, better effort in October: will be
better suited by 1¼m +. *I. A. Balding.*

RELIEF MAP 2 ch.f. (Apr 19) Relkino 131–Montania 68 (Mourne 126) [1989   **63 p**
a8g⁴] sparely-made filly: half-sister to several winners, including middle-distance
performers High Tension (by Vitiges) and Base Camp (by Derring-Do): dam won
over 7f: green, around 2 lengths fourth of 10, slowly away, to Calgary Redeye in
maiden at Lingfield: will stay 1¼m: should improve. *W. Hastings-Bass.*

Mrs John Wallinger's "Relief Pitcher"

RELIEF PITCHER   3 b.c. Welsh Term 126–Bases Loaded (USA) (Northern **120**
Dancer) [1988 7d⁴ 8.2d 1989 9g⁵ 10g² 11.7m³ 10f² 10f* 12f³ 12m² 12f² 10g* 11.1m²
10d⁴] big, deep-girthed colt: won maiden at Kempton in June and listed race (making
all) at Deauville in August: ran very well when head second of 5, leading over 2f out
until close home, to Assatis in BonusPrint September Stakes at Kempton: modest
fourth of 5 in Group 3 event at Goodwood 13 days later: stays 1½m: acts on firm
going, possibly unsuited by a soft surface: has run well when sweating and on toes:
very smart: reportedly remains in training. *P. T. Walwyn.*

REMEDY FOR LOVE   2 ch.c. (Feb 4) Cure The Blues (USA)–Oatlands (USA)   **51**
(Secretariat (USA)) [1989 5m⁴ 6f 5.1m 7.6m⁵ 8.2g] neat, good-topped colt:
half-brother to several winners in Ireland and France, including Irish 1½m and 2m
winner Reap The Harvest (by Ela-Mana-Mou): dam, Irish 1¼m winner, is
half-sister to very useful French middle-distance filly Gamberta: plating-class
maiden: probably stays 1m: blinkered second outing: reportedly gurgled second outing: sold
7,200 gns Newmarket Autumn Sales. *C. E. Brittain.*

REMEMBER WHEN   3 b.c. Taufan (USA) 119–Patiala (Crocket 130) [1988 6g³   **57** §
6f 6d 1989 7g 8f⁶ 7m 8m³ a8g⁴] strong, long-backed colt: moderate walker: quite
modest maiden: first form in handicaps and claimers as 3-y-o only when in frame at
Chepstow and Lingfield (visored) in October: stays 1m: blinkered third and fourth outings:
blinkered third and fourth outings, on first of them taking keen hold and wandering
under pressure: appears highly-strung, and is one to have reservations about. *R.
Hannon.*

REMTHAT NASER   2 b.f. (Apr 11) Sharpo 132–Warning Sound (Red Alert 127) **100**
[1989 5d* 6g² 7g² 7g⁵ 6g] IR 16,000Y: neat filly: second foal: half-sister to Irish
3-y-o 1¼m winner Second Guess (by Ela-Mana-Mou): dam Irish 5f to 1¼m winner:
won maiden at Warwick in May in good style: ran well in Ireland on next 2 starts,
particularly when beaten 1½ lengths by Wedding Bouquet in C L Weld EBF Park

734

Stakes at Phoenix Park: respectable fifth to Negligent in Bottisham Heath Stud
Rockfel Stakes at Newmarket in October: suited by 7f: sold 40,000 gns Newmarket
December Sales. *G. A. Huffer.*

REMWOOD GIRL   3 b.f. Remainder Man 126§–Aliwood Girl 64§ (Broxted 120)   **44**
[1988 5f⁴ 5g⁵ 5f² 6f³ 6g 6m 6s 7f 8m 1989 6s² 7.5d* 7f 8.2g 8v 8m] small, plain filly:
keen walker: plater: best efforts first 2 outings, winning at Beverley (no bid) in
April: showed little in non-selling events after: should stay beyond 7.5f: goes well
on a soft surface: sometimes edgy: tried in blinkers as 2-y-o when tended to hang
badly left. *W. Bentley.*

RENDEZVOUS BAY   3 b.f. Mill Reef (USA) 141–Figure de Proue (FR) (Petingo   —
135) [1988 7m 8s² 8g⁵ 1989 10m 10.6g 12.2m a 13g a 14g] leggy filly: modest maiden at
2 yrs: no form as 3-y-o, mostly in handicaps: should stay 1¼m: acts on soft going. *J.
L. Dunlop.*

RENTINA   2 b.f. (Mar 3) Adonijah 126–Gay Charlotte 95 (Charlottown 127) [1989   **57** p
7m⁶] 31,000Y: half-sister to several winners, including very smart 1¼m to 1½m
winner Upend (by Main Reef) and fairly useful middle-distance performer High Gait
(by High Top), dam of top-class stayer Royal Gait: dam, winner over 7.5f at 2 yrs in
Ireland and over 1m at 3 yrs in USA, is daughter of Irish Oaks winner Merry Mate:
odds on, over 7 lengths sixth of 12 to Pencarreg in maiden at Lingfield in September,
hard ridden over 2f out and never able to challenge: clearly thought capable of
better. *H. R. A. Cecil.*

REPACKER   3 ch.f. Aragon 118–Golden October 62 (Young Generation 129)   —
[1988 NR 1989 7m a 10g] 3,600Y: leggy filly: first foal: dam won over 6f: well beaten
in seller (bandaged), wore tongue strap and very green) at Leicester in August and
maiden claimer at Lingfield in December. *C. N. Allen.*

REPERCUTIONIST (USA)   2 b.f. (May 4) Beaudelaire (USA) 125–Reper-   **111**
cussion (USA) (Tatan (USA)) [1989 6d⁴ 7d* 7g⁵ 5g* 6m⁴] 210,000 francs (approx
£19,200, privately) Y: leggy filly: half-sister to several winners, including 3 in stakes
company: dam won maiden at around 5f at 2 yrs: successful in maiden in French
Provinces, and in Prix d'Arenberg (by 2 lengths from Rich And Famous) at
Longchamp in September: bandaged, over a length fourth of 11, keeping on well
towards finish, to Dead Certain in Tattersalls Cheveley Park Stakes at Newmarket:
best form at sprint distances. *A. J. Falourd, France.*

REPRIMAND   4 b.c. Mummy's Pet 125–Just You Wait (Nonoalco (USA)   **122**
131) [1988 7d² 8g* 1989 9g* 8s* 8f³ 10f³ 8f² 8m³ 8g³]
    Reprimand was restricted to just five races in his first two seasons by
one problem or another. As a two-year-old he had held a favourite's chance in
the Dewhurst only for the race to be abandoned because of severe gales, and
had been kept off the track in 1988 until October. He quickly made up for lost
time as a four-year-old and by the end of April his tally to six wins
from seven outings with successes in the Earl of Sefton EBF Stakes at
Newmarket and the Trusthouse Forte Mile at Sandown. In beating French
Stress and Most Welcome in the Trusthouse Forte Mile Reprimand achieved
more than when accounting for an essentially uncompetitive field in a
slowly-run affair at Newmarket. Of his seven opponents in the Earl of Sefton
Stakes only the half-length runner-up Petrullo and Llyn Gwynant went on to
win a race. Reprimand shared favouritism at Sandown with French Stress, the
only other one of the five runners to have been out already. The outcome was
decided when Cauthen, already in front, sent Reprimand on two furlongs out;
neither French Stress nor Most Welcome could peg them back and were
beaten by a length and two lengths.
    Cecil always maintained that Reprimand went best at home on top-
of-the-ground. Reprimand encountered such conditions for the first time on
the racecourse on his next start when he went off second favourite of four in
the Juddmonte Lockinge Stakes at Newbury. He ran creditably, but was
outpaced by Most Welcome (who reopposed on better terms) and Warning
inside the final furlong and was beaten two lengths and three quarters of a
length. The rest of the season saw a gradual decline in Reprimand's form.
After finishing a close third in the slowly-run Brigadier Gerard Stakes at
Sandown, his only try at a mile and a quarter, and second to the most
impressive Warning in the Queen Anne Stakes at Royal Ascot, he was off the
track for two months. On his remaining two starts he was held up, a somewhat

Sheikh Mohammed's "Reprimand"

surprising change in tactics in view of his lack of a top-class turn of foot. On the first one he tended to carry his head high, failed to respond to pressure and was a most disappointing favourite in the Beefeater Gin Celebration Mile at Goodwood, whilst in the Premio Vittorio di Capua at Milan he was a never-nearer two-and-three-quarter-length third of ten to Just A Flutter, whom he had easily disposed of in the Trusthouse Forte Mile and who in the meantime had been sold to a German stable.

Reprimand (b.c. 1985)	Mummy's Pet (b 1968)	Sing Sing (b 1957)	Tudor Minstrel Agin The Law
		Money For Nothing (br 1962)	Grey Sovereign Sweet Nothings
	Just You Wait (b 1980)	Nonoalco (b 1971)	Nearctic Seximee
		Sleat (ch 1969)	Santa Claus Belle of Athens

Reprimand is set to join Chilibang, Petoski, Rousillon and Jalmood at the National Stud, where he'll stand at a fee of £4,500, with an October 1st concession. Twenty-five of the forty shares were made available at £14,000 each, with the National Stud agreeing to buy five shares. Reprimand's pedigree has been covered at some length in the last two *Racehorses*. He is from the third-last crop of the high-class sprinter Mummy's Pet, known primarily as a sire of two-year-olds and of sprinters. That Reprimand stayed further than the majority of his sire's progeny was due in part to his relaxed

736

manner of racing—he was a lazy individual who needed plenty of driving. And there is some stamina on the dam's side. Although Just You Wait never ran, his grandam Sleat was a very useful winner at a mile and a quarter, notably in the Sun Chariot Stakes. Sleat, a half-sister to the St Leger winner Athens Wood, bred four winners, the best of them the fairly useful mile-and-a-quarter winner Kristana, the dam of Prix Robert Papin winner Ozone Friendly. Sleat is also the grandam of the useful two-year-old Fawzi and the very useful French miler Soft Currency. Just You Wait's first foal and only other winner is Another Rhythm (by Music Boy), a modest sprinter at his best, but also highly-strung and ungenuine.

Reprimand, a good walker, usually impressed in appearance; he is a strong, rangy colt tending to carry plenty of condition. He seemed to stay a mile and a quarter in a slowly-run race. His form was just as good on firm going as it was on soft, although at times he gave the impression he wasn't at ease on firm. He was seen to best advantage ridden close to the pace. *H. R. A. Cecil.*

RE-RELEASE 4 ch.f. Baptism 119–Release Record (Jukebox 120) [1988 8d⁵ 7g³   **91** 1989 7g⁴ 8s⁶ 8.5d⁵ 8f² 8.2m²ᵈⁱˢ 8.2g³ 9g³ 12d²] rangy, angular filly: fair handicapper: placed at Chepstow, Haydock (twice, disqualified first time for interference, most unlucky second time), Newmarket and Thirsk: ran very well at last 2 behind Rambo's Hall in William Hill Cambridgeshire Handicap and Firelight Fiesta in William Hill November Handicap: stays 1½m: acts on any going: visored last 2 outings: blinkered previous 5: trained until after third start by M. H. Easterby. *M. C. Pipe.*

RES IPSA LOQUITUR 2 b.c. (Mar 21) Law Society (USA) 130–Bubbling   **92** (USA) (Stage Door Johnny) [1989 6m⁴ 7g⁴ 7g⁴ 10g] IR 52,000Y: well-made, useful-looking colt: has plenty of scope: half-brother to useful Irish 7f and 1¼m winner Raconteur and useful 7.6f and 1m winner Midnight Tiger (both by The Minstrel): dam half-sister to high-class 6.5f and 1½m winner Effervescing, was smart stakes winner over 1m: put up much improved effort when around 5 lengths fourth of 7 to Free At Last in listed race at Newmarket in October, running on well last 2f: ran poorly in similar event won by Rock Hopper there following month, dropping away last 3f: should be suited by further than 7f. *R. Hollinshead.*

RESOLUTE BAY 3 b.g. Crofthall 110–Spinner 59 (Blue Cashmere 129) [1988   **91** 5g² 5m² 5f² 5m* 5m* 6m* 6g⁴ 6f 6g⁶ 1989 5g 6m⁵ 6m 5f⁴ 6m⁴ 6f* 6m* 6f 6m 6f] lengthy gelding: has a rather round action: fairly useful handicapper: easy winner at Redcar and dead-heated in £11,400 contest at Newcastle 8 days later: below form later in summer, soon hard driven in rear in £16,500 event final start: suited by 6f: appears ideally suited by top-of-the-ground: visored fifth to eighth outings. *R. M. Whitaker.*

RESPECTABLE JONES 3 ch.g. Tina's Pet 121–Jonesee 64 (Dublin Taxi)   **69** [1988 6m 6g² 6s 7s⁴ 1989 6m⁶ 5g³ 5f⁴ 6g 6g 7.6m 5d* 5d⁴] leggy, lengthy gelding: 25/1, led on line in 27-runner handicap at Newbury in October: well below form previous 3 starts: stays 6f: acts on any going: visored last 2 outings. *G. B. Balding.*

RESPRAY 3 gr.f. Rusticaro (FR) 124–Nye (FR) (Sanctus II 132) [1988 5d 7.5f³ 6m   **—** 7d 7g 1989 10.6g 8h 9f⁴ 8.5m] lengthy, good-topped filly: quite modest maiden at best: tubed in 1989 and showed little: wandered badly under pressure fourth start: should stay 1¼m: acts on firm going and a soft surface. *M. Johnston.*

RESTLESS DON 4 b.c. Mandrake Major 122–La Fille 58 (Crooner 119) [1988   **80** 5m² 5s 5f 5m³ 5g⁴ 5m² 5m* 5g 5s⁶ 5f 5f 5g 5m 1989 5g 5f4 5f 5m* 5g³ 6m 5g⁴ 5m 5m⁵ 5m 5m] lengthy, dipped-backed colt: fair handicapper: won at Haydock in May: suited by 5f and a sound surface: has shown a tendency to hang: inconsistent. *D. W. Chapman.*

RESTLESS RHAPSODY 6 ch.g. Young Generation 129–Bohemian Rhapsody   **40** 86 (On Your Mark 125) [1988 6v² 6f⁵ 6m 6d² 5.1g² 6m⁶ 5m 6g 6m 8g 1989 5m 5f 6m 7m 7g²] robust gelding: quite modest handicapper at best: showed he retained a little ability on final outing when neck second of 10 in apprentice event at Lingfield: stays 7f: possibly suited by an easy surface nowadays: effective with or without blinkers: has won for apprentice: usually bandaged off-fore nowadays: sold to join K. White, 2,400 gns Ascot September Sales. *W. J. Haggas.*

RESTLESS STAR 2 ch.f. (Apr 12) Star Appeal 133–Restive 96 (Relic) [1989 6m   **—** 7m 7g] rather leggy, unfurnished filly: half-sister to several winners, including useful sprinters Sharpish (by Sharpen Up) and Respect (by Mummy's Pet) and 1½m

*Paul Caddick And MacGay Sprint Trophy (Handicap), York—
blinkered Restore holds on from Duckington*

winner Rest (by Dance In Time): dam suited by 7f: behind in big fields of maidens:
went very freely to post final start. *G. A. Pritchard-Gordon.*

RESTORE 6 ch.g. Habitat 134–Never So Lovely 87 (Realm 129) [1988 5d² 6m⁵ **104**
5s⁵ 6m* 5g⁴ 6m 6m* 6m⁵ 6g* 6s 6s⁴ 6d 6f* 6g 1989 6v⁴ 5s 6f* 6f* 6f 6m 6m 6m 6g³
6g] useful-looking gelding: had much better season as 5-y-o having been hobdayed
(was so again at end of season) and improved again when winning listed event at
Lingfield in June by ¾ length from Green's Canaletto: beat Duckington a neck in
valuable handicap at York nearly 3 weeks earlier: creditable third to Corwyn Bay in
listed event at the Curragh, only form in second half of season: suited by 6f: well
suited by sound surface: has worn visor, blinkered nowadays: unsuited by track at
Epsom: often on edge: usually taken early or quietly to post (went down very freely
final outing): best with strong handling. *G. Lewis.*

RESTOWEST 2 ch.c. (Mar 3) Hotfoot 126–Mondoodle 63 (Monsanto (FR) 121) —
[1989 6s] 2,500Y, 11,500 2-y-o: first foal: dam 6f winner at 2 yrs: 50/1, tailed off in
Hamilton claimer: sold 625 gns Ascot November Sales. *R. J. Holder.*

RESTRAINED (USA) 3 b.f. Robellino (USA) 127–For The Flag (USA) 66 **98**
(Forli (ARG)) [1988 NR 1989 8f⁴ 8.5g* 9.5s* 10g³ 8g³ 11.5s³ 12g³] sister to a minor
winner in USA and half-sister to smart filly On The Staff and useful colt National
Service (both by Master Willie), all successful at around 1¼m: dam, from good
family, plating-class maiden here later won at 1m in USA: successful twice at
Cagnes-sur-Mer in February: in need of race on first run of 7 months, ran well in
apprentice event at Ascot fifth outing: third after in listed races at Rouen and
Toulouse: probably stays 1½m: goes well on soft going: sold 40,000 gns Newmarket
December Sales. *W. Hastings-Bass.*

RESUCADA 3 b.g. Red Sunset 120–Camden Dancer (Camden Town 125) [1988 **72**
5g* 6f⁵ 6s 1989 6s 5s 6d 6m³ 6f 6f⁴ 6m* 5f⁵ 6h⁴ 5m] lengthy, quite useful-looking
gelding: moderate walker: modest handicapper: ridden by 5-lb claimer, made all in
£6,800 event at Epsom in June: stays 6f: needs a sound surface, and acts on hard
ground: blinkered last 4 outings: bought out of G. Lewis' stable 17,500 gns
Newmarket July Sales before final one. *T. Fairhurst.*

RETOUCH 3 b.c. Touching Wood (USA) 127–Nelly Do Da 78 (Derring-Do 131)   **87**
[1988 6m⁴ 7m* 8s⁵ 9m² 8g² 1989 10g 12f 10f* 13.8g² 11.7f³ 14m⁵] workmanlike, rather sparely-made colt: favourite, won claimer at Nottingham in September: ran well after in similar event and handicaps: stays 1¾m: acts on firm going: has run creditably for 5-lb claimer. *P. F. I. Cole.*

RETRENCHMENT 3 b.f. Royal Match 117–Enchanted Evening (Warpath 113)   **—**
[1988 NR 1989 6f 7f4 9f 9f] 300F: sturdy filly: fourth foal: dam poor on flat later successful over hurdles: no form in maiden and sellers: bred to stay 1¼m + , but has pulled hard. *G. M. Moore.*

RETRIEVE 6 b.g. High Top 131–Front Row 111 (Epaulette 125) [1988 5d⁶ 6g³   **—**
6g⁵ 5f 6d 6m⁵ 6m 6s 6s 1989 6d 8d 7d] compact, robust gelding: moderate mover: one-time fair handicapper: easily best effort in spring (not seen out after April) on second outing: best form at 6f or 7f: unsuited by soft going, acts on any other: blinkered final appearance at 5 yrs. *W. Jarvis.*

RETURN FAIR 3 ch.f. Beldale Lark 105–Moonsail (Windjammer (USA)) [1988   **—**
5f 5f 5g 5g 1989 5g] workmanlike filly: of little account. *J. Mackie.*

RETURN TO ROMANCE 3 b.f. Trojan Fen 118–Honest Penny (USA) (Honest   **71**
Pleasure (USA)) [1988 7f 7v* 8.2v⁵ 1989 8.2v 7g* 8m² 8.3m 11.7g 11.5m 7.6m³ 8f 10f* 12.5f*] good-bodied, workmanlike filly: carries condition: very useful plater: won at Doncaster (no bid) in May, Nottingham (bought in 4,750 gns) in September and Wolverhampton (sold 6,000 gns) in October: held up in rear when gaining last 2 successes: suited by 1½m: acts on any going: claimed out of Sir Mark Prescott's stable £6,300 third start: winning hurdler for F. Jordan. *C. A. Horgan.*

RETURN TO SENDER 2 b.c. (Apr 10) Auction Ring (USA) 123–Tarte Tatin   **—**
(FR) (Busted 134) [1989 7g] 21,000F, 50,000Y: second foal: half-brother to Irish 7f winner Sallustar (by Sallust): dam, French maiden, is half-sister to Noir Et Or: 33/1, soundly beaten in maiden at Newmarket in November. *R. J. R. Williams.*

REVARO 3 b.g. Corvaro (USA) 122–Quick Dream (Crepello 136) [1988 6g 6s 7m   **70**
7f 8v⁴ 1989 10.2g* 10v* 10.6s³ 12.3m 12d 10s 10.6m⁵ 15s] medium-sized gelding: has a round action: modest handicapper: justified favouritism at Newcastle and Ayr early in season: below form last 5 outings: should stay 1½m: suited by plenty of give in the ground. *Mrs J. R. Ramsden.*

REVOKE (USA) 2 ro.f. (Apr 21) Riverman (USA) 131–Queens Only (USA)   **64**
(Marshua's Dancer (USA)) [1989 6f³ 5g³ 5m² 5m⁶ 6g⁴] smallish, unfurnished filly: seventh foal: half-sister to 4 winners, including smart 1982 American 2-y-o 1m and 9f winner Only Queens (by Transworld) and quite useful 1988 2-y-o 6f winner Roback (by Roberto): dam, 6f to 1m winner in USA, is closely related to Native Royalty, smart at around 9f: quite modest maiden: bred to need further than 6f: very edgy and gave trouble stalls at Catterick second start. *B. W. Hills.*

RHAPSODY IN RED 3 ch.c. Song 132–Embarrassed 81 (Busted 134) [1988 5d²   **50**
6m³ 6f⁶ 7s 1989 7s 7s 6m⁴ 7f 7f 7f⁶] strong colt: maiden handicapper: easily best effort as 3-y-o on third start: ran in seller final one: probably doesn't stay 7f: acts on firm going and a soft surface: trained most of season by M. Usher. *C. C. Elsey.*

RHUM BAY 4 ch.c. Buzzards Bay 128§–Czar's Diamond 66 (Queen's Hussar   **—**
124) [1988 10g 12f 16s 1989 10d 12.5g⁴ 12f 14.8m] stocky, plain colt: little sign of ability: looked difficult ride final outing. *H. J. Collingridge.*

RIBOKEYES BOY 7 b.g. Riboboy (USA) 124–Molvitesse 75 (Molvedo 137)   **39**
[1988 10m* 10d* 10d⁶ 12f⁶ 10m² 10m 1989 10s³ 10s⁵ 10f] close-coupled gelding: poor plater: stays 1¼m well: acts on top-of-the-ground and soft going: usually bandaged nowadays: occasionally slowly away: has run creditably for apprentice: winning hurdler. *A. R. Davison.*

RIBO MELODY 6 b.m. Riboboy (USA) 124–Sovereign Melody 89§ (Fortino II   **—**
120) [1988 12s 13.8g³ 12g 16m⁵ 1989 13f4] light-framed mare: poor maiden: probably best at 1½m to 1¾m: acts on firm going: often sweats: bandaged first 2 starts at 5 yrs: winning hurdler. *B. McLean.*

RICH AND FAMOUS (FR) 2 b.f. (Feb 17) Deep Roots 124–Paraxelle (FR)   **111**
(Poleax (USA)) [1989 5g⁴ 5g* 5g² 5g] 70,000 francs (approx £6,400) Y: half-sister to several winners in France and USA, notably useful French 1984 2-y-o Loucoum (by Iron Duke), later 6.5f to 8.5f winner in USA, and French 3-y-o 9f winner Bellara (by Bellman): dam won at 9f and 1¼m in France: very useful filly: won Prix du Bois at Longchamp in June by a short head: beaten 2 lengths by Repercutionist in Prix d'Arenberg there over 2 months later: ran respectably behind Silver Fling in Prix de l'Abbaye de Longchamp in October: should stay beyond 5f. *P. Bary, France.*

739

RICHARDS PET 3 ch.g. Noalto 120–Whipalash 73 (Stephen George 102) [1988   **59**
5d 5g[4] 6d[3] 6d[6] 7g[5] 8f 6d 8g 1989 8f 7h 7f 9f[2] 10g 10f] good-topped, close-coupled,
workmanlike gelding: has a roundish action: second in claimer at Wolverhampton in
July, only worthwhile form as 3-y-o: should stay 1¼m: acts on firm going and a soft
surface: has joined Miss G. Dollar. *L. G. Cottrell.*

RICHMOND PARK 2 b.c. (Feb 27) Aragon 118–The Ranee (Royal Palace 131)   **51**
[1989 6m[6] 6f[5] 8m 7d[5] 8g[5]] 3,400F, 5,800Y: sparely-made colt: second foal:
half-brother to modest 7f and 1m winner Alipura (by Anfield): dam behind in modest
company: fair plater: best efforts final 2 starts: suited by forcing tactics: best form on an easy
surface: blinkered third start: sold to join L. Barratt 2,100 gns Newmarket Autumn
Sales. *A. Bailey.*

RICMAR (USA) 6 ch.g. Lydian (FR) 120–Regency Tale (CAN) (Vice Regent   —
(CAN)) [1988 NR 1989 14s 16f 16f[4]] small gelding: quite modest handicapper at his
best: not seen out after June: stays 2m: probably acts on any going: wears blinkers:
bandaged last 2 starts: suited by forcing tactics. *J. R. Jenkins.*

RIDGEPOINT 2 ch.c. (Mar 15) Gorytus (USA) 132–Cooliney Princess 98 (Bruni   **83** p
132) [1989 8m[4] 8.2d*] IR 37,000F, 18,000Y: strong, lengthy colt: second foal:
half-brother to fair 1988 2-y-o 6f winner Prince of The Glen (by Glenstal): dam, Irish
2-y-o 7f and 1½m winner, is half-sister to Irish St Leger winner Conor Pass: won
maiden at Haydock in October by a short head from Adding, leading 2f out having
been hampered shortly before and running on well: will stay 1¼m: may well
improve again. *C. E. Brittain.*

RIDGIDUCT 5 ch.m. Ahonoora 122–Salique (Sallust 134) [1988 5s[2] 5g 5g 6m 5f[5]   **51**
5f 5f[2] 5f[3] 5s[5] 5d 1989 5f[3] 5m[5] 5. 1f[2] 5f* 5m 5d[6] 5.3f[2] 5f 5m[3] 5g] workmanlike mare:
favourite, won (for first time) handicap at Thirsk in July by ½ length, running on
despite tending to edge left and carry head awkwardly: easily best efforts after when
placed: suited by 5f: acts on any going: blinkered twice at 4 yrs, edgy second time:
bandaged near-hind fifth start: suitable mount for apprentice: sold 3,400 gns Ascot
December Sales. *J. Wharton.*

RIESENER 3 ch.c. Touching Wood (USA) 127–Sharp Run (Sharpen Up 127)   —
[1988 8f 7m 1989 9g 10.6m 16.2g 12.4m 8g[5] 10g] poor maiden: has joined Mrs P.
Barker. *R. Hollinshead.*

RIEVAULX 3 b.g. Petorius 117–Sister Sala (Double-U-Jay 120) [1988 NR 1989   —
8f[4] 10.6g 8g[6] 8m] IR 4,000Y: lengthy, plain gelding: third living foal: half-brother to
1985 Irish 2-y-o 1m winner Dalsala (by Dalsaan): dam champion 2-y-o in Norway, is
sister to Norsk 2000 Guineas winner Opatia: quite modest form at best in varied
events: may do better at 7f. *W. J. Pearce.*

RIFADA 3 b.f. Ela-Mana-Mou 132–Rilasa (FR) (St Paddy 133) [1988 NR 1989 8m[3]   **103**
12f* 12.2m*dis 12g* 12g* 12f[4] 12m[3]] leggy, sparely-made filly: third living foal:
half-sister to useful 1m and 1¼m winner Riyda (by Be My Guest) and French 1¼m
winner Rakisa (by Thatch): dam lightly raced but very useful performer at up to 9.5f:
won maiden at Chepstow in May, 4-runner minor event (disqualified over 5 months
later after testing positive) at Warwick in June and £8,000 handicap (showing
improved form and making all) at Newbury in August: will stay 1¾m: acts on firm
going: ran creditably when sweating sixth start: useful and genuine. *R. F. Johnson
Houghton.*

RIGHT ON CUE 3 b.g. Taufan (USA) 119–Cigarette 61 (Miralgo 130) [1988 NR   —
1989 9f 8.2f[4] 12g[5]] 13,000Y: angular gelding: half-brother to 5 winners here and
abroad, including useful 1974 Irish 2-y-o Say Cheese (by Polyfoto): dam plater: no
sign of ability in minor events. *B. A. McMahon.*

RIGHT PATH 4 b.g. Ya Zaman (USA) 122–Our Ena (Tower Walk 130) [1988   **48**
8.5m[6] 8f 9f[4] 10m 8s[4] 8g 7g 1989 8s[4] 7g 6d 8.3m[4] 8m[2] 8m 8m[3] 8f[3] 8g] close-coupled,
workmanlike gelding: tubed: poor mover: modest plater: good third at Edinburgh
and Pontefract (handicap, claimed out of J. Spearing's stable £6,050) in June: needs
further than 6f and stays 1m well: acts on any going. *N. Tinkler.*

RIGHT STEP (FR) 4 ch.g. Noalcoholic (FR) 128–Right Dancer 97 (Dance In   **45**
Time (CAN)) [1988 8g 10m 1989 10f[3] 12f* 12h] lengthy, good-topped gelding:
moderate mover: won strongly-run seller (no bid) at Thirsk in May: well beaten,
facing stiff task, in handicap at Carlisle 2 weeks later: suited by 1½m: acts on firm
going: winning hurdler. *R. J. O'Sullivan.*

RINCON 3 b.c. Nicholas Bill 125–Floricelle 92 (Derring-Do 131) [1988 7f 7g* 7g   **81**
7m 1989 8d[2] 10v[3] 10g[3] 12.4m[2] 12g* 11.7m[4] 15s[2] 13.8g[3] 12g] strong, lengthy colt:
has a markedly round action: fair handicapper: won at Edinburgh in July: soundly
beaten in amateurs event final outing: stays 1½m: acts on top-of-the-ground and
heavy going: sold 19,000 gns Newmarket Autumn Sales. *Sir Mark Prescott.*

RING APPEAL 2 ch.g. (Mar 8) Star Appeal 133–Sally Gal 101 (Lord Gayle (USA) —
124) [1989 5.8m 8g a7g] IR 6,800Y, 28,000 2-y-o: small, sparely-made gelding:
half-brother to Irish 1½m winner Sallytude (by Tudor Music) and 3 winners in
Germany: dam won at 7.5f (at 2 yrs) and 1½m: well beaten in maidens, including an
auction event: pulled hard, hung right and looked irresolute second outing. *C. E.
Brittain.*

RING ME BACK 4 b.f. Ring Bidder 88–Snippet (Ragstone 128) [1988 6g 7f⁶ 6m —
8g 8g³ 8g⁵ 9g 8s 1989 7d] leggy, rather close-coupled filly: poor maiden: taken early
and quietly to post, tailed off in seller at Catterick in March: stays 1m: sold 1,600 gns
Doncaster April Sales: resold 1,075 gns Ascot November Sales. *D. McCain.*

RINGMORE 7 ch.g. Porto Bello 118–Dirrie Star 78 (Dunoon Star 110) [1988 12f⁴ 50
10f³ 8.5g² 8d⁵ 10g³ 10f³ 10g⁶ 1989 10.2g 10d² 8d⁶ 10d 9f 9f 10.6g² 10.6d 10f 10.6m]
dipped-backed, good-quartered gelding: poor mover: plating-class handicapper:
stays 10.6f: acts on firm going and a soft surface: usually claimer ridden: usually held
up, often given lot to do: winning hurdler/chaser. *J. Parkes.*

RING OF THE SOUTH 2 b.g. (Feb 25) Jalmood (USA) 126–Saturne (Bellypha —
130) [1989 a7g⁶ a7g] 6,800Y: compact gelding: first foal: dam unraced: backward,
poor form in late-year maidens at Lingfield: will stay 1¼m. *R. F. Johnson Houghton.*

RING RACECALL 2 b.g. (May 2) Montekin 125–Right Minx (Right Tack 131) 54
[1989 6m 7m 6f² 6f³ 6f⁶ 7g] IR 8,000F, IR 4,600Y: compact, rather sparely-made
gelding: has a quick action: sixth reported foal: closely related to 1983 2-y-o 1m
winner Spiv's Right (by Mount Hagen) and half-brother to 2 other winners,
including 1m seller winner Everloft (by Camden Town): dam won 7 times at up to 9f
in France: plating-class maiden: ran poorly on last 2 starts: should stay 7f: blinkered
final outing: subsequently gelded. *J. W. Hills.*

RINJA (USA) 2 b.c. (Apr 2) Robellino (USA) 127–Dijla 82 (Hittite Glory 125) 72
[1989 6m⁵ 6f 7.6m* 8g⁶ 7g⁶] $9,000F: workmanlike, angular colt: has scope: third
foal: dam 7f and 1m winner here later successful in USA, is half-sister to Ibn Majed:
well-backed co-favourite, won maiden at Lingfield in September by 2 lengths from
Tuwittuwittuwoo: ran well in nurseries afterwards: stays 1m: bandaged behind last
3 starts. *D. W. P. Arbuthnot.*

RINTINTIN 2 ch.c. (Apr 22) Tina's Pet 121–Countess Down (Roan Rocket 128) —
[1989 8v 8g] unfurnished colt: third foal: dam never ran: prominent over 5f in minor
event at Newbury and maiden at Leicester late in season. *G. Lewis.*

RIO PIEDRAS 5 b.m. Kala Shikari 125–Glory Isle 60 (Hittite Glory 125) [1988 74
10s³ 11.7f 11.7d² 10m³ 10m² 10v⁶ 10s² 8f² 10g³ 1989 10s² 9v* 8.5d 8g 8f 9m³ 10m
10m² 8m⁴ 10g⁶ a10g 10g*] smallish, lightly-made mare: modest performer: often in
frame, but her wins in handicaps at Kempton (girl apprentices) in April and Redcar
in November have been her only successes since debut at 2 yrs: ideally suited by
around 1¼m: acts on any going: ran poorly when visored fourth outing: blinkered
seventh: sometimes sweats and gets on edge: suitable mount for inexperienced
rider: has looked none too keen. *A. Bailey.*

RIOSAMBA (USA) 3 b.f. Caerleon (USA) 132–Immensity (BRZ) (Zenabre) 88
[1988 7g 1989 7g⁴ 8m* 10m 10m³ 10m] sparely-made, angular filly: moderate
mover: stayed on strongly to lead close home in Newmarket maiden in May: good
third in handicap at Newbury, no extra and edging left inside final 1f: behind in listed
race and £8,000 handicap starts either side: stays 1¼m. *C. F. Wall.*

RIPTIDE 3 ch.f. Mill Reef (USA) 141–Mighty Fly 117 (Comedy Star (USA) 121) 77
[1988 7m 7f⁶ 1989 10f⁴ 9f 8m⁵ 9m 9m 9g⁵ 8m* 9d* 10g³ 8m³] rather unfurnished
filly: won handicap (blinkered, making all) at Wolverhampton and minor event at
Ostend in August: blinkered, ran creditably in handicaps last 2 starts: should prove
best short of 1¼m: acts on firm going and a soft surface: sometimes apprentice
ridden. *I. A. Balding.*

RISATINA 3 ch.f. Sallust 134–Saga's Humour 61 (Bustino 136) [1988 7g 1989 7s 45
10s 12f 10.2f³ 10f³ 11.7f⁵ a12g a10g] small filly: moderate mover: poor maiden: form
only at 1¼m on firm going: blinkered last 5 outings: bandaged near-hind on
reappearance: trained until after fourth start by A. Lee. *Mrs A. Knight.*

RISEN MOON (USA) 2 b.c. (May 6) Hawaiian Sound (USA) 129–Uvula (USA) 63 p
(His Majesty (USA)) [1989 7g] $13,000Y: tall, leggy colt: looks weak: sixth foal:
half-brother to a minor winner: dam minor winner in USA, is sister to good-class
middle-distance filly Ribbon and very useful Polar Gap: 6/1, around 10 lengths tenth
of 29, fading final 2f, to Lord of The Field in maiden at Newmarket in November:
sure to do better over further. *B. W. Hills.*

RISE OVER 3 ch.f. Smackover 107–Stewart's Rise 52 (Good Bond 122) [1988 NR 1989 8.5d 8d⁴ 10.6g 8m⁵] big, unfurnished filly: has scope: has a round action: first foal: dam plater, won from 1m to 1½m: sweating and ridden by 5-lb claimer, strong-finishing fourth in maiden at Warwick, easily best effort: bandaged and tailed off next start 5 months later: should stay 1¼m. *K. White.* —

RISK FACTOR 3 b.g. Auction Ring (USA) 123–Flying Anna (Roan Rocket 128) [1988 NR 1989 10s 12m 9m⁶ 8.2d] IR 42,000Y: sturdy, workmanlike gelding: sixth foal: brother to Irish 1½m winner Sotheby Sound and half-brother to 2 winners in Ireland, notably useful Irish 1m to 9f winner Alianna (by Nebbiolo): dam Irish 5f and 1m winner: never-nearer sixth in maiden at Mallow when trained by T. Stack: tailed off in Haydock claimer over 4 months later. *D. Moffatt.* —

RISLAN (USA) 3 b.c. Diesis 133–Sanctum Sanctorum (USA) (Secretariat (USA)) [1988 NR 1989 8v³ 8.5f³ 8m⁴ 11.5g⁶] fifth foal: half-brother to 1¼m winner Gulf Palace (by Green Dancer), and 2 winners in North America, one stakes placed: dam, minor winner in USA, is closely related to a good stakes winner and half-sister to 2 others: quite modest maiden: fourth at Edinburgh, best effort: should stay beyond 1m: possibly needs top-of-the-ground: sold to join G. Enright 9,000 gns Newmarket July Sales: winning juvenile hurdler. *P. F. I. Cole.* 57

RIVART (FR) 6 ch.g. River River (FR) 117–Artillerie (FR) (Crocket 130) [1988 12m 10.2m⁵ 1989 12m* 12m² 12m 14m² 14m⁵] tall, leggy gelding: moderate mover: quite modest handicapper: won (for first time) at Brighton in April: creditable second, hanging left, at same course and Yarmouth: stays 1¾m: acts on top-of-the-ground and soft going: blinkered once (tailed off): tends to carry head high, and is ungenuine. *P. A. Kelleway.* 61 §

RIVA (USA) 2 b.f. (Mar 30) Riverman (USA) 131–Valderna (FR) (Val de Loir 133) [1989 5f³] smallish, close-coupled filly: keen walker: sister to American 9f winner Fame and half-sister to 1m winner Alderney (by Great Nephew) and 2 winners in France, including 5f to 1m winner Travolta (by Targowice): dam, useful 10.5f winner at 3 yrs in France, is half-sister to Durtal and Detroit (by Riverman): favourite and on toes, over 3 lengths third of 6, not handling final turn and unable to quicken last furlong, to Susha in maiden at Chester in May. *B. W. Hills.* 42

RIVERBANK (USA) 2 b.c. (Mar 13) Robellino (USA) 127–River Crana (USA) (Cyane) [1989 6f 8m 9g] sturdy, good-quartered colt: moderate walker: shows knee action: first foal: dam unraced daughter of Fred Darling winner and Champion Stakes runner-up Northern Gem: well beaten in maidens and a claimer (blinkered): sold 5,600 gns Newmarket Autumn Sales. *I. A. Balding.* —

RIVER DRAGON 4 b.g. Rarity 129–Wet Powder (Above Suspicion 127) [1988 10g 12f⁶ 10m 12m 12d² 1989 12s 12s⁵ 16g* 16f² 16.5g³ 16g⁵ 16.5m² 16m³] sturdy gelding: carries plenty of condition: moderate mover: won handicap at Doncaster in May, ducking left after quickening into lead 1f out: placed after, running creditably, in similar company at Redcar, Doncaster (twice) and Warwick: better suited by 2m than 1½m and should stay further: acts on firm going and a soft surface: probably needs strong handling: has joined N. Henderson. *J. W. Payne.* 59

RIVER FOYLE 3 b. or br.f. Irish River (FR) 131–Royal Saint (USA) (Crimson Satan) [1988 NR 1989 10f⁴ 12g] strong, angular filly: third foal: dam, winner from 1m to 1¼m in USA, is half-sister to dam of Mount Livermore and Magical Wonder: no worthwhile form in maidens in the summer: sold 6,400 gns Newmarket December Sales. *G. Harwood.* —

RIVER GOD (USA) 2 b.c. (Jan 26) Val de L'Orne (FR) 130–Princess Morvi (USA) (Graustark) [1989 7g³] 74,000Y: useful-looking colt: has plenty of scope: brother to Japan Cup winner Pay The Butler and half-brother to winners in France and USA: dam 1m and 11f winner in France: 5/1 and green, 7½ lengths third of 28, staying on in excellent style towards finish, to Rami in maiden at Newmarket in November: will be well suited by middle distances: interesting prospect, sure to win races. *H. R. A. Cecil.* 78 p

RIVERHEAD (USA) 5 b.h. Riverman (USA) 131–Tertiary (USA) (Vaguely Noble 140) [1988 8.5g³ 8m 8g 8m³ 1989 8g⁶ 12g⁵ 10v² 10g 10g 8g] good-topped, attractive ex-French horse: has a quick action: second foal: half-brother to Tote Ebor winner Primary (by Green Dancer) and good-class 4-y-o Kefaah (by Blushing Groom): dam, second over 10.5f in France, is sister to high-class filly Nobiliary and half-sister to Lyphard: won handicap at Longchamp as 3-y-o: showed ability on first 4 outings in 1989: should stay 1½m: acts on any going: wears bandages. *D. R. C. Elsworth.* 93

RIVER OF HOPE (USA) 3 ch.f. Irish River (FR) 131–Bonnie Hope (USA) 73
(Nijinsky (CAN) 138) [1988 NR 1989 7f² 6f 8f² 10m² 8f 9f³ 8.2m] leggy, rather
shallow-girthed filly: has a free, rather round action: fifth foal: half-sister to 1½m
and 1¾m winner Raahin (by Super Concorde) and modest 1986 2-y-o maiden Bois
de Boulogne (by Green Forest), later winner in USA: dam ran only at 2 yrs, when
successful at around 1m: modest maiden: stays 1¼m: ran creditably for apprentice
sixth start, but wandered under pressure. *A. A. Scott.*

RIVER OF LIGHT (USA) 2 ch.c. (Jan 25) Irish River (FR) 131–Boreale (FR) **108**
115 (Bellypha 130) [1989 5g* 5g³ 6.5m² 7g⁵] 2,600,000 francs (approx £237,900) Y:
second foal: brother to 3-y-o Riviere Boreale, placed several times: dam French 6.5f
to 1m winner, is closely related to very useful French 1m and 9f winner Cabbaliste
and half-sister to high-class 1974 French 2-y-o Princesse Lee, herself dam of
Princesse Lida: successful in 5-runner newcomers race at Chantilly in June: placed
subsequently in Prix du Bois (2½ lengths third to Rich And Famous) at Longchamp
and listed race at Evry: ran moderately in Criterium de Maisons-Laffitte in October:
should stay 7f. *A. Fabre, France.*

RIVER REEF 3 b. or br.c. Dunphy 124–Zarinia (FR) (Right Royal V 135) [1988 7g   —
1989 8s 10.8m³] medium-sized, workmanlike colt: no form in maidens and 3-runner
minor event: sold 1,150 gns Ascot September Sales. *B. Gubby.*

RIVER SPIRIT (USA) 4 ch.g. Arts And Letters–Norma Teagarden (Jukebox   —
120) [1988 10m 12m 16m⁶ 1989 12d] lengthy, workmanlike gelding: has shown signs
of only a modicum of ability: sold 6,000 gns Doncaster August Sales. *P. Monteith.*

RIVERS RHAPSODY 2 b.f. (Feb 22) Dominion 123–Trwyn Cilan 89 (Import **84 p**
127) [1989 5m³ 6m² 5m³ 5m*] angular filly: first foal: dam best at 5f: showed
improved form when winning nursery at Newbury in September, quickening in good
style, by ¾ length from India's Twist: speedy: will improve again. *G. B. Balding.*

RIVER'S RISING (FR) 3 gr.f. Mendez (FR) 128–Dry Land 84 (Nonoalco **88**
(USA) 131) [1988 NR 1989 7d⁵ 8m* 8m⁶ 8d 7g] angular, workmanlike filly: second
foal: half-sister to fairly useful 7f winner Trojan Desert (by Troy): dam,
granddaughter of very smart sprinter Lucasland, won over 5f: won maiden at
Newbury in July, leading well inside final furlong: below form in listed race
(favourite) and handicaps after, twice leading then one pace final 1f: stays 1m. *J.
Tree.*

RIVERS SECRET 5 b.m. Young Man (FR) 73–Pendle's Secret 73 (Le Johnstan **36**
123) [1988 15m⁶ 1989 13.8d⁴] workmanlike mare: poor handicapper: stays 13.8f: acts
on any going: blinkered or visored on 4 of last 5 outings on flat: fair winning hurdler.
Denys Smith.

RIVER WARDEN (USA) 3 b.c. Riverman (USA) 131–Sweet Simone (FR) **114**
(Green Dancer (USA) 132) [1988 8s² 9s² 1989 10s² 10.5s* 10m⁴ 10m* 10f] fifth
reported foal: half-brother to French 1986 2-y-o 6f winner Sweettuc (by Spectacular
Bid), also Grade 3 8.5f winner in USA as 2-y-o: dam, placed 3 times from as many
starts at 2 yrs, is out of half-sister to top-class middle-distance horse Sigebert:
successful at Saint-Cloud in maiden in May and slowly-run Group 2 Prix Eugene
Adam (showing improved form to beat Creator a head, leading close home) in July:
co-favourite, behind in Arlington Million in September: stays 10.5f: possibly suited
by top-of-the-ground. *A. Fabre, France.*

RIVIERA MAGIC 2 ch.c. (Mar 2) Niniski (USA) 125–Miss Beaulieu 106 **79**
(Northfields (USA)) [1989 6m⁴ 6f² 7g⁴] compact colt: moderate walker: shows a
quick action: second foal: half-brother to disappointing 3-y-o French Riviera (by
Teenoso): dam 6f and 1¼m winner: fair maiden: will stay 1¼m. *G. Wragg.*

RIVIERA SCENE 6 gr.g. Mummy's Pet 125–Pariscene 86 (Dragonara Palace **53**
(USA) 115) [1988 7g 6m⁵ 6g 6m 1989 6f⁶ 6m³] tall gelding: modest maiden at his
best: ridden by 7-lb claimer, showed he retained some ability in handicap at
Chepstow and claimer at Windsor in summer: stays 6f: acts on firm going: blinkered
once: has shown a tendency to edge left: often sweating and on toes: tail swisher. *P.
J. Makin.*

RIYADH LIGHTS 4 b.g. Formidable (USA) 125–Rivers Maid 83 (Rarity 129)   — §
[1988 10m³ 14f 1989 12f⁴ 15.5f 14m] compact gelding: moderate mover: poor maiden:
well tailed off in handicaps at Folkestone (blinkered, flashed tail) and Yarmouth last
2 outings: stays 1¼m: seems to act on any going: early-season winning hurdler: one
to leave alone on flat. *J. B. Sayers.*

ROAD TO REASON 3 b.c. Known Fact (USA) 135–Road To The Top 84 **91**
(Shirley Heights 130) [1988 6d* 6f² 1989 9d⁴ 10.4f³ 10f 12m⁴ 12m³ 10m] leggy,
rather sparely-made colt: fluent mover: fairly useful: in frame in listed races at

Francis Lever (Partners)'s "Robellation"

Newmarket and Chester and minor events at Leicester: stays 1½m: acts on firm going and a soft surface: blinkered as 3-y-o, except for first and fourth starts: may prove suited by galloping track: lacks turn of foot: sold 25,000 gns Newmarket Autumn Sales. *Major W. R. Hern.*

ROBBIE BURNS 3 br.c. Daring March 116–Gangawayhame 91 (Lochnager 132) **61**
[1988 NR 1989 6v 7s⁵ 8s 10g] second foal: brother to 5.8f winner Awa'wi'ye: dam won over 6f at 2 yrs and stayed 7f: quite modest form at best: appears suited by 1¼m. *R. V. Smyth.*

ROBCHRIS 3 b. or br.c. Dunphy 124–Whispering Star 78 (Sound Track 132) **59**
[1988 NR 1989 6d³ 6f³ 6h⁴] IR 4,000Y, 1,550 2-y-o: leggy, close-coupled colt: half-brother to numerous winners, including very useful performers Seadiver, Pearl Star and Portese (all by Gulf Pearl) and smart sprinter Blue Star (by Majority Blue): dam won over 5f on only start: quite modest maiden: hung left when below form second start: sweating and edgy final one (June): will probably stay 7f: claimer ridden. *M. O'Neill.*

ROBELLATION (USA) 2 b.c. (Mar 19) Robellino (USA) 127–Vexation (USA) **112**
(Vice Regent (CAN)) [1989 5g² 6f* 6f 7f² 7f* 7m² 8d² 8m⁵ 7.3d²] quite attractive colt: good mover: first foal: dam unraced half-sister to useful 1985 2-y-o 6f winner Chalk Stream (by Robellino) and smart 1m to 1¼m performer Baronet: very useful performer: successful in minor events at Kempton in May and Lingfield in August: best efforts when beaten narrowly in pattern races at Goodwood, Sandown and Newbury (head second to Tirol in Vodafone Horris Hill Stakes on final outing): sweated up when below-form fifth in Royal Lodge EBF Stakes at Ascot: suited by 7f or 1m: yet to race on very soft ground, acts on any other. *G. Harwood.*

ROBERT DEAR (USA) 3 gr.c. Caro 133–Marketess (USA) (To Market) [1988 **78**
6g 7m⁵ 7m 1989 8g 7d 11.7m⁵ 10g³ 8f* 8h* 8f 8g³] rangy colt: fair handicapper:

744

successful at Goodwood and Bath in June: worth another try over bit further: acts on firm going. *P. F. I. Cole.*

ROBERTET (USA)   3 b.f. Roberto (USA) 131–Ethics (USA) (Nijinsky (CAN) **118** 138) [1988 NR 1989 10d³ 10g* 12g³ 12g² 12.5m² 15.5g³] $37,000Y: first foal: dam unraced sister to high-class middle-distance colt Solford: won maiden at Deauville: placed after in listed races then Prix de Royallieu (coming from well off pace) and Prix Royal-Oak (3½ lengths third to Top Sunrise) at Longchamp: better at 15.5f than shorter: acts on top-of-the-ground. *E. Lellouche, France.*

ROBERTS PRIDE   3 b.f. Roberto (USA) 131–Glowing With Pride 114 (Ile de **62 +** Bourbon (USA) 133) [1988 NR 1989 8m 10.4m³ 8m 10g 12g 13.3d⁶ a16g⁴] big, angular filly: first foal: dam 7f and 10.5f winner, runner-up in Park Hill Stakes and St Simon Stakes: quite modest form: ran creditably facing stiff tasks in handicaps last 2 outings, disputing lead 3f out then weakening when fourth at Lingfield, leaving impresssion will be suited by return to shorter: acts on top-of-the-ground and a soft surface: acted as pacemaker third and fourth starts: bandaged all starts: lacks turn of foot: sold 15,000 gns Newmarket December Sales. *G. Wragg.*

ROBIN DES BOIS (USA)   2 b.c. (Feb 9) Nureyev (USA) 131–Rare Mint (USA) **106** (Key To The Mint (USA)) [1989 5g³ 6g² 5.5g² 6.5m* 7g³] closely related to good-class French 1m (at 2 yrs) to 1½m winner Mystery Rays and 1¾m winner Dragon's Blood (both by Nijinsky) and half-brother to useful French winner Juba Dollar (by Upper Nile), successful at up to 10.5f: dam unplaced daughter of half-sister to dams of Be My Guest and Golden Fleece: useful colt: won listed race at Evry in September: 4 lengths third to Septieme Ciel in Criterium de Maisons-Laffitte following month: will stay 1m: has raced only on a sound surface. *F. Boutin, France.*

ROBINIA (USA)   3 ch.f. Roberto (USA) 131–Royal Graustark (USA) (Graustark)   **90** [1988 7g* 7g 1989 12f4 9.2f5 9f6] rangy filly: good mover, with a light action: fairly useful at best: fifth at Goodwood, easily best effort in handicaps: made most 6f and found little final start (July): headstrong, and should prove best short of 1½m: acts on firm going: sold 7,000 gns Newmarket December Sales. *G. Harwood.*

ROBLET (USA)   3 b.c. Roberto (USA) 131–Valse Noble (USA) (Nijinsky (CAN) **105** 138) [1988 NR 1989 8g³ 10s* 10.1m³ 10.1m² 12m* 12m*] strong, good-bodied colt: third foal: dam, lightly raced, placed over 1m at 2 yrs in France: progressive form: set pace or ridden close to it when winning maiden at Nottingham in May and minor events at Leicester and Newmarket in July: will stay 1¾m: acts on top-of-the-ground and soft going: game and genuine. *H. R. A. Cecil.*

ROBORE (FR)   4 br.c. Zino 127–Mona Mou (FR) (Luthier 126) [1988 **124** 10.5v² 11d⁶ 10.5d⁴ 10.5s² 10.5s³ 10.5g² 10m³ 10s² 10.5s* 12d* 12g² 1989 10.5v³ 12d* 12m² 12d² 12g⁴ 12d² 12g⁶ 12m*]

In October Robore added his name to the considerable list of horses to have gained compensation in the Group 2 Prix du Conseil de Paris at Longchamp two weeks after being beaten in the Prix de l'Arc de Triomphe. He was the fourth to do so in the 'eighties, following Rahotep (nineteenth to Gold River), Sagace (eleventh to All Along) and Jupiter Island (eighth to demoted Sagace). Robore finished closer in the Arc than any of those three and, on his first venture into Group 1 company, acquitted himself extremely well. He was one of many who didn't get a clear run in a rough race. Soon switched inside from his wide draw, he remained boxed in towards the back of the field until the straight when, pulled out, he stayed on well without ever looking likely to reach the principals. At the post he was three lengths down on Carroll House in sixth place. Top Class, twelfth of nineteen, was the only other Arc participant to take his place in the eight-runner Prix du Conseil de Paris, for which Robore went off at odds on. Robore was held up as usual, made up his ground easily and quickened to the front a furlong out. He held off Louis Chypre comfortably by a length, with the three-year-old Ode and Deliorman in close attention. Top Class, blinkered for the first time, finished sixth.

In many ways Robore's career has been similar to that of another recent Conseil de Paris winner—Village Star. Bought cheaply as yearlings, they both improved considerably as four-year-olds, particularly in the second half of the year. In the first half both ran in the Prix d'Hedouville at Longchamp, the Prix Jean de Chaudenay at Saint-Cloud, the Grand Prix d'Evry and La Coupe at Longchamp. Village Star found one too good for him in all four; Robore also

Prix du Conseil de Paris, Longchamp—
Arc sixth Robore finds the opposition less exacting;
Louis Cyphre (No. 5) finishes well for second

filled the runner-up spot in the Prix Jean de Chaudenay and the Grand Prix d'Evry, but went one better in the Prix d'Hedouville, beating Boyatino by two lengths. Boyatino, who was making his reappearance and giving weight at Longchamp, reversed the placings in the Chaudenay five weeks later. In the Grand Prix d'Evry Robore finished a length and a half behind Star Lift in receipt of 6 lb. On terms 4 lb worse, Robore halved Star Lift's advantage in the Prix Foy at Longchamp in September (the pair were ten lengths clear of Apache) on his first run for almost three months.

			Welsh Pageant	Tudor Melody
	Zino		(b 1966)	Picture Light
	(b 1979)	Cyriana	Salvo
Robore (FR)			(b 1972)	Cynara
(br.c. 1985)			Luthier	Klairon
	Mona Mou (FR)		(b or br 1965)	Flute Enchantee
	(ch 1976)	East Hampton	Marino
			(b 1968)	Winchester

Robore, who is to stay in training, is from the second crop of the Two Thousand Guineas winner Zino and is easily his best runner to date. Bought for 110,000 francs (approximately £11,100) as a yearling at Deauville, Robore is the fourth foal of the unraced Mona Mou, the first of whom Posso Kani (by Brinkmanship) was successful in Belgium and the second Poros (by Sharpman) a winner from nine furlongs to a mile and a half in France. Robore's grandam East Hampton won four times in France at up to a mile and three quarters and stayed extreme distances, finishing runner-up to the British horse Hickleton in the Prix Gladiateur in the days when the race was staged over three miles. She produced several winners in France, none of them of any great significance. The leggy Robore, splendidly tough and consistent, is much better suited by a mile and a half than shorter. He has yet to race on firm going, but acts on any other. There may be a little more improvement in him yet. *N. Pelat, France.*

ROCHALLOR 3 ch.g. Dara Monarch 128–Ballymaloe Girl (Nonoalco (USA) 131) **66**
[1988 5m⁵ 5f 6f 6m 9m⁶ 1989 12d³ 12v³ 10f 10.2h*] compact, rather plain gelding:
moderate walker: has a round action: blinkered and apprentice ridden, won claimer
(claimed to join M. Pipe £12,300) at Bath in June by 5 lengths, leading over 1f out:
well beaten otherwise as 3-y-o: stays 1¼m well: acts on hard going: winning
juvenile hurdler. *R. Hannon.*

ROCHE 3 b.g. Balliol 125–Pink Stripes (Pyjama Hunt 126) [1988 7g 6d 6v 1989 8d —
12m 10f 10.1m 12h 8f] small gelding: keen walker: has a round action: little
worthwhile form, including in seller: probably doesn't stay 1½m: blinkered fourth
outing: trained until after fifth by N. Callaghan. *J. L. Spearing.*

ROCKARIA 4 b.c. Ballad Rock 122–Grazia 90 (Aureole 132) [1988 7d 8m 8.5m 7f —
8s* 7f⁵ 8d 1989 8m 8.2g 8m 7s 8.2d] sturdy, good-topped colt: quite modest winner
as 3-y-o: little show in varied events in 1989: suited by 1m: probably acts on any
going: blinkered final 3 outings at 3 yrs: sold to join M. Pipe 10,000 gns Newmarket
Autumn Sales. *G. B. Balding.*

ROCK CITY 2 br.c. (Mar 8) Ballad Rock 122–Rimosa's Pet 109 (Petingo **113**
135) [1989 5s* 6f* 6f* 6g* 6m* 7g⁴ 6m²]
Defeat in the Prix de la Salamandre and the Tattersalls Middle Park
Stakes in the autumn tarnished in the eyes of many the reputation that Rock
City had built up with a five-race unbeaten run which did much to enliven what
was a rather humdrum season for two-year-olds. There's no doubt that Rock
City was the best English two-year-old colt around in the summer, one who
was really thriving on his racing, and by the time of his clash with the leading
French colt Machiavellian in the Salamandre he had compiled a record which
bore close enough inspection to dent even the confidence of Machiavellian's
trainer Boutin. The possibility exists, however, that Rock City might not have
been right on his last two starts—his connections were swift to point to
physical problems of an unspecified nature—and if that's the case then all the
more credit to him, for, in our opinion, he lost no caste in defeat, anyway.
Come the autumn several two-year-olds made much greater strides than
Rock City, and in all likelihood he just wasn't good enough to complete his
first season unbeaten. Nonetheless, that shouldn't detract from his achieve-
ments at two: he's already one of the few horses who've won more in prize
money than they've cost, and he seems likely to pay his way again at three.
We doubt very much whether Rock City will emulate Mon Fils and Don't
Forget Me, two former inmates of Hannon's stable, and go on to success in the
Two Thousand Guineas, for which he's 20/1 at the time of writing.
The compact, good-quartered Rock City first rose to prominence in the
Coventry Stakes at Royal Ascot, where he lined up as one of four unbeaten
colts in a field of sixteen, having won a maiden at Sandown in April by a length
and a half from Brown Carpet and a minor event at York the following month
by three lengths from Regal Thatch. The betting at Ascot suggested that the
highly-regarded Wadood, who'd done remarkably well to come from last to
first in a maiden at York on his only start, the dual winner Candy Glen and the
five-length Kempton winner Robellation would fight out the finish, but in the
event it was the 9/1-shot Rock City who came home on his own, running on
really strongly in the final furlong to account for Wadood and Candy Glen by

Anglia Television July Stakes, Newmarket—Rock City dominates the four-runner race

three lengths and two with Bold Russian well back in fourth. Six years earlier
another son of Ballad Rock, Chief Singer, had won the Coventry in similarly
impressive fashion before going on to run in the Anglia Television July Stakes
at Newmarket. Whereas Chief Singer ran unaccountably badly, the progressive Rock City enhanced his reputation with a decisive victory. Conceding 5 lb
to his three opponents, among whom were Wadood, a strongly-backed
favourite, and the much improved northern-trained colt Champagne Gold,
Rock City made every post a winning one, smoothly stepping up a gear
approaching the final furlong and coming clean away to put five lengths
between himself and Champagne Gold; Wadood, whose last race of the season
it was to be, ran as if something was troubling him and finished a length behind
in third. Rock City was the fourth horse to complete the Coventry-July double
in the last twenty years, and the second since the Coventry was demoted to
Group 3 status in 1984. Only Horage, in 1982, of the other trio went on to
success in the Scottish Equitable Gimcrack Stakes at York in August—Primo
Dominie in 1984 and Perdu in 1972 both bypassed the race—but the four
runners that opposed Rock City at York didn't look strong enough to prevent
his completing the treble and predictably he started a very short-priced
favourite. Taking up the running from Olympic Hero at halfway Rock City
readily shook off the Ascot maiden winner Swiss Affair inside the penultimate
furlong and had only to be shown the whip in the last two hundred yards to
fend off the useful Book The Band by a length and a half; Champagne Gold,
who'd veered to his right leaving the stalls and interfered with Swiss Affair
and Olympic Hero, never got into the hunt and was defeated as comprehensively as he had been at Newmarket.

It's a consequence of the modern pattern of racing two-year-olds that the
order of merit among them changes briskly in the autumn as the late
developers come through, and though Rock City had strong claims to being
regarded as the best around in the summer his standing had diminished by the
close of the year. He continued to run creditably, though his three-length
fourth to Machiavellian in the Salamandre was widely regarded as a
disappointment. Approaching the final quarter of a mile Rock City held every
chance, but he was unable to quicken as Machiavellian and Qirmazi
accelerated past, and lost third place near the line. His rider Carson, who'd
partnered him in all his races except his first, reported that he'd gurgled on
the way to post and failed to respond in his usual manner when the race
developed. Much the same comments were forthcoming after Rock City's
two-length second to a much-improved Balla Cove in the Middle Park at
Newmarket in October, leaving his connections to mull over his future. On
our figures, however, Rock City ran just about up to his best in a strongly-run
race, and we're satisfied to accept that he was beaten simply by a better horse
on the day. If so, there are going to be more days like that for him in the
coming season.

The Airlie Stud stallion Ballad Rock has had a rather chequered career
since he retired from the racecourse in 1979. A good-class sprinter, much
better than when British racegoers saw him virtually tailed off in the Cork and

A. F. Budge (Equine) Ltd's "Rock City"

Rock City (br.c. Mar 8, 1987)	Ballad Rock (ch 1974)	Bold Lad (b 1964)	Bold Ruler
			Barn Pride
		True Rocket (gr 1967)	Roan Rocket
			True Course
	Rimosa's Pet (b 1976)	Petingo (b 1965)	Petition
			Alcazar
		Rimosa (br 1960)	Mossborough
			Rosy Dolly

Orrery Stakes at Royal Ascot on his only venture outside Ireland, Ballad Rock was afflicted by equine metritis in his early days at stud, badly affecting his health and fertility. He'd made a full recovery by the mid-'eighties when he was represented by his best son to date, the aforementioned Chief Singer, who recovered his form at three when he developed into a top-class sprinter/miler. Since Chief Singer's retirement in 1984 Ballad Rock's name has rather faded from the spotlight, but his fortunes revived in 1989 when Rock City and Balla Cove helped him to finish the season as fourth leading sire of two-year-olds. Ballad Rock is the first sprinting mate for Rock City's dam Rimosa's Pet. She made a slow start to her days as a broodmare—neither of her first two foals, both by Northern Baby, made the racecourse—but came good in 1988, when Kerrera (by Diesis) won the Cherry Hinton Stakes, and did well again in 1989 when besides Rock City and Kerrera, who finished second in the One Thousand Guineas, her third foal Secretariat's Pet (by Secretariat) showed useful form when successful at around a mile and a quarter in France. Rock City was obtained for much less than the reputed seven-figure sum which Kerrera fetched in a private deal and still less than the 200,000 guineas that Rimosa's Pet was sold for at the end of her time in training—at 35,000 guineas as a foal and 50,000 guineas at the Tattersalls October Yearling Sales. Rimosa's Pet was a talented filly, not so good as Rock City or Kerrera, but good enough to win three races from six furlongs to a mile and a quarter, including in the Princess Elizabeth Stakes and the Musidora Stakes. Her dam Rimosa, who was racing as far back as the early-'sixties, also won three races, coming into her own when encountering middle distances and soft ground. A daughter of a half-sister to Dante and Sayajirao, Rimosa bred several winners besides Rimosa's Pet, including the Blue Seal winner Denosa. Most members of the family have stayed a mile and Rock City, who has a much more placid temperament than Kerrera, certainly shouldn't have any trouble with that distance; though the fact that he was put back to six furlongs for his final race of the season suggests that connections feel sprinting might be his forte. He acts on any going. *R. Hannon.*

ROCK FACE 2 b.f. (Mar 3) Ballad Rock 122–Misty Halo 93 (High Top 131) [1989 **52**
7g a7g6 a8g] unfurnished filly: first foal: dam prolific winner at 1m to 2¼m: plating-class maiden: best effort second outing: never travelling particularly well final one. *Sir Mark Prescott.*

ROCK HOPPER 2 b.c. (Jun 9) Shareef Dancer (USA) 135–Cormorant **104 p**
Wood 130 (Home Guard (USA) 129) [1989 8.2f5 10g* 10g*]
Defoe wrote over two-hundred-and-fifty years ago about Nottingham races 'Tis a most glorious show they have here when the running season begins; for here is such an assembly of gentlemen of quality, that not Bansted Down, or New Market Heath, produces better company, better horses, or shows the horse and master's skill better'. Nowadays, as regards the quality of the horses at any rate, it's unlikely anyone would claim on Nottingham's behalf that it rivals Epsom or Newmarket since like most of the Midlands tracks the emphasis is generally placed on quantity with sizeable fields running for relatively modest prizes. Nevertheless, the Nottingham regulars saw some interesting horses in action in the latest season: Michelozzo, who ran away with a minor event in April, was one and there were several noteworthy performances in the two-year-old races. Salsabil, Something-different and Argentum all used wins against largely modest opponents as a stepping stone to success in pattern races either here or abroad, while Snurge passed the post first in the Group 1 Criterium de Saint-Cloud only to be controversially demoted, less than three weeks after being beaten in a Nottingham maiden event. Rock Hopper, was one of the vast majority of Nottingham winners who didn't go on to compete in pattern company. He did improve significantly to win the listed Jennings The Bookmakers Zetland Stakes though, and the manner of his victory in that race stamped him as a very useful middle-distance stayer in the making.

Rock Hopper's first two outings were both in Nottingham maiden events. Greenness and a very slow start meant he never reached the leaders in the first. He missed the break again in the second, but soon recovered and a sustained challenge in the straight saw him get up on the line to touch off Adding, who was being beaten by a short head for the third consecutive outing, with ten others well strung out behind. That win indicated stamina was very much Rock Hopper's strong suit, and his performance in the Zetland Stakes at Newmarket in November confirmed that in no uncertain manner. In a thirteen-runner field the pace was strong throughout. Rock Hopper, who'd been held up until after halfway, produced a promising challenge with two furlongs to run. He veered noticeably left both approaching and inside the final furlong, but despite this he continued to stay on really strongly, so much so that on reaching the post he'd forged six lengths clear of Access Sun (the judge gave five) with Laxey Bay a length and a half back in third. Admittedly, with fancied contenders like Almuinjjid and another Shareef Dancer colt Primacy running way below expectations the Zetland Stakes wasn't quite so informative as it might have been. Still, Rock Hopper could do no more than win handsomely, and further improvement looks assured especially if his steering problems can be ironed out.

*Jennings The Bookmakers Zetland Stakes, Newmarket—
a fine performance from a progressive staying two-year-old*

Rock Hopper turned out to be Greville Starkey's last winner in Britain. He retires with a tremendous record: in a career which spanned four decades he rode almost two thousand winners on the flat (plus a handful over hurdles), and races won included a Derby and Prix de l'Arc as mentioned in Cacoethes' commentary, a Two Thousand Guineas on Dancing Brave and another on To-Agori-Mou, and the Oaks on Homeward Bound and Fair Salinia. One of Starkey's main roles in the coming season will be to act as chief work rider for Rock Hopper's stable.

	Shareef Dancer (USA) (b 1980)	Northern Dancer (b 1961)	Nearctic Natalma
		Sweet Alliance (b 1974)	Sir Ivor Mrs Peterkin
Rock Hopper (b.c. Jun 9, 1987)			
	Cormorant Wood (b 1980)	Home Guard (ch or br 1969)	Forli Stay At Home
		Quarry Wood (b 1968)	Super Sam Phrygia

Rock Hopper's sire Shareef Dancer hasn't made the sort of start to his stud career that many people expected of him. His best representative so far is probably the good-class French middle-distance filly Colorado Dancer; he's also the sire of the One Thousand Guineas runner-up Dabaweyaa, and besides Rock Hopper he was responsible for a couple of other useful two-year-olds in 1989 in Shamshoon and the French filly Noble Ballerina. The dam will need little introduction to anyone who's followed racing closely during the 'eighties. Cormorant Wood was a top-class filly over a mile and a quarter. As a three-year-old she came out just on top in a thrilling three-horse finish to the Champion Stakes, and in the Benson and Hedges Gold Cup at York the following season she produced a splendid burst of speed to beat Tolomeo, Chief Singer and Sadler's Wells emphatically, in doing so becoming the first filly to win that particular race since Dahlia in 1975. Unfortunately, Cormorant Wood sustained an injury at York which brought her racing days to an end. She's since produced two foals of racing age. Rock Hopper is the second following his unraced brother Waaria, and Cormorant Wood's third foal, who'll be a two-year-old in 1991, is a filly by the Irish Derby winner Law Society. There's plenty of stamina in this family. Quarry Wood, who won at up to a mile and three quarters, is the dam of the good-class hurdler River Ceiriog, while Rock Hopper's third dam Phrygia has produced several staying types. Rock Hopper is a well-made colt with the scope to go on. At present it's hard to assess what type of ground he'll prove best on, though it is worth noting that his sire and dam both seemed best on a sound surface. *M. R. Stoute.*

ROCKMARTIN 7 b.g. Fair Season 120–Aunt Eva 99 (Great Nephew 126) [1988 NR 1989 10.6d] robust, well-made gelding: carries plenty of condition: modest handicapper in 1987: needed race only subsequent outing on flat: effective from 1m to 1½m: acts on firm going and a soft surface: inconsistent, and hasn't won on flat since first outing as 3-y-o: winner over hurdles: sold 7,200 gns Doncaster November Sales. *C. W. Thornton.* —

ROCK PULSE 3 ch.g. Ballad Rock 122–Muscadina (Major Portion) 129) [1988 NR 1989 12.2d 8m 8f 10g 7.5m] 22,000Y, 920 2-y-o: sparely-made, plain gelding: poor walker: moderate mover: brother to useful miler Hajes and half-brother to —

Irish 1¼m winner Muscadier (by Sassafras): dam French 7.5f winner: poor plater: stays 7.5f (pulled hard over 1¼m). *Ronald Thompson.*

ROCK SALT 7 ch.g. Ballad Rock 122–Sea Music 108 (Atan) [1988 NR 1989 7m] — big gelding: poor walker: of little account: wore visor and tongue strap final outing at 5 yrs. *P. Butler.*

ROCKSAVAGE 4 ch.g. Formidable (USA) 125–Seven Seas (FR) 76 (Riverman — (USA) 131) [1988 8d 8g 8g⁶ 7f 8m 8m 1989 10g 12m] good-bodied gelding: poor maiden: possibly temperamental: sold 2,300 gns Ascot September Sales. *M. H. Tompkins.*

ROCKY RAJAH 3 b.g. Indian King (USA) 128–Mountain High 79 (Mount Hagen — (FR) 127) [1988 7g 1989 10s] big, strong, good-topped gelding: well beaten in maidens: dead. *W. J. Haggas.*

ROCKY'S MATE 2 b.f. (Mar 19) Young Man (FR) 73–Gold Spangle 97 — (Klondyke Bill 125) [1989 6g] 700Y: half-sister to winning 3-y-o sprint plater Ever Reckless (by Crever) and several other winners, including fair 6f and 7f winner Kakisa (by Forlorn River): dam won over 5f at 2 yrs: 33/1 and ridden by 7-lb claimer, in rear in 19-runner maiden at Redcar in November: has joined J. Czerpak. *W. Wilson.*

ROCQUAINE 3 ch.g. Ballad Rock 122–Lola Sharp (Sharpen Up 127) [1988 7g 7g 65 6d 1989 8.2s⁶ 6m* 6f⁵ 6m³ 8m 8.2g⁴ 7g⁴ 7s] well-made gelding: moderate walker: quite modest handicapper: 20/1, won at Brighton in May: stays 7f: suited by a sound surface: blinkered once at 2 yrs: ran well when edgy and sweating, moderately for amateur. *Mrs J. Pitman.*

RODCHENKO (USA) 4 b.c. Run The Gantlet (USA)–Golden Jolie (USA) — (Royal Serenade 132) [1988 12.2f3 12f² 13.3g² 14.6g* 16m* 14.6f* 13.3f 1989 14g 14g 16f] rather lightly-made, quite attractive colt: fairly useful winner (including for amateur) as 3-y-o when trained by B. Hills: well beaten in handicaps in first half of 1989: needs at least 1¾m: acts on firm going: usually sweats *W. J. Haggas.*

RODEO STAR (USA) 3 ch.c. Nodouble (USA)–Roundup Rose (USA) — (Minnesota Mac) [1988 NR 1989 10.6g⁵] workmanlike, plain colt: half-brother to 4 winners in USA, notably high-class Codex (by Arts And Letters), winner of Hollywood Derby, Santa Anita Derby and Preakness Stakes: dam 2-y-o 6f winner on only start, from highly successful family: 20/1 and mulish in paddock, 13 lengths fifth of 10 to Sartorius in maiden at Haydock in August, staying on well having been slowly away and soon pushed along in rear: will be suited by 1½m+. *J. H. M. Gosden.*

ROGERS PRINCESS 7 b.m. Owen Anthony 102–Ask For Roger (Menelek 114) — [1988 NR 1989 16.2d] fair staying hurdler: backward, tailed off in handicap at Haydock in October, only run on flat since 1984. *M. Tate.*

ROKALA 4 b.f. Kalaglow 132–Romantiki (USA) (Giboulee (CAN)) [1988 10g 10g — 10.2f⁵ 10.2g 12f⁵ 8f² 10g 8h² 8s³ 10s 1989 8d 10f⁵ 12f⁴] tall, lengthy filly: modest maiden as 3-y-o: long way below her best in first half of 1989: possibly didn't stay 1½m: ideally suited by firm going: often blinkered or visored: winning selling hurdler: dead. *N. Tinkler.*

ROKER ROAR 5 b.g. Taufan (USA) 119–Harp Song 64 (Auction Ring (USA) 123) — [1988 5d 7g⁵ 5m 6g 5f⁶ 6h 5g⁵ 6g⁴ 6g* 6m³ 5f 6d 6g⁵ 5g* 5s* 5s 6g 1989 5g 6f 6m 5m 6g] compact gelding: tubed: poor walker: plating-class winner (including for apprentice) as 4-y-o: not discredited from moderate draw at Thirsk second outing in 1989: well beaten after, twice rearing as stalls opened: suited by 6f or stiff 5f: best form on an easy surface: sometimes blinkered or visored: often slowly into stride: has found little off bridle: one to treat with caution. *M. H. Easterby.*

ROKER ROYALE 3 ch.f. Dara Monarch 128–Simbella (Simbir 130) [1988 5g⁴ 53 5f² 7f² 7g 7m⁴ 6g 8g⁶ 7g 1989 8g⁶ 8s 8d⁴ 7.5d⁴ 8g 8f² 8.5m² 7m 8f³] sparely-made, plain filly: has a quick action: fair plater: stays 1m: acts on firm going and a soft surface: blinkered last 7 outings: sweating fifth start: sometimes edgy: has run creditably for apprentice: sold 1,700 gns Doncaster November Sales: found little on occasions, and is possibly ungenuine. *M. H. Easterby.*

ROLFESON 5 b.h. Rolfe (USA) 77–Do Something 77 (Pardao 120) [1988 8g 10g 67 7.5m 8g⁴ 10g⁴ 8g 10f 10m 8g 8.2d⁴ 1989 10m⁴ 10m² 9g* 10.6d⁵ 9m⁶ 11s 10g³ 8f] sturdy, good-quartered horse: good mover: quite modest handicapper: favourite, won apprentice event at Wolverhampton in July: effective at 1m to 1¼m: well suited by an easy surface (possibly unsuited by very soft going): blinkered twice. *B. C. Morgan.*

ROLIAD 5 br.g. Rolfe (USA) 77–Clear Whistle 80 (Tin Whistle 128) [1988 NR 1989 17.4s] workmanlike gelding: modest maiden as 3-y-o: 33/1, remote eighth of 15 in handicap at Ayr in September: stays 13f: acts on a soft surface: winning selling hurdler. *J. J. O'Neill.* —

ROLL A DOLLAR 3 b.g. Spin of A Coin 88–Handy Dancer 87 (Green God 128) [1988 NR 1989 10g 10.1m* 10.1m3 11.7m*] tall, leggy gelding: good mover: fourth foal: half-brother to 1¾m winner Gydaros (by Ardross) and 1986 2-y-o 5f and 6f winner Mr Grumpy (by The Brianstan), later successful in Belgium: dam won 3 times over 1¼m: successful in Windsor minor events in July and August: stays 1½m: has plenty of scope and can continue to improve. *D. R. C. Elsworth.* 99 p

ROMAN BEACH 9 b.g. Averof 123–Lovage (Linacre 133) [1988 9g 8g6 8g 8.2d 1989 8g 8d 8.2d] lengthy gelding: one-time fairly useful handicapper: lightly raced and little form nowadays: stays 1¼m: used to be well suited by a soft surface: suited by waiting tactics: sold 1,075 gns Ascot November Sales. *W. J. Musson.* —

ROMAN CRACKSHOT 5 b.g. Roman Glory–Ogeno (Rugantino 97) [1988 NR 1989 12f] second foal: dam poor novice hurdler/chaser: 33/1, tailed off in ladies event at Lingfield in June. *J. O'Donoghue.* —

ROMAN JOY 4 b.f. Le Johnstan 123–Silk Willoughby (Pirate King 129) [1988 10f 8f 1989 9m] of little account. *B. E. Wilkinson.* —

ROMANOVNA 2 b.f. (May 6) Mummy's Pet 125–Empress of Russia 79 (Royal Palace 131) [1989 7g 6g] smallish, sparely-made filly: seventh foal: sister to 3-y-o Mrs Wing Commander and modest staying maiden Naabi and half-sister to quite modest 1½m winners Empress Catherine and National Dress (both by Welsh Pageant): dam, half-sister to Connaught, won over 1½m at 4 yrs: poor form in late-season maidens at Folkestone and Leicester. *T. Thomson Jones.* —

ROMAN PROSE 4 ch.g. Sallust 134–Mothers Girl (Huntercombe 133) [1988 6m* 5.6m* 5g4 6m5 1989 7.2g 6f 6m4] workmanlike, sparely-made gelding: active type: has scarred knees: fairly useful performer: visored and facing stiffish task, ran easily best race as 4-y-o when fourth of 9 to Alo Ez in strongly-run listed contest at Newmarket in August: suited by sprint distances: acts on top-of-the-ground. *L. G. Cottrell.* 97

ROMANTIC MELODY 3 ch.f. Battle Hymn 103–Love Patrol 71 (Green God 128) [1988 5g 7m 6g 1989 7.5d3 7.5d2 8m5 8.2f2 7m2 8m 8f 8f] leggy filly: plating-class form: has run in sellers: consistent until sixth start: stays 1m: acts on firm going and a soft surface: usually sweating. *K. S. Bridgwater.* 56

ROMANTIC PAST (USA) 3 b.f. Miswaki (USA) 124–Ruth Pitcher (USA) (Ack Ack (USA)) [1988 7d4 6s3 1989 8m* 8g 7m] $225,000Y: leggy, quite good-topped filly: fourth foal: half-sister to Coastal Connection (by Coastal) and Outlaws Sham (by Sham), both stakes winners at about 1m: dam winner at up to 9f: on toes, won apprentice maiden at Yarmouth in August: well beaten in handicaps at Ripon (didn't get clear run) and Redcar (soon outpaced) following month: stays 1m well: acts on top-of-the-ground: trained at 2 yrs by J. Oxx in Ireland: sold 60,000 gns Newmarket December Sales. *J. Gosden.* 82

ROMANTIC SAGA 2 b.f. (Apr 25) Prince Tenderfoot (USA) 126–Sirena 70 (Red Alert 127) [1989 5f3 6m3 5m2 5g2] IR 1,500Y, 8,600 2-y-o: strong, good sort: has plenty of scope: has a quick action: fifth foal: dam middle-distance winner: quite modest form in varied races: looked ungenerous last 2 outings: stays 6f: sweating last 3 starts, and edgy final one: one to be bit wary of. *Denys Smith.* 69

ROMAN WALK 2 b.f. (Apr 28) Petorius 117–Plum Bold 83 (Be My Guest (USA) 126) [1989 6f4 6f2 6g2 6g* 6g] angular filly: fourth foal: half-sister to 1987 2-y-o Irish 5f winner Very Welcome (by Main Reef) and 1m winner Kaleidophone (by Kalaglow): dam 6f winner: showed improved form when winning maiden at Newmarket by a neck from Spoof, making most and running on gamely: ran poorly in listed race at York later in October. *Lord John FitzGerald.* 80

ROMANY BELLE 4 br.f. Bay Express 132–Petulengra (Mummy's Pet 125) [1988 6v 5g3 6g 5g5 6d 1989 5f 7f] small, sparely-made filly: poor mover: plating-class maiden at best: form only at 5f: possibly unsuited by firm going: blinkered and bandaged off-fore final outing: sold 1,700 gns Newmarket July Sales. *P. F. I. Cole.* —

RON'S GUEST 2 ch.g. (Feb 10) Be My Guest (USA) 126–Al Nuwaibi (USA) 71 (Sir Ivor 135) [1989 6f5 6g 7.6m6 7f] IR 2,400Y: compact gelding: first foal: dam won over 6f on debut but showed nothing after: poor maiden: best effort third start: dead. *M. E. D. Francis.* 48

ROOF GHOST 5 b.g. Thatching 131–Vital Spirit 65 (Tachypous 128) [1988 6g 52
6m⁵ 6g⁵ 7.5g⁴ 7.5f² 8f 7.6s 8g⁵ 7m* 7g⁵ 7.5f⁵ 8g⁴ 8d 7d⁵ 1989 6g⁶ 6f 7m⁴ 8f² 6g³
7m* 7m³ 7g⁵ 6m³ 7.5m²] lengthy, workmanlike gelding: moderate walker and
mover: poor handicapper: won selling event (bought in 5,200 gns) at Edinburgh in
July: effective at 6f and stays 1m: best on a sound surface: has run well for
apprentice: sold to join R. Bennett 4,200 gns Doncaster September Sales: none too
genuine. *Capt. J. Wilson.*

ROOSTERS TIPPLE 3 b.g. Henbit (USA) 130–Amiel (Nonoalco (USA) 131) —
[1988 8s 8m² 6g⁶ 1989 10.6g 8g 8m] big, lengthy, angular gelding: no form since
second in maiden auction race as 2-y-o: should stay 1¼m: changed hands 4,600 gns
Newmarket Autumn Sales. *M. W. Easterby.*

ROPE TRICK 2 br.c. (Apr 29) Indian King (USA) 128–Trickster 92 (Major 80
Portion 129) [1989 6f³ 7f² 7g⁶ 5m⁴ 6f² 6m⁵ 5g*] 13,500Y: lengthy, good-quartered
colt: half-brother to smart sprinter Jester and fairly useful 1987 2-y-o sprinter
Tricky Note (both by Song), fair 6f winner Bretton Park and fair 7f and 1m winner
Hooligan (both by Mummy's Pet), and to 2 other winners: dam sprinter: modest
performer: made all in nursery at Redcar in November, beating Monkey Love by a
length: stays 6f: blinkered last 3 starts: ran freely and hung right on sixth outing.
Mrs N. Macauley.

ROSEATE LODGE 3 b.g. Habitat 134–Elegant Tern (USA) 102 (Sea Bird II 83
145) [1988 NR 1989 8s 8g* 9f² 8g* 8.2g* 8m 8s 8g²] compact, workmanlike gelding:
eighth foal: half-brother to several winners, including fairly useful 10.2f and 13.4f
winner Nemesia and useful 5f and 7f winner Fairy Tern (both by Mill Reef): dam
won 3 times at around 1m and stayed 1½m: won maiden at Carlisle in April and
handicaps at Pontefract in May and Haydock in June: ran moderately when unplaced
in valuable handicaps: stays 9f: acts on firm going: hung left when beaten short head
third outing: has joined M. Tompkins and has been gelded. *J. W. Watts.*

ROSEATE TERN 3 b.f. Blakeney 126–Rosia Bay 102 (High Top 131) [1988 123
7g² 7g² 8f² 8g⁴ 1989 10g³ 12m³ 12f² 12g* 12f* 14.6s³]

From maiden status in July to a sale-tag of 1,100,000 guineas in
December—that's one, somewhat sensational, way to summarise Roseate
Tern's three-year-old season. She'd shown she was a likely contender for the
top fillies' middle-distance races much earlier when beaten a short head by
Tessla in the May Hill Stakes at Doncaster as a two-year-old but for a long
time it looked as though she lacked the vital turn of foot to win one of them. In
the circumstances, it might have seemed most appropriate to have plenty of

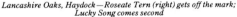

*Lancashire Oaks, Haydock—Roseate Tern (right) gets off the mark;
Lucky Song comes second*

Aston Upthorpe Yorkshire Oaks, York—another win,
as she stays on strongly from the grey Alydaress, Petite Ile and Lady Shipley

use made of her, but after the Hoover Fillies' Mile in which Roseate Tern had helped to force the pace before finishing fourth, she was invariably held up in 1989. Another innovation for 1989 was the application of blinkers. A mile and a quarter for the Pretty Polly Stakes at Newmarket in May was certainly on the sharp side for her and having been pushed along some way out and tended to hang, Roseate Tern only began to gain ground well inside the final furlong, eventually beaten a neck and a head behind the demoted Rambushka. Roseate Tern was duly stepped up in distance and showed improved form but again put in her best work at the finish—and much too late; she followed Aliysa through on the inside in the Oaks but lost a length on her approaching the final two furlongs before staying on steadily to finish third at 25/1, beaten about three lengths behind the favourite and a short head behind Snow Bride. In the Ribblesdale twelve days later she was beaten two and a half lengths by Alydaress, checked over a furlong out and then making inroads on Alydaress' advantage only close home.

Roseate Tern must have been a strong choice for the best maiden in training at that stage but a drop in class for the Group 3 Lancashire Oaks showed that she wasn't just good at chasing horses. With Braiswick not so effective at the trip and ground conditions probably not ideal for Knoosh, Roseate Tern was able to overcome a sedate early gallop to get to the enterprisingly-ridden Lucky Song entering the final furlong and win by half a length with the Italian Oaks second Wrapping a further two and a half lengths back in third. Ives, who took the ride that day, reported that Roseate Tern had idled once hitting the front. The Aston Upthorpe Yorkshire Oaks provided tougher opposition and Roseate Tern's crowning moment. Alydaress was again in opposition following her Irish Oaks triumph over Aliysa, and was joined by the Curragh third Petite Ile and the Oaks d'Italia and Lupe Stakes winners Nydrion and Lady Shipley. Despite a steady pace again early on, Roseate Tern surprised many, including her regular jockey Carson who was back in the saddle, with the way she came from last to first in the final two and a half furlongs, turning over a deficit of some five lengths to win by a length and a half from Alydaress, who looked to have struggled on the firm ground, and a further head to Petite Ile who'd travelled best of all until asked for her effort at the furlong marker. Afterwards Carson was quoted as saying 'I did not think she had that much speed but she went for kindness today and seemed to appreciate that more than the stick'. The one race which kept coming to mind for Roseate Tern was the Park Hill Stakes but the stable mistakenly failed to enter her and she took on the colts instead in the St Leger. The extra distance seemed sure to suit but although the transfer from Doncaster to Ayr produced a depleted field in which Roseate Tern had a good chance on form, it also brought soft ground. Like her dam before her, Roseate

Tern seemed unsuited by such conditions; she was never going particularly well and was beaten eight and a half lengths behind Michelozzo, reaching the frame however for the tenth time in as many starts.

Following Roseate Tern's sale for 1,100,000 guineas (the second highest price for a three-year-old filly sold in Europe following Ravinella's 1,400,000 guineas twelve months earlier) to Peter Brant at the Newmarket December Sales, her breeder Lord Carnarvon no longer has any of Rosia Bay's seven foals. Rosia Bay herself is now owned by Sheikh Hamdan Al-Maktoum's Shadwell Estates which bought her for 600,000 dollars in foal to Diesis when she was sent up by Lane's End Farm to the Keeneland November Sales in 1988. Rosia Bay has produced three fillies of modest ability at best in the 1984 two-year-old five-furlong winner Cerise Bouquet (by Mummy's Pet) and the maidens Mary Sunley (by Known Fact) and Tea Rose (by Moorestyle) but in most years it would be difficult to match her successes in 1989 when she was represented not only by Roseate Tern but by the high-class five-year-old Ibn Bey (by Mill Reef) as well. Her 1987 foal Barakat (by Bustino) was sold for 135,000 guineas at the Highflyer Sales, also to Shadwell Estates, and is in training with Stewart. Rosia Bay was barren in 1988, had a colt by Diesis in 1989 when she was due to visit El Gran Senor, and will visit Nashwan in 1990. It's interesting to reflect that Lord Carnarvon obtained her for just 6,200 guineas after her racing days when she showed fairly useful form in winning twice at around a mile. She's the first foal out of the useful mile winner Ouija but the family has achieved a great deal more to recommend it since Rosia Bay went to the December Sales as she's a half-sister to the Queen Elizabeth II Stakes and Arlington Million winner Teleprompter. Ouija's latest representative Message Pad made a most promising debut in winning a minor event at Doncaster in September but disappointed on his only subsequent start. As was pointed out in the entry on Ibn Bey, there are similarities between the careers of Ibn Bey, Teleprompter and Roseate Tern in the application of blinkers or a visor and their not always looking the easiest of rides, although Roseate Tern is seemingly best with waiting tactics whereas Teleprompter, and now Ibn Bey, have gone well ridden from the front. Rosia Bay incidentally, was blinkered when winning the Atalanta Fillies Stakes as a three-year-old despite hanging right.

		Hethersett	Hugh Lupus
	Blakeney	(b 1959)	Bride Elect
	(b 1966)	Windmill Girl	Hornbeam
Roseate Tern		(b 1961)	Chorus Beauty
(b.f. 1986)		High Top	Derring-Do
	Rosia Bay	(b 1969)	Camenae
	(b 1977)	Ouija	Silly Season
		(b or br 1971)	Samanda

So what of Roseate Tern's prospects for 1990 when she'll be trained by Cumani who, interestingly, seems loath to fit any of his runners in blinkers? A large number of the latest season's leading three-year-old middle-distance performers are due to remain in training and she could well find the competition too hot in the top races at a mile and a half. The valuable North American turf races in the second half of the season are also under consideration. Looking further ahead, several commentators observed forebodingly that Blakeney has hardly excelled as a broodmare sire. Roseate Tern is a good-topped filly with plenty of scope. She should stay a mile and three quarters; she acts on firm going and appears to be unsuited by soft. *Major W. R. Hern.*

ROSEBERY AVENUE 3 b.f. Sadler's Wells (USA) 132–Waterway (FR) 112 73 (Riverman (USA) 131) [1988 NR 1989 9f 8m⁴ 10.6g³ 10m] rangy, rather unfurnished filly: has scope: fourth live foal: half-sister to Irish Oaks winner Helen Street (by Troy): dam, from family of Sun Prince, very useful at up to 1m in France: modest maiden: wandered under pressure when third at Haydock: worth another try over shorter. *M. R. Stoute.*

ROSE BOUQUET 4 ch.f. General Assembly (USA)–Premier Rose 117 (Sharp — Edge 123) [1988 6g 6m³ 6m 7g³ 6m 1989 6f 6f] big, angular, dipped-backed filly: modest winner as 2-y-o: burly, well below form in handicaps in first half of 1989:

stayed 7f well: acted on top-of-the-ground and soft going: in foal to Dominion. *P. W. Harris.*

ROSE CAMPION 3 b.f. Mill Reef (USA) 141–Rose Bowl (USA) 131 (Habitat 134)   80
[1988 6d³ 6g² 6d² 7.3s³ 1989 8f 9.2f⁴ 10g* 10m⁶] leggy filly: ridden by 5-lb claimer, won handicap at Newbury in June: should have stayed 1½m: acted on soft going and possibly unsuited by top-of-the-ground: dead. *I. A. Balding.*

ROSEFAIR LADY 3 b.f. What A Guest 119–Lake Constance 85 (Star Gazer 123)   47
[1988 5g 6g⁵ 6m 8v 1989 8m 10f] sparely-made filly: keen walker: poor maiden: stays 1¼m: acts on firm going. *M. H. Tompkins.*

ROSE FESTIVAL 3 br.f. Ile de Bourbon (USA) 133–Vendemmia (Silly Season   59
127) [1988 NR 1989 10.2g⁶ 12.2g² 12g⁴ a12g⁴] leggy, rather sparely-made filly: sister to quite modest maiden Festival Fanfare and smart 1984 French staying 2-y-o Bourbonel and half-sister to 2 winners: dam poor maiden: easily best effort in maidens on debut: blinkered, well beaten in handicap at Lingfield in December, travelling well long way: worth another try over 1¼m: sold out of Sir Mark Prescott's stable 6,000 gns Newmarket Autumn Sales after third start. *R. J. O'Sullivan.*

ROSE GLEN 3 b.f. Lochnager 132–Phoenix Rose 85 (Frankincense 120) [1988   86
NR 1989 7g* 8s⁵ 6d⁴ 7m⁵ 7f² 7f² 7m a7g⁴ a8g] 16,000Y: big, workmanlike filly: has a rather round action: half-sister to 9f winner Arcville Fred (by Miami Springs) and fairly useful 1985 2-y-o 1m winner Open Hero (by Imperial Fling): dam won sellers over 9f and 10.6f: fair performer: won newcomers race at Doncaster in April: first run for 4½ months, good fourth in handicap at Southwell in December: suited by 7f: acts on firm going. *A. Bailey.*

ROSEN (USA) 3 ch.c. Northern Baby (CAN) 127–Rosespray (USA) (Bagdad)   94
[1988 NR 1989 10g³ 12f* 11.7d 12f* 10g⁶] $180,000Y: leggy, close-coupled colt: sixth foal: half-brother to 3 winners in USA, notably Boutinierre (by Bold Forbes), prolifically successful at up to 1¼m: dam won once at around 1m at 3 yrs in USA: short-priced favourite, made virtually all to win maiden at Folkestone in May and handicap (much improved form, by 8 lengths) at Salisbury in October: well beaten in handicaps third (took hold) and final (£10,300 contest, never going well and eased considerably) starts: suited by 1½m: possibly unsuited by a soft surface: sold 27,000 gns Newmarket Autumn Sales. *G. Harwood.*

ROSE OF HIGH LEGH 3 b.f. Martinmas 128–Halka (Daring March 116) [1988   59
5g⁴ 5g² 5f 5d² 7d⁴ 6d* 6g³ 6g⁴ 6s² 6g² 1989 7d* 6s* 6g 6f 7s⁵ 6g 6s⁵ 6g] leggy, angular filly: moderate mover: behind at halfway when winning seller (no bid) at Catterick in March and claimer (apprentice ridden) at Nottingham in April: easily best effort after, appearing to run very well, when fifth in 7f minor event at Ayr: stays 7f: goes well with plenty of give in the ground: blinkered last 2 starts and 3 times in 1988 (won in blinkers at 2 yrs): sometimes slowly away, very much so for apprentice final outing: game. *J. Berry.*

ROSE OF MIAMI 2 b.c. (Mar 29) Crofter (USA) 124–Rose Mullion 82 (Tudor   89
Melody 129) [1989 5g⁴ 5f³ 5f⁶ 6m* 6m* 7.5m⁶ 6m² 6g⁴ 6g* 6s 6v] IR 5,000Y, 18,000 2-y-o: close-coupled colt: moderate walker: has a quick action: half-brother to 2 winners, including staying handicapper Marlion (by Julio Mariner): dam won over 5f at 2 yrs: fair performer: won claimers at Yarmouth and Hamilton in summer and at Haydock, by 6 lengths from Facility Letter, in September: much better suited by 6f than 5f, and should stay further: possibly unsuited by soft going: blinkered last 5 starts: tends to hang: often on toes: sold to race in Norway 18,000 gns Doncaster November Sales. *T. D. Barron.*

ROSE OF TOUGET 2 b.f. (Apr 8) Dreams To Reality (USA) 113–Loredana 64   —
(Grange Melody) [1989 5f⁴ 5g 6m] 500F: small filly: poor mover: first foal: dam 7f and 1m winner: poor maiden: best effort in seller on debut. *J. Ringer.*

ROSES IN MAY 3 b.f. Mummy's Game 120–Ma Famille 90 (Welsh Saint 126)   —
[1988 5m 6d⁶ 1989 6f] workmanlike filly: moderate mover: well beaten in sellers at 2 yrs and claimer (unruly in paddock) in July, only start in 1989: should stay at least 6f. *C. J. Hill.*

ROSE'S PRIDE 3 b.f. Ballacashtal (CAN)–Tropingay (Cawston's Clown 113)   —
[1988 NR 1989 8m 10m 10.4m³ 10g 10g] sturdy filly: first foal: dam well beaten: plating-class maiden: apparently best effort when third at Chester having set modest pace: may be worth another try over 1m: sold 2,400 gns Ascot December Sales. *Capt. R. M. Smyly.*

ROSIE POTTS 3 b.f. Shareef Dancer (USA) 135–Much Pleasure (Morston (FR)   83
125) [1988 6f* 7.3s 1989 8f*] neat, good-quartered filly: looking particularly well,

won handicap at York in May: well beaten in listed race at Newbury at 2 yrs: bred to stay 1¼m: sold 48,000 gns Newmarket December Sales. *H. R. A. Cecil.*

ROSTOVOL 4 b.g. Vaigly Great 127–Emerin 85 (King Emperor (USA)) [1988 6v 6g 7s* 7g⁵ 7f 1989 8.5f 9f] leggy gelding: moderate mover: quite modest winner as 3-y-o: apprentice ridden, well beaten in handicaps in autumn: stays 7f: probably acts on any going: blinkered final 3 outings in 1988, finding nothing when headed last 2 occasions: inconsistent. *D. H. Topley.* —

ROSY DIAMOND 3 ch.f. Jalmood (USA) 126–Sun Approach 84 (Sun Prince 128) [1988 6g 6g 7d 1989 7.5g⁵ 6m³ 7f 6f 9m⁴ 11m 9.1f 6m* 6g 6f] angular filly: poor walker: well drawn and tenderly handled when winning handicap at Thirsk in September, best effort: effective at 6f and probably stays 9f: best form on top-of-the-ground: unseated apprentice 1f out on seventh outing having taken strong hold and run wide. *C. C. Elsey.* 57

ROTHERFIELD GREYS 7 b. or br.g. Mummy's Pet 125–Relicia (Relko 136) [1988 7.6g⁶ 6f⁴ 6g* 5d 6m 5d⁶ 1989 5m 6f 6f³ 6m³ 6m 6s 5m] strong, good-bodied gelding: carries plenty of condition: useful handicapper: won William Hill Stewards' Cup (Handicap) at Goodwood as 6-y-o: showed he retained his ability when third at same course in same event and in £14,800 contest in summer: suited by sprint distances: best on a sound surface: good mount for apprentice: often sweats and gets on toes: best with waiting tactics: has joined D. Browne. *C. F. Wall.* 103

ROTHKO 8 b.g. Ile de Bourbon (USA) 133–Scala di Seta 85 (Shantung 132) [1988 NR 1989 13v* 13v² 21.6d* 16d² 17.4s 18g] lengthy gelding: has been fired: did well in spring, winning handicaps at Hamilton and Pontefract: hopelessy tailed off at Ayr (first run for nearly 5 months) and Newmarket (Tote Cesarewitch, finished badly lame) in autumn: suited by test of stamina: acts very well in the mud: blinkered both starts at 3 yrs. *G. M. Moore.* 71

ROUGE ROI 4 b.g. Hays 120–Restless Morn (Morston (FR) 125) [1988 7d 8m⁵ 9g 8g³ 10.4d⁵ 1989 8m³ 9f 8g⁶] rather sparely-made gelding: poor mover: poor maiden: probably stays 1¼m: acts on top-of-the-ground and a soft surface: sometimes blinkered: bandaged at 4 yrs. *P. D. Evans.* 48

ROUNDELAY 5 ch.h. Song 132–Flying Portion 72 (Major Portion 129) [1988 8d³ 8s⁶ 8f 1989 10s 12d 7d 7.5g 8.2f 6m² 5f 6g 7f] good-topped horse: moderate mover: poor maiden: probably needs further than 5f and stays 1m: acts on firm going and a soft surface: blinkered last 6 outings: often wears bandages: occasionally slowly away: inconsistent: sold 950 gns Doncaster November Sales. *S. R. Bowring.* 36

ROUPALA (USA) 3 b.f. Vaguely Noble 140–Cairn Rouge 127 (Pitcairn 126) [1988 NR 1989 8m* 10g 10g⁶] stocky filly: has a round action: third foal: half-sister to useful 6f and 7f winner Ajuga (by The Minstrel): dam won Irish 1000 Guineas, Coronation Stakes and Champion Stakes: favourite, won Newmarket Challenge Whip in May: 25/1 and still green on first run for 4 months, strong-finishing sixth to If Memory Serves in minor event at Leicester in November, given plenty to do: stays 1¼m well: may well improve again. *B. W. Hills.* 75 p

ROUSHAYD 5 ch.h. Known Fact (USA) 135–Rosy Moon (FR) (Sheshoon 132) [1988 12g³ 13.3f⁴ 12m⁶ 12g* 12s 13.4s⁵ 12m 11s 1989 12m 14m⁴ 14f 13s 12m⁴ 11v] big, rather leggy, attractive horse: carries plenty of condition: has a long stride: useful performer: ran best race as 5-y-o when fourth of 17, tending to edge right 2f out, to Braashee in £71,300 Tote Festival Handicap at Ascot in September: stays 1¾m: has won on soft going, but needs a sounder surface nowadays: takes a good hold and best racing up with pace: has appeared unsuited by Epsom track: sold, probably for export, 38,000 gns Newmarket Autumn Sales. *R. F. Johnson Houghton.* 101

ROUSKI 2 b.c. (Apr 30) Rousillon (USA) 133–Missy Baldski (USA) (Baldski (USA)) [1989 7g⁴ 7g 7m 6m² 6m 6g] 7,000 2-y-o: angular, lengthy colt: moderate walker: has a long stride: second foal: dam champion 2-y-o in Norway in 1983: quite modest maiden: best effort fourth outing: takes a keen hold, and is none too easy a ride. *J. W. Payne.* 66

ROUTE MARCH 10 ch.g. Queen's Hussar 124–Wide of The Mark 91 (Gulf Pearl 117) [1988 NR 1989 10.1m 12m 12g] compact, round-barrelled gelding: of little account. *P. A. Pritchard.* —

ROUTILANTE 2 b.f. (Jan 22) Rousillon (USA) 133–Danseuse Classique (CAN) (Northern Dancer) [1989 6g* 6m² 6m²] 31,000F, 60,000Y: leggy, workmanlike filly: sixth foal: half-sister to 3-y-o Seulma (by Pas de Seul) and 3 winners, including 1985 Irish 2-y-o 6f winner Classic Style (by Thatching), later successful in USA: dam once-raced half-sister to high-class Canadian colt Son of Briartic: fairly useful filly: won maiden at Newbury in June: better efforts when second of 6 to Pharaoh's 96

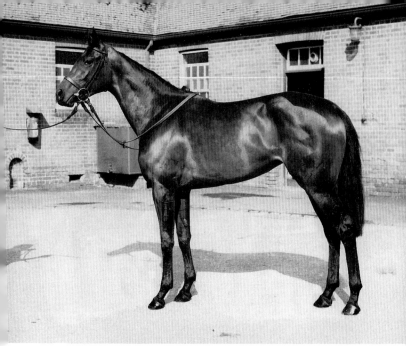

George Strawbridge's "Routilante"

Delight in Princess Margaret Stakes at Ascot and to Dead Certain in 'The Pacemaker Update' Lowther Stakes at York: will probably stay 7f. *I. A. Balding.*

ROUYAN 3 b.g. Akarad (FR) 130–Rosy Moon (FR) (Sheshoon 132) [1988 NR 1989 **89** 12m⁴ 12g⁴ 14d* 15s⁶] rangy, good-bodied gelding: has plenty of scope: fifth foal: half-brother to useful 1½m winner Roushayd (by Known Fact) and fairly useful but unreliable 1½m winner Rasmara (by Kalaglow): dam French 10.5f winner: won maiden at Haydock in September by a neck, running on well despite wandering: favourite, ran badly in minor event at Ayr 3 weeks later: stays 1¾m well: takes keen hold and will prove best with strong handling: sold to join R. Simpson 28,000 gns Newmarket Autumn Sales, and subsequently gelded. *R. F. Johnson Houghton.*

ROWDY 3 bl.g. Lucky Wednesday 124–Angel Row 96 (Prince Regent (FR) 129) **40** [1988 6m 7m 7g⁶ 1989 7.5d 10m 7m⁵ 6f 12m 8g⁶ 6f⁵ 8f 7m] leggy, medium-sized gelding: poor form, including in sellers: stays 1m (stumbled and unseated rider over 1¼m): sold to join R. Barr 1,400 gns Doncaster August Sales and subsequently gelded. *S. R. Bowring.*

ROXBY MELODY 4 b.f. Song 132–Quenlyn (Welsh Pageant 132) [1988 6f 6m⁵ **—** 5f* 5g⁵ 5m 5m⁴ 6g⁶ 5m 6s 5f 1989 5d 5m 5m 6f 5m 5f 6h 5f] sparely-made filly: plating-class winner as 3-y-o: no form in 1989: struck into, severed tendon and destroyed at Thirsk in July: best at 5f: acted on firm going and was possibly unsuited by soft surface: blinkered once: often started slowly and wandered. *Mrs G. R. Reveley.*

ROYAL ACADEMY (USA) 2 b.c. (Feb 21) Nijinsky (CAN) 138–Crimson **107** p Saint (USA) (Crimson Satan) [1989 6g* 7g⁶]
The numerous shareholders that make up Classic Thoroughbreds Plc, the ambitious Irish-based ownership group which was launched in 1987, will

759

Classic Thoroughbreds Plc's "Royal Academy"

want to forget the 1989 Flat racing season as swiftly as the market value of their stock depreciated during the year. In the spring the outlook for the company, which had Classic Fame and Saratogan among several promising three-year-olds, looked healthy as shares reached an all-time high of 41p on the stock market in expectation of a bold showing from Saratogan in the Two Thousand Guineas; but by December, following a dispiriting and largely anonymous season, they'd slumped dramatically to 11p, necessitating an urgent rights issue. Saratogan's comprehensive defeat at Newmarket was the turning point in the company's fortunes. Optimism gave way to despondency as results on the racecourse didn't pick up and by mid-summer Classic Thoroughbreds' share-price had settled near its previous low. It wasn't until October, after a period of relative inactivity on the stock market as well as the racecourse, that shares began to rally again as anticipation grew that the highly-regarded Royal Academy, who'd hacked up by ten lengths in a maiden at Phoenix Park on his only start, would spark a revival by becoming his trainer Vincent O'Brien's first Dewhurst winner since El Gran Senor in 1983 and his seventh in all. The increasing confidence behind Royal Academy, boosted by impressive gallop reports, ensured that he started an even-money favourite at Newmarket even though his form, which was well short of the standard usually required to win the Dewhurst, had been let down in the interim. For a brief moment over a furlong out Royal Academy threatened to burst into the reckoning, but he was unable to quicken under pressure and showed signs of reluctance before finishing around four lengths sixth of seven behind Dashing Blade. While the Dewhurst represented significant improve-

760

ment on Royal Academy's behalf it couldn't prevent shares in Classic Thoroughbreds from plunging even further. As few of their other two-year-olds made much of a name for themselves in the autumn, and less was spent than in the past on yearlings at the sales, the future for the company looks a whole lot less rosy than it did twelve months previously.

			Northern Dancer	Nearctic
Royal Academy (USA) (b.c. Feb 21, 1987)	Nijinsky (CAN) (b 1967)		(b 1961)	Natalma
			Flaming Page	Bull Page
			(b 1959)	Flaring Top
	Crimson Saint (USA) (ch 1969)		Crimson Satan	Spy Song
			(ch 1959)	Papila
			Bolero Rose	Bolero
			(b 1958)	First Rose

At 3,500,000 dollars, the rangy, rather unfurnished Royal Academy was the most expensive yearling purchased at public auction in 1988. His dam Crimson Saint has bred several other winners, notably the good-class sprinter Pancho Villa and the very smart 1978 two-year-old filly Terlingua (both by Secretariat). Terlingua, who won three Grade 2 events at two, including the six-furlong Hollywood Juvenile Championship, has since foaled the Breeders' Cup Juvenile runner-up Storm Cat and his three-parts sister Chapel of Dreams, whose four Graded Stakes victories to the end of 1988 came over eight and a half and nine furlongs. Crimson Saint won seven of her eleven races, including the Grade 3 five-and-half-furlong Hollywood Express Handicap, and is one of several winners from the useful filly Bolero Rose.

There was much talk after the Dewhurst of Royal Academy's reverting to sprinting in the coming season. True, there's plenty of speed in his pedigree, but he doesn't strike us as a colt with an abundance of pace and we feel he'll be seen to better advantage over longer distances. He's good enough to win more races as a three-year-old, assuming he's not too highly tried; if he doesn't, he'll no doubt be found a place at stud. *M. V. O'Brien, Ireland.*

ROYAL ACCLAIM 4 ch.g. Tender King 123–Glimmer 58 (Hot Spark 126) [1988 **60** 6d 6g 7m* 7m³ 8g³ 7g 6m 7m⁴ 7f² 6d 1989 7.6h² 7.6m² 8m⁶ 8m² 7.6f³ 7m⁶] sturdy gelding: carries condition: quite modest handicapper: runner-up at Lingfield (twice, amateurs event first time, apprentice ridden second) in June and Newmarket (invitation race) in August: stays 1m: yet to race on soft going, acts on any other: has raced with head high: often blinkered or visored. *A. Hide.*

ROYAL ALASKA 3 br.c. Hotfoot 126–Snow Damsel (Mandamus 120) [1988 5m⁶ **51** d 6g 7d 7s 1989 10.8s⁵ 12s 10.1m 10f 10.2h 10.1m 10.8f⁵ 10f] small, lengthy colt: plating-class maiden: third at Folkestone in April: well beaten after, including in sellers: visored and slowly away seventh start: will stay beyond 1½m: acts on soft going. *P. J. Arthur.*

ROYAL ANNOUNCEMENT 3 ch.g. Tina's Pet 121–Kimble Girl 80 (Some **—** Hand 119) [1988 NR 1989 10g 9d 10s] lengthy, sparely-made gelding: first reported foal: dam twice second over 5f at 2 yrs: no form in maiden and sellers: broke pastern and destroyed at Nottingham in May. *W. J. Musson.*

ROYAL ARCHIVE (USA) 2 b.f. (Apr 5) Shadeed (USA) 135–Round Tower 93 **76** (High Top 131) [1989 6g⁴ 6m³ 8f⁵] rangy, good-quartered filly: fourth foal: half-sister to 3-y-o 1¼m and 1½m winner Windsor Park (by Bold Forbes), 1½m winner Water Splash (by Little Current) and useful 1986 2-y-o 7f winner Roundlet (by Roberto): dam, winner at 10.1f and 10.6f, is out of half-sister to 1000 Guineas and French Oaks winner Highclere: modest form in Newmarket maidens on first 2 starts: pulled hard final start: should stay 1m. *Major W. R. Hern.*

ROYAL ASSIGNMENT (USA) 3 b. or br.c. Star de Naskra (USA)–Royal Kin **87** (USA) (Sir Gaylord) [1988 7g⁴ 7d* 7d³ 1989 8h² 8m³ 9f* 10f² 12m⁴ 10.5m⁶] $225,000Y: leggy, quite good-topped colt: half-brother to several winners, notably Taisez Vous (by Silent Screen), a high-class winner at up to 9f: dam stakes-placed winner of 3 sprint races at 2 yrs: fair performer: won maiden (made all, trained by J. Oxx) at Tipperary at 2 yrs and strongly-run apprentice race at Ripon in August: ran well in minor event and apprentice handicap fourth and fifth starts, in latter giving impression would have gone close set less to more: stays 1½m: yet to race on very soft going, probably acts on any other: visored 4 times in 1989, including at Ripon: wore crossed noseband last 3 starts. *J. Gosden.*

ROYAL ASTRONAUT (USA) 5 ch.g. Grey Dawn II 132–Short Stanza (USA) 70
(Verbatim (USA)) [1988 NR 1989 14s* 16d*] lengthy gelding: showed improved
form in spring, winning handicaps at Nottingham (fit from hurdling) and Ripon: will
stay beyond 2m: goes very well with plenty of give in the ground. *R. Akehurst.*

ROYAL BEAR 7 gr.g. Rupert Bear 105–Queens Leap 54 (King's Leap 111) [1988 38
5s⁶ 5d⁴ 5g² 5s⁶ 5g⁶ 5.8f⁵ 5g 5g* 5m³ 5f 5d³ 5s⁴ 5g 5g 5m 1989 5s³ 5d 5d 6g⁴ 5f⁶ 5f
5f 5m 5m⁴ 6m] rangy gelding: poor handicapper: stays 6f: acts on any going: ran
poorly when blinkered: suitable mount for apprentice. *J. M. Bradley.*

ROYAL BEQUEST (CAN) 3 b.c. Mill Reef (USA) 141–Regal Heiress 81 87
(English Prince 129) [1988 NR 1989 12g⁵ 12m³ 14f⁴ 11.7m²] compact, well-made
colt: fourth foal: brother to once-raced Bawareq: dam 1½m and 13f winner, is
half-sister to Shirley Heights (by Mill Reef): fair form in Newmarket maidens, minor
event at York and moderately-run handicap at Windsor: should prove best at around
1½m: gives impression won't prove best on very firm going: sold to join N. Tinkler
19,000 gns Newmarket Autumn Sales. *M. R. Stoute.*

ROYAL-BLUE BELLE 3 b.f. Castle Keep 121–Pat Pong 62 (Mummy's Pet —
125) [1988 6s 1989 12g 10f 8g] seems of little account. *T. Kersey.*

ROYAL BOROUGH 4 b.g. Bustino 136–Lady R B (USA) (Gun Shot) [1988 10v⁶ 90
11.7g* 12m² 1989 12m⁵ 12f⁶ 12m 12g³ 12g4* 12.4g* 12g²] rather leggy, useful-looking
gelding: fair handicapper: won at Newcastle in October in good style: favourite, good
second of 21, clear, to First Victory at Leicester over week later: stays 12.4f: acts on
top-of-the-ground, and a soft surface: hung left final outing (June) as 3-y-o and
wandered under pressure fourth one in 1989: has joined Miss H. Knight. *J. L.
Dunlop.*

ROYAL BRINK (BEL) 2 ch.c. (Apr 25) Ginger Brink (FR) 117–Royal Track 98 69
(Track Spare 125) [1989 a7g²] good-quartered Belgian-bred colt: dam best at 5f:
won at around 7.5f in Belgium in 1989: slow-starting second of 14, beaten 6 lengths,
to Orchard Court in claimer at Southwell in December. *M. J. Ryan.*

ROYAL CLOVER 3 ch.f. Mansingh (USA) 120–Resurgence (Runnymede 123) —
[1988 5f 5f* 6m 5s 1989 6m 7.5f] leggy filly: quite modest winner at 2 yrs: sweating,
tailed off in handicaps in spring as 3-y-o: gave trouble at stalls on reappearance:
form only at 5f: appears to act on any going. *J. M. Jefferson.*

ROYAL COQUELIN 2 b.g. (May 19) Coquelin (USA) 121–Demeter 83 (Silly 41
Season 127) [1989 6m 6g 7m] 8,200F, 7,000Y: leggy, rather sparely-made gelding:
half-brother to useful 5f to 7f performer Mother Earth (by Jukebox) and 1½m winner
Gilt Star (by Star Appeal): dam 7f winner as 2-y-o: poor form in maidens and when
not knocked about in a seller. *C. Tinkler.*

ROYAL COURSE 4 ch.g. On Your Mark 125–Debnic 86 (Counsel 118) [1988 8g — §
8m 8f⁵ 9g 8d 8g² 8f 8d 1989 7.5g 8f 10f 8m] lengthy, plain gelding: moderate mover:
plater: won twice at 2 yrs: very little subsequent form: tailed off final 3 outings in
1989: visored second start: trained until after then by J. Wainwright: has looked
reluctant, and is unreliable. *G. P. Kelly.*

ROYAL DARTMOUTH (USA) 4 ch.g. Czaravich (USA)–Blushing Emy 58
(USA) (Blushing Groom (FR) 131) [1988 5g⁵ 5.8g⁵ 7m³ 6f 6d⁴ 5.8f² 5d³ 6d* 1989
6v³ 7g³ 6f⁴ 6m 7.6m 6m 8f] tall, lengthy gelding: plating-class handicapper: off
course 3 months after fourth outing, and didn't recapture his form: stays 7f: acts on
any going: didn't find great deal second start. *L. G. Cottrell.*

ROYAL DERBI 4 b.g. Derrylin 115–Royal Birthday (St Paddy 133) [1988 10.1m —
7m 10m 8.3d* 8.2m² 1989 10f] leggy, angular gelding: winning plater as 3-y-o:
moved badly to post, well beaten in non-selling handicap at Nottingham (10/3 from
7/4) in June: should stay beyond 1m: acts on top-of-the-ground (possibly unsuited by
very firm going) and a soft surface: didn't handle track at Epsom: leading juvenile
hurdler in 1988/9: changed hands 47,000 gns Newmarket July Sales. *N. A.
Callaghan.*

ROYAL DESTINY 3 b.f. King of Spain 121–Avon Belle 75 (Balidar 133) [1988 —
NR 1989 8m 7f 7f 11s a8g] strong filly: second foal: dam best at sprint distances: no
worthwhile form in varied events, in need of race first 4 outings then leading long
way in Lingfield claimer on final one: will prove best short of 11f: sold 1,450 gns
Ascot December Sales. *P. J. Makin.*

ROYAL DIGGER 3 ch.c. Sharpo 132–Canasta Girl 90 (Charlottesville 135) 64
[1988 6f 7g⁵ 7m⁶ 6f⁴ 7g 1989 6g 8f⁶ 8g⁵] rather leggy, angular colt: quite modest
maiden: not discredited facing stiff tasks in handicaps first and final starts: probably
stays 1m. *J. P. Hudson.*

ROYAL ESTIMATE 3 br.g. Tender King 123–Nistona (Will Somers 114§) [1988 80
5f⁴ 5g³ 6g 7f⁴ 7f 7g² 7d² 8f⁶ 1989 8g 6m² 6h² 7m* 8f* 9m⁵ 9g⁴ 10f⁶ 8m⁵ 8m⁴ 8g*
8s² 9g⁵] big, strong gelding: carries condition: keen walker: fair handicapper:
narrow winner at York and Ayr in June, held up and leading close home, and at Ripon
in September, making virtually all: suited by forcing tactics over 1m nowadays, and
stays 9f: acts on any going: usually blinkered, but wasn't last 3 starts: consistent. *M.
W. Easterby.*

ROYAL FAN 6 br.g. Taufan (USA) 119–Miss Royal (King's Company 124) [1988 78
5g² 5m² 6g 5f³ 5g* 5g 5.6m 5f 6g 1989 6d⁴ 5f⁴ 5m 5f⁵ 5m⁶ 5m⁴ 5m 5m 5.6g 6g³ 5d²]
tall, good-quartered gelding: has a round action: fair handicapper: ideally suited by
5f and a bit of give in the ground: ran moderately when blinkered ninth start. *M. H.
Easterby.*

ROYAL FI FI (USA) 2 b.f. (Apr 1) Conquistador Cielo (USA)–Apple Betty 94
(USA) (Best Turn (USA)) [1989 5m* 6m* 6f* 6s⁴ 7g² 7g⁴] leggy, quite good-topped
filly: has scope: did well physically: fifth foal: sister to 2 minor winner in USA and
half-sister to another: dam won at up to 1m: sire top class at up to 1½m: successful in
late-summer in maiden at Pontefract and minor events at Windsor and Chepstow:
ran well afterwards in Oh So Sharp Stakes (beaten 7 lengths by Va Toujours) and
Bottisham Heath Stud Rockfel Stakes (8 lengths fourth to Negligent) at
Newmarket: suited by 7f: races keenly. *Mrs L. Piggott.*

ROYAL GROOM 4 b.g. Coquelin (USA) 121–Adorable Princess 91 (Royal Palace —
131) [1988 10.1g⁴ 1989 10.1m⁶ 8m 10.2h⁶ 10f] quite good-topped gelding: poor
maiden: pulled up lame final outing: stays 1¼m: blinkered last 2 outings: sold to join
C. Horgan 1,050 gns Ascot November Sales. *I. A. Balding.*

ROYAL HUNT 4 b.g. Mill Reef (USA) 141–Glass Slipper 100 (Relko 136) [1988 38
9f³ 8g⁶ 1989 12g 10m³] leggy, quite good-topped gelding: lightly-raced maiden:
dropped to selling company and well-backed favourite, 1½ lengths third of 22 in
handicap at Brighton in April: should stay 1½m: acts on firm going: bought 2,500 gns
Ascot February Sales. *M. Madgwick.*

ROYALIST (CAN) 3 b.c. Commemorate (USA)–Hangin Round (USA) (Stage 82
Door Johnny) [1988 NR 1989 8m⁵ 8f² 10g² 10m] $148,395Y: strong, good sort:
carries condition: tenth reported living foal: half-brother to several winners,
including best Canadian 2-y-o filly of 1980 Rainbow Connection (by Halo), later
runner-up in Rothmans International, and Hangin On A Star (by Vice Regent), a
Canadian Grade 1 winner at 1½m: dam ran 5 times unplaced: sire runner-up in
Breeders' Cup Sprint: second in maidens at Ayr and Ripon: ran moderately in
£8,000 handicap at Newmarket: better at 1¼m than 1m, and should stay 1½m. *J. W.
Watts.*

ROYAL JIVE 3 b.c. Sadler's Wells (USA) 132–Chemise 75 (Shantung 132) [1988 —
NR 1989 12d] 175,000Y, 155,000Y: half-brother to very smart middle-distance
performer Erin's Isle (by Busted), smart 1m to 1¼m winner Erin's Hope (by
Manado) and a winner in Malaysia: dam won over 1¼m: 25/1, tailed off in minor
event at Thirsk in November: collapsed and died shortly after. *H. R. A. Cecil.*

ROYAL MAC 2 br.c. (Mar 19) Pas de Seul 133–Royal Wolff (Prince Tenderfoot —
(USA) 126) [1989 8g 8d] IR 9,500F, IR 4,500Y, 6,400 2-y-o: first foal: dam Irish
sprinter: always behind in large-field maidens at Leicester and Thirsk in November.
N. Tinkler.

ROYAL MEETING 5 b.m. Dara Monarch 128–Press Luncheon 100 (Be —
Friendly 130) [1988 NR 1989 11.7m⁵] good-topped mare: winning plater as 3-y-o:
20/1, sweating and carrying condition, about 7 lengths fifth of 12, slowly away, in
handicap at Windsor in July: should stay 1½m: acts on firm going. *D. J. G.
Murray-Smith.*

ROYAL PASSION 2 ch.f. (Apr 10) Ahonoora 122–Courtesy Call (Northfields 75
(USA)) [1989 6g² 6m² 7m³ 8g² 8g⁶] IR 52,000Y: rangy filly: shows a quick action:
third foal: half-sister to modest 6f winner Courtoisie (by Thatching) and Irish
hurdles winner Joshua Tree (by Hello Gorgeous): dam thrice-raced half-sister to
smart 1976 2-y-o 5f performer Piney Ridge and very useful 1¼m winner Hill's
Yankee: modest form in varied events: stays 1m. *M. A. Jarvis.*

ROYAL PENNY 3 ch.f. Thatching 131–Cardinal Palace 85 (Royal Palace 131) 67
[1988 6m 8.2m 1989 8s² 10s⁵ 11.7m 12.4g* 12g a11g] big, rather sparely-made filly:
has a round action: quite modest performer: won seller (bought in 8,400 gns) at
Newcastle in October: ran poorly in handicaps previous start and both since, moving
moderately down then hanging under pressure on first occasion, off course over 5
months after: suited by 1½m: possibly best on an easy surface. *M. J. Ryan.*

763

ROYAL PIRANA 3 ch.f. Royal Match 117–Pirana (High Hat 131) [1988 NR 1989 —
10f³ 12m] IR 5,000Y, 8,000 2-y-o: sturdy filly: half-sister to several winners here
and abroad, including Royal Hunt Cup winner Tender Heart (by Prince Tenderfoot):
dam never ran: 22/1, always last when beaten 3½ lengths behind odds-on Jungle
Rose in minor event at Lingfield: still bit backward, tailed off in Salisbury maiden
later in August. *C. V. Bravery.*

ROYAL RESORT 2 b.f. (Apr 3) King of Spain 121–Regency Brighton (Royal 57
Palace 131) [1989 6m⁵ 8m⁵ 7m 6g] leggy, angular filly: second reported foal:
half-sister to poor plater Dyfed (by Daring March): dam showed little on flat:
plating-class maiden: needs further than 6f and stays 1m: races keenly. *P. Calver.*

ROYAL SCOTS GREYS 2 ch.f. (May 2) Blazing Saddles (AUS)–Relicia (Relko —
136) [1989 a7g a8g⁶] half-sister to several winners, including useful sprinter
Rotherfield Greys (by Mummy's Pet) and fair miler Scottish Fling (by Imperial
Fling): dam, from very successful family, showed smart form over middle distances
in France: well beaten in maidens at Lingfield and Southwell. *J. Ringer.*

ROYAL SQUARE (CAN) 3 ch.c. Gregorian (USA) 115–Dance Crazy (USA) 100
(Foolish Pleasure (USA)) [1988 8m* 1989 8s⁴ 10.1m² 12m³ 12f 13.3m 16.2m* 16f*
18g 14g³] big, strong colt: successful in moderately-run races in August for
amateurs event (9/2 on) at Beverley and 4-runner minor contest at Redcar: ran
poorly in Cesarewitch (sweating) at Newmarket next start but creditably in minor
event at Redcar on final one: stays 2m: acts on firm going: suited by a galloping
track: ran creditably when sweating third start: useful. *G. Harwood.*

ROYAL STING 3 b.g. Prince Bee 128–Dolly-Longlegs 74 (Majority Blue 126) —
[1988 5g 6f 8s 7m 1989 12s 12f 14g³] rather leggy gelding: little worthwhile form in
quite modest company: sold to join M. Robinson 2,200 gns Ascot July Sales. *M. J.
Fetherston-Godley.*

ROYAL SUPREME 2 b.c. (Jan 18) Another Realm 118–La Crima 63 (Runny- 67
mede 123) [1989 5s 5s* 5f⁶] 13,000Y: rather leggy, close-coupled colt: has a short,
quick action: half-brother to 7f winner Optimistic Dreamer (by Full of Hope), good
jumper Voice of Progress (by Matahawk) and several minor winners abroad: dam
won over 7.6f in French Provinces: on toes, won 5-runner maiden at Epsom in April:
well beaten, struggling by halfway, in similar event at Pontefract following month,
not seen out again: gives impression requires soft surface. *G. Lewis.*

ROYAL TOUCH 4 b.f. Tap On Wood 130–Sovereign Dona 117 (Sovereign Path 121
125) [1988 7d² 8m* 7m* 8g² 1989 7m⁴ 6g⁵ 8s³ 8f* 8.5s* 7m² 8f⁴ 9f³] workmanlike
filly: improved into good-class performer late in year, reaching frame in Prix de la
Foret (beaten short head by Gabina) at Longchamp, Breeders' Cup Mile (around 1½
lengths fourth to Steinlen, staying on strongly after being hampered early in
straight) at Gulfstream Park and Matriarch Stakes at Hollywood Park: earlier won
listed event at Cologne and Group 2 Grosser Preis von Dusseldorf (by 5 lengths):
effective at 7f to 9f: acts on any going. *J. E. Hammond, France.*

ROYAL TOWER 5 b.g. Tower Walk 130–Molvitesse 75 (Molvedo 137) [1988 NR —
1989 12f⁶ 12h] lengthy, good-quartered gelding: moderate mover: poor performer:
probably doesn't stay 1½m: blinkered final 3 appearances at 3 yrs: sold 1,500 gns
Doncaster June Sales: subsequently gelded. *P. A. Blockley.*

ROYAL TREATY 5 ch.g. Tower Walk 130–Covenant 75 (Good Bond 122) [1988 —
NR 1989 10m 10.4m 8.2d] leggy gelding: moderate mover: appears no longer of
much account: bandaged nowadays. *R. E. Peacock.*

ROYAL VERSE (FR) 2 b.c. (May 13) Recitation (USA) 124–Sauce Royale 88
(Royal Palace 131) [1989 5s 6m 7m* 7g 8f² 8g² 8f² 10g] 100,000 francs (approx
£9,100) Y: good-topped, angular colt: half-brother to several winners here and
abroad, including French 3-y-o 12.5f winner Akadya (by Akarad), 1¼m winner at 2
yrs, and fair 1m winner Copt Hall Royale (by Right Tack): dam poor half-sister to
very smart 1m to 1¼m filly Sauceboat: fair performer: won maiden at Kempton in
June by 7 lengths from Verro, making virtually all: ran well in nurseries and a minor
event on fifth to seventh starts, moderately in listed race at Newmarket on final one:
should be suited by 1¼m: game and genuine. *P. A. Kelleway.*

ROYAL VOTE (USA) 3 b.c. Deputy Minister (CAN)–La Belle Fleur (USA) 105
(Vaguely Noble 140) [1988 NR 1989 10f² 12m² 14m* 16g* 18g] $550,000Y:
good-topped colt: fourth foal: half-brother to 2 winners, including Chase The Dream
(by Sir Ivor), stakes winner at up to 9f: dam unraced half-sister to good American
filly Cascapedia: sire champion American 2-y-o, later stayed 1¼m: won maiden
(odds on, easily) at Yarmouth in August and £9,600 handicap (leading over 4f out and
keeping on strongly) at Ascot in October: 11/1, below best facing stiffish task in

Cesarewitch at Newmarket 8 days after Ascot: well suited by 2m: sold 72,000 gns Newmarket Autumn Sales: useful. *G. Harwood.*

ROYAL WARRANT (USA) 2 ch.g. (Feb 8) Wavering Monarch (USA)–Gay **58** Lady J (USA) (Forli (ARG)) [1989 6m 6m⁵ 5g 8m⁶ 6s] $23,000Y: rangy, well-made gelding: good mover, with a long stride: first foal: dam placed once at 4 yrs in USA: plating-class maiden: races keenly, and may prove best short of 1m: sweating fourth start. *J. W. Watts.*

ROYAL WONDER 3 b.f. Welsh Saint 126–Collectors' Item 96 (Run The Gantlet **54** (USA)) [1988 7f 8.2m 1989 10s⁵ 12s³ 14m⁵ 14m⁶ 14g*] leggy, unfurnished filly: ridden by 7-lb claimer, won claimer (claimed to join M. Pipe £6,111) at Yarmouth in July, leading until well over 3f out and staying on strongly: will stay well: acts on top-of-the-ground: no form when twice sweating: winning novice hurdler. *M. J. Ryan.*

ROY HOBBS 2 b.c. (Jan 31) Glint of Gold 128–Glory of Hera 99 (Formidable **69** (USA) 125) [1989 6f⁴ 7m 6g] 30,000Y: strong colt: has plenty of scope: poor walker: first foal: dam fairly useful sprinter at 2 yrs well beaten as 3-y-o: bit backward, around 3 lengths fourth of 6, keeping on well after slow start, to Rock City in minor event at York in May when trained by M. Brittain: well beaten over 3 months later in £15,300 event there and claimer at Haydock. *C. Spares.*

ROYSIA BOY 9 b.g. African Sky 124–For Keeps 57 (Track Spare 125) [1988 5.1g **41** d 7f 6g 6m 6d 1989 6f³ 6f 6m 5.1f⁵ 6m 6f] big, good-bodied gelding: tends to look dull in coat: poor walker and mover: one-time fair handicapper: advantageously drawn when third at Thirsk in May: no form after, blinkered once: best at 6f: suited by a sound surface: has pulled hard: bandaged and ridden by 7-lb claimer first 2 starts. *J. Pearce.*

ROZALA (USA) 3 ch.f. Roberto (USA) 131–Golden Highlights (USA) (Secre- — tariat (USA)) [1988 NR 1989 8.5m⁶] $385,000Y: third foal: half-sister to fairly useful 1987 2-y-o 6f winner Fariedah (by Topsider) and to a winner in USA by In Reality: dam stakes winner at up to 1m: 25/1 and in need of race, 16½ lengths sixth of 12 to Al Najah in maiden at Epsom in June, soon behind and pushed along vigorously: wore tongue strap. *M. Moubarak.*

RUADH ADHAR 3 b.f. Heroic Air 96–Rosemarkie 75 (Goldhill 125) [1988 NR — 1989 8.2g⁴ 7s⁶] ninth foal: half-sister to 3 winners, including quite modest 1981 2-y-o 7.2f winner Market Rose (by Most Secret): dam 13f winner: 50/1, showed signs of ability in maiden and minor events in Scotland in September: very slowly away first outing. *J. S. Wilson.*

RUBELITE 3 gr.f. Kalaglow 132–Jacinth 133 (Red God 128§) [1988 NR 1989 10s **87** 11.5m* 11.7m³ 12m⁵ 14.6g³ 13.3d] big, angular filly: has plenty of scope: half-sister to 4 winners, including fair 1½m winner Spinelle (by Great Nephew) and fairly useful 6f winner Jacquinta (by Habitat): dam best 2-y-o of 1972 and high-class miler at 3 yrs: won maiden at Yarmouth in June: good third in moderately-run handicap at Windsor and 4-runner Park Hill Stakes (beaten about 10 lengths by Lucky Song) at Doncaster: well behind facing stiff task in handicap final start: probably stays 1¾m: acts on top-of-the-ground: sold 30,000 gns Newmarket December Sales. *A. C. Stewart.*

RUBICUND 2 b.c. (Mar 27) Niniski (USA) 125–Rosananti 107 (Blushing Groom **76** p (FR) 131) [1989 8.2d²] lengthy colt: fourth foal: half-brother to modest 1m winner Persian Emperor (by Persepolis): dam, half-sister to good English and German performer Claddagh, won from 6f to 1m and stayed 1½m: 25/1 and backward, short-head second of 11 to Almuinjjid in maiden at Haydock in October, running on from 3f out and quickening in tremendous style last furlong (would have won in another stride) after running very green in rear early: sure to improve, and could make useful 3-y-o over further. *J. L. Dunlop.*

RUBINKA 3 b.f. Bustino 136–Relkina (FR) 85 (Relkino 131) [1988 7f 1989 7d⁵ 6s — 7.5d 8.2f 9f 10f 7f 6f 6g] leggy filly: poor plater: should be suited by 1¼m: possibly needs a soft surface: often apprentice ridden: sold 1,200 gns Doncaster August Sales. *D. W. Chapman.*

RUBY DAVIES 3 b.f. Ya Zaman (USA) 122–Tarpon Springs (Grey Sovereign — 128§) [1988 NR 1989 7g 8f 8m 8h 8m] IR 1,000Y, resold 475Y: workmanlike filly: half-sister to several winners, including fairly useful 1978 2-y-o 6f winner Fair Mark (by On Your Mark): dam closely related to No Mercy: little worthwhile form in sellers and a claimer: often sweats: sold 1,600 gns Ascot August Sales. *Capt. J. Wilson.*

RUBY REALM   2 ch.f. (Apr 28) Valiyar 129–Mai Pussy 91 (Realm 129) [1989 6g]   —
sixth foal: half-sister to 3 winners, including smart 7f to 1¼m performer Beau Sher
(by Ile de Bourbon): dam stayed 6f: 33/1, always behind in 23-runner maiden at
Newbury in August. *B. Hanbury.*

RUBY SETTING   2 b.f. (Apr 20) Gorytus (USA) 132–Sun Princess 130 (English   73 p
Prince 129) [1989 6g⁵] medium-sized filly: second foal: half-sister to 3-y-o 1¼m
winner Prince of Dance (by Sadler's Wells), high-class 7f winner at 2 yrs: dam won
Oaks and St Leger: 7/1, around 5 lengths fifth of 6, one pace last 2f, to Alwathba in
Blue Seal Stakes at Ascot in September: will be better suited by 7f+: sure to
improve. *Major W. R. Hern.*

RUBY SHOES   3 b.f. Day Is Done 115–Very Seldom (Rarity 129) [1988 7g 7g 1989   46
7s 8d⁴ 8g 10.6s] plain filly: has a quick action: moderate plater: best effort (well
backed) when staying-on fourth at Bath in April: off course 3 months before final
start: should stay 1¼m: trained first 3 starts by W. Wilson. *R. Bastiman.*

RUBY TIGER   2 gr.f. (Apr 8) Ahonoora 122–Hayati 94 (Hotfoot 126) [1989 6g⁴   92 p
7g* 8g*] 33,000F: first foal: dam 7f and 1¼m winner: won minor event at Epsom in
August by a neck from Rafha, staying on strongly to lead near line, and Premio
Dormello at Milan in October by 2½ lengths from Kerama: suited by 1m: should
make useful 3-y-o. *P. F. I. Cole.*

RUDDA CASS   5 b.g. Rapid River 127–Glaven (Blakeney 126) [1988 7.5m 10g*   —
11m 10f 8m 10m 8g 1989 12g 10f] smallish, workmanlike gelding: winning plater as
4-y-o: no form in subsequent handicaps: stays 1¼m: acts on top-of-the-ground:
blinkered twice at 4 yrs: has won for apprentice. *W. W. Haigh.*

RUDDA FLASH   5 b.m. General David–Palinode 98 (Pall Mall 132) [1988 NR   —
1989 8.5f 12.3f] sturdy, plain mare: poor mover: half-sister to 3 winners, including
fairly useful 6f and 1m winner Sky Mill (by Sky Gypsy): dam fairly useful at up to
1½m: appears of little account. *W. W. Haigh.*

RUDDY CHEEK (USA)   2 b.c. (Apr 20) Blushing Groom (FR) 131–Hail Maggie   76
(USA) (Hail To Reason) [1989 7s³ 8m⁴ 8g³] 98,000Y: close-coupled, sparely-made
colt: half-brother to 2 winners, notably fairly useful 1984 2-y-o 7f winner Sabona (by
Exclusive Native), later Grade 1-placed winner at up to 1m in USA: dam once-raced
sister to top-class middle-distance mare Trillion (dam of Triptych) and smart
Margravine: modest maiden: flashed tail when length third to High Beacon at
Leicester final start: will stay 1¼m: capable of winning a race. *J. L. Dunlop.*

RUDDY LUCKY   3 b.c. Gorytus (USA) 132–Quelle Chance 81 (General   101
Assembly (USA)) [1988 5m 7m² 7d 8.2m² 8h⁴ 8m² 1989 10g⁵ 11f* 12f² 12m² 12f]
workmanlike, angular colt: won maiden at Redcar in May: good second in King
George V Stakes (Handicap) at Royal Ascot and 4-runner minor event at Leicester:
suited by 1½m: best efforts on top-of-the-ground: sold to race in Saudi Arabia
43,000 gns Newmarket Autumn Sales. *J. W. Hills.*

RUDJIG (USA)   3 b.c. Secreto (USA) 128–Chic Belle (USA) (Mr Prospector   103
(USA)) [1988 7s³ 1989 9g⁶ 10.4m² 12m⁶] good-topped, attractive colt: first foal:
dam, winner of 4 stakes races at up to 7f at 4 yrs in USA, is out of half-sister to very
useful sprinter Northern Prospect (by Mr Prospector), Monmouth Oaks winner
Sharp Belle and the dam of Irish Derby winner Sir Harry Lewis: placed in maidens at
Leopardstown (trained by D. O'Brien) and Chester: improved again when about 4½
lengths sixth of 18 to Prorutori in Derby Italiano at Rome in May: suited by 1½m:
acts on top-of-the-ground: likely to prove suited by galloping track. *J. Gosden.*

RUDY'S FANTASY (USA)   2 b.c. (Mar 7) Nureyev (USA) 131–Rainbow's Edge   93 p
(USA) (Creme dela Creme) [1989 7m⁴ 7g³] IR 660,000Y: angular, attractive colt:
closely related to 1½m to 13.8f winner Kaprielian (by The Minstrel) and winner in
France and North America: dam, 2-y-o 5f winner, is half-sister to smart
middle-distance fillies Sweet Rhapsody and Sisterhood: fairly useful form at
Newmarket in October in maiden (very green) won by Mukddaam and £10,000 event
(keeping on strongly) won by Duke of Paducah: sure to win races at 1m+. *L.
Cumani.*

RUGADAY   3 br.g. Milford 119–Relma (Relko 136) [1988 5m 5g 7g 7g 1989 6f 7h³   50 §
7m⁴ 8.3m⁶ 8f 8.3d 7.6m] leggy, close-coupled gelding: fair plater: ran moderately
last 2 starts: stays 1m: acts on hard going: probably ungenuine. *J. H. Baker.*

RUIZ MIGUEL   3 br.g. Precocious 126–Lakshmi 83 (Tribal Chief 125) [1988 6d   —
6d⁵ 1989 8s⁵] strong, deep-girthed gelding: quite modest form in maidens at 2 yrs:
66/1, on toes and burly, faced very stiff task when remote last of 5 in minor event in
April at Sandown, only start in 1989: not bred to stay 1m. *L. G. Cottrell.*

RULE BY FEAR 3 ch.g. Pas de Seul 133–Okavango 90 (Homeric 133) [1988 6m 7m⁵ 7f⁶ 1989 10h 10m a8g] angular gelding: has a long, slightly round stride: quite modest maiden at 2 yrs: always behind as 3-y-o, including in claimer: should be suited by further than 7f: sold 660 gns Newmarket Autumn Sales. *D. J. G. Murray-Smith.* —

RULING DYNASTY 5 br.g. Ile de Bourbon (USA) 133–Bahariva (FR) (Sir Gaylord (USA)) [1988 17g 1989 12m⁵] sparely-made, quite attractive gelding: fair winner as 3-y-o: never-dangerous fifth of 10 in handicap at Brighton in May, only second subsequent outing on flat: stays 1½m: acts on firm going: blinkered only start at 4 yrs: has run well when sweating: winning hurdler/chaser: has joined M. Pipe. *R. J. O'Sullivan.* —

RULING PASSION 2 b.c. (Apr 20) Bairn (USA) 126–Unbidden Melody (USA) (Chieftain II) 68,000Y: rather unfurnished, useful-looking colt: good walker: second foal: half-brother to 3-y-o Ulting Wick (by Brave Shot): dam half-sister to Faustus: 11/2 from 2/1 and green, won 11-runner maiden at Nottingham in May by 1½ lengths from Lars Porsena: looked sure to improve but wasn't seen out again. *M. R. Stoute.* **70 p**

RUMBA ROYALE 5 b.g. Ela-Mana-Mou 132–Regal Way (Sovereign Path 125) [1988 NR 1989 14s 12s 21.6d 16g 12m] bad maiden: probably doesn't stay extreme distances: blinkered once: wears bandages: pulls hard, and wears a crossed noseband. *S. R. Bowring.* —

RUMBOOGIE 5 ch.g. Sharpo 132–Santa Musica (Luthier 126) [1988 8s 7m 8g 8f 1989 8d 7d 5s 10f 8.3m⁶ 8m 6m] good-topped, attractive gelding: poor mover: useful 2-y-o: reportedly split a pastern early in 1987 and little subsequent form: stays 7f: best form with give in the ground: blinkered twice at 4 yrs: sweating fifth and sixth outings: sold 1,000 gns Newmarket Autumn Sales. *C. A. Austin.* —

RUM CAY (USA) 4 ch.f. Our Native (USA)–Oraston 115 (Morston (FR) 125) [1988 NR 1989 14.6g*] 2,000 3-y-o: leggy, angular filly: third foal: half-sister to a winner in Italy by To The Quick: dam won 1¼m Premio Lydia Tesio, and is half-sister to smart French 1m and 1¼m performer The Abbot: won 20-runner maiden at Doncaster in April: sold 28,000 gns Newmarket December Sales in foal to Rousillon. *R. Curtis.* **75**

RUNCIBLE CAT (USA) 3 b.c. J O Tobin (USA) 130–Beau Cougar (USA) (Cougar (CHI)) [1988 6g⁴ 6m⁶ 6d⁴ 6g⁴ 7g⁴ 1989 8d 6d 6f 7g 7m⁴ 7g⁶ 7m³ 7g 6f⁴ 8f³ 8m² 6g⁵] small, lengthy colt: is tubed: quite modest maiden: ran well in seller on tenth start: stays 1m: acts on firm ground: sweating third (also edgy) and sixth outings: below form for 7-lb claimer. *C. E. Brittain.* **67**

RUN DON'T FLY (USA) 3 b.c. Lear Fan (USA) 130–Gantlette (Run The Gantlet (USA)) [1988 7g⁶ 7g³ 7g² 8.2d⁵ 1989 10m³ 12m* 12f* 12m* 12m³] sturdy, **102**

Sun Life of Canada Garrowby Stakes (Limited Handicap), York—
third win in a row for Run Don't Fly who has plenty in hand of Dance Spectrum

quite attractive colt: carries condition: useful handicapper: won at Epsom in June, £11,800 contest at Goodwood in July and £14,200 event at York in September: heavily-backed favourite, creditable third to Braashee in £71,300 Tote Festival Handicap at Ascot in September, always close up and leading briefly inside final 1f: stays 1½m well: best efforts on a sound surface: takes keen hold. *P. F. I. Cole.*

RUN FOR JOYCE 3 br.f. My Dad Tom (USA) 109–Assel Zawie (Sit In The **41** Corner (USA)) [1988 5m 5f 6g 5f⁴ 5g³ 5g⁴ 5g⁴ 5.1f² 5g 1989 5m 5m⁵ 5m 5m² 5m⁴ 5f 6f³ 5m 5f 5f] smallish, close-coupled filly: carries plenty of condition: bad walker: poor maiden: best at 5f: acts on firm going: ridden by 7-lb claimer: inconsistent. *J. Balding.*

RUN FREE 4 b.g. Julio Mariner 127–Lucky Appeal 36 (Star Appeal 133) [1988 8m **54** 10g 11.5d 11.7m 14g 14.5g 10d² 1989 14s⁶ 12s* 12s² 16g₂12g] smallish, leggy gelding: won 22-runner handicap at Leicester in April in good style: tailed off in similar company at Lingfield final outing, first for 6 months: suited by forcing tactics at 1½m: seems to need soft going: blinkered once at 3 yrs: sold 4,400 gns Doncaster November Sales. *R. Guest.*

RUN HIGH 6 b.g. Thatch (USA) 136–Fleet Noble (USA) (Vaguely Noble 140) **68** [1988 12s 16s⁵ 16g⁶ 14d³ 18.4v 14d 14g 13g² 13s² 15.8d⁴ 12m 15.5g⁶ 12g³ 12.2g* 12d² 12g² 1989 12v⁵ 14s⁵ 14f* 12f⁵ 12m⁵ 14f² 14f³ 13m* 15f² 13g⁴ 12g*] strong, medium-sized gelding: moderate mover: quite modest handicapper: won at Sandown in May, Ayr in July and Epsom (apprentices) in August: needs at least 1½m and stays 2m: acts on any going: good mount for inexperienced rider: tough and genuine. *P. Mitchell.*

RUN HOME 2 b.c. (May 9) Homeboy 114–Chiparia 82 (Song 132) [1989 6m 6m **67** 7f⁵ 7g⁵ a6g] small, close-coupled colt: seventh foal: half-brother to 6f winner Young Tearaway (by Young Generation) and 2 other winners, including 1985 2-y-o 6f winner Our Tilly (by Grundy): dam best at 5f: quite modest maiden: best effort (Leicester nursery) penultimate start: never travelling well at Lingfield final one: better suited by 7f than 6f. *R. Akehurst.*

RUNNER DUCK 3 ch.g. On Your Mark 125–Khaki Campbell (USA) (Quack — (USA)) [1988 5g 5f³ 6m 5.8g 6m 7m 7f 1989 7f 8.3m 7f] neat, good-quartered gelding: moderate walker: plating-class maiden in 1988: no worthwhile form in handicaps as 3-y-o: bred to stay 1m: visored once at 2 yrs. *G. B. Balding.*

RUNNETT FOR CASH 3 b.f. Runnett 125–Melissa Claire (Camden Town 125) **46** § [1988 5d 5s 6m 5f² 5g⁴ 5.3f⁴ 5m² 6g³ 7g³ 6d 6g⁴ 6g³ 1989 8g⁴ 7.5d 8m² 8h⁵ 7m⁴ 8m⁴ 7m 8g* 8.2f 7g 10m³ 8f⁶ 10g⁴ 12g³] small, workmanlike filly: moderate mover: modest plater: dead-heated in apprentice handicap at Newcastle in August, switched inside final 1f and joining Not Yet on post: set plenty to do when creditable third final start: stays 1½m: acts on top-of-the-ground: tends to carry head high and hang left: blinkered when trained first 7 starts by M. Fetherston-Godley: difficult ride: none too genuine. *Mrs J. R. Ramsden.*

RUNNING FLUSH 7 ch.g. Lord Gayle (USA) 124–Hidden Hand (USA) — (Ribocco 129) [1988 10d 10f³ 10f* 10f⁶ 10f 10m 10f 11.5m 12g 1989 10g] tall, lightly-made gelding: quite modest winner as 6-y-o: has completely lost his form: tailed off at Folkestone in October: suited by 1¼m: acts on any going: visored nowadays: suited by strong handling: inconsistent. *P. Howling.*

RUNNING HOME 2 b.c. (Apr 2) Homing 130–Canvas Shoe 57 (Hotfoot 126) — [1989 5f 6f 8m 8f5] 6,800Y: smallish, well-made colt: third foal: half-brother to 3-y-o Ward One (by Mr Fluorocarbon), successful at 7f (at 2 yrs) and 8.2f, and poor plater on flat but winning hurdler Sabdabeani (by Good Times): dam won 6f seller at 2 yrs: poor form in varied races, including a seller: blinkered last 2 starts: sold 1,300 gns Doncaster October Sales. *S. G. Norton.*

RUN TO JENNY 3 b.f. Runnett 125–Loch Leven 87 (Le Levanstell 122) [1988 **105** 5g⁵ 6m³ 5m* 6g² 6s 1989 7s³ 8m³ 8f 7f² 8g⁵ 7g³ 6g 7d5] medium-sized, lengthy filly: third in Goffs Irish 1000 Guineas at the Curragh (beaten 2¾ lengths by Ensconce) and seventh in Coronation Stakes (on toes) at Royal Ascot second and third starts: blinkered, third to Twilight Agenda in listed race at Leopardstown, best effort after: ran moderately when fourth in Ladbroke Sprint Cup (visored) at Haydock and IR £11,500 listed event at the Curragh: suited by 1m: acts on any going. *Kevin Connolly, Ireland.*

RUN TO WORK 5 b.g. Workboy 123–Runasca 49 (Runnymede 123) [1988 8.5m — 8f 10g 1989 7f] small, good-quartered gelding: no longer of any account: blinkered twice. *T. Kersey.*

Whyte & Mackay Scotch Stakes (Handicap), Ascot—
Runun (light colours) finds his best form;
the eventual second Baldomero (blinkered) is making ground in fourth place

RUNUN 3 br.c. Sharpo 132–Silent Movie (Shirley Heights 130) [1988 NR 1989 **94**
8m⁴ 7f² 7f⁵ 7m³ 8m⁴ 7m* 6g] lengthy, rather sparely-made colt: moderate mover:
first foal: dam, half-sister to very smart 7f to 1¼m performer Noalto, showed little
worthwhile form from 10.6f to 15.8f: 12/1, won £49,600 Whyte & Mackay Scotch
Stakes (Handicap) at Ascot in September by ¾ length from Baldomero, always
prominent: 100/1, 9 lengths fifth of 12 to Zilzal in Jersey Stakes at Royal Ascot, easily
best other effort: moved badly down fifth and final (soon struggling) starts: should
stay 1m: sold 16,000 gns Newmarket Autumn Sales: quite useful but inconsistent. *C.
E. Brittain.*

RUNWAY ROMANCE (FR) 2 gr.c. (Apr 29) Julius Caesar (FR) 115–Airstrip **66 p**
(Warpath 113) [1989 7f³] first reported foal: dam unraced: 11/4 and ridden by
apprentice, under 3 lengths third of 12 to Beehive Boy in claimer at Salisbury in
September: bred to stay quite well: sure to improve, and win a similar event. *P. J.
Makin.*

RUPPLES 2 b.g. (Apr 30) Muscatite 122–Miss Annie 73 (Scottish Rifle 127) [1989 **—**
6m a6g a7g] 2,700Y, 7,600 2-y-o: leggy, workmanlike gelding: second foal:
half-brother to 3-y-o Joshykin (by Montekin): dam 7f and 1¾m winner: well beaten
in seller at Leicester and claimers at Southwell. *M. J. Ryan.*

RUSCAROFF 3 gr.c. Rusticaro (FR) 124–Fair Or Foul (Patch 129) [1988 8s 1989 **65**
9g 8f⁴ 8m 9m 8.2f 11.7f³ 12.5f² 12.5f³ 12.4g³] leggy, good-topped colt: quite modest
maiden: tailed off as though something amiss in handicaps third to fifth starts, ran
creditably in sellers last 3: stays 1½m: acts on firm ground: ran moderately when
sweating and edgy seventh outing: sometimes taken down early: sold to join G.
Moore 11,000 gns Newmarket Autumn Sales. *J. W. Hills.*

RUSCINO 2 br.c. (Apr 7) Rousillon (USA) 133–Eastern Shore 70 (Sun Prince **67 p**
128) [1989 6d⁵] finely-made, useful-looking colt: fourth foal: half-brother to 3-y-o
Siokra (by Kris), 6f and 1m winner Abu Muslab (by Ile de Bourbon) and French 1½m
winner Carmita (by Caerleon): dam, stayed 11.7f, is granddaughter of very smart
sprinter Lucasland: 8/1, 8½ lengths fifth of 24, making eye-catching late headway
not at all knocked about, to Notley in maiden at Newbury in October: will stay 1m:
sure to improve and win a maiden. *G. Harwood.*

RUSHANES 2 ch.c. (Apr 13) Millfontaine 114–Saulonika 94 (Saulingo 122) [1989 **73**
6f 5m⁴ 6f⁴ 5g⁵ a6g⁵ a5g*] small, sturdy colt: fifth reported foal: brother to modest
3-y-o sprinter Aughfad: dam 2-y-o 5f winner: modest performer: best effort when
winning late-year claimer at Southwell: seems better suited by 5f than 6f: ran in
Chesham Stakes on debut when trained by D. O'Donnell. *R. Hannon.*

RUSHLUAN 5 gr.g. Kalaglow 132–Labista 116 (Crowned Prince (USA) 128) **53**
[1988 12g⁴ 12m* 10d 10m³ 8s 1989 8f² 10.2f 10.6m 12f⁴] leggy, good-topped gelding:
has a quick action: one-time fair performer, only plating class at best nowadays: best

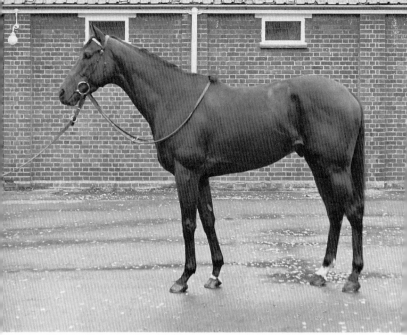

Sheikh Mohammed's "Russian Bond"

form at 1½m: acts on firm going and is probably unsuited by soft surface: ran creditably in visor: apprentice ridden first 3 starts. *R. J. Hodges.*

RUSHMORE (USA) 2 b.c. (Mar 15) Mt Livermore (USA)–Super Act (USA) 71 **104** (Native Royalty (USA)) [1989 7f³ 6m* 6f³ 7m²] $85,000Y: rangy, angular colt: has scope: moderate walker: third reported foal: dam best at 2 yrs here, won at up to 9f in USA: sire won over 1m but better at shorter: made all in 5-runner listed race at Newbury in July and won by ½ length from Dayjur: ¾-length second of 6 to Candy Glen in minor event at Sandown in September: probably better suited by 7f than 6f. *C. E. Brittain.*

RUSSBOROUGH 8 ch.g. Astrapi 85–Melpo 73 (Hook Money 124) [1988 15.5g — 1989 15.5s] lengthy, plain gelding: quite modest handicapper at 3 yrs: bandaged and needed race at Folkestone in April, only second subsequent outing on flat. *R. Voorspuy.*

RUSSIAN BOND (USA) 3 b.c. Danzig (USA)–Somfas (USA) (What A **113** Pleasure (USA)) [1988 6m* 6f* 1989 6f 7g²] tall, well-made, good sort: long odds on, successful at 2 yrs in maiden at Yarmouth and slowly-run Rokeby Farms Mill Reef Stakes at Newbury: 5 lengths second of 4 to Zilzal in moderately-run Van Geest Criterion Stakes at Newmarket in July: never dangerous or knocked about when in need of race in Cork and Orrery Stakes at Royal Ascot 9 days earlier: should have stayed 1m: smart: reportedly sold to stand in Japan in 1990. *H. R. A. Cecil.*

RUSSIAN EXPRESS 3 b.f. Bay Express 132–Zarnina 56 (The Brianstan 128) — [1988 5f 5g 5g³ 5d 5m 5m 5d 1989 5m 5m 5f] good-quartered, workmanlike filly: has shown little for some time: seems unlikely to stay beyond 5f. *D. W. Chapman.*

RUSSIAN FRONTIER 2 gr.c. (Apr 4) Nureyev (USA) 131–Lovelight 112 **83 p**
(Bleep-Bleep 134) [1989 6d³] lengthy, rather unfurnished colt: brother to very
useful 1m and 9f winner Literati and half-brother to several other winners, including
very smart 6f to 1m winner Motavato (by Apalachee), later successful in USA: dam
very game sprinter: 5/1, wearing dropped noseband and bit backward, one-paced
third of 24, beaten 3 lengths, to Notley in maiden at Newbury in October: sure to
improve and win a race. *B. W. Hills.*

RUSSIAN IVORY (USA) 3 b.c. Nureyev (USA) 131–Dame Ivor (USA) (Sir Ivor **— §**
135) [1988 NR 1989 6f⁶ 7m] small colt: first foal: dam unraced half-sister to
high-class 1971 US 2-y-o Rest Your Case and to dam of Horris Hill winner Super
Asset, high-class 8.5f to 1¼m winner Bates Motel (both by Sir Ivor) and high-class
middle-distance colt Hatim: soundly beaten in maidens at Brighton (visored) and
Thirsk (blinkered and wearing crossed noseband, very reluctant on way to post and
on bend in race) in the autumn: sold 1,700 gns Newmarket Autumn Sales: one to
avoid. *J. H. M. Gosden.*

RUSSIAN RED 2 ch.c. (Mar 16) Kind of Hush 118–Green Diamond (Green God **72**
128) [1989 5s 5g 6f⁶ 7m⁵ 7g³ 7f 7m³ 7m a8g] strong, lengthy colt: has scope:
moderate mover: half-brother to 3-y-o Jewel In The Storm and half-brother to 1989
2-y-o 8. 2f seller winner Ribogirl (by Riboboy) and a winner in Italy by Green-
jammer: dam placed over hurdles: modest maiden: should be suited by further than
7f: inconsistent. *W. G. R. Wightman.*

RUSSIAN ROYAL (USA) 3 gr.f. Nureyev (USA) 131–Princess Karenda (USA) **108**
(Gummo (USA)) [1988 6m* 1989 7.3s² 8m 7f* 7f² 7f² 6g 7g⁴] big, angular filly: has a
rather round action: easily landed odds (made all) in minor event at Chepstow in
May: in frame in Fred Darling Stakes at Newbury, Jersey Stakes (on toes) at Royal
Ascot, Beeswing Stakes (edgy, held up and pulling hard) at Newcastle and Supreme
Stakes at Goodwood: suited by 7f: acts on any going: gives impression best with
forcing tactics: useful. *M. R. Stoute.*

RUSTIC TRACK 9 b.g. Palm Track 122–Polly-Ann Tanja (Cletus) [1988 10m **—**
12d⁶ 12f⁶ 12f 12f⁵ 12m 12m 13.8g 1989 11d¹⁴] lengthy, sparely-made gelding: bad
handicapper nowadays: stays 1½m: acts on any going: has won for apprentice: has
worn blinkers: often gets well behind. *Denys Smith.*

RUSTINO 3 ch.c. Bustino 136–Miss Britain (Tudor Melody 129) [1988 NR 1989 **64**
8s 8d⁶ 8.5g⁵ 11f⁵ 12g 12.3g⁵ 9f 10.6d] workmanlike colt: has a round action:
half-brother to 5f to 8.5f winner Inishpour (by Nishapour): dam poor sister to very
smart 1973 2-y-o Welsh Harmony: modest maiden: tailed off final start: will prove
suited by 1½m: probably unsuited by very firm going: winning hurdler for A.
Robson. *Mrs R. Wharton.*

RUSTLE 7 b.g. Homeboy 114–Plunder 77 (Tamerlane 128) [1988 NR 1989 16d⁶] **—**
big, rangy gelding: half-brother to a winner in Norway and to 4 winners over jumps,
including staying chasers Never Tamper (by Never Say Die) and John Silver (by
Pieces of Eight): dam ran twice: high-class hurdler, winner of Waterford Crystal
Stayers' Hurdle at Cheltenham in March: 20/1 and visored, chased leaders until 3f
out when well-beaten sixth of 10 to Travel Mystery in Insulpak Sagaro EBF Stakes
at Ascot in April: will be suited by extreme test of stamina. *N. J. Henderson.*

RUST PROOF 2 gr.c. (May 22) Rusticaro (FR) 124–Grecian Charter (Runny- **—**
mede 123) [1989 7m] workmanlike, angular colt: fifth live foal: half-brother to
winning stayer Ribo Charter (by Ribero), 6f and 8.2f winner Qemlas (by Town Crier)
and a winner in Italy: dam never ran: 100/1, well beaten in 20-runner maiden at
Lingfield in September. *M. Blanshard.*

RUTHLESS BOY 2 ch.g. (Mar 21) Precocious 126–Bushy Top 83 (Thatching **58**
131) [1989 6f⁴ 6h⁵ 7g⁵ 7g³ 6f² 8.2f⁶ 7g⁴ 6m] 23,000Y: leggy, rather unfurnished
gelding: turns fore-feet out: has a roundish action: first foal: dam 6f winner stayed
7f: plating-class form, including in sellers: really needs further than 6f: looked ill at
ease on hard ground second outing: blinkered sixth and seventh starts: sold 4,800
gns Newmarket Autumn Sales. *N. A. Callaghan.*

RYAN'S GIFT (USA) 3 b.c. Nijinsky (CAN) 138–On The Bench (USA) (Good **72**
Behaving (USA)) [1988 NR 1989 8d 11.7m⁴ 10.1m⁴] sturdy, lengthy, angular colt:
first reported foal: dam won at up to 1m: modest form at best in maidens and minor
event: may prove best at short of 1½m: sold 4,200 gns Newmarket Autumn Sales.
Major W. R. Hern.

RYAN'S GIRL 3 br.f. Tanfirion 110–Lost Path (Sovereign Path 125) [1988 5m **58**
5g* 6m³ 6m² 6m* 6g* 6d³ 7.5m³ 8.2m 8s 8.2s 9f 1989 8s 7g 6m³ 6g] workmanlike,
good-quartered filly: carries condition: poor walker: has a roundish action: useful

plater at 2 yrs: easily best effort as 3-y-o when creditable third in claimer at Haydock in May: stays 1m: probably unsuited by soft going: blinkered fifth to tenth starts at 2 yrs: has run creditably for apprentice but tends to wander: sold 3,250 gns Doncaster October Sales. *C. Tinkler.*

RYAN'S WAY 3 br.g. Kafu 120–Tassie (Lochnager 132) [1988 5g² 5f 6m³ 6g⁴ 7f 8g 6s 1989 8.5d 8.2f⁶ 8g 8.2g] leggy, close-coupled gelding: quite modest maiden as 2-y-o: no form in handicaps and claimer in 1989: best form at 6f and not sure to stay 1m: sold 1,600 gns Doncaster November Sales, probably to race in Scandinavia. *C. Tinkler.* —

S

SAALIB 6 b.g. Tyrnavos 129–Velvet Habit 89 (Habitat 134) [1988 7.6g 10f 7m⁴ 6m⁶ 6g⁶ 7m⁵ 7.6f 1989 6v 7m⁴ 7m 7g⁶ 7m 6m⁴ 7m⁴ 7g⁵ 5m 8f] sturdy gelding: carries plenty of condition: usually looks well: poor performer: effective at 6f and stays 1m: acts on any going: has worn blinkers, visored third outing: often apprentice ridden nowadays. *Pat Mitchell.* **34**

SABARAB 3 b.c. Sayf El Arab (USA) 127–Miss Speak Easy (USA) (Sea Bird II 145) [1988 NR 1989 8s² 8d⁴ 8.5f⁴ 10.1m⁶ 12.3g³ 10m* 12f* 14f 12d³ 10f* 10g⁵ 11v] 3,300Y, 18,000 2-y-o: compact colt: has a quick action: half-brother to several winners, including very useful French middle-distance winner Natchitoches (by Pontifex): dam minor French 9f winner: won claimers at Sandown in July and Salisbury (short-priced favourite) in August and October: good fifth at Ascot, easily better effort in quite valuable handicaps last 2 outings: stays 1½m: acts on firm going and a soft surface: blinkered last 3 starts. *K. O. Cunningham-Brown.* **80**

SABI JAI 3 ch.f. Adonijah 126–Sharai Jill (Scorpio (FR) 127) [1988 5g⁵ 6f 6f 8m 7m 7d⁵ 1989 8s] lengthy, workmanlike filly: plating-class maiden: shaped quite well in seller at Ripon in April, only start as 3-y-o: best form at 7f. *P. Calver.* —

SABINE'S GULL (USA) 2 br.f. (Apr 14) Arctic Tern (USA) 126–Altesse de Loir (USA) (Vaguely Noble 140) [1989 7g] 10,500Y: sturdy filly: half-sister to minor winner in USA by Overskate: dam, placed once in France from 7 starts, out of top-class French middle-distance performer Comtesse de Loir: backward, last of 12 in maiden at Leicester in August. *M. Blanshard.* —

SABONIS (USA) 2 b.f. (Mar 2) The Minstrel (CAN) 135–Journey (USA) (What A Pleasure (USA)) [1989 6f* 7m⁵ 6g⁶] $130,000Y: quite attractive filly: has a round action: closely related to 3-y-o 1m winner Lambourn Citizen (by L'Emigrant) and half-sister to 4 winners in North America: dam never ran: won maiden at Chepstow in June by short head: creditable sixth in nursery at Nottingham in October: should stay 1m: sold 6,000 gns Newmarket December Sales. *D. J. G. Murray-Smith.* **68**

SABOTAGE (FR) 3 ch.c. Kris 135–Subject To Change (USA) (Buckpasser) [1988 NR 1989 8g* 10.5f⁵ 8f* 8m* 9g² 8g⁶] 170,000Y: leggy, quite good-topped, attractive colt: easy walker: half-brother to 5 winners in France, including 9.5f and 1¼m winner Salute (by Luthier): dam placed in USA: justified favouritism in Johansens Guides Wood Ditton Stakes at Newmarket in April, 2-runner minor event at Goodwood in July and 5-runner £9,200 contest (made all) at Newmarket in October: good head second to Princess Accord easily better effort after in listed races at Newmarket, making most until line: stays 9f: very useful. *M. R. Stoute.* **114**

SABOTEUR 5 ch.g. Pyjama Hunt 126–Frondia 76 (Parthia 132) [1988 7m* 7f 1989 7m 7g² 7g 7g] lengthy, dipped-backed gelding: bad mover: poor handicapper: made all at Yarmouth at 3 yrs and 4 yrs: ridden by 7-lb claimer, good second at same course in July: well beaten other 3 outings in 1989: suited by 7f and a sound surface: blinkered once: inconsistent. *I. Campbell.* **44**

SABRE LONG 3 ch.c. Young Man (FR) 73–Honey Palm 86 (Honeyway 125) [1988 NR 1989 10.1g 10f⁵ 7f] sparely-made colt: half-brother to 4 winners, including 1m and 1¼m winner Honegger (by King's Troop) and winner at up to 2m and high-class hurdler Floyd (by Relko): dam sprinter best at 2 yrs: tailed off in minor events: has joined R. Holder. *J. M. Bradley.* —

SACOSHE 2 b.f. (Apr 21) Swing Easy (USA) 126–Just Irene 50 (Sagaro 133) [1989 5g] 840Y: second foal: sister to a 3-y-o in Belgium: dam, plater, won over 1¼m: backward, slowly away and always behind in 23-runner maiden at Redcar in October. *M. P. Naughton.* —

Main Reef Stakes, Newmarket—Sabotage dictates thoroughout.
Behind come Charmer, hard-ridden Hello Vaigly and Double Encore

SACRED NOTARY 2 b.c. (Mar 18) Blushing Scribe (USA) 107–Blesseen 71 (So **44**
Blessed 130) [1989 5d 5s 5f 5m⁵] 1,450F, 5,600Y: good-topped colt: has a round
action: brother to 3-y-o Blushing Bunny and half-brother to 1983 2-y-o 7f winner
Quiet Solicitor (by Roan Rocket) and a winner in Scandinavia: dam raced only at
sprint distances: poor maiden: best effort third start: blinkered final one: sold 1,700
gns Newmarket Autumn Sales. *M. J. Haynes.*

SACRE D'OR (USA) 4 b.g. Lemhi Gold (USA) 123–Dedicated To Sue (USA) **77**
(Su Ka Wa) [1988 10.1g³ 12g⁵ 1989 10.2g⁴ 10s* 11.7d² 12d 11s⁵ 12g] rangy,
useful-looking gelding: has a markedly round action: fair handicapper: showed much
improved form when winning 22-runner event at Nottingham in April: off course
over 4 months after next outing: stays 1½m: goes well with plenty of give in the
ground: winning hurdler. *J. Mackie.*

SADDLE BOW 2 b.f. (Jan 15) Sadler's Wells (USA) 132–Charming Life 88 **82 p**
(Habitat 134) [1989 6m 7g³] 165,000F, 200,000Y: leggy, sparely-made filly: second
foal: dam won over 7f as a 4-y-o: still in need of race, 2½ lengths third of 24, staying
on quite strongly, to Sardegna in maiden at Newmarket in November: will be suited
by 1m: likely to improve further. *J. Gosden.*

SADEEM (USA) 6 ch.h. Forli (ARG)–Miss Mazepah (USA) (Nijinsky **122**
(CAN) 138) [1988 16g³ 20f* 21m* 15m⁵ 18f² 20m* 15.5s 1989 16f* 20f* 21f²]
For those who prefer their England green and pleasant the summer of
1989 is probably best forgotten. The sunniest summer in living memory made
things particularly difficult for racehorse trainers among others. Very few
horses are really at home on the extremes of going and many trainers were
reluctant to run some of their horses on the widely-prevailing firm. However,
the summer-long drought provided good opportunities for the top-of-
the-ground performers. Conditions were ideal on Gold Cup day for Sadeem
who followed up his victory the previous year—achieved in controversial
circumstances—with a scintillating eight-length success, pulling up, over his
stable-companion Mazzacano and six others. Sadeem was in his element on
the firm going, and, forcefully ridden, he left his rivals toiling after being sent
to the front rounding the turn into the final straight. A steady early gallop
resulted in Sadeem's winning time being over seven seconds outside that of
first-past-the-post Royal Gait's the previous year. It was Sadeem's third Gold
Cup—he was also second to Paean in 1987—and, all being well, he will be in

773

Gold Cup, Ascot — no danger to odds-on Sadeem

the field again in 1990 when he will have a chance to emulate Sagaro's unequalled feat of winning the Gold Cup three years in a row. Sadeem added to his Gold Cup victory in the Goodwood Cup as a five-year-old but he went down by a neck at Goodwood in the latest season to Mazzacano, to whom he conceded 7 lb. Sadeem wasn't seen out again. He was down to contest the Jockey Club Cup in October, but was withdrawn late on after rain.

With Royal Gait off the course for the season injured and Sadeem's 1988 Doncaster Cup conqueror Kneller sadly dead, it always seemed on the cards that the leading Cup horses of 1989 might turn out to be a moderate collection. Sadeem started at 11/8-on for the Gold Cup after winning the Mappin & Webb Henry II Stakes at Sandown on his reappearance from another stable-companion Zero Watt, and Zaffaran (the first three all owned by Sheikh Mohammed). The added money for the Gold Cup was raised to £100,000 in 1989 and, for the time being at least, its distance is to remain two and a half miles. There is a strong body of opinion, however, which favours reducing the distances of the Cup races and the Jockey Club conducted a survey into their future in the latest season. Sadeem's trainer is among those who believe the Gold Cup, for example, would be better as a two-mile race (with the Queen Alexandra Stakes retained at the Royal meeting for the out-and-out stayers). There is no doubt that the quality of fields for the Cup races has declined significantly over the years. The editor of *The Sporting Life* went so far as to write that they had 'no part in a sensible pattern-race programme aimed at improving the thoroughbred racehorse'. But who says racing should be run in the interests of breeders? Racing is essentially an entertainment industry and there's no reason why important races over two miles and upwards shouldn't have a prominent place in the racing programme. Of course, it has to be accepted that the majority of breeders don't want out-and-out stayers as stallions, but there will always be horses who stay extreme distances and it's only fair that they should have big prizes to aim at. Long distance races can provide magnificent entertainment for the spectators. Offer substantial prizes for the Cup races—the Goodwood and Doncaster Cups should be worth £100,000 too—with possibly a bonus for winning all three and you'll attract some of the good-class stayers that are nowadays campaigned over distances at which they are not fully effective but at which there is currently more prize-money and greater prestige to be earned. It is questionable whether running the Cup races over shorter distances would help to restore their relevance as a proving ground for potential stallions; there are already pattern races run over two miles and there is no evidence that their winners have any more appeal to commercial breeders. No recommendations about the future of the Cup races had been published by the Jockey Club at the time of going to press, but Ascot had officially confirmed that the Gold Cup would be run over two and a half miles in 1990.

	Forli (ARG) (ch 1963)	Aristophanes (ch 1948)	Hyperion
			Commotion
		Trevisa (ch 1951)	Advocate
Sadeem (USA) (ch.h. 1983)			Veneta
	Miss Mazepah (USA) (b 1972)	Nijinsky (b 1967)	Northern Dancer
			Flaming Page
		Monade (br 1959)	Klairon
			Mormyre

The big, strong, workmanlike Sadeem carries plenty of condition;he's a moderate mover in all his paces. There's little to add to the details given about Sadeem's pedigree in previous Annuals. Most of the offspring of his sire the Argentinian triple crown winner Forli, now dead, have shown more speed than stamina (Thatch, Posse, Home Guard, Boone's Cabin and Gay Fandango

Sheikh Mohammed's "Sadeem"

are among the best of his progeny to race in Europe and none of them won beyond a mile). Sadeem's dam Miss Mazepah, a daughter of Oaks winner Monade, has bred three other winners including the useful middle-distance winner Formaz, a full brother to Sadeem. Sadeem tends to get on edge and sometimes sweats. He needs strong handling and has been well ridden by his now-retired regular partner Starkey and by Carson, who partnered Sadeem to his latest Gold Cup victory. *G. Harwood.*

SADLER'S LAD 3 b.c. Sadler's Wells (USA) 132–Ukraine Girl 121 (Targowice **92** (USA) 130) [1988 NR 1989 10v⁴ 10v⁵ 10f² 12f* 12g* 16f] IR 410,000Y: rangy colt: fourth foal: closely related to Irish 1¼m winner Ukraine Dancer (by Shareef Dancer) and half-brother to 1985 Irish 2-y-o 6f winner Sherkraine (by Shergar): dam won Poule d'Essai des Pouliches: favourite, successful in June in maiden at the Curragh and minor event at Leopardstown: 12/1 and on toes, chased leaders (taking keen hold early) long way when behind in Queen's Vase at Royal Ascot: stays 1½m, not 2m: acts on firm going: visored final outing: blinkered previous three. *D. K. Weld, Ireland.*

SAFARI KEEPER 3 b.g. Longleat (USA) 109–Garden Party 111 (Reform 132) — [1988 NR 1989 7f a6g] useful-looking gelding: half-brother to a winner in Belgium: dam won 5 times at up to 7.2f: bit backward, slowly away and showed little in minor event at Warwick and claimer at Southwell 2½ months later. *M. J. Wilkinson.*

SAFAWAN 3 ch.c. Young Generation 129–Safita 117 (Habitat 134) [1988 7g 7g² **106** 6d* 1989 7g 7m* 8.2m* 8f*] lengthy, robust colt: has a roundish action: useful handicapper: progressed well, winning at Newmarket and Haydock (Tote Credit Handicap) in May and £57,500 Schweppes Golden Mile at Goodwood (ran on gamely when beating Serious Trouble by a head) in July: 11/2, always close up, led over 2f out and ran on gamely when beating Serious Trouble by a head at Goodwood: suited by 1m and top-of-the-ground. *M. R. Stoute.*

SAFE 3 b.c. Kris 135–Carnival Dance 69 (Welsh Pageant 132) [1988 7m⁶ 8g⁶ 1989 **78** 10h⁵ 12.2m* 14m 12m³ 11.7m³ 14m 12f⁵] angular, close-coupled colt: turns near-fore in: shows plenty of knee action: won handicap at Catterick in June: third in amateurs race at Newmarket and moderately-run handicap at Windsor, easily best other efforts: suited by around 1½m: acts on top-of-the-ground. *P. F. I. Cole.*

SAFETY (USA) 2 b.c. (Apr 26) Topsider (USA)–Flare Pass (USA) (Buckpasser) — [1989 6m 6f] lengthy colt: half-brother to several winners here and abroad, including useful 1m winner Slaney (by Irish River): dam, placed twice, is sister to very smart American colt Buckaroo: no worthwhile form in minor events at Windsor in August and Nottingham in September. *B. W. Hills.*

SAFFAANH (USA) 3 b.f. Shareef Dancer (USA) 135–Give Thanks 123 (Relko **87** 136) [1988 7g² 7.3s⁶ 1989 10f⁴ 10m⁴ 12.2m*] medium-sized filly: moderate mover, with a roundish action: fair performer: in frame in listed races at Newbury and 4-runner minor event (tending to hang left and carry head bit awkwardly) at Warwick in the summer: awarded last-named on technicality over 5 months later: stayed 1½m: acted on firm ground: visits Riverman. *Major W. R. Hern.*

Schweppes Golden Mile (Handicap), Goodwood—Safawan (rails) holds on gamely from Serious Trouble (No. 11) and Mirror Black

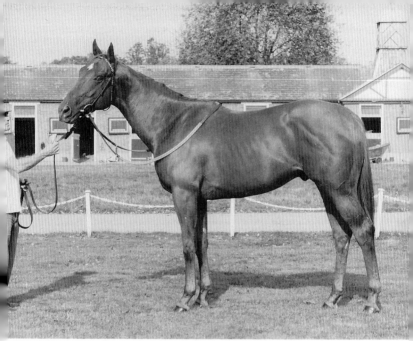

H. H. Aga Khan's "Safawan"

SAFFRON LACE 2 b.f. (May 8) Rabdan 129–French Music (French Beige 127) **43**
[1989 5m⁴ 5m 5.1f 7m 5.1m 8g 6m a6g a7g a8g] 3,000Y, 6,000 2-y-o: smallish,
sparely-made filly: poor walker: half-sister to several winners here and abroad,
including fair 1981 2-y-o 6f and 7f winner Lively Rhythm (by Sharpen Up), later
successful in Germany: dam ran once: poor form, including in sellers: took good
hold after slow start when blinkered fifth start: looks a difficult ride: trained first 5
outings by E. Eldin. *C. F. Wall.*

SAFFRON VENTURE 2 b.f. (Apr 4) Mufrij–New Saffron (New Member 119) —
[1989 6m 7f] third foal: dam showed no ability in point-to-points: well beaten in
maidens at Ripon in August and Redcar in September. *M. Avison.*

SAFWAH 3 ch.f. Ahonoora 122–Lough Graney (Sallust 134) [1988 5m² 6m* 6f* —
6g 1989 6m] workmanlike, angular filly: moderate mover: fair winner as 2-y-o: ran
poorly in handicaps afterwards: should have been suited by 7f + : visits Master
Willie. *R. W. Armstrong.*

SAGAMAN (GER) 3 b.g. Solo Dancer (GER)–Scholastika (GER) (Alpenkonig **57**
(GER)) [1988 6g 8s⁶ 8.2m⁴ 8.2s 1989 10s⁶ 12g 8.2s⁶ 12h³ 12f⁶ 12h² 12f 10g] strong,
heavy-topped gelding: quite modest maiden: stays 1½m: possibly needs top-of-the-
ground: blinkered third to seventh starts: virtually tailed off in visor once at 2 yrs:
trained until after penultimate outing by K. Brassey: winner over hurdles. *L. J.
Codd.*

SAGAMORE (USA) 3 b.c. Simply Great (FR) 122–Vallee Secrete (USA) **108**
(Secretariat (USA)) [1988 6g² 5d* 6d² 6d 1989 7v⁵ 8s* 7v* 6m⁵ 8g⁵ 8g² 8g⁴]
ex-Irish colt: third living foal: half-brother to fairly useful 1985 2-y-o 5f winner
Kombus (by Known Fact), later winner abroad: dam, from excellent family, won
over 1m at 3 yrs in France: successful in minor event at Leopardstown and listed
Harp Lager EBF 2000 Guineas Trial at Phoenix Park in April: in frame in pattern

events at Phoenix Park (very good 2 lengths second to Distant Relative) and Cologne in July: stays 1m: acts on top-of-the-ground and heavy going: useful: has joined Hans Blume in Germany. *K. Prendergast, Ireland.*

SAGAR ISLAND (USA)   2 b. or br.f. (Feb 5) Sagace (FR) 135–Star River (FR)   **74** p
(Riverman (USA) 131) [1989 7f³] 94,000Y: close-coupled, angular, sparely-made filly: third foal: half-sister to 7f winner Saraa-Ree and French 1m winner Sir Bruce (both by Caro): dam, winner at up to around 9f in France, is sister to top-class Irish River: 12/1 and very green, 2 lengths third of 8, slowly away, hanging left over 2f out then running on strongly, to Star of The Future in maiden at Leicester in October: will stay 1¼m: sure to improve. *M. R. Stoute.*

SAGE BRUSH   3 ch.f. Sagaro 133–Tentwort 79 (Shiny Tenth 120) [1988 NR 1989   —
11g] first foal: dam staying handicapper: 50/1, green, backward and never dangerous in claimer at Redcar in October. *C. W. C. Elsey.*

SAGITTA'S BELLE   3 b.f. Belfort (FR) 89–Cassiar 84 (Connaught 130) [1988   **44**
NR 1989 6s 5s⁵ 6m 5g⁴ 6m⁵ 6m 5m] sparely-made filly: moderate mover: seventh foal: sister to fair 6f winner Persistent Bell and half-sister to a winner in Mexico by Direct Flight: dam, daughter of very speedy Fortune's Darling, won over 11.5f: poor form, including in handicaps: may well stay beyond 6f: acts on soft ground. *G. Blum.*

SAGLAWY   3 ch.c. Krayyan 117–Willow Bird 74 (Weepers Boy 124) [1988 5m 5g⁵   —
6g 6g 6f 7f 8s 7f 10m 7g 1989 12s⁶ 10g] lengthy, good-topped colt: has shown nothing since sixth start at 2 yrs, off course over 6 months after reappearance: not bred to stay middle distances: blinkered once at 2 yrs, visored twice. *J. P. Hudson.*

SAHARA BALADEE (USA)   2 b.f. (Mar 15) Shadeed (USA) 135–Splendid Girl   **79**
(USA) (Golden Eagle (FR)) [1989 6f² 7m²] angular, sparely-made filly: has a roundish action: fifth foal: half-sister to top-class French 1m and 9f winner Thrill Show (by Northern Baby), later a good winner in USA, David's Bird (by Storm Bird), a good winner at up to 1¼m at 2 yrs, and 3-y-o Miss Fancy That (by The Minstrel), 7f winner at 2 yrs: dam won 7 races at up to 1m: second in September maidens at Nottingham and Lingfield: will stay 1m: capable of winning a race. *M. R. Stoute.*

SAHARA BREEZE   3 b.f. Ela-Mana-Mou 132–Diamond Land (Sparkler 130)   **85**
[1988 7f² 7s³ 1989 10.5f 8m³] leggy filly: has a roundish action: taken down early and edgy, best effort when third in maiden at Yarmouth in June, pulling hard: should stay 1¼m: sold 4,200 gns Newmarket December Sales. *B. Hanbury.*

SAILING AROUND   4 b.f. Viking (USA)–Shining Jenny (Timmy My Boy 125)   —
[1988 10g 12m 1989 10f] ex-Irish filly: half-sister to 4 winners, including useful Irish 1986 2-y-o 1m and 9f winner Bobsbent (by Taufan), successful over 9f and placed at up to 1½m at 3 yrs: dam never ran: modest form at best as 2-y-o: very lightly raced on flat and well beaten subsequently: should stay 1¼m: best form on a soft surface: blinkered once at 3 yrs: visored (tailed off) only start at 4 yrs. *P. D. Evans.*

SAILOR BOY   3 b.c. Main Reef 126–Main Sail 104 (Blakeney 126) [1988 6m⁵ 7g⁴   **84**
1989 10.1m 12m* 13.1f³ 17.1f*] smallish, quite attractive colt: easy mover, with a light action: fair handicapper: narrow winner at Leicester in July and Bath in October: stays 17f: acts on firm ground: ran creditably in blinkers third start: not an easy ride: sold to join R. Akehurst 30,000 gns Newmarket Autumn Sales. *Major W. R. Hern.*

SAILOR MILAN   2 ch.c. (Mar 1) Pas de Seul 133–Sweet Home (Home Guard   —
(USA) 129) [1989 6m 7f 7v] leggy, sparely-made colt: first foal: dam, 6f winner in USA, daughter of half-sister to Irish 1000 Guineas winner Miralla: well beaten in varied events, including a seller. *N. Bycroft.*

SAIL (USA)   3 b.c. Topsider (USA)–Bar J Gal (USA) (Key To The Mint (USA))   **75**
[1988 6g³ 6d⁶ 6m⁴ 7d 1989 8d³ 8f⁶ 10m 10.2g⁴] tall, lengthy colt: moderate mover with a quick action: modest handicapper: not seen out after June: lacks turn of foot and will be suited by more forcing tactics over 1¼m +: best on an easy surface: may be worth a try in blinkers: didn't handle Epsom track third start: sold 18,000 gns Newmarket Autumn Sales. *H. Thomson Jones.*

SAINT ANDREWS (FR)   5 b.h. Kenmare (FR) 125–Hardiona (FR) (Hard   **128** §
To Beat 132) [1988 10v³ 10s³ 12d³ 10.5d* 9.2d² 12s² 12m⁵ 11s* 12g 1989 10v*
10s² 10.5s* 9.2g⁶ 12d 12g³ 12s]
    There were times as a five-year-old when Saint Andrews, the epitome of consistency for so long, cried enough's enough. His season wasn't one of total disappointment, however, for in the Prix Ganay and Ciga Prix de l'Arc de Triomphe he produced the best performances of his twenty-six-race career. He was available at 50/1 for the Prix de l'Arc with bookmakers in Britain (on

Prix Ganay, Longchamp—Saint Andrews (left) beats Star Lift to land his second Ganay

the pari-mutuel he was coupled with Young Mother and went off second favourite at 5/1) after finishing last in the Prix d'Ispahan (the first time he carried the colours of his new owner Frank Stronach, who also bought Alwuhush, amongst others, in 1989) and not finishing at all in the Prix Foy on his two outings after the Prix Ganay. In the Prix d'Ispahan he broke sluggishly and was ridden along throughout after behaving very badly in the preliminaries and proving troublesome at the stalls. In the Prix Foy he was again slowly away and after a few yards declined to go any further. He had to pass a stalls test before being allowed to take his chance in the Arc, but in the race itself his attitude couldn't be faulted. Blinkered for the first time in a long while, he soon took up a prominent position tracking Harvest Time and Star Lift, and went to the front before the final turn. He remained in the lead until Carroll House went on over a furlong out. Saint Andrews was caught by Behera for second only in the dying strides, on the line a length and a half down on Carroll House, with Young Mother a neck away in fourth. If the Arc saw the best side of Saint Andrews, then the Rothmans International at Woodbine provided further evidence of his worst. Starting favourite at a shade of odds against, he was kept away from the others in the build-up but in the race again showed little interest, virtually pulling himself up and finishing tailed off along with Tralos. His jockey Legrix observed afterwards, 'After the start, no gas, no action, very bad'.

Whereas Saint Andrews and Star Lift finished far apart in the Prix Foy and Prix de l'Arc, there was little to separate them in the Prix d'Harcourt and Prix Ganay at Longchamp in the spring. After running away with the Prix Exbury at Saint-Cloud in March on his reappearance, Saint Andrews took on Star Lift and Fijar Tango, both having their first run of the season, in the Prix d'Harcourt. Star Lift was sent to the front leaving the stalls and was never headed, Saint Andrews getting the better of Fijar Tango late on for second, two and a half lengths behind the winner. The first two home were the first two in the betting for the seven-runner Prix Ganay three weeks later, with Star Lift odds on. It wasn't just a two-horse race, however, for the Arc third Boyatino was also in the field and had run encouragingly behind Robore in the Prix d'Hedouville a fortnight earlier. Mansonnien took them along until Star Lift went by on his outside over a furlong out. Saint Andrews, having made his move up the rails, caught Star Lift well inside the final furlong and held him by half a length, the two pulling four lengths clear of Mansonnien. Boyatino was another four adrift in fifth. Saint Andrews had beaten Grand Fleuve in the race twelve months previously and became the first to win the Prix Ganay in successive seasons since Allez France, who died in December, in the mid-'seventies.

Kenmare, now standing in Australia, was the leading sire in France for the fourth consecutive year thanks mainly to Saint Andrews and the Dubai Poule d'Essai des Poulains winner Kendor. The distaff side of Saint Andrews' pedigree isn't so impressive and accounts mainly for the modest sum (106,000

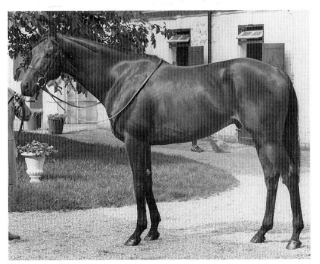

Mr F. Stronach's "Saint Andrews"

Saint Andrews (FR) (b.h. 1984)	Kenmare (FR) (gr 1975)	Kalamoun (gr 1970)	Zeddaan Khairunissa
		Belle of Ireland (ch 1964)	Milesian Belle of The Ball
	Hardiona (FR) (ch 1976)	Hard To Beat (b 1969)	Hardicanute Virtuous
		Mapiona (b 1970)	Tompion Marion Delorme

francs) he fetched as a yearling and his relatively low stud fee for one of his ability of 60,000 francs (October 1st terms). His dam, Hardiona, a winner over ten and a half furlongs, has bred four other winners, but none in the same class as Saint Andrews. Three of them are minor winners by King of Macedon, the other the three-year-old Patty Rose (by Iron Duke), a winner of three races as a two-year-old, including a listed event at Marseilles, as well as a mile-and-a-quarter handicap at Deauville in the latest season. The next three dams Mapiona (a winner over a mile at Cagnes-sur-Mer), Marion Delorme (a thrice-placed maiden) and Fiorenza (a winner of the Prix de la Grotte and placed in the Poule d'Essai des Pouliches and Prix de Diane), have failed to produce a good winner between them. Saint Andrews, a tall, attractive horse, was effective at a mile and a quarter to a mile and a half. He was well suited by give in the ground. He is to stand at the Haras de Victot. *J-M. Beguigne, France.*

SAINT JOACHIM   3 b.c. Thatching 131–Malossol 62 (Gulf Pearl 117) [1988 7m² **91** 7g³ 6.3d⁶ 5v⁴ 7g 1989 6v 5v³ 5m⁵ 5m 5g* 5g⁴ 5m⁴ 5d⁴ 5g 5d³ 6g* 6d* 5g⁶] IR 15,500F, IR 43,000Y: rather leggy colt: half-brother to 3 winners, including 1987 2-y-o 5f winner Caviar Blini (by What A Guest) and 1985 2-y-o 7f winner Ghika (by Star Appeal): dam sister to top-class sprinter Deep Diver and half-sister to Irish 2000 Guineas winner King's Company: won maiden at Bellewstown in July and minor event and handicap at the Curragh in September: 20/1 and bandaged off-fore, fair sixth to Lugana Beach in strongly-run listed race at Newmarket in October: stays 6f: acts on top-of-the-ground and a soft surface: ran moderately in blinkers ninth start. *M. Kauntze, Ireland.*

SAINTLY LAD 7 b.g. Derrylin 115–Saintly Miss 63 (St Paddy 133) [1988 16d 1989 14s 12m 11.7m] strong, chunky gelding: carries condition: modest maiden as 3-y-o: very lightly raced and well beaten subsequently: stays 11f: acts on soft going: usually bandaged. *P. D. Cundell.* —

SAINT NAVARRO 4 ch.f. Raga Navarro (ITY) 119–Saint Motunde 84 (Tyrant (USA)) [1988 6g 5g* 6d 5g 6m⁶ 5f⁴ 6m 5g* 6d⁴ 1989 5f 6f⁶ 6f⁵ 5f* 5m⁴ᵈⁱˢ 5g* 5g* 5f² 5m 5g⁵ 5.6g] rather leggy, plain, close-coupled filly: has a round action: modest performer: won claimer at Chepstow and handicaps at Chester and Pontefract in first half of season: best efforts at 5f: probably acts on any going: wears blinkers: hung left (as she did on reappearance) and disqualified for interference fifth outing: has swished tail. *B. A. McMahon.* 70

SAINT SYSTEMS 3 b.f. Uncle Pokey 116–Fire Mountain 87 (Dragonara Palace (USA) 115) [1988 5m⁴ 5f⁴ 5f⁶ 5g* 5m* 5g⁴ 5g 5g⁴ 5d⁴ 5m 5m 1989 6m 6g 5f 5m 5h 5m³ 6f 5g 5m⁶] angular, sparely-made filly: poor handicapper nowadays, best effort when well-backed third at Warwick: best at 5f on sound surface: below form in blinkers once at 2 yrs: has run creditably for apprentice. *C. J. Hill.* 45

SAINT TRISTAN 5 b.g. Tyrnavos 129–Greyburn 85 (Saintly Song 128) [1988 NR 1989 9f] good-bodied gelding: little worthwhile form in modest company: backward, tailed off in handicap at Redcar in May. *W. W. Haigh.* —

SAIYYAAF 6 b.g. Thatching 131–Nana's Girl 109 (Tin Whistle 128) [1988 9g 1989 7f 8f 10m 8g 10.4m 8f] compact, good-bodied gelding: poor maiden: probably stays 1m: acts on top-of-the-ground: bandaged, trained on reappearance by I. Campbell. *D. W. Chapman.* —

SAJJAYA (USA) 2 ch.f. (Mar 26) Blushing Groom (FR) 131–Lady Cutlass (USA) (Cutlass (USA)) [1989 7f² 7s* 7g⁶] leggy, attractive filly: good walker: fluent mover: fourth foal: half-sister to Umaimah (by Halo), 7f winner at 2 yrs in 1988, and 2 other winners, including 1985 Irish 2-y-o 1m winner Lady of The North (by Northern Baby): dam, 5f to 7f winner in North America, is half-sister to high-class middle-distance performer General Holme: odds on, won 10-runner maiden at Ayr in September by 3 lengths, making most and running on well: respectable sixth of 12 to Negligent in Bottisham Heath Stud Rockfel Stakes at Newmarket following month: will be suited by 1m. *J. L. Dunlop.* 84

SAKKBAH 3 b.f. Wassl 125–Silojoka 95 (Home Guard (USA) 129) [1988 NR 1989 7d 6s 5h⁶ 6m⁴ 5m] quite good-topped filly: moderate walker and mover: third foal: closely related to 1m to 11.5f winner Yamrah (by Milford): dam sprinting daughter of half-sister to very smart Golden Horus: plating-class maiden: sweating, ran moderately in apprentice handicap final start: should be suited by further than 5f: form only on top-of-the-ground: sold 1,150 gns Newmarket Autumn Sales. *C. J. Benstead.* 52

SAKURA DANCER 2 ch.f. (Apr 27) Viking (USA)–Serenesse (Habat 127) [1989 5h⁶ 6g⁶ 6f⁵ 5g] 3,500Y: compact filly: moderate walker: second foal: half-sister to 3-y-o 1¼m winner Towny Boy (by Camden Town): dam listed winner in Italy: poor form in quite modest company. *J. M. Bradley.* 32

SALADAN KNIGHT 4 b.g. Dalsaan 125–Exciting Times (Windjammer (USA)) [1988 5g⁴ 5m* 5m* 5m⁴ 5g 5f 1989 5m 5f a5g* a6g*] leggy, lengthy gelding: moderate mover: neck winner of handicaps at Southwell in December: effective at 5f and 6f: best on a sound surface: slowly away second start: tends to wander, but has run well for apprentice: often on toes. *J. G. FitzGerald.* 92

SALAR'S SPIRIT 3 ch.c. Salmon Leap (USA) 131–Indigine (USA) 71 (Raise A Native) [1988 NR 1989 10.2g 10g] IR 15,000Y: robust colt: fourth foal: closely related to fair 7f to 1m winner Below Zero (by Northfields) and half-brother to 7f winner In Glory (by Dalsaan): dam lightly-raced 2-y-o 6f winner: backward and never dangerous in summer maidens, showing signs of ability in £5,700 contest at Newmarket final start: sold to join C. C. Elsey 2,100 gns Newmarket Autumn Sales. *W. Jarvis.* —

SALAX (USA) 4 b.g. Monteverdi 129–Salacious (Sallust 134) [1988 5m⁴ 5g 6d⁶ 6s 1989 6f] workmanlike gelding: poor maiden: best effort on debut at 3 yrs: dead. *M. H. Easterby.* —

SALESMAN 2 b.c. (Mar 22) Starch Reduced 112–Miss Purchase 62 (Sterling Bay (SWE)) [1989 5g] leggy colt: second reported foal: dam plating-class maiden on flat —

781

won over hurdles: slowly away and always behind in 17-runner maiden at Leicester in April. *B. Palling.*

SALINE 4 ch.f. Sallust 134–Silk Rein 107 (Shantung 132) [1988 8s⁴ 10f 11.5m⁵ 50 14g⁵ 12m 1989 17.1f 10m⁴ 11g 10.8m² 10f² 10.4m⁵ 12g⁶] angular, workmanlike filly: moderate mover: plating-class maiden: best at 1¼m: acts on firm going: blinkered twice at 3 yrs and on last 4 starts: had tongue tied down second outing: slowly away on fourth and sixth: bought 3,100 gns Doncaster April Sales. *J. Mackie.*

SALLY DELIGHT 3 b.f. Homing 130–Noorina (Royal And Regal (USA)) [1988 — NR 1989 10g 10g 10g] rangy filly: moderate mover: third foal: half-sister to 5f to 8.2f winner Urray On Harry (by Anfield): dam never ran: behind all starts, including in seller: trained first 2 by J. Mackie. *D. J. Wintle.*

SALLY FORTH 3 b.g. Sallust 134–Sally Knox (Busted 134) [1988 6m⁴ 6g 7g 59 1989 8.5g 8g³ 8m²] angular, deep-girthed gelding: quite modest maiden: placed, running well and staying on in good style, in Newmarket claimers in the summer: claimed to join J. Bostock £10,561 after last of them: will stay further: acts on top-of-the-ground. *G. A. Pritchard-Gordon.*

SALLY ROUS 2 br.f. (Mar 10) Rousillon (USA) 133–Sassalya (Sassafras (FR) 78 P 135) [1989 6g*] leggy, workmanlike filly: has scope: eighth foal: half-sister to 3-y-o 10.4f winner Krisalya (by Kris) and 4 other winners, including very useful middle-distance stayer Chauve Souris (by Beldale Flutter), useful middle-distance performer Assemblyman (by General Assembly) and useful 7f to 1¼m performer Bold Indian (by Bold Lad, IRE): dam useful Irish 7f and 1¼m winner: 9/2 but bit backward, won 12-runner maiden at Leicester in November by 2 lengths, quickening in good style around 1f out having been slowly away and green: will stay at least 1m: sure to improve considerably. *G. Wragg.*

SALLY SQUASH (USA) 3 ch.f. Fit To Fight (USA)–On Second Thought — (USA) (Raise A Native) [1988 5.8d² 6f³ 6f* 6g* 1989 7.6f 9.2f] rather unfurnished filly: modest winner at 2 yrs: soundly beaten facing stiff tasks in handicaps as 3-y-o: should be suited by 7f+: acts on firm ground and a soft surface. *R. V. Smyth.*

SALLY'S SON 3 b.c. Beldale Flutter (USA) 130–Sally Chase 101 (Sallust 134) 59 [1988 6m 1989 6f⁵ 7f 5.1m⁴ 6m a6g a6g⁴ a7g⁴] strong, good-bodied colt: moderate walker: quite modest form at best: fair fourth in December handicaps at Lingfield, visored first time, blinkered second: should stay 7f: slowly away second start. *W. A. O'Gorman.*

SALLYS WON 5 b.g. Free State 125–Arbatina (Sallust 134) [1988 NR 1989 56 10.2g² 10g³] rangy gelding: moderate mover: plating-class maiden: placed in amateurs handicap at Doncaster (sweating and carrying considerable overweight) and apprentice event at Brighton (taking keen hold) in first weeks of season: stays 1¼m. *R. Curtis.*

SALMAN (USA) 3 b.c. Nain Bleu (FR)–H M S Pellinore (USA) (King Pellinore 87 (USA)) [1988 6f³ 7d 6g² 7g* 1989 8.2m 8.5f² 8m*] strong, good-topped colt: fair performer: won 14-runner minor event at Edinburgh in October: stays 8.5f: acts on firm ground. *S. G. Norton.*

SALMIYA 2 b.f. (May 10) Superlative 118–The Firebird (Busted 134) [1989 7m⁶ 58 7m] 10,000Y: sturdy filly: has scope: first live foal: dam ran twice: plating-class form in summer maidens at Newmarket and Yarmouth: sent to J. Czerpak. *G. A. Huffer.*

SALMONID 3 ch.c. Salmon Leap (USA) 131–Persian Polly 99 (Persian Bold 123) 80 [1988 6s⁶ 7s² 1989 10s⁶ 10g⁴ 7.6f⁵ 8f 7f² 10g* 10g*] sturdy, lengthy colt: carries plenty of condition: modest handicapper: always close up and led over 3f out when winning amateurs events at Salisbury (threw rider in preliminaries) and Ayr (moderately-run race) in July: suited by 1¼m and an easy surface. *P. F. I. Cole.*

SALMON PRINCE 3 ch.g. Salmon Leap (USA) 131–Princesse Anglaise — (Crepello 136) [1988 7m 8.2d⁵ 1989 12d⁴ 12d⁵ 10g] workmanlike gelding: quite modest maiden: not entirely discredited when fifth in Goodwood handicap in September: ran poorly in apprentice handicap 3 weeks later: probably stays 1½m: best effort on a soft surface: trained reappearance by R. Akehurst. *Miss B. Sanders.*

SALMON SPARKLE 2 ch.c. (Mar 23) Salmon Leap (USA) 131–Sparkling Air 66 (Malinowski (USA) 123) [1989 a7g⁶ a8g⁴] leggy colt: third foal: brother to a winner in Sweden: dam, unplaced in 5 starts in Ireland, is half-sister to Sparkler: under 4 lengths fourth of 11 to Blake's Treasure, better effort in December maidens at Lingfield: will probably stay further. *P. T. Walwyn.*

SALOONATIC (USA) 2 b.c. (Mar 21) Do Tell George (USA)–Spiked Dancer — (USA) (Levee Dancer (USA)) [1989 5m] angular colt: fourth reported foal: brother to a winner at around 1m in USA and half-brother to another winner: dam ran 3 times: sire won minor 1m stakes: last of 8, virtually pulled up final 1f, in maiden at Newcastle in July: dead. *S. G. Norton.*

SALRAMIC   2 ch.g. (Apr 7) Salmon Leap (USA) 131–Ceramic (USA) (Raja Baba   47 (USA)) [1989 7m 7m³ 7g 7m 10.6d 7g] 2,600Y: leggy, angular gelding: first foal: dam, ran once in Ireland, is granddaughter of top-class 4.5f to 9f winner Furl Sail: modest plater: best effort third in Yarmouth claimer: sold privately, probably to race in Scandinavia, 1,000 gns Doncaster November Sales. *R. Guest.*

SALSABIL   2 b.f. (Jan 18) Sadler's Wells (USA) 132–Flame of Tara 124 **116 p** (Artaius (USA) 129) [1989 6f* 7m² 8g*]

With Ashayer and now Salsabil the owner-trainer-jockey combination of Hamdan Al-Maktoum, John Dunlop and Willie Carson have won the Prix Marcel Boussac, France's premier test for two-year-old fillies, twice in the last three years. Unfortunately for her connections the 1988 Guineas and Oaks came and went without Ashayer, and although she was returned to France to win a Group 3 race later on it's fair to say that on the whole she didn't quite live up to the promise of her win in the Boussac. However, it's unlikely the latter remark will be applicable to Salsabil at the end of her second season. Salsabil's emphatic defeat of a field comprising fourteen other winners in the latest running of the Boussac suggests she has all the makings of a very good three-year-old. Salsabil made her debut in a maiden event at Nottingham in September with quite a reputation to live up to. She was sent off at odds on, and the way she quickened to draw clear of eleven opponents was the highlight of an otherwise routine Monday card. Salsabil was also odds on for a graduation race at Newbury later in the month where, after making most, she couldn't quite produce enough to fend off the sustained challenge thrown down by Free At Last, going down by a short head with the rest well strung out. Defeat in such a race—albeit a valuable one by the narrowest of margins—is seldom the prelude to victory in Group 1 company. Nevertheless, the Newbury form received a boost when Free At Last came out to win the Somerville Tattersall Stakes at Newmarket two days prior to the Boussac, and Salsabil was the subject of plenty of support at Longchamp, eventually starting at 13/2. The Fabre-trained Qirmazi, runner-up behind Machiavellian in the Prix Morny and the Prix de la Salamandre, headed the market on 17/10 coupled with Sheikh Mohammed's other runner, Yarmouth winner Wajna, who'd been supplemented for the Boussac on the strength of recent homework; Rive du Sud, a Nureyev filly who'd won a minor event over course and distance on her debut, came next on 6/1, followed by Salsabil, Qirmazi's stable-companion Houseproud, a daughter of Riverman who'd beaten the useful Robin des Bois over five and a half furlongs at Evry in September, and

Prix Marcel Boussac, Longchamp—first of three Group 1 pattern-race victories for British-trained horses on Arc day.
Salsabil wins decisively from Houseproud (centre),
Alchi (rails), Zinarelle (No. 14), Qirmazi and Wajna

the Prix d'Aumale winner Mackla. The pace set by Cauthen on Wajna was much stronger than is often seen in the important French races, and there was soon at least a dozen lengths between first and last. Wajna still held the lead early in the straight, but it was clear she was almost at full stretch to do so. Salsabil, on the other hand, had travelled smoothly just behind the leaders from the start. She took a few strides to respond once asked to accelerate, then with a furlong and a half to run produced a decisive burst of speed, in doing so securing a two-length advantage which she sustained despite tending to run a shade lazily in front. Houseproud kept on strongly to finish an excellent second, narrowly in front of the highly-rated Alchi, who raced prominently throughout and battled on in the manner of one who'll be very well suited by a longer trip at three. Qirmazi, never nearer, was disappointing in fifth; Wajna in sixth ran a fine race for one so inexperienced, but the two other English-trained runners Palace Street and Native Guile finished soundly beaten. In post-race interviews Dunlop said that he thought Salsabil's improvement was due at least in part to being held up, while Carson stated that he thought the filly also well served by the slightly easier surface. Doubtless the extra furlong played its part. With only three runs behind her Salsabil is almost certainly capable of improving again; she looks to hold sound each-way credentials for the General Accident One Thousand Guineas.

Along with the hitherto-unraced South Shore (by Caerleon out of Shore Line), Salsabil was the highest-priced filly sold at the Highflyer Sale in 1988. The pair fetched 440,000 guineas each, and even in the unlikely event of her failing to win another race Sheikh Hamdan will surely consider Salsabil worth every penny. Sadler's Wells continues to give the impression he's heading for the top as a stallion. In the latest season only Blushing Groom's progeny won more money in Great Britain and Ireland; only Caerleon and Taufan sired the winners of more races—an excellent feat considering Sadler's Wells had just two crops representing him—and all this was achieved despite the fact that the dual classic winner Old Vic was missing through injury for half the season and the admirable Prince of Dance had to be put down due to cancer soon after the Derby. Naturally, the highly promising start Sadler's Wells has made to his stud career has also been reflected in the sales ring. His sons and daughters continued to be extremely popular in 1989, and besides Salsabil the likes of Old Vic, Dolpour, Braashee, Scenic and the good French colt In The Wings all promise to advertise his prowess further in the coming season. Salsabil didn't attract such interest at the sales solely because of her sire. Her dam Flame of Tara, much the best runner sired by the largely disappointing stallion Artaius, was a good-class Irish filly, winning eight times from six furlongs to a mile and a half and running a tremendous race to finish a close third, promoted to second, in Cormorant Wood's Champion Stakes. Although it's early days Flame of Tara looks all set to be just as successful at stud as she was on the track. Salsabil is her second foal. Her first, Nearctic Flame, also by Sadler's Wells, showed very useful form over middle distances for Stoute in the latest season; her third, a colt from the first crop sired by Last Tycoon, went to the Shadwell Estates' bid of 440,000 guineas at the latest Irish National Yearling Sale, a figure bettered at the same sale only by the Sadler's Wells colt out of Forlene. Further back in the pedigree, Salsabil's second dam Welsh Flame, a useful miler, is also the grandam of the high-class stayer Kneller, while the third and fourth dams, Electric Flash and Lightning, are half-sisters to the Derby winner Parthia and the top-notch middle-distance stayer Alcide respectively.

Salsabil is a lightly-made, attractive filly, a fluent mover with a rather quick action. She's also a free-running sort, and it could be that this will count against her if and when she's tried over longer distances. However, on pedigree there's little doubt that Salsabil will stay beyond a mile; if she stays a mile and a half she looks set to become a leading candidate for the Gold Seal Oaks. *J. L. Dunlop.*

SALTESSA 2 b.f. (Mar 1) Thatching 131–Bebe Altesse (GER) (Alpenkonig (GER)) [1989 6h* 5g³ 6f² 7.3v] 72,000Y: workmanlike, rather angular filly: shows a free, rather round action: first reported foal: dam, winner in Germany, is out of good German mare Bebe Girl: won 5-runner maiden at Brighton in June: stays 6f: races keenly: sold 15,000 gns Newmarket December Sales. *B. Hanbury.*   78

SALUTI TUTTI 3 b.f. Trojan Fen 118–Moat (USA) (Sir Ivor 135) [1988 6m⁵ 1989 7s⁵ 5d² 5g² 6g⁵ 6m⁴ 6m² 8.3m 6f²] compact, workmanlike filly: modest maiden: led 5f and wandered under pressure when running creditably in handicap final start (July): best at sprint distances: acts on firm ground. *W. A. O'Gorman.*   77

SAMARZANA (USA) 3 b.f. Blushing Groom (FR) 131–Samata (FR) (Rheffic (FR) 129) [1988 7g 1989 10f² 9m³ 10m³ 12.5m* 12g³ 10g⁶] sparely-made filly: has a rather round action: fairly useful performer: easily landed odds in maiden at Wolverhampton in August: good third at Goodwood, easily better effort in handicaps after: will stay further than 1½m: acts on top-of-the-ground. *M. R. Stoute.*   95

SAMAZA (USA) 3 ch.f. Arctic Tern (USA) 126–Itsamaza (USA) (Limit To Reason (USA)) [1988 7m* 7d⁴ 1989 10f] lengthy, good-quartered, attractive filly: fairly useful at 2 yrs, making all in £8,500 event at Newbury and fourth in Group 3 event (spoiling chance by pulling hard and becoming unbalanced 1f out) at Newmarket: 4/1, well-beaten last of 7 in listed race at Newbury in May, only start in 1989: bred to stay 1¼m. *J. Tree.*   —

SAM COCKTAIL 3 ch.c. Be My Guest (USA) 126–Marylove (Kalydon 122) [1988 NR 1989 8g 8m³ 8m 8f⁶ 8f³ 9.2m³ 12m* 12.2g⁴ 12.5f² 12g⁴ᵈⁱˢ] IR 32,000Y: sparely-made, angular colt: has a quick action: brother to 1983 2-y-o 7f winner Petrodollar and half-brother to 1985 2-y-o 5f winner Blessed Aisle (by Godswalk) and winners in Australia by Solinus and Home Guard: dam, Irish middle-distance winner, is closely related to very smart Ksar: fair form: ridden by 7-lb claimer, won claimer at Thirsk in September: ran creditably after but disqualified in apprentice handicap final start after veering left 2f out: stays 1½m: acts on firm ground: has wandered under pressure and found little: not one to trust implicitly. *L. M. Cumani.*   84

SAMHAAN 7 ch.h. Niniski (USA) 125–Mai Pussy 91 (Realm 129) [1988 9d 10d 11f³ 11.1m³ 10f* 12f 10m 10g³ 10m⁵ 10.2g 11.7m 10.5f⁴ 10v³ 11s 1989 10f⁵ 10m⁶ 10m⁵ 11.5g 12f³] lengthy horse: has a quick action: modest handicapper: needs at least 1m and stays 11f: well suited by top-of-the-ground: wears blinkers or visor: very good mount for inexperienced rider. *M. McCormack.*   72

SAMHOI (USA) 3 b.c. Nijinsky (CAN) 138–Strictly Raised (USA) (Raise A Native) [1988 8s⁴ 1989 10g⁵ 9f4] lengthy, leggy colt: has a quick action: fair form: fifth in £6,200 event at Newmarket in May, easily better effort as 3-y-o: bit edgy and taken very quietly to post before minor event 5½ months later: stays 1¼m: sold 11,000 gns Newmarket Autumn Sales. *M. R. Stoute.*   84

SAMLEON 5 gr.g. Kind of Hush 118–Perlesse 88 (Bold Lad (USA)) [1988 5s⁴ 6d⁶ 5s* 5g 5d 1989 5f] moderate mover: quite modest winner (apprentice ridden) as 4-y-o: bandaged, ran badly in claimer at Wolverhampton in May: stays 6f: well suited by an easy surface: blinkered once: sold 1,100 gns Ascot September Sales: has looked ungenuine. *K. G. Wingrove.*   — §

SAMMY'S STAR 3 gr.g. Comedy Star (USA) 121–Sammy Bear 69 (Rupert Bear 105) [1988 5f 5g 6d 6d⁶ 1989 6m 5m 7.5m] leggy, close-coupled gelding: of little account: sold 1,500 gns Doncaster September Sales. *W. Bentley.*   —

SAMOAAN CHARGER 3 b.g. Aragon 118–Sea Charm 70 (Julio Mariner 127) [1988 6g 7.5m⁵ 8m 7g 10d 1989 8g² 10g 10.2h a10g a14g] sturdy gelding: quite modest performer: ran well in handicap on reappearance, poorly after: should stay 1¼m: likely to prove best with strong handling: bandaged near-hind at 2 yrs: trained first 3 outings by R. J. R. Williams. *R. Voorspuy.*   62

SAMOAN (USA) 3 b.c. Diesis 133–Pago Dancer (USA) (Pago Pago) [1988 7f* 7d* 8g² 7d⁶ 1989 7d⁶ 7m² 8m* 8m⁴] good-topped, lengthy colt: very useful performer: 25/1, best effort when 4 lengths fourth of 5 to Distant Relative in Beefeater Gin Celebration Mile at Goodwood in August, always close up and keeping on well: 9/4 on, won minor event at Newcastle in June by a neck, pushed out   113

vigorously: stays 1m: best form on a sound surface: reportedly sold to Allen Paulson to race in USA. *H. R. A. Cecil.*

SAMSON-AGONISTES 3 b.c. Bold Fort 100–Hello Cuddles 99 (He Loves Me 120) [1988 5d³ 5g⁴ 5f 5f⁴ 5g⁵ 5s 5g* 5d 5g⁴ 5g⁵ 5d 1989 5.8m 5f⁵ 5m² 6m 5.1m 5m 5.8h 5g 7.6m⁵ 8m] leggy colt: poor walker and mover: quite modest performer: has run in seller: below form after third outing: stays 7.5f: acts on top-of-the-ground. *B. Preece.* **53**

SAMSOVA 2 b.f. (Mar 24) Shareef Dancer (USA) 135–Deadly Serious (USA) 113 (Queen's Hussar 124) [1989 7m³ 7m³] 38,000F: workmanlike filly: fifth living foal: half-sister to 3-y-o Stormy Reef (by Mill Reef) and 9f winner Sparkling Fire (by Sparkler): dam, daughter of very smart Joking Apart, won Galtres Stakes: third, keeping on strongly, in £8,200 event at Newbury and maiden at Chepstow in the autumn: will be much better suited by 1m + . *I. A. Balding.* **71**

SAM THE MAN 2 b.g. (Feb 28) Aragon 118–First Temptation (USA) 67 (Mr Leader (USA)) [1989 6f] first foal: dam, maiden on flat suited by test of stamina, won juvenile hurdle: well beaten in 10-runner maiden at Lingfield in October. *Miss B. Sanders.* **—**

SANAWI 2 b.c. (Mar 21) Glenstal (USA) 118–Russeting 76 (Mummy's Pet 125) [1989 6m⁴ 5m⁵ 6m⁵ 6m⁵ a6g] 53,000Y: strong, medium-sized, attractive colt: has a round action: fourth foal: half-brother to 3-y-o 1m winner Fisherman's Croft (by Dunbeath), a prolific winning hurdler: dam, 5f winner at 2 yrs, lightly-raced sister to high-class sprinter Runnett and very useful 1977 2-y-o 5f performer Cala-Vadella: quite modest maiden: ran moderately in nursery at Lingfield final start, first since July: will stay 7f: sold 4,200 gns Doncaster November Sales. *C. J. Benstead.* **63**

SAN CARLOS 7 b.g. Formidable (USA) 125–Omentello 91 (Elopement 125) **45**
[1988 12f 12s 14d* 16m 15.5f² 14d³ 14g⁵ 17.1f² 12f² 16g⁵ 12m 11.7g 12m⁴ 15.5g* 1989
12s⁶ 17.1m⁶ 15.5f 14f⁶ 12h⁴ 12h² 12h³ 16.5f⁶] close-coupled gelding: moderate
mover: modest at his best: effective at 1½m and stayed 17f: acted on any going:
blinkered fourth outing: won for amateur: none too reliable: dead. *A. P. Ingham.*

SAND CASTLE 8 ch.g. Tap On Wood 130–Pacific Sands (Sandford Lad 133) **55**
[1988 10f⁴ 8m⁵ 1989 10m⁶ 12f⁶ 12.4m⁴] compact, well-made gelding: plating-class
handicapper: not seen out after June: stays 1½m: acts on any going: used to wear
blinkers: suitable mount for inexperienced rider: winning hurdler/chaser. *M. J.
Ryan.*

SAND-DOLLAR 6 ch.h. Persian Bold 123–Late Spring 101 (Silly Season 127) **—**
[1988 7f⁴ 8.5m 8f* 8f* 8g³ 8.5m³ 7.6m³ 8m⁴ 1989 8d 8h⁶ 10.6s] leggy, sparely-made
horse: quite modest winner as 5-y-o: lightly raced and well below his best in 1989:
best at 7f or 1m: acts well on firm going: wore crossed noseband first 2 outings:
sweating final one, first for over 4 months: well served by forcing tactics. *J. A. B.
Old.*

SANDFORD SPRINGS (USA) 2 b.f. (Mar 18) Robellino (USA) 127–Tiger **67**
Scout (USA) 86 (Silent Screen (USA)) [1989 6g 7f⁵] medium-sized, quite attractive
filly: third foal: half-sister to 3-y-o Tiger Claw (by Diamond Shoal), a winning
hurdler: dam, 2-y-o 7f winner later winner over further in USA, is daughter of
half-sister to high-class 6f to 8.5f winner Screen King: around 8½ lengths fifth of 7,
never dangerous not knocked about, to Zawahir in maiden at Goodwood in July,
better effort: gave trouble stalls and slowly away on debut. *I. A. Balding.*

SANDHURST LASS 2 ch.f. (May 1) Sandhurst Prince 128–Exmoor Lass (FR) **43 §**
86 (Exbury 138) [1989 5s 5d 5g 7f* 7m⁴ 7.5g 7m⁴ 7f⁶ 6g⁴ 6m 7m⁴ 6g 8.5f⁵ 10.6d 10f]
IR 2,600Y: small, shallow-girthed filly: half-sister to 3-y-o Birmingham's Glory (by
Hays) and a winner in South Africa by Wolver Hollow: dam 2-y-o 7f winner: modest
plater: won at Redcar (no bid) in June when trained by M. W. Easterby: usually ran
moderately afterwards: slowly away twice, and hung badly on 3 occasions: one to
be wary of. *D. Yeoman.*

SANDICLIFFE STAR 3 b.c. High Top 131–Georgina Park 88 (Silly Season **92**
127) [1988 6d⁵ 7m 1989 8.5g* 8.2g 8f* 8m⁴ 8.2d] workmanlike colt: shade
unfurnished: has a rather round action: fairly useful performer: won maiden at
Beverley in May and handicap at Kempton in July: looking very well, ran as though
something amiss in £8,300 handicap final outing: likely to prove best over 7f or 1m:
goes well on firm going. *B. W. Hills.*

SANDITTON PALACE 6 gr.g. Dragonara Palace (USA) 115–Petona **77 d**
(Mummy's Pet 125) [1988 5g 5m 5d⁶ 5f⁵ 5g 5f 5m* 5m⁶ 5g 5s 5f³ 5s 6d* 5m 1989 5g
6f* 6f 6f⁵ 6m 6m⁴ 6g² 6m 7g 6m⁶] tall gelding: carries plenty of condition: fair
handicapper on his day: 20/1-winner at Pontefract in May: effective at 5f and 6f:
unsuited by soft going, acts on any other: visored once at 5 yrs: sweating on
reappearance: sometimes on toes: needs very strong handling: has looked reluctant
and is unreliable. *P. S. Felgate.*

SANDMOOR COTTON 3 b.c. Sayf El Arab (USA) 127–Dog's Bay (Tumble **—**
Wind (USA)) [1988 5m⁵ 5g² 5f² 5m* 5m³ 6m² 5g 5g² 5f⁵ 5f⁵ 1989 5g⁵ 5s⁶ 5d⁵ 5f 6m
6m 6f] neat, good-quartered colt: modest winner at 2 yrs: little form in 1989: stays
6f: possibly unsuited by soft going. *D. W. Chapman.*

SANDMOOR DENIM 2 b.g. (Apr 14) Red Sunset 120–Holernzaye 93 (Sallust **60**
134) [1989 6g² 6h² 6m 5m a6g] 11,500Y: close-coupled gelding: sixth foal: brother to
7.5f (in Ireland) and 9f winner Eye In The Sky, and half-brother to 3-y-o Sky
Watcher (by Skyliner) and a winner abroad by Busted: dam, half-sister to Rheingold,
won over 5f and 6f at 2 yrs: quite modest maiden: stays 6f: blinkered third (ran
freely) and fourth starts: trained first 4 outings by M. H. Easterby. *S. R. Bowring.*

SANDMOOR JACQUARD 2 ch.c. (Feb 10) Noalto 120–Grand Opera 92 (Great **62**
Nephew 126) [1989 5d⁴ 6m 5f³ 7g 6g⁵ 7m⁵ 7f² 6g* 6g³ 7m 6g] 7,600Y: workmanlike
colt: fifth foal: half-brother to fair 1¼m performer Operatic Score (by Kind of Hush),
also successful hurdler, and modest 1984 2-y-o 7f winner Dame Nellie (by
Dominion): dam 7f winner at 2 yrs: quite modest performer: won nursery at
Catterick in August: stays 7f: blinkered fifth outing and last 5: lazy type, suited by
strong handling. *M. H. Easterby.*

SANDS OF TIME 5 ch.g. Dance In Time (CAN)–Sarah Siddons (Reform 132) **—**
[1988 NR 1989 7f] compact, sturdy gelding: winning plater at 2 yrs: little subsequent

worthwhile form: best form at 6f: acts on firm going: sold 725 gns Ascot December Sales. *D. R. Tucker.*

SANDSUMO 2 ch.g. (Apr 16) Sandhurst Prince 128–Mursuma (Rarity 129) [1989 5m 6m 7m 5m 6f] IR 4,200Y, 3,600 2-y-o: lengthy, unfurnished gelding: moderate mover: first foal: dam, Irish 1m winner from only 3 starts, half-sister to high-class hurdler Galmoy: poor maiden: best form at 7f. *M. H. Tompkins.* 47

SANDSWALLOW 3 ch.c. Sandhurst Prince 128–La Calera (GER) (Caracol (FR)) [1988 6f 6d4 7.5f 8f 1989 11m] leggy, rather angular colt: plating-class maiden in 1988: last in handicap in May, only start as 3-y-o: should stay beyond 6f: possibly unsuited by top-of-the-ground: hung left and ran wide once at 2 yrs. *C. Tinkler.* —

SAN FELICE (USA) 2 b.c. (Mar 16) Forli (ARG)–Plutomania (USA) (Groton) [1989 5.1m4 6f2 6m3] 40,000Y: medium-sized colt: has scope: half-brother to several minor winners in North America, one in minor stakes: dam showed little ability: modest performer: placed in July in maiden (odds on) at Redcar and £11,800 event (visored) at Salisbury: stays 6f. *W. Hastings-Bass.* 79

SAN GIOVANNI 4 br.f. Strong Gale 116–Simmay (Simbir 130) [1988 5g 7f 12m 9m 10f6 13f2 12m3 12d2 16g5 1989 14.8d6] lengthy, sparely-made filly: has a quick action: quite modest maiden at best: co-favourite, ran poorly in handicap at Warwick in May: stays 13f: acts on firm going and a soft surface. *R. Akehurst.* —

SANGLAMORE (USA) 2 ch.c. (Mar 1) Sharpen Up 127–Ballinderry 112 (Irish River (FR) 131) [1989 8g2] good-bodied colt: has scope: first foal: dam, Ribblesdale winner, is half-sister to French Derby third Sharpman (by Sharpen Up) and very smart French middle-distance winner Lydian: 5/1, 3 lengths second of 17 to Lover's Moon in maiden at Leicester in November, disputing lead until 1f out and weakening and eased close home: sure to improve, and win a race. *J. Tree.* 84 p

SAN GRECO 2 b.g. (Mar 4) Mandrake Major 122–Rich Lass (Broxted 120) [1989 6f3 7g2] 7,800Y: quite attractive, close-coupled gelding: second foal: half-brother to fairly useful 1987 2-y-o 6f winner Fortinbras (by Junius): dam poor daughter of half-sister to smart miler Richboy: favourite, hung left under pressure when beaten head in 20-runner maiden auction event at Doncaster in June: subsequently gelded. *J. W. Watts.* 76

SAN PIER NICETO 2 b.c. (Jan 23) Norwick (USA) 120–Langton Herring (Nearly A Hand 115) [1989 7m6 7g3 6m a8g* a8g* a7g2] 6,400F, 5,800Y: third foal: half-brother to quite moderate 1987 2-y-o 5f winner Sleep Easy (by Ballacashtal): dam unraced half-sister to very useful sprinter Sylvan Barbarosa: smallish, lengthy colt: moderate walker: progressive colt: successful in maiden and a nursery (by ¾ length from Bardolph, pair clear) at Lingfield in November: creditable second of 8 to Corrin Hill in nursery there final start: will stay 1¼m. *R. Boss.* 84

SAN ROQUE 4 b.g. Aragon 118–Arch Sculptress 85 (Arch Sculptor 123) [1988 7d 7.6g 8m 7g 8g* 8f* 9d 8s 1989 10s5 8f 9.2f5 8.2f 8m* 8.2g3 8m4 8m5 10.2f* 10.6m] close-coupled, angular gelding: moderate walker: has a quick action: modest handicapper: won at Chepstow in July and Bath in September: seems suited by 1¼m: acts on firm going and is unsuited by soft surface: blinkered fourth outing: has won for apprentice, but has looked not the easiest of rides: sold to join D. Morley 13,500 gns Newmarket Autumn Sales. *J. L. Dunlop.* 75

SANSOOL 3 b.g. Dominion 123–Young Diana (Young Generation 129) [1988 7m 8s 7g 1989 12h 12h3 11.5g 11.7h3] small, good-bodied gelding: plating-class maiden: swished tail under pressure on reappearance: stays 1½m: acts on hard going: sold 3,200 gns Newmarket September Sales: resold 3,000 gns Doncaster November Sales. *N. A. Callaghan.* 58

SANSSONG 2 ch.f. (Feb 3) Song 132–Saniette (Crystal Palace (FR) 132) [1989 6g 6m4 7f3] rather unfurnished filly: has scope: second foal: sister to unreliable 3-y-o 13.1f winner Shoe Tapper: dam ran once in France: plating-class maiden: third of 28 to Orchard Court in seller at Redcar in October: will stay further: sold 1,250 gns Ascot October Sales. *Lord John FitzGerald.* 52

SANTAC 4 b.g. Tachypous 128–Sandy Keerie (Sandy Creek 123) [1988 9g 10g5 12f2 12f5 12.3s5 17g 13.8f6 1989 12.5f] good-bodied, workmanlike gelding: moderate mover: poor maiden: should stay beyond 1¾m: best form on top-of-the-ground. *D. McCain.* —

SANTA TECLA 3 ch.c. Habitat 134–San Salvador (GER) (Klairon 131) [1988 6g2 6f4 6m4 1989 8v 7.6m2 8m3 8m* 8f2 9m* 9f2 8g4] rather leggy colt: has fluent action: made virtually all to win apprentice maiden (odds on) at Warwick in July and minor event at Wolverhampton in August: probably set too strong a pace in apprentice contest penultimate start: stays 9f: acts on any going: goes well with 93 forcing tactics: found nothing off bridle fifth start and hung left seventh: probably best with strong handling. *B. W. Hills.*

SANTELLA BOBKES (USA) 4 b.c. Solford (USA) 127–Ambiente (USA) **86** (Tentam (USA)) [1988 12g² 12m 12m³ 12s² 12d* 1989 12m 20f² 19f⁵ 18m*] good-topped colt: fair handicapper: favourite, well ridden by G. Starkey when winning at Ripon in August by 4 lengths: ran creditably earlier when second to stable-companion Arizelos in Ascot Stakes (Handicap) at Royal Ascot and fifth to Late Cut in Pimm's Goodwood Stakes (Handicap): suited by extreme distances: acts on any going: blinkered last 3 outings: has won for amateur: suited by forcing tactics: very useful winning hurdler. *G. Harwood.*

SANTELLA BOY 7 b.h. Sparkler 130–Hors Serie (USA) 103 (Vaguely Noble **—** 140) [1988 NR 1989 11.7g 12h 14g] quite attractive, close-coupled horse: turns near-fore in: moderate walker and mover: soundly beaten in handicaps in summer: stays 2m: acts on top-of-the-ground and soft going: bandaged last 2 starts. *J. R. Jenkins.*

SANTELLA PAL (USA) 8 b.g. Effervescing (USA)–Hempens Pal (USA) **—** (Hempen) [1988 9f 12f³ 8g² 10m 1989 12f] workmanlike gelding: has been operated on for wind infirmity: poor handicapper: stays 1½m: acts on hard going and a soft surface: suitable mount for inexperienced rider: winning hurdler. *D. R. C. Elsworth.*

SAO PAULO (USA) 3 ch.c. El Gran Senor (USA) 136–Millingdale Lillie 119 **87 d** (Tumble Wind (USA)) [1988 6d 6m⁴ 1989 10g⁶ 10f² 10g² 10.2g⁵ 10.4m² 9.2m⁴ a12g⁴ a10g⁴] rangy colt: has a quick action: fair maiden: second at Lingfield and Epsom second and third starts: ran moderately after, sweating and edgy first 3 occasions: stays 1¼m: acts on firm going: found little off bridle sixth outing: sold out of B. Hills's stable 6,200 gns Newmarket Autumn Sales after sixth. *C. N. Allen.*

SAPIENCE 3 ch.c. Niniski (USA) 125–Claretta (USA) 82 (Roberto (USA) **117** 131) [1988 5g⁴ 7d* 8.5m* 8s 1989 12m² 12f 14f* 14.6s² 16g² 15.5g⁶]
It went to the last possible opportunity before the North sent out its first placed horse in a British classic in the 'eighties, Jimmy FitzGerald's Sapience finishing second in the St Leger. Though far more sparingly campaigned than the North's last St Leger winner Peleid who'd run nine times before his triumph in 1973, Sapience took a similar route (to Ayr, though, not Doncaster) to the final classic comprising the King George V Stakes at Royal Ascot and the Tote Ebor at York. Having shown fairly useful form in winning a maiden at Chester and a minor event at Epsom as a two-year-old, Sapience had just one run before Royal Ascot, not given a hard race in going down by a neck to Northants in a minor contest at Beverley. Two weeks later the two of them were in opposition again in the King George V Handicap and this time they were quickly at the wrong end of the field as Northants ran one of his moodiest races while Sapience, some way ahead of him but at least a dozen lengths behind the leaders, couldn't improve his position at the back of the main body of runners having been steadied at the start. The way Sapience stayed on in the straight to finish eighth behind Carlingford suggested a mile and three quarters would suit him better and, with early offers of 33/1 quickly taken, an Ebor gamble gathered force. From a stable particularly adept in preparing horses for the big races, on a handicap mark 15 lb lower than at the start of the season and with Pat Eddery booked to ride, it wasn't surprising that Sapience captured the imagination of the betting public. Lightly raced three-year-olds had provided three of the past five Ebor winners and in 1989 they provided three of the first four finishers. Horn Dance, favourite at the off after Sapience had headed the morning betting, was the definitive lightly-raced animal having won a Newmarket maiden on his two-year-old debut and not been seen out since. Together with the second favourite, the Magnet Cup runner-up Afriyd, he and Sapience were kept close to the pace from the start. Afriyd was the first to go for home in the straight but with Horn Dance quickly under pressure it was Sapience who came with a steady run to lead at the two-furlong marker. 50/1-shot Bush Hill's sustained challenge proved the most dangerous but Sapience held him by half a length, with Horn Dance third and Afriyd fourth. It was an improved effort after which Sapience was kept to pattern company and progressed again. In a weakened field for the St Leger at Ayr he was a 15/1-chance with only the ex-French handicapper Blazing Touch and pacemaker Skisurf at longer odds. The Bill Watts-trained Abbeydale had

*Tote Ebor (Handicap), York — improving three-year-old Sapience (noseband)
holds on from 50/1-shot Bush Hill*

been the last northern horse to be placed in a British classic when she ran One
In A Million to a length and a half in the 1979 One Thousand Guineas. In the
1989 St Leger nothing held a candle to Michelozzo but Sapience finished
closest (at eight lengths) and gave a really game display under his young
stable jockey Fallon who'd put him in the race with every chance until
Michelozzo was given the office two furlongs out. Roseate Tern was half a
length further back in third. Sapience's next start, in the Jockey Club Cup at
Newmarket two weeks later, saw an equally creditable performance but he
almost certainly reached the limits of his stamina, for having led over three
furlongs out looking the likely winner, he'd been headed again by Weld at the
furlong pole and was beaten a length and a half. Over a marginally shorter trip
in the Prix Royal-Oak at Longchamp, Sapience's strenuous autumn seemed to
have got the better of him and he finished a below-par sixth, over ten lengths
behind Top Sunrise.

		Niniski (USA) (b 1976)	Nijinsky (b 1967)	Northern Dancer Flaming Page
Sapience (ch.c. 1986)			Virginia Hills (b 1971)	Tom Rolfe Ridin' Easy
		Claretta (USA) (ch 1976)	Roberto (b 1969)	Hail To Reason Bramalea
			Clarina (ch 1969)	Klairon Athanasia

If confirmation were needed that Sapience would stay a mile and three
quarters after Royal Ascot then plenty of encouragement could be gleaned
from the record of his sire Niniski who was third to Son of Love in the St Leger
before going on to win the Irish version (by ten lengths) and the Royal-Oak.
After Kala Dancer and Petoski in his first crop, Niniski's subsequent offspring
might be described as somewhat disappointing in quality terms but one thing
he definitely has passed on is stamina. Minster Son, Sergeyevich and Princess
Sobieska are testament to that. The dam's family's greatest successes
hitherto had all come abroad. For Claretta's previous four foals it's a case of
only successes; Autolycus (by Bold Lad) didn't cut much ice here before
winning four times in Belgium and Bluebell Copse (by Formidable) won in
Jersey in 1988. Two foals by Thatching died before they could be put into
training. Claretta won a seven-furlong maiden race at Brighton as a two-
year-old but didn't progress. She's out of the dual Irish mile-and-a-half winner
Clarina and is half-sister to two useful performers in Claddagh and Rosananti.
Claddagh was a mile-and-a-quarter handicapper here before winning the

790

Stockholm Cup as a five-year-old while Rosananti's best efforts probably came in winning the Premio Regina Elena then finishing second in the Oaks d'Italia and third to Swiftfoot in the Irish Oaks.

Sapience was bought for 26,000 guineas as a foal and owned by the Marquesa de Moratalla until another of FitzGerald's patrons purchased him after the Jockey Club Cup. He will be a difficult horse to place as a four-year-old though, as he's clearly better at a mile and three quarters than a mile and a half but, as Weld showed, he isn't going to prove suited by an extreme test of stamina. Ground conditions will be less problematical as he acts on any. A leggy, rather angular colt, Sapience doesn't carry much condition. He looked very well at York and Ayr and, all in all, is a credit to his trainer. *J. G. Fitz-Gerald.*

SAPPHO COMET 3 b.c. Habitat 134–Sunbittern 112 (Sea Hawk II 131) [1988 7d⁵ 7d² 6m² 6f⁶ 8g⁵ 1989 8m 7.3m² 7f* 8f³ 7g a7g*] good-quartered, quite attractive colt: good walker: has a rather round action: won maiden at Lingfield (odds on) in October and handicap (staying on really well from a poor position) at Southwell in December: ran poorly penultimate start: should stay 1m: acts on firm going: seems rather moody. *J. L. Dunlop.*   **93**

SARAA-REE (USA) 3 b.f. Caro 133–Star River (FR) (Riverman (USA) 131) [1988 NR 1989 7g* 10.5f⁵ 8m² 8f 6m] 96,000Y: strong, workmanlike filly: has plenty of scope: moderate walker: second foal: sister to French 1m winner Sir Bruce: dam, winner twice at around 9f in French Provinces at 3 yrs, is sister to top-class Irish River: won Newmarket maiden in May: useful performances when fifth in Musidora Stakes at York and second in £7,700 event (pulling hard) at Newbury: 33/1, tailed off   **102**

Sonic Lady Stakes, Newmarket—Saraa-Ree makes a winning debut

Classic Thoroughbreds Plc's "Saratogan"

in Coronation Stakes at Royal Ascot: probably in need of race in £7,900 handicap 3½ months later: may prove best at around 1m: gives strong impression will be suited by an easy surface. *B. Hanbury.*

SARAH CARTER 2 b.f. (May 7) Reesh 117–Second Swallow 55 (My Swallow 134) [1989 5s* 6f³ 6f⁵ 5m a6g⁶] 3,100Y: leggy, useful-looking filly: fifth live foal: dam sprint maiden half-sister to high-class Gold Rod: fair plater: bought in 4,000 gns after winning early-season event at Nottingham: claimed out of J. Berry's stable £10,500 after similar event second start: off course 5 months before running creditably final outing: stays 6f. *R. W. Stubbs.*   **57**

SARAH GEORGINA 2 b.f. (Jan 31) Persian Bold 123–Dance By Night 84 (Northfields (USA)) [1989 5d 6g* 6m⁴ 7g³] workmanlike filly: first foal: dam won twice at 7f at 2 yrs: won 14-runner minor event at Windsor in July by 3 lengths, leading over 1f out and running on well: creditable fourth, staying on, to Pharaoh's Delight in Princess Margaret Stakes at Ascot later in the month, better subsequent effort: should stay 1m. *R. Akehurst.*   **79**

SARAH'S FANTASY 3 b.f. Uncle Pokey 116–Lynsey-Louise (Three Sevens 103) [1988 5f 5g⁵ 7f 8.5f 8m 1989 9f 12f] leggy, lightly-made filly: appears of little account. *M. W. Ellerby.*   **—**

SARATOGAN (USA) 3 ch.c. El Gran Senor (USA) 136–Patia 119 (Don (ITY) 123) [1988 7v² 7d³ 1989 6v* 7s* 8m 8m⁶ 8g⁵] medium-sized, good-quartered colt: good 2-y-o, beaten ½ length in Dewhurst Stakes at Newmarket: landed odds at the Curragh in April in maiden and Group 3 Dermot McCalmont Tetrarch EBF Stakes, in latter beating Sylvan Tempest comfortably by 2 lengths, leading 1f out and tending to carry head high: below form after in 2000 Guineas at Newmarket, Irish   **109**

792

2000 Guineas (blinkered) at the Curragh and Phoenix International Stakes at Phoenix Park: stays 7f: best form on a soft surface: to be trained by G. Jones in California. *M. V. O'Brien, Ireland.*

SARDEGNA 2 b.f. (Apr 11) Pharly (FR) 130–Sandy Island 110 (Mill Reef (USA) 141) [1989 7g*] leggy, quite attractive filly: shade unfurnished: second foal: sister to 3-y-o Scarpanto: dam, closely related to Slip Anchor, won Pretty Polly Stakes and Lancashire Oaks: well-backed favourite but green, won 24-runner maiden at Newmarket in November by ½ length from Narwala, leading 3f out and keeping on well hand ridden: will be well suited by 1m + : sure to improve and win more races. *H. R. A. Cecil.* **90 p**

SARHAN 3 ch.c. Ahonoora 122–Rosserk (Roan Rocket 128) [1988 6d⁴ 6f 1989 8m⁴ 8.5f³ 7f 6f⁵ 6f⁶ 8g 6m 6f 6g⁴ a6g²] rangy, useful-looking colt: has scope: quite modest maiden at best: sold out of P. Walwyn's stable 6,600 gns Newmarket July Sales after fourth start and easily best effort after when second in claimer at Southwell in December: unlikely to stay beyond 8.5f: blinkered eighth outing, visored previous 2: needs strong handling. *G. Blum.* **55**

SARMATARA (USA) 2 gr.f. (Feb 10) Roberto (USA) 131–Samata (FR) (Rheffic (FR) 129) [1989 6g 8.5f³ 8f⁴ 8.2g⁴] medium-sized, close-coupled filly: fifth foal: half-sister to 3-y-o 12.5f winner Samarzana and useful but inconsistent 6f to 1¼m winner Samarid (both by Blushing Groom) and fair 1¾m winner Samatarana (by Alleged): dam very useful middle-distance performer: modest maiden: good fourth to Chou-Chou Royale in nursery at Nottingham in October: one paced: will be better suited by 1¼m + . *M. R. Stoute.* **72**

SARNIA 2 b.g. (May 9) Bold Owl 101–Oceania (Aureole 132) [1989 6m 7f] 3,000F, 5,800Y: workmanlike, plain gelding: brother to poor middle-distance winner Needwood Nymph and half-brother to 1½m winner Mareth Line (by Royal Palace) and 2 minor winners: dam unraced daughter of Coronation Stakes winner Ocean: well beaten in big fields of platers at Redcar in the autumn: sold 2,700 gns Newmarket Autumn Sales. *Sir Mark Prescott.* **—**

SARNIA HOLLOW 3 b.f. Wolver Hollow 126–Northampton (Northfields (USA)) [1988 6m 8.5f⁶ 9g 7g 1989 11.7m 8g 8m 8g] small, leggy filly: moderate mover: plating-class form at best: well beaten, including in seller, as 3-y-o: stays 8.5f: sold 1,050 gns Newmarket Autumn Sales. *M. H. Tompkins.* **—**

SARNIA SOUND 4 ch.g. Music Boy 124–St Pauli Girl 114 (St Paddy 133) [1988 5g 7g⁶ 7g 8.2g³ 8g⁴ 10m 10f⁶ 12f⁵ 12s⁵ 12.2f 8s 6g 1989 8g 10d⁴ 10f³ 10m 10. 1m² 10g⁶ 13f³] lengthy, angular gelding: has a quick action: poor maiden: stays 13f: acts on firm going and a soft surface: sometimes blinkered: sweating last 2 outings: has looked a difficult ride: sold to join Mrs P. Barker 1,900 gns Ascot November Sales. *W. J. Musson.* **44**

SARRAM (USA) 2 b.c. (Feb 13) Sharpen Up 127–Delphinskaa 110 (Green Dancer (USA) 132) [1989 7g⁶ 6g⁴ 6g 8.2g] 60,000Y: tall, leggy colt: has a roundish action: first foal: dam, French 1¼m to 12.5f winner, is half-sister to smart French middle-distance performer Darly: plating-class maiden: best effort first outing: looked bit temperamental final one: better suited by 7f than 6f, and should stay 1m. *G. A. Huffer.* **60**

SARTORIUS 3 b.c. Henbit (USA) 130–Salvationist (Mill Reef (USA) 141) [1988 NR 1989 10g⁵ 10.6g*] 10,000Y: lengthy colt: has scope: half-brother to fair 1m to 13.3f winner Failiq (by Bustino) and French 7.5f winner Salonique (by Nadjar): dam, winner at 11f and 11.5f in France, is half-sister to Marquis de Sade out of half-sister to Lorenzaccio: 11/10 on, won maiden at Haydock in August by 4 lengths, always prominent, one pace 3f out then running on strongly to lead inside last: will be suited by 1½m and forcing tactics: sold to join P. Bailey's stable 13,000 gns Newmarket Autumn Sales: may improve again: winning hurdler. *H. R. A. Cecil.* **93**

SARUM 3 b.g. Tina's Pet 121–Contessa (HUN) (Peleid 125) [1988 6f 7f⁵ 7g 6g⁶ 1989 6m* 5.8m 6f 6m⁵ a8g⁴ a7g⁶ a6g²] tall, leggy, rather narrow gelding: poor mover: quite modest handicapper: 25/1, won at Brighton in April: ran well in Lingfield claimers fifth (first start for nearly 5 months) and final outings: effective at 6f and stays 1m: acts on top-of-the-ground. *C. P. Wildman.* **62**

SASAKI 2 b.c. (Apr 6) Sadler's Wells 132–Sairshea (Simbir 130) [1989 7f*] IR 470,000Y: leggy, quite attractive colt: has scope: fifth living foal: closely related to 3-y-o 1½m winner La Rosette (by Lomond), smart 1¼m and 1½m winner Santiki (by Be My Guest), later winner in USA, and half-brother to Derby third Shearwalk (by Godswalk): dam won 3 times over 1½m in Ireland: second favourite but very green, won 10-runner maiden at Leicester in October by 5 lengths, running green 2f **85 P**

out then staying on strongly despite edging right: will be suited by 1m+: sure to improve considerably and win more races. *M. R. Stoute.*

SASHTAL 2 ch.c. (Feb 8) Ballacashtal (CAN)–Salala 83 (Connaught 130) [1989 71 7f² 7g] strong, sturdy colt: first foal: dam, won once at 7f, is half-sister to Beau Sher: modest form in autumn maidens at Leicester (backed from 10/1 to 4/1) and Newmarket: will stay 1m: may be capable of improvement. *B. Hanbury.*

SATIN LAKE (USA) 2 b.f. (Jan 23) Well Decorated (USA)–Bunny Lake 61 (Northern Baby (CAN) 127) [1989 6f⁴ 7f⁵ 7g] $12,500Y: first foal: dam, placed once in USA, is sister to top-class middle-distance performer Orange Bay: quite modest maiden: best effort first outing: ran poorly final one: will stay 1m. *S. G. Norton.*

SATIN SILK (USA) 3 gr.f. Al Nasr (FR) 126–Toveris 91 (Homing 130) [1988 NR — 1989 8m⁵ 7f 10.2f⁶ 8g 10m 10f⁵ 12g 12.5f a8g] leggy, angular filly: first foal: dam, 2-y-o 7f winner, didn't recover form: poor on most form: easily best effort on second start: blinkered, well beaten in seller on penultimate one: probably stays 1¼m: often bandaged: sold out of B. Hills's stable 1,900 gns Newmarket July Sales after fourth start: resold 1,000 gns Ascot December Sales. *J. L. Harris.*

SATIN WOOD 2 b.c. (May 2) Darshaan 133–Satanella (GER) (Pentathlon) [1989 106 7m² 7m* 8m⁴ 8g²] sturdy, useful-looking colt: eighth foal: half-brother to 2 Group-placed winners in Germany: dam, from good German family, won over 1¼m from 3 starts: put up useful performances when fourth of 9 to Digression in Royal Lodge EBF Stakes at Ascot in September and second of 16 to stable-companion Belmez in minor event at Newmarket in November: earlier won Yarmouth maiden in a canter: will be better suited by 1¼m. *H. R. A. Cecil.*

SATIS DANCER 2 br.f. (Apr 22) Mashhor Dancer (USA)–Chrisanthy 81 (So 72 Blessed 130) [1989 6m² 6m⁴ 6m² 7m² 7g* 7.3m³ 7g 7g⁵] 5,000Y: compact filly: moderate walker: third reported foal: half-sister to 3-y-o King Toh-Toh (by Simply Great) and a winner in Hong Kong by Sayyaf: dam 2-y-o 5f winner failed to train on: won 8-runner nursery at Yarmouth in September: ran well afterwards in similar events: better suited by 7f than 6f, and may stay 1m: has run creditably for inexperienced apprentice. *M. J. Ryan.*

SATURN MAN 3 b.g. Dalsaan 125–Pale Moon 58 (Jukebox 120) [1988 6d 5f³ 5m⁶ 65 5g 6g⁵ 5g³ 5m² 1989 5g 6m⁶ 6f 6f 5m² 5f 6g* 5m 6m⁴ 6g 6g] lengthy, dipped-backed gelding: won seller (no bid) at Newcastle in August in very good style having been last at halfway: mostly below form after: suited by 6f: acts on top-of-the-ground: blinkered third and last 5 starts: below form when sweating and edgy sixth: probably not entirely genuine. *M. W. Easterby.*

SATURN MOON 4 ch.f. Monsanto (FR) 121–Riturda (USA) 95 (Roi Dagobert 46 128) [1988 10v³ 9v⁴ 11g 12g⁴ 12f² 12m⁵ 12m 12h 12.2g² 12g³ 12d³ 16.5g³ 12s 12d⁵ 1989 12d 12d 12f 13f⁵ 12f 12g* 12f⁶] small, sturdy filly: sometimes unimpressive in coat: poor mover: won for first time in poorly-contested amateurs handicap at Carlisle in June, only form in 1989: best form at 1½m on an easy surface: has worn blinkers and visor, including at Carlisle: suitable mount for inexperienced rider: sold to join Mrs A. Knight 3,400 gns Doncaster August Sales. *J. S. Wilson.*

SAUCY SAINT 2 b.g. (Feb 24) Show-A-Leg 107–Stolen Halo 52 (Manacle 123) — [1989 5h 6f⁴ 5f 7f a6g 5g] leggy gelding: second reported foal: dam ran best race at 1¼m: little worthwhile form in varied races, including a seller: hung left and looked none too keen when blinkered third start: trained first 3 outings by P. Blockley. *M. Johnston.*

SAULIRE 4 b.g. High Top 131–Strathoykel 94 (Aberdeen 109) [1988 8d 8m 10g 46 8m 1989 8m⁵ 7f 7m 10m⁵] big, lengthy gelding: moderate mover: poor maiden: stays 1m: didn't handle turn and hung left at Edinburgh third start: has joined S. Dow. *Sir Mark Prescott.*

SAUMAREZ 2 b. or br.c. (Mar 28) Rainbow Quest (USA) 134–Fiesta Fun 105 74 P (Welsh Pageant 132) [1989 7g⁴] 45,000Y: tall colt: has scope: third living foal: half-brother to 3-y-o 1m winner Carnival Spirit (by Kris) and 1986 2-y-o 5f and 6f winner Vivienda (by Known Fact): dam, 1m and 1¼m winner, is half-sister to smart 6f and 7f winner Derrylin: 9/4 but very green, over 6 lengths fourth of 10, keeping on final 2f, to Abs in maiden at Leicester in September: will be better suited by 1m+: sure to improve considerably, and win a similar event. *H. R. A. Cecil.*

SAVAHRA SOUND 4 b.c. Song 132–Savahra 82 (Free State 125) [1988 8s⁴ 7g 111 6f* 6m⁵ 6f⁴ 6d 7d⁴ 7m³ 6g 1989 6g 6f* 6g* 6f³ 6s* 7f³ 6s² 6m 6.5s* 7d² 6v⁴] tall, rather dipped-backed colt: has a round action: very useful performer: successful in same minor event at Brighton (for second year running) and listed Benazet-Rennen at Baden-Baden in May, Group 3 De Kuyper-Sprinter-Preis at Hamburg in July and listed Grosser Sprint Preis der Electronic 2000 at Munich in October: 33/1 and bandaged behind, excellent third to Danehill in Cork and Orrery Stakes at Royal Ascot, fourth outing: best form at around 6f: acts on any going: game and consistent. *R. Hannon.*

SAVERNAKE (USA) 2 b.g. (Mar 18) Green Forest (USA) 134–Radiant (USA) — (Foolish Pleasure (USA)) [1989 8v] unfurnished gelding: first foal: dam, minor winner at around 6f, is half-sister to good-class middle-distance colt Gold And Ivory: 20/1 and bit backward, prominent over 5f in 23-runner minor event at Newbury in October: sold 4,900 gns Newmarket Autumn Sales. *I. A. Balding.*

SAVILLE WAY 2 ch.g. (Apr 24) Gorytus (USA) 132–Claretta (USA) 82 (Roberto 57 (USA) 131) [1989 6g⁶ 6m⁶ 7m 7g 7g] 14,000Y: strong, workmanlike gelding: keen walker: sixth foal: closely related to smart 3-y-o Sapience (by Niniski), winner from 7f (at 2 yrs) to 1¾m and second in St Leger, and half-brother to winners in Belgium and Jersey: dam, 2-y-o 7f winner, is half-sister to Italian 1000 Guineas winner Rosananti and good English and German performer Claddagh: plating-class maiden: will be better suited by 1m +: should win seller. *W. J. Musson.*

SAVO 2 b.f. (May 15) Norwick (USA) 120–Honiara 86 (Pitcairn 126) [1989 8m] — 1,550Y: fourth foal: half-sister to 3-y-o Florida Island (by Miami Springs): dam 2-y-o 5f winner: 14/1 and bandaged behind, well beaten in 23-runner seller at Newmarket in October. *P. F. I. Cole.*

SAWAIK 3 ch.g. Dominion 123–Cutlers Corner 111 (Sharpen Up 127) [1988 6f⁴ 6f⁴ 5f* 5g* 1989 7f] medium-sized, angular gelding: fairly useful winner in summer at 2 yrs: 20/1, moved moderately down and ran as if something amiss in £16,800 handicap at York in May, only start in 1989: best form at 5f: sold 2,700 gns Newmarket September Sales and subsequently gelded. *R. W. Armstrong.*

SAWAKI 2 br.f. (Apr 4) Song 132–Roxy Hart (High Top 131) [1989 6g] IR 80,000Y: — p sister to fair 6f and 7.6f winner Farras and half-sister to 7f and 1m winner Super Lunar (by Kalaglow): dam unraced half-sister to good sprinter Music Maestro and smart 1975 2-y-o Outer Circle: 20/1, in mid-division, slowly away, in 19-runner maiden at Redcar in November: should do better. *H. Thomson Jones.*

SAWSAN 2 b.f. (Feb 2) Top Ville 129–Al Washl (USA) 79 (The Minstrel (CAN) — 135) [1989 6g] lengthy, shallow-girthed, sparely-made filly: third foal: half-sister to fairly useful 3-y-o sprinter Hufoof (by Known Fact): dam placed over 5f and 6f at 3 yrs: 10/1 and in need of experience, slowly away and well behind last 2f in 12-runner maiden at Leicester in November: constantly swished tail beforehand. *P. T. Walwyn.*

SAXBY STORM 2 ch.f. (May 11) Northern Tempest (USA) 120–Rigton Sally 59 (Joshua 129) [1989 7f³ 8g] first reported foal: dam winning staying hurdler: 100/1, around 8 lengths third of 10, keeping on, to Hasbah in maiden at Redcar in October, much better effort: should stay 1m. *Mrs R. Wharton.*

SAXON COURT 3 b.g. Mummy's Game 120–Blickling 64 (Blakeney 126) [1988 83 d 5f 7m 7m³ 8g 8d 12.5f* 15.5f² 12f² 14f⁴ 17.1f⁶ 12m⁶ 12g 14f⁵ 12f] strong, good-bodied gelding: carries condition: fair handicapper: held up when winning at Wolverhampton in May: stays 15.5f well: acts on firm going: blinkered. *K. M. Brassey.*

SAXON LAD (USA) 3 b.c. Lear Fan (USA) 130–Presto Youth (USA) (Youth 68 (USA) 135) [1988 7m 7s 1989 7m⁴ 7f² 7m* 6f* 7.6f² 7d] leggy colt: progressive form in handicaps until running poorly final start: favourite, won at Yarmouth in August and Pontefract in September: effective at 6f and should stay 1m: acts on firm ground: tends to hang left and likely to prove best with waiting tactics: trained reappearance by N. Gaselee. *Mrs L. Piggott.*

SAYALOT 3 b.g. Sayyaf 121–Lottie's Charm (Charlottesville 135) [1988 5m 6d 46 8.2m⁵ 1989 12.2d* 12.5f 12.2m 12g⁵] smallish, sparely-made gelding: modest plater: won at Catterick (no bid) in April by short head: suited by 1½m: acts on a soft surface, possibly unsuited by top-of-the-ground: blinkered second and third starts: sold to join K. Ryan 1,400 gns Newmarket Autumn Sales. *M. L. W. Bell.*

SAY A PRAYER 2 ch.f. (May 4) Sayf El Arab (USA) 127–Careless Flyer 66 57 (Malicious) [1989 5m² 5m⁴ 6f³ 6g] 4,000Y: workmanlike filly: half-sister to 1983 2-y-o 7f seller winner Miss A Beat (by Song), later winner in Italy, and a winning hurdler: dam 6f winner: plating-class maiden: easily best effort first outing: should stay 6f. *Denys Smith.*

SAYMORE 3 ch.c. Seymour Hicks (FR) 125–Huahinee (FR) 94 (Riverman (USA) 96 131) [1988 5.8g 8m 1989 8f² 10f³ 10m 8m* 8m 8.2d 8m 8d*] tall, leggy, close-coupled colt: won handicaps at Salisbury (made virtually all) in June and Newbury

(27-runner £6,100 contest, always prominent and best effort) in October: effective at 1m and 1¼m: acts on firm and dead ground: takes keen hold: sold to join C. Brooks 40,000 gns Newmarket Autumn Sales. *M. E. D. Francis.*

SAYNETE 3 b.g. Night Shift (USA)–Allander Girl (Miralgo 130) [1988 5f² 5m⁶ 5g 1989 8m* 8.5f² 8f 8.5g* 7.5f⁴ 9g 8m 8m*] useful-looking gelding: hobdayed before 3-y-o season: moderate walker: quite useful handicapper: won at Ripon in May, Beverley in July and Thirsk in September: below form fifth to seventh starts when on toes first time, sweating second and reportedly gurgled third: stays 8.5f: acts on firm going: takes strong hold, and suited by good pace and strong handling: wore severe noseband as 3-y-o: sold to race in Middle East 35,000 gns Newmarket Autumn Sales. *J. G. FitzGerald.* **94**

SAYSANA 2 b.f. (Mar 31) Sayf El Arab (USA) 127–Rosana Park 83 (Music Boy 124) [1989 5d 5.3m⁴ 5.3h* 6m⁶ 5f* 5.3h² 5f⁴ 5f⁴ 5.3f³] 11,000Y: leggy, quite good-topped filly: keen walker: second foal: half-sister to 3-y-o Angelica Park (by Simply Great): dam, 6f winner, stayed 7f: successful in 5-runner sellers at Brighton (bought out of R. Smyth's stable 4,400 gns) in June and Folkestone (retained 3,500 gns) in July: ran well afterwards in nurseries and minor events: best at 5f: acts well on hard going. *A. Moore.* **63**

SAY SHANAZ 3 b. or br.f. Tickled Pink 114–Wild Pumpkin (Auction Ring (USA) 123) [1988 5m³ 5g⁴ 5m 1989 5.3h 6f 6h 5g 5m 5.3h 7m⁵ 7g a8g] leggy filly: poor maiden: suited by 7f: possibly unsuited by very firm ground: blinkered fourth to eighth outings: gave trouble at stalls and withdrawn on intended reappearance. *R. Voorspuy.* **—**

SAYSUKI 3 b.f. Sayf El Arab (USA) 127–Miss Suki 57 (Upper Case (USA)) [1988 5f9g 10d² 1989 10s 12m² 11.5g 11.7h⁴ 12f⁴ 10f] leggy filly: stays 1¼m: best effort on a soft surface: blinkered on debut: sweating final outing. *C. P. Wildman.* **42**

SAYYAF'S LAD 4 ch.c. Sayyaf 121–Opinebo 82 (Nebbiolo 125) [1988 5g* 6s⁴ 5g⁴ 5d 5g 5d⁵ 6g 6m 6m 5m 7g 1989 6d 5f⁵ 5g 5g 7m 7g] good-quartered colt: plating-class winner early as 3-y-o: little subsequent worthwhile form: stays 6f: needs give in the ground: has worn severe bridle and been taken down early. *C. Spares.* **45**

SAY YOU 5 b.g. Sayyaf 121–Braida (FR) (Tissot 131) [1988 10f⁴ 12f* 12f⁵ 10f5 12f* 13.3m 12f 12f 12f⁶ 12g 12d 1989 12g 12m 12m 11.7g 12m] tall, leggy gelding: usually looks well: moderate mover: no form since winning handicaps at Brighton (second time in apprentice event) early in 1988: effective from 1¼m to 1¾m: possibly unsuited by soft going, acts on any other: visored fourth outing (first for 3 months), blinkered and bandaged final one. *P. Howling.* **—**

SAY YOU WILL 5 b.g. Riboboy (USA) 124–Polita 86 (Constable 119) [1988 9d⁴ 9s⁴ 8d² 8g 8g⁵ 7f 7f 8v 6g² 1989 6d 6g 6g² 8.5d 7m* 7.5f* 7.6m* 7m⁵ 6m* 6f 7m 6s 7m 7g* 6g 7d²] robust gelding: carries condition: has a quick action: modest handicapper: had not won before June, but was then successful at Catterick, Beverley, Lingfield and twice at Newmarket: other form on last 7 outings only when second of 27, caught final stride, in apprentice race at Newbury: effective at 6f and probably best at up to 1m: possibly unsuited by soft going nowadays, acts on any other: has worn blinkers, usually visored nowadays: sometimes apprentice ridden: sometimes looks unenthusiastic: inconsistent. *M. P. Naughton.* **76**

SAYYURE (USA) 3 b.c. Lydian (FR) 120–Periquito (USA) (Olden Times) [1988 7g 1989 10s 9s 10d 16.2g³ 13.8f² 16.2g⁴] good-topped colt: has a round action: quite modest handicapper: given plenty to do when running creditably last 2 outings, sweating and edgy first of them: will be suited by extreme test of stamina: acts on firm going: useful hurdler. *N. Tinkler.* **61**

SCALES OF JUSTICE 3 br.f. Final Straw 127–Foiled Again 110 (Bold Lad (IRE) 133) [1988 NR 1989 10.6g 9g 10d a12g⁵ a12g* a12g] big, rangy filly: has plenty of scope: half-sister to Cut No Ice (by Great Nephew), 7f winner here and 1m listed winner in 1989, useful middle-distance performer Gillson (by High Top) and a minor winner in France: dam won from 6f to 1¼m: little worthwhile form apart from winning Lingfield claimer (second favourite) in November, always close up: stays 1½m. *J. W. Hills.* **62**

SCANDAL (USA) 3 b.g. Blood Royal (USA) 129–Affair 78 (Bold Lad (IRE) 133) [1988 NR 1989 12f* 12f 14f] big, good-topped gelding: has plenty of scope: first foal: dam, 6f winner at 2 yrs who showed little subsequently, is daughter of useful 7f and 9f winner Guest Night and granddaughter of high-class Mesopotamia: green, created good impression when winning maiden at York in July, quickening well from rear to lead 2f out: well behind in £12,000 handicaps at Goodwood (didn't handle **88**

descent) and York (moved moderately down, never going well): subsequently gelded: gives impression will be suited by easier surface. *C. W. C. Elsey.*

SCANNER LAD 3 br.c. Mansingh (USA) 120–Immodest Miss 73 (Daring Display (USA) 129) [1988 6g 5f 6d 1989 6s 8f 7h 8m 8.3m] leggy colt: little worthwhile form, including in sellers: blinkered final outing: bandaged and visored previous 2, not looking keen on second of them. *J. A. Bennett.* —

SCAPIN 3 gr.c. Scallywag 127–Green Room (Crooner 119) [1988 NR 1989 13.3m⁵] big, deep-girthed colt: third foal: dam never ran: 20/1, backward and green, looked likely to improve when about 20 lengths fifth of 15 to Musaahim in maiden at Newbury in June, keeping on steadily. *R. F. Johnson Houghton.* —

SCARLET CREST 5 b.g. High Top 131–Red Ruby 113 (Tudor Melody 129) [1988 10d 1989 10m⁶ 11.7m³] good-topped gelding: has ability, but is very lightly raced nowadays: stays 11.7f well: acts on top-of-the-ground and heavy going: mulish in preliminaries on reappearance: pulled hard both times at 5 yrs. *Lady Herries.* 75

SCARLET EXPRESS 2 b.c. (Feb 6) Precocious 126–Scarlet Slipper (Gay Mecene (USA) 128) [1989 6m⁶ 7g 7g⁵] 29,000F, 420,000 francs (approx £38,500) Y: quite attractive colt: first foal: dam, winner at 1m in France, is half-sister to useful 7f and 1¼m winner Golden Braid: plating-class form in fair company. *P. A. Kelleway.* 59

SCARLET LEGEND 3 b.g. Legend of France (USA) 124–Orillia (Red God 128§) [1988 NR 1989 10s 10s 12f⁶ 11m 10m] 4,000Y: workmanlike, good-bodied gelding: half-brother to useful Irish 1¼m winner Catherine Mary (by Ela-Mana-Mou) and French provincial 7.5f to 1¼m winner Ortrud (by Bay Express): dam unraced daughter of smart French middle-distance filly Relicia: behind in maidens and handicaps: bandaged and very edgy on debut. *Mrs L. Piggott.* —

SCARLETT HOLLY 2 b.f. (Apr 16) Red Sunset 120–Wilderness 88 (Martinmas 128) [1989 6f* 6v] 22,000Y: medium-sized filly, rather unfurnished: fourth foal: sister to fair 8.2f winner Positive Attitude and fair 1986 2-y-o 5f winner Sameek, and half-sister to a winner in Barbados: dam won over 7f: won 12-runner maiden auction race at Newbury in May by 4 lengths: edgy, very good eighth of 23, fading final furlong, to Altered Beast in nursery at Newbury over 5 months later: will stay 1m: likely to improve further. *P. J. Makin.* 79 p

SCARLET VEIL 3 b.f. Tyrnavos 129–Red Velvet 114 (Red God 128§) [1988 7m 1989 10m⁶ 10h²] close-coupled, plain filly: modest form in maidens: given plenty to do when beaten length in apprentice event at Brighton in June: stays 1¼m. *W. Jarvis.* 75

SCARPANTO 3 ch.g. Pharly (FR) 130–Sandy Island 110 (Mill Reef (USA) 141) [1988 NR 1989 8g⁵ 11f⁴] tall, close-coupled gelding: first foal: dam, closely related to Slip Anchor, won Pretty Polly Stakes and Lancashire Oaks: 14/1, 10½ lengths fifth of 20 in £8,300 newcomers race at Newmarket in April, racing keenly in lead 5f and keeping on quite well: favourite, failed to confirm that promise in maiden (showed a round action) at Redcar 6 weeks later, leading 1m: sold to join R. Stubbs 3,600 gns Newmarket September Sales and subsequently gelded. *W. Jarvis.* 81

SCARRON (USA) 3 b.c. Storm Bird (CAN) 134–Asoka (USA) (Youth (USA) 135) [1988 7m 6m² 1989 8f* 8.2m² 8.2g⁶ 8m 7g²] robust, round-barrelled colt: carries plenty of condition: moderate mover: won minor event at Sandown in May: creditable second in similar events at Haydock (on toes) and Catterick in the summer: probably needs a strongly-run race at 7f and stays 1m: has raced only on a sound surface: has worn severe noseband: sold A. Falourd 9,000 gns Newmarket Autumn Sales. *H. R. A. Cecil.* 89

SCATTER 2 b.c. (Mar 16) Sharpo 132–Visitation 84 (Tarqogan 125) [1989 5f 6m* 6g* 6g 7g] 24,000Y: good-topped colt: half-brother to several winners, including fairly useful 1985 2-y-o 5f winner Little Pipers (by Music Boy): dam stayed 1½m: fairly useful performer: won maiden at Lingfield in June and nursery (sweating) at Windsor in August: ran moderately afterwards in nurseries at Ascot: stays 6f: tends to hang. *G. Harwood.* 93

SCENIC 3 b.c. Sadler's Wells (USA) 132–Idyllic (USA) (Foolish Pleasure (USA)) [1988 6d² 7d* 7d* 7d* 1989 8f³ 10m* 10g 10g⁴ 12f] 125

While Scenic, thankfully, didn't suffer the fate of his fellow Three Chimneys Dewhurst dead-heater Prince of Dance, who was diagnosed as having cancer of the spine and put down in June, his season was one affected by ill health and injury. Found to be running a very high temperature and coughing two days before his scheduled reappearance in the 'Back A Winner By Train' Classic Trial at Thirsk, Scenic missed the Guineas and wasn't seen out until Royal Ascot. His three-length third to the same owner's Shaadi in the Group 1 St James's Palace Stakes was encouraging, though did little to alter the conclusion reached at the end of his first season that Scenic might prove ideally suited by a mile and a quarter and some give in the ground. However, he put up a good performance on firmish going when contesting Scotland's sole scheduled pattern race, the mile-and-a-quarter William Hill Classic at Ayr three and a half weeks later. In a three-cornered affair, Ile de Chypre, penalised for his Group 2 success in Ireland, and High Estate, one of the previous season's top two-year-olds who was still bidding to re-establish himself, shared favouritism at 6/4 while Scenic figured on 5/2. Ile de Chypre seemed to play into his rivals' hands by setting a sedate gallop, restrained in front to the home turn. Scenic, displaying a smart turn of foot, came from last to lead at the distance and prevail by a length, given just a couple of reminders to make sure, with High Estate possibly flattered by the slow pace in finishing only two and a half lengths further back. Scenic's season finally looked to be taking off. Not so. A bruised foot put it on 'hold' again—the Juddmonte International Stakes at York was run without him, and won, incidentally, under a more positive ride than at Ayr, by Ile de Chypre—then, when he did make the line-up for the Phoenix Champion Stakes, for which he was the clear favourite at 5/4, Scenic performed abysmally, beaten soon after the turn, and was later reported to be coughing once more. Thus Scenic's final outing of a light British season, in the Dubai Champion Stakes at Newmarket, became something of a reputation-restoring exercise. His fourth, beaten around a length and a half by the trio involved in a photo, Legal Case, Dolpour and Ile de Chypre, was indeed a gallant effort; he improved to hold every chance in the Dip but was just beginning to give best when slightly impeded a hundred yards out, nevertheless finishing six lengths clear of the remainder who were headed by Charmer, and included Ile de Nisky and High Estate. In the post-race inquest, Scenic's connections felt strongly that their charge would now be suited by a mile and a half, and certainly there was little harm in trying him at the trip. Anyway, his subsequent eleventh of fourteen in the Breeders' Cup Turf at Gulfstream Park was below his best. Whether lack of stamina was to blame is hard to say—on breeding it's touch and go whether he'll stay so far. Scenic had already given the impression that a galloping track suited him, so it's also a possibility that the American circuit wasn't in his favour.

		Northern Dancer	Nearctic
	Sadler's Wells (USA)	(b 1961)	Natalma
	(b 1981)	Fairy Bridge	Bold Reason
Scenic		(b 1975)	Special
(b.c. 1986)		Foolish Pleasure	What A Pleasure
	Idyllic (USA)	(b 1972)	Fool-Me-Not
	(b or br 1982)	Where You Lead	Raise A Native
		(ch 1970)	Noblesse

Scenic's pedigree is detailed in *Racehorses of 1988*, while an update on the impressive progress of his sire Sadler's Wells can be found in the essay on Salsabil. A rather leggy, useful-looking colt, Scenic is the first foal of the unraced but well-bred Idyllic, a granddaughter of the outstanding filly Noblesse; the second foal is a filly named Quixotic, by Caerleon and stabled with Cecil. To complete, Scenic is a keen walker and a fluent mover with a slightly rounded action. He stays in training, and, we're bound to say, has to make more than normal improvement unless he is to fall short of top honours again. *B. W. Hills.*

SCENT OF SUCCESS (USA) 3 b. or br.c. Seattle Song (USA) 130–Sancta Rose (Karabas 132) [1988 NR 1989 12m⁵] $400,000Y: good-topped colt: fifth foal: closely related to fair 6f and 8.5f winner Seattle Rose (by Seattle Slew) and half-brother to Derby third Mashkour (by Irish River): dam Irish 7.5f and 1¼m winner: backward and very lethargic in paddock, never going well when about 11 lengths last of 5 in minor event at Newmarket in July: has plenty of scope. *H. R. A. Cecil.*   —

SCHADENFREUDE 3 b.g. Valiyar 129–Shorthouse 102 (Habitat 134) [1988 7m 7m 8d 1989 8.5d 10g] neat, workmanlike gelding: good mover: behind in maidens and handicaps. *A. C. Stewart.*   —

SCHHH YOU-KNOW-WHO   3 b.c. Longleat (USA) 109–Kabylia (FR) (Dancer's Image (USA)) [1988 7g 6g* 7g³ 7m 1989 6m⁶ 7m³ 8m 8m⁵ 8d⁴ 8f* 8g² 7d⁴] well-made, useful-looking colt: fair handicapper: sweating, made all at Salisbury in October: stays 1m: acts on firm going: has run creditably for apprentice: changed hands 19,000 gns Newmarket Autumn Sales. *R. J. R. Williams.*   81

SCHOOL DINNERS   3 ch.f. Sharpo 132–Patois (I Say 125) [1988 NR 1989 7d 7m² 8m] 26,000F, IR 62,000Y: smallish filly: half-sister to several winners here and abroad, including middle-distance winner La Bandera (by Morston): dam twice-raced half-sister to smart stayer Petty Officer: 33/1-second in minor event at Salisbury, always in touch and easily best effort in first half of season: should stay 1m. *C. A. Horgan.*   74

SCHWEPPES TIME   3 b.c. Formidable (USA) 125–Hi There 89 (High Top 131) [1988 7m 7g⁴ 8d³ 1989 10s] rather unfurnished colt: plating-class maiden: gave impression should stay 1¼m only start as 3-y-o (April). *Mrs N. Macauley.*   —

SCHWEPPES TONIC   3 br.c. Persian Bold 123–Gay Shadow 99 (Northfields (USA)) [1988 7f⁴ 7g 7.5m⁴ 6s 6d 1989 6s 8s⁴ 10.6s 10.4m 7.5f⁶ 8m 12g⁶ 12m⁶ 12g a11g* a14g a11g³] close-coupled, rather plain colt: has a round action: 25/1, best effort as 3-y-o when winning claimer at Southwell by 10 lengths: fair third in similar event in month: stays 11f: possibly unsuited by a soft surface. *B. A. McMahon.*   69

SCOBIE DOUGH   3 br.g. Over The River (FR)–Clerihan Miss (Tarqogan 125) [1988 NR 1989 8.5f 7m] small, workmanlike gelding: first reported foal: dam unraced: no promise in claimer and seller. *Miss S. J. Wilton.*   —

SCORCHED EARTH (USA)   2 ch.c. (Apr 25) Private Account (USA)–Sun Valley Linda (USA) (Prince John) [1989 7m³ 7f² 8m² 8f] $92,000Y: useful-looking colt: has scope: seventh foal: half-brother to 6 winners, including useful French 7f and 1m winner Princely Ruler (by Foolish Pleasure) and 2 placed in minor stakes: dam never ran: sire 9f and 1¼m stakes winner: quite modest maiden: best effort 2½ lengths second of 8 to Bold Passion at Chepstow in August: better suited by 1m than 7f: sold 15,000 gns Newmarket Autumn Sales. *P. F. I. Cole.*   68

SCORPIO LADY   2 ch.f. (Apr 4) Vaigly Great 127–Buy G'S 60 (Blakeney 126) [1989 6m⁵ 6f² 6m⁶ 6g² 6m³ 7g⁶ 6v* a7g² 7g³] 2,200Y: sparely-made filly: has a round action: first foal: dam 12.2f winner: modest performer: won autumn auction at Ayr by 2½ lengths: ran creditably in nurseries final 2 starts: will stay 1m: best form on an easy surface: visored on debut: usually sweats: consistent. *G. Blum.*   76

SCOTCH DOUBLE (USA)   3 b.c. Duns Scotus (CAN)–Role Twice (USA) (Droll Role) [1988 7g 8d 8m 1989 11.7d 11.7m 13.1h² 14f 16.2g² 16m* 16.2g³ 16m³ 21f4] sturdy, compact colt: made all and battled on well when winning maiden at Nottingham in June: creditable third in handicaps then out of depth in Goodwood Cup later in summer: will be suited by thorough test of stamina: acts on hard going and a soft surface: blinkered last 5 starts: sold 13,000 gns Newmarket Autumn Sales. *M. E. D. Francis.*   81

SCOTCH IMP   5 ch.m. Imperial Fling (USA) 116–Bunduq 67 (Scottish Rifle 127) [1988 7m² 6g² 7g 6s³ 7.5m 6m² 7m⁵ 6g³ 7m* 6h* 7.6s⁴ 6d² 6m⁴ 6d³ 8g⁴ 7d 6s* 6g* 6s⁵ 6g 7m 1989 6f 6m⁴ 6m⁶ 6g³ 6f⁵ 6f⁵ 6m 6m² 6m 6f⁴ 6g 7g a7g a8g a6g] workmanlike mare: modest handicapper: good second at Ripon in August: reportedly struck into next outing: well beaten last 4, on final one badly hampered early: suited by 7f or stiff 6f: acts on any going: sometimes blinkered, but wasn't in 1989: has worn dropped noseband: good mount for apprentice. *D. W. Chapman.*   77

SCOTGAVOTTE (FR)   3 b.f. Dunbeath (USA) 127–French Minuet (FR) (Jim French (USA)) [1988 8.5f 9f 8m⁵ 1989 10.2g² 9v³ 9g 10m 10f⁴ 10f 10f6] leggy filly: carries condition: has a moderate, quick action: poor form: ran moderately in sellers last 2 starts: bred to stay 1½m: appears to act on any going: moved badly down third start, first for almost 4 months: took keen hold in visor final one: sold to join F. Jackson 4,700 gns Doncaster November Sales. *M. J. Camacho.*   42

SCOTONI   3 ch.c. Final Straw 127–Damiya (FR) (Direct Flight) [1988 6m⁶ 6g 8s 6g 8d 1989 8.3m 8m²] close-coupled, rather sparely-made colt: edgy, easily best effort when beaten ¾ length in apprentice handicap at Salisbury in August, running on strongly: may well stay further. *R. J. O'Sullivan.*   60

SCOTS LAW   2 b.c. (May 3) Law Society (USA) 130–Tweedling (USA) (Sir Ivor 135) [1989 6m⁵ 7f* a8g6] IR 5,000Y: compact, quite attractive colt: second foal: dam won at around 1m in USA: quite modest performer: won 4-runner maiden auction event at Catterick in July: carried head awkwardly after slow start when respectable sixth in nursery at Lingfield around 5 months later: will stay 1¼m. *C. E. Brittain.*   65

SCOTTISH FLING 5 ch.g. Imperial Fling (USA) 116–Relicia (Relko 136) [1988 **64**
11s⁴ 8.5m² 9m³ 8.2m² 8f* 12f³ 9g⁶ 8.2d 1989 8f⁶ 9f* 8.2f³ 8f² 10f⁵ 12.3m⁵ 9f⁶ 10.2g⁵
10.6d⁵ 8m² 9f3] workmanlike gelding: moderate mover: quite modest handicapper:
won slowly-run event at Redcar in June: ideally suited by slightly shorter than 1¼m:
best form on top-of-the-ground: has worn blinkers and visor, but didn't at 5 yrs: has
won when sweating: good mount for inexperienced rider: bought 12,000 gns
Doncaster April Sales: tough. *J. Berry.*

SCOTTISH REFORM 2 b.c. (Jun 4) Night Shift (USA)–Molvitesse 75 (Mol- **67**
vedo 137) [1989 6m² 6f³ 7m⁶ 8g4] 7,000Y: lengthy colt: moderate walker: turns
fore-feet in: has plenty of scope: half-brother to several winners, including 1982
2-y-o 6f winner Auburn Hill (by Silly Season) and 1¼m seller winner Riboeyes Boy
(by Riboboy): dam won over 1m: quite modest maiden: suited by 1m. *J. Berry.*

SCRATCHING CAT 2 br.f. (Apr 24) Mansingh (USA) 120–Sweet Helen (No —
Mercy 126) [1989 6g 5f6] sturdy, deep-girthed filly: fifth foal: sister to a poor animal
and half-sister to 6f winner Grange Farm Lady and 5f winner Grange Farm Lad (both
by Faraway Times): dam ran once: blinkered, well beaten in seller at Doncaster and
6-runner maiden at Wolverhampton in the autumn. *J. R. Jenkins.*

SCRIBBLING 2 b.f. (Feb 6) Blushing Scribe (USA) 107–Captain Bonnie 60 **38**
(Captain James 123) [1989 5s 5g 5.3m⁵ 5.8h 6f 6m⁵ 5g⁶ 7f⁴ 7m 6m 5m⁵ 5m] 1,200F,
700Y: smallish, sturdy filly: poor walker: second living foal: dam ran only at 2 yrs,
placed over 5f: poor plater: stays 7f: blinkered fifth to seventh outings, visored
eleventh: has sweated up: has run creditably for 7-lb claimer: trained until after
ninth outing by D. Wintle. *J. D. Czerpak.*

SEABTIC 2 br.c. (May 11) Sayf El Arab (USA) 127–Tickled To Bits (Sweet **40**
Revenge 129) [1989 5f⁵ 6m³ 5g⁵ 7f6] 500F, 7,000Y: medium-sized colt: brother to
3-y-o Barale and half-brother to a winner in Norway by Hittite Glory: dam of little
account: poor form in varied events, including sellers: not seen out after July: stays
6f: visored last 3 outings: sent to P. Wigham. *Mrs N. Macauley.*

SEA BUCK 3 b.g. Simply Great (FR) 122–Heatherside 80 (Hethersett 134) [1988 —
7m 8m⁴ 7g 8d 10d 1989 11m 14m 13.3d] useful-looking gelding: quite modest
maiden: below form since third outing at 2 yrs: bred to stay middle distances:
visored 3 times as a 2-y-o: winning hurdler. *G. B. Balding.*

SEA DEVIL 3 gr.g. Absalom 128–Miss Poinciana 78 (Averof 123) [1988 5g⁵ 6g 6g **63**
6s 6f 1989 5g⁴ 6d² 7.5f⁴ 6m 5s 6s⁴ 6s] lengthy, good-quartered gelding: moderate
walker and mover: maiden handicapper: appears suited by 6f and a soft surface:
tends to wander under pressure. *M. J. Camacho.*

SEAMERE 6 b.g. Crofter (USA) 124–Whistling Waltz (Whistler 129) [1988 8m⁵ **60**
7g⁴ 5g* 5g* 6d 5g⁶ 5f 1989 5f 6f 5m³ 5g⁵ 5g⁴ 5g 5g² 5m⁴ 5f* 5f² 5f³ 5g]
workmanlike, deep-bodied gelding: carries plenty of condition: moderate mover:
quite modest handicapper: won apprentice event at Pontefract (rider fined for
coming out of wrong stall) in September: ran well next 2 outings: best at 5f
nowadays: best form on a sound surface: often used to wear a visor, but hasn't since
1987: blinkered last 6 starts: excellent mount for inexperienced rider. *B. R.
Cambidge.*

SEAMROG 3 b. or br.f. Be My Native (USA) 122–Coup de Veine (FR) (Gift Card **68**
(FR) 124) [1988 6d⁴ 1989 8d⁵ 8m 7m] rather leggy, workmanlike filly: turns off-fore
in: quite modest form at best: showed little in maiden final start (August): may stay
beyond 1m: bandaged behind on debut, off-hind on reappearance. *H. Candy.*

SE-AQ 4 b.c. Krayyan 117–Messie (Linacre 133) [1988 8.2v 8g 8.5m³ 8g⁶ 8m* **72**
1989 7m² 7m* 7.5m 7s 8s 7m 8.2d³ 8g] lengthy colt: has a quick action: favourite,
led close home when winning claimer at Ayr (claimed out of J. W. Watts's stable
£6,575) in July: form after only on penultimate outing: stays 8.5f: acts on top-of-the-
ground and a soft surface: blinkered once at 3 yrs: bandaged off-hind third outing:
has looked a difficult ride: inconsistent. *J. S. Wilson.*

SEARCH THE WIND 5 b.g. Wind And Wuthering (USA) 132–Single Gal 97 —
(Mansingh (USA) 120) [1988 NR 1989 10.6m] sparely-made gelding: has a round
action: poor maiden: blinkered once: sold 1,250 gns Ascot November Sales. *M. J.
Haynes.*

SEA SHARK 2 ch.f. (Mar 12) Gorytus (USA) 132–Sharrara (CAN) 61 (Blushing —
Groom (FR) 131) [1989 7g] second foal: half-sister to 3-y-o 1m winner Juvenara (by
Young Generation): dam, lightly-raced maiden, stayed 1¼m: always in rear in
17-runner maiden at Folkestone in October: sold 800 gns Newmarket December
Sales. *C. E. Brittain.*

SEA SIESTA 3 b.f. Vaigly Great 127–Janlarmar 69 (Habat 127) [1988 NR 1989 8f] —
4,000F: third foal: sister to 6f seller winner Crimpsall and half-sister to a poor
animal by Monsanto: dam won 6f seller: 100/1, well-beaten seventh of 12 in minor
event at Warwick in October. *Miss A. J. Whitfield.*

SEATTLE PRIDE (CAN) 3 b.c. Seattle Song (USA) 130–Minstrelsy (USA) —
(The Minstrel (CAN) 135) [1988 NR 1989 10f⁴ 10.1g⁴ 8g 9m 12.2d] $195,000Y:
leggy, quite attractive colt: has a fluent, round action: third foal: half-brother to
11.7f winner Mr Minstrel (by Master Willie): dam, 4-y-o 1m winner, is half-sister to
Kentucky Oaks winner Sweet Alliance, dam of Shareef Dancer: ran poorly after
second start, edgy and blinkered penultimate one: has worn tongue strap: trained
until after fourth outing by M. Moubarak. *M. H. Tompkins.*

SEA VENTURE (USA) 3 b.c. Storm Bird (CAN) 134–Heat of Holme (USA) 76
(Noholme II) [1988 6d 6v⁵ 1989 6m⁴ᵈⁱˢ 5g³ 6m 7f⁴] lengthy colt: modest maiden:
should be suited by further than 6f: acts on top-of-the-ground: visored final outing
(June). *M. R. Stoute.*

SECONDS 3 br.f. Lucky Wednesday 124–Hitravelscene (Mansingh (USA) 120) §§
[1988 5g 5g 5g 8m 1989 7g] leggy filly: of little account and temperamental: has been
tried in blinkers, including when unseated rider and withdrawn final appearance
(May). *J. Balding.*

SECOND TO NONE 2 b.g. (Apr 28) Superlative 118–Matinata (Dike (USA)) 58
[1989 5f³ 5m³ 5d⁶] 30,000Y: strong, quite attractive gelding: half-brother to useful
1¼m to 11.5f winner Early Call (by Kind of Hush), quite modest 1985 2-y-o 6f seller
winner Lydia Languish (by Hotfoot) and winners in France and Italy: dam ran once:
plating-class maiden: will stay 6f. *J. Berry.*

SECRETAIRE (USA) 2 b.f. (Jan 4) Secretariat (USA)–Dame Margot (USA) 61
(Northern Dancer) [1989 8m 8f⁶ 8.2f⁴ 8.2g] $250,000Y: medium-sized, leggy filly,
rather unfurnished: has scope: sixth named foal: half-sister to 2 winners in USA,
including stakes winner at up to 9f Lord of The Night (by Lord Avie): dam unraced:
quite modest maiden: best effort on third outing, edging left and taking keen hold:
looked reluctant to race when blinkered final one. *P. F. I. Cole.*

SECRET ARCH 4 b.c. Starch Reduced 112–Lana's Secret 79 (Most Secret 119) —
[1988 6d 8g 7d 6m 6g⁴ 6f⁵ 6d 8d 1989 7f 7m 7f] compact colt: poor maiden: 33/1,
tailed off in handicaps at Leicester (selling event) and Chepstow (blinkered) last 2
outings: form only at 6f on a sound surface: often sweats. *B. Palling.*

SECRETARY OF STATE 3 b.c. Alzao (USA) 117–Colonial Line (USA) 75 95
(Plenty Old (USA)) [1988 NR 1989 10s 8m* 8.2m³ 7f⁵ 8.3g 8m* 9g*] 2,600F:
strong, workmanlike colt: carries condition: good mover: third foal: half-brother to
poor maiden Gold Collar (by Sayyaf): dam, best at 2 yrs, won over 5f at 3 yrs and 4
yrs: stayed on well when winning maiden at Brighton in April, claimer at Chepstow
in October and £15,400 handicap at Newmarket in November: 10/1 and looking really
well, one of 2 to race stand side when winning 17-runner event at Newmarket by 5
lengths, leading 2f out: better at 9f than 1m: probably acts on firm going. *P. F. I. Cole.*

SECRET CONTRACT 4 b.g. Caruso 112–Sealed Contract 76 (Runnymede 123) —
[1988 6g⁶ 7m 8f⁴ 6m⁵ 7g 1989 8g 8h⁵ 8f] leggy, light-framed gelding: poor plater.
Mrs G. R. Reveley.

SECRET DANCER 3 ch.g. Last Fandango 125–Secret Isle (USA) (Voluntario 61
III) [1988 8m 7g⁵ 8d⁶ 1989 11f 8m 12f 10f⁴ 12.2m 13.6g] robust, lengthy gelding:
moderate mover: quite modest maiden: fourth in seller at Redcar in May, best effort
as 3-y-o: tailed off in handicap final start, first for 4½ months: stays 1¼m: best form
on a soft surface: visored third start: tends to carry head high and often looks none
too keen. *R. M. Whitaker.*

SECRET FAVOR (USA) 3 b.f. Secreto (USA) 128–Irish Party (USA) (Irish 69
Lancer) [1988 6m⁵ 1989 10d] smallish filly: moderate mover: beaten about 8 lengths
in Blue Seal Stakes at Ascot and maiden (running on) at Newbury 13 months later:
will stay 1½m: may improve. *B. W. Hills.*

SECRET LEAH 2 b.f. (Apr 29) Gorytus (USA) 132–Phoenicia (USA) (Forli 31
(ARG)) [1989 5m⁵ 5f 7m] compact, good-quartered filly: sprint type: second foal:
half-sister to a winner in Germany: dam never ran: poor form in a maiden and
sellers: flashed tail and looked reluctant second start. *M. D. I. Usher.*

SECRET LIASON 3 b.g. Ballacashtal (CAN)–Midnight Mistress (Midsummer 68
Night II 117) [1988 7m 1989 7.5d 6f* 6f* 7m 7m* 6f 7m⁵ 7g4] angular gelding:
moderate walker: smart plater: won at Folkestone (no bid) and Hamilton (bought in
3,200 gns) in June and Warwick (bought in 8,200 gns) in July: good fourth in

non-selling handicap at Catterick: stays 7f: acts on firm going: raced freely in blinkers on reappearance: has won for 5-lb claimer. *W. G. M. Turner.*

SECRET OBSESSION (USA) 3 b.f. Secretariat (USA)–Ann Stuart (USA) 89 (Lyphard (USA) 132) [1988 6g 1989 10f6 10g3 10m* 12m] leggy, close-coupled filly: hard ridden to lead close home in £6,000 handicap at Newmarket in July: again favourite and ridden by 5-lb claimer, never dangerous in strongly-run £19,100 handicap at same course following month, pushed along over 4f out, getting poor run 2f out then staying on steadily: should prove suited by 1½m + . *M. R. Stoute.*

SECRET SOCIETY 2 b. or br.c. (Apr 1) Law Society (USA) 130–Shaara (FR) 76 (Sanctus II 132) [1989 8s 8.2d3 8d] big, deep-girthed colt: has scope: eighth foal: half-brother to several winners, including smart 5f to 1m winner Shasavaan (by Red God): dam placed at up to 11f in French Provinces: very close third of 11, keeping on strongly in moderately-run race, to Almuinjjid in maiden at Haydock in October, easily best effort: will stay 1¼m. *I. V. Matthews.*

SECRET TURN (USA) 3 b.c. Secreto (USA) 128–Changing (USA) (Forli 96 (ARG)) [1988 NR 1989 10.1m3 10.1m3 12m] $50,000Y: lengthy, useful-looking colt: carries condition: second foal: dam never ran: fairly useful form when third in Windsor minor events: took keen hold and prominent until running wide on home turn when well beaten in maiden at Kempton in July: should stay 1½m but needs to become more tractable: sold to join A. Turnell 16,000 gns Newmarket Autumn Sales, gelded after. *P. F. I. Cole.*

SECRET WATERS 2 b.f. (Mar 9) Pharly (FR) 130–Idle Waters 116 (Mill Reef 61 (USA) 141) [1989 6g 7f6 8g4] leggy, close-coupled, quite attractive filly: half-sister to 3-y-o Desert Bluebell, smart 1986 2-y-o Shining Water (both by Kalaglow) and modest staying handicapper Ancient Mariner (by Wollow): dam smart 1½m to 14.6f winner: quite modest maiden: best effort 6½ lengths fourth of 15, staying on steadily, to Advie Bridge at Leicester in September: will be well suited by further: may improve. *R. F. Johnson Houghton.*

SEENACHANCE 2 ch.f. (Apr 2) King of Clubs 124–Masina (Current Coin 118) 69 [1989 5d 7m5 7m4 7f5] 13,000Y: leggy, sparely-made filly: moderate walker: half-sister to Irish 1½m winner Sindara (by Dara Monarch) and a winner in South Africa by Malinowski: dam, Irish 9f winner, half-sister to Champion Stakes winner Giacometti: quite modest maiden: best effort third outing: will stay 1¼m. *R. J. R. Williams.*

SEE NOW 4 ch.g. Tumble Wind (USA)–Rosie O'Grady (Barrons Court) [1988 8g — 7d3 7g* 8g 7f 1989 7d 7f] medium-sized gelding: fairly useful winner of minor event at Lingfield as 3-y-o: no worthwhile form since, lightly raced and generally highly tried: stays 7f: hooded final outing. *J. R. Shaw.*

SEE THE LIGHT 2 b.f. (Feb 26) Relkino 131–Sun Worshipper (Sun Prince 128) — [1989 6m 8f] 3,100Y: leggy filly: second reported foal: dam unraced half-sister to smart 6f and 7f performer Columnist: apparently of little account. *C. B. B. Booth.*

SELDOM IN 3 ch.c. Mummy's Game 120–Pinzamber (Pinicola 113) [1988 6m 7f4 48 8g 8g 1989 8m 7m6 8m 9f a11g4] leggy, angular colt: poor maiden: stays 11f: sweated fourth start: tended to hang fifth one: has swished tail. *J. Wharton.*

SELF IMPROVEMENT (USA) 3 b.c. Sharpen Up 127–Imaflash (USA) 75 (Reviewer (USA)) [1988 NR 1989 11.5m4 10f* 14m] good-topped colt: has scope: sixth foal: half-brother to 3 minor winners in USA: dam stakes-placed winner 10 times at up to 9f: won strongly-run maiden at Folkestone in July, running in snatches and leading well inside final 1f: prominent 1¼m when tailed off in handicap 2½ months later: sour in appearance and found little in amateurs maiden (visored) on debut: suited by 1¼m: trained first 2 starts by J. Gosden. *N. Tinkler.*

SEMINOFF (FR) 3 b.g. In Fijar (USA) 121–Borjana (USA) (To The Quick — (USA)) [1988 NR 1989 7m5 10.1m] sparely-made gelding: first foal: dam, fourth on only start at 2 yrs, is daughter of half-sister to Verbatim: well beaten in summer maidens: bandaged second start: has joined T. Craig. *M. Moubarak.*

SENDFORTHEBOBBIE'S 2 b.f. (Feb 27) Relkino 131–Louise 71 (Royal — Palace 131) [1989 5f 7m6] 2,000Y: sparely-made, rather dipped-backed filly: half-sister to 3 winners, including 7f winner Acapulco (by Music Boy): dam 1½m winner: apparently of little account. *Ronald Thompson.*

SENOJOJ 4 b.g. Tachypous 128–Merency 75 (Meldrum 112) [1988 11.7m 12g — 11.7d3 11.7g3 1989 10d4] workmanlike gelding: has a round action: plating-class maiden: suited by 1½m: acts on a soft surface: visored last 4 appearances: difficult ride. *J. R. Jenkins.*

SEPTIEME CIEL (USA)   2 b.c. (Apr 25) Seattle Slew (USA)–Maximova **119** p
(FR) 121 (Green Dancer (USA) 132) [1989 6d⁵ 7.5s* 8d⁴ 7.5g*]
During the late-'seventies and early-'eighties Francois Boutin monopolised the Criterium de Maisons-Laffitte, his representatives—among them
Zino, Cresta Rider, L'Emigrant and Procida—passing the post first every year
from 1977 to 1983. However, the last six years have seen the stable's grip on
the race loosened somewhat. True, Boutin did win a sub- standard running
with Corviglia in 1988, but the trainer with the best record in the race in
recent years is Criquette Head, who first took the prize in 1984 with the filly
Rapide Pied, then with the Seattle Slew filly Bitooh in 1987, and Septieme
Ciel, also by Seattle Slew, in 1989. Septieme Ciel's record in his first season
was one of constant improvement. He began in early-August with a promising
fifth of eight behind Machiavellian and Jade Robbery in the Prix Yacowlef
at Deauville, confirmed that by winning a minor event on the same course
later in the month, and in the Group 3 Prix La Rochette at Longchamp in
September he ran a sound race, keeping on steadily having pulled hard under
restraint, to finish four lengths fourth of seven behind Linamix, Jade Robbery
and Honor Rajana. The form of the Rochette was made to look very useful
indeed when the first three home went on to dominate the Grand Criterium
three weeks later. Septieme Ciel gave it a further boost with a smooth victory
over five opponents in the Group 3 Prix Thomas Bryon at Saint-Cloud on his
next appearance. Then came the Criterium de Maisons-Laffitte where in a
field of five Septieme Ciel was sent off third favourite at a shade under 5/2. As
a pattern-race winner Septieme Ciel had to concede 3 lb and upwards all
round, yet the penalty proved of little consequence. Indeed, Septieme Ciel put
up one of the best performances by a two-year-old all season, travelling
comfortably just off the pace, quickening immediately when given reminders
at the distance and running on strongly to win in thoroughly convincing
fashion; Sharp Sass, an impressive winner over course and distance on her
only previous start, made most and kept on to finish two lengths away in
second with the Boutin runner Robin des Bois the same distance away in
third. Although it's difficult to say for certain, Septieme Ciel's striking
progress on his final two starts may have had something to do with the
ground: those were the only two occasions on which he raced on a sound
surface. Whatever the reason, Septieme Ciel definitely ended 1989 very much
on the upgrade, and is one to watch out for.
  Seattle Slew had a good year with his two-year-olds. In addition to
Septieme Ciel he was also responsible for the Royal Lodge winner Digression

*Prix Thomas Bryon, Saint-Cloud—
an easy win for Septieme Ciel in this Group 3 race*

and the Remsen Stakes winner Yonder; the achievements of this trio made him the only stallion in 1989 to sire pattern-race or graded two-year-old winners in Britain, France and America. Septieme Ciel is the third foal produced by his dam Maximova and the second winner following the Blushing Groom filly Balchaia, who showed quite useful form to win a listed race over a mile and a quarter at Longchamp in 1988. Maximova was close to the best of her sex in both the seasons she raced; at two she won five out of six, including a dead-heat for the Prix de la Salamandre, and ended the year inferior only to her stable-companion Ma Biche; the following year she finished placed in the French and Irish One Thousand Guineas and also won pattern races at Deauville and Maisons-Laffitte when brought back to six furlongs. There's a reasonable amount of stamina in Maximova's pedigree, enough to suggest that Septieme Ciel has prospects of staying beyond a mile. Green Dancer sires plenty of horses who stay well, and Maximova is a sister to a mile and a half winner out of a dam, the useful miler Baracala, who's a half-sister to both the Guineas winner Nonoalco and Stradavinsky, who showed very smart form at up to a mile and a half. Baracala has made quite a name for herself at stud in the last few years; besides Maximova she's also produced the Nureyev fillies Vilikaia, a good-class sprinter and miler, and Navratilovna, who won the Prix d'Astarte and acquitted herself with credit in several other good mile races in 1989.

		Bold Reasoning	Boldnesian
Seattle Slew (USA)		(b or br 1968)	Reason To Earn
(b or br 1974)	My Charmer	Poker
Septieme Ciel (USA)		(b 1969)	Fair Charmer
(b.c. Apr 25, 1987)		Green Dancer	Nijinsky
	Maximova (FR)	(b 1972)	Green Valley
	(b 1980)	Baracala	Swaps
		(ch 1972)	Seximee

It's clear, then, that Septieme Ciel has plenty going for him on both form and breeding. Add to this the fact that he's a most attractive colt from an excellent stable, and it's clear he has excellent prospects of adding to his successful record as a three-year-old. *Mme C. Head, France.*

SEQUANA (USA) 3 br.f. Critique (USA) 124–Marie de Sarre (FR) (Queen's   —
Hussar 124) [1988 7g 1989 8m 11.5m a10g] leggy, workmanlike filly: no worthwhile form in maidens and minor event: should be suited by middle distances: bandaged at 3 yrs. *D. R. C. Elsworth.*

SEQUESTRATOR 6 b.g. African Sky 124–Miss Redmarshall 80 (Most Secret   —
119) [1988 7g 7f 8f 7m 7f⁴ 7f 7f 1989 10.8m] small, light-framed gelding: poor handicapper: suited by 7f: acts on firm going: inconsistent. *P. D. Evans.*

SEREMO 3 gr.g. Morston (FR) 125–Serenata (Larrinaga 97) [1988 7m 7f 7m 10s*   59
10m* 1989 10s* 10v⁴ 10.6s 12g 10.6s⁴] leggy, sparely-made, angular gelding: enterprisingly ridden to make all in moderately-run handicap at Kempton in March: favourite, fair fourth at Lingfield, easily best effort in handicaps and seller after: should stay 1½m: acts on top-of-the-ground and soft going: suited by forcing tactics. *Mrs N. Macauley.*

SERENADER (FR) 2 b.c. (Feb 21) Ela-Mana-Mou 132–Seattle Serenade (USA)   76
82 (Seattle Slew (USA)) [1989 7m² 8.2g²] angular, good-quartered colt: has scope: first foal: dam, second over 6f at 2 yrs, is from family of top-class Majestic Light: second in September maidens at Chester (favourite) and Haydock: will stay 1¼m. *Major W. R. Hern.*

SERENE SONG 3 br.f. Dominion 123–Dash On 93 (Klairon 131) [1988 6m 1989   —
8m 8f] sparely-made filly: no worthwhile form in maidens though has shown signs of ability: should stay further: sold 6,600 gns Newmarket December Sales. *B. Hanbury.*

SERENIKI 2 b.f. (Apr 15) Dublin Taxi–Highdrive (Ballymore 123) [1989 5f 5m⁵   42
6f a6g⁵ a7g] 1,200Y: leggy filly: poor mover: first foal: dam well beaten in varied races at 3 yrs and 4 yrs: bandaged behind, poor form in varied events: stays 7f. *W. Wilson.*

SERGEANT MERYLL 5 b.g. Marching On 101–Mistress Meryll 61 (Tower   —
Walk 130) [1988 9d 7.6d 7m 7.6g* 8d* 8f⁶ 7m 8g⁶ 8.3m 8g 8m⁵ 8.5m 8m 10g 8g 7g*
1989 7v 8f] sturdy, quite attractive gelding: moderate mover: quite modest winner

Mr G. Moore's "Serious Trouble"

(including for apprentice) as 4-y-o: never dangerous both starts in spring: effective at 7f and 1m: seems to need an easy surface nowadays: visored once. *P. Howling.*

SERGEYEVICH 5 b.h. Niniski (USA) 125–Rexana (Relko 136) [1988 16m* 16g⁴ **109** 20f² 21m⁵ 16f³ 18f³ 20m⁴ 1989 16d 16g² 22.2f² 14m² 16g³ 15g*] lengthy, rather sparely-made horse: very useful performer: favourite, made all in listed event at Milan in October: runner-up in Irish Mutual Building Society Saval Beg EBF Stakes at Leopardstown, Queen Alexandra Stakes at Royal Ascot and listed EBF Curragh Cup (beaten ¾ length by Tyrone Bridge, pair clear) earlier in season: tailed-off last of 3 in Jockey Club Cup at Newmarket, first outing for nearly 3 months: suited by a test of stamina: well suited by a sound surface: occasionally sweats: suited by enterprising tactics: tough and genuine: sold to race in Saudi Arabia 78,000 gns Newmarket December Sales. *J. L. Dunlop.*

SERIOUS BLUE 2 b.c. (Mar 21) Valiyar 129–Blue Linnet 96 (Habitat 134) [1989 — 6m⁶ 5m 6m a7g a8g] strong, good-bodied colt: sixth living foal: half-brother to winners abroad: dam won 4 times over 5f: soundly beaten in maidens and a seller: trained first 2 starts by A. Ingham: sold out of C. Elsey's stable 1,050 gns Ascot October Sales after third outing. *G. G. Gracey.*

SERIOUS TROUBLE 3 ch.c. Good Times (ITY)–Silly Woman (Silly Season **104** 127) [1988 6f² 6m* 6h² 7m³ 7d² 7g⁵ 7g⁴ 1989 8g² 8s⁵ 7f* 7f* 7f² 8m² 8f² 8m* 7g⁴ 8g*] strong, good-topped colt: carries condition: useful performer: justified favouritism in apprentice event at Lingfield and handicap (making all, 2 days later) at Doncaster at end of May and in minor event (long odds on) at Salisbury in August: drifted right and below best when winning apprentice event at Ascot in October:

St Simon Stakes, Newbury—apprentice-ridden Sesame (left)
and Sudden Victory handle the conditions best

worth a try over further: acts on any going: good mount for apprentice: game and consistent. *Sir Mark Prescott.*

SERLBY CONNECTION 4 ch.c. Crofthall 110–Well Connected (Bold And   **56**
Free 118) [1988 7g 10g 7.5g⁶ 8m⁵ 8g* 7.5s* 7m² 8m 7g 8g 6m 8m⁶ 8g 12m³ 12v 1989
10d 12f⁶ 12g⁵ 10m 8f 8.2g 8g 8.5f 7m 10.6d⁶ 8f* 8g* 8g] big, lengthy colt: carries
plenty of condition: has a slightly round action: plating-class handicapper on his day:
successful at Leicester and Carlisle (unseated rider before start) in October: best at
around 1m: acts on any going: ran wide at Pontefract (ridden by 7-lb claimer)
seventh start: slowly away on ninth: has swished tail under pressure: inconsistent.
S. R. Bowring.

SERRANILLA 4 b.f. Tap On Wood 130–Antilla 87 (Averof 123) [1988 10.1m 9g²   **—**
9f⁵ 8g² 1989 8f⁴ 8m 7f 10f] neat filly: quite modest maiden at best: stays 9f: best with
give in the ground: bandaged behind nowadays. *W. G. A. Brooks.*

SESAME 4 b.f. Derrylin 115–Hot Spice (Hotfoot 126) [1988 8m* 8g³ 10.2m*   **113**
10m* 10m² 10.5g⁴ 12s* 11s⁴ 12.5m⁵ 1989 10m 14f⁴ 12g⁵ 11f⁴ 12f* 12m³ 13.5g 10.2m²
14d⁵ 12m² 12v*] strong, lengthy filly: carries condition: very useful performer: 14/1
and ridden by apprentice unable to claim, ran best race of season when winning
11-runner St Simon Stakes at Newbury in October by neck, clear, from Sudden
Victory, rallying inside final 1f: earlier successful in apprentice race at Chepstow:
suited by 1½m: acts on any going, but particularly well on very soft: takes good hold
and has worn a dropped noseband: suited by extreme waiting tactics. *M. F. D.
Morley.*

SETONGO 3 gr.f. Petong 126–Najd 86 (St Chad 120) [1988 NR 1989 7g 7m 7m 8m   **—**
7m 10f] smallish, workmanlike filly: half-sister to 3 winners, including 1986 2-y-o 5f
winner Copper Red (by Song) and French middle-distance winner Akaria (by
Vitiges): dam 5f winner: appears of little account: sold 1,400 gns Newmarket
Autumn Sales. *D. T. Thom.*

SETTLEMENT (USA) 3 ch.f. Irish River (FR) 131–Glad Tidings (FR) 85   **75**
(Pharly (FR) 130) [1988 6g 6g 1989 8.5m 10.2f* 9g 10.2f 9m] rather unfurnished filly:

moderate mover: apparently best effort when making all in maiden at Bath in July, at modest pace initially: behind in handicap and claimer last 2 starts: may stay 1½m: sold 9,500 gns Newmarket December Sales. *I. A. Balding.*

SET YOUR MARK 2 b.c. (Mar 7) On Your Mark 125–Obsession (Wolver Hollow 126) [1989 6f3 6f3 6m5 5m6] IR 1,600Y, IR 4,600Y: lengthy, rather sparely-made colt: keen walker: first foal: dam unraced half-sister to Molecomb Stakes winner Miss Slip: plating-class maiden: best effort second start: unseated rider to post, and got loose final one: sold 6,200 gns Newmarket Autumn Sales. *D. Haydn Jones.* **60**

SEULMA 3 b.f. Pas de Seul 133–Danseuse Classique (CAN) (Northern Dancer) [1988 6f 7m 6g3 1989 8m6 8g 10m 7m 7m] leggy, quite attractive filly: quite modest maiden at best: showed little after reappearance: should stay at least 1m: possibly suited by some give in the ground. *M. E. D. Francis.* **—**

SEVENS ARE WILD 3 b.f. Petorius 117–Northern Glen (Northfields (USA)) [1988 NR 1989 8m] IR 13,000Y: sixth foal: half-sister to Irish 1987 2-y-o 6f winner Rustic Glen (by Rusticaro) and Irish listed-placed sprinter Wolverglen (by Wolverlife): dam unraced half-sister to very useful 1971 2-y-o 5f winner Pert Lassie: well beaten in maiden (moved poorly down) at Yarmouth in June: has joined A. Lee. *J. A. R. Toller.* **—**

SEVEN SONS 2 b.g. (May 11) Absalom 128–Archaic 65 (Relic) [1989 5s6 5m* 6f6 7m4 6g 5f5 7g 6f] 11,500Y: small, close-coupled gelding: half-brother to several winners, including very smart 1978 2-y-o 5f performer Schweppeshire Lad (by Decoy Boy), subsequently a leading sprinter in New Zealand: dam poor maiden: quite modest performer: won maiden auction race at Bath in May: ran poorly in selling nursery final start: subsequently gelded: likely to prove best at up to 6f: best form on top-of-the-ground. *J. Berry.* **61**

SEVEN VEILS 2 b.f. (May 10) Crofthall 110–Casbar Lady 79 (Native Bazaar 122) [1989 5g 6h4 5g 5v 6s] 1,000Y: small, lengthy filly: sixth foal: half-sister to 3 sprint winners, one 2 yrs the other also successful over hurdles: dam won 5 times over 5f: poor plater: form only on fourth outing: sold 450 gns Doncaster November Sales. *E. J. Alston.* **33**

SEVERS 6 br.g. Ballad Rock 122–Courting (Quorum 126) [1988 NR 1989 8g 6d 8.2f] rangy gelding: fair winner in 1986 when trained by H. Cecil: bandaged, tailed off in handicaps (last 2 selling) as 6-y-o: stays 9f: blinkered final outing. *M. W. Easterby.* **—**

SEW HIGH 6 b.g. Nicholas Bill 125–Sew Nice 71 (Tower Walk 130) [1988 6g 6g 6d 5f 7m5 6s5 8g5 8m 6d2 6g4 6g 5s3 5g 6g 1989 5s5 6m* 6f6 5f 6f5] close-coupled, lightly-made gelding: poor mover: quite modest handicapper nowadays: 20/1, made all in 20-runner event at Leicester in June: ran moderately afterwards: suited by sprint distances: not at his best on firm going, acts on any other: bandaged off-hind final outing: suited by forcing tactics: good mount for apprentice: usually taken down steadily: sold to join Mrs J. Wonnacott 1,900 gns Ascot September Sales. *B. A. McMahon.* **59**

SEXY MOVER 2 ch.c. (Feb 12) Coquelin (USA) 121–Princess Sinna (Sun Prince 128) [1989 7g5 8g6] IR 13,500Y: fifth foal: half-brother to Irish 3-y-o 1½m winner Midsummer Fun (by Trojan Fen), a winner in USA by Kampala and 2 poor maidens by Hard Fought: dam once-raced half-sister to Bay Express: plating-class form in late-season maidens at Folkestone and Edinburgh. *J. P. Hudson.* **53**

SHAADI (USA) 3 b.c. Danzig (USA)–Unfurled (USA) (Hoist The Flag (USA)) [1988 7m* 7g* 1989 8d* 8m 8m* 8f* 8f 7m5] **126**
Having asked the trainer to explain his horse's much improved running, the stewards accepted his explanation that he had no explanation. This pragmatic response was elicited from the Curragh stewards in May following Shaadi's consummate revival in the Airlie/Coolmore Irish Two Thousand Guineas. What couldn't be explained was Shaadi's lamentable showing in the General Accident Two Thousand Guineas two weeks earlier in which he'd started third favourite and finished about twenty lengths behind Nashwan, Swinburn reporting afterwards that Shaadi 'never gave him any feel going down to the start and never appeared with any chance in the race'. Stoute told the Irish stewards that the colt had been well guarded before the Newmarket Guineas and had been in fine form immediately before and after the race. Shaadi's performances in the Charles Heidsieck Craven Stakes and the Irish Guineas, his starts either side of the Two Thousand, and in the St James's Palace Stakes at Royal Ascot, all within the space of two months, would have

Airlie/Coolmore Irish Two Thousand Guineas, the Curragh—
Shaadi makes amends for a disappointing effort at Newmarket.
Great Commotion just gets the better of Distant Relative (rails) for second

entitled him to finish close up to Nashwan. In the Craven Stakes, the best guide to the Two Thousand Guineas in recent years, Shaadi was made favourite following good home reports and won decisively, followed in by two other unexposed colts in Exbourne and Citidancer. The only runner who had contested one of the major two-year-old prizes, the William Hill Futurity winner Al Hareb, ran badly. There seemed no obvious reason why Exbourne (on whom late replacement Starkey carried 1 lb overweight) should overturn his two-and-a-half-length beating; Shaadi had joined him on the bridle three furlongs out and though taking time to go on he'd drawn clear in good style in the last hundred yards. Exbourne was beaten a length by Nashwan in the Guineas. Another form line of scant consolation to Shaadi's Guineas supporters were the performances of Danehill who was beaten a length and a half by Nashwan then four and a half lengths by Shaadi at the Curragh. Saratogan's running in the two races tells a different story of course and the problems settling Danehill clearly affected him more in Ireland, but regardless of that Shaadi's Guineas victory was a high-class performance, make no mistake. He got a nice lead from Danehill's pacemaker Tatsfield, went on three furlongs out and was never seriously challenged; Great Commotion chased him throughout and was beaten two and a half lengths with Distant Relative staying on from the rear half a length behind him.

There are few things in racing to which the general public latches on so readily as possible malpractice and skullduggery, and in 1989 Shaadi's somewhat inconsistent record inspired such images just about as effectively as any other horse in training which lacked the aid of a sonic gun. His Guineas aberration still fresh in the mind, Shaadi's fourth appearance of the season in the St James's Palace Stakes was preceded by his ominous drifting in the betting from 11/8 on to 6/4. He promptly demonstrated how ridiculous such apparently, we're told, apocalyptic signals can be. Shaadi set a sound pace to Scenic (on his seasonal debut) and the hard-pulling duo Great Commotion and Thorn Dance, then ran on splendidly under pressure in the straight with the outsider Greensmith staying on best of the others to be beaten two lengths. Favourable comparisons were made afterwards between Shaadi and the stable's 1985 Two Thousand Guineas winner Shadeed but these looked hasty at the time and many observers, ourselves included, had already revised Stoute's table of merit to Shaadi's detriment twenty hours later after Zilzal's

St James's Palace Stakes, Ascot—an all-the-way win for Shaadi

sparkling triumph in the Jersey Stakes. After Royal Ascot, Shaadi fell very much beneath his stable-companion's shadow. In the Sussex Stakes he helped force the pace before dropping away pretty tamely over two furlongs out to finish a well-beaten seventh of eight behind Zilzal. Shaadi's two-and-a-half-length fifth of eight to Gabina in the Prix de la Foret was a much better effort but still a bit below his best.

Shaadi (USA) (b.c. 1986)	Danzig (USA) (b 1977)	Northern Dancer (b 1961)	Nearctic Natalma
		Pas de Nom (b or br 1968)	Admiral's Voyage Petitioner
	Unfurled (USA) (b 1974)	Hoist The Flag (b 1968)	Tom Rolfe Wavy Navy
		Lemon Souffle (br 1958)	Johns Joy Miel

In Shaadi's entry in *Racehorses of 1988* we mentioned the promise shown by several Danzig two-year-olds and in 1989 we can report that in nearly all cases that promise reached fruition. The latest season also provided probably the clearest demonstration yet that Danzig is a marked influence for speed. A nomination to Danzig went for 250,000 dollars at the Matchmaker Breeders' Exchange's January (1990) Sale. Shaadi is the ninth foal out of the U.S. two-year-old six-furlong maiden race winner Unfurled. Unfurled's was hitherto a solid if unspectacular producing record. Her first seven foals were winners, the first Unbiased (by Foolish Pleasure) winning a seven-furlong Newmarket maiden at three years, Xannax (by The Minstrel) a mile race at Vichy in 1988 as a four-year-old and all the rest gaining their victories in North America, the best of them being Pleasure Cay (by Foolish Pleasure) who won two Grade 3 handicaps over seven furlongs and an extended mile. The next two dams Lemon Souffle and Miel both won in minor company, but only once and twice

Sheikh Mohammed's "Shaadi"

respectively, and although Lemon Souffle is half-sister to several stakes winners she produced only one herself in the three-year-old six-furlong Miss Woodford Stakes winner Wageko. Another of her foals is Sanquirico's maternal grandsire Lanyon but this isn't an outstanding pedigree by any means. Anything is possible by Danzig though and Shaadi fetched 900,000 dollars at Keeneland as a yearling, the fifth-highest price paid for a Danzig yearling that year.

Shaadi's physique will certainly have had quite a bearing on that purchase price; he's a big, lengthy colt who had plenty of scope. He also has a quick action. One most likely explanation for Shaadi's drift in the betting at Royal Ascot was his pre-race demeanour. He was on his toes, swishing his tail and in a lather before the parade began. It was much the same story during the parade for the Sussex Stakes (though not before the Guineas), in the paddock at Ascot before the second of his two victories as a two-year-old and to a lesser extent during his other appearances in the latest season. He was suited by a mile and acted on firm going and a soft surface, although his participation on the firm ground at Goodwood was in doubt until the morning of the race. Shaadi is to stand at the Kildangan Stud, County Kildare, in 1990 at a fee of IR £20,000. *M. R. Stoute.*

SHABANAZ 4 b.c. Imperial Fling (USA) 116–Claironcita 97 (Don Carlos) [1988 7d 8g 7g⁵ 7g* 8f² 7g* 8g 7s⁵ 7f² 7g* 7g⁴ 7d 1989 8g³ 8d 8m² 8f 8f⁶ 8.5g⁶ 8f] rangy, angular colt: good mover: useful winner as 3-y-o: placed in listed event at Doncaster and minor contest at Brighton (beaten 5 lengths by Luzum) in 1989: never a threat

93

in handicaps or in Diomed Stakes (out of his depth) at Epsom on other 5 outings: not seen out after June: effective at 7f and 1m: well suited by a sound surface: often wears a dropped noseband. *R. Hannon.*

SHACKMAN 3 ch.g. Shack (USA) 118–Peperonia (Prince Taj 123) [1988 6f 1989 — 7m 7m 12.3f⁵] leggy gelding: poor maiden. *J. H. Johnson.*

SHADEUX 3 ch.g. Valiyar 129–A Deux (FR) 80 (Crepello 136) [1988 5g⁶ 6f² 6h* **73** 7.5s² 7m⁵ 7s 8s 7.5f⁴ 8.2m 1989 8g 12.3s 11f⁵ 13m 12.2m² 12f*] leggy, quite good-topped gelding: moderate mover: modest performer: won claimer (claimed to join M. Pipe £15,530) at Goodwood in June: may prove as effective over 1¼m as 1½m: acts on any going: blinkered last 4 starts: winning juvenile hurdler. *C. W. Thornton.*

SHADOW BIRD 2 b.f. (Apr 26) Martinmas 128–In The Shade 89 (Bustino 136) — [1989 7m 7m 7g] IR 13,000Y: leggy, workmanlike filly: first foal: dam won from 1½m to 14.8f: well beaten in maidens. *G. A. Pritchard-Gordon.*

SHADOW BOXER 3 ch.g. Absalom 128–Loup de Mer 86 (Wolver Hollow 126) **71** [1988 6d 6d 1989 6v 6m 7h* 8m* 8m⁴ 8.3m*] rather sparely-made gelding: has a moderate, quick action: modest handicapper: successful at Brighton (gambled on and first form) and Kempton (odds on) in June then Windsor (visored, having been outpaced and had plenty to do) in August: sweating, ran well in between: may well stay beyond 1m: acts on hard ground: needs plenty of driving. *J. Sutcliffe.*

SHADY HEIGHTS 5 b.h. Shirley Heights 130–Vaguely 92 (Bold Lad (IRE) 133) **118** [1988 8v4 9g³ 8d² 10g* 9.2d⁵ 10g² 10g* 10.5f* 10d² 12s 10g⁴ 12f 1989 9g⁵ 10s⁵ 10.5f³ 10f 9.7m⁵] sparely-made, angular horse: moderate walker: has a round, scratchy action: high class as 4-y-o, second in Coral-Eclipse Stakes at Sandown, International Stakes (awarded race having been beaten on merit) at York and Phoenix Champion Stakes: generally well below his best subsequently: ran best race in 1989 when third of 7, staying on steadily without being a threat, to Ile de Chypre in Juddmonte International Stakes at York, first outing for nearly 4 months: ran poorly in Arlington Million (reportedly broke blood vessel) at Chicago next outing: best forcing pace over 1¼m: unsuited by soft going, acts on any other. *R. W. Armstrong.*

SHADY STAR 3 b.f. Lochnager 132–Shady Desire 88 (Meldrum 112) [1988 NR — 1989 7g 11g] strong filly: fifth foal: half-sister to 6f and 7f winner Ben Jarrow (by Roman Warrior) and fair 6f winner Jarrovian (by Moorestyle): dam won from 5f to 1m: very burly, no sign of ability in maiden and claimer. *P. Liddle.*

SHADY VALLEY (USA) 3 b.f. Solford (USA) 127–Paille (USA) 77 (Bold — Bidder) [1988 NR 1989 12.2g] 17,000Y: fifth foal: half-sister to Andrew Wong (by Irish River), winner in France from 1m to 10.5f: dam, 1¼m winner, daughter of Prix Vermeille winner Paulista: well behind in maiden at Catterick in September: sold 1,900 gns Newmarket December Sales. *R. J. R. Williams.*

SHAGUDINE (USA) 2 ch.f. (Mar 15) Shadeed (USA) 135–Lady Norcliffe (USA) **86** (Norcliffe (CAN)) [1989 5m* 5f 6g³ 7g*] 120,000Y: small, good-quartered filly: lacks scope: has a quick action: second foal: half-sister to 3-y-o La Minor (by The Minstrel): dam good winner at up to 11f: won 13-runner maiden at the Curragh in May and 17-runner minor event at Phoenix Park in September: last of 13 in Queen Mary Stakes at Royal Ascot: will stay 1m. *D. K. Weld, Ireland.*

SHAHRAYAR (MOR) 3 b.f. Happy Lord (FR)–Bellinga (FR) (Violon d'Ingres) — [1988 NR 1989 10.2f 8m] half-sister to 3 winners in Morocco: dam French 9.5f to 10.5f winner: sire French 1m and 9f winner, later successful at up to 1½m in Morocco: always always behind in maidens: sold to join K. Morgan 1,400 gns Doncaster August Sales. *G. Lewis.*

SHAHRIZA 2 br.f. (Mar 4) Persian Bold 123–Amalee 57 (Troy 137) [1989 6d 6g] — 8,000Y: leggy, angular filly: has a round action: second foal: half-sister to 3-y-o Musil (by Mummy's Pet), 6f winner at 2 yrs: dam, maiden and possibly temperamental, stayed 14.6f: well beaten in late-season maidens at Newbury and Leicester (gave trouble stalls). *C. C. Elsey.*

SHALBOOD 3 b.c. Runnett 125–Deer Park (FR) (Faraway Son (USA) 130) [1988 — § 6g 6f⁶ 6d 7g* 1989 6d⁶ 7f⁶ 7g 9m 8.2d⁵] big, good-bodied colt: fair winner at 2 yrs: well below form in varied events as 3-y-o, showing plenty of temperament: refused to do his best in claimer final start: probably stays 9f: blinkered second outing: has given trouble at stalls and refused to enter them in early-September (bandaged): sold to join C. Spares 7,500 gns Newmarket Autumn Sales: one to avoid. *Mrs L. Piggott.*

SHALFLEET 3 b.g. Sharpo 132–River Lane (Riverman (USA) 131) [1988 6d² 6g²   **99**
1989 5s* 6g] well-made gelding: won minor event at Haydock, leading 1f out then
weakening close home, by neck from Habitancy: favourite, ran poorly in £8,900
handicap at Newmarket 9 days later in October: stays 6f: acts on soft going: gave
trouble at stalls at Haydock: sold 7,200 gns Newmarket Autumn Sales. *B. W. Hills.*

SHAMAL 2 b.f. (May 5) Exhibitioner 111–Kilpeacon (Florescence 120) [1989 6g]   **—**
IR 6,300Y: half-sister to several winners, including Irish 1½m winner Tracy's
Sundown (by Red Sunset) and 1987 2-y-o 5f seller winner Peaconpala (by Kampala):
dam won from 5f to 7f in Ireland: last of 19 in maiden at Redcar in November. *G. P.
Kelly.*

SHAMBO 2 b.c. (May 10) Lafontaine (USA) 117–Lucky Appeal 36 (Star Appeal   **72**
133) [1989 6f⁵ 6f⁶ 7g 7g³ 8.2d 10g⁶] strong, quite attractive colt: moderate walker:
third foal: brother to a winner in Norway and half-brother to 4-y-o 1½m winner Run
Free (by Julio Mariner): dam half-sister to very useful sprinter Lucky Hunter:
modest maiden: easily best efforts fourth start and final one: gives impression will
stay well. *C. E. Brittain.*

SHAMIRANI 3 gr.g. Darshaan 133–Sharmada (FR) 113 (Zeddaan 130) [1988 8g⁶   **107**
1989 8m* 11.5m² 10f²] leggy, good-topped gelding: won maiden at Yarmouth in
June: creditable second following month in minor event at Yarmouth and Extel
Stakes at Goodwood: stays 11.5f: acts on firm going: has twice flashed tail: sold to
join J. H. Johnson 40,000 gns Newmarket Autumn Sales and subsequently gelded:
useful. *M. R. Stoute.*

SHAMSHOON 2 b.c. (Jan 31) Shareef Dancer (USA) 135–Bentinck Hotel 74   **102**
(Red God 128§) [1989 5f² 5.1m² 5.8h* 5g* 5g⁴ 5f⁴ 6g³ 6g⁵] 43,000F, 62,000Y:
smallish, lengthy colt: closely related to 1m winner Maysara and 5f winner Conrad
Hilton (both by Be My Guest) and half-brother to several winners, including fairly
useful 1¼m winner Benzina (by Jaazeiro) and fair 5f and 6f winner Latch String (by
Thatch): dam 2-y-o 5f winner: useful performer: won early-summer minor events at
Bath and Sandown: good fifth in Racecall Gold Trophy at Redcar in October: suited
by 6f: tends to hang. *Mrs L. Piggott.*

SHAMYL 2 ch.c. (Apr 28) Ahonoora 122–Salidar (Sallust 134) [1989 6f⁵ 6f⁶ 7f a7g   **63**
a7g⁵ a6g] 90,000F, 76,000Y: small, lengthy colt: third reported foal: half-brother to
3-y-o 6f and 7f winner Budapest (by Diesis): dam winner over 9.5f in Ireland,
half-sister to Park Appeal, Nashamaa (both by Ahonoora) and Desirable: quite
modest maiden: bred to stay 1m but may prove better at shorter. *J. L. Dunlop.*

SHANAKEE 2 b.c. (Apr 14) Wassl 125–Sheeog 80 (Reform 132) [1989 5s⁶ 6f⁴ 6h⁴   **56**
6m⁵ 6f⁵] medium-sized colt: has scope: second foal: brother to 3-y-o Shillelagh: dam
5f and 6f winner, from very good German family: plating-class maiden: blinkered
final start: sold 1,600 gns Ascot August Sales. *C. R. Nelson.*

SHANNON EXPRESS 2 gr.g. (Jan 31) Magic Mirror 105–Tatisha (Habitat 134)   **59**
[1989 6m⁴ 7m⁴ 6g a6g⁶] 1,100F: leggy, angular, plain gelding: fifth foal: half-brother
to modest 1½m and 2¼m winner Relkisha (by Relkino): dam, French 1m winner, is
half-sister to high-class sprinter Green God: quite modest form in maidens: stays
7f: bandaged final start. *P. A. Kelleway.*

SHARARDOUN 3 gr.c. Sharpen Up 127–Shannfara (FR) (Zeddaan 130) [1988   **99**
6d³ 1989 10.4m* 10.2m² 8f 8g] leggy, close-coupled, rather sparely-made colt: has a
fluent, rather round action: favourite, won maiden at Chester in May: again well
supported, below form in valuable handicaps at York and Ascot (wore net muzzle)
last 2 outings: stays 1¼m: acts on top-of-the-ground: sold 21,000 gns Newmarket
Autumn Sales. *M. R. Stoute.*

SHARAZARI 4 gr.c. Kings Lake (USA) 133–Sharmada (FR) 113 (Zeddaan 130)   **106**
[1988 10g⁵ 1989 8.5g² 8f 9m⁵ 8.5g* 8m* 8g⁶] tall, leggy, useful-looking colt:
favourite, successful in 6-runner minor event at Beverley: much better effort when
winning £5,000 ladies race at Ascot later in July by length from Serious Trouble:
co-favourite, moderate last of 6 in £7,100 contest at Kempton: should stay 1¼m: has
often hung: has joined J. Gosden: useful. *M. R. Stoute.*

SHARBLASK 5 b.h. Sharpo 132–Blaskette 99 (Blast 125) [1988 8d 8d 7g² 8d*
8s⁴ 8g 8v⁴ 8f⁴ 8d 10.2g 10m 8m 9g⁴ 11m 8.2d³ 8g a8g] leggy, quite good-topped
horse: moderate mover: useful performer at his best: well below form in 1989,
taking little interest and soon tailed off at Southwell final outing: suited by 1m: used
to go particularly well on a soft surface: usually blinkered or visored: one to be wary
of: sold 2,700 gns Doncaster November Sales. *C. W. Thornton.*

SHARENARA (USA) 3 ch.f. Vaguely Noble 140–Shademah 88 (Thatch (USA)   **—**
136) [1988 8m 1989 10f⁴] smallish, angular, sparely-made filly: third foal: half-sister

to dual Derby winner Shahrastani (by Nijinsky): dam, won from 7f to 8.2f, is half-sister to Shakapour: plating-class form in maidens: not seen out after fourth at Beverley in May. *M. R. Stoute.*

SHAREUBELLE 2 b.f. (May 3) Saher 115–Blue Kingsmill 69 (Roi Soleil 125) — [1989 5f 8g] IR 1,250Y: half-sister to 3-y-o City Native (by Be My Native) and Irish 9f winner Queen of Wolves (by Wolver Hollow): dam, third over 6f at 2 yrs, is granddaughter of Irish Oaks winner Agar's Plough: behind last 2f in maidens at Chepstow in May and Leicester in November. *E. A. Wheeler.*

SHARI LOUISE 6 br.m. Radetzky 123–Jenny Splendid 101 (John Splendid 116) — [1988 7d 6g³ 6s³ 7f 6d* 6s 6d³ 7g 6d⁶ 5v 1989 6d 6g 5f 7f 7m⁵ 6g 6s 6s] sturdy, workmanlike mare: bad mover: poor handicapper: stays 6f: best on a soft surface: usually blinkered: good mount for apprentice: refused to enter stalls fourth intended outing: sold 1,050 gns Doncaster November Sales. *J. L. Spearing.*

SHARINSKI 2 ch.g. (May 14) Niniski (USA) 125–Upanishad 85 (Amber Rama 58 (USA) 133) [1989 7f⁵ 7g³ 7.5f⁶ 7m 9g] IR 28,000Y: lengthy, workmanlike gelding: closely related to modest maiden Flaming Dancer (by Ile de Bourbon), best at 1¼m, and half-brother to 3-y-o 1m winner Fenfire (by Trojan Fen), useful 1¼m winner Goody Blake (by Blakeney) and middle-distance winner Diwali (by Great Nephew): dam, 1¼m winner, is half-sister to smart sprinter Bas Bleu: plating-class maiden: had stiff task and was never going well when visored in a nursery final start: will probably be suited by a test of stamina. *M. H. Easterby.*

SHARKA 3 b.f. Shareef Dancer (USA) 135–Ghaiya (USA) 110 (Alleged (USA) 138) 97 [1988 6m⁵ 8m* 8s* 1989 8.5s* 11.3m³ 8f³] leggy, quite good-topped filly: won listed race at Epsom in April, one of only 2 on far side: favourite, 4½ lengths third to both Braiswick in Cheshire Oaks (odds on) and Comic Talent in listed event at Sandown in May: should be suited by further than 1m: probably acts on any going. *H. R. A. Cecil.*

SHARLIE'S WIMPY 10 ch.g. Tumble Wind (USA)–Sweet Sharlie 77 (Fighting 47 d Charlie 127) [1988 6g 6m⁴ 7f³ 7m⁶ 7d⁴ 7.5f 7m 8m 6g 1989 6m² 6f⁶ 5f³ 7f⁴ 7m² 7m⁴ 7g³ 5f 8f⁶] strong, attractive gelding: carries plenty of condition: good mover: poor handicapper: best at 6f or 7f: well suited by a sound surface: has worn blinkers: has won for apprentice: finds little and well served by waiting tactics. *W. J. Pearce.*

SHARON'S ROYALE 6 ch.g. Royal Match 117–Rose Amber (Amber Rama 74 (USA) 133) [1988 8m 8g⁵ 8f⁵ 8.5m 8f⁵ 8.5g² 8g³ 8g² 10s² 8g³ 8d 8s⁴ 9s* 9g 8f* 8g⁵ 1989 11m 10m 9f⁴ 8g² 9m⁵ 8s 8f³ 8g⁴ 8f] workmanlike, close-coupled gelding: poor mover: modest performer: effective at 1m and stays 1¼m: acts on any going: good mount for inexperienced rider: sold to join A. Jones 9,200 gns Doncaster October Sales. *R. M. Whitaker.*

SHARPALTO 2 br.c. (Jun 4) Noalto 120–Sharp Venita 84 (Sharp Edge 123) [1989 67 7.3g 5m 6m 5m³ 5m 5m³ 5g⁵ 6m⁴ 5f⁵] rather unfurnished colt: third foal: half-brother to 3-y-o Honey Mill (by Milford) and quite modest 6f and 7f winner Sharp Times (by Faraway Times): dam sprinter: quite modest maiden: ran best races in nurseries last 4 outings: should stay 7f. *E. A. Wheeler.*

SHARP ANNE 2 gr.f. (Jan 20) Belfort (FR) 89–Princess Sharpenup 63 (Lochna- 82 ger 132) [1989 5g* 5f* 5f² 5f 6m* 6f³ 6g³ 5m³ 6g³ 5g³ 6s⁵ 6v] 4,000Y: leggy, quite good-topped filly: progressed well physically: moderate mover: second foal: sister to 3-y-o My Concordia: dam third over 5f at 2 yrs on only outing: fair performer: successful in maiden at Carlisle in April, minor event at Pontefract in May and claimer at Newcastle in July: stays 6f: acts on firm going, and seems unsuited by soft: sold 5,000 gns Doncaster October Sales. *J. Berry.*

SHARP CHARTER 3 ch.c. Kris 135–Centrocon 112 (High Line 125) [1988 NR 84 1989 10.1m 14f³ 16.5g² 14d⁵ 16m³ 18.1g²] strong, angular colt: half-brother to top-class Time Charter (by Saritamer) and Known Charter (by Known Fact), a 6f winner at 2 yrs who stayed 1¼m: dam, 1m to 2m winner, is sister to Nicholas Bill and Centroline: fair maiden: stays 2m: acts on top-of-the-ground: probably best with visor: wandered under pressure for lady rider, and is difficult ride: sold 19,000 gns Newmarket Autumn Sales. *M. R. Stoute.*

SHARPER BLUE 2 b.c. (Mar 18) Sharpo 132–Riverlily (FR) (Green Dancer — p (USA) 132) [1989 8v] 29,000Y: useful-looking colt: fourth foal: half-brother to 3-y-o 1¼m winner Steel Spark (by Persepolis), 1986 2-y-o 7f winner Lord Westgate (by Hello Gorgeous) and a winner over jumps in France: dam, placed over middle distances in France, is half-sister to high-class French 1972 2-y-o Robertino: 25/1, shaped well in 23-runner minor event at Newbury in October, keeping on well not knocked about: will improve. *P. J. Makin.*

SHARPGUN (FR) 3 ch.c. Sharpo 132–Whitegun (FR) (Carwhite 127) [1988 5m⁶ **70**
6d² 7s⁶ 1989 6d 6v⁴ 8g³ 7m⁴ 7s 8.2g] tall, rather leggy colt: moderate walker:
modest on most form: should prove best at up to 1m: yet to race on very firm going,
probably acts on any other: ran badly in blinkers on reappearance: sold to join V.
Young 10,000 gns Newmarket Autumn Sales. *P. A. Kelleway.*

SHARP INVITE 2 ch.f. (Feb 22) Sharpo 132–Invitation 107 (Faberge II 121) **43**
[1989 5g 5d] 6,000F, 5,800Y: leggy filly: seventh living foal: half-sister to modest
11.5f winner Quickstep (by Hotfoot), also successful over hurdles: dam, sister to
Rheingold, won at up to 13f: poor form in early-season maidens: sent to J. Eustace.
P. J. Feilden.

SHARP JUSTICE 3 ch.c. Sharpo 132–Lady Justice 90 (Status Seeker) [1988 **103**
5m* 6m² 5g³ 6g* 6g* 6g⁵ 6f 1989 8s 7g⁵ 6f 7.6f 6m* 6g 7f⁴ 7.6m 7g⁵ 7g²] well-
made, close-coupled colt: moderate mover: useful at best: dead-heated in £11,400
handicap at Newcastle in July, rallying well: ran well last 2 outings: stays 7f: acts on
firm going: visored final start at 2 yrs: inconsistent. *M. J. Ryan.*

SHARP MOVER 2 b.f. (Feb 16) Sharpo 132–Matoa (USA) (Tom Rolfe) [1989 5s* **78**
6f²] sparely-made filly: half-sister to several winners, including fairly useful 1m to
15f winner Prince Spruce (by Big Spruce) and 6f and 1m winner Rear Action (by
Home Guard): dam won twice at up to 1m in USA: heavily-backed favourite, won
8-runner maiden at Sandown in April by 12 lengths: long odds on, beaten ¾ length
by Tribal Lady in 3-runner minor event at Newbury following month: stays 6f. *B. W.
Hills.*

SHARP N' EARLY 3 b.c. Runnett 125–Irish Kick (Windjammer (USA)) [1988 **110**
5s* 5m³ 5g⁴ 6f³ 6g⁵ 7m⁴ 6f* 1989 7d⁵ 8v⁴ 8m 6m⁶ 6.5d³ 8s 7g⁶] rangy colt:
moderate mover: won Scottish Equitable Gimcrack Stakes at York as 2-y-o: 66/1,
about 5½ lengths sixth to Cadeaux Genereux in July Cup at Newmarket: fair third to
Cricket Ball in Prix Maurice de Gheest (again never nearer) at Deauville, easily best
effort after: best form over 6f, though gives impression may prove suited by 7f: acts
on any going: smart at his best. *R. Hannon.*

SHARP N' EASY 2 b.f. (Feb 3) Swing Easy (USA) 126–Dulcidene 71 (Behistoun **62**
131) [1989 5m⁵ 5f² 6g⁴ 6g⁴ a7g a8g a7g⁶] sixth reported foal: half-sister to 13.8f
seller winner Co-Tack (by Connaught) and 2 other winners: dam won sellers at
around 1¼m: quite modest maiden: ran moderately last 3 starts. *R. Hannon.*

SHARP'N SHINE (USA) 3 b.c. Sharpen Up 127–Repetitious 103 (Northfields **— §**
(USA)) [1988 7f⁴ 8f* 8.2d 1989 8s 11.7m] strong, rangy colt: has a long, rather round
stride: fair winner at 2 yrs: showed unsatisfactory temperament when well beaten in
handicaps in spring as 3-y-o: should stay 1¼m: possibly unsuited by soft surface:
tends to sweat: sold 13,500 gns Newmarket Autumn Sales: one to treat with caution.
M. R. Stoute.

SHARP N' SMOOTH 2 ch.c. (Feb 28) Sharpo 132–Winning Look 71 (Relko **58**
136) [1989 5d⁴ 5m² 5m] 4,600F, 13,000Y: close-coupled, workmanlike colt: has a
quick action: half-brother to winners in USA and Italy: dam, ungenerous maiden
stayed 1¾m, from good family: plating-class maiden: not raced after July. *R.
Hannon.*

SHARPO'S LAD 4 ch.c. Sharpo 132–Hissy Missy 70 (Bold Lad (IRE) 133) [1988 **—**
8m 8f⁶ 7f 5.3f 8g 6g 1989 6f] sturdy, good-bodied colt: behind in varied events,
including seller: blinkered 3 times: visored once. *J. P. Hudson.*

SHARP REMINDER 5 b.h. Sharpo 132–Fallen Rose (Busted 134) [1988 6g⁴ **110**
7g* 6d⁴ 6s⁴ 6g⁶ 6m 6s 6g 6m 1989 6d² 6g² 7.2s³ 6m 6g 6d⁶] lengthy, quite attractive
horse: carries condition: poor mover: useful performer: good second in £6,000
event at Kempton and listed race at Newmarket in spring: off course over 5 months
after fourth outing: modest sixth in Thirsk listed contest: effective at 7f, but
probably better suited by 6f when conditions are testing: best with give in the
ground: visored once at 4 yrs. *C. N. Williams.*

SHARP ROMANCE (USA) 7 ch.h. Sharpen Up 127–Sir Ivor's Favour (USA) **— §**
(Sir Ivor 135) [1988 6f 5m⁵ 5f 6d 6g 5m 7.3g 5d 6s 6g 5m 6s 1989 6v 8d 6s 6f 8f⁴] big,
strong, quite attractive horse: carries condition: one-time smart sprinter: well
beaten vast majority of starts (often facing stiff task) since finishing second in
Vernons Sprint Cup in 1987: has been tried in blinkers and visor: finds little off
bridle. *J. P. Hudson.*

SHARP RUNNER (FR) 2 gr.c. (Mar 14) Star Appeal 133–Assembly Day 66 **70**
(General Assembly (USA)) [1989 6f³ 6h⁶ 6m³ 7f⁶ 9g 8f a7g] 2,600F, 15,500Y:
workmanlike colt: second foal: half-brother to 1988 2-y-o 5f winner Parton Express
(by Bay Express): dam ran 4 times as 2-y-o: modest maiden: creditable sixth of 13 to

Native Tribe in nursery at Goodwood fourth outing: ran poorly final 2 starts: stays 7f. *J. L. Dunlop.*

SHARP SALUTE (USA)   2 ch.c. (Mar 10) Sharpen Up 127–Topolly (USA)   **74 p**
(Turn-To) [1989 7g 8.2g4] tall, leggy colt: half-brother to several winners, including 3-y-o Continental Claire (by Peterhof), 5f winner at 2 yrs, and very smart French middle-distance colt Coquelin (by Blushing Groom): dam, French 9f winner, is granddaughter of top-class Bella Paola: 13/2, fourth of 14 finishers behind very easy winner Golan Heights in maiden at Haydock in September: favourite in big field at Newbury 6 weeks previously: stays 1m: likely to improve further. *B. W. Hills.*

SHARP SASS (USA)   2 b.f. (Feb 22) Sharpen Up 127–Village Sass (USA) **107**
(Sassafras (FR) 135) [1989 7s* 7g2] $575,000Y: first foal: dam, winner at up to 9f, including in minor stakes: won 11-runner maiden at Longchamp by 2½ lengths: 2 lengths second to Septieme Ciel in Criterium de Maisons-Laffitte: will stay 1m: useful. *J. E. Pease, France.*

SHARP SHAPE (USA)   4 ch.c. Sharpen Up 127–Love That Girl (USA) (High   —
Echelon) [1988 8m2 8m 7f6 10g6 1989 9d 10s 12m] useful-looking colt: second in valuable maiden at York as 3-y-o, only form: blinkered last 2 outings: sold to join D. Bell, 2,900 gns Newmarket July Sales. *R. Hannon.*

SHARP STEVEN   3 b.c. Balliol 125–Cheb's Honour 70 (Chebs Lad 120) [1988   **66**
5s6 5d4 6f 6g 1989 6v 5m 6f5 5.8h3 5.8m3 5.8h* 5.3h* 6g5 5m 5m] leggy colt: successful in maiden at Bath in July and handicap at Brighton in August: stays 6f: acts on hard ground and possibly needs a sound surface: blinkered third start (slowly away, found little) and last 5: sometimes wears a tongue strap: sold 3,800 gns Doncaster September Sales. *J. Berry.*

SHARP THISTLE   3 b.f. Sharpo 132–Marphousha (FR) (Shirley Heights 130)   **78**
[1988 5g5 5g3 6f 7m* 8s4 7.5g4 8m4 1989 7.3s 8.5s 7f6 7f2 7m5 6m 7f6 7g3 8m 7s6 8g4 a8g4] leggy, light-framed filly: turns near-fore out: moderate mover: modest performer: below form last 4 outings: likely to stay middle distances: probably acts on any going: has run creditably for 5-lb claimer: sometimes on toes. *W. J. Musson.*

SHARP TIMES   6 b.g. Faraway Times (USA) 123–Sharp Venita 84 (Sharp Edge   **66**
123) [1988 7m* 6m6 6m* 7m2 6d* 6m 6s 6d 6s2 1989 6s 6v6 6d* 6f 6f 6m 6m6 5g3 6g 6d2 6m] lengthy, shallow-girthed gelding: modest handicapper: well-backed favourite, confirmed promise of previous outing when winning at Ripon in April: gambled on again, very good second of 24, leading final 1f, to Dawn's Delight at Haydock in October: effective at 5f and stays 7f: acts on any going: has won for apprentice: wanders in front, usually held up and ideally suited by strong gallop. *W. J. Musson.*

SHARQUIN   2 b.c. (May 3) Indian King (USA) 128–Lady of The Land 75 (Wollow   **48**
132) [1989 7g 8d] 7,200Y: unfurnished colt: second foal: dam won over 1m and is half-sister to very useful 1976 2-y-o Easy Landing: always behind in modest company at Leicester and Thirsk in November. *M. Brittain.*

SHATTERED DREAMS   2 ch.c. (Mar 11) Sharpo 132–Only A Dream (FR)   **72 p**
(Green Dancer (USA) 132) [1989 5m4 5m*] IR 160,000Y: close-coupled, quite attractive colt: has a quick, moderate action: first foal: dam, 11f winner at 4 yrs in France, is half-sister to 2 useful or better middle-distance performers in France and a daughter of a smart winner at up to 1½m in France: won 22-runner maiden at Windsor in July by a short head, running on strongly from 2f out: will be suited by 6f. *J. Gosden.*

SHAVIAN   2 b.c. (Mar 31) Kris 135–Mixed Applause (USA) 101 (Nijinsky **106 p**
(CAN) 138) [1989 7g2 7m*]
   Although it carries upwards of £10,000 in added prize money nowadays, the EBF Mornington Stakes, a graduation event for two-year-old colts and geldings, is not regarded as one of the more important races run at Ascot's September meeting. However, the subsequent achievements of its recent winners have been impressive. Ajdal started the ball rolling; he followed his win in 1986 with another in the Dewhurst three weeks later and became top sprinter the following year; Sheriff's Star, the 1987 winner, continued the good work by becoming one of the best middle-distance colts around in both the next two seasons; then Shaadi, who only scrambled home, proved himself a good-class miler in 1989 with victories in the Irish Two Thousand Guineas and the St James's Palace Stakes. So Shavian has something to live up to. Shavian made his debut in another race that's lately gained a reputation as a starting point for potentially smart performers, the EBF Queens Own

EBF Mornington Stakes, Ascot—strong-galloping Shavian impresses

Yorkshire Dragoons Stakes at Doncaster in September. He was a short-priced favourite despite looking a little less forward than one or two of his opponents; considering he also ran green he shaped with plenty of promise to go down by a neck to the 25/1-chance Message Pad. On the strength of that effort Shavian was sent off at odds on in a field of five at Ascot. As at Doncaster he was asked to make all, and this time he dominated throughout, responding impressively when shaken up approaching the two-furlong pole then drawing clear without being asked a serious question to beat the newcomer Kaheel by a long-looking three lengths. Racegoers were denied an opportunity to see Shavian in action against some of the better two-year-olds when a plan to run him in the Vodafone Horris Hill Stakes at Newbury in October was scrapped. However, we saw enough of him to convince us he's capable of holding his own in stronger company; we'll be watching his progress with interest.

	Kris (ch 1976)	Sharpen Up (ch 1969)	Atan Rocchetta
Shavian (b.c. Mar 31, 1987)		Doubly Sure (b 1971)	Reliance II Soft Angels
	Mixed Applause (USA) (b 1976)	Nijinsky (b 1967)	Northern Dancer Flaming Page
		My Advantage (b 1966)	Princely Gift My Game

Shavian took the eye in the paddock both times—he's a lengthy, good-bodied sort with plenty of scope. He's also well bred. His sire Kris hasn't had a really outstanding representative in the last couple of years but he's had plenty of more-than-useful ones, and in the latest season his daughters Rafha and Moon Cactus both won two-year-old pattern races for the Cecil stable. Shavian's dam Mixed Applause, a half-sister to the dam of Be My Chief, who won the seven-furlong Sweet Solera Stakes as a two-year-old in her only season to race, was also trained by Cecil, and so were her four previous foals. All four won at least once, the best of them being Paean (by Bustino), who romped away with the 1987 Gold Cup only to be forced into retirement by injury a few days later. While it's not to be anticipated that Shavian will have Paean's stamina, he'll be well suited by a mile early on as a three-year-old and is likely to stay a mile and a half in due course. His brother, the hard-pulling Tempering, has won at a mile and a quarter and stays further; his sister Khandjar won over nine furlongs, the longest distance she tackled. Shavian, a strong-galloping type with a powerful action, has yet to race on ground softer than good. *H. R. A. Cecil.*

SHAWINIGA 3 b.f. Lyphard's Wish (FR) 124–Shining Bright (USA) (Bold **58** Bidder) [1988 5.5g3 6g* 6g4 6g2 7.5g* 8g3 1989 8g5 8s 7m2 7m2 9f2 7m3 7.5m6 10f3 8.2g2 8m] IR 2,000F, 65,000 francs (approx £6,560) Y: sparely-made filly: first foal: dam unraced: successful in minor events at Bordeaux and Dax as 2-y-o: quite modest form in sellers and claimers here: claimed out of N. Tinkler's stable £5,300 penultimate start: sweating, ran moderately in amateurs handicap final one: stays 9f: carried head high and gave impression ill at ease on firm ground eighth outing: trained until after fourth by J. Rouget. *J. S. Wilson.*

SHAYNOOR 3 ro.c. Niniski (USA) 125–Shaiyneen (Kalamoun 129) [1988 7g⁵ **89**
1989 9f² 10.6g³ 10.2f* 10m 12m³ 12g⁶] angular, unfurnished colt: easily landed odds
in maiden at Bath in September: good third in handicap at Chepstow penultimate
start: ran moderately in similar events either side, well-backed favourite and
travelling strongly 1m in £8,000 race at Newmarket then blinkered at Carlisle: stays
1½m: acts on firm ground: sold 30,000 gns Newmarket Autumn Sales. *R. F. Johnson
Houghton.*

SHAYRAZ 3 b.f. Darshaan 133–Shaiyra (Relko 136) [1988 NR 1989 8d* 10.5f² **110**
12m* 12f⁴ 13.4m⁴] leggy, good-topped, attractive filly: has plenty of scope:
moderate mover: fifth foal: half-sister to 3 winners, including smart miler Shaikiya
(by Bold Lad, IRE) and useful 1987 2-y-o 8.2f winner Shehiyr (by Hotfoot): dam
unraced half-sister to high-class French stayer Shafaraz: won maiden at Warwick in
May and minor event at Leicester in June: in frame in £5,600 event (staying on
strongly) at York, moderately-run Ribblesdale Stakes (hanging throughout final
2½f) at Royal Ascot and listed event (favourite) at Chester: should prove suited by
1½m and an easy surface. *R. F. Johnson Houghton.*

SHEBA'S PAL 2 b.f. (Mar 8) Claude Monet (USA) 121–Bread 'n Honey 51 **—**
(Goldhills Pride 105) [1989 5s 5d] 2,600Y: first foal: dam, placed once from 4 races at
2 yrs, is half-sister to smart sprinter Prince Reymo: well beaten in April maiden
auctions at Leicester and Pontefract. *G. Blum.*

SHEEN CLEEN LAD 2 ch.c. (Mar 14) On Your Mark 125–Mishcasu (Majority **57**
Blue 126) [1989 5f* 5m 6f⁶ 7.5m⁶ 8f⁴ 8.2s 8f a6g² a7g] IR 4,000Y, 12,500 2-y-o:
lengthy, rather angular colt: fourth reported foal: dam won over 9f at 4 yrs in Ireland
and is half-sister to dam of very useful middle-distance staying filly Senorita
Poquito: plating-class performer: made all in maiden at Doncaster: good second in
late-year claimer at Southwell: ran poorly final outing: stays 1m: possibly unsuited
by soft ground: visored last 2 outings: races keenly. *Ronald Thompson.*

SHEER PRECOCITY 2 b.c. (Apr 11) Precocious 126–Age of Elegance (Troy **110**
137) [1989 6m* 6m* 7f⁴ 6m⁵ 7g 6g³] IR 54,000Y: strong, useful-looking colt: first
foal: dam French 11f and 1½m winner, is half-sister to Elegant Air: showed much
improved form when always-prominent third of 25, beaten 5½ lengths, by Osario in
Racecall Gold Trophy at Redcar in October: earlier successful in maiden at Haydock
and minor event at York, and fourth of 5 to Be My Chief in Lanson Champagne
Vintage Stakes at Goodwood: evidently best at 6f: ran poorly fourth outing. *F. H.
Lee.*

SHEIKH'S PET 3 b.c. Mummy's Pet 125–Parlais 101 (Pardao 120) [1988 5g⁶ 5g⁵ **70**
5g⁴ 6f 6f⁶ 6s 5g 6m 1989 5s³ 5s 6m³ 6f* 7h² 6h⁴ 6m³ 6f⁶ 6g⁶ 6f] small colt:
moderate walker: poor mover: modest handicapper: won at Brighton in May: stays
7f: acts on any going: visored in 1989, except for third outing: ran moderately in
blinkers final 4 starts at 2 yrs. *J. P. Hudson.*

SHEILA SHALLOT (USA) 3 br.f. Green Dancer (USA) 132–Evening Belle **—**
(USA) 97 (Damascus (USA)) [1988 7g⁶ 1989 8m⁴] compact filly: 50/1, 9½ lengths
fourth of 18, leading 7f, to Shieling in maiden at Bath in May. *C. R. Nelson.*

SHEILAS HILLCREST 3 b.c. Hotfoot 126–Be Honest 95 (Klairon 131) [1988 **—**
8f 1989 16.2f] leggy, sparely-made colt: poor walker: bit backward, never placed to
challenge in maidens in the North. *N. Tinkler.*

SHELBERRY 3 b.f. Jester 119–Dainty Eden 53 (Orbit 106) [1988 5f 5f 1989 5d **—**
6f⁶] angular filly, somewhat sparely-made: moderate mover: poor form in sellers
then maidens: should be best at 5f: sold 900 gns Doncaster November Sales. *J.
Berry.*

SHELBOURNE 7 br.g. Shirley Heights 130–Super Dancer 72 (Taj Dewan 128) **—**
[1988 13s⁶ 1989 14g] ex-Irish gelding: extremely lightly raced on flat nowadays. *J. S.
Haldane.*

SHELBOURNE LADY 3 ch.f. Coquelin (USA) 121–La Vosgienne (Ashmore **51**
(FR) 125) [1988 5g 6f 6m 7d⁵ 7m* 7d⁵ 7m 8g² 1989 12s⁵ 8g⁶ 8m 8m³ 10m 8.3m 10g⁶
8.2f 7f] leggy, close-coupled filly: moderate mover: plating-class performer: best
form at 1m: possibly unsuited by extremes of going: sold to Horse France 1,500 gns
Newmarket Autumn Sales. *R. Hannon.*

SHELLAC 3 b.c. What A Guest 119–Lacquer 118 (Shantung 132) [1988 NR 1989 **109**
10f* 10.5m⁴ 10f* 11s* 9g 12v] sturdy, good sort: really good walker: has a quick
action: half-brother to several winners, including good middle-distance colt Shining Finish and very smart stayer Bright Finish (both by Nijinsky): dam won
Cambridgeshire and Irish 1000 Guineas: short-priced favourite, won maiden at
Sandown in June and Nottingham minor event and listed Doonside Cup (by 6 lengths

Doonside Cup, Ayr—Shellac wins easily;
the other in the picture, Operation Wolf, lost second place to Sudden Victory

from Sudden Victory) at Ayr in September: ran on strongly from impossible position for eighth place in Cambridgeshire Handicap at Newmarket: co-second favourite, headway then soon beaten 3f out when tailed off in Group 3 event at Newbury 3 weeks later: stays 11f: possibly unsuited by heavy going, acts on any other: has turn of foot: very useful: remains in training. *L. M. Cumani.*

SHELTER   2 b.c. (Feb 19) Teenoso (USA) 135–Safe House 81§ (Lyphard (USA)   **46** 132) [1989 5f 7m] robust, useful-looking colt: fourth foal: half-brother to French 4-y-o 7.5f winner Highest Risk (by High Top) and 1986 2-y-o 6f winner Safety Pin (by Grundy): dam, temperamental, won at 10.8f: poor form in maidens at Newbury in May and Wolverhampton in June. *R. J. R. Williams.*

SHEMALEYAH   2 b.f. (Feb 15) Lomond (USA) 128–Burghclere 86 (Busted 134)   **—** [1989 7f] robust, useful-looking filly: fifth foal: closely related to 3-y-o 2m winner Invite (by Be My Guest) and half-sister to smart 6f and 1¼m winner Capo di Monte (by Final Straw) and 1¾m winner Kingsmill (by Kings Lake): dam, 1¾m winner, is daughter of Highclere: weak 5/1, green and in need of race, slowly away and never going well in 8-runner maiden at Leicester in October: showed a quick action. *Major W. R. Hern.*

SHERARDA (FR)   3 b.f. Glenstal (USA) 118–Sherniya (USA) 82 (Empery (USA)   **114** 128) [1988 7.5d³ 1989 12.5d* 12g³ 12g6 10g5 10g5 8g² 9.2g² 8g* 10g6] second foal: half-sister to French provincial 1¼m winner Shansadasi (by Vayrann): dam, twice-raced over 7f at 2 yrs, is out of smart French performer at around 1½m Sherkala: won maiden at Maisons-Laffitte in June and listed race at Longchamp in October: placed in Prix de Malleret at Longchamp, listed race at Evry and Prix de l'Opera (beaten head by Athyka) at Longchamp: not discredited in Yellow Ribbon Stakes at Santa Anita in November: stays 1½m, and effective at 1m: acts on a soft surface. *A. de Royer-Dupre, France.*

SHERIFF'S BAND   2 ch.g. (May 4) Posse (USA) 130–Willis (FR) (Lyphard   **58** (USA) 132) [1989 5s³ 6m] 2,100F: tall, unfurnished gelding: has scope: shows knee action: third living foal: brother to French 1m and 10.5f winner Gambero and half-brother to Irish 3-y-o Tinakilly (by Scorpio): dam, placed once in France at 3 yrs, is half-sister to North American winner at up to 7f Play The King: placed in maiden at Thirsk in April: showed little in similar event same course nearly 5 months later. *M. H. Easterby.*

SHERIFF'S STAR   4 gr.c. Posse (USA) 130–Castle Moon 79 (Kalamoun   **125** 129) [1988 10m² 12m6 12f* 12f* 14.6g³ 1989 12m4 12g* 12g* 12m4 12s³]
Although Sheriff's Star failed to meet his early-season objective, the Tancred Stakes at Rosehill in Australia, and wasn't invited to take part in his

proposed late-season one, the Japan Cup, he still managed to earn over £250,000 in prize money and fully vindicate connections' decision to keep him in training. As in 1988, Sheriff's Star ran five times and won twice. But whereas the previous year his successes were achieved in Group 2 races, in the latest season they came in a higher grade.

Sheriff's Star's season started quietly—he looked short of his peak and proved one paced when beaten seven lengths into fourth behind Unfuwain in the General Accident Jockey Club Stakes at Newmarket in May. That didn't prevent his being sent off a well-backed favourite in his next race, the Hanson Coronation Cup at Epsom, where he faced eight rivals. Apart from Saint Estephe's year, 1986, this was the biggest field assembled for the race since Oncidium came out on top in a field of ten in 1965. Sheriff's Star, held up as usual, was left with a fair bit to do when the tempo quickened entering the straight, but he responded gamely to pressure and stayed on strongly to gain the upper hand a hundred yards or so from the post. He had half a length to spare on the line, with the stable-companions Ile de Chypre and Green Adventure filling the minor places and Mountain Kingdom, unable to cope with the step back in distance, a soundly-beaten sixth. It was then announced that the Grand Prix de Saint-Cloud—a race which his half-brother Moon Madness won in 1987—would be Sheriff's Star's next target.

French-trained horses have found the Grand Prix de Saint-Cloud difficult to win in recent seasons, Village Star and Strawberry Road being the only successful candidates in the last eight years; and Sheriff's Star was the fifth British-trained winner in the 'eighties, following Glint of Gold, Diamond

Hanson Coronation Cup, Epsom —
a good finish between the grey Sheriff's Star and Ile de Chypre

Grand Prix de Saint-Cloud—even closer between Sheriff's Star, Golden Pheasant (No. 6) and Boyatino; Mill Pond finished fourth but was relegated to fifth

Shoal, Teenoso and Moon Madness, to lift this prestigious prize. Sheriff's Star was the sole overseas contender in a field of six when Love The Groom was a late withdrawal due to a high temperature, and he started third favourite behind the odds-on Star Lift and Boyatino, winner of the Grand Prix d'Evry and Prix Jean de Chaudenay, respectively, on their latest starts. The Derby fifth Mill Pond, seven-year-old Vaguely Pleasant and ex-British Golden Pheasant, runner-up to Old Vic in the Chester Vase, completed the field. The feature of the race was the very slow gallop set by Mill Pond for over a mile. Sensibly, Ives had moved Sheriff's Star up before the final straight and he was in prime position when the race began in earnest. Sheriff's Star took it up at the furlong marker and held on by a head from Golden Pheasant, with Boyatino a short head away in third. Mill Pond came next but was disqualified and placed fifth for interfering with Star Lift a furlong and a half out. Bearing in mind the ground was good, just how slowly the race was run can be gauged by the fact that Exceller, who holds the fastest time for the race, took three seconds less to cover an extra half furlong—the race distance was reduced to a mile and a half in 1987—and in the circumstances that less than two and a half lengths covered the entire field wasn't surprising. Sheriff's Star was Lady Herries' first winner with her first runner in France and he provided Ives with his first success in a French Group 1 race. Ives left Britain in August to continue his riding career in Hong Kong, after partnering nearly a thousand winners since his first in 1971. He's probably best known for his victory on Teleprompter in the 1985 Budweiser Million and for his record-breaking partnership with 1984 Horse of the Year Provideo.

The King George VI and Queen Elizabeth Diamond Stakes at Ascot three weeks later was Sheriff's Star's next race, but on this occasion he wasn't ridden to best advantage in a moderately-run race and merely stayed on steadily from the rear to finish fourth, beaten eight lengths by Nashwan and Cacoethes. Sheriff's Star was a below-par third on his final outing, beaten over seven lengths by Ibn Bey in the R & V Europa-Preis at Cologne in September. Two nights of heavy rain in Cologne had made the ground soft and connections reported Sheriff's Star was never going well. He did return home with an injury but is reported likely to stay in training as a five-year-old.

820

		Forli	Aristophanes
	Posse (USA)	(ch 1963)	Trevisa
	(ch 1977)	In Hot Pursuit	Bold Ruler
Sheriff's Star		(b 1971)	Lady Be Good
(gr.c. 1985)		Kalamoun	Zeddaan
	Castle Moon	(gr 1970)	Khairunissa
	(ro 1975)	Fotheringay	Right Royal V
		(b 1964)	La Fresnes

Sheriff's Star was the fourth successive winner out of Castle Moon, herself a winner three times at up to thirteen furlongs, following Moon Parade, Moon Madness and Wood Chanter. The last-named now stands at stud following an injury-restricted career. The sequence wasn't maintained in the latest season as Moon Mystery (by Mummy's Pet) failed to win for Dunlop, who also has in his care the once-raced two-year-old Lucky Moon (by Touching Wood). Castle Moon also has a yearling filly by Be My Guest: she wasn't covered in 1988. The genuine Sheriff's Star, a leggy, sparely-made colt and a good walker, has a round action when galloping. He has done nearly all his racing on a sound surface and his performance in Germany suggests that soft doesn't suit him, but he did come a good second to Emmson on dead in the William Hill Futurity as a two-year-old. Sheriff's Star has given trouble at the stalls in the past and occasionally used to be loaded early, but that problem seems to have been overcome. *Lady Herries.*

SHERNA LAVENDER (DEN) 2 b.f. (Mar 25) Shernazar 131–Cotton Lavender 52 (Sassafras 135) [1989 5g] angular filly: half-sister to 2 winners abroad and a winner over hurdles: dam, half-sister to smart stayer Realistic, never raced beyond 7f: always behind in 13-runner Newmarket maiden in April. *R. Guest.* —

SHERPAMAN 7 b.g. Northfields (USA)–McCoy (USA) (Hillsdale) [1988 10.2d 10v 7m 10m 12.2f⁵ 16m 1989 8m] smallish, strong, sturdy gelding: of little account: has worn visor and blinkers. *G. P. Kelly.* —

SHERTANGO (USA) 4 b.f. Khatango (USA)–Native Sherry (USA) 78 (Raise A Native) [1988 10m 12f 10m 8m 8m 7d 1989 8.2f 8f³ 8g 8f 7.6m⁶ 7m 8h*] angular filly: poor handicapper: won 4-runner apprentice event at Carlisle (second outing in 2 days) in July: stays 1m: acts on hard going: blinkered once. *C. W. Thornton.* 44

SHERWOOD FOREST 7 ch.g. Vaigly Great 127–Roanello 102 (Roan Rocket 128) [1988 NR 1989 7g 10s 10f] sturdy gelding: behind in selling handicaps in spring: wears bandages: sold 1,500 gns Ascot 2nd June Sales. *J. B. Sayers.* —

SHERZINE 3 br.f. Gorytus (USA) 132–Tableline (USA) (Round Table) [1988 6g⁴ 6s⁴ 6m 7m 1989 10d 11g 12f* 12.2m 12h⁴ 12m⁴] lengthy, workmanlike filly: plating-class performer: favourite, won seller (no bid) at Thirsk in May: mostly below form otherwise: stays 1½m well: acts on any going: blinkered once at 2 yrs: ran poorly for 7-lb claimer and when edgy: sold to join Mrs J. Retter 3,900 gns Doncaster October Sales. *M. H. Easterby.* 49

SHESHELLS 4 b.f. Zino 127–Sandy Doll (Thatching 131) [1988 8f 10g 7m² 7m³ 7f 7f 1989 7d 9f³ 8m] leggy, sparely-made filly: poor mover: poor maiden: should stay 1¼m: seems unable to take much racing on firm ground: blinkered once at 3 yrs: has flashed tail and is a difficult ride: winning hurdler (broke down in October). *G. M. Moore.* 35

SHEWHOMUSTBEOBEYED 2 ch.f. (Mar 21) Miami Springs 121–Sleepline Promise 63 (Record Token 128) [1989 5d³ 5g 5m⁶ 5f 5m⁵] 580Y: workmanlike filly: third foal: half-sister to a poor plater by Kind of Hush: dam showed some ability at 2 yrs: poor maiden: visored final start: unsatisfactory temperamentally: one to leave alone. *A. W. Jones.* 44 §

SHIELING 3 b.f. Persian Bold 123–Geldar Shiel (Grundy 137) [1988 NR 1989 8m* 8.2m⁶ 8.5m² 8f 7g² 8m⁵ 8f* 9g³] leggy, sparely-made filly: good mover: third foal: half-sister to very useful French 7.5f to 1½m winner Takfa Yahmed (by Main Reef), thrice successful over 7f here as 2-y-o in 1985, and to a winner in Denmark by Try My Best: dam unraced daughter of useful 1¼m filly Crofting: won maiden at Bath in May and minor event (edging left in front) at Warwick in October: on toes nd bit mulish at stalls, good third in £15,400 handicap at Newmarket in November, set plenty to do: should stay 1¼m: acts on firm going: sold 50,000 gns Newmarket December Sales. *L. M. Cumani.* 96

SHIFNAL 4 ch.g. Tower Walk 130–Leitha (Vienna 127) [1988 NR 1989 10.2g — 16.2d 10f 15.3f] leggy gelding: half-brother to a winning plater and a winner abroad: dam never ran: no sign of ability. *A. P. James.*

SHIFTING BREEZE 2 ch.f. (Mar 13) Night Shift (USA)–Easterly Wind 94 **69** (Windjammer (USA)) [1989 7f 8m² 8g* a8g⁴] 1,800F, 7,600Y: workmanlike filly: fifth foal: half-sister to fair sprinter Northern Trust (by Music Boy): dam sprinter: won maiden at Edinburgh in November by 1½ lengths: modest fourth in nursery at Lingfield later in month. *T. Thomson Jones.*

SHIFT OVER (USA) 2 b.f. (Apr 18) Night Shift (USA)–Becky Branch (Run The 62 Gantlet (USA)) [1989 5m⁵ 6f³ 6f 6g] leggy, close-coupled filly: second foal: dam once-raced sister to top-class middle-distance filly April Run: quite modest maiden: best effort second start: will be better suited by 7f+: sold 3,600 gns Newmarket December Sales. *R. V. Smyth.*

SHIFT SURPRISE (USA) 2 ch.f. (May 15) Night Shift (USA)–Al-Burak — p (Silver Shark 129) [1989 a7g⁴] neat filly: sister to 3-y-o Evening Shift and half-sister to several winners, including 7f to 1¾m winner Eastern Palace (by Habitat): dam won at up to 1¼m in Ireland and France: bit backward and ridden by 7-lb claimer, around 9 lengths fourth of 13, running wide into straight, to Petite Butterfly in maiden at Lingfield. *R. V. Smyth.*

SHIFTY ALBERT 3 ch.g. Morston (FR) 125–Miss Shifter (Realm 129) [1988 — 7m 7g 6d 1989 8f] rather sparely-made gelding: no sign of ability, including in seller: once blinkered: sold 750 gns Ascot October Sales. *J. E. Long.*

SHIKABELL 5 br.m. Kala Shikari 125–Betbellof 65 (Averof 123) [1988 12f² 17g — 1989 14.6g⁴ 12m 17.1m] leggy mare: in frame in maidens at Brighton and Doncaster: soundly beaten in handicaps other on 3 starts on flat in last 2 seasons: stays 1¾m: acts on firm going and probably unsuited by heavy: inconsistent. *P. J. Jones.*

SHIKARI KID 2 b.g. (Apr 19) Kala Shikari 125–Muffet 75 (Matador 131) [1989 **52** 5g⁶ 6m⁶ 7m 7m⁵ 8g⁴ a7g] 9,400Y: smallish, angular gelding: has a round action: half-brother to several winners here and abroad, including sprinters Captain's Bidd (by Captain James) and Feather Sound (by Be My Guest): dam (known as Matty) won over 5f: plating-class maiden: stays 1m: blinkered or visored last 2 outings. *S. G. Norton.*

SHIKARI'S SON 2 br.c. (Apr 26) Kala Shikari 125–Have Form (Haveroid 122) 62 [1989 6m⁶ 7g⁴ 6g] 4,400Y, 17,000 2-y-o: leggy colt: first foal: dam stayed 7f: quite modest form in varied company, best effort second start: may do better in handicaps. *S. T. Harris.*

SHIKARI SUNSHINE 2 b.g. (Mar 11) Kala Shikari 125–Sunshine Holyday 96 — (Three Wishes 114) [1989 5g⁵ 6f⁴ 6f 6m 7m] 7,000Y: small, workmanlike gelding: has a round action: half-brother to fairly useful 1982 2-y-o 7f winner Wargame, out-and-out stayer Image of War (both by Warpath) and 3 other winners, including fairly useful 1977 2-y-o 1m winner Westwood Boy (by Saintly Song): dam stayer: soundly beaten in maidens and a claimer: visored penultimate start. *J. S. Wilson.*

SHILLELAGH 3 b.f. Wassl 125–Sheeog 80 (Reform 132) [1988 5d⁴ 5m 5g⁴ 1989 **68** 6m² 6f 7.3m³ 7m⁴ 7f⁴ 8g⁵ 8f 10g] smallish, workmanlike filly: modest handicapper: stays 1m: acts on top-of-the-ground: constantly swished tail before race penultimate start: sold 1,200 gns Newmarket Autumn Sales. *D. W. P. Arbuthnot.*

SHINE FOR SURE 3 b.f. Song 132–Annie Get Your Gun 69 (Blakeney 126) — [1988 5f⁶ 5m² 5s³ 5g 6f 6g 6m 8d 6g 1989 8g⁵ 8g 5m] neat filly: poor form, including in sellers: appears not to stay 1m: sold 1,200 gns Doncaster October Sales. *B. A. McMahon.*

SHINING JEWEL 2 b.c. (Apr 17) Exhibitioner 111–Vaguely Jade (Corvaro — (USA) 122) [1989 7g] IR 3,800F, IR 6,400Y: medium-sized colt: second foal: half-brother to 3-y-o 1m winner Aardvark (by On Your Mark): dam never ran: well beaten, slowly away, in maiden at Newmarket in July. *E. Eldin.*

SHINING STEEL 3 b.c. Kris 135–Lady Moon 101 (Mill Reef (USA) 141) [1988 **123** 7g* 7m² 7g² 7.3s⁵ 1989 7g⁶ 8.5s* 7m⁴ 8.5g*] rangy, good-bodied colt: carries condition: usually impressive in appearance: good walker: made virtually all at Epsom when winning £10,300 contest in April and Group 3 Diomed Stakes (by neck and the same from Beau Sher and Greensmith) in June: well below his best, unable to dominate, at Newmarket otherwise as 3-y-o: suited by around 1m and forcing tactics: acts on soft going: very smart: sold to be trained by C. Whittingham in USA and was unplaced in Hollywood Derby in November. *H. R. A. Cecil.*

Diomed Stakes, Epsom—left to right, Greensmith, Shining Steel and Beau Sher

SHINNEL WATER 3 b.c. Rolfe (USA) 77–Linda Dudley 81 (Owen Dudley 121) —
[1988 NR 1989 11m 7m 8.2g⁵ 7g 6s⁵] workmanlike colt: first living foal: dam
lightly-raced half-sister to William Hill Futurity winner Count Pahlen: plating class
at best: should stay further than 1m: possibly suited by an easy surface. *T. Craig.*

SHINY PENNY 4 b.f. Glint of Gold 128–Luck Penny 87 (Bustino 136) [1988 **63**
10m² 10f⁶ 10m⁴ 11.7m 12.2d³ 1989 13.6f 12g³ 14f⁴ 12m 12g 12.2g] neat filly: quite
modest maiden: probably stays 1¾m: acts on firm going and a soft surface: has been
bandaged: ridden by 7-lb claimer at 4 yrs. *J. A. Glover.*

SHIP OF GOLD 3 b.f. Glint of Gold 128–Sally Rose 92 (Sallust 134) [1988 7m⁶ **78**
1989 10.1g⁴ 12g³ 10d] compact filly: moderate mover: modest form when in frame in
minor event at Windsor and maiden at Haydock, in latter taking strong hold to post
and in race then hanging in straight: blinkered and edgy, well beaten in Newbury
maiden nearly 3 months later: stays 1½m: one to have reservations about. *Major W.
R. Hern.*

SHMAME (USA) 3 ch.c. Topsider (USA)–Golden Cay (Habitat 134) [1988 6g² **75**
1989 6d* 6m 8d] leggy, close-coupled colt: won maiden at Pontefract in April: easily
better effort in handicaps when running creditably (bit coltish, facing stiff task) next
start: off course nearly 6 months after: should stay beyond 6f: acts on
top-of-the-ground and a soft surface: sold 13,000 gns Newmarket Autumn Sales. *C.
R. Nelson.*

SHOCKING AFFAIR 2 ch.f. (Apr 18) Electric 126–Bedspring 67 (Pyjama Hunt —
126) [1989 6g a6g] small, light-framed filly: first foal: dam half-sister to useful 1982
2-y-o sprinter Carolside: behind in November maidens at Leicester and Lingfield. *J.
W. Payne.*

SHOEHORN 2 br.c. (Jan 26) Prince Tenderfoot (USA) 126–Relkalim 102 (Relko —
136) [1989 7g] IR 17,000F, IR 50,000Y: half-brother to several winners abroad: dam,
useful at up to 1¼m, is half-sister to top-class 2-y-o and Coronation Stakes winner
Sovereign: 25/1, soon behind and ridden along in 28-runner maiden at Newmarket in
November. *B. W. Hills.*

SHOE TAPPER 3 b.g. Song 132–Saniette (Crystal Palace (FR) 132) [1988 5m³ **48** d
7m 1989 7s 8g 7g 7h 10f⁴ 9f⁵ 13.1h* 14m 14m 15.3g 15.3f⁶ 12.5f] workmanlike
gelding: won handicap at Bath in July: little other form, in mid-division in Wolverhampton seller last time: stays 13f: acts on hard ground: blinkered at 2 yrs and on
third and penultimate outings in 1989: sweating (twice edgy) eighth to eleventh
starts, taking keen hold first 3 of them: sold 2,600 gns Newmarket Autumn Sales:
unreliable. *L. G. Cottrell.*

SHOKRAN 4 b.g. Top Ville 129–Celtic Twilight 111 (Varano) [1988 10v² 8g⁴ —
10.1m 13.3d 1989 14g 10m] leggy gelding: moderate mover: modest maiden at his
best: slowly away and tailed off in handicap at Yarmouth final outing: stays 1¼m:
needs give in the ground: sold to join R. Simpson 3,000 gns Ascot July Sales. *J. B.
Sayers.*

SHOO BEE DOO 2 gr.c. (Apr 29) Absalom 128–Campagna (Romulus 129) [1989 **64**
6m 7f⁶ 6m 7m³ 7f⁴ 7m 8s⁵] 21,000Y: quite good-topped colt: shows a round action:
half-brother to several winners, including quite useful middle-distance filly
Carlingford Rose (by Dance In Time): dam won over 1¼m in France: quite modest
maiden: probably stays 1m: sold 7,600 gns Newmarket Autumn Sales. *N. Tinkler.*

SHOOT AHEAD 3 b.c. Shirley Heights 130–Shoot Clear 111 (Bay Express 132) **98**
[1988 7m² 7f³ 1989 10g² 12.3m* 12.3g* 13.3m³] lengthy colt: favourite at Ripon,
won maiden (odds on, made all) in August and handicap in September: co-favourite,
creditable third of 16 in 'Coral' Autumn Cup (Handicap) at Newbury: reportedly
chipped knee bone on reappearance, and off course over 4 months after: lacks turn
of foot, and should be suited by further. *M. R. Stoute.*

SHOOT TO KILL 2 ch.f. (May 23) Posse (USA) 130–Sorata (FR) (Sodium 128) **64**
[1989 5g 6f³] tall, leggy, sparely-made filly: half-sister to numerous winners abroad,
including useful Italian miler Mantero (by Derrylin): dam won from 6f to 11f in
France: sweating, 7 lengths third of 12 to Salsabil in maiden at Nottingham in
September: gave trouble at stalls on debut: will be suited by 7f +. *J. G. FitzGerald.*

SHOREHAM LADY 4 br.f. Strong Gale 116–Tarpon Springs (Grey Sovereign **35**
128§) [1988 12g 12g⁵ 12d⁴ 16m 12g 1989 10d 10f 12g 13f³] leggy, lengthy filly: poor
maiden: suited by around 1½m: sold to join S. Cole 6,800 gns Ascot August Sales. *H.
P. Rohan.*

SHOREHAM MARINA 3 ch.f. Horage 124–Miss Duckins (Simbir 130) [1988 **75**
7d⁶ 8s 1989 8m* 8m² 9.2f 10g 9m] leggy, good-topped filly: 25/1, made virtually all
to win maiden at Brighton in May: good second in minor event at Edinburgh, easily
best effort after: stays 1m: acts on top-of-the-ground: sweating fourth start: on toes
final one. *M. McCormack.*

SHORT BLADE 4 ch.f. Wattlefield 117–Couteau 92 (Nelcius 133) [1988 10v 8s —
11.7g 10s 1989 14s] sturdy, dipped-backed filly: little sign of ability: probably doesn't
stay 1¾m: sweated only outing (March) at 4 yrs. *M. J. Ryan.*

SHORT ENCOUNTER 2 b.c. (Jan 31) Blakeney 126–Double Stitch 74 (Wolver —
Hollow 126) [1989 7g 7m] 6,600Y: workmanlike colt: has a quick action: second foal:
dam 8.2f winner: backward, well beaten in fair company at Kempton and Lingfield in
September. *D. T. Thom.*

SHORT SHOT 3 b.c. Young Generation 129–Blessed Damsel 99 (So Blessed **86** d
130) [1988 8d⁶ 7g³ 7s⁵ 1989 9s⁴ 10.1m² 10m⁵ 10.6s 10g] useful-looking colt: shade
unfurnished: best effort when beaten head in handicap at Windsor in June: ran
moderately in similar company after, finding little third start: suited by 1¼m: best
form on top-of-the-ground: sweating and on toes final outing: lacks turn of foot: sold
to join J. Jenkins 16,500 gns Newmarket Autumn Sales. *W. Hastings-Bass.*

SHORT STRAW 2 b.c. (Apr 30) Thatching 131–Makeacurtsey (USA) (Herbager — p
136) [1989 7g] 50,000Y: medium-sized, sturdy, lengthy colt: closely related to very
useful 1¼m winner Hill's Yankee (by Thatch) and half-brother to 3 other winners,
all at least useful, including smart 1976 2-y-o 5f performer Piney Ridge (by Native
Prince): dam, placed in USA, is half-sister to 3 good stakes winners, including very
smart turf horse Knightly Manner: 33/1, with leaders to halfway in 13-runner
£10,000 event at Newmarket in October. *R. Hannon.*

SHOT AND SHELL (USA) 4 b.g. Damascus (USA)–Leap Lively (USA) 116 —
(Nijinsky (CAN) 138) [1988 8d 10.2g³ 11.5g 1989 12.5g 10m⁶ 12f] leggy, sparely-
made gelding: moderate mover: poor maiden: soon tailed off in handicap at Folkestone final outing: stays 1¼m: seems unsuited by firm going: has given trouble in
preliminaries: visored first 2 starts. *G. P. Enright.*

SHOTICHE (USA) 3 b.c. Northern Dancer–Nimble Folly (USA) (Cyane) [1988   93
7g³ 1989 10g* 12f⁴ 12m⁶ 10m* 10f² 9m⁵ 10.2g] medium-sized colt: fairly useful
handicapper: won at Salisbury (maiden) in May and Leicester in July: got no sort of
run penultimate start: well-beaten last of 7 in £21,000 limited handicap at Newcastle
over 2 months later: should prove at least as effective over 9f as 1¼m: acts on firm
going. *J. Tree.*

SHOUT AND SING (USA) 2 ch.c. (May 5) The Minstrel (CAN) 135–Godetia   86 p
(USA) 119 (Sir Ivor 135) [1989 7g⁵] strong, compact, attractive colt:
half-brother to moderate 8.5f winner Norquay (by Arctic Tern) and quite useful 1986
2-y-o maiden Castle Creek (by Sharpen Up), later winner in USA: dam won Irish
1000 Guineas and Oaks: 8/1, around 2 lengths fifth of 29, staying on well having run
green, to Lord of The Field in maiden at Newmarket in November: will be suited by
1m +: sure to improve. *G. Harwood.*

SHOUT FORE 2 gr.c. (Mar 23) Petong 126–Mavahra 93 (Mummy's Pet 125)   88
[1989 5d⁶ 5s⁵ 6f* 6m 7m² 7g 5m⁵ 6g² 6m²] 13,500F, 11,000Y: close-coupled,
sparely-made colt: first foal: dam, 5f and 6f winner stayed 7f, is sister to fairly useful
sprinter Pavahra: fair performer: won 4-runner maiden at Hamilton in July by 5
lengths: excellent second in nurseries at York and Newmarket in October: best
form at 6f: acts well on firm going: has run respectably for 7-lb claimer. *N. A.
Callaghan.*

SHOUT OUT 2 b.c. (Mar 11) Auction Ring (USA) 123–Manora (USA) (Stop The   72
Music (USA)) [1989 6f³ 6m³] rangy colt, rather dipped-backed: moderate mover:
first foal: dam unplaced in 2 starts in France at 3 yrs: placed in fair company at York
and Doncaster in May: drifted left each time. *C. R. Nelson.*

SHOWDOWN 3 ch.g. Final Straw 127–Sideshow 103 (Welsh Pageant 132) [1988   75
8f⁵ 10g 1989 8.2v³ 10f 8m* 8m³ 8.3g* 8.3m³ 8d] strong, heavy-bodied colt: good
walker: modest handicapper: always prominent, won at Yarmouth in July and
Windsor (tending to hang left) in August: suited by 1m: acts on top-of-the-ground,
probably unsuited by soft: trained first 6 outings by Sir Mark Prescott. *A. Moore.*

SHOWMANSHIP 2 b.g. (Apr 7) Shernazar 131–Melodramatic 112 (Tudor   —
Melody 129) [1989 7g] rather sparely-made gelding: closely related to Irish 8.5f and
11.5f winner Overplay and Irish 1½m winner Overcall (both by Bustino) and
half-brother to several other winners, including useful miler Crown Witness (by
Crowned Prince): dam won at 7f and 9f: bit backward, faded soon after halfway in
15-runner maiden at Newmarket in July. *C. F. Wall.*

SHOW US GLORY 3 b.f. Show-A-Leg 107–Transonic 60 (Continuation 120)   —
[1988 NR 1989 7s 7.5d 7g 6m 6m 12f] small, lengthy filly: first foal: dam sprinter: no
sign of ability, including in sellers. *R. Thompson.*

SHREAKE 3 b.g. Shirley Heights 130–Creake 80 (Derring-Do 131) [1988 NR   84
1989 14m² 17.6m² 14g² 16m⁶] leggy, angular gelding: half-brother to 1m winner
Affaire de Coeur (by Imperial Fling) and 2 winners in Ireland, including 6f and 7f
winner Creake's Pet (by Mummy's Pet): dam, 1½m winner from 3 starts, is
daughter of half-sister to Blakeney and Morston: fair maiden: soundly beaten in
£7,400 handicap at Newmarket: should be suited by test of stamina. *A. C. Stewart.*

SHRRAAR 3 b.c. Lomond (USA) 128–Cairnfold (USA) 68 (Never Bend) [1988 NR   —
1989 12m 17.6f 16f²] IR 170,000Y: lengthy, good-bodied colt: closely related to a
winner in USA by Northfields: dam, 11.7f winner, is half-sister to dam of Cheshire
Oaks winner Malaak and Crowning Honors, a Grade 1 winner in Canada: soundly
beaten in maidens (reluctant to race early on first of them) and 2-runner minor
event: should stay 1½m: sold to join B. Stevens 6,000 gns Newmarket Autumn
Sales. *A. C. Stewart.*

SHUNT 2 ch.f. (Mar 9) Bay Express 132–Flying Sovereign 74 (Sovereign Bill 105)   77
[1989 5m* 6f* 6g⁵ 6m⁵ 7g] 8,000Y: quite good-topped filly: half-sister to
1984 2-y-o 1m seller winner Flying Scarlet (by Crimson Beau): dam 5f winner at 2
yrs: won early-season auction events at Newmarket and Kempton, showing fine
turn of foot: off course for over 2 months after fourth outing: not discredited in listed
race at Phoenix Park in September on return: probably stays 7f: acts on firm going.
G. A. Pritchard-Gordon.

SHUTAFUT 3 b.c. Tachypous 128–Declamation 93 (Town Crier 119) [1988 NR   83
1989 10.1g 12m 10.8m³] good-bodied colt: has scope: has a quick action: seventh
foal: half-brother to 3 winners, including useful middle-distance mare Aim To
Please (by Gunner B): dam second of 26 over 6f on only start: taken down steadily,
keeping-on third of 6 in minor event at Warwick in October, best effort: took keen

hold and gave trouble at stalls first 2 starts: has joined T. Forster. *R. F. Johnson Houghton.*

SHUTTLECOCK CORNER (USA) 3 b.c. Cresta Rider (USA) 124–Sweet **114** Ellen (USA) (Vitriolic) [1988 5g 5g* 5m* 5g² 5d³ 5d⁶ 5f* 5d³ 5g* 1989 6s* 5m 6f⁶ 5m² 5f⁴ 5₁₁₁ 6g⁵ 5m³] chunky, sprint type: carries condition: poor walker: moderate mover: very useful performer: won minor event at Folkestone in April: ran well in King's Stand Stakes at Royal Ascot, William Hill Sprint Championship at York and Ladbroke Sprint Cup at Haydock fifth to seventh outings: suited by strongly-run race at 5f and stays 6f: acts on any going. *P. S. Felgate.*

SHY MISTRESS 6 b.m. Cawston's Clown 113–Shy Talk 93 (Sharpen Up 127) **45** § [1988 6g 6g 6m⁶ 6m⁴ 7m² 8.2d 7f⁶ 8s 6g 7g⁶ 8d 6v⁴ 1989 8m⁴ 6f* 7f 6g⁵ 8g⁵ 7f] smallish mare: moderate mover: appeared to show much improved form when winning amateurs handicap at Redcar in May by 5 lengths, leading 1f out having drifted right and been last at halfway: failed to reproduce that run by some way in handicaps and claimer: best form at 6f on firm going: often slowly away and not the easiest of rides: sold 900 gns Doncaster November Sales: not one to trust. *A. W. Jones.*

SHYOUSHKA 3 ch.f. Shy Groom (USA)–Capsville (USA) (Cyane) [1988 6s* **107** 6m⁴ 7g² 6g⁴ 1989 8d⁴ 10f³ 10m* 10d] IR 5,600F, IR 7,600Y: strong, lengthy ex-Irish filly: carries condition: has a quick action: half-sister to numerous winners, including stayer Harlyn Bay (by Wolver Hollow) and fairly useful 9f and 1¼m winner Willieswrightoncue (by Red Sunset): dam, placed in USA, is sister to smart stakes winner Pinch Pie: trained at 2 yrs in Ireland by Peter Hill, winning maiden at Phoenix Park: showed improved form when winning listed race at Newbury in June, quickening clear in good style inside final 1f: favourite, finished lame in Pretty Polly Stakes at the Curragh following month: will stay 1½m: easily best form on top-of-the ground, though has won on soft: continually hung left and carried head awkwardly second start: reportedly to remain in training. *H. R. A. Cecil.*

SIAN'S LADY 2 b.f. (May 2) Dunbeath (USA) 127–Hawaiian Joss (USA) (Hawaii) **56** [1989 5g 5g⁵ 5g⁴ 6m² 7f* 6m² 7m] 2,200Y: angular, fair sort: did well physically: second foal: half-sister to 3-y-o Permanently Pink (by Auction Ring), 7f seller winner at 2 yrs: dam unraced: won 13-runner seller (bought in 4,200 gns) at Wolverhampton in July by 7 lengths: good second to Tarnside Club in nursery at Pontefract following month: should stay at least 1m: acts on firm going. *D. Haydn Jones.*

SIBERIAN STEPPES 2 b. or br.f. (Apr 3) Siberian Express (USA) 125–La **45** Palma (Posse (USA) 130) [1989 5v 5s⁶ 5g 5f 6v 6g⁵] 4,000Y: leggy filly: first foal: dam, placed at 9f in France at 3 yrs, is granddaughter of Carrozza: poor maiden: best effort in claiming nursery final start: should stay further. *P. Mitchell.*

SICILIAN DREAMS 2 b.c. (Apr 23) Dreams To Reality (USA) 113–Trapani **40** (Ragusa 137) [1989 5d⁶ 5d] smallish, sparely-made colt: poor walker: has a round action: seventh foal: half-brother to 3-y-o 7f winner Miss Skindles (by Taufan), fairly useful 5f and 1m winner Prince Ragusa (by English Prince) and prolific winners in Norway and Italy: dam ran 3 times: poor maiden: not raced after May: wears blinkers: sold 1,200 gns Ascot December Sales. *P. F. I. Cole.*

SICILIAN SWING 4 b.g. Swing Easy (USA) 126–Mab (Morston (FR) 125) [1988 — 8.2v 6g 1989 8f 9s] big, workmanlike gelding: little sign of ability, including in seller. *W. Holden.*

SICILIAN VESPERS 4 b.f. Mummy's Game 120–Orange Silk 68 (Moulton 128) **44** [1988 7d 8f 8m 9g 6m 7g 6d 1989 8s 7g* 7m 8h 7.5m⁴ 7h 7m 8.3g] small, workmanlike filly: dropped to selling company, won handicap (no bid) at Brighton in April: form after only on fifth outing: stays 7f: probably unsuited by hard going: slowly away third and sixth starts: sweating and edgy final one: inconsistent: winning selling hurdler with J. White. *M. Blanshard.*

SIDELOADER SPECIAL 3 b.f. Song 132–Hellene (Dominion 123) [1988 6s⁵ **66** 1989 5d⁶ 5m² 6g⁴ 6g* 6g] small filly: favourite, won handicap at Catterick in August by head after saddle slipped inside last: behind facing stiffish task in similar event 11 days later: stays 6f: best efforts on a sound surface: sold 4,800 gns Doncaster November Sales. *Miss S. E. Hall.*

SIDI BARANI 2 br.g. (Apr 12) Coded Scrap 90–Merrywren (Julio Mariner 127) — [1989 8f 8.2g 8.2g] angular gelding: first foal: dam, maiden, suited by test of stamina on flat won over hurdles: well beaten in varied company. *J. H. Johnson.*

SIERRA ROBERTA (FR)   3 ch.f. Don Roberto (USA)–Sierra Morena **129**
(ITY) (Canisbay 120) [1988 7.5g* 7d⁵ 8g³ 8m⁵ 1989 9d⁴ 10g³ 10g* 12d² 12g⁵
12f²]

After Trempolino's half-length defeat by Theatrical in 1987, the de
Moussac-Fabre-Eddery team came even closer to winning the 2,000,000-
dollar Breeders' Cup Turf with Sierra Roberta in 1989. Unfancied by the locals
at 25/1, Sierra Roberta was some way off the pace set by Ile de Chypre and
Caltech early on but made good headway with half a mile to run so that she
took the final turn in fourth or fifth. It was readily apparent that she'd get the
measure of the leaders but Sierra Roberta also had a slight disadvantage with
the turf-debutant Prized and, though staying on gamely, could only reduce
that deficit to a head at the line. Luck in running played an excessive role in
deciding this year's Breeders' Cup honours but there was some justice in
Sierra Roberta's getting it on this occasion while Behera (just over a length
back in fourth) did not, for it had been the other way round in the Arc de
Triomphe at Longchamp five weeks earlier. At 15/1, Sierra Roberta was
coupled in the betting on the Arc on the French Tote with the same owner's
Harvest Time but, ironically, it was Harvest Time who caused her and
Freddie Head the most problems. Sierra Roberta turned into the straight in
about eighth position on the rails but Harvest Time was weakening up front
and, as Head tried to go past him first on the inside then on the outside two
hundred metres out, Boisnard in the same colours vigorously applied his whip
four times just in front of Sierra Roberta before finally dropping out of
contention. Sierra Roberta was about six lengths behind Carroll House when
she got through but, having taken a while to get into her stride, she'd cut that
to about two and a half lengths at the post and finished fifth. The sight of Sierra
Roberta staying on at the finish was a familiar one. She'd not got the best of
runs in either the Prix Chloe at Longchamp in July or the Prix de Psyche at
Deauville in August but then, really starting to come into her own in the
autumn, she won the Prix de la Nonette and was second in the Vermeille, both
at Longchamp. The Nonette provided her first meeting with Behera and, a
little surprisingly considering her lack of a recent outing, the Aga Khan's filly
was strongly supported to odds on with Sierra Roberta, who received 7 lb,
second favourite. This time, and indeed in the Vermeille, Sierra Roberta was
steered clear of any trouble in running and switched to the wide outside early
in the straight, a manoeuvre which is far from easy to execute in the much
larger field for the Arc. In the Nonette these tactics brought Sierra Roberta to
the front about half way through the final furlong and she won by a length and a
half from stable-mate Nadina with Behera the same distance back in third, but
in the Vermeille two weeks later she couldn't make much impression on

*Prix de la Nonette, Longchamp — Sierra Roberta and Nadina give their stable
the first two places as Behera (No. 1) makes an encouraging return*

Young Mother having gone second at about the same stage, and was herself beaten a length and a half.

```
                        ┌Don Roberto (USA)  ┌Roberto      ┌Hail To Reason
                        │  (ch 1977)        │  (b 1969)   │Bramalea
                        │                   │Exit Smiling ┌Stage Door Johnny
Sierra Roberta (FR)   ┤                   │  ( 1970)    └Chandelier
  (ch.f. 1986)          │                   ┌Canisbay     ┌Doutelle
                        │Sierra Morena (ITY) │  (ch 1961)  │Stroma
                        └  (ch 1973)        │Saigon       ┌Mossborough
                                            └  (ch 1965)  └Savona II
```

Sierra Roberta's sire Don Roberto is virtually unheard of in Britain where he's been represented by two fairly useful performers in the Gordon Stakes fourth Kaliberto and the unreliable Off The Record and only one winner—a very useful two-year-old plater called Tear It Down. Before Sierra Roberta came along he'd hardly captured the imagination in his adopted country France either, and stood at a fee of a little over £1,000 in the latest season before being exported to Spain. Don Roberto did all his racing in the USA, showing smart form in winning six of twenty-four starts (including stakes at a mile and a quarter and eleven furlongs on turf), and was a regular competitor in some of the best turf handicaps as a five-year-old; receiving 1 lb, he was beaten two lengths into second by the ex-Irish Erins Isle in the Grade 1 mile-and-a-half Sunset Handicap. When Sierra Roberta was foaled, the dam Sierra Morena, quite unlike Don Roberto, had already established a good producing record with her first two foals Port Saigon (by What A Pleasure) and Morespeed (by Pharly), both fairly useful winners at around a mile and a quarter. Her next three offspring were the useful French seven-furlong to a mile-and-a-quarter winner Port Etienne (by Mill Reef), a minor winner by Dom Racine and the smart mile-and-a-half winner Port Lyautey (by Shirley Heights). Sierra Morena's unraced two-year-old of 1989 is called Port Arthur, by Miller's Mate who stands at Paul de Moussac's Haras du Mezeray as did Don Roberto. Sierra Morena was the joint-second highest-rated three-year-old filly of 1976 in Italy. She was reportedly best when delivering a late challenge and hit the front too soon when second in the Oaks d'Italia and Premio Lydia Tesio. Sierra Morena also filled the same position in the Gran Premio del Jockey Club. She's a half-sister to Suffolk, who won a substandard Derby Italiano two years earlier, and a daughter of the Premio Regina Elena second and Oaks d'Italia third Saigon.

Sierra Roberta remains in training and improvement is not out of the question as she was definitely on the upgrade at the end of the latest season. She stays a mile and a half well and is likely to prove best in a strongly-run race at that distance. Very soft going is something Sierra Roberta hasn't come across yet but she acts on any other. *A. Fabre, France.*

SIERRA SNOW   4 br.f. King of Spain 121–Snow Rum (Quorum 126) [1988 6g⁵   **46** §
7g³ 7g⁶ 8d² 7m 8f³ 10g² 10m 1989 12d 10m 10f⁴ 8h² 8h 8h⁵ 10h 8f⁶ 10f⁴] leggy, lightly-made filly: has a quick action: poor maiden nowadays: stays 1¼m: yet to race on soft going, acts on any other: blinkered final 3 starts as 3-y-o, visored 5 of last 6 outings: has given trouble at stalls, started slowly and looked difficult ride: unreliable. *S. Dow.*

SIERRA STAR   3 b.c. Mill Reef (USA) 141–New Chant (CAN) (New Providence)   **76**
[1988 NR 1989 12m³ 15.3f³ 12g⁶ 14.5g*] lengthy colt: half-brother to 4 winners, including Casual (by Caro), a stakes-placed winner at up to 9f: dam, 2-y-o 6f winner, is half-sister to top Canadian colt Giboulee: won 5-runner St Leger Italiano at Turin in July by 2 lengths from Annio Chilone: third in maidens at Newmarket and Wolverhampton: well beaten in Bankverein Swiss Derby at Frauenfeld: will stay 2m. *M. A. Jarvis.*

SIESTA KEY   4 b.g. Glint of Gold 128–Petite Hester 85 (Wollow 132) [1988 11g   **87**
11.7f³ 11.7g² 13.1f* 13.1f* 13.3g 14g* 14f 1989 14g 13.3m⁵ 16m³] leggy, attractive gelding: usually looks well: fair handicapper: favourite, best effort in 1989 when third of 5, no extra final 1f after travelling best most of way, in quite valuable event at Ascot in July: stays 2m: acts on firm going: goes well with forcing tactics: suitable mount for apprentice: gelded after final outing. *I. A. Balding.*

SIGAMA (USA)   3 ch.g. Stop The Music (USA)–Lady Speedwell (USA)   **75**
(Secretariat (USA)) [1988 6s 5d³ 5m* 5g⁵ 6g 5d⁵ 1989 5g² 5d³ 5g 5m³ 5m 5f 5m 5g]

828

sturdy, dipped-backed gelding: has a quick action: modest performer at his best: ran well first 4 starts but moderately after, giving impression something amiss: speedy: acts on a soft surface and top-of-the-ground: tends to hang: blinkered once at 2 yrs: gelded after final start. *F. H. Lee.*

SIGGLESTHORNE 2 ch.f. (Mar 13) Claude Monet (USA) 121–Le Levandoll 92 **42** (Le Levanstell 122) [1989 6f⁵ 5g⁵ 6f 5g] 4,000Y: close-coupled, sparely-made filly: half-sister to a minor 2-y-o winner by Supreme Sovereign and 2 winners abroad: dam won from 6f to 1½m: poor form in minor events and maidens: reluctant at stalls on debut: bred to be better suited by 7f +. *P. A. Blockley.*

SIGNORE ODONE 7 b.g. Milford 119–Duchy 99 (Rheingold 137) [1988 7.5m 7f — §
8f⁴ 9f³ 8h⁵ 8.5g⁶ 8g 1989 10m 8f] workmanlike, lengthy gelding: modest at best: stayed 8.5f: didn't race on soft going, acted on any other: best allowed to stride on (ran too freely in blinkers): winning hurdler/novice chaser: dead. *M. H. Easterby.*

SIGN PEOPLE 3 ch.c. Sayyaf 121–Maura Paul (Bonne Noel 115) [1988 6m* 6m² **92** 6m* 6g³ 6m 1989 7m³ 8.2m 7m⁴ 8m² 8m⁵ 7m 7f⁴ 9g] smallish, quite good-topped colt: fairly useful handicapper: good second in £22,000 Foodbrokers Trophy at Newmarket in July: below form last 3 outings: stays 1m: acts on top-of-the-ground. *Dr J. D. Scargill.*

SIGWELL'S GOLD 2 b.f. (Mar 8) Sonnen Gold 121–Manna Green (Bustino **59** 136) [1989 6f² 7m² 7m⁵] 2,000 (privately) Y: rather leggy, unfurnished filly: fourth foal: sister to 3-y-o Merry Marigold, 6f and 7f winner at 2 yrs, and half-sister to 9f claiming race winner Taxi Man (by Dublin Taxi): dam ran twice: runner-up, beaten a length, in maidens at Hamilton and Warwick: not raced after July: bred to stay 1m: sent to R. Holder. *W. G. M. Turner.*

SIKESTON (USA) 3 b.c. Lear Fan (USA) 130–Small Timer (USA) (Lyphard **113** (USA) 132) [1988 7f² 7g² 7g³ 8s* 1989 7d 8v* 12m] robust, deep-bodied, good sort: won Premio Parioli at Rome in April by 1¼ lengths from Lioubovnik: well below form in Derby Italiano at Rome month later: probably doesn't stay 1½m: best form on very soft ground: has joined C. Brittain. *J. L. Dunlop.*

SILCA AN' KEY 2 b.c. (Mar 12) Commanche Run 133–Miss Silca Key 102 **75 p** (Welsh Saint 126) [1989 6g⁶ 7g⁴] 36,000Y: rangy, good-topped colt: has plenty of scope: second foal: half-brother to useful 3-y-o 6f winner Silca Supreme (by Chief Singer): dam won 7f Jersey Stakes: 9 lengths fourth of 28, going on in good style, to Rami in maiden at Newmarket in November: slowly away and never travelling well on debut: will be suited by 1m: sure to do better. *D. R. C. Elsworth.*

SILCA SUPREME 3 b.g. Chief Singer 131–Miss Silca Key 102 (Welsh Saint 126) **103** [1988 5g 5g 1989 6m* 6f² 7f 6g² 7.3g] big, rangy, unfurnished gelding: won Newmarket maiden in May: good second in £6,100 event at Newbury and strongly-run £7,700 handicap at Newmarket: ran poorly in Jersey Stakes at Royal Ascot and Hungerford Stakes at Newbury otherwise in summer: suited by 6f: acts on firm going: on toes and looked extremely well first 2 and fourth starts: bandaged third outing and on debut. *D. R. C. Elsworth.*

SILENT DREAMS 4 b.f. Day Is Done 115–Ciao (Mandamus 120) [1988 10g 8m —
6g⁵ 7d 8g² 8g⁴ 9v 1989 8d] medium-sized ex-Irish filly: half-sister to 2 winners, including 1983 2-y-o 6f winner Flingamus (by Imperial Fling): dam Irish 5f winner: in frame in handicaps at Laytown and Leopardstown as 3-y-o: well beaten in Edinburgh maiden in April: probably best at 1m: possibly unsuited by soft going: often apprentice ridden. *P. A. Blockley.*

SILENT GIRL 2 ch.f. (Apr 10) Krayyan 117–Silent Pearl (USA) (Silent Screen **68** (USA)) [1989 6m⁶ 8g⁶ 8m* 8s⁵ a7g] tall, useful-looking filly: fourth foal: half-sister to 3-y-o 6f (at 2 yrs) and 1¼m winner Always Valiant (by Valiyar) and modest and inconsistent staying maiden Glint of Pearl (by Glint of Gold): dam won twice in USA at up to 7f, and is daughter of sister to high-class middle-distance stayer Hopeful Venture: favourite and lowered in class, won 23-runner seller (retained 5,500 gns) at Newmarket by 7 lengths: will stay 1¼m. *N. A. Callaghan.*

SILENT LOCH 2 b.f. (May 14) Lochnager 132–Keep Silent 83 (Balidar 133) —
[1989 a7g a6g] angular filly: third reported foal: half-sister to 3-y-o Silentina (by Tina's Pet) and a winner in Denmark by Blue Cashmere: dam won 6f seller at 2 yrs: bit backward, soundly beaten in Southwell claimers. *M. Johnston.*

SILENT ORDER 2 b.c. (Mar 28) Kind of Hush 118–Cateryne (Ballymoss 136) —
[1989 8.2g] 5,500Y, 11,000 2-y-o: half-brother to 3 modest winners at up to 8.2f: dam ran once: broke a leg at Haydock in September: dead. *N. Tinkler.*

SILENT PRINCESS 3 b.f. King of Spain 121–Silent Dancer 76 (Quiet Fling —
(USA) 116) [1988 7m 1989 10.1m 12f⁵ 14f 12m 17.1f⁴ 16f⁶] poor form at best: will be
suited by return to shorter: blinkered fourth start: visored after: sold 2,500 gns
Ascot November Sales. *P. T. Walwyn.*

SILENT RING (USA) 3 b. or br.g. Silent Cal (USA)–Rafters Ring (USA) (Delta 42
Judge) [1988 8.2m 8m 9f 1989 12.2d³ 12s⁶ 11v³ 16.2d⁵ 11g 12.3m 12.2f 15g] lengthy,
angular gelding: moderate walker and mover: poor maiden: will prove suited by test
of stamina: acts on heavy going: visored second start, blinkered final one: sold to
join P. Hedger 3,400 gns Newmarket July Sales: winning novice hurdler. *S. G.
Norton.*

SILENT SISTER 4 gr.f. Kind of Hush 118–Little Mercy 90 (No Mercy 126) 49
[1988 8s⁶ 7g 6m 7h³ 8g 1989 7m 7f⁵ 7m 6f³] lengthy, angular filly: powerful galloper:
modest winner at 2 yrs: showed she retained some ability on second and final
(blinkered) outings: stays 7f: acts on hard going and a soft surface: often used to
make running. *R. Hannon.*

SILENT STEPS 2 ch.c. (Mar 4) Kind of Hush 118–On The Turn 87 (Manacle —
123) [1989 6m 7m] 7,800Y: leggy, angular colt: half-brother to fair miler It's My
Turn (by Palm Track): dam 5f sprinter: never dangerous in maidens at Newbury in
July and Chepstow in October. *M. McCormack.*

SILICON LADY (FR) 3 br.f. Mille Balles (FR) 124–Siliciana 113 (Silly Season 116
(USA) 127) [1988 7m³ 7.5g³ 8d* 7m² 6.5d² 7.5g* 1989 8g⁴ 8g* 9.2g 8v² 8d²]
700,000 francs (approx £70,700) Y: closely related to 3 winners here and in France,
including French 1½m winner Silicon King (by Shirley Heights), half-sister to 3
other winners and also to dam of Risk Me: dam won Cambridgeshire: useful at 2 yrs,
winning listed race and Prix Thomas Bryon: not seen out until September in 1989:
won listed race at Evry that month: good 2 lengths second to Miss Kenmare in
Group 3 Prix Perth at Saint-Cloud in November on penultimate outing: should stay
1¼m: best form on an easy surface, and acts on heavy going. *J. Pease, France.*

SILK BRAID (USA) 3 b.f. Danzig (USA)–Ribbon (USA) (His Majesty (USA)) 105 p
[1988 NR 1989 8m 9g* 12v*] rather leggy filly: fourth living foal: half-sister to 1988
Belmont and Preakness Stakes winner Risen Star (by Secretariat) and a winner in
USA by Bold Forbes: dam prolific winner from 6f to 11f at 3 yrs in USA: won maiden
(gambled on favourite though still green) at York in October and listed race (by 12
lengths) at Milan in November: suited by 1½m: acts on heavy going: may well
improve again. *J. Gosden.*

SILK DEGREES 3 gr.g. Dunbeath (USA) 127–Bustling Nelly 94 (Bustino 136) 55
[1988 8g⁶ 1989 12g 10f 12h 10f⁶ 8s 12f⁶ 16f*] rather plain gelding: only worthwhile
form as 3-y-o when making all in handicap at Warwick in October: stays 2m well:
sold to join D. Wintle 9,000 gns Newmarket Autumn Sales. *C. A. Cyzer.*

SILK DYNASTY 3 b.g. Prince Tenderfoot (USA) 126–Mountain Chase (Mount —
Hagen (FR) 127) [1988 6g⁴ 6g⁶ 8g⁵ 8d 1989 12d² 10g 8.5d 8g a10g⁶] small, compact
gelding: shade unfurnished: turns near-fore out: moderate mover: modest maiden
at 2 yrs: well beaten in 1989, off course 6 months before final start: pulled hard in
blinkers previous 2 outings: possibly not genuine. *M. E. D. Francis.*

SILK 'N' STUFF 2 ch.f. (Mar 4) Vaigly Great 127–Remould 83 (Reform 132) 41
[1989 5m 6m³ 6m 6f 6g 7d] 4,000Y: small, sparely-made filly: half-sister to
middle-distance winner Deal On (by Quiet Fling) and 2 winners abroad: dam won
over 5f at 2 yrs: moderate plater: better suited by 6f than 5f: best form on
top-of-the-ground: sweating third and fourth starts: blinkered fifth: wears bandage
behind: sold 1,300 gns Doncaster November Sales. *C. W. Thornton.*

SILKOND 3 b.f. Lomond (USA) 128–Silk Sari (USA) 101 (Raja Baba (USA)) [1988 —
8g² 1989 8.5s⁵ 8m 10.2f⁶] sturdy, angular filly: modest maiden at best: stays 8.5f:
possibly needs an easy surface: sweating penultimate start. *P. T. Walwyn.*

SILK PETAL 3 b.f. Petorius 117–Salabella 64 (Sallust 134) [1988 NR 1989 7d³ 105
7f* 7s* 8g³ 7d²] 17,500Y: workmanlike filly: second foal: half-sister to useful 1986
2-y-o 6f winner Rockfella (by Ballad Rock): dam, half-sister to Irish St Leger winner
M-Lolshan, stayed 11f: favourite, won 17-runner maiden at Wolverhampton in May
and minor event (6/5 on) at Ayr in September: ran well after in listed races won by
Light of Morn at Newmarket and Milieu at Leopardstown: suited by 1m: acts on any
going: useful. *J. L. Dunlop.*

SILKS DOMINO 4 ch.g. Dominion 123–Bourgeonette 81 (Mummy's Pet 125) —
[1988 8d 9d 7.6g 10m 12f³ 13s* 12d* 18d 12g 1989 12s 12g 16m 12d⁶ 13s 12.2m]
medium-sized, rather plain gelding: has a long stride: quite modest winner as 3-y-o:
no worthwhile form in 1989: sweating fourth start, first for 4 months: stays 13f: best

form on a soft surface: blinkered final 4 outings in 1988 and fifth one in 1989: visored final start: best forcing the pace. *M. J. Ryan.*

SILK SLIPPERS (USA) 2 b.f. (Feb 21) Nureyev (USA) 131–Nalee's **104** p Fantasy (USA) (Graustark) [1989 7m* 8m*]

Owner Robert Sangster could well be forgiven for looking back on 1989 with mixed feelings. His large collection of mainly lightly-raced and well-bred three-year-olds stabled at the Manton complex mustered just a single success between them—in a minor event at Catterick—and their owner had his least profitable year in terms of both winners and prize money for over a decade. In October came the announcement that the superbly-equipped Manton estate was on the market for a sum reportedly in the region of £15,000,000. Sangster is adamant he has no intention of cutting back on his bloodstock interests, and 1990 ought to see his familiar colours much more to the fore. Observation Post, for example, is more than capable of doing well provided he's none the worse for whatever kept him off the track after the Irish Derby; so is the two-year-old Victory Piper, who followed up a highly promising debut at Newbury by winning the Group 2 Juddmonte EBF Beresford Stakes at the Curragh in October. And then there's the two-year-old Silk Slippers, who ended her first season unbeaten and gave the impression she'd be even better granted a winter in which to mature. Silk Slippers was made evens favourite for her debut in a six-runner minor event at York in September. Despite showing clear signs of greenness she justified the support, albeit by the narrowest of margins, and connections then decided to step her up in distance for the Group 2 Hoover Fillies' Mile at Ascot, a race won by Diminuendo, Untold and Oh So Sharp in three of its previous five runnings. In the paddock prior to the race the paying public were given precious little opportunity to see the eight runners—a poor show even allowing that the previous race had been late getting under way—but only the briefest inspection was needed to see that Silk Slippers, an easy-to-back 10/1 chance, dwarfed her rivals. A big, lengthy filly with any amount of scope, she really did take the eye, and in a moderately-run race she put up a fine performance. Switched left with a plenty to do early in the straight, she temporarily looked uncertain of what was required, but produced a good turn of foot to beat the heavily-backed odds-on chance Moon Cactus by a head. Fujaiyrah was two and a half lengths away in third with the Prix du Calvados winner Arousal a head back in fourth. The form is probably unexceptional by this race's particular standards. Moon Cactus, who'd looked assured of victory until Silk Slippers found full stride, had shown useful form, no better, in winning her two previous races, and both she and Arousal were conceding the winner 3 lb as a result of having won Group 3 contests. However, that doesn't dampen our enthusiasm for Silk Slippers at all: unless we're very much mistaken she'll be much better at three than she was at two, and she has classic potential.

Hoover Fillies' Mile, Ascot—Silk Slippers (right) gets up on the line to beat Moon Cactus

Nureyev's exceptional success as a stallion has come to a large extent through horses who've been best at up to a mile. However, Alwuhush, Theatrical and Stately Don have all shown high-class form over a mile and a half, and the odds are that Silk Slippers will stay at least a mile and a quarter. Silk Slippers' dam Nalee's Fantasy, whose second reported foal she is, won twice at up to a mile and a quarter. Her dam Nalee is a sister to Shuvee, twice champion handicap mare in the United States and twice a winner of the two-mile Jockey Club Gold Cup. Nalee herself wasn't far behind the best, a winner three times in stakes company, and her record at stud is tremendous. The runaway Irish St Leger winner Meneval is probably the best of her ten winners; she's also the dam of the unraced Nalees Flying Flag, whose produce include such as the Belmont Stakes runner-up Johns Treasure and the champion three-year-old filly Sacahuista.

		Northern Dancer	Nearctic
	Nureyev (USA)	(b 1961)	Natalma
	(b 1977)	Special	Forli
Silk Slippers (USA)		(b 1969)	Thong
(b.f. Feb 21, 1987)		Graustark	Ribot
	Nalee's Fantasy (USA)	(ch 1963)	Flower Bowl
	(b 1977)	Nalee	Nashua
		(b 1960)	Levee

Silk Slippers was quoted at around 16/1 for the One Thousand Guineas on the strength of her Ascot win. She'll probably lack the pace to trouble the best in that race, but at this early stage she has to rate fairly highly on the short list of Oaks candidates. She was bought for 325,000 dollars at Keeneland as a yearling, and her year-younger brother fell to a bid of 400,000 dollars from the Darley Stud Management at the same sale in 1989. *B. W. Hills.*

SILKS PRINCESS 3 b.f. Prince Tenderfoot (USA) 126–Pitlessie 75 (Hook **96** Money 124) [1988 5g* 5f2 6d6 6m2 6f2 6m3 1989 6s* 6s2 6s* 6m4 6g 6s 6m 6g] lengthy, good-bodied filly: useful form first 2 starts, winning handicap at Kempton in March: didn't run to that form after, though won minor event (moved moderately down) at Nottingham in May: bred to stay further: has form on firm going but best efforts on soft: blinkered or visored final 2 outings at 2 yrs. *M. J. Ryan.*

SILKS VENTURE 4 br.c. Lochnager 132–Honey Thief 77 (Burglar 128) [1988 — 5g 5m3 5f4 5f4 5g* 5s* 5g* 5s2 5g6 6s 5m 5.6m 5d 1989 a5g] rather leggy colt: moderate mover: modest winner (including for apprentice) as 3-y-o: has since lost his form: bandaged, tailed off in Southwell handicap in December: best at 5f, with give in the ground: blinkered once at 3 yrs. *P. A. Blockley.*

SILK THREAD 6 ch.g. Relkino 131–Silken Way (FR) 103 (Shantung 132) [1988 **64** 13v* 12.3s* 12g3 16g2 18.4v 15s5 13s 15.8g* 14.7d* 12m 1989 12.4g2 13v* 14g5 16d6 12g 17.4s 13s 15s] workmanlike gelding: quite modest handicapper: well ridden when winning corresponding race at Ayr in April for second year running, holding on by ¾ length after being sent clear early in straight: off course nearly 4 months after fourth outing and below his best subsequently: stays 2m: suited by an easy surface and goes well in the mud: blinkered once: has worn bandages behind: races up with pace. *R. M. Whitaker.*

SILKWORM 3 b.f. Czaravich (USA)–Jemeela 90 (Windjammer (USA)) [1988 NR — 1989 8d 10.6s 12.2d 12m] 14,000Y: lengthy filly: moderate walker: first foal: dam, 6f winner at 2 yrs, is half-sister to numerous winners, including the dam of good sprinter Miami Springs: sire high-class performer from 7f to 11f: no sign of ability, including in sellers: off course over 5 months and sold out of W. O'Gorman's stable 1,550 gns Newmarket July Sales after debut. *R. Bastiman.*

SILLARS SANDPIPER 2 ch.f. (Apr 6) Burslem 123–Cress (Crepello 136) — [1989 7m 7g 8g] IR 1,500F, IR 7,000Y: close-coupled filly: half-sister to 3 winners, including speedy Self Portrait (by Jukebox) and 1¼m winner Dhofar (by Octavo): dam ran 3 times: poor form in maidens and a claimer: sold 1,000 gns Doncaster November Sales. *Mrs J. R. Ramsden.*

SILLY HABIT (USA) 3 b.f. Assert 134–Habitassa 100 (Habitat 134) [1988 7d3 **68** 1989 11.7h6 12f2 10.1m2 12f2] workmanlike filly: modest form: second in claimer (claimed out of B. Hills's stable £15,000), minor event and maiden in the summer: stays 1½m. *R. Akehurst.*

SILLY'S BROTHER 3 ch.g. Longleat (USA) 109–Scilly Isles 54 (Silly Season **72** 127) [1988 7g 7g 7g2 1989 7g 7v2 7m4 7f 9s 7g] heavy-topped gelding: modest maiden: easily best effort as 3-y-o when leading until post at Ayr in April: keen sort, may prove best at 7f: acts on heavy going, possibly unsuited by top-of-the-ground: usually makes running. *N. Bycroft.*

SILVER AGE (USA) 3 b.c. Silver Hawk (USA) 123–Our Paige (USA) (Grand —
Revival (USA)) [1988 NR 1989 a10g⁶ a14g⁶] 1,300 2-y-o: sixth foal: half-brother to
very useful French 9f winner Ginger Lass (by Elocutionist): dam, 6f winner, is
half-sister to very smart 6f to 11f winner Lyphard's Special and champion sprinter
My Juliet: beaten about 10 lengths in maiden at Lingfield and claimer at Southwell:
should be suited by return to shorter. *J. M. Bradley.*

SILVER ARCH 4 b.c. Starch Reduced 112–Slightly Saucy 74 (Galivanter 131) —
[1988 7d 8g⁵ 10v 12g 12f⁵ 8f² 8f² 10f⁶ 8m 10m 8s⁶ 10m 12g 1989 10d 15.3m
16.5g 15.8f⁴ 15.3f⁶ 15.3g⁶ 17.6f⁴] neat colt: poor maiden: should stay 2m: acts on
firm going: possibly ungenuine. *R. Hollinshead.*

SILVER CLEF 3 b.c. Reesh 117–Ullapool (Dominion 123) [1988 NR 1989 6v 8g] —
4,200Y, 12,000 2-y-o: leggy, good-topped colt: first foal: dam unraced: always behind
in minor event and claimer in the spring. *D. J. G. Murray-Smith.*

SILVERDALE FOX 2 ch.c. (May 7) Sweet Monday 122–Its My Turn 80 (Palm 82
Track 122) [1989 6m 7f⁶ 7m 6m* 7m 6v*] plain colt: first foal: dam miler: fair
performer: successful in nurseries at Haydock in September and Ayr in October:
sweating and edgy, ran poorly in similar event at York in between: should stay 7f:
hampered stalls third outing: slowly away first 2 appearances. *R. Hollinshead.*

SILVER FLING (USA) 4 br.f. The Minstrel (CAN) 135–Royal Dilemma 120
(USA) (Buckpasser) [1988 6f* 7.3g⁵ 5m² 6f² 6m² 5g* 5m* 5d² 6s² 5m³ 1989
6g* 5m* 5f⁴ 5m² 6g⁴ 6m² 5g*]

If ever a horse deserved to end its career on a high note it was Silver
Fling, who in the final stride of her final race got up to beat an international
field in the Ciga Prix de l'Abbaye de Longchamp. In her previous nineteen
races she had only twice been beaten more than three lengths, the first time
when slowly away on her debut as a two-year-old, the second on her only
excursion outside sprinting in the Fred Darling Stakes at Newbury. Since
finishing second to Cadeaux Genereux in the William Hill Golden Spurs
Trophy Handicap at York later as a three-year-old, she had run in listed or
pattern company, never out of the frame. On her three attempts over the
minimum trip as a four-year-old prior to the Abbaye she had found the pace
too hot in the early stages, then come with a tremendous late flourish. She
edged ahead in the last few yards to pip Superpower and Access Travel in the
Palace House Stakes at Newmarket in May, but on the sharper track at
Goodwood and on the firm ground at York she failed to catch all those in front

Palace House Stakes, Newmarket—
Silver Fling pips the blinkered runners Superpower (right) and Access Travel

Ciga Prix de l'Abbaye de Longchamp—Silver Fling's last race.
Right to left it's Whippet, the winner, Canadian challenger Zadracarta,
Nabeel Dancer, Statoblest and Point of Light

of her in the King George Stakes and William Hill Sprint Championship, respectively. At Goodwood she was returning from a near three-month break, an injury to a hock causing her to miss the King's Stand Stakes at Royal Ascot and the July Cup at Newmarket. At York she got to within three quarters of a length of Cadeaux Genereux despite sustaining a cut to her off-fore, as a result of which she spent four days confined to her box before taking her place in the Ladbroke Sprint Cup field at Haydock just over a week later. This time the six furlongs proved just beyond her and, as in the Krug Diadem Stakes at Ascot on her next outing, she was run out of it having led briefly inside the final furlong; at Haydock she was beaten three lengths by Danehill, at Ascot three parts of a length by Chummy's Favourite. Back in April though, she had managed to hang on to her advantage over six furlongs in the listed Cammidge Trophy at Doncaster on her reappearance when, despite drifting right, she accounted for Mac's Fighter by a length and a half.

The latest running of the Ciga Prix de l'Abbaye de Longchamp wasn't up to standard, with the one-time leading contenders Cadeaux Genereux, Danehill and Indian Ridge already retired, but the British nevertheless mounted their usual strong challenge and Statoblest, Nabeel Dancer, Chummy's Favourite, Green's Canaletto and Point of Light all joined Silver Fling in the field of sixteen. Cricket Ball headed the home defence and was the only French runner to start at less than 10/1. The field was more international than usual. Rainbow Brite travelled from Belgium, but her journey was nothing compared to those of Zadracarta and Graphus, prolific winners in Canada and Brazil respectively. Whether Silver Fling would be able to take advantage of her opportunity depended largely upon her luck in running, for over Longchamp's sharp five furlongs she was always going to struggle early on. At halfway she'd got to within two and a half lengths of the leaders, but still had half the field in front of her. The gaps appeared at the right time, though Silver Fling needed all her battling qualities to catch Zadracarta and Nabeel Dancer virtually on the line, jockey Matthias using his whip almost twenty times in the last two furlongs. It wasn't just the first three that were concerned in the finish, as the next four Point of Light, Or Acier (the best-placed French runner), Whippet and favourite Statoblest were all within two lengths of the winner at the post. Silver Fling survived an objection, lodged by Whippet's rider, to ensure the continued dominance of British and Irish runners over the French for at least another year; it's now eleven years since Sigy last kept France's only Group 1 sprint at home.

The Minstrel continues to sire winners over a wide range of distances, in the latest season with Silver Fling at one extreme and the Northumberland

George Strawbridge's "Silver Fling"

Plate winner Orpheus at the other. Royal Dilemma has proved an excellent broodmare, for besides Silver Fling she has produced six other winners. Her first foal Imperial Fling (by Northern Dancer) won the Group 3 mile-and-a-half Bayerisches Zuchtrennen at Munich, her second Imperial Dilemma (by Damascus) a seven-furlong minor event at Redcar as a two-year-old before going on to be a graded-placed winner in North America. The best of the lot, however, is Silver Fling's sister Silverdip, a high-class winner over seven furlongs as a three-year-old, including in the Salisbury One Thousand Guineas Trial and the Strensall Stakes at York. Royal Dilemma, twice successful over sprint distances and placed in stakes company in the States, is a daughter of Queen Empress, the champion two-year-old filly in America in 1964, when she crossed the line first in nine (once disqualified) of her fourteen races. The winner of over 400,000 dollars in total prize money Queen Empress is a sister to the stakes-winning King Emperor.

Silver Fling (USA) (br.f. 1985)	The Minstrel (CAN) (ch 1974)	Northern Dancer (b 1961)	Nearctic
			Natalma
		Fleur (b 1964)	Victoria Park
			Flaming Page
	Royal Dilemma (USA) (br 1971)	Buckpasser (b 1963)	Tom Fool
			Busanda
		Queen Empress (b 1962)	Bold Ruler
			Irish Jay

Silver Fling, a lengthy, useful-looking filly with a quick action, acted on any going. She sweated up at Goodwood, was taken down early at York and was mounted outside the paddock at Newmarket and Goodwood. That shouldn't in any way cast doubts over her temperament; once racing she was splendidly game and genuine. She visits Kris. *I. A. Balding.*

835

SILVER HAZE 5 gr.g. Absalom 128–Chance Belle 85 (Foggy Bell 108) [1988 8d² 87
7d* 10d 8g 7f* 8f⁴ 7f³ 8m 8d 7d* 9g⁵ 1989 8g⁶ 8s² 7d 8g⁴] workmanlike,
good-bodied gelding: carries plenty of condition: has a round action: fairly useful
winner (including for apprentice) as 4-y-o: ran well when in frame in handicap at
Thirsk (caught final strides) and Badener-Meile at Baden-Baden (never nearer) in
spring: subsequently sent to race in Switzerland: effective at testing 6f and probably
barely stays 9f: acts on any going: on toes on reappearance: tough and genuine. *Miss
S. E. Hall.*

SILVER HELLO 3 gr.g. Nishapour (FR) 125–Si (Ragusa 137) [1988 7m⁵ 7g 8m 78
1989 8g⁴ 10m 12.4m³ 10.2f³ 10g³ 12g³ 12g 10v 12g*] rather leggy, quite good-topped
gelding: showed improved form when winning claimer at Edinburgh in November,
running on well: stays 1½m: acts on firm going, possibly unsuited by heavy. *P. S.
Felgate.*

SILVER ORE (FR) 2 ch.f. (Apr 7) Silver Hawk (USA) 123–Forever Mary 81 79
(Red Alert 127) [1989 6m* 6g⁶] quite attractive filly: shade unfurnished: second
foal: dam, sprint maiden here later successful at up to 7f in USA, is out of half-sister
to very smart Greenland Park, dam of Fitnah: won 6-runner minor event at Windsor
in July: carried head awkwardly when sixth of 13 in nursery at Newmarket
almost 3 months later: should stay 7f. *W. A. O'Gorman.*

SILVER OWL 3 gr.c. Daring March 116–Bird's Custard 80 (Birdbrook 116) [1988 88
6d 6d⁴ 1989 7d 6g⁵ 6m 12h* 12f* 12f² 12f* 12h² 12h* 12g* 12g⁴] leggy,
close-coupled colt: progressive handicapper: successful twice at both Brighton and
Folkestone and in £7,800 amateurs event at Epsom in the summer: should stay
further: acts on hard ground. *R. V. Smyth.*

SILVER PATROL 4 gr.g. Rusticaro (FR) 124–Goccia d'Oro (ITY) (Bolkonski —
134) [1988 6v² 7d² 7f 7g* 7v³ 8d 8v 1989 10d⁴ 7.2s 12m 8m 8.2g 9g 11s] angular,
sparely-made ex-Irish gelding: first foal: dam placed over 1m in Ireland from 3
starts: won maiden at Sligo as 3-y-o: on toes, 9 lengths fourth to Lazaz in minor
event at Pontefract in April, leading until over 3f out: well beaten after in varied
events, including handicaps: stays 7f: acts on heavy going: taken early to post. *A. P.
Stringer.*

SILVER'S GIRL 4 b.f. Sweet Monday 122–Persian Silver 61 (Cash And Courage 58
116) [1988 7g⁶ 8g² 7.5m 8m 8.2s³ 9v 1989 9v* 10v* 12g 8.2g⁴ 10.6d 12g 9g 10v] plain
filly: much improved in spring, winning maiden claiming event at Hamilton and
apprentice handicap at Ayr: well below her best last 4 outings, very slowly away first
of them: stays 1¼m well: needs give in the ground: blinkered once at 3 yrs. *D.
Moffatt.*

SILVER SHIFTER 2 b.f. (Apr 10) Night Shift (USA)–The Silver Darling 75 —
(John Splendid 116) [1989 6g] workmanlike, angular filly: has scope: half-sister to
several winners, including very useful sprinter Sylvan Barbarosa (by Native Bazaar): dam second in Britain before winning in Belgium: 9/1, prominent until beaten
and eased considerably after 4f in 12-runner maiden at Leicester in November. *A. C.
Stewart.*

SILVER SINGING (USA) 2 gr.f. (Feb 7) Topsider (USA)–Early Rising (USA) 69
(Grey Dawn II 132) [1989 6m³ 6g⁵] leggy, sparely-made filly: has a quick action:
third foal: half-sister to minor winner in USA by Timeless Moment: dam, minor
winner in USA at about 1m, out of half-sister to top-class Key To The Mint: quite
modest form in maidens at Newbury and Newmarket (favourite) in the autumn: will
be better suited by 7f. *I. A. Balding.*

SILVER STICK 2 gr.g. (May 4) Absalom 128–Queen's Parade (Sovereign Path 49
125) [1989 6f 6f 6f] leggy, rather angular gelding: sixth foal: brother to 7f winner Life
Guard and half-brother to winning hurdler Rowlandsons Trophy (by Vaigly Great):
dam poor maiden: plating-class maiden: not raced after June. *J. W. Watts.*

SILVER STRINGS 9 b.g. Blakeney 126–Melody Hour 105 (Sing Sing 134) [1988 47
NR 1989 10s⁴ 14s⁶ 14.8m* 12f 16m⁴ 15.3f* 15.3g² 17.6g⁵ 14f* 12.2m 15.8g⁶] rangy
gelding: poor handicapper: won at Warwick in May, Wolverhampton in July and
Nottingham in September: suited by around 1¾m: acts well on firm going: genuine.
B. Palling.

SILVER THORN 5 b.m. Record Run 127–Victory Corner 68 (Sit In The Corner 49
(USA)) 1988 NR 1989 16m² 18.8f* 17.6m⁴ 16m²] leggy, sparely-made mare: won
slowly-run handicap at Warwick in July: stays 2¼m: acts on firm going: visored final
2 appearances at 3 yrs. *R. J. Holder.*

SILVERWALTZ 4 gr.g. Lord Gayle (USA) 124–Languid (English Prince 129) —
[1988 8v⁵ 12d 1989 9s 12m 10g⁶] strong gelding: well beaten in modest company. *H.
P. Rohan.*

SIMASCALA 3 b.g. Electric 126–Elegida 93 (Habitat 134) [1988 7.5f 7m 7g² 7m* **60** 8.2m 8.2s 7g 1989 8s 10s 12s 8m 10f⁵ 8.2m 10g⁵] angular, workmanlike gelding: ridden by 5-lb claimer, easily best effort as 3-y-o when leading 1m in claimer at Yarmouth in August, final start: probably stays 1¼m: best form on a sound surface: visored last 3 starts. *W. Wilson.*

SIMJOUR 3 ch.c. Adonijah 126–Sellasia (FR) (Dankaro (FR) 131) [1988 7d* 1989 **92** 8g* 12f² 12f⁶ 12m³ 12m⁴] angular colt: fairly useful handicapper: justified favouritism at Brighton in April: ran well in fair company in the summer, including when third in listed event at Haydock: stays 1½m well: acts on firm going: hung right second start: visored final one. *R. F. Johnson Houghton.*

SIMON'S SONG 3 b.c. Reesh 117–Queen Swallow 58 (Le Levanstell 122) [1988 **—** NR 1989 6s 6f⁶ 6f] 13,000Y: sturdy colt: fourth reported foal: half-brother to 5f and 6f winner Monswart (by Sonnen Gold) and a winning plater by The Brianstan: dam, closely related to My Swallow, unplaced from 5f to 2m: poor maiden: best effort in apprentice claimer (sweating) final start (June): sold to join J. Thomas 1,300 gns Ascot October Sales. *K. M. Brassey.*

SIMPLY A WINNER 2 br.f. (May 15) Simply Great (FR) 122–Veruschka (USA) **41** (Turn-To) [1989 5f 6f³ 7m⁴ 6m⁵ 7g³] 2,000Y: leggy, small, light-framed filly: has a quick action: half-sister to several winners, including Cambridgeshire winner Sagamore (by Sagaro): dam French 2-y-o 6f winner: moderate plater: blinkered, went left start and swerved badly soon after, at Yarmouth in July on final appearance: best form at 6f. *W. Wilson.*

SIMPLY BLUE 2 ch.f. (Mar 15) Simply Great (FR) 122–Bluethroat 95 (Bally- **70** more 123) [1989 5.1f³ 6h* 7m⁴ 8f* 8f] IR 7,200Y: first foal: dam successful over 6f and 8.2f at 2 yrs here and over 1½m at 3 yrs in Ireland: modest performer: won 5-runner maiden auction race at Brighton in August and 7-runner nursery at Bath in September: ran as though something amiss final start: will be suited by 1¼m. *M. Bell.*

SIMPLY DES 2 b.f. (Mar 9) Simply Great (FR) 122–Kashida 68 (Green Dancer **55** (USA) 132) [1989 5h 5f⁴ 6m 7g 5m 6f⁴ 6m⁴ 6m 6m⁴ 6g 8m* 8g³ 8.2s] IR 2,000F, IR 3,900Y: neat filly: has a round action: second foal: half-sister to a winner in Belguim by Coquelin: dam lightly-raced daughter of Buz Kashi: fair plater: won 17-runner apprentice event at Warwick (bought in 6,200 gns) in October: good third to Integrity Boy in nursery at Carlisle later in month: suited by 1m: possibly unsuited by soft going: visored ninth outing: trained first 6 by N. Tinkler: sold 2,000 gns Ascot November Sales. *R. M. Whitaker.*

SIMPLY FIRST CLASS 3 b.g. Tower Walk 130–Duchy 99 (Rheingold 137) **—** [1988 8m⁶ 8m 1989 12.2m 12f 10m] workmanlike gelding: plating-class form at 2 yrs: well beaten in 1989, unseating apprentice over 4f out on final start: should stay at least 1¼m. *W. J. Pearce.*

SIMPLY HENRY 3 b.c. Simply Great (FR) 122–Salique (Sallust 134) [1988 6f³ **101** 6f² 6f* 7s 1989 8f² 8.5g³ 7h* 7f³ 7h* 7g*] lengthy, rather unfurnished colt: good mover: won apprentice claimer (sweating badly and hanging left) at Lingfield in July and, making all, handicap at Brighton and minor event at Catterick in August: stays 8.5f: acts on hard ground, ran poorly on soft: difficult ride, possibly suited by enterprising tactics: useful. *Sir Mark Prescott.*

SIMPLY PERFECT 3 b.c. Wassl 125–Haneena 118 (Habitat 134) [1988 6f 7g⁴ **69** 1989 10s⁶ 12f 14m 9g 12g 14g³] modest form at best: stays 1¾m: best efforts with some give in the ground: edgy final start: later bought out of H. Thomson Jones's stable 8,000 gns Newmarket July Sales. *M. Johnston.*

SIMPLY SPIM 2 b.f. (Mar 4) Simply Great (FR) 122–Spimpinina (Be My Guest **65** (USA) 126) [1989 6g 7m⁵ 6f³ 6v] strong, good-topped filly: second foal: dam won in Italy at 3 yrs: quite modest maiden: will stay at least 1¼m: acts on firm going. *W. G. R. Wightman.*

SIMPLY SWELL 3 br.g. Simply Great (FR) 122–Nelly Gail (Mount Hagen (FR) **75** 127) [1988 7m⁶ 8g 1989 14f³ 16.2g 14m³ 14m⁴ 14f² 14m² 14m³ 14m 15.3f² 16f⁴ 15.8g⁵ a12g⁴] small, leggy, close-coupled colt: modest maiden: below form last 3 outings and when finding little under pressure seventh and eighth: suited by 1¾m: acts on firm going: blinkered. *Lord John FitzGerald.*

SIMPLY TERRIFIC 2 b. or br.c. (Feb 7) Simply Great (FR) 122–Sweet Repose **93** (High Top 131) [1989 6m 6f² 6g 7f² 8f* 7m* 7g² 8d⁴ 7g 8.5g⁴] IR 30,000Y: second living foal: dam unraced daughter of champion 2-y-o filly of 1971 Rose Dubarry: improved colt: under a length fourth in Panasonic Smurfit EBF Futurity Stakes at the Curragh in September on eighth start: earlier won maiden at Killarney and nursery at Galway: around 11 lengths fourth of 9 to Go And Go in Laurel Futurity at Laurel on final start: stays 1m. *T. Stack, Ireland.*

SINCERELY YOURS 2 gr.f. (Feb 16) Kind of Hush 118–Mallihouana 84 — (Bustino 136) [1989 7f] lengthy, unfurnished filly: first foal: dam, 7f winner, sister to useful 1985 2-y-o 7f winner Normanby Lass: bit backward, slowly away and always behind in maiden at Leicester in October: moved moderately down. *R. Hollinshead.*

SINCLAIR BOY 3 b.c. Aragon 118–Amber Flyer 91 (Amber Rama (USA) 133) 66 [1988 5g³ 6d* 7m⁵ 5m⁵ 6g⁴ 1989 6d⁶ 8g⁶ 6m³ 6f² 7.6g⁵ 7.6f⁶ 9f² 9g 12.3m⁴ 8f 8.2f²] rather leggy, attractive colt: quite modest performer: stays 9f: acts on firm going and a soft surface: ran well when sweating final start: sold 6,400 gns Newmarket Autumn Sales: of questionable attitude. *R. Hollinshead.*

SINCLAIR LADY 5 gr.m. Absalom 128–Katsue 98 (King's Leap 111) [1988 5d 43 § 7g 5g 5g 6f 1989 5d² 6d³ 6m 5m⁵ 6m] neat, strong mare: quite useful winner at 2 yrs: has deteriorated considerably and is temperamental: effective at 5f and 6f: has got on toes: bolted on way down on reappearance in 1988 and on final outing: usually taken down early or very steadily. *M. Brittain.*

SINCLAIR PRINCE 2 ch.c. (Apr 8) Local Suitor (USA) 128–Mothers Girl — (Huntercombe 133) [1989 6m 6g] 15,500Y: sixth foal: half-brother to 3-y-o Nipotina (by Simply Great), fairly useful sprinter Roman Prose (by Sallust) and French 1¼m and 11.7f winner Wolver Knight (by Wolver Hollow): dam unraced half-sister to North Stoke and Anfield: poor form in August maidens at Ripon and Hamilton. *R. Hollinshead.*

SINGH HOLME 2 br.c. (May 6) Mansingh (USA) 120–Ivy Holme (Silly Season 48 127) [1989 5g 5d 5f] IR 4,000Y, 13,500 2-y-o: sparely-made colt: second foal: brother to a 2-y-o winner in Italy: dam ran once: poor maiden: showed ability only on second outing: off course for over 3 months after debut. *L. G. Cottrell.*

SINGH'S LADY 2 ch.f. (May 20) Mansingh (USA) 120–Deep Lady 78 (Deep — Diver 134) [1989 5m 5g⁶ 7m 8f] 1,150F: leggy filly: poor mover: sister to 1986 2-y-o 6f winner Green's Herring and half-sister to 1984 2-y-o 6f winner and fair hurdler Ballyarry (by Balliol): dam 2-y-o 5f winner: of little account and temperamental. *E. J. Alston.*

SINGING DETECTIVE 2 gr.c. (Mar 27) Absalom 128–Smoke Creek 67 64 (Habitat 134) [1989 5s³ 5g 5f² 6g⁶ 7g⁵ 7f⁶ 7g 7g 7g⁶] 10,000Y: rangy, rather angular colt: moderate walker: has a round action: second foal: half-brother to untrustworthy 3-y-o 16.5f winner Ardoran (by Little Wolf): dam maiden suited by 1½m: quite modest maiden: probably stays 7f: acts on any going: blinkered final appearance. *M. Brittain.*

SINGING GOLD 3 b.c. Gold Claim 90–Gellifawr 80 (Saulingo 122) [1988 NR — 1989 7f 6g a6g] sturdy colt: second foal: dam best at 5f: won twice (over 6f and 7f) in Belgium: no form here in late-season minor event and claimers, on final start carrying condition, chasing leaders 4f and eased: trained until after second start here by C. Guest in Belgium. *R. Guest.*

SINGING STAR 3 b.g. Crooner 119–Wild Jewel (Great Heron (USA) 126) [1988 62 5g 5g² 5g² 5g² 5g² 5g⁵ 6s 5g 5m⁶ 5g 1989 5g 5d⁴ 5f³ 6g⁵ 6f⁶ 6h⁴ 6f 6f² 5m⁶ 5f] close-coupled gelding: quite modest maiden: below form in claimer (not finding much under pressure) and handicap (moved badly to post, sweating and bandaged) in August last 2 starts: stays 6f: acts on hard going and a soft surface: blinkered fifth to ninth outings and twice at 2 yrs: gelded after final start. *J. Balding.*

SINGING STEVEN 5 b.h. Balliol 125–Cheb's Honour 70 (Chebs Lad 120) [1988 — 5g 5f 6f⁴ 5m 5m⁶ 5g 5g 5f 5g 5g 5d⁵ 6g 5s 5m 1989 5g 6f 5f 6m 5f⁶ 6f⁵ 5m 5m] strong, lengthy horse: poor mover: very useful sprinter at his best: well beaten majority of starts after 1987: best form on a sound surface: had been tried in blinkers and visor: retired to West Nesbit Stud, Jedburgh, fee £750 (Oct 1st). *D. W. Chapman.*

SINGING STREAM 3 b.f. Chief Singer 131–Sandstream 72 (Sandford Lad 133) — [1988 6d⁶ 6d 1989 7f 6f⁵ 6f] rather leggy, good-topped filly: poor maiden: stays 7f. *R. Hannon.*

SINGING SUZY 3 ch.f. Music Maestro 119–High Button Boots (Tower Walk 40 130) [1988 NR 1989 5s 5f⁶ 5f 5m⁴ 5.8h 6m] small, good-quartered filly: first living foal: dam ran 3 times: poor form, including in seller: best effort fourth start: sweating on debut: should stay beyond 5f: sold 1,050 gns Doncaster August Sales. *G. Blum.*

SINGING (USA) 2 b.f. (Feb 22) The Minstrel (CAN) 135–Social Column (USA) 70 p (Swoon's Son) [1989 7f⁴] close-coupled, good-quartered filly: closely related to

Mondanite (by Lyphard), disappointing here at 3 yrs later winner in USA, and half-sister to very smart 3-y-o 1¼m winner Two Timing (by Blushing Groom) and a winner in France over 1¼m: dam, placed at 6f, is half-sister to champion 3-y-o Chris Evert: co-favourite but better for race and green, 7 lengths fourth of 7, ridden 3f out no headway, to Zawahir in maiden at Goodwood in July: sure to improve. *B. W. Hills.*

SINGLE 7 gr.g. Jellaby 124–Miss Solo (Runnymede 123) [1988 8d 8g⁶ 8f 8.3m 8d³ 8g⁴ 8g² 9g⁶ 8d 8s⁶ 1989 8d 8g² 7.6f 8m 8m⁴ 8g 8g⁵ 9g 8m a8g⁶ a10g⁵] leggy, sparely-made gelding: fair handicapper: effective at 7f to 9f: possibly ideally suited by an easy surface nowadays: has won for apprentice: pulled up (broke blood vessel) fourth appearance in 1988: bandaged then and on fifth outing in 1989: none too consistent nowadays. *W. G. R. Wightman.* **90 d**

SINGLE COMBAT (USA) 2 b.c. (Mar 19) Nijinsky (CAN) 138–La Dame du Lac (USA) (Round Table) [1989 6.3g² 6.3g*] 90,000Y: brother to useful 1987 Irish 2-y-o 6f winner Lake Como, winner at 1m in France in 1989, and a minor winner in USA, closely related to a winner in USA by Storm Bird, and half-brother to a stakes-placed winner by Exceller: dam, unraced, from excellent family: won 10-runner Dunmurry Stud EBF Anglesey Stakes at the Curragh in August by a neck from Tenderetta, with Absolutely Perfect ½ length away: will be much better suited by 7f+: useful 3-y-o in the making. *T. Stack, Ireland.* **92 p**

SINGLE SHOOTER (USA) 4 b.g. Nodouble (USA)–Irish Sister (USA) (Needles) [1988 10f⁵ 1989 8m³ 7f⁵ 10m³ 10h² 11.7m 9g] close-coupled gelding: plating-class maiden: stays 11.7f: acts on hard going: blinkered second outing: has sweated: winning hurdler. *R. J. O'Sullivan.* **57**

SING THE BLUES 5 b.g. Blue Cashmere 129–Pulcini 61 (Quartette 106) [1988 10.1m 11.7m 10.1m 12g 12d 1989 12g 16.5f³ 14f⁶ 16f* 16m² a16g⁶ a16g⁶] big, lengthy gelding: won strongly-run handicap at Lingfield in August: well beaten at same course last 2 starts: will stay beyond 2m: acts on firm going: bandaged behind final outing: winning hurdler. *C. J. Benstead.* **33**

SINGULAR RUN 3 b.g. Trojan Fen 118–Needy (High Top 131) [1988 7f* 7g³ 7g* 7s 7f² 1989 11d³ 10.2d⁴ 12m³ 10m³] lengthy, good-quartered, workmanlike gelding: carries condition: fair performer: not seen out after running creditably in minor event and slowly-run handicap in the summer: stays 1½m: acts well on firm going and possibly unsuited by a soft surface. *P. F. I. Cole.* **84**

SINK THE FLEET (USA) 2 b.g. (Apr 25) Cutlass (USA)–Noontime Splendor (USA) (Diplomat Way) [1989 5g² 5s⁴ 5f² 5m³ 5g⁴ 7m² 7m* 7f³ 7f²] $20,000Y: compact gelding: good mover: half-brother to a minor winner in North America by Star de Naskra: dam second once from 17 starts: modest performer: won 6-runner maiden at Ayr in July: will stay 1m: ran moderately when blinkered. *J. Etherington.* **77**

SINODOS 3 b.f. Ela-Mana-Mou 132–Safety Measure 68 (Home Guard (USA) 129) [1988 7g 1989 8m³ 8g⁶ 8s] lengthy, angular filly: showed signs of ability in maidens first 2 outings: may stay further: possibly unsuited by soft ground: takes keen hold: edgy penultimate start: bandaged off-hind final one: sold 3,900 gns Newmarket Autumn Sales. *W. Jarvis.* **—**

SIOKRA 3 ch.f. Kris 135–Eastern Shore 70 (Sun Prince 128) [1988 NR 1989 8.5m³ 10f⁴ 9g⁴] leggy, angular filly: third foal: half-sister to French 1½m winner Carmita (by Caerleon) and 6f and 1m winner Abu Muslab (by Ile de Bourbon): dam stayed 11.7f: progressive form in maidens: took strong hold and wandered under pressure second start: should be suited by 1¼m: twice awkward at stalls. *A. C. Stewart.* **67**

SIR ANDREW LEWIS 3 br.g. Petorius 117–Spooning (Ashmore (FR) 125) [1988 7g 6m 6g 7f 7m 7v⁶ 1989 7s³ 10m 7g² 7.5d 7h] rather narrow, sparely-made gelding: poor mover: poor form, including in sellers: stays 7f well: acts on heavy going: bandaged reappearance: sold to join D. R. Wellicome 1,000 gns Newmarket September Sales. *C. N. Allen.* **50**

SIR ARTHUR HOBBS 2 b.c. (Apr 15) Lyphard's Special (USA) 124–Song Grove 61 (Song 132) [1989 6m² 6f 6g⁶ 5g* 5d² 6g* 5m³ 5d³ 6g⁵ 6g] 26,000Y: lengthy, round-barrelled colt: progressed well physically: moderate mover: seventh foal: half-brother to moderate 1984 2-y-o 5f winner Call of The Wild (by Thatching), and several winners abroad: dam, successful over 5.8f at 4 yrs in Ireland, is half-sister to dam of good Australian sprinter Getting Closer: fairly useful performer: won 18-runner maiden at Ripon in July and 8-runner nursery at Newcastle in August: ran creditably next 3 starts (one in Ireland), moderately final one: stays 6f: used to be awkward at stalls, and was withdrawn at Chester in July. *F. H. Lee.* **96**

SIR CROON 3 ch.g. Crooner 119–Sirette 42 (Great Nephew 126) [1988 8s 7d — 1989 7s⁶ 10d⁶ a10g] compact gelding: has a quick action: sign of ability only in Epsom maiden on reappearance: off course nearly 5 months after: should stay at least 1m. *L. G. Cottrell.*

SIR EDWARD 4 b.g. Formidable (USA) 125–Pearl Wedding 86 (Gulf Pearl 117) — [1988 NR 1989 16.5g] 1,100 4-y-o: workmanlike gelding: seventh foal: half-brother to Cambridgeshire winner Century City (by High Top): dam won over 1¼m and 1½m: 66/1, backward and bandaged, tailed off in ladies maiden at Doncaster in June. *T. Kersey.*

SIREESH 2 b.c. (Mar 5) Reesh 117–Record Lady (Record Token 128) [1989 5f⁴ 5d **48** 5f⁴ 5f 6g] leggy, sparely-made colt: has a round action: first foal: dam unraced daughter of half-sister to Chellaston Park (by Record Token): plating-class maiden: stays 6f: sweating third start. *M. Brittain.*

SIRGAME 3 b.c. Thatching 131–Vaunt (USA) (Hill Rise 127) [1988 6m 6m 1989 8f — 12g⁶] good-bodied, rather leggy colt: no worthwhile form in maidens and a minor event: tailed off in visor final start. *Mrs N. Macauley.*

SIR NICK 2 gr.g. (Apr 4) Sandhurst Prince 128–Silecia (Sky Gipsy 117) [1989 6m **69** 8.2f⁴ 8m⁴ 8f⁴ 8g a7g² a7g² a8g³] 10,000Y: leggy, lengthy, angular gelding: half-brother to several winners, including quite useful 7f and 1¼m winner Hayati (by Hotfoot): dam never ran: modest maiden: looked temperamental final outing: will stay 1¼m: blinkered fifth appearance. *N. A. Callaghan.*

SIROCCO SPRITE 4 b.f. Sayyaf 121–Kitty Frisk 64 (Prince Tenderfoot (USA) — 126) [1988 7d 9g 12f 10g⁶ 13.8d 13.8f⁵ 1989 10s] plain filly: poor plater. *P. S. Felgate.*

SIR PERCY 6 b.h. Blakeney 126–Nicoletta 81 (Busted 134) [1988 10.2s 1989 — a10g] tall, quite attractive horse: moderate mover: one-time fairly useful performer: tailed off only start at 5 yrs and 6 yrs: stays 1¾m: acts on any going: ran poorly when blinkered. *Mrs N. Macauley.*

SIR RUFUS 3 ch.c. Thatching 131–La Melodie 77 (Silly Season 127) [1988 8.2m⁶ **70** 8f* 1989 10g 9f 10g⁵ 10f⁴ a10g a11g³ a14g a12g³] good-bodied, quite attractive colt: moderate mover: modest handicapper: placed at Southwell and Lingfield (blinkered) in the winter: stays 1½m: acts on firm ground: also blinkered fourth to sixth outings, sour in appearance on first of them: has looked difficult ride, and should be best with strong handling. *C. R. Nelson.*

SIRSE 2 gr.f. (Mar 11) Enchantment 115–Sea Farer Lake 74 (Gairloch 122) [1989 **61** 5d 5d 6m 6m³ 6f³ 6f⁴ 6f* 6f⁵ 6g* 8g] close-coupled, rather lightly-made filly: poor mover: first foal: dam 1m and 1¼m winner: useful plater: bought in 6,200 gns then 4,200 gns after winning at Lingfield in summer: ran poorly last 3 starts: should stay 7f: races freely: has worn bandages. *M. D. I. Usher.*

SIR TOM 2 ch.g. (Apr 13) Adonijah 126–Speed Baby (USA) 76 (Diplomat Way) **63** [1989 5s³ 6m* 6m³ 6g³ 6m³ 6f 6g] 10,000Y: leggy, quite good-topped gelding: easy mover: third foal: dam won over 5f on debut showed little after: quite modest performer: won 5-runner minor event at Thirsk in May: off course for nearly 3 months after fifth outing: ran poorly on return: suited by 6f: acts on top-of-the-ground. *J. Berry.*

SI SAWAT 2 ch.g. (Feb 11) Superlative 118–Soft Chinook (USA) (Hitting Away) **42** [1989 5g⁵ 6g² 6m 8.2f 7g] 2,000F, 580Y: medium-sized, deep-girthed gelding: has scope: half-brother to 5 winners including 3-y-o 9f winner Tarlogie (by Touching Wood) and fair 1980 2-y-o 5f winner Swinging Rhythm (by Swing Easy): dam French plater: moderate plater: stays 1m: visored fourth start. *S. J. Muldoon.*

SISTER CHABRIAS 4 b.f. Chabrias (FR) 103–Ginger Tart 87 (Swing Easy **71** (USA) 126) [1988 8.2v⁴ 6m 8.5m 6g² 6m* 6g² 6m 6g² 6g 6s⁴ 1989 7g⁶ 7f 7m³ 8f⁶] lengthy filly: modest handicapper: not seen out after July: stays 7f: acts on top-of-the-ground and soft going: apprentice ridden as 4-y-o except on third outing: slowly away on reappearance: sometimes wears a visor. *M. C. Pipe.*

SISTER CHERYL 4 ch.f. Vaigly Great 127–Miss Merlin 79 (Manacle 123) [1988 **48** 5m 6g⁶ 6g⁶ 6f⁴ 6f 6m 8.5f 1989 10m 5f² 5f 7m² 7f 8f a7g] tall, angular filly: moderate mover: poor performer: sweating, ran poorly fifth start: stays 7f: acts on firm going. *R. G. Frost.*

SISTER SAL 2 ch.f. (Mar 7) Bairn (USA) 126–Mercy Cure 81 (No Mercy 126) **74** [1989 5m 5m 5f 6f² 6m* 6g*] 8,000Y: lengthy filly: fifth foal: half-sister to 3-y-o Champion Girl (by Blazing Saddles), 5f winner at 2 yrs, and 5f to 7f winner Last Recovery (by Final Straw): dam firm-ground sprinter: smart plater: bought in 5,000 gns after winning 28-runner event at Newmarket in October: won 30-runner claiming nursery same course following month by 3 lengths: better suited by 6f than 5f, and may stay 7f: often sweats and on toes. *J. Sutcliffe.*

SITEX 11 b.h. Record Run 127–Glorious Light 53 (Alcide 136) [1988 7f 6f⁵ 6m 6f²   **32** 5g⁵ 5g 5g 6m⁵ 5.8f⁴ 1989 5s 6f⁵ 6f 5f 6f 6m³ 5f] lengthy horse: poor walker and mover: poor performer: best at sprint distances: acts on firm going and soft surface: has run creditably in blinkers: usually gets long way behind: inconsistent. *M. J. Bolton.*

SIXSLIP (USA) 3 ch.f. Diesis 133–Oxslip 106 (Owen Dudley 121) [1988 7f 1989   **94** 10s* 10.5f 13.3g⁴ 14f⁴ 14.6g⁴ 14m] rangy, angular filly: good walker: won maiden at Sandown in April and handicap (showing improved form) at Kempton in September: will stay 2m: best form on an easy surface: not discredited after on toes and swishing tail in paddock fourth start: fairly useful. *H. Candy.*

SIXTEEN ACRES 3 b.g. Welsh Term 126–Lamya 73 (Hittite Glory 125) [1988   **—** 7g 1989 12s⁵ 12f 12m 10g] medium-sized, quite well-made gelding: signs of ability in varied events only on reappearance: should be suited by further: has joined D. Welsh. *P. Howling.*

SKAZKA (USA) 3 b.f. Sir Ivor 135–Winter Words (USA) (Northern Dancer)   **84** [1988 6d² 7d³ 8s⁵ 7.3m* 8g 1989 8g 10.2m² 8f* 10m⁴ 10m² 10f⁶ 12g 10m] sturdy, good-bodied filly: moderate mover, with a round action: fair handicapper: won at Salisbury in May: ran moderately in quite valuable events last 2 outings: stays 1¼m: best form on top-of-the-ground: often ridden by 5-lb claimer. *I. A. Balding.*

SKELLIG 3 ch.g. Day Is Done 115–Window Box (Swing Easy (USA) 126) [1988   **63** 6s⁵ 7d⁵ 6s² 7f* 6s⁴ 1989 7g 6d 8m 7m⁵ 7m 6g 8v 8.2g] lengthy, shallow-girthed gelding: fair winner as 2-y-o: below form in 1989 when best efforts second (edgy) and fourth outings: moved badly down on sixth and ran badly after: stays 7f: acts on any going: sometimes edges left: visored fifth start: not discredited when sweating once at 2 yrs. *J. S. Wainwright.*

SKI CAPTAIN 5 b.g. Welsh Captain 113–Miss Nelski 84 (Most Secret 119) [1988   **92** 5g 5v⁵ 5g⁵ 5g* 5m³ 5f* 5g 5g³ 5m³ 5g⁴ 5g³ 5f* 5g 5g 1989 5f 5f⁵ 5f⁵ 5g² 6f⁴ 5g² 5m* 5g⁴ 5f⁵ 5g⁶ 5g⁴ 5m⁶ 5g 5m³ 5g* 5m 5m⁵ 5g² 5d] strong, workmanlike gelding: usually looks well: moderate mover: successful in June in £7,600 Northern Rock Gosforth Park Cup (Handicap) at Newcastle for second year running and in October in 9-runner handicap (racing alone far side) at Goodwood: 33/1, appeared to run a tremendous race when ¾-length second to Lugana Beach in listed event at Newmarket later in October: suited by 5f: best form on a sound surface: has worn blinkers and a visor, but not since 1987: has won when sweating and for an apprentice: splendidly tough and consistent. *P. Howling.*

SKIMMING 4 b.c. Mill Reef (USA) 141–Mighty Fly 117 (Comedy Star (USA) 121)   **51** [1988 10.8d⁶ 10g 1989 10v⁶ 12f⁴ 13g* 12m 11s²] sparely-made colt: 25/1, made most, setting moderate pace, when winning 4-runner handicap at Ayr in July: sweating, creditable second of 15, rallying, in seller at same course in October: little other worthwhile form: stays 13f: acts on soft going: bandaged last 4 outings: has joined J. Gillen. *G. M. Moore.*

SKIPLAM WOOD 3 b.f. Cree Song 99–Mab (Morston (FR) 125) [1988 6f⁵ 6f   **57** 1989 7m³ 7f³ 6f⁵ 9.1f⁴ 8f⁵] compact, plain filly: turns fore-feet in: quite modest maiden: third at Edinburgh, second and best effort despite swerving left to stand rail: pulled hard in crossed noseband fourth outing: stays 7f. *D. Lee.*

SKIRBECK 3 b.c. Ahonoora 122–Grecian Sky (African Sky 124) [1988 7g 7g² 8g   **67** 1989 8d⁶ 8f 10m⁶ 8.3g⁴] leggy, rather unfurnished colt: poor mover: quite modest maiden: best effort staying on well at 1m on good ground. *J. A. R. Toller.*

SKISURF 3 b.c. Niniski (USA) 125–Seasurf 106 (Seaepic (USA) 100) [1988 NR   **80** 1989 12m⁵ 11f 14m³ 13.3m⁵ 14.6s] close-coupled, workmanlike colt: fourth foal: brother to 7f and 2m winner Janiski and half-brother to winning juvenile hurdler Crested (by Busted): dam won over 7f at 2 yrs and useful over 1m at 3 yrs: fair maiden: best effort on third start: set pace in St Leger at Ayr final one: will stay beyond 1¾m: acts on top-of-the-ground. *C. E. Brittain.*

SKOLERN 5 b.g. Lochnager 132–Piethorne 86 (Fine Blade (USA) 121) [1988 8g⁵   **76** 8m 7.5f* 7.5m² 7s² 7m³ 7d² 6d 7f² 7d* 1989 8.5d 8m² 7m 8.2d] rather leggy, good-topped gelding: carries plenty of condition: fair handicapper: effective at 7f and 1m: acts on any going: visored third to sixth starts in 1988: sometimes sweats (badly so when running moderately third outing): suitable mount for apprentice: goes well with enterprising tactics: sold privately to join Mrs P. Barker 5,000 gns Doncaster October Sales: winning hurdler. *R. M. Whitaker.*

SKY CAT 5 b.g. Skyliner 117–Spring Kitten (Pitcairn 126) [1988 8s² 8m² 10s 1989   **67**
8g⁶ 8g² 8s4] leggy gelding: quite modest handicapper: blinkered, in frame in spring
at Doncaster and Thirsk, setting strong gallop on each occasion: stays 1m: acts on
top-of-the-ground and soft going: sometimes sweats: seems best with strong
handling. *M. H. Easterby.*

SKY CLOUD 3 ch.g. Formidable (USA) 125–Cloud Nine 97 (Skymaster 126)   **73**
[1988 5m 6f 5g 5f⁵ 7d 1989 7d² 7m 6m 7m⁶ 8f³ 7m² 7s 6f³ 7g² 7d* a6g³] stocky
gelding: moderate walker: won handicap at Catterick in October: effective at 6f to
1m: acts on firm going and a soft surface: ridden by 7-lb claimer first 3 starts: best
ridden close to pace. *W. G. A. Brooks.*

SKY CONQUEROR (USA) 4 ch.c. Conquistador Cielo (USA)–Blushing Cathy   **93**
(USA) (Blushing Groom (FR) 131) [1988 10m* 10f² 9m* 10g² 10g⁶ 1989 10g 10f 10g³
8f* 9m⁴ 10g 8m³ 10f] sparely-made, rather angular colt: fairly useful performer:
made all in handicap at Sandown in June, keeping on gamely to beat Spanish Heart
1½ lengths: creditable third to Sharazari in £5,000 ladies event at Ascot following
month: better suited by 1m than 1¼m: acts on firm going: probably needs to
dominate: often wears crossed noseband: has had tongue tied down: has been taken
very quietly to post. *A. A. Scott.*

SKY FIGHTER 2 b.f. (Apr 19) Hard Fought 125–Sky Valley 101 (Skymaster 126)   **43**
[1989 5d 5f³ 6m 5m³ 7m⁴ 8g⁵] IR 2,400F, IR 5,600Y: rather leggy filly: moderate
mover: sister to a winner in Belgium, closely related to Belgian 1000 Guineas
second Hot Valley (by Hot Spark) and half-sister to 4 winners: dam sprinting
half-sister to Owen Anthony: poor maiden: not discredited in selling nurseries last 2
starts: stays 1m. *Capt. J. Wilson.*

SKY SINGER 3 b.f. Kafu 120–Singalong Lass 63 (Bold Lad (IRE) 133) [1988 5g   —
5m 5.1g 5.8d 7g 1989 7d 6g] workmanlike filly: plating-class maiden: not seen out
until late-season, showing speed 4f in apprentice seller final start: should stay 7f:
acts on soft surface. *D. W. Chapman.*

SKY WATCHER 3 b.g. Skyliner 117–Holernzaye 93 (Sallust 134) [1988 6m 5g⁶   **54**
5h⁴ 7g⁵ 7m⁵ 7f 8s 1989 7g⁶ 6v⁴ 6v⁵ 8.2m 10f² 8h* 10f³ 11g⁴ 10m a8g] compact,
workmanlike gelding: good second in summer sellers at Redcar and Carlisle,
awarded latter race on technicality: below form after: should prove suited by 1¼m:
acts on any going: has run well for apprentice and when sweating: lacks turn of foot.
Denys Smith.

SLADES HILL 2 b.c. (Apr 2) Lochnager 132–Mephisto Waltz 98 (Dancer's   **64**
Image (USA)) [1989 5f⁴ 5g] 22,000Y: smallish, good-quartered colt: fifth foal:
half-brother to 3 sprint winners,including 4-y-o Cumbrian Waltzer (by Stanford),
and a winner in Spain by Cut Above: dam won over 5f and 6f at 2 yrs: quite modest
form in autumn maidens at Nottingham (bandaged) and Redcar: sold to join Miss S.
Hall 13,000 gns Doncaster November Sales. *I. V. Matthews.*

SLAVE TO LOVE 2 ch.f. (Apr 15) Song 132–Presentable 60 (Sharpen Up 127)   —
[1989 6m 7m] 7,600F, 10,000Y: smallish filly: moderate mover: half-sister to 3-y-o
9f and 1¼m seller winner Blakesware Gold (by Vaigly Great) and 2 other winners,
including 1985 2-y-o 1m winner Centrepoint (by Reform): dam, half-sister to
Gimcrack winner Wishing Star, was placed over 1½m: well beaten in summer
maidens at Yarmouth (unruly stalls) and Warwick (slowly away). *Mrs L. Piggott.*

SLEEKBURN LADY 2 b.f. (Jun 10) Rapid River 127–Sophia Western (Steel   —
Heart 128) [1989 5g⁴ 5g] stocky filly: third living foal: half-sister to 3-y-o 1m seller
winner Week St Mary (by Warpath) and 1985 2-y-o 5f seller winner Dolly Dare (by
Daring March): dam well beaten all starts: soundly beaten in 4-runner minor event
at Carlisle and 23-runner maiden at Redcar in October. *R. O'Leary.*

SLEEPERS 5 br.m. Swing Easy (USA) 126–Jenny's Rocket (Roan Rocket 128)   **53** §
[1988 5m⁵ 6g 6f 5f 5f 7f⁵ 7m 5d⁶ 6m 5m 6g⁴ 5s⁴ 5f* 6m⁻5g 5s⁴ 1989 5f 5f 5f⁴ 5f² 5f
5f⁵ 6f 5f 5m⁶ 5m⁴ 5f⁴ 5m⁶ 5f⁴ 5f⁵] lengthy, rather angular mare: poor mover:
plating-class performer: stays 6f: acts on any going: has worn blinkers, but not last 7
starts: has worn bandages behind: tends to get behind and ideally needs strong
handling: sold 1,350 gns Ascot November Sales: unreliable. *C. B. B. Booth.*

SLEEPLINE FANTASY 4 ch.c. Buzzards Bay 128§–Sleepline Princess 86   **82**
(Royal Palace 131) [1988 6s* 6d⁵ 5.8g² 6m 5g 7m 7d³ 6s 1989 6v 7s⁴ 7g² 8.2m⁵ 8f⁵
7.6m⁵ 8m* 8.2d⁶ 7m 8m⁴ 8d] leggy, sparely-made colt: fair handicapper: won
£10,100 Crocker Bulteel Stakes (Handicap) at Ascot in July by 2 lengths, drifting
left, from Vague Shot: didn't get clear run next 3 starts, on last occasion fourth of 16,
checked 2f out, to Aradu in £11,100 event at Ascot: stays 1m: acts on any going:
sometimes sweats, and has got on edge. *R. J. Holder.*

SLEEPLINE PALACE 2 b.f. (May 6) Homing 130–Sleepline Princess 86 **60**
(Royal Palace 131) [1989 6f⁵ 5h* 5g] leggy, lengthy filly: third foal: half-sister to
3-y-o 7f winner Sleepline Royale and fair 4-y-o Sleepline Fantasy (both by Buzzards
Bay), successful at up to 1m: dam won over 6f at 2 yrs: won 6-runner maiden at Bath
in June by short head: creditable seventh in listed race at Newbury 6 weeks later:
bred to stay 1m. *R. J. Holder.*

SLEEPLINE ROYALE 3 ch.g. Buzzards Bay 128§–Sleepline Princess 86 **62**
(Royal Palace 131) [1988 5d 5.8g⁴ 5f 1989 6s³ 7d* 7g 7h 11m 10m⁴ 8h⁴ 8.2d⁵ 10.2f]
leggy gelding: quite modest handicapper: sweating, won at Warwick in good style in
early-May: easily best efforts after on sixth and eighth starts: stays 1¼m: acts on
top-of-the-ground but goes well on a soft surface. *R. J. Holder.*

SLEEPY HEAD 3 b.f. Shirley Heights 130–Idle Days 80 (Hittite Glory 125) **81**
[1988 8s⁵ 8g 1989 14d³ 13v] tall, leggy filly: has a powerful, round action: third in
maiden at Haydock in September, only worthwhile form: should be suited by test of
stamina: on toes as 3-y-o: sweating final start and when withdrawn (gave trouble at
stalls) on intended reappearance. *W. Hastings-Bass.*

SLEEPY MOUNTAIN 4 b.c. Young Generation 129–Super Anna (Super Sam **103**
124) [1988 6g* 6d* 5m⁶ 6m* 5m⁴ 6g⁴ 6.5g³ 1989 6g 6m 7g 6m 6m 8m* 7g⁵ 7g⁴ 8d]
tall, quite attractive colt: moderate walker: has a quick, powerful action: useful
performer: won strongly-run 5-runner handicap at Goodwood in August: ran well
when fifth to Kerita in Supreme Stakes at same course in October: found little next
outing: stays 1m: acts on top-of-the-ground and a soft surface: blinkered third (on
toes, free to post and in race) and fifth starts: sold to race in Middle East 23,000 gns
Newmarket Autumn Sales. *B. Hanbury.*

SLENDER BENDER 3 b.f. Gorytus (USA) 132–Addison's Jubilee 73 (Sparkler **82**
130) [1988 6f⁴ 5m 6m⁶ 6m 7g⁵ 1989 8g² 8f⁶ 9f* 10m⁵ 8g³ 8g⁶] workmanlike
filly: fair handicapper: won at Hamilton in June and Yarmouth (in good style) in July:
stays 9f: acts on firm going. *G. A. Pritchard-Gordon.*

SLENDER STYLE (USA) 3 b.f. Alleged (USA) 138–Cold Buns (USA) (Far **111**
North (CAN) 120) [1988 NR 1989 8s* 10d² 11m³ 10d³ 12g*] $100,000Y: second foal:
sister to a winner in North America in 1989: dam, minor 1m stakes winner in USA, is
half-sister to top-class 5f to 9f winner Raise Your Skirts, the dam of Big Shuffle: won
maiden (favourite) at Leopardstown in April and Group 3 EBF Meld Stakes (by 2
lengths from Noora Abu) at the Curragh in August: placed in listed races and Group
2 contest: stays 1½m: yet to race on very firm going, probably acts on any other. *D.
K. Weld, Ireland.*

SLEW THE SLEWOR (USA) 2 b.c. (Apr 25) Slew O'Gold (USA)–Featherhill **111**
(USA) (Lyphard (USA) 132) [1989 7d⁴ 7g 8g³ 7s*] 1,800,000 francs (approx
£167,800) Y: fourth foal: half-brother to high-class 1m to 10.5f winner Groom Dancer
(by Blushing Groom), also successful from 6f to 9f at 2 yrs, and French 3-y-o Tagel
(by Cox's Ridge), smart stayer at 2 yrs: dam, French 1¼m and 1½m performer, is
daughter of Prix Royal-Oak winner Lady Berry: won maiden at Saint-Cloud in
October: under 2 lengths third to Funambule in Group 3 Prix des Chenes there
earlier in month: will stay 1¼m: yet to race on firm going. *F. Boutin, France.*

SLICK CHERRY 2 b.f. (Feb 16) Noalto 120–Slick Chick 89 (Shiny Tenth 120) **66**
[1989 6m⁶ 6g³ 7g] 2,400F: workmanlike, good-quartered filly: has a round action:
seventh living foal: half-sister to several winners here and abroad, including quite
useful 5f to 1¼m winner Basil Boy (by Jimsun), later successful in USA: dam stayed
13f: quite modest maiden: should stay at least 1m. *D. R. C. Elsworth.*

SLIGHT INDULGENCE 2 br.c. (May 19) Runnett 125–Bellagold (Rheingold –
137) [1989 5s 5m 6m] IR 4,400F, 6,000Y: compact, good-bodied colt: third foal:
half-brother to sprint maiden Ration of Passion (by Camden Town): dam Irish 9f and
1¼m winner: well beaten in maidens and a seller: slowly away first 2 starts: sold
1,900 gns Ascot July Sales. *L. J. Holt.*

SLIP-A-SNIP 2 b.f. (Apr 2) Wolverlife 115–Stramenta (Thatching 131) [1989 6m –
6m 5m] IR 1,400Y: lengthy, sparely-made, dipped-backed filly: moderate mover:
second foal: dam unraced: apparently of little account. *N. R. Mitchell.*

SLIPPEROSE 2 gr.f. (Apr 23) Persepolis (FR) 127–Scholastika (GER) **72**
(Alpenkonig (GER)) [1989 6g⁶ 6g³ 6g²] compact, workmanlike filly: good walker:
has a roundish action: second known foal: dam German bred: modest maiden: best
effort final start: will probably be better suited by 7f + . *J. W. Hills.*

SLIP UP 9 b.g. Quiet Fling (USA) 124–Artemis 91 (King Emperor (USA)) [1988 –
NR 1989 18.8f] apparently no longer of much account on flat: winning hurdler. *G. P.
Enright.*

SLOE BERRY 3 b.f. Sharpo 132–Native Berry (FR) 76 (Ribero 126) [1988 NR 82 1989 6m 6m⁵ 6f* 5f⁵ 5f⁶ 6m 6m² 5m² 6m³ 5m 5d a5g²] close-coupled, rather sparely-made filly: moderate walker and mover: sixth foal: half-sister to some poor animals: dam, who raced in Britain and France, won at up to 6f: fair handicapper: won maiden at Lingfield in July: ran creditably when placed, beaten neck at Southwell in December: stays 6f: acts on firm going: tailed off at Chester sixth start. *C. E. Brittain.*

SLOW EXPOSURE 2 b.c. (Apr 25) Pharly (FR) 130–Armure Bleue (FR) 65 p (Riverman (USA) 131) [1989 8g⁴ 8v] 2,600Y: close-coupled colt: second live foal: dam once-raced half-sister to Ashmore: well beaten, not knocked about, in autumn minor events at Sandown and Newbury: likely to do better. *K. O. Cunningham-Brown.*

SMALL FEE 4 ch.f. Blue Cashmere 129–Gay Picture 62 (Linacre 133) [1988 5s² 68 5g 5s⁶ 5d³ 6g 6m 6g² 5d* 5g² 5g 6f 6s⁵ 5s 6f⁵ 5d 1989 6d⁶ 6g 6g² 6d 6s a7g³ a7g² a7g a6g² a6g⁴ a6g⁶] angular, sparely-made filly: often unimpressive in appearance: poor mover: modest performer: needs testing conditions at 5f and stays 7f: suited by an easy surface: suitable mount for apprentice: has been bandaged off-fore and visored: inconsistent. *M. Brittain.*

SMALL WIND 3 b.f. Tumble Wind (USA)–Small Is Beautiful (Condorcet (FR)) — [1988 6m 6s 6m 1989 7f 6m 6f 7.5m 6f 6g] smallish, workmanlike filly: quite moderate plater: should prove better at 7f than 6f: blinkered fourth and final starts: visored, broke out of stalls and withdrawn fifth one: took keen hold and hung on fourth: sold 700 gns Ascot November Sales. *C. W. C. Elsey.*

SMART COPPER 4 ch.f. Floriferous–Our Quest (Private Walk 108) [1988 NR — 1989 10.1m] smallish filly: first foal: dam last in Irish 7f maiden on only outing: blinkered, dwelt badly and tailed off from halfway in claimer at Windsor in May: sold 1,200 gns Ascot July Sales. *Miss L. Bower.*

SMARTIE LEE 2 ch.f. (Feb 9) Dominion 123–Nosy Parker (FR) (Kashmir II 66 125) [1989 5d⁶ 6m³ 6m³ 7f⁵ 7m* 8.2f* 8f³ 8f⁴] 15,500F, 12,500Y: small, close-coupled filly: keen walker: fourth foal: half-sister to winning French middle-distance stayer The Searcher (by Bellman): dam never ran: quite modest performer: won selling nursery (changed hands 10,000 gns) at Sandown in August and nursery at Nottingham in September: suited by 1m: consistent. *P. F. I. Cole.*

SMART IN BLACK 7 b. or br.h. Roscoe Blake 120–Cool Down (Warpath 113) — [1988 NR 1989 12.2m⁶] workmanlike horse: poor maiden on flat: winning hurdler/novice chaser: dead. *G. Richards.*

SMART MART 10 ch.g. Jimmy Reppin 131–Fochetta (Fortino II 120) [1988 8m — 8f⁴ 8g⁵ 1989 10.2f a8g] workmanlike, sturdy gelding: poor handicapper: stays 1¼m: acts on any going: often visored or blinkered: finds little off bridle. *J. M. Bradley.*

SMART MOVE 4 b.c. Try My Best (USA) 130–Rheinbloom (Rheingold 137) — [1988 7g 8f⁴ 8.2g² 10.1m⁴ 1989 12s] medium-sized, good-topped colt: well beaten in varied events: bandaged and sweating only start at 4 yrs: sold 1,750 gns Ascot September Sales. *I. P. Wardle.*

SMART PERFORMER 4 b.g. Formidable (USA) 125–Brilliant Rosa 91 80 § (Luthier 126) [1988 8m³ 9s² 10g² 1989 10.2g* 8f] strong, deep-girthed gelding: moderate mover: won slowly-run maiden at Newcastle (swished tail) in March: soon refused to race in handicap at York 2 months later: stays 1¼m: acts on top-of-the-ground and soft going: one to treat with caution. *N. Tinkler.*

SMART SLAVE 6 b.g. Smartset 100–Slave Trade (African Sky 124) [1988 12m⁴ — 12s⁴ 1989 19g] ex-Irish gelding: second foal: half-brother to winning hurdler Fine Slave (by Fine Blade): dam won point-to-point in Ireland: dead-heated in NH Flat race at Killarney at 5 yrs: in frame in celebrity race at Dundalk and maiden at Killarney later in season: 100/1, well tailed off in minor event at Goodwood in October: stays 1½m. *Miss L. Bower.*

SMART TURN 2 b.f. (Mar 21) His Turn 82–Smashing Pet (Mummy's Pet 125) 67 p [1989 7g] leggy, close-coupled filly: second foal: dam half-sister to good-class 1m and 1¼m winner Broken Hearted: 50/1 and ridden by 7-lb claimer, eleventh of 24, never dangerous, in maiden at Newmarket in November: should do better. *G. A. Huffer.*

SMILE OF FORTUNE 2 ch.f. (Apr 24) Nodouble (USA)–Embraceable Slew — (USA) (Seattle Slew (USA)) [1989 5.8m 7f 7m 7m] 1,800Y: lengthy, angular filly: first foal: dam won over 7f at 4 yrs in USA: apparently of little account. *C. A. Cyzer.*

SMILING BEAR (USA) 6 b.g. Nikoli 125–Share A Smile (USA) (Hagley —
(USA)) [1988 12d 1989 10m 8g 8.5f] angular, sparely-made gelding: quite modest
performer in 1987: tailed off in handicaps 4 subsequent outings on flat: visored
second start: sold 850 gns Doncaster August Sales. *M. C. Chapman.*

SMITH'S PEAK 5 ro.g. Alias Smith (USA)–Sacred Mountain 74 (St Paddy 133) —
[1988 NR 1989 7g 7f⁶ 8g] workmanlike gelding: half-brother to several winners,
including useful Irish 1983 2-y-o 6f winner Mount Imperial (by Imperial Fling) and
4-y-o 7f and 9f winner Sobriety (by Noalcoholic): dam sister to very smart 1m to
1¼m performer Calpurnius: winner 3 times in Italy, twice as 2-y-o and once (over
7.5f) in 1987: never dangerous in apprentice events at Ascot and minor race at
Warwick in autumn. *R. V. Smyth.*

SMOKEY NATIVE (USA) 2 b.c. (Mar 19) Our Native (USA)–Smokey Spender 87
(USA) (Bold Bidder) [1989 7m⁴ 7m² 7g] $85,000Y: well-made, attractive colt: has
scope: fifth reported foal: half-brother to 2 minor winners in USA: dam unplaced on
only start: fair performer: best effort 2 lengths second of 11, making most and
running on well, to Aquatic (USA) in £15,300 event at York in August: ninth of 10 to
Dashing Blade in GPA National Stakes at the Curragh following month: will stay 1m:
sure to win a maiden. *C. R. Nelson.*

SMOKIN JOSIE 4 ch.f. Longleat (USA) 109–Sallusteno 80 (Sallust 134) [1988 —
NR 1989 6f 5g 5m 6f] sturdy, good-quartered filly: poor form in varied company,
including selling: has sweated. *D. W. Chapman.*

SMOOTH FINISH 2 b.g. (Jun 1) Welsh Term 126–Chantry Pearl (Gulf Pearl —
117) [1989 5m⁵ 5f] IR 2,700F, 5,000 2-y-o: sparely-made gelding: half-brother to 3
winners, including fairly useful 5f and 7f winner Jewelled Turban (by Mansingh):
dam of little account: well beaten in June maidens at Catterick and Redcar. *M. P.
Naughton.*

SMOOTH FLIGHT 3 ch.f. Sandhurst Prince 128–Female Mudwrestler 63
(Ahonoora 122) [1988 NR 1989 10m 10m 7m 8.2f³ 8f³ 8m* 7.5m² 8.2f⁶ 8m² 8g³ 8d³
8f⁴] IR 3,600Y: angular, sparely-made filly: first foal: dam once-raced half-sister to
useful 1½m winner Saint Osyth: made all in maiden at Edinburgh in June: below
form in handicaps at Goodwood (raced alone far side) and Bath last 2 outings: seems
suited by forcing tactics at around 1m: acts on top-of-the-ground: blinkered fifth
start. *R. W. Stubbs.*

SNAFEE 2 b.c. (Apr 19) Mummy's Pet 125–Miss Kuta Beach 91 (Bold Lad (IRE) 65
133) [1989 6f³ 6g] 27,000Y: leggy colt: second foal: dam, 6f and 1¼m winner, is
half-sister to very useful 1m and 9f winner Bali Dancer: quite modest form, keeping
on last 2f, in late-season maidens at Redcar and Newmarket. *M. F. D. Morley.*

SNAKE EYE 4 b.g. Tina's Pet 121–Dingle Belle 72 (Dominion 123) [1988 8g⁶ 7v² 59 §
8f⁴ 7g⁴ 7g⁵ 7m⁵ 6m 6m⁶ 7g 1989 9f 9f³ 10.8m 8.2f] smallish, sturdy gelding:
moderate mover: quite modest performer: found little when third in claimer at
Wolverhampton in May: tailed off in handicaps afterwards: stays 9f: acts on any
going: blinkered once at 3 yrs: sweating and edgy on reappearance: not one to trust.
J. Wharton.

SNAKE SONG 3 br.f. Mansingh (USA) 120–Boa (Mandrake Major 122) [1988 5f³ 72
5m² 5g⁴ 5g* 5g⁶ 5g² 5m⁶ 1989 5d⁵ 6m 5g 5m 5m 6g 5f⁴ 6g* a6g] strong, sturdy filly:
carries condition: modest handicapper: well drawn, won claimer at Nottingham in
October, quickening well to lead inside final 1f: again favourite and blinkered, below
form at Southwell following month: stays 6f: possibly unsuited by top-of-the-
ground. *J. Wharton.*

SNAPPY DATE (USA) 3 ch.c. Blushing Groom (FR) 131–Mystery Mood 70
(USA) (Night Invader (USA)) [1988 6m⁶ 7m⁴ 1989 10s 8.5g²] rather sparely-made,
angular colt: has a quick action: modest maiden: visored-second at Beverley, better
effort in the spring: bred to stay bit further than 1m: acts on top-of-the-ground:
ridden by 7-lb claimer on reappearance: sold 7,400 gns Newmarket Autumn Sales.
M. R. Stoute.

SNIGGY 3 b.f. Belfort (FR) 89–Firey Kim (CAN) (Cannonade (USA)) [1988 6f 46
5.8g⁵ 1989 5f 6f⁴] leggy filly: poor maiden: visored, fourth in apprentice handicap at
Ayr in June, clear on stand side and staying on despite edging left and swishing tail:
stays 6f: bandaged reappearance: trained by C. Wall, broke out of stalls and
withdrawn in July: has joined D. Browne. *D. T. O'Donnell.*

SNO PROBLEM 4 b.g. Be My Native (USA) 122–Regal Ray 107 (Prince Regent —
(FR) 129) [1988 7d 8g 6m 12m 7m³ 7f³ 7.6s² 8.5m⁶ 7g 1989 8m] tall, close-coupled
gelding: good mover: quite modest handicapper in 1988: edgy, didn't get clear run
only outing at 4 yrs: suited by 7f or 1m: acts on any going. *R. Boss.*

SNO SERENADE   3 b.g. Song 132–When The Saints (Bay Express 132) [1988 5v **84**
5g³ 5f* 6m* 6f⁶ 6m 7s⁴ 8.5m⁴ 6g 1989 7g 7.6f⁶ 8.5g* 9f* 10.2g 10h³ 10g³ 8.2f⁵ 8f*
7.6f] tall, leggy, quite attractive gelding: has a quick action: fair performer: made
virtually all when successful in claimer at Epsom and handicap at Sandown in June
and handicap at Brighton in September: stays 9f well: acts on any going except
perhaps heavy: below form in visor eighth start: suited by forcing tactics. *R. Boss.*

SNOW BRIDE (USA)   3 ch.f. Blushing Groom (FR) 131–Awaasif (CAN) **121**
130 (Snow Knight 125) [1988 7g* 8g* 1989 10g⁵ 10.5f* 12m² 12d⁴ 12m*]
    Snow Bride collected two hard-fought Group 3 victories in 1989 but her
short-head defeat of Roseate Tern for second place in the Oaks may yet yield
officially her greatest triumph if Aliysa is disqualified following the detection
of camphor in her routine test. Though Snow Bride has many qualities to be
admired in a racehorse, her tenacity at the head of them, she would be clearly
a substandard Oaks 'winner', the worst of the decade by our reckoning; on the
two occasions she contested Group 1 events, she ran to just about the top of
her form but was comprehensively put in her place.
    Snow Bride started 13/2 third favourite at Epsom following her win in the
Tattersalls Musidora Stakes at York, very much the better of her runs in May
after she'd been a heavily-backed favourite but finished only fifth of seven in
the Pretty Polly Stakes at Newmarket, the explanation being that she was in
season. At York, her Oaks challenge was put firmly back on the rails. Cauthen
rode one of his almost inimitable races from the front, steadily increasing the
pace in the straight and then getting the gamest response from his mount as
Pilot, an even-money favourite after her Newmarket maiden race victory,
challenged strongly approaching the distance. Snow Bride looked sure to be
beaten at that point but kept on the stronger to be well on top at the finish
where her advantage was half a length. Further back in the field were two of
the leading two-year-old fillies of 1988 in Pick of The Pops and Lucky Song,
both making their reappearance. Cecil's yard contained the filly with perhaps
the strongest claims for middle-distance honours among the previous
season's two-year-olds in Tessla but Snow Bride now surpassed her as the

Tattersalls Musidora Stakes, York—
Snow Bride (right) redeems her reputation by beating Pilot

Princess Royal Stakes, Ascot—Snow Bride wears down Princess Sobieska

stable's number-one hope for the Oaks. Cecil had sent out three of the previous five Musidora winners in Fatah Flare, Indian Skimmer and the 1988 Oaks winner Diminuendo. Cauthen always had Snow Bride in the front rank in the 1989 Oaks but they never really looked like repeating Diminuendo's success; Snow Bride was pushed along firmly to go in pursuit of Mamaluna three furlongs out but at the two-furlong marker Aliysa, challenging between horses, had already got Snow Bride's measure and the battle, a dogged one at that, was only for second. Following that hard race, Snow Bride was rested for nearly three months before taking on France's leading fillies in the Prix Vermeille but she didn't find this new company any easier to live with. Young Mother led her into the straight and although Snow Bride stayed on gamely, the leader stretched away and beat her four and a half lengths—a length and a half more than Aliysa had done. Sierra Roberta and Colorado Dancer passed Snow Bride for the minor places.

The Princess Royal Stakes at Ascot in October often provides an intriguing clash between established fillies seeking compensation for their efforts in better company—Group 1 winners are not qualified—and those that have only come into their own in the autumn. Snow Bride and the York-shire Oaks fourth Lady Shipley fell into the former category while Quiet Awakening, Dazzling Heights, Destiny Dance and Nesaah were numbered amongst the less exposed fillies in a ten-runner field. Snow Bride proved much better than those but Princess Sobieska, narrowly beaten in both the Goodwood Cup and Park Hill, made a tremendous race of it with her, setting a strong pace to bring her stamina into play and stretching the field virtually from the start. Snow Bride was the only one to mount an effective challenge; she began to stay on under pressure on the turn, cut Princess Sobieska's lead to a length and a half before the distance and got her head in front about a hundred and fifty yards out before going on to win by a length and a half, the pair having drawn five lengths clear of the remainder headed by Lady Shipley. The Princess Royal Stakes demonstrated Snow Bride's strength to the full; she doesn't have much in the way of a turn of foot but has plenty of guts and

Saeed Maktoum Al-Maktoum's "Snow Bride"

sees out the mile and a half very well. Both Snow Bride and her dam would have been interesting prospects over a mile and three quarters had they been given the chance.

Snow Bride (USA) (ch.f. 1986)	Blushing Groom (FR) (ch 1974)	Red God (ch 1954)	Nasrullah / Spring Run
		Runaway Bride (b 1962)	Wild Risk / Aimee
	Awaasif (CAN) (b 1979)	Snow Knight (ch 1971)	Firestreak / Snow Blossom
		Royal Statute (b 1969)	Northern Dancer / Queen's Statute

Snow Bride is the second foal out of Awaasif, among the first horses to carry Sheikh Mohammed's colours with distinction in top-class European competition. The year 1982, when Awaasif won the Yorkshire Oaks and was third in the Arc de Triomphe and fourth in the Oaks, was also the first season that Sheikh Mohammed featured in the leading twelve owners in Britain; he finished seventh with twenty horses winning thirty races and £142,760. Things change. The Sheikh was leading owner in Britain for the fifth year in succession in 1989, when ninety of his horses won a hundred and thirty races and £1,296,052. Awaasif was kept in training as a four-year-old when she came fourth in the King George VI and Queen Elizabeth Diamond Stakes and won the Gran Premio del Jockey Club. Her first foal Salaadim (by Seattle Slew) won his first race, a seven-furlong Yarmouth maiden, most impressively as a two-year-old but didn't go on and ran only twice more here before being sent back to the USA where he was a winner in the latest season. Snow Bride is followed by Jarraar (by Mr Prospector), a colt by Blushing Groom and filly by Kris; Awaasif visited Kris again in 1989 and is reported to be a probable mate

848

for Nashwan in 1990. Awaasif is from a good family, her dam Royal Statute having produced the One Thousand Guineas second Konafa and very smart American colt Akureyri before her and the very useful mile and mile-and-a-quarter winner Royal Lorna after. Konafa has foaled several above-average winners in France, including the high-class Prix de Seine-et-Oise winner Proskona, and an unraced half-sister to Awaasif has produced the Prix de la Jonchere winner Majuscule and a Graded-placed winner in the USA. Royal Statute was a three-year-old five-furlong winner and is out of the unraced Queen's Statute who, having been exported from England to Canada in 1956, went on to foal thirteen winners from as many runners, including Royal Statute's brother the twice Champion Canadian Handicap Horse Dance Act.

Snow Bride has been retired. She is a smallish, rather sparely-made filly with a fluent, quick action who never raced on very soft ground but acted on any other. *H. R. A. Cecil.*

SNOW GLINT 3 ch.f. Glint of Gold 128–Snow Habit (Habitat 134) [1988 NR 1989   **86** 11.5m² 12m² 12.2m*] small, sparely-made filly: has a quick action: seventh living foal: half-sister to several winners, including 7f winner Snow Maid (by High Top) and 2 winners in Italy: dam, placed over 6f at 2 yrs in France, is half-sister to dam of Count Pahlen: favourite, won maiden at Catterick in July, racing keenly and close up, leading 1½f out and running on strongly: may stay further. *L. M. Cumani.*

SNOW HARBOR (USA) 3 br.f. Northjet 136–Royal Dilemma (USA)   **61** (Buckpasser) [1988 6d 6s² 6m⁴ 6s⁵ 1989 7f 6g4] lengthy, good-quartered filly: quite modest maiden: ran creditably last 2 starts, in space of 3 days in May, sweating final one: may prove suited by 6f: acts on any going: suitable mount for apprentice. *I. A. Balding.*

SNOW HUNTRESS 5 b.m. Shirley Heights 130–Head Huntress 106 (Upper   **69** Case (USA)) [1988 12d 12m² 11.7g 13.1g 12h 1989 10s* 10.2g4 10.6g] leggy, shallow-girthed, lightly-made mare: modest performer: won ladies event at Nottingham in March: headstrong when well beaten in amateurs handicap at Haydock final outing: stays 1½m: acts on top-of-the-ground and soft going: occasionally blinkered: awkward in preliminaries first 2 starts: sold 10,000 gns Newmarket July Sales. *D. Marks.*

SNOWMAN 3 b.c. Kris 135–Anzeige (GER) (Soderini 123) [1988 NR 1989 10.6g   **—** 14g] strong, good sort: half-brother to several winners here and abroad, including useful 7f winner Flower Bowl (by Homing): dam, daughter of German Oaks runner-up Ankerette, won over 1m in Germany: well beaten in summer maidens, making most 11f and eased inside last on second of them: may do better in time. *A. C. Stewart.*

SNOW SHY 2 gr.f. (Mar 14) Shy Groom (USA)–Snow Maid 90 (High Top 131)   **—** [1989 6m⁶ 6f a6g] IR 3,400Y: workmanlike filly: moderate mover: fifth foal: half-sister to 1986 2-y-o 5f winner Artful Maid (by Artaius) and Irish 3-y-o 1½m winner Dublin's Fair City (by Henbit): dam, out of half-sister to dam of Count Pahlen, ran once at 3 yrs, winning over 7f: well beaten in maidens and a claimer. *Pat Mitchell.*

SNOWSPIN 2 b.f. (Feb 20) Carwhite 127–Spin (High Top 131) [1989 7f] smallish,   **54** p close-coupled filly: third live foal: half-sister to quite useful 1m to 1¼m winner Girotondo (by Young Generation) and very useful 7f and 12.3f winner Salchow (by Niniski): dam never ran: 6/1 from 2/1, over 9 lengths seventh of 8, not knocked about, to Star of The Future in maiden at Leicester in October: should improve. *Major W. R. Hern.*

SNOW WONDER 3 gr.f. Music Boy 124–Grey Charter 58 (Runnymede 123)   **—** [1988 6g⁶ 1989 6d⁴ 7s 6g 7h 6f⁵ 6m 6g a6g] sparely-made, plain filly: has a rather round action: plating class at best: mostly below form after reappearance, including in sellers: should stay 7f: best effort on a soft surface. *P. Howling.*

SNUGFIT'S IMAGE 3 b.g. Music Boy 124–Sinzinbra 112 (Royal Palace 131)   **—** [1988 5g 5g 5d³ 1989 6m 10s 8.2g 5g] strong, rather dipped-backed gelding: has a rather round action: behind in handicaps as 3-y-o, ridden by 7-lb claimer and sweating on reappearance: should stay beyond 5f: best effort on a soft surface: has joined O. Sherwood. *J. Berry.*

SNUGGLE 2 ch.f. (May 11) Music Boy 124–Sinzinbra 112 (Royal Palace 131) [1989   **75** 5f4 5h* 6m² 5m 6m⁶ 6v] 7,800Y: sister to 3-y-o Snugfit's Image, and sprint winners Young Snugfit (useful jumper) and Superb Singer, closely related to Grand National runner-up Mr Snugfit (by Jukebox) and half-brother to 2 winners: dam won at up to

1¼m: modest performer: made all in 9-runner maiden at Carlisle in May: creditable sixth to Night At Sea in nursery at Newmarket in October: better suited by 6f than 5f, and will probably stay 7f: off course over 3 months after third start. *M. H. Tompkins.*

SNURGE 2 ch.c. (Mar 12) Ela-Mana-Mou 132–Finlandia (FR) (Faraway Son **118** ? (USA) 130) [1989 8m³ 10g² 10v²]

Rule 153 again came under the spotlight in Britain in 1989 but even under our Rules there was no harsher decision than that taken by the French stewards at Saint-Cloud in November to disqualify Snurge from a fairly-earned first place in the Group 1 Criterium de Saint-Cloud. In the opinion of the stewards Snurge interfered with the runner-up Intimiste inside the final furlong and despite running on strongly to win by three lengths was demoted to second while his rider Quinn incurred a four-day suspension. There's no doubt that Snurge steered an erratic course in the last two furlongs and did cross in front of Intimiste, but Quinn did all that was possible to prevent his colt hanging in the heavy ground and any interference that did take place was marginal and had no effect upon the placings. Close inspection of the video reveals clearly that Intimiste was a spent force at the moment Snurge, who'd begun to veer to his right as soon as he'd entered the straight wide of the other runners, drifted across him with less than two hundred yards to run; Intimiste only just held off the closing Guiza as Snurge pulled clear. Intimiste's connections took the view that the rules of racing had been breached, but to argue that Snurge's antics had lost them the race was ludicrous. Trainer Cole immediately lodged an appeal with the Societe d'Encouragement, but when the French Stewards convened in December to review the decision the revised result was allowed to stand. Connections' disappointment at the outcome will be mitigated by the performance of this lightly-raced colt. Although Snurge didn't have to show anything like top-class form to beat a non-vintage field (the odds-on Dr Somerville seemed not to cope with the testing conditions) it still represented a considerable improvement on his earlier form, which had seen him placed behind Tanfith in the Haynes, Hanson and Clark Stakes at Newbury and Blue Stag in a maiden at Nottingham. Hopefully, the wayward tendencies that he displayed at Saint-Cloud, where he also reared in the stalls, can be attributed to inexperience: he'd lost no ground at the start and kept as straight as a gun-barrel in his earlier races. It would be unfortunate if temperament were to get the better of the well-grown, workmanlike Snurge, for he's got plenty of scope and looks altogether the sort to develop into a grand three-year-old. Assuming he progresses the right way he'll be a good middle-distance stayer in time.

Snurge (ch.c. Mar 12, 1987)	Ela-Mana-Mou (b 1976)	Pitcairn (b 1971)	Petingo Border Bounty
		Rose Bertin (ch 1970)	High Hat Wide Awake
	Finlandia (FR) (b 1977)	Faraway Son (b 1967)	Ambiopoise Locust Time
		Musical II (ch 1961)	Prince Chevalier Musidora

At 36,000 guineas from the Irish National Yearling Sale, Snurge cost more than the average for a yearling by Ela-Mana-Mou in 1988. The former top-class middle-distance colt Ela-Mana-Mou has sired a string of good performers since being retired to stud in 1981, notably Eurobird, Sumayr, Almaarad and Emmson, who, rather ironically, was at the centre of another controversial incident with the French Stewards in 1989 when his rider Carson was suspended for reckless riding. Snurge's dam Finlandia, a daughter of the top-class miler Faraway Son, has produced only one other winner, the useful Irish mile-and-a-half winner Faraway Pastures (by Northfields), fourth in Unite's Irish Oaks, from five living foals. Finlandia was one of the less talented members of her well-known family. Her dam Musical, a useful filly in France, has produced the Irish Sweeps Derby third Master Glory, the very useful French middle-distance filly Musique Royale and the dam of the high-class two-year-old and miler Horage; and her grandam Musidora was the champion three-year-old filly in 1949, when she won the One Thousand Guineas and Oaks, and can be found in the pedigrees of the Princess Royal winner Heavenly Thought, the top-class miler Homing and the St Leger runner-up Water Mill. *P. F. I. Cole.*

SOBER MIND (USA) 2 b.c. (Mar 23) Caro 133–Lolly Dolly 104 (Alleged (USA) 91 p
138) [1989 7g² 7m*] 32,000Y: good-quartered colt: first foal: dam, useful 2-y-o 1m winner in France successful in USA at 4 yrs, is out of very useful French middle-distance performer Lady Gold: 5/1, won 6-runner £8,300 event at Newbury in July by a length, staying on well to lead last 100 yds: will be suited by 1m + : should improve further. *P. A. Kelleway.*

SOBRIETY 4 b.c. Noalcoholic (FR) 128–Sacred Mountain 74 (St Paddy 133) 56
[1988 7f⁴ 8g⁴ 1989 8d⁵ 8f 10f 8m 10g 10m 8h² 10f 9m* 10g² 10.6d 7d*] leggy colt: plating-class handicapper: won apprentice events at Kempton in September and Newbury in October: stays 1¼m: acts on hard going and a soft surface. *G. B. Balding.*

SO CAREFUL 6 br.h. Dalsaan 125–Miss Carefree 99 (Hill Clown (USA)) [1988 81
6v 7g² 7f⁶ 7f⁶ 7m⁴ 6f 6s* 6d² 6f⁶ 5g* 6s 6s* 6d 6g 6g 1989 6d³ 6v⁵ 6s⁵ 7f 6f 6f² 6m 6g⁴ 6m⁶ 6s 6d 6m*] lengthy, rather angular horse: usually looks very well: fair handicapper: 16/1, won 19-runner ladies event at Chepstow in October: suited by 6f: acts on any going: sometimes blinkered or visored: none too consistent. *J. Berry.*

SOCIAL BUTTERFLY 3 b.f. Mr Fluorocarbon 126–Orange Tip 77 (Orange —
Bay 131) [1988 7m 7s 1989 11.5m 14g⁴ 12m] workmanlike filly: little sign of ability, tailed off in seller final outing. *G. A. Pritchard-Gordon.*

SOCIAL SECRET 3 b.f. Secreto (USA) 128–Expediency (USA) (Vaguely Noble 52
140) [1988 7m⁶ 1989 10f 10f 10.1m 11.5m⁵] small filly: quite modest form at best in maidens (best effort penultimate start) and a handicap: probably doesn't stay 1½m: sold 7,000 gns Newmarket December Sales. *I. A. Balding.*

SOCIETY BALL 2 b.f. (Mar 8) Law Society (USA) 130–Mariakova (USA) 84 62 p
(The Minstrel (CAN) 135) [1989 8f⁴] third foal: dam, placed on her only 2 starts, suited by 1m: 12/1, around 3 lengths fourth of 5 finishers, staying on having been outpaced soon after halfway, to Pay The Bank in maiden at Redcar in October: will stay 1¼m: should improve. *J. W. Watts.*

SOCIETY GUEST 3 ch.g. High Line 125–Welcome Break (Wollow 132) [1988 72
8m⁵ 7g 8s³ 10d³ 1989 12d³ 10d⁵ 10s 8f⁵ 12.2m⁶ 10f² 8.2g] big, workmanlike colt: carries condition: good mover: modest maiden: seems suited by middle distances: acts on firm going and a soft surface: probably set too strong a pace in blinkers fourth outing: one paced: sold A. Turnell 24,000 gns Doncaster November Sales. *I. V. Matthews.*

SOCKEM 2 b.g. (Mar 14) Nordico (USA)–Floating Petal 90 (Wollow 132) [1989 58
6m⁶ 6f⁶ 6f⁶ 6h² 5m⁵ 6f³ 6f 5.3h⁴ 8.2f⁴ 8m 7d a6g⁴ a6g² a6g a6g a8g] IR 12,500Y: compact, rather sparely-made gelding: moderate mover: third foal: dam won over 1m at 4 yrs in Ireland: plater, useful on his day: easily best effort ¾-length second to Green's Corot in late-year maiden at Lingfield: best at 6f: showed nothing when blinkered: has sweated up: inconsistent. *C. N. Williams.*

SOFTLY SPOKEN 6 b.m. Mummy's Pet 125–Tender Answer 80 (Prince —
Tenderfoot (USA) 126) [1988 7f 6d³ 6g² 6f³ 6d⁵ 6m² 6f⁴ 6s² 6g* 6m² 6g 6f² 6g⁵ 6m 1989 5s⁶ 6g] tall, leggy mare: tubed: fair winner of handicap as 5-y-o: 25/1, never able to challenge when sixth of 15 at Ayr in September: slowly away and soon tailed off at Newcastle over month later: suited by 6f: acts on any going: occasionally sweats: has given trouble at stalls: best covered up and suited by good gallop. *M. W. Easterby.*

SOFT SHOE SHUFFLE 6 b.g. Hard Fought 125–Carroldance (FR) (Lyphard 36
(USA) 132) [1988 9g 12g⁶ 11.7g 11.7m 1989 11.1f⁴ 11.7m 12h⁴ 10h² 12f⁴] tall, leggy, close-coupled gelding: winning plater in 1986: subsequent form only on fourth outing: stays 1½m: acts on hard going: apprentice ridden first 4 starts: has worn bandages. *Miss B. Sanders.*

SO GIFTED 3 b.f. Niniski (USA) 125–Maybe So 90 (So Blessed 130) [1988 7g 6d 54
1989 5m 8.5f 7g³ 10m 8m] leggy, quite attractive filly: plating-class maiden: should be suited by further than 7f: best effort with give in the ground: hung right 2f out when blinkered final start: sold to join J. Norton 3,000 gns Doncaster September Sales. *J. W. Watts.*

SO KNOWLEDGEABLE 2 b.f. (Mar 10) Night Shift (USA)–Sister Hannah 70 — p
(Monseigneur (USA) 127) [1989 6s⁴] 7,000Y: second foal: half-sister to 3-y-o

Summit Reached (by Homing): dam, 5f winner, is daughter of half-sister to 1000 Guineas winner Mrs McArdy: 20/1, around 7 lengths fourth of 13, keeping on, to Albert in minor event at Ayr in September: should do better. *N. Tinkler.*

SOLA MIA 3 b.f. Tolomeo 127–Be My Sweet 78 (Galivanter 131) [1988 6f* 7g³ 6g **72** 7d⁴ 6s 1989 8g⁶ 11f 8.5m² 9g 10f 9f⁵ 8f 10s 8.2g 7m⁴] lengthy filly: moderate mover: modest handicapper: in frame at Beverley (sweating badly) in July and Edinburgh in October: best short of 1¼m: probably acts on any going: usually held up in rear prior to last 2 outings (blinkered) when made the running: rather inconsistent. *W. J. Pearce.*

SOLDIER BOY 3 b.c. Sandhurst Prince 128–War Ballad (FR) (Green Dancer **58** (USA) 132) [1988 6g 1989 7g⁶ 7f 8s 7f 8m a10g⁴] angular, plain colt: quite modest form: fourth in maiden at Lingfield, first show since reappearance: should be suited by at least 1m: sold 2,200 gns Ascot November Sales. *J. L. Dunlop.*

SOLDIER BRAVE 3 b.g. Persian Bold 123–Gilwanigan (Captain's Gig (USA)) **57** [1988 7s 1989 8g⁵ 8m 8m 8f*] leggy, close-coupled gelding: improved form when winning seller (bought in 6,600 gns) at Bath in August: will stay further: acts on firm going: has joined R. Manning. *I. A. Balding.*

SOLDIER EVE 3 ch.f. Soldier Rose 98–Jubilee Eve (Royalty 130) [1988 NR 1989 — 8.2f 10f] small, sturdy filly: third reported foal: half-sister to a poor maiden by Decoy Boy: dam poor on flat and over jumps: no sign of ability in claimer and seller (sweating). *J. R. Bosley.*

SOLDIERS DUTY (USA) 5 b.g. Golden Act (USA)–Fuzier (USA) (Crozier **50** § (USA) 117) [1988 15.5d 13.8g 12f 14m 12d⁵ 12f* 14m⁵ 12d² 10v⁶ 1989 15.3m³] small, quite attractive gelding: winning plater (apprentice ridden) as 4-y-o: refused to race on another occasion in 1988 and reluctant to do so on another: carrying condition, creditable third of 7 in Wolverhampton handicap in July: stays 2m: possibly unsuited by soft going, acts on any other: often sweats: not to be trusted. *J. Mackie.*

SOLEIL GRAND 2 b.g. (Feb 24) Red Sunset 120–Becassine (El Gallo 122) **83** [1989 6m³ 6m 7g⁴ 7g* 7m⁶ 8f⁴ 7g] 10,500F, 13,000Y: lengthy, robust gelding: turns off-fore out: has a round action: closely related to fairly useful middle-distance winner Nonsense (by Stanford) and half-brother to several winners, including useful Irish sprinter Entre Fancy (by Entre Chat): dam ran only at 2 yrs: made all in 8-runner maiden at Yarmouth in August: best form at 7f on good ground: gelded after final outing. *M. McCormack.*

SOLENT SUN 4 b.g. Undulate (USA)–River Palace (Royal Palace 131) [1988 — 10m⁵ 12d 12d 1989 10s] workmanlike gelding: has a round action: little sign of ability, including in selling handicap (bandaged) in April. *B. Stevens.*

SOLINSKY 4 ch.f. Bali Dancer 107–Sailor's Sol (The Bo'sun 114) [1988 NR 1989 **36** 10.2m⁴ 10m] angular filly: half-sister to 2 winning hurdlers: dam, raced only at 4 yrs, half-sister to some useful chasers: about 5 lengths fourth of 7 in amateurs event at Doncaster in July: slowly away when tailed off in seller at Nottingham 2 weeks later. *G. H. Jones.*

SOLITARY REAPER 4 b.c. Valiyar 129–Fardella (ITY) (Molvedo 137) [1988 **47** 11.7f 10f⁶ 12f⁴ 12.3s³ 11g⁵ 10d⁵ 12d 1989 12f⁴ 12f⁶] leggy colt: poor maiden: stays 1½m: acts on firm going: sometimes visored or blinkered: ridden by claimer at 4 yrs. *Miss B. Sanders.*

SOLO ACT 3 b.c. Chief Singer 131–La Creperie 70 (Crepello 136) [1988 NR 1989 **97** 8d 10.1m² 10.1g² 12m* 12.3g* 14f³ 12m 12s] 47,000Y: useful-looking colt: has scope: half-brother to 1½m winner Brandon Creek (by Be My Guest) and a winner in Yugoslavia: dam stayed well: rallied well when winning maiden at Newbury and handicap at Ripon in July: never going particularly well when below form in handicaps last 2 outings: stays 1¾m: acts on firm going: ran creditably when on toes sixth start: sold 43,000 gns Newmarket Autumn Sales. *B. W. Hills.*

SOLO ARTIST 4 ch.g. Young Generation 129–Jubilee Song 71 (Song 132) [1988 **83** 8.2v* 8d⁵ 11.7g⁶ 10g³ 10d⁴ 1989 9d 12v 10d* 10.4m* 11f 10f²] strong, rangy gelding: fair handicapper: successful in spring at Beverley and Chester: excellent second to Oh Danny Boy at former course in September, first outing for 4 months: suited by 1¼m: acts on any going: blinkered last 7 outings: often forces pace: has joined R. Simpson. *I. V. Matthews.*

SOLO COURT 2 ch.f. (May 1) King of Clubs 124–Mrs Tittlemouse (Nonoalco **79** (USA) 131) [1989 6m² 6m⁵ 6f³] 19,000F, IR 8,500Y: second living foal: dam unraced half-sister to high-class miler Bairn: modest performer: best effort around a length third of 5 to May Hinton in £8,500 event at Salisbury in September: will be better suited by 7f + . *Dr J. D. Scargill.*

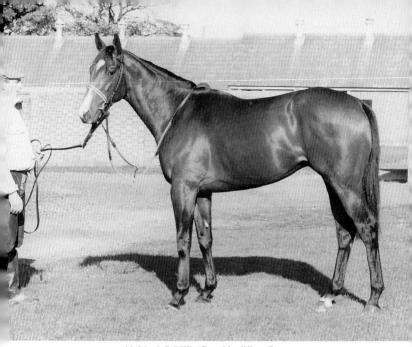

Mr John A. Bell III's "Somethingdifferent"

SOLOMON'S SONG 3 b.g. Night Shift (USA)–Judeah 69 (Great Nephew 126) **62**
[1988 7m 7m⁴ 6g 7d 7m 1989 8m* 8.3m⁶ 7g² 7m 6m⁶ 6g* 7m] strong, good-bodied
gelding: has been hobdayed: moderate mover: won seller (bought in 7,700 gns) at
Leicester in July, making virtually all, and handicap at Hamilton in August, always
front rank: ran moderately fourth and final (looking very well) starts: appears suited
by 6f: acts on top-of-the-ground. *M. Johnston.*

SOLWAY MIST 3 ch.f. Sagaro 133–Helewise 76 (Dance In Time (CAN)) [1988 **35**
NR 1989 12f 10g⁵ 12.2g 12g⁵ 18g] small filly: first foal: dam 2-y-o 1m winner: poor
maiden: form only on fourth start: sweating final one. *E. Weymes.*

SOMEBODY 5 b.h. Bustino 136–Kashmir Lass 118 (Kashmir II 125) [1988 12s* **65**
12g³ 14d⁴ 14g² 14d⁴ 12m 14d⁴ 13s 10d 1989 13v² 16s⁴ 15.5s²] strong, stocky horse:
carries condition: usually looks really well: poor mover: quite modest handicapper:
not seen out after April: probably best at up to 1¾m: well suited by soft surface:
doesn't find great deal and probably needs blinkers nowadays. *J. White.*

SOMETHINGDIFFERENT (USA) 2 b.c. (Feb 9) Green Forest (USA) 134– **113**
Try Something New (USA) (Hail The Pirates (USA) 126) [1989 5.1m⁵ 5f* 6f² 5g²
6g* 6g* 6m² 5m² 8g*] compact colt: moderate walker: first foal: dam good-class
winner at up to 1¼m: progressive colt: won $50,000 Manila Stakes at Gulfstream
Park in November by 3½ lengths: previously successful in maiden at Nottingham,
minor event at Windsor and Moet et Chandon-Rennen (by a short head) at
Baden-Baden: beaten 1½ lengths by Welney in Rokeby Farms Mill Reef Stakes at
Newbury in September on seventh outing: better suited by 1m than by shorter
distances: acts on firm going: genuine. *J. H. M. Gosden.*

SONALTO 3 br.c. Noalto 120–Sanandrea (Upper Case (USA)) [1988 6m⁶ 6d⁴ 6g⁴ **60**
7g 1989 8g² 8s⁵ 8.2s³ 8.5d 8m² 9m⁵ 9m 12m] leggy, lengthy, quite attractive colt:

has a rather round action: quite modest maiden: ran poorly last 3 starts, racing too keenly in handicap final one: suited by 1m: yet to race on very firm going, probably acts on any other: has run creditably for 7-lb claimer and when sweating. *Denys Smith.*

SONAR 3 b. or br.c. Pitskelly 122–Diana's Choice (Tudor Music 131) [1988 5g 5f 6f 7m⁵ 7m 8g 1989 7g 8g 12m 10m 10m 10m² 10f³ 12m⁶ 10g 12g 10g⁶] leggy colt: has a round action: capable of quite modest form but is temperamental: found little when good second in claimer at Newmarket: suited by 1¼m: acts on top-of-the-ground: blinkered last 6 outings: has sweated: one to treat with caution. *Pat Mitchell.* **57 §**

SONBERE 4 ch.f. Electric 126–Miellita 98 (King Emperor (USA)) [1988 10s 7g 7f⁵ 8d 12f⁵ 1989 10v 8.5d*] workmanlike filly: moderate mover: 25/1, won apprentice handicap at Beverley in May: stays 8.5f: acts on a soft surface: blinkered once at 3 yrs. *P. Calver.* **56**

SONEETO 3 b.g. Teenoso (USA) 135–Flying Bid 71 (Auction Ring (USA) 123) [1988 7m 8m⁶ 8g⁶ 1989 11f 13.3m 13.3g 8g 10m] tall, close-coupled gelding: modest form as 2-y-o: often took keen hold and looked temperamentally unsatisfactory in varied events in 1989: should stay middle distances: joined S. Woodman and subsequently gelded: winning hurdler. *R. Hannon.* **— §**

SONGBIRD MIRACLE 3 ch.g. Music Maestro 119–Mallow 70 (Le Dieu d'Or 119) [1988 NR 1989 6m⁶ 5f 6f⁶ 7f 6f 6m 5m] 6,000Y: big, plain gelding: fifth foal: brother to 1985 2-y-o 6f seller winner Meneghini Rose and half-brother to 1986 2-y-o 5f seller winner Gardenia Lady (by Mummy's Game): dam, winner twice over hurdles, is half-sister to smart sprinter Bream: poor form in varied events: may prove best over 5f. *M. H. Easterby.* **—**

SONG FOR EUROPE (USA) 2 b.c. (Feb 27) Seattle Song (USA) 130–Doing It My Way (USA) (Exclusive Native (USA)) [1989 6f 7m*] $152,000Y: strong, rangy colt: has plenty of scope: first known foal: dam, stakes winner at up to 9f, is half-sister to 3 winners very useful or better, including 1m winner Mennea: second favourite but still green, won 9-runner maiden at Sandown in July by 3 lengths, leading over 2f out: will be suited by 1m+: likely to improve further. *G. Harwood.* **88 p**

SONG OF GYMCRAK 2 b.f. (Mar 5) Chief Singer 131–Dusty Letter (USA) 78 (Run Dusty Run (USA)) [1989 5d 7g³ 8f] IR 15,000Y: angular, workmanlike filly: has scope: second foal: dam, maiden, stayed 1¼m, is daughter of half-sister to Irish 1000 Guineas winner Favoletta and Teenoso's dam Furioso: burly, over 2 lengths third of 14, staying on strongly, to Hot Performer in seller at Catterick in August, only indication of merit: not at all knocked about in maiden auction event at Redcar later in month: should stay 1m: one to keep an eye on in sellers. *M. H. Easterby.* **40 p**

SONG OF HOPE 3 b.f. Chief Singer 131–Penny Blessing 112 (So Blessed 130) [1988 6g³ 5g* 5g* 6d² 7d 1989 6s³ 8m³ 8g² 7m⁶ 7.6m 7s] smallish, quite attractive filly: bit below best as 3-y-o, second in minor event at Ayr: not discredited in listed race and £5,600 handicap (faced stiff task) last 2 outings: stays 1m: acts on a soft surface: blinkered last 4 starts: sold 21,000 gns Newmarket December Sales. *M. H. Easterby.* **86**

SONG OF SIXPENCE (USA) 5 b.g. The Minstrel (CAN) 135–Gliding By (USA) (Tom Rolfe) [1988 11.7f² 11.7d* 12m 12d³ 12f 12m² 11.7g* 14f 12g⁵ 12s³ 1989 12.3s² 11f⁵ 10.6d⁶] big, strong, close-coupled gelding: has a round action: fairly useful handicapper: good second to Taylormade Boy at Ripon in April: very much caught the eye on final outing: stays 1½m well: not at best on firm going and well suited by an easy surface: sweated badly eighth start at 4 yrs: has run creditably for apprentice. *I. A. Balding.* **88**

SONGSTEAD 3 b.f. Song 132–Skysted (Busted 134) [1988 6m³ 6f* 6m⁵ 6g⁶ 6f⁴ 6d⁶ 1989 6m* 6m⁶ 6f* 6f 6m⁶ 7g⁶ 6g 6f*] workmanlike filly: fairly useful handicapper: disputed lead throughout when winning at Haydock in May and York in July: best effort after when winning claimer at Newcastle in October, leading post as Letsbehonestaboutit turned it in: bolted before start and withdrawn seventh intended outing: stays 6f well: needs top-of-the-ground. *M. J. Camacho.* **92**

SONIC LORD 4 b.c. Final Straw 127–Lucent 117 (Irish Ball (FR) 127) [1988 9g 10m³ 10d 10m 10f⁵ 10d² 10g⁴ 12f³ 12m 1989 12g 12m 10.1m* 10f 10f 10m 10h⁵ 10m* 10f 12m a11g] strong colt: carries condition: poor mover: won claimer at Windsor in May and handicap at Yarmouth (25/1, first run for 2 months) in August: stays 1½m: yet to race on soft going, acts on any other: best visored or blinkered: sweating fourth start: has swished tail in paddock: unreliable. *A. Hide.* **57 §**

SONIC SIGNAL 3 b.f. Trojan Fen 118–Danger Signal 106 (Red God 128§) [1988 7v 8v⁶ 1989 8s 11m* 9m 12m 10d⁶dis 8m 11.7g² 12g* 10d² 14m] 23,000Y: small, **75**

sparely-made filly: half-sister to fair 1982 2-y-o 5f winner Red Roman (by Solinus) and 7f winner Green For Danger (by Formidable): dam, speedy 2-y-o, is half-sister to dam of Roland Gardens: won maiden at Killarney in May and claimer (by 6 lengths, showing improved form) at Newmarket in August: very good second in handicap at Goodwood penultimate start: stays 1½m: acts on a soft surface and top-of-the-ground: sold out of M. Kauntze's stable 1,500 gns Newmarket July Sales after fifth outing. *M. J. Haynes.*

SONILLA 4 b.f. Son of Shaka 119–Il Piccolo (Ribston 104) [1988 6g 5s 5d 5f 5g 5f⁵ 5f⁶ 6g⁵ 5d 5s 1989 5.8h⁵ 6f³ 6m 5.8h 5h² 5f 5g 7m* 7m* 7g⁴ 7s* 6m* 5m 6g 7g] **90** smallish filly: has a quick action: fairly useful handicapper: in tremendous heart in second half of season, winning at Chepstow in August, York and Ayr in September and Newmarket in October: led well inside final 1f when beating Young Tearaway by neck in strongly-run £7,900 event at last-named: never able to challenge last 3 outings: ideally suited by 7f: acts on any going: has sweated and often got on toes. *R. J. Holder.*

SONNY HILL LAD 6 ch.g. Celtic Cone 116–Honey Dipper (Golden Dipper 119) — [1988 14.6d 18.8d³ 1989 16.2m³] sturdy, workmanlike gelding: poor maiden on flat: probably stays 2¼m: winning hurdler. *R. J. Holder.*

SONOMA MISSION 4 b.g. Glenstal (USA) 118–Sun Lassie (FR) (King **40 §** Emperor (USA)) [1988 8d⁶ 8d⁶ 8m* 11.5g 10d 8g³ 8.2m 10.2g 1989 10s⁴ 12.5g⁵] big, angular gelding: moderate mover: plating-class winner as 3-y-o: hung left and didn't look keen when well-beaten fifth in claiming event at Wolverhampton in May: stays 1¼m: yet to race on firm going, acts on any other: sold 1,350 gns Ascot September Sales: unreliable. *J. S. King.*

SOOTY AUSTIN 2 b.g. (Mar 21) Electric 126–Partridge Brook 109 (Birdbrook — 110) [1989 a7g] sixth live foal: brother to poor 1987 2-y-o Abhainn and half-brother to 4 winners, including plater Topsoil (by Relkino), successful from 1m to 1½m and also over hurdles: dam won from 5f to 1¼m: slowly away and soon tailed off in late-year maiden at Southwell. *R. T. Juckes.*

SOOTY TERN 2 br.c. (Mar 19) Wassl 125–High Tern 93 (High Line 125) [1989 8s — 6d 6g] compact, quite attractive colt: first foal: dam, 14.7f and 2m winner, is half-sister to high-class middle-distance stayer High Hawk and to dam of Infamy: poor form in modest company: stumbled bend at Catterick second start. *J. W. Watts.*

SOPHIA GARDENS 2 gr.f. (May 8) Kalaglow 132–Mint Julep (Mill Reef (USA) **54 p** 141) [1989 7m⁶] 10,000Y: fifth reported foal: dam unraced half-sister to Bedtime, high-class 1¼m to 1½m performer: 14/1, over 5 lengths sixth of 17, one pace final 2f, to Mull House in maiden at Chepstow in October: will be better suited by 1m +: should improve. *I. A. Balding.*

SOPORIFIC 3 b.f. Pharly (FR) 130–Shuteye 91 (Shirley Heights 130) [1988 7d⁴ **79** 7g³ 1989 10g 9.1f² 12f⁵ 12g] big, workmanlike filly: has a long stride: fair form when beaten head in maiden at Newcastle in July, wandering and looking ill at ease on firm ground: taken very quietly and last to post, faced stiff task next outing: ran moderately in handicap final one: stays 9f well: may prove best on an easy surface: sold 11,500 gns Newmarket Autumn Sales. *W. Hastings-Bass.*

SORCERESS (FR) 2 b.f. (Apr 9) Fabulous Dancer (USA) 126–Lilac Charm 87 **108** (Bustino 136) [1989 8g* 8g³ 8g] 550,000 francs (approx £50,300) Y: lengthy, good sort: third foal: half-sister to 6f to 1¼m winner Heard It Before (by Pharly) and a winner in Italy: dam 1½m winner, is daughter of Rose Dubarry: won newcomers race at Deauville by ¾ length from Mackla: close third to same horse in Prix d'Aumale at Longchamp following month: well beaten in Prix Marcel Boussac at Longchamp in October: will stay 1¼m. *D. Smaga, France.*

SO RHYTHMICAL 5 b.g. Dance In Time (CAN)–So Lyrical 68 (So Blessed 130) **79** [1988 5d 5g 6f 7f⁴ 7m² 8g 6m* 1989 5s 6f* 6f* 7f* 8f 7.6m] sturdy gelding: modest handicapper: made virtually all at Kempton (comfortably) and Goodwood in early-summer: beat Cape Pigeon a head in £8,100 Samsung Electronics Stakes (Handicap) at Goodwood in late-July: below form last 2 outings: effective at 6f and 7f: best on top-of-the-ground: sometimes sweats and gets on edge: usually bandaged off-hind. *A. Hide.*

SORONET 2 b.f. (May 11) Superlative 118–Safe Passage (Charlottown 127) [1989 — 7g] 1,300F, 3,000 2-y-o: half-sister to 8.2f winner Lots of Luck (by Neltino), Norsk 1000 Guineas and Norsk Oaks winner Lots of Skill (by Record Run), and a winning hurdler: dam never ran: always towards rear in 24-runner maiden at Newmarket in November. *J. Pearce.*

SOUND MUSIC 3 b.f. Music Boy 124–Kanvita (Home Guard (USA) 129) [1988 —
NR 1989 7g 7g a8g a6g a8g] IR 13,500F, 26,000Y: shallow-girthed, angular filly:
half-sister to 3 winners, including useful sprinter Alpine Strings (by Stradavinsky)
and fair 1986 2-y-o 5f winner Demderise (by Vaigly Great): dam never ran: no
worthwhile form though showed signs of ability (sweating) second and third
outings: will prove best at up to 7f. *R. W. Armstrong.*

SOUND OF VICTORY 4 b.c. Thatching 131–Bugle Sound 96 (Bustino 136) —
[1988 6v* 7s 7d 6g5 5d 6v4 6v 1989 6d6 6s 7g 8g 7.6m 8g6] good-bodied ex-Irish colt:
poor mover: third reported foal: half-brother to 1984 Irish 2-y-o 1¼m winner Over
The Waves (by Main Reef): dam, daughter of smart Melodina, the dam of Dubian and
See You Then, stayed 1¾m: won maiden at Naas early as 3-y-o: beaten fair way in
varied contests, including seller, in 1989: suited by 6f: acts on heavy going:
sometimes blinkered: visored final outing, first for 3½ months. *J. P. Hudson.*

SOUPCON 3 b.f. King of Spain 121–Duck Soup 55 (Decoy Boy 129) [1988 6g 6s* —
1989 7g5] rather leggy filly: moderate walker: modest form when winning maiden at
Hamilton at 2 yrs, having been behind and ridden along early: below form but shaped
fairly well in handicap in April, only start in 1989: should stay 7f: has joined Miss B.
Sanders. *J. Glover.*

SOUTH CROSS (USA) 4 ch.g. Valdez (USA) Blue Cross Nurse (USA) —
(Needles) [1988 12s5 10.2f3 10m5 1989 16.2d6] well-made gelding: moderate mover:
quite modest maiden as 3-y-o: well-beaten sixth of 15 at Beverley in April: subsequently gelded: best form at 1¼m: possibly unsuited by soft going: winning
hurdler. *G. M. Moore.*

SOUTHEND SCALLYWAG 3 b.f. Tina's Pet 121–By The Lake 48 (Tyrant 53
(USA)) [1988 6d 6g 6s 5g2 5d6 1989 8.2m 8f5 7f6 8m* 8.2m] lengthy, sparely-made
filly: has a round action: 20/1, appeared to show improved form when making all in
maiden at Edinburgh in July: stays 1m: acts on firm ground: winning hurdler. *G. M.
Moore.*

SOUTHERN BEAU (USA) 2 b.c. (Mar 22) Dixieland Band (USA)–Love For 88
Love (USA) (Cornish Prince) [1989 6f5 7g* 7m4 8g6 7.3m5] $130,000Y: useful-
looking colt: sixth named foal: half-brother to a winner in USA: dam winner twice
over 6f, is daughter of half-sister to top-class Jaipur: fair performer: won 20-runner
maiden at Newbury in August: stays 1m, but may prove ideally suited by 7f:
blinkered last 2 starts: has suspect temperament. *C. R. Nelson.*

SOUTHERN SKY 4 b.f. Comedy Star (USA) 121–Starky's Pet (Mummy's Pet 89
125) [1988 7f* 7g2 7m2 7d2 8d 1989 8d 7g4 7g* 8m2 7g5 8m3 7f2 7m* 8f] rather
leggy, angular filly: fair handicapper: led well inside final 1f when winning £8,700
event at Epsom in June and 7-runner contest at Goodwood (favourite, by neck from
Cape Pigeon) in August: effective at 7f and 1m: acts on firm going and a soft surface:
has run well when sweating: hung right seventh outing: game and consistent. *D. R.
C. Elsworth.*

SOUTH LONDON 3 ch.g. Bustino 136–Crimson Lake (FR) 71 (Mill Reef (USA) —
141) [1988 6d 1989 8m 6f 10f] useful-looking gelding: no sign of ability in maiden and
sellers: bred to need middle distances: blinkered debut: twice sweating, also on toes
on reappearance. *R. P. C. Hoad.*

SOUTHROP 3 b.c.c. Auction Ring (USA) 123–Giovinezza (FR) (Roi Dagobert 128 69
[1988 6g 6g6 5g2 1989 5s2 5s 6f 6f 7m 5m6 6m 8.2g] lengthy, quite attractive colt:
modest handicapper: ran fairly well at Goodwood and Warwick fourth and sixth
starts: showed little after: should be better at 6f than 5f: acts on any going. *M.
Blanshard.*

SOUTH SANDS 3 ch.g. Sayf El Arab (USA) 127–Collegian 90 (Stanford 121§) 78
[1988 5.1f5 6f* 7f5 8s6 7m 8g 1989 9f6 9f* 9m6 11f5 10f4 12m2 12f* 10.6m2 12.2d6
12g2] sparely-made gelding: fair handicapper: won at Redcar in June and Beverley
(claimer) in September: stays 1½m: best on a sound surface: ran creditably when
sweating and edgy sixth start: sold 15,000 gns Doncaster November Sales. *M. J.
Camacho.*

SOUTH STACK 3 b.g. Daring March 116–Lady Henham 92 (Breakspear II) 59
[1988 7g 8g5 1989 10s 8s 7g* 12f 11s] strong, lengthy gelding: has a round action:
looking really well, game winner of seller (sold out of D. Morley's stable 8,800 gns)
at Doncaster in May, leading inside final 1f: off course 4½ months (gelded) and
below form after: will be suited by return to around 1m: ridden by 5-lb claimer until
third start. *Ronald Thompson.*

SOVEREIGN HILL 2 ch.f. (Mar 9) Dominion 123–Tuft Hill 92 (Grundy 137) 44
[1989 5m 5f6 7f 6g] 15,000Y: sparely-made filly, slightly dipped-backed: second foal:

dam, 2-y-o 6f winner, is half-sister to 10.5f Prix Corrida winner Bonshamile: poor form in varied races: sweating badly, swished tail and looked temperamental final start: should stay at least 1m: one to treat with caution. *M. H. Easterby.*

SOVEREIGN ROCKET (USA) 4 b.c. Sovereign Dancer (USA)–Jeffs Miss Rocket (USA) (Jeff D) [1988 8d⁴ 8f² 8.5m* 1989 8m 8f 8m³ 10m⁵] strong, good-topped, quite attractive colt: moderate walker: has a quick action: fair handicapper: well beaten final outing (July): should stay 1¼m: has won when sweating. *G. Harwood.* 87

SOVIET SAINT 2 gr.f. (Mar 16) Siberian Express (USA) 125–Halo 51 (Godswalk (USA) 130) [1989 6d⁴ 6g] 6,800F, IR 2,000Y: sparely-made filly: first foal: dam poor daughter of sister to high-class performers Thatching and Golden Thatch: slowly away and always behind in 5-runner minor event at Goodwood and 11-runner claimer at Catterick in the autumn: sold 650 gns Ascot December Sales. *P. Mitchell.* —

SOY ROBERTO (USA) 2 ch.c. (May 2) Roberto (USA) 131–Ocean's Answer (USA) (Northern Answer (USA)) [1989 7m² 6g²] $225,000Y: close-coupled, rather leggy, attractive colt: good mover: brother to French provincial 11f winner Tiramisu and half-brother to 3 winners, including smart sprinter Al Zawbaah (by Mr Prospector): dam, very useful 2-y-o 1m stakes winner, is closely related to Storm Bird: 7/2 but very green, 2 lengths second of 19, leading over 1f out but unable to quicken again last 75 yds, to Mukddaam in maiden at Newmarket in October: carried head high closing stages when beaten ¾ length by Alidiva in similar event same course later in month: will be suited by 1m + : sure to win a race or two. *B. Hanbury.* 99 p

SPANISH EMPIRE (USA) 2 b.c. (Mar 18) El Gran Senor (USA) 136–Tea And Roses (USA) (Fleet Nasrullah) [1989 8v⁴] $700,000Y: rangy, angular colt: third foal: closely related to fairly useful 7f and 1m winner Jerwah (by Nureyev) and half-brother to a winner in USA by Assert: dam, half-sister to high-class sprinter Faliraki, placed at up to 1m in Ireland prior to winning in USA: 10/1, under 5 lengths fourth of 23, keeping on well having been very slowly away, to Tyburn Tree in minor event at Newbury in October: sure to improve, and win a race. *B. W. Hills.* 87 p

SPANISH ENVOY 2 br.g. (Apr 2) King of Spain 121–Queen's Herald (King's Leap 111) [1989 6m 5f 5m 7g a8g] tall gelding: sixth foal: half-brother to useful sprinter Deccan Queen (by Decoy Boy) and quite modest sprinter Queen of Aragon (by Aragon): dam Irish 2m winner: of little account. *M. C. Chapman.* —

SPANISH HARLEM 3 br.c. King of Spain 121–Luscinia 73 (Sing Sing 134) [1988 5m⁴ 5f² 5f² 1989 5m 6f* 6g] medium-sized, good-bodied colt: won handicap at Hamilton: never dangerous in similar event later in July: suited by 6f: acts on firm going: twice tended to hang as 2-y-o, looking temperamentally unsatisfactory final start. *W. J. Pearce.* 72

SPANISH HEART 4 b.f. King of Spain 121–Hearten (Hittite Glory 125) [1988 7s 6f² 7m² 7g² 7g* 7f² 7m* 8m⁵ 1989 7g 8.5m 8f² 8g³ 7f* 8m² 7.6m⁴ 8f²] medium-sized filly: fair handicapper: led over 1f out and ran on well when winning at Salisbury in August: good second of 15 at same course in October: withdrawn after getting upset in stalls at Ascot (apprentices) later in month: effective at 7f and 1m: acts on firm going. *P. J. Makin.* 86

SPANISH LOVE 3 b. or br.f. Precocious 126–San Marguerite 80 (Blakeney 126) [1988 5g 7d⁴ 6m 1989 7f² 7.3m 7f 7f⁶ a8g³ a8g⁶ a8g] close-coupled, workmanlike filly: plating-class form: best efforts when placed in maiden at Goodwood amd claimer (slowly away and well beaten) at Lingfield: will probably stay beyond 1m. *M. McCormack.* 56

SPANISH MOU 4 b.f. King of Spain 121–Baggage 86 (Zeus Boy 121) [1988 9d 10g 7.5f 6m 1989 8s 6m] workmanlike filly: moderate mover: plater: little form since 2 yrs: visored once in 1988. *M. W. Eckley.* —

SPANISH OAK 3 b.c. King of Spain 121–Hearten (Hittite Glory 125) [1988 5f⁴ 5m* 5.3f⁵ 5.8g 5g 7m 8f 8d 1989 7h 5f 5m] leggy, unfurnished colt: quite modest winner as 2-y-o: well beaten since, showing signs of retaining ability at 3 yrs only on second start: not sure to stay 1m: acts on top-of-the-ground: has worn tongue strap. *P. J. Makin.* —

SPANISH PINE 4 b.c. King of Spain 121–Pine Ridge 80 (High Top 131) [1988 7g⁶ 7d 10d³ 9m⁵ 8g* 8g 8g⁵ 8v³ 9f 1989 8g 7g] rangy, useful-looking colt: quite useful winner in 1988: apprentice ridden, never dangerous in Newmarket handicaps as 4-y-o: needed good gallop at 1m, but barely stayed 1¼m: needed give in the ground: dead. *B. Hanbury.* —

SPANISH PRINCESS 5 b.m. King of Spain 121–Doogali 93 (Doon 124) [1988 —
14m⁶ 1989 10.1m 14f] strong, workmanlike mare: shows plenty of knee action: well
beaten in varied company. *G. P. Enright.*

SPANISH REALM 2 b.f. (Feb 22) King of Spain 121–Miss Realm 86 (Realm 69
129) [1989 5s 5d* 5f⁵ 5d* 6f⁴ 6g³ 6m⁵ 6g² 6g⁴ 5m*] 720Y: small, sparely-made filly:
second foal: dam 2-y-o 5f winner: quite modest filly: won maiden auction event at
Catterick in April, claimer at Beverley in May, and 11-runner nursery at Windsor in
August: stays 6f: acts on top-of-the-ground and a soft surface: tends to hang:
bandaged third and last 2 (off-hind only) starts: good mount for inexperienced
apprentice. *M. Brittain.*

SPANISH REEL 7 b.g. Gay Fandango (USA) 132–De Nada 79 (Ragusa 137) 51
[1988 NR 1989 10d 10.8m⁴ 10.8m* 11.7m⁵] good-bodied gelding: plating-class
handicapper: sweating profusely, won at Warwick in June: stays 11.7f: acts on any
going: visored once: has worn crossed noseband: winning hurdler. *J. A. C. Edwards.*

SPANISH SONG 4 br.g. King of Spain 121–Rock Concert 76 (Star Appeal 133) —
[1988 8m 8d 1989 8.5d 8g 8m 8f] leggy, lengthy gelding: shows signs of stringhalt:
poor mover: poor maiden: bandaged second outing. *M. C. Chapman.*

SPANISH VERDICT 2 b.c. (Apr 16) King of Spain 121–Counsel's Verdict 70
(Firestreak 125) [1989 6f³ 6f⁴ 6g² 6g⁴ 6v⁵] 1,500F, 6,000Y: sturdy, good-quartered
colt: has scope: fifth foal: half-brother to 4-y-o Emma Tom Bay (by Bay Express):
dam of little account: quite modest maiden: will stay 7f: probably acts on any going:
visored final outing. *Miss S. E. Hall.*

SPANISH WHISPER 2 b.c. (May 11) Aragon 118–Whisper Gently 91 (Pitskelly 55
122) [1989 6m 6f 6m⁵ 6g a7g a7g] medium-sized colt: third foal: half-brother to 1m
seller winner Mascalls Lady (by Nicholas Bill): dam Irish 9.5f to 1½m winner: best
effort fifth of 28 to Sister Sal in seller at Newmarket: blinkered, ran moderately final
outing: should be suited by 7f. *P. J. Makin.*

SPARE US ALL 5 b.g. Moorestyle 137–Second Generation 95 (Decoy Boy 129) —
[1988 6s⁶ 10g 8.5m 6f 1989 10s⁵] big, strong, workmanlike gelding: lightly-raced
maiden, no worthwhile form. *B. J. Curley.*

SPARKLER GEBE 3 b.c. Be My Native (USA) 124–Siliferous (Sandy Creek 79 d
123) [1988 NR 1989 11.7m² 12f 10f⁴ 13.3d] 3,300F, 7,800Y: tall, leggy colt: first foal:
dam, unplaced 4 times at 2 yrs, is closely related to useful 1m to 1½m performer
Kahaila: staying-on second in maiden at Bath in May, tending to edge left but easily
best effort: suited by 1½m. *P. G. Bailey.*

SPARKLING DANCER 4 b.g. Sparkling Boy 110–Tea Dance (Vitiges (FR) —
132) [1988 10m 12m 10s 1989 9s] of little account. *J. S. Wainwright.*

SPARKLING NECTAR 2 b.f. (May 5) Thatching 131–Baby Brew 123 (Green 70
God 128) [1989 6g 6m⁵ 6g] 54,000Y: useful-looking filly: has scope: shows a fluent
action: sixth foal: half-sister to Irish 3-y-o 1m winner Small Scotch (by Lomond), 1m
winner Ashwa (by Golden Fleece) and moderate 7f winner Feydan (by Double
Form): dam very smart sprinter from family of Deep River and King's Company: 12
lengths fifth of 6 to Dead Certain in 'The Pacemaker Update' Lowther Stakes at
York in August, only indication of merit: stays 6f. *R. Hannon.*

SPARK OF WIT 3 b.g. Comedy Star (USA) 121–Rekindle 70 (Relkino 131) [1988 —
NR 1989 9f 7f 10.2h 12m 8f] sparely-made gelding: first foal: dam, poor maiden, is
half-sister to useful 1½m to 2m winner No Bombs: well beaten in varied events,
including seller: should be suited by 1½m+: visored final start: sold 2,400 gns
Ascot August Sales. *R. J. Holder.*

SPARKY LAD 6 b.h. Hot Spark 126–Rather Warm 103 (Tribal Chief 125) [1988 —
7.6d* 7g 7g² 7.6f* 6g 6f* 6m⁵ 7d 7.6m 7d 8s 6s 1989 7s 7.6f 7m a7g] slightly
dipped-backed horse: moderate walker and mover: quite modest winner as 5-y-o:
has lost his form completely: better suited by 7f than 6f: acts on any going: blinkered
once: occasionally sweats. *J. R. Jenkins.*

SPATE (FR) 4 b.g. Shareef Dancer (USA) 135–Riverina (FR) (Snob II 130) [1988 49
12g³ 12s⁴ 12.5g² 12.5g⁵ 1989 9v² 11g²] ex-French gelding: closely related to 2
winners in France, including smart middle-distance winner Lys River (by Lyphard):
dam, placed over 1½m, is half-sister to good staying 2-y-o's Riverton and
Robertshaw: in frame in French maidens as 3-y-o and in maiden claiming events at
Hamilton in spring: stays 1½m: acts on heavy going: winning selling hurdler. *N.
Tinkler.*

SPECIAL FRED 3 b.c. Lyphard's Special (USA) 122–Vienna Girl (Ballymore 85
123) [1988 7g³ 7s* 7m⁴ 1989 9d⁶ 8m 7g⁴] lengthy, attractive colt: carries condition:

fluent mover: fair performer: not discredited in listed race at Newmarket in April and moderately-run minor event at Leicester in May, first and final starts: awkward at stalls, unseated rider and withdrawn at Newmarket in July: bred to stay 9f: acts on soft going and top-of-the-ground: tends to take strong hold, though settled better at Leicester. *P. T. Walwyn.*

SPECIALISED BOY 3 ch.c. Mummy's Game 120–Nasty Niece (CAN) (Great 75 Nephew 126) [1988 6g² 6d* 7f⁶ 6g 1989 7g 7s² 8g 8m 7m 8.2f 8g⁴ 8g⁵] leggy, close-coupled colt: modest handicapper: below form after second start, though not entirely discredited penultimate one: should stay 1m: possibly needs a soft surface: blinkered (moved moderately down) sixth start: changed hands 9,400 gns Newmarket Autumn Sales after seventh. *C. F. Wall.*

SPECIAL RESERVE 4 b.g. Auction Ring (USA) 123–Grande Madame 64 37 (Monseigneur (USA) 127) [1988 8.2v* 8g⁴ 10g⁴ 8m* 8m² 8.2s 9s³ 8.2s 1989 8s 8v 8m 8g 8m* 8m⁶ 8g* 8m 7g 8f⁶ 8f² 8f a8g] smallish, plain, lightly-made gelding: moderate mover: poor plater: won handicaps at Bath (no bid) in July and Yarmouth (no bid, apprentice ridden) in August: best at up to 9f: acts on any going: sweating and blinkered fourth outing: has worn bandages: inconsistent: sold 2,000 gns Ascot December Sales. *P. J. Feilden.*

SPECIFIC IMPULSE 2 b.c. (May 31) Star Appeal 133–Lead Me On (King's 55 Troop 118) [1989 8f⁴ 8.2g 8g] seventh foal: brother to 1¼m winner Burning Bright and half-brother to winning stayer Chasing The Dragon (by Moulton) and a winning plater: dam never ran: plating-class maiden: best effort second outing. *M. Johnston.*

SPECKLED BRAID (USA) 2 b.f. (Feb 20) Miswaki (USA) 124–Petes Lucky 72 p Lady (USA) (Droll Roll) [1989 6g²] $50,000Y: angular, sparely-made filly: moderate walker: half-sister to a minor winner in USA: dam half-sister to Noble Nashua, a leading 3-y-o in USA in 1981 when dual Grade 1 1¼m winner: favourite but bit green, ½-length second of 8, staying on well, to Walkern Witch in maiden at Yarmouth in September: sure to do better over further. *H. R. A. Cecil.*

SPECKYFOUREYES 6 b.m. Blue Cashmere 129–Sprightly Sprite 80 (Babur — 126) [1988 NR 1989 12m⁴ 16.2m⁶ 18f⁵] half-sister to minor winners here and abroad: dam middle-distance performer: bandaged, well beaten in amateur events and in £7,000 contest (soon tailed off) at Pontefract: winning hurdler. *J. Pearce.*

SPEEDY BOY 7 ch.g. Tachypous 128–Grandpa's Legacy 102 (Zeus Boy 120) — [1988 17.1g 16m 1989 12m] workmanlike gelding: poor maiden: has been visored. *G. P. Enright.*

SPEEDY SNAPS LAD 4 b.g. Magnolia Lad 102–Parton Gold 74 (The — Go-Between 129) [1988 5g 8.2d⁴ 1989 8g 7.5f 6f⁶ 8.3m] angular, sparely-made gelding: bad mover: bad plater: probably best at sprint distances: blinkered 4 times: looked difficult ride second start. *K. S. Bridgwater.*

SPENDOMANIA (USA) 2 b.f. (Mar 13) Roberto (USA) 131–La Trinite (FR) 107 112 (Lyphard (USA) 132) [1989 7d⁵ 7m* 6d² 6g⁵ 8m⁴ 8m⁵] half-sister to Prix Morny winners Seven Springs (by Irish River) and Regal State (by Affirmed), French 3-y-o 6.5f and 7f winner Neptune's Wonder (by Irish River) and a winner abroad: dam won twice at around 6f at 2 yrs in France and is out of sister to Oaks winner Pia: useful filly: successful in maiden at Saint-Cloud: ½-length second to Qirmazi in Prix de Cabourg at Deauville and over 5 lengths fourth to Jade Robbery in Ciga Grand Criterium at Longchamp, best subsequent efforts: stays 1m. *J. Fellows, France.*

SPHINX 5 b.g. Auction Ring (USA) 123–The Yellow Girl 102 (Yellow God 129) 60 [1988 8d* 10g² 10.8s 10f⁴ 8g 8g⁵ 7f 8g 8g 10d³ 1989 10.8s² 8d² 10.8d 8g² 8.2g² 8v⁴ a11g⁴ a12g] lengthy, robust gelding: plating-class handicapper: stays 11f: probably unsuited by firm going: acts on any other: blinkered once: has won for apprentice. *J. R. Jenkins.*

SPICA (USA) 2 b.f. (May 2) Diesis 133–Giboulee Era (USA) (Giboulee (CAN)) 70 p [1989 6g³] $225,000Y: leggy, angular filly: third foal: sister to French 7f winner Baino Charm: dam won at up to 9f: 20/1, 3 lengths third of 22, headway 2f out and staying on strongly, to Lip Sing in maiden at Leicester in November: will be much better suited by 7f+: sure to improve, and should win a race. *J. Tree.*

SPIDER WOMAN 2 b.f. (Apr 25) Touching Wood (USA) 127–Red Spider 78 — (Red God 128§) [1989 6m⁶] leggy, rather lengthy filly: has scope: sister to 3-y-o 1¼m winner Volcanoes Spark and half-sister to November Handicap winner Abu Kadra (by Blakeney), middle-distance performer Blushing Spy (by Great Nephew) and a winner over jumps: dam won over 1m: 14/1, backward, green and ridden by 7-lb claimer, well-beaten sixth of 7 in maiden at Nottingham in August: sold K. Cunningham-Brown 3,100 gns Newmarket Autumn Sales. *B. Hanbury.*

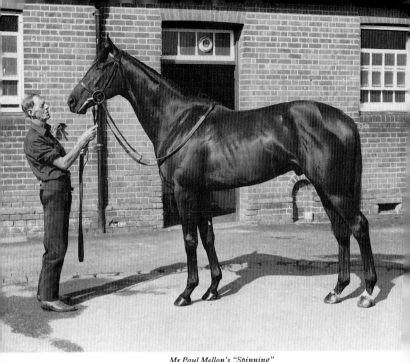

Mr Paul Mellon's "Spinning"

SPINNING 2 b. or br.c. (Mar 14) Glint of Gold 128–Strathspey 105 (Jimmy Reppin **110** 131) [1989 8g* 8d³ 8m] tall, rather leggy, useful-looking colt: easy mover: sixth living foal: brother to 3-y-o Sun On The Spey, closely related to quite useful 1986 2-y-o 6f winner Dunninald, useful 1984 2-y-o 7.3f winner River Spey and a winner in Belgium (all by Mill Reef) and half-brother to modest 10.2f winner Bastinado (by Bustino): dam, winner from 6f to 1m, is sister to very smart Joking Apart: won listed Danepak Bacon Stakes at Newmarket in August by 7 lengths, drawing quickly away 1f out despite drifting markedly left: failed to confirm favourable impression made that day in Country Lady Stardom Stakes (third of 4) at Goodwood and Royal Lodge Stakes (virtually pulled up after hanging badly left from 3f out) at Ascot: will stay 1¼m: one to treat with caution. *I. A. Balding.*

SPIRIT AWAY 2 b.f. (Mar 14) Dominion 123–Jove's Voodoo (USA) 74 (Northern — Jove (CAN)) [1989 6f] smallish, sturdy filly: second foal: sister to 3-y-o 1m winner Zamore, winning juvenile hurdler: dam 6f winner: unruly in stalls and slowly away in maiden at Redcar in May. *S. G. Norton.*

SPIRIT SAM 4 ch.c. Music Boy 124–Kalia (Wollow 132) [1988 7s 7s⁵ 8f 10g⁴ 12m — 10.2f 12d 8g 7m 1989 6v 6m 9f 8.3m] robust, angular colt: moderate mover: poor maiden: blinkered on 5 of last 6 outings: sold 800 gns Newmarket Autumn Sales: difficult ride. *W. Carter.*

SPIRITUALIST 3 ch.c. Simply Great (FR) 122–Parima 72 (Pardao 120) [1988 **73** 7g⁴ 8v⁵ 10.2m 1989 12g² 12.3m 13.6f² 12g a16g²] angular colt: second in handicaps at Leicester, Redcar and Lingfield: stays 2m: acts on firm ground: sold out of S. Norton's stable 11,000 gns Newmarket Autumn Sales after fourth start. *Dr J. D. Scargill.*

860

SPITFIRE 3 b.c. Shirley Heights 130–Home Fire 99 (Firestreak 125) [1988 6f² **107** 7g* 7m² 8m² 8g⁴ 1989 10.2d* 12f³ 10f* 12m⁵ 10m³ 10g³ 9m⁵] medium-sized, useful-looking colt: successful in small fields for minor events at Bath (hanging left) in April and Lingfield in June: ran creditably most other starts, including in 3 pattern events, though below best (finding little) in listed event at York final outing: stays 1½m: acts on firm going and a soft surface: has sweated, and did so at York: sometimes bit edgy: looks difficult ride: useful. *C. R. Nelson.*

SPITFIRE JUBILEE 3 b.c. Chief Singer 131–Altana 71 (Grundy 137) [1988 NR — 1989 8d⁶ 8s 8m] leggy, workmanlike colt: first foal: dam 1½m and 1¾m winner: easily best effort in maidens and claimer in the spring in 22-runner Newbury maiden on debut: will be suited by 1¼m: sold to join R. Hodges 5,600 gns Ascot June Sales. *I. A. Balding.*

SPITTIN MICK 5 b.g. The Brianstan 128–La Fille 58 (Crooner 119) [1988 5m 6g **48** 5m 5m⁶ 6d 5g 6d 1989 5m 5m 6m³ 5f⁴ 6g³ 5f⁶ 5g⁴ 6h² 6m 6m 6f 6g 5f⁶ 7m³ a7g] lengthy, smallish gelding: moderate mover: poor handicapper: stays 7f: best on a sound surface: occasionally sweats: has run creditably for apprentice. *G. M. Moore.*

SPITZABIT 5 br.g. Pitskelly 122–Marsabit (Martinmas 128) [1988 5d⁵ 6g 6g⁵ **44** 5d⁵ 6f³ 6f⁴ 6f³ 6m 5d 1989 5d⁶ 6m] leggy gelding: moderate mover: poor handicapper nowadays: not seen out after May: stays 6f: best on an easy surface: sometimes on toes: inconsistent. *Pat Mitchell.*

SPLASHMAN (USA) 3 ch.c. Riverman 131–L'Extravagante (Le Fabuleux 133) **82** [1988 NR 1989 10.1g 10.1m⁴ 10.6g⁴ 10.6s² 12.4g] $160,000Y: big, angular colt: poor mover: ninth foal: half-brother to 5 winners, including lightly-raced Gallinule Stakes winner Montelimar (by Alleged): dam, winner 3 times at up to 1m at 3 yrs, is from excellent family: fair form when in frame in minor event, maiden and handicap: very upset in stalls, hampered first bend and virtually pulled up in straight when favourite for handicap final outing: should be suited by further than 1¼m: acts on soft going: sold to join J. Jenkins 36,000 gns Newmarket Autumn Sales. *L. M. Cumani.*

SPLENDID CAREER (USA) 3 ch.c. Northern Baby (CAN) 127–Sir Ivor's **105** Sorrow (USA) (Sir Ivor 135) [1988 8g 8d 1989 7d 8f* 8m⁴ 10m* 10.1m* 10m 10f⁵ 10.6d* 10m² 9g] big, strong, useful-looking colt: has plenty of scope: has a powerful, rather round action: useful handicapper: justified favouritism in summer events at Kempton (apprentices), Yarmouth and Windsor: showed improved form in September when making most at strong pace and winning £8,000 event at Haydock then second in £24,200 event at Newbury: favourite and looking very fit, led 7f when well beaten in Cambridgeshire at Newmarket final start: suited by 1¼m: acts on firm going and a soft surface. *L. M. Cumani.*

SPLINTERING 3 ch.f. Sharpo 132–Fall To Pieces (USA) 101 (Forli (ARG)) **97** [1988 5d 6s⁴ 1989 5s* 6s³ 6f* 6m* 6m⁴ 6f⁴ 6m 5.6g] leggy filly: won maiden at Folkestone in April and handicaps at Goodwood in May and Newbury in June: fourth in listed race at Newbury and Stewards' Cup at Goodwood: looking lean, ran moderately in listed event and £25,000 event after: stays 6f: acts on any going: tends to hang and carry head awkwardly: unseated 5-lb claimer at stalls on debut. *P. T. Walwyn.*

SPOFFORTH 2 b.g. (Feb 5) Jalmood (USA) 126–Visible Form 99 (Formidable **50** (USA) 125) [1989 7m 8m 8.2f 8s] 18,500F, IR 25,000Y: close-coupled gelding: good walker: has a round action: second foal: half-brother to 3-y-o Azeb (by Young Generation), 6f winner at 2 yrs: dam, 6f and 1¼m winner, is out of half-sister to very smart stayer Raise You Ten: plating-class maiden: will be suited by 1¼m + . *G. A. Pritchard-Gordon.*

SPOILT SON 3 b.c. Mummy's Pet 125–Lady Hester (Native Prince) [1988 NR **72** 1989 6s³ 6m⁵ 6m 5f] 80,000Y: sturdy colt: has a round action: moderate walker: eighth foal: half-brother to several winners, notably smart French 1m and 9f performer L'Irresponsable (by Ile de Bourbon): dam, granddaughter of excellent broodmare Zanzara, winner over 5f and 6f in Ireland: long odds on, hung left throughout when unimpressive winner of minor event at Thirsk in April: ran moderately last 2 starts, on final one (July) blinkered: likely to prove best at 6f: acts on soft ground: sold 900 gns Newmarket Autumn Sales, resold 2,600 gns Ascot December Sales. *A. A. Scott.*

SPOOF 2 b.f. (Jan 20) Precocious 126–Thimblerigger 62 (Sharpen Up 127) [1989 **79** 6g² 7g] 26,000F, 28,000Y: unfurnished filly: has scope: sixth foal: half-sister to winning 4-y-o stayer Cleavers Gate (by Touching Wood), Italian 6f and 7f winner Hopeless Devoted (by Vitiges) and a winner in North America by Bold Lad (IRE): dam won over 1¼m: 8/1, beaten a neck by Roman Walk in 16-runner maiden at

Newmarket in October: favourite, found little when ninth of 24 in similar event there following month: should stay 7f. *W. Jarvis.*

SPORTING IDOL 4 b.g. Mummy's Game 120–Village Idol 74 (Blakeney 126) [1988 7d* 7d* 10g3 11d 10d6 8f 8f3 8m 7.6d 1989 8s6 7v5 8h 7f 7m 10.1m a8g5 a7g] leggy, workmanlike gelding: has a round action: plater: probably best at up to 1m: suited by plenty of give in the ground: visored final outing: often flashes tail: sold 3,000 gns Ascot December Sales. *T. M. Jones.* **49 d**

SPORTING SIMON 4 ch.g. Vaigly Great 127–City Link Lass 92 (Double Jump 131) [1988 7g 8g 8g 8g4 8.2g4 9s2 8m 9s4 8v2 1989 12f 10m 8g5 7f3 7f 7g6] workmanlike, plain gelding: moderate mover: quite modest maiden: stays 9f: acts on any going: has appeared difficult ride, including when blinkered. *L. G. Cottrell.* **62**

SPORTING WEDNESDAY 4 b.g. Martinmas 128–Philogyny 94 (Philip of Spain 126) [1988 8f 10g 10d5 7m* 7f4 8.3m4 7g5 8g 1989 8.3m 7.6m] quite modest winner as 3-y-o: eased once beaten when behind at Windsor and Lingfield in 1989: best form at 7f: acts on top-of-the-ground. *C. A. Horgan.* **—**

SPOT ON ANNIE 3 gr.f. Miami Springs 121–Hallo Rosie 67 (Swing Easy (USA) 126) [1988 6f3 5g 5f4 5g6 5d* 1989 6m 6m 5.3h3 5f 5g* 6m4 5f4] leggy filly: quite modest handicapper: won at Windsor in July: ideally suited for 5f: acts on hard going and a soft surface. *M. Madgwick.* **59**

SPRINGFIELD MATCH 4 b.f. Royal Match 117–Petoria 74 (Songedor 116) [1988 9g 7.5m2 8f3 7.5s 7.5m2 10g3 12.2f4 10d 1989 8.5g 8f 8.5m 8m 8.5m6 12.3m 11s 10f5 12.5f a11g] sparely-made, angular filly: has a round action: poor maiden: soundly beaten last 5 outings: best at up to 1¼m: needs a sound surface: visored once at 3 yrs: blinkered final start: has worn severe bridle. *P. Wigham.* **33**

SPRING FORWARD 5 b.h. Double Form 130–Forward Princess (USA) 45 (Forward Pass) [1988 11g 12h 15g* 15.5m5 14.8s* 16.5m2 15.8d2 18g3 15m 16m3 15d 1989 18g5 16s 18s3 18.4m 19f4 15.8m3 17.1h4 16g* 18.4f2 15.3m5 16m4 16.2f5] small, leggy horse: usually looks well: poor handicapper: well ridden by S. Wood when winning 6-runner event at Chester in June: ran badly final outing: suited by a test of stamina: probably not ideally suited by firm going, acts on any other: has worn blinkers, visored eighth to tenth starts: often apprentice ridden: has sweated and got on edge. *R. E. Peacock.*

SPRING HARMONY 2 b. or br.f. (May 1) Daring March 116–Heavenly Chord 89 (Hittite Glory 125) [1989 5m 7f 7m 8.5f] 6,400Y: workmanlike, good-bodied filly: has scope: fifth foal: closely related to winner in Norway by Dominion and half-sister to 3 other winners, including 7.5f to 8.5f winner Heavenly Hoofer (by Dance In Time): dam 6f winner at 2 yrs: of little account: trained first 3 outings by P. Felgate. *M. W. Easterby.* **—**

SPRING HAY 3 gr.c. Wassl 125–Spring Silver (Palestine 133) [1988 NR 1989 10s3 10s2 12f 10.6g4 12f3 10g5 10g4] 70,000Y: leggy, quite good-topped colt: half-brother to 3 winners in Ireland, including 11.9f winner Brown Pearl (by Tap On Wood) and 1¾m winner Eyre Court (by Pollerton): dam, placed in Irish bumpers, is half-sister to Cesarewitch winner Scoria and Champion Hurdle winner Lanzarote: led long way when beaten under 5 lengths behind Old Vic in Guardian Classic Trial at Sandown and Cacoethes in moderately-run King Edward VII Stakes at Royal Ascot second and fifth outings: other form bears no comparison: in need of race in minor event final start (November), first since Eclipse Stakes: will stay beyond 1½m: acts on any going: has joined D. Nicholson. *C. E. Brittain.* **106 ?**

SPRING HIGH 2 b.f. (Apr 1) Miami Springs 121–High Voltage 82 (Electrify) [1989 5d5 5m3 5f4 5m3 6f* 5f2 5m2 6m 5f3 5f] tall, leggy, lengthy filly: fifth living foal: half-sister to 3-y-o Yeoman Force (by Crofter), fair 5f winner at 2 yrs, and fairly useful sprinter Dorking Lad (by Cawston's Clown): dam won 3 times over 5f: modest performer: made virtually all in 5-runner maiden at Folkestone in July: ran well afterwards in nurseries and minor events: best form at 5f: twice blinkered: has given impression possibly ungenuine. *K. T. Ivory.* **74**

SPRINGLAKE'S LADY 3 b.f. Music Boy 124–North Pine (Import 127) [1988 5m6 5m5 5g* 6f 1989 8m 8m 8.3g 9f3 9f 7m] lengthy filly: fair plater: third at Hamilton in July, easily best effort as 3-y-o: stays 9f: acts on firm going: sold to join J. Forte 2,000 gns Doncaster September Sales. *W. J. Pearce.* **50**

SPRINGMAN 5 b.g. Young Man (FR) 73–Spring Secret (USA) 71 (Hillary) [1988 8.5f4 10.2m 8.5g5 8g 10f6 10s 1989 6f4 7.5m5 a8g5] narrow, rather leggy, plain gelding: has a round action: poor maiden: stays 1m: acts on firm going: has run well for amateur. *A. Smith.* **50**

862

SPRING MORN (USA) 4 b.g. Alleged (USA) 138–Valenciennes (USA) —
(Northern Dancer) [1988 10g³ 1989 10.2m³ 8.2g⁵] lengthy ex-Irish gelding: second
foal: brother to Irish 1¼m winner Temple Bar: dam unraced daughter of half-sister
to Artaius: third in maiden at the Curragh as 3-y-o when trained by M. V. O'Brien
and in 3-runner slowly-run minor event at Newcastle (backward, beaten 8½ lengths
by High Estate) in June: never placed to challenge in maiden at Hamilton over 2
months later: will be suited by return to 1¼m. *A. P. Stringer.*

SPRING RAG 3 b.g. Raga Navarro (ITY) 119–Spring Music (Silly Season 127) —
[1988 6m⁵ 7g 7d 1989 7m 10f⁴ 8m] leggy, workmanlike gelding: moderate mover: no
worthwhile form, though showed signs of ability on reappearance: had no chance
final start: bred to stay beyond 7f. *G. B. Balding.*

SPRING RUN 2 ch.c. (Apr 3) Salmon Leap (USA) 131–Quick Burn 64 (Carnival **46**
Dancer 117) [1989 5g² 7g⁴] 11,000Y: angular colt: moderate walker: half-brother to
several winners, including 1981 2-y-o 5f winner Swing Fire (by Swing Easy), later
good sprinter in Italy, and fair 1980 2-y-o 5f winner Miss Quaver (by Averof): dam
winning sister to smart sprinter Ubedizzy and half-sister to Cajun: poor form in
quite modest company at Beverley (odds on) and Ayr in July. *J. Berry.*

SPRING SPARKLE 3 ch.f. Lord Gayle (USA) 124–Friendly Ann (Artaius **95** d
(USA) 129) [1988 6s² 1989 7.3s³ 8g⁵ 7g⁵ 10g] lengthy, medium-sized filly: has a
quick action: stayed on well having been last over 4f out when 7½ lengths third to
Pass The Peace in Group 3 event at Newbury in April: ran poorly after in maidens
(favourite, off course 6 months in between) and handicap: likely to prove best at up
to 1m: possibly needs a soft surface: sold 14,000 gns Newmarket December Sales. *B.
W. Hills.*

SPRINGS WELCOME 3 b.f. Blakeney 126–Tomfoolery 73 (Silly Season 127) **86**
[1988 NR 1989 10f 12f⁵ 11.5m 12.5f* 12f⁵ 14.8m⁵ 10.4m* 10g⁴ 13.3m 12.2d³] 5,000Y:
workmanlike filly: seventh living foal: half-sister to 3 winners in Belgium: dam ran
only at 2 yrs: fair handicapper: won at Wolverhampton (hanging left) in July and
Chester (apprentices) in September: rider lost irons in £20,000 event penultimate
start: ran well outings either side, on first of them (ridden by 7-lb claimer) beaten
short head but demoted for interference: effective at 1¼m and should stay 1¾m:
acts on top-of-the-ground and a soft surface: sold 16,000 gns Newmarket Autumn
Sales. *C. A. Cyzer.*

SPRING TO GLORY 2 b.c. (Apr 18) Teenoso (USA) 135–English Spring (USA) —
116 (Grey Dawn II 132) [1989 7g] first foal: dam, smart performer at about 1m, is
half-sister to winners in USA by Forli and Foolish Pleasure: always behind in
28-runner maiden at Newmarket in November. *I. A. Balding.*

SPRITSAIL 3 b.c. Kalaglow 132–Set Sail 64 (Alpenkonig (GER)) [1988 7g* **117**
1989 9s* 12f* 12d³ 12f* 12f* 12m⁴ 12m* 12v³]
Spritsail put up a smart performance in winning the listed Hewitson,
Becke & Shaw Godolphin Stakes at Newmarket in October, leading going into
the Dip and just being pushed along to beat Sesame in good style by two
lengths. Post-race media comment, however, centred on the absence of a
stewards inquiry into the supposed dramatic improvement Spritsail had
shown compared with his finishing last of four when odds on for the Group 3
Cumberland Lodge Stakes at Ascot a week earlier. We find it hard to believe
that Spritsail's running could raise serious questions. At Ascot, on his first
outing for two and a half months, he had quite a stiff task at the weights
against the older Tralos—the terms were 4 lb worse than weight for age—and
the two other three-year-olds, Husyan and Warrshan, weren't exactly
pushovers. Every chance in the race, he lost little caste in being beaten under
five lengths. Though Spritsail had run well on his only previous outing in
pattern company to finish under three lengths third behind Harvest Time and
Golden Pheasant in the Group 3 Prix du Lys at Chantilly in June—his
otherwise-unbeaten record had been gained in a slightly lower grade. Still
green when winning early-season minor events at Ripon and Lingfield,
Spritsail was successful in the summer in the Churchill Stakes at Ascot
(beating Derby-sixth Gran Alba by three lengths) and the Welsh Brewers
Premier Stakes at Chepstow. The last-named event, formerly the Welsh
Derby, disappointingly attracted only one older horse in a field of five under
its new conditions: Spritsail quickened clear under two furlongs out to win
easily by five lengths from Polar Run.

Hewitson, Becke & Shaw Godolphin Stakes, Newmarket—
Spritsail runs on strongly from Sesame

Spritsail's grandam is the distinguished, now deceased, broodmare Sayonara. Dam of the German Two Thousand Guineas winner Swazi, she was imported by Lord Howard de Walden in the late-'seventies and subsequently produced Slip Anchor and Lancashire Oaks winner Sandy Island. The last-named is starting to make her own mark at stud, her second foal Sardegna making a winning debut in a Newmarket maiden in November. Spritsail's dam Set Sail was a plating-class performer, sold for 1,600 guineas at Newmarket as a two-year-old. (Spritsail runs in the colours of Lady Howard de Walden having been bought back privately after a foal-share arrangement). Set Sail's first foal was Comedy Sail (by Comedy Star), a plating-class winner at up to seventeen furlongs. Set Sail's only other produce prior to private sale to New Zealand is the unraced two-year-old Emperor Fountain (by Chief Singer), a 100,000-guinea yearling in training with Toller. Set Sail's first foal to Southern Hemisphere time, a filly by Gold And Ivory, was bought for around £45,000 at the National Yearling Sale at Karaka and is to be trained by Mayfield-Smith in Sydney.

Spritsail (b.c. 1986)	Kalaglow (gr 1978)	Kalamoun (gr 1970)	Zeddaan Khairunissa
		Rossitor (ch 1970)	Pall Mall Sonia
	Set Sail (b 1979)	Alpenkonig (b 1967)	Tamerlane Alpenlerche
		Sayonara (b 1965)	Birkhahn Suleika

A tall, still rather leggy colt, with a quick action, Spritsail remains in training and may well improve enough to win a pattern race. He still looked less than the finished article at Newmarket. Though he was below his best when third behind Sesame in the St Simon Stakes at Newbury on his final start, the chances are that he was unsuited by the heavy going: he seems to act on any other. Invariably held up, Spritsail stays a mile and a half well. *H. R. A. Cecil.*

SPROUTING VENTURE 2 ch.f. (Mar 16) Crooner 119–Two Diamonds **59** (Double Jump 131) [1989 a7g a8g5] sparely-made filly: first foal: dam no sign of ability on flat or over hurdles: under 5 lengths fifth of 11 to Blake's Treasure, better effort in December maidens at Lingfield: slowly away on debut: ridden by 7-lb claimer. *R. Curtis.*

SPS CREATIVE 3 gr.f. Petong 126–Rosalina 71 (Porto Bello 118) [1988 5g6 5f5 **51** d 5.8g2 6g5 5s4 5f 1989 6s 6m 5m3 6f2 6f3 7m 6m 7f5 7m 7m] leggy, light-framed filly: moderate walker: poor maiden: ridden by 5-lb claimer, always-prominent second in handicap at Redcar in early-June, easily best effort: has run in sellers: stays 6f: best form on firm going: sold to join M. Barnes 750 gns Doncaster November Sales. *M. Brittain.*

SPURNED (USA) 2 b.f. (Feb 20) Robellino (USA) 127–Refill 88 (Mill Reef **91** (USA) 141) [1989 6g³ 7m* 7g⁵ 8g⁶] lengthy, rather angular filly: first known foal: dam, placed over 6f here later successful at up to 11f in USA, is half-sister to useful 1981 2-y-o sprinter Corley Moor: favourite, won 7-runner £5,600 event at Sandown in July by ¾ length from Fujaiyrah, quickening well to lead final furlong: fifth in EBF Silver Flash Stakes at Pheonix Park in September, better subsequent effort: should stay at least 1¼m. *I. A. Balding.*

SQUARE DATA DYNAMO 3 b.c. Swing Easy (USA) 126–Ringaround — (Martinmas 128) [1988 NR 1989 7g⁴ 8.2v 6g 6g 6m 8.2d] 1,700Y: tall, lengthy, sparely-made colt: half-brother to 1984 Irish 2-y-o 1m winer Lady Connaught (by Connaught) and a winner in Austria by Reliance II: dam unraced close relation of Horris Hill winner Fair Season: plating-class maiden: ran moderately after fourth outing: best form over 6f. *M. Brittain.*

SQUEAKY WHEEL (USA) 4 b.c. Riverman (USA) 131–Grease 125 (Filiberto **98** (USA) 123) [1988 7.5g* 8v² 10v⁴ 9v* 1989 10d² 9s*] leggy, useful-looking colt: first foal: dam very smart French winner from 5f (as 2-y-o) to 1¼m, later successful in USA: successful at Rome and Milan (4-runner event) in first half of 1988 and at Turin in November: carried head awkwardly under pressure when 5 lengths second to odds-on Lazaz in minor event at Pontefract in April when trained by C. Brittain: stays 1¼m: acts on heavy going. *F. Turner, Italy.*

SQUEEZE ME 3 b.f. Creetown 123–Queezy 86 (Lear Jet 123) [1988 6f 6m 5s⁶ — 1989 10g] tall filly: poor maiden: led over 6f when behind in September handicap, only start in 1989: should stay 1m: sold to join L. Wordingham 1,100 gns Newmarket Autumn Sales. *I. V. Matthews.*

SQUIDGELY (USA) 3 ch.f. London Bells (CAN) 109–Choctaw Goddess (Crow — (FR) 134) [1988 NR 1989 10f² 12m 7g] workmanlike filly: half-sister to 1987 Irish 2-y-o 6f winner Malihouna (by Recitation): dam unraced: comfortably beaten by long odds-on Jungle Rose in 3-runner minor event at Lingfield in July: tailed off in Salisbury maiden (still bit backward) and prominent 5f when in mid-division in similar event at Lingfield later in month. *R. J. Hodges.*

SQUILL (USA) 4 b.c. Stop The Music (USA)–River Rose (FR) 116 (Riverman **122** (USA) 131) [1988 7.5d* 8d* 8m* 10m⁴ 10m³ 9.7m* 10f³ 1989 8s⁶ 8d* 8g⁶ 8g² 8g⁴] French colt: successful in June in Premio Emilio Turati at Milan easily by 4½

Mme Arpad Plesch's "Squill"

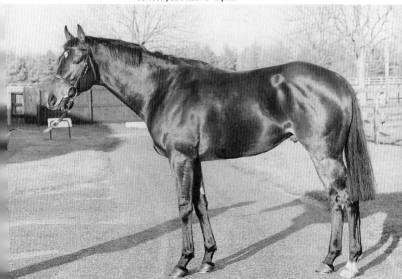

Classic Thoroughbreds Plc's "Stadler"

lengths: 16/1, put up good-class performance when 2 lengths second of 11 to Polish
Precedent in Prix du Moulin de Longchamp in September, running on from over 1f
out without having any chance with winner: below-form fourth of 10, nearest at
finish, to Just A Flutter in Premio Vittorio di Capua at Milan 6 weeks later: stayed
1¼m: possibly not at his best on soft going, acted on any other: scratched to post
third outing: retired to Aston Park Stud, Oxon, fee £5,000 (Oct 1st). *Mme C. Head,
France.*

SQUIRE JIM 5 b.g. Jimsun 121–Squiffy (Articulate 121) [1988 12g⁵ 1989 11.7g⁵] —
strong, good-bodied gelding: winning hurdler: little worthwhile form on flat, slowly
away. *R. G. Brazington.*

SQUIRSKY 3 b.c. Tina's Pet 121–Targos Delight (Targowice (USA) 130) [1988 —
5s⁴ 5g³ 6g³ 5d 5m 1989 6m 6f 6g] good-topped, workmanlike colt: carries condition:
plating-class form at best: showed nothing as 3-y-o: stays 6f: best efforts on an easy
surface: visored last 3 outings at 2 yrs: possibly ungenuine. *R. Hollinshead.*

STADLER 2 b.c. (Feb 1) Sadler's Wells (USA) 132–Santa Roseanna 111 (Caracol **86 p**
(FR)) [1989 8d*] 250,000F, IR 400,000Y: fourth foal: half-brother to 7f winner Mulia
and very useful 6f winner King's College (both by Golden Fleece): dam, from good
family, won from 7f to 9f in Ireland and stayed 1½m: 6/4 from 5/4 on, won 15-runner
maiden at Leopardstown in October by ½ length: will stay 1¼m: should go on to
better things. *M. V. O'Brien, Ireland.*

STAFF APPROVED 3 b.f. Teenoso (USA) 135–Klairlone 116 (Klairon 131) —
[1988 8g* 1989 12m³ 11v] leggy, lengthy, rather sparely-made filly: comfortable
winner of maiden at Leicester at 2 yrs: well beaten in 3-runner £7,300 event at
Kempton and £8,800 handicap (tailed off) at Newbury in autumn as 3-y-o: should
stay middle distances: sold 9,000 gns Newmarket December Sales. *M. R. Stoute.*

STAFFORD LAD 3 b.c. Tachypous 128–Frizzante 73 (Varano) [1988 5m 5m⁴ 7f —
1989 8.2g] workmanlike colt: poor mover: poor form at best in varied company: sold
to join P. Rodford 1,450 gns Ascot August Sales. *T. Fairhurst.*

STAGECRAFT 2 b.c. (Mar 16) Sadler's Wells (USA) 132–Bella Colora 119   87 p
(Bellypha 130) [1989 7d²] 520,000Y: first foal: dam, third in 1000 Guineas and
winner at 6f to 1¼m, is half-sister to Irish Oaks winner Colorspin (by High Top) and
very useful Rappa Tap Tap (by Tap On Wood): odds on, beaten a head by Bold
Performer in 11-runner minor event at Thirsk in November, keeping on well: will be
suited by 1m + : sure to improve. *M. R. Stoute.*

STAGE PLAYER 3 b.g. Ile de Bourbon (USA) 133–Popkins 120 (Romulus 129)   87
[1988 6m³ 8d* 1989 10s 10.6s 12f⁶ 9f³ 10m* 10g* 10m⁴ 10g 10g] workmanlike,
deep-girthed gelding: fair handicapper: ridden by 5-lb claimer, showed improved
form when winning at Ripon in August and Yarmouth (4-runner £9,200 contest) in
September: ran moderately in quite valuable events after: stays 1¼m: ·acts on
top-of-the-ground and a soft surface: winning novice hurdler. *I. V. Matthews.*

STAGE QUEEN 3 br.f. Dawn Johnny (USA) 90–Queen of The Kop 60 (Queen's   36
Hussar 124) [1988 5m 6m 5g⁶ 1989 10f³ 9f] smallish, workmanlike filly: poor plater:
suited by 1¼m: tends to wander, and swerved stalls once at 2 yrs. *F. Jordan.*

STAGE VILLAIN 4 b.c. Mummy's Pet 125–Toccata (USA) 64 (Mr Leader   — §
(USA)) [1988 8m* 7g⁵ 8.5m 7g³ 8g 1989 8f] stocky colt: poor mover: fair winner at
3-y-o when trained by B. Hills: behind in Sandown apprentice handicap in May:
stays 1m: acts on top-of-the-ground: looks ungenerous. *Mrs N. Macauley.*

STAGS LANE 4 b.g. Magnolia Lad 102–Larullah (Lorenzaccio 130) [1988 NR   —
1989 12m] rather leggy gelding: third reported live foal: half-brother to a bad animal
by Streetfighter: dam ran twice: 100/1, slowly away and tailed off in minor event at
Leicester in June. *P. Hayward.*

STAND AT EASE 4 b.g. The Brianstan 128–Plush 75 (Lombard (GER)) [1988   64
8.2v³ 8m⁵ 8.5m 8.5f 8v³ 8g 10g 1989 8.5d 8.5d2] quite modest maiden: 16/1, neck
second of 16 in apprentice handicap at Beverley in May: doesn't stay 1¼m: acts well
in the mud: sold privately to join P. Liddle 4,000 gns Doncaster May Sales. *Mrs J. R.
Ramsden.*

STANDING COUNT 3 ch.g. Stanford 121§–Barefoot Contessa (Homeric 133)   71
[1988 6f 6g 7m⁶ 8m 7m³ 6s* 1989 7s² 8g³ 7f² 8f⁶ 8g² 8.2g³ 8.2g 10.2g] leggy,
angular gelding: good mover: modest handicapper: ran well when placed as 3-y-o:
effective at 7f and 1m: acts on any going: bolted to post and withdrawn intended
fourth start: taken very quietly down after: has run creditably for apprentice. *Mrs J.
R. Ramsden.*

STANDING ROOM ONLY 2 b.g. (Mar 2) Stalwart (USA)–Mary Mary Mouse   64
(USA) (Valdez (USA)) [1989 7m⁴ 6m 7g 6f⁴] 9,400Y: lengthy gelding: has scope: has
a quick action: first foal: dam unraced half-sister to dam of Contract Law and from
family of Law Society and Legal Bid: blinkered, fourth in selling nursery at Lingfield
in October, easily best effort: should stay 7f: sold 1,200 gns Ascot October Sales:
subsequently gelded. *H. Candy.*

STANFORD BOY 4 b.g. Stanford 121§–Gothic Lady (Godswalk (USA) 130)   —
[1988 8v 7d 7.5m 8m 8.2m⁵ 8f 7m 8f⁴ 8g 8m⁵ 8g 1989 8.2v] lengthy, angular gelding:
moderate mover: inconsistent plater: stays 1m: acts on firm going: sometimes
blinkered or visored: sold 1,550 gns Ascot May Sales: best treated with caution. *J.
Parkes.*

STANFORD'S JOY 3 b.f. Stanford 121§–Ottoline 59 (Brigadier Gerard 144)   —
[1988 NR 1989 7.5d 7g 7.5d] IR 6,000Y: sister to 1984 2-y-o 5f and 7f winner
Standing Order and half-sister to 3 winners: dam stayed 1½m: no sign of ability in
sellers: blinkered final start. *M. F. D. Morley.*

STANHOPE 4 ch.f. Music Boy 124–Omnia 80 (Hill Clown (USA)) [1988 10f³ 7d*   —
9g⁶ 7g⁶ 7s⁶ 1989 10m 10g 7f 8.5m 8.2d] tall, leggy filly: modest winner as 3-y-o:
below form subsequently: hampered in selling handicap (gambled on) fourth outing:
hung left final one: unlikely to stay 1¼m: acts on soft surface: sweating on
reappearance: sold 4,000 gns Newmarket December Sales. *J. A. Glover.*

ST ANLO 7 b.m. Sir Nulli 87–Bridport 69 (Porto Bello 118) [1988 NR 1989 15.5f]   —
workmanlike mare: well beaten in varied company. *W. G. Morris.*

STANSTED FLYER 3 b.g. Rabdan 129–Maputo Princess (Raga Navarro (ITY)   —
119) [1988 5s² 6g⁵ 5m 6m 7.5g 7g⁵ 6g 1989 7.5d⁴ 8.2g² 7m 8g 9s 12g] small,
sparely-made gelding: poor mover with a quick action: plater: should be suited by
further than 7.5f: suited by a soft surface: blinkered last 2 starts and 4 times at 2 yrs:
trained until after third outing by K. Stone. *J. F. Bottomley.*

STANWAY 2 b.g. (Apr 1) Sandhurst Prince 128–Spring Bride 57 (Auction Ring   66
(USA) 123) [1989 6m 7m³ 7m² 7h⁵ 7m⁴] IR 13,500F, IR 36,000Y: strong,

good-topped gelding: has plenty of scope: half-brother to useful 3-y-o sprinter Hafir (by Tender King) and 1986 2-y-o 7f winner Lightning Laser (by Monseigneur): dam, raced only at 2 yrs, is sister to very useful 1979 2-y-o Highest Bidder and half-sister to good American horse Peregrinator and smart sprinter Royal Ride: quite modest maiden: will probably stay 1m: acts on hard going: slowly away when blinkered fourth start. *R. Hannon.*

STANWELL (CAN) 3 ch.c. The Minstrel (CAN) 135–Star Game (USA) (Pia **81** Star) [1988 8g 8s* 1989 8s 8m⁶ 8f 10m² 10m⁴ 10f⁴] strong, good sort: has a powerful, rather round action: fair handicapper: good second in £6,000 event at Newmarket, leading 2f out until close home: ran moderately at Kempton (last, visored) and Salisbury (took keen hold to post, drifted right under pressure) later in summer: stays 1¼m: acts on soft going and top-of-the-ground: has run creditably for apprentice: sold to race in Saudi Arabia 42,000 gns Newmarket Autumn Sales. *J. Tree.*

STAPEHILL 3 b.c. Bon Sang (FR) 126–Native Bride 101 (Native Prince) [1988 — 5g⁶ 5m 6f 7g 7f 1989 7g 12.5f 16f] leggy colt: moderate walker and mover: well beaten in sellers: reportedly cracked pelvis after second run at 2 yrs: dead. *S. J. Muldoon.*

STAR BLAZE 2 b.f. (Mar 5) Alzao (USA) 117–Space Mark (On Your Mark 125) **62** [1989 6m 5m⁴ 5g⁶] small filly: first foal: dam winner at 7f at 4 yrs in Ireland: quite modest maiden: should stay 6f: sent to M. Bolton. *S. G. Norton.*

STARCH EXPRESS 3 b.g. Starch Reduced 112–Roxemma (Broxted 120) [1988 **54** 6g 6m³ 7d 1989 6g³ 6s⁵ 5s⁶] angular, deep-bodied gelding: plating-class maiden: ran well early on as 3-y-o, including in handicaps: will be suited by return to 6f and should stay 7f: acts on soft going: slowly away final start. *R. Curtis.*

STAR CHILD (USA) 2 b.f. (Jan 20) Our Native (USA)–Ice Princess (USA) **68** (Icecapade (USA)) [1989 6m⁴ 7m* 7m 6g 7g] $35,000Y: smallish, workmanlike filly: good walker: second named foal: half-sister to a winner in USA: dam Grade 1 stakes-placed winner at up to 9f: made all in 10-runner maiden at Wolverhampton in July: ran well in nursery next start, then poorly: better suited by 7f than by 6f: visored final outing. *J. Gosden.*

STARCHY BELLE 2 b.f. (Mar 18) Starch Reduced 112–Ty-With-Belle (Pamroy **47** 99) [1989 5f* 6m 7f] dipped-backed, unfurnished filly: second foal: half-sister to 3-y-o plater Bellhopper (by Sacrilege): dam modest maiden at 2 yrs later placed over hurdles: 33/1, won 6-runner seller (retained 4,400 gns) at Wolverhampton in May by head, easily best effort: off course for 4 months after second outing: should stay beyond 5f. *B. Palling.*

STARCHY COVE 2 br.f. (Mar 3) Starch Reduced 112–Rosey Covert (Sahib 114) **61** [1989 5g⁶ 5d⁶ 5f² 5m⁵ 5g⁵ 5f⁵ 5f³ 6m³ 5f* 6g a5g⁴ a6g⁶ a5g²] leggy filly: third reported foal: sister to poor 3-y-o Star Cover: dam won over hurdles: quite modest performer: won nursery at Wolverhampton: ran creditably in late-year nurseries at Southwell on eleventh and final starts: better suited by 5f than 6f: has sweated up: has run creditably for 7-lb claimer. *R. Hollinshead.*

STAR COVER 3 b.f. Starch Reduced 112–Rosey Covert (Sahib 114) [1988 5d⁶ **37** 5g² 5f⁴ 6s 5d 6g 5d 1989 8.2s 6s 5m 6g⁶ 7m³ 6f 7m 7m 5f 5f⁵ 7g 5f] lengthy, workmanlike filly: good walker: poor maiden: stays 7f: acts on top-of-the-ground and a soft surface: blinkered last 3 outings: got loose in paddock and slowly away final one: bandaged fourth to sixth: usually ridden by 7-lb claimer. *S. R. Bowring.*

STAR EXHIBIT 2 ch.c. (Apr 9) Exhibitioner 111–Star Bound (Crowned Prince — (USA) 128) [1989 a8g] IR 4,000Y: workmanlike colt: fifth foal: half-brother to 3-y-o Starwar (by Trojan Fen) and Irish 4-y-o Martian Princess (by Cure The Blues): dam Irish 7f to 9f winner: bit backward and green, always behind in late-year maiden at Southwell. *R. Hollinshead.*

STAR HILL 2 b.c. (Apr 23) Star Appeal 133–Pook's Hill (High Top 131) [1989 5f² **97** 6f* 6m² 6h* 6f* 6g* 6g⁶ 7.3d⁴] workmanlike colt: shows a quick action: second foal: half-brother to 3-y-o New Start (by Absalom): dam unraced daughter of very smart 1972 2-y-o Silver Birch: successful in maiden at Goodwood in June, nurseries at Lingfield and Goodwood in July and BonusPrint Sirenia Stakes (comfortably by 1½ lengths from Daawi) at Kempton in September: fair fourth of 8, keeping on, to Tirol in Vodafone Horris Hill Stakes at Newbury in October: bred to stay 1m: acts on hard going and a soft surface: tends to wander: genuine. *W. G. R. Wightman.*

STARK REALITY (USA) 5 b. or br.g. Graustark–Laser Belle (Laser Light — 118) [1988 12d 12g⁵ 12m 10f⁵ 1989 10.2g 10v 12s 11.5f] lengthy, medium-sized gelding: maiden race winner in Ireland as 3-y-o: soundly beaten in handicaps and minor event in first half of 1989: raced too freely for amateur on reappearance: probably better suited by 1¼m than 1½m: acts on firm going: visored 3 times, blinkered twice: sold 1,000 gns Ascot July Sales: resold 775 gns Ascot October Sales. *P. Howling.*

STAR LEADER   2 b.f. (Apr 9) Kafu 120–Sweet Relief 90 (Sweet Revenge 129)   53
[1989 5f 5m6 5m4 5m4 6d a6g] 880F: tall, short-backed filly: moderate mover: half-sister to 1983 2-y-o 7f winner Forge Close (by Swing Easy) and a winner in Italy: dam won three 6f races: plating-class maiden: best efforts (at Wolverhampton) on third and fourth starts: tailed off in Southwell nursery on final outing: better suited by 5f than 6f. *R. Hollinshead.*

STARLET   3 b.f. Teenoso (USA) 135–Pas de Deux 80 (Nijinsky (CAN) 138) [1988   —
8g* 7m* 1989 11v 12d6] sparely-made filly: fairly useful winner at 2 yrs: ridden by 5-lb claimer, 13 lengths sixth of 19 to Firelight Fiesta in November Handicap at Thirsk, better effort in autumn as 3-y-o: probably stays 1½m. *W. Hastings-Bass.*

STAR LIFT   5 ch.h. Mill Reef (USA) 141–Seneca (FR) (Chaparral (FR) 128)   127
[1988 10.5v* 12d2 12.5d2 13.5g5 10.5d* 15.5s* 1989 10s* 10.5s2 12d* 12g4 12d* 12g 12f3 12f]
Star Lift showed himself to be better than ever as a five-year-old but it wasn't plain sailing for him all the way. First there was his misfortune in the Grand Prix de Saint-Cloud in July when interference almost certainly denied him another Group 1 victory to add to that in the Prix Royal-Oak as a four-year-old. The Grand Prix was run at a sedate pace until Mill Pond quickened entering the straight. About two furlongs out Mill Pond began to drift away from the rail and Star Lift was aimed at the gap, apparently still full of running. As Mill Pond's rider attempted to correct his mount, however, he cut back towards the rail, causing Star Lift to be snatched up and forfeit all chance. Star Lift eventually finished only about two lengths behind Sheriff's Star and was subsequently promoted from fifth to fourth on Mill Pond's disqualification. Then there was Star Lift's accident in the Ciga Prix de l'Arc de Triomphe: he was struck into, and after holding a forward position starting the home turn he dropped out to last. Of those involved in the finish, Star Lift had already beaten Saint Andrews and Robore, third and sixth respectively— and subsequently beat the runner-up Behera when third to Prized in the

*Prix Foy, Longchamp—Star Lift beats Robore
in this traditional Prix de l'Arc trial*

M D. Wildenstein's "Star Lift"

Breeders' Cup Turf at Gulfstream Park in November, which suggests he might have been involved in the battle for the places with normal luck in running. In more propitious circumstances Star Lift managed three victories. On his reappearance in April he took the Prix d'Harcourt at Longchamp by two and a half lengths from Saint Andrews (who narrowly reversed the placings in the Prix Ganay later in the month). Star Lift's other wins were both at the chief expense of Robore: he gave him 6 lb and a length-and-a-half beating in the Grand Prix d'Evry in June, and 2 lb and a three-quarter-length beating in the Prix Foy at Longchamp in September, the latter a race in which the English challenger Apache was ten lengths behind in third. After the Breeders' Cup Star Lift joined D. Wayne Lukas and finished ninth of ten to Frankly Perfect in the Grade 1 Hollywood Turf Cup on his first outing for his new stable.

Star Lift (ch.h. 1984)	Mill Reef (USA) (b 1968)	Never Bend (b 1960)	Nasrullah
			Lalun
		Milan Mill (b 1962)	Princequillo
			Virginia Water
	Seneca (FR) (b 1973)	Chaparral (b 1966)	Val de Loir
			Niccolina
		Schonbrunn (b 1966)	Pantheon
			Scheherezade

By an Arc winner, Mill Reef, and half-brother to another Arc winner, Sagace (by Luthier), Star Lift could hardly have been better bred for that race. He's also a brother to Mecca-Dante winner Simply Great out of Seneca, who won at twelve and a half furlongs on her only start. Full details of Star Lift's pedigree can be found in *Racehorses of 1988*. A leggy, rather sparely-made horse, Star Lift is effective at a mile and a quarter when conditions are testing and stays fifteen and a half furlongs. In Europe he seemed suited by an easy surface, but he ran very well on firm at Gulfstream Park. *A. Fabre, France.*

STARLIGHT WONDER 3 ch.f. Star Appeal 133–My Lady Muriel (USA) 40
(Visible (USA)) [1988 6m 7m 1989 7g 7m 7g 7m 7m 6g4] smallish, unfurnished filly: 33/1 and well drawn, first worthwhile form when staying-on fourth in claimer at Nottingham in October: should stay 7f: sold 1,050 gns Newmarket Autumn Sales. *E. Eldin.*

STAR LORD 3 b.c. Lord Gayle (USA) 124–Crack of Light 95 (Salvo 129) [1988 98 p
NR 1989 11.7m2 12m2 14m* 11v2] IR 18,000F, 36,000Y: angular, sparely-made colt: good mover with a long stride: half-brother to useful 11f and 1½m winner Debach Delight (by Great Nephew) and to a winner each in France and Italy: dam, middle-distance stayer, won 8 times from 14 starts: won moderately-run 4-runner minor event at York: beaten short head in £8,800 handicap at Newbury later in October, leading 3f out until post: probably stays 1¾m: acts on top-of-the-ground and heavy: takes keen hold: may well improve further as 4-y-o. *A. C. Stewart.*

STAR MAESTRO 7 br.g. Music Maestro 119–Maryland Star 76 (I Say 125) [1988 —
8g 10d4 9m 12f6 8g* 10m6 8s6 8g2 8d 1989 8d 8.2f 7m 10.8m 12m 8m] sparely-made gelding: poor mover: poor plater: best at short of 1½m: suited by give in the ground nowadays: often wears severe bridle. *J. Pearce.*

STAR MOON 3 b.c. Tyrnavos 129–Lady of The Manor 78 (Astec 128) [1988 NR —
1989 8.5d 10f 10g 12f] 700Y: long, dipped-backed colt: has a round action: second reported foal: half-brother to Tirso (by Niniski), winner 3 times at around 1½m in Belgium in 1988: dam, half-sister to very smart stayer Ragstone, placed at 1¼m: no sign of ability in maidens and claimer: needs to settle. *N. Bycroft.*

STAR OF A GUNNER 9 ch.g. Gunner B 126–Starkist 81 (So Blessed 130) 68
[1988 8d6 8s3 8d 7.6v 8s 1989 8g 8d 10.8d3 10f6 8f 10f6] strong gelding: usually dull in coat: modest handicapper nowadays: worthwhile form as 9-y-o only on third outing: best form at 1m: revels in the mud: has been taken down steadily: bandaged off-hind final appearance at 8 yrs. *R. J. Holder.*

STAR OF FASHION 2 b.f. (Apr 9) Comedy Star (USA) 121–Fashion Lover 70 45
(Shiny Tenth 120) [1989 5f 5g] 3,800Y: close-coupled, good-topped filly: second foal: sister to a winner in Malaya: dam 1m seller winner: poor form in claimer at Redcar in May and maiden at Hamilton in October: sold 1,750 gns Doncaster October Sales. *J. Berry.*

STAR OF IRELAND 9 b.g. Star Appeal 133–Belligerent 74 (Roan Rocket 128) 67
[1988 12v 12d4 10s 11.7f 10.8s* 12g 10d 8g 1989 10.8s* 12s 10s 10.8d5] good-topped, quite attractive gelding: poor walker: a grand old servant who won early in season at Warwick for the third time in March: below his best later in spring: stays 1½m: needs a soft surface: blinkered twice: often wears bandages: well suited by strong handling: has joined W. Sheedy. *G. Price.*

STAR OF THE FUTURE (USA) 2 b.f. (Feb 27) El Gran Senor (USA) 136– 79
Promising Girl (USA) (Youth (USA) 135) [1989 7f* 7.3v4] IR 275,000Y: smallish, angular filly: moderate mover: first foal: dam stakes-placed winner at up to around 1m in USA and half-sister to very smart 6f to 1¼m performer Beau's Eagle: 11/2 from 3/1, won 8-runner maiden at Leicester in October by 1½ lengths: modest fourth of 12 to Berry's Dream in listed race at Newbury later in month: should stay at least 1¼m. *B. W. Hills.*

STAR OF THE GLEN 3 b.c. Glenstal (USA) 118–Bamstar 70 (Relko 136) [1988 —
7g6 7g6 8m 1989 8f 11m 13.3g] angular, lengthy colt: little worthwhile form: should stay at least 1m: winning hurdler. *C. A. Horgan.*

STAR OF THE SEA 2 gr.f. (May 21) Absalom 128–River Chimes 43 (Forlorn 43
River 124) [1989 5g 5m4 6m 5s] small, lengthy filly: has a round action: sixth foal: sister to speedy 1984 2-y-o Absent Chimes and quite modest 1987 2-y-o Rapid Chimes: dam sister to high-class Rapid River: poor maiden: best effort second start: sent to N. Chamberlain. *W. A. Stephenson.*

STAR PLAYER 3 ch.c. Simply Great (FR) 122–Star Girl (Sovereign Gleam 117) 72
[1988 NR 1989 14m2] IR 30,000F, 46,000Y: closely related to poor 1m winner Star Reef (by Main Reef) and half-brother to several winners, including fairly useful Irish 1m winner Star Spartan and Irish and German middle-distance winner Star Spark (both by Sparkler): dam once-raced half-sister to Star Appeal: 4/1 from evens, beaten 8 lengths by Hateel in 5-runner maiden at York in June, leading 4f out until

2½f out, hanging and carrying head awkwardly: sold to join J. Baker 9,000 gns Newmarket Autumn Sales. *G. Harwood.*

STARRLYN 3 ch.f. Star Appeal 133–Petingalyn (Petingo 135) [1988 7g 8.2m 7s **51** 1989 8.5s 10.2m⁵ 10f⁴ 12m⁵ 10m³ 9g 10g⁵] tall, rather leggy filly: plating-class maiden: best form over 1¼m, but worth another try over 1m: acts on firm going: ran creditably when edgy and pulling hard second outing. *S. Dow.*

STAR SHAREEF 3 b.c. Shareef Dancer (USA) 135–Anne Stuart (FR) (Bolkon- **105** ski 134) [1988 7g³ 8m* 8s² 1989 12f⁵ 12m³] well-made colt: useful performer: 3¼ lengths third to Prorutori in Derby Italiano at Rome in May: carrying plenty of condition, appeared completely unsuited by track when fifth of 6 in minor event (showed a sharp action) at Lingfield: stays 1½m: acts on top-of-the-ground and soft going. *J. L. Dunlop.*

STAR STORM (USA) 3 br.c. Storm Bird (CAN) 134–Affenpinscher (USA) — (Affirmed (USA)) [1988 NR 1989 10f⁵] 420,000 francs (approx £40,000) 2-y-o: angular, useful-looking colt: first foal: dam unraced daughter of sister to Gyr and Berkut, latter dam of Alydar's Best: never placed to challenge or knocked about when last of 5 in maiden at Nottingham in July: moved poorly when taken very steadily to post. *N. A. Callaghan.*

STARSTREAK 2 b.c. (Mar 14) Comedy Star (USA) 121–Kochia 54 (Firestreak **89** 125) [1989 6m⁶ 6g² 6m* 6m 7g*] rangy colt: has scope: easy mover: third foal: dam 1m seller winner: made all in maiden at Pontefract in July and 17-runner minor event at Leicester in November: better suited by 7f than 6f, and will stay 1m. *M. Johnston.*

STAR TRACKER 2 br.f. (May 24) Lochnager 132–Star Attention 91 — (Northfields (USA)) [1989 6g 6g] fourth living foal: dam best at sprint distances: well beaten in late-season maidens at Newcastle and Redcar. *W. A. Stephenson.*

STATE BANK 3 b.g. Kampala 120–Lily Bank 73 (Young Generation 129) [1988 **64** 8d 7s⁶ 8m 1989 9g 10g 12m⁶ 10m 12g² 11s 12g⁴] rather leggy gelding: quite modest maiden: ran fairly well in seller final start: stays 1½m: best form on an easy surface: blinkered second start: visored third. *M. J. Ryan.*

STATE JESTER 6 b.g. Free State 125–Mirthful 73 (Will Somers 114§) [1988 — 14.7d 15d 1989 12.3f⁵] medium-sized gelding: plating-class handicapper in first half of 1987: favourite, wearing crossed noseband and taken steadily to post, last of 5, taking keen hold, at Chester in May: stays 1½m: acts well on top-of-the-ground: effective with or without blinkers: vastly improved hurdler in 1988/9. *C. W. C. Elsey.*

STATEN ISLAND 4 b.c. Town And Country 124–Regal Wonder 74 (Stupen- **96** dous) [1988 10m* 12d* 10m* 12f* 12f* 16f 11.7g³ 12f⁴ 12d 10m³ 1989 12d⁶ 12m* 12f³ 12f³ 12f* 12m² 12m* 12f² 12h⁴] big, close-coupled colt: carries plenty of condition: fairly useful handicapper: better than ever as 4-y-o, making all at Brighton (twice) and Lingfield: suited by 1½m: yet to race on soft going and well suited by top-of-the-ground: excellent mount for apprentice: suited by forcing tactics and goes particularly well left-handed: splendidly tough, game and genuine: sold to race in Saudi Arabia 41,000 gns Newmarket Autumn Sales. *N. A. Callaghan.*

STATE OF AFFAIRS 2 b.c. (May 14) Free State 125–Trigamy 112 (Tribal Chief **72** 125) [1989 6g³ 6f⁴ 8d] 27,000Y: medium-sized, sturdy colt: brother to 7f to 1¼m winner New Mexico and half-brother to 5 other winners, including 7f winner Mango Manilla (by Martinmas): dam 5f performer: 3 lengths third of 12 to Champagne Gold in minor event at Epsom in June, easily best effort: off course for almost 5 months after next outing. *R. Hollinshead.*

STATOBLEST 3 b.c. Ahonoora 122–Statira 103 (Skymaster 125) [1988 6f² **120** 6m⁶ 1989 6g* 6m³ 6m² 5m* 5f² 5f* 5m³ 5g* 5g]

Good three-year-old sprinters were few and far between in 1989, and the pick of them, Danehill and Golden Opinion, the latter tried at short of a mile only once, were both retired due to injury late in the season. Of those who remain in training Statoblest was about the best. Statoblest came up through maiden, minor and handicap races, showing improved form when put back to five furlongs, having begun by winning over six at Newmarket in April. Indeed, he proved speedy enough to win on two of the sharpest courses in the country, in a handicap at Epsom in June and the King George Stakes at Goodwood the following month, in the latter getting the better of Princess Athena, Carol's Treasure and Silver Fling in a tight finish. After this Statoblest continued to run well to the end of the season. He reached new heights next time out when sent to York to contest the William Hill Sprint

*King George Stakes, Goodwood—a competitive race goes to Statoblest (No. 11)
from Princess Athena (check cap)*

Championship, surprisingly his trainer's first runner in a Group 1 sprint since
1981. Statoblest, who started 9/1, was held up but came through strongly in the
second half of the race until unable to match Cadeaux Genereux's acceleration
approaching the final furlong, and was also run out of second close home by
Silver Fling. Tigani, about the equal of Statoblest among the three-year-olds,
was a head behind in fourth. On this, Statoblest had a favourite's chance in the
listed Doncaster Bloodstock Sales Scarbrough Stakes in September and took
it by two lengths from Green's Canaletto. Back in the top grade he came
seventh of sixteen to Silver Fling when favourite in the Ciga Prix de l'Abbaye
de Longchamp, looking likely to take a hand in the finish a furlong out and
beaten only around two lengths in the end. Statoblest flashed his tail under
pressure in these last two events, as he'd also done on his third start when
also wandering. He's genuine enough, though.

Mr Richard L. Duchossois' "Statoblest"

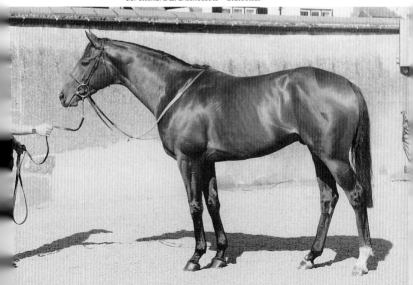

Statoblest (b.c. 1986)	Ahonoora (ch 1975)	Lorenzaccio (ch 1965)	Klairon
			Phoenissa
		Helen Nichols (ch 1966)	Martial
			Quaker Girl
	Statira (b 1969)	Skymaster (ch 1958)	Golden Cloud
			Discipliner
		Parysatis (b 1960)	Darius
			Leidenschaft

Statoblest's sire and dam both died in 1989. Ahonoora's career is detailed in the essays on Indian Ridge and Negligent. Statira produced only eight foals in sixteen years at stud, though five of the seven to race so far are winners. Apart from Statoblest they include Ludova (by Right Tack), a winner at six furlongs in France at two years and subsequently a stakes-placed winner in America, and the German four-year-old Stockrose (by Horage), a winner from six furlongs to a mile. Statira's final foal, a yearling by King of Clubs, was sold for IR21,000 guineas at the latest Irish National Yearling Sale. In her racing days Statira was a useful two-year-old sprinter who failed to train on; she's a half-sister to the smart northern sprinters Artaxerxes and Most Secret—the latter the sire of Soba. The grandam Parysatis was unraced, but her dam Leidenschaft was a top-class winner in Germany. Statoblest is a strong-quartered, useful-looking colt who acts well on firm going; he's yet to race on a soft surface. Five furlongs is his best distance. *L. M. Cumani.*

STAUNCH RIVAL (USA) 2 b.c. (Jan 31) Sir Ivor 135–Crystal Bright 75 (Bold Lad (IRE) 133) [1989 8.2g⁶ 8g³] IR 50,000Y: leggy, close-coupled colt: fourth foal: dam, placed at 5f at 2 yrs, later winner at about 1m in USA: 4/1 but looking weak, under 3 lengths third to Bawbee in 16-runner maiden at Leicester in November: will probably stay 1¼m: likely to improve further. *J. Gosden.*   **76 p**

STAY AWAKE 3 ch.g. Anfield 117–Djimbaran Bay (Le Levanstell 122) [1988 5g* 5m* 5g 7d 6g 1989 6d 6m 7f⁵ 6m⁵ 8g 7f³] rangy gelding: quite modest handicapper: ran creditably most starts in first half of 3-y-o season: stays 7f (didn't get clear run over 1m): acts on top-of-the-ground and a soft surface: appeared bit temperamental last 3 starts at 2 yrs: consistent: winning novice hurdler for J. J. O'Neill. *H. P. Rohan.*   **59**

ST CADOC 4 ch.g. Caerleon (USA) 132–Melody (USA) 96 (Lord Gayle (USA) 124) [1988 8.5s² 8g 12d² 10.1d³ 11.7m² 1989 8g⁶ 11m³ 12d⁴ 13s 17.6f² 13.8d a14g] sturdy, good-quartered gelding: one-time useful performer, only fair at best nowadays: soundly beaten in handicaps last 2 outings: seems to stay 17.6f: best form on an easy surface: looked difficult ride final start at 3 yrs: somewhat disappointing. *J. W. Hills.*   **79**

STEADY LOVE 4 br.f. Swing Easy (USA) 126–Lucky Love 65 (Mummy's Pet 125) [1988 6m 7d 6d⁵ 1989 7f 6m 6m 7d] smallish, sparely-made filly: poor maiden: saddle slipped and pulled up final outing. *P. Hayward.*   **—**

STEALTHY 2 ch.f. (Apr 13) Kind of Hush 118–Misty Cat (USA) (Misty Flight) [1989 6f² 6f 6d] rangy filly: has scope: half-sister to 2 minor winners here and in Norway: dam, half-sister to high-class sprinter Caerphilly, won 1m claimer in USA: modest maiden: easily best effort on debut: off course over 2½ months after next outing: should stay 1m. *I. A. Balding.*   **73**

STEAMING 2 b.f. (Mar 29) Lord Gayle (USA) 124–Scalded (Hotfoot 126) [1989 5g⁶ 6g] IR 12,000F, IR 4,300F: sparely-made filly: first foal: dam unraced half-sister to good Italian sprinter Swing Fire: apparently of little account. *M. Bell.*   **—**

STEEL CYGNET 6 gr.g. Taufan (USA) 119–Swan Girl (My Swanee 122) [1988 10g⁵ 12g⁶ 12d 10d⁶ 1989 10d² 10s⁶ 10f⁶ 10.2h* 10g] small, light-framed gelding: plating-class handicapper nowadays: 9/1 from 20/1, won 17-runner selling event at Bath (bandaged, bought in 4,700 gns) in June easily by 6 lengths: below form in apprentice race nearly 4 months later: effective at 1¼m and 1½m: probably acts on any going: blinkered 3 times, including first 2 starts: visored next 2: sometimes apprentice ridden. *G. P. Enright.*   **51**

STEEL RIVER 2 b.c. (Mar 29) Be My Native (USA) 122–Oystons Propweekly 74 (Swing Easy (USA) 126) [1989 6f 6g] second reported foal: half-brother to 1987 Irish 2-y-o 6f winner Glowing Tribute (by Taufan): dam, 2-y-o 5f winner, is grand-daughter of very useful Paresseuse: plating-class form in October maidens at Redcar (slowly away) and Newcastle. *A. M. Robson.*   **53**

STEEL SPARK 3 br.c. Persepolis (FR) 127–Riverlily (FR) (Green Dancer (USA) 132) [1988 NR 1989 8g⁴ 10g³ 11f² 10.5m⁵ 10.2g 10.2g a10g*] 35,000Y: **90**

lengthy, dipped-backed colt: good walker and mover: third foal: half-brother to 1986 2-y-o 7f winner Lord Westgate (by Hello Gorgeous) and a winner over jumps in France: dam, placed over middle distances in France, is half-sister to high-class French 1972 2-y-o Robertino: favourite, won maiden at Lingfield in October: other form only when in frame in competitive events at Newmarket and maiden (wandering under pressure) at Newbury: will stay 1½m: acts on firm going: blinkered last 3 starts: sold 20,000 gns Newmarket Autumn Sales: possibly unsatisfactory. *P. T. Walwyn.*

STEFFI 3 ch.f. Precocious 126–Western Gem 86 (Sheshoon 132) [1988 6m⁶ 7m 8s⁶ 1989 8m 9m 8g* 8g 10m² 11.5m⁴ 10m⁴ 9m² 8g⁶ 9g] sturdy filly: modest handicapper: won at Doncaster in July: good second in claimer at Newmarket in October, best later effort: should prove best at up to 1¼m: acts on top-of-the-ground and soft going: blinkered last 3 outings: sold 6,200 gns Newmarket December Sales. *G. A. Pritchard-Gordon.* **67**

STELBY 5 ch.h. Stetchworth (USA) 120–Little Trilby 107 (Tyrant (USA)) [1988 6g 7g 5f 6g* 6m* 7.5m 6s 7f⁶ 6g⁵ 6d 7m 1989 7m⁶ 6m⁶ 7f³ 6m² 6g³ 6m⁵ 6m⁴ 7g² 8f⁶ 7f⁵ 8g] small, quite well-made horse: good mover: quite modest handicapper: best at 6f or 7f: best on a sound surface: wears dropped noseband: has hung and usually gets behind. *O. Brennan.* **66**

STELLA BIANCA (USA) 2 b.f. (Apr 22) Vaguely Noble 140–Cahard (USA) (Lyphard (USA) 132) [1989 6m² 7m⁴ 7m³] $50,000Y: leggy filly: first foal: dam unraced: quite modest form in varied company: will be better suited by 1m +. *C. E. Brittain.* **69**

STELLAJOE 3 b.f. Le Dauphin 73–Right Shady (Right Tack 131) [1988 6m 6m⁵ 6d⁵ 1989 10m] neat filly: poor form at best: hampered early and not knocked about in seller in April, only start as 3-y-o: should stay beyond 6f: difficult at stalls and withdrawn once at 2 yrs. *A. R. Davison.* **—**

ST ELMO'S FIRE 4 b.c. Electric 126–Sealady (Seaepic (USA) 100) [1988 8d* 9g² 8f 8g⁴ 7g² 8d⁵ 10g⁴ 10m⁶ 8g* 1989 8f² 8f 8.2d 8g⁶ 9g 8d] sturdy colt: fair handicapper: 20/1, good second of 16 to True Panache at York in May: off course 3 months after next outing: easily best subsequent effort on fourth start (sweating): stays 9f: yet to race on soft going, possibly can't take much racing on firm: blinkered final outing: has run creditably for amateur: sold to join C. Brooks 18,000 gns Newmarket Autumn Sales. *Sir Mark Prescott.* **85**

STEP IN TIME 6 br.g. Bellypha 130–Sometime Lucky 89 (Levmoss 133) [1988 12g⁴ 12m⁴ 12f⁶ 1989 12d] tall, heavy-topped gelding: turns fore feet out: moderate mover: modest handicapper: not seen out in 1988 after Royal Ascot: subsequently gelded: 20/1, never dangerous in 9-runner event at Newmarket in April: probably stays 1¾m: acts well on top-of-the-ground and possibly unsuited by soft going: not an easy ride. *P. J. Makin.* **—**

STEPPEY LANE 4 b.f. Tachypous 128–Alpine Alice 94 (Abwah 118) [1988 8s³ 8m 10g⁶ 7f 7f 1989 8s 10d³ 10.2g⁴ 12f⁵ 12m⁴ 12.4m³ 12d 12.3g⁴ 13.8d* 12.4g³ 14g⁴] leggy, workmanlike filly: has a round action: fair handicapper nowadays: 14/1, won 18-runner event at Catterick in October by 5 lengths: good third of 19 to Royal Borough at Newcastle later in month, staying on from 3f out without reaching leaders: stays 1¾m: acts on any going: has got on edge: has been mounted on track and taken down early. *W. W. Haigh.* **83**

STEREO (USA) 2 b.c. (Apr 16) The Minstrel (CAN) 135–Silver In Flight (USA) (Silver Series (USA)) [1989 8g²] strong, good-topped, attractive colt: has plenty of scope: second foal: dam graded stakes-place winner at up to 11f: favourite, ½-length second of 16, keeping on well, to My Lord in maiden at Leicester in November: will stay at least 1¼m: sure to improve, and win a race. *G. Harwood.* **82 p**

STERLING BUCK (USA) 2 b.c. (May 27) Buckfinder (USA)–Aged (USA) (Olden Times) [1989 6d 7g] $6,500Y: leggy, close-coupled colt: second foal: dam, winner at around 6f, is half-sister to useful Irish 6f and 1¼m winner Curio: tailed off in large-field autumn maidens at Newbury and Newmarket. *M. D. I. Usher.* **—**

STETCHWORTH LADY 3 b.f. Tolomeo 127–Royal Yacht (USA) 65 (Riverman (USA) 131) [1988 8d⁵ 1989 10s⁵ 8h³ a12g] tall, rather leggy, unfurnished filly: moderate walker and mover: fifth in maiden at Newmarket at 2 yrs: below that form in varied events as 3-y-o, tailed off in Lingfield handicap on final start, first for over 5 months: should be suited by further than 1m (pulled hard in moderately-run race over 1¼m): possibly unsuited by extremes of going: sold 4,500 gns Newmarket December Sales. *B. W. Hills.* **60**

STEVEJAN 7 b.g. Bivouac 114–Stick'Em Up (Burglar 128) [1988 6h 6g⁶ 6d³ 6s* — 6m 6f 6d² 6s 6d 6g 6d 1989 6v 8v] small, plain gelding: poor handicapper: tailed off both starts in spring: suited by 6f and suited by plenty of give nowadays: usually apprentice ridden, often at overweight: best without blinkers: sold 1,000 gns Ascot June Sales: inconsistent. *J. J. O'Neill.*

STEVEN JOHN 2 b. or br.g. (May 4) Carriage Way 107–Harmony Thyme 73   **49** (Sing Sing 134) [1989 8m 8g] leggy gelding: half-brother to 3 minor winners by Mansingh and one by Tribal Chief: dam 5f winner at 2 yrs: poor form in autumn maidens at Edinburgh (slowly away) and Leicester. *D. H. Topley.*

STIG 2 b.c. (Apr 6) The Brianstan 128–The Crying Game 55 (Manor Farm Boy 114)   — [1989 7m 7g 6d 5g] leggy, sparely-made colt: turns fore-feet out: first reported foal: dam, plater, stayed 1m: well beaten in varied races: unseated rider, and bolted, before second outing. *B. C. Morgan.*

STILL BATTLING 2 ch.g. (Apr 23) Hard Fought 125–Heartland 72 (North-   **43** fields (USA)) [1989 5g⁶ 5g³ 5m⁵ 5f⁵ 6m 6m] IR 4,200Y: leggy gelding: moderate mover: first foal: dam placed over 1¼m at 3 yrs: modest plater: blinkered second outing and last two. *J. S. Wainwright.*

STILL SURPRISED 4 ch.g. Nicholas Bill 125–Noammo (Realm 129) [1988 8g   **85** 1989 10f 9f⁴ 8f* 8m⁵ 8f 7s] big, lengthy, angular gelding: fair handicapper: won at York in July by length from disqualified Northern Printer, travelling really well much of way, but idling once quickening into lead 1f out: ran poorly final outing: suited by 1m: probably unsuited by soft going, acts on any other: visored at York and on last 2 starts: keen sort, who carries head high: ideally suited by strong handling and good gallop: a difficult ride. *R. M. Whitaker.*

STILL TIME LEFT 3 b.c. Teenoso (USA) 135–Peculiar One (USA) (Quack   **52** (USA)) [1988 NR 1989 12g 16d⁵ 13.3m] big, good-topped colt: moderate mover: third foal: half-brother to useful 8.2f to 1½m winner Grand Tour (by Troy) and to 1½m winner Hats High (by High Top): dam unraced daughter of sister to very smart 1977 American 2-y-o filly Stub: plating-class maiden: only form at 2m on a soft surface: sold 4,600 gns Newmarket Autumn Sales. *W. Hastings-Bass.*

STILVELLA 2 ch.f. (Mar 11) Camden Town 125–Sinella 93 (Sing Sing 134) [1989   — 5m⁶ 6g] half-sister to 2 winners and to dam of smart 1977 sprinting 2-y-o Hawkins: dam, winner over 5f at 2 yrs, is half-sister to top-class sprinter and broodmare Stilvi: well beaten in maiden (slowly away) at Warwick in July and claimer at Goodwood in October. *S. Dow.*

STISTED PARK 4 b.g. Be My Native (USA) 122–Up To You (Sallust 134) [1988   **50** 8.2v 10v⁵ 12f* 13f⁴ 12g 12m⁴ 14m⁶ 12h* 1989 12g 10f³ 12f² 12m³ 12f⁶ 14m] lightly-made gelding: moderate mover: fair plater: suited by 1½m: acts on hard going: has won for apprentice: didn't handle bend at Lingfield second start. *M. H. Tompkins.*

ST JAMES'S RISK 6 b.g. Captain James 123–Queen's Bazaar (Queen's Hussar   — 124) [1988 7d 1989 8.2v] quite attractive gelding: fair winner at 2 yrs: retains little ability nowadays: blinkered once: sold to join J. Bridger 1,850 gns Ascot June Sales. *R. D. E. Woodhouse.*

ST LOUIS BLUES 4 b.c. Cure The Blues (USA)–Flaretown 63 (Town Crier   — 119) [1988 8.5m⁴ 9f³ 10g⁴ 8.2g* 8g³ 8g 1989 10.1m⁴ 10f 12f 12m] workmanlike colt: moderate mover: modest winner as 3-y-o: well below his best in first half of 1989: needs forcing tactics at 1m: acts on firm going: suited by strong handling: has joined J. Edwards. *R. Curtis.*

ST NINIAN 3 ch.c. Ardross 134–Caergwrle 115 (Crepello 136) [1988 8.2m³ 8s³   **86** 1989 8s* 10.6s⁴ 10.2f⁴] useful-looking colt: made all in maiden at Thirsk in April: ran creditably in minor event and handicap later in spring: stays 1¼m: acts on any going: strong-running type and may prove best with forcing tactics. *M. H. Easterby.*

STOCIOUS 3 br.f. Petong 126–Moonlight Serenade 66 (Crooner 119) [1988 6m⁵   **79** 6f 5f* 1989 6f 5m⁵ 5m* 5f⁵ 5g³ 5f⁶ 5f³ 6m 5d] small filly: has a quick action: fair handicapper: successful at York in June: stays 6f: acts on any going: ran creditably in visor seventh start, and when sweating and edgy on eighth: sold 10,000 gns Newmarket Autumn Sales. *D. J. G. Murray-Smith.*

STOCKAIR 3 ch.c. Air Trooper 115–Fair Nic (Romancero 100) [1988 5m³ 6m 6g   **53** 1989 6m⁵ 6f 6m a8g⁵] leggy, light-framed colt: plating-class form: best effort in handicaps and claimer as 3-y-o on reappearance: stays 6f: trained until after third outing by G. Cottrell. *J. Sutcliffe.*

STOCK PILE 2 b.f. (Feb 9) Galveston 114–Yen (AUS) (Biscay (AUS)) [1989 7m 39 8.2f 7d] good-topped filly: first known foal: dam ran without success in Australia: poor plater: stays 1m: visored final outing: sold 420 gns Ascot November Sales. *W. Hastings-Bass.*

STOCKTINA 2 ch.f. (Apr 22) Tina's Pet 121–Mrewa (Runnymede 123) [1989 5f5] — smallish filly: sixth foal: sister to useful sprinter Ashtina and half-sister to 3-y-o Sunwind (by Windjammer): dam thrice-raced maiden: under 7 lengths fifth of 8 to Nobodys Sweetheart in maiden at Warwick in July: showed a round action. *J. White.*

STOLON TIME 3 ch.f. Good Times (ITY)–Stolen Love 85 (Alcide 136) [1988 — 5m3 6f4 6d3 6s* 6g 6s* 7f 1989 7g5 6m 6m 8g 6g] sturdy filly: fair winner at 2 yrs: fair fifth at Newcastle, easily best effort in handicaps as 3-y-o: best form at 6f though bred to stay at least 1m: acts well on soft going, and possibly unsuited to top-of-the-ground: active type. *J. A. Glover.*

STONEBROKER 7 ch.m. Morston (FR) 125–Overspent 85 (Busted 134) [1988 45 9f3 10d5 8g2 8f 12.3s5 9g 10.2g 10g 9g5 10g2 10m2 12.2d6 8g 10d 1989 8s2 10.8d 9f 10f 8.3m 10m 8f5 a11g] workmanlike mare: poor handicapper: effective at 1m and stays 1½m: acts on any going: visored once at 6 yrs: blinkered (hung right) sixth start: doesn't find great deal off bridle and is a difficult ride: inconsistent. *D. Haydn Jones.*

STONE FLAKE (USA) 3 ch.c. Diesis 133–Wyandra (So Blessed 130) [1988 6f* 101 d 6f4 7d2 7m3 7d3 7m 8g6 1989 7d4 8m 10.5f 8m5 7.3g5 7g 7m] neat colt: useful at his best: ran well in pattern company first 2 starts and in £7,700 event on fourth one: sweating freely, bit below best in Hungerford Stakes at Newbury fifth outing: showed nothing after in Group 3 contest and £8,800 handicap: stays 1m: acts on top-of-the-ground and a soft surface: also sweating (bit edgy, ran poorly) third outing: changed hands 22,000 gns Newmarket December Sales. *P. A. Kelleway.*

STONE FOREST 4 b. or br.c. Thatching 131–Senta's Girl (Averof 123) [1988 8d — 8s* 1989 8g 8d 11.5g 12d] strong, rangy colt: has a quick action: landed the odds very easily in maiden at Haydock early as 3-y-o when trained by B. Hills: lightly raced and little show subsequently: stays 1m: acts on soft going. *Miss A. J. Whitfield.*

STONEYTHORPEWONDER 2 b.c. (Feb 4) Smackover 107–Holloway Won- 74 der 93 (Swing Easy (USA) 126) [1989 5d* 5d 5g* 6g 5g] lengthy, rather sparely-made colt: poor mover: dam effective at 5f and stayed 1m: modest performer: won 8-runner maiden at Ripon in April and 14-runner nursery at Hamilton (first run since mid-May) in September: likely to prove best at 5f. *P. A. Blockley.*

STOP DAY (USA) 4 b.f. Stop The Music (USA)–Yellow Serenade (USA) 93 (Graustark) [1988 7g4 8g 6f* 6f 6m 6g 1989 6g 5s3 6g 6g* 5m 6v] strong-quartered, quite attractive filly: good mover, with a quick action: fairly useful performer: won £5,500 5-runner event at Goodwood in October by length from Young Tearaway, first run for nearly 5 months: around 3½ lengths seventh of 11 to Or Acier in Premio Omenoni at Milan, better subsequent effort in Italy: ideally suited by 6f: acts on any going except heavy: fell third outing. *J. L. Dunlop.*

STOP HIGH 2 ch.f. (Mar 16) Crofthall 110–Portvally (Import 127) [1989 5m6 6m2 48 6f* 6f3 5g2 6g2 6m] 800Y: leggy, narrow filly: poor walker: quite good mover: third foal: dam never ran: fair plater: made all at Nottingham (no bid) in June: seems equally effective at 5f and 6f: sold 1,100 gns Doncaster October Sales. *J. Berry.*

STORM CONE 3 ch.g. Northern Tempest (USA) 120–Be Royal 97 (Royal Palm — 131) [1988 NR 1989 8m] 23,000Y: workmanlike gelding: fourth reported foal: half-brother to useful 6f and 7f winner Native Oak (by Tower Walk): dam, 5f winner at 2 yrs, is half-sister to dam of Pas de Seul: very slowly away, behind in minor event at Carlisle in June: dead. *M. H. Easterby.*

STORM FORCE (USA) 5 b.h. Storm Bird (CAN) 134–Kittyhawk 113 (Bustino 82 136) [1988 12f4 10f* 10g 12f3 1989 12s 10f2 10h* 10h* 10f* 10f* 10g] small, quite attractive horse: fair handicapper: in tremendous form for much of season, making all or virtually all when winning once at Brighton (third course victory and second in Channel Handicap) and 3 times at Lingfield: well below his best in apprentice race at Goodwood final outing, first for 2 months: suited by 1¼m and very firm going: sweating final start at 4 yrs: suited by forcing tactics and a switchback track: genuine and consistent. *R. Akehurst.*

STORM FREE (USA) 3 b.c. Storm Bird (CAN) 134–No Designs (USA) 72 80 (Vaguely Noble 140) [1988 6d2 1989 8s 8g5 10.6g6 10v] rather leggy, angular colt: fair maiden: best effort after debut when sixth at Haydock in September, brief effort over 2f out and not given hard race: should stay 1m: probably unsuited by very soft going: sold to join G. Cottrell 15,000 gns Newmarket Autumn Sales. *M. R. Stoute.*

STORM JIB 2 b.c. (Apr 19) Elegant Air 119–Calvet 62 (Thatch (USA) 136) [1989 **65**
7f³ 7g⁶ 7g⁶ 8.2g a7g⁶ a7g⁵] IR 8,800F, IR 7,200Y: quite attractive colt: first foal:
dam placed from 7f to 1¼m, is daughter of Coronation Stakes winner Calve, herself
a daughter of St Leger runner-up Patti: quite modest form in varied races: should be
suited by 1m + . *J. L. Dunlop.*

STORMLINE (USA) 4 b.c. The Minstrel (CAN) 135–In The Offing (USA) **?**
(Hoist The Flag (USA)) [1988 10d* 10g 10m² 1989 8m⁴ 10m²] big, good-topped colt:
good mover: useful winner as 3-y-o: long way below his best when in frame in
£5,000 ladies event at Ascot (sweating, on toes, badly hampered 3f out) and
amateurs race at Sandown (moving smoothly into lead 2f out, edging right and
caught well inside last) in summer: stays 1¼m: acts on top-of-the-ground and a soft
surface: usually takes keen hold: sold 11,000 gns Newmarket Autumn Sales: a
difficult ride. *G. Harwood.*

STORM RUNNER 4 b.f. Runnett 125–Glimmer of Hope (USA) (Never Bend) **65**
[1988 6v⁵ 6g³ 6g 6d⁴ 6f* 7m* 7m⁵ 6g⁶ 6g* 7g³ 5g³ 6g⁵ 5g 6f⁶ 6s 6g 6d⁴ 6g 1989 8s
7s 7.6f* 8h 8h⁶ 7.6f5] leggy, shallow-girthed filly: sometimes dull in coat: has a
round action: quite modest handicapper: won 20-runner event at Lingfield in May:
below form later in summer: stays 1m: goes well on top-of-the-ground: blinkered
once: has worn bandages behind: has run creditably when sweating: has won 3 times
at Catterick. *J. P. Hudson.*

STORM WARRIOR 4 b.g. Main Reef 126–Spadilla 59 (Javelot 124) [1988 10.8d **—**
12g 10m 12.3s 10.1g 8.3g 1989 12.5f⁵ 15.3g] close-coupled, quite attractive gelding:
moderate mover: bad maiden: stays 1½m: blinkered on reappearance: has started
very slowly: apprentice ridden at 4 yrs: winning selling hurdler. *B. Preece.*

STORMY BELLE 2 ch.f. (Feb 4) Tumble Wind (USA)–Never So Lovely 87 **76**
(Realm 129) [1989 5g² 5d³ 5m* 5g⁶ 5m 6g] IR 10,000Y: big, rather angular filly: has
plenty of scope: moderate walker: fifth foal: half-sister to 4 winners, including very
useful sprinter Restore and fair 1¼m winner Zabeel (both by Habitat): dam 6f
winner: modest performer: won maiden at Wolverhampton in June: ran well next 2
starts in listed race at Newmarket in July and Cornwallis Stakes at Ascot in October:
speedy: may be capable of improvement. *M. A. Jarvis.*

STORMY PRAISE (USA) 5 ch.h. Storm Bird (CAN) 134–Prayers'n Promises **56**
(USA) (Foolish Pleasure (USA)) [1988 7g³ 7f⁴ 6m⁴ 6f 6g⁵ 5m 5g 7m 6s 1989 5.8h 6f⁴
6f⁴ 7f 7f 6f⁶] lengthy, angular horse: quite modest maiden: ran poorly fourth and
fifth outings: effective at 6f and 7f: acts on firm going: wore hood and blinkers third
and fourth starts: has worn cross noseband: often taken down quietly: headstrong
and not an easy ride: highly-strung: sold 2,500 gns Ascot October Sales. *C. James.*

STORMY REEF 3 ch.f. Mill Reef 126–Deadly Serious (USA) 113 **75**
(Queen's Hussar 124) [1988 7.3s 1989 11s⁶ 9m⁴ 12g⁶ 12m³] big, lengthy, angular
filly: modest form in maidens at Newbury and Salisbury (leading over 1¼m) on last 2
outings: will stay further: lacks turn of foot, and should prove best with forcing
tactics. *I. A. Balding.*

STRADBROKE 2 b.c. (Mar 1) Fairy King (USA)–Mattira (FR) (Rheffic (FR) 129) **—**
[1989 7m] IR 5,900 (privately) F, 19,000Y: big, strong, lengthy colt: keen walker:
closely related to 10.2f winner and successful hurdler Viking Venture (by Viking)
and half-brother to a winner in Ireland by Acamas: dam never ran: 20/1, burly and
very green, very slowly away and always behind, not knocked about, in 19-runner
maiden at Newmarket in October. *R. Boss.*

STRAIGHT GOLD 4 ch.f. Vaigly Great 127–Merokette 83 (Blast 125) [1988 **64**
8.5s³ 10.2g⁴ 8f⁶ 7.3m 7f⁶ 7.6f 7m⁵ 7g 1989 7s⁵ 8d⁶ 8m 8f² 8m² 8h⁶ 8f⁴ 9m⁶ 7s³
10.2f² 12g²] tall filly: quite modest handicapper: seems to stay 1½m: acts on any
going: visored 3 times as 3-y-o: has started slowly, got long way behind and found
little: a difficult ride: sold to join S. Cole 12,500 gns Newmarket Autumn Sales. *I. A.
Balding.*

STRANGER STILL 2 b.f. (Feb 6) Cragador 110–No Relation 94 (Klairon 131) **58**
[1989 6g 6g] leggy, sparely-made filly: has a quick action: sister to 3-y-o Relative
Stranger and half-sister to several winners, including fairly useful middle-distance
handicapper Warbeck (by Royal Palace): dam stayed 1m: plating-class form, slowly
away, in autumn maidens at Yarmouth and Leicester. *G. Wragg.*

STRANGER TO FEAR 2 ch.f. (Feb 18) Never So Bold 135–Acadie (FR) 80 **—**
(Caracolero (USA)) [1989 6g] 34,000Y: leggy, unfurnished filly: first reported foal:
dam 7f winner at 2 yrs showed little form subsequently, including in USA: always
behind in 29-runner maiden at Newmarket in November. *R. F. Johnson Houghton.*

STRATFORD PONDS 4 b.c. High Top 131–Opinion 71 (Great Nephew 126) **96**
[1988 10.1d⁵ 10.1m² 11.5d* 12f³ 10d 14g³ 1989 14g² 16g⁴ 14m³ 12f* 12g³ 12m] big,
angular colt: has a quick action: fairly useful handicapper: won £12,000 Bessborough
Stakes (Handicap) at Royal Ascot by 1½ lengths from Butlers Wharf, soon
recovering after slow start and leading before halfway: good third to Nickle Plated in
£24,300 event at Haydock over 2 weeks later: best at 1½m: has won on a soft
surface, but best form on a sound one: lacks turn of foot and best ridden close to the
pace: sold to join O. Sherwood 40,000 gns Newmarket Autumn Sales. *J. L. Dunlop.*

STRAT'S LEGACY 2 b.g. (Feb 18) Chukaroo 103–State Romance 67 (Free **—**
State 125) [1989 6g a6g] small, light-framed gelding: second reported foal: brother to
fairly useful sprinter Very Adjacent: dam won at 7f and 1m: well beaten in claimer at
Goodwood and maiden (bandaged behind) at Lingfield. *D. W. P. Arbuthnot.*

STRAW BLADE 3 ch.f. Final Straw 127–Little Niece 79 (Great Nephew 126) **66**
[1988 6g 7d 1989 8m⁶ 10.2m³ 9.2f⁶ 10.6g*] leggy, rather sparely-made filly: won
claimer (claimed £12,501) at Haydock in July, driven along vigorously early in
straight and leading inside final 1f: suited by 1¼m: well below form on very firm
going: winning novice hurdler for M. Pipe. *J. L. Dunlop.*

STRAW BOWLER 4 b.g. Thatching 131–Final Game 83 (Pardao 120) [1988 NR **—**
1989 10g 8m 12.5g 12f 11.7g 10.8m⁵ 12m] sturdy, lengthy gelding: half-brother to 2
winners, including very smart sprinter Mummy's Game (by Mummy's Pet): dam
won over 1¼m: poor plater: blinkered last 2 outings: sold 1,250 gns Ascot October
Sales. *C. P. Wildman.*

STRAW CASTLE 4 ch.f. Final Straw 127–Candy Castle 82 (Habitat 134) [1988 **—**
6m⁵ 8f 7f⁴ 7g⁴ 8m⁵ 8g 1989 7g 10s 9f⁶ 8.3m 8m⁶ 8f] workmanlike filly: moderate
mover: poor maiden: stays 1m: acts on firm going: blinkered 3 times: has sweated,
and usually gets on toes: finds little and best treated with caution: bought out of W.
Haggas's stable 2,000 gns Doncaster May Sales after third outing. *T. B. Hallett.*

STREET LEVEL 8 b.m. Swing Easy (USA) 126–Street Vendor 60 (High Perch **—**
126) [1988 5s 6d 7g 7.6f 1989 5d] leggy, lightly-made, angular mare: bad handicapper: stays 7.6f: goes well in the mud. *H. O'Neill.*

STREET PARTY 5 b.m. General Assembly (USA)–Chalkey Road 100 (Relko **—**
136) [1988 10g³ 8f 8f* 8d 7m⁵ 8f⁶ 7f 1989 8f] tall, leggy mare: has a short, sharp
action: quite modest winner (making all) as 4-y-o: backward only outing in 1989
(May): best at 7f to 9f: acts on firm going and a soft surface: sometimes sweats: has
looked none too keen. *N. Tinkler.*

STRIDE HOME 4 ch.f. Absalom 128–Another Treat 82 (Derring-Do 131) [1988 **62**
8.2v 7g⁵ 8.5m⁴ 10d 10g² 10g⁶ 10m* 10m⁶ 10g³ 1989 10.1m 12f 10h⁴ 12m⁴ 11.7m²
11.7m² 10f 9m 12f⁵] neat filly: has a quick action: quite modest handicapper: needs
further than 9f and stays 1½m: seems to act on any going: often blinkered or
visored: bandaged second start: inconsistent. *M. Madgwick.*

STRIKE FOR HOME 2 b.c. (Feb 28) Glint of Gold 128–Home And Away **67**
(Home Guard (USA) 129) [1989 7g 7m⁶ 8.2d⁶ a7g] 19,000Y: small, lengthy colt: sixth
foal: half-brother to 3-y-o Good Point (by Chief Singer), 1984 2-y-o 7f winner Top of
The League (by High Top) and fair 11f and 1½m winner First Division (by Wolver
Hollow): dam unraced half-sister to high-class American middle-distance performer
Galaxy Libra: quite modest performer: blinkered, ran moderately in nursery at
Lingfield on final outing: will be suited by middle distances: sold 7,000 gns
Newmarket Autumn Sales. *P. T. Walwyn.*

STRING PLAYER 7 ch.g. Orchestra 118–Ghana's Daughter 93 (Sallust 134) **—**
[1988 12v⁵ 18m 16g 1989 18m] workmanlike, deep-girthed gelding: moderate walker: has a slightly round action: plating-class handicapper on flat: burly, hopelessly
tailed off at Ripon in August: stays 1½m: acts on any going: has run respectably for
apprentice: sometimes sweats: winning chaser in 1988/9. *F. H. Lee.*

STRIPANOORA 4 ch.f. Ahonoora 122–Strip Fast 71 (Virginia Boy 106) [1988 8m **—**
8m² 7g⁶ 7m 1989 8s 8d 7.6f 8g⁶] big, lengthy, angular filly: has a quick action: quite
modest maiden at best: blinkered, weakened quickly final 2f when tailed-off last of 6
in handicap at Edinburgh in July, first outing for 2 months: stays 1m: acts on
top-of-the-ground. *M. L. W. Bell.*

STRONG LANGUAGE 4 ch.f. Formidable (USA) 125–Linguistic 95 (Porto **52**
Bello 118) [1988 8d²8.2m⁴ 10m³ 12.2g⁴ 13g* 12m² 15.5g 1989 11v⁵ 10m⁴ 12.5g⁴ 12h³
12f⁴ 12f 10.1m* 10f⁵ 10.1m 10f⁴ 12m⁴ 12g] compact filly: plating-class performer:
favourite and apprentice ridden, won 23-runner selling handicap at Windsor (bought
in 2,600 gns) in June: stays 13f: acts on firm going and unsuited by heavy: edged left

and didn't find great deal third outing: slowly away sixth and final starts: winning selling hurdler. *J. White.*

STRONGLY FAVOURED (USA) 2 ch.g. (May 11) Miswaki (USA) 124–Bag of Tunes (USA) (Herbager 136) [1989 7g6 7m4] closely related to poor 1985 3-y-o Busca (by Mr Prospector) and half-brother to several winners here and abroad, notably useful 7f and 1½m winner Andaleeb (by Lyphard): dam won Kentucky Oaks and second in CCA Oaks: quite modest form in maidens at Newbury in August and Chepstow in October: sold 15,500 gns Newmarket Autumn Sales. *J. Tree.* **69**

STUBBS ROAD 2 b.c. (Mar 26) Blushing Scribe (USA) 107–Rheinza 66 (Rheingold 137) [1989 7g 8.5f] 500F: sturdy colt: poor mover: third living foal: half-brother to Italian 1¼m winner Glinza (by Glint of Gold): dam, middle-distance maiden, half-sister to high-class miler Belmont Bay: well beaten in minor event at Doncaster and maiden at Beverley in September. *R. Champion.* **—**

ST VILLE 3 b.c. Top Ville 129–Dame Julian 84 (Blakeney 126) [1988 7m 7g 1989 11.7d 12g 15.3m3 17.6g6 16f5 15.8g2 a14g a16g5] good-bodied colt: poor walker and moderate mover: plating class: led close home in handicap at Lingfield in November: well beaten at Southwell and Lingfield following month: suited by test of stamina: acts on firm going: edgy, below form in moderately-run race fourth start. *J. D. Bethell.* **60**

STYLISH GENT 2 br.g. (Feb 10) Vitiges (FR) 132–Squire's Daughter (Bay Express 132) [1989 6g* 6g5 7m*] IR 6,500Y: useful-looking gelding: first foal: dam 5.5f winner at 2 yrs in France: won 18-runner maiden auction at Haydock (fractious stalls) in August and 15-runner listed race at Fairyhouse in September: ran moderately in nursery at Newmarket in between: better suited by 7f than 6f: acts on top-of-the-ground. *W. Hastings-Bass.* **87**

SUBOOK 3 ch.f. Salmon Leap (USA) 131–Dellie Douglass (USA) (Mongo) [1988 8s 1989 10.1m 10.1m 12m 10f] compact, plain filly: no form in varied events: trained until after second outing by G. Lewis. *J. D. Czerpak.* **—**

SUBURBIA 3 b.f. Another Realm 118–Leaplet (Alcide 136) [1988 NR 1989 7g 9s] fifth foal: half-sister to 2 winning platers, including 1984 2-y-o 6f winner Full of Ale (by Full of Hope): dam unraced: 100/1, no sign of ability in claimer (moved easily down) and seller in Scotland. *F. Watson.* **—**

SUDDEN IMPACT (FR) 3 ch.c. Crystal Glitters (USA) 127–Simple Simone (FR) (Arctic Tern (USA) 126) [1988 7f4 1989 10g 10.5f6 8f4] quite attractive, angular colt: rather unfurnished: poor mover: modest maiden: stays 1m: bandaged all round last 2 outings. *C. E. Brittain.* **72**

SUDDEN LOVE (FR) 4 b.f. Kris 135–Sudden Glory (FR) 98 (Luthier 126) [1988 7g3 10f* 12m2 10d2 12f2 10g* 12m2 10f* 10f5 1989 9g* 10f4] rather sparely-made filly: has a powerful, slightly round action: smart 3-y-o, successful in listed races at Newbury and Newcastle and in E P Taylor Stakes at Woodbine: long odds on, won minor event at Ripon in July by 2½ lengths from Eradicate: favourite, modest fourth of 5, never able to challenge, to Mamaluna in Vodafone Nassau Stakes at Goodwood later in month: suited by 1¼m to 1½m: acts on firm going and a soft surface: has run creditably when sweating and on edge: game. *L. M. Cumani.* **107**

SUDDEN VICTORY 5 ch.g. Kings Lake (USA) 133–Shebeen 124 (Saint Crespin III 132) [1988 14g5 14f3 16.1d* 14g* 13.4s* 13.5g2 16g5 15.5s 1989 13.3g5 11s2 11s* 12v2 14g2] tall, top-topped gelding: turns near-fore out: poor mover in slower paces: smart performer: comfortably landed the odds in claimer at Ayr in September: 14/1, very good neck second of 11, clear, battling on well, to Sesame in St Simon Stakes at Newbury following month: odds on, well below his best when second in minor event at Redcar final outing: stays 1¾m: best with plenty of give in the ground. *B. W. Hills.* **115**

SUE FOREVER 5 b.m. Riboboy (USA) 124–Lucy Martin 73 (Forlorn River 124) [1988 NR 1989 11.7g 10.8m] lengthy mare: poor performer: stays 1m: acts on firm going and is possibly unsuited by a soft surface: bandaged at 5 yrs. *Mrs A. Knight.* **—**

SUGAR PLUM FAIRY 3 b.f. Sadler's Wells (USA) 132–Epithet 105 (Mill Reef (USA) 141) [1988 6g4 7m6 1989 8.5m 12h3 10.8f* 9.2d* 10g5 8g] leggy, lengthy, rather shallow-girthed filly: won maiden (idling, by a neck) at Warwick in July and £7,300 handicap (by 7 lengths) at Goodwood in September: never able to challenge in listed events after: may prove suited by around 1¼m: acts on firm going and clearly goes well on a soft surface. *W. Jarvis.* **91**

SUGAR THE PILL 2 b.g. (Apr 3) Blue Cashmere 129–Maple Syrup 89 (Charlottown 127) [1989 5s 5g3 6f 7f5 7f 8.2s a7g] 7,000Y: lengthy gelding: has scope: half-brother to Irish 9f and 11f winner Fish Merchant (by Night Shift) and 2 **52**

other winners: dam, placed over 6f and 1¼m, is daughter of Sweet Solera: moderate walker and mover: plating-class maiden: ran very well when sweating fourth start: well beaten in nurseries afterwards. *T. Fairhurst.*

SUGGIA 2 b.f. (Mar 29) Alzao (USA) 117–Marthe Meynet (Welsh Pageant 132) [1989 6f 5m] half-sister to several winners, including fair sprinter Batoni (by Realm) and 6f and 1m winner and quite useful jumper Antinous (by Hello Gorgeous): dam never ran: well beaten in August maidens at Redcar and Newcastle. *M. H. Easterby.*   —

SUGO 2 ch.f. (Apr 8) Prince Ragusa 96–Lucky Friend (Galivanter 131) [1989 5s 5m⁵] 500Y: lengthy, angular filly: first living foal: dam no sign of ability on flat or over hurdles: of little account. *Ronald Thompson.*   —

SUHAIL DANCER 3 b.c. Shareef Dancer (USA) 135–Fluctuate 87 (Sharpen Up 127) [1988 6m* 6m³ 7m³ 6g* 1989 7g³ 6f² 7m⁶ 8h³ 7.6g 7.6f³ 6f 6m²] useful-looking colt: fair performer: effective at 6f to 1m: acts on firm ground: blinkered fourth and last 3 outings: usually takes a good hold: sweating, edgy and mulish before running creditably fourth start: sold 12,000 gns Newmarket Autumn Sales: appears somewhat temperamental and not one to rely on. *Mrs L. Piggott.*   84

SUHAM 3 ch.f. Kris 135–Amatrice (Appiani II 128) [1988 NR 1989 10f4] 165,000Y: workmanlike filly: half-sister to 3 winners, including fairly useful Irish 7f winner Soluce (by Junius) and Irish middle-distance filly Cienaga (by Tarboosh): dam won over 1½m in Ireland: 9/2 and green, 12 lengths fourth of 7 in maiden at Chepstow in July, one pace 3f out and eased: sold 7,000 gns Newmarket December Sales. *H. Thomson Jones.*   —

SUIVEZ MOI 5 ch.g. Pas de Seul 133–Reparata (Jukebox 120) [1988 18d4 14v 13.8g 18m³ 16g⁵ 15.8m⁶ 14.8d³ 18.8d² 12g 17.1g4 17.1g⁶ 18g 14.7d³ 1989 14s² 21.6d 16g⁶ 18.4m 14.8m4 14m⁵ 14m⁶ 15.3m* 15.3m⁵ a16g² a16g4 a16g⁵] small, light-framed gelding: poor mover: poor handicapper: dropped again to selling company, won 14-runner event (bought in 8,000 gns) at Wolverhampton in June: stays well: acts on any going, except possibly heavy: went too fast when visored sixth and seventh starts: suitable mount for apprentice: sometimes sweats: genuine. *C. N. Allen.*   35

SUKAAB 4 gr.g. Nishapour (FR) 125–Nye (FR) (Sanctus II 132) [1988 10m 12d 1989 12d 8f 8.5d] tall, close-coupled gelding: little sign of ability in maidens or handicaps. *B. McLean.*   —

SUKEY TAWDRY 3 gr.f. Wassl 125–Jenny Diver (USA) (Hatchet Man (USA)) [1988 6g 5g³ 6f⁵ 7g 6g 1989 7.5d⁵ 8h 10f4 12m 12f² 8.5m* 18.1g4 8.5f 10m 10f] leggy filly: fair plater at best: bandaged, plenty to do on turn when winning at Beverley (sold out of P. Calver's stable 3,000 gns) in August: well behind (twice out of handicap in non-selling event) after: may prove ideally suited by 1¼m: acts on firm going: ran creditably when edgy fifth start: visored eighth and ninth: sold 1,800 gns Doncaster November Sales. *M. C. Chapman.*   46

SULCIS 4 ch.g. Castle Keep 121–Skiboule (BEL) (Boulou) [1988 10g 10g² 10m 9.5m 8g⁶ 10m⁵ 10v 12d4 12d 14.6m4 1989 13f 12g 15s* 14g⁵ 15.5s 14s 15.5f³ 16.2m² 15.3m⁶ 12g⁵] well-made gelding: has a fluent action: plating-class handicapper: won at Cagnes-sur-Mer in February: stays 2m: seems to act on any going: trained first 6 starts in 1988 and first 7 in 1989 by C. Milbank in France: winning hurdler. *R. Hollinshead.*   55

SULLY'S CHOICE (USA) 8 b.g. King Pellinore (USA) 127–Salute The Coates (USA) (Solar Salute (USA)) [1988 6g 6g² 6g 6m³ 5f4 5m³ 6g4 5m 6f4 6d4 6g 6m4 6f² 6g² 5f⁵ 5g 5f 6f 6d 1989 5m 6f 6m 6f⁵ 6h³ 6f* 5g⁶ 6m² 6m² 6m* 6f³ 6m* 6m² 5.6g 6s 6m 6g 6f 6g 5d a6g a6g⁵ a6g³ a6g] small, sturdy gelding: carries plenty of condition: usually looks very well: in excellent form in summer, winning handicaps at Redcar, Ripon and York (beating Dorking Lad a length in £12,300 event): well below his best after next outing: effective at 5f to 6f: acts on any going: visored twice: effective with or without blinkers: suitable mount for apprentice: suited by forcing tactics. *D. W. Chapman.*   92 d

SULTANS GIFT 3 ch.f. Homing 130–Suzannah's Song (Song 132) [1988 6d 6g 6g 1989 6f⁶ 5m³ 6f 5.8h² 5g 6f 6f 6g] small filly: poor mover: plating-class maiden: should be suited by 6f: acts on hard ground: often ridden by claimer: also bandaged sixth outing: blinkered seventh: changed hands 1,050 gns Newmarket September Sales. *C. N. Allen.*   47

SULUK (USA) 4 b.c. Lypheor 118–Cheerful Heart (Petingo 135) [1988 10d⁵ 10g 12m³ 12g* 14d4 12g4 9g³ 10s³ 9d⁶ 9m⁵ 9v 8s 1989 10s 10v 12.5g 12f 12g 12h* 12.3m* 16g⁶ 12g³ 12.3m² 12h* 12f* 12m* 12f 12.2f 12f⁵ 12g 12g] strong, dipped-backed, good-quartered ex-Irish colt: carries condition: half-brother to 3-y-o 1¼m winner   72

Momtaaz (by Diesis), successful over 1m at 2 yrs: dam 1½m winner in Ireland, is half-sister to Gift Wrapped, dam of Royal Lodge winner Reach: in excellent form in summer, making all or virtually all when winning handicaps at Carlisle (twice), Ripon, Thirsk (2-runner event) and Beverley: well below his best last 5 outings: best form at 1½m: acts very well on top-of-the-ground: goes very well with forcing tactics: genuine. *R. Hollinshead.*

SUMAN 2 b.c. (Jun 9) Remainder Man 126§–Camdamus 83 (Mandamus 120) [1989   **43** 5d 6f⁴ 6m⁶ 6m⁴ 6f 7m 8g] 2,000F, 1,900Y: small colt: half-brother to 7f and 1m winner Smokey Shadow (by Dragonara Palace): dam best at up to 1¼m: modest plater: should stay at least 1m: twice wandered when blinkered: looks awkward ride: sent to A. W. Jones. *Mrs N. Macauley.*

SUMMA CUM LAUDE 3 ch.f. Superlative 118–Bas Bleu 117 (Abernant 142)   **87** [1988 NR 1989 7d² 7.6m 6g* 6m 6g 7g 6v] close-coupled filly: has a markedly round action: half-sister to 2 winners, including useful miler Baccalaureate (by Crowned Prince): dam, best at sprint distances, stayed 1m: won minor event at Leicester in May: faced stiff tasks in quite valuable handicaps after, running poorly first 2 occasions and off course 3 months after: suited by 6f: best efforts on an easy surface: sold 21,000 gns Newmarket December Sales. *G. Wragg.*

SUM MEDE 2 b.c. (Apr 7) King Persian 107–Brun's Toy (FR) (Bruni 132) [1989   **70** 5m² 5m⁶ 6m 6f* 7f 8m 8m² 8f² 8f²] IR 5,000F, 5,000Y, resold 6,000Y, 19,500 2-y-o: workmanlike colt: has a quick action: second foal: dam minor winner at 9f at 4 yrs in France: quite modest performer: won nursery at Warwick in July: ran well afterwards in similar events: will stay 1¼m: acts on firm going. *R. Hannon.*

SUMMER FASHION 4 b.f. Moorestyle 137–My Candy 81 (Lorenzaccio 130)   **82** [1988 7f 7f 7g² 8d* 9m⁶ 8g 10m³ 8g* 9g⁴ 1989 8h² 8.5m 10m* 8f³ 10f* 10m* 9g 11v] leggy filly: moderate mover: fair handicapper: successful at Goodwood in June and Salisbury (twice) in August: fair ninth of 34 in William Hill Cambridgeshire Handicap at Newmarket: ideally suited by 1¼m: probably unsuited by soft going, acts on any other: wears bandages behind: genuine. *D. R. C. Elsworth.*

SUMMERHILL IVORY 3 gr.f. Camden Town 125–For Sure 88 (Fortino II 120)   **—** [1988 NR 1989 8m 10f] IR 7,600Y: leggy, angular filly: half-sister to useful 1976 2-y-o 6f winner Sal (by Sallust), dam of good Australian performer Special, and a winner abroad: dam, who appeared to stay 1m, is half-sister to high-class sprinter Monet: never placed to challenge or knocked about in maidens at Newmarket and Kempton in first half of season: may do better. *J. L. Dunlop.*

SUMMERHILL SALLY 3 b.f. Dunbeath (USA) 127–Sharper Still (Sharpen Up   **53** 127) [1988 6f 1989 7s 8m 10m² 10.2h 8m 7h] medium-sized filly: second in claimer at Nottingham in June: below form in similar events after: best form at 1¼m: takes keen hold: has found little: sold to join P. Leach 5,400 gns Ascot August Sales. *J. L. Dunlop.*

SUMMER TRIP (USA) 4 b. or br.f. L'Emigrant (USA) 129–Summer Review **114** (USA) (Graustark (USA)) [1988 8v² 10d³ 10v² 12s³ 10.5m⁴ 12g⁴ 13.5d³ 12g³ 12.5m* 12s 1989 12s 10.5v 12d 10.5g² 12g³ 13.5g² 12g³ 12.5m⁴ 12g⁴] French filly: very useful performer: regularly raced in good company and has won only once: in frame as 4-y-o in Prix Fille de l'Air at Saint-Cloud, Grosser Preis der Berliner Bank at Dusseldorf, Prix de Pomone (short-head second to Colorado Dancer) at Deauville, Grosser Preis von Baden (beaten length and neck by Mondrian and Per Quod) at Baden-Baden, Ciga Prix de Royallieu at Longchamp and listed event at Saint-Cloud: stays 13.5f: yet to race on firm going, acts on any other: has been tried in blinkers: tough. *J. Fellows, France.*

SUMMIT REACHED 3 b.f. Homing 130–Sister Hannah 70 (Monseigneur   **—** (USA) 127) [1988 7m 7s 1989 8m 10m 14g⁵ 14m³ 15.3g⁴ 16f 14m] lengthy, useful-looking filly: poor maiden: should stay well: tailed off in blinkers last 2 outings: sold 1,500 gns Newmarket Autumn Sales. *R. J. R. Williams.*

SUM MUSIC 4 b.f. Music Boy 124–Sum Star 67 (Comedy Star (USA) 121) [1988   **—** 5f 5f⁵ 6d 5m 5s 5f 6m 1989 5m⁵ 5m⁶ 5m 5f] leggy filly: has a round action: bad sprint maiden. *J. S. Wainwright.*

SUNDANCE KID (USA) 2 b.c. (Apr 3) Fappiano (USA)–Gallanta (FR) 112   **91** p (Nureyev (USA) 131) [1989 6f* 6g] angular, useful-looking colt: has scope: first foal: dam, 5.5f to 1m winner in France, is half-sister to Gay Mecene, also family of Raja Baba: long odds on, won 8-runner maiden at Newcastle in October readily by 2 lengths, quickening well final furlong: 13 lengths tenth of 25, never dangerous, to Osario in Racecall Gold Trophy at Redcar later in month: will be better suited by 7f: sure to improve further. *H. R. A. Cecil.*

SUNDAY SPORT'S PET   2 b.f. (Apr 19) Mummy's Pet 125–My Princess (King   58
Emperor (USA)) [1989 5g⁴ 5m⁴ 6g⁴] 22,000Y: sparely-made filly: good walker:
moderate mover: ninth reported foal: sister to 1985 2-y-o 5f winner Moonlight Lady,
later much better at 7f and 1m, and half-sister to several other winners: dam won at
2 yrs in Italy: plating-class maiden: easily best effort on debut: not raced after July. *J.
Berry.*

SUNDAY SPORT STAR   4 b.f. Star Appeal 133–Justine (GER) (Luciano) [1988   86 d
12d³ 12g⁴ 12m 16f 10m² 9s* 12f⁶ 10g² 10f 12g 1989 10d³ 8g 12d⁶ 10.5f 10m] rather
sparely-made filly: good mover: fairly useful at her best: stayed on strongly final 2f
after losing place under halfway when third to Queens Tour in valuable handicap at
Kempton in March: well below form afterwards, and not seen out after July: needed
further than 1m and stayed 1½m: seemed to act on any going: usually blinkered:
occasionally sweated: inconsistent: stud. *P. A. Kelleway.*

SUNFLOWER SEED   2 b.f. (Feb 21) Mummy's Pet 125–Bright Sun (Mill Reef   70
(USA) 141) [1989 7f² 6g] IR 42,000Y: first foal: dam unraced sister to Milford and
half-sister to Height of Fashion, dam of Unfuwain and Nashwan: 4 lengths second of
7 to Anshan in maiden at Sandown in July: co-favourite, poor seventh of 18 in similar
event at Hamilton following month: better suited by 7f than 6f. *W. Hastings-Bass.*

SUNGROVE PRIDE   3 b.g. Chukaroo 103–Judann (Some Hand 119) [1988 5f³   —
7g 1989 7h 6h 7m 6m 6m 5m] leggy gelding: plating-class maiden: has shown little
since debut: should stay 7f. *L. J. Holt.*

SUNIRAM   3 b. or br.f. Marching On 101–Wellington Bear (Dragonara Palace   50
(USA) 115) [1988 6m⁶ 1989 5m⁶ 7m 5g 5g] workmanlike filly: plating-class maiden:
behind after reappearance, including in handicaps: suited by sprint distances: tends
to sweat and get on edge. *J. M. Jefferson.*

SUNLEY PRINCESS   4 ch.f. Ballad Rock 122–Silk Blend (Busted 134) [1988 8d   —
7g⁶ 7f⁴ 8d⁴ 7d³ 7m² 7m 7f⁵ 7g 8d 1989 8.2g 7g 10m] lightly-made filly: quite modest
maiden at her best: suited by 7f: acts on top-of-the-ground and a soft surface:
sweating on reappearance. *J. A. C. Edwards.*

SUNLEY SUNSHINE   3 b.f. Sunley Builds 102–Brown Velvet 68 (Mansingh   66
(USA) 120) [1988 6g 7m⁵ 1989 11f 8f⁶ 10.2h³ a10g] big, leggy filly: has scope: quite
modest maiden: creditable third at Bath: facing stiff task, always struggling in
Lingfield handicap over 4 months later: stays 1¼m. *J. L. Dunlop.*

SUNNY JORVIK   3 b.c. Mansingh (USA) 120–Melowen 75 (Owen Dudley 121)   — §
[1988 5f 5g 7g⁶ 7g 1989 8s 7.5d] small, angular colt: little worthwhile form, including
in sellers: tried in blinkers and a visor at 2 yrs: sold 750 gns Doncaster May Sales:
temperamental, and one to avoid. *M. Brittain.*

SUNNYSIDE   2 ch.f. (Apr 30) Doulab (USA) 115–Sunny Look 91 (Lombard (GER)   50
126) [1989 5f² 5h² 5m³ 5m 6g 5g] IR 5,000Y: leggy, sparely-made filly: third foal:
half-sister to Belgian winner Some of These Days (by Coquelin): dam 1¼m and 2m
winner: plating-class maiden: should stay 6f: tends to get on toes. *R. Hollinshead.*

SUNNYSIDE JOHN   3 b.c. Monsanto (FR) 121–Ribellina (Ribero 126) [1988 5g³   62
5m 5m² 5d* 6g² 6g⁶ 6f 6g² 6m⁵ 6s⁶ 5d⁴ 6g³ 5m 1989 7m⁶ 8.5d²] strong, compact,
rather dipped-backed colt: carries condition: moderate mover: quite useful plater:
ran creditably in non-selling handicaps in spring as 3-y-o, despite drifting badly right
final start: should stay 1¼m: acts on top-of-the-ground but most effective with a bit
of give: best form at 2 yrs when visored. *Mrs N. Macauley.*

SUN ON THE SPEY   3 ch.f. Glint of Gold 128–Strathspey 105 (Jimmy Reppin   —
131) [1988 NR 1989 12m 12g] lengthy, angular filly: fifth living foal: closely related to
quite useful 1986 2-y-o 6f winner Dunninald, useful 1984 2-y-o 7.3f winner River
Spey and a winner in Belgium (all by Mill Reef) and half-sister to 1¼m winner
Bastinado (by Bustino): dam, 6f to 1m winner, is sister to very smart Joking Apart:
soundly beaten in maidens at Newbury: pulled hard on debut: sold 20,000 gns
Newmarket December Sales. *I. A. Balding.*

SUNSET REINS FREE   4 b.c.c. Red Sunset 120–Free Rein (Sagaro 133) [1988   69
6g 8m² 7f² 8.2g* 8d* 8.2d* 9s 9f 9g 1989 8s 12d⁵ 12g³ 10m 8.2g 12.3m 17.6g⁴ 17.4s]
big, good-bodied colt: carries plenty of condition: moderate mover: modest handicapper: below form after third outing: stays 1½m: best on an easy surface (yet to
show his form on very soft going): withdrawn 3 times after early-August, once after
breaking blood vessel, once after breaking out of stalls and once after unseating
rider and bolting: usually visored nowadays (blinkered when withdrawn on third
occasion): winning hurdler. *E. J. Alston.*

SUNSET ROSE   2 b.f. (May 19) Shirley Heights 130–Rose Bowl (USA) 131   —
(Habitat 134) [1989 7.3v] closely related to 3-y-o 1¼m winner Rose Campion, 7f and

1¼m winner Antigua Rose and Irish 7f to 1¼m winner Rose Reef (all by Mill Reef) and half-sister to very useful 7f and 1½m winner Golden Bowl (by Vaguely Noble): dam, outstanding 1m to 1¼m performer, is half-sister to top-class Ile de Bourbon: 14/1, slowly away and always behind in 12-runner listed race at Newbury in October. *I. A. Balding.*

SUNSET RULER 2 b.c. (Jan 14) Red Sunset 120–Swift Verdict 89 (My Swallow 56 134) [1989 6m⁴ 6m 7m⁵ 8.2d⁵ 8.2g a7g] 8,600Y: compact colt: has scope: good walker: seventh foal: dam Irish 1¼m winner: plating-class maiden: ran creditably in blinkers final start: stays 1m: on toes third outing: sold 4,900 gns Doncaster November Sales. *E. Eldin.*

SUNWIND 3 b.g. Windjammer (USA)–Mrewa (Runnymede 123) [1988 6f 5g³ 6d² 70 6m² 1989 7s 7g 7f 6h 6m 6m⁶ 6f 6g²] stocky gelding: modest maiden: best efforts in handicaps after reappearance when staying on at Ascot (£7,600 event) and Folkestone (beaten short head) fifth and final outings: best form at 6f: acts on top-of-the-ground and a soft surface: trained until after fifth outing by A. Ingham. *J. Sutcliffe.*

SUPER BENZ 3 ch.g. Hello Gorgeous (USA) 128–Investiture 62 (Welsh 77 Pageant 132) [1988 5d* 7.5f* 7.5g³ 7g² 7g³ 7g 6s 1989 8.2s⁶ 10.6s 8.5d⁴ 8m⁴ 6f* 6m⁴ 6g³ 6m 5m 6g] leggy, lengthy, useful-looking gelding: has a roundish action: fair handicapper: made all, unchallenged on stand side, in apprentice claimer at Nottingham in June: ran moderately in claimers last 2 starts: seems suited by 6f: best form on a sound surface: visored once at 2 yrs, on reappearance and eighth outing: tends to put head in air. *M. H. Easterby.*

SUPERBRAVE 3 b.c. Superlative 118–Tribal Feast 100 (Tribal Chief 125) [1988 — p NR 1989 7g] strong, lengthy colt: seventh living foal: half-brother to smart 1984 2-y-o Brave Bambino (by Jaazeiro) and 11f winner Tribal Pageant (by Welsh Pageant): dam speedy half-sister to high-class sprinter Runnett: 12/1 from 50/1 but green and backward, about 9 lengths ninth of 16 to Breezed Well in minor event at Leicester in November: should improve. *J. Etherington.*

SUPERCHIP 2 ch.c. (Mar 19) Superlative 118–Crockfords Green 73 (Roan — Rocket 128) [1989 8f 7.5f 8f] 6,600Y: good-topped colt: fourth foal: dam 1m winner: poor form in maiden auction races. *J. Etherington.*

SUPERCOOMBE 6 gr.g. John de Coombe 122–Petalina 93 (Mummy's Pet 125) — [1988 10s 7f 1989 8m 7.6h 12m 10g 11.7m 8.3m] lengthy gelding: poor maiden: well beaten in handicaps and a claimer in 1989: probably stayed 1m: unsuited by firm going, acted on any other: occasionally slowly away: dead. *P. Butler.*

SUPER DEB 2 ch.f. (May 12) Superlative 118–Debutina Park 87 (Averof 123) 70 [1989 6m³ 5f² 5m* 6g] 22,000Y: third foal: half-sister to poor 3-y-o Trojan Debut (by Trojan Fen) and 5f winner Avidal Park (by Horage): dam 2-y-o 6f winner ran only once afterwards: won 8-runner maiden at Chester in September: had very stiff task when favourite in nursery at York month later: stays 6f. *B. Hanbury.*

SUPERENFER 2 b.c. (Mar 13) Superlative 118–Moment In Time 91 (Without 69 Fear (FR)) [1989 6g³ 6m³ 6s² 6m] 22,000F: strong, lengthy colt: third foal: dam 7f winner at 2 yrs: quite modest maiden: acts on top-of-the-ground and soft going: visored final appearance. *J. G. FitzGerald.*

SUPERETTA 2 ch.f. (Apr 11) Superlative 118–Brown's Cay (Formidable (USA) 65 p 125) [1989 7g⁴ 6g⁵] IR 10,000Y: angular, sparely-made filly: second foal: half-sister to poor 1988 2-y-o Situation (by Noalto): dam, placed over 1m at 2 yrs, is half-sister to smart stayer Antler and daughter of Jockey Club Stakes winner Queen of Twilight: around 5 lengths fifth of 22 to Lip Sing in maiden at Leicester in November, better effort: likely to improve bit further. *J. W. Hills.*

SUPER GUNNER 4 ch.g. Busted 134–Lunaria (USA) (Twist The Axe (USA)) — [1988 9g³ 10f 10s 8g 13.1f 12d³ 12d³ 12v⁶ 1989 11.7d 12d⁴] lengthy gelding: poor mover: poor maiden: stays 1½m: acts on firm going and a soft surface: has run creditably for amateur. *M. J. Fetherston-Godley.*

SUPER JULES (FR) 4 ch.g. Trio (FR)–Silver Plate (FR) (Son of Silver 123) — [1988 NR 1989 a10g] first foal: dam unplaced 3 times as 2-y-o in France: 25/1, slowly away and always tailed off in maiden at Lingfield in October: winning hurdler in France. *J. A. B. Old.*

SUPERLASSIE 3 b.f. Superlative 118–Brig of Ayr 90 (Brigadier Gerard 144) — [1988 6f⁶ 6f 1989 7s 8g 6f 7h 7f 8g⁶ 7g 7f] medium-sized filly: moderate walker: has a round action: bad plater: may stay beyond 1m: showed little in blinkers penultimate start: sold 1,100 gns Ascot October Sales. *P. Howling.*

SUPER LUNAR 5 gr.g. Kalaglow 132–Roxy Hart (High Top 131) [1988 6g 7g⁴ **75**
8d⁴ 8g 8f⁵ 7m⁵ 8f³ 8g* 10d⁵ 7m* 1989 7s⁵ 8g³ 9.2f⁴ 8f 8m⁴ 8m² 9f* 8.5g⁵ 8m³ 8g³
11v⁴ 10g²] strong, close-coupled gelding: modest handicapper: won at Sandown in
July, quickening clear 2f out then tending to idle: placed after, running creditably, at
Sandown, Newmarket and Redcar: stays 1¼m: seems not at his best on soft going,
acts on any other: ran moderately in blinkers: has run well for apprentice: often
takes good hold: hung right fourth appearance. *L. G. Cottrell.*

SUPERMATE 2 b.f. (Apr 6) Superlative 118–Stately Girl (Free State 125) [1989 **53**
5m 5m² 6f⁵ 6d 5g 6g] 6,000F: small, workmanlike filly: third foal: dam won 6 races in
Italy: plating-class maiden: stays 6f: blinkered final start: sold 2,400 gns Doncaster
November Sales. *J. Etherington.*

SUPER MORNING 3 b.c. Martinmas 128–Super Lady (Averof 123) [1988 6m **62**
6s* 6m² 8f 6f⁵ 1989 8s 7s⁵ 8.5d 7g 7g²ᵈⁱˢ 7m 7m 7m⁴ 8f⁵ 8m] tall, good-bodied colt:
moderate walker: quite modest handicapper: beaten short head in £6,000 event at
Newbury in August, hanging left (saddle reportedly slipped) and disqualified: stays
1m: acts on any going: blinkered or visored last 7 starts. *M. J. Fetherston-Godley.*

SUPER NEON 3 b.g. Dominion 123–Super Anna (Super Sam 124) [1988 5f² 5d⁵ **68**
6d 1989 7m² 8.5g 7m 8m 7.6m* 7s⁵] good-topped gelding: showed improved form
when winning claimer at Chester, leading well inside final 1f: co-favourite, well
beaten in amateurs handicap week later in September: suited by 7f: possibly needs
top-of-the-ground. *Mrs L. Piggott.*

SUPER ONE 2 b.g. (Apr 25) Superlative 118–Josephine Gibney (High Top 131) **75**
[1989 5d 6m² 5f* 6f³ 5f⁴ 7m 6g 6m* 6s 6m 7m] 30,000Y: compact gelding: moderate
mover: first foal: dam, winner in Italy, from family of high-class sprinter Green God:
modest performer: successful in maiden at Lingfield in June and valuable seller
(bought out of B. Hanbury's stable 21,000 gns) at York in August: free runner, best
at sprint distances: possibly unsuited by a soft surface: effective with blinkers or
without: has worn a tongue strap: gelded after final appearance. *T. D. Barron.*

SUPEROO 3 b.g. Superlative 118–Shirleen (Daring Display (USA) 129) [1988 6f **88**
1989 7f⁶ 10.1m 8f⁶ 7m* 7m* 7g* 7g] big, workmanlike gelding: fair handicapper:
won at Leicester and Newmarket in July and Doncaster (£5,500 race) in September:
favourite, ran poorly in £8,600 contest at Newmarket final start: well-backed
favourite, withdrawn (lame) at start for £49,600 event at Ascot 6 days earlier: should
stay 1m: acts on top-of-the-ground: gelded after final start. *J. Sutcliffe.*

SUPERPOWER 3 b.c. Superlative 118–Champ d'Avril 89 (Northfields (USA)) **113**
[1988 5g* 5d* 5m* 5f* 5g* 5f* 5d² 5.5d³ 6g* 5d² 5g⁴ 1989 5m² 5f⁴ 5f 6m⁶] big,
strong, lengthy colt: has a rather round action: very useful sprinter, highly successful at 2 yrs: beaten head by Silver Fling in Palace House Stakes at Newmarket in
May: off course 2 months between outings after, running fairly well in pattern
events at Sandown, Goodwood and Ascot: stayed 6f well: didn't race on very soft
going, acted on any other: tended to run lazily, and wore blinkers as 3-y-o and twice
at 2 yrs: usually looked very well: to stand at Ballykisteen Stud, Co. Tipperary, fee
IR £4,000 (Oct 1st). *W. A. O'Gorman.*

SUPER RELATIVE 3 b.g. Superlative 118–Breton's Sister 58 (Relko 136) **53**
[1988 7g 7g 1989 7f 7m 7m² 9f³ 6g] deep-girthed gelding: placed in claimer (easily
best effort, claimed out of I. Balding's stable £8,256) at Newmarket and seller
(leading over 6f) at Redcar: will prove best short of 9f. *N. Tinkler.*

SUPERSINGLE LADY 3 b.f. Kafu 120–Giddy Lyn (USA) (Relko 136) [1988 —
5g⁶ 5g 5m 5f* 5f* 5m⁶ 5m² 5g 5m 1989 5f 5g 5g 5m 6g 5f] small, dipped-backed filly:
carries plenty of condition: has a quick action: quite modest seller winner as 2-y-o:
well behind in handicaps in 1989: best at 5f: possibly requires firm ground: wore
visor final start: also tried in one and blinkered at 2 yrs. *C. Tinkler.*

SUPER TRIP 8 b.g. Windjammer (USA)–Esker Rose (Sunny Way 120) [1988 —
7.5g* 8d 1989 7f 8f⁴] well-made gelding: carries plenty of condition: poor mover:
modest winner as 7-y-o: better effort in 1989 when never-nearer fourth of 10 at
Chepstow in June: best at around 1m: best form on a sound surface: suitable mount
for apprentice: suited by a strongly-run race and waiting tactics: often wears
bandages. *M. J. Fetherston-Godley.*

SUPER TRUCKER 6 b.g. Lochnager 132–The Haulier 53 (Pitskelly 122) [1988 —
7.5g 8g 8g² 9s* 10g 8g 1989 8h] leggy gelding: has a round action: poor handicapper:
stays 9f: goes well on soft going: occasionally sweats: has won for apprentice:
inconsistent. *W. W. Haigh.*

SUPER VIRTUOSA 2 b.f. (Feb 3) Wassl 125–Resolve (Reform 132) [1989 5s² **59**
5g³ 5m⁴ 6g⁶ 7m⁴ 8m⁵ 7g] 3,600Y: leggy filly: shows a quick action: moderate

mover: fourth foal: half-sister to prolific Italian winner Luvi Ullman (by Thatching): dam unraced half-sister to Homing and Water Mill: plating-class maiden: stays 1m. *M. J. Haynes.*

SUPERWHITE 2 gr.f. (Mar 7) Superlative 118–Blanche Neige 75 (Forlorn River 124) [1989 5v⁶ 5f 7f] 7,200Y: rather unfurnished filly: third foal: dam, half-sister to high-class French sprinter Kind Music and very useful 5f performer Boy Trumpeter, won over 5f on debut at 2 yrs but failed to progress: poor maiden: sold 1,100 gns Ascot November Sales. *Mrs N. Macauley.* —

SUPREME BLUES 3 b.c. Cure The Blues (USA)–Court Barns (USA) 101 (Riva Ridge (USA)) [1988 6d⁴ 5m² 1989 8d 8g a8g⁴ a10g³ a8g] angular, sparely-made colt: moderate mover: plating-class form at best: in frame in claimer and handicap at Lingfield, making most and wandering under pressure penultimate start: sweating, lean in appearance and below form final one: seems to stay 1¼m: blinkered last 2 outings. *M. Brittain.* 57

SUPREME COURT 2 b.g. (Apr 15) Yashgan 126–My Natalie 64 (Rheingold 137) [1989 5d⁴ 5f⁴ 6g 7.5g³ 7g 7m³ 7m 6m⁶ 10.6d a6g] 5,800F, 7,200Y: dipped-backed gelding: poor mover: fifth foal: half-brother to Irish 1m and 1¼m winner Myliege (by Lord Gayle), fair 7f and 7.5f winner Ned's Aura (by Dalsaan) and a winner in Italy: dam 1m winner: quite modest plater: seems not to stay 10.6f: acts on firm going and a soft surface: visored fourth to sixth starts: has given trouble at stalls: usually on toes or edgy: has given impression hasn't ideal attitude. *S. J. Muldoon.* 44

SUPREME DANCER (FR) 2 b.g. (Feb 23) Alzao (USA) 117–Supreme Solar (Royal Captive 116) [1989 6g] 60,000 francs (approx 5,500) Y: quite attractive gelding: fifth foal: dam ran twice at 4 yrs in Ireland: slowly away and always behind in 29-runner maiden at Newmarket in November: subsequently gelded. *W. Jarvis.* —

SUPREME GUEST 3 gr.g. What A Guest 119–Fortune's Lady 93 (Fortino II 120) [1988 7m³ 8.2s⁵ 1989 11f 10g] close-coupled gelding: failed to confirm debut promise in maidens and amateurs handicap: should stay at least 1m: gelded after final start (July). *C. R. Nelson.* —

SUPREME HEIGHTS 3 b. or br.f. Valiyar 129–Coral Heights 86 (Shirley Heights 130) [1988 7m 8g² 1989 12.2m⁴] good-topped filly: quite modest form in maidens: took keen hold only start as 3-y-o, in June: stays 12.2f: sold 800 gns Newmarket December Sales. *C. E. Brittain.* 66

SUPREME NEPHEW 5 b.g. Sallust 134–Country Niece (Great Nephew 126) [1988 10m 12m 12m 10f 8m 8f 1989 12m] close-coupled, smallish gelding: of little account: blinkered once. *J. C. Fox.* —

SUPREME OPTIMIST 5 b.g. Absalom 128–Cachucha (Gay Fandango (USA) 132) [1988 6g 6f⁶ 7f 6g 5g⁵ 6g 6s⁵ 6m 7.6s 10m 7g⁵ 7f⁴ 6s 6g 7d³ 5v 1989 6d⁶ 7d* 6g* 7.5g⁴ 6f³ 7f³ 5g² 7.6m 5m] small, workmanlike gelding: poor mover: apprentice ridden, made all in handicaps at Edinburgh (20/1) and Carlisle (favourite) in April: placed, running well, in amateur events afterwards: stays 7f: acts on any going: best form in blinkers: has worn tongue strap and crossed noseband: excellent mount for inexperienced rider. *R. E. Peacock.* 52

SUPREME ROSE 5 b.m. Frimley Park 109–Ragtime Rose (Ragstone 128) [1988 6m 6f 6g 5g 5g⁴ 6s 6g 6d³ 5v⁴ 1989 5g 5m 6m] leggy, workmanlike mare: one-time fairly useful performer: ran poorly last 2 outings: needs stiff 5f and stays 6f well: acts on any going: visored once at 4 yrs: has worn bandages: inconsistent. *E. A. Wheeler.* —

SUPREME WARRIOR 3 b.c. Simply Great (FR) 122–Sindo 91 (Derring-Do 131) [1988 8g 1989 12m⁶ 11f² 10.4g⁶ 13f² 16f⁴ 12m⁴ 11.7f² 14m² 12m 10.2f] workmanlike colt: has a long stride: quite modest maiden: should stay well: best efforts on firm going: often makes running: claimed out of R. Hollinshead's stable £8,055 eighth start. *P. J. Hobbs.* 61

SUPRETTE 2 b.f. (Feb 12) Superlative 118–Blaskette 99 (Blast 125) [1989 6g⁴] 27,000Y: good-quartered filly: has scope: half-sister to 3-y-o Castoret (by Jalmood) and several winners, including useful 6f and 1m winner Sharblask (by Sharpo): dam middle-distance handicapper: 7/2 but bit backward and green, about 4 lengths fourth of 14, one pace final 1f, to Sarah Georgina in minor event at Windsor in July: has joined J. Hills. *P. F. I. Cole.* 68 p

SURCOAT 2 b.c. (Apr 9) Bustino 136–Mullet 75 (Star Appeal 133) [1989 6f 7f⁵ 8m⁵ 8.2g a7g⁶] sturdy colt: carries condition: second foal: dam, 1¼m winner, is half-sister to very smart 7f to 13.3f winner Consol: plating-class maiden: wore net muzzle when running well in nursery at Nottingham on fourth start: will be suited by 1¼m: sent to C. W. C. Elsey. *P. Walwyn.* 58

SUREFOOT SILLARS 2 ch.c. (Feb 19) Hotfoot 126–Make A Signal 76 (Royal   **60**
Gunner (USA)) [1989 7g 6f⁶ 6d⁶ 7g] 6,400F, 11,000Y: neat colt: sixth foal: half-
brother to a winner in Italy by African Sky and a winner in France by Owen Dudley:
dam, successful stayer (won 7 races), from family of Raise You Ten: quite modest
performer: easily best effort in Catterick maiden on third start: should stay at least
1¼m. *Mrs J. R. Ramsden.*

SURE GOLD 3 b.f. Glint of Gold 128–Carolside 108 (Music Maestro 119) [1988   **100**
6f² 6d³ 6f* 7m³ 6f⁵ 1989 6m² 6g² 6m* 7g⁴ 7f³ 6g⁵ 6g³] lengthy, workmanlike filly:
good mover, with a long stride: won William Hill Golden Spurs Trophy (Handicap) at
York in June: creditable third in listed race at Goodwood, best subsequent effort:
slowly away and ran poorly last 2 outings, looking reluctant to race on final one:
stays 7f: acts on firm going: sometimes goes freely to post, and refused to settle in
moderately-run race fourth outing: best with waiting tactics: one to be wary of. *P. T.
Walwyn.*

SURELY GREAT 5 b.m. Vaigly Great 127–Niorkie (FR) (My Swallow 134)   **46** §
[1988 6m⁴ 6g 6g⁴ 6f⁵ 7m 6m 7.6f 5s³ 5g 6m 6m³ 6f³ 6d 6g 1989 6f⁶ 6f⁴] big, lengthy
mare: has a quick action: still a maiden and is not resolute: effective at 5f given
testing conditions and stays 7f: acts on any going: effective with or without blinkers
or visor: has sweated: reluctant to race once in 1988: not to be trusted. *J. R. Jenkins.*

SURE SHARP (USA) 2 b.c. (Feb 16) Sharpen Up 127–Double Lock 104 (Home   **97** p
Guard (USA) 129) [1989 6g⁵ 6g*] big, good-topped colt: has plenty of scope: brother
to quite useful Only A Pound, a winner from 1m to 1¼m and later at 6f in South
Africa, closely related to top-class miler Sure Blade (by Kris), and half-brother to
Sure Locked (by Lyphard), 1m winner in France: dam won over 1¼m: co-favourite,
made most in 29-runner maiden at Newmarket in November, beating Rahaam
comfortably by 2½ lengths: very slowly away on debut 2 weeks previously: will be
better suited by 7f+: likely to improve again, and win more races. *B. W. Hills.*

SUREST DANCER (USA) 3 b.c. Green Dancer (USA) 132–Oopsie Daisy   **73**
(USA) (Dewan) [1988 NR 1989 7d 10m³ 10m 10.8f³ 12m 17.6m⁴ 16f⁴ 15.3f a12g⁶]
16,500Y: medium-sized, rather finely-made colt: has a fluent, slightly round action:
half-brother to 3 winners in USA, including Dark Accent (by Pretense), stakes-
placed winner at up to 1¼m: dam unraced sister to Grade 1 winner Afifa, close
relation of Auction Ring and half-sister to Alias Smith: modest maiden: below form
last 5 starts: should stay 1½m: blinkered last 3 starts: lacks turn of foot: sold to join
Mrs P. Barker 8,000 gns Newmarket Autumn Sales: possibly irresolute. *P. T.
Walwyn.*

SURF BIRD 3 b.f. Shareef Dancer (USA) 135–Britannia's Rule 108 (Blakeney   **—**
126) [1988 NR 1989 12f 12f 10.1m 12m] sturdy filly: sixth foal: half-sister to several
winners, including 4-y-o middle-distance stayer Clifton Chapel (by High Line), very

*William Hill Golden Spurs Trophy (Handicap), York—
Sure Gold wins the feature race on the nineteenth Timeform Charity Day
which raised a total of £90,000 for Cancer Relief and other charities*

useful 1½m and 2m winner Guarde Royale (by Ile de Bourbon) and useful 7f to 1½m winner Henry The Lion (by Great Nephew): dam, out of half-sister to Vaguely Noble, was third in Oaks: sign of ability only when beaten about 7½ lengths in maiden at Newbury in July final start, making steady headway despite being bumped 2f. *H. Candy.*

SURPASSING 2 ch.f. (May 10) Superlative 118–Catherine Howard 68 (Tower 79 Walk 130) [1989 5f4 6f2 5f4 5f 7g* 7m5 9g3 8m] lengthy, rather sparely-made filly: has scope: good walker: has a fluent action: sixth foal: half-sister to 3-y-o Head-strong (by Precocious), plating-class stayer Goodtime Hal (by Good Times) and 2 winners, including fair 5f winner Breakaway (by Song): dam placed over 1¼m: modest performer: won 12-runner maiden at Leicester in August: ran well after-wards in nurseries and Hoover Fillies' Mile: needs at least 7f and stays 9f: blinkered and edgy fourth outing. *C. E. Brittain.*

SURPRISE GAME 3 b.f. Mummy's Game 120–Record Surprise 78 (Record Run — 127) [1988 5m 5g 6d5 5.8d4 5g 1989 5.8h] medium-sized filly: has a round action: little worthwhile form, including in sellers. *C. J. Hill.*

SURREAL 4 ch.f. Bustino 136–Swiftacre (Bay Express 132) [1988 8d5 7d5 7.6g 59 d 6f6 6m4 5m3 5.3f3 5m* 5m 1989 5s2 5d 5s 5.8h6 5.1m 5.8h6 5m6 5m] rangy filly: plating-class handicapper: generally well below her best after first outing: best at sprint distances: acts on any going: wears blinkers: possibly needs strong handling: often sweats: sold 1,000 gns Newmarket Autumn Sales. *K. M. Brassey.*

SURSAS 2 b.c. (Jan 20) Chief Singer 131–Dignified Air (FR) 70 (Wolver Hollow 50 126) [1989 6m4 5m5 6g 8.2s6 7g] 48,000Y: strong, medium-sized, quite attractive colt: second foal: dam, 6f winner at 4 yrs, out of a half-sister to very smart Joking Apart: plating-class maiden: best effort on debut: looked ungenerous when blinkered final start: should stay further than 6f: one to be wary of. *J. G. FitzGerald.*

SUSAN HENCHARD 5 b.m. Auction Ring (USA) 123–Let Slip 77 (Busted 134) 32 [1988 10.2s6 8.5m6 9d 7m 8f 8g 8m 8g 10d2 1989 10.2g3 11v3 11d 8f 10f 11f6 a11g] rather angular, deep-girthed mare: moderate mover: poor performer: stays 11f: acts on heavy going, seems unsuited by firm nowadays: blinkered once at 4 yrs and on third and fifth outings: visored sixth: has started slowly: has given trouble in preliminaries. *M. Avison.*

SUSANNA'S SECRET 2 b.c. (Apr 28) Superlative 118–Queens Welcome 60 — (Northfields (USA)) [1989 6g 6g a6g] 9,000Y: strong, close-coupled colt: first foal: dam, ran only at 2 yrs, is half-sister to high-class 1973 2-y-o sprinter The Blues: poor form in maidens. *Mrs L. Piggott.*

SUSAN'S REEF 4 b.g. Main Reef 126–Susan's Way (Red God 128§) [1988 6g6 7g 58 7d4 1989 5g 9f 8m 8.3d 8f 6s2] workmanlike gelding: has a long stride: plating-class maiden nowadays: 12/1 from 33/1, form as 4-y-o only when neck second of 12 in seller at Hamilton in November: stays 7f: best with plenty of give in the ground: blinkered final 3 starts at 2 yrs. *J. M. Bradley.*

SUSHA 2 gr.f. (Mar 28) Bay Express 132–Gem-May 71 (Mansingh (USA) 120) 59 [1989 5d5 5f* 6m 5g3 5g] neat filly: moderate mover: first foal: dam, maiden plater, stayed 1½m: plating-class performer: made all in 6-runner maiden at Chester in May: speedy, and likely to prove best at 5f: bandaged last 2 starts. *A. M. Robson.*

SUSPECT DEVICE 2 ch.c. (Mar 24) Dublin Taxi–Kimstar 61 (Aureole 132) 50 [1989 6g 7.5f4 8f6] IR 3,100F, 3,000Y: half-brother to 1m seller winner Pale Star (by Kampala) and winning Irish middle-distance stayer Tawkin (by Taufan): dam, maiden, stayed 12f: poor maiden: stays 7.5f. *A. M. Robson.*

SUTOSKY 5 b.m. Great Nephew 126–Butosky 71 (Busted 134) [1988 10d4 9f2 78 10f3 8.2s* 10.2g3 10m* 8g2 10d* 8s* 1989 10d6 10g* 10m 8f 9g] leggy, sparely-made mare: fair handicapper: successful at Newmarket in April: ran poorly next 2 outings and off course over 4 months afterwards: badly hampered leaving stalls and never a threat in William Hill Cambridgeshire Handicap at Newmarket: suited by 1m to 1¼m: has won on top-of-the-ground, but best form on an easy surface: sometimes sweats: genuine. *I. V. Matthews.*

SUZY LORENZO 4 b. or br.f. Swing Easy (USA) 126–Love Beach 75 59 (Lorenzaccio 130) [1988 8g6 11f 10g 10g 10.2f 7g 8g 1989 a8g6 a10g] tall, leggy filly: plating-class maiden: best form at 1m: visored twice at 3 yrs: blinkered in 1989. *R. J. O'Sullivan.*

SVELTISSIMA 3 b.f. Dunphy 124–Night Vision 100 (Yellow God 129) [1988 5d6 50 6m5 7f 7g 7d4 7m 7g3 8.2s 10s 1989 8.2v* 11v2 8d6 8m 8.2m2 8f2 10.6g6 9g] lengthy, workmanlike filly: carries condition: moderate mover: fair plater: won at Hamilton (no bid) in April: effective at 1m and probably stays 11f: acts on top-of-the-ground and heavy going: trained until after penultimate start by J. Berry. *G. R. Oldroyd.*

SWANK GILBERT 3 b.g. Balliol 125–Song To Singo 63 (Master Sing 109) [1988   **31** 7g⁵ 7f 7f 5g 1989 8h 8g³ 8f⁴ 7m 8.2g⁴] workmanlike gelding: moderate walker: poor plater: ridden by 5-lb claimer and blinkered, ran creditably and claimed £2,100 final start: seems suited by 1m: may prove suited by easy surface: sometimes very edgy, and gives impression may be temperamental. *J. Etherington.*

SWATTLING THOMAS 2 ch.g. (Apr 14) Ballacashtal (CAN)–Princess Xenia   **53** (USA) (Transworld (USA) 121) [1989 5g 5f 5m⁴ 6m³ 7f³ 6f² 6m* 6m 6g 6g 7d³ a6g³ a6g a7g] workmanlike gelding: third foal: half-brother to poor animal by Tower Walk: dam never ran: fair plater: won at Ripon (no bid) in August: ran moderately last 2 starts: better suited by 6f and 7f than 5f: blinkered third to fifth outings, visored final one: sometimes on toes. *J. Berry.*

SWEENY TODD 2 b.c. (Apr 29) Mansingh (USA) 120–La Brigitte 87 (Gulf Pearl   **47** 117) [1989 5m 6m⁶ 7m 6f] 4,000F: lengthy, dipped-backed colt: half-brother to 1986 2-y-o 7f seller winner Shade of Pale (by Kind of Hush) fair 1978 2-y-o 5f and 6f winner Great Wonder (by Miracle) and to a winner in USA: dam won over 5f at 2 yrs: poor maiden: appeared to drop himself out second outing: slowly away final one: may do better in blinkers: one to be wary of. *K. M. Brassey.*

SWEEPING 3 b.f. Indian King (USA) 128–Glancing 113 (Grundy 137) [1988 6f*   **104** 6f² 7g³ 1989 8.5s² 8f⁴ 8.5m³ 9d⁵ 10f] lengthy, good-topped filly: has a long stride: useful performer: ran well in listed race, handicaps then Group 3 Prix Chloe at Evry first 4 outings: sweating, prominent 1m when below form in Extel Stakes at Goodwood in July, final start: suited by 9f: acts on any going: sold 92,000 gns Newmarket December Sales. *J. Tree.*

SWEET ALMA 2 b.f. (Feb 6) Alzao (USA) 117–Sweet Relations (Skymaster 126)   **67** [1989 6m⁴ 8f³ 8g³ 8f³ 7g² a8g²] leggy filly: sixth foal: half-sister to several winners, including very useful 1985 2-y-o 5f to 7f winner Mazaad (by Auction Ring), later graded winner in USA, and very smart performer at up to 1¼m Montekin (by Mount Hagen): dam lightly-raced daughter of 1000 Guineas winner Night Off: quite modest form in maidens: caught on line by Calgary Redeye at Lingfield in November on final start: stays 1m. *P. F. I. Cole.*

SWEET CHESNE (FR) 4 b.c. R B Chesne 123–Sweetilda (FR) (Sandford Lad   **115** 133) [1988 8d² 8g* 8m* 8d⁵ 8g* 8m² 1989 7g⁴ 10f* 8f³ 8g² 10d² 8g 10d] strong, good-topped colt: moderate mover: very useful performer: won moderately-run listed Festival Stakes at Goodwood in May by length from Hibernian Gold: placed after in Queen Anne Stakes at Royal Ascot, Prix Messidor at Maisons-Laffitte and Prix Gontaut-Biron (beaten ¾ length by Emmson) at Deauville: beaten fair way in Prix du Moulin de Longchamp (stiff task) and La Coupe de Maisons-Laffitte: stays 1¼m well: yet to race on soft going, acts on any other: tends to idle and goes well with waiting tactics: trained until after third outing by H. Cecil: genuine. *J. E. Hammond, France.*

SWEET DRAGON 3 ch.f. Sweet Monday 122–Gay Desire (Dragonara Palace   **58** (USA) 115) [1988 5v⁴ 5d³ 5f⁶ 5f* 5g³ 5m⁵ 5f² 6d² 6d 1989 6s 6g 6m 6g⁶ 6f³ 6f³ 5g 6m² 6g⁵ 7g] small, plain filly: usually looks dull in coat: plater: second at Windsor in August: soundly beaten after: stays 6f: acts on firm going and a soft surface: sold 2,000 gns Doncaster October Sales. *J. Berry.*

SWEET EIRE 7 br.m. On Your Mark 125–Cool Melody 65 (Right Boy 137) [1988   **42** NR 1989 5g² 7d⁵ 6g² 6m⁴ 6m 5f 5m⁶ 5m³ 5m 5f 5f] small mare: poor maiden in Britain: better suited by 6f than 5f: possibly unsuited by soft going: sometimes visored as 7-y-o, and has been tried in blinkers: has worn bandages: often apprentice ridden, usually at overweight: sold 1,700 gns Doncaster August Sales: subsequently a winner in Belgium. *P. Monteith.*

SWEETEN GALE 3 ch.f. On Your Mark 125–Betty Bun (St Chad 120) [1988 5g 5g³ 5m⁵ 1989 5g 10f 8.2g] smallish, sparely-made filly: has a quick action: plating-class maiden: tailed off as 3-y-o, bandaged in seller final start. *T. Kersey.*

SWEET ENOUGH 4 b.f. Caerleon (USA) 132–Pampalina 119 (Bairam II 101)   **74** [1988 7d 10d³ 12f⁵ 10.4s³ 12g⁴ 15.8f² 17.1g* 16d* 1989 16s 16s 16g 12f* 11.1f² 20f⁶ 16.1g⁵ 16f²] close-coupled, sparely-made filly: poor walker: moderate mover, with a quick action: modest handicapper: returned to form when winning strongly-run event at Kempton in May: ran creditably next 2 and final outings: suited by good gallop at 1½m and stays very well: acts on any going. *C. E. Brittain.*

SWEET FORM 2 b.f. (Apr 10) Formidable (USA) 125–Sweet Emma 108 (Welsh   **51** Saint 126) [1989 6f⁴ 5m] 35,000Y: rangy filly: third foal: half-sister to sprint winner

Love Legend (by Glint of Gold): dam best at 2 yrs, winning 3 times over 5f in Ireland: plating-class maiden: not raced after June: better suited by 6f than 5f: sold 5,400 gns Newmarket Autumn Sales. *B. W. Hills.*

SWEETINGS OYSTER 3 b.f. Camden Town 125–Miss Cella 89 (Polyfoto 124) 57 [1988 NR 1989 6s⁶] IR 2,600Y: fifth reported living foal: dam won three 5f races at 2 yrs: running-on sixth in maiden at Nottingham in March: dead. *M. H. Easterby.*

SWEET KAFU . 2 b.f. (May 4) Kafu 120–Peach Melba 96 (So Blessed 130) [1989 45 5f³ 5m 5d 5m 5v] 5,700Y: leggy, close-coupled filly: has a quick action: sixth foal: half-sister to fair 1983 2-y-o 5f winner Llandwyn (by Jaazeiro): dam won over 5f at 2 yrs: poor maiden: showed nothing after second start: blinkered and wore crossed noseband in seller final one: sold 1,750 gns Doncaster October Sales. *J. Etherington.*

SWEET 'N' LOW 2 b.c. (Apr 14) Kampala 120–Karin Maria 86 (Double Jump — 131) [1989 a7g] IR 7,800Y: sparely-made colt: half-brother to 2 winners in Ireland, including 1980 2-y-o 5f winner Theme Music (by Tudor Music): dam 6f winner, raced only at 3 yrs: 16/1, very slowly away and always behind in Lingfield maiden in December. *M. H. Tompkins.*

SWEET 'N' SHARP 3 ch.f. Sharpo 132–Smagiada (Young Generation 129) — [1988 5d² 5d² 5f⁵ 5g³ 5f 5m* 6g⁵ 1989 7g] leggy, angular filly: moderate mover, with a quick action: ridden by 5-lb claimer, modest winner at 2 yrs: raced stiff task in £6,000 handicap in August, only start in 1989: probably stays 6f: acts on top-of-the-ground and a soft surface: tends to be on toes. *J. P. Hudson.*

SWEET N' TWENTY 3 b.f. High Top 131–Royal Home 69 (Royal Palace 131) 69 [1988 NR 1989 8s² 8d 8m⁴ 10f 10h³ 12h⁵ 11.7m* 11.7m 12m⁴ 14f² 14m 13.8d] 7,400Y: sturdy, lengthy filly: moderate mover: third foal: half-sister to 4-y-o sprint winner Erris Express (by Bay Express): dam 9f winner: modest handicapper: won at Windsor in July: below form last 2 outings, tailed off final one: suited by 1¾m: probably acts on any going: sold to join R. Whitaker 9,200 gns Newmarket Autumn Sales. *C. A. Cyzer.*

SWEET ON WILLIE (USA) 3 ch.f. Master Willie 129–Maryland Cookie 37 (USA) 101 (Bold Hour) [1988 6f 7s 8.5f⁵ 1989 8m⁴ 7m 10m 7m 12g] small, angular filly: has a slightly round action: poor maiden: below form as 3-y-o, including in sellers: stays 8.5f: headstrong and has looked temperamentally unsatisfactory: sold 840 gns Newmarket July Sales. *C. N. Allen.*

SWEET THURSDAY 3 ch.f. Sunley Builds 102–Adrift (Acrania 110) [1988 6m — 8d 1989 12g 10m 10.1m 10f] sturdy filly: third foal: dam ran once: no worthwhile form, including in sellers. *B. Stevens.*

SWEET VOILA 2 b.f. (Apr 14) Sayyaf 121–Sweet Princess (Prince Regent (FR) — 129) [1989 5m⁶] IR 3,200F, 8,400Y: leggy filly: half-sister to 3 winners here and abroad, including 1½m winner Far Too Much (by Windjammer): dam unraced sister to useful filly Brightelmstone: 14/1 and backward, tailed off from halfway in 6-runner minor event at Windsor in May. *R. A. Bennett.*

SWEET WYN 2 ch.f. (Mar 25) Sweet Monday 122–Wyn-Bank 82 (Green God — 128) [1989 5g 5f 5m] 600Y: angular filly: fifth foal: dam won from 6f to 1¼m and also won over hurdles: of little account. *A. Smith.*

SWELL ROMANCE 4 b.g. Formidable (USA) 125–Geopelia 109 (Raffingora — 130) [1988 8d⁴ 6m 7f 8.2m 6s 1989 6m 6m 8.2g 6g 10m 16f⁶ 17.6f³ 17f] lengthy, dipped-backed gelding: moderate mover: bad maiden: blinkered once at 3 yrs. *J. L. Harris.*

SWIFT CHANTER 2 ch.c. (Mar 15) Hotfoot 126–Chantal 74 (Charlottesville — 135) [1989 6f 7f⁵ 5g] 6,200F, 14,000Y: sparely-made, angular colt: half-brother to Derby third Scintillating Air (by Sparkler), 3-y-o 17.1f winner Chance of Stardom (by Star Appeal) and a Belgian middle-distance winner: dam placed at 1¼m: apparently of little account. *M. H. Easterby.*

SWIFT PURSUIT 4 ch.f. Posse (USA) 130–Hants 111 (Exbury 138) [1988 8.5f 57 10d⁵ 1989 8h²] workmanlike filly: carrying plenty of condition and gave bit of trouble going down, ¾-length second of 6 in apprentice race at Carlisle in June. *W. Jarvis.*

SWIFT WATERS 3 b.c. Sadler's Wells (USA) 132–Rapids (USA) 112 (Head of — The River (USA)) [1988 NR 1989 10.6g 9f⁵] 50,000Y: rangy colt: leggy, good walker: closely related to smart French 1984 2-y-o 1m winner River Express (by Northfields) and French 1m winner Baino Bluff (by Be My Guest), and half-brother to 1½m winner No Chili (by Glint of Gold): dam 1½m winner, fifth in 1000 Guineas and half-sister to Hawaiian Sound: well beaten in maiden (took good hold, found nothing final 3f) and minor event in the autumn. *Mrs J. Pitman.*

SWINGIN DUSTY (USA) 3 ch.f. Dust Commander (USA)–Swingin Gossip — (USA) (Grey Dawn II 132) [1988 7g 6m 1989 8s 8f 7g 5s] good-topped filly: well beaten in maidens and handicap in the North. *S. G. Norton.*

SWINGING NOE JOE 3 b.g. Swing Easy (USA) 126–Palace Pet (Dragonara 51 Palace (USA) 115) [1988 5g 5g 5g 5g 5g6 6m 8f6 7d3 1989 8g 6g3 7f 7f 7d] rangy gelding: plating-class maiden: best form at 7f on a soft surface: blinkered once at 2 yrs: on toes on reappearance: has worn bandage near-hind. *N. R. Mitchell.*

SWINGING PARTNER 3 b.f. Young Generation 129–Saint Cynthia (Welsh — Saint 126) [1988 6g 1989 7m 7m 7m 7m] workmanlike filly: signs of ability in varied events as 3-y-o only on reappearance: will be suited by return to shorter: blinkered final start (July). *Capt. R. M. Smyly.*

SWING LUCKY 4 b.g. Swing Easy (USA) 126–Bounding (Forlorn River 124) 67 [1988 5s5 5v2 5v2 5g 7.6g5 6g6 5g 5d* 5g2 5g3 5f3 5.6m 6s 6g3 8g4 8g 1989 8g 7v 8f 6f3 6m 6m3 6g5 5m3 5f4 5m 5.6g 5s 8s* 7g6 8.2g a6g4 a8g] rather leggy, workmanlike gelding: moderate mover: quite modest handicapper on his day: 50/1 and ridden by 7-lb claimer, won 24-runner £17,600 Ladbrokes Ayrshire Handicap in September, clear 4f out: effective at 5f and stays 1m: acts on any going: usually blinkered nowadays: occasionally bandaged and slowly away: inconsistent. *K. T. Ivory.*

SWING NORTH 2 b.c. (Apr 12) Night Shift (USA)–Run For Her Life 75 (Runny- 78 mede 123) [1989 5s4 5m5 5m4 5f2 6f5 5g2 5.8h2 6m6 6g 6g5 7d4 5m* 5g3 a6g* 5g3 a5g6 a7g3 a7g2 a5g*] 13,000Y: strong, dipped-backed colt: fifth foal: half-brother to fair 1985 2-y-o 6f winner Seclusive (by Good Times): dam won 1¼m seller: former plater: improved towards end of year and won modest non-selling nurseries at Edinburgh and Southwell (2): stays 7f: easily best form on good ground: effective with or without blinkers. *D. W. Chapman.*

SWING SHIFT 3 ch.c. Night Shift (USA)–Summersault (USA) (Vaguely Noble 95 140) [1988 6m3 8h* 1989 7g 7f2 8.2g2 8h2 10m2] compact colt: good mover: fairly useful performer: second in apprentice race (unlucky) at Lingfield and handicaps at Haydock and Brighton: 6/5 on and sweating slightly, below form in 3-runner handicap in June, final start: stays 1m: acts on hard going. *L. M. Cumani.*

SWISS AFFAIR (USA) 2 ch.c. (Mar 19) Private Account (USA)–Ten Cents A 101 p Kiss (USA) (Key To The Mint (USA)) [1989 7m* 6m3 6m4] $525,000Y: medium-sized, attractive colt: shows a quick action: sixth foal: closely related to 3 winners by Damascus, including 9f Grade 3 winner Drachma, and half-brother to a winner by Irish Castle: dam won at up to 6f: won 4-runner maiden at Ascot in July by a head from Lift And Load: ran well afterwards in Scottish Equitable Gimcrack Stakes at York and Rokeby Farms Mill Reef Stakes (4½ lengths fourth to Welney) at Newbury: likely to improve further. *A. A. Scott.*

SWISS BALL 4 b.g. Ballacashtal (CAN)–Sister Rosarii (USA) (Properantes — (USA)) [1988 7v 6g 6d 7.5f 8d 8f5 8g 8m6 8g4 8g 1989 10.2g4 7s 8f6 9f5 10f] sturdy, quite attractive gelding: bad mover: poor maiden: probably needs further than 7f: blinkered once. *J. Parkes.*

SWITCHED ON 3 b.f. Known Fact (USA) 135–Light Duty 113 (Queen's Hussar 84 124) [1988 7g 8g4 1989 9m* 10m4 10g] angular, workmanlike filly: won minor event at Wolverhampton in June: well beaten in other events, carrying head high final start: stays 9f: acts on top-of-the-ground. *W. Hastings-Bass.*

SWOOPING 4 b.g. Kings Lake (USA) 133–High Hawk 124 (Shirley Heights 130) — [1988 12d5 14f 1989 10s 8d] good-bodied, attractive gelding: moderate mover: only a little sign of ability in modest company. *J. R. Bosley.*

SWORDSMITH (USA) 2 b.c. (Apr 4) Diesis 133–Lettre d'Amour (USA) (Caro 95 133) [1989 7.3g 7g2 7g* 7m* 7g*] 50,000Y: lengthy, rather sparely-made colt: has a round action: fourth living foal: closely related to 3-y-o Mira Adonde (by Sharpen Up) and temperamental maiden Encore L'Amour (by Monteverdi): dam unraced daughter of top-class 4.5f to 1m winner Lianga: progressive colt: successful in minor event at Wolverhampton in July and nurseries at Salisbury in August and Newmarket in October: will stay 1m. *B. W. Hills.*

SWYNFORD DUTCHESS 4 ch.f. Wattlefield 117–Maputo Princess (Raga — Navarro (ITY) 119) [1988 6s 7d 7.5m 10f 10g6 1989 12s 12.5f 13m] smallish, sparely-made filly: of little account: blinkered once at 3 yrs. *K. Stone.*

SYBILLIN 3 b.g. Henbit (USA) 130–Tea House 107 (Sassafras (FR) 135) [1988   —
6m⁴ 7d 8m* 7d 1989 12m 8f 8m] rather leggy, close-coupled gelding: moderate
walker: has a quick action: modest winner at 2 yrs: well beaten otherwise, taking
keen hold in handicaps in summer as 3-y-o: bred to stay beyond 1m, but needs to
settle: on toes last 2 outings: winning novice hurdler. *J. G. FitzGerald.*

SYCALUS 3 b.c. Sicyos (USA) 125–Alcassa (FR) (Satingo 129) [1988 NR 1989 8g   —
10s a8g a8g] 5,800F, 5,600Y: second foal: dam 11f winner at 4 yrs in France: beaten
about 5¾ lengths in maiden at Southwell in November, final start: no form in varied
events previously, including seller. *C. B. B. Booth.*

SYCODELIC (FR) 3 ch.c. Sicyos (USA) 125–St Cordelia (FR) (Roi Lear (FR)   —
126) [1988 NR 1989 10f 12m] 70,000 francs (approx £7,100) Y: rather sparely-made
colt: fourth foal: half-brother to 2 winners in France, including minor 1986 2-y-o
1¼m winner Pelos Bank (by Zino): dam French 9.1f and 11f winner: in need of race,
well beaten in maidens: sold 680 gns Newmarket Autumn Sales. *Capt. R. M. Smyly.*

SYLOW 3 b.c. Beldale Flutter (USA) 130–Fleet Noble (USA) (Vaguely Noble 140)   **56**
[1988 5g³ 1989 8g 9s 8h 7.5f³ 9f³ 8g³ 9m⁴ 8m 8m⁴] rather leggy colt: plating-class
handicapper: stays 9f: acts on firm going: has carried head bit high: raced too freely
in lead on third start: sold 6,000 gns Doncaster November Sales: one to be wary of.
M. H. Easterby.

SYLVAN MISTRAL 3 ch.c. Aragon 118–Bauhinia 70 (Sagaro 133) [1988 6m³   **95**
5g⁵ 6g³ 5g* 5d³ 5m* 5s⁵ 5g² 5g 1989 6d 6m 6f* 6m* 6g⁶ 6m⁵ 6m] lengthy, good-
quartered colt: has a roundish action: made virtually all when winning handicap at
Lingfield and listed Scherping-Rennen at Baden-Baden in May: stayed 6f: probably
acted on any going: dead. *P. Mitchell.*

SYLVAN TEMPEST 3 b. or br.g. Strong Gale 116–Hedwige (African Sky 124) **104** d
[1988 5g² 5d* 6m² 7m⁴ 6f 6s⁵ 1989 6v* 7s² 8m 7.2g 6.3g 7g 7m 6v 7g⁶ 7d] leggy,
useful-looking gelding: keen walker: moderate mover: won minor event at Lingfield in April by 10 lengths: 2 lengths second to Saratogan in Group 3 event at the
Curragh 2 weeks later: generally lost form in face of stiff tasks afterwards: stays 7f:
needs a soft surface. *P. Mitchell.*

SYMPATHY 3 ch.f. Precocious 126–Antilla 87 (Averof 123) [1988 NR 1989 7f*]   **77** p
27,000Y: third foal: half-sister to 1986 2-y-o 6f winner Uniformity (by Formidable):
dam, 2-y-o 5f winner, is half-sister to very smart John French and daughter of
half-sister to Derrylin: 3/1, comfortably won 6-runner minor event at Kempton in
July, leading over 4f out. *H. R. A. Cecil.*

SYRIAN SPIRIT (USA) 3 ch.c. Nureyev (USA) 131–Willing Maid (USA)   —
(Olden Times) [1988 NR 1989 10g] tall colt: eighth foal: half-brother to 2 minor
winners in USA by Inverness Drive: dam French 9.5f to 11f winner: 50/1 and bit
backward, showed signs of ability though well beaten in £6,200 event at Newmarket
in May, travelling strongly 7f. *B. Hanbury.*

SYRING (FR) 2 ch.c. (Mar 31) Sicyos (USA) 125–Lady Ring (Tachypous 128)   —
[1989 6g 7m] 110,000 francs (approx £10,100) Y: sparely-made colt: fourth foal:
half-brother to French 10.5f winner Run Ring (by In Fijar): dam from family of Sun
Princess: well beaten in maidens: sold 820 gns Newmarket Autumn Sales. *R. Guest.*

SYRTOS 2 b.c. (May 5) Shareef Dancer (USA) 135–Wayward Lass (USA) (Hail   **81**
The Pirates (USA) 126) [1989 7f² 10g⁴] fourth foal: closely related to winning hurdler Zamil (by Lyphard) and half-brother to Waywardly (by In Reality), successful at
up to 7f in USA: dam champion 3-y-o filly in 1981 in USA: 1½ lengths second to easy
winner El Paso in 14-runner maiden at Salisbury in October: took keen hold, had
poorish run and faded last furlong in Nottingham maiden won by Rock Hopper later
in month: may prove best at short of 1¼m. *J. L. Dunlop.*

SYRUS P TURNTABLE 3 b.g. King of Spain 121–Lizabeth Chudleigh   **57**
(Imperial Fling (USA) 116) [1988 5g 5d³ 5m⁴ 6m⁶ 6f* 6m* 7g⁵ 1989 8m⁶ 9m 8.2g 8g
8h³ 7m 7m] strong, deep-bodied gelding: capable of quite modest form but generally
disappointing as 3-y-o, including in seller: best efforts over 6f: acts on firm going
and a soft surface: blinkered twice at 2 yrs: not an easy ride, and may well prove best
with waiting tactics: sold to join M. Clutterbuck 2,700 gns Ascot August Sales: not
one to rely on. *C. Tinkler.*

T

TABDEA (USA) 2 b.f. (Mar 21) Topsider (USA)–Madame Secretary (USA) **103**
(Secretariat (USA)) [1989 6m³ 6m* 6g⁶ 6s* 6m] $160,000Y: strong, sturdy filly: has

scope: has a quick action: first foal: dam, successful at up to 9f, is half-sister to Stewards' Cup winner Green Ruby and useful stayer Zero Watt: useful performer: impressive winner of maiden at Ripon in August and listed event (beat Performing Arts comfortably by 6 lengths) at Ayr following month: creditable seventh, keeping on well from rear last furlong, to Dead Certain in Tattersalls Cheveley Park Stakes at Newmarket: will stay 7f: likely to win more races. *A. A. Scott.*

TABYAN (USA) 2 b.f. (May 20) Topsider (USA)–Wink (USA) 101 (Forli (ARG)) **62** [1989 5m⁵ 5m⁵ 6g] $170,000Y: leggy filly: has scope: half-sister to quite useful 1m winner Dwell (by Habitat): dam won over 6f at 2 yrs and placed over 1m: quite modest maiden: hung badly when favourite on debut: off course 4 months afterwards. *P. T. Walwyn.*

TACHYON PARK 7 b.h. Frimley Park 109–Frimley's Alana 73 (Lear Jet 123) **87** [1988 5s 5f⁶ 5m 5.8g 5m² 5d⁵ 5m* 5g 6m 5m 5f 5.8f³ 5g⁴ 5d 5d* 5m* 1989 5g² 5s 5m 5f² 5g 5.8h³ 5g⁶ 5m⁴ 5m* 5f* 5g⁴ 5m 5m 5m⁶ 5f² 5m 5d] strong, good-quartered horse: fair handicapper: made all or virtually all in 7-runner race at Newbury and £7,500 event at Newcastle in July: good second to Clarentia at Lingfield, easily best subsequent effort: speedy, and best at 5f: not at his best on soft going and well suited by top-of-the-ground: usually blinkered or visored: has run well for apprentice, but has also hung under pressure: withdrawn after unseating rider and bolting fourth intended outing: tough. *P. J. Arthur.*

TACOMA HEIGHTS 3 b.c. Taufan (USA) 119–Good Relations (Be My Guest **79** (USA) 126) [1988 5g⁶ 6d⁴ 6m⁴ 6g⁶ 6f² 6d³ 7m 1989 8g* 8g 10f³ 8.5g 10g] leggy colt: moderate walker: won maiden at Doncaster in March: third in handicap at Chepstow, easily best effort after: stays 1¼m: acts on firm going and a soft surface: blinkered third and fourth outings: has tended to hang: off course 5 months, and bought out of R. Hannon's stable 15,000 gns Ascot 2nd June Sales, after fourth start: not one to trust implicitly. *B. A. McMahon.*

TADBIR 4 b.g. Try My Best (USA) 130–La Grange 79 (Habitat 134) [1988 8g² 8g² **—** 10g⁶ 10s 1989 10.2g 10s 10.1m⁶ 10f 11.7g⁶ 10.1m 12g 9s] close-coupled, good-bodied gelding: fair maiden early as 3-y-o: subsequently long way below his best: unlikely to stay 1½m: possibly unsuited by soft going: occasionally sweating and on toes: pulled hard fourth and sixth starts. *W. J. Musson.*

TADEUS 2 b.c. (Feb 2) Final Straw 127–Lost Splendour (USA) (Vaguely Noble **69** 140) [1989 5g 5v⁵ 5s² 5m* 5g³ 6f⁵ 7g⁶ 6m 7g a6g*] IR £12,500Y: medium-sized colt: shows a quick action: fourth foal: closely related to minor Irish 7f winner Izba (by Thatching) and half-brother to 1m and 1¼m winner Count Nulin (by Pas de Seul): dam unraced daughter of Roussalka, sister to Our Home and half-sister to Oh So Sharp: quite modest performer: successful in maiden at Chester and claimer at Lingfield: best form at up to 6f: trained first 7 outings by R. Hollinshead: inconsistent. *M. A. Jarvis.*

TADWIN 2 ch.f. (Apr 13) Never So Bold 135–Songs Jest (Song 132) [1989 5g³ 5m* **94** 5s²] 62,000Y: lengthy, attractive filly: has plenty of scope: seventh foal: closely related to 3-y-o Wakayi (by Persian Bold), 5f winner at 2 yrs, and half-sister to 3 other sprint winners, best of them Reesh (by Lochnager): dam unraced half-sister to dam of smart sprinter Jester (by Song): fairly useful performer: made all in minor event at Warwick in August: better form when placed in listed races, 2 lengths second of 7 to Mademoiselle Chloe at Ayr following month: unseated rider in stalls and was withdrawn from Cornwallis Stakes at Ascot in October. *P. T. Walwyn.*

TAFFETA AND TULLE (USA) 3 ch.f. Nureyev (USA) 131–Miss Nymph **91** (ARG) (Perugin (ARG)) [1988 NR 1989 8m⁶ 8m² 7.6m* 9.2g⁴] $200,000Y: small, sparely-made filly: third foal: half-sister to modest 1½m winner Al Shamikh (by Czaravich): dam, champion 2-y-o filly in Argentina, is half-sister to smart sprinting 2-y-o Enchanted: favourite, won maiden at Lingfield in September by a head, making all far side: beaten 5½ lengths in listed race at Le Croise-Laroche 6 weeks later: may well prove suited by further than 1m. *J. Gosden.*

TAFFIDALE 4 ch.f. Welsh Pageant 132–Ashdale (Busted 134) [1988 7g 12g⁴ **—** 12.2g³ 1989 11.7m 14.8f⁵ 12g⁶] big, rangy filly: quite modest maiden as 3-y-o: well beaten in handicaps in 1989: stays 1½m. *A. W. Denson.*

TAFFY JONES 10 br.g. Welsh Pageant 132–Shallow Stream 100 (Reliance II **—** 137) [1988 12s 1989 12m 12h] big gelding: carries plenty of condition: poor handicapper: probably stays 1¾m: best on top-of-the-ground: suitable mount for inexperienced rider: usually races up with pace: has worn blinkers: ran too keenly when visored: winning chaser. *M. McCormack.*

893

TAFILA 3 ch.f. Adonijah 126–Brigata (Brigadier Gerard 144) [1988 7g³ 1989 8d² **84**
10f² 10f* 8f⁶] sturdy, good-topped filly: has a round action: odds on, won maiden at
Beverley in May by a head having led virtually on bridle 1f out: bit below form in
£9,200 handicap at Ascot following month: should be at least as effective over 1m as
1¼m: acts on firm going and a soft surface: races keenly. *W. Jarvis.*

TAFTAZANI (USA) 4 b.c. Roberto (USA) 131–La Toulzanie (FR) (Sanctus II —
132) [1988 8g 10.5d 12g² 12s³ 12f² 16.5g³ 1989 14.6g 17.6f 11.1f⁵] big, angular colt:
poor walker: has a rather round action: modest maiden at his best: well beaten in
spring: needs at least 1½m, but barely stays 2m: probably unsuited by soft going:
blinkered last 2 outings. *I. P. Wardle.*

TAGIO 9 b.g. Martinmas 128–Harford Belle 97 (Track Spare 125) [1988 12g 1989 **37**
8m⁶ 10.6g4] workmanlike gelding: poor performer nowadays: stays 10.6f: possibly
not at best on soft going, acts on any other: has won for apprentice. *M. Tate.*

TAHADDI (USA) 2 ch.f. (Mar 11) Northern Baby (CAN) 127–Nofertiti (FR) **59 p**
(Exbury 138) [1989 6m³] leggy, angular, light-framed filly: fifth known foal:
half-sister to 4 winners, including very useful middle-distance performer Hawa
Bladi (by Nishapour): dam, second over 1½m in France, is half-sister to high-class
1m to 1¼m performer Nadjar: 16/1, 6 lengths third of 7, keeping on after slow start,
to very easy winner Fire And Shade in maiden at Nottingham in August: should
improve. *N. A. Callaghan.*

TAHIYR (USA) 3 b.c. Riverman (USA) 131–La Toulzanie (FR) (Sanctus II 132) —
[1988 NR 1989 8f 10.1g] lengthy, angular colt: fifth foal: half-brother to useful 1m to
1¼m performer Tamourad (by Blushing Groom), 1¼m winner Tabadar (by The
Minstrel) and modest maiden Taftazani (by Roberto): dam won 3 times at around
1½m: well beaten in maiden at Pontefract in May and minor event at Windsor in
July: sold 2,300 gns Newmarket July Sales. *M. R. Stoute.*

TAILSPIN 4 b.g. Young Generation 129–Mumtaz Flyer (USA) (Al Hattab (USA)) **81 §**
[1988 12g4 14.7f* 16g4 14.8d4 14f² 14.6f³ 16g 1989 12f 16.2m⁵ 16m 14g⁶ 14f 16m³]
big, lengthy gelding: moderate mover: capable of fair form: hung left and found
nothing fourth start: tended to run in snatches final one: stays 2m: suited by a sound
surface: blinkered twice at 3 yrs and third to fifth starts in 1989: has got on edge: not
to be trusted. *B. W. Hills.*

TAITTINGER ROSE (DEN) 2 ch.f. (May 18) Pelton Lad–Shadow Rose 112 —
(Dancer's Image (USA)) [1989 5d 7s] sparely-made, plain filly: seventh foal:
half-sister to useful 1982 2-y-o 7f winner Sangrador (by Thatch): dam very useful
Irish sprinter: well beaten in maidens: dead. *J. Mackie.*

TAJIKA 3 gr.f. Rusticaro (FR) 124–Taj Princess 88 (Taj Dewan 128) [1988 6d⁵ 7f **79**
8m⁴ 1989 8m 10f 10f⁵ 9g⁶ 9g a11g* a11g⁵] plain, angular filly: poor mover: 12/1,
comfortable winner of handicap at Southwell in November, leading over 1f out: little
other form as 3-y-o: will stay 1½m: acts on top-of-the-ground. *J. L. Dunlop.*

TAJROBA (USA) 4 b.g. Solford (USA) 127–You're So Vain (USA) (Pardallo II —
124) [1988 8g 11.5g* 12m² 10m⁵ 12f⁵ 1989 12g⁶ 12m³] leggy gelding: moderate
walker: modest winner (for amateur) as 3-y-o when trained by A. Stewart: well
beaten in handicaps at Doncaster in first half of 1989: stays 1½m: acts on firm going:
winning hurdler. *J. R. Jenkins.*

TAKDEER 3 ch.c. Sharpo 132–Red Gloves 83 (Red God 128§) [1988 NR 1989 6v* **95**
6s³ 7s⁶ 8m 8m⁴ 6s a8g* a8g4] leggy, rather sparely-made colt: third reported foal:
half-brother to fairly useful 6f and 7f winner Master Palehouse (by Moorestyle):
dam, placed over 6f and 7f at 2 yrs, is out of unraced half-sister to 1969 Criterium des
Pouliches winner Vela: won maiden at Naas in March and claimer at Lingfield in
November: below best in Lingfield handicap final start, giving impression worth
another try over 7f: yet to race on firm going, probably acts on any other: bought out
of K. Prendergast's stable 3,000 gns Newmarket Autumn Sales after sixth outing.
W. A. O'Gorman.

TAKE A BATH 2 b.c. (Apr 17) Pitskelly 122–Ebullient (Darius 129) [1989 5h⁴ **53**
5.8m⁶ 6f³ 7m⁴ 8g] IR 8,000Y: neat colt: half-brother to Irish 7f and 8.5f winner Old
Faithful (by Red Regent) and a winner in France: dam, Irish 7f winner, comes from
family of Zeddaan: fair plater: should stay 1m: sold 3,600 gns Newmarket Autumn
Sales. *M. J. Fetherston-Godley.*

TAKEALL 2 b.f. (Mar 7) Another Realm 118–Cratloe (African Sky 124) [1989 5d³ **72**
5d² 5f4 5.3h² 5m² 5g* 5m* 5g 5m*] 2,600Y: rather leggy, unfurnished filly: sixth
reported foal: half-sister 2 winning 2-y-o sprinters: dam never ran: improved filly:
successful in seller (bought in 4,100 gns) and a nursery at Wolverhampton in

summer and an auction event (by 2 lengths from Young India) at Redcar in September: speedy: didn't handle Brighton track fourth start. *J. Berry.*

TAKE EFFECT 5 b.g. Tap On Wood 130–Welsh Partner 91 (Welsh Saint 126) [1988 5d 6f 5f 6g² 7m⁶ 6d² 5g² 5m 5g* 5g² 5s⁶ 5f 6s 5m 6d 1989 6v⁵ 6d³ 6f 6f 6f⁴ 6f² 6m⁶ 7f⁶ 7.6m⁶ 6g⁵ 7f⁴ 6m 7f 6s² a7g] leggy, lightly-made gelding: tubed: plating-class performer: best form at 5f and 6f: has form on firm going, but particularly well suited by give in the ground: best in blinkers: suitable mount for apprentice: unsuited by sharp track: inconsistent. *M. Brittain.*   52

TAKE HEART 3 b.f. Electric 126–Hollow Heart 89 (Wolver Hollow 126) [1988 NR 1989 8.5m⁵ 10.2f⁵ 7m* 8g] workmanlike filly: third foal: half-sister to 7f and 1m winner Aradu (by Posse): dam, 5f winner at 2 yrs, is closely related to smart middle-distance handicapper Royal Match: wearing severe noseband, won maiden at Goodwood in August, going keenly to post and in race, leading 5f, switched and quickening well to lead again close home: taken quietly to post, never dangerous in listed event at Ascot 7 weeks later: appears suited by 7f. *D. R. C. Elsworth.*   77

TAKE ISSUE 4 b.g. Absalom 128–Abstract 73 (French Beige 127) [1988 10m 13.1f⁴ 11.5d 12f 14m 12g³ 1989 16s 14s⁴ 9m 14g] well-made gelding: plating-class handicapper: stays 1¾m: acts on any going: winning hurdler. *J. Sutcliffe.*   59

TAKENHALL 4 b.g. Pitskelly 122–Great Dora (Great Nephew 126) [1988 7f⁴ 6d* 6g* 6m* 5.6m 7.3m³ 1989 7d 8s 7m 8m 6f* 6f 6f⁵ 6m⁵ 7m⁴ 7m² 7m⁴ 7.3m⁴] lengthy, workmanlike gelding: moderate mover: modest handicapper: won at Kempton in June by 2 necks, quickening really well to lead close home: ran creditably last 4 outings: stays 7.3f: acts on firm going and a soft surface: has won for apprentice, but not an easy ride and usually gets behind: worth a try in blinkers or visor. *M. J. Fetherston-Godley.*   68

TAKE NO NOTICE 4 b.g. Indian King (USA) 128–Amiga Mia 71 (Be Friendly 130) [1988 8v 10d 8s 10g 7g 8g⁵ 8s² 7s³ 8m 10g⁵ 1989 8m³] sturdy, workmanlike gelding: modest maiden: stays 1m: acts on top-of-the-ground and soft going. *R. Akehurst.*   72

TAKE ONE 3 b.c. Teenoso (USA) 135–Old Kate 110 (Busted 134) [1988 NR 1989 12f⁴ 14g⁴ 13s² 12g] lengthy, robust colt: third foal: half-brother to useful 11f and 1½m winner Kalakate (by Kalaglow) and Irish 1¼m winner Keepcalm (by Auction Ring), later a listed winner in Italy: dam 9f and 10.2f winner, is sister to very smart soft-ground stayer Old Bill: modest form in varied events: on toes, set strong pace facing stiff task in handicap final start: moved poorly down on second: probably stays 13f: can do better. *G. Wragg.*   75 p

TAKEOVER TALK (USA) 2 b.c. (Mar 21) Conquistador Cielo (USA)–Love Words (USA) (Gallant Romeo (USA)) [1989 8g] $120,000Y: strong, lengthy colt: has scope: easy mover: fifth foal: half-brother to 3-y-o 10.6f winner Aljarih (by Nijinsky), fairly useful 7f winner Dwonedd (by Nureyev) and a French middle-distance winner: dam lightly-raced sister to Elocutionist: 50/1, slowly away and never dangerous or knocked about behind Belmez in 16-runner minor event at Newmarket in November: should improve. *G. Harwood.*   71 p

TAKE YOUR PICK 4 b. or br.f. Gorytus (USA) 132–Takealetter (Wolver Hollow 126) [1988 7f 11m 1989 12m⁵ 8.5f 8.2g 5f] ex-Irish filly: first foal: half-sister to a 3-y-o winner in Italy by Try My Best: dam placed over middle distances in Ireland: no form in varied events, including seller, as 4-y-o: stays 7f: blinkered final start: trained first 2 outings by P. Blockley: sold 1,150 gns Doncaster September Sales. *M. Johnston.*   —

TAKWIM 2 br.f. (Mar 26) Taufan (USA) 119–Brush Away (Ahonoora 122) [1989 5v* 6m² 5f 6g² 7g 6d⁶] IR 17,000Y: small, leggy filly: first foal: dam unraced half-sister to useful stayer Princess Genista and from family of Teenoso: won maiden at the Curragh in March by 3 lengths: around 8 lengths eighth of 13 to Dead Certain in Queen Mary Stakes at Royal Ascot: below form final 2 starts: best form at 6f. *K. Prendergast, Ireland.*   85

TALABAYRA 2 b.f. (May 18) Darshaan 133–Takariyna (Grundy 137) [1989 7g³] first foal: dam, French 1¼m winner, is half-sister to Top Ville: 9/4, over 4 lengths third of 13 to Flying Diva in minor event at Carlisle in October: will stay 1½m: sure to improve. *M. R. Stoute.*   71 p

TALASEA 2 b.f. (Mar 26) Lear Fan (USA) 130–Joyful Lass (USA) (Danzig (USA)) [1989 6f⁴ 6f 6m³] 7,000F: medium-sized, lengthy, good-bodied filly: first foal: dam ran 6 times in North America: in frame in minor event at Goodwood in May and listed contest (beaten 6 lengths) at Milan: remained with O. Pessi in Italy, and won over 5f at Naples in July. *J. L. Dunlop.*   ?

TALES OF EIRANN 3 b.f. Dara Monarch 128–Shenachie 79 (Sheshoon 132) 59
[1988 NR 1989 17.6m 12f³ 14g 12.2g⁵ 10f] lengthy, workmanlike filly: poor walker:
seventh reported living foal: half-sister to quite modest 12.2f winner Strathdearn
(by Saritamer) and Irish 5f (at 2 yrs) to 1¼m winner Warning Sound (by Red Alert):
dam stayer: quite modest maiden: soundly beaten last 3 outings, including in
claimer: stays 1½m: blinkered. *A. Bailey.*

TALIANNA 3 b.f. Kind of Hush 118–Friths Folly 62 (Good Bond 122) [1988 5g —
5m⁶ 5d 5g 6g 6s 6g 8m 1989 7g⁶ 7.5d 8m 7m 7m⁶ 8.2f⁴ 7m 7.5m 6m 7g] workmanlike
filly: has a round action: plater: little form after fifth (unruly on way down) start:
stays 7f: acts on top-of-the-ground: blinkered once at 2 yrs: taken down early
seventh and ninth outings: sweating, edgy and pulled hard in between. *J. Balding.*

TALITHA 3 b.f. Auction Ring (USA) 123–Double Celt 93 (Owen Dudley 121) 87
[1988 7m⁴ 1989 9g² 12f³ 9g] small, sparely-made filly: moderate walker: fair maiden:
off course 5 months before running poorly final start: should be suited by 1¼m +:
best effort on an easy surface: sold 3,000 gns Newmarket December Sales. *H. R. A.
Cecil.*

TALK OF GLORY 8 b.g. Hittite Glory 125–Fiddle-Faddle 85 (Silly Season 127) —
[1988 8g 8g 8m³ 8g⁶ 8f² 8.3m 8m 8f⁵ 8g³ 8g⁴ 1989 8m⁴ 8m 8.3m 10h 8f a11g] strong,
rangy gelding: quite modest handicapper in 1988: no form in varied contests,
including sellers, as 8-y-o: stays 1¼m: used to be well suited by top-of-the-ground:
has won for apprentice. *J. White.*

TALL MEASURE 3 b.g. High Top 131–Millimeter (USA) (Ribocco 129) [1988 6f 72
6d³ 7m⁶ 7.5g 7g⁴ 7s 8s 8m 1989 10.6m 10f³ 12.4m⁵ 10g⁵ 12.4f* 12m⁵ 11m⁴ 12g² 12g
13s 12g] robust, round-barrelled gelding: modest handicapper: awarded race at
Newcastle in July: very good second at Hamilton, easily best effort after: best at up
to 1½m: acts on firm going, probably unsuited by soft: visored fourth and last 4
starts: blinkered once at 2 yrs. *F. H. Lee.*

TALONS TALE 3 b.g. Windjammer (USA)–Babe In The Wood (Athens Wood 58
126) [1988 5f⁶ 5f² 6s 6m 6g⁴ 6m 7g 7g 7d⁵ 1989 6s 8g 7g² 8m* 8f² 8m³ 8h² 9m 8f]
strong, compact gelding: has a quick action: useful plater: won at Brighton (no bid)
in May: ran well next 3 starts: stays 1m well: acts on hard going and a soft surface:
usually blinkered: suited by strong handling. *R. Hannon.*

TAMAHAN (USA) 2 b.c. (Apr 16) Riverman (USA) 131–Taduska (FR) (Daring 84
Display (USA) 129) [1989 7m⁶ 7.5f* 8g] quite attractive colt: has a quick action:
fourth foal: half-brother to 3-y-o 1¼m winner Toushtari (by Youth) and 1¾m winner
Tamatour (by Caro): dam won at around 1m in France: long odds on following
eye-catching debut, won maiden at Beverley in August easily by ¾ length, clear,
from Trainglot: ran poorly in nursery at Goodwood final start: should stay 1m: has
given trouble stalls each outing: sold 27,000 gns Newmarket Autumn Sales. *M. R.
Stoute.*

TAMARA'S TWINKLE (USA) 2 ch.f. (Apr 6) Sharpen Up 127–Lady Tamara 71
114 (Kenmare (FR) 125) [1989 5m* 5f 5f*] compact, robust filly: not a good walker:
first foal: dam French 1m to 1½m performer: successful in maiden at Catterick in
May and 2-runner minor event at Newcastle, swishing tail final furlong, in July: still
green when in rear in Windsor Castle Stakes (awkward stalls) at Royal Ascot in
between: will be suited by 6f. *J. Berry.*

TAMBORA 2 b.f. (May 20) Darshaan 133–Tameen (FR) (Pharly (FR) 130) [1989 64 p
7g] strong, deep-girthed, lengthy filly: third foal: half-sister to 1¼m winner Talukdar
(by Forli): dam French 1m and 1¼m winner: very weak 14/1-shot
and in need of experience, never dangerous in 24-runner maiden at Newmarket in
November: should improve. *L. M. Cumani.*

TAMERTOWN LAD 8 b.g. Creetown 123–Gay Tamarind (Tamerlane 128) —
[1988 14g³ 12m³ 13s* 12g 14.6g* 1989 12m 12d² 13s⁶ 16.2d⁶ 12d] strong, quite attractive gelding: carries condition: well
beaten as 8-y-o, including in sellers on last 2 starts: slowly away when blinkered:
has worn a tongue strap. *A. W. Potts.*

TAMI 4 ch.f. Miami Springs 121–Tenoria 82 (Mansingh (USA) 120) [1988 5g 6f —
5.8f³ 6m 6g 6m³ 6m 6g⁵ 1989 8.3m] small, sturdy filly: poor plater: sweating and
backward, badly hampered after 2f and pulled up final 2f (rider lost irons) in handicap
at Windsor in May: stays 6f well: acts on any going: best in blinkers or visor. *M.
McCourt.*

TANCRED SAND 6 ch.g. Nicholas Bill 125–Another Move 67 (Farm Walk 111) 82
[1988 14g³ 12m³ 13s* 12g 14.6g* 1989 12m 12d² 13s⁶ 16.2d⁶ 12d] lengthy, rather
sparely-made gelding: shows knee action: fair handicapper: best effort in second
half of season when second to Mrs Pistol at Haydock: ran poorly in William Hill

November Handicap at Thirsk: stays 1¾m: well suited by an easy surface: winning hurdler. *J. M. Jefferson.*

TANFEN 8 b.g. Tanfirion 110–Lady Mary (Sallust 134) [1988 7d 6m 6g 6f³ 6h³ 6g⁵ **44** 6d 5m⁵ 6s 6g⁶ 5d⁶ 1989 6g 6m⁵ 6h³ 6f 5m⁴ 6f* 6h⁵ 6m] strong, workmanlike gelding: has been hobdayed: poor handicapper: won at Catterick in July: best at sprint distances: acts on any going: has worn visor and blinkers, but didn't in 1989: often bandaged nowadays: suitable mount for apprentice: sometimes sweats: suited by forcing tactics. *T. Craig.*

TANFITH (CAN) 2 b.c. (Mar 1) Chief's Crown (USA)–Foxy Olympia (USA) **97 p** (Stage Door Johnny) [1989 7g* 8m*] $200,000Y: medium-sized, rather sparely-made colt: half-brother to a minor winner in USA: dam never ran: sire champion 2-y-o colt later stayed 1½m: successful in September in maiden at Yarmouth and £7,100 event (by a neck from Waki Gold, keeping on strongly) at Newbury: will stay 1¼m: sure to win more races. *R. W. Armstrong.*

TANGLE FREE 2 b.f. (Apr 25) Absalom 128–Freely Given 69 (Petingo 135) **50** [1989 6f⁶ a7g] sixth foal: half-sister to 3-y-o 1m winner Command Performer (by Comedy Star), 1½m winner New Zealand (by Dominion) and fair 7f to 15f winner Bloodless Coup (by Free State): dam highly-raced half-sister to very useful stayer Tom Cribb: poor form in maidens at Chepstow in June and Southwell in November: sold 1,300 gns Doncaster November Sales. *P. T. Walwyn.*

TANODA 3 b.f. Tyrnavos 129–Anoda (FR) (Amber Rama (USA) 133) [1988 5g* 5g **67** 7d* 6g⁵ 8s³ 8s* 8v⁵ 8.2d 1989 10s³ 10v 10.6g 8.5g⁴ 9m 10f 10.2g] leggy filly: moderate walker: has a round action: modest handicapper: stays 1¼m: needs give in the ground, and goes well on soft: has run creditably when on toes: tends to edge left (hung badly sixth outing): often apprentice ridden. *M. Brittain.*

TANTUM ERGO 3 br.f. Tanfirion 110–Cathedra (So Blessed 130) [1988 5m 6m* **—** 7g* 1989 8m 7.2g] Irish filly: successful at Phoenix Park as 2-y-o in restricted IR £14,600 event and C L Weld Park Stakes: eleventh of 16 in Poule d'Essai des Pouliches at Longchamp and well-beaten eighth of 13, front rank until weakening final 1f, in listed race at Haydock in first half of 1989 season: should stay 1m: moved moderately to post at Haydock. *Edward Lynam, Ireland.*

TANWI 2 br.f. (Mar 27) Vision (USA)–Shine The Light (Home Guard (USA) 129) **95** [1989 5v* 5m² 6g³ 6d 6g⁵ 6g* 5d² 7d*] IR 26,000Y: half-sister to a winner in Australia: dam, who has been in Australia, won over 5f at 2 yrs in Ireland: won minor event at Phoenix Park in April, nursery at the Curragh in September and Ardenode Stud EBF Leopardstown Stakes (by 2 lengths) in October: good second to Wedding Bouquet in listed race at the Curragh penultimate outing: will stay 1m: acts on heavy going, and has yet to race on firm. *K. Prendergast, Ireland.*

TANYA'S PRINCESS 6 b.m. Imperial Fling (USA) 116–Princess Kofiyah 72 **—** (High Line 125) [1988 NR 1989 5m] lightly-built mare: poor maiden: 66/1, last of 11 in selling handicap at Edinburgh in June: best form at 7f: acts on firm going. *J. H. Johnson.*

TAP DANCING 3 ch.c. Sallust 134–Amarok 85 (Wolver Hollow 126) [1988 6m **55** 7.5m 7m 6g⁵ 6s 1989 7m 8.5f 8.2f³ 10m³ 10f] leggy colt: has a round action: plating-class maiden: may prove suited by return to 1m: acts on firm going: has joined M. O'Neill. *R. F. Casey.*

TARANGA 6 b.g. Music Boy 124–Emblazon 91 (Wolver Hollow 126) [1988 6v³ **45** 6v⁴ 6d⁵ 6g 7g⁴ 8f 8f* 8f³ 7.6m 8g⁴ 7m 10.2g⁶ 10g⁶ 1989 8s* 8.2v⁶ 8d 8m³ 8g* 8.3m a6g⁴ a7g] strong, workmanlike gelding: moderate mover: won handicaps at Warwick (edged left) in March and Pontefract (selling event, bought in 4,000 gns) in July: suited by 1m: acts on any going: has run creditably when visored: has won for apprentice and when sweating: has been taken down early: inconsistent. *J. White.*

TARA'S DELIGHT 2 b.f. (Apr 3) Dunbeath (USA) 127–Tickton Bridge (Grundy **50** 137) [1989 6m³ 6m 8g] 4,200Y: deep-girthed filly: first foal: dam unraced half-sister to Connaught Bridge and Rhein Bridge: plating-class form in maidens, one an auction event: bred to stay beyond 1m. *M. J. Ryan.*

TARA'S GIRL 2 b.f. (May 14) Touching Wood (USA) 127–Esquire Lady (Be My **—** Guest (USA) 126) [1989 a6g] 8,000Y: small filly: second foal: dam won at 1m and 9.5f at 3 yrs in Ireland: slowly away and never able to challenge in claimer at Southwell: bred to need further. *W. A. O'Gorman.*

TARA'S VISION 3 b.f. Vision (USA)–Crimson Kiss (USA) (Crimson Satan) **41** [1988 5f 5f⁵ 7d⁵ 1989 8m⁶ 8m 9f⁴ 8f 8f⁶ 10f] sparely-made filly: rather inconsistent plater: stays 9f: sold 1,500 gns Newmarket Autumn Sales. *R. Hollinshead.*

TARAZED (ITY) 2 ch.f. (Apr 9) Spring Heights–Dark Angel (Sole Mio (USA)) **61**
[1989 7f³ 7f⁶ 7f² 7g⁶] third living foal: half-sister to Italian winner Erco Strong (by
Ercolano): dam won 5 times at 2 yrs in Italy: quite modest maiden: will be suited by
1m + . *J. L. Dunlop.*

TARIKHANA 2 gr.f. (Apr 26) Mouktar 129–Tremogia (FR) (Silver Shark 129) **69 P**
[1989 7g⁶] lengthy, rather sparely-made filly: half-sister to several winners here
and in France, including Princess Royal winner Tashtiya (by Shergar) and useful 7f
and 1m winner Taysha (by Habitat): dam unraced half-sister to very smart
middle-distance stayer Sauvage and daughter of Prix Saint-Alary winner Tonnera:
12/1 and green, 8 lengths sixth of 24, slowly away and keeping on steadily, to
Sardegna in maiden at Newmarket in November: should improve. *M. R. Stoute.*

TARISTEAC 9 ch.g. Be My Guest (USA) 126–Sans Culotte (FR) (Roi Dagobert **—**
128) [1988 6d 6g⁵ 6f 6g² 6m² 7m² 8f² 6h⁴ 8g³ 6d* 7d² 8d 8m 7m 6m 6m 8.2s 7g 7d
1989 10m 12g 12.2m 7f] small, strong gelding: poor mover: poor handicapper: no
form since July, 1988: stays 1m: acts on hard going and a soft surface: occasionally
blinkered nowadays: wears bandages: has won for apprentice: often gets well
behind. *S. R. Bowring.*

TARLETON'S OAK 6 br.g. Town Crier 119–Stately Gala (Gala Performance **—**
(USA) [1988 10f⁴ 10g 10m³ 12h⁶ 12g 1989 10.8m] rangy gelding: quite modest
handicapper at his best: raced too keenly when tailed off at Warwick in May: stays
1¼m: seems to require top-of-the-ground: good mount for inexperienced rider: sold
to join J. Love 5,000 gns Doncaster August Sales. *K. S. Bridgwater.*

TARLOGIE 3 b.c. Touching Wood (USA) 127–Soft Chinook (USA) (Hitting **66 d**
Away) [1988 5f⁶ 7m 8m 10s 1989 12.2d³ 9d* 10d 8h⁶ 11f 12.3g 9.1f⁶ 11s⁵ 12.4g] leggy
colt: has a round, moderate action: won seller (no bid) at Ripon in April: little form
after: stays 1½m: suited by a soft surface: has been tried in a visor. *S. J. Muldoon.*

TARN PURE 4 ch.g. Blue Refrain 121–Sterling Kate (Sterling Bay (SWE)) [1988 **48**
8d⁵ 8d⁵ 7.6m 8g 10m⁶ 10.2f 10g⁴ 8d 1989 11.5f⁵ 8f³ 12f² 10h* 12f⁵] lengthy,
workmanlike gelding: poor handicapper: won (for first time) at Brighton in August:
well-beaten fifth of 6 at same course 2 weeks later: stays 1½m: acts on hard going:
visored or blinkered final 4 starts at 3 yrs. *A. Moore.*

TARNSIDE CLUB 2 br.c. (May 4) Mummy's Game 120–Alison Rose 58 **84**
(Jaazeiro (USA) 127) [1989 5g⁴ 5m² 5g² 6f* 5f² 6m* 6g³ 6f⁶ 7m] 12,500Y: leggy
colt: carries condition: second living foal: half-brother to 1m winner Turbo Rose (by
Taufan): dam lightly raced at 2 yrs and seemingly a short runner, is daughter of
speedy half-sister to Runnett: progressive colt: successful in summer in maiden at
Hamilton and nursery at Pontefract: probably stays 7f: sometimes wanders. *J.
Etherington.*

TAROOM 2 b.c. (Feb 12) Lomond (USA) 128–Gallic Pride (USA) (Key To The **— P**
Kingdom (USA)) [1989 7m] 19,500F: fourth foal: dam, daughter of Ribblesdale
winner Gallina, showed little ability: 33/1, beaten over 12 lengths behind Mull
House in maiden at Chepstow in October: may improve. *J. L. Dunlop.*

TARSHO 3 ch.c. Lomond (USA) 128–Hogan's Sister (USA) (Speak John) [1988 **93**
6m³ 7m 7g 1989 8m² 10g* 12m] sturdy, good-topped colt: carries condition: made
virtually all to win £5,700 maiden at Newmarket in July by a short head, rallying
well: chased leaders 1m when behind in strongly-run £19,100 handicap there
following month: suited by forcing tactics over 1¼m. *H. R. A. Cecil.*

TARTAR'S BOW 2 b.c. (Apr 21) Gorytus (USA) 132–Sweet Eliane (Birdbrook **—**
110) [1989 6g] 18,000Y: unfurnished colt: half-brother to 3-y-o Maple Hayes and 2
winners, including 1983 2-y-o 6f winner Sir Humpherson (by Music Boy): dam poor
maiden: backward and green, struggling when hampered slightly 2f out in 29-runner
maiden at Newmarket in November. *M. A. Jarvis.*

TARTAS (FR) 3 ch.c. Maelstrom Lake 118–Association (FR) (Margouillat (FR) **113**
133) [1988 NR 1989 8v⁶ 8m² 8.5g² 8g* 10m³ 9g* 9.7m⁶ 11g²] fourth foal:
half-brother to 3 colts by Tip Moss, including smart 11f and 1½m winner Mansonnien and quite useful 1½m winner Merano: dam French 9f winner: won maiden
at Saint-Cloud and Group 3 Prix Daphnis at Evry in July: narrowly beaten in Prix
Eugene Adam at Saint-Cloud in between: stays 11f: acts on top-of-the-ground. *N.
Pelat, France.*

TARTIQUE TWIST (USA) 3 b.f. Arctic Tern (USA) 126–Professional Dance **70 P**
(USA) (Nijinsky (CAN) 138) [1988 NR 1989 8g 12g⁶ 12f⁵ a12g a16g*] 15,000Y:
strong, rangy, attractive filly: has a quick action: third reported foal: dam unraced
half-sister to dam of good French performers L'Emigrant and Salpinx: confirmed

earlier promise when winning 5-runner handicap at Lingfield in December: stays 2m: can improve again. *J. L. Dunlop.*

TARVISIO 2 b.c. (Mar 29) Northern Baby (CAN) 127–Bold And Bright (FR) **102** (Bold Lad (USA)) [1989 7.5d5 8g3 8d* 9m3] third foal: half-brother to 2 animals by Arctic Tern, including modest 1½m handicapper Frangnito: dam, successful twice at around 1¼m, is daughter of half-sister to Irish Ball and Irish Bird, the dam of Bikala, Assert and Eurobird: progressive form: won maiden at Maisons-Laffitte in September: 5 lengths third of 4 to Dr Somerville in Prix de Conde at Longchamp in October: will stay 1¼m. *F. Boutin, France.*

TASARLY 2 b.f. (Apr 2) Miller's Mate 116–Formido 61 (Formidable (USA) 125) **74** [1989 6m2 6g6 7g*] smallish, sparely-made filly: first foal: dam, 7f winner, is granddaughter of 1000 Guineas winner Fleet: showed improved form when winning 12-runner maiden at Catterick in October: will stay 1m: sold 8,600 gns Newmarket Autumn Sales. *A. A. Scott.*

TASHANITZA 2 b.f. (Feb 5) Starch Reduced 112–Mrs Dumbfounded (Adropejo **49** 114) [1989 5d 6f2] IR 2,600Y: lengthy, plain filly: fifth foal: sister to a poor maiden and half-sister to 8.2f winner Baker's Double (by Rapid River): dam bad plater: 33/1, 2 lengths second of 6, taking good hold then running on well despite drifting left final 1f, to Dancing Tender in claimer at Chepstow in July. *B. Palling.*

TASHONYA 7 b.g. Grundy 137–Explorelka (Relko 136) [1988 NR 1989 12f] — leggy, close-coupled gelding: former plater: tailed off in amateurs handicap at Goodwood in June, only outing on flat since 1986: stays 1¼m: acts on firm going: has sweated. *W. G. Morris.*

TASKALADY 3 b.f. Touching Wood (USA) 127–Damaska (USA) (Damascus **47** (USA)) [1988 6g 6g 6f4 7m 1989 11f 10m 10.6s5 11s*] small, leggy, plain filly: modest plater: first form as 3-y-o when winning at Ayr (no bid) in October: stays 11f: acts on soft ground: sold to join Mrs A. Knight 2,000 gns Doncaster November Sales. *M. Brittain.*

TASKFORCE FIXED IT 2 b.g. (Mar 12) Aragon 118–Broken Accent (Busted **65** 134) [1989 5m 7f4 7m2 8.2f 8f] 10,000Y: compact gelding: second foal: dam ran twice: quite modest performer: stays 7f: sometimes bandaged: looked hard ride fourth start: gelded after final one. *Dr J. D. Scargill.*

TATOUMA (USA) 3 ch.f. The Minstrel (CAN) 135–Sheer Fantasy (USA) — (Damascus (USA)) [1988 5g* 6g* 6m 5g 1989 5f 6f] leggy, sparely-made filly: modest winner as 2-y-o: little worthwhile form since, facing stiff tasks in handicaps in summer as 3-y-o: bred to stay much further than 6f: has given trouble at stalls: on toes and moved keenly down final start. *B. W. Hills.*

TATSFIELD 3 b.c. Habitat 134–Sephira (Luthier 126) [1988 6g* 7f* 1989 8.5s3 **107** 8m 8m* 7f 7.6h2 7m2] lengthy, leggy colt: won £7,700 event at Newbury in June: 6 lengths second of 3 to Markofdistinction in 7.6f listed race at Lingfield: ran poorly in Jersey Stakes at Royal Ascot and below-form second to Magical Strike in August listed race at York starts either side: stays 1m: goes well on top-of-the-ground: blinkered when pacemaker second outing. *J. Tree.*

TATWIJ (USA) 2 b.f. (Feb 28) Topsider (USA)–Infantes (USA) (Exclusive **94 p** Native (USA)) [1989 5g* 5s*] $475,000Y: leggy filly: second foal: half-sister to Tejano (by Caro), second best 2-y-o in USA in 1987 and graded-stakes placed several times at 3 yrs: dam won at around 1m at 2 yrs: favourite, won maiden at Hamilton and (long odds on) minor event at Ayr in October: slowly away when beating Homosassa by 7 lengths on first occasion, made all when beating Western Music easily by 5 lengths on second: will stay 6f: sure to go on to better things. *H. Thomson Jones.*

TAUBER 5 b.g. Taufan (USA) 119–Our Bernie (Continuation 120) [1988 6g 7m 6g **83** 6g 7d 8s 7d 1989 7v* 6d5 7g* 7f4 7f 7m 7m 7m 7g4 8f3 7m* a6g* a6g3 a8g2 a8g] rather leggy gelding: has a markedly round action: fair handicapper: won at Lingfield and Wolverhampton in spring and at Edinburgh and Lingfield (twice, both times from Tyrian Belle) in autumn: effective at 6f and stays 1m: acts on any going: suitable mount for apprentice. *Pat Mitchell.*

TAULELA 2 b.f. (Apr 12) Taufan (USA) 119–Balela (African Sky 124) [1989 5f2 **61** 5m4 6g6] 16,000Y: leggy, unfurnished filly: first foal: dam unraced half-sister to dam of Geoffrey Freer winner Top Class: quite modest maiden: best effort on debut. *D. R. C. Elsworth.*

TAUVALERA 2 b.f. (Feb 8) Taufan (USA) 119–Halva (Troy 137) [1989 7g 7d] — 14,000Y: first foal: dam unraced, from good family: well beaten in maiden auction race and seller: sold 1,700 gns Newmarket Autumn Sales. *W. Jarvis.*

TAVOLARA 2 ch.f. (Mar 1) Superlative 118–Sardinia (Romulus 129) [1989 5m⁴ 5m⁶ 6g⁴ 6s⁶] small, good-quartered filly: half-sister to several minor winners here and abroad: dam Irish 5f and 1m winner: raced alone and showed improved form when over 4 lengths fourth of 28 to Alidiva in maiden at Newmarket in October: ran moderately from poor draw following month: better suited by 6f than 5f. *W. Jarvis.* **62 ?**

TA WARDLE 5 ch.g. Import 127–Zephyr Lady 59 (Windjammer (USA)) [1988 12d⁴ 8m³ 1989 12m³ a11g] tall, leggy gelding: poor maiden: finds 1m on short side and stays 1½m: acts on top-of-the-ground and a soft surface: ran creditably for apprentice on reappearance. *M. J. Bolton.* **40**

TAWJIH (USA) 2 b.c. (Feb 9) Lyphard's Wish (FR) 124–Chop Towhee (USA) (Hatchet Man (USA)) [1989 6m⁶ 7.6m³] $77,000Y: third foal: brother to American 3-y-o Cut A Wish, 7.5f stakes winner at 2 yrs: dam minor winner at up to 7f: co-favourite, over 2 lengths third of 12, always prominent, to Rinja in maiden at Lingfield in September, better effort: sold to join R. Guest 21,000 gns Newmarket Autumn Sales. *R. W. Armstrong.* **64**

TAWNY 3 ch.f. Grey Ghost 98–Trim Taxi 87 (Dublin Taxi) [1988 5g⁴ 5g³ 5m² 5f* 5m* 5s⁶ 6f* 6g² 5m⁴ 1989 5f² 6m² 6f⁵ 5m⁶ 5g] leggy, lightly-made filly: moderate walker: modest handicapper: below form last 2 outings and not seen out after July: suited by 6f: acts on firm going: blinkered once at 2 yrs: best on galloping track: sometimes wanders and has looked an awkward ride. *T. D. Barron.* **69**

TAXI MAN 6 ch.g. Dublin Taxi–Manna Green (Bustino 136) [1988 NR 1989 5f 8.2f 10m] moderate mover: quite modest winner as 3-y-o: behind all starts in 1989: stays 1¼m: acts on firm going and a soft surface: blinkered once: pulled hard in hood final outing (July). *D. Burchell.* **—**

TAYLORMADE BOY 6 b.g. Dominion 123–Ash Gayle 49 (Lord Gayle (USA) 124) [1988 12s 12g⁴ 12s² 12f² 12g 1989 12.3s* 12d⁶ 16.2g³] rather leggy, work-manlike gelding: poor mover: very well treated on best form and fit from hurdling, won handicap at Ripon in April: stays 2m: acts on any going: blinkered once: has run creditably for lady. *Denys Smith.* **56**

TAYLORS CASTLE 2 b.f. (Apr 1) Castle Keep 121–How Audacious (Hittite Glory 125) [1989 5m³ 6m 5m⁶ 7m] 1,500Y: compact filly: carries condition: third foal: dam unraced half-sister to Royal Hunt Cup winner Tender Heart: poor maiden: best efforts first and third starts: should stay at least 7f. *E. Eldin.* **46**

TAYLORS PET 4 b.f. Tina's Pet 121–Quick Kick (Saritamer (USA) 130) [1988 6d⁶ 10f⁶ 10g⁵ 11m² 10.8g³ 11g 11.5g⁴ 1989 8d 10.8d 10m² 8g 9s] tall, sparely-made filly: plating-class maiden: form in handicaps as 4-y-o only when 3 lengths second to Firelight Fiesta at Yarmouth in June: off course nearly 5 months afterwards: stays 11.5f: acts on firm going and unsuited by soft: has joined J. Gillen. *H. J. Collingridge.* **47**

TAYLORS PRINCE 2 ch.c. (Apr 25) Sandhurst Prince 128–Maiden's Dance 65 (Hotfoot 126) [1989 7g 8g] 9,400Y: strong, workmanlike colt: third foal: half-brother to 3-y-o Vision's Dance (by Vision) and 1m and 9f winner Dancing Monarch (by Dara Monarch): dam, possibly temperamental, half-sister to very useful 1m to 1½m winners Tudor Rhythm and Rhineland, stayed 1m: soundly beaten in £10,000 event at Newmarket and maiden at Leicester late in season. *H. J. Collingridge.* **50**

TAYLORS QUEEN 3 b.f. Tender King 123–Fenland Queen (King's Troop 118) [1988 6d 1989 10g 8.5g 8m* 8.5g 9m 10m 7.5m⁴ 7m 8m³ 8m⁴ 10f 9m 8.2d⁶ 8.2g] useful-looking filly: moderate mover: 33/1, won claimer at Warwick in May: well beaten in claimers and apprentice seller last 4 starts: best at up to 1m: acts on top-of-the-ground: blinkered 3 of last 5 starts: sold 1,200 gns Newmarket December Sales. *H. J. Collingridge.* **59**

TAYLOR'S REALM 3 gr.f. Another Realm 118–Sweet Rosina 61 (Sweet Revenge 129) [1988 6m 6g 7m³ 7f* 8f* 8.2m³ 7g 7d 1989 8d⁴ 8.5d 8g 8m 8g⁵ 8m⁵ 11.5m* 12m 12g 14f 12g⁵ 12g] leggy, angular filly: has a quick action: quite modest performer: won handicap at Yarmouth in August: below form after, including in seller: appears suited by 1½m: acts well on firm going. *H. J. Collingridge.* **63**

TAY PEARL 3 b.f. Formidable (USA) 125–Lasani (FR) (Appiani II 128) [1988 7g⁶ 1989 8m⁶ 6s] third foal: dam French 1m to 10.5f winner: sixth in maiden at Compiegne in July as 2-y-o when trained by A. Fabre and in claimer (leading 5f out until 2f out) at Chepstow in October: always behind in seller at Hamilton: will be suited by return to further. *M. Johnston.* **—**

TAY WHARF 4 b.c. High Top 131–Brigata (Brigadier Gerard 144) [1988 8g* 8m³ 10.5f 10g 8m⁴ 7s³ 8g 1989 8g³ 7g³ 7.3g⁶ 9g] strong, good-topped colt: carries plenty of condition: powerful galloper, with a round action: one-time smart performer, third in Dubai Poule d'Essai des Poulains at Longchamp: well below his best last 6 **100**

Brendan O'Byrne's "Teach Dha Mhile"

starts: soundly-beaten last of 11 in listed event at Newmarket final one: stays
1¼m: unsuited by firm going: sold 17,000 gns Newmarket Autumn Sales. *C. E.
Brittain.*

TAYYBAH 2 ch.f. (Feb 12) Local Suitor (USA) 128–Rozeyneh 69 (Thatch (USA) **61**
136) [1989 6m⁶ 7m³ 7f⁴ 8g] leggy, shallow-girthed filly: first foal: dam, 7f winner, is
daughter of half-sister to very useful racemare and broodmare Miss Petard: quite
modest maiden: ran poorly in Yarmouth nursery final start: should be suited by 1m:
withdrawn after giving trouble at stalls fourth intended outing: sold 2,000 gns
Newmarket Autumn Sales. *D. Morley.*

TEACH DHA MHILE 2 b.c. (Apr 26) Kampala 120–Mittens (Run The **95**
Gantlet (USA)) [1989 6f⁴ 8f* 6d* 8d*]
  Belief in the power of the Almighty is something the parishioners of Two
Mile House in County Kildare won't be short of after the engaging tale of
events which unfolded around their horse Teach Dha Mhile, who went on to answer
everyone's prayers by bringing in enough money to ensure its existence long
beyond its bi-centenary in 1990. Teach Dha Mhile, the Gaelic name for the
parish between Naas and Kilcullen in which the church is situated, was
purchased at the 1988 Irish National Open Yearling Sale for 8,400 guineas by
leading trainer Dermot Weld, whose father is buried in the parish, with a
benevolent view to offering the colt as the prize. Fortuitously for all involved,
the winner of the raffle decided to take cash instead, leaving the parishioners
to keep the horse in training with Weld and run it in the colours of the local
priest Father Brendan O'Byrne. After coming fourth on his debut at Naas,

earning IR £200, Teach Dha Mhile went on to win a maiden at Killarney before boosting the church coffers significantly by winning the Sportsman's Challenge Perpetual Cup (restricted to graduates of the sale at which he was bought) at Phoenix Park in August and the Group 3 Panasonic Beresford EBF Futurity Stakes, by a neck from Annie Laurie in a bunched finish, at the Curragh in September. The success of the raffle and the publicity it engendered inspired the purchase of another yearling at Goffs in October for a similar venture on behalf of the De La Salle Boys Primary School in Kildare: the colt, by Glenstal out of Shikari Lady, is eligible to run in the next Cartier Million and will be trained by former school pupil John Oxx. Teach Dha Mhile, meanwhile, has been sold to Italian interests, reportedly for in excess of IR £100,000, and will be aimed at the Italian Two Thousand Guineas and Derby, though still remaining in training with Weld.

			Kalamoun	Zeddaan
	Kampala		(gr 1970)	Khairunissa
	(br 1976)		State Pension	Only For Life
Teach Dha Mhile			(b 1967)	Lorelei
(b.c. Apr 26, 1987)			Run The Gantlet	Tom Rolfe
	Mittens		(b 1968)	First Feather
	(b 1977)		Aunt Eva	Great Nephew
			(b 1971)	Calleva

Teach Dha Mhile is by the Hungerford Stakes winner Kampala, sire of the Arc winner Tony Bin, out of the Irish bumpers and hurdles winner Mittens. He is her fourth foal; the others include the staying handicapper Green Archer (by Hardgreen) and the bumpers and novice hurdle winner Remittance Man (by Prince Regent). This is also the family of the Cesarewitch winner Centurion and the Irish Two Thousand Guineas runner-up Martinmas. There's plenty of stamina on both sides of Teach Dha Mhile's pedigree, and he should have little difficulty staying a mile and a half. Teach Dha Mhile, who wore blinkers on his last two outings, acts on firm ground, but has shown his best form on good to soft. *D. K. Weld, Ireland.*

TEACHER'S DRAM 3 b.f. Strong Gale 116–Top Marks 61 (Breakspear II) — [1988 NR 1989 8.2m 10d 10g] ninth living foal: dam only form as 2-y-o when 5f seller winner: little sign of ability in minor events and a maiden, off course 5 months after debut. *R. Dickin.*

TEAMSTER 3 b.c. Known Fact (USA) 135–Rosetta Stone 89 (Guillaume Tell 97 (USA) 121) [1988 8m³ 1989 12s* 12.3m⁴ 12f 14f* 14.8m² 17.6d* 18g] good-bodied colt: good mover with a quick action: useful handicapper: progressed well when winning at Folkestone (maiden) in April, Kempton in July and Haydock (£14,500 event) in September: 10/1 and looking very well, not discredited in Cesarewitch at Newmarket final start: should prove suited by long distances: acts on any going: genuine. *M. R. Stoute.*

TEARS OF HAPPINESS 2 ch.c. (Feb 19) Rousillon (USA) 133–Shadiliya 90 76 (Red Alert 127) [1989 5d 6m² 7m* 7f²] 50,000Y: strong, workmanlike colt: has plenty of scope: second foal: half-brother to 3-y-o Galwex Lady (by Mendez): dam, 7f winner at 2 yrs, is closely related to very useful 5f to 1m winner Shasavaan: modest performer: won maiden at Warwick in June: very good ¾-length second of 5 to Front Line Romance in moderately-run minor event at Redcar following month, running on having been checked over 1f out: suited by 7f. *G. A. Huffer.*

TEBITTO 6 b.g. Derrylin 115–Over Beyond 78 (Bold Lad (IRE) 133) [1988 NR — 1989 10f] stocky, workmanlike gelding: carries plenty of condition: moderate walker and mover: modest handicapper in 1987: tailed off at Salisbury in May: stays 1½m: suited by top-of-the-ground: suited by forcing tactics: has run creditably in blinkers: winning hurdler/novice chaser. *Andrew Turnell.*

TECHNOLOGY (FR) 3 b.f. Top Ville 129–Luoyang (FR) (Devon III 125) [1988 73 d 8d⁴ 1989 10s* 13.1h 10m 10m] leggy, lightly-made filly: made most when justifying favouritism in minor event at Nottingham in March: well beaten in handicaps and claimer, running as if something amiss on first occasion: lacks turn of foot and should be suited by 1½m: possibly unsuited by top-of-the-ground: raced too freely in blinkers final start (July). *N. A. Callaghan.*

TEEMING SHORE (USA) 4 b.f. L'Emigrant (USA) 129–Molly (USA) 100 110 (Christopher R (USA)) [1988 5g* 5.8g* 6f 5f⁴ 5g* 5s 5g* 5g* 5g² 1989 5f 6m* 5g²

5m⁵] strong filly: usually looks well: beat sole opponent easily by 7 lengths in minor event at Yarmouth in August: showed improved form when head second of 9, always disputing lead, to Handsome Sailor in Waterford Foods EBF Phoenix Flying Five: favourite, below-form fifth of 11, hampered leaving stalls, to Poyle George in listed race at Newmarket in October: best at 5f: best efforts on good going: usually sweats and gets on toes: game and genuine. *Sir Mark Prescott.*

TEE WALL 3 b.c. Tampero (FR) 115–Wallpark Princess (Balidar 133) [1988 5g* 5f 5g⁶ 5g³ 5s⁴ 5d 1989 5s⁵ 6d⁵ 5m 6m 5.3h 5d a6g] neat colt: keen walker: poor mover: plating-class handicapper: below form after second outing: stays 6f: probably requires easy surface. *B. A. McMahon.*   **54**

TELEGRAPH CALLGIRL 2 b.f. (Apr 13) Northern Tempest (USA) 120– Northgate Lady 54 (Fordham (USA) 117) [1989 5f⁴ 5f⁴ 6m 6g a6g⁵ a8g² a7g² a8g²] 620Y: strong, compact filly: moderate mover: second foal: half-sister to a modest plater: dam poor: quite modest performer: stays 1m: best form on good ground: good mount for a claimer. *M. Brittain.*   **63**

TELETRADER 8 ch.g. Nearly A Hand 115–Miss Saddler (St Paddy 133) [1988 NR 1989 10.2g² 10v 12d²] workmanlike gelding: first foal: dam won over hurdles: fit from hurdling, 3 lengths second of 19 in maiden at Doncaster in March: beaten 15 lengths by long odds-on Dance Spectrum in 3-runner minor event at Beverley following month: should stay beyond 1¼m: has given bit of trouble at stalls. *R. J. Hodges.*   **57**

TELL'S TOWER 3 b.f. Dunbeath (USA) 127–Gallatin Valley (USA) (Apalachee (USA) 137) [1988 NR 1989 10g] leggy filly: fifth foal: half-sister to 7f winner Raja Moulana (by Raja Baba) and useful 1½m winner Devizes (by Kris): dam won at up to 1m: 50/1, bit backward, very mulish at stalls and always behind in minor event at Nottingham in October. *R. Hollinshead.*   **—**

TEMPERABLE 5 ch.g. Touching Wood (USA) 127–On Demand 80 (Mandamus 120) [1988 16s⁶ 14.6g 16d 1989 14s 17f⁴] sturdy, good-bodied gelding: moderate mover: quite modest handicapper in 1987: lightly raced and well below his best on flat in last 2 seasons: suited by a test of stamina: acts on any going: blinkered 4 times, including both starts in spring: sold to join J. Thomas 4,000 gns Ascot August Sales. *M. H. Tompkins.*   **—**

TEMPERING 3 b.g. Kris 135–Mixed Applause (USA) 101 (Nijinsky (CAN) 138) [1988 NR 1989 9g 10f* 12f³ 11m²] strong, good-bodied gelding: has plenty of scope: has a powerful, round action: fourth foal: brother to 9f winner Khandjar and half-brother to Gold Cup winner Paean (by Bustino) and 6f (at 2 yrs) and 1m winner Grand Tier (by Habitat): dam won at up to 7f at 2 yrs: favourite, made all in maiden at Redcar in May: placed, making most, in £6,000 handicap at Newbury and minor event at Wolverhampton in the summer: sweating, very unruly, got loose and bolted when withdrawn at Newmarket in late-August: subsequently gelded: should be suited by return to 1½m: acts on firm going: takes keen hold: has joined W. Jarvis. *H. R. A. Cecil.*   **90**

TEMPESTOSA 2 b.f. (May 21) Northern Tempest (USA) 120–Lucky Candy 61 (Lucky Wednesday 124) [1989 7f⁶ 6g 8g⁵] first foal: dam, form only at 2 yrs, is out of half-sister to Gunner B: poor maiden: best form at 1m: soundly beaten in a seller on debut. *W. J. Pearce.*   **41**

TEMPLE REEF 5 ch.g. Mill Reef (USA) 141–Makura (Pampered King 121) [1988 16g 18.4v 16m² 18m 17.1g⁴ 16m³ 16m⁵ 17g² 16f⁴ 16f⁵ 17.1g 1989 19f³] smallish, compact gelding: quite modest handicapper on his day, but is thoroughly inconsistent and of doubtful temperament: needs test of stamina: well suited by top-of-the-ground: blinkered or visored last 5 outings: winning hurdler. *M. C. Pipe.*   **— §**

TEMPTING ODDS 2 ch.f. (Apr 15) Smackover 107–Pass No Remarks 78 (Wolverlife 115) [1989 5s³ 5d 5f³ 5g⁶ 5m 5f⁴] 1,000Y: small, sparely-made filly: moderate mover: second foal: dam 5f winner at 2 yrs: poor maiden: blinkered fourth start. *B. A. McMahon.*   **49**

TEMPTING OFFER 3 b.f. Raga Navarro (ITY) 119–Strawberry Ice (Arctic Storm 134) [1988 7.5s 7m 6g 1989 7.5d 12.5f 14f 11m⁴ 12g 12.2d 12m⁴ 12g⁶ 12g a16g] rather leggy, close-coupled filly: poor handicapper: suited by 1½m: acts on firm going. *N. Bycroft.*   **39**

TEN CENTS A DANCE 2 b.f. (Feb 25) Mashhor Dancer (USA)–Gold Rupee 86 (Native Prince) [1989 6g] quite attractive filly: half-sister to several winners, notably fairly useful sprinter Alakh (by Sharpen Up): dam won twice over 6f: 50/1, never a factor in 28-runner maiden at Newmarket in October. *B. Hanbury.*   **—**

TENDENCY 4 ch.f. Ballad Rock 122–Clover Hollow (Wolver Hollow 126) [1988 **71**
7m⁵ 7f⁴ 7g 6m 6m 1989 6g* 6m 6g] strong, workmanlike filly: 20/1-winner of
21-runner handicap at Leicester in September: ran moderately in similar company
afterwards: suited by 6f: blinkered and sweating, appeared ungenuine final start in
1988: inconsistent. *A. Hide.*

TENDER BID 3 ch.g. Tender King 123–Princess Biddy 86 (Sun Prince 128) **68**
[1988 6m 6m 1989 8.2s⁵ 7m⁴ 6m⁴ 7m* 7m² 7f 7g] good-topped gelding: moderate
walker: quite modest handicapper: won at Edinburgh in June, running on strongly:
creditable second at Wolverhampton, easily best effort later in summer: suited by
7f: easily best form on top-of-the-ground. *F. H. Lee.*

TENDER CHARM 2 ch.g. (Feb 16) Tumble Wind (USA)–Best Bidder 72 **62**
(Auction Ring (USA) 123) [1989 5f² 5m² a6g⁵] smallish, sparely-made gelding: third
foal: dam sprinter: quite modest performer: runner-up in maidens at Wolverhampton and Catterick when trained by R. Hollinshead: ran respectably on return 6
months later. *Mrs L. Piggott.*

TENDER DEALER 3 b.g. Tender King 123–Drora (Busted 134) [1988 6d⁶ 6d **61**
1989 6f² 6m⁵ 7.6m 6d] sturdy gelding: second of 5 in minor event at Folkestone in
July, steadied stalls, staying on strongly and easily best effort: should stay 7f: acts
on firm ground: sweating third start. *E. Eldin.*

TENDERLOIN 2 b.g. (Apr 25) Tender King 123–Samkhya (Crocket 130) [1989 **65**
5g² 5s⁶ 5d⁴ 7m⁴ 7m² 6g 7f² 7d* 7g⁶ a6g⁵ a8g²] IR 6,000Y: leggy, close-coupled
gelding: sixth living foal: half-brother to winners abroad by Ashmore and Miami
Springs: dam won in Italy: useful plater: won 17-runner event (no bid) at Catterick in
October: good second in Southwell claimer final outing: better suited by 7f and 1m
than by shorter. *N. Tinkler.*

TENDER SPENDER 3 br.g. Tender King 123–Sigtrudis (Sigebert 131) [1988 —
6s 8m 1989 7g] leggy gelding: soundly beaten, including in seller: blinkered final
outing at 2 yrs. *A. P. Stringer.*

TENDER TILLY 3 b.f. Tender King 123–Nightly Dip (Wollow 132) [1988 5m³ **57**
5d⁴ 1989 5m 6m² a6g] leggy, quite good-topped filly: quite modest maiden: second
of 4 in minor event at Thirsk in September: always behind in Southwell claimer 3½
months later: slowly away on reappearance: worth a try at 7f. *W. W. Haigh.*

TENDER TRAIL 2 ch.f. (Apr 26) Tender King 123–Trail (Thatch (USA) 136) **63**
[1989 5v 5s 5f⁶ 5m² 5f⁴ 5f⁵ 5m⁴ 5g 5m 5m² 5f⁴] IR 4,500F, 7,000Y: smallish, lengthy
filly: has a round action: half-sister to 2 winners, including French 3-y-o Fanfare du
Roi (by Rusticaro), 7f winner at 2 yrs: dam never ran: quite modest performer: best
effort in nursery at Sandown seventh start: worth a try at 6f: usually sweats: has
joined J. Benstead. *G. Blum.*

TENDER TYPE 6 b.g. Prince Tenderfoot (USA) 126–Double Type (Behistoun **71**
131) [1988 12f* 12g² 16g³ 13f* 12g⁴ 13d* 15g* 14.7m² 14f³ 1989 13m⁵ 15f⁴ 12.3g⁵
12f² 14f] strong, lengthy gelding: modest handicapper: best effort as 6-y-o when
equal-second to Waterlow Park in ladies event at Beverley, staying on well having
been slowly into stride and hampered early: eased considerably last 2f when behind
in Tote Ebor (Handicap) at York 2 weeks later: ideally suited by around 1¾m: acts
on firm going and a soft surface: has won for apprentice and when sweating. *R. M.
Whitaker.*

TENDER WHISPER 4 b.f. Tender King 123–Queens Message 93 (Town Crier —
119) [1988 7d⁶ 8d⁴ 6f⁴ 6f⁵ 1989 8h 5f a8g] sturdy, angular filly: sustained small
fracture of cannon bone at 2 yrs: plating-class maiden: needed race final outing, first
for 6 months: trained first 2 starts by B. Palling. *D. Burchell.*

TENTER CLOSE 3 b.g. Gorytus (USA) 132–Love Land (FR) (Kautokeino (FR)) **75**
[1988 5m 5g² 6d² 6f 6g 6g³ 6d² 7d 1989 8m* 8m 8.5f⁶ 9g 10f* 12m⁴ 13.8g⁴ 10m⁴
11f*] leggy gelding: has a rather round action: won claimer at Carlisle in May and
sellers (favourite, led close home, bought in 8,800 gns then sold 8,000 gns) at Ripon
in August and Redcar in October: bandaged, ran moderately in apprentice handicap
penultimate outing: stays 13.8f: acts on firm ground and a soft surface: reluctant at
stalls and ran badly in visor final start at 2 yrs. *R. M. Whitaker.*

TEREBRID 2 ch.c. (Apr 16) Coquelin (USA) 121–Hone 79 (Sharpen Up 127) **58**
[1989 5d⁴ 6f³ 6g] 21,000F, 27,000Y: leggy, sparely-made colt: poor walker: sixth
living foal: half-brother to 3-y-o 1m winner Hawwam (by Glenstal), quite useful 7f
winner in 1988, and to 3 good winners in Belgium, including middle-distance
performer Balkan Prince (by King of Macedon): dam 2-y-o 5f winner here, did well
in Belgium after: plating-class maiden: bred to stay 1m: on toes and moved freely to
post final start. *C. R. Nelson.*

TERIMON 3 gr.c. Bustino 136–Nicholas Grey 100 (Track Spare 125) [1988 **119**
6f 6g^2 7g^4 6g^6 1989 7g^2 8s^2 10.4m^3 10m* 12g^2 12f^2 14.6s^4]

Trainer Clive Brittain's quixotic approach to campaigning his horses
once again paid good dividends in 1989, notably through the Ever Ready
Derby second placing of Terimon. Terimon's record prior to Epsom was that
of a third-division horse. He failed to win from four starts at two years,
including a last-of-six placing in the Middle Park Stakes, and was having his
eighth outing when a narrow winner of a division of the mile-and-a-quarter
Groby Maiden Stakes at Leicester nine days before the Derby. His prospects
of success at Epsom looked minimal and the starting price of 500/1 an accurate
reflection of his chance. However, Terimon ran an excellent race. Held up at
the back of the field, he was still last but one turning for home. He began to
stay on very well once switched off the rails and, driven out to the line, passed
Cacoethes towards the finish to pick up £111,000, five lengths behind
Nashwan, two lengths ahead of Cacoethes. This performance represented
going on for 28 lb improvement on the part of Terimon and isn't easy to
explain. Indeed some wags, who thought it apt that Terimon is an anagram of
'no merit', chose to regard his performance as some sort of fluke. The most
likely explanation seems that a very strongly-run mile and a half suited him.
He had improved when, on testing ground, he tackled a mile for the first time
and had sustained his progress over a mile and a quarter. Given his pedigree,
his improvement at a mile and a half shouldn't have been surprising even if the
amount of improvement he made was.

Brittain announced after Epsom that Terimon would go for either the
Gordon Stakes or the Great Voltigeur as a preparatory race for the St Leger.
After a brief flirtation with the Eclipse (he was left in at the five-day stage),
Terimon missed the Gordon, apparently because he hadn't been pleasing in
his work, and went to York where he came a half-length second of three to
Zalazl. Terimon ran well, looking a shade burly, probably as well as he'd run at
Epsom. He was supplemented for the St Leger but wasn't able to reproduce
his best on the soft ground at Ayr and was quickly in trouble once Michelozzo
went for home, finishing ten lengths fourth of eight.

		Busted	Crepello
	Bustino	(b 1963)	Sans Le Sou
	(b 1971)	Ship Yard	Doutelle
Terimon		(ch 1963)	Paving Stone
(gr.c. 1986)		Track Spare	Sound Track
	Nicholas Grey	(b 1963)	Rosy Myth
	(gr 1976)	Rosy Morn	Roan Rocket
		(gr 1970)	Golden Pride

Terimon should stay a mile and three quarters. His sire Bustino is a
notable sire of stayers and middle-distance horses—Paean, Bedtime, Easter
Sun and Nashwan's dam Height of Fashion among the best. Terimon's dam
Nicholas Grey has a plebeian pedigree but has done little but good for any of
her owners. She won four races in Britain as a two-year-old, was sold to Italy
where she won another four and finished second in the Oaks d'Italia as a
three-year-old, then returned to Britain for a successful stud career. Her four
foals prior to Terimon have all won. Young Nicholas (by Young Generation)
was a fairly useful mile and a quarter winner; Dyscolos (by Dance In Time)
quite useful at up to a mile in Italy; Butsova (by Formidable) the winner of a
six-furlong listed race; and Terimon's close relation Nicolaki (by Busted) a
fairly useful winner over a mile and a half as a three-year-old. Nicholas Grey's
1987 Dominion foal, named Nidomi, ran once for Sir Mark Prescott in 1989.
Nicholas Grey herself is half-sister to three winners in Scandinavia, including
Baccarat Rose, placed in the quaintly-named graded race, the Lovey-Dovey
Cup. The second dam Rosy Morn showed little on the racecourse though she
was a half-sister to the fair hurdler Flatbush.

Terimon, a 140,000-guinea purchase at the Newmarket October Sales, is
a good-topped colt who walks well but moves with a slightly round action. He
is to stay in training with a programme of good-class mile-and-a-quarter and
mile-and-a-half races. He is likely to prove better at the longer distance. His
best performances have been on a sound surface and it seems probable soft
ground isn't ideal for him. Terimon will need to improve to win a top race but

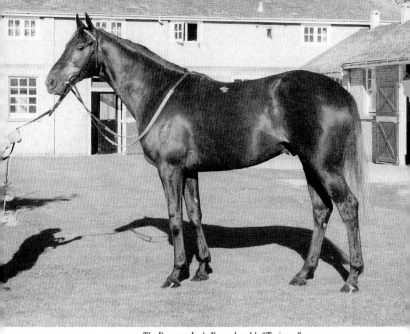

The Dowager Lady Beaverbrook's "Terimon"

progress from three to four isn't out of the question given his breeding and his record to date. If he shows the improvement from three to four that the Dowager Lady Beaverbrook's previous Derby second Relkino did he could have a cracking season. *C. E. Brittain.*

TERMALIEN (USA) 4 br.g. Arctic Tern (USA) 126–Laquiola (FR) 113 —
(Lyphard (USA) 132) [1988 11d² 10m⁴ 10s 1989 12m 12m 16.5g 12g] sparely-made ex-French gelding: third reported foal: half-brother to winning hurdler Mausolee (by Val de L'Orne): dam, French winner at up to 11f, is half-sister to Prix du Jockey Club winner Roi Lear: poor maiden: blinkered, always behind in varied events in 1989: has looked difficult ride over hurdles: sold 2,000 gns Newmarket Autumn Sales. *C.P. Wildman.*

TERNIMUS (USA) 2 ch.c. (Mar 21) Arctic Tern (USA) 126–Lustrious (USA) **64 p**
(Delaware Chief (USA)) [1989 8m 8g] $90,000Y: rather leggy, quite attractive colt: third reported foal: half-brother to minor winners in USA by Monteverdi and Stalwart: dam, winner 5 times at up to 9f, is half-sister to smart U.S. 2-y-o of 1980 Astrious: showed some ability in mid-division in late-season maidens won by Defensive Play at Newmarket and Lover's Moon at Leicester: probably capable of better. *M. A. Jarvis.*

TESEKKUREDERIM 2 b. or br.g. (Apr 18) Blazing Saddles (AUS)–Rhein —
Symphony 74 (Rheingold 137) [1989 7g] fifth living foal: brother to winning Norwegian 3-y-o Lovers Lullaby: dam won at 1½m: 25/1, slowly away and always behind in 17-runner maiden (hooded) at Folkestone in October. *J. Pearce.*

TESORA 2 ch.f. (Apr 20) Busted 134–Savahra 82 (Free State 125) [1989 7g⁴] **84 p**
27,000Y: good-bodied filly: good walker: fourth foal: half-sister to very useful

sprinter Savahra Sound and a winner in Belgium (both by Song): dam 11f and 13f winner: 25/1 and better for race, shaped promisingly when around 10 lengths fourth of 8, keeping on not knocked about, to Va Toujours in £8,000 event at Newmarket in October: will be suited by middle distances: will improve, and win races. *W. Jarvis.*

TESSLA (USA) 3 b.f. Glint of Gold 128–Chellita (Habitat 134) [1988 7m* 8f* **112** 8g* 1989 10.5g² 12m⁶ 8f⁴ 10f³ 10g 10g⁴] rather leggy, attractive filly: has a quick action: very useful performer: leading 2-y-o filly of 1988, winner of Hoover Fillies' Mile: in frame, running creditably, in Prix de Royaumont at Longchamp, Coronation Stakes at Royal Ascot and Nassau Stakes at Goodwood: below form last 2 outings in Prix de Psyche (setting good pace) at Deauville and Sun Chariot Stakes at Newmarket: will prove best at around 1¼m: acts on firm going: lacks turn of foot and should be suited by forcing tactics: sold to Japanese interests. *H. R. A. Cecil.*

TEST CASE 4 b.f. Busted 134–Wolverhants 79 (Wolver Hollow 126) [1988 8f* 12f **90** 1989 10m 8f⁵] rangy filly: moderate mover: fairly useful winner as 3-y-o: 20/1, soon pushed along in last when never-nearer fifth of 7 to Comic Talent in listed event at Sandown in May: should prove suited by 1¼m +: acts on firm going. *W. Jarvis.*

TEXAS BLUE 2 ch.f. (Feb 2) Jalmood (USA) 126–Laurel Express 76 (Bay **51** Express 132) [1989 6m 6m⁵ 6g 7f⁵ 5v 6g³ 6g a6g a7g a7g] IR 10,500Y: small, angular filly: second foal: half-sister to 3-y-o Belle Express (by Music Boy): dam second over 7f from 2 starts: fair plater on her day: ran poorly last 3 starts, first 2 within space of 40 mins: should stay 7f: has run respectably for 7-lb claimer: sold 1,600 gns Doncaster November Sales. *M. Brittain.*

THABEH 3 b.f. Shareef Dancer (USA) 135–Loveshine (USA) (Gallant Romeo **57** (USA)) [1988 7d⁵ 7g 1989 8m⁴ 7m⁶ a10g⁵] fourth foal: sister to 7f and 1½m winner Hug Me and half-sister to French 7f and 9f winner Touching Love (by Touching Wood): dam, 1m stakes winner, is half-sister to very smart Clever Trick: quite moderate form in maidens at Leopardstown and Galway in July: probably in need of race in Lingfield claimer 5 months later: should stay beyond 1m: bought of J. Bolger's stable 3,600 gns Newmarket Autumn Sales. *K. O. Cunningham-Brown.*

THAKHAYR 3 b.f. Sadler's Wells (USA) 132–Turkish Treasure (USA) 111 (Sir Ivor 135) [1988 NR 1989 10f] rather unfurnished, leggy filly: eighth foal: closely related to useful Irish 2-y-o's Treasure Trove (by Try My Best), successful over 6f and 7f, and Magic Mirror (by Nureyev), successful over 5f, and half-sister to 2 winners, including smart Irish 7f to 13f winner The Miller (by Mill Reef): dam won over 6f and 7f at 2 yrs: slowly away, very green early (carrying head high) and not knocked about in maiden at Sandown in May. *A. C. Stewart.*

THAKIB (USA) 2 b.c. (Mar 31) Sovereign Dancer (USA)–Eternal Queen (USA) **66 p** (Fleet Nasrullah) [1989 7m⁴] $175,000Y: leggy colt: has scope: closely related to 2 minor winners by Barachois and half-brother to several other winners, notably Eternal Prince (by Majestic Prince), good class at up to 1¼m: dam ran only at 2 yrs when successful at around 6f: sire useful at up to 1½m in France at 4 yrs: 8/1, green and carrying condition, over 6 lengths fourth of 5, slowly away and weakening over 1f out, to Western Ocean in maiden at Yarmouth in August: likely to improve. *J. Gosden.*

THAMESDOWN TOOTSIE 4 b.f. Comedy Star (USA) 121–Lizzie Lightfoot — (Hotfoot 126) [1988 NR 1989 7h 10.1g 8f] workmanlike filly: half-sister to 2 winners by Bay Express, including 7f and 1m winner Neds Expressa: dam unraced close relative of very useful Light Fire: little sign of ability, including in seller. *S. Mellor.*

THANKS A MILLION 3 ch.f. Simply Great (FR) 122–Friendly Thoughts **52** (USA) (Al Hattab (USA)) [1988 6m 1989 8f⁶ 8f 10m 10.1m² 10f*] lengthy, workmanlike filly: sweating and edgy, won seller (sold to join W. G. M. Turner 8,200 gns) at Lingfield in August, leading 2½f out and holding on by a neck: blinkered previous 2 starts: only form over 1¼m. *J. W. Hills.*

THARROS 3 b.c. Nishapour (FR) 125–Bold Maiden (USA) 71 (Bold Lad (USA)) **64** [1988 6d 8s 1989 9f 9f³ 10g] workmanlike colt: last of 3 in handicap at Kempton in June, first form: bit backward, faced stiff task in minor event 5 months later: stays 9f: takes keen hold. *M. E. D. Francis.*

THARSIS 4 ch.g. What A Guest 119–Grande Promesse (FR) (Sea Hawk II 131) — [1988 8v 9g 9g 12.8g⁵ 16g² 14f⁴ 16f⁴ 14f 12g³ 12g² 14v 12g 1989 14.6g] sparely-made ex-Irish gelding: brother to a winner in Spain and half-brother to 2 other winners abroad: dam won over 10.5f in France: quite modest maiden as 3-y-o: well beaten at Doncaster in April: stays 2m: acts on firm going: blinkered last 8 outings in 1988: has run creditably for apprentice. *W. Bentley.*

THATCHED MILL 3 b.g. Thatching 131–Gay France (FR) 91 (Sir Gaylord) — [1988 NR 1989 10.1m 10.1g 8m 6m] 16,000Y: rather sparely-made gelding: has a roundish action: fifth foal: closely related to a winner in West Indies by Thatch and half-brother to 3 winners, notably very useful 1985 2-y-o 7f winner Lucayan Princess (by High Line): dam 2-y-o 6f winner: no form in minor events and claimers in the summer. *P. F. I. Cole.*

THAT'S MOTORING 5 b.m. Andy Rew 103–Small Hope Bay (The Brianstan — 128) [1988 NR 1989 6g] small, sturdy mare: appears of little account: refused to enter stalls on intended reappearance: mounted on track only subsequent outing. *B. Preece.*

THAT'S THE ONE 3 br.g. Known Fact (USA) 135–Kesarini (USA) 87 (Singh 96 (USA)) [1988 5m* 5g* 5f³ 6g² 5s² 5d 5g⁴ 1989 7g 5m 6m⁵ 5m⁵ 6m 6s 5m 6g⁴ 5d] medium-sized, close-coupled gelding: moderate walker: poor mover: fairly useful performer: 40/1, creditable fourth of 21 in £8,900 handicap at Newmarket in October: below form previous 3 and final starts: stays 6f: likely to prove best on easy surface: has hung markedly on occasions, and is a difficult ride: gelded after final start. *I. V. Matthews.*

THEATRE CRITIC 2 b.c. (Apr 25) Sadler's Wells (USA) 132–Querida (Habitat 101 p 134) [1989 7d² 8s*] IR 340,000Y: half-brother to several winners, including fairly useful 1987 2-y-o 7f winner Huldine (by Cure The Blues) and Irish 1m winner Quintillon (by Rusticaro): dam, 7.9f winner at 2 yrs in Ireland, is half-sister to Chief Singer: successful in 10-runner maiden at Maisons-Laffitte in October by 1½ lengths and 5 lengths: will probably stay 1¼m: sure to improve. *A. Fabre, France.*

THE BAIRD 4 ch.g. Monsanto (FR) 121–Louisa Anne 73 (Mummy's Pet 125) — [1988 10s⁵ 8f 11.7m 11.7g 1989 10d 10s 8.3m] leggy, lengthy, sparely-made gelding: no longer of much account: blinkered, sweating and on toes final outing. *C. P. Wildman.*

THE BANK (USA) 3 br.c. Clever Trick (USA)–Quick Reason (USA) (Hail To — Reason) [1988 7m⁴ 1989 8s⁶ 9m³] rather leggy colt: modest form at best in varied events: not seen out after apprentice event (no extra 1f out) in June: should be suited by return to 1m: sold to join F. Jordan 1,200 gns Doncaster November Sales. *B. W. Hills.*

THE BARON GREY 3 gr.g. Baron Blakeney 83–I-Ching 66 (No Mercy 126) — [1988 NR 1989 8d 10.1m 7f 7m 7m 8f 9f] 420Y: small, plain gelding: second foal: dam 1m and 1¼m seller winner: no worthwhile form, including in sellers: should stay middle distances: blinkered final outing: trained first 5 by J. Perrett. *O. O'Neill.*

THE BURDEN 4 br.f. Kafu 120–Winter Sunshine 76 (Crisp And Even 116) [1988 49 5s 5f⁵ 6g* 6f* 5.8g⁴ 6g 6g 1989 5.8h 6h⁴ 6f⁶ 7f] sparely-made filly: moderate mover, with a quick action: plating-class winner as 3-y-o: ran poorly at Chepstow in July, and not seen out again: suited by 6f: acts on any going: visored once: slowly away on reappearance: looked unenthusiastic next time: sold 2,800 gns Newmarket Autumn Sales: inconsistent. *D. J. G. Murray-Smith.*

THE CAN CAN MAN 2 b.c. (Mar 16) Daring March 116–Dawn Ditty 100 (Song 41 132) [1989 7g 6m⁵ 6f] 3,000Y: big, rangy colt: carries condition: third foal (all by Daring March): brother to 3-y-o How's Yer Father: dam sprinter: little worthwhile form (though shaped quite well first 2 starts) in auction races: hung badly right final outing. *J. W. Blundell.*

THE CARETAKER 2 b.f. (Feb 14) Caerleon (USA) 132–Go Feather Go 113 p (USA) (Go Marching (USA)) [1989 6g² 7g* 7g*]

Very much against the trend, which dishearteningly for the home-trained contingent has seen virtually every worthwhile prize in Ireland plundered from abroad, the Irish managed to keep the most valuable jewel in their crown, the Cartier Million at Phoenix Park, at home for the second time in as many runnings. The Million, which is confined to graduates of selected sessions of the Irish National Yearling Sale, looked a more strongly-contested event than its predecessor won by Corwyn Bay, yet The Caretaker put three lengths between herself and a field which wouldn't have been out of place in the two-year-old pattern. At 25/1, she's an attractive each-way outsider for the One Thousand Guineas.

The Million, which because of its restricted nature carries only listed status, was The Caretaker's third and final race in a season which had begun with second place behind Aminata in the listed Smurfit Italia EBF Stakes at Leopardstown in June, but didn't continue until the EBF Silver Flash Stakes

Cartier Million, Phoenix Park — The Caretaker draws away from (left to right) Cullinan, Anshan and Book The Band

over the Million course and distance in September. Backed down from 7/2 to 7/4 favourite The Caretaker landed some substantial bets with a fairly useful performance, coming through in the final furlong to account for Missing You by a length with the Newmarket-trained raider Endless Joy a neck away in third. The Caretaker was the best supported of the home defence (which made up just under half of the maximum permitted twenty runners) in the Million in October and shared third spot at 8/1 with the useful Book The Band in a market dominated by the Sheikh Mohammed-owned pair of Anshan (who started 5/2 favourite) and Cullinan, both of whom had shown plenty of promise when successful against minor opposition. The Caretaker's success was the initial leg of a marvellous weekend double for her rider Kinane; at Longchamp the following afternoon he partnered Carroll House to victory in the Arc. Favourably drawn towards the inside—the course bends sharply right shortly after the start—The Caretaker was always able to hold a position close to the leaders; she drew level with Cullinan and Anshan two furlongs out and ran on strongly, despite changing her legs in the last hundred and fifty yards, to settle the issue convincingly; Cullinan deprived Anshan of second spot by a head. Incidentally, it's rather incongruous that an event as valuable as the Million—the first prize was IR £500,000—should be prey to the luck of the draw. As was Corwyn Bay the year before, the first three home were all drawn among the high numbers, a clear advantage given the shape of the track; and connections of fourth-placed Book The Band, who finished well clear of those other runners drawn low, can count themselves unfortunate to have been burdened with an outside stall. Nevertheless, all credit to The Caretaker, who showed much the best turn of foot in a race run at a true gallop. Though The Caretaker wasn't seen out again, the form was done no harm by the subsequent performances of those that finished behind her—Anshan ran a close third in the Dewhurst with Cullinan not far behind—and she, at least, looks to have a bright future. The prospects for Goffs, the Irish bloodstock sales company which co-stages the Million, however, at times in the latest season appeared less bright. Average returns for the Million sale fell in 1989, the managing director Jonathan Irwin, inaugurator of the Million and instrumental in the upturn of the company's fortunes, resigned in a boardroom row over the role played by Cartier, who, it's said, may soon pull out.

Being catalogued among the last dozen lots of the five-day Irish National Yearling Sale seemed not to affect The Caretaker's sale price adversely; at IR 100,000 guineas it comfortably exceeded the average for the two-hundred-and-fifty-one sold lots which made up the select Million section in 1988. There's plenty in The Caretaker's pedigree to explain why she should attract attention. Her sire Caerleon, who had a fairly quiet time in 1989 when his only

Mount Juliet Ltd's "The Caretaker"

pattern winners came in France and Italy, was responsible for Corwyn Bay; and several of her dam's other foals have shown well-above-average form in various parts of the world. The most familiar among them are the useful Irish sprinter Fearless Lad (by Sandford Lad) and the quite useful six-furlong to one-mile winner Moujik (by Ela-Mana-Mou); though the less well-known Go Honey Go (by General Assembly) won a Grade 3 event over eight and a half furlongs in the States in 1988 having spent the earlier part of her career in France. The Caretaker's dam Go Feather Go, a winner over five furlongs at two years in Ireland, is one of numerous winners produced by Feather Bed in a breeding career that has spanned twenty years. None of her winners in the States are of any great importance, but Go Feather Go's full sister Tepatitlan made a name for herself over hurdles in France where she won the Grande Course des Haies de Quatre Ans in 1977.

The Caretaker (b.f. Feb 14, 1987)	Caerleon (USA) (b 1980)	Nijinsky (b 1967)	Northern Dancer
			Flaming Page
		Foreseer (b or br 1969)	Round Table
			Regal Gleam
	Go Feather Go (USA) (b 1972)	Go Marching (b 1965)	Princequillo
			Leallah
		Feather Bed (br 1961)	Johns Joy
			Silly Sara

The Caretaker will find a mile easily within her compass at three, and will probably stay a mile and a quarter. Together with her stable-companion Go And Go, who took the Laurel Futurity in 1989, she looks at this juncture the best Irish hope for classic success in 1990. *D. K. Weld, Ireland.*

THE

THE COTTAGE 4 ch.g. Thatching 131–Brave Lass 114 (Ridan (USA)) [1988 9d — 5g 8f 7m 7d 6m 6m 5f 1989 8d 10f 8m] small, dipped-backed gelding: poor plater: blinkered once at 3 yrs: often bandaged off-fore. *P. J. Feilden.*

THE DARA QUEEN 2 b.f. (Apr 3) Dara Monarch 128–Ladyfish 79 (Pampapaul 58 p 121) [1989 8g] 27,000Y: leggy, sparely-made filly: third foal: half-sister to 3-y-o Fishki (by Niniski) and a winner in Italy: dam, 1m winner, is half-sister to Carroll House: 33/1, around 6 lengths seventh of 16, keeping on steadily after swerving start, to High Beacon in maiden at Leicester in November: should improve. *M. A. Jarvis.*

THE DARING SPORT 2 b.g. (May 6) Daring March 116–Hot Bird 98 52 (Birdbrook 110) [1989 5d⁵ 5d 5m 5f 5f² 5f⁶ 6m³ 7f 6m⁵] 3,500Y: lengthy, rather dipped-backed gelding: turns fore-feet in: fifth foal: brother to 3-y-o Migration Bird, quite modest 5.1f winner Charm Bird and 2 winners in Belgium: dam sprinter: fair plater: stays 6f: blinkered fourth outing: sweating and edgy sixth: tends to wander: likely to win soon with strong handling: gelded after final outing. *M. W. Easterby.*

THE DEVIL'S MUSIC 5 ch.h. Music Boy 124–Obergurgl 69 (Warpath 113) 65 [1988 6g 6g⁴ 6g 6f⁵ 6d* 6g 5m⁶ 5f⁶ 6g* 6g 6g⁵ 7d² 6f⁴ 6g 7s 5s 6s⁶ 6g 1989 5g* 6d² 6v 6d 6.1f 6h⁶ 6m 6m 8.2m 6m⁴ 6m 5s⁵ 5g 6d 6s a6g] robust horse: carries plenty of condition: turns fore-feet out: shows a quick action: quite modest handicapper on his day: comfortable length winner at Newcastle in March: best efforts after on next and tenth outings: best at sprint distances: not at his best on very soft going, acts on any other: has run creditably in blinkers, but almost bolted to post and tailed off in visor: has got on toes: sweated profusely eighth start: inconsistent. *N. Bycroft.*

THE DOODLER 3 b.g. Marching On 101–River Belle 72 (Divine Gift 127) [1988 — NR 1989 8.2m 9f 8f] 480F: quite good-topped gelding: fourth live foal: dam 7f winner, successful over hurdles: tailed off in claimers and a seller: blinkered, pulled hard last 2 starts. *T. Craig.*

THE FLYING FOUR 2 b.f. (Mar 18) Sayf El Arab (USA) 127–Bar Gold 80 44 (Lucky Brief 128) [1989 5d 5g 7m] 9,000Y: close-coupled filly: half-sister to several winners here and abroad over wide range of distances, including fair 1985 2-y-o Lily Fogg (by Swing Easy) and stayer Gold Rifle (by Scottish Rifle): dam won twice at around 1¼m: well beaten in maidens. *W. Carter.*

THE FOALICULE 4 b.f. Imperial Fling (USA) 116–Reita 87 (Gilles de Retz 132) — [1988 7m 7f⁵ 10.2g 12m⁵ 11.7g⁵ 1989 12g a12g] workmanlike filly: poor maiden: 33/1, tailed off in claimer at Leicester and handicap at Lingfield (blinkered, on toes) as 4-y-o: best effort at 1½m. *S. Christian.*

THE FOOTMAN 7 br.h. Hotfoot 126–Philogyny 94 (Philip of Spain 126) [1988 56 10.2s* 13v³ 10.8d* 10s⁶ 10m² 10f³ 10g 1989 10.8s³ 10.2g 10s⁴ 10v³ 8d⁵ 7.5d⁴ 8d 9f² 8f 8f 8h 7.5m 10m⁴ 9m 10f⁵ 10.6m] lengthy, good-quartered horse: good walker: poor mover: plating-class handicapper: off course almost 3 months after eleventh outing: never a threat all subsequent starts: better suited by 1¼m than 1m: acts on any going: visored twice: usually bandaged: has won for apprentice: has worn a tongue strap: invariably held up. *R. W. Stubbs.*

THE FRESHES 4 ch.g. Good Times (ITY)–Town Lady 93 (Town Crier 119) 88 [1988 8m³ 10g⁶ 10m² 12f³ 10m* 10m 12f* 11s 1989 10m⁵ 12m* 12m⁴ 16.1g³ 14m⁵ 12g] lengthy gelding: fairly useful handicapper: won at Doncaster in May: ran moderately at Haydock final outing: seems to stay 2m: possibly unsuited by soft going, acts on any other: suitable mount for apprentice: lacks a turn of foot: sold 27,000 gns Newmarket Autumn Sales: game. *W. Jarvis.*

THE GANNOCHY (USA) 3 ch.g. Coastal (USA)–Bright View 110 (Hot Spark 58 § 126) [1988 5d 6f 7m⁴ 8f 1989 11f⁶ 14f 12.2m² 12h] leggy, close-coupled gelding: quite modest maiden: second in Catterick handicap, easily best effort in first half of season: acts on top-of-the-ground: sometimes blinkered: won selling hurdle for L. Wordingham: has looked ungenuine and is one to avoid. *J. W. Watts.*

THE GOOFER 2 b.g. (May 12) Be My Native (USA) 122–Siliferous (Sandy 72 Creek 123) [1989 8s³ 8.2d⁵ 10g] 5,500F: leggy gelding: has a round action: second foal: brother to 3-y-o Sparkler Gebe: dam unplaced 4 times at 2 yrs, is closely related to useful 1m to 1¼m performer Kahaila: 50/1, 2½ lengths third of 15, keeping on well last 2f, to Ile de Roma in maiden at Ayr in September: well beaten in minor event at Redcar final start: should stay 1¼m. *A. P. Stringer.*

THE HEALY 2 b.f. (Jan 28) Blushing Scribe (USA) 107–Smitten 72 (Run The — Gantlet (USA)) [1989 5g 5v] 420F, 1,500Y: small filly: third foal: sister to 3-y-o 1¼m winner Auto Connection: dam ran only at 2 yrs when placed at 6f and 7f from 3 starts: slowly away and always behind in maiden and seller. *R. M. Whitaker.*

THEHOOL (USA) 2 gr.c. (Apr 26) Nureyev (USA) 131–Benouville (FR) (Caro 82 p
133) [1989 6f* 6m*] $600,000Y: unfurnished colt: closely related to a winner by
Northern Baby and half-brother to 2 other winners: dam lightly-raced half-sister to
good French sprinter/miler Boitron: favourite, successful in maiden at Goodwood in
July by 4 lengths from Waki Gold and slowly-run minor event at Chester in
September by ½ length from Galactic Scheme: may well stay further: sure to make
fairly useful performer. *M. R. Stoute.*

THE HOUGH 8 b.g. Palm Track 122–Dunoon Twinkle (Dunoon Star 110) [1988 40
11m 12.3f 11g⁵ 11g³ 11d⁴ 1989 13.8d⁴ 16.2g* 15.8m³ 16m⁴] workmanlike gelding:
poor handicapper: wearing crossed noseband, won at Beverley in July: suited by 2m:
often apprentice ridden: winning hurdler. *Mrs G. R. Reveley.*

THE IRISH SHEIK 2 ch.c. (Apr 9) Sayf El Arab (USA) 127–Melindra 83 (Gold 82
Form 108) [1989 5g³ 5g³ 5v³ 5f* 5f⁵ 5m² 5g] 6,000F, 15,500Y: good-quartered,
attractive colt: second living foal: half-brother to 1988 2-y-o 5f seller winner Mia
Scintilla (by Blazing Saddles): dam sprinter: fair performer: made all, beating
Shamshoon 6 lengths easing up, in maiden at Lingfield in May: speedy: blinkered
and on toes final start: sent to Italy. *M. McCormack.*

THE ISLAND 2 ch.f. (May 15) Bairn (USA) 126–Redhead 66 (Hotfoot 126) [1989 68
5d⁴ 5v* 5d⁶ 5m³ 7m³ 8m 8.5g⁶] 6,000Y: small, light-framed filly: moderate mover:
half-sister to several winners here and abroad, including 1986 2-y-o 6f winner
Lucianaga (by King of Spain): dam won 9f seller: quite modest performer: won
early-season maiden at Lingfield: best subsequent efforts on fifth and sixth starts:
suited by 1m. *M. J. Haynes.*

THE JONES BOY (FR) 2 b.g. (Apr 9) Top Ville 129–Rythmique (CAN) (The —
Minstrel (CAN) 135) [1989 7f 8f 8.2s] 5,000Y: lengthy, good-bodied, angular gelding:
third foal: half-brother to French 3-y-o 1½m winner City Ex (by Ardross): dam,
French 2-y-o winner, is from excellent family: well beaten in auction events and a
maiden. *J. Berry.*

THE KINGS DAUGHTER 3 b.f. Indian King (USA) 128–Burnished (Form- 79
idable (USA) 125) [1988 6g 5d⁴ 5g⁵ 6d² 6d⁵ 1989 5s⁴ 5.8m⁵ 6f* 5f² 5f* 6g² 5g² 6m]
strong, rather plain filly: successful in July in minor event (always front rank) at
Folkestone and claimer (running on well from off pace) at Sandown: stays 6f: acts on
firm going: has run creditably for an apprentice. *P. F. I. Cole.*

THEKKIAN 5 ch.h. Thatching 131–Debian 71 (Relko 136) [1988 7g 5g 6g² 6f⁵ 6d⁴ 63
6g³ 7d² 6d 6d⁴ 5m² 6g 5f* 5g* 6d⁴ 5m 1989 6s 6v 6s² 6f⁵ 5.8h³ 5.8h² 6f* 6m⁴ 6g⁵
6h⁴ 6g 6f 5f² 6d 6g⁶ 5s 7g a6g] tall, narrow horse: quite modest handicapper: won
strongly-run event at Thirsk in June, leading last 50 yds: effective at 5f and stays 7f:
acts on any going: often used to wear blinkers or visor, but hasn't for long time:
usually bandaged nowadays: sometimes slowly away: has looked irresolute and
needs exaggerated waiting tactics: particularly well handled by A. Culhane. *R.
Hollinshead.*

THE LIGHTER SIDE 3 br.g. Comedy Star (USA) 121–Moberry 54 (Mossberry 61
97) [1988 6f 6d 1989 8.2g³ 10v 8g 9s] neat, good-bodied gelding: worthwhile form
only when third in maiden at Hamilton: faced stiff tasks in handicaps after: stays 1m:
sold to join B. Preece after winning selling hurdle. *W. J. Pearce.*

THE MAGUE 5 br.g. Bold Owl 101–Silvery Moon (Lorenzaccio 130) [1988 10m 64
10d³ 10m 10.8m* 10m³ 10.8g* 10m⁵ 10.2g 10m 10g 10g⁵ 9d³ 10.2f⁵ 10f 10.5f 1989
10m⁴ 10.8m* 9f³ 10f² 10.8m⁶ 10.2m⁵ 9m] neat gelding: quite modest handicapper:
won same race at Warwick (fourth course victory) in May narrowly for second year
running: ran moderately last 2 outings: suited by around 1¼m: acts on firm going
and a soft surface: usually blinkered (also tried in hood): has got no edge: sometimes
starts slowly: probably needs strong handling: doesn't find much in front and well
suited by tracks with short straights: none too reliable. *Miss L. C. Siddall.*

THE MAIN MAN 5 b.h. Main Reef 126–Lady Westleigh 76 (St Paddy 133) [1988 —
NR 1989 14.8s 15.5s 14s 17.6f 19f 12h] moderate mover: modest winning stayer as
3-y-o: lost his form completely in first half of 1989: blinkered final start: has sweated
and got on toes: has pulled hard. *H. O'Neill.*

THE MALDIVE LADY 3 b.f. Oats 126–Kaotesse (Djakao (FR) 124) [1988 NR —
1989 10.1g 10.1m 10.2f] lengthy filly: ninth foal: half-sister to plating-class maiden
Blue Disc (by Disc Jockey): dam placed in France: behind in minor event and
maidens, taking good hold second start. *J. R. Jenkins.*

THE MAZALL 9 br.g. Persian Bold 123–Dance All Night 106 (Double-U-Jay 120) 59
[1988 7g⁵ 7.5m 7m* 7g³ 7.5f 7m 7d³ 7f 7s³ 7m⁶ 7f² 7f 1989 7m⁵ 7f⁴ 7m³ 7f 6g 7m²
7g² 8m 7g 7m 8.2g⁶] small gelding: poor mover: quite modest handicapper on his

day: suited by 7f: acts on any going: has worn blinkers: has sweated (did so profusely fourth outing): has reportedly suffered back trouble: none too reliable. *Miss L. C. Siddall.*

THE MINDER (FR)   2 b. or br.g. (Apr 3) Miller's Mate 116–Clarandal 80 (Young   —
Generation 129) [1989 7m⁶] rather leggy gelding: first foal: dam 1m winner: last to Closed Shop in claimer at Yarmouth in July. *W. Hastings-Bass.*

THE MISSISSIPPIAN   8 b.g. Tumble Wind (USA)–Dolly-Longlegs 74   —
(Majority Blue 126) [1988 NR 1989 12d 10.6g⁵] strong, workmanlike gelding: not discredited in handicaps at Haydock in first half of 1989, on second outing (still carrying condition) never-nearer fifth of 20, soon pushed along, in amateurs event: suited by 1½m to 1¾m: best with give in the ground: blinkered once: good mount for apprentice. *B. A. McMahon.*

THE MONEYS GONE   2 b.f. (May 11) Precocious 126–Be Merry 104   —
(Charlottown 127) [1989 6f 6m 6g 7f] 10,000Y: sturdy, lengthy filly: half-sister to several winners, including 1978 2-y-o 5f winner Just Married (by Habitat), later successful in Norwegian 1000 Guineas: dam, half-sister to very smart May Hill, stayed at least 13f: well beaten in varied races: usually blinkered or visored: sold 1,250 gns Newmarket Autumn Sales. *M. J. Fetherston-Godley.*

THE NASH   2 ch.c. (May 19) Joshua 129–Dawn Affair 77 (Entanglement 118)   —
[1989 10g] sixth living foal: half-brother to poor 3-y-o Arrandale (by Tickled Pink): dam ran 49 times without success on flat and over hurdles: 100/1, slowly away and soon tailed off in minor event at Redcar in November. *J. Mulhall.*

THE OIL BARON   3 gr.g. Absalom 128–Ruby's Chance 71 (Charlottesville 135)   55
[1988 5d⁴ 5s² 5.3f² 7f³ 6g⁴ 7d⁵ 6s 7s 1989 10v 8g 10f² 12h² 11m 11.7m 12m⁵ 12h] leggy gelding: plating-class maiden: staying-on second in handicaps at Lingfield and Brighton: below form later in summer: stays 1½m well: acts on hard going: has joined R. Akehurst. *R. Hannon.*

THE OVERNIGHT MAN   4 ch.c. Smackover 107–Highland Rossie 67   32 §
(Pablond 93) [1988 12d 10g⁵ 12.2g⁵ 12g⁶ 12f⁶ 16g 12m 13.8d² 12d 12g⁵ 1989 14s 12.5f³ 12f] leggy colt: has a round action: plater: well beaten at Thirsk in May, and not seen out again: stays 1¾m: acts on any going: sometimes blinkered: often appears reluctant. *B. A. McMahon.*

THE PRODIGAL   2 b.g. (Feb 24) Aragon 118–Patois (I Say 125) [1989 7g⁵ 6f³   72
8m a8g³] 16,500F, 12,000Y, 3,000 2-y-o: rangy, useful-looking gelding: has scope: half-brother to 3-y-o School Dinners (by Sharpo) and several winners here and abroad, including middle-distance winner La Bandera (by Morston): dam twice-raced half-sister to smart stayer Petty Officer: modest maiden: best effort final start: suited by 1m. *R. Hannon.*

THE PRUSSIAN (USA)   3 b.c. Danzig (USA)–Miss Secretariat (USA)   93
(Secretariat (USA)) [1988 NR 1989 10g² 10m³ 12.4g*] $375,000Y: compact, rather angular colt: moderate mover: fifth foal: half-brother to 3 winners in USA, 2 by Roberto, including 8.5f stakes winner Uno Roberto: dam, unplaced in 5 starts, is out of 1963 Selima Stakes winner My Card: comfortably landed odds in maiden at Newcastle in August: placed in quite valuable maidens at Newmarket and Ascot, in latter hanging when ridden along 2f out: should prove better at 1½m than 1¼m. *M. R. Stoute.*

THE QUEEN OF SOUL   3 b.f. Chief Singer 131–Catriona 96 (Sing Sing 134)   75
[1988 5m⁵ 5m⁴ 5g 6g 1989 6f* 6m³ 5f* 5f⁶ 5f] leggy filly: made all or most to win apprentice maiden at Pontefract in June and handicap at Sandown in July: ran moderately in handicaps last 2 outings: stays 6f: acts on firm going. *J. A. R. Toller.*

THE REFRIGERATOR   5 b.g. Shirley Heights 130–Nip In The Air (USA) 114   59
(Northern Dancer) [1988 12f 14f 17.1g⁵ 12d⁶ 16d 1989 14g⁵ 14m⁵ 14m⁵ 16m⁶ 16g⁴ 18g⁵] rangy gelding: has a slightly round action: plating-class maiden: faced stiff tasks in handicaps as 5-y-o: 100/1, good fifth of 21 finishers, leading much of way, to Double Dutch in Tote Cesarewitch (Handicap) at Newmarket final outing: suited by good test of stamina: acts on firm going and possibly unsuited by soft: one paced and best with forcing tactics: has seemed a difficult ride and may do better in blinkers or a visor. *L. G. Cottrell.*

THERE YOU ARE   3 b.f. Kings Lake (USA) 133–Occupation (Homing 130)   59
[1988 7g 6g 7g⁴ 8d⁴ 1989 8g² 10v 8d 8m⁶ 12m* 14f 14f 12h 12m⁵ 13.8g⁶] workmanlike filly: 20/1 and ridden by 5-lb claimer, won claimer at Edinburgh in May: well beaten in handicaps and claimer after: suited by 1½m: best efforts on a sound surface: ran poorly when visored ninth start: blinkered next: has run creditably when sweating: sold 2,700 gns Doncaster October Sales. *M. Brittain.*

THE RIGHT TIME 4 b.g. King of Spain 121–Noddy Time 97 (Gratitude 130) 56
[1988 7m⁵ 8.2s 8d⁴ 1989 7.5g 7.5m 7f* 6m⁶ 6f⁴ 6g⁶ 6g* 6s³ 7g] robust gelding: fair
plater: ridden by 5-lb claimer, won handicaps at Redcar (no bid) in July and Hamilton
(no bid) in October: best form at 6f or 7f: acts on any going: visored debut, usually
blinkered nowadays. *J. Parkes.*

THE SCARLET DRAGON 3 b.f. Oats 126–Dragon Fire 67 (Dragonara Palace —
(USA) 115) [1988 NR 1989 9m⁶ 8m] strong, close-coupled filly: first foal: dam 1m to
1½m winner: seems of little account. *M. W. Eckley.*

THE SHANAHAN BAY 4 b.c. Hays 120–Tanala Bay (Sterling Bay (SWE)) 70
[1988 7m 8m 8m⁵ 8f² 1989 7m 7m³ 6g 5m³ 5f* 5m 6s⁴ a6g* a6g⁵ a6g* a6g*]
angular colt: poor walker: made all or virtually all in all-aged seller (no bid) at
Beverley and claimers at Southwell (twice) and Lingfield in second half of season:
suited by 6f: acts on any going: blinkered last 5 starts: has run well for apprentice:
suited by forcing tactics: goes very well on turning track: has looked none too keen.
E. Eldin.

THE STAMP DEALER 6 b. or br.g. Runnett 125–Royal Meath 83 (Realm 129) —
[1988 NR 1989 5m⁵ 5m 6f 7.6m 5m 6m 5f 5m] rangy gelding: no longer of much
account: has been tried in blinkers and visor. *A. W. Jones.*

THE SWAMP FOX 2 b.c. (Feb 25) Mummy's Pet 125–River Maiden (FR) 86 46
(Riverman (USA) 131) [1989 5s 6f⁵] 40,000Y: leggy colt: second foal: dam 7f winner:
over 9 lengths fifth of 6, outpaced from halfway, to Born To Swing in minor event at
Lingfield in August: off course 4 months after debut. *K. M. Brassey.*

THE SWINGE 2 b.c. (Feb 18) Thatching 131–Hi Gorgeous (Hello Gorgeous 57
(USA) 128) [1989 6f⁵ 6g] 2,400Y: first foal: dam never ran: backward and green,
about 8 lengths fifth of 12 to Eurolink The Lad, easily better effort in October
maidens at Folkestone: should stay 7f. *P. Mitchell.*

THE TANSEY MAN 3 ch.g. Millfontaine 114–Kindle (Firestreak 125) [1988 5g 52
5m⁴ 5.8g⁵ 6f⁶ 5d³ 6s³ 6m² 5.8d⁴ 5g⁵ 5f⁴ 8.2m⁶ 6d 7d 1989 6s 6m 7d 6m 6g⁴ 6f⁴ 7h³
6m 8.3m 5f 7f³] smallish, lightly-made gelding: plating-class maiden: in frame in
sellers: effective at 6f and 7f: acts on any going: blinkered thrice as 2-y-o: tends
to wander: has run well when sweating: active type, often on toes. *K. O.
Cunningham-Brown.*

THETHINGABOUTITIS (USA) 4 gr.c. Fluorescent Light (USA)–Croquet 95
(USA) (Court Martial) [1988 9d* 8f⁴ 11.7m* 10m² 12f* 10g³ 13.1g³ 11d² 12g² 14f²
1989 12s 7m⁵ 12m 12f⁴ 16f* 16g* 10.1d 18g²] lengthy, dipped-backed colt: has a
round action: fairly useful performer: successful in summer in quite valuable
handicaps at Ascot and at Sandown: 9/2, no extra final 1f when beaten 6 lengths by
long-odds-on Weld in 3-runner Doncaster Cup: suited by test of stamina: acts on
firm going and a soft surface: sometimes bandaged nowadays: game and genuine. *G.
Lewis.*

THE WEIR 2 ch.g. (May 3) Salmon Leap (USA) 131–Galka 98 (Deep Diver 134) —
[1989 8g] smallish, stocky gelding: half-brother to several winners, including 1m
winner Guess Again (by Stradavinsky): dam, half-sister to top-class sprinter Double
Form and good-class filly Scimitarra, won twice at 5f at 2 yrs: 50/1, soundly beaten in
17-runner maiden at Leicester in November: subsequently gelded. *A. N. Lee.*

THE WHITE LION 5 b.m. Flying Tyke 90–Comedy Spring (Comedy Star 68
(USA) 121) [1988 7g 9g* 8g 10d² 9m* 8f⁴ 8.2m* 8.5g* 8g³ 10m⁶ 8g²ᵈⁱˢ 8g³ 10.2f
10s⁶ 8g³ 1989 8g 8.2v² 8d⁴ 11.7m 12.8m⁵ 8m³ 8.2g³] leggy, quite good-topped mare:
poor mover: quite modest handicapper: not seen out after July: best form at around
1m: well suited by an easy surface: good mount for apprentice: genuine. *J. A. Glover.*

THEY ALL FORGOT ME 2 b.g. (Apr 25) Tender King 123–African Doll —
(African Sky 124) [1989 7m 7g 7f] 80,000F, IR 20,000Y: smallish, rather sparely-
made gelding: half-brother to Don't Forget Me (by Ahonoora) and a winning
middle-distance plater: dam Irish 1½m winner: poor form in Salisbury maidens. *R.
Hannon.*

THE YOKEL 3 b.g. Hays 120–Some Dame 72 (Will Somers 114§) [1988 NR 1989 43
6m 7m 8g 8g 10m⁵ 10m² 11.7f] 8,800Y: lengthy gelding: moderate mover:
half-brother to very useful sprinter Reggae (by Gay Fandango), sprint handicapper
Farmer Jock (by Crofter) and winners in France and Belgium: dam, half-sister to
high-class Record Run, won over 1¼m: plating-class form at best: stays 1¼m: best
efforts on top-of-the-ground: sold to join R. Manning 2,600 gns Ascot October Sales.
G. A. Pritchard-Gordon.

THE YOMPER (FR) 7 ch.g. Arctic Tern (USA) 126–Grundylee (FR) (Grundy —
137) [1988 10.2d* 10d² 10.4s 10m 1989 12s⁵ 10g] sturdy gelding: won amateurs

handicap at Doncaster in March, 1988: appeared to show considerable improvement next time but failed to reproduce that running: stays 1½m: suited by easy surface: suited by forcing tactics: sweating on reappearance. *R. Curtis.*

THIMBALINA 3 ch.f. Salmon Leap (USA) 131–Maestrette 77 (Manado 130) 57 [1988 6g⁶ 7s⁵ 6s 1989 6m 7f⁶ 7g 9g⁵ a12g] leggy, lightly-made filly: lacks scope: moderate walker: plating-class maiden: has run in seller: bred to stay 1m +, but may not do so: acts on soft ground. *L. G. Cottrell.*

THIN RED LINE 5 b. or br.g. Brigadier Gerard 144–Golden Keep 77 (Worden II 66 129) [1988 10g⁴ 10g* 11.7d 10m 12f 12m 12g 12d⁶ 1989 10m 10m 11.5f 11f* 10g² 11.7g⁴ a11g] leggy gelding: first form for some time when easily winning poor claimer at Hamilton in July: in frame, finding little, in similar events at Ayr and Windsor (bandaged) afterwards: stays 11f: acts on firm going: visored last 4 outings: often sweating and edgy: winning selling hurdler: none too genuine. *J. R. Jenkins.*

THIRTY FIRST 4 gr.g. Castle Keep 121–January (FR) (Sigebert 131) [1988 11.7f 88 § 11.7g 12.2f* 16.1m² 19v 1989 14s⁶ 18.4m 18f² 19f² 17.1f⁴ 18g] lengthy, angular gelding: fairly useful winner as 3-y-o: runner-up in subsequent handicaps, on last occasion putting head in air and finding little under pressure in uncompetitive event at Goodwood in June: suited by test of stamina: acts well on firm going and is probably unsuited by soft: one to treat with caution. *J. L. Dunlop.*

THOMAS LENG 4 ch.c. Homing 130–Fast Asleep (Hotfoot 126) [1988 7v* 7d² 67 § 8g* 6v⁴ 7g⁶ 8m² 8f⁵ 8g 7f 7g 1989 8s 8.5d⁶ 8.2g 8.2g⁴ 8v] leggy, rather sparely-made colt: moderate mover: modest handicapper on his day: didn't look keen and tended to hang left final outing: stays 1m: acts on top-of-the-ground and heavy going: has worn blinkers and visor: has got on toes: usually makes running at strong pace (went too fast second start): unreliable. *M. Brittain.*

THORESBY 2 ch.c. (Feb 4) Thatching 131–Nana's Queen 86 (Ridan (USA)) [1989 6g 6g] IR 11,500F, IR 13,000Y: workmanlike colt: has scope: fifth living foal: dam, half-sister to good 6f and 7f colt Royal Boy, won over 7f at 2 yrs and stayed 1m: soundly beaten in large-field maidens at Newmarket late in season. *R. J. R. Williams.*

THORN DANCE (USA) 3 b.c. Northern Dancer–Barb's Bold (USA) 112 (Bold 107 Forbes (USA)) [1988 6m* 7f* 1989 6m² 8f⁵ 6m³] strong, good-bodied colt: successful in summer as 2-y-o in maiden at Newmarket and Acomb Stakes at York before sustaining knee injury: beaten ½ length by Kerrera in listed race at Haydock in May, keeping on strongly despite edging left: looked very well but moved poorly down when well-beaten last of 5 in St James's Palace Stakes at Royal Ascot and about 6 lengths third of 5 to Green's Canaletto in July listed race (leading 4f and again drifting left) at Newbury: should be suited by further than 6f: yet to race on an easy surface: reportedly to join N. Drysdale in USA. *H. R. A. Cecil.*

THORNFIELD BOY 3 b.g. Homeboy 114–Pink Blues 103 (Tickled Pink 114) 105 [1988 5d⁵ 6m² 6d³ 6m⁴ 6d* 6s⁴ 1989 6f² 6g* 6f⁶ 6f* 6m⁴ 6s 6m] workmanlike,

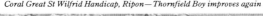

Coral Great St Wilfrid Handicap, Ripon—Thornfield Boy improves again

good-bodied gelding: carries condition: won £7,700 handicap at Newmarket in July and Coral Great St Wilfrid Handicap (well-backed favourite, making all to win by 3 lengths) at Ripon in August: behind in Ayr Gold Cup (moderately drawn) and Group 3 event at Ascot last 2 starts: will prove suited by strongly-run race or stiff track over 6f: probably acts on any going: won for 5-lb claimer as 2-y-o: useful. *R. Akehurst.*

THORNPUSS 3 b.f. Tachypous 128–Kiki Mouse 66§ (Song 132) [1988 5m 1989 8m] lengthy, sparely-made filly: bit backward, behind in maidens. *J. J. Bridger.* —

THORNYLEE 3 ch.c. Ballachstal (CAN)–Miss Worth 73 (Streak 119) [1988 NR 1989 5m] 4,000Y, 25,000 2-y-o: third foal: half-brother to 1m seller winner Inner Calm (by Jellaby): dam 5f winner: 25/1, slowly away and always behind in apprentice maiden at Edinburgh in July. *W. D. Fairgrieve.* —

THORNZEE 2 gr.f. (Mar 26) Belfort (FR) 89–Trackally 95 (Track Spare 125) [1989 5f6 5m6 5m 5f] 900F: leggy filly: half-sister to a winner abroad by Free State: dam quite useful at 5f and 6f: little worthwhile form in maidens and a claimer: pulled very hard final start, and headstrong to post previous 2 outings. *J. J. Bridger.* —

THOU FEEAL 2 b.f. (Feb 7) Mr Fluorocarbon 126–Jose Collins 91 (Singing Bede 122) [1989 5d 5g 6g 7f] 450F, 780Y: third live foal: dam best at 5f: little worthwhile form in maiden auction events and sellers: has joined Miss S. Williamson. *M. W. Easterby.* —

THRESHFIELD (USA) 3 b.c. Northern Prospect (USA)–French Cutie (USA) 76 p (Vaguely Noble 140) [1988 NR 1989 7m2] $72,000Y: tall, quite good-topped colt: sixth foal: brother to 2 winners in USA at up to 9f, including stakes-placed Ice Cold Gold, and closely related to Cadillac Ranch (by Distinctive Pro), successful in USA at up to 7f: dam unraced: 10/1, green, on toes and in need of race, neck second of 11, tending to edge left, to Lust of Love in maiden at Thirsk in September: took keen hold to post and in race: should improve. *W. J. Haggas.*

THRINTOFT 3 ch.c. Sandhurst Prince 128–Finlarrig (Thatching 131) [1988 7d4 57 7f 6g6 6s 7m* 7d4 7m 1989 7m4 6f 7m 6g2 6f2 8f6 7.5m3 8.2g 8.2f 7g4 8m4 8f2 8.2g3 8g] leggy colt: poor mover: placed in handicap and sellers: stays 1m: acts on firm ground: not particularly consistent. *T. D. Barron.*

THUNDERING 4 b.g. Persian Bold 123–Am Stretchin' (USA) (Ambiorix II 130) — [1988 10f 7m 7.5f3 10s5 1989 7s 7.6m 6m 7m5 8.5g 7m 12m 8.2d 8m] lengthy gelding: has a round action: poor maiden: very little form in 1989: stays 7.5f: acts on firm going and a soft surface: blinkered sixth outing. *A. W. Jones.*

THURBER 2 b.c. (Apr 10) Vision (USA)–Peas-Blossom 79 (Midsummer Night II 75 117) [1989 5d5 5d* 6m5 6m3 5d5 5g] IR 10,500Y: smallish, angular colt: moderate mover: half-brother to several winners in Scandinavia, including Danish and Swedish Oaks and Derby winner Rossard (by Glacial): dam, maiden, stayed 1m, is half-sister to very useful stayer Hickleton and daughter of smart 2-y-o 5f and 6f winner Fan Light: modest performer: won maiden at Catterick and minor event at Beverley in spring: best subsequent effort in nursery at Pontefract on fourth start: bred to stay further than 6f: acts on top-of-the-ground and a soft surface. *M. H. Easterby.*

TICKLE TOUCH (USA) 2 b.f. (Feb 4) Stop The Music (USA)–Abeesh (USA) 75 77 (Nijinsky (CAN) 138) [1989 7m* 8.2d5] workmanlike, good-quartered filly: first foal: dam lightly-raced middle-distance maiden: ridden by 7-lb claimer, won 10-runner maiden at Yarmouth in August (gave trouble at stalls) by ½ length from Totham: over 4 lengths fifth of 11 to Laird of Balmoral in minor event at Haydock following month: stays 1m. *B. Hanbury.*

TICKLE TRAP 4 b.f. Homing 130–Palace Travel (High Top 131) [1988 7g 7f 7f4 — 8f 7g 8d 10f6 1989 10.6g] compact, useful-looking filly: moderate mover: quite modest maiden at best: carrying condition, tailed off in amateurs handicap at Haydock in June: stays 7f: acts on firm going: blinkered once: sometimes bandaged. *Mrs J. Pitman.*

TICKLE YOUR FANCY 3 b.g. Tickled Pink 114–Florries Fancy (Breeders — Dream 116) [1988 6d 1989 8g 6f 7m 5.8h 8m 9f 10f] rather leggy, plain gelding: has a markedly round action: probably of little account: sold 925 gns Ascot October Sales. *J. A. Bennett.*

TIDDLY WINKS 2 b.c. (Mar 4) Daring March 116–Party Game 70 (Red Alert 56 127) [1989 5m 6m 6g 5f6 6f 6m4 6g] medium-sized, heavy-topped colt: first foal: dam 6f winner stayed 7f: showed improved form when always-prominent 3 lengths fourth of 28 to Sister Sal in seller at Newmarket in October: ran moderately in claiming nursery there following month: will be better suited by 7f. *R. V. Smyth.*

TIDEMARK (USA)   2 b.c. (Apr 13) Riverman (USA) 131–Remarkably (USA)   **89** ?
(Prince John) [1989 6g* 7g] $65,000Y: good-bodied, quite attractive colt: seventh
foal: half-brother to 3 winners in North America, one in minor stakes: dam unraced:
favourite but very green, won 4-runner maiden at Ascot in September by length
from Eye of The Tiger, running on well: well-backed favourite, stumbled and never
in contention in 18-runner nursery at Newmarket following month: bred to stay 1m.
L. M. Cumani.

TIDY SUM   2 ch.f. (Apr 16) Mansingh (USA) 120–Wayleave (Blakeney 126) [1989   —
5g⁶] 3,400Y: workmanlike filly: fifth living foal: half-sister to 3-y-o Jindabyne (by
Good Times) and a winning middle-distance plater: dam ran once: 10/1, green and
backward, well-beaten sixth of 7, hanging badly left, to You Sure in seller at
Haydock in July: reared in stalls: sold 700 gns Doncaster November Sales. *S. J.
Muldoon.*

TIE BACK   3 b. or br.f. Tender King 123–Grattan Princess (Tumble Wind (USA))   —
[1988 6s 6g 8m 1989 10.2f 10g⁶ 11g] quite good-topped filly: poor at best: pulled hard
in seller penultimate start: very slowly away final one. *M. J. Camacho.*

TIEMPO   3 b.f. King of Spain 121–Noddy Time 97 (Gratitude 130) [1988 NR 1989   **50**
6m⁵ 6m⁵ 7f 6d⁴ 5s⁵] compact, workmanlike filly: has scope: sister to modest maiden
The Right Time and quite useful maiden Father Time, and half-sister to
several winners, including smart 5f to 7f winner Grey Desire (by Habat) and smart
1¼m performer The Dunce (by High Hat): dam stayed 1m: ridden by 5-lb claimer,
strong-finishing fourth of 24 in handicap at Haydock in October, best effort:
favourite, well beaten in similar event at Hamilton 3 weeks later: likely to prove
best at 6f: acts on a soft surface. *M. H. Tompkins.*

TIFFIN TIME   2 b.f. (May 2) Lochnager 132–Mashin Time 73 (Palm Track 122)   **52**
[1989 5d³ 5f 6g 5m⁶] leggy filly: has a roundish action: fourth foal: sister to a poor
maiden: dam 6f and 1m winner: plating-class maiden: easily best effort on debut:
acts on a soft surface, and seems unsuited by firm. *M. H. Easterby.*

TIGANI   3 b.c. Good Times (ITY)–She Who Dares (Bellypha 130) [1988 5g* 6m*   **120**
6f⁶ 7f³ 8g⁵ 5d² 1989 5f* 5g⁶ 5f² 5m⁴] big, good-topped colt: carries condition: very

Capt M. Lemos' "Tigani"

smart performer: always close up and battled on gamely when running very well last 2 starts in King's Stand Stakes (beaten a neck) won by Indian Ridge at Royal Ascot and William Hill Sprint Championship (beaten around a length) won by Cadeaux Genereux at York: won minor event (went down really well) at Kempton in May: suited by 5f: acts on a soft surface, and goes very well on firm going. *G. Lewis.*

TIGER CLAW (USA) 3 b.c. Diamond Shoal 130–Tiger Scout (USA) 86 (Silent **65** Screen (USA)) [1988 7m⁴ 7g 8g 1989 8g⁵ 10.6m² 10g² 11m 11.7f⁴ a12g] good-bodied colt: quite modest handicapper: second at Haydock (apprentices) and Leicester within 4 days in May: claimed £21,000 when running fairly well penultimate start: possibly suited by around 1¼m: acts on top-of-the-ground: raced too keenly in blinkers fourth outing: visored final one: winning novice hurdler. *I. A. Balding.*

TIGHT REIN 2 b.g. (May 27) Muscatite 122–Rathlin Sound (Margouillat (FR) **55** 133) [1989 6m 6m 6f* 6m⁶ 6m] IR 4,000F, IR 4,400Y, 5,000 2-y-o: tall, lengthy gelding: fourth foal: half-brother to poor 1987 2-y-o The Watfordian (by Stanford): dam ran 4 times in Ireland: fair plater: successful at Nottingham in August (no bid) by a neck from Give In: ran well last 2 starts. *K. M. Brassey.*

TIGNANELLO 2 ch.c. (Apr 9) Burslem 123–Ms Yvonne (Morston (FR) 125) **53** [1989 6f⁵ 6m 7m⁴ 7f 8f] IR 3,800F, 11,000Y: workmanlike colt: has scope: second foal: dam placed from 7f to 1½m in Ireland: plating-class maiden: ran moderately in nurseries final 2 starts: stays 7f: edgy second and third starts: tended to hang left third. *G. A. Pritchard-Gordon.*

TILLY TAVI 7 gr.m. Welsh Pageant 132–Princess Tavi (Sea Hawk II 131) [1988 **74** 16f 18.4s* 15g 16f⁴ 15.8d* 16f³ 16m 1989 18.4m 12m* 14g 16g² 18.4f⁴ 12m 16m] workmanlike mare: good mover: modest handicapper: well ridden to make all at Edinburgh in May: very good second to Spring Forward at Chester, best subsequent effort: suited by enterprising tactics at 1½m and stays very well: acts on any going: has won for apprentice: tough and genuine. *J. Mackie.*

TILSTONE LODGE 4 br.g. Try My Best (USA) 130–Sabirone (FR) (Iron Duke — (FR) 122) [1988 10m 10.4d 1989 9g a11g⁴ a14g] lengthy gelding: 33/1, sign of ability only when 10 lengths fourth of 13, staying on strongly, in handicap at Southwell in December: sweating, edgy and backward on reappearance: should be suited by 1½m + : visored last 2 outings. *T. H. Caldwell.*

TILT TECH FLYER 4 b.g. Windjammer (USA)–Queen Kate 52 (Queen's **68** Hussar 124) [1988 7d 7.6s* 7.6f 8m 7.6m⁵ 8f 7.6d* 1989 7v³ 8g* 7.6f 7g 7m 7.6m 8f] big, leggy, sparely-made gelding: quite modest handicapper: won at Salisbury in May ridden by 2 lengths: well beaten last 3 outings: stays 1m: acts on heavy going and unsuited by top-of-the-ground nowadays: has run creditably for apprentice: occasionally sweats and gets on edge: winning hurdler. *R. Akehurst.*

TIMBER'S GIRL 3 b.f. Southern Arrow (USA) 106–Vignargenta (Absalom 128) §§ [1988 6f 7m 7d⁶ 1989 12m⁴] unfurnished filly: no worthwhile form in auction events and a minor contest: refused to race (blinkered) then virtually refused last 2 starts at 2 yrs: one to leave alone. *J. Ringer.*

TIME BANDIT 4 ch.c. Bold Lad (IRE) 133–Flo Kelly (Florescence 120) [1988 — NR 1989 5f 9m] lengthy, good-quartered colt: seventh foal: half-brother to 3 winners, including useful 5f and 7f winner Kellord (by Lord Gayle): dam fairly useful Irish sprinter: soundly beaten in claimer at Sandown (tailed off) and ladies race at Kempton: sold 840 gns Newmarket September Sales. *R. J. R. Williams.*

TIME FOR JOY 5 b.m. Good Times (ITY)–Cry of Joy 50 (Town Crier 119) [1988 — 6v² 6v 6g 7m 6f 5g 5f 1989 7f 5f 7f] lengthy, leggy mare: poor handicapper: no form since first outing (tended to hang left and carry head high) as 4-y-o: not seen out after July: stays 6f: well suited by the mud: often apprentice ridden. *Mrs N. Macauley.*

TIMELESS LAND 4 ch.f. Bay Express 132–Australia Fair (AUS) (Without Fear — (FR) 128) [1988 6d 1989 6d 8d 8.3m 5f 7m] sparely-made filly: no longer of much account. *B. Forsey.*

TIME ON MY HANDS 3 ch.f. Warpath 113–Midsummer Madness 66 (Silly **59** Season 127) [1988 6s 1989 8g² 8.2m⁵ 13f⁵ 9f* 9f] leggy, sparely-made filly: made virtually all when comfortable winner of seller (no bid) at Redcar: again favourite, travelled well to dispute lead 3f out then found little and eased in similar event three 4 days later in August: may prove best short of 13f: sold to join Mrs A. Knight 5,800 gns Doncaster October Sales. *C. W. Thornton.*

TIMES ARE HARD 5 b.g. Bay Express 132–Raffinrula 75 (Raffingora 130) **37** [1988 7g⁶ 12g 9g³ 8g³ 1989 a10g³] close-coupled gelding: poor maiden: stays 1¼m: suitable mount for apprentice. *D. Burchell.*

TIMES GIFT 2 ch.c. (Feb 1) Burslem 123–Sun Gift (Guillaume Tell (USA) 121) 80
[1989 6m³ 6m* 6m⁶ 6m] 10,500F, 14,000Y: lengthy colt: has scope: second foal: dam
never ran: sweating slightly, won maiden at Windsor in July by 4 lengths from
Copperbottom: in need of race and not at all knocked about in nursery at Newmarket
final start: ran poorly in between: bred to stay 7f +. *W. A. O'Gorman.*

TIME TO REIGN 3 b.f. Ya Zaman (USA) 122–Barrera Queen (USA) (Barrera —
(USA)) [1988 6m 7f² 1989 7f⁵ 8f 7f⁴] fair at best: well below form in maidens and
handicap in 1989: may been suited by return to shorter: dead. *M. H. Tompkins.*

TIMOTHY'S TOY 4 b.c. High Top 128–Current Pattie (USA) 102 (Little 94
Current (USA)) [1988 10d² 10m* 10g⁵ 12g³ 12g³ 12s 1989 12d⁵ 10.4m⁶ 12m* 12f³
12m 10g³ 12v] rangy, angular, useful-looking colt: returned to his best when
winning strongly-run £19,100 handicap at Newmarket in August by head from Gulf
Palace: better suited by 1½m than 1¼m: acts on firm going and probably unsuited by
heavy: takes keen hold: genuine: sold to race in Saudi Arabia 50,000 gns Newmarket
Autumn Sales. *C. E. Brittain.*

TIMOURTASH (USA) 3 ch.c. Riverman (USA) 131–Tikarna (FR) (Targowice 104
(USA) 130) [1988 6f² 6g* 7g² 1989 8s² 8.5s⁴ 10.1m* 12m³ 12v] rather sparely-made,
attractive colt: won minor event at Windsor in May: good third in listed race at
Newmarket 5 months later: tailed off in Group 3 event at Newbury final start: stays
1½m: acts on soft going and top-of-the-ground: sold 42,000 gns Newmarket Autumn
Sales for export to Saudi Arabia. *R. F. Johnson Houghton.*

TIMSOLO 6 ch.g. Remainder Man 126§–Miss Tehran 73 (Manacle 123) [1988 44
16m⁵ 15s 15v² 15d* 1989 14s* 13v⁶ 12d⁵ 15g⁵ 13s⁶ 13.6f⁴ 15s 15g* a16g⁶ a14g³]
sturdy gelding: poor handicapper: won at Nottingham in March and Edinburgh in
November: stays 15f: goes particularly well on an easy surface: good mount for
apprentice: best racing up with pace: winning hurdler. *C. Tinkler.*

TIMUR'S KING 2 b.g. (May 24) King of Spain 121–Timur's Daughter 103 —
(Tamerlane 128) [1989 7g] big, lengthy gelding: half-brother to several winners,
including useful 6f to 1¼m winner Heir Presumptive (by Habitat): dam stayed at
least 9f: 33/1 and very green, swerved right stalls and never in contention in
29-runner maiden at Newmarket in November. *R. F. Johnson Houghton.*

TINA'S ANGEL 2 b.f. (May 7) Martinmas 128–Tina's Magic (Carnival Night) —
[1989 5f 7f⁵ 6g] leggy, sparely-made filly: third foal: half-sister to 3-y-o Jomana (by
Roman Warrior), 5f winner at 2 yrs: dam won novice selling hurdle: well beaten in
maidens, twice ridden by 7-lb claimer. *J. C. Fox.*

TINA'S GIFT 3 ch.g. Tina's Pet 121–Floral Gift 84 (Princely Gift 137) [1988 5g⁵ 52
5g² 5m⁵ 5d⁵ 5g 5d³ 7.5m⁶ 6g 7f⁵ 5g³ 6g 1989 7d² 7.5d³ 6f 6g 7m] rather
sparely-made gelding: moderate mover: plating-class maiden: has put up best
performances when placed at Catterick: suited by 7f: acts on top-of-the-ground and
a soft surface: sometimes visored: inconsistent. *Ronald Thompson.*

TINAS LAD 6 b.g. Jellaby 124–Arbatina (Sallust 134) [1988 13m* 15.8m² 12m² —
12g² 12m* 12m* 13.3f 12.2d⁵ 1989 12.2m] big gelding: carries plenty of condition:
has a round action: quite modest winner (including for amateur) as 5-y-o: in need of
race only start in 1989: suited by around 1½m: acts well on top-of-the-ground: races
up with pace. *J. A. C. Edwards.*

TINA'S MOMENTO 2 b.f. (Mar 3) Tina's Pet 121–Mio Mementa 61 (Streak 119) 47
[1989 5s³ 5v* 5s 5g⁵] 720F, 1,050Y: leggy, sparely-made filly: has a round action:
second foal: sister to smart 3-y-o 7f and 7.6f winner Just Three: dam sprint maiden:
early-season plater: 6-length winner at Hamilton (no bid). *W. G. M. Turner.*

TINA'S SONG 4 b.f. Tina's Pet 121–Chinese Falcon 81 (Skymaster 126) [1988 37
5m⁴ 5m 5d³ 5s⁶ 6m 6f⁴ 6f 7g 6m⁶ 7f 7m³ 6m 7f⁴ 6d 6g 8m⁶ 1989 8m⁴ 8.3m³ 8m
7.6h⁶ 8.3g⁴ 8g² 8.3m 8.3d⁶ 8f] strong, compact filly: usually looks well: moderate
mover: poor plater: stays 1m: acts on any going: has run creditably in blinkers and
visor: sold 1,150 gns Doncaster November Sales. *P. Howling.*

TINKERBIRD 2 b.f. (Feb 28) Music Boy 124–Quaranta 83 (Hotfoot 126) [1989 68
6d³ 6g⁶] 15,000Y: angular filly: has scope: moderate mover: closely related to fair
1984 2-y-o maiden What A Record (by Record Token) and half-sister to 3 winners,
latest Cambridgeshire winner Quinlan Terry (by Welsh Pageant), later successful at
1½m: dam 2-y-o 5f winner, is half-sister to smart 5f to 7f performer Quy: quite
modest form, fading final furlong, in late-season maidens won by Heart of Joy at
Newbury and Lip Sing at Leicester. *W. Jarvis.*

TIPPY TIPPY TOE (USA) 2 b.f. (May 23) Nureyev (USA) 131–Belle Of Dodge 60
Me (Creme Dela Creme) [1989 6g⁶ 5f] $270,000Y: smallish, workmanlike filly:
seventh foal: closely related to useful 1984 2-y-o 7f winner Gallant Archer (by

Nijinsky), later Grade 3 11f winner in USA: dam smart winner at up to 1m, is sister to high-class filly Barely Even: around 5 lengths sixth of 8, taking good hold and unable to quicken last 2f, to Walkern Witch in maiden at Yarmouth: prominent 3f, not clear run and not knocked about, in similar event at Beverley later in September: bred to stay 7f + . *M. R. Stoute.*

TIPTONIAN   10 gr.g. Royalty 130–Pretty Fast 52 (Firestreak 125) [1988 NR 1989   —
14f⁶] poor performer: tailed off in 6-runner handicap at Nottingham in July, only outing on flat since 1985: has worn bandages: winning chaser. *K. S. Bridgwater.*

TIROL   2 br.c. (Mar 16) Thatching 131–Alpine Niece 87 (Great Nephew 126) **112** p
[1989 6m³ 6m² 6g* 7.3d*]
    No winner of the Horris Hill Stakes since Efisio in 1984 has gone on to further success. Celtic Heir, who sprang a 20/1 surprise in 1985, was beaten on all his three outings the following year; so was the 1988 winner Gouriev, who ended up being sold for just 23,000 guineas at the July Sales; Naheez and Glacial Storm, Horris Hill winners in 1986 and 1987 respectively, both showed good-class form as three-year-olds to reach a place in two Derbys but couldn't manage a win. It now falls to the progressive Tirol to attempt to end the sequence in 1990. Tirol never looked back after failing to justify strong support in maiden events at Newbury and Newmarket on his first two starts. His first win came in a ten-runner graduation race on the third day of Doncaster's St Leger meeting. Able Player's fall passing the two-furlong pole and the subsequent discovery of subsidence which caused the rest of the fixture to be abandoned claimed the vast majority of the headlines that day. Nevertheless, Tirol's half-length defeat of the subsequent Newmarket winner Cutting Note was significant, and represented clear improvement on his previous form; in a field of eight for the Vodafone-sponsored Horris Hill he was sent off the 6/1 fourth choice. Missionary Ridge headed the market at 9/4 after his runaway win in a maiden event at Leicester earlier in October, followed by the Washington Singer Stakes winner Karinga Bay on 3/1 and the useful though seemingly-exposed Robellation on 9/2. It was evident early in the home straight that Karinga Bay's journey from County Durham was going to prove a wasted one, but at that point the three other fancied contenders were all handily positioned travelling well within themselves; with a furlong to run there was virtually nothing to separate the trio, and in a thrilling finish

Vodafone Horris Hill Stakes, Newbury—little between Tirol (left) and Robellation

Tirol just proved the strongest, battling on tenaciously under strong pressure from Pat Eddery to beat Robellation by a head with Missionary Ridge two and a half lengths away in third.

			Thatch	Forli
	Thatching		(b 1970)	Thong
Tirol	(b 1975)		Abella	Abernant
(br.c. Mar 16, 1987)			(ch 1968)	Darrica
			Great Nephew	Honeyway
	Alpine Niece		(b 1963)	Sybil's Niece
	(b 1972)		Fragrant Morn	Mourne
			(ch 1966)	Alpine Scent

A tall, leggy colt, Tirol cost 13,000 guineas as a foal and four times that amount when re-sold as a yearling at the Highflyer Sales. His pedigree is sound rather than spectacular. Thatching developed into a top-class racehorse once switched to sprinting and fitted with blinkers in 1979; his impact as a stallion hasn't been quite so significant, but he has sired plenty of useful performers. The July Stakes winner Mansooj and the Gimcrack winner Wiganthorpe are two of his best representatives; another is the unbeaten Irish colt Puissance, who looked to be making up into a good sprinter until injury ended his season prematurely. Tirol's dam Alpine Niece finished placed over six furlongs and a mile and a half but was largely disappointing on the racecourse. She's produced a couple of fair sprinters at stud, notably the Gosforth Park Cup winner Relatively Sharp (by Sharpen Up); and her dam Fragrant Morn, also a sprinter, is responsible for several winners: one of them, Alpine Niece's brother Alpine Nephew, was a very useful staying two-year-old, while another, the Matahawk colt Minatzin, wasn't far behind the best French two-year-olds of 1985 when his two wins included the nine-furlong Prix de Conde. Going back further it's interesting to note that Fragrant Morn's grandam is Fragrant View, a Cheveley Park runner-up and also a half-sister to the Derby and St Leger winner Airborne.

Tirol's current odds of 33/1 for the Two Thousand Guineas look a reasonable reflection of his chance—his form as a two-year-old was almost a stone inferior to the best colts, and it's also worth noting that his stable houses several other Guineas hopefuls, notably Rock City and the impressive Racecall Gold Trophy winner Osario. As for Tirol's stamina potential: his trainer reportedly thinks he'll prove effective over a mile and a half in due course, but we wouldn't be so sure. Admittedly, Tirol did improve markedly when stepped up in distance for the Horris Hill, but most of Thatching's progeny have shown their best form at a mile or shorter. Whatever his distance turns out to be Tirol does possess the scope to improve further; on the evidence of his first season it seems some give in the ground suits him particularly well. *R. Hannon.*

TISSERAND (ITY) 4 gr.c. Nadjar (FR) 128–Tandina (ITY) (Claude (ITY)) [1988 **116** 10.5g* 10s* 11g* 12s* 12s² 1989 9g* 10v* 10g³ 12m² 12m 12m 10s] big, lengthy, good-bodied colt: half-brother to a winner in Italy by Ercolano: dam, won 5 races and runner-up in Premio Roma, is daughter of Italian Oaks runner-up Tejada: winner of 8 races in Italy, notably Derby Italiano at Rome in 1988 when beating Carroll House a short neck: placed as 4-y-o behind Alwuhush in Premio Presidente della Repubblica at Rome and Gran Premio di Milano: well beaten after in King George VI and Queen Elizabeth Diamond Stakes at Ascot and in Group 1 events at Milan and Rome: stays 1½m: acts on top-of-the-ground and heavy going. *M. Vincis, Italy.*

TITCHWELL 3 b.g. Thatching 131–Bird Reserve 74 (Blakeney 126) [1988 6s 6f* **73** 6s 1989 8s 8m 10f 8.5g⁴ 11m 10m*] stocky gelding: won claimer at Nottingham in June by a neck, given plenty to do then holding on well: stays 1¼m: acts on firm going, possibly unsuited by soft: blinkered third outing: inconsistent. *J. D. Bethell.*

TITE SPOT 2 ch.f. (Apr 1) Muscatite 122–Luan Causca 70 (Pampapaul 121) [1989 **55** 5f³ 5g³ 6m 5f⁶ 6m² 6m⁶ 5m a6g* a5g] IR 2,300Y: narrow, sparely-made filly: third reported foal: half-sister to a winner in Norway: dam 2-y-o 5f winner: fair plater: won late-season claimer at Southwell: better suited to 6f than 5f: blinkered third outing: sometimes sweating and edgy. *N. Tinkler.*

TITIAN MIST 3 ch.f. Town And Country 124–Artracin (High Line 125) [1988 5m — 5d 1989 8s⁶ 8s] leggy filly: behind in varied events, including seller: bred to stay at least 1m: tends to give deal of trouble at stalls. *J. M. Jefferson.*

TIT WILLOW 7 b.g. He Loves Me 120–Willow Bird 74 (Weepers Boy 124) [1988   39 §
6m 7f² 8f 7g³ 8g 7d 8d 8m⁵ 8.2s⁴ 1989 8m⁶ 7m³ 7m³] sparely-made gelding: poor
handicapper: not seen out after July: stays 1m: acts on any going: wears blinkers:
bandaged at 7 yrs: often slowly away: best with strong handling: inconsistent and
not one to trust. *T. Craig.*

TL QUARTER PINT 3 b.c. Prince Tenderfoot (USA) 126–Tumble Royal   —
(Tumble Wind (USA)) [1988 6g 1989 7f 8f⁵] well beaten in maidens. *M. J.
Fetherston-Godley.*

TOAD ALONG 4 b.g. Daring March 116–Fille de Phaeton (Sun Prince 128) [1988   —
7g 6f 6f⁴ 7g 1989 7g 7f 6f⁶] workmanlike gelding: quite modest maiden at best: races
freely, but stays 7f: acts on heavy going: blinkered once at 3 yrs: has joined O.
Sherwood. *L. G. Cottrell.*

TOAST THE HOST 2 gr.c. (Apr 30) Elegant Air 119–Alhargah (Be My Guest   73
(USA) 126) [1989 5f 5f³ 7g⁵ 7m⁴ 8m⁵ 8.5g* 8g 8.2f] 12,000 2-y-o: lengthy colt: has
scope: keen walker: moderate mover: second foal: half-brother to a winner in Italy:
dam poor daughter of half-sister to high-class middle-distance colt Pelerin: modest
performer: won nursery at Epsom in August, making all and running on well: ran
moderately last 2 starts, seeming to take little interest when held up on final one:
will stay middle distances: suited by forcing tactics: hung markedly fourth outing. *R.
Hannon.*

TOBACCO ROAD 2 ch.c. (May 15) Burslem 123–Ishtar (Dike (USA)) [1989 8g   64
8d a8g⁴ a8g⁶] 8,800Y: sparely-made colt: fourth foal: dam ran several times in
Ireland: quite modest maiden, best efforts last 2 starts. *R. W. Armstrong.*

TO BE FAIR 2 ch.c. (Mar 28) Adonijah 126–Aquarula 88 (Dominion 123) [1989 6f   —
8m⁶ 8g] 24,000Y: workmanlike colt: first foal: dam 2-y-o 5f and 6f winner, is
half-sister to 2 useful or better 2-y-o winners: well beaten in maidens. *Dr J. D.
Scargill.*

TOBERMORY BOY 12 b.g. Mummy's Pet 125–Penny Pincher 95 (Constable   61
119) [1988 6g 6m 6f³ 6f 6m 6f⁴ 6m² 6g 6f⁴ 6f⁴ 7f³ 6m* 6f 7d 1989 6.1f⁶ 6m 6f⁵ 6m 6m
7f 7f⁴ 6m 6g³ 6f⁴ 6m 7f² 7m 7g 6g⁵ 8g] neat, strong gelding: carries plenty of
condition: moderate mover: quite modest handicapper on his day: stays 7f: best on a
sound surface: visored once: often gets outpaced: tough. *R. M. Whitaker.*

TOD 2 gr.c. (Feb 27) Petorius 117–Mainly Dry (The Brianstan 128) [1989 6h² 6m²   97
6m* 6m⁴ 6m² 6f* 5m] 29,000Y: good-topped colt: has scope: good walker: has a

*Timeform Futurity, Pontefract—game efforts from these two-year-olds.
Tod wins from King Al and La Galerie*

quick action: third foal: half-brother to 3-y-o Mainly Sunset (by Red Sunset) and quite useful sprinter Great Chaddington (by Crofter): dam never ran: quite useful performer: successful in maiden at Goodwood in June and minor event (by a neck from King Al) at Pontefract in September: short-head second to Green's Belle in listed race at Ripon on fifth start: never travelling well in blinkers final start: suited by 6f: tends to wander. *J. Berry.*

TODA 2 ch.f. (Apr 7) Absalom 128–Lambay 88 (Lorenzaccio 130) [1989 6g] leggy filly: fourth foal: half-sister to useful 1m to 11f performer My Lamb (by Relkino) and 3-y-o 7.6f winner Bay Bay (by Bay Express): dam 7f winner at 2 yrs: always behind in 15-runner maiden at Newbury in June. *R. F. Johnson Houghton.*   —

TOKANDA 5 ch.g. Record Token 128–Andalucia 57 (Rheingold 137) [1988 12m 1989 14.8m 15.3m³ 12g² 16f⁵ 12m⁵ 12m⁶] workmanlike gelding: has a round action: bad performer: stays 15.3f: acts on any going: often blinkered at 2 yrs. *F. J. Yardley.*   30

TOLEDO (USA) 2 b.c. (Mar 12) Fappiano (USA)–Visual Emotion (USA) (King Emperor (USA)) [1989 8g²] $525,000Y: leggy, finely-made, quite attractive colt: poor walker: second foal: half-brother to a minor winner in USA: dam winner at up to 1m: favourite but very green, 4 lengths second of 17, edging left 2f out and one pace final furlong, to Castle Courageous in maiden at Leicester in November: sure to improve, and win a maiden. *H. R. A. Cecil.*   80 p

TOLMOSS 2 ch.c. (Mar 15) Night Shift (USA)–Viennese Waltz 85 (High Top 131) [1989 6f⁴] 17,000Y: sturdy colt: second foal: dam suited by a test of stamina: carrying condition, soundly-beaten last of 4 in claimer at Hamilton in July: has joined L. Barratt. *J. Berry.*   —

TOLO 4 b.g. Bold Lad (IRE) 133–Thessaloniki 94 (Julio Mariner 127) [1988 8s⁵ 6d 6f⁴ 6m⁶ 6m 6m 6g 6m 1989 6d 7s 7g 6f 6f* 6m⁴ 6m 5.6g 7m 7g 6f] small, good-topped gelding: usually looks well: good mover: fair handicapper: led close home when winning at Kempton in July: below form after next outing: brought down eighth start: effective at 6f and stays 1m: probably needs a sound surface: tailed off when blinkered on reappearance: trained first 3 outings by G. Lewis: sold to join W. Carter 5,000 gns Newmarket Autumn Sales: subsequently gelded: inconsistent. *C. E. Brittain.*   78

TOLOMENA 3 b.f. Tolomeo 127–Meg's Pride (Sparkler 130) [1988 5f⁴ 5g⁵ 6g 6f⁶ 1989 8m 10.1m⁶ 7g 12f³ 16f² 18g] lengthy, workmanlike filly: showed improved form when second in handicap at Warwick in October, staying on well having run in snatches: ran badly 2 weeks later: stays 2m: acts on firm ground. *W. G. R. Wightman.*   61

TOMAHAWK 2 ch.c. (Apr 16) Be My Guest (USA) 126–Siouan 78 (So Blessed 130) [1989 6s] sixth foal: half-brother to 3 winning middle-distance performers, notably very smart 4-y-o Apache (by Great Nephew): dam won over 1½m, and is half-sister to high-class middle-distance stayer Dakota and very useful Warpath: 6/1, well beaten in 13-runner minor event at Ayr in September. *C. W. Thornton.*   —

TOM CLAPTON 2 b.g. (Apr 14) Daring March 116–Embroideress 80 (Stanford 121§) [1989 7m 6g 8g] close-coupled gelding: first foal: dam 5f to 7f winner: behind in big fields of maidens at Newmarket and Leicester late in season. *D. Morley.*   53

TOMMY DALY 4 b.g. Dunphy 124–Bit of A Fiddle (Stradavinsky 121) [1988 6d 5f 6m⁶ 6m 6d⁴ 7m⁴ 7h⁴ 7g 7f 7d 6s 1989 9d⁶ 12v 10.8d 7f 7g 8f] sturdy, good-topped gelding: carries condition: poor mover: quite modest handicapper on his day: not seen out after June: should stay beyond 7f, but unlikely to stay 1½m: probably unsuited by soft going, acts on any other: often blinkered or visored: difficult ride: unreliable. *W. Carter.*   — §

TOM RUM 6 b.g. Liboi (USA) 76–Snow Rum (Quorum 126) [1988 9g 8g 8g 9f 8.2m³ 8m² 8f³ 8g 8.5f² 8g 1989 8f⁶ 7f⁵ 7.5m* 8.2f 8m] leggy gelding: poor walker: plating-class handicapper: won at Beverley in June: best at around 1m: well suited by top-of-the-ground: often wears a crossed noseband: sometimes sweats: good mount for inexperienced rider. *H. Candy.*   51

TOM TOWLEY 3 b.g. Reformed Character 107–Darwin Tulip (Campaign 106) [1988 NR 1989 14g] half-brother to sprint plater Royal Darwin (by Royal Palm) and 2 middle-distance winners, including modest 1½m to 2m winner High Rainbow (by High Line): dam never ran: 100/1, slowly away and tailed off in minor event at Redcar in November. *A. Smith.*   —

TONGADIN 3 b.g. Petong 126–River Vixen (Sagaro 133) [1988 5g 8.5f 6g⁶ 8m 1989 8.2v⁵ 8s* 8g² 8.2m⁴ 10.6m 9f 8g³ 8g² 8m 8.2g 8.2d 10g 9s⁵ 8.2g* 8g 8g] sparely-made, angular gelding: won sellers at Ripon (on toes, bought in 5,000 gns) in April and Nottingham (sweating, apprentice race and no bid) in October: stays 9f: 57 acts on soft going and top-of-the-ground: claimer ridden: inconsistent, difficult ride (tends to hang and has run in snatches) and not one to trust implicitly. *M. J. O'Neill.*

TONGUE TIED JOHNNY (USA) 3 b.c. Sir Ivor 135–Tongue Tied Muse (USA) (Stage Door Johnny) [1988 8.2d 10.2m² 1989 11f⁴ 11.5f 13.3d⁴ 14g⁵] strong, chunky colt: modest maiden at best: probably stays 13f (faced stiff task over 1¾m): best effort on top-of-the-ground: changed hands 21,000 gns Newmarket Autumn Sales after third start. *R. J. R. Williams.* —

TONKAWA 4 b.g. Indian King (USA) 128–Lady Tycoon 67 (No Mercy 126) [1988 8g 8d⁴ 7g⁴ 1989 6f 8f 10f* 10f 13.1f* 17.1f²] big, robust gelding: good mover, with a long stride: fairly useful handicapper: won at Kempton in July and Bath (beating Lady Rosanna ¾ length) in August: good neck second of 4 in a slowly-run event at Bath in October: probably stays 17.1f: acts on firm going and a soft surface. *G. Harwood.* 97

TOO EAGER 3 b.g. Nishapour (FR) 125–Double Habit (Double Form 130) [1988 5m 5g 7g⁶ 5g 6g⁴ 6m⁶ 6s 7m 1989 7m⁶ 8.2f 7f 7f* 7g² 6g* 7m² 6g⁶ 6g 7m³] lengthy, dipped-backed gelding: quite modest handicapper: led inside final 1f when winning twice at Ayr within 6 days in July: suited by 7f: acts on firm going, unsuited by soft: best in blinkers: changed hands 3,800 gns Doncaster May Sales. *M. W. Easterby.* 64

TOPASANNAH 2 b.f. (Mar 7) Commanche Run 133–Princess Tracy 111 (Ahonoora 122) [1989 6g 6g⁵] rather unfurnished filly: first foal: dam useful Irish sprinter stayed 7f: around 12 lengths fifth of 15 to Childrey at Folkestone, easily better effort in October maidens. *B. W. Hills.* 55

TOP BERRY 2 b.f. (Mar 9) High Top 131–Falcon Berry (FR) (Bustino 136) [1989 7m 8f²] close-coupled, good-bodied filly: second foal: half-sister to 3-y-o 13f winnner Beaumood (by Jalmood): dam lightly-raced daughter of Cheveley Park runner-up Red Berry: weak 5/1, 2½ lengths second of 6, one pace last 2f, to Pay The Bank in maiden at Redcar in October: hampered start and ran green on debut: will be suited by 1¼m +. *L. Cumani.* 63

TOP-BOOT 3 b.c. High Top 131–Sauceboat 120 (Connaught 130) [1988 7d⁶ 7m² 7m² 8d* 1989 7g⁴ 8s* 8.2m² 8g² 10v²] lengthy, quite attractive colt: has a quick, sharp action: won Esher Cup (Handicap) at Sandown in April, rallying well: second after in £19,300 handicap (hanging left) at Haydock, listed race (below form on first run for 4 months) at the Curragh and Group 3 contest at Milan: probably stays 1¼m: yet to race on very firm going, probably acts on any other: useful. *J. L. Dunlop.* 108

TOP CLASS 4 b.c. High Top 131–Cassina 91 (Habitat 134) [1988 10d5 12g⁴ 10m⁵ 12d 12m* 13.3g* 14.6g⁶ 12m² 1989 12s² 12s² 12f² 12g⁵ 12m³ 12g 12m⁶] lengthy, good-topped colt: grand walker: moderate mover: runner-up in N E Manion Cup (Handicap) and Tancred International Stakes at Rosehill, Australia, within a week in March and in 4-runner Hardwicke Stakes at Royal Ascot: given enterprising ride when third of 7, beaten over 7 lengths, tending to hang, to Nashwan in King George VI and Queen Elizabeth Diamond Stakes at Ascot: below form at Longchamp in autumn in Ciga Prix de l'Arc de Triomphe (50/1) and in Prix du Conseil de Paris (blinkered): stays 13.3f: appears to act on any going: game. *C. E. Brittain.* 120

TOPCLIFFE 2 b.f. (Mar 7) Top Ville 129–Sandford Lady 116 (Will Somers 114§) [1989 7m 8.2f³ 7g⁶] leggy filly: half-sister to Irish 3-y-o 1¼m winner Love That Mac (by Niniski) and 3 other winners, including useful sprinter Gaius (by Sallust) and 1987 2-y-o 1m winner Sandford Prince (by Tap On Wood): dam, half-sister to top-class sprinter Sandford Lad, won 6 times at around 6f: 6 lengths third of 6, not handling bend, to Tasarly in minor event at Nottingham in September: better suited by 1m than 7f. *D. Morley.* 66

TOP COMPANY (FR) 2 b.c. (May 2) Lomond (USA) 128–Highest (FR) (High Top 131) [1989 7s] 580,000 francs (approx £53,100) Y: first foal: dam, winner in Italy, is half-sister to Highest Honor: 20/1, over 8 lengths seventh of 10 to Bondstone in maiden at Goodwood in September. *P. A. Kelleway.* 61 p

TOP DREAM 4 br.c. High Top 131–Pleasant Dream 89 (Sharpen Up 127) [1988 7g² 7g³ 7.6g* 8f⁵ 7g* 7.6g* 1989 8g 7d* 7.6f⁴ 7g 7m 7g 7m] smallish, strong, close-coupled, attractive colt: good walker: moderate mover with a quick, round action: reportedly chipped bone in knee final start (July) as 3-y-o: showed himself as good as ever when winning £17,100 Insulpak Victoria Cup (Handicap) at Ascot in April: well below his best last 4 outings: suited by 7f: best on an easy surface (possibly unsuited by very soft going): has run creditably for apprentice: keen type. *M. A. Jarvis.* 98

TOPEKA EXPRESS (USA) 6 b.g. Topsider (USA)–Watch Out 99 (Blakeney 126) [1988 8g 8.5m 8f* 8f⁵ 8g⁶ 8g⁴ 8m⁶ 8g 10m 8m 1989 8g³ 8s 8f 8f⁴ 8.2f* 10.8f* 67

8m[6] 8.2f[2] 8.2f[4] 10f[4] 8.2d[3] 9m[4]] smallish, sturdy gelding: carries plenty of condition: moderate mover: quite modest handicapper: successful from small fields at Hamilton and Ayr in June: stays 10.8f: not at his best on soft going: effective with blinkers or without: has won for apprentice. *C. Tinkler.*

TOPGLOW   5 ro.h. Kalaglow 132–Lady Gaylass (USA) (Sir Gaylord) [1988 12f* — 12g 1989 12g[6] 16s 12f 12f[6] 14f 12.2g 8g a10g] lengthy horse: poor mover: suffered hairline fracture of near-hind as 3-y-o and has enlarged joint: little show since winning maiden at Brighton early in 1988: stays 1½m: acts on firm going: blinkered last 2 outings: reluctant at stalls second start: trained first 5 by H. O'Neill. *W. J. Pearce.*

TOPHAMS   3 b. or br.c. Good Times (ITY)–Sun Lamp 76 (Pall Mall 132) [1988 5m   65 1989 6d 5g 6f5 8m 8.2g[6] 8f[6] 6g[2] a6g[4] a6g[2] a6g[3]] big colt: poor mover: quite modest maiden: seems suited by 6f: acts on firm going: trained first 2 starts by Ronald Thompson. *R. Hollinshead.*

TOPHARD   3 b.g. Lyphard's Special (USA) 122–Tomard (Thatching 131) [1988 5d   53 5g 6f 8d 1989 12f 14f 12f[3] 12m[4] 15g* 12f[3] 13f[5] 12m 15g[6] 18g] leggy, workmanlike gelding: won claimer at Edinburgh in July: ran well in claimer (leading 1m) next start, poorly on last 3: best form at around 1½m: acts on firm going: usually blinkered: tends to hang under pressure: sold to join R. Lee 6,000 gns Newmarket Autumn Sales. *W. J. Pearce.*

TOP KNOT   3 b.f. High Top 131–Fiddle-Faddle 85 (Silly Season 127) [1988 NR   — 1989 10s[6] 11.5m 12g[5] 17.4s] 40,000Y: big, lengthy, full-quartered filly: sixth foal: half-sister to 3 winners, including useful stayer El Conquistador (by Shirley Heights) and quite modest 7f and 1m winner Talk of Glory (by Hittite Glory): dam, half-sister to Cesarewitch and Irish St Leger winner Mountain Lodge, won over 1½m and 2m: little worthwhile form, including in handicaps: reluctant at stalls second outing. *J. W. Hills.*

TOP OF THE BILL   2 b.c. (Apr 12) Star Appeal 133–Cash Limit 62 (High Top   70 131) [1989 7m[6] 7m[5] 8g* 7g] 5,200F, 18,000Y: small, rather sparely-made colt: brother to 3-y-o Hand In Glove and half-brother to fair 1984 2-y-o 7f and 8.2f winner Double Limit (by Roan Rocket) and a winner in Italy by Hotfoot: dam lightly raced: won maiden at Edinburgh in September by a neck from Allez-Oops, staying on strongly last 3f: ran creditably in mid-division in nursery at Newmarket following month: shapes like a stayer: ran well for 7-lb claimer second start. *N. A. Callaghan.*

TOP OF THE WORLD   2 b.c. (Apr 22) Top Ville 129–Une Florentine (FR)   — p (Pharly (FR) 130) [1989 7m[3]] 36,000Y: tall colt: second foal: half-brother to French 3-y-o Un Brigand (by Vayrann), 7f claimer winner at 2 yrs: dam French 5.5f and 9f winner, is half-sister to high-class French 1m to 1¼m performer Un Desperado: 13/2, bit backward and green, remote last of 3 in minor event at Ascot in October: should do better. *C. E. Brittain.*

TOP ONE   4 ch.g. Sallust 134–Light Diamond (Florescence 120) [1988 6s 6d 7g   67 6m* 7m 1989 9f 5f[6] 7f 6f*] close-coupled, useful-looking gelding: very much caught the eye (20/1 from 10/1, running subject to stewards inquiry) in handicap at Chepstow in July and 9 days later landed gamble in similar company at same course: suited by 6f: acts on any going: usually bandaged nowadays: pulls hard. *C. J. Hill.*

TOPPER TWO   3 br.c. High Top 131–Polly Packer 81 (Reform 132) [1988 NR   — 1989 10m[3] 12.5f[4] 19f[4]] sturdy, good-topped colt: has plenty of scope: fifth foal: brother to 2m winner Upton Park and half-brother to stayer Sun Street (by Ile de Bourbon) and 1½m to 2¼m winner Regal Reform (by Prince Tenderfoot): dam, daughter of very useful miler Vital Match, won second over 7f and 1m: well beaten in maidens and slowly-run minor event: sold 6,400 gns Newmarket Autumn Sales. *C. E. Brittain.*

TOP ROW   6 b.g. Beldale Flutter (USA) 130–Connaught Nymph 71 (Connaught   — 130) [1988 8.2v[2] 7d[6] 8.2s 7d 1989 8.2d 8m a8g] robust gelding: carries condition: poor walker and mover: poor maiden: best at 7f or 1m: well suited by the mud: has run well for amateur. *A. W. Jones.*

TOPS ALL (USA)   3 b.c. Topsider (USA)–Tell Me All (USA) (Cyane) [1988 7g*   95 1989 8g[5] 8s[2] 8.2m[4] 8.3m[3] 8f] sparely-made, useful-looking colt: fairly useful handicapper: in frame in valuable events at Sandown and Haydock and when sweating and edgy at Windsor: looking very fit, ran poorly in Schwepps Golden Mile at Goodwood in July: stays 1m: acts on soft going and top-of-the-ground. *J. W. Hills.*

TOP SCALE   3 b.g. Tower Walk 130–Singing High 87 (Julio Mariner 127) [1988 7g   47 7g 8m 1989 8m 8.2f[6] 8m 8f[2]] good-topped gelding: poor maiden: stays 1m: acts on firm ground: apprentice or amateur ridden as 3-y-o. *A. Hide.*

925

TOP SUMMIT   3 b.f. Head For Heights 125–Hayloft (FR) 111 (Tudor Melody 129)   —
[1988 NR 1989 10.6m⁵ 10.1m] smallish, lengthy filly: half-sister to Irish 2000
Guineas winner Wassl (by Mill Reef) and a winner over hurdles: dam won 3 races
over 5f at 2 yrs, including Molecomb Stakes: quite modest form in maidens at
Haydock and Windsor (ran in snatches) in the summer: will be well suited by
1½m + : sold 27,000 gns Newmarket December Sales. *Major W. R. Hern.*

TOP SUNRISE (FR)   4 b.c. Top Ville 129–Marie de Russy (FR) (Sassafras **122**
(FR) 135) [1988 12s 12s³ 12s* 15d* 15m⁴ 15s* 15m³ 12s⁶ 1989 15.5s* 15d*
13.5s 15.5g* 12f]
    Wins in the Prix de Barbeville at Longchamp, Prix Kergorlay at
Deauville and Prix Royal-Oak at Longchamp established Top Sunrise as
comfortably the best stayer in a weak older-horse division in France. It
emerged that he needed to be fresh to produce his running: each of his wins
came after a lengthy absence from the track and his two poor efforts on the
second of two runs in a month. Unusually for a race in France, the runners
were well strung out at the finish of the Prix de Barbeville in April and Top
Sunrise accounted for Vaguely Pleasant and Rachmaninov easily by three
lengths and the same. A shoulder injury ruled out trips to Ascot for the Sagaro
Stakes and Gold Cup and four months passed by before Top Sunrise reached
the course again in a substandard running of the Prix Kergorlay. The sole
British challenger, the Northumberland Plate winner Orpheus, headed the
market and also the race until two furlongs out. Top Sunrise, held up last of
seven, was switched to the outside in the straight, passed the field in a matter
of a hundred yards and, without Asmussen applying much pressure, held the
challenge of the Prix de l'Esperance winner Turgeon by a length and a half.
Taking weight-for-age into account, Top Sunrise received a 7-lb beating from
Turgeon, but it would be unwise to interpret his performance strictly on
figures because he looked to have plenty in reserve.
    A two-month break followed Top Sunrise's poor showing in the Grand
Prix de Deauville Lancel. On his return he was well supported for the Prix
Royal-Oak, close up behind the coupled Noble Savage and Mardonius in the
betting. The St Leger runner-up Sapience joined Noble Savage from Britain,
with the German St Leger winner Britannia completing the foreign challenge.
The Prix Royal-Oak went very much the same way as the Prix Kergorlay, with

Prix Royal-Oak, Longchamp—Top Sunrise wins from Turgeon

the Harwood-Sheikh Mohammed three-year-old representative Noble Savage taking them along and Top Sunrise (ridden by Head in place of the injured Asmussen) bringing up the rear. Noble Savage, at one time well clear, hung on to his lead until Top Sunrise, almost tailed off early on, quickened in excellent style to hit the front over a furlong out and ran on well to beat Turgeon (again the better horse at the weights) by two lengths and Robertet another one and a half. Top Sunrise found conditions much too quick in the mile-and-a-half Japan Cup; badly outpaced for much of the way he did pass five in the home straight. For long enough the Gold Cup was talked of as his main target in 1990 granted some give in the ground, but soon after the Japan Cup he was sold, reportedly for 700,000 dollars, to join the growing band of ex-European horses now racing in Saudi Arabia.

		High Top	Derring-Do
	Top Ville	(b 1969)	Camenae
	(b 1976)	Sega Ville	Charlottesville
Top Sunrise (FR)		(b 1968)	La Sega
(b.c. 1985)		Sassafras	Sheshoon
	Marie de Russy (FR)	(b 1967)	Ruta
	(ch 1979)	Primula	Petingo
		(ch 1972)	Valrose

Top Sunrise's sire, the Prix du Jockey-Club winner Top Ville, is set to return to France after spending the last four years at Dalham Hall, Newmarket. His fee at the Haras d'Etreham is to be 150,000 francs. Top Sunrise is the second foal and only winner to date of Marie de Russy, the winner of a maiden race over an extended ten furlongs at Saint-Cloud and a half-sister to the Prix Morny winner Sakura Reiko and to Dom d'Albignac, a smart winner in France at up to ten and a half furlongs. Primula, a winner over a mile at two and three years, including in the listed Prix de la Calonne at Deauville, is probably the best of several winners produced by the Prix de Minerve winner Valrose. Top Sunrise, whose best form is with give in the ground, runs as though fifteen and a half furlongs isn't his limit. He is usually held up and has a good turn of foot. *A. Fabre, France.*

TOP VILLAIN 3 b.g. Top Ville 129–Swan Ann 84 (My Swanee 122) [1988 NR 1989 8g 10g⁵] 300,000Y: rangy gelding: keen walker: half-brother to 5 winners, including very smart sprinter Primo Dominie (by Dominion) and Salisbury 2000 Guineas Trial winner Poyle Crusher (by Sweet Revenge): dam won at 6f: no worthwhile form in newcomers race (tenderly handled) at Newmarket in April and minor event (smooth headway then hung badly left final 2f) at Nottingham in October: sold to join A. Turnell 34,000 gns Newmarket Autumn Sales, and gelded: one to be wary of. *Major W. R. Hern.* —

TORCELLO 2 b.c. (Mar 12) Procida (USA) 129–Millieme 107 (Mill Reef (USA) 141) [1989 7g] medium-sized, attractive colt: fifth foal: half-brother to 4 winners in France, including smart 3-y-o middle-distance performer Myth To Reality (by Sadler's Wells) and useful 1987 2-y-o 1m winner Titus Groan (by Gorytus): dam, fourth in 1m Prix des Reservoirs at 2 yrs in France, is sister to Shirley Heights: 33/1, slowly away and never dangerous or knocked about in 21-runner all-aged event at Newmarket in November: will improve. *G. Harwood.* — p

TORGHIA 2 b.f. (Mar 10) Taufan (USA) 119–Brave Louise 76 (Brave Shot) [1989 5f⁵ 6f² 7f⁴ 7m] 5,800F: leggy, angular filly: has a round action: first foal: dam, 6f to 1½m winner, is daughter of half-sister to Irish Oaks winner Aurabella: plating-class maiden: stays 7f. *S. Dow.* 59

TORIUS 3 b.g. Petorius 117–Princess Martina 64 (English Prince) 129) [1988 6d⁶ 6m 1989 7s 6s 5s⁵ 5.8m⁴ 5f* 6f⁶ 5f 5m* 5m 5m 5.8f⁴ 5f a6g⁵ a6g³] strong, lengthy, good-quartered gelding: moderate mover: modest handicapper: successful at Wolverhampton in May and in claimer (33/1) at Sandown in August: creditable third at Lingfield in December, staying on well from rear: stays 6f: acts on any going: blinkered in 1989, except first and sixth outings: rather inconsistent. *R. Simpson.* 67

TORJOUN (USA) 3 ch.c. Green Dancer (USA) 132–Tarsila (High Top 131) [1988 8g² 1989 9f* 10.5f* 12g] 122

End to end, Torjoun's three-year-old racing career lasted just thirty-one days, taking in three starts. On his only start at two years the lengthy Torjoun had been a promising head second to Warrshan in an October minor event at

William Hill Dante Stakes, York — Torjoun books his place in the Derby field;
Observation Post follows him home

Newmarket, and his fifteen-length victory in a sixteen-runner graduation event at Wolverhampton in May amply confirmed that potential. Although an easy victory, this Wolverhampton performance was no meaningless canter over poor opposition: Torjoun was pushed along throughout the final three furlongs, and the manner of his success impressed connections sufficiently to send him for the William Hill Dante Stakes at York where he started at 6/1 third favourite behind Observation Post and Zalazl in a seven-runner field. He hardly advertised his chances beforehand, sweating and becoming very much on edge in the paddock, but temperament didn't get the better of him in the race. Racing keenly in the lead, Torjoun started to quicken entering the straight and gradually got the other runners off the bridle before coming home two lengths clear, staying on strongly, of Observation Post, with Zalazl a two-and-a-half-length third. The Dante is often an informative Derby trial but the latest edition looked below standard and only Torjoun and the no-hoper Flockton's Own went on to Epsom. Once again Torjoun was sweating and on his toes in the preliminaries. In the race he took up the running at halfway, maintaining the very strong gallop, but was headed early in the straight and dropped away to finish a well-beaten eighth. It may be that in attempting to sap Nashwan's stamina Torjoun over-used his own resources, though he should stay a mile and a half. Whatever the reason for Torjoun's below-par performance his trainer reported that he did not come out of the race well, and although an autumn campaign was suggested no more was heard of him until it was announced that he'd be sent to Neil Drysdale in the United States.

Torjoun's dam Tarsila is said to have been inclined to sweat up in her racing days; there were also slight doubts about the temperament of her brother, the top-class middle-distance performer Top Ville, towards the end of his career. Tarsila won at a mile and nine furlongs in France, and Torjoun is her second foal. The first, Torkabar (by Vaguely Noble), is a modest staying maiden on the flat and a winning hurdler. Tarsila has a two-year-old by Sir Ivor

928

H. H. Aga Khan's "Torjoun"

	Green Dancer (USA) (b 1972)	Nijinsky (b 1967)	Northern Dancer Flaming Page
Torjoun (USA) (ch.c. 1986)		Green Valley (br 1967)	Val de Loir Sly Pola
	Tarsila (b 1980)	High Top (b 1969)	Derring-Do Camenae
		Sega Ville (b 1968)	Charlottesville La Sega

in training at Bedford House. Both her dam and grandam were good winners in France. Sega Ville won the Prix de Flore over ten and a half furlongs whilst La Sega won nine races, including five-furlong events at two years and later the Poule d'Essai de Pouliches, the Prix Saint-Alary and the Prix de Diane. La Sega is also a sister to the top-class stayer Danseur. *L. M. Cumani.*

TORKABAR (USA) 4 ch.c. Vaguely Noble 140–Tarsila (High Top 131) [1988 10.1g⁶ 12g² 12.2d³ 1989 14.6g² 16.2d² 14s] medium-sized, sparely-made colt: moderate mover: modest maiden: didn't find great deal in front and caught last strides at Beverley in April: always behind in Sandown handicap later in month: stays 2m: acts on a soft surface: winning hurdler: has joined G. Ham. *R. J. Holder.* **74**

TORMENTED (USA) 3 br.f. Alleged (USA) 138–Lauromeo (USA) (Gallant Romeo (USA)) [1988 NR 1989 10.1g 12m 12f a16g] leggy, sparely-made filly: has a round action: third reported foal: dam stakes winner at up to 9f: quite modest form at best in the autumn but deteriorated. *B. W. Hills.* **—**

TORRANCE 5 br.g. Niels 107–Aurambre (FR) (Sicambre 135) [1988 7.6d 7g 7f 7f 7m 7.6f 7.6m 8d⁵ 7m² 8f³ 8f 7f* 8m³ 7h* 8g 8d⁶ 7g 1989 7m 7f 6h⁵ 8f 7m 7m 7m*] good-topped gelding: quite modest handicapper on his day: none too reliable, but goes very well at Brighton (has gained all his 4 successes there) and showed only form as 5-y-o when beating Beechwood Cottage there by 2½ lengths in September, **56**

929

leading inside last after hanging right and looking reluctant 2f out: best at 7f or 1m: goes very well on top-of-the-ground: effective with or without blinkers: usually taken down early or steadily: usually wears crossed noseband: highly-strung: sold to join Mrs J. Wonnacott 5,000 gns Ascot September Sales. *D. A. Wilson.*

TORVILLE GOLD 3 b.f. Aragon 118–Lady Doubloon (Pieces of Eight 128) [1988 7g 1989 8.5f 7m 6g 6g⁶ 6m] sparely-made, close-coupled filly: no worthwhile form, including in seller: takes keen hold. *J. G. FitzGerald.* —

TORY CONQUEST (FR) 2 b.c. (Mar 21) Rainbow Quest (USA) 134–Princesse Tora (FR) (Prince Taj 123) [1989 8f² 8m*] 52,000Y: good-topped colt: has scope: half-brother to several winners, including high-class 1974 French 2-y-o Princesse Lee (by Habitat), herself dam of leading French 2-y-o Princesse Lida, and smart French 6.5f to 1m winner Boreale (by Bellypha): dam, very useful at around 1m, is half-sister to top-class miler Carlemont: odds on, won 5-runner maiden at Warwick in October by ½ length from Daromann, staying on strongly: will stay 1¼m: fairly useful colt in the making. *G. Harwood.* **79 p**

TOSCANA 8 ch.m. Town And Country 124–Constanza 94 (Sun Prince 128) [1988 12g 12m 12f 12f* 15.5m⁴ 12m 12f 1989 12f⁴ 12.3m⁶ 12m⁶ 12m⁶] hollow-backed mare: poor performer: creditable fourth to Waterlow Park at Goodwood, easily best effort in amateur races in 1989: suited by 1½m: acts on firm going and a soft surface: winning hurdler: inconsistent. *D. Marks.* **42 d**

TOSHIBA COMET 2 b.c. (Feb 28) Noalto 120–Silk Lady 97 (Tribal Chief 125) [1989 5d⁵ 5g³ 5m³ 6f² 7f⁴ 7.5m 6g⁴ 6g* 5s³ 5g] 14,000Y: sturdy colt: moderate walker: sixth living foal: half-brother to 3-y-o 5f and 6f winner Mzeff (by Ahonoora) and 4 other winners, including 5f and 7f winner Mister Colin (by Lord Gayle): dam won three 5f races at 2 yrs: showed much improved form when winning minor event at Hamilton in September by 3 lengths from Razzberry: ran very well from unfavourable draw when third to Lake Mistassiu in nursery at Haydock next outing: stays 6f: seems suited by an easy surface. *W. J. Pearce.* **78**

TOSS OF THE COIN 2 ch.g. (Mar 8) Rabdan 129–Cedees 48 (Habat 127) [1989 5g⁴ 6g 5f⁵ 6g 6m² 6g* 6s 8.2f³ 5m² 7g 7g a7g] 3,400Y, 7,200 2-y-o: sturdy gelding: first foal: dam stayed 6f: very useful plater: won at Ripon (no bid) in August: ran well when placed in nurseries after, poorly last 3 starts: really needs further than 5f, and stays 1m: appears unsuited by soft ground: sometimes hangs. *D. W. Chapman.* **70**

TOTAL CLEARANCE 3 ch.f. Stanford 121§–Morcal 56 (Dragonara Palace (USA) 115) [1988 5g 6f 6m 7m 1989 7f 8h 6h 6m] small, lengthy filly: poor mover: little sign of ability: visored second outing: blinkered last two. *A. W. Denson.* —

TOTEM MAJOR 2 br.f. (Feb 5) Shy Groom (USA)–Persian Wind (Windjammer (USA)) [1989 8.2f 8m 8m] IR 4,600F, IR 6,000Y: angular, sparely-made filly: fourth foal: half-sister to a bumpers winner: dam never ran: well beaten in sellers: looked reluctant to race final start: sold 800 gns Newmarket Autumn Sales. *Dr J. D. Scargill.* —

TOTHAM 2 b.f. (Apr 14) Shernazar 131–Susanna (USA) 81§ (Nijinsky (CAN) 138) [1989 7g 7m³ 7m³ 7g] useful-looking filly: has scope: fifth foal: half-sister to 2 winners, including useful 7f and 1¼m winner Sue Grundy (by Grundy): dam, daughter of 1000 Guineas winner Full Dress II, was placed 5 times over 1m but became disappointing: progressive form in fair company first 3 starts: not entirely discredited in face of very stiff task in Bottisham Heath Stud Rockfel Stakes at Newmarket final start: will be suited by 1m. *G. Wragg.* **74**

TOUCAN 2 b.c. (Jan 12) King of Clubs 124–Yellow Plume (Home Guard (USA) 129) [1989 7m 8g³ 8.2d⁴ 7g] IR 34,000Y: medium-sized, quite good-topped colt: sixth foal: dam, daughter of Prix de Diane winner Sweet Mimosa, won over 7.9f at 2 yrs in Ireland: modest performer: looks a thorough stayer: sold 15,000 gns Newmarket Autumn Sales. *L. M. Cumani.* **74**

TOUCH ABOVE 3 b.c. Touching Wood (USA) 127–B A Poundstretcher 82 (Laser Light 118) [1988 6f 6g 6g 8.2s⁴ 8v 1989 8s² 8g³ 10d 8m³ 8.5f³ 10f* 10g³ 10.2f⁵ 9g 10m⁴ 12g⁶ 10f⁵ 10m⁶] leggy colt: good mover: quite modest handicapper: won at Beverley in June by short head: went very freely to post and chased leaders when below form in apprentice event final start: probably suited by 1¼m: acts on any going: ran creditably when sweating and in crossed noseband tenth outing: usually given plenty to do: consistent. *T. D. Barron.* **65**

TOUCHING STAR 4 b.g. Touching Wood (USA) 127–Beaufort Star 95 (Great Nephew 126) [1988 10g⁵ 8f⁴ 8m⁴ 10d⁶ 10g 8g 8m⁴ 12d 10d³ 8g² 1989 8m* 10.6g* 10m] leggy, useful-looking gelding: won amateur events at Warwick in May and Haydock (handicap) following month: apprentice ridden, well below form in **75**

Salisbury handicap in June: subsequently gelded: stays 10.6f: acts on firm going: blinkered twice at 3 yrs: sometimes sweats: has hung badly left. *F. Jordan.*

TOUCHLIN PRIDE   3 b.c. Touch Boy 109–Lindrake's Pride (Mandrake Major   66
122) [1988 NR 1989 8f⁶ 7m⁵ 8g 7m⁴ 7m] small colt: first foal: dam never ran: quite modest maiden: better suited by 7f than 1m: sometimes sweats. *Miss L. C. Siddall.*

TOUCH OF WHITE   3 ch.f. Song 132–Cayla (Tumble Wind (USA)) [1988 NR   86
1989 5g* 5f4] 6,000Y: second foal: half-sister to poor maiden Akaylaah (by Valiyar): dam, from successful family, showed signs of ability: 10/1 and ridden by 5-lb claimer, won maiden at Beverley in May, drifting left: under 4 lengths fourth of 12 in £12,500 handicap at Ascot following month, racing keenly on stand side and running on steadily. *G. A. Huffer.*

TOUCH THE CLOUDS   2 b.f. (Mar 22) Precocious 126–Siouxsie 90 (Warpath   53
113) [1989 5d 7s⁶ 7v⁵] 14,000F, 23,000Y: rather leggy, good-topped, attractive filly: sister to unreliable 3-y-o 9f seller winner Pretty Precocious and half-sister to 5 winners by Mandrake Major, including 1m winner Last Stand and fairly useful 1983 2-y-o Sajeda: dam 2-y-o 6f winner: on toes, over 12 lengths fifth of 17, one pace final 2f, to Barakish at Ayr in October, best effort in maidens: will stay 1m. *C. W. Thornton.*

TOUCHWOOD (FR)   5 b.g. Gay Mecene (USA) 128–Ribaude (USA) (Ribot 142)   —
[1988 12.2g⁵ 1989 14.6g] leggy, workmanlike gelding: poor maiden: best form at 1¼m: acts on heavy going: has sweated: has worn a crossed noseband: sold 2,300 gns Ascot June Sales. *J. A. C. Edwards.*

TOUGH COOKIE   4 gr.g. Lochnager 132–Jovenita (High Top 131) [1988 11v⁴ 8d   —
8.2s 8g 1989 11v⁴] big, rangy gelding: poor maiden: blinkered twice. *R. Allan.*

TOUGH LITTLE NUT   2 gr.f. (Mar 21) Afzal 83–Rest Hill Dolly (Balinger 116)   —
[1989 5m⁵ 5.1m⁵ 6f⁵ 6g] sparely-made, plain filly: first foal: dam unraced half-sister to smart handicapper Pipedreamer: little worthwhile form in a minor event and in sellers: slowly away first 2 starts. *T. M. Jones.*

TOUR DE FORCE   9 ch.g. Reliance II 137–Set To Work (Workboy 123) [1988   —
NR 1989 12s] lengthy, workmanlike gelding: poor mover: quite modest handicapper in 1985: well beaten only 2 subsequent outings on flat: best form at 1½m: acts on any going: has often worn blinkers: not an easy ride. *P. J. Makin.*

TOURMALIEN   4 ch.g. Caerleon (USA) 132–Jacinth 133 (Red God 128§) [1988   —
8g⁶ 10.1m⁶ 10g 1989 12f] strong gelding: showed ability in fair company first 2 outings as 3-y-o: well beaten subsequently in claimer and amateurs handicap: sold to join R. Hoad 2,100 gns Ascot May Sales. *A. Moore.*

TOUSHTARI (USA)   3 b.g. Youth (USA) 135–Taduska (FR) (Daring Display   80 +
(USA) 129) [1988 NR 1989 10d* 10.6g⁵] 2,800 2-y-o: big, workmanlike gelding: moderate walker: third reported foal: half-brother to 1¾m winner Tamatour (by Caro): dam won at around 1m in France: 8/1, won maiden at Beverley in May, leading inside final 1f after losing position on home turn: still in need of experience, shaped well when fifth of 12, staying on strongly, in £7,800 handicap at Haydock 11 days later: will be very well suited by 1½m. *M. F. D. Morley.*

TOWN ATHLETE   4 b.c. Camden Town 125–War Lass 100 (Whistler 129) [1988   —
NR 1989 10f 12d 8g 10v] rather leggy, unfurnished colt: brother to 1¼m winner Beau Benz and 3-y-o Northern Line, 5f winner in 1988, and half-brother to several winners, including useful 1976 Irish 2-y-o 5f winner Tamariscifolia (by Ridan): dam won twice over 5f at 2 yrs: well beaten in varied company: sold 3,000 gns Doncaster November Sales. *M. J. O'Neill.*

TOWN MEETING   5 ch.g. General Assembly (USA)–La Marne (USA) (Nashua)   52
[1988 10.2s 8d 10g² 8.5f 8g³ 8g 8.5g⁴ 8.2g⁶ 8.2d⁶ 8.2s⁶ 10v⁴ 8s³ 9v 1989 10.2g* 10s* 8.2v 8d 10f⁴ 10.6d³ 10v³] close-coupled gelding: plating-class handicapper: won at Doncaster (strongly-run apprentice event) in March and Leicester in April: best effort after on sixth start: suited by testing conditions at 1¼m and will stay 1½m: not at his best on firm going and acts on soft: visored last 3 starts in 1988: bandaged fifth outing, first for nearly 4 months. *M. Brittain.*

TOWN PATROL   3 br.g. Town And Country 124–Swing Gently 78 (Swing Easy   —
(USA) 126) [1988 8d 8g 8g⁵ 1989 10s 10v 8f 10.1g 10f 7m 12f⁵ 10g] big, workmanlike gelding: well beaten in 1989, including in handicaps and seller: should stay 1¼m: best form on good ground: visored seventh outing: sold 1,300 gns Newmarket Autumn Sales. *M. D. I. Usher.*

TOWNY BOY   3 b.g. Camden Town 125–Serenesse (Habat 127) [1988 6m 6s³ 6m   81
8v² 1989 10v⁴ 10s* 13v⁴] leggy gelding: poor mover, with a round action: 25/1, first

931

*Hoover Cumberland Lodge Stakes, Ascot—a good close up of Tralos,
ahead of Warrshan (rails) and Husyan*

run for 5 months and ridden by 5-lb claimer, won handicap at Ayr in September by a
neck, always close up: well beaten otherwise as 3-y-o: suited by 1¼m: probably
requires soft ground. *J. M. Jefferson.*

TOW-STAR'S LADY   3 b.f. On Your Mark 125–Miss Tehran 73 (Manacle 123)   51
[1988 6f 6g⁴ 6g² 5g³ 6s 6f 7g 1989 7.5d 6m³ 6f 8f 7m 6m⁵ 6f* 6f 6f 5m³ 6g 7m 5f³ 6f]
sparely-made filly: fair plater: won at Hamilton (no bid) in July: suited by 6f: acts on
firm ground: visored: has run well when sweating and edgy: hung left in ladies event
ninth start: inconsistent: sold to join J. Norton 2,000 gns Doncaster November
Sales. *M. P. Naughton.*

TOXOTIS   3 ch.c. Pharly (FR) 130–Stilvi 126 (Derring-Do 131) [1988 6g 1989 8m   86
6f² 6m* 6g⁵ 6m 6f²] sturdy, quite attractive colt: bad mover: fair handicapper: won
at Windsor in June: good short-head second at Salisbury in August having quickened
clear 1½f out: better at 6f than 1m: acts on firm going. *Lord John FitzGerald.*

TRACE OF IRONY (USA)   3 b. or br.f. Cannonade (USA)–Tracy L (USA)   61
(Bold Favorite (USA)) [1988 5f³ 6f 6m 7f 7g⁴ 1989 5f 6m 8.2f 6g⁵ a8g⁵ a10g a7g⁴]
quite good-topped filly: has a quick action: quite modest maiden: probably stays 1m:
blinkered final outing at 2 yrs: below form when twice sweating in 1989. *C. F. Wall.*

TRACEY'S LADD   3 b.c. Raga Navarro (ITY) 119–Lutescens (Skymaster 126)   57
[1988 5v 5s² 5g 5m 5m 5f⁴ 5.8g 5g⁵ 5g 1989 5v² 5s⁴ 5d 5d* 5g 6m⁵ 6g] small,
lightly-made colt: has a very round action: ridden by 7-lb claimer, won strongly-run
handicap at Beverley in April: appears suited by testing conditions at 5f: quite
blinkered at 2 yrs: inconsistent: sold 750 gns Doncaster November Sales. *M.
Brittain.*

TRAFALGAR BOOKSHOP   3 b.f. Windjammer (USA)–Boston Flyer 57   58 d
(Mansingh (USA) 120) [1988 NR 1989 7f 6g² 6f⁶ 7m 6f 6f³ 6f² 7m 7m 6f 7g] lengthy,
angular filly: seventh foal: half-sister to tough 1981 2-y-o 5f winner She's My Girl
(by Mandamus) and a winner in Hong Kong: dam 2-y-o 5f winner: quite modest at
best: strong-finishing second in seller at Leicester second start: well below that
form after, including in sellers: should stay further than 6f: seems to need give in
the ground: blinkered fifth start. *M. F. D. Morley.*

TRAINGLOT   2 ch.c. (May 6) Dominion 123–Mary Green 81 (Sahib 114) [1989 6f   83
6m 7.5f² 8.2s* 10g³] compact colt: half-brother to useful stayer Destroyer (by

Lombard) and fair 2m winner Stan The Man (by Tachypous): dam won from 1½m to 17f: progressive colt: stayed on strongly when winning maiden at Hamilton in September by 4 lengths from Corporate Member: ridden by 7-lb claimer, good third of 18, keeping on despite wandering, to Adding in minor event at Redcar: shapes like a thorough stayer: acts on any going. *J. G. FitzGerald.*

TRALOS (USA) 4 b.c. Roberto (USA) 131–Solartic (CAN) (Briartic (CAN)) **118** [1988 10m* 8m* 8m⁶ 8d 1989 10v 12m³ 12m⁴ 12g 11.1m³ 12m* 12s] big, strong colt: carries condition: has a low action: smart performer: 10/1, won 4-runner Hoover Cumberland Lodge Stakes at Ascot in September, quickening very well to lead over 1f out, by 2 lengths from Husyan: ran creditably when in frame behind Unfuwain in General Accident Jockey Club Stakes at Newmarket, Boyatino in Prix Jean de Chaudenay at Saint-Cloud and stable-companion Assatis in BonusPrint September Stakes at Kempton: tailed off in Rothmans International at Woodbine final start: stays 1½m: acts on firm going and is unsuited by soft: to continue career in Canada. *G. Harwood.*

TRANQUIL WATERS (USA) 3 ch.c. Diesis 133–Ebbing Tide (USA) (His **94 p** Majesty (USA)) [1988 NR 1989 10f² 10.2g³ 12.2g*] $140,000Y: rather unfurnished colt: fourth foal: half-brother to 1m and 8.5f winner Ice Chocolate (by Icecapade): dam half-sister to Oh So Fair, the dam of Oh So Sharp (by Kris) and Roussalka: won apprentice race at Catterick in October by 7 lengths, leading 4f out: better at 1½m than 1¼m: sold to join N. Tinkler 30,000 gns Newmarket Autumn Sales. *H. R. A. Cecil.*

TRANSCRIBER (USA) 2 b.c. (Apr 20) Transworld (USA) 121–Scrabbler **66** (USA) (Verbatim (USA)) [1989 6f² 6m 7f 6g⁵ 8g⁵ a6g⁶ a7g²] $2,200Y, resold $12,000Y: angular, useful-looking colt: has scope: first foal: probably stays 1m: blinkered last 3 starts. *A. Bailey.*

TRANSITIONAL 2 b.c. (Mar 16) Dalsaan 125–Parkeen Princess (He Loves Me **— p** 120) [1989 6d] good-topped colt: third foal: brother to 3-y-o 1m to 10.2f winner Nobby and closely related to a winner in Malaysia: dam never ran: 25/1 and very green to post, about 16 lengths tenth of 24, outpaced then making steady late headway, in maiden at Newbury in October: can improve. *P. J. Makin.*

TRAPEZE ARTIST 8 b.h. High Line 125–Maternal 93 (High Top 131) [1988 14g **53 §** 14d⁶ 14g 14d⁴ 14f⁴ 18m² 20f 16g⁴ 16g 16f 14m 14.5g 198f 14s² 15.5s] small horse: quite useful handicapper at his best: became most temperamental: suited by test of stamina: acted on any going: had worn a visor (did so both starts in spring) and blinkers: suited by strong gallop: retired to Wood End Stud, Evesham, fee £250 + £250 (Oct 1st). *P. J. Jones.*

TRAVEL BYE 2 b.f. (May 29) Miller's Mate 116–Travel Again 67 (Derrylin 115) **62** [1989 6d⁵ 5f⁴ 6d] 18,000Y: angular filly: first foal: dam probably stayed 1¼m: quite modest maiden: best effort second start: bred to stay at least 1m: bandaged off-hind. *L. G. Cottrell.*

TRAVELLING LIGHT 3 b.g. Electric 126–La Levantina (Le Levanstell 122) **95** [1988 5g 6m 1989 6v⁵ 6d 7m 8g 12f* 11f* 12f* 12.3m⁵ 14g* 17.4s* 18g³] quite good-topped gelding: moderate mover: progressive handicapper: won at Pontefract, Hamilton and Edinburgh within 7 days (well-backed favourite each time) in June then at Haydock in August and Ayr (most impressively by 15 lengths) in September: heavily-backed favourite, narrowly-beaten third of 22 to Double Dutch in Tote Cesarewitch at Newmarket, staying on very strongly only inside final 1f: suited by thorough test of stamina: goes very well on soft going. *Mrs J. R. Ramsden.*

TRAVELLING TRYST (USA) 3 ch.c. Pilgrim (USA) 108–King's Courtesan **83** (USA) (Kauai King) [1988 7f² 8m² 1989 8s³ 8m 10g 8m³ 10.1m³ 10m⁵ 14g³ 13.8g*

Eglinton And Winton Memorial Handicap, Ayr—
Travelling Light looks a strong Cesarewitch candidate

16m⁶ 13v²] rangy, rather sparely-made colt: fair performer: ridden by 7-lb claimer, won claimer at Catterick in September: hung left and appeared not to go through with effort in similar event final start: tailed off (lame) in 2000 Guineas on second: stays 1¾m: probably acts on any going: takes keen hold and pulled hard in visor third start: sold 27,000 gns Newmarket Autumn Sales. *R. J. R. Williams.*

TRAVEL MYSTERY 6 b.m. Godswalk (USA) 130–Sugar Cookie 71 (Crepello **110** 136) [1988 12f⁶ 12g⁴ 1989 16d* 18.4m²] lengthy mare: fit from hurdling, showed improved form when winning strongly-run Insulpak Sagaro EBF Stakes at Ascot in April, enterprisingly ridden to beat Mazzacano ½ length: favourite, beaten a neck by Grey Salute in Ladbroke Chester Cup (Handicap) over 2 weeks later, hampered slightly 2f out: suited by test of stamina: acts on firm going and a soft surface: lazy sort, who needs plenty of driving: genuine. *M. C. Pipe.*

TRAVEL STORM 3 b.f. Lord Gayle (USA) 124–Starlust 79 (Sallust 134) [1988 **77** NR 1989 8m 10h² 10h* 12f⁵] 8,000F, 31,000Y: angular filly: third foal: half-sister to useful 6f and 1m winner Bronzewing (by Beldale Flutter): dam, 2-y-o 5f winner, is half-sister to Welsh Pearl, very useful winner at up to 1m: won apprentice maiden at Brighton in June, taking good hold and making virtualy all: faced very stiff task following month: stays 1¼m. *M. C. Pipe.*

TREACLE MINE 2 ch.c. (Apr 14) Ballacashtal (CAN)–Miss Anniversary **67** (Tachypous 128) [1989 5m 6m 6f⁴ 6g a7g³ a6g a6g] strong, close-coupled colt: poor mover: second foal: dam temperamental sprint maiden banned from racing as 3-y-o: quite modest maiden: best effort fifth start: suited by 7f: has worn bandages behind. *M. D. I. Usher.*

TREAD LIKA PRINCE 3 b.c. Prince Tenderfoot (USA) 126–Flat Refusal **57** (USA) (Ribero 126) [1988 5g 5v⁶ 5g 6f³ 5f 6g 5m* 5m⁵ 5g 5g 1989 8.2s⁴ 11.7m] compact, workmanlike colt: moderate mover: quite modest winner at 2 yrs: fair fourth at Nottingham, plenty to do 2f out then staying on well, easily better effort in handicaps in May as 3-y-o: stays 1m: visored and blinkered once at 2 yrs: often on toes: tends to hang, and is difficult ride. *J. P. Hudson.*

TREBLE EIGHT 2 ch.c. (May 13) Kings Lake (USA) 133–Persian Polly 99 **100** p (Persian Bold 123) [1989 8m*] 13,500Y: sturdy, angular colt: has scope: fourth foal: half-brother to 3-y-o 1¼m winner Salmonid (by Salmon Leap) and 2 other winners, including 10.2f winner Persian Tapestry (by Tap On Wood): dam, Irish 2-y-o 7f winner, is out of half-sister to dam of Perion: 9/1, won 8-runner maiden at Newmarket in October going away by 1½ lengths from Eton Lad, showing fine turn of foot: will stay 1¼m: sure to improve. *M. A. Jarvis.*

TREBROOK (FR) 5 ch. or br.h. Trepan (FR) 133–Bambrook (FR) (Hauban **112** (FR) 132) [1988 12d⁴ 15m² 15s² 20m² 15.5s 1989 14d* 15.5s² 20m* 20f] good-topped horse: has a round action: very useful performer: won 90,000-franc event at Saint-Cloud and 3-runner Prix du Cadran at Longchamp in spring, in latter beating Vaguely Pleasant 1½ lengths: sweating, bit edgy and swishing tail in paddock, well-beaten seventh of 8 to Sadeem in Gold Cup at Royal Ascot: stays extreme distances: possibly unsuited by firm going, acts on any other: consistent. *J. Lesbordes, France.*

TREMEIRCHION 3 b.c. Teenoso (USA) 135–Lady Waverton (Huntercombe — 133) [1988 7g 1989 12g 10g] big, lengthy colt: poor mover: 33/1 and still carrying condition, seventh of 17 at Salisbury in May, chasing leaders 1m, third and easily best effort in maidens. *J. A. R. Toller.*

TRES AMIGOS 2 b.g. (Feb 18) Norwick (USA) 120–Safeguard 77 (Wolver **43** Hollow 126) [1989 5m 5d 6m 7.5f 8f 7g] 5,000Y: good-bodied gelding: has scope: third live foal: half-brother to winning jumper Star of Kinloch (by Comedy Star): dam, stayer, won over hurdles: poor maiden: had stiff tasks in nurseries on last 2 outings. *D. W. Chapman.*

TREVOSE 4 br.g. Penmarric (USA) 111–Belle Year (Quorum 126) [1988 NR 1989 — 8s 7m] sparely-made gelding: poor form in varied company: tailed off in selling handicap final outing: probably suited by shorter than 1m. *P. D. Cundell.*

TREYARNON (USA) 7 b.g. Superbity (USA)–Lagrange Belle (USA) (True — Knight (USA)) [1988 10v* 11v³ 12d³ 12m 8.2g² 11g² 9s² 11d² 1989 10v 7d⁴ 8f 12m⁶] lengthy gelding: poor handicapper: not seen out after June: ideally needs further than 7f and stays 1½m: possibly needs an easy surface nowadays: has run fairly well in blinkers and visor: good mount for apprentice: often bandaged nowadays: suited by forcing tactics. *P. Monteith.*

TRIBAL LADY 2 b.f. (Mar 9) Absalom 128–Placid Pet 65 (Mummy's Pet 125) **80** [1989 5d² 5d⁴ 5d* 6f* 6f³ 5f⁵ 6m³ 6v] 13,500Y: medium-sized, angular filly: good mover: sixth live foal: half-sister to 3-y-o 6f winner Boules (by Petong) and 1984 2-y-o 5f winner Doppio (by Dublin Taxi): dam, 1m winner, sister to Runnett: modest performer: won maiden at Haydock and minor event (beating long odds-on Sharp Mover ¾ length in 3-runner race) at Newbury in May: ran creditably in minor events next 3 starts: off course over 4 months before final one: better suited by 6f than 5f. *M. McCormack.*

TRIBAL MASCOT (USA)   4 b.g. Our Native (USA)–Little Lady Luck (USA) — (Jacinto) [1988 10g² 10m* 10g⁶ 1989 11.7d 12f] tall, close-coupled gelding: quite modest winner as 3-y-o when trained by L. Cumani: ran badly in handicaps in 1989: stays 1¼m: acts on top-of-the-ground: blinkered twice at 2 yrs: winning hurdler. *D. R. Gandolfo.*

TRIBUTARY (USA)   2 b.f. (Apr 21) Seattle Slew (USA)–Woodstream (USA) 113   74 p (Northern Dancer) [1989 6g*] $140,000Y: fourth foal: sister to Irish 3-y-o Seattle Centre, 6f winner at 2 yrs: dam, half-sister to Jaazeiro, won over 6f and 7f at 2 yrs, including in Cheveley Park, and was second in Irish 1000 Guineas: 11/10, won 11-runner maiden at Phoenix Park in September by a neck: should go on to better things. *M. V. O'Brien, Ireland.*

TRIBUTE TO DAD   2 b.g. (Mar 14) Aragon 118–Bourienne 58 (Bolkonski 134) — [1989 5m⁶ 7g] 10,500F, 5,600Y: third foal: half-brother to poor maiden Jollienne (by Absalom): dam won sellers over 1m and 9f: well beaten in maiden at Warwick in July and claimer (never placed to challenge) at Leicester 2 months later. *D. Haydn Jones.*

TRICOTRIC   2 br.f. (Apr 20) Electric 126–Orpheline 76 (Thatch (USA) 136) [1989   58 8.2g 7g] 5,200Y: good-topped filly: fifth foal: half-sister to fair 1984 2-y-o 5f winner Landspeed (by Hot Spark): dam 1¼m winner: around 13 lengths eleventh of 24, fading final furlong, to Sardegna in maiden at Newmarket in November, better effort: slowly away on debut: bred to stay beyond 7f. *P. S. Felgate.*

TRIKKALA STAR   7 b.m. Tachypous 128–Emma Chizzet 59 (High Top 131) — [1988 NR 1989 8m 16f] rangy, plain mare: no longer of much account: blinkered twice. *B. R. Cambidge.*

TRIMLINES   3 b.g. Sallust 134–Euphoria (Prince Tenderfoot (USA) 126) [1988 — NR 1989 7g] IR 1,600Y, resold 4,700Y: half-brother to a winner abroad: dam never ran: ridden by 7-lb claimer, tailed off from halfway in seller at Doncaster in May: has joined P. Feilden. *W. Wilson.*

TRING PARK   3 b.c. Niniski (USA) 125–Habanna 107 (Habitat 134) [1988 8d 1989   74 10g 10m⁶ 15s 9m 12f² 18g] big, leggy colt: easily best effort when running-on second in handicap at Leicester: 20/1 and looking very well, always in rear in Cesarewitch Handicap at Newmarket 5 days later in October: odds-on favourite in claimer there fourth start: stays 1½m well: acts on firm ground. *M. H. Tompkins.*

TRIODE (USA)   3 ch.f. Sharpen Up 127–Triple Tipple (USA) 111 (Raise A Cup   105 (USA)) [1988 NR 1989 8m² 8m* 7f² 10g^wo 9m⁴ 10g⁶ 8f² 8g³] rangy filly: first foal: dam, 7f to 1m winner later stakes winner in USA, is daughter of half-sister to very useful middle-distance filly Trillionaire: won maiden at Kempton in July and walked over in minor event at Lingfield in August: ran well after when in frame in listed event at York, minor contest at Leicester and Group 3 event at Milan: stays 9f: acts on firm going: useful. *L. M. Cumani.*

TRIOMPHE MODEST   2 b.f. (Mar 11) Petorius 117–Tinktura 92 (Pampapaul   64 12 f) [1989 5v² 5d³ 6g² 5d 7m⁴ 6f* 7f 6g⁶] IR 10,000F, 4,800Y: angular filly: fourth foal: dam 2-y-o 7f winner from 3 starts: ridden by 7-lb claimer, made most in auction event at Nottingham in September: better suited by 6f than 5f, but yet to show she stays 7f. *C. A. Cyzer.*

TRIPLE BARREL (USA)   2 b.c. (Feb 18) Sharpen Up 127–Galexcel (USA)   60 p (Exceller (USA) 129) [1989 7g a8g⁶] $100,000Y: smallish, dipped-backed colt: first foal: dam, placed twice in USA, from good family: over 6 lengths sixth to Blake's Treasure in late-season maiden at Lingfield, better effort: likely to improve again. *N. A. Callaghan.*

TRIPLE DIAMOND   3 b.f. Youth (USA) 135–Latch The Hatch (Thatch (USA) — 136) [1988 6m 6m 5g 1989 7m 5m] neat filly: no sign of ability. *Mrs Barbara Waring.*

TRIPLE TOP   4 b.g. High Top 131–Dalmally 89 (Sharpen Up 127) [1988 8g 10g 8g   53 8m 8g⁶ 1989 8h⁴ 10f⁶ 9g³ 8.5f 8f] good-bodied gelding: plating-class maiden: stays 9f: acts on hard going. *Miss L. C. Siddall.*

TRIPLE WISH   4 ch.f. Lyphard's Wish (FR) 124–Glorious Fate (Northfields   54 (USA)) [1988 6g⁵ 6d 1989 7f⁶ 7h 7m⁵ 8g⁴ 8.2f 8f³ 10g 9f² 10g] small, sparely-made filly: moderate walker: poor handicapper: ran in sellers last 4 starts, creditably when staying on well to be placed: hampered final outing: should be suited by 1¼m: acts on firm going: blinkered, ran poorly seventh start. *R. F. Johnson Houghton.*

TRIPLICATE 3 b.c. Mill Reef (USA) 141–Triple First 117 (High Top 131) [1988 **75** 7g 1989 8s⁴ 8f] small colt: always-prominent fourth of 21 at Kempton, only form in maidens: never dangerous facing stiff task in handicap later in May: should stay beyond 1m: evidently suited by soft going: bandaged near-fore at 3 yrs: sold 6,200 gns Newmarket Autumn Sales. *J. L. Dunlop.*

TRIP THE DAISEY 3 gr.f. Touching Wood (USA) 127–Easymede 85 (Runny- **53** mede 123) [1988 5f⁶ 6g 1989 6s 7d 9m⁶ 10.2f⁴ 8.3m 10m*] sparely-made filly: awarded seller (sold to join K. Ryan 4,600 gns) at Nottingham in August having been beaten short head, well behind 4f out then staying on well from 2f out: other worthwhile form only on third start: will stay beyond 1¼m. *H. Candy.*

TRIP TO THE MOON 3 b.c. Red Sunset 120–Mile By Mile 92 (Milesian 125) **62** [1988 NR 1989 7g⁴ 8.2g² 8m⁵] IR 11,000F, 12,000Y: lengthy colt: has scope: half-brother to several winners, including fair sprinter Numismatist (by Vitiges) and fair miler Be Cheerful (by Sayyaf): dam won over 6f at 2 yrs: quite modest form in modest company in the North: off course over 5 months after debut: uncertain to stay much further. *C. W. Thornton.*

TRIREME 2 ch.c. (Mar 12) Rainbow Quest (USA) 134–Bireme 127 (Grundy 137) **92 p** [1989 7g*] rangy, rather sparely-made colt: half-brother to winning hurdler Dhoni (by Bustino): dam, half-sister to high-class middle-distance stayer Buoy, won Oaks: 4/1, won 15-runner maiden at Newmarket in July by 2½ lengths from Lift And Load, always travelling smoothly and quickening to front 1½f out: reportedly split a pastern subsequently: bred to stay middle distances: sure to improve and win again if recovering from injury. *Major W. R. Hern.*

TRISTAN'S COMET 2 br.c. (Mar 28) Sayf El Arab (USA) 127–Gleneagle 91 **63** (Swing Easy (USA) 126) [1989 7g a7g⁵] 5,200F, 7,800Y: half-brother to winner in Italy by Coquelin: dam won at 5f and 6f: 11/2, over 2 lengths fifth of 13 to Majesty's Room in late-season maiden at Southwell, better effort: may stay 1m. *M. A. Jarvis.*

TRISTIORUM 2 ch.g. (Feb 17) Crofthall 110–Annie-Jo (Malicious) [1989 6g] **— p** half-brother to 1986 2-y-o 7f seller winner Melgrove (by Marching On): dam showed no ability: 33/1, showed signs of ability in 19-runner maiden at Redcar in November: subsequently gelded. *J. Etherington.*

TRIUMPHAL SONG 2 ch.c. (Mar 28) Caerleon (USA) 132–Zither 72 (Vienna **71** 127) [1989 6m 7f³] 10,000Y: workmanlike colt: half-brother to numerous winners, notably high-class stayer Zimbalon (by Ragusa): dam won at 1¼m: 5½ lengths third of 7, leading 3f out, to Anshan in maiden at Sandown in July, better effort. *B. W. Hills.*

TRIXIE'S GUEST 2 gr.f. (Mar 23) What A Guest 119–Winter Lady (Bonne Noel **58** 115) [1989 5m³ 6g 6f³ 7m⁶ 5m⁶ 7g⁴] IR 6,000Y: leggy, angular, plain filly: third reported foal: sister to French 9f winner Decathlon: dam unraced sister to Noelino and Irish Oaks runner-up Little Bonny: plating-class maiden: will stay 1m. *S. G. Norton.*

TROJAN DEBUT 3 b.g. Trojan Fen 118–Debutina Park 87 (Averof 123) [1988 7d **60 d** 6s 6m 8d 1989 7g² 6f 6h⁶ 6m 7g 7f⁵ a8g⁶] robust, round-barrelled gelding: carries condition: keen walker: poor mover: moderate plater: suited by 7f: possibly best with give in the ground: sweating fifth start: not knocked about in blinkers third: very slowly away time before. *M. J. Ryan.*

TROJAN EXCEL 2 b.f. (Apr 2) Trojan Fen 118–War Ballad (FR) (Green Dancer **75** (USA) 132) [1989 5m 5m² 5f* 6m* 7.5f⁵ 7.5m³ 7f³ 7f* 7f* 6d 8.2f⁵] IR 1,300Y: strong, compact filly: carries condition: good mover: second foal: half-sister to 3-y-o Soldier Boy (by Sandhurst Prince): dam placed over 10.5f in France: improved filly: best effort when beating Gymcrak Lovebird by a head, clear, in nursery at Thirsk in August, staying on strongly last 1½f: earlier successful in sellers at Beverley (no bid) and Warwick (bought in 6,000 gns) and a nursery (by 5 lengths from Dawson City) at Redcar: below best last 2 starts: needs further than 6f, and should stay 1m. *C. Tinkler.*

TROJAN GENERAL 2 gr.c. (Mar 29) Trojan Fen 118–Lady Regent (Wolver **58 p** Hollow 126) [1989 6m⁴ 6g] 11,000F, 6,000Y: smallish, workmanlike colt: third foal: half-brother to moderate plater Foot Perfect (by Pas de Seul): dam won over 7f at 3 yrs in Ireland: shaped well, not unduly knocked about, in minor event at Windsor and maiden auction event at Haydock within a week in summer: gives impression capable of better. *D. J. G. Murray-Smith.*

TROJAN GOD 7 b.g. Tyrnavos 129–My Lynnie 74§ (Frankincense 120) [1988   —
NR 1989 10.2f] small, short-backed gelding: poor performer: 33/1, always behind in
apprentice handicap at Bath in July: stays 1½m: acts on firm going. *G. H. Jones.*

TROJAN HEART 3 b.c. Trojan Fen 118–Heavenly Spark (Habitat 134) [1988   67
7m⁵ 7g 1989 7m²] rangy colt: quite modest maiden: favourite, beaten 6 lengths by If
Memory Serves at York in July: uncertain to stay much beyond 7f: sold 8,000 gns
Newmarket Autumn Sales. *P. T. Walwyn.*

TROJAN LANCER 3 b.c. Trojan Fen 118–Dunster's Cream 51 (Sharpen Up   59
127) [1988 6f⁶ 7m⁵ 8f³ 1989 9g 10f 10m⁶ 12m 12g 10m³ 10v 9s4] sturdy,
close-coupled colt: moderate mover: quite modest maiden: suited by 1¼m: possibly
needs top-of-the-ground: bandaged off-hind second outing: wandered under
pressure when running well on next. *Dr J. D. Scargill.*

TROJAN PLEASURE 2 br.f. (Apr 18) Trojan Fen 118–Sweet Pleasure 88   — p
(Sweet Revenge 129) [1989 8g] leggy, lengthy filly: half-sister to useful
1986 French 2-y-o sprinter Ma Colombine and 1¼m winner Jaaziel (both by
Jaazeiro): dam 6f winner at 2 yrs: 33/1, 14 lengths seventh of 15 in maiden at
Leicester in November. *D. J. G. Murray-Smith.*

TROJAN RIVER (USA) 3 ch.f. Riverman (USA) 131–Troyanna 109 (Troy 137)   96 p
[1988 NR 1989 10.6m³ 10d4 14g* 10d*] medium-sized filly: moderate mover: first
foal: dam 7f winner at 2 yrs and fourth in Irish Oaks: is out of half-sister to very
smart 1963 American 2-y-o Traffic: won minor events at Redcar and Leopardstown
within 9 days in November: stays 1¾m: acts on a soft surface: progressive. *L. M.
Cumani.*

TROJAN WAY 7 ch.g. Troy 137–Sea Venture (FR) 98 (Diatome 132) [1988 NR   —
1989 12f 12g 16f 12m⁶ 10m 12f 16.2m⁵ 18m] strong, heavy-topped gelding: carries
plenty of condition: virtually no form (mainly in amateur events) in summer. *R.
Hollinshead.*

TROPICAL ACE 2 b.f. (Apr 30) Final Straw 127–Rampage 93 (Busted 134)   —
[1989 7g⁵ 8m 8g] 2,300Y: strong, sturdy filly: has scope: half-sister to 3 winners
including 3-y-o 1½m winner Rambo Castle (by Castle Keep) and French 11.7f
winner Catalogue (by Auction Ring): dam, out of half-sister to 1000 Guineas winner
Full Dress II, won from 11f to 1¾m: no worthwhile form in maidens. *R. Voorspuy.*

TROPICAL RAGS 3 br.f. Mummy's Game 120–Gay Tamarind (Tamerlane 128)   —
[1988 6m 6d 1989 5g 12g 10g a12g⁶] has shown signs of ability but no worthwhile
form, including in seller: sold 925 gns Ascot December Sales. *P. J. Makin.*

TROWBRIDGE (USA) 3 ch.c. Sauce Boat (USA)–Not A Clue (USA) (Carle-   —
mont 132) [1988 7s 1989 12h 10.8m4 12.4g] workmanlike colt: has a quick action:
well beaten in maidens and handicap: didn't handle descent at Lingfield on reappearance: sold 9,200 gns Newmarket Autumn Sales. *G. Harwood.*

TRUCE 3 gr.c. Martinmas 128–Queendom 109 (Quorum 126) [1988 7g 7m 8g 8.2v²   61
1989 10v 8d 8.2s⁴ᵈⁱˢ 10f³ 10g 12f* 12.3g 12g 11.7m 14g] close-coupled colt: very easy
winner of handicap at Chepstow in June: ridden by 5-lb claimer and 18 lb out of
handicap, eighth and best subsequent effort when running creditably in £8,000
Newbury handicap: iron broke final outing: suited by 1½m: acts on any going: edged
badly left for amateur, and isn't an easy ride. *D. A. Wilson.*

TRUCKHAVEN TRIBUNE 3 ch.c. Glenstal (USA) 118–Greek Gift (Acropolis   —
132) [1988 6m⁵ 7m⁶ 7d⁵ 1989 12m 10g 12.4f5] chunky, workmanlike colt: poor
maiden: fifth in handicap at Newcastle in July, given a lot to do and only show as
3-y-o: appears to stay 1½m: blinkered on debut: twice edgy at 3 yrs, pulling hard for
apprentice on reappearance: sold 1,250 gns Newmarket Autumn Sales. *M. F. D.
Morley.*

TRUDO 2 br.c. (Mar 20) Tudorville 80–Dominique III (Evening Trial 94) [1989 5g   41
6f⁵ 7m³ 7m a8g] leggy, close-coupled non-thoroughbred colt: has a quick action:
third reported foal: dam never ran: poor plater: stays 7f: sweating second outing. *B.
A. McMahon.*

TRUE ANNIE 3 b.f. Head For Heights 125–Swiss Domain (Dominion 123) [1988   —
6g 1989 7f 7m⁶ 10m 8.2m 12f 12g 10g⁶] quite attractive filly: plating-class maiden:
showed little after second start: should stay beyond 7f: sometimes pulls hard:
sweating and edgy fourth start: sold 1,450 gns Ascot December Sales. *J. D. Bethell.*

TRUE DIVIDEND (USA) 3 ch.c. Blushing Groom (FR) 131–Singing Rain   —
(USA) (Sensitivo) [1988 NR 1989 8g] good-topped colt: half-brother to numerous
winners, including good French 1m winner Hail To Roberto (by Roberto) and a
minor stakes winner: dam, from family of Prix de Diane and Prix Vermeille winner

Royal Hunt Cup, Ascot—the far side just has it.
Favourite True Panache (No. 9) wins gamely from Wood Dancer (noseband);
on this side are third-placed Cuvee Charlie (No. 15) and sixth-placed Milieu (No. 2)

Mrs Penny, was high class at around 1m: favourite but green, soundly beaten in apprentice event at Ascot in October: gave trouble at stalls. *L. M. Cumani.*

TRUE GENT (USA)   5 b.h. Lord Gaylord (USA)–Glamour Girl (ARG) (Mysolo 120) [1988 8d⁶ 7g 8d 8m 8g⁶ 8g 8d⁶ 1989 10f 8.2g 7f 8.5f] rangy horse: tubed: poor mover: fairly useful winner only start at 2 yrs: has deteriorated considerably: visored last 3 outings: has worn a crossed noseband: sometimes wears tongue strap nowadays. *S. J. Muldoon.* —

TRUE GEORGE   2 ch.g. (Apr 12) King of Clubs 124–Piculet 69 (Morston (FR) 125) [1989 5g⁶ 6g* 5f 6m 6v a8g] 10,000Y: smallish, shallow-girthed gelding: moderate mover: fourth living foal: half-brother to Italian 3-y-o 7f winner Elsa Morante (by Rusticaro): dam half-sister to Dominion and Prominent: showed modest form when winning auction race at Epsom in June: ran poorly afterwards, virtually pulling up fourth start. *J. D. Bethell.* **71**

TRUE PANACHE (USA)   4 b.c. Mr Prospector (USA)–Durtal 121 (Lyphard (USA) 132) [1988 11f² 12g⁴ 10m² 1989 8s⁶ 8f* 8f*] quite attractive colt: showed improved form when winning £6,700 limited handicap at York and £33,300 Royal Hunt Cup (Handicap) at Royal Ascot, in latter (favourite of 27) always close up when beating Wood Dancer gamely by a length: suited by 1m: best on top-of-the-ground: sweated at 4 yrs: genuine: sustained leg injury and retired to stud. *J. Tree.* **94**

TRUG   3 gr.f. Final Straw 127–Trestle 57 (Three Legs 128) [1988 8g 1989 7f 8f 10m 9f] leggy filly: well beaten, including in claimer: sold 740 gns Newmarket September Sales. *R. F. Casey.* —

TRUSS   2 b.g. (Mar 15) Lyphard's Special (USA) 122–Trestle 57 (Three Legs 128) [1989 7m 8.2f] 12,500Y: neat gelding: moderate mover: third living foal: half-brother to 3-y-o Trug (by Final Straw): dam lightly-raced half-sister to very useful 1975 2-y-o 5f winner Grey Home: visored, soundly beaten in September sellers at Thirsk (mulish, slowly away) and Nottingham: sold to join A. Leighton 940 gns Newmarket Autumn Sales. *J. H. M. Gosden.* —

TRUST TROY   3 br.c. Gorytus (USA) 132–Gay Fantasy (Troy 137) [1988 6m⁴ 7g³ 7m* 7m 1989 8f⁶ 8f² 9f* 8d³ 9g⁶] lengthy, rather angular colt: fair handicapper: won at Redcar in October: creditable third of 27 at Newbury, better subsequent effort: may well stay beyond 9f: acts on firm and dead going: has given impression may prove best on galloping track. *J. L. Dunlop.* **87**

TRYING DAYS   2 b.c. (Apr 19) Teenoso (USA) 135–April Days 75 (Silly Season 127) [1989 7g⁵ 8f²] tall, good-topped colt: seventh living foal: half-brother to 3-y-o Lucy's Day (by Anfield), 7f winner at 2 yrs, and several winners here and abroad, including a 1¼m winning plater by Bay Express: dam, daughter of Oaks second Maina, won over 10.4f: ½-length second of 7, finishing strongly, to Myhamet in minor event at Bath in October: will be suited by 1¼m. *P. T. Walwyn.* **79**

TRYING FOR GOLD (USA) 3 b.f. Northern Baby (CAN) 127–Expansive 111 **103** p (Exbury 138) [1988 8d 1989 12m* 12.5g* 12d²] leggy, quite attractive filly: favourite, won maiden (outpaced then staying on strongly to lead post) at Salisbury in August and minor event (odds on, made all) at Wolverhampton in September: 4/1, beaten 2½ lengths by odds-on Per Quod in minor event at Thirsk in November: will be suited by further: progressive. *Major W. R. Hern.*

TRY ME NOW 3 b.g. Try My Best (USA) 130–Sapientia (FR) (Prudent II 133) **56** [1988 6d 8d 8g 1989 8m 8g⁴ 8m²] strong, rangy gelding: plating-class maiden: claimed to join J. Upson £10,050 when running-on second in claimer at Leicester in July, best effort: stays 1m: blinkered once at 2 yrs: carried head awkwardly in 1989: has worn net muzzle. *Mrs L. Piggott.*

TRY SCORER 7 b.g. Gulf Pearl 117–Just Frolicking (Pals Passage 115) [1988 8d **44** 8m⁶ 8.5m 9d 9f⁶ 8f⁶ 8g² 8g 8d² 8s 8d 8m⁶ 8g 8g 1989 8g⁴ 8.5d 8f⁴ 8.5d⁴ 8f 8h² 8f 8.5g³ 8h² 8f³ 8m³ 8.5f 8g³ 8m⁶ 8m 8f 8g] sparely-made gelding: shows traces of stringhalt: bad mover: poor handicapper: ran creditably (including for apprentice and amateur) numerous times as 7-y-o, but has not won since August, 1987: stays 11f, but raced only at around 1m nowadays: acts on any going: sometimes blinkered or visored: sweats badly: best held up as long as possible. *Denys Smith.*

TRY VICKERS (USA) 4 b. or br.f. Fuzzbuster (USA)–J A's Joy (USA) (Johns **49** Joy) [1988 8h³ 8g³ 9d⁴ 10g⁶ 10g 1989 12m⁴ 12f 12m 10f⁵ 10.4m³ 10.6d] leggy, angular filly: poor maiden: probably doesn't stay 1½m: acts on hard going and probably unsuited by soft surface: visored second outing: often pulls hard: one to have reservations about. *S. G. Norton.*

TTAYWEN 2 br.f. (Mar 5) Noalto 120–Scotch Thistle 73 (Sassafras (FR) 135) **49** [1989 8g 9f³ a8g] 2,000Y: angular, sparely-made filly: half-sister to modest 1m to 10.4f winner Flying Scotsman (by Tower Walk) and 7f winner Scotch Rocket (by Roan Rocket): dam placed at up to 1½m: plating-class maiden: refused to enter stalls, and was withdrawn at Brighton in September. *J. A. Bennett.*

TUCK BOX 3 ch.g. Bustino 136–Sweet Hour 91 (Primera 131) [1988 6f 6g² 1989 **75** 8f 10m⁵] smallish, rather sparely-made gelding: modest maiden: co-favourite, fair fifth in handicap at Nottingham, easily better effort as 3-y-o: bred to be suited by middle distances but takes keen hold and may prove suited by return to 1m: sold to join J. White 2,500 gns Ascot July Sales. *Major W. R. Hern.*

TUDOR ACE 2 b.g. (May 26) Stanford 121§–Lusaka (Wolver Hollow 126) [1989 **41** 5.1m 6m 5.1f 5g 5f 6f 5m] IR 3,200Y: good-topped, rather dipped-backed gelding: has a quick action: fifth foal: half-brother to 3-y-o Indicative (by Shy Groom) and useful 5f to 1m winner Individualist (by Viking): dam placed twice in Ireland at 7f: poor form in varied company, including selling: had stiff task when blinkered in nursery at Edinburgh final start: gelded after. *Pat Mitchell.*

TUDOR PILGRIM 4 ch.f. Welsh Pageant 132–Pilley Green 100 (Porto Bello **58** 118) [1988 7g 7f 10g 8.3g² 8m⁵ 9g 10.2g 1989 7d* 8f 8g³ 7s 8.2g² a10g³ a8g] lengthy, angular filly: plating-class handicapper: won (for first time) at Catterick in April, leading final strides: good second to Habeta at Nottingham, best subsequent effort: co-favourite, badly hampered and placing best ignored final outing: possibly best at short of 1¼m: probably needs an easy surface: has run creditably for apprentice. *Lady Herries.*

TUFTY LADY 5 b.m. Riboboy (USA) 124–War Talk (USA) 90 (Assagai) [1988 6g **45** 9g 8f* 8f² 8f³ 8f⁵ 8g³ 8.2d 1989 8s 7v 10s 8m 7f³ 10f 12f a8g] smallish, workmanlike mare: carries condition: good mover: made all in seller at Brighton as 4-y-o: worthwhile form in 1989 only on fifth outing: suited by 1m: best on a sound surface: blinkered twice: often visored: has run well for apprentice: sold 2,000 gns Ascot December Sales. *I. Campbell.*

TUGBOAT 10 ch.g. Grundy 137–Pirate Queen 77 (Pirate King 129) [1988 18d **55** 21.6g⁴ 16d 19m³ 16f* 20.4d⁴ 1989 19f* 17.1h³] lengthy, rather dipped-backed gelding: plating-class handicapper: won uncompetitive event at Goodwood in June: suited by a stiff test of stamina: acts on any going: effective with or without blinkers: has won when sweating: has won William The Lion Handicap at Ayr 3 times. *P. J. Makin.*

TULUM 4 b.g. Blakeney 126–Inca Girl (Tribal Chief 125) [1988 12g 12f 1989 12s **—** 13m 14m] has shown only a modicum of ability. *Mrs G. R. Reveley.*

TUMBLECOMBE 2 b.c. (Apr 13) Tumble Wind (USA)–Ching A Ling (Pam- **—** papaul 121) [1989 5g 5g] IR 5,000Y, 20,000 2-y-o: strong, lengthy colt: keen walker: third foal: dam Irish 5f winner at 4 yrs: no sign of ability in maiden and minor event: edgy, ran freely and tended to wander final start (July). *N. R. Mitchell.*

TUNEFUL CHARTER 2 gr.g. (Feb 3) Song 132–Martin-Lavell Star 64   **44**
(Godswalk (USA) 130) [1989 5m 5f⁶ 5m 6m 6g 5v a7g] 2,000F, 1,100Y: quite
good-topped gelding: first foal: dam 6f winner from 2 starts at 2 yrs: poor form,
including in sellers: often blinkered: usually sweats. *T. Fairhurst.*

TUPPENNY BIT 2 ch.f. (Apr 3) Godswalk (USA) 130–Blue Cloak (Majority   —
Blue 126) [1989 5s 5d] IR 1,000Y: close-coupled filly: first foal: dam unraced:
soundly beaten in seller and maiden auction event (ridden by 7-lb claimer) early in
season. *J. G. M. O'Shea.*

TUPPENNY RED 3 ch.g. Sallust 134–Red For Go (Tanfirion 110) [1988 NR 1989   **83**
7s 8m 8g* 10m² 10m* 12m² 11v] IR 3,200F, 7,200Y: unfurnished gelding: moderate
mover: second foal: half-brother to 4-y-o maiden Far Too Risky (by Prince Tenderfoot): dam never ran: successful at Salisbury in claimer (dead-heated) in May and
handicap in June: good second to Bay Bird in Kempton handicap penultimate start:
tailed off in similar event at Newbury 3½ months later: stays 1½m: has run
creditably when sweating: blinkered last 3 outings. *J. Sutcliffe.*

TURBINE BLADE 4 b.c. Kings Lake (USA) 133–Mountain Lodge 120   **83**
(Blakeney 126) [1988 11.5d⁴ 1989 10f⁴ 10g* 10.6g² 11d* 11.5g⁴ 9g] sturdy, lengthy
colt: fair handicapper: favourite, narrow winner of 6-runner event at Yarmouth
in July and Grand Handicap International d'Ostende in August: never a threat
last 2 outings: will stay 1½m: probably acts on any going: usually bandaged: moved
down moderately fifth start: sold 15,000 gns Newmarket Autumn Sales. *Mrs L.
Piggott.*

TURBO SPEED 4 b.c. Be My Native (USA) 122–Irish Summer (Sun Prince 128)   **99**
[1988 7g⁶ 6m⁴ 6f² 6g³ 6f³ 5m* 5s⁴ 6m⁴ 5m⁴ 6d* 5g⁴ 6g 1989 7s² 6g 7.6m³ 8m³
8.5m* 8f³ 8h⁵ 8g⁵ 8.2d² 7.6m] lengthy colt: turns fore-feet in: has a quick action:
fairly useful handicapper: first past the post in quite valuable events at Epsom in
June and Haydock (edged left and demoted to second) in September: soon pushed
along in rear at Chester week later: stays 8.5f: acts on any going except hard: has
worn blinkers: often bandaged: apprentice ridden fifth and sixth (slowly away)
outings: difficult ride, and probably best with considerate handling. *B. Hanbury.*

TURGEON (USA) 3 gr.c. Caro 133–Reiko (Targowice (USA) 130) [1988 NR   **123**
1989 10s⁵ 12m⁶ 15d* 15g* 15d² 15m³ 15.5g²] first reported foal: dam French 1m to
11f winner: won maiden at Chantilly in June and Group 2 Prix de L'Esperance
(beaten short head by demoted Noble Savage) at Longchamp in August: placed,
running well, in Prix Kergorlay at Deauville and Prix de Lutece and Prix Royal-Oak
(best effort, beaten 2 lengths by Top Sunrise) at Longchamp: suited by around 2m:
acts on top-of-the-ground and a soft surface. *J. E. Pease, France.*

TURGOT 5 ro.h. Ardross 134–Halton Hills (Sovereign Path 125) [1988 10g⁴ 16m³   **90**
11f* 12g³ 11g³ 14f 14.8m⁶ 12g 1989 12m⁶ 12f 12g⁴ 11f⁴ 12f⁶] compact, good-bodied
horse: chipped bone in knee final start at 3 yrs: moderate mover: fairly useful
performer: beaten 5 lengths when fourth to Highland Chieftain in 11f Grand Prix
Prince Rose at Ostend in July: modest sixth of 12 in £8,100 handicap at York month
later: ideally needs good gallop at 1½m, but seems best at short of 2m: acts on any
going, but can't take much racing on firm nowadays: sold 12,500 gns Newmarket
Autumn Sales. *G. A. Huffer.*

TURKISH TOURIST 4 b.g. Busted 134–Kalazero 96 (Kalamoun 129) [1988 8g
1989 10.8m⁶] big, rangy gelding: well beaten in newcomers race at Newmarket
(trained by B. Hanbury) early as 3-y-o and in minor event (backward, bandaged
near-hind, slowly away) at Warwick in October. *B. J. Curley.*

TURMALIN (USA) 3 ch.c. Mill Reef (USA) 141–Port Ahoy 93 (Petingo 135)   **69**
[1988 NR 1989 10s⁴ 11d⁵] 40,000Y: lengthy, rather angular colt: eighth foal:
half-brother to several winners, including 1m and 1¼m winner Pretty Pol (by Final
Straw), 1981 2-y-o 7f winner Top Hope (by High Top) and middle-distance colt Wylfa
(by Formidable), all at least useful: dam, 2-y-o 6f and 7f winner, is half-sister to dam
of Pebbles: showed ability in minor event at Nottingham (edging left) and £6,000
event at Newbury in the spring: gives impression needs strong handling: sold 7,000
gns Newmarket Autumn Sales. *W. Hastings-Bass.*

TURMERIC 6 ch.g. Alias Smith (USA)–Hot Spice (Hotfoot 126) [1988 13.8g*   **78**
12g⁶ 12f4 12.2g⁶ 15.8m² 12f 15.8g* 15.8g* 12m³ 15.8f² 14f 16m 15.8g⁵ 15d 1989
13.8d³ 12g² 15.8m³ 12m 15.8m* 13f³ 15.8f* 15.8m* 14f³ 14m⁴ 12.2g² 13.8d³] leggy,
sparely-made gelding: modest handicapper: has gained 8 of his 10 wins at Catterick,
beating Eurocon there in June and Cleavers Gate (easily by 5 lengths) and Impunity
in July: stays 2m: acts on any going: visored twice: bandaged behind nowadays: has a
turn of foot and usually held up: best with strong handling. *M. F. D. Morley.*

TURN FOR TH'BETTER 6 b.g. Tyrnavos 129–Connaught Crescent 102 —
(Connaught 130) [1988 NR 1989 10s] workmanlike gelding: no worthwhile form on
flat: bandaged and visored, soundly beaten in selling handicap at Folkestone in
April: sold 1,200 gns Doncaster August Sales. *J. Ffitch-Heyes.*

TURS 2 br.c. (Apr 8) Precocious 126–Splendid Chance (Random Shot 116) [1989 **63**
5m⁴ 6g] IR 95,000Y: good-topped colt: closely related to good 1985 2-y-o Luqman
(by Runnett) and half-brother to French 1¼m winner Splendid Day (by Day Is
Done): dam, stoutly-bred Irish 1¼m winner, stayed 1¾m: green, over 4 lengths
fourth of 6 in maiden at Newmarket in May: again in need of race, slow-starting last
of 9 in listed race at Kempton 4 months later: sold 9,000 gns Newmarket Autumn
Sales. *P. T. Walwyn.*

TURSANAH (USA) 3 br.f. Roberto (USA) 131–Farouche (USA) (Northern **112**
Dancer) [1988 6g* 6s⁴ 7s* 1989 7v* 8m 10d⁵ 10g⁵ 12s² 10v⁵] very useful Irish filly:
won listed Harp Lager EBF 1000 Guineas Trial at Phoenix Park in April: ran well
fourth and fifth starts in EBF Phoenix Champion Stakes at same course and Group 2
EBF Blandford Stakes (beaten ½ length by Indian Queen) at the Curragh but
moderately at 5/4 on in Group 3 contest at Milan on final one: stayed 1½m: acted on
heavy going, possibly unsuited by top-of-the-ground: visits Nashwan. *K. Prendergast, Ireland.*

TUWITTUWITTUWOO 2 b.c. (May 28) Vaigly Great 127–More Or Less 64 **64**
(Morston (FR) 125) [1989 7.6m² 8f⁵] 15,500Y: brother to 7f to 1¼m winner Goscar
and half-brother to 3 other winners, including middle-distance performer Dipyn
Bach (by Welsh Pageant) and quite useful 11.1f and 11.7f winner Queen Angel (by
Anfield): dam winning stayer: 2 lengths second of 12, staying on, to Rinja in maiden
at Lingfield in September: never able to challenge in Bath minor event won by
Myhamet following month: will be suited by middle distances: sold 6,200 gns
Doncaster November Sales. *I. V. Matthews.*

TWIGGERS 3 gr.g. Petong 126–Petulengra 98 (Mummy's Pet 125) [1988 NR —
1989 8s 8d] 16,000Y: leggy, sparely-made gelding: fourth foal: half-brother to poor
maiden Romany Belle (by Bay Express): dam 5f and 6f winner at 2 yrs: well behind
in maidens at Warwick and Newbury: sold to join J. Baker 2,200 gns Ascot 2nd June
Sales. *K. M. Brassey.*

TWILIGHT FALLS 4 ch.g. Day Is Done 115–Grattan Princess (Tumble Wind **56**
(USA)) [1988 5g 6g 6d⁶ 7m 6m⁶ 6g 1989 7g 6d* 6g⁶ 6g 6g] good-topped gelding: poor
mover: gambled on, won selling handicap (bought in 4,200 gns) at Pontefract in
April: no worthwhile form after, on final outing (first for over 3 months) poorly
drawn and well beaten in 25-runner handicap at Nottingham: keen sort, suited by 6f:
acts on a soft surface. *M. J. Camacho.*

TWILIGHT FANTASY 3 b.f. Red Sunset 120–Imagination 91 (Relko 136) **52**
[1988 5d 1989 7m⁴ 7f 7m 7.6m⁵ 6f³ 8f⁴ 8m⁴] light-framed filly: plating-class maiden:
stays 1m well: acts on firm ground. *M. Blanshard.*

TWIN JET (USA) 3 b.c. Lear Fan (USA) 130–Twice A Fool (USA) (Foolish **104**
Pleasure (USA)) [1988 7m² 1989 8d² 8.2d³ 8m* 8f* 9f] rangy, good sort: has plenty
of scope: made all or most to win maiden (odds on, easily) at Yarmouth and 4-runner
minor event (rallying well, by neck from Santa Tecla) at Thirsk in July: heavily-
backed favourite, led 6f when below form in Andy Capp Handicap at York in August:
will be suited by 1¼m: acts well on firm going: bandaged and edgy, ran poorly
second outing: should prove best on a galloping track. *H. R. A. Cecil.*

TWIST AND SHOUT 3 b.f. Cure The Blues (USA)–Tulalanee (Habitat 134) —
[1988 NR 1989 11.5m 8m] sister to plating-class 1987 2-y-o Zazu and half-sister to 2
winners, including useful Irish 7f and 1½m winner Inisheer (by Be My Guest): dam,
half-sister to Derby second Cavo Doro, showed only a little ability: scant promise in
maidens at Yarmouth in the summer: in foal to Adonijah. *Mrs L. Piggott.*

TWO LEFT FEET 2 b.c. (May 22) Petorius 117–Whitstar 93 (Whitstead 125) **95** p
[1989 7m² 8f* 8.2g* 7g*] 12,000Y: lengthy, good-bodied colt: good walker: first
living foal: dam, 10.2f winner at 2 yrs, half-sister to very useful 6f to 1¼m winner
Homeboy: progressive colt: successful in second half of season in auction events at
Redcar and Hamilton and all-aged event (by a neck, rallying splendidly, from Donna
Elvira) at Newmarket: stays 1m: potentially useful. *Sir Mark Prescott.*

TWO MOONS 3 ch.f. Bold Lad (IRE) 133–Shoshoni 72 (Ballymoss 136) [1988 7s —
1989 8.5d 12g 16f] compact, plain filly: bit backward, no sign of ability in maidens and
a handicap. *C. W. Thornton.*

TWO REALMS 3 b.f. Another Realm 118–Two Shots (Dom Racine (FR) 121) —
[1988 6f 6g⁵ 6m⁴ 6m² 6s⁴ 7m⁶ 7m 6g⁵ 6f⁴ 7d⁴ 1989 8g⁶ 9f 8g 10g 10f² 12m 10f⁴ 9f

a8g] close-coupled, good-bodied filly: poor maiden: below form in selling events and claimer last 4 starts: appears to stay 1¼m: acts on any going: blinkered eighth start: has raced with head in air: takes keen hold and has worn pricker. *K. O. Cunningham-Brown.*

TWO STRIDES 2 ch.g. (May 8) Mansingh (USA) 120–Saratoga Chip (USA) 59 — (Plenty Old (USA)) [1989 6f 5g 5f] 960F, 5,400Y: close-coupled, rather plain gelding: third foal: dam won 7f seller: little worthwhile form in maidens, including auction event. *M. W. Ellerby.*

TWOTIME BID 3 b.g. Taufan (USA) 119–Avebury Ring (Auction Ring (USA) 72 123) [1988 6f 7f⁴ 6d 1989 9g 9f⁶ 8s* 8g² 8g*] quite good-topped gelding: has a round, fluent action: won claimers at Ayr in October and Leicester in November: may prove best at 1m: goes well on soft ground. *Miss S. E. Hall.*

TWO TIMING (USA) 3 b.c. Blushing Groom (FR) 131–Social Column 124 (USA) (Vaguely Noble 140) [1988 7g² 1989 10.5f⁴ 10m* 10m* 10f* 10.5f⁶]
Jeremy Tree retired at the end of the latest season, handing over control at Beckhampton to his long-time assistant Roger Charlton. Having first taken out a licence in 1952, Tree sent out four British classic winners in Only For Life (1963 Two Thousand Guineas), Juliette Marny (1975 Oaks), Scintillate (1979 Oaks) and Known Fact (1980 Two Thousand Guineas) along with a champion sprinter Sharpo, the high-class stayer John Cherry, a champion two-year-old in Double Jump and, possibly best of the lot, the Prix de l'Arc de Triomphe winner Rainbow Quest, among a host of good-class wins. Surprisingly perhaps, Tree's best seasonal total was forty winners in 1985, partly a reflection of the patience he showed with his charges. In his final season, for instance, just two of his twenty-nine wins came from two-year-olds. In the week following the announcement of his retirement, Tree sent out three winners at Royal Ascot: Two Timing in the Prince of Wales's Stakes, True Panache in the Royal Hunt Cup and Danehill in the Cork and Orrery. All three take a strong hold and their careers have had to be reshaped as a consequence. For the last two this entailed a step down in distance but with Two Timing that wasn't necessary, they simply gave up attempting to settle him behind horses and allowed the colt to stride on and make his own pace. The first two occasions these tactics were employed Two Timing would most probably have won whatever the tactics so modest was the opposition in the Flying Horse Maiden at Nottingham and the Tipsters Table Stakes at Leicester eight days later. Landing the odds there took very little, if anything, out of him because in the Prince of Wales's Stakes Two Timing took on and beat almost as contrasting a set of opponents as one could find for his third race in eighteen days. Eddery almost immediately had Two Timing in a clear lead in front of the usually front-running Brigadier Gerard Stakes winner Hibernian Gold before giving him a breather and allowing the others to close up before the turn. Once sent on again Two Timing produced a game response and, despite hanging away from the rail and not being subjected to anything like his jockey's maximum pressure, held off first Hibernian Gold and the subsequent Eclipse runner-up Opening Verse then the three-time listed-race winner Beau Sher to win by a length. The Lockinge winner Most Welcome had been made an odds-on favourite but found

Prince of Wales's Stakes, Ascot—a high-class performance from the three-year-old Two Timing against Beau Sher and Most Welcome (almost hidden)

Mr K. Abdulla's "Two Timing"

disappointingly little once getting a clear run at the distance and was beaten another length in third.

The idea that Two Timing would be capable of holding his own in such company was clearly not a new one to connections as they had chosen the William Hill Dante Stakes for his reappearance, and only second race all told, in fact, after his neck second to Observation Post in a big field of maidens at Newmarket. Although there was a good pace at York, Two Timing still took a strong hold under restraint about four lengths behind the rest of the field before staying on to finish a never-dangerous fourth to Torjoun, beaten five and a quarter lengths. In August, Two Timing was returned to York for the Juddmonte International Stakes ridden in very different fashion but he couldn't shake off the close attentions of Ile de Chypre and dropped away steadily once headed early in the straight to finish well beaten. In October it was reported that Two Timing had been sold to race in the USA where he'll be trained by Neil Drysdale.

Two Timing (USA) (b.c. 1986)	Blushing Groom (FR) (ch 1974)	Red God (ch 1954)	Nasrullah
			Spring Run
		Runaway Bride (b 1962)	Wild Risk
			Aimee
	Social Column (USA) (b 1976)	Vaguely Noble (b 1965)	Vienna
			Noble Lassie
		Miss Carmie (b 1966)	T V Lark
			Twice Over

Two Timing is the fifth foal and third winner out of the twice-raced Social Column following Mondanite (by Lyphard), disappointing here before winning five times in the USA, and the four-year-old filly Liaison (by Blushing Groom) who won a mile-and-a-quarter listed race at Longchamp in May. Her 1987 foal is a filly by The Minstrel called Singing. Social Column made 600,000 dollars then 425,000 dollars when sent to public auction at Keeneland in November 1980 and 1982. By Vaguely Noble but officially described as being by Vaguely Noble or Swoon's Son, Social Column possibly wouldn't have been so valuable

943

a property if by the latter but would have been a sister to the champion U S three-year-old filly of 1974 Chris Evert. Their dam Miss Carmie, a six-furlong stakes winner at two years, also produced All Rainbows, useful herself on the racecourse but more notably the dam of only the third filly to win the Kentucky Derby, Winning Colors. Chris Evert is the dam of Six Crowns who produced Chiefs Crown, the champion U S two-year-old of 1984, later placed in all legs of the triple crown and the outstanding first-season sire of 1989. With ten of Miss Carmie's first fourteen foals being fillies, most superbly bred, we're sure to hear a lot more of this family.

Two Timing is a tall, leggy, attractive colt. Everything about his race-course appearances was determined by his headstrong nature; sometimes edgy in the paddock, he was almost habitually so when mounted and taken to post and wore a net muzzle in the preliminaries throughout his three-year-old season. Two Timing is clearly best when able to dominate his races from the front, stays a mile and a quarter and acts on firm ground. He's never raced on a soft surface. *J. Tree.*

TWO TOFFS 2 gr.g. (Feb 18) Another Realm 118–Two Shots (Dom Racine (FR) **61** 121) [1989 5f* 5m² 5.1m* 5m4 5f* 5f² 5m³ 5m² 5f4 5g] 1,050Y, 5,100 2-y-o: smallish, sparely-made gelding: moderate mover: third foal: brother to 3-y-o Two Realms: dam ran twice at 2 yrs: useful plater: successful in June at Redcar (retained 3,100 gns) and Yarmouth (retained 5,200 gns) and in claimer at Ayr following month: mostly ran well in nurseries afterwards: will stay 6f: tends to hang. *C. Tinkler.*

TWO WORLDS (USA) 3 ch.f. Diesis 133–Sweet Ramblin Rose (USA) (Turn- **68** To) [1988 5d³ 6g 1989 7m4 7h] useful-looking filly: shows traces of stringhalt: modest at best: 25/1, 4½ lengths fourth of 5 to impressive Kerita in minor event at Leicester: ran moderately facing stiff task in Brighton handicap later in June: suited by 7f. *P. F. I. Cole.*

TYBURN LAD 2 gr.c. (Apr 3) Belfort (FR) 89–Swing Is Back (Busted 134) [1989 **51** 5s 7g 7.5f6 8f 7g 6f 6g] 4,000Y: lengthy, rather angular colt: has a round action: brother to 3-y-o Balizara, fairly useful 5f to 1m winner: dam French 1¼m winner: plating-class maiden: best effort on third start: needs further than 6f: trained by R. Stubbs on debut. *H. J. Collingridge.*

TYBURN TREE 2 b.c. (Apr 7) High Top 131–Catalpa 115 (Reform 132) [1989 **96 p** 8v*] compact colt: half-brother to 5 winners, including 3-y-o middle-distance stayer Knifeboard, 11.5f and 1½m winner Kenanga (both by Kris) and Ribblesdale Stakes winner Strigida (by Habitat): dam and grandam won Ribblesdale Stakes: 13/2, won 23-runner maiden at Newbury in October in good style by 4 lengths from Quest For Fame, leading 2f out: will be well suited by middle distances: sure to improve, and win more races. *H. R. A. Cecil.*

TYLERS WOOD 4 br.g. Homing 130–Beryl's Jewel 86 (Siliconn 121) [1988 5d **67** 5.3f² 5m5 6f² 5.3f5 5g* 5g 5g³ 5d4 1989 5g 6h³ 5.1m5 6m6 5g6 5f* 6h] smallish, compact gelding: quite modest handicapper: co-favourite, returned to form when winning at Sandown in July: slowly away and always behind at Brighton 2 weeks later: stays 6f: yet to race on soft going, acts on any other: has run well when edgy and sweating. *W. J. Haggas.*

TYRIAN 2 b.f. (Mar 4) Elegant Air 119–Character Builder 92 (African Sky 124) **—** [1989 6g 7g 6g] fourth foal: half-sister to a winner in Italy by Milford: dam best at 2 yrs, when successful from 5f to 7f: soundly beaten in maidens. *Sir Mark Prescott.*

TYRIAN BELLE 4 b.f. Enchantment 115–Chasten (Manacle 123) [1988 6s* 5g* **77** 6d5 5m³ 6f 6s 1989 5s³ 5f6 5g4 6f4 6g4 a6g² a6g²] workmanlike filly: modest handicapper: stays 6f: probably not at her best on firm going, acts on any other: bandaged final outing. *P. F. I. Cole.*

TYRIAN PRINCE 2 b.g. (May 27) Norwick (USA) 120–Chasten (Manacle 123) **65** [1989 6f4] 8,800Y: leggy, rather unfurnished gelding: half-brother to 3 winning 2-y-o's, latest modest sprinter Tyrian Belle (by Enchantment): dam never ran: 13/2, under 7 lengths fourth of 12, keeping on, to Scarlett Holly in maiden auction race at Newbury in May: subsequently gelded. *P. F. I. Cole.*

TYRNIPPY 3 b.c. Tyrnavos 129–Floral 82 (Floribunda 136) [1988 5g 5f 5m³ 5g* **80** 5s* 6g² 7g 6g 6s 6s4 6s6 1989 7g4 7g* 6s² 7g6 8d* 8.5d5 7f 7f6 8.2g 8m 8.2g 8.2d 7g 7g] smallish, sparely-made colt: has a round action: fair handicapper: won at Doncaster (idled in front) and Bath in April: below form last 6 outings: suited by 1m: may prove suited by an easy surface: has run creditably for apprentice. *M. Brittain.*

TYRONE BRIDGE 3 b.g. Kings Lake (USA) 133–Rhein Bridge 107 **120**
(Rheingold 137) [1988 7d 7g² 1989 10v* 14m* 16f 14m* 12m² 14d² 12s³]
  Don't judge Tyrone Bridge on his only outing in Britain in the Queen's
Vase at Royal Ascot—held up, he was never able to challenge and was beaten
around twenty lengths behind Weld in seventh place. His form in his native
country entitles Tyrone Bridge to be regarded as one of the top two
three-year-olds to be trained in Ireland in the latest season. Successful in a
maiden at Phoenix Park and minor event at Leopardstown earlier, Tyrone
Bridge showed further improvement in winning the listed Curragh Cup three
weeks after Royal Ascot. Always tracking front-running Sergeyevich, he
moved up to challenge a furlong out and battled on gamely to establish a
three-quarter-length advantage by the line, the pair drawing ten lengths clear.
Tyrone Bridge subsequently failed twice by only a short head to win a pattern
race. In the Group 3 Royal Whip Stakes over a mile and a half he couldn't quite
catch enterprisingly-ridden Beyond The Lake. Returned to a mile and three
quarters on the same course the following month Tyrone Bridge put up a
better effort in the Jefferson Smurfit Memorial Irish St Leger. Taking up the
running from Lazaz with under two furlongs to go, Tyrone Bridge just got the
worse of a sustained duel in the closing stages with the filly Petite Ile, who
was receiving the 3-lb sex allowance. A seemingly-modest third behind Indian
Queen when favourite for the mile-and-a-half Group 2 EBF Blandford Stakes
at the Curragh on his final start can probably be excused. Ridden with more
restraint than usual, he finished strongly having been given a lot to do in a
race run at none too strong a pace and was beaten under a length. British
racegoers are likely to see more of Tyrone Bridge in 1990 when he's
reportedly to be trained for the Cup races. He'll miss penalties in races such
as the Yorkshire Cup and the Sagaro Stakes, and should pay his way.

		⎡Nijinsky	⎡Northern Dancer
	⎡Kings Lake (USA)	⎨ (b 1967)	⎨Flaming Page
	⎜ (b 1978)	⎣Fish-Bar	⎣Baldric
Tyrone Bridge	⎨	(b 1967)	⎡Fisherman's Wharf
(b.g. 1986)	⎜	⎡Rheingold	⎨Faberge II
	⎜Rhein Bridge	⎨ (br 1969)	⎣Athene
	⎣ (b 1978)	⎣Fishermans Bridge	⎡Crepello
		(b 1970)	⎣Riva

  There's a fair amount of stamina in Tyrone Bridge's pedigree. Though
Kings Lake showed his best form at a mile, he was bred to stay middle
distances and has sired several winners over further, including smart
two-mile winner Sudden Victory. Rhein Bridge, a very game short-head
winner of the Lancashire Oaks in 1981, stayed a mile and a half well though
she was below her best on her only run over further. She's a half-sister to
Yorkshire Oaks winner Connaught Bridge. Their dam, the determined and
very useful front-runner Fishermans Bridge, never ran beyond a mile and a
quarter. Further back this is the family of St Leger winner Cantelo. Tyrone
Bridge is Rhein Bridge's third foal and first winner. Her yearling of 1989, a
sister to Tyrone Bridge, was sold for IR 16,000 guineas at Goffs in October.
Tyrone Bridge was bought for IR 28,000 guineas at the same venue in 1987.
He was purchased privately by Mr Paul Green prior to the Irish St Leger, with
the reported original intention of joining his new owner's string of jumpers
with Pipe. Needless to say, he'd have been a high-class recruit to National
Hunt racing. A leggy sort, gelded as a two-year-old, Tyrone Bridge has shown
his form on ground ranging from heavy through to good to firm. He's
thoroughly genuine. *K. Prendergast, Ireland.*

U

ULANOVA (USA) 3 b.f. Barachois (CAN)–Theron (USA) (Sea Bird II 145) [1988 **77**
5m*dis 5s* 6g³ 7m 6f³ 6g 1989 8f 7m⁶ 6m⁶ 7.5m* 7.5f⁴ 8m* 8g⁶] smallish,
close-coupled filly: good mover: modest performer: won claimer at Beverley in July
and handicap at Thirsk in September: ran moderately final start: stays 1m: probably
acts on any going: ridden by 7-lb claimer last 2 starts. *J. Etherington.*

ULTIMATE DREAM   3 b.f. Kafu 120–Fortera (FR) (Sanctus II 132) [1988 5g⁶   —
5f* 5g* 5g⁵ 6f 1989 7.3m 6f 5m 6g] useful-looking filly: has a rather round action:
modest winner at 2 yrs: behind in handicaps and claimer in 1989: stays 6f: acts on
firm going: pulled hard on reappearance: sweating and edgy final start. *R. Hannon.*

ULTING WICK   3 b.f. Brave Shot–Unbidden Melody (USA) (Chieftain II) [1988   **68**
NR 1989 7m³ 8s 8.2m] leggy filly: first foal: dam, half-sister to smart 6f and
1m winner Faustus, ran twice in USA: easily best effort in September maidens on
debut: hampered early on final start: should stay at least 1m. *W. J. Haggas.*

ULTRA LIGHT   3 b.c. Superlative 118–High Explosive (Mount Hagen (FR) 127)   **87**
[1988 6f 6d* 6g 1989 7g 8d² 9s* 10.6g 10.1m³ 10.2g³ 10.6d 10g⁵ 9g³] compact,
useful-looking colt: poor walker and mover: fair handicapper: led on line at Kempton
in May: below form seventh and eighth outings, checked 6f out then only one pace
on second of them: possibly suited by 1¼m: acts on top-of-the-ground and soft
going: blinkered last 7 outings: sold 35,000 gns Newmarket Autumn Sales. *M. A.
Jarvis.*

ULTRA MAGIC   2 b.f. (Mar 4) Magic Mirror 105–Cardane (FR) (Dan Cupid 132)   **59**
[1989 6m³ 6f4 6m² 6g 5g⁶] leggy, sparely-made, plain filly: half-sister to French
1¼m winner Adalia (by Owen Dudley) and some moderate jumpers in France: dam
ran once at 2 yrs in France: plating-class maiden: should be suited by much further
than 6f: acts on firm going: gave trouble going down final outing. *A. C. Stewart.*

UNCLE BOBBY   2 ch.g. (May 11) King Persian 107–Honi Soit (Above Suspicion   **59**
127) [1989 6m 7g²] 6,000 2-y-o: close-coupled, sparely-made gelding: has a quick
action: half-brother to 3 winners by Welsh Saint, including 7f and 1½m winner
Susan's Sunset and 1977 Irish 2-y-o 5f winner Clanrickard, and 2 other winners:
dam poor Irish maiden: 10 lengths second of 4 to Swordsmith in minor event at Wolverhampton in July: subsequently gelded: will be suited by 1m +. *Miss S. J. Wilton.*

UNCLE ERNIE   4 b.g. Uncle Pokey 116–Ladyfold 60 (Never Dwell 89) [1988 8d   **71**
7d4 6f⁵ 7g 8d 8g² 8g³ 8m 6s* 6s 8v* 8g 1989 10.2g 12.3s³ 10s² 12d³ 12.3f² 14g]
leggy, workmanlike gelding: has a round action: modest handicapper: best at 1¼m
to 1½m nowadays: acts on any going: winning hurdler with J. FitzGerald. *Mrs J. R.
Ramsden.*

UNDER THE STARS   7 ch.g. Ahonoora 122–Moonlight Night (Huntercombe   —
133) [1988 NR 1989 10s] light-framed gelding: poor maiden: blinkered for second
time, well beaten in selling handicap at Folkestone in April, only outing on flat since
1986: stays 1¼m: acts on firm going. *R. J. Hodges.*

UNDER THE WING   2 b.f. (Apr 23) Aragon 118–Royal Custody (Reform 132)   **69**
[1989 5f³ 6g⁶ 6f² 7f³ 7m4 8m] leggy, quite attractive filly: second foal: dam unraced
half-sister to several winners, including Ragstone, Castle Keep and Castle Moon
(dam of Moon Madness and Sheriff's Star): quite modest maiden: best effort
penultimate start: should stay 1m: usually sweating and on toes. *Lady Herries.*

UNDERTONES   2 b.f. (Mar 16) Song 132–Tattle 61 (St Paddy 133) [1989 5m⁵ 5f³   **58**
5g⁶ 5d 6g 5g a6g4] rather leggy, fair sort: third foal: sister to a winner in
Scandinavia: dam lightly-raced sister to useful middle-distance performer King's
General and from family of Espresso: plating-class maiden: ran well for 7-lb claimer
final start: better suited by 6f than 5f. *J. A. Glover.*

UNEXPECTED GUEST   4 b.f. Be My Guest (USA) 126–Elevated (USA) (Stop   **61**
The Music (USA)) [1988 7d 8f 8f 10m 10.1g* 10m 10g 1989 12m² 11.5g² 11.7m4 12f²]
compact, quite attractive filly: has a long stride: good second, nearest at finish, in
handicaps at Salisbury (amateurs), Sandown and Folkestone: will stay beyond 1½m:
probably acts on any going: best in blinkers or visor: bandaged off-hind third start
(on toes), in front final one: sold 7,600 gns Newmarket Autumn Sales. *D. R. C.
Elsworth.*

UNFUWAIN (USA)   4 b.c. Northern Dancer–Height of Fashion (FR) 124 **126**
(Bustino 136) [1988 12d* 12.3s* 12m 12d* 12d² 12m4 1989 12d* 12m*]

Unfuwain was kept in training as a four-year-old primarily with the aim of
improving on his second and fourth placings in the King George VI and Queen
Elizabeth Diamond Stakes and the Ciga Prix de l'Arc de Triomphe respectively. He ran in neither and made his final appearance at Newmarket in
early-May, twenty-four hours before his half-brother Nashwan embarked on
his three-year-old campaign in the Two Thousand Guineas. The firm ground
that prevailed virtually throughout the summer made it very difficult to train
Unfuwain, and so what might have been a hard decision whether to allow him
to take on Nashwan never had to be faced. As for the Arc, he was stated as a

General Accident Jockey Club Stakes, Newmarket—
Unfuwain goes three lengths clear of Glacial Storm before being eased

probable non-runner more than three weeks beforehand, the rain apparently arriving too late for him to be able to take his chance in his intended prep race—the Prix Foy at Longchamp—from which he was withdrawn at the first-forfeit stage. The announcement of his retirement to the Nunnery Stud, Thetford, where he'll stand alongside Nashwan and Green Desert, came shortly afterwards, his valuation set at £2.7 million with his owner retaining twenty-three of the forty-five shares. His first-season fee will be £15,000 with an October 1st concession.

If Unfuwain's season ended in disappointment, it began most encouragingly with wins in the Lanes End John Porter EBF Stakes at Newbury and the General Accident Jockey Club Stakes at Newmarket, successes achieved in similar style to his clear-cut victories as a three-year-old—keeping up a relentless gallop after being sent for home a fair way out. In beating Glacial Storm in the Jockey Club Stakes he went one better than his brother, the now-exported Alwasmi, who was beaten by Almaarad twelve months previously having taken the John Porter Stakes on his reappearance at 25/1. Unfuwain was sent off at odds on at both Newbury and Newmarket. He looked as though he'd be better for the race at Newbury, whereas his two main rivals (to whom he gave 3 lb) had already had an outing and shown themselves suited by the conditions. Per Quod had trounced his opposition in the Magnolia Stakes at Kempton; Apache had also passed the post first on his reappearance in the Doncaster Shield. Unfuwain raced ahead of the chasing group and came through to take the lead off his pacemaker Ghadbbaan four furlongs out. He first repelled the challenge of Apache, then gradually quickened the pace and found extra in the final furlong to keep Per Quod at bay by a length and a half. At Newmarket three weeks later Unfuwain was opposed by five, including his pacemaker Misbah. The best backed of his rivals was Sheriff's Star, even though he looked short of his peak on his first run since the St Leger. Two others, Red Glow and Glacial Storm, were becoming disappointing, while Tralos had been well beaten in the mud at Kempton on his only previous run of the season. The field wasn't so competitive as it might have been, then, but Unfuwain was still impressive. He took up the running under four furlongs out, soon had his rivals toiling and kept on strongly until eased close home; his winning margin of a length over Glacial Storm could have been at least three.

		Nearctic	Nearco
	Northern Dancer	(br 1954)	Lady Angela
	(b 1961)	Natalma	Native Dancer
Unfuwain (USA)		(b 1957)	Almahmoud
(b.c. 1985)		Bustino	Busted
	Height of Fashion (FR)	(b 1971)	Ship Yard
	(b 1979)	Highclere	Queen's Hussar
		(b 1971)	Highlight

Unfuwain, a good walker with a quick, rather round action, is a rangy, strong, most attractive colt. His family's record is an outstanding one that may well be enhanced in 1990 by Mukddaam (by Danzig), the winner of his only race as a two-year-old. Unfuwain acted on soft going and, while never risked on very firm going, he showed in the Arc and the Jockey Club Stakes

947

Hamdan Al-Maktoum's "Unfuwain" (W. Carson)

that he was capable of producing his form when the ground was on the firm side. He was suited by a good gallop at a mile and a half and would have stayed further. Unfuwain was tough, genuine and consistent. *Major W. R. Hern.*

UNIROYAL WINDWAY 3 b.c. Runnett 125–Monaco Lady 83 (Manado 130) **52** [1988 5g³ 5m⁵ 6g⁴ 6m³ 6m 6d 1989 5d⁶ 5m 6f³ 6m³ 6f 9f² 7m 7.5m⁵ 6g 6g 10f² 10m* 10f⁵ 10f⁴ 10g] leggy, sparely-made colt: fairly useful plater: favourite, won at Redcar (bought in 3,700 gns) in October: ran poorly final start: will prove best at up to 1¼m: acts on firm going, possibly unsuited by a soft surface: takes good hold: goes well with forcing tactics: trained first 5 outings by C. Nelson: sold 3,000 gns Doncaster October Sales. *D. W. Chapman.*

UNKNOWN QUANTITY 4 b.g. Young Generation 129–Pas de Deux 80 **114** (Nijinsky (CAN) 138) [1988 8g⁴ 7f 8m³ 10m⁴ 10m⁵ 9g 1989 7.6f* 10g* 10s* 12f⁶]
    While the British raid on Breeders' Cup day once again drew a blank, Unknown Quantity, Braiswick and Somethingdifferent all managed to win in North America. Unknown Quantity and Braiswick both won Grade 1 events, Braiswick the E P Taylor Stakes at Woodbine, Canada, and Unknown Quantity the Arlington Handicap at Arlington Park. Unknown Quantity's victory was the more unlikely. The winner of the £9,200 Daily Mail Casino Stakes (Handicap) at Lingfield and the £27,600 Royal Hong Kong Jockey Club Trophy (Handicap) at Sandown on his only two previous runs of the season, he

Royal Hong Kong Jockey Club Trophy (Handicap), Sandown—a valuable win in the Royal colours for Unknown Quantity (left); Gulf Palace (centre) and Main Objective run him close

took on apparently stronger opposition at Arlington. His four rivals, all major contenders for the Arlington Million three weeks hence, were Blushing John, the top older handicap horse in the States, the Breeders' Cup Turf winner Great Communicator, the King Edward Gold Cup winner Frosty The Snowman and Delegant, a son of Dahlia. Unknown Quantity, receiving weight all round (12 lb from Blushing John), started fourth favourite at 10/1. Great Communicator set the early pace, chased by Blushing John. Unknown Quantity, racing on soft ground for the first time, tracked the pair down the back straight, challenged full of running a quarter of a mile out and drew clear to beat Frosty The Snowman three lengths. Great Communicator, having his first run for nearly two months, weakened into fourth, with Blushing John, eased considerably, tailed-off last. Unknown Quantity, who nearly trebled his earnings, was the Queen's first winner in a Graded or pattern race since 1982, when Height of Fashion won the Princess of Wales's Stakes, and her first winner in the States. The Queen's only previous runner Landau, whom she leased from the National Stud, finished unplaced in the 1954 Washington DC International. Unknown Quantity's trainer does seem more adept than most at beating the Americans, for in 1988 he sent over Luge to land the Laurel Futurity. Unknown Quantity had not been nominated for the Arlington Million, and rather than pay the 50,000-dollar supplementary fee connections chose the Summer Tan Handicap for his next race, run at Arlington the day after the Million. On his first attempt at a mile and a half, Unknown Quantity failed to settle and weakened in the straight to finish more than eight lengths behind Delegant, whom he'd beaten almost five lengths in the Arlington Handicap.

Unknown Quantity (b.g. 1985)	Young Generation (b 1976)	Balidar (br 1966)	Will Somers
			Violet Bank
		Brig O'Doon (ch 1967)	Shantung
			Tam O'Shanter
	Pas de Deux (ch 1974)	Nijinsky (b 1967)	Northern Dancer
			Flaming Page
		Example (ch 1968)	Exbury
			Amicable

Pas de Deux's first seven foals have all been winners, the best of them besides Unknown Quantity being Insular (by Moulton), successful ten times on the flat at up to two miles, as well as twice over hurdles, including in the William Hill Imperial Cup, and on his only outing over fences. Pas de Deux's last two foals to race Starlet and Once Upon A Time (both by Teenoso) won as two-year-olds, the latter in a maiden race over an extended mile at Beverley in September. A winner as a three-year-old over a mile and a quarter, Pas de Deux is a daughter of the Park Hill Stakes winner Example, a half-sister to the Lancashire Oaks winner Amphora and the Ribblesdale Stakes winner Expansive. Unknown Quantity's great-grandam Amicable, a daughter of the Queen Mary Stakes winner Amy Leigh, ran five times, winning the Nell Gwyn Stakes on her debut and finishing runner-up in the Yorkshire Oaks. Unknown Quantity's sire Young Generation, who died in 1986, was also represented in the latest season by the leading sprinter Cadeaux Genereux. The leggy, quite attractive Unknown Quantity, a fluent mover, has shown his best form at a mile and a quarter. He acts on any going. *W. Hastings-Bass.*

UNPAID MEMBER 5 b.g. Moorestyle 137–Sunningdale Queen 88 (Gay — Fandango (USA) 132) [1988 8s 12d* 1989 10.2g6] smallish, workmanlike gelding: has a round action: won maiden at Galway as 4-y-o: sixth of 30 in amateurs handicap at Doncaster in March: stays 1½m: acts on a soft surface, but probably not at best on very soft going: winning hurdler. *P. A. Blockley.*

UNWANTED GIFT 3 b.g. Auction Ring (USA) 123–Carioca (Gala Performance **74** (USA)) [1988 7d 6m 1989 7s4 8d] leggy, sparely-made gelding: modest maiden: good fourth at Epsom in April: 10/1, last of 10 in handicap at Goodwood 5 months later, close up 6f: stays 7f: acts on top-of-the-ground and soft going: has joined D. Barons. *L. G. Cottrell.*

UPPER STRATA 4 b.f. Shirley Heights 130–Bright Landing 78 (Sun Prince 128) **109** [1988 NR 1989 8f3 12m4 12g4 13.4m3 14d4 16g*] lengthy filly, rather sparely-made: moderate mover: useful performer: won maiden and listed race as 2-y-o: reportedly injured tendon behind and was unraced in 1988: successful on final outing in listed George Stubbs EBF Stakes at Newmarket in November by 4 lengths, quickening clear 4f out, from Patience Camp: earlier in frame in varied events, on fifth start fourth of 10, leading until under 2f out, to Petite Ile in Jefferson Smurfit Memorial Irish St Leger at the Curragh: lacked turn of foot, and suited by enterprising tactics over 1½m+: stud. *L. M. Cumani.*

UP THE WAGON 2 ch.c. (Apr 2) Formidable (USA) 125–Skiboule (BEL) — (Boulou) [1989 8m a8g] 5,000Y, 9,600 2-y-o: small, workmanlike colt: poor walker: ninth foal in Britain: half-brother to 3-y-o La Gloriosa (by Ardross) and several winners, including useful middle-distance fillies Rollrights and Rollfast (both by Ragstone): dam won in Belgium: well beaten in seller at Warwick and claimer at Southwell. *C. N. Allen.*

UPTON PARK 4 br.g. High Top 131–Polly Packer 81 (Reform 132) [1988 12m3 **77** 16m* 16.5m6 1989 12m5 14g3 16.1g4 17.4s3 16.2d3 18g] leggy gelding: easy mover: fair handicapper: very good third at Haydock in October on fifth outing: 20/1, close up until badly hampered 4f out in Tote Cesarewitch (Handicap) at Newmarket later in month: suited by a test of stamina: acts on top-of-the-ground and soft going. *J. W. Watts.*

UPTOWN GIRL 9 br.m. Caruso 110–Sealed Contract 76 (Runnymede 123) [1988 — 5f* 5g5 5f* 5m 5g2 5m3 5g 5.1g* 5g4 5g 5m 5g4 5s 5f 6f4 5g 5d4 1989 5m 5m 5f 6f 5g] compact, good-quartered mare: poor walker: quite modest winner as 8-y-o when trained by D. Chapman: no worthwhile form in 1989: best at 5f: acts on any going: blinkered last 3 starts at 8 yrs: often sweats: suited by forcing tactics. *Miss L. C. Siddall.*

UPWARD TREND 3 ch.f. Salmon Leap (USA) 131–Ivory Home (FR) (Home **112** Guard (USA) 129) [1988 7g* 10g 1989 9v2 10s* 10d* 10g2 10m5 8g* 8g2 8g2 9g* 8g* 9.2g] IR 53,000Y: fourth foal: closely related to a winning stayer in Belgium by Try My Best and half-sister to fair 1¼m winner Manjaniq (by Kings Lake): dam, unraced, is from family of Glad Rags: successful in 2 listed races at both the Curragh and Phoenix Park, and then Group 3 Mount Coote Stud EBF Matron Stakes (by 2 lengths from Awayed) at the Curragh: not discredited, staying on after modest run, in Group 2 contest at Longchamp final start: effective at 1m to 1¼m: best form on an easy surface: consistent. *J. S. Bolger, Ireland.*

UP WEST 3 b.g. King of Spain 121–Shaky Puddin (Ragstone 128) [1988 6m 8d 7g — 1989 8f 8m 7.6m] strong, workmanlike gelding: no form in varied events: changed hands 2,800 gns Doncaster February Sales: dead. *S. G. Norton.*

URFAN 2 br.c. (Mar 29) Valiyar 129–Nafla (FR) (Arctic Tern (USA) 126) [1989 5f5 **42** 5f4 6m5] smallish, rather sparely-made colt: first foal: dam French 7f to 1¼m winner, is granddaughter of Park Hill winner Cursorial: quite modest plater: not raced after June: visored second start (bought out of J. Dunlop's stable 1,150 gns): somewhat temperamental. *K. White.*

URIZEN 4 ch.g. High Line 125–Off The Reel (USA) 81 (Silent Screen (USA)) [1988 10g⁵ 12f² 13.3d* 14.8d⁵ 14g* 14f⁶ 1989 14g] rather leggy, good-topped gelding: fairly useful winner as 3-y-o: led until 4f out when well beaten in Newmarket handicap in April: stays 1¾m well: yet to race on soft going, acts on any other: races up with pace. *D. R. C. Elsworth.* —

URRAY ON HARRY 5 b.g. Anfield 117–Noorina (Royal And Regal (USA)) [1988 12f 10d 10g 7d* 7f² 7m 8s 1989 8s 8d 8d 7f⁴ 8.2g* 7.6m⁴ 8m* 8.2g² 8.2d² 9f⁶ 10.6s⁵ 8v² 8g a8g⁵] smallish, workmanlike gelding: poor mover: modest handicapper: successful in apprentice event at Haydock and 17-runner contest at Doncaster: ran well most starts after, but below his best last 2: should prove as effective at 1¼m as at 1m: probably acts on any going: sweating final outing: tends to idle: best with strong handling and waiting tactics. *R. Hollinshead.* **71**

USA DOLLAR 2 b.c. (Apr 28) Gabitat 119–Burglars Girl 63 (Burglar 128) [1989 6g 7m 8g] strong colt: fifth foal: half-brother to 3-y-o Dollar's Sister (by Mandrake Belle), 7f winner Red Dollar (by Tachypous) and fairly useful 5f and 6f winner Green Dollar (by Tickled Pink): dam sprinter: poor form in modest company. *B. Gubby.* **45**

USAYLAH 2 ch.f. (Mar 23) Siberian Express (USA) 125–Nawara 75 (Welsh Pageant 132) [1989 7m 8g 6g²] lengthy, sturdy, medium-sized filly: third foal: half-sister to useful 3-y-o 1¼m to 13f winner Usran and 1987 2-y-o 6f winner Irnan (both by Valiyar): dam 10.2f winner: length second of 9, going on strongly, to Jacomino in maiden at Goodwood in October, easily best effort: should stay at least 1m. *J. L. Dunlop.* **69**

USEFUL ADDITION 7 b.m. Royalty 130–Facade 99 (Double Jump 131) [1988 NR 1989 16.2d] well beaten in varied company. *M. Tate.* —

USRAN 3 b.c. Valiyar 129–Nawara 75 (Welsh Pageant 132) [1988 7m³ 7d² 7g² 1989 8g³ 10m³ 10h* 12d* 13s* 11g³ 14s⁶] tall, close-coupled colt: useful performer: won handicaps at Lingfield in July and Goodwood and Ayr in September: not **109**

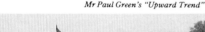

Mr Paul Green's "Upward Trend"

discredited after in Group 3 events at Lyon and Rome: should be suited by 1¾m: acts on any going. *J. L. Dunlop.*

UXONTORIUS 3 b.c. Petorius 117–Regency Gold (Prince Regent (FR) 129) **64** [1988 6d 1989 6f* 7h⁵ 7f] strong, rangy colt: has plenty of scope: game winner of minor event at Goodwood in May: better effort in the summer when creditable fifth in similar event at Brighton: probably stays 7f: acts on hard ground. *R. Hannon.*

V

VAGUE DANCER 3 b.c. Vaigly Great 127–Step You Gaily 71 (King's Company **96** 124) [1988 6f³ 6g* 6g² 1989 6m* 6m³ 7f 6m⁶ 6m⁶ 7m] leggy, rather angular colt: has a powerful, roundish action: won minor event at Thirsk in May: better efforts in listed race at Haydock and £16,300 handicap at York second and fifth outings: tailed off in Jersey Stakes (sweating and edgy) at Royal Ascot and well behind in £8,800 Newmarket handicap on third and final ones: should be suited by 7f: acts on top-of-the-ground. *E. Weymes.*

VAGUE DISCRETION 4 b.g. Vaigly Great 127–Discreet 104 (Jukebox 120) **90** [1988 8s⁵ 1989 7d⁴ 8s 7m 6g⁶ 7g] strong, sturdy gelding: carries condition: moderate walker and mover: quite useful winner at 2 yrs: first outing for year (chipped bone in knee only start in 1988) when fourth to Top Dream in Insulpak Victoria Cup (Handicap) at Ascot in April: well below form in subsequent handicaps: suited by 7f: possibly needs a soft surface nowadays: changed hands 3,100 gns Newmarket Autumn Sales. *R. J. R. Williams.*

VAGUELY GOLD 3 ch.f. Vaigly Great 127–Golden Samantha 88 (Sammy Davis **37** 129) [1988 5m 6m 8g 1989 7s² 8s 8g 6f] workmanlike filly, rather unfurnished: moderate mover: poor plater: favourite, second at Warwick in March, easily best effort: tailed off facing stiff task in ladies event final start: has taken good hold: best form on soft going: often sweating and edgy: sold 1,800 gns Ascot August Sales. *H. P. Rohan.*

VAGUELY PLEASANT (FR) 7 ch.h. Fabulous Dancer (USA) 124–Pleasant **110** Noble (USA) (Vaguely Noble 140) [1988 12s³ 12g 10.5g³ 12m 15s³ 11s* 15.5s³ 12g⁵ 1989 15.5s² 15.5s³ 20m² 12g² 12g⁶ 12d⁴ 15.5g] French horse: very useful performer: placed as 7-y-o in Prix de Barbeville, Prix Vicomtesse Vigier, 3-runner Prix du Cadran and La Coupe, all at Longchamp: beaten under 3 lengths when last in Grand Prix de Saint-Cloud (had stiff task) and in listed event at Saint-Cloud next 2 outings: well beaten in Prix Royal-Oak at Longchamp in autumn: seems to stay 2½m: goes particularly well on soft ground. *P. L. Biancone, France.*

VAGUE MELODY 7 ch.g. Vaigly Great 127–Shangara (Credo 123) [1988 10.2d **66** 12.2d⁴ 10.8s³ 10.8m² 10m⁶ 12f² 11.5g⁵ 12m⁴ 10m 12g⁵ 12.2f⁵ 12.2d² 12m 1989 10.8d* 10.8m] quite attractive, close-coupled gelding: moderate mover: quite modest handicapper: won at Warwick in May: struck into and pulled up lame at same course almost month later: needed testing conditions at around 1m and stayed 1½m: acted on any going: excellent mount for inexperienced rider: dead. *Mrs L. Piggott.*

VAGUE SHOT 6 ch.h. Vaigly Great 127–Cease Fire 112 (Martial 131) [1988 8s* **106** 9g⁵ 8d⁴ 8.5m⁴ 8g⁵ 9d⁶ 10g⁶ 1989 8g⁵ 8d 7.2s 8m² 8f 8g⁴ 8s⁴ 8.5s⁵ 8g] smallish, useful sort: usually looks well: has a quick action: useful performer: best efforts as 6-y-o when fifth to Fact Finder in William Hill Lincoln Handicap at Doncaster, second to Sleepline Fantasy in £10,100 handicap at Ascot and equal-fourth (on seventh outing) in Group 2 Elite Preis at Cologne: ran moderately in Newmarket listed event final outing: stays 9f: not ideally suited by firm going and goes very well with plenty of give: blinkered once: has worn bandages, including on fourth and fifth starts: trained until after third outing by J. White. *R. F. Casey.*

VAIG APPEAL 2 b.c. (May 18) Star Appeal 133–Dervaig 90 (Derring-Do 131) **—** [1989 6g] brother to smart sprinter Vaigly Star and half-brother to several winners, including high-class sprinter Vaigly Great (by Great Nephew) and useful 7f and 1m winner Hello Vaigly (by Hello Gorgeous): dam, won over 5f at 2 yrs: never dangerous and tended to wander in 29-runner maiden at Newmarket in November. *M. R. Stoute.*

VAIGLY BLAZED 5 ch.g. Vaigly Great 127–Monkey Tricks 85 (Saint Crespin **—** III 132) [1988 NR 1989 14.6g 16g 14f 11.7m 11.7m 14m 16f] workmanlike gelding: poor maiden. *C. A. Horgan.*

VAIGLY GREEN 2 ch.g. (May 2) Vaigly Great 127–Crimbourne 83 (Mummy's **45** Pet 125) [1989 5m 5f⁵] leggy, lengthy, rather unfurnished gelding: first foal: dam maiden best at 7f, is daughter of smart 1m to 1½m winner Lucent, daughter of very good sprinter Lucasland: speed 4f in maiden at Bath and seller (favourite) at Wolverhampton in April. *M. McCormack.*

VAIGLY KATE 3 b.f. Vaigly Great 127–Gold Cheb 88 (Chebs Lad 120) [1988 NR 1989 6s 10d 5m 7g] rangy, workmanlike filly: half-sister to 1985 2-y-o 6f winner Jays Special (by Monsanto) and 1981 2-y-o 5f winner Gold Key and winning sprinter Lady Cara (both by Lochnager): dam won three 7f races: plating-class form but gave indications of better, particularly on debut: should have proved best beyond sprint distances: sweating third start: dead. *M. W. Easterby.* —

VAIGLY PERCEPTIVE 3 b.c. Vaigly Great 127–Ash Gayle 49 (Lord Gayle (USA) 124) [1988 6m⁴ 6s³ 7g 7g⁶ 6d³ 1989 10s 7d⁶ 6m² 6m 6m 8.3m 6m 6g 6g²] smallish colt: well below 2-y-o form but easily best efforts in 1989 when second in handicap in May and apprentice seller (blinkered, wandering early then running on well) in November: suited by 6f: best form on a soft surface: sweating badly seventh start: winning claiming hurdler. *B. Stevens.* 52

VAIGLY VISIBLE 4 b.f. Vaigly Great 125–Sea Aura 89 (Roi Soleil 125) [1988 8f⁴ 7f⁶ 8f⁵ 8.2g 1989 7m 8h 7.5m 7f⁴ 7f 5m] lengthy, workmanlike filly: poor maiden: blinkered last 3 outings, racing freely first 2 occasions. *Denys Smith.* —

VAIGRANT WIND 3 ch.f. Vaigly Great 127–Silent Prayer 58 (Queen's Hussar 124) [1988 6g² 6f* 6f³ 7d 6g 7.3m 8g 7d 1989 6m 6m 6f⁴ 7f] workmanlike filly: modest performer as 2-y-o: below form in 1989: should stay beyond 6f: runs freely: blinkered last 2 starts: has joined D. Gandolfo. *R. Hannon.* —

VAIN PRINCE 2 b.c. (May 15) Sandhurst Prince 128–Vain Deb 66 (Gay Fandango (USA) 132) [1989 8.2g 8.2g 10g] rangy colt: second foal: half-brother to modest 3-y-o sprinter Red Rosein (by Red Sunset): dam 1m to 9f winner stayed 1¼m: plating-class form in maidens: probably stays 1¼m. *N. Tinkler.* 52

VAIN SEARCH (USA) 2 gr.f. (Mar 28) Vigors (USA)–Hunt The Thimble (USA) 86 (Turn And Count (USA)) [1989 7g⁶ 10g] $50,000Y: rangy filly: third foal: half-sister to useful Irish sprinter Astraeus (by Star de Naskra): dam placed twice at 6f (at 2 yrs) from 4 starts here and won at up to 1m in USA: sire top-class over middle distances: showed up in first of 2 races in quite useful company at Newmarket at the back-end: should stay at least 1m. *M. A. Jarvis.* 67

VALCENA 2 ch.f. (Apr 15) Glint of Gold 128–Baltimore Belle 95 (Bold Lad (IRE) 133) [1989 6g 7g] 17,000Y: sturdy filly: third foal: sister to twice-raced Kentucky Belle, placed over 1½m and 14.7f: dam winner over 6f (at 2 yrs) to 7.3f, is half-sister to Wollow: little form in large-field autumn maidens at Newmarket. *W. Jarvis.* —

VAL DES BOIS (FR) 3 gr.c. Bellypha 130–Vallee des Fleurs 116 (Captain's Gig (USA)) [1988 7m⁵ 8g³ 9s* 10v⁵ 1989 9.2s* 10m* 8g 9.7m³ 8v³] smart French colt: won Group 3 events at Longchamp for Prix de Guiche in April and Prix La Force in May: creditable third in Prix Dollar (3 lengths behind Creator) at Longchamp and Prix Perth at Saint-Cloud: suited by 1¼m: yet to race on very firm ground, acts on any other. *Mme C. Head, France.* 119

VAL GARDENA 2 b.f. (May 15) Ahonoora 122–Caralia 77 (Caracolero (USA) 131) [1989 7m⁴] IR 12,000Y: leggy, sparely-made filly: turns fore-feet in: fourth foal: half-sister to Irish 9f winner Buttons And Bows (by Northern Treat): dam, best at 2 yrs later in frame over 1½m, is half-sister to Katies and Millfontaine: 9/2 but bit backward and very green, swerved stalls and behind from 2f out in 6-runner minor event at Doncaster in July: sold 3,200 gns Doncaster November Sales. *S. J. Muldoon.* —

VALIANT BOY 3 b.g. Connaught 130–Irish Amber (Amber Rama (USA) 133) [1988 NR 1989 10m⁵ 8.2f³] sparely-made, workmanlike gelding: second reported foal: dam never ran: evens, 7¾ lengths third of 4 to Bold Mac in minor event at Nottingham in June: shaped well in maiden at Ripon: winning selling hurdler for S. Kettlewell. *J. Mackie.* —

VALIANT DASH 3 b.g. Valiyar 129–Dame Ashfield 90 (Grundy 137) [1988 7d⁴ 6m 6g 1989 10f 8.2m⁶ 12m⁶ 10f 12f³ 12m⁶ 13.8g² 16.2m⁵] workmanlike gelding: has a round action: appeared to put up easily best effort as 3-y-o when staying-on second in seller at Catterick: lacks turn of foot, and should stay well: blinkered fifth and sixth starts, visored previous 3: sometimes claimer ridden: sold out of J. Norton's stable 4,000 gns Doncaster June Sales after sixth outing: winning juvenile hurdler. *S. E. Kettlewell.* 41

VALIANT HOPE 2 ch.f. (Apr 21) Valiyar 129–Lucky Fingers 81 (Hotfoot 126) [1989 6g⁵] 1,000F, 9,400Y: workmanlike filly: second foal: half-sister to a listed winner in Spain: dam maiden suited by 1½m: green and slowly away, about 10 — p lengths fifth of 14, running on strongly, in minor event at Windsor in July: moved poorly down: will be much better suited by 7f +: sure to improve. *T. Thomson Jones.*

VALIANT RED 3 ch.c. Blushing Scribe (USA) 107–Corvelle (Reliance II 137) 52 [1988 5m⁴ 6f⁴ 5f⁶ 6s 5d 7g 1989 8g 7h 6f⁵ 7m 6f³ 7m* 7.5f⁵ 7g] good-topped colt: won claimer at Newmarket in July, running on strongly to lead close home: ran moderately in handicaps after: stays 7f: acts on firm ground: visored fourth outing: possibly best on galloping track. *D. J. G. Murray-Smith.*

VALIANT SAINT 4 b.c. Welsh Saint 126–Corvelle (Reliance II 137) [1988 6s⁴ — 6d* 7g 8m 1989 7v 6f a6g a6g] good-bodied colt: quite modest winner early as 3-y-o: lightly raced and little subsequent worthwhile form: best form at 6f with bit of give in the ground: blinkered once at 3 yrs. *D. J. G. Murray-Smith.*

VALIANT VICAR 2 b.g. (Mar 3) Belfort (FR) 89–Shagra (Sallust 134) [1989 67 6m³ 6g⁶ 8.2s³ 7m] 5,000F, 11,000Y: rather sparely-made gelding: brother to 3-y-o Gratclo, winner at 6f (at 2 yrs) and 7f, and half-brother to 2 winners in Norway: dam of no account: quite modest maiden: suited by 1m: acts on top-of-the-ground and soft going. *C. W. Thornton.*

VALIANT WORDS 2 br.c. (Apr 13) Valiyar 129–Wild Words 76 (Galivanter 131) 62 [1989 7g 8f⁵ 8g] leggy colt: half-brother to several winners, including useful 7f to 1m winner Chukaroo (by Kibenka) and useful sprinter Battle Hymn (by Music Boy): dam half-sister to very useful sprinter Sound Barrier: quite modest form, apparently backward, in maidens: off course for over 2 months after debut: may do better. *R. Akehurst.*

VALIKA 4 b.f. Valiyar 129–Double Finesse 97 (Double Jump 131) [1988 8m⁶ 8g² — 10m³ 12g³ 10h⁵ 10f 1989 10f] sparely-made filly: modest maiden at best: below form as 3-y-o after third outing and looked difficult ride final one: 20/1 and in need of race, last of 17 in handicap at Nottingham in June: suited by 1¼m: acted on top-of-the-ground: sold 5,200 gns Newmarket December Sales in foal to Primo Dominie. *W. J. Haggas.*

VALIRA (USA) 2 ch.f. (Feb 27) Nijinsky (CAN) 138–Condessa 121 (Condorcet 82 p (FR)) [1989 7m²] $400,000Y: lengthy, well-made filly: has scope: fourth foal: dam won Yorkshire Oaks: odds on but bit backward, 8 lengths second of 3 to Dovekie in minor event at Ascot in October: should stay 1½m: sure to improve. *B. W. Hills.*

VALLDEMOSA 3 ch.f. Music Boy 124–Astral Suite 82 (On Your Mark 125) 78 [1988 5g² 5g⁴ 5m⁵ 5g* 6g⁵ 5d² 5g² 5d 1989 5f 5f⁴ 5m 5f* 5g 5g⁴ 5m³ 5f 5f⁶ 5g⁵] compact filly: has a quick action: fair performer: won handicap at Warwick in July: ran fairly well in similar events at Pontefract and Catterick last 2 outings: likely to prove best at 5f: acts on firm going and a soft surface: suitable mount for 7-lb claimer. *J. Berry.*

VALLEY OF DANUATA 4 b.g. Taufan (USA) 119–Dane Valley (Simbir 130) — [1988 10m² 13.1f³ 12f 16d⁴ 1989 12f⁶ 12g] leggy, lengthy gelding: fair handicapper at his best: ran poorly at Goodwood and Haydock (took good hold) in 1989: stays 13f: looks ill at ease on firm going. *F. Jordan.*

VALLS D'ANDORRA 3 b.f. Free State 125–Valley Farm 88 (Red God 128§) 75 [1988 6g 8.2s³ 6m 1989 10g* 11m⁶ 12m² 11.7m³ 14f* 15.8g* 15s³] good-topped filly: good mover: modest handicapper: won at Leicester in May, Sandown in July and Catterick in August: edgy, ran fairly well final start: stays 15.8f: acts on top-of-the-ground and soft going: sometimes sweating: suited by firm handling. *P. J. Makin.*

VALOUROUS 2 b.f. (Apr 7) Bold Lad (IRE) 133–Midsummer Madness 66 (Silly — Season 127) [1989 6f] IR 6,800Y, 24,000 2-y-o: half-sister to 5 winners by Warpath, including 3-y-o 9f winner Time On My Hands, 1983 2-y-o 1m winner July and 1½m winners Dangerous Moonlite and Indian Moonshine, and a winner by So Blessed: dam 1½m winner: well beaten in 10-runner maiden at Lingfield in October. *P. Mitchell.*

VAL RECIT (FR) 3 b.c. Recitation (USA) 124–Valdecka (FR) (Val de L'Orne 99 (FR) 130) [1988 8d⁴ 1989 8.2s³ 11f* 12f⁵] big, strong, good sort: made all and ran on well in maiden at Newbury in May: 13/2 and again looking very well, 7¾ lengths fifth of 6 to Cacoethes in moderately-run King Edward VII Stakes at Royal Ascot month later: stays 1½m: acts on firm going: remains in training. *R. W. Armstrong.*

VALTAKI 4 b.g. Valiyar 129–Taqa 85 (Blakeney 126) [1988 8d 7g 8f⁶ 8.5m 8.3m 57 10m⁴ 9s 10g 1989 12.4g⁴ a10g] small, quite attractive gelding: bad mover: fair winner at 2 yrs: 20/1, over 7 lengths fourth of 11, sent clear entering straight, in seller at Newcastle in October: hampered early when well beaten in handicap month later:

should stay 1½m: best effort on a soft surface: winning selling hurdler with J. Baker. *L. J. Codd.*

VA LUTE (FR) 5 b.g. No Lute (FR) 129–Viverba (FR) (Sanctus II 132) [1988 — 15.5m 1989 12g 8.2d 9s] leggy, lightly-made gelding: has a round action: no worthwhile form in varied company on flat: winning selling hurdler. *W. Holden.*

VALVILLE (FR) 3 gr.c. Top Ville 129–Valse Exquise (FR) (Zeddaan 130) [1988 **95** 8s⁴ 8.2d 1989 13.3m 13.3g³ 14g* 14.6g³ 15s² 16m* 16.2d²] lengthy, deep-girthed colt: won maiden at Nottingham in July and £7,400 handicap at Newmarket in October: good head second of 15, keeping on well despite tending to edge left, in Haydock handicap final outing: looks an out-and-out stayer: yet to race on very firm going, acts on any other. *J. L. Dunlop.*

VALYASH 3 b.f. Valiyar 129–Badwell Ash (Morston (FR) 125) [1988 NR 1989 — 8m⁵ 8.2m³ 10f⁴ 10f] workmanlike, good-quartered filly: fifth foal: sister to useful 8.5f and 1¼m winner Validate and half-sister to fairly useful 1m winner New Tick (by Young Generation) and a winner in Scandinavia: dam unraced close relative of Cheshire Oaks winner Hunston: plating-class maiden, form only on debut: always behind in seller final start: should stay 1¼m: sold 6,000 gns Ascot September Sales. *Sir Mark Prescott.*

VANISHED LAND (USA) 3 b.c. Green Dancer (USA) 132–Land Girl (USA) — (Sir Ivor 135) [1988 7d² 7.5f* 8s* 10g⁵ 1989 10m⁴] angular, quite attractive colt: fairly useful winner as 2-y-o: well-beaten last of 4, facing stiff task, to Prince of Dance in listed event at Newmarket in May, only start in 1989: seems to stay 1¼m and act on any going. *H. R. A. Cecil.*

VANISHING SPIRIT 4 b.f. Crofter (USA) 124–Fearless Felon (USA) **63** (Bailjumper (USA)) [1988 6v⁶ 5g³ 6g 6m 6g³ 6m⁵ 6g⁵ 5.8d² 5m 6g 5m³ 6h⁶ 6g 6d⁶ 1989 8m* 10f⁵ 7m* 7h² 8h³ 7m 7g⁴ 7.6f⁶ 7f* 8m 7f 7m⁴ 8f] leggy, sparely-made filly: quite modest performer: won sellers at Brighton (no bid) in May and Leicester (bought in 6,250 gns) in June and apprentice handicap at Folkestone in July: ran moderately in seller at Brighton final outing: suited by 7f or 1m: acts particularly well on top-of-the-ground: tailed off in visor: blinkered final 4 outings in 1988: usually apprentice ridden nowadays: sold 5,400 gns Newmarket Autumn Sales. *C. A. Cyzer.*

VANROY 5 b.g. Formidable (USA) 125–Princess Tavi (Sea Hawk II 131) [1988 **76** 12g⁴ 8g* 11m⁶ 8g* 8g* 7m* 8m 1989 8s 7.6m 7m² 7g² 8.5m⁶ 8f 8f⁶ 8f⁴ 8g a10g a8g* a8g] sturdy gelding: has a rather round action: modest handicapper: 20/1, led last stride when winning at Lingfield in November: bandaged, well beaten at same course 2 weeks later: suited by 7f to 1m: acts on firm going: good mount for apprentice. *J. R. Jenkins.*

VANTIFANTAY 3 b.f. Castle Keep 121–Sule Skerry 78 (Scottish Rifle 127) — [1988 6f⁶ 6f⁶ 6g 8s 7g 1989 7.5d⁵ 8g] smallish, leggy filly: poor maiden: better effort in May sellers on reappearance: bred to stay beyond 1m. *N. Tinkler.*

VARNISH 2 ch.f. (Mar 17) Final Straw 127–Rainbow's End 83 (My Swallow 134) **85** [1989 7g² 7m* 8g⁴] 40,000Y: unfurnished filly: has scope: good walker and mover: eighth foal: sister to fairly useful 1986 2-y-o 5f winner Chasing Moonbeams and half-sister to 3 other winners, including fairly useful stayer Cap del Mond (by Troy): dam 2-y-o 6f winner: won 13-runner maiden at Ayr in August: took keen hold when well beaten in May Hill EBF Stakes at Doncaster following month: bred to stay 1m. *W. Hastings-Bass.*

VASCO (USA) 3 b.c. Nijinsky (CAN) 138–Klaizia (Sing Sing 134) [1988 NR 1989 — 10m⁶ 10f⁴ 8m⁴] 62,000Y: angular, rather sparely-made colt: poor mover: closely related to smart French miler Lypheor (by Lyphard) and half-brother to a minor winner at up to 1m in USA by General Assembly: dam, smart sprinter, is half-sister to good French performers Kebah and L'Ensorceleur, and to the dam of Al Nasr: well beaten in maidens and a minor event in the summer: should stay beyond 1m: bandaged near-fore final outing: sold 7,600 gns Newmarket Autumn Sales. *R. F. Casey.*

VASSAL 4 ro.g. Kalaglow 132–Vresia 78 (Vitiges (FR) 132) [1988 8d 8g⁴ 10.1m **54** 10.1g 1989 10.8d 12m⁴ 14f⁴ 14m⁵ 14f³ 14m 12m 12g] big, workmanlike gelding: moderate mover: plating-class maiden: ran poorly in seller final outing: should stay 2m: tailed off when blinkered sixth start: has often got worked up in preliminaries: sold to join M. Chapman 6,600 gns Newmarket Autumn Sales. *H. Candy.*

VA TOUJOURS 2 b.f. (Feb 25) Alzao (USA) 117–French Princess 94 (Prince **109** Regent (FR) 129) [1989 6g* 7g* 7g³] strong, workmanlike filly: has plenty of scope: seventh foal: half-sister to 11.7f winner King Among Kings (by Dara Monarch), 1½m winner French Flutter (by Beldale Flutter) and French provincial 8.5f and 9.5f winner Kind Guest (by Be My Guest): dam stayed well: put up very useful performance on second outing (successful in Newmarket maiden 6 weeks previously) winning Oh So Sharp Stakes at Newmarket in October in fast time by 7 lengths from Royal Fi Fi: well-backed favourite, third of 12 behind very easy winner Negligent in Bottisham Heath Stud Rockfel Stakes on same course 2 weeks later: will probably stay at least 1¼m: sure to win more races. *H. J. Collingridge.*

VAULT (USA)   3 b.c. Golden Act (USA)–Open Gate (USA) (Dr Fager (USA))   95
[1988 7m² 7m³ 1989 7d² 8f 7g⁴] good-bodied, useful-looking colt: fairly useful maiden: beaten 5 lengths by Great Commotion at Newmarket in April, becoming unbalanced and tending to hang right approaching final 1f: co-favourite, ran creditably in mid-division in Britannia Stakes (Handicap) at Royal Ascot, taking keen hold early: second favourite, below form in all-aged event at Newmarket over 4 months later: should be well suited by 1m or 1¼m: has joined O. Sherwood. *L. M. Cumani.*

VAX LADY   2 ch.f. (Apr 19) Millfontaine 114–Opinebo 82 (Nebbiolo 125) [1989 5d²   91
5m* 5m* 6g² 6g³ 6g] small, rather lightly-made filly: second reported foal: half-sister to 5f winner Sayyaf's Lad (by Sayyaf): dam winning stayer: fairly useful performer: successful in maiden at Edinburgh in June and nursery (beating Madam Tudor in good style by 4 lengths) at Wolverhampton in August: excellent third behind Montendre and Daarik in listed race at York in October: likely to prove best at sprint distances. *J. L. Spearing.*

VELTION   3 b.c. Tyrnavos 129–Lefki 99 (Red God 128§) [1988 6f⁶ 6d⁵ 7s⁵ 1989 8g   76
8d 10g⁴ 9f 10f* 9m² 9m² 8m⁶ 8g] workmanlike colt: modest performer: won claimer at Folkestone in May: good second in handicaps at Wolverhampton and York: probably needs further than 1m, and should stay 1½m: acts on firm going: blinkered last 7 outings, except at Folkestone: made most last 3 starts: consistent: sold 8,800 gns Newmarket Autumn Sales. *Lord John FitzGerald.*

VELVET FALLS (USA)   3 b.f. Diamond Shoal 130–Albany Girl (USA) (Alydar   —
(USA)) [1988 7d³ 7g 8s 9f 1989 8m 11m 15g⁶ 12f 16.2m 9f 8f] smallish, attractive filly: plating-class maiden: little worthwhile form as 3-y-o: pulled hard in ladies handicap fourth start: should stay at least 1m: blinkered third and final outings: sold 1,200 gns Newmarket Autumn Sales. *J. L. Spearing.*

VENCEREMOS   3 ch.c. Longleat (USA) 109–Agreloui 59 (Tower Walk 130)   66
[1988 NR 1989 7g⁶ 8m 8m² 8f³ 8m⁵ 10f³ 9m³ 10.6d] sparely-made colt: second reported living foal: dam, from family of Sing Sing and Burglar, lightly-raced maiden best over 5f: quite modest maiden: stays 1¼m: acts on firm going: sold to join J. McConnochie 15,500 gns Newmarket Autumn Sales. *R. J. R. Williams.*

VENDREDI TREIZE   6 b. or br.g. Lucky Wednesday 124–Angel Row 96   —
(Prince Regent (FR) 129) [1988 7m⁴ 6f² 8f 7g⁵ 7m³ 7f 8s 6v 1989 8v⁶ 8m 7f 7m 6g 7f] tall gelding: moderate mover: no worthwhile form in handicaps (4 of them selling events) in 1989: stays 7f: acts on firm going and a soft surface: sometimes blinkered: sweating third outing. *Ronald Thompson.*

VENT DE MER   3 b.c. Tumble Wind (USA)–Ocean Boulevard (Pitskelly 122)   75
[1988 5m⁵ 6s⁶ 6f⁵ 5m 1989 5s² 5f] strong, lengthy, good-quartered colt: 20/1, showed much improved form when second in handicap at Sandown in April, always prominent and running on well: still carrying plenty of condition, ran poorly in similar event following month: easily best form over 5f on soft ground. *A. P. Ingham.*

VENTO   4 gr.c. Tumble Wind (USA)–Courting (Quorum 126) [1988 5m³ 5m 1989   53
5d⁵ 6m 6f 6h 5f 5m 5g⁶ 5m⁵ 5f⁴ 5g⁶ 5f* 5g 5m³] smallish, close-coupled colt: poor mover: successful in all-aged seller (no bid) at Beverley in September: creditable third of 16 in handicap at Edinburgh following month: form only at 5f: probably acts on any going: blinkered twice: suitable mount for apprentice: sold 4,200 gns Doncaster November Sales. *R. Hollinshead.*

VENTRY   2 b.f. (May 2) Stanford 121§–Lisahunny (Pitskelly 122) [1989 6m] IR   —
2,200Y: fourth foal: half-sister to Irish middle-distance winner Desert Gale (by Taufan): dam won over 5f in Ireland: always behind in 18-runner seller at Ripon in August. *J. S. Wainwright.*

VERBARIUM (USA)   9 br.g. Verbatim (USA)–Havre (Mister Gus) [1988 8s*   53
8g 8f⁶ 1989 8g⁵ 8g 8v² 10s⁴ 10m⁵ 10f* 12h³ 12.3m⁴ 10.8m* 11s] close-coupled, workmanlike gelding: plating-class handicapper: won selling events at Beverley (apprentices, no bid) in June and Warwick (apprentice ridden, well-backed favourite, no bid) in August: probably best at up to 1¼m: acts on any going: genuine. *Mrs J. R. Ramsden.*

VERDANT BOY   6 br.g. Green Dancer (USA) 132–Favorite Prospect (USA) (Mr   84
Prospector (USA)) [1988 NR 1989 8g 6d 6.1f⁴ 6f 6g⁶ 6f 6g* 6m 7g⁶ 6m a8g* a7g*]
lightly-made, quite attractive gelding: moderate walker: one-time useful performer,
only fair at best nowadays: won apprentice handicap at Ripon in September and
claimers at Lingfield (slowly away, easily by 8 lengths) in October and Southwell in
November: effective at 6f and stays 1m: best form on a sound surface: sweating
tenth outing. *D. W. Chapman.*

VERDEUSE (FR)   2 ch.f. (Apr 23) Arctic Tern (USA) 126–Toujours Vert 73   75
(Northfields (USA)) [1989 5m⁵ 7g 7m²] 74,000F, 78,000Y: medium-sized, close-
coupled filly: moderate mover: second foal: sister to Italian 3-y-o 7.5f winner Lady
Sapience: dam, 1m winner later won at 6f and 1m in USA, is half-sister to good Italian
1974 2-y-o Godzilla, dam of Observation Post and Colchis: 14/1 from 25/1, length
second of 17, leading until inside final 1f, to Zoman in maiden at Chepstow in
October, easily best effort: will stay 1¼m. *B. W. Hills.*

VERMONT   2 b.c. (May 20) Montekin 125–Bluemore (Morston 125) [1989 5m 5f*   67
5m² 5g⁶ 6g⁴ 5f⁶] 5,000Y, 4,000 2-y-o: good-topped colt: carries condition: has
scope: moderate walker and mover: half-brother to Irish 7f and 1m winner He's A
Flyer (by Whistling Deer): dam never ran: quite modest performer: made all,
hanging badly left from halfway, in 16-runner maiden auction at Beverley in May:
creditable fourth in nursery at Catterick in August: should stay at least 1m: acts on
firm going. *Ronald Thompson.*

VERRO (USA)   2 ch.c. (Mar 12) Irish River (FR) 131–Royal Rafale (USA)   63
(Reneged) [1989 7m²] sturdy colt: half-brother to several winners worldwide,
including Irish 1¾m winner Fortold (by Forli) and American 5.5f to 8.5f winner
Flama Ardiente (by Crimson Satan), dam of Breeders' Cup Sprint third Mt
Livermore and good French miler Magical Wonder: 5/2, 7 lengths second of 7 to
Royal Verse in maiden at Kempton in June: sold 8,200 gns Newmarket Autumn
Sales. *G. Harwood.*

VERSAILLES ROAD (USA)   6 b.h. Blushing Groom (FR) 131–Lucinda Lea   89
(USA) (Best Turn (USA)) [1988 10v 12f* 12m⁶ 1989 12m⁴ 11.7m⁵ 10m³ 12m² 12.8m*
12m* 12m² 12f 12m* 12.3g⁶ 12m⁴ 10m⁴] strong, angular horse: easy mover: has had
operations for soft palate: fair handicapper: had good season, winning at Ripon,
Leicester (beating My Lamb 1½ lengths in £7,500 event) and Beverley (3-runner
event): ran well most other outings, but long way below his best on final one: suited
by 1½m and top-of-the-ground: has worn blinkers: good mount for inexperienced
rider: often has tongue tied down nowadays: races up with pace. *Mrs L. Piggott.*

VERY ADJACENT   4 b.c. Chukaroo 103–State Romance 67 (Free State 125)   88
[1988 7g 7m⁶ 6m* 6f³ 6m⁴ 6m³ 6f* 7g 6g⁵ 6m⁶ 7g⁶ 1989 5s 5m 6m 5.8h⁵ 6f⁵ 6f⁴ 6f*
6h³] leggy, lengthy colt: has a quick action: backed at long odds, well handled by
Dale Gibson when winning £52,400 William Hill Stewards' Cup (Handicap) at
Goodwood in July by short head from Plain Fact, always prominent, leading over 1f
out and running on well despite tending to drift left: good third, under 7 lb penalty, in
£7,400 handicap at Brighton over week later: suited by 6f: goes particularly well on
top-of-the-ground: visored last 2 starts: has joined G. Cottrell. *G. Lewis.*

VESTIGE   2 ch.c. (Feb 27) Remainder Man 126§–Starchy (Crisp And Even 116)   70
[1989 7.5f 7m 8.2g⁴ 10g] 3,600F: workmanlike colt: brother to modest maiden
stayer Lysways: dam well beaten both outings: 7 lengths fourth of 5 behind Chirone
in minor event at Haydock in September, easily best effort: should stay 1½m. *R.
Hollinshead.*

VESTRIS ABU   3 b.c. Lyphard's Special (USA) 122–Ishtar Abu (St Chad 120) 105
[1988 6d² 6m⁴ 7g² 8g² 8s* 7d³ 7d⁶ 8v 1989 7v* 7v² 7s⁴ 8d² 8m 10m⁵ 11m* 8.5m
9g² 7d⁶ 11g⁵ 12d⁵ 7d] useful Irish colt: won minor events at Leopardstown in March
and Phoenix Park (odds on in 3-runner race) in July: easily beaten 6 lengths by
odds-on Citidancer in Group 3 contest at Leopardstown ninth start: ran moderately
in listed races after: seems to stay 11f: probably best with plenty of give in the
ground. *J. Bolger, Ireland.*

VIA VERITAS   5 ch.m. Vicomte 104–Red Ragusa 62 (Homeric 133) [1988 NR   —
1989 17.6f 15.8m] leggy mare: poor maiden: soundly beaten in handicaps at
Wolverhampton and Catterick in May. *R. Hollinshead.*

VICEROY   2 b.c. (Feb 27) Indian King (USA) 128–Bold Polly 67 (Bold Lad (IRE)   92
133) [1989 5g* 5m* 6f² 5d* 5m⁵] 18,000Y: medium-sized, quite well-made colt:
third foal: half-brother to 7f winner Sir Arnold (by Mummy's Pet) and moderate 1987
2-y-o sprinter Chummy's Great (by Tender King), both later successful in Italy:
dam won twice at 5f: fairly useful performer: successful in maiden at Carlisle in
June, minor event (comfortably by 3 lengths from Judgement Call) at Hamilton in

July and auction race at Haydock in August: creditable fifth of 9 to Old Alliance in listed race at York later in August: stays 6f: wore crossed noseband last 2 outings: often unimpressive in appearance. *W. J. Pearce.*

VICEROY AGAIN 4 ch.g. Krayyan 117–Regal Step 101 (Ribero 126) [1988 10g — 8m 6m 1989 10.1m] angular gelding: of little account: has been visored and blinkered. *W. J. Musson.*

VICEROY EXPRESS 2 ch.f. (Apr 15) Jalmood (USA) 126–Viceroy Princess 65 — (Godswalk (USA) 130) [1989 6m 5f⁵ 5f 6g 7g a7g a7g] strong, compact filly: third foal: half-sister to Irish 3-y-o 7f winner Moments Peace (by Adonijah) and useful 1987 2-y-o Classic Ruler (by Dominion): dam showed form only when winning 7f seller at 2 yrs: little worthwhile in maidens and nurseries. *J. R. Jenkins.*

VICEROY JESTER 4 br.g. Jester 119–Midnight Patrol (Ashmore (FR) 125) **73** [1988 8.5m 6g 8m 6d* 6f 7m 6m 6s³ 6d⁵ 6s 1989 6s² 7v² 7d 7g⁵ 7f 8f 7g 7g] leggy gelding: modest handicapper on his day: below form last 4 outings: should stay 1m: suited by plenty of give in the ground: blinkered when successful at 2 yrs and on first 3 starts in 1988: often sweats: gave trouble at stalls third outing. *R. J. Holder.*

VICEROY MAJOR 6 ch.g. Bay Express 132–Lady Marmalade (Hotfoot 126) — [1988 10.1d⁶ 12f* 12.2d 15.5m⁶ 12s⁴ 1989 12m] good-bodied gelding: winning plater: 20/1, tailed-off last of 20 in amateurs handicap at Salisbury in June: stays 1½m: acts on any going: blinkered twice: has run well for apprentice. *W. G. Turner.*

VICKENDA 4 ch.f. Giacometti 130–Phlox 101 (Floriana 106) [1988 7f 6m 7g 6s² **44** 6d³ 6g 1989 6g 6m 7m² 7f⁵ 7.6h 8.3g³ 8g⁶ 7m* 7m 7g⁵] angular, sparely-made filly: poor mover: poor handicapper: won at Catterick in July: suited by 7f: acts on any going: often visored nowadays: has worn bandages: has run creditably for inexperienced rider: sometimes slowly away. *C. N. Allen.*

VICKI-VICKI VEE 4 ch.f. Busted Fiddle 90–Olymena (Royalty 130) [1988 NR — 1989 10f 6f 10.1m 8f] lightly-made filly: moderate mover: second reported living foal: dam unraced: of little account. *J. M. Bradley.*

VICKSTOWN 7 b.h. Town And Country 124–Empress Victoria (Brave Invader — (USA)) [1988 12s 13v 12g 10.8s⁴ 10m⁵ 10m 12m⁴ 12g⁶ 12d⁵ 11m 12d 1989 13.8d] workmanlike horse: poor handicapper: best form at 1½m: suited by a sound surface: has won for apprentice: sometimes wears a tongue strap. *B. C. Morgan.*

VICO EQUENSE 4 gr.f. Absalom 128–Miss Diaward 82 (Supreme Sovereign — 119) [1988 10m 12g 12.3g 12d 10f⁴ 10s 1989 16g] lengthy filly: poor plater: best effort when visored on firm going. *S. G. Payne.*

VICTORIA MILL 3 b.f. Free State 125–Island Mill 79 (Mill Reef (USA) 141) **59** [1988 5.8g⁴ 6d 1989 8m 8f⁵ 10h² 10f² 10f⁶ 10f³ 12g⁶ 10g³ a10g] smallish, sparely-made filly: quite modest maiden: placed in handicaps at Brighton, Lingfield, Folkestone and Goodwood: suited by 1¼m: acts on hard ground: has run well for 5-lb claimer. *I. A. Balding.*

VICTORIA PRINCESS 2 b.f. (Mar 11) King of Spain 121–Renira 60 (Relkino — p 131) [1989 6g 6g] 4,400Y: compact, workmanlike filly: poor mover: first foal: poor maiden: poor form in maidens at Folkestone and Leicester (eased after being hampered) in the autumn: probably capable of better. *D. R. C. Elsworth.*

VICTORIOUS KING 3 b.g. Petorius 117–Petit Secret 64 (Petingo 135) [1988 — NR 1989 10g 8g 12m 7m] 8,400Y: quite attractive gelding: half-brother to 4 winners, including rair 6f to 1¼m winner Terminator (by Tachypous) and useful 1982 2-y-o 5f and 6f winner Secret Miracle (by Abwah): dam placed over 1m: well beaten in maiden, claimers and a seller: sold to join M. Pipe 1,600 gns Newmarket July Sales. *P. F. I. Cole.*

VICTORY LANE 3 b.g. Valiyar 129–Open Country (Town And Country 124) — [1988 7g⁶ 8s 7s⁵ 1989 10.1m 8g 12m] medium-sized gelding: worthwhile form only on debut: edgy, took strong hold in handicap final outing: should stay 1m: has joined P. Jones: one to be wary of. *R. Hannon.*

VICTORY PARADE (USA) 3 b.f. Peterhof (USA) 115–Wave In Glory (USA) — (Hoist The Flag (USA)) [1988 NR 1989 7s⁶ 8m] leggy filly: moderate mover: third foal: half-sister to smart 6f to 1¼m winner Conquering Hero (by Storm Bird): dam won twice at up to 7f at 2 yrs: well beaten in maidens at Folkestone and Bath in the spring. *B. W. Hills.*

VICTORY PIPER (USA) 2 ch.c. (Mar 21) Nijinsky (CAN) 138–Arisen (USA) **100** p (Mr Prospector (USA)) [1989 7g⁴ 8s*] $325,000F, $285,000Y: fifth named foal: brother to modest 1¾m winner Badeel and half-brother to a modest 6f winner by Seattle Slew: dam, twice a stakes winner at around 1m, is half-sister to smart middle-distance performer Pair of Deuces: second favourite, won 11-runner Juddmonte EBF Beresford Stakes at the Curragh in October by ¾ length, staying on strongly, from Armanesco: will stay 1½m: sure to improve further. *B. W. Hills.*

VICTORY TORCH (CAN) 4 b.g. Majestic Light (USA)–Victory Songster **44** (USA) (Stratus 122) [1988 10g 11.7f 10m⁴ 12f⁶ 12.2d² 12.2g³ 14.5g⁵ 1989 13.8d 11g³ 12m 13f⁶ 12m 8g² 9f⁵ 9g 12g 9s] close-coupled gelding: has been hobdayed: moderate mover: modest maiden as 3-y-o when trained by J. Dunlop: well below his best in 1989, including in selling company: virtually pulled up final 3f eighth outing: fell next time, and tailed off final start: stays 1½m: best on an easy surface, but possibly unsuited by very soft going. *D. W. Chapman.*

VICTORY WIND 4 ch.g. Asdic 94–Cool Wind 64 (Windjammer (USA)) [1988 5d —
5.8f 7d³ 5d⁵ 9g 7m⁶ 1989 8f 8f 12.5f] angular, workmanlike gelding: plater: tailed off in handicaps last 2 outings: suited by 7f: acts on soft going: sweating final start. *G. Price.*

VIEW FROM ABOVE 3 b.f. Dara Monarch 128–Organdy 84 (Blakeney 126) **91**
[1988 6m 1989 7m* 7f² 8m³] strong filly: odds on, won maiden at Kempton in July, battling on well: ran well after in minor event (odds on) at Folkestone and handicap at Kempton: stays 1m: has raced only on top-of-the-ground. *G. Harwood.*

VIGANO (USA) 3 ch.c. Lyphard (USA) 132–Pasadoble (USA) (Prove Out —
(USA)) [1988 NR 1989 8m 8m 8m] $375,000Y: medium-sized colt: third foal: closely related to outstanding miler Miesque (by Nureyev): dam very useful French miler out of half-sister to top-class 1½m filly Comtesse de Loir: easily best effort in maidens at Newbury second start: drifted left in apprentice race on final one: sold to join K. Bailey 10,000 gns Newmarket Autumn Sales. *H. R. A. Cecil.*

VIKING ROCKET 5 ch.m. Viking (USA)–Calcine 75 (Roan Rocket 128) [1988 —
NR 1989 16g³] half-sister to several minor winners: dam placed twice over 6f at 2 yrs: led until 3f out when 13 lengths third to easy winner Dhakrah in poorly-contested minor event at Carlisle in October: fair winning hurdler. *C. Parker.*

VIKING VENTURE 4 ch.c. Viking (USA)–Mattira (FR) (Rheffic (FR) 129) —
[1988 8d 8f² 8g 10.2g* 10.2m³ 10m 10g³ 10g⁴ 10.1m⁶ 10m 1989 12m 9f 12f] small, lengthy, workmanlike colt: quite modest winner as 3-y-o: never dangerous in handicaps in 1989: off course 4½ months before final outing: races keenly, but stays 1¼m: possibly unsuited by soft going, acts on any other: sweating and on toes second outing. *D. A. Wilson.*

VILANDRADO 3 b.c. Vayrann 133–Vieille Villa (FR) (Kashmir II 125) [1988 **103**
7m* 7.5g⁵ 8d 1989 8s⁵ 9d 10g 12f⁶ 12m⁵] rather leggy, fair sort: moderate walker and mover: has a round action: fairly useful performer: below form at 3 yrs prior to finishing 4¼ lengths fifth of 18, making most, to Prorutori in Derby Italiano at Rome: subsequently remained in Italy and made all in listed 1¼m event at Naples in June: gives impression may prove best at short of 1½m: best form on a sound surface. *P. A. Kelleway.*

VILANIKA (FR) 3 b.f. Top Ville 129–Kamanika (FR) (Amber Rama (USA) 133) **79**
[1988 7g⁴ 7g 7.3s 1989 8v² 9g⁵ 11.5m 8m⁴ 7m² 9m⁴ 7.6m² 8m² 8g] tall, leggy filly: fair maiden: second in handicaps at Doncaster, Lingfield (edgy and sweating) and Ascot (£11,700 event, beaten short head), best efforts: always behind in listed race final start: stays 1m (pulled hard and tailed off over 11.5f): yet to race on very firm going, acts on any other: swished tail fourth start. *C. E. Brittain.*

VILLA BIANCA 3 b.f. Mummy's Game 120–Belinda (Ragusa 137) [1988 6d 7m **61**
6d 1989 6s³ 8.2s 9m 7f 9m⁵ 8m 8f 9s*] sparely-made, angular filly: poor walker, turns fore-feet in: moderate mover: 20/1, easily best effort after reappearance when winning handicap at Hamilton in November by 10 lengths: stays 9f: needs the mud: blinkered fifth and sixth (edgy) outings: often ridden by 7-lb claimer. *M. J. Ryan.*

VILLAGE DANCER 2 b.g. (Mar 22) Creetown 123–Autumn Ballet (Averof —
123) [1989 5m⁶] first reported foal: dam winning hurdler: soundly-beaten sixth of 7 in minor event at Windsor in June. *A. W. Denson.*

VILLEROI 2 ch.c. (Feb 15) Kris 135–Vilikaia (USA) 125 (Nureyev (USA) 131) **86 p**
[1989 6g 5g*] angular colt: first foal: dam, effective from 5f (best sprinter in France) to 1m, is half-sister to good filly at up to 1m Maximova and daughter of half-sister to 2000 Guineas winner Nonoalco and very smart Stradavinsky: 9/1, won 23-runner maiden at Redcar in October by 2½ lengths from Katzakeena, leading 2f out: should stay at least 1m: probably useful 3-y-o in making, and looks sure to win more races. *G. Harwood.*

VILVEAER 3 br.f. Tachypous 128–Sera Sera 88 (Hill Clown (USA)) [1988 5m 5f — 6g 1989 8g 12m⁶ 10f] compact filly: no sign of ability: blinkered and very slowly away in seller final start. *S. Woodman.*

VINEGAR BOB 2 b.g. (May 19) Blushing Scribe (USA) 107–Gentle Gypsy 94 — (Junius (USA) 124) [1989 5s] workmanlike gelding: has scope: first foal: dam 2-y-o 5f winner seemed not to train on: slowly away and always behind in 13-runner maiden at Thirsk (unruly paddock) in April. *M. W. Easterby.*

VINSTAN 3 gr.c. Rabdan 129–Pretty Fast 52 (Firestreak 125) [1988 NR 1989 8f⁵ 85 10.2m³] big, lengthy colt: half-brother to poor animals by Royal Palace and Royalty: dam won over 1¼m and also over hurdles: bit backward and ridden by 7-lb claimer, showed promise both starts, particularly when staying-on third to Ile de Nisky in minor event at Doncaster in May: should be suited by 1½m. *Denys Smith.*

VINTAGE 4 b.g. Noalcoholic (FR) 128–Good To Follow 82 (Wollow 132) [1988 8g 89 10g* 10m⁴ 11d 10.1m 1989 10s 10f³ 12m² 10m² 10f* 11.7g* 11.7m* 12m* 11.7d⁴ 12f²] strong, lengthy gelding: fairly useful handicapper: had excellent season, winning at Pontefract, Windsor (twice) and Leicester: favourite, in frame, running well, at Windsor and Salisbury last 2 outings: better suited by 1½m than 1¼m: acts on firm going and a soft surface: wears a crossed noseband: apprentice ridden first 3 starts: sometimes sweats and gets on toes: usually held up: consistent. *Major W. R. Hern.*

VINTAGE PORT (USA) 7 b.g. Blood Royal (USA) 129–Port Au Pass (USA) 62 (Pass (USA)) [1988 NR 1989 12f a14g² a16g² a14g²] leggy gelding: quite modest performer: stays 2m: acts on firm going. *R. Akehurst.*

VINTAGE TYPE 2 b.g. (Feb 10) Import 127–Marock Morley 59 (Most Secret 65 119) [1989 5m² 5m² 5m³] 5,800Y: workmanlike gelding: has scope: fifth foal: half-brother to 1982 2-y-o 5f winner Pip'em (by Jimmy Reppin) and 9f winner Absurd (by Absalom): dam won over 5f at 5 yrs: quite modest maiden: takes a keen hold: has worn a crossed noseband. *J. W. Watts.*

VINTON VA 4 b.f. Crofter (USA) 124–Bold Flirt (USA) (Bold Ruler) [1988 8.2v 56 8g⁵ 7.5f⁶ 12f⁶ 10g 10d³ 8g³ 8g 9s* 9d 9g 10s 10g⁴ 9g 1989 10s 10d 9g⁶ 10.6d 12d 9g* 8s] rather leggy, close-coupled filly: 16/1 and apprentice ridden, easily best effort as 4-y-o when winning 18-runner handicap at Hamilton in September: faced stiff task final outing: stays 1¼m: suited by give in the ground: sweating third start: has given trouble at stalls (withdrawn once): sold to join R. Bennett 4,600 gns Doncaster September Sales: inconsistent. *Capt. J. Wilson.*

VIRGIN GORDA 2 b.f. (Feb 25) Law Society (USA) 130–Betsy Bay (FR) 107 67 p (Bellypha 130) [1989 8g³ 7g] 11,000Y: second foal: dam, 6f to 7.3f winner at 2 yrs, stayed 1m: beaten at least 12 lengths in minor event at Sandown in September and maiden at Newmarket in November: likely to do better. *M. A. Jarvis.*

VIRGINIA'S BAY 3 b.g. Uncle Pokey 116–Carnation 64 (Runnymede 123) [1988 — 6f⁴ 6f⁴ 6m* 6f³ 7m⁴ 1989 7s 7g 9f⁴ 8f⁵ 7f a12g] lengthy, useful-looking gelding: quite modest winner as 2-y-o: generally below form in handicaps in 1989: stays 7f: tends to carry head high: sometimes blinkered: once visored: winning hurdler. *Miss B. Sanders.*

VIRKON 2 ch.c. (Mar 12) King Persian 107–Beyond The Rainbow (Royal Palace 53 131) [1989 5.3g⁶ 5f³ 5m⁴ 5f² 5.1m³ 7f² 7m 6m] IR 1,500F, IR 2,800Y: leggy, sparely-made colt: moderate walker: sixth foal: half-brother to 3-y-o Heemee (by On Your Mark), fair 5f winner at 2 yrs, and winning hurdler Hobournes (by Stanford): dam unraced: fair plater: best form at 5f: trained first 7 outings by M. Tompkins. *Mrs N. Macauley.*

VISAGE 2 b.f. (Apr 22) Vision (USA)–Be Tuneful 130 (Be Friendly 130) [1989 7m 75 p 8g³] 19,000Y: big, strong, lengthy filly: has scope: fifth foal: closely related to Italian 3-y-o Yellow King (by Kings Lake), successful from 1m to 1¼m, including at 2 yrs, and half-sister to 11.7f winner Sexton (by Beldale Flutter) and 13.8f winner Blakey Bank (by Blakeney): dam top class at up to 7f: still in need of race, over 3 lengths third of 17, keeping on strongly despite flashing tail, to Lover's Moon in maiden at Leicester in November: should improve further. *D. W. P. Arbuthnot.*

VISION OF INDIA 2 b.f. (Feb 25) Vision (USA)–Flying Bid 71 (Auction Ring 67 p (USA) 123) [1989 7f⁴] IR 160,000Y: workmanlike filly: fifth foal: half-sister to temperamental 3-y-o Soneeto (by Teenoso) and 3 winners, including useful 1987 Irish 2-y-o 5f and 6f winner Flutter Away (by Lomond) and Rawah (by Northern Baby), successful over 1½m: dam, sister to Prix Robert Papin winner Maelstrom Lake, won over 1¼m in Ireland: sire, brother to Caerleon, won Grade 1 1½m Secretariat Stakes: weak 8/1, 4½ lengths fourth of 8, unable to quicken, to Star of The Future in maiden at Leicester in October: should improve. *P. T. Walwyn.*

VISION OF WONDER   5 b.g. Tyrnavos 129–Valeur (Val de Loir 133) [1988   38
12f⁶ 15.5f⁶ 14.8m⁵ 14m⁴ 16g³ 14.8s² 14.5g 15.5g 1989 16m 17.1f* 14.8f⁴] angular
gelding: poor handicapper: apprentice ridden, returned to form when winning
uncompetitive event at Bath in July: favourite, moderate fourth of 6 at Warwick 10
days later: suited by a test of stamina: acts on any going: didn't find great deal sixth
start at 4 yrs. *J. S. King.*

VISION'S DANCE   3 b.c. Vision (USA)–Maiden's Dance 65 (Hotfoot 126) [1988   —
6m 1989 6f 7h] rather leggy, good-topped colt: no sign of ability in minor events: sold
800 gns Newmarket July Sales. *G. Lewis.*

VISON GRIS   4 gr.g. Lord Gayle (USA) 124–Roof (Thatch (USA) 136) [1988 8d²   —
8f 9g⁵ 12m 8d² 10.8s² 10.2f4 10g⁵ 1989 10s] sparely-made colt: quite modest maiden
as 3-y-o when trained by B. Hills: fit from hurdling, always behind in handicap at
Leicester in April: stays 10.8f: acts on any going. *D. J. Wintle.*

VISUAL STAR   3 b.c. Vision (USA)–Eternal Tam (USA) (Tentam (USA)) [1988   54
8s 8g 8f 1989 8.5f4 10f 11m³ 10m³ 10g 10m⁶ 10m 8.2f⁵ 8.2g 8s a8g² 8g] rather leggy
colt: plating-class maiden: probably best at around 1m: acts on firm going, probably
unsuited by soft: blinkered seventh (pulled hard) and last 2 outings: sold 7,600 gns
Doncaster November Sales. *M. Brittain.*

VITAL CLUE (USA)   2 b.c. (May 23) Alleged (USA) 138–Where You Lead   — P
(USA) (Raise A Native) [1989 8.2g] 52,000Y: lengthy colt: has scope: half-brother
to 3 winners, including Rainbow Quest's dam I Will Follow (by Herbager) and
Warning's dam Slightly Dangerous (by Roberto), runner-up in Oaks: dam, Musidora
Stakes winner and Oaks runner-up, is daughter of Oaks winner Noblesse: 20/1 and
very green, over 13 lengths eighth of 20, eased noticeably when beaten approaching
final furlong, to Elmuraqash in minor event at Nottingham in October: looked weak:
sort to do considerably better in time. *J. L. Dunlop.*

VITALITY   3 b.f. Young Generation 129–Blaze of Glory 92 (Queen's Hussar 124)   98
[1988 6g* 1989 8d⁵ 10m⁵ 10g⁵ 9m 8g³ 9g⁵] big, rangy filly: keen walker: has a good,
easy action: fairly useful performer: best efforts in listed event (staying on strongly
from rear) at Ascot and £15,400 handicap (led over 7f) at Newmarket last 2 starts:
stays 9f: acts on top-of-the-ground and a soft surface: sweating and bit edgy third
start: races keenly. *I. A. Balding.*

VITE VITE   3 ch.g. Kind of Hush 118–Swiftacre (Bay Express 132) [1988 7m 7s⁶   74
1989 7d 7s³ 8f4 7f 7m* 7m⁵ 8.5g³ 8f³ a10g* a8g⁵] strong, workmanlike gelding:
modest handicapper: won at Salisbury in June and Lingfield in November: will be
suited by return to 1¼m: acts on firm ground: sweating, edgy and hung under
pressure when below form sixth start. *J. Sutcliffe.*

VIVA ZAPATA (USA)   3 ch.f. Affirmed (USA)–Viva Aviva (USA) (Secretariat 116
(USA) [1988 6.5d² 7d* 1989 7v4 6.5s² 5m³ 5g*] $135,000Y: fourth foal: half-sister
to 3 minor winners in USA: dam, lightly-raced winner at around 6f in USA, is
daughter of Grade 3 6f to 7f winner Viva La Vivi: successful in maiden at Deauville
as 2-y-o and in Group 2 Prix du Gros Chene, narrowly from Holst and Cricket Ball,
at Chantilly in June: best other effort about 2 lengths third to Holst in Prix de
Saint-Georges at Longchamp: appeared suited by sprint distances and an easy
surface: blinkered at Chantilly: has been retired. *J. E. Pease, France.*

VIVIENDA   4 br.f. Known Fact (USA) 135–Fiesta Fun 105 (Welsh Pageant 132)   71
[1988 8s³ 8.5d4 7g 7d 8.5m³ 9g 7.6d 6s 6m 1989 5g 5m4 6m] smallish filly: moderate
mover, with quick action: modest performer: ridden by 7-lb claimer, tended to carry
head high in handicaps at Newbury on first 2 starts: stays 8.5f: acts on top-
of-the-ground and soft going: gave trouble at stalls and withdrawn once at 3 yrs:
inconsistent. *P. Arbuthnot.*

VOGOS ANGEL   2 b.f. (May 7) Song 132–Lovage (Linacre 133) [1989 7f³ 7f4   54
8g⁵] 10,000Y: sister to fairly useful 7f (at 2 yrs) and 1¼m winner Melody Maker,
closely related to speedy filly Chain Lady (by Manacle) and half-sister to 3 other
winners here and abroad: dam of little account: plating-class form in maidens: stays
1m. *Sir Mark Prescott.*

VOILA TOUT   3 b.c. Glint of Gold 128–Another Way 68 (Wolverlife 115) [1988 7m   —
7m⁶ 8g 1989 7s 7d 10g] good-quartered, useful-looking colt: has a quick action: quite
modest maiden in 1988: well beaten as 3-y-o, in minor event at Baden-Baden in May
final outing: gives impression will stay well. *M. J. Ryan.*

VOLCANOES SPARK   3 ch.c. Touching Wood (USA) 127–Red Spider 78 (Red   83 §
God 128§) [1988 NR 1989 10g* 9.2m² 12m³ 10g] angular colt: half-brother to 1½m
winner Blushing Spy (by Great Nephew) and very useful 1m to 1½m winner Abu
Kadra (by Blakeney), later an ungenuine winning hurdler/chaser: dam won over 1m:

won claimer at Yarmouth in August, always front rank: looked very hard ride, wandering and reluctant under pressure, when placed in similar events at Goodwood and Thirsk: ran poorly final start: may well stay beyond 1½m: sold 9,000 gns Newmarket Autumn Sales: very much one to be wary of. *B. Hanbury.*

VOLTAGE   4 b.g. Electric 126–Clouded Vision 74 (So Blessed 130) [1988 11g 10g   — 12m* 13.8f² 12m 1989 12d 12d 12m 14.8m] rangy, angular gelding: modest winner as 3-y-o when trained by R. Sheather: well below form in first half of 1989: barely stayed 1¾m: acted on firm going and possibly unsuited by soft surface: taken down early third outing: went well forcing pace: dead. *F. Jordan.*

VOLTZ   3 b.g. Electric 126–Follow Me Follow 92 (Wollow 132) [1988 NR 1989 8.2s   — 8g] 1,800Y: sparely-made gelding: second foal: closely related to modest 4-y-o maiden Mountain Shadow (by Tyrnavos): dam 5f winner at 2 yrs, is from family of Honeyblest: well behind in claimers in the spring. *R. Hannon.*

VOTE IN FAVOUR   2 b.f. (Apr 1) General Assembly (USA)–Favoridge (USA)   **71 p** 122 (Riva Ridge (USA)) [1989 6g²] leggy, rather shallow-girthed filly: third foal: half-sister to 3-y-o Abberton (by Ile de Bourbon) and a winner in Holland: dam high-class sprinting 2-y-o later stayed 1m, is from excellent family: 9/2, 2½ lengths second of 22 to Lip Sing in maiden at Leicester in November, headway halfway (after slow start) but unable to quicken approaching final 1f: should improve, and win a race. *G. Wragg.*

VOUCHSAFE   7 b.h. Bustino 136–Gracious Consent 89 (Prince Regent (FR)   **86** 129) [1988 12g² 12g⁵ 12m 12f* 12g³ 1989 12m³] well-made, attractive horse: fair handicapper: won Bessborough Stakes (Handicap) at Royal Ascot as 6-y-o: not seen out again in 1988 after following month: carrying plenty of condition, good third, not having clear run, to Versailles Road in £7,500 event at Leicester in June: stayed 1½m: acted on any going: retired to Oxstalls Farm Stud, Stratford-on-Avon, fee £650 (Oct 1st). *Major W. R. Hern.*

VUCHTERBACHER   3 b.c. Longleat (USA) 109–Queensbury Star 76 (Wishing   — Star 117) [1988 6m 7g 1989 10g 7.5g 8g⁶ 7m 7g] leggy, close-coupled colt: has a round action: poor maiden: visored, tailed off in seller final outing: may prove best over sprint distances: bandaged third and fourth starts. *C. Spares.*

VULCANIST   2 ch.g. (May 11) Posse (USA) 130–Neptune's Treasure 65 (Gulf   **55** Pearl 117) [1989 5s 6m 6m⁵ 5f² 6f⁶ 5f² 5m³] 2,000Y: leggy, unfurnished gelding: has a roundish action: sixth foal: half-brother to quite modest 1½m winner Hidden Planet (by Star Appeal): dam best at 1¼m: plating-class maiden: best form at 5f: often hangs: has been awkward in preliminaries: blinkered fifth and final outings. *M. W. Easterby.*

W

WAAFI   7 b.g. Wolver Hollow 126–Geraldville (Lord Gayle (USA) 124) [1988 14g⁴   **42** 14f² 15.5g⁴ 14f 18g 1989 14f 16f⁴ 15.3f⁴ 12f⁵ 14m⁵] lengthy gelding: good walker and mover: has had soft palate operation: poor handicapper: barely stays 2m: acts on firm going and soft surface: has sweated: suitable mount for inexperienced rider: winning hurdler. *K. C. Bailey.*

WABENZI   3 b.f. Niniski (USA) 125–Winterlude (Wollow 132) [1988 NR 1989   — 10.2h⁶] 7,000Y: third living foal: half-sister to a winner in Norway by Rusticaro: dam twice-raced half-sister to smart stayer Hazy Idea: well-beaten sixth of 7 in maiden at Bath in June: sold 800 gns Newmarket December Sales. *Mrs L. Piggott.*

WABIL (USA)   4 b.c. Far North (CAN) 120–Kushka (USA) (First Landing) [1988   **105** 7g 7g³ 8g* 9d* 10.2g² 10d² 10.2g² 1989 12d 8m⁴ 10m* 10.5m] leggy, angular colt: moderate walker: useful performer: odds on, made most, beating Polemos by short head, in 6-runner private sweepstakes at Ascot in September: favourite, ran moderately in handicap at York following month: stays 1¼m: yet to race on extremes of going: off course 5 months after reappearance: suited by forcing tactics: sold 30,000 gns Newmarket Autumn Sales: game. *R. W. Armstrong.*

WACE (USA)   2 b.c. (Apr 24) Nijinsky (CAN) 138–La Mesa (USA) (Round Table)   **69 p** [1989 8f⁴] $1,100,000Y: rangy colt: half-brother to 6 winners in North America, notably top 1984 American 2-y-o filly Outstandingly (by Exclusive Native): dam placed in USA at 2 yrs: weak 5/2 and very green, under 11 lengths fourth of 10, unable to quicken 2f out and eased inside last, to Missionary Ridge in maiden at Leicester in October: showed a quick action: will be suited by 1¼m+: sure to improve. *M. R. Stoute.*

WADOOD (USA) 2 b.c. (Feb 14) Danzig (USA)–Foreign Missile (USA) **97** (Damascus (USA)) [1989 6f* 6f² 6g³] $1,300,000Y: leggy, good-topped, attractive colt: has plenty of scope: moderate mover, with a rather round action: half-brother to useful 1982 Irish 2-y-o 7f winner Heron Bay (by Alleged) and several other winners, including prolific stakes winner Squan Song (by Exceller): dam 7f winner from one of America's finest families: placed behind Rock City in Coventry Stakes at Royal Ascot and Anglia Television July Stakes (gave impression all was not well, and afterwards looked very stiff) at Newmarket: had finished lame when winning maiden at York on debut: will be suited by 7f. *M. R. Stoute.*

WAGON LOAD 4 ch.g. Bustino 136–Noble Girl (Be Friendly 130) [1988 7v⁶ 10s — 12f⁶ 14g⁵ 12m 14d⁶ 9g⁵ 12d⁴ 14s⁵ 14s 12g⁶ 12v* 1989 8m 10.1m 8m] compact gelding: won listed race at Leopardstown as 2-y-o: not so good since, and well behind in varied events in 1989: stays 1¾m: probably acts on any going: blinkered twice. *J. Ffitch-Heyes.*

WAJNA (USA) 2 b.f. (Feb 24) Nureyev (USA) 131–Wind Spirit (USA) (Round **108** Table) [1989 7g* 8g⁶] $575,000Y: half-sister to modest maiden Alleged Spirit (by Alleged) and several winners, notably smart turf winner at up to 1½m Moon Spirit (by Hatchet Man): dam won 3 minor sprints: odds on, made all in 8-runner maiden at Yarmouth in July, beating Varnish by a length: excellent sixth of 15, headed 1f out and beaten around 3 lengths, to Salsabil in Ciga Prix Marcel Boussac at Longchamp over 2½ months later: stays 1m. *H. R. A. Cecil.*

WAKAYI 3 br.f. Persian Bold 123–Songs Jest (Song 132) [1988 5d⁵ 5g* 5f* 5f⁴ 6d **76** 1989 6s⁶ 6s⁴ 5f 5d 5g] strong, sprint type: fair winner as 2-y-o: not entirely discredited in listed event at Leopardstown on reappearance: well beaten in handicaps at Goodwood (£12,800 event), Phoenix Park and the Curragh last 3 starts: best form at 5f: possibly required sound surface: trained until after third outing by P. Walwyn: visits Cadeaux Genereux. *K. Prendergast, Ireland.*

WAKE UP 2 ch.c. (Feb 11) Night Shift (USA)–Astonishing (Jolly Good 122) [1989 **76** 5g³ 5f* 6m³ 6h 7m⁵ 8m 7g] sturdy colt: has a long stride: second foal: dam poor half-sister to very smart stayer Mr Bigmore: modest performer: won maiden at Wolverhampton in May: mixed form afterwards, best effort in Newmarket nursery fifth start: should stay 1m: sent to J. Eustace. *W. Jarvis.*

WAKI GOLD (USA) 2 ch.c. (Feb 13) Miswaki (USA) 124–Sainte Croix (USA) **91** (Nijinsky (CAN) 138) [1989 6f² 6g 8m² 7g] IR 40,000Y: big, rangy colt: has plenty of

EBF Cotman Maiden Fillies Stakes, Yarmouth—Wajna, pictured beating Varnish,
is yet another very useful two-year-old to make its debut on this course

scope: first foal: dam, French maiden, is sister to smart Irish middle-distance stayer Empire Glory and half-sister to Irish 1000 Guineas winner Gaily and high-class American 6f to 9f winner King's Bishop: showed improved form when beaten a neck by Tanfith in £7,100 event at Newbury, keeping on well (despite carrying head high) having taken good hold: well beaten in Cartier Million at Phoenix Park final start: will stay at least 1¼m. *P. A. Kelleway.*

WAKI RAINBOW (USA) 3 ch.f. Miswaki (USA) 124–Seek A Rainbow (USA) 82 (Bolero) [1988 5d* 6f² 5m* 5f⁵ 5f⁵ 1989 5m 5g 5m 7f⁵ 5g⁶ 6f 5g 5g] sturdy filly: good walker: fairly useful as 2-y-o: fifth in handicap at Lingfield, only form (faced stiff tasks previously) in 1989: best form at 5f: blinkered final start: underwent operation on near-fore after final start at 2 yrs: sometimes sweating at 3 yrs: sold 31,000 gns Newmarket December Sales. *P. A. Kelleway.*

WALKERN WITCH 2 b.f. (Mar 20) Dunbeath (USA) 127–Emblazon 91 (Wolver 72 Hollow 126) [1989 6m⁵ 7m 7m 6g* 6g 8s 7d³ a8g] 7,200Y: strong, workmanlike filly: carries condition: fifth foal: half-sister to 3-y-o Broderie Anglaise (by Night Shift) and 3 winners here and abroad, including modest 6f and 1m winner Taranga (by Music Boy): dam, daughter of good staying 2-y-o Slip Stitch, won at up to 1½m: 50/1, won September maiden at Yarmouth by ½ length, making all: over 2 lengths third of 11 to Himmah in minor event at Thirsk, only other form: stays 7f: sweating third start: bandaged behind final outing. *D. T. Thom.*

WALKERWAY BOY 2 b.c. (Apr 19) Muscatite 122–Hadala (Le Levanstell 122) 60 [1989 7m⁵ 7g 7h⁴ 8g⁶ 8f] IR 6,800F, 8,400Y: workmanlike, dipped-backed colt: moderate mover: half-brother to 2-y-o winner in Norway and winning French hurdler: dam, daughter of Cheveley Park winner Opaline II, winner at 11.5f in France: plating-class maiden: easily best effort third outing: should stay at least 1¼m: blinkered final start. *A. Bailey.*

WALKING SAINT 2 b.f. (May 3) Godswalk (USA) 130–Saintly Tune (Welsh 71 Saint 126) [1989 6g 7g* 7m² 7g] sparely-made, angular filly: third foal: half-sister to poor maiden Donna Immobile (by Don): dam won at up to 1¾m on flat and up to 2½m over hurdles at 4 yrs in Ireland: won 15-runner seller (bought in 22,500 gns) at Newmarket in July in good style by 4 lengths: demoted for hampering runner-up after passing post first, head in front of Mogul Prince, in 12-runner nursery on same track under 2 weeks later: off course for over 3 months afterwards: will stay at least 1m. *R. Hannon.*

WALK IN THE WOODS 2 b.f. (Apr 22) Elegant Air 119–Red Roses (FR) (Roi 40 Dagobert 128) [1989 5.3g⁵ 5d 5g 6m 6h⁵ 5.3h 6g] 2,700Y: good-bodied filly: fourth foal: half-sister to 3 winners abroad: dam won at up to 6f in France: quite modest plater: form only on debut: tends to flash tail. *C. A. Cyzer.*

WALK WELL 2 b.f. (Jan 31) Sadler's Wells (USA) 132–Walkyria (Lord Gayle 67 p (USA) 124) [1989 8f³] tall, leggy, quite attractive filly: second foal: dam Irish middle-distance winner, from family of Slip Anchor: 8/1, 3 lengths third of 9, staying on well, to Hafhafah in maiden at Wolverhampton in October: will be suited by 1¼m: should improve. *J. L. Dunlop.*

WALL STREET SLUMP 3 gr.g. Belfort (FR) 89–Running Dancer (FR) 45 § (Dancer's Image (USA)) [1988 6f⁵ 6s⁵ 8f 1989 6f⁵ 7m 7m 8f 6f⁴ 5m 9f 7m⁵ 7.5m 8.2g 12g 12m⁶] leggy gelding: plating class at best nowadays and looks temperamentally unsatisfactory: will be suited by a return to shorter: appears to act on any going: blinkered sixth (sweating) and ninth starts: visored, claimed out of W. Pearce's stable £2,000 on tenth: best left alone. *P. Monteith.*

WALTZING HOME 2 b.c. (Apr 17) Habitat 134–State Ball 61 (Dance In Time 84 p (CAN)) [1989 6m³] quite attractive colt: third foal: half-brother to 3-y-o Lutine Royal (by Formidable) and quite modest maiden Matlub (by Valiyar): dam, placed 5 times at around 1½m, is half-sister to Royal Palace and Glass Slipper, latter dam of Fairy Footsteps and Light Cavalry: 16/1, burly and green, 2½ lengths third to Muwfiq in 10-runner maiden at York in October, keeping on well after being hampered around 1f out: will be better suited by 7f+: sure to improve. *R. F. Johnson Houghton.*

WALTZING WEASEL 2 b.f. (May 5) Nemorino (USA) 81–Branston Express 50 (Bay Express 132) [1989 5s² 5d 5m 7g a7g a7g] leggy filly: poor mover: first foal: dam half-sister to useful sprinter Tuxford Hideaway: plating-class maiden: best effort on debut. *J. Wharton.*

WALTZ ON AIR 3 b.f. Doc Marten 104–Young Romance (King's Troop 118) 82 [1988 5f⁶ 5m* 6g⁵ 6s² 1989 6d 6d* 8f 8g 7g 7g 8v⁵ 7g] compact filly: poor walker: has a roundish action: fair performer at best: won minor event at Thirsk in April, running on strongly: below form in handicaps after: best form at 6f on a soft surface. *C. Tinkler.*

WANDA   2 b.f. (Mar 13) Taufan (USA) 119–Pitaka (Pitskelly 122) [1989 5s² 5g* 5f²   **66**
5f² 6g⁵ 6d 5g²] IR 5,400Y: smallish, angular filly: fourth foal: half-sister to Italian
3-y-o Paris Sunset (by Red Sunset) and poor and inconsistent maiden Puno (by
Aragon): dam never ran: won maiden auction event at Doncaster in May by short
head: ran well in nurseries: stays 6f: acts on any going: blinkered final appearance:
has had tongue tied down: has sweated up and got on edge. *M. W. Easterby.*

WANTAGE PARK   5 b.m. Pas de Seul 133–Bourgeonette 81 (Mummy's Pet   **100**
125) [1988 6g³ 6d³ 6f³ 7d* 7f⁵ 7.6g⁵ 7.3g 7d³ 6m⁶ 7m⁴ 7g⁴ 8g⁵ 1989 6g⁶]
close-coupled, angular mare: has a quick action: useful winner as 4-y-o: 33/1,
creditable sixth of 13 in handicap at Newmarket (ridden by 5-lb claimer) in May:
stays 7f: acts on firm going and a soft surface: sometimes bandaged. *M. J. Ryan.*

WAR CHILD   5 b.m. Welsh Chanter 124–Winter Sunshine 76 (Crisp And Even   **—**
116) [1988 NR 1989 10d] compact mare: plater: bandaged, always behind in Folkestone handicap in April: best form at 1¼m: acts on any going. *A. Moore.*

WARD ONE   3 b.f. Mr Fluorocarbon 126–Canvas Shoe 57 (Hotfoot 126) [1988 5m   **68**
6f² 7g* 7d* 7m³ 1989 7f⁵ 7f³ 7.5m³ 7g⁴ 8.2g* 9g a7g] workmanlike filly: keen
walker: modest performer: co-favourite, won 17-runner handicap at Hamilton in
October, leading inside final 1f: behind in handicaps at Newmarket (£15,400 event)
and Southwell after: suited by 1m: yet to race on very soft ground, acts on any other:
has run creditably for 5-lb claimer: occasionally slowly away: refused to enter stalls
once. *M. J. Camacho.*

WARM FEELING   2 b.c. (Mar 20) Kalaglow 132–Height of Passion (Shirley   **65 p**
Heights 130) [1989 7g] 46,000Y: first foal: dam thrice-raced half-sister to middle-
distance performer Prince Carl and 5. 1f to 7f winner Rising Dexy, both fairly useful:
14/1, around 9 lengths seventh of 29, running on well, to Lord of The Field in maiden
at Newmarket in November: will be suited by 1¼m + : sure to improve. *B. W. Hills.*

WARM WINTER   3 gr.f. Kalaglow 132–Fair Head 87 (High Line 125) [1988 7m⁶   **61**
8s 8m 1989 7f 7f⁵] rangy, rather angular filly: quite modest maiden: creditable
staying-on fifth at Chepstow in July: should stay 1¼m: sold 1,350 gns Newmarket
December Sales. *H. Candy.*

WARNING   4 b.c. Known Fact (USA) 135–Slightly Dangerous (USA) 122 **130**
(Roberto (USA) 131) [1988 8g² 7.6g* 8g* 8m² 8g* 8g 1989 8f² 8f* 10g⁴ 8f⁶]
    Warning's career record raises the question of how much the standing of
a horse is affected by such matters as its consistency and versatility. In truth,
Warning became a somewhat exasperating individual towards the end of his
racing days. The ability was there all right, it was more a question of when he
would show it. The champion two-year-old of 1987, he put up a performance of
superlative merit when running away with the Queen Elizabeth II Stakes at
Ascot's Festival of British Racing towards the end of his second season.

Queen Anne Stakes, Ascot—a top-class performance from Warning

Many, ourselves included, considered that performance the best at weight-for-age by any horse in Europe in 1988. But, far from proving the point, Warning flopped dismally in the Breeders' Cup Mile, for which he started favourite, on his only subsequent appearance. Still, excuses were made, largely because of the slippery ground, and at least it was revealed that Warning would get the chance to make amends as a four-year-old. In fact, Warning ran only four times more, winning once in tremendous fashion again, but running below his best in defeat on the three other occasions. That victory came in the Queen Anne Stakes at Royal Ascot. Looking on good terms with himself, Warning started at 5/2 on, despite giving weight to all six of his rivals, who included the Cecil-trained pair Reprimand and Sweet Chesne and the very smart foreign challenger French Stress. Niggled along two furlongs out on the outside of the field, Warning took up the running at the distance and quickly strode clear, reaching the line four lengths and a further two lengths clear of Reprimand and Sweet Chesne. No excuses needed this time. But they were much in evidence after Warning's other starts of the year. He was said to have needed the run on his reappearance, when a two-length second of four to Most Welcome in the Juddmonte Lockinge Stakes at Newbury in May. It was suggested that he was unsuited to the going (some even blamed the trip) when a most disappointing twenty-length fourth of six behind Nashwan in the Coral-Eclipse Stakes at Sandown in July. And he was excused in some quarters on the grounds that he received a moderate ride when only nine lengths sixth of eight behind Zilzal in the Swettenham Stud Sussex Stakes at Goodwood later in July. The point about his fitness at Newbury might have had some validity for he ran as if a shade rusty, getting outpaced inside the final furlong, having been niggled at shortly after halfway. To blame the ground at Sandown was possibly unreasonable as, although a shade loose on top, it was by no means soft, and to blame the trip definitely was unreasonable, for Warning was beaten turning for home, much too far out to be attributable

Mr K. Abdulla's "Warning"

to lack of stamina. Finally, to blame Pat Eddery for Warning's defeat at Goodwood is overly-harsh; he was uneasy on the horse early in the straight and what trouble the pair met by coming up the inside made little difference to the result.

While admitting that consistency was not Warning's strong suit, we are convinced that he was a top-class performer at his best. Who could argue with that in view of his win in the 1988 Queen Elizabeth, in which he brushed aside horses of the calibre of Salse, Persian Heights and Soviet Star and recorded an exceptional timefigure into the bargain? Who could deny that even on the basis of his win in the latest Queen Anne? There were those that could it seems. Writing in *The Sporting Life* after the Eclipse, Geoff Lester praised Nashwan to the skies but attempted to dismiss Warning with the oft-used remark 'top-class horses should go on any ground'. What nonsense! Why anyone should think that 'top-class' racehorses are an entirely different breed from their lesser counterparts is a mystery. They are subject to conditions such as going, trip, course, luck in running, and so on, no less and no more than are run-of-the-mill performers, though their superior ability sometimes disguises this fact from the less discerning. If Warning needed a particular set of conditions to show his best form then this reflects upon his versatility, not his merit. However, it is surely inevitable that a horse's overall reputation will suffer as a consequence of lack of versatility or, for that matter, consistency. In this respect, Warning may well not receive the credit that his better performances, taken in isolation, deserve.

Warning (b.c. 1985)	Known Fact (USA) (b 1977)	In Reality (b 1964)	Intentionally / My Dear Girl
		Tamerett (b or br 1962)	Tim Tam / Mixed Marriage
	Slightly Dangerous (USA) (b 1979)	Roberto (b 1969)	Hail To Reason / Bramalea
		Where You Lead (ch 1970)	Raise A Native / Noblesse

As far as Warning the racehorse is concerned these matters are largely academic now. Warning was prepared for a second attempt on the Breeders' Cup Mile but injured himself on the journey over and has been retired to the Banstead Manor Stud near Newmarket at a fee of £15,000 with the October 1st concession. He is easily the best of his sire's numerous winning offspring. In the latest season Known Fact was also represented by the likes of the Guineas fourth Markofdistinction, the St James's Palace Stakes runner-up Greensmith (a stable-companion of Warning's and the early pacemaker in the Eclipse) and the useful performers Known Ranger, Ajanac and Plain Fact. Known Fact was the best miler of 1980 when he won the Waterford Crystal Mile, the Kiveton Park Steel Stakes, the Queen Elizabeth II Stakes and was awarded the Two Thousand Guineas on the disqualification of Nureyev. After a spell in Britain he was moved to Juddmonte Farms in Kentucky, USA. Warning's dam, Slightly Dangerous, a daughter of the Oaks runner-up Where You Lead and granddaughter of the Oaks winner Noblesse, was herself second (to Time Charter) in the Epsom classic, having won the Fred Darling Stakes. Warning is her second foal, after the very useful middle-distance performer Timefighter, and was followed by colts by Shirley Heights—the unraced Highly Dangerous and the promising two-year-old of the latest season Deploy—and a filly by Dancing Brave.

A good-topped colt and a quick-actioned mover, Warning usually got on his toes (he did so noticeably before the Queen Anne Stakes and proved a difficult subject to photograph when we visited Coombelands in the autumn—hence the less than classical pose in the accompanying portrait). While his career ended under a bit of a cloud, he deserves to be remembered as a top-notch performer on his day, certainly one of the best milers of recent years. *G. Harwood.*

WARRSHAN (USA) 3 b.c. Northern Dancer–Secret Asset (USA) (Graustark) **117** [1988 7m* 8g* 1989 12.3m³ 10f* 12g 12f* 12f³ 12m³ 12f] lengthy, rather dipped-backed, attractive colt: turns fore-feet in: good mover: didn't find much in front when successful at Goodwood in N M Financial Predominate Stakes in May

Gordon Stakes, Goodwood—Warrshan has to be driven along to beat Alphabel, N C Owen (rails) and Greenwich Papillon

and Gordon Stakes (beat Alphabel a head) in July: creditable third after in small fields for Great Voltigeur Stakes at York, outpaced then staying on, and Cumberland Lodge Stakes at Ascot, leading long way: last of 9 in Grade 1 event at Santa Anita: stays 1½m: acts on firm going: possibly swallowed tongue when virtually pulled up in Ever Ready Derby at Epsom, and wore tongue strap afterwards: usually held up prior to Ascot: reportedly to be trained by C. Whittingham. *M. R. Stoute.*

WARTHILL GIRL 4 b.f. Anfield 117–Rosy Lee (FR) (Le Haar 126) [1988 5v³ 5m³ 6g 6f 6m⁴ 7g 7g⁵ 1989 7d 7s⁴ 7.5d⁵ 7d³ 7m 6f 7f 8.5m] lengthy, workmanlike filly: has a round action: poor handicapper: tubed final start: will stay 1m: seems to need an easy surface nowadays: inconsistent. *M. Brittain.* **50 d**

WARWICK SUITE 7 b.g. Orchestra 118–Place To Place (USA) (No Robbery) [1988 NR 1989 15s] lengthy, workmanlike gelding: very lightly raced on flat nowadays: stays 1¼m: acts on soft going: usually blinkered or visored: winning hurdler. *M. P. Naughton.* **—**

WASHITA 2 b.f. (Apr 28) Valiyar 129–Ardneasken 84 (Right Royal V 135) [1989 7v] small filly: half-sister to poor 3-y-o Campfire (by Auction Ring) and numerous winners, including high-class middle-distance stayer Dakota (by Stupendous) and very useful middle-distance performer Warpath (by Sovereign Path): dam out-and-out stayer: tailed off in 17-runner maiden at Ayr in October. *C. W. Thornton.* **—**

WASIMAH 3 b.f. Caerleon (USA) 132–Pennycuick 101 (Celtic Ash) [1988 5g² 5s² 5f* 5g⁶ 5g* 5g 1989 5f 5m 5f 5m⁵] neat filly: good walker: has a quick action: fair performer as 2-y-o, twice making all: well below form in handicaps in 1989, racing much too freely final outing (June): suited by sharp 5f: best form on a sound surface: blinkered last 6 starts, except for reappearance: often taken down steadily: inconsistent: sold 23,000 gns Newmarket December Sales. *B. Hanbury.* **—**

WASNAH (USA) 2 b.f. (Feb 17) Nijinsky (CAN) 138–Highest Trump (USA) 112 (Bold Bidder) [1989 7g²] $850,000Y: rather angular filly: eighth foal (including twins): closely related to very useful Irish 6f and 7f winner Northern Plain, smart Irish 7f and 11.5f winner Dance Bid and Irish 7f to 9f winner Jugah (all by Northern Dancer): dam won Queen Mary Stakes and stayed 1m: 13/2, 2½ lengths second of 5, staying on well, to Atoll in minor event at York in October: will be better suited by 1m+: should improve. *J. L. Dunlop.* **90 p**

WASSELNI 3 br.g. Wassl 125–Monongelia 98 (Welsh Pageant 132) [1988 NR 1989 8h⁵ 12h⁴ 14g²] lengthy, angular gelding: first foal: dam 9f and 1¼m winner at 3 yrs, later successful at 1m in Ireland: progressive form in summer maidens: will be **83**

968

Sheikh Mohammed's "Warrshan"

suited by good test of stamina: sold to join K. Morgan 14,500 gns Newmarket July Sales and subsequently gelded. *M. A. Jarvis.*

WASSLING 3 b.c. Wassl 125–Sarissa 105 (Reform 132) [1988 7g* 1989 8s 10.6s³] 91
angular colt: rather unfurnished: has a round action: won maiden at 2 yrs: 16/1, staying-on third of 7 in minor event at Haydock in April: well behind in listed race at Kempton: stays 10.6f: acts on soft going. *Lord John FitzGerald.*

WASSL PORT 3 b.c. Wassl 125–Sea Port (Averof 123) [1988 NR 1989 7g³ 8.2m⁴ 91
8.5m* 8g* 8d⁵] 58,000Y: attractive colt: good mover: second foal: half-brother to lightly-raced Fayidah (by Glenstal): dam, fourth on only start, is half-sister to high-class stayer Sea Anchor: led around 2f out when winning maiden (easily) at Beverley and handicap at Newmarket in August: favourite, creditable fifth of 27 in handicap at Newbury in October: stays 8.5f: acts on top-of-the-ground and a soft surface. *B. W. Hills.*

WATER CANNON 8 b.g. Gunner B 126–Awash (Busted 134) [1988 18v 17.1g 42
16m 1989 21.6d⁴ 18s 17.6f³ 18f 18h 20.4g³] compact gelding: poor handicapper: not seen out after July: out-and-out stayer: sometimes wears a visor (did so only once in 1989): often wears a tongue strap: inconsistent. *F. H. Lee.*

WATERFIELD 5 ch.h. Le Moss 135–Shannon Princess (Connaught 130) [1988 **107**
12d⁴ 16m³ 16g⁶ 14g* 12g³ 13.3g³ 14v 1989 12g* 16d⁴ 16g⁵] lengthy, good-bodied

horse: moderate mover: useful performer: fortunate winner of £10,500 Doncaster Shield in April having been beaten ¾ length by demoted Apache, staying on strongly to get second close home: in frame in Insulpak Sagaro EBF Stakes at Ascot (fourth to Travel Mystery), travelling well in strongly-run race for much of way: one-paced fifth in Oleander-Rennen at Baden-Baden in May: has won at 2m, but best at 1½m to 1¾m, particularly when ridden with enterprise and when conditions are testing: probably unsuited by firm going, acts on any other: sold 22,000 gns Newmarket December Sales. *P. T. Walwyn.*

WATER GOD   2 b.c. (Feb 19) Dominion 123–Silent Pool 68 (Relkino 131) [1989   —
6g] 8,400Y: smallish, quite attractive colt: second living foal: brother to quite modest 1987 2-y-o Demerger: dam slow daughter of Park Hill Stakes winner Idle Waters: burly, well beaten in 29-runner maiden at Newmarket in November. *R. F. Johnson Houghton.*

WATERLOW PARK   7 ch.g. Wollow 132–Caraquenga (USA) 92 (Cyane) [1988   78
10f* 12g* 12f* 10s⁵ 10g 1989 10.2g³ 12g³ 12m* 12f² 12f* 12h* 12m² 12f* 11d 12d
10.6m] big gelding: good mover: modest handicapper: an excellent mount for in-experienced rider, and in tremendous form for much of season, winning apprentice event at Leicester, amateurs contest at Goodwood, 8-runner race at Brighton and ladies event (leading on line in very close finish) at Beverley: better at 1½m than 1¼m and stays well: suited by a sound surface nowadays: has broken blood vessels (did so final outing): genuine. *I. A. Balding.*

WATERSHED   3 b.c. Blakeney 126–Anadyomene 101 (Sea Hawk II 131) [1988 7g   62
10d 1989 10g 12f³ 12f⁴ 14m 11.3f*] strong, lengthy colt: favourite, won maiden claimer (claimed to join N. Tinkler £10,500) at Chester in July, always prominent and staying on well: should be suited by further than 1½m: acts on firm going and a soft surface: ran creditably in blinkers third outing. *Mrs L. Piggott.*

WATER WELL   2 b.f. (Jan 28) Sadler's Wells (USA) 132–Soba 127 (Most Secret   85
119) [1989 6g⁴ 6m⁶ 6g 6m 8f³ 7g³] 70,000Y: well-made, attractive filly: third foal: closely related to minor 7f and 1½m winner Gold Dust (by Golden Fleece): dam high-class sprinter: fair performer: best efforts tenth of 11 to Dead Certain in Tattersalls Cheveley Park Stakes at Newmarket on fourth start and always-prominent third to Katsina in maiden on same course on final one: ran moderately (held up in slowly-run race) in weak field at Redcar in between: stays 7f: possibly unsuited by very firm ground. *C. E. Brittain.*

WATTLEMEADE   4 b.g. Wattlefield 117–Maymede 79 (Runnymede 123) [1988   52
6v* 6g 5.8g⁶ 6g 1989 6f 7.5g 7f 7m⁵ 7h] rangy, rather dipped-backed gelding: quite modest winner early in 1988: below form subsequently, but showed he retained a little ability when fifth in apprentice handicap at Yarmouth in June: best form at 6f on heavy going: blinkered once at 3 yrs: sold 520 gns Doncaster August Sales. *M. C. Chapman.*

WAVE MASTER   2 b.c. (Apr 1) Chief Singer 131–Sea Fret 96 (Habat 127) [1989   82
5.1m* 6m² 5g 6f⁵ 8f⁵ 7g] 42,000Y: sturdy, close-coupled colt: sprint type: has a roundish action: third foal: half-brother to a winner in Holland: dam, 2-y-o 6f winner, is daughter of smart Fluke, a half-sister to Buoy and Bireme: won 8-runner maiden at Yarmouth in June: second to easy winner Qui Danzig in minor event at Windsor later in month, best subsequent effort: off course around 3 months after fourth start: should stay further than 6f: blinkered final outing. *G. A. Pritchard-Gordon.*

WAVERLEY GIRL   3 b.f. Seymour Hicks (FR) 125–Iamstopped (Furry Glen   —
121) [1988 7s 8f 7m 1989 8s 12m⁵ 14f⁶ 8f 9f 12m 12g] rather sparely-made filly: poor mover: little sign of ability on flat. *J. S. Wainwright.*

WAVERLEY HEIGHTS   3 b.f. Shirley Heights 130–More Heather 97   —
(Ballymore 123) [1988 6f⁶ 7f 7s 7d⁴ 8.2v* 1989 12d⁴ 8d] small, lightly-made filly: turns off-fore in: modest winner as 2-y-o: well below form in handicaps in April: should be suited by 1¼m +: acts well on heavy ground: sold 6,000 gns Newmarket December Sales. *I. V. Matthews.*

WAVERLEY STAR   4 br.g. Pitskelly 122–Quelle Blague (Red God 128§) [1988   58
5s 7m 8g⁶ 6d² 6m* 6g⁴ 5g 6f² 5m² 6m² 6g 5g 7m 6d 1989 5g³ 5g⁴ 6v 6.1f⁵ 7.5g 5f*
6m 6f⁴ 5f 5m 5f⁴ 6f⁵ 8m 6m³ 6f 6g⁴ 7m] big, workmanlike gelding: poor mover, with a round action: quite modest handicapper: led close home when winning at Hamilton (gained only previous victory there) in May: best effort after when third of 24 at Ripon: suited by 6f or stiff 5f: possibly unsuited by soft going, acts on any other: probably best in blinkers and has been tried in visor: has sweated, and often gets on toes: a difficult ride, who often hangs, and ideally needs strong handling: in-consistent. *J. S. Wainwright.*

WAY TOO MUCH   2 b.c. (Mar 12) Doulab (USA) 115–Fire Flash 74 (Bustino 136)   **70**
[1989 5m 6h³ 6m⁴ 7m 7.5m² 8f⁶ 8f⁶ 9g⁴] IR 13,000Y: small, sparely-made colt: first
foal: dam, never tried beyond 1¼m, is daughter of smart 7f and 1m performer
Dazzling Light, a half-sister to Welsh Pageant: modest maiden: best effort short-
head second of 8 to Eire Leath-Sceal in nursery at Beverley in August: may prove
best at around 1m: visored sixth outing: twice slowly away. *M. A. Jarvis.*

WEAREAGRANDMOTHER   2 b.f. (Apr 2) Prince Tenderfoot (USA) 126–   **65**
Lady Bettina (Bustino 136) [1989 6g 6m 7m⁶ 8m* 9g 7g] IR 7,400Y: workmanlike
filly: third foal: sister to a winner in Italy and half-sister to another: dam ran once:
quite modest performer: won 7-runner nursery at York in September by a short
head, leading last stride: suited by 1m. *G. A. Pritchard-Gordon.*

WEDDING BOUQUET   2 b.f. (Feb 3) Kings Lake (USA) 133–Doff The Derby   **104**
(USA) (Master Derby (USA)) [1989 6g* 6d³ 6g³ 7g² 5d* 7g*] IR 120,000F: second
foal: half-sister to a winner at up to 1m in USA: dam unraced half-sister to Trillion,
dam of Triptych: useful filly: successful in maiden and a listed race (by 1½ lengths
from Tanwi) at the Curragh and CL Weld EBF Park Stakes (by 1½ lengths from
Remthat Naser) at Phoenix Park: ¾-length second to Dashing Blade in GPA
National Stakes at the Curragh, best other effort: should stay at least 1m: yet to race
on top-of-the-ground. *M. V. O'Brien, Ireland.*

WEEKENDER   2 ch.f. (Apr 16) Mummy's Game 120–Antique Bloom 101   **41**
(Sterling Bay (SWE)) [1989 6m⁴ 6m⁴ 7f] IR 2,000Y: fifth living foal: half-sister to a
winner abroad: dam 5f winner at 2 yrs didn't train on: poor maiden: ran in sellers
first 2 starts, trained by J. White: better suited by 7f than 6f. *T. Thomson Jones.*

WEEK ST MARY   3 gr.f. Warpath 113–Sophia Western (Steel Heart 128) [1988   **42**
5g 6m 5g 5g² 5m³ 8.2m⁴ 6d 1989 7s 10m 10.2h 9g 8m 8f⁵ 8f* 10.2f 8f 8.2g] sturdy
filly: carries condition: moderate mover: modest plater: won at Bath (bought in
2,900 gns) in September, running on strongly to lead post: only other show as 3-y-o
on previous start, again having had plenty to do: stays 1m well: acts on firm going:
trained until after Bath by C. Hill. *R. J. Hodges.*

WEFFIE   3 ch.f. On Your Mark 125–Catch Crop (Capistrano 120) [1988 5.1m³ 6m⁵   **44**
6m⁵ 6m⁶ 8m* 8v 7g 8.2v 1989 7.5d⁶ 8g⁴ 10f 12.2f⁶ 8g 8.5m] sparely-made, rather

Mrs M. V. O'Brien's "Wedding Bouquet"

leggy filly: modest plater: best form at 1m (not discredited over 1¼m) on a sound surface: blinkered last 2 outings and once at 2 yrs: bought out of A. Bailey's stable 3,000 gns Doncaster February Sales: sold 2,000 gns Doncaster September Sales. *R. O'Leary.*

WELD   3 ch.c. Kalaglow 132–Meliora 73 (Crowned Prince (USA) 128) [1988 **122** 7g 1989 10s⁴ 14m* 16f* 16f* 18g* 16g*]

Report has it that Bruce Raymond's succinct post-race assessment of Weld on his only appearance at two years was 'slow'. Well, Weld is no champion sprinter, but it's a fair bet that the veteran jockey is looking forward with eagerness to resuming the partnership in the forthcoming season, as Weld emerged as a very smart young stayer in 1989, beaten only once—over an inadequate trip at Wolverhampton first time out—from six starts and collecting £91,000 in prize money. Weld made a greater impact when sent over an extra half mile on his second start, landing some sizeable wagers in a maiden at Newmarket, but not enough to bring him in to shorter than 16/1 when lining up for the listed Queen's Vase at Royal Ascot. Weld caused an upset, winning in track-record time to give Lord Howard de Walden a third success in the race following Falkland in 1972 and Arden in 1987. Held up pulling hard as his owner's 5/2-chance Konigsberg took the field along at a strong gallop, Weld could be named the winner once in line for home. Driven along, he quickened to the front at the furlong pole and readily put five lengths between himself and his closest pursuer, the 13/8 favourite Demawend, and another two to the Derby-pacemaker Polar Run, Konigsberg having faded into fifth. Weld's trainer, who had witnessed at first hand the preparations of the great stayers Le Moss and Ardross during the five years-plus he spent as assistant at Warren Place, forecast that Weld could well return twelve months hence as a serious contender for the Gold Cup. The rest of Weld's campaign, kept to conditions events, added more substance to his prediction.

After two months off, partly due to sore shins, and a much narrower defeat of Demawend (4 lb better off) in a moderately-run Lonsdale Stakes at York, Weld wound up by completing the Doncaster Cup-Jockey Club Cup double. That he had to beat only four rivals so to do—including the handicappers Ecran and Thethingaboutitis at Doncaster—is ready ammunition for those detractors of staying races. On the other side of the coin, the Jockey Club Cup at Newmarket in October provided an exciting spectacle, as

Jockey Club Cup, Newmarket—Weld stays on from Sapience

Doncaster Cup — Weld brushes aside his two opponents

had the Mappin & Webb Henry II Stakes and the Goodwood Cup earlier in the season. The late withdrawal of Sadeem owing to the rain-softened ground left evens-favourite Weld to do battle with St Leger second Sapience and the five-year-old Sergeyevich, 2/1 and 7/2 respectively. Sergeyevich offered token resistance, losing touch fully six furlongs out, but Sapience proved an altogether sterner opponent. Indeed, Sapience looked more than Weld could cope with when moving into the lead approaching the Bushes but he didn't quite see out the longer trip, allowing Weld, who for his part rallied splendidly, to regain the initiative a furlong out and score by a length and a half.

What chance does Weld have of lifting the 1990 Gold Cup? A very good one, we should think. Firstly, he's probably already the equal of the top older stayers Sadeem and Top Sunrise, while, from his own generation, he's likely to be weakly opposed if Michelozzo, as intended, is kept at middle distances. Irish St Leger second Tyrone Bridge would seem to be the best of the other prospects from the three-year-olds of 1989. Weld's victory over two vastly inferior rivals at Doncaster can't be regarded as conclusive evidence that he

Lord Howard de Walden's "Weld"

stays two and a quarter miles but, for all that he takes a keen hold, he runs like one suited by a thorough test and it will be surprising if the distance at Ascot proves his undoing.

		Kalamoun	Zeddaan
Weld (ch.c. 1986)	Kalaglow (gr 1978)	(gr 1970)	Khairunissa
		Rossitor	Pall Mall
		(ch 1970)	Sonia
	Meliora (b 1976)	Crowned Prince	Raise A Native
		(ch 1969)	Gay Hostess
		Grecian Craft	Acropolis
		(b 1971)	Kyak

In the current climate in which very few breeders set out to produce out-and-out stayers, an examination of a Gold Cup candidate's pedigree is often discouraging. At first glance, Weld's pedigree would seem that of a middle-distance colt in that he's by the Eclipse and King George VI and Queen Elizabeth Stakes winner Kalaglow out of a mare, Meliora, who gained her sole success in a Leicester maiden over seven furlongs and stayed a mile. However, Weld is also from Dick Hollingsworth's famous Felucca family which has yielded a recent Gold Cup winner in Longboat; Meliora was the first foal of Grecian Craft, an ultimately disappointing sister to the smart stayer Mariner. Grecian Craft, also the dam of the good French performer Nemr, is a half-sister to the exceptional broodmare Ripeck, whose offspring included Bireme and Buoy. Ripeck is additionally the grandam of Sea Anchor, a fine third to Sagaro and Crash Course in the 1976 Gold Cup. Meliora's maternal grandam Kyak was also a racehorse of some note, forming the middle leg of a treble of Park Hill successes for daughters of Felucca in the 'fifties. Meliora's first live foal was the modest two-and-a-quarter-mile winner Lhasa (by Top Ville). Before Weld she also produced Upper (by Cure The Blues), who made a winning debut over five furlongs at two but died that year, and Gild The Lily (by Ile de Bourbon), successful at nine furlongs in 1988, while since she has foaled the unraced Shareef Dancer filly Mevlevi who's in training with Cecil. Weld is quite an imposing individual, though big and rather leggy as a three-year-old; he should strengthen with another year on him. Round actioned, he acts on firm going. *W. Jarvis.*

WELDNAAS (USA) 3 ch.c. Diesis 133–Bank On Love (USA) (Gallant Romeo **112** (USA)) [1988 6f² 6m* 6g³ 6f³ 1989 9d³ 8v⁵ 7f⁶ 7.2g*] deep-girthed colt: really good mover: very useful performer: 20/1, best effort when winning listed race at Haydock in June by 2 lengths from Always Fair, getting good run (always prominent) and leading 2½f out: races freely and may prove suited by racing up with pace at 7f: probably acts on any going: wears tongue strap: has joined N. Drysdale in USA. *B. Hanbury.*

WELL FURNISHED 2 ch.c. (May 4) Salmon Leap (USA) 131–Mimicry (Thatch **68** (USA) 136) [1989 6m 7g⁴ 7g] IR 8,000Y: rangy colt: has plenty of scope: fourth foal: closely related to Irish 3-y-o 9f winner George Phillips and Irish 7f winner Naoko (both by Glenstal): dam unraced half-sister to Triumph Hurdle winner Solar Cloud: quite modest maiden: form only on second start: will be better suited by 1m + . *A. A. Scott.*

WELLOW WINE (USA) 4 b.g. Sensitive Prince (USA)–Tempting Lady (USA) — (L'Enjoleur (CAN)) [1988 6v² 5g 6g⁵ 7f 6m⁴ 5g 6g⁵ 6m⁶ 5.1m³ 6g 5g³ 6d 6m 1989 5s a6g] tall, leggy, sparely-made gelding: plating-class maiden: off course 9 months between starts at 4 yrs: stays 6f: probably acts on any going: often bandaged: blinkered once, visored once. *R. A. Bennett.*

WELLSY LAD (USA) 2 ch.c. (Apr 10) El Baba (USA)–Iwishiknew (USA) **76** (Damascus (USA)) [1989 6g a6g⁵ a6g² a7g* a8g²] $28,000Y: fourth reported foal: half-brother to a winner in USA: dam won at around 6f: modest performer: won late-season claimer at Southwell: better suited by 7f and 1m than 6f: blinkered on debut: bought afterwards out of W. O'Gorman's stable 2,500 gns Newmarket Autumn Sales. *D. W. Chapman.*

WELNEY 2 b. or br.c. (Feb 20) Habitat 134–On Show 92 (Welsh Pageant **113** 132) [1989 6m⁴ 6g* 6m* 7g⁴]
Welney is a puzzle. First of all there's his physical description. When we saw him make a promising debut at Newbury in July we thought him a well-

Rokeby Farms Mill Reef Stakes, Newbury—
Welney wins going away from Somethingdifferent and Old Alliance

grown, attractive colt; but by the time of the Three Chimneys Dewhurst Stakes at Newmarket in October, his final outing of the season, we'd altered our opinion more than once, and, though we were still of the persuasion that he was good-bodied, he was reminding us more and more of his diminutive half-sister Inchmurrin. Then there are his performances. He showed such improvement between winning a maiden race at Yarmouth and the Rokeby Farms Mill Reef Stakes at Newbury within nine days in September that we felt certain he'd continue progressing and take all the beating in the Dewhurst; but in the event he failed to reveal the sparkle that had characterised his display at Newbury, and his fourth of seven behind Dashing Blade, beaten nearly two lengths, raises the possibility that he was slightly flattered by his length-and-a-half defeat of Somethingdifferent, two lengths ahead of Old Alliance, in the Mill Reef. Certainly, the leaders went off very fast that day, and Welney, who looked much tighter in condition than he had at Yarmouth, Somethingdifferent and fourth-placed Swiss Affair occupied the last three positions at halfway. What was so impressive about Welney at Newbury, and made his subsequent run hard to grasp, was the short, sharp burst of acceleration he unleashed in the final furlong, having had nothing but a troubled run in the previous three hundred yards. That finishing speed hadn't been in evidence at Yarmouth where, on his first run for two months, he made all the running and just held on from the subsequent listed winner Montendre, nor was it in the Dewhurst where waiting tactics were again adopted. All things considered we ended the season with the view that Welney may prove best waited with in a strongly-run race over six or seven furlongs, possibly when the ground is on top. But Inchmurrin went on to prove us wrong at the same stage of her career, and we won't be too surprised if Welney continues to bewilder us in the coming season!

		Sir Gaylord	Turn-To
	Habitat	(b 1959)	Somethingroyal
	(b 1966)	Little Hut	Occupy
Welney		(b 1952)	Savage Beauty
(b. or br.c. Feb 20, 1987)		Welsh Pageant	Tudor Melody
	On Show	(b 1966)	Picture Light
	(br 1978)	African Dancer	Nijinsky
		(b 1973)	Miba

Welney is the fourth foal from his dam On Show following the poor animal Pete Marsh (by Grundy), the smart miler Inchmurrin (by Lomond) and her close relative Guest Artiste (by Be My Guest), a very useful winner of two minor events at a mile in the latest season. On Show stayed further than any of her winning offspring, running second in the mile-and-a-half November Handicap after winning over a mile and a quarter at Nottingham. The next dam

975

African Dancer came third in the Oaks and stayed well enough to go two places better than her dam Miba and win the Park Hill Stakes over an extended mile and three quarters. Quick-actioned Welney has raced only on a sound surface. *G. Wragg.*

WELSH BLUEBELL 7 b.m. Manado 130–Welsh Sapphire (Welsh Saint 126) [1988 15.5f 1989 14.8d] leggy, workmanlike mare: poor mover: 100/1-second in Sandown claimer as 5-y-o: well beaten subsequently in maidens and handicaps: very one paced: acts on firm going: has worn blinkers and bandages. *G. Roe.* —

WELSH COLUMN 3 b.f. Welsh Captain 113–Bally's Step (Ballynockan 112) [1988 5d² 5f 5m 6g⁶ 7f³ 7g 7s² 7g⁵ 8f 8.2s* 8.2s⁵ 1989 7d⁴ 8s* 8g 8.2g⁴ 9g 8.2g 8v 8g] small, angular filly: poor walker: quite modest handicapper: won at Ripon in April: well below form (including in seller) after, off course over 4 months before fifth start: should stay beyond 1m: sometimes on toes: sold 3,100 gns Ascot November Sales. *R. M. Whitaker.* 59

WELSH FLUTE 3 b.f. Welsh Captain 113–Spanish Flute 55 (Philip of Spain 126) [1988 5g 5g⁶ 6d 6g 6m 1989 8g 5s 6s 6f 6f 8f] workmanlike, sparely-made filly: plating-class maiden: ran poorly as 3-y-o, including in sellers: slowly away and ran wide on turn at Catterick and Thirsk (blinkered) last 2 outings. *R. Thompson.* —

WELSH GOVERNOR 3 b.g. Welsh Term 126–The Way She Moves (North Stoke 130) [1988 7m* 1989 10m] leggy gelding: modest form when making all in claimer at Yarmouth as 2-y-o: burly, prominent 7f in similar event at Newbury in June, only start in 1989: should stay beyond 7f. *R. Boss.* —

WELSH KING 3 ch.g. Kings Lake (USA) 133–Daffodil Day (Welsh Pageant 132) [1988 NR 1989 10m] smallish, sparely-made gelding: third live foal: dam twice-raced half-sister to Connaught: 8/1, about 14 lengths seventh of 12 in maiden at Leicester in May, edging right: sold to join K. Morgan 2,600 gns Ascot July Sales and subsequently gelded. *H. R. A. Cecil.* —

WELSHMAN 3 ch.g. Final Straw 127–Joie de Galles 72 (Welsh Pageant 132) [1988 7g 7m 1989 8s⁶ 12v* 12g 12s] close-coupled, workmanlike gelding: won claimer at Lingfield in April, always prominent and keeping on gamely: below form later in spring in handicap and claimer: suited by 1½m: goes well in the mud. *M. Blanshard.* 71

WELSH MANSION 3 b.c. Longleat (USA) 109–La Gallia 70 (Welsh Saint 126) [1988 6d 6f² 6f³ 7m⁴ 7d 1989 8f 7f 8m² 7m 8.2f* 8.2m⁶ 8.2d² 8.2d 8.2g*] lengthy, workmanlike colt: made all at Hamilton in maiden claimer in July and claimer (visored) in September: stays 1m: acts on firm going and a soft surface: also visored when running creditably eighth start: has joined P. Davis. *C. Tinkler.* 66

WELSHMANS PRIDE 3 ch.g. Skyliner 117–Material 107 (Song 132) [1988 5f 5m⁵ 5f³ 5g 1989 6m 5f 5f] good-quartered gelding: poor walker: quite modest maiden as 2-y-o: well beaten in first half of 1989: best at 5f: acts well on firm going: visored last 2 starts at 2 yrs: slowly away for apprentice final start: subsequently gelded. *J. White.* —

WELSH PAGEANTRY 6 b.m. Welsh Pageant 132–Sacred Mountain 74 (St Paddy 133) [1988 9f* 10m² 8m³ 9d 10f³ 10m³ 10.2f³ 10f 1989 10h⁵ 9m 10f⁶ 8f] lengthy, quite attractive mare: quite modest winner as 5-y-o: form in 1989 only on first outing (would probably have won but for being badly hampered): better suited by 1¼m than 1m: yet to show her best form on soft going, acts on any other: blinkered once: occasionally sweats: has won for apprentice. *M. E. D. Francis.* 50 +

WELSH ROSE 3 b.f. Mummy's Game 120–Welsh Flower (Welsh Saint 126) [1988 5s 5f⁴ 6f³ 5.1f 6m 5g 1989 5s] leggy filly: bad plater. *Pat Mitchell.* —

WELSH SIREN 3 b.f. Welsh Saint 126–Kalonji (Red Alert 127) [1988 5g³ 5g² 6g⁵ 6s 1989 8f 7f⁴ 7m⁵ 7g² 6f⁵ 8f² 10.2g 10s⁴ 9m⁴ 9f⁴ 10f⁴] workmanlike filly: keen walker: modest maiden: stays 9f: acts on firm going: sweating fifth (edgy) and ninth starts: sold 5,000 gns Newmarket December Sales. *C. W. C. Elsey.* 68

WENSLEYDALEWARRIOR 5 ro.g. Alias Smith (USA)–Foolish Heroine 78 (Brigadier Gerard 144) [1988 10.2d 9d⁶ 7g⁴ 7m⁶ 7m³ 1989 8m⁵ 8g 7g 8m 8g⁴ 7f 8.2g] sturdy, workmanlike gelding: fair winner as 3-y-o: generally well below form subsequently: best at up to 1m: best form with give in the ground: often bandaged nowadays: suitable mount for apprentice: often gets on toes. *G. M. Moore.* 55

WENTBRIDGE GIRL 3 gr.f. Petong 126–Naughty Party (Parthia 132) [1988 6m⁵ 7g⁵ 6g⁶ 6g⁶ 7m 5g 1989 8.5m 10f a11g] rather leggy filly: moderate mover: poor maiden: showed little in 1989, including in seller: best form at 6f: blinkered last 3 starts at 2 yrs. *Ronald Thompson.* —

WE'RE IN 2 ch.f. (Feb 23) Superlative 118–Almond Blossom 69 (Grundy 137) **43**
[1989 5g⁴ 5.1f 5g] 5,000Y: sparely-made filly: second foal: dam 1½m winner and
daughter of Lingfield Oaks Trial winner Riboreen: poor maiden: off course long time
between races: sold 1,100 gns Doncaster October Sales. *J. Berry.*

WESSEX 7 b.h. Free State 125–Bonandra 82 (Andrea Mantegna) [1988 13s 12s **57**
15v³ 12g 1989 13v⁵ 13v⁴ 13f⁵ 16.5g⁴ 13m 20.4g² 15s⁶] strong horse: shows traces of
stringhalt: plating-class handicapper: shapes like out-and-out stayer nowadays: acts
on any going: effective with blinkers or without: good mount for apprentice: winning
hurdler. *N. Tinkler.*

WEST BECK 3 ch.f. Mr Fluorocarbon 126–Hod On 67 (Decoy Boy 129) [1988 5s² **64**
6g 7g⁴ 1989 7.5d* 7g* 7m* 7.6f 7d a7g] lengthy, rather angular filly: turns fore-feet
in: won seller (retained 1,800 gns) at Beverley in April and claimers at Carlisle
(bandaged behind) in April and Epsom (making virtually all) in June: ran poorly in
handicaps after: stays 7.5f well: possibly unsuited by very firm going. *M. J.
Camacho.*

WEST CHINA 5 b.h. Habitat 134–Sorbus 121 (Busted 134) [1988 10g⁶ 9m³ 12m³ **107**
12g² 14g⁴ 12d³ 14g² 14s* 12s⁴ 15.5s 1989 12v² 12d⁵ 13.4f³ 16f 12m] angular,
sparely-made ex-Irish horse: moderate mover: brother to Irish 7f winner Klarifi and
half-brother to smart Irish miler Captivator (by Artaius) and to very useful
middle-distance stayer Bahamian (by Mill Reef): dam disqualified winner of Irish
Guinness Oaks: much improved in first half of 1989, running well when fifth in
Lanes End John Porter EBF Stakes at Newbury and when last of 3 in slowly-run
Ormonde EBF Stakes at Chester: well beaten in Mappin & Webb Henry II Stakes at
Sandown and listed event at Newmarket (tailed off) last 2 outings, and not seen out
after early-July: stays 1¾m: acts on heavy going and seems unable to take much
racing on top-of-the-ground: blinkered nowadays: trained until after reappearance
by D. K. Weld. *J. P. Hudson.*

WESTERN DANCER 8 b.g. Free State 125–Polyandrist 92 (Polic 126) [1988 **69**
12g⁶ 12m 12f³ 13.3m 12g³ 14g³ 16d⁴ 16m* 14f 14.8m² 19v² 16d⁶ 1989 16s⁴ 12v⁴ 14f⁴
16m⁵ 14g 16.2d*] lengthy gelding: usually looks well: good mover: modest
handicapper: won at Haydock in October by head from Valville, leading 3f out and
battling on splendidly under strong pressure (rider suspended for excessive use of
whip): suited by good test of stamina: acts on any going: well served by strong
gallop. *C. A. Horgan.*

WESTERN DIVIDE (USA) 4 b.g. Sharpen Up 127–River Nile (USA) —
(Damascus (USA)) [1988 8d³ 10g 1989 10.2g 10s 12g] compact gelding: bad mover:
lightly raced and soundly beaten since finishing third in minor event at Sandown
early as 3-y-o: gelded after second start. *J. Perrett.*

WESTERN DYNASTY 3 ch.g. Hotfoot 126–Northern Dynasty 65 (Breeders —
Dream 116) [1988 8g 8d 7g 1989 12g⁴ 14f4] big, lengthy gelding: moderate mover:
quite modest maiden: fourth in handicaps at Leicester and Nottingham in the
summer: stays 1½m: acts on a soft surface. *M. J. Ryan.*

WESTERN GUN (USA) 4 b.c. Lypheor 118–Fandangerina (USA) (Grey Dawn **101**
II 132) [1988 8m² 8.5m⁵ 8.5f⁶ 9f 1989 8g⁵] lengthy, good-bodied colt: has a sharp,
slightly round action: useful performer: ran creditably in first half of 1988 in
3-runner listed event at Kempton and Diomed Stakes at Epsom: later raced twice in
USA: led until over 1f out when over 5 lengths fifth of 6 in £7,100 contest at Kempton
in September: stays 8.5f: acts on firm going and a soft surface: forces pace: has
joined S. Christian. *R. W. Armstrong.*

WESTERN MUSIC 2 ch.f. (Mar 20) Music Boy 124–Tripolitaine (FR) (Nono- **77**
alco (USA) 131) [1989 5f* 5m³ 6m⁵ 5s⁴ 5s⁴ 5s² 5g³ 7d] compact, workmanlike filly: fifth living foal: half-sister to 1986 2-y-o 6f winner Welsh Arrow (by
Welsh Pageant) and a winner abroad: dam won twice at around 11f in France: modest
performer: won 3-runner maiden at Ayr in June: probably stays 7f: acts on any
going: consistent. *J. S. Wilson.*

WESTERN OCEAN 2 ch.c. (Feb 6) Pharly (FR) 130–Pretty Pol 102 (Final **86**
Straw 127) [1989 7m² 7m* 8g⁴] medium-sized, lengthy colt: first foal: dam 1m and
1¼m winner: won 5-runner maiden at Yarmouth in August: good fourth of 12 to
Platonique in nursery at Doncaster following month: will stay at least 1¼m. *M. R.
Stoute.*

WESTERN SECRET 2 br.g. (Mar 23) Kind of Hush 118–My Ginny 83 —
(Palestine 133) [1989 6s] 10,000F, 12,000Y: closely related to a winner in Spain and
half-brother to several other winners, including winning stayer and fair hurdler

Mariner's Dream (by Julio Mariner): dam 2-y-o 6f winner: well beaten in 13-runner minor event at Ayr in September. *J. S. Wilson.*

WESTERN WOLF 4 ch.c. Wolverlife 115–Sweet Kate (Slippered 103) [1988 7s² 7v³ 7d³ 7g 5g⁴ 5m 6.3m 6v⁵ 6s 8v 10s⁵ 9s 1989 8v 10f4 8f⁵ 8.5g 10m4 12g 8.3m⁵ 8.5f* 8g* 8m 8d] plain ex-Irish colt: half-brother to Irish 9f winner Saintly Things (by Welsh Saint) and to a bumpers winner: dam placed over hurdles in Ireland: fair handicapper: successful in September in 18-runner event at Beverley and £10,000 contest at Ascot, in latter tending to idle when beating Northern Printer ½ length: ran moderately in well-contested events last 2 outings: best at up to 1¼m: probably acts on any going: ran poorly in blinkers: trained on reappearance by N. Meade and on next 5 starts by R. Curtis. *W. Carter.* **88**

WESTGATE ROCK 2 b.c. (Feb 25) Jalmood (USA) 126–Westgate Sovereign 89 (Sovereign Path 125) [1989 7g⁶] IR 19,000Y: half-brother to 3-y-o Gorgeous Style (by Sharpo) and 3 winners, including fairly useful 1986 Irish 2-y-o 5f winner Harry Quinn (by Jaazeiro): dam 2-y-o 5f winner: 10/1, under 6 lengths sixth of 17, staying on, to Starstreak in minor event at Leicester in November: should improve. *L. M. Cumani.* **65 p**

WEST WITH THE WIND 2 b. or br.c. (Apr 11) Glint of Gold 128–Mighty Fly 117 (Comedy Star (USA) 121) [1989 8m 8v⁶] workmanlike colt: third foal: closely related to 3-y-o 1m and 9f winner Riptide and 13f winner Skimming (both by Mill Reef): dam won Lincoln Handicap and Royal Hunt Cup: better effort around 15 lengths sixth of 23, running green 2f out and drifting left, to Tyburn Tree in minor event at Newbury in October: will be suited by 1¼m+: likely to improve. *I. A. Balding.* **59 p**

WHAT A GUY 5 b.g. What A Guest 119–Khadija 69 (Habat 127) [1988 6f* 6f² 6m 6m³ 5g⁵ 5m 6m⁵ 5f³ 6d 1989 6f 6m 6f4 5m⁶] lengthy, medium-sized gelding: quite modest winner as 4-y-o: apprentice ridden at overweight, form in 1989 (not seen out after July) only when fourth of 6 at Lingfield: suited by 6f or stiff 5f: best on top-of-the-ground: has run well when sweating: has worn crossed noseband: has got on toes, and been taken down early. *P. Mitchell.* **57**

WHAT A LINE 7 ch.g. High Line 125–Something To Hide 66 (Double-U-Jay 120) [1988 12d⁵ 12g³ 12g* 12m⁵ 11f³ 12.3f* 10g 12g² 10g 14m 12m⁵ 12m⁵ 1989 12m² 12h4 12f4 13.6f³ 12.4m⁶ 12g³] small, lightly-built gelding: plating-class handicapper: needs further than 1¼m and probably stays 15f: acts on any going: suited by waiting tactics (takes strong hold) and strong gallop: particularly well ridden by J. Lowe: often sweats and gets on edge: winning hurdler. *Mrs G. R. Reveley.* **52**

WHAT A ROWLEY 3 ch.g. What A Guest 119–Lady Rowley 114 (Royal Levee (USA)) [1988 6m² 6g⁶ 6d² 6g* 1989 6m 6m 6m 6m 6m 6g] strong, lengthy gelding: capable of fair form but thoroughly unreliable: gelded after fourth outing and refused to race after: should have stayed 7f: blinkered after penultimate outing at 2 yrs except when visored fourth start: dead. *G. A. Huffer.* **§§**

WHAT A SAVE 2 b.f. (May 21) Law Society (USA) 130–Merriment (Kings Lake (USA) 133) [1989 6m 6g³] 64,000F, 33,000Y: leggy filly: first foal: dam, remote third over 1½m at 3 yrs in Ireland, is half-sister to a champion filly in Japan and daughter of outstanding American mare Typecast: still bit backward, over 3 lengths third of 12, staying on strongly despite flashing tail, to Himmah in maiden at Leicester in November: will be much better suited by 7f+. *R. Hannon.* **63 p**

WHAT A SNIP (USA) 4 b.g. Water Bank (USA)–Snip (Shantung 132) [1988 10m⁶ 12f 12g 9f 10.4d 8.2s 12.2g* 10d 12g 1989 12g 12h 12h4 13.8m³] lengthy, rather sparely-made gelding: winning plater as 3-y-o: 3 lengths third of 6 in apprentice claiming event at Catterick in July, only subsequent worthwhile form: probably stays 13.8f: visored once at 3 yrs: blinkered (unseated rider going down, very slowly away) third start: tends to get on edge. *D. H. Topley.* **35**

WHAT HAPPENS NEXT 2 ch.c. (Jan 14) Lucky Wednesday 124–Delayed Action 113 (Jolly Jet 111) [1989 5f³ 5h⁶ 7f a6g] useful-looking colt: sixth living foal: half-brother to fairly useful sprinter Force of Action (by Galivanter) and Manx 1m winner Rapid Action (by Gunner B): dam won seven 5f races: poor form in sellers and a maiden. *W. J. Pearce.* **40**

WHATS YOURS CALLED 3 ch.f. Windjammer (USA)–Thorganby Melody (Highland Melody 112) [1988 5g 5g 8m 8g⁶ 1989 8.2m³ 9f* 11f4 10f a10g] leggy, angular filly: moderate walker: won claimer at Hamilton in June: good fourth at same course (off course 4 months after) easily best effort in handicaps subsequently: stays 11f: acts on firm going. *W. J. Pearce.* **64**

WHEATSHEAF 3 ch.c. Final Straw 127–Paperwork (Brigadier Gerard 144) 77 [1988 7m 6m² 6g³ 1989 8d³ 7m² 7f 8.2m 7m⁴ 7.5f² 8m³] leggy, workmanlike colt: modest maiden: not seen out after running moderately at Edinburgh (odds on) in July: should stay 1m: best form on top-of-the-ground: inconsistent: sold 7,400 gns Newmarket Autumn Sales. *Capt. J. Wilson.*

WHERE IS SHE 3 b.f. Beldale Flutter (USA) 130–Touraine (FR) (Luthier 126) 84 [1988 NR 1989 8.5m³ 10m* 9m² 8g² 9g] lengthy, workmanlike filly: half-sister to fair 1m and 1¼m winner Farm Club (by Kris) and to a winner in Italy: dam French 2-y-o 7f winner: evens, won slowly-run maiden at Pontefract in August: good running-on second in Sandown handicaps: best form over 1m: sold 24,000 gns Newmarket December Sales. *J. W. Hills.*

WHERE'S THE MONEY 3 b.f. Lochnager 132–Balearica 90 (Bustino 136) 71 [1988 5d 5g* 6s⁶ 5g* 6d⁶ 6s² 1989 5s³ 5g 5d 6s 5m 5d] sturdy, workmanlike filly: fair performer at best: off course 4 months after reappearance (moved poorly down but ran creditably) then well beaten: stays 6f: acts on soft going: retained 6,200 gns Newmarket December Sales. *M. J. Fetherston-Godley.*

WHIPPER IN 5 b.g. Bay Express 132–Whip Finish 77 (Be Friendly 130) [1988 63 § 6m 6g 5m 6f 1989 6f 5f⁴ 6f 6g 5m⁶ 5m⁵ 6m² 6g 5d] tall, good-topped gelding: poor mover: very useful at his best, but has deteriorated considerably: wearing crossed noseband, 1½ lengths second of 17, racing virtually alone, in seller at York in October: well beaten in handicaps afterwards: effective at 5f and 6f: best form on a sound surface: blinkered once at 4 yrs and on fifth outing, visored third: sometimes slowly away: not to be trusted. *J. Etherington.*

WHIPPET 5 b.h. Sparkler 130–St Louis Sue (FR) 79 (Nonoalco (USA) 131) [1988 115 6g³ 5g 6d⁶ 8g 6f 5g 5g⁶ 6g 5m 7g 5d 5g⁶ 6s 6m 1989 5g* 6.5g⁴ 6s⁴ 6s* 5m⁶ 5g⁵ 5m* 6d² 5f⁵ 5g² 6g⁴ 5g⁶ 5g⁴] lengthy, good-quartered horse: bad walker and moderate mover: successful at Cagnes-sur-Mer and in listed events at Evry and Milan: showed improved form when second to Cricket Ball in Prix de Ris-Orangis at Evry: ran well after when fifth in King George Stakes at Goodwood, second in listed event at Deauville and sixth in Prix de l'Abbaye de Longchamp: suited by sprint distances: acts on any going: has worn blinkers and visor: tough and smart. *J. E. Hammond, France.*

WHIPPOORWILL 2 ch.g. (Apr 10) Bold Owl 101–Whipalash 73 (Stephen 42 George 102) [1989 5f⁶ 6m⁶ 6m 7m 5m 6g] 4,600Y: plain gelding: has a markedly round action: sixth foal: brother to modest sprint maiden James Owl and half-brother to 3-y-o Richards Pet (by Noalto): quite modest plater: stays 6f: has worn bandages. *M. W. Easterby.*

WHIPP'S CROSS 4 gr.f. Kris 135–Be Easy 110 (Be Friendly 130) [1988 8d³ 7f 89 7m 10g* 10g⁶ 10m³ 10s³ 10g 10s* 11s* 1989 10v 10d³ 10d⁴ 10f⁶] close-coupled, sparely-made filly: fairly useful performer: in frame in minor event at Pontefract and listed race at Phoenix Park in spring: wearing severe bridle and mounted on track, soundly-beaten last of 6 in listed contest at Goodwood in May: stayed 11f: suited by plenty of give in the ground: usually held up: virtually bolted before fifth appearance at 3 yrs and taken early or quietly to post subsequently: in foal to Petoski. *C. F. Wall.*

WHIRLYGIGGER 3 b.f. Taufan (USA) 119–Pavella (Palestine 133) [1988 NR 69 1989 7g⁵ 8m 10.6m⁴ 12g⁴ 14g] IR 7,500Y, 3,600 2-y-o: close-coupled, workmanlike filly: half-sister to numerous winners, including useful middle-distance stayer Dowdall (by Dike) and useful 1980 Irish 2-y-o 7.9f winner Tumblella (by Tumble Wind): dam won Madrid Free Handicap and fourth in Irish 1000 Guineas: modest maiden: moved poorly down and ran poorly final start: probably stays 1½m: sweating third start: sold 5,200 gns Newmarket Autumn Sales. *C. E. Brittain.*

WHISPERING HEIGHTS 3 ch.f. Kind of Hush 118–Horton Line 89 (High — § Line 125) [1988 7m 8h 1989 8.5f] has shown plenty of temperament but no ability in maiden events: sold 780 gns Doncaster June Sales: one to avoid. *J. A. Glover.*

WHISPERING SEA 2 b.f. (Apr 25) Bustino 136–Sound of The Sea 91 52 p (Windjammer (USA)) [1989 8g] IR 20,000Y: first reported foal: dam stayed 7f but better at shorter: 14/1 and very green, around 10 lengths eighth of 16, fading final furlong and eased, to Bawbee in maiden at Leicester in November: likely to improve. *P. T. Walwyn.*

WHISPER THE WIND 3 b.f. Night Shift (USA)–Mossage 75 (Ballymoss 136) 64 [1988 5f² 5m⁶ 5m² 5g⁶ 6m⁵ 6g⁶ 6g⁶ 1989 8.5d 8g 6f² 5m⁴ 6f 6m⁵ 6g 6f⁵ 6f* 6f] sturdy, workmanlike filly: has a round action: 16/1, made all in maiden at Folkestone in August: generally well below that form otherwise except when second in claimer (claimed out of Lord John FitzGerald's stable £12,127) at Nottingham: suited by 6f:

acts on firm going: usually blinkered: doubtful temperamentally: sold to race in Saudi Arabia 2,800 gns Newmarket Autumn Sales. *R. W. Stubbs.*

WHISTLE THE WIND 3 ch.f. Dara Monarch 128–Headin' Home 105 (Habitat 134) [1988 6m⁴ 7g⁴ 8g³ 1989 8g 8m] close-coupled, angular filly: keen walker: has a quick action: quite modest maiden at 2 yrs: soundly beaten in handicap (sweating and backward) in May and maiden (didn't take eye in preliminaries, pulled hard) in September: better suited by 1m than shorter. *G. A. Pritchard-Gordon.*

WHISTLING BLUES 3 ch.f. Stanford 121§–Whistling Girl 68 (Whistling Wind 123) [1988 6d 5m 6d 1989 8.2s 6d 7g⁵ 5g² 5g⁶ 5m 7.6m] rangy filly: has a roundish action: plating-class maiden: showed nothing in handicap and seller last 2 outings: best efforts over 5f (should be suited by further) on good ground. *H. P. Rohan.* 48

WHISTLING GALE 2 ch.f. (May 11) Whistling Deer 117–Velpol (Polyfoto 124) [1989 6f 5f 6m⁴ 7m⁵ 7d 6s⁶] IR 2,800Y: small filly: half-sister to Irish 9f and 1½m winner Woodview Gold (by Condorcet): dam never ran: quite modest plater: best effort in claimer final start: will probably stay 1m: changed hands 1,000 gns Doncaster October Sales after fifth outing. *M. Brittain.* 38

WHISTLING WILDE 2 br.f. (May 18) Whistling Deer 117–Deviation (Petingo 135) [1989 6m 7m⁵ 7.5g⁶ 7f] IR 2,100Y: leggy filly: half-sister to fair 1981 2-y-o 5f winner Kash-In (by Kashiwa) dam unraced: poor form in sellers: usually edgy. *T. D. Barron.* 32

WHITCOMBE PRINCE 2 b.c. (May 25) Anita's Prince 126–Hello Stranger (Milesian 125) [1989 5m 5h⁵ 6m 5.8f⁵ 5f 8f] IR 2,000F, IR 1,100Y, 8,000 2-y-o: small colt: half-brother to several winners, notably useful middle-distance stayer Grey Thunder (by Sea Hawk II): dam useful winner over 1m in Ireland: of little account. *N. R. Mitchell.* —

WHITCOMBE WARRIOR 3 b.g. Tina's Pet 121–Minuetto 59 (Roan Rocket 128) [1988 5g⁵ 1989 7s] smallish gelding: poor form in maidens at Bath (beaten about 4 lengths) in May, 1988, and Epsom nearly year later. *N. R. Mitchell.* —

WHITE CLOUD 2 ro.c. (May 7) Vaigly Great 127–Cheyenne 83 (Sovereign Path 125) [1989 6g] 2,000F, 17,500Y: closely related to 1½m winner Choctaw (by Great Nephew) and half-brother to 2 winners abroad and a winning hurdler: dam, 6f winner at 2 yrs, is sister to very useful stayer Warpath: fifteenth of 19 in maiden at Redcar in November. *C. W. Thornton.* —

WHITE GLOW 3 b.c. Kalaglow 132–Bianca Lancia (FR) (Mill Reef (USA) 141) [1988 NR 1989 10g⁴ 10g] 74,000Y: smallish, rather sparely-made colt: first foal: dam never ran: green, modest form but shaped well, making smooth headway 3f out, in late-season minor events at Nottingham and Leicester, in last-named eased right down when one pace 2f out: changed hands 35,000 gns Newmarket Autumn Sales in between: has plenty of ability and is sure to win a race or two. *A. C. Stewart.* 79 p

WHITEHOUSE GEM 6 ch.m. Amboise 113–Golden Pinelopi 62 (Sovereign Lord 120) [1988 NR 1989 10.2m³] seventh reported live foal: dam half-sister to very smart Relpin: 4½ lengths third of 7 in amateurs event at Doncaster in July: poor hurdler. *Miss S. J. Wilton.* 30

WHITE JASMIN 3 ch.f. Jalmood (USA) 126–Willowbed 66 (Wollow 132) [1988 6s 7s 8m³ 8g 1989 12.2m³ 12f 12m⁵ 12.2m⁴ 16f* 19f³ 16m⁵] angular filly: plating-class handicapper: won moderately-run race at Thirsk in July: stays 19f: best efforts on top-of-the-ground: flashes tail under pressure: changed hands 3,000 gns Ascot September Sales after sixth start. *C. W. Thornton.* 51

WHITE RIVER 3 ch.c. Pharly (FR) 130–Regain 86 (Relko 136) [1988 7m 7g 7g 1989 6d 8.2s 8g 9f⁶ 12m² 17.6m⁵ 12g a12g⁶ a16g] smallish, lengthy colt: edgy, easily best effort as 3-y-o when beaten neck in handicap at Pontefract in August having been pushed along and well behind 3f out: moved poorly down next start: stays 1½m well: worth a try in blinkers or visor. *D. Haydn Jones.* 58

WHITE SAPPHIRE 4 b.c. Sparkler 130–On A Bit 66 (Mummy's Pet 125) [1988 10g* 10d³ 9m* 8d⁴ 10s 9f⁴ 9g⁶ 1989 9m⁶ 9g³ 10.2m³ 10m* 9f 10.6m 9g] good-topped colt: moderate mover: fair handicapper: won at Ripon in August: well beaten last 3, though not entirely discredited in William Hill Cambridgeshire Handicap at Newmarket on final one: suited by around 1¼m: acts on any going: wandered and found little when blinkered final outing at 3 yrs: gave trouble at stalls once on reappearance: not the easiest of rides: sold to race in Middle East 40,000 gns Newmarket Autumn Sales. *J. G. FitzGerald.* 88

WHITE SQUIRREL 2 b.f. (Feb 23) Noalto 120–Lovely Lassie (Connaught 130) [1989 6f 5m⁶ 7m⁶] 2,200Y: angular, dipped-backed filly: fifth foal: half-sister to a 59

winner in Italy: dam unraced daughter of half-sister to Lacquer and Sovereign: plating-class form in fair company, best effort final start: will stay at least 1m. *W. Carter.*

WHITE-WASH 4 b.f. Final Straw 127–Cecilia Bianchi (FR) (Petingo 135) [1988 **92** 8s* 7f² 8f⁴ 9m⁴ 10g* 10m 1989 12d³ 12.3f³ 12m⁵ 10.5f³ 10g⁴ 10g] smallish, quite well-made filly: has a quick action: fairly useful performer: creditable third to Icona in £32,000 handicap at York in July, edging left and weakening over 1f out: 33/1, carrying condition and facing stiff task, not discredited when fourth of 5 in listed event won by Monastery at Goodwood nearly 3 months later: ran moderately in Ascot handicap final outing: ideally suited by 1¼m: acts on any going. *J. L. Dunlop.*

WHITEWEBB 2 br.g. (Apr 13) Carwhite 127–Mrs Webb (Sonnen Gold 121) **47** [1989 5s⁶ 5g⁶ 6m 6v 8g] 2,600Y: leggy, sparely-made gelding: second foal: dam ran 3 times, well beaten, at 2 yrs: poor maiden: off course 5 months after third outing: sold to join J. Wainwright 1,250 gns Doncaster November Sales. *C. Tinkler.*

WHO GIVES A DONALD 2 bl.g. (Feb 10) King of Spain 121–Minuetto 59 **50** (Roan Rocket 128) [1989 5d 5g³ 6m] 3,700Y: small, sparely-made gelding: fifth foal: half-brother to 3-y-o Whitcombe Warrior (by Tina's Pet): dam placed at 5f at 2 yrs, only season: modest plater: not raced after June. *C. Tinkler.*

WHYBROWS 3 b.g. Star Appeal 133–Haida (Astec 128) [1988 8m 7.5f³ 8g⁴ 8g 8g **62** 1989 8s⁵ 8s⁴ 12.2d⁴ 12m 12f⁵ 12.3m³ 10g² 10m 12f4] medium-sized, well-made gelding: quite modest performer: claimed out of F. Durr's stable third start: contested amateurs events after, running poorly (wandered under pressure) penultimate start but creditably otherwise last 5 outings: 14 lb overweight, narrowly beaten at Beverley final start, in August: stays 1½m: probably acts on any going: blinkered once at 2 yrs: sold to join R. Lee 13,000 gns Doncaster September Sales and subsequently gelded. *Denys Smith.*

WICK POUND 3 b.c. Niniski (USA) 125–Hors Serie (USA) 103 (Vaguely Noble **76** 140) [1988 7g⁴ 8g 7g 1989 10.1m⁶ 10m 12.2m*] small, lightly-made colt: has a quick action: first run for over 4 months, showed improved form when winning handicap at Warwick in October by 4 lengths, quickening well 1½f out and soon clear: stays 1½m well: sold to join J. Old 23,000 gns Newmarket Autumn Sales. *Major W. R. Hern.*

WIG (USA) 3 b.f. Clever Trick (USA)–Noble Damsel (USA) (Vaguely Noble 140) **—** [1988 NR 1989 8m 10m] $50,000Y: rather leggy filly: first reported living foal: dam winner at up to 11f in USA, very useful turf performer at 4 yrs, is daughter of smart 2-y-o sprinter Tender Camilla: sire very smart sprinter/miler: always behind in Newmarket maiden and claimer (pulling hard) at Newbury in the summer: sold 3,000 gns Newmarket December Sales. *B. Hanbury.*

WILD DANCER 2 br.g. (Feb 10) Gorytus (USA) 132–Rosserk (Roan Rocket **69** 128) [1989 6m* 7g³ 7m⁴ 7f4] IR 10,500Y: good-topped gelding: has scope: good mover with long stride: fifth foal: brother to a poor sprint maiden and half-brother to 3-y-o Sarhan (by Ahonoora): dam, lightly raced in Ireland, is sister to very speedy 1969 Irish 2-y-o True Rocket, dam of Ballad Rock: won maiden at Carlisle in May: not raced after July: stays 7f. *C. Tinkler.*

WILD MOON (USA) 4 b.f. Arctic Tern (USA) 126–Wild Lover (USA) (Lyphard **—** (USA) 132) [1988 8g* 10m⁶ 10s 8g² 8g 9.5m³ 8d³ 1989 8g 10v 7g] sparely-made ex-French filly: first foal: dam, French 10.5f winner, daughter of half-sister to Dahlia: won handicap at Evry as 3-y-o when trained by Mme C. Head: well beaten in listed races at Doncaster and Leicester (reluctant to go down) and in minor event at Kempton in spring: stays 9.5f: acts on top-of-the-ground and a soft surface. *K. T. Ivory.*

WILD REVENGE 3 ch.f. Krayyan 117–Prodigality (Mount Hagen (FR) 127) **—** [1988 NR 1989 8.3m 8.3m] 5,800 2-y-o, resold 400 2-y-o: small, plain filly: fourth foal: dam plating-class maiden: behind in claimer and seller at Windsor within 5 days in July. *K. O. Cunningham-Brown.*

WILD SAGE 2 ch.f. (Mar 20) Noalto 120–Jenny's Rocket 90 (Roan Rocket 128) **46** [1989 5m 7g] 4,000Y: plain filly: fourth foal: half-sister to 5f winner Sleepers (by Swing Easy): dam, 6f winner at 2 yrs, also won over hurdles: well beaten in summer maidens at Windsor (slowly away) and Leicester. *P. Mitchell.*

WILD WARRIOR 2 b.c. (Apr 21) Trojan Fen 118–Mary Mitsu 110 (Tarboosh **47** (USA)) [1989 7g 8.2g 6s a7g] IR 8,400Y: good-bodied colt: half-brother to 3-y-o Malham Tarn (by Riverman): dam very useful 5f and 1m winner: poor form in maidens and a claimer: sold 1,850 gns Doncaster November Sales. *C. Tinkler.*

WILLBUTWHEN 2 ch.c. (Feb 8) Nicholas Bill 125–Henceforth 58 (Full of Hope **88**
125) [1989 5s* 5m⁴ 5g²] neat, good-quartered colt: good walker: third foal: brother
to 4-y-o 1¼m winner William Four and 9f winner Bildad: dam won once over 5f from
3 races at 2 yrs: won 10-runner maiden at Nottingham in May: ran very well in
late-season nurseries at Newmarket: will be well suited by 6f: should win another
race. *H. Candy.*

WILLIAM FOUR 4 b.g. Nicholas Bill 125–Henceforth 58 (Full of Hope 125) **74**
[1988 7d² 8m⁴ 1989 8m³ 10f⁵ 10m* 10.2g² 10g³ a10g⁶] leggy, quite good-topped
gelding: modest handicapper: co-favourite and ridden by 7-lb claimer, won slowly-
run 6-runner event at Chepstow in August: placed, running well, at Doncaster
(sweating) and Newmarket (apprentices) afterwards: will stay 1½m: yet to race on
soft going, acts on any other: has run creditably for amateur: consistent. *H. Candy.*

WILLIE MCGARR (USA) 4 ch.g. Master Willie 129–Pay T V (USA) (T V —
Commercial (USA)) [1988 NR 1989 8.3m] medium-sized gelding: half-brother to 2
winners in USA: dam won 10 races, including in minor stakes company at 6 yrs, at up
to 1m: 16/1, lost place 4f out in seller at Windsor in July: poor hurdler. *B. Palling.*

WILLILOV 3 ch.g. Rabdan 129–Miss Love 58 (Ragstone 128) [1988 NR 1989 7m⁵ —
8.5f⁵ 10f³ 10m 8f⁴ 10m] leggy gelding: second foal: dam, suited by 1½m on flat, won
over hurdles: little worthwhile form, including in handicaps: mulish at stalls and
withdrawn fifth intended start: should stay beyond 1m: has looked ill at ease on firm
going. *Denys Smith.*

WILL JAMES 3 ch.g. Raga Navarro (ITY) 119–Sleekit 78 (Blakeney 126) [1988 —
NR 1989 10h 7m⁵ 7m] sturdy gelding: fourth foal: half-brother to 1¼m winner Kitty
Clare (by Milford): dam winner at 1½m: well beaten in maidens and claimer. *Andrew
Turnell.*

WILLOW GORGE 6 ch.g. Hello Gorgeous (USA) 128–Willowy (Mourne 126) —
[1988 NR 1989 15.5f] tall, quite attractive gelding: poor maiden on flat: stays 13f:
probably acts on any going: has run well for apprentice: tailed off in blinkers:
winning hurdler. *Miss B. Sanders.*

WILL RAINE 5 ch.g. Nicholas Bill 125–Chinese Falcon 81 (Skymaster 126) —
[1988 NR 1989 14m 10f] smallish, workmanlike gelding: showed signs of ability as
3-y-o, but seemed a difficult ride and possibly isn't genuine: tailed off both outings in
1989: blinkered once: has sweated. *I. Campbell.*

WILVICK 2 ch.c. (Mar 7) Gabitat 119–Pas de Chat (Relko 136) [1989 5h⁵ 6m³ 5m³ **68**
5.3h* 6g⁶] compact colt: moderate mover: fifth foal: half-brother to 3-y-o Carvick
and thoroughly unreliable 5f and 7f winner Jovick (both by Swing Easy): dam ran
twice: won 5-runner nursery at Brighton in August, showing much improved form:
bred to stay beyond 6f: sweating third outing, went freely down last two. *R.
Akehurst.*

WIMBORNE 4 ro.c. What A Guest 119–Khadija 69 (Habat 127) [1988 10g 10m 8v **39**
1989 8.2v³ 10d 12.5f 8.2f 8h* 8f* 9m² 11f² 10f⁵ 8.2d] lengthy, rather angular colt: has
a rather round action: won selling handicaps at Carlisle (no bid) and Pontefract
(bought in 5,000 gns) in June: stays 11f, at least in slowly-run race: acts on any going:
slowly away last 2 outings, hanging badly right first time and facing very stiff task on
second: usually taken down early nowadays. *R. Bastiman.*

WINDATUM 4 gr.c. Windjammer (USA)–Raffinata (Raffingora 130) [1988 6s 5g³ **65** §
6v5 5g⁴ 6d 5.3f⁵ 6m 6f* 6g 6g 6m² 6g 6m 6m⁵ 7g* 8m 7g 7g³ 6m 1989 6s 7g 7.6m³
9m⁵ 8m⁵ 7.6f* 8m 7.6f² 8g⁴ 8m 7.6m² 7.6m] tall, sparely-made colt: poor mover:
quite modest handicapper: has gained 2 of his 4 wins at Lingfield, and won there
in July: stays 9f: acts on any going: has worn blinkers and visor, but not when
successful: has worn bandages, but didn't in 1989: has won for apprentice: unreliable. *Mrs N. Macauley.*

WINDBOUND LASS 6 ch.m. Crofter (USA) 124–Nevilles Cross (USA) 67 **53**
(Nodouble (USA)) [1988 12f* 12f³ 13.3m⁵ 12g² 1989 12g⁵ 12g³ 11.5f³ 17.1h² 13.1h²
12f² 12m] leggy, plain mare: plating-class handicapper: ran as though something
amiss final start: suited by strongly-run race at 1½m and seems to stay 17f: acts well
on top-of-the-ground: successful hurdler: consistent. *R. J. Holder.*

WINDBURN 3 b.f. Windjammer (USA)–Bourges (FR) (Luthier 126) [1988 6m 7g —
6m 1989 7h 8m 7h] big, workmanlike filly: no worthwhile form: well-backed
favourite in seller second outing: blinkered once at 2 yrs. *G. B. Balding.*

WIND OF FLOWER (FR) 3 ch.f. Pharly (FR) 130–Flower Parade (Mill Reef **66**
(USA) 141) [1988 7m² 1989 8d³ 9m] angular, sparely-made filly: placed in maidens at
Leicester (beaten short head) and Ripon: moved poorly down and ran poorly, never

982

striding out well, in minor event at Wolverhampton: stayed 1m: dead. *M. H. Tompkins.*

WINDSOR PARK (USA) 3 br.c. Bold Forbes (USA)–Round Tower 93 (High 85 Top 131) [1988 5g² 5m³ 1989 5g 7h⁵ 8m³ 10m² 12g 10g⁴ 10g* 10g² a12g* a12g* a12g²] leggy, quite attractive colt: good walker: comfortable winner of slowly-run claimer (claimed out of W. Hastings-Bass's stable £18,000) at Goodwood and handicaps (ridden by 5-lb claimer) at Lingfield towards end of season: stays 1½m: acts on top-of-the-ground: taken down early third start. *R. J. O'Sullivan.*

WINDWARD ARIOM 3 ch.c. Pas de Seul 133–Deja Vu (FR) (Be My Guest — (USA) 126) [1988 6g 6f 7m 7g 1989 9f 8h 8m 8g 12.2m⁵] leggy, close-coupled colt: has a roundish action: little worthwhile form, including in handicaps: probably stays 1½m: blinkered once at 2 yrs. *D. H. Topley.*

WINE CELLAR 2 br.f. (May 30) Muscatite 122–Passage Falcon (Falcon 131) 62 [1989 5s³ 5d² 5f³ 6m³ 6f* 7f* 6f² 6f* 7.5m⁴] IR 2,500Y: smallish, close-coupled filly: half-sister to successful Irish 5f performer Just A Shadow (by Laser Light) and 1983 2-y-o 6f and 7f winner Lawnswood Avenger (by Gulf Pearl): dam unplaced 4 times in Ireland: useful plater: successful (no bid) at Thirsk and Redcar in the summer, and in claimer at Redcar in between: good fourth in nursery at Beverley in August: stays 7.5f: best form on firm going: game and genuine. *M. H. Easterby.*

WINGED FOOT 3 b.f. Tap On Wood 130–Goirtin (Levmoss 133) [1988 6m 6f⁶ 56 1989 12.2d⁶ 8d⁴ 12d⁵ 10f³ 11f³ 11.3f⁶ 10g⁵ 11f³ 10.6d 10m 10f⁶] IR 17,000Y: small, quite well-made filly: has a round action: third living foal: sister to modest 9.4f winner Lyapkin-Tyapkin: dam Irish 1¼m winner: plating-class maiden: below form at Beverley last 2 outings: stays 1½m: acts on firm going and a soft surface: trained at 2 yrs by M. Kauntze in Ireland. *J. Parkes.*

WINGED MELODY 3 gr.f. Song 132–Fancy Flight (FR) 74 (Arctic Tern (USA) — 126) [1988 NR 1989 6f⁴ 6m 6m] leggy filly: first foal: dam 1¼m winner: no worthwhile form in maiden (bandaged, hung throughout), claimer and seller (moved poorly down) in the summer. *D. R. C. Elsworth.*

WINGED PHARAOH 5 b.g. Beldale Flutter (USA) 130–Fly For Home 78 — (Habitat 134) [1988 14.6d 1989 12d] no form in maidens or handicap. *S. G. Norton.*

WING OF FREEDOM 5 ch.m. Troy 137–Marablue 86 (Bold Lad (IRE) 133) — [1988 16m³ 1989 14.6g 16.2d 17f⁶ 17.6f⁶ 14.8m] sturdy mare: in frame in maidens: bandaged, soundly beaten, including in handicaps, in 1989: blinkered once. *A. P. James.*

WING PARK 5 ch.h. Golden Dipper 119–Puente Primera 90 (Primera 131) [1988 — 7g 7m* 7.6f 6f² 6g² 5d⁵ 5g⁵ 7s 1989 6m 6f] lengthy horse: made up into useful 4-y-o, running a tremendous race when fifth in William Hill Sprint Championship at York: facing stiff tasks, prominent until 2f out in £8,000 handicap at York and Cork and Orrery Stakes (well beaten, reportedly jarred up) at Royal Ascot within a week in 1989: best form at 5f: acts on firm going and a soft surface: suited by forcing tactics: genuine: remains in training. *A. Bailey.*

WINKING WINNER 4 ch.c. Vaigly Great 127–Toccatina 79 (Bleep-Bleep 134) 79 [1988 7g 6d⁶ 6g³ 7g⁶ 6m* 6m³ 6d⁵ 7m 7.6f³ 8.3m² 8g⁴ 7.6m* 7d 7g 1989 7g³ 7d³ 7.6m 7.6m*] strong, workmanlike colt: fair handicapper: first outing for 4 months, won at Lingfield in September, leading final stride: stays 1m: acts on firm going and a soft surface: good mount for apprentice: genuine and consistent: sold to race in Saudi Arabia 17,000 gns Newmarket Autumn Sales. *N. A. Callaghan.*

WINMOSS 4 b.g. Windjammer (USA)–Mossy Girl (Ballymoss 136) [1988 8.2v* — 9d² 8g⁶ 8.2m 9f 10.2g 1989 8s 10s 11.7d⁵ 8.3m⁴ 8.5f⁶ 9g 12s⁴] workmanlike gelding: has lost his form: stays 9f: used to go particularly well with plenty of give in the ground: suitable mount for apprentice: usually visored at 2 yrs: has worn bandages: sold 600 gns Ascot December Sales: inconsistent. *M. Brittain.*

WINNIES LUCK 5 b.m. Music Boy 124–Home Sweet Home (Royal Palace 131) — [1988 7g 8s⁵ 10g³ 7m 10v 1989 10d⁶ 16.2g] smallish, workmanlike mare: moderate mover: poor plater: best form at 1m: suited by give in the ground, but not heavy going: dead. *G. H. Jones.*

WINNING GALLERY 4 b.c. Giacometti 130–Balnespick 101 (Charlottown 94 127) [1988 14f* 1989 13.3m² 16f 16m⁵ 16.1g* 14m] lightly-raced performer: won handicap at Newmarket in July, hanging right once leading 1½f out: pulled up very lame 6f out in similar event at Sandown week later: stays 2m: bandaged at 4 yrs: whipped round from flag start and soon pulled up second outing: seems suited by waiting tactics: difficult to train. *N. A. Callaghan.*

WINSLOW LAD 2 br.g. (Feb 27) Horage 124–Rathcoffey Daisy (Pampapaul 121) **55**
[1989 7m⁵ 7f⁶ 8.2f 8m 8m³ 10f⁶ 8g⁴] IR 1,600Y: angular, sparely-made gelding:
moderate mover: second foal: dam never ran: fair plater: suited by 1m: showed
nothing when blinkered: best form ridden by 7-lb claimer. *R. W. Stubbs.*

WINTER STORM 4 b.g. Formidable (USA) 125–December Rose (Silly Season
127) [1988 8.5m 12m⁶ 14.7f 12.3f⁶ 13g⁵ 9g³ 11g* 10m 10g 10m 10m² 12f² 1989 12s 12d
12.3f⁶ 12.3m 14f] good-topped gelding: poor mover: quite modest winner as 3-y-o:
well below form in handicaps in 1989: stays 1½m, at least in moderately-run race:
acts on firm going: blinkered twice at 3 yrs: bandaged behind final outing: suited by
front-running tactics: sold to join K. Oliver 1,600 gns Doncaster October Sales. *T. D.
Barron.*

WISCONSIN 5 b.m. Mummy's Game 120–Montana (Mossborough 126) [1988 —
12g 12m 8f⁴ 12g⁵ 14g⁵ 1989 16m 14m 12h 12h⁶] big, rangy, workmanlike mare:
moderate mover: no longer of much account on flat: sometimes visored nowadays:
occasionally sweats: winning hurdler. *M. C. Chapman.*

WISECOURSE (USA) 5 b.g. Irish River (FR) 131–Strigida 120 (Habitat 134) —
[1988 10.8d 10s 12d 10g² 10f 9g 9g⁵ 9g 8.2s⁴ 1989 9v³ 10h] strong, workmanlike
gelding: poor maiden: tailed off virtually throughout in handicap at Brighton in May:
better suited by 1¼m than 1m: acts on heavy going and seems unsuited by hard:
visored once at 4 yrs: sold 1,500 gns Ascot December Sales. *C. C. Trietline.*

WISE TIMES 5 b.m. Young Generation 129–Ballinkillen (Levmoss 133) [1988 7g —
1989 8m 8m 10g] strong, close-coupled mare: has a round action: modest maiden at 2
yrs: very little subsequent form: stays 7f: acts on top-of-the-ground and a soft
surface. *D. R. C. Elsworth.*

WISHAWAY (USA) 3 b.g. Lyphard's Wish (FR) 124–Hy Carol (USA) (Hy **77 +**
Frost) [1988 6m⁴ 8d 8m 6d* 1989 7g* 7g] lengthy, good-bodied gelding: won £6,000
handicap (carrying condition) at Newbury in August by short head having been last
over 2f out and checked approaching final 1f: favourite and ridden by 7-lb claimer,
ran moderately in similar event 3 weeks later: will probably stay 1m: acts well
on a soft surface: sold 30,000 gns Newmarket Autumn Sales and gelded. *R. W.
Armstrong.*

WISHIAH 3 b.f. Persian Bold 123–Last Request 92 (Dancer's Image (USA)) **90**
[1988 6f⁵ 8s⁶ 8h⁵ 9g⁴ 10d* 10.2m⁴ 1989 10.2m 10.2f 9f² 8g⁴ 8m 9m* 10f* 10g] leggy,
close-coupled filly: moderate mover with a roundish action: fair handicapper: well
backed, successful twice at Redcar in the autumn: bit edgy, ran moderately there in
£8,900 event final start: suited by 1¼m: acts on firm going and a soft surface: used
to make running but didn't last 4 starts: visits Warning. *H. Thomson Jones.*

WISHLON (USA) 6 b.h. Lyphard's Wish (FR) 124–Swiss Swish (USA) (Wajima **85**
(USA)) [1988 7.6g⁶ 10m 14f 12g² 12g 1989 10g⁶ 12d* 8f 14f⁵ 12m⁵] very tall, leggy
horse: has a round action: fair handicapper: won strongly-run apprentice event at
Ascot in April: needed further than 1¼m and probably stayed 1¾m: acted on any
going, but went particularly well on an easy surface: sometimes sweated: usually
held up: smart hurdler: retired to Church Farm Stud, Leighton Buzzard, fee £400
(Oct 1st). *R. V. Smyth.*

WISH YOU WELL 3 b.f. Sadler's Wells (USA) 132–Happy Thought (FR) (Kauai **78**
King) [1988 NR 1989 12m⁵ 12g 14d⁶ 14g] 190,000Y: angular, medium-sized filly:
half-sister to 2 winners, notably very smart 1983 2-y-o Creag-An-Sgor (by Captain
James): dam slow half-sister to smart stayer Stetchworth: modest maiden: will be
suited by an extreme test of stamina. *C. R. Nelson.*

WITH GUSTO 2 b.c. (Mar 25) Taufan (USA) 119–Finesse 87 (Miralgo 130) [1989 —
7m 7g] 16,500F, 34,000Y: good-topped colt: half-brother to several winners,
including very useful Irish sprinter Princess Seal and Irish 1½m winner South
Meadow (both by Prince Tenderfoot): dam won over 1½m: poor form in summer
maidens at Newmarket and Yarmouth: sold 4,500 gns Newmarket Autumn Sales. *R.
J. R. Williams.*

WITHIN REASON 2 ch.f. (Apr 12) Reasonable (FR) 119–Nom de Plume 70 —
(Aureole 132) [1989 6m⁶ 5m 5g 6g] lengthy, sparely-made filly: half-sister to 3-y-o
Brinksway (by Electric) and 4 winners, including useful French Gent (by Sassafras),
5f to 7f winner at 2 yrs who stayed 1½m: dam ran only at 2 yrs, winning over 7f: no
form: probably needs further. *P. S. Felgate.*

WITHOUT EQUAL (USA) 2 ch.c. (Apr 16) Sharpen Up 127–Key Tothe **71 p**
Minstrel (USA) 108 (The Minstrel (CAN) 135) [1989 6m⁶ 8g⁴] 200,000Y:
medium-sized, quite powerful colt: second foal: closely related to 3-y-o 1m winner
Go On Smile (by Diesis): dam, 2-y-o 6f winner fourth in Hoover Fillies' Mile, is out

of unraced half-sister to top-class Fort Marcy and Key To The Mint: modest form, running on well not knocked about, in maidens at Newmarket in July and Leicester in November: will probably stay 1¼m: likely to improve: should win a maiden. *M. R. Stoute.*

WITHY BANK 7 b.g. Blakeney 126–Chiltern Lass 100 (High Hat 131) [1988 18g² **72** 19v⁶ 17.4s⁶ 1989 18g³ 21.6d² 16d³ 18.4m] well-made gelding: good walker: modest handicapper: suited by a good test of stamina: ideally suited by an easy surface: genuine: winning hurdler/chaser. *M. H. Easterby.*

WIZARDRY 3 b.f. Shirley Heights 130–Merlins Charm (USA) 113 (Bold Bidder) **83** [1988 NR 1989 8g 11.3m⁴ 12f⁵ 14.6g⁴ a10g³ a12g⁶] rangy filly: has a round action: has plenty of scope: poor walker: third foal: half-sister to 8.5f winner Island Charm (by Golden Fleece) and Black Sabbath (by Be My Guest), once-raced here later 1989 7f and 1m winner in Belgium: dam won Jersey Stakes: fair form: best effort in Cheshire Oaks second start, running in snatches: 3½ lengths third of 13 to New Arrangement in maiden at Lingfield: may be suited by around 1¼m: looked ill at ease on firm ground: sweating and edgy, ran poorly third start: flashed tail at Chester and did so constantly in 4-runner 14.6f Park Hill Stakes at Doncaster: sold 36,000 gns Newmarket December Sales. *B. W. Hills.*

WIZZARD ARTIST 4 b.c. Electric 126–Polly Darling 80 (Darling Boy 124) **63** [1988 12d 12m⁵ 12g² 10g⁵ 12g 12g* 12m⁶ 12g 1989 12g 12s 11.7m 14f⁴ 14f⁵ 16m* 18.8f² 16.5m* 16f⁵ 12m⁵ 16f a16g] small, workmanlike colt: moderate mover: quite modest handicapper: successful in July at Chepstow and Doncaster: stayed 2¼m: acted on firm going: winning hurdler: dead. *M. J. Haynes.*

WIZZARD MAGIC 6 ch.h. Ahonoora 122–Siofra Beag (Steel Heart 128) [1988 7f **55** 8f⁴ 8m³ 8g 8g³ 9.3g⁴ 1989 8g 9d⁵ 10f⁶ 9.2f 9m 8m² 10m⁵ 10g⁴ 7s a8g* a10g⁶] good-topped horse: plating-class performer: best on line when winning claimer at Lingfield in October: stays 1¼m: acts on firm going and possibly unsuited by soft: has worn blinkers, visored nowadays: suitable mount for inexperienced rider: sometimes sweats. *M. J. Haynes.*

WOLVER GEM 3 b.c. Wolver Hollow 126–Perle's Fashion (Sallust 134) [1988 — 7.5m 8m 8s 1989 8f 10g 10m 10m 8.2g] leggy, angular colt: has a round action: quite modest maiden as 2-y-o: showed little in 1989: bred to stay 1¼m: blinkered fourth start: has joined Mrs G. Reveley. *J. A. Glover.*

WOLVER GOLD 2 b.f. (Apr 1) Wolverlife 115–Mahele (USA) (Hawaii) [1989 6f **73** 6g 5f² 5.8f² 5f* 6g 5f] 1,000F: tall, leggy filly: sixth reported foal: sister to Gold Bondage, winner at up to 6f in USA: dam showed poor form: modest performer: won nursery at Chepstow in September: best form at 5f: sometimes troublesome at stalls. *J. D. Roberts.*

WONDER DANCER (USA) 3 b.c. Raise A Native–White Reason (USA) (Hail **111** To Reason) [1988 6m* 6g* 5s⁴ 6g⁴ 1989 5m 6m 5f² 5f⁶ 5f 5m 5m] useful-looking colt: very useful performer: ran creditably third to sixth outings in pattern events at Sandown (2½ lengths second to Dancing Dissident in Sears Temple Stakes), Royal Ascot, Goodwood and York: visored, raced alone when behind in Newmarket listed race on final one: will probably prove best at 5f on a sound surface: blinkered first 2 (edgy and below form) and fifth starts. *A. Bailey.*

WONDER MAN (FR) 4 ch.g. The Wonder (FR) 129–Juvenilia (FR) (Kashmir II — 125) [1988 10g² 8g² 9g* 9g* 8g* 10g² 10g6 10.1m 9s⁵ 10d 8s 1989 10m] big, strong, good-topped gelding: usually looks well: successful 3 times in French Provinces as 3-y-o: 33/1 in need of race, not discredited when eighth of 16 in £24,200 handicap at Newbury in September, running on strongly from rear then not getting clear run 2f out and not knocked about: probably stays 1¼m: edgy and carried head awkwardly final outing at 3 yrs: winning hurdler with Mrs J. Pitman. *H. Candy.*

WONDERMENT 2 b.f. (Apr 15) Mummy's Pet 125–Baffle 87 (Petingo 135) — [1989 7f] compact filly: sister to very useful 6f and 7f winner Mister Wonderful, later a good winner in USA, and half-sister to several winners, including 3-y-o 1½m and 1¾m winner Castle Secret (by Castle Keep): dam, from good staying family, won over 13.3f: 11/2 from 10/1 but very green, last of 8, soon behind, in maiden at Leicester in October: gave trouble at stalls. *Lady Herries.*

WOODCOCK WONDER 2 ch.c. (May 16) Royal Vulcan 83–Deandar **53** (Communication 119) [1989 6m 7m 6g a8g⁶ a7g⁴ a7g] rather sparely-made colt: first foal: dam of no account over jumps: plating-class maiden: sweating final start: will be better suited by 1¼m +. *J. R. Jenkins.*

WOOD DANCER (USA) 4 br.g. Malinowski (USA) 123–Tiger Trap (USA) 80 **110** (Al Hattab (USA)) [1988 6f² 6m² 8f* 9g 1989 8s² 8f² 8g* 9m* 8.5f] big, workmanlike gelding: has a long stride: useful performer: favourite, won strongly-run £27,100 Sandown EBF Stakes (limited handicap) gamely by ½ length from Hello Vaigly and listed race (better effort) at Leopardstown by 6 lengths from Lone Runner in July: behind in valuable handicap at Gulfstream Park in November: stays 9f: acts on any going: has run well when sweating: slowly away on reappearance: withdrawn after bolting next intended outing: taken down early nowadays: genuine. *W. Hastings-Bass.*

WOOD HOLLOW 2 b.f. (Mar 17) Chukaroo 103–Belle Year (Quorum 126) [1989 8.2g 6g] medium-sized, quite attractive filly: moderate mover: half-sister to several winners here and abroad: dam apparently of no account: tailed off in 20-runner minor event at Nottingham and 12-runner maiden at Leicester in the autumn. *R. Dickin.* —

WOODHOOPOE 3 ch.f. Touching Wood (USA) 127–Good Try 92 (Good Bond 122) [1988 NR 1989 10g 12.2m 10.2h⁵ 8m⁵ 7m 7s⁶ 8.2g² a11g a11g*] medium-sized, rather sparely-made filly: seventh foal: half-sister to several winners, including quite useful 1984 2-y-o 6f winner Sergeant Gerard (by Brigadier Gerard) and 1½m winner Castle Heights (by Shirley Heights): dam 2-y-o 5f winner: made all in claimer at Southwell in December: will stay 1½m+: has sweated and got on edge: sold out of A. Stewart's stable 4,100 gns Newmarket Autumn Sales after seventh outing. *C. J. Bell.* 63

WOODLANDS CROWN 6 ch.g. Milford 119–Town Girl 99 (Town Crier 119) [1988 10.8m⁴ 12m 10.8g 10d 1989 11.7d³ 11.7m 8.5g⁶] leggy, quite good-topped gelding: poor handicapper: not seen out after May: should stay further than 1½m: acts on top-of-the-ground and a soft surface: has run well for apprentice. *D. C. Tucker.* 45

WOODLANDS GREY 3 gr.c. Nishapour (FR) 125–Topling 85 (High Top 131) [1988 NR 1989 7g 8d 8g 8f] IR 8,200F, 14,500Y: close-coupled, workmanlike colt: brother to Italian 6f winner Shatop and half-brother to 7f winner Kenooz (by Mummy's Pet) and a winner in Italy: dam won over 7f and 1¼m: little worthwhile form in varied events in first half of season, showing promise on debut: should stay at least 1m: bandaged behind second and final starts: has joined P. Pritchard. *C. A. Horgan.* —

WOODSIDE HEATH 2 ch.c. (Apr 15) King Persian 107–Saga's Humour 61 (Bustino 136) [1989 6h³ 5f³ 7h³ 6g³ a7g* a8g³] 8,000F, 11,000Y: small, sparely-made colt: fourth foal: half-brother to 3-y-o Risatina (by Sallust), 1¼m winner Haygate Park (by Final Straw) and a winner in Scandinavia: dam best at 6f: modest performer: won late-year nursery at Lingfield by 2 lengths: probably stays 1m: has worn bandages. *R. Hannon.* 75

WOODSIDE MILL 3 ch.c. Millfontaine 114–Warbiola (Nebbiolo 125) [1988 6m⁵ 6f² 6m⁶ 6g 8f* 8g* 1989 10s 8f² 7f* 8f 7m² 8m 8f⁵ 8d⁵ 8f³ 7m³ 8d] tall, rather sparely-made colt: fairly useful handicapper: won at Sandown in May: good third at Bath and Newmarket: may prove ideally suited by 7f: acts on firm going: ran badly sixth start and looked unsatisfactory on next: takes keen hold and is held up. *R. Hannon.* 95

WOODURATHER 3 br.c. Touching Wood (USA) 127–Rather Warm 103 (Tribal Chief 125) [1988 NR 1989 8g² 8f4] small, light-framed colt: fifth foal: brother to 1987 2-y-o 7f winner Rather Touching, and half-brother to 2 winners, including 5f to 7f winner Sparky Lad (by Hot Spark): dam won at up to 7.6f at 2 yrs: weak 14/1, beaten length in claimer (moved poorly down) at Newmarket, keeping on well: co-favourite, one-paced fourth of 7 in apprentice claimer at Warwick later in July. *P. F. I. Cole.* 56

WOOLY RAGS 3 ch.f. Raga Navarro (ITY) 119–Woolcana 71 (Some Hand 119) [1988 5m⁵ 6m 6d* 6m⁴ 6m 1989 8d 6g 7m 6m] close-coupled filly: poor walker and mover: quite moderate winning plater as 2-y-o: well beaten in 1989 and not seen out after July: suited by 6f: acts on top-of-the-ground and a soft surface: has joined P. Pritchard. *M. Fetherston-Godley.* —

WOOTTON (USA) 3 ch.c. Secreto (USA) 128–Writin' Mama (USA) (Gleaming (USA)) [1988 7g³ 7g⁴ 1989 12g 11.7m⁵ 12f³ 14g⁵] workmanlike colt: fair maiden: third in handicap at Salisbury in September, best effort: stays 1½m: acts on firm ground: lacks a turn of foot: sold to race in France 25,000 gns Newmarket Autumn Sales. *J. Tree.* 83

WORKADAY 7 gr.m. Workboy 123–Courting Day 90 (Right Boy 137) [1988 NR 1989 a7g a6g a6g] leggy mare: modest handicapper in 1986: no form in claimers and handicap at Southwell as 7-y-o: has been tried in visor: has been to stud. *A. Smith.* —

986

WORK ON AIR 3 ch.g. Doc Marten 104–Set To Work (Workboy 123) [1988 5m⁶ **54**
6s 6m 6g 1989 5m³ 5f 5f 6f² 6m 6g 6g⁴ 6m⁴ 8f³ 7g 6g a6g⁴] plain, angular gelding:
has a quick action: plating-class handicapper: should prove as effective over 7f as
1m: acts on firm going: ran creditably in visor ninth outing, fairly well in blinkers
final one: trained until final start by C. Tinkler. *W. A. O'Gorman.*

WORLD PARTY (FR) 3 ch.f. Esprit du Nord (USA) 126–Happy River **68**
(Riverman (USA) 131) [1988 6d 7m 6g 1989 10g 11m³ 14.8m* 16f⁴ 18g⁵] leggy,
close-coupled, sparely-made filly: won handicap at Warwick in July, always
prominent and staying on well: in need of race, not discredited in similar event final
start: stays 15f: acts on top-of-the-ground (looked ill at ease on firm): often claimer
ridden: sold 4,000 gns Newmarket December Sales. *J. W. Hills.*

WORLDSPORTFLYER 3 b.c. Hays 120–Arabian Pearl (Deep Diver 134) **48**
[1988 NR 1989 9g 12s 12f² 12m 12m⁴ 15.3g 10g] IR 1,800F, 8,000Y: rangy, angular
colt: half-brother to Irish 1¼m winner Going West (by Runnett) and a winner in
Malaysia: dam of little account: modest plater: worth another try over shorter: acts
on firm going: blinkered final start, disputing lead long way: sold to join M. Chapman
1,700 gns Newmarket Autumn Sales. *A. N. Lee.*

WORTHY PRINCE 5 b.g. Balliol 125–Princess Vronski (The Brianstan 128) **—**
[1988 10.8s 10.4m 14.8m 1989 7m] close-coupled gelding: well beaten since 2 yrs: stays
7f: acts on firm going: blinkered only outing at 5 yrs: sold, probably to race in
Scandinavia, 1,500 gns Newmarket Autumn Sales. *C. N. Williams.*

WRAPPING 3 b.f. Kris 135–Gift Wrapped 116 (Wolver Hollow 126) [1988 NR **108** §
1989 8s² 12f² 12g² 12g³ 10m² 12g³ 10g³ 10d] big, angular filly: has long stride: fifth
foal: sister to Royal Lodge Stakes winner Reach and half-sister to 1¼m seller
winner Fusion (by Mill Reef): dam won Lingfield Oaks Trial but best at up to 1¼m:
placed first 6 starts, showing very useful form, in listed race, £6,800 event and four
1½m pattern races (including Italian Oaks, beaten only a head): below form last 2
outings, particularly so when favourite and looking ungenerous under pressure in
Newbury maiden final one: suited by 1½m: has swished tail in preliminaries:
disappointing and not one to trust. *P. F. I. Cole.*

WRITE THE MUSIC 8 b.g. Riboboy (USA) 124–Zither 72 (Vienna 127) [1988 **—**
21.6g 1989 21.6d³] big, close-coupled gelding: winning handicapper in 1985: lightly
raced on flat subsequently: out-and-out stayer: acts on any going: has run well in
blinkers and a visor. *P. S. Felgate.*

WRYBILL 2 b.c. (Mar 10) Sharpo 132–Wryneck 89 (Niniski (USA) 125) [1989 6m⁴ **73** p
6g³] close-coupled, useful-looking colt: grand walker: first foal: dam won over 7f at
2 yrs on only start: modest form in fair maiden company at York in August and
Newmarket in November: will be better suited by 7f: should improve. *J. Tree.*

WYARDS WONDER 3 b.g. Hotfoot 126–Tenth Hussar 73 (Shiny Tenth 120) **—**
[1988 5d⁶ 5m⁶ 1989 12d⁶] workmanlike gelding: well beaten in maidens and seller:
not bred to stay middle distances. *Miss B. Sanders.*

WYKEHAMIST 6 ch.g. Blue Refrain 121–Flying Portion 72 (Major Portion 129) **62**
[1988 9d 8g 8m 10g* 8g³ 10f³ 9g* 10g³ 10.2g³ 10d² 1989 9d⁴ 9v⁵ 8g a10g⁴ a12g a10g
a12g²] rangy gelding: carries plenty of condition: moderate mover: quite modest
handicapper: stays 1½m: acts on any going: has won for apprentice: occasionally
sweats: usually held up. *C. J. Benstead.*

WYLAM 2 b.g. (Mar 18) What A Guest 119–Wish You Wow (Wolver Hollow 126) **—**
[1989 7m⁴] IR 10,000Y, 13,000 2-y-o: lengthy, attractive gelding: fifth foal: half-
brother to Irish 9f winner Sherman Gutrey (by Ardoon) and a winning hurdler in
Ireland: dam ran once at 3 yrs in Ireland: 10/1, bit backward and very green, 13
lengths fourth of 8 to Kadim in maiden at Redcar in September: sold 9,000 gns
Newmarket Autumn Sales: to be trained by M. H. Tompkins in 1990. *J. W. Watts.*

WYNCKY 3 b.g. Lucky Wednesday 124–Wynburry 70 (No Mercy 126) [1988 6g **—**
8.2s⁴ 8m 1989 8.2v 6s 7.5d] robust gelding: quite modest plater at 2 yrs: well beaten
in 1989, on second start sweating, edgy and moved moderately down: stays 1m: acts
on soft going: sold 1,950 gns Doncaster June Sales. *W. J. Pearce.*

WYNS VISION 2 br.f. (Mar 12) Vision (USA)–First Round 97 (Primera 131) **—**
[1989 6f⁴ 6g 6g⁶] 13,500F: leggy filly: half-sister to numerous winners, including
smart 5f and 7f winner Glenturret (by Habitat) and useful sprinter Rollahead (by
Tower Walk): dam won at up to 1¼m: appeared to show ability in slowly-run race
first outing: tailed off afterwards, on first occasion after bolting to post and on
second (on toes and taken down steadily) giving impression something amiss. *D. T.
Thom.*

X

XAFU XAFU   3 b.c. Kafu 120–On The Road (On Your Mark 125) [1988 6g³ 5g⁵   67
6m³ 6m³ 5s² 6s 1989 6m 8h³ 7.5f² 8m³ 6m² 6m² 6g 6s 6g 8g] tall, leggy colt: modest
maiden: ran moderately last 4 starts, on penultimate one swishing tail and hanging
under pressure: kicked at start next intended appearance: effective over 6f and 1m:
acts on any going: sometimes blinkered or visored. *M. H. Tompkins.*

XAI-TANG   2 gr.g. (Apr 11) Petong 126–Northern Dynasty 65 (Breeders Dream   43
116) [1989 5m⁶ 5m 7m 7m⁵ 6g] 8,400Y: small, compact gelding: fourth reported live
foal: half-brother to fair middle-distance winner Southern Dynasty (by Gunner B)
and 3-y-o Western Dynasty (by Hotfoot): dam won over 1m: poor maiden: bought
out of K. Brassey's stable 1,400 gns Ascot July Sales after fourth outing. *K. White.*

XEROMEDE   5 b.g. Runnymede 123–Nervous Cough (New Linacre 82) [1988   —
NR 1989 5f 10m⁶ a10g] non-thoroughbred gelding: dam unraced: of little account:
wears bandage on off-hind: withdrawn after giving trouble at stalls on intended
debut. *N. Kernick.*

XHAI   7 b.g. Brave Shot–Wild Thyme 63 (Galivanter 131) [1988 NR 1989 8g 8f⁴ 8m   61
8m² 8m⁶ 8f 8g⁶ 10m² 10m⁶ 8f 8f⁴ 8.2g] angular, workmanlike gelding: quite modest
handicapper nowadays: stays 1¼m: acts on any going: blinkered once: bandaged
nowadays: suitable mount for apprentice. *R. Simpson.*

XHUBE   2 b.c. (Apr 15) Reasonable (FR) 119–Mooned 64 (Fair Season 120) [1989   57
5.3m³ 5f⁶ 5f⁶ 6f⁵ 6g⁵ 6m⁵ 8s 7g a6g³] IR 900F, IR 4,100Y: small, sturdy colt: not a
good walker: moderate mover: first foal: dam daughter of half-sister to Irish Oaks
winner Celina, also the family of Dubian, See You Then and Sure Blade: fair plater:
should stay at least 7f: blinkered penultimate appearance: inconsistent. *M. H.
Tompkins.*

XYLOPHONE   7 b.m. Tap On Wood 130–Cecily (Prince Regent (FR) 129) [1988   40
10m 8g⁶ 10m 12f⁶ 1989 9v⁴ 10.1m 10g] leggy, close-coupled mare: has a round
action: poor handicapper: tailed off final outing, first for 5 months: stays 1¼m:
probably best on a soft surface nowadays: occasionally sweats: suitable mount for
inexperienced rider. *Miss L. Bower.*

Y

YAAZI   2 b.c. (Apr 21) Mummy's Pet 125–Ica (Great Nephew 126) [1989 6m*]   82 p
150,000Y: medium-sized, attractive colt: brother to Aragon, smart at up to 1m,
closely related to a winner in France and USA by African Sky and half-brother to
several winners and 3-y-o Ice Queen (by Kings Lake): dam unraced half-sister to
Song: 11/8 favourite, won 8-runner minor event at Newmarket in August by 3
lengths from Royal Passion, making all: moved moderately down: sure to improve
and win again. *A. C. Stewart.*

YABREEN (USA)   3 b.c. Lypheor 118–Noble Mistress (USA) (Vaguely Noble   —
140) [1988 6d⁶ 1989 8m] smallish, sparely-made colt: modest form in Newmarket
maiden at 2 yrs: 25/1 and wearing dropped noseband, raced keenly and well beaten
in similar event there in May, only start in 1989. *H. R. A. Cecil.*

YAHALABEAK   2 b. or br.c. (Mar 24) Glint of Gold 128–Spring Rose (Blakeney   — p
126) [1989 8m 8g] 11,000Y: sturdy, angular, medium-sized colt: first foal: dam poor
half-sister to good sprinters Saulingo and Music Maestro and smart 1975 2-y-o
Outer Circle: never dangerous, not knocked about, in large-field maidens at
Newmarket and Leicester late-season: looks sort to do better in time. *B. Hanbury.*

YAHALOM (USA)   3 b.f. Diamond Prospect (USA) 126–Mysia (FR) (Lyphard   51
(USA) 132) [1988 NR 1989 8f 8h² 8m⁵ 6f⁴ 7g 6g] close-coupled, angular filly: turns
near-fore out: fourth foal: sister to a winner in North America at around 5f: dam, who
showed a little ability at 3 yrs in France, is half-sister to very smart middle-distance
stayer Midshipman: plating-class maiden: stays 1m: acts on hard ground: takes
strong hold. *S. G. Norton.*

YAJIB (USA)   2 b.c. (Apr 11) El Gran Senor (USA) 136–Chocolate Puff (USA)   51 p
(Hawaii) [1989 7m 8.2g] IR 260,000Y: quite attractive colt: first foal: dam
lightly-raced half-sister to good Canadian horse Royal Chocolate: in mid-division,
not unduly knocked about, in fair company at Newmarket (coltish and on toes) and
Nottingham in October: likely to do better. *J. L. Dunlop.*

YAMASHITA (USA) 4 b.g. Vaguely Noble 140–Princesse Aglae (FR) 68
(Crowned Prince (USA) 128) [1988 12f 1989 12h² 12m² 16.1g 10f³ 8f 10f⁴] robust,
angular, attractive gelding: good walker: has a rather round action: quite modest
maiden: placed in 4-runner events at Thirsk (minor contest), Lingfield and Redcar:
well beaten other starts in 1989, poorly treated in handicaps third and fifth ones:
stays 1½m: acts on hard going: blinkered final appearance: keen sort: has joined F.
Jordan. *Mrs N. Macauley.*

YAMRAH 5 b.m. Milford 119–Silojoka 95 (Home Guard (USA) 129) [1988 7f 8f* 70
10f² 10f² 10f* 11.5g* 10g² 12f³ 12m² 12h² 12g 1989 10m² 11.5g⁴ 10m⁴ 10f³ 12h⁶]
lengthy mare: quite modest handicapper: ran moderately final outing (early-
August): stays 1½m: acts on hard going and a soft surface: good mount for apprentice: consistent. *Miss B. Sanders.*

YA MUNA 4 ch.f. Vitiges (FR) 132–La Vosgienne (Ashmore (FR) 125) [1988 10d —
12f³ 12g⁵ 14m* 11.5f³ 14m 1989 10.2g 12m] useful-looking, rather leggy filly: won
4-runner claimer at Yarmouth as 3-y-o: soundly beaten in handicaps in spring:
stayed 1¾m: acted on firm going: blinkered last 6 outings: tended to get on toes:
difficult ride: dead. *J. Ffitch-Heyes.*

YANABEE 2 b.f. (Mar 24) Doulab (USA) 115–Johara (USA) 92 (Exclusive Native 61
(USA)) [1989 6f* 8.2f] angular, sparely-made filly: third foal: half-sister to 1¼m
winner Kashshaf (by Tap On Wood) and 3-y-o 2m winner Ashal (by Touching
Wood): dam won over 6f on debut at 2 yrs: long odds on, beat sole rival Cannon's
Spirit by 2 lengths after slow start in maiden at Thirsk in July: well beaten in nursery
at Nottingham nearly 2 months later: sold 10,500 gns Newmarket Autumn Sales. *H.
Thomson Jones.*

YANBU 4 b.g. Artaius (USA) 129–Belle Bretonne 90 (Celtic Ash) [1988 12d⁶ 12d 59
10v 12m⁴ 14m 16f⁴ 12m 1989 15.5s 12.5g* 12f⁴ 15.3m] angular gelding: moderate
mover: won claiming event at Wolverhampton in May: ridden virtually throughout
in selling races afterwards: stays 2m: possibly unsuited by top-of-the-ground
nowadays: blinkered as 4-y-o: has worn a tongue strap: winning hurdler: none too
genuine. *J. R. Jenkins.*

YANKEE TRADER 2 b.f. (Jan 18) Stanford 121§–Amboselli 73 (Raga Navarro 44
(ITY) 119) [1989 5f 6f 6g] medium-sized, rather unfurnished filly: has scope: second
reported foal: half-sister to modest 3-y-o sprinter Nikki Dow (by Tanfirion): dam
placed over 5f at 2 yrs: poor form in late-season maidens. *Sir Mark Prescott.*

YARRA GLEN 2 ch.f. (Jan 22) Known Fact (USA) 135–Sloane Ranger 84 67
(Sharpen Up 127) [1989 8m³ 8f² 8.5f²] IR 20,000Y: leggy, lengthy filly: fourth
reported living foal: half-sister to 6f to 1m winner Liffey Reef (by Main Reef) and 6f
to 8.5f winner Bold Sea Rover (by Viking): dam won at up to 1m: quite modest
maiden: stays 1m. *C. R. Nelson.*

YARRAMAN 2 b.g. (Apr 26) Ya Zaman (USA) 122–Isa (Dance In Time (CAN)) 57
[1989 6s 6g a8g⁶ a6g⁶ a7g³] IR 8,200Y: leggy gelding: third foal: half-brother to poor
maiden Rillandel (by Wolver Hollow) and prolific 1988 2-y-o sprint winner Time To
Go Home (by Day Is Done), listed winner in Germany at 3 yrs: dam never ran:
showed improved form when 8 lengths third of 14 to Orchard Court in late-year
claimer at Southwell: should stay 1m. *R. Hollinshead.*

YASLOU 2 ch.g. (Feb 28) Yashgan 126–Lough Graney (Sallust 134) [1989 5f⁶ 6m⁴ 65
6m⁴ 7f⁶] IR 17,500F: good-quartered gelding: poor mover: third foal: half-brother to
3-y-o Safwah (by Ahonoora), fair 6f winner at 2 yrs, and Irish 7f winner Indian
Lagoon (by Indian King): dam, Irish 1½m winner, is half-sister to Tap On Wood:
quite modest maiden: best effort second start: will stay 1¼m. *M. E. D. Francis.*

YASSOO MANA MOU 4 gr.c. Ela-Mana-Mou 132–Brenda (Sovereign Path —
125) [1988 8m 8f 8m 10m² 1989 8s] good-topped colt: moderate mover: second in
seller at Leicester as 3-y-o, only form: backward only outing (April) in 1989: stays
1¼m: acts on top-of-the-ground. *B. Preece.*

YEARSLEY 3 b.g. Anfield 117–Mantina (Bustino 136) [1988 6m⁴ 6f⁵ 7.5g³ 6g 87
1989 7m 7m 7f* 7.5f* 8f* 8.2d⁵] rangy gelding: good walker and mover: fair
handicapper: successful in July at Catterick, Beverley and Thirsk (sweating),
making all first 2 occasions: led over 6f when below-form fifth at Haydock in August:
should prove best at around 7f: goes well on firm going: suited by forcing tactics. *M.
H. Easterby.*

YELLOW RING 3 b.f. Auction Ring (USA) 123–The Yellow Girl 102 (Yellow 51
God 129) [1988 6g 6g 7s 1989 8g⁵ 8.2f⁴] quite good-looking filly: plating-class
maiden: best form over 1m: looked ill at ease on firm ground final outing, in June. *G.
A. Pritchard-Gordon.*

YEOMAN BID 2 b.c. (Feb 16) Longleat (USA) 109–Bounding (Forlorn River 70 124) [1989 5s 5f⁵ 8.2d a6g a7g³ a8g²] big, angular colt: has a roundish action: fifth living foal: half-brother to several winners, including sprinter Pendor Dancer (by Piaffer): dam never ran: modest performer: best effort final outing: stays 1m: has been bandaged behind. *K. T. Ivory.*

YEOMAN FORCE 3 b.c. Crofter (USA) 124–High Voltage 82 (Electrify) [1988 81 5f³ 5m* 5f⁶ 5g⁴ 1989 6s³ 5g 6d⁴ 6m⁶ 6f 8m⁶ 6m 6d 5d a6g³ 5d a6g² a6g² a7g²] tall, angular colt: rather unfurnished: has a long stride: fair handicapper: easily best efforts after fourth start when placed, running well, at Lingfield in late-season: effective at 6f and 7f: probably acts on any going: often visored: not entirely discredited in blinkers. *K. T. Ivory.*

YERIF NOGARD 3 b. or br.f. Don 128–Firey Dragon (Tarboosh (USA)) [1988 57 NR 1989 8g⁵] IR 800Y: rangy, rather leggy filly: third foal: sister to Irish 6f and 7f winner Maldive: dam unraced: 9/2, about 3½ lengths fifth of 13 in claimer at Salisbury in May, staying on despite edging left. *R. W. Stubbs.*

YER-NO-PUGGY 2 ch.c. (Apr 13) Stanford 121§–Picnic Time (Silly Season 127) 38 [1989 5s 5d 6f 6m 7f 10f] IR 4,000Y: rather sparely-made colt: half-brother to 3 winners, including by Prince Tenderfoot and Godswalk, over 1m or more: dam poor maiden: poor maiden: sweated badly third start: edgy, and fractious stalls, fourth: sold 900 gns Newmarket Autumn Sales. *R. Hollinshead.*

YESICAN 3 gr.c. Kalaglow 132–Geoffrey's Sister 102 (Sparkler 130) [1988 NR 73 p 1989 7g⁴] 22,000F, 43,000Y: lengthy, workmanlike colt: fourth foal: half-brother to good-class 6f and 7f winner Mac's Fighter (by Hard Fought) and 12.2f winner Keep Hoping (by Busted): dam miler: 10/1 from 33/1 though bit backward, showed plenty of promise when 7 lengths fourth of 10 in minor event at Yarmouth in September, green and well behind then running on well final 3f: moved moderately down: will stay 1m: sold to join N. Tinkler 9,600 gns Newmarket Autumn Sales: should improve. *L. M. Cumani.*

YET 4 gr.f. Last Fandango 125–Rana of Coombe (Moulton 128) [1988 6s 10.2m³ 9f 42 10m* 11.7m³ 10f⁴ 12g⁴ 12m 1989 12g 10m 12g 10m⁴ 12g 12.2f⁶] workmanlike filly: has a quick action: poor handicapper: suited by 1¼m: acts on firm going: blinkered once at 3 yrs and on second outing (sweating, edgy, mulish at stalls and slowly away) in 1989: sometimes wanders and not the easiest of rides. *M. J. Ryan.*

YONGE TENDER 2 b.f. (Mar 27) Tender King 123–St Clair Star (Sallust 134) 70 [1989 5m⁶ 5g 6g⁵ a5g³ a5g⁴] close-coupled filly: moderate walker: has a quick action: first foal: dam unraced half-sister to smart 5f to 7f winner Superlative: modest performer: best form at 5f: off course 4 months after debut. *J. Wharton.*

YORK GLASS 3 b.f. Ampney Prince 96–Lingala (Pinturischio 116) [1988 7m — 7.5m 8.2m³ 8m 1989 10f 12f⁵ 10f 9s 10f 15.8g 12m] small, workmanlike filly: moderate walker and mover: modest plater: below form as 3-y-o: sweating on reappearance: trained until after third outing by Miss L. Siddall. *A. P. Stringer.*

YORKSHIRE HOLLY 6 br.g. Bivouac 114–Holly Doon (Doon 124) [1988 NR 74 1989 10g 10m 14f⁴ 15f* 16f⁴ 16.2m² 19f² 16.2m* 18m⁵] smallish, workmanlike gelding: half-brother to 3 winners, including temperamental stayer Holly Buoy and 11f winner Christmas Holly (both by Blind Harbour): dam poor plater: won handicaps at Edinburgh in June and Beverley (in very good style by 3 lengths) in August: weakened final 1f when fifth of 10 at Ripon 2 weeks later: suited by 2m: acts on firm going: ridden by claimer: held up: winning hurdler. *Mrs G. R. Reveley.*

YORKSHIRE PRINCESS 4 ch.f. Junius (USA) 124–Magic Lady (Gala — Performance (USA)) [1988 8g³ 10v³ 8.3m 10f³ 10d⁵ 1989 8s 9f] leggy, sparely-made filly: quite moderate plater as 3-y-o: well beaten in spring: seems to act on any going: blinkered last 2 outings in 1988 and on reappearance: difficult ride: bought out of P. Rohan's stable 675 gns Ascot May Sales after first outing. *D. R. Tucker.*

YOU ARE A STAR 3 b.c. Persian Bold 123–Flinging Star (USA) (Northern Fling 76 (USA)) [1988 6g 7d 5m⁵ 1989 7d 7s³ 8g* 7.6f³ 7g* 7f² 7h 8d] big, rangy colt: carries condition: modest handicapper: successful at Salisbury in May and Epsom in June: effective at 7f and 1m: probably acts on any going: ran moderately in visor eighth start. *R. Hannon.*

YOU KNOW THE RULES 2 b.f. (May 13) Castle Keep 121–Falls of Lora 107 67 (Scottish Rifle 127) [1989 6f 7f⁵ 6m⁴ 8f⁴ 8g⁴ 8.2f* 7f³ 8f³] sparely-made filly: has a quick action: fifth live foal: dam won from 6f to 1½m: quite modest performer: won 20-runner seller (no bid) at Nottingham in September: afterwards ran well in nurseries: will stay 1½m: acts on firm going. *K. O. Cunningham-Brown.*

YOU MISSED ME 3 b.c. Known Fact (USA) 135–Milk And Honey 102 (So **82**
Blessed 130) [1988 6m⁴ 6d³ 1989 6s² 7g³ 8f⁵ 7f³ 8m* 8g* 8.3g⁶ 9g⁵ 9g] leggy,
angular colt: has a quick action: fair handicapper: won at Kempton in July and
Leicester in August: 50/1 and 5 lb out of handicap, creditable fifth of 34 in
Cambridgeshire Handicap at Newmarket penultimate start: below form outings
either side: stays 9f: acts on any going. *D. W. P. Arbuthnot.*

YOUNG ASPIRATION 3 ch.g. Coquelin (USA) 121–Persian Case (Upper Case **–**
(USA)) [1988 15g 6m 1989 12f 7f⁶ 6f a10g] workmanlike gelding: well beaten,
including in sellers: blinkered once in 1988: dead. *N. Kernick.*

YOUNG BENZ 5 ch.g. Young Generation 129–Cavalier's Blush (King's Troop **–**
118) [1988 10g 9f 9d 10.5f⁶ 10s⁴ 12m* 1989 12d⁴ 12.3f⁴ 11s 12s 10g] workmanlike
gelding: usually dull in coat: moderate mover: fair handicapper in 1988: lightly raced
on flat as 5-y-o, but gave indications on last 2 outings of retaining plenty of his
ability: stays 1½m: probably acts on any going: best in blinkers: has run well for
apprentice, but is not the easiest of rides and possibly best covered up: smart novice
hurdler in 1988/9. *M. H. Easterby.*

YOUNG CHRISTOS 2 b.c. (May 3) Sayf El Arab (USA) 127–Pahaska 86 **–**
(Wolver Hollow 126) [1989 6d 6g 6g] leggy colt: half-brother to 3 minor
winners here and abroad, including sprinter Corrals Joy (by Absalom): dam stayed
1¼m: well beaten in late-season maidens. *C. N. Allen.*

YOUNG COMMANDER 5 br.g. Bustino 136–Bombshell 76 (Le Levanstell **67**
122) [1988 11g 11g³ 8.2s 8f⁵ 8m* 8d³ 1989 8g³ 8d³ 8f³ 8m⁵ 9f² 7m² 12m⁵ 8f⁶ 8g²
8.2f* 8.2f* 8m⁶ 8.2g 8.5f⁴ 8f* 8g 8g] lengthy, medium-sized gelding: has been
hobdayed: won handicaps at Hamilton within 6 days in July and at Newcastle in
October: generally ran creditably in similar company otherwise, though often found
little off bridle: effective at 7f to 9f: possibly unsuited by soft going, acts on any
other: visored nowadays: has swished tail: best with waiting tactics. *M. P.
Naughton.*

YOUNG GENERAL 3 br.c. Young Generation 129–Amerella (Welsh Pageant **89**
132) [1988 NR 1989 10g² 10.1g³ 12m² 12g² 12g² 10m⁵ 10.6m 12m⁴ 13.3d] 23,000Y:
lengthy, angular colt: sixth foal: half-brother to 1988 French 1m to 11.5f winner
Honest Word (by Touching Wood) and 3 other winners, including Cragside (by Hot
Spark), a smart sprinter in 1985: dam, daughter of Molecomb Stakes winner Lowna,
won over 1¼m in Ireland: fair maiden: moved moderately down and ran badly in
handicap final outing: should prove better at 1½m than shorter: acts on firm ground:
has run creditably for claimer, and when sweating and on toes: has joined M.
Robinson. *P. F. I. Cole.*

YOUNG GEORGE 2 b.g. (May 20) Camden Town 125–Young Grace (Young **44 p**
Emperor 133) [1989 6f 7g 7f⁶ 6f] IR 4,000Y: good-topped, close-coupled gelding:
third reported foal: dam placed at 1½m in Ireland: showed signs of ability,
particularly so last 2 starts, when shaping much better than mid-field position in
sellers suggests: should stay 1m: on toes final outing: one to watch out for in sellers.
C. Tinkler.

YOUNG HAL 4 b. or br.c. Young Generation 129–Klaire 85 (Klairon 131) [1988 **105**
7g⁶ 7d 6m⁴ 5f³ 5g⁴ 6g 6f² 6f* 6m² 5m* 6g⁴ 1989 6g⁵ 6g⁶ 6m³ 6m⁴ 5f 6f⁴ 5g⁴ 6m 5m]
tall, rather leggy colt: good mover: very useful performer in 1988: generally
disappointing in 1989: best effort when third to Puissance in EBF Greenlands
Stakes at the Curragh in May: finds easy 5f on sharp side and stays 6f: acts on firm
going and a soft surface: blinkered seventh (slowly away) and final outings:
sometimes sweating and edgy: needs strong handling: sent to join J. Russell in
California: none too reliable. *P. T. Walwyn.*

YOUNG INCA 11 gr.g. Young Emperor 133–Sunny Eyes (Reliance II 137) [1988 **76**
6m 6m 6m* 6f 6m⁶ 6m³ 6g⁴ 6g 6m 5f 5d² 6s 1989 7g 6f 6f² 7g 6f² 6m 6m⁴ 6m* 6f⁶
5m⁵ 6m⁵ 6s⁴ 5m 6g] big, strong gelding: good mover: modest handicapper: won
£7,600 event at Ascot in July by neck from Chummy's Favourite: ran creditably at
Goodwood (3 times) and Sandown on next 4 outings: below form last 2, on final one
rearing in stalls and bumped shortly after leaving them: best at 6f: acts on any going:
has won in blinkers, but better without: often starts slowly: tough. *L. G. Cottrell.*

YOUNG INDIA 2 br.f. (Apr 20) Indian King (USA) 128–Marfisa (Green God 128) **75**
[1989 5g 5g² 6m* 5g* 5m²] IR 3,700Y: well-grown, workmanlike filly: fifth foal:
half-sister to fairly useful 1986 2-y-o 7f seller winner Gillot Bar (by Rarity) and a
winner in Italy: dam won 6 races in Italy: made all in 23-runner maiden auction race
at Ripon in August and 14-runner nursery (flashed tail) at Edinburgh in September:
stays 6f: wears a bandage near-hind. *T. D. Barron.*

YOUNG JASON   6 ch.g. Star Appeal 133–Smarten Up 119 (Sharpen Up 127)   **83**
[1988 8g* 7g² 9f⁵ 8f² 8m* 7m³ 10g³ 9f 8s 8f⁵ 10.2m 1989 10.2g 7.6m* 8m* 8.2m⁶
8m⁵ 8m⁵ 8.5m* 8m² 8.2d⁴ 8m⁴ 7.6m² 8.5f 8g] small, good-bodied gelding:
moderate mover: fair handicapper: won at Chester and Carlisle within 4 days in May
and at Beverley in July: ideally suited by strong gallop at around 1m: acts on any
going: blinkered once: goes well on turning track: tough. *F. H. Lee.*

YOUNG JAZZ   3 b.c. Young Generation 129–River Music (Riverman (USA) 131)   **— p**
[1988 NR 1989 7d⁶] IR 180,000Y: big, close-coupled, attractive colt: fourth living
foal: half-brother to useful 1983 2-y-o 5f winner Time Machine (by Connaught): dam
won over 5f from 3 starts at 2 yrs in Ireland: favourite but bit burly and very green,
over 11 lengths sixth of 20 to Great Commotion in maiden at Newmarket in April,
unable to quicken over 1f out then eased considerably: found to have split a pastern:
sure to improve if recovering from his injury. *G. Harwood.*

YOUNG MONTY   2 b.g. (Feb 25) Montekin 125–Bective Baby 57 (Nebbiolo 125)   **65**
[1989 5g⁵ 5v³ 5.3m³ 6f² 5f³ 5f* 5f² 5m² 5m³] IR 2,000F, IR 3,500Y, resold 8,400Y:
sturdy gelding: keen walker: first foal: dam placed at 5f and 6f: ridden by 7-lb
claimer, made all in 7-runner claimer at Goodwood in June: seems better suited by
5f than 6f: effective with or without blinkers: looked none too keen final outing
(July). *R. Hannon.*

YOUNG MOTHER (FR)   3 b.f. Youth (USA) 135–Santa Tina 123 (Santa   **128**
Claus 133) [1988 NR 1989 10.7g* 12s* 12g* 12g* 13.5g³ 12d* 12g⁴]
    Snow Bride ran a brave race in the Prix Vermeille at Longchamp in
September only to be beaten by three better fillies, Young Mother, Sierra
Roberta and Colorado Dancer, all of them French trained. Young Mother was
her young trainer's second winner in this important race following Indian
Rose in 1988, and she went on to perform with much more credit than her
predecessor in the Ciga Prix de l'Arc de Triomphe, finishing under two
lengths fourth of nineteen to Carroll House, just in front of Sierra Roberta
who next time out came within a head of winning the Breeders' Cup Turf.
    Trainer Beguigne worked his way up from the bottom as a stable lad with
Pollet, via a spell with jumping trainer Laumain and another as assistant to
Mathet. Young Mother (whom he owns as well as trains) also set off well down
the racing ladder, in a maiden at the provincial track at Le Croise-Laroche in
April, starting at odds against when winning; then she was upgraded so
successfully that she went to Deauville for the Prix de Pomone still unbeaten
after visits to Evry, Chantilly and Longchamp. The weights for the Pomone
favoured Colorado Dancer, who'd finished a half-length second to Young
Mother at Longchamp in the Group 2 Prix de Malleret, by 3 lb, and Young
Mother ran well over the longer distance even though defeated at last. She
was always prominent and kept on well, two short heads behind Colorado
Dancer and the back-to-form four-year-old Summer Trip. Defeat, however
honourable, cost Young Mother favouritism in the Vermeille. The very

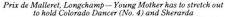

*Prix de Malleret, Longchamp — Young Mother has to stretch out
to hold Colorado Dancer (No. 4) and Sherarda*

Prix Vermeille, Longchamp — Young Mother never looks like being caught;
Colorado Dancer is third this time, beaten by Sierra Roberta

good-looking Colorado Dancer was considered to be improving the faster and in a field of seven she started at evens; Young Mother started at 21/10 coupled with pacemaker Nuance Pale; Snow Bride was 4/1, Sierra Roberta 19/4, Sudaka 20/1 and the maiden Zartota 89/1. In the race Young Mother always had the upper hand over the other fancied runners. She went on from the pacemaker round the last turn and, driven along, ran on really well the rest of the way home. Snow Bride, Sudaka and Zartota tried to hang on, but having established a two-length advantage Young Mother never looked like being pulled back. She held the late challenges of Colorado Dancer and Sierra Roberta with a degree of comfort to run out the winner by a length and a half and the same. In the Arc Young Mother held a good place throughout. This time though she never reached the front, for when she made the attempt out of the last turn stable-companion Saint Andrews, Carroll House and Behera all accelerated better. It was fairly late on before she began to pull any of them back; staying on strongly, she went down by a length and a half, a short neck and a neck. A good and genuine filly, obviously, but not yet of the standard of some Vermeille winners of the 'seventies and 'eighties, five of whom also won the Arc.

Young Mother (FR) (b.f. 1986)	Youth (USA) (b 1973)	Ack Ack (b 1966)	Battle Joined / Fast Turn
		Gazala II (br 1964)	Dark Star / Belle Angevine
	Santa Tina (br 1967)	Santa Claus (br 1961)	Chamossaire / Aunt Clara
		Reine des Bois (b 1950)	Bois Roussel / Queen of Shiraz

The passage of time hasn't been kind to the reputations of Young Mother's sire and dam, Youth and Santa Tina. Neither has enjoyed the success at stud that might have been anticipated from their racing records. Youth rates among the best Prix du Jockey-Club winners but was very disappointing as a sire in the USA and is now in Brazil: take away Teenoso, Young Mother and his other Vermeille winner Sharaya and there's not much left. The Irish Guinness Oaks winner Santa Tina reached the age of nineteen before she produced a foal anywhere near her own ability in Young Mother. Five of her previous offspring were successful in a minor way, and an unraced daughter, her first foal Zonta, is the dam of stakes winners, notably the Canadian Turf Handicap winner Equalize. Santa Tina is a granddaughter of another Irish Oaks winner in Queen of Shiraz, and is sister to the 1969 Irish St Leger winner Reindeer and half-sister to the 1967 Irish Two Thousand Guineas winner Atherstone Wood. Santa Tina had good form at a mile and a quarter but Young Mother runs as though she needs at least a mile and a half in top company. Her chances in the Prix Ganay, which could well be on her agenda in the first part of 1990, would be much improved by testing conditions. *J.-M. Beguigne, France.*

YOUNG OAK   3 b.c. Young Generation 129–Angel Beam (SWE) 115 (Hornbeam   **98** 130) [1988 6m³ 6s 1989 6h* 5f 5m* 6f] good-topped colt: moderate mover, with a quick action: odds on, made virtually all to win 4-runner races for maiden at Carlisle and minor event at Chepstow in the summer: ran well in £12,500 Ascot handicap in between but poorly when blinkered in similar event at Ayr in July: bred to stay further: possibly unsuited by soft going: sold 5,800 gns Newmarket Autumn Sales. *C. R. Nelson.*

YOUNG TEARAWAY   4 br.f. Young Generation 129–Chiparia 82 (Song 132)   **90** [1988 6f⁴ 6d* 6g 6m 1989 5s 6f² 6m 5f 6s⁶ 6m² 6g² 6g 6d] good-quartered filly: fair performer: runner-up to Sonilla in handicap at Newmarket and Stop Day in £5,500 event at Goodwood on consecutive days in October: below form last 2 starts, visored final one: suited by 6f: acts on any going. *R. Boss.*

YOUNG TURPIN   3 b.g. Young Generation 129–Tura (Northfields (USA)) [1988   **86** 6f³ 7m³ 7g² 6f³ 7g⁴ 1989 8f³ 10f 8.5g 6f* 7.6f⁶] quite attractive gelding: good mover: fair at best: ran on strongly to lead close home in handicap at Salisbury in August: again ridden by 7-lb claimer, ran moderately in similar event at Lingfield 2 months later, leading 5f: stays 1m but may prove ideally suited by 6f: acts on firm going: below form in blinkers once at 2 yrs: didn't handle turn at Epsom third outing: takes a keen hold: sold 15,000 gns Newmarket Autumn Sales: not one to trust implicitly. *D. R. C. Elsworth.*

YOUNG WOODLEY (USA)   3 b.c. Lyphard (USA) 132–Friendswood (USA)   **94** (Vaguely Noble 140) [1988 6g⁵ 1989 8.2m² 9f² 10g³] good-topped colt: carries condition: good mover: battled on well when second in minor events at Nottingham then Wolverhampton 5 months later: fair third in similar contest at Leicester: probably stays 1¼m: acts on firm going: taken quietly to post and made running last 2 starts: fairly useful. *H. R. A. Cecil.*

YOU'RE THE TOPS   3 b.c. Head For Heights 125–Relatively Sharp 86 (Shar-   **—** pen Up 127) [1988 6m 6g 1989 8s 10m] sturdy, good-quartered colt: well beaten, including in handicap. *C. W. Thornton.*

YOU SURE   2 ch.f. (Apr 28) Buzzards Bay 128§–Firbeck 78 (Veiled Wonder   **55** (USA)) [1989 5d 5d⁴ 5g² 5f² 5f* 5f³ 5g* 6d] 1,000Y: lengthy, rather sparely-made filly: fourth foal: dam 5f sprinter: won sellers (no bid) at Redcar in May and Haydock in July: suited by a sound surface: trained first 4 starts by W. G. M. Turner. *M. H. Easterby.*

YOUTHFUL PIP   4 b.g. Young Generation 129–Pipina (USA) 81 (Sir Gaylord)   **—** [1988 NR 1989 8.5g 10.2g 9.1f³ 8.5f 12.4g⁴ 12s] rangy gelding: showed promise in fair company on 3 outings as 2-y-o: well beaten in varied company in 1989: on toes and bandaged second outing. *M. W. Easterby.*

YSATIROUS   2 gr.c. (Mar 20) Ahonoora 122–Amalancher (USA) 85 (Alleged   **78 p** (USA) 138) [1989 7g²] big, good-topped, lengthy colt: first foal: dam, French 2-y-o 1m winner, half-sister to William Hill Futurity runner-up Cock Robin: weak 9/2 and green, shaped well after starting slowly, running on strongly from halfway, when length second of 17 to Starstreak in minor event at Leicester in November: sure to improve and win a race. *M. R. Stoute.*

YUAN PRINCESS   4 ch.f. Tender King 123–Skyey 70 (Skymaster 126) [1988 7f 10.2g⁶ 10f³ 13.8d⁴ 12f² 10.8f 13.8f* 1989 10m 12f 10.8m 15.3g³ 12g 12.2f] sturdy filly: winning plater as 3-y-o: well below her best in 1989: best form at up to 1¾m: acts on firm going: twice blinkered and edgy at 3 yrs: often sweats: sold 1,750 gns Ascot October Sales. *J. M. Bradley.*

YUFFROUW ANN   4 b.f. Tyrnavos 129–Recline 70 (Wollow 132) [1988 7d 10s 8g 8f 8f 8.2m 6m 7m² 7g⁶ 7g 7m² 1989 9f] small filly: won 3 races (2 sellers) as 2-y-o: has deteriorated since: stays 7f: acts on any going: seems best in a visor: bandaged and edgy only outing at 4 yrs: unreliable. *K. G. Wingrove.*

YUKON RUSH (USA)   3 b.c. Mr Prospector (USA)–Northernette (CAN) (Northern Dancer) [1988 NR 1989 8f 10m⁴] $550,000Y: big, rather leggy, quite attractive colt: has a free, rather round action: sixth foal: brother to 2 winners, notably very smart 1984 Irish 2-y-o 7f and 1m winner Gold Crest, and half-brother to Irish 7f winner Snowdonia (by Alydar): dam, sister to Storm Bird, was top Canadian filly at 2 yrs and 3 yrs, successful in 9f Canadian Oaks: well beaten in minor event (very green) at Sandown and maiden (wearing crossed noseband) at Ripon in May, in latter looking a difficult ride, hanging left and appearing none too keen. *M. R. Stoute.*

YUKOSAN 2 ch.f. (Mar 9) Absalom 128–K-Sera 95 (Lord Gayle (USA) 124) [1989   **69** 5g* 6g a6g² a6g* a5g³ a8g⁵] 3,700Y: lengthy filly: fourth foal: half-sister to 1m winner Willbe Willbe (by Music Boy) and modest sprinter Will Be Bold (by Bold Lad, IRE): dam 7f winner at 2 yrs: won seller (bought in 3,200 gns) at Wolverhampton and late-year claimer (claimed out of J. Wharton's stable £6,600) at Southwell: also ran well third start: probably better suited by 6f than 5f: bandaged and slowly away on debut. *Ronald Thompson.*

YUNG CHAN 3 ch.g. Netherkelly 112–Changan 59 (Touch Paper 113) [1988 NR   **42** 1989 10.8s 10s 8g 12g⁴] strong, deep-girthed gelding: third foal: dam stayed 7f at 2 yrs, ran only once at 3 yrs: 33/1, fourth in claimer at Newmarket in August: bandaged, withdrawn lame at Leicester following month: suited by 1½m: tailed off on soft going. *R. Hollinshead.*

YUNO WHY 3 gr.g. Horage 124–Pete's Money (USA) (Caucasus (USA) 127)   **57** [1988 5m 5g⁴ 5g 6f 1989 8.5d 8g** 8.5d 8m] workmanlike, good-quartered gelding: moderate mover: plating-class handicapper: won at Doncaster in May by a head, staying on well having been driven along early in straight: showed little final start later in same month: stays 1m well: blinkered once at 2 yrs. *J. Etherington.*

Z

ZABARRJAD (USA) 2 b.f. (May 27) Northern Dancer–Smooth Bore (USA)   **— p** (His Majesty (USA)) [1989 8g⁶] medium-sized, sturdy filly: fifth foal: closely related to lightly-raced So Smooth (by Nijinsky) and half-sister to 3 winners, notably Midway Lady (by Alleged): dam very useful stakes winner at around 1m as 4-y-o: favourite though very green, around 13 lengths sixth of 15, ridden 2f out and one pace, to Azadeh in maiden at Leicester in November. *M. R. Stoute.*

ZACCIUS 2 ch.c. (Mar 29) Burslem 123–Vesperale (Rarity 129) [1989 6h 7m 6g   **—** 7f] IR 1,100Y, resold IR 2,700Y: compact colt: first foal: dam Irish maiden: of little account: blinkered last 2 starts. *D. H. Topley.*

ZADRACARTA (CAN) 4 b. or br.f. Bold Ruckus (USA)–Montmorency (USA) **117** (Selari (USA)) [1988 6f* 6f5 6f* 6f2 6f4 1989 6f4 6f5 6f* 6f3 6f2 6f2 5g2] Canadian sprinter: sixth foal: half-sister to a winner by Royal Chocolate: dam won 4 times at up to 7f: winner 8 times at Woodbine, including in Grade 3 events: successful in Whimsical Stakes in April: 40/1, bandaged and blinkered, disputed lead throughout when short-head second to Silver Fling in Ciga Prix de l'Abbaye de Longchamp in October: effective on dirt as well as turf: very speedy. *P. J. Collins, Canada.*

ZAFFARAN (USA) 4 b.c. Assert 134–Sweet Alliance (USA) (Sir Ivor 135) [1988 **115** 10g* 12f 12g* 12g* 14m* 14.6g⁴ 14v 1989 16d³ 14f² 16f³] tall colt: has a long, rather round stride: placed in spring (not seen out after May) in Insulpak Sagaro EBF Stakes at Ascot, Coloroll Yorkshire Cup at York (quickening clear over 3f out and battling on well when beaten neck by Mountain Kingdom, pair clear) and Mappin & Webb Henry II EBF Stakes (close up travelling well and leading over 3f out until over 1f out) at Sandown: ideally suited by 1¾m: unsuited by heavy going and acts well on top-of-the-ground: lacks a turn of foot: gave trouble at stalls first 2 appearances in 1988. *M. R. Stoute.*

ZAFIRO 3 br.g. Starch Reduced 112–Miss Admington 71 (Double Jump 131) [1988   **43** 5g 5m 6g 7g 1989 5m 6m⁴ 6m 5m⁵ 5f² 5g 5f⁴ 7m 6f 5f 8f 5g⁴] sturdy gelding: poor maiden: keen sort, best form at 5f: acts on firm going: sweating on reappearance. *B. Preece.*

ZAFOD 2 b.c. (May 30) Silly Prices 110–Coatham 81 (Divine Gift 127) [1989 5g 5g   **—** 7m] 320F, 420Y: small colt: poor mover: brother to quite moderate sprinter Bargain Pack: dam won 5f seller at 2 yrs: of no account. *B. Preece.*

ZAGADKA (FR) 4 gr.f. Carwhite 127–Fille du Roi (FR) (Roi Dagobert 128)   **—** [1988 8d 6m 1989 16f] tall, leggy, close-coupled filly: no form. *T. Kersey.*

ZAKHIR (USA) 3 b.c. Topsider (USA)–Ambassador of Luck (USA) (What Luck   **94** (USA)) [1988 6f* 6g* 6g² 1989 7g 8m⁵ 8.2m] neat, quite attractive colt: good walker: has a quick, rather round action: fairly useful performer: ran creditably in competitive handicaps at Newmarket first 2 starts, moderately at Haydock on final one (May): stays 1m: has won on firm going, yet to race on a soft surface: sold 33,000 gns Newmarket Autumn Sales. *H. Thomson Jones.*

ZALALI   2 b.f. (Mar 1) Blakeney 126–Antarna (FR) 95 (Filiberto (USA) 123) [1989 **56** 7m⁶ 7.5f⁴ 7m²] 15,000Y: leggy, angular filly: has a quick action: third reported foal: half-sister to a winner in Italy: dam, successful from 9f to 10.8f, is half-sister to very good middle-distance performers Ashmore and Acoma: ridden by 7-lb claimer, 5½ lengths fourth to very easy winner Tamahan in maiden at Beverley in August, best effort: odds on, 1½ lengths second to Orchard Court in seller at Thirsk following month: will be suited by 1¼m+: sold 3,500 gns Newmarket Autumn Sales. *B. Hanbury.*

ZALAZL (USA)   3 b.c. Roberto (USA) 131–Salpinx (USA) 123 (Northern **120** Dancer) [1988 6m* 6f 7g* 7g* 8m* 8g² 1989 10d* 10.5f³ 12f*]

The Great Voltigeur Stakes at York's Ebor meeting attracts the fewest runners of all British pattern races nowadays: the last five renewals have attracted just twenty-one participants, the latest only three. At least the field was more evenly matched than when Reference Point—at odds of 14/1 on—beat two opponents in 1987. The favourite was Warrshan, winner of the Predominate Stakes and Gordon Stakes at Goodwood, who started 13/8; Zalazl started at 7/4, with Derby runner-up Terimon completing the trio at 9/4. Zalazl had not been seen out since May. On his reappearance in the White Rose Stakes at Ascot in April he had given 12 lb and a short-head beating to Demawend, just getting the better of a driving finish. Zalazl was then sent for the William Hill Dante Stakes at York, and though failing to strengthen his Derby claims he finished a creditable third behind Torjoun and Observation Post. The extra distance of the Great Voltigeur Stakes seemed likely to suit Zalazl, and his rider set out to make the running on him, though at a sedate pace initially. Zalazl quickened early in the straight and although Terimon challenged from three furlongs out the lead never looked in serious danger of changing hands; Zalazl kept on to win by half a length, with Warrshan a further length and a half behind. The St Leger was announced as Zalazl's next target but he was withdrawn from the five-day acceptors, reportedly due to soreness in a check ligament, and wasn't seen out again.

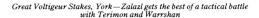

Great Voltigeur Stakes, York—Zalazl gets the best of a tactical battle with Terimon and Warrshan

			Hail To Reason		Turn-To
		Roberto (USA)	(br 1958)		Nothirdchance
		(b 1969)	Bramalea		Nashua
Zalazl (USA)			(b or br 1959)		Rarelea
(b.c. 1986)			Northern Dancer		Nearctic
		Salpinx (USA)	(b 1961)		Natalma
		(b 1976)	Suprina		Vaguely Noble
			(b 1970)		Perfecta

Zalazl is the fourth foal and third winner out of the high-class French middle-distance mare Salpinx. Zalazl's brother Caillebotte was placed at nine furlongs in Ireland as a two-year-old, Synefos (by Irish River) was a very useful performer at a mile and nine furlongs in France and Severini (by Tom Rolfe) won at a mile and a half, also in France. Al Batal, her two-year-old by Blushing Groom, is in training with Dunlop. The grandam Suprina is an unraced daughter of seven-furlong winner Perfecta, herself a daughter of the excellent broodmare Cosmah. Further details of Zalazl's pedigree can be found in *Racehorses of 1988*. Zalazl is a close-coupled, good-quartered, medium-sized colt with a short, quick action. He's better suited by a mile and a half than shorter and acts on firm and dead going. He's thoroughly game and genuine. *H. R. A. Cecil.*

ZAMBOANGA 2 br.f. (May 11) Blazing Saddles (AUS)–Maid of The Manor (Hotfoot 126) [1989 5f] 1,800Y: second foal: dam never ran: 20/1, backward and green, slowly away and soon behind in 16-runner maiden auction race at Beverley in May. *M. J. Camacho.* —

ZAMMAH 2 b.f. (Mar 12) Jalmood (USA) 126–Petrol 73 (Troy 137) [1989 6f⁴ 8m⁴ 7m³ 8.2f²] compact filly: second foal: half-sister to 3-y-o 2m winner Dhakrah (by Touching Wood): dam won at 1m and stayed 1¼m: modest maiden: length second to Bimbo in nursery at Nottingham in September: will stay well. *P. T. Walwyn.* 70

ZAMORE 3 b.g. Dominion 123–Jove's Voodoo (USA) 74 (Northern Jove (CAN)) [1988 5g 5g³ 6f⁶ 7g 6m⁶ 7d 1989 8s³ 8d*] small gelding: modest walker: made all in seller (sold to join M. Pipe 6,600 gns) at Bath in April: suited by 1m and a soft surface: winning novice hurdler: dead. *R. F. Johnson Houghton.* 64

ZANOBA 2 ch.f. (Apr 19) Precocious 126–Zanubia 81 (Nonoalco (USA) 131) [1989 6g 5m 5m⁵ 5m³ 5f] 27,000Y: workmanlike filly: fourth foal: half-sister to Italian 3-y-o 7f and 1m winner Sharp N Blunt (by Beldale Flutter) and 1986 2-y-o 5f winner Bothy Ballad (by Final Straw): dam, 7f winner, is half-sister to dam of Knockando out of a half-sister to Connaught: showed improved form when 2 lengths third to Number One Son in nursery at Warwick in October: soon outpaced in similar event at Wolverhampton: should stay 6f. *F. Durr.* 59

ZANONI 2 b.c. (Apr 20) Mummy's Pet 125–Princely Maid 71 (King's Troop 118) [1989 6m² 6d²] leggy, quite attractive colt: brother to 3-y-o Aonia, fairly useful 5f winner at 2 yrs, and plating-class maiden Irenic and half-brother to several winners, including Forzando (by Formidable), good performer at up to 8.5f here and in USA: dam 5f winner at 2 yrs: fair form in October maidens won by Muwfiq at York and by Heart of Joy at Newbury: sure to win a race. *M. A. Jarvis.* 89 p

ZANUSSI LINE 5 b.g. High Line 125–Angelica (SWE) (Hornbeam 130) [1988 NR 1989 15.5s] form on flat only on debut at 2 yrs: sold 5,200 gns Doncaster May Sales: resold 1,850 gns Ascot 2nd June Sales. *M. J. Wilkinson.* —

ZANUSSI SATELLITE 3 b.g. Formidable (USA) 125–Varushka 74 (Sharpen Up 127) [1988 6f 5f³ 5.8g² 6f⁴ 1989 8d⁵ 7d 8.3m] smallish gelding: quite modest maiden at 2 yrs: below form in sellers and handicap as 3-y-o: should be suited by further than 6f: possibly unsuited by a soft surface: visored second outing: tends to play up: sold 2,100 gns Ascot June Sales. *D. W. P. Arbuthnot.* 47

ZARNA 2 ro.f. (May 18) Shernazar 131–Zahra (Habitat 134) [1989 7m² 7g³ 6g] compact, workmanlike filly: moderate mover: sixth foal: half-sister to 7f winner Zariya (by Blushing Groom) and fairly useful 1½m winner Zareef (by Top Ville), later successful in Italy: dam, placed in France from 1m to 11f, is daughter of top-class Petite Etoile: quite modest form when in frame in maiden at Yarmouth and minor event at Kempton: never placed to challenge or knocked about in maiden at Leicester in November, catching eye running on strongly towards finish: will be suited by 1m+: one to keep an eye on in handicap company. *M. R. Stoute.* 68 p

ZARRARA (USA) 3 b.f. Desert Wine (USA)–Surera (ARG) (Sheet Anchor) [1988 6d* 7m 1989 8.5s³ 10.2m 11.5f⁵ 12f 10g 10f³ a12g⁶ a10g] strong, 64

good-quartered filly: quite modest handicapper: below form at Lingfield last 2 starts, bit backward on first of them: should stay 1½m: best effort on soft going: has twice failed to handle turn: bandaged final outing. *P. F. I. Cole.*

ZAWAHIR (USA) 2 ch.f. (May 11) Nureyev (USA) 131–Solariat (USA) **88** (Secretariat (USA)) [1989 6m² 7f* 7m⁶] rangy, rather unfurnished filly: has scope: fifth foal: sister to useful Italian 7f and 9f winner Alex Nureyev and quite useful 1987 2-y-o 6f winner Angelina Ballerina, later stakes placed in USA: dam unraced daughter of half-sister to Try My Best and El Gran Senor: co-favourite, won maiden at Goodwood in July comfortably by 2½ lengths from Platinum Dancer: on toes and unruly at stalls, well-beaten sixth of 7, racing keenly, finding little and tending to edge right final 2f, to Moon Cactus in Black Bottle Scotch Whisky Prestige Stakes there month later: bred to stay 1m. *J. L. Dunlop.*

ZAYYANI 3 b.c. Darshaan 133–Zariya (USA) 88 (Blushing Groom (FR) 131) [1988 **119** 7m* 7d⁴ 1989 7d* 8m 12f² 12g⁶ 10g⁵] medium-sized, attractive colt: has a quick action: smart performer: won Singer & Friedlander Greenham Stakes at Newbury in April: 8/1, ¾-length second to 6 to Cacoethes in moderately-run King Edward VII Stakes at Royal Ascot, last entering straight and running on well: below best in 2000 Guineas at Newmarket, Irish Derby at the Curragh and Prix Guillaume d'Ornano at Deauville: stays 1½m: acts on firm going and a soft surface: edgy at start before Greenham and final start at 2 yrs: sent to N. Drysdale in USA. *R. F. Johnson Houghton.*

ZEBOIM 3 ch.g. Stanford 121§–Solarina (Solinus 130) [1988 NR 1989 8.2s 5f 6f 6f⁶ **56** 5g⁵ 6m* 5f* 6m⁵ 5m] IR 2,600F, 5,000Y: big, lengthy, workmanlike gelding: first living foal: dam placed over 7f on first of only 2 starts in Ireland as 3-y-o: won apprentice seller (sweating, bought in 7,200 gns) at Windsor and handicap at Lingfield in July: below form in handicaps following month: stays 6f: acts on firm going: blinkered last 5 outings: suitable mount for apprentice. *K. M. Brassey.*

ZEFFIRELLA 3 b.f. Known Fact (USA) 135–Lyric Dance 106 (Lyphard (USA) **84** 132) [1988 6g 7g² 1989 7f² 7f² 8f⁴ 7f* 7f⁵ 7g² 6f²] leggy, lengthy filly: turns off-fore in: has a quick action: won maiden at Chepstow in July: good third (promoted) in £6,000 handicap at Newbury on sixth start, edging left but best effort after: stays 1m: acts on firm going. *W. G. A. Brooks.*

ZENELLA 2 b.f. (Apr 20) Precocious 126–Zepha 88 (Great Nephew 126) [1989 **—** 7g] fifth foal: half-sister to 3-y-o 7f winner Fedoria (by Formidable) and 3 other winners, including 1987 2-y-o 1m winner Great Prospector (by Glint of Gold), later middle-distance winner in Italy: dam won from 1m to 9.4f: 20/1 and ridden by 7-lb claimer, hampered around halfway and never dangerous in 24-runner maiden at Newmarket in November: changed hands 2,200 gns Newmarket December Sales. *W. Jarvis.*

ZEPHYR NIGHTS (USA) 2 b.c. (May 20) Grey Dawn II 132–Vaslava (Habitat **—** 134) [1989 7g 7g] $5,000Y: leggy, angular colt: second foal: dam French 1½m winner: well beaten in autumn maidens at Yarmouth and Goodwood (auction event). *I. Campbell.*

ZERO TIME 2 br.f. (Feb 16) Alzao (USA) 117–Queen of Time (USA) (Roi **52** Dagobert 128) [1989 5s³ 6f³ 6g] 32,000Y: compact, good-bodied filly: has scope: has a roundish action: half-sister to 6f winner Time-Table (by Mansingh) and several winners abroad: dam poor maiden: plating-class form in maiden at Sandown and minor event at Folkestone in first half of season: carrying condition, well beaten in Leicester maiden in November. *P. F. I. Cole.*

ZERO WATT (USA) 5 b.h. Little Current (USA)–Ruby Tuesday (USA) (T V **107** Lark) [1988 16g⁵ 20f* 16f² 16.1d⁴ 18g 1989 16f² 22.2f³] big, strong, close-coupled horse: carries deal of condition: has a long, rather round stride: favourite, stayed on strongly to win Ascot Stakes (Handicap) at Royal Ascot as 4-y-o: ran very well when neck second to stable-companion Sadeem in Mappin & Webb Henry II EBF Stakes at Sandown in May, making most: long odds on, ran in snatches and hung badly over 1f out when 4½ lengths third to Ala Hounak in Queen Alexandra Stakes at Royal Ascot over 3 weeks later: out-and-out stayer: probably needed top-of-the-ground: retired to Louella Stud, Leicestershire, fee £250 + £350 (Oct 1st). *G. Harwood.*

Sheikh Mohammed's "Zero Watt"

ZHIVAGO'S PASSION 2 gr.f. (Mar 13) Another Realm 118–Crystal Gael 79 **60**
(Sparkler 130) [1989 5g² 5m⁶ 5m⁵ 5g] 4,700F, 4,800Y: workmanlike filly: half-sister
to 3 minor winners, including 1986 2-y-o 5f winner On Notice (by Song): dam won
over 1m at 2 yrs: quite modest performer: best effort third start: may be better
suited by 6f. *J. J. Bridger.*

ZIA (USA) 3 b.f. Shareef Dancer (USA) 135–Diomedia (USA) (Sea Bird 145) [1988 **88**
6m² 7m⁵ 8.2m² 1989 12.5f² 11.5f⁶ 10f² 12m² 12.2g* 14m³] close-coupled,
workmanlike filly: favourite, won maiden at Catterick in September by 15 lengths:
good third in £6,400 handicap at Newmarket following month: stays 1¾m: lacks
turn of foot and likely to prove suited by forcing tactics. *C. E. Brittain.*

ZILZAL (USA) 3 ch.c. Nureyev (USA) 131–French Charmer (USA) (Le **137**
Fabuleux 133) [1988 NR 1989 7g* 7f* 7g* 8f* 8m* 8f⁶]
Will Britain ever win a Breeders' Cup Mile? Six years of trying has met
with no better reward than third place from Shadeed in 1985, Sonic Lady in
1987 and Most Welcome in 1989, while horses of the calibre of Lear Fan,
Rousillon, Milligram, Warning and Zilzal all finished out of the first five. The
American press (and the critics at home) have tended to see the many and
varied explanations for defeat more as excuses for failure, but there was a
general consensus after the latest running that Zilzal had seriously under-
mined his chance by missing the break from what had already been regarded
as an unfavourable outside draw. Zilzal was last away from his nine-of-eleven
stall and was never able to get back on terms with the leaders, virtually forced
to race wide all the way in a rough race run at a cut-throat pace on the very
tight track. By the last bend he'd improved four places without recovering
much ground; making the turn he halved the deficit to about three lengths
without improving his placing; he made a bit more progress in the short
straight until hampered by Most Welcome close home and eventually finished
sixth to Steinlen, beaten no more than two lengths.
At evens Zilzal started the shortest-priced favourite in the Mile so far.
Arguably Britain has never fielded a stronger candidate. He went as champion
European miler, unbeaten, widely held to be an exceptional colt after his
defeat of the French three-year-old Polish Precedent in the Queen Elizabeth
II Stakes at Ascot in September last time out. The Queen Elizabeth II Stakes
has usually been won by a top-class miler, occasionally by an exceptional one,
since its inception in 1955. The handsome increase in the prize money
resulting from the establishment of the Festival of British Racing has been
responsible for attracting fields well up to standard in the last three years; the
latest running was preceded by Warning's spectacular victory, and before that
by Milligram's defeat of Miesque. Zilzal had three other opponents, of whom
Distant Relative and Green Line Express also have form in the best company,
but Polish Precedent seemed easily the biggest threat. He'd won all his seven
races in 1989 including the most important over the distance in France, the
Prix Jacques le Marois at Deauville and the Prix du Moulin at Longchamp. He

Jersey Stakes, Ascot—Zilzal reveals himself top class

Van Geest Criterion Stakes, Newmarket—Zilzal impresses again

was a very good-looking animal and had been winning very impressively, showing a turn of foot that Zilzal would do well to cope with where such as Citidancer, the filly Magic Gleam, Cadeaux Genereux and Green Line Express had failed. Under conditions ideal for both, Zilzal beat Polish Precedent hands down by three lengths. The early pace was just ordinary, which probably accounts for the fact that Cottenham could keep in touch and be beaten under six lengths in last place at the finish. Zilzal made the pace tracked by Polish Precedent, and stayed in front all the way. The field turned into the straight in a bunch. Soon afterwards Zilzal began to stretch them, and though Polish Precedent managed to stick close for a while Zilzal had him in trouble over a furlong out and, continuing to quicken under driving, was able to put three lengths between himself and his main rival by the line. The consistent Distant Relative finished another two lengths back in third, never having been able to land a blow.

After this performance the case against sending Zilzal to Gulfstream Park rested on his inexperience, his temperament and the supposition that he had another season in front of him. Zilzal's lack of experience was incontrovertible—he'd run in only five races, none further afield than Goodwood where he'd won the Swettenham Stud Sussex Stakes in July, whereas Steinlen, for instance, had already run twenty-four times in the States following a career in France. As for his temperament, while Zilzal was a very free-sweater and could be a real handful to get down to the start, everything had gone smoothly in his races so far. We expected him both to travel well and run well. However, his boiling over just prior to loading in the Breeders' Cup, having been taken down early to lessen the chances of that happening, may well have contributed to his poor start. Almost as soon as the race ended the world learned that Zilzal did not have another season in front of him; not on the track anyway, he'd been packed off to stud in Kentucky. Whether a lack of confidence in his prospects of going the right way from three to four played any part in the decision to retire him is unclear. That would seem a shade more plausible a reason for doing so than his defeat, for surely concrete plans would have had to be made well in advance of the

Breeders' Cup. The news of the retirement brought down adverse, even hostile, criticism on Zilzal's connections, some of it completely undeserved. Breaking faith with the public was one of the milder sentiments expressed. Actually, the horse was as much a loser as the public. Zilzal had been deprived of the chance to re-establish himself, not to say prove himself further. He will not be at the Breeders' Cup in 1990, which will be run on the biggest turf track in the States at Belmont Park in temperatures almost certain to be less oppressive than those found in Florida in early-November. Though he was undoubtedly one of the outstanding milers of the decade his reputation is diminished by his having run only six times.

Zilzal's entire racing career ran only from May 30th to November 4th and took in only four important events; his first race, in a minor contest at Leicester, and his third, in the Van Geest Stakes at Newmarket, both won by wide margins (the latter from Russian Bond), were largely for educational purposes. For a horse having only his second run, Zilzal's performance when odds on in the Jersey Stakes at Royal Ascot was exceptional. The way he moved up to lead two furlongs out in a fast-run affair and came right away from Russian Royal, Distant Relative and the rest of a fair Jersey Stakes field showed him a rival to his stable companion Shaadi, the previous day's St James's Palace Stakes winner. The pair met on Shaadi's next appearance, in the Sussex Stakes. In what looked the most competitive mile race of the season up to that stage Zilzal started 5/2 second favourite behind Warning, and Shaadi at 7/1. Markofdistinction (3/1), Most Welcome (20/1), Opening Verse (40/1), Green Line Express (100/1) and the pacemaker Hilton Brown completed the line-up. The race turned out less competitive than anticipated when Warning and Shaadi ran below form. Nevertheless there is no reason to suppose that the other horses of established merit, in fourth and fifth, Most Welcome and Opening Verse, did not give their running, and in beating them at least four and a half lengths Zilzal confirmed himself among the best in training. He was very impressive again, especially in the way he quickened in another strongly-run race. Despite the pace, he kept up easily and went on from Opening Verse well over a furlong out; once in front, ridden along to make sure, he kept on finding more and won with complete authority by three lengths and one and a half from Green Line Express and Markofdistinction. His timefigure of 1.52 fast, the equivalent to a timerating of 138, was the best of any horse running in Britain in 1989. That Zilzal's pre-race humour needn't be detrimental to his performance was clearly illustrated here—he sweated badly in the parade and showed a reluctance to go down. After these four quick outings he waited for Ascot and the meeting with Polish Precedent.

In the meantime came an announcement potentially of great significance to everyone concerned with a racehorse anywhere near as good as Zilzal: a world-wide handicap for all rated at 110 or higher is proposed for the mid-'nineties, following talks held at the Arlington Million meeting between the official handicappers of Britain, Ireland and France, and others representing Victoria State in Australia and four of the main racetracks in America. It's a project which is unlikely to meet with general acceptance for

Swettenham Stud Sussex Stakes, Goodwood—
the winner quickens away from Green Line Express, Markofdistinction,
Opening Verse (rails) and Most Welcome

Queen Elizabeth II Stakes, Ascot—Zilzal ends Polish Precedent's run in the day's show-piece; Distant Relative is a good third

there is no way it can achieve its objective of 'enabling precise comparisons to be made between the best performers across the globe'. How can you achieve 'a full integration of the international classifications of the thirteen principal racing countries' when those countries race under such variable conditions and when so little inter-continental competition takes place? And if by some miracle enough competition could be brought about to enable some sort of comparisons to be drawn, the figures would still be the result of that unsatisfactory process, handicapping by committee, with the suspicion of horse-trading behind closed doors as each country fights its corner. The day must be a long way off when, as proposed, the commercial sales companies agree to publish these ratings in their catalogues 'to bring an end to exaggerated or misleading claims about the merits of horses going through the ring'. All that said, it would be of considerable academic interest to know how the assorted officials view the scene worldwide in any particular year, just as it was to read senior handicapper Gibbs's opinion, which probably wouldn't go down too well in the States, that 'Steinlen is not a bad horse. He's about a 128-130 horse, and the best miler since the International Classification began was El Gran Senor who was rated 138. He was a really brilliant horse. But in US conditions it is different. Take the case of Zilzal. I would have thought that he was 5 lb-6 lb in front of Steinlen purely on his Ascot and Goodwood form, but Steinlen beat him. You need to have 5 lb or 6 lb in hand to be confident of winning'. For the record, Zilzal was rated at 134 in the International Classification in Europe, joint-top with Old Vic and 3 lb ahead of Nashwan.

Zilzal (USA) (ch.c. 1986)	Nureyev (USA) (b 1977)	Northern Dancer (b 1961)	Nearctic / Natalma
		Special (b 1969)	Forli / Thong
	French Charmer (USA) (ch 1978)	Le Fabuleux (ch 1961)	Wild Risk / Anguar
		Bold Example (b 1969)	Bold Lad / Lady Be Good

Zilzal and Polish Precedent are closely related on both sides: their sires are sons of Northern Dancer while their dams are half-sisters by staying sires out of Bold Example, a stakes-placed sprint winner bred in Ireland. Polish Precedent's dam never ran, but French Charmer figured only 10 lb behind the best of her sex on turf in the *Daily Racing Form* Free Handicap in 1981, the year she won the nine-furlong Del Mar Oaks. Before Zilzal—her third foal—French Charmer produced two fillies, both of whom were still winning as four-year-olds. The first Taras Charmer (by Majestic Light) raced in the States; the second Charmante (by Alydar) showed useful form at up to a mile over here, and she was successful in the States in 1989. French Charmer's two-year-old of 1989 is a colt by Mr Prospector called Really Awesome.

On looks the 750,000-dollar yearling Zilzal has to give best to Polish Precedent: he's a leggy, rather angular colt. The actions of the two are similar, rather short and quick as often associated with firm-ground specialists. Zilzal raced only on a sound surface and acted well on firm. His covering fee to begin with will be 60,000 dollars, live foal. *M. R. Stoute.*

ZINARELLE (FR) 2 b.f. (Apr 15) Zino 127–Liberale (FR) (Fabulous Dancer **110**
(USA) 126) [1989 5.5g* 5.5d* 5.5g² 8g 8g⁴ 7g⁴] 65,000 francs (approx £5,900) Y:
small, compact filly: first foal: dam won from 6f (at 2 yrs) to 1½m in France:
successful in maiden and a listed race (by 1½ lengths) at Maisons-Laffitte: length
second to Ozone Friendly in Prix Robert Papin at Maisons-Laffitte on third start,
over 2 lengths fourth of 15 to Salsabil in Prix Marcel Boussac at Longchamp on fifth:
ran poorly final one: stays 1m. *J. Laumain, France.*

ZINBAQ 3 ch.c. Ahonoora 122–Zaiyundeen (FR) (Exbury 138) [1988 5m 5m² —
5.8g² 6g⁴ 6g⁶ 8g 6s 1989 6d 6m 7g 6m 6g 7g] quite attractive colt: moderate mover:
modest maiden at 2 yrs: well beaten as 3-y-o: takes good hold, and will probably
prove best at short of 1m. *C. J. Benstead.*

ZINGALONG 2 b.f. (Feb 2) Dominion 123–Lady Acquiesce 67 (Galivanter 131) —
[1989 6m 6f⁵] 15,000F: workmanlike, sparely-made filly: first foal: dam, 2-y-o 5f
winner, is half-sister to smart sprinter Chellaston Park: well beaten in minor event
at Windsor and maiden at Brighton: sold 1,800 gns Ascot November Sales. *R. V.
Smyth.*

ZIO PEPPINO 8 ch.g. Thatch (USA) 136–Victorian Habit 101 (Habitat 134) [1988 —
8g 7m 7m 7d4 6d⁵ 8d 6s 1989 8g 8.5d 8m 8.2f⁶ 8m 8m 7g 10.8m 8f 10f a12g] sturdy
gelding: poor handicapper: stays 9f: unsuited by soft going and used to act well on
top-of-the-ground: blinkered 5 times: has worn bandages: suitable mount for
apprentice. *J. P. Smith.*

ZIPPERTI DO 3 ch.f. Precocious 126–Doobie Do 106 (Derring-Do 131) [1988 NR **70**
1989 7g a8g*] deep-girthed filly: fourth foal: half-sister to 2m winner Gold Tint (by
Glint of Gold) and a winner in Norway: dam, second in Cherry Hinton, is out of
half-sister to smart stayer Almeira: 14/1 and reluctant at stalls, won maiden at
Southwell in December by 3 lengths, outpaced early: slowly away and no show in
all-aged event at Newmarket 4 weeks earlier. *P. J. Makin.*

ZIZANIA 2 ch.f. (Feb 27) Ahonoora 122–Bolkonskina (Balidar 133) [1989 6g 6g **77**
7f⁶ 6g⁴ 6g⁶] 50,000Y: medium-sized, quite good-topped filly: has knee action: sixth
foal: half-sister to 3 modest animals: dam, sister to Bolkonski, won twice at 2 yrs in
Italy: showed improved form when around length fourth of 16, always prominent, to
Roman Walk in maiden at Newmarket in October: not discredited in big field there
month later: seems better suited by 6f than 7f. *C. E. Brittain.*

ZODE 3 b.c. Simply Great (FR) 122–Star Face (African Sky 124) [1988 7g⁶ 1989 7d] —
good-topped, attractive colt: 50/1, about 14 lengths eighth of 20 in maiden at
Newmarket in April, running on steadily from rear after saddle slipped: sold 6,400
gns Newmarket Autumn Sales. *H. R. A. Cecil.*

ZODIAC BOY 4 b.g. Monseigneur (USA) 124–Hannie Caulder (Workboy 123) —
[1988 8g 7m 6g 6s 6g 1989 10s 12.5f 12m 12h] close-coupled, workmanlike gelding: of
little account: bandaged off-hind at 4 yrs. *J. Pearce.*

ZOMAN (USA) 2 ch.c. (Mar 16) Affirmed (USA)–A Little Affection (USA) (King **83** p
Emperor (USA)) [1989 7m*] $300,000Y: fourth foal: closely related to American
3-y-o Love And Affection (by Exclusive Era), smart winner at 2 yrs: dam won at up
to 1m: favourite, won 17-runner maiden at Chepstow in October by a length from
Verdeuse, held up then making steady headway final 2f to lead inside last: sure to
improve. *P. F. I. Cole.*

ZUBROVKA (FR) 2 b.c. (Mar 18) Law Society (USA) 130–Czar's Bride (USA) **92** P
78 (Northern Dancer) [1989 7g⁴] medium-sized, attractive colt: has plenty of scope:
fourth foal: half-brother to 3 winners in France, including 1½m winner Stolichinaya
(by Known Fact): dam middle-distance maiden, out of half-sister to top-class filly
and broodmare Fanfreluche and good Canadian colt Barachois (both by Northern
Dancer): 15/2 but very green, shaped most promisingly when under 2 lengths fourth
of 13 to Duke of Paducah in £10,000 event at Newmarket in October, leading 2f out
until 1f out and eased closing stages: will stay 1¼m: an interesting prospect, sure to
win races. *J. Tree.*

ZUCCHINI 3 ch.g. Absalom 128–Hot Spice (Hotfoot 126) [1988 7d⁶ 7m⁵ 7f 8g **70**
1989 12d 12f 8m³ 8.2g⁵ 7f² 7m² 7.5f* 7.5m] strong, rangy gelding: modest
handicapper: favourite, moved moderately down when winning at Beverley in
August: ran well previous 2 outings but moderately on final one: effective at 7f and
1m: acts on firm going: blinkered fourth and fifth outings: sold 13,500 gns
Newmarket Autumn Sales. *M. F. D. Morley.*

ZULU PAGEANT 4 ch.f. Son of Shaka 119–Have A Good Day (Red Alert 127) —
[1988 NR 1989 6d 6v 5f] plain filly: first foal: dam unraced: no form in modest
company. *R. W. Stubbs.*

TIMEFORM CHAMPIONS OF 1989

HORSE OF THE YEAR (RATED AT 137)

ZILZAL (USA)
3 ch.c. Nureyev–French Charmer (Le Fabuleux)
Owner Mana Al-Maktoum   Trainer M. Stoute

BEST TWO-YEAR-OLD COLT (RATED AT 123p)

BE MY CHIEF (USA)
2 b.c. Chief's Crown–Lady Be Mine (Sir Ivor)
Owner Mr P. Burrell   Trainer H. Cecil

BEST TWO-YEAR-OLD FILLY (RATED AT 118p)

NEGLIGENT
2 gr.f. Ahonoora–Negligence (Roan Rocket)
Owner Mrs J. M. Corbett   Trainer B. Hills

BEST SPRINTER (RATED AT 131)

CADEAUX GENEREUX
4 ch.c. Young Generation–Smarten Up (Sharpen Up)
Owner Maktoum Al-Maktoum   Trainer A. Scott

BEST MILER (RATED AT 137)

ZILZAL (USA)
3 ch.c. Nureyev–French Charmer (Le Fabuleux)
Owner Mana Al-Maktoum   Trainer M. Stoute

BEST MIDDLE-DISTANCE HORSE (RATED AT 136)

OLD VIC
3 b.c. Sadler's Wells–Cockade (Derring-Do)
Owner Sheikh Mohammed   Trainer H. Cecil

BEST STAYER (RATED AT 127p)

MICHELOZZO (USA)
3 b.c. Northern Baby–Tres Agreable (Luthier)
Owner Mr C. A. B. St George   Trainer H. Cecil

THE TIMEFORM 'TOP HUNDRED'

Here are listed the 'Top 100' two-year-olds, three-year-olds and older horses in the annual.

Two-Year-Olds

123p	Be My Chief
122p	Machiavellian
121p	Jade Robbery
119p	Linamix
119p	Septieme Ciel
119	Balla Cove
119	Osario
118p	Negligent
118	Pole Position
118?	Snurge
117p	Elmaamul
117	Dashing Blade
116p	Bleu de France
116p	Digression
116p	Salsabil
116	Anshan
116	Argentum
116	Call To Arms
115p	Funambule
114	Dead Certain
113p	The Caretaker
113	Golden Era
113	Horatio Luro
113	Pont-Aven
113	Qirmazi
113	Rock City
113	Somethingdifferent
113	Welney
113?	Intimiste
112p	Line of Thunder
112p	Tirol
112	Alchi
112	Baligh
112	Chimes of Freedom
112	Cordoba
112	Dr Somerville
112	Ernani
112	Honor Rajana
112	Houseproud
112	Miss Afrique
112	Robellation
111	Qathif
111	Repercutionist
111	Rich And Famous
111	Slew The Slewor
110	Follidays
110	Haunting Beauty
110	Sheer Precocity
110	Spinning
110	Zinarelle
109p	Belmez
109	Mackla
109	Va Toujours
109?	Guiza
108p	Filago
108p	Montendre
108	Bridal Toast
108	Catherine Parr
108	Contract Law

108	Mabrova
108	Pharaoh's Delight
108	Rafha
108	River of Light
108	Sorceress
108	Wajna
107p	Gharam
107p	Moon Cactus
107p	Raj Waki
107p	Royal Academy
107	Air Music
107	Boston Two Step
107	Cullinan
107	Daarik
107	Duck And Dive
107	Ozone Friendly
107	Sharp Sass
107	Spendomania
106 +	Champagne Gold
106p	Dorset Duke
106p	Mademoiselle Chloe
106p	Missionary Ridge
106p	Shavian
106	Book The Band
106	Candy Glen
106	Dictator's Song
106	Knight's Baroness
106	Robin des Bois
106	Satin Wood
105p	Dovekie
105p	In Excess
105p	Noble Patriarch
105	Athauf
105?	Pictorial
104p	Makbul
104p	Rock Hopper
104p	Silk Slippers
104	Loch Fruin
104	Rushmore
104	Wedding Bouquet
103p	Dayjur
103	Barouf
103	Cutting Note
103	Dancing Music
103	Harbour Bar
103	Old Alliance
103	Tabdea

Three-Year-Olds

137	Zilzal
136	Old Vic
135	Nashwan
131	Polish Precedent
130	Cacoethes
129	Behera
129	Sierra Roberta
128	Dolpour
128	Legal Case
128	Young Mother

127p	Michelozzo
127	Dancehall
127	Distant Relative
127	Golden Opinion
127	Lady In Silver
126	Aliysa
126	Creator
126	Danehill
126	Green Line Express
126	Shaadi
125	Exbourne
125	Mondrian (Ger)
125	Scenic
124	Alydaress
124	Borromini
124	Gold Seam
124	In The Wings
124	Two Timing
123	Louveterie
123	Markofdistinction
123	Norberto
123	Prince of Dance
123	Roseate Tern
123	Shining Steel
123	Turgeon
122	Aliocha
122	Colorado Dancer
122	Local Talent
122	Louis Cyphre
122	Magic Gleam
122	Opening Verse
122	Torjoun
122	Weld
122?	Le Voyageur
121	Deliorman
121	Filia Ardross
121	Greensmith
121	Kendor
121	Observation Post
121	Petite Ile
121	Snow Bride
120	Braiswick
120	Citidancer
120	Relief Pitcher
120	Statoblest
120	Tigani
120	Tyrone Bridge
120	Zalazl
119	Dancing Dissident
119	Golden Pheasant
119	Harvest Time
119	Icona
119	Navratilovna
119	Passionaria
119	Terimon
119	Val des Bois
119	Zayyani
118	Drum Taps
118	Galetto
118	Great Commotion
118	Mardonius

118	Ode	121	Royal Touch	110	Sharp Reminder
118	Or Acier	120	Chummy's Favourite	110	Teeming Shore
118	Pearl Bracelet	120	Executive Perk	110	Travel Mystery
118	Pirate Army	120	Fijar Tango	110	Vaguely Pleasant
118	Robertet	120	Kefaah	110	Wood Dancer
117	Ensconse	120	Nabeel Dancer	109	Al Mufti
117	Fieldwork	120	Silver Fling	109	Alquoz
117	Light of Morn	120	Top Class	109	Hoy
117	Lucky Song	119	Beau Sher	109	Insan
117	Monsagem	119	Green Adventure	109	My Lamb
117	Musical Bliss	119	Holst	109	Sergeyevich
117	Pilot	119	Mansonnien	109	Upper Strata
117	Sapience	119	Per Quod		
117	Spritsail	119	Princess Athena		
117	Warrshan	118	A Prayer For Wings		
116p	Bex	118	Malaspina		
116	Alphabel	118	Red Glow		
116	Free Sweater	118	Shady Heights		
116	French Glory	118	Tralos		
116	High Estate	117	Athyka		
116	Ile de Nisky	117	Carol's Treasure		
116	Just Three	117	Gallic League		
116	Nadina	117	Hibernian Gold		
116	Pass The Peace	117	Mazzacano		
116	Rain Burst	117	Petrullo		
116	Silicon Lady	117	Point of Light		
116	Viva Zapata	117	Zadracarta		
115p	Husyan	116	Albadr		
115	Braashee	116	Big Shuffle		
115	Corwyn Bay	116	Emmson		
115	Dancing Tribute	116	Hello Calder		
115	Kerrera	116	Mac's Fighter		
115	Lady Winner	116	Miss Kenmare		
115	Lugana Beach	116	Mountain Kingdom		
115	Monastery	116	Pelorus		
115	N C Owen	116	Rambo's Hall		
115	Porter Rhodes	116	Tisserand		
115	Princess Accord	116§	Rachmaninov		
115	Princess Sobieska	115	Firelight Fiesta		
		115	Just A Flutter		
		115	Sudden Victory		
Older Horses		115	Sweet Chesne		
		115	Whippet		
132	Carroll House	115	Zaffaran		
131	Cadeaux Genereux	114	Charmer		
130	Warning	114	Summer Trip		
128	Ile de Chypre	114	Unknown Quantity		
128§	Saint Andrews	114§	Glacial Storm		
127	Star Lift	113	Arden		
126	Ibn Bey	113	Handsome Sailor		
126	Unfuwain	113	Lazaz		
125	Assatis	113	Noora Abu		
125	French Stress	113	Poyle George		
125	Sheriff's Star	113	Sesame		
124	Boyatino	112	Astronef		
124	Cricket Ball	112	Elementary		
124	Most Welcome	112	Llyn Gwynant		
124	Robore	112	Luzum		
123	Indian Ridge	112	Trebrook		
122	Reprimand	112?	Ala Hounak		
122	Sadeem	111	Indian Queen		
122	Squill	111	Milieu		
122	Top Sunrise	111	Nemesia		
121	Alwuhush	111	Savahra Sound		
121	Apache	110	Atlaal		
121	Gabina	110	Dust Devil		
121	Highland Chieftain	110	Hello Vaigly		
121	Indian Skimmer	110	Main Objective		

1989 STATISTICS

The following tables show the leading owners, trainers, breeders, jockeys, horses and sires of winners during the 1989 season, under Jockey Club Rules. The tables are reproduced by permission of *The Sporting Life*.

OWNERS

		Horses	Races Won	Stakes £
1.	Sheikh Mohammed	90	130	1,296,052
2.	Hamdan Al-Maktoum	65	98	1,226,358
3.	K. Abdulla	40	61	683,586
4.	Maktoum Al-Maktoum	21	32	484,693
5.	H. H. Aga Khan	33	48	480,433
6.	Mana Al-Maktoum	1	5	397,607
7.	Sir Gordon White	13	20	337,714
8.	C. A. B. St George	13	17	250,071
9.	Athos Christodoulou	5	8	213,797
10.	Commander G. G. Marten	1	4	198,544
11.	Peter Burrell	1	6	187,900
12.	Lord Howard de Walden	14	19	152,868

TRAINERS

		Horses	Races Won	Stakes £
1.	M. R. Stoute	82	117	1,469,171
2.	H. R. A. Cecil	71	116	1,175,054
3.	W. R. Hern	28	45	1,100,369
4.	G. Harwood	69	109	1,070,827
5.	L. M. Cumani	51	88	822,032
6.	B. W. Hills	50	73	479,676
7.	D. R. C. Elsworth	21	35	418,006
8.	R. Hannon	40	53	360,262
9.	J. Tree	18	29	323,208
10.	A. A. Scott	17	24	314,289
11.	I. A. Balding	26	41	295,433
12.	W. Jarvis	21	32	258,204

BREEDERS

		Horses	Races Won	Stakes £
1.	Hamdan Al-Maktoum	7	12	853,781
2.	H. H. Aga Khan	33	48	480,433
3.	Kentucky Select Bloodstock I	2	6	400,181
4.	Ovidstown Investments Ltd	1	4	277,924
5.	R. F. Johnson Houghton	2	8	229,304
6.	Juddmonte Farms	14	21	229,278
7.	Peter E. Burrell Trust	1	6	187,900
8.	Charles Rowe	1	3	184,163
9.	Mrs R. B. Kennard	4	9	182,310
10.	Lord Porchester	5	10	177,173
11.	Darley Stud Management Co Ltd	6	7	175,784
12.	White Lodge Stud Ltd	6	11	156,819

		JOCKEYS				*Total*	*Per*
		1st	*2nd*	*3rd*	*Unpl*	*Mts*	*Cent*
1.	Pat Eddery	171	126	91	449	837	20.4
2.	S. Cauthen	163	92	65	341	661	24.7
3.	W. Carson	138	126	121	483	867	15.9
4.	R. Cochrane	120	97	85	379	682	17.6
5.	M. Roberts	107	106	88	522	823	13.0
6.	W. R. Swinburn	94	92	91	375	652	14.4
7.	M. Birch	91	61	75	465	692	13.2
8.	Dean McKeown	86	77	64	498	725	11.9
9.	J. Reid	84	71	68	364	587	14.3
10.	G. Duffield	78	66	63	475	682	11.4
11.	M. Hills	77	61	57	299	494	15.6
12.	L. Dettori	75	59	56	284	474	15.8

HORSES

		Races Won	*Stakes £*
		---	---
1.	Nashwan 3 ch.c. Blushing Groom–Height of Fashion	4	772,046
2.	Zilzal 3 ch.c. Nureyev–French Charmer	5	397,607
3.	Legal Case 3 b.c. Alleged–Maryinsky	4	277,924
4.	Dead Certain 2 b.f. Absalom–Sirnelta	4	198,544
5.	Be My Chief 2 b.c. Chief's Crown–Lady Be Mine	6	187,900
6.	Michelozzo 3 b.c. Northern Baby–Tres Agreable	3	184,163
7.	Cadeaux Genereux 4 ch.c. Young Generation–Smarten Up	2	162,399
8.	Dashing Blade 2 b.c. Elegant Air–Sharp Castan	3	144,908
9.	Shaadi 3 b.c. Danzig–Unfurled	2	136,053
10.	Danehill 3 b.c. Danzig–Razyana	3	127,501
11.	Ile de Chypre 4 b.c. Ile de Bourbon–Salamina	1	125,348
12.	Aliysa 3 b.f. Darshaan–Alannya	2	122,030

SIRES OF WINNERS

		Horses	*Races Won*	*Stakes £*
		---	---	---
1.	Blushing Groom (1974) by Red God	13	22	922,163
2.	Nureyev (1977) by Northern Dancer	22	35	636,813
3.	Danzig (1977) by Northern Dancer	17	29	427,003
4.	Alleged (1974) by Hoist The Flag	9	19	365,701
5.	Young Generation (1976) by Balidar	10	16	311,601
6.	Absalom (1975) by Abwah	18	30	271,027
7.	Sadler's Wells (1981) by Northern Dancer	14	25	270,673
8.	Northern Baby (1976) by Northern Dancer	6	18	261,049
9.	Known Fact (1977) by In Reality	18	27	241,529
10.	Habitat (1966) by Sir Gaylord	15	24	227,410
11.	The Minstrel (1974) by Northern Dancer	10	16	223,238
12.	Ile de Bourbon (1975) by Nijinsky	14	23	219,673

THE FREE HANDICAPS

TWO-YEAR-OLDS

The following are the weights allotted in the Ladbroke European Free Handicap published on 11th January. The race is to be run over seven furlongs at Newmarket on 18th April, 1990.

	st	lb		st	lb		st	lb
Machiavellian	9	7	Rafha	8	7	Atoll	8	2
Argentum	9	2	Repercutionist	8	7	Dancing Music	8	2
Digression	9	2	Alchi	8	6	Fujaiyrah	8	2
Jade Robbery	9	2	Book The Band	8	6	Golan Heights	8	2
Contract Law	9	1	Duck And Dive	8	6	Jovial	8	2
Be My Chief	9	0	Filago	8	6	Lord Glen	8	2
Elmaamul	9	0	Go And Go	8	6	Missionary Ridge	8	2
Linamix	9	0	Haunting Beauty	8	6	Noble Patriarch	8	2
Negligent	9	0	Houseproud	8	6	Old Alliance	8	2
Rock City	9	0	Intimiste	8	6	Qathif	8	2
Blue de France	8	13	Miss Afrique	8	6	Ridgepoint	8	2
Dead Certain	8	12	Osario	8	6	Rock Hopper	8	2
Qirmazi	8	12	Ozone Friendly	8	6	Rushmore	8	2
Septieme Ciel	8	12	Pont-Aven	8	6	Alidiva	8	1
Balla Cove	8	11	Robellation	8	6	Blue Stag	8	1
Funambule	8	11	Roi de Rome	8	6	Dayjur	8	1
The Caretaker	8	11	Slew The Slewor	8	6	Drayton Special	8	1
Bridal Toast	8	10	Tirol	8	6	Harbour Bar	8	1
Moon Cactus	8	10	Defensive Play	8	5	Marquetry	8	1
Qui Danzig	8	10	Dorset Duke	8	5	Princess Taufan	8	1
Salsabil	8	10	Duke of Paducah	8	5	Red Henry	8	1
Snurge	8	10	Fearless Revival	8	5	Tabdea	8	1
Somethingdifferent	8	10	Makbul	8	5	Berry's Dream	8	0
Welney	8	10	Mukddaam	8	5	Daarik	8	0
Air Music	8	9	Raj Waki	8	5	Green's Leader	8	0
Dashing Blade	8	9	Treble Eight	8	5	Grey Duster	8	0
Free At Last	8	9	Wadood	8	5	Heart of Joy	8	0
Pharaoh's Delight	8	9	Arousal	8	4	In The Groove	8	0
Anshan	8	8	Belmez	8	4	Marienski	8	0
Call To Arms	8	8	Candy Glen	8	4	Message Pad	8	0
Chimes of Freedom	8	8	Cordoba	8	4	Naval Party	8	0
Curia Regis	8	8	Knight's Baroness	8	4	Notley	8	0
Dr Somerville	8	8	Montendre	8	4	Olympic Hero	8	0
Epicarmo	8	8	Routillante	8	4	Palace Street	8	0
Ernani	8	8	Spinning	8	4	Petillante	8	0
Gharam	8	8	Trireme	8	4	Please Believe Me	8	0
Honor Rajana	8	8	Va Toujours	8	4	Remthat Naser	8	0
Horatio Luro	8	8	Akamantis	8	3	Royal Academy	8	0
Line of Thunder	8	8	Baligh	8	3	Royal Fi Fi	8	0
Pole Position	8	8	Karinga Bay	8	3	Ruby Tiger	8	0
Rich And Famous	8	8	Mademoiselle			Sardegna	8	0
Satin Wood	8	8	Chloe	8	3	Shavian	8	0
Silk Slippers	8	8	Native Twine	8	3	Sheer Precocity	8	0
Champagne Gold	8	7	Tanfith	8	3	Soy Roberto	8	0
Cullinan	8	7	Wajna	8	3	Swiss Affair	8	0
Follidays	8	7	Zoman	8	3	Tod	8	0
Golden Era	8	7	Adding	8	2	Victory Piper	8	0

THREE-YEAR-OLDS

14 furlongs plus	111 Princess	100 Ashal	122 Aliysa
123 Michelozzo	Sobieska		120 Roseate Tern
116 Weld	110 Demawend	**11 furlongs plus**	119 Observation Post
113 Lucky Song	105 Noble Savage	134 Old Vic	119 Terimon
112 Sapience	105 Orpheus	128 Cacoethes	118 Alydaress

<table>
<tr><td>117 Snow Bride</td><td>122 Dolpour</td><td>100 Marcinkus</td><td>107 Folly Foot</td></tr>
<tr><td>117 Zalazl</td><td>120 Opening Verse</td><td>100 Marine Diver</td><td>107 Kerita</td></tr>
<tr><td>116 Golden Pheasant</td><td>119 Citidancer</td><td>100 Prince Ibrahim</td><td>107 Mon Tresor</td></tr>
<tr><td>116 Petite Ile</td><td>119 Prince of Dance</td><td></td><td>107 Muhbubh</td></tr>
<tr><td>116 Pirate Army</td><td>119 Scenic</td><td>**7 furlongs plus**</td><td>106 Safawan</td></tr>
<tr><td>115 Ile de Nisky</td><td>119 Torjoun</td><td>134 Zilzal</td><td>105 Just Three</td></tr>
<tr><td>114 Prorutori</td><td>118 Braiswick</td><td>129 Polish Precedent</td><td>105 Polar Boy</td></tr>
<tr><td>113 Warrshan</td><td>118 Two Timing</td><td>126 Golden Opinion</td><td>105 Triode</td></tr>
<tr><td>113 Zayyani</td><td>114 Mamaluna</td><td>124 Distant Relative</td><td>104 Known Ranger</td></tr>
<tr><td>112 Artic Envoy</td><td>114 Pilot</td><td>123 Green Line</td><td>104 Moviegoer</td></tr>
<tr><td>112 Spritsail</td><td>113 Alcando</td><td>   Express</td><td>104 Sharka</td></tr>
<tr><td>111 Braashee</td><td>113 High Estate</td><td>122 Exbourne</td><td>103 Awayed</td></tr>
<tr><td>111 Knoosh</td><td>113 Porter Rhodes</td><td>120 Markof-</td><td>103 Guest Artiste</td></tr>
<tr><td>111 Nearctic Flame</td><td>112 Batshoof</td><td>   distinction</td><td>103 Serious Trouble</td></tr>
<tr><td>110 Alphabel</td><td>111 Brush Aside</td><td>120 Shaadi</td><td>102 Sure Gold</td></tr>
<tr><td>110 Husyan</td><td>111 Greenwich</td><td>119 Magic Gleam</td><td>100 Malevich</td></tr>
<tr><td>109 Free Sweater</td><td>   Papillon</td><td>118 Shining Steel</td><td>100 Tatsfield</td></tr>
<tr><td>109 N C Owen</td><td>111 Lady Shipley</td><td>117 Ensconse</td><td></td></tr>
<tr><td>108 Polar Run</td><td>111 Life At The Top</td><td>116 Greensmith</td><td>**5 furlongs plus**</td></tr>
<tr><td>108 Shayraz</td><td>111 Monastery</td><td>116 Pass The Peace</td><td>123 Danehill</td></tr>
<tr><td>107 Gran Alba</td><td>111 Relief Pitcher</td><td>115 Gold Seam</td><td>119 Statoblest</td></tr>
<tr><td>105 By Charter</td><td>111 Tessla</td><td>115 Great</td><td>119 Tigani</td></tr>
<tr><td>105 Konigsberg</td><td>110 Bex</td><td>   Commotion</td><td>116 Dancing</td></tr>
<tr><td>105 Quiet</td><td>110 Drum Taps</td><td>115 Monsagem</td><td>   Dissident</td></tr>
<tr><td>   Awakening</td><td>110 Icona</td><td>115 Musical Bliss</td><td>112 Shuttlecock</td></tr>
<tr><td>105 Shellac</td><td>110 Shyoushka</td><td>113 Kerrera</td><td>   Corner</td></tr>
<tr><td>104 Destiny Dance</td><td>109 Mysteries</td><td>113 Lunar Mover</td><td>112 Superpower</td></tr>
<tr><td>104 Timourtash</td><td>108 Rambushka</td><td>113 Magical Strike</td><td>110 Green's</td></tr>
<tr><td>104 Wrapping</td><td>108 Spitfire</td><td>113 Mirror Black</td><td>   Canaletto</td></tr>
<tr><td>103 Trying For Gold</td><td>107 If Memory</td><td>112 Aldbourne</td><td>109 Lugana Beach</td></tr>
<tr><td>102 Elmayer</td><td>   Serves</td><td>112 Cottenham</td><td>107 Wonder Dancer</td></tr>
<tr><td>102 Val Recit</td><td>106 Arsaan</td><td>112 Princess Accord</td><td>106 Thorn Dance</td></tr>
<tr><td>101 Jehol</td><td>105 Always On A</td><td>112 Russian Bond</td><td>104 Didicoy</td></tr>
<tr><td>101 Prime Display</td><td>   Sunday</td><td>112 Samoan</td><td>103 Access Travel</td></tr>
<tr><td>101 Roblet</td><td>105 Dimmer</td><td>111 Dancing Tribute</td><td>103 Blyton Lad</td></tr>
<tr><td>100 Fair Prospect</td><td>105 Flamingo Pond</td><td>111 Weldnaas</td><td>103 Desert Dawn</td></tr>
<tr><td>100 Operation Wolf</td><td>105 Really Brilliant</td><td>110 Light of Morn</td><td>102 Hadif</td></tr>
<tr><td>100 Rifada</td><td>104 Always Valiant</td><td>110 Rain Burst</td><td>101 Almost Blue</td></tr>
<tr><td></td><td>104 Nangarar</td><td>110 Russian Royal</td><td>101 Paley Prince</td></tr>
<tr><td>**9½ furlongs plus**</td><td>104 Top Boot</td><td>110 Sabotage</td><td>101 Silca Supreme</td></tr>
<tr><td>131 Nashwan</td><td>101 Jungle Pioneer</td><td>109 Comic Talent</td><td>100 Four-Legged</td></tr>
<tr><td>123 Legal Case</td><td>100 Green Flag</td><td>107 Bequest</td><td>   Friend</td></tr>
</table>

FOUR-YEAR-OLDS AND UPWARDS

<table>
<tr><td>**14 furlongs plus**</td><td>121 Assatis</td><td>**9½ furlongs plus**</td><td>120 French Stress</td></tr>
<tr><td>118 Sadeem</td><td>120 Sheriff's Star</td><td>123 Ile de Chypre</td><td>118 Reprimand</td></tr>
<tr><td>112 Mountain</td><td>119 Highland</td><td>119 Kefaah</td><td>117 Beau Sher</td></tr>
<tr><td>   Kingdom</td><td>   Chieftain</td><td>114 Petrullo</td><td>111 Luzum</td></tr>
<tr><td>111 Mazzacano</td><td>117 Top Class</td><td>113 Emmson</td><td>111 Sweet Chesne</td></tr>
<tr><td>111 Zaffaran</td><td>116 Per Quod</td><td>112 Pelorus</td><td>110 Charmer</td></tr>
<tr><td>109 Lazaz</td><td>114 Tralos</td><td>112 Shady Heights</td><td>109 Alquoz</td></tr>
<tr><td>108 Zero Watt</td><td>113 Apache</td><td>111 Hibernian Gold</td><td>109 Rambo's Hall</td></tr>
<tr><td>105 Ala Hounak</td><td>112 Green</td><td>109 Insan</td><td>108 Always Fair</td></tr>
<tr><td>104 Arden</td><td>   Adventure</td><td>108 Sudden Love</td><td>108 Hoy</td></tr>
<tr><td>104 Arizelos</td><td>111 Albadr</td><td>105 Dust Devil</td><td>105 Hello Vaigly</td></tr>
<tr><td>102 Sergeyevich</td><td>109 Indian Queen</td><td>105 Lapierre</td><td>105 Vague Shot</td></tr>
<tr><td>102 Upper Strata</td><td>109 Waterfield</td><td>103 Main Objective</td><td>103 Point House</td></tr>
<tr><td>101 Lauries Crusador</td><td>108 Atlaal</td><td>100 Unknown</td><td>103 Wood Dancer</td></tr>
<tr><td>100 Nomadic Way</td><td>108 Glacial Storm</td><td>   Quantity</td><td>101 Colway Rally</td></tr>
<tr><td></td><td>108 Sudden Victory</td><td></td><td>101 Tay Wharf</td></tr>
<tr><td>**11 furlongs plus**</td><td>106 Sesame</td><td>**7 furlongs plus**</td><td>100 Electric Lady</td></tr>
<tr><td>128 Carroll House</td><td>105 Nemesia</td><td>127 Warning</td><td></td></tr>
<tr><td>127 Unfuwain</td><td>104 Firelight Fiesta</td><td>123 Most Welcome</td><td>**5 furlongs plus**</td></tr>
<tr><td>124 Ibn Bey</td><td>103 My Lamb</td><td>121 Indian Skimmer</td><td>124 Cadeaux Gen.</td></tr>
</table>

122 Indian Ridge	114 A Prayer For	113 Princess Athena	106 Sharp Reminder
120 Cricket Ball	Wings	112 Carol's Treasure	106 Teeming Shore
118 Gallic League	114 Mac's Fighter	112 Savahra Sound	102 Ajanac
116 Nabeel Dancer	114 Point of Light	106 Intimidate	100 Perion
116 Silver Fling	113 Chummy's Fav.	106 Poyle George	

INTERNATIONAL CLASSIFICATIONS

The following were published for information only on 11th January, 1989. The figure allotted to each horse is that which the Official Handicappers, having regard to previous Classifications, consider to represent its overall racing merit. Horses racing over different distances and being top rated, are credited with those performances by inclusion in the appropriate division.

TWO-YEAR-OLDS

125 Machiavellian	114 Bridal Toast	112 Curia Regis	111 Repercutionist
120 Argentum	114 Moon Cactus	112 Dr Somerville	110 Alchi
120 Digression	114 Qui Danzig	112 Epicarmo	110 Book The Band
120 Jade Robbery	114 Salsabil	112 Ernani	110 Duck And Dive
119 Contract Law	114 Snurge	112 Gharam	110 Filago
118 Be My Chief	114 Something-	112 Honor Rajana	110 Go And Go
118 Elmaamul	different	112 Horatio Luro	110 Haunting Beauty
118 Linamix	114 Welney	112 Line of Thunder	110 Houseproud
118 Negligent	113 Air Music	112 Pole Position	110 Intimiste
118 Rock City	113 Dashing Blade	112 Rich And Famous	110 Miss Afrique
117 Bleu de France	113 Free At Last	112 Satin Wood	110 Osario
116 Dead Certain	113 Pharaoh's	112 Silk Slippers	110 Ozone Friendly
116 Qirmazi	Delight	111 Champagne Gold	110 Pont-Aven
116 Septieme Ciel	112 Anshan	111 Cullinan	110 Robellation
115 Ball Cove	112 Call To Arms	111 Follidays	110 Roi de Rome
115 Funambule	112 Chimes of	111 Golden Era	110 Slew The Slewor
115 The Caretaker	Freedom	111 Rafha	110 Tirol

THREE-YEAR-OLDS

14 furlongs plus	120 Roseate Tern	113 Taishan	119 Scenic
123 Michelozzo	119 Observation Post	113 Warrshan	119 Torjoun
116 Turgeon	119 Terimon	113 Zayyani	118 Braiswick
116 Weld	118 Alydaress	112 Artic Envoy	118 Filia Ardross
115 Mardonius	118 Colorado Dancer	112 Ode	118 In The Wings
113 Lou Biella	117 Snow Bride	112 Spritsail	118 Two Timing
113 Lucky Song	117 Zalazl		117 Galetto
113 Tyrone Bridge	116 Borromini	**9½ furlongs plus**	117 Yellow King
112 Sapience	116 Golden Pheasant	131 Nashwan	115 River Warden
112 Sharnfold	116 Louis Cyphre	125 Dancehall	115 Val de Bois
	116 Petite Ile	124 Creator	114 Along All
11 furlongs plus	116 Pirate Army	123 Legal Case	114 Mamaluna
134 Old Vic	115 Deliorman	122 Dolpour	114 Pilot
128 Cacoethes	115 Ile de Nisky	121 Lady In Silver	114 Premier Amour
124 Mondrian	115 Passionaria	121 Norberto	114 Rose de Crystal
123 Behera	114 Prorutori	120 Louveterie	114 Sovereign Water
122 Aliysa	114 Sherada	120 Opening Verse	114 Turfkonig
122 Sierra Roberta	113 French Glory	119 Citidancer	113 Alcando
122 Young Mother	113 Mill Pond	119 Prince of Dance	113 Bellarida

113 High Estate	122 Exbourne	115 Go Milord	112 Lightning Fire
113 Phantom Breeze	120 Local Talent	115 Gold Seam	112 Lioubrovnik
113 Porter Rhodes	120 Markof-	115 Great Com.	112 Princess Accord
113 Tartas	distinction	115 Monsagem	112 Russian Bond
112 Batshoof	120 Shaadi	115 Musical Bliss	112 Samoan
112 J'Ai Deux	119 Aliocha	114 Lady Winner	
Amours	119 Goldneyev	114 Lowell	**5 furlongs plus**
	119 Magic Gleam	114 Silkeston	123 Danehill
7 furlongs plus	119 Ocean Falls	113 Keniant	119 Statoblest
134 Zilzal	119 Pearl Bracelet	113 Kerrera	119 Tigani
129 Polish Precedent	118 Shining Steel	113 Lunar Mover	116 Dancing Dis.
128 Golden Opinion	117 Ensconse	113 Magical Strike	112 Or Acier
124 Distant Relative	116 Greensmith	113 Mirror Black	112 Puissance
124 Kendor	116 Navratilovna	112 Aldbourne	112 Shuttlecock
123 Green Line	116 Pass The Peace	112 Be Exclusive	Corner
Express	116 Star Touch	112 Cottenham	112 Superpower

FOUR-YEAR-OLDS AND UPWARDS

14 furlongs plus	117 Top Class	112 Love The Groom	**5 furlongs plus**
119 Top Sunrise	116 Per Quod	112 Noora Abu	124 Cadeaux
118 Sadeem	114 Britannia	112 Pelorus	Genereux
115 Rachmaninov	114 Luigi	112 Shady Heights	122 Indian Ridge
114 Trebrook	114 Tralos		120 Cricket Ball
112 Mountain	113 Apache	**7 furlongs plus**	118 Gallic League
Kingdom	113 Knight Line	127 Warning	116 Nabeel Dancer
112 Vaguely	Dancer	124 Most Welcome	116 Silver Fling
Pleasant	113 Summer Trip	122 Squill	115 Big Shuffle
	112 Green	121 Indian Skimmer	115 Zadracarta
11 furlongs plus	Adventure	120 French Stress	114 A Prayer For
128 Carroll House		120 Gabina	Wings
127 Unfuwain	**9½ furlongs plus**	119 Royal Touch	114 Mac's Fighter
125 Boyatino	123 Ile de Chypre	118 Athyka	114 Point of Light
125 Saint Andrews	119 Kefaah	118 Reprimand	113 Chummy's
124 Ibn Bey	118 Mansonnien	117 Beau Sher	Favourite
123 Star Lift	118 Welsh Guide	117 Just A Flutter	113 Holst
122 Robore	117 Fijar Tango	115 In Extremis	113 Princess Athena
121 Alwuhush	115 Executive Perk	114 Red Glow	112 Astronef
121 Assatis	115 Hello Calder	114 Zampano	112 Carol's Treasure
120 Sheriff's Star	114 Elementary	113 Miss Kenmare	112 Savahra Sound
119 Highland	114 Petrullo	112 Alkalde	
Chieftain	113 Emmson	112 Malaspina	
117 Tisserand	113 Medicus	112 Val des Pres	

IRISH CLASSIFICATIONS

TWO-YEAR-OLDS

115 The Caretaker	104 Aminata	99 Teach Dha Mhile	96 Thetford Forest
113 Dashing Blade	104 Royal	98 Quebec	95 Annie Laurie
113 Pharaoh's Del.	Academy	97 Legal Verdict	95 Ereng
112 Chimes of	104 Victory Piper	97 Missing You	95 Gilt Note
Freedom	102 Armanasco	97 Simply Terrific	95 Music Prospector
110 Go And Go	102 Mr Brooks	97 Single Combat	95 Neat Dish
109 Pictorial	101 Polar Bird	96 Endless Joy	95 Sadlers Congress
108 Wedding Bou.	99 Hero's Welcome	96 Tanwi	95 War Chest

THREE-YEAR-OLDS

14 furlongs plus
113 Tyrone Bridge

11 furlongs plus
134 Old Vic
118 Alydaress
116 Petite Ile
107 Beyond The
      Lake
107 Gran Alba
105 Classic Sport

9½ furlongs plus
119 Citidancer
113 Phantom Breeze
113 Porter Rhodes
110 Bex
108 Tursanah
106 Slender Style
102 Lone Runner

7 furlongs plus
124 Distant Relative

120 Shaadi
117 Ensconse
108 Classic Fame
108 Run To Jenny
108 Upward Trend
106 Honoria
106 Saratogan
105 Elegance In
      Design
105 Just Three

104 Tantum Egro
103 Awayed
103 Kyra
102 Great Lakes
102 Pirouette
101 Blasted Heath

5 furlongs plus
112 Puissance
111 Corwyn Bay
109 Eloquent Min.

FOUR-YEAR-OLDS AND UPWARDS

11 furlongs plus
128 Carroll House
109 Indian Queen

9½ furlongs plus
123 Ile de Chypre
115 Executive Perk

114 Elementary
112 Noora Abu
109 Little
      Bighorn

7 furlongs plus
108 Milieu

108 Llyn Gwynant
105 Cielamour
103 Wood Dancer

5 furlongs plus
118 Gallic League
115 Big Shuffle

114 A Prayer For
      Wings
114 Point of Light
110 Handsome Sailor
105 Astraeus

FRENCH CLASSIFICATIONS

TWO-YEAR-OLDS

Kilos

Kilos							
125	Machiavellian	112	Horatio Luro	110	Pont Aven	109	Lituanien
120	Jade Robbery	112	Pole Position	110	Roi de Rome	109	Mackla
118	Linamix	112	Rich And	110	Slew The	109	Noblely
118	Rock City		Famous		Slewor	109	Pagan Gold
117	Bleu de France	111	Follidays	109	Anna's Honor	109	Pas Facile
116	Qirmazi	111	Golden Era	109	Boston Two	109	Princess Player
116	Septieme Ciel	111	Repercutionist		Step	109	River of Light
115	Funambule	110	Alchi	109	Boxing Day	109	Robin des Bois
114	Salsabil	110	Filago	109	Company	109	Sharp Sass
114	Snurge	110	Houseproud	109	Evocatrice	109	Sifting Gold
112	Dr Somerville	110	Intimiste	109	Goofalik	109	Theatre Critic
112	Ernani	110	Miss Afrique	109	Houmayoun	109	Zinarelle
112	Honor Rajana	110	Ozone Friendly	109	King White		

SELECTED BIG RACES 1989

Prize money for racing abroad has been converted to £ Sterling at the exchange rate current at the time of the race. The figures are correct to the nearest £.

1   LANES END JOHN   1½m
PORTER EBF STAKES
(Gr 3)
£24,741   Newbury   15 April
Unfuwain (USA) 4-8-13
   WCarson 1
Per Quod (USA) 4-8-10
   BRaymond 1½.2
Apache 4-8-10 PatEddery ... 3.3
Mountain Kingdom (USA)
   5-8-10 MRoberts 1.4
West China 5-8-10
   RCochrane s.hd.5
Sunday Sport Star 4-8-7
   CAsmussen 15.6
Ghadbbaan 5-8-10 BProctor 7

4/9 UNFUWAIN, 5/1 Apache, Per Quod, 12/1 Mountain Kingdom, 100/1 Ghadbbaan, Sunday Sport Star, West China
   Mr Hamdan Al-Maktoum (Major W. R. Hern) 7ran 2m40.85 (Dead)

2   GORDON RICHARDS   1¼m
EBF STAKES (Gr 3)
£22,599   Sandown   29 April
Indian Skimmer (USA) 5-9-0
   SCauthen 1
1²   **Per Quod (USA)** 4-8-10
   BRaymond hd.2
Carroll House 4-9-3
   WRSwinburn hd.3
Petrullo 4-8-10 BRouse 2.4
Shady Heights 5-9-3
   MRoberts 15.5
Emmson 4-8-10
   WCarson s.hd.6
Galitzin 4-8-13 GDuffield 7
Alwuhush (USA) 4-8-10
   PatEddery 8
La Vie En Primrose 4-8-7
   MHills 9

8/15 INDIAN SKIMMER, 7/2 Per Quod, 10/1 Shady Heights, 12/1 Emmson, 16/1 Petrullo, 20/1 Alwuhush, 33/1 Carroll House, Galitzin, 66/1 La Vie En Primrose
   Sheikh Mohammed (H. R. A. Cecil) 9ran 2m18.57 (Soft)

3   PRIX GANAY (Gr 1)   1m2½f
(4y + c + f)
£48,723   Longchamp   30 April
Saint Andrews (Fr) 5-9-2
   ABadel 1
Star Lift 5-9-2
   CAsmussen ½.2
Mansonnien (Fr) 5-9-2
   DBoeuf 4.3
Nerio 4-9-2 FHead 2½.4

Boyatino 5-9-2 ELegrix 1½.5
Sakura Patrick 4-9-2
   GMoore 1½.6
Chevron 4-9-2 ACruz 2.7

7/10 Star Lift, 22/10 SAINT ANDREWS, 9/2 Boyatino, 14/1 Chevron, Nerio, 24/1 Mansonnien, 26/1 Sakura Patrick
   Mme Volterra (J. Beguigne) 7ran 2m20.8 (Soft)

4   GENERAL ACCIDENT   1m
1,000 GUINEAS STAKES
(Gr 1) (3y f)
£98,260   Newmarket   4 May
Musical Bliss (USA) 9-0
   WRSwinburn 1
Kerrera 9-0 PatEddery ¾.2
Aldbourne 9-0
   PHamblett 1.3
Ensconse (USA) 9-0
   RCochrane hd.4
Pass The Peace 9-0
   TQuinn nk.5
Bequest (USA) 9-0
   GStarkey 2.6
Muhbubh 9-0
   RHills s.hd.7

7/4 Ensconse, 7/2 MUSICAL BLISS, Pass The Peace, 9/1 Kerrera, 10/1 Bequest, 16/1 Muhbubh, 20/1 Aldbourne
   Sheikh Mohammed (M. R. Stoute) 7ran 1m42.69 (Good)

5   GENERAL ACCIDENT   1m
2,000 GUINEAS STAKES
(Gr 1) (3y c + f)
£103,263   Newmarket   6 May
Nashwan (USA) 9-0
   WCarson 1
Exbourne (USA) 9-0
   CAsmussen 1.2
Danehill (USA) 9-0
   PatEddery ½.3
Markofdistinction 9-0
   RCochrane nk.4
Monsagem (USA) 9-0
   SCauthen 3.5
Lunar Mover (USA) 9-0
   PaulEddery 1.6
Pure Genius (USA) 9-0
   GStarkey s.hd.7
Zayyani 9-0 WNewnes nk.8
Saratogan (USA) 9-0 JReid ... 3.9
Sharp N' Early 9-0
   BRouse ½.10
Shaadi (USA) 9-0
   WRSwinburn 10.11
Greensmith 9-0 MHills ... 2½.12
Mon Tresor 9-0 MRoberts .. 8.13

Travelling Tryst (USA) 9-0
　TIves dist.14

3/1 NASHWAN, 7/2 Saratogan, 5/1 Shaadi, 9/1 Danehill, Zayyani, 10/1 Exbourne, 14/1 Markofdistinction, 20/1 Monsagem, Pure Genius, 40/1 Mon Tresor, 50/1 Lunar Mover, 100/1 Greensmith, Sharp N' Early, 200/1 Travelling Tryst

Mr Hamdan Al-Maktoum (Major W. R. Hern) 14ran 1m36.44 (Good to Firm)

| 6 | DUBAI POULE D'ESSAI DES POULAINS (Gr 1) (3y c) | 1m |
| £93,110 | Longchamp | 7 May |

Kendor (Fr) 9-2
　MPhilipperon 1
Goldneyev (USA) 9-2
　GGuignard 2.2
Ocean Falls 9-2
　CAsmussen s.nk.3
Star Touch (Fr) 9-2
　ASCruz ¾.4
Great Commotion (USA) 9-2
　PatEddery 1½.5
Corviglia (USA) 9-2 GMosse
　.......................... 1½.6
Tagel (USA) 9-2 FHead hd.7
Stone Flake (USA) 9-2
　SCauthen s.hd.8
Sylvan Tempest 9-2
　WRSwinburn 20.9
Ours Blanc (Fr) 9-2
　CAubert 1½.10

Evens KENDOR, 11/4 Great Commotion, 4/1 Ocean Falls, 13/2 Goldneyev, 7/1 Tagel, 14/1 Star Touch, 31/1 Corviglia, 39/1 Sylvan Tempest, 54/1 Stone Flake, 60/1 Ours Blanc

A. Bader (R. Touflan) 10ran 1m36.1 (Good to Firm)

| 7 | DUBAI POULE D'ESSAI DES POULICHES (Gr 1) (3y f) | 1m |
| £93,110 | Longchamp | 14 May |

Pearl Bracelet (USA) 9-2
　AGibert 1
Pass The Peace 9-2
　TQuinn ¾.2
Golden Opinion (USA) 9-2
　CAsmussen ¾.3
Keniant (Fr) 9-2
　GWMoore ¾.4
La Plumita (USA) 9-2
　GDubroeucq 1.5
Charara (USA) 9-2
　ELegrix 1½.6
Tersa (USA) 9-2 GMosse ½.7
Oczy Czarnie (USA) 9-2
　SCauthen nk.8
Russian Royal (USA) 9-2
　WRSwinburn nk.9
Lightning Fire 9-2 FHead . ns.10
Tantum Ergo 9-2 DGillespie ... 0

Irish Order (USA) 9-2 DBoeuf . 0
Mary Linoa (USA) 9-2
　ALequeux 0
Rose de Thai (USA) 9-2
　GGuignard 0
Miss Manila (USA) 9-2
　PBodin 0
Lakila (Fr) 9-2 J-LKessas 0

5/4 Golden Opinion, Miss Manila and Russian Royal, 9/2 Pass The Peace, 29/4 Keniant and Lakila 9/1 Oczy Czarnie, 10/1 Mary Linoa, 13/1 Rose de Thai, 15/1 Lightning Fire, 18/1 Irish Order, 20/1 Tersa, 21/1 Charara, 44/1 La Plumita, 50/1 PEARL BRACELET, 52/1 Tantum Ergo

Écurie Fustok (R. Wojtowiez) 16ran 1m37.1 (Good to Firm)

| 8 | WILLIAM HILL DANTE STAKES (Gr 2) (3y) | 1¼m 110y |
| £74,232 | York | 17 May |

Torjoun (USA) 9-0
　RCochrane 1
Observation Post 9-0
　MHills 2.2
Zalazl (USA) 9-0
　SCauthen 2½.3
Two Timing (USA) 9-0
　PatEddery ¾.4
Sabotage (Fr) 9-0
　WRSwinburn ¾.5
Flockton's Own 9-0
　GCarter 2.6
Stone Flake (USA) 9-0 JReid ... 7

11/10 Observation Post, 9/2 Sabotage, 5/1 Zalazl, 6/1 TORJOUN, 8/1 Two Timing, 100/1 Flockton's Own, Stone Flake

H. H. Aga Khan (L. M. Cumani) 7ran 2m06.98 (Firm)

| 9 | COLOROLL YORKSHIRE CUP (Gr 2) | 1¾m |
| £31,428 | York | 18 May |

Mountain Kingdom (USA)
　5-8-9 SCauthen 1
Zaffaran (USA) 4-8-9
　WRSwinburn nk.2
Mazzacano 4-8-9
　GStarkey 7.3
Sesame 4-8-6 MBirch 8.4
Al Mufti (USA) 4-8-9 RHills .. 5.5
Polemos 5-8-9 NCarlisle 25.6

2/1 MOUNTAIN KINGDOM, 9/4 Mazzacano, 10/3 Zaffaran, 8/1 Al Mufti, 12/1 Sesame, 200/1 Polemos

Mr David Thompson (C. E. Brittain) 6ran 2m52.92 (Firm)

| 10 | DUKE OF YORK STAKES (Gr 3) | 6f |
| £19,156 | York | 18 May |

Indian Ridge 4-9-4
　SCauthen 1

Gallic League 4-9-0
WCarson 1½.**2**
Nabeel Dancer (USA) 4-9-0
PatEddery s.hd.**3**
Point of Light 4-9-0
PaulEddery ½.**4**
Hadif (USA) 3-8-5
MRoberts **3.5**
Shuttlecock Corner (USA) 3-8-9
GDuffield nk.**6**
Chummy's Favourite 4-9-0
BRaymond **7**
Sharp Romance (USA) 7-9-0
SKeightley **8**
Handsome Sailor 6-9-12
MHills **9**
Petrillia 3-7-12 RHills **10**

7/2 INDIAN RIDGE, 4/1 Point of Light,
5/1 Gallic League, 11/2 Handsome Sailor,
10/1 Hadif, Nabeel Dancer, 12/1 Shuttlecock Corner, 25/1 Chummy's Favourite,
Petrillia, Sharp Romance
Mrs Anne Coughlan (D. R. C. Elsworth) 10ran 1m10.17 (Firm)

11   JUDDMONTE   1m
      LOCKINGE STAKES
      (Gr 2)
£33,786   Newbury   19 May
Most Welcome 5-9-1
PaulEddery **1**
Warning 4-9-6 PatEddery ... 2.**2**
Reprimand 4-9-4
SCauthen ¾.**3**
Hilton Brown 8-9-1 AClark . 20.**4**

8/15 Warning, 2/1 Reprimand, 9/1 MOST
WELCOME, 50/1 Hilton Brown
Sir Philip Oppenheimer (G. Wragg)
4ran 1m36.52 (Firm)

12   AIRLIE/COOLMORE   1m
      IRISH 2,000 GUINEAS
      (Gr 1) (3y c + f)
£112,941   Curragh   20 May
5   **Shaadi (USA)** 9-0
      WRSwinburn **1**
6   **Great Commotion (USA)** 9-0
      WCarson 2½.**2**
      Distant Relative 9-0
      MHills ½.**3**
5³   Danehill (USA) 9-0
      PatEddery 1½.**4**
      Classic Fame (USA) 9-0
      DGillespie 1½.**5**
5   Saratogan (USA) 9-0 JReid .. ¾.**6**
      Takdeer 9-0 DParnell **4.7**
      Corwyn Bay 9-0 SCraine 2.**8**
      Vestris Abu 9-0 CRoche 2.**9**
      Twilight Agenda (USA) 9-0
      MJKinane nk.**10**
      August Agent (USA) 9-0
      PShanahan ½.**11**
      Tatsfield 9-0 SRaymont 8.**12**

6/4 Danehill, 7/2 SHAADI, 13/2
Saratogan, 8/1 Classic Fame, 10/1 Great
Commotion, 20/1 Corwyn Bay, Twilight
Agenda, 25/1 August Agent, Distant
Relative, 66/1 Takdeer, Vestris Abu,
150/1 Tatsfield
Sheikh Mohammed (M. R. Stoute)
12ran 1m37.5 (Good to Firm)

13   TATTERSALLS EBF   1¼m
      ROGERS GOLD CUP
      STAKES (Gr 2)
£36,366   Curragh   20 May
Ile de Chypre 4-8-12 AClark .. **1**
Executive Perk 4-8-12
MJKinane 3.**2**
2³   **Carroll House** 4-9-4
      WRSwinburn 1½.**3**
2²   Per Quod (USA) 4-8-12
      BRaymond 4.**4**
      Causa Sua 4-8-9 DParnell 4.**5**
      Maiden Fair 6-8-9 SCraine **6**
      Secret Appeal 5-8-12 JTHyde .. **7**
      Project Manager 4-9-1
      CRoche **8**
      Kris Kringle 4-9-1 JReid **9**

15/8 Executive Perk, 3/1 Per Quod, 6/1
Carroll House, 7/1 ILE DE CHYPRE, 8/1
Kris Kringle, 10/1 Project Manager, 20/1
Secret Appeal, 25/1 Maiden Fair, 33/1
Causa Sua
Mr Athos Christodoulou (G. Har-
wood) 9ran 2m03.5 (Good to Firm)

14   PRIX SAINT-ALARY   1¼m
      (Gr 1) (3y f)
£43,622   Longchamp   21 May
Behera 9-2 ALequeux **1**
Louveterie (USA) 9-2
CAsmussen s.hd.**2**
Lady In Silver (USA) 9-2
ACruz ½.**3**
Rose de Crystal (Fr) 9-2
ELegrix 1½.**4**
Restikala 9-2 GMosse ½.**5**
Vieille France 9-2
PBodin 2½.**6**
Franc Argument 9-2 FHead .. 8.**7**

Evens Louveterie and Vieille France,
6/4 Rose de Crystal, 43/10 BEHERA,
11/1 Franc Argument, 13/1 Lady In
Silver, 14/1 Restikala
H. H. Aga Khan (A. de Royer-Dupre)
7ran 2m2.1 (Good to Firm)

15   GOFFS IRISH 1,000   1m
      GUINEAS (Gr 1) (3y f)
£110,483   Curragh   27 May
4   **Ensconse (USA)** 9-0
      RCochrane **1**
4³   **Aldbourne** 9-0 PHamblett ... 2.**2**
      Run To Jenny 9-0
      PaulEddery ¾.**3**
      Honoria (USA) 9-0 CRoche .. 1.**4**
      Elegance In Design 9-0
      MJKinane hd.**5**
      Dance Festival 9-0
      WRSwinburn 1.**6**
      Kyra 9-0 JReid s.hd.**7**

1018

Glenbeigh Summer 9-0
 DGillespie 3.8
Pirouette 9-0 SCraine nk.9
Tursanah (USA) 9-0
 DParnell 2½.10
Blasted Heath 9-0
 PShanahan s.hd.11
Try My Rosie 9-0
 KJManning 6.12
Flamenco Wave (USA) 9-0
 RQuinton 6.13

13/8 ENSCONSE, 9/2 Dance Festival, Pirouette, 9/1 Tursanah, 10/1 Aldbourne, 14/1 Blasted Heath, 25/1 Elegance In Design, Flamenco Wave, Kyra, 33/1 Glenbeigh Summer, Run To Jenny, 40/1 Honoria, 66/1 Try My Rosie
 Sheikh Mohammed (L. M. Cumani) 13ran 1m38.5 (Good to Firm)

16 PRIX D'ISPAHAN 1m1f55y
 (Gr 1)
£41,744 Longchamp 28 May
2* **Indian Skimmer (USA)** 5-8-13
 SCauthen 1
 Gabina (USA) 4-8-13
 ELegrix ½.2
 French Stress (USA) 4-9-2
 CAsmussen 2.3
3³ Mansonnien (Fr) 5-9-2
 DBoeuf 2.4
 In Extremis (USA) 4-9-2
 FHead ¾.5
3* Saint Andrews (Fr) 5-9-2
 ABadel 5.6

7/10 INDIAN SKIMMER, 13/4 Saint Andrews, 7/2 French Stress, 27/4 Gabina, 15/1 In Extremis, Mansonnien
 Sheikh Mohammed (H. R. A. Cecil) 6ran 1m52.3 (Good)

17 PRIX JEAN PRAT 1m1f55y
 (Gr 1) (3y c + f)
£46,382 Longchamp 28 May
 Local Talent (USA) 9-2
 CAsmussen 1
6* **Kendor (FR)** 9-2
 MPhilipperon ½.2
5 **Monsagem (USA)** 9-2
 SCauthen 2.3
6 Corviglia (USA) 9-2
 FHead 2½.4
 Some Forest (USA) 9-2
 ELegrix 1½.5
 Chivalrous (Fr) 9-2
 WMongil 2½.6

3/10 Kendor, 19/10 LOCAL TALENT and Monsagem, 11/1 Chivalrous, 16/1 Corviglia, 18/1 Some Forest
 Sheikh Mohammed (A. Fabre) 6ran 1m59.5 (Good)

18 PRIX DU JOCKEY-CLUB 1½m
 LANCIA (Gr 1) (3y)
£318,394 Chantilly 4 June
 Old Vic 9-2 SCauthen 1

Dancehall (USA) 9-2
 CAsmussen 7.2
Galetto (FR) 9-2 ELegrix ... 8.3
Norberto (Can) 9-2
 DBoeuf 1½.4
Louis Cyphre 9-2 FHead 1½.5
Sovereign Water (Fr) 9-2
 ASCruz 2.6
Rainibik (Fr) 9-2 GMosse 7.7
Miserden (USA) 9-2
 PatEddery s.hd.8
Elmayer (USA) 9-2 MHills ... 3.9
Edimbourg 9-2 ALequeux .. 10.0
Atakad (Fr) 9-2 AJunk 20.0
6 Ours Blanc (Fr) 9-2
 DManning 20.0

6/4 Galetto, 7/2 Dancehall, 4/1 Louis Cyphre, 47/10 OLD VIC, 10/1 Norberto, 13/1 Sovereign Water, 29/1 Miserden, 30/1 Edimbourg, 38/1 Rainibik, 39/1 Atakad, 84/1 Elmayer, 96/1 Ours Blanc
 Sheikh Mohammed (H. R. A. Cecil) 12ran 2m28.7 (Good)

19 EVER READY DERBY 1½m
 (Gr 1) (3y c + f)
£296,000 Epsom 7 June
5* **Nashwan (USA)** 9-0
 WCarson 1
 Terimon 9-0 MRoberts 5.2
 Cacoethes (USA) 9-0
 GStarkey 2.3
 Ile de Nisky 9-0 GDuffield ... ½.4
 Mill Pond (Fr) 9-0
 PatEddery 2.5
 Gran Alba (USA) 9-0
 BRouse 2.6
12 Classic Fame (USA) 9-0
 JReid 6.7
8* Torjoun (USA) 9-0
 RCochrane ¾.8
8 Flockton's Own 9-0 RHills ... 3.9
 Prince of Dance 9-0
 SCauthen hd.10
 Warrshan (USA) 9-0
 WRSwinburn 15.11
 Polar Run (USA) 9-0
 AClark 25.12

5/4 NASHWAN, 3/1 Cacoethes, 11/2 Prince of Dance, 11/1 Torjoun, 13/1 Warrshan, 16/1 Mill Pond, 20/1 Ile de Nisky, 33/1 Classic Fame, 80/1 Gran Alba, 250/1 Polar Run, 500/1 Flockton's Own, Terimon
 Mr Hamdan Al-Maktoum (Major W. R. Hern) 12ran 2m34.9 (Good)

20 HANSON CORONATION 1½m
 CUP (Gr 1)
£78,480 Epsom 8 June
 Sheriff's Star 4-9-0
 RCochrane 1
13* **Ile de Chypre** 4-9-0
 GStarkey ½.2
 Green Adventure (USA)
 4-9-0 CAsmussen 2½.3

Glacial Storm (USA) 4-9-0
MHills 3.4
9 Sesame 4-8-11 MBirch 3.5
9* Mountain Kingdom (USA) 5-9-0
SCauthen ¾.6
Tralos (USA) 4-9-0
PatEddery 5.7
9 Al Mufti (USA) 4-9-0
RHills 1½.8
Lazaz (USA) 4-9-0
WRSwinburn 1½.9

11/4 SHERIFF'S STAR, 7/2 Glacial Storm, Mountain Kingdom, 6/1 Ile de Chypre, 9/1 Lazaz, 11/1 Green Adventure, 16/1 Tralos, 25/1 Al Mufti, 33/1 Sesame
Lavinia Duchess of Norfolk (Lady Herries) 9ran 2m35.49 (Good)

21 GOLD SEAL OAKS (Gr 1) 1½m (3y f)
£108,450 Epsom 10 June
Aliysa 9-0 WRSwinburn 1
Snow Bride (USA) 9-0
SCauthen 3.2
Roseate Tern 9-0
WCarson s.hd.3
Mamaluna (USA) 9-0
GStarkey 2½.4
Knoosh (USA) 9-0 JReid ¾.5
Tessla (USA) 9-0
PaulEddery 2½.6
4* Musical Bliss (USA) 9-0
MRoberts 2½.7
Always On A Sunday 9-0
BThomson 10.8
Rambushka (USA) 9-0
PatEddery 2½.9

11/10 ALIYSA, 4/1 Musical Bliss, 13/2 Snow Bride, 7/1 Tessla, 16/1 Knoosh, Rambushka, 25/1 Roseate Tern, 50/1 Always On A Sunday, Mamaluna
H. H. Aga Khan (M. R. Stoute) 9ran 2m34.22 (Good to Firm)

22 PRIX DE DIANE 1¼m 110y HERMES (Gr 1) (3y f)
£132,827 Chantilly 11 June
14³ **Lady In Silver (USA)** 9-2
ASCruz 1
14² **Louveterie (USA)** 9-2
CAsmussen s.nk.2
Premier Amour 9-2
DBoeuf 2½.3
Sentimental Side (USA) 9-2
ALequeux 2.4
Glenbelle 9-2 GMosse 1½.5
15* Ensconse (USA) 9-2
PatEddery nk.6
Bellarida (Fr) 9-2
GGuignard nk.7
Akadya (Fr) 9-2
MPhilliperon 1½.8
Reine du Ciel (Fr) 9-2
SCauthen ½.9
7 Tersa (USA) 9-2 FHead .. 2½.10
Belle Tempete (Fr) 9-2

AGibert 4.11
7² Pass The Peace 9-2
TQuinn ½.12
14 Rose de Crystal (Fr) 9-2
ELegrix s.hd.13
Sudaka (Fr) 9-2
GDubroeucq 3.14

2/1 Ensconse, 13/4 Louveterie, 10/1 Rose de Crystal, 11/1 Premier Amour and Sentimental Side, 14/1 LADY IN SILVER, 15/1 Reine du Ciel, 16/1 Pass The Peace, 17/1 Tersa, 25/1 Akadya, Belle Tempete, 32/1 Glenbelle, 38/1 Sudaka
M. Abdul Karim (R. Wojtowiez) 14ran 2m10.5 (Dead)

23 QUEEN ANNE 1m (Str.) STAKES (Gr 2)
£49,324 Ascot 20 June
11² **Warning** 4-9-8 PatEddery 1
11³ **Reprimand** 4-9-5
SCauthen 4.2
Sweet Chesne (FR) 4-9-2
PaulEddery 2.3
16³ French Stress (USA) 4-9-2
CAsmussen ½.4
Always Valiant 3-8-2
WCarson 7.5
11 Hilton Brown 8-9-2
AClark s.hd.6
Bocas Rose 3-7-13 AMcGlone . 7

2/5 WARNING, 6/1 Reprimand, 13/2 French Stress, 11/1 Sweet Chesne, Always Valiant, 100/1 Bocas Rose, 300/1 Hilton Brown
Mr K. Abdulla (G. Harwood) 7ran 1m39.95 (Firm)

24 PRINCE OF WALES'S 1¼m STAKES (Gr 2)
£52,604 Ascot 20 June
8 **Two Timing (USA)** 3-8-4
PatEddery 1
Beau Sher 6-9-4
BRaymond 1.2
11* **Most Welcome** 5-9-6
PaulEddery 1.3
Opening Verse (USA) 3-8-3
WRyan 4.4
Lapierre 4-9-8 MRoberts .. 2½.5
2 Petrullo 4-9-4 JReid hd.6
Hibernian Gold (USA) 4-9-4
SCauthen 1½.7
2 Galitzin 4-9-4 RCochrane 8

4/6 Most Welcome, 5/1 Hibernian Gold, TWO TIMING, 12/1 Beau Sher, 20/1 Opening Verse, 25/1 Petrullo, 50/1, Lapierre, 66/1 Galitzin
Mr K. Abdulla (J. Tree) 8ran 2m04.9 (Firm)

25 ST JAMES'S PALACE 1m STAKES (Gr 1) (3y c + f)
£113,994 Ascot 20 June
12* **Shaadi (USA)** 9-0
WRSwinburn 1

5 **Greensmith** 9-0
   PatEddery 2.2
   Scenic 9-0 MHills 1.3
12² Great Commotion (USA) 9-0
   WCarson 2½.4
   Thorn Dance (USA) 9-0
   SCauthen 10.5

6/4 SHAADI, 9/4 Thorn Dance, 6/1 Great
Commotion, Scenic, 10/1 Greensmith
   Sheikh Mohammed (M. R. Stoute)
5ran 1m39.33 (Firm)

26 CORONATION   1m
    STAKES (Gr 1) (3y f)
£111,947   Ascot   21 June
7³ **Golden Opinion (USA)** 9-0
    CAsmussen 1
    Magic Gleam (USA) 9-0
    PatEddery ½.2
    Guest Artiste 9-0
    PaulEddery 4.3
21 Tessla (USA) 9-0
    SCauthen ½.4
    Rain Burst 9-0 LDettori nk.5
15² Aldbourne 9-0 PHamblett 1.6
    Pick of The Pops 9-0
    WRSwinburn nk.7
15³ Run To Jenny 9-0
    MJKinane dh.7
    Comic Talent 9-0
    RCochrane ½.9
    Kerita 9-0 WCarson 2.10
    Saraa-Ree (USA) 9-0
    BRaymond 11
15 Honoria 9-0 CRoche ... 12

7/2 GOLDEN OPINION, 6/1 Aldbourne,
Comic Talent, Tessla, 9/1 Guest Artiste,
10/1 Kerita, 11/1 Pick of The Pops, 12/1
Rain Burst, 16/1 Magic Gleam, 20/1 Run
To Jenny, 33/1 Saraa-Ree, 50/1 Honoria
   Sheikh Mohammed (A. Fabre) 12ran
1m39.6 (Firm)

27 CORK AND ORRERY   6f
    STAKES (Gr 3)
£31,300   Ascot   22 June
12 **Danehill (USA)** 3-8-0
    WCarson 1
10³ **Nabeel Dancer (USA)** 4-8-10
    PatEddery 3.2
    Savahra Sound 4-8-10
    BRouse 1½.3
    Dancing Dissident (USA) 3-8-8
    WRSwinburn hd.4
10 Hadif (USA) 3-8-4
    WShoemaker 1½.5
10 Point of Light 4-8-10
    PaulEddery 1.6
    Russian Bond 3-8-8
    SCauthen hd.7
    Green's Canaletto (USA) 3-8-0
    MRoberts 7.8
    Bay Bay 3-7-12 KDarley 8.9
    Wing Park 5-8-10 WNewnes . 10
    Paddy Chalk 3-8-0 NAdams ... 11
    Restore 6-8-10 RCochrane 12

11/8 DANEHILL, 7/2 Dancing Dissi-
dent, 10/1 Nabeel Dancer, Russian Bond,
12/1 Point of Light, 25/1 Green's
Canaletto, Paddy Chalk, Restore, 33/1
Hadif, Savahra Sound, Wing Park, 100/1
Bay Bay
   Mr K. Abdulla (J. Tree) 12ran 1m12.95
(Firm)

28 GOLD CUP (Gr 1)   2½m
£79,740   Ascot   22 June
    Sadeem (USA) 6-9-0
    WCarson 1
9³ **Mazzacano** 4-9-0
    PatEddery 8.2
    Lauries Crusador 4-9-0
    MRoberts ¾.3
    Nomadic Way (USA) 4-9-0
    MHills 1½.4
20³ Green Adventure (USA) 4-9-0
    WRSwinburn 3.5
    Bold Stranger 4-9-0
    JReid 8.6
    Trebrook (Fr) 5-9-0
    ELegrix 2½.7
    Arden 5-9-0 SCauthen 15.8

8/11 SADEEM, 4/1 Green Adventure,
9/1 Arden, 10/1 Trebrook, 12/1 Mazzacano, Nomadic Way, 66/1 Bold Stranger,
Lauries Crusador
   Sheikh Mohammed (G. Harwood)
8ran 4m22.68 (Firm)

29 RIBBLESDALE STAKES   1½m
    (Gr 2) (3y f)
£57,232   Ascot   22 June
    Alydaress (USA) 8-9
    SCauthen 1
21³ **Roseate Tern** 8-8
    WCarson 2½.2
    Nearctic Flame 8-8
    WRSwinburn 1½.3
    Shayraz 8-8 PatEddery ¾.4
    Braiswick 8-8
    PaulEddery 1½.5
    Boldabsa 8-8 PShanahan 15.6

9/4 Nearctic Flame, 3/1 Roseate Tern,
7/2 Shayraz, 4/1 ALYDARESS, 8/1 Braiswick, 33/1 Boldabsa
   Sheikh Mohammed (H. R. A. Cecil)
6ran 2m31.95 (Firm)

30 HARDWICKE STAKES   1½m
    (Gr 2)
£47,493   Ascot   23 June
    Assatis (USA) 4-8-9
    PatEddery 1
    Top Class 4-8-12
    MRoberts 3.2
2   **Emmson** 4-8-9 WCarson 1.3
20 Glacial Storm (USA) 4-8-9
    MHills 5.4

4/11 ASSATIS, 11/2 Glacial Storm, 13/2
Emmson, 8/1 Top Class
   Mr K. Abdulla (G. Harwood) 4ran
2m29.04 (Firm)

31   KING'S STAND STAKES   5f
    (Gr 2)
£60,532   Ascot   23 June
10*   **Indian Ridge** 4-9-3
    SCauthen 1
    Tigani 3-8-9 RCochrane nk.2
10[2]   **Gallic League** 4-9-3
    MHills hd.3
10   Shuttlecock Corner (USA) 3-8-9
    GDuffield 1½.4
    Desert Dawn 3-8-6 TIves ¾.5
    Wonder Dancer (USA) 3-8-9
    ACruz s.hd.6
4[2]   Kerrera 3-8-6 WRSwinburn . 3.7
    Cadeaux Genereux 4-9-3
    PatEddery ½.8
    Perion 7-9-3 PaulDavy . s.hd.9
10   Handsome Sailor 6-9-3
    WCarson hd.10
    Eloquent Minister (USA) 3-8-6
    SCraine 1.11
    Carol's Treasure 5-9-3
    WShoemaker ¾.12
    Astronef 5-9-3
    CAsmussen s.hd.13
    Access Travel 3-8-9
    MRoberts 14
    Paley Prince (USA) 3-8-9
    AMcGlone 15

9/4 INDIAN RIDGE, 7/2 Cadeaux Genereux, 5/1 Kerrera, 6/1 Gallic League, 14/1 Carol's Treasure, 16/1 Handsome Sailor, 25/1 Astronef, Shuttlecock Corner, Tigani, 33/1 Access Travel, Eloquent Minister, 50/1 Perion, Wonder Dancer, 100/1 Desert Dawn, Paley Prince
    Mrs Anne Coughlan (D. R. C. Elsworth) 15ran 1m01.36 (Firm)

32   GRAND PRIX DE PARIS   1¼m
    LOUIS VUITTON (Gr 1)
    (3y c + f)
£144,614   Longchamp   25 June
18[2]   **Dancehall (USA)** 9-2
    CAsmussen 1
18   Norberto (Can) 9-2
    PatEddery 2.2
    Creator 9-2 WRSwinburn .. nk.3
17[2]   Kendor (Fr) 9-2
    MPhilipperon s.nk.4
    Citidancer 9-2 SCauthen ½.5
18[3]   Galetto (Fr) 9-2 ELegrix 1.6
    Rasi Brasak 9-2 ACruz 2½.7
17   Corviglia (USA) 9-2
    GDubroeucq 3.8

9/10 DANCEHALL, 2/1 Kendor and Corviglia, 13/1 Rasi Brasak, 14/1 Citidancer, Norberto, 25/1 Creator
    T. Wada (A. Fabre) 8ran 2m3.6 (Good)

33   BUDWEISER IRISH   1½m
    DERBY (Gr 1) (3y c + f)
£321,491   Curragh   2 July
18*   **Old Vic** 9-0 SCauthen 1

8[2]   **Observation Post** 9-0
    WCarson 4.2
19   **Ile de Nisky** 9-0
    PatEddery 2½.3
    Phantom Breeze 9-0
    MKinane 5.4
    Glowing Star 9-0 CRoche ... 2½.5
5   Zayyani 9-0 WRSwinburn ... hd.6
    Stone Drum 9-0 SCraine 8.7
    Galliero 9-0 JReid 15.8

4/11 OLD VIC, 5/1 Ile de Nisky, 10/1 Zayyani, 12/1 Observation Post, 20/1 Phantom Breeze, 33/1 Glowing Star, 100/1 Galliero, 250/1 Stone Drum
    Sheikh Mohammed (H. R. A. Cecil) 8ran 2m29.8 (Good)

34   GRAND PRIX DE SAINT-   1½m
    CLOUD (Gr 1)
£158,528   Saint-Cloud   2 July
20*   **Sheriff's Star** 4-9-8 TIves 1
    Golden Pheasant (USA) 3-8-9
    ACruz hd.2
3   **Boyatino** 5-9-8 ELegrix .. s.hd.3
3[2]   Star Lift 5-9-8 CAsmussen 4
19   Mill Pond (Fr) 3-8-9 GMoore ... 5
    Vaguely Pleasant 7-9-8
    GMosse ½.6

Mill Pond was fourth past the post, a length behind Boyatino and ¾ length in front of Star Lift. After a stewards inquiry Mill Pond was relegated for interference

7/10 Star Lift, 15/4 Boyatino, 48/10 SHERIFF'S STAR, 7/1 Mill Pond, 3¼1 Golden Pheasant, 20/1 Vaguely Pleasant
    Lavinia Duchess of Norfolk (Lady Herries) 6ran 2m35.8 (Good)

35   CORAL-ECLIPSE   1¼m
    STAKES (Gr 1)
£154,695   Sandown   8 July
19*   **Nashwan (USA)** 3-8-8
    WCarson 1
24   Opening Verse (USA) 3-8-8
    NDay 5.2
16*   Indian Skimmer (USA) 5-9-4
    SCauthen s.hd.3
23*   Warning 4-9-7 PatEddery ... 15.4
    Spring Hay 3-8-8
    WNewnes 1½.5
25[2]   Greensmith 3-8-8
    GStarkey 20.6

2/5 NASHWAN, 7/2 Warning, 11/2 Indian Skimmer, 80/1 Greensmith, 200/1 Opening Verse, Spring Hay
    Mr Hamdan Al-Maktoum (Major W. R. Hern) 6ran 2m07.38 (Good)

36   PRINCESS OF WALES'S   1½m
    STAKES (Gr 2)
£47,813   Newmarket   11 July
13[3]   **Carroll House** 4-9-5
    WRSwinburn 1
30*   **Assatis (USA)** 4-9-3
    PatEddery nk.2

Michelozzo (USA) 3-8-0
    PaulEddery 3.3
    Upper Strata 4-8-11
    RCochrane 2½.4
30² Top Class 4-9-3
    MRoberts 5.5

4/11 Assatis, 8/1 Michelozzo, 17/2 Top Class, 10/1 CARROLL HOUSE, 20/1 Upper Strata
    Mr Antonio Balzarini (M. A. Jarvis)
5ran 2m33.23 (Good)

| 37 | CHILD STAKES (Gr 2) | 1m |
| £36,210 | Newmarket | 12 July |

26² **Magic Gleam (USA)** 3-8-6
    PatEddery 1
22 **Ensconse (USA)** 3-8-12
    RCochrane 4.2
26³ **Guest Artiste** 3-8-6
    PaulEddery 2½.3
23 Bocas Rose 3-8-6
    WCarson 2½.4
    Arsaan (USA) 3-8-6
    WRSwinburn 8.5
    Racing Home (Fr) 3-8-6
    MRoberts 6.6

13/8 Ensconse, 15/8 MAGIC GLEAM, 10/3 Guest Artiste, 9/1 Arsaan, 33/1 Bocas Rose, 66/1 Racing Home
    Maktoum Al-Maktoum (A. A. Scott)
6ran 1m37.5 (Good)

| 38 | CARROLL FOUNDATION JULY CUP (Gr 1) | 6f |
| £101,112 | Newmarket | 13 July |

31 **Cadeaux Genereux** 4-9-6
    PaulEddery 1
26* **Golden Opinion (USA)** 3-8-8
    CAsmussen hd.2
27* **Danehill (USA)** 3-8-11
    PatEddery 2½.3
31 Kerrera 3-8-8
    WRSwinburn 1½.4
27 Point of Light 4-9-6
    SCauthen ¾.5
5 Sharp N' Early 3-8-11
    BRouse ½.6
31³ Gallic League 4-9-6
    MHills ¾.7
5 Mon Tresor 3-8-11
    MRoberts ¾.8
    Big Shuffle (USA) 5-9-6
    MKinane 1½.9
31 Handsome Sailor 6-9-6
    TIves 4.10
    Magical Strike (USA) 3-8-11
    RCochrane s.hd.11

Evens Danehill, 11/4 Golden Opinion, 9/1 Kerrera, 10/1 CADEAUX GENE-REUX, 12/1 Gallic League, 25/1 Big Shuffle, Magical Strike, 33/1 Handsome Sailor, Mon Tresor, Point of Light, 66/1 Sharp N' Early
    Maktoum Al-Maktoum (A. A. Scott)
11ran 1m09.82 (Good to Firm)

| 39 | KILDANGAN STUD IRISH OAKS (Gr 1) (3y f) | 1½m |
| £106,315 | Curragh | 15 July |

29* **Alydaress (USA)** 9-0
    MJKinane 1
21* **Aliysa** 9-0
    WRSwinburn ¾.2
    Petite Ile 9-0 RQuinton hd.3
    Royal Climber 9-0
    CRoche 10.4
    Caerless Writing 9-0
    WJSupple 5

4/7 Aliysa, 7/4 ALYDARESS, 14/1 Petite Ile, 50/1 Royal Climber, 100/1 Caerless Writing
    Sheikh Mohammed (H. R. A. Cecil)
5ran 2m31.2 (Good to Firm)

| 40 | KING GEORGE VI AND QUEEN ELIZABETH DIAMOND STAKES (Gr 1) | 1½m |
| £218,088 | Ascot | 22 July |

35* **Nashwan (USA)** 3-8-8
    WCarson 1
19³ **Cacoethes (USA)** 3-8-8
    GStarkey nk.2
36 **Top Class** 4-9-7
    MRoberts 7.3
34* Sheriff's Star 4-9-7 TIves 1.4
36* Carroll House 4-9-7
    WRSwinburn 3.5
9 Polemos 5-9-7 RHills 1½.6
    Tisserand (Ity) 4-9-7
    LSorrentino ¾.7

2/9 NASHWAN, 6/1 Cacoethes, 10/1 Sheriff's Star, 33/1 Carroll House, 50/1 Tisserand, Top Class, 500/1 Polemos
    Mr Hamdan Al-Maktoum (Major W. R. Hern) 7ran 2m32.27 (Good to Firm)

| 41 | SWETTENHAM STUD SUSSEX STAKES (Gr 1) | 1m |
| £192,150 | Goodwood | 26 July |

    Zilzal (USA) 3-8-10
    WRSwinburn 1
    Green Express (USA)
    3-8-10 ACruz 3.2
5 **Markofdistinction** 3-8-10
    RCochrane 1½.3
24³ Most Welcome 5-9-7
    PaulEddery s.hd.4
35² Opening Verse (USA) 3-8-10
    WRyan ½.5
35 Warning 4-9-7 PatEddery 4.6
25* Shaadi (USA) 3-8-10
    SCauthen 3.7
23 Hilton Brown 8-9-7
    AClark 25.8

7/4 Warning, 5/2 ZILZAL, 3/1 Markof-distinction, 7/1 Shaadi, 20/1 Most Welcome, 40/1 Opening Verse, 100/1 Green Line Express, 500/1 Hilton Brown
    Mr Mana Al-Maktoum (M. R. Stoute)
8ran 1m36.77 (Firm)

42   LANSON CHAMPAGNE   7f
VINTAGE STAKES (Gr 3)
(2y)
£18,008   Goodwood   27 July

Be My Chief (USA) 9-0
  SCauthen 1
Robellation (USA) 8-11
  GStarkey ½.2
Dashing Blade 8-11
  JMatthias 1.3
Sheer Precocity 8-11
  WCarson 6.4
Lifewatch Vision 9-0
  RPElliott 1½.5

8/15 BE MY CHIEF, 5/2 Dashing Blade,
11/1 Sheer Precocity, 25/1, Lifewatch
Vision, Robellation
Mr Peter Burrell (H. R. A. Cecil) 5ran
1m26.61(Firm)

43   WALMAC   1m5f60y
INTERNATIONAL
GEOFFREY FREER
STAKES (Gr 2)
£43,750   Newbury   12 August

Ibn Bey 5-9-8 TQuinn 1
1³ **Apache** 4-9-2 PatEddery hd.2
Alphabel 3-8-3 MRoberts 3.3
30 Glacial Storm (USA) 4-9-2
  MHills ½.4
Sudden Victory 5-9-2 JReid .. 6.5
Prorutori (USA) 3-8-9
  WRSwinburn ½.6

11/8 Apache, 7/4 Alphabel, 9/2 IBN BEY,
10/1 Prorutori, 14/1 Glacial Storm, 25/1
Sudden Victory
Mr Fahd Salman (P. F. I. Cole) 6ran
2m50.62 (Good)

44   PRIX DU HARAS DE   1m
FRESNEY-LE-BUFFARD
JACQUES LE MAROIS
(Gr 1)
£107,401   Deauville   13 August

Polish Precedent (USA) 3-8-9
  CAsmussen 1
23 **French Stress (USA)** 4-9-2
  DBoeuf 2.2
37* **Magic Gleam (USA)** 3-8-6
  PatEddery 2.3
16² Gabina (USA) 4-8-13
  ELegrix nk.4
Navratilovna (USA) 3-8-6
  FHead dh.4
Squill (USA) 4-9-2
  GGuignard 1.6
22 Tersa (USA) 3-8-6 GMosse ... 5.7
21 Musical Bliss (USA) 3-8-6
  WRSwinburn 3.8
Hibouni (Fr) 4-9-2
  GDubroeucq 8.9
41 Most Welcome 5-9-2
  SCauthen 1½.10

11/10 Musical Bliss and POLISH
PRECEDENT, 7/4 Magic Gleam, 6/1
Gabina, 17/2 Navratilovna, 12/1 Squill,

15/1 Most Welcome, 19/1 French Stress,
20/1 Tersa, 42/1 Hibouni
Sheikh Mohammed (A. Fabre) 10ran
1m37.3 (Good)

45   HEINZ 57 PHOENIX   6f
STAKES (Gr 1) (2y c + f)
£106,130 Phoenix Park 13 August

Pharaoh's Delight 8-11
  RCochrane 1
Duck And Dive 9-0
  BRouse 1.2
Wedding Bouquet 8-11
  JReid 1.3
Aminata 8-11 CRoche 3.4
Princess Taufan 8-11
  WNewnes 3.5
Gilt Note 9-0 PShanahan .. s.hd.6
Poke The Fire 9-0 MHills 7
Tanwi 8-11 DParnell 8
Regal Peace 8-11 DGillespie ... 9
Red Henry (USA) 9-0 TIves ... 10

2/1 PHARAOH'S DELIGHT, 3/1 Wed-
ding Bouquet, 13/2 Princess Taufan, 8/1
Red Henry, 9/1 Aminata, 10/1 Duck And
Dive, 14/1 Poke The Fire, 25/1 Tanwi,
33/1 Gilt Note, Regal Peace
Al-Deera Bloodstock Holdings Ltd (J.
P. Hudson) 10ran 1m11.6 (Dead)

46   PRIX DE MEAUTRY   6f
(Gr 3)
£19,507   Deauville   15 August

Cricket Ball (USA)
  6-9-5 GMosse 1
27² **Nabeel Dancer (USA)** 4-8-11
  WRSwinburn s.nk.2
32 **Corviglia (USA)** 3-8-7
  GDubroeucq 2.3
7 Oczy Czarnie (USA) 3-8-7
  ELegrix ns.4
Save Me The Waltz 3-8-5
  ALequeux nk.5
Or Acier (USA) 3-8-10
  FHead 1½.6
Simon Rattle 4-8-11 ACruz .. ¾.7
Canango 5-9-3 GGuignard 6.8
Umbelata 6-8-11
  MPhilipperon hd.9
Villa d'Orleans 5-8-11
  ABadel ¾.10
Holst (USA) 5-9-3
  CAsmussen 11

7/10 CRICKET BALL, 2 1/4 Or Acier and
Save Me The Waltz, 8/1 Oczy Czarnie,
17/2 Holst, 9/1 Nabeel Dancer, 13/1
Corviglia, Umbelata, 16/1 Canango, 18/1
Villa d'Orleans, 22/1 Simon Rattle
R. Scully (J. Fellows) 11ran 1m12.2
(Good)

47   IMRY SOLARIO STAKES   7f
(Gr 3) (2y)
£25,331   Sandown   18 August

42* **Be My Chief (USA)** 9-0
  SCauthen 1

42² **Robellation (USA)** 8-11
GStarkey ¾.**2**
Balla Cove 8-11
PatEddery 3.**3**
1/3 BE MY CHIEF (USA), 100/30
Robellation, 12/1 Balla Cove
P. Burrell (H. R. A. Cecil) 3ran
1m29.38 (Good to Firm)

48 PRIX MORNY AGENCE 6f
FRANCAISE (Gr 1)
(2y c + f)
£96,525 Deauville 20 August
Machiavellian (USA) 8-11
FHead **1**
Qirmazi (USA) 8-8
CAsmussen 2.**2**
Mill Lady (Fr) 8-8
GDubroeucq 4.**3**
Ozone Friendly (USA) 8-8
PatEddery nk.**4**
Spendomania 8-8
ALequeux 2.**5**
Age of Miracles 8-11
GMoore hd.**6**
Waki Gold (USA) 8-11
GCarter 10.**7**
9/10 MACHIAVELLIAN, 5/2 Qirmazi,
13/4 Ozone Friendly, 5/1 Spendomania,
23/1 Mill Lady, 25/1 Waki Gold, 38/1 Age
of Miracles
S. Niarchos (F. Boutin) 7ran 1m12.8
(Good)

49 JUDDMONTE 1¼m110y
INTERNATIONAL
STAKES (Gr 1)
£125,348 York 22 August
20² **Ile de Chypre** 4-9-6
AClark **1**
40² **Cacoethes (USA)** 3-8-10
GStarkey 1½.**2**
2 **Shady Heights** 5-9-6
WCarson 4.**3**
44³ Magic Gleam (USA) 3-8-7
SCauthen 2½.**4**
Batshoof 3-8-10
BRaymond ½.**5**
24* Two Timing (USA) 3-8-10
PatEddery 4.**6**
24 Lapierre 4-9-6
MRoberts 6.**7**
2/5 Cacoethes, 11/2 Two Timing, 9/1
Magic Gleam, 16/1 ILE DE CHYPRE,
20/1 Shady Heights, 25/1 Batshoof, 80/1
Lapierre
Mr Athos Christodoulou (G. Harwood) 7ran 2m06.91(Firm)

50 GREAT VOLTIGEUR 1½m
STAKES (Gr 2) (3y c + g)
£39,915 York 22 August
8³ **Zalazl (USA)** 8-9 SCauthen **1**
19² **Terimon** 8-9 MRoberts ½.**2**
19 **Warrshan (USA)** 8-9
WRSwinburn 1½.**3**

13/8 Warrshan, 7/4 ZALAZL, 9/4 Terimon
Mr M. Al-Maktoum (H. R. A. Cecil)
3ran 2m30.61(Firm)

51 ASTON UPTHORPE 1½m
YORKSHIRE OAKS (Gr 1)
(3y f)
£57,614 York 23 August
29² **Roseate Tern** 9-0
WCarson **1**
39* **Alydaress (USA)** 9-0
SCauthen 1½.**2**
39³ **Petite Ile** 9-0 RQuinton hd.**3**
Lady Shipley 9-0
WRSwinburn 1½.**4**
Nydrion (USA) 9-0
PatEddery 10.**5**
1/2 Alydaress, 11/2 ROSEATE TERN,
7/1 Petite Ile, 13/1 Lady Shipley, 14/1
Nydrion
Lord Carnarvon (Major W. R. Hern)
5ran 2m31.58 (Firm)

52 SCOTTISH EQUITABLE 6f
GIMCRACK STAKES
(Gr 2) (2y c + g)
£37,170 York 23 August
Rock City 9-3 WCarson **1**
Book The Band 9-0
MRoberts 1½.**2**
Swiss Affair (USA) 9-0
PatEddery 3.**3**
Olympic Hero 9-0
SCauthen nk.**4**
Champagne Gold 9-0
RCochrane ¾.**5**
1/2 ROCK CITY, 4/1 Book The Band,
10/1 Olympic Hero, Swiss Affair, 12/1
Champagne Gold
A. F. Budge (Equine) Limited (R.
Hannon) 5ran 1m10.97 (Good to Firm)

53 WILLIAM HILL SPRINT 5f
CHAMPIONSHIP (Gr 1)
£61,287 York 24 August
38* **Cadeaux Genereux** 4-9-6
PatEddery **1**
Silver Fling (USA) 4-9-3
JMatthias ¾.**2**
Statoblest 3-9-2
RCochrane s.hd.**3**
31² Tigani 3-9-2 BRaymond hd.**4**
27 Dancing Dissident (USA) 3-9-2
WRSwinburn 2.**5**
31 Eloquent Minister (USA)
3-8-13 SCraine ½.**6**
31 Shuttlecock Corner (USA) 3-9-2
GDuffield s.hd.**7**
31 Wonder Dancer (USA) 3-9-2
SCauthen 2.**8**
Petillante 2-7-8 WCarson 3.**9**
31 Desert Dawn 3-8-13
RHills hd.**10**
Hinari Televideo 3-8-13
RPElliott 1½.**11**

1025

11/10 CADEAUX GENEREUX, 5/1
Silver Fling, 9/1 Dancing Dissident,
Statoblest, 10/1 Tigani, 12/1 Petillante,
20/1 Eloquent Minister, Shuttlecock
Corner, 25/1 Hinari Televideo, 33/1
Desert Dawn, Wonder Dancer,
  Maktoum Al-Maktoum (A. A. Scott)
11ran 57.67 (Good to Firm)

54	BEEFEATER GIN	1m
	CELEBRATION MILE	
	(Gr 2)	
£47,095	Goodwood	26 August
12³	**Distant Relative** 3-8-12	
	MHills 1	
25	**Great Commotion (USA)**	
	3-8-9 PatEddery 2½.2	
23²	**Reprimand** 4-9-6	
	SCauthen 1.3	
	Samoan (USA) 3-8-9	
	WRyan ½.4	
	Point House 4-9-3 JReid 6.5	

6/4 Reprimand, 2/1 DISTANT RELA-
TIVE, 5/2 Great Commotion, 25/1 Point
House, Samoan
  Mr Wafic Said (B. W. Hills) 5ran
1m40.08 (Good to Firm)

55	LADBROKE SPRINT	6f
	CUP (Gr 1)	
£74,422	Haydock	2 September
38³	**Danehill (USA)** 3-9-5	
	PatEddery 1	
46*	**Cricket Ball (USA)** 6-9-10	
	WCarson 2.2	
	A Prayer For Wings 5-9-10	
	MRoberts 1.3	
53²	Silver Fling (USA) 4-9-7	
	JMatthias s.hd.4	
53	Shuttlecock Corner (USA)	
	3-9-5 MBirch 3.5	
	Mansion House 3-9-5	
	DeanMcKeown 4.6	
38	Kerrera 3-9-2 WRSwinburn . 2.7	
26	Run To Jenny 3-9-2	
	LDettori ½.8	
46	Holst (USA) 5-9-10	
	PaulEddery nk.9	

7/4 Silver Fling, 3/1 DANEHILL, 7/2
Cricket Ball, 7/1 Kerrera, 15/2 A Prayer
For Wings, 33/1 Holst, Shuttlecock
Corner, 100/1 Mansion House, Run To
Jenny
  Mr K. Abdulla (J. Tree) 9ran 1m12.75
(Good)

56	EBF PHOENIX	1¼m
	CHAMPION STAKES	
	(Gr 1)	
£104,783	Phoenix Park	2 September
40	**Carroll House** 4-9-6	
	MJKinane 1	
32	**Citidancer** 3-8-11	
	SCauthen ¾.2	
24	Petrullo 4-9-6 JReid 1.3	
21	Mamaluna (USA) 3-8-8	
	GStarkey ¾.4	

15	Tursanah (USA) 3-8-8	
	DParnell ¾.5	
	Little Bighorn 4-9-6	
	SCraine ¾.6	
	Alcando 3-8-8 AMcGlone 2.7	
25³	Scenic 3-8-11 MHills 2½.8	
	Noora Abu 7-9-3 CRoche 5.9	

5/4 Scenic, 5/1 CARROLL HOUSE,
Citidancer, 11/2 Mamaluna, 12/1 Noora
Abu, 16/1 Tursanah, 20/1 Alcando, 25/1
Petrullo, 66/1 Little Bighorn
  Mr Antonio Balzarini (M. A. Jarvis)
9ran 2m04.0 (Good)

57	ARLINGTON MILLION	1¼m
	(Gr 1)	
£379,747	Arlington	3 September
	Steinlen 6-9-0 JSantos 1	
22*	**Lady In Silver (USA)** 3-8-5	
	LPincay ½.2	
	Yankee Affair (USA) 7-9-0	
	PDay ½.3	
	El Senor (USA) 5-9-0	
	HMcCauley hd.4	
	Kefaah (USA) 4-9-0	
	RCochrane 2.5	
	Frosty The Snowman (USA)	
	4-9-0 JVelasquez 1¼.6	
	Pleasant Variety (USA) 5-9-0	
	FToro ns.7	
	Great Communicator (USA) 6-9-0	
	RSibille 8.8	
	Fijar Tango (Fr) 4-9-0	
	ACordero 2.9	
	Nasr El Arab (USA) 4-9-0	
	PValenzuela 2.10	
	River Warden (USA) 3-8-8	
	SCauthen 2½.11	
	Pay The Butler (USA) 5-9-0	
	RDavis 3½.12	
49³	Shady Heights 5-9-0	
	WCarson 3½.13	

31/10 Nasr El Arab, River Warden, 47/10
Frosty The Snowman, 53/10 STEIN-
LEN, 58/10 Great Communicator, 79/10
Fijar Tango, 89/10 Kefaah, 13/1 Yankee
Affair, 132/10 Shady Heights, 14/1 El
Senor, 23/1 Lady In Silver, 34/1 Pay The
Butler and Pleasant Variety
  Wildenstein Stable (D. Lukas) 13ran
2m3.6 (Firm)

58	PRIX DU MOULIN DE	1m
	LONGCHAMP (Gr 1)	
£86,957	Longchamp	3 September
44*	**Polish Precedent (USA)** 3-8-11	
	CAsmussen 1	
44	**Squill (USA)** 4-9-2	
	GGuignard 2.2	
53*	**Cadeaux Genereux** 4-9-2	
	PatEddery s.hd.3	
41²	Green Line Express (USA)	
	3-8-11 ASCruz s.hd.4	
44²	French Stress (USA) 4-9-2	
	ALequeux 2.5	
44	Navratilovna (USA) 3-8-8	
	FHead ¾.6	

Good Example (Fr) 3-8-8
  GDubroeucq 2.7
Val des Bois (Fr) 3-8-11
  GMosse 1.8
23³ Sweet Chesne (Fr) 4-9-2
  MRoberts 2.9
46³ Corviglia (USA) 3-8-11
  MPhilipperon 2.10
Nursery Slope (USA) 3-8-11
  PBodin 11

2/5 Nursery Slope and POLISH PRE-CEDENT, 13/4 Good Example and Green Line Express, 9/1 French Stress, Sweet Chesne, Cadeaux Genereux, 14/1 Navratilovna, 16/1 Squill, 31/1 Val des Bois, 38/1 Corviglia
Sheikh Mohammed (A. Fabre) 11ran
1m38.5 (Good)

59 G.P.A. NATIONAL   7f
   STAKES (Gr 1) (2y c + f)
£84,173   Curragh   9 September
42³ **Dashing Blade** 9-0
  JMatthias 1
45³ **Wedding Bouquet** 8-11
  JReid ¾.2
52² **Book The Band** 9-0
  MRoberts nk.3
Pictorial (USA) 9-0
  SCraine nk.4
Legal Verdict 9-0
  PShanahan 6.5
Missionary Ridge 9-0
  MHills hd.6
Go And Go 9-0 MJKinane ¾.7
Janubi 9-0 DParnell 8
Smokey Native (USA) 9-0
  SWhitworth 9
Crystal Beam 9-0 IJohnson 10

2/1 Book The Band, 3/1 DASHING BLADE, 4/1 Go And Go, 9/2 Missionary Ridge, 6/1 Wedding Bouquet, 10/1 Smokey Native, 12/1 Pictorial, 16/1 Janubi, 20/1 Crystal Beam, 33/1 Legal Verdict
Mr J. C. Smith (I. A. Balding) 10ran
1m25.2 (Good)

60 MOYGLARE STUD   6f
   STAKES (Gr 1) (2y f)
£84,173   Curragh   10 September
Chimes of Freedom (USA)
  8-11 SCauthen 1
45* **Pharoah's Delight** 8-11
  PatEddery 6.2
Annie Laurie 8-11
  PBGilson 1½.3
Tenderetta 8-11 MJKinane ... 1.4
Felin Special 8-11 SCraine 3.5
Artistic Idea (USA) 8-11
  JReid ¾.6
Geht Schnell 8-11 DGillespie .. 7

Evens Pharoah's Delight, 6/4 CHIMES OF FREEDOM, 10/1 Artistic Idea, Felin Special, 12/1 Tenderetta, 33/1 Annie Laurie, 50/1 Geht Schnell

Mr S. S. Niarchos (H. R. A. Cecil) 7ran
1m10.8 (Good)

61 PRIX DE LA   7f
   SALAMANDRE (Gr 1)
   (2y c + f)
£43,273   Longchamp   10 September
48* **Machiavellian** (USA) 8-11
  FHead 1
48² **Qirmazi** (USA) 8-8
  CAsmussen ½.2
Ernani 8-11 ALequeux 2.3
52² Rock City 8-11 WCarson ½.4
El Quahirah (Fr) 8-8
  GDubroeucq 5.5
Tulsa Time 8-11 CPiccioni 4.6

7/10 MACHIAVELLIAN and Tulsa Time, 9/4 Rock City, 4/1 Qirmazi, 25/4 Ernani, 28/1 El Quahirah
Mr S. S. Niarchos (F. Boutin) 6ran
1m24.0 (Good)

62 KIVETON PARK   7f
   STAKES (Gr 3)
£22,950   Doncaster   14 September
Gold Seam (USA) 3-8-7
  WCarson 1
41³ **Markofdistinction** 3-8-7
  LDettori 2.2
26 **Kerita** 3-8-5 PatEddery 2.3
Rasheek (USA) 3-8-7
  GBaxter ½.4
55³ A Prayer For Wings 5-9-0
  MWigham 3.5
Cottenham 3-8-7 JReid s.hd.6

8/11 Markofdistinction, 9/4 GOLD SEAM, 10/1 A Prayer For Wings, 14/1 Kerita, 25/1 Cottenham, Rasheek
Mr Peter M. Brant (Major W. R. Hern) 6ran 1m27.26 (Good)

63 PRIX FOY (Gr 3) (4y +)   1½m
£18,898   Longchamp   17 September
34 **Star Lift** 5-9-2 DBoeuf 1
Robore (Fr) 4-9-0
  AGibert ¾.2
43² **Apache** 4-8-12 PatEddery . 10.3
Augias (Ger) 4-8-12
  ELegrix 2½.4
16 Saint Andrews (Fr) 5-9-4
  ABadel .... pu

6/10 STAR LIFT, 5/2 Saint Andrews, 7/2 Apache, 13/2 Robore, 16/1 Augias
D. Wildenstein (A. Fabre) 5ran
2m32.8 (Dead)

64 PRIX NIEL (Gr 2) (3y)   1½m
£38,055   Longchamp   17 September
34² **Golden Pheasant** (USA) 8-11
  ASCruz 1
French Glory 8-11
  PatEddery 1½.2
40* **Nashwan** (USA) 9-4
  WCarson ½.3
Reliable (Fr) 8-11
  CAsmussen snk.4

1027

Along All 9-2 DBoeuf 5.5
Lights Out (Fr) 8-11
WMongil 1½.6
34   Mill Pond (Fr) 8-11 ELegrix .. 4.7
Nad Elshiba (USA) 8-11
BProcter 10.8

2/10 Nashwan and Nad Elshiba, 25/4
Reliable, 7 1/10 GOLDEN PHEASANT,
10/1 Lights Out, Mill Pond, 14/1 Along
All, 2 1/1 French Glory
   Mr B. McNall (J. Pease) 8ran 2m32.5
(Dead)

65   PRIX VERMEILLE (Gr 1) 1½m
   (3y f)
£74,666   Longchamp   17 September
   Young Mother (Fr) 9-2
ABadel **1**
Sierra Roberta (Fr) 9-2
PatEddery 1½.**2**
Colorado Dancer 9-2
CAsmussen 1½.**3**
21²   Snow Bride (USA) 9-2
SCauthen 1½.4
22   Sudaka (Fr) 9-2
GDubroeucq 3.5
Zartota (USA) 9-2 DBoeuf . 1½.6
Nuance Pale (Fr) 9-2
ELegrix dist.7

Evens Colorado Dancer, 2 1/10 YOUNG
MOTHER and Nuance Pale, 4/1 Snow
Bride, 19/4 Sierra Roberta, 20/1 Sudaka,
89/1 Zartota
   Mr J-M Beguigne (Owner) 7ran
2m33.1(Dead)

66   REFERENCE POINTER   1m
   STAKES (2y)
£3,600   Sandown   19 September
   Elmaamul (USA) 9-4
WCarson **1**
Air Music (Fr) 8-12
PatEddery 7.2
Virgin Gorda 8-4
BMarcus 5.3
Slow Exposure 8-9
GStarkey 1½.4
Needham Hope 9-4
PatEddery ¾.5
Mieka 8-9 BRaymond 5.6
USA Dollar 8-12 JWilliams 4.7
Laser Contact (Ity) 8-9
AClark 6.8

2/5 ELMAAMUL, 11/2 Air Music, 8/1
Needham Hope, 16/1 Laser Contact, 20/1
Mieka, 25/1 Virgin Gorda, 33/1 Slow
Exposure, 50/1 USA Dollar
   Hamdan Al-Maktoum (Major W. R.
Hern) 8ran 1m43.5 (Good)

67   ST LEGER STAKES 1¾m 127y
   (Gr 1) (3y c + f)
£170,774   Ayr   23 September
36³   **Michelozzo (USA)** 9-0
SCauthen **1**
Sapience 9-0 KFallon 8.**2**

51*   **Roseate Tern** 8-11
WCarson ½.**3**
50²   Terimon 9-0 MBirch 1½.4
Blazing Touch (USA) 9-0
MHills 2½.5
N C Owen 9-0 LDettori 6.6
43³   Alphabel 9-0 ASCruz 5.7
Skisurf 9-0 JLowe 2.8

6/4 MICHELOZZO, 5/2 Roseate Tern,
7/2 Terimon, 12/1 N C Owen, 14/1
Alphabel, 15/1 Sapience, 100/1 Blazing
Touch, 250/1 Skisurf
   Mr C. A. B. St George (H. R. A. Cecil)
8ran 3m20.72 (Soft)

68   ROKEBY FARMS MILL   6f
   REEF STAKES (Gr 2)
   (2y)
£41,130   Newbury   23 September
   Welney 8-11 GCarter **1**
Somethingdifferent (USA)
9-1 GStarkey 1½.**2**
Old Alliance (USA) 8-11
PatEddery 2.**3**
52³   Swiss Affair (USA) 8-11
PaulEddery 1.4
45²   Duck And Dive 8-11
BRouse 4.5
53   Petillante 8-6 RHills s.hd.6
Candy Glen 8-11 NDay 3.7

5/2 Old Alliance, 4/11 Candy Glen, Duck
And Dive, 7/1 Swiss Affair, 8/1 Somethingdifferent, 9/1 WELNEY, 10/1 Petillante
   Sir Philip Oppenheimer (G. Wragg)
7ran 1m12.11 (Good to Firm)

69   JEFFERSON SMURFIT 1¾m
   MEMORIAL IRISH ST
   LEGER (Gr 1)
£91,435   Curragh   23 September
51³   **Petite Ile** 3-8-9
RQuinton **1**
Tyrone Bridge 3-8-12
DParnell s.hd.**2**
20   Lazaz (USA) 4-9-8
WRSwinburn 3.3
36   Upper Strata 4-9-5
DGillespie 4.4
20   Sesame 4-9-5 CRoche 1.5
33   Phantom Breeze 3-8-12
MJKinane 1.6
Beyond The Lake 3-8-12
RCarroll 3.7
Daarkom 6-9-8 JReid 6.8
13   Maiden Fair 6-9-5
SCraine s.hd.9
Smaoineamh 3-8-9
WJSupple 8 10

3/1 PETITE ILE, 4/1 Phantom Breeze,
6/1 Daarkom, Lazaz, 8/1 Tyrone Bridge,
Upper Strata, 12/1 Sesame, 16/1 Beyond
The Lake, 20/1 Smaoineamh, 66/1
Maiden Fair
   Mr J. F. Malle (J. Oxx) 10ran 3m05.0
(Dead)

70 R + V PREIS VON   1½m
    EUROPA (Gr 1)
£76,797   Cologne   24 September
43* **Ibn Bey** 5-9-6 TQuinn 1
    Mondrian 3-8-10
     KWoodburn 6.2
40   **Sheriff's Star** 4-9-6
     JReid 1½.3
     Britannia (Ger) 4-9-2
     LMader 2½.4
     Expertiello 3-8-10
     ABoschert 7.5
     Turfkonig 3-8-10
     WNewnes dist.6

Evens Mondrian, 22/10 Sheriff's Star,
42/10 Turfkonig, 74/10 Britannia, IBN
BEY, 94/10 Expertiello
    F. Salman (P. Cole) 6ran 2m34.57
(Soft)

71   PRIX DU PRINCE   1¼m
     D'ORANGE (Gr 3)
£23,185   Longchamp   24 September
     In The Wings 3-8-9
     CAsmussen 1
16   **Mansonnien (Fr)** 5-8-13
     ELegrix ½.2
     Athyka 4-8-12 GGuignard . ¾.3
18   Louis Cyphre 3-8-9
     GMosse hd.4
3   Chevron 4-8-13 ABadel 1½.5

Evens Athyka, 11/4 Mansonnien, 31/10
IN THE WINGS, 15/4 Louis Cyphre, 12/1
Chevron
    Sheikh Mohammed (A. Fabre) 5ran
2m12.5 (Good to Soft)

72   KRUG DIADEM STAKES   6f
     (Gr 3)
£44,010   Ascot   30 September
10   **Chummy's Favourite** 4-9-2
     LDettori 1
55   **Silver Fling (USA)** 4-8-13
     JMatthias ¾.2
46² **Nabeel Dancer (USA)** 4-9-2
     PatEddery 2.3
53   Dancing Dissident (USA) 3-9-2
     WRSwinburn hd.4
27   Green's Canaletto (USA)
     3-8-12 WCarson 2½.5
     Superpower 3-8-12
     CAsmussen ½.6
27³ Savahra Sound 4-9-2
     BRouse hd.7
     Hafir 3-8-12 TQuinn 1.8
38   Point of Light 4-9-2
     PaulEddery 9
     Young Hal 4-9-2 MRoberts 10
     Thornfield Boy 3-8-12
     SCauthen 11

As they passed the post. Third and
fourth placings were later reversed by
the stewards

13/8 Silver Fling, 7/1 Dancing Dissident,
Green's Canaletto, 15/2 Nabeel Dancer,

Superpower, Point of Light, 25/1 Young
Hal, 33/1 Thornfield Boy, 40/1 CHUM-
MY'S FAVOURITE, 66/1 Hafir
    Mr Michael Hill (N. A. Callaghan)
11ran 1m14.25 (Good to Firm)

73   QUEEN ELIZABETH II   1m
     STAKES (Gr 1)
£153,000   Ascot   30 September
41* **Zilzal (USA)** 3-8-11
     WRSwinburn 1
58* **Polish Precedent (USA)**
     3-8-11 CAsmussen 3.2
54* **Distant Relative** 3-8-11
     MHills 2.3
58   Green Line Express (USA)
     3-8-11 PatEddery nk.4
62   Cottenham 3-8-11
     SCauthen nk.5

Evens ZILZAL, 11/8 Polish Precedent,
10/1 Distant Relative, 20/1 Green Line
Express, 66/1 Cottenham
    Mr Mana Al-Maktoum (M. R. Stoute)
5ran 1m40.57 (Good to Firm)

74   ROYAL LODGE EBF   1m
     STAKES (Gr 2) (2y c + g)
£60,939   Ascot   30 September
     Digression (USA) 8-10
     PatEddery 1
     Bridal Toast 8-10 LDettori . 3.2
66² **Air Music (Fr)** 8-10
     MRoberts ½.3
     Satin Wood 8-10 SCauthen . nk.4
47² Robellation (USA) 8-10
     GStarkey 3.5
     Marienski (USA) 8-10
     WCarson 3.6
     Aquatic (USA) 8-10
     WRSwinburn s.hd.7
     Glazerite 8-10 PaulEddery ... 2.8
     Spinning 8-10 JMatthias 9

4/1 DIGRESSION and Satin Wood, 9/2
Bridal Toast, 5/1 Marienski, 6/1
Spinning, 7/1 Aquatic, 15/2 Robellation,
66/1 Air Music, Glazerite
    Mr K. Abdulla (G. Harwood) 9ran
1m42.2 (Good to Firm)

75   TATTERSALLS   6f
     CHEVELEY PARK
     STAKES (Gr 1) (2y f)
£133,695   Newmarket   4 October
     Dead Certain 8-11
     CAsmussen 1
     Line of Thunder (USA)
     8-11 RCochrane ¾.2
60* **Chimes of Freedom (USA)**
     8-11 SCauthen hd.3
     Repercutionist (USA) 8-11
     ASCruz hd.4
     Haunting Beauty (USA) 8-11
     MRoberts ½.5
     Mademoiselle Chloe 8-11
     KHodgson 1½.6
     Tabdea (USA) 8-11 MBirch ... 1.7

Kissogram Girl (USA) 8-11
WRSwinburn 1.8
48 Ozone Friendly (USA) 8-11
MHills 9
Water Well 8-11 TQuinn 10
In The Papers 8-11 MWigham 11

Evens Chimes of Freedom, 11/2 DEAD
CERTAIN, 13/2 Kissogram Girl, 8/1
Mademoiselle Chloe, 10/1 Line of Thunder, 12/1 In The Papers, 16/1 Ozone
Friendly, Tabdea, 20/1 Haunting
Beauty, 50/1 Repercutionist, 100/1
Water Well
   Commander G. G. Marten (D. R. C.
Elsworth) 11ran 1m 14.25 (Good to Firm)

76   TATTERSALLS MIDDLE   6f
     PARK STAKES (Gr 1)
     (2y c)
£79,131   Newmarket   5 October
47³   Balla Cove 9-0 SCauthen 1
61   Rock City 9-0 WCarson 2.2
     Cordoba (USA) 9-0
       WRSwinburn 1½.3
     Croupier 9-0 MRoberts 5.4
68   Duck And Dive 9-0
       BRouse nk.5
     Batzushka (USA) 9-0
       PatEddery 1½.6

8/13 Cordoba, 9/4 Rock City, 10/1
Batzushka, 14/1 Duck And Dive, 20/1
BALLA COVE, 40/1 Croupier
   Mr Harvey Cohen (R. Boss) 6ran
1m 10.62 (Good to Firm)

77   CHEVELEY PARK STUD   1¼m
     SUN CHARIOT STAKES
     (Gr 2) (3y + f + m)
£32,670   Newmarket   7 October
29   Braiswick 3-8-7 GCarter 1
     Life At The Top 3-8-7
       BRaymond 7.2
22   Pass The Peace 3-8-7
       GDuffield 1½.3
26   Tessla (USA) 3-8-7
       PaulEddery 4.4
21   Always On A Sunday 3-8-7
       RHills 2½.5
     Triode (USA) 3-8-7
       AMunro 1½.6
21   Rambushka (USA) 3-8-7
       PatEddery 10.7
56   Mamaluna (USA) 3-8-10
       GStarkey hd.8
     Mary Gee 3-8-7 WRyan 9

10/3 Mamaluna, 7/2 Rambushka, 4/1
BRAISWICK, 11/2 Pass The Peace,
Tessla, 12/1 Triode, 14/1 Life At The
Top, 25/1 Always On A Sunday, 66/1
Mary Gee
   White Lodge Stud (G. Wragg) 9ran
2m05.79 (Good)

78   JOCKEY CLUB CUP   2m
     (Gr 3)
£28,351   Newmarket   7 October
     Weld 3-8-7 BRaymond 1

67   Sapience 3-8-4 KFallon 1½.2
     Sergeyevich 5-9-5
       PatEddery 25.3

Evens WELD, 2/1 Sapience, 7/2
Sergeyevich
   Lord Howard de Walden (W. Jarvis)
3ran 3m34.82 (Good)

79   CARTIER MILLION (2y)   7f
£438,114   Phoenix Park   7 October
     The Caretaker 8-11
       MKinane 1
     Cullinan (USA) 9-0
       LDettori 3.2
     Anshan 9-0 SCauthen hd.3
59³ Book The Band 9-0
       PShanahan hd.4
     Jovial 9-0 WSwinburn 2.5
     Dashing Senor 9-0
       MRoberts 6.6
     Sadlers Congress 9-0
       RCarroll ½.7
42   Sheer Precocity 9-0
       WCarson hd.8
     Simply Terrific 9-0
       RQuinton ½.9
     Missing You 8-11 SCraine . hd.10
59   Legal Verdict 9-0
       DParnell nk.11
     Bastille Day 9-0 WNewnes 12
     Petite Mou 8-11 DGillespie ... 13
     Super Flame (Can) 9-0
       CRoche 14
     Loch Fruin 9-0 MHills 15
48   Waki Gold (USA) 9-0 MBirch   16
     Time Slot (USA) 9-0 JReid 17
     Chipandabit 9-0 MWigham 18
     Going Supersonic (USA) 9-0
       PGilson 19
     Avoca Holmes 8-11 TQuinn ... 20

5/2 Anshan, 9/2 Cullinan, 8/1 Book The
Band, THE CARETAKER, 10/1 Missing
You, 12/1 Loch Fruin, 14/1 Bastille Day,
16/1 Jovial, Time Slot, 20/1 Dashing
Senor, Legal Verdict, Petite Mou,
Simply Terrific, 25/1 Waki Gold, 33/1
Avoca Holmes, Chipandabit, Going
Supersonic, Sadlers Congress, Sheer
Precocity, Super Flame
   Mount Juliet Ltd (D. Weld) 20ran
1m20.1 (Good)

80   CIGA GRAND   1m
     CRITERIUM (Gr 1)
     (2y c + f)
£116,845   Longchamp   7 October
     Jade Robbery (USA) 8-11
       CAsmussen 1
     Linamix (Fr) 8-11
       GMosse ¾.2
     Honor Rajana (USA) 8-11
       ELegrix 4.3
48   Spendomania (USA) 8-8
       GWMoore ½.4
     Filago (USA) 8-11
       GGuignard 1.5
     Snow Bowl (Fr) 8-11 DBoeuf 2.6

Victory Chorus 8-8
ALequeux 5.7
Bold Ambition 8-11
ASCruz 6.8

2/1 Filago, Linamix, 22/10 JADE
ROBBERY, 8/1 Bold Ambition, Honor
Rajana, 18/1 Victory Chorus, 40/1 Spend-
omania, 58/1 Snow Bowl,
 Z. Yoshida (A. Fabre) 8ran 1m40.6
(Good to Firm)

81   CIGA PRIX DOLLAR   1m 1f 165y
     (Gr 2)
£38,230   Longchamp   7 October
32³   **Creator** 3-9-0
       CAsmussen 1
       Hello Calder 4-8-13
       DBoeuf 2.2
58   **Val des Bois (Fr)** 3-8-12
       FHead 2.3
       Neskimo (Fr) 4-8-13
       TJarnet 1.4
57   Shady Heights 5-8-13
       GBaxter hd.5
       Tartas (Fr) 3-8-12
       GGuignard hd.6
       Light of Morn (USA) 3-8-9
       ASCruz hd.7
18   Rainibik (Fr) 3-8-9
       GMosse nk.8
       Silver Lane (USA) 4-8-10
       GDubroeucq 4.9

9/10 CREATOR, 41/10 Light of Morn,
49/10 Val des Bois, 73/10 Shady Heights,
96/10 Tartas, 12/1 Silver Lane, 22/1
Neskimo, 26/1 Hello Calder, 40/1
Rainibik
 Sheikh Mohammed (A. Fabre) 9ran
2m04.1 (Good to Firm)

82   CIGA PRIX DU ROND-   1m
     POINT (Gr 3)
£33,646   Longchamp   8 October
38²   **Golden Opinion (USA)** 3-9-1
       CAsmussen 1
58   **Good Example (Fr)** 3-8-8
       GDubroeucq 6.2
6   Star Touch (Fr) 3-8-11
       ACruz hd.3
       Go Milord 3-9-0 FHead ½.4
       Cielamour 4-8-10
       CRoche 1½.5
57   Kefaah (USA) 4-9-0
       LDettori 1.6
       Oberruti 3-8-8
       MPhilipperon 6.7
       Gulf Star 4-9-0
       GAlmeida hd.8
       Girl of France 3-8-8
       WLequeux 2.9

4/10 GOLDEN OPINION, 4/1 Kefaah, 8/1
Good Example, Star Touch, 9/1 Go
Milord, 12/1 Girl of France, 27/1 Gulf
Star, 42/1 Cielamour, 46/1 Oberruti
 Sheikh Mohammed (A. Fabre) 9ran
1m38.4 (Good)

83   PRIX MARCEL   1m
     BOUSSAC (Gr 1)(2y f)
£68,160   Longchamp   8 October
       Salsabil 8-9 WCarson 1
       Houseproud (USA) 8-9
       PatEddery 2.2
       Alchi (USA) 8-9
       GMosse s.hd.3
       Zinarelle (Fr) 8-9 AGibert ... nk.4
61²   Qirmazi (USA) 8-9
       CAsmussen ½.5
       Wajna (USA) 8-9 SCauthen .. ½.6
       Mackla 8-9 FHead 1½.7
       Luring (USA) 8-9
       ASCruz s.hd.8
       Rive du Sud (USA) 8-9
       GGuignard 3.9
       Sorceress (Fr) 8-9
       ALequeux 3.10
       Appealing Missy (USA) 8-9
       GWMoore 1½.11
       Palace Street (USA) 8-9
       WRSwinburn nk.12
48³   Mill Lady (Fr) 8-9
       GDubroeucq 2.13
45   Aminata 8-9 CRoche 4.14
       Native Guile 8-9 MHills hd.15

7/10 Qirmazi and Wajna, 5/1 Rive du Sud,
13/2 SALSABIL, 17/2 Houseproud, 10/1
Mackia, 17/1 Luring, 29/1 Palace Street,
41/1 Native Guile, 47/1 Sorceress, 55/1
Alchi, 65/1 Appealing Missy, 77/1 Zinarelle, 93/1 Aminata, 96/1 Mill Lady
 Mr Hamdan Al-Maktoum (J. Dunlop)
15ran 1m40.3 (Good)

84   PRIX DE L'ABBAYE DE   5f
     LONGCHAMP (Gr 1)
£68,160   Longchamp   8 October
72²   **Silver Fling (USA)** 4-9-8
       JMatthias 1
       Zadracarta (Can) 4-9-8
       ASCruz s.hd.2
72³   **Nabeel Dancer (USA)** 4-9-11
       PatEddery hd.3
72   Point of Light 4-9-11 JReid 1.4
46   Or Acier (USA) 3-9-11
       CAsmussen nk.5
       Whippet 5-9-11 ELegrix ½.6
53³   Statoblest 3-9-11
       WRSwinburn nk.7
72*   Chummy's Favourite 4-9-11
       LDettori 2.8
       Graphus (Brz) 5-9-11
       JRicardo hd.9
55²   Cricket Ball 6-9-11
       GMosse 2.10
72   Green's Canaletto (USA)
       3-9-11 SCauthen 1½.11
       Rich And Famous (Fr) 2-8-5
       WCarson 1½.12
58   Navratilovna (USA) 3-9-8
       FHead 1½.13
       Rainbow Brite (Bel) 3-9-8
       EHavegheer 1½.14
       Pellezzano (Fr) 3-9-11
       DLawniczak s.hd.15

31 Astronef 5-9-11 A Lequeux . 1.16

2/1 Statoblest, 3/1 SILVER FLING, 17/4 Cricket Ball, 11/1 Astronef and Or Acier, 12/1 Chummy's Favourite, Nabeel Dancer, 16/1 Navratilovna, Rich And Famous, 18/1 Whippet, 30/1 Green's Canaletto, 38/1 Graphus, 40/1 Zadracarta, 58/1 Point of Light, Rainbow Brite, 81/1 Pellezzano

Mr G. Strawbridge (I. A. Balding) 16 ran 59.9 secs (Good)

| 85 | CIGA PRIX DE L'ARC DE | 1½m |
| | TRIOMPHE (Gr 1) | |

£486,855   Longchamp   8 October

56*	**Carroll House** 4-9-4	
	MJKinane 1	
14*	**Behera** 3-8-8 A Lequeux ... 1½.2	
63	**Saint Andrews (Fr)** 5-9-4	
	ELegrix s.nk.3	
65*	Young Mother (Fr) 3-8-8	
	ABadel nk.4	
65²	Sierra Roberta (Fr) 3-8-8	
	FHead ¾.5	
63²	Robore (Fr) 4-9-4 A Gibert ... ½.6	
32²	Norberto (Can) 3-8-11	
	GWMoore 1.7	
	Legal Case 3-8-11 L Dettori . ¾.8	
70	Britannia (Ger) 4-9-1	
	TQuinn hd.9	
39²	Aliysa 3-8-8	
	WRSwinburn hd.10	
71*	In The Wings 3-8-11	
	CAsmussen ½.11	
40³	Top Class 4-9-4	
	MRoberts ¾.12	
71²	Mansonnien (Fr) 5-9-4	
	GMosse 1.13	
64*	Golden Pheasant (USA) 3-8-11	
	ASCruz 3.14	
	Harvest Time (Fr) 3-8-11	
	JBoisnard 1.15	
49²	Cacoethes (USA) 3-8-11	
	SCauthen 1½ 16	
56³	Petrullo 4-9-4 G Guignard ... 3.17	
64²	French Glory 3-8-11	
	PatEddery 3.18	
63*	Star Lift 5-9-4 DBoeuf 19	

15/4 In The Wings, 5/1 Saint Andrews and Young Mother, Cacoethes, 6/1 Aliysa and Behera, 13/2 Star Lift, 10/1 Golden Pheasant, 15/1 Harvest Time and Sierra Roberta, 16/1 French Glory, 19/1 CARROLL HOUSE, Legal Case, 24/1 Norberto, 25/1 Mansonnien and Robore, 50/1 Top Class, 87/1 Britannia, 107/1 Petrullo

Mr A. Balzarini (M. Jarvis) 19 ran 2m30.8 (Good)

| 86 | CORNWALLIS STAKES | 5f |
| | (Gr 3) (2y) | |

£23,571   Ascot   14 October

	Argentum 8-13 J Reid 1	
68²	**Somethingdifferent (USA)**	
	9-5 WCarson 6.2	

	Dancing Music 8-13	
	JCarroll ¾.3	
52	Olympic Hero 8-13	
	SCauthen ¾.4	
	Deux Anes 9-0 LMcGarrity .. 2.5	
	Love Returned 8-8	
	PaulEddery 2.6	
	Stormy Belle 8-8	
	MRoberts 2.7	
75	Kissogram Girl (USA) 8-8	
	WSwinburn 7.8	
75	Haunting Beauty (USA) 8-11	
	PatEddery 10.9	

5/2 Haunting Beauty, 11/4 Kissogram Girl, 9/2 ARGENTUM, 13/2 Somethingdifferent, 7/1 Olympic Hero, 10/1 Dancing Music, 12/1 Deux Anes, Love Returned, 14/1 Stormy Belle

K. F. Khan (L. J. Holt) 9 ran 1m1.65 (Good to Firm)

| 87 | PRIX DE LA FORET | 7f |
| | (Gr 1) (2y + c + f) | |

£49,128   Longchamp   15 October

44	**Gabina (USA)** 4-9-11	
	ELegrix 1	
	Royal Touch 4-9-11	
	GDubroeucq s.hd.2	
	Aliocha 3-9-12 A Cruz 1½.3	
	Malaspina 5-10-0	
	GMosse ¾.4	
41	Shaadi (USA) 3-9-12	
	WSwinburn s.hd.5	
84	Navratilovna (USA) 3-9-9	
	FHead 1½.6	
62*	Gold Seam (USA) 3-9-12	
	WCarson 1½.7	
6³	Ocean Falls 3-9-12	
	DBoeuf 15.8	

5/2 Royal Touch and Shaadi, Gold Seam, 3/1 Ocean Falls, 7/2 GABINA, 11/1 Malaspina, 14/1 Navratilovna, 15/1 Aliocha

J. D. Schiefelbein (J. Cunnington) 8 ran 1m21.0 (Good to Firm)

88	BISQUIT COGNAC	7f
	CHALLENGE STAKES	
	(Gr 2)	

£32,490   Newmarket   19 October

73³	**Distant Relative** 3-8-13	
	MHills 1	
	Dancing Tribute (USA)	
	3-8-7 GStarkey 1½.2	
62³	**Kerita** 3-8-7 PatEddery 2.3	
	Milieu 4-9-0 MKinane 1½.4	
38	Magical Strike (USA) 3-8-10	
	WSwinburn ¾.5	
54	Point House 4-9-0	
	SCauthen 6.6	

Evens DISTANT RELATIVE, 9/2 Magical Strike (USA), 11/2 Kerita, 6/1 Dancing Tribute (USA), 11/1 Milieu, 20/1 Point House

Wafic Said (B. W. Hills) 6 ran 1m25.13 (Good to Firm)

89 BOTTISHAM HEATH   7f
    STUD ROCKFEL
    STAKES (Gr 3) (2y f)
£26,649   Newmarket   20 October
    Negligent 8-8 MHills **1**
    Fearless Revival 8-8
      WSwinburn 5.**2**
    Va Toujours 8-8
      MRimmer 1½.**3**
    Royal Fi Fi (USA) 8-8
      RCochrane 1½.4
    Remthat Naser 8-8
      PaulEddery s.hd.5
    Sajjaya (USA) 8-8 WCarson .. 4.6
    Lady of Persia (USA) 8-8
      BRaymond ¾.7
    Endless Joy 8-11 JReid ¾.8
    Long Island 8-8 LDettori ½.9
    Idle Chat (USA) 8-10
      SCauthen 3.10
    Totham 8-8 GCarter 11
    Fujairyah 8-8 PatEddery 12

15/8 Va Toujours, 100/30 NEGLIGENT,
5/1 Sajjaya (USA), 9/1 Fujaiyrah, 11/1
Fearless Revival, 12/1 Idle Chat (USA),
Remthat Naser, 16/1 Endless Joy, 25/1
Royal Fi Fi (USA), 33/1 Lady of Persia
(USA), Long Island, Totham
  Mrs J. M. Corbett (B. W. Hills) 12ran
1m24.42 (Good)

90 THREE CHIMNEYS   7f
    DEWHURST STAKES
    (Gr 1) (2y c + f)
£128,513   Newmarket   20 October
59* **Dashing Blade** 9-0 JMatthias **1**
    Call To Arms 9-0
      MRoberts nk.**2**
79³ **Anshan** 9-0 SCauthen s.hd.**3**
68* Welney 9-0 GCarter 1½.4
76³ Cordoba (USA) 9-0
      WSwinburn hd.5
    Royal Academy (USA) 9-0
      JReid 2.6
79² Cullinan (USA) 9-0
      LDettori s.hd.7

Evens Royal Academy, 7/2 Welney, 5/1
Cordoba, 8/1 DASHING BLADE, 12/1
Anshan, 14/1 Cullinan, 66/1 Call To Arms
  J. C. Smith (I. A. Balding) 7ran
1m25.43 (Good)

91 DUBAI CHAMPION   1¼m
    STAKES (Gr 1)
£255,745   Newmarket   21 October
85   **Legal Case** 3-8-10
      RCochrane **1**
    Dolpour 3-8-10
      WSwinburn hd.**2**
49* Ile de Chypre 4-9-3
      WCarson s.hd.3
56   Scenic 3-8-10 MHills 1½.4
    Charmer 4-9-3 TQuinn 6.5
33³ Ile de Nisky 3-8-10 ACruz ... nk.6
    Braashee 3-8-10
      PatEddery nk.7

High Estate 3-8-10
      SCauthen 3.8
77² Life At The Top 3-8-7
      MRoberts 9
    Monastery 3-8-10 LDettori ... 10
85   Petrullo 4-9-3 DMcKeown 11

4/1 Dolpour, 5/1 Ile de Chypre, LEGAL
CASE, 6/1 Scenic, 13/2 Braashee, 9/1
High Estate, 16/1 Ile de Nisky, 20/1
Petrullo, 25/1 Life At The Top,
Monastery, 33/1 Charmer
  Sir G. White (L. Cumani) 11ran 2m2.35
(Good)

92   GRAN PREMIO DEL   1½m
    JOCKEY CLUB E COPPA
    D'ORO (Gr 1)
£145,968   San Siro   21 October
36² **Assatis (USA)** 4-9-3
      GBaxter **1**
51² **Alydaress (USA)** 3-8-8
      WRyan ½.**2**
    Yellow King 3-8-11
      GDettori 4½.**3**
    Artic Envoy (USA) 3-8-11
      GMoore 2½.4
    Jung 5-9-3 BJovine s.hd.5
    Love The Groom (USA) 5-9-3
      ALequeux 3.6
40   Tisserand (Ity) 4-9-3
      LSorrentino 10.7
    Cunizza da Romano 5-9-0
      SDettori 8.8

Tote odds to a ten lira stake: WIN 17: PL:
11-12-19
  Y. Ito (G. Harwood) 8ran 2m28.0
(Good to Firm)

93   PRIX DU CONSEIL DE   1½m
    PARIS (Gr 2) (3y +)
£36,385   Longchamp   22 October
85   **Robore (Fr)** 4-9-4 AGibert **1**
71   **Louis Cyphre** 3-8-9 FHead . 1.**2**
    Ode (USA) 3-8-6
      DBoeuf s.nk.**3**
    Deliorman 3-8-9 ACruz ns.4
    Lesotho (USA) 6-9-0
      GMoore 1½.5
85   Top Class 4-9-0 MRoberts .. nk.6
    Shades of Peace (USA) 3-8-6
      MKinane nk.7
    Myth To Reality (Fr) 3-8-6
      ESaint-Martin 3.8

8/10 ROBORE, 4/1 Top Class, 17/4 Ode,
11/2 Louis Cyphre and Myth To Reality,
7/1 Deliorman, 10/1 Shades of Peace, 14/1
Lesotho
  Marquis de Geoffre (N. Pelat) 8ran
2m30.4 (Good to Firm)

94   RACING POST TROPHY   1m
    (Gr 1) (2y c + f)
£118,952   Newcastle   28 October
47* **Be My Chief (USA)** 9-0
      SCauthen **1**
    Baligh 9-0 WCarson 4.**2**

```
        Qathif (USA) 9-0 RHills .... nk.3
79    Loch Fruin 9-0 MHills ........... 3.4
      Cutting Note (USA) 9-0
        DMcKeown ........................ ½.5
4/7 BE MY CHIEF (USA), 5/1 Qathif,
11/2 Cutting Note (USA), 11/1 Baligh,
25/1 Loch Fruin
    P. Burrell (H. R. A. Cecil) 5ran
1m42.99 (Good)

95    PRIX ROYAL-OAK (Gr 1) 1m7½f
£36,836    Longchamp    29 October
      Top Sunrise (USA) 4-9-3
        FHead ................................. 1
      Turgeon (USA) 3-8-11
        ACruz ................................. 2.2
      Robertet (USA) 3-8-8
        DBoeuf ........................... 1½.3
      Rachmaninov (Fr) 4-9-3
        ELegrix ........................... ¾.4
      Mardonius 3-8-11 SCauthen . 1.5
78²   Sapience 3-8-11 WCarson ..... 5.6
34    Vaguely Pleasant (Fr) 7-9-3
        GMosse ........................ s.hd.7
      Noble Savage 3-8-11
        AClark ............................ 2½.8
85    Britannia (Ger) 4-9-0
        MRimmer ............................ 6.9
2/1 Mardonius and Noble Savage, 28/10
TOP SUNRISE, 57/10 Robertet, 58/10
Sapience, Turgeon, 66/10 Rachmaninov,
14/1 Britannia, 20/1 Vaguely Pleasant
    C. Schmidt (A. Fabre) 9ran 3m22.0
(Good)

96    RACECALL GOLD            6f
      TROPHY (Gr 3)
£100,523    Redcar    31 October
      Osario 8-4 BRouse ................. 1
90²   Call To Arms 8-4
        MRoberts ...................... 2½.2
79    Sheer Precocity 8-12
        BRaymond ....................... 3.3
      In Excess 8-10 WSwinburn ... 1.4
      Shamshoon 9-0
        RCochrane .................... 2½.5
      Lakeland Beauty 8-9
        WNewnes ....................... ½.6
      Addison's Blade 8-4
        TQuinn ............................ 1.7
86³   Dancing Music 8-7
        JCarroll ...................... s.hd.8
      Ayr Raider 8-2
        DMcKeown ................... 1½.9
      Sundance Kid (USA) 9-0
        SCauthen ...................... 1.10
      Green's Belle 8-6
        PatEddery ..................... nk.11
86    Olympic Hero 8-1
        WCarson ......................... 1.12
      La Domaine 8-7
        SWhitworth ................. 1½.13
      Vax Lady 8-0 KDarley ....... nk.14
      Lyndseylee 7-10
        AMackay ........................ ½.15
      Sir Arthur Hobbs 8-4
        GCarter ......................... ½.16
```

```
86    Stormy Belle 7-13
        GDuffield ...................... nk.17
42    Lifewatch Vision 8-10
        RElliott ......................... ¾.18
      Flower Girl 8-2 RHills ....... hd.19
      All Fired Up 7-13 David
        Eddery .......................... nk.20
86*   Argentum 8-9 JReid ......... 1½.21
      King Al 8-4 WRyan ........... ½.22
89    Remthat Naser 8-5
        PaulEddery .................... ½.23
      Brisas 8-7 MBirch .............. 3.24
      Broughton Bay 8-4
        MWigham ........................... 25
2/1 Argentum, 9/2 Sundance Kid, 8/1 Call
To Arms, 10/1 Broughton Bay, Olympic
Hero, Remthat Naser, 12/1 OSARIO,
14/1 Flower Girl, 16/1 Green's Belle, In
Excess, 20/1 Lakeland Beauty, 25/1 Vax
Lady, 33/1 King Al, Lyndseylee, 50/1
Addison's Blade, All Fired Up, Ayr
Raider, Brisas, Dancing Music, La
Domaine, Lifewatch Vision, Sham-
shoon, Sheer Precocity, Sir Arthur
Hobbs, Stormy Belle
    J. G. Davis (R. Hannon) 25ran 1m10.58
(Good)

97    BREEDERS' CUP TURF      1½m
      (Gr 1)
£569,620    Gulfstream    4 November
      Prized (USA) 3-8-10
        EDelahoussaye ................... 1
85    Sierra Roberta (Fr) 3-8-7
        PatEddery ...................... hd.2
85    Star Lift 5-9-0 GStevens ...... 1.3
85²   Behera 3-8-7 ALequeux ...... nk.4
      Caltech (USA) 3-8-10
        RDouglas .......................... 3.5
57    Pleasant Variety (USA) 5-9-0
        ASolis ............................ ¾.6
57    El Senor (USA) 5-9-0
        WMcCauley .................. 1¼.7
      Green Barb (USA) 4-9-0
        JVelasquez ...................... hd.8
91³   Ile de Chypre 4-9-0
        AClark ........................... nk.9
      Milesius (USA) 5-9-0
        RMigliore ...................... hd.10
91    Scenic 3-8-10 MHills ........ nk.11
57²   Lady In Silver (USA) 3-8-7
        LPincay ........................ 3½.12
      Hodges Bay (USA) 4-9-0
        JCruguet ...................... 3½.13
      Sunshine Forever (USA) 4-9-0
        ACordero ....................... ½.14
34/10 El Senor, 38/10 Behera, 42/10
Caltech, 6/1 Lady In Silver, 64/10 Ile de
Chypre, 88/10 PRIZED, 18/1 Sunshine
Forever, 19/1 Hodges Bay, 25/1 Sierra
Roberta, 26/1 Scenic, 36/1 Green Barb
and Milesius and Pleasant Variety, 52/1
Star Lift
    Clover Racing Stable & Meadow-
brook Farms (N. Drysdale) 14ran
2m28.0 (Firm)
```

BREEDERS' CUP MILE   1m
(Gr 1)
£284,810   Gulfstream   4 November

57*	**Steinlen** 6-9-0 JSantos 1	
	Sabona (USA) 7-9-0	
	CMcCarron ¾.2	
44	**Most Welcome** 5-9-0	
	GCarter ½.3	
87²	Royal Touch 4-8-11	
	GStevens nk.4	
	Simply Majestic (USA) 5-9-0	
	ACordero hd.5	
73*	Zilzal (USA) 3-8-11	
	WSwinburn nk.6	
	Highland Springs (USA) 5-9-0	
	KDesormeaux hd.7	
	Quick Call (USA) 5-9-0	
	PDay 3.8	
16	In Extremis (USA) 4-9-0	
	LPincay 4½.9	
	Little Bold John (USA) 7-9-0	
	DMiller 3½.10	
73	Green Line Express (USA)	
	3-8-11 CPerret 1¼.11	

Evens Zilzal, 18/10 STEINLEN, 48/10
Simply Majestic, 2 1/2 Sabona, 35/1
Highland Springs, 39/1 Quick Call, Little
Bold John and Royal Touch, 59/1 Green
Line Express, 65/1 In Extremis, 93/1
Most Welcome

Wildenstein Stable (D. Lukas) 11 ran
1m37.2 (Firm)

99   CRITERIUM DE SAINT-   1¼m
CLOUD (Gr 1) (2y c + f)
£50,403   Saint-Cloud   11 November

	Intimiste (USA) 8-11	
	GMosse 1	
	Snurge 8-11 RQuinn 2	
	Guiza (USA) 8-8	
	ELegrix hd.3	
	Houmayoun (Fr) 8-11	
	ACruz 1½.4	
	Anna's Honor (USA) 8-8	
	AGibert 1½.5	
	Noble Ballerina 8-8	
	ABadel 2½.6	
	Mahshari 8-11 WMongil hd.7	
	Dr Somerville (USA) 8-11	
	FHead ½.8	
	Comte du Bourg (Fr) 8-11	
	GDubroecq 20.9	
	Anidal (Fr) 8-11	
	DBoeuf 2½.10	

Snurge finished first 3 lengths ahead of
Intimiste. However, after a stewards
inquiry Snurge was found to have caused
interference to Intimiste and the
placings were reversed

7/10 Dr Somerville, 5/2 Houmayoun and
Mahshari, 17/2 Comte du Bourg, 12/1
Snurge, 16/1 INTIMISTE, 17/1 Anna's
Honor, 19/1 Noble Ballerina, 29/1 Anidal,
Guiza

N. Incisa della Rocchetta (F. Boutin)
10 ran 2m 19.3 (Heavy)

100   JAPAN CUP (Gr 1)   1½m
£589,162   Tokyo   26 November

	Horlicks (NZ) 6-8-9	
	LO'Sullivan 1	
	Oguri Cap (Jpn) 4-9-0	
	KMinai nk.2	
57	**Pay The Butler (USA)** 5-9-0	
	CMcCarron 3.3	
	Super Creek (Jpn) 4-9-0	
	YTake nk.4	
	Hawkster (USA) 3-8-9	
	RBaze 1.5	
70*	Ibn Bey 5-9-0 TQuinn 2.6	
	Running Free (Jpn) 6-9-0	
	YSuguwara nk.7	
	Kiri Power (Jpn) 4-9-0	
	YShibata 1.8	
	Fresh Voice (Jpn) 6-9-0	
	HMatoba ns.9	
95*	Top Sunrise (Fr) 4-9-0	
	FHead ns.10	
	Inari One (Jpn) 5-9-0	
	MShibata 2.11	
92*	Assatis (USA) 4-9-0	
	RCochrane 1.12	
	Bamboo Memory (Jpn) 4-9-0	
	MMatsunaga 1½.13	
85*	Carroll House 4-9-0	
	MKinane 4.14	
	Rosita (Jpn) 3-8-5	
	TNozaki dist.15	

36/10 Super Creek, 43/10 Oguri Cap,
46/10 Hawkster, 63/10 Ibn Bey, 76/10
Pay The Butler, 13/2 Assatis, 79/10
Carroll House, 13/1 Inari One, 19/1
HORLICKS, 25/1 Top Sunrise, 37/1 Kiri
Power, 42/1 Rosita, 48/1 Bamboo
Memory, 62/1 Fresh Voice, 84/1
Running Free

G. W de Gruchy (D. O'Sullivan) 15 ran
2m22.2 (Firm)

TRAINERS

The figures in brackets are the number of winners each trainer has had in Britain over the past five seasons from 1985 to 1989 inclusive. Quarters and telephone numbers are given.

Akehurst, R. P. J.   (6:16:27:25:32)
Epsom   Epsom (03727) 27596
Allan, A. R.   (0:0:1:1:1)
Cornhill-on-Tweed
          Crookham (089082) 581
Allen, C. N.   (—:—:2:7:8)
Newmarket
          Newmarket (0638) 76767 and
          667870
Alston, E. J.   (2:1:1:10:1)
Preston   Longton (0772) 612120
Anderson, P. J.   (—:—:—:—:0)
Church Stretton
          Longville (06943) 387
Arbuthnot, D. W. P.   (13:8:17:3:10)
Newbury   Newbury (0635) 578427
Armstrong, R. W.   (22:31:25:36:20)
Newmarket
          Newmarket (0638) 663333 or
          663334
Armytage, Mrs S.   (—:—:—:0:1)
East Ilsley   East Ilsley (063 528) 203
Arthur, P. J.   (—:2:4:5:6)
Abingdon   Abingdon (0235) 850669
Austin, C. A.   (2:3:0:0:1)
Wokingham
          Wokingham (0734) 786 425
Avison, M.   (—:—:—:1:0)
Nawton   Helmsley (0439) 71672

Bailey, A.   (11:19:30:21:9)
Newmarket
          Newmarket (0638) 661537
Bailey, K. C.   (0:1:0:0:1)
Lambourn   Lambourn (0488) 71483
Bailey, P. G.   (0:1:2:2:0)
Salisbury
          Amesbury (0980) 22964 (home) and
          22682 (office)
Baker, J. H.   (0:0:0:2:0)
Dulverton
          Bampton (0398) 31646 (home) and
          31355 (stables)
Balding, G. B.   (4:13:13:7:15)
Weyhill   Weyhill (026 477) 2278
Balding, I. A.   (59:48:31:43:41)
Kingsclere   Kingsclere (0635) 298210
Balding, J.   (—:—:1:2:5)
Doncaster
          Doncaster (0302) 710096 and
          Retford (0777) 818407 (stable)
Barons, D. H.   (0:0:0:0:0)
Kingsbridge
          Kingsbridge (0548) 550326 and
          550411
Barratt, L. J.   (1:2:0:4:0)
Oswestry   Queens Head (069188) 209
Barron, T. D.   (26:13:19:18:19)
Thirsk   Thirsk (0845) 587 435

Barrow, A. K.   (0:0:—:—:0)
Bridgwater   Bridgwater (0278) 732522
Bastiman, R.   (—:—:1:3:7)
Wetherby   Wetherby (0937) 63050
Beaumont, P.   (—:—:—:0:0)
Brandsby   Brandsby (03475) 208
Beever, C. R.   (—:—:—:—:0)
Doncaster   Doncaster (0302) 725939
Bell, C. J.   (—:—:0:0:0)
Nantwich   Nantwich (0270) 623604
          and carphone (0836) 273153
Bell, M. L. W.   (—:—:—:—:18)
Newmarket
          Newmarket (0638) 666567
Bennett, J. A.   (—:—:0:0:0)
Sparsholt   Childrey (023559) 635
Bennett, R. A.   (—:—:—:0:1)
Maidenhead
          Maidenhead (0628) 30290
Benstead, C. J.   (13:14:12:14:9)
Epsom   Ashtead (037 22) 73152
Bentley, W.   (7:1:8:0:1)
Middleham Wensleydale (0969) 22289
Berry, J.   (19:21:31:70:92)
Lancaster   Forton (0524) 791179
Bethell, J. D. W.   (4:6:2:4:11)
Didcot   Abingdon (0235) 834333
Bevan, P. J.   (5:2:4:0:0)
Kingstone
          Dapple Heath (088 921) 647 (yard)
          or 670 (home)
Bill, T. T.   (1:0:1:0:0)
Ashby-de-la-Zouch
          Ashby-de-la-Zouch (0530) 415881
Bishop, K. S.   (0:0:0:0:0)
Bridgwater   Holford (027 874) 255
Blanshard, M. T. W.   (15:4:5:3:8)
Lambourn   Lambourn (0488) 71091
Blockley, P. A.   (—:0:0:3:2)
Rise Park
          Hornsea (0964) 542583 (home) and
          562440 (stable)
Blum, G.   (3:8:2:3:1)
Newmarket
          Newmarket (0638) 713916
Blundell J. W.   (—:—:—:0:0)
Grimsby
          Grimsby (0472) 840256 and 840494
Bolton, M. J.   (0:3:0:0:0)
East Grinstead
          Shrewton (0980) 621059
Booth, C. B. B.   (8:5:6:7:4)
Flaxton
          Whitwell-on-the-Hill (065 381) 586
Bosley, J. R.   (2:2:1:0:0)
Bampton
          Bampton Castle (0993) 850 212
Boss, R.   (17:21:19:23:22)
Newmarket
          Newmarket (0638) 661335

1040

Bottomley, J. F.   (—:—:—:—:3)
Malton   Malton (0653) 693511
Bowden, P. A.   (—:0:1:0:0)
Brokerswood
          Westbury (0373) 864665
Bower, Miss L. J.   (—:2:0:0:0)
Alresford   Bramdean (096 279) 552
Bowring, S. R.   (—:0:2:7:2)
Mansfield   Mansfield (0623) 822451
Bradley, J. M.   (1:0:2:2:1)
Chepstow   Chepstow (029 12) 2486
Bradstock, M. F.   (—:—:—:0:0)
East Garston
          Great Shefford (048839) 258
Brassey, K. M.   (25:17:14:16:13)
Lambourn   Lambourn (0488) 71508
Bravery, C. V.   (—:—:—:0:1)
Jevington   Polegate (032 12) 3662
Brazington, R. G.   (0:0:0:0:0)
Redmarley, Glos.
          Staunton Court (045 284) 384
Brennan, O.   (0:1:1:2:0)
Newark   Caunton (063 686) 332
Bridger, J. J.   (2:0:0:0:0)
Chichester   Liphook (0428) 722528
Bridgwater, K. S.   (0:2:0:1:0)
Solihull   Lapworth (05643) 2895
Brittain, C. E.   (51:39:38:40:36)
Newmarket
          Newmarket (0638) 663739 and
                              664347
Brittain, M. A.   (22:24:57:44:25)
Warthill
          Stamford Bridge (0759) 71472 and
                              71781
Brooks, C. P. E.   (—:—:—:0:1)
Lambourn
          Lambourn (0488) 72077 (office) and
                              72909 (home)
Brooks, W. G. A.   (—:2:5:4:5)
Lambourn   Lambourn (0488) 72140
Brown, A. D.   (—:—:—:0:0:0)
Kirkbymoorside
          Pickering (075 1) 31066
Browne, D. W. P.   (—:—:—:—:—)
Lambourn
          Lambourn (0488) 39706 and
          carphone (0860) 398166
Burchell, W. D.   (—:0:0:0:1)
Ebbw Vale   Ebbw Vale (0495) 302551
Burgoyne, P. V. J. P.   (0:0:3:0:0)
Sparsholt   Childrey (023 559) 688
Butler, P.   (2:1:0:0:0)
Lewes   Plumpton (0273) 890124
Bycroft, N.   (6:6:10:10:2)
Brandsby   Brandsby (034 75) 641

Caldwell, T. H.   (—:—:—:—:0)
Warrington   Arley (056585) 275
Callaghan, N. A.   (15:25:20:27:29)
Newmarket
          Newmarket (0638) 664040
Calver, P.   (2:9:7:7:7)
Ripon   Ripon (0765) 700313
Camacho, M. J. C.   (7:6:6:8:12)
Malton   Malton (0653) 694901

Cambidge, B. R.   (0:1:0:2:1)
Shifnal
          Weston-under-Lizard (095 276) 249
Campbell, I.   (—:—:1:4:2)
Newmarket
          Newmarket (0638) 660829
Candy, H. D. N. B.   (33:27:33:20:16)
Wantage   Uffington (036 782) 276
Carter, W. Y.   (—:—:—:2:21)
Leatherhead
          Leatherhead (0372) 377209
Casey, R. F.   (—:—:2:6:0)
Newmarket
          mobilephone (0831) 104775
Casey, W. T.   (—:2:1:3:1)
Banbury
          Banbury (0295) 711006 and 711686
Castell, M.   (—:0:0:0:0)
Knightwick   Knightwick (0886) 21538
Cecil, H. R. A.   (132:115:180:112:116)
Newmarket
          Newmarket (0638) 662192 or
                              662387 (home)
Chamberlain, N.   (0:0:1:0:0)
West Auckland
          Bishop Auckland (0388) 832 465
Champion, R.   (0:0:0:0:1)
Newmarket
          Newmarket (0638) 666546
Chapman, D. W.   (30:14:13:36:27)
Stillington · Easingwold (0347) 21683
Chapman, M. C.   (1:1:0:0:0)
Market Rasen
          Market Rasen (0673) 843663
Charles, M. J.   (—:—:0:0:0)
Warwick   Warwick (0926) 493878
Charlton, J. I. A.   (0:0:0:0:0)
Stocksfield Stocksfield (066 1) 843 247
Christian, S. P. L.   (0:0:1:1:0)
Kinnersley
          Severn Stoke (090567) 233
Clay, W.   (0:0:0:0:0)
Fulford
          Stoke-on-Trent (0782) 392 131
Codd, L. J.   (—:—:—:—:3)
Redditch   Inkberrow (0386) 793263
Cole, P. F. I.   (54:64:55:43:50)
Whatcombe
          Chaddleworth (04882) 433 or 434
Collingridge, H. J.   (3:4:6:7:12)
Newmarket
          Newmarket (0638) 665454
Cottrell, L. G.   (12:8:23:19:12)
Cullompton Kentisbeare (088 46) 320
Craig, T.   (7:4:6:1:4)
Dunbar   Dunbar (0368) 62583
Cumani, L. M.   (60:67:83:73:88)
Newmarket
          Newmarket (0638) 665432
Cundell, P. D.   (9:13:8:5:1)
Newbury   Newbury (0635) 578267
Cunningham, T. W.   (—:—:0:0:0)
Northallerton
          East Harlsey (060982) 695
Cunningham-Brown, K. O. (0:0:1:0:7)
Stockbridge   Andover (0264) 781 611
Curley, B. J.   (—:—:0:1:0)
Newmarket   Exning (063877) 645

1041

Curtis, R. (—:—:—:3:3)
Epsom (0372) 277645
Cyzer, C. A. (—:—:—:—:14)
Horsham Southwater (0403) 730255
Czerpak, J. D. (—:—:—:—:0)
Farnham
Frensham (Surrey) (025125) 3505

Davies, J. D. J. (2:0:2:0:0)
Dymchurch
Folkestone (0303) 874089
Davison, A. R. (1:1:0:2:0)
Caterham Caterham (0883) 44523
Denson, A. W. (—:—:0:0:1)
Epsom Epsom (03727) 29398
Dickin, R. (—:0:0:0:0)
Dymock Dymock (053185) 644
Dooler, J. (—:—:—:—:0)
Goole Goole (0405) 861903
Douglas-Home, J. T. A. (6:2:3:4:1)
Wantage Abingdon (0235) 833247
Dow, S. L. (—:3:0:6:7)
Guildford
Epsom (03727) 21490 (stable) and
Ashtead (03722) 75878 (home)
Dunlop, J. L. (62:106:61:66:61)
Arundel
Arundel (0903) 882194 (office) or
882106 (home)
Durr, F. (22:4:10:2:10)
Newmarket
Newmarket (0638) 662090

Earnshaw, R. (—:—:0:0:3)
Harrogate Harrogate (0423) 567790
Easterby, M. H. (29:49:68:64:57)
Malton
Kirby Misperton (065 386) 600
Easterby, M. W. (31:33:12:25:19)
Sheriff Hutton
Sheriff Hutton (03477) 368
Eckley, M. W. (3:4:5:4:1)
Ludlow Brimfield (058 472) 372
Edwards, J. A. C. (1:1:5:6:1)
Ross-on-Wye
Harewood End (098987) 259 and
639 (home)
Eldin, E. (11:17:6:10:7)
Newmarket
Newmarket (0638) 662036 or
663217
Ellerby, M. W. (—:0:0:0:1)
Pickering Pickering (0751) 74092
Elsey, C. C. (—:—:—:—:2)
Lambourn Lambourn (0488) 71242
Elsey, C. W. C. (12:7:13:10:10)
Malton Malton (0653) 693149
Elsworth, D. R. C. (22:31:31:28:35)
Fordingbridge
Rockbourne (07253) 220 (home) or
528 (office)
Enright, G. P. (—:—:—:0:1)
Haywards Heath
Bolney (044482) 761
Etherington, J. (25:16:11:11:18)
Malton Malton (0653) 692842

Etherington, T. J. (—:—:—:—:0)
Beare Green Newdigate (030677) 529
Eustace, J. M. P. (—:—:—:—:0)
Newmarket
Evans, P. D. (—:—:—:—:0)
Welshpool Trewern (093874) 288

Fairgrieve, W. D. (—:—:—:—:0)
Galashiels Selkirk (0750) 22110
Fairhurst, T. (12:16:8:10:11)
Middleham Wensleydale (0969) 23362
Fanshawe, J. R. (—:—:—:—:0)
Newmarket
Newmarket (0638) 660153 and
664523
Feilden, P. J. (1:2:0:1:7)
Newmarket Exning (063877) 637
Felgate, P. S. (5:11:8:17:12)
Melton Mowbray
Melton Mowbray (0664) 812019
Fetherston-Godley, M. J.
(—:9:6:10:2)
East Ilsley East Ilsley (063 528) 250
Ffitch-Heyes, J. R. (0:0:2:0:0)
Lewes Brighton (0273) 477529
Fisher, R. F. (7:2:4:2:1)
Ulverston
Ulverston (0229) 55664 and
55819 (office)
FitzGerald, J. G. (23:17:7:20:18)
Malton Malton (0653) 692718
FitzGerald, Lord J. (—:11:11:9:11)
Newmarket
Newmarket (0638) 660605
Forsey, B. (0:0:0:1:0)
Crowcombe Crowcombe (098 48) 270
Forster, T. A. (0:0:0:0:0)
Letcombe Bassett
Wantage (023 57) 3092
Fox, J. C. (0:2:0:1:3)
Amesbury Shrewton (0980) 620 861
Francis, M. E. D. (7:7:8:8:4)
Lambourn Lambourn (0488) 71700
Francis, R. B. (3:0:0:0:0)
Malpas
Tilston (082 98) 208 (stable) and
515 (home)
Frost, R. G. (—:0:1:0:0)
Buckfastleigh
Buckfastleigh (03644) 2267

Gandolfo, D. R. (0:0:0:0:0)
Wantage Wantage (023 57) 3242
Gaselee, N. A. D. C. (0:0:1:3:2)
Lambourn Lambourn (0488) 71503
Gifford, J. T. (0:0:0:0:0)
Findon (0903) 872226
Glover, J. A. (1:3:8:12:3)
Worksop
Worksop (0909) 475962 or
475425 (stable)
Gosden, J. H. M. (—:—:—:—:28)
Newmarket Newmarket (0638)
669944
Gracey, G. G. (0:1:0:0:0)
Caterham Caterham (0883) 40922

1042

Graham, N. A.   (—:—:—:11:—)
Newmarket
          Newmarket (0638) 665202
Green, Miss Z. A.   (0:0:0:0:0)
Carlisle   Low Ireby (09657) 219
Grissell, D. M.   (0:0:0:—:0)
Heathfield   Brightling (042 482) 241
Gubby, B.   (3:0:0:1:0)
Bagshot   Bagshot (0276) 63282 and
          71030 (evenings)
Guest, R.   (—:—:—:—:7)
Newmarket
          Newmarket (0638) 661508

Haggas, W. J.   (—:0:17:14:16)
Newmarket
          Newmarket (0638) 667013
Haigh, W. W.   (4:7:7:3:2)
Malton   Malton (0653) 694428
Haine, Mrs D. E. S.   (—:—:—:0:1)
Newmarket   Exning (063877) 719
Haldane, J. S.   (1:1:1:1:0)
Kelso   Kelso (0573) 24956
Hall, Miss S. E.   (19:12:9:7:6)
Middleham   Wensleydale (0969)
          40223
Hallett, T. B.   (0:4:0:0:0)
Saltash   Saltash (075 55) 6829
Hanbury, B.   (20:24:31:40:41)
Newmarket
          Newmarket (0638) 663193 (stable)
          and Wickhambrook (0440) 820396
          (home)
Hanley, D. L.   (1:1:1:0:0)
Marlborough
          Marlborough (0672) 40646 and
          40130
Hannon, R. M.   (37:56:33:43:53)
Marlborough
          Collingbourne Ducis (026 485) 254
Hanson, J.   (—:3:1:1:2)
Wetherby   Wetherby (0937) 62841 and
          66776 (yard)
Harris, J. L.   (1:0:0:0:0)
Melton Mowbray   Harby (0949) 60671
Harris, P. W.   (—:0:0:0:2)
Berkhamsted
          Hemel Hempstead (0442) 842 480
Harris, S. T.   (0:0:0:0:0)
Amersham   Chesham (0494) 715446
Harwood, G.   (84:112:67:73:109)
Pulborough   Pulborough (079 82)
          3011 or 3012
Hastings-Bass, W. E. R. H.
          (15:30:15:31:25)
West Ilsley
Haynes, M. J.   (10:5:10:11:6)
Epsom   Burgh Heath (073 73) 51140
Hayward, P. A.   (—:—:2:0:1)
Netheravon   Netheravon (09807) 585
Henderson, N. J.   (0:0:0:0:0)
Lambourn   Lambourn (0488) 72259
Hern, W. R.   (53:45:36:30:45)
West Ilsley
          East Ilsley (063 528) 219 and 251
Herries, Lady   (0:2:6:6:6)
Arundel   Patching (090674) 421

Hetherton, J.   (—:—:—:—:2)
Malton   Malton (0653) 696778
Hide, A. G.   (5:9:8:8:11)
Newmarket
          Newmarket (0638) 662063
Hill, C. J.   (2:3:2:5:3)
Barnstaple   Barnstaple (0271) 42048
Hills, B. W.   (68:55:96:93:73)
Marlborough
          Marlborough (0672) 54901 (office)
          and 54871 (home)
Hills, J. W.   (—:—:13:14:15)
Lambourn   Lambourn (0488) 71548
Hoad, R. P. C.   (1:1:0:1:0)
Lewes   Brighton (0273) 477124
Hobbs, P. J.   (—:0:0:0:0)
Watchet   Washford (0984) 40366
Hodges, R. J.   (1:5:2:8:12)
Somerton
          Charlton Mackrell (045822) 3922
Holden, W.   (5:6:5:4:3)
Newmarket   Exning (063 877) 384
Holder, R. J.   (10:8:13:8:17)
Portbury Pill (027 581) 2192 and 9881
Hollinshead, R.   (40:28:28:33:30)
Upper Longdon
          Armitage (0543) 490298 and 490490
Holmes, C. J.   (0:0:0:0:0)
Gerrards Cross
          Chalfont St Giles (02407) 5964
Holt, L. J.   (7:9:9:6:13)
Tunworth Basingstoke (0256) 463376
Horgan, C. A.   (21:15:1:6:8)
Billingbear
          Winkfield Row (0344) 425382
Houghton, R. F. J.   (17:34:26:36:24)
Blewbury   Blewbury (0235) 850480
Howling, P.   (—:—:5:9:5)
Brook
          Haslemere (0428) 792996 (home)
          and 794065 (stable)
Hudson, J. P.   (—:—:—:—:10)
Lambourn   Lambourn (0488) 71485
Huffer, G. A.   (30:17:23:12:16)
Newmarket
          Newmarket (0638) 667997

Incisa, D. E.   (3:1:1:2:0)
Leyburn   Wensleydale (0969) 40653
Ivory, K. T.   (7:9:18:7:7)
Radlett   Radlett (092 76) 6081

Jackson, C. F. C.   (—:0:3:2:0)
Malvern   Malvern (088684) 463
James, A. P.   (0:0:0:0:0)
Bosbury
          Bosbury (053186) 264
James, C. J.   (2:1:4:6:1)
Newbury
          Great Shefford (048 839) 280
James, M. B. C.   (2:1:0:2:0)
Whitchurch   Whitchurch (0948) 4067
Jarvis, M. A.   (21:30:19:31:28)
Newmarket
          Newmarket (0638) 661702 and
          662519
Jarvis, W.   (12:16:27:26:32)
Newmarket

Newmarket (0638) 669873 (office)
or 662677 (home)
Jefferson, J. M.   (4:2:5:4:1)
Malton   Malton (0653) 697225
Jenkins, J. R.   (2:1:8:15:7)
Royston
Royston (0763) 41141 (office) and
46611 (home)
Jermy, D. C.   (1:0:0:0:0)
Warminster
Warminster (0985) 213155
Johnson, J. H.   (0:0:0:0:0)
Bishop Auckland
Bishop Auckland (0388) 762113 and
730872
Johnston, M. S.   (—:—:1:5:15)
Middleham Wensleydale (0969) 22237
Jones, A. W.   (2:1:1:0:1)
Oswestry   Oswestry (0691) 659 720
Jones, D. H.   (11:13:4:6:2)
Pontypridd Pontypridd (0443) 202515
Jones, Mrs G. E.   (—:—:—:0:0)
Upton-on-Severn
Upton-on-Severn (06846) 2691
Jones, G. H.   (—:—:0:0:0)
Tenbury Wells
Leysters (056887) 676 and
305 (stable)
Jones, H. Thomson   (55:43:30:41:37)
Newmarket
Newmarket (0638) 664884
Jones, P. J.   (—:0:0:0:0)
Marlborough
Lockeridge (067286) 427
Jones, T. M.   (0:0:0:4:0)
Guildford   Shere (048 641) 2604
Jones, T. Thomson   (—:—:—:—:6)
Lambourn
Lambourn (0488) 71596 and 72933
Jordan, F. T. J.   (0:1:3:1:3)
Leominster
Steens Bridge (056 882) 281
Juckes, R. T.   (—:0:0:0:0)
Abberley, Worcs.
Great Witley (0299) 896471

Kelleway, P. A.   (17:18:12:16:13)
Newmarket
Newmarket (0638) 661461
Kelly, G. P.   (—:—:0:0:0)
Sheriff Hutton
Sheriff Hutton (03477) 518
Kemp, W. T.   (—:1:0:0:0)
Ashford, Kent   Ashford (0233) 72525
Kernick, N.   (0:0:0:0:0)
Kingsteignton
Newton Abbot (0626) 65899
Kersey, T.   (0:0:0:0:1)
West Melton
Rotherham (0709) 873166
Kettlewell, S. E.   (—:—:1:0:0)
Middleham Wensleydale (0969) 40295
King, Miss A. L. M.   (0:1:3:0:0)
Stratford-on-Avon
Stratford-on-Avon (0789) 298346
King, J. S.   (0:1:2:0:4)
Swindon Broad Hinton (0793) 731481

Knight, Mrs A. J.   (—:—:0:0:0)
Cullompton   Hemyock (0823) 680959

Leach, M. R.   (2:0:0:1:0)
Newark
Fenton Claypole (063684) 518
Leach, P. S.   (—:—:—:—:0)
Taunton
Bishop's Lydeard (0823) 433249
Leadbetter, S. J.   (0:0:0:0:0)
Ladykirk
Berwick-Upon-Tweed (0289) 82519
Lee, A. N.   (—:—:—:2:8)
Newmarket
Newmarket (0638) 662734 (home)
and 669783 (stable)
Lee, D.   (—:0:0:0:0)
Pickering   Pickering (0751) 32425
Lee, F. H.   (—:—:2:8:27)
Wilmslow
Wilmslow (0625) 529672 and
533250 (stud)
Lee, R. A.   (—:—:0:0:0)
Presteigne
Presteigne (0544) 267672 and
mobilephone (0836) 537145
Leigh, J. P.   (1:0:3:3:0)
Willoughton, Lincs.
Hemswell (042 773) 210
Lewis, G.   (29:25:25:32:23)
Epsom
Ashtead (037 22) 77662 or 77366
Liddle, P.   (—:—:—:—:0)
Chester-le-Street
Wearside 091-410-2072
Long, J. E.   (0:0:1:0:0)
Plumpton   Plumpton (0273) 890244

Macauley, Mrs N. J.   (2:4:7:6:12)
Sproxton
Grantham (0476) 860578 and
860090 (office)
Mackie, W. J. W.   (0:1:0:9:6)
Derby   Sudbury (028378) 604
Madgwick, M. J.   (5:2:1:2:3)
Denmead   Horndean (0705) 258313
Makin, P. J.   (24:19:18:24:27)
Ogbourne Maisey
Marlborough (0672) 52973
Marks, J.   (4:3:3:1:2)
Lambourn   Lambourn (0488) 71767
Matthews, I. V.   (—:7:12:21:10)
Newmarket
Newmarket (0638) 669637 and
662420
McCain, D.   (1:0:0:0:0)
Birkdale
Southport (0704) 66007 or 69677
McConnochie, J. C.   (—:—:—:—:0)
Stratford-on-Avon
Alderminster (078987) 607
McCormack, M.   (22:16:7:4:12)
Wantage   Childrey (023 559) 433
McCourt, M.   (14:8:4:1:3)
Letcombe Regis
Wantage (023 57) 4456

McLean, B. (0:0:0:0:0)
Morpeth   Felton (067 087) 478
and 314 (home)
McMahon, B. A. (19:8:6:20:19)
Tamworth   Tamworth (0827) 62901
Mellor, S. T. E. (9:8:3:2:2)
Wanborough   Swindon (0793) 790230
Millman, B. R. (—:—:—:—:—)
Cullompton
Mitchell, N. R. (0:0:0:0:0)
Sherborne   Dorchester (0305) 251429
Mitchell, P. (15:9:5:12:14)
Epsom   Ashtead (037 22) 73729
Mitchell, P. (Pat) K. (8:4:6:2:6)
Newmarket
Newmarket (0638) 660013
Moffatt, D. (1:3:2:0:2)
Cartmel
Cartmel (05395) 36689 and 36236
Monteith, P. (0:1:2:3:1)
Rosewell   Edinburgh (031-440) 2309
Moore, A. (8:5:1:0:4)
Woodingdean   Brighton (0273) 681679
Moore, G. M. (7:10:18:12:18)
Middleham   Wensleydale (0969) 23823
Morgan, B. C. (3:1:6:6:3)
Barton-under-Needwood
Hoar Cross (028 375) 304
Morgan, K. A. (0:0:0:0:0)
Waltham-on-the-Wolds
Waltham-on-the-Wolds (066478) 711
Morley, M. F. D. (14:16:19:30:26)
Newmarket
Newmarket (0638) 667175
Morris, D. (—:—:—:—:—)
Newmarket
Morris, W. G. (1:0:0:0:0)
Hartlebury   Hartlebury (0299) 250686
Moubarak, M. Y. (—:—:—:1:1)
Newmarket
Newmarket (0638) 666553
Muldoon, S. J. (—:—:1:9:4)
Malton   Malton (0653) 693795 and
696409 (office) and
(0836) 652729 (mobile)
Mulhall, J. L. (2:2:0:0:0)
York   York (0904) 706321
Murphy, M. P. F. (—:—:—:—:0)
Bury St Edmunds
Murray-Smith, D. J. G. (1:4:2:9:8)
Upper Lambourn
Lambourn (0488) 71041
Musson, W. J. (19:21:14:10:6)
Newmarket
Newmarket (0638) 663371

Naughton, M. P. (2:3:7:8:19)
Richmond, N. Yorks
Richmond (0748) 2803
Nelson, C. R. (18:26:26:22:19)
Lambourn   Lambourn (0488) 71391
Nicholson, D. (1:1:0:0:0)
Condicote
Stow-on-the-Wold (0451) 30417
Norton, J. (—:0:0:2:0)
Barnsley   Barnsley (0226) 387633

Norton, S. G. (35:21:33:33:11)
Barnsley   Wakefield (0924) 830450
and 830406 (office)

O'Donoghue, J. (0:0:0:0:0)
Reigate   Reigate (073 72) 45241
O'Gorman, W. A. (15:20:10:24:9)
Newmarket
Newmarket (0638) 663330
Old, J. A. B. (0:0:1:1:0)
Ditcheat   Ditcheat (074986) 656 and
carphone (0836) 721459
Oldroyd, G. R. (1:3:1:2:0)
Malton
Malton (0653) 695991 (home) and
Burythorpe (065385) 224 (stable)
O'Leary, R. M. (—:—:0:1:2)
Malton Kirby Misperton (065386) 684
and 404
Oliver, Miss S. (—:—:0:1:0)
Suckley   Suckley (08864) 539 and 271
Oliver, Mrs S. (—:1:1:0:1)
Himley
Wombourne (0902) 892648 (stable)
and 892017 (home)
O'Neill, J. J. (—:0:0:1:0)
Penrith   Skelton (08534) 555
O'Neill, M. J. (—:—:—:—:9)
Lydiate
Liverpool 051-531 9616 (office),
6887 (home) and 526 9115 (evening)
O'Neill, O. (0:0:0:1:0)
Cheltenham
Bishops Cleeve (024 267) 3275
O'Shea, J. G. M. (—:—:0:0:0)
Droitwich   Hartlebury (0299) 250905
O'Sullivan, R. J. (—:—:—:0:6)
Bogner   Pagham (02432) 67563
Owen, E. H. (0:0:0:0:1)
Denbigh
Llandyrnog (08244) 264 and 356

Palling, B. (0:2:1:1:4)
Cowbridge   Cowbridge (044 63) 2089
Parker, C. (0:0:0:0:0)
Lockerbie   Kettleholme (05765) 232
Parkes, J. E. (1:0:0:1:6)
Malton   Malton (0653) 697570
Payne, J. W. (—:2:9:9:5)
Newmarket
Newmarket (0638) 668675
Payne, S. G. (—:—:—:—:0)
Carlisle   Aspatria (0965) 20010
Peacock, R. E. (0:2:0:2:3)
Tarporley   Tarporley (082 93) 2716
Pearce, J. N. (—:—:3:3:5)
Newmarket
Newmarket (0638) 664669
Pearce, W. J. (10:7:8:18:23)
Hambleton   Thirsk (0845) 597373
Perrett, A. C. J. (0:0:0:0:0)
Cheltenham
Andoversford (0242) 820244 and
820841
Piggott, Mrs S. E. (—:—:1:17:33)
Newmarket
Newmarket (0638) 660229

1045

Pipe, M. C. (8:4:16:5:2)
Wellington, Somerset
Craddock (0884) 40715
Pitman, Mrs J. S. (0:0:0:2:2)
Lambourn   Lambourn (0488) 71714
Popham, C. L. (—:—:0:0:0)
Bishop's Lydeard
Bishop's Lydeard (0823) 432769
Potts, A. W. (1:1:0:0:0)
Barton-on-Humber
Saxby All Saints (065 261) 750
Preece, W. G. (—:0:1:2:0)
Telford   Uppington (095 286) 249
Prescott, Sir Mark (17:39:26:34:40)
Newmarket
Newmarket (0638) 662117
Price, G. H. (3:5:1:10:1)
Leominster
Steens Bridge (056 882) 235
Pritchard-Gordon, G. A.
(38:37:35:20:16)
Newmarket
Newmarket (0638) 662824
Pritchard, P. A. (—:—:—:0:0)
Shipston-on-Stour
Tysoe (029588) 689

Ramsden, Mrs L. E. (4:—:11:14:32)
Sandhutton   Thirsk (0845) 587226
Reveley, Mrs G. (12:6:20:12:15)
Malton   Malton (0653) 600295
Richards, G. W. (0:0:1:1:0)
Greystoke   Greystoke (085 33) 392
Richmond, B. A. (0:0:1:0:0)
Wellingore   Lincoln (0522) 810578
Ringer, D. J. (—:—:—:0:0)
Newmarket
Newmarket (0638) 662653
Roberts, J. D. (0:0:0:0:1)
Tiverton   Bampton (0398) 31626
Robinson, M. H. B. (—:—:1:0:0)
Wantage   Wantage (0235) 835050
Robinson, W. R. (0:0:0:0:0)
Scarborough
Scarborough (0723) 862162
Robson, A. M. (2:2:1:3:5)
Middleham Wensleydale (0969) 40431
Roe, C. G. A. M. (—:—:0:0:0)
Chalford   Brimscombe (0453) 885487
Ryan, M. J. (23:33:29:22:13)
Newmarket
Newmarket (0638) 664172

Sanders, Miss B. V. J. (—:1:5:14:7)
Epsom   Ashtead (03722) 78453
Sayers, J. B. (—:—:—:0:0)
Findon   Findon (090671) 2610
Scargill, Dr J. D. (—:—:—:9:8)
Newmarket
Newmarket (0638) 663254
Scott, A. A. (—:—:—:—:24)
Newmarket
Newmarket (0638) 661998
Scudamore, M. J. (0:0:0:0:0)
Hoarwithy   Carey (043 270) 253

Semple, I. (—:—:—:—:0)
Crossford
Carluke (0555) 71994 (office),
50910 (home) and 50660
Sharpe, Mrs N. S. A. (—:—:0:0:0)
Leominster   Leominster (0568) 2673
Shaw, J. R. (—:6:4:1:2)
Newmarket
Newmarket (0638) 661680
Sherwood, O. M. C. (0:0:0:2:0)
Upper Lambourn
Lambourn (0488) 71411
Siddall, Miss L. C. (3:7:2:9:8)
York Appleton Roebuck (090 484) 291
Simpson, R. (9:14:14:8:7)
Upper Lambourn
Lambourn (0488) 72688
Smart, B. (—:0:0:0:0)
Lambourn   Lambourn (0488) 71632
Smith, A. (2:1:1:3:1)
Beverley   Beverley (0482) 882520
Smith, D. (15:20:16:14:15)
Bishop Auckland
Bishop Auckland (0388) 603317 and
606180
Smith, J. P. (0:0:2:0:1)
Rugeley   Burntwood (054 36) 6587
Smyly, R. M. (4:6:2:3:1)
Lambourn   Lambourn (0488) 71408
Smyth, R. V. (17:9:6:12:10)
Epsom   Epsom (037 27) 20053
Spares, C. W. (0:0:3:2:0)
Aslockton   Whatton (0949) 50099
Spearing, J. L. (5:5:5:3:8)
Alcester
Bidford-on-Avon (0789) 772639
Stephenson, W. A. (6:4:1:0:0)
Bishop Auckland
Rushyford (0388) 720213 and
720432 (hostel)
Stevens, B. (4:7:1:0:2)
Winchester
Winchester (0962) 883030
Stewart, A. C. (22:26:37:40:30)
Newmarket
Newmarket (0638) 667323
Storey, W. L. (0:3:1:0:0)
Consett   Edmundbyers (0207) 55259
Stoute, M. R. (120:76:105:99:117)
Newmarket
Newmarket (0638) 663801
Stringer, A. P. (—:—:—:—:2)
Carlton Husthwaite
Thirsk (0845) 401329
Stubbs, R. W. (7:10:9:12:8)
Newmarket
Newmarket (0638) 560014
Sutcliffe, J. R. E. (17:16:13:12:17)
Epsom   Ashtead (037 22) 72825

Tate, F. M. (0:0:0:0:0)
Kidderminster
Chaddesley Corbett (056 283) 243
Thom, D. T. (7:7:12:10:6)
Newmarket   Exning (063 877) 288
Thompson, R. (3:0:2:0:3)
Grantham
Castle Bytham (0780) 410812

Thompson, Ronald (6:6:8:7:5)
Doncaster   Doncaster (0302) 842 857,
845904 and 840174
Thompson, V. (0:0:0:0:0)
Alnwick   Embleton (066 576) 272
Thorne, Miss J. C. (—:0:0:0:1)
Bridgwater   Holford (027 874) 216
Thorner, G. E. (0:0:0:0:0)
Letcombe Regis
Wantage (023 57) 3003
Thornton, C. W. (15:5:14:15:12)
Middleham
Wensleydale (0969) 23350
Tinkler, C. H. (20:21:31:24:34)
Malton   Malton (0653) 695981
Tinkler, N. D. (14:30:31:24:24)
Malton
Burythorpe (065 385) 245 and 512
Toller, J. A. R. (4:7:15:6:7)
Newmarket
Newmarket (0638) 668503
Tompkins, M. H. (17:19:24:16:44)
Newmarket
Newmarket (0638) 661434
Topley, D. H. (—:—:—:—:1)
Esh   Wearside 091-373 5460 (office),
0312 (home) and 091-384 0989
Tree, A. J. (40:35:32:30:29)
Beckhampton
Avebury (067 23) 204 and 244
Trietline, C. C. (0:0:0:0:0)
Welford-on-Avon
Stratford-on-Avon (0789) 750 294
Tucker, D. C. (0:2:0:0:0)
Frome   Frome (0373) 62383
Tucker, D. R. (0:0:1:0:0)
Cullompton   Hemyock (0823) 680159
Turnell, A. (1:1:1:2:4)
East Hendred
East Hendred (0235 833) 297
Turner, W. G. (0:0:—:0:0)
Tavistock   Mary Tavy (082 281) 237
Turner, W. (Bill) G. M.
(2:1:5:3:6)
Corton Denham
Corton Denham (096322) 523
Twiston-Davies, N. A. (—:—:—:—:0)
Cheltenham
Guiting Power (04515) 278

Usher, M. D. I. (19:16:15:8:14)
East Garston
Lambourn (0488) 398953/4 (office)
and 71307 (home)

Voorspuy, R. (1:2:3:2:0)
Polegate   Polegate (032 12) 7133

Wainwright, J. S. (—:—:2:2:4)
Malton   Burythorpe (065385) 537
Wall, C. F. (—:—:9:13:9)
Newmarket
Newmarket (0638) 661999
Walwyn, P. T. (42:43:36:30:35)
Lambourn   Lambourn (0488) 71347

Wardle, I. P. (0:0:0:1:0)
Newmarket
Newmarket (0638) 667320
Waring, Mrs B. H. (0:1:0:2:1)
Malmesbury   Crudwell (066 67) 238
Watson, F. (1:0:0:0:1)
Sedgefield   Sedgefield (0740) 20582
Watts, J. W. (34:24:32:23:24)
Richmond   Richmond (0748) 850444
Weaver, R. J. (—:—:0:—:0)
Leicester   Markfield (0530) 243105
Webber, J. H. (0:0:0:0:0)
Banbury   Cropredy (0295) 750226
and 750466 (stable)
and mobilephone (0836) 580129
Weymes, F. (2:5:4:10:6)
Leyburn   Wensleydale (0969) 40229
Wharton, J. (—:—:—:9:12)
Melton Mowbray
Melton Mowbray (0664) 78334
(stable) and 65225 (home)
Wharton, Mrs R. T. (—:—:—:—:0)
Middleham
Wensleydale (0969) 23173
Wheeler, E. A. (—:0:3:4:2)
Lambourn   Lambourn (0488) 71650
Whitaker, R. M. (11:27:33:49:29)
Wetherby   Leeds (0532) 892265 and
Wetherby (0937) 62122
White, J. R. (—:—:—:—:0:5)
Wendover   Wendover (0296) 623387
White, K. B. (1:0:2:1:0)
Craven Arms   Munslow (058 476) 200
Whitfield, Miss A. J. (—:—:—:—:0)
Lambourn   Lambourn (0488) 72342
Wigham, P. (0:2:0:0:0)
Malton   Rillington (094 42) 332
Wightman, W. G. R. (3:3:7:3:8)
Upham
Bishop's Waltham (048 93) 2565
Wildman, C. P. (5:0:3:1:3)
Salisbury
Durrington Walls (0980) 52226
Wilkinson, B. E. (0:0:0:0:0)
Middleham   Wensleydale (0969) 23385
Wilkinson, M. J. (—:0:0:0:0)
Chipping Warden
Chipping Warden (029586) 713
Williams, C. N. (1:1:1:1:2)
Newmarket
Newmarket (0638) 665116
Williams, D. L. (—:0:0:0:0)
Broadway   Broadway (0386) 852569
Williams, R. J. R. (18:25:26:18:17)
Newmarket
Newmarket (0638) 663 218
Williamson, Miss S. L. (—:—:0:0:0)
Piercebridge
Piercebridge (032574) 839
Wilson, A. J. (—:0:0:0:0)
Cheltenham
Cheltenham (0242) 244713
Wilson, D. A. (2:1:9:7:14)
Headley
Ashtead (03722) 78327 (office)
and 73839 (home)
Wilson, Capt. J. H. (3:8:5:11:8)
Preston Hesketh Bank (0772) 812780

Wilson, J. S. (4:13:7:8:13)
Ayr   Ayr (0292) 266232
Wilson, W. T. J. (—:—:—:2:0)
Newmarket
      Newmarket (0638) 661393
Wilton, Miss S. J. (—:—:—:0:0)
Stoke-on-Trent
      Stoke-on-Trent (0782) 550861
Wingrove, K. G. (—:—:—:—:0)
Rugby   Southam (092 681) 3958
Wintle, D. J. (1:0:1:0:0)
Westbury-on-Severn
      Westbury-on-Severn (045 276) 459
                         and 825
Wise, B. J. (2:2:0:0:0)
Polegate
      Polegate (032 12) 3331 and 2505
Woodhouse, R. D. E. (3:4:0:0:0)
York
      Whitwell-on-the-Hill (065 381) 637
Woodman, S. (—:—:2:0:0)
Chichester Chichester (0243) 527136
Wragg, G. (26:32:27:31:25)
Newmarket
      Newmarket (0638) 662328

Yardley, F. J. (8:1:1:1:1)
Ombersley Worcester (0905) 620477
Yeoman, D. (0:0:1:0:0)
Richmond, N. Yorks.
      Richmond (0748) 811756

The following relinquished their
licence during the season

Costello, J. J. (—:—:—:0:0)

Crump, N. F. (0:0:0:0:0)

Eddy, D. (—:—:—:0:0)

Fleming, H. (0:0:0:0:0)

Ingham, A. P. (9:7:11:5:2)

Kindersley, G. (0:4:0:0:0)

O'Donnell, D. T. (0:3:3:0:0)

Rimell, Mrs M. (1:0:0:0:0)

Rohan, H. P. (15:12:14:5:1)

Stone, K. (18:13:10:5:2)

Wharton, H. the late (1:1:3:5:1)

JOCKEYS

The figures in brackets show the number of winners each jockey has
ridden in Britain during the past five seasons from 1985 to 1989 inclusive.
Also included are telephone numbers and riding weights.

Adams, J. A. (4:2:4:1:0) 8 0
Walton-on-Thames (0932) 243913
Adams, N. M. (13:21:21:17:20) 7 7
Lambourn (0488) 72004 and
Worthing (0903) 873780 (agent)

Bacon, A. E. (2:0:6:8:8) 7 11
c/o Wensleydale (0969) 22237
Banner, M. A. (3:0:1:1:0) 8 6
Newmarket (0638) 751517
Bardwell, G. S. (1:9:27:39:9) 7 7
Newmarket (0638) 660621 (home) and
668484 (agent)
Baxter, G. E. (37:29:22:19:21) 8 1
Worthing (0903) 873780 (agent)
Berry, R. J. (—:—:—:—:0) 8 2
Ashstead (0372) 386167
Birch, M. (46:53:92:95:91) 8 3
Hovingham (065 382) 578 and
carphone (0860) 245768
Bleasdale, J. (15:7:13:11:6) 8 0
Bedale (0677) 22222 and

Wensleydale (0969) 23350 and
Richmond (0748) 5640 (agent)
Bloomfield, P. S. (1:3:12:14:10) ... 8 3
Newmarket (0638) 731113 (home) and
667624 (agent)
Bond, A. M. (7:6:0:1:1) 8 0
Newmarket (0638) 76681
Bradshaw, K. (10:8:10:7:4) 8 1
Brennan, M. J. (1:2:0:—:0) 8 10
Brown, D. L. (5:2:0:—:0) 7 7
Rockbourne (07253) 657 (home) and
528 (office)
Brown, G. (6:5:3:0:1) 7 13
c/o Newmarket (0638) 669944
Brown, J. H. (5:14:3:3:3) 8 0
Malton (0653) 697768
Buckton, S. A. (1:0:3:0:0) 7 12
c/o Brandsby (03475) 641

Carlisle, N. A. (21:14:6:9:17) 7 7
(0827) 880652

Newmarket (0638) 666431 (agent) and
carphone (0860) 392889
Carr, J. M. (1:6:4:8:5) 8   0
Malton (0653) 692695, 693356 and
York (0904) 647213 (agent)
Carroll, J. (4:9:24:49:62) 7 13
Forton (0524) 791697 and
carphone (0836) 238602 and (agent)
Coxwold (03476) 482,
carphone (0836) 326084
Carson, W. F. H.
(125:130:100:130:138) 7 10
Newmarket (0638) 660947,
East Ilsley (063528) 348,
Cirencester (0285) 658919 and
(agent) 01-748-9746 or (0836) 315000
Carter, G. A. (37:34:50:42:45) 7 10
Newmarket (0638) 665950 (home) and
668484 (office)
Carter, J. P. (3:4:8:9:4) 7   7
Lambourn (0488) 39384 and
Rillington (09442) 419 and 8879 (agent)
Cauthen, S. M.
(195:149:197:104:163) 8   7
Abingdon (0235) 833544 and
Newmarket (0638) 768262 and
(0860) 565111 (agent's mobile)
Clark, A. S. (16:28:18:20:38) 8   0
Pulborough (07982) 3028 and (0788)
832958 (office)
Cochrane,   **R.**
(51:89:111:120:120) 8   4
Newmarket (0638) 743045
Cook, P. A. (51:41:36:33:28) 8   4
Marlborough (0672) 20265 (home) and
Worthing (0903) 873780 (agent)
Crossley, B. G. (0:11:12:9:15) 7 10
Newmarket (0638) 751367 (home) and
667624 (agent)
Cruz, A. S. (0:1:4:1:2) 8   3
01-3819318 (agent)
Curant, R. D. (9:16:16:5:0) 8   2
Hawthorn (0225) 810171

D'Arcy, P. W. (6:6:4:7:5) 7 12
Newmarket (0638) 750005 and
(agent) 76686 (24 hours) or
Witney (0993) 772671
Darley, K. P. (30:30:55:38:68) 7 13
Easingwold (0347) 22588 and
carphone (0860) 231240 and (agent)
Stamford Bridge (0759) 71586 or
carphone (0836) 753052
Dawson, S. (15:20:15:14:16) 7   7
Lambourn (0488) 72261 (home) and
Worthing (0903) 873780 (agent)
Day, N. P. (21:14:17:26:17) 8   2
Newmarket (0638) 730012 (home)
(0638) 660258 and 660811 (office)
Dicks, A. C. (0:2:1:1:0) 8   4
Bristol (0272) 519184 and
Pill (027581) 2192
Duffield, G. P. (61:94:64:77:78) ... 8   0
Newmarket (0638) 668484 (agent) and
76544 (home)
Dwyer, C. A. (13:6:6:3:2) 8   6
Newmarket (0638) 665533 (home)

Eddery, Paul A.
(50:49:37:52:44) 8   0
Newmarket (0638) 714672 and 712426
Eddery, P. J. J.
(162:176:195:183:171) 8   4
Haddenham (0844) 290282 and
201427
Elliott, R. P. (12:8:8:10:19) 8   0
Wensleydale (0969) 22884

Fallon, K. F. (—:—:—:31:27) 8   2
York (0904) 647213 (agent)
Fox, R. D. S. (27:9:20:16:11) 7   9
Newmarket (0638) 778188
Fozzard, M. G. (0:0:0:1:0) 7   7
Grantham (0476) 870178
Fry, M. J. (11:22:13:15:13) 7   7
(0737) 246416 (home) and
(0932) 243913 (agent)

Gibson, D. J. (1:2:0:16:0) 8   0
Newmarket (0638) 665512
Griffiths, S. P. (4:6:0:0:0) 7   2
Tadcaster (0937) 835541
Guest, E. J. (19:15:0:—:1) 8   6
(0524) 792367

Hayes, W. J. (0:2:0:2:2) 8   0
Lambourn (0488) 72649
Higgins, J. J. (0:—:0:—:0) 8   6
Newmarket (0638) 720723 (agent)
Hills, M. P. (45:40:75:76:77) 8   0
Newmarket (0638) 750379 and
751421 (office)
Hills, R. J. (39:42:46:52:59) 8   0
Newmarket (0638) 750379 and 751421
(office)
Hindley, M. G. (26:3:2:0:1) 8   4
Malton (0653) 693628
Hodgson, K. (33:19:4:10:5) 8   6
Malton (0653) 696651
Hood, W. (—:0:2:1:4) 8   4
Newmarket (0638) 778366
Horsfall, S. S. (3:1:3:0:0) 8   3
c/o Doncaster (0302) 710096
Howard, P. T. (—:—:—:0:0) 7   7
Newmarket (0638) 660013
Howe, N. J. (13:12:7:5:4) 7 13
Wantage (02357) 68227 (home) and
69742 (office)

James, Miss S. E. (1:2:0:0:0) 8 11
Whitchurch (0948) 4067
Johnson, E. (12:—:5:10:4) 7   8
Cirencester (0285) 5020
Johnson, I. E. (13:8:9:20:14) 8   4
Kintbury (0488) 58749
Jones, L. (2:6:2:2:0) 8   1
Andover (0264) 333520

Keightley, S. L. (5:4:4:3:6) 8 11
Newmarket (0638) 666070
Kennedy, J. B. (1:2:0:0:0) 8   2
Lambourn (0488) 72734
King, G. N. (0:7:5:0:0) 7   7
Newmarket (0638) 668163 and
(agent) 76686 (24 hours) or
Witney (0993) 772671

Lang, T. L. (0:3:0:0:1) 8   2
   Kentisbeare (08846) 419
Lawes, S. D. (0:0:1:0:0) 8   3
   Beverley (0482) 869885
Lowe, J. J. (42:38:60:41:36) 7   8
   York (0904) 708871 and
   (0347) 810103 and
   carphone (0860) 244284

Mackay, A. (25:47:21:36:7) 7   8
   Newmarket (0638) 662036 and 730306
Matthias, J. J. (29:14:11:7:22) 8   6
   Kingsclere (0635) 298423
McAndrew, M. A. (1:0:0:0:0) 7   12
McGhin, R. (4:0:0:1:2) 8   3
   Newmarket (0638) 660920
McGlone, A. D. (23:28:9:16:14) ... 7   12
   (0264) 790421,
   carphone (0836) 242788 and
   Harrogate (0423) 871624 (agent)
McKay, D. J. (12:6:9:5:3) 7   9
   Marlborough (0672) 40802 (home)
McKeown, D. R. (1:21:20:59:86) . 8   1
   Wetherby (0937) 63301 and
   01-381-9318 (agent)
McKeown, T. P. (—:—:—:—:0) .. 7   10
   Newmarket (0638) 661589
McNamee, C. J. (—:0:0:0:0) 8   0
   Marlborough (0672) 55453
Montgomery, D. J. (0:0:0:0:0) 6   7
Morris, S. D. (0:2:2:7:2) 7   12
   Malton (0653) 692098
Morse, R. R. (11:10:10:2:4) 7   9
Murray, J. G. (0:0:0:4:3) 8   4
   c/o Southwater (0403) 730255

Nesbitt, H. A. (—:—:—:—:0) 7   7
   Newmarket (0638) 730703 (home) and
   663801 (yard)
Newnes, W. A. P.
   (—:15:48:44:39) 8   2
   c/o H. Candy,
   Uffington (036782) 276 (home) and
   (agent) London 01-674 3673 and
   (0271) 883813
Nicholls, A. (44:38:33:32:28) 8   6
   Coxwold (03476) 622 and
   York (0904) 647213 (agent) and
   carphone (0836) 713418
Nutter, C. (0:2:2:1:2) 8   0
   Newmarket (0638) 668153

Perks, S. J. (30:19:18:18:31) 8   5
   Armitage (0543) 491594
Procter, B. T. (2:0:2:2:4) 8   3
   East Ilsley (063528) 596
Proud, A. (10:6:10:12:7) 7   10
   Bingham (0949) 43350 (home) and
   50099 (office)

Quinn, T. R. (47:69:55:46:60) 8   0
   Lambourn (0488) 72576 (home) and
   carphone (0860) 287172

Radcliffe, K. (7:2:0:—:0) 8   0
   c/o Liverpool 051-531 9616
Rate, C. (2:0:4:9:0) 8   4
   c/o Newmarket (0638) 665432

Raymond, B. H.
   (38:—:45:77:66) 8   4
   Newmarket (0638) 730387 (home) and
   666431 (agent)
Raymont, S. J. (2:0:2:1:1) 8   1
   Avebury (06723) 573
Reid, J. A. (53:60:81:79:84) 8   5
   Uffington (036782) 214
Richardson, M. A. (2:2:1:2:0) 8   4
   c/o Coxwold (03476) 622
Rimmer, M. E. (2:14:6:11:11) 8   4
   Newmarket (0638) 666581
Roberts, M. L.
   (—:42:74:121:107) 8   0
   Newmarket (0638) 661026 (home) and
   East Ilsley (063528) 331 (office)
Rouse, B. A. (31:34:50:51:51) 8   2
   Ruster (0293) 871547
Rutter, C. L. P. (20:30:27:15:14) .. 7   10
   Uffington (036 782) 276 (office),
   Wantage (02357) 65263 (home),
   (0836) 760769 (mobile) and
   (0295) 68619 (agent)
Ryan, M. J. (—:—:—:—:1) 8   0
   Newmarket (0638) 66547
Ryan, W. (37:56:69:58:49) 8   2
   Newmarket (0638) 717236 (home),
   (0860) 243295 (carphone) and
   (0223) 892783) (sundays) and
   Harrogate (0423) 871624 (agent)

Sedgwick, P. (—:—:—:—:0) 8   4
   c/o Stamford Bridge (0759) 71472
Sexton, G. C. (5:8:6:1:0) 8   3
   Newmarket (0638) 660252 (home)
Shoults, A. F. (23:22:11:4:3) 7   12
   Newmarket (0638) 730371
Smith, V. (0:1:1:3:0) 8   4
   Newmarket (0638) 668972
Starkey, G. M. W.
   (81:102:55:48:52) 8   6
   Newmarket (0638) 751256 and 750847
Still, R. W. (1:0:0:0:0) 7   6
   Newmarket (0638) 750755
Street, R. (10:5:8:6:3) 7   7
   Lambourn (0488) 71412 and 71548
   and (0865) 61666 (office)
Swinburn, W. R. J.
   (75:83:92:88:94) 8   6
   Wickhambrook (0440) 820277 (home)
   and Newmarket (0638) 660811 and
   660258 (agent)

Thomas, M. L. (26:7:—:7:0) 7   7
   Newmarket (0638) 666431
   and 720723 (agent)
Thomson, B. P. (64:67:32:—:0) ... 8   3
Tinkler, Mrs K. A.
   (2:18:21:16:12) 7   7
   Burythorpe (065385) 245 and 512

Walsh, M. P. (—:—:—:1:1) 7   10
   c/o Melton Mowbray (0664) 65225
Webster, S. G. (18:8:3:19:22) 8   0
   Elvington (090485) 458
Wernham, R. A. (11:12:3:12:6) ... 8   3
   Abingdon (0235) 833754
Wharton, W. J. (0:3:0:0:1) 8   5
   Uffington (036782) 710

Whitehall, A. J. (2:1:3:8:0) 7 10
  Kingsclere (0635) 298598
Whitelam, S. M. (0:0:0:—:0) 8 2
Whitworth, S. J.
  (30:28:22:31:24) 8 0
  (0860) 342314 (portable phone) and
  01-9693517 (agent)
Wigham, M. (18:32:28:23:32) 8 2
  York (0904) 488008 and
  carphone (0836) 229685
Wigham, R. (—:—:—:—:0) 8 7
  Grantham (0476) 860090
Williams, J. A. N.
  (6:14:15:25:34) 8 2
  Badminton (045421) 622
Williams, T. L. (31:50:53:28:34) .. 7 10
  Lambourn (0488) 72734 (home)
Wood, M. (18:15:10:1:2) 8 0
  Burythorpe (065385) 412 and
  Coxwold (03476) 482 or
  carphone (0836) 326084 (agent)

The following relinquished their
licence during the season

Burke, P. A.   (2:4:4:23:14)

Carter, Miss W. J.   (3:0:2:—:0)

Charnock, L.   (32:22:24:18:15)

Connorton, N. B.   (26:27:46:34:21)

Curant, J. A.   (—:—:2:2:2)

Fry, M. J.   (11:22:13:15:13)

Hamblett, P. A.   (4:6:1:3:2)

Ives, T. A.   (77:72:70:62:30)

Mercer, A.   (0:4:6:2:5)

APPRENTICES

The following list shows the employer and riding weight of every
apprentice who holds a current licence to ride on the flat, and the number of
winners he or she has ridden in Britain, wins in apprentice races being
recorded separately.

Apprentices may claim 7 lb until they have won 10 races, 5 lb until they
have won 50 races and 3 lb until they have won 75 races. Apprentice races are
excepted in all these cases. The allowance each apprentice is entitled to
claim is shown in brackets. The claim may be exercised in all handicaps and
selling races, and in all other races with guaranteed prize money of not more
than £8,000.

Allen R. J. (7) 7 13
  (Sir Mark Prescott)
Armes, Miss A. C. (7) 7 0
  (H. Candy)
Arrowsmith, F. P. (7) 1 + 5 ap 8 0
  (I. Balding)
Ashley, T. L. (7) 7 0
  (J. Glover)
Aspell, J. S. (7) 7 10
  (J. Pitman)
Avery, C. M. (7) 1 + 1 ap 7 8
  (L. Holt)

Baird, P. J. (7) 7 2
  (M. Ryan)
Balding, Miss C. (7) 1 + 5 amt 7 4
  (J. Balding)
Barnard, P. J. (5) 16 + 5 ap 8 10
  (S. Mellor)
Barrett, D. J. P.(7) 7 4
  (F. Lee)
Bentley, E. (7) 2 .... 7 12
  (M. Morley)
Berry, R. (7) 7 7
  (G. Lewis)

Biggs, D. D. (5) 11 + 9 ap 7 4
  (R. Williams)
  Newmarket (0638) 663218
Bithell, D. P. (7) 7 0
  (K. Bridgwater)
Bowker, Miss J. (5) 14 + 4 ap 7 7
  (N. Tinkler)
Brace, Miss D. A. (7) 8 8
  (L. Holt)
Bradley, M. P. (7) 7 12
  (I. Balding)
Bray, V. (7) 7 4
  (M. Stoute)
Brette, P. (7) 4 + 2 ap 8 0
  (R. Guest)
Bridger, Miss R. J. (7) 7 9
  (J. Bridger)
Brislen, P. (7) 1 .... 7 10
  (H. Candy)
Brown, G. (7) 7 12
  (R. Whitaker)
Brown, Miss T. (7) 7 10
  (C. Tinkler)
Brownsword, K. (7) 3 .... 7 6
  (T. Fairhurst)

Burns, A. C. (7) 7 10
  (J. Hudson)
Buxton, Miss W. H. (7) 7   7
  (A. Bailey)

Cairns, S. (7) 2 ap 7   7
  (P. Mitchell)
Campbell, C. (7) 1 + 1 ap 7   4
  (S. Dow)
Carter, L. A. (7) 7   0
  (R. Akehurst)
Cassidy, M. P. (7) 1 ap 7 12
  (A. Stewart)
Chambers, Miss L. (7) 7   7
  (P. Howling)
Clark, A. A. (7) 7 12
  (C. Horgan)
Clayton, W. (7) 7   7
  (W. Pearce)
Clements, Miss E. D. (7) 7   0
  (Miss S. Oliver)
Corrigan, J. A. P. (7) 8   0
  (G. Harwood)
Cosgrove, D. W. (7) 6 10
  (C. W. C. Elsey)
Coulter, Miss R. E. (7) 6 12
  (J. Berry)
Cripps, D. (7) 8   0
  (J. Sutcliffe)
Culhane, P. A. 89 + 5 ap 7 12
  (R. Hollinshead)
  Stamford Bridge (0759) 7 1586 and
  carphone (0836) 753052 (agent)

Dace, L. A. (7) 9   0
  (R. Smyth)
Dacombe, Miss M. (7) 7   7
  (R. Armstrong)
Dalton, P. J. (7) 5 + 1 ap 7   2
  (D. Smith) York (0904) 6472 13 (agent)
D'Arcy, D. J. (7) 4 ap 7   7
  (J. Gosden)
  Newmarket (0638) 76686 (24 hours) or
  Witney (0993) 772671 (agent)
Davies, L. (7) 7   4
  (C. Nelson)
Davies, S. G. (7) 2 ap 7   2
  (H. Cecil)
Deacon, Miss D. (7) 7   7
  (P. Howling)
Deering, M. V. (7) 1 + 2 ap 7 12
  (J. FitzGerald)
Denaro, M. J. (7) 9   7
  (C. Allen)
Dettori, L. 112 + 10 ap 7 11
  (L Cumani)
  Newmarket (0638) 666431 (agent)
Dobbin, A. G. (7) 7 10
  (J. O'Neill)
Doyle, B. (7) 1 ap 6   4
  (C. Brittain)
Drowne, S. J. (7) 7   0
  (C. Spares)
Drugan, M. J. J. (7) 8   0
  (S. Norton)
Dunnachie, D. D. (7) 2 + 3 ap 7 10
  (L. Cumani)

Eddery, J. D. (3) 57 + 5 ap 7 10
  (R. Williams)
  Newmarket (0638) 663218 and
  (0748) 5640 (agent)
Eeles, J. S. (7) 7   0
  (A. Robson)
Eiffert, S. (7) 7   0
  (R. Guest)
Ennis, P. J. (7) 8   4
  (H. Cecil)

Fahey, R. A. (7) 8 + 9 ap 8 12
  (S. Muldoon)
  York (0904) 647213 (agent)
Fallon, D. (7) 7   7
  (J. Berry)
Ferguson, I. (7) 7   5
  (C. Williams)
Ferriday, J. D. (7) 7   0
  (B. Preece)
Fordham, J. R. (7) 7   0
  (R. Hollinshead)
Forster, G. (7) 2 + 2 ap 8   0
  (J. Etherington)
Fortune, J. J. (5) 30 + 7 ap 7   7
  (M. O'Neill)
  Coxwold (03476) 482 or
  carphone (0836) 326084 (agent)

Garth, A. R. (7) 6   2
  (R. Hollinshead)
Gibson, D. R. (5) 49 + 21 ap 7   4
  (W. Hastings-Bass)
  Newmarket (0638) 665202,
  667851 and 730284 (home)
Giles, M. A. (5) 10 + 6 ap 7   7
  (Mrs L. E. Ramsden)
  Thirsk (0845) 587226
Giles, S. M. (7) 2 + 5 ap 7 13
  (W. Haggas)
Granger, R. Y. (7) 1 ap 7   7
  (H. Collinridge)
Gray, S. A. (7) 6   7
  (T. Barron)
Greaves, Miss A. A. (7) 3 8   7
  (T. Barron)
Gurney, Miss K. A. (7) 1 8   0
  (K. White)
Gwilliams, N. L. (5) 10 + 1 ap 7 10
  (M. Ryan)
  Newmarket (0638) 668484 (agent)

Haigh, I. N. (7) 7   2
  (P. Rohan)
Hall, N. V. (7) 1 ap 7   9
  (R. Whitaker)
Harper, Miss A. M. (7) 3 + 3 ap 7 12
  (R. Williams)
Harrison, D. P. (7) 6   0
  (W. Hastings-Bass)
Harte, P. G. (7) 9   0
  (Mrs R. Wharton)
Hawkes, S. R. (7) 7   2
  (M. Brittain)
Hawksley, C. L. (7) 7   0
  (H. Cecil)
Haworth, S. M. (7) 1 7   2
  (N. Callaghan)

O'Gorman, S. M. (5) 24 + 2 ap 7 8
(I. Balding)
O'Neill, G. J. (7) 7 7
(G. Harwood)
O'Reilly, M. G. (7) 1 ap 8 0
(M. O'Neill)

Perham, R. (7) 7 + 2 ap 7 12
(R. Hannon)
Perry, N. L. (7) 7 12
(J. Hills)
Pollard, C. (7) 7 7
(E. Eldin)
Popely, A. M. (7) 1 ap 7 9
(Miss L. Siddall)
Porter, J. J. (7) 7 7
(J. Watts)
Porter, S. P. (7) 7 3
(M. Ryan)
Price, R. W. (7) 8 + 5 ap 7 4
(M. Bell)
Newmarket (0638) 76686 (24 hours)
and Witney (0993) 77267 1 (agent)
Priest, C. (7) 8 3
(N. Bycroft)
Procter, A. R. (7) 1 + 4 ap 7 12
(D. Arbuthnot)
Newmarket (0638) 76686 (24 hours)
and Witney (0993) 77267 1 (agent)
Prys-Jones, Miss B. L. (7) 7 8
(K. Ivory)
Purseglove, Miss T. N. (7) 8 0
(G. Balding)

Quane, S. H. N. (5) 10 + 9 ap 8 0
(I. Matthews)
Newmarket (0638) 664568 and
(0993) 72671
Quinn, J. A. (3) 67 + 12 ap 7 7
(A. Bailey)
Newmarket (0638) 662287 (home) and
York (0904) 6472 13 (office)

Rabjohn, S. D. (7) 8 2
(M. Johnston)
Riding, A. (5) 15 + 5 ap 7 12
(J. White)
Newmarket (0638) 6602 12 (agent)
Riggio, L. F. (5) 14 + 5 ap 7 12
(E. Wheeler)
Roberts, Miss C. (7) 7 12
(Miss L. Siddall)
Roberts, C. N. (7) 6 10
(Capt. J. Wilson)
Roffey, P. (7) 7 12
(D. Arbuthnot)
Rollingson, G. (7) 8 0
(J. Etherington)
Rourke, R. R. (7) 7 11
(J. Jenkins)
Russell, B. J. (7) 7 4
(W. Holden)
Rutter, K. (7) 7 10
(J. Scargill)
Ryan, J. B. (5) 1 + 5 amt 8 5
(M. Ryan)

Scally, C. (7) 1 ap 7 9
(K. Ivory)
Simpson, A. J. (7) 7 9
(P. Cole)
Simpson, Miss C. A. (7) 7 7
(F. Jordan)
Simpson, M. (7) 8 0
(W. Hastings-Bass)
Skelton, P. R. (7) 1 ap 7 12
(M. Blanshard)
Slattery, J. V. (7) 8 7
(O. O'Neill)
Smith, M. J. J. (7) 1 .... 8 0
(K. Bridgwater)
Smith-Eccles, P. (7) 7 4
(G. Pritchard-Gordon)
Smith, R. O. (7) 1 + 1 ap 7 10
(B. Hanbury)
Smith, S. J. (7) 7 6
(T. Fairhurst)
Snowdon, Miss V. F. (7) 7 10
(D. Elsworth)
Spence, A. J. (7) 1 ap 7 10
(W. Musson)
Spence, S. D. (7) 7 4
(J. Wilson)
Sprake, T. J. (5) 10 + 8 ap 7 10
(P. Makin)
Stannard, Miss E. C. (7) 8 0
(M. Stoute)
Stather, D. M. (7) 3 ap 8 0
(G. Harwood)
Stenning, J. (7) 8 0
(J. Long)
Stoddart, Miss A. L. (7) 7 7
(R. Whitaker)
Strange, G. (7) 7 7
(Ronald Thompson)
Strickland, Miss C. L. (7) 6 7
(D. Haydn Jones)
Surrey, D. (7) 1 + 3 ap 7 12
(G. Wragg)

Tate, A. B. (7) 7 6
(M. Usher)
Tate, J. D. (7) 7 2
(P. Arthur)
Taylor, C. (7) 7 10
(H. Collingridge)
Taylor, S. D. (7) 7 0
(G. Moore)
Tebbutt, M. J. (5) 10 + 2 ap 8 2
(W. Jarvis)
Tervit, B. G. (7) 1 + 1 ap 7 12
(W. Jarvis)
Thomas, B. (7) 7 2
(R. Simpson)
Thomas, Miss N. J. (7) 7 10
(M. Ryan)
Tierney, D. P. (7) 1 ap 7 11
(G. Balding)
Timms, C. C. (7) 6 0
(D. Haydn Jones)
Todd, A. W. (7) 7 0
(D. Chapman)
Town, Miss M. (7) 1 + 3 ap 8 0
(A. Bailey)

Tucker, A. P. (7) 1 + 5 ap 7   7
  (M. McCormack)
  Newmarket (0638) 76686 (24 hours) or
  Witney (0993) 772671 (agent)
Turner, P. J. (7) 6   7
  (M. Tompkins)
Turner, R. D. (7) 7   0
  (C. W. Elsey)

Vale, J. (7) 7 12
  (I. Matthews)

Want, D. (7) 2 7   7
  (R. Thompson)
  Stamford (0780) 4 108 12
Weaver, J. C. (7) 7   7
  (L. Cumani)
Webster, Miss S. (7) 8   0
  (O. Brennan)
Wentworth, Miss T. A. (7) 1 ap 7 10
  (Mrs M. Reveley)
White, P. A. (7) 7 13
  (E. Eldin)
Whitham, A. D. (7) 8   0
  (R. Earnshaw)
Widger, G. (7) 7   7
  (P. Burgoyne)
Widger, M. (7) 7   0
  (P. Cole)
Williams, D. J. (5) 24 + 5 ap 7 10
  (H. Candy)
  (0748) 5640 and
  Uffington (036782) 276
Williams, J. (7) 7 10
  (G. Lewis)
Williams, S. D. (7) 3 + 2 ap 8   0
  (J. Glover)
Wilson, C. J. (7) 8   0
  (P. Feilden)
Wood, S. (5) 36 + 3 ap 7   2
  (D. Chapman)

  Coxwold (03476) 482 and
  carphone (0836) 326084
Woodall, N. C. (7) 8   4
  (J. Wainwright)
Wright, M. G. (7) 7   0
  (P. Cole)

The following winning apprentices relinquished their licence during the season

Birch, J. 2 + 2 ap

Cahill, W. 1 ap

Foster, G. N. 1 + 9 ap

Gallagher, M. A. 11 + 3 ap

Hegarty, P. E. 1 + 3 ap

Hillis, R. P. 45 + 2 ap

Hind, G. E. P. 35 + 5 ap

Lappin, R. T. 22 + 10 ap

Lees, D. W. 1 + 3 ap

Lynch, P. P. 1 ap

Martinez, F. 1 ap

Swift, J. C. 4 ap

Thompson, G. 3 ap

Thompson, T. P. 2 + 1 ap

1990 FLAT RACING FIXTURES

(a)   Denotes All-Weather meeting

*   Denotes evening meeting

March

1 Thu.	Lingfield (a)
3 Sat.	Southwell (a)
6 Tue.	Lingfield (a)
8 Thu.	Southwell (a)
10 Sat.	Lingfield (a)
22 Thu.	Doncaster
23 Fri.	Doncaster
24 Sat.	Doncaster
26 Mon.	Folkestone, Leicester
27 Tue.	Leicester
28 Wed.	Catterick
29 Thu.	Newcastle
30 Fri.	Beverley
31 Sat.	Beverley, Warwick

April

2 Mon.	Folkestone, Nottingham
3 Tue.	Hamilton
4 Wed.	Hamilton
5 Thu.	Brighton
6 Fri.	Kempton
7 Sat.	Lingfield (a)
9 Mon.	Wolverhampton
10 Tue.	Pontefract, Wolverhampton
11 Wed.	Ripon
12 Thu.	Ripon
14 Sat.	Haydock, Kempton, Newcastle
16 Mon.	Kempton, Newcastle, Nottingham, Warwick
17 Tue.	Newmarket, Warwick
18 Wed.	Ayr, Newmarket, Pontefract
19 Thu.	Ayr (mixed), Newmarket
20 Fri.	Newbury, Thirsk
21 Sat.	Newbury, Thirsk
23 Mon.	Brighton, Edinburgh
24 Tue.	Epsom
25 Wed.	Catterick, Epsom
26 Thu.	Beverley
27 Fri.	Carlisle, Sandown
28 Sat.	Leicester, Ripon, Sandown (mixed)
30 Mon.	Pontefract, Windsor*, Wolverhampton

May

1 Tue.	Bath, Nottingham, Redcar
2 Wed.	Ascot
3 Thu.	Newmarket, Salisbury
4 Fri.	Hamilton, Newmarket
5 Sat.	Haydock, Newmarket, Thirsk
7 Mon.	Doncaster, Haydock (mixed), Kempton, Warwick
8 Tue.	Chester, Folkestone*, Salisbury
9 Wed.	Chester, Salisbury, Sandown*
10 Thu.	Carlisle, Chester
11 Fri.	Beverley, Carlisle, Lingfield
12 Sat.	Bath, Beverley, Lingfield
14 Mon.	Hamilton, Windsor*, Wolverhampton

15 Tue.	Brighton*, Nottingham*, York
16 Wed.	Kempton*, York
17 Thu.	York
18 Fri.	Newbury, Newmarket, Thirsk
19 Sat.	Hamilton*, Lingfield*, Newbury, Newmarket, Southwell*, Thirsk
21 Mon.	Bath, Edinburgh, Wolverhampton
22 Tue.	Beverley, Salisbury
23 Wed.	Goodwood
24 Thu.	Catterick, Goodwood
25 Fri.	Haydock, Pontefract*
26 Sat.	Doncaster, Haydock, Kempton, Lingfield*, Southwell*, Warwick*
28 Mon.	Chepstow, Doncaster, Leicester, Redcar, Sandown
29 Tue.	Leicester, Redcar, Sandown*
30 Wed.	Brighton, Ripon*
31 Thu.	Brighton, Carlisle

June

1 Fri.	Goodwood*, Hamilton, Nottingham
2 Sat.	Edinburgh, Lingfield
4 Mon.	Edinburgh*, Leicester, Redcar
5 Tue.	Folkestone, Yarmouth
6 Wed.	Beverley*, Epsom, Yarmouth
7 Thu.	Beverley, Epsom
8 Fri.	Catterick, Epsom, Goodwood*, Haydock*, Southwell
9 Sat.	Carlisle*, Catterick, Epsom, Haydock, Leicester*
11 Mon.	Brighton*, Nottingham, Pontefract
12 Tue.	Goodwood, Pontefract
13 Wed.	Beverley, Hamilton*, Kempton*, Newbury
14 Thu.	Chepstow*, Hamilton, Newbury
15 Fri.	Doncaster*, Goodwood*, Sandown, Southwell, York
16 Sat.	Bath, Lingfield*, Nottingham*, Sandown, York
18 Mon.	Brighton, Edinburgh, Windsor*, Wolverhampton*
19 Tue.	Royal Ascot, Thirsk
20 Wed.	Ripon, Royal Ascot
21 Thu.	Ripon, Royal Ascot
22 Fri.	Ayr, Redcar, Royal Ascot, Southwell
23 Sat.	Ascot, Ayr, Lingfield*, Redcar, Warwick*
25 Mon.	Edinburgh, Nottingham, Windsor*
26 Tue.	Brighton, Newbury*, Yarmouth
27 Wed.	Carlisle, Chester*, Kempton*, Salisbury
28 Thu.	Carlisle, Salisbury

29 Fri.	Bath*, Doncaster, Goodwood*, Lingfield, Newcastle*, Newmarket
30 Sat.	Chepstow, Doncaster*, Lingfield*, Newcastle, Newmarket, Warwick*

July

2 Mon.	Edinburgh, Pontefract, Windsor*, Wolverhampton*
3 Tue.	Chepstow, Folkestone
4 Wed.	Catterick*, Warwick, Yarmouth
5 Thu.	Brighton*, Catterick, Haydock*, Yarmouth
6 Fri.	Beverley*, Haydock, Sandown, Southwell
7 Sat.	Bath, Beverley, Haydock, Nottingham*, Sandown
9 Mon.	Edinburgh, Leicester, Ripon*, Windsor*
10 Tue.	Newmarket, Pontefract
11 Wed.	Bath, Kempton*, Newmarket, Redcar*
12 Thu.	Chepstow*, Hamilton*, Kempton, Newmarket
13 Fri.	Chester*, Hamilton*, Lingfield, Warwick, York
14 Sat.	Ayr, Chester, Lingfield, Salisbury, Southwell*, York
16 Mon.	Ayr, Beverley*, Windsor*, Wolverhampton
17 Tue.	Ayr, Beverley, Folkestone*, Leicester*
18 Wed.	Catterick, Hamilton, Sandown*, Yarmouth
19 Thu.	Catterick, Chepstow*, Hamilton, Sandown
20 Fri.	Ayr, Newbury, Newmarket*, Thirsk
21 Sat.	Ayr, Lingfield*, Newbury, Newmarket, Ripon, Southwell*
23 Mon.	Ayr, Bath, Nottingham*, Windsor*
24 Tue.	Folkestone, Redcar*, Yarmouth
25 Wed.	Doncaster*, Redcar, Sandown*, Yarmouth
26 Thu.	Brighton, Doncaster
27 Fri.	Ascot, Carlisle, Pontefract*
28 Sat.	Ascot,, Hamilton, Newcastle, Southwell*, Warwick*
30 Mon.	Lingfield, Newcastle, Windsor*, Wolverhampton*
31 Tue.	Beverley, Goodwood, Leicester*

August

1 Wed.	Catterick, Goodwood, Southwell*
2 Thu.	Goodwood, Yarmouth
3 Fri.	Edinburgh*, Goodwood, Newmarket*, Thirsk
4 Sat.	Goodwood, Newmarket, Thirsk, Windsor*
6 Mon.	Nottingham*, Ripon
7 Tue.	Brighton, Nottingham*, Redcar
8 Wed.	Brighton, Kempton*, Pontefract
9 Thu.	Brighton, Pontefract

10 Fri.	Haydock*, Newmarket*, Redcar
11 Sat.	Haydock, Lingfield*, Newmarket, Redcar, Southwell*
13 Mon.	Leicester*, Thirsk*, Windsor
14 Tue.	Bath, Catterick*, Yarmouth
15 Wed.	Beverley, Folkestone*, Salisbury, Southwell
16 Thu.	Beverley, Salisbury, Southwell
17 Fri.	Haydock*, Newbury, Southwell
18 Sat.	Lingfield*, Newbury, Ripon, Wolverhampton*
20 Mon.	Hamilton, Windsor
21 Tue.	Folkestone, York
22 Wed.	Yarmouth, York
23 Thu.	Salisbury*, Yarmouth, York
24 Fri.	Goodwood, Newmarket
25 Sat.	Goodwood, Newcastle, Newmarket, Windsor*
27 Mon.	Chepstow, Newcastle, Ripon, Sandown, Warwick, Wolverhampton
28 Tue.	Ripon
29 Wed.	Brighton, Redcar
30 Thu.	Lingfield
31 Fri.	Chester, Sandown, Thirsk

September

1 Sat.	Chester, Ripon, Sandown
3 Mon.	Nottingham
4 Tue.	Brighton, Pontefract
5 Wed.	York
6 Thu.	Salisbury, York
7 Fri.	Haydock, Kempton
8 Sat.	Haydock, Kempton, Southwell, Thirsk
10 Mon.	Hamilton, Wolverhampton
11 Tue.	Carlisle, Leicester, Lingfield
12 Wed.	Doncaster
13 Thu.	Doncaster, Folkestone
14 Fri.	Doncaster, Goodwood
15 Sat.	Chepstow, Doncaster, Goodwood
17 Mon.	Bath, Edinburgh, Leicester
18 Tue.	Sandown, Yarmouth
19 Wed.	Ayr, Beverley, Sandown, Yarmouth
20 Thu.	Ayr, Beverley, Lingfield, Yarmouth
21 Fri.	Ayr, Newbury, Southwell
22 Sat.	Ayr, Catterick, Newbury
24 Mon.	Folkestone, Hamilton, Nottingham
25 Tue.	Kempton, Nottingham, Pontefract
26 Wed.	Brighton
27 Thu.	Ascot
28 Fri.	Ascot, Haydock, Redcar
29 Sat.	Ascot, Haydock, Redcar

October

1 Mon.	Bath, Wolverhampton
2 Tue.	Brighton, Newcastle, Wolverhampton
3 Wed.	Newmarket, Salisbury
4 Thu.	Lingfield, Newmarket
5 Fri.	Goodwood, Newmarket
6 Sat.	Goodwood, Newmarket

8 Mon.	Pontefract, Warwick		**November**
9 Tue.	Folkestone, Redcar, Warwick	1 Thu.	Newmarket
10 Wed.	Haydock, York	2 Fri.	Lingfield (a), Newmarket
11 Thu.	Haydock, York	3 Sat.	Newmarket
12 Fri.	Ascot	5 Mon.	Newcastle
13 Sat.	Ascot, York	6 Tue.	Hamilton
15 Mon.	Ayr, Leicester	7 Wed.	Southwell (a)
16 Tue.	Ayr, Chepstow, Leicester	8 Thu.	Lingfield (a)
17 Wed.	Redcar, Wolverhampton	9 Fri.	Doncaster
18 Thu.	Newmarket	10 Sat.	Doncaster
19 Fri.	Catterick, Newmarket	12 Mon.	Folkestone
20 Sat.	Catterick, Newmarket	13 Tue.	Southwell (a)
22 Mon.	Folkestone, Nottingham	20 Tue.	Southwell (a)
23 Tue.	Chepstow, Chester, Nottingham	22 Thu.	Lingfield (a)
24 Wed.	Chester, Edinburgh	30 Fri.	Southwell (a)
25 Thu.	Newbury, Pontefract		
26 Fri.	Doncaster		**December**
27 Sat.	Doncaster, Newbury	6 Thu.	Lingfield (a)
29 Mon.	Bath, Leicester, Lingfield	13 Thu.	Southwell (a)
30 Tue.	Leicester, Redcar, Salisbury	15 Sat.	Lingfield (a)
31 Wed.	Edinburgh, Yarmouth	27 Thu.	Lingfield (a)
		29 Sat.	Southwell (a)

ERRATA & ADDENDA

'RACEHORSES OF 1988'

Allazzaz	fourth foal
Assatis	P77. One of dam's previous foals unplaced in USA
Avonmouthsecretary	dam ran twice in Ireland
Azeb	Raise You Ten not French
Bell Tower	third foal: half-sister to a winner in USA by Diamond Prospect
Blue Book	P116. Phountzi fetched 420,000 guineas
First Victory	sixth foal: two of previous ones won in West Indies
Frankly Perfect	dam also French 2-y-o 6f winner
Glenbeigh Summer	also half-sister to Irish 1985 2-y-o 6f winner Williamsburg (by Cure The Blues)
Green's Still Life	delete reference to Fluteau
Heard It Before	Carlisle, not Beverley
Johns Valentine	fifth foal: half-brother to 3 winners abroad
Lapierre	P455 finished seventh in Guineas
Lazy Rhythm	dam winning sprinter
Louis Cyphre	Louis Cyphre
Luge	P484 beat James Payne, not Paddy Chalk, at Salisbury
Musical Bliss	P567 Lucky Round, P568 Safe Play
Nomadic Way	Haydock in September
Old Vic	dam won over 1m at Salisbury
Puppet Dance	foaled Mar 15, trainer D. Sepulchre
Seldom Blue	dam never ran
Swooping	trainer J. L. Dunlop
Tony Bin	P871 Eddery did not ride Indian Rose in Vermeille
Val des Bois	is a colt
What A Line	Newcastle, not Nottingham

1059

CHARACTERISTICS OF RACECOURSES

ASCOT—The Ascot round course is a right-handed, triangular circuit of 1m 6f and 34 yds, with a run-in of 2½f. There is a straight mile course, over which the Royal Hunt Cup is run, and the Old mile course which joins the round course in Swinley Bottom. All races shorter than a mile are decided on the straight course. From the 1½-mile starting gate the round course runs downhill to the bend in Swinley Bottom, where it is level, then rises steadily to the turn into the straight, from where it is uphill until less than a furlong from the winning post, the last hundred yards being more or less level. The straight mile is slightly downhill from the start and then rises to the 5f gate, after which there is a slight fall before the junction with the round course. Despite the downhill run into Swinley Bottom and the relatively short run-in from the final turn, the Ascot course is galloping in character; the turns are easy, there are no minor surface undulations to throw a long-striding horse off balance, and all races are very much against the collar over the last half-mile. The course is, in fact, quite a testing one, and very much so in soft going, when there is a heavy premium on stamina. In such circumstances races over 2 miles to 2¾ miles are very severe tests.
DRAW: The draw seems of little consequence nowadays.

AYR—The Ayr round course is a left-handed, oval track, about twelve furlongs in extent, with a run-in of half a mile. Eleven-furlong races start on a chute, which joins the round course after about a furlong. There is a straight six-furlong course of considerable width. The course is relatively flat, but there are gentle undulations throughout, perhaps more marked in the straight. It has a good surface and well-graded turns, and is a fine and very fair track, on the whole galloping in character.
DRAW: In races over seven furlongs and a mile a low number is desirable. On the straight course a low draw seems an advantage when the ground is soft.

BATH—The Bath round course is a left-handed, oval track, just over a mile and a half in extent, with a run-in of nearly half a mile. There is an extension for races over five furlongs and five furlongs and 167 yards. The run-in bends to the left, and is on the rise all the way. The mile and the mile-and-a-quarter courses have been designed to give over a quarter of a mile straight at the start, and the track generally is galloping rather than sharp. The course consists of old downland turf.
DRAW: The draw seems of little consequence nowadays.

BEVERLEY—The Beverley round course is a right-handed, oval track, just over a mile and three furlongs in extent, with a run-in of two and a half furlongs. The five-furlong track bends right at halfway. The general galloping nature of the track is modified by the downhill turn into the straight and the relatively short run-in. The five-furlong course is on the rise throughout, and so is rather testing even in normal conditions; in soft going it takes some getting, particularly for two-year-olds early in the season.
DRAW: High numbers have an advantage over the five-furlong course.

BRIGHTON—The Brighton course takes the shape of an extended 'U' and is 1½ miles in length. The first three furlongs are uphill, following which there is a slight descent followed by a slight rise to about four furlongs from home; the track then runs more sharply downhill until a quarter of a mile out, from where it rises to the last hundred yards, the finish being level. The run-in is about 3½ furlongs, and there is no straight course. This is essentially a sharp track. While the turns are easy enough, the pronounced gradients make Brighton an unsuitable course for big, long-striding horses, resolute gallopers or round-actioned horses. Handy, medium-sized, fluent movers, and quick-actioned horses are much more at home on the course. There are no opportunities for long-distance plodders at Brighton.
DRAW: In sprint races a low number is advantageous, and speed out of the gate even more so.

CARLISLE—Carlisle is a right-handed, pear-shaped course, just over a mile and a half in extent, with a run-in of a little more than three furlongs. The six-furlong course, of which the five-furlong course is a part, the mile course, and the mile-and-a-half course start on three separate off-shoot extensions. For the first three furlongs or so the course runs downhill, then rises for a short distance, levelling out just beyond the mile post. From there until the turn into the straight the course is flat, apart from minor undulations. The six-furlong course, which bears right soon after the start, and again at the turn into the straight, is level for two furlongs, then rises fairly steeply until the distance, from which point it is practically level. The track is galloping in character, and the six-furlong course is a stiff test of stamina for a two-year-old.

DRAW: High numbers have an advantage which is more marked in the shorter races.

CATTERICK—The Catterick round course is a left-handed, oval track, measuring one mile and 180 yards, with a run-in of three furlongs. The five-furlong course bears left before and at the junction with the round course. From the seven-furlong starting gate the round course is downhill almost all the way, and there is a sharp turn on the falling gradient into the straight. The five-furlong course is downhill throughout, quite steeply to start with, and less so thereafter. Catterick is an exceedingly sharp track with pronounced undulations of surface, and it is therefore an impossible course for a big, long-striding animal. Experience of the track counts for a great deal, and jockeyship is of the utmost importance.

DRAW: A low number gives a slight advantage over five furlongs, but in races over six furlongs and seven furlongs a slow beginner on the inside is almost certain to be cut off.

CHEPSTOW—The Chepstow round course is a left-handed, oval track, about two miles in extent, with a run-in of five furlongs. There is a straight mile course, over which all races up to a mile are run. The round course has well-marked undulations, and the straight course is generally downhill and level alternately as far as the run-in, thereafter rising sharply for over two furlongs, and then gradually levelling out to the winning post. Notwithstanding the long run-in and general rise over the last five furlongs, this is not an ideal galloping track because of the changing gradients.

DRAW: Of little consequence nowadays.

CHESTER—Chester is a left-handed, circular course, only a few yards over a mile round, the smallest circuit of any flat-race course in Great Britain. It is quite flat and on the turn almost throughout, and although the run-in is nearly straight, it is less than two furlongs in length. Apart from extreme distance events, such as the Chester Cup and other 2¼m races, the course is against the long-striding, resolute galloper and greatly favours the handy, medium-sized, sharp-actioned horse.

DRAW: Given a good start, the draw is of little consequence. A slow start is virtually impossible to overcome in sprint races.

DONCASTER—Doncaster is a left-handed, pear-shaped course, over 15 furlongs round and quite flat, except for a slight hill about 1¼ miles from the finish. There is a perfectly straight mile, and a round mile starting on an off-shoot of the round course. The run-in from the turn is about 4½ furlongs. This is one of the fairest courses in the country, but its flat surface and great width, its sweeping turn into the straight, and long run-in, make it galloping in character, and ideal for the big, long-striding stayer.

DRAW: The draw is of no importance on the round course. On the straight course high numbers used to have a considerable advantage, but nowadays low numbers are usually favoured.

EDINBURGH—The Edinburgh round course is a right-handed oval track, nearly a mile and a quarter in extent, with a run-in of half a mile. There is a straight five-furlong course. The track is flat, with slight undulations and a gentle rise from the distance to the winning post. The turns at the top end of the course and into the straight are very sharp, and handiness and adaptability to negotiate the bends is of the utmost importance. The big, long-striding, cumbersome horse is at a distinct disadvantage on the round track, especially in races at up to a mile and three furlongs, but to a lesser extent in races over longer distances.

DRAW: Over five furlongs low numbers have a considerable advantage when the stalls are on the stand side and high numbers have a slight advantage when the stalls are on the far side. High numbers have an advantage in seven-furlong and mile races.

EPSOM—Epsom is a left-handed, U-shaped course, 1½ miles in extent. The Derby course is decidedly uphill for the first half-mile, level for nearly two furlongs and then quite sharply downhill round the bend to Tattenham Corner and all the way up the straight until approaching the final furlong, from where there is a fairish rise to the winning post. The run-in is less than four furlongs. The 7f and 6f courses start on tangential extensions. The 5f course is quite straight and sharply downhill to the

FLAT RACING FIXTURES 1990

APRIL
14th Sat.
Field Marshal Stakes; Turfcall Handicap.

MAY
5th Sat.
Fairey Spring Trophy.

7th Mon. Mixed
Swinton Insurance Hurdle.

25th & 26th Fri. and Sat.
Daresbury Handicap (Friday); Tote Handicap, Sandy Lane Stakes (Saturday).

JUNE
8th & 9th Fri. (Eve) & Sat.
Burtonwood Brewery Handicap (Friday); John of Gaunt Stakes (Saturday).

JULY
5th, 6th & 7th Thur. (Eve), Fri. & Sat.
July Trophy (Thursday); Samsung Handicap (Friday); Lancashire Oaks, Old Newton Cup, Cock of the North Stakes (Saturday).

AUGUST
10th & 11th Fri. (Eve) & Sat.
Haydock Park Leisure Company Handicap (Friday); Burtonwood Brewery Rose of Lancaster Stakes, Coral Bookmakers Handicap (Saturday).

17th Fri. (Eve)
Racing Post Handicap.

SEPTEMBER
7th & 8th Fri. & Sat.
Henriot Champagne Handicap (Friday); Ladbroke Sprint Cup, Juddmonte Claiming Stakes Final (Saturday).

28th & 29th Fri. & Sat.
Stanley Leisure Organisation Dream Mile (Friday); Bucklow Hill Handicap, Brooke Bond Foods Amateur Riders Final (Saturday).

OCTOBER
10th & 11th Wed. & Thur.
Oak Handicap (Wednesday); Hornbeam Handicap (Thursday).

N.B. The details given above are correct at the time of going to press, but factors outside the control of the Haydock Park Executive may result in alterations having to be made.

For enquiries and special group prices please contact:
HAYDOCK PARK RACECOURSE, NEWTON-LE-WILLOWS,
MERSEYSIDE WA12 0HQ
Phone: Ashton-in-Makerfield (0942) 725963

HAYDOCK PARK .... LEADING THE FIELD

junction with the round course. Races over 1½ miles can be testing if the pace over the first uphill four furlongs is strong, as it frequently is in the Derby. Otherwise the track is not really testing in itself, and races up to 8½ furlongs are very sharp indeed, the sprint courses being the fastest in the world. Owing to its bends and pronounced downhill gradients, Epsom favours the handy, fluent-actioned, medium-sized horse: big horses sometimes handle the course well enough, but cumbersome horses, long-striding gallopers, or those with pronounced 'knee-action' are not suited by it and are frequently quite unable to act upon it, especially when the going is firm or hard. Any hesitation at the start or slowness into stride results in considerable loss of ground over the first furlong in sprint races. For this reason Epsom is no course for a green and inexperienced two-year-old, slow to realise what is required.

DRAW: Nowadays a high draw is a considerable advantage over five furlongs and a slight advantage over six. A low number is an advantage over distances of seven furlongs to a mile and a quarter. A quick start is desirable at up to seven furlongs at least.

FOLKESTONE—The Folkestone round course is a right-handed, pear-shaped track, about ten and a half furlongs in extent, with a run-in of two and a half furlongs. There is a straight six-furlong course. The course is undulating, with the last part slightly on the rise, but notwithstanding its width, the easy turns, and the uphill finish, it is by no means a galloping track.

DRAW: No advantage on the straight course. Middle to high numbers have a slight advantage over seven furlongs. High numbers seem to have an advantage over a mile and a quarter and a mile and a half.

GOODWOOD—The Goodwood track consists of a nearly straight 6f course, with a triangular right-handed loop circuit. The Goodwood Cup, run over about 2m 5f, is started by flag in front of the stands: the horses run the reverse way of the straight, branch left at the first or lower bend, go right-handed round the loop and return to the straight course via the top bend. Races over 2m 3f, 1¾m, 1½m and 1¼m are also run on this course, but 1m races rejoin the straight course via the lower bend. Although there is a 5f run-in for races of 1¼m and upwards, the turns and, more specially, the pronounced downhill gradients from the turn, make Goodwood essentially a sharp track, favouring the active, handy, fluent mover rather than the big, long-striding horse. This is of lesser importance in 2m 3f and 2m 5f races, where the emphasis is on sound stamina, and of greater importance in the shorter distance races, particularly in sprints and especially when the going is on top. The 5f course is one of the fastest in the country.

DRAW: A low number is regarded as advantageous in sprint races, but the advantage is not great. Alacrity out of the gate is certainly of importance in five-furlong races.

HAMILTON—The Hamilton track is a perfectly straight six-furlong course, with a pear-shaped, right-handed loop, the whole being a mile and five furlongs in extent from a start in front of the stands, round the loop and back to the winning post. The run-in is five furlongs. The turns are very easy, and the course is undulating for the most part, but just over three furlongs from the winning post there are steep gradients into and out of a pronounced hollow, followed by a severe hill to the finish.

DRAW: Middle to high numbers have an advantage in races over the straight course.

HAYDOCK PARK—Haydock Park is a left-handed, oval-shaped course, about thirteen furlongs round, with a run-in of 4½ furlongs, and a straight 6-furlong course. The alternative 6-furlong course and all races of 1½ miles start on tangential extensions to the round course. Haydock is rather galloping in character.

DRAW: When conditions are testing there is a considerable advantage in racing close to the stand rail in the straight. Whatever the conditions, in races over 7 furlongs and a mile a good start and a handy position on the home turn are important.

KEMPTON—Kempton is a right-handed, triangular course, just over 13 furlongs round. The ten-furlong Jubilee Course starts on an extension to the round course. Sprint races are run over a separate diagonal course. The Kempton track is perfectly flat with normal characteristics, being neither a sharp track nor a galloping one.

DRAW: On the sprint course a draw near the rails is advantageous when the ground is soft; when the stalls are placed on the far side a high draw is an enormous advantage nowadays whatever the going.

LEICESTER—The Leicester round course is a right-handed, oval track, about a mile and three quarters in extent, with a run-in of four and a half furlongs. The straight mile course, on which all races of up to a mile are run, is mainly downhill to halfway, then rises gradually for over two furlongs, finishing on the level. The course is well-drained, the bends into the straight and beyond the winning post have been eased and cambered, and the track is galloping. For two-year-olds early in the season it poses quite a test of stamina.

DRAW: Low numbers have an advantage in races at up to a mile and the advantage seems to be more marked when the going is on the soft side.

LINGFIELD (Turf)—The Lingfield Park round course is a left-handed loop, which intersects the straight of seven furlongs and 140 yards nearly half a mile out. For nearly half its length the round course is quite flat, then rises with easy gradients to the summit of a slight hill, after which there is a downhill turn to the straight. The straight course has a considerable downhill gradient to halfway, and is slightly downhill for the rest of the way. The straight course is very easy, and the track as a whole is sharp, putting a premium on speed and adaptability, and making relatively small demands upon stamina, though this does not, of course, apply to races over two miles. The mile and a half course, over which the Derby Trial is run, bears quite close resemblance to the Epsom Derby course.

DRAW: On the straight course high numbers have a quite marked advantage.

LINGFIELD (All-Weather)—The all-weather track is laid out inside the turf track, following much the same line in the straight and the back straight then turning sharply for home at the top corner, so that it is only a mile and a quarter in extent, a chute in the straight providing a thirteen-furlong start. There is no straight sprint course, the fields at five furlongs and six furlongs having two bends to negotiate. The surface is Equitrack, whereas Southwell's is Fibresand.

DRAW: Early results show that despite the sharp nature of the track a high draw can be overcome.

NEWBURY—The Newbury round course is a left-handed, oval track, about a mile and seven furlongs in extent, with a run-in of nearly five furlongs. There is a straight mile course, which is slightly undulating throughout. Races on the round mile and over the extended seven furlongs start on an extension from the round course. Notwithstanding the undulations this is a good galloping track.

DRAW: A high number used to be a fairly considerable advantage over the straight course, but since the narrowing of the track the advantage seems to have disappeared.

NEWCASTLE—Newcastle is a left-handed, oval-shaped course of 1m 6f in circumference. There is also a straight course, over which all races of seven furlongs or less are run. The course is decidedly galloping in character, and a steady climb from the turn into the straight makes Newcastle a testing track, particularly for two-year-olds early in the season. Ability to see the journey out thoroughly is most important.

DRAW: The draw is of no particular consequence on a sound surface. On the straight course, the softer the ground the bigger the advantage the lower numbers enjoy.

NEWMARKET ROWLEY MILE COURSE—The Cesarewitch course is two and a quarter miles in extent, with a right-handed bend after a mile, the last mile and a quarter being the straight Across the Flat. From the Cesarewitch start the course runs generally downhill to a sharp rise just before the turn. There are undulations throughout the first mile of the straight, then the course runs downhill for a furlong to the Dip, and uphill for the last furlong to the winning post. This is an exceedingly wide, galloping track, without minor irregularities of surface, so it is ideal for the big, long-striding horse, except for the descent into the Dip, which is more than counterbalanced by the final hill.

DRAW: The draw confers little advantage.

NEWMARKET SUMMER COURSE—The Newmarket Summer Course is two miles and twenty-four yards in extent, with a right-handed bend at halfway, the first mile being part of the Cesarewitch course, and the last the straight Bunbury Mile. The course runs generally downhill to a sharp rise just before the turn. There are undulations for the first three quarters of a mile of the straight, then the course runs downhill for a furlong to a dip and uphill for the last furlong to the winning post. This is an exceedingly wide, galloping track, ideal for the big, long-striding horse, except for the descent into the dip, which is more than counterbalanced by the final hill.

DRAW: The draw confers little advantage.

NOTTINGHAM—The Nottingham round course is a left-handed, oval track, about a mile and a half in extent, with a run-in of four and a half furlongs. There is a straight

6f course, but no longer a straight mile. The course is flat and the turns are easy.
DRAW: In sprints when the stalls are placed on the stand side high numbers have a clear advantage, increasing as the ground softens. With the stalls on the far side low numbers are preferred.

PONTEFRACT—Pontefract is a left-handed, oval track, about two miles in extent. There is no straight course, and the run-in is only just over two furlongs. There are considerable gradients and a testing hill over the last three furlongs. The undulations, the sharp bend into the straight, and the short run-in disqualify it from being described as a galloping track, but there is a premium on stamina.
DRAW: A low number is advantageous particularly over five furlongs but it becomes a decided disadvantage if a horse fails to jump off well.

REDCAR—Redcar is a narrow, left-handed, oval track, about a mile and three quarters in extent, with a run-in of five furlongs, which is part of the straight mile course. The course is perfectly flat with normal characteristics, and provides an excellent gallop.
DRAW: Middle to high numbers have a big advantage on the straight course.

RIPON—The Ripon course is a right-handed, oval circuit of 13 furlongs, with a run-in of 5f, and a straight 6f course. Owing to the rather cramped bends and the surface undulations in the straight, the Ripon track is rather sharp in character.
DRAW: On the straight course the draw is of no importance but in races on the mile course, horses drawn in the high numbers seem to have an advantage.

SALISBURY—The Salisbury track is a right-handed loop course, with a run-in of seven furlongs, which, however, is not straight, for the mile course, of which it is a part, has a right-handed elbow after three furlongs. For races over a mile and three quarters horses start opposite the Club Enclosure, and running away from the stands, bear to the left, and go round the loop. The course, which is uphill throughout the last half-mile, is galloping and rather testing.
DRAW: Low numbers are favoured in sprints when the going is soft.

SANDOWN—Sandown is a right-handed, oval-shaped course of 13 furlongs, with a straight run-in of 4f. There is a separate straight course which runs across the main circuit over which all 5f races are decided. From the 1¼m starting gate, the Eclipse Stakes course, the track is level to the turn into the straight, from where it is uphill until less than a furlong from the winning post, the last hundred yards being more or less level. The 5f track is perfectly straight and rises steadily throughout. Apart from the minor gradients between the main winning post and the 1¼m starting gate, there are no undulations to throw a long-striding horse off balance, and all races over the round course are very much against the collar from the turn into the straight. The course is, in fact, a testing one, and over all distances the ability to see the trip out well is of the utmost importance.
DRAW: On the five-furlong course high numbers have a considerable advantage in big fields when the ground is soft.

SOUTHWELL—The left-handed course is laid out in a tight, level, mile-and-a-quarter oval, a spur to the three-furlong run-in providing a straight five furlongs. There are two types of surface, the all-weather track on the outside of the turf track. The all-weather surface is Fibresand, whereas Lingfield's is Equitrack.
DRAW: Early results suggest the track is very fair.

THIRSK—The Thirsk round course is a left-handed, oval track, just over a mile and a quarter in extent, with a run-in of half a mile. There is a straight six-furlong course, which is slightly undulating throughout. The round course itself is almost perfectly flat, but though the turns are relatively easy and the ground well levelled all round, the track is on the sharp side and by no means ideal for a horse that requires time to settle down, and time and space to get down to work in the straight.
DRAW: High numbers have a big advantage on the straight course.

WARWICK—Warwick is a broad, left-handed, oval track, just over a mile and three quarters in extent, with a run-in of about three and a half furlongs. There is no straight course, the five-furlong course having a left-hand elbow at the junction with the round course. Mile races start on an extension from the round course, the first four and a half furlongs being perfectly straight. This is a sharp track, with the emphasis on speed and adaptability rather than stamina. The laboured galloper is at a disadvantage, especially in races at up to a mile.

1066

DRAW: A high number is advantageous in races up to a mile when the ground is soft, but a quick beginning is also important.

WINDSOR—Windsor racecourse, laid out in the form of a figure eight, is 12½ furlongs in extent. In races of around 1½ miles both left-handed and right-handed turns are met. The last five furlongs of the course are straight, except for a slight bend to the right three furlongs from the finish. The six-furlong start is now on an extension of the straight. Although perfectly flat throughout, the bends make this track rather sharp in character. However, as there is a nearly straight 5f run-in the relative sharpness of the track is of no consequence in the longer races. Big, long-striding horses which normally require a more galloping course are at little or no disadvantage over these trips.
DRAW: No material advantage.

WOLVERHAMPTON—The Wolverhampton round course is a left-handed, pear-shaped or triangular track, just over a mile and a half in extent, with a run-in of five furlongs. There is a straight course of five furlongs. The course is level throughout, with normal characteristics.
DRAW: The draw confers no advantage.

YARMOUTH—The Yarmouth round course is a narrow, left-handed, oval track, about thirteen furlongs in extent, with a run-in of five furlongs. There is a straight mile course. Apart from a slight fall just before the run-in, the track is perfectly flat, with normal characteristics.
DRAW: High numbers used to be favoured on the straight course; in 1989 a position in the middle of the track seemed a great advantage.

YORK—York is a left-handed, U-shaped course, 2 miles in extent, and quite flat throughout. There is also a perfectly flat straight course, over which all 5f and 6f races are run. 7f races start on a spur which joins the round course after about two furlongs. The run-in from the turn is nearly 5 furlongs. This is one of the best courses in the country, of great width throughout and with a sweeping turn into the long straight. The entire absence of surface undulations makes it ideal for a long-striding, resolute galloper, but it is really a splendid track, bestowing no great favour on any type of horse.
DRAW: The draw used to be of no consequence, but recently low numbers have had a marked advantage, particularly when the ground has been on the soft side.

STALLION
SECTION

Timeform Ratings quoted in the Stallion Section are those which appeared in the 'Racehorses' annuals except where otherwise stated

DOMINION
SEVEN TIMES A CHAMPION

ELEGANT AIR
CHAMPION FIRST SEASON SIRE 1989

SQUILL (USA)
TOP CLASS MILER WITH A CLASSIC PEDIGREE

Winning lines

ASTON PARK STUD. ASTON ROWANT. OXFORDSHIRE OX9 5SS. ENGLAND
ENQUIRIES TO: MRS A J CUTHBERT. TELEPHONE 0844 51492 (OFFICE)
0844 28417 (HOME)   FAX 0844 51091   TELEX 27822

LONDON
THOROUGHBRED
SERVICES LTD.

Purchases · Sales · Shares · Nominations
Stallion Management · Valuations · Transport · Insurance

1990 STALLION FEES

EXACTLY SHARP	**IR£5,000 S.L.F.**
FORZANDO	**£3,000 N.F.N.F. October 1st**
KRIS	**£40,000 July 15th + £40,000 N.F.N.F. October 1st**
PHARLY	**£10,000 N.F.N.F. October 1st**
ROBELLINO	**£5,000 N.F.N.F. October 1st**
SHARPO	**£12,000 N.F.N.F. October 1st**
SHARROOD	**£6,000 N.F.N.F. October 1st**
SLIP ANCHOR	**£20,000 N.F.N.F. October 1st**

APPROVED MARES ONLY
All nominations subject to availability

Enquiries to:
London Thoroughbred Services Ltd.,
7, Phene Street, Chelsea, London SW3 5NZ.
Telephone: 01-351-2181. Telex: 916950 (LONTSL G).
Fax: 01-352-8958.

EXACTLY SHARP(USA)

Chesnut 1985, by Sharpen Up out of Exactly So by Caro

Group 1 winner in record time over 10½F at Longchamp

at 2 years
Won Prix Catari 7F at Maisons-Laffitte on his debut.
Won Prix des Foals (**LR**) 7F at Deauville,
beating multiple Group 1 winner **FIJAR TANGO**.

at 3 years
Won Prix Lupin (**Gr.1**) 10½F at Longchamp. Race and track record.
Won Grosser Preis der Steigenberger Hotels (**Gr.3**) 10F
4th Prix du Jockey Club (**Gr.1**) 12F at Longchamp. Beaten sh hd,
3/4L, short nk, flying at the finish, *"in one of the closest finishes to a
European Classic in recent years"* Thoroughbred Breeder, July 1988.

Total Prize Money £117,499.

Group winners or dams of Group winners in foal include:
**BHAMA, RACQUETTE, FLAMME D'AMOUR,
FLEUR D'ORANGER, DRAMA, ROSE DE SARON**
Timeform Racehorses of 1988 rated **121**.

Only five **Gr.1**. winning sons of **SHARPEN UP** at stud **KRIS, DIESIS,
SHARPO, TREMPOLINO, EXACTLY SHARP**

Fee £IR£5,000 S.L.F.

Enquiries to: **LONDON THOROUGHBRED SERVICES LTD.,**
7 Phene Street, Chelsea, London SW3 5NZ.
Telephone: 01–351–2181. Fax: 01–352–8958. Telex: 916950 LONTSL G.
Brendan Hayes, **KILFRUSH STUD,** Knocklong, Co. Limerick, Ireland.
Telephone: (062) 53352/53104. Telex: 70145. Fax: (062) 53255.

PHARLY

Multiple Group 1 winning son of LYPHARD

From his first 8 crops sire of 49% Winners to Foals
in 1989 Sire of 40 individual winners of 57 races and £380,431
including 10 individual 2-y-old winners
**ACCESS SUN, BETWEEN THE STICKS, BOCA LAD,
FLOWER GIRL, FRENCH BAY, NOBODYS SWEETHEART,
NORTHERN HEIGHTS, PHARLEY HILL, SARDEGNA** and
WESTERN OCEAN.

**Fee £10,000 N.F.N.F. Oct. 1st
Standing at Woodland Stud, Newmarket in 1990**

Enquiries to: **LONDON THOROUGHBRED SERVICES LTD.,**
7 Phene Street, Chelsea, London SW3 5NZ.
Telephone: 01-351-2181. Fax: 01-352-8958. Telex:916950 LONTSL G

ROBELLINO

Bay 1978 by Roberto - Isobelline by Pronto

Won 5 races, 6-8F, and £60,064 inc. Royal Lodge S. **Gr.2** (7F), course
record, Seaton Delaval S. **Gr.3** (7F) top weight, won by 4l
Timeform rated **127** Racehorses of 1980.
Third in International 2-y-old Classification
Champion First Season Sire in England 1985
Sire of 8 winners from 13 runners in Europe including
FAUSTUS, CHALK STREAM, LOCAL HERBERT, Hello Ernani.

1st crop 69% Winners to Runners · 2nd crop 63% Winners to Runners
3rd crop 62% Winners to Runners

1989 Runners Worldwide 25 individual winners of 53 races and £300,000
including **ROBELLATION, BORN TO SWING, RINJA,
SPURNED** etc.

Fee: £5,000 N.F.N.F. Oct. 1st

Enquiries to: **LONDON THOROUGHBRED SERVICES LTD.,**
7 Phene Street, Chelsea, London SW3 5NZ.
Tel: 01-351-2181. Fax: 01-352-8958. Telex: 916950 LONTSL G.
or Jeff Smith, **LITTLETON STUD,** Winchester, Hants. SO21 2QF.
Tel: (0962) 880210

SHARPO

Chesnut, 1977, by Sharpen Up - Moiety Bird, by Falcon

Champion European Sprinter 1981/2

WON Gr.1 William Hill July Cup

WON Gr.1 Prix de l'Abbaye de Longchamp

WON Gr.2 William Hill Sprint Championship (1980, 81, 82)

WON Gr.3 Temple Stakes

1986 **LEADING FIRST SEASON SIRE**

1987 Sire of dual Group 1 winner **RISK ME,** winner of Grand Prix de Paris **Gr.1,** Prix Jean Prat Ecurie Fustok **Gr.1**

1988 Sire of 27 individual winners of 39 races and £264,661 incl. **SWs SHARP GAIN, SHARP JUSTICE, SHARP REMINDER**

1989 Sire of 33 individual winners of 49 races and £331,248 including 2-y-old Group winner **POLE POSITION** and Group/Listed performers **CHASEN'S, POYLE GEORGE, REMTHAT NASER, SHARP REMINDER, TAKDEER.**

Sire in 1989 of 10 individual 2-y-old winners.

FEE: £12,000 N.F.N.F. Oct. 1st.

Standing at Woodland Stud, Newmarket.

Enquiries to: **LONDON THOROUGHBRED SERVICES LTD.,**
7 Phene Street, Chelsea, London SW3 5NZ.
Tel: 01–351–2181. Fax: 01–352–8958. Telex: 916950 LONTSL G.

Standing at Highclere Stud, Nr. Newbury, Berkshire.

SHARROOD

Grey 1983, 16h.1in., by **CARO** ex **ANGEL ISLAND** by **COUGAR II**

Winner of 7 races from 2-4 years and £355,193

At 2 years	**WON**	4 consecutive races 6-7F.
At 3 years	**2nd**	Waterford Crystal Mile **Gr.2,**
	2nd	Prix Eugene Adam **Gr.2**
	3rd	Airlie/Coolmore Irish 2000 Gns **Gr.1.**
	3rd	St James's Palace S. **Gr.2**
	4th	General Accident 2000 Gns **Gr.1.**
At 4 years	**WON**	Eddie Read H. **Gr.2** (turf) 9F course record
	WON	Stars and Stripes H. **Gr.2** (turf) 8½F
	2nd	Budweiser-Arlington Million **Gr.1** (to **MANILA**, beating **THEATRICAL**)

First Yearlings 1990

Fee: £6,000 N.F.N.F. Oct 1st (limited to 50 mares)

Enquiries to: **LONDON THOROUGHBRED SERVICES LTD.,**
7 Phene Street, Chelsea, London SW3 5NZ.
Tel: 01-351-2181. Fax: 01-352-8958. Telex: 916950 LONTSL G.
or **HIGHCLERE STUD,** Highclere, Newbury, Berks RG15 9LT.
Tel: (0635) 253212.

SLIP ANCHOR

Bay 1982 by **SHIRLEY HEIGHTS** out of **SAYONARA,** by **BIRKHAHN**

Champion European 3-y-old of 1985

WON Ever Ready Derby **Gr.1** by 7 lengths.
WON Highland Spring Derby Trial Stakes, **Gr.3** by 10 lengths
WON Heathorn Stakes **LR.**
2nd Dubai Champion Stakes **Gr.1** beaten by 4-y-old Pebbles.

His first Yearlings at Deauville, Tattersalls Highflyer and Goffs
averaged £108,684 (10 sold)

Fee £20,000 N.F.N.F. Oct 1st

Enquiries to: **LONDON THOROUGHBRED SERVICES LTD.,**
7 Phene Street, Chelsea, London SW3 5NZ.
Telephone: 01–351–2181. Fax: 01–352–8958. Telex: 916950 LONTSL G.
Leslie Harrison, **PLANTATION STUD,** Exning, Newmarket, Suffolk.
Telephone: Exning (063877) 341

THE BLOODSTOCK AGENCY WITH MORE HORSEPOWER

STALLIONS FOR 1990

ARAGON
(1980 by Mummy's Pet)
Standing at Lavington Stud

ELEGANT AIR
(1981 by Shirley Heights)
Standing at Aston Park Stud

BALIDAR
(1966 by Will Somers)
Standing at Meddler Stud

FAUSTUS (USA)
(1983 by Robellino)
Standing at Fawley Stud

BLUSHING SCRIBE (USA)
(1981 by Blushing Groom)
Standing at Theakston Stud

GLINT OF GOLD
(1978 by Mill Reef)
Standing at Eagle Lane Farm

BUSTINO
(1971 by Busted)
Standing at Wolferton Stud

HADEER
(1982 by General Assembly)
Standing at Stetchworth Park Stud

CHIEF SINGER
(1981 by Ballad Rock)
Standing at Side Hill Stud

INSAN (USA)
(1985 by Our Native)
Standing at Sledmere Stud

CLAUDE MONET (USA)
(1981 by Affirmed)
Standing at Sledmere Stud

JALMOOD (USA)
(1979 by Blushing Groom)
Standing at The National Stud

DAMISTER (USA)
(1982 by Mr. Prospector)
Standing at Woodditton Stud

KALAGLOW
(1978 by Kalamoun)
Standing at Brook Stud

DOMYNSKY
(1980 by Dominion)
Standing at Easthorpe Hall Stud

K-BATTERY
(1981 by Gunner B)
Standing at Chesters Stud

DREAMS TO REALITY (USA)
(1982 by Lyphard)
Standing at Wood Farm Stud

LOCHNAGER
(1972 by Dumbarnie)
Standing at Ticklerton Stud

MANSINGH (USA)
(1969 by Jaipur)
Standing at Red House Stud

MASHHOR DANCER (USA)
(1983 by Northern Dancer)
Standing at Littleton Stud

MAZILIER (USA)
(1984 by Lyphard)
Standing at Barleythorpe Stud

MIDYAN (USA)
(1984 by Miswaki)
Standing at Whitsbury Manor Stud

MINSTER SON
(1985 by Niniski)
Standing at Longholes Stud

MOST WELCOME
(1984 by Be My Guest)
Standing at Meddler Stud

NIGHT SHIFT (USA)
(1980 by Northern Dancer)
Standing at Barton Stud

NINISKI (USA)
(1976 by Nijinsky)
Standing at Lanwades Stud

NOMINATION
(1983 by Dominion)
Standing at Limestone Stud

NORTHERN STATE (USA)
(1985 by Northern Dancer)
Standing at Barleythorpe Stud

PETONG
(1980 by Mansingh)
Standing at Barleythorpe Stud

PETOSKI
(1982 by Niniski)
Standing at The National Stud

PRECOCIOUS
(1981 by Mummy's Pet)
Standing at Ashley Heath Stud

REPRIMAND
(1985 by Mummy's Pet)
Standing at The National Stud

SAYF EL ARAB (USA)
(1980 by Drone)
Standing at Woodditton Stud

SHIRLEY HEIGHTS
(1975 by Mill Reef)
Standing at Sandringham Stud

SIZZLING MELODY
(1984 by Song)
Standing at Gazeley Stud

SUPERLATIVE
(1981 by Nebbiolo)
Standing at Woodditton Stud

For further details of nomination fees
and availability please contact
Simon Morley or **Martin Percival**, BBA Stallion Dept. on
Newmarket (0638) 665021

The BRITISH
BLOODSTOCK AGENCY plc

Queensberry House, High Street, Newmarket, Suffolk CB8 9BD
Tel: (0638) 665021 Telex: 817157 BBA NKT G Fax: (0638) 660283

STALLIONS FOR 1990
AL HAREB
ALZAO
BARBAROLLI
BE MY GUEST

BLUEBIRD
CAERLEON
COMMANCHE RUN
DANEHILL
DON'T FORGET ME

ENTITLED
GALLIC LEAGUE
GLENSTAL
HIGH ESTATE
LAST TYCOON

LAW SOCIETY
LOMOND
PERSIAN HEIGHTS
SADLER'S WELLS
SALMON LEAP

Europe's finest source of proven stallions drawn from the world's greatest racing bloodlines.

COOLMORE

Contact: **Bob Lanigan** or **Christy Grassick.**

Coolmore Stud, Fethard, Co. Tipperary, Ireland. Tel: 353-52-31298. Telex: 80695. Fax: 353-52-31382.

	U.S.A. STALLIONS	**NATIONAL HUNT**	EXECUTIVE PERK
TATE GALLERY	ASSERT	**STALLIONS**	HENBIT
THATCHING	EL GRAN SENOR	BUCKSKIN	LANCASTRIAN
TRY MY BEST	SEATTLE DANCER	CARLINGFORD CASTLE	LE MOSS
VACARME	STORM BIRD	ELECTRIC	SUPREME LEADER
WAAJIB	WOODMAN		

DARLEY STUD

MANAGEMENT

Stallions

FOR 1990

- **DANCING BRAVE 1983** *by Lyphard - Navajo Princess by Drone*
  Champion European 3-year-old of 1986. First crop 2-year-olds in 1990.

- **POLISH PRECEDENT 1986** *by Danzig - Past Example by Buckpasser*
  Won Prix du Moulin de Longchamp **G.1**, Prix du Haras de Fresnay-le-Buffard Jacques le Marois **G.1**. Retires to Stud in 1990.

- **REFERENCE POINT 1984** *by Mill Reef - Home on the Range by Habitat*
  Champion European 2 and 3 year old. First crop yearlings in 1990.

- **SHAREEF DANCER 1980** *by Northern Dancer - Sweet Alliance by Sir Ivor*
  Sire of **COLORADO DANCER, DABAWEYAA, NEDIYM, NOBLE BALLERINA, RASLAAN, ROCK HOPPER, SHAMSHOON, SHARKA, STAR SHAREEF, TRIPLE KISS** etc.

- **SOVIET STAR 1984** *by Nureyev - Veruschka by Venture*
  Champion European Sprinter 1988. Won 5 Group 1 races. First crop foals in 1990.

- **MTOTO 1983** *by Busted - Amazer by Mincio*
  Champion European 4 and 5-year-old in 1987. First crop foals in 1990.

- **SHAADI 1986** *by Danzig - Unfurled by Hoist The Flag*
  Unbeaten 2-y-old, won Airlie/Coolmore Irish 2000 Guineas **G.1**, St James's Palace S. **G.1**. Retires to Stud in 1990.

- **SURE BLADE 1983** *by Kris - Double Lock by Home Guard*
  Won St James's Palace S. **G.2**, Queen Elizabeth II S. **G.2**, Laurent Perrier Champagne S. **G.2**, Coventry S. **G.3**. First Crop 2-year-olds in 1990.

- **DUNBEATH 1980** *by Grey Dawn - Priceless Fame by Irish Castle*
  Won William Hill Futurity **G.1**. Sire in 1989 of 18 individual winners from his first crop, and 9 from his second crop.

- **JALMOOD 1979** *by Blushing Groom - Fast Ride by Sicambre*
  Group 1 winner. Sire of winners of 95 races and over £500,000 from 3 crops.

- **MASHHOR DANCER 1983** *by Northern Dancer - Zonely by Round Table*
  Won his only race at 2 years. First season sire 1989 of 2 winners from 6 runners.

- **TEENOSO 1980** *by Youth - Furioso by Ballymoss*
  Champion Older Horse in Europe at 4. Won Derby **G.1**, King George VI & Queen Elizabeth S. **G.1**. Sire of winners in England and Italy from his first 2 crops.

- **MILLER'S MATE 1982** *by Mill Reef - Primatie by Vaguely Noble*
  Won Wood Ditton Stakes. First season sire 1989 with 7 individual winners.

- **LOCAL SUITOR 1982** *by Blushing Groom - Home Love by Vaguely Noble*
  Won Rokeby Farms Mill Reef Stakes **G.2**, beaten a head and same in Dewhurst Stakes **G.1**. First Crop 3-year-olds 1990.

- **TOP VILLE 1976** *by High Top - Sega Ville by Charlottesville*
  Sire of Group 1 winners **DARARA, PRINCESS PATI, SAINT ESTEPHE, SHARDARI** and **TOP SUNRISE**.

Darley Stud Management Company Ltd.,
Dalham Hall Stud, Duchess Drive, Newmarket, Suffolk
Telephone: Newmarket (0638) 730070. Telex: 818823 (DALHAM G).
Fax: (0638) 730167.

1086

ADVERTISERS

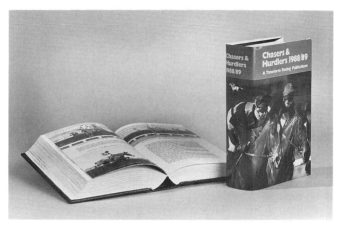

The Timeform Annual for the jumpers

This magnificent volume is the complete
annual review of the National Hunt season.
It contains Timeform Ratings and Commentaries
for every horse that ran during the British season,
plus the best of the Irish.
All the top horses are dealt with
in essay form

1000 pages   350 photographs

On Sale October

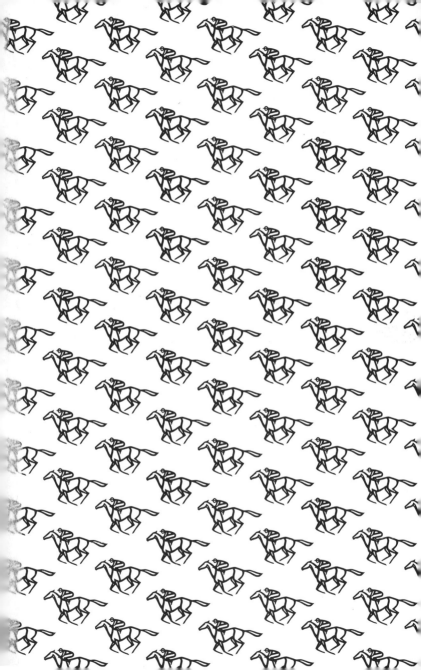

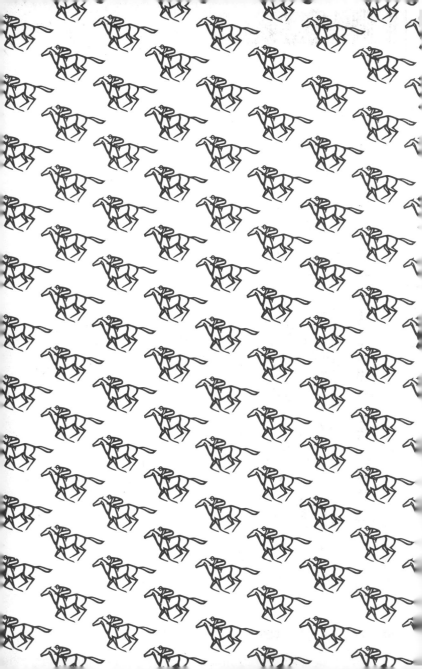